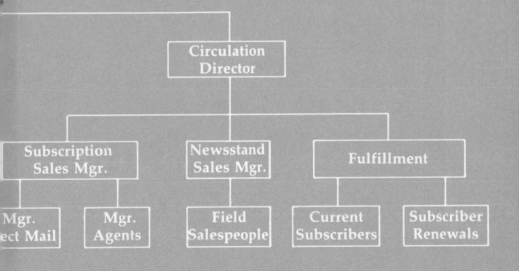

taff Services
Printing
Research
blic Relations
ccounting, etc.

Circulation
Director

Subscription
Sales Mgr.

Newsstand
Sales Mgr.

Fulfillment

Mgr.
ect Mail

Mgr.
Agents

Field
Salespeople

Current
Subscribers

Subscriber
Renewals

1985 WRITER'S MARKET®

WHERE TO SELL WHAT YOU WRITE

Edited by Paula Deimling

Writer's
Digest
Books

Cincinnati, Ohio

Acknowledgments

The editor wishes to acknowledge Bernadine Clark (*Writer's Market* editor, 1983-84) for her contributions in planning this edition.

Distributed in Canada by Prentice-Hall of Canada Ltd., 1870 Birchmount Road, Scarborough, Ontario M1P 2J7, and in Australia and New Zealand by Bookwise (Aust.) Pty. Ltd., Box 296, Welland, S.A. 5007, Australia.

Library of Congress Catalog Number 31-20772

International Standard Serial Number 0084-2729
International Standard Book Number 0-89879-151-0

Contents

The Profession

The Markets

The Profession

Introduction

Authorship is, according to the spirit
in which it is pursued, an infamy, a pastime,
a day-labor, a handicraft, an art, a science, or a
virtue.
> —A.W. Schlegel

The spirit in which you pursue authorship *decides* your future as a writer.

You can't write a book by keeping only a diary; you can't be a published writer if you don't pursue markets for your work. If selling what you write is your goal, *Writer's Market* and day (and night) labor for years must be your pursuit.

In this 56th edition, you'll meet ten writers who pursue this goal. Their essays (chosen from the 159 essays we received) tell you how *they* write, sell, and use *Writer's Market* to do both. Reading the essays will show you uses for this book you may never have thought of.

For some, *Writer's Market* "works" as an inspiration; for others, it's a tool for earning reprint checks. And writers visit these pages annually to learn what's happening in the freelance writing world. They discover new markets and rediscover old ones with new changes because we contact editors, publishers, producers, and cartoonists year-round about editorial needs and changes that might affect freelance writers. We query new publishers to see if they buy freelance material. Here, we share this information with you.

So much information did we find, in fact, that this year's *Writer's Market* is the largest edition ever—larger by 96 pages.

We've reinstated sections on authors' agents, contests and awards, gag writing, and syndicates. A double dagger (‡) denotes the hundreds of new markets in this book, with the exception of these four sections where all listings are new for 1985. If a market isn't listed, there may be several reasons why; see page four for an explanation of our selection process.

New(s) this year. The following are additional or expanded features that will help you think and write like a pro.

● What Editors Say. Editors tell you their side of the story on writing, editing and selling. Their quotes will teach and inspire you.

● Section introductions with industry tips and trends. In many cases this year, we've used editors' colorful ways of expressing their points.

● "Close-up" interviews with editors and writers. Many of our Close-up interviewees like William Zinsser and Ray Robinson work in both capacities.

● Submissions recordkeeper. Now you can record your submissions and sales on the inside cover.

● Symbol chart. This key (on page four) will help you to interpret various symbols used before listings throughout the book.

New(s) classics. We've updated, revised, and brought back again these helpful sections.

● Book Publisher Subject Index of over 90 categories to aid you in your search for a publisher.

● Appendix of updated information on manuscript mechanics, submission procedures, query letter, postal chart, and payment rates for writing jobs from critiques to speeches.

● Glossary. Concise definitions of writing terms used throughout the book and in the publishing world.

Start tapping these resources and your typewriter or PC keys if you want your writing to be more than a handicraft. Writing can be your livelihood or a celebration of your *living* (even if you don't sell your work). But that depends on your goals—and the spirit in which you pursue your writing.

—*Paula Deimling*

Using Writer's Market

Careful writers read and reread each listing. They also respect editors' needs and send *only* the type of material that is requested.

• Information regarding the emphasis and audience of a publication gives important clues to the slant and style your submissions should take.

• Figures listing the number of freelance manuscripts purchased are approximations, but they indicate a market's openness. With new magazines, these figures may change dramatically, depending on the submissions they receive or sudden changes in policy.

• Figures for manuscript lengths preferred by editors are limits to keep in mind when submitting material or suggesting manuscript length in a query letter. However, a story should be told in the space it requires—no more and no less.

• Look for markets that pay on acceptance, *not* "on publication." Payment here is immediate, and not dependent on when your story appears in print. Also, some magazines pay more for assigned stories than for complete manuscripts sent over the transom. Querying for an assignment in these cases is the best move.

• Look, too, for markets that don't buy all rights, and don't make "work-for-hire" contract agreements (in which the market, and not the author, owns the article's copyright). Retain rights you might be able to resell. (Information regarding a publication's openness to previously published work is also listed.)

• Don't abuse openness to simultaneous submissions or phone queries. Use these routes only when your "hot" story will be chilled by usual submission procedures. Also, openness to photocopied submissions *does not* imply that simultaneous submissions are OK.

• Check a market's receptiveness to computer printout and electronic submissions, as well as preference for letter-quality over dot-matrix type. If no mention is made of printout or disk submissions, the editor prefers not to get them.

• Times listed are approximate. When an editor gave us a range of reporting and publishing times, say four to six weeks, we listed the time as six weeks. Give editors about six extra weeks on reporting time before following up politely on queries or submissions.

• Enclose a self-addressed, stamped envelope (SASE) in *any* correspondence with editors. Remember that enclosing a SASE without enough postage to get a manuscript back to its owner is like not sending a SASE—and that's poor etiquette for a writer. Use International Reply Coupons (IRCs) with a return envelope for all Canadian and foreign submissions. U.S. (return) postage is useless in Canada and foreign countries.

• If a listing instructs you to query, please query. If it instructs you to send a complete manuscript, send a complete manuscript.

• Address a cover letter or query to a specific editor by name. If the name is not easily recognizable as to gender, use the full name (without the titles—Mr., Mrs., or Ms.) on both the envelope and the letter (e.g., Dear Dale Smith:).

• Don't abuse the editor's willingness to distribute free sample copies. Purchase samples at newsstands if possible. *Always* read a sample copy before querying or making a submission.

• If the editor advises in the listing that a sample copy is available for a price and a SASE—but does not specify the size of the SASE—look at the publication's description. If it is a tabloid, newspaper or magazine, you'll need to enclose a 9x12 SASE with three first class stamps affixed. If the publication is a newsletter, chances are it will weigh less than an ounce, so a business-size SASE with one first class stamp affixed should be sufficient. Generally speaking, if a sample copy is available for a price (without SASE), assume that postage is included in the price quoted. Most guidelines are available for a business-size envelope with one first class stamp (unless otherwise specified).

Key to Symbols Used in *Writer's Market* Listings:

‡ New listing in all sections
* Subsidy publisher in Book Publishers section
● Company publication in Consumer and Trade, Technical, and Professional Journals sections
□ Cable TV market in Scriptwriting section

Urgent

● Listings are based on editorial questionnaires and interviews. They are *not* advertisements, *nor* are markets endorsed by *WM* editors.

● Information in listings is as current as possible, but editors change jobs, companies and publications move, and editorial needs change between the publication date of *Writer's Market* and the day you buy it. Listings for new markets and changes in others can be found throughout the year in *Writer's Digest*, the monthly magazine for freelancers. If you know of a market not listed in this book, send us the market's name and address; we will solicit it for the next edition.

● When looking for a specific market, check the index. A market might not be listed for one of these reasons: 1) It doesn't solicit freelance material. 2) It has gone out of business. 3) It doesn't pay for material (we have, however, included nonpaying listings in the journalism, lifestyles, and poetry categories because publication in these magazines could be valuable to a writer). 4) It has failed to verify or update its listing for the 1985 edition. 5) It requests not to be listed. 6) Complaints have been received about it, and it hasn't answered *Writer's Market* inquiries satisfactorily. (To the best of our ability—and with our readers' help—we try to screen out any dishonest listings.) 7) It buys few manuscripts, thereby constituting a very small market for freelancers. 8) It was in the midst of being sold at press time, and rather than disclose premature details, we chose not to list it.

● *Writer's Market* reserves the right to exclude any listing.

What Writers Say . . .

"The sailor hoisting his sail against a blue sky; the kid dropping a freshly hooked worm into the bayou; the writer cranking an 8½x11 battle zone into his typewriter—they're all living on hope," says writer Don M. Aycock. "Hope is what the *Writer's Market* symbolizes to me."

To others, it symbolizes a meeting place (for ideas and conversations with other writers). Many call it a writer's Bible. And one writer suggests 101 uses for the book.

Here at *Writer's Market*, we *found* 159 ways of looking at the book. That's how many essays we received from readers when we asked for essays on writing and *Writer's Market*.

Writers working for their first bylines and writers with published books and many bylines responded. Essays came from small towns, big cities, Canada, Hawaii, Switzerland and Singapore. It took days (and nights) of reading and rereading, comparing, and looking for fresh ideas expressed in fresh ways. The difficult part was selecting the ten *best* essays, because each writer shared a part of his life with us; we hated to *judge* work that inspired us so deeply.

You'll see, though, we did decide. We also decided to publish the essays as the writers wrote them (without extensive editing).

We now pass these essays to you for your scrutiny and enjoyment. Learn from each writer's ideas. Observe how writers cover the same subject in ten (actually 159) different ways. And, above all, see how you too—with practice, research, and hope—can hoist a sail on a writing career.

Lead Me to the Candy!

By Barbara Weston, Miami, Florida

Every time I open a new edition of *Writer's Market*, I feel like a kid turned loose in a candy store. I open it excitedly, thinking that with all those markets out there, there MUST be a place for me.

Once the initial euphoria passes, I get down to some serious planning and noble intentions. A small file cabinet holds sample copies of magazines, filed alphabetically. Some of these I sent for; many were purchased for half-price at local paperback discount stores. This latter is an excellent source, frequently carrying hard-to-find publications—and the price is *right*. I then mark the *WM* index, indicating that a particular magazine is in my file. The essential writer's guidelines I can get for a SASE is well worth the 20¢ investment. Current information from *Writer's Digest*, etc., concerning changes in policies or staff, contributors' complaints, or other details of a specific publication are noted under that particular listing in *WM*. When a query letter or manuscript receives an editor's personal comment, this is also noted. (Those water stains come from joyous tears—someone has actually READ my efforts.)

One of my files is marked simply "Possibilities"; it contains suggestions for getting editors' attention. One idea concerns the "Letters to the Editor" section of a magazine. I scan current issues of publications for controversial articles. A brief but thoughtful comment about such an article often interests an editor and may even lead to further communication. I've found this a successful maneuver—well worth the small amount of time and effort. I may include suggestions for additional pieces along similar lines—which I would *gladly* supply, if asked—or just generally comment on the subject.

Other letters I find indispensable are those written to editors thanking them for accepting a manuscript, followed by notes of appreciation after publication—indicating your satisfaction at the presentation. It's one more way to keep your name in the editors' minds. In this case, familiarity definitely does NOT breed contempt—only sales.

My first sale was totally unexpected. *Writer's Digest* announced that a popular magazine was planning a 50th anniversary issue. Being familiar with the publication, I wrote a short, congratulatory note and enclosed a 26-line poem, praising its achievements through the years. It was printed in its anniversary issue, complete with artwork and byline. Not only was I thrilled by the sale, but I had established contact with an editor. I've discovered there are many such occasions: change of format, publications resuming publication (*Saturday Evening Post*, for example), new editors, etc. Any of these events might provide the opportunity for a short, congratulatory letter.

My *WM* from a previous year has its special advantage. I note changes: Are certain editors paying more now—or less? Have their types of readers changed? Are policies different from last year? This comparison gives a valuable insight into the publication—where it WAS and where it is NOW.

Whether it's last year's copy or one just off the press, the feeling is the same whenever I flip through the 1,000 or so pages. I still feel like that kid in the candy store, and I'm still sure there *MUST* be a place for me.

101 Uses for *Writer's Market*

By Barbara Herigstad, Spearfish, South Dakota

My list of 101 uses for *Writer's Market* began on a jet airplane over Colorado several years ago. I was reading the newest edition when a stranger, noticing the book, began a conversation about writing. He then presented me with a detailed plot for a short story which he did not feel qualified to write.

That conversation heads my list of the ways in which I use *Writer's Market*:

1. Conversation starter. Carrying it in public places may result in friendships, plots, and contacts.
2. Resource list for names, spellings, and addresses of periodicals and publishers.
3. Self-education. Each edition is a mini-course in how-to, copyright, and writing advice.
4. Impressing visitors to my study. Awestruck upon seeing the book, they ask, "Are you a writer?"
5. Income tax deduction when old editions are donated to school or library.
6. Income tax deduction when profits from manuscripts finally began to arrive.
7. Three editions wrapped in plastic make an adequate booster chair for small children.
8. Locating subscription information and subject matter of periodicals or subject matter in which a publisher specializes.
9. Reference for proper form and style of manuscript preparation.
10. Weight to hold scrapbook of clippings while paste is drying.
11. Locating obscure books. By writing directly to the most-likely publisher in *Writer's Market*, I recently found a book for which I had searched for months.
12. Gift to friends who are would-be writers.
13. Filling the mailbox with writer's guidelines for which I have sent SASE. I have also discovered this brings catalogs and advertising materials from strange and varied sources.
14. Stepstool, adding old editions as needed, for reaching top shelves, especially for us "shorties."
15. Visual aid and background information for assignment in creative writing class.
16. Keeping current on latest changes in copyright laws, trends and editors.
17. Swatting mosquitos which invade the study in summer.

18. Browsing and daydreaming of those editors who will one day recognize my genius.
19. Indexing articles in old editions to create a reference source.
20. Pressing corsages presented at local writers' group meetings.
21. Building morale when I read blurbs from editors such as: "we *do* read unsolicited mss" or "we are looking for *undiscovered* authors."
22. Propping up the corner of the typing table.
23. Conceiving ideas for articles or stories based on needs listed by publishers.
24. Paperweight to hold down pages of "great American novel" as I finish writing them.
25. to 101. Last, but far from least, I even use *Writer's Market* to locate buyers for my writings. I make a list of potential buyers for each story I finish. I send the story off to the first publisher on the list. If and when the story is rejected, I mail it off to the next potential buyer on the *same day* it is returned.

Thus, out of *Writer's Market* come answers to problems, practical helps, new knowledge and inspiration. What else can one ask of a book?

Highlighting *Writer's Market* Highlights

By J.F. Peirce, Bryan, Texas

Each year *Writer's Market* gets bigger and bigger, and unless one uses it systematically, he or she can waste precious time. Obviously, many of the markets listed are not of use to the average writer, so the trick is how to find one's way through the maze of unusable markets to those that are usable as quickly as possible.

When I get a new *WM*, I go through it, market by market, with a highlighter and colored pens in hand. Those markets I am interested in, I highlight. I also highlight the facts in the write-up that are important to me: the word lengths and rights bought, the payment made and when, etc.

In the margins, I indicate with colored ink the kind(s) of manuscripts that I write that the market buys. I'm primarily a writer of mystery and suspense stories and logic puzzles. I also write stories and articles about knives. If a magazine uses mystery or suspense stories, I put a red star in the margin. If it uses logic puzzles, I put a blue star in the margin, and so forth. I indicate high paying markets with a +, poor paying markets with a -, and average paying markets with a *.

I highlight the reference to the market in the index to help me locate it more quickly.

If I'm positive a market has nothing to offer me, I draw a line through it.

I add tabs to those sections of *WM* that I use frequently. And I update my *WM* each month as I go through the market information in *Writer's Digest*, crossing out those markets that have folded and adding (in the blank pages at the back) any markets in which I'm interested. At times, I cut the market listings out of *WD* and insert them in their proper place in my *WM*.

I keep my *WM* on a table next to my easy chair, and anytime I have a few minutes to spare, I dip into it to better familiarize myself with my markets. This is especially helpful when I'm writing something different for which I don't have a market in mind. A write-up about a market may help me focus the piece, say, by giving it a female rather than a male slant.

Once my *WM* is properly highlighted, I can flip through it, checking for the proper colored stars. When I come to one, I check the word-lengths bought, which I've highlighted. If the maximum length manuscript bought is 3,000 words and my story is 5,000, I skip to the next market. If my story is 3,500 words long, however, I make a note of the market and return to it if I cannot find a suitable market to decide whether I can cut the story to the length bought.

Remember: the time you save by using your *WM* effectively can be used to write or make love or do whatever else that interests you.

How I Harvest Cash with My *Writer's Market*

By Edith Flowers Kilgo, Forest Park, Georgia

Considering my passion for reading everything (even telephone directories and dictionaries), it was inevitable my first encounter with *Writer's Market* would be love at first sight.

And a profitable affair it has been, too. This object of my affection has, in eight years, guided me through the publication of hundreds of magazine articles, three books, and into becoming a columnist for two national magazines and a book reviewer for a third.

My house went undusted and my family unhugged as I, an unpublished would-be writer, read my first *Writer's Market* cover to cover, all the while underlining and taking notes. Certainly, I already knew about such publications as *Redbook* and *McCall's*, but my *Writer's Market* introduced me to the possibilities of such magazines as *Listen*, *Home Cooking*, and *The Good News Broadcaster*—all of which bought my articles the first time out.

Looking back on the experience, I realize now my cover-to-cover approach was a sound one. Through it I found markets I never knew existed—markets especially favorable to beginners—but better yet, along the way I learned to write.

Even if a publication listed in *Writer's Market* was out of my field I still read and tried to heed the applicable advice from hundreds of editors. For me, these nuggets were more beneficial than anything else I'd ever read. Here, I learned to "write tight" and to "use active verbs" and to "limit use of the first-person approach." Fascinated, I frequently forgot to thaw something for dinner.

Weeks passed and my relationship with my *Writer's Market* matured. Patiently, my mentor explained the mysterious process by which plain white bond is turned into green spending money. Understanding increased. Soon we had formulated Kilgo's Law of Moving Up.

I'd begin by locating a lesser known publication where submissions were undoubtedly lower than, say, *Reader's Digest*. Following the advice of my *Writer's Market*, I'd send for guidelines and a sample copy. Thoroughly I'd study the publication as my teacher directed: word by word, even ad by ad. Timidly the thick yellow envelopes went out. Increasingly, the long thin, white ones came back in their place.

My guide explained slant. Suddenly I comprehended that I could write a basic story, sell it, and then search my *Writer's Market* for other noncompeting publications requiring a different approach. The result? Minimum work. Growing income. Maximum credentials. From a starting pay of $16 for my first article I saw the numbers leap to $50, $100, $200, even $500.

And finally the ultimate recycle: a book. I turned to my proven friend. The advice was sound. Not only was the manuscript accepted by that publisher but two other books followed thereafter. Ironically, the next edition of *Writer's Market* mentioned my first book by title as being representative of the kind of material my publisher was seeking. Our relationship was now mutually beneficial—I had finally given something back.

Is Bigger Better? Not for Beginners.

By Eric Lenaburg, Phoenix, Arizona

Like most writers, I always think my stories should be published in *Esquire*, or the *Atlantic*, or *The New Yorker*.

I have yet to crack any of those tough cookies.

But I keep selling freelance articles. I consult *Writer's Market* religiously, and keep up with the markets in *Writer's Digest* every month. I make notations in the book. My '84 edition of *Writer's Market* is jammed with index cards, scrawled with the names of new editors, rates and fees.

The Gary Provosts, Hal Higdons and Jay Stullers can afford to start at the top, and pick and choose their markets. But I'm a freelancer with a handful of major credits. As far as most editors know, I'm only as reliable as my query letter. I'm a risk.

For two years, I worked as a reporter for a small-town daily newspaper. During that time, I frequently came across stories that begged to be rewritten and submitted to national markets.

I started reading *Writer's Market* at the library. The logical choice for my first piece was *Grit*. As it says in the weekly tabloid's market listing, "Small-town and rural America." They buy a lot of manuscripts, a healthy sign, and they're willing to work with new, unknown freelancers.

The pay is 12 cents a word. Not earth-shattering, certainly nothing to quit your job for. But it helps, and it gives you those important clips.

Pecking away at the low-pay market can help defray the costs of important trips, when you need to expand your contacts and climb the ladder into the next area of markets.

Before making a trip to Los Angeles (which set me back about $200), I phoned publicity agents at all three major TV networks, searching for performers available for interviews.

I wound up selling a piece on Danielle Brisebois ("Archie Bunker's Place") to *Young Miss* for $225. Also, I talked with Ed Marinaro ("Hill Street Blues") and Marla Gibbs ("The Jeffersons"), and later sold freelance pieces on both.

You don't have to live in Hollywood or Manhattan to be a successful writer.

But before you begin, know the magazine. Those guidelines and editors' comments aren't included just to fill space. If they say they don't want humor, quit trying to prove you're the next Robin Williams. If they want light features, for God's sake, don't send them a 3,000-word think piece on nuclear war.

The best advice I ever received came to me from another freelancer, about five years ago:

"You can talk about it all you want. You can complain about editors. You can cry about your hard luck. While you're doing that, I'm going to write another article."

Sweeping Up More Assignments

By George Sheldon, Hershey, Pennsylvania

While most writers—including me—use the *Writer's Market* for the purpose of finding new markets for their work, I also use the listings to locate markets where I can achieve *additional* sales of material already completed for other purposes.

Simply, this is making maximum sales from the same information. By making some simple changes, writing a separate story with a different slant, or by just writing two different articles, double sales can easily be achieved.

For example, I recently did a story on a local chimney sweep for a nearby newspaper. This colorful character dresses up as the sweeps did years ago, wearing a tall top hat, tuxedo coat, a full beard, and always has a corn cob pipe clenched between his teeth.

This particular chimney sweep also just happened to be using a Volkswagen to drive from job to job.

By using the *Writer's Market*, I located a listing for *Small World*, which was looking for stories on the use of Volkswagens. I put together a different story than the one I did for the newspaper. I submitted some photos, and called my new article, "A Sweep in A Rabbit," and it was quickly sold to *Small World* for $100.

By using the *Writer's Market* to locate additional markets for similar sales, a writer's income can be greatly increased.

I have used this same approach to make sales to *Police Product News*, *The Farm Journal*, *Giftware News*, and *Mature Living*, to name a few.

My best advice is to spend some time reading the listings of the markets you know nothing about. Study their needs. Make notes, either mental or perhaps in your notebook, of the types of articles these particular markets, usually specialty publications, are indicating that they need. Then, when you are writing about any topic, remember these listings, and ask yourself: how can I adapt this material to make sales to these other markets?

This same technique can be used very successfully to market fillers, short-shorts, and news items. By keeping tabs on events, news, and what's happening in your area, and reporting these bits of information to the specialty markets, a writer will suddenly find that he or she has: (1) become published; (2) has lots of credits; (3) has an "in" with lots of editors for both query go-aheads, and lucrative assignments.

So it pays to study the listings, and particularly the listings of little known, or highly specialized markets. Don't forget a good slant is all it takes to make sales. For example, if there is a local wood carver in your area, consider the kind of vehicle he uses, his tools, his clothing, how to decorate an office or home with wood carving, how to get started with wood carvings, and the history of wood carving. Where can you send these story ideas? To those listings, right here in *Writer's Market*, after, of course, you studied the needs of the editors.

The end result will be more sales, more checks in the mail box, more credits, and eventually, more assignments.

Behind Every Successful Freelancer There's A. . .*Writer's Market*

By Eddie Osborne, Miami, Florida

You have a hot article idea, and you want to identify an appropriate market. What do you do?

If you're like I was when I began freelancing back in 1972, you'll probably pick up copies of several publications you feel would be interested, jot down the editor's name and address as given in the masthead of the best prospect, and fire off your sure-fire query letter.

You'd be making a big mistake.

Sure, having a copy of the publication for which you hope to write before you is always a good idea (the masthead, for example, will tell you who's who and where to send your submission, and an analysis of the articles will give you an idea of the type of material preferred), but a publication alone is hardly enough.

For one thing, a magazine won't tell you what kind of people make up its reader-ship (unless you're the perceptive type who can discern this from the ads being run), how material should be submitted or what rights they buy. Nor will it tell you how long articles should run or whether you'll be paid upon acceptance or on publica-tion.

For the answer to those and the host of other questions that will influence your marketing decision, you'll need *Writer's Market*.

I discovered *Writer's Market* some 12 years ago when William and Ellen Hartley, a widely-published husband and wife freelance team who taught a magazine-writing course at Miami-Dade Community College, brought their dog-eared copy to class one evening for us to check out. The next day I went to a local bookstore and bought a copy for my own library.

I've studied the book religiously ever since and have been richly rewarded for my efforts. Over the years, by coupling the tips given in *Writer's Market* with careful analysis of my intended markets, I've succeeded in selling to a number of nationally- and regionally-circulated publications (*Essence, Encore American & Worldwide News, Sepia, Hip, Black Stars* among them), and I keep adding new ones to that list with each passing month.

Writer's Market has helped my writing career along in other ways as well. For ex-ample, in the course of thumbing through its pages in search of market information,

I've discovered that there are quite a few publications that pay in the four figures. The prospect of hitting these high-paying markets acts as an incentive for me to continue refining my writing skills and to come up with ever better story ideas.

Actually, *Writer's Market* itself has proved an invaluable source of ideas for various money-making projects. I've often gotten article ideas while mulling over editors' needs in the listings. And one particular section of the book ("How Much Should I Charge?") has helped me by not only providing a standard on which to base my prices for publicity and other writing tasks I perform for local businesses and politicians but also has given me ideas for jobs that I had not previously considered.

If you make a habit of studying *Writer's Market*, you too can learn how to tailor your writing to suit your buyers' needs. Remember, the successful writer isn't necessarily the fellow who knows the most about a given subject, but rather the one who knows *where* to find information on those things he doesn't know.

A Free Lunch for Freelancers: Going on the Reprint Circuit

By LindaAnn Loschiavo, New York City

Last year *Writer's Market* helped me earn over $1,000—and all I had to write was a few letters. These queries sold "second rights" to manuscripts I had already published elsewhere. Here's a sample:

Dear Name-of-the-Editor:
According to the current *Writer's Market*, you purchase reprints. The enclosed tearsheet, "Engaged Encounter: Preparing for a Lifetime Love," was initially published in the April/May 1983 *Modern Bride*. Since I sold Ziff-Davis Publications first rights only, I'm free to resell my work.
Would you consider reprinting it?
If not, please return my clipping in the attached SASE.

With *Writer's Market* detailing who buys second rights, and what types (and lengths) of pieces these publishers are seeking, I resold my first-person account of an Engaged Encounter three times. Other stories have done even better.

Some titles have more reprint potential than others. Time-dated features, for instance, go stale quickly. Interviews of a person in the news *that moment*, but whose "star status" is fleeting, may fizzle after the first sale.

Which features are forever? Manuscripts that *can* be recycled include how-to features and pieces about health (mental and physical), or relationships, or self-development. For example, two of my most popular reprints are: "Romance: How to Keep the Magic Alive" and "Towards a New Understanding of Pain."

Writer's Market offers helpful information not only about reselling an *entire* article—but also when it pays to divide and conquer. Armed with this knowledge, I sold *Cosmopolitan* the last five paragraphs of a lengthy medical article originally done for *USAir*; it was reprinted as an end-of-column filler. I sold *Woman* a shortie on sharing housework, one whole section lifted from my 1,500-worder written for King Features on handling stressful marital situations. (Again: health features and how-tos sell and re-sell swiftly.)

Recycling your work—in whole or in part—brings several bonuses. There's a financial benefit: the joy of earning a check for an article you merely photocopy and mail with a cover letter and an SASE. When Gannett News Service reprinted four titles of mine, the check tided me over until I received another publisher's payment for just-completed work.

Here are five other professional advantages:

● Introducing yourself to an editor through a reprint, which highlights your track record, often leads to future assignments.

• Reprints fatten up your list of editorial credits, making you seem prolific and popular with publishers.

• With your byline getting double-exposure (or more), you'll increase your chances of being noticed; other contacts will come your way.

• Receiving a rejection is less hard to bear when your mailbox contains another editor's acceptance of your reprint.

Whenever I get a new article idea, I flip through *Writer's Market* for details on how to hone that topic for a particular magazine. But my mind runs on two tracks: simultaneously, I'm assessing what oldies-but-goodies might hit pay-dirt with this publication (if the *WM* listing states the editor uses reprints).

There may be no free lunch for freelancers. But for less than a dollar's worth of postage and duplicating, and 15 minutes with *Writer's Market*, you, too, can turn tearsheets into greenbacks. Why not flip through your file cabinet right now and see if you can find publishing success the second time around?

My Anecdote Agent and Constant Companion

By Connon Edward Barclay, Holland, Michigan

Freelance writers often use agents for fiction and nonfiction work of some length. Frequently these agents are worth the cost, however what assistance in marketing is best for the anecdote/filler writer? *Writer's Market* is the answer. . .at least it has been for me. . .and for a number of years.

Often I ride trains, subways, airplanes, buses, taxis, and even on occasion a rickshaw. Knowing full well that almost anybody has a story, an amusing or inspirational anecdote to share. . .the trick for filler writers is to HEAR these tales. And the magic wand (*Writer's Market*) has been my constant traveling partner for any number of years.

With credits in some 87 publications for fillers, etc., I would strongly suggest you carry the *Writer's Market* everywhere you go. History would tell almost any soul that when one carries a Bible a certain respect and usually a certain distance is accorded. If one carried the other extreme: a well-known men's magazine another attitude or several could be displayed by strangers. . .and here again. . .perhaps a certain distance.

However, if you carry and occasionally open—as if to be reading—a *Writer's Market*, watch the people gain entrance to your writing world. People have been and probably always will be fascinated by writers. As Saul Bellows once said, "All a writer has to do to get a woman is say he's a writer; it's an aphrodisiac." The men I know are equally fascinated when meeting female writers.

Hand-in-hand with that theme is the reason for making *Writer's Market* your "public agent." Strangers will approach and feel comfortable asking if you are a writer. . .and any writer worth genderless salt only needs the door open a crack to make entry into new worlds, research, news, new stories and tales. People love to tell their tales to writers, yet they rarely know any such creative forces. So even if standing in line at a bank, waiting in line with your children to see Santa Claus, buying first-come World Series tickets, having your transmission repaired or even picking up your unemployment check, let the public see your agent.

This filler writer could almost guarantee that before much traveling time together . . . you and your hardbound agent will have the world you travel in knocking at your ears.

The Professional Approach

By Ellen M. Kozak, Milwaukee, Wisconsin

I made the transition from the amateur to professional writer very quickly. I've always been convinced that *Writer's Market*—and my professional approach to its use—have been largely responsible for my ability to *sell* my work.

I purchase each annual volume as soon as it arrives in my bookstore. I read it through immediately—usually in one marathon session—to see what changes in format have been made. Then I decide what sections of the book I am most likely to use.

I index these by typing a one-word tab ("Women's" or "Travel," for example) and taping it to the edge of the first page of that section. Staggering these tabs on the edge of the book makes them easier to read. Then, having marked the categories I am likely to be able to sell to, I begin my *serious* perusal of the listings.

I first look to see how much a publication pays, and *when* it pays for an article. Then I check out the kind of rights they say they purchase (although I've found this may often be negotiable). I save publications that pay too little, or too late, for reprint sales, and never touch those that make "work-for-hire" assignments.

If a publication pays enough, and preferably does so on acceptance, I look for an offer of guidelines, sample copies or both. I send for these to discern whether I can, indeed, match their style and give them the kind of article they want.

Only then do I send a query letter (most listings suggest querying, and it pays to pay attention to this), and these queries often garner assignments.

When I get an assignment, I usually ask whether there's a kill fee (or, where they mention one in their listing, ask them to verify that it will be in effect). That way I know I'll be paid something for my efforts, even if new management takes over and rejects my story.

All this may seem more pragmatic than romantic, but starving isn't really romantic. This approach assures that I will seldom expend postage or typewriter ribbons without getting a monetary return. I have learned that, while it may be very gratifying to see your work in print, it's even more so when you know you've been paid for the piece. Like the commercial suggests, "I'm worth it." If you can write well, so are you.

What Editors Say . . .

If a writer's only contact with editors has been form-letter rejections, he might think editors work six-hour days, take frequent trips, and two-hour lunches.

Let's see the other side of the story. A typical day's mail at some offices brings ten queries and eight manuscripts. In another office, an editor photocopies and edits 60 pages of a book manuscript before meeting with a copy editor in two hours. There are other endless editorial deadlines too—four hours, four days, and four weeks from now.

Writers (who might feel overlooked by editors) *must* understand that editors are outnumbered by the volume of writers. Thus, we've asked editors to talk about writing, selling, and editing material for their publications. Here we share their side of the story with you.

On Writing

Writing is work, not a form of self-indulgence (except perhaps in the rough-draft stage); it should be approached in a disciplined way.

> —Millea Kenin, *Empire*
> quoting Marion Zimmer Bradley

State your thesis; explain what impact it has on your readers; use expert testimony or documentable facts to prove your thesis; provide a possible solution, again using expert testimony; sum up and shut up. Also, every time you write a sentence that seems especially brilliant, strike it out.

> —Daniel S. Wheeler
> *The American Legion Magazine*

Many writers seem to think if they send in a brilliant 6,000-word manuscript, the editor will make amends. Sorry. If we only have room for 1,500 words and Norman Mailer sends us a 3,000-word Pulitzer Prize-winner, then Norman Mailer will lose 1,500 Pulitzer Prize-winning words.

> —John Wood
> *Dynamic Years*

. . . Grammatical expertise makes all the difference to me; if a writer doesn't demonstrate good writing skills, I tend to doubt his/her credibility.

> —Kathleen M. Horrigan
> *Family Journal*

Probably the best advice [that brought about "a turning point" in my career] was from a newspaper editor—"Write about everything you can get your hands on, keep writing, and then write some more."

> —Jill-Marie Jones
> *Horse Illustrated*

You'll have to face this piece of writing the rest of your life—make it the best.
> —Richard L. Knudson
> *The Dossier*

Brevity was the advice of Frank Garafalo—"Even the second coming of Christ doesn't merit more than 600 words."

> —*Entrepreneur Magazine*

On Selling

The selling writer *knows* his subject matter and presents it in such a way that I know he *knows*. Editors of specialty magazines come to know that special subject exceptionally well. The nonselling writer attempts to fool the old hand, which he cannot do.

—Dave Epperson
Survival Guide

I am interested in reading only the submission, not those long lists of previous sales elsewhere.

—Dorothy Harvey
Capper's Weekly

Your book is one of several hundred we produce each year. We have well thought-out procedures; follow them and your book will do much better than if you try to create your own systems.

—Lynne A. Lumsden
Prentice-Hall, Inc.

. . . Sometimes writers don't read what you have published [in *Writer's Market*], and we get material on a subject such as "How to Cultivate Your Garden" or something just as far afield.

—James C. Vebeck
Plan and Print

We've changed our name in the past two years as well as many editorial staffers, yet we frequently get queries from people who are unaware of our name and address change and personnel changes, although they took place some time ago.

—Pam Greenberg
Cable Television Business

Sounds nitpicking, but it's very important for me to be able to read something clearly and quickly without struggling over a coffee stain or fingerprints of brownies.

—Nancy Adams
Antiques Dealer

Little magazines keep material too long at times, especially if they are considering it. . . . A frantic letter will always get material bounced back to you, even if it was under serious consideration.

—Earl R. Snodgrass
Japanophile

Being too general or too technical is a fatal mistake. Readers subscribe to our magazine to get specialized information not found anywhere else—but they have to be able to *understand* what they read.

—Kay Melchisedech Olson
Garden Supply Retailer

On Editing

Our founding editor, Dr. Garry C. Myers, wrote the following sentences which are still included on our rejection form: "All editors have preferences. Our wisdom and judgment are limited. What we reject here may be eagerly accepted elsewhere. Many a noted writer has climbed to success on steps built with early rejection slips. . . ."

—Constance McAllister
Highlights for Children

Editors are not whimsical ogres who are just waiting for a stray typo to permit them to toss aside the manuscript, partially read. We look very hard to try to spot promise in stories.

—Mimi Jones
formerly of *Redbook*

. . . Most editors do not enjoy rejecting submissions. Good editors *want* to find a publishable piece. They find it very pleasant to say "Yes" to a writer—and painful to say "No." Editors—at least most of them—are not the enemy.

—Lauren Barnett Scharf
Lone Star

Editing is not done (or should not be done) to personally invalidate the writer's efforts but rather to accommodate necessary realities of the publishing process—i.e., money, space, etc.

—C.L. Morrison
Format: Art and the World

Don't worry about what an editor does with your words, leads, summaries, heads. The editor knows the readers better than you do—and knows how to get them into the article. No editor intentionally weakens a story.

—Dick Hale
Dental Economics

An editor tries to help the writer say what he wants to say.

—John Fink
Chicago Magazine

The articles we dread the most are the ones that are poorly-written treatments of a great idea. We hate these because we cannot reject them outright, yet it takes us so much time and money to put them into presentable form that we almost wish we had never received them.

—Louise Allen Zak
The Herb Quarterly

The Markets

Book Publishers

Every great book is an action,
and every great action is a book.
> —Martin Luther

Good isn't enough in book publishing, because thousands of *greats* compete each day. Readers will buy great books, not good ones. So will editors, and that's why they continually read manuscripts in the office and sometimes by their fireplaces late in the evening.

There is plenty of talent for editors to choose from; the problem is finding *books that will sell* from among the stacks (yes, stacks) of good manuscripts.

"The average book only sells 5,000-10,000 copies a year," says one Prentice-Hall vice president. "That hasn't changed in the twelve years and three companies I've worked for in the business."

Great books defy the average. The ultimate challenge then for the writer is to write great literature that sells.

Approximately 46,000 new titles roll off presses each year. Yours can be one of them—if you can write what publishers want.

First, though, you must know the audience you're writing for and the publishers who reach this audience. *Writer's Market* is the first step to finding out who they are—coupled with your own delving into publishers' titles in book stores and libraries. Then you can narrow down the nearly endless choices to a few choices.

Some writers get manuscripts in the door at new, small, and/or close-to-home publishers. Here, the writer and publisher are usually looking for a loyal readership. Small, independent presses and regional publishers, for example, attract such audiences.

Regional publishers are a bit like resorts, drawing people to a particular area. Readers want books to take them to Florida's beaches and Arizona's deserts. They also want to learn about country inns and out-lying areas.

If you live in a region that readers long to visit, you can research the area without the expense of traveling to it.

As some writers use regional publishing to gain national reputations, some publishers do likewise. "We anticipate success in both regional publishing and in entering the national market with our novels and nature nonfiction," says one Florida publisher.

Small presses, on the other hand, don't cover a region per se, but cater to areas not explored by commercial presses.

Some publishers believe today's Shakespeares are writing for small presses. At the same time, publishing costs threaten to slow down small presses.

"Publishers are not able to finance all the books that they would like to produce," says one small press editor. He predicts there will be more cooperative efforts between authors and publishers.

Other publishers, however, say that presses dependent on grants and author subsidies will fade from the marketplace.

One major boost to small presses is R.R. Bowker's bimonthly *Small Press, The Magazine of Independent Book Publishing*. Such "press" promotes more awareness of literary independence. The image of small presses producing obscure, bizarre works is fading too. Readers are learning what writer Alexander Pope knew more than 200 years ago: "To buy books only because they were published by an eminent printer, is much as if a man should buy clothes that did not fit him, only because [they were] made by some famous tailor."

At major publishing houses, editors are replacing the multimillion-dollar competitions of several years ago with more cautious buying. Publishers today will pay several million for a book, but only for the *right* book.

Other publishing trends that writers should know (especially when deciding what kind of book to write) include the following:

● educational books. Readers want to learn new skills without taking expensive, time-consuming classes. One publisher reports that books with English as a second language and foreign language markets are showing an increase.

● specialty books. Self-help, diet, exercise and health books continue to sell well. Celebrities and people who can *model* the results of their advice are especially well suited to write these books.

● computer books. "Computer how-to books are still good, but purchasers have become more selective," says one publisher. The same is true for most computer books.

● books for children under three. As more children spend their pre-school days away from home, parents and pre-school programs are emphasizing early, early learning.

● romance. The passion for romances is still sweeping away heroines and readers— the more romances they read, the more they want to read.

● books as films. A century ago, a writer's work appeared only on printed pages. Now with film versions of *Winds of War, Thorn Birds* and other books, publishers and writers can't help but think of this as a possibility. Highly introspective books with little action will never become candidates for the screen.

● nonfiction. Writing in science, communication, and technology draws a loyal readership. The author with several popular books on a subject will have fans waiting for the next book two hours after reading the latest book.

● fiction. "The market is overloaded with fiction which merely tells a story rather than focusing on the consequences of human motives and action," says one publisher. Fiction that gives the reader insight into humanity *in a special way* will get special treatment from publishers.

● quality of life. Some readers want to probe the social, political, and economic issues of the day. Others want to learn more about nuclear power and war and how to combat crime in their neighborhood.

● interactive books. Readers, especially children, are enjoying this new type of computer book with a choice of multiple endings.

● biography or autobiography. Whether authorized or unauthorized by their subjects, people want to read about people, especially the famous and infamous. The stories of athletes, rock stars, public officials, and celebrities sell books.

● headline-inspired books. Yesterday's front-page news story may be today's bestseller. Stories on mass murders and political scandals sell newspapers and books.

● the latest craze. As a writer, you can analyze the latest craze or perhaps start one. As the jitterbug becomes disco or break dancing, readers turn to authors to learn more about these fads. Start thinking *in the future*, so you'll be ready to write about the next craze.

Once you have an idea for a book, you must find a publisher for it. Don't assume you're the only person with such a mindstorm. The *Subject Guide to Books in Print* in libraries tells you what has been written on each subject. Studying this resource and reading the books on *your idea* keep you from submitting a proposal exactly like a book already in print. In fact, some publishers want writers to explain how their proposed book is similar *and* different from specific books on the market.

Read *Publishers Weekly* for information on industry trends, problems, and not-yet-released titles. Read *Writer's Digest* magazine. Study book titles and the layout of book stores. What do colorful displays in front aisles tell you about book buyers? If you're not sure, visit book stores in non-rush hours. Become friends with book store managers and librarians.

Also, send for book catalogs and writer's guidelines—they're clues to the audiences a publisher hopes to reach. What does the publisher emphasize in explaining each book? Emphasize those aspects in your proposal.

One drawback to the would-be author is that each publisher prefers different ways of receiving submissions. Some want complete manuscripts; others want one-page proposals. The more than 800 publishers in this book tell you how to submit material; do it *their* way. Keep in mind also that a change of editors may mean policy changes.

Above all, *don't wait idly* for a reply. Many writers lose three months of writing time, thinking they deserve a vacation for shipping a bestseller to a publisher. Few writers make the lists. *If* your book does become a bestseller, publishers will fight over your next book, so write it as if this is your last chance at the keyboard.

One publisher suggests that writers start with short works and "master the details of producing them first. Keep extending the length of works you can handle until you achieve your goal."

The writer must be a lifelong student. If you've chosen to write books because it's a prestigious career entailing less time than, perhaps, earning a law degree, you've chosen the wrong field. As an author, you'll always be *pursuing* some degree (of success with book publishers).

The process of writing, editing, and publishing will go on for ages. Modern technology speeds up the sequence, but the art of creating worlds from words gets no simpler. It takes *great* effort.

ABBEY PRESS, St. Meinrad IN 47577. (812)357-8011. Publisher: Keith McClellan, OSB. Publishes original paperbacks. Averages 8 titles/year. Pays definite royalty on net sales. Publishes book an average of 9 months after acceptance. Computer printout submissions acceptable; prefers letter-quality to dot-matrix. Query with outline and sample chapter. Reports in 3 weeks. SASE.
Nonfiction: "Primarily books that contribute to the healing, support, enrichment and celebration of marriage and family life. Mainline Christian perspective."
Recent Nonfiction Title: *From This Day Forward: The Challenges and Gifts of the Early Years of Marriage*, by Jon Nilson.

ABBOTT, LANGER & ASSOCIATES, 548 1st St., Crete IL 60417. (312)672-4200. Managing Consultant: Dr. Steven Langer. Publishes trade paperback originals and loose-leaf books. Averages 12 titles/year. Pays 10-15% royalty; no advance. Publishes book an average of 3 months after acceptance. Photocopied submissions OK. Computer printouts submissions acceptable. SASE. Reports in 2 weeks on queries; 1 month on mss.
Nonfiction: How-to, reference, technical on some phase of personnel administration or industrial relations. Especially needs "a very limited number (3-5) of books dealing with very specialized topics in the field of personnel management, wages and salary administration, training, recruitment, selection, labor relations, etc." Publishes for personnel directors, wage and salary administrators, training directors, etc. Query.
Recent Nonfiction Title: *Compensation of Industrial Engineers (8th Ed.)*, by S. Langer (pay survey report).

Asterisk preceding a listing indicates that individual subsidy publishing or co-publishing (where author pays part or all of publishing costs) is also available. Those firms that specialize in total subsidy publishing are listed at the end of the book publishers' section.

ABC-CLIO INFORMATION SERVICES, (formerly ABC-CLIO, Inc.), 2040 A.P.S., Santa Barbara CA 93103. (805)963-4221. Vice President and General Manager: Dr. Gail Schlachter. Publishes hardcover originals (95%) and paperback reprints (5%). Averages 25-30 titles/year. Pays 10-15% royalty on net price. Photocopied submissions OK. Disk submissions "must be compatible with our equipment; check with us first." Computer printout submissions acceptable. Reports in 2 months. SASE. Free book catalog.
Nonfiction: Bibliographic guides, dictionaries, directories, handbooks, serials, and other reference tools (specifically in political science, history, library science, art and women's studies). Mss on comparative politics should be forwarded directly to the series editor, Prof. Peter H. Merkl; bibliographies on war/peace issues may be forwarded to Prof. Richard D. Burns; other reference guides may be forwarded to Dr. Gail Schlachter; dictionaries in political science may be forwarded to Jack C. Plano. Query or submit outline/synopsis and 2-3 sample chapters. Reviews artwork/photos as part of ms package.
Recent Nonfiction Title: *Directory of Financial Aids for Minorities 1984-1985*; by Gail A. Schlachter.

ABINGDON PRESS, 201 8th Ave. S., Box 801, Nashville TN 37202. (615)749-6403. Editorial Director: Ronald P. Patterson. Managing Editor: Robert Hill Jr. Editor/Professional Books: R. Donald Hardy. Senior Editor/Reference Books: Carey J. Gifford. Editor of Lay Books: Mary Ruth Howes. Editor of Academic Books: Pierce S. Ellis Jr. Editor of Family Books: Ernestine Calhoun. Publishes paperback originals and reprints. Published 100 titles last year. Pays royalty. Publishes book an average of 18 months after acceptance. Computer printout submissions acceptable. Query with outline and samples. Write for ms submission guide. Reports in 6 weeks. SASE.
Nonfiction: Religious-lay and professional, children's books and academic texts. Length: 32-300 pages.
Recent Nonfiction Title: *When a Friend Is Dying*, by Edward F. Dobihal, Jr. and Charles W. Stewart.
Fiction: Juveniles only.
Recent Fiction Title: *Humbug Potion*, by Lorna Balian.
Tips: "A short, pithy book is ahead of the game. Long, rambling books are a luxury few can afford."

HARRY N. ABRAMS, INC., 100 5th Ave., New York NY 10011. (212)206-7715. Subsidiary of Times Mirror Co. President, Publisher and Editor-in-Chief: Paul Gottlieb. Publishes hardcover and "a few" paperback originals. Averages 65 titles/year. "We are one of the few publishers who publish almost exclusively illustrated books. We consider ourselves the leading publishers of art books and high quality artwork in the US." Offers variable advance. Prefers no simultaneous submissions; photocopied submissions OK. SASE. Reports in 3 months. Free book catalog.
Nonfiction: Art, nature and science and outdoor recreation. Needs illustrated books for art and art history, museums. Submit outline/synopsis and sample chapters and illustrations.
Recent Nonfiction Title: *Renoir, His Life, Art, and Letters*, by Barbara Ehrlich White.

ABT BOOKS, Subsidiary of Abt Associates, Inc., 55 Wheeler St., Cambridge MA 02138. (617)492-7100. Editor-in-Chief: Clark C. Abt. Publishes hardcover and trade paperback originals. Averages 30 titles/year. Pays 10-15% royalty on receipts; offers negotiable advance. Photocopied submissions OK. SASE. Reports on queries in 3 weeks; 1 month on mss. Free book catalog.
Nonfiction: Business and world economy, social science and social issues. Subjects include business and economics, crime, housing, health, military, politics, psychology, sociology and research methods. "Social policy studies based on extensive research; how-to books on research methods; and business strategy. Our readers are professional and business groups with the 'need to know'; e.g., how housing programs work, how to conduct survey research, how to meet the public-involvement requirements under state and federal law." No belles-lettres. Submit outline/synopsis and sample chapters.
Recent Nonfiction Title: *Coalition Strategy*, by Robert Komer.

ACADEMIC PRESS, INC., Harcourt Brace Jovanovich Bldg., Orlando FL 32887. Editorial Vice President: E.V. Cohen. Pays variable royalty. Publishes over 400 titles/year. Reports in 1 month. SASE.
Nonfiction: Specializes in scientific, mathematical, technical and medical works. Textbooks and reference works only in natural, behavioral-social sciences at college and research levels. Submit outline, preface and sample chapter. Books for researchers only, not general public.
Recent Nonfiction Title: *Nonlinear Laser Spectroscopy*.

ACADEMY CHICAGO, 425 N. Michigan Ave., Chicago IL 60611. (312)644-1723. Editorial Director/Senior Editor: Anita Miller. Publishes hardcover and paperback originals (35%) and reprints (65%). Averages 40 titles/year. Pays 7-10% royalty; no advance. Publishes book an average of 1 year after acceptance. Photocopied submissions OK. Computer printout submissions acceptable; no dot-matrix. Reports in 2 months. SASE.
Nonfiction: Adult, travel, and historical. No how-to, cookbooks, self-help, etc. Query or submit sample chapters. "Do *not* send whole books. We find synopses defeating. We look first of all for good writing style, professional organization; after subject matter, that's important. Sample chapters are most helpful."
Recent Nonfiction Title: *Behind the Front Page*, by A. A. Dornfeld.

Fiction: "We would consider mysteries with one detective for series." No "romantic" fiction, or religious or sexist material; nothing avant-garde. "We can no longer do children's books or young adults."
Recent Fiction Title: *The Cold Stove League*, by Thomas Boyle.
Tips: "We are very interested in good nonfiction history and biography. We are also interested in quality fiction and will consider once-published books that deserve reprinting."

ACCELERATED DEVELOPMENT, INC., 3400 Kilgore Ave., Muncie IN 47304. (317)284-7511. President: Dr. Joseph W. Hollis. Executive Vice President: Mrs. Lucile Hollis. Publishes textbooks/paperback originals and software. Averages 6-8 titles/year. Electronic submissions OK if compatible with CPT equipment (schedule needs to be arranged), but requires hard copy also. Computer printout submissions acceptable; prefers letter-quality to dot-matrix. Pays 6-15% royalty on net price. Publishes book an average of 1 year after acceptance. SASE. Reports in 3 months. Free book catalog.
Nonfiction: Reference books and textbooks on psychology, counseling, guidance and counseling, teacher education and death education. Especially needs "psychologically-based textbook or reference materials, death education material, theories of counseling psychology, techniques of counseling, and gerontological counseling." Publishes for professors, counselors, teachers, college and secondary students, psychologists, death educators, psychological therapists, and other health-service providers. "Write for the graduate level student." Submit outline/synopsis and 2 sample chapters.
Recent Nonfiction Title: *Enhancing Self Esteem*, by D. Trey and J. Carlock.
Software: Contact Lucille U. Hollis, executive vice president. Needs courseware in "the helping professions."
Tips: "Freelance writers should be aware of American Psychological Association style of preparing manuscripts."

ACCENT BOOKS, A division of Accent Publications, 12100 W. 6th Ave., Box 15337, Denver CO 80215. (303)988-5300. Executive Editor: Jerry A. Wilke. Managing Editor: Robert R. Cook. Publishes evangelical Christian paperbacks, the majority of which are nonfiction (including teacher training books), though superior fiction books are considered if they contain underlying Christian message. Averages 18 titles/year. Pays royalty on cover price. Publishes book an average of 1 year after acceptance. Computer printout submissions acceptable; no dot-matrix. Query or submit 2 sample chapters and a brief synopsis of each chapter, together with contents page. SASE. Do not submit full ms unless requested. Reports in 2 months. Free author's information sheet upon request.
Recent Nonfiction Title: *Computer Bible Games*.

ACE SCIENCE FICTION, The Berkley Publishing Group, 200 Madison Ave., New York NY 10016. (212)686-9820. Publishes paperback originals and reprints. Publishes 160 titles/year.
Fiction: Science fiction and fantasy. Query with outline and 3 sample chapters. Reports in 2 months. SASE.

‡ACHERON PRESS, Bear Creek at the Kettle, Friendsville MD 21531. (301)746-5885. Publisher: R.E. Pletta. Publishes trade paperback originals, and hardcover, and trade and mass market paperback reprints. Averages 1-2 titles/year. Pays standard 7.5% royalty on sales, makes outright purchase, or makes purchase agreement with author. Simultaneous and photocopied submissions OK. SASE. Reports in 3 weeks. Book catalog for SASE.
Nonfiction: Textbook and literary. Subjects include art, history, philosophy, religion, academic and children's. "Will consider other categories with financial agreements." Especially looking for 2-3 poetry anthologies; about 4-6 serious monographs. Query or submit outline/synopsis and sample chapters.
Recent Nonfiction Title: *The Choice of Emptiness*, by Jim Ralston.
Fiction: Adventure, confession, experimental, gothic, historical, mainstream (sometimes), mystery, religious (if serious), romance (possibly), science fiction (if serious), short fiction. Prefers serious ideas in all formats. "Our fiction possibilities already exceed our resources." Query or submit outline/synopsis and sample chapters.
Recent Fiction Title: *Sylvia's Father*, by Joan Nevry and Jim Ralston (adult/childrens books).
Poetry: "As many as we accept and thus can afford." Submit collections.
Recent Poetry Title: *Many Times of Year*, by Frank B. Ebersole (philosophic nature).
Tips: "Our audience is generally formally educated, but also those who think."

ACROPOLIS BOOKS, LTD., Subsidiary of Colortone Press, 2400 17th St. NW, Washington DC 20009. (202)387-6805. Publisher: Alphons J. Hackl. Publishes hardcover and trade paperback originals. Averages 25 titles/year. Pays individually negotiated royalty. Publishes book an average of 7 months after acceptance. Electronic submissions OK, but requires hard copy also. Computer printout submissions acceptable; prefers letter-quality to dot-matrix. SASE. Reports in 2 months. Free book catalog.
Nonfiction: How-to, reference and self-help. Subjects include health, beauty/fashion and money management. "We will be looking for manuscripts dealing with fashion and beauty, and self development. We also

will be continuing our teacher books for early childhood education. Our audience includes general adult consumers, professional elementary school teachers and children." Submit outline/synopsis and sample chapters. Reviews artwork/photos as part of ms package.

Recent Nonfiction Title: *Xanadu—The Computerized Home of Tomorrow*, by Roy Mason (computerized housekeeping technology).

‡**ACS PUBLICATIONS, INC.**, Box 16430, San Diego CA 92116-0430. (619)297-9203. Editorial Director: Maritha Pottenger. Publishes trade paperback originals (70%) and reprints (30%). Averages 10 titles/year. Pays 15-20% royalty "on monies received through wholesale and retail sales." No advance. Publishes book an average of 18 months after acceptance. Photocopied submissions OK "if neat." Electronic submissions OK if CP/M compatible with Cromemco, DEC VT180, IBM CPM-86, Osborne, Xerox. 5¼" diskettes. 9 track, 800 bpi, ½ inch magnetic tape; ASCII also acceptable. Computer printout submissions acceptable. SASE. Reports in 4 weeks on queries; 2 months on mss. Free book catalog. Writer's guidelines for 9x12 SAE.

Nonfiction: Self-help, astrology and New Age. Subjects include holistic health alternatives, psychology, numerology, and psychic understanding. "Our most important market is astrology. We are seeking pragmatic, useful, immediately applicable contributions to field; prefer psychological approach. Specific ideas and topics should enhance people's lives. Research also valued. No determinism ('Saturn made made me do it.') No autobiographies. No airy-fairy 'space cadet' philosophizing. Keep it grounded, useful, opening options (not closing doors) for readers." Query or submit outline/synopsis and 3 sample chapters.

Recent Nonfiction Title: *Expanding Astrology's Universe*, by Zipporah Dobyns.

Tips: "Our readers are astrology students and professionals plus the general public interested in increased fulfillment through nontraditional paths."

BOB ADAMS, INC., 2045 Commonwealth Ave., Brighton MA 02135. (617)782-5707. Contact: Submissions Editor. Publishes hardcover and trade paperback originals and software. Averages 10 titles/yr. Pays variable royalty. Publishes book an average of 3 months after acceptance. Simultaneous and photocopied submissions OK. Electronic submissions OK, but requires hard copy also. Computer printout submissions acceptable. SASE. Reports in 1 month on queries; 2 months on mss.

Nonfiction: Specializes in career and job-hunting books. "We are interested in seeing outlines of all manuscripts related to careers, career planning, and job-hunting. We have also published books in other subject areas and will consider titles in all categories of nonfiction. Please submit query first and only send manuscript upon request. We cannot assume responsibility for unsolicited manuscripts." Reviews artwork/photos as part of ms package.

Recent Nonfiction Title: *The Greater Atlanta Job Bank*, by Adams and Fiedler (local employment guide in series).

Software: Career/job-hunting related. Send query letter.

ADDISON-WESLEY PUBLISHING CO., INC., General Books Division, Jacob Way, Reading MA 01867. Publisher: Ann Dilworth. Executive Editor: Dorothy Coover. Publishes hardcover and paperback originals. Publishes 50 titles/year. Pays royalty. Simultaneous and photocopied submissions OK. SASE. Reports in 3-4 weeks. Free book catalog.

Nonfiction: Biography, business/economics, health, how-to, nature, photography, politics, psychology, recreation, science, self-help, sociology and sports. "Also needs books on 'tools for living' related to finance, everyday law, health, education, and parenting by people well-known and respected in their field. No cookbooks or books on transactional analysis." Query, then submit outline/synopsis and 1 sample chapter.

Recent Nonfiction Title: *100 Best Companies to Work for in America*, by Levering, Moskowitz, and Katz.

Tips: Queries/mss may be routed to other editors in the publishing group.

AGLOW PUBLICATIONS, Subsidiary of Women's Aglow Fellowship, Box I, Lynnwood WA 98046-1557. (206)775-7282. Editor: Gwen Weising. Publishes mass market paperback originals. Averages 2-3 books, 2-3 minibooks, 3-4 booklets/year. Pays up to 7½% maximum royalty on retail price "depending on amount of editorial work needed"; buys some mss outright. No advance. Publishes book 12 months after acceptance. Photocopied submissions OK. Computer printout submissions acceptable. SASE. Reports in 1 month on queries; 1½ months on mss. Free book catalog.

Nonfiction: Bible studies, self-help and cookbook. Subjects include religion (Christian only). Accepts nonfiction and fiction translations. "We also publish Bible studies, booklets and mini-books. Please familiarize yourself with our materials before submitting. Our needs and formats are very specific." Query or submit outline/synopsis and first 3 sample chapters or complete ms.

Recent Nonfiction Title: *The Successful Life*, by George Wood.

Fiction: Religious. "We are a Christian women's publishing house. We do not publish secular material or material directed toward a men's audience." No Christian romance. Query or submit outline/synopsis and sample chapters or complete ms.

Recent Fiction Title: *Love Is for Tomorrow*, by Hope Traver (gothic-Christian).

Tips: "Our books are largely bought by evangelical, charismatic Christian women, although many of our books, especially cookbooks have a much larger audience. Because of the increased cost of paper and postage, we are printing shorter publications than previously."

AHSAHTA PRESS, Boise State University, Dept. of English, 1910 University Dr., Boise ID 83725. (208)385-1246. Co-Editor: Tom Trusky. Publishes trade paperback originals. Averages 3 titles/year. Pays 25% royalty on retail price. "Royalty commences with 3rd printing." Publishes books an average of 10 months after acceptance. Simultaneous and photocopied submissions OK. Computer printout submissions acceptable; prefers letter-quality to dot-matrix. SASE. Reports in 2 weeks on queries; 3 months on mss.
Poetry: Contemporary Western American poetry collections. No "rhymed verse; 'songs of the sage'; 'buckaroo ballads'; purple mountain's majesty; coyote wisdom; Jesus-in-the-prairie; or 'nice' verse." Accepts poetry translations from native American languages, Spanish and Basque. Submit 15 samples with SASE between February and April. "Write incredible, original poetry."
Recent Poetry Title: *Hannah's Travel*, by Richard Speakes (Western woman's diary)

*ALASKA NATURE PRESS, Box 632, Eagle River AK 99577. Editor/Publisher: Ben Guild. Publishes hardcover and paperback originals. Plans to offer subsidy publishing "as needed—estimated 10%." Averages 2 titles/year. Pays 10% royalty on retail price; no advance. Publishes book an average of 1 year after acceptance. Simultaneous and photocopied submissions OK. Computer printout submissions acceptable; prefers letter-quality to dot-matrix. SASE. Reports in 2 months.
Nonfiction: Alaska material only: animals, biography, history, how-to, juveniles, nature, photography, poetry, recreation, wildlife, nature and self-help. No hunting or fishing tales. Query or submit outline/synopsis and 2-3 sample chapters or complete ms. Reviews artwork/photos as part of ms package. "As a specialty publishing house (we take *only* Alaskans material) the work *must* have an impact on Alaska or people interested in Alaska—for Alaska."
Fiction: Alaska material only: adventure, historical, romance and suspense. Query editor/publisher. "SASE, please." Reports in 2 months.

ALASKA NORTHWEST PUBLISHING CO., Box 4-EEE, Anchorage AK 99509. Editor and Publisher: Robert A. Henning. Publishes primarily paperback originals. Averages 12 titles/year. Most contracts call for straight 10% royalty. Free book catalog. "Rejections are made promptly, unless we have 3 or 4 possibilities in the same general field, and it's a matter of which one gets the decision. That could take 3 months." Publishes books an average of 2 years after acceptance. Computer printout submissions acceptable; prefers letter-quality to dot-matrix. SASE.
Nonfiction: "Alaska, northern British Columbia, Yukon, Northwest Territories and northwest United States are subject areas. Emphasis on life in the last frontier, history, biography, cookbooks, travel, field guides, juveniles and outdoor subjects. Writer must be familiar with area first-hand. We listen to any ideas." Query with outline, sample chapters, and any relevant photographs preferred. Reviews artwork/photos as part of ms package.

ALBA HOUSE, 2187 Victory Blvd., Staten Island, New York NY 10314. (212)761-0047. Editor-in-Chief: Anthony L. Chenevey. Publishes hardcover and paperback originals (90%) and reprints (10%). Specializes in religious books. "We publish shorter editions than many publishers in our field." Pays 10% royalty on retail price. Averages 15 titles/year. Query. State availability of photos/illustrations. Simultaneous and photocopied submissions OK. Reports in 2-4 weeks. SASE. Free book catalog.
Nonfiction: Publishes philosophy, psychology, religion, sociology, textbooks and Biblical books. Accepts nonfiction translations from French, German or Spanish. Submit outline/synopsis and 1-2 sample chapters.
Recent Nonfiction Title: *The Making of a Pastoral Person*, by Gerald Niklas.
Tips: "We look to new authors." Queries/mss may be routed to other editors in the publishing group.

ALFRED PUBLISHING CO., INC., 15335 Morrison St., Box 5964, Sherman Oaks CA 91413. (818)995-8811. Senior Editor: Joseph Cellini. Publishes Alfred Handy Guides, full-size trade paperbacks and software. Averages 40 titles/year. Pays variable royalty; buys some mss outright; offers negotiable advance. Publishes book an average of 8 months after acceptance. Simultaneous submissions OK. Electronic submissions OK on either double-sided, double-density IBM configured disk or capture keystrokes via modem from author; but requires hard copy also. Computer submissions acceptable; "use good ribbon." SASE. Reports in 2 months. Free book catalog.
Nonfiction: How-to. Subjects include computers and business; will look at other nonfiction titles. Length: 15,000 words minimum. Submit outline/synopsis and 1 sample chapter. Reviews artwork/photos as part of ms package.
Recent Nonfiction Title: *How to Use the IBM Personal Computer*, by Manus.
Software: Contact Joseph Cellini, senior editor.
Tips: "Freelance writers should be aware of the sudden tightening of the computer book market. Publishers with whom I've spoken are being much more selective because booksellers no longer can stock everything."

ALLEGHENY PRESS, Box 220, Elgin PA 16413. Editor: Bonnie Henderson. Publishes hardcover originals, trade paperback originals and reprints. Averages 4 titles/year. Pays 10-20% royalty on wholesale price. Publishes book an average of 4 months after acceptance. Simultaneous and photocopied submissions OK. Computer printout submissions acceptable. SASE. Reports in 2 weeks on queries; 1 month on mss.
Nonfiction: How-to, self-help, textbook on animals, hobbies, nature, recreation, and travel. Especially needs college lab manuals and texts and nature/outdoor books. Publishes for college students, outdoor enthusiasts, and armchair geographers. Submit outline/synopsis and sample chapters.
Recent Nonfiction Title: *Alaska Highway Journal*, by Tomikel (travelogue).

ALLEN & UNWIN, INC., 9 Winchester Terrace, Winchester MA 01890. (617)729-0830. Vice President/ General Manager: Katherine L. Zarker. Publishes hardcover and paperback originals. Averages 150 titles/year. Publishes book an average of 1 year after acceptance. Simultaneous and photocopied submissions OK. Computer printout submissions acceptable. SASE. Reports in 2-3 weeks. Book catalog for SASE.
Nonfiction: Business/economics, history, literature, literary criticism, philosophy, politics, reference, science, sociology, technical, and textbooks. Especially needs advanced university material; must be of international interest. Submit outline/synopsis and sample chapters.

ALLEN PUBLISHING CO., 7324 Reseda Blvd., Reseda CA 91335. Publisher: Michael Wiener. Publishes paperback originals. Averages 3 titles/year. Pays 10% royalty on net price; no advance. Publishes book an average of 6 months after acceptance. Simultaneous and photocopied submissions OK. Computer printout submissions acceptable; prefers letter-quality to dot-matrix. "Author queries welcome from new or established writers. Do not send manuscript or sample chapter." Reports in 2 weeks. SASE "essential." One-page author guidelines available for SASE.
Nonfiction: "Self-help material, 25,000-50,000 words, aimed at wealth-builders. We want to reach the vast audience of opportunity seekers who, for instance, purchased *Lazy Man's Way to Riches*, by Joe Karbo. Material must be original and authoritative, not rehashed from other sources. Most of what we market is sold via mail order in softcover book form. No home fix-it, hobby hints, health or 'cure' books, or 'faith' stories, poetry or fiction. We are a specialty publisher and will not consider any book not fitting the above description." Reviews artwork/photos as part of ms package.
Recent Nonfiction Title: *The Incredible Money Game*.
Tips: "Self-help books are always needed. There never seems to be enough."

ALMAR PRESS, 4105 Marietta Dr., Binghamton NY 13903. (607)722-0265. Editor-in-Chief: A.N. Weiner. Managing Editor: M.F. Weiner. Publishes hardcover and paperback originals and reprints. Averages 6 titles/ year. Pays 10% royalty; no advance. Publishes book an average of 6 months after acceptance. Prefers exclusive submissions; however, simultaneous (if so indicated) and photocopied submissions OK. Electronic submissions OK if compatible with IBM-PC. Reports in 1 month. SASE must be included. Catalog for SASE.
Nonfiction: Publishes business, technical, and consumer books and reports. "These main subjects include general business, financial, travel, career, technology, personal help, hobbies, general medical, general legal, and how-to. *Almar Reports* are business and technology subjects published for management use and prepared in 8½x11 and book format. Publications are printed and bound in soft covers as required. Reprint publications represent a new aspect of our business." Submit outline/synopsis and sample chapters. Reviews artwork/photos as part of ms package. Looks for information in the proposed book that makes it different or unusual enough to attract book buyers.
Recent Nonfiction Title: *How to Buy, Install and Maintain Your Own Telephone Equipment*, by La Carrubba and Zimmer.
Tips: "We look for timely subjects. We do not publish poetry or fiction."

*ALPINE PUBLICATIONS, INC., 1901 S. Garfield St., Loveland CO 80537. Managing Editor: B.J. McKinney. Publishes hardcover and paperback originals. Averages 4 titles/year. Subsidy publishes 25% of books. Pays 7-15% royalty. Publishes book an average of 18 months after acceptance. Simultaneous and photocopied submissions OK. Computer printout submissions acceptable. SASE. Reports in 6 weeks. Free catalog and guidelines for SASE.
Nonfiction: "Alpine Publications is seeking book-length nonfiction mss with illustrations on the care, management, health, training or characteristics of various breeds of dogs, horses and cats. We specialize in books for the owner/breeder, so they must be written by persons knowledgeable in these fields or be well-researched and documented. Our books provide in-depth coverage, present new techniques, and specific 'how-to' instruction. We are not interested in books about reptiles or exotic pets." Reviews artwork/photos as part of ms package. Query with SASE. Prefers outline/synopsis and 3-5 chapters or complete ms.
Recent Nonfiction Title: *The Arabian Horse* by Byford.

*ALYSON PUBLICATIONS, INC., Box 2783, Boston MA 02208. (617)542-5679. Publisher: Sasha Alyson. Publishes trade paperback originals and reprints. Averages 12 titles/year. Subsidy publishes 5% of books.

Pays 8-15% royalty on net price; buys some mss outright for $200-1,000; offers average $600 advance. Publishes book an average of 1 year after acceptance. Computer printout submissions acceptable; prefers letter-quality to dot-matrix. SASE. Reports in 2 weeks on queries; 5 weeks on mss. Looks for "writing ability and content suitable for our house." Book catalog for business-size SAE and 3 first class stamps.

Nonfiction: Subjects include gay/lesbian. "We are especially interested in nonfiction providing a positive approach to gay/lesbian issues." Accepts nonfiction translations. Submit one-page synopsis. Reviews artwork/photos as part of ms package.

Recent Nonfiction Title: *The Men With the Pink Triangle*, by Heinz Heger (history).

Fiction: Gay novels. Accepts fiction translations. Submit one-page synopsis.

Recent Fiction Title: *Between Friends*, by Gillian E. Hanscombe (lesbian fiction).

Tips: "We publish many books by new authors."

AMERICAN ASTRONAUTICAL SOCIETY, (Univelt, Inc., Publisher), Box 28130, San Diego CA 92128. (619)746-4005. Editorial Director: H. Jacobs. Publishes hardcover originals. Averages 8-10 titles/year. Pays 10% royalty on actual sales; no advance. Publishes book an average of 4 months after acceptance. Simultaneous and photocopied submissions OK. Computer printout submissions acceptable. Reports in 4 weeks. SASE. Free book catalog.

Nonfiction: Proceedings or monographs in the field of astronautics, including applications of aerospace technology to Earth's problems. "Our books must be space-oriented or space related. They are meant for technical libraries, research establishments and the aerospace industry worldwide." Submit outline/synopsis and 1-2 sample chapters. Reviews artwork/photos as part of ms package.

Recent Nonfiction Title: *Soviet Lunar and Planetary Exploration*, by N.L. Johnson.

*AMERICAN ATHEIST PRESS, Subsidiary of Society of Separationists, Inc., Box 2117, Austin TX 78768. (512)485-1244. Editor/Director: Jon G. Murray. Publishes trade paperback and mass market paperback originals (50%) and reprints. Averages 15 titles/year. Subsidy publishes 5% of books (100% cost of first printing). Pays 7% royalty on wholesale price. Publishes book an average of 8 months after acceptance. Simultaneous and photocopied submissions OK. Computer printout submissions acceptable. SASE. Reports in 1 week on queries; 1 month on mss. Free book catalog.

Nonfiction: Biography and atheism. Publishes books based on solid research in atheism for "anyone interested in finding out the truth about religion. Accepts nonfiction translations. Reprints of atheist classics do well. We envision more of these, as well as up-to-date refinements on the position of atheism in the world. Synthesize science and atheism, including accurate, detailed biographies of the most significant people and descriptions of the most significant developments. No promotions of religious or superstitious beliefs." Submit the complete ms. Reviews artwork/photos as part of ms package.

Recent Nonfiction Title: *Ingersoll the Magnificent*, by Joseph Lewis.

AMERICAN CATHOLIC PRESS, 1223 Rossell Ave., Oak Park IL 60302. (312)386-1366. Editorial Director: Father Michael Gilligan. Publishes hardcover originals (90%) and hardcover and paperback reprints (10%). "Most of our sales are by direct mail, although we do work through retail outlets." Pays by outright purchase of $25-100; no advance. Publishes book an average of 8 months after acceptance. Simultaneous and photocopied submissions OK. Computer printout submissions acceptable. Reports in 2 months. SASE. Free book catalog.

Nonfiction: "We publish books on the Roman Catholic Liturgy, for the most part books on religious music and educational books and pamphlets. We also publish religious songs for church use, including Psalms, as well as choral and instrumental arrangements. We are very interested in new music, meant for use in church services. Books, or even pamphlets, on the Roman Catholic Mass are especially welcome. We have no interest in secular topics and are not interested in religious poetry of any kind." Query.

Recent Nonfiction Title: *The Role of Music in the New Roman Liturgy*, by W. Herring (educational).

AMERICAN COUNCIL FOR THE ARTS, 570 7th Ave., New York NY 10018. (212)354-6655. Manager of Publishing: Robert Porter. Publishes hardcover and trade paperback originals. Averages 5-8 titles/year. Pays 10-15% royalty on wholesale or retail price. Simultaneous and photocopied submissions OK. Electronic submissions OK if compatible with DECmate II; requires hard copy also. Computer printout submissions acceptable. SASE. Reports in 4 weeks on queries; 2 months on mss. Publishes book an average of 9 months after acceptance. Free book catalog.

Nonfiction: How-to, reference, technical, textbook and professional books on business and economics—nonprofit management, recreation, sociology, travel—all as they pertain to the arts. Books on the arts in areas of management, reference, public policy, and role in society (i.e., city life, travel, recreation, education, etc.). Especially needs books on nonprofit management skills, especially the arts (i.e., marketing, planning); public policy in the arts; resource directories for the arts; and practical discussions of ways the arts can be integrated into specific aspects of everyday life. Publishes for artists, professionals, and trustees of arts organizations and

agencies; university faculty and students; professionals and trustees of nonprofit institutions. No mss on the aesthetics of specific arts disciplines or biographies. Query or submit outline/synopsis and 3-4 sample chapters. Reviews artwork/photos as part of ms package.
Recent Nonfiction Title: *Cultivating the Wasteland: Can Cable Put the Vision Back in TV?*, by Kirsten Beck (reference-media-arts).

AMERICAN PHILATELIC SOCIETY, Box 8000, State College PA 16803. (814)237-3803. Editor: Richard L. Sine. Publishes hardcover originals (85%), and softcover originals (15%). Averages 2 titles/year. Pays 5-10% royalty. Publishes book an average of 2 years after acceptance. Photocopied submissions OK. Electronic submissions OK if compatible with 5¼ disk to Osborne EX I spec. or after approval via telephone on 300 band; requires hard copy also. Computer printout submissions acceptable; prefers letter-quality to dot-matrix. SASE. Reports in 2 weeks on queries; 3+ months on mss. Free book catalog.
Nonfiction: How-to, reference and technical. Subjects include stamp collecting. Accepts nonfiction translations. "We're interested in anything showing solid research into various areas of stamp collecting." Query "if not a member of our society" or submit complete ms or at least 3 sample chapters. Reviews artwork/photos as part of ms package.
Recent Nonfiction Title: *100 Trivia Quizzes on Stamp Collecting*, by Bill Olcheski.

AMERICAN PRESS, 520 Commonwealth Ave., #416, Boston MA 02215. (617)247-0022. Executive Editor: Malcolm Fox. Publishes college level text books and ancillary material. Average 150 titles/year. Pays 5-15% royalty on wholesale price; offers average $200 advance "for typing and/or illustrations." Publishes book an average of 6 months after acceptance. Simultaneous and photocopied submissions OK. Computer printout submissions acceptable; no dot-matrix. SASE. Reports in 6 weeks.
Nonfiction: Everything except modern languages and music. Query or submit outline/synopsis and 1 sample chapter. Reviews artwork/photos as part of ms package.
Recent Nonfiction Title: *Meat Science*, by Smith (text and lab).

‡THE AMERICAN PSYCHIATRIC PRESS, INC., (associated with the American Psychiatric Association), 1400 K St. NW, Washington DC 20005. (202)682-6268. Editor: Tim Clancy. Publishes hardcover and trade paperback originals and software. Averages 35 titles/year, 6-10 trade books/year in its new line. Pays 10% minimum royalty based on all money actually received, maximum varies; offers average $10,000-15,000 advance (depending on subject and nature of book). Publishes book an average of 1 year after acceptance. Simultaneous and photocopied submissions OK (if made clear in cover letter). Electronic submissions OK but requirements vary depending on type of project. Requires hard copy also. Computer printout submissions acceptable; prefers letter-quality to dot-matrix. SASE. Reports in 6 weeks "in regard to an *initial* decision regarding our interest. A *final* decision requires more time (8-12 weeks)." Book catalog for business-size SAE and 1 first class stamp.
Nonfiction: Reference, self-help, technical, textbook, and general nonfiction. Subjects include psychology/psychiatry and sociology (as it relates to psychiatry). Especially looking for books that discuss major psychiatric topics for the general public. Also interested in books for children. No first-person accounts of mental illness or anything not clearly related to psychiatry. Query with outline/synopsis and sample chapters.
Recent Nonfiction Title: *Depression and Its Treatment*, by John H. Greist, M.D., and James W. Jefferson, M.D.
Software: Contact: editor. "We need psychiatric-application software written (and perhaps by) psychiatrists. We are still in the exploratory phase."
Tips: "Our trade line is aimed at the educated lay reader—people who need help dealing with the psychiatric problems that can plague them and their friends and family. These problems range from drug abuse to anorexia nervosa to major psychiatric disorders. Besides these trade books, we publish many professional titles. The purpose of the trade books is to communicate with and educate the public. Since the reading public has become increasingly aware of psychiatric disorders, we anticipate healthy sales. If I were a writer trying to market a book today, I would make absolutely sure I am writing about an important topic and my approach is fresh and innovative. Authors should have a professional background in social science or health (preferably an M.D.). Professional writers may wish to approach a psychiatrist to be a co-author."

AMPHOTO, 1515 Broadway, New York NY 10036. (212)764-7300. Editorial Director: David Lewis. Publishes hardcover and paperback originals. Averages 20 titles/year. Pays royalty, or by outright purchase; offers variable advance. Publishes book an average of 9 months after acceptance. Simultaneous and photocopied submissions OK. Electronic submissions OK, but requires hard copy also. Computer printout submissions acceptable; prefers letter-quality to dot-matrix. Reports in 1 month. SASE. Free book catalog.
Nonfiction: "Photography instruction only. We cover all technical and how-to aspects. Few portfolios or picture books." Submit outline/synopsis, sample chapters and sample photos. Reviews artwork/photos as part of ms package. Looks for "practical value to the readers, marketing info."
Recent Nonfiction Title: *The Fashion Photographer*, by Robert Farber.
Tips: "Consult the photo magazines for book ideas."

*AND BOOKS, 702 S. Michigan, South Bend IN 46618. (219)232-3134. Editor: Janos Szebedinszky. Assistant Editor: Patricia Walsh. Publishes trade paperback originals. Averages 15-25 titles/year. Subsidy publishes 5% of books. Pays standard royalty on retail price. Publishes book an average of 9 months after acceptance. Electronic submissions OK from some systems; query. Computer printout submissions acceptable. Simultaneous and photocopied submissions OK. Disk submissions OK. SASE. Reports in 2 weeks on queries; 5 weeks on mss. Free book catalog.
Nonfiction: Subjects include: current affairs, computers, business, economics, music, philosophy, sociology, media, self-help, natural living, and women's issues. "All material must be literate and salable." No college theses, found-out descriptions, diaries, autobiographies of civil servants, pet stories, hunting and fishing guides, technical journals, investment guides or family genealogies." Query (preferred) or submit 2-3 sample chapters/complete ms. Reviews artwork/photos as part of ms package.
Recent Nonfiction Title: *Black Book of Polish Censorship*, by A. Niczow (current affairs).
Tips: Queries/mss may be routed to other editors in the publishing group.

‡ANDERSEN PRESS, 19-21 Conway St., London, W1P 6BS England. 01-380-0438. Editor: Audrey Adams. Averages 25 titles/year. SASE. Reports in 1 week on queries; 3 weeks on mss. Free book catalog.
Fiction: Children's. Especially looking for children's picture books, about 2,000 words, and short novels for 7-12 age group, about 20,000 words. Query or submit outline/synopsis and sample chapters or complete ms.
Recent Fiction Title: *I Hate My Teddy Bear*, by David McKee (children's picture book).
Tips: "Our books are likely to appeal to parents and children with a lively mind and an eye for the unusual."

*ANDERSON PUBLISHING CO., Suite 501, 602 Main St., Cincinnati OH 45201. (513)421-4393. Editorial Director: Jean Martin. Publishes hardcover, paperback originals, journals and software (75%) and reprints (25%). Publishes 14 titles/year. Subsidy publishes 10% of books. Pays 15-18% royalty; "advance in selected cases." Publishes book an average of 7 months after acceptance. Simultaneous and photocopied submissions OK. Computer printout submissions acceptable; prefers letter-quality to dot-matrix. Reports in 2 months. SASE. Free book catalog.
Nonfiction: Law, and law-related books, and criminal justice criminology texts (justice administration legal series). Query or submit outline/chapters with vitae.
Recent Nonfiction Title: *Biology, Crime and Ethics*, by Janet Katz and Frank Marsh.
Software: Contact Rick Adams.

*AND/OR PRESS, Box 522, Berkeley CA 94701. For information, contact Ronin Publishing, Box 1035, Berkeley CA 94201. (415)540-6278. Publisher: Sebastian Orfali. Publishes paperback originals (95%); and hardcover and paperback reprints (5%). Specializes in "nonfiction works with young urban professional interest. We function as an alternative information resource. 25% are funded by investors and author receives small advance. 75% are funded by author; Ronin works with author to produce, promote and distribute. Also obtains foreign and domestic subsidy rights." Pays 5-10% royalty; offers average advance of 10% of first print run. Averages maximum of 8 titles/year. Publishes ms an average of 6 months after acceptance. Disk submissions OK. Computer printout submissions acceptable. Reports in 2 weeks to 3 months. SASE. Prefers outline with 1-3 sample chapters.
Nonfiction: Publishes appropriate technology, human potential, the future, health and nutrition, travel and psycho-pharmacology books. Also alternative lifestyle books. Reviews artwork/photos as part of ms package.
Recent Nonfiction Title: *The IBM-Personal Computer Handbook*, by Dzintar Draunieks.
Tips: "Ronin recognizes that the author is not merely an outside vendor but is an integral part of all phases of the publishing process. Ronin uses a decentralized form—relying on freelance professionals: artists, editors, etc. Ronin uses a novel distribution approach in addition to the traditional"

ANDREWS AND McMEEL, INC., 4400 Johnson Dr., Fairway KS 66205. Editorial Director: Donna Martin. Publishes hardcover and paperback originals. Publishes 30 titles annually. Pays royalty on retail price. Computer printout submissions acceptable; prefers letter-quality to dot-matrix. "Not currently reading unsolicited mss. Publishing program mainly related to features of Universal Press Syndicate, parent company of Andrews & McMeel."

*ANGEL PRESS/PUBLISHERS, 561 Tyler, Monterey CA 93940. (408)372-1658. Associate Editor: Ruby Grace. Publishes hardcover originals and reprints and mass market paperback originals. Averages 2-4 titles/year. Subsidy publishes 50% of books. Pays negotiable royalty; cash return (actual). No advance. Computer printout submissions acceptable; prefers letter-quality to dot-matrix. Simultaneous and photocopied submissions OK. SASE. Reports in 3 weeks on queries; "several" months on mss.
Nonfiction: Biography, how-to, humor, self-help and spiritual/metaphysical. Subjects include Americana, animals, health, history, hobbies, nature, philosophy, photography, politics, psychology, recreation, religion and sociology. Especially needs "well-written, well-conceived books in the areas of controversy, erotica, feminist, humor, satire; plus any book that is unusually well written and is potentially a good seller in its field."

Query before submitting ms. Reviews artwork/photos as part of ms package.
Recent Nonfiction Title: *Living with Angels*, by Dorie D'Angelo (spiritual/inspirational).
Fiction: Adventure, confession, erotica, fantasy, humor, mainstream, religious, metaphysical, and human potential. "Fiction is not our main thrust. No out-and-out pornography. Professionalism is the key word." Query before submitting ms.
Recent Fiction Title: *Re'lize Whut Ahm Talkin' 'Bout?*, by Steve Chennault (black English).

*ANNA PUBLISHING, INC., Box 218, Ocoee FL 32761. Book publisher and independent book producer/packager. President: Darrell K. Wolfe. Publishes hardcover originals and trade paperback originals and reprints. Averages 20 titles/year. Subsidy publishes 2 books/year, based on subject matter. "We do not solicit subsidized books." Pays 10-20% royalty on wholesale or retail price; buys some mss outright for $250-1,500. No advance. Photocopied submissions OK. No simultaneous submissions. SASE. Reports in 2 weeks on queries; 1 month on mss. Book catalog for 6x9 SAE and 35¢ postage.
Nonfiction: Cookbook, how-to, illustrated book, reference (psychology) and physical fitness. Subjects include cooking and foods, health and sports medicine. Publishes for college instructors, professionals, and advanced or advancing physical fitness experts. Query or submit outline/synopsis and sample chapters.
Recent Nonfiction Title: *The Irrepressible Saint*, by Harriet Mead.

APPLE PRESS, 5536 SE Harlow, Milwaukie OR 97222. (503)659-2475. Senior Editor: Judith S. Majors. Publishes trade paperback originals. Averages 3-5 titles/year. Pays 7-10% royalty on retail price; offers average advance $200-500. Publishes book an average of 6 months after acceptance. Computer printout submissions acceptable "as long as they're legible." Prefers letter-quality to dot-matrix. SASE. Reports in 4-6 weeks.
Nonfiction: Health and self-help. Query first. Looks for "well-done research and accuracy." SASE.
Recent Nonfiction Title: *Sugar Free Kid's Cookery*, (calculated youth cookbook).

APPLE-WOOD BOOKS, INC., Box 2870, Cambridge MA 02139. (617)923-9337. Editorial Director: Phil Zuckerman. Publishes hardcover and trade paperback originals. Averages 12 titles/year. Pays 10-15% royalty on wholesale price; offers $250-2,500 advance. Publishes book an average of 18 months after acceptance. Simultaneous and photocopied submissions OK. Computer printout submissions acceptable. SASE. Reports in 3 weeks on queries; 3 months on mss. Book catalog for 8½x11 SAE and 2 first class stamps.
Nonfiction: Subjects include biography, history, politics, literature and humor. "We publish books for people who grew up in the 50s and 60s."
Recent Nonfiction Title: *A Guide to Writer's Homes in New England*, by Miriam Levine (guidebook).
Fiction: "We don't consider fiction by category, but by quality. We publish the future great American writers." Query or submit outline/synopsis, sample chapters and SASE.
Recent Fiction Title: *The Personal History, Adventures, Experiences & Observations of Peter Leroy*, by Eric Kraft.

ARBOR HOUSE, Subsidiary of Hearst Corp., 235 E. 45th St., New York NY 10017. Publisher: Eden Collinsworth. Editorial Director: Bill Thompson. Publishes hardcover and trade paperback originals and selected reprints. Pays standard royalty; offers negotiable advance. Publishes book an average of 9 months after acceptance. Computer printout submissions acceptable; prefers letter-quality to dot-matrix. SASE. Free book catalog.
Nonfiction: Autobiography, cookbook, how-to, and self-help. Subjects include Americana (possibly), art (possibly), business and economics, cooking and foods, health, history, politics, psychology, recreation, inspiration and sports. Query or submit outline/synopsis and sample chapters to "The Editors". Reviews artwork/photos as part of ms package.
Recent Nonfiction Title: *Tennessee Williams: An Intimate Biography*, by Dakin Williams.
Fiction: "Quality fiction—everything from romance to science fiction, fantasy, adventure and suspense." Query or submit outline/synopsis and sample chapters to "The Editors."
Recent Fiction Title: *Murder on Embassy Row*, by Margaret Truman.
Tips: "Freelance writers should be aware of a greater emphasis on agented properties and market resistance to untried fiction."

ARCHITECTURAL BOOK PUBLISHING CO., INC., 10 E. 40th St., New York NY 10016. (212)689-5400. Editor: Walter Frese. Averages 10 titles/year. Royalty is percentage of retail price. Prefers queries, outlines and 2 sample chapters with number of illustrations. Reports in 2 weeks. SASE.
Nonfiction: Publishes architecture, decoration, and reference books on city planning and industrial arts. Accepts nonfiction translations. Also interested in history, biography, and science of architecture and decoration.

ARCO PUBLISHING, INC., 215 Park Ave. S., New York NY 10003. Senior Editor, Consumer Books (trade): Madelyn Larsen. Pays advance against royalties. Simultaneous submissions OK; "inform us if so." Computer printout submissions acceptable; no dot-matrix. Materials submitted without sufficient postage will not be returned.

Nonfiction: Publishes business; needle crafts; pet care and training; horses (all aspects); science (young adult); how-to; and militaria. "Our readers are people who want information, instruction and technical know-how from their books. They want to learn something tangible." No fiction, poetry, cookbooks, biographies, auto-biographies, religion or personal "true" accounts of persons or pets. Prefers letter of inquiry with a contents page and 1 sample chapter. Educational Books, Linda Bernbach, Editor; Career guidance, test preparation and study guides, Ellen Lichtenstein, Editor. Same requirements as for consumer books.

ARCsoft PUBLISHERS, Box 132, Woodsboro MD 21798. (301)845-8856. Publisher: Anthony R. Curtis. Publishes trade paperback originals and software. Averages 20 titles/year. Pays 10% royalty on net sales; offers variable advance. Publishes book an average of 3 months after acceptance. Computer printout submissions acceptable; no dot-matrix. SASE. Reports in 1 month on queries; 10 weeks on mss. Free book catalog.
Nonfiction: Technical. "We publish books in personal computing, especially for beginners. In computers we need books of programs for as many different brand names of computers as are on the market." Accepts nonfiction translations. Query or submit outline/synopsis and 1 sample chapter. Reviews artwork/photos as part of ms package. Looks for "ability to cover (our desired) subject thoroughly, writing quality and interest."
Software: Publishes brief programs for beginners.
Recent Nonfiction Title: *IBM PCjr Games Programs*, by Howard Bridges.

*M. ARMAN PUBLISHING, INC., Suite 200, 175 W. Granada Blvd., Ormond Beach FL 32074. (904)673-5576. Mailing address: Box 785, Ormond Beach FL 32074. Contact: Mike Arman. Publishes trade paperback originals, reprints and software. Averages 6-8 titles/year. Subsidy publishes 20% of books. Pays 10% royalty on wholesale price. No advance. Publishes book (on royalty basis) an average of 6 months after acceptance; 6 weeks on subsidy basis. Electronic submissions OK on 5¼ disk, WordStar or Kaypro format; requires hard copy also. Photocopied submissions OK. Computer printout submissions acceptable. SASE. Reports in 1 week on queries; 3 weeks on mss. Book catalog for business-sized SASE with 37¢ postage.
Nonfiction: How-to, reference, technical, textbook on hobbies, recreation, sports, and travel. Accepts nonfiction translations. "Motorcycle and aircraft technical books only." Publishes for enthusiasts. Submit complete ms. Reviews artwork/photos as part of ms package.
Recent Nonfiction Title: *A Guide to Autogyros*, by Crowe (construction, flight training, operation of autogyros).
Fiction: "Motorcycle or aircraft-related only." Accepts fiction translations. Immediate needs are "slim," but not non-existent. Submit complete ms.
Recent Fiction Title: *Motorcycle Summers*, by Gately (G-rated short stories about motorcycling).

*‡JAMES ARNOLD & CO., Suite 138, 18533 Burbank Blvd., Tarzana CA 91356. (818)888-4883. Publisher: James A. Arnold. Averages 6 titles/year. Subsidy publishes 25% of books depending on proposed market and money needed for development. Pays 10% maximum royalty on retail price. Photocopied submissions OK. Computer printout submissions acceptable. SASE. Reports as soon as possible on queries, 1 month on mss. Free book catalog.
Nonfiction: How-to and self help. Subjects include business and economics, hobbies, psychology and recreation. Especially looking for how-to subject matter: gambling, business, and general instructional material. Not interested in cookbooks. Query or submit outline/synopsis and sample chapters.
Recent Nonfiction Title: *Come Seven: The Crap Shooters Manual*, by Frank Hanback (gambling).
Fiction: Erotica. Query. All unsolicited mss are returned unopened.
Tips: "Our books are written in easy-to-understand language. We want to reach the non-reader or occasional reader. We also specialize in books on tape accompanied with a conventional-type, fully illustrated book."

‡ARROW PRESS, Suite 251, 239 Washington St., Boston MA 02108. Publishes hardcover and mass market paperback originals. Averages approximately 48 titles/year. Makes outright purchase, $1,500 minimum; offers average 20% advance. Simultaneous and photocopied submissions OK. Computer printout submissions acceptable. Include 20 *loose* first class stamps with each MS submitted. Reports in 1 month. Book catalog for 6x9 SAE, and 5 *loose* first class stamps.
Nonfiction: "Adult love."
Fiction: Erotica, fantasy, historical, horror, mystery, romance and suspense. Submit complete ms.
Tips: Audience is 16 years old and well educated.

ART DIRECTION BOOK COMPANY, 10 E. 39th St., New York NY 10016. (212)889-6500. Editorial Director: Don Barron. Senior Editor: Lawrence Oberwager. Publishes hardcover and paperback originals. Publishes 15-20 titles/year. Pays 10% royalty on retail price; offers average advance: $1,000. Publishes book an average of 1 year after acceptance. Photocopied submissions OK. SASE. Computer printout submissions acceptable; no dot-matrix. Reports in 3 months. Free book catalog.
Nonfiction: Commercial art, ad art how-to, and textbooks. Reviews artwork/photos as part of ms package.

Query first with outline/synopsis and 1 sample chapter. "We are interested in books for the professional advertising art field—that is, books for art directors, designers, et. al; also entry level books for commercial and advertising art students in such fields as typography, photography, paste-up, illustration, clip-art, design, layout and graphic arts."

Recent Nonfiction Title: *Art as a Living*, by Ruth Corbett.

*ARTECH HOUSE, INC., 610 Washington St., Dedham MA 02026. (617)326-8220. Editor: Dennis Ricci. Publishes hardcover originals and software. Averages 15-18 titles/year. Subsidy publishes 7% of books. Offers 10-15% royalty on net price; no advance. Publishes book an average of 6 months after acceptance. Simultaneous and photocopied submissions OK. Electronic submissions OK on disk or tape only, but requires hard copy also. "No telecommunications capability." Computer printout submissions acceptable. SASE. Reports in 6 months. Catalog available.

Nonfiction: Technical. "High quality treatments of the state-of-the-art in electronic technologies, including radar, microwave, telecommunications, computers and medical technology subjects. We do *not* want anything non scientific or technical in any area not cited above." Submit outline/synopsis and sample chapters or complete ms. Reviews artwork/photos as part of ms package.

Recent Nonfiction Title: *Introduction to Microwaves*, by Fred Gardiol.

Software: Publishes software "only as a supplement to a book. Software must be machine specific and be produced and tested by the author." Contact: William M. Bazzy.

Tips: Publishes software "only as a supplement to a book. Software must be machine-specific and be produced and tested by the author."

‡ASHTON-TATE PUBLICATIONS GROUP, Division Ashton-Tate, 10150 W. Jefferson Blvd., Culver City CA 90230. (213)204-5570. Editor: Bill Jordan. Publishes trade paperback originals. Averages 30 titles/year. Pays royalty on actual cash received. Simultaneous and photocopied submissions OK. SASE. Reports in 3 weeks on query; 1 month on mss. Free book catalog.

Nonfiction: Technical, microcomputer-related. Especially looking for microcomputer hardware and software topic areas for introductory through advanced readers. No non-computer related material. Submit outline/synopsis and sample chapters.

Recent Nonfiction Title: *Everyman's Database Primer*, by Robert Byers (computer language).

Tips: Audience is "specific software end-users, software application developers, and general audience/microcomputer enthusaists."

ASSOCIATED BOOK PUBLISHERS, INC., Box 5657, Scottsdale AZ 85261-5657. (602)998-5223. Editor: Ivan Kapetanovic. Publishes hardcover and paperback originals and software. "Offer outright payment or standard minimum book contract. We have not made a practice of giving advances." Averages 3-4 titles/year. Will consider photocopied submissions. Computer printout submissions acceptable. Submit outline and 1 sample chapter, or submit complete ms. Reports in 3 weeks. "We are not responsible for unsolicited materials unless return postage is enclosed."

Nonfiction: "We would especially consider publication of books suitable for elementary, junior high and high school students, in the field of guidance, including occupational information, college entrance and orientation, personal and social problems and how to pass tests of all kinds. In addition to the categories listed below, we are interested in bibliographies in all subject areas and in textbooks for elementary through high school grades. Books published in following categories: economics, linguistics, dictionaries, education, children's books, cooking and nutrition, gardening, history, hobby and crafts, self-help and how-to, sociology and guidance. Accepts nonfiction translations. No strict length requirements." Reviews artwork/photos as part of ms package.

Recent Nonfiction Title: *Croatia and the Croatians*, by Prpic.

Software: Publishes educational software.

*ASSOCIATED BOOKSELLERS, 147 McKinley Ave., Bridgeport CT 06606. (203)366-5494. Editor-in-Chief: Alex M. Yudkin. Hardcover and paperback originals. Averages 8 titles/year. Pays 10% royalty on wholesale or retail price; advance averages $500. Subsidy publishes 10% of books. Subsidy publishing is offered "if the marketing potential is limited." Query. Simultaneous and photocopied submissions OK. Computer printout submissions acceptable; no dot-matrix. Reports in 2-4 weeks. SASE. Book catalog for SASE.

Nonfiction: Publishes how-to, hobbies, recreation, self-help, and sports books.

Recent Title: *Kashi-No-Bo*, by Claude St. Denise.

ATHENEUM PUBLISHERS, 597 5th Ave., New York NY 10017. Editor-in-Chief: Thomas A. Stewart. Simultaneous and photocopied submissions OK. Electronic submissions OK, but requires hard copy also. Computer printout submissions acceptable. Reports in 6 weeks. Publishes book an average of 9 months after acceptance. SASE.

Nonfiction: General trade material dealing with politics, psychology, history, cookbooks, sports, biographies

and general interest. Length: 40,000 words minimum. Query or submit outline/synopsis and a sample chapter.
Recent Nonfiction Title: *Son*, by Jack Olsen.
Tips: "We would prefer not to have artwork or photographs accompany unsolicited manuscripts."

ATHENEUM PUBLISHERS, INC., Juvenile Department, 597 5th Ave., New York NY 10017. Editor: Jean Karl. Publishes hardcover originals and paperback reprints. Averages 55 titles/year. Publishes book an average of 18 months after acceptance. Computer printout submissions acceptable. Reports in 6 weeks. SASE.
Nonfiction: Juvenile books for ages 3-16. Picture books for ages 3-8. "We have no special needs; we publish whatever comes in that interests us." Accepts artwork/photos "of professional quality."
Tips: "Most submissions are poorly conceived, poorly written. Think deeper and learn to put words on paper in a way that conveys that depth to readers, without being didactic."

ATHLETIC PRESS, Box 80250, Pasadena CA 91108. (213)283-3446. Editor-in-Chief: Donald Duke. Publishes paperback originals. Specializes in sports conditioning books. Pays 10% royalty; no advance. Publishes book an average of 1 year after acceptance. Averages 3 titles/year. Query or submit complete ms. "Illustrations will be requested when we believe ms is publishable." Simultaneous and photocopied submissions OK. Computer printout submissions acceptable. Reports in 4 weeks. SASE. Free book catalog.
Nonfiction: Publishes sports books.

ATLANTIC MONTHLY PRESS, 8 Arlington St., Boston MA 02116. (617)536-9500. Director: Upton Birnie Brady. Associate Director, Children's Books: Melanie Kroupa. Managing Editor: Natalie Greenberg. Senior Editor: Peter Davison. Averages 36 titles/year. "Advance and royalties depend on the nature of the book, the stature of the author, and the subject matter." Computer printout submissions acceptable. SASE.
Nonfiction: Publishes general nonfiction, biography, autobiography, science, philosophy, the arts, belles lettres, history and world affairs. Looks for "intelligence, coherence, organization, good writing (which comes first), neatness of presentation—and a covering letter." Length: 70,000-200,000 words.
Recent Nonfiction Title: *What Men Don't Tell Women*, by Roy Blount Jr.
Fiction: Publishes general fiction, juveniles and poetry. Length: 70,000-200,000 words.
Recent Fiction Title: *The Collected Stories of Sean O'Faolain*, distributed by Little, Brown and Company.

‡***ATLANTIS PUBLISHING COMPANY**, 5432 Hallandale Beach Blvd., Hollywood FL 33023. (305)981-1009. President: Dr. Arthur G. Haggis. Publishes hardcover, trade paperback and mass market paperback originals. Averages 5 titles/year. Subsidy publishes 10% of books based on "book subjects and how well written." Pays 7-15% royalty on wholesale price. Offers no advance. Simultaneous submissions OK with notation as to other publishers contacted. Computer printout submissions acceptable; no dot-matrix. SASE. Reports in 1 month. Free book catalog.
Nonfiction: How-to, self-help, and textbooks. Subjects include health, spelling, beginning language and numbers, computers. "We have no plans to publish nonfiction books other than present series of health, spelling, beginning language and number development, and computer texts." Submit outline/synopsis and sample chapters or complete ms.
Recent Nonfiction Title: *Atlantis Beginning Language and Number Development Program Book 1*, by Dr. Arthur G. Haggis and Lewanna S. Haggis (pre-kindergarten-grade 1).
Tips: "Our books are for preschool through grades 12, remedial education, adult basic education, and home study programs (book style)."

AUGSBURG PUBLISHING HOUSE, 426 S. 5th St., Box 1209, Minneapolis MN 55440. (612)330-3432. Director, Book Department: Roland Seboldt. Publishes hardcover and paperback originals (95%) and paperback reprints (5%). Publishes 45 titles/year. Pays 10-15% royalty on retail price; offers variable advance. Simultaneous and photocopied submissions OK. Computer printout submissions acceptable; prefers letter-quality to dot-matrix. Reports in 6 weeks. SASE.
Nonfiction: Health, psychology, religion, self-help and textbooks. "We are looking for manuscripts that apply scientific knowledge and Christian faith to the needs of people as individuals, in groups and in society." Query or submit outline/synopsis and a sample chapter or submit complete ms.
Recent Nonfiction Title: *The Caring Question*, by Don and Nancy Tubesing.
Tips: "We are looking for good contemporary stories with a Christian theme for the young readers in age categories 8-11, 12-14, and 15 and up." Submit complete ms.

The double dagger (‡) before a listing indicates that the listing is new in this edition. New markets are often the most receptive to freelance contributions.

‡**AUGUST HOUSE, INC.**, Box 3223, Little Rock AR 72203-3223. (501)376-4516. Associate Director: Liz Smith Parkhurst. Publishes hardcover and trade paperback originals and hardcover and trade paperback reprints. Averages 6-8 titles/year. Pays 6-10% royalty on wholesale price. Simultaneous and photocopied submissions OK. Computer printout submissions acceptable; prefers letter-quality to dot-matrix. SASE. Reports in 3 weeks on queries; 3-9 months on mss. Book catalog for 6x9 SAE and 3 first class stamps.

Nonfiction: Biography, "coffee table" book, how-to and humor. Subjects include Americana, history, politics and folklore. Especially looking for Southern history and folklore, and "how-to" books on specific crafts. Query.

Recent Nonfiction Title: *Africa Alone: Odyssey of an American Traveler*, by Sandy McMath (recit de voyage).

Fiction: Adventure, ethnic, experimental, fantasy, historical, humor, mainstream, mystery, religious, suspense and western. Especially looking for novels set in specific Southern cities. No romance, gothic, horror or erotica. Query.

Recent Fiction Title: *Pardon My Pandemonium*, by Dee Brown (mystery).

Poetry: Submit complete ms.

Recent Poetry Title: *Journey of the Medicine Man*, by Red Hawk (modern).

Tips: "If I were a writer trying to market a book today, I would at least *try* to get an agent, especially if I had some publishing credit. Failing that, I would send out queries, not asking permission to send a ms but asking for submission guidelines. Queries should be directed personally to publishers and should not look like form letters."

AVALON BOOKS, Thomas Bouregy & Co., Inc., 22 E. 60th St., New York NY 10022. Editor: Rita Brenig. "We like the writers to focus on the plot, drama, and characters, not the background." Publishes hardcover originals. Publishes 60 titles/year. Pays $400 advance which is applied against sales of the first 3,500 copies of the book. Computer printout submissions acceptable; no dot-matrix. SASE. Reports in 12 weeks. Free book list for SASE.

Fiction: "We want well-plotted, fast-moving light romances, romance-mysteries, gothics, westerns, and nurse-romance books of about 50,000 words." Submit one-page synopsis or submit complete ms. No sample chapters or long outlines. SASE.

Recent Fiction Title: *Magic Island*, by Louise Bergstrom.

AVANT BOOKS, 3719 Sixth Ave., San Diego CA 92103. Publisher: Michael Gosney. Publishes trade paperback originals. Averages 8 titles/year. Pays 9-20% royalty on wholesale price. Submit outlines and 2 sample chapters only. Simultaneous (if so advised) and photocopied submissions OK. Electronic submissions OK if compatible with IBM PC or Kaypro 4. Computer printout submissions acceptable; prefers letter-quality to dot-matrix. SASE. Reports in 2 months on queries. Book catalog $1.50.

Nonfiction: Subjects include art, health, nature, philosophy, psychology and social commentary. "Books dealing with contemporary thought, global culture, consciousness, vital ecological issues, social movements, 'new renaissance' art and writing. Also some 'how-to' and 'self-help' titles." No overly esoteric, political, single-group or viewpoint orientation (as opposed to more universal, holistic, planetary). Submit outline/synopsis and sample chapters only. Reviews artwork/photos as part of ms package.

Recent Nonfiction Title: *Arcosanti*, by Paolo Soleri.

Fiction: "Some experimental fiction. Titles which represent the creative leading edge, East/West synthesis, ecological awareness, consciousness, and 'new renaissance' mythologies. No '60s throwbacks, overly narcissistic works, overly specialized subjects, or scenarios." Submit outline/synopsis and sample chapters only.

Recent Fiction Title: *Buddha*, by Nikos Kazantzakis (drama).

*****AVI PUBLISHING CO.**, 250 Post Rd. E., Box 831, Westport CT 06881. (203)226-0738. Editor-in-Chief: James R. Ice, Ph.D. Hardcover and paperback originals. Specializes in publication of books in the fields of food science and technology, food service, nutrition, hospitality, health, agriculture and aquaculture. Pays 10% royalty, based on list price on the first 3,000 copies sold; $500 average advance (paid only on typing and art bills). "Subsidy publishes symposia; subject matter within the areas of food, nutrition, agriculture and health, endorsed by appropriate professional organizations in the area of our specialty." Publishes 30 titles/year. Subsidy publishes 10% of books. Publishes book an average of 1 year after acceptance. Electronic submissions OK "with permission," but requires hard copy also. Computer printout submissions acceptable; prefers letter-quality to dot-matrix. Reports in 1 month. SASE. Free book catalog.

Nonfiction: Publishes books on foods, agriculture, nutrition and health, scientific, technical, textbooks and reference works. Accepts nonfiction translations. Query or "submit a 500-word summary, a preface, a table of contents, estimated number of pages in manuscript, 1-2 sample chapters, when to be completed and a biographical sketch." Reviews artwork/photos as part of ms package.

Recent Nonfiction Title: *Leaf Protein Concentrates*, by Telck and Graham.

*AVIATION BOOK CO., 1640 Victory Blvd., Glendale CA 91201. (213)240-1771. Editor: Walter P. Winner. Publishes hardcover and paperback originals and reprints. Averages 5 titles/year. Subsidy publishes 2% of books. Pays royalty on retail price. No advance. Query with outline. Publishes book an average of 6 months after acceptance. Computer printout submissions acceptable; prefers letter-quality dot-matrix. Reports in 2 months. SASE. Free book catalog.
Nonfiction: Aviation books, primarily of a technical nature and pertaining to pilot training. Young adult level and up. Also aeronautical history. Asks of ms, "Does it fill a void in available books on subject?" or, "Is it better than available material?" Reviews artwork/photos as part of ms package.
Recent Nonfiction Title: *Airmen's Information Manual*, by Winner (pilot training).

AVON BOOKS, 1790 Broadway, New York NY 10019. President/Publisher: Walter Meade. Editorial Director: Page Cuddy. Publishes paperback originals (48%) and paperback reprints (52%). Averages 300 titles/year. Pay and advance are negotiable. Publishes ms an average of 2 years after acceptance. Simultaneous and photocopied submissions OK. Computer printout submissions acceptable; prefers letter-quality to dot matrix. SASE. Reports in 8 weeks. Buys 10-20 unsolicited mss/year. Free book catalog for SASE.
Nonfiction: Animals, biography, business/economics, cookbooks/cooking, health, history, hobbies, how-to, humor, juveniles, music, nature, philosophy, photography, politics, psychology, recreation, reference, religion, science, self-help, sociology, and sports. No textbooks. Submit outline/synopsis and first three chapters. SASE.
Recent Nonfiction Title: *Adams Companion*, by Ramsey J. Benson and Jack B. Rochester.
Fiction: Adventure, fantasy, gothic, historical, mainstream, mystery, religious, romance, science fiction, suspense, and western. Submit outline/synopsis, first three sample chapters and SASE.
Recent Fiction Title: *Stormfire*, by Christine Monson.

AZTEX CORP., 1126 N. 6th Ave., Box 50046, Tucson AZ 85703. (608)882-4656. Publishes hardcover and paperback originals. Averages 15 titles/year. Pays 10% royalty. Publishes book an average of 18 months after acceptance. Computer printout submissions acceptable; prefers letter-quality to dot-matrix. Electronic and disk submissions OK but inquire about compability; requires hard copy also. SASE. Reports in 3 months. Free catalog. *Author-Publisher Handbook* $3.95.
Nonfiction: "We specialize in transportation subjects (how-to and history) and early childhood education." Accepts nonfiction translations. Submit outline/synopsis and 2 sample chapters or complete ms. Reviews artwork/photos as part of ms package. Looks for "accuracy, thoroughness, and interesting presentation."
Recent Nonfiction Title: *MGA—A History and Restoration Guide* , by Robert Vitrikas.

BAHAMAS INTERNATIONAL PUBLISHING CO., LTD., Box 1914, Nassau, The Bahamas. (809)322-1149. Editorial Director: Michael A. Symonette. Publishes paperback originals. Averages 18-24 titles/year. Buys mss outright for $250-1,000; offers average $250 advance. Publishes ms an average of 6 months after acceptance. Simultaneous and photocopied submissions OK. Electronic submissions OK "only when we request them." Computer printout submissions acceptable; prefers letter-quality to dot-matrix. SASE. Reports in 6 weeks. Book catalog $3. Sample copies of books $6.95 postpaid.
Imprints: The Island Press, Ltd., The Herald, Ltd., Inter-Continental Publishing Co., and The Lighthouse Press.
Nonfiction: Biography. Subjects include history. Query. "Unsolicited mss are not accepted."
Recent Nonfiction Title: *Discovery of a Nation* (illustrated history of The Bahamas).
Fiction: Mainstream. "We will consider only mainstream fiction of the highest literary quality, suitable for European as well as North American readers. We are not really interested in fiction built around the standard commercial formula of today. We are concerned with substantial themes and the development of ideas. There should be strong characterization and a meaningful story line. Ours is a limited but highly literate international market. *Absolutely no* romances, gothics, science fiction, confessions, occult, fantasy, or variations on these themes in any form." Query. "Unsolicited mss are not accepted."
Recent Fiction Title: *The Best of the Herald* (anthology).
Tips: "We are currently accepting short fiction for a monthly international review. The same guidelines apply with approximately 6-8 stories per issue and payment on publication. Query first. As publishers of the city magazine, *Nassau*, we are also looking for short stories and articles set in the Bahamas or other islands of the Caribbean. Query first."

BAKER BOOK HOUSE COMPANY, Box 6287, Grand Rapids MI 49506. (616)676-9185. Editorial Director: Dan Van't Kerkhoff. Publishes hardcover and paperback originals (40%) and paperback reprints (60%). Averages 100 titles/year. Pays 5-10% royalty. Also buys booklet-length mss by outright purchase: $250-500. No advance. Simultaneous and photocopied submissions OK. Computer printout submissions acceptable "if legible"; prefers letter-quality to dot-matrix. SASE. Reports in 4 weeks. Book catalog for large SASE.
Nonfiction: Humor, juvenile, philosophy, psychology, religion, self-help; and textbook. "All must be of religious nature." Submit outline/synopsis and 2-3 sample chapters (more, if chapters are brief) or submit complete ms.

Recent Nonfiction Title: *Shaping Your Child's Sexual Identity*, by George A. Rekers.
Fiction: "Juvenile adventure with religious flavor." Submit complete ms.
Recent Fiction Title: *Uncle Jask Stories*, by Helen Noordewier.

BALE BOOKS, Box 2727, New Orleans LA 70176. Editor-in-Chief: Don Bale Jr. Publishes hardcover and paperback originals and reprints. Offers standard 10-12½-15% royalty contract on wholesale or retail price; no advance. Sometimes purchases mss outright for $500. Averages 10 titles/year. Publishes book an average of 3 years after acceptance. "Most books are sold through publicity and ads in the coin newspapers." Book catalog for SASE. Will consider photocopied submissions. Computer printout submissions acceptable. "Send ms by registered or certified mail. Be sure copy of ms is retained." Reports usually within several months. SASE.
Nonfiction: "Our specialty is coin and stock market investment books; especially coin investment books and coin price guides. We are open to any new ideas in the area of numismatics. The writer should write for a teen-age through adult level. Lead the reader by the hand like a teacher, building chapter by chapter. Our books sometimes have a light, humorous treatment, but not necessarily." Looks for "good English, construction and content, and sales potential." Submit outline/synopsis and 3 sample chapters.
Recent Nonfiction Title: *How to Find Valuable, Old Scarce Coins.*

BALLANTINE BOOKS, Division of Random House, 201 E. 50th St., New York NY 10022. "Science fiction and fantasy should be sent to Judy Lynn, Del Rey editor-in-chief, Del Rey Books. Proposals for trade books, poster books, calendars, etc., should be directed to Joelle Delbourgo, editor of trade books. Proposals including sample chapters for contemporary and historical fiction and romances should be sent to Pamela Strickler, senior editor of Ballantine or Barbara Dicks, senior editor of Fawcett." Publishes trade and mass market paperback originals and reprints. Royalty contract varies. Published 350 titles last year; about 25% were originals.
Nonfiction: General nonfiction. "Not interested in poetry; books under 50,000 words are too short for consideration. Since we are a mass market house, books which have a heavy regional flavor would be inappropriate for our list."
Fiction: General fiction, science fiction and fantasy.
Recent Title: *Banker*, by Dick Francis.

BALLINGER PUBLISHING CO., 54 Church St., Harvard Square, Cambridge MA 02138. (617)492-0670. Editor: Carol Franco. Publishes hardcover originals. Averages 70 titles/year. Pays royalty by arrangement. Simultaneous and photocopied submissions OK. Computer printout submissions acceptable; prefers letter-quality to dot-matrix. SASE. Reports in 1 month. Free book catalog.
Nonfiction: Professional and reference books in social and behavioral sciences, energy, economics, business, finance, high technology, and international relations. Submit outline/synopsis and sample chapters or submit complete ms.
Recent Nonfiction Title: *Global Stakes: The Future of High Technology in America*, by James Botkin, Dan Dimancescu and Ray Stata.

BANKERS PUBLISHING CO., 210 South St., Boston MA 02111. (617)426-4495. Executive Editor: Robert I. Roen. Publishes hardcover originals. Averages 7 titles/year. Publishes book an average of 8 months after acceptance. Pays 10-15% royalty on both wholesale and retail price; buys some mss outright for negotiable fee. SASE. Computer printout submissions acceptable. Reports in 2 months. Book catalog for 5½x8½ SAE and 1 first class stamp.
Nonfiction: How-to reference texts on banking only for banking professionals. "Because of their nature, our books remain useful for many years (it is not unusual for a title to remain in print for 5-10 years). However, some of our technical titles are revised and updated frequently." Looks for "the ability of the author to communicate practical, how-to technical knowledge to the reader in an understanding way." Submit outline/synopsis and 2 sample chapters.
Recent Nonfiction Title: *Bank Audits and Examination*, by John Savage.
Tips: "As long as a book contains technical, necessary information about doing a particular banking job, it does well. We try to provide bankers with information and guidance not available anywhere else. Most of our writers are experienced bankers, but we are willing to consider a professional researcher/writer for some projects. We seek to work with new authors."

BANTAM BOOKS, INC., 666 5th Ave., New York NY 10103. Imprints include Skylark, For Young Readers, Sweet Dreams, Peacock Press, Loveswept, New Age Books, Windstone, and Bantam Classics. (212)765-6500. President/CEO: Lou Wolfe. Executive Vice President/COO: Alberto Vitale. Vice President/Publisher: Jack Romanos. Editorial Director/Vice President, Adult Fiction and Nonfiction Books: Linda Grey. Publishes mass market, trade paperback, and hardcover books for adults, young adults (ages 12-17), and young readers (ages 8-12), fiction and nonfiction reprints and originals. Pays variable royalty and advance. Publisher does not accept queries or unsolicited manuscripts.

Nonfiction: Brad Miner, Senior Editor, Religious and Inspirational Books; Toni Burbank, Executive Editor (women's studies, school and college); Fred Klein, Vice President and Executive Editor/Media; Senior Editors: Linda Price (cookbooks, mysteries, health); Linda Cunningham (business, finance); LuAnn Walther (school and college, classics); Tobi Sanders (science); Nessa Rapoport (Bantam Jewish Bookshelf).
Fiction: Irwyn Applebaum, Publishing Manager (westerns); Peter Guzzardi (sports and general fiction); Carolyn Nichols (Loveswept); Brad Miner (war series); Lou Aronica, Editor, Science Fiction and Fantasy; Kate Miciak, Administrative Editor (general fiction, mysteries); Elizabeth Barrett, Associate Editor, Loveswept. Young Adult titles: Ron Buehl, Vice President/Editorial Director; Ann Martin, books for young readers.

*BANYAN BOOKS, INC., Box 431160, Miami FL 33243. (305)665-6011. Director: Ellen Edelen. Publishes hardcover and paperback originals (90%) and reprints (10%). Averages 6 titles/year. Specializes in Florida regional and natural history books. Pays 10% royalty on retail price; no advance. Subsidy publishes 10% of books; "worthwhile books that fill a gap in the market, but whose sales potential is limited." Send prints if illustrations are to be used with ms. Photocopied submissions OK. Computer printout submissions acceptable; no dot-matrix. Reports in 1 month. SASE. Free book catalog.
Nonfiction: Publishes regional history and books on nature and horticulture. Submission of outline/synopsis, sample chapters preferred, but will accept queries.
Recent Nonfiction Title: *Cracker Florida: Some Lives and Times*, by Ray Washington.
Tips: "Look for gaps in material available in bookstores and libraries; ask booksellers and librarians what they are asked for that is not readily available. Be aware of trends and what is being accepted for publication."

A.S. BARNES AND CO., INC., 9601 Aero Dr., San Diego CA 92123. (619)560-5163. President: Robert Jackman. Editorial Director: Modeste Williams. Publishes hardcover and paperback originals and reprints. Contract negotiable. Pays 10-15% royalty. Advance varies, depending on author's previous works and nature of book. Averages 10-25 titles/year. Will send a catalog. Query or submit outline, synopsis and sample chapters, plus SASE. Reports in 6-8 weeks.
Nonfiction: Adult nonfiction on general interest subjects with special emphasis on cinema and performing arts, contemporary issues, US history (particularly Civil War and WW II), sports, collecting and crafts. Looks for "market identification, synopsis with rationale for book, unique features, sample chapters to demonstrate writing style and subject development, commentary on strengths and weaknesses of competing titles."
Recent Nonfiction Title: *Cagney*, by Patrick McGilligan.

BARNES & NOBLE, Division of Harper & Row, 10 E. 53rd St., New York NY 10022. (212)593-7000. Editorial Director: Irving Levey. Editor: Jeanne Flagg. Assistant Editor: Daniel Bial. Special Projects: Lourdes Font. Publishes paperback originals (50%) and paperback reprints (50%). Averages 40 titles/year. Pays standard paperback royalties for reprints; offers variable advance. Simultaneous and photocopied submissions OK. Computer printout submissions acceptable. SASE. Reports in 1 month.
Nonfiction: Education paperbacks including "College Outline Series" (summaries of college subjects) and Everyday Handbooks (self-teaching books on academic subjects, and skills and hobbies). Query or submit outline/synopsis and sample chapters. Looks for "an indication that the author knows the subject he is writing about and that he can present it clearly and logically."
Recent Nonfiction Title: *Changing Memories into Memoirs*.

BASIC BOOKS, INC., 10 E. 53rd St., New York NY 10022. (212)207-7057. Editorial Director: Martin Kessler. Publishes hardcover originals, and paperback reprints from its backlist only. Publishes approximately 60 titles/year. Pays standard royalty; negotiates advance depending on projects. SASE. Reports in 3 months.
Nonfiction: Political science, economics, behavioral sciences, and some popular science for universities and trade. Prefers submission of propectus, outline, synopsis, and/or sample chapters.
Recent Nonfiction Title: *The Social Transformation of American Medicine*, by Paul Starr.

‡BC STUDIO PUBLICATIONS, Bill Camp Graphics and Copywriting, Box 5908, Huntington Beach CA 92615. Executive Editor: Shirleen Kaye. Publishes booklets and reports. Averages 50/year. Pays 8-10% on wholesale price; will possibly negotiate outright purchase; buys b&w art for $10-250. No advance. Simultaneous submissions OK; photocopied submissions preferred. SASE, but prefers photocopy for permanent file. Reports in 1 month on queries; 6 weeks on mss. Samples and art and writers guidelines for $2, business size SAE and 2 loose first class stamps.
Nonfiction: Softcover booklets up to 28 pages: business directory, cookbook, how-to, juvenile, mail order, reference, self-help, technical and textbook. Subjects include art, business and economics, cooking and foods, diets, health, hobbies, philosophy, psychology, recreation and travel. "We are interested in any short report from 2-28 pages that shows people how to solve a problem, make more money, start a business, build something, improve themselves or their lives, or find sources for their needs through low cost softcover directories. No sex, partisan politics, religion, fiction or purely recreational type reading." Query acceptable but prefers complete ms.

Recent Title: *325 Ways to Make Money Living in the Country*, by B. Camp (paperback report 8x11").
Tips: "Our booklets and reports are for ordinary people who are interested in self-improvement, income improvement, dollar streching, and those interested in mailorder or small business. We also will publish for some hobbyists and collectors."

BEACON HILL PRESS OF KANSAS CITY, (formerly Nazarene Publishing House), Box 527, Kansas City MO 64141. Book division of Nazarene Publishing House. Coordinator: Betty Fuhrman. Editorial Associate: Evelyn Stenbock. Publishes hardcover and paperback originals. Offers "standard contract (sometimes flat rate purchase). Advance on royalty is paid on first 1,000 copies at publication date. On standard contract, pays 10% on first 10,000 copies and 12% on subsequent copies at the end of each calendar year." Averages 65-70 titles/year, 5-10 of them freelance. Publishes book an average of 2 years after acceptance. Computer printout submissions acceptable; prefers letter-quality to dot-matrix. SASE. Reports in 4-8 months unless immediately returned. "Book Committee meets quarterly to select from the mss which will be published."
Nonfiction: Inspirational, Bible-based. Doctrinally must conform to the evangelical, Wesleyan tradition. Conservative view of Bible. No autobiography, poetry, devotional collections, or children's picture books. Accent on holy living; encouragement in daily Christian life. Popular style books usually under 128 pages. Query. Textbooks "almost exclusively done on assignment." Full ms or outline/sample chapters. Length: 20,000-40,000 words.
Recent Nonfiction Title: *The Towel and the Cross*, by John B. Nielson.

BEACON PRESS, 25 Beacon St., Boston MA 02108. (617)742-2110. Director: Wendy J. Strothman. Publishes hardcover originals (50%) and paperback reprints (50%). Averages 32 titles/year. Offers royalty on net retail price; advance varies. Simultaneous and photocopied submissions OK. Computer printout submissions acceptable; prefers letter-quality to dot-matrix. Reports in 2 months. Query or submit outline/synopsis and sample chapters to Nancy Lattanzio, editorial assistant. Return of materials not guaranteed without SASE.
Nonfiction: General nonfiction including works of original scholarship, religion, current affairs, communications, sociology, psychology, women's political science, art, literature, philosophy, history and some counseling.
Recent Nonfiction Title: *Our Right to Choose: Toward a New Ethic of Abortion*, by Beverly Wildung Harrison.
Tips: "No fiction or poetry submissions invited. No children's books."

‡*BEAR AND CO., INC.**, Drawer 2860, Santa Fe NM 87504-2860. (505)983-9868. Acquisitions/PR: Barbara Clow. Publishes trade paperback originals and trade paperback reprints. Averages 9 titles/year. Subsidy publishes 10% of books. Pays 8-10% royalty on wholesale price; offers no advance. Publishes book an average of 1 year after acceptance. No simultaneous or photocopied submissions. Computer printout submissions acceptable; prefers letter-quality to dot-matrix. SASE. Reports in 2 weeks on queries; 2 months on mss. Free book catalog.
Nonfiction: Reference. Subjects include theology, philosophy, art, history, music, politics, psychology, religion, sociology and science. "We publish works coming out of Matthew Fox's creation-centered theology, a school of contemporary Catholicism. We are looking for books on creation-centered mystics 0D-2,000 AD. Write to Bear for specific sources we want to publish. No lightweight theology, history, new-science or art books. No classical Catholic religious works." Query only with outline/synopsis and sample chapters. Reviews artwork/photos as part of ms package.
Recent Nonfiction Title: *Original Blessing*, by Matthew Fox, OP (theology).
Tips: "Books with depth and quality are sought now. Our audience is comprised of individuals from all cultures who are seriously investigating sources of spirituality from Western roots."

BEAUFORT BOOKS, INC., 9 E. 40th St., New York NY 10016. (212)685-8588. Editorial Director: Susan Suffes. Publishes hardcover and trade paperback originals. Averages 70-80 titles/year. Pays 7½-15% royalty on retail price; offers variable advance. Publishes book an average of 1 year after acceptance. Simultaneous and photocopied submissions OK. Computer printout submissions acceptable; no dot-matrix. SASE. Reports in 2 weeks on queries; 1 month on mss. Book catalog for 6x9 SAE and 2 first class stamps.
Nonfiction: Subjects include cooking and foods, health, business, sports, humor, history, hobbies, psychology and recreation. Query, or submit outline synopsis and 3 sample chapters or complete ms.
Recent Nonfiction Title: *A View of the Mountain*, by Morris Gibson, author of *One Man's Medicine*.
Fiction: Adventure, and literary novels. "No first novels, no science fiction." Accepts fiction translations from French. Query or submit complete ms.
Recent Fiction Title: *Impressionist*, by Joan King (adult novel, based on the life of the artist Mary Cassatt).

THE BENJAMIN COMPANY, INC., One Westchester Plaza, Elmsford NY 10523. (914)592-8088. President: Ted Benjamin. Publishes hardcover and paperback originals. Averages 10-12 titles/year. Buys mss by outright purchase. Offers advance. Simultaneous and photocopied submissions OK. Computer printout sub-

missions acceptable; prefers letter-quality to dot-matrix. Reports in 2 months.
Nonfiction: Business/economics, cookbooks, cooking and foods, health, hobbies, how-to, self-help, sports and consumerism. "Ours is a very specialized kind of publishing—for clients (industrial and association) to use in promotional, PR, or educational programs. If an author has an idea for a book, and close connections with a company that might be interested in using that book, we will be very interested in working together with the author to 'sell' the program and the idea of a special book for that company. Once published, our books do get trade distribution through a distributing publisher, so the author generally sees the book in regular book outlets as well as in the special programs undertaken by the sponsoring company. Normally we do not encourage submission of mss. We usually commission an author to write for us. The most helpful thing an author can do is to let us know what he or she has written, or what subjects he or she feels competent to write about. We will contact the author when our needs indicate that the author might be the right person to produce a needed ms." Query. Submit outline/synopsis and 1 sample chapter. Looks for "possibility of tie-in with sponsoring company or association."
Recent Nonfiction Title: *The Goodyear Story*, for Goodyear Tire & Rubber Company.

BENNETT & MCKNIGHT PUBLISHING CO., (formerly Bennett Publishing Company), 809 W. Detweiller Dr., Peoria IL 61615. (309)691-4454. Editorial Director: Michael Kenny. Publishes hardcover and paperback originals. Specializes in textbooks and related materials. Pays 10% royalty for textbooks "based on cash received, less for supplements"; no advance. Publishes book an average of 2 years after acceptance. Averages 30 titles/year. Query "with 1-2 sample chapters that represent much of the book; not a general introduction if the ms is mostly specific 'how-to' instructions." Photocopied submissions OK. Computer printout submissions acceptable. Reports in 2-4 weeks. SASE. Free book catalog.
Nonfiction: Publishes textbooks and related items for home economics, industrial education, and art programs in schools, junior high and above. Wants "content with good coverage of subject matter in a course in one of our fields; intelligent organization; and clear expression." Prefers author to submit art and/or prints with text matter.
Recent Nonfiction Title: *Furniture and Cabinet Making*, by Dr. John L. Feirer.

THE BERKLEY PUBLISHING GROUP, (publishers of Berkley/Berkley Trade Paperbacks/Jove/Charter/Second Chance at Love/To Have and To Hold/Tempo young adult fiction/Ace Science Fiction), 200 Madison Ave., New York NY 10016. (212)686-9820. Vice President/Editorial Director: Roger Cooper. Editor-in-Chief: Nancy Coffey. Publishes paperback originals (60%) and reprints (40%). Publishes approximately 800 titles/year. Pays 6-10% royalty on retail price; offers advance. Publishes book an average of 18 months after acceptance. Computer printout submissions acceptable; prefers letter-quality to dot-matrix. SASE. Reports in 6 months.
Nonfiction: How-to, inspirational, family life, philosophy and nutrition.
Recent Nonfiction Title: *Danse Macabre*, by Stephen King.
Fiction: Adventure, historical, mainstream men's adventure, young adult, suspense, western, occult, romance and science fiction. Submit outline and first 3 chapters.
Recent Fiction Title: *Floating Dragon*, by Peter Straub.
Young Adult Fiction Title: *Before Love*, by Gloria Mikowitz.

BETHANY HOUSE PUBLISHERS, 6820 Auto Club Rd., Minneapolis MN 55438. (612)944-2121. Managing Editor: Carol Johnson. Publishes hardcover and paperback originals (85%) and paperback reprints (15%). "Contracts negotiable." Averages 50 titles/year. Publishes book an average of 18 months after acceptance. Simultaneous and photocopied submissions OK. Computer printout submissions acceptable. Reports in 1-2 months. Free book catalog on request.
Nonfiction: Publishes reference (lay-oriented), devotional (evangelical, charismatic) and personal growth books. "No poetry, please." Submit outline and 2-3 sample chapters. Reviews artwork/photos as part of ms package. Looks for "provocative subject, quality writing style, authoritative presentation, unique approach, sound Christian truth."
Recent Nonfiction Title: *The Bethany Parallel Commentary* (reference).
Fiction: Well-written stories with a Christian message. Submit synopsis and 2-3 sample chapters. SASE. Guidelines available. SASE.
Recent Fiction Title: *Jenny*, by Marcia Mitchell (young adult romance).

BETTER HOMES AND GARDENS BOOKS, 1716 Locust St., Des Moines IA 50336. Editor: Gerald Knox. Publishes hardcover originals and reprints. Publishes 20 titles/year. "Ordinarily we pay an outright fee for work (amount depending on the scope of the assignment). If the book is the work of one author, we sometimes offer royalties in addition to the fee." Prefers outlines and 1 sample chapter, but will accept complete ms. Will consider photocopied submissions. Reports in 6 weeks. SASE.
Nonfiction: "We publish nonfiction in many family and home service categories, including gardening, decorating and remodeling, sewing and crafts, money management, entertaining, handyman's topics, cooking and

nutrition, and other subjects of home service value. Emphasis is on how-to and on stimulating people to action. We require concise, factual writing. Audience is primarily husbands and wives with home and family as their main center of interest. Style should be informative and lively with a straightforward approach. Stress the positive. Emphasis is entirely on reader service. We approach the general audience with a confident air, instilling in them a desire and the motivation to accomplish things. Food book areas that we have already dealt with in detail are currently overworked by writers submitting to us. We rely heavily on a staff of home economist editors for food books. We are interested in nonfood books that can serve mail order and book club requirements (to sell at least for $9.95 and up) as well as trade. Rarely is our first printing of a book less than 100,000 copies. Publisher recommends careful study of specific *Better Homes and Gardens* book titles before submitting material."
Tips: Queries/mss may be routed to other editors in the publishing group.

BETTERWAY PUBLICATIONS, INC., General Delivery, White Hall VA 22987. (804)823-5661. Senior Editor: Robert F. Hostage. Publishes hardcover and trade paperback originals. Averages 10-12 titles/year. Pays 10-15% royalty on wholesale price. Advance averages $500. Publishes book an average of 9 months after acceptance. Simultaneous and photocopied submissions OK. Computer printout submissions acceptable; prefers letter-quality to dot-matrix. SASE. Reports in 3 weeks on queries; 1 month on mss. Free book catalog.
Nonfiction: Cookbook, how-to, illustrated book, juvenile, reference, self-help, health and crafts. Subjects include small business and economics, cooking and foods, health, childcare and parenting, and homemaking. Especially wants "small and home business books; practical and inspirational books for women who want personal/business fulfillments and a strong home and family life; how-to books for juveniles and adolescents; books on parenting and child care; health and nutrition; and contemporary issues affecting personal and family lives." Submit outline/synopsis and sample chapters. Reviews artwork/photos as part of ms package.
Recent Nonfiction Title: *Homemade Money—The Definitive Guide to Success in a Home Business*, by Barbara Brabec.
Tips: Trends in book publishing that freelance writers should be aware of include "the dynamically increasing number of book published and publishing ventures founded every month, and the resulting need for aspiring authors to research their subject category markets, to ensure that there is a market niche for their proposed work."

‡BIBLI O'PHILE PUBLISHING CO., Box 5189, New York NY 10022. (212)888-1008. Vice President/ General Manager: Howard Barbanel. Publishes hardcover and trade paperback originals. Averages 2-3 titles/ year. Pays 5-10% royalty on wholesale price. Offers average $2,000 advance. Computer printout submissions acceptable; no dot-matrix. SASE. Reports in 2 months. Free book catalog.
Nonfiction: Biography, cookbook, how-to and self-help. Subjects include business and economics (lay person's guide); cooking and food; and health. Especially looking for biographies, autobiographies, self-help, financial guides for laypersons, books on inner and outer beauty, and health/vegetarian cookbooks. No baby books, religion, text or juvenile. Submit complete ms.
Recent Nonfiction Title: *The Hip High-Prote, Low Cal, Easy-Does-It Cookbook*, by Hayden (cookbook).
Tips: "Our books are for educated people of all ages. Earthy, well written self-help books are doing well for us in today's market. We're looking for plenty of substance."

BILINGUAL EDUCATIONAL SERVICES, INC., 2514 S. Grand Ave., Los Angeles CA 90007. (213)749-6213. General Manager: Joann N. Baker. Publishes hardcover and paperback originals. Averages 2 titles/year. Negotiates royalty; offers no advance. Simultaneous and photocopied submissions OK. Computer printout submissions acceptable; no dot-matrix. SASE. Reports in 3 months. Book catalog for 9x12 SASE.
Nonfiction: Publishes adult and juvenile nonfiction. Interested in "anything which will appeal to Spanish-speaking people, especially Chicano and Southwest US topics—high-interest low-vocabulary—easy to translate into Spanish." Also interested in English as a second language materials. Submit outline/synopsis and sample chapters. Submit complete ms if intended for translation.
Recent Nonfiction Title: *450 Years of Chicano History*.
Fiction: Publishes adult and juvenile fiction. Same subject requirements as nonfiction.

***BINFORD & MORT PUBLISHING**, 2536 SE 11th Ave., Box 42368, Portland OR 97242. (503)238-9666. Publisher: James Gardenier. Publishes hardcover and paperback originals (80%) and reprints (20%). Pays 10% royalty on retail price; offers variable advance (to established authors). Publishes about 24 titles annually. Occasionally does some subsidy publishing (100%), "when ms merits it, but it does not fit into our type of publishing." Reports in 2-4 months. Electronic submissions OK ("inquire for compatibility of systems"), but requires hard copy also. Computer printout submissions acceptable. SASE. Free book catalog.
Nonfiction: Publishes books about the Pacific Northwest, mainly in the historical field. Also Americana, biography, cookbooks, cooking and foods, history, nature, photography, recreation, reference, sports, and travel. Query. Reviews artwork/photos as part of ms package.
Recent Nonfiction Title: *Yukon Solo*, by Karel Dohnal.
Fiction: Publishes historical and western books. Must be strongly laced with historical background.

BIOMEDICAL PUBLICATIONS, Box 8209, Foster City CA 94404. (415)573-6222. General Manager: L. Mak. Averages 3-5 titles/year. Pays 10-20% royalty on wholesale or retail price; offers negotiable advance. Publishes book an average of 6 months after acceptance. Simultaneous and photocopied submissions OK. Electronic submissions OK; but requires hard copy also. Computer printout submissions acceptable; prefers letter-quality to dot-matrix. SASE. Reports in 1 week on queries; 3 weeks on mss. Free book catalog.
Nonfiction: Reference, technical and textbook. Subjects include occupational health and biomedical sciences. Accepts nonfiction translations from German, French and Spanish. "Manuscripts on industrial toxicology, environmental contamination, drug and chemical toxicology, pharmacology and pharmacokinetics, clinical chemistry, and forensic science. Our readers include toxicologists, pharmacologists, clinical pharmacists, pathologists, forensic scientists and attorneys." Query or submit outline/synopsis and 1-2 sample chapters.
Recent Nonfiction Title: *Forensic Toxicology*, by Cravey (textbook).

*BIWORLD PUBLISHERS, INC., 671 N. State, Orem UT 84057. (801)224-5803. Vice President: Al Lisonbee. Publishes hardcover and trade paperback originals. Averages 12-20 titles/year. Subsidy publishes 10% of books, based on each individual case. Pays 8-12% royalty on net price; no advance. Publishes book an average of 6 months after acceptance. Computer printout submissions acceptable; prefers letter-quality to dot-matrix. SASE. Reports in 2 weeks on queries; 1 month on mss. Free book catalog.
Nonfiction: Cookbook, how-to, reference, self-help and textbook. Subjects include cooking and foods, health and nature. "We're looking for reputable, professionally-done, well-researched manuscripts dealing in health, natural medicine, etc." Submit outline/synopsis and sample chapters or complete ms. Reviews artwork/photos as part of ms package.
Recent Nonfiction Title: *Healing Energies*, by Stephen Shepard.
Tips: "The health field is just now dawning. Health-related books of quality research are in demand."

THE BLACKSBURG GROUP, INC., Box 242, Blacksburg VA 24060. (703)951-9030. President: Jonathan A. Titus, Ph.D. Editorial Director: Christopher A. Titus, Ph.D. Senior Editor: J.R. Smallwood. "Our group writes and edits books and software from outside authors. Our books are published by technical publishers. We offer competitive royalties, advances for technical works, and we offer our writers many advantages not found with most technical publishers. We also act as agents but usually do not take any portion of the author's royalties for our publishing efforts." Publishes paperback originals. Averages 20 titles/year. Pays 10-15% royalty; offers advance. Publishes book an average of 6 months after acceptance. Photocopied submissions OK. Electronic submissions OK, "but call us first;" requires hard copy also. Computer printout submissions acceptable; prefers letter-quality to dot-matrix. "Authors should call first to see if formats for disk submissions are the same." SASE. Reports in under 1 month. Free book catalog.
Nonfiction: Computers and electronics; how-to (electronic projects); reference, technical and textbooks (computers, electronics, and computer programming). Especially interested in "microcomputer applications (hardware and software) from Commodore 64 and other computer applications and programs, digital and analog electronics, books with experiments/projects/hands-on learning." Query, submit outline/synopsis introduction and sample chapter or complete ms. Looks for "complete coverage of the material at a level suitable for the reader to whom the book is directed. Careful organization and attention to detail, and technically correct and timely (up-to-date) material. At least three people look at our incoming book proposals."
Recent Nonfiction Title: *Local Area Network Book*, by E.G. Brooner.
Software: Scientific, engineering, mathematics and other application programs for college-level and professional use. Contact: Dr. C.A. Titus.
Tips: "Writers should be aware of the *glut* of computer books. We are particularly interested in books about specific applications and uses of computers. Only the best books will survive the coming fall-out."

JOHN F. BLAIR, PUBLISHER, 1406 Plaza Dr., Winston-Salem NC 27103. (919)768-1374. Editor-in-Chief: John F. Blair. Publishes hardcover originals, trade paperbacks and occasionally reprints. Royalty to be negotiated. Free book catalog. Submit synopsis/outline and first 3 chapters or complete ms. Computer printout submissions acceptable; no dot-matrix. Reports in 3 months. SASE.
Nonfiction: Especially interested in well-researched adult biography and history. Preference given to books dealing with Southeastern United States. Also interested in environment and Americana; query on other nonfiction topics. Looks for utility and significance. Reviews artwork/photos as part of ms package.
Recent Nonfiction Title: *Cruising Guide to Coastal North Carolina*, by Claiborne Young.
Fiction: "We are most interested in serious novels of substance and imagination. Preference given to material related to Southeastern United States. No category fiction. Juveniles should be for ages 9-14; no picture books. We are accepting few poetry mss at this time."
Recent Fiction Title: *Tales of the South Carolina Low Country*, by Nancy Rhyne.

THE BOBBS-MERRILL CO., INC., 630 3rd Ave., New York NY 10017. Editor-in-Chief: Margaret B. Parkinson. Publishes hardcover originals, some trade paper originals and reprints. Pays 10-15% royalty on retail price and variable advances depending on author's reputation and nature of book. Publishes 22 titles/year.

Publishes book an average of 6 months after acceptance. Simultaneous and photocopied submissions OK. Electronic submissions OK, but requires hard copy also. Computer printout submissions acceptable. Reports in 1 month on queries; 2 months on mss. SASE.

Nonfiction: Biography, cookbook, how-to, self-help, psychology, and medicine. Subjects include parenting, cooking and foods, health, diet, and sports. Query through agent only. All unsolicited mss are returned unopened.

Recent Nonfiction Title: *Fathers Are People Too*, by D.L. Stewart.

BOOKCRAFT, INC., 1848 W. 2300 South, Salt Lake City UT 84119. (801)972-6180. Managing Editor: H. George Bickerstaff. Publishes (mainly hardcover) originals and reprints. Pays standard 10-12½-15% royalty on retail price; "we rarely give a royalty advance." Averages 25-30 titles/year. Will send general information to prospective authors on request. Query. Publishes book an average of 6 months after acceptance. Will consider photocopied submissions. Computer printout submissions acceptable; prefers letter-quality to dot-matrix. "Include contents page with ms." Reports in about 2-4 months. SASE.

Nonfiction: "We publish for members of The Church of Jesus Christ of Latter-Day Saints (Mormons) and do not distribute to the national market. All our books are closely oriented to the faith and practices of the LDS church, and we will be glad to review such mss. Mss which have merely a general religious appeal are not acceptable. Ideal book lengths range from about 64 to 176 pages or so, depending on subject, presentation, and age level. We look for a fresh approach—rehashes of well-known concepts or doctrines not acceptable. Mss should be anecdotal unless truly scholarly or on a specialized subject. Outlook must be positive. We do not publish anti-Mormon works. We don't publish poetry, plays, personal philosophizings, family histories, or personal histories. We also publish short and moderate length books for Mormon youth, about ages 14 to 19, mostly nonfiction. These reflect LDS principles without being 'preachy'; must be motivational. 20,000-30,000 words is about the right length, though good longer mss are not entirely ruled out. This is a tough area to write in, and the mortality rate for such mss is high. We publish only 1 or 2 new juvenile titles annually."

Recent Nonfiction Title: *Marriage & Family: Gospel Insights*, by Stephen R. Covey and Truman G. Madsen.

Fiction: Must be closely oriented to LDS faith and practices.

Recent Fiction Title: *Keeping Score*, by George D. Durrant.

BOREALIS PRESS, LTD., 9 Ashburn Dr., Nepean, Ontario K2E 6N4 Canada. Editorial Director: Frank Tierney. Senior Editor: Glenn Clever. Publishes hardcover and paperback originals. Averages 10 titles/year. Pays 10% royalty on retail price; no advance. Publishes book an average of 2 years after acceptance. "No multiple submissions or electronic printouts on paper more than 8½ inches wide." Computer printout submissions acceptable; prefers letter-quality to dot-matrix. Reports in 4 months. SAE and IRCs. Book catalog $1.

Nonfiction: "Only material Canadian in content." Query. Reviews artwork/photos as part of ms package. Looks for "style in tone and language, reader interest, and maturity of outlook."

Recent Nonfiction Title: *The Canadian Parliamentary Handbook 1983-84*, by John Bejermi.

Fiction: "Only material Canadian in content and dealing with significant aspects of the human situation." Query.

Recent Fiction Title: *The Trouble with Heroes and Other Stories*, by Guy Vanderhaeghe.

THE BORGO PRESS, Box 2845, San Bernardino CA 92406. (714)884-5813. Publisher: Robert Reginald. Editor: Mary A. Burgess. Publishes hardcover and paperback originals. Averages 35 titles/year. Pays royalty on retail price: "10% of gross, with a 12% escalator." No advance. Publishes book an average of 1-2 years after acceptance. "Most of our sales are to the library market." Computer printout submissions acceptable; no dot-matrix. "Will accept diskettes compatible with IBM PC or DOS 2.0." Reports in 2 months. SASE. Free book catalog for SASE.

Nonfiction: Publishes literary critiques, historical research, film critiques, interview volumes, biographies, social studies, political science, and reference works for library and academic markets. Query with letter or outline/synopsis and 1 sample chapter. Accepts nonfiction translations. "We appreciate people who've looked at our books before submitting proposals; all of the books in our Milford series, for example, are based around a certain format that we prefer using."

Recent Nonfiction Title: *Anti-Sartre, With an Essay on Camus*, by Colin Wilson.

*DON BOSCO PUBLICATIONS, 475 N. Ave., Box T, New Rochelle NY 10802. (914)576-0122. Subsidiaries include Salesiana Publishers. Editorial Director: James Hurley. Publishes hardcover and trade paperback originals. Averages 6-10 titles/year. Subsidy publishes 10% of books. "We judge the content of the manuscript and quality to be sure it fits the description of our house. We subsidy publish for nonprofit and religious societies." Pays 5-10% royalty on retail price; offers average $100 advance. Publishes book an average of 9 months after acceptance. Computer printout submissions acceptable; no dot-matrix. SASE. Reports in 2 weeks on queries; 2 months on mss. Free book catalog.

Nonfiction: Biography, juvenile, textbook on Roman Catholic religion and sports. "Biographies of outstanding Christian men and women of today. Sports for youngsters and young adults. We are a new publisher with

wide experience in school marketing, especially in religious education field." Accepts nonfiction translations from Italian and Spanish. Query or submit outline/synopsis and 2 sample chapters.
Recent Nonfiction Title: *The Spiritual Writings of Saint John Bosco*, edited by Joseph Aubry.
Fiction: "We are not considering fiction in the coming year."
Tips: Queries/mss may be routed to other editors in the publishing group.

THOMAS BOUREGY AND CO., INC., 22 E. 60th St., New York NY 10022. Editor: Rita Brenig. Offers advance on publication date. Averages 60 titles/year. Reports in 3 months. Computer printout submissions acceptable; no dot-matrix. SASE.
Imprints: *Avalon Books* (fiction).
Fiction: Romances, nurse/romances, westerns and gothic novels. Avoid sensationalist elements. Send one-page query with SASE. No sample chapters. Length: about 50,000 words.
Recent Fiction Title: *Hand of Evil*, by Juanita Tyree Osborne.

R.R. BOWKER CO., 205 E. 42nd St., New York NY 10017. (212)916-1600. Editor-in-Chief, Professional Books: Paul Doebler. Pays negotiable royalty. Reports in 2 months. SASE.
Nonfiction: Publishes books for the book trade and library field, professional books, reference books and bibliographies. Query; "send in with your idea a very thoroughly developed proposal with a table of contents, representative chapters, and analysis of the competition."

‡MARION BOYARS INC., 262 W. 22nd St., New York NY 10011. (212)807-6574. Managing Editor: Ken Hollings. Publishes hardcover and trade paperback originals and hardcover and trade paperback reprints. Averages 40 titles/year. "Standard advance against royalty on retail price is the only method we employ." Pays 15% maximum royalty on retail price; offers ⅓ of royalty on first printing as advance. SASE. "All submissions must be through a recognized literary agent." Computer printout submissions acceptable; no dot-matrix. Book catalog for 9x12 SAE and 2 first class stamps.
Nonfiction: Biography, belles lettres. Subjects include business and economics, history, music, nature, philosophy, politics, psychology, and sociology. Especially looking for materials on "serious topical issues and matters of international concern in feminisim, health, energy, literature, sociology, language." No cookery, biographies. Query to Marion Boyars, 18 Brewer St., London W.1, England through agent only.
Recent Nonfiction Title: *The Road to Lagoa Santa*, by Henrik Stangerup.
Fiction: Ethnic, experimental, general and thrillers. Query through agent only.
Recent Fiction Title: *Peggy Salte*, by Page Edwards.

BRADBURY PRESS, INC., 2 Overhill Rd., Scarsdale NY 10583. (914)472-5100. Editor-in-Chief: Richard Jackson. Publishes hardcover originals for children and young adults. Averages 25 titles/year. An affiliate of Macmillan, Inc. Pays 10% royalty or 5% on retail price to author, 5% to artist; advance averages $2,000. Reports in 3 months. SASE. Book catalog for 37¢
Fiction: Contemporary fiction, adventure and humor. Also "stories about real kids; special interest in realistic dialogue." No adult manuscripts. No fantasy or religious material. Submit complete ms.
Recent Fiction Title: *God's Radar*, by Fran Arrick.
Tips: "Blockbusters make it *possible* to take risks; we still do first novels."

*BRADSON PRESS, INC., 120 Longfellow St., Thousand Oaks CA 91360. (805)496-8212. President: Donn Delson. Publishes trade paperback originals and reprints. Averages 3 titles/year. Subsidy publishes 50% of books "depending on quality of work and market potential." Pays 5-12% royalty. Publishes book an average of 6 months after acceptance. Simultaneous and photocopied submissions OK. Computer printout submissions acceptable. SASE. Reports in 6 weeks. Free book catalog.
Nonfiction: Humor, juvenile, reference, self-help and technical covering health, hobbies, psychology, sociology, sports, entertainment and communications. "Self-help and how-to books are our primary focus—also interested in unique humorous concepts for mass market." No history, politics, religion. Submit outline/synopsis and sample chapters. Reviews artwork/photos as part of ms package.
Recent Nonfiction Title: *Motion Picture Distribution: An Accountant's Perspective*, by D. Leedy.
Fiction: Humor. No religious or western material. Submit outline/synopsis and sample chapters.

‡BRANDEN PRESS, INC., 21 Station St., Box 843, Brookline Village MA 02147. (617)734-2045. President: Adolph Caso. Subsidiaries include International Pocket Library, Popular Techology. Publishes hardcover and trade paperback originals, hardcover and trade paperback reprints and software. Averages 15 titles/year. Pays 10-5% royalty on wholesale price; offers $1,000 maximum advances. Publishes book an average of 10 months after acceptance. Electronic submissions must be compatible with in-house system and be accompanied by a hard copy. Computer printout submissions acceptable. Inquiries only with SASE. Reports in 1 week on queries; 2 months on mss. Free book catalog.
Nonfiction: Biography, illustrated book, juvenile, reference, technical, and textbook. Subjects include

Americana, art, health, history, music, photography, politics, sociology, and classics. Especially looking for "about 10 mss on national and international subjects, including biographies of well-known individuals." No religion or philosophy. Query. Reviews artwork/photos as part of ms package.

Recent Nonfiction Title: *Einstein and the Poet*, by William Hermanns.

Fiction: Adventure (well-written, realistic); ethnic (histories, integration); historical (especially biographies); mainstream (emphasis on youth and immigrants); religious (historical-reconstructive); romance (novels with well-drawn characters); and books about computers and software. No science, mystery or pornography. Query.

Recent Fiction Title: *Erebus Child of Chaos*, by Sam Saladino.

Poetry: No religious, humorous or autobiographical poetry books. Submit 5 poems.

Recent Poetry Title: *Words Ready for Music*, by Rachel Hazen.

Software: Contact Popular Technology. Needs task-results oriented material; has to solve problems for practical applications.

Tips: "Branden publishes only mss determined to have a significant impact on modern society. Our audience is a well-read general public, professionals, college students, and some high school students. If I were a writer trying to market a book today, I would thoroughly investigate the number of potential readers interested in the content of my book."

CHARLES T. BRANFORD CO., Box 41, Newton Centre MA 02159. (617)964-2441. Editor-in-Chief: I.F. Jacobs. Hardcover and paperback originals (80%) and reprints (20%). Offers 10% royalty on retail price. No advance. Publishes about 4 titles annually. Photocopied submissions OK. Computer printout submissions acceptable; no dot-matrix. Reports in 2 weeks. SASE. Free book catalog.

Nonfiction: Hobbies, how-to, recreation, and self-help. Accepts nonfiction translations. Query first. Reviews artwork/photos as part of ms package.

Recent Nonfiction Title: *Technique of Metal Thread Embroidery*, by B. Dawson.

GEORGE BRAZILLER, INC., 1 Park Ave., New York NY 10016. Offers standard 10-12½-15% royalty contract; offers variable advance depending on author's reputation and nature of book. Computer printout submissions acceptable; prefers letter-quality to dot-matrix. No unsolicited mss. Reports in 6 weeks. SASE.

Fiction and Nonfiction: Publishes general fiction and nonfiction; literature, art, philosophy, and history. Accepts nonfiction, fiction and poetry translations "provided clearance from foreign publisher is obtained." Query. Accepts outline/synopsis and 2 sample chapters.

Recent Nonfiction Title: *Childhood*, by Nathalie Sarrante.

Recent Fiction Title: *Flying to Nowhere*, by John Fuller.

BREVET PRESS, INC., Box 1404, Sioux Falls SD 57101. Editor-in-Chief: Donald P. Mackintosh. Managing Editor: Peter E. Reid. Publishes hardcover and paperback originals (67%) and reprints (33%). Specializes in business management, history, place names, and historical marker series. Pays 5% royalty; advance averages $1,000. Query; "after query, detailed instructions will follow if we are interested." Send copies if photos/illustrations are to accompany ms. Simultaneous and photocopied submissions OK. Reports in 1-2 months. SASE. Free book catalog.

Nonfiction: Publishes Americana (A. Melton, editor); business (D.P. Mackintosh, editor); history (B. Mackintosh, editor); and technical books (Peter Reid, editor).

Recent Nonfiction Title: *Challenge*, by R. Karolevitz (history).

BRIARCLIFF PRESS PUBLISHERS, 11 Wimbledon Ct., Jericho NY 11753. Editorial Director: Trudy Settel. Senior Editor: J. Frieman. Publishes hardcover and paperback originals and software. Averages 5-7 titles/year. Pays $4,000-5,000 by outright purchase; average advance of $1,000. Publishes book an average of 90 days after acceptance. "We do not use unsolicited manuscripts. Ours are custom books prepared for businesses, and assignments are initiated by us." Computer printout submissions acceptable. No dot-matrix.

Nonfiction: How-to, cookbooks, sports, travel, fitness/health, business and finance, diet, gardening, and crafts. "We want our books to be designed to meet the needs of specific business." Query. Accepts outline and 2 sample chapters. Reviews artwork/photos as part of ms package. Accepts nonfiction translations from French, German, and Italian.

Recent Nonfiction Title: *Amana Microwave Oven Cookbook*, by C. Adams.

Software: Publishes computer-oriented texts. "We're interested in new ideas."

‡***BRIDGE PUBLISHING, INC.**, 2500 Hamilton Blvd., South Plainfield NJ 07080. (201)754-0745. Executive Editor: Lloyd B. Hildebrand. Imprints include Logos (pentecostal/charismatic), Haven (evangelical), and Open Scroll (pentecostal/charismatic and evangelical). Contact Drew Thomas, assistant editor for imprint submissions. Publishes trade and mass market paperback originals and trade and mass market paperback reprints. Averages 25 titles/year. Subsidy publishes 5% of books. "We determine whether an author should be subsidy published based on if the ms is publishable, although we cannot offer marketing services, and if the au-

thor can market his/her own book." Pays negotiable royalty or makes outright purchase. Offers finder's fees for books in public domain (if we publish them). "We buy American rights on books published abroad; we assign projects to writers." Offers negotiable advances. Photocopied submissions OK. Computer printout submissions acceptable; prefers letter-quality to dot-matrix. SASE. Reports in 4 weeks on queries; 2 months on mss. Free book catalog.
Nonfiction: How-to, self-help and religious/Christian (nondenominational). Subjects include health, religion, and personal testimony written in a "teaching," self-help style. Especially looking for books with spiritual emphasis. Query with outline/synopsis and at least 3 sample chapters or submit complete ms.
Recent Nonfiction Title: *A Christian View of Russia*, by David Ziomek (current events).
Fiction: Religious and inspirational. Query.
Recent Fiction Title: *The Marriage License*, by Joanna Hager-Smith (contemporary).
Tips: "If I were a writer trying to market a book today, I would write personal letters to one editor at a time on my list.The letter would tell what audiences the ms is addressed to and would explain the theme and other pertinent information."

BROADMAN PRESS, 127 9th Ave. N, Nashville TN 37234. Editorial Director: Thomas L. Clark. Publishes hardcover and paperback originals (85%) and reprints (15%). Averages 100 titles/year. Pays 10% royalty on retail price; no advance. Photocopied submissions OK "only if they're sharp and clear." Computer printouts acceptable; prefers letter-quality to dot-matrix. SASE. Reports in 2 months.
Nonfiction: Religion. "We are open to freelance submissions in the children's and inspirational area. Materials in both areas must be suited for a conservative Protestant readership. No poetry, biography, sermons, or anything outside the area of the Protestant tradition." Query, submit outline/synopsis and sample chapters, or submit complete ms. Reviews artwork/photos as part of ms package.
Fiction: Religious. "We publish almost no fiction—less than five titles per year. For our occasional publication we want not only a very good story, but also one that sets forth Christian values. Nothing that lacks a positive Christian emphasis; nothing that fails to sustain reader interest." Submit complete ms with synopsis.
Tips: "Bible study is very good for us, but our publishing is largely restricted in this area to works that we enlist on the basis of specific author qualifications. Preparation for the future and living with life's stresses and complexities are trends in the subject area."

‡**BROADSIDE PRESS**, 12651 Old Mill Place, Detroit MI 48238. (313)935-1188. Editor: Dudley Randall. Imprints include Broadside Poets and Broadside Critics. Publishes hardcover and trade paperback originals. Averages 3 titles/year. Pays royalty (1/10 of printing, in books). Publishes book an average of 1 year after acceptance. Computer printout submissions acceptable; no dot-matrix. SASE. Reports in 3 months. Free book catalog.
Nonfiction: Biography, criticism of poets. Query.
Recent Nonfiction Title: *Song for Maya*, by Melba Boyd (poetry).
Poetry: Especially looking for "1 16-page chapbook by an unpublished black poet." No "bad poetry." Submit 3-10 poems.
Recent Poetry Title: *Sketches from Home*, by Michele Gibbs (lyric).
Tips: "We publish only poetry, biography or criticism of poets. Broadside Press publishes the best black poetry."

WILLIAM C. BROWN CO., PUBLISHERS, 2460 Kerper Blvd., Dubuque IA 52001. President, College and Professional Division: Lawrence E. Cremer. Publishes 110 titles/year. Pays variable royalty on net price. SASE. Query. Accepts outline/synopsis and 2 sample chapters. Electronic submissions OK. Computer printout submissions acceptable.
Nonfiction: College textbooks. Reviews photos/artwork as part of ms package. "Be aware of the reading level for the intended audience."
Recent Nonfiction Title: *Learning to Use Pocket Computers*, by Zimmerman/Conrad.
Tips: Queries/mss may be routed to other editors in the publishing group.

****BRUNSWICK PUBLISHING CO.**, Box 555, Lawrenceville VA 23868. (804)848-3865. Publisher: Marianne S. Raymond. Publishes hardcover originals, trade and mass market paperback originals. Averages 5-6 titles/year. Subsidy publishes 90% of books based on "author-publisher dialogue." Payment is based on "individual contracts according to work." Publishes ms an average of 6 months after acceptance. Photocopied submissions OK. Computer printout submissions acceptable. SASE. Reports in 2 weeks on queries; 3 weeks on mss. Book catalog for business size SAE.
Nonfiction: Biography, "coffee table" book, cookbook, how-to, humor, illustrated book, juvenile, reference, self-help, technical and textbook. Subjects include Americana, animals, business and economics, cooking and foods, health, history, hobbies, music, nature, philosophy, politics, psychology, religion, sociology, travel, biography, black experience and ethnic experience. "Not limited to any particular subject, but interested in Third World authors and subjects to continue Third World Monograph series." Query or submit outline/synop-

sis and sample chapters. Reviews artwork/photos as part of ms package. Looks for "quality, originality, utility."

Recent Nonfiction Title: *The Lagos Plan of Action vs. the Berg Report*, by Robert S. Browne and Robert J. Cummings.

Fiction: "Will consider fiction mainly on subsidy basis—not limited to special topics." Adventure, erotica, ethnic, historical, humor, mainstream and romance. Query or submit outline/synopsis and sample chapters.

Poetry: "Poetry published only on subsidy basis as of now—not limited to any particular subject."

Recent Poetry Title: *Johnny Boy*, by Al Lies.

Tips: "Try to be very original in material or presentation. Offer your readers excellent advice (how-to, self-help). Don't take one person's opinion of what constitutes a 'good' or 'bad' manuscript as final."

BUCKNELL UNIVERSITY PRESS, Lewisburg PA 17837. (717)524-3674. Distributed by Associated University Presses. Director: Mills F. Edgerton Jr. Publishes hardcover originals. Averages 18-20 titles/year. Pays royalty. Publishes book an average of 2 years after acceptance. Photocopied submissions OK. Computer printout submissions acceptable. Reports in 2-4 weeks on queries; 3-6 months on mss. Book catalog free on request.

Nonfiction: Scholarly art, history, music, philosophy, politics, psychology, religion, and sociology. "In all fields, our criterion is scholarly presentation; mss must be addressed to the scholarly community." Query.

Recent Nonfiction Title: *New Americans: The Westerner and the Modern Experience in the American Novel*, by Glen A. Love

*BYLS PRESS, Department of Bet Yoatz Library Services, 6247 N. Francisco Ave., Chicago IL 60659. (312)262-8959. President: Daniel D. Stuhlman. Publishes trade paperback originals. Averages 3 titles/year. Subsidy publishes variable percentage of books. Pays 7½-15% on wholesale price; no advance. Photocopied submissions OK. Electronic submissions OK, if North Star 5¼" SD, Apple 5½" BASIC, or Pascal, Applewriter. Computer printout submissions acceptable. SASE. Reports in 1 week on queries; reporting time on mss "depends on material." Free book catalog.

Nonfiction: How-to (for teachers); and juvenile. Subjects include baking and religion ("stories aimed at children for Jewish holidays"). "We're looking for children's books for Jewish holidays that can be made into computer personalized books. In particular we need books for Sukkot, Shabbat, and Purim. We need titles for our teacher education series." Query; "no agents, authors only. Do not submit ideas without examining our books and ask yourself if a book idea fits what we are looking for."

Recent Nonfiction Title: *My Own Hanukah Story*, by D. Stuhlman (children's).

Fiction: Religious (stories for Jewish children). No expository fiction. "All unsolicited mss are returned only if return postage is included."

C Q PRESS, (formerly Congressional Quarterly Press), 1414 22nd St. NW, Washington DC 20037. (202)887-8642. Director: Joanne Daniels. Publishes hardcover and paperback originals. Pays standard college royalty on wholesale price; offers college text advance. Simultaneous and photocopied submissions OK. SASE. Reports in 3 months. Free book catalog on request.

Nonfiction: "We are the most distinguished publisher in the area of Congress and US government." College texts in most areas of political science. Submit outline and prospectus.

Recent Nonfiction Title: *Bringing Back the Parties*, by David Price.

CALIFORNIA INSTITUTE OF PUBLIC AFFAIRS, Box 10, Claremont CA 91711. (714)624-5212. President/Director: T.C. Trzyna. Publishes paperback originals. Averages 6-8 titles/year. Negotiates royalties and outright purchases; also for some types of mss authors are not paid. Rarely offers advance. "In the few cases in which outside submissions are accepted, the time publishing the book is about 9 months average." Simultaneous and photocopied submissions OK. Computer printout submissions acceptable. SASE. Reports in 3 weeks. Free book catalog.

Nonfiction: "The California Institute of Public Affairs is a research foundation affiliated with the Claremont Colleges. Most of our books are written by our staff; however, we are open to publishing material by other writers that fits into our program, and several titles have come to us 'over the transom.' Our list is very specialized. We do not want to see mss that do not fit exactly into our very specialized fields of interest and format. We publish in two fairly narrow fields and all submissions must fit into one of them: (1) California reference books, that is, either directories or bibliographies relating to California, and (2) reference books on world peace and global environmental and natural resource problems. Several titles have been co-published with such houses as Marquis Who's Who, Inc. and the Sierra Club. A prospective author should request and examine our list before submitting an idea or outline." Query or submit outline/synopsis and sample chapters (biographic information useful).

Recent Nonfiction Title: *The United States and the Global Environment: A Guide to American Organizations*, by staff (information guide).

CAMARO PUBLISHING CO., 90430 World Way, Los Angeles CA 90009. (213)837-7500. Editor-in-Chief: Garth W. Bishop. Publishes hardcover and paperback originals. Pays royalty on wholesale price. "Every contract is different. Many books are bought outright." Published 14 titles last year. Query. SASE.
Nonfiction: Books on travel, food, wine, health and success.
Recent Nonfiction Title: *California Red Wine Book*.

CAMBRIDGE BOOK COMPANY, 888 7th Ave., New York NY 10106. (212)957-5300. Vice President Editorial: Brian Schenk. Publishes paperback originals in adult education. Averages 25 titles/year. Pays usually flat fee only; occasionally pays 6% royalty on institutional net price; offers small advance. Publishes book an average of 1 year after acceptance. Photocopied submissions OK. Computer printout submissions acceptable; prefers letter-quality to dot-matrix. SASE. Reports in 1 month. Free book catalog.
Nonfiction: Basic skills—adult education only—emphasizing alternative programs. Vocational, pre-GED, and ESL. Submit prospectus and sample lesson only. No phone calls. Looks for "marketability (how broad and how stable the market is for the program); understanding of adult students (learning styles and needs); thoroughness of design of program (will it require substantial editing? How does the design relate to current educational practice); and cost factors, possible production problems." Reviews artwork/photos as part of ms package. Best known for GED preparation material.
Recent Nonfiction Title: *English Spoken Here* (ESL program).

CAMBRIDGE UNIVERSITY PRESS, 32 E. 57th St., New York NY 10022. Editorial Director: Colin Day. Publishes hardcover and paperback originals. Publishes 500 titles/year. Pays 10% royalty on retail price; 6% on paperbacks; no advance. Query. Computer printout submissions acceptable. Reports in 2 weeks to 6 months. SASE.
Nonfiction: Anthropology, archeology, economics, life sciences, mathematics, psychology, upper-level textbooks, academic trade, scholarly monographs, biography, history, and music. Looking for academic excellence in all work submitted. Department Editors: Elizabeth Maguire (humanities), Susan Milmoe (psychology), Frank Smith (history, political science), David Tranah (mathematics, physical sciences), Richard Ziemacki (history of science, life sciences), Susan Allen-Mills (social anthropology, sociology), Ellen Shaw (English as second language), Colin Day (economics).
Recent Nonfiction Title: *The Cliffs of Solitude: A Reading of Robinson Jeffers*, by Robert Zaller.

CAMELOT BOOKS, Children's Book Imprint of Avon Books, a division of the Hearst Corp., 1790 Broadway, New York NY 10019. (212)399-1384. Editorial Director: Judy Gitenstein. Publishes paperback originals (25%) and reprints (75%). Averages 36 titles/year. Pays 6-8% royalty on retail price; minimum advance $1,500. Query or submit entire ms. Simultaneous and photocopied submissions OK. Computer printout submissions acceptable. SASE. Reports in 10 weeks. Free book catalog.
Fiction: Adventure, fantasy, humor, mainstream, mystery, science fiction, and suspense.
Recent Fiction Title: *Howliday Inn*, by James Howe.

CAPRA PRESS, Box 2068, Santa Barbara CA 93120. (805)966-4590. Editor-in-Chief: Noel Young. Publishes hardcover and paperback originals. Lifestyle books, fiction and regional nonfiction. Pays 8% royalty on wholesale price; advance averages $1,000. Averages 14 titles/year. State availability of photos and/or illustrations to accompany ms. Simultaneous submissions OK "if we are told where else it has been sent." Reports in 1 month. Looks for "coherent and original ideas, good writing, with California origination, yet having national appeal." SASE. Book catalog for SASE.
Nonfiction: Publishes Western contemporary nonfiction (30,000 words); how-to; and nature books "for the more serious reader with an exploring mind." Submit outline/synopsis and sample chapters.
Recent Nonfiction Title: *In Praise of Wild Herbs*, by Ludo Chardenon, Introduction by Lawrence Durrell.
Fiction: Submit outline/synopsis and sample chapters.
Recent Fiction Title: *El Moro*, by Lawrence Clark Powell.

*ARISTIDE D. CARATZAS, PUBLISHER, Box 210, 481 Main St., New Rochelle NY 10802. (914)632-8487. Managing Director: Marybeth Sollins. Publishes hardcover and paperback originals (80%) and hardcover and paperback reprints (20%). Averages 20 titles/year. Subsidy publishes 5% of books based on ms "commercially marginal, though of importance to a particular field." Photocopied submissions OK. Computer printout submissions acceptable; no dot-matrix. Disk submissions OK "if compatible with our equipment," but requires hard copy also. SASE. Reports in 3 months. Free book catalog on request.
Nonfiction: Subjects include art, history, philosophy and religion. Query first. Unsolicited mss are not returned; "we cannot be responsible for lost unsolicited mss." Looks for "suitability with our publications program; credentials of the author; and quality and economic justification of the work." Accepts nonfiction translations from German, French, Italian and modern Greek.
Recent Nonfiction Title: *The Rediscovery of Greece*, by F. M. Tsigakou.

CAREER PUBLISHING, INC., 936 N. Main St., Box 5486, Orange CA 92667. (714)771-5155. Contact: Senior Editor. Publishes paperback originals and software. Averages 6-23 titles/year. Pays 10% royalty on wholesale price; no advance. Publishes book an average of 2 months after acceptance. Simultaneous (if so informed with names of others to whom submissions have been sent) and photocopied submissions OK. Computer printout submissions acceptable. Reports in 2 months. SASE. Book catalog 25¢.

Nonfiction: Microcomputer material, educational software, word processing, guidance material, allied health, dictionaries, etc. "Textbooks should provide core upon which class curriculum can be based: textbook, workbook or kit with 'hands-on' activities and exercises, and teacher's guide. Should incorporate modern and effective teaching techniques. Should lead to a job objective. We also publish support materials for existing courses and are open to unique, marketable ideas with schools in mind. Reading level should be controlled appropriately—usually 8th-9th grade equivalent for vocational school and community college level courses. Any sign of sexism or racism will disqualify the work. No career awareness masquerading as career training." Submit outline/synopsis and 2 sample chapters and table of contents or complete ms. Reviews artwork/photos as part of ms package.

Recent Nonfiction Title: *Motorcycle Dictionary/Terminology*, by Willam H. Kosbab.

Software: Contact Sherry Robson. Needs educational software for gifted children, junior high, senior high, community colleges, universities, vocational and adult education.

Tips: "Authors should be aware of vocational/career areas with inadequate or no training textbooks, submit ideas and samples to fill the gap. Trends in book publishing that freelance writers should be aware of include education—especially for microcomputers."

CAROLINA BIOLOGICAL SUPPLY CO., 2700 York Rd., Burlington NC 27215. (919)584-0381. Head, Scientific Publications: Dr. Phillip L. Owens. Publishes paperback originals. Averages 15 titles/year. Pays 10% royalty on sales. Simultaneous and photocopied submissions OK. SASE. Reports in 2 weeks on queries.

Nonfiction: Self-help, technical, textbook on animals, health, nature, biology, and science. "Will consider short (10,000 words) mss of general interest to high school and college students on health, computers, biology, physics, astronomy, microscopes, etc. Longer mss less favored but will be considered." Query first. Reviews photos/artwork as part of ms package.

Recent Nonfiction Title: *Microfilaments*, by Vivianne T. Nachmias.

CAROLRHODA BOOKS, INC., 241 1st Ave. N., Minneapolis MN 55401. (612)332-3345. Editor: Susan Pearson. Publishes hardcover originals. Averages 30-40 titles/year. Pays negotiable royalty; buys new authors' mss outright. Publishes book an average of 18 months after acceptance. Simultaneous and photocopied submissions OK. Computer printout submissions acceptable; prefers letter-quality to dot-matrix. SASE. Reports in 3 months. Book catalog for 9x12 SAE and 88¢ postage.

Nonfiction: Juvenile (easy to read, grades 1-2) on early American history. Submit complete ms. Reviews artwork/photos as part of ms package.

Recent Nonfiction Title: *Cornstalks & Cannonballs*, by Barbara Mitchell (history for young readers).

Fiction: Humor, mystery, and science fiction. "Light fiction for 7-11 year olds." Submit outline/synopsis and 2 sample chapters.

Recent Fiction Title: *A Matter of Pride*, by Emily Crofford.

‡**CARPENTER PRESS**, Route 4, Pomeroy OH 45769. (614)992-7520. Publisher: Robert Fox. Publishes trade paperback originals. Averages 0-4 titles/year. Pays 10% minimum royalty on wholesale price. Publishes book an average of 1 year after acceptance. Simultaneous and photocopied submissions OK. Computer printout submissions acceptable; no dot-matrix. SAE. Reports in 1 week on queries; 3 months on mss. Book catalog for business-size SAE and 1 first class stamp.

Fiction: Experimental, fantasy, mainstream, and science fiction. "We are backlogged for at least 2 years and cannot consider new mss for that time." No genre fiction. Query.

Recent Fiction Title: *Leviathan*, by Hugh Fox (novel).

‡**CARROLL & GRAF PUBLISHERS, INC.**, 260 5th Ave., New York NY 10001. (212)889-8772. Contact: Kent Carroll. Publishes hardcover, trade paperback, and mass market paperback originals, and hardcover, trade paperback, and mass market paperback reprints. Averages 60 titles/year. Pays 6-10% royalty on retail price. Publishes book an average of 1 year after acceptance. Photocopied submissions OK. Computer printout submissions acceptable; prefers letter-quality to dot-matrix. SASE. Reports in 2 weeks on queries; 1 month on mss. Free book catalog.

Nonfiction: Biography and fiction. Query. Reviews artwork/photos as part of ms package. All unsolicited mss are returned unopened.

Fiction: Adventure, erotica, fantasy, humor, mainstream, mystery, and suspense. Query. All unsolicited mss are returned unopened.

CARSTENS PUBLICATIONS, INC., Hobby Book Division, Box 700, Newton NJ 07860. (201)383-3355. Publisher: Harold H. Carstens. Publishes paperback originals. Averages 5 titles/year. Pays 10% royalty on retail price; offers average advance. SASE. Electonic submissions OK if compatible with ASCII-5¼" floppy disk, TRS 80 or Modem. Computer printout submissions acceptable; prefers letter-quality to dot-matrix. Book catalog for SASE.
Nonfiction: Model railroading, toy trains, model aviation, railroads and model hobbies. "We have scheduled or planned titles on several railroads as well as model railroad and model airplane books. Authors must know their field intimately since our readers are active modelers. Our railroad books presently are primarily photographic essays on specific railroads. Writers cannot write about somebody else's hobby with authority. If they do, we can't use them." Query. Reviews artwork/photos as part of ms package.
Recent Nonfiction Title: *Electrical Handbook for Model RR*, by Paul Mallery.
Tips: "No fiction. We need lots of good b&w photos. Material must be in model, hobby, railroad field only."

CATHOLIC TRUTH SOCIETY, 38/40 Eccleston Square, London SW1V 1PD England. (01)834-4392. Editorial Director: David Murphy. Publishes hardcover and paperback originals (70%) and reprints (30%). Averages 80 titles/year. Pays in outright purchase of $50-400; no advance. Simultaneous and photocopied submissions OK. Computer printout submissions acceptable; prefers letter-quality to dot-matrix. Reports in 4 weeks. SASE. Free book catalog.
Nonfiction: Books dealing with how to solve problems in personal relationships, parenthood, teen-age, widowhood, sickness and death, especially drawing on Christian and Catholic tradition for inspiration; simple accounts of points of interest in Catholic faith, for non-Catholic readership; and books of prayer and devotion. Reviews artwork/photos as part of ms package. Query, submit outline/synopsis and sample chapter, or submit complete ms.
Recent Nonfiction Title: *Disabled from Birth—What Parents Should Know*, by Prof. R.B. Zachary.

CATHOLIC UNIVERSITY OF AMERICA PRESS, 620 Michigan Ave. NE, Washington DC 20064. (202)635-5052. Director: Dr. David J. McGonagle. Marketing Manager: Cynthia Miller. Averages 5-10 titles/year. Pays 10% royalty on net receipts. Query with sample chapter plus outline of entire work, along with curriculum vitae and list of previous publications. Publishes book an average of 1 year after acceptance. Computer printout submissions acceptable; prefers letter-quality to dot-matrix. Reports in 2 months. SASE.
Nonfiction: Publishes history, biography, languages and literature, philosophy, religion, church-state relations, and social studies. No doctoral dissertations. Length: 200,000-500,000 words.
Recent Nonfiction Title: *Metaphysical Themes in Thomas Aquinas*, by John F. Wippel.

THE CAXTON PRINTERS, LTD., 312 Main St., Box 700, Caldwell ID 83605. (208)459-7421. Vice President: Gordon Gipson. Publishes hardcover and trade paperback originals. Averages 6-8 titles/year. Audience includes Westerners, students, historians and researchers. Pays royalty; advance $500-2,000. Publishes book an average of 18 months after acceptance. Simultaneous and photocopied submissions OK. Computer printout submissions acceptable; no dot-matrix. SASE. Reports in 2 weeks on queries; 8 weeks on mss. Free book catalog.
Nonfiction: "Coffee table," Americana and Western Americana. "We need good Western Americana, preferably copiously illustrated with unpublished photos." Query. Reviews artwork/photos as part of ms package.
Recent Nonfiction Title: *Tillamook Burn Country*, by Ellis Lucia.

CEDARSHOUSE PRESS, 406 W. 28th St., Bryan TX 77801. (713)822-5615. Editor: Paul Christensen. Publishes hardcover originals and trade paperback reprints. Averages 4-8 titles/year. Pays 5-8% royalty on retail price. Photocopied submissions OK. SASE. Reports in 6 weeks on queries; 4 months on mss.
Nonfiction: Biography, reference, belles lettres on Americana, history, philosophy, politics, and travel. "Studies of neglected American authors, fiction, poetry, nonfiction; controversial historical subjects—race relations, leftist political systems in US, generation studies of Americans in 20th century, commentary on contemporary society, etc." Publishes for Southwestern readers interested in the lore and mythology of the region; readers of innovative and experimental fiction and verse; historical and critical writing appealing to writers, social observers, general interest audiences." No pop studies, slick prose, magazine writing, superficial surveys, trendy concepts, "coffee table" book writing, photo books, private journals and survival memoirs, etc. Query or submit outline/synopsis and 3 sample chapters.
Recent Nonfiction Title: *A Bibliography of Texas Poets 1945-1982*, by S. Turner.
Fiction: "Very low priority; no particular needs at this time except for distinguished mss of experimental prose." No conventional fiction of any type. Query.
Poetry: "Long poems of an experimental attitude; regional poetry stressing unique perception of land and people; Southwestern topics; books tightly ordered and innovative." Accepts poetry translations from French and Spanish. No conventional lyrics, collections of verse, theme books, confessional writing, memoirs, travelogues, scenic poems, anthologies. Submit 6-10 samples.
Recent Poetry Title: *Old and Lost Rivers* , by Christensen (lyric poetry).
Tips: Queries/mss may be routed to other editors in the publishing group.

CELESTIAL ARTS, Box 7327, Berkeley CA 94707. (415)524-1801. Editorial Director: George Young. Publishes paperback originals, adult and children's books. Publishes 20 titles/year. Simultaneous and photocopied submissions OK. Computer printout submissions acceptable; prefers letter-quality to dot-matrix. SASE. Reports in 3 months. Book catalog for $1.
Nonfiction: Publishes biography, cookbooks/cooking, health, humor, psychology, recreation and self-help. No poetry. "Submit 2-3 sample chapters and outline; no original copy. If return requested, include postage."
Recent Nonfiction Title: *Love Is Letting Go of Fear*, by Jerry Jampolsky.

CHAMPION ATHLETE PUBLISHING COMPANY, Box 2936, Richmond VA 23235. Editor: Dr. George B. Dintiman. Publishes hardcover and paperback originals. Averages 3 titles/year. Pays 15% royalty on wholesale or retail price. Simultaneous and photocopied submissions OK. Computer printout submissions acceptable. SASE. Reports in 4 weeks. Brochure for $1.
Nonfiction: Health, sports and textbooks (physical education/athletics). Exercise texts for the college class market and other texts targeted for a specific course. Accepts nonfiction translations from Spanish. Books are published for the participant and not the coach. "We are only interested in health and sports areas or texts designed for physical education service or major classes." Submit outline/synopsis and 1 sample chapter or submit complete ms.
Recent Nonfiction Title: *Doctor Tennis*, by J. Myers (tennis conditioning and injury prevention guide).

‡**CHARLES RIVER BOOKS**, Box 65, Charlestown MA 02129. Editorial Director: Bruce Crabtree. Publishes hardcover and trade paperback originals, hardcover and trade paperback reprints and software. Averages 20 titles/year. "We certainly do not rule out subsidized publishing, although we are not a vanity press." Pays 5-15% royalty, negotiable on retail price or makes outright purchase; offers average $1,000 advance for completed ms. Publishes book an average of 9 months after acceptance. Simultaneous and photocopied submissions OK. Electronic submissions OK; send printed ms first. Computer printout submissions acceptable. SASE. Reports in 1 week on queries; 2 weeks on mss. Free book catalog.
Nonfiction: Biography, how-to, humor, reference (New England guides), self-help, and calendars. Subjects include Americana (New England especially), art, business and economics, health, history, hobbies, nature, nautical, philosophy, politics, psychology, recreation, religion, sociology, social work, sports, and travel. "We are looking for good general interest nonfiction. Nothing too technical or specialized. Books on New England are especially welcome." Query with outline/synopsis and sample chapters or submit complete ms. Reviews artwork/photos as part of ms package.
Recent Nonfiction Title: *Sell Your Own Home*, by Thomas Tammany (how-to).
Fiction: Adventure, confession, ethnic, experimental, historical, humor, religious, political/sociological, nautical and translations. "All quality fiction will be considered. We publish new authors." Query or submit complete ms.
Recent Fiction Title: *January's Dream*, by John Robinson (novel).
Poetry: Submit complete ms.
Recent Poetry Title: *Sweet Wild World*, by William White (selections from the journals of Thoreau arranged as poetry).

CHARTER BOOKS, The Berkley Publishing Group, 200 Madison Ave., New York NY 10016. (212)686-9820. Publishes paperback originals and reprints. Publishes over 100 titles/year. Publishes book an average of 18 months after acceptance.
Fiction: General fiction, suspense, adventure, espionage, epic/saga, westerns, and romances. No short stories or novellas. Reviews artwork/photos as part of ms package. No unsolicited mss accepted.
Recent Fiction Title: *The Butcher's Boy*, by Thomas Perry.

THE CHATHAM PRESS, a subsidiary of Devin-Adair Publishers, Box A, Old Greenwich CT 06870. Publishes hardcover and paperback originals, reprints and anthologies relating to New England and the Atlantic coastline. "Standard book contract does not always apply if the book is heavily illustrated. Average advance is low." Averages 14 titles/year. Electronic submissions OK. Computer printout submissions acceptable. Free book catalog. Query with outline and 3 sample chapters. Reports in 2 weeks. SASE.
Nonfiction: Publishes mostly "regional history and natural history, involving mainly Northeast seaboard and the Carolinas, mostly illustrated, with emphasis on conservation and outdoor recreation." Reviews artwork/photos as part of ms package. Accepts nonfiction translations from French and German.
Recent Nonfiction Title: *A Beachcomber's Companion*, by Ted Wesemann.
Tips: Manufacturing quality and design standards are of major importance."

*****CHICAGO REVIEW PRESS**, 213 W. Institute Place, Chicago IL 60610. (312)337-0747. Editor: Linda Matthews. Publishes hardcover and trade paperback originals. Averages 12 titles/year. Subsidy publishes 3% of books. Pays 7-15% royalty on retail price; offers average $2,000 advance. Publishes book an average of 8

months after acceptance. Simultaneous and photocopied submissions OK. Electronic submissions OK, but editor wants to discuss format in advance; requires hard copy also. Computer printout submissions acceptable; prefers letter-quality to dot-matrix. SASE. Reports in 3 weeks on queries; 2 months on mss. Free book catalog.
Nonfiction: Cookbook, how-to, reference, self-help and guidebooks. Subjects include cooking and foods, health, hobbies, recreation, sports and travel. "We especially need Chicago guidebooks, national-interest, popular how-to or self-help books, career guides, books on writing, and trendy nonfiction with strong subrights possibilities." Query or submit outline/synopsis and 2-3 sample chapters. Looks for "clear thinking, lively writing, salable idea."
Recent Nonfiction Title: *Hearts and Dollars: How to Beat the High Cost of Falling In and Out of Love*, by Steven R. Lake (popular self-help).

CHILDRENS PRESS, 1224 W. Van Buren St., Chicago IL 60607. (312)666-4200. Editorial Director: Fran Dyra. Pays in outright purchase or offers small advance against royalty. Averages 80 titles/year. Reports in 12 weeks. SASE. Simultaneous submissions OK. Computer printout submissions acceptable.
Juveniles: For supplementary use in elementary and secondary schools; picture books for early childhood and beginning readers; high-interest, easy reading material. Specific categories include social studies and science. Especially wants new biographies. Length: 50-10,000 words. For picture books, needs are very broad. They should be geared from preschool to grade 3. "We have a strong tendency to publish books in series. Odds are against a single book that couldn't, if sales warrant, develop into a series." Length: 50-1,000 words. Send outline with 1 sample chapter; complete ms for picture books. Accepts translations. Reviews artwork and photos as part of ms package, "but best to submit ms first." Do not send finished artwork with ms.
Recent Nonfiction Title: *People of Distinctions*, (biography series).
Fiction: For supplementary use in elementary and secondary schools. Length: 50-10,000 words. Picture books from preschool to grade 3. Length: 50-1,000 words. Send outline with sample chapters; complete ms for picture books. Do not send finished artwork with ms.
Tips: Submissions often "lack originality. Too often authors talk 'down' to young readers. First it must be a good story, then it can have an educational or moral point. We're looking for writers in the science and technology areas."

CHILTON BOOK CO., Chilton Way, Radnor PA 19089. Editorial Director: Alan F. Turner. Publishes hardcover and trade paperback originals. Publishes 90 titles/year. Pays royalty; average advance. Simultaneous and photocopied submissions OK. Electronic submissions OK, decided "case by case." Computer printout submissions acceptable. SASE. Reports in 3 weeks.
Nonfiction: Business/economics, computers, crafts, how-to and technical. "We only want to see any manuscripts with informational value." Query or submit outline/synopsis and 2-3 sample chapters.
Recent Nonfiction Title: *The Small Business Computer Handbook*.

*CHINA BOOKS, 2929 24th St., San Francisco CA 94110. (415)282-2994. Editorial Director: Foster Stockwell. Publishes trade paperback originals. Averages 6 titles/year. Subsidy publishes 20% of books. Pays average 8% royalty; offers negotiable advance. Publishes book an average of 1 year after acceptance. Simultaneous and photocopied submissions OK. Computer printout submissions acceptable; prefers letter-quality to dot-matrix. SASE. Reports in 2 weeks. Book catalog $1.
Nonfiction: Biography, cookbook, illustrated book, reference on Chinese history, travel, and things related to the People's Republic of China. Reviews artwork/photos as part of ms package. "Books about China or things Chinese that are new or unusual." Query. Accepts Chinese translations.
Recent Nonfiction Title: *Bridge to China*, by Donald Gledhill (travel).
Tips: Queries/mss may be routed to other editors in the publishing group.

CHOSEN BOOKS, Lincoln VA 22078. (703)338-4131. Associate Publisher: Leonard E. LeSourd. Hardcover and paperback originals. Averages 12 titles/year. Publishes book an average of 1 year after final ms is accepted. Computer printouts in Courier 72, 10 pitch acceptable; prefers letter-quality to dot-matrix. Free book catalog for SASE.
Nonfiction: Seeks out teaching and personal experience books of Christian content with high quality. Length: 40,000-60,000 words. Query. Submit 1-2 page synopsis. Reviews artwork/photos as part of ms package.
Recent Nonfiction Title: *Story Bible*, by Catherine Marshall.
Tips: "Write a book that grips the reader in the first pages and then holds him through all chapters. Give the reader a 'you are there feeling.' "

*CHRISTIAN CLASSICS, Box 30, Westminster MD 21157. (301)848-3065. Director: John J. McHale. Publishes hardcover originals (5%), and hardcover reprints (95%). Averages 10 titles/year. Subsidy publishes 1% of books. Pays 10% royalty; buys some mss outright for $500-2,000. Publishes book an average of 6 months after acceptance. Photocopied submissions OK. Computer printout submissions acceptable; no dot-matrix. SASE. Reports in 2 months. Free book catalog.

Nonfiction: Subjects include psychology and religion. "We're looking for general books of religious interest. Authors should be aware of latest theological trends and major influences."Query. Reviews artwork/photos as part of ms package.

Recent Nonfiction Title: *The Angels and Their Mission*, by Jean Danielou, S.J. (religious).

Tips: "Think about mass market paperback possibilities."

‡**CHRISTIN PUBLICATIONS & STUDIOS**, 6034 E. State Blvd., Box 5492, Ft. Wayne IN 46895. (219)749-8139. Executive Director/Editor: Terrence R. Campbell. Publishes mass market paperback originals. Averages 5-8 titles/year. Pays 15-30% royalty on wholesale price; offers no advance. Simultaneous submissions OK. Electronic submissions compatible with IBM or Apple hardware OK. Computer printout submissions acceptable. SASE. Reports in 1 month on queries; 2 months on mss. Book catalog for 6½x9½ SAE and 40¢ postage.

Nonfiction: How-to, juvenile and self-help. Subjects include business and economics; cooking and foods (health foods); health (holistic); philosophy; religion (ecumenical only); and "new age consciousness. we specialize in books adaptable to video cassette workshops. Subjects include children, family, relationships, harmony and understanding, global transformation, spiritual growth, ecumenical religious, gardening, holistic medicine and diet, management, success/motivation. We are not interested in traditional religious dogma, coffee table treatments, nationalistic doctrine or poetry." Query. All unsolicited mss are returned unopened. opened.

Recent Nonfiction Title: *How To Confront and Treat Teen Alcohol-Drug Abuse*, by J. Stuart Rahrer (instructional how-to).

Fiction: New Age Consciousness—fiction that gives a "what if" approach to the consciousness movement. Query. All unsolicited mss are returned unopened.

Tips: "Our books are for people who attend workshops for information and self improvement, usually some college and family. Books that deal with improving relationships with other people and the environment are doing well in today's market, and I feel this will continue into the future."

CHRONICLE BOOKS, 870 Market St., San Francisco CA 94102. Editorial Director: Larry L. Smith. Publishes hardcover and paperback originals. Publishes 25 titles annually. Pays 6-10% royalty on retail price; negotiates advance. Publishes book an average of 1 year after acceptance. Simultaneous and photocopied submissions OK. Computer printout submissions acceptable. SASE. Reports in 1 month.

Nonfiction: West Coast regional and recreational guidebooks, West Coast regional histories, art and architecture, and natural history. No fiction, science fiction, drama or poetry. Query or submit outline/synopsis and 2 sample chapters. Reviews artwork/photos as part of ms package.

Recent Nonfiction Title: *A Vineyard Year*.

CITADEL PRESS, 120 Enterprise Ave., Secaucus NJ 07094. (212)736-0007. Editorial Director: Allan J. Wilson. Publishes hardcover originals and paperback reprints. Pays 10% royalty on hardcover, 5-7% on paperback; offers average $2,000 advance. Simultaneous and photocopied submissions OK. Computer printout submissions acceptable; prefers letter-quality to dot-matrix. Reports in 2 months. SASE.

Nonfiction: Biography, film, psychology, humor and history. Also seeks "off-beat material," but no "poetry, religion, politics." Accepts nonfiction and fiction translations. Query. Accepts outline/synopsis and 3 sample chapters.

Recent Nonfiction Title: *Moe Howard and the Three Stooges*, by M. Howard (filmography).

CLARION BOOKS, Ticknor & Fields: a Houghton Mifflin Company. 52 Vanderbilt Ave., New York NY 10017. Editor and Publisher: James C. Giblin. Senior Editor for Nonfiction: Ann Troy. Publishes hardcover originals. Averages 30-32 titles/year. Pays 5-10% royalty on retail price; $1,000-3,000 advance, depending on whether project is a picture book or a longer work for older children. Photocopied submissions OK. No multiple submissions. Computer printout submissions acceptable; no dot-matrix. SASE. Reports in 6-8 weeks. Publishes book an average of 18 months after acceptance. Free book catalog.

Nonfiction: Americana, biography, holiday, humor, nature, photo essays and word play. Prefers books for younger children. Reviews artwork/photos as part of ms package. Query.

Recent Nonfiction Title: *Junk Food, Fast Food, Health Food*, by Lila Perl (nutrition).

Fiction: Adventure, fantasy, humor, mystery, strong character studies, and suspense. "We would like to see more humorous contemporary stories that young people of 8-12 or 10-14 can identify with readily." Accepts fiction translations. Query on ms of more than 50 pages. Looks for "freshness, enthusiasm—in short, life" (fiction and nonfiction).

Recent Fiction Title: *Lindsay, Lindsay, Fly Away Home*, by Stella Pevsner (teenage story).

*****ARTHUR H. CLARK CO.**, Box 230, Glendale CA 92109. (213)245-9119. Editorial Director: Robert A. Clark. Publishes hardcover originals. Averages 8 titles/year. Subsidy publishes 10% of books based on whether they are "high-risk sales." Pays 10% minimum royalty on wholesale prices. Publishes book an average of 9

Close-up

William Zinsser
Author

The writer needs energy, originality, an ear for language, and *trust*. Yes, trust, says author William Zinsser. "If the material is very rich, trust the material and don't explain it."

Look at his *New Yorker* piece (4-23-84) on musician Willie Ruff. "Nowhere do I say, 'isn't it amazing' or explain what it is. A lot of writers today are writing what they call color as if it could be separated from the facts. The facts are the color," he says. "Practice the craft in a way that does homage to the material."

Writers' attitudes in approaching their material concern Zinsser; it's a concept he explores in the third edition of *On Writing Well* (Harper & Row).

"I've learned more in the last five years about attitudes that go into writing, many of which are quite injurious—pomposity, genteelism, pretentiousness, intrusiveness," says this author of eleven books. "I've also given more thought to the positive attitudes that ought to go into writing like confidence, ego, tone—more subjective matters."

Before starting to write, Zinsser reads E.B. White "to get into this deceptively casual style that I try to effect which is actually the result of so much effort."

He writes for himself, *then* thinks about how he will sell the piece. "I am very crotchety about editors changing anything I write," says Zinsser. "I will fight for a semicolon." He has bought back the rights to articles when magazines have tampered too much with his words.

Zinsser advises writers to decide where they want to go with their writing. "You don't want to go through life writing for someone else's formula," says the executive editor of the Book-of-the-Month Club. "You eventually want to break out of that, so that ought to be at least a goal when you can afford it.

"The only way you're going to suc-ceed as a writer is to write differently from all the people who are writing in clichés," says Zinsser whose Yale University writing classes inspired him to write *On Writing Well*. "Originality has to be finally the difference."

Read your material aloud, suggests Zinsser. "If it's as ponderous as what everybody else is writing, you'll hear it, or at least you should. It'll sound plodding. Once you begin to hear that in your writing, then you should start looking for some way to introduce anecdote, humor, detail, surprise."

Interviewed by the writer, most people will explain a point to him in three different ways. "The reader only wants it one way, so pick; let one example suffice for three. Every component in a piece of writing should be doing some useful work by which I mean *new* work."

The writer must also search for new material. When Willie Ruff traveled to Venice, Zinsser asked to join him. "People say 'how lucky you were to have gone off to Venice'," says Zinsser. "It isn't luck; you make your own luck."

Finding rich material worth trusting became part of the trip and later the *New Yorker* article. The author's travels also inspired his *Willie and Dwike: An American Profile* (Harper & Row).

What is Zinsser's next destination, readers might ask.

"I have no ideas for a next book," he says, "but maybe like the trip to Venice it will surprise me."

months after acceptance. Photocopied submissions OK. Computer printout submissions acceptable; prefers letter-quality to dot-matrix. SASE. Reports in 1 week on queries; 2 months on mss. Free book catalog.
Nonfiction: Biography, reference and historical nonfiction. Subjects include Americana and history. "We're looking for documentary source material in Western American history." Query or submit outline/synopsis and 3 sample chapters. Looks for "content, form, style." Reviews artwork/photos as part of ms package.
Recent Nonfiction Title: *The Custer Trail*, by John Carroll.

T&T CLARK LTD., 36 George St., Edinburgh, EH2 2LQ Scotland. (031)225-4703. Editorial Director: Geoffrey Green. Publishes hardcover and paperback originals (25%) and reprints (75%). Averages 50 titles/ year. Pays 5-10% royalty based on wholesale or retail price. May offer 500 pounds advance. Simultaneous and photocopied submissions OK. Electronic submissions OK, but requires hard copy also. Computer printout submissions acceptable. SASE. Reports in 4 weeks. Free book catalog.
Nonfiction: Religion, law, philosophy, and history. Accepts translations. Top level academic. Query first.
Recent Nonfiction Title: *A History of Christian Doctrine*, by H. Cunliffe-Jones (religion/theology/history student textbook).

CLIFFS NOTES, INC., Box 80728, Lincoln NE 68501. (402)477-6971. Editor: Michele Spence. Publishes trade paperback originals. Averages 10 titles/year. Pays royalty on wholesale price. Buys some mss outright; "full payment on acceptance of ms." SASE. Reports in 1 month. Free book catalog.
Nonfiction: Self-help, and textbook. "We publish self-help study aids directed to junior high through graduate school audience. Publications include *Cliffs Notes*, *Cliffs Test Preparation Guides*, *Cliffs Speech and Hearing Series*, and other study guides. Most authors are experienced teachers, usually with advanced degrees. Some books also appeal to a general lay audience." Query.

COBBLESMITH, Box 191, RFD 1, Freeport ME 04032. Editor-in-Chief: Gene H. Boyington. Publishes hardcover and paperback originals (90%) and hardcover and paperback reprints (10%). Averages 3 titles/year. Pays 10% royalty on list price; no advance. Publishes book an average of 2 years after acceptance. Simultaneous and photocopied submissions OK. Computer printout submissions acceptable; no dot-matrix. SASE. Query first. *"Unsolicited mss often are treated as though only a little better than unsolicited third class mail."* Reports in 4 months minimum. Free book-catalog.
Nonfiction: Americana and art topics (especially New England and antiques); law (popular, self-help); cookbooks, cooking and foods; gardening; psychology (applied—not theory); how-to (home and homestead crafts); philosophy (educational and new developments); sociology (applied—not theory); material on alternative lifestyles; nature, travel (offbeat guide books); and self-help. Accepts nonfiction, fiction and poetry translations. Reviews artwork/photos as part of ms package.
Recent Nonfiction Title: *Prejudice Against Nature* (environmental education).

COLLECTOR BOOKS, Box 3009, Paducah KY 42001. Editor: Steve Quertermous. Publishes hardcover and paperback originals. Pays 5% royalty on retail; no advance. Publishes book an average of 8 months after acceptance. Publishes 25-30 titles/year. Send prints or transparencies if illustrations are to accompany ms. Computer printout submissions acceptable; no dot-matrix. SASE. Reports in 2-4 weeks. Free book catalog.
Nonfiction: "We only publish books on antiques and collectibles. We require our authors to be very knowledgeable in their respective fields and have access to a large representative sampling of the particular subject concerned." Query. Accepts outline/synopsis and 2-3 sample chapters. Reviews artwork/photos as part of ms package.
Recent Nonfiction Title: *Character Toys*, by D. Longest.

COLLEGE-HILL PRESS, 4284 41st St., San Diego CA 92105. (619)563-8899. Promotions Manager: Karen Jackson. Publishes hardcover and trade paperback originals. Averages 25 titles/year. Pays average 10% royalty on retail price. Reports in 1 week. SASE. Free book catalog.
Nonfiction: Reference, textbook, and medical. Subjects include speech, hearing, language, special education, and medicine. Query and request "editorial and marketing questionnaire."
Recent Nonfiction Title: *Birth Defects and Speech and Hearing Problems*, by Shirley Sparks.

COLLIER MACMILLAN CANADA, INC., 50 Gervais Dr., Don Mills, Ontario M3C 3K4 Canada. Publishes both originals and reprints in hardcover and paperback. Advance varies, depending on author's reputation and nature of book. Published 15 titles last year. Reports in 6 weeks. SAE and IRCs.
General Nonfiction: "Topical subjects of special interest to Canadians." Query.
Textbooks: Mathematics, language arts, and reading: mainly texts conforming to Canadian curriculum requirements. Also resource books, either paperback or pamphlet for senior elementary and high schools. Length: open.

‡*WILLIAM COLLINS & CO. LTD., 8 Grafton St., London, W1X 3LA England. (01)493-7070. Subsidiaries include The Harvill Press, Fontana Paperbacks and Granada Publishing. Publishes hardcover, trade paperback, and mass market paperback originals and hardcover, trade paperback, and mass market paperback reprints. "We determine whether an author should be subsidy published based upon the quality of the ms and strength of market for the book." Pays royalty (against advance) or makes outright purchase. Simultaneous and photocopied submissions OK. SASE.
Nonfiction: Biography, "coffee table" book, cookbook, how-to, humor, illustrated book, juvenile, reference, self-help, and textbook. Subjects include Americana, animals, art, business and economics, cooking and foods, health, history, hobbies, music, nature, philosophy, photography, politics, psychology, recreation, religion, sociology, sports, and travel. Looking for "cogent, well-written and interesting material." No "highly technical or academic. No personal reminiscences and philosophizings of adult people." Submit outline/synopsis and sample chapters through agent only.
Recent Nonfiction Title: *The Year of Three Kings*, by Giles St. Aubyn (history).
Fiction: Adventure, confession, ethnic, experimental, fantasy, gothic, historical, horror, humor, mainstream, mystery, religious, romance, science fiction (Granada), suspense, Western. Submit through agent only.
Recent Fiction Title: *The Far Side of the World*, by Patrick O'Brian (historical novel).

COLORADO ASSOCIATED UNIVERSITY PRESS, Box 480, 1338 Grandview Ave., University of Colorado, Boulder CO 80309. (303)492-7191. Editor: Frederick Rinehart. Publishes hardcover and paperback originals. Averages 10 titles/year. Pays 10-12½-15% royalty contract on wholesale or retail price; "no advances." Publishes book an average of 18 months after acceptance. Will consider photocopied submissions "if not sent simultaneously to another publisher." Electronic submissions OK but "inquire first;" requires hard copy also. Computer printout submissions acceptable. Reports in 3 months. SASE. Free book catalog.
Nonfiction: "Scholarly and regional." Length: 250-500 ms pages. Query first with table of contents, preface or opening chapter. Reviews artwork/photos as part of ms package.
Recent Nonfiction Title: *Chemicals and Cancer*, by Matthew S. Meselson (biology).

*COLUMBIA PUBLISHING CO., INC., Frenchtown NJ 08825. (201)996-2141. Editorial Director: Bernard Rabb. Publishes hardcover originals. Pays 10% royalty; offers average advance. "Subsidy publishing is rarely offered and then only if we feel the book to be worthy to have our name on it." Subsidy publishes 5% of books. Publishes book an average of 9 months after acceptance. Simultaneous and photocopied submissions OK. Electronic submissions OK; but requires hard copy also. Computer printout submissions acceptable; no dot-matrix. Reports in 6 months or longer. SASE.
Nonfiction: Biography, theater, film, dance, classical music, political science, business, recreation, and nature/ecology. Accepts nonfiction and fiction translations from French and German. "We do not want spy novels, westerns, romances, science fiction, mysteries, fad books, religious titles or academic books not applicable to a lay audience." Submit complete ms. Reviews artwork/photos as part of ms package.
Recent Nonfiction Title: *New York and the China Trade*, by Howard.
Fiction: Literary novels—serious fiction only. Submit complete ms.
Recent Fiction Title: *Odyssey of Revenge*, by Diamond.

COLUMBIA UNIVERSITY PRESS, 562 W. 113th St., New York NY 10025. Director: John D. Moore. Editor-in-Chief: William P. Germano. Publishes hardcover and paperback originals and reprints. Pays negotiable royalty. Query. Computer printout submissions acceptable "if high quality". SASE.
Nonfiction: "General interest nonfiction of scholarly value." Scholarly books in the fields of literature, philosophy, fine arts, Oriental studies, history, social sciences, science and law.
Fiction: Serious fiction in translation, of scholarly interest.

COMMONERS' PUBLISHING, 432 Rideau St., Ottawa, Ontario K1N 5Z1 Canada. (613)233-4997. Editorial Director: Glenn Cheriton. Senior Editors: Lucille Shaw, Bruce Brown. Publishes hardcover and paperback originals and software. Royalties paid yearly based on 10% of sales, list. Publishes book an average of 4 months after acceptance. Photocopied submissions OK. "We do not like simultaneous submissions." Computer printout submissions acceptable. Reports in 4 months. SAE and IRCs. Book catalog for SAE and IRC.
Nonfiction: Self-help, alternative lifestyles and crafts books. Reviews artwork/photos as part of ms package. Submit complete ms. Accepts translations from French.
Recent Nonfiction Title: *Kidding Around Ottawa*, by Gold and McDuff.
Fiction: Canadian short stories, plays and fiction; also full-length novels with Canadian themes, locations, and authors; and Canadian poetry. Submit complete ms.
Recent Fiction Title: *Still Close to the Island*, by Dabydeen (short stories).
Software: Contact editor for specific needs.
Tips: Queries/mss may be routed to other editors in the publishing group.

COMMUNICATION SKILL BUILDERS, INC., Box 42050, Tucson AZ 85733. (602)323-7500. Acquisitions/Editorial Manager: Ellen B. North. Publishes paperback originals, kits, games, software and audio cassettes. 60 titles for 1984. Pays negotiable royalty on wholesale or retail price. Publishes book an average of 9 months after acceptance. No simultaneous submissions; photocopied submissions OK. Electronic submissions OK, if IBM-PC compatible or telecommunicated through modem, but requires hard copy also. Computer printout submissions acceptable. SASE. Reports in 4 months. Free book catalog—Speech-Lanugage/Special Education.

Nonfiction: Speech-Language/Special Education material: Articulation therapy, language remediation and development; hearing impaired; adult communicative disorders; physically handicapped/developmentally delayed; early childhood education; professional resource's assessment materials. Reviews artwork/photos as part of ms package. "If a material is illustrated, costs for the photographs or drawings are the responsibility of the author."

Recent Nonfiction Title: *Shape Up Your Language*.
Software: Contact Ellen B. North.

COMMUNICATIONS PRESS, INC., 1346 Connecticut Ave. NW, Washington DC 20036. (202)785-0865. President: Mary Louise Hollowell. Publishes hardcover, trade paperback, and professional/text paperback originals. Averages 6-10 titles/year. Pays royalty or honorarium; offers "nominal, if any" advance. Publishes book an average of 9 months after acceptance. Computer printout submissions acceptable; no dot-matrix. SASE. Reports in 1 month. Free book catalog.

Nonfiction: Reference, technical and textbook. Subjects include business and economics (communications); journalism and communications; performing arts; and politics and sociology (science/technology, public affairs and communications). Accepts outline/synopsis and 2 sample chapters.

Recent Nonfiction Title: *Acting in the Million Dollar Minute: The Art and Business of Performing in TV Commercials*, by Tom Logan.

COMPACT BOOKS, 3014 Willow Lane, Hollywood FL 33021. (305)983-6464. Editor: Wendy V.B. Rappoport. Publishes trade paperback originals. Averages 20 titles/year. Buys mss outright for $3,000 minimum (average 10¢/word) or negotiable royalty. Publishes book an average of 1 year after acceptance. Electronic submissions OK on double-sided/double-density floppy disks using WordStar, but requires hard copy also. Computer printout submissions acceptable; prefers letter-quality to dot-matrix. SASE. Reports in 1 month.

Nonfiction: How-to, self-help and diet and health guides. Subjects include others with mass market appeal. Query.

Recent Nonfiction Title: *Herpes: Prevention and Treatment*, by Donald Kullman, MD and Joel Klass, MD.

COMPCARE PUBLICATIONS, 2415 Annapolis Lane, Minneapolis MN 55441. Publisher: Arnold Keuning. Publishes hardcover and trade paperback originals and reprints. Averages 6-8 titles/year. Pays negotiable royalty; offers negotiable advance. Simultaneous and photocopied submissions OK. Electronic submissions OK, but requires hard copy also. Computer printout submissions acceptable. SASE. Reports in 2 months. Free book catalog.

Nonfiction: Personal growth books on alcoholism/chemical dependency, weight control, personal relationships, stress management, and parenting. "Prefer to hear from writers with credentials in the field they are writing about. Very little chance of publication for divorce experiences or personal recovery from alcoholism or drug addiction." Query.

Recent Nonfiction Title: *Welcome Stress*, by William D. Brown, Ph.D.

‡COMPUTE! BOOKS, A Division of COMPUTE! Publications, Inc., Affiliate of ABC Publishing Companies, Box 5406, Greensboro NC 27403. (919)275-9809. Book editor: Steven Levy. Publishes trade paperback originals and software. Averages 36-48 titles/year. Pays 15% of gross wholesale receipts as royalty on one-author books; pro rata (per page) share of 7½% of gross receipts, plus one-time fee as royalty on collections. "Advances are always paid, but vary according to expected earnings—unlikely to be less than $3,000; can be much higher." Photocopied submissions OK. Publishes ms an average of 6 months after acceptance. Electronic submissions OK if prior arrangements made. Computer printout submissions acceptable (dot-matrix OK if clear). Reports in 4 weeks.

Nonfiction: Books on computers. "We publish books for the home computer user and are always looking for reference books, teaching books, and books of useful programs for small computers. Books must be aimed at the users of a *specific* computer with a specific and limited purpose in mind. For instance, our *Mapping the 64* covers Commodore 64 memory locations clearly and completely with general tips for using them but does not attempt to provide any full-fledged programs. If you have unusual expertise or inside knowledge of a particular subject, then we might well be interested in a highly technical reference book on the order of *Atari BASIC Sourcebook*, but usually we try to aim our books at nontechnical users who are learning programming in their own way and at their own pace. Writers should think of their audience as intelligent people who want their computers to improve their lives and the lives of their loved ones. We are also interested in entertainment programs and programming; home applications; educational programs; and books that teach programming at different levels—if a family or individual would find them useful and interesting. Business applications, obscure languages and expensive computers are generally outside our market, although we will carefully read any proposal." No highly technical books or hardware books. Submit proposal first, which may be a phone call, letter, or outline and synopsis with sample chapters. "We will always require a detailed outline before we issue a contract, but we like to start at the proposal stage and sometimes work with promising authors to develop the outline we want to see. Writers who are known to us through articles in *COMPUTE! Magazine, COMPUTE!'s Gazette* and *Compute!'s PC and PCjr* magazine already have our trust—we know they can come through with the right material—but we have often bought from writers we did not know, and from writers who had never published anything before."

Recent Nonfiction Title: *Compute!'s Reference Guide to Commodore 64 Graphics*, by John Heilborn.
Software: Contact: Randy Fosner.
Tips: "If I were trying to create a marketable computer book today, I would become intimately familiar with one computer, then define a specific area to explain to less-familiar computer users, and write a clear, concise outline of the book I meant to write, along with a sample chapter from the working section of the book (not the introduction). Then I would send that proposal to a publisher whose books you believe are excellent and who targets the same audience you are aiming at. Once the proposal was in the mail, I'd forget about it. Keep learning more about the computer and develop another book proposal. *Don't write a book without a go-ahead from a publisher*. The chances are too great that you will spend 6 months writing a book, only to discover that there are nine on the market with the same concept by the time your ms is ready to send out."

COMPUTER SCIENCE PRESS, INC., 11 Taft Ct., Rockville MD 20850. (301)251-9050. President: Barbara B. Friedman. Editor-in-Chief: Dr. Arthur D. Friedman. Director, Acquisitions: Elizabeth Mergner. Publishes hardcover and paperback originals and software. Averages 20 titles/year. Pays royalty on net price; no advance. Publishes book an average of 1 year after acceptance. Simultaneous and photocopied submissions OK. Computer printout submissions acceptable. Reports ASAP. SASE. Free book catalog.
Nonfiction: "Technical books in all aspects of computer science, computer engineering, computer chess, electrical engineering, computers and math, and telecommunications. Both text and reference books. Will also consider public appeal 'trade' books in computer science, mss and diskettes for computer education at all levels: elementary, secondary and college." Also publishes bibliographies in computer science areas and the quarterly *Journal of VLSI Systems & Computations* and *Journal of Telecommunication Networks*. Query or submit complete ms. "We prefer 3 copies of manuscripts." Looks for "technical accuracy of the material and reason this approach is being taken. We would also like a covering letter stating what the author sees as the competition for this work and why this work is superior."
Recent Nonfiction Title: *Computational Aspects of VLSI*, by Jeff Ullman.
Software: Contact Betty Rouse.

COMPUTER SKILL BUILDERS, Box 42050, Tucson AZ 85733. (602)323-7500. Managing Editor: Ronald H. Weintraub. Publishes educational, trade and mass market paperback originals and software. Averages 10 titles/year. Pays negotiable royalty. No advance. Publishes book an average of 6 months after acceptance. Electronic submissions OK, but requires hard copy also; "inquire first." Computer printout submissions OK; prefers letter-quality to dot-matrix. SASE. Reports in 2-3 weeks on queries; 3 months on mss. Book catalog for 9x12 SAE and 2 first class stamps.
Nonfiction: How-to, reference, self-help, technical and textbook on computers. Interested in "anything to do with computers." Query or submit outline/synopsis and sample chapters. Reviews artwork/photos as part of ms package.
Recent Nonfiction Title: *Math Skill Builders* (software).
Software: Contact Ronald Weintraub. Inquire first before sending software.

CONCORDIA PUBLISHING HOUSE, 3558 S. Jefferson Ave., St. Louis MO 63118. Pays royalty on retail price; outright purchase in some cases. Averages 62 titles/year. Submit outline and sample chapter for nonfiction; complete ms for fiction. Reports in 3 months. SASE. Free book catalog.
Nonfiction: Publishes Protestant, general religious, theological books and periodicals, music works and juveniles. "As a religious publisher, we look for mss that deal with ways that readers can apply Christian beliefs and principles to daily living. Any ms that deals specifically with theology and/or doctrine should conform to the tenets of the Lutheran Church-Missouri Synod. We suggest that if authors have any doubt about their submissions in light of what kind of mss we want, they should first correspond with us."
Fiction: Publishes juvenile picture and beginner books. "We look for mss that deal with Bible stories, Bible history and Christian missions." Looking for novels based on true life stories from the Bible.
Recent Fiction Title: *Sarah*.

CONGDON & WEED, INC., 298 5th Ave., New York NY 10001. (212)736-4883. Assistant Editor: Leslie Garisto. Publishes hardcover and trade paperback originals and trade paperback reprints. Averages 30-35 titles/year. Pays royalty on retail price. Simultaneous and photocopied submissions OK. SASE. Reports in 3 months. Book catalog for 7x10 SAE and 54¢ postage.

Nonfiction: Biography, "coffee table" book, cookbook, humor, illustrated book, and guide book. Subjects include Americana, art, business and economics, cooking and foods, health, history, music, philosophy, politics, psychology and travel. No inspirational books. Submit query letter only.

Recent Nonfiction Title: *Growing Up,* by Russell Baker (autobiography).

Fiction: No genre books of any description. Submit query letter only.

Recent Fiction Title: *A View from the Square,* by John Trenhaile (espionage).

CONSUMER REPORTS BOOKS, Subsidiary of Consumers Union. Subsidiaries include *Consumer Reports* magazine and *Penny Power,* (magazine for children 8-14). 256 Washington St., Mt. Vernon NY 10550. (914)667-9400. Contact: Director, Consumer Reports Books. Publishes trade paperback originals (50%), and trade paperback reprints (50%). Averages 5-10 titles/year. Pays variable royalty on retail price; buys some mss outright. Simultaneous and photocopied submissions OK. Reports in 1 month on queries; 2 months on mss. Free book listing.

Nonfiction: Cookbook, how-to, reference, self-help and technical, and how-to books for children. Subjects include business and economics, cooking and foods, health, music and consumer guidance. Submit outline/synopsis and 1-2 sample chapters.

Recent Nonfiction Title: *Guide to Used Cars.*

CONTEMPORARY BOOKS, 180 N. Michigan Ave., Chicago IL 60601. (312)782-9181. Publisher: Harvey Plotnick. Executive Editor: Nancy Crossman. Adult Education Director: Wendy Harris. Publishes hardcover and trade paperbacks. Averages 110 titles/year. Pays sliding scale of royalties for cloth; most frequently 7½% for paperback. Offers small advance. Simultaneous submissions OK, if so advised. Reports in 3 weeks, longer on complete ms.

Nonfiction: Sports instructional, fitness and health, how-to, self improvement, leisure activities, hobbies, practical business, women's interest, and cookbooks. Also publishes GED and adult basic education materials. Prefers query first with outline/synopsis and sample chapter. "We look at everything; and we do, in fact, publish occasional titles that come in over the transom." Looks for "clarity, insight, high regard for the reader."

Recent Nonfiction Title: *The Official Gourmet Handbook,* by Pat Bruno.

THE CONTINUUM PUBLISHING CORPORATION, 370 Lexington Ave., New York NY 10017. (212)532-3650. Contact: The Editors. Publishes hardcover and paperback originals (85%) and paperback reprints (15%). Publishes 30 titles/year. Pays average 10-12½-15% royalty on hardcover; 7½% on retail paperback; offers an advance. Photocopied submissions OK. SASE. Reports in 2 months. Free book catalog.

Nonfiction: Current affairs, social and educational concerns, psychology, philosophy, sociology, literary criticism, history, biography and self help. Query.

Recent Nonfiction Title: *Talking to Children About Nuclear War,* by William and Mary Van Ormun.

DAVID C. COOK PUBLISHING CO., Chariot Books, 850 N. Grove, Elgin IL 60120. (312)741-2400. Managing Editor: Catherine L. Davis. Associate Editor: Julie Smith. Publishes hardcover and paperback originals and paperback reprints for children and teens. Averages 30-35 titles/year. Pays royalty on retail price. No unsolicited ms. Query only. Computer printout submissions acceptable; prefers letter-quality to dot-matrix. SASE required. Reports in 3 months. Writer's guidelines for 9x12 SASE.

Nonfiction: "We're particularly interested in books that teach the child about the Bible in fun and interesting ways—not just Bible story rehashes. Also books that help children understand their feelings and problems; books about animals, sports, science, or true stories of young people whose Christian faith is a vital part of an interesting life." Query. "We prefer a 2- to 4-page synopsis and first 2 chapters." No unsolicited mss.

Recent Nonfiction Title: *Abram, Abram, Where Are We Going?,* by Fred and Pat McKissack.

Fiction: "We want books with a spiritual dimension that is an integral inevitable part of the story. The plot should involve spiritual as well as external conflict, and the characters should resolve these conflicts through faith in God. Yet the stories should be entertaining and compelling. We are always looking for books that are humorous and books that can be part of a series. For the Pennypincher series we need sports or space fiction for the 10- to 14-year-old boy, and romances for 10- to 14-year-old girls. Also need more titles for the Making Choices series for both 9-12 year-olds and 6-8 year-olds, in which reader is main character, and story has many possible endings.

Recent Fiction Title: *Tales of the Kingdom,* by Karen and David Mains.

Tips: "The author should sell us his manuscript, not only providing a sampling of the book, but also explaining the book's uniqueness, why the book will sell, and why the author is qualified to write it."

COPLEY BOOKS, Subsidiary of The Copley Press, Inc., (Copley Newspapers), Box 957, La Jolla CA 92038. (619)454-1842, 454-0411. Manager: Jean I. Bradford. Publishes hardcover originals. Averages 1-2 titles/year. Pays royalty; "individual agreement with author for each publication." Publishes book a minimum of 1 year after acceptance. Simultaneous and photocopied submissions OK. SASE. Reports in "a few weeks." Free book catalog.

Nonfiction: Biography, "coffee table" book, illustrated book on Americana, art or Western history. Needs mss on "the history of California (including Baja) and the West; aspects of Western contemporary and earlier history, not widely covered previously; diaries, letters of Western pioneers; ecology; water needs in the West, and solutions; Indian lore; Hispanic history and contemporary status." Query or submit outline/synopsis and sample chapters. "If we are really interested in a manuscript and know illustrations are available, we look into artwork/photos in depth. Our publications must be well illustrated!"

Recent Nonfiction Title: *The California to Remember*, by Richard F. Pourade (nostalgic view of old places and old scenes).

CORDOVAN PRESS, Division of Cordovan Corp., Publishers, 5314 Bingle Rd., Houston TX 77092. (713)688-8811. Director: Delton Simmons. Publishes hardcover and paperback originals and reprints. Pays negotiable royalty. Averages 5 titles/year. Publishes book an average of 1 year after acceptance. Computer printout submissions acceptable.

Nonfiction: Professional business and finance, and business self-help. General interest and regional trade, on Texana, Western and Southwestern history, Texas and Southwestern travel and guidebooks. Query.

THE CORINTHIAN PRESS, Subsidiary of EDR Corp., 3592 Lee Rd., Shaker Heights OH 44120. (216)751-7300. Editor: Dave Cockley. Publishes hardcover and trade paperback originals. Averages 3-4 titles/year. Pays 10-15% royalty on wholesale price. Publishes book an average of 1 year after acceptance. Simultaneous and photocopied submissions OK; prefers originals. Computer printout submissions acceptable; no dot-matrix. SASE. Reports in 1 month on queries; 2 months on mss. Free book catalog.

Nonfiction: How-to, juvenile, self-help, technical, and books of regional interest. Subjects include business and economics, health and travel. "We are primarily interested in business books targeted to highly specialized audiences and books of regional interest." Submit outline/synopsis and sample chapters. Reviews artwork/photos as part of ms package.

Recent Nonfiction Title: *Your Skin & How to Live In It*, by Dr. Jerome Z. Litt (self-help).

CORNELL MARITIME PRESS, INC., Box 456, Centreville MD 21617. Managing Editor: Willard A. Lockwood. Publishes original hardcover and quality paperbacks. Averages 10 titles/year. Payment is negotiable but royalties do not exceed 10% for first 5,000 copies, 12½% for second 5,000 copies, 15% on all additional. Revised editions revert to original royalty schedule. Publishes book an average of 1 year after acceptance. Electronic submissions OK "under some circumstances; inquire first." Requires hard copy also. Computer printout submissions acceptable; prefers letter-quality to dot-matrix. Send queries first, accompanied by writing samples and outlines of book ideas. Reports in 1 month. SASE. Free book catalog.

Nonfiction: Marine subjects (highly technical); manuals; and how-to books on maritime subjects. Tidewater Publishers imprint publishes books on regional history, folklore and wildlife of the Chesapeake Bay and the Delmarva Peninsula.

Recent Nonfiction Title: *Nautical Rules of the Road* (2nd ed.).

CORTINA LEARNING INTERNATIONAL, INC., (formerly R.D. Cortina Co., Inc.), 17 Riverside Ave., Westport CT 06880. (203)227-8471. General Editor: MacDonald Brown. Pays on a fee or a royalty basis. Published 27 titles last year. "Do not send unsolicited mss; send outline and sample chapter." Reports in 2 months or less.

Nonfiction: Publishes foreign language and ESL teaching textbooks for self-study and school; language teaching phonograph records and tapes; materials of special ESL interest; and how-to books on writing fiction and nonfiction, writing for radio and TV, photography and art. New titles are published each year in each area. Word length varies.

COWARD McCANN, INC., Imprint of G.P. Putnam's Sons, 200 Madison Ave., New York NY 10016. (212)576-8900. President: Peter Israel. Publisher: Phyllis Grann. Publishes hardcover originals. "We publish about 60 adult titles a year." Pays 10-15% royalty on retail prices. No unsolicited mss. No response without SASE.

Nonfiction: Animals, biography, health, history, how-to, juveniles, nature, politics, psychology, recreation, science, self-help, sociology and sports. "We are looking for nonfiction books on topics of current and/or lasting popular interest, for general, not specialized audiences. Our scope is broad; our needs are for quality manuscripts marketable in the hardcover arena. We do not want manuscripts in specialized or technical fields that require extensive design and art work that lead to high cover prices." Query with SASE only.

Recent Nonfiction Title: *Great Expectations*, by Landon Jones.

Fiction: Adventure, mainstream, mystery, romance and suspense. "We also want espionage thrillers and mysteries, although the market for these is not as strong as it once was. We do not want science fiction, fantasy or experimental novels." Query with SASE only.

Recent Fiction Title: *The Danger*, by Dick Francis.

CRAFTSMAN BOOK CO. OF AMERICA, 6058 Corte Del Cedro, Box 6500, Carlsbad CA 92008. (714)438-7828. Editor-in-Chief: Laurence D. Jacobs. Publishes paperback originals. Pays royalty of 12½% of gross revenues, regardless of quantity sold. Averages 10 titles/year. "More than 60% of our sales are directly to the consumer, and since royalties are based on gross revenues the author's share is maximized." Publishes book an average of 1 year after acceptance. Will send free catalog and author's submission guide on request. Will consider photocopied submissions. Computer printout submissions acceptable. Electronic submissions OK "if compatible with our computers." Submit query or outline. Reports in 2 weeks. SASE.
Nonfiction: "We publish practical references for professional builders and are aggressively seeking manuscripts related to construction, the building trades, civil engineering, construction cost estimating and construction management. Ours are not how-to books for homeowners. Emphasis is on step-by-step instructions, illustrations, charts, reference data, checklists, forms, samples, cost estimates, estimating data, rules of thumb, and procedures that solve actual problems in the field or in the builder's office. Each book covers a limited subject fully, becomes the owner's primary reference on that subject, has a high utility-to-cost ratio, and helps the owner make a better living in his profession. We like to see ideas and queries for books in their early stages; we work with first-time authors, prefer an outline or query, and look for completeness in the coverage of the topic, and clear, simple writing." Reviews artwork/photos as part of ms package.
Recent Nonfiction Title: *Contractor's Guide to the Building Code*, by Jack Hageman.

CRAIN BOOKS, 740 Rush St., Chicago IL 60611. Director: Jack Graham. Publishes hardcover and paperback originals. Averages 12-18 titles/year. Pays royalty on net revenues; makes an advance only under exceptional circumstances. Publishes book an average of 1 year after acceptance. Send contact sheet if photos/illustrations are to accompany ms. Reports in 2 months. SASE. Free book catalog.
Nonfiction: Publishes business books exclusively both for the professional and academic markets. Subject areas: advertising and marketing, insurance, finance and investment, business management, and international business. Basically interested in "practical, nuts-and-bolts, how-to approach by experts in the field." Wants to see "outline, table of contents (down to B heads), and 2-3 sample chapters." Reviews artwork/photos as part of ms package.
Recent Nonfiction Title: *Marketing Research People*, by Jack J. Honomichl.

CREATIVE ARTS BOOK COMPANY, Donald S. Ellis, San Francicso; Black Lizard Books; Life and Health Books; CA Communications Books. 833 Bancroft Way, Berkeley CA 94710. (415)848-4777. Publisher: Donald S. Ellis. Senior Editor: Barry Gifford. Sales Director: Katherine Kruse. Publishes hardcover and paperback originals (50%) and paperback reprints (50%). Averages 16 titles/year. Pays 5-10% royalty on retail price or buys some mss outright for $500-$10,000. Offers minimum $500 advance. Publishes book an average of 18 months after acceptance. Simultaneous and photocopied submissions OK. Computer printout submissions acceptable. SASE. Reports in 3 weeks. Free book catalog.
Nonfiction: Alternative health and foods, cookbooks, how-to, biographies and essays, but open to anything *brilliant* (except poetry). Reviews artwork/photos as part of ms package.
Recent Nonfiction Title: *Getting in Shape*, by Cindy Pemberton.
Fiction: "Looking for serious literary fiction of broad appeal."
Recent Fiction Title: *An Unfortunate Woman*, by Barry Gifford.

CREATIVE BOOK CO., 8210 Varna Ave., Van Nuys CA 91402. (818)988-2334. Editor-in-Chief: Sol H. Marshall. Publishes paperback originals. Full schedule for 1985. Do not submit until late 1985. Pays $50-200 in outright purchase. Publishes book an average of 3 months after acceptance. Simultaneous and photocopied submissions OK. SASE. Reports in 2 weeks. Catalog for SASE.
Nonfiction: Cookbooks/cooking and fund raising and public relations for education and community services. Query or submit outline/synopsis.
Recent Nonfiction Title: *Recipes My Milwaukee Mother Taught Me*, by Dolly Medress.

CRESCENDO PUBLISHING, 132 W. 22nd, New York NY 10011. Address submissions to Gerald Krimm. Publishes hardcover and paperback originals and reprints. Offers standard 10-12½-15% royalty contract; "advances are rare; sometimes made when we seek out an author." Published 20 titles last year. Will look at queries or completed mss. Computer printout submissions acceptable; no dot-matrix. SASE. Reports in 6 weeks.
Nonfiction: Tradebooks in music. Length: open.

THE CROSSING PRESS, Box 640, Trumansburg NY 14886. Co-Publishers: Elaine Gill or John Gill. Publishes hardcover and trade paperback originals. Averages 10-12 titles/year. Pays royalty. Simultaneous and photocopied submissions OK. Electronic submissions acceptable if 8" disks, but requires hard copy also. Computer printout submissions acceptable. Reports in 1 month on queries; 2 months on mss. Publishes book an average of 1 year after acceptance. Free book catalog.
Nonfiction: Cookbook, how-to, literary and feminist. Subjects include cooking, health, gays and feminism.

Accepts nonfiction, fiction and poetry translations. Submissions to be considered for the feminist series must be written by women. Submit outline and sample chapter. Reviews artwork/photos as part of ms package.
Recent Nonfiction Title: *Reclaiming Birth.*
Fiction: Feminism (good literary material). Submit outline and sample chapter.
Recent Fiction Title: *Abeng, Connecticut Countess.*

CROSSWAY BOOKS, 9825 W. Roosevelt Rd., Westchester IL 60153. Subsidiary of Good News Publishers. Editor-in-Chief: Jan P. Dennis. Publishes hardcover and trade paperback originals. Averages 25 titles/year. Pays negotiable royalty; offers negotiable advance. Simultaneous and photocopied submissions OK. SASE. Reports in 6-8 weeks. Book catalog for 9x12 SAE and 2 first class stamps.
Nonfiction: Subjects include issues on Christianity in contemporary culture, Christian doctrine, and church history. Accepts translations from European languages. "All books must be written out of Christian perspective or world view." Query by phone or letter with 3-5 sample chapters or submit complete ms. Accepts artwork/photos.
Recent Nonfiction Title: *A Christian Manifesto,* by Frances Schaeffer.
Fiction: Mainstream; science fiction; fantasy (genuinely creative in the tradition of C.S. Lewis, J.R.R. Tolkien and Madeleine L'Engle); and juvenile age 6 and up to young adult. No formula romance. Submit complete ms. "All fiction must be written from a genuine Christian perspective."
Recent Fiction Title: *Alpha Centauri,* by Robert Siegel.

CROWN PUBLISHERS, INC., 1 Park Ave., New York NY 10016. (212)532-9200. Imprints include Clarkson N. Potter/Arlington House, Barre, Harmony and Julian Press. Editor-in-Chief: Betty A. Prashker. Publishes hardcover and paperback originals. Publishes 250 titles/year. Simultaneous submissions OK. Computer printout submissions acceptable; no dot-matrix. SASE. Reports in 6 weeks.
Nonfiction: Americana, animals, art, biography, cookbooks/cooking, health, history, hobbies, how-to, humor, juveniles, music, nature, philosophy, photography, politics, psychology, recreation, reference, science, self-help and sports. Query with letter only.
Recent Title: *Mistral's Daughter,* by Judith Krantz.

THE CUMBERLAND PRESS, INC., Box 296, Freeport ME 04032. (207)865-6045. Editor: Mary Louise Bridge. Pays 10% royalty on retail price. No advance. Averages 4-6 titles/year. Publishes book an average of 2 years after acceptance. Computer printout submissions acceptable. SASE.
Nonfiction: "We are interested in nonfiction books for national market (especially how-to, calligraphy and philosophy) and regional manuscripts, particularly New England." Looks for marketability, quality, organization. Query.
Recent Nonfiction Title: *These I Do Remember: Fragments From the Holocaust,* by Gerda Haas.

DANTE UNIVERSITY OF AMERICA PRESS, INC., Box 635, Weston MA 02193. Contact: Manuscripts Editor. Publishes hardcover originals and reprints, and trade paperback originals and reprints. Averages 3-5 titles/year. Pays royalty; offers negotiable advance. Publishes book an average of 10 months after acceptance. Simultaneous and photocopied submissions OK. Electronic submissions OK if compatible with in-house systems, but requires hard copy also. Computer printout submissions acceptable. SASE. Reports in 6 weeks on queries; 2 months on mss. Book catalog for business size SAE and 1 first class stamp.
Nonfiction: Biography, reference, reprints and nonfiction and fiction translations from Italian and Latin. Subjects include general scholarly nonfiction, Renaissance thought and letter, Italian language and linguistics, Italian-American history and culture and bilingual education. Query first with SASE. Reviews artwork/photos as part of ms package.
Recent Nonfiction Title: *The Inferno,* by Dante (new translation by Nicholas Kilmer; 34 modern illustrations by Benjamin Martinez).
Poetry: "There is a chance that we would use Renaissance poetry translations."

‡**DAPHNEAN PRESS**, Suite 301, 737 N. LaSalle St., Chicago IL 60610. (312)944-2525. President: Michael Gross. Publishes hardcover and trade paperback originals and hardcover and trade paperback reprints. Averages 5-10 titles/year. Pays 5-10% royalty on paperback wholesale price and hardcover retail price. Simultaneous and photocopied (if good quality) submissions OK. Electronic submissions OK if IBM PC compatible, but requires hard copy also. Computer printout submissions acceptable, preferably double-struck. SASE. Reports in 4 weeks on queries; 10 weeks on mss. Free book catalog.
Nonfiction: General and scholarly academic. Subjects include Americana, biography, reference, anthropology, history, philosophy, photography, political science, psychology, religion, sociology and Judaica. "We are particularly interested in the humanities and the social sciences. We are also looking for manuscripts in a specialized nonfiction field which might be called 'academic hobbies.' This field includes reference works for those who pursue an academic field such as history, or psychology as a hobby. In other words, we are looking for academic level books that would be marketable to a more general audience. Nonfiction of academic, schol-

arly and textbook quality is also of great interest." No how-to, occult or martial arts. Query or submit complete ms.

Fiction: Full-length historical novels. "We are primarily a nonfiction house but will consider historical fiction."

Tips: "Our audience is academic and semi academic. The niche that we see for ourselves is between scholarly and popular, emphasizing quality nonfiction."

DARTNELL CORP., 4660 N. Ravenswood Ave., Chicago IL 60640. (312)561-4000. Senior Vice-President: John P. Steinbrink. Publishes manuals, reports, hardcovers. Royalties: sliding scale based "usually on retail price. Published 7 titles last year." Publishes book an average of 1 year after acceptance. Computer printout submission acceptable; no dot-matrix. Send outline and sample chapter. Reports in 4 weeks. SASE.
Nonfiction: Interested in new material on business skills and techniques in management, supervision, administration, advertising sales, etc.
Recent Nonfiction Title: *Wage and Salary Administration*, by William Davidson.

DARWIN PUBLICATIONS, 850 N. Hollywood Way, Burbank CA 91505. (818)848-0944. Executive Editor: Victoria Darwin. Publishes hardcover and trade paperback originals and reprints. Averages 3-4 titles/year. Pays 10% royalty on retail price. Simultaneous and photocopied submissions OK. Computer printout submissions acceptable (printout paper should be separated and collated with sprocket holes detached); "only letter-quality is acceptable." SASE. Reports in 2 weeks on queries; 1 month on mss. Free book catalog.
Nonfiction: "Coffee table" book, how-to, illustrated book, reference and technical. Subjects include Americana, regional history, hobbies, nature, railroading and recreation. "Manuscripts on adventurous topics, with interesting photos, (mostly b&w). In-depth research with casual writing style." Query. Accepts outline/synopsis and 1-2 sample chapters. "We look at overall scope and treatment of the topic, the author's writing style, how photos and illustrations complement the text, and how much editing it will require in light of its salability (its editorial cost-effectiveness). Author is expected to contribute marketing input." Reviews artwork/photos as part of ms package.
Recent Nonfiction Title: *Recreational Gold Prospecting*, by Jim Martin (how-to).
Tips: "It is increasingly expensive to produce hardcover, illustrated books that pertain to limited audiences. Writer should either broaden their scope for such books or lower their expectations for production specifications."

DATA AND RESEARCH TECHNOLOGY CORP., D.A.R.T. Corp., 1102 McNeilly Ave., Pittsburgh PA 15216. Editor: Frank X. McNulty. Pays 10% royalty; buys some mss outright. Computer printout submissions acceptable. SASE. Reports in 3 weeks.
Nonfiction: Publishes the "Answers:" (series of select bibliographies). Current and original bibliographies as reference sources for specific audiences like telecommunications managers, condominium owners, or people interested in computer applications, etc. "To be accepted for publication, the quality must meet the approval of any serious researcher or librarian. The references must include a brief abstract, title, publisher, pages, price. The bibliography should include not only books, but periodicals, tapes, any audiovisuals, videotapes and discs, trade associations, etc." Also looks at any authoritative, specific manuscripts in the field of bibliography. Query with SASE. Accepts outline/synopsis and 1 sample chapter.

DAVIS PUBLICATIONS, INC., 50 Portland St., Worcester MA 01608. (617)754-7201. Acquisitions Editor: Wyatt Wade. Averages 5-10 titles/year. Pays 10-15% royalty. Publishes book an average of 1 year after acceptance. Computer printout submissions acceptable; prefers letter-quality to dot-matrix. Write for copy of guidelines for authors. Submit outline, sample chapters and illustrations. Enclose return postage.
Nonfiction: Publishes art, design and craft books. Accepts nonfiction translations. "Keep in mind the intended audience. Our readers are *viewers*, as well. All illustrations should be collated separately from the text, but keyed to the text. Photos should be good quality original prints. Well selected illustrations should explain, amplify, and enhance the text. We average 2-4 photos/page. We like to see technique photos as well as illustrations of finished artwork. Recent books have been on papermaking, airbrush painting, jewelry, design, puppets, programs for the artistically gifted, quilting, and watercolor painting." Reviews artwork/photos as part of ms package.

STEVE DAVIS PUBLISHING, Box 190831, Dallas TX 75219. Publisher: Steve Davis. Publishes trade paperback originals and software. Averages 6-8 titles/year. Pays 10-15% royalty on net price. Publishes book an average of 3 months after acceptance. "Disk submissions compatible with TI Professional (MS-DOS, CPM-86 or P-system ASCII files) preferred, but should be accompanied by hardcopy printout and should not use extensive special formatting codes." Computer printout submissions acceptable. "We expect manuscripts to be professionally proofed for style, grammar and spelling before submission." SASE. Reports in 3 weeks on queries; 1 month on mss.
Nonfiction: Specializes in personal computer topics. "We want to see a unique approach to timely information

for computer users." Query or submit outline/synopsis and sample chapter. Reviews artwork/photos as part of ms package.
Recent Nonfiction Title: *Programs for the PCjr*, by David Migicovsky, Brian Madigan and Steve Davis.
Fiction: Experimental, fantasy, humor and science fiction. "We do not expect to publish primarily fiction. However, would consider something fresh and unique." No mass market westerns, romance, religious, etc. Query or submit outline/synopsis and sample chapters.

DAW BOOKS, INC., 1633 Broadway, New York NY 10019. Editor: Donald A. Wollheim. Publishes science fiction paperback originals and reprints and software. Publishes 62 titles/year. Pays 6% royalty; $2,500 advance and up. Simultaneous submissions "returned at once, unread." Computer printout submissions acceptable; prefers letter-quality to dot-matrix. SASE. Reports in 6 weeks. Free book catalog.
Fiction: "We are interested in science fiction and fantasy novels only. We do not publish any other category of fiction. We are not seeking collections of short stories or ideas for anthologies. We do not want any nonfiction manuscripts." Submit complete ms.
Recent Fiction Title: *Thendara House*, by Marion Zimmer Bradley.

DBI BOOKS, INC., 1 Northfield Plaza, Northfield IL 60093. Subsidiary of Dun & Bradstreet, Technical Publishing Co. (312)441-7010. Vice President, Publisher: Sheldon L. Factor. Publishes trade paperback originals. Averages 15-20 titles/year. Pays negotiable royalty on retail price; buys some mss outright. Reports in 2 weeks on queries; 3 weeks on mss. SASE. Free book catalog.
Nonfiction: Subjects include recreation and sports. Specifically needs how-to books on guns, hunting, fishing, camping and various participant sports. No spectator sports. Query or submit outline/synopsis and sample chapters.
Recent Nonfiction Title: *Gun Digest*, edited by Ken Warner (annual technical gun book).

JOHN DE GRAFF, INC., Distributed by International Marine Publishing Co., Camden ME 04843. Editorial: Clinton Corners NY 12514. (914)266-5800. President: John G. DeGraff. Publishes hardcover originals. Averages 2-3 titles/year. Pays 10% royalty on retail price. Publishes book an average of 10 months after acceptance. Simultaneous and photocopied submissions OK. Computer printout submissions acceptable. SASE. Reports in 2 weeks on queries; 1 month on mss. Free book catalog.
Nonfiction: Nautical (pleasure boating). "Our books are for yachtsmen, boat builders and naval architects. We're interested in the how-to aspects rather than boating experiences." Submit complete ms. Reviews artwork/photos as part of ms package.
Recent Nonfiction Title: *Yachtsmen's Legal Guide to Co-ownership*, by Odin.

DELACORTE PRESS, 245 E. 47th St., New York NY 10017. (212)605-3000. Editor-in-Chief: Jackie Farber. Publishes hardcover originals. Publishes 30 titles/year. Pays 10-12½-15% royalty; average advance. Publishes book an average of 18 months after acceptance. Simultaneous and photocopied submissions OK. Computer printout submissions acceptable; prefers letter-quality to dot-matrix. SASE. Reports in 2 months.
Fiction and Nonfiction: Query, outline or brief proposal, or complete ms accepted only through an agent; otherwise returned unopened. No mss for children's or young adult books accepted in this division.
Recent Nonfiction Title: *Go For It!*, by Dr. Irene C. Kassorla.
Recent Fiction Title: *Changes* by Danielle Steel.

DELAIR PUBLISHING COMPANY, INC., 420 Lexington Ave., New York NY 10170. (212)867-2255. Imprints include Culinary Arts Institute (cookbooks). Editor: Louise L. Apfelbaum. Executive Editor: Edward T. Finnegan. Publishes hardcover and paperback originals (80%) and reprints (20%). Averages 45 titles/year. Pays royalty; offers advance; other arrangements, depending on work. SASE. Simultaneous and photocopied submissions OK. Computer printout submissions acceptable.
Nonfiction: Cookbooks; women's interest; consumerism; how-to; juvenile to age 9 (with art only); reference and self-help books about cooking, entertaining and foods; crafts; home maintenance, decorating and improvement; health; medicine; and travel. Accepts nonfiction translations. Query or submit outline/synopsis and 2 sample chapters. Reviews artwork/photos with ms package.
Recent Nonfiction Title: *Chinese Cuisine: Cooking for Health and Happiness*, by Eva Lee Jen.
Tips: "We are actively looking for manuscripts with very broad mass appeal (primarily to homemakers). Heavily illustrated books OK; cookbooks should contain a minimum of 200 recipes, though can be much longer."

DELL PUBLISHING CO., INC., 1 Dag Hammarskjold Plaza, New York NY 10017. Imprints include Dell, Delacorte Press, Delta Books, Dell Trade Paperbacks, Laurel, Delacorte Press Books for Young Readers, Candlelight Books, Yearling and Laurel Leaf. Publishes hardcover and paperback originals and reprints. Publishes 500 titles/year. Pays royalty on retail price. "General guidelines for unagented submissions. Please adhere strictly to the following procedure: 1) Do not send manuscript, sample chapters or art work; 2) Do not register, certify or insure your letter; 3) Send only a 4-page synopsis or outline with a cover letter stating previous work published or relevant experience." Simultaneous and photocopied submissions OK. Reports in 3 months. SASE.

Nonfiction: "Because Dell is comprised of several imprints, each with its own editorial department, we ask you to carefully review the following information and direct your submission to the appropriate department. Your envelope must be marked, Attention: (blank) Editorial Department—Proposal. Fill in the blank with one of the following: Delacorte: Publishes in hardcover. Looks for popular nonfiction (*Indecent Exposure*). Delta and Dell Trade: Publishes in trade paperback; rarely publishes original fiction; looks for useful, substantial guides (*Feed Your Kids Right*); entertaining, amusing nonfiction (*Cult Movies*); serious work in the area of modern society (*Killing Our Own*). Yearling and Laurel Leaf: Publishes in paperback and hardcover for children and young adults, grades 7-12. Purse: Publishes miniature paperbacks about 60 pages in length on topics of current consumer interest, e.g., diet, exercise, coin prices, etc."

Fiction: Refer to the above guidelines. Delacorte: Publishes top-notch commercial fiction in hardcover (e.g., *Changes*). Dell: Publishes mass-market paperbacks; rarely publishes original nonfiction; looks for family sagas, historical romances, sexy modern romance, adventure and suspense, thrillers, occult/horror and war novels. Especially interested in submissions for our Candlelight Ecstasy Line. Not currently publishing original mysteries, westerns or science fiction.

DELMAR PUBLISHERS, INC., 2 Computer Dr., W., Box 15-015, Albany NY 12212. (518)459-1150. Director of Publishing: G.C. Spatz. Publishes hardcover and paperback textbooks and educational sofware. Averages 50 titles/year. Pays royalty on wholesale price. SASE. Reports in 2 weeks on queries; 2 months on submissions. Free book catalog.

Nonfiction: Subjects include business and data processing, allied health/nursing, childcare, mathematics, agriculture/horticulture texts, and textbooks for most vocational and technical subjects. Reviews artwork/photos as part of ms package. Books are used in secondary and postsecondary schools. Query and submit outline/synopsis and 2-3 sample chapters.

Recent Nonfiction Title: *Fundamentals of Numerical Control*, by William Luggen.

Software: Developing educational software in the same areas as nonfiction above.

Tips: Queries/mss may be routed to other editors in the publishing group.

DELTA BOOKS, Division of Dell Publishing Co., 1 Dag Hammarskjold Plaza, New York NY 10017. (212)605-3000. Editor-in-Chief: Jackie Farber. Publishes trade paperback reprints and originals. Averages 10 titles/year. Pays 6-7½% royalty; average advance. Simultaneous and photocopied submissions OK. Computer printout submissions acceptable; prefers letter-quality to dot-matrix. SASE. Reports in 2 months. Book catalog for 8½x11 SASE.

Nonfiction: Consciousness, health, how-to, humor, music, New Age, photography, politics, recreation, reference, science, self-help and sports. "We would like to see books on the arts, social history, social criticism and analysis, and child care. We do not want to see biography, philosophy, academic books, textbooks, juveniles, or poetry books." Query or submit outline/synopsis and sample chapters. Prefers submissions through agents.

Recent Nonfiction Title: *Holy Terror*, by Flo Conway and Jim Siegelmann.

Fiction: "We are looking for original, innovative and contemporary novels." Submit through an agent.

Recent Fiction Title: *The Feud*, by Thomas Berger.

DEMBNER BOOKS, 1841 Broadway, New York NY 10023. (212)265-1250. Subsidiary of Red Dembner Enterprises Corp. Editorial Director: S. Arthur Dembner. Senior Editor: Anna Dembner. Publishes hardcover and trade paperback originals. Averages 10 titles/year. Offers royalty on invoice list price. "Advances are negotiable—from bare bones on up." Publishes book an average of 1 year after acceptance. Simultaneous and photocopied submissions OK. Computer printout submissions acceptable; no dot-matrix. SASE. Reports in 2-3 weeks.

Nonfiction: Biography, business/economics, health, history, hobbies, how-to, nature, philosophy, politics, psychology, recreation, reference, science, and self-help. "We're interested in upbeat, intelligent, informative manuscripts. No cult, fad, or sex books. We prefer books that are worth reading, and even keeping." Submit outline/synopsis and sample chapters with SASE. Reviews artwork/photos as part of ms package "if it is pertinent."

Recent Nonfiction Title: *The Singing Voice*, by R. Rushmore (history of singing).

Fiction: Adventure, historical, mainstream, mystery, and suspense. "We are prepared to publish a limited number of well-written, nonsensational works of fiction." Submit outline/synopsis and sample chapters with SASE.

Recent Fiction Title: *D.E.A.D. (A Medical Mystery)*, by E. Whitmore.

DENEAU PUBLISHERS & CO. LTD., 411 Queen St., Ottawa, Ontario K1R 5A6 Canada. (613)233-4075. Editorial Director: Barbara Stevenson. Publishes 93% hardcover and paperback originals and 7% paperback reprints. Averages 12 titles/year. Negotiates royalty and advance. Simultaneous and photocopied submissions

OK. Computer printout submissions acceptable; prefers letter-quality to dot-matrix. SASE. Reports in 2 months. Free book catalog.
Nonfiction: Business/economics, social issues, politics, recreation and travel. Submit outline/synopsis and 1-2 sample chapters.
Recent Nonfiction Title: *A Very Public Life-Volume I-Far from Home*, by Paul Martin.
Fiction: Literary. Submit outline and 1-2 sample chapters.
Recent Fiction Title: *Hix Nix Stix & Pix*, by David Burdett.

T.S. DENISON & CO., INC., 9601 Newton Ave., S. Minneapolis MN 55431. Editor-in-Chief: W.E. Rosenfelt. Publishes teacher aid materials. Royalty varies, usually $80-100 per 1,000 sold, 8-10% on occasion; no advance. Send prints if photos are to accompany ms. Photocopied submissions OK. Computer printout submissions acceptable; no dot-matrix. Reports in 2-4 weeks. SASE. Book catalog for SASE.
Nonfiction: Specializes in early childhood books. Submit complete ms. Reviews artwork/photos as part of ms package.

DENLINGER'S PUBLISHERS, LTD., Box 76, Fairfax VA 22030. (703)631-1500. Publisher: William W. Denlinger. Publishes hardcover and trade paperback originals, mass market paperback originals and hardcover and trade paperback reprints. Averages 12 titles/year. Pays variable royalty. No advance. Simultaneous and photocopied submissions OK. SASE. Reports in 1 week on queries; 6 weeks on mss.
Nonfiction: Biography, "coffee table" book, how-to and technical books on Americana and animals. Query.
Recent Nonfiction Title: Bird Dogs and Upland Game Birds, by Jack Stuart.
Fiction: Historical and animal (dog). Query.
Recent Fiction Title: *Mandingo*.

DETSELIG ENTERPRISES LTD., Box G399, Calgary, Alberta T3A 2G3 Canada. President: T.E. Giles. Publishes hardcover and trade paperback originals. Averages 6-8 titles/year. "The quality of the material and writing must be of a very high standard." Pays 8-13% royalty on wholesale price. No advance. Publishes book an average of 10 months after acceptance. Simultaneous and photocopied submissions OK. Computer printout submissions acceptable; prefers letter-quality to dot-matrix. SASE. Reports in 1 month on queries; 4 months on mss. Free book catalog.
Nonfiction: Biography, "coffee table" book, cookbook, reference, technical and textbook. Subjects include business and economics, cooking and foods, health, history, hobbies, psychology and sociology. "Most of our books will emphasize the Canadian scene." Immediate needs are university and college textbooks. No radical politics and religion. Query.
Recent Nonfiction Title: *The Canadian Coal Industry*, by F. Anton.

*DEVIN-ADAIR PUBLISHERS, INC., Subsidiary: The Chatham Press, 6 N. Water St., Greenwich CT 06830. (203)531-7755. Editor: Jane Andrassi. Publishes hardcover and paperback originals, reprints and software. . Royalty on sliding scale, 5-25%; "average advance is low." Averages 20 titles/year. Subsidy publishes 5% of books. Publishes book an average of 1 year after acceptance. No simultaneous submissions. Electronic submissions OK on disk compatible with present system, but requires hard copy also. Computer printout submissions acceptable. SASE. Free book catalog.
Nonfiction: Publishes Americana, business, how-to, conservative politics, history, medicine, nature, economics, sports and travel books. New lines: personal computer books and homeopathic books. Accepts translations. Query or submit outline/synopsis and sample chapters. Reviews artwork/photos as part of ms package. Looks for "early interest, uniqueness, economy of expression, good style, and new information."
Recent Nonfiction Title: *A Defense that Defends*, by Lt. Gen. Daniel O. Graham.
Tips: "We purposely seek to publish books of high quality manufacture. We spend 8% more on production and design than necessary to insure a better quality book. Trends include increased specialization and a more narrow view of a subject. General overviews in computer publishing are now a thing of the past. Better a narrow subject in depth than a wide superficial one."

*DHARMA PUBLISHING, 2425 Hillside Ave., Berkeley CA 94704. (415)548-5407. Editor: Betty Cook. Publishes hardcover and paperback originals (90%) and paperback reprints (10%). Publishes 10 titles/year. Pays 5-7% royalty on retail price; no advance. Subsidy publishes 5% of books. Computer printout submissions acceptable. SASE. Reports in 1-2 months. Free book catalog.
Nonfiction: Art (Tibetan and other Buddhist); biography (Buddhist); history (Asia and Buddhism); philosophy

(Buddhist); photography (Buddhist); psychology (Buddhist); religion (Buddhism); and self-help. "We want translations of Buddhist texts from Tibetan or Sanskrit. Please—no original discussions of Buddhist topics." Query.
Recent Nonfiction Title: *The Voice of the Buddha (Buddhist Sutra).*

‡**DIAL BOOKS FOR YOUNG READERS**, Subsidiary of E.P. Dutton, Inc., 2 Park Ave., New York NY 10016. (212)725-1818. Assistant Editor: Paula Wiseman. Imprints include Dial Easy-to-Read Books, Out-and-About Books, and Dial Very First Books. Publishes hardcover originals. Averages 50 titles/year. Pays variable royalty and advance. Simultaneous and photocopied submissions OK. Computer printout submissions acceptable; no dot-matrix. SASE. Reports in 2 weeks on queries; 3 months on mss. Free book catalog.
Nonfiction: Juvenile picture books and young adult books. Subjects include animals, history and nature. Especially looking for "quality picture books and well-researched young adult and middle-reader mss." Not interested in alphabet books, riddle and game books, and early concept books." Query with outline/synopsis and sample chapters.
Recent Nonfiction Title: *Mountains*, by Clive Catchpole (picture book).
Fiction: Adventure, fantasy, historical, humor, mystery, romance (appropriate for young adults), and suspense. Especially looking for "lively and well written novels for middle grade and young adult children involving a convincing plot and believable characters. The subject matter or theme should not already be overworked in previously published books. The approach must not be demeaning to any minority group, nor should the roles of female characters (or others) be stereotyped, though we don't think books should be didactic, or in any way message-y." No "topics inappropriate for the juvenile, young adult, and middle grade audiences. No plays or poetry." Submit complete ms.
Recent Fiction Title: *The Man in the Woods*, by Rosemary Wells (novel).
Tips: "Our readers are anywhere from preschool age to teenage. Picture books must have strong plots, lots of action, unusual premises, or universal themes treated with freshness and originality. Humor works well in these books."

THE DIAL PRESS, Doubleday, Inc., 245 Park Ave., New York NY 10167. (212)953-4561. Publishes hardcover and paperback originals. Averages 60 titles/year. Pays royalty on retail price. Simultaneous and photocopied submissions OK. Reports in 6 weeks. SASE.
Nonfiction: "All general trade nonfiction is of interest." Submit outline/synopsis and sample chapters.
Recent Nonfiction Title: *Sensing the Enemy*, by Lady Borton.
Fiction: All general adult categories. Submit outline/synopsis and sample chapters.
Recent Fiction Title: *Deadlock*, by Sara Paretsky.

‡**DIGITAL PRESS, Digital Equipment Corp.**, 30 North Ave., (FPD/B9), Burlington MA 01803. (617)273-6252. Managing Editor: John Osborn. Imprints include DEC books. Averages about 16 titles/year. Pays 7½-20% royalty. Offers average $5,000 advance. Simultaneous submissions OK. Computer printout submissions acceptable, but must be double-spaced. SASE. Reports in 1 month. Free book catalog.
Nonfiction: How-to, reference, technical and textbook. Subjects include computer systems and applications. "For Digital Press, we're especially looking for texts for students in intermediate and advanced undergraduate computer and information science courses. Also, exercise texts for new technologies for practicing hardware and software engineers. For DEC books, how-to books for uses of Digital Equipment products that help readers work more effectively at their jobs. No elementary or humorous books; no documentation." Submit outline synopsis and sample chapters.
Recent Nonfiction Titles: *Going-Online*, by Alfred Grossbrenner.
Tips: Our audiences are undergraduate computer science students and practicing engineers (Digital Press); and DEC customers, especially VAX PDP-11 and Rainbow (DEC Books). Our most successful titles are those that are either concise (yet comprehensive) introductions to new technologies (office automation, communications, AI) or product specific guides.

DILITHIUM PRESS, Box 606, Beaverton OR 97075. (503)646-2713. Editorial Director: Merl Miller. Publishes paperback originals and software. Averages 25-30 titles/year. Pays 5-25% royalty on wholesale or retail price; average advance. Photocopied submissions OK. Electronic submissions OK, if compatible with IBM. Computer printout submissions acceptable. SASE. Reports in 2 months. Free book catalog.
Nonfiction: Textbooks and books about microcomputers. "We are looking for manuscripts in the field of microcomputers. Topics should be geared to general information, hardware and software." Accepts outline/synopsis and 4-5 sample chapters. Reviews artwork/photos as part of ms package. Query.
Recent Nonfiction Title: *Bits, Bytes and Buzzwords*, by Mark Garetz.
Software: Contact Gary Swanson.

DILLON PRESS, INC., 500 S. 3rd St., Minneapolis MN 55415. (612)333-2691. Editorial Director: (Ms.) Uva Dillon. Senior Editor: Tom Schneider. Juvenile Fiction Editor: (Mr.) Terry Hopkins. Publishes hardcover originals. Averages 25-30 titles/year. Pays royalty and by outright purchase. Publishes book an average of 9 months after acceptance. Submit complete ms or outline and 1 sample chapter. Computer printout submissions acceptable; no dot-matrix. Reports in 6 weeks. SASE.

Nonfiction: "We are actively seeking manuscripts for the juvenile educational market." Areas of interest: science, wildlife, environment, biography, heritage, crafts and outdoor activities, and contemporary issues. Reviews artwork/photos as part of ms package.

Recent Nonfiction Title: *China: From Emperors to Communes*, by Chris and Janie Filstrap (juvenile).

Fiction: We are looking for engaging stories that will appeal to K-6 readers. Areas of interest: animal/nature tales, mysteries, science fiction, and stories that focus on the lifestyles, problems, and experiences of today's young people.

Tips: "Writers can best tailor their material to our needs by making themselves aware of the subjects and people who appeal to today's youngsters."

DIMENSION BOOKS, INC., Box 811, Denville NJ 07834-0811. (201)627-4334. Contact: Thomas P. Coffey. Publishes 35 titles/year. Pays "regular royalty schedule" based on retail price; advance is negotiable. Book catalog for SASE. Reports in 1 week on receipt of mss. SASE.

General Nonfiction: Publishes general nonfiction including religion, principally Roman Catholic. Also psychology. Accepts nonfiction translations. Query. Accepts outline/synopsis and 3 sample chapters. Length: 40,000 words minimum.

Recent Nonfiction Title: *Looking for Jesus*, by A. van Kaam

*DODD, MEAD & CO., 79 Madison Ave., New York NY 10016. (212)685-6464. Includes Everest House imprint. Senior Editors: Jerry Gross, Nancy Crawford, Allen T. Klots, Margaret Norton, Cynthia Vartan. Managing Editor: Chris Fortunato. Royalty basis: 10-15%. Advances vary, depending on the sales potential of the book. A contract for nonfiction books is offered on the basis of a query, a suggested outline and a sample chapter. Write for permission before sending mss. Averages 200 titles annually. Subsidy publishes 1% of books. Adult fiction, history, philosophy, the arts, and religion should be addressed to Editorial Department. Publishes book an average of 9 months after acceptance. Electronic submissions OK "only on exceptional occasions when submission can be used on equipment of our suppliers." Reports in 1 month. SASE.

Fiction and Nonfiction: Publishes book-length mss. Length: 70,000-100,000 words average. Fiction and nonfiction of high quality, mysteries and romantic novels of suspense, biography, popular science, travel, yachting and other sports, music and other arts. Very rarely buys photographs or poetry. Publishes books for juveniles. Children's Books Editor: Mrs. Jo Ann Daly. Length: 1,500-75,000 words.

Tips: "Freelance writers should be aware of trends toward nonfiction and the difficulty of publishing marginal or midlist fiction."

DOLL READER, Subsidiary of Hobby House Press, Inc., 900 Frederick St., Cumberland MD 21502. (301)759-3770. Subsidiaries include *Doll Reader*, *The Teddy Bear and Friends Magazine*, and *Dolls Values Quarterly*. Publisher: Gary R. Ruddell. Publishes hardcover originals. Averages 18 titles/year. Pays royalty. Simultaneous and photocopied submissions OK. Computer printout submissions acceptable. SASE. Reports in 2 weeks. Free book catalog.

Nonfiction: Doll related books. "We publish books pertaining to dolls and teddy bears as a collector's hobby; we also publish pattern books. The *Doll Reader* is published 8 times a year dealing with the hobby of doll collecting. We appeal to those people who are doll collectors, miniature collectors, as well as people who sew for dolls. Our magazine has a worldwide circulation of close to 50,000." Query or submit outline/synopsis. Reviews artwork/photos as part of ms package. *The Teddy Bear and Friends Magazine* is published quarterly.

Recent Nonfiction Title: *5th Blue Book of Dolls and Values*, by Jan Foulke (price guide for dolls).

THE DONNING COMPANY/PUBLISHERS, INC., 5659 Virginia Beach Blvd., Norfolk VA 23502. Editorial Director: Robert S. Friedman. Publishes hardcover and paperback originals. Averages 30-35 titles/year. Pays 10-12½-15% royalty on retail price, up to 50% discount (hardcover titles); 8-10-12% royalty on paperback; advance "negotiable." Simultaneous (if so informed) and photocopied submissions OK. Computer printout submissions acceptable. Reports in 3 months. SASE. Book catalog for SASE.

Nonfiction: Wants material for 3 series: 1) Portraits of American Cities Series (pictorial histories of American cities with 300 illustrations, primarily photographs, with fully descriptive captions and historical overview text of approximately 10,000 words. "The intent is to capture the character of a community in transition, from earliest known settlers to the present. Author need not be a professional historian, but must have close ties to the community and cooperation of local historians and private and public photo archives); 2) Regional Specialty Books (specialty, regional cookbooks, popular history and art collections); and 3) Unilaw Library imprint (Editor: Richard Horwege. Religious, inspirational, metaphysical subjects and themes). Accepts nonfiction translations. "Prefer complete manuscript, if not a thorough outline and 3 sample chapters. We look for professionally presented material, with helpful marketing and promotion suggestions if author has any." Accepts artwork/photos.

Recent Nonfiction Title: *Worlds Beyond: The Art of Chesley Bonestell.*
Fiction: Starblaze Editions imprint. Editor: Kay Reynolds.
Recent Fiction Title: *Hit or Myth*, by Robert Asprin (science fiction/fantasy).
Tips: "Beginning writers are finding it harder to get published because of the increasing number of copies needed to break even. Regional appeal books are easier to place, and authors should consider doing more of them to break into print." Queries/mss may be routed to other editors in the publishing group.

DOUBLEDAY & CO., INC., 245 Park Ave., New York NY 10167. (212)953-4561. Publishes hardcover and paperback originals; publishes paperback reprints under Anchor, Dolphin and Image imprints. Offers royalty on retail price; offers variable advance. Reports in 2½ months. Publishes over 400 titles/year. Query with outline and sample chapters for both fiction and nonfiction to editorial department. Enclose return postage. "Doubleday has a policy concerning the handling of unsolicited manuscripts. We return unopened and unread all complete manuscripts, accompanied by a form telling how we would like submissions made. However, in 2 areas, we will accept complete manuscripts: mysteries and science fiction. These mss should be addressed to the appropriate editor (for example, Science Fiction Editor) and not just to Doubleday. We presently have a moratorium on books for young readers, and poetry publishing and are not accepting proposals."

DOUBLEDAY CANADA, LTD., 105 Bond St., Toronto, Ontario M5B 1Y3 Canada. (416)977-7891. Senior Editor: Janet Turnbull. Publishes hardcover originals. Publishes 15-20 titles/year. Pays royalty on retail price; advance "varies." Publishes book an average of 6 months after acceptance. Simultaneous and photocopied submissions OK. Computer printout submissions acceptable. Reports in 3 months. Free book catalog.
Nonfiction: General interest. "We do not specialize, but the major part of our list consists of biography, popular history, and subjects of contemporary interest. Our main concern is to publish books of particular interest to the Canadian market, although our books are published in the US as well. We will consider any nonfiction proposal." Query or submit outline/synopsis and 3 or 4 sample chapters. Reviews artwork/photos as part of ms package "if pertinent, but photocopies will suffice—*do not* send original artwork in the mail."
Recent Nonfiction Title: *Glenn Gould Variations*, by Himself and His Friends.
Fiction: "No particular preferences as to style or genre. We publish both 'literary' and 'commercial' books. Once again, we are most interested in adult fiction with a Canadian angle (author, setting, subject). Of course, we hope they have North American potential as well." Query or submit outline/synopsis and opening chapters.
Recent Fiction Title: *Among Friends*, by L.R. Wright.
Tips: Looks for "identification of genre of work; straightforward description of what book is about; indication of whether work is completed or in progress; covering letter detailing writer's publishing history, any credentials or experience that particularly qualifies him/her to do the proposed book." In fiction, studies plot summary and brief sketch of major characters. Queries/mss may be routed to other editors in the publishing group.

DOW JONES-IRWIN, (Business and Finance) 1818 Ridge Rd., Homewood IL 60430. (312)798-6000. Executive Editor: Ralph Rieves. Publishes originals only. Royalty schedule and advance negotiable. Publishes 85 titles annually. Reports in 2 weeks. SASE.
Nonfiction: Business and financial subjects. Query with outline.
Recent Nonfiction Title: *Money Market: Myth, Reality and Practice*, by Marcia Stigum.
Tips: Queries/mss may be routed to other editors in the publishing group.

DOWN EAST BOOKS, Subsidiary of Down East Enterprise, Inc., Box 679, Camden ME 04843. (207)594-9544. Editor: Karin Womer. Publishes hardcover and trade paperback originals and hardcover and trade paperback reprints. Averages 10-16 titles/year. Pays 10-15% on wholesale price. Offers average $200 advance. Publishes book an average of 18 months after acceptance. Simultaneous and photocopied submissions OK. Computer printout submissions acceptable. SASE. Reports in 2 weeks on queries; 2 months on mss. Free book catalog.
Nonfiction: Biography, "coffee table" book, cookbook, illustrated book, juvenile, reference and textbook. Subjects include Americana, art, cooking and foods, history, nature, traditional crafts, photography and recreation. "Our books have a Maine or New England emphasis." Query. Reviews artwork/photos as part of ms package.
Recent Nonfiction Title: *Our Home Made of Stone*, by Helen Nearing.
Fiction: "We publish no fiction except for an occasional juvenile title (average 1/year)."
Recent Fiction Title: *The Circus Boat*, by John Hooper.

***DRAGON'S TEETH PRESS**, El Dorado National Forest, Georgetown CA 95634. (916)333-4224. Editor: Cornel Lengyel. Publishes trade paperback originals. Averages 6 titles/year. Subsidy publishes 25% of books; applies "if book has high literary merit, but very limited market." Pays 10% royalty on retail price, or in copies. Publishes book an average of 4 months after acceptance. Simultaneous and photocopied submissions OK. Computer printout submissions acceptable. SASE. Reports in 2 weeks on queries; 1 month on mss. Book catalog for SASE with 63¢ postage.

Nonfiction: Music and philosophy. Publishes for 500 poets, or potential poets. Query or submit outline/synopsis and sample chapters. Reviews artwork/photos as part of ms package.

Poetry: "Highly original works of potential literary genius. No trite, trivial or trendy ego exhibitions." Submit 10 samples or the complete ms.

Recent Poetry Title: *The Liam Poems*, by Thomas Heffernan (lyric poetry).

THE DRAGONSBREATH PRESS, 10905 Bay Shore Dr., Sister Bay WI 54234. Editor: Fred Johnson. Publishes hardcover and trade paperback originals. "The Dragonsbreath Press is a small press producing handmade limited edition books including original artwork meant for collectors of fine art and books who appreciate letterpress printing. This audience accepts a handmade book as a work of art." Averages 1 title/year. Payment conditions "to be arranged"; no advance. Simultaneous and photocopied submissions OK. Computer printout submissions acceptable; prefers letter-quality to dot-matrix. SASE. Reports in 2 months on queries; 3 months on mss.

Nonfiction: Biography, humor, illustrated book. Subjects include Americana, art, history and photography. "We're interested in anything suited to handmade book production—short biography, history, original artwork, photography." Query first; do not submit ms. Reviews artwork/photos as part of ms package.

Fiction: Adventure, erotica, experimental, fantasy, horror, humor, mystery, science fiction. "We are looking for short, well written stories which lend themselves to illustration and deserve to be made into fine, handmade books." *No long, novel length manuscripts or children's books.* Query first; do not submit ms.

Recent Fiction Title: *How I Became Popular Overnight*, by F.W. Johnson (mystery/humor).

Poetry: "We're looking for good readable poetry that is unique. No religious, sweet Hallmark style or divorce poems." Submit 3 samples with query; submit complete ms "only when requested."

Tips: "We are not currently reading any manuscripts. Please do not submit mss unless they have been requested."

DRAMA BOOK PUBLISHERS, 821 Broadway, New York NY 10003. (212)228-3400. Contact: Ralph Pine or Judith C. Rudnicki. Publishes hardcover and paperback originals and reprints and software. Royalty varies; advance varies; negotiable. Publishes book an average of 9 months after acceptance. Electronic submissions for Read CP/M (kaypro) OK; but requires hard copy also. Computer printout submissions acceptable; "but query first." Averages 15 titles/year. Reports in 4 to 8 weeks. SASE.

Nonfiction: Books—texts, guides, manuals, directories, reference—for and about performing arts theory and practice: acting, directing; voice, speech, movement, music, dance, mime; makeup, masks, wigs; costumes, sets, lighting, sound; design and execution; technical theatre, stagecraft, equipment; stage management; producing; arts management, all varieties; business and legal aspects; film, radio, television, cable, video; theory, criticism, reference; playwriting; theatre and performance history. Accepts nonfiction, drama, and technical works in translations also. Query; accepts 1-3 sample chapters; no complete mss. Reviews artwork/photos as part of ms package.

Fiction: Plays and musicals.

Software: Contact Ralph Pine. Publishes software for performing arts-related programs.

*DUCK DOWN PRESS, Box 1047, Fallon NV 89406. (702)423-6643. Editor/Publisher: Kirk Robertson. Imprints: Windriver Series (fiction and poetry). Publishes trade paperback originals. Averages 3-5 titles/year. Subsidy (combination of NEA and private funds) publishes 50% of books. Pays in copies and royalties on "amount of sales above expenses." Computer printout submissions acceptable; prefer letter-quality to dot-matrix. Publishes book an average of 1 year after acceptance. SASE. Reports in 1 week on queries; 3 weeks on mss. Book catalog for 6x9 SAE and 2 first class stamps.

Nonfiction: Art and photography, especially collage. Reviews artwork/photos as part of ms package.

Fiction: Quality post modern literature. Query with outline/synopsis and sample.

Recent Fiction Title: *The Chase*, by Gerald Locklin (novel).

Poetry: Publishes 2-4 titles/year. No juvenile, rhymed or metrical. Submit 5-10 poems.

Recent Poetry Title: *The Broken Face of Sommer*, by Michael Hogan.

‡DUNDURN PRESS LTD., Box 245, Station F, Toronto, Ontario, M4Y 2L4 Canada. (416)368-9390. Publisher: Kirk Howard. Editor: Bernice Lever. Publishes hardcover, trade paperback and mass market paperback reprints and hardcover, trade paperback, and mass market paperback reprints. Averages 6-12 titles/year. Pays 10% royalty on wholesale price; 8% royalty on some paperback children's books. Publishes book an average of 1 year after acceptance. "Easy-to-read" photocopied submissions OK. Computer printout submissions acceptable; prefers letter-quality to dot-matrix.

Nonfiction: Biography, "coffee table" book, how-to, juvenile, literary, and reference. Subjects include Canadiana, art, history, hobbies, Canadian history and literary criticism. Especially looking for Canadian biographies. No religious or soft science topics. Query with outline/synopsis and sample chapters. Reviews artwork/photos as part of ms package.

Recent Nonfiction Title: *Dolls in Canada.*

Fiction: Looking for fiction dealing with Canadian historical topics. No "usual mass market sex, crime and romance, etc., books." Query with outlines/synopsis and sample chapters.
Recent Fiction Title: *Laura Secord.*
Tips: "Publishers want more factual books written in better prose styles. If I were a writer trying to market a book today, I would visit book stores and watch what readers buy and what company prints that type of book 'close' to my ms."

DUQUESNE UNIVERSITY PRESS, 600 Forbes Ave., Pittsburgh PA 15282. (412)434-6610. Averages 9 titles/year. Pays 10% royalty on net sales; no advance. Publishes book an average of 1 year after acceptance. Query. Reports in 3 months. Enclose return postage.
Nonfiction: Scholarly books in the humanities, social sciences for academics, libraries, college bookstores and educated laypersons. Length: open. Looks for scholarship.
Recent Nonfiction Title: *Contemporary Psychology: Revealing and Obscuring the Human*, by Maurice Friedman (psychology).

DURST PUBLICATIONS, 29-28 41st Ave., Long Island City NY 11101. (212)706-0303. Owner: Sanford Durst. Publishes hardcover and trade paperback originals (30%) and reprints. Averages 20+ titles/year. Pays variable royalty. Publishes book an average of 6 months after acceptance. Computer printout submissions acceptable; no dot-matrix. SASE. Reports in 1 month. Book catalog for business-size SAE and 75¢ postage.
Nonfiction: How-to and reference on Americana, art, business and economics, cooking and foods, hobbies—primarily coin collecting, stamp collecting, antiques and legal. Especially needs reference books and how-to on coins, medals, tokens, paper money, art, antiques—illustrated with valuations or rarities, if possible. Publishes for dealers, libraries, collectors and attorneys. Submit outline/synopsis and sample chapters. Reviews artwork/photos as part of ms package.
Recent Nonfiction Title: *Buying & Selling Country Land*, by D. Reisman (practical/legal).
Tips: "Write in simple English. Do not repeat yourself. Present matter in logical, orderly form. Try to illustrate."

DUSTBOOKS, Box 100, Paradise CA 95969. (916)877-6110. Publisher: Len Fulton. Publishes hardcover and paperback originals. Averages 7 titles/year. Offers 15% royalty. Offers average $500 advance. Simultaneous and photocopied submissions OK if so informed. Computer printout submissions acceptable. SASE. Reports in 1-2 months. Free book catalog.
Nonfiction: Technical. "DustBooks would like to see manuscripts dealing with microcomputers (software, hardware) and water (any aspect). Must be technically sound and well-written. We have at present no titles in these areas. These represent an expansion of our interests." Submit outline/synopsis and sample chapters.

E.P. DUTTON, 2 Park Ave., New York NY 10016. (212)725-1818. Publisher, Children's Books: Ann Durell. Senior Editor: Julie Amper. Averages 50 titles/year. Pays royalty on list price; offers variable advance. Considers unsolicited mss. Computer printout submissions acceptable; prefers letter-quality to dot-matrix. "Please send query letter first on all except picture book mss."
Fiction: Picture books; Smart Cats (beginning readers); stories for ages 8-12; Skinny Books (Hi-lo for ages 12 and up). Reviews artwork/photos as part of ms package. Emphasis on books that will be current and popular as well as well written.
Recent Fiction Title: *The Kestrel*, by Lloyd Alexander.
Tips: Queries/mss may be routed to other editors in the publishing group.

EAKIN PUBLICATIONS, INC., Box 23066, Austin TX 78735. (512)288-1771. Imprints include Nortex. Editorial Director: Edwin M. Eakin. Publishes hardcover and paperback originals (95%) and reprints (5%). Averages 40 titles/year. Pays 10-12-15% in royalty. Simultaneous and photocopied submissions OK. SASE. Reports in 3 months. Free book catalog sent on request.
Nonfiction: History, juvenile history and folklore. Specifically needs biographies of well-known Texas people, current Texas politics and history for grades 3-9. Query first or submit outline/synopsis and sample chapters.
Recent Nonfiction Title: *Marble Dust: Biography of Elizabeth Ney.*
Fiction: Historical fiction for school market. Specifically need juveniles that relate to Texas. Query or submit outline/synopsis and sample chapters.
Recent Fiction Title: *Bluebonnet at the Alamo*, by Mary Brooke Casad (juvenile).

EAST WOODS PRESS, (Trade name of Fast & McMillan Publishers, Inc.), 429 East Blvd., Charlotte NC 28203. (704)334-0897. Editorial Director: Sally Hill McMillan. Publishes hardcover and paperback originals and hardcover and paperback reprints. Publishes 10-15 titles/year. Pays 5-12% royalty on retail price. "Submissions must be on hard copy. If accepted, we can work with disks to edit and produce." Computer printout submissions acceptable. Reports in 4 weeks on queries; 6-8 weeks on mss. Average advance $500. SASE. Book catalog for 9x12 SAE and 40¢ postage.

Nonfiction: "Coffee table" book, cookbook, how-to, self-help and travel guides. No business or humor. "We are mainly interested in travel and the outdoors. Regional guidebooks are our specialty, but anything on travel and outdoors will be considered." Query. "A list of competitive books should be submitted, along with specific reasons why this manuscript should be published. Also, maps and art should be supplied by the author."
Recent Nonfiction Title: *Wildflower Folklore*, by Laura C. Martin.

*EASTVIEW EDITIONS, INC., Box 783, Westfield NJ 07091. (201)233-0474. Subsidiary includes Glenn Associates. Manager: Mr. N. Glenn. Publishes hardcover and trade paperback originals (90%) and reprints. Averages 12 titles/year. Pays standard royalty contract. Simultaneous and photocopied submissions OK. Computer printout submissions acceptable. SASE. Reports in 6 weeks. Free book catalog.
Nonfiction: Illustrated books on the arts, history, hobbies, music, nature, photography, design, dance and antiques. Also does limited editions of nature and art books. Considers all material for domestic and international publication. Submit outline and 2-3 sample chapters, table of contents; "description of the book, what the author envisions." Reviews artwork/photos as part of ms package. Will distribute to book trade and libraries; (national and international) books privately printed. Will cooperate with author/artist/photographer in producing mss and books for publication and distribution.
Recent Nonfiction Title: *Enchanting Hungary*, by Lau.

THE ECCO PRESS, Subsidiaries include *Antaeus*, 18 W. 30th St., New York NY 10001. (212)685-8240. Editor: Daniel Halpern. Associate and Managing Editor: Megan Ratner. Publishes hardcover and trade paperback originals and reprints. Averages 12 titles/year. Pays 5-15% royalty on retail price; offers average $300 advance. Photocopied submissions OK. SASE. Reports in 1 week on queries; 2 months on mss. Free book catalog.
Nonfiction: Cookbook and literary criticism. "Can do only 1 or 2 books." No scientific, historical or sociological mss. Query.
Recent Nonfiction Title: *Twentieth Century Pleasures*, by Robert Hass.
Fiction: Experimental, mainstream and serious or 'literary' fiction. "Can do 1 or possibly 2 novels or short story collections." Query.
Recent Fiction Title: *The Crush*, by Gary Gildner (short story).
Poetry: One or two new collections. No religious, inspirational, etc. Submit 4-6 samples.
Recent Poetry Title: *History of My Heart*, by Robert Pinsky.

*EDUCATION ASSOCIATES, Box 8021, Athens GA 30603. (404)542-4244. Editor, Text Division: D. Keith Osborn. Publishes hardcover and trade paperback originals. Averages 2-6 titles/year. Subsidy publishes 50% of books. "We may publish a textbook which has a very limited audience . . . but we still believe that the book will make a contribution to the educational field." Buys mss "on individual basis." Photocopied submissions OK. Computer printout submissions acceptable; prefers letter-quality to dot-matrix. SASE. Reports in 3 weeks on queries.
Nonfiction: How-to and textbook. Subjects include psychology and education. "Books in the fields of early childhood and middle school education. Do not wish basic textbooks. Rather, are interested in more specific areas of interest in above fields. We are more interested in small runs on topics of more limited nature than general texts." Query with one-page letter. If interested will request synopsis and sample chapters. No reply unless SASE is enclosed.
Recent Nonfiction Title: *Creative Activities for Preschoolers*, by A. Hendrickson (supplemental college text).

WILLIAM B. EERDMANS PUBLISHING CO., Christian University Press, 255 Jefferson Ave. SE, Grand Rapids MI 49503. (616)459-4591. Editor-in-Chief: Jon Pott. Publishes hardcover and paperback originals (80%) and reprints (20%). Averages 55 titles/year. Pays 7½-10% royalty on retail price; usually no advance. Simultaneous and photocopied submissions OK. Computer printout submissions acceptable; prefers letter-quality to dot-matrix. SASE. Reports in 3 weeks for queries and 4 months for mss. Looks for "quality and relevance." Free book catalog.
Nonfiction: History, philosophy, psychology, reference, religion, sociology and textbooks, regional history, geography and tourists guidebooks. "Approximately 80% of our publications are religious—specifically Protestant and largely of the more academic or theological (as opposed to devotional, inspirational or celebrity-conversion type of book) variety. Our history and 'social studies' titles aim, similarly, at an academic audience; some of them are 'documentary' histories. We prefer that writers take the time to notice if we have published anything at all in the same category as their manuscript before sending it to us." Accepts nonfiction translations. Query. Accepts outline/synopsis and 2-3 sample chapters.
Recent Nonfiction Title: *The Naked Public Square*, by Richard John Neuhaus.

‡EMC PUBLISHING, EMC Corporation, 300 York Ave., St. Paul MN 55101. (612)771-1555. Editor: Rosemary J. Barry. Publishes hardcover originals and software. Averages 20 titles/year. Publishes book an average of 1 year after acceptance. Pays variable royalty or makes variable outright purchase. Simultaneous and photocopied submissions OK. Computer printout submissions acceptable; prefers letter-quality to dot-matrix. Reports in 2 weeks on queries; 1 month on mss.

Nonfiction: Textbook. Subjects include business and economics, career/consumer education, language arts and foreign language. Especially looking for "language arts skill material. No religious or adult material. We strictly publish for schools." Query. All unsolicited mss are returned unopened.

Recent Nonfiction Title: *Decisions*, by Brenneke and Hamill (consumer economics textbook).

Fiction: "No religious or adult material; we publish *only* for schools." Query. All unsolicited mss are returned unopened.

Software: Language arts, science and math for educational market.

ENSLOW PUBLISHERS, Bloy St. and Ramsey Ave., Box 777, Hillside NJ 07205. (201)964-4116. Editor: Ridley Enslow. Publishes hardcover and paperback originals. Averages 30 titles/year. Pays 10-15% royalty on retail price or net price; offers $500-5,000 advance. Publishes book an average of 8 months after acceptance. Query. Photocopied submissions OK. Computer printout submissions acceptable. SASE. Reports in 2 weeks. Free book catalog.

Nonfiction: Biography, business/economics, health, hobbies, how-to, juveniles, philosophy, psychology, recreation, reference, science, self-help, sociology, sports and technical. Accepts nonfiction translations. Submit outline/synopsis and 2 sample chapters. Reviews artwork/photos as part of ms package.

Recent Nonfiction Title: *Complete Handbook of Speed Skating*, by Holum (sports).

ENTERPRISE PUBLISHING CO., INC., 725 Market St., Wilmington DE 19801. (302)654-0110. Editor/Publisher: T.N. Peterson. Publishes hardcover and paperback originals, "with an increasing interest in newsletters and periodicals." Averages 4 titles/year. Pays royalty on wholesale or retail price. Advance averages $1,000. Publishes book an average of 6 months after acceptance. Simultaneous and photocopied submissions OK, but "let us know." Computer printout submissions acceptable; prefers letter-quality to dot-matrix. SASE. Catalog and writer's guidelines for SASE.

Nonfiction: "Subjects of interest to small business owners/entrepreneurs. They are highly independent and self-sufficient, and of an apolitical to conservative political leaning. They need practical information, as opposed to theoretical: self-help topics on business, including starting and managing a small enterprise, advertising, marketing, raising capital, public relations, tax avoidance and personal finance." Business/economics, legal self-help and business how-to. Query. All unsolicited mss are returned unopened.

Recent Nonfiction Title: *The Complete Credit and Collections System*, by Arnold S. Goldstein.

ENVIRONMENTAL DESIGN & RESEARCH CENTER, 261 Port Royal Ave., Foster City CA 94404. Contact: Dr. Kaiman Lee. Publishes hardcover originals. Averages 5 titles/year. Pays 15-18% royalty. SASE. Free book catalog.

Nonfiction: Reference, technical, textbook and encyclopedic. Subjects include business and economics (personal finance); architecture; energy; and environment. "We're looking for manuscripts on personal financial and survival planning. Our books are highly technical but of current material." Submit complete ms.

Recent Nonfiction Title: *Encyclopedia of Financial and Personal Survival: 650 Coping Strategies*, by K. Lee and R. Yang.

*PAUL S. ERIKSSON, PUBLISHER, Battell Bldg., Middlebury VT 05753. (802)388-7303, (802)247-8415. President: Paul S. Eriksson. Publishes hardcover and paperback trade originals (99%) and paperback trade reprints (1%). Averages 5-10 titles/year. Pays 10-15% royalty on retail price; advance offered if necessary. Subsidy publishes 5% of books. "We have to like the book and probably the author." Photocopied submissions OK. SASE. Reports in 3 weeks. Free book catalog.

Nonfiction: Americana, birds (ornithology), art, biography, business/economics, cookbooks/cooking/foods, health, history, hobbies, how-to, humor, music, nature, philosophy, photography, politics, psychology, recreation, self-help, sociology, sports and travel. Submit outline/synopsis and sample chapters. Looks for "intelligence, excitement and salability."

Recent Nonfiction Title: *Steinbeck and Covici*, by Thomas Fensch.

Fiction: Mainstream. Submit outline/synopsis and sample chapters.

Recent Fiction Title: *The Headmaster's Papers*, by Richard A. Hawley.

ESSCO, Akron Airport, Akron OH 44306. (216)733-6241. President/Editorial Director: Ernest Stadvec. Publishes paperback originals. Averages 14 titles/year. Pays 10% royalty on retail price for the first 1,000 and 15% thereafter; no advance. Simultaneous and photocopied submissions OK. SASE. Reports in 2 weeks. Free book catalog.

Nonfiction: Biography, history, hobbies, how-to, technical and textbooks, all on aviation. Specifically needs aviation-related subjects, aircraft guide books, training manuals, aircraft picture books, historical books and military aviation. Query.

Recent Nonfiction Title: *The Eternal Twin Beech*, by E. Stadvec (historical).

*ETC PUBLICATIONS, Drawer ETC, Palm Springs CA 92263. (619)325-5352. Editorial Director: LeeOna S. Hostrop. Senior Editor: Dr. Richard W. Hostrop. Publishes hardcover and paperback originals. Subsidy publishes 5-10% of books. Averages 12 titles/year. Offers 5-15% royalty, based on wholesale and retail price. No advance. Publishes book an average of 1 year after acceptance. Simultaneous and photocopied submissions OK. Computer printout submissions acceptable. SASE. Reports in 3 weeks. Book catalog $2.
Nonfiction: Business/economics, how-to, library science, reference, education, sports, technical, and textbooks. Reviews artwork/photos as part of ms package. Accepts nonfiction translations. Submit complete ms.
Recent Nonfiction Title: *The Fans Vote! 100 Baseball Superstars*, by R. Bartlett (sports).
Tips: "ETC is particularly interested in textbook titles for use in college courses in professional education—also reference titles in all areas."

EVANS AND CO., INC., 216 E. 49 St., New York NY 10017. Editor-in-Chief: Herbert M. Katz. Publishes hardcover originals. Royalty schedule to be negotiated. Averages 30 titles annually. Will consider photocopied submissions. Computer printout and disk submissions OK. "No mss should be sent unsolicited. A letter of inquiry is essential." Reports in 8 weeks. SASE.
General Nonfiction and Fiction: "We publish a general trade list of adult fiction and nonfiction, cookbooks and semi-reference works. The emphasis is on selectivity since we publish only 30 titles a year. Our fiction list represents an attempt to combine quality with commercial potential. Our most successful nonfiction titles have been related to health and the behavioral sciences. No limitation on subject. A writer should clearly indicate what his book is all about, frequently the task the writer performs least well. His credentials, although important, mean less than his ability to convince this company that he understands his subject and that he has the ability to communicate a message worth hearing." Accepts artwork/photos.
Tips: "Writers should review our catalog (available for 9x12 envelope with 2 stamps) or the *Publishers Trade List Annual* before making submissions."

EXANIMO PRESS, 23520 Hwy. 12, Segundo CO 81070. Editor: Dean Miller. Publishes hardcover and trade paperback originals. Averages 6-10 titles/year. Pays 10% minimum royalty on retail price; buys some mss outright for $500-1,500; no advance. Publishes ms an average of 6 months after acceptance. Photocopied submissions OK. Computer printout submissions acceptable; prefers letter-quality to dot-matrix. SASE. Reports in 1 month on queries; 2 weeks on mss. Book catalog for SAE and 1 first class stamp.
Nonfiction: How-to and technical. Subjects include prospecting; small mining; treasure hunting; self-employment; dowsing (water witching); and self or family improvement from an economical point of view. Accepts nonfiction translations from German or French (on dowsing and mining only). "We would like to publish one book per month in our particular field which is mining, prospecting and treasure hunting. Our style and format is approximately 8x10" pages with books running from 40 to 104 pages. We prefer a profusely illustrated book, and our artist will make finished sketches from rough drawings. Our books are aimed at the adventuresome person or family and people who want to get out of the rat race and into a profitable activity that relieves them of audits, inspections and red tape. No copy artistry, please, and no read-and-rewrites; we want hard core mining material from people with at least ten full years of experience." Query. Accepts outline/synopsis, 1 sample chapter and intended table of contents. Reviews artwork/photos as part of ms package.
Recent Nonfiction Title: *Midas Manual—How to Earn Money as Your Own Boss.*
Tips: "Investigate the market and find a publisher whose specialty is in accord with your proposed book or books. Most try to create a good working relationship and pave the way for future books which will obviously pave the way for a higher financial return for you. The secret is to get a first book published in order to give leverage for future books. Specialize in one field and develop a reputation for technically accurate books and get two or three titles into print and then look forward to an ascending career in writing."

‡FABER & FABER, INC., Division of Faber & Faber, Ltd., London, England; 39 Thompson St., Winchester MA 01890. (617)721-1427. Editorial Director: Dennis M. Campbell. Publishes hardcover and trade paperback originals, and hardcover and trade paperback reprints. Averages 20 titles/year. Pays 7½-15% royalty on wholesale or retail price, offers average $1,500 advance. Publishes book an average of 9 months after acceptance. Simultaneous and photocopied submissions OK. Computer printout submissions acceptable; prefers letter-quality to dot-matrix. SASE. Reports in 3 weeks on queries; 6 weeks on mss. Book catalog for 8½x11 SAE and 3 first class stamps.
Nonfiction: Biography, "coffee table" book, how-to, humor, illustrated book, juvenile, self-help, and technical. Subjects include Americana, animals, art, health, history, hobbies, music, philosophy, photography, politics, sociology and travel. Query. Reviews artwork/photos as part of ms package.
Recent Nonfiction Title: *Mysterious America*, by Loren Coleman.
Fiction: Ethnic, experimental, historical, mainstream, mystery and regional. No historical/family sagas. Query.
Recent Fiction Title: *Last Dance*, by Lee Grove.
Tips: "If I were a writer trying to market a book today, I would go with an established small press if it were my first work."

‡**FABLEWAVES PRESS**, Box 7874, Van Nuys CA 91409. (213)322-0236. Editor: Tina Harris. Publishes trade paperback originals. Averages 3 titles/year. Pays 6-7½% royalty on retail price. Simultaneous and photocopied submissions OK. Computer printout submissions acceptable; prefers letter-quality to dot-matrix. SASE. Reports in 6 weeks on queries; 4 months on mss. Free book catalog.
Fiction: Adventure, experimental, fantasy, humor/satire, mainstream, and science fiction (creatures that look human; no hard-core science or machinery). Also short stories and literary—"to encourage creative writing for our offbeat/bizarre Anthology series; fiction of 'electrifying literary merit' for our highly selective Where Does Literary Acclaim Originate in America? series." Send for free guidelines catalog. "Present needs: well-crafted novels that reflect the vices and follies of our time. Don't send deadwood-formula type manuscripts if you want to catch our interest. Be inventive at heart. Project your soul and guts. No pro-macho, pro-war, pro-wealth, pro-power or pro-materialistic visions." Query or submit outline/synopsis and sample chapters.
Recent Fiction Title: *Hollyhell*, by Felix DeSicilia (mainstream novel).
Tips: "Our audience is young and old; curious and progressive."

*****FAIRCHILD BOOKS & VISUALS**, Book Division, 7 E. 12th St., New York NY 10003. Manager: E.B. Gold. Publishes hardcover and paperback originals. Offers standard minimum book contract; no advance. Pays 10% of net sales distributed twice annually. Published 12 titles last year. Subsidy publishes 5% of books. Publishes book an average of 1 year after acceptance. Photocopied submissions OK. Enclose return postage. Free book catalog.
Nonfiction: Publishes business books and textbooks relating to fashion, electronics, marketing, retailing, career education, advertising, home economics and management. Length: open. Query, giving subject matter, brief outline and at least 1 sample chapter. Reviews artwork/photos as part of ms package.
Recent Nonfiction Title: *Fairchild's Designer's/Stylist's Handbook*, by Gioello.

‡*****FAIRLEIGH DICKINSON UNIVERSITY PRESS**, 285 Madison Ave., Madison NJ 07940. (201)377-4050. Chairperson, Editorial Committee: Harry Keyishian. Subsidy publishes less than 10% of books. Publishes hardcover originals. Averages 35 titles/year. "Contract is arranged through Associated University Presses. We are a *selection* committee only." Computer printout submissions acceptable. Reports in 2 weeks on queries; 4 months on mss. Publishes book an average of 18 months after acceptance. Free book catalog.
Nonfiction: Reference and scholarly books. Subjects include art, business and economics, history, music, philosophy, politics, psychology and sociology. Looking for scholarly books in all fields. No non scholarly books. Query with outline/synopsis and sample chapters. Reviews artwork/photos as part of ms package.
Recent Nonfiction Title: *Beyond the Ballot Box: A Social History of the Boston Irish*, by Dennis Ryan.

*****FALCON PRESS PUBLISHING CO., INC.**, 324 Fuller, Box 731, Helena MT 59624. (406)442-6597. Publisher: Bill Schneider. Publishes hardcover and trade paperback originals. Averages 5-8 titles/year. Subsidy publishes 30% of books. Pays 8-15% royalty on net price. Publishes book an average of 6 months after ms is in final form. Simultaneous and photocopied submissions OK. Computer printout submissions acceptable. SASE. Reports in 3 weeks on queries; 6 weeks on mss. Free book catalog.
Nonfiction: "Coffee table" book, cookbook, how-to and self-help. Subjects include Americana, cooking and foods, health, history, hobbies, nature, photography, recreation, sports and travel. "We're primarily interested in recreational guidebooks." No fiction or poetry. Query only. Do not send ms.
Recent Nonfiction Title: *The Floater's Guide to Colorado*, by Doug Wheat.

*****THE FAMILY ALBUM**, Rt. 1, Box 42, Glen Rock PA 17327. (717)235-2134. Contact: Ron Lieberman. Publishes hardcover originals and reprints and software. Averages 4 titles/year. Subsidy publishes 20% of books. Pays royalty on wholesale price. Publishes book an average of 6 months after publication. Simultaneous and photocopied submissions OK. Electronic submissions OK on 5¼ floppy disk—CP/M. Computer printout submissions acceptable. SASE. Reports in 2 months.
Nonfiction: "Significant works in the field of (nonfiction) bibliography. Worthy submissions in the field of Pennsylvania-history, biography, folk art and lore. We are also seeking materials relating to books, literacy, and national development. Special emphasis on Third World countries, and the role of printing in international development." No religious material. Submit outline/synopsis and sample chapters.
Software: Bibliography and library/bookselling.

*****FARNSWORTH PUBLISHING CO., INC.**, 78 Randall Ave., Rockville Centre NY 11570. (516)536-8400. President: Lee Rosler. Publishes hardcover and paperback originals. "Standard royalty applies, but 5% is payable on mail order sales." Publishes 20 titles/year. Subsidy publishes 15% of books. Publishes book an average of 1 year after acceptance. Computer printout submissions accepted "for consideration"; prefers letter-quality to dot-matrix. Reports in 2 months. SASE.
Nonfiction: "Our books generally fall into 2 categories: books that appeal to executives, lawyers, accountants, life underwriters, financial planners and other salespeople (subject matter may cover selling techniques, estate and financial planning, taxation, money management, etc.); and books that appeal to the general popula-

tion—generally in the financial area—and are marketable by direct mail and mail order, in addition to bookstore sales." Submit outline/synopsis and 3 sample chapters.

Recent Nonfiction Title: *The Financial Planner's Handbook to Regulation and Successful Practice*, by Jeffrey B. Kelvin, JD, LL.M, CLU.

FARRAR, STRAUS AND GIROUX, INC., 19 Union Square West, New York NY 10003. Children's Editor: Stephen Roxburgh. Publishes hardcover originals. Pays royalty; advance. Publishes book an average of 18 months after acceptance. Photocopied submissions OK. Computer printout submissions acceptable. SASE. Reports in 3 months. Catalog for SASE.

Nonfiction and Fiction: "We are interested in fiction picture books, and nonfiction for ages 10 and up. Submit outline/synopsis and sample chapters. Reviews artwork/photos as part of ms package.

Recent Nonfiction Title: *Upon the Head of the Goat: A Childhood in Hungary 1939-1944*, by Aranka Siegal.

Recent Fiction Title: *The Witches*, by Roald Dahl.

Recent Picture Book Title: *It Happened in Pinsk*, by Arthur Yorinks.

*FREDERICK FELL PUBLISHERS, INC., 386 Park Ave., S., New York NY 10016. (212)685-9017. Editor: Ms. Mercer Warriner. Publishes hardcover and paperback originals (95%) and reprints (5%). Pays 10% royalty, based on wholesale or retail price. Publishes 20 titles/year. Subsidy publishes 1% of books. Send sample prints or contact sheet if photos/illustrations are to accompany ms. Publishes book an average of 1 year after acceptance. Photocopied submissions OK. Computer printout submissions acceptable; no dot-matrix. Reports in 2 months. SASE. Free book catalog.

Nonfiction: Diet, business, hobbies, how-to, medicine and psychiatry, psychology, recreation, inspiration, self-help and sports books. Query with outline and 3 sample chapters. Reviews artwork/photos as part of ms package.

Recent Nonfiction Title: *Food Allergy Detection Program*, by Terry Traub.

THE FEMINIST PRESS, Box 334, Old Westbury NY 11568. (516)997-7660. Publishes paperback originals and reprints of literature. Averages 12-15 titles/year. Pays 10% royalty on net sales; no advance. Simultaneous and photocopied submissions OK. Reports in 3 months. Query or submit outline/synopsis and sample chapters.

Nonfiction: Florence Howe, Editor. Feminist books for a general trade and women's studies audience. "We publish biographies, reprints of lost feminist literature, women's history, bibliographies and educational materials. No material without a feminist viewpoint. No contemporary adult fiction, drama, or poetry." Looks for "feminist perspective, interesting subject, potential use in women's studies classroom, sensitivity to issues of race and class, clear writing style, general grasp of subject."

Recent Nonfiction Title: *Lesbian Studies*, edited by Cruikshauh, (anthology).

Tips: "Submit a proposal for an important feminist work that is sophisticated in its analysis, yet popular in its writing style. Both historical and contemporary subjects will be considered. We are especially interested in works that appeal to both a trade audience and a women's studies classroom market."

‡*FICTION COLLECTIVE, INC., c/o Department of English, Brooklyn College, Brooklyn NY 11210. (212)780-5547. All ms queries should be addressed to Fiction Collective Manuscript Central, c/o Department of English, Illinois State University, Normal IL 61761. Publishes hardcover and trade paperback originals. Averages 4 titles/year. "When we have accepted a ms for publication, and if we have funds to subsidize publication, these funds are used to subsidize production costs. If no subsidy or other funds are available, we must postpone publication." Pays in books. Publishes book an average of 1 year after acceptance. Simultaneous and photocopied submissions OK. Computer printout submissions acceptable; no dot-matrix. SASE. Reports in 2 weeks on queries; 6 months on mss. Free book catalog.

Fiction: "We will consider any genre of fiction that is innovative and of high quality. Structure and language, not genre, are our considerations. We are always interested in high quality, innovative fiction whether it's a novel, short story collection or novella. We would not consider any ms that did not meet our criteria—innovative, first rate, interest and emphasis on language, style, structure, tone, not genre or topic. Query.

Recent Fiction Title: *I Smell Esther Williams*, by Mark Leyner (collection of short fiction).

Tips: "In book publishing in general, the large companies continue to publish predictable books, usually by established authors. Fear of the new continues. There seems to be a large, for the most part, untapped black audience for high quality fiction by black writers. Fiction Collective books seem to do well, considering the relatively small audience for experimental, contemporary fiction."

FIESTA CITY PUBLISHERS, 740 Sky View Dr., Box 5861, Santa Barbara CA 93108. (805)969-2891. President: Frank E. Cooke. Publishes hardcover and mass market paperback originals. Averages 3 titles/year. Pays 5-15% royalty on retail price. No advance. Publishes book on average of 3 months after acceptance. Simultaneous and photocopied submissions OK. Computer printout submissions acceptable; prefers letter-quality to dot-matrix. SASE. Reports in 2 weeks on queries; 1 month on mss. Book catalog for 4x9½ SAE.

Nonfiction: Cookbook, self-help and musical subjects. "How-to books on playing instruments, writing music, marketing songs; any music-related material (including bios or autobios of famous music world personalities. Nothing personalized or dull." Query or submit complete ms. Reviews artwork/photos as part of ms package.
Recent Nonfiction Title: *Write That Song!*, by Frank E. Cooke (self-help).
Tips: "Know what is commercial; attempt to understand what subjects and methods have lasting value; avoid short-term fads."

*THE FILTER PRESS, Box 5, Palmer Lake CO 80133. (303)481-2523. Editorial Director: Gilbert L. Campbell. Senior Editor: Lollie W. Campbell. Publishes hardcover and paperback originals (50%) and reprints (50%). Publishes 8 titles/year. Subsidy publishes 25% of books. "These are usually family histories in short runs, although subjects have ranged from preaching, ranching, history debunking, to a study of UFOs. If we feel we can market a book profitably for us and the author, and it is a good book and the author feels he needs it published, we will consider it." Pays 10% royalty on net price; no advance. Publishes book an average of 8 months after acceptance. Simultaneous and photocopied submissions OK. Reports in 2-3 weeks. "Must have SASE." Book catalog for SASE.
Nonfiction: "Cookbooks must appeal to Westerners, campers, and tourists. Accepts nonfiction translations. We have one cookbook on game cookery, one on pancakes, one on camp cooking, one on Southwestern Indian recipes, two on Mexican cooking for the Anglo bride. Also Western legends, Indians, ghost towns, and other Western Americana, as we are quite regional. We must stay at or near our 64-page limit, as most booklets are sold softbound, saddle stitched. We have done some verse of Western interest. Our morgue of antique wood engravings is used extensively, so books with a Western Victorian feel fit in best. Western Americana on our list includes Indians, explorations, lawmen, and bandits. We have Butch Cassidy and Pat Garrett. Family histories and very local history have not done well for us. Writers must remember we are small, publish few books, and they must be things that a tourist will buy to take home, although we are in many Eastern bookstores." Query; "it is much cheaper and safer to send a query and SASE than to send the manuscript to us cold." Reviews artwork/photos as part of ms package.
Recent Nonfiction Title: *The West on Wood*, by Kelly Choda.

FJORD PRESS, Box 615, Corte Madera CA 94925. (415)924-9566. Editors: Steven T. Murray and Susan Doran. Publishes clothbound and trade paperback originals and reprints. Averages 6-8 titles/year. Pays 1-7½% royalty on retail price (to translators only); sometimes offers advance. Simultaneous (if so advised) and photocopied submissions OK. Computer printout submissions acceptable; prefers letter-quality to dot-matrix. SASE. Reports in 6-8 weeks on queries. Book catalog for 2 first class stamps.
Nonfiction: Subjects include cooking and foods (European); history (European); nature (European ecology, animals, natural history); travel (literary only); and women (European). "Acquired through European publishers, but open to suggestions from translators." No original American mss. Query first with resume and submit outline/synopsis and sample chapter. Looks "first for an interesting style. Second, a good story. Third, the magic ingredient that makes the book worth translating and publishing here." Reviews artwork/photos as part of ms package.
Recent Nonfiction Title: *Poff the Cat*, by Hartmut von Hentig.
Fiction: Mainstream (modern European literature and 19th century classics); suspense; and women's mainstream from any language. "Translations of modern or contemporary European novels that have not been done in English before; or of modern classics that should be reprinted." Interested in ethnic American fiction. Query first with resume, and submit outline/synopsis.
Recent Fiction Title: *The First Polka*, by Horst Bienek.
Poetry: "Limited to one book per year, modern classics only (European)." No American mss. Submit 5 to 10 samples.
Recent Poetry Title: *Love & Solitude*, by Edith Sodergran (Finnish-Swedish classic).
Tips: Accepts translations; "our specialty is Germanic, but we are looking for others (mainly European and Latin American)."

FLARE BOOKS, Young Adult Imprint of Avon Books, a division of the Hearst Corp., 1790 Broadway, New York NY 10019. (212)399-1384. Editorial Director: Judy Gitenstein. Publishes mass market paperback originals (50%) and reprints (50%). Pays 6-8% royalty; offers average $2,000 advance. Simultaneous and photocopied submissions OK. Computer printout submissions acceptable. SASE. Reports in 10 weeks.
Nonfiction: General. Query or submit outline/synopsis and 6 sample chapters. "We are *very* selective with young adult nonfiction."
Recent Nonfiction Title: *Dear Diary*, by Jeann Betancourt.
Fiction: Adventure, ethnic, experimental, fantasy, humor, mainstream, mystery, romance, suspense and contemporary. Mss appropriate to ages 12-18. Query or submit complete ms.
Recent Fiction Title: *Facing It*, by Julian Thompson.

FLEET PRESS CORP., 160 5th Ave., New York NY 10010. (212)243-6100. Editor: Susan Nueckel. Publishes hardcover and paperback originals and reprints. Royalty schedule and advance "varies." Publishes book an average of 1 year after acceptance. Free book catalog. Reports in 6 weeks. Enclose return postage with ms.
Nonfiction: History, biography, arts, religion, general nonfiction and sports. Length: 45,000 words. Query with outline; no unsolicited mss. Publishes juveniles. Stress on social studies and minority subjects; for ages 8-15. Length: 25,000 words. Query with outline; no unsolicited mss.

‡FLORA AND FAUNA PUBLICATIONS, 2406 NW 47th Terrace, Gainesville FL 32606. (904)371-9858. Editor/Publisher: Ross H. Arnett, Jr. Book publisher/packager producing 8-10 titles/year. Publishes hardcover and trade paperback originals. Pays 10-15% royalty on wholesale price; offers average $500 advance. Publishes book an average of 1 year after acceptance. Photocopied submissions OK. Computer printout submissions acceptable; prefers letter-quality to dot-matrix. SASE. Reports in 2 weeks on queries; 3 months on mss. Free book catalog.
Nonfiction: Reference, technical, textbook and directories. Subjects include animals (for amateur and professional biologists), and nature. Looking for "books dealing with kinds of plants and animals, especially insects. No nature stories or "Oh My" nature books." Query with outline/synopsis and sample chapters. Reviews artwork/photos as part of ms package.
Recent Nonfiction Title: *Plants and Insects*, by P. Jolivet (natural history).
Tips: "If I were a writer trying to market a book today, I would pick a publisher that knows the special market of my book. Don't send queries unless data can be documented."

FOCAL PRESS, Division of Butterworth Publishers, 80 Montvale Ave., Stoneham MA 02180. (617)438-8464. General Manager/Editor: Arlyn S. Powell. Publishes hardcover and paperback originals. Publishes 20 titles/year. Offers royalty; rate negotiable. Advances paid. Publishes book an average of 1 year after acceptance. Simultaneous and photocopied submissions OK. SASE. Reports in usually 6 weeks. Free book catalog.
Nonfiction: "We publish only in the fields of photography, cinematography, audiovisual and broadcasting—how-to books for beginning amateur to advanced level research monographs." Does *not* want to see books of pictures or portfolios. Submit outline/synopsis and sample chapters or complete ms. Reviews artwork/photos as part of ms package. "We look for a logical format, strong writing and an *organized*, well-planned presentation."
Recent Nonfiction Title: *The Life of a Photograph*, by Keefe and Inch.

FODOR'S TRAVEL GUIDES, 2 Park Ave., New York NY 10016. (212)340-9800. President and Publisher: James Louttit. Vice President/Editorial: Alan Tucker. Publishes paperback travel guides. Averages 85 titles/year.
Nonfiction: "We are the publishers of dated travel guides—regions, countries, cities, and special tourist attractions. We do not solicit manuscripts on a royalty basis, but we are interested in travel writers and/or experts who will and can cover an area of the globe for Fodor's for a fee." Submit credentials and samples of work.
Recent Nonfiction Titles: *Fodor's Good Time Travel Guides to Montreal, Oahu, Acapulco and San Francisco*.

FOLCRAFT LIBRARY EDITIONS/NORWOOD EDITIONS, 842 Main St., Darby PA 19023. (215)583-4550. President: Hassie Weiman. Publishes hardcover originals (library bound). Publishes 300 titles/year. Pays standard royalty rates; offers variable advance. Simultaneous and photocopied submissions OK. SASE. Reports in 3 months.
Nonfiction: Scholarly materials in the humanities by scholars and active researchers associated with universities. Submit complete ms.
Recent Nonfiction Title: *Democracy and Change: The Kibbutz and Social Theory*, by Rosner.

*FORDHAM UNIVERSITY PRESS, University Box L, Bronx NY 10458. (212)579-2320. Director: H.G. Fletcher. Averages 8 titles/year. Subsidy publishes 0-5% of books. Pays royalty on sales income. Send written queries only; do not send unsolicited manuscripts. Publishes book an average of 2 years after acceptance. Computer printout submissions acceptable; no dot-matrix. SASE. Reports in 1 week. Free book catalog.
Nonfiction: Humanities. "We would like the writer to use the *MLA Style Sheet*, latest edition. We do not want dissertations or fiction material."
Recent Nonfiction Title: *Evil and a Good God*, by Bruce Reichenbach.

FORMAN PUBLISHING INC., Suite 206, 11661 San Vicente Blvd., Los Angeles CA 90049. (213)820-8672. President: Len Forman. Publishes hardcover and mass market paperback originals. Averages 6 titles/year. Pays standard royalty. Photocopied submissions OK. SASE. Reports in 1 month.
Nonfiction: Cookbook, how-to, and self-help. Accepts nonfiction translations. Submit outline/synopsis and 3 sample chapters.
Recent Nonfiction Title: *A Woman's Guide to Feeling Good All Month*, by Dr. Susan Lark.

FORTRESS PRESS, 2900 Queen Lane, Philadelphia PA 19129. (215)848-6800. Editorial Director: Norman A. Hjelm. Publishes hardcover and paperback originals. Specializes in general religion for laity and clergy; academic texts and monographs in theology (all areas). Pays 7½% royalty on paperbacks; 10% on hardcover; modest advance. Mss must follow Chicago *Manual of Style* (13th edition). Publishes book an average of 1 year after acceptance. Photocopied submissions OK. Computer printout submissions acceptable. Reports in 90 days. SASE. Free book catalog.
Nonfiction: Publishes theology, religious and counseling books. Accepts nonfiction translations. Query. Accepts outline/synopsis and 2 sample chapters. No religious poetry or fiction.
Recent Nonfiction Title: *A Gathering of Hope*, by Helen Hayes.

FRANCISCAN HERALD PRESS, 1434 W. 51st St., Chicago IL 60609. (312)254-4462. Editor: The Rev. Mark Hegener, O.F.M. Senior Editor: Marion A. Habig. Imprints include Synthesis Booklets and Herald Biblical Booklets. Publishes hardcover and paperback originals (90%) and reprints (10%). Averages 40 titles/year. Pays 8-12% royalty on both wholesale and retail price; offers $200-1,000 advance. Photocopied submissions OK. Computer printout submissions acceptable; disk submissions "only after acceptance of the work." SASE. Reports in 2 weeks. Free book catalog.
Nonfiction: "We are publishers of Franciscan literature for the various branches of the Franciscan Order: history, philosophy, theology, Franciscan spirituality and biographies of Franciscan saints and blessed." Accepts nonfiction translations from German, French, Italian and Spanish. Query or submit outline/synopsis and 1 sample chapter. Reviews artwork/photos as part of ms package.
Recent Nonfiction Title: *The Principles of Catholic Moral Life*, edited by William E. May.

THE FREE PRESS, Division of the Macmillan Publishing Co., Inc., 866 3rd Ave., New York NY 10022. President/Publisher: Erwin A. Glikes. Averages 65 titles/year. Royalty schedule varies. Publishes book an average of 9 months after acceptance. Send 1-3 sample chapters, outline, and query letter before submitting mss. "Prefers camera-ready copy to machine-readable media." SASE. Reports in 3 weeks.
Nonfiction: Professional books and textbooks. Publishes college texts, adult nonfiction, and professional books in the social sciences, humanities and business, and software. Reviews artwork/photos as part of ms package "but we can accept no responsibility for photos or art." Looks for "identifiable target audience, evidence of writing ability." Accepts nonfiction translations. Reviews artwork/photos as part of ms package, "but we can accept *no* responsibility for photos or art."
Software: Contact editor-in-chief. Business and management.

FRONT ROW EXPERIENCE, 540 Discovery Bay Blvd., Byron CA 94514. (415)634-5710. Editor: Frank Alexander. Publishes trade paperback originals. Averages 2-3 titles/year. Pays 5-10% royalty on net sales. Publishes book an average of 1 year after acceptance. Simultaneous and photocopied submissions OK. Computer printout submissions acceptable; prefers letter-quality to dot-matrix. "We return submissions but not without a SASE." Reports in 1 week on queries; 1 month on mss. Free book catalog.
Nonfiction: How-to, reference, curriculum guides for movement education, and perceptual-motor development. Especially needs innovative curriculum guides. Publishes for elementary physical education directors, elementary and preschool teachers, YMCA activity directors, occupational therapists, physical therapists and childhood development professionals in general. Accepts nonfiction translations from any language in subject areas we specialize in. No mss outside of movement education, special education, and perceptual-motor development. Reviews artwork/photos as part of ms package. Query. Accepts outline/synopsis and 3 sample chapters.
Recent Nonfiction Title: *Parachute Movement Activities*, by Ron French and Michael Horvat.

GAMBLING TIMES, 1018 N. Cole, Hollywood CA 90038. (213)466-5261. Associate Publisher, Book Division: Arnold L. Abrams. Publishes hardcover and softcover. Averages 35 titles/year. Pays 9-11% royalty on retail price for hardcover; 4-6% on softcover. Simultaneous and photocopied submissions OK. SASE. Reports in 1 month.
Nonfiction: How-to. "Straight gambling material related to gambling systems, betting methods, etc. Also interested in political, economic and legal issues surrounding gambling inside and outside the US." Submit sample chapters. Gambling-related books only.

GAMING BOOK DISTRIBUTORS, (formerly SRS Enterprises, Inc./Scientific Research Services), Division of Gambling Times, Inc., 1018 N. Cole Ave., Hollywood CA 90038. (213)466-5261. Nationally distributed by Lyle Stuart Inc., Secouse NJ. Director of Publishing: Arnold L. Abrams. Publishes hardcover and trade paperback originals. Averages 40 titles/year. Pays 4-10% royalty on retail price; no advance. Publishes book an average of 1 year after acceptance. Computer printout submissions acceptable. SASE. Reports in 6 weeks on queries; 3 months on mss.
Nonfiction: How-to. Subjects cover only gambling. "We're looking for books on all types of gambling and gambling-related activities." Submit outline/synopsis and sample chapters. Reviews artwork/photos as part of ms package.

Recent Nonfiction Title: *Million Dollar Blackjack*, by Ken Uston (how to play and win at 21).
Fiction: Query.

GUY GANNETT BOOKS, Subsidiary of Guy Gannett Publishing Co., 390 Congress St., Portland ME 04101. (207)775-5811. Editorial Director: Allan A. Swenson. Publishes hardcover originals and trade paperback originals and reprints. Averages 10 titles/year. Pays 6-14% royalty on retail price; offers average $1,500 advance. Publishes book an average of 1 year after acceptance. Simultaneous and photocopied submissions OK. Computer printout submissions acceptable; no dot-matrix. SASE. Reports in 1 month on queries; 6 weeks on mss. Free book catalog.
Nonfiction: Biography, cookbook, how-to, humor, juvenile and self-help. Subjects include Americana, animals, cooking and foods, history, nature and travel. "We're looking for books of wide appeal based on Maine and New England themes and topics. We publish the 'Best of Maine' books—expanding to be the 'Best of New England.' Our audience is a broad base of readers interested in New England history, traditions, folklore, heritage and outdoors." Reviews artwork/photos as part of ms package. Submit outline/synopsis and 3-4 sample chapters.
Recent Nonfiction Title: *Islands of Maine, Where America Really Began*, by Bill Caldwell (history).
Tips: Queries/mss may be routed to other editors in the publishing group.

GARBER COMMUNICATIONS, INC., (affiliates: Steinerbooks, Spiritual Fiction Publications, Spiritual Science Library, Rudolf Steiner Publications, Freedeeds Books, Biograf Publications), 5 Garber Hill Rd., Blauvelt NY 10913. (914)359-9292. Editor: Bernard J. Garber. Publishes hardcover and paperback originals and reprints. Averages 15 titles/year. Pays 5-7% royalty on retail price; advance averages $500. Publishes book an average of 1 year after acceptance. Query with outline and first, middle and last chapters for nonfiction. Will consider photocopied submissions. Computer printout submissions acceptable; no dot-matrix. Reports in 2 months. SASE. Free book catalog.
Nonfiction: Spiritual sciences, occult, philosophical, metaphysical, and ESP. These are for our Steiner Books division only. Serious nonfiction. Philosophy and Spiritual Sciences: Bernard J. Garber.
Recent Nonfiction Title: *The American Mercury: Facsimile Edition of Volume I*, by H.L. Mencken and George Jean Nathan, editors.
Fiction: Patricia Abrams, editor. The new genre called Spiritual Fiction™ Publications. "We are now looking for original manuscripts or rewrites of classics in modern terms."
Recent Fiction Title: *Legend*, by Barry Maher.

GARDEN WAY PUBLISHING, Storey Communications, Inc., Schoolhouse Rd., Pownal VT 05261. (802)823-5811. Editor: Roger Griffith. Publishes hardcover and paperback originals. Publishes 12 titles/year. Offers a flat fee arrangement varying with book's scope, or royalty, which usually pays author 6% of book's retail price. Advances are negotiable, but usually range from $1,500 to $3,000. "We stress continued promotion of titles and sales over many years." Emphasizes direct mail sales and sales to specialty stores, plus sales to bookstores through Harper and Row. Photocopied submissions OK. Computer printout submissions acceptable; prefers letter-quality to dot-matrix. Publishes book an average of 9 months after acceptance. Enclose return postage.
Nonfiction: Books on gardening, cooking, animal husbandry, homesteading, country living, country business, house and small building construction and energy conservation. Accepts artwork/photos. Emphasis should be on how-to. Length requirements are flexible. "The writer should remember the reader will buy his book to learn to do something, so that all information to accomplish this must be given. We are publishing specifically for the person who is concerned about natural resources and a deteriorating life style and wants to do something about it." Query with outline and 2-3 sample chapters. Reviews artwork/photos as part of ms package.
Recent Nonfiction Title: *Cookbook*, by Janet Ballantyne.

*GARLAND PUBLISHING, INC., 136 Madison Ave., New York NY 10016. (212)686-7492. Senior Editor: Gary Kuris. Publishes hardcover originals and software. Averages 120 titles/year. Subsidy publishes 50% of books. Pays 10-15% royalty on wholesale price. "Depending on marketability, authors may prepare camera-ready copy." Publishes book an average of 3 months after acceptance. Simultaneous and photocopied submissions OK. Computer printout submissions acceptable; prefers letter-quality to dot-matrix. Reports in 2 weeks on queries; 1 month on mss. Free book catalog.
Nonfiction: Reference books for libraries. Humanities and social sciences. Accepts nonfiction translations. "We're interested in reference books—bibliographies, sourcebooks, indexes, etc.—in all fields." Submit outline/synopsis and 1-2 sample chapters. Reviews artwork/photos as part of ms package.
Recent Nonfiction Title: *America's White Working-Class Women: A Historical Bibliography*, by Kennedy.
Software: Educational material.

GASLIGHT PUBLICATIONS, 112 E. 2nd St., Bloomington IN 47401. (812)332-5169. Publisher: Jack Tracy. Publishes hardcover originals (50%) and hardcover reprints (50%). Averages 6-8 titles/year. Pays 10% minimum royalty on retail price; no advance. Publishes book an average of 1 year after acceptance. Simultaneous and photocopied submissions OK. Computer printout submissions acceptable. SASE. Reports in 1 month.
Nonfiction: "Studies in A. Conan Doyle, Sherlock Holmes and related Victoriana. Serious, well-researched, not necessarily for the specialist. 12,000 words minimum. Our publications are usually heavily illustrated, and a generous number of appropriate illustrations will materially enhance a book's chances for acceptance." No ephemera, parodies, pastiches or "untold tales." Query or submit outline/synopsis, sample chapters or complete ms. Reviews artwork/photos as part of ms package.
Recent Nonfiction Title: *Origins of Sherlock Holmes*, by Walter Klinefelter (literary history).

*GENEALOGICAL PUBLISHING CO., INC., 1001 N. Calvert St., Baltimore MD 21202. (301)837-8271. Editor-in-Chief: Michael H. Tepper, Ph.D. Publishes hardcover originals and reprints. Offers straight 10% royalty on retail price. Subsidy publishes 10% of books. Averages 80 titles/year. Publishes book an average of 6 months after acceptance. Photocopied submissions OK. Computer printout submissions acceptable. Prefers query first, but will look at outline and sample chapter or complete ms. Reports "immediately." Enclose SAE and return postage.
Nonfiction: Reference, genealogy, and immigration records: "Our requirements are unusual, so we usually treat each author and his subject in a way particularly appropriate to his special skills and subject matter. Guidelines are flexible, but it is expected that an author will consult with us in depth. Most, though not all, of our original publications are offset from camera-ready typescript. Since most genealogical reference works are compilations of vital records and similar data, tabular formats are common. We hope to receive more ms material covering vital records and ships' passenger lists. We want family history compendia, basic methodology in genealogy, heraldry, and immigration records. Reviews artwork/photos as part of ms package.
Recent Nonfiction Title: *Genealogical Research in New England*.

THE J. PAUL GETTY MUSEUM, Subsidiary of The J. Paul Getty Museum Trust, Box 2112, Santa Monica CA 90406. (213)459-2306. Editor: Sandra Knudsen Morgan. Publishes hardcover and trade paperback originals (80%) and reprints. Averages 10 titles/year. Pays 6-12% royalty on retail price; buys some mss outright; offers average $500 advance. Publishes book an average of 18 months after acceptance. SASE. Photocopied submissions OK. Computer printout submissions acceptable. SASE. Reports in 1 month. Free book catalog.
Nonfiction: Reference and scholarly on art and history. "Scholarly titles and well-researched general and children's titles on topics related to the museum's five collections: Greek and Roman art and architecture (especially the Villa dei Papiri), Old Master paintings of the Renaissance and Baroque, European decorative arts of the Regence through Napoleonic periods, Old Master drawings and illuminated manuscripts." No non European art. Query. Reviews artwork/photos as part of ms package.
Recent Nonfiction Title: *Selections from the Decorative Arts in the JPGM*, by G. Wilson.

THE K.S. GINIGER CO., INC., 235 Park Ave., S., New York NY 10003. (212)533-5080. President: Kenneth Seeman Giniger. Book publisher and independent book producer/packager. Publishes hardcover, trade, and paperback originals. Averages 8 titles/year. Pays royalty on wholesale or retail price. Publishes book an average of 1 year after acceptance. Computer printout submissions acceptable; prefers letter-quality to dot-matrix. SASE. Reports in 2 weeks.
Nonfiction: Biography, cookbook, how-to, juvenile, reference and self-help. Subjects include Americana, art, cooking and foods, health, history, hobbies, religion, sports and travel. Query with SASE. Accepts outline/synopsis; 1 sample chapter. Reviews artwork/photos as part of ms package. All unsolicited mss are returned unread "if postage is enclosed." Looks for "good idea and power of expressing it with clarity and interest."
Recent Nonfiction Title: *Churchill and the Generals*, by Barrie Pitt (history).

GLOBE MINI MAGS, 2112 S. Congress Ave., West Palm Beach FL 33406. (305)433-1551. Associate Editor: Toby Donahue. Averages 120 titles/year. Buys some mss outright; "negotiated individually." No advance. Publishes book an average of 6 months after acceptance. Computer printout submissions acceptable; prefers letter-quality to dot-matrix. SASE. Reports in 1 month.
Nonfiction: "We publish 64-page mini mag handbooks sold at variety stores, supermarkets, and gift shops." Subjects include nutrition and foods, health, diets and exercises. Reviews artwork/photos as part of ms package. "We prefer a query letter with the writer's credentials and a *brief* description of the proposed mini mag."
Recent Nonfiction Title: *Aerobic Dancing* (exercise).
Tips: Queries/mss may be routed to other editors in the publishing group.

THE GLOBE PEQUOT PRESS, INC., Old Chester Rd., Box Q, Chester CT 06412. (203)526-9571. Vice President/Publications Director: Linda Kennedy. Publishes hardcover and paperback originals (95%) and paperback reprints (5%). Averages 15 titles/year. Offers 7½-10% royalty on net price; advances offered "for specific expenses only." Simultaneous and photocopied submissions OK. SASE. Reports in 3 weeks. Book catalog for SASE.

Nonfiction: The Northeast: Americana; recreation (outdoor books); and travel (guide books). Some regional history and cookbooks. "Guide books are especially promising today; with a guide book people can plan travel itineraries in advance, save time and money. Books with a New England or northeastern focus will be considered most seriously." No doctoral theses, genealogies or textbooks. Submit outline/synopsis and sample chapters.

Recent Nonfiction Title: *Bed and Breakfast in the Northeast: From Maine to Washington, DC, 300 Selected B&Bs,* by Bernice Chester.

GMG PUBLISHING, 25 W. 43rd St., New York NY 10036. (212)354-8840. President: Gerald Galison. Publishes hardcover and trade paperback originals (90%) and reprints (10%), illustrated and text only. Averages 10 titles/year. Pays negotiable royalty; offers negotiable advance. Simultaneous submissions OK. Computer printout submissions acceptable; prefers letter-quality to dot-matrix. SASE. Reports in 2 weeks.

Nonfiction: Soft science, natural history, and the arts. Accepts nonfiction translations. "Open to quality projects in topics of current interest." Query. Accepts outline/synopsis and 1 sample chapter.

Recent Nonfiction Title: *The Smithsonian Family Learning Project—Things to Do, See, Learn and Make.*

GOLDEN BOOKS, Western Publishing Co., Inc., 850 3rd Ave., New York NY 10022. Publisher, Adult Books: Jonathan P. Latimer. Publisher, Children's Books: Doris Duenewald. Averages 200 titles/year. Pays royalty; buys some mss outright.

Nonfiction: Adult nonfiction, especially family-oriented how-to subjects. Children's books, including picturebooks, concept books, novelty books, and information books. Query before submitting ms. Looks for "completeness, an indication that the author knows his subject and audience."

Fiction: Children's picturebooks and young fiction. Query before submitting ms.

*****THE GOLDEN QUILL PRESS,** Avery Rd., Francestown NH 03043. (603)547-6622. Owner: Edward T. Dell Jr. Publishes hardcover originals. Averages 25 titles/year. Subsidy publishes 90% of books "depending on past sales records." Pays 10% maximum royalty on retail price. Photocopied submissions OK. Electronic submissions OK, 1200 Baud—modem supplied, but requires hard copy. Computer printout submissions acceptable. SASE. Reports in 2 weeks on queries; 1 month on mss. Free book catalog.

Nonfiction: Biography. Query or submit complete ms. Reviews artwork/photos as part of ms package.

Poetry: All types. Submit complete ms.

GOLDEN WEST BOOKS, Box 80250, San Marino CA 91108. (213)283-3446. Editor-in-Chief: Donald Duke. Managing Editor: Jeff Dunning. Publishes hardcover and paperback originals. Pays 10% royalty contract; no advance. Simultaneous and photocopied submissions OK. Reports in 2-4 weeks. SASE. Free book catalog.

Nonfiction: Publishes selected Western Americana and transportation Americana. Query or submit complete ms. "Illustrations and photographs will be examined if we like ms."

Recent Nonfiction Title: *Tehachapi,* by John Signor.

GOLDEN WEST PUBLISHERS, 4113 N. Longview, Phoenix AZ 85014. (602)265-4392. Editor: Hal Mitchell. Publishes trade paperback originals. Averages 4 titles/year. Pays 6-10% royalty on retail price or makes outright purchase of $500-2,500. No advances. Publishes book an average of 6 months after acceptance. Simultaneous and photocopied submissions OK. Computer printout submissions acceptable; no dot-matrix. Prefers query letter first. SASE. Reports in 2 weeks on queries; 1 month on mss. Book catalog for business-size SAE and 1 first class stamp.

Nonfiction: Cookbooks, how-to, humor, guide books and self-help books. Subjects include cooking and foods, health, history, the outdoors, travel and the West or Southwest. Query or submit outline/synopsis and sample chapters. Reviews artwork/photos as part of ms package.

Recent Title: *Mexican Family Favorites Cook Book,* by Maria Teresa Bermudez.

GRAPHIC ARTS CENTER PUBLISHING CO., 3019 NW Yeon Ave., Box 10306, Portland OR 97210. (503)226-2402. President: Betty A. Sechser. Editor: Douglas Pfeiffer. Publishes hardcover originals. Averages 3-6 titles/year. Pays outright purchase averaging $3,000 (less for paperbacks); small advance. Simultaneous and photocopied submissions OK. Reports in 3 weeks. SASE. Free book catalog.

Nonfiction: "All titles are pictorials with text. Text usually runs separately from the pictorial treatment. All of the new series of pictorial books are more flexible in style." Query.

*****GRAPHIC IMAGE PUBLICATIONS,** Box 1740, La Jolla CA 92038. (619)457-0344. President: Hurb Crow. Publishes trade and mass market paperback originals and software. Averages 5 titles/year. Subsidy publishes 10% of books based on "length of experience and success of prior works." Pays 5-15% royalty on wholesale price; advance negotiable. Publishes book an average of 1 year after acceptance. Query with outline/synopsis and 2 sample chapters to the attention of Judy Delp, managing editor. Must have SASE for response. Reports in 2 months. Simultaneous and photocopied submissions OK. Computer printout submissions acceptable; no dot-matrix.

Nonfiction: How-to, computer software programs and travel. "We publish for people with a desire to learn on their own; and for people who love to travel and to know about the areas they visit."

Recent Nonfiction Title: *Cabo San Lucas—A Place in the Sun*, by Susan H. Crow.

Fiction: Romance.

Recent Fiction Title: *Night Vision*, by Erin Hahn (suspense).

Software: Needs "informative, easy-to-understand computer books." Contact R. Wallace.

Tips: "Be professional in your query, and let us know a little about yourself, be positive." Queries/mss may be routed to other editors in the publishing group.

GRAY'S PUBLISHING, LTD., Box 2160, Sidney, BC V8L 3S6 Canada. (604)652-5911. Editor: Maralyn Horsdal. Publishes hardcover and paperback originals and reprints. Offers standard royalty contract on retail price. Averages 4 titles/year. Query with outline and 3-4 sample chapters. Reports in 6-10 weeks. SAE and IRCs.

Nonfiction: Wants "nonfiction, Canadiana," especially Pacific Northwest. Biography, natural history, history and nautical. Looks for "good writing and worthwhile marketable topic." Reviews artwork/photos as part of ms package. Length: 60,000-120,000 words.

Recent Nonfiction Title: *The Columbia Is Coming!*, by Doris Andersen (history).

‡**GRAYWOLF PRESS**, Box 142, Port Townsend WA 98368. (206)385-3643. Editor/Publisher: Scott Walker. Imprints include Graywolf Short Fiction Series. Publishes hardcover and trade paperback originals, and trade paperback reprints. Averages 6-12 titles/year. Pays 7-10% royalty on retail price. Photocopied submissions OK. SASE. Reports in 2 weeks on queries; 1 month on mss. Free book catalog.

Fiction: Short fiction collections. "Limited to direct solicitation only." Query through agent only.

GREAT OCEAN PUBLISHERS, 1823 N. Lincoln St., Arlington VA 22207. (703)525-0909. President: Mark Esterman. Publishes hardcover and trade paperback originals (90%) and hardcover reprints (10%). Averages 3 titles/year. Pays 8-10% hardcover royalty; 6-8% paperback on retail price; occasionally offers advance. Publishes book an average of 1 year after acceptance. Simultaneous (if so indicated) and photocopied submissions OK. Computer printout submissions acceptable; prefers letter-quality to dot-matrix. Reports in 3 weeks.

Nonfiction: Biography, how-to, illustrated book, reference, self-help, and technical. Subjects include art, business and economics, child care/development, health, history, music, philosophy, politics, and religion. "Any subject is fine as long as it meets our standards of quality." Submit outline/synopsis and sample chapters. "SASE *must* be included with all material to be returned." Looks for "1) good writing, 2) clear evidence that ms is intended as a *book*, not a long collection of weakly organized small pieces, and 3) good organization. Not to mention a worthwhile, interesting subject." Accepts nonfiction translations—query first.

Recent Nonfiction Title: *Essays on Marriage*, by Seikan Hasegawa.

Fiction: Not seeking fiction mss at this time.

*****GREEN HILL PUBLISHERS, INC.**, 722 Columbus St., Ottawa IL 61350. (815)434-7905. (Distributed by Caroline House). Publisher: Jameson G. Campaigne. Senior Editor: Richard S. Wheeler. Publishes hardcover and mass market paperback originals. Publishes 12-14 titles/year. "We have co-published with foundations." Pays 6-15% royalty. Advance averages $2,500. Simultaneous and "clean" photocopied submissions OK. Electronic submissions OK but query first; requires hard copy also. Computer printout submissions acceptable; prefers letter-quality to dot-matrix. Reports in 2 months on queries; 4 months on mss. SASE. Book catalog for SASE.

Nonfiction: Reference, self-help, how-to and biography (of major subjects). Subjects include business and economics, history, nature, politics, recreation and sports. Query or submit complete ms.

Recent Nonfiction Title: *Reagan Electionomics*, by Donald Devine (Reagan election data).

Fiction: Adventure, ethnic (American Indian), historical, mainstream, Western and business fiction, especially "mountain man, early fur trade stories." Query or submit complete ms.

Recent Fiction Title: *Carry the Wind*, by Terry Johnston (Western/historical).

Tips: "Concentrate on *literacy*, vocabulary, grammar, basic story telling and narrative skills."

*****WARREN H. GREEN, INC.**, 8356 Olive Blvd., St. Louis MO 63132. Editor: Warren H. Green. Imprints include Fireside Books. Publishes hardcover originals. Offers "10-20% sliding scale of royalties based on quantity distributed. All books are short run, highly specialized, with no advance." Subsidy publishes about 5% of books, e.g., "books in philosophy and those with many color plates." Averages 30 titles/year. "37% of total marketing is overseas." Will send a catalog to a writer on request. Publishes book an average of 9 months after acceptance. Will consider simultaneous and photocopied submissions. Computer printout submissions

acceptable; no dot-matrix. Query or submit outline and sample chapters. "Publisher requires 300-500-word statement of scope, plan, and purpose of book, together with curriculum vitae of author." Reports in 60-90 days. SASE.
Nonfiction: Medical and scientific. "Specialty monographs for practicing physicians and medical researchers. Books of 160 pages upward. Illustrated as required by subject. Medical books are non-textbook type, usually specialties within specialties, and no general books for a given specialty. For example, separate books on each facet of radiology, and not one complete book on radiology. Authors must be authorities in their chosen fields and accepted as such by their peers. Books should be designed for all doctors in English speaking world engaged in full or part time activity discussed in book. We would like to increase publications in the fields of radiology, anesthesiology, pathology, psychiatry, surgery and orthopedic surgery, obstetrics and gynecology, and speech and hearing." Also interested in books on health, philosophy, psychology and sociology. Reviews artwork/photos as part of ms package.
Recent Nonfiction Title: *Diseases of the Stump*, by Dr. S. William Levy (orthopedic surgery).

GREEN TIGER PRESS, 1061 India St., San Diego CA 92101. (619)238-1001. Editor: Harold Darling. Imprints include Star & Elephant (nonfiction and fiction). Publishes hardcover and trade paperback originals and reprints. Averages 12 titles/year. Pays 10% minimum royalty on retail price; offers average $350 advance. Simultaneous and photocopied submissions OK. SASE. Reports in 2 weeks on queries; 2 months on mss. Free book catalog.
Nonfiction: Illustrated book and juvenile. Subjects include illustrations and fantasy.
Recent Nonfiction Title: *The World of Carl Larsson* (commentary on life and work of illustrator includes over 400 illustrations).
Fiction: Juvenile, fantasy, myth, art.
Recent Fiction Title: *The Teddy Bears' Picnic*, by Jimmy Kennedy.
Poetry: Submit 3 samples.
Recent Poetry Title: *Lost Wine*, by John Theobald (7 centuries of French/English lyric poetry).
Tips: "We look for manuscripts containing a romantic, visionary or imaginative quality, often with a mythic feeling where fantasy and reality co-exist. Since we are a visually-oriented house, we look for manuscripts whose texts readily conjure up visual imagery."

THE STEPHEN GREENE PRESS/LEWIS PUBLISHING, Box 1000, Brattleboro VT 05301. (802)257-7757. Editorial Director: Thomas Begner. Publishes hardcover and paperback originals (99%); hardcover and paperback reprints (1%). Averages 30 titles/year. Royalty "variable; advances are small." Send contact sheet or prints to illustrate ms. Photocopied submissions OK. Reports in 6 weeks. SASE. Book catalog for SASE.
Nonfiction: How-to (self-reliance); nature and environment; recreation; self-help; sports (outdoor and horse); popular technology; popular psychology and social science; and regional (New England). "We see our audience as mainly college-educated men and women, 30 and over. They are regular book buyers and readers. They probably have pronounced interests, hobby or professional, in subjects that our books treat. Authors can assess their needs by looking critically at what we have published."
Recent Nonfiction Title: *Improving Your Running*, by Bill Squires and Ray Krise.

GREENLEAF CLASSICS, INC., Box 20194, San Diego CA 92120. Managing Editor: Ralph Vaughan. Publishes paperback originals. Specializes in adult erotic fiction. Publishes 450 titles/year. Pays by outright purchase about 3 months after acceptance. Publishes book an average of 4 months after acceptance. Photocopied submissions OK. Reports in 2-4 weeks. "No mss will be returned unless accompanied by return postage." Writer's guidelines for SASE.
Fiction: Erotic novels. "All stories must have a sexual theme. They must be contemporary novels dealing with the serious problems of everyday people. All plots are structured so that characters must get involved in erotic situations. Write from the female viewpoint (third person). *Request our guidelines before beginning any project for us.*" Preferred length: 35,000 words. Send complete ms (preferred); or at least 3 sample chapters.

GREGG DIVISION, McGraw-Hill Book Co., 1221 Avenue of the Americas, New York NY 10020. Vice President/General Manager: David H. Weaver. Publishes hardcover and softcover instructional material for secondary and post-secondary education market. "Contracts negotiable; no advances." Query. "We accept very few unsolicited mss." Publishes books on typewriting, office education, shorthand, accounting and data processing, distribution and marketing, trade and industrial education, health and consumer education and word processing. Reports in 1-2 months. Enclose return postage with query.
Recent Nonfiction Title: *Gregg Shorthand for the Electronic Office, Parts 1 and 2*, by Leslie, Zoubek, and Condon.

GROUPWORK TODAY, INC., Box 258, South Plainfield NJ 07080. Editor-in-Chief: Harry E. Moore Jr. Publishes hardcover and paperback originals. Averages 4-6 titles/year. Offers $100 advance against royalties on receipt of contract and completion of ms ready for publication; 10% of gross receipts from sale of book.

Publishes book an average of 3 months after acceptance. Books are marketed by direct mail to Groupwork Agency executives and professionals (YMCA, YWCA, Scouts, Salvation Army, colleges, directors of organized camps, and libraries). Will send catalog to a writer for SASE with 37¢ in stamps. "Also will answer specific questions from an author considering us as a publisher." Will not consider simultaneous submissions. Reports in 6-8 weeks. Enclose return postage.

Nonfiction: "We are publishers of books and materials for professionals and volunteers who work with people in groups. Titles are also used by colleges for texts and resources. Some of our materials are also suited to the needs of professionals who work with individuals. Groupwork agency management, finance, program development and personnel development are among the subjects of interest to us. Writers must be thoroughly familiar with 'people work' and have fresh insights to offer. New writers are most welcome here. Lengths are open but usually run 40,000-60,000 words." Readers are mainly social agency administrators and professional staff members. Groupwork materials are also read by volunteers serving in the social agencies. Mss are judged by experienced professionals in social agencies. The company is advised on policy direction by a council of advisors from national agencies and colleges across the nation. "We also are publishing our 'monogram' series to deal with the most important problems with which social work agencies must deal today. We are also in the market for papers, 15-35 double-spaced pages, for a Management Workbook Series. Papers must deal with finance, program development, communication, organizational planning or some other subject directed to the problems of nonprofit, human services organizations. We pay a $35 advance against a 10% royalty on gross sales." Submit outline and 3 sample chapters for nonfiction. Reviews artwork/photos as part of ms package.

Recent Nonfiction Title: *Helping Women: Counseling Girls and Women in a Decade of Change*, by Gloria Sklansky and Linda Algazi.

Tips: "If a writer will send material only on which he or she has done as much work as possible to make a good outline, a sample chapter or two to indicate writing ability, and the idea is a contribution to our field, we will spend all kinds of time guiding the author to completion of the work.

GROVE PRESS, 196 W. Houston St., New York NY 10014. Editorial Director: Barney Rosset. Imprints include Evergreen and Black Cat books. Publishes hardcover and paperback originals (50%) and paperback reprints (50%). Averages 80 titles/year. Simultaneous and photocopied submissions OK. Electronic submissions OK on ASC II, CP/M-based 5¼" floppy, but requires hard copy also. Computer printout submissions acceptable; prefers letter-quality to dot-matrix. SASE. "We accept no phone calls concerning mss, requests for catalogs and other information." Free book catalog.

Nonfiction: Biography, health, history, how-to, philosophy, politics, psychology, self-help, and sports. Accepts nonfiction translations. Accepts outline/synopsis and 3 sample chapters. Reviews artwork/photos as part of ms package.

Recent Nonfiction Title: *Memory Babe: A Biography of Jack Kerouac*, by Gerald Nicosia (literary biography).

Fiction: Novels.

Recent Fiction Title: *Great Expectations*, by Kathy Acker.

*GUERNICA EDITIONS, Box 633, Station N.D.G., Montreal, Quebec H4A 3R1 Canada. (514)481-5569. President/Editor: Antonio D'Alfonso. Publishes hardcover and trade paperback originals, hardcover and trade paperback reprints and software. Averages 10 titles/year. Subsidy publishes 50% of titles. "Subsidy in Canada is received only when the author is established, Canadian-born and active in the country's cultural world. The others we subsidize ourselves." Pays 3-10% royalty on retail price. Makes outright purchase of $200-5,000. Offers 7¢/word advance for translators. Photocopied submissions OK. IRCs required. "American stamps are of no use to us in Canada." Reports in 1 month on queries; 6 weeks on mss. Free book catalog.

Nonfiction: Biography, humor, juvenile, reference and textbook. Subjects include art, history, music, nature, philosophy, photography, politics, psychology, recreation, religion and Canadiana. "We are looking for essays on history, philosophy, religion, politics, film, and other topics which can be used as discussion books." Query.

Fiction: Erotica, ethnic, historical, mystery, science fiction and suspense. "We wish to open up into the fiction world. No country is a country without its fiction writers. Canada is growing some fine fiction writers. We'd like to read you. No first novels." Query.

Poetry: "We wish to have writers in translation. Any writer who has translated Italian poetry is welcomed. Full books only. Not single poems by different authors, unless modern, and used as an anthology. First books will have no place in the next couple of years." Submit samples.

Recent Poetry Title: *Black Tongue*, by Antonio D'Alfonso.

Software: Contact Antonio D'Alfonso and Marco Fraticelli.

GUIDANCE CENTRE, Faculty of Education, University of Toronto, 10 Alcorn Ave., Toronto, Ontario M4V 2Z8 Canada. (416)978-3210. Editorial Director: L. Miller. Coordinating Editor: Hazel Ross. Publishes hardcover and paperback originals. Averages 15 titles/year. Pays in royalties. Reports in 1 month. Submissions returned "only if Canadian postage is sent." Free book catalog.

Nonfiction: "The Guidance Centre is interested in publications related to career planning and guidance and in measurement and evaluation. Also general education. No manuscripts which have confined their references and illustrations to United States material." Submit complete ms. Consult Chicago *Manual of Style*.
Recent Nonfiction Title: *Studying Effectively and Efficiently*, by MacFarlon and Hodson.

*GULF PUBLISHING CO., Box 2608, Houston TX 77001. (713)529-4301. Vice President: C.A. Umbach Jr. Editor-in-Chief: William J. Lowe. Imprints include Lone Star Books (regional Texas books). Publishes hardcover and large format paperback originals and software. Pays 10% royalty on net income; advance averages $300-2,000. Averages 40-50 titles/year. Subsidy publishes 5% of books. Publishes book an average of 1 year after acceptance. Simultaneous and photocopied submissions OK. Computer printout submissions OK; no dot-matrix. Reports in 1-2 months. SASE. Free book catalog.
Nonfiction: Business, reference, regional trade, and scientific and self-help. "We are the world's largest specialized publisher to the energy industries." Submit outline/synopsis and 1-2 sample chapters. Reviews artwork/photos as part of ms package.
Recent Nonfiction Title: *Negotiating with the Japanese*, by R. Moran.
Software: Engineering. Contact W.J. Lowe.

H.P. BOOKS, Subsidiary of Knight-Ridder Newspapers, Box 5367, Tucson AZ 85703. Executive Editor: Rick Bailey. Publishes hardcover and paperback originals. Specializes in how-to books in several fields, all photo-illustrated. Pays royalty on wholesale price; advance negotiable. Averages 40-45 titles/year. Publishes ms an average of 9 months after acceptance. Simultaneous and photocopied submissions OK. "We delight in disk submissions but must be 8" diskette compatible with Wang VS 100 system or transfer directly to computer via telephone modem." Reports in 2-4 weeks. SASE. Free book catalog.
Nonfiction: Cookbooks, cooking and foods, gardening, hobbies, how-to, leisure activities, photography, automotive, health, recreation, self-help, art techniques, computer and technical books. Most books are 160 pages minimum; "word count varies with the format." Query and state number and type of illustrations available. Accepts introdution and 1 sample chapter. "We *require* author to supply photos and illustrations to our specifications."
Recent Nonfiction Title: *Best of International Cooking*, by Woltner/Teubner.

‡*ROBERT HALE LIMITED, Clerkenwell House, 45/47 Clerkenwell Green, London EC1R 0HT England. (01)251-2661. Managing Director: John Hale. Chief Editor: Jill Norman. Imprints include Jill Norman. Publishes hardcover and trade paperback originals, and hardcover reprints. Averages 800 titles/year. Subsidy publishes 5% of books. Pays royalty on retail price. Publishes book an average of 9 months after acceptance. Photocopied submissions OK. Computer printout submissions acceptable. SASE. Reports in 1 week on queries; 6 weeks on mss. Book catalog for $1 (postage).
Nonfiction: Biography, "coffee table" book, cookbook, how-to, humor, illustrated book, reference, and self-help. Subjects include animals, art, cooking and foods, health, history, hobbies, music, nature, photography, politics, recreation, religion, sports, and travel. No autobiography of unknown persons, verse, philosophy, American history, education or technical material. Submit outline/synopsis and sample chapters. Reviews artwork/photos as part of ms package.
Recent Nonfiction Title: *Ava*, by Roland Flamini (biography).
Fiction: Adventure, gothic, historical, mainstream, mystery, romance, suspense, and western. "We are seeking anything between the lengths of 40,000 and 100,000 words for the adult reader." No Americana, confession, erotica, ethnic, experimental, fantasy, horror, humor, religious or science fiction. Submit outline/synopsis and sample chapters.
Recent Fiction Title: *The Shadow King*, by Roberta J. Dewa (historical).

HAMMOND, INC., 515 Valley St., Maplewood NJ 07040. (201)763-6000. General Trade Editor: Dorothy Bacheller. Hardcover and paperback originals. "Books are negotiated from flat fee for outright purchase to advances against standard royalties, depending on subject." Published 12 titles in 1983. Submit outline/synopsis and sample chapters. State availability of photos/illustrations. Simultanous submissions OK. Reports in 2-4 weeks. SASE. Book catalog for SASE.
Nonfiction: Publishes Americana, art, business, cookbooks, history, hobbies, how-to, nature, recreation, reference, sports and travel books.
Recent Nonfiction Title: *Dinosaurs-An Illustrated History*, by Dr. Edwin Colbert.

HANCOCK HOUSE PUBLISHERS LTD., 1431 Harrison Ave., Blaine WA 98230. Editor-in-Chief: David Hancock. Hardcover and paperback originals (85%) and reprints (15%). Pays 10% royalty on list price; $500 minimum advance. Publishes 40 titles/year. State availability of photos and/or illustrations to accompany ms. Computer printout submissions acceptable; prefers letter-quality to dot-matrix. Reports in 1-2 months. SASE. Free book catalog.
Nonfiction: Publishes (in order of preference): craft, anthropology, sport, nature, history, biography, refer-

ence, Americana and Canadian, cookbooks, cooking and foods, hobbies, how-to, photography, recreation, self-help, and travel books. Needs 25 new titles on Northwestern history and nature; 25 titles on small farm crops and animals. Query or send complete ms including photos. Looks for "a very complete outline and table of contents."

Recent Nonfiction Title: *My Spirit Soars*, by Chief Dan George.

HARCOURT BRACE JOVANOVICH, 1250 6th Ave., San Diego CA 92101. Director of Trade Books Department: Peter Jovanovich. Publishes hardcover and paperback originals and reprints. SASE.

HARCOURT BRACE JOVANOVICH LEGAL & PROFESSIONAL PUBLICATIONS, INC., Subsidiary of Harcourt Brace Jovanovich, Inc., 14415 S. Main St., Gardena CA 90248. (213)321-3275. Subsidiaries include Law Distributors, Gilbert Printing, Gilbert Law & Legalines, Bar/Bri Law Reviews. President: Meyer Fisher. Publishes trade paperback originals, trade paperback reprints and software. Averages 6 titles/year. Pays 7-10% royalty on wholesale price. Offers $1,000-6,000 advance. Publishes ms an average of 6 months after acceptance. Simultaneous submissions OK. Electronic submissions OK, but requires hard copy also. Computer printout submissions acceptable. SASE. Reports in 3 weeks on queries; 2 months on mss. Free book catalog.
Nonfiction: How-to, reference law books for minors, self-help, technical, textbook, law outlines and study aids. Subjects include business and economics, psychology, professional law, C.P.A., and criminal justice. Especially needs books on "juvenile laws, psychology for law people, law for law people. Does not want biography, cookbooks, health, humor, politics, or religious books. Submit outline/synopsis and 6 sample chapters. Reviews artwork/photos as part of ms package.
Recent Nonfiction Title: *Gilbert Law Summaries: California Bar Performance Test Skills.*
Software: Contact Law Distributors.
Tips: Queries/mss may be routed to other editors in the publishing group.

‡**HARCOURT BRACE JOVANOVICH, PUBLISHERS,** Children's Books, 1250 Sixth Ave., San Diego CA 92101. (619)231-6616. Contact: Maria Modugno, manager, or Kathleen Krull, senior editor. Publishes hardcover originals and trade paperback reprints. Averages 30 titles/year. Pays royalty; terms vary. Offers variable advance. No simultaneous submissions; photocopied submissions OK. Computer printout submissions acceptable; no dot-matrix. SASE. Reports in 8 weeks. Free book catalog.
Nonfiction: Juvenile books on topics of interest to children ages 1-14. Query.
Recent Nonfiction Title: *Winners and Losers: How Elections Work in America*, by Jules Archer.
Fiction: Fiction categories of interest to children ages 1-14. No series fiction or teen romance. Submit outline/synopsis and sample chapters.
Recent Fiction Title: *Bailey's Window*, by Anne Lindbergh.
Poetry: Submit complete ms.
Recent Poetry Title: *Crickets and Bullfrogs and Whispers of Thunder*, by Harry Behn, edited by Lee Bennett Hopkins.
Tips: "We are looking for good books for children that combine high commercial appeal with solid backlist potential. We strongly recommend that writers study the HBJ list, particularly of the last two years before submitting manuscripts."

HARLEQUIN BOOKS, 225 Duncan Mill Rd., Don Mills, Ontario M3B 3K9 Canada. (416)445-5860. Imprints include Harlequin Romance, Harlequin Presents, Superromances, Harlequin American Romance, Worldwide Bestsellers, Harlequin Temptation and Harlequin Intrigue. Publishes paperback originals. Pays royalty on retail price; offers advance. Publishes book an average of 18 months after acceptance. Photocopied submissions OK. SAE and IRCs. Reports in 2-3 months.
Fiction: For Harlequin Romance and Harlequin Presents submit to Maryan Gibson, senior editor. Outline/synopsis and sample chapters OK. For Superromance submit to Lauren Bauman, senior editor. Outline/synopsis and sample chapters OK. For Temptation submit to Margaret Carney. For Bestsellers submit to Star Helmer, editorial director. For Harlequin American Romance and Harlequin Intrique submit to Hilari Cohen or Debra Matteucci, senior editors, Harlequin Books, 919 3rd Ave., 15th Floor, New York NY 10022. Complete mss only.

HARPER & ROW JUNIOR BOOKS GROUP, 10 E. 53rd St., New York NY 10022. (212)207-7044. Imprints include: Harper & Row Junior Books, including Charlotte Zolotow Books; T.Y. Crowell and Lippincott Junior Books. Publisher: Elizabeth Gordon. Editors: Charlotte Zolotow, Nina Ignatowitz, Marilyn Kriney, Barbara Fenton, Lucille Schultz, Laura Geringer, Robert O. Warren. Publishes hardcover originals and paperback reprints—picture books, easy-to-read, middle-grade, teenage, and young adult novels. Published 73 titles in 1984 (Harper, cloth); 38 titles (Harper-Trophy, paperback); 26 titles (Crowell); 17 titles (Lippincott). Query; submit complete ms; submit outline/synopsis and sample chapters; or submit through agent. SASE.

Photocopied submissions OK. "Please identify simultaneous submissions." Reports in 2-3 months. Pays average royalty of 10%. Royalties on picture books shared with illustrators. Offers advance. Book catalog for self-addressed label.

Nonfiction: Science, history, social studies, and sports.

Fiction: Fantasy, animal, spy/adventure, science fiction, problem novels, contemporary. Needs picture books, easy-to-read, middle-grade, teenage and young adult novels.

Recent Titles: *Fire! Fire!*, written and illustrated by Gail Gibbons (Crowell); *In the Year of the Boar and Jackie Robinson*, written by Betty Bao Lord and illustrated by Marc Simont (Harper and Row); *More Scary Stories to Tell in the Dark*, written by Alvin Schwartz and illustrated by Steven Gammell (Lippincott); and *Hold On to Love*, by Mollie Hunter (A Charlotte Zolotow book).

Tips: "Write from your own experience and the child you once were. Read widely in the field of adult and children's literature. Realize that writing for children is a difficult challenge."

HARPER & ROW PUBLISHERS, INC., 10 E. 53rd St., New York NY 10022. (212)207-7000. Imprints include Barnes & Noble; Harper & Row-San Francisco (religious books only); Perennial; Colophon; and Torchbooks. Contact: Managing Editor. Publishes hardcover and paperback originals, and paperback reprints. Publishes 300 titles/year. Pays standard royalties; advances negotiable. No unsolicited queries or mss. Reports on solicited queries in 6 weeks.

Nonfiction: Americana, animals, art, biography, business/economics, cookbooks, health, history, how-to, humor, music, nature, philosophy, photography, poetry, politics, psychology, reference, religion, science, self-help, sociology, sports and travel. "No technical books."

Fiction: Adventure, fantasy, gothic, historical, mainstream, mystery, romance, science fiction, suspense, western and literary. "We look for a strong story line and exceptional literary talent."

‡HART PUBLISHING CO., INC., 24 Fifth Ave., New York NY 10011. (212)982-0190. Book packagers. Hardcover and paperback originals. Pays royalty on list price for paperbacks and hardcovers. Averages 30 titles/year. Reports in 2-3 weeks. SASE.

Nonfiction: Publishes only nonfiction books on education, hobbies, how-to, psychology, recreation, reference, self-help and sociology. Query, submit outline and sample chapter or submit complete ms.

Recent Nonfiction Title: *Mammoth Book of Fun & Games*.

Tips: "We need crossword puzzles with reproduciable art, quizzes, puzzles and original word games. We pay anywhere from $10-25 per piece, depending on length and merit. Payment is made immediately upon acceptance. All material must be accompanied by SASE. Replies will be made within 3 weeks."

THE HARVARD COMMON PRESS, 535 Albany St., Boston MA 02118. (617)423-5803. Editorial Director: Kathleen Cushman. Publishes hardcover and trade paperback originals and reprints. Averages 16 titles/year. Pays royalty; offers average $1,000 advance. Simultaneous and photocopied submissions OK. Electronic submissions OK. Computer printout submissions acceptable; prefers letter-quality to dot-matrix. SASE. Reports in 1 month. Catalog for 9x11½ SAE and 2 first class stamps.

Nonfiction: Biography, cookbook, how-to, humor, reference and self-help. Subjects include Americana, business and economics, cooking and foods, health, history, hobbies, music, nature, politics, psychology, recreation, sociology, sports and travel. "We want strong, practical books with an idealistic bias—books that help people gain control over a particular area of their lives, whether it's family matters, business or financial matters, health, travel, or careers. We're open to any good nonfiction proposal that shows evidence of strong organization and writing. First-time authors are welcome." Accepts nonfiction translations. Submit outline/synopsis and 1-3 sample chapters.

Recent Nonfiction Title: *Helping Children Cope With Separation and Loss*, by Claudia Jewett (family matters).

HASTINGS HOUSE PUBLISHERS, INC., 10 E. 40th St., New York NY 10016. (212)689-5400. Editor: Walter Frese. Hardcover and paperback originals (80%) and reprints (20%). Averages 60 titles/year. 10% minimum royalty. Reports in 1-2 weeks. SASE. Free book catalog.

Nonfiction: Publishes Americana, graphic arts, biography, cookbooks, cooking and foods, history, juveniles, photography, recreation, sports and travel. Accepts nonfiction translations. Query or submit outline/synopsis and 2 sample chapters. Reviews artwork/photos as part of ms package.

Recent Nonfiction Title: *Graphic Designers Production Handbook*, by Sanders/Bevington.

*HAWKES PUBLISHING, INC., 3775 S. 5th W., Salt Lake City UT 84115. (801)262-5555. President: John Hawkes. Publishes hardcover and trade paperback originals. Averages 24 titles/year. Subsidy publishes 25% of books/year based on "how promising they are." Pays varying royalty of 10% on retail price to 10% on wholesale; no advance. Photocopied submissions OK. SASE. Reports in 1 month on queries; 3 months on mss. Free book catalog.

Nonfiction: Cookbook, how-to and self-help. Subjects include cooking and foods, health, history, hobbies and psychology. Query or submit outline/synopsis and sample chapters.
Recent Nonfiction Title: *Migrant's Road*, by Reba Lazenby.

HAYDEN BOOK CO., 10 Mulholland Dr., Hasbrouck Heights NJ 07604. (201)393-6000. Editorial Director: Michael Violano. Publishes hardcover and paperback originals. Publishes 125 titles/year. Pays 12-15% royalty; offers advance. Simultaneous (if so identified) and photocopied submissions OK. Reports in 4-6 weeks. SASE. Free book catalog.
Nonfiction: Publishes technician-level and engineering texts and references on microcomputers, digital electronics, electricity and robotics; computer science; texts; and books on programming and applications for popular microcomputers; children's books on computers and technology.

HAZELDEN FOUNDATION, Dept. of Educational Materials, Box 176, Center City MN 55012. (612)257-4010. Managing Editor: Linda Peterson. Publishes hardcover and trade paperback originals. Predominantly direct mail. Averages 40 titles/year. Pays 7-9% royalty on retail price; buys some mss outright; offers $150-300+ advance. Publishes ms an average of 10 months after acceptance. Simultaneous and photocopied submissions OK. Computer printout submissions acceptable. SASE. "We immediately acknowledge receipt. A decision is usually made within 2 months."
Nonfiction: Reference, self-help, technical on philosophy, psychology, sociology, and addictions. "We are seeking mss of pamphlet or booklet length. The subject matter, ideally, will center around alcoholism, drug abuse or other addictions. The focus would be on the prevention, recovery from, or understanding of an addiction." Publishes for people recovering from an addiction and those close to them; people seeking information about alcoholism/drug abuse; and professionals who help such people. No personal stories or poetry. Submit outline/synopsis, introduction and 2 sample chapters.
Recent Nonfiction Title: *Women in Treatment: Creating a New Self-Image*, by Barbara McFarland, Ed.D. (booklet).

HEALTH PROFESSION DIVISION, McGraw-Hill Book Co., 1221 Avenue of the Americas, New York NY 10020. General Manager: Robert P. McGraw. Publishes 60 titles/year. Pays on royalty basis. SASE.
Textbooks: Publishes textbooks, major reference books and continuing education materials in the field of medicine.
Recent Nonfiction Title: *Harrison's Principles of Internal Medicine*, 10th Edition, by Petersdorf, et al.

*HEART OF THE LAKES PUBLISHING, 2989 Lodi Rd., Interlaken NY 14847-0299. (607)532-4997. Contact: Walter Steesy. Publishes hardcover and trade paperback originals and hardcover and trade paperback reprints. Averages 10-15 titles/year. Subsidy publishes 50% of books, "depending on type of material and potential sales." Payment is "worked out individually." Publishes book an average of 1 year after acceptance. Simultaneous and photocopied submissions OK. Electronic submissions OK; contact in advance for information. Computer printouts acceptable. SASE. Reports in 1 week on queries; 2 weeks on mss. Current books flyer for busness size SAE and 1 first class stamp; full catalog $3.
Nonfiction: New York state and New England history and genealogy. Query.
Recent Nonfiction Title: *Their Own Voices: Oral History Recorded in 1840 in Washington County, New York*, by Asa Fitch, c 1840 (edited by Wiston Adler).
Fiction: "Not looking for any, but will review any that deal with New York state historical subjects."

D.C. HEATH & CO., 125 Spring St., Lexington MA 02173. (617)862-6650. College Division Editorial Director—Softside: Barbara Piercecchi. Division Editor-in-Chief: Robert Marshall. Vice President/General Manager: Robert D. Bovenschulte. Collamore Press General Manager: Geoff Gunn. College Div. Editorial Director—Hardside: Thomas Flaherty. Publishes hardcover and paperback textbooks, professional scholarly, medical books and software. Averages 300 titles/year. Offers standard royalty rates. Query. Publishes book an average of 1 year after acceptance. Electronic submissions OK if compatible with Wang and IBM. Computer printout submissions acceptable; prefers letter-quality to dot-matrix. SASE.
Textbooks: "Texts at the college level in psychology, history, political science, chemistry, math, biology, physics, economics, modern languages, English, business, and computer science. Also publishes professional reference books: "Advanced-level research studies in the social sciences, library science, and in technical fields (Lexington Books) and medical books (The Collamore Press)." Length varies.
Software: Contact Thomas Haver.
Tips: Queries/mss may be routed to other editors in the publishing group.

HEINLE & HEINLE PUBLISHERS, INC., Subsidiary of Linguistics International, Inc., 286 Congress St., Boston MA 02210. (617)451-1940. President: Charles H. Heinle. Editor: Stanley Galek. Averages 15 titles/year. Pays 6-15% royalty on net price; no advance. SASE. Reports in 3 weeks on queries; 3 months on mss. Free book catalog.

Nonfiction: Textbook. "Foreign language and English as a second or foreign language text materials. Before writing the book, submit complete prospectus along with sample chapters, and specify market and competitive position of proposed text."
Recent Nonfiction Title: *Allons-y! Le Français Par Etapes*, by Jeannette D. Bragger and Donald B. Rice.

‡**HENDRICKSON PUBLISHERS, INC.**, 1 Scouting Way, Box 3473, Peabody MA 01961-3473. (617)535-6437. General Editor: Dr. Ben Aker. Publishes hardcover and trade paperback originals, and hardcover and trade paperback reprints. Averages 6-12 titles/year. Pays 5-15% royalty on wholesale and retail price. Average advance depends on project. Publishes book an average of 6 months after acceptance. Simultaneous (if so notified) and photocopied submissions OK. Computer printout submissions acceptable. SASE. Reports in 4 weeks on queries; 6 weeks on mss. Free book catalog.
Nonfiction: Religious. "We will consider any quality mss within the area of religion, specifically related to Biblical studies and related fields." Submit outline/synopsis and sample chapters or complete ms.
Recent Nonfiction Title: *Music and Ministry: A Biblical Counterpoint*, by Calvin Johansson.

*HERALD PRESS, Mennonite Publishing House, 616 Walnut Ave., Scottdale PA 15683. (412)887-8500. Book Editor: Paul M. Schrock. Publishes hardcover and paperback originals and reprints. Averages 35 titles/year. Several titles a year are subsidized by church organizations. "Subsidy is accepted only for books sponsored by an official board or committee of the Mennonite Church to meet discriminating needs when a book is not otherwise economically feasible." Pays 10-15% royalty on retail price; no advance. Electronic submissions OK. Photocopied submissions OK. Computer printout submissions acceptable; prefers letter-quality to dot-matrix. SASE. Catalog 50¢. Reports in 3 weeks.
Nonfiction: Biography (religious); cookbooks; history (church); how-to; juveniles; devotional/inspirational; psychology (religion); reference (Mennonite); religion; missions and evangelism; self-help (Christian); sociology (of religion); peace and social issues; and textbooks (Christian). Query. Accepts outline/synopsis and 1 sample chapter. Looks for "a fresh perspective; competence of the writer in the subject treated (professional credentials if applicable); crisp use of language; neatness of manuscript; ability of author/manuscript to immediately capture attention and sustain interest."
Recent Nonfiction Title: *Faith in a Nuclear Age*, by Dave Beachey.
Fiction: Adventure (juvenile); historical and religious. Query.
Recent Fiction Title: *Crisis at Pemberton Dike*, by Rachel Sherwood Roberts (juvenile).

HERE'S LIFE PUBLISHERS, INC., Subsidiary of Campus Crusade for Christ, Box 1576, San Bernardino CA 92404. (714)886-7981. Editorial Director: Les Stobbe. Publishes hardcover and trade paperback originals and mass market paperback originals. Averages 40 titles/year. Pays 15% royalty on wholesale price. Offers $1,000-2,000 advance. Simultaneous and photocopied submissions OK. SASE. Reports in 1 month on queries; 3 months on mss. Book catalog for 8½x11 SAE and $2 postage. Writer's guidelines available.
Nonfiction: Biography, how-to, illustrated book, reference and self-help. Subjects include religion and sports (religious). Needs "books in the areas of evangelism, Christian growth and family life; must reflect basic understanding of ministry and mission of Campus Crusade for Christ. No metaphysical or missionary biography." Query or submit outline/synopsis and sample chapters.
Recent Nonfiction Title: *First We Have Coffee*, by Margaret Jensen.

*HERITAGE BOOKS, INC., 3602 Maureen, Bowie MD 20715. (301)464-1159. Editorial Director: Laird C. Towle. Publishes hardcover and paperback originals (20%) and reprints (80%). Averages 8 titles/year. Subsidy publishes 5% of books. "Quality of the book is of prime importance; next is its relevance to our fields of interest." Pays 10% royalty on retail price; occasional advance. Publishes book an average of 9 months after acceptance. Simultaneous and photocopied submissions OK. Computer printout submissions acceptable; prefers letter-quality to dot-matrix. Reports in 1 month. SASE. Free book catalog.
Nonfiction: "We particularly desire nonfiction titles dealing with history and genealogy including how-to and reference works, as well as conventional histories and genealogies. The titles should be either of national interest or restricted to New England. Other subject matter will be considered provided that it is of either national or New England interest. We prefer writers to query, submit an outline/synopsis, or submit a complete ms, in that order, depending on the stage the writer has reached in the preparation of his work."
Recent Nonfiction Title: *Abstracts of the Probate Records of Strafford County, N.H., 1771-1799*, by Evans.

*HIGH/COO PRESS, Route #1, Battle Ground IN 47920. (317)567-2596. Editors: Randy and Shirley Brooks. Publishes originals. Averages 5 titles/year. Subsidy publishes 5% of books. Pays 15% minimum royalty on retail price saddle-stitched after production expenses. SASE. Publishes book an average of 1 year after acceptance. Reports in 2 weeks on queries; 2 months on mss. Book catalog for business-size SAE and 1 first class stamp. Sample chapbook $3.50 postpaid.
Nonfiction: Reference. Subjects include haiku books. "Every two years we publish a directory of haiku in English called *Haiku Review*. We list and review haiku books in print along with other haiku bibliography in-

formation. We have an international audience of poets and haiku enthusiasts. We do not seek or desire any mass market, but rather an informed, astute readership." Query.
Recent Nonfiction Title: *Haiku Review '84*, edited by Randy and Shirley Brooks (haiku directory).
Poetry: "We publish a chapbook of short poetry every 6 months. Each chapbook is 24-48 pages. We also publish 3-4 mini-chapbooks every year. Each mini is 12-24 pages. No poems with more than thirteen lines." Submit complete ms. "Sample our publications before submitting."
Recent Poetry Title: *Cicada Voices*, by Eric Amann.

HOLIDAY HOUSE, 18 E. 53rd St., New York NY 10022. (212)688-0085. Editorial Director: Margery Cuyler. Publishes hardcover originals. Averages 30-35 titles/year. Pays in royalties based on retail price; offers variable advance. Photocopied submissions OK. Computer printouts submissions acceptable. Reports in 2 months. SASE.
Nonfiction and Fiction: General fiction and nonfiction for young readers—pre-school through high school. "It's better to submit the ms without art." Submit outline/synopsis and 3 sample chapters or complete ms. "No certified, insured or registered mail accepted."
Recent Nonfiction Title: *Whales: Giants of the Deep*, by Dorothy Hinshaw Patent.
Recent Fiction Title: *The Doll House Murders*, by Betty Ren Wright.

HOLLOWAY HOUSE PUBLISHING CO., 8060 Melrose Ave., Los Angeles CA 90046. (213)653-8060. Editorial Director: Robert Leighton. Publishes paperback originals (95%) and reprints (5%). Averages 30 titles/year. Pays royalty based on retail price. Photocopied submissions OK. Prefer outline and 3 sample chapters. SASE. Reports in 6 weeks. Free book catalog for SASE.
Nonfiction: Gambling and game books—from time to time publishes gambling books along the line of *How to Win*, *World's Greatest Winning Systems*, *Backgammon*, *How to Play and Win at Gin Rummy*, etc. Send query letter and/or outline with one sample chapter. SASE. Length: 60,000 words.
Recent Nonfiction Title: *Jesse Jackson*, by Eddie Stowe (biography).
Fiction: "Holloway House is the largest publisher of Black Experience literature. We are in the market for hard-hitting contemporary stories with easily identifiable characters and locations. Dialogue must be realistic. A strain of sex is acceptable but not essential. Action, people and places must be thoroughly depicted and graphically presented." Black romance line newly launched—Holloway House Heartline Romances, designed to appeal to middle class black women paralleling other romance lines designed for white readers.
Recent Fiction Title: *Delta Crossing*, by Joe Nazch (political novel set in modern South).

*HOLMES & MEIER PUBLISHERS, INC., 30 Irving Place, New York NY 10003. (212)254-4100. Publisher: Max J. Holmes. Associate Publisher: Barbara Lyons. Editor: Naomi Lipman. Publishes hardcover and paperback originals (50%) and reprints (50%). Publishes 80 titles/year. Subsidy publishes 2% of books. Pays variable royalty. Publishes book an average of 8 months after acceptance. Computer printout submissions acceptable; prefers letter-quality to dot-matrix. SASE. Reports in 3 months. Free book catalog.
Nonfiction: Americana, Africana, art, biography, business/economics, education, history, Judaica, Latin American studies, literary criticism, music, nature, politics, psychology, reference, sociology, textbooks and women's studies. Accepts nonfiction translations. "We are noted as a scholarly publishing house and are pleased with our reputation of excellence in the field. However, while we will continue to publish books for academic and professional audiences, we are expanding our list to reach the broader non-academic intellectual community. We will continue to build on our strengths in the social sciences, humanities and natural sciences. We do not want how-to and self-help material." Reviews artwork/photos as part of ms package. Query first and submit outline/synopsis, sample chapters, curriculum vitae and idea of intended market/audience.
Recent Nonfiction Title: *The Destruction of the European Jews*, by Raul Hilberg.

‡HOLT, RINEHART & WINSTON, Trade Division (General Books), 521 Fifth Ave., New York NY 10175. Imprints include Owl. Publishes hardcover and trade paperback originals and hardcover and trade paperback reprints.
Nonfiction: Biography, cookbook, how-to, humor, juvenile, reference, self-help and technical. Subjects include Americana, animals, art, business and economics, cooking and foods, health, history, hobbies, music, nature, philosophy, photography, politics, psychology, recreation, religion, sociology, sports and travel. "Unsolicited mss not accepted." Submit through agent only. All unsolicited mss are returned unopened.
Fiction: Submit through agent only. All unsolicited mss are returned unopened.
Poetry: "Unsolicited mss not accepted."

HOLT, RINEHART & WINSTON OF CANADA, LTD., 55 Horner Ave., Toronto, Ontario M8Z 4X6, Canada. (416)255-4491. School Editor-in-Chief: William Park. College Editor-in-Chief: Ron Munro. Publishes hardcover and paperback text originals for the El-Hi, community college and university markets. Royalty varies according to type of book; pays $200-500 for anthologies. No advance. Simultaneous and photocopied submissions OK. Reports in 1-3 months. SAE and IRCs. Free book catalog.

Nonfiction: Education texts. Query.
Recent Nonfiction Title: *Music Canada*, general editor, Penny Louise Brooks.

HORIZON PRESS, 156 5th Ave., New York NY 10010. Pays royalty based on both wholesale and retail price. Royalty schedule standard scale from 10% to 15%. Averages 24 titles/year. Free book catalog. Reports in 3 months. SASE.
Nonfiction: History, literature, science, biography, the arts, general. Length: 40,000 words and up. Accepts nonfiction and fiction translations. Reviews artwork/photos as part of ms package. Query with full description.
Recent Nonfiction Title: *William Glackens and "The Eight"*.
Fiction: Query with full description. "We rarely publish fiction."
Recent Fiction Title: *Countrymen of Bones*.

HOUGHTON MIFFLIN CO., 2 Park St., Boston MA 02108. (617)725-5000. Editor-in-Chief: Nan A. Talese. Managing Editor: Linda Glick Conway. Hardcover and paperback originals (90%) and paperback reprints (10%). Royalty of 6% on retail price for paperbacks; 10-15% on sliding scale for standard fiction and nonfiction; advance varies widely. Publishes book an average of 18 months after acceptance. Publishes 110 titles/year. Simultaneous submissions and photocopied submissions OK. Computer printout submissions acceptable; no dot-matrix. "Proposals will not be returned without SASE." Reports in 6-8 weeks. SASE.
Nonfiction: Americana, natural history, animals, biography, cookbooks/cooking/food, health, history, how-to, juveniles, poetry, politics, psychology and self-help. Query.
Recent Nonfiction Title: *Kingdom by the Sea*, by Paul Theroux.
Fiction: Historical, mainstream, mystery, science fiction and suspense. Query.
Recent Fiction Title: *August*, by Judith Rossner.

HOUGHTON MIFFLIN CO., Children's Trade Books, 2 Park St., Boston MA 02108. Contact: Editor. Publishes hardcover originals and trade paperback reprints (some simultaneous hard/soft). Averages 45-50 titles/year. Pays standard royalty; offers advance. Computer printout submissions acceptable; no dot-matrix. SASE. Reports in 1 month on queries; 2 months on mss. Free book catalog.
Nonfiction: Submit outline/synopsis and sample chapters. Reviews artwork/photos as part of ms package.
Fiction: Submit complete ms.

HOUNSLOW PRESS, A Division of Anthony R. Hawke Limited, 124 Parkview Ave., Willowdale, Ontario M2N 3Y5 Canada. (416)225-9176. President: Anthony Hawke. Publishes hardcover and trade paperback originals and reprints. Averages 6 titles/year. Pays 5-15% royalty on retail price; offers average $500 advance. Simultaneous and photocopied submissions OK. Reports in 1 week on queries; 2 weeks on mss. Free book catalog.
Nonfiction: Biography, "coffee table" book, cookbook, how-to, humor, illustrated book, juvenile, reference, self-help on animals, art, business and economics, cooking and foods, health, history, hobbies, nature, philosophy, photography, politics, psychology, recreation, religion, and travel. Publishes for a general audience. "We do well with cookbooks and photography books about Canadian themes." Query. Accepts outline/synopsis and 4 sample chapters.
Recent Nonfiction Title: *Sorry Daddy—A Father's Guide to Toddlers*, by Marvin Ross and David Shaw.
Fiction: Adventure, humor, and mainstream. Query.
Poetry: Submit 20 samples.
Recent Poetry Title: *Mirages*, by Ludwig Zeller and Susanna Wald.

HOUSE OF COLLECTIBLES, INC., 1900 Premier Row, Orlando FL 32809. Publishes hardcover and trade paperback originals. Royalty is based on the stature of the author, the subject and the ms. Average advance is $1,000. Published 50 titles last year. Exclusive publisher of official price guides. Complete distribution and marketing range in all fields with heavy coverage on the collectible markets. Will consider photocopied submissions. Mss must be typed, double spaced with sample illustrations, when necessary. Reports in 2 months. Enclose return postage. Will send catalog to writer on request.
Nonfiction: "On the subject of collectibles (antiques, numismatics, philatelics) and how-to-do books, we prefer an author who knows his or her subject thoroughly. Any special treatment of emphasis is a matter of decision for the author." Submit outline and sample chapters.

HOWARD UNIVERSITY PRESS, 2900 Van Ness St. NW, Washington DC 20008. (202)686-6696. Managing Editor: Renee Mayfield. Publishes hardcover and paperback originals (90%), and hardcover reprints (10%). Averages 14 titles/year. Pays 5-15% royalty; offers average $500 advance. Simultaneous and photocopied submissions OK. SASE. Reports in 2 months. Free book catalog.
Nonfiction: Biography and reference. Subjects include Americana, art, business and economics, health, history, music, philosophy, photography, politics, psychology, religion, sociology, sports, science and literary

criticism. "We would be pleased to receive inquiries concerning projects of an original, scholarly, conceptual nature on the above subjects as they pertain to minorities in the US or to people in the Third World. In Black studies, works that relate Black Americans to the Diaspora and, continually, works that serve to integrate Black history from slavery to WWII." No textbooks or personal revelations having no foundation in scholarly or journalistic methods.

Recent Nonfiction Title: *Mental Health and People of Color: Curriculum Development and Change*, edited by Joy C. Chunn, Patricia Dunston and Fariyal Ross-Sheriff.

Fiction: Experimental and mainstream. "Our needs in this area are minimal. We will probably be aware of and seek out any projects we would do in this area." Query.

Recent Fiction Title: *And Then We Heard the Thunder*, by John Oliver Killens.

Tips: "Visit bookstores and college campuses, and tune in to what is being bought, read, researched and argued."

HUDSON HILLS PRESS, INC., Suite 301, 220 5th Ave., New York NY 10001. (212)889-3090. President/Editorial Director: Paul Anbinder. Publishes hardcover and paperback originals. Averages 6-8 titles/year. Offers royalties of 5-8% on retail price. Average advance: $5,000. Publishes book an average of 1 year after acceptance. Simultaneous and photocopied submissions OK. Computer printout submissions acceptable; prefers letter-quality to dot-matrix. SASE. Reports in 4 weeks. Free book catalog.

Nonfiction: Art and photography. "We are only interested in publishing books about art and photography, or collections of photographs (photo essays or monographs)." Query first, then submit outline/synopsis and sample chapters including illustrations.

Recent Nonfiction Title: *Photography in California 1945-80*, by Louis Katzman.

HUMANICS LIMITED, 1182 W. Peachtree St. NE, Atlanta GA 30309. (404)874-2176. President: Gary B. Wilson. Publishes softcover, educational and trade paperback originals and software. Averages 10 titles/year. Pays average 10% royalty on net sales; buys some mss outright. Publishes book an average of 6 months after acceptance. Reports in 8 weeks. Free book catalog.

Nonfiction: Juvenile, self-help, textbook and teacher resource books. Subjects include cooking and foods, health, psychology, sociology, education, parenting and New Age.. Submit outline/synopsis and at least 3 sample chapters. Reviews artwork/photos as part of ms package.

Recent Nonfiction Title: *Love Notes*, by Angie Rose (parenting).

Software: Pre-school and early elementary. Commodore 64, Apple, and IBM.

‡**HUNTINGTON HOUSE, INC.**, 1200 N. Market St., Shreveport LA 71107. (318)221-2767. President: Bill Keith. Publishes hardcover, trade paperback, and mass market paperback originals, and trade paperback reprints. Averages 10-20 titles/year. Pays 10-15% royalty on wholesale and retail price, or makes outright purchase of $50; offers $100-2,500 advance. Simultaneous and photocopied submissions OK. SASE. Reports in 2 weeks on queries; 6 weeks on mss. Free book catalog.

Nonfiction: Biography, self-help, and religious. Subjects include religion. "We publish self-help books and Christian growth books oriented to the Christian community." No "New Age," occult, humanism or liberal theology. Query.

Recent Nonfiction Title: *The Hidden Dangers of the Rainbow*, by Constance Cumbey.

Fiction: Religious. Especially looking for evangelical Christian romance, mystery and historical biography. No nonreligious material. Query.

Tips: "Write clear, crisp, exciting self-help or teaching mss."

HURTIG PUBLISHERS LTD., 10560 105th St., Edmonton, Alberta T5H 2W7, Canada. (403)426-2359. Editor-in-Chief: Elizabeth Munroe. Hardcover and paperback originals (80%) and reprints (20%). Averages 12 titles/year. Typically pays 10% royalty on first 7,500 copies; 12% on next 7,500; 15% thereafter. Advance averages $500-1,000. State availability of photos and/or illustrations to accompany ms. Photocopied submissions OK. Computer printouts acceptable; "will read anything legible—must be hard copy printout. Prefers letter of inquiry first. Reports in 2-3 months. SASE. Free book catalog.

Nonfiction: Publishes biographies of well-known Canadians, Canadian history, humor, nature, topical Canadian politics and economics, reference (Canadian), and material about native Canadians "aimed at the nationalistic Canadian interested in politics, the North and energy policy." No poetry or original fiction. Query or submit outline/synopsis and 1-2 sample chapters; or submit complete ms. Very few unsolicited manuscripts published. Looks for "suitability of topic to general publishing program; market interest in topic; qualifications of writer to treat that topic well; quality of writing."

Recent Nonfiction Title: *Pitseolak: A Canadian Tragedy*, by David F. Raine.

ICARUS PRESS, INC., Suite 906, 120 W. LaSalle St., Box 1225, South Bend IN 46624. (219)233-6020. Editorial Director: Bruce M. Fingerhut. Publishes hardcover and paperback originals. Averages 20 titles/year. Offers 12-17% royalty based on wholesale price. Average advance: $2,000. Simultaneous and photocopied submissions OK (if so indicated). SASE. Reports in 1 month. Free book catalog.

Nonfiction: Americana, biography, history, recreation, sports, and travel (regional). Accepts nonfiction translations. "Our interests in sports, whether of the self-help, coaching, or history genre, remain high. As to history, biography, current affairs, etc., such manuscripts as we publish must be real trade titles—with national appeal. We do *not* want to see poetry, photography, art, hobbies (other than those immediately connected with sports), or cookbooks." Reviews artwork/photos as part of ms package. Query first, then submit outline/synopsis and 2-4 sample chapters. Looks for "originality, flair of style, writing competence."

Recent Nonfiction Title: *Beating the Bushes*, by Frank Dolson (sports).

*IDEAL WORLD PUBLISHING CO., Box 1237-EG, Melbourne FL 32936-1237. New Idea Publishing Co. is a division of Ideal World Publishing Co. Publisher: Harold Pallatz. Publishes hardcover and paperback originals and reprints. Averages 3 titles/year. 90% subsidy published. Offers subsidy publication of "difficult-to-place" manuscripts. "If your book has marketing potential which major publishers have failed to recognize due to their own business strategy, we can help you get published. We offer you a special subsidy plan which includes typing, printing, binding and distribution. Fee starts at $50 for short runs, depending upon number of pages, copies, etc. Publishes ms an average of 10 weeks after acceptance. Photocopied submissions OK. Computer printout submissions acceptable. "Query, first, please." Reports in 2-4 weeks. *"No material will be returned unless SASE is attached."*

Nonfiction: "Natural approaches to good health through nutrition, herbs, vegetarianism, vitamins, and unusual medical approaches for specific ailments, particularly from authorities in the field. Any style is acceptable, but it must hold the reader's attention and make for fairly smooth nonintensive (no brain taxation) requirements. Ideas should be in a simple, easygoing pace." Also publishes energy-related books: alternative energy themes, particularly do-it-yourself hybrid vehicles. "The scope of our publishing is confined to health and energy nonfiction; we do not accept fiction or poetry." Reviews artwork/photos as part of ms package.

Recent Nonfiction Title: *Hybrid Manual*, by Harold Pallatz (electric cars).

IDEALS PUBLISHING CORP., 11315 Watertown Plank Rd., Milwaukee WI 53226. Director, Publishing: Patricia Pingry. Publishes hardcover and paperback juvenile books, cookbooks, greeting booklets, and *Ideals* periodical. Pays on royalty and buyout basis; offers advance only on assigned projects. Photocopied submissions OK. SASE. Reports in 4-6 weeks.

Nonfiction: Cookbooks. Length: 300 recipes.

Recent Nonfiction Title: *Wok Cookbook*.

Fiction: "Juveniles fall into one of 3 categories: seasonal (holiday theme), religious or of some educational or moral value. They must stress the same traditional values as *Ideals* periodicals." Query. Length varies.

ILLUMINATI, Suite 204, 8812 W. Pico Blvd., Los Angeles CA 90035. (213)271-1460. Editor: P. Schneidre. Publishes hardcover and trade paperback originals. Imprints include tadbooks (poetry). Averages 10 titles/year. Pays 12½% royalty on retail price. Offers average $150 advance. Photocopied submissions OK. SASE. Reports in 2 weeks on queries; 3 weeks on mss. Book catalog for 9x12 SAE and 37¢ postage.

Nonfiction: Literature and art. Submit complete ms.

Poetry: "We will be needing several 'tadbooks'—i.e., small book mss comprised, probably, of a single long poem, an illustrated poem or a sequence of poems." No light verse or haiku. Submit complete ms.

Recent Poetry Title: *A Horse of a Different Color*, by Greg Kuzma.

‡INCENTIVE PUBLICATIONS, INC, 3835 Cleghorn Ave., Nashville TN 37215. (615)385-2934. Editor: Susan C. Oglander. Publishes trade paperback originals. Averages 15-20 titles/year. Pays royalty on retail price or makes outright purchase. Publishes book an average of 1 year after acceptance. Photocopied submissions OK. Computer printout submissions acceptable; prefers letter-quality to dot-matrix. SASE. Reports in 2 weeks on queries; 3 weeks on mss. Free book catalog.

Nonfiction: Juvenile, teacher resources, and books on all areas relating to children. Especially looking for nonfiction in "all basic areas of education, perhaps with a new twist. Also computers in the classroom and early learning materials." Submit outline/synopsis and sample chapters. Reviews artwork/photos as part of ms package.

Recent Nonfiction Title: *The Puppet Factory*, by Forte (teacher reproducible book).

Tips: "The parent market for educational activity books will expand tremendously. Solid educational books that appeal to parents working at home with their children, and supplementary materials for teachers are doing well for us in today's market."

*INDEPENDENT PUBLISHING SERVICES, (formerly Lame Johnny Press), Rt. 3, Box 9A, Hermosa SD 57744. (605)255-4466. Publisher: Linda M. Hasselstrom. Publishes hardcover and trade paperback originals, and hardcover reprints. Subsidy publishes 98% of books. Averages 2-5 titles/year. Pays 30-50% royalty on wholesale price. Publishes book an average of 6 months after acceptance. Computer printout submissions acceptable; prefers letter-quality to dot-matrix. SASE. Reports in 6 weeks. Book catalog for business size SASE and 2 first class stamps.

Nonfiction: How-to and self-help. Subjects include Americana and history. Accepts nonfiction translations. "We do not search for nonfiction titles; accept only occasional rare ones that originate in the Great Plains." Looks for "enough of a sample of the writing to determine quality of the work—sample chapters should accompany synopsis or outline. Simply—good writing without bombast, or obtuseness; clear characters in whom the reader can develop an interest." Reviews artwork/photos as part of ms package. Submit complete ms.
Recent Nonfiction Title: *Next-Year Country: One Woman's View*, by Alma Phillip (informal history).
Fiction: Historical (on the Great Plains only). "We consider only works by/about Great Plains, loosely defined or works with a geographically western subject matter, but not shoot-em-ups, love-my-gun, love-my-horse books. Quality determines acceptance." Submit complete ms or extensive plot outline.
Recent Fiction Title: *A Country for Old Men and Other Stories*, by Zietlow (Great Plains short stories).
Poetry: "Quality determines acceptance; must be by/about the Great Plains." Submit complete ms.
Recent Poetry Title: *Where Is Dancer's Hill?*, by Robert Schuler (short poems, influenced by Indian history and myth).
Tips: "Our readers in the Great Plains seek cultural pride. Readers outside the plains seek information, entertainment, and high-quality writing. Our authors participate in the publishing of their books; sometimes by helping finance the book (but we're *not* a subsidy publisher); sometimes in other ways. The entire process remains personal, with the writer involved in every step if he/she wishes to be."

*INDIANA UNIVERSITY PRESS, 10th & Morton Sts., Bloomington IN 47405. (812)337-4203. Director: John Gallman. Publishes hardcover and paperback originals (75%) and paperback reprints (25%). Averages 80-90 titles/year. Subsidy publishes 10% of books. Pays maximum 10% royalty on retail price; offers occasional advance. Publishes book an average of 1 year after acceptance. Photocopied submissions OK. Computer printout submissions acceptable; no dot-matrix. Reports in 2 months. SASE. Free book catalog.
Nonfiction: Scholarly books on humanities, history, philosophy, translations, semiotics, public policy, film, music, linguistics, social sciences, regional materials, African studies, women's studies, and serious nonfiction for the general reader. Query or submit outline/synopsis and sample chapters. "Queries should include as much descriptive material as is necessary to convey scope and market appeal to us."
Recent Nonfiction Title: *Semiotics and the Philosophy of Language*, by Umberto Eco.
Fiction: Query or submit outline/synopsis.

‡INDUSTRIAL PRESS INC., 200 Madison Ave., New York NY 10157. (212)889-6330. Director of Marketing: Woodrow Chapman. Publishes hardcover originals. Averages 3 titles/year. Publishes book an average of 8 months after acceptance of finished ms. Electronic submissions OK if "compatible with composition material." Computer printout submissions acceptable; no dot-matrix. Reports in 4 weeks. Free book catalog.
Nonfiction: Reference and technical. Subjects include business and economics, science and engineering. "We envision professional engineers, plant managers, on-line industrial professionals responsible for equipment operation, professors teaching manufacturing, engineering, technology related courses as our audience." Especially looking for material on manufacturing technologies and titles on specific areas in manufacturing and industry. Computers in manufacturing are a priority. No energy-related books or how-to books. Query.
Recent Nonfiction Title: *Industrial Robotic Handbook*, by V. Daniel Hunt (guide to current industrial robotics).

‡INFOSOURCE, INC., 1909 NW 12th Rd., Gainesville FL 32605. (904)373-7984. Book packager producing 10 titles/year. President: D. Michael Werner. Publishes hardcover and trade paperback originals. Pays 10-20% on retail price or makes outright purchase of $100-5,000. Offers average $50-2,000 advance. Publishes book an average of 6 months after acceptance. Simultaneous and photocopied submissions OK. Electronic submissions OK via The Source (i.d. is STN 733), but requires hard copy also. Computer printout submissions acceptable. SASE. Report in 2 weeks on queries; 1 month on mss. Book catalog for legal-size SAE and 3 first class stamps.
Nonfiction: How-to, reference and technical. Subjects include business and computers. "We envision sophisticated business managers with no computer background as our audience for computer books, and middle-level managers as our audience for business books. Looking immediately for contributors for volumes on Apple and IBM-PC computers and on all business topics. Looking in the next 1-2 years for books on portable computers, public data bases, small business and marketing, and for contributors for volumes on Apple and IBM-PC computers and on business topics." Query.
Recent Nonfiction Title: *Micros, Minis and Mainframes*, by Werner/Warrner (how-to).
Tips: "If I were a writer trying to market a book today, I would concentrate 100% of my time on writing 'how-to' and instructional materials geared to increased productivity on a personal computer."

INSTITUTE FOR BUSINESS PLANNING, Division of Prentice-Hall, Sylvan Ave., Englewood Cliffs NJ 07632. (201)592-3080. Managing Editor: Anthony Vlamis. Publishes hardcover originals and paperback reprints. Averages 15 titles/year. "No subsidy but we are open to considering such arrangement." Pays 5% maximum royalty (direct mail) and 15% royalty (trade retail). Average advance: $2,500. Publishes book an average of less than a year after acceptance. No simultaneous submissions; photocopied submissions OK. Electronic submissions OK "if accompanied by hard copy for review purposes." Computer printout submissions acceptable; prefers letter-quality to dot-matrix. SASE. Reports in 4-6 weeks. Free book catalog.

Nonfiction: Business/economics; how-to ("high level professional audience; not how to make money in mail order or other pedestrian books"); and reference. "We seek practical professional reference books in the following areas: accounting, business management, estate planning and administration, real estate, law, especially trial related subjects, taxation and finance. Areas open for future considerations are: banking, insurance, and financial planning." Does *not* want inspirational and selling mss. Query first or submit outline/synopsis and sample chapters. Reviews artwork/photos as part of ms package. Looks for "a unique salable central idea or unusual presentation of familiar material that makes it easily understandable and applicable."

Recent Nonfiction Title: *Desk Book for Setting Up a Closely-Held Corporation*, by R. Hess (law).

Tips: "Freelance writers should be aware that publishers in general are paying less and taking fewer fully exposed risks/chances than just a few years ago."

*INSTITUTE FOR THE STUDY OF HUMAN ISSUES, (ISHI Publications), 3401 Market St., Philadelphia PA 19104. (215)387-9002. Director of Publications: Betty Crapivinsky-Jutkowitz. Associate Director: Edward A. Jutkowitz. Managing Editor: Brad Fisher. Publishes hardcover and paperback originals (85%) and paperback reprints (15%). Averages 18 titles/year. Publishes 10% of books by partial subsidy. Pays 10-12½% royalty on wholesale price; no advance. Photocopied submissions OK. Computer printout submissions acceptable; no dot-matrix. Reports in 3 months. SASE. Free book catalog.

Nonfiction: Books on political science, history, anthropology, folklore, sociology, economics and drug studies, suitable for students and scholars in these fields. Accepts nonfiction translations. Submit outline/synopsis for initial consideration. Reviews artwork/photos as part of ms package.

Recent Nonfiction Title: *The US and the Philippines*, by Stephen Rosskamm Shalom (political science/foreign affairs).

INTERCULTURAL PRESS, INC., Box 768, Yarmouth ME 04096. (207)846-5168. Contact: David S. Hoopes, Editor-in-Chief, 130 North Rd., Vershire VT 05079. (802)685-4448. Publishes hardcover and trade paperback originals. Averages 5-15 titles/year. Pays royalty; occasionally offers small advance. Simultaneous and photocopied submissions OK. Computer printout submissions acceptable; prefers letter-quality to dot-matrix. SASE. Reports in "several weeks" on queries; 2 months on mss. Free book catalog and writer's guidelines.

Nonfiction: How-to, reference, self-help, textbook and theory. Subjects include business and economics, philosophy, politics, psychology, sociology, travel, or "any book with an international or domestic intercultural, multicultural or cross-cultural focus, i.e., a focus on the cultural factors in personal, social, political or economic relations. We want books with an international or domestic intercultural or multicultural focus, especially those on business operations (how to be effective in intercultural business activities) and education (textbooks for teaching intercultural subjects, for instance). Our books are published for educators in the intercultural field, business people who are engaged in international business, and anyone else who works in an international occupation or has had intercultural experience. No mss that don't have an intercultural focus." Accepts nonfiction translations. Query "if there is any question of suitability (we can tell quickly from a good query)," or submit outline/synopsis. Do not submit mss unless invited.

Recent Nonfiction Title: *Survival Kit for Overseas Living*, by Robert Kohls (how-to).

INTERNATIONAL MARINE PUBLISHING CO., 21 Elm St., Camden ME 04843. President: Roger C. Taylor. Publishes hardcover and paperback originals. Averages 15 titles/year. "Standard royalties, based on retail price, with advances." Free mail-order catalog. "Material in all stages welcome. We prefer queries first with 2-3 sample chapters. Publishes book an average of 9 months after acceptance. Computer printout submission acceptable; prefers letter-quality to dot-matrix. Reports in 6 weeks. Return postage necessary.

Nonfiction: "Marine nonfiction only—but a wide range of subjects within that category: boatbuilding, boat design, yachting, seamanship, boat maintenance, maritime history, etc." All books are illustrated black and white only. Reviews artwork/photos as part of ms package.

Recent Nonfiction Title: *Dr. Cohen's Healthy Sailor Book*, by Michael Martin Cohen, M.D.

Tips: "Freelance writers should be aware of the need for clarity, accuracy and interest."

INTERNATIONAL PUBLISHERS CO., INC., #1301, 381 Park Ave. S., New York NY 10016. (212)685-2864. President: Betty Smith. Publishes hardcover and trade paperback originals and trade paperback reprints. Averages 10-20 titles/year. Pays 5% royalty on paperbacks; 10% royalty on cloth. No advance. Publishes book an average of 6 months after acceptance. Simultaneous and photocopied submissions OK. SASE. Computer printout submissions acceptable; prefers letter-quality to dot-matrix. Reports in 1 month on queries; 6 months on mss. Free book catalog.

Nonfiction: Biography, reference and textbook. Subjects include Americana, economics, history, philosophy, politics, social sciences, and Marxist-Leninist classics. "Books on labor, black studies and women's studies

based on Marxist science have high priority." Query or submit outline/synopsis and sample chapters. Reviews artwork/photos as part of ms package.
Recent Nonfiction Title: *Cuba at 25*, by Gil Green.
Fiction: "We publish very little fiction. We are considering an anthology of original short stories and a novel on working class life." Query or submit outline/synopsis and sample chapters.
Poetry: "We rarely publish individual poets, usually anthologies."
Recent Poetry Title: *Leaving the Bough*, ed. by Roger Gaess (anthology of newer poets).

INTERNATIONAL SELF-COUNSEL PRESS, LTD., 306 W. 25th St., North Vancouver, British Columbia V7N 2G1 Canada. (604)986-3366. President: Diana R. Douglas. Editor-in-Chief: Lois Richardson. Publishes trade paperback originals. Publishes 50 titles/year. Pays 10% royalty on wholesale price; no advance. Publishes book an average of 6 months after acceptance. Simultaneous and photocopied submissions OK. Computer printout submissions acceptable; prefers letter-quality to dot-matrix. Reports in 4-6 weeks. SAE,IRCs. Free book catalog.
Nonfiction: "Books only on law and business for the layperson (how-to)." Submit outline/synopsis and sample chapters. Follow Chicago *Manual of Style*.
Recent Nonfiction Title: *Medical Law Handbook*, by T. David Marshall.

*THE INTERNATIONAL UNIVERSITY PRESS, Subsidiary of The International University Foundation, 1301 S. Noland Rd., Independence MO 64055. (816)461-3633. Editor: Dr. John Wayne Johnston. Publishes hardcover originals and trade and mass market paperback originals. Averages 100 titles/year. Subsidy publishes 30% of books. "Such decisions are made by a committee based on internal criteria." Pays "percentage, based on size of first run." Publishes book an average of 3 months after acceptance. Simultaneous and photocopied submissions OK. Computer printout submissions acceptable; prefers letter-quality to dot-matrix. SASE. Reports in 2 weeks on queries; 2 months on mss.
Nonfiction: Biography, reference, technical, textbook on art, business and economics, health, history, music, philosophy, politics, psychology, religion, sociology, and sports. Especially needs "any manuscript that exhibits coherence, originality, adequate command of the language, and few, if any, mechanical errors. Must have serious intent and some market appeal." Publishes for a "small, select group of readers of quality work." No poorly written work on any topic. Submit complete ms. Reviews artwork/photos as part of ms package. Accepts poetry translations from Spanish.
Recent Nonfiction Title: *Playwriting Principles*, by Philip P. Shaps.
Fiction: Fantasy, gothic, historical, horror, humor, mainstream, mystery, romance, science fiction, suspense, and western. "We hope to review a large number of fiction mss with an eye to publishing a growing volume of such works. No erotica or any work of questionable general interest to a sober, serious reading audience." Submit complete ms.
Poetry: "We will consider poetry mss of 50 pages or more either in form of long, epic poems or a collection of shorter works." Submit complete ms. Accepts poetry translations from Spanish.

*THE INTERSTATE PRINTERS & PUBLISHERS, INC., 19-27 N. Jackson St., Box 594, Danville IL 61832-0594. (217)446-0500. Acquisitions: Russell L. Guin. Managing Editor: Ronald L. McDaniel. Hardcover and paperback originals. Usual royalty is 10% of wholesale price; no advance. Publishes about 50 titles/year. Subsidy publishes 5% of books. Markets books by mail and exhibits. Publishes book an average of 9 months after acceptance. Computer printout submissions acceptable; prefers letter-quality to dot-matrix. Reports in 1-2 months. SASE. Free book catalog.
Nonfiction: Publishes high school and college textbooks, agriculture, special education, trade and industrial, home economics, athletics, career education, outdoor education, school law, marriage counseling, and learning disabilities books. "We favor, but do not limit ourselves to, works which are designed for class—quantity rather than single-copy sale." Reviews artwork/photos as part of ms package. Query or submit outline/synopsis and 2-3 sample chapters.
Recent Nonfiction Title: *Photo Articulation Test, 1984 edition*, by Kathleen Pendergast, et al.
Tips, "Freelance writers should be aware of strict adherence to the use of nonsexist language; fair and balanced representation of the sexes and of minorities in both text and illustrations; and discussion of computer applications wherever applicable."

‡INTERURBAN PRESS/TRANS ANGLO BOOKS, Box 6444, Glendale CA 91205. (213)240-9130. President: Mac Sebree. Publishes hardcover and trade paperback originals. Averages 10 titles/year. Pays 5-10% royalty on retail price; offers no advance. SASE. Reports in 2 weeks on queries; 2 months on mss. Free book catalog.
Nonfiction: Western Americana and transportation. Subjects include Americana, business and economics, history, hobbies, and travel. "We are interested only in mss about railroads, local transit, local history, and Western American (gold mining, logging, early transportation, etc.). Also anything pertaining to preservation movement, nostalgia." Query.

Recent Nonfiction Title: *Silver Short Line*, by Demoro/Wurm (history).
Tips: "We stick strictly to the topics already enumerated. Our audience is comprised of hobbyists in the rail transportation field ("railfans"); those interested in Western Americana (logging, mining, etc.); and students of transportation history, especially railroads and local rail transit (streetcars)."

INTERVARSITY PRESS, Box 1400, Downers Grove IL 60515. (312)964-5700. Editorial Director: James W. Sire. Publishes hardcover and paperback originals. Averages 40 titles/year. Pays 10% royalty on retail price; advance averages $750. Publishes book an average of 1 year after acceptance. "Indicate simultaneous submissions." Computer printout submissions acceptable; prefers letter-quality to dot-matrix. Reports in 16 weeks. SASE. Free book catalog.
Nonfiction: "InterVarsity Press publishes books geared to the presentation of Biblical Christianity in its various relations to personal life, art, literature, sociology, psychology, philosophy, history and so forth. Though we are primarily publishers of trade books, we are cognizant of the textbook market at the college, university and seminary level within the general religious field. The audience for which the books are published is composed primarily of university students and graduates; stylistic treatment varies from topic to topic and from fairly simple popularizations for college freshmen to scholarly works primarily designed to be read by scholars." Accepts nonfiction translations. Query or submit outline/synopsis and 2 sample chapters.
Recent Nonfiction Title: *The Gravedigger File*, by Os Guinness.

*IOWA STATE UNIVERSITY PRESS, 2121 S. State Ave., Ames IA 50010. (515)294-5280. Director: Merritt Bailey. Managing Editor: Judith Gildner. Hardcover and paperback originals. Pays 10-12½-15% royalty on wholesale price; no advance. Subsidy publishes 10-50% of titles, based on sales potential of book and contribution to scholarship. Averages 35 titles/year. Send contrasting b&w glossy prints to illustrate ms. Simultaneous submissions OK, if advised; photocopied submissions OK. Reports in 2-4 months. SASE. Free book catalog.
Nonfiction: Publishes biography, history, scientific/technical textbooks, the arts and sciences, statistics and mathematics, and medical and veterinary sciences. Accepts nonfiction translations. Submit outline/synopsis and several sample chapters, preferably not in sequence; must be double-speaced throughout. Looks for "unique approach to subject; clear, concise narrative; and effective integration of scholarly apparatus."
Recent Nonfiction Title: *Roswel Garst: A Biography*, by Harold Lee.

‡ISHIYAKU EUROAMERICA, INC., Subsidiary of Ishiyaku Publishers, Inc., Tokyo, Japan: 11559 Rock Island Court, St. Louis MO 63043. (314)432-1933. President: Manuel L. Ponte. Publishes hardcover originals. Averages 5 titles/year. Pays 10% minimum royalty on retail price or pays 35% of all foreign translation rights sales. Offers average advance of $1,000. Simultaneous submissions OK. Computer printout submissions acceptable. SASE. Reports in 2 weeks on queries; 1 week on mss. Free book catalog.
Nonfiction: Reference and medical/dental/nursing textbooks. Subjects include art; health (medical and dental); psychology (nursing); and psychiatry. Especially looking for "all phases of nursing education, administration and clinical procedures. I do not wish to see additional dental books in 1985." Query, or submit outline/synopsis and sample chapters or complete ms.
Recent Nonfiction Title: *Pathology of the Extremely Aged*, by Oota and Ohtsu (medical reference).
Tips: "The export market for professional books continues to grow, while confusing the 'international' publishers who don't know how to treat it."

ISLAND PRESS, Star Route 1, Box 38, Covelo CA 95428. Executive Director: Barbara Dean. Publishes paperback originals. Publishes 4 titles/year. Pays 8-10% royalty on retail price; offers $500 average advance. Publishes book an average of 1 year after acceptance. Computer printout submissions acceptable. SASE. Reports in 3 months. Free book catalog for 8½x11 SASE.
Nonfiction: "We specialize in books on the environment and on human experience. We would welcome well-researched, technically accurate material on particular aspects of nature, conservation, animal life; also on true, personal experience in nature or personal growth. Emphasis on protection of wilderness, living with nature and human experience as means of spiritual growth. No poetry, science fiction, historical romance, children's books or textbooks. Also we are not interested in new age fads or trendy material." Query or submit outline/synopsis and 2 sample chapters. Reviews artwork/photos as part of ms package.
Recent Nonfiction Title: *Tree Talk: The People and Politics of Timber*, by Ray Raphael (voices from industry and environmentalists).
Fiction: "We are interested only in the unusual fiction that would merge with our primarily nonfiction list; fiction dealing with environmental consciousness or with human experience leading to personal/spiritual growth." No gothic, science fiction, romance, confession, etc. Query or submit outline/synopsis and 2 sample chapters.
Recent Fiction Title: *No Substitute for Madness*, by Ron Jones (six stories from a teacher and his unusual kids).

‡ITHACA HOUSE, 108 N. Plain St., Ithaca NY 14850. (607)272-1233. Subsidiaries include *Chiaroscuro: A Magazine of Poetry*. Editor: John Latta. Publishes trade paperback originals. Averages 3-5 titles/year. Pays in copies; 40% discount on purchases. Publishes book an average of 1 year after acceptance. Simultaneous and photocopied submissions OK (if notified). Computer printout submissions acceptable; no dot-matrix. SASE. Reports in 3 weeks on queries; 4 months on mss. Free book catalog.

Poetry: "We will publish 3-5 volumes of contemporary poetry—literary work of the highest order." Submit 5-10 poems.

Recent Poetry Title: *All That Autumn*, by Eileen Silver-Lillywhite (contemporary).

JALMAR PRESS, INC., B.L. Winch & Associates, 45 Hitching Post Dr., Bldg. 2, Rolling Hills Estates CA 90274. (213)547-1240. Editor: Suzanne Mikesell. Publishes trade paperback originals. Averages 6 titles/year. Pays 5-15% on net sales. Publishes book an average of 18 months after acceptance. Simultaneous and photocopied submissions OK. Electronic submissions OK via WP disks; but requires hard copy also. Computer printout submissions acceptable. SASE. Reports in 1 month on queries; 3 months on mss. Free book catalog on request.

Nonfiction: Psychological, self-help, parenting and educational. Helpful, purposeful books for schools, families, adults and children, that assist positive mental health, self-esteem development. No technical, academic-oriented manuscripts. Must be practical—reach a wide audience. Reviews artwork/photos as part of ms package. Query or submit outline synopsis and 2 sample chapters or complete ms.

Recent Nonfiction Title: *Whose Child Cries: Children of Gay Parents Talk About Their Lives*, by Joe Gantz.

JAMESTOWN PUBLISHERS, INC., Box 6743, Providence RI 02940. (401)351-1915. Senior Editor: Ted Knight. Publishes paperback supplementary reading text/workbooks and software. Averages 25-30 titles/year. Pays 10% royalty on retail price; buys some mss outright; offers variable advance. Publishes book an average of 1 year after acceptance. Computer printout submissions acceptable; prefers letter-quality to dot-matrix. SASE. Reports in 1 month. Free book catalog.

Nonfiction: Textbook. "Materials for improving reading and study skills for K-12, college, or adult education." Submit outline/synopsis and sample chapters. Reviews artwork/photos as part of ms package.

Recent Nonfiction Title: *How to Study in High School*, by Jean Snider.

Fiction: "We occasionally use original fiction as the basis for comprehension exercises and drills." Submit outline/synopsis and sample chapters.

Software: Reading—remedial and developmental. Study skills.

JH PRESS, Box 294, Village Station, New York NY 10014. (212)255-4713. Publisher: Terry Helbing. Publishes trade paperback originals. Averages 3 titles/year. Pays 6-10% royalty on retail price; offers average $100 advance. Publishes book an average of 9 months after acceptance. Simultaneous and photocopied submissions OK. SASE. Reports in 2 weeks. Free book catalog.

Nonfiction: Subjects include drama and theater. "Studies of gay theater or gay plays." Query. Reviews artwork/photos as part of ms package.

Recent Nonfiction Title: *Gay Theatre Alliance Directory of Gay Plays*, by Terry Helbing.

Fiction: Drama and theater. "Gay plays that have been produced but not previously published." Query.

Recent Fiction Title: *Forever After*, by Doric Wilson (play).

JOHNS HOPKINS UNIVERSITY PRESS, Baltimore MD 21218. Editorial Director: Anders Richter. Publishes mostly clothbound originals and paperback reprints; some paperback originals. Publishes 100 titles/year. Payment varies; contract negotiated with author. Publishes book an average of 10 months after acceptance. Electronic submission OK but requires hard copy also. Computer printout submissions acceptable; prefers letter-quality to dot-matrix. SASE. Reports in 2 months.

Nonfiction: Publishes scholarly books and journals, biomedical sciences, history, literary theory and criticism, wildlife biology and management, psychology, political science, regional material, and economics. Accepts nonfiction translations. Query. Accepts outline/synopsis and 2-3 sample chapters. Reviews artwork/photos as part of ms package. Length: 50,000 words minimum.

Recent Nonfiction Title: *Without Honor: Defeat in Vietnam and Cambodia*, by Arnold R. Isaacs.

Fiction: Occasional fiction by invitation only.

JOHNSON BOOKS, 1880 S. 57th Ct., Boulder CO 80301. (303)443-1576. Editorial Director: Michael McNierney. Publishes hardcover and paperback originals and reprints. Publishes 8-10 titles/year. Royalties vary. Publishes book an average of 1 year after acceptance. Computer printout submissions acceptable; prefers letter-quality to dot-matrix. SASE. Reports in 1-2 months. Free book catalog.

Nonfiction: General nonfiction, cookbooks, how-to, Western regional history, environmental subjects, science, geology, nature, outdoor recreation and sports. Accepts nonfiction translations. "We are primarily interested in books for the informed popular market, though we will consider vividly written scholarly works. As a small publisher, we are able to give every submission close personal attention." Query first or call. Accepts outline/synopsis and 3 sample chapters. Reviews artwork/photos as part of ms package. Looks for "good writing, thorough research, professional presentation and appropriate style. Marketing suggestions from writers are helpful."

Recent Nonfiction Title: *The Tribal Living Book: 150 Things to Do and Make from Traditional Cultures Around the World,* by David Levinson and David Sherwood.

JONATHAN DAVID PUBLISHERS, 68-22 Eliot Ave., Middle Village NY 11379. (212)456-8611. Editor-in-Chief: Alfred J. Kolatch. Publishes hardcover and paperback originals. Averages 25-30 titles/year. Pays standard royalty. Reports in 3 weeks. SASE.
Nonfiction: Adult nonfiction books for a general audience. Americana, cookbooks, cooking and foods, how-to, recreation, reference, self-help and sports. "We specialize in Judaica." Query.
Recent Nonfiction Title: *Cooking Kosher: The Natural Way,* by Jane Kinderlehrer.

JOSSEY-BASS, INC., PUBLISHERS, 433 California St., San Francisco CA 94104. (415)433-1740. Editorial Director: Allen Jossey-Bass. Publishes hardcover and paperback originals. Averages 100 titles/year. Pays 10-15% royalty on net receipts; no advance. Computer printout submissions acceptable; no dot-matrix. Reports in 4 weeks. SASE. Free book catalog.
Nonfiction: Professional, scholarly books for senior administrators, faculty, researchers, graduate students, and professionals in private practice. Research-based books developed for practical application. "We do not want undergraduate texts or collections of previously published materials." Submit outline/synopsis and 3-4 sample chapters.
Recent Nonfiction Title: *Ordeal Therapy,* by Jay Haley.

JUDSON PRESS, Valley Forge PA 19481. (215)768-2116. General Manager: Harold L. Twiss. Publishes hardcover and paperback originals. Generally 10% royalty on retail price. "Payment of an advance depends on author's reputation and nature of book." Averages 40 titles/year. Free book catalog. Publishes book an average of 10 months after acceptance. Computer printout submissions acceptable; no dot-matrix. Query with outline and 2-3 sample chapters. Reports in 3 months. Enclose return postage.
Nonfiction: Adult religious nonfiction of 30,000-80,000 words. "Our audience is mostly church members who seek to have a more fulfilling personal spiritual life and want to do a better job as Christians in their church and other relationships." Reviews artwork/photos as part of ms package.
Recent Nonfiction Title: *How to Stay Christian,* by John Galloway Jr.

‡**KALIMAT PRESS,** Suite 700, 10889 Wilshire Blvd., Los Angeles CA 90024. (213)208-8559. Managing Editor: Anthony A. Lee. Publishes hardcover and trade paperback originals and hardcover reprints. Averages 10 titles/year. Pays 10% minimum royalty on wholesale price; offers average $1,000 advance. Publishes book an average of 1 year after acceptance. Photocopied submissions OK. Computer printout submissions acceptable; prefers letter-quality to dot-matrix. SASE. Reports in 3 weeks on queries; 6 weeks on mss. Free book catalog.
Nonfiction: Biography, juvenile and academic. Subjects include history (Middle East) and religion (Baha'i faith). "We want Baha'i books only. No non-baha'i books." Submit outline/synopsis and sample chapters. Reviews artwork/photos as part of ms package.
Recent Nonfiction Title: *The Diary of Juliet Thompson,* by Thompson (casebound).
Fiction: Adventure, confession, historical, humor, religious, romance and suspense (Baha'i orientation *only*). Submit outline/synopsis and sample chapters.
Recent Fiction Title: *Fire and Blood,* by Garlington.

KALMBACH PUBLISHING CO., 1027 N. 7th St., Milwaukee WI 53233. (414)272-2060. Editorial Director: David P. Morgan. Books Editor: Bob Hayden. Publishes hardcover and paperback originals (80%) and paperback reprints (20%). Averages 6 titles/year. Offers 5-8% royalty on retail price. Average advance: $1,000. Publishes book an average of 18 months after acceptance. Electronic submissions OK "if compatible with our Atex system," but requires hard copy also. Computer printout submissions acceptable. SASE. Reports in 8 weeks. Free book catalog.
Nonfiction: Hobbies, how-to, and recreation. "Our book publishing effort is in railroading and hobby how-to-do-it titles *only*." Query first. "I welcome telephone inquiries. They save me a lot of time, and they can save an author a lot of misconceptions and wasted work." In written query, want to see "a detailed outline of two or three pages and a complete sample chapter with photos, drawings, and how-to text."
Recent Nonfiction Title: *18 Tailor-Made Model Railroad Track Plans,* by John Armstrong (model railroading).
Tips: "Our books are about half text and and half illustrations. Any author who wants to publish with us must be able to furnish good photographs and rough drawings before we'll consider contracting for his book."

‡**KAR-BEN COPIES INC.,** 11216 Empire Lane, Rockville MD 20852. (301)984-8733. President: Judy Groner. Publishes hardcover and trade paperback originals. Averages 6 titles/year. Pays 3-10% on retail price; makes negotiable outright purchase; offers average $1,000 advance. Publishes book an average of 1 year after acceptance. Computer printout submissions acceptable. SASE. Reports in 1 week on queries; 4 weeks on mss. Free book catalog.

Nonfiction: Jewish juvenile. Subjects include religion and Jewish history texts. Especially looking for books on Jewish history, holidays, and customs for children—"early childhood and elementary." Nothing not in above category. Query with outline/synopsis and sample chapters or submit complete ms. Reviews artwork/photos as part of ms package.
Recent Nonfiction Title: *What's an Israel*, by Chaya Burstein (travelog/activity book).
Fiction: Adventure, fantasy, historical and religious (all Jewish juvenile). Especially looking for Jewish holiday and history-related fiction for young children. Submit outline/synopsis and sample chapters or complete ms.
Recent Fiction Title: *Poppyseeds, Too*, by D. Miller (juvenile fiction).
Tips: "We envision Jewish children and their families and juveniles interested in learning about Jewish subjects as our audience."

WILLIAM KAUFMANN, INC., 95 1st St., Los Altos CA 94022. Editor-in-Chief: William Kaufmann. Hardcover and paperback originals (90%) and reprints (10%). "Generally offers standard minimum book contract of 10-12½-15% but special requirements of book may call for lower royalties"; no advance. Averages 15 titles/year. State availability of photos and/or illustrations to accompany ms. Simultaneous and photocopied submissions OK. Computer printout submissions acceptable. Reports in 1-2 months. SASE. Free book catalog.
Nonfiction: "We specialize in not being specialized; we look primarily for originality and quality." Publishes Americana, art, biography, business, computer science, economics, history, how-to, humor, medicine and psychiatry, nature, psychology, recreation, scientific, sports, and textbooks. Does not want to see cookbooks, novels, poetry, inspirational/religious or erotica. Query.
Recent Nonfiction Title: *Authors by Profession*, 2 volumes, by Victor Bonham-Carter.

KAV BOOKS, INC., Box 1134, New York NY 10159. (212)505-6076. President: Dr. T.M. Kemnitz. Publishes hardcover and trade paperback originals. Averages 53 titles/year. Pays 5-10% royalty on wholesale price. Photocopied submissions OK. SASE. Reports in 3 weeks. Free book catalog.
Nonfiction: Cookbook, how-to, juvenile, self-help on Americana particularly crafts/how-to, cooking and foods—canning, preservation, growing; games, puzzles, and brain teasers. Query or submit outline/synopsis and sample chapters or complete ms.
Fiction: Mainstream, mystery.

KENT STATE UNIVERSITY PRESS, Kent State University, Kent OH 44242. (216)672-7913. Director: Paul H. Rohmann. Publishes hardcover and paperback originals and some reprints. Standard minimum book contract on net sales; rarely offers advance. Averages 12-15 titles/year. "Always write a letter of inquiry before submitting mss. We can publish only a limited number of titles each year and can frequently tell in advance whether or not we would be interested in a particular ms. This practice saves both our time and that of the author, not to mention postage costs. If interested we will ask for complete ms. Decisions based on in-house readings and two by outside scholars in the field of the study." Computer printout submissions acceptable; prefers letter-quality to dot-matrix. Reports in 10 weeks. Enclose return postage. Free book catalog.
Nonfiction: Especially interested in "scholarly works in history of high quality, particularly any titles of regional interest for Ohio. Also will consider scholarly biographies, literary studies, archeological research, the arts, and general nonfiction."
Recent Nonfiction Title: *First Lady: The Life of Lucy Webb Hayes*, by Emily Geer (biography, history).

‡**KIDS CAN PRESS**, 585½ Bloor St. W., Toronto, Ontario M6G 1K5 Canada. (416)534-3141. Contact: Ricky Englander. Publishes hardcover and trade paperback originals. Averages 8 titles/year. Pays 10% maximum royalty on retail price. Publishes book an average of 1 year after acceptance. Computer printout submissions acceptable. SASE. Reports in 2 months on mss. Free book catalog.
Nonfiction: Juvenile. Subjects include Canadiana, cooking and foods, health, history, hobbies, music, and nature. Readers range from preschoolers to 15-year-olds. Reviews artwork/photos as part of ms package.
Fiction: Adventure, historical (Canadian), humor, mystery, romance, and science fiction. Submit complete ms.
Tips: "All material must be authored by Canadian citizen or landed immigrant and be from Canadian view."

B. KLEIN PUBLICATIONS, Box 8503, Coral Springs FL 33065. (305)752-1708. Editor-in-Chief: Bernard Klein. Hardcover and paperback originals. Specializes in directories, annuals, who's who type of books, bibliography, business opportunity, reference books. Averages 15-20 titles/year. Pays 10% royalty on wholesale price, "but we're negotiable." Advance "depends on many factors." Markets books by direct mail and mail order. Simultaneous and photocopied submissions OK. Reports in 1-2 weeks. SASE. Catalog for SASE.
Nonfiction: Business, hobbies, how-to, reference, self-help, directories and bibliographies. Query or submit outline/synopsis and sample chapters or complete ms.
Recent Nonfiction Title: *Guide to American Directories*.

‡**THE KNAPP PRESS**, Knapp Communications Corp., 5900 Wilshire Blvd., Los Angeles CA 90036. (213)937-3454. Editor: Norman Kolpas. Publishes hardcover originals. Averages 20 titles/year. Pays royalty, makes outright purchase or combination payment depending on the book. Simultaneous and photocopied submissions OK. SASE. Reports in 1 month. Free book catalog.
Nonfiction: Large format illustrated books, cookbooks and how-to. Subjects include Americana, animals, art, cooking and entertaining, collecting, hobbies, photography, interior design, architecture, home redecorating and remodeling, and travel. "We are expanding our program of original cookbooks for the *Bon Appetit* audience. We also need high quality art, photography, travel and design books aimed toward *Architectural Digest* audience, *GEO* and *Home* subscribers.
Recent Nonfiction Title: *The Best of Bon Appetit*, Vol. II.
Tips: "Our audience is educated, curious, with high standards for quality books; discriminating. Books are aimed toward subscribers of Knapp magazines, *Architectural Digest*, *Bon Appetit*, *Home* and *GEO*."

ALFRED A. KNOPF, INC., 201 E. 50th St., New York NY 10022. (212)751-2600. Senior Editor: Ashbel Green. Children's Book Editor: Ms. Frances Foster. Publishes hardcover and paperback originals (90%) and paperback reprints (10%). Published 173 titles in 1983. Royalties and advance "vary." Simultaneous (if so informed) and photocopied submissions OK. Reports in 2-4 weeks. Book catalog for SASE.
Nonfiction: Book-length nonfiction, including books of scholarly merit. Preferred length: 40,000-150,000 words. "A good nonfiction writer should be able to follow the latest scholarship in any field of human knowledge, and fill in the abstractions of scholarship for the benefit of the general reader by means of good, concrete, sensory reporting." Query.
Recent Nonfiction Title: *The March of Folly*, by B. Tuchman (history).
Fiction: Publishes book-length fiction of literary merit by known or unknown writers. Length: 30,000-150,000 words. Submit complete ms.
Recent Fiction Title: *A Choice of Enemies*, by G.V. Higgins.

KNOWLEDGE INDUSTRY PUBLICATIONS, INC., 701 Westchester Ave., White Plains, NY 10604. (914)328-9157. Vice President/Executive Director: Barbara Miller. Publishes hardcover and paperback originals. Averages 40 titles/year. Offers 5-10% royalty on wholesale price; also buys mss by outright purchase for minimum $500. Offers negotiable advance. Publishes book an average of 6 months after acceptance. Photocopied submissions OK. Computer printout submissions acceptable; prefers letter-quality to dot-matrix. SASE. Reports in 2 weeks. Free book catalog.
Nonfiction: Business and economics. Especially needs "communication and information technologies, TV and video, library and information science, office automation and office productivity." Query first, then submit outline/synopsis and sample chapters. Reviews artwork/photos as part of ms package.
Recent Nonfiction Title: *The Executive's Guide to On-line Information Services*, by Ryan E. Hoover.

JOHN KNOX PRESS, 341 Ponce de Leon Ave. NE, Atlanta GA 30365. (404)873-1549. Editorial Director: Walter C. Sutton. Acquisitions Editor: John G. Gibbs. Publishes 24 nonfiction titles/year. Pays royalty on income received; no advances. Free catalog and "Guidelines for a Book Proposal" on request with SASE.
Nonfiction: "We publish textbooks, resource books for ministry, and books to encourage Christian faith, in subject areas including biblical studies, theology, ethics, psychology, counseling, worship, and the relationship of science and technology to faith." Query or submit outline/synopsis and sample chapters.

KARL KRAMER VERLAG GMBH & CO., Rotebuhlstrasse 40, D-7000, Stuttgart, Germany. 49-711-62-08-93. President/Editorial Director: Karl H. Kramer. Publishes hardcover and paperback originals. Averages 15 titles/year. Pays 10% minimum royalty; offers $500-$1,000 average advance. SASE. Reports in 2 months. Free book catalog.
Nonfiction: Architecture. Submit outline/synopsis and sample chapters or complete ms.
Recent Nonfiction Title: *Frank Lloyd Wright and Europe*, by Heidi Kief-Niederwöhrmeier.

THE KRANTZ COMPANY PUBLISHERS, 2210 N. Burling, Chicago IL 60614. (312)472-4900. Publisher: L. Krantz. Publishes hardcover and trade paperback originals. Averages 4-5 titles/year. Pays royalty or makes outright purchase. Simultaneous submissions OK. SASE. Reports in 4 weeks. Free book catalog.
Nonfiction: Coffee table book, how-to, reference, self-help and general nonfiction in the areas of art and photography, and some science. Query. Accepts artwork/photos. No unsolicited mss accepted.
Recent Title: *Antiques—Best of the Best*, by Marjorie Glass (general nonfiction).

‡**ROBERT E. KREIGER PUBLISHING CO. INC.**, Box 9542, Melbourne FL 32902-9542. (305)724-9542. Executive Assistant: Ann M. Krieger. Publishes hardcover and paperback originals as well as reprints. Averages 120 titles/year. Pays royalty on net realized price. Electronic submissions OK if IBM. Computer printout submissions acceptable; prefers letter-quality to dot-matrix. Reports in 1 month. Free book catalog.
Nonfiction: College reference, technical, and textbook. Subjects include business and economics, history,

music, philosophy, psychology, recreation, religion, sociology, sports, chemistry, physics, engineering and medical.
Recent Nonfiction Title: *The Life Table*, by Chiang (technical statistics).

‡**LACE PUBLICATIONS**, Box 10037, Denver CO 80210-0037. (303)221-4405. Managing Editor: Artemis OakGrove. Publishes trade paperback originals and reprints. Plans to publish 5 titles in 1985. Pays royalty. "Each project is negotiated on an individual basis. We will eventually offer advances." Simultaneous and photocopied submissions OK. Computer printout submissions acceptable; prefers letter-quality to dot-matrix. SASE. Reports in 1 month on queries; 2 months on mss.
Fiction: Adventure, erotica, ethnic, fantasy, gothic, historical, humor, mystery, romance, science fiction and western. "All submissions must have lesbian themes and main characters. We would like to publish a total of fifteen books in the next two years, including reprints. Erotica for our Lady Winston series is especially appreciated. We plan to do some quality erotic art and photography and will be looking for work to fill that need. We would like at least one good work in each of the fiction categories mentioned. Entertainment is our main emphasis." No poetry or horror. "We specifically wish to avoid material that is political in nature or designed to make our readers question their inner needs or selves and be left with a negative sense about their lifestyles." Query or submit outline/synopsis and sample chapters.
Recent Fiction Title: *The Raging Peace*, by Artemis OakGrove (lesbian erotic romance).
Tips: "Audience consists of lesbians and all other women interested in sexuality out of the norm. It isn't likely that our books will appeal to men accept in the prurient sense. We would like to capture some of the romance market as well as mystery and science fiction and fantasy. We are going to market exclusively to women."

LAKE VIEW PRESS, Box 25421, Chicago IL 60625. (312)935-2694. Director: Paul Elitzik. Publishes hardcover and paperback originals. Averages 6 titles/year. Pays 8-10% royalty on retail price. No advance. Publishes book an average of 1 year after acceptance. Computer printout submissions acceptable; no dot-matrix. SASE. Reports in 2 months. Free catalog with SASE.
Nonfiction: Films, Middle East, Afro-American, labor, women, and Asia. Accepts nonfiction translations. "Our audience interest is current affairs, politics and the contemporary cultural scene." Submit outline, 2 sample chapters and author biography. Reviews artwork/photos as part of ms package.
Recent Nonfiction Title: *Reflections: A Writer's Life, A Writer's Work*, by Harry Mark Petrakis.

LAKEWOOD BOOKS, 4 Park Ave., New York NY 10016. Editorial Director: Donald Wigal, PhD. Publishes 64-page paperback originals. Publishes up to 38 titles/year. Pays on a "qualified" work-for-hire basis. "Few exceptions." Publishes book an average of 2 years after acceptance. Simultaneous and photocopied submissions OK. Electronic submissions OK if prearranged, but requires hard copy also. Computer printout (letter-quality) submissions acceptable. Reports in 2 months. SASE.
Nonfiction: "Our books are apparently bought by women who have families, or are attracted to a rather middle-of-the-road life style. Our titles are mainly self-help (exercise, diet) and informational (finances, how-to). We avoid controversial topics. Nonfiction which ties in with specific products welcomed by query (e.g., '100 Tips on Using Brand X in the Garden')." No fiction, poetry, astrology, puzzle, cookbook or sport titles needed at present (1984-5). Query. Author should have "an awareness of our format (limitations and potential), and sensitivity to the mass market. Concise overview best." Reviews artwork/photos as part of ms package.
Recent Nonfiction Title: *Shape Up Hips and Thighs*.
Tips: "Freelance writers should be aware that "an author's word processing ability is becoming standard and presumed by editors. I have to be assured the work is on tape or disk ready for fast editing and that revised copy is quickly available. Freelance editing is becoming more popular."

LANCASTER MILLER & SCHNOBRICH PUBLISHERS, Box 3056, Berkeley CA 94703. (415)652-6004. Editor and Publisher: Thomas Miller. Imprints include Asian Humanities (scholarly books, art and thought). Publishes trade hardcover, paperback originals and software. Averages 6-7 titles/year. Pays 6-8% royalty on paperbacks; 10-12% on hardcover; offers $1,000-30,000 advance. Computer printout submissions acceptable. SASE. Reports in 2 weeks. Free book catalog.
Nonfiction: Computer books only.
Recent Nonfiction Title: *LMS Instant Access Guide Series to Popular Computers and Computer Software*.
Software: Educational only. No games.

***LANCELOT PRESS LTD.**, Box 425, Hantsport, Nova Scotia B0P 1P0, Canada. (902)684-9129. Editor: William Pope. Publishes trade paperback originals. Averages 18 titles/year. Pays 10% royalty on retail price. Photocopied submissions OK. SASE. Reports in 3 weeks on queries; 1 month on mss. Free book catalog.
Nonfiction: Biography, "coffee table" book, cookbook, humor, illustrated book, juvenile, regional on art, cooking and foods, health, history, hobbies, nature, politics, recreation, religion, sports, and travel. "We consider any good book of its kind, but more success has been achieved with books of regional interest. We do well

with books pertaining to the sea." No technical or specialized subjects. Query or submit outline/synopsis and sample chapters.
Recent Nonfiction Title: *The Electric City*, by Paul Stehlin.

LANDMARK BOOKS, 2200 66th St. W., Minneapolis MN 55423. Editor-in-Chief: Joyce Hovelsrud. Publishes hardcover and paperback originals. Pays standard royalty. Averages 6-10 titles/year. Publishes book an average of 18 months after acceptance. Computer printout submissions acceptable. SASE. Reports in 6 weeks. Free book catalog and writer's guidelines.
Nonfiction: "We're a religious market looking for manuscripts on subjects of current issues and interest, which are appropriate for both religious and general markets. Material must be scripturally sound. We do not publish watered down religion and are interested in material with impact." Looks for "subjects that are timely and timeless." Want to see "the thrust of the subject in synopsis; the comment the author is making; where he is going with a subject and how he's going to develop it in his outline." In the completed ms wants "something of impact, order, relevance, *good* writing, and a recognizable style." Accepts translations. Query or submit complete ms. Reviews artwork/photos as part of ms package.
Recent Nonfiction Title: *A Flower and Prayer for the Hurting Hour*, by Ruth Grant.

LARANMARK PRESS, Box 253, Neshkoro WI 54960. (414)293-4377. President/Editor-in-Chief: Larry D. Names. Contact: Peggy Eagan or Rob Precourt. Publishes hardcover and paperback originals and fiction reprints. Averages 6-12 titles/year. Pays 6% royalty on the first 50,000 copies; 8% on the next 50,000; 10% thereafter; 12% on hardcover; sometimes offers $150-1,000 advance. Computer printout submissions acceptable; prefers letter-quality to dot-matrix.
Nonfiction: Adult books for hardcover line on sports, cooking, Americana, history, and how-tos. Accepts nonfiction translations. Query with outline/synopsis and 3 sample chapters, or submit through agent. Reviews artwork/photos as part of ms package.
Recent Nonfiction Title: *Summer Sail*, by John Torinus.
Fiction: "We are not accepting *any* fiction until January 1986. We are booked up. We are concentrating on good nonfiction."
Recent Fiction Title: *The PK Factor*, by C.H. Martin.
Tips: "We are looking for nonfiction that can be aimed at a specific group of people, i.e., sailors."

LARKSDALE, 133 S. Heights Blvd., Houston TX 77007. (713)869-9092. Publisher: James Goodman. Editor-in-Chief: Nancy B. Adleman. Imprints include The Linolean Press (religious), The Lindahl Press (general), Harle House (mass market paperback). Publishes hardcover and paperback originals. Averages 30 titles/year. Pays standard royalty contract; no advance. Publishes book an average of 18 months after acceptance. Computer printout submissions acceptable. "SASE, means stamped container for return, not a check for postage." Reports in 3 months.
Nonfiction: Religion (Christian doctrine). General trade publisher. No off-color work accepted. Submit *complete* ms to publisher. Looks for "an uplifting moral purpose, quality writing, salability in mss." Reviews artwork/photos as part of ms package.
Recent Nonfiction Title: *Two Birds Flying*, by Phyllis Prokop (inspirational).
Recent Fiction Title: *The Temptation*, by Jack D. Coombe (religious).

LARKSPUR PUBLICATIONS, Box 211, Bowmansville NY 14026. (716)684-0762. Editorial Director: Judith E. Donaldson. Publishes hardcover, and trade and mass market paperback originals. Averages 12 titles/year. Pays 3-5% royalty on wholesale price; makes outright purchase, $200-500; and pays in books. Simultaneous and photocopied submissions OK. SASE. Reports in 1 month on queries; 3 months on mss.
Nonfiction: Illustrated books, juvenile, self-help. Subjects include animals, religion, (Protestant-Christian) and sports. "We will consider manuscripts, from freelance writers, suitable for the protestant christian reader in the following categories." Adult: Bible puzzles and quizzes suitable for mass market paperback, 132 pages in length; family life: self help; understanding teens, divorce, death etc. Teenagers: Self help and gudiance. Children: Activity books, ages 4-7 years, dealing with Bible characters; coloring and follow the dot, 16 pages, 8x10. Submit outline/synopsis and sample chapters.
Recent Nonfiction Title: *Doodles, Diddles Sports Fan*, by G. Brown (game book, trade size).
Fiction: Adult wholesome romance novels, and children's stories (true to life, must teach some helpful lesson). Especially looking for adult christian romance—wholesome, clean love stories.
Tips: "We will consider manuscripts suitable for the Protestant Christian reader for our new Christian book division."

‡**LARSON PUBLICATIONS, INC.**, Subsidiary of Bokforlaget Robert Larson A.B., Sweden; 4936 Route 414, Burdett NY 14818. (607)546-9342. Director: Paul Cash. Publishes hardcover and trade paperback originals and hardcover and trade paperback reprints. Averages 8-10 titles/year. Pays 10% minimum royalty of cash received, flexible maximum on wholesale price. Offers advance of ⅓ of first year's expected royalty on some

titles. Photocopied submissions OK. Electronic submissions OK if compatible with IBM-PC. Computer print-out submissions acceptable. SASE. Reports in 2 weeks. Free book catalog.
Nonfiction: How-to and self-help. Subjects include alternative education, astrology, cooking and foods, health, parenting, philosophy and religion. Query.
Recent Nonfiction Title: *Better than School*, by Nancy Wallace (parenting/education/home schooling).
Fiction: Fantasy, mystical allegory, religious and science fiction. "We are just beginning to explore this area." No mss unrelated to spiritual self-discovery. Query.
Tips: "Our audience is independent, spiritually-minded, all ages."

LAW-ARTS PUBLISHERS, Suite 500, 2001 Wilshire Blvd., Santa Monica CA 90403. Editorial Director: Joseph Taubman. Publishes hardcover and paperback originals (90%) and paperback reprints (10%). Pays 10% royalty; no advance. Simultaneous and photocopied submissions OK. Reports in 3 months. SASE.
Nonfiction: Legal-related, in-depth textbooks; books on creative work, audiovisual techniques, management, publicity, etc. No photography books. Submit outline/synopsis and sample chapters.
Recent Nonfiction Title: *Video for Lawyers*, by Ellen Miller.

LE BEACON PRESSE, Dept. WM 84, Suite 7, 2921 E. Madison St., Seattle WA 98112. (206)322-1431. Coordinator: Keith S. Gormezano. Publishes trade and mass market paperback originals and reprints. Averages 5-10 titles/year. Pays 20-25% royalty; buys some mss outright for $100-1,000. Simultaneous and photo-copied submissions OK. SASE.
Nonfiction: Humor, reference and technical. Subjects include Americana, art, business and economics, cooking and foods, photography, politics, recreation and travel. Accepts translations. "In the near future we will need 5 reference books, 3 with political themes and 1 autobiographical novel." All unsolicited mss are returned unopened. Query first.
Recent Nonfiction Title: *Name Identification*, by Keith S. Gormezano (political).
Fiction: Adventure, erotica, ethnic, experimental, historical, horror, humor, mystery, science fiction and suspense. Query. All unsolicited mss are returned unopened.
Poetry: "Will publish 3, 36-page poetry books." Submit maximum 3 poems with cover letter.
Recent Poetry Title: *Mongrel Harmony*, by Davis.

LEARNING PUBLICATIONS, INC., Box 1326, Holmes Beach FL 33509. (616)372-1045. Editor: Danna Downing. Publishes hardcover and trade paperback originals. Averages 15 titles/year. Pays 5% royalty on income received from sales. No advance. Publishes book an average of 18 months after acceptance. Photocopied submissions OK. Computer printout submissions acceptable. SASE. Reports in 3 weeks on queries; 3 months on mss. Free book catalog.
Nonfiction: How-to, reference, self-help, technical, textbook on art, psychology, sociology, reference books for counselors, teachers, and school administrators. Books to help parents of children with reading problems and special needs (impaired, gifted, etc.); or art activity books for teachers. Query or submit outline synopsis and sample chapters.
Recent Nonfiction Title: *Teaching Basic: Thirty Lesson Plans, Activities and Quizzes*, by Vonk and Erickson.

*LEATHER STOCKING BOOKS, Box 19746, West Allis WI 53219. (414)778-1120. Editor: Carlton Sitz. Publishes hardcover and original paperbacks. Average 3-5 titles/year. Subsidy publishes 1% of books. Pays 10% royalty on wholesale price; no advance. Publishes book an average of 2 years after acceptance. Electronic submissions OK, but requires hard copy also. Computer printout submissions acceptable. SASE. Reports in 2 months.
Nonfiction: Frontier history, guns, outdoor (how-to), and military. Reviews artwork/photos as part of ms package. Query.
Recent Nonfiction Title: *Famous Guns & Gunners*, by Virines.

LEBHAR-FRIEDMAN, 425 Park Ave., New York NY 10022. (212)371-9400. Chief Editor: Barbara Miller. Publishes hardcover and paperback originals. Pays royalty on wholesale price; no advance. Photocopied sub-missions OK. Reports in 4-8 weeks. SASE. Book catalog for SASE.
Nonfiction: "Most of our books published are for the retail business field (food service and supermarket). Our market is directed at both the retailer, administrator, and the college and junior college student wishing to enter the field and needing a good hard look at the facts and how-to's of the business. We are not interested in the generalist approach but with specifics that will be of importance to the business person." Submit outline/synopsis and 1-3 sample chapters.
Recent Nonfiction Title: *Restaurant Survival Kit for the 80s*, by David Seltz.

LEE'S BOOKS FOR YOUNG READERS, 813 West Ave., Box 111, O'Neil Professional Bldg., Wellington TX 79095. (806)447-5445. Independent book producer/packager. Publisher: Lee Templeton. Publishes hard-cover originals. Averages 8 titles/year. Pays 10% minimum royalty on wholesale price. No advance. Publishes book an average of 1 year after acceptance. Computer printout submissions acceptable; no dot-matrix. SASE. Free book catalog.

Nonfiction: Biography. "Our books are nonfiction history of young heroes. All our books are written for 'reluctant' readers in junior high school market (10-14 age group), to be sold to junior (middle) school libraries. We will consider queries about young American heroes, male or female, that historians overlooked." All unsolicited mss are returned unopened.

Recent Nonfiction Title: *Cannon Boy of the Alamo*, by Lee Templeton.

THE LEWIS PUBLISHING CO., 15 Muzzey St., Lexington MA 02173. (617)861-0170. Publisher: Thomas Begner. Publishes hardcover and trade paperback originals. Averages 10 titles/year. Pays negotiable royalty; offers variable advance. Reports in 3 months. Book catalog 50¢.

Nonfiction: Popular social science. Submit outline/synopsis and 3 sample chapters.

Recent Nonfiction Title: *The Kids Book of Divorce*, by The Unit at the Fairweather School.

‡**LEXIKOS**, #208, 703 Market St., San Francisco CA 94103. (415)495-3493. Co-publisher: Tom Cole. Publishes hardcover and trade paperback originals and trade paperback reprints. Averages 5-7 (growing each season) titles/year. Royalties vary from 8-12½% according to book sold. "Authors asked to accept lower royalty on high discount (50% plus) sales." Offers average $1,000 advance. Simultaneous and photocopied submissions OK. SASE. Reports in 1 month. Book catalog for 6x9 SAE and 2 first class stamps.

Nonfiction: "Coffee table" book, illustrated book. Subjects include regional outdoors, Americana, history, nature, sports, and travel. Especially looking for 50,000-word "city and regional histories, anecdotal in style for a general audience; books of regional interest about *places*; adventure and wilderness books; annotated reprints of books of Americana; Americana in general; and travel." No health, sex, diet, broad humor, quickie books (we stress backlist vitality), religion or nutrition. Submit outline/synopsis and sample chapters.

Recent Nonfiction Title: *High and Wild*, by Galen Rowell (essays).

Tips: "Submit a short, cogent proposal; follow up with letter queries. Give publisher reason to believe you will help him *sell* the book (identify the market, point out availability of mailing lists, distinguish book from competition. Avoid grandiose claims. Establish faith (in letters, proposals) of your ability to *write*, take editing. We stress high production values, durability and intelligent writing."

LIBERTY PUBLISHING COMPANY, INC., 50 Scott Adam Rd., Cockeysville MD 21030. (301)667-6680. Publisher: Jeffrey B. Little. Imprints include Liberty Personal Counsel Library, J. Little, publisher. Publishes hardcover and mostly trade paperback originals. Averages 10-15 titles/year. Pays 6-12% royalty on wholesale or retail price; buys some mss outright for $500-1,500; offers typical $400 advance. Publishes book an average of 9 months after acceptance. Computer printout submissions acceptable; prefers letter-quality to dot-matrix. Reports in 3 weeks on queries; 1-2 months on mss. "Exclusive distribution arrangements with self-publishers possible."

Nonfiction: Biography, cookbook, how-to, illustrated book, and self-help. Subjects include Americana, business and economics, cooking and foods, history, hobbies, photography (b&w only), recreation, sports, travel; educational, and parent guides. Accepts nonfiction translations. "How-to or self-help books dealing with concrete advice written by people qualified to address the subject. Extensive graphic possibilities preferred. No self improvement books dealing with psychology and mind improvement. No poetry, please." Query with author biography or submit outline/synopsis and 3 sample chapters. Reviews artwork/photos as part of ms package.

Recent Nonfiction Title: *Understanding Wall Street*, by J. Little (business guide for the layman investor).

*****LIBRA PUBLISHERS, INC.**, 391 Willets Rd., Roslyn Heights NY 11577. (516)484-4950. Contact: William Kroll. Publishes hardcover and paperback originals. Specializes in the behavioral sciences. Averages 15 titles/year. 10-15% royalty on retail price; no advance. Subsidy publishes 15% of books (those which have obvious marketing problems or are too specialized). Publishes book an average of 8 months after acceptance. Computer printout submissions acceptable; prefers letter-quality to dot-matrix. Reports in 1-2 weeks. SASE. Free book catalog.

Nonfiction: Mss in all subject areas will be given consideration, but main interest is in the behavioral sciences. Submit outline/synopsis and 3 sample chapters. Reviews artwork/photos as part of ms package.

Recent Nonfiction Title: *The Rhythm Factor in Human Behavior*, by Salvatore J. Garzino.

LIBRARIES UNLIMITED, Box 263, Littleton CO 80160. (303)770-1220. Editor-in-Chief: Bohdan S. Wynar. Publishes hardcover and paperback originals (95%) and hardcover reprints (5%). Averages 30-40 titles/year. Specializes in library science and reference books. 10% royalty on net sales; advance averages $500. Publishes book an average of 9 months after acceptance. Marketed by direct mail to 40,000 libraries and schools in this country and abroad. Query or submit outline/synopsis and sample chapters. All prospective authors are required to fill out an author questionnaire. Query if photos/illustrations are to accompany ms. Reports in 2 months. SASE. Free book catalog.

Nonfiction: Publishes reference and library science text books. Looks for professional experience.
Recent Nonfiction Title: *Guide to American Literature*, by Valmai Kirkham Fenster.

LIGHTBOOKS, Box 1268, Twain Harte CA 95383. (209)533-4222. Publisher: Paul Castle. Publishes hardcover and paperback originals. Averages 4-6 titles/year. Pays 10-15% royalty on wholesale or retail price; no advance. Publishes book an average of 6 months after acceptance. Simultaneous and photocopied submissions OK. SASE. Reports in 4 weeks.
Nonfiction: Photography. "We are always interested in good mss on technique and/or business of photography. We especially want mss on *marketing* one's photography. We don't want mss on art criticism of photography, collections of art photos, basic photo teaching books, or anything other than books on the technique and/or business of photography. Query; if the idea is good, we'll ask for outline/synopsis and sample chapters." Reviews artwork/photos as part of ms package.
Recent Nonfiction Title: *Outdoor Photography How to Shoot It, How to Sell It*, by Robert McQuilkin.
Tips: "We need more anecdotes and illustrations (word) to amplify the writer's points. We particularly look for skilled photographers who are doing something very well and can communicate their expertise to others. We are willing to work with such individuals on extensive re-write and editing, if what they have to say is valuable."

LIGUORI PUBLICATIONS, Book and Pamphlet Dept., 1 Liguori Dr., Liguori MO 63057. (314)464-2500. Editor-in-Chief: Rev. Christopher Farrell, C.SS.R. Managing Editor: Roger Marchand. Publishes paperback originals. Specializes in Catholic-Christian religious materials. Averages 30 titles/year. Pays royalty on books; flat fee on pamphlets and teacher's guides. Publishes book an average of 6 months after acceptance. Electronic submissions on TRS-80 Model III in a 1.3 system/1.0 version OK "if sent with computer printout." Computer printout submissions acceptable. Query or submit outline/synopsis and 1 sample chapter; "never submit total book." State availability of photos and/or illustrations. Reports in 3-5 weeks. SASE. Free book catalog.
Nonfiction: Publishes doctrinal, inspirational, Biblical, self-help and educational materials. Looks for "thought and language that speak to the basic practical and religious concerns of contemporary Catholic Christians."
Recent Nonfiction Title: *How to Forgive Yourself and Others*.
Tips: "People seek light on real-life concerns. Writers lead and educate in light of Good News shared in faith-community."

LINCH PUBLISHING, INC., Box 75, Orlando FL 32802. (305)647-3025. President: Barbara Linch. Publishes hardcover and trade paperback originals. Pays 10-15% royalty on wholesale price. Offers variable advance. Simultaneous and photocopied submissions OK. Reports in 2 weeks. Book catalog for $1 and regular size SAE with 37¢ postage.
Nonfiction: Specializes in how-to books on estate planning, legal procedures and financial planning. Subjects include record keeping book for heirs, settling an estate and funeral arrangements, and specific titles in the financial area, such as convertible bonds (the how-to's for the average investor), financial planning for the individual, etc. "Call before submitting a manuscript to be sure we are still interested in that Title or subject—we could have already accepted a manuscript from another writer and be in the process of publishing it."
Recent Nonfiction Title: *It's Easy to Avoid Probate*.

LIPPINCOTT JUNIOR BOOKS, see Harper & Row Junior Books Group.

LITTLE, BROWN AND CO., INC., 34 Beacon St., Boston MA 02106. Contact: Editorial Department, Trade Division. Publishes hardcover and paperback originals and paperback reprints. Publishes 100 titles/year. "Royalty and advance agreements vary from book to book and are discussed with the author at the time an offer is made." Submissions only from authors who have had a book published or have been published in professional or literary journals, newspapers or magazines." Computer printout submissions acceptable; prefers letter-quality to dot-matrix. Reports in 10-12 weeks for queries/proposals. SASE.
Nonfiction: "Some how-to books, distinctive cookbooks, biographies, history, science and sports." Query or submit outline/synopsis and sample chapters.
Recent Nonfiction Title: *Blue Highways*, by William Moon.
Fiction: Contemporary popular fiction as well as fiction of literary distinction. "Our poetry list is extremely limited; those collections of poems that we do publish are usually the work of poets who have gained recogni-

Market conditions are constantly changing! If this is 1986 or later, buy the newest edition of *Writer's Market* at your favorite bookstore or order directly from Writer's Digest Books.

tion through publication in literary reviews and various periodicals." Reviews artwork/photos as part of ms package. Query or submit outline/synopsis and sample chapters.

Recent Fiction Title: *The Auerbach Will*, by Stephen Birmingham.

‡*THE LITTLE HOUSE PRESS, 2544 N. Monticello Ave., Chicago IL 60647. (312)342-3338. Senior Editor: Gene Lovitz. Publishes hardcover and trade paperback originals and hardcover and trade paperback reprints. "Our first list will be either four or five books, but we'll expand that for the right manuscript. The following two lists will probably be at the same rate. We do not expect to do subsidy books that normally go to vanity sources. We do expect to establish a line where a worthy self-publishing book can get professional handling from editing, design, manufacture, promotion, advertising and good distribution and order fulfillment." Pays 10% minimum royalty on hardcover retail price; maximum royalty negotiable. Average advance varies with author or quality of book and market. Simultaneous and photocopied submissions OK. Computer printout submissions acceptable. SASE. Reports in 2 weeks on queries; 4 weeks on mss. Book catalog for SAE with 4 first class stamps (available in spring of 1985).

Nonfiction: Biography, how-to, humor, juvenile, reference and self-help. Subjects include Americana, animals, business and economics, cooking and foods, health, history, hobbies, nature, politics, recreation, religion, sports and travel. "No scholary books with limited sale, cookbooks and travel by unknown authors." Query by letter only. "We will advise what we wish to see."

Fiction: Adventure, confession, ethnic, fantasy, gothic, historical, horror, humor, mainstream, mystery, religious, romance, suspense and western. "All fiction must be strong candidates with wide appeal. Fiction ms needs depend on the quality of the ms. We will be flexible for a book of quality and salability." Query by letter only.

Poetry: "Highly selective with emphasis on humorous light poetry of excellence; concise and strong imagery." No obscure and trite or epic poetry. Submit 5 samples.

Tips: "Our audience is people of all ages and occupations who appreciate excellence. We are particularly interested in the 50-plus age reader which has been so ignored by general publishing. The proliferation of small presses is the result of the failure of general publishing to risk publishing first book manuscripts and worthy books of modest but respectable prospects. We are a new publisher with all the attendent problems of getting established. We are part of a movement to establish an association of small publishers and related services to offer support and common services to each other, concentrating buying power, warehouse and order fulfillment, and all other editorial and publishing services."

‡LIVE OAK PUBLICATIONS, Box 2193, Boulder CO 80306. (303)530-1087. Publisher: Tom Ellison. Publishes trade paperback originals. Averages 3-6 titles/year. Negotiable payment, depending on the work. Offers average $1,000 advance. Photocopied submissions OK. SASE. Reports in 2 weeks. Free book catalog.

Nonfiction: How-to. Subjects include business and self-help. "We need manuscripts for how-to books on specific self-employment opportunities, preferably including interviews with people who are successfully self-employed in interesting businesses. We also could use more general manuscripts on work satisfaction and changing work patterns." Query.

Recent Nonfiction Title: *Freelance Foodcrafting*, by Janet Shown (how to).

Tips: "Our readers want books which can show them how to assume more control over their lives. If you have any ideas let us hear from you."

‡LIVING POETS PRESS, Subsidiary of Mandelbaum and Tree, 26 Court St., Brooklyn NY 11242. (212)875-9545. Advisor: Leo Connellan. Publishes trade paperback originals. Averages 10 titles/year. Pays 5-15% royalty on wholesale price; buys some mss outright for $5,000-10,000. Offers average $5,000 advance. Photocopied submissions OK. SASE. Reports in 1 month on queries; 3 months on mss. Free book catalog.

Nonfiction: Art. Submit outline/synopsis and sample chapters or complete ms.

Fiction: Adventure, erotica and experimental. Submit outline/synopsis and sample chapters or send complete ms.

Poetry: No religious poetry. Submit complete ms.

Recent Poetry Title: *Another Poet in New York*, by Leo Connellan.

LODESTAR BOOKS, Division of E. P. Dutton, 2 Park Ave., New York NY 10016. (212)725-1818. Editorial Director: Virginia Buckley. Hardcover originals. Publishes juveniles, young adults, fiction and nonfiction; no picture books. Averages 25 titles/year. Pays royalty on list price; advance offered. State availability of photos and/or illustrations. Publishes book an average of 18 months after acceptance. Photocopied submissions OK. Electronic submissions OK, but requires hard copy also. Computer printout submissions acceptable. Reports in 2-4 months. SASE.

Nonfiction: Query or submit outline/synopsis and 2-3 sample chapters including "theme, chapter-by-chapter outline, and 1 or 2 completed chapters." Reviews artwork/photos as part of ms package.

Fiction: Publishes only for young adults and juveniles: adventure, fantasy, humorous, contemporary, mystery, science fiction, suspense and western books. Submit complete ms.

Tips: Queries/mss may be routed to other editors in the publishing group.

LOIRY PUBLISHING HOUSE, Suite 6, 635 S. Orange Ave., Sarasota FL 33577. (813)365-1959. Executive Editor: William S. Loiry. Publishes hardcover and trade paperback originals. Pays negotiable royalty. No advance. Simultaneous and photocopied submissions OK. SASE. Reports in 1 month.
Nonfiction: How-to, juvenile, reference, self-help, and textbook. Human Relations: effective living, sexuality, male/female relations, parenting, race relations; children and youth: conditions of youth, youth policy, youth programs, youth activism; politics: what's really going on in politics and government and why. Query.
Recent Nonfiction Title: *A History of Children and Youth with Recommendations for the Future*.

*LONE STAR PUBLISHERS, INC., Box 9774, Austin TX 78766. (512)255-2333. Editorial Director: A.J. Lerager. Publishes hardcover and paperback originals. Averages 3 titles/year. Subsidy publishes approximately 1 title/year based on "the subject matter, the author's reputation, the potential market, the capital investment, etc." Pays 12½-15% royalty on wholesale or retail price; no advance. Simultaneous and photocopied submissions OK. Computer prinout submissions acceptable. Reports in 3 weeks. SASE. Free book catalog.
Nonfiction: College textbooks. No poetry. Query.
Recent Nonfiction Title: *Texas Real Estate Law, 2nd Edition*, by Eugene W. Nelson.

LONGMAN GROUP U.S.A., INC., (formerly Development Systems Corp.), 500 N. Dearborn, Chicago IL 60610. (312)836-0466. Acquisitions Coordinator, Real Estate/Business/Professional Books, Real Estate Textbooks: Bobbye Middendorf. Acquisitions Editor, Financial Services Textbooks: Ivy Lester. Imprints include Real Estate Education Co., Educational Methods, Inc., Longman Financial Services Publishing. Publishes hardcover and paperback originals. Averages 50 titles/year. Pays 5-15% royalty; no advance. Simultaneous and photocopied submissions OK. Computer printout submissions acceptable. SASE. Reports in 2 months. Free book catalog.
Nonfiction: "Publishes books for real estate professionals and other financial services professionals (banking, insurance, securities). Any topics appropriate for this market are of interest." Submit outline and 1-3 sample chapters (but not the first chapter) or complete ms.
Recent Nonfiction Title: *The Buyer's Guide to Financial Services Software* (reference book).

LONGMAN, INC., 1560 Broadway, New York NY 10036. (212)764-3950. Executive Vice President: Bruce Butterfield. Publishes hardcover and paperback originals. Publishes 60 titles/year. Pays variable royalty; offers average $1,000 advance. Photocopied submissions OK. SASE. Reports in 6 weeks.
Nonfiction: Textbooks only (college and professional). History, politics, psychology, reference, sociology, and English as a second language. No trade, art or juvenile, El-hi texts. Query.

‡LOOMPANICS UNLIMITED, Box 1197, Port Townsend WA 98368. Book Editor: Michael Hoy. Publishes trade paperback originals. Publishes 12 titles/year. Pays 7½-20% royalty on wholesale or retail price; or makes outright purchase of $100-1,200. Offers average advance of $500. Simultaneous and photocopied submissions OK. Computer printout submissions acceptable. SASE. Reports in 6 weeks. Free book catalog.
Nonfiction: How-to, reference and self-help. Subjects include business and economics, philosophy, politics, travel, and "beat the system" books. "We are looking for how-to books in the fields of espionage, investigation, the underground economy, police methods, how to beat the system, crime and criminal techniques. No cookbooks, inspirational, travel, or cutesy-wutesy stuff." Query, or submit outlines/synopsis and sample chapters.
Recent Nonfiction Title: *Methods of Disguise*, by John Sample (how-to).
Tips: "Our audience is young males looking for hard-to-find information on alternatives to 'The System'."

‡*LORIEN HOUSE, Box 1112, Black Mountain NC 28711. Editor: David A. Wilson. Publishes hardcover and trade paperback originals. Averages 2-4 titles/year. Subsidy publishes 20% of books. "Rather than subsidy, we do a co-op publishing, sharing costs with the author. If it is a poetry book, it has to be done this way." Pays 10-15% royalty on retail price. No advance. Publishes book an average of 18 months after acceptance. Computer printout submissions acceptable. SASE. Reports in 1 week on queries; 1 month on mss. Book catalog 50¢.
Nonfiction: How-to, technical and literary. Subjects include history (as related to metaphysics); nature (wild foods, ecology); and philosophy (metaphysics). "We are open to any subject as long as it is well done and treated as a literary and technical piece at the same time." No photo essays or children's books. Submit outline/synopsis and sample chapters. Reviews artwork/photos as part of ms package.
Recent Nonfiction Title: *Gemstones, Crystals & Healing*, by Thelma Isaacs (geology/metaphysics).
Fiction: Fantasy, historical, mainstream, and science fiction. "I want to see a work with plenty of 'meat' in it, something that gets the reader to think—an in-depth work. No horror, shock effect, four letter words, or sex and violence mss. A *quality* work could have some of each of these but they detract from the main plot (and upset the editor)." Submit complete ms of 150-200 pages.
Recent Fiction Title: *Al Hadj, The Pilgrimage*, by David Wilson (symbolism).

Poetry: Very limited interest. "Poetry is very difficult to sell." Submit complete ms.
Recent Poetry Title: *Solstice Poems*, by Charles Baar.

LOTHROP, LEE & SHEPARD BOOKS, Division of William Morrow Company, 105 Madison Ave., New York NY 10016. (212)889-3050. Editor-in-Chief: Dorothy Briley. Hardcover original children's books only. Royalty and advance vary according to type of book. Averages 55 titles/year. State availability of photos to accompany ms. Publishes book an average of 18 months after acceptance. Photocopied submissions OK, but originals preferred. Computer printout submissions acceptable; prefers letter-quality to dot-matrix. Reports in 4-6 weeks. SASE. Free book catalog.
Juveniles: Publishes picture books, general nonfiction, and novels. Submit outline/synopsis and sample chapters for nonfiction. Juvenile fiction emphasis on contemporary novels, but also includes adventure, fantasy, historical, humorous, mystery, science fiction and suspense. Submit complete ms for fiction. Looks for "organization, clarity, creativity, literary style." Reviews artwork/photos as part of ms package.
Recent Title: *Sugar Blue*, by Vera Cleaver.
Tips: "Trends in book publishing that freelance writers should be aware of include the demand for books for children under age 3 and the shrinking market for young adult books, especially novels."

LOUISIANA STATE UNIVERSITY PRESS, Baton Rouge LA 70803. (504)388-6618. Associate/Executive Editor: Beverly Jarrett. Director: L.E. Phillabaum. Averages 60 titles/year. Pays royalty on wholesale price; no advance. Photocopied submissions OK. Computer printout submissions acceptable; no dot-matrix. SASE. Reports in 1 month on queries; 1-6 months on mss. Free book catalog.
Nonfiction: "We would like to have mss on humanities and social sciences, with special emphasis on Southern history and literature; Southern studies; French studies; political philosophy; and music, especially jazz." Query.
Recent Nonfiction Title: *George Washington: A Biography*, by John Alden.

*THE LOWELL PRESS, INC., 115 E. 31st St., Box 1877, Kansas City MO 64141. (816)753-4545. Editor: Barbara Funk. Publishes hardcover and trade paperback originals (50%) and reprints. Averages 5-10 titles/year. Subsidy publishes 33% of books. Simultaneous submissions OK. Publishes book an average of 6 months after acceptance. SASE. Reports in 1 month. Free book catalog.
Nonfiction: "Coffee table" book, western American, humor, illustrated book on Americana, animals, art, nature, photography, and travel. Query. Reviews artwork/photos as part of ms package.
Recent Nonfiction Title: *Missouri*, by Bill Nunn (nature, travel).

‡NICK LYONS BOOKS, 212 5th Ave., New York NY 10010. (212)689-9580. Book packager producing 15-20 titles/year. Editor: Peter Burford. Publishes hardcover and trade paperback originals and trade paperback reprints. Pays royalty. Simultaneous and photocopied submissions OK. Computer printout submissions acceptable; prefers letter-quality to dot-matrix. SASE. Reports in 1 week on queries; 4 weeks on mss. Free book catalog.
Nonfiction: How-to. Subjects include conservation, nature/ecology, sports, fly fishing and outdoor leisure sports. "We need 20-30 mss (on subjects listed above) by serious authors—preferably those with magazine or book experience." Query.
Recent Nonfiction Title: *Acid Rain*, by R. Boyle (conservation).
Tips: If I were a writer trying to market a book today, I would write about something important to society and write it well."

McCLELLAND AND STEWART, LTD., 25 Hollinger Rd., Toronto, Ontario M4B 3G2 Canada. Publisher: L.E. McKnight. Publishes hardcover and paperback originals. Offers sliding scale of royalty on copies sold. Advance varies. Free book catalog. Submit outline and 3 sample chapters for nonfiction and fiction. Reports in 6 weeks, average. SAE and IRCs.
Nonfiction, Poetry and Fiction: Publishes "Canadian fiction and poetry. Nonfiction in the humanities and social sciences, with emphasis on Canadian concerns. "Coffee table" books on art, architecture, sculpture and Canadian history." Reviews artwork/photos as part of ms package. Will also consider general adult trade fiction, biography, history, nature, photography, politics, sociology, and textbooks. Accepts nonfiction and fiction translations.

MARGARET K. McELDERRY BOOKS, Atheneum Publishers, Inc., 597 5th Ave., New York NY 10017. Editor: Margaret K. McElderry. Publishes hardcover originals. Publishes 20-25 titles/year. Pays royalty on retail price. Publishes book an average of 1 year after acceptance. Reports in 6 weeks. Computer printout submissions acceptable; no dot-matrix. SASE.
Nonfiction and Fiction: Quality material for preschoolers to 16-year-olds. Looks for "originality of ideas, clarity and felicity of expression, well-organized plot (fiction) or exposition (nonfiction) quality." Reviews artwork/photos as part of ms package.

Recent Title: *Seaward*, by Susan Cooper.

Tips: Freelance writers should be aware of the swing away from teen-age problem novels to books for young readers.

McFARLAND & COMPANY, INC., PUBLISHERS, Box 611, Jefferson NC 28640. (919)246-4460. President: Robert Franklin. Publishes hardcover and "quality" paperback originals; a non-"trade" publisher. Averages 40 titles/year. Pays 10-12½% royalty on gross receipts; no advance. Publishes book an average of 14 months after acceptance. Computer printout submissions acceptable; prefers letter-quality to dot-matrix. Reports in 2 weeks.

Nonfiction: Scholarly monographs, reference, technical and professional. Subjects include Americana, art, business and economics, chess, drama/theatre, health, cinema/radio/TV (very strong here), history, literature, librarianship (very strong here), music, parapsychology, religion, sociology, sports/recreation, women's studies, and world affairs. "We will consider *any* scholarly book—with authorial maturity and competent grasp of subject." Reference books are particularly wanted—fresh material (i.e., not in head-to-head competition with an established title). We don't like mss of fewer than 200 double-spaced typed pages. Our market consists mainly of libraries, and a few college textbooks. Our film books make it into book clubs frequently. They are the only ones we send to bookstores." No memoirs, poetry, children's books, or personal essays. Query or submit outline/synopsis and sample chapters. Reviews artwork/photos as part of ms package.

Recent Nonfiction Title: *Sports Quotations*, by Andrew J. Maikovich (reference).

Tips: "Possibly because of the approach of the year 2000, writings in the milleniumism vein are *heavily* on the upswing—e.g., end of the world, end of mankind, the second coming, ultra-profound impending courage, etc. Don't worry about writing skills—we have editors. What we want is well-organized *knowledge* of an area in which there is not good information coverage at present. Plus reliability so we don't feel we have to check absolutely everything."

McGRAW-HILL BOOK CO., College Textbooks Division, 1221 Avenue of the Americas, New York NY 10020. (212)997-2271. Editorial Director: William J. Willey. Editor-in-Chief, Engineering, Math and Science: B.J. Clark. Editor-in-Chief, Social Sciences and Humanities: Philip Butcher. Publishes hardcover and softcover technical material and software for the college market.

Nonfiction: The College Division publishes textbooks. The writer must know the college curriculum and course structure. Also publishes scientific texts and reference books in business and economics, computers, engineering, social sciences, physical sciences, nursing, and mathematics. Material should be scientifically and factually accurate. Most, but not all, books should be designed for existing courses offered in various disciplines of study. Books should have superior presentations and be more up-to-date than existing textbooks.

*McGRAW-HILL BOOK CO., Professional and Reference Division, 1221 Avenue of the Americas, New York NY 10020. General Manager: Peter Nalle. Multi/Volume Encyclopedia Editor-in-Chief: Sybil Parker. Business Editor-in-Chief: William Sabin. Handbooks and Technical Books Editor-in-Chief: Harold B. Crawford. Computing and Software Editor-in-Chief: Tyler G. Hicks. Publishes hardcover and paperback originals and software. Pays 10-12½-15% royalty on net price on hardcover and 7½% royalty on retail price on paperback. Subsidy publishes 5% books. Publishes book an average of 18 months after acceptance. Electronic submissions OK, but requires hard copy also. Computer printout submissions acceptable; prefers letter-quality to dot-matrix. Reports in 3 weeks. SASE.

Nonfiction: Publishes books for engineers, architects, scientists and business people who need information on the professional level. Some of these books also find use in college and technical institute courses. This division also publishes multi-volume encyclopedias (which are usually staff-prepared using work from outside contributors who are specialists in their fields) and one-volume encyclopedias prepared by experts in a given field. The professional books are usually written by graduate engineers, architects, scientists or business people (such as accountants, lawyers, stockbrokers, etc.). Authors of the professional books are expected to be highly qualified in their fields. Such qualifications are the result of education and experience in the field; these qualifications are prerequisite for authorship. The multi-volume encyclopedias rarely accept contributions from freelancers because the above education and experience qualifications are also necessary. Single-volume encyclopedias are usually prepared by subject specialists; again freelancers are seldom used unless they have the necessary experience and educational background.

Software: Contact: J. Robinson, Professional and Reference Division.

DAVID McKAY CO., INC., 2 Park Ave., New York NY 10016. Editor: James Louttit. Publishes hardcover and paperback originals. Averages 20 titles/year. "No unsolicited manuscripts or proposals considered or acknowledged."

*MACMILLAN OF CANADA, Suite 685, 146 Front St. W., Toronto, Ontario M5J 1G2 Canada. Publisher: Douglas M. Gibson. Editor-in-Chief: Anne Holloway. Publishes hardcover originals and paperback reprints. Averages 25 titles/year. Subsidy publishes 5% of books. 10% royalty on retail price. Sample chapters and outlines only acceptable form of submission. Publishes book an average of 1 year after acceptance. Computer printout submissions acceptable; prefers letter-quality to dot-matrix. Reports in 10 weeks. SAE and IRCs. Book catalog for SAE and IRCs.

Nonfiction: "We publish Canadian authors on all sorts of subjects and books of all sorts that are about Canada. Biography, history, art, current affairs, how-to, and juveniles. Particularly looking for good topical nonfiction." Reviews artwork/photos as part of ms package. Accepts translations. Accepts outline/synopsis and 3, 4 or 5 sample chapters "depending on length of total manuscript."

Recent Nonfiction Title: *The Game*, by Ken Dryden (sports biography).

Fiction: Query.

Recent Fiction Title: *A Tune for Judas*, by Morley Callaghan.

MACMILLAN PUBLISHING COMPANY, 866 3rd Ave., New York NY 10022. Publishes hardcover and paperback originals and reprints. Averages 130 titles/year. Will consider juvenile submissions only. Address mss to Children's Book Department. Enclose return postage.

Nonfiction: Publishes children's books only.

MCPHERSON & COMPANY, Box 638, New Paltz NY 12561. Editor: Bruce McPherson. Imprints include: Treacle Press, Documentext. Publishes hardcover and paperback originals, and paperback reprints. Averages 5 titles/year. Pays royalty. No unsolicited manuscripts—query first with SASE. Reports in 3 weeks to 2 months.

Fiction and Nonfiction: "We issue novels, anthologies, books of literary criticism, anthropology, film studies, etc., and plan to expand into the areas of alternative lifestyle and contemporary politics." Accepts fiction translations.

Recent Nonfiction Title: *Anticipation*, by Frederick Ted Castle.

MADRONA PUBLISHERS, INC., Box 22667, Seattle WA 98122. (206)325-3973. President: Daniel J. Levant. Editorial Director: Sara Levant. Publishes hardcover and paperback originals (90%) and paperback reprints (10%). Averages 6 titles/year. Pays 7½-15% royalty on wholesale or retail price; offers $1,000 average advance. Publishes book an average of 1 year after acceptance. Computer printout submissions acceptable. SASE. Reports in 8 weeks.

Nonfiction: Americana, biography, cookbooks, cooking and foods, health, history, hobbies, how-to, humor, photography, politics, psychology, recreation, self-help and travel. Query, submit outline/synopsis and at least 2 sample chapters or complete ms. Accepts nonfiction and fiction translations. Reviews artwork/photos as part of ms package.

Recent Nonfiction Title: *Eating Right to Live Sober*, by Katherine Ketcham and Dr. Anne Mueller.

*MANYLAND BOOKS, INC., 84-39 90th St., Woodhaven NY 11421. (212)441-6768. Editor-in-Chief: Stepas Zobarskas. Publishes hardcover and paperback originals. Pays 5-10-12½-15% royalty on wholesale price; no advance. Subsidy publishes 5% of books. Photocopied submissions OK. Submit complete ms. Reports in 8-10 weeks. Enclose return postage with ms.

Fiction, Nonfiction, and Poetry: "Manyland is concerned primarily with the literature of the lesser known countries. It has already published a score of novels, collections of short stories, folk tales, juvenile books, works of poetry, essays, and historical studies. Most of the publications have more than local interest. Their content and value transcend natural boundaries. They have universal appeal. We are interested in both new and established writers. We will consider any subject as long as it is well-written. No length requirements. We are especially interested in memoirs, biographies, anthologies." Accepts translations.

Recent Fiction Title: *Two Hearts In a Melting Pot*, by Paul Kolesar.

Recent Poetry Title: *Mayaag*, by William A. Evans.

Tips: Queries/mss may be routed to other editors in the publishing group.

MARATHON INTERNATIONAL PUBLISHING COMPANY, INC., Dept. WM, Box 33008, Louisville KY 40232. (502)245-1566. President: Jim Wortham. Publishes hardcover originals, trade paperback originals, trade paperback reprints. Averages 10 titles/year. Pays 10% royalty on wholesale. Publishes book an average of 10 months after acceptance. Simultaneous and photocopied submissions OK. Computer printout submissions acceptable. SASE. Reports in 1 week on queries; 2 weeks on mss. Book catalog for 6x9 SAE and 4 first class stamps.

Nonfiction: Cookbooks, how-to, self-help on business and economics, and offbeat humor. Especially needs how-to make extra money-type manuscripts; self-improvement; how a person can be happier and more prosperous. Does not want biography or textbooks. Query. Reviews artwork/photos as part of ms package.

Recent Nonfiction Title: *How to Make Money in Penny Stocks*, by Jim Scott (financial).

Poetry: Will consider poetry manuscripts for subsidy publication only.

‡MCN PRESS, Box 52033, Tulsa OK 74152. (918)743-6048. Publisher: Jack Britton. Publishes hardcover and trade paperback originals. Averages 5-7 titles/year. Pays 10% royalty on wholesale or retail price; offers **no**

advance. Computer printout submissions acceptable. SASE. Reports in 10 weeks. Free book catalog.
Nonfiction: Biography, illustrated book, and reference. Subjects include history and hobbies. "Our audience includes collectors, military personnel and military fans." Submit outline/synopsis and sample chapters or complete ms.
Recent Nonfiction Title: *Medals, Military and Civilian of U.S.* by Borthick and Britton (reference).

MEDICAL ECONOMICS BOOKS, Division of Medical Economics Co., 680 Kinderkamack, Oradell NJ 07649. Acquisitions Director: Elizabeth A. Stueck. Editor: Reuben Barr. Publishes hardcover, paperback, and spiral bound originals. Company also publishes magazines and references for doctors, nurses, pharmacists, laboratorians. Averages 36 titles/year. Pays by individual arrangement. Publishes book an average of 11 months after acceptance. Simultaneous and photocopied submissions OK. Electronic submissions "accepted on selective basis; inquire first," but requires hard copy also. Computer printout submissions acceptable. SASE. Reports in 6 weeks. Free book catalog. Tests freelancers for rewriting and editing assignments.
Nonfiction: Clinical and practice-financial management references, handbooks, and manuals. Medical—primary care—all fields; obstetrics and gynecology, pathology and laboratory medicine. Nursing for the practicing nurse. Submit table of contents and prospectus. Reviews artwork/photos as part of ms package.
Recent Nonfiction Title: *RN's Survival Sourcebook: Coping with Stress*, by Gloria F. Donnelly, RN, MSN.
Tips: "Our mission is to provide the practicing health care professional with high quality, clearly-written, practical, useful books." Queries/mss may be routed to other editors in the publishing group.

*MEDICAL EXAMINATION PUBLISHING CO., INC., 3003 New Hyde Park Rd., New Hyde Park NY 11042. Editors: Janice Resnick and Esther Gumpert. Publishes software. Subsidy publishes 1-5% of books. Royalty schedule is negotiable. Publishes book an average of 9 months after acceptance. Computer printout submissions acceptable; no dot-matrix. Reports in 1 month. Free catalog.
Nonfiction: Medical texts, reference works, and review books; monographs and training material for the medical, nursing and allied health professions. Submit outline. Reviews artwork/photos as part of ms package.
Software: Nursing and medical programmed learning. Contact: Maizie Reagan.

*MED-PSYCH PUBLICATIONS, Box 19746, West Allis, WI 53219. (414)778-1120. Aquisitions Editor: Marilyn A. Brilliant. Publishes hardcover and paperback originals. Averages 6-8 titles/year. Subsidy publishes 1% of books. Pays 10% royalty on wholesale price; no advance. Publishes book an average of 2 years after acceptance. Electronic submissions OK, but requires hard copy also. Computer printout submissions acceptable. SASE. Reports in 2 months. Book catalog $1.
Nonfiction: Health, how-to psychology, and self-help. "We would like to see more para-psychology, folk medicine and counseling material. We do not want any text books." Reviews artwork/photos as part of ms package. Query.
Recent Nonfiction Title: *Second Chance*, by Sydney Banks.

‡MENASHA RIDGE PRESS, INC., Rt. 3, Box 450, Hillsborough NC 27278. (919)732-6661. Managing Editor: R.W. Sehlinger. Publishes hardcover and trade paperback originals. Averages 10-15 titles/year. Pays 10% royalty on wholesale price or purchases outright; offers average $1,000 advance. Simultaneous and photocopied submissions OK. SASE. Reports in 1 month. Free book catalog.
Nonfiction: How-to, reference, self-help, consumer, outdoor recreation, travel guides and small business. Subjects include business and economics, health, hobbies, recreation, sports, travel and consumer advice. Especially looking for manuscripts in small business, how-to and consumer affairs. No biography or religious copies. Submit outline/synopsis and sample chapters.
Recent Nonfiction Title: *Home Buyers, Lambs to the Slaughter*, by Bashinsky (how-to/real estate).
Tips: Audience: age 25-60, 14-18 years' education, white collar and professional, $22,000+ median income, 75% male, 75% east of Mississippi River.

*MERCER UNIVERSITY PRESS, Macon GA 31207. (912)744-2880. Director: Edd Rowell. Publishes hardcover originals. Averages 60 titles/year. Subsidy publishes 90% of books. Pays royalty. Publishes book an average of 9 months after acceptance. Computer printout submissions acceptable; prefers letter-quality to dot-matrix. SASE. Reports in 3 weeks. Free book catalog.
Nonfiction: Reference and textbook. Subjects include history (of the American South); philosophy; religion, theology and biblical studies. Accepts nonfiction translations (German theology). Query. Accepts outline/synopsis and 2 sample chapters. Reviews artwork/photos as part of ms package.
Recent Nonfiction Title: *No Place to Hide: the South and Human Rights*, by Ralph McGill.

‡*MERCURY HOUSE INC., Suite 700, 300 Montgomery St., San Francisco CA 94104. (415)981-1434. President: William M. Brinton. Publishes hardcover originals. Averages 6 titles/year. Subsidy publishes "only if there is a good market and author has something to say and can say it well." Pays standard royalties; advances negotiable. "Will consider negotiating with author who pays a percentage of cost of printing, publishing, sell-

ing book, a tax-oriented transaction." Simultaneous and photocopied submissions OK. SASE. Reports in 3 weeks on queries; 6 weeks on mss.
Nonfiction: Subjects include business and economics and politics. Nonfiction needs are very limited. "We do not want to see nonfiction topics unless written by well-known author." Query with outline synopsis and sample chapters. All unsolicited mss are returned unopened.
Fiction: Political and financial world and suspense. Query with outline/synopsis and sample chapters. All unsolicited mss are returned unopened.
Recent Fiction Title: *The Alaska Deception*.
Tips: "Our audience is adult laymen and professionals. Mercury House expects to use electronic marketing of its titles through computer users, thus reducing need for distributors and retail outlets."

MERIWETHER PUBLISHING LTD., 885 Elkton Dr., Colorado Springs CO 80907. Editor-in-Chief: Arthur L. Zapel. Publishes paperback originals on how-to subjects relating to youth activities or communication arts. Averages 10 book titles and 35 plays (1-act and 3-act)/year. Payment by royalty arrangement, based on wholesale and retail price. Publishes book an average of 6 months after acceptance. Marketed by direct mail. Computer printout submissions acceptable; no dot-matrix. Book catalog $1. Editorial guidelines also available. Query, or a "brief synopsis or outline together with a brief page or two of writing style. Do not send ms until after response from us." Reports in about 1 month. Enclose return postage.
Nonfiction: Mss for educational use in schools and churches. Subjects include speech, drama and English. Religious, self-help, how-to, and Bible-study books are also published. Accepts translations. Reviews artwork/photos as part of ms package.
Recent Nonfiction Title: *Designing Small Theatres*, by James Hull Miller.
Drama: Plays, satire and comedy. "We publish 25-35 plays yearly."
Tips: Trends in book publishing that freelance writers should be aware of include "brief and stylish writing, even in nonfiction. Books shouldn't try to be fully comprehensive in nonfiction formats; books should motivate the pursuit of knowledge—let Britannica cover subjects in depth."

CHARLES E. MERRILL PUBLISHING CO., a Bell & Howell Co., 1300 Alum Creek Dr., Columbus OH 43216. (614)890-1111. Publishes hardcover and paperback originals. "Royalties and contract terms vary with the nature of the material. They are very competitive within each market area. Some projects are handled on an outright purchase basis." Publishes approximately 200 titles/year. Will accept simultaneous submissions if notified. SASE. Submit outline/synopsis and 3 sample chapters. Reports in 4-12 weeks.
Education Division: Editor: Ann Turpie. Publishes texts, workbooks, instructional tapes, overhead projection transparencies and programmed materials for elementary, junior high and high schools in all subject areas, primarily language arts and literature, mathematics, science and social studies (no juvenile stories or novels).
College Division: Editor-in-Chief, Education, Special Education and Humanities, Business, Mathematics, Science and Technology: Alan B. Borne. Publishes college texts and multimedia programs.

JULIAN MESSNER,(Division of Simon & Schuster Inc.), 1230 Avenue of the Americas, New York NY 10020. Editor-in-Chief: Iris Rosoff. Senior Editor for junior and senior high school: June Steltenpohl. Hardcover originals. Averages 70 titles/year. Royalty varies. Advance averages $2,000. State availability of photos and/or illustrations to accompany ms. "Propose book ideas to start with. If the editor is interested, we will ask for detailed outline and sample chapters." Reports in 2-3 months. SASE. Free book catalog.
Nonfiction: Nonfiction books only for young people.
Recent Nonfiction Title: *Why Are They Starving Themselves?: Understanding Anorexia Nervosa and Bulimia*, by Elaine Landau.

*METAMORPHOUS PRESS, Subsidiary of Metamorphosis, Inc., 7 Mt. Jefferson Terrace, Box 1712, Lake Oswego OR 97034. (503)635-6709. Editor: Victor Roberge. Publishes hardcover, trade paperback originals and hardcover and trade paperback reprints. Averages 6-8 titles/year. Subsidy publishes 10% of books. Pays 5-10% royalty on wholesale prices. No advance. Publishes book an average of 8 months after acceptance. Simultaneous and photocopied submissions OK. Electronic submissions OK, but requires hard copy also. Computer printout submissions acceptable; prefers letter-quality to dot-matrix. SASE. Free book catalog.
Nonfiction: Biography, how-to, illustrated book, reference, self-help, technical and textbook—all related to behavioral science and personal growth. Subjects include business and economics, health, psychology, sociology, science and new ideas in behavioral science. "We are interested in any well-proven new idea or philosophy in the behavioral science areas." Submit idea, outline, and table of contents only. Reviews artwork/photos as part of ms package.
Recent Nonfiction Title: *Alchemy of Intelligence*, by Warren Doheman (mind and education).

MICROTREND, INC., 3719 6th Ave., San Diego CA 92103. (619)295-0473. Publisher: Leslie S. Smith. Publishes trade paperback originals and software. Averages 12 titles/year. Pays 10-20% royalty on wholesale price. Offers variable advance. Publishes book an average of 6 months after acceptance. Simultaneous and photocopied submissions OK. Computer printout submissions acceptable. SASE. Reports in 2 weeks on queries; 1 month on mss. Write for book catalog.

Nonfiction: How-to, self-help, and technical—only microcomputer subjects. Query. Reviews artwork/photos as part of ms package.

Recent Nonfiction Title: *Programming in the C Language for the IBM PC*, by Pollack and Cummings.

Software: "We publish special market items."

MILLER BOOKS, 2908 W. Valley Blvd., Alhambra CA 91803. (213)284-7607. Subsidiaries include *San Gabriel Valley Magazine*, Miller Press and Miller Electric. Publisher: Joseph Miller. Publishes hardcover and trade paperback originals, hardcover reprints and software. Averages 4 titles/year. Pays 10-15% royalty on retail price; buys some mss outright. Simultaneous and photocopied submissions OK. Computer printout submissions acceptable. SASE ("no returns on erotic material"). Reports in 2 weeks on queries; 2 months on mss. Free book catalog.

Nonfiction: Cookbook, how-to, self-help, textbook and remedial textbooks. Subjects include Americana, animals, cooking and foods, history, philosophy and politics. "Remedial manuscripts are needed in most fields." No erotica. Submit complete ms. Reviews artwork/photos as part of ms package. "Please don't send letters. Let us see your work."

Recent Nonfiction Title: *Republican Chaos*, by J. Miller (political textbook).

Fiction: Adventure, historical, humor, mystery and western. No erotica. Submit complete ms.

Recent Fiction Title: *The Magic Story*, by F.V.R. Dey (positive thinking).

Software: Contact: Editor.

Tips: "Write something good about people, places and our country. Avoid the negative—it doesn't sell."

*MIMIR PUBLISHERS, INC., Box 5011, Madison WI 53705. Editor-in-Chief: Henry H. Bakken. Hardcover and paperback originals. Specializes in books in the social sciences at college level, and software. Averages 3-10 titles/year. 15% royalty on list price, "but nearly all titles are determined on a special contract." No advance. Subsidy publishing is offered "if the author wishes to proceed on our 50/50 type contract and share in the proceeds. Under this contract the author gets all the proceeds until he recovers his venture capital." Query or submit complete ms. Computer printout submissions acceptable; prefers letter-quality to dot-matrix. Reports in 2-4 months. SASE. Free book catalog.

Nonfiction: Publishes Americana, biography (limited), business, economics, history, law, philosophy, politics, sociology, and textbooks. Reviews artwork/photos as part of ms package.

Recent Nonfiction Title: *The Hills of Home*, by Bakken.

*MIT PRESS, 28 Carleton St., Cambridge MA 02142. (617)253-1693. Acquisitions Coordinator: Cristina Sanmartin. Averages 100 titles/year. "Subsidies are sometimes provided by cultural agencies but not by author." Pays 8-10% royalty on wholesale or retail price; $500-1,000 advance. Publishes book an average of 18 months after acceptance. Electronic submissions OK "if compatible with our computer graphics equipment," but requires hard copy also. Computer printout submissions acceptable; prefers letter-quality to dot-matrix. SASE. Reports in 4-6 weeks. Free book catalog.

Nonfiction: Computer science/artificial intelligence, civil engineering/transportation, neuroscience, linguistics/psychology/philosophy, architecture, design, visual communication, economics, physics, math, and history of science and technology. "Our books must reflect a certain level of technological sophistication. We do not want fiction, poetry, literary criticism, education, pure philosophy, European history before 1920, belles-lettres, drama, personal philosophies, or children's books." Submit outline/synopsis, c.v. and sample chapters.

Recent Nonfiction Title: *Memories That Shaped an Industry*, by Emerson Pugh.

MONITOR BOOK CO., INC., 195 S. Beverly Dr., Beverly Hills CA 90212. (213)271-5558. Editor-in-Chief: Alan F. Pater. Hardcover originals. Pays 10% minimum royalty or by outright purchase, depending on circumstances; no advance. Send prints if photos and/or illustrations are to accompany ms. Reports in 2-4 months. SASE. Book catalog for SASE.

Nonfiction: Americana, biographies (only of well-known personalities), law and reference books.

Recent Nonfiction Title: *Yearbook of American Poetry for 1984*.

‡MOON PUBLICATIONS, Subsidiaries include Travel & Leisure Press, Box 1696, Chico CA 95927. (916)345-5473/345-5413. Editors: Deke Castleman and Bill Dalton. Publishes trade paperback originals. Averages 3 titles/year. Pays 10-12½% royalty on retail price; offers average $700-1,500 advance. Photocopied and electronic submissions OK if compatible with CPM; prefers disk submissions. Computer printout submissions acceptable. SASE. Reports in 3 weeks. Publishes book an average of 6 months after acceptance. Free book catalog.

Nonfiction: Travel guidebook titles. Subjects include recreation and travel. "We will consider any guidebook, designed after our format and 'writing style' on virtually any country or travel destination area in the world.

Writers should first write for a copy of our writer's guidelines. We specialize in Asia and the Pacific. No travelogue or super-subjective travel writing or 'narrative' travel writing.'' Query with outline/synopsis and sample chapters.
Recent Nonfiction Title: *South Pacific Handbook*, by David Stanley (guidebook).
Tips: "Our books are for the general public. We find all socio-economic classes buying them. They are aimed for the independent, budget-minded, do-it-yourself traveler but appeal to all travelers because they tend to be the comprehensive guides to the areas they cover.''

MOREHOUSE-BARLOW CO., INC., 78 Danbury Rd., Wilton CT 06897. Editorial Director: Stephen S. Wilburn. Publishes hardcover and paperback originals. Averages 20 titles/year. Pay 10% royalty on retail price. Publishes book an average of 8 months after acceptance. Computer printout submissions acceptable; prefers letter-quality to dot-matrix. SASE.
Nonfiction: Specializes in Anglican religious publishing. Theology, ethics, church history, pastoral counseling, liturgy and religious education. Accepts outline/synopsis and 3-5 sample chapters. No fiction, poetry or drama. Reviews artwork/photos as part of ms package.
Recent Nonfiction Title: *Anglicanism and the Bible*, ed. Frederick H. Borsch.

WILLIAM MORROW AND CO., 105 Madison Ave., New York NY 10016. Publisher: Sherry W. Arden. Imprints include Greenwillow Books (juveniles), Susan Hirschman, editor. Lothrop, Lee and Shephard (juveniles), Dorothy Briley, editor. Morrow Junior Books (juveniles), David Reuther, editor. Quill (trade paperback), James D. Landis, publisher. Affiliates include Hearst Books (trade). Editorial Director: Joan Nagy. Hearst Marine Books (nautical). Publisher: Paul Larsen. Payment is on standard royalty basis. Publishes book an average of 18 months after acceptance. Query letter on all books. No unsolicited mss or proposals. Mss and proposals should be submitted through a literary agent. Computer printout submissions acceptable.
Nonfiction: Publishes adult fiction, nonfiction, history, biography, arts, religion, poetry, how-to books and cookbooks. Length: 50,000-100,000 words.
Recent Title: *On Wings of Eagles*, by Ken Follett.

MORROW JUNIOR BOOKS, 105 Madison Ave., New York NY 10016. (212)889-3050. Editor-in-Chief: David L. Reuther. Senior Editors: Pamela Pollack and Andrea Curley. Publishes hardcover originals. Publishes 50 titles/year. All contracts negotiated separately; advance varies. No simultaneous or photocopied submissions. Computer printout submissions acceptable; prefers letter-quality to dot-matrix. SASE. Reports in 6 weeks. Free book catalog.
Nonfiction: Juveniles (trade books). No textbooks. Query. Reviews artwork/photos as part of ms package.
Fiction: Juveniles (trade books).

MOSAIC PRESS, 358 Oliver Rd., Cincinnati OH 45215. (513)761-5977. Publisher: Miriam Irwin. Publishes hardcover originals. Averages 11 titles/year. Buys mss outright for $50. Publishes book an average of 2 years after acceptance. Computer printout submissions acceptable. SASE. Reports in 2 weeks; "but our production, if ms is accepted, often takes 2 or 3 years.'' Book catalog $3.
Nonfiction: Biography, cookbook, humor, illustrated book and satire. Subjects include Americana, animals, art, business and economics, cooking and foods, health, history, hobbies, music, nature, sports and travel. Interested in "beautifully written, delightful text. If factual, it must be extremely correct and authoritative. Our books are intended to delight, both in their miniature size, beautiful bindings and excellent writing.'' No occult, pornography, science fiction, fantasy, haiku, or how-to. Query or submit outline/synopsis and sample chapters or complete ms. Reviews artwork/photos as part of ms package.
Recent Nonfiction Title: *Healing and Belief*, by Norman Cousins.

MOTORBOOKS INTERNATIONAL PUBLISHERS & WHOLESALERS, INC., Box 2, Osceola WI 54020. Director of Publications: William F. Kosfeld. Senior Editor: Barbara K. Harold. Hardcover and paperback originals. Offers 7-15% royalty on wholesale or retail price. Average advance: $1,500. Averages 10-12 titles/year. Publishes book an average of 8 months after acceptance. Simultaneous and photocopied submissions OK. Computer printout submissions acceptable. Reports in 2-3 months. SASE. Free book catalog.
Nonfiction: Publishes biography, history, how-to, photography, and motor sports as they relate to cars, trucks, motorcycles, motor sports and aviation (domestic and foreign). Submit outline/synopsis, 1-2 sample chapters and sample of illustrations. Accepts nonfiction translations from German/Italian. "State qualifications for doing book.'' Reviews artwork/photos as part of ms package. Prefers not to see repair manuals.

The double dagger (‡) before a listing indicates that the listing is new in this edition. New markets are often the most receptive to freelance contributions.

Recent Nonfiction Title: *The Harley-Davidson Motor Company*, by David Wright.
Tips: "Trends in book publishing that freelance writers should be aware of include higher trade discounts resulting in less total royalties."

MOTT MEDIA, INC., PUBLISHERS, 1000 E. Huron, Milford MI 48042. Senior Editor: Leonard George Goss. Associated with Evangelical Book Club. Hardcover and paperback originals (75%) and paperback reprints (25%). Averages 20-25 titles/year. Specializes in religious books, including trade and Christian school textbooks. Pays variable royalty on retail, depending on type of book. Computer printout submissions acceptable. Query or submit outline/synopsis and sample chapters. Reports in 1 month. SASE. Free book catalog.
Nonfiction: Publishes Americana (religious slant); biography (for juveniles on famous Christians, adventure-filled; for adults on Christian people, scholarly, new slant for marketing); how-to (for pastors, Christian laymen); juvenile (biographies, 30,000-40,000 words); politics (conservative, Christian approach); religious (conservative Christian); self-help (religious); and textbooks (all levels from a Christian perspective, all subject fields). No preschool materials. Main emphasis of all mss must be religious. Wants to know "vocation, present position and education of author; brief description of the contents of the book; basic readership for which the mss. was written; brief explanation of why the ms differs from other books on the same subject; the author's interpretation of the significance of this ms."
Recent Nonfiction Title: *Social Justice and the Christian Church*, by Ronald Nash.
Fiction: "We're beginning to consider a limited amount of fiction for the Christian consumer. No overt moral or crisis decision necessary, but fiction must demonstrate a Christian perspective."

*MOUNTAIN PRESS PUBLISHING CO., 1600 North Ave. W, Missoula MT 59806. Publisher: David P. Flaccus. Hardcover and paperback originals (90%) and reprints (10%). Royalty of 12% of net amount received; no advance. Subsidy publishes less than 5% of books. "Top-quality work in very limited market only." Averages 12 titles/year. State availability of photos and/or illustrations to accompany ms. Publishes book an average of 6 months after acceptance. Computer printout submissions acceptable. Reports in 2-4 weeks. SASE. Free book catalog.
Nonfiction: Publishes history (western Americana); hobbies; how-to (angling, hunting); nature (geology, habitat and conservation); outdoor recreation (backpacking, fishing, etc.); technical (wood design and technology); and textbooks. Looks for "target audience, organization, quality of writing and style compatibility with current list and goals." Accepts nonfiction translations. Reviews artwork/photos as part of ms package.
Recent Nonfiction Title: *Death, Too, for the Heavy-Runner*, by Ben Bennett.

THE MOUNTAINEERS BOOKS, 715 Pike St., Seattle WA 98101. (206)682-4636. Manager: Donna DeShazo. Publishes hardcover and paperback originals (85%) and reprints (15%). Averages 10-15 titles/year. Offers 10-15% royalty based on wholesale or retail price. Offers advance on occasion. Publishes book an average of 1 year after acceptance. Computer printout submissions acceptable. SASE. Reports in 6-8 weeks. Free book catalog.
Nonfiction: Recreation, sports, and outdoor how-to books. "We specialize only in books dealing with mountaineering, hiking, backpacking, skiing, snowshoeing, canoeing, bicycling, etc. These can be either how-to-do-it, where-to-do-it (guidebooks), or accounts of mountain-related experiences." Does *not* want to see "anything dealing with hunting, fishing or motorized travel." Submit outline/synopsis and minimum of 2 sample chapters. Accepts nonfiction translations. Looks for "expert knowledge, good organization." Reviews artwork/photos as part of ms package.
Recent Nonfiction Title: *Trekking in Nepal*, by Stephen Bezruchka (guidebook).
Fiction: "We might consider an exceptionally well-done book-length manuscript on mountaineering. It could be humorous and/or could be aimed at the juvenile audience." Does *not* want poetry or mystery. Query first.

JOHN MUIR PUBLICATIONS, Box 613, Santa Fe NM 87501. (505)982-4078. Project Co-ordinator: Lisa Cron. Publishes trade paperback originals. Averages 6 titles/year. Pays 8-12% royalty; offers variable advance. Publishes book an average of 1 year after acceptance. Simultaneous and photocopied submissions OK. Computer printout submissions acceptable; no dot-matrix. SASE. Reports in 1 month on queries; 2 months on mss. Free book catalog.
Nonfiction: How-to, illustrated book and self-help. Subjects include automobile repair manuals, health, music, and travel. "We are interested in manuscripts written with warmth, wit, humor and accuracy and which help promote self-sufficiency. The topic of such a submission is open; we'll look at almost anything except cookbooks. We're particularly interested in manuscripts pertaining to automobile repair and maintenance. However, we don't publish theory books or political treatises or books like 'The History of Tennis Memorabilia'; in other words, we want manuscripts that offer practical applications." Submit outline/synopsis and at least 3 sample chapters. Reviews artwork/photos as part of ms package.
Recent Nonfiction Title: *A Guide to Midwifery*, by Elizabeth Davis.
Tips: Readers include "counterculture people and those in the mainstream who have become dissatisfied with the status quo. *Please* take a look at our books before submitting a manuscript. We continue to get textbook-

type submissions—dryly written, and with no practical application. It is friendliness and humor that set our books apart. Also we often get queries for 'the children's book editor' or 'the poetry editor' when a bit of research would reveal we publish neither children's nor poetry books."

MUSEUM OF NEW MEXICO PRESS, Box 2087, Santa Fe NM 87503. (505)827-2352. Director: James Mafchir. Editor-in-Chief: Sarah Nestor. Hardcover and paperback originals (90%) and reprints (10%). Averages 4-6 titles/year. Royalty of 10% of list after first 1,000 copies; no advance. Publishes book an average of 1 year after acceptance. Prints preferred for illustrations; transparencies best for color. Sources of photos or illustrations should be indicated for each. Computer printout submissions acceptable; prefers letter-quality to dot-matrix. Query or submit outline/synopsis and sample chapters to Sarah Neston, Editor-in-Chief. Mss should be typed double-spaced, follow Chicago *Manual of Style*, and be accompanied by information about the author's credentials and professional background. Reports in 1-2 months. SASE. Free book catalog.
Nonfiction: "We publish both popular and scholarly books on regional anthropology, history, fine and folk arts; geography, natural history, the Americas and the Southwest; regional cookbooks; art, biography (regional and Southwest); music; nature; reference, scientific and technical. Accepts nonfiction translations. Reviews artwork/photos as part of ms package.

MUSIC SALES CORP., 24 E. 22nd St., New York NY 10010. (212)254-2100. Imprints include Acorn, Amsco, Anfor, Ariel, Award, Consolidated, Embassy, Oak, Yorktown, Music Sales Ltd., London; Wise Pub., Ashdown Ltd., and Music Sales, Australia. Editor-in-Chief: Eugene Weintraub. Contact: Barry Edward, President (NY office). Publishes paperback originals (95%) and reprints (5%). Publishes 75 titles/year. Standard publishing contracts. Simultaneous and photocopied submissions OK.
Nonfiction: Instructional music books on blues, bluegrass, classical, folk and jazz; also technical, theory, reference and pop music personalities. Music Sales Corporation publishes and distributes a complete line of quality music instruction books for every musician from beginner to professional.
Recent Nonfiction Title: *Guitar Gadgets*, by Craig Anterton.

THE NAIAD PRESS, INC., Box 10543, Tallahassee FL 32302. (904)539-9322. Editorial Director: Barbara Grier. Publishes paperback originals. Averages 12 titles/year. Pays 15% royalty on wholesale or retail price; no advance. Publishes book an average of 1 year after acceptance. Reports in 8 weeks. SASE. Book catalog for SASE.
Fiction: "We publish lesbian fiction, preferably lesbian/feminist fiction. We are not impressed with the 'oh woe' school and prefer realistic (i.e., happy) novels." Query. "We emphasize fiction, and are now heavily reading manuscripts in that area. We are working in a lot of genre fiction—mysteries, science fiction, short stories, fantasy—all with Lesbian themes, of course."
Recent Fiction Title: *Curious Wine*, by Katherine V. Forrest.

NATIONAL BOOK COMPANY, 333 SW Park Ave., Portland OR 97205. (503)228-6345. Imprints include Halcyon House. Editorial Director: Carl W. Salser. Senior Editor: John R. Kimmel. Manager of Copyrights: Lucille Fry. Publishes hardcover and paperback originals (95%), paperback reprints (2%), and software. Averages 28 titles/year. Pays 5-15% royalty on wholesale or retail price; no advance. Publishes book an average of 1 year after acceptance. Computer printout submissions acceptable. SASE. Reports in 2 months. Free catalog for 9"x12", 24¢ SASE.
Nonfiction: Only materials suitable for educational uses in all categories. Art, business/economics, health, history, music, politics, psychology, reference, science, technical and textbooks. "The vast majority of titles are individualized instruction/Mastery Learning programs for educational consumers. Prospective authors should be aware of this and be prepared for this type of format, although content, style and appropriateness of subject matter are the major criteria by which submissions are judged. We are most interested in materials in the areas of the language arts, social studies and the sciences." Query, submit outline/synopsis and 2-5 sample chapters or complete ms. Reviews artwork/photos as part of ms package.
Recent Nonfiction Title: *Using Ten-Key Electronic Desktop Calculators*, by J. Kimmel.

THE NATIONAL GALLERY OF CANADA, Publications Division, Ottawa, Ontario K1A 0M8 Canada. (613)995-6526. Head: Peter L. Smith. Publishes hardcover and paperback originals. Averages 15 titles/year. Pays in outright purchase of $1,500-2,500; advance averages $700. Photocopied submissions OK. Reports in 3 months. SASE. Free sales catalog.
Nonfiction: "In general, we publish only *solicited* manuscripts on art, particularly Canadian art, and must publish them in English and French. Exhibition catalogs are commissioned, but we are open (upon approval by Curatorial general editors) to mss for the various series, monographic and otherwise, that we publish. All mss should be directed to our Editorial Coordinator, who doubles as manuscript editor. Since we publish translations into French, authors have access to French Canada and the rest of Francophonia. Because our titles are distributed by University of Chicago Press, authors have the attention of European as well as American markets."
Recent Nonfiction Title: *Cultural Engineering*, by Tom Sherman.

NATIONAL PUBLISHERS OF THE BLACK HILLS, INC., Box 288, Rapid City SD 57709. (605)394-4993. Editorial Director: Jean Babrick. Publishes trade and mass market paperback originals and trade paperback reprints. Averages 10 titles/year. Pays negotiable royalty; offers negotiable advance. Computer printout submissions acceptable; no dot-matrix. SASE. Reports in 3 weeks on queries; 5 weeks on mss.
Nonfiction: Technical, business and economics texts, medical administrative assisting, computer science texts, travel, and English texts. Immediate needs include basic electronics texts, basic geophysical surveying texts, and remedial math. Query or submit outline/synopsis and 3 sample chapters or complete ms. Reviews artwork/photos as part of ms package.
Recent Nonfiction Title: *Sales and Marketing for Travel and Tourism*, by Philip and Doris Davidoff.

NATIONAL TEXTBOOK CO., 4255 W. Touhy Ave., Lincolnwood IL 60646-1975. (312)679-5500. Editorial Director: Leonard I. Fiddle. Mss purchased on either royalty or buy-out basis. Averages 9 titles/year. Publishes book an average of 1 year after acceptance. Computer printout submissions acceptable. Free book catalog and writer's guidelines. Send sample chapter and outline or contents. Reports in 4 months. Enclose return postage.
Nonfiction: Textbook. Major emphasis being given to language arts area, especially secondary level material. Gay E. Menges, Language Arts Editor.
Recent Nonfiction Title: *Building Real Life English Skills*, by Penn and Storkey (survival reading and writing).
Software: Contact editors. Foreign language and ESL.

NATUREGRAPH PUBLISHERS, INC., Box 1075, Happy Camp CA 96039. (916)493-5353. Editor: Barbara Brown. Quality trade books. Averages 5 titles/year. "We offer 10% of wholesale; 12½% after 10,000 copies are sold. To speed things up, queries should include: 1)summary, 2)detailed outline, 3)comparison to related books, 4)2 sample chapters, 5)availability and samples of any photos or illustrations, and 6)author background. Send ms only on request." Publishes book an average of 18 months after acceptance. Photocopied submissions OK. Computer printout submissions acceptable; prefers letter-quality to dot-matrix. Reports in 1-2 months. SASE. Free book catalog.
Nonfiction: Primarily publishes nonfiction for the layman in 7 general areas: natural history (biology, geology, ecology, astronomy); American Indian (historical and contemporary); outdoor living (backpacking, wild edibles, etc.); land and gardening (modern homesteading); crafts and how-to; holistic health (natural foods and healing arts); and PRISM Editions (Baha'i and other new age approaches to harmonious living). All material must be well-grounded; author must be professional, and in command of effective style. Our natural history and American Indian lines can be geared for educational markets."
Recent Nonfiction Title: *All the World Is Kin*, by Bernice Espy Hicks.

THE NAUTICAL & AVIATION PUBLISHING CO. OF AMERICA, INC., 8 Randall St., Annapolis MD 21401. (301)267-8522. President: Mr. Jan Snouck-Hurgronje. Publishes hardcover originals (50%) and reprints (25%) and imported books (25%). Pays 14-18% royalty on net selling price; sometimes offers advance. Simultaneous and photocopied submissions OK. Computer printout submissions acceptable; no dot-matrix. Reports in 2 weeks.
Nonfiction: History, biography, and reference. Accepts nonfiction translations from Russian, German, and Japanese. Especially needs mss on military topics, history, and reference. Looking for books on individual aircraft and Marine Corps history. Submit outline/synopsis, 2-3 sample chapters and table of contents. Reviews artwork/photos as part of ms package.
Recent Nonfiction Title: *A Battlefield Atlas of the Civil War*.
Fiction: Military. "Would consider reprinting of original novels." Submit complete ms.

NAVAL INSTITUTE PRESS, Annapolis MD 21402. Acquisitions Editors: Richard R. Hobbs, and Deborah P.O. Guberti. Press Director: Thomas F. Epley. Averages 30 titles/year. Pays 14-18-21% royalty based on net sales; modest advance. Publishes book an average of 1 year after acceptance. Computer printout submissions acceptable. SASE. Reports in 2 weeks (queries); 6 weeks (others). Free book catalog.
Nonfiction: "We are interested in naval and maritime subjects: navigation, naval history, biographies of naval leaders and naval aviation." Reviews artwork/photos as part of ms package.
Fiction: Limited, very high quality fiction on naval and maritime themes.
Recent Title: *U.S. Aircraft Carriers: An Illustrated Design History*, by Norman Friedman.

NC PRESS, 31 Portland St., Toronto, Ontario M5V 2V9 Canada. (416)593-6284. Editorial Director: Caroline Walker. Publishes hardcover and paperback originals and reprints and a full line of children's books. Averages 10-15 titles/year. Pays royalty on list under 50% discount. Electronic submissions OK on CP/M 8" diskettes, but requires hard copy also. Computer printout submissions acceptable. SASE.
Nonfiction: "We generally publish books of social/political relevance either on contemporary topics of concern (current events, ecology, etc.), or historical studies. We publish primarily Canadiana. US authors must

have US co-publisher—i.e., we're only interested in Canadian rights and cannot publish US authors without US co-publisher." Accepts nonfiction translations from French. Submit outline/synopsis and 1-2 sample chapters.
Recent Nonfiction Title: *This Thing of Darkness*, by Norman Elder (travel/anthropology).

THOMAS NELSON PUBLISHERS, Nelson Place at Elm Hill Pike, Nashville TN 37214. (615)889-9000. Editor: Lawrence M. Stone. Publishes hardcover and paperback originals (95%) and reprints (5%). Averages 125 titles/year. Pays royalty or by outright purchase; sometimes an advance. Publishes book an average of 1 year after acceptance. Computer printout submissions acceptable. SASE. Reports in 6-8 weeks. Book catalog for SASE.
Nonfiction: Reference and religious (must be orthodox Christian in theology). Accepts outline/synopsis and 3 sample chapters. Reviews artwork/photos as part of ms package. Looks for "orthodoxy, honesty, quality, validity."
Recent Nonfiction Title: *The Complete Concordance to the Bible (NKJV)* (reference).
Recent Fiction Title: *Chase the Wind*, by Deborah Lawrence and Aggie Villanueva.

NELSON-HALL PUBLISHERS, 111 N. Canal St., Chicago IL 60606. (312)930-9446. Editorial Director: Harold Wise, PhD. Publishes hardcover and paperback originals. Averages 105 titles/year. Pays 15% maximum royalty on retail price; average advance. Photocopied submissions OK. SASE. Reports in 1 month. Free book catalog.
Nonfiction: Textbooks and general scholarly books in the social sciences. Query.
Recent Nonfiction Title: *Fundamentals of Abnormal Psychology*, by Richard Suinn.

NEW AMERICAN LIBRARY, 1633 Broadway, New York NY 10019. (212)397-8000. Imprints include Signet, Mentor, Signet, Classic, Plume, Meridian, and NAL Books. Publisher: Elaine Koster. Editor-in-Chief/ Paperback: Maureen Baron. Editor-in-Chief/Hardcover: Michaela Hamilton. Publishes hardcover and paperback originals and hardcover reprints. Publishes 350 titles/year. Royalty is "variable;" offers "substantial" advance. Simultaneous and photocopied submissions OK. Computer printout submissions acceptable. Reports in 2 months. SASE. Free book catalog.
Tips: Queries/mss may be routed to other editors in the publishing group.

NEW LEAF PRESS, INC., Box 1045, Harrison AR 72061. Editor-in-Chief: Bertha Sprenger. Hardcover and paperback originals. Publishes 10 titles/year. Specializes in charismatic books. Pays 10% royalty on first 10,000 copies, paid once a year; no advance. Send photos and illustrations to accompany ms. Simultaneous and photocopied submissions OK. Computer printout and disk submissions acceptable. SASE. Reports in 3 months. Free book catalog.
Nonfiction: Biography and self-help. Charismatic books; life stories, and how-to live the Christian life. Length: 100-400 pages. Submit complete ms.
Recent Nonfiction Title: *Can Reagan Beat the Zero Course?*, by David A. Lewis.

NEW READERS PRESS, Publishing division of Laubach Literacy International, Box 131, Syracuse NY 13210. Assistant Editorial Director: Kay Koschnick. Publishes paperback originals. Averages 15 titles/year. "Most of our sales are to public education systems, including adult basic education programs, with some sales to volunteer literacy programs, private human-services agencies, prisons, and libraries with outreach programs for poor readers." Pays royalty on retail price, or by outright purchase. "Rate varies according to type of publication and length of ms." Advance is "different in each case, but does not exceed projected royalty for first year." Publishes book an average of 1 year after acceptance. Photocopied submissions OK. Computer printout submissions acceptable; prefers letter-quality to dot-matrix. Reports in 2 months. SASE. Free book catalog.
Nonfiction: "Our audience is adults and older teenagers with limited reading skills (6th grade level and below). We publish basic education materials in reading and writing, math, social studies, health, science, and English-as-a-second-language for double illiterates. We are particularly interested in materials that fulfill curriculum requirements in these areas. Mss must be not only easy to read (3rd-6th grade level) but mature in tone and concepts. We would consider submissions in the curriculum areas of reading skills development, composition, grammar, practical math, social studies (economics, geography and U.S. history), science, self-awareness and human relations, and adapting to U.S. culture (for functionally illiterate English-as-a-second language students). We would also consider materials for specialized audiences of nonreaders, such as the learning disabled or speakers of nonstandard dialects. We are not interested in biography, poetry, or anything at all written for children." Accepts outline/synopsis and 1-3 sample chapters depending on how representative of the total they are." Reviews artwork/photos as part of ms package.
Recent Nonfiction Title: *Earth Below and Sky Above*, by Marilynne Mathias and Robert Johnson.
Fiction: "We are not currently accepting fiction submissions."

NEW YORK UNIVERSITY PRESS, Washington Square, New York NY 10003. (212)598-2886. Contact: Editor. Publishes hardcover and scholarly paperback originals. Averages 50 titles/year. Pays negotiable royalty. No advance. Reports in 3 weeks. Free book catalog.
Nonfiction: Scholarly works in the areas of art history, history, New York City regional history, philosophy, politics, and literary criticism. Submit precis and vita.
Recent Nonfiction Title: *Super Chief Earl Warren: A Judicial Biography*, by Bernard Schwartz.

NEW YORK ZOETROPE, INC., 80 E. 11th St., New York NY 10003. (212)254-8235. Contact: James Monaco. Publishes hardcover and trade paperback originals, hardcover and trade paperback reprints and software. Averages 25 titles/year. Pays 10-20% royalty on wholesale prices or makes outright purchase of $500-1,000. Offers average $200 advance. Publishes book an average of 1 year after acceptance. Simultaneous and photocopied submissions OK. Computer printout submissions acceptable. SASE. Reports in 2 weeks on queries; 2 months on mss.
Nonfiction: "Coffee table" book, reference, technical and textbook. Subjects include business and economics, travel and media. Interested especially in film and computer subjects. No fiction. Query.
Recent Nonfiction Title: *Hollywood: The First 100 Years*, by Torrence (art).
Software: Contact James Monaco.

NEWCASTLE PUBLISHING CO., INC., 13419 Saticoy, North Hollywood CA 91605. (213)873-3191. Editor-in-Chief: Alfred Saunders. Publishes trade paperback originals and trade paperback reprints. Averages 8 titles/year. Pays 5-10% royalty on retail price; no advance. Simultaneous and photocopied submissions OK. SASE. Reports in 3 weeks on queries; 6 weeks on mss. Free book catalog.
Nonfiction: How-to, self-help, metaphysical, and new age. Subjects include health (physical fitness, diet and nutrition); psychology; and religion. "Our audience is made up of college students and college-age non-students; also, adults aged 25 and up." No biography or travel. Query or submit outline/synopsis and sample chapters. Looks for "something to grab the reader so that he/she will readily remember that passage."
Recent Nonfiction Title: *Handwriting Analysis: The Complete Basic Book*, by Amend & Ruiz (occult/psychology).

NICHOLS PUBLISHING CO., Box 96, New York NY 10024. Editorial Director: Linda Kahn. Publishes hardcover originals. Averages 25-30 titles/year. Simultaneous and photocopied submissions OK. Computer printout submissions acceptable. Reports in 6 weeks. SASE. Book catalog for SASE.
Nonfiction: Professional/academic materials in architecture, business, education, engineering, international affairs, investment, and energy topics. Reviews artwork/photos as part of ms package. Query with outline, table of contents, 2 sample chapters.
Recent Nonfiction Title: *The Financing and Financial Control of Small Enterprise Development*, by Ray and Hutchison.

NIMBUS PUBLISHING LIMITED, Subsidiary of H.H. Marshall Ltd., Box 9301, Station A, Halifax, Nova Scotia B3K 5N5 Canada. (902)454-8381. Contact: Elizabeth Eve. Imprints include: Petheric Press (nonfiction and fiction). Publishes hardcover and trade paperback originals (90%) and trade paperback reprints. Averages 5 titles/year. Pays 4-10% royalty on retail price. Publishes book an average of 1 year after acceptance. Photocopied submissions OK. Computer printout submissions acceptable. SAE, IRCs. Reports in 2 months on queries; 4 months on mss. Free book catalog.
Nonfiction: Biography, "coffee table" books, cookbooks, how-to, humor, illustrated books, juvenile, books of regional interest on art, cooking and foods, history, nature, travel, and regional. "We do some specialized publishing; otherwise, our audience is the tourist and trade market in Nova Scotia." Query or submit outline/synopsis and a minimum of 1 sample chapter. Reviews artwork/photos as part of ms package.
Recent Nonfiction Title: *Halifax*, by Hines (96-page book of colored pictures of the city).

NORTH LIGHT, Imprint of Writer's Digest Books, 32 Berwick Court, Fairfield CT 06430. (203)336-4225. Editor/Design Director: Fritz Henning. Publishes hardcover originals and trade paperback originals. Averages 8-10 titles/year. Pays 10% royalty on net receipts. Offers $1,000-3,000 advance. Simultaneous submissions and photographs of artwork OK. SASE. Reports in 3 weeks on queries; 2 months on mss. Free book catalog.
Nonfiction: How-to and reference art books. Subjects include instructional art. Interested in books on acrylic painting; oil painting, basic drawing, and pen and ink watercolor. Does not want "prestige-type art books not focusing on how-to art instruction." Query or submit outline/synopsis and examples of artwork.
Recent Nonfiction Title: *Concept and Composition*, by Fritz Henning (art instruction-all levels).

*NORTHEASTERN UNIVERSITY PRESS, 17 Cushing Hall, Northeastern University, 360 Huntington Ave., Boston MA 02115. (617)437-2783. Editors: Deborah Kops and Dana Rowan. Publishes hardcover originals, and hardcover and paperback reprints. Averages 10 titles/year. Subsidy publishes 20% of books. Pays 7-10% royalty on wholesale price. Publishes book an average of 1 year after acceptance. SASE. Reports in 1 month on queries; 3 months on mss.

Close-up

Mary Cunnane
Editor, W.W. Norton & Co., Inc.

When Norton editor Mary Cunnane reads a manuscript, she knows it is the most important thing in that writer's life at the time. "Whether that book ever gets published or not, that's still a tremendous achievement, and I have nothing but admiration for writers."

Norton is one of the large publishing houses where editors still read unsolicited manuscripts. Why Norton editors spend time *in the transom* has never been articulated, she says, but most likely "out of respect for writers.

"If someone has worked hard enough to write a book or proposal, we as publishers have a responsibility to at least consider it," says Cunnane, who has worked for Norton for eight years. "Publishing is a two-way street; we have to be open to the submission of books and ideas from the outside. Closing off one avenue for those books would be narrowing the flow of ideas; I don't think we want to do that," she says.

Cunnane works as an acquiring editor in the trade book department and also as British rights manager.

"Working with an author on a book is the most pleasurable part of the whole process, but that is only one part of the publishing process," she says. "This is a business; money has to be made not just for the publisher but for the author. It's not just editing; it's publishing."

Like most trade editors, Cunnane handles mail and phone communication with authors and agents, meets with the art department, helps promote the books she edits. "The person who is the inhouse advocate for the author and who is ultimately responsible for the success of the book is the editor," she points out.

Such responsibilities leave little time for reading manuscripts in the office. "All that reading has to be done at night and on the weekends," she says. "I'm not complaining; if that is really

Photo by Hugh O'Neill

burdensome, then you shouldn't be in this business."

Cunnane wants writers to say in their queries "why my book will fit Norton's list" and to show how the proposed book compares with ones on the market. Find out from publicity departments which editor is responsible for the books similar to the one you propose; tell that editor (in a letter, of course) why you enjoy or don't enjoy these books, she suggests.

Above all, Cunnane likes "writing that shows the author is thinking all the time of whom their potential readers are—writing not for themselves but for their readers.

"If the writer is good, knows his or her subject, knows there is a market for the nonfiction book he wants to write, his chances are very good indeed," she says.

Cunnane also believes the public wants good literary fiction. "You've heard for years about the death of the novel and the first novel and that everyone is looking at computers and TV and nobody's interested in good writing. I don't think that's true. There is a substantial market for well-published, well-written work," she says. "It's literary fiction that made me and probably most people love books.

"You really have to fall in love with books to work with them and writers all day," points out Cunnane.

That love fills some evenings too when she takes another manuscript from her briefcase.

Nonfiction: Biography, reference and scholarly. Subjects include history, music, politics, criminal justice, literary criticism, women's studies, New England regional and scholarly material. "We are looking for scholarly works of high quality, particularly in the fields of American history, criminal justice, literary criticism, French literature, music and women's studies. Our books are read by scholars, students, and a limited trade audience." Submit outline/synopsis and 2-3 sample chapters. Reviews artwork/photos as part of ms package.
Recent Nonfiction Title: *Legal Homicide: Death as Punishment in America, 1864-1982*, by William J. Bowers (criminal justice).
Poetry: "We will consider translations, particularly of French poetry." Submit complete ms.
Recent Poetry Title: *Renard the Fox*, by Patricia Terry (translation from the Old French).

NORTHERN ILLINOIS UNIVERSITY PRESS, DeKalb IL 60115. (815)753-1826. Director: M.L. Livingston. Pays 10-15% royalty on wholesale price. SASE. Free catalog.
Nonfiction: "The NIU Press publishes mainly history, literary criticism and regional studies. It does not consider collections of previously published articles, essays, etc., nor do we consider unsolicited poetry." Accepts nonfiction translations. Query with outline/synopsis and 1-3 sample chapters.

*NORTHLAND PRESS, Box N, Flagstaff AZ 86002. (602)774-5251. Hardcover and paperback originals (80%) and reprints (20%). Advance varies. Averages 5 titles/year. Subsidy publishes 25% of books. Pays royalty on wholesale or retail price. Transparencies and contact sheet required for photos and/or illustrations to accompany ms. Publishes book an average of 8 months after acceptance. Computer printout submissions acceptable; no dot-matrix. Simultaneous and photocopied submissions OK. Reports in 6-8 weeks. SASE. Free book catalog.
Nonfiction: Publishes western Americana, Indian arts and culture, Southwestern natural history and fine photography with a western orientation. Query. "Submit a proposal including an outline of the book, a sample chapter, the introduction or preface and sample illustrations. Include an inventory of items sent." Looks for "clearly developed treatment of subject; tightly constructed presentation; an outline of author's background; pertinent research reference. Author should include assessment of intended audience (potential buyers and market) and other books published on same subject matter."
Recent Nonfiction Title: *CO Bar: Bill Owen Depicts the Historic Babbitt Ranch*, by Marshall Tiemble.

‡NORTHWOODS PRESS, Box 88, Thomaston ME 04861. (207)354-6550. Editor-in-Chief: R.W. Olmsted. Publishes hardcover and trade paperback originals. Averages 30 titles/year. Pays 10% royalty on amount received by publisher. Offers no advance. Simultaneous submissions OK; photocopied submissions on plain bond only. Electronic submissions OK if compatible with Compugraphic Editwriter, Sanyo computer or TI 99/HA. Computer printout submissions acceptable. SASE. Reports in 3 weeks. Book catalog for 6x9 SAE and 1 first class stamp.
Nonfiction: Biography, cookbook, and how-to. Subjects include Americana, cooking and foods, history, hobbies, nature, philosophy, politics, psychology, recreation, sociology and travel. "We consider anything but pornographic and evangelical material."
Recent Nonfiction Title: *Appalachian Trail: History, Humanity and Ecology*, by Robert A. Browne (hiking trip). Submit complete ms.
Poetry: Good, serious work. No "Edgar A. Guest type poetry, no versy stuff that rhymes—no 'typewriter' poetry."
Recent Poetry Title: *Sleeping Through Seasons*, by Stuart Bartow Jr.

W.W. NORTON CO., INC., 500 5th Ave., New York NY 10110. (212)354-5500. Managing Editor: Sterling Lawrence. Royalty varies on retail price; advance varies. Publishes 213 titles/year. Photocopied and simultaneous submissions OK. Computer printout submissions acceptable. Submit outline and/or 2-3 sample chapters for fiction and nonfiction. Return of material not guaranteed without SASE. Reports in 4 weeks.
Nonfiction and Fiction: "General, adult fiction and nonfiction of all kinds on nearly all subjects and of the highest quality possible within the limits of each particular book." Last year there were 56 book club rights sales; 30 mass paperback reprint sales; "innumerable serializations, second serial, syndication, translations, etc." Looks for "clear, intelligent, creative writing on original subjects or with original characters."
Recent Nonfiction Title: *The Minimal Self: A Psychic Survival in Troubled Times*, by Christopher Lash.
Recent Fiction Title: *Under the Lake*, by Stewart Woods.
Tips: "Long novels are too expensive—keep them under 350 pages (manuscript pages)."

NOYES DATA CORP., (including Noyes Press and Noyes Publications), Noyes Bldg., Park Ridge NJ 07656. Publishes hardcover originals. Averages 60 titles/year. Pays 10%-12% royalty on retail price; advance varies, depending on author's reputation and nature of book. Free book catalog. Query Editorial Department. Reports in 1-2 weeks. Enclose return postage.
Nonfiction: (Noyes Press) "Art, classical studies, archeology, and history. Material directed to the intelligent adult and the academic market." Technical: (Noyes Publications) Publishes practical industrial processing sci-

ence; technical, economic books pertaining to chemistry, chemical engineering, food, textile, energy, electronics, pollution control—primarily those of interest to the business executive. Length: 50,000-250,000 words.

NURSECO, INC., Box 145, Pacific Palisades CA 90272. (213)454-6597. Publisher: Margo Neal. Publishes hardcover and trade paperback originals and textbooks. Averages 15 titles/year. Pays 6% minimum royalty; offers negotiable advance. Simultaneous and photocopied submissions OK. SASE. Reports in 2 months. Free book catalog.
Nonfiction: Reference on nursing. Resources for working nurses. No medical mss. Submit outline/synopsis.
Recent Nonfiction Title: *Nursing Care Planning Guide 1-6*, by Margo Neal.

OAK TREE PUBLICATIONS, INC., 9601 Aero Dr., San Diego CA 92123. (619)560-5163. Editorial Assistant: Modeste Williams. Publishes hardcover and paperback originals. Averages 15-25 titles/year. Offers variable advance. SASE. Reports in 2 months.
Nonfiction: Adult books on current social, adult, and parenting concerns; juvenile nonfiction (7-11): books that inform in entertaining format. Unique craft, activity, science, and aid-in-development (i.e., parent participation) books.
Recent Nonfiction Title: *What You Think of Me Is None of My Business*, by Rev. T. Cole-Whittaker.
Fiction: Educational and informational children's books.
Recent Fiction Title: *Where the Deer and the Cantaloupe Play*, by T. Ernesto Bethancourt.

OCCUPATIONAL AWARENESS, Box 948, Los Alamitos CA 90720. Editor-in-Chief: Edith Ericksen. Publishes originals and software. Averages 10 titles/year. Offers standard contract. Average advance $1,500. Publishes book an average of 1 year after acceptance. Photocopied submissions OK. Electronic submissions OK, but requires hard copy also. Computer printout submissions acceptable. Submit outline and 3 sample chapters for professional books and textbooks. SASE.
Nonfiction: Materials on behavior/adjustment (no TA), textbooks, workbooks, kits, career guidance, relating careers to curricula, special education, tests. Reviews artwork/photos as part of ms package.
Software: Publishes career, special education, and subject area programs (supplementary).

OCTAMERON ASSOCIATES, 820 Fontaine St., Alexandria VA 22302. (703)836-1019. Editorial Director: Karen Stokstad. Publishes trade paperback originals. Averages 10 titles/year. Pays 10-15% royalty on wholesale price. Publishes book an average of 2 months after acceptance. Simultaneous submissions OK. SASE. Computer printout submissions acceptable; no dot-matrix. Reports in 1 week. Free book catalog.
Nonfiction: Reference and self-help, post-secondary education subjects. Especially interested in "paying-for-college and college admission guides." Does not want books unrelated to postsecondary education. Query. Accepts outline/synopsis and 2 sample chapters.
Recent Nonfiction Title: *How We Do It*, by Ed Wall.

OCTOBER PRESS, INC., 200 Park Ave. S., Suite 1320, New York NY 10003. (212)477-1251. President: Mark Iocolano. Book and software producer, co-publishing programs. "Currently, October Press is developing several business and technical books for photographers, designers, and other users of photography." Pays variable rate, depending upon project. Publishes book an average of 6 months after acceptance. Query first. "We cannot handle unsolicited proposals." Electronic submissions OK; requirements to be arranged, but requires hard copy also. Computer printout submissions acceptable; prefers letter-quality to dot-matrix. Reports in 3 weeks.
Nonfiction: How-to, illustrated book, juvenile, technical on hobbies, photography, professional handbooks.
Software: Contact Mark Iocolano.

ODDO PUBLISHING, INC., Box 68, Beauregard Blvd., Fayetteville GA 30214. (404)461-7627. Managing Editor: Genevieve Oddo. Publishes hardcover and paperback originals. Scripts are usually purchased outright. "We judge all scripts independently." Royalty considered for special scripts only. Send complete ms, typed clearly. Publishes book an average of 2 years after acceptance. Computer printout submissions acceptable; prefers letter-quality to dot-matrix. Reports in 3-4 months. Book catalog 50¢. "Ms will not be returned without SASE."
Nonfiction: Publishes juvenile books in language arts, workbooks in math, writing (English), photophonics, science (space and oceanography), and social studies for schools, libraries, and trade. Interested in children's supplementary readers in the areas of language arts, math, science, social studies, etc. "Texts run from 1,500 to 3,500 words. Ecology, space, oceanography and pollution are subjects of interest. Books on patriotism. Ms must be easy to read, general, and not set to outdated themes. It must lend itself to full color illustration. Reviews artwork/photos as part of ms package. No stories of grandmother long ago. No love angle, permissive language, or immoral words or statements."
Recent Nonfiction Title: *Bobby Bear Meets Cousin Boo*.

OHARA PUBLICATIONS, INC., 1813 Victory Place, Box 7728, Burbank CA 91510-7728. Contact: Editor. Publishes trade paperback originals. Averages 12 titles/year. Pays royalty. Photocopied submissions OK. SASE. Write for guidelines. Reports in 3 weeks on queries; 6 weeks on mss. Free book catalog.
Nonfiction: Martial arts. "We decide to do a book on a specific martial art, then seek out the most qualified martial artist to author that book. 'How to' books are our mainstay, and we will accept no ms that does not pertain to martial arts systems (their history, techniques, philosophy, etc.)" Query first, then submit outline/synopsis and sample chapter.
Recent Nonfiction Title: *Championship Kenpo*, by Steve Sanders and Donnie Williams.

OHIO STATE UNIVERSITY PRESS, 1050 Carmack Rd., Columbus OH 43210. (614)422-6930. Director: Weldon A. Kefauver. Pays royalty on wholesale or retail price. Averages 20 titles/year. Query letter preferred with outline and sample chapters. Reports in 2 months. Ms held longer with author's permission. Enclose return postage.
Nonfiction: Publishes history, biography, science, philosophy, the arts, political science, law, literature, economics, education, sociology, anthropology, geography, and general scholarly nonfiction. No length limitations.

*OHIO UNIVERSITY PRESS, Scott Quad, Ohio University, Athens OH 45701. (614)594-5505. Imprints include *Ohio University Press* and *Swallow Press*. Director: Patricia Elisar. Associate Director: Holly Panich. Publishes hardcover and paperback originals (97%) and reprints (3%). Averages 40-45 titles/year. Subsidy publishes 6% of titles, based on projected market. Pays in royalties starting at 1,500 copies based on wholesale or retail price. No advance. Photocopied submissions OK. Reports in 3-5 months. SASE. Free book catalog.
Nonfiction: "General scholarly nonfiction with particular emphasis on 19th century literature and culture. Also history, social sciences, philosophy, business, western regional works and miscellaneous categories." Query.
Recent Nonfiction Title: *The Wilson Sisters-A Biographical Study of Upper Middle Class Victorian Life*, by Martha Westwater.

101 PRODUCTIONS, 834 Mission St., San Francisco CA 94103. (415)495-6040. Editor-in-Chief: Jacqueline Killeen. Publishes paperback originals. Offers standard minimum book contract on retail prices. Averages 12 titles/year. Free book catalog. Publishes book an average of 1 year after acceptance. Photocopied submissions OK. "We are equipped to edit and typeset from electronic disks, providing the software is compatible with Wordstar"; requires hard copy also. Computer printout submissions acceptable. Query. No unsolicited mss will be read. SASE.
Nonfiction: All nonfiction, mostly how-to: cookbooks, the home, gardening, outdoors, and travel. Heavy emphasis on graphics and illustrations. Reviews artwork/photos as part of ms package. Most books are 192 pages.
Recent Nonfiction Title: *Cook's Marketplace, New York*, by Irene Sax.

OPEN COURT PUBLISHING CO., Box 599, LaSalle IL 61301. Publisher: M. Blouke Carus. Textbook General Manager: James S. Heywood. Director, General Books: Dr. Andre Carus. Averages 5-10 titles/year. Royalty contracts negotiable for each book. Computer printout submissions acceptable; prefers letter-quality to dot-matrix. Query. Accepts outline/synopsis and 2-3 sample chapters. Enclose return postage.
Nonfiction: Philosophy, psychology, mathematics, comparative religion, education, chemistry, orientalia, and related scholarly topics. Accepts nonfiction translations from German and French. "This is a publishing house run as an intellectual enterprise, to reflect the concerns of its staff and as a service to the world of learning." Reviews artwork/photos as part of ms package.
Recent Nonfiction Title: *The Inward Journey: Art As Therapy*, by Margaret Frings Keyes (psychology).

OPTIMUM PUBLISHING INTERNATIONAL INC., 2335 Sherbrooke St., West Montreal, Quebec H3H 1G6 Canada. (514)932-0666 or 932-0776. Managing Director and Editor-in-Chief: Michael S. Baxendale. Hardcover and paperback originals and reprints. Averages 21 titles/year. Publishes in both official Canadian languages (English and French). Query or submit outline/synopsis and sample chapters. Photocopied submissions OK. Reports in 4-6 weeks. SAE and IRCs.
Nonfiction: Biography; cookbooks, cooking and foods; gardening; history; natural history; how-to; health; nature; crafts; photography; art; self-help; crime; sports; and travel books.
Recent Nonfiction Title: *Creative Parenting*, by William Sears.

ORBIS BOOKS, Maryknoll NY 10545. (914)941-7590. Editor: Philip Scharper. Publishes paperback originals. Publishes 30 titles/year. 7-8½-10% royalty on retail prices; advance averages $1,000. Query with outline, 2 sample chapters, and prospectus. Disk submissions OK. Reports in 4 to 6 weeks. Enclose return postage.
Nonfiction: "Religious developments in Asia, Africa and Latin America. Christian missions. Justice and peace. Christianity and world religions."
Recent Nonfiction Title: *The Power of the Poor in History*, by Gustavo Gutierrez.

OREGON STATE UNIVERSITY PRESS, 101 Waldo Hall, Corvallis OR 97331. (503)754-3166. Hardcover and paperback originals. Averages 5-10 titles/year. Pays royalty on wholesale price. No advance. Submit contact sheet of photos and/or illustrations to accompany ms. Publishes book an average of 9 months after acceptance. Computer printout submissions acceptable; no dot-matrix. SASE. Reports in 4 months. Free book catalog for SASE.
Nonfiction: Publishes Americana, biography, economics, history, nature, philosophy, energy and recreation, reference, scientific (biological sciences only), technical (energy), and American literary criticism books. Emphasis on Pacific or Northwestern topics. Submit outline/synopsis and sample chapters. Reviews artwork/photos as part of ms package.
Recent Nonfiction Title: *Contemporary Northwest Writing*, by R. Carlson (anthology).

ORYX PRESS, 2214 N. Central Ave., Phoenix AZ 85004. (602)254-6156. President/Editorial Director: Phyllis B. Steckler. Publishes hardcover and paperback originals. Averages 35 titles/year. Pays 10-15% royalty on net receipts; no advance. Publishes book an average of 6 months after acceptance. Electronic submissions OK, but requires hard copy also. Computer printout submissions acceptable; prefers letter-quality to dot-matrix. SASE. Reports in 8 weeks. Queries/mss may be routed to other editors in the publishing group. Free book catalog.
Nonfiction: Bibliographies, directories, education, general reference, library and information science, and agriculture monographs. Publishes nonfiction for public, college and university, junior college and special libraries; education faculty members; agriculture specialists. Reviews artwork/photos as part of ms package. Query or submit outline/synopsis and 1 sample chapter, or complete ms.
Recent Nonfiction Title: *Evolution vs Creationism: The Public Education Controversy*, ed. by Zetterberg (resource for teachers and librarians).

‡OSBORNE/MCGRAW-HILL, Division of McGraw-Hill, Inc., 2600 10th St., Berkeley CA 94710. (415)548-2805. Editor-in-Chief: Judith Ziajka. Publishes trade paperback originals. Pays royalty on wholesale price. Publishes book an average of 5 months after acceptance. Electronic submissions OK, but requires hard copy also. Computer printout submissions acceptable. SASE. Reports in 1 week on queries; 2-3 weeks on mss. Free book catalog.
Nonfiction: Technical. "We are interested in books about popular microcomputer hardware and software, especially those written for beginning users." Submit outline/synopsis and sample chapters.
Recent Nonfiction Title: *Apple II User Guide*, by Lon Poole (technical).
Tips: "We envision home and business users of microcomputers, programmers and aspiring programmers as our audience."

OTTENHEIMER PUBLISHERS, INC., 300 Reisterstown Rd., Baltimore MD 21208. (301)484-2100. President: Allen T. Hirsh Jr. Managing Editor: Emmeline Kroiz. Publishes hardcover and paperback originals. Publishes 250 titles/year. Negotiates royalty and advance. Photocopied submissions OK. Reports in 1 month.
Nonfiction: Cookbooks, reference, gardening, home repair and decorating, automotive and medical for the layperson. Submit outline/synopsis and sample chapters or complete ms.

OUR SUNDAY VISITOR, INC., 200 Noll Plaza, Huntington IN 46750. (219)356-8400. Managing Editor: Robert Lockwood. Publishes paperback originals and reprints. Pays variable royalty on net receipts; offers average $500 advance. Averages 20-30 titles a year. Reports in 1 month on most queries and submissions. SASE. Free author's guide and catalog.
Nonfiction: Catholic viewpoints on current issues, reference and guidance, Bibles and devotional books, and Catholic heritage books. Prefers to see well-developed proposals as first submission with "annotated outline, three sample chapters, definition of intended market."
Recent Nonfiction Title: *Strange Gods: Contemporary Religious Cults in America*, by William Whalen.

OUTBOOKS INC., 217 Kimball Ave., Golden CO 80401. Contact: William R. Jones. Publishes trade paperback originals and reprints. Averages 10 titles/year. Pays 5% royalty on retail price. Computer printout submissions acceptable; no dot-matrix. SASE. Reports in 1 month on queries; 2 months on mss. Free book catalog "as available."
Nonfiction: Cookbook, how-to, regional books on Americana, animals, cooking and foods, history, hobbies, nature, photography, recreation, sports, and travel. Reviews artwork/photos as part of ms package. Publishes for "lay enthusiasts in American history, outdoors, and natural history, ecology, and conservation." Query.
Recent Nonfiction Title: *Evidence and the Custer Enigma*, by Jerome A. Greene.

*OUTDOOR EMPIRE PUBLISHING, INC., Box C-19000, Seattle WA 98109. Associate Publisher: Fay Ainsworth. Publishes trade paperback originals (25%) and reprints (75%). Averages 25 titles/year. Subsidy publishes 50% of books based on market potential of subject. Buys some mss outright for $500, or by special contract depending upon project. Publishes book an average of 3 months after acceptance. Computer printout submissions acceptable "if good quality." SASE. Reports in 1 month. Book catalog for business size SAE and 1 first class stamp.

Nonfiction: How-to, self-help, textbook, and workbook-texts on recreation and sports for ages 10 through adult. "Contemporary how-to treatment of various subjects in the areas of outdoor recreation: boating, fishing, hunting, camping, bicycling, mopeds, 4-wheel drives, survival, and emergency preparedness." No mss on professional team sports, or outdoor travel journals. Reviews artwork/photos as part of ms package. Query or submit outline/synopsis and sample chapters or complete ms.

Recent Nonfiction Title: *Better Boating—A Guide to Safety Afloat.*

OUTDOOR LIFE BOOKS, Book Division, Times Mirror Magazines (subsidiary of Times Mirror Co.), 380 Madison Ave., New York NY 10017. Editor: John Sill. Publishes books for Outdoor Life Book Club that are also distributed by major trade publishers. Pays royalty and advance relative to book list price. SASE.

Nonfiction: Guides on hunting, fishing, firearms, outdoor lore, and wildlife—all of broad appeal to national sportsman audience. Submit author resume, outline, sample chapters, and sample illustrations for heavily illustrated small books to 35,000 words and large books to 150,000 words. Looks for "either a description of each chapter's contents or a subject-by-subject breakout. Sample rough drawings and photographs: either color transparencies, any size or 8x10 b&w glossies."

‡THE OVERLOOK PRESS, Distributed by Viking/Penguin, 12 W. 21st St., New York NY 10010. (212)807-7300. Editor-in-Chief: Mark Gompertz. Imprints include Tusk Books. Publishes hardcover and trade paperback originals and hardcover reprints. Averages 25 titles/year. Pays 3-15% royalty on wholesale or retail price. Simultaneous and photocopied submissions OK. SASE. Reports in 2 months on queries; 3 months on mss. Free book catalog.

Nonfiction: "Coffee table" book, cookbook, how-to, humor (serious), illustrated book, juvenile, reference, self-help, and technical. Subjects include Americana, animals, art, business and economics, cooking and foods, health, history, hobbies, music, nature, philosophy, photography, politics, psychology, recreation, religion, sociology, sports, and travel. No pornography. Query or submit outline/synopsis and sample chapters. Reviews artwork/photos as part of ms package.

Recent Nonfiction Title: *Cradle of Mankind*, by Mohamed Amin (photography).

Fiction: Adventure, confession, erotica, ethnic, experimental, fantasy/science fiction, historical, mainstream, mystery/suspense. "We tend not to publish commercial fiction." Submit outline/synopsis and sample chapters.

Recent Fiction Title: *The Radetzsky March*, by Joseph Roth (historical fiction).

Poetry: "We like to publish poets who have a strong following—those who read in New York City regularly or publish in periodicals regularly." No poetry from unpublished authors. Submit complete ms.

Recent Poetry Title: *To an Idea*, by David Shapiro.

Tips: "We are a very small company that will never publish more than 15-25 books each year. If authors want a very quick decision, they should go to another company first and come back to us. We try to be as prompt as possible, but it sometimes takes over 3 months for us to get to a final decision."

OXFORD UNIVERSITY PRESS, INC., 200 Madison Ave., New York NY 10016. (212)679-7300. Publishes hardcover originals and paperback reprints. Publishes over 100 titles/year. Pays standard royalty; offers variable advance. Photocopied submissions OK. SASE. Free book catalog.

Nonfiction: American history, music, political science, and reference books. Submit outline/synopsis and sample chapters.

Recent Nonfiction Title: *Franklin D. Roosevelt and American Foreign Policy* (political history).

OXMOOR HOUSE, (Division of The Southern Progress Corp.), Box 2262, Birmingham AL 35201. Editor-in-Chief: John Logue. Vice President/General Manager: Tom Angelillo. Publishes hardcover and paperback originals. Pays on royalty basis or fee. Averages 13 titles/year. Submit outline and sample chapter. Reports in 1 month. SASE.

Nonfiction: "Publishes books of general interest to Southern readers—cookbooks, garden books, books on crafts, sewing, photography, art, outdoors, antiques and how-to topics.

Recent Nonfiction Title: *The Southern Heritage Cookbook Library.*

‡P.P.I. PUBLISHING, 7016 Corporate Way, Box 335, Dayton OH 45459. (513)433-2709. Vice President: Kim Brooks. Publishes mass market paperback originals. Averages 30-50 titles/year. Pays 10% on invoice amount with or without discount or as actual selling price (average $3.29). Publishes book an average of 3 months after acceptance. Computer printout submissions acceptable; no dot-matrix. Reports in 2 weeks on queries; 12 weeks on mss. Free book catalog with writer's guidelines.

Nonfiction: How-to (small percentage), juvenile, and self-help. Subjects include health. Especially looking for "items of controversy, current events, items in the news, items dealing with children and teens, some health issues, but not very technical items." No how-to items on the above topics. No autobiographies, no historical material. "We will give some outside topics an editorial review." Query or submit complete ms of 13,000-15,000 words. Reviews artwork/photos as part of ms package.

Recent Nonfiction Title: *Childhood and Teen Suicide*, by Laura Deni.

Tips: "If I were a writer trying to market a book today, I would aim for current events—what the junior or senior high school student wants to know along with the library patron. Concentrate on what's wrong in society, world events, health problems and trends, teen problems, issues facing society today."

THE PAGURIAN CORPORATION LIMITED, 13 Hazelton Ave., Toronto, Ontario M5R 2E1 Canada. (416)968-0255. Editor-in-Chief: Christopher Ondaatje. Publishes paperback and hardcover originals and reprints. Offers negotiable royalty contract. Advance negotiable. Averages 2 titles/year. Publishes book an average of 6 months after acceptance. Photocopied submissions OK. Computer printout submissions acceptable; prefers letter-quality to dot-matrix. Submit 2-page outline, synopsis or chapter headings and contents. Reports "immediately." SAE and IRC.

Nonfiction: Publishes general interest trade and art books. Will consider fine arts, outdoor and cookbooks. Length: 40,000-70,000 words. Reviews artwork/photos as part of ms package.

Tips: "We are publishing *fewer* books, and all are Canadian art or art history themes."

PALADIN PRESS, Box 1307, Boulder CO 80306. (303)443-7250. President/Publisher: Peder C. Lund. General Manager: Kim R. Hood. Editorial Director: Virginia Thomas. Publishes hardcover and paperback originals (80%) and paperback reprints (20%). Averages 22 titles/year. Pays 10-12-15% royalty on net sales. Publishes book an average of 1 year after acceptance. Simultaneous and photocopied submissions OK. Computer printout submissions acceptable. Reports in 1 month. SASE. Free book catalog.

Nonfiction: "Paladin Press primarily publishes original manuscripts on military science, weaponry, self-defense, the martial arts, survival, police science, guerrilla warfare and fieldcraft, and within the last two years, humor. How-to manuscripts, as well as pictorial histories, are given priority. Manuals on building weapons, when technically accurate and cleanly presented, are encouraged. If applicable, send sample photographs and line drawings with outline and sample chapters." Query or submit outline/synopsis and sample chapters. Reviews artwork/photos as part of ms package.

Recent Nonfiction Title: *Fallout Survival, A Guide to Radiological Defense*, by Bruce Clayton.

Tips: "We need concise, instructive material aimed at our market and accompanied by sharp, relevant illustrations and photos."

‡*PANJANDRUM BOOKS, Suite 1, 11321 Iowa Ave., Los Angeles CA 90025. (213)477-8771. Subsidiaries include Panjandrum Books Inc. Editor and Publisher: Dennis Koran. Publishes hardcover and trade paperback originals. Averages 4-5 titles/year. Subsidy publishes 20% of books (National Endowment for the Arts). Computer printout submissions acceptable. SASE. Reports in 2 weeks on queries; 2 months on mss. Book catalog for 7x10 SAE and 2 first class stamps.

Nonfiction: Biography, cookbook, how-to, juvenile, reference, and self-help. Subjects include cooking and foods, health, history, hobbies, music, philosophy, recreation, theater and drama, herbs, vegetarianism, and childhood sexuality. "We're looking for mss of cookbooks, health books, music (how-to), drama (how-to), and critical/history, and are open to queries on other subjects." No religious or humorous material. Query or submit outline/synopsis and sample chapters.

Recent Nonfiction Title: *Four Seasons Cookbook*, by Gershen (cookbook written in calligraphy).

Fiction: Avant-garde, experimental, fantasy, gothic (not romance), and translations of European literature (not previously translated into English). Query with sample chapter.

Recent Fiction Title: *Fighting Men*, by Manus (post-Vietnam novel).

Poetry: Submit 5 poems.

Recent Poetry Title: *Visions of the Fathers of Lascaux*, by Eshleman.

PANTHEON BOOKS, Division of Random House, Inc., 201 E. 50th St., New York NY 10022. Managing Editor: Betsy Amster. Published more than 90 titles last year. Publishes book an average of 1 year (longer if ms not written/completed when contract is signed). Pays royalty on retail price. Address queries to Don Guttenplan, Adult Editorial Department (15th Floor). Computer printout submissions acceptable; prefers letter-quality to dot-matrix. Enclose return postage.

Nonfiction: Emphasis on Asia, international politics, radical social theory, history, medicine, women's studies, and law. Recreational guides and practical how-to books as well. Query letters only. No manuscripts accepted. Publishes some juveniles. Address queries to Juvenile Editorial Department (6th floor).

Recent Nonfiction Title: *Secrets*, by Sissela Bok.

Fiction: Publishes fewer than 5 novels each year, primarily mysteries. Queries on fiction not accepted.

Tips: Queries/mss may be routed to other editors in the publishing group.

PARADOX PUBLISHING CO., 2476 Buttonwood Court, Florissant MO 63031. (314)838-0241. Subsidiary of Paradox Enterprises, Inc. Senior Editor: Curt Scarborough. Publishes hardcover and trade paperback originals. Averages 12 titles/year. No advance. Publishes book an average of 1 year after acceptance. Computer printout submissions acceptable. SASE. Reports in 2 weeks on queries; 1 month on mss.

Nonfiction: How-to and self-help on health, philosophy, psychology, religion, and sociology. "We specialize in Christian how-to books—self-help, ethics, psychology, etc. Looking for promising how-to books for paperback line: 64-page books; approximately 20,000 words. Also interested in original ideas for full-length hardback books." Query. Reviews artwork/photos as part of ms package.

PARENTS MAGAZINE PRESS, A division of Parents Magazine Enterprises, Inc., 685 3rd Ave., New York NY 10017. (212)878-8612. Editorial Director: Stephanie Calmenson. Publishes hardcover originals. Averages 14 titles/year. Pays flat fee for Parents book club edition; royalty for trade and library editions which are distributed by E.P. Dutton. Computer printout submissions acceptable. SASE. Reports in 6-8 weeks.

Nonfiction: "We are not doing any nonfiction at this time."

Fiction: "We are publishing only easy-to-read, full color picture books for children 2-7. Average text/art pages about 38, in a 48-page self-ended book. Approximately 400-600 words. Emphasis is on humor, action, and child appeal. No message stories." Submit complete ms. Reviews artwork/photos as part of ms package.

Recent Title: *Cats! Cats! Cats!*, by Bernard Wiseman.

PARKER PUBLISHING CO., West Nyack NY 10994. Publishes hardcover originals and paperback reprints. Pays 10% royalty; 5% mail order and book clubs. Publishes 85 titles/year. Will send catalog on request. Reports in 3-5 weeks.

Nonfiction: Publishes practical, self-help, and how-to books. Subject areas include popular health, letterwriting, electronics, education, secretarial, selling, and personal and business self-improvement. Length: 65,000 words.

Recent Nonfiction Title: *The Complete Secretary's Handbook*, by Lillian Doris and Besse Mae Miller and revised by Mary DeVries.

PAULIST PRESS, 545 Island Road, Ramsey, NJ 07446. (201)825-7300. Publisher: Rev. Kevin A. Lynch. Managing Editor: Donald Brophy. Publishes hardcover and paperback originals (90%) and paperback reprints (10%). Averages 100 titles/year. Pays royalty on retail price; sometimes an advance. Photocopied submissions OK. SASE. Reports in 4 weeks.

Nonfiction: Philosophy, religion, self-help, and textbooks (religious subject). Accepts nonfiction translations from German, French and Spanish. "We would like to see theology (Catholic and ecumenical Christian), popular spirituality, liturgy, and religious education texts." Submit outline/synopsis and 2 sample chapters.

Recent Nonfiction Title: *The Churches the Apostles Left Behind*, by Raymond Brown.

‡**PEACHTREE PUBLISHERS, LTD.**, 494 Armour Circle NE, Atlanta GA 30324. (404)299-2610. Executive Editor: Chuck Perry. Publishes hardcover and trade paperback originals. Averages 12-15 titles/year. Publishes book an average of 1 year after acceptance. Computer printout submissions acceptable. Reports in 1 week on queries; 3 months on mss. Free book catalog.

Nonfiction: Cookbook and humor. Subjects include cooking and foods, history, recreation and religion. No business, technical, reference, art and photography, juvenile or animals. Submit outline/synopsis and sample chapters.

Recent Nonfiction Title: *If Love Were Oil, I'd Be About a Quart Low*, by Lewis Grizzard (humor).

Fiction: Historical, humor and mainstream. "We are particularly interested in fiction with a Southern angle." No fantasy, juvenile, science fiction or romance. Submit outline/synopsis and sample chapters.

Recent Fiction Title: *Run with the Horsemen*, by Ferrol Sams (general fiction).

‡**PEGASUS PRESS**, Subsidiary of Pegasus Publishers, Inc., Box 1350, Vashon WA 98070. (206)567-5224. Chief Editor: J.H. Raymond. Publishes hardcover and trade paperback originals. Averages 8-10 titles/year. Pays 7½-15% royalty on retail price. Offers average $1,500 advance. Simultaneous and photocopied submissions OK. SASE. Reports in 2 weeks on queries; 1 month on mss. Free book catalog.

Nonfiction: Biography, how-to, reference and self-help. Subjects include biography, autobiography and bibliography related to authors, publishing and book collecting. Query, or submit outline/synopsis and sample chapters or complete ms.

Recent Nonfiction Title: *International Book Collectors Directory*, by J.H. Raymond (reference directory).

Tips: "We have three major markets: libraries, book collectors and booksellers."

****PELICAN PUBLISHING CO., INC.**, 1101 Monroe St., Box 189, Gretna LA 70053. (504)368-1175. Imprints include Pelican Publishing House, Dixie Press, Friends of the Cabildo, and Jackson Square Press. Editor-in-Chief: James Calhoun. Editor: Karen Trahan. Publishes hardcover and paperback originals (90%) and reprints (10%). Publishes 50-75 titles/year. Subsidy publishes 4% of books. Pays 10-15% royalty on wholesale price; sometimes offers advance. "Please send us a photocopy and retain the original. Exclusive submissions preferred. SASE if ms to be returned; otherwise it will be discarded if not accepted. Electronic submissions

OK, but requires hard copy also. Computer printout submissions acceptable; no dot-matrix. Reports in 3 months. While we will use care, we accept no responsibility for unsolicited manuscripts."
Nonfiction: Art; cookbooks/cooking; self-help (especially motivational); inspirational; and travel (guidebooks). Accepts nonfiction translations. Submit outline/synopsis and sample chapters. "We look for clarity and conciseness of expression and presentation in a synopsis/outline, and we ask to see those that will most likely yield proposals that will fit our list and that we feel we can market successfully. We look for completed manuscripts that are well written and will require little editing, that contain subject matter that is in line with our publishing program." Reviews artwork/photos as part of ms package.
Recent Nonfiction Title: *Dear Family*, by Zig Ziglar.
Fiction: Novels. "We are actively seeking well-written fiction."
Recent Fiction Title: *Henry Hamilton, Graduate Ghost*, by Marilyn Redmond (juvenile/adult fiction).

THE PENNSYLVANIA STATE UNIVERSITY PRESS, 215 Wagner Bldg., University Park PA 16802. (814)865-1327. Editor-in-Chief: Jack Pickering. Hardcover and paperback originals. Specializes in books of scholarly value, and/or regional interest. Averages 40 titles/year. Pays 10% royalty on wholesale price; no advance. Maintains own distribution company in England which serves the British Empire, Europe, etc. Submit outline/synopsis and 2 sample chapters plus endorsement by a scholar at a university or research institution. Publishes book an average of 8 months after acceptance. Electronic submissions OK, but requires hard copy also. Computer printout submissions acceptable; prefers letter-quality to dot-matrix. Reports in 2-4 months. SASE. Free book catalog.
Nonfiction: Publishes scholarly books on agriculture, art, business, economics, history, medicine and psychiatry, music, nature, philosophy, politics, psychology, religions, science, sociology, technology, women's studies, black studies, and *Keystone Books* (a paperback series concentrating on topics of special interest to those living in the mid-Atlantic states.) Accepts nonfiction translations. Reviews artwork/photos as part of ms package. Looks for "content and form acceptable to scholars (as attested by a recognized scholar)."
Recent Nonfiction Title: *Rivers of Pennsylvania*, by T. Palmer (nature, conservation, history).

PENNWELL BOOKS, Box 1260, Tulsa OK 74101. (918)663-4220. Acquisitions Editor: Kathryn Pile. Publishes hardcover originals on petroleum/energy. Averages 30 titles/year. Pays 10-15% royalty on net receipts. No advance. SASE. Reports in 1 week on queries; 2 weeks on mss. Free book catalog.
Nonfiction: Technical books on petroleum engineering, dental practice management, computer technology and laser technology. No "novel, alternative energy (solar, hydrogen) or fiction with an oilfield topic." Submit outline/synopsis and sample chapters.

***PEREGRINE SMITH BOOKS**, Box 667, Layton UT 84041. (801)544-9800. Editorial Director: Buckley C. Jeppson. Publishes hardcover and paperback originals (80%) and reprints (20%). Subsidy publishes 10% of books. Pays 10% royalty on wholesale price; no advance. Publishes book an average of 1 year after acceptance. Photocopied submissions OK. Computer printout submissions acceptable; no dot-matrix. Reports in 3 months. SASE. Book catalog 37¢.
Nonfiction: "Western American history, natural history, American architecture, art history and fine arts. We consider biographical, historical, descriptive and analytical studies in all of the above. Much emphasis is also placed on pictorial content. Many of our books are used as university texts." Query or submit outline/synopsis and 2 sample chapters. Reviews artwork/photos as part of ms package. Accepts nonfiction translations from French. Consult *Chicago Manual of Style*.
Recent Nonfiction Title: *Spectacular Vernacular*, by J. Bourgeois.
Fiction: "We mainly publish reprints or anthologies of American writers." Query or submit outline/synopsis and 2 sample chapters. "No unsolicited manuscripts accepted. Query first." Looks for "style, readable, intelligent, careful writing. Must be geared to a competitive commercial market." Accepts fiction translations from French.
Tips: "Write seriously. If fiction, no potboilers, bestseller movie tie-in type hype books and no science fiction. We like Pynchon and Gaddis. If nonfiction, only serious, well-researched critical, historical or craft-related topics."

THE PERFECTION FORM CO., Suite 15, 8350 Hickman Rd., Des Moines IA 50322. (515)278-0133. Editor: M. Kathleen Myers. Publishes paperback originals for sale in secondary schools and software. Publishes 10 titles/year. Pays royalty; offers small advance on publication. Publishes book an average of 2 years after acceptance. Computer printout submissions acceptable. SASE. Reports in 12 weeks. Free book catalog.
Fiction: Original mss of approximately 20,000-30,000 words written for young adult audiences ages 12-18. Wholesome, high interest books. Adventure stories, humor, mystery, supernatural, personal conflict and choice, sports, family, courage and endurance. Submit chapter and outline or complete ms.
Software: CAI language arts and social studies.

PERSEA BOOKS, 225 LaFayette St., New York City NY 10012. (212)431-5270. Editorial Director: Karen Braziller. Publisher: Michael Braziller. Publishes hardcover and paperback originals and reprints. Averages 10 titles/year. Pays 6-15% royalty. Offers average $500 advance. Publishes book an average of 2 years after acceptance. Computer printout submissions acceptable; no dot-matrix. SASE. Reports in 2 months.
Nonfiction: Poetry, critical essays and literary criticism. "Authors must send query letters first. If no query letter is sent unsolicited manuscripts will not be considered."
Recent Nonfiction Title: *The Book of the City of Ladies*, by Christine de Pizan.
Fiction: Experimental, historical, and mainstream. Query.
Recent Fiction Title: *A Meditation*, by Juan Benet.

PETERSON'S GUIDES, INC., Box 2123, Princeton NJ 08540. (609)924-5338. Publisher/President: Peter W. Hegener. Editorial Director: Karen C. Hegener. Publishes paperback originals and software. Averages 25 titles/year. Pays 5-10% royalty on net sales; offers advance. Publishes book an average of 1 year after acceptance. Photocopied submissions OK. Computer printout submissions acceptable. Reports in 3 months. Free catalog.
Nonfiction: Educational and career reference and guidance works for professionals, libraries, and trade. Submit complete ms or detailed outline and sample chapters. Looks for "appropriateness of contents to our market, accuracy of information and use of reliable information sources, and writing style suitable for audience." Reviews artwork/photos as part of ms package.
Recent Nonfiction Title: *Athlete's Game Plan for College and Career*, by Howard and Stephen Figler.
Software: Publishes material for the educational/guidance market.

PETROCELLI BOOKS, INC., Research Park, 251 Wall St., Princeton NJ 08540. (609)924-5851. Editorial Director: O.R. Petrocelli. Senior Editor: Rick Batlan. Publishes hardcover and paperback originals. Publishes 20 titles/year. Offers 12½-18% royalties. No advance. Simultaneous and photocopied submissions OK. Computer printout submissions acceptable; prefers letter-quality to dot-matrix. SASE. Reports in 4 weeks. Free book catalog.
Nonfiction: Business/economics, reference, technical, and textbooks. Submit outline/synopsis and 1-2 sample chapters.
Recent Nonfiction Title: *Effective Structured Programming*, by Lem O. Ejiogu.

PHILOMEL BOOKS, Division of The Putnam Publishing Group, 51 Madison Ave., New York NY 10010. (212)689-9200. Editor-in-Chief: Ann Beneduce. Managing Editor: Chandler Varona-Dixon. Editor: Christine Grenz. Publishes quality hardcover originals. Publishes 15-30 titles/year. Pays standard royalty. Advance negotiable. SASE. Reports in 1 month on queries. Free book catalog on request.
Nonfiction: Young adult and children's picture books. Does not want to see alphabet books or workbooks. Query first. Looks for "interesting theme; writing quality; suitability to our market."
Recent Nonfiction Title: *Sight and Seeing: A World of Light and Color*, by Hilda Simon.
Fiction: Young adult and children's book on any topic. Query to Christine Grenz.
Recent Fiction Title: *A Little Love*, by Virginia Hamilton.
Tips: Unsolicited manuscripts will be returned unopened. "We regret this change in procedure; we cannot afford the time required to process manuscripts unless we have authorized their submission in response to a previously submitted query letter."

‡JUDY PIATKUS (PUBLISHER) LTD., 40 Hanway St., London, England WIP 9DE. (01)637-4816. Managing Director: Judy Piatkus. Publishes hardcover and trade paperback originals and hardcover reprints. Averages 80 titles/year. Pays royalty. Offers negotiable advance. Computer printout submissions acceptable; no dot-matrix. Photocopied submissions OK. SAE, IRCs. Reports in 1 week on queries; 2 months on mss. Book catalog $1.
Nonfiction: Cookbook, how-to and self-help. Subjects include cooking and foods, health, hobbies and women's interest. Query.
Recent Nonfiction Title: *Children's Parties*, by Hollest and Gaine (general).
Fiction: Adventure, historical, mainstream and romance. "Any good stories." Submit outline/synopsis and sample chapters.
Recent Fiction Title: *No Time for Tears*, by Cynthia Freeman (general).
Tips: "Our audience is middle of the road, mainly women."

PICKWICK PUBLICATIONS, 4137 Timberlane Dr., Allison Park PA 15101. Editorial Director: Dikran Y. Hadidian. Publishes paperback originals and reprints. Averages 3-6 titles/year. Pays 8-10% royalty on wholesale or retail price; no advance. Publishes book an average of 18 months after acceptance. Photocopied submissions OK. Computer printout submissions acceptable. Reports in 4 months. SASE. Free book catalog.
Nonfiction: Religious and scholarly mss in Biblical archeology, Biblical studies, church history and theology. Also reprints of outstanding out-of-print titles and original texts and translations. Accepts nonfiction transla-

tions from French or German. No popular religious material. Query. Accepts outline/synopsis and 2 sample chapters. Consult *MLA Style Sheet* or Turabian's *A Manual for Writers*.
Recent Nonfiction Title: *Social Concern in Calvin's Geneva*, by William C. Innes.

PILOT BOOKS, 103 Cooper St., Babylon NY 11702. (516)422-2225. Publishes paperback originals. Offers standard royalty contract based on wholesale or retail price. Usual advance is $250, but this varies, depending on author's reputation and nature of book. Averages 20-30 titles/year. Send outline. Publishes book an average of 6 months after acceptance. Computer printout submissions acceptable. Reports in 4 weeks. Enclose return postage.
Nonfiction: "Publishes financial, business, travel, career, personal guides and training manuals. Our training manuals are utilized by America's giant corporations as well as the government." Directories and books on moneymaking opportunities. Wants "clear, concise treatment of subject matter." Length: 8,000-30,000 words. Reviews artwork/photos as part of ms package.
Recent Nonfiction Title: *The Senior Citizen's 10-Minutes-A-Day Fitness Plan*, by Paige Palmer.

*PINE MOUNTAIN PRESS, INC., Box 19746, West Allis WI 53219. (414)778-1120. President: Robert W. Pradt. Aquisitions Editor: Marilyn A. Brilliant. Imprints include: Leatherstocking (frontier history, firearms, outdoor how-to's) and Med-Psych Publications (psychology and [folk] medicine text books to popular markets). Publishes hardcover and quality paperback originals. Averages 8 titles/year. Subsidy publishes 1% of books. (We may help one a year with self publishing, but we discourage it.) Pays 10-12% royalty on wholesale price. No advance. Publishes book an average of 2 years after acceptance. Electronic submissions OK, but requires hard copy also (author will be prepared to transmit by phone to typesetter). Computer printout submissions acceptable. SASE. Reports in 3 months. Book catalog for business size SAE and 1 first class stamp.
Nonfiction: Inspirational. Query or submit outline/synopsis and 2 sample chapters. Reviews artwork/photos as part of ms package.
Recent Nonfiction Title: *Sanity, Insanity and Common Sense*, by Enrique Suarez and Roger Mills.
Tips: "Once we start working with a writer we look for ideas only, not complete manuscripts." Queries/mss may be routed to other editors in the publishing group.

‡PINEAPPLE PRESS, INC., Box 314, Englewood FL 33533. (813)475-2238. Editor: June Cussen. Publishes hardcover and trade paperback originals and hardcover and trade paperback reprints. Averages 5-10 titles/year. Pays 7½-15% royalty on retail price. Publishes book an average of 1 year after acceptance. Simultaneous and photocopied submissions OK. Computer printout submissions acceptable; prefers letter-quality to dot-matrix. SASE. Reports in 3 weeks on queries; 6 weeks on mss. Free book catalog.
Nonfiction: General nonfiction, illustrated book, juvenile and reference. Subjects include Americana, Floridiana, animals, art, health, history (Florida), hobbies, nature (Florida and other), sports and travel. Especially looking for material for Florida Living Series and for books on nature, conservation and the environment. Query with outline/synopsis and sample chapters or submit complete ms. Reviews artwork/photos as part of ms package.
Recent Nonfiction Title: *Florida Discount Shopping: A Bargain Hunter's Guide to Florida*, by Stephen Kaplan.
Fiction: Adventure, experimental, historical, humor, mainstream and juvenile. "Our upcoming novels deal in some way with Florida, nature or Indians—though this is not necessary." Query or submit complete ms.
Recent Fiction Title: *The Seminole Seed*, by Robert Newton Peck (novel).
Tips: "We anticipate success in both regional publishing (Florida) and in enticing the national market with our novels and nature nonfiction. If I were a writer trying to market a book today, I would learn as much as I could about the realities of the publishing industry and learn how to participate effectively in publicizing my book."

PINNACLE BOOKS, 1430 Broadway, New York NY 10018. President/Publisher: Sondra Ordover. Publishes paperback originals and reprints. "Contracts and terms are standard and primarily competitive." Publishes 160 titles/year. Pays royalty on retail price. Catalog and requirements memo for SASE. "Will no longer accept unsolicited mss. Most books are assigned to known writers or developed through established agents. However, an intelligent, literate and descriptive letter of query will often be given serious consideration." SASE.
Nonfiction: "Books range from general nonfiction to commercial trade fiction in most popular categories. Pinnacle's list is aimed for wide popular appeal, with fast-moving, highly compelling escape reading, adventure, espionage, historical intrigue and romance, western, popular sociological issues, and topical nonfiction. Seems to be a better acceptance of nonfiction and good commercial contemporary romance—both in the Helen Van Slyke and Jacqueline Susann style."
Tips: "Become familiar with our list of published books and follow our instructions. It is a difficult market—paperbacks—with publishers competing for rack space. Watch what sells best and follow the trends as closely as possible. Study the original books that work, as well as the reprints. Good, persuasive query letters are the best and fastest tools you have to get an editor's attention. The idea, or angle is vital . . . then we trust the author has or can complete the manuscript."

PITMAN LEARNING, 19 Davis Dr., Belmont CA 94002. Publisher, Book Publishing Division: Mel Cebulash. Averages 50-80 titles/year. Pays royalty or fee outright. Photocopied submissions OK. Computer printout submissions acceptable; prefers letter-quality to dot-matrix. SASE. Query or submit outline/synopsis for nonfiction. Submit ms for fiction. Reports in 1 month. Free book catalog.
Recent Nonfiction Title: *Management by Guilt*, by Iuppa (trade hardcover).
Fiction: "We are looking for easy-to-read fiction suitable for middle school and up. We prefer the major characters to be young adults or adults. Solid plotting is essential." Length: 20,000 words maximum.
Recent Fiction Title: *The Intruder*, by Richard Laymon.

PLATT & MUNK PUBLISHERS, Division of Grosset & Dunlap, 51 Madison Ave., New York NY 10010. Editor-in-Chief: Bernette G. Ford. Publishes hardcover and paperback originals. Averages 10-20 titles/year. Pays $1,000-3,500 in outright purchase; advance negotiable. Simultaneous and photocopied submissions OK. SASE. Reports in 6 weeks.
Nonfiction: Juveniles. Submit proposal or query first. "We are particularly interested in series proposals rather than individual manuscripts. Nature, science, and light technology type books are all of interest." Looks for "new ways of looking at the world of children; no cutesy stuff."
Recent Nonfiction Title: *Mysterious Seas*, by Mary Elting.
Fiction: Juvenile—all types, picture books for 3-7 age group and some higher. Also interested in anthology-type works and collections with a fresh approach.
Recent Fiction Title: *The Illustrated Treasury of Fairy Tales*, edited by T. Kennedy.
Tips: "We want something new—a proposal for a new series for the ordinary picture book. You have a better chance if you have new ideas."

PLENUM PUBLISHING CORP., 233 Spring St., New York NY 10013. Imprints include Da Capo Press, Consultants Bureau, IFI/Plenum Data Corporation, Plenum Press, Plenum Medical Book Company, and Plenum Scientific. President: Martin Tash. Executive Vice President: Mark Shaw. Publishes hardcover and paperback reprints. Publishes 300 titles/year.
Nonfiction: Scientific, medical and technical books including the social and behavioral sciences, physics, engineering and mathematics. Da Capo division publishes art, music, photography, dance and film.

PLURIBUS PRESS, INC., Division of Teach'em, Inc., 160 E. Illinois St., Chicago IL 60611. Associate Editor: Ellen Slezak. Publishes hardcover and trade paperback originals. Averages 15 titles/year. Pays royalty. Simultaneous and photocopied submissions (if so advised) OK. Will consider computer printout submissions. SASE. Reports in 1 month.
Nonfiction: How-to, self-help, technical, textbooks on business and economics, health, psychology, sports, management "for adult professionals interested in improving the quality of their work and home life. In particular we want material that shows how to or is in self-help, technical, or textbook form with emphasis on health and education administration. Will consider proposals in the following areas: business/management, psychology, and sports. We will consider humorous treatment. No fiction, poetry, art, nature, history, juvenile, politics, religion, travel, biography or autobiography considered." Query or submit outline/synopsis and 3 sample chapters.
Recent Nonfiction Title: *The Healing Mission and the Business Ethic*, by Robert M. Cunningham Jr. (health care).

POCKET BOOKS, 1230 Avenue of the Americas, New York NY 10020. Imprints include Washington Square Press (high-quality mass market), Timescape (science fiction and fantasy), Archway (children and young adults), Poseidon Press (hardcover fiction and nonfiction), Tapestry (historical romance), Wallaby (trade paperbacks), and Long Shadow Books (novelty trade paperbacks). Paperback originals and reprints. Published 300 titles last year. Pays royalty on retail price. Query only; include SASE. No unsolicited mss, except for imprints which follow: Tapestry, Archway.
Nonfiction: History, biography, general nonfiction and adult fiction (mysteries, science fiction, romance, westerns). Reference books.
Recent Nonfiction Title: *The Invisible Bankers*, by Andrew Tobias.
Recent Fiction Title: *Lace*, by Shirley Conran.

POLARIS PRESS, 16540 Camellia Terrace, Los Gatos CA 95030. (408)356-7795. Editor: Edward W. Ludwig. Paperback originals; considers reprints, depending upon reputation of author. Specializes in science fiction and college-level books with appeal to general public. Averages 3 titles/year. Pays 6% royalty on retail price; advance averages $300-500. Publishes book an average of 1 year after acceptance. Send contact sheets or prints if photos and/or illustrations are to accompany ms. Computer printout submissions acceptable; no dot-matrix. Reports in 1-2 weeks. SASE. Free book catalog with 50¢ postage.
Fiction: Fantasy and science fiction 60,000-90,000 words. "Please, *no* mss which require extensive (and expensive) use of color in inner pages." No juvenile or general fiction. Reviews artwork/photos as part of ms package. Query.

Recent Fiction Title: *The Seven Shapes of Solomon*, by Ludwig (anthology of previously published science and science fantasy stories).

Tips: "Query to determine immediate needs, which are usually specialized. List briefly main interests and qualifications. Will accept 2 sample chapters plus synopsis. There is little chance that a nonsolicited manuscript will be accepted spontaneously."

POPULAR SCIENCE BOOKS, Book Division, Times Mirror Magazines, Inc., (subsidiary of Times Mirror Co.), 380 Madison Ave., New York NY 10017. Editor: John Sill. Publishes books for Popular Science Book Club that are also distributed by major trade publishers. Pays royalty and advance relative to book list price. SASE.

Nonfiction: Do-it-yourself guides on home and shop how-to, wood-working, cabinet making, housebuilding, and home repairs. Submit author resume, outline, sample chapters, and sample illustrations for heavily illustrated small books to 35,000 words and large books to 150,000 words. Looks for "either a description of each chapter's contents or a subject-by-subject breakout. Sample rough drawings and photographs: either color tranparencies, any size, or 8x10 b&w glossies."

PORTER SARGENT PUBLISHERS, INC., 11 Beacon St., Boston MA 02108. (617)523-1670. Publishes hardcover and paperback originals, reprints, translations and anthologies. Averages 4 titles/year. Pays royalty on retail price. "Each contract is dealt with on an individual basis with the author." Free book catalog. Send query with brief description, table of contents, sample chapter and information regarding author's background. Computer printout submissions acceptable. Enclose return postage. Looks for "originality and clear and concise treatment and availability of subject."

Nonfiction: Reference, special education and academic nonfiction. "Handbook Series and Special Education Series offer standard, definitive reference works in private education and writings and texts in special education. The Extending Horizons Series is an outspoken, unconventional series which presents topics of importance in contemporary affairs and the social sciences." This series is particularly directed to the college adoption market. Accepts nonfiction translations from French and Spanish. Contact: Christopher Leonesio.

Recent Nonfiction Title: *Social Power and Political Freedom*, by G. Sharp (political science).

‡POSEIDON PRESS, Division of Pocket Books, 1230 Avenue of the Americas, New York NY 10020. (212)246-2121. Editor-in-Chief: Ann E. Patty. Publishes hardcover and trade paperback originals (100%). Averages 10-12 titles/year. Pays 10-15% royalty on hardcover retail price. Simultaneous and photocopied submissions OK. Electronic submissions OK. Computer printout submissions acceptable; no dot-matrix. SASE. Reports in 1 month.

Nonfiction: Biography, cookbook, reference and self-help. Subjects include business and economics, health, history, politics, psychology and sociology. No religious/inspiration, humor. Query or submit outline/synopsis and sample characters.

Recent Nonfiction Title: *Is That All There Is?*, by Dr. David Brandt (psychology/self-help).

Fiction: Literary, historical, contemporary and mainstream. Query or submist outline/synopsis and sample chapters.

Recent Fiction Title: *Possessions*, by Judith Michael.

POTENTIALS DEVELOPMENT FOR HEALTH & AGING SERVICES, 775 Main St., Buffalo NY 14203. (716)842-2658. Editor: Mary V. Kirchhofer. Publishes paperback originals. Averages 6 titles/year. Pays 5-10% royalty on retail price. Publishes book an average of 1 year after acceptance. Computer printout submissions acceptable; prefers letter-quality to dot-matrix. SASE. Reports in 6 weeks. Free book catalog for SASE.

Nonfiction: Human development mss with emphasis on mental, physical and emotional health for older adults. "We seek material of interest to those working with elderly people in the community and in institutional settings. We need tested, innovative and practical ideas." Query or submit outline/synopsis and 3 sample chapters. Reviews artwork/photos as part of ms package. Looks for "suitable subject matter, writing style and organization."

Recent Nonfiction Title: *Where In the World?* by C. Suchan (quiz).

CLARKSON N. POTTER, INC., 1 Park Ave., New York NY 10016. (212)532-9200. Editorial Director: Carol Southern. Director of Operations: Michael Fragnito. Publishes hardcover and trade paperbacks. Pays 10% royalty on hardcover; 5-7½% on paperback; 5-7% illustrated hardcover, varying escalations; advance depends on type of book and reputation or experience of author. Averages 35 titles/year. Regretfully, no unagented manuscripts can be considered. Photocopied submissions OK. Reports in 2-4 weeks. SASE. Free book catalog.

Nonfiction: Publishes Americana, art, autobiography, biography, cooking and foods, history, how-to, humor, juvenile, nature, photography, self-help, style and annotated literature. "Mss must be cleanly typed on 8½x11 non-erasable bond; double-spaced. Chicago *Manual of Style* is preferred." Reviews artwork/photos as part of

ms package. Query or submit outline/synopsis and sample chapters. Accepts nonfiction translations.
Recent Nonfiction Title: *Why Can't Men Open Up?*, by Steven W. Naifeh and Gregory W. Smith.
Fiction: Quality.
Recent Fiction Title: *Arcadio*, by William Goyen.

‡**THE PRAIRIE PUBLISHING COMPANY**, Box 264, Postal Station C, Winnipeg, Manitoba R3M 3S7, Canada. (204)885-6496. Publisher: Ralph Watkins. Publishes trade paperback originals. Averages 4 titles/ year. Pays 10% royalty on retail prices. Computer printout submissions acceptable; prefers letter-quality to dot-matrix. Photocopied submissions OK. SASE. Reports in several weeks. Free book catalog.
Nonfiction: Biography, cookbook and others. Subjects include cooking and foods. "We would look at any submissions."
Recent Nonfiction Title: *My Name Is Marie Anne Gabaury*, by Mary Jordan.

PRENTICE-HALL, Children's Book Division, Englewood Cliffs NJ 07632. Editor-in-Chief: Barbara Francis. Manuscripts Editor: Rose Lopez. Publishes hardcover and paperback originals and paperback reprints. Publishes "roughly 30 hardcovers, and about 15 paperbacks/year. Pays royalty; average advance. SASE. Reports in 6 weeks. Book catalog for SASE.
Nonfiction: All subjects, all age groups but special interest in topical science and technology, art, social sciences, "star" biography (7-10 of outlaws, magicians and other characters), current events (7-10 and 9-12), health (teenage problems by MDs only), history (any unusual approaches), humor (no jokes or riddles but funny fiction), music (keen interest in basic approaches, no biographies), sociology (8-12), and sports (6-9), puzzle and participation (6-8). Query. Accepts outline/synopsis and 5-6 sample chapters from published writers; entire ms from unpublished writers. Prefers to see portfolio separate from ms except when illustrator is making the submission or when clarity requires that ms be accompanied by photos or rough illustrations.
Recent Nonfiction Title: *The Robots Are Here*, by Dr. Alvin and Virginia B. Silverstein.
Fiction: Gothic, humor, mainstream and mystery. Submit outline/synopsis and sample chapters.
Recent Fiction Title: *Rickshaw to Horror: A Miss Mallard Mystery*, by Robert Quackenbush (detective mystery, ages 6-9).
Picture Books: Accent on humor.
Recent Picture Book: *Alistair's Elephant*, by Marilyn Sadler, illustrated by Roger Bollen.

‡**PRENTICE-HALL CANADA, INC.**, College Division, 1870 Birchmount Road, Scarborough, Ontario M1P 2J7, Canada. (416)293-3621. Executive Editor: Cliff Newman. Publishes hardcover and paperback originals and software. Pays 10-15 royalty on net price. Publishes book an average of 3 months after acceptance. Electronic submissions OK, but requires hard copy also. Computer printout submissions acceptable.
Nonfiction: The College Division publishes textbooks suitable for the community college and large university market. Most submissions should be designed for existing courses in all disciplines of study. Canadian content is important.
Recent Nonfiction Title: *Contemporary Business Mathematics with Canadian Applications*, by Hummelbrunner.
Software: Will consider software in most disciplines especially business and sciences.

‡**PRENTICE-HALL CANADA, INC.**, Educational Book Division, 1870 Birchmount Road, Scarborough, Ontario M1P 2J7, Canada. (416)293-3621. Executive Editor: Rob Greenaway.
Nonfiction: Publishes texts, workbooks, and instructional media including computer courseware for elementary, junior high and high schools. Subjects include business, computer studies, geography, history, language arts, mathematics, science, social studies, technology and French as a second language.

PRENTICE-HALL CANADA, INC., Trade Division, 1870 Birchmount Road, Scarborough, Ontario M1P 2J7 Canada. (416)293-3621. Acquisitions Editor: Janice Whitford. Publishes hardcover and trade paperback originals and software. Averages 10 titles/year. Negotiates royalty and advance. Publishes book an average of 9 months after acceptance. Computer printout submissions acceptable; prefers letter-quality to dot-matrix. Send sample chapters or outlines. SAE and IRCs. Reports in 10 weeks.
Nonfiction: Subjects of Canadian and international interest; art, politics and current affairs, business, travel, health, and food.
Recent Nonfiction Title: *Contenders*, by Patrick Martin, Allan Gregg, and George Perlin (politics).

PRENTICE-HALL, INC., General Publishing Division, Englewood Cliffs NJ 07632. Editorial Director: Lynne A. Lumsden. Publishes hardcover and simultaneous trade paperback originals and software. Publishes book an average of 9 months after acceptance. Electronic submissions OK depending on project. Will consider unsolicited photocopied submissions on nonfiction topics, but not responsible for returning unsolicited manuscripts. Computer printout submissions acceptable; prefers letter-quality to dot-matrix. SASE must be included in order to receive a response in 6-8 weeks. "No responses will be sent nor materials returned on proposals

for fiction, poetry, romances, westerns, personal life stories, or for other subjects we do not publish."
Nonfiction: Educational, professional, or how-to subjects like computers (books and software), business, health, music and other performing arts, psychology, science, art, travel, nature, religion, sports, self-help, vocational-technical subjects, hobbies, recreation, and reference. Length 60,000 words. Accepts nonfiction translations. Submit outline and 2-3 sample chapters.
Software: For software, submit demo disk with draft of the documentation. Contact technical editors.
Tips: "The writer should submit his/her work professionally prepared and typewritten." Queries/mss will be routed to other editors in the publishing group.

THE PRESERVATION PRESS, National Trust for Historic Preservation, 1785 Massachusetts Ave. NW, Washington DC 20036. Editor: Diane Maddex. Publishes nonfiction books and periodicals on historic preservation (saving and reusing the "built environment"). Averages 6 titles/year. Books are often commissioned by the publisher. Subject matter encompasses architecture and architectural history, neighborhood preservation, regional planning, building restoration and rural area conservation. No local history. Query. Looks for "relevance to national preservation-oriented audience; educational or instructional value; depth; uniqueness; need in field."
Recent Nonfiction Title: *What Style Is It?: A Guide to American Architecture.*

PRESIDIO PRESS, 31 Pamaron Way, Novato CA 94947. (415)883-1373. Editor-in-Chief: Adele Horwitz. Senior Editor: Joan Griffin. Publishes hardcover and paperback originals. Pays 15% on net price royalty; offers nominal advance. Publishes book an average of 18 months after acceptance. Photocopied submissions OK. Electronic submissions OK once book has been accepted for publication. Computer printout submissions acceptable; prefers letter-quality to dot-matrix. SASE. Reports in 3 months. Free book catalog.
Nonfiction: California, regional, contemporary and military history. No scholarly mss. Fiction with military background considered. Accepts nonfiction translations. Query or submit outline/synopsis and 3 sample chapters. Reviews artwork/photos as part of ms package.
Recent Nonfiction Title: *San Francisco: Story of a City*, by J. McGloin (history).

PRESSWORKS, INC., Box 12606, Dallas TX 75225. (214)369-3113. President: Anne Dickson. Publishes hardcover originals. Averages 17 titles/year. Pays variable royalty on retail price; offers variable advance. Simultaneous and photocopied submissions OK. Computer printout submissions OK; prefers letter-quality to dot matrix. SASE. Reports in 1 month on queries; reporting time varies on mss. Free book catalog.
Nonfiction: Reference. Subjects include Americana, art, business and economics, history, and other branches of the humanities. Consumers are libraries and scholars, trade bookstores, and rare book dealers. Submit outline/synopsis and 3 sample chapters. Looks for "good, clean style and timely subject." Accepts nonfiction translations.
Recent Nonfiction Title: *Engineer Babies*, by Emily Williams.
Fiction: Humor and/or intense feeling with well-developed dialogue. Accepts fiction translations.
Recent Fiction Title: *The Krone Experiment: A Space Adventure*, by J. Craig Wheeler.

PRICE/STERN/SLOAN INC., PUBLISHERS, 410 N. La Cienega Blvd., Los Angeles CA 90048. Imprints include Cliff House Books, Serendipity Books, Troubador Press and Laughter Library. Editorial Director: Lawrence S. Dietz. Publishes trade paperback originals. Averages 100-120 titles/year. Pays royalty on wholesale price, or by outright purchase; small or no advance. Simultaneous and photocopied submissions OK. Computer printout submissions acceptable; no dot-matrix. SASE. Reports in 3-4 months.
Nonfiction: Humor; self-help (limited); and satire (limited). Submit outline/synopsis and sample chapters only. "Most titles are unique in concept as well as execution and are geared for the so-called gift market."

*PRINCETON UNIVERSITY PRESS, 41 William St., Princeton NJ 08540. (609)542-4900. Associate Director/Editor: R. Miriam Brokaw. Publishes hardcover and trade paperback ("very few") originals and reprints. Averages 130 titles/year. Subsidy assists 50% of books, "when we don't break even on the first printing." Pays 15% maximum royalty on retail price; offers advances ("but rarely"). Simultaneous and photocopied submissions OK, if notified. SASE. Reports in 1 week on queries; 1 month on mss "if unsuitable" or 4 months "if suitable."
Nonfiction: Biography, reference and technical. Subjects include art, literature, history, science, music, politics, religion sociology and poetry. "We're looking for any scholarly book with an importance of subject, clear writing." Query.
Recent Nonfiction Title: *The Collected Letters of William Morris*, edited by Norman Kelvin.
Poetry: "Poetry submissions (original and in translation) are judged in competition. Contact Robert Brown." Submit complete ms.

PRINTEMPS BOOKS, INC., Box 746, Wilmette IL 60091. (312)251-5418. Secretary/Treasurer: Beatrice Penovich. Publishes trade paperbacks. Averages 3 titles/year. Pays royalty or buys some mss outright, "to be agreed upon." No advance. SASE. Reports in 1 month on mss.

Fiction: Adventure, ethnic, fantasy, humor, mystery, suspense, and children's stories (short). "Our aim is to both entertain and educate students who have less than average reading skills. We envision publication of a collection of stories suitable for high school students who have a very limited vocabulary." Publishes for school systems and over-the-counter purchases. Submit complete ms.

PROMETHEUS BOOKS, INC., 700 E. Amherst St., Buffalo NY 14215. (716)837-2475. Editor-in-Chief: Paul Kurtz. Director of Advertising and Promotion: Victor Gulotta. Publishes hardcover and trade paperback originals. Averages 26 titles/year. Pays 5-10% royalty on wholesale price; offers negotiable advance. Computer printout submissions acceptable. SASE. Reports in 2 months. Free book catalog.

Nonfiction and Fiction: Textbook and trade. Subjects include philosophy, science, psychology, religion, sociology, medical ethics, biography, literature and criticism. "Prometheus is an independent publishing house with a commitment to maximizing the availability of books of high scholarly merit and popular intrigue. We welcome manuscript proposals suitable to our publishing program, which focuses on the humanities and social and natural sciences. One area of specialization in which we have experienced tremendous growth is scientific criticism of 'paranormal phenomena.' We also are interested in examining proposals for competitive college texts, both primary and supplementary." Accepts nonfiction translations. Submission of popular trade nonfiction is also encouraged. Submit outline/synopsis and "at least the first few" chapters. Reviews artwork/photos as part of ms package.

Recent Title: *The Roving Mind*, by Isaac Asimov (science).

*PRUETT PUBLISHING CO., 2928 Pearl, Boulder CO 80301. Managing Editor: Gerald Keenan. Publishes software. Averages 20 titles/year. Subsidy publishes 1% of books. Royalty contract on wholesale price. No advance. "Most books that we publish are aimed at special interest groups. As a small publisher, we feel most comfortable in dealing with a segment of the market that is very clearly identifiable, and one we know we can reach with our resources." Mss must conform to the Chicago *Manual of Style*. Publishes book an average of 1 year after acceptance. Legible photocopies acceptable. Any disk submissions would have to interface with present typesetting system; query, but requires hard copy also. Computer printout submissions acceptable; no dot-matrix. Reports in 2-4 weeks. SASE. Free catalog on request.

Nonfiction: Publishes general adult nonfiction and textbooks. Subjects include: Pictorial railroad histories, outdoor activities related to the Intermountain West, and some Western Americana. Textbooks with a regional (intermountain) aspect for pre-school through college level. Does not want to see anything with the personal reminiscence angle or biographical studies of little-known personalities. "Like most small publishers, we try to emphasize quality from start to finish, because, for the most part, our titles are going to a specialized market that is very quality conscious. We also feel that one of our strong points is the personal involvement ('touch') so often absent in a much larger organization." Accepts outline/synopsis and 3 sample chapters. Reviews artwork/photos as part of ms package.

Recent Nonfiction Title: *San Juan Country*, by Griffiths.

Software: At this point, limited to a previously published work. Contact: Gerald Keenan.

PSG PUBLISHING CO., INC., (formerly John Wright/PSG Inc.), 545 Great Rd., Littleton MA 01460. (617)486-8971. President/Publisher: Frank Paparello. Hardcover and paperback originals. Pays royalty on net revenues. Specializes in publishing medical and dental books, newsletters, and journals for the professional and student markets. Pays 10-15% royalty. Simultaneous submissions OK. Reports in 2-4 weeks. SASE. Free book catalog.

Nonfiction: Medical, dental books, newsletters, and journals. Reviews artwork/photos as part of ms package. Request proposal form. Query or submit complete ms.

Recent Nonfiction Title: *Clinical Psychopharmacology*, by Jerrold Bernstein, MD.

Tips: Queries/mss may be routed to other editors in the publishing group.

‡PUCKERBRUSH PRESS, 76 Main St., Orono ME 04473. (207)581-3832/866-4808. Publisher/Editor: Constance Hunting. Publishes trade paperback and mass market paperback originals (75%) and trade paperback reprints (25%). Averages 2-3 titles/year. Pays 10-15% royalty on retail price. Simultaneous submissions OK. Computer printout submissions acceptable; no dot-matrix. SASE. Reports in 1 month. Free book catalog.

Nonfiction: Literary. Subjects include religion ("lively, interesting"). Submit outline/synopsis and sample chapters or complete ms.

Recent Nonfiction Title: *The Rocking Horse*, by Douglas Young (sermons for children).

Fiction: Literary—"anything fresh, written (as opposed to confused or automated)." No California fantasy or Midwest realism. Submit outline/synopsis and sample chapters or complete ms.

Recent Fiction Title: *The Police Know Everything*, by Sanford Phippen (downeast, bizarre stories).

Poetry: "Anything non-temporary." No "confessional, feminist, or 20th century imitation." Submit complete ms.

Recent Poetry Title: *Dead of Winter*, by Michael McMahon (delicate, timeless).

Tips: "We have a small, literate, widely-read audience."

PURDUE UNIVERSITY PRESS, South Campus Courts, D., West Lafayette IN 47907. (317)494-2035. Director: William J. Whalen. Managing Editor: Verna Emery. Publishes hardcover and paperback originals. Specializes in scholarly books from all areas of academic endeavor. Pays 10% royalty on list price; no advance. Publishes 6 titles/year. Publishes book an average of 1 year after acceptance. Photocopied submissions OK "if author will verify that it does not mean simultaneous submission elsewhere." Computer submissions acceptable; no dot-matrix. Reports in 2-4 months. SASE. Free book catalog.
Nonfiction: Publishes agriculture, Americana, art (but no color plates), biography, communication, economics, engineering, history, horticulture, literature, philosophy, political science, psychology, scientific, sociology, and literary criticism. "Works of scholarship only." Submit complete ms only.
Recent Nonfiction Title: *My Amiable Uncle: Recollections about Booth Tarkington*, by Susanah Mayberry.

Q.E.D. INFORMATION SCIENCES, INC., 170 Linden St., Box 181, Wellesley MA 02181. (617)237-5656. Manager of Publication: Jerry Murphy. Publishes trade paperback originals and software. Averages 10 titles/year. Pays 10-15% royalty on retail price. Publishes book an average of 3 months after acceptance. Electronic submissions OK on IBM PC and Apple. Computer printout submissions acceptable. SASE. Reports in 1 week on queries; 3 weeks on mss. Free book catalog.
Nonfiction: Technical. Subjects include computers, personal computing, and database technology. "Our books are read by data processing managers and technicians." Submit outline/synopsis and 2 sample chapters. Reviews artwork/photos as part of ms package.
Recent Nonfiction Title: *Data Analysis: The Key to Data Base Design*, by R. Perkinson.
Software: PC training and PC utilities.

QUALITY PUBLICATIONS, INC., Box 2633, Lakewood OH 44107. Executive Editor: Gary S. Skeens. Associate Editor: Robin S. Moser. Publishes trade paperback originals. Averages 7 titles/year. Pays 10-20% royalty on retail price. No advance. Computer printout submissions acceptable. SAE. Reports in 1 week on queries; 2 months on mss. Book catalog for 6x9 SAE and 3 first class stamps.
Fiction: Adventure, erotica, mainstream, and western. Accepts fiction and poetry translations from French, Spanish and Russian. Publishes for an "open audience: wide range of backgrounds, experiences, education; those who feel to the very marrow of their bone. No weak plot or character development, dishonesty with writers' work or themselves, pornography." Query. "We will not be actively seeking manuscripts between 1983 and 1985, though we will look at any strong queries that might be sent in."
Recent Fiction Title: *As Any Mountain of Its Snows*, by Joseph Davey.
Poetry: No "pornography, weak style, development lapses, poor image usage." Submit 10-15 samples.
Recent Poetry Title: *Animal Acts*, by Alan Catlin.

‡**QUARTET BOOKS INC.**, Subsidiary of The Namara Group. 13th Floor, 360 Park Ave. S, New York NY 10010. (212)684-2233. Director: Marilyn Warnick. Subsidiaries include The Womens Press and Namara Publications. Publishes hardcover and trade paperback originals and hardcover and trade paperback reprints. Averages 40 titles/year in US, 200 in UK. Pays 6-12% royalty; offers average $2,000 advance. Simultaneous submissions OK. SASE. Reports in 3 weeks on queries; 6 weeks on mss. Book catalog for 7x9 SAE and 2 first class stamps.
Nonfiction: Biography, "coffee table" book, and illustrated book. Subjects include animals, business and economics, history, philosophy, photography, politics, psychology, sociology and Middle Eastern politics, culture and society. Especially looking for "well-written, thoroughly researched books on most serious topics and people who will be of interest to both the English and American reader. No World War II experiences, cookery, health, do-it-yourself, keep-fit, astrology, or anything sexist or racist. Submit outline/synopsis and sample chapters.
Recent Nonfiction Title: *Kennedy: A Time Remembered*, by Jacques Lowe (photography/history).
Fiction: Adventure, erotica (only if very literary), mainstream, crime, and feminist. No romances, science fiction, westerns, horror, or any genre books other than crime. Submit though agent only.
Tips: "If I were a writer trying to market a book today, I would try to come up with something fresh rather than imitating current bestsellers. We are looking for titles that can be published by our sister company, Quartet Books Ltd. in London, as well as by the US company so the books must appeal to both markets."

QUE CORPORATION, 7999 Knue Rd., Indianapolis IN 46250. (317)842-7162. Editorial Director: David F. Noble. Publishes trade paperback originals, hardware and software products guides, software for books on computer spreadsheets, and software. Published 28 titles in 1983; 45 titles anticipated in 1984. Pays 7-10% escalating royalty on wholesale price; buys some manuscripts outright. Query or submit outline/synopsis and sample chapters, or complete ms. Simultaneous (if so advised) and photocopied submissions OK. Electronic disk submissions should be CP/M 8" or IBM PC-compatible; requires hard copy also. Computer printout submissions acceptable. SASE. Reports in 1 month. Free book catalog and guidelines for authors.
Nonfiction: How-to, technical, and reference books relating to microcomputers; textbooks on business use of microcomputers; software user's guides and tutorials; operating systems user's guides; computer programming

language reference works; books on microcomputer systems, spreadsheet software business applications, word processing, data base management, time management, popular computer programs for the home, computer graphics and game programs, hobbies (microcomputers), networking, communications, educational uses of microcomputers, computer-assisted instruction in education and business and course-authoring applications. "We will consider books on most subjects relating to microcomputers."
Recent Nonfiction Title: *Introducing IBM PCjr*, by Cobb and DeVoney.
Software: Contact: Chris DeVoney. Companion software to our books on spreadsheets programs.

QUINTESSENCE PUBLISHING CO., INC., 8 S. Michigan Ave., Chicago IL 60603. (312)782-3221. Publisher: H.W. Haase. Vice President, Editorial: Tomoko Tsuchiya. Publishes hardcover and trade paperback originals. Averages 22 titles/year. Pays average 10% royalty. Computer printout submissions acceptable. SASE. Reports in 2 weeks.
Nonfiction: Technical (on all aspects of dentistry). Reviews artwork/photos as part of ms package. Submit outline/synopsis and 2-4 sample chapters.

R & E PUBLISHERS, INC., (formerly R&E Research Assoc.), Box 2008, Saratoga CA 95070. (415)494-1112. Publisher: R. Reed. Publishes trade paperback originals. Averages 60 titles/year. Pays 10-15% royalty on retail price; no advance. Query letter first. Photocopied submissions OK. SASE. Reports in 3 months. Free book catalog.
Nonfiction: How-to, reference, self-help, textbook and scholarly. Subjects include Americana, business and economics, health, history, politics, psychology, sociology and education. "We would like how-to books, manuals for educators, self-help books, and reference materials." Query or submit outline/synopsis and sample chapters.
Recent Nonfiction Title: *The Middle Class Credo: 1000 All-American Beliefs?*, by T.L. Brink.

R & R NEWKIRK, ITT Publishing, Box 1727, Indianapolis IN 46206. (317)297-4360. Editor: Anne Shropshire. Publishes trade paperback, hardbound originals and software. Averages 6 titles/year. Pays 10-15% royalty on retail price. Publishes book an average of 6 months after acceptance. Computer printout submissions acceptable; prefers letter-quality to dot-matrix. SASE. Reports in 2 weeks on queries; 1 month on mss. Free book catalog.
Nonfiction: Technical, training, and sales technique/methods. Subjects include how-to for life insurance selling and financial planning. "Our books are written for life insurance agents, managers and trainers, and financial planners. We publish one book approximately every other month—have scheduled prospective mss through January 1985, but this is not an inflexible schedule and we can alter it in consideration of a publishable ms. Material must pertain to sales and/or financial services." Submit outline/synopsis and 3 sample chapters or complete ms. Reviews artwork/photos as part of ms package. Looks for "clear, crisp writing; a fully developed theme with a 'how-to' slant."
Recent Nonfiction Title: *Become Famous then Rich: How to Promote Yourself and Your Business*, by Dennis Hensley (how-to).
Software: Life insurance product orientation and financial planning orientation. Contact: Leo C. Hodges, Vice President; Product Development.
Tips: "Research thoroughly your intended audience and direct your work to its needs. Subject should be appropriate to the life insurance (particularly sales) market, and the financial planning industry. The more defined the subject matter, the better."

‡*RAINBOW BOOKS/BETTY WRIGHT, Betty Wright & Associates, Creative Consultants, Box 1069, Moore Haven FL 33471. (813)946-0293. Book publisher/packager producing 8-10 titles/year. Publisher: Betty Wright. Publishes hardcover and trade paperback originals and software. Subsidy publishes 50% of books. Pays 2-5% on retail price; average $100+ advance. Electronic submissions OK. Computer printout submissions acceptable. SASE. Reports in 1 week on queries; 2 weeks on mss. Book catalog for $1.
Nonfiction: How-to, humor, reference and self-help. "We will package any type of book." Subjects include Americana, history, politics, psychology, sociology, astonomy and UFO genre. "We are interested in reaching science and science fiction fans and futurists and in broadening our reference and resource audience. We are particularly interested in reference and resource books. Also, we'd like to see some entertaining science fiction and UFO books." Reviews artwork/photos as part of ms package. Query.
Recent Nonfiction Title: *Retirement Tracks*, by Dr. Georgia B. Watson (humor/nonfiction).
Fiction: Adventure, ethnic, historical, humor, mainstream, mystery, religious, romance, science fiction, suspense, western and astronomy/UFO. "We're most interested in seeing science fiction at this time. However, we're open to all fiction." Query.
Recent Fiction Title: *A Taste of Red Onion*, by Paul Olear (historical).
Poetry: Limited. Submit 3 poems.
Recent Poetry Title: *Running the River*, by John Hendricks.
Tips: "We are interested in seeing work by unpublished authors. We want to find and develop the new writer."

We have highly sophisticated equipment which can read and translate diskettes through our word processor which is interfaced to typesetter—a book packager plus!''

‡**RAINTREE PUBLISHERS INC.**, 205 W. Highland Ave., Milwaukee WI 53203. (414)273-0873. Editor-in-Chief: Richard D. Hawthorne. Publishes hardcover originals. Averages 20-50 titles/year. Pays royalty or makes outright purchase. Simultaneous and photocopied submissions OK. Computer printout submissions acceptable; prefers letter-quality to dot-matrix. SASE. Reports in 8 weeks. Free book catalog.
Nonfiction: Juvenile and reference. Subjects include animals, health, history, nature and photography. "We publish school and library books in series." Query with outline/synopsis and sample chapters. Reviews artwork/photos as part of ms package.
Fiction: Adventure, historical and science fiction. Query with outline/synopsis and sample chapters.

RAND McNALLY & CO. PUBLISHING GROUP, Box 7600, Chicago IL 60680. Managing Editor: Robert J. Garlock. Variable royalty and advance schedule. Some outright purchases. Photocopied submissions OK. SASE.
Nonfiction: Juvenile: Picture books, young information books. Travel and other reference works. Focus on geographically-related subjects. Query first.
Recent Nonfiction Title: *This Great Land: Scenic Splendor of America.*

RANDOM HOUSE, INC., 201 E. 50th St., New York NY 10022. Also publishes Vintage Books. Publishes hardcover and paperback originals and reprints. Payment as per standard minimum book contracts. Query. SASE.
Fiction and Nonfiction: Publishes fiction and nonfiction of the "highest standards."
Poetry: Some poetry volumes.

RANDOM HOUSE, INC., School Division, 201 E. 50th St., New York NY 10022. Managing Editor: Gerry Gabianelli. Publishes textbooks, paperbacks, and worktexts for school market. Averages 40 titles/year. Pays royalty or buys ms outright; "depending on the nature of the project." Reports in 2 months.
Nonfiction: Textbooks and workbooks in reading, language arts and math—K-8, English and social studies for secondary level. Submit outline/synopsis and 2-3 sample chapters.

REALTORS NATIONAL MARKETING INSTITUTE, Affiliate of National Association of Realtors, 430 N. Michigan Ave., Chicago IL 60611. (312)670-3780. Director of Publishing: Barbara Gamez-Craig. Publishes hardcover and trade paperback originals. Averages 3 titles/year. Pays 10% maximum on retail price; offers advance: "50% of estimated royalties from sales of first printing." Simultaneous and photocopied submissions OK. SASE. Reports in 2 months. Free book catalog.
Nonfiction: How-to, reference, self-help and technical. Subjects include business and economics (realty-oriented) and professional real estate. "We're interested in real estate oriented mss on commercial-investment (basic how-to); residential-creative; and management strategies and motivation for real estate professionals." Submit outline/synopsis and sample chapter.
Recent Nonfiction Title: *The Real Estate Sales Handbook.*

REGAL BOOKS, Division of Gospel Light Publications, 2300 Knoll Dr., Ventura CA 93003. Senior Editor: Donald E. Pugh. Publishes hardcover and paperback originals. Averages 40 titles/year. Pays 10% royalty on paperback titles, 10% net for curriculum books. Publishes book an average of 11 months after acceptance. Computer printout submissions acceptable. Reports in 3 months. SASE.
Nonfiction: Missions, Bible studies (Old and New Testament), Christian living, counseling (self-help), contemporary concerns, evangelism (church growth), marriage and family, youth, communication resources, teaching enrichment resources, Bible commentary for Laymen Series, and fiction. Query or submit detailed outline/synopsis and 2-3 sample chapters.
Recent Nonfiction Title: *In Search of Dignity,* by R.C. Sproul.
Recent Fiction Title: *Some Strange Joy,* by Laurie B. Clifford.
Recent Young Adult Title: *When Someone Really Loves You,* by Carolyn Phillips.
Tips: Queries/mss may be routed to other editors in the publishing group.

REGENTS PUBLISHING CO., INC., 2 Park Ave., New York NY 10016. Averages 50 titles/year. ESL Acquisitions Editor: John Chapman. Spanish Language Editor: Lolita Koch. Computerized Instruction Editor: David Tillyer. Publishes English as a second language and Spanish language textbooks, as well as computer-assisted instruction programs for the same market and software. Prefers complete proposals, including description of target market, comparison with similar materials already on the market, description of age/grade/difficulty level, as well as table of contents and at least 3 sample units. Publishes book an average of 1 year after acceptance. Electronic submissions OK if compatible with Apple or IBM PC, but requires hard copy also. Computer printout submissions acceptable.

Nonfiction: Textbooks. Publishes ESL/EFL and Spanish language textbooks for all ages. Produces ESP materials for business, science, etc. Reviews artwork/photos as part of ms package.
Recent Nonfiction Title: *Spectrum* (an adult notional/functional ESL series).
Software: Contact: David Tillyer, computerized instruction editor. English as a second language instruction, and foreign language instruction (Spanish). Produces ESL practice materials for use with microcomputers in home and school settings.
Tips: "Freelance writers should be aware of English as a second language trend and foreign language market needs in the educational marketplace."

REGNERY/GATEWAY, INC., 360 W. Superior St., Chicago IL 60610. President: Clyde P. Peters. Chairman: Henry Regnery. Publishes hardcover and paperback originals (50%) and paperback reprints (50%). Averages 12-15 titles/year. Pays royalty. Simultaneous and photocopied submissions OK. Computer printout submissions acceptable. SASE. Reports in 1 month. Free book catalog.
Nonfiction: Biography, economics, history, philosophy, politics, psychology, religion, science, sociology, and education (teaching). Accepts nonfiction translations. "We are looking for books on current affairs—of either political, legal, social, environmental, educational or historical interest. Books heavy on sex and obscene brutality should not be submitted. Please, no fiction, verse, or children's literature." Inquiries preferred. Additional information if requested. No unsolicited mss accepted. Looks for "a novel approach to the subject, expertise of the author, clean, respectable writing, salability of the proposed work."
Recent Nonfiction Title: *The Coercive Utopians*, by Rael Jean Isaac.

‡**RENAISSANCE PUBLISHING, INC.**, 239 Washington St., Boston MA 02108. Editor: R.E. Rambo. Publishes hardcover and mass market paperback originals. Averages 125 titles/year. Makes outright purchase. Simultaneous and photocopied submissions OK. Computer printout submissions acceptable. SASE. Reports in 1 month.
Nonfiction: Biography, how-to, humor, illustrated book, self-help and adult. Subjects include photography and erotica. Plans to publish approximately 20 nonfiction books this year. Submit complete ms. "Must have complete postage SAE or box for return of ms."
Fiction: Erotica, fantasy, humor, mainstream, mystery and romance. Plans 100-150 fiction books this year. Submit complete ms including return SAE or box with full postage.
Tips: "Our books are intended for mass audience appeal—ages 18-49, male and female."

*****RESOURCE PUBLICATIONS, INC.**, #290, 160 E. Virginia St., San Jose CA 95112. Associate Editor: James K. Nageotte. Publishes paperback originals and software. Publishes 8 titles/year. Subsidy publishes 25% of books. "If the author can present and defend a personal publicity effort or otherwise demonstrate demand and the work is in our field, we will consider it." Pays 8% royalty; no advance. Publishes book an average of 1 year after acceptance. Photocopied submissions (with written assurance that work is not being submitted simultaneously) OK. Electronic submissions OK if CP/M 8" single density disks, but requires hard copy also. Computer printout submissions acceptable. Reports in 2 months. SASE.
Nonfiction: "We look for creative source books for the religious education, worship, religious art, and architecture fields. How-to books, especially for contemporary religious art forms, are of particular interest (dance, mime, drama, choral reading, singing, music, musicianship, bannermaking, statuary, or any visual art form). No heavy theoretical, philosophical, or theological tomes. Nothing utterly unrelated or unrelatable to the religious market as described above. "We're starting a new line of how-to books for personal computer applications." Query or submit outline/synopsis and sample chapters. "Prepare a clear outline of the work and an ambitious schedule of public appearances to help make it known and present both as a proposal to the publisher. With our company a work that can be serialized or systematically excerpted in our periodicals is always given special attention." Accepts translations. Reviews artwork/photos as part of ms package.
Recent Nonfiction Title: *Banners and Such*, by Ortegel (how-to).
Fiction: "Light works providing examples of good expression through the religious art forms. Any collected short works in the areas of drama, dance, song, stories, anecdotes or good visual art. Long poems or illustrated light novels which entertain while teaching a life value which could be useful in religious education or to the religious market at large." Query or submit outline/synopsis and sample chapters.
Recent Fiction Title: *Parables for Little People*, by Larry Castagnola (stories).
Tips: "We are opening an editorial department for books dealing with small computers. It represents a real opportunity for the author active in small computers."

RESTON PUBLISHING CO., Subsidiary of Prentice-Hall, 11480 Sunset Hills Rd., Reston VA 22090. President: David M. Ungerer. Publishes hardcover and trade paperback originals and software. Offers standard minimum book contract of 10-12-15% on net sales; advance varies. Publishes book an average of 7 months after acceptance. Averages 300 titles/year. Will consider photocopied submissions. Computer printout submissions acceptable; prefers letter-quality to dot-matrix. Electronic submissions OK on disk that can be used or converted by suppliers or submitted via modem, but requires hard copy also. Submit outline and a minimum of

2 sample chapters. Looks for "rationale for writing book, writing style, market." Reports immediately. Enclose return postage. Free catalog on request.
Nonfiction: Textbooks. "We look for titles in agriculture, business and real estate, engineering, finance, computer science, paramedical field, and nursing. Primarily for the junior college and vocational/technical school market, computer titles for trade market and professionally oriented books for in-service practitioners and professionals. All material should be written in style and subject to appeal to these markets. We are able to attract to write our books the best experts in all phases of academic and professional life. But we are always seeking new material in all areas of publishing, any area that is represented by courses at any post-secondary level." Reviews artwork/photos as part of ms package.
Recent Nonfiction Title: *Power of Money Dynamics*, by Van Caspal.
Software: Contact Carol King.
Tips: "Freelance writers should be aware of the new computers coming onto market."

FLEMING H. REVELL CO., Central Ave., Old Tappan NJ 07675. Imprints include Power Books and Spire. Vice President/Editor-in-Chief: Gary A. Sledge. Managing Editor: Norma F. Chimento. Publishes hardcover and paperback originals and reprints. Publishes 80 titles/year. Pays royalty on retail price; sometimes an advance. Simultaneous and photocopied submissions OK. SASE. Reports in 2 months. Book catalog for SASE.
Nonfiction: Religion and inspirational. "All books must appeal to Protestant-evangelical readers." Query. No poetry.
Recent Nonfiction Title: *The Encyclopedia of Christian Marriage*, edited by Cecil Murphey.
Fiction: Protestant-evangelical religion and inspiration. Query or submit 3-6 sample chapters or complete ms. No poetry.
Recent Fiction Title: *The Thirteenth Disciple*, by Bette M. Ross.

REVIEW AND HERALD PUBLISHING ASSOCIATION, 55 West Oak Ridge Dr., Hagerstown MD 21740. Vice President for Editors: Richard W. Coffen. Publishes hardcover and paperback originals. Specializes in religiously oriented books. Averages 30-40 titles/year. Pays 5-10% royalty on retail price; advance averages $100. Publishes book an average of 1 year after acceptance. Computer printout submissions acceptable; prefers letter-quality to dot-matrix. SASE. Reports in 2-4 months. Free brochure.
Nonfiction: Juveniles (religiously oriented only; 20,000-60,000 words; 128 pages average); nature (128 pages average); and religious (20,000-60,000 words; 128 pages average). Query or submit outline/synopsis and 2-3 sample chapters. Reviews artwork/photos as part of ms package. Looks for "literary style, constructive tone, factual accuracy, compatibility with Adventist theology and life style, and length of manuscript."
Recent Nonfiction Title: *To Know God*, by Morris L. Venden.
Software: Bible games for Radio Shack Co-Co, Commodore 64, Adam, and Atari. Contact: Gail Hunt.
Tips: "Familiarize yourself with Adventist theology because Review and Herald Publishing Association is owned and operated by the Seventh-day Adventist Church. We are accepting fewer but better-written manuscripts."

REYMONT ASSOCIATES, 6556 SW Maple Lane, Boca Raton FL 33433. Editor-in-Chief: D.J. Scherer. Managing Editor: Felicia Scherer. Paperback originals. Pays 10-12-15% royalty on wholesale price; no advance. Publishes book an average of 3 months after acceptance. Submit outline/synopsis and 2 sample chapters. Computer printout submissions acceptable. Reports in 2 weeks. SASE. Report catalog for SASE.
Nonfiction: Publishes business reports, how-to, unique directories, and bibliographies. " 'Net' writing; no rhetoric. Aim for 7,500-10,000 words."
Recent Nonfiction Title: *Improving EDP Software Production*.
Tips: "Trends in book publishing that freelance writers should be aware of include the need for sharply focused single-subject reports of 700-800 words in length.

RICHBORO PRESS, Box 1, Richboro PA 18954. (215)364-2212. Editor: George Moore. Publishes hardcover, trade paperback originals and software. Averages 6 titles/year. Pays 10% royalty on retail price. Publishes book an average of 1 year after acceptance. Electronic submissions OK (query), but requires hard copy also. Computer printout submissions acceptable. Query encouraged on DOS required for floppy modern transmission. SASE. Reports in 6 weeks on queries; 3 months on mss. Free book catalog.
Nonfiction: Cookbook, how-to, and gardening. Subjects include cooking and foods. Query.
Recent Nonfiction Title: *Italian Herb Cooking*, by Daneo.
Software: Professional (CMD, DVM, DDS, Atty), and vertical (farm, small business, wholesale); query on need and language.

THE RIVERDALE COMPANY, INC., PUBLISHERS, #102, 5506 Kenilworth Ave., Riverdale MD 20737. (301)864-2029. President: John Adams. Publishes hardcover originals. Averages 6-8 titles/year. Pays 15% maximum royalty on wholesale price. Publishes book an average of 6 months after acceptance. Computer printout submissions acceptable; prefers letter-quality to dot-matrix. SASE. Reports in 1 week on queries; 1 month on mss. Free book catalog.

Nonfiction: "We publish technical and social science textbooks for scholars, students, policy makers; and tour, restaurant and recreational guides for the mass market." Subjects include economics, history, politics, psychology, sociology, and travel. Especially needs "social science manuscripts on South Asia or South Asia-Africa. Will consider college text proposals in economics and South Asian studies; travel guides for Washington DC and immediate area." Query. Accepts outline/synopsis and 2-3 sample chapters.

THE ROSEN PUBLISHING GROUP, 29 E. 21st St., New York NY 10010. (212)777-3017. President: Roger Rosen. Imprints include Pelion Press (music titles). Publishes hardcover originals. Entire firm averages 46 titles/year; young adult division averages 35 titles/year. Pays royalty or makes outright purchase. Simultaneous and photocopied submissions OK. Computer printout submissions acceptable; prefers letter-quality to dot-matrix. SASE. Reports in 3-4 weeks. Free book catalog.
Nonfiction: Young adult, reference, self-help and textbook. Subjects include art, health, coping, and music. "Our books are geared to the young adult audience whom we reach via school and public libraries. Most of the books we publish are related to guidance career and personal adjustment. We also publish material on the theater, music and art, as well as journalism for schools. Interested in supplementary material for enrichment of school curriculum. Manuscripts in the young-adult nonfiction areas of vocational guidance, personal and social adjustment, journalism, and theater. Reviews artwork/photos as part of ms package. For Pelion Press, mss on classical music, emphasis on opera and singing." Query or submit outline/synopsis and sample chapters.
Recent Nonfiction Title: *Coping with Academic Anxiety*, by Ottens.

ROSS BOOKS, Box 4340, Berkeley CA 94704. President: Franz Ross. Publishes hardcover and paperback originals (85%), paperback reprints (15%), and software. Averages 7-10 titles/year. Offers 8-12% royalties on net price. Average advance: 10% of the first print run. Publishes book an average of 10 months after acceptance. Simultaneous and photocopied submissions OK. Electronic submissions on disk for TRS80 OK. Computer printout submissions acceptable. SASE. Reports in 1 month. Free book catalog.
Nonfiction: General career finding, bicycle books, popular how-to science, garden books, music, general how-to, some natural foods and Eastern religion. Especially wants general career finding, popular how-to science and how-to's. No political, fiction, poetry or children's books. Accepts nonfiction translations. Reviews artwork/photos as part of ms package. Submit outline/synopsis and 2 sample chapters with SASE.
Recent Nonfiction Title: *300 Years at the Keyboard*.
Software: Send description of program (what it does) and machines it will run on.

ROSSEL BOOKS, 44 Dunbow Dr., Chappaqua NY 10514. (914)238-8954. President: Seymour Rossel. Publishes hardcover originals, trade paperback originals, reprints and software. Averages 6-8 titles/year. "We subsidy publish only books which have been sponsored by foundations, organizations, etc." Pays royalty on wholesale or retail price. Negotiates advance. Publishes book an average of 1 year after acceptance. Photocopied submissions OK. Electronic submissions OK on IBM PC Readable: 5¼" diskette. Computer printout submissions acceptable. SASE. Reports in 2 weeks on queries; 1 month on mss. Book catalog for business-size SAE and 37¢ postage.
Nonfiction: Cookbook, how-to, illustrated book, juvenile, reference, textbook, and Judaica in all fields—art, cooking and foods, history, philosophy, photography, politics, psychology, religion, sociology, and travel. "We currently seek juvenile nonfiction manuscripts on Jewish subjects; adult manuscripts on being Jewish in America, Jews on the frontier, interesting anecdotal histories with Jewish content, and collections of American Jewish photos. We do not publish adult Jewish fiction. However, we do wish to see juvenile fiction in the Judaica field." Submit outline/synopsis and sample chapters. Reviews artwork/photos as part of ms package.
Recent Nonfiction Title: *Torah From Our Sage*, by J. Nevsner (commentary on Jewish classic, Pirke Avot).
Fiction: Juvenile Jewish adventure, ethnic, historical, mystery, religious, romance and science fiction. Submit outline synopsis and sample chapters.
Software: Jewish subject matter only. Contact: S. Rossel.
Tips: "Within the next year, Rossel Books will be initiating a new publishing imprint, Longhorn Books. Longhorn will seek to do Texas-oriented material for the Texas regional marketplace. We would be glad to see submissions for this new imprint as well."

*ROSS-ERIKSON, INC., PUBLISHERS, 223 Via Sevilla, Santa Barbara CA 93109. (805)962-1175. Editor: Roy (Buzz) Erikson. Managing Editor: Shelley Lowenkopf. Publishes hardcover and trade paperback originals, and hardcover and trade paperback reprints. Averages 6 titles/year. Subsidy publishes 15-20% of books. Pays 7-10% royalty; offers average $500 advance. Publishes book an average of 18 months after acceptance. Simultaneous and photocopied submissions OK. Computer printout submissions acceptable; no dot-matrix. SASE. Reports in 2 months on queries; 6 months on mss. Book catalog for 50¢.
Nonfiction: How-to, self-help, anthropology, philosophy, and comparative religion. Accepts nonfiction translations from German and Spanish. Subjects include art, health, philosophy, psychology and religion (comparative). Query or submit outline/synopsis and 1-2 sample chapters. Looks for "strength of style, accuracy in nonfiction works, talent." Reviews artwork/photos as part of ms package.

Recent Nonfiction Title: *The Don Juan Papers*, by Richard deMille (anthropology, philosophy and science).
Fiction: No fiction or poetry being considered this year.
Tips: "Trends in book publishing that freelance writers should be aware of include co-publishing—where part of risk is taken by writers—particularly where market is unstable (fiction and poetry)."

ROUTLEDGE & KEGAN PAUL, INC., 9 Park St., Boston MA 02108. Director: Bob Paul. Editor: Stratford Caldecott. Imprints include Pandora Press. Publishes hardcover and paperback originals and reprints. Pays standard 10-12½-15% wholesale royalty contract "on clothbound editions, if the books are not part of a series"; usual advance is $1,000-3,000. Averages 200 titles/year. Query with outline and sample chapters. Submit complete ms "only after going through outline and sample chapters step." Reports in 2-3 months. Enclose check for return postage.
Nonfiction: "Academic, reference, and scholarly levels: social sciences, philosophy and logic, psychology, parapsychology, oriental religions, history, political science and education. Our books generally form a reputable series under the general editorship of distinguished academics in their fields. The approach should be similar to the styles adopted by Cambridge University Press, Harvard University Press and others." Interested in material for the International Library of Sociology, International Library of Philosophy, International Library of Psychology and US Policy and Welfare. Length: 50,000-150,000 words.

RPM PRESS, INC., 221½ N. Jefferson, Wadena MN 56482. (218)631-4707. Publisher: David A. Hietala. Publishes trade paperback originals (90%), trade paperback reprints (10%), and audio-cassette (with workbook) training programs. Averages 18-24 titles/year. Pays 5-15% royalty on retail price or makes outright purchase of $300-1,500. Average advance to established authors is $500. Simultaneous and photocopied submissions OK. Computer printout submissions acceptable. SASE. Reports in 5 weeks on queries; 2 months on mss (usually sooner). Pubishes book an average of 6 months after acceptance. Book catalog for 9x12 SAE and 54¢ postage.
Nonfiction: How-to-do-it, reference and technical books and audio-cassette training programs on business, applied management, finance, and engineering geared toward managing the nonprofit sheltered workcenter (for the handicapped). "We are looking for how-to books and audio-cassette programs that tell how to set up new business ventures, or how to improve present business management practice. For example, a how-to book on setting up a profitable micrographics operation would catch our eye. Or, something on setting up QC or Inventory procedures (that work) would also get our interest going. People who buy our books and tape packages are managers and concerned professionals looking to improve the management practice of their nonprofit business enterprises, so we obviously like to hear from writers who have spent some time in the management of business organizations. We know that few writers can write the kind of stuff we need—and even fewer know the marketplace we serve, so we offer new authors extensive editorial assistance to make sure that they address the special needs of the marketplace. We are entirely receptive to hearing all ideas and are interested in working with authors who—once they establish themselves with us—are willing to work with us on long-term basis." Query.
Recent Nonfiction Title: *The Direct Mail Marketing Handbook*, D. Hietala (marketing).

RUSSICA PUBLISHERS, INC., 799 Broadway, New York NY 10003. (212)473-7480. Contact: Valery Kuharets. Publishes trade paperback originals (50%) and reprints (50%). Averages 15 titles/year. Pays 10-15% royalty on retail price. Photocopied submissions OK. SASE. Reports in 2 weeks. Free book catalog.
Nonfiction: Biography and humor. Subjects include history. "We're looking for biographies of prominent Russians or Slavs written in English. All other mss must be in Russian only."
Recent Nonfiction Title: *Uncensored Russian Limericks*, by V. Kozlovsky (folklore).
Fiction: Adventure, erotica, ethnic, horror, humor, mystery and suspense. "Russian language manuscripts only." Submit complete ms.
Recent Fiction Title: *Poetry*, by Marina Tsvetaeva.
Poetry: Modern Russian poetry. Submit complete ms.
Recent Poetry Title: *Roman Elegies*, by Joseph Brodsky.

RUTGERS UNIVERSITY PRESS, 30 College Ave., New Brunswick NJ 08903. Averages 50 titles/year. Pays royalty on retail price. Publishes book an average of 1 year after acceptance. Computer printout submissions acceptable; no dot-matrix. Final decision depends on time required to secure competent professional reading reports. Enclose return postage. Free book catalog.
Nonfiction: Scholarly books in history, literary criticism, anthropology, sociology, women's studies and criminal justice. Regional nonfiction must deal with mid-Atlantic region with emphasis on New Jersey. Length: 60,000 words minimum. Query. Reviews artwork/photos as part of ms package.
Recent Nonfiction Title: *Joseph Conrad*, by Zdzislaw Nadjer.

S. C. E.-EDITIONS L'ETINCELLE, 65 Hillside Ave., Westmount, Montreal, Quebec H3Z 1W1 Canada. (514)935-1314. President: Robert Davies. Imprints include L'Etincelle (nonfiction and fiction) and Memoire

Vive (microcomputer books). Publishes trade paperback originals. Averages 12 titles/year. Pays 8-12% royalty on retail price; offers average $1,000. Simultaneous and photocopied submissions OK. SASE. Reports in 8 weeks on queries; 3 months on mss. Free book catalog.

Nonfiction: Biography, cookbook, how-to, humor, reference and self-help. Subjects include animals, business and economics, cooking and foods, health, history, hobbies, microcomputers, nature, philosophy, politics, psychology, recreation, sociology, sports and travel. Accepts nonfiction translations. "We are looking for about 5 translatable works of nonfiction, in any popular field. Our audience includes French-speaking readers in all major markets in the world." No "topics of interest only to Americans." Query or submit outline/synopsis and 3 sample chapters.

Recent Nonfiction Title: *Commodore 64 Handbook.*

ST. ANTHONY MESSENGER PRESS, 1615 Republic St., Cincinnati OH 45210. Editor-in-Chief: The Rev. Norman Perry, O.F.M. Publishes paperback originals. Averages 12 titles/year. Pays 6-8% royalty on retail price; offers $500 average advance. Publishes book an average of 8 months after acceptance. Books are sold in bulk to groups (study clubs, high school or college classes) and in bookstores. Will consider photocopied submissions if they are not simultaneous submissions to other publishers. Electronic submissions OK, but requires hard copy also. Computer printout submissions acceptable; prefers letter-quality to dot-matrix. Query or submit outline and 2 sample chapters. Enclose return postage. Will send free catalog to writer on request.

Nonfiction: Religion. "We try to reach the Catholic market with topics near the heart of the ordinary Catholic's belief. We want to offer insight and inspiration and thus give people support in living a Christian life in a pluralistic society. We are not interested in an academic or abstract approach. Our emphasis is on popular writing with examples, specifics, color and anecdotes." Length: 25,000-40,000 words.

Recent Nonfiction Title: *Six Ways to Pray from Six Great Saints*, by Gloria Hutchinson.

Tips: "Trends in book publishing that freelance writers should be aware of include publishers interest in word processing/typesetting interface. Therefore, format of book is more important than ever."

ST. LUKE'S PRESS, Mid-Memphis Tower, 1407 Union, Memphis TN 38104. (901)357-5441. Subsidiaries include Raccoon Books, Inc. (literary non-profit), and American Blake Foundation (scholarly non-profit). Managing Editor: Roger Easson, PhD. Averages 5-6 titles/year. Pays 10% minimum royalty on invoice; offers average $100-200. Publishes book an average of 18 months after acceptance. Electronic submissions OK for Apple II on TRS 80, but requires hard copy also. Computer printout submissions acceptable. SASE. Reports in 3 months. Book catalog $1.

Nonfiction: Biography. "The author must have some logical connection with the mid-South region." Submit story line and 3 sample chapters. Accepts translations.

Recent Nonfiction Title: *Absolutely, Positively Overnight*, by Robert Sigafoos.

Fiction: Submit story line and 3 sample chapters.

Recent Fiction Title: *Covenant at Coldwater*, by John Osier.

Recent Poetry Title: *Poetry Is You*, by Douglas Hinkle.

ST. MARTIN'S PRESS, 175 5th Ave., New York NY 10010. Averages 550 titles/year. SASE. Reports "promptly."

Nonfiction: General and textbook. Publishes general fiction and nonfiction; major interest in adult fiction and nonfiction, history, self-help, political science, popular science, biography, scholarly, popular reference, etc. "No children's books." Query. "It takes very persuasive credentials to prompt us to commission a book or outline." Electronic submissions OK, but requires hard copy also. Computer printout submissions acceptable.

Recent Title: *Death in Kasmir*, by M.M. Kaye.

Tips: "We do every kind of book there is, all adult trade; everything except children's books."

HOWARD W. SAMS & CO., INC., 4300 W. 62nd St., Indianapolis IN 46268. (317)298-5400. Manager of Acquisitions: C.P. Oliphant. Payment depends on quantity, quality, and salability. Offers both royalty arrangements or outright purchase. Prefers queries, outlines, and sample chapters. Usually reports within 30 days. SASE.

Nonfiction: Technical and engineering books on computers, electronics, security, robots, video and telecommunications.

‡**SAYBROOK PUBLISHING CO.**, 3518 Armstrong, Dallas TX 75205. (214)521-3757. Managing Editor: Pat Howell. Publishes hardcover and trade paperback originals and reprints. Averages 4-5 titles/year. Pays 6-12% royalty on retail price. Simultaneous and photocopied submissions OK. Electronic submissions OK for WordStar simplified type language, or any system that will interface with a composer printer. Computer printout submissions acceptable. SASE. Reports in 1 month. Free book catalog.

Nonfiction: Biography, juvenile, and literary human science. Subjects include Americana, art, business and economics, health, nature, philosophy, politics, psychology, religion, sociology, women's studies, and envi-

ronmental studies. "Especially interested in scholarly studies in the human sciences which are also exciting, marketable literature written for the trade, e.g., Rollo May and Loren Eisley." No books written to advance the writer's academic reputation. Submit outline/synopsis and sample chapters.
Recent Nonfiction Title: *Embodied Mind*, by R. Patton (physiology).
Fiction: Scholarly work in the human sciences. Especially looking for "books which reveal in a scholarly way specific, essential truths about human beings, e.g., Issac Basevitch Singer. No books whose *only* purpose is to sell." Submit outline/synopsis and sample chapters.
Tips: "Our books are for the intelligent, curious, general reader. We only publish freelance submissions. Seek to tell the truth about human beings by any means. The times in which we live demand it. There are enough readers who hunger for it."

SCARECROW PRESS, INC., 52 Liberty St., Metuchen NJ 08840. Senior Editor: Bill Eshelman. Editors: Barbara Lee and Beth Ellis. Publishes hardcover originals. Averages 110 titles/year. Pays 10% royalty on list price of first 1,500 copies; 15% on list price thereafter. No advance. Publishes book an average of 11 months after acceptance. Photocopied submissions OK. SASE. Reports in 2 weeks. Free book catalog.
Nonfiction: Books about music. Needs reference books, annotated bibliographies, indexes, women's studies, and movies. Query.

*SCHENKMAN PUBLISHING CO., INC., 190 Concord Ave., Cambridge MA 02138. (617)492-4952. Editor-in-Chief: Alfred S. Schenkman. Publishes hardcover and paperback originals. Specializes in textbooks and professional and technical books. Averages 60 titles/year. Subsidy publishes 3% of books. Royalty varies on net sales, but averages 10%. "In some cases, no royalties are paid on first 2,000 copies sold." No advance. State availability of photos and/or illustrations. Publishes book an average of 6 months after acceptance. Computer printout submissions acceptable. Reports in 1-2 months. SASE. Free book catalog.
Nonfiction: Publishes economics, history, psychology, sociology, textbooks and professional and technical books. Reviews artwork/photos as part of ms package. Query.
Recent Nonfiction Title: *The Compleat University*, by Hermanns et al.

SCHIRMER BOOKS, Macmillan Publishing Co., Inc., 866 3rd Ave., New York NY 10022. Senior Editor: Maribeth Payne. Publishes hardcover and paperback originals, paperback reprints and software. Pays royalty on wholesale or retail price; small advance. Publishes 20 books/year. Subsidy publishes 5-10% of books. Submit photos and/or illustrations "if central to the book, not if decorative or tangential." Publishes book an average of 1 year after acceptance. Electronic submissions OK, but requires hard copy also. Computer printout submissions acceptable. Reports in 6 weeks. SASE. Book catalog for SASE.
Nonfiction: Publishes books on the performing arts specializing in music, dance and theater, college texts, "coffee table" books, biographies, reference, and how-to. Submit outline/synopsis and sample chapters and current vita. Reviews artwork/photos as part of ms package.
Recent Nonfiction Title: *A Moment's Notice: Portraits of American Jazz Musicians*, by Carol Friedman.

SCHOCKEN BOOKS, INC., 200 Madison Ave., New York NY 10016. (212)685-6500. Managing Director: Emile Capouya. Publishes hardcover and paperback originals and paperback reprints and simultaneous. Publishes 56 titles/year. Pays standard royalty; offers variable advance. Photocopied submissions OK. SASE. Reports in 6 weeks. Free book catalog.
Nonfiction: Needs books of Jewish interest, academic sociology, and children's (mythology and folktales). Submit outline/synopsis and sample chapters.
Recent Nonfiction Title: *Women's Diaries of the Westward Journey*, by Lillian Schlissel.

SCHOLARLY RESOURCES, INC., 104 Greenhill Ave., Wilmington DE 19805. (302)654-7713. Managing Editor: Philip G. Johnson. Publishes hardcover and trade paperback originals. Averages 15 hardcover titles/year. Pays 5-15% royalty on retail price. Simultaneous and photocopied submissions OK. Computer printout submissions acceptable. SASE. Reports in 2 weeks on queries; 2 months on mss. Free book catalog.
Nonfiction: Reference. Subjects include history, sociology and political science. "We are interested in bibliography and other reference material as well as historical research and interpretative works on modern America, modern China, and diplomatic history. Our audience includes university and public libraries; some course adoption." Query or submit outline/synopsis and sample chapters. Reviews artwork/photos as part of ms package.
Recent Nonfiction Title: *North Korea: A Political Handbook*, by Tai Sung An.

SCHOLASTIC, INC., 730 Broadway, New York NY 10003. (212)505-3000. Editor: Ann Reit. Imprints include Wildfire, Windswept and Sunfire. Publishes trade paperback originals and software. Averages 36 titles/year. Pays 6% royalty on retail price. Computer printout submissions acceptable; no dot-matrix. Reports in 3 months. Tip sheet for business-sized SASE with 20¢ postage.
Fiction: Gothic (Windswept line); romance (Wildlife line); and historical romance (Sunfire). "Windswept and

Wildlife books should be 40,000-45,000 words and Sunfire 85,000 words for 12 to 15 year old girls who are average to good readers." Query. Request tip sheet and follow guidelines carefully before submitting outline and three sample chapters.
Software: Contact Deb Kovacs.
Tips: Queries/mss may be routed to other editors in the publishing group.

SCHOLASTIC, INC., Pretzel Books, 730 Broadway, New York NY 10036. (212)505-3000. Editor: Molly Harrington. Publishes trade paperback and book club originals. Averages 6-8 titles/year. Pays 6% royalty on retail price; buys some mss outright for $3,000-4,000; $2,500 advance. Photocopied submissions OK. SASE. Reports in 1 month.
Nonfiction: Juvenile and puzzle books. "Puzzle manuscripts containing one kind of puzzle (crosswords, word finds mazes, etc.) or manuscripts containing all different kinds of puzzles. Manuscripts written with a specific theme in mind (joke-puzzles, space, video, etc.) will also be considered. The puzzles should be geared for children ages 9-12. I'm looking for a fun, humorous, snappy approach, as well as good puzzle-making." No mss where the puzzles are fashioned around a licensed character (Superman, Peanuts, etc.) or a particular movie (*Star Wars*, *Raiders of the Lost Ark*, etc.). Submit puzzle and samples or complete ms.
Recent Nonfiction Title: *Pig Jokes and Puzzles*, by Lisa Eisenberg and Katy Hall.

SCHOLASTIC-TAB PUBLICATIONS, 123 Newkirk Rd., Richmond Hill, Ontario L4C 3G5 Canada. (416)883-5300. Subsidiary of Scholastic, Inc. Acquisitions Editor: Sandra B. Johnston. Imprints include North Winds Press (nonfiction and fiction). Publishes hardcover, trade paperback and mass market paperback originals (80%), and paperback reprints (20%). Averages 35 titles/year in English and French. Pays royalty on list price; advance "depends on probable print run." Publishes book an average of 18 months after acceptance. Computer printout submissions acceptable; prefers letter-quality to dot-matrix. SASE. Reports in 3 weeks on queries; 3 months on mss.
Nonfiction: How-to, humor and juvenile. Subjects include animals, hobbies, crafts, puzzle books, mystery and adventure stories; Canadian authors preferred. Submit outline/synopsis and sample chapters with basic storyline; looking for "an engaging story with a compelling and imaginative storyline, strong and convincing characters, and an immediate, lively writing style," or complete ms. Reviews artwork/photos as part of ms package.
Recent Nonfiction Title: *Seeds & Weeds, A Book of Country Crafts*, by Mary Alice Downie and Jillian Gilliland.
Fiction: Adventure, fantasy, humor, mainstream, mystery, romance, science fiction and suspense, suitable for ages 4-16, Canadian authors preferred. Submit outline/synopsis and sample chapters or complete ms.
Recent Fiction Title: *The Seventh Princess*, by Nick Sullivan.

CHARLES SCRIBNER'S SONS, 597 5th Ave., New York NY 10017. Director of Trade Publishing: Jacek K. Galazka. Publishes hardcover originals and hardcover and paperback reprints. Averages 300 titles/year. "Our contract terms, royalties and advances vary, depending on the nature of the project." Computer printout submissions acceptable; prefers letter-quality to dot-matrix. Reports in 1-2 months. Enclose return postage.
Nonfiction: Publishes adult general fiction and nonfiction, practical books, science for the layman, and health and business books. Queries only.
Recent Fiction Title: *Mediations in Green*, by Stephen Wright (novel).

CHARLES SCRIBNER'S SONS, Children's Books Department, 597 5th Ave., New York NY 10017. (212)486-4035. Editorial Director, Children's Books: Clare Costello. Publishes hardcover originals and paperback reprints of own titles. Averages 40 titles/year. Pays royalty on retail price; offers advance. Publishes book an average of 1 years after acceptance. Computer printout submissions acceptable. SASE. Free book catalog.
Nonfiction: Animals, art, biography, health, hobbies, humor, nature, photography, recreation, science and sports. Reviews artwork/photos as part of ms package. Query.
Recent Nonfiction Title: *Wolfman*, by Lawrence Pringle.
Fiction: Adventure, fantasy, historical, humor, mainstream, mystery, science fiction and suspense. Submit outline/synopsis and sample chapters.
Recent Fiction Title: *The Wild Children*, by Felice Holmen.

SECOND CHANCE AT LOVE, 200 Madison Ave., New York NY 10016. (212)686-9820. Subsidiary of Berkley Publishing Group. Senior Editor: Ellen Edwards. Publishes mass market paperback original category romances. Averages 72 titles/year. Pays 2-6% royalty; averages $5,000 advance. Photocopied submissions OK. Computer printout and disk submissions acceptable; prefers letter-quality to dot-matrix. Reports in 6 weeks.
Fiction: Contemporary romance. Accepts 3 sample chapters and detailed chapter-by-chapter outline. Query and request writer's guidelines.
Recent Fiction Title: *Kisses From Heaven*, by Jeanne Grant.

‡**SECOND CHANCE PRESS/PERMANENT PRESS**, Rd. #2, Noyac Rd., Sag Harbor NY 11963. (516)725-1101. Editor: Judith Shepard. Publishes hardcover and trade paperback originals, hardcover trade paperback, and mass market paperback reprints. Averages 12 titles/year. Pays 10% maximum royalty on wholesale price; offers average $200 advance. Publishes book an average of 18 months after acceptance. Simultaneous and photocopied submissions OK. Computer printout submissions acceptable; prefers letter-quality to dot-matrix. SASE. Reports in 2 weeks on queries; 3 months on mss. Free book catalog.
Nonfiction: Biography, "coffee table" book, cookbook, how-to, humor, illustrated book, juvenile (young adult), and self-help. Subjects include Americana, cooking and foods, health, history, philosophy, politics, psychology, and religion. No scientific and technical material or academic studies. Query.
Recent Nonfiction Title: *Hamptons Health Spa Diet Cookbook*, by Matthews and Kulick (cookbook).
Fiction: Adventure, confession, erotica, ethnic, experimental, fantasy, gothic, historical, humor, mainstream, mystery, religious, romance, and suspense. Especially looking for fiction with a unique point of view—"original and arresting", suitable for college literature classes. No mass-market romance. Query.
Recent Fiction Title: *The Sorcerer*, by Anne Crompton (young adult).

SELF-COUNSEL PRESS, INC., Subsidiary of International Self-Counsel Press, Ltd., 1303 N. Northgate Way, Seattle WA 98133. (206)522-8383. Editor-in-Chief: Lois Richardson. Publishes trade paperback originals. Averages 15 new titles/year. Pays 10% royalty on wholesale price. Publishes book an average of 7 months after acceptance. Computer printout submissions acceptable; prefers letter-quality to dot-matrix. SASE. Reports in 6 weeks on queries; 2 months on mss. Free book catalog.
Nonfiction: How-to and reference on law, business and economics. Books on starting and running specific businesses applicable to both Canada and the US. Do-it-yourself and self-help law books for laypeople. No general "how to start a business" books. Query or submit outline/synopsis and sample chapters.
Recent Nonfiction Title: *Collection Techniques for the Small Business*, by Tim Paulsen.

SERVANT PUBLICATIONS, 840 Airport Blvd., Box 8617, Ann Arbor MI 48107. (313)761-8505. Editor: Ann Spangler. Publishes hardcover, trade and mass market paperback originals, and trade paperback reprints. Averages 25 titles/year. Pays 10% royalty on retail price. Computer printout submissions acceptable. Reports in 1 month. Free book catalog.
Nonfiction: Subjects include religion. "We're looking for practical Christian teaching, scripture, current problems facing the Christian church, and inspiration." No heterodox or non-Christian approaches. Query or submit brief outline/synopsis and 1 sample chapter. Reviews artwork/photos as part of ms package. All unsolicited mss are returned unopened.
Recent Nonfiction Title: *On Christian Truth*, by Harry Blamires.

SEVEN SEAS PRESS, Subsidiary of Davis Publications, 524 Thames St., Newport RI 02840. (401)847-1683. Editor: James Gilbert. Publishes hardcover originals. Averages 12 titles/year. Pays 8-12½% on gross receipts. Offers average $1,500 advance. Publishes book an average of 1 year after acceptance. Computer printout submissions acceptable "if legible." SASE. Reports in 1 month.
Nonfiction: "Coffee table" book, cookbook, how-to, humor, illustrated book, reference and technical. "All our titles are in the nautical/marine field. We specialize in informative books that help cruising sailors, in particular, enjoy their sport." Not interested in any nonfiction that is not of use or benefit to the cruising sailor. Query or submit outline/synopsis and sample chapters. Reviews artwork/photos as part of ms package.
Recent Nonfiction Title: *Spurr's Boatbook*, by Dan Spurr (projects to help boatowners upgrade their boats).

HAROLD SHAW PUBLISHERS, 388 Gundersen Dr., Box 567, Wheaton IL 60189. (312)665-6700. Managing Editor: Megs Singer. Publishes hardcover and paperback originals (80%) and paperback reprints (20%). Averages 24 titles/year. Offers 5-10% royalty on retail price. Average advance (only with established authors): $300-400. Publishes book an average of 2 years after acceptance. Computer printout submissions acceptable; prefers letter-quality to dot-matrix. SASE. Reports in 1 month. Free book catalog.
Nonfiction: How-to, juveniles, poetry, literary, religion, and self-help. Especially needs "manuscripts dealing with the needs of Christians in today's changing world that give Christians practical help and challenge for living out their faith. If it is not for the Christian market, we don't want to see it. We do not want to see poetry unless the poet is already established and has a reading audience. Mss must be high in quality and creativity." Query first, then submit outline/synopsis and 2-3 sample chapters.
Recent Nonfiction Title: *Finders Keepers*, by Dee Brestin (personal and small group evangelism).
Tips: "Trends in book publishing that freelance writers should be aware of include the need to use non-sexist language without going to extremes.

THE SHOE STRING PRESS, (Archon Books, Linnet Books, Library Professional Publications), 995 Sherman Ave., Hamden CT 06514. (203)248-6307. Distributor for the Connecticut Academy of Arts and Sciences. President: James Thorpe III. Publishes 60 titles/year. Royalty on net; no advance. Publishes book an average of 1 year after acceptance. Electronic submissions OK, but requires hard copy also. Computer printout submis-

sions acceptable; prefers letter-quality to dot-matrix. Reports in 4-6 weeks. SASE.
Nonfiction: Publishes scholarly books: history, biography, literary criticism, reference, geography, bibliography, military history, information science, library science, education and general adult nonfiction. Accepts nonfiction translations. Preferred length: 40,000-130,000 words, though there is no set limit. Query with table of contents and 2-3 sample chapters. Reviews artwork/photos as part of ms package.
Recent Nonfiction Title: *Both Sides of the Ocean: A Biography of Henry Adams: His First Life, 1838-1862*, by Edward Chalfan.
Tips: Queries/mss may be routed to other editors in the publishing group.

SIERRA CLUB BOOKS, 2034 Fillmore St., San Francisco CA 94115. (415)931-7950. Editor-in-Chief: Daniel Moses. Publishes hardcover and paperback originals (95%) and reprints (5%). Averages 20 titles/year. Offers 7-12½% royalty on retail price. Average advance: $5,000. Computer printout submissions acceptable. SASE. Reports in 2 months. Free book catalog.
Nonfiction: Animals, health, history (natural), how-to (outdoors), juveniles, nature, philosophy, photography, recreation (outdoors, nonmechanical), science, sports (outdoors), and travel (by foot or bicycle). "The Sierra Club was founded to help people to explore, enjoy and preserve the nation's forests, waters, wildlife and wilderness. The books program looks to publish quality trade books about the outdoors and the protection of natural resources. Specifically, we are interested in undeveloped land (not philosophical but informational), nuclear power, self-sufficiency, natural history, politics and the environment, and juvenile books with an ecological theme." Does *not* want "personal, lyrical, philosophical books on the great outdoors; proposals for large color photographic books without substantial text; how-to books on building things outdoors; books on motorized travel; or any but the most professional studies of animals." Query first, submit outline/synopsis and sample chapters.
Recent Nonfiction Title: *A Bitter Fog: Herbicides and Human Rights*, by Carol Van Strum (a book about the affects of pesticide spraying on a rural community in Oregon).
Fiction: Adventure, historical, mainstream, and science fiction. "We do very little fiction, but will consider a fiction manuscript if its theme fits our philosophical aims: the enjoyment and protection of the environment." Does *not* want "any ms with animals or plants that talk; apocalyptic plots." Query first, submit outline/synopsis and sample chapters, or submit complete ms.
Recent Fiction Title: *The River Why*, by David James Duncan.

SIGNPOST BOOKS, 8912 192nd SW, Edmonds WA 98020. Editor-in-Chief: Cliff Cameron. Publishes paperback originals. Averages 3-4 titles/year. Offers standard minimum book contract of 6% on retail price. Publishes book an average of 1 year after acceptance. Computer printout submissions acceptable "if good quality". Query. Accepts outline/synopsis and 2-3 sample chapters. Reports in 3 weeks. SASE. Free book catalog.
Nonfiction: "Books on outdoor subjects emphasizing self-propelled activity such as hiking, canoeing, bicycling, camping and related interests. Books should have strong environmental material for a general audience, where applicable." Reviews artwork/photos as part of ms package.
Recent Nonfiction Title: *Stehekin: The Enchanted Valley*, by Fred Darvill Jr. (hiking and nature guide).
Tips: Queries/mss may be routed to other editors in the publishing group.

SILHOUETTE BOOKS, Subsidiary of Simon & Schuster/Pocket Books, 1230 Avenue of the Americas, New York NY 10020. (212)586-6151. Editor-in-Chief: Karen Solem. Publishes mass market paperback originals. Averages 336 titles/year. Pays royalty; buys some mss outright. Publishes book an average of 1 year after acceptance. Photocopied submissions OK. Computer printout submissions acceptable; no dot-matrix. SASE. Reports in 5 weeks on queries; 3 months on mss. "Tip-sheets are available upon request."
Imprints: Silhouette Romances (contemporary adult romances), Patricia Smith, editor; 50,000-55,000 words. Silhouette Special Editions (contemporary adult romances), Mary Clare Kersten, editor: 75,000-80,000 words. Silhouette Desires (contemporary adult romances), Isabel Swift, editor: 55,000-65,000 words. Silhouette First Loves (contemporary young adult romances), Nancy Jackson, editor: 35,000-40,000 words. Silhouette Intimate Moments (contemporary adult romances), Leslie Wainger, editor: 75,000-85,000 words. Silhouette Inspirations (contemporary adult religious romances), Roz Noonan, editor: 55,000-60,000 words.
Fiction: Romance (contemporary romance for adults and young adults). "We are particularly interested in seeing material for the Silhouette Romance, Silhouette Desire and Silhouette Inspiration lines, though we will consider submissions for all lines. No mss other than contemporary romances of the type outlined above." Submit one-page queries only; "follow our general format, yet have an individuality and life of its own that will make it stand out in the readers' minds."
Recent Fiction Title: *Controlling Interest*, by Janet Joyce.
WM Editor's Note: As of press time, Torstar Corporation, owner of Harlequin Books, had announced the acquisition of Silhouette Books *subject* to a definitive agreement.

Close-up

Mary Clare (Susen) Kersten
Senior Editor, Silhouette Books

If you want to make money writing, don't write a romance novel—unless you *love* the genre. "Our ideal romance writers are those writers who enjoy romances, who have read them for a long time, and are very interested in them," says Silhouette senior editor Mary Clare (Susen) Kersten.

It *is* a lucrative undertaking for the writer who can publish two to three books annually. "Hopeful romance writers who don't make it are either those who have no talent for the language or those who don't like romances but are looking for a way to make money in writing," she says.

Thousands of submissions arrive each year at the Silhouette offices where each editor edits four to six titles a month. Editors no longer accept unsolicited (complete or partial) manuscripts but do review one-page queries for Silhouette's six lines: Contemporary Romances, Desire, First Love, Inspirations, Intimate Moments, and Special Editions.

Silhouette is open to ideas and will respond to query letters (target them for a particular line), Kersten stresses. "It is imperative that we work on manuscripts that are promising.

"We used to look at a lot of potential partials which would be flops when they came in as complete manuscripts," says Kersten, in charge of Silhouette Special Editions.

For category romances, editors would rather reject a manuscript than make extensive changes. "When I edit, I don't get down to the very, very fine points of writing because quite frankly the readers aren't interested in perfect literary style—they're interested in good stories," says Kersten, who joined Silhouette five years ago as Simon & Schuster was initiating romance lines.

She checks the plot lines and looks for inaccuracies. "We just make sure that when that book goes out to the public it's a fun book, it's readable, and it makes a lot of sense."

There is no typical Silhouette author. They range in age from the late 20s to the 60s; some are happily or unhappily married, and some rich, some poor. What they have in common is an understanding of romances' two main ingredients: "a lot of passion and romantic tension combined with a good, sympathetic story."

By passion, Kersten means "falling in love with the heart," not explicit scenes.

The number of brand-name contemporary category romances (excluding historicals) published *each month* industry-wide has gone from 30 to 140. As readers clamor for more romances, the writing and the stories get better, believes Kersten.

Potential writers—already more than 4,200 of them—have learned the latest Silhouette *news* at its "How to Write a Romance" Workshops. Editors traveled to 15 American cities to give 21 workshops in 1983.

The writer who repeatedly cannot break in to the romance market might want to try another genre. "Not everybody can write a romance," she says. "I don't buy books on taste; I buy books that I know our readers are going to like."

SILVER BURDETT, Subsidiary of SFN Companies, Inc., 250 James St., Morristown NJ 07960. Editor-in-Chief: Charlotte Gemmel. Publishes hardcover and paperback originals, and software. Publishes 180 titles/year. "Textbook rates only, el-hi range." Publishes book an average of 3 years after acceptance. Electronic submissions OK, but requires hard copy also. Computer printout submissions acceptable. Query. SASE.
Nonfiction: Education. Produces educational materials for preschoolers, elementary and high school students. Among materials produced: textbooks, teachers' materials, other print and nonprint classroom materials including educational courseware, manipulatives and audiovisual aids (silent and sound 16mm films and filmstrips, records, multimedia kits, overhead transparencies, tapes, etc.). Assigns projects to qualified writers on occasion. Writer must have understanding of school market and school learning materials. Reviews artwork/photos as part of ms package.
Software: Elementary and high school, all basal academic areas. Contact: Jeanne Gleason.
Tips: Queries/mss may be routed to other editors in the publishing group.

SIMON & SCHUSTER, Trade Books Division, 1230 Avenue of the Americas, New York NY 10020. "If we accept a book for publication, business arrangements are worked out with the author or his agent and a contract is drawn up. The specific terms vary according to the type of book and other considerations. Royalty rates are more or less standard among publishers. Special arrangements are made for anthologies, translations and projects involving editorial research services. All unsolicited mss will be returned unread. Only mss submitted by agents or recommended to us by friends or actively solicited by us will be considered. In such cases, our requirements are as follows: All mss submitted for consideration should be marked to the attention of a specific editor. It usually takes at least three weeks for the author to be notified of a decision—often longer. Sufficient postage for return by first-class registered mail, or instructions for return by express collect, in case of rejection, should be included. Mss must be typewritten, double-spaced, on one side of the sheet only. We suggest margins of about one inch all around and the standard 8"x11" typewriter paper." Prefers complete mss. Computer printout submissions acceptable; prefers letter-quality to dot-matrix.
Nonfiction and Fiction: "Simon and Schuster publishes books of general adult fiction, history, biography, science, philosophy, the arts and popular culture, running 50,000 words or more. Our program does not, however, include school textbooks, extremely technical or highly specialized works, or, as a general rule, poetry or plays. Exceptions have been made, of course, for extraordinary mss of great distinction or significance."
Tips: Queries/mss may be routed to other editors in the publishing group.

*SLAVICA PUBLISHERS, INC., Box 14388, Columbus OH 43214. (614)268-4002. President/Editor: Charles E. Gribble. Publishes hardcover and paperback originals, reprints and software. Averages 20 titles/year. Subsidy publishes 33-50% of books. "All manuscripts are read for quality; if they pass that test, then we talk about money. We *never* accept full subsidies on a book, and we *never* publish anything that has not passed the scrutiny of expert readers. Most subsidies are very small (usually in the range of $200-800)." Offers 10-15% royalty on retail price; "for some books, royalties do not begin until specified number has been sold." Publishes book an average of 1 year after acceptance. Computer printout submissions acceptable. "Only in exceptional circumstances will we consider simultaneous submissions, and only if we are informed of it. We strongly prefer good photocopied submissions rather than the original." Query first. SASE. Reports in 1 week to 4 months (more in some cases). Free book catalog.
Nonfiction: Biography, history, reference, textbooks, travel, language study, literature, folklore, and literary criticism. "We publish books dealing with almost any aspect of the peoples, languages, literatures, history, cultures of Eastern Europe and the Soviet Union, as well as general linguistics and Balkan studies. We do not publish original fiction and in general do not publish books dealing with areas of the world other than Eastern Europe, the USSR and the Balkans (except for linguistics, which may deal with any area)." Accepts nonfiction translations from Eastern European languages. Query first. Looks for authors of scholarly and textbooks who know their fields and write clearly.
Recent Nonfiction Title: *Guide to the Slavonic Languages (3rd Edition)*, by R.G.A. de Bray (language study and linguistics).
Software: Foreign language teaching and research.
Tips: "A large percentage of our authors are academics, but we would be happy to hear from other authors as well. Very few of our books sell well enough to make the author much money, since the field in which we work is so small. The few that do make money are normally textbooks."

THE SMITH, 5 Beekman St.; New York NY 10038. Publishes hardcover and paperback originals. The Smith is owned by the Generalist Association, Inc., a nonprofit organization which gives to writers awards averaging $500 for book projects. Averages 5 titles/year. Publishes book an average of 1 year after acceptance. Publishing relationship usually first established through magazine, *Pulpsmith*, which includes stories, poetry, novel excerpts, and essays. Computer printout submissions acceptable. Send query first for nonfiction; sample chapter preferred for fiction. Reports in 2 months. SASE. Free book catalog.
Nonfiction and Fiction: "Original fiction—no specific schools or categories; for nonfiction, the more controversial, the better." Reviews artwork/photos as part of ms package. Managing Editor: Tom Tolnay.
Recent Title: *Two Friends*, by Menke Katz and Henry Smith (poet friends speak in verse).

SOCIAL SCIENCE EDUCATION CONSORTIUM, INC., (SSEC), 855 Broadway, Boulder CO 80302. (303)492-8154. Publications Manager: Laurel R. Singleton. Publishes trade paperback originals. Averages 8-10 titles/year. Pays up to $600 honorarium. Photocopied submissions OK. Computer printout submissions acceptable. SASE. "At the end of each calendar year we establish a forthcoming list for the whole year. Before that time, we can only respond tentatively to prospective authors. Definite 'nos' receive responses within 30 days." Free book catalog.

Nonfiction: Reference and professional books for educators. Subjects include economics, history, politics, psychology, sociology and education. "We are always looking for useful, original resources that social studies educators can use in the classroom and in planning curriculum and staff-development programs. We also publish some scholarly research in social science education." Looks for material "that would be of direct interest to social studies educators, administrators, teacher educators, and preservice teachers." Query or submit outline/synopsis and 2 sample chapters. Also, tight organization, up-to-date information and references, reasonable length (200-400 pages)."

Recent Nonfiction Title: *Teachers Have Rights, Too: What Educators Should Know About School Law*, by Leigh Stelzer and Joanna Banthin (review of educators' legal rights, status).

Tips: "The SSEC is a not-for-profit educational service organization. One of our ongoing activities is a small, short-run publications program. All of our publications are designed for professionals in some aspect and at some level of education, particularly social studies/social science education. In fact, without exception, all of our publications are written and edited by people who fit that description. Our books are sold exclusively by direct mail. Thus, a freelance writer whose main motivation is to make money by selling manuscripts probably would not find us to be an attractive market. We pay only a modest honorarium, although some royalty arrangements will also be forthcoming; most of our authors are motivated by desire for professional growth, prestige, and service."

SOS PUBLICATIONS, Subsidiary of Bradley Products, 4223-25 W. Jefferson Blvd., Los Angeles CA 90016. (213)730-1815. Publisher: Paul Bradley. Publishes trade paperback originals. Averages 4 titles/year. Pays royalty on wholesale price. Photocopied submissions OK. Computer printout submissions acceptable; no dot-matrix. SASE, which will *enclose* the manuscript, must accompany submission. Any queries must also include SASE. Due to both the large number of manuscripts received and our limited reading staff, we report as soon as possible, but allow approximately 3-4 months.

Fiction: Contact Fiction Editor. Mystery, romance and suspense. Send complete ms for publisher's review.

Tips: "We are enlarging our scope of publishing to the novel form with special attention to mysteries, thrillers, romance stories and new traditional fiction."

SOUTH END PRESS, 302 Columbus Ave., Boston MA 02116. (617)266-0629. Publishes trade paperback and hardcover originals and trade paperback reprints. Averages 22 nonfiction titles/year. Pays 8% royalty on retail price. Simultaneous submissions OK. Computer printout submissions acceptable; no dot-matrix. Reports in 6-8 weeks. Free book catalog.

Nonfiction: Subjects include politics, economics, feminism, social change, radical cultural criticism, explorations of race, class, and sex oppression and liberation. No conservative political themes. Submit outline/synopsis and 1-2 sample chapter(s).

Fiction: Not accepting unsolicited fiction manuscripts or queries.

SOUTHERN ILLINOIS UNIVERSITY PRESS, Box 3697, Carbondale IL 62901. (618)453-2281. Director: Kenney Withers. Averages 50 titles/year. Pays 10-12½% royalty on net price. Publishes book an average of 1 year after acceptance. Computer printout submissions acceptable; no dot-matrix. SASE. Reports in 6 weeks. Free book catalog.

Nonfiction: "We are interested in humanities, social sciences and contemporary affairs material. No dissertations or collections of previously published articles." Accepts nonfiction translations from French, German, Scandinavian and Hebrew. Query.

Recent Nonfiction Title: *Thomas Pynchon*, by Cowart (literary criticism).

SOUTHERN METHODIST UNIVERSITY PRESS, Dallas TX 75275. (214)692-2263. Director: Trudy McMurrin. Averages 7 titles/year. Payment is on royalty basis; contracts variable. No advance. Computer printout submissions acceptable "as long as copy is clear and double-spaced." Requires query letter with outline, vita, and 1-2 sample chapters. Reports "tend to be slow for promising mss requiring outside reading by authorities." Enclose return postage. Free book catalog.

Nonfiction: Regional and scholarly nonfiction. History, biography, folklore literature, anthropology, geology, international and constitutional law, American studies, and performing arts. Length: open.

Recent Nonfiction Title: *Talking with Ingmar Bergman*, edited by G. William Jones.

SOVEREIGN PRESS, 326 Harris Rd., Rochester WA 98579. Senior Editor: Marguerite Pedersen. Publishes hardcover and trade paperback originals. Averages 5 titles/year. Pays by individual agreements. "Payments before publishing are bonus rather than advance." Simultaneous and photocopied submissions OK. Computer printout submissions acceptable. SASE. Reports in 1 month on queries and mss. Book catalog $1. "We have a unique dedication to the culture of individual sovereignty and put out a special catalog that gives full details of our publishing policy. We want no inquiries and no submissions from anyone not acquainted with our unique orientation."

Nonfiction: Social orientation books on history, philosophy, politics, and religion (individual sovereignty only). Publishes for "those seeking a way to integrate personal ideals with universal realities." Especially needs "works effectively promoting the *culture* of individual sovereignty." Submit complete ms.

Recent Nonfiction Title: *Valoric Fire*, from the Valorian Society.

Fiction: "Historical novels and fictional projections that promote individual sovereignty." Especially needs "perceptively conceived historical novels of Northern European life before individual sovereignty was corrupted by theocracy; fictional projections for a *practical* society of sovereign individuals." Submit complete ms.

Recent Fiction Title: *Camp 38*, by Jill von Konen.

*SPECIAL LIBRARIES ASSN., 235 Park Ave. S., New York NY 10003. (212)477-9250. Editor, Nonserial Publications: Michael J. Esposito. Publishes hardcover originals. Averages 10 titles/year. Pays 15% royalty on income over expenses. No advance. "Since we are an association publisher, subisdy arrangements are usually made with our chapter and divisions, not individual authors." Computer printout submissions acceptable; prefers letter-quality to dot-matrix. SASE. Reports in 1 month on queries; 3 months on mss. Free book catalog.

Nonfiction: Reference, technical, textbooks, and professional development for librarians and information managers. Query or submit outline/synopsis and 3 sample chapters.

Recent Nonfiction Title: *Mapping Your Business*, by Barbara Shupe and Colette O'Connell.

STACKPOLE BOOKS, Box 1831, Harrisburg PA 17105. Editorial Director: Chet Fish. Publishes hardcover and quality paperback originals. Publishes approximately 50 titles/year. "Proposals should begin as a one-page letter, leading to chapter outline only on request. If author is unknown to Stackpole, supply credentials." Publishes book an average of 9 months after acceptance. Computer printout submissions acceptable; prefers letter-quality to dot-matrix. SASE. Free author's guidelines.

Nonfiction: Outdoor-related subject areas—firearms, fishing, hunting, military, wildlife, and outdoor skills. Reviews artwork/photos as part of ms package.

*STANDARD PUBLISHING, 8121 Hamilton Ave., Cincinnati OH 45231. (513)931-4050. Publisher/Vice President: Ralph M. Small. Publishes hardcover and paperback originals (85%) and reprints (15%). Specializes in religious books. Averages 60 titles/year. Subsidy publishes 5% of books. Pays 10% usual royalty on wholesale price. Advance averages $200-1,500. Publishes book an average of 1 year after acceptance. Query or submit outline/synopsis and 2-3 sample chapters. Reviews artwork/photos as part of ms package. Reports in 1-2 months. SASE.

Nonfiction: Publishes how-to; crafts (to be used in Christian education); juveniles; reference; Christian education; quiz; puzzle and religious books; and college textbooks (religious). All mss must pertain to religion.

Recent Nonfiction Title: *Older, Wiser, Better in Almost Every Way*, by Jeanette Lockerbie.

Fiction: Publishes religious, devotional books.

Recent Fiction Title: *The Bradford Adventure Series*, by Jerry Jenkins.

STANFORD UNIVERSITY PRESS, Stanford CA 94305. (415)497-9434. Editor: J.G. Bell. Averages 45 titles/year. Pays 10-15% royalty; "rarely" offers advance. Photocopied submissions OK. SASE. Reports in 3 weeks. Free book catalog.

Nonfiction: Books on European history, the history of China and Japan, anthropology, psychology, taxonomy, literature and Latin American studies. Query.

Recent Nonfiction Title: *The Letters of Anthony Trollope*, edited by John Hall.

STEIN AND DAY PUBLISHERS, Scarborough House, Briarcliff Manor NY 10510. Averages 100 titles/year. Offers standard royalty contract. No unsolicited mss without querying first. Nonfiction, send outline or summary and sample chapter. *Must* furnish SASE with all fiction and nonfiction queries.

Nonfiction & Fiction: Publishes general adult fiction and nonfiction books; no juveniles or college. All types of nonfiction except technical. Quality fiction. Minimum length: 65,000 words.

Recent Nonfiction Title: *Princess Grace*, by Sarah Bradford.

Recent Fiction Title: *The Judas Code*, by Derek Lambert.

‡STEMMER HOUSE PUBLISHERS, INC., 2627 Caves Rd., Owings Mills MD 21117. (301)363-3690. President: Barbara Holdridge. Publishes hardcover originals. Averages 25 titles/year. Pays royalty on wholesale price. Publishes book an average of 18 months after acceptance. Computer printout submissions acceptable. SASE. Reports in 2 weeks on queries; 3 months on mss. Book catalog for 9x12 SAE and 1 first class stamp.

Nonfiction: Biography, cookbook, illustrated book, juvenile, and design books. Subjects include Americana, animals, art, cooking and foods, history, nature. Especially looking for "literary novels of sustained quality, biography, history, and art and design." No humor. Query or submit outline/synopsis and sample chapters. Reviews artwork/photos as part of ms package.

Recent Nonfiction Title: *Seasons of Heron Pond*, by Mary Leister (natural history).

Fiction: Adventure, ethnic, historical, mainstream, and philosophical. "We want only mss of sustained literary merit. No popular-type mss written to be instant bestsellers." Query.

Recent Fiction Title: *Paradise*, by Dikkon Eberhart (philosophical adventure).

Tips: "If I were a writer trying to market a book today, I would not imitate current genres on the bestseller lists, but strike out with a subject of intense interest to me."

STERLING PUBLISHING, 2 Park Ave., New York NY 10016. (212)532-7160. Acquisitions Manager: Sheila Anne Barry. Publishes hardcover and paperback originals (75%) and reprints (25%). Averages 80 titles/year. Pays royalty; offers advance. Publishes book an average of 8 months after acceptance. Computer printout submissions acceptable; prefers letter-quality to dot-matrix. Reports in 4-6 weeks. SASE. Book catalog for SASE.

Nonfiction: Alternative lifestyle, fiber arts, games, health, Americana, business, foods, economics, hobbies, how-to, humor, medicine, music, occult, pets, photography, psychology, recreation, reference, self-help, sports, theater (how-to), technical, wine and woodworking. Query or submit complete chapter list, detailed outline/synopsis and 2 sample chapters with photos if necessary. Reviews artwork/photos as part of ms package.

Recent Nonfiction Title: *Hardcore Bodybuilding*, by Robert Kennedy.

*STIPES PUBLISHING CO., 10-12 Chester St., Champaign IL 61820. (217)356-8391. Contact: Robert Watts. Publishes hardcover and paper originals. Averages 25 titles/year. Subsidy publishes 2% of books, "determined by scholarly contribution of the book." Pays 15% maximum royalty on retail price. Computer printout submissions acceptable. SASE. Reports in 2 weeks on queries; 2 months on mss.

Nonfiction: Technical (some areas), textbooks on business and economics, music, agriculture/horticulture recreation and physical education. "All of our books in the trade area are books that also have a college text market." No "books unrelated to educational fields taught at the college level." Submit outline/synopsis and 1 sample chapter.

Recent Nonfiction Title: *Manual of Woody Landscape Plants*, by Michael Dirr (college text and general reference).

‡STOEGER PUBLISHING COMPANY, 55 Ruta Court, S. Hackensack NJ 07606. (201)440-2700. Subsidiary includes Stoeger Industries. Publisher: Robert E. Weise. Publishes trade paperback originals. Averages 12-15 titles/year. Royalty varies, depending on ms. Simultaneous and photocopied submissions OK. SASE. Reports in 1 month on queries; 3 months on mss. Free book catalog.

Nonfiction: Cookbook, how-to, and self-help. Subjects include sports, outdoor sports, cooking and foods, and hobbies. Especially looking for how-to books relating to hunting, fishing, or other outdoor sports. Submit outline/synopsis and sample chapters.

Recent Nonfiction Title: *Advanced Bow Hunting Guide*, by Roger Maynard.

STONE WALL PRESS, INC., 1241 30th St., NW, Washington DC 20007. President/Publisher: Henry Wheelwright. Publishes hardcover and trade paperback originals. Averages 2-5 titles/year. Pays standard royalty; offers minimal advance. Publishes book an average of 6 months after acceptance. Computer printout submissions acceptable; no dot-matrix. SASE. Reports in 2 weeks. Book catalog for business size SAE and 1 first class stamp.

Nonfiction: How-to and environmental/outdoor. "Unique, practical, illustrated how-to outdoor books (nature, camping, fishing, hiking, hunting, etc.) and environmental books for the general public." Query. Looks for "concise, sharp writing style with humorous touches; a rough table of contents for an idea of the direction of the book, a new approach or topic which hasn't been done recently." Accepts outline/synopsis and several sample chapters. Reviews artwork/photos as part of ms package.

Recent Nonfiction Title: *Vanishing Fishes of North America*, by Oro, Williams, and Wagner.

STONEYDALE PRESS PUBLISHING CO., 304 Main St., Stevensville MT 59870. (406)777-2729. Publisher: Dale A. Burk. Publishes hardcover and trade paperback originals. Averages 6-8 titles/year. Pays 10-12% on wholesale price or makes outright purchase. Offers average $500 advance. SASE. Reports in 1 month. Book catalog for SAE and 1 first class stamp.

Nonfiction: Biography, "coffee table" book and how-to on Americana, art, history, nature, recreation, travel and Montana topics. "We're looking for good outdoor recreation book ideas for our area (Northern Rocky Mountains, Pacific Northwest); historical ideas from the same region not overly done in the past. Also open to 'coffee table' format books, if we can be convinced a market exists for a specific idea." Query.

Recent Nonfiction Title: *Young People's Guide to Yellowstone Park*, by Robin Tawney (recreation/travel guide).

STRAWBERRY HILL PRESS, 2594 15th Ave., San Francisco CA 94127. President: Jean-Louis Brinda-mour, Ph.D. Senior Editors: Donna L. Osgood, Gretchen Stengel, Robin Witkin. Publishes paperback originals. Publishes 12 titles/year. "We are a small house, proud of what we do, and intending to stay relatively small (that does not mean that we will do a less-than-professional job in marketing our books, however). The author-publisher relationship is vital, from the moment the contract is signed until there are no more books to sell, and we operate on that premise. We do no hardcovers, and, for the moment at least, our format is limited strictly to 6x9 quality paperbacks, prices between $4.95-10.95. We never print fewer than 5,000 copies in a first printing, with reprintings also never falling below that same figure." Pays 10-20% royalty on wholesale price; no advance. Photocopied submissions OK. Electronic submissions OK on TRS 80 system. Computer printout submissions acceptable. Reports in 2 months. SASE. Book catalog for SASE.
Nonfiction: Self-help, inspiration (not religion), cookbooks, health and nutrition, aging, diet, popular philosophy, metaphysics, alternative life style,; Third World, minority histories, oral history and popular medicine. Accepts nonfiction and fiction translations. No religion, sports, craft books, photography or fine art material. Submit outline/synopsis and 1 sample chapter.
Recent Nonfiction Title: *Believe The Heart*, by Elizabeth Fleming.
Recent Fiction Title: *Dowry of Death*, by Melvin A. Casberg, M.D.

LYLE STUART, INC., 120 Enterprise Ave., Secaucus NJ 07094. (201)866-0490, (212)736-1141. Subsidiaries include Citadel Press and University Books. President: Lyle Stuart. Editor-in-Chief: Alan J. Wilson. Publishes hardcover and trade paperback originals, and trade paperback reprints. Averages 70 titles/year. Pays 10-12% royalty on retail price; offers "low advance." SASE.
Nonfiction: Biography, "coffee table" book, how-to, humor, illustrated book and self-help. Subjects include Americana, art, business and economics, health, history, music and politics. "The percentage of acceptable over-the-transom mss has been so low during the years that we are no longer reading unsolicited material."
Recent Nonfiction Title: *The Films of Dustin Hoffman*.

SHERWOOD SUGDEN & COMPANY, PUBLISHERS, 1117 8th St., La Salle IL 61301. (815)223-1231. Publisher: Sherwood Sugden. Publishes hardcover and trade paperback originals and reprints. Averages 8 titles/year. Pays 4-12% royalty. Simultaneous and photocopied submissions OK. Computer printout submissions acceptable. SASE. Reports in 3 weeks on queries; 3 months on mss. Book catalog for business-size SAE.
Nonfiction: Subjects include history, philosophy, politics, religion (Christian, especially Roman Catholic), and literary criticism. "We're looking for lucid presentations and defenses of orthodox Roman Catholic doctrine, Church history and lives of the Saints aimed at the average intelligent reader. (Possibly one or two scholarly works of the same sort as well.) Works of criticism of British or American authors: perhaps a biography or two; also a work in elementary syllogistic logic. The audience for our books ranges from the bright high school student with a curiosity about ideas through the mature general reader. Certain of our titles (perhaps 30% of our annual output) will appeal chiefly to the advanced student or scholar in the relevant disciplines." Submit outline/synopsis and 1 sample chapter.
Recent Nonfiction Title: *Escape from Scepticism: Liberal Education as if Truth Mattered*, by Christopher Derrick.

*SUN PUBLISHING CO., Box 4383, Albuquerque NM 87196-4383. (505)255-6550. Editor-in-Chief: Skip Whitson. Publishes hardcover and paperback originals (20%) and reprints (80%). Averages 30 titles/year. Pays 8% royalty; no advance. Will subsidy publish "if we think the book is good enough and if we have the money to do it, we'll publish it on our own; otherwise, the author will have to put up the money." Query or submit outline/synopsis, 2 sample chapters and table of contents. "Do not send complete ms unless requested to do so." Send photocopies if photos/illustrations are to accompany ms. Simultaneous and photocopied submissions OK. Computer printout submissions acceptable; prefers letter-quality to dot-matrix. Reports in 2-4 months. SASE. Book list for SASE.
Nonfiction: Metaphysical, Oriental and new age books. "40-200-page lengths are preferred." Looks for brevity and clarity.
Recent Title: *Earth Changes Survival Handbook*, by Page Bryant.
Tips: "We are looking for manuscripts on the coming earth changes, for outright purchase."

THE SUNSTONE PRESS, Box 2321, Santa Fe NM 87504. (505)988-4418. Editor-in-Chief: James C. Smith Jr. Publishes paperback originals; "sometimes hardcover originals." Averages 16 titles/year. Pays royalty on wholesale price. Free book catalog. Query. Looks for "strong regional appeal (Southwestern). Computer printout submissions acceptable. Reports in 2 months. Enclose return postage.
Nonfiction: How-to series craft books. Books on the history of the Southwest; poetry. Length: open.
Recent Nonfiction Title: *How to Paint and Sell Your Art*, by Marcia Muth (how-to).

Fiction: Publishes "for readers who use the subject matter to elevate their impressions of our world, our immediate society, families and friends."
Recent Fiction Title: *Curandero*, by Jose Ortiz y Pino (Southwest fiction).
Poetry: *Stone Run: Tidings*, by Cynthia Grenfell.

SYBEX, INC., 2344 6th St., Berkeley CA 94710. (415)848-8233. Editor-in-Chief: Dr. Rudolph S. Langer. Acquisitions Editor: Jim Hill. Publishes hardcover and paperback originals. Averages 60 titles/year. Royalty rates vary. Average $3,500 advance. Publishes book an average of 6 months after acceptance. Simultaneous and photocopied submissions OK. "We prefer hard copy for proposal evaluations and encourage our authors to submit Wordstar diskettes upon completion of their manuscripts. Wordstar word processor diskettes preferred. Computer printout submissions acceptable. Reports in 2 months. Free book catalog.
Nonfiction: Computer and electronics. "Manuscripts most publishable in the field of microprocessors, microcomputers, hardware, LSI, programming, programming languages, applications, automation, and telecommunications." Submit outline/synopsis and 2-3 sample chapters. Accepts nonfiction translations from French or German. Looks for "clear writing; technical accuracy; logical presentation of material; and good selection of material, such that the most important aspects of the subject matter are thoroughly covered; well-focused subject matter; and well-thought-out organization that helps the reader understand the material. And marketability." Reviews artwork/photos as part of ms package.
Recent Nonfiction Title: *Practical WordStar*, by Julie A. Arca.
Tips: Queries/mss may be routed to other editors in the publishing group.

*SYMMES SYSTEMS, Box 8101, Atlanta GA 30306. Editor-in-Chief: E. C. Symmes. Publishes hardcover and paperback originals. Pays 10% royalty on wholesale price. "Contracts are usually written for the individual title and may have different terms." No advance. Does 40% subsidy publishing. Will consider photocopied and simultaneous submissions. Computer printout submissions acceptable; no dot-matrix. Acknowledges receipt in 10 days; evaluation within 1 month. Query. SASE.
Nonfiction: Nature. "Our books have mostly been in the art of bonsai (miniature trees). We are publishing quality information for laypersons (hobbyists). Most of the titles introduce information that is totally new for the hobbyist." Clear and concise writing style. Text must be topical, showing state-of-the-art. All books so far have been illustrated with photos and/or drawings. Would like to see more material on bonsai and other horticultural subjects; also photography and collecting photographica. Length: open. Reviews artwork/photos as part of ms package.
Recent Nonfiction Title: *The Physician's Guide to Nutritional Therapy*, by Anderson.

SYRACUSE UNIVERSITY PRESS, 1600 Jamesville Ave., Syracuse NY 13210. (315)423-2596. Director/Editor: Arpena Mesrobian. Averages 25 titles/year. Pays royalty on net sales. Simultaneous and photocopied submissions OK "only if we are informed." Computer printout submissions acceptable. SASE. Reports in 2 weeks on queries; "longer on submissions." Free book catalog.
Nonfiction: "The best opportunities in our nonfiction program for freelance writers are of books on New York state. We have published regional books by people with limited formal education, but they were thoroughly acquainted with their subjects, and they wrote simply and directly about them. No vague descriptions or assumptions that a reference to a name (in the case of a biography) or place is sufficient information. The author must make a case for the importance of his subject." Query. Accepts outline/synopsis and at least 2 sample chapters.
Recent Nonfiction Title: *Joseph Brant, 1743-1807: Man of Two Worlds*, by Isabel Thompson Kelsay.

T.F.H. PUBLICATIONS, INC., 211 W. Sylvania Ave., Neptune City NJ 07753. (201)988-8400. Managing Editor: Neal Pronek. Publishes hardcover originals. Averages 30 titles/year. Buys most mss outright. Publishes book an average of 8 months after acceptance. Simultaneous and photocopied submissions OK. Computer printout submissions acceptable; prefers letter-quality to dot-matrix. SASE. Reports "immediately." Book catalog for 9x12 SAE with $1.90 postage.
Nonfiction: How-to on animals (especially pets) and nature, illustrated book, juvenile, reference, technical (fish taxonomy) for owners of pet animals, tropical fish hobbyists, and textbook. Especially needs "books that tell people how to care for and (where applicable) breed animals (dogs, cats, fresh and saltwater fish, and birds) kept as pets." Query or submit outline/synopsis and 1 sample chapter.
Recent Nonfiction Title: *The Book of the Cocker Spaniel*, by Joan Brearley.
Tips: "Nonfiction manuscript needs for the next year or two include pet books on marketable subjects (dogs, cats, birds, fish) suitable as pets. We must have *photo* illustrations, preferably in color."

TAB BOOKS, INC., Blue Ridge Summit PA 17214. (717)794-2191. Vice President: Ray Collins. Publishes hardcover and paperback originals and reprints. Publishes 200 titles per year. Pays variable royalty and advance. Buys some mss outright for a negotiable fee. Photocopied submissions OK (except for art). Computer printout submissions acceptable; prefers letter-quality to dot-matrix. Reports in 6 weeks. SASE. Free book catalog and manuscript preparation guide.

Nonfiction: TAB publishes titles in such fields as computer hardware, computer software, solar and alternate energy, marine line, aviation, automotive, music technology, consumer medicine, electronics, electrical and electronics repair, amateur radio, shortwave listening, model railroading, toys, hobbies, drawing, animals and animal power, practical skills with projects, building furniture, basic how-to for the house, building large structures, calculators, robotics, telephones, model radio control, TV servicing, audio, recording, hi-fi and stereo, electronic music, electric motors, electrical wiring, electronic test equipment, video programming, CATV, MATV and CCTV, broadcasting, photography and film, appliance servicing and repair, advertising, antiques and restoration, bicycles, crafts, farmsteading, hobby electronics, home construction, license study guides, mathematics, metalworking, reference books, schematics and manuals, small gasoline engines, two-way radio and CB, and woodworking. Accepts nonfiction translations.

TAPLINGER PUBLISHING CO., INC., 132 W. 22nd, New York NY 10011. (212)741-0801. Imprints include Crescendo (music), Pentalic (calligraphy). Editors: Ms. Bobs Pinkerton and Roy E. Thomas. Publishes hardcover originals. Publishes 75 titles/year. Pays standard royalty; offers variable advance. Publishes book an average of 1 year after acceptance. Simultaneous and photocopied submissions OK. Reports in 10 weeks. Computer printout submissions acceptable; no dot-matrix. SASE.
Nonfiction: Art, biography, history, theatre, general trade and belles-lettres. No juveniles. Query.
Fiction: Serious contemporary quality fiction. Accepts fiction translations. No juveniles.

JEREMY P. TARCHER, INC., 9110 Sunset Blvd., Los Angeles CA 90069. (213)273-3274. President and Editor-in-Chief: Jeremy P. Tarcher. Publishes hardcover and trade paperback originals. Pays 10-12½-15% royalty on hardcover list price; offers advance "competitive in the industry." Averages 35 titles/year. State availability of photos and/or illustrations to accompany ms. Publishes book an average of 7 months after acceptance. Simultaneous and photocopied submissions OK. Reports in 6 weeks. SASE. Free book catalog.
Nonfiction: Publishes popular psychology, sociology, health and fitness, alternative medicine, consciousness, gardening, cooking, and humor. Submit outline/synopsis and sample chapters.
Recent Nonfiction Title: *America II*, by Richard Lou.

‡*ALISTER TAYLOR PUBLISHERS**, The Mall, Russell, Bay of Islands, New Zealand. Subsidiaries include Glenbervie Press, Student Publications Ltd. Managing Director: Alister Taylor. Publishes hardcover and trade paperback originals and software. Averages 15-20 titles/year. Subsidy publishes 20% of books. Pays 7½-15% royalty on retail price; buys some mss outright for $5,000-75,000. Advance "depends on the project." Publishes ms an average of 4 months after acceptance. Photocopied submissions OK, "but no invited multiple submissions considered." Electronic submissions OK if compatible with Epson or Apple. Computer printout submissions acceptable. SAE and IRCs. Reports in 2 weeks on queries; 3 months on mss. Free book catalog.
Nonfiction: Biography, "coffee table" books, fine edition books, illustrated books, juvenile, reference books, and self-help on art, history, photography, politics and sports. Publishes for "literate audience interested in definitive quality books." Especially needs "illustrated catalogues raisonne of major painters; major books on the thoroughbred and Arab horse." Query or submit outline/synopsis and sample chapters. Reviews artwork/photos as part of ms package.
Recent Nonfiction Title: *Gauguin in the Pacific* (biography and catalogue raisonne).
Fiction: New Zealand/Australian fiction only. Query or submit outline/synopsis and sample chapters.
Recent Fiction Title: *Pet Shop*, by Ian Middleton (novel).
Poetry: New Zealand poetry only. Submit complete ms.
Recent Poetry Title: *Collected Poems 1947-83*, by Alistair Campbell.
Software: Australasian-oriented.

TAYLOR PUBLISHING CO., Subsidiary of Insilco, Box 597, Dallas TX 75221. (214)637-2800. Assistant Editor: Candace Albertson. Editorial Director: J. Nelson Black. Publishes hardcover and trade paperback originals. Advance varies. Pays 10-12½-15% royalties. Publishes book an average of 6 months after acceptance. Averages 10-20 titles/year. Computer printout submissions acceptable. SASE. Reports in 6 weeks on queries; 4 months on mss. Free book catalog.
Nonfiction: Biography, "coffee table" book, cookbook, how-to, humor, illustrated book, reference, self-help, technical and textbook. Subjects include Americana, art, business and economics, cooking and foods, health, history, nature, photography, recreation, and sports. Interested in gardening, sports and business (sales and management) books—nonfiction with a regional slant and a national appeal. Query or submit outline/synopsis and sample chapters. Reviews artwork/photos as part of ms package.
Recent Nonfiction Title: *The Adolphus Cookbook*, by Joanne Smith.
Tips: "At Taylor our market seems to be moving more and more toward books on specific subjects targeted at smaller segments of the population. Instead of publishing one general interest title not aimed at anyone in particular, while hoping to sell 50,000 copies, we are now tending toward publishing five books with each aimed at a specific segment, such as fly tying or how to ride a unicycle, with hopes of selling 10,000 of each. Our market is also moving toward books with less copy and more illustrations and photos."

TEACHER UPDATE, INC., Box 205, Saddle River NJ 07458. (201)327-8486. Editorial Director: Donna Papalia. Senior Editor: Nick Roes. Editorial Assistant: Nancy Roes. Publishes hardcover and paperback originals. Averages 6 titles/year. Pays royalty; buys some mss outright by arrangement; offers variable advance. Photocopied submissions OK. Computer printout submissions acceptable. SASE. Reports in 1 month. Free book catalog for SASE.
Nonfiction: Education, consumer and general interest. Reviews artwork/photos as part of ms package. Queries only.
Recent Nonfiction Title: *Helping Children Watch TV*, by N. Roes (handbook).

*TEACHERS COLLEGE PRESS, 1234 Amsterdam Ave., New York NY 10027. (212)678-3929. Director: Carole P. Saltz. Publishes hardcover and paperback originals (90%) and reprints (10%). Royalty varies; offers advance. Averages 75 titles/year. Subsidy publishes 20% of books. Publishes book an average of 1 year after acceptance. Reports in 3-6 months. SASE. Free book catalog.
Nonfiction: "This university press concentrates on books in the field of education in the broadest sense, from early childhood to higher education: good classroom practices, teacher training, special education, innovative trends and issues, administration and supervision, film, continuing and adult education, all areas of the curriculum, comparative education, dental, guidance and counseling and the politics, economics, nursing, philosophy, sociology and history of education. The press also issues classroom materials for students at all levels, with a strong emphasis on reading and writing." Submit outline/synopsis and sample chapters.
Recent Nonfiction Title: *Observing and Recording the Behavior of Young Children*, 3rd edition, by Dorothy H. Cohen, Virginia Stern and Nancy Balaban.

‡TECHWRITE CORPORATION, 7940 Zionsville Rd., Indianapolis IN 46268. (317)875-5232. Chief Technical Editor: Lucy Spurgeon. Publishes trade paperback originals and trade paperback reprints. Averages 10-20 titles/year. Pays 10-5% royalty on wholesale price or makes outright purchase ($5/page minimum, $10/page maximum). Simultaneous and photocopied submissions OK. SASE. Reports in 4 weeks on queries; 2 weeks on mss.
Nonfiction: Cookbook, how-to, reference, technical, textbook and computer documentation. Subjects include cooking and foods and technical information. "Some of *TECHwrite*'s specialty areas include electronics, computers, industrial equipment and machinery, robotics, medical equipment, security systems, communication systems, and aerospace." Especially looking for books involving state-of-the-art technology. Query with outline/synopsis and sample chapters, or submit complete ms.
Recent Nonfiction Title: *Heat Transfer Pump Handbooks*, by Dean Brothers (reference manual).
Fiction: Experimental fiction mss "as long as they are technically oriented."
Tips: "We envision persons desiring information on various technical subjects, involving new developments and/or innovative procedures of computer technology and other sciences as our audience. If I were a writer trying to market a book today, I would check out and target the high-technology market."

TEMPLE UNIVERSITY PRESS, Broad and Oxford Sts., Philadelphia PA 19122. (215)787-8787. Editor-in-Chief: Michael Ames. Publishes 35 titles/year. Pays royalty on wholesale price. Publishes book an average of 9 months after acceptance. Electronic submissions OK, but requires hard copy also. Computer printout submissions acceptable. SASE. Reports in 3 months. Free book catalog.
Nonfiction: American history, public policy and regional (Philadelphia area). "All books should be scholarly. Authors are generally connected with a university. No memoirs, fiction or poetry." Uses Chicago *Manual of Style*. Reviews artwork/photos as part of ms package. Query.
Recent Nonfiction Title: *Charlotte Perkins Gilman*, by Mary A. Hill.

TEMPO BOOKS, A division of The Berkley Publishing Group, 200 Madison Ave., New York NY 10016. (212)686-9820. Publishes hardcover reprints and paperback originals. Nonfiction and fiction titles for young adults. Buys manuscripts on royalty basis. Submit 3 chapters and synopsis. SASE. Reports in 5-8 weeks.
Fiction: Contemporary romances and problem novels for ages 11 to 18. "We are looking for contemporary young adult fiction dealing in all subjects." Submit outline/synopsis and sample chapters.
Recent Fiction Title: *S.W.A.K. Sealed With a Kiss*, by Judith Enderle (a Caprice Romance).

TEN SPEED PRESS, Box 7123, Berkeley CA 94707. Editor: P. Wood. Publishes hardcover and paperback originals, reprints and software. Offers royalty of 8% of list price; 12½% after 100,000 copies are sold. Offers average $3,000 advance. Averages 15 titles/year. Submit outline and sample chapters for nonfiction. Electronic submissions OK, but requires hard copy also. Computer printout submissions acceptable. Reports in 1 month. Publishes book an average of 6 months after acceptance. Enclose return postage. Will send catalog to writer on request for SASE.
Nonfiction: Americana, gardening, cookbooks, cooking and foods, history, humor, law, nature, self-help, how-to, sports, hobbies, recreation and pets and travel. Publishes mostly trade paperbacks. Subjects range from bicycle books to William Blake's illustrations. "We will consider any first-rate nonfiction material that

we feel will have a long shelf life and be a credit to our list." No set requirements. Some recipe books and career development books. Reviews artwork/photos as part of ms package.
Recent Nonfiction Title: *How To Get The Degree You Want*, by John Bear.
Software: Contact Phil Wood, editor.

‡*TENSLEEP PUBLICATIONS**, Box 925, Aberdeen SD 57401. (605)226-0488. Publisher: Ken Melius. Publishes trade paperback originals. Averages 3-4 titles/year. "We will consider cooperative publishing arrangements." Pays 5-10% royalty on retail price; offers average $500-1,000 advance. Publishes book an average of 4 months after acceptance. Simultaneous and photocopied submissions OK. Computer printout submissions acceptable. SASE. Reports in 3 weeks on queries; 1 month on mss. Free book catalog.
Nonfiction: How-to, reference, and self-help. "We envision an audience interested in recreation and travel. Most of the works are aimed at individuals who participate in outdoor recreation. How-to books are designed for those who want to enjoy recreation, travel and hobbies." Subjects include hobbies, nature, recreation, travel and regional. "We want mss which describe a recreational activity on a national scale or mss which describe a specific area or recreation in a specific area of the US or the world. We need how-to mss on subject such as travel, recreation and hobbies." Will also consider regional histories and educational self-help works. No art, music or religious submissions. Query with outline/synopsis and sample chapters. Reviews artwork/photos as part of ms package.
Recent Nonfiction Title: *Cloud Peak Primitive Area: Trail Guide, History and Photo Odyssey.*
Tips: "We see a trend toward regional publications and more interest in local histories or histories about specific areas. We have also noticed a need for books which are very eye-appealing. In the future we plan to continue publishing books which are very carefully constructed and which appeal to a specific audience. If I were a writer trying to market a book today, I would submit a carefully prepared query or proposal and would try to do as much market research for the editor as possible."

TEXAS A&M UNIVERSITY PRESS, Drawer C, College Station TX 77843. (409)845-1436. Director: Lloyd G. Lyman. Publishes 30 titles/year. Pays in royalties. Publishes book an average of 9 months after acceptance. Electronic submissions OK, but requires hard copy also. Computer printout submissions acceptable; prefers letter-quality to dot-matrix. SASE. Reports in 1 week (queries); 1 month (submissions). Free book catalog.
Nonfiction: History, natural history, environmental history, economics, agriculture and regional studies. Receives artwork/photos as part of ms package. "We do not want poetry." Query. Accepts outline/synopsis and 2-3 sample chapters. Reviews artwork/photos as part of ms package.
Recent Nonfiction Title: *Growing Old at Willie Nelson's Picnic and Other Sketches of Life in the Southwest*, edited by Ronald B. Querry (nonfiction).

TEXAS CHRISTIAN UNIVERSITY PRESS, Box 30783, TCU, Fort Worth TX 76129. (817)921-7822. Associate Director: Keith Gregory. Editor: Judy Alter. Publishes hardcover originals, some reprints. Averages 12 titles/year. Pays royalty. Publishes book an average of 1 year after acceptance. Computer printout submissions acceptable; prefers letter-quality to dot-matrix. Reports "as soon as possible."
Nonfiction: American studies, Texana, theology, literature and criticism, and young adult regional fiction. "We are looking for good scholarly monographs, other serious scholarly work and regional titles of significance." Reviews artwork/photos as part of ms package. Query.
Recent Nonfiction Title: *Cowboys and Cattleland*, by Halsell.
Recent Fiction: *War Pony*, by Worcester.

‡**TEXAS INSTRUMENTS LEARNING CENTER**, Subsidiary of Texas Instruments Inc., Box 225012, M/S 54, Dallas TX 75265. (214)995-5516. Manager, Product Development: Gerald Luecke. Publishes hardcover, trade paperback originals and software. Averages 3-6 titles/year. Pays fixed fee per printed page for each book. Publishes book an average of 9 months after acceptance. Free book catalog. Photocopied submissions OK. Computer printout submissions acceptable; prefers letter-quality to dot-matrix. SASE. Reports in 2 weeks on queries; 1 month on mss.
Nonfiction: Reference books, self-help, technical, textbooks on semiconductor technology, electronics, computers and their application. Publishes for hobbyists, technicians, continuing education, vocational schools, community colleges, industrial learning and training centers. "We publish books that enhance the understanding and use of the technologies that Texas Instruments uses for its products and for the extended use of the products that result from those technologies." No nontechnical or unrelated themes. Submit outline/synopsis and 1 sample chapter. Reviews artwork/photos as part of ms package. "We normally work from outline agreed on for contract before writing begins. We would accept submissions but disclosure form needs to be signed to protect both parties."
Recent Nonfiction Title: *Understanding Electronic Control of Automation Systems*, by N.M. Schmitt and R.F. Farwell.
Software: Support TZPC.

TEXAS MONTHLY PRESS, INC., Subsidiary of Mediatex Communications Corp., Box 1569, Austin TX 78767. (512)476-7085. Editorial Director: Scott Lubeck. Publishes hardcover and trade paperback originals (80%), and trade paperback reprints (20%). Averages 16-20 titles/year. Pays royalty; offers average $2,500 advance. Publishes book an average of 18 months after acceptance. Simultaneous and photocopied submissions OK. Electronic submissions OK, but requires hard copy also. Computer printout submissions acceptable. SASE. Reports in 2 weeks on queries; 2 months on mss. Free book catalog.

Nonfiction: Biography, "coffee table" book, cookbook, humor, guidebook, illustrated book and reference. Subjects include Texana, art, business and economics, cooking and foods, history, nature, photography, politics, recreation, sports and travel. Texas-related subjects only. "Especially interested in biographies of distinguished Texans in all fields." Query or submit outline/synopsis and 3 sample chapters. Reviews artwork/photos as part of ms package.

Recent Nonfiction Title: *American Gumbo*, by Linda Eckhardt.

Fiction: Adventure, ethnic, historical, mainstream, mystery, suspense and western. "All stories must be set in Texas." No experimental, erotica, confession, gothic, romance or poetry. Query or submit outline/synopsis and 3 sample chapters. No unsolicited mss.

Recent Fiction Title: *A Family Likeness*, by Janis Stout (generational saga).

TEXAS WESTERN PRESS, The University of Texas at El Paso, El Paso TX 79968. (915)747-5688. Director/Editor: Hugh W. Treadwell. Publishes hardcover and paperback originals. Publishes 9-10 titles/year. "We are a university press, not a commercial house; therefore, payment is in books and prestige more than money. We sell to libraries and serious readers of serious nonfiction." Will consider photocopied submissions. Will send a catalog to a writer on request. Query. Follow *MLA Style Sheet*. Reports in 1 to 3 months.

Nonfiction: "Scholarly books. Historic and cultural accounts of the Southwest (west Texas, southern New Mexico, northern Mexico and Arizona). Some literary works, occasional scientific titles. Our *Southwestern Studies* use mss of 20,000 words. Our hardback books range from 30,000 words up. The writer should use good exposition in his work. Most of our work requires documentation. We favor a scholarly, but not overly pedantic, style. We specialize in superior book design."

Recent Nonfiction Title: *American Indian Ecology*, by J. Donald Huges.

*THE THEOSOPHICAL PUBLISHING HOUSE, Subsidiary of The Theosophical Society in America, 306 W. Geneva Rd., Wheaton IL 60189. (312)665-0123. Senior Editor: Shirley Nicholson. Imprints include Guest (nonfiction). Publishes trade paperback originals. Averages 12 titles/year. Subsidy publishes 40% of books based on "author need and quality and theme of manuscript." Pays 10-12% royalty on retail price; offers average $1,500 advance. Publishes book an average of 8 months after acceptance. Simultaneous and photocopied submissions OK. Computer printout submissions acceptable; prefers letter-quality to dot-matrix. SASE. Reports in 1 week on queries, 2 months on mss. Free book catalog.

Nonfiction: Subjects include self-development, self-help, philosophy (holistic), psychology (transpersonal), Eastern and Western religions, comparative religion, holistic implications in science, health and healing, yoga, meditation, and astrology. "TPH seeks works which are compatible with the theosophical philosophy. Our audience includes the 'new age' consciousness community seekers in all religions, general public, professors, and health professionals. No material which does not fit the description of needs outlined above." Accepts nonfiction translations. Query or submit outline/synopsis and sample chapters. Reviews artwork/photos as part of ms package. SASE required.

Recent Nonfiction Title: *The Healing Energies of Music*, by Hal Lingerman.

‡THISTLEDOWN PRESS, 668 E. Place, Saskatoon, Saskatchewan S7J 2Z5, Canada. (306)477-0556. Editor-in-Chief: Paddy O' Rourke. Publishes hardcover and trade paperback originals. Average 6-8 titles/year. Pays standard royalty on retail price. Publishes book an average of 18 months after acceptance. Computer printout submissions acceptable; no dot-matrix. SASE. Reports in 2 weeks on queries; 8 weeks on mss. Free book catalog.

Fiction: Literary. Solicited fiction only. All unsolicited mss are returned unopened.

Recent Fiction Title: *The Way to Always Dance*, by Gertrude Story (literary—short stories).

Poetry: "Author should make him/herself familiar with our publishing program before deciding whether or not her/his work is appropriate." No poetry by people *not* citizens and residents of Canada. Submit complete ms.

Recent Poetry Title: *Fielding*, by Dennis Cooley (contemporary Canadian).

THORNDIKE PRESS, One Mile Rd., Box 157, Thorndike ME 04986. (207)948-2962. Senior Editor: Timothy A. Loeb. Publishes hardcover and paperback originals (25%) and reprints (75%). Averages 100 titles/year. Offers 10-15% of wholesale receipts; also buys mss by outright purchase: $500-2,000. Average advance: $1,000. Publishes book an average of 1 year after acceptance. Computer printout submissions acceptable; prefers letter-quality to dot-matrix. SASE. Reports in 2 months. Free book catalog.

Nonfiction: Americana (especially Maine and the Northeast), animals, humor, nature, and all subjects of regional interest. Especially needs "manuscripts relating to the wilderness and oudoor recreation (hunting, fishing, etc.) in the Northeast US." No poetry, young adult or children's books. Submit outline/synopsis and 2-3 sample chapters. Reviews artwork/photos as part of ms package.

Recent Nonfiction Title: *Fly Fishing in Maine*, by A. Raychard (guide).

Fiction: Mystery, humor (New England), nostalgia, and regional interests (Maine and New England). "We will always consider exceptional manuscripts in our areas of interest, but 80% of submissions we receive are not appropriate to our line." Prefer short works." No young adult or children's books; no poetry. Submit outline/synopsis and 2-3 sample chapters.

Recent Fiction Title: *Adventure in a Model T*, by Arthur Macdougall (Dud Dean stories).

Tips: "We are moving away from Maine-only books and looking for a wider audience. The majority of our publishing consists of large print editions of current best sellers for the visually impaired (88 titles a year). For original books, we seek outdoors/nature guides, New England humor, nostalgia, mystery and general fiction of a high degree of literary merit. We are *not* publishing poetry, children's or young adult, adventure/suspense, cookbooks, science fiction, erotica, or mass-market fiction, or romances."

THORSONS PUBLISHERS, LTD, Denington Estate, Wellingborough, Northamptonshire NN8 2RQ England. Editor-in-Chief: J.R. Hardaker. Publishes hardcover and paperback originals and reprints. Pays 7½-10% royalty. Publishes book an average of 9 months after acceptance. Photocopied submissions OK. Computer printout submissions OK; prefers letter-quality to dot-matrix. SAE and IRCs. Reports in 2-4 weeks. Free book catalog.

Nonfiction: Natural health and healing, natural food and vegetarian cookery, alternative medicine, hypnotism and hypnotherapy, practical psychology, inspiration, mind training, personal improvement, self-help themes, books for women, special diets, animal rights, public speaking topics, yoga and related disciplines. Submit outline/synopsis and 3 sample chapters. Reviews artwork/photos as part of ms package.

Tips: Queries/mss may be routed to other editors in the publishing group.

THREE CONTINENTS PRESS, 1346 Connecticut Ave. NW, Washington DC 20036. Publisher/Editor-in-Chief: Donald E. Herdeck. General Editor: Norman Ware. Publishes hardcover and paperback originals (90%) and reprints (10%). Pays 10% royalty; advance "only on delivery of complete ms which is found acceptable; usually $300." Prefers photocopied submissions. State availability of photos/illustrations. Simultaneous submissions OK. Reports in 6 months. SASE. Free book catalog.

Nonfiction and Fiction: Specializes in African, Caribbean and Middle Eastern (Arabic and Persian) literature and criticism and translation, third world literature and history. Scholarly, well-prepared mss; creative writing. Fiction, poetry, criticism, history and translations of creative writing. "We search for books which will make clear the complexity and value of African literature and culture, including bilingual texts (African language/ English translations) of previously unpublished authors from less well-known areas of Africa. We are always interested in genuine contributions to understanding African and Caribbean culture." Length: 50,000-125,000 words. Query. "Please do not submit ms unless we ask for it."

Recent Nonfiction Title: *So Spoke the Uncle*, by Jean Price-Mars.

Recent Fiction Title: *The Web: Stories by Argentine Women*, edited by E. Lewald.

THUNDER'S MOUTH PRESS, Box 780, New York NY 10025. (212)866-4329. Publisher: Neil Ortenberg. Publishes hardcover and trade paperback originals and reprints. Averages 6 titles/year. Pays 5-10% royalty on retail price; offers average $200 advance. Publishes book an average of 8 months after acceptance. Computer printout submissions acceptable; no dot-matrix. Reports in 3 weeks on queries; 2 months on mss. Book catalog for SAE with 20¢ postage.

Nonfiction: Biography, cookbook, how-to, self-help on cooking and foods, history, philosophy, politics, and sociology. Publishes for "college students, academics, politically left of center, ethnic, social activists, women, etc. We basically do poetry and fiction now, but intend to start doing nonfiction over the next few years. How-to books, or biographies, history books, cookbooks would be fine." No cat books. Query or submit outline/synopsis and sample chapters.

Fiction: Erotica, ethnic, experimental, historical, humor, science fiction, and political. "We are interested in doing anywhere from 3-5 novels per year, particularly highly literary or socially relevant novels." No romance novels. Query or submit outline/synopsis and sample chapters.

Recent Fiction Title: *The Red Menace*, by Michael Anania.

Poetry: "We intend to publish 3-5 books of poetry per year." No elitist poetry, rhymes poetry, religious poetry." Submit complete ms.

Recent Poetry Title: *Echoes Inside the Labyrinth*, by Tom McGrath.

TIMBER PRESS, Box 1631, Beaverton OR 97075. (503)292-2606. Editor: Richard Abel. Publishes hardcover and paperback originals. Publishes 20 titles/year. Pays 10-20% royalty; "sometimes" offers advance to cover costs of artwork and final ms completion. Publishes book an average of 8 months after acceptance. Electronic submissions OK, but requires hard copy also. Computer printout submissions acceptable. SASE. Reports in 2 months. Free book catalog.

Nonfiction: Arts and crafts, natural history, Northwest regional material, forestry and horticulture. Accepts nonfiction translations from German. Query or submit outline/synopsis and 3-4 sample chapters. Reviews artwork/photos as part of ms package.
Recent Nonfiction Title: *Complete Book of Roses*, by Krussmann (horticulture).

TIME-LIFE BOOKS INC., 777 Duke St., Alexandria VA 22314. (703)838-7000. Editor: George Constable. Publishes hardcover originals. Publishes 40 titles/year. "We have no minimum or maximum fee because our needs vary tremendously. Advance, as such, is not offered. Author is paid as he completes part of contracted work." Books are almost entirely staff-generated and staff-produced, and distribution is primarily through mail order sale. Query to the Director of Corporate Development. SASE.
Nonfiction: "General interest books. Most books tend to be heavily illustrated (by staff), with text written by assigned authors. We very rarely accept mss or book ideas submitted from outside our staff." Length: open.
Recent Nonfiction Title: *Solar System* (Planet Earth series).

TIMES BOOKS, The New York Times Book Co., Inc., 130 Fifth Ave., New York NY 10011. (212)620-5900. Vice President, Editor-in-Chief: Jonathan B. Segal. Senior Editors: Kathleen Moloney, Elisabeth Scharlatt and Hugh O'Neill. Publishes hardcover and paperback originals (75%) and reprints (25%). Publishes 45 titles/year. Pays royalty; average advance. Publishes book an average of 1 year after acceptance. Computer printout submissions acceptable.
Nonfiction: Business/economics, science and medicine, history, biography, women's issues, the family, cookbooks, current affairs, cooking, self-help and sports. Accepts only solicited manuscripts. Reviews artwork/photos as part of ms package.
Recent Nonfiction Title: *Russia: Broken Idols, Solemn Dreams*, by David K. Shipler.

T.L. ENTERPRISES, INC., **Book Division**, 29901 Agoura Rd., Agoura CA 91301. (818)991-4980. Editor-in-Chief: Michael Schneider. Administrative Assistant: Gail Lerman. Publishes trade and mass market paperback originals. Averages 2 titles/year. Pays 5-10% royalty on retail price. Publishes book an average of 1 year after acceptance. Computer printout submissions acceptable; no dot-matrix. Reports in 1 month.
Nonfiction: Cookbook, how-to, reference, technical and travel/touring. Subjects include cooking and foods, hobbies, nature, recreation and travel. "We *do* read all queries and we will mail-test titles of promise; test winners will receive an immediate home. At present, our book market consists of RV owners and motorcycle touring enthusiasts. We would, however, like to expand our audience. For now, our book audience is our magazine audience—the million or more people who read *Trailer Life, Motor Home, Rider*, et al—together with the 450,000 families who belong to our Good Sam (RV owners) Club." Query with outline/synopsis. Reviews artwork/photos as part of ms package.
Recent Nonfiction Title: *RV Repair & Maintenance Manual*, by John Thompson.

‡**TO HAVE AND TO HOLD**, 200 Madison Ave., New York NY 10016. (212)686-9820. Subsidiary of Berkley Publishing Group. Senior Editor: Ellen Edwards. Publishes mass market paperback original category romances. Averages 36 titles/year. Pays 2-6% royalty; averages $5,000 advance.
Fiction: Contemporary category romances about married love. Will look at 3 sample chapters and detailed chapter-by-chapter outline. Query and request writer's guidelines.
Recent Fiction Title: *The Testimony*, by Robin James.

***TOMPSON & RUTTER INC.**, Box 297, Grantham NH 03753. (603)863-4392. President: Frances T. Rutter. Publishes trade paperback originals. Averages 4 titles/year. Subsidy publishes 5% of books. Pays average 10% royalty on wholesale price. No advance. Publishes book an average of 1 year after acceptance. Simultaneous submissions OK. Computer printout submissions acceptable; prefers letter-quality to dot-matrix. Reports in 1 month. Included in Shoe String Press catalog.
Nonfiction: Local history and New England folklore. Query with one-page sample of published writing.
Recent Nonfiction Title: *It Happened in New Hampshire*, by Fairfax Downey.

TOR BOOKS, 8-10 W. 36th St., New York NY 10018. (212)564-0150. Managing Editor: Elizabeth Fanger. Publishes mass market and trade paperback originals (75% "and growing") and reprints (25%). Averages 72 books/year. Pays 6-8% royalty; offers negotiable advance.
Fiction: Horror, science fiction, occult, and some fantasy. In the near future: thrillers. Prefers agented mss or proposals.
Recent Fiction Title: *Kahawa*, by Donald Westlake.
Tips: "We're pretty broad in the occult, horror and fantasy but more straightforward in science fiction and thrillers, tending to stay with certain authors and certain types of work."

***THE TOUCHSTONE PRESS**, Box 81, Beaverton OR 97075. (503)646-8081. Editor-in-Chief: Thomas K. Worcester. Publishes paperback originals. Specializes in field guide books. "Not seeking manuscripts at this time." Royalty of 10% of retail price; seldom offers an advance. Averages 3 titles/year. Subsidy publishes 10% of books. Photocopied submissions OK, "but don't expect response without SASE." Computer printout submissions acceptable; prefers letter-quality to dot-matrix. Reports in 1-2 months. SASE. No fiction or poetry.

Nonfiction: Cookbooks, cooking and foods; history, hobbies, how-to, recreation, sports and travel books. "Must be within the range of our outdoor styles." Query with "synopsis: the idea, and sample chapters. Query should demonstrate the skill to accomplish what the idea suggests." Reviews artwork/photos as part of ms package.

Recent Nonfiction Title: *35 Hiking Trails, Columbia River Gorge*, by Don and Roberta Lowe.

*TRANSACTION BOOKS, Rutgers University, New Brunswick NJ 08903. (201)932-2280. President: I.L. Horowitz. Publisher: Scott Bramson. Book Division Director: Dalia Buzin. Publishes hardcover and paperback originals (65%) and reprints (35%). Specializes in scholarly social science books. Averages 85 titles/year. Subsidy publishes 10% of books. Royalty "depends almost entirely on individual contract; we've gone anywhere from 2-15%." No advance. Publishes book an average of 6 months after acceptance. Electronic submissions OK, but requires hard copy also. Computer printout submissions acceptable; prefers letter-quality to dot-matrix. Reports in 1-4 months. SASE. Free book catalog.

Nonfiction: Americana, art, biography, economics, history, law, medicine and psychiatry, music, philosophy, politics, psychology, reference, scientific, sociology, technical and textbooks. "All must be scholarly social science or related." Query or submit outline/synopsis. Do not submit sample chapters. We evaluate complete manuscripts only. Accepts nonfiction translations. Use Chicago *Manual of Style*." Looks for "scholarly content, presentation, methodology, and target audience." State availability of photos/illustrations and send one photocopied example.

Recent Nonfiction Title: *Politics of Defense Contracting*, by Gordon Adams (international relations).

‡TREE BY THE RIVER PUBLISHING, 4375 Highland Place, Riverside CA 92506. (714)682-8942. Editor: Bill Dalton. Imprint includes Music Business Books. Publishes hardcover and trade paperback originals. Averages 5 titles/year. Pays 5% royalty on retail price or makes outright purchase of $300-2,000. No advance. Publishes book an average of 1 year after acceptance. Simultaneous and photocopied submissions OK. Computer printout submissions acceptable; no dot-matrix. SASE. Reports in 2 months. Free book catalog.

Nonfiction: How-to, Western Americana, history, music and the music business and travel. "Writers should first query. When the writer receives permission to mail his manuscript, he need only include the first and second chapter with a brief outline of remaining chapters. We also invite writers to send us their ideas for a new book on a subject we cover. *All unsolicited mss are returned unopened.*" Reviews artwork/photos as part of ms package.

Recent Nonfiction Title: *Rosa May: The Search for a Mining Camp Legend*, by George Williams III.

TREND HOUSE, Box 611, St. Petersburg FL 33731. (813)893-8111. Chairman: Eugene C. Patterson. President: Clifton D. Camp Jr. Publisher: Andrew P. Corty. Publishes hardcover and paperback originals and reprints. Specializes in books on Florida—all categories. Pays royalty; no advance. Books are marketed through *Florida Trend* magazine. Publishes book an average of 8 months after acceptance. Computer printout submissions acceptable; no dot-matrix. Reports in 2-4 weeks. SASE.

Nonfiction: Business, economics, history, law, politics, reference, textbooks and travel. "All books pertain to Florida." Query. Reviews artwork/photos as part of ms package.

‡TRIBECA COMMUNICATIONS INC., Suite 1907, 401 Broadway, New York NY 10013. (212)226-6047. Editor: Geraldine Ivins. Book publisher/packager producing 25 titles/year. Publishes hardcover and trade paperback originals. Royalty and advance negotiable. Publishes book an average of 18 months after acceptance. Simultaneous and photocopied submissions OK. Computer printout submissions acceptable; prefers letter-quality to dot-matrix. SASE. Reports in 2 weeks on queries; 2 months on mss. Free book catalog.

Nonfiction: "Coffee table" book, cookbook, humor, and juvenile. Subjects include animals, business and economics, cooking and foods, health, history, recreation, sports, travel and computers. Especially looking for "original ideas for computer books, humor books, children's books that 'teach' some kind of skill; we are interested in almost all nonfiction areas. No 'real' books (Real Women Don't) or *knock off* books of any kind." Sumbit outline/synopsis and sample chapters, and sample art.

Recent Nonfiction Title: *The Second Nine Months*, by Judith Gansberg and Arthur Mostel, M.D.

TROUBADOR PRESS, Suite 205, 1 Sutter St., San Francisco CA 94104. (415)397-3716. Editorial Director: Malcolm K. Whyte. Publishes paperback originals (occasional hardcover editions). Averages 10 titles/year. Pays royalty. Advance averages $500-1,000. Publishes book an average of 6 months after acceptance. Electronic submissions OK, but requires hard copy also. Computer printout submissions acceptable. Reports in 1 month. SASE. Book catalog for SASE.

Nonfiction: "Troubador Press publishes project, activity, entertainment, art, game, nature, craft and hobby books. All titles feature original art and exceptional graphics. Primarily nonfiction. Current series include creative cut-outs and paper dolls; mazes and other puzzle books; color and story books; how-to-draw and other art and entertainment books. Interested in expanding on themes of 80 current titles. We like books which have the potential to develop into series.'' Query or submit outline/synopsis and 2-3 sample chapters with conciseness and clarity of a good idea. Reviews artwork/photos as part of ms package.

Recent Nonfiction Title: *Everything for Your Birthday Party Book*, by Chad.

Tips: ''We have always and will continue to publish new, unpublished authors along with established writers/artists and licensed properties. We feel the mix is good and healthy.'' Queries/mss may be routed to other editors in the publishing group.

TURNSTONE PRESS LTD., Denington Estate, Wellingborough, Northamptonshire NN8 2RQ England. Editors: John Hardaker and Michael Cox. Hardcover and paperback originals and reprints. 7½% royalty on paperbacks; 10% on hardcovers. Photocopied submissions OK. Computer printout submissions acceptable; prefers letter-quality to dot-matrix. SAE. Reports in 1-2 months. Free book catalog.

Nonfiction: Pre-history, archaeology (alternative), earth mysteries, psychology, personal development, health and healing, ecology, lifestyle, new age topics and social issues. Submit outline/synopsis and 3 sample chapters.

Tips: Queries/mss may be routed to other editors in the publishing group.

*CHARLES E. TUTTLE CO., INC., Publishers & Booksellers, Suido 1-chome, 2-6, Bunkyo-ku, Tokyo, Japan 112. Publishes originals and reprints. ''Handles all matters of editing, production and administration including royalties, rights and permissions.'' Pays $500 against 10% royalty on retail price; advance varies. Averages 30 titles/year. Subsidy publishes 30% of books. Send complete mss or queries accompanied by outlines or sample chapters and biographical data to Tokyo. US and Canada distributors: Publishers and Booksellers, Drawer F, 26-30 Main St., Rutland VT 05701. Publishes book an average of 2 years after acceptance. Computer printout submissions acceptable; no dot-matrix. Reports in 4-6 weeks. SASE. Book catalog $1.

Nonfiction: Specializes in publishing books about Oriental art, culture, language and sociology as well as history, literature, cookery, sport, martial arts, and children's books which relate to Asia, the Hawaiian Islands, Australia and the Pacific areas. Also interested in Americana, especially antique collecting, architecture, genealogy and Canadiana. No poetry and fiction except that of Oriental themes. Accepts translations. Normal book length only. Looks for ''subject matter related to Asia, particularly Japan; authority of the author; balance and logical order in the structure of the ms; presentation—minimum of spelling/grammatical errors, double-spaced typing.'' Reviews artwork/photos as part of ms package.

Recent Nonfiction Title: *The Book of Topiary*, by Charles H. Curtis and W. Gibson.

TWAYNE PUBLISHERS, A division of G.K. Hall & Co., 70 Lincoln St., Boston MA 02111. (617)423-3990. Editor: Caroline L. Birdsall. Payment is on royalty basis. Publishes 120 titles/year. Electronic submissions OK, but requires hard copy also. Computer printout submissions acceptable; prefers letter-quality to dot-matrix. Query. Reports in 5 weeks. Enclose return postage.

Nonfiction: Publishes scholarly books and volumes for the general reader in series. Literary criticism, biography, American history, studies of film music, dance; women's studies; and art history.

Recent Nonfiction Title: *Louisa May Alcott*, by Ruth K. MacDonald.

Tips: Queries/mss may be routed to other editors in the publishing group.

TWENTY-THIRD PUBLICATIONS, INC., 185 Willow St., Box 180, Mystic CT 06355. (203)536-2611. Acquisitions: Neil Kluepfel. Publishes trade paperback originals. Averages 8 titles/year. Pays average 10% royalty on wholesale price. Publishes book an average of 18 months after acceptance. SASE. Reports in 3 weeks. Book catalog for 9x12 SAE and 2 first class stamps.

Nonfiction: Religious education, and adult education (Roman Catholic). ''Our audience is teachers, mainstream and educators.'' Query.

Recent Nonfiction Title: *Jesus in Focus, A Life in Its Setting*, by Gerard Sloyan.

*TYNDALE HOUSE PUBLISHERS, INC., 336 Gundersen Dr., Wheaton IL 60187. (312)668-8300. Editor-in-Chief/Acquisitions: Wendell Hawley. Publishes hardcover and trade paperback originals (90%) and hardcover and mass paperback reprints (10%). Publishes 100 titles/year. Subsidy publishes 2% of books. Pays 10% royalty; negotiable advance. Publishes book an average of 10 months after acceptance. Electronic submissions OK, but requires both floppy disk and hard copy. Computer printout submissions acceptable; prefers letter-quality to dot-matrix. Reports in 6 weeks. SASE. Free book catalog.

Nonfiction: Religious books only: personal experience, family living, marriage, Bible reference works and commentaries, Christian living, devotional, inspirational, church and social issues, Bible prophecy, theology and doctrine, counseling and Christian psychology, Christian apologetics and church history. Submit table of contents, chapter summary, preface, first two chapters and one later chapter.

Fiction: Bible and contemporary novels. Christian romances, westerns, and adventure. Junior high fiction. Submit outline/synopsis and sample chapters.

U.S. GAMES SYSTEMS, INC., 38 E. 32nd St., New York NY 10016. (212)685-4300. President: Stuart Kaplan. Publishes hardcover and trade paperback originals. Averages 10 titles/year. Pays royalty. Simultaneous and photocopied submissions OK. SASE. Reports in 1 month. Book catalog $1.
Nonfiction: Reference on tarot cards, history of playing cards. "Must be something new, different, and worthwhile limited to those subjects." Submit outline/synopsis and sample chapters.
Recent Nonfiction Title: *The Encyclopedia of Tarot*, by Stuart Kaplan.
Tips: Prefers publishing books when accompanied by artwork for new tarot cards.

‡ULTRALIGHT PUBLICATIONS, INC., Box 234, Hammelstown PA 17036. (717)566-0468. Editor: Michael A. Markowski. Imprints includes Aviation Publishers. Publishes hardcover and trade paperback originals. Averages 8 titles/year. Pays 10-15% royalty on wholesale price; buys some mss outright; offers average $1,000 advance. Simultaneous and photocopied submissions OK. SASE. Reports in 3 weeks on queries; 2 months on mss. Free book catalog.
Nonfiction: How-to, technical on hobbies (model airplanes) and aviation. Publishes for "aviation buffs, dreamers and enthusiasts. We are looking for titles in the homebuilt, ultralight, sport and general aviation fields. We are interested in how-to, technical and reference books of short to medium length that will serve recognized and emerging aviation needs." We are also interested in automotive historical, reference and how-to titles. Query or submit outline/synopsis and 3 sample chapters.
Recent Nonfiction Title: *Composite Construction*, by Lambie (how-to).

‡UMI RESEARCH PRESS, University Microfilms International, Xerox, 300 N. Zeeb Road, Ann Arbor MI 48106. Contact: Subject Acquisitions Editor. Publishes hardcover originals and revised dissertations. Averages 100 titles/year. Pays 5% royalty on net sales. Offers average $100 advance. Accepts photocopied and electronic submissions via disk or modem (contact publisher for details); no simultaneous submissions. Computer printout submissions acceptable "if good quality."
Nonfiction: Christine B. Hammes, acquisition editor. Scholarly and professional research, history and critical studies. Subjects include architecture; cinema, (theory and aesthetics); art; theatre (history and theory); business and economics, musicology; computer science; photography (theory); popular culture; cultural anthropology; nursing management; psychology (clinical); urban planning and history; and literary criticism. Especially looking for "scholarly works, original conclusions resulting from careful academic research. Primarily aimed at graduate, post-graduate and professional level. Academics, research librarians, art and music communities, business and nursing professionals are our audience." No mass market books. Query.
Recent Nonfiction Title: *Essays in Performance Practice*, by F. Neumann (musicology essays).
Tips: "Send letters of inquiry to appropriate publishers *before* devoting hours to a manuscript. Get feedback at the outline/prospects stage."

‡UNDERGROUND REPORTS, Suite 144, 4418 E. Chapman Ave., Orange CA 92669. (714)538-5390. Editor: David Lopez. Publishes mass market paperback originals (80%) and mass market paperback reprints (20%). Averages 6-10 titles/year. "We do no subsidy publishing but will consider distributing subsidy books if in our interest range." Pays 10% maximum royalty on retail price; sometimes buys outright. Offers no advance. Photocopied submissions OK. Computer printout submissions acceptable; prefers letter-quality to dot-matrix. SASE. Reports in 1 month on queries; 3 months on mss.
Nonfiction: How-to, reference and self-help. Subjects include tax rebellion, barter, occult, hard money, holistic health, libertarianism, survival, supressed information, unpopular viewpoints, alternative schools, alternative banking (exchanges), anti-establishment and pro-free market. "We need original works of 30,000 or more words written from the pro-Freedom (Free Market) point of view. They must be *PRACTICAL*. They might show the reader how to set up a part-time business—written in a step-by-step format. No flag-waving, vague, general, pro-establishment, liberal, pro-communist, pro-socialist material. Query or submit outline/synopsis and sample chapters.
Recent Nonfiction Title: *Underground Car Dealer*, by DeSoto (how-to).
Tips: "We expect more people to be aware of alternative (Free Market) activities. Our audience is middle-class males who are tired of being taxed to death; people who want to develop their own businesses; and people who want to restore the US Constitution."

UNDERWOOD-MILLER, Brandywyne Books, 651 Chestnut St., Columbia PA 17512. Editorial Director: Chuck Miller. Publishes hardcover and trade paperback originals and hardcover reprints. Averages 20 titles/year. Pays 10% royalty on retail price. Publishes book an average of 1 year after acceptance. Photocopied submissions OK. Electronic submissions via modem OK. Computer printout submissions acceptable. Query or submit outline/synopsis and sample chapters. SASE. Reports in 2 months. Free book catalog.
Nonfiction: Reference bibliography; critical studies of science fiction, horror and fantasy authors. Also critical review anthologies and single-author critical review volumes. "In the next year or two, we will be seeking single-author critical volumes on authors like James Clavell, etc., and annotated bibliographies on popular authors such as Louis L'Amour." Publishes for "hard-core science fiction and fantasy collectors and institutional

libraries. Our books are full cloth, smyth-sewn and made with acid-free paper. We are looking for specific studies of science fiction and fantasy authors. We also publish illustrated bibliographies of SF authors." Query. Reviews artwork/photos as part of ms package.

Recent Nonfiction Title: *Fear Itself—The Fiction of Stephen King*, edited by Tim Underwood and Chuck Miller (critical study of King).

Fiction: Fantasy, horror, and science fiction. "We publish limited edition SF and fantasy novels and collections for the collectors and library markets." All of our fiction is reprints (for libraries) of existing books. Query.

Recent Fiction Title: *Gilden-Fire*, by Stephen R. Donaldson (fantasy).

UNIVELT, INC., Box 28130, San Diego CA 92128. (619)746-4005. Editorial Director: H. Jacobs. Publishes hardcover originals. Averages 8 titles/year. Pays 10% royalty on actual sales; no advance. Publishes book an average of 4 months after acceptance. Computer printout submissions acceptable. Reports in 4 weeks. SASE. Free book catalog.

Nonfiction: Publishes in the field of aerospace, especially astronautics, and technical communications, but including application of aerospace technology to Earth's problems. Submit outline/synopsis and 1-2 sample chapters. Reviews artwork/photos as part of ms package.

Recent Nonfiction Title: *Handbook of Soviet Manned Space Flight*.

Tips: Queries/mss may be routed to other editors in the publishing group.

UNIVERSE BOOKS, 381 Park Ave. S., New York NY 10016. (212)685-7400. Editorial Director: Louis Barron. Publishes hardcover and paperback originals (95%) and reprints (5%). Averages 45 titles/year. Offers 10-15% royalty on retail price (hardbound books). "On a few extra-illustrated art books and on special studies with a limited market we may pay a smaller royalty." Average advance: $1,000-4,000. "If a book makes a genuine contribution to knowledge but is a commercial risk, we might perhaps accept a subsidy from a foundation or other organization, but not directly from the author." Publishes book an average of 9 months after acceptance. Simultaneous and photocopied submissions OK. Computer printout submissions acceptable; prefers letter-quality to dot-matrix. "Will not return material without postage-paid SAE." Reports in 2 weeks. Book catalog if 55¢ in stamps (not SASE) is enclosed.

Nonfiction: Animals, art, economics, history, nature, performing arts, politics, reference and science. Universe also pays secondary attention to biography, health and how-to. Also uses "discussions of specific animal, bird or plant species; social histories of specific types of artifacts or social institutions; art histories of specific types of artifacts or symbols. We publish books in the following categories: antiques, crafts and collectibles, art, architecture and design, history, life, physical and agricultural sciences, ballet, music, contemporary problems, and social sciences (especially books on survival, appropriate technology, and the limits to growth). We do not publish fiction, poetry, cookbooks, criticism or belles lettres." Reviews artwork/photos as part of ms package. Accepts artwork/photos. Submit outline/synopsis and 2-3 sample chapters. Accepts nonfiction French and German translations.

Recent Nonfiction Title: *The Ballerina* and *Pas de Deux*, by S. Montague.

UNIVERSITY ASSOCIATES, INC., 8517 Production Ave., San Diego CA 92121. (619)578-5900. President: J. William Pfeiffer. Publishes paperback originals (65%) and reprints (35%). Specializes in practical materials for human resource development, consultants, etc. Pays average 10% royalty; no advance. Publishes book an average of 6 months after acceptance. Markets books by direct mail. Simultaneous submissions OK. Computer printout submissions acceptable; no dot-matrix. SASE. Reports in 2-4 months. Free book catalog.

Nonfiction: Marion Mettler, Vice-President, Publications. Publishes (in order of preference) human resource development and group-oriented material, management education and community relations and personal growth, and business. No materials for grammar school or high school classroom teachers. Use *American Psychological Association Style manual*. Query. Send prints or completed art or rough sketches to accompany ms.

Recent Nonfiction Title: *The 1984 Annual for Human Resource Development*, by J.W. Pfeiffer and L.D. Goodstein.

UNIVERSITY OF ALABAMA PRESS, Box 2877, University AL 35486. Director: Malcolm MacDonald. Publishes hardcover originals. Published 31 titles last year. "Maximum royalty (on wholesale price) is 10%; no advances made." Computer printout submissions acceptable. Enclose return postage. Free book catalog.

Nonfiction: Biography, business and economics, history, music, philosophy, politics, religion and sociology. Considers upon merit almost any subject of scholarly interest, but specializes in linguistics and philology, political science and public administration, literary criticism and biography, philosophy, and history. Accepts nonfiction translations.

Recent Nonfiction Title: *A History of Metals in Colonial America* (US history).

‡THE UNIVERSITY OF ALBERTA PRESS, 450 Athabasca Hall, Edmonton, Alberta T6G 2E8 Canada. (403)432-3662. Subsidiary includes Pica Pica Press. Director: Norma Gutteridge. Imprint includes Pica Pica

Press. Publishes hardcover and trade paperback originals, and trade paperback reprints. Averages 10 titles/year. Pays 10% royalty on retail price. Publishes book an average of 1 year after acceptance. Computer printout submissions acceptable; no dot-matrix. SASE Reports in 1 week on queries; 3 months on mss. Free book catalog.

Nonfiction: Biography, how-to, reference, technical textbook, and scholarly. Subjects include art, history, nature, philosophy, politics, and sociology. Especially looking for "biographies of Canadians in public life, and works analyzing Canada's political history and public policy, particularly in international affairs. No pioneer reminiscences, literary criticism (unless in Canadian literature), reports of narrowly focused studies, unrevised theses." Reviews artwork/photos as part of ms package. Submit complete ms.

Recent Nonfiction Title: *Generalissimos of the Western Roman Empire*, by John O'Flynn (ancient history).

Tips: "Technical and business books are a growing market. If I were a writer trying to market a book today, I would concentrate on an area of expertise and write to inform people, whether in law, human relationships, gardening, or whatever. I would first become an acknowledged expert in that area. Trends in book publishing that freelance writers should be aware of include increased cost of production, which means that shorter books (under 500 typescript pages) will have more chance of acceptance than longer ones." A foot high stack of paper means an immediate minimum on editor's mind.

UNIVERSITY OF ARIZONA PRESS, 1615 E. Speedway, Tucson AZ 85719. (602)621-1441. Director: Stephen Cox. Publishes hardcover and paperback originals and reprints. "Contracts are individually negotiated, but as a 'scholarly publishing house' operating primarily on informational works, does not pay any advances. Also, royalty starting point may be after sale of first 1,000 copies, by virtue of the nature of the publishing program." Averages 25-30 titles/year. Publishes book an average of 1 year after acceptance. Will consider photocopied submissions if ms is not undergoing consideration at another publishing house. "Must have this assurance." Computer printout submissions acceptable; no dot-matrix. Query and submit outline and sample chapters. Reports on material within 90 days. SASE. Free catalog and editorial guidelines.

Nonfiction: "Significant works of a regional nature about Arizona, the Southwest and Mexico; and books of merit in subject matter fields strongly identified with the universities in Arizona; i.e., anthropology, arid lands studies, space sciences, Asian studies, Southwest Indians, Mexico, etc. No "personal diary types of Western Americana, mainly directed only toward family interest, rather than broad general interest." Reviews artwork/photos as part of ms package.

Recent Nonfiction Title: *Hopi Photographers/Hopi Images*, compiled by Victor Masayesva and Erin Younger.

*THE UNIVERSITY OF ARKANSAS PRESS, 201 Ozark St., Fayetteville AR 72701. (501)575-3246. Director: Miller Williams. Contact: Jeanie Pittman. Publishes hardcover and trade paperback originals and reprints. Averages 6-10 titles/year. Subsidy publishes 30% of our authors by means of various institutional grants, which partially underwrite publisher's costs. Pays 10% royalty on wholesale price. No advance. Publishes book an average of 9 months after acceptance. Computer printout submissions acceptable; no dot-matrix. SASE. Reports in 2 weeks on queries; 3 months on mss. Free book catalog.

Nonfiction: Biography, literary criticism, regional studies. Publishes for "educated humanist, generalist." Especially needs "critical works on modern American writers; Southern, British and intellectual history; general Southern regional studies." Accepts translations. No non-books, how-to, juvenile, self-help, technical or textbooks. Submit outline/synopsis and 3-5 sample chapters. Reviews artwork/photos as part of ms package.

Recent Nonfiction Title: *The Hound of Conscience: WWI Draft Resistance in England*, by Thomas Kennedy (history).

Fiction: Mainstream. "We are primarily interested in high-energy short stories." No confession, erotica, religious, romance, or western. Submit outline/synopsis and sample chapters.

Recent Fiction Title: *In The Land of Dreamy Dreams*, by Ellen Gilchrist (short stories).

Poetry: "We are eclectic in our view of poetry and are willing to read most any submission, but are more often convinced by the short lyric, formal or free, original or in translation." No "rant or cant." Submit complete ms.

Recent Poetry Title: *Life On the Edge Of the Continent*, by Ronald Koertge (lyric, free verse).

UNIVERSITY OF CALIFORNIA PRESS, 2120 Berkeley Way, Berkeley CA 94720. Director: James H. Clark. Assistant Director: Leroy T. Barnes Jr. Los Angeles office: Suite 613, 10995 Le Conte Ave., UCLA, Los Angeles CA 94995. New York office: Room 513, 50 E. 42 St., New York NY 10017. London office: University Presses of California, Chicago, Harvard and MIT, 126 Buckingham Palace Rd., London SW1W 9SD England. Publishes hardcover and paperback originals and reprints. "On books likely to do more than return their costs, a standard royalty contract beginning at 10% is paid; on paperbacks it is less." Published 201 titles last year. Queries are always advisable, accompanied by outlines or sample material. Accepts nonfiction translations. Send to Berkeley address. Reports vary, depending on the subject. Enclose return postage.

Nonfiction: "It should be clear that most of our publications are hardcover nonfiction written by scholars." Publishes scholarly books including art, literary studies, social sciences, natural sciences and some high-level popularizations. No length preferences.

Fiction and Poetry: Publishes fiction and poetry only in translation, usually in bilingual editions.

‡*UNIVERSITY OF ILLINOIS PRESS, 54 E. Gregory, Champaign IL 61820. (217)333-0950. Director/
Editor: Richard L. Wentworth. Publishes hardcover and trade paperback originals, and hardcover and trade paperback reprints. Averages 50-60 titles/year. Subsidy publishes 20-25% of books. "We decide whether an author should be subsidy published by determining which mss can't be published without the expectation of defi-
cite larger that we can afford." Pays 0-15% royalty on net sales; offers average 1,000-1,500 advance (rarely).
Simultaneous and photocopied submissions OK. Computer printout submissions acceptable; prefers letter-
quality to dot-matrix. SASE. Reports in 1 week on queries; 4 months on mss. Free book catalog.
Nonfiction: Biography, reference and scholarly books. Subjects include Americana, business and economics,
history (especially American history), music (especially American music), politics, sociology, sports, and lit-
erature. Always looking for "solid scholarly books in American history, especially social history; books on
American popular music, and books in the broad area of American studies." Query with outlines/synopsis.
Recent Nonfiction Title: *Theirs Be the Power:The Moguls of Eastern Kentucky*, by Harry M. Caudill (polemical history).
Fiction: Ethnic, experimental, and mainstream. "We publish four collections of stories by individual writers
each year. We do not publish novels." Query.
Recent Fiction Title: *Home Fires*, by David Long (short stories).
Tips: "Serious scholarly books that are broad enough and well written enough to appeal to non-specialists are
doing well for us in today's market. Writers of nonfiction trying to determine where to submit a ms are advised
to try at least a dozen commercial publishers before thinking about offering the work to a university press."

UNIVERSITY OF IOWA PRESS, Graphic Services Bldg., Iowa City IA 52242. (319)353-3181. Editor: Art
Pflughaupt. Publishes hardcover and paperback originals. Averages 7 titles/year. Pays 10% royalty on retail
price. Subsidy publishing is offered "if a scholarly institution will advance a subsidy to support publication of a
worthwhile book. We market mostly by direct mailing of fliers to groups with special interests in our titles."
Publishes book an average of 1 year after acceptance. Query or submit outline/synopsis and 3 sample chapters.
Use Chicago *Manual of Style*. Electronic submissions OK for tape, but requires hard copy also. Computer
printout submissions acceptable; prefers letter-quality to dot-matrix. Reports in 2-4 months. SASE. Free book
catalog.
Nonfiction: Publishes art, economics, history, music, philosophy, reference, and scientific books. Accepts
nonfiction, fiction and poetry translations. "We do not publish children's books, or any poetry or short fiction
except the Iowa Translation Series and the Iowa School of Letters Award for short fiction." Looks for "evidence of original research; reliable sources; clarity of organization, complete development of theme with documentation and supportive footnotes and/or bibliography; and a substantive contribution to knowledge in the
field treated." Reviews artwork/photos as part of ms package.
Recent Nonfiction Title: *Crisis and Conflict: World News Reporting Between Two Wars*, by Robert W. Des-
mond.

UNIVERSITY OF MASSACHUSETTS PRESS, Box 429, Amherst MA 01004. (413)545-2217. Director:
Bruce Wilcox. Acquisitions Editor: Richard Martin. Publishes hardcover and paperback originals (95%) reprints and imports (5%). Averages 25-30 titles/year. "Royalties depend on character of book; if offered, generally at 10% of list price. Advance rarely offered." No author subsidies accepted. Publishes book an average of
10 months after acceptance. Electronic submissions OK, but requires hard copy also. Computer printout submissions acceptable; prefers letter-quality to dot-matrix. Preliminary report in 6 weeks. SASE. Free book catalog.
Nonfiction: Publishes Afro-American studies, art and architecture, biography, criticism, history, natural history, philosophy, poetry, psychology, public policy, sociology and women's studies in original and reprint editions. Accepts nonfiction translations. Reviews artwork/photos as part of ms package. Submit outline/synop-
sis and 1-2 sample chapters.
Recent Nonfiction Title: *Thoreau's Seasons*, by Richard Lebeaux (criticism).
Tips: "As members of AAUP, we sometimes route (queries/mss) to other university presses."

UNIVERSITY OF MICHIGAN PRESS, 839 Greene St., Ann Arbor MI 48106. (313)764-4394. Editorial
Director: Walter E. Sears. Senior Editor: Mary C. Erwin. Publishes hardcover and paperback originals (95%)
and reprints (5%). Averages 35-40 titles/year. Pays 10% royalty on retail price but primarily on net; offers advance. Electronic submissions OK, but requires hard copy also. Computer printout submissions acceptable; no
dot-matrix. SASE. Reports in 2 weeks. Free book catalog.
Nonfiction: Americana, animals, art, biography, business/economics, health, history, music, nature, philosophy, photography, psychology, recreation, reference, religion, science, sociology, technical, textbooks, and
travel. No dissertations. Query first.
Recent Nonfiction Title: *Nuclear Power: Technology on Trial*, by J. Duderstadt and C. Kikuchi.

UNIVERSITY OF MISSOURI PRESS, 200 Lewis Hall, Columbia MO 65211. (314)882-7641. Director:
Edward D. King. Associate Director: Susan McGregor Denny. Publishes hardcover and paperback originals

and paperback reprints. Averages 30 titles/year. Pays 10% royalty on net receipts; no advance. Publishes book an average of 2 years after acceptance. Photocopied submissions OK. Electronic submissions OK, but requires hard copy also. Computer printout submissions acceptable. Reports in 6 months. SASE. Free book catalog.

Nonfiction: "Scholarly publisher interested in history, literary criticism, political science, social science, music, art, art history, and original poetry." Also regional books about Missouri and the Midwest. "We do not publish mathematics or hard sciences." Query or submit outline/synopsis and sample chapters. Consult Chicago *Manual of Style.*

Recent Nonfiction Title: *Painters of the Humble Truth: Masterpieces of American Still Life 1901-1939,* by William H. Gerdts.

Fiction: "Fiction, poetry, and drama manuscripts are taken into submission only in February and March of odd-numbered years. We publish original short fiction in Breakthrough Series, not to exceed 35,000 words. May be short story collection or novella. We also publish poetry and drama in the same series. No limitations on subject matter." Query.

Recent Fiction Title: *Winter Weeds,* by Harry Humes.

UNIVERSITY OF NEBRASKA PRESS, 901 N. 17th St., Lincoln NE 68588-0520. Editor-in-Chief: Willis G. Regier. Publishes hardcover and paperback originals (60%) and hardcover and paperback reprints (40%). Specializes in scholarly nonfiction, some regional books; reprints of Western Americana; and natural history. Royalty is usually graduated from 10% on wholesale price for original books; no advance. Averages 50 new titles, 30 paperback reprints (*Bison Books*)/year. Computer printout submissions acceptable. SASE. Reports in 2-4 months. Free book catalog.

Nonfiction: Publishes Americana, biography, history, nature, photography, psychology, sports, literature, agriculture and American Indian themes. Accepts nonfiction and fiction translations. Query. Accepts outline/synopsis, 2 sample chapters and introduction. Looks for "an indication that the author knows his subject thoroughly and interprets it intelligently."

Recent Nonfiction Title: *Shawnee Prophet,* by David Edmunds.

UNIVERSITY OF NEVADA PRESS, Reno NV 89557. (702)784-6573. Director: John Stetter. Editor: Nicholas M. Cady. Publishes hardcover and paperback originals (90%) and reprints (10%). Averages 6 titles/year. Pays 10% royalty on retail price. Publishes book an average of 2 years after acceptance. Computer printout submissions acceptable; prefers letter-quality to dot-matrix. Preliminary reports in 2 months. Free book catalog.

Nonfiction: Specifically needs regional history and natural history, anthropology, biographies and Basque studies. "We are the first university press to sustain a sound series on Basque studies—New World and Old World." No juvenile books. Submit complete manuscript.

Recent Nonfiction Title: *Walter Van Tilburg Clark: Critiques,* ed. by Charlton Laird.

‡*UNIVERSITY OF NEW MEXICO PRESS, Journalism 220, Albuquerque NM 87131. (505)277-2346. Senior Editor: Elizabeth C. Hadas. Publishes hardcover and trade paperback originals and hardcover and trade paperback reprints. Averages 60 titles/year. Subsidy publishes 5% of books "depending upon nature of ms." Pays maximum 10% royalty on wholesale price. Publishes book an average of 18 months after acceptance. Electronic submissions OK, but requires hard copy also. Computer printout submissions acceptable. SASE. Reports in 2 weeks on queries; 6 months on mss. Free book catalog.

Nonfiction: Scholarly and regional books covering Americana, art, history, nature and photography. Reviews artwork/photos as part of ms package. Query.

Recent Nonfiction Title: *Textiles of the Prehistoric Southwest,* by Kate Kent (illustrated monograph).

Fiction: "No original fiction. Any fiction mss will be returned unread if accompanied by SASE. Otherwise, they will be discarded."

THE UNIVERSITY OF NORTH CAROLINA PRESS, Box 2288, Chapel Hill NC 27514. (919)966-3561. Editor-in-Chief: Iris Tillman Hill. Publishes hardcover and paperback originals. Specializes in scholarly books and regional trade books. Royalty schedule "varies." No advance. Averages 50 titles/year. "As a university press, we do not have the resources for mass marketing books." Send prints to illustrate ms only if they are a major part of the book. Photocopied submissions OK. Reports in 2-5 months. SASE. Free book catalog.

Nonfiction: "Our major fields are American and European history." Also scholarly books on Americana, classics, oral history, political science, urban studies, religious studies, psychology and sociology. History books on law and music. Books on nature, particularly on the Southeast; literary studies. Submit outline/synopsis and sample chapters. Must follow Chicago *Manual of Style.* Looks for "intellectual excellence and clear writing."

Recent Nonfiction Title: *Turing's Man: Western Culture in the Computer Age,* by J. David Bolter.

UNIVERSITY OF NOTRE DAME PRESS, Notre Dame IN 46556. Editor: Ann Rice. Publishes hardcover and paperback originals and paperback reprints. Pays 10-12½-15% royalty, no advance. Publishes 30-35 titles/

year. Will consider photocopied submissions. Query. Reports in 2 months. SASE. Free book catalog.
Nonfiction: "Scholarly books, serious nonfiction of general interest, book-length only. Especially in the areas of philosophy, theology, history, sociology, English literature (Middle English period, and modern literature criticism in the area of relation of literature and theology), government, international relations, and Mexican-American studies.
Recent Nonfiction Title: *After Virtue*, by Alasdair MacIntyre.

UNIVERSITY OF OKLAHOMA PRESS, 1005 Asp Ave., Norman OK 73019. (405)325-5111. Editor-in-Chief: John Drayton. Publishes hardcover and paperback originals (85%); and reprints (15%). Averages 50 titles/year. Royalty ranges from 0-15% on wholesale price, "depending on market potential"; no advance. Publishes book an average of 18 months after acceptance. Electronic submissions OK, but requires hard copy also. Computer printout submissions acceptable; prefers letter-quality to dot-matrix. Reports in 2-4 months. SASE. Book catalog for SASE.
Nonfiction: Publishes North American Indian studies, Western history, Americana and art (Indian and Western), Mesoamerican studies, Oklahoma, classical studies, literary criticism, and philosophy. Poetry and fiction not invited. Query, including outline, 1-2 sample chapters and author resume. Accepts nonfiction translations from Spanish, German and French. Reviews artwork/photos as part of ms package.
Recent Nonfiction Title: *The Rocky Mountains: A Vision for Artists in the Nineteenth Century*, by Patricia Trenton and Peter Hassrick (Western history).

*UNIVERSITY OF PENNSYLVANIA PRESS, 3933 Walnut St., Philadelphia PA 19104. (215)243-6261. Director: Thomas M. Rotell. Hardcover and paperback originals (90%) and reprints (10%). Pays 10% royalty on wholesale price for first 5,000 copies sold; 12½% for next 5,000 copies sold; 15% thereafter; no advance. Averages 45 titles/year. Subsidy publishes 10% of books. Subsidy publishing is determined by: evaluation obtained by the press from outside specialists; work approved by Press Editorial Committee; subsidy approved by funding organization. State availability of photos and/or illustrations to accompany ms, with copies of illustrations. Photocopied submissions OK. Computer printout submissions acceptable; no dot-matrix. Reports in 1-3 months. SASE. Free book catalog.
Nonfiction: Publishes Americana, biography, business, economics, medicine, biological sciences, computer science, physical sciences, law, anthropology, folklore and literary criticism. "Serious books that serve the scholar and the professional." Follow the Chicago *Manual of Style*. Query with outline and 1-4 sample chapters addressed to the editor.
Recent Nonfiction Title: *Passing the Time in Ballymenone*, by Henry Glassie.
Tips: Queries/mss may be routed to other editors in the publishing group.

UNIVERSITY OF PITTSBURGH PRESS, 127 N. Bellefield Ave., Pittsburgh PA 15260. (412)624-4110. Director: Frederick A. Hetzel. Managing Editor: Catherine Marshall. Publishes hardcover and paperback originals. Publishes 32 titles/year. Pays 12½% royalty on hardcover, 8% on paperback; no advance. Photocopied submissions OK. Computer printout submissions acceptable; prefers letter-quality to dot-matrix. Reports in 1-4 months. SASE. Free book catalog.
Nonfiction: Scholarly nonfiction. No textbooks or general nonfiction of an unscholarly nature. Submit outline/synopsis and 1 sample chapter.
Recent Nonfiction Title: *Cuba Between Empires, 1878-1902*, by Louis A. Pérez Jr..

THE UNIVERSITY OF TENNESSEE PRESS, 293 Communications Bldg., Knoxville TN 37996. Contact: Acquisitions Editor. Averages 30 titles/year. Pays negotiable royalty on retail price. Photocopied submissions OK. "We can only review hard copy." Computer printout submissions acceptable; no dot-matrix. Reports in 2 week on queries; "in 1 month on submissions we have encouraged." Free catalog and writer's guidelines.
Nonfiction: American history, political science, film studies, sports studies, literary criticism, anthropology, folklore and regional studies. Prefers "scholarly treatment and a readable style. Authors usually have PhDs." Submit outline/synopsis, author vita, and 2 sample chapters. No fiction, poetry or plays.
Recent Nonfiction Title: *Miners, Millhands, and Mountaineers*, by Ronald D. Eller (history).
Tips: "Our market is in several groups: scholars; educated readers with special interests in given scholarly subjects; and the general educated public interested in Tennessee, Appalachia and the South. Not all our books appeal to all these groups, of course, but any given book must appeal to at least one of them."

UNIVERSITY OF TEXAS PRESS, Box 7819, Austin TX 78712. Managing Editor: Barbara Spielman. Averages 60 titles/year. Pays royalty usually based on net income; occasionally offers advance. Publishes book an average of 3 years after acceptance. Electronic submissions OK, but requires hard copy also. Computer printout submissions acceptable; no dot-matrix. SASE. Reports in 8 weeks. Free catalog and writer's guidelines.
Nonfiction: General scholarly subjects: astronomy, natural history, economics, Latin American and Middle Eastern studies, native Americans, classics, films, medical, biology, contemporary architecture, archeology, Chicano studies, physics, health, sciences, international relations, linguistics, photography, twentieth-century

and women's literature. Also uses specialty titles related to Texas and the Southwest, national trade titles, and regional trade titles. Reviews artwork/photos as part of ms package. Query or submit outline/synopsis and 2 sample chapters. Accepts nonfiction and fiction translations.
Recent Nonfiction Title: *The Greeks*, by Ken Dover.
Tips: "It's difficult to make a ms over 400 double spaced pages into a feasible book. Authors should take special care to edit out extraneous material." Looks for sharply focused, in-depth treatments of important topics.

UNIVERSITY OF UTAH PRESS, University of Utah, 101 University Services Bldg., Salt Lake City UT 84112. (801)581-6771. Director: Stephen H. Hess. Publishes hardcover and paperback originals and reprints. Pays 10% royalty on net income on first 2,000 copies sold; 12% on 2,001 to 4,000 copies sold; 15% thereafter. Royalty schedule varies on paperback editions. Averages 12 titles/year. Free book catalog. Publishes book an average of 1 year after acceptance. Electronic submissions OK, but requires hard copy also. Computer printout submissions acceptable; prefers letter-quality to dot-matrix. Query with outline and 3 sample chapters. Author should specify page length in query. Reports in 6-8 weeks. SASE.
Nonfiction: Scholarly books on Western history, philosophy, anthropology, Mesoamerican studies, folklore, and Middle Eastern studies. Accepts nonfiction translations. Annual poetry competition, accepting mss of more than 60 pages in March.
Recent Nonfiction Title: *Conversations with Wallace Stegner*, by Wallace Stegner and Richard W. Etulain.

UNIVERSITY OF WISCONSIN PRESS, 114 N. Murray St., Madison WI 53715. (608)262-4928 (telex: 265452). Director: Allen N. Fitchen. Acquisitions Editors: Peter J. Givler and Gordon Lester-Massman. Publishes hardcover and paperback originals, reprints and translations. Pays standard royalties on retail price. Averages 40-50 titles/year. Send complete ms. Follow Chicago *Manual of Style*. Reports in 3 months. Enclose return postage with ms.
Nonfiction: Publishes general nonfiction based on scholarly research. "Among university publishers, geographical orientation and environmental emphasis distinguishes this university press." Looks for "originality, significance, quality of the research represented, literary quality, and breadth of interest to the educated community at large." Accepts nonfiction translations.
Recent Nonfiction Title: *A Century of American Print Making, 1880-1980*, by James Watrous.

UNIVERSITY PRESS OF AMERICA, 4720 Boston Way, Lanham MD 20706. (301)459-3366. Editorial Director: James E. Lyons. Publishes hardcover and paperback originals (95%) and reprints (5%). Averages 450 titles/year. Pays 5-15% royalty on wholesale price; no advance. Computer printout submissions acceptable. Reports in 6 weeks. SASE. Free book catalog.
Nonfiction: Scholarly monographs, college, and graduate level textbooks in history, economics, business, psychology, political science, African studies, black studies, philosophy, religion, sociology, music, art, literature, drama, and education. No juvenile or el-hi material. Submit outline.
Recent Nonfiction Title: *Vietnam as History*, by Peter Braestrup.

UNIVERSITY PRESS OF KANSAS, (formerly Regents Press of Kansas), 303 Carruth, Lawrence KS 66045. (913)864-4154. Editor: Fred Woodward. Hardcover and paperback originals. Averages 20 titles/year. Royalties negotiable. No advance. Markets books by advertising and direct mail, chiefly to libraries and scholars. "State availability of illustrations if they add significantly to the ms." Publishes book an average of 10 months after acceptance. Computer printout submissions acceptable; no dot-matrix. Reports in 2-4 months. SASE. Free book catalog.
Nonfiction: Publishes biography, history, psychology, philosophy, politics, regional subjects, and scholarly nonfiction books. Reviews artwork/photos as part of ms package. Query.
Recent Nonfiction Title: *The Presidency of Lyndon B. Johnson* (history).

UNIVERSITY PRESS OF KENTUCKY, 102 Lafferty Hall, Lexington KY 40506-0024. (606)257-2951. Director: Kenneth Cherry. Editor-in-Chief: Jerome Crouch. Managing Editor: Evalin F. Douglas. Hardcover originals (95%) and paperback reprints (5%). Pays 10% royalty after first 1,000 copies; no advance. State availability of photos and/or artwork to accompany ms. "Author is ultimately responsible for submitting all artwork in camera-ready form." Computer printout submissions acceptable; prefers letter-quality to dot-matrix. Reports in 2-4 months. SASE. Free book catalog.
Nonfiction: Publishes (in order of preference): history, political science, literary criticism and history, politics, anthropology, law, philosophy, medical history and nature. "All mss must receive an endorsement (secured by the press) from a scholar in the appropriate area of learning and must be approved by an editorial board before final acceptance." No original fiction, poetry, drama or textbooks. Query or submit outline/synopsis with 1 sample chapter. Reviews artwork/photos as part of ms package.
Recent Nonfiction Title: *Generations*, by John Egerton.
Tips: Queries/mss may be routed to other editors in the publishing group.

UNIVERSITY PRESS OF MISSISSIPPI, 3825 Ridgewood Rd., Jackson MS 39211. (601)982-6205. Director: Barney McKee. Publishes hardcover and paperback originals (90%) and reprints (10%). Averages 18 titles/year. Pays 10% net royalty on first printing and 12% net on additional printings. No advance. Publishes book an average of 9 months after acceptance. Computer printout submissions acceptable. SASE. Reports in 1 month. Free book catalog.
Nonfiction: Americana, art, biography, business and economics, history, philosophy, politics, psychology, sociology, literary criticism, and folklore. Especially needs regional studies and literary studies, particularly mss on William Faulkner and Eudora Welty. Submit outline/synopsis and sample chapters and curriculum vita. Reviews artwork/photos as part of ms package.
Recent Nonfiction Title: *The South and Film*, edited by Warren French.

*UNIVERSITY PRESS OF NEW ENGLAND, 3 Lebanon St., Hanover NH 03755. (603)646-3349. "University Press of New England is a consortium of university presses. Some books—those published for one of the consortium members—carry the joint imprint of New England and the member: Dartmouth, Brandeis, Brown, Tufts, Clark, Universities of New Hampshire, Vermont and Rhode Island." Director and Editor: Thomas L. McFarland. Publishes hardcover and trade paperback originals (90%) and trade paperback reprints (10%). Averages 30 titles/year. Subsidy publishes 80% of books. Pays standard royalty; occasionally offers advance. Electronic submissions OK, but requires hard copy also. Computer printout submissions acceptable. SASE. Reports in 1 month. Free book catalog.
Nonfiction: Americana (regional—New England), art, biography, business and economics, history, music, nature, philosophy, politics, psychology, reference, science, sociology, technical, textbooks and regional (New England). No festschriften, memoirs or unrevised doctoral dissertations. Only a few symposium collections accepted. Accepts nonfiction translations. Submit outline/synopsis and 1-2 sample chapters.
Recent Nonfiction Title: *The Work of Augustus Saint Gaudens*, by John H. Dryfhout (art).

UNIVERSITY PRESS OF THE PACIFIC, INC., Box 66129, Seattle WA 98166. Publishes hardcover and paperback originals (50%) and reprints (50%). Averages 10 titles/year. Pays 5-10% royalty; buys some mss outright; no advance. Publishes book an average of 2 years after acceptance. Simultaneous and photocopied submissions OK. Computer printout submissions acceptable; prefers letter-quality to dot-matrix. SASE. Reports "very slowly."
Nonfiction: Business and economics, history, politics, reference, science, technical and textbooks. We are looking for scholarly and reference books which are unique in content. Our advertising media concentrates on the library marketplace, yet we do sell some to the trade. We are not interested in popular trade books." Query.
Recent Nonfiction Title: *World Within Worlds*, by I. Asimov (historical account of science).
Tips: "We will also consider text for specialized courses where a professor can identify a specific market at his own or at other institutions; however, we will be buying very little in 1985. We are in the process of changing our method of operation to specialize in producing on-demand and very short-run reference publications for the academic community."

*UNIVERSITY PRESS OF VIRGINIA, Box 3608, University Station, Charlottesville VA 22903. (804)924-3468. Editor-in-Chief: Walker Cowen. Publishes hardcover and paperback originals (95%) and reprints (5%). Averages 45 titles/year. Royalty on retail depends on the market for the book; sometimes none is made. "We subsidy publish 40% of our books, based on cost vs. probable market." Publishes book an average of 9 months after acceptance. Electronic submissions OK, but requires hard copy also. Computer printout submissions acceptable; no dot-matrix. Returns rejected material within a week. Reports on acceptances in 1-2 months. SASE. Free catalog.
Nonfiction: Publishes Americana, business, history, law, medicine and psychiatry, politics, reference, scientific, bibliography, and decorative arts books. "Write a letter to the director, describing content of the manuscript, plus length. Also specify if maps, tables, illustrations, etc., are included. Please, no educational or sociological or psychological manuscripts." Accepts nonfiction translations from French. Reviews artwork/photos as part of ms package.
Recent Nonfiction Title: *The Space of Death*, by Michel Ragon.

‡*UNIVERSITY PRESSES OF FLORIDA, 15 NW 15th St., Gainesville FL 32603. (904)392-1351. Director: Phillip Martin. Publishes hardcover and trade paperback originals and trade paperback reprints. Averages 30 titles/year. Subsidy publishes 15% of books. "We must break even on direct costs of manufacture." Pays 0-12½% royalty on net sales receipts; offers no advance. Simultaneous and photocopied submissions OK. Electronic submissions OK, but confer with editor in advance. Computer printout submissions acceptable. SASE. Reports in 4 weeks on queries; 6 months on mss. Free book catalog.
Nonfiction: Biography, "coffee table" book, cookbook, reference, and scholarly monographs. Subjects include Americana, animals, art, business and economics, cooking and foods, health, history, nature, philosophy, photography, politics, psychology, religion, sociology, sports (history), archaeology and literary theory. Especially looking for "learned works on serious subjects lucidly written for the general, educated reader. No

astrology, faith healing, folk medicine, handicraft or education textbooks." Query.
Recent Nonfiction Title: *Philosophy of the Literary Symbolic*, by Hazard Adams (literary theory).

UTAH STATE UNIVERSITY PRESS, Utah State University, Logan UT 84322. (801)750-1362. Director: Linda Speth. Publishes hardcover and trade paperback originals and hardcover and trade paperback reprints. Averages 6 titles/year. Pays 10-15% royalty on retail price. No advance. Computer printout submissions acceptable. SASE. Reports in 2 weeks on queries; 2 months on mss. Free book catalog.
Nonfiction: Biography, reference and textbook on Americana, history, politics and science. "Particularly interested in book-length scholarly manuscripts dealing with Western history, Western literature (Western Americana). All manuscript submission must have a scholarly focus." Submit complete ms.
Recent Nonfiction Title: *Diary of Charles Lowell Walker*, by Karl and Katherine Larsen (diary).
Poetry: "At the present time, we have accepted several poetry mss and will not be reading poetry submissions for one year."
Recent Poetry Title: *Stone Roses: Poems from Transylvania*, by Keith Wilson.

VANCE BIBLIOGRAPHIES, 112 N. Charter, Box 229, Monticello IL 61856. (217)762-3831. Editor: Mary Vance. Imprints include Architecture Series: Bibliography and Public Administration Series: Bibliography, Mary Vance, editor. Publishes trade paperback originals. Averages 480 titles/year, 240/imprints. Pays $100 honorarium, 10-20 author's copies. Publishes book an average of 4 months after acceptance. Photocopied submissions OK. Computer printout submissions acceptable. SASE. Reports in 1 week on queries; 2 weeks on mss. Free book catalog.
Nonfiction: Reference bibliographies on public administration and/or architecture and related subject areas. Publishes for "graduate students and professionals in the field; primary customers are libraries." Query or submit complete ms.
Recent Nonfiction Title: *Pedestrian Facilities Design in Architecture*, by R.B. Harmon.

VANGUARD PRESS, INC., 424 Madison Ave., New York NY 10017. Editor-in-Chief: Mrs. Bernice S. Woll. Publishes hardcover originals and reprints. Publishes 20 titles/year. Offers 7½-15% royalty on retail price; also buys mss outright; pays variable advance. Simultaneous and photocopied submissions OK. SASE. Reports in 8 weeks.
Nonfiction: Animals; art; biography (especially of musicians, artists and political figures); business (management, making money, how-to); cookbooks (gourmet and diet books); cooking and foods; history (scholarly, but written with flair); hobbies (crafts, especially sewing); how-to; humor; juveniles (folk stories, nature and art topics); music (no scores, but anything pertaining to the field—also, jazz); nature (ecology and nature adventure); philosophy; poetry; politics (current issues); psychology; religion in literature and society (no tracts); current sociology studies; sports; travel; juvenile science; and literary criticism. "No textbooks, reference books or technical material." Query or submit outline/synopsis and sample chapters.
Recent Nonfiction Title: *Iwo Jima*, by Bill Ross.
Fiction: Believable adventure, experimental, humor, mystery, modern suspense and "good literature." No confessions, erotica or gothics. Query or submit outline/synopsis and sample chapters.
Recent Fiction Title: *Go, Go, Said the Bird*, by Anne Stallworth.

‡**VEHICULE PRESS**, Box 125, Station "La Cite," Montreal, Quebec H2W 2M9 Canada. (514)844-6073. President/Publisher: Simon Dardick. Imprints include Signal Editions (poetry). Publishes trade paperback originals. Average 8 titles/year. Pays 10-15% royalty on retail price; offers average $200-500 advance. Photocopied submissions OK. SAE. "We would appreciate receiving IRCs rather than US postage stamps which we cannot use." Reports in 2 weeks on queries; 2 months on mss. Free book catalog.
Nonfiction: Biography and cookbook. Subjects include Canadiana, cooking and foods, history, politics, social history and literature. Especially looking for Canadian social history. Query. Reviews artwork/photos as part of ms package.
Recent Nonfiction Title: *The Life of a Document: A Global Approach to Archives and Records Management*, by Carol Couture and J-Y Rousseau.
Fiction: Historical, mainstream and mystery. Query.
Recent Fiction Title: *The Bequest & Other Stories*, by Jerry Wexler (short stories).
Poetry: Contact Michael Harris, editor. Especially looking for Canadian authors. Submit complete ms.
Recent Poetry Title: *Veiled Countries*, by Marie-Clair Blais.
Tips: "We are predominantly interested in Canadian authors but will look at work by other authors."

***VESTA PUBLICATIONS, LTD.**, Box 1641, Cornwall, Ontario K6H 5V6 Canada. (613)932-2135. Editor-in-Chief: Stephen Gill. Paperback and hardcover originals. 10% minimum royalty on wholesale price. Subsidy publishes 5% of books. "We ask a writer to subsidize a part of the cost of printing; normally, it is 50%. We do so when we find that the book does not have a wide market, as in the case of university theses and the author's first collection of poems. The writer gets 25 free copies and 10% royalty on paperback editions." No advance.

Publishes 16 titles/year. State availability of photos and/or illustrations to accompany ms. Simultaneous submissions OK if so informed. Photocopied submissions OK. Reports in 1 week on queries; 1 month on mss. SAE and IRCs. Free book catalog.

Nonfiction: Publishes Americana, art, biography, cookbooks, cooking and foods, history, philosophy, poetry, politics, reference, and religious. Accepts nonfiction translations. Query or submit complete ms. Looks for knowledge of the language and subject. "Query letters and mss should be accompanied by synopsis of the book and biographical notes."

Recent Nonfiction Title: *Famine*, by Edward Pike.

VGM CAREER HORIZONS, (Division of National Textbook Co.), 4255 W. Touhy Ave., Lincolnwood IL 60646-1975. (312)679-4210. Editorial Director: Leonard Fiddle. Senior Editor: Barbara Wood Donner. Publishes hardcover and paperback originals. Averages 20-30 titles/year. Mss purchased on either royalty or buy-out basis. Computer printout submissions acceptable. SASE. Reports in 6 weeks. Book catalog for large SASE.

Nonfiction: Publishes career guidance books. "We are interested in all professional and vocational areas. Our titles are marketed to a senior high school, college and trade audience, so readability and reading level (10-12) of books in the series is especially important. VGM books are used by students and others considering careers in specific areas, and contain basic information of the history and development of the field; its educational requirements; specialties and working conditions; how to write a resume, interview, and get started in the field; and salaries and benefits. Additionally, we expect to be producing more general career guidance and development materials in the next year or two. We are open to all suggestions in this area, although all proposals should be of relevance to young adults, as well as to older career changers. Since our titles are largely formatted, potential writers should always query first, requesting information on already-published titles and format and structure." Looks for "a comprehensive, orderly synthesis of the material, and an interesting presentation that is clear and accurate."

Recent Nonfiction Title: *Opportunities in Film*, by Jan Bone.

Tips: "On most projects, we prefer writers who have considerable personal background and knowledge of their subjects, although freelance writers who research well are also considered. Although the content of most titles is similar, the ability to present fairly cut-and-dried information in an upbeat, interesting manner is particularly in an author's favor."

VICTOR BOOKS, Box 1825, Wheaton IL 60187. (312)668-6000. Executive Editor: James R. Adair. Publishes trade paperbacks, mass market paperbacks and hardcover originals. Averages 50 titles/year. Pays "competitive royalties on retail price with advances." Publishes book an average of 1 year after acceptance. Computer printout submissions acceptable; prefers letter-quality to dot-matrix. Prefers outline/synopsis and sample chapters, but queries are acceptable. Reports in 1-2 months. SASE. Free book catalog and author's brochure.

Nonfiction: Only religious themes. "Writers must know the evangelical market well and their material should have substance. Many of our books are by ministers, Bible teachers, seminar speakers, counselors and subject experts. Freelancers can team with nonwriting experts to ghost or co-author books to fit our line. We prefer to see a brief outline to show where the book is going, accompanied by at least 2 sample chapters to give an indication of writing and content. Writing must have a popular touch, clearly communicate, and be biblically based." Also publishes reference books with religious themes for children and adults.

Recent Nonfiction Title: *With Liberty and Justice*, by Lynn Buzzard.

Fiction: "Fiction queries are being considered, both children and adults."

THE VIKING PENGUIN INC., 40 W. 23rd St., New York NY 10010. Imprints include Viking (adult hardcover books); Penguin (adult paperbacks); Viking Kestrel (children's hardcover books); and Puffin (children's paperbacks). Published over 300 titles last year. Pays royalty. Query letter only. Manuscripts considered only when sent through agent or intermediary to specific editor. SASE. Reports in 6 weeks.

VISION HOUSE PUBLISHERS, INC., 2300 Knoll Dr., Ventura CA 93003. (805)644-9721. Senior Editor: Donald Pugh. Publishes hardcover, trade and mass market paperback originals. Averages 6-10 titles/year. Pays 5-10% on retail price. Publishes book an average of 9 months after acceptance. Photocopied submissions OK. Computer printout submissions acceptable. SASE. Reports in 3 months. SASE. Book catalog for 9x12 SAE and 4 first class stamps.

Market conditions are constantly changing! If this is 1986 or later, buy the newest edition of *Writer's Market* at your favorite bookstore or order directly from Writer's Digest Books.

Nonfiction: Biography, how-to, humor, reference, and self-help. Subjects include family, psychology, religion (Christian) and comparative religion. "The thrust of Vision House over the next year will be nonfiction, with a heavy emphasis on books that lend themselves to total media packages (i.e., books that are adaptable to audio and video cassettes or film)." Query or submit outline/synopsis and 2-3 sample chapters.
Recent Nonfiction Title: *Steve McQueen: The Final Chapter*, by Grady Ragsdale (biography).

J. WESTON WALCH, PUBLISHER, Box 658, Portland ME 04104. (207)772-2846. Managing Editor: Richard S. Kimball. Senior Editor: Jane Carter. Computer Editor: Robert Crepeau. Publishes paperback originals. Averages 120 titles/year. Offers 10-15% royalty on gross receipts. Buys some titles by outright purchase; offers $100-1,000. No advance. Publishes book an average of 1 year after acceptance. Electronic submissions OK, but requires hard copy also. Computer printout submissions acceptable. SASE. Reports in 3 weeks. Free book catalog.
Nonfiction: Subjects include art, business, computer education, economics, English, foreign language, government, health, history, mathematics, music, psychology, recreation, science, social science, sociology, special education, and sports. "We publish only supplementary educational material for sale to secondary schools throughout the United States and Canada. Formats include books, posters, ditto master sets, visual master sets (masters for making transparencies), cassettes, filmstrips, microcomputer courseware, and mixed packages. Most titles are assigned by us, though we occasionally accept an author's unsolicited submission. We have a great need for author/artist teams and for authors who can write at third- to tenth-grade levels. We do *not* want basic texts, anthologies or industrial arts titles. Most of our authors—but not all—have secondary teaching experience. I cannot stress too much the advantages that an author/artist team would have in approaching us and probably other publishers." Query first. Looks for "sense of organization, writing ability, knowledge of subject, skill of communicating with intended audience." Reviews artwork/photos as part of ms package.
Recent Nonfiction Title: *Efficient Reading: 50 Steps to Increased Reading Rate*, by Fred Pyrczak (spirit masters for high school use).

WALKER AND CO., 720 5th Ave., New York NY 10019. Contact: Managing Editor. Hardcover and paperback originals (90%) and reprints (10%). Averages 150 titles/year. Pays 10-12-15% royalty on retail price or by outright purchase; advance averages $1,000-2,500 "but could be higher or lower." Query or submit outline/synopsis and sample chapters. Submit samples of photos/illustrations to accompany ms. Photocopied submissions OK. SASE. Free book catalog.
Nonfiction: Publishes Americana, art, biography, business, histories, how-to, juveniles, science and history, medicine and psychiatry, music, nature, parenting, pets, psychology, recreation, reference, popular science, and self-help books.
Recent Nonfiction Title: *How to Make Your Child a Winner*, by Dr. Victor B. Cline (parenting).
Fiction: Mystery, romance, suspense, regency romance, historical romance, western, and men's action.
Recent Fiction Title: *Murder Among Friends*, by Frank McConnell.

WALLACE—HOMESTEAD BOOK CO., Suite 501, 1501 42nd St., West Des Moines IA 50265. (515)224-6028. Editorial Director: Liz Fletcher. Publishes hardcover and paperback originals. Averages 20 titles/year. Offers 10% royalty on net price. No advance. Simultaneous and photocopied submissions OK. SASE. Reports in 6 weeks. Free book catalog.
Nonfiction: Antiques, collectibles and needlecraft. Query first, submit outline/synopsis and sample chapters or submit complete ms. Reviews artwork/photos as part of ms package.
Recent Nonfiction Title: *American Oak Furniture*, by Robert and Harriett Swedberg.

WANDERER BOOKS, Division of Simon & Schuster, 1230 Avenue of the Americas, New York NY 10020. (212)245-6400. Editorial Director: Wendy Barish. Publishes hardcover, trade and mass market paperback originals. Averages 60 titles/year. Pays 2-6% royalty on retail price; buys some mss outright. Simultaneous submissions OK. SASE. Reports in 2 weeks on queries. Accepts no unsolicited ms. Book catalog for SAE.
Nonfiction: Juvenile. Subjects include art, health, hobbies and recreation. "We are looking for solid backlist nonfiction for the next year or so, for ages 8-14. No science, nature, history, or other school- and library-oriented nonfiction. We are a trade and mass market publishing imprint for children."
Recent Nonfiction Title: *Michael Jackson*, by Gordon Matthews.
Fiction: Adventure, humor, mystery and science fiction.

FREDERICK WARNE & CO., INC., 2 Park Ave., New York NY 10016. Assistant Editor, Books for Young People: Colleen Mehegan. Publishes hardcover originals. Offers 10% royalty contract. Averages 15-20 titles/year. Minimum advance is $1,000. Submit outline and 3-4 sample chapters for nonfiction and fiction. Computer printout submissions acceptable; no dot-matrix. "Ms will not be considered unless requested." Reports in 10 weeks.
Fiction & Nonfiction: Juveniles. Hardcover trade books for children and young adults. Picture books (ages 4-7), fiction and nonfiction for the middle reader (ages 7-12) and young adults (ages 11 and up). Mss must com-

bine a high-interest level with fine writing. Prefers to see fewer picture books and more submissions for 8- to 12-year-olds. Reviews artwork/photos as part of ms package.

Recent Nonfiction Title: *Doodlebugging—The Treasure Hunt for Oil*, by Elaine Scott.

Recent Fiction Title: *My Mom Travels a Lot*, by Caroline Seller Bauer.

‡**WARNER PRESS, INC.**, Owned and operated by the Church of God, 1200 E. 5th St., Box 2499, Anderson IN 46018. (317)644-7721. Editor-in-Chief: Arlo F. Newell. Publishes hardcover and trade paperback originals. Averages 10 titles/year. Publishes book an average of 1 year after acceptance. Makes negotiable outright purchase, offers negotiable advance. Electronic submissions OK for CPM. Computer printout submissions acceptable. SASE. Reports in 8 weeks.

Nonfiction: Biography, "coffee table" book, cookbook, how-to, humor, illustrated book, reference, self-help, and textbook. Subjects include religion. Especially looking for religious books: "Bible study helps, 'how-to' spiritual growth books, personal experience books, doctrinal books (Wesleyan/Armenian), and inspirational, devotional material." Submit outline/synopsis and sample chapters or complete ms.

Recent Nonfiction Title: *The Miracle and Power of Blessing*, Maurice Berquist.

Fiction: Religious. Especially looking for "religious humor, religious mystery, religious adventure, historical and religious novels." All material must have a religious viewpoint. Submit outline/synopsis and sample chapters.

Recent Fiction Title: *Trace of Perfume*, by Esther Vogt (religious).

Tips: "Religious self-help books are our fastest growing market. We published our first religious fiction last year, and based on its success, plan more. If I were a writer trying to market a book today, I would not overlook smaller publishers as they are more likely to give an untried writer a chance; I would push publishers to explain their marketing strategy."

WATSON-GUPTILL PUBLICATIONS, 1515 Broadway, New York NY 10036. Imprints include Watson-Guptill, Amphoto, Whitney Library of Design, and Billboard Books. Publishes originals. Pays 10-12½-15% royalty; usual advance is $1,000, but average varies depending on author's reputation and nature of book. Averages 60 titles/year. Address queries (followed by outlines and 1-3 sample chapters) to David E. Lewis, editorial director. Publishes book an average of 9 months after acceptance. Electronic submissions OK, but requires hard copy also. Computer printout submissions acceptable; prefers letter-quality to dot-matrix. Reports on queries within 1 month. Enclose return postage.

Nonfiction: Art. Publishes art instruction, photography and architecture books. Interested only in how-to books in any field of painting, graphic design, and photography and professional books in architecture and interior design. Looks for "a strong concept or theme that is carried out in a thoughtful, well-organized manner." Length: open. Reviews artwork/photos as part of ms package.

Tips: "We often put together the book that we want for a particular market and hire freelance writers (nonroyalty) to write all or parts of it." Queries/mss may be routed to other editors in the publishing group.

WAYNE STATE UNIVERSITY PRESS, 5959 Woodward Ave., Detroit MI 48202. (313)577-4606. Director: B.M. Goldman. Editor: J. Owen. Publishes hardcover and paperback originals. "Standard royalty schedule" on wholesale price; no advance. Publishes 30 titles/year. Publishes book an average of 20 months after acceptance. Computer printout submissions acceptable; no dot-matrix. Reports in 1-6 months. SASE. Free book catalog.

Nonfiction: Publishes Americana, biography, economics, history, law, medicine and psychiatry, music, philosophy, politics, psychology, and literature books. Submit outline/synopsis and sample chapters. "Do not send photos unless requested, or send photocopies."

Recent Nonfiction Title: *Long Night's Journey Into Day*, by Eckardt and Eckardt.

WEBSTER DIVISION, McGraw-Hill Book Co., 1221 Avenue of the Americas, New York NY 10020. General Manager: Jack L. Farnsworth. Royalties vary. "Our royalty and advance schedules are competitive with the industry." Photocopied submissions OK. Reports in 2-4 weeks. SASE.

Nonfiction: Textbooks. Publishes software and instructional materials for elementary and secondary schools. Subject areas served include social studies, science, reading and language arts, home economics, health, foreign languages, computer literacy and mathematics. "Material is generally part of a series, system, or program done in connection with other writers, teachers, testing experts, et al. Material must be matched to the psychological age level, with reading achievement and other educational prerequisites in mind."

WESLEYAN UNIVERSITY PRESS, 110 Mt. Vernon, Middletown CT 06457. Director: Jeannette Hopkins. Publishes 25-30 titles/year. Photocopied submissions OK. SASE. Reports in approximately 4 months.

Nonfiction: Concentration on American history and American studies, public affairs, poetry and theater. Accepts poetry translations. Query.

‡**WESTERN MARINE ENTERPRISES INC.**, Box Q, Ventura CA 93002. (805)644-6043. Editor: William Berssen. Publishes hardcover and trade paperback originals. Averages 6 titles/year. Pays 15% royalty on net price. Offers no advance. Computer printout submissions acceptable; prefers letter-quality to dot-matrix. SASE. Reports in 3 week.

Nonfiction: Boating. Subjects include recreation, sports and travel. "We specialize in boating books—mainly how-to and where-to." No "simple narrative accounts of how someone sailed a boat from here to there." Submit outline/synopsis and sample chapters or complete ms.

Recent Nonfiction Title: *Cruising Guide to California's Channel Islands*, by Brian M. Fagan (sail and power-boat guide).

WESTERN PRODUCER PRAIRIE BOOKS, Box 2500, Saskatoon, Saskatchewan S7K 2C4 Canada. Manager: Rob Sanders. Publishes hardcover and paperback originals (95%) and reprints (5%). Specializes in nonfiction historical and natural history works set in western Canada. Pays negotiable royalty on list price. Averages 15 titles/year. Submit contact sheets or prints if illustrations are to accompany ms. Publishes book an average of 20 months after acceptance. Electronic submissions OK, but requires hard copy also. Computer printout submissions acceptable. Reports in 2-4 months. SAE and IRCs. Free book catalog.

Nonfiction: Publishes history, nature, photography, biography, reference, agriculture, economics, politics and cookbooks. Submit outline, synopsis and 2-3 sample chapters. Accepts nonfiction and fiction translations. Reviews artwork/photos as part of ms package.

Recent Nonfiction Title: *Riel and the Rebellion*, by T. Flanagan.

WESTERN TANAGER PRESS, 1111 Pacific Ave., Santa Cruz CA 95060. (408)425-1111. Publisher: Hal Morris. Publishes hardcover and trade paperback originals (50%), and hardcover and trade paperback reprints (50%). Averages 3 titles/year.

Nonfiction: Biography and history. "We are looking for works of local and regional history dealing with California. This includes biography, natural history, art and politics. Also interested in travel." Query. Looks for "a well-written, well-thought-out project with a specific audience in mind."

WESTERNLORE PRESS, Box 35305, Tucson AZ 85740. Editor: Lynn R. Bailey. Publishes 6-12 titles/year. Pays standard royalties on retail price "except in special cases." Query. Reports in 60 days. Enclose return postage with query.

Nonfiction: Publishes Western Americana of a scholarly and semi-scholarly nature: anthropology, history, biography, historic sites, restoration, and ethnohistory pertaining to the greater American West. Republication of rare and out-of-print books. Length: 25,000-100,000 words.

WESTIN COMMUNICATIONS, Suite 31, 5760 Owensmouth Ave., Woodland Hills CA 91367. (313)340-6515. Acquisitions Editor: Carla M. Klein. Publishes trade paperback originals. Averages 15 titles/year. Pays royalty; buys some mss outright. Computer printout submissions acceptable; prefers letter-quality to dot-matrix. SASE. Reports in 1 week on queries; 1 month on mss. Book catalog for business size SAE and 1 first class stamp.

Nonfiction: How-to, reference books, technical, textbooks, test preparations on business and economics, and computer science. Especially needs "college-level study review books in science, business and economics, mathematics, computers as part of Westin Study Review Series; career evaluation and test preparation books for college students; dictionaries in selected technical fields. No topic which cannot successfully be marketed to college students through college stores or to professionals by direct mail." Query or submit outline/synopsis and 1 sample chapter.

Recent Nonfiction Title: *Cost Accounting*, by G. Klein (study review books).

THE WESTMINSTER PRESS, Department CBE, 925 Chestnut St., Philadelphia PA 19107. (215)928-2700. Children's Book Editor: Barbara S. Bates. Publishes hardcover originals. Publishes 10 juveniles. Royalty on retail price and advance "vary with author's experience and credentials, and the amount of illustration needed." Publishes book an average of 9 months after acceptance. Photocopied submissions OK if not simultaneous. Computer printout submissions acceptable; prefers letter-quality to dot-matrix. Reports in 3 months. SASE. Book catalog for SASE.

Nonfiction: Juvenile only, for readers 8-14. Consumer education, self-help, self-awareness, social studies, recreation and how-to, and sports and hobbies. Query or submit outline/synopsis and 2-3 sample chapters. Accepts photos. Looks for "originality, relevance, author reputation, quality."

Recent Nonfiction Title: *My Diary—My World*, by Elizabeth Yates (social studies/career).

Fiction: Juvenile only, for ages 8-13. Adventure, humor, mystery, family, and suspense. No picture books or stories in verse. Submit outline/synopsis and sample chapters.

Recent Fiction Title: *Meet Me in the Park, Angie*, by Phyllis Anderson Wood.

*WESTVIEW PRESS, 5500 Central Ave., Boulder CO 80301. (303)444-3541. Publisher/President: F.A. Praeger. Associate Publisher/Vice President: Lynne Rienner. Hardcover and paperback originals (90%), lecture notes, reference books, and paperback texts (10%). Specializes in scholarly monographs or conference reports with strong emphasis on applied science, both social and natural. Zero to 12% royalty on net price, depending on market. Accepts subsidies for a small number of books, "but only in the case of first class scholarly material for a limited market when books need to be priced low, or when the manuscripts have unusual difficulties such as Chinese or Sanskrit characters; the usual quality standards of a top-flight university press apply, and subsidies must be furnished by institutions, not by individuals." Averages 200 titles/year. Markets books mainly by direct mail. State availability of photos and/or illustrations to accompany manuscript. Reports in 1-4 months. SASE. Free book catalog.
Nonfiction: Agriculture/food, public policy, energy, natural resources, international economics and business, international relations, area studies, geography, science and technology policy, sociology, anthropology, reference, military affairs, and health. Looks for "scholarly excellence and scientific relevance." Query and submit 2 sample chapters. Use Chicago *Manual of Style*. "Unsolicited manuscripts receive low priority; inquire before submitting projects."
Recent Nonfiction Title: *The Road to Berlin*, by John Erickson.

WETHERALL PUBLISHING CO., 510 1st Ave. N., Minneapolis MN 55403. (612)339-3363. Director of Acquisitions: Judy Galbraith. Publishes trade paperback originals. Averages 6 titles/year. Pays 6-12% royalty on retail price or makes outright purchase. SASE. Reports in 2 weeks on queries; 3 weeks on mss.
Nonfiction: How-to, humor, juvenile and self-help. Subjects include business and economics, health, education, books for gifted children and parents. "We expect to be publishing more titles for small business and considerably more for gifted children and parents. These in addition to some humor, health and diet, and other general subject areas." Query or submit outline/synopsis and sample chapters.
Recent Nonfiction Title: *Quit*, by Charles F. Wetherall (psychology, how to stop smoking).

*WHITAKER HOUSE, Pittsburgh and Colfax Sts., Springdale PA 15144. (412)274-4440. Managing Editor: Donna C. Arthur. Paperback originals (40%) and reprints (60%). Subsidy publishes 25% of books. "We publish only Christian books." Royalty negotiated based on the cover price of the book. Publishes about 30-35 titles annually. "We market books in Christian book stores and in rack-jobbing locations such as supermarkets and drug stores." Looking for teaching books with illustrations, antecdotes, and personal experiences used throughout, typed, double-spaced, about 300 pages in length. Publishes book an average of 6 months after acceptance. Query first. Unsolicited mss returned. Computer printout submissions acceptable; prefers letter-quality to dot-matrix. SASE.
Nonfiction: Publishes mostly how-to books ("how to move on in your Christian walk", 90,000 words); and religious ("don't want heavy theology", 90,000 words). Accepts outline/synopsis and 2-3 sample chapters. Reviews artwork/photos as part of ms package. "Please note that we want teaching books that give the author's life experiences as well as solid Christian teaching." Looks for "well-written informative work that *follows our specifications*."
Recent Nonfiction Title: *Revival*, by Winkie Pratney.

THE WHITSTON PUBLISHING CO., Box 958, Troy NY 12181. (518)283-4363. Editorial Director: Jean Goode. Publishes hardcover originals. Averages 20 titles/year. Pays 10-12-15% royalty on wholesale price; no advance. Publishes book an average of 2 years after acceptance. Computer printout submissions acceptable; no dot-matrix. Reports in 1 year. SASE.
Nonfiction: "We publish scholarly and critical books in the arts, humanities and some of the social sciences. We also publish reference books, bibliographies, indexes and checklists. We do not want author bibliographies in general unless they are unusual and unusually scholarly. We are, however, much interested in catalogs and inventories of library collections of individuals, such as the catalog of the Evelyn Waugh Collection at the Humanities Research Center, the University of Texas at Austin; and collections of interest to the specific scholarly community, such as surveys of early black newspapers in libraries in the US, etc." Query or submit complete ms. Reviews artwork/photos as part of ms package. Accepts poetry translations from French and Spanish.
Recent Nonfiction Title: *Marcel Duchamp: Eros C'est la Vie*, by A. Marquis (biography).

WILDERNESS PRESS, 2440 Bancroft Way, Berkeley CA 94704. (415)843-8080. Editorial Director: Thomas Winnett. Publishes paperback originals. Averages 4 titles/year. Pays 8-10% royalty on retail price; advance averages $200. Publishes book an average of 6 months after acceptance. Computer printout submissions acceptable. Reports in 2 weeks. SASE. Book catalog for SASE.
Nonfiction: "We publish books about the outdoors. Most of our books are trail guides for hikers and backpackers, but we also publish how-to books about the outdoors and perhaps will publish personal adventures. The manuscript must be accurate. The author must thoroughly research an area in person. If he is writing a trail guide, he must walk all the trails in the area his book is about. The outlook must be strongly conservationist. The style must be appropriate for a highly literate audience." Query, submit outline/synopsis and sample chap-

ters, or submit complete ms demonstrating "accuracy, literacy, and popularity of subject area." Reviews artwork/photos as part of ms package.
Recent Nonfiction Title: *Point Reyes*, by Dorothy Whitnah.

JOHN WILEY & SONS, INC., 605 3rd Ave., New York NY 10158. (212)850-6000. Publishes hardcover and paperback originals and software. Publishes 1000 titles/year. Pays variable royalties on wholesale price. Follow *MLA Style Sheet*. Simultaneous and photocopied submissions OK. Electronic submissions OK. "We are actively seeking software authors." Reports in 6 months. SASE. Free book catalog.
Nonfiction: Publishes college textbooks, professional reference titles, trade books, journals. Query or submit outline/synopsis and 2 sample chapters.
Recent Nonfiction Title: *"The Coming Computer Industry Shakeout*, by Steven T. McClellan.
Software: Publishes software in engineering, social science, computer science, business, life science, politics, law and medicine.
Tips: Queries/mss may be routed to other editors in the publishing group.

‡WILLIAMSON PUBLISHING CO., Box 185, Church Hill Rd., Charlotte VT 05445. (802)425-2102. Editorial Director: Susan Williamson. Publishes trade paperback originals. Averages 12-15 titles/year. Pays 10-12% royalty "on sales dollars received" or makes outright purchase if favored by author; offers average $1,000-1,500 advance. Publishes book an average of 1 year after acceptance. Simultaneous and photocopied submissions OK. SASE. Reports in 2 weeks on queries; 3 weeks on mss. Free book catalog.
Nonfiction: Cookbook, how-to, humor, illustrated book and self-help. Subjects include animals, business and economics, cooking and foods, health, hobbies, nature, recreation, sports and travel. "Our areas of concentration are cookbooks, people-oriented business books, small-scale livestock raising, family housing (all aspects), health and sports books." No children's books, photography, politics, religion, history, art or biography. Query with outline/synopsis and sample chapters. Reviews artwork/photos as part of ms package.
Recent Nonfiction Title: *Home Tanning of Leathers*, by Kathy Kellogg (how-to).
Tips: "In our specialized area, the more solid how-to information on important subjects in people's lives the better."

WILSHIRE BOOK CO., 12015 Sherman Rd., North Hollywood CA 91605. (213)875-1711. Editorial Director: Melvin Powers. Publishes paperback originals (50%) and reprints (50%). Publishes 50 titles/year. Pays 5% minimum royalty; "advance varies with nature of the book." Computer printout submissions acceptable. SASE. Reports in 2 weeks. Catalog for SASE.
Nonfiction: Calligraphy, health, hobbies, how-to, psychology, recreation, self-help and mail order. "We are always looking for self-help and psychological books, such as *Psycho-Cybernetics* and *Guide to Rational Living*. We need manuscripts teaching mail order and advertising. We publish 70 horse books. "All that I need is the concept of the book to determine if the project is viable. I welcome phone calls to discuss manuscripts with authors."
Recent Nonfiction Title: *How to Self-Publish Your Book and Have the Fun and Excitement of Being a Best-Selling Author*, by Melvin Powers.

*WIMMER BROTHERS BOOKS, 4210 B.F. Goodrich Blvd., Box 18408, Memphis TN 38118. (901)362-8900. Editorial Director: Richard Anderson. Senior Editor: Jane Coward. Publishes hardcover and paperback originals. Averages 4-5 titles/year. Subsidy publishes 50% of books. Offers 10-15% royalty on wholesale price. No advance. Publishes book an average of 15 months after acceptance. Computer printout submissions acceptable; no dot-matrix. SASE. Reports in 2 months. Book catalog for SASE.
Nonfiction: Cookbooks, cooking and foods, and how-to. Especially needs specialized cookbooks and how-to books dealing with home entertainment. Submit complete ms. Reviews artwork/photos as part of ms package. Looks for "interesting angle, well-edited recipes in the book and good grammar."
Recent Nonfiction Title: *The Pastors' Wives Cookbook*, by S. DuBose (cookbook).

B.L. WINCH & ASSOCIATES, 45 Hitching Post Dr., Bldg. 2, Rolling Hills Estates CA 90274. (213)539-6430. Editorial Director: B.L. Winch. Production Editor: J. Lovelady. Senior Editor: Suzanne Mikesell. Publishes paperback originals and reprints. Averages 4-8 titles/year. Offers 5-15% royalty on net receipts. Publishes book an average of 18 months after acceptance. Simultaneous and photocopied submissions OK. SASE. Reports in 3 months. Free book catalog.
Nonfiction: Parent-oriented enabling self-help materials (infant to teen), material for the gifted, affective curriculum, guidebooks and strategies, classroom management, guidebooks, and right brain learning materials. Reviews artwork/photos as part of ms package. "Prefer completed ms."
Recent Nonfiction Title: *SAGE: Self-Awareness Growth Experiences*, by V. Alex Kehayan, Ed.D.

WINCHESTER PRESS, Imprint of New Century Publishers, Inc., 220 Old New Brunswick Rd., Piscataway NJ 08854. Consulting Editor: Robert Elman. Publishes hardcover and paperback originals. Pays 10-12½-15%

royalty on retail price; offers $2,500 average advance. Averages 15-20 titles/year. "Submit sample photos and some idea of total number projected for final book." Simultaneous and photocopied submissions OK. Reports in 3 months. Looks for "good organization, defined audience potential, original and accurate information and good photographs." SASE. Free book catalog.

Nonfiction: Main interest is in leisure activities, outdoor sports, crafts and related subjects. Publishes cookbooks related to fish and game; how-to (sports and sporting equipment); pets (hunting dogs); recreation (outdoor); sports (hunting, fishing, etc.); and technical (firearms, boats and motors, fishing tackle, etc.). Submit outline/synopsis and sample chapters.

Recent Nonfiction Title: *All-American Deer Hunter's Guide*, by Jim Zumbo and Robert Elman.

Tips: "The writing of leisure-activities books—particularly how-to books—has vastly improved in recent years. Mss must now be better written and must reflect new ideas and new information if they are to be considered for publication by Winchester Press. Recreational equipment and opportunities have expanded, and writers must also be up-to-date journalists."

WINDSOR PUBLICATIONS, 21220 Erwin St., Box 1500, Woodland Hills CA 91365. Senior Publications Editor: Rita Johnson. "We publish pictorial civic publications, business directories, and relocation guides for chambers of commerce, boards of realtors, etc. Our audience is anyone considering relocating or visiting another part of the country, and our publications document in pictures and words every aspect of a city or area. Writers and photographers work on assignment only, after having demonstrated ability through samples. Publications are annual or biennial, vary in size and are titled with the name of a city. Circulation is controlled. Writers and writer/photographers with strong interview, reporting and travel writing experience are especially sought." Queries, stating writing and/or photography experience and including tearsheets, are welcome.

Nonfiction: "All mss assigned. Unsolicited manuscripts and/or photos not wanted." Length: 3,000-10,000 words. Pays $500-2,400 on acceptance for all rights. Photos: Photography for each publication usually assigned to photographer on per-day rate plus expenses. Also purchase stock, speculative and existing photos on one-time use basis if they pertain to future publications. 35mm and larger color transparencies, b&w contact sheets and negatives or b&w prints (5x7 to 8x10) are acceptable; no color prints. Complete captions required.

WINGBOW PRESS, Subsidiary of Bookpeople, 2929 Fifth St., Berkeley CA 94710. (415)549-3030. Editor: Randy Fingland. Publishes hardcover and trade paperback originals and trade paperback reprints. Averages 3-4 titles/year. Pays 7-10% royalty on retail price; offers average $500 advance. Publishes book an average of 18 months after acceptance. Computer printout submissions acceptable. SASE. Reports in 3 weeks on queries; 9 weeks on mss. Free book catalog.

Nonfiction: "Coffee table" books, how-to, illustrated books, reference books, self-help on business and economics, hobbies, psychology, and sociology. Especially needs regional guides to San Francisco Bay area. Reviews artwork/photos as part of ms package. No psychology, cooking, gardening or textbooks. Query or submit outline/synopsis and 1-5 sample chapters.

Recent Nonfiction Title: *Bargain Hunting in Bay Area*, by Sally Socolich (consumer reference).

Poetry: "Strongly written, usually not rhyming, modern verse. No philosophical or political diatribes." Submit complete ms.

Recent Poetry Title: *Hello La Jolla*, by Edward Dorn (free verse).

Tips: Queries/mss may be routed to other editors in the publishing group.

‡**WINGRA WOODS PRESS**, Box 9601, Madison WI 53715. (608)256-2578. Acquisitions Editor: M.G. Mahoney. Book packager producing 6-10 titles/year. Publishes trade paperback originals. Pays 10-12% royalty on retail price. Simultaneous and photocopied submissions OK. Computer printout submissions acceptable. SASE. Reports in 2 weeks on queries; 1 month on mss. Book catalog $1.

Nonfiction: Cookbook, how-to, juvenile and self-help. Subjects include Americana, animals, art, cooking and foods, nature, psychology and travel. Especially looking for popularized book-length treatments of specialized knowledge; particularly interested in proposals from academics and professionals. Query or submit outline/synopsis and sample chapters.

Recent Nonfiction Title: *Financial Independence with Style* (self-help).

WINSTON PRESS, INC., CBS Educational Publishing, 430 Oak Grove, Minneapolis MN 55403. (612)871-7000. Trade Books Editorial Director: Wayne Paulson. Curriculum Editorial Director: Dee Ready. Publishes hardcover and paperback originals (90%) and reprints (10%). Publishes 40 trade titles/year. Pays royalty on net; advance varies. Publishes book an average of 14 months after acceptance. Photocopied submissions OK. Computer printout submissions acceptable. SASE. Reports in 2 months. Writer's guidelines for SASE.

Nonfiction: "Religion and human development. Curriculum materials for preschool through adult education. Specialized and general trade books, gift and photography books." Query or submit outline/synopsis. Looks for "a clear, popular writing style, responsible scholarship (but not a scholarly style), and fresh ideas." Accepts artwork/photos. Accepts nonfiction translations.

Recent Nonfiction Title: *Baby Hunger*, by Lois Davitz.

*WINSTON-DEREK PUBLISHERS, Pennywell Dr., Box 90883, Nashville TN 37209. (615)329-1319 or 356-7384. Publisher: James W. Peebles. Publishes hardcover, trade and mass market paperback originals. Averages 25-35 titles/year. "We will co-publish exceptional works of quality and style only when we reach our quota in our trade book division." Pays 10-15% royalty on retail price; advance varies. Simultaneous and photocopied submissions OK. SASE. Reports in 1 month on queries; 6 weeks on mss.
Nonfiction: Biography, behavioral science and health. Subjects include Americana; philosophy (contemporary format); cookbooks; religion (noncultism); and inspirational. Length: 50,000 words or less. Submit outline/first 2 or 4 consecutive chapters. Reviews artwork/photos as part of ms package. No political or technical material.
Recent Nonfiction Title: *To Be the Bridge: Black/White Catholicism, U.S.A.*, by Sandra Smithson, O.S.F.
Fiction: Ethnic (non-defamatory); religious (theologically sound); suspense (highly plotted); and Americana (minorities and whites in positive relationships). Length: 50,000 words or less. "We can use fiction with a semi-historical plot; must be based or centered around actual facts and events—Americana, religion, gothic, and science fiction. Juvenile: "We are looking for books on relevant aspects of growing up and understanding life's situations. No funny animals talking." Children's books must be of high quality. Submit outline/synopsis and first 2 or 4 consecutive chapters. Reviews artwork/photos as part of ms package. Unsolicited manuscripts will be returned unopened. "We do not discuss manuscripts via telephone."
Recent Fiction Title: *Night Wood*, by Darlene Goodenow (an Althea Bantree mystery selection).
Recent Children's Book Title: *The Hey God Series*, by Roxie Cawood Gibson.
Poetry: "Should be inspirational and divine—poetry that is suitable for meditation. We will accept unusual poetry book of exceptional quality and taste." Submit complete ms for all poetry.
Recent Poetry Title: *Thoughts From a Friend*, by Eric Dlugokinski.
Tips: "The American audience is looking for less violent material. Outstanding biographies are quite successful, as are books dealing with the simplicity of man and his relationship with his environs. Our new imprint is *Scythe Books*, the children's division of Winston-Derek Publishers. We need material for adolescents within the 9-13 age group. These manuscripts should help young people with motivation for learning and succeeding, goal setting and character building. Biographies of famous women and men are always welcome. Stories must have a new twist."

ALAN WOFSY FINE ARTS, Box 2210, San Francisco CA 94126. Publishes hardcover and paperback originals (50%) and hardcover reprints (50%). Specializes in art reference books, specifically catalogs of graphic artists; bibliographies related to fine presses and the art of the book. Pays negotiable fee on retail price; offers advance. Publishes 5 titles annually. SASE. Reports in 2-4 weeks. Free book catalog.
Nonfiction: Publishes reference books on art. Seeking catalogues of (i.e., reference books on) collectibles. Query. Reviews artwork/photos as part of ms package.

WOLF HOUSE BOOKS, Box 6657, Grand Rapids MI 49506. (616)245-8812. Editorial Director: Richard Weiderman. Publishes hardcover and paperback originals (50%) and reprints (50%). Published 5 titles in 1979. Offers 10% royalty. No advance. Computer printout submissions acceptable. Reports in 4 weeks. SASE. Book catalog for SASE.
Nonfiction: Literary criticism and biography and other studies (e.g., bibliography, etc.) on Jack London. Reviews artwork/photos as part of ms package. Query.
Recent Nonfiction Title: *Alien Worlds of Jack London*, by D.L. Walker.

WOODBRIDGE PRESS PUBLISHING CO., Box 6189, Santa Barbara CA 93111. Editor-in-Chief: Howard B. Weeks. Publishes hardcover and paperback originals. Standard royalty contract. Rarely gives an advance. Will consider photocopied submissions. Computer printout submissions acceptable. Query. Returns rejected material and reports on material accepted for publication as soon as possible. Accepts no responsibility for such material other than as may be stated in a written publishing agreement. Enclose return postage with query.
Nonfiction: General. "How-to books on personal health and well-being. Should offer the reader usable new information or insights on anything from recreation to diet to mental health that will enable him to achieve greater personal fulfillment, with emphasis on that goal. Should minimize broad philosophy and maximize specific, useful information." Length: Books range from 96 to 300 pages. Also publishes cookbooks and gardening books and humor. Reviews artwork/photos as part of ms package.
Recent Nonfiction Title: *Anyone for Insomnia?*, by Armour.

*WOODSONG GRAPHICS, INC., Stoney Hill Rd., Box 231, New Hope PA 18938. (215)794-8321. Editor: Ellen P. Bordner. Publishes hardcover and trade paperback originals. Averages 6 titles/year. Subsidy publishes 15% of books. Will occasionally consider subsidy publishing based on "quality of material, motivation of author in distributing his work, and cost factors (which depend on the type of material involved), plus our own feelings on its marketability." Pays royalty on net price; offers average $100 advance. Publishes book an average of 1 year after acceptance. Simultaneous submissions OK. Computer printout submissions acceptable. SASE. Reports in two weeks on queries; reports on full manuscripts *can* take several months, depending on the amount of material already in the house. "We do everything possible to facilitate replies, but we have a small staff and want to give every manuscript a thoughtful reading."

Nonfiction: Biography, cookbook, how-to, humor, illustrated book, juvenile, reference, and self-help. Subjects include cooking and foods, hobbies, philosophy, and psychology. "We're happy to look at anything of good quality, but we're not equipped to handle lavish color spreads at this time. Needs are very open, and we're interested in seeing any subject, provided it's handled with competence and style. Good writing from unknowns is also welcome." No pornographic mss; only minimal interest in technical manuals of any kind. Query or submit outline/synopsis and at least 2 sample chapters. Reviews artwork/photos as part of ms package.

Fiction: Adventure, experimental, fantasy, gothic, historical, humor, mainstream, mystery, romance, science fiction, suspense, and western. "In fiction, we simply are looking for books with good, solid characterizations and well-thought-out plots. I find it difficult to define what they should be, but look forward to recognizing such material when it comes." No pornography or "sick" material. Submit outline/synopsis and sample chapters.

Poetry: "Again, serious pornography is about the only taboo here." Submit 6 samples or complete ms.

‡**WORD BEAT PRESS**, Box 10509, Tallahassee FL 32302-2509. Editor: Allen Woodman. Publishes trade paperback originals and trade paperback reprints. Averages 3-5 titles/year. Pays 10% royalty on wholesale price. Offers average $100 advance. Publishes book an average of 6 months after acceptance. Computer printout submissions acceptable; prefers letter-quality to dot-matrix. SASE. Reports in 5 weeks on queries; 3 months on mss. Book catalog for legal-size SAE and 1 first class stamp.

Nonfiction: "We will look at any book that would be of interest to fiction writers, how-to, self-help, reference, and other books about writing." Reviews artwork/photos as part of ms package.

Fiction: Short story collections and novellas; "open to fine writing in any category. We are planning a series of perfect-bound short story collections and novellas of between 40-90 typed, double-spaced ms pages." Query first.

Tips: "We are also planning a new line of children's books. We hold annual fiction book competitions judged by nationally recognized writers. Query with SASE first."

‡**WORDWARE PUBLISHING, INC.**, Suite 104, 1104 Summit Ave., Plano TX 75074. (214)423-0090. Editor: Thomas H. Berliner. Publishes mass market paperback originals. Averages 100 titles/year. Pays 7.5% minimum royalty, negotiable maximum. Advance negotiated. "We have a wide variety of alternatives for electronic submissions. They can be tailored to the individual author. He/she should contact us." Computer printout submissions acceptable. SASE. Reports in 2 weeks.

Nonfiction: How-to, illustrated book, reference, self-help, technical and textbook. Subjects include business and economics, history, hobbies, politics, and computers. "In general, our books are aimed at self-help and education. However, we are evolving our editorial direction and wish to avoid restricting genre."

Recent Nonfiction Title: *Writing And Publishing On Your Microcomputer*, by R.A. Stultz (computer how-to).

Tips: "Basically, we seek to appeal to the individual who is interested in a variety of subjects and wishes to have them provided to him/her in easy-to-understand terms."

WORLD ALMANAC PUBLICATIONS, 200 Park Ave., New York NY 10166. (212)557-2333. Editor-in-Chief: Hana Umlauf Lane. Senior Editor: Rob Fitz. Publisher of *The World Almanac*. Publishes hardcover and trade paperback originals. Averages 20 titles/year. Pays 5-15% on retail price. Publishes book an average of 1 year after acceptance. Computer printout submissions acceptable; prefers letter-quality to dot-matrix. SASE. Reports in 3 weeks. Free book catalog, if requested.

Nonfiction: Reference. "We look for information books, like *The World Almanac*, but popular and entertaining. We expect at least a synopsis/outline and sample chapters, and would like to see completed manuscript." Reviews artwork/photos as part of ms package.

Recent Nonfiction Title: *The World Almanac Dictionary of Dates*.

WORLD NATURAL HISTORY PUBLICATIONS, Division of Plexus Publishing, Inc., 143 Old Marlton Pike, Medford NJ 08055. (609)654-6500. Editorial Director: Thomas Hogan. Publishes hardcover and paperback originals. Averages 4 titles/year. Pays 10-20% royalty on wholesale price, buys some booklets outright for $250-1,000; offers average $500-1,000 advance. Simultaneous and photocopied submissions OK. SASE. Reports in 2 months. Book catalog for SASE.

Nonfiction: Animals, biography of naturalists, nature and reference. "We are looking for mss of about 300-400 pages for our series *Introduction to ...* some group of plants or animals designed for high school and undergraduate college use and for amateur naturalists. We will consider any book on a nature/biology subject, particularly those of a reference (permanent) nature. No philosophy or psychology; no gardening; generally not interested in travel, but will consider travel that gives sound ecological information." Also interested in mss of about 20 to 40 pages in length for feature articles in *Biology Digest* (guidelines for these available with SASE). Always query.

Recent Nonfiction Title: *Working for Life: Careers in Biology.*
Tips: "Write a book that is absolutely accurate and that has been reviewed by specialists to eliminate misstatement of fact."

‡*WRIGHT PUBLISHING COMPANY, INC., Suite 303, 1422 W. Peachtree St., Atlanta GA 30309. (404)876-1900. Editor-in-Chief: Yvonne Bowman Wright. Publishes hardcover, trade paperback, and mass market paperback originals, and hardcover, trade paperback, and mass market paperback reprints. Averages 10 titles/year. Subsidy publishes 75% of books. "We determine whether an author should be subsidy published based on the book's potential marketability and the author's financial resources." Pays 12-17% royalty on wholesale price, makes outright purchase of $5,000 maximum, or author pays for production. Offers average 20% advance. Publishes book an average of 4 months after acceptance. Computer printout submissions acceptable; prefers letter-quality to dot-matrix. SASE. Reports in 1 month on queries; 2 months on mss.
Nonfiction: Biography, cookbook, how-to, humor, illustrated book, juvenile, self-help, technical, and textbook. Subjects include business and economics, cooking and foods, health, and sports. "We are especially interested in technical, business, economics, juvenile, sports, health and beauty, and cookbooks. Also, biographies and/or autobiographies." Submit outline/synopsis and sample chapters or complete ms. Reviews artwork/photos as part of ms package.
Recent Nonfiction Title: *Fundamentally Yours, Pete Dimperio,* by John Wilborn (biography/sports).
Fiction: Adventure, confession, erotica, ethnic, fantasy, horror, humor, mainstream, mystery, romance, science fiction, and suspense. Submit outline/synopsis and sample chapters or complete ms.

WRITER'S DIGEST BOOKS, 9933 Alliance Rd., Cincinnati OH 45242. (513)984-0717. Editor-in-Chief: Carol Cartaino. Publishes hardcover and paperback originals (nonfiction only) about writing, photography, music, and other creative pursuits; as well as general-interest subjects. Pays advance and variable royalty depending upon type of book. Published 29 titles in 1984. Simultaneous (if so advised) and photocopied submissions OK. "Computer printout submissions fine, especially if on double-wide paper so we have a huge right-hand margin." Prefers letter-quality to dot-matrix. Publishes book an average of 6 months after acceptance. Enclose return postage. Book catalog for SASE.
Nonfiction: "We're seeking up-to-date, instructional treatments by authors who can write from successful experience. Should be well-researched, yet lively and anecdotal. Query or submit outline/synopsis and sample chapters. Be prepared to explain how the proposed book differs from existing books on the subject. We are also very interested in republishing self-published nonfiction books. No fiction or poetry! Send sample copy, sales record, and reviews if available." Reviews artwork/photos as part of ms package. Reports in 3 months—"or more, or less—depending on the priority of a topic in our publishing program, the research necessary on the subject, and our workload at the time. Please be patient—if you haven't heard from us, it probably means we're trying to give it further consideration."
Recent Nonfiction Title: *If I Can Write, You Can Write,* by Charlie Shedd.

YALE UNIVERSITY PRESS, 92A Yale Station, New Haven CT 06520. Editor-in-Chief: Edward Tripp. Publishes hardcover and paperback originals (96%) and reprints (4%). Averages 120 titles/year. Pays 5-10% royalty on retail price. Computer printout submissions acceptable. Reports in 2-3 months. SASE. Book catalog for SASE.
Nonfiction: Works of original scholarship in the humanities, social sciences and hard sciences. No fiction, cookbooks or popular nonfiction. Query or submit outline/synopsis and sample chapters.
Recent Nonfiction Title: *Hannah Arendt: For Love of the World,* by Elizabeth Young-Bruehl.

YANKEE BOOKS, Main St., Dublin NH 03444. (603)563-8111. Subsidiary of Yankee Publishing Inc. Editor: Clarissa M. Silitch. Publishes trade paperback and hardcover originals. Averages 8-10 titles/year. Royalty with $1,000-1,500 advance. Publishes book an average of 1 year after acceptance. Electronic submissions OK if floppy compatible with BMPC, DD, DS, but requires hard copy also. Computer printout submissions acceptable. SASE. Reports in 3-4 weeks on queries; 4-6 weeks on mss. Free book catalog.
Nonfiction: Cookbooks, how-to, country matters, nature, subjects related in one way or another to New England: nostalgia, Americana antiques, cooking, crafts, house and home, gardening, the outdoors, essays, folklore and popular history, photographs, today and old-time, travel (solely New England), the sea, boats, sailors, et al. No scholarly history, even slightly off-color humor, highly technical works, or biographies of persons not strikingly interesting. Query or submit outline/synopsis and sample chapters or complete ms. Reviews artwork/photos as part of ms package.
Recent Nonfiction Title: *Moving Upcountry.*

ZEBRA BOOKS, Subsidiary of Norfolk Publishing Co., 475 Park Ave. S., New York NY 10016. (212)889-2299. Editorial Director: Leslie Gelbman. Publishes mass market paperback originals and reprints. Averages 150 titles/year. Pays royalty on retail price or makes outright purchase. Simultaneous and photocopied submissions OK. SASE. Reports in 2 months on queries; 3 months on mss. Book catalog for business-size SAE and 37¢ postage.

Nonfiction: Biography, how-to, humor and self-help. Subjects include health, history and psychology. "We are open to many areas, especially self-help, stress, money management, child-rearing, health, war (WWII, Vietnam), and celebrity biographies." No nature, art, music, photography, religion or philosophy. Query or submit outline/synopsis and sample chapters.

Recent Nonfiction Title: *The Telephone Survival Guide*, by Dawn B. Sova.

Fiction: Adventure, confession, erotica, gothic, historical, horror, humor, mainstream, romance and suspense. Tip sheet on historical romances, gothics, family sagas, adult romances and women's contemporary fiction is available. No poetry or short story collections. Query with synopsis and several sample chapters. SASE is a must.

Recent Fiction Title: *Betray Not My Passion*, by Sylvie F. Sommerfield.

CHARLOTTE ZOLOTOW BOOKS, see Harper & Row Junior Books group.

THE ZONDERVAN CORP., 1415 Lake Drive, SE, Grand Rapids MI 49506. (616)698-6900. Executive Editor: Cheryl Forbes. Publishes hardcover and trade and mass market paperback originals (60%), and trade and mass market paperback reprints (40%). Averages 100 titles/year. Pays royalty of 14% of the net amount received on sales of cloth and softcover trade editions and 12% of net amount received on sales of mass market paperbacks; offers variable advance. Computer printout submissions are acceptable, but the author should separate the perforated pages. SASE. Reports in 8 weeks on queries. Catalog for 9x12 SAE and $1.22 postage.

Nonfiction: Biography, "coffee table" book, how-to, humor, illustrated book, reference, devotional and gift, self-help, textbook on philosophy, psychology, religion, and sociology. "All from religious perspective (evangelical, protestant)." Immediate needs include "books that take a fresh approach to issues and problems in protestant, evangelical community; books that offer new insights into solving personal and interpersonal problems; books that encourage readers to mature spiritually." No mss written from a mystical or occult point of view. Query or submit outline/synopsis and 2 sample chapters. Reviews artwork/photos as part of ms package.

Recent Nonfiction Title: *Forgive and Be Free*, by Richard P. Walters (personal development).

Fiction: "Books that deal realistically and creatively with relevant social and religious issues." No mss for new children's books. Query or submit outline/synopsis and 2 sample chapters.

Recent Fiction Title: *MacIntosh Mountain*, by Vic Kelly (contemporary/family issues).

Subsidy Book Publishers

The following listings are for book publishing companies which are totally subsidy publishers, meaning they do no standard trade publishing, and will publish a work only if the author is willing to underwrite the entire amount of the venture. This may cost thousands of dollars, usually returning less than 25% of the initial investment.

Read any literature or contracts carefully and thoroughly, being sure that all conditions of the venture (binding, editing, promotion, number of copies to be printed, number of copies to be bound, etc.) are spelled out specifically.

Dorrance & Company, 828 Lancaster Ave., Bryn Mawr PA 19010.

Mojave Books, 7118 Canby Rd., Reseda CA 91335.

Vantage Press, 516 W. 34th St., New York NY 10001.

Book Publishers Subject Index

Nonfiction

This subject index will help you locate book publishers interested in your writing topic. The parenthetical phrases following publishers' names give you an additional clue to the type of book (within that writing topic) that a publisher needs. Clarion, for example, is listed in the Americana subject area. Its editors though, want books for children on the subject so you'll see the word, juvenile, in parentheses. When you find a publisher that seems "right" for your book idea or manuscript, read the corresponding market listing carefully. A publisher may be categorized as publishing ethnic nonfiction. But unless you read through the entire *Writer's Market* entry, you will not know that only Greek-related manuscripts or materials on the history of southwestern American Indians are welcome.

Agriculture/Horticulture. Allen & Unwin; AVI (textbook); Banyan; Delmar (textbook); Hancock; Interstate (textbook); Oryx (reference); Pennsylvania State (scholarly); Purdue (scholarly): Reston (textbook); Stipes (textbook); Texas A&M; Universe; University of Nebraska (scholarly); University Press of America (scholarly); Western Producer Prairie; Westview (scholarly).

Alternative Lifestyles. Arid; And/Or; Avant; Cobblesmith; Commoners'; Ideal World; McPherson; Naturegraph; South End; Sterling; Strawberry Hill; Thorsons; Turnston; Underground Reports.

Americana. Allegheny(textbook); American(textbook); Angel; August; Binford & Mort; John F. Blair; Branden; Brevet; Brunswick; Caxton; Cedarshouse; Charles River; Clarion (juvenile); Arthur H. Clark; Cobblesmith; William Collins; Congdon & Weed; Copley; Coward McCann; Crown; Daphnean; Darwin (reference); Denlinger's; Devin-Adair; Dragonsbreath; Durst (reference); Paul S. Eriksson; Faber & Faber; Falcon; Filter; Guy Gannett; K.S. Giniger; Globe Pequot; Golden West Books; Hammond; Hancock; Harper & Row; Harvard Common; Hastings; Holmes & Meier; Holt, Rinehart & Winston; Hounslow; Howard (scholarly); Icarus; Independent; International; Interurban/Trans Anglo; Jonathan David; William Kaufmann; Laranmark; Le Beacon; Lexikos; Liberty; Little; Lowell; McFarland (reference); Madrona; Miller; Mimir; Monitor; Mosaic; Mott Media; Northland; Oregon State; Outbooks; Overlook; Pineapple; Clarkson N. Potter; Pressworks (reference); Purdue (scholarly); R & E; Rainbow/Betty Wright; Saybrook; Second Chance/Permanent; Stemmer; Sterling; Stoneydale; Lyle Stuart; Sun; Taylor; Ten Speed; Thorndike; Transaction; Tree by the River; Charles E. Tuttle; University of Illinois; University of Michigan (scholarly); University of Nebraska (scholarly); University of New Mexico (scholarly); University of North Carolina (scholarly); University of Pennsylvania (scholarly); University Press of Mississippi; University Press of New England (scholarly); University Press of Virginia (scholarly); University Presses of Florida; Utah State (scholarly); Vesta; Walker; Westernlore (scholarly); Wingra Woods; Yankee (reference).

Animals. Alaska Nature; Alpine; American (textbook); Angel; Arco (how-to); Avon; Brunswick; Carolina Biological Supply (textbook); William Collins; David C. Cook (juvenile); Crown; Dial (young adult & juvenile); Dillon (juvenile); Paul S. Eriksson; Faber & Faber; Fjord; Flora and Fauna; Guy Gannett; Garden Way; Robert Hale; Hancock; Harper & Row; Holt; Rinehart & Winston; Houghton Mifflin; Iowa State (textbook); Island; Larkspur; Little; Lowell; Miller; Mosaic; Overlook; Pineapple; Quartet; S.C.E.-Editions; Scholastic-Tab; Scribner's, Children's (juvenile); Sierra Club; Stemmer; T.F.H. (technical & how-to); Tab; Ten Speed; Thorndike; Thorsons; Tribeca; Universe; University of Michigan (scholarly); University Presses of Florida; Vanguard; Walker; Williamson; Wingra Woods; World Natural History (reference).

Anthropology/Archaeology. Cambridge University (textbook); Daphnean; Hancock; Institute for the Study of Human Issues; McPherson; Museum of New Mexico (scholarly); Noyes Data (scholarly); Ohio State (scholarly); Ross-Erikson; Rutgers (scholarly); Southern Methodist (scholarly); Stanford; Trado-Medic (reference); Turnstone; University of Arizona (scholarly); University of Nevada (scholarly); University of Tennessee (scholarly); University of Texas (scholarly); University of Utah (scholarly); University Press of Kentucky (scholarly); University Presses of Florida; Westernlore (scholarly); Westview (scholarly).

Art and Architecture. Harry N. Abrams; Acheron; American (textbook); Architectural; Art Director (how-to & textbook); Avant; BC Studio; Beacon; Bear; Bennett & McKnight (textbook); Branden; George Braziller; Bucknell (scholarly); Aristide D. Caratzas; Charles River; Chronicle; Cobblesmith; William Collins; Columbia (scholarly); Congdon & Weed; Copley; Crown; Davis (reference); Delta; Denlinger's Dharma; Donning; Dragonsbreath; Duck Down; Dundurn; Durst (how-to); Eastview; Environmental Design & Research Center (reference); Faber & Faber; Fairleigh Dickinson; J. Paul Getty Museum (scholarly & reference); K.S. Giniger; Great Ocean; Guernica; H.P. Books; Robert Hale; Hammond; Harper & Row; Hastings; Holmes & Meier; Holt, Rinehart & Winston; Hounslow; Howard (scholarly); Hudson Hills; Illuminate; International University (textbook); William Kaufman; Karl Kramer Verlag GMBH; Krantz (reference); Lancaster Miller & Schnobrich (scholarly); Lancelot; Le Beacon; Learning (how-to & textbook); Living Poets; Lowell; McFarland (reference); McGraw-Hill, Professional & Reference (reference); Macmillan of Canada; MIT (scholarly); William Morrow; Mosaic; National (textbook); National Gallery of Canada; New York University (scholarly); North Light (how-to & reference); Noyes Data (scholarly); Ohio State (scholarly); Optimum; Overlook; Oxmoor; Pagurian; Pelican; Pennsylvania State (scholarly); Peregrine Smith; Pineapple; Clarkson N. Potter; Prentice-Hall (juvenile); Prentice-Hall, General; Preservation; Pressworks (reference); Princeton (scholarly); Purdue (scholarly); Resource; Rossel; Ross-Erikson; Saybrook; Scribner's, Children's (juvenile); Simon & Schuster; Stemmer; Sterling; Stoneydale; Lyle Stuart; Sun; Taplinger; Taylor; Ten Speed; Transaction; Troubador; Charles E. Tuttle; Universe; University of Alberta; University of California (scholarly); University of Iowa (scholarly); University of Massachusetts (scholarly); University of Michigan (scholarly); University of Missouri (scholarly); University of New Mexico (scholarly); University Press of Mississippi; University Press of New England (scholarly); University Presses of Florida; Vance Bibliographies (bibliography); Vanguard (history); Vesta; Viking Penguin; J. Weston Walch (textbook); Walker; Wanderer (juvenile); Watson-Guptill (how-to); Western Tanager; Whitston (scholarly); Wingra Woods; Winston-Derek; Alan Wofsy Fine Arts (reference & bibliographies).

Astrology/Psychic Phenomena. ACS; ASI; Front Row Experience; Garber; Intercultural; Larson; Newcastle; Pitman Learning; Porter Sargent; Regal; Sterling; Strawberry Hill; Sun; Theosophical; Turnstone; U.S. Games Systems; Underground Reports.

Autobiography. Arbor; Artech; Atlantic Monthly; Pegasus.

Bibliography. Associated; R.R. Bowker; Data and Research Technology; Family Album; Feminist; Garland; Klein; Oryx; Reymont; Scarecrow; Shoe String (scholarly); University Press of Virginia (scholarly); Whitston (scholarly).

Biography. Academy Chicago; Addison-Wesley; Alaska Nature; Alaska Northwest; American Atheist; Apple-Wood; Architectural; Atheneum; Atlantic Monthly; August; Avon; Bahamas International; Bibli O' Phile; Binford & Mort; John F. Blair; Bobbs-Merrill; Borgo; Don Bosco; Marion Boyars; Branden; Broadside; Brunswick; Cambridge University; Capra; Carroll & Graf; Catholic University (scholarly); Cedarshouse; Celestial Arts; Charles River; China; Citadel; Clarion (juvenile); Arthur F. Clark; William Collins; Columbia; Congdon & Weed; Continuum; Copley; Coward McCann; Creative Arts; Crown; Dante University; Daphnean; Dembner; Detselig; Dharma; Dillon (juvenile); Dodd, Mead; Doubleday Canada; Dragonsbreath; Dundurn; Enslow; Paul S. Eriksson; Essco; Faber & Faber; Family Album; Feminist (juvenile); Fiesta City; Fleet; Franciscan Herald; Guy Gannett; K.S. Giniger; Golden Quill; Gray's; Great Ocean; Green Hill; Grove; Guernica; Robert Hale; Hancock House; Harper & Row; Harvard Common; Hastings House; Holmes & Meier; Holt, Rinehart & Winston; Horizon; Houghton Mifflin; Hounslow; Howard University (scholarly); Huntington House; Hurtig; Icarus; International; International University (scholarly); Iowa State University; Kalimat; William Kaufman; Lancelot; Lee's (juvenile); Liberty; Little, Brown; Little House; Macmillan of Canada; MCN; Madrona; Manyland; Metamorphous; Mimir; Monitor; William Morrow; Mosaic; Motorbooks; Mott Media (juvenile); Nautical & Aviation; Naval Institute; Nimbus; Northeastern; Ohio State (scholarly); Optimum; Oregon State; Panjandrum; Pegasus; Pocket Books; Poseiden; Clarkson N. Potter; Prairie, Prentice-Hall (juvenile); Princeton; Prometheus; Purdue (scholarly); Quartet; Regnery/Gateway; Russica; S.C.E.-Editions; St. Luke's; St. Martin's; Saybrook; Schirmer; Scribner's, Children's (juvenile); Second Chance/Permanent; Shoe String (scholarly); Simon & Schuster; Slavica; Southern Methodist (scholarly); Stemmer; Stoneydale; Lyle Stuart; Sun; Taplinger; Texas Monthly; Thunder's Mouth; Transaction; Twayne; Universe; University of Alabama; University of Alberta; University of Arkansas; University of Illinois; University of Massachusetts (scholarly); University of Michigan (scholarly); University of Nebraska (scholarly); University of Nevada (scholarly); University of Pennsylvania(scholarly); University Press of Kansas (scholarly); University Press of Mississippi; University Press of New England(scholarly); University Presses of Florida; Vanguard; Vehicule; Vesta; Vision House; Walker; Warner; Wayne State (Americana); Western Producer Prairie; Western Tanager; Westernlore (scholarly); Winston-Derek; Wolf; Woodsong; World Natural History; Wright; Zondervan.

Business and Economics. ABT (reference); Bob Adams (reference); Addison-Wesley; Alfred (how-to); Allen & Unwin; Allen (how-to); Almar; American Council for the Arts (reference); American (textbook); And; Arbor; Arco (how-to); Associated; Avon; Ballinger (reference); Bankers (reference); Bantam; Basic; BC Studio; Benjamin; Better Way; Bibli O' Phile; Marion Boyars; Brevet; Briarcliff; Brunswick; Cambridge (textbook); Charles River; Charter; Chilton; William Collins; Columbia; Communications (reference); Congdon & Weed; Consumer Reports (reference); Cordovan; Corinthian; Crain (textbook); Cumberland; Dartnell; Delmar (textbook); Dembner; Deneau; Devin-Adair; Dow Jones-Irwin; Durst (reference); EMC; Enslow; Enterprise; Environmental Design & Research Center (reference); Paul S. Eriksson; ETC; Exanimo; Fairchild (textbook); Fairleigh Dickinson; Farnsworth; Frederick Fell; Free Press (textbook & reference); Great Ocean; Gregg (textbook); Gulf; Hammond; Harcourt Brace Jovanovich Legal & Professional (reference); Harper & Row; Harvard Common; D.C. Health (textbook); Holmes & Meier; Holt, Rinehart & Winston; Hounslow; Howard University (scholarly); Industrial; Infosource; Institute for Business Planning (how-to & reference); Institute for the Study of Human Issues; Intercultural (how-to); International; International Self-Counsel (how-to); International University (textbook); Interurban/Trans Anglo; Johns Hopkins (scholarly); William Kaufmann; Klein; Knowledge Industry; Robert E. Kreiger; Le Beacon; Liberty; Linch; Little House; Live Oak; McFarland (reference); McGraw-Hill (reference); McGraw-Hill, Professional & Reference (reference); Marathon International (self-help); Menasha Ridge; Charles E. Merrill (textbook); Metamorphous; Mimir; MIT (scholarly); Mosaic; National (textbook); National Publishers of the Black Hills (textbook); New York Zoetrope (textbook & reference); Noyes Data (technical); Ohio University (scholarly); Oregon State; Overlook; Parker (how-to); Pennsylvania State (scholarly); Petrocelli; Pilot (reference); Pluribus (how-to); Poseidon; Prentice-Hall Canada, Educational (juvenile); Prentice-Hall Canada, Trade; Prentice-Hall, General; Pressworks (reference); Purdue (scholarly); Quartet; R & E; R & R Newkirk (technical); Realtors National Marketing Institute (how-to); Regnery/Gateway; Reston (textbook); Reymont; Riverdale (textbook); RPM; S.C.E.-Editions; Saybrook; Schenkman (textbook); Scribner's; Self-Counsel (how-to & reference); Social Science Education Consortium (reference); South End (government & politics); Southern Methodist (scholarly); Sterling; Stipes (textbook); Lyle Stuart; Taylor; Teachers College; Texas A&M (scholarly); Times; Transaction; Trend House; Tribeca; Universe; University Associates; University of Alabama (scholarly); University of Illinois; University of Iowa (scholarly); University of Michigan (scholarly); University of Pennsylvania (scholarly); University of Texas (scholarly); University Press of America (scholarly); University Press of Mississippi; University Press of New England (scholarly); University Press of the Pacific (scholarly); University Press of Virginia (scholarly); University Presses of Florida; Vanguard (how-to); G. Weston Walch (textbook); Walker; Wayne State University; Western Producer Prairie; Westin Communications (textbook & reference); Wetherall (how-to); John Wiley (reference); Williamson; Wingbow (self-help); Wordware; Wright.

Calendars. Charles River.

Career Guidance. Bob Adams (reference); Almar; Arco; Associated; Career; Chatham; Chicago Review; Fairchild; Guidance Center; Interstate (textbook); Peterson's Guides (reference); Pilot (reference); Rosen (young adult); Ross; Teachers College; VGM Career Horizons; Westin Communications.

Communications. And; Avant; Bradson; Career; Chicago Review; College-Hill (reference); Communication Skill Builders; Communications (reference); Drama (reference); Focal (how-to); Knowledge Industry; Law-Arts (textbook); Meriwether (juvenile & textbook); National Publishers of the Black Hills (textbook); New York Zoetrope (reference); Oryx; Random House (textbook); Regal; Shoe String (scholarly); Special Libraries (textbook & reference); Univelt; University Associates; Writer's Digest (how-to & reference).

Community/Public Affairs. A.S. Barnes; Communications; Continuum; Creative; Deneau; Groupwork Today; Indiana University; Loiry (reference); Macmillan of Canada; NC; Temple (scholarly); Trado-Medic (health & medicine); University Associates; Vance Bibliographies (bibliography); Wesleyan (scholarly); Westview (scholarly).

Computers. Alfred (how-to); And; ARCsoft; Artech; Ashton-Tate; Atlantis; Blacksburg (textbook & reference); Career; Carolina Biological Supply; Chilton; Compute!; Computer Science (general, bibliographies, textbook & reference); Computer Skill Builders; Steve Davis (how-to, technical, & reference); Delmar (textbook); Dustbooks; Fairchild (textbook); Hayden (reference); D.C. Heath (textbook); Incentive; Infosource; Intervarsity (textbook); William Kaufmann; Lancaster Milles & Schnobrich; McGraw-Hill (reference); Microtrend; MIT (scholarly); National Publishers of the Black Hills (textbook); New York Zoetrope (technical & reference); Noyes Data (technical); Osborn/McGraw-Hill; Prentice-Hall, Canada Educational (juvenile); Prentice-Hall, General; Q.E.D. Information Sciences (technical); Que (educational);

Regents (textbook); Resource (how-to); Reston (textbook); Sybex; Tab; Techwrite; Texas Instruments (technical & reference); Tribeca; University Press of Virginia (scholarly); J. Weston Walch (textbook); Webster (how-to); Westin Communications (textbook & reference); John Wiley; Wordware.

Consumer Affairs. Almar; Consumer Reports (reference); Delair; Dell; Gregg (textbook); Menasha Ridge; Teacher Update; Westminster (juvenile).

Cooking/Foods/Nutrition. Aglow; Alaska Northwest; Angel; Anna; Apple; Arbor; Associated; Atheneum; AVI (textbook); Avon; Bantam; BC Studio; Beaufort; Benjamin; Berkley; Better Homes and Gardens; Bibli O' Phile; Binford & Mort; Biworld; Bobbs-Merrill (how-to); Briarcliff; Brunswick; Byls; Camaro; Celestial Arts; Chicago Review; China; Christin; Cobblesmith; William Collins; Compact; Congdon & Weed; Consumer Reports (how-to); Contemporary; Creative Arts; Creative; Crossing; Crown; Delair; Detselig; Durst (how-to); Ecco; Paul S. Eriksson; Evans; Falcon; Frederick Fell; Filter; Forman; Guy Gannett; Garden Way; K.S. Giniger; Globe Mini Mags; Globe Pequot; Golden West; Graphic Image; H.P. Books; Robert Hale; Hammond; Hancock; Harper & Row; Harvard Common; Hastings; Hawkes (how-to); Hayden (textbook); Herald; Holt, Rinehart & Winston; Houghton Mifflin; Hounslow; Humanics; Ideals; Johnson; Jonathan David; Kav (how-to); Kids Can (juvenile); Lancelot; Laranmark; Larson; Le Beacon; Liberty; Little, Brown; Little House; Lone Star; Madrona; Marathon International; Miller (how-to); William Morrow; Mosaic; Nimbus; 101 Productions (how-to); Optimum; Ottenheimer; Outbooks; Overlook; Oxmoor House; Pagurian; Panjandrum; Peachtree; Pelican; Judy Piatkus; Pluribus (how-to); Poseidon; Clarkson N. Potter; Prairie; Prentice-Hall Canada, Trade; Richboro; Ross; Rossel; S.C.E.-Editions; Second Chance/Permanent; Seven Seas; Stackpole; Stemmer House; Sterling; Stoeger; Strawberry Hill; Sun; Jeremy P. Tarcher; Taylor; Techwrite; Ten Speed; Texas Monthly; Thorsons; Thunder's Mouth; Times; T.L. (how-to); Tribeca; Touchstone; Troubador; University Press of Virginia (scholarly); University Presses of Florida; Vanguard; Vehicule; Vesta; Walker; Warner; Western Producer Prairie; Williamson; Wimmer; Winchester; Wingra Woods; Woodbridge; Woodsong Graphics; Wright; Yankee.

Counseling. Accelerated Development (reference & textbook); Career; Consumer Reports (how-to); Edits (reference); Groupwork Today; Interstate (textbook); Learning (reference); Med-Psych; Morehouse-Barlow; Mott Media; New Leaf; Occupational Awareness; Teachers College; Tynedale.

Crafts. Arco (how-to); Associated; A.S. Barnes; Better Homes and Gardens; Betterway; Charles T. Branford (how-to); Briarcliff; Chilton; Collector; Commoner's; Davis (reference); Delair (how-to); Dillon (juvenile); Doll Reader; Hancock House; House of Collectibles (how-to); Kav (how-to); Naturegraph; Oak Tree (how-to); Optimum; Oxmoor House; Popular Science (how-to); Scholastic Tab; Stackpole; Standard (how-to); Sunstone (how-to); Tab; Timber; Troubador; Universe; Vanguard; Wallace-Homestead; Winchester (how-to); Yankee.

Education(al). Accelerated Development (reference & textbook); Acheron; Acropolis; Addison-Wesley; American Catholic; Arco; Associated; Aztex; Bantam; Barnes & Noble; Bilingual Educational (juvenile); John F. Blair; Byls; Cambridge; Career; Cliffs Notes; Communication Skill Builders; Computer Skill Builders; Continuum; Dante; T.S. Denison; Edits (reference); Education Associates (textbook); EMC (recreation); ETC; Feminist; Gregg; Guidance Centre; Holmes & Meier; Holt, Rinehart & Winston of Canada (textbook); Humanics; Incentive; Interstate (textbook); Jalmar; Jamestown; Larson; Learning (reference); Liberty; Liguori; Meriwether (juvenile); Charles E. Merrill (textbook); Morehouse Barlow; National; New Readers; Occupational Awareness; Octameron; Ohio State (scholarly); Open Court; Oryx; Parker (how-to); R & E; Regents; Regnery/Gateway; Resource; Routledge & Kegan Paul (scholarly); Shoe String (scholarly); Silver Burdett; Social Science Education Consortium (reference); Teacher Update; Teachers College; Twenty-Third; University Press of America (scholarly); J. Weston Walch; Webster (how-to); Wetherall; B.L. Winch; Winston.

Ethnic. ABC-Clio (reference); And; Bilingual Educational (juvenile); Borealis; Brunswick; Byls; China; Columbia University (scholarly); Dante; Dharma; Fleet (juvenile); Genealogical; Guernica; Heart of the Lakes; Heritage; Holloway House; Institute for the Study of Human Issues; International; Kar-Ben (juvenile); Manyland; Museum of New Mexico (scholarly); Naturegraph; Northland; Pennsylvania State (scholarly); Precedent (scholarly); Rossel; Schocken; Slavica; Strawberry Hill; Sun; Texas Western (scholarly); Three Continents; Charles E. Tuttle; University of Arizona (scholarly); University of Massachusetts (scholarly); University of Nebraska (scholarly); University of Nevada (scholarly); University of Oklahoma (scholarly); University of Pennsylvania (scholarly); University of Utah (scholarly); University Press of America (scholarly); Westernlore (scholarly); Yankee.

Fashion/Beauty. Acropolis (how-to & reference); Fairchild (textbook).

Film/Cinema. Atlantic Monthly; A.S. Barnes; Borgo; Bradson; Citadel; Columbia; Communications; Drama (reference); Indiana University; JH; Lake View; Law-Arts (textbook); McFarland (reference); McPherson; Panjandrum; Scarecrow; Schirmer; Sterling; Tab; Taplinger; Twayne; University of Tennessee (scholarly); Wesleyan University (scholarly).

Games and Entertainment. Contemporary; Dell; Gaming; Gambling Times; H.P. Books; Holloway; Kav; Knowledge Industry; Larkspur; McFarland (reference); Scholastic (juvenile); Scholastic-Tab; Sterling; Tab; Troubador; U.S. Games Systems; Winchester.

Gardening and Plants. Associated; Banyan; Better Homes and Gardens; Betterway (how-to); Briarcliff; Cobblesmith; Cortina Learning; Delmar (textbook); Garden Way; Gulf; H.P. Books; Keats; Naturegraph; 101 Productions (how-to); Optimum; Ottenheimer; Richboro; Ross; Symmes; Jeremy P. Torcher; Taylor; Timber; Universe; Walker; Woodbridge; Yankee.

Gay and Lesbian. Alyson; Crossing; JH; Thorsons (how-to).

General Nonfiction. Academy Chicago; American Psychiatric; Atheneum; Ballantine; A.S. Barnes; Beacon; Charter; Delacorte; Dell; Doubleday Canada; Evans; William Morrow; New American Library; W.W. Norton; Pineapple; Pinnacle; Pocket Books; Pruett; Random House; St. Martin's; Scribner's; Shoe String; The Smith; Stein & Day; Taplinger; Teacher Update; Time-Life; Viking Penguin.

Government and Politics. ABC-Clio (reference); ABT; Addison-Wesley; Allen & Unwin; American (textbook); Angel; Apple-Wood; Arbor; Atheneum; August; Avon; Basic; Beacon; Bear; John F. Blair; Borgo; Marion Boyars; Branden; Brunswick; Bucknell (scholarly); CQ; Cedarshouse; Charles River; William Collins; Columbia; Communications; Congdon & Weed; Coward McCann; Crown; Daphnean; Delta; Dembner; Deneau; Devin-Adair; Paul S. Eriksson; Faber & Faber; Fairleigh Dickinson; Great Ocean; Grove; Guernica; Robert Hale; Harper & Row; Harvard Common; D.C. Heath (textbook); Holmes & Meier; Holt, Rinehart & Winston; Houghton Mifflin; Hounslow; Howard University (scholarly); Hurtig; Institute for the Study of Human Issues; Intercultural (reference); International; International University (scholarly); Johns Hopkins (scholarly); Le Beacon; Little House; Loiry (reference); Longman (textbook); Louisiana State University; McPherson; Madrona; Miller; Mimir; Mott Media; National (textbook); NC; New York University (scholarly); Northeastern (reference); Ohio State (scholarly); Overlook; Oxford (scholarly); Pantheon; Pennsylvania State (scholarly); Poseidon; Prentice-Hall Canada, Trade; Princeton (scholarly); Quartet; R & E; Rainbow/Betty Wright; Regnery/Gateway; Riverdale (textbook); Rossel; Routledge & Kegan Paul (scholarly); S.C.E.-Editions; St. Martin's; Saybrook; Scholarly Resources (scholarly); Second Chance/Permanent; Social Science Education Consortium (reference); Sovereign; Lyle Stuart; Sherwood Sugden; Sun; Teachers College; Texas Monthly; Thunder's Mouth; Transaction; Trend House; Universe; University of Alabama (scholarly); University of Alberta; University of Illinois; University of Massachusetts (scholarly); University of North Carolina (scholarly); University of Notre Dame (scholarly); University of Pennsylvania (scholarly); University of Tennessee (scholarly); University of Texas (scholarly); University Press of America (scholarly); University Press of Kansas (scholarly); University Press of Kentucky (scholarly); University Press of Mississippi; University Press of New England (scholarly); University Press of the Pacific (scholarly); University Press of Virginia (scholarly); University Presses of Florida; Utah State (scholarly); Vanguard; Vehicule; Vesta; J. Weston Walch (textbook); Wayne State; Western Tanager; John Wiley (reference); Wordware.

Health and Medicine. ABT; Academic (scholarly); Acropolis (how-to & reference); ACS; Addison-Wesley; Almar; American (textbook); American Psychiatric; And/Or; Angel; Anna (reference); Apple; Arbor; Arco (reference); Artech (technical); ASI; Atlantis; Augsburg; Avant; AVI (textbook); Avon; Bantam; BC Studio; Beaufort; Benjamin; Better Homes and Gardens; Betterway; Bibli O' Phile; Biomedical (textbook & reference); Biworld (reference & self-help); Bobbs-Merrill; Bradson; Branden; Briarcliff; Bridge; Brunswick; Camaro; Cambridge University (textbook); Career; Carolina Biological Supply (textbook); Celestial Arts; Champion Athlete; Charles River; Christin; College-Hill (textbook & reference); William Collins; Compact; Compcare (self-help); Congdon & Weed; Computer Reports (reference); Contemporary; Copley; Corinthian; Coward McCann; Creative Arts; Crossing; Crown; Delair (how-to); Delmar (textbook); Delta; Dembner; Detselig; Devin-Adair; Enslow; Paul S. Eriksson; Evans; Faber & Faber; Falcon; Frederick Fell; Flare (young adult); K.S. Giniger; Globe Mini Mags; Golden West; Great Ocean; Warren H. Green (scholarly); Gregg (textbook); Grove; H.P. Books; Robert Hale; Harper & Row; Harvard Common; Hawkes (how-to); Hazelden; Health Profession (textbook & reference); D.C. Heath (reference); Holt, Rinehart & Winston; Houghton Mifflin; Hounslow; Howard University (scholarly); Humanics; Ideal World; International University Press (textbook); Iowa State University (textbook); Johns Hopkins (scholarly); William Kaufmann; Kids Can (juvenile); Larson; Little House; McFarland (reference); Madrona; Medical Economics (reference); Medical Examination (textbook); Med-Psych; Menasha Ridge; Metamorphous; Mosaic; John Muir (how-to); National (textbook); Naturegraph;

Newcastle; Nuresco (reference); Optimum; Ottenheimer; Overlook; P.P.I.; Panjandrum; Pantheon; Parker (how-to); Pennsylvania State University (scholarly); Pineapple; Plenum; Pluribus (reference); Poseidon; Potentials Development for Health & Aging Services; Prentice-Hall (juvenile); Prentice Hall Canada, Trade; PSG (reference); Quintessence (technical); R & E; Reston (textbook); Rosen (young adult); Ross-Eriksson; S.C.E.-Editions; Saybrook; Scribner's; Scribner's, Children's (juvenile); Second Chance/Permanent; Sierra Club; Sterling; Strawberry Hill; Lyle Stuart; Jeremy P. Tarcher; Teachers College; Theosophical; Thorsons; Trado-Medic (reference); Transaction; Tribeca; Turnstone; Underground Reports; Universe; University Presses of Florida; J. Weston Walch (textbook); Walker; Wanderer (juvenile); Wayne State; Westview (scholarly); Wetherall (self-help); John Wiley (reference); Williamson; Wilshire; Woodbridge (how-to); Wright; Zebra.

History. ABC-Clio (reference); Academy Chicago; Acheron; Alaska Northwest; Allen & Unwin; American (textbook); Angel; Apple-Wood; Arbor; Associated; Atheneum; Atlantic Monthly; August; Avon; Aztex; Bahamas International; Banyan; A.S. Barnes; Bear; Binford & Mort (travel); John F. Blair; Borgo; Marion Boyars; Branden; George Braziller; Brevet; Brunswick; Bucknell (scholarly); Cambridge University; Aristide O. Caratzas; Carolrhoda (juvenile); Catholic University (scholarly); Cedarshouse; Charles River; China; Citadel; Arthur H. Clark; William Collins; Columbia University (scholarly); Congdon & Weed; Continuum; Cordovan; Coward McCann; Crossway; Crown; Daphnean; Darwin (reference); Dembner; Detselig; Devin-Adair; Dharma; Dial (juvenile & young adults); Dillon; Donning; Doubleday Canada; Dragonsbreath; Dundurn; Eastview; William B. Eerdmans; Paul S. Eriksson; Essco; Faber & Faber; Fairleigh Dickinson; Falcon; Farrar, Straus and Giroux (young adult); Fjord; Fleet; Franciscan Herald; Guy Gannett; Gaslight; Genealogical; J. Paul Getty Museum (scholarly & reference); K.S. Giniger; Globe Pequot; GMG; Golden West; Gray's; Great Ocean; Grove; Guernica; Robert Hale; Hammond; Hancock House; Harper & Row Junior Books (juvenile); Harper & Row; Harvard Common; Hastings House; Hawkes; Heart of the Lakes; D.C. Heath (textbook); Herald; Heritage; Holmes & Meier; Holt, Rinehart & Winston; Horizon; Houghton Mifflin; Hounslow; Howard University; Hurtig; Icarus; Independent; Indiana University; Institute for the Study of Human Issues; International Marine; International; International University (textbook); Interurban/Trans Anglo; Iowa State; Johns Hopkins (scholarly); Johnson; Kalimat; Kar-Ben; William Kaufmann; Kent State (scholarly); Kids Can (juvenile); Robert E. Kreiger; Lancelot; Laranmark; Leather Stocking; Lexikos; Liberty; Little, Brown; Little House; Longman (textbook); Lorien; Louisiana State; McFarland (reference); Macmillan of Canada; MCN; Madrona; Mercer University (reference); Miller; Mimir; William Morrow; Mosaic; Motorbooks International; Mountain; Museum of New Mexico (scholarly); National (textbook); Naturegraph; Nautical & Aviation; NC; New Readers; New York University (scholarly); Nimbus; Northeastern (reference); Northern Illinois (scholarly); Noyes Data (scholarly); Ohio State (scholarly); Ohio University (scholarly); Optimum; Oregon State; Outbooks; Overlook; Oxford University (scholarly); Paladin; Panjandrum; Pantheon; Peachtree; Pennsylvania State (scholarly); Peregrine Smith; Pine Mountain; Pineapple; Pocket Books; Poseidon; Clarkson N. Potter; Precedent (scholarly); Prentice-Hall (juvenile); Prentice-Hall, Canada, Educational (juvenile); Preservation; Presidio; Pressworks (reference); Princeton (scholarly); Purdue (scholarly); Quartet; R & E; Rainbow/Betty Wright; Regnery/Gateway; Riverdale (textbook); Rossel; Routledge & Kegan Paul (scholarly); Russica; Rutgers (scholarly); S.C.E.-Editions; St. Martin's; Schenkman (textbook); Scholarly Resources (scholarly, bibliographies); Second Chance/Permanent; Shoe String (scholarly); Simon & Schuster; Slavica; Social Science Education Consortium (reference); Southern Methodist (scholarly); Sovereign; Stanford; Stemmer House; Stoneydale; Strawberry Hill; Sherwood Sugden; Sun; Sunstone; Taplinger; Temple (scholarly); Ten Speed; Texas A&M (scholarly); Texas Monthly; Texas Western (scholarly); Three Continents; Thunder's Mouth; Thompson & Rutter; Touchstone; Transaction; Tree by the River; Trend House; Tribeca; Turnstone; Charles E. Tuttle; Universe; University of Alabama (scholarly); University of Alberta; University of Arkansas (scholarly); University of Illinois; University of Iowa (scholarly); University of Massachusetts (scholarly); University of Missouri (scholarly); University of Nebraska (scholarly); University of Nevada (scholarly); University of New Mexico (scholarly); University of North Carolina (scholarly); University of Notre Dame (scholarly); University of Oklahoma (scholarly); University of Pennsylvania (scholarly); University of Tennessee (scholarly); University of Utah (scholarly); University Press of America (scholarly); University Press of Kansas (scholarly); University Press of Kentucky (medical & scholarly); University Press of Mississippi; University Press of New England; University Press of the Pacific (scholarly); University Press of Virginia (scholarly); University Presses of Florida (sport); Utah State (scholarly); Vanguard; Vehicule; Vesta; J. Weston Walch (textbook); Walker; Wayne State; Wesleyan (scholarly); Western Producer Prairie; Western Tanager; Westernlore (scholarly); Wordware; Yankee; Zebra.

Hobby. Allegheny (how-to); Almar; American Philatelic (how-to); Angel; Arco (how-to); M. Arman (how-to, textbook & reference); Associated; Associated Booksellers (how-to); Avon; Bale; Barnes & Noble (how-to); BC Studio; Beaufort; Benjamin; Bradson; Charles T. Branford (how-to); Brunswick; Carstens; Charles River; Chicago Review (reference); Collector; William

Collins; Contemporary (how-to); Crown; Darwin (how-to); Dembner; Detselig; Doll Reader; Dundurn; Durst (how-to); Eastview; Enslow; Paul S. Eriksson; Essco; Faber & Faber; Falcon; Frederick Fell; K.S. Giniger; H.P. Books; Robert Hale; Hammond; Hancock House; Harvard Common; Hawkes; Holt, Rinehart & Winston; Hounslow; House of Collectibles (how-to); Interurban/Trans Anglo; Kalmbach (how-to); Kids Can (juvenile); Klein; Liberty; Little House; MCN; Madrona; Menasha Ridge; Mosaic; Mountain; October (technical); Outbooks; Overlook; Oxmoor House; Panjandrum; Pineapple; Popular Science (how-to); Prentice-Hall, General; S.C.E.-Editions; Scholastic-Tab; Scribner's, Children's (juvenile); Sterling; Stoeger; Lyle Stuart; Tab; Ten Speed; Tensleep; T.L. (how-to); Touchstone; Ultralight (technical); Walker; Wallace-Homestead; Wanderer (juvenile); Williamson; Wilshire; Wingbow (how-to); Woodsong Graphics; Wordware.

Home and Family Life. Abbey; Addison-Wesley; Aztex; Bennett & McKnight(textbook); Berkley; Better Homes & Gardens; Better Way (how-to & reference); Bobbs-Merrill (how-to); Career; Catholic Truth Society (how-to); Cobblesmith (how-to); Compcare (how-to); Delair (how-to); Delmar (textbook); Delta; Fairchild (textbook); Great Ocean; Here's Life; Humanics; Ideals; Interstate (textbook); John Knox; Lakewood (self-help); Larkspur; Loiry (reference); Oak Tree; 101 Productions (how-to); Ottenheimer; Popular Science (how-to); Regal; Harold Shaw; Sterling; Tab (how-to); Tyndale House; Vision House; Williamson; Wimmer (how-to); B.L. Winch (self-help).

How-to. Addison Wesley; Angel; Anna; James Arnold; Atlantis; August; Barnes & Noble; BC Studio; Berkley; Bibli O' Phile; Biworld, Briarcliff; Bridge; Capra; Charles River; Chicago Review; Chilton; Christin; William Collins; Computer Skill Builders; Corinthian; Coward McCann; Creative Arts; Crown; Dell; Delta; Dembner; Devin-Adair; Digital; Dundurn; Enslow; Paul S. Eriksson; Essco; ETC; Exanimo; Faber & Faber; Falcon; Frederick Fell; Forman; Front Row Experience; Gambling Times; K.S. Giniger; Graphic Image; Green Hill; Grove; H.P. Books; Robert Hale; Hammond; Hancock House; Harcourt Brace Jovanovich Legal & Professional; Harper & Row; Harvard Common; Herald; Here's Life; Holt, Rinehart & Winston; Ideals; Independent; Infosource; Johnson; Jonathan David; William Kaufmann; Klein; Laranmark; Larson; Liberty; Linch; Little, Brown; Little House; Loiry; Lone Star; Lorien; Nick Lyons; Macmillan of Canada; Madrona; Meriwether (juvenile); Metamorphous; William Morrow; Motorbook International; Naturegraph; Newcastle; Nimbus; Optimum; Outbooks; Outdoor Empire; Overlook; Oxmoor; PPI; Panjandrum; Pantheon; Pegasus; Judy Piatkus; Pluribus; Clarkson N. Potter; Prentice-Hall, General; Que; R & E; Rainbow/Betty Wright; Reymont; Richboro; Rossel; RPM; Scholastic-Tab; Second Chance/Permanent; Harold Shaw; Sierra Club; Stoeger; Stoneydale; Sun; Taylor; Techwrite; Ten Speed; Tensleep; Thunder's Mouth; Touchstone; Ultralight; Underground Reports; University of Alberta; Vision House; Warner; Western; Westminster (juvenile); Williamson; Wilshire; Wingra Woods; Woodsong Graphics; Wordware; Wright; Yankee; Zebra; Zondervan.

Humanities. American Council for the Arts (reference); Duquesne (scholarly); Folcraft/Norwood (scholarly); Fordham (scholarly); Tree Press (textbook & reference); Garland (reference); Holmes & Meier; Indiana University; Louisiana State; Pressworks (reference); Prometheus; Southern Illinois; University of Texas (scholarly); Whitston (scholarly).

Humor. Angel; Apple-Wood; August; Avon; Baker; John F. Blair; Bradson; Celestial Arts; Charles River; Citadel; Clarion (juvenile); William Collins; Cortina Learning (language & literature textbooks); Crown; Delta; Dragonsbreath; Paul J. Eriksson; Faber & Faber; Farrar, Straus & Giroux (young adult); Golden West, Guernica; Robert Hale; Harper & Row; Harvard Common; Holt, Rinehart & Winston; Hounslow; Hurtig; William Kaufmann; Lancelot; Le Beacon; Little House; Lowell; Madrona; Marathon International; Mosaic; Nimbus; Overlook; Paladin; Peachtree; Pine Mountain; Pineapple; Clarkson N. Potter; Prentice-Hall (juvenile); Price/Stern/Sloan; Princeton; Rainbow/Betty Wright; Russica; S.C.E.-Editions; Scholastic (juvenile); Scholastic-Tab; Scribner's Children's (juvenile); Second Chance/Permanent; Sterling; Lyle Stuart; Jeremy P. Tarcher; Ten Speed; Texas Monthly; Thorndike; Tribeca; Vanguard; Vision House; Warner; Wetherall (home & family life); Woodbridge; Woodsong; Wright; Zebra; Zondervan.

Juvenile. Abingdon; Alaska Nature; Alaska Northwest; Angel; Apple; Associated; Atheneum; Augsburg; Avon; Baker; Bantam; BC Studio; Better Way (how-to); Bookcraft; Don Bosco; Bradson; Branden; Broadman; Brunswick; William Collins; Concordia; Corinthian; Coward McCann; Crown; Delair; Dell; T.S. Denison; Dial; Dundurn; Dutton; Enslow; Faber & Faber; Farrar, Straus & Giroux; Guy Gannett; K.S. Giniger; Guernica; Harcourt, Brace Jovanovich, Children's; Hastings; Herald; Holiday; Holt, Rinehart & Winston; Houghton Mifflin, Children's; Houghton Mifflin; Hounslow; Incentive; Kalimat; Kav; Kids Can; Lancelot; Larkspur; Little House; Lodestar; Loiry; Lothrop, Lee & Shepard; Margaret K. McElderry; Macmillan; Macmillan of Canada; Julian Messner; Morrow Junior; Nimbus; Oak Tree; October; Overlook; P.P.I.; Panjandrum; Pantheon; Philomel; Pineapple; Clarkson N. Potter;

Prentice-Hall, Canada, Educational (juvenile); Rossel; Saybrook; Schocken; Scholastic; Scholastic-Tab; Harold Shaw; Sierra Club; Standard; Stemmer; Tribeca; Viking Penguin; Walker; Frederick Warne; Wetherall; Wingbow; Wingra Woods; Winston-Derek; Woodsong; Wright.

Labor and Management. Abbott, Langer (reference; Crain (textbook); Dartnell; Groupwork Today; International; Lake View; MIT (scholarly); Realtors National Marketing Institute (reference); RPM; University Associates.

Language and Literature. Allen & Unwin; Apple-Wood; Associated; Atlantis; Bantam; Beacon; Branden; George Braziller; Cambridge; Catholic University; College-Hill (reference); Collier Macmillan Canada (textbook); Columbia University (scholarly); Communication Skill Builders; Continuum; Creative Arts; Crossing; Dante; EMC; Gaslight; Hayden (textbook); D.C. Heath (textbook); Heinle & Heinle (textbook); High/Coo (reference); Horizon; Illuminati; Indiana University; Johns Hopkins (scholarly); Longman (textbook); Lorien; Louisiana State; McFarland (reference); Charles E. Merrill (textbook); MIT (scholarly); National (textbook); National Publishers of the Black Hills (textbook); New Readers; New York University; Oddo (juvenile); Ohio State (scholarly); Oregon State; Prentice-Hall Canada, Educational (juvenile); Princeton (scholarly); Prometheus; Purdue (scholarly); Random (textbook); Regents; Slavica; Southern Methodist (scholarly); Stanford; Taplinger; Texas Christian; Three Continents; Charles E. Tuttle; Underwood-Miller (reference); University of Alabama (scholarly); University of Arkansas (scholarly); University of Illinois; University of Nebraska (scholarly); University of Notre Dame (scholarly); University of Texas (scholarly); University Press of America (scholarly); University Press of Mississippi; Utah State University (scholarly); Vehicule; J. Weston Walch (textbook); Webster (textbook); Word Beat (how-to, self-help & reference).

Literary Criticism. Allen & Unwin; Borgo; Broadside; Dundurn; Ecco; Holmes & Meier; Howard University; McPherson; Northern Illinois; Persea; Prometheus; Rutgers; Shoe String; Slavica; Sherwood Sugden; Texas Christian; Three Continents; Twayne; Underwood-Miller; University of Alabama; University of Arkansas; University of Massachusetts; University of Missouri; University of North Carolina; University of Notre Dame; University of Oklahoma; University of Tennessee; University Press of Kentucky; University Presses of Florida; Vanguard; Wolf.

Marine Subjects. Charles River; Cornell Maritime (how-to & technical); Gray's; International Marine; Lancelot; Naval Institute (history); Seven Seas (reference).

Military. ABT; Arco; Beaufort; Essco; Leather Stocking; Nautical & Aviation (reference); Paladin; Presidio; Shoe String (scholarly); Stackpole; Westview (scholarly).

Money and Finances. Acropolis (how-to & reference); Addison-Wesley; Almar; Bale; Bankers (reference); Bantam; Benjamin; Better Homes & Gardens; Contemporary (how-to); Cordovan; Dow Jones-Irwin; Enterprise; Environmental Design (reference); Farnsworth; Institute for Business Planning (reference); International Self-Counsel (how-to); Lakewood (self-help) Linch; Longman Group USA; Marathon International (self-help); Medical Economics (reference); Pilot (reference); R&R Newkirk; Realtors National Marketing Institute (self-help); Vanguard (how-to).

Music and Dance. American Catholic; And; Atlantic Monthly; Avon; Bear; Marion Boyars; Branden; Brunswick; Bucknell (scholarly); Cambridge; William Collins; Columbia; Columbia University (scholarly); Communications; Concordia; Congdon & Weed; Consumers Reports (reference); Crescendo; Delta; Dodd, Mead; Dragon's Teeth (reference); Eastview; Paul S. Eriksson; Faber & Faber; Fairleigh Dickinson; Fiesta City (self-help & how-to); Front Row Experience; Guernica; Robert Hale; Harvard Common; Kids Can (juvenile); Robert E. Kreiger; Longman (textbook); Louisiana State; McFarland (reference); William Morrow; Mosaic; John Muir; Music Sales (how-to); National (textbook); Northeastern (reference); Ohio State (scholarly); Oxford (scholarly); Pagurian; Panjandrum; Pennsylvania State (scholarly); Prentice-Halle (juvenile); Prentice-Hall, General; Princeton (scholarly); Resource; Rosen (young adult); Ross; Scarecrow; Schirmer (reference & textbook); Simon & Schuster; Sterling; Stipes (textbook); Lyle Stuart; Transaction; Tree by the River (how-to); Twayne (scholarly); Universe; University of Alabama (scholarly); University of Illinois; University of Iowa; University of Missouri (scholarly); University of North Carolina (scholarly); University Press of America (scholarly); University Press of New England (scholarly); Vanguard; J. Weston Walch (textbook); Walker; Wayne State; Whitston (scholarly).

Nature and Environment. ABC-Clio (reference); Harry N. Abrams; Addison-Wesley; Alaska Nature; Alaska Northwest; Allegheny (textbook); Angel; Avant; Avon; Banyan; Binford & Mort; Biomedical (reference); Biworld (reference); John F. Blair; Marion Boyars; Brunswick;

California Institute of Public Affairs (reference); Capra; Carolina Biological Supply (textbook); Charles River; Chatham; Chronicle; Clarion (juvenile); Cobblesmith; William Collins; Columbia; Coward McCann; Crown; Darwin (reference); Dembner; Devin-Adair; Dial (history & young adult); Dillon (juvenile); Dustbooks; East Woods; Eastview; Environmental Design (reference); Paul S. Eriksson; Falcon; Fjord; Flora and Fauna; Guy Gannett; Garden Way; GMG; Gray's; Stephen Green/Lewis; Guernica; Robert Hale; Hammond; Hancock; Harper & Row; Harvard Common; Holmes & Meier; Holt, Rinehart & Winston; Hounslow; Hurtig; Ideal World; Island; Johns Hopkins (scholarly); Johnson; William Kaufmann; Kids Can (juvenile); Robert E. Kreiger; Lancelot; Lexikos; Little House; Lorien; Lowell; Nick Lyons; Mosaic; Mountain; Museum of New Mexico (scholarly); National Publishers of the Black Hills; Naturegraph; NC; Nimbus; Northland; Noyer Data (technical); Oddo (juvenile); Optimum; Oregon State; Outlooks; Outdoor Life; Overlook; Pagurian; Pennsylvania State (scholarly); Penwell (reference & technical); Peregrine Smith; Pineapple; Platt & Munk (juvenile); Clarkson N. Potter; Prentice-Hall, General; Purdue (scholarly); Regnery/Gateway; Review & Herald (juvenile); S.C.E.-Editions; Saybrook; Scribner's, Children's (juvenile); Sierra Club; Signpost; Stackpole; Stemmer; Stipes (textbook); Stone Wall (how-to); Stoneydale; Symmes; T.F.H. (how-to); Ten Speed; Tensleep; Texas A&M; Texas Monthly; Thorndike; Timber; T.L.; Troubador; Turnstone; Universe; University of Alberta; University of Massachusetts (scholarly); University of Michigan (scholarly); University of Nebraska (scholarly); University of Nevada (scholarly); University of New Mexico (scholarly); University of North Carolina (scholarly); University of Wisconsin (scholarly); University Press of Kentucky (scholarly); University Press of New England (scholarly); University Presses of Florida; Vanguard (juvenile); Walker; Western Producer Prairie; Western Tanager; Westview (scholarly); Wilderness; Wingra Woods; World Natural History (reference).

Philosophy. Acheron; Alba; Allen & Unwin; American Atheist; Aud; And/Or; Angel; Atlantic Monthly; Avant; Avon; Baker; BC Studio; Beacon; Bear; Berkley; Marion Boyars; George Braziller; Brunswick; Bucknell (scholarly); Aristide D. Caratzas; Catholic University (scholarly); Cedarshouse; Charles River; Christin; Cobblesmith; William Collins; Columbia (scholarly); Congdon & Weed; Continuum; Crown; Cumberland; Dante University; Daphnean; Dembner; Dharma; Dragon's Teeth; William B. Eerdmans; Enslow; Paul S. Eriksson; Faber & Faber; Fairleigh Dickinson; Farrar, Straus and Giroux; Franciscan Herald; Garber; Great Ocean; Grove; Guernica; Harper & Row; Hazelden (technical); Holt, Rinehart & Winston; Hounslow; Howard University (scholarly); Indiana University; Intercultural (reference); International; International University (textbook); Robert E. Kreiger; Larson; Lorien; Louisiana State; Mercer University (textbook & reference); Miller; Mimir; New York University (scholarly); Ohara; Ohio State (scholarly); Ohio University (scholarly); Open Court; Oregon State; Overlook; Panjandrum; Paradox (self-help); Paulist; Pennsylvania State (scholarly); Precedent (scholarly); Prometheus; Purdue (scholarly); Quartet; Regnery/Gateway; Rossel; Ross Erikson; Routledge & Kegan Paul (scholarly); S.C.E.-Editions; Saybrook; Sierra Club; Simon & Schuster; South End; Sovereign; Strawberry Hill; Sherwood Sugden; Teachers College; Theosophical; Thunder's Mouth; Transaction; University of Alabama (scholarly); University of Alberta; University of Iowa (scholarly); University of Massachusetts (scholarly); University of Michigan (scholarly); University of Notre Dame (scholarly); University of Oklahoma (scholarly); University of Pennsylvania (scholarly); University of Utah (scholarly); University Press of America (scholarly); University Press of Kansas (scholarly); University Press of Kentucky (scholarly); University Press of Mississippi; University Press of New England (scholarly); University Presses of Florida; Vanguard; Vesta; Wayne State; Winston-Derek; Woodsong; Zondervan (textbook).

Photography. Addison-Wesley; Alaska Nature; Amphoto (how-to & technical); Angel; Art Direction (how-to); Avon; Binford & Mort; Branden; Charles River; William Collins; Crown; Daphnean; Delta; Dharma; Dodd, Mead; Dragonsbreath; Duck Down; Eastview; Paul S. Eriksson; Faber & Faber; Falcon; Focal (how-to); Graphic Image; Guernica; H.P. Books; Robert Hale; Hancock; Harper & Row; Hastings; Holt, Rinehart & Winston; Hounslow; Howard University (scholarly); Hudson Hills; Krantz (reference); Lancaster Miller & Schnobrich; Le Beacon; Liberty; Lightbooks (how-to); Lowell; Madrona; Motorbooks International; Northland; October (technical); Optimum; Outbooks (how-to); Overlook; Oxmoor House; Clarkson N. Potter; Quartet; Rossel; Scribner's, Children's (juvenile); Sierra Club; Sterling; Tab; Taylor; Texas Monthly; University of Michigan (scholarly); University of Nebraska (scholarly); University of New Mexico (scholarly); University of Texas (scholarly); University Presses of Florida; Viking Penguin; Watson-Guptill (how-to); Western Producer Prairie; Winston; Writer's Digest (how-to & reference); Yankee.

Psychology. ABT; Accelerated Development (reference & textbook); ACS; Addison-Wesley; Alba; American (textbook); American Psychiatric; Angel; Anna (reference); Arbor; Atheneum; Augsburg; Avant; Avon; Baker; Basic; BC Studio; Beacon; Bear; Beaufort; Bobbs-Merrill; Marion Boyars; Bradson; Brunswick; Bucknell (scholarly); Cambridge (textbook); Celestial Arts; Charles River; Christian Classics; Citadel; Cobblesmith; William Collins; Congdon & Weed; Continuum; Coward McCann; Crown; Daphnean; Dembner; Detselig; Dharma;

Dimension; Edits (reference); Education Associates (textbook); William B. Eerdmans; Enslow; Paul S. Eriksson; Fairleigh Dickinson; Farrar, Straus and Giroux; Frederick Fell; Flare (young adult); Stephen Green/Lewis; Grove; Guernica; Harcourt Brace Jovanovich Legal & Professional (reference); Harper & Row; Harvard Common; Hawkes (self-help); Hazelden (technical); D.C. Heath (textbook); Herald; Holmes & Meier; Holt, Rinehart & Winston; Houghton Mifflin; Hounslow; Howard University (scholarly); Humanics; Intercultural (reference); International; International University (textbook); Jalmar; Johns Hopkins (scholarly); William Kaufmann; Robert E. Kreiger; Learning (reference); Libra; Longman (textbook); McFarland (reference); Madrona; Med-Psyche (how-to); Metamorphous; MIT (scholarly); National (textbook); Newcastle; Open Court; Overlook; Paradox (self-help); Pine Mountain; Pluribus (how-to); Poseidon; Precedent (scholarly); Prentice-Hall, General; Prometheus; Purdue University (scholarly); Quartet; R&E; Rainbow/Betty Wright; Regnery/Gateway; Riverdale (textbook); Rossel; Ross-Erikson; Routledge & Kegan Paul (scholarly); S.C.E.-Editions; Saybrook, Schenkman (textbook); Second Chance/Permanent; Social Science Education (reference); Stanford; Sterling; Jeremy P. Tarcher; Theosophical; Transaction; Turnstone; University of Massachusetts (scholarly); University of Michigan (scholarly); University of Nebraska (scholarly); University of North Carolina (scholarly); University of Pennsylvania (scholarly); University Press of America (scholarly); University Press of Kansas (scholarly); University Press of Mississippi; University Presses of Florida; Vision House; J. Weston Walch (textbook); Walker; Wayne State; Wilshire; Wingra Woods; Woodsong; Zebra; Zondervan (textbook).

Real Estate. Longman Group USA.

Recreation. Harry N. Abrams; Addison Wesley; Alaska Nature; Allegheny (textbook); American Council for the Arts (reference); Angel; Arbor; M. Arman (how-to, textbook & reference); Associated Booksellers (how-to); Avon; BC Studio; Beaufort; John F. Blair; Charles T. Branford; Celestial Arts; Charles River; Chicago Review (reference); Chronicle; William Collins; Columbia; Coward McCann; Crown; Darwin (reference); DBI; John De Graff (how-to); Delta; Dembner; Deneau; Dillon (juvenile); East Woods; Enslow; Paul S. Eriksson; Falcon; Frederick Fell; Front Row Experience; Guy Gannett; Globe Pequot; Stephen Green/Lewis; Guernica; H.P. Books; Robert Hale; Hammond; Hancock; Harvard Common; Hastings; Holt, Rinehart & Winston; Hounslow; Icarus; International Marine; Johnson; Jonathan David; William Kaufmann; Le Beacon; Leather Stocking; Liberty; Little House; Nick Lyons; McFarland (reference); Madrona; Menosha Ridge; Moon; Mountain; Mountaineers (how-to); Occupational Awareness; Oregon State; Outbooks; Outdoor Empire (textbook); Overlook; Panjandrum; Pantheon (reference); Peachtree; Prentice-Hall, General; Riverdale; Ross; S.C.E.-Editions; Scribner's, Children's (juvenile); Sierra Club; Signpost; Stackpole; Sterling; Stipes (textbook); Stone Wall (how-to); Stoneydale; Taylor; Ten Speed; Tensleep; Texas Monthly; Thorndike; T.L.; Touchstone; Tribeca; University of Michigan (scholarly); J. Weston Walch (textbook); Walker; Wanderer (juvenile); Westminster (juvenile); Wilderness; Williamson; Wilshire; Winchester (how-to); Woodbridge (how-to).

Reference. Allen & Unwin; American Psychiatric; Bear; Bethany; Binford & Mort; Borgo; R.R. Bowker; Bradson; Branden; Brunswick, Career; Cedarshouse; Charles River; Arthur F. Clark; William Collins; Compute!; Computer Skill Builders; Craftsman; Crown; Dante; Daphnean; Delair; Delta; Dembner; Detselig; Dundurn; William B. Eerdmans; Enslow; ETC; Fairleigh Dickinson; Flora and Fauna; Front Row Experience; Genealogical; K.S. Giniger; Great Ocean; Guernica; Gulf; Robert Hale; Hammond; Hancock; Harper & Row; Harvard Common; Hazelden; Holmes & Meier; Holt, Rinehart & Winston; Howard University (scholarly); Hurtig; Industrial; Infosource; International; International University; Jonathan David; Klein; Robert E. Kreiger; Le Beacon; Libraries Unlimited; Little House; Loiry; MCN; Metamorphous; Monitor; National; Thomas Nelson; Octameron; Oregon State; Ottenheimer; Overlook; Oxford (scholarly); Panjandrum; Pegasus; Petrocelli; Pineapple; Pocket Books; Poseidon; Prentice-Hall, General; Princeton; Que; R&E; Rainbow/Betty Wright; Rosen (young adult); Rossel; RPM; S.C.E.-Editions; St. Martin's; Scarecrow; Shoe String (scholarly); Slavica; Social Science Education; Standard; Sterling; Taylor; Techwrite; Tensleep; Texas Monthly; Transaction; Trend House; Underground Reports; Universe; University of Alberta; University of Illinois; University Press of New England (scholarly); University Press of the Pacific (scholarly); Vesta; Vision House; Warner; Western Producer Prairie; Windsor; Woodsong; Wordware.

Regional. Alaska Northwest; Apple-Wood; Banyan; Binford & Mort; Borealis; California Institute of Public Affairs (reference); Capra; Caxton; Chatham; Chronicle; Collier Macmillan Canada; Colorado Associated University; Copley; Cordovan; Corinthian; Cumberland; Donning; Doubleday Canada; Dundurn; East Woods; Family Album; Filter; Guy Gannett; Globe Pequot; Golden West; Graphic Arts Center; Gray's; Stephen Green/Lewis; Guernica; Gulf; Hancock; Heart of the Lakes; Heritage; Holmes & Meier; Hurtig; Indiana University; Johns Hopkins (scholarly); Johnson; Kent State; Lancelot; Lexikos; Louisiana State; Macmillan of

Canada; Moon; Mountain; Museum of New Mexico (scholarly); NC; New York University (scholarly); Nimbus; Northeastern; Northern Illinois (scholarly); Northland; Ohio University; Outbooks; Oxmoor House; Pennsylvania State; Peregrine Smith; Pineapple; Prentice-Hall Canada, Trade; Preservation; Presidio; Pruett; Quartet; St. Luke's; Southern Methodist; Stoneydale; Sunstone; Syracuse University; Taylor; Temple (scholarly); Tensleep; Texas A&M; Texas Christian; Texas Monthly; Texas Western (scholarly); Thorndike; Timber; Thompson & Rutter; Charles E. Tuttle; University of Arizona (scholarly); University of Arkansas; University of Illinois; University of Nevada; University of New Mexico; University of Tennessee (scholarly); University of Texas (scholarly); University of Wisconsin (scholarly); University Press of Kansas (scholarly); University Press of Mississippi; University Press of New England (scholarly); Utah State (scholarly); Westernlore (scholarly); Wingbow; Yankee.

Religion. ABC-Clio; Abingdon; Accent; Acheron; Aglow; Alba; American (textbook); American Atheist; American Catholic; Angel; Augsburg; Avon; Baker (textbook); Bantam; Beacon; Beacon Hill; Bear; Bethany; Bookcraft; Don Bosco (textbook); Bridge; Broadman; Brunswick; Bucknell University (scholarly); Byls; Aristide D. Caratzas; Catholic Truth Society; Catholic University (scholarly); Charles River; Chosen; Christian Classics; Christin; William Collins; Concordia; Cook (juvenile); Crossway; Daphnean; Dharma; Dimension; Donning; William B. Eerdmans; Fleet; Fortress; Franciscan Herald; K.S. Giniger; Great Ocean; Guernica; Robert Hale; Hendrickson; Here's Life; Holmes & Meier; Holt, Rinehart & Winston; Hounslow; Howard University (scholarly); Huntington House; International University (textbook); Judson; Kalimat; Kar-Ben; John Knox; Robert E. Kreiger; Lancelot; Landmark; Larksdale; Larkspur; Larson; Liguori; Little House; McFarland (reference); Mercer University (reference); Meriwether (juvenile); Morehouse-Barlow; William Morrow; Mott Media; Thomas Nelson; New Leaf; Newcastle; Open Court; Orbis; Our Sunday Visitor; Overlook; Paradox (how-to & self-help); Paulist (textbook); Peachtree; Pennsylvania State (scholarly); Precedent (scholarly); Prentice-Hall, General; Princeton University (scholarly); Prometheus; Regal; Regnery/Gateway; Resource; Fleming H. Revell; Review & Herald (juvenile); Ross; Rossel; Ross-Erikson; Routledge & Kegan Paul (reference); St. Anthony Messenger; Saybrook; Second Chance/Permanent; Servant; Harold Shaw; Sovereign; Standard (textbook); Sherwood Sugden; Theosophical; Twenty-Third; Tyndale; University of Alabama (scholarly); University of Michigan (scholarly); University of North Carolina (scholarly); University of Notre Dame (scholarly); University Press of America (scholarly); University Press of New England (scholarly); University Presses of Florida; Vesta; Victor; Vision; Warner; Wayne State; Whitaker (biography); Winston; Winston-Derek; Zondervan (textbook & reference).

Scholarly. Cambridge; Colorado Associated University; Columbia University; Dante University; Daphnean; Indiana University; Interurban/Trans Anglo; Jossey-Bass; Kalimat; Knopf; Louisiana State; McFarland; Northeastern; Open Court; R&E; St. Martin's; Saybrook; Social Science Education Consortium; Texas Christian University; Twayne; University of Alberta; University of Illinois; University of Pittsburgh; University Presses of Florida; Wayne State; Western Tanager.

Science and Technology. Harry N. Abrams; Academic (scholarly); Addison-Wesley; Allen & Unwin; Almar; American (textbook); American Aeronautical Society; And/Or; Arco; Artech; Atlantic Monthly; Avon; Ballinger (reference); Bantam; Bear; Biomedical (textbook & technical); Balcksburg; Cambridge (textbook); Carolina Biological Supply (textbook); Childrens (juvenile); Coles; Collier Macmillan Canada (textbook); Columbia University (scholarly); Computer Science (technical); Cook (juvenile); Coward McCann; Crown; Steve Davis (reference); Delmar (textbook); Delta; Dembner; Digital; Dillon (juvenile); Dodd, Mead; Enslow; Farrar, Straus & Giroux; Warren H. Green; Gulf; Harper & Row Junior Books (juvenile); Harper & Row; Hayden (reference); D.C. Heath (textbook); Holmes & Meier; Horizon; Howard University (scholarly); Industrial; Iowa State (textbook); Johnson; William Kaufmann; Knowledge Industry; Krantz (reference); Robert E. Kreiger; Little Brown; McGraw-Hill (reference); McGraw-Hill, Professional & Reference (reference); Charles E. Merrill (textbook); MIT (scholarly); National (textbook); New Readers; Noyes Data (technical); Oddo (juvenile); Open Court; Oregon State; Parker (how-to); Pennsylvania State (scholarly); Platt & Munk (juvenile); Plenum; Prentice-Hall (juvenile); Prentice-Hall, General; Prometheus; Purdue (scholarly); Rainbow/Betty Wright; Regnery/Gateway; Resource (how-to); Reston (textbook); Ross (how-to); St. Martin's Press; Scribner's; Scribner's, Children's (juvenile); Sierra Club; Simon & Schuster; Sun; Tab; Texas Instruments (textbook); Transaction; Univelt; Universe; University of Arizona (scholarly); University of California (scholarly); University of Iowa (scholarly); University of Michigan (scholarly); University of Pennsylvania (scholarly); University of Texas (scholarly); University Press of New England (scholarly); University Press of the Pacific (scholarly); Utah State (scholarly); J. Weston Walch (textbook); Walker; Webster (textbook); John Wiley (reference); Wordware.

Self-Help. ACS; Addison-Wesley; Aglow; Alaska Nature; Allen; American Psychiatric; And; Angel; Apple; Arbor; James Arnold; ASI; Associated; Associated Booksellers; Atlantis;

Augsburg; Avon; Baker; BC Studio; Beacon; Benjamin; Bethany; Betterway; Bibli O' Phile; Bobbs-Merrill; Bradson; Charles T. Branford; Bridge; Brunswick; Carolina Biological Supply; Celestial Arts; Charles River; Chicago Review; Christin; Cliffs Notes (textbook); Cobblesmith; William Collins; Commoners'; Consumer Reports; Contemporary; Continuum; Corinthian; Coward McCann; Crown; Delair; Delta; Dembner; Dharma; Enslow; Paul S. Eriksson; Examino; Faber & Faber; Falcon; Frederick Fell; Flare (young adult); Forman; Fortress; Guy Gannett; K.S. Giniger; Great Ocean; Stephen Green/Lewis (how-to); Grove; Gulf; H.P. Books; Hancock; Harcourt Brace Jovanovich Legal & Professional; Harper & Row; Hazelden; Here's Life; Holt, Rinehart & Winston; Houghton Mifflin; Huntington House; Jalmar; Jonathan David; Kav; Klein; Larkspur; Larson; Learning; Liguori; Little House; Live Oak; Loiry; Lone Star; Madrona; Med-Psych; Metamorphous; John Muir; New Leaf; Newcastle; Octameron; Ohara; Ohio State (scholarly); Optimum; Outdoor Empire; P.P.I.; Paladin; Panjandrum; Parker; Paulist; Pegasus; Pelican; Judy Piatkus; Pluribus; Poseidon; Clarkson N. Potter; Prentice-Hall, General; Price/Stern/Sloan; R&E; Rainbow/Betty Wright; Rosen (young adult); St. Martin's; Second Chance/Permanent; Harold Shaw; Sterling; Stoeger; Strawberry Hill; Sun; Ten Speed; Tensleep; Texas Instruments; Thorsons; Times; Underground Reports; Vision; Walker; Warner; Westminster (juvenile); Wetherall; Whitaker (religion); Williamson; Wilshire; Wingra Woods; Woodsong; Wordware; Wright; Yankee; Zebra; Zondervan.

Social Sciences. ABT; Academic (scholarly); Avant; Ballinger; Catholic University (scholarly); Columbia University; Continuum; Delta; Duquesne (scholarly); Edits (reference); Evans; Free Press (textbook & reference); Garland (reference); GMG; Stephen Green/Lewis; Groupwork Today; Harper & Row Junior Books (juvenile); Heath (reference); Holmes & Meier; Indiana University; Iowa State (textbook); Lewis; McGraw-Hill (reference); Nelson-Hall (textbook & scholarly); Oak Tree; Oddo (juvenile); Ohio University (scholarly); Plenum; Porter Sargent; Prentice-Hall (juvenile); Random House (textbook); Riverdale (textbook); Routledge & Kegan Paul (scholarly); Southern Illinois; Transaction (scholarly); Turnstone; Twayne; University of Arkansas (scholarly); University of Missouri (scholarly); University of Texas (scholarly); J. Weston Walch (textbook); Webster (textbook); Westminster (juvenile); Westview (scholarly); Whitston (scholarly); John Wiley (reference).

Sociology. Addison-Wesley; Alba; American Council for the Arts (reference); American Psychiatric; And; Angel; Apple-Wood; Associated; Avon; Basic; Beacon; Bear; Marion Boyars; Bradson; Branden; Brunswick; Bucknell (scholarly); Charles River; Cobblesmith; William Collins; Communications; Continuum; Coward McCann; Daphnean; Detselig; William B. Eerdmans; Enslow; Paul S. Eriksson; Faber & Faber; Fairleigh Dickinson; Farrar, Straus & Giroux; Harper & Row; Harvard Common; Hazelden (technical); Herald; Holmes & Meier; Holt, Rinehart & Winston; Howard University (scholarly); Humanics; Institute for the Study of Human Issues; Intercultural (reference); International; International University (textbook); Robert E. Kreiger; Learning (reference); Longman (textbook); McFarland (reference); Meriwether (juvenile); Metamorphous; Mimir; Ohio State (scholarly); Overlook; Paradox (self-help); Pennsylvania State (scholarly); Poseidon; Prentice-Hall (juvenile); Princeton (scholarly); Prometheus; Purdue (scholarly); Quartet; R&E; Rainbow/Betty Wright; Regnery/Gateway; Riverdale (textbook); Rossel; Rutgers (scholarly); S.C.E.-Editions; Saybrook; Schenkman (textbook); Schocken (scholarly); Scholarly Resources (scholarly); Social Science Education Consortium (reference); Jeremy P. Tarcher; Teachers College; Thunder's Mouth; Transaction; Charles E. Tuttle; University of Alberta; University of Illinois; University of Massachusetts (scholarly); University of Michigan (scholarly); University of North Carolina (scholarly); University of Notre Dame (scholarly); University Press of Mississippi; University Press of New England (scholarly); University Presses of Florida; Vehicule; J. Weston Walch (textbook); Wayne State; Wingbow (reference); Zondervan (textbook).

Sports. Addison-Wesley; Almar; American (textbook); Anna (reference); Arbor; M. Arman (how-to, reference & textbook); Associated Booksellers; Atheneum; Athletic; Avon; A.S. Barnes; Benjamin; Binford & Mort; Bobbs-Merrill; Don Bosco; Bradson; Briarcliff; Champion Athlete (textbook); Charles River; William Collins; Contemporary (how-to); Cook (juvenile); Coward McCann; Crown; DBI; Delta; Devin-Adair; Dodd, Mead; Enslow; Paul S. Eriksson; ETC; Falcon; Frederich Fell; Fleet; K.S. Giniger; Green Hill; Stephen Green/Lewis; Grove; Robert Hale; Hammond; Hancock; Harper & Row; Harper & Row Junior Books (juvenile); Harvard Common; Hastings; Holt, Rinehart & Winston; Howard University (scholarly); Icarus; International University (textbook); Interstate (textbook); Johnson; Jonathan David; William Kaufmann; Robert E. Kreiger; Lancelot; Laranmark; Larkspur; Lexikos; Liberty; Little, Brown; Little House; Lone Star; Nick Lyons; McFarland (reference); Menasha Ridge; Mosaic; Motorbooks International; Mountain (how-to); Mountaineers (how-to); Ohio State (scholarly); Optimum; Outbooks; Outdoor Empire (textbook); Outdoor Life; Overlook; Pineapple; Pluribus; Prentice-Hall (juvenile); Prentice-Hall, General; S.C.E.-Editions; Scribner's, Children's (juvenile); Sierra Club; Sterling; Stoeger; Stone Wall (how-to); Jeremy P. Tarcher; Taylor; Ten Speed; Texas Monthly; Times; Touchstone; Tribeca; Ultralight; University of Illinois; University of Nebraska (scholarly); University of Tennesse (scholarly); J. Weston Walch (textbook); Walker; Western; Wilshire; Winchester; Wright.

Technical. Allen & Unwin; Almar; American Psychiatric; Artech; Ashton-Tate; BC Studio; Bradson; Branden; Brevet; Brunswick; Carolina Biological Supply; Chilton; Compute!; Computer Skill Builders; Corinthian; Craftsman; Enslow; Environmental Design & Research Center; Essco; ETC; Faber & Faber; Flora and Fauna; Great Ocean; H.P. Books; D.C. Heath (reference); Industrial; Infosource; Iowa State (textbook); Robert E. Kreiger; Le Beacon; Lorien; Metamorphous; Mountain; National Publisher of the Black Hills; Oregon State; Osborn/McGraw Hill; Petrocelli; Plenum; Que; R&R Newkirk; Riverdale; RPM; Schenkman; Taylor; Techwrite; Texas Instruments; T.L.; Univelt; University of Alberta; University of Michigan (scholarly); University Press of New England (scholarly); University Press of the Pacific (scholarly); Westin Communications; Wright.

Textbook. Abingdon; Acheron; Alba; Allen & Unwin; American Psychiatric; Atlantis; Augsburg; BC Studio; Branden; William C. Brown; Career; Computer Skill Builders; Detselig; Digital; William B. Eerdmans; EMC; Essco; ETC; Flora and Fauna; Ginn; Graphic Image; Gregg; Guernica; Holmes & Meier; International; Interstate; Jamestown; William Kaufmann; Robert E. Kreiger; Libraries Unlimited; Loiry; Lone Star; McGraw-Hill; Charles E. Merrill; Metamorphous; Mimir; Mott Media; Mountain; National; Occupational Awareness; Petrocelli; Potentials Development for Health & Development; Prentice-Hall Canada, College Div.; Prometheus; Pruett; Que; R&E; Regents; Rosen (young adult); Silver Burdett; Slavica; Taylor; Techwrite; Trend House; University of Alberta; University of Michigan; University Press of New England (scholarly); University Press of the Pacific (scholarly); Warner; John Wiley; Wordware; Wright.

Transportation. American Aeronautical Society; Aviation (technical); Aztex (how-to); Darwin (reference); John De Graff (how-to); Golden West Books; H.P. Books; International Marine; Kalmbach (reference); MIT (scholarly); Motorbooks International; John Muir (how-to); Nautical & Aviation; Outdoor Empire; Pruett; Ross; Tab; Ultralight.

Travel. Academy Chicago; Alaska Northwest; Allegheny (reference); Almar; American Council for the Arts (reference); And/Or; M. Arman (how-to, textbook & reference); BC Studio; Briarcliff; Brunswick; Camaro; Cedarshouse; China; Cobblesmith; William Collins; Congdon & Weed; Corinthian; Darwin (reference); Delair; Deneau; Devin-Adair; Dodd, Mead; East Woods; William B. Eerdmans; Paul S. Eriksson; Faber & Faber; Falcon; Fjord; Fodor's Travel Guide; Guy Gannett; K.S. Giniger; Globe Pequot; Golden West; Graphic Image; Robert Hale; Hammond; Hancock; Harper & Row; Harvard Common; Hastings; Holt, Rinehart & Winston; Hounslow; Icarus; Intercultural (reference); Interurban/Trans Anglo; Lancelot; Le Beacon; Lexikos; Liberty; Little House; Lowell; Madrona; Menasha Ridge; Moon; Mosaic; John Muir; National Publisher of the Black Hills; New York Zoetrope; Nimbus; 101 Productions; Optimum; Outbooks; Overlook; Pelican; Pilot (reference); Pineapple; Prentice-Hall Canada, Trade; Prentice-Hall, General; Regnery/Gateway; Riverdale; Rossel; S.C.E.-Editions; Sierra Club; Slavica; Stoneydale; Ten Speed; Tensleep; Texas Monthly; T.L.; Touchstone; Tree by the River; Trend House; Tribeca; University of Michigan; Walker; Western; Wingra Woods; Winston-Derek; Yankee.

Women's Studies/Feminism. ABC-Clio (reference); And; Bantam; Beacon; Contemporary; Crossing; Delair; Feminist; Holmes & Meier; Indiana University; International; Lake View; Northeastern (reference); Pantheon; Pennsylvania State (scholarly); Rutgers University (scholarly); Saybrook; Scarecrow; South End; Thorsons; Thunder's Mouth; Twayne (scholarly).

World Affairs. ABC-Clio (reference); ABT; And; Atlantic Monthly; Avant; Ballinger (reference); Beacon; California Institute of Public Affairs (reference); China; Family Album; Intercultural (how-to); Lake View; Manyland; NC; Open Court; Orbis; Pantheon; Prentice-Hall Canada, Trade; Regnery/Gateway; Routledge & Kegan Paul (scholarly); Southern Illinois; Stanford; Strawberry Hill; University of Notre Dame (scholarly); University of Utah (scholarly); Westview (scholarly).

Young Adult. Arco; Dell; Dial; Graphic Image; Harper & Row Junior Books; Holiday; Larkspur; Lodestar; Second Chance/Permanent (juvenile); Tempo; Frederick Warne.

Fiction

Use this subject index to identify book publishers devoted completely to fiction or publishing fiction in addition to their nonfiction lines. Notice parenthetical phrases (following publishers' names) that offer more information about the kind of fiction manuscripts (juvenile, young adult, etc.) accepted.

As with the nonfiction markets, read the complete editorial listing. In addition to telling you exactly what they like to see in fiction manuscripts, editors often include tips and advice for writers interested in submitting material to them. For a comprehensive list of fiction publishers, consult *Fiction Writer's Market* (Writer's Digest Books).

Adventure. Acheron; Alaska Nature; Angel; Arbor; M. Arman; Avon; Baker (juvenile); Berkley; Bookcraft; Bradbury (young adult); Branden; Brunswick; Camelot; Carroll & Graf; Charter; Clarion (juvenile); William Collins; Coward McCann; Dell; Dembner; Dial (young adult & juvenile); Dragonsbreath; Farrar, Straus & Giroux (young adult & juvenile); Flare (young adult); Robert Hale; Harper & Row Junior Books (juvenile); Harper & Row; Herald (juvenile); Hounslow; Kalimat; Kar-Ben (juvenile); Kids Can (juvenile & young adult); Laranmark; Le Beacon; Little House; Living Poets; Lodestar (juvenile); Lothrop, Lee & Shepard (juvenile); Miller; Mountaineers; New Readers; Overlook; Peregrine Smith (young adult); Judy Piatkus; Pineapple; Pinnacle; Printemps (young adult); Quality; Quartet; Rainbow/Betty Wright; Rossel (juvenile); Russica; Scribner's, Children's (juvenile); Second Chance/Permanent; Seven Seas; Sierra Club; Stemmer House; Texas Monthly; Vanguard; Wanderer; Westminster (juvenile); Wingbow; Woodsong Graphics; Wright; Zebra.

Confession. Acheron; Angel; William Collins; Kalimat; Little House; Overlook; Scholastic-Tab (juvenile); Second Chance/Permanent; Wingbow; Wright; Zebra.

Erotica. Angel; James Arnold; Arrow; Brunswick; Carroll & Graf; Dragonsbreath; Graphic Image; Greenleaf Classics; Guernica; Le Beacon; Living Poets; Overlook; Quality; Quartet; Russica; Second Chance/Permanent; Thunder's Mouth; Wingbow; Wright; Zebra.

Ethnic. Bilingual Educational Services (juvenile); Borealis; Marion Boyars; Branden; Brunswick; William Collins; Faber & Faber; Flare (young adult); Guernica; Le Beacon; Little House; Overlook; Printemps (young adult); Rainbow/Betty Wright; Rossel (juvenile); Russica; Second Chance/Permanent; Stemmer House; Texas Monthly; Thunder's Mouth; University of Illinois; Winston-Derek; Wright.

Experimental. Acheron; Avant; Marion Boyars; William Collins; Dragonsbreath; Ecco; Faber & Faber; Flare (young adult); Howard University; Le Beacon; Living Poets; Overlook; Panjandrum; Persea; Pineapple; Second Chance/Permanent; Techwrite; Thunder's Mouth; University of Illinois; Vanguard; Woodsong Graphics.

Fantasy. Ace Science Fiction; Angel; Arbor; Arrow; Avon; Ballantine; Camelot; Carroll & Graf; Clarion (juvenile); William Collins; Daw; Dial (young adult & juvenile); Dragonsbreath; Farrar, Straus & Giroux (juvenile); Flare (young adult); Graphic Image; Harper & Row Junior Books (juvenile); Harper & Row; International University; Kar-Ben (juvenile); Larson; Little House; Lodestar (juvenile); Lothrop, Lee & Shepard (juvenile); Overlook; Panjandrum; Polaris; Printemps (young adult); Scholastic-Tab (juvenile); Scribner's, Children's (juvenile); Second Chance/Permanent; Tor; Wingbow; Woodsong Graphics; Wright.

Feminist. Crossing; Quartet; South End.

Gay/Lesbian. Alyson; JH; Lace; Naiad.

Gothic. Acheron; Avalon; Avon; Bethany; Thomas Bouregy; Charter; William Collins; Robert Hale; Harper & Row; International University; Little House; Panjandrum; Prentice-Hall (juvenile); Scholastic (young adult); Second Chance/Permanent; Woodsong Graphics; Zebra.

Historical. Acheron; Alaska Nature; Arrow; Avon; Ballantine; Berkley; Branden (ethnic & religious); Brunswick; William Collins; Daphnean; Dell; Dembner; Denlinger's; Dial (young adult & juvenile); Dundurn; Faber & Faber; Farrar, Straus & Giroux (juvenile); Guernica; Robert Hale; Harper & Row; Herald; Houghton Mifflin; Huntington House; Independent; International University; Kalimat; Kar-Ben (juvenile); Kids Can (juvenile & young adult); Laranmark; Le Beacon; Little House; Lothrop, Lee & Shepard (juvenile); Miller; Overlook; Peachtree; Persea; Judy Piatkus; Pineapple; Pinnacle; Poseidon; Rainbow/Betty Wright; Rossel (juvenile); Scribner's, Children's (juvenile); Second Chance/Permanent; Sierra Club; Sovereign; Stemmer House; Texas Monthly; Thunder's Mouth; Vehicule; Wingbow; Woodsong Graphics; Zebra.

Horror. Arrow; William Collins; Dragonsbreath; International University; Laranmark; Le Beacon; Little House; Lodestar (young adult); Russica; Second Chance/Permanent; Seven Seas; Tor; Wright; Zebra.

Humor. Angel; Bradbury (young adult); Bradson; Brunswick; Camelot; Carolrhoda (juvenile); Carroll & Graf; Clarian (juvenile); William Collins; David C. Cook (juvenile); Dial (young adult & juvenile); Dragonsbreath; Farrar, Straus & Giroux (juvenile); Flare (young adult); Hounslow; International University; Kalimat; Kids Can (juvenile & young adult); Laranmark; Le Beacon; Little House; Lothrop, Lee & Shepard (juvenile); Miller; Mountaineers; Parents Magazine (juvenile); Peachtree; Peregrine Smith (young adult); Pineapple; Prentice-Hall (juvenile); Pressworks; Printemps (young adult); Rainbow/Betty Wright; Russica; Scholastic-Tab (juvenile); Scribner's, Children's (juvenile); Second Chance/Permanent; Thorndike; Thunder's Mouth; Vanguard; Wanderer; Westminster (juvenile); Woodsong Graphics; Wright; Zebra.

Juvenile. Abingdon; Andersen; Bantam; John F. Blair; Bradbury; Crossway; Dial; Dutton; Feminist; Graphic Image; Harcourt Brace Jovanovich, Children's; Holiday House; Houghton Mifflin; Ideals; Kids Can; Larkspur; Margaret K. McElderry; Macmillan; Oak Tree; Philomel; Pineapple; Platt & Munk; Printemps; Victor; Frederick Warne.

Literary. Columbia; Creative Arts; Deneau; Doubleday Canada; Ecco; Great Ocean; Harper & Row; Knopf; Little, Brown; Poseidon; Puckerbrush; Stemmer House; Taplinger; Thistledown; Thunder's Mouth.

Mainstream. Acheron; Angel; Avon; Bahamas International; Berkley; John F. Blair; Branden; George Braziller; Brunswick; Camelot; Carroll & Graf; Charter; Christin; William Collins; Coward McCann; Crossway; Dell; Delta; Dembner; Dillon (juvenile); Doubleday Canada; Ecco; Evans; Faber & Faber; Farrar, Straus & Giroux (juvenile); Fjord; Flare (young adult); Forman; Grove; Robert Hale; Harper & Row; Harper & Row Junior Books (juvenile); Houghton Mifflin; Hounslow; Howard University; Icarus; International University; Kav; Little, Brown; Little House; Morrow; Norton; Overlook; Peachtree; Pelican; Persea; Judy Piatkus; Pineapple; Poseidon; Prentice-Hall (juvenile); Quality; Quartet; Rainbow/Betty Wright; Random House; Scholastic-Tab (juvenile); Scribner's; Scribner's, Children's (juvenile); Second Chance/Permanent; Sierra Club; Simon & Schuster; The Smith; Stein & Day; Stemmer House; Texas Monthly; University of Arkansas; University of Illinois; Vehicule; Viking Penguin; Wingbow; Woodsong Graphics; Wright; Zebra.

Military. Bantam; Dell; Nautical & Aviation.

Mystery. Academy Chicago; Acheron; Arrow; Avalon; Avon; Camelot; Carolrhoda (juvenile); Carroll & Graf; Charter; Clarion (juvenile); William Collins; Coward McCann; Dembner; Dial (young adult & juvenile); Dillon (juvenile); Dodd, Mead; Doubleday; Dragonsbreath; Faber & Faber; Farrar, Straus & Giroux (young adult); Flare (young adult); Guernica; Robert Hale; Harper & Row; Houghton Mifflin; Huntington House; International University; Kav; Kids Can (juvenile & young adult); Laranmark; Le Beacon; Little House; Lodestar (young adult); Lothrop, Lee & Shepard (juvenile); Miller; New Readers; Overlook; Pantheon; Pocket Books; Prentice-Hall (juvenile); Printemps (young adult); Rainbow/Betty Wright; Rossel (juvenile); Russica; Scholastic-Tab (juvenile); Scribner's, Children's (juvenile); Second Chance/Permanent; Seven Seas; SOS; Texas Monthly; Thorndike; Vanguard; Vehicule; Walker; Wanderer; Westminster (juvenile); Wingbow; Woodsong Graphics; Wright.

Nostalgia. Dell; Thorndike; Tor.

Occult. Berkley.

Picture Books. Childrens (juvenile); Concordia; Dial (young adult & juvenile); Dutton; Harper & Row Junior Books; Parents Magazine (juvenile); Platt & Munk; Prentice-Hall (juvenile); Frederick Warne (juvenile).

Plays. Commoners'; JH; Living Poets.

Poetry. Ahsahta; Avon; Branden; Broadside; Brunswick; Cedarshouse; Commoners'; Dragon's Teeth; Dragonsbreath; Duck Down; Ecco; Golden Quill; Graphic Image; Guernica; High/Coo; Houghton Mifflin; Illuminati; Independent; International University; Ithaca; Le Beacon; Living Poets; Marathon International; William Morrow; Northeastern; Overlook; Panjandrum; Persea; Princeton; Puckerbrush; Quality; Random House; Resource; St. Luke's; Harold Shaw; Sunstone; Thistledown; Three Continents; University of Arkansas; University of Missouri; Vanguard; Vehicule; Vesta; Wesleyan; Wingbow; Winston-Derek; Woodsong Graphics.

Regional. Commoners'; Doubleday Canada; Dundurn; Faber & Faber; Garber; Island; Peachtree; St. Luke's; Sunstone; Thistledown; Thorndike.

Religious. Acheron; Aglow; Angel; Avon; Baker (juvenile); Bookcraft; Don Bosco; Branden; Bridge; Broadman; Byls (juvenile); William Collins; Concordia; David C. Cook (juvenile); Herald; Huntington House; Kalimat; Kar-Ben (juvenile); Larson; Little House; Mott Media; Rainbow/Betty Wright; Resource; Fleming H. Revell; Rossel (juvenile); Second Chance/Permanent; Standard; Tyndale House; Victor; Warner (humor, mystery, adventure & historical); Winston-Derek; Zondervan.

Romance. Acheron; Alaska Nature; Arbor; Arrow; Avalon; Avon; Ballantine; Berkley; Bethany (young adult); Thomas Bouregy; Branden; Brunswick; Charter; William Collins; David C. Cook (young adult); Coward McCann; Dell; Dial (young adult & juvenile); Dodd, Mead; Farrar, Straus & Giroux (young adult); Flare (young adult); Graphic Image; Robert Hale; Harlequin; Harper & Row; Holloway House; Huntington House (Christian); International University; Kalimat; Kids Can (young adult); Larkspur (religious); Little House; New Readers; Judy Piatkus; Pinnacle; Pocket Books; Rainbow/Betty Wright; Rossel (juvenile); Scholastic (young adult); Scholastic-Tab (young adult); Second Chance at Love; Second Chance/Permanent; Seven Seas; Silhouette (young adult); SOS; To Have and To Hold (mainstream); Walker; Woodsong Graphics; Wright; Zebra.

Science Fiction. Ace Science Fiction; Acheron; Alaska Nature; Avon; Ballantine; Bantam; Berkley; Camelot; Carolrhoda (juvenile); Charter; William Collins; Crossway; Daw; Dillon (juvenile); Donning; Doubleday; Dragonsbreath; Farrar, Straus & Giroux (young adult); Flare (young adult); Guernica; Harper & Row Junior Books (juvenile); Harper & Row; Houghton Mifflin; International University; Kids Can (juvenile & young adult); Larson; Le Beacon; Lodestar (young adult); Lothrop, Lee & Shepard (juvenile); Overlook; Pinnacle; Pocket Books; Polaris; Rainbow/Betty Wright; Rossel (juvenile); Scholastic-Tab (juvenile); Scribner's, Children's (juvenile); Second Chance/Permanent; Sierra Club; Thunder's Mouth; Tor; Wanderer; Westminster (juvenile); Wingbow; Woodsong Graphics; Wright.

Spiritual. Larson.

Sports. Bantam; Cook (juvenile); Peregrine Smith (young adult).

Suspense. Arbor; Arrow; Avon; Berkley; Marion Boyars; Camelot; Carroll & Graf; Charter; Clarion (juvenile); William Collins; Coward McCann; Dell; Dembner; Dial (young adult & juvenile); Farrar, Straus & Giroux (young adult); Fjord; Flare (young adult); Guernica; Robert Hale; Harper & Row; Houghton Mifflin; International University; Kalimat; Le Beacon; Little House; Lodestar (young adult); Lothrop, Lee & Shepard; Overlook; Printemps (young adult); Rainbow/Betty Wright; Russica; Scholastic-Tab (juvenile); Scribner's, Children's (juvenile); Second Chance/Permanent; Seven Seas; SOS; Texas Monthly; Vanguard; Walker; Westminster (juvenile); Wingbow; Winston-Derek; Woodsong Graphics; Wright; Zebra.

Western. Avalon; Avon; Bantam; Berkley; Thomas Bouregy; Charter; William Collins; Farrar, Straus & Giroux (young adult); Robert Hale; Harper & Row; International University; Laranmark; Little House; Lodestar (young adult); Miller; Pinnacle; Pocket Books; Quality; Rainbow/Betty Wright; Texas Monthly; Walker; Woodsong Graphics.

Young Adult. Bantam; Berkley; Branden (mainstream); Crossway; Dial; Harper & Row Junior Books (juvenile); Holiday House; Kids Can; Margaret K. McElderry; Morrow Junior; Philomel; Pitman Learning; Tempo; Frederick Warne.

Consumer Publications

"The two most engaging powers of an author
are to make new things *familiar* and *familiar*
things new."
—Dr. S. Johnson

As a writer you witness new and familiar things every day—break dancing, sunsets, people laughing or in tears. You write and send your work to editors.

But since all writers see these things, you must *capture* them in a new way.

Editors expect these powers of you: originality, knowledge, vitality, a command of language. But, without originality, new and familiar things have no power—your manuscript becomes just a page of often-said words.

"Freelance writers who can go beyond the ordinary in their ideas and in their writing won't have trouble marketing their work," says one editor, who used to freelance.

Create atmospheres that readers will want to loiter in, and they won't set your work aside. Neither will editors. Editors want to amuse, inform, and inspire readers. That's why they read hundreds of manuscripts they will never buy, looking for that one manuscript that *is* right. That's why they've agreed to be listed in this book. Don't disappoint them.

Based on what editors have told us, we've compiled a list of industry trends that affect what editors buy for their publications.

● emphasis on "people" stories. Celebrity interviews in print and on TV are clues to what people are interested in. Editors of large and small magazines want people-oriented stories; the *people* can be celebrities or your next-door neighbors. "Our readers like to know about people—their neighbors—and what they're doing that's interesting and worthwhile (not necessarily unusual)," says *BitterSweet* editor-in-chief Harry Bee.

● documentation. Because editors don't use footnotes in their magazines does not mean they are not interested in a writer's sources. Some editors want documentation of sources for their files; all editors want accurate information.

● specialty magazines. Fans in each field turn to (and sometimes start) specialty magazines. Some editors know more about the subject of their magazine than about the publishing world; most editors are pros in both areas. New computer magazines arrive at our offices each week, though editors predict that only the best will survive—once the market reaches a plateau. Health magazines are still strong as are lifestyle and romance publications. Sprinting into this year's spotlight are magazines geared to the tri-athlete and persons seeking super-human strengths. Regional entertainment guides need writers who live minutes from the subjects they cover. Check hotel and restaurant lobbies for these free handouts (some not listed in *WM*); they could lead to a writing assignment.

● an eye for graphics. More editors than ever are viewing stories and photos as a total package to lure the reader. The popular "look" of *USA Today* and design changes in other newspapers and magazines are prompting "word-type" editors to see the graphics side of a story. In some cases, editors will reject a good story with poor pictures. "Photos are essential," say some editors. "Learn to use a camera well."

● shorter articles. Articles short in length—but stuffed with details—have a greater chance of acceptance. Today's readers have more diversions and less time to read. "The secret of successful writing is to leave out each and every word that does not belong in the particular story you're working on," *Yankee* editor-in-chief

Judson Hale tells writers. ". . . You also have all the words you didn't use available for future stories."

Being a professional writer means studying magazine racks in libraries and waiting rooms. Reading a magazine's table of contents is not enough. Read every story, every advertisement. When you know the audience, the slant, and what sets this magazine apart from all others, then you will be ready to write for it.

Other aspects of writing professionalism include:

● query letter. Make it original in its message and its wording. Editors will infer what kind of writer you are from this letter. Don't give a sloppy performance. A query letter that alludes to a magazine in specifics tells its editor, "This query is *for* you." The practice of querying the one magazine you want to write for is still best. (Refer to the Appendix for more details on how to write effective queries.)

● simultaneous submissions. Word processors make it easier for writers to drown the market with material. Many editors find that printouts *are* simultaneous submissions. Writers who mass-produce queries without research are writing their own rejection slips.

● SASE. Send a self-addressed, stamped envelope with all submissions.

● organization and rewriting. Editors do not have time to rework your writing; that's your job.

● proofreading. Proofread your work letter by letter. Double-check proper names. Typos may give editors a quick laugh, but certainly won't sell your manuscript. (We received one letter at our office with the salutation, Dear Sit.)

● computer printout submissions. Editors are becoming more receptive to printouts, but some refuse to read dot-matrix submissions. If a listing does not mention printout or disk preferences, then its editors do *not* want to get such submissions.

● word count. If *Writer's Market* guidelines specify that 2,000-word articles are preferred, don't try to market a 4,000-word piece.

● slant. You cannot write about (child) discipline for parents, teachers, babysitters, and children with the same set of research and words. Each story is a new adventure—you cannot focus a story in four directions without making it a general overview suited for no one in particular.

● editor-writer relations. Contrary to what some writers think, editors are a writer's best friend. A rejection note might be tactless, but it might also be telling you how unprofessional your work is. Some editors view the form-letter rejection as a kind way of telling a writer, "no, thanks." Says one editor, "If I told some writers how hopeless their writing is, they would never write again. It's not my place to make such judgments." At the same time, brilliant writers also receive rejection letters. An editor's main responsibility is pleasing his readers. When you send a query letter, wait patiently for a reply to the first query before sending four more queries on other subjects to the same editor. If (by chance) there is an extra hour in a day, the editor will spend it on the magazine, not hunting for the five queries you sent to the office last year.

● "alienable" rights. We asked editors this year to clarify the rights they buy. Based on their comments, we find that certain rights for one editor do not mean the same rights to another editor. Make sure you get a written agreement from editors as to which rights they are buying.

● pay variations. Magazines like the *Young Ambassador* have two pay scales—one for unsolicited manuscripts and one for assigned manuscripts. Sometimes assigned manuscripts merit higher per-word rates. Don't shortchange yourself by always submitting complete manuscripts. Editors encourage queries; they want to discuss with writers story slants to fit the magazine, even if it costs the magazine a few more cents per word.

● new magazines. "The average life of some magazines is 45 minutes," said one editor, jokingly. The fact is some magazines *don't* survive beyond the premier edition. But new magazines (some of them, a lifetime dream for their publishers) continue to spring up. If you query a magazine established in 1983 or 1984, be aware that the address and policies might change overnight. The good news is that a new editor may be establishing a corps of dependable freelancers. And remember, some *new* magazines have lasted a century.

● updates. *Writer's Digest* magazine lists the latest editorial needs and changes in the magazine world. The monthly publication features The Markets column, New York Market Letter, The West Market Report, Poetry Notes, and Market Update.

The more you know about writing markets, the better prepared you will be to face the keyboard or notebook. After all, you want this publishing world to be familiar and this familiar world to be as new as the sunsets you hope to write about.

Animal

Studying magazines geared to the animal owner or trainer, the writer soon learns that dogs are not man's *only* best friends. "We're starting to see a lot more caring (not anthropomorphism) in owners' attitudes toward their animals," says one animal magazine editor. Recent research on the human/animal companionship bond is among trends that may affect what animal publications buy in 1985.

The publications in this section deal with pets, racing and show horses, other pleasure animals and wildlife. Magazines about animals bred and raised for the market are classified in the Farm category. Publications about horse racing will be found in the Sports section.

‡**AMERICAN FARRIERS JOURNAL**, The Laux Company Publishers, Inc., Box L, Harvard MA 01451. (617)456-8000. Editor: Fran Garvan. Bimonthly (with an additional annual edition) magazine coving horseshoeing, horse health related to legs and feet of horses and metalworking for a professional audience of full-time horseshoers, veterinarians and horse trainers. Circ. 5,000. Pays on publication. Byline given. Buys all rights. Submit seasonal/holiday material 6 months in advance. No simultaneous queries, or simultaneous, photocopied or previously published submissions. Computer printout submissions acceptable; dot-matrix submission accepted only when double spaced. Reports in 4 weeks on queries; 2 weeks on mss. Sample copy $6; writer's guidelines for SAE and 1 first class stamp.
Nonfiction: Book excerpts, general interest, historical/nostalgic, how-to, interview/profile, new product, personal experience, photo feature and technical. No material about horseshoers that is degrading or negative. Buys 30 mss/year. Send complete ms. Length: 800-3,000 words. Pays $50-450.
Photos: Send photos with ms. Reviews b&w contact sheets, b&w negatives, 35mm color transparencies, and 8x10 b&w or color prints. Captions and identification of subjects required. Buys one-time rights.

ANIMAL KINGDOM, New York Zoological Park, Bronx NY 10460. (212)220-5121. Editor: Eugene J. Walter Jr. Bimonthly magazine for members of zoological societies, individuals interested in wildlife, zoos and aquariums. Buys all rights. Usually pays 25% kill fee but it varies according to length, amount of work involved, etc. Byline given. Pays on acceptance. Reports in 8 months. SASE.
Nonfiction: Wildlife articles dealing with wildlife, natural history, conservation or behavior. Also included are articles about animals in history, art and culture. Articles must be scientifically well-grounded, but written for a general audience, not scientific journal readers. Recent article example: "Kangaroos: Too many or Too Few?" (February-March 1984). No pets, domestic animals, or botany. Length: 1,000-2,500 words. Pays $350-850. State availability of photos. Payment for photos purchased with mss is negotiable.
Tips: "It helps to be a working scientist dealing directly with animals in the wild, or a scientist working in a zoo such as a staff member here at the New York Zoological Society. I cannot be too encouraging to anyone who lacks field experience. Many authors who send us unsolicited mss are nonscientists who are doing their research in libraries. They're simply working from scientific literature and writing it up for popular consumption. There are a fair number of others who are backyard naturalists, so to speak, and while their observations may be personal, they are not well grounded scientifically. It has nothing to do with whether or not they are good or bad writers. In fact, some of our authors are not especially good writers, but they are able to provide us with fresh, original material and new insights into animal behavior and biology. That sort of thing is impossible from someone who is working from books."

● Bullet preceding a listing indicates a company publication.

ANIMALS, MSPCA, 350 S. Huntington Ave., Boston MA 02130. Editor: Susan Burns. Bimonthly magazine for members of the MSPCA. 40 pages. Circ. 15,000. Pays on publication. Buys one-time rights. Photocopied and previously published submissions (accepted but infrequently) OK. Computer printout submissions acceptable; prefers letter-quality to dot-matrix. Reports in 2 weeks. Sample copy $1.75 with 8½x11 SASE; writer's guidelines for SASE.
Nonfiction: Uses practical articles on animal care; humane/animal protection issues; animal profiles; true pet stories (*not mawkish*) and research essays on animal protection. Nonsentimental approach. Length: 300-3,000 words. Pays 2¢/word.
Photos: Pays $10 for 5x7 or larger b&w prints; $30 for color transparencies with accompanying ms or on assignment. Uses photo essays and original photos of artistic distinction for "Gallery" department.

‡**APPALOOSA RACING RECORD**, Appaloosa Racing Record, Inc., Box 1709, Norman OK 73070. (405)364-9444. Editor: G.D. Hollingsworth. A monthly magazine covering Appaloosa horse racing and breeding for horse owners, trainers and breeders who raise, train and race Appaloosa horses. Circ. 2,000. Pays on publication. Byline given. Offers 50% kill fee. Not copyrighted. Buys first North American serial rights. Submit seasonal/holiday material 3 months in advance. Computer printout submissions acceptable. SASE. Photocopied and previously published submissions OK. Reports in 1 month on queries; 2 weeks on mss. Sample copy $3; free writer's guidelines.
Nonfiction: Book excerpts, historical/nostalgic, interview/profile, new product, photo feature and technical. Buys 20 mss/year. Query with published clips. Length: 1,000-3,000 words. Pays $50-200.
Photos: State availability of photos. Pays $15-25 for b&w prints; $75 for color. Captions and identification of subjects required. Buys all rights.
Tips: "Many articles that are acceptable for publication in other horse racing magazines will also apply to *Appaloosa Racing*. Some articles used in *Derby* magazine are also used in *Appaloosa Racing Record* for additional fee."

‡**BIRD TALK, Dedicated to Better Care for Pet Birds**, Fancy Publications, Box 6050, Mission Viejo CA 92690. (714)240-6001. Editor: Linda W. Lewis. Bimonthly magazine covering the care and training of cage birds for men and women who own any number of pet or exotic birds. Estab. 1984. Circ. 10,000. Pays latter part of month in which article appears. Byline given. Buys first North American serial rights. Submit seasonal/holiday material 4 months in advance. Simultaneous queries, and photocopied and previously published submissions OK. SASE. Reports in 3 weeks on queries; 6 weeks on mss. Sample copy $3; writer's guidelines for 9x12 SAE and 1 first class stamp.
Nonfiction: General interest (anything to do with pet birds); historical/nostalgic (of bird breeds, owners, cages); how-to (build cages, aviaries, playpens and groom, feed, breed, tame); humor; interview/profile (of bird and bird owners); new product; how-to (live with birds—compatible pets, lifestyle, apartment adaptability, etc.); personal experience (with your own bird); photo feature (humorous or informative); travel (with pet birds or to see exotic birds); and articles giving medical information, legal information, and description of breeds. No juvenile or material on wild birds not pertinent to pet care; everything should relate to *pet* birds. Buys 30 mss/year. Query or send complete ms. Length: 500-3,000 words. Pays 3¢/word and up.
Photos: State availability of photos. Reviews b&w contact sheets. Pays $50-100 for color transparencies; $10 minimum for 8x10 b&w prints. Model release and identification of subjects required. Buys one-time rights.
Columns/Departments: Editorial (opinion on a phase of owning pet birds); "Small Talk" (short news item of general interest to bird owners). Buys 4 mss/year. Send complete ms. Length: 100-250 words. Pays 3¢/word and up.
Fiction: "Only fiction with pet birds as primary focus of interest." Adventure, fantasy, historical, humorous, mystery, suspense. No juvenile, and no birds talking unless it's their trained vocabulary. Buys 6 mss/year. Send complete ms. Length: 2,000-3,000 words. Pays 3¢/word and up.
Tips: "Send grammatical, clean copy on a human-interest story about a pet bird or human/pet bird relationship. We also need how-tos on feather crafts, cage cover making, aviary, perch and cage building, and planting plants in aviaries safe and good for birds. Keep health, nutrition, lack of stress in mind regarding pet birds. Study issues of *Cat Fancy*, *Dog Fancy* or *Horse Illustrated* to learn our style."

CALIFORNIA HORSE REVIEW, The Largest All-Breeds Horse Magazine in the Nation, Box 646, North Highlands CA 95660. (916)485-4301. Editor: Kate Riordan. 50-60% freelance written. Monthly magazine covering all equines, for "professional trainers, breeders and amateurs whose main interest is in caring for, breeding, showing and riding their horses. Articles provide entertainment and factual information to these readers. Emphasis is on equines in the West and most particularly in California." Circ. 8,500. Pays on publication. Publishes ms an average of 3 months after acceptance. Byline given. Pays $50 kill fee. Buys first North American serial rights. Submit seasonal/holiday material 3 months in advance. Photocopied submissions OK. Computer printout submissions acceptable. SASE. Reports in 4 weeks. Sample copy $1; writer's guidelines for business size SAE and 1 first class stamp.
Nonfiction: Historical/nostalgic, how-to, veterinary medicine, humor, inspirational, interview/profile, per-

sonal experience, photo feature, technical and travel. "We want material for major articles concerning health, training, equipment, breeding, and interviews with well-known personalities in the equine field. No general-interest articles or articles not aimed at Western horse owners, trainers or breeders." Buys 200 mss/year. Query. Length: 1,200-3,000 words. Pays $35-125.

Photos: "Photos are purchased usually as a part of the editorial package; however, we do buy cover photos for $75."

Fiction: Adventure, historical, humorous, mainstream, novel excerpts and western. No general interest fiction; must be horse-oriented. Buys 12 mss/year. Length: 1,200-2,500 words. Pays $45-125.

Tips: "We are more apt to purchase material from horsemen who have some writing skill than from writers who have little horse knowledge. Interviews of trainers, breeders or others well known in the horse world are always sought. Readers want factual information written in clear, understandable fashion. Photos are necessary to illustrate many nonfiction articles. A writer in this field should also be a photographer and should continually work to sharpen writing skills."

CANINE CHRONICLE, Routledge Publications, Inc., Box 115, Montpelier IN 47359. (317)728-2464. Publisher: Ric Routledge. Editor: Francis M. Bir. 10% freelance written. Twice weekly tabloid covering pure-bred dogs for people who breed and show them. Circ. 7,000. Publishes mss an average of 2 weeks after acceptance. Pays on acceptance. Byline given. Buys all rights. Submit seasonal/holiday material 3 months in advance. Simultaneous queries and photocopied and previously published submissions OK. Computer printout submissions acceptable; no dot-matrix. SASE. Reports in 3 weeks on queries and mss. Free sample copy.

Nonfiction: How-to (on grooming, feeding, handling, breeding, kennels); history; interviews and features about the people behind the dogs. Buys 25 mss/year. Send complete ms. Pays average of $100 for 1,500 words, "though we are not a stickler on length if the subject is covered."

Photos: State availability of photos. "Technical how-tos should be illustrated if possible." Reviews 5x7 b&w prints. Captions and identification of subjects required. Buys all rights.

Columns/Departments: Query or send complete ms.

Fiction: "We use a limited amount of fiction. Stay away from 'Boy meets dog.'" Buys 5 mss/year. Send complete ms.

CAT FANCY, Fancy Publications, Inc., Box 6050, Mission Viejo CA 92690. (714)240-6001. Editor: Linda W. Lewis. 75% freelance written. Monthly magazine for men and women of all ages interested in all phases of cat ownership. 64 pages. Circ. 100,000. Pays after publication. Publishes ms an average of 9 months after acceptance. Buys first American serial rights. Byline given. Submit seasonal/holiday material 4 months in advance. Computer printout submissions acceptable. SASE. Reports in 6 weeks. Sample copy $3; writer's guidelines for SASE.

Nonfiction: Historical, medical, how-to, humor, informational, personal experience, photo feature and technical. Buys 5 mss/issue. Query or send complete ms. Length: 500-3,000 words. Pays 3-5¢/word.

Photos: Photos purchased with or without accompanying ms. Pays $10 minimum for 8x10 b&w glossy prints; $50-100 for 35mm or 2¼x2¼ color transparencies. Send prints and transparencies. Model release required.

Fiction: Adventure, fantasy, historical and humorous, nothing written with cats speaking. Buys 1 ms/issue. Send complete ms. Length: 500-3,000 words. Pays 3¢/word.

Poetry: Avant-garde, free verse, haiku, light verse and traditional. Buys 5 poems/issue. Length: 5-50 lines. Pays $10.

Fillers: Newsworthy or unusual; items with photo and cartoons. Buys 10 fillers/year. Length: 100-500 words. Pays $20-35.

Tips: "Writers' resistance to writing well-researched articles is frustrating."

CATS MAGAZINE, Box 4106, Pittsburgh PA 15202. Executive Editor: Jean Amelia Laux. (412)766-1662. Co-Editor: Linda J. Walton, Box 37, Port Orange FL 32019. Monthly magazine for men and women of all ages; cat enthusiasts, vets and geneticists. Circ. 75,000. Buys first North American serial rights and Japanese first rights. Byline given. Buys 50 mss/year. Pays on publication. Free sample copy. Submit seasonal/Christmas material 6 months in advance. Reports in 6-8 weeks. SASE.

Nonfiction: "Cat health, cat breed articles, articles on the cat in art, literature, history, human culture, cats in the news. Cat pets of popular personalities. In general how cats and cat people are contributing to our society. We're more serious, more scientific, but we do like an occasional light or humorous article portraying cats and humans, however, as they really are. No talking cats! Would like to see something on psychological benefits of cat ownership; how do cat-owning families differ from others?" Length: 800-2,500 words. Pays $15-75. Photos purchased with or without accompanying ms. Captions optional. Pays $10 minimum for 4x5 or larger b&w photos; $150 minimum for color (cover). Prefers 2x2 minimum, but can use 35mm (transparencies only). "We use color for cover only. Prefer cats as part of scenes rather than stiff portraits." Send transparencies to Box 37, Port Orange FL 32019. Please mark each transparency with name and address.

Fiction and Poetry: Science fiction, fantasy and humorous fiction; cat themes only. Length: 800-2,500

words. Pays $15-$100. Poetry in traditional forms, blank or free verse, avant-garde forms and some light verse; cat themes only. Length: 4-64 lines. Pays 50¢/line.
Tips: "We sometimes hold articles due to a backlog. Please advise if you have a time limit."

‡**DERBY**, Derby Publishing Corp., Box 5418, Norman OK 73070. (405)364-9444. Editor: G.D. Hollingsworth. A monthly magazine covering thoroughbred horses; racing and breeding, and dedicated to the sport of thoroughbred racing in the central and southwestern states. Estab. 1983. Circ. 5,000. Pays on acceptance for writers previously published in *Derby*; all others on publication. Byline given. Offers 50% kill fee. Buys first North American serial rights. Submit seasonal/holiday material 3 months in advance. Computer printout submissions acceptable. SASE. Photocopied submissions OK. Reports in 1 month on queries; 2 weeks on mss. Sample copy $3; free writer's guidelines.
Nonfiction: Historical/nostalgic, interview/profile, photo feature and technical. All material must be of regional significance. Buys 20 mss/year. Query with published clips. Length: 1,200-5,000 words. Pays $100-500.
Photos: State availability of photos. Pays $25 for 8x10 b&w prints; $75 for color transparencies. Captions and identification of subjects required. Buys all rights.
Fillers: Newsbreaks. Buys 24/year. Length: 500 words maximum. Pays $75 maximum.
Tips: "*Derby* is a horse *business* magazine that is read by experienced professional breeders. Knowledge of the horse business as it relates specifically to thoroughbred horses is almost essential. Historical articles about people and places important to the thoroughbred industry, and medical research papers on horses are areas most open to freelancers.

DOG FANCY, Fancy Publications, Inc., Box 6050, Mission Viejo CA 92690. (714)240-6001. Editor: Linda Lewis. Managing Editor: John Riise. 75% freelance written. Monthly magazine for men and women of all ages interested in all phases of dog ownership. Circ. 80,000. Pays after publication. Buys first American serial rights. Byline given. Submit seasonal/holiday material 4 months in advance. Publishes ms an average of 9 months after acceptance. Sample copy $3; free writer's guidelines. Computer printout submissions acceptable. SASE.
Nonfiction: Historical, medical, how-to, humor, informational, interview, personal experience, photo feature, profile and technical. Buys 5 mss/issue. Query or send complete ms. Length: 500-3,000 words. Pays 3¢/word.
Photos: Photos purchased with or without accompanying ms. Pays $10 minimum for 8x10 b&w glossy prints; $50-100 for 35mm or 2¼x2¼ color transparencies. Send prints and transparencies. Model release required.
Fiction: Adventure, fantasy, historical and humorous. Buys 5 mss/year. Send complete ms. Length: 500-3,000 words. Pays 3¢/word.
Fillers: "Need short, punchy photo fillers and cartoons." Buys 10 fillers/year. Pays $20-35.
Tips: "The most rewarding aspect of working with freelance writers is finding a writer who not only knows how to write, but does it with feeling, conviction and sensitivity to his audience. Freelance writers should be aware of long lead times for seasonal material."

‡**GONE MATCHIN'**, Box 436, New Haven IN 46774. (219)632-5508. Editor: Linda F. Hein. Managing Editor: Sherrie L. Lewis. A monthly magazine about purebred dogs for owners who are interested in showing them, especially those owners just starting out. Most readers live in Midwest. Estab. 1984. Circ. 1,000 + . Pays on publication. Byline given. Offers 13½% kill fee. Buys first North American serial rights. Submit seasonal/holiday material 3 months in advance. Simultaneous queries and submissions OK if so advised. Computer printout submissions acceptable. SASE. Reports in 2 weeks on queries; 1 month on mss. Sample copy $1.75; free writer's guidelines.
Nonfiction: How-to (show, breed, groom, etc.); humor (life with puppies and dogs, my first match, my first show, etc.); interview/profile (breeders, handlers, judges); personal experience (exhibiting, breeding, judging, etc.). "Writers may send for a list of planned breed articles. All articles should be geared to the novice. We do *not* want to see negative articles on the sport of dog showing which might be discouraging to the novice." Buys 12-24 mss/year. Query or send complete ms. Length: 750-2,500 words. Pays $25 minimum. "Payment will be determined more by quality and content of the article than the length."
Photos: State availability of photos with query or send photos with ms. Reviews b&w prints, 3x5 preferred. "We prefer pictures of dogs and puppies only. Captions should include the name of the dog or puppy, his age, his accomplishments, and the name of his owner." Buys one-time rights. "Most departments are open to subscriber contributions only. We would be open to new column proposals especially from breeders, judges, groomers or trainers.
Fillers: Newsbreaks on new dog products, laws affecting dogs and their owners. Pays $5-10.
Tips: "If the writer does not have a lot of experience, the best way to break in is with a profile piece. The subject does not have to live in the Midwest, if very well established in his field. We are very interested in articles on different dog organizations and services such as the American Dog Breeders Association, Hearing Ear Dogs, Breeders Registry services, etc. Writers should always remember to gear their articles to the novice per-

son. At present there is only one edition of *Gone Matchin'*, the Midwest edition. Plans are underway to start a Southwest edition by the end of 1985, and regional editions for the rest of the country by 1988."

‡**GREYHOUND RACING RECORD**, Greyhound Publications, Box 611919, N. Miami FL 33261-1919. (305)893-2101. Editor: Dave Kaiser. A monthly magazine covering grehyound racing, handicapping, general news and features related to greyhound owners, trainers and fans. Circ. 15,000. Pays on acceptance. Byline given. Offers negotiable kill fee. Buys first rights. Submit seasonal/holiday material 3 months in advance. Simultaneous queries and previously published submissions OK. Computer printout submissions acceptable; prefers letter-quality to dot-matrix. Reports in 1 week. Free sample copy and writer's guidelines.
Nonfiction: Book excerpts, how-to, interview/profile, new product, personal experience, photo feature and travel. "We would appreciate queries about any topic which would interest our readers: the basics of the sport, handicapping methods, tax angles, trainers, kennel owners, prominent industry personalities, and special programs. Topics which have run recently or will soon be featured are: greyhound racing vacations, how to set up your computer to handicap the dogs; University of Florida program to study greyhound breeding, novice takes a look at the sport, and numerous interviews with prominent kennel owners, track owners, and handicappers." No outdated information or race results. Buys 50+ mss/year. Query with published clips. Length: 300 or less-1,500 words. Pays $30-450.
Photos: State availability of photos with query; send photos with ms. "We use color extensively, both inside the magazine and on the cover, so slides and b&w prints are encouraged." Reviews b&w contact sheets. Pays $15-25 for 5x7 or larger b&w prints and 35mm or any size color transparency. Captions and identification of subjects required. Buys one-time rights.
Columns/Departments: Query with or without published clips. Length: 500-1,000 words. Pays $50-100.
Tips: "All areas are open to freelancers. Average story length is from 300-1,000 words. Material should be tightly written, but there is no constraint in case it is over 1,000 words; while 3,000 words would be pushing it, nothing says we couldn't run two installments. 'Track' stories involving actual news events and race results are prepared by track pr persons; no reason, however, that a writer shouldn't contact these people to find out what stories they are sending and what feature spin-offs could be done."

THE GREYHOUND REVIEW, Official Publication of the National Greyhound Association, National Greyhound Association, Box 543, Abilene KS 67410. (913)263-4660. Executive Editor: Gary Guccione. Monthly magazine covering greyhound breeding and racing for greyhound owners. Circ. 4,200. Pays on acceptance. Byline given. Not copyrighted. Buys first North American serial rights. Submit seasonal/holiday material 3 months in advance. Publishes ms an average of 3 months after acceptance. Simultaneous queries and photocopied and previously published submissions OK. Computer printout submissions acceptable; prefers letter-quality to dot-matrix. SASE. Reports in 1 month. Free sample copy and writer's guidelines.
Nonfiction: Jane E. Allen, articles and managing editor. Book excerpts; general interest; historical/nostalgic; how-to (train greyhounds, better care for greyhounds, etc.); humor; interview/profile; opinion; personal experience; photo feature; technical. Not interested in articles of general interest that greyhound owners will find too fundamental. Buys 60 mss/year. Send complete ms. Length: 1,000-10,000 words. Pays $40-100 and contributor's copies.
Photos: Send photos with ms. Pays $10-50 for 5x7 b&w and color prints. Identification of subjects required. "When submitting photos for cover (preferably color), leave ample cropping space on all margins around the subject in the picture. We like to use a full-bleed photo on our cover."
Columns/Departments: Jane E. Allen, column/department editor. "Our Readers Write"—consideration of all mss relevant to all pertinent greyhound issues. Buys 10 mss/year. Send complete ms. Length: 1,000-5,000 words. Pays $40-100 and contributor's copies.
Tips: "When a freelancer brings a story to light and to our readers in a clean, tight package, it has a place in our book. We are a record of our industry and we want to present the correct information. It helps when writers submit exceptional manuscripts, professionally prepared, thoroughly researched, facts checked. A writer can't only *wish* to be published; his manuscript should convey all the elements (punctuation, spellng, style, originality) to *warrant* publication. Then comes the nurturing, the start, we hope, of a worthwhile association."

HORSE AND HORSEMAN, Box HH, Capistrano Beach CA 92624. Editor: Mark Thiffault. 75% freelance written. For owners of pleasure horses; predominantly female with main interest in show/pleasure riding. Monthly magazine; 74 pages. Circ. 96,000. Buys all rights. Byline given. Buys 40-50 mss/year. Pays on acceptance. Sample copy $1.50; writer's guidelines for SASE. Submit special material (horse and tack care; veterinary medicine pieces in winter and spring issues) 3 months in advance. Reports in 1 month. Query or submit complete ms. SASE.
Nonfiction: Training tips, do-it-yourself pieces, grooming and feeding, stable management, tack maintenance, sports, personalities, rodeo and general horse-related features. Emphasis must be on informing, rather than merely entertaining. Aimed primarily at the beginner, but with information for experienced horsemen. Subject matter must have thorough, in-depth appraisal. Interested in more English (hunter/jumper) riding/training copy, plus pieces on driving horses and special horse areas like Tennessee Walkers and other gaited

breeds. More factual breed histories. Uses informational, how-to, personal experience, interview, profile, humor, historical, nostalgia, successful business operations, technical articles. Length: 2,500 words average. Pays $75-200.

Photos: B&w photos (4x5 and larger) purchased with or without mss. Pays $4-10 when purchased without ms. Uses original color transparencies (35mm and larger). No duplicates. Pays $100 for cover use. Payment for inside editorial color is negotiated.

HORSE ILLUSTRATED, Fancy Publications, Inc., Box 6050, Mission Viejo CA 92690. (714)240-6001. Editor: Linda Lewis. Managing Editor: Jill-Marie Jones. 90% freelance written. Monthly magazine for men and women of all ages interested in all phases of horse ownership. Circ. 50,000. Pays after publication. Publishes ms an average of 4 months after acceptance. Buys first North American serial rights. Submit seasonal/holiday material 4 months in advance. Computer printout submissions acceptable. Sample copy $3; free writer's guidelines. SASE.

Nonfiction: Medical, how-to, humor, informational, interview, photo feature, profile, technical and sport. Buys 5 mss/issue. Length: 500-2,500 words. Pays 3-5¢/word.

Photos: Photos purchased with or without accompanying ms. Pays $10 minimum for 8x10 b&w glossy prints; $50-100 for 35mm 2¼x2¼ color transparencies. Send prints and transparencies. Model release required.

Fiction: Adventure and humor. Buys 5 mss/year. Send complete ms. Length: 500-2,000 words. Pays 3¢/word.

Fillers: Newsworthy or unusual items with photo and cartoons. Buys 10/year. Pays $20-35.

Tips: ''The most rewarding aspect of working with freelance writers is watching a writer grow in his/her craft. We believe very strongly in working with new/young journalists with talent, and support them by giving them more and more assignments. The most annoying aspect of working with freelance writers is not meeting deadlines. Writers often don't realize editors/publishers have unforgiving timetables, and if a writer misses a deadline even once we are very gun shy about using him/her again.''

HORSE WOMEN, Rich Publishing, Inc., 41919 Moreno Rd., Temecula CA 92390. Editor: Ray Rich. Annual magazine covering western and English riding for those interested in taking better care of their horse and improving their riding. Magazine is tailored for working women and family women who are interested in riding or caring for equines. Circ. 80,000. Pays on publication. Buys all rights. Offers 100% kill fee. Byline given. Phone queries OK. Submit seasonal/holiday material 3 months in advance. SASE. Reports in 1 month. Sample copy $3; free writer's guidelines.

Nonfiction: How-to (anything relating to western and English riding, jumping, barrel racing, etc.); humor; interview (with well-known professional trainers); new product (want new product releases, description of the product and b&w photo, featuring the latest in western and English tack and clothing); and photo feature (preferably foaling). Buys 10-15 mss/issue. Query or send complete ms. Length: 1,000-2,500 words. Pays $40-60/printed page depending on quality and number of photos.

Photos: Send photos with ms. Offers no additional payment for 5x7 or 8x10 b&w glossy prints. Pays extra for color photos. Captions preferred.

HORSEMAN MAGAZINE, 5314 Bingle Rd., Houston TX 77092. (713)688-8811. Editor: Linda Blake. 60% freelance written. Monthly magazine for people who own and ride horses for pleasure and competition. Majority own western stock horses and compete in western type horse shows as a hobby or business. Many have owned horses for many years. Circ. 192,926. Rights purchased vary with author and material. Buys first North American serial rights. Byline given. Pays on publication. Computer printout submissions acceptable; no dot-matrix. Free sample copy and writer's guidelines. Submit seasonal material 4 months in advance. Reports in 3 weeks. Query. SASE.

Nonfiction: ''How-to articles on horsemanship, training, grooming, exhibiting, horsekeeping, and history dealing with horses. We really like articles from professional trainers, or articles about their methods written by freelancers. The approach is to educate and inform readers as to how they can ride, train, keep and enjoy their horses more.'' Length: 1,000-2,500 words. Pays up to 7-10¢/word.

Photos: Photos purchased with accompanying ms or on assignment. Captions required. Pays $10 minimum for 5x7 or 8x10 b&w prints; 35mm or 120 negatives. Pays $25 for inside color. Prefers transparencies. Buys all rights.

Tips: ''Send article ideas with very narrow focus. Indicate depth. Use know-how from top experts or send us good, concise articles about specific training problems with detailed explanation of correction. Otherwise, stick to fringe articles: humor, photo essay, Horseman Travelog. The articles need to be packed with information, but we don't always mean step-by-step how to. Make them readable.''

HORSEMEN'S YANKEE PEDLAR NEWSPAPER, Box 785 Southbridge St., Auburn MA 01501. (617)832-9638. Publisher: Nancy L. Khoury. Editor: Judith Francisco. 40% freelance written. ''All-breed monthly newspaper for horse enthusiasts of all ages and incomes, from one-horse owners to large commercial stables. Covers region from New Jersey to Maine.'' Circ. 12,000. Pays on publication. Buys all rights for one year. Submit seasonal/holiday material 3 months in advance of issue date. SASE. Reports in 1 month.

Publishes ms an average of 6 months after acceptance. Sample copy $1.75.

Nonfiction: Humor, educational and interview about horses and the people involved with them. Pays $2/published inch. Buys 50 mss/year. Submit complete ms or outline. Length: 1,500 words maximum.

Photos: Purchased with ms. Captions and photo credit required. Buys 1 cover photo/month; pays $10. Submit b&w prints. Pays $5.

Columns/Departments: Area news column. Buys 85-95/year. Length: 1,200-1,400 words. Pays 75¢/column inch. Query.

Tips: "Query with outline of angle of story, approximate length and date when story will be submitted. Stories should be people oriented and horse focused. Send newsworthy, timely pieces, such as stories that are applicable to the season, for example: foaling in the spring or how to keep a horse healthy through the winter. We like to see how-to's, features about special horse people and anything that has to do with the preservation of horses and their rights as creatures deserving a chance to survive."

HORSEPLAY, Box 545, Gaithersburg MD 20877. (301)840-1866. Editor: Cordelia Doucet. 20% freelance written. Monthly magazine covering horses and horse sports for a readership interested in horses, and show jumping, dressage, combined training, hunting, and driving. 60-80 pages. Circ. 46,000. Pays after publication. Publishes ms an average of 3 months after acceptance. All rights reserved. Pays kill fee. Byline given. Phone queries OK. Computer printout submissions acceptable. Submit all material 2 months in advance. SASE. Reports in 6 weeks. Sample copy $2.50; free writer's and photographer's guidelines.

Nonfiction: How-to (various aspects of horsemanship, course designing, stable management, putting on horse shows, etc.); humor; interview; photo feature; profile and technical. Length: 1,000-3,000 words. Pays 6¢/word.

Photos: Cathy Mitchell, art director. Purchased on assignment. Captions required. Query or send contact sheet, prints or transparencies. Pays $10 for 8x10 b&w glossy prints; $125 for color transparencies for cover; $35 for inside color.

Tips: "No fiction, western riding, or racing articles."

HORSES ALL, Rocky Top Holdings, Ltd., Box 550, Nanton, Alberta, Canada T0L 1R0. (403)646-2144. Editor: Jacki French. 5% freelance written. Monthly tabloid for horse owners, 75% rural, 25% urban. Circ. 11,200. Pays on publication. Publishes ms an average of 3 months after acceptance. Buys one-time rights. Phone queries OK. Submit seasonal material 3 months in advance. Simultaneous, photocopied (if clear), and previously published submissions OK. Computer printout submissions acceptable. Reports on queries in 5 weeks; on mss in 6 weeks. Sample copy $2.

Nonfiction: Interview, humor and personal experience. Query. Pays $20-100.

Photos: State availability of photos. Captions required.

Columns/Departments: Length: 1-2 columns. Query. Open to suggestions for new columns/departments. Query Doug French.

Fiction: Historical and western. Query. Pays $20-100.

‡**LONE STAR HORSE REPORT**, 5129 E. Belknap, Fort Worth TX 76117. (817)834-3951. Editor: Henry L. King. Managing Editor: Byron Travis. 15-20% freelance written. Monthly magazine on horses and horse people in and around Dallas/Ft. Worth metroplex. Estab. 1983. Circ. 5,346. Pays on publication. Publishes ms an average of 2 months after acceptance. Byline given. Buys first rights and second serial (reprint) rights to material originally published elsewhere. Submit seasonal/holiday material 2 months in advance. Photocopied and previously published submissions OK. Computer printout submissions acceptable. SASE. Reports in 2 weeks on queries; 4 weeks on mss. Sample copy $1; free writer's guidelines.

Nonfiction: How-to (how a specific horseman trains horses for specific events); interview/profile (horsemen living in trade area); photo feature (horses, farms, arenas, facilities, people in trade area). Buys 30-40 mss/year. Query with published clips or send complete ms. Length: 200-2,000 words. Pays $15-60.

Photos: State availability of photos. Pays $5 for 5x7 b&w prints. Buys one-time rights.

Tips: "We need reports of specific horse-related events in north Texas area such as trail rides, rodeos, play days, shows, etc., and also feature articles on horse farms, outstanding horses and/or horsemen. Emphasis on local events as opposed to events which would attract national coverage is a trend that writers should be aware of."

THE MORGAN HORSE, American Morgan Horse Association, Box 1, Westmoreland NY 13490. (315)735-7522. Acting Editor: Avo Kiviranna. Article Contact: Marcia Werts. Monthly breed journal covering the training, showing, and vet care of Morgan horses. Circ. 9,000. Pays on publication. Byline given. Buys all rights. Submit seasonal/holiday material 3 months in advance. Simultaneous queries and simultaneous, photocopied, and previously published submissions OK (subject to editor's discretion). SASE. Reports in 3 months. Sample copy $2 (price may vary with issue); writer's guidelines for business size SAE and 1 first class stamp.

Nonfiction: How-to (trailering, driving, training, etc.); human interest (if highly unusual); interview/profile (of respected Morgan personalities); veterinary articles. Special issues include January-Morgan Grand National; February-Stallions; March-Versatility; April-Driving; May-Mare; June-Youth; August-Western; September-Gelding; October-Foal; November-International; December-Horse Buying. "No articles with less-than-national interest or material dealing with half-bred Morgans." Buys 15-20 mss/year. Query with clips of published work. Length: 500-3,000 words. Pays 5¢/word.

Photos: Send photos with ms. Pays $5 minimum for 8x10 b&w prints. Captions, model release, and identification of subjects required.

Tips: "We like to see completed manuscripts from new writers and welcome articles on veterinary breakthroughs and training."

PAINT HORSE JOURNAL, American Paint Horse Association, Box 18519, Fort Worth TX 76118. (817)439-3400. Managing Editor: Phil Livingston. For people who raise, breed and show paint horses. Monthly magazine. Circ. 12,000. Pays on acceptance. Normally buys all rights. Pays negotiable kill fee. Byline given. Phone queries OK. Submit seasonal/holiday material 3 months in advance. Photocopied and previously published submissions OK. SASE. Reports in 1 month. Free sample copy and writer's guidelines.

Nonfiction: General interest (personality pieces on well-known owners of paints); historical (paint horses in the past—particular horses and the breed in general); how-to (train and show horses); and photo feature (paint horses). Buys 4-5 mss/issue. Send complete ms. Pays $50-250.

Photos: Send photos with ms. Offers no additional payment for photos accepted with accompanying ms. Uses 3x5 or larger b&w glossy prints; 3x5 color transparencies. Captions preferred. Normally buys all rights.

Tips: "*PHJ* needs breeder-trainer articles from areas far-distant from our office. Photos with copy are almost always essential. Well-written first person articles welcome. Humor, too. Submit well-written items that show a definite understanding of the horse business. Use proper equine terminology and proper grounding in ability to communicate thoughts."

PERFORMANCE HORSEMAN, Gum Tree Store Press, Inc. Gum Tree Corner, Unionville PA 19375. (215)857-1101. Editor-in-Chief: Pamela Goold. 33% freelance written. Monthly magazine covering Western horsemanship and horse care. Circ. 35,000. Pays on acceptance. Byline given. Offers negotiable kill fee. Buys all rights. Computer printout submissions acceptable. SASE. Reports in 2 months on queries and mss. Sample copy for 9x12 SAE; free writer's guidelines.

Nonfiction: Miranda Lorraine, articles editor. How-to (on riding, training, horse care, horse health); interviews (with top western riders and trainers, and researchers or veterinarians on breakthroughs, new developments/methods); photo feature (must be how-to of a specific stable skill). "Be familiar with our format and content. Query with name and credentials of a trainer or top horseman, along with slant for the story. Personal experience stories must contain how-to information. We are not interested in writer's own opinion or method; interview must be with proven trainer. No puff pieces on a horseman, yarns, tales of the Old West—must be how-to material." Buys 25 mss/year. Query.

Photos: State availability of photos. Identification of subjects required.

Tips: "First person training articles are most open to freelancers. Keep stories in first person with subject of story 'I'; accompany with colorful biography."

PURE-BRED DOGS AMERICAN KENNEL GAZETTE, American Kennel Club, Inc., 51 Madison Ave., New York NY 10010. (212)696-8330, ext. 8331 or 8332. Editor: Ms. Pat Beresford. Official publication of the American Kennel Club, a monthly magazine covering dogs. "Reaches pure-bred dog breeders, owners. All articles published must be related to the pure-bred dog fancy—dog showing, judging, breeding, health and medicine, grooming, training, the dog in art or literature as well as some personal experience pieces." 80% freelance written. Circ. 48,000. Pays on publication. Byline given. Buys all rights. Submit seasonal/holiday material 6 months in advance. Simultaneous queries and photocopied and previously published submissions OK "on rare occasions." Reports in 1 month. Publishes ms an average of "up to a year after acceptance, depending on subject matter." Free sample copy and writer's guidelines.

Nonfiction: General interest, historical/nostalgic, how-to, humor, personal experience, photo feature, technical, medical. No personal experience or opinion that is not of interest to the pure-bred dog fancier. Buys about 50 mss/year. Send complete ms. Length: 750-3,000 words. Pays $50-250 and up "depending on article."

Photos: Send photos with accompanying query or ms. Reviews 8x10 b&w and color prints or slides. Pay depends on entire article. Model release and identification of subjects required.

Fiction: Adventure, humorous stories related to dogs. Buys about 2 mss/year. Send complete ms. Length: 750-3,000 words. Pays $50-250, depending on ms.

Fillers: Anecdotes, short humor, newsbreaks. Length: 750 words maximum. Pays $50 maximum.

Tips: "We simply like to have complete outlines of manuscripts on any ideas submitted. If we like the work or see potential, we will contact the writer. Most of the editorial features section is open to freelancers. We like to see in-depth coverage with good photo illustrations."

‡PURRRRR! THE NEWSLETTER FOR CAT LOVERS, The Meow Company, Suite 187, 89 Massachusetts Ave., Boston MA 02115. Editor: Carol Frakes. A bimonthly newsletter for the average cat owner, *not* breeders. "The publication is designed to amuse while providing cat lovers with information about the care, feeding and enjoyment of house cats." Circ. 2,000 + . Pays on publication. Byline given. Buys first North American serial rights. Submit seasonal/holiday material 6 months in advance. Photocopied and previously published submissions OK. SASE. Reports in 2 weeks. Sample copy $2; writer's guidelines fro business size SAE and 1 first class stamp.

Nonfiction: General interest; historical/nostalgic; how-to; literary cat lovers (have featured Colette, Mark Twain and May Sarton); humor; interview/profile; new product; travel. "We want a humorous slant wherever possible; writing should be tight and professional. Avoid the first person." Special Christmas issue. No shaggy cat stories, sentimental stories, "I taught Fluffy to roll over" cutsie material. Buys 50/mss year. Query with published clips, or send complete ms. Length: 250-1,500 words. Pays: $15-100.

Photos: Avoid "cute" photos. State availability of photos. Pays $5-10 for 5x8 b&w prints. Model release and identification of subjects required. Buys one-time rights.

Fillers: Clippings, anecdotes, short humor, newsbreaks. Buys 5/year. Length: 25-75 words. Pays $5.

Tips: "All sections are open to freelancers who follow our guidelines. We want practical articles, such as recent articles on pet insurance, pros and cons of declawing, etc."

THE QUARTER HORSE JOURNAL, Box 9105, Amarillo TX 79105. (806)376-4811. Editor-in-Chief: Audie Rackley. 10% freelance written. Official publication of the American Quarter Horse Association. Monthly magazine; 650 pages. Circ. 89,000. Pays on acceptance. Publishes ms an average of 60 days after acceptance. Buys all rights or first rights. Submit seasonal/holiday material 2 months in advance. SASE. Reports in 2 weeks. Free sample copy and writer's guidelines.

Nonfiction: Historical ("those that retain our western heritage"); how-to (fitting, grooming, showing, or anything that relates to owning, showing, or breeding); informational (educational clinics, current news); interview (feature-type stories—must be about established people who have made a contribution to the business); new product; personal opinion; and technical (medical updates, new surgery procedures, etc.). Buys 30 mss/year. Length: 800-2,500 words. Pays $50-250.

Photos: Purchased with accompanying ms. Captions required. Send prints or transparencies. Uses 5x7 or 8x10 b&w glossy prints; 2¼x2¼ or 4x5 color transparencies. Offers no additional payment for photos accepted with accompanying ms.

Tips: "Freelance writers should be aware of the electronic age and how it affects people and their business."

‡**TROPICAL FISH HOBBYIST**, 211 W. Sylvania Ave., Neptune City NJ 07753. Editor: Edward C. Taylor. Monthly magazine for tropical fish keepers. Circ. 52,000. Rights purchased vary with author and material. Usually buys all rights. Byline given. Buys 50 mss/year. Pays on acceptance. Query or submit complete ms. Computer printout submissions acceptable; prefers letter-quality to dot-matrix. SASE. Sample copy $2.

Nonfiction and Photos: "Don't submit material unless you're an experienced keeper of tropical fishes and know what you're talking about. Offer specific advice about caring for and breeding tropicals, amphibians, reptiles and about related topics. Study the publication before submitting." Informal style preferred. Can use personality profiles of successful aquarium hobbyists, but query first on these.

Photos: Submit b&w prints or color transparencies.

THE WESTERN HORSEMAN, Box 7980, Colorado Springs CO 80933. Editor: Chan Bergen. 40% freelance written. Monthly magazine covering western horsemanship. Circ. 170,000. Pays on acceptance. Buys first-time rights. Byline given. Submit seasonal/holiday material 3 months in advance. SASE. Reports in 3 weeks. Publishes ms an average of 4 months after acceptance. Sample copy $1.75.

Nonfiction: How-to (horse training, care of horses, tips, etc.); and informational (on rodeos, ranch life, historical articles of the West emphasizing horses). Length: 1,500 words. Payment begins at $175; "sometimes higher by special arrangement."

Photos: Send photos with ms. Offers no additional payment for photos. Uses 5x7 or 8x10 b&w glossy prints and 35mm transparencies. Captions required.

Tips: "Submit clean copy with professional quality photos. Stay away from generalities. Writing style should show a deep interest in horses coupled with a wide knowledge of the subject."

Art

　　Like artists and art patrons, art magazines demand originality from their writers. ". . . Submit work that represents an individual viewpoint, not merely a rehash of the 'current accepted thinking'," says one art magazine editor. Listed here are publications of and about art, art history, and specific art forms written for art patrons and artists. Publications addressing the business and management concerns of the art industry are listed in the Art, Design, and Collectibles category of the Trade Journals section.

THE AMERICAN ART JOURNAL, Kennedy Galleries, Inc., 40 W. 57th St., 5th Floor, New York NY 10019. (212)541-9600. Editor-in-Chief: Jane Van N. Turano. Scholarly magazine of American art history of the 17th, 18th, 19th and 20th centuries, including painting, sculpture, architecture, decorative arts, etc., for people with a serious interest in American art, and who are already knowledgeable about the subject. Readers are scholars, curators, collectors, students of American art, or persons who have a strong interest in Americana. Quarterly magazine; 96 pages. Circ. 2,000. Pays on acceptance. Buys all rights. Byline given. Photocopied submissions OK. SASE. Reports in 2 months. Sample copy $7.
Nonfiction: "All articles are historical in the sense that they are all about some phase or aspect of American art history." No how-to articles or reviews of exhibitions. No book reviews or opinion pieces. No human interest approaches to artists' lives. No articles written in a casual or "folksy" style. *Writing style must be formal and serious*. Buys 25-30 mss/year. Submit complete ms "with good cover letter." Length: 2,500-8,000 words. Pays $300-400.
Photos: Purchased with accompanying ms. Captions required. Uses b&w only. Offers no additional payment for photos accepted with accompanying ms.
Tips: "Actually, our range of interest is quite broad. Any topic within our time frame is acceptable if it is well researched, well written, and illustrated. Whenever possible, all mss must be accompanied by b&w photographs which have been integrated into the text by the use of numbers."

AMERICAN INDIAN ART MAGAZINE, American Indian Art, Inc., 7314 E. Osborn Dr., Scottsdale AZ 85251. (602)994-5445. Managing Editor: Roanne P. Goldfein. 97% freelance written. Quarterly magazine covering Native American art, historic and contemporary, including new research on any aspect of Native American art. Circ. 15,000. Pays on publication. Publishes ms an average of 8 months after acceptance. Byline given. Buys one-time and first rights. Submit seasonal/holiday material 6 months in advance. Simultaneous queries OK. Reports in 2 weeks on queries; 2 months on mss. Writer's guidelines available.
Nonfiction: New research on any aspect of Native American art. No previously published work or personal interviews with artists. Buys 12-18 mss/year. Query. Length: 1,000-2,500 words. Pays $75-300.
Tips: "We are devoted to the great variety of textiles, ceramics, jewelry and artifacts of Native American artists—in articles (with bibliographies) appealing to lay men and professionals."

ART & ARTISTS, Oil Pastel Association, 304 Highmount Terrace, Upper-Nyack-on-Hudson NY 10960. Editor: Sheila Elliot. 50% freelance written. Quarterly magazine covering art and artists. "Our artists are either working in or interested in oil pastel; we will always be interested in articles with a slant toward this medium. We are, however, open to and interested in all well-researched articles with any art subject matter." Estab. 1983. Circ. under 1,000. Pays on publication. Publishes ms an average of 5 months after acceptance. Byline given. Buys first North American serial rights, first rights and second serial (reprint) rights to material originally published elsewhere. Submit seasonal/holiday material 3 months in advance. Simultaneous queries, and simultaneous, photocopied and previously published (specify where published) submissions OK. Electronic submissions OK if compatible to TRS 80 color tape system, but requires hard copy also. Computer printout submissions acceptable, "if dark enough to read." SASE. Will return mss only if adequate postage and envelope is provided. Reports in 1 month on queries; 2 months on mss. Sample copy for $3, 9x12 SAE and 4 first class stamps; writer's guidelines for 5x9 SAE and 2 first class stamps.
Nonfiction: Historical/nostalgic (interviews of persons close to historic art scene or who knew prominent artists); how-to (art or art-related, such as marketing your art, legal, etc.); humor (art-related, short); interview/profile (artists or fine arts figures such as influential museum directors, art consultants, etc.); new product (art materials); opinion (art issues); personal experience; photo feature; technical; travel (good art locations and inexpensive hotels, hostels, etc.). Buys 50 mss/year. Query. Length: 500-7,500 words. Pays $5 minimum.
Photos: State availability of photos. Pays $1 for b&w contact sheets and 5x7 or 8x10 prints; $1 for 35mm color transparencies and 5x7 or 8x10 color prints. Captions, model release and identification of subjects required. Buys one-time rights.
Columns/Departments: Book reviews are staff written. Interested in teacher feature contributions. Buys 50 mss/year. Send complete ms. Length: 25-800 words. Pays $1 "for 25 words and up."
Fiction: "We would consider fiction that dealt with inner struggles of artists, such as 'why am I painting' or 'can I have children and do art, too?' Not interested in experimental depression; tone must be upbeat. We would also consider art-related humor. Although we do not plan to use fiction regularly, if you have something you are really excited about, consider submitting to us." Will consider high-quality shorts and short shorts. Send complete ms. Pays up to $25 for short stories.

Poetry: Free verse, haiku, light verse, traditional. "Nothing overly long." Buys 15 poems/year. Submit maximum 10 poems. Length: 2-24 lines. Pays $1. "Should not 'knock' art—must be positive in outlook."

Fillers: Clippings, anecdotes, short humor, newsbreaks. Buys 50/year. Length: 25-500 words. Pays $1.

Tips: "We are a fledgling magazine that needs all kinds of material. Study the art magazines that are currently on the market, especially *American Artist* for practicing artist articles, and *Art in America* and other expensive glossies for 'think' pieces and reviews. We are inclined to be indulgent of relatively weak writing techniques, provided the writer has something to say and is willing to work with us and accept extensive editing. Hence, we are an excellent submission ground for new, as yet, 'un-polished' writers. Whenever possible, we will request revisions of the writer, or submit our own revisions to author for approval. We will continue to need art exhibition reviews, especially in USA outside New York City area, Canada and foreign art capitals. Reviews should be informed and scholarly, and show clearly the theoretical context from which the reviewer analyzes. A brief credentials page should accompany queries and reviews."

ART NEW ENGLAND, A Resource for the Visual Arts, 353 Washington St., Brighton MA 02135. (617)782-3008. Editors: Carla Munsatand, Stephanie Adelman. Visual arts tabloid published 10 times/year. Provides "a comprehensive index for regional exhibitions, lectures and films. Articles focus on different aspects of painting, sculpture, graphics, crafts, photography, and architecture; features include interviews and profiles on new or established artists, curators and other leaders in the art community. Articles on the business of art and collecting are also included." Circ. 15,000. Pays on publication. Byline given. Submit seasonal/holiday material 2 months in advance. SASE. Sample copy $1.75; free writer's guidelines.

Nonfiction: Book excerpts and book reviews (fine arts, photography, crafts, architecture); interview/profile (on new and established artists, curators and other members of the art community); opinion (on artists' rights, etc.); personal experience (from artist's or curator's point of view); and photo feature (art). No articles or reviews *not* related to the visual arts. "We are only interested in art-related subjects." Buys 30 mss/year. Query with resume and clips. Length: 900-1,500 words (features only). Pays $50 maximum features only; reviews less.

Tips: "Features and reviews are most open to freelancers."

ART WEST MAGAZINE, The Foremost Western Art Journal, Art West, Inc., 303 E. Main St., Box 1799, Bozeman MT 59715. (406)586-5411. Editor: Helori M. Graff. 50% freelance written. Bimonthly publication covering Western and wildlife art. "In addition to keeping our readers informed of trends in the Western and wildlife art scenes, our major form of presentation is profiles of the individual artists—covering everything—technique, philosophies, lifestyle, etc." Circ. 38,500. Pays on acceptance. Publishes ms an average of 1 year after acceptance. Byline given. Offers 50% kill fee. Buys first North American serial rights. Submit seasonal/holiday material 8 months in advance. Electronic submissions OK on 5¼ WordStar floppy disk, but requires hard copy also. Computer printout submissions acceptable. SASE. Reports in 2 months. Sample copy for 9x12 SAE and $2.50 postage; writer's guidelines for business-size SAE and 1 first class stamp.

Nonfiction: Expose (art market, re: Western and wildlife art); historical (Western artists); interview/profile (artists/gallery owners); opinion (forum for opinions on art-related topics); photo feature (artists, techniques, museum and gallery openings); technical (methods artists employ); travel (towns considered havens for artists). "Don't complete a profile on an artist before Editorial Board makes the decision to publish feature on that artist (send query with photographs of artist's work first)." Buys 50 mss/year. Query with published clips. Length: 1,200-3,000 words.

Columns/Departments: Art Tomes (reviews of Western, wildlife, or general art, art publications); In Review (reviews of art shows); Art Events (events, trends in Western, wildlife art). Buys 20-30 mss/year. Query with published clips. Length: 200-1,500 words.

Tips: "*Art West* profiles are typically written in clear, lively and unaffected prose which entertains as well as informs readers of the artist's background, personality, interests, artistic methods, style, philosophies, hopes for the future. Readers have indicated a desire to know about each artist's techniques. Relate why writer is interested, qualified for this type of subject. Come to us with a story idea—not entire manuscript. If writer is proposing a particular artist as topic of article, please query first and enclose varied sampling of that artist's work (photographs, transparencies, brochure, etc.)."

THE ARTIST'S MAGAZINE, F&W Publications, Inc., 9933 Alliance Rd., Cincinnati OH 45242. Editor: Michael Ward. Monthly (12 times/year) magazine covering art instruction. "Ours is a highly visual approach to teaching the serious amateur artist techniques that will help him improve his skills and market his work. The style should be crisp and immediately engaging." Estab. 1984. Circ. 110,000. Pays on acceptance. Byline given. Offers 20% kill fee. Buys first North American serial rights and second serial (reprint) rights. Submit seasonal/holiday material 6 months in advance. Simultaneous queries, and photocopied and previously published submissions OK "as long as noted as such." Computer printout submissions acceptable; no dot-matrix. SASE. Reports in 3 weeks. Sample copy for 9x12 SAE plus postage; free writer's guidelines.

Nonfiction: Book excerpts; historical/nostalgic; how-to (every aspect of technique for painting, drawing and the business of art); inspirational (how an artist may have succeeded through hard work, determination, etc.);

opinion; interview/profile; new product. "Every article type must instruct the reader in some way." Special issues include: educational issue (the virtues of training, workshops, etc.) and artists' tools issue (perhaps an historical view). No unillustrated articles. Buys 50 mss/year. Query. Length: 500-2,500 words. Pays $50-350.
Photos: "Photos are purchased with every sort of article, but are essential in any instructional piece." Pays $5-35 for b&w contact sheet; $25-100 for 35mm color transparencies. Captions required. Buys one-time rights.
Columns/Departments: Book reviews; The Artist's Life (brief items about art and artists); The Artist's Market (galleries and markets for artists). Buys 300 mss/year. Send complete ms. Length: 25-250 words. Pays $5-50.
Tips: "Look at several issues carefully and read the author's guidelines carefully. We are especially happy to get excellent visuals which illustrate the article and the 4-color separations for such visuals."

ARTS MAGAZINE, 23 E. 26th St., New York NY 10010. (212)685-8500. Editor: Richard Martin. A journal of contemporary art, art criticism, analysis and history, particularly for artists, scholars, museum officials, art teachers and students, and collectors. Monthly, except July and August. Circ. 28,500. Buys all rights. Pays on publication. Query. SASE.
Nonfiction and Photos: Art criticism, analysis and history. Topical reference to museum or gallery exhibition preferred. Length: 1,500-2,500 words. Pays $100, with opportunity for negotiation. B&w glossies or color transparencies customarily supplied by related museums or galleries.

CRAFT RANGE, The Mountain Plains Crafts Journal, 6800 W. Oregon Dr., Denver CO 80226. (303)986-4891. Editor: Blu Wagner. 90% freelance written. Bimonthly tabloid covering criticism, review, artists, shows, galleries, institutions and issues related to contemporary crafts and arts in areas west of the Mississippi River, excluding the West Coast states. Circ. 2,000. Pays on publication. Publishes ms an average of 2 months after acceptance. Byline given. Buys one-time rights. Queries, photocopied and previously published submissions OK. Computer printout submissions acceptable; prefers letter-quality to dot-matrix. SAE. Reports on queries and mss in 1 month. Sample copy $2; writer's guidelines free for business size SAE and 1 first class stamp.
Nonfiction: Seeking human interest; unique, unusual, interesting work in crafts (clay, glass, metal, fiber, paper, plastic, wood, etc.) of fine art quality; general interest (craft related); interview/profile (artists); personal experience; photo feature; and book reviews. No how-to-do crafts, or business/marketing. Query. Length: 250-1,500 words. Pays $30-50/article.
Photos: State availability of photos. Reviews 5x7 or larger b&w glossy prints. Cost of photos are reimbursed. Model release and identification of subjects required. "Try to get public relations photos from the gallery or artist."

FORMAT: ART & THE WORLD, Seven Oaks Press, 405 S. 7th St., St. Charles IL 60174. (312)584-0187. Editor: Ms. C.L. Morrison. Quarterly magazine covering art and society. "Our audience consists of three groups: artists wanting to know more about survival and the effectiveness in the current art system (visual and other arts); women exploring their role, opportunities, and situation in the art world; and writer/editors involved in the small-press literary community. We are practical, straight-talking and non-sexist—not a glossy coffee-table art magazine, but instead a budget-conscious vehicle by which creative people can communicate ideas, experiences and proposals for change. Subscribers are 30% Midwest, 20% West Coast, 20% East Coast, with the rest scattered in the US and a tiny segment of Europe." 50% freelance written. Circ. 700. Buys first rights. Pays on publication. Byline given. "We copyright for the author; some assignments are on a work-for-hire basis." Photocopied submissions OK. SASE. Reports in 1 month. Publishes ms an average of 6 months after acceptance. Sample copy $3.
Nonfiction: Opinion, personal experience, and some historical subjects involving a new interpretation. "Subjects we are particularly interested in now include: artists as workers (self-employment and being an employee); artist's social role; proposals for education of artists; how do artists make their work known; using art-knowledge in everyday life; how artists can affect the direction of industry and consumer preference; opinions about government funding; how current society affects current art; how past society and living conditions affected past art; and artists' personal experiences with one thing or another—i.e., real life episodes. No articles that say, 'I don't understand modern art—it's all a bunch of ridiculous stuff,' or murder mysteries in which the hard working cop is uplifted by the artist-victim's work." Send complete ms. Length: 300-3,000 words. Pays $5-15 plus up to 1 pound of contributor's copies.
Fiction: "Art-related, or 'odd' subjects." Buys 10 mss/year. Length: 250-1,000 words. Pays $5-15 and/or 1 pound of contributor's copies.
Poetry: Avant-garde, free verse and traditional. Poetry should be subject-oriented. Subjects are social critique, art and sex-role identity. No "romantic, organic sense-impressions, word-pictures, pure language, and so forth." Buys 25 mss/year. Submit maximum 10 poems. Length: 8-40 lines. Pays 1 pound of contributor's copies.
Tips: "A writer can break in with us by being straightforward, outspoken, original, well informed, individualistic, concerned. Our general tone, however, is not angry. We are often quite light and humorous. Try to avoid

'complaining' and feature concrete observation, evaluation and proposals. We would like to receive more articles and interviews—well written and not repeats of information published 1,000 times before. If the writer has no real-life experience, i.e., is all textbooks and academia, forget it. Material should be knowledgeable, but not so remote as to lack everyday application."

GLASS, Box 23383, Portland OR 97223. Contact: Editor. A fine arts quarterly publication that showcases all aspects of glass art as well as artists, collectors, museum exhibits, etc. Appeals to artists, hobbyists, museums, galleries, collectors and anyone else interested in looking at glass art. Circ. 30,000. Pays 1 month after publication.
Nonfiction: "This magazine showcases glass as a fine art, showing only the best. We are looking for artists' profiles, exhibit reviews, special features. Writing for this publication requires considerable knowledge about the medium." Pays $400 maximum.

‡GLASS CRAFT NEWS, [The Monthly Magazine for Stained Glass Enthusiasts], Edge Publishing Group, Room 1310, 270 Lafayette St., New York NY 10012. (212)966-6694. Editor: David Ostiller. Monthly magazine covering stained glass. "Our readers are stained glass hobbyists. We are interested in articles that are useful to them, rather than merely interesting." Estab. 1983. Circ. 40,000. Pays on publication. Byline given. Offers $25 kill fee. Buys first North American serial rights. Simultaneous queries, and simultaneous, photocopied and previously published submissions OK. Computer printout submissions acceptable. SASE. Reports in 2 weeks on queries; 1 month on mss. Sample copy for 9x12 SAE and 71¢ postage; writer's guidelines for 4x9½ SAE and 1 first class stamp.
Nonfiction: How-to (anything related to stained glass); interview/profile (of stained glass craftsmen); new product; and technical. "We like articles on techniques, features on individuals who are doing interesting work in glass (with emphasis on the technical aspects of their work), and marketing tips. We also want articles on subjects other than glass, which would be of use to hobbyists, e.g., cabinet making, lighting techniques and glass photography. We are not interested in non practical articles, such as stories about church windows or Louis Tiffany." Buys 30 mss/year. Query. Length: 500-2,000 words. Pays $50-200.
Photos: State availability of photos. Pays $5-25 for color contact sheets, transparencies and 8x10 prints. Identification of subjects required. Buys one-time rights.
Tips: "Freelancers should have a reasonable understanding of the crafts field, particularly stained glass. We get too many articles from people who are not familiar with their subject."

GLASS STUDIO, Box 23383, Portland OR 97223. Contact: Editor. For artists, craftspeople, and hobbyists working in blown glass, stained glass, conceptual glass, as well as collectors, museum curators, gallery and shop owners, students in the arts, and anyone else interested in glass art. Monthly. Circ. 30,000. Computer printout submissions acceptable; prefers letter-quality to dot-matrix. Pays 1 month after publication.
Nonfiction: "We are looking for technical articles, how-to articles from people who know what they're talking about. Also, features on artists, glass companies, and unusual stories related to glass art. Remember, you are writing for a specific audience that either works with glass or collects it." Pays $200 maximum.
Photos: No additional payment for photos used with mss.

METALSMITH, Society of North American Goldsmiths, 6707 N. Santa Monica Blvd., Milwaukee WI 53217-3940. Editor: Sarah Bodine. Editorial address: 1 Penn Lyle Rd., Princeton Jct. NJ 08550. Quarterly magazine covering craft metalwork and metal arts for people who work in metal and those interested in the field, including museum curators, collectors and teachers. The magazine covers all aspects of the craft including historical and technical articles, business and marketing advice and exhibition reviews. Circ. 3,000. Pays on publication. Byline given. Buys first North American serial rights. Submit seasonal/holiday material 6' months in advance. Photocopied and previously published submissions (foreign) OK. Computer printout submissions acceptable; prefers letter-quality to dot-matrix. SASE. Reports in 1 month on queries; 6 weeks on mss.
Nonfiction: Expose (metals, markets, theft); historical/nostalgic; how-to (advanced-level metalsmithing techniques); humor; inspirational; interview/profile; opinion (regular column); personal experience; photo feature; technical (research); and travel (Metalsmith's Guides to Cities). Special issues include Annual Summer Program Listing and Suppliers Listing. Buys 15 mss/year. Recent article example: "Beyond the Bench: Production Jewelers and How They Survive" (1984). Query with clips of published work and indicate "experience in the field or related fields." Length: 1,000-3,500 words. Pays $25-100/article.
Columns/Departments: Exhibition reviews; Issues: Galleries, Marketing and Business Advice, Metalsmith's Guides to Cities and Regions, and Book Reviews. Buys 20 mss/year. Query with clips of published work. Length: 250-3,000 words. Pays $10-50/article.
Tips: "The discovery of new talent is a priority—queries about innovative work which has not received much publicity are welcome. Almost all our writing is done by freelancers. Those knowledgeable in the field and who have previous experience in writing analysis and criticism are most sought after. *Metalsmith* is looking to build a stable of crafts writers and so far have found these few and far between. Those who have both a feeling

for metalwork of all kinds and a sharp pencil are sought. Articles must have some substance. We do not go for two-page spreads, so an idea submitted must have thematic unity and depth. We are not looking for pretty pictures of metalwork, but analysis, presentation of new or undiscovered talent and historical documentation. A few lines of explanation of a story idea are therefore helpful.''

THE ORIGINAL ART REPORT, Box 1641, Chicago IL 60690. Editor and Publisher: Frank Salantrie. 1% freelance written. Emphasizes ''visual art conditions from the visual artists', and general public's perspective.'' Newsletter; 6 pages. Pays on publication. Publishes ms an average of 1 month after acceptance. SASE. Reports in 2 weeks. Sample copy $1.25

Nonfiction: Exposé (art galleries, government agencies ripping off artists, or ignoring them); historical (perspective pieces relating to now); humor (whenever possible); informational (material that is unavailable in other art publications); inspirational (acts and ideas of courage); interview (with artists, other experts; serious material); personal opinion; technical (brief items to recall traditional methods of producing art); travel (places in the world where artists are welcome and honored); philosophical, economic, aesthetic, and artistic. ''No vanity profiles of artists, arts organizations, and arts promoters' operations.'' Buys 4-5 mss/year. Query or submit complete ms. Length: 1,000 words maximum. Pays 1¢/word.

Columns/Departments: New column: In Back of the Individual Artist. ''Artists express their views about non-art topics. After all, artists are in this world, too!''; WOW (Worth One Wow), Worth Repeating, and Worth Repeating Again. ''Basically, these are reprint items with introduction to give context and source, including complete name and address of publication. Looking for insightful, succinct commentary.'' Submit complete ms. Length: 500 words maximum. Pays ½¢/word.

Tips: ''I get excited when ideas are proposed which address substantive problems of individual artist in the art condition and as they affect the general population. Send original material that is direct and to the point, opinionated and knowledgeable. Write in a factual style with clarity. No straight educational or historical stuff, please.'' Recent article example: ''The Best May Be Illusory'' (Vol. 7, No. 7). Send SASE for free sample.

PLATE WORLD, The Magazine of Collector's Plates, Plate World Ltd., 6054 W. Touhy, Chicago IL 60648. (312)763-7773. Editor: Jane Grant Tougas. Associate Editor: Alyson Wycoff. 5% freelance written. Bimonthly magazine. ''We write exclusively about limited-edition collector's plates/artists/makers. Our audience is involved in plates as collectors or retailers, makers or producers.'' Circ. 75,000. Pays on publication. Publishes ms an average of 3 months after acceptance. Byline given. Offers 50% kill fee. Buys first and second rights to the same material. Makes work-for-hire assignments. Submit seasonal/holiday material 5 months in advance. Computer printout submissions acceptable; prefers letter-quality to dot-matrix. Reports in 2 weeks on queries; 1 week on mss. Sample copy $3.50; free writer's guidelines.

Nonfiction: Interview/profile (how artists create, biography of artist); photo feature (about artist or plate manufacturer). No critical attacks on industry. Buys 10 mss/year. Query. Pays $100-400.

Photos: Ingeborg Jakobson, art director. Human interest, technical. State availability of photos. Reviews transparencies. Pays negotiable rate. Identification of subjects required. Buys all rights.

Tips: Profiles of artists working in plates is the area most open to freelancers.

SOUTHWEST ART, Box 13037, Houston TX 77219. (713)850-0990. Editor: Susan Hallsten McGarry. Emphasizes art—painting and sculpture. Monthly. Pays on 10th of the month of publication. Buys first rights. Photocopied submissions OK. SASE. Reports in 3 months. Sample copy $6.

Nonfiction: Informational, interview, personal opinion, and profile. ''We publish articles about artists and art trends, concentrating on a geographical area west of the Mississippi. Articles should explore the artist's personality, philosophy, media and techniques, and means by which they convey ideas.'' Buys approximately 100 mss/year. Must submit 20 color prints/transparencies along with a full biography of the artist. If artist is accepted, article length is 1,800-2,000 words minimum. Pays $300 base.

Tips: ''Submit both published and unpublished samples of your writing. An indication of how quickly you work and your availability on short notice is helpful.''

WESTART, Box 1396, Auburn CA 95603. (916)885-0969. Editor-in-Chief: Martha Garcia. Emphasizes art for practicing artists and artist/craftsmen; students of art and art patrons. Semimonthly tabloid; 20 pages. Circ. 7,500. Pays on publication. Buys all rights. Byline given. Phone queries OK. Photocopied submissions OK. SASE required for reply and return of material. Sample copy 50¢; free writer's guidelines.

Nonfiction: Informational; photo feature and profile. No hobbies. Buys 6-8 mss/year. Query or submit complete ms. Length: 700-800 words. Pays 30¢/column inch.

Photos: Purchased with or without accompanying ms. Send b&w prints. Pays 30¢/column inch.

Tips: ''We publish information which is current—that is, we will use a review of an exhibition only if exhibition is still open on date of publication. Therefore, reviewer must be familiar with our printing deadlines and news deadlines.''

Association, Club, and Fraternal

Association publications link members who may live nearby or sometimes continents from one another. These publications keep members, friends and institutions informed of the ideals, objectives, projects, and activities of the sponsoring club or organization. Club-financed magazines that carry material not directly related to the group's activities (for example, *The American Legion Magazine* in the General Interest section) are classified by their subject matter in the Consumer and Trade Journals sections of this book.

CALIFORNIA HIGHWAY PATROLMAN, California Association of Highway Patrolmen, 2030 V St., Sacramento CA 95818. (916)452-6751. Editor: Carol Perri. 100% freelance written. Monthly magazine; 100 plus pages. Circ. 20,000. Pays on publication. Buys all rights. Computer printout submissions acceptable. SASE. Reports in 2 months. Free sample copy and writer's guidelines.
Nonfiction: Publishes articles on transportation safety and driver education. "Topics can include autos, boats, bicycles, motorcycles, snowmobiles, recreational vehicles and pedestrian safety. We are also in the market for California travel pieces and articles on early California. We are *not* a technical journal for teachers and traffic safety experts, but rather a general interest publication geared toward the layman." Pays 2½¢/word.
Photos: "Illustrated articles always receive preference." Pays $2.50/b&w photo. Captions and model releases required.

‡**CATHOLIC FORESTER**, Catholic Order of Foresters, 425 W. Shuman Blvd., Naperville IL 60540. Editor: Barbara Cunningham. A bimonthly magazine of short, general interest articles and fiction for members of the Order which is a fraternal insurance company. Family type audience, middle class. Circ. 150,000. Pays on acceptance. Byline given. Buys all rights. Submit seasonal/holiday material 3 months in advance. Simultaneous queries, and simultaneous, photocopied, and previously published submissions OK. Computer printout submissions acceptable; no dot-matrix. SASE. Reports in 3 weeks on queries; 6 weeks on ms. Sample copy for 8½x11 SASE; free writer's guidelines.
Nonfiction: General interest; historical/nostalgic; how-to (carpentry, cooking, repairs, etc.) humor; inspirational; interview/profile; new product; opinion; personal experience; photo feature; technical (depends on subject); and travel. No blatant sex nor anything too violent. Query with or without published clips, or send complete ms. Length: 1,000-3,000 words. Pays $50 minimum.
Photos: Prefers something of unusual interest or story-telling. State availability of photos, or send photos with query or ms. Reviews any size b&w and color prints. Payment to be determined. Captions, model releases, and identification of subjects required. Buys one-time rights.
Columns/Departments: Needs unusual items on what is going on in the world; new, interesting products or discoveries. Query or send complete ms. Length: 1,000 words. Payment to be determined.
Fiction: Adventure, historical, humorous, mainstream, mystery, religious (Catholic), romance, suspense and western. No sex or extreme violence. Length: 1,200-5,000 words. Pays $50 minimum.
Poetry: Free verse, Haiku, light verse, traditional. Submit maximum 5 poems. Payment to be determined.
Fillers: Jokes, anecdotes, short humor. Length: 300-500 words. Payment to be determined.
Tips: "Short feature articles of interest to the all-American type are most open to freelancers."

‡**CBIA NEWS, Journal of the Connecticut Business and Industry Association**, CBIA Service Corp., 370 Asylum St., Hartford CT 06103. (203)547-1661. Editor: Mara Braverman. A monthly tabloid (except combined July/August issue) covering business in Connecticut for approximately 6,500 member companies. Half of the *News* is about the association and written in-house. Other half is about how to run your business better; interesting businesspeople in Connecticut, and business trends here. These are sometimes written by freelancers. Circ. 7,200. Pays on acceptance. Byline given. Offers 20% kill fee. Buys variable rights; can be negotiable. Photocopied and previously published submissions OK. Computer printout submissions acceptable. SASE. Reports in 2 weeks. Free sample copy.
Nonfiction: Book excerpts, how-to (how to run your business better in some specific way); interview/profile (must be a Connecticut person). Buys approximately 20 mss/year. Query with published clips. Length and payment vary with the subject.
Photos: State availability of photos with query or ms. Reviews b&w contact sheets. Pays negotiable rate. Model release and identification of subjects required.
Tips: Write to me including resume and clips. They do *not* have to be from business publications. If I'm interested, I'll contact you and describe fees, rules, etc. You can include ideas, but it's not necessary. I'm most interested in writers who live in or near Connecticut, since everything must be applicable to Connecticut business."

‡**CHARIOT**, Ben Hur Life Association, Box 312, Crawfordsville IN 47933. (317)362-4500. Editor: Loren Harrington. A quarterly magazine covering fraternal activities plus general interest items. Circ. 12,000. Pays on acceptance. Byline given. Not copyrighted. Buys variable rights. Submit seasonal/holiday material 8-10 months in advance. Simultaneous queries, and simultaneous and photocopied submissions OK. Computer printout submissions acceptable. SASE. Reports in 2 weeks on queries; 1 month on mss. Sample copy for 8½x11 SAE and 4 first class stamps—for *serious* inquiries only; writer's guidelines for 8½x11 SAE and 2 first class stamps.
Nonfiction: General interest, historical and how-to. "Absolutely *nothing* of a smutty, sexually-oriented, gay, etc. nature. Only items of benefit to our readers and/or family would be considered." Rarely buys mss. Query with or without published clips, or send complete ms. Length: 300-10,000 words. Pays 3-20¢/word.
Photos: State availability of photos with query letter or ms. "We would like to have quality photo with query. We will return if rejected." Reviews b&w and color contact sheets and b&w and color prints. Payment for photos included in payment for mss. Captions, model release and identification of subjects required. Buys one-time rights.
Columns/Departments: Columns are editorial or insurance-related. "Would consider a query piece, but it would have to be extremely applicable."
Fiction: "Absolutely *nothing* of a smutty, sexually-oriented, gay etc. nature. Only stories of benefit to our readers and/or family would be considered." Query with or without published clips or send complete ms. Length: 300-10,000 words. Pays 3-20¢/word.
Poetry: Light verse and traditional. "Poetry not normally used, but would consider short snappy poems as filler material." Length: open. Pays 3-20¢/word.
Fillers: Clippings, jokes, gags, anecdotes, short humor and newsbreaks. Rarely buys fillers. Length: open. Pays $1-20.
Tips: "Our requirements are very tightly edited and professionally written with a wide appeal to our particular audience, self-help volunteer and charity. Those items that we can give our local units to encourage their fraternal practiciation and projects would be considered more than any other single submitted features. Only on rare occasions in the past have we looked to outside submitted features. Our current procedures, however, will probably tend to encourage such things in the future."

THE ELKS MAGAZINE, 425 W. Diversey, Chicago IL 60614. Managing Editor: Herbert Gates. 50% freelance written. Emphasizes general interest with family appeal. Magazine published 10 times/year. 56 pages. Circ. 1,600,000. Pays on acceptance. Publishes mss an average of 6 months after acceptance. Buys first North American serial rights. Computer printout submissions acceptable; prefers letter-quality to dot-matrix. SASE. Reports in 6 weeks. Free sample copy and writer's guidelines.
Nonfiction: Articles of information, business, contemporary life problems and situations, or just interesting topics, ranging from medicine, science, and history, to sports. "The articles should not just be a rehash of existing material. They must be fresh, provocative, thought provoking, well researched and documented. No fiction, travel or political articles, fillers or verse. Buys 2-3 mss/issue. Written query a must. No phone queries. Length 2,000-3,000 words. Pays $150-500.
Photos: Purchased with or without accompanying manuscript (for cover). Captions required. Query with b&w photos or send transparencies. Uses 8x10 or 5x7 b&w glossies and 35mm or 2¼x2¼ color transparencies (for cover). Pays $250 minimum for color (cover). Offers no additional payment for photos accepted with mss.
Tips: "Since we continue to offer sample copies and guidelines for the asking there is no excuse for being unfamiliar with *The Elks Magazine*. A submission, following a query letter go-ahead would do best to include several b&w prints, if the piece lends itself to illustration."

‡**FEDCO REPORTER, A Publication Exclusively for FEDCO Members**, 9300 Santa Fe Springs Rd., Santa Fe Springs CA 90670. (213)946-2511. Articles Editor: Francine Buschel. A monthly catalog/magazine for FEDCO department store members, covering FEDCO merchandise and including "articles designed to help members improve their homes, lower their cost of living, develop new skills, and learn about new trends." Circ. 1,800,000. Pays on acceptance. Byline given. Offers $50 kill fee. Buys all rights but will reassign rights to author upon request. Photocopied and previously published submissions OK. SASE. Reports in 6 weeks. Sample copy for 9x12 SASE; writer's guidelines for SASE.
Nonfiction: General interest, how-to, interview/profile, new product, travel, electronics, stereos, photography, family finances and automotive. No first person narrative. Buys 50 mss/year. Query with published clips. Length: 300-1,000 words. Pays $100-350.
Photos: State availability of photos. Reviews b&w and color slides. Pays negotiable fee.
Columns/Departments: Spotlight (bimonthly column on celebrities with special emphasis on recipes, tips, fitness routines and fashion), and You and Your Car. Buys 12 mss/year. Query with or without published clips. Length: 350-1,000 words. Pays $50-350.
Fillers: Historical anecdotes or everyday information.
Tips: "The entire editorial content of our publication is based on freelance submissions. Articles should be of topical interest to consumers. How-tos are very popular."

‡● **GRACE DIGEST**, W.R. Grace & Co., 1114 Avenue of Americas, New York NY 10036. (212)819-6003. Editor: Joyce Cole. A semiannual magazine covering Grace products and people; company divisions and subsidiaries. "Articles are written in lay terms for shareholders and all Grace employees." Circ. 10,000. Computer printout submissions acceptable; no dot-matrix. SASE. Free sample copy.
Nonfiction: Interview/profile, technical (in lay terms). Buys 5-10 mss/year. Query with published clips. Pays competitive rates.
Photos: State availability of photos. Captions, model release and identification of subjects required.

‡**HCA COMPANION**, Hospital Media, Inc., Box 2733, Knoxville TN 37901. (615)523-4301. Editor: A. Richard Johnson. A general interest magazine for Hospital Corporation of America patients, visitors and staff. Estab. 1983. Circ. 700,000. Pays on acceptance. Computer printout submissions acceptable. SASE. Reports in several weeks. Sample copy $2; writer's guidelines for SAE and 1 first class stamp.
Nonfiction: General interest; how-to (gardening); humor; inspirational; travel; recreation; nature; entertainment; essay; and Americana. No health or diet-related articles. Buys 32 mss/year. Query with clips of published work. Length: 500-2,500 words. Pays $250-2,500; "depends on length of article, value of submission, experience of author."

THE KIWANIS MAGAZINE, 3636 Woodview Trace, Indianapolis IN 46268. Executive Editor: Scott Pemberton. 95% of feature articles freelance written. Magazine published 10 times/year for business and professional men and their families. Circ. 300,000. Buys first North American serial rights. Pays 20-40% kill fee. Byline given. Pays on acceptance. Publishes ms an average of 6 months after acceptance. Free sample copy and writer's guidelines with large SASE. Computer printout submissions acceptable "if clear, paper is of good quality, and print is of typewriter quality. Prefer writers separate sheets before submission." Reports in 1 month. SASE.
Nonfiction and Photos: Articles about social and civic betterment, business, education, religion, family, sports, health, recreation, etc. Emphasis on objectivity, intelligent analysis and thorough research of contemporary problems. Concise, lively writing, absence of cliches, and impartial presentation of controversy required. Especially needs "articles on business and professional topics that will directly assist the readers in their own businesses (generally independent retailers and companies of less than 25 employees) or careers. We have an increasing need for articles of international interest and those that will enlighten our readers about the problems of underprivileged children and the handicapped." Length: 1,500-3,000 words. Pays $300-750. "No fiction, personal essays, fillers or verse of any kind. A light or humorous approach welcomed where subject is appropriate and all other requirements are observed. Detailed queries can save work and submission time. We often accept photos submitted with mss, but we do not pay extra for them; they are considered part of the price of the ms. Our rate for a ms with good photos is higher than for one without." Query.
Tips: "Freelance writers should be aware of a trend toward more stories of shorter length in a publication."

‡**LEFTHANDER MAGAZINE, Membership Publication of Lefthanders International**, Lefthanders International, 3601 SW 29th St., Topeka KS 66614. (913)273-0680. Executive Director: Carol O'Donnell. Managing Editor: Mary Betzen. 90% freelance written. Magazine covering handedness/brain dominance. "Our readers are lefthanded people of all ages and interest in 50 US states and 10 foreign countries. The one thing they have in common is a pride and interest in lefthandedness as a way of life, as a personal asset, and as a common bond with other members." Circ. 4,000. Pays on publication. Publishes ms an average of 2 months after acceptance. Byline given. Offers 25% kill fee. Buys all rights. Submit seasonal/holiday material 6 months in advance. Simultaneous queries, and simultaneous, photocopied and previously published work OK. Computer printout submissions acceptable; prefers letter-quality to dot-matrix. SASE. Reports in 4 weeks on queries. Sample copy for 8½x11 SAE and 5 first class stamps; writer's guidelines for legal-size SAE and 25¢ postage.
Nonfiction: Book excerpts, expose, general interest, how-to (sports and crafts for lefthanded people), humor, interview/profile, new product and personal experience. All articles should relate to lefthandedness. Buys 30-40 mss/year. Query with published clips. Length: 250-1,000 words. Pays $50-100.
Photos: State availability of photos. Pays $10-50 for 8x10 b&w prints. Captions, model release and identification of subjects required. Buys variable rights.
Fiction: Adventure (lefthandedness), humorous (lefthandedness). No confession, erotic, horror or religious material. Buys fewer than 10 mss/year. Query with published clips. Length: 250-1,000 words. Pays $50-100.
Fillers: Clippings, jokes, gags, anecdotes, short humor. Buys fewer than 10 mss/year. Length: 10-100 words. Pays $20-50.
Tips: "Freelance writers should be aware of the movement toward quick, practical, self-help and self-awareness types of editorial content. We look for pieces about discrimination in the workplace, research, and 'lefty' celebrity interviews. We prefer brief, light, general interest topics and consumer information, education and product pieces. Query with specific article proposals. Being lefthanded helps, but isn't required."

THE LION, 300 22nd St., Oak Brook IL 60570. (312)986-1700. Editor-in-Chief: Roy Schaetzel. Senior Editor: Robert Kleinfelder. 40% freelance written. Covers service club organization for Lions Club members and their families. Monthly magazine; 36 pages. Circ. 670,000. Pays on acceptance. Publishes ms an average of 5 months after acceptance. Buys all rights. Byline given. Phone queries OK. Photocopied submissions OK. SASE. Reports in 2 weeks. Free sample copy and writer's guidelines.
Nonfiction: Informational (stories of interest to civic-minded men) and photo feature (must be of a Lions Club service project). No travel, biography, or personal experiences. No sensationalism. Prefers anecdotes in articles. Buys 4 mss/issue. Query. Length: 500-2,200. Pays $50-400.
Photos: Purchased with or without accompanying ms or on assignment. Captions required. Query for photos. B&w and color glossies at least 5x7 or 35mm color slides. Total purchase price for ms includes payment for photos, accepted with ms. "Be sure photos are clear and as candid as possible."
Tips: "Trends in magazine publishing that freelance writers should be aware of include more specialization and less personal experience and biographical material."

NATIONAL 4-H NEWS, 7100 Connecticut Ave., Chevy Chase MD 20815. (301)656-9000, ext. 203. Editor: Suzanne C. Harting. 20% freelance written. For "volunteers of a wide range of ages who lead 4-H clubs; most with high school, many with college education, whose primary reason for reading us is their interest in working with kids in informal youth education projects, ranging from aerospace to sewing, and almost anything in between." Monthly. Circ. 70,000. Buys first serial or one-time rights. Computer printout submissions acceptable. Buys about 1-2 unsolicited mss/year. Pays on acceptance. Publishes ms an average of 6 months after acceptance. Free sample copy and writer's guidelines. Query with outline. "We are very specialized, and unless a writer has been published in our magazine before, he more than likely doesn't have a clue to what we can use. When query comes about a specific topic, we often can suggest angles that make it usable." Submit seasonal material 1 year in advance. Reports in 1 month. SASE.
Nonfiction: "Education and child psychology from authorities, written in light, easy-to-read fashion with specific suggestions how the layman can apply principles in volunteer work with youth; how-to-do-it pieces about genuinely new and interesting crafts of any kind. Craft articles must be fresh in style and ideas, and tell how to make something worthwhile . . . almost anything that tells about kids having fun and learning outside the classroom, including how they became interested, most effective programs, etc., always with enough detail and examples, so reader can repeat project or program with his or her group, merely by reading the article. Speak directly to our reader (you) without preaching. Tell him in a conversational manner how he might work better with kids to help them have fun and learn at the same time. Use lots of genuine examples (although names and dates are not important) to illustrate points. Use contractions when applicable. Write in a concise, interesting way. Our readers have other jobs and not a lot of time to spend with us. Will not print personal reminiscences, stories on 'How this 4-H club made good' or about state or county fair winners." Length: 3-8 pages, typewritten, doublespaced. Payment up to $200, depending on quality and accompanying photos or illustrations.
Photos: State availability of photos. "Photos must be genuinely candid, of excellent technical quality and preferably shot 'available light' or in that style; must show young people or adults and young people having fun learning something. How to photos or drawings must supplement instructional texts. Photos do not necessarily have to include people. Photos are usually purchased with accompanying ms, with no additional payment. Captions required. If we use an excellent single photo, we generally pay $25 and up."
Tips: There will be "more emphasis on interpersonal skills, techniques for working with kids, more focus on the family. Familiarity with the 4-H program and philosophy is most helpful. Write for sample copy. I judge a writer's technical skills by the grammar and syntax of query letter; seldom ask for a ms I think will require extensive reorganization or heavy editing." Recent article example: "Raise a Champion" (November 1983.)

THE OPTIMIST MAGAZINE, Optimist International, 4494 Lindell Blvd., St. Louis MO 63108. (314)371-6000. Editor: Dennis R. Osterwisch. Assistant Editor: Kathy Robertson. 20% freelance written. Monthly magazine about the work of Optimist clubs and members for the 148,000 members of the Optimist clubs in the United States and Canada. Circ. 148,000. Pays on acceptance. Publishes ms an average of 4 months after acceptance. Buys first North American serial rights. Submit seasonal material 3 months in advance. Photocopied and previously published submissions OK. SASE. Reports in 1 week. Free sample copy and writer's guidelines.
Nonfiction: General interest (people, places and things that would interest men dedicated to community service through volunteer work); interview (members who have in some way distinguished themselves). No articles of a negative nature. "A well-written article on some unusual Optimist-related activity with good action photos will probably be purchased, as well as upbeat general interest articles that point out the good side of life, anything that promotes fellowship, international understanding, respect for the law, and anything that highlights what's good about the youth of today." Buys 2-3 mss/issue. Query. "Submit a letter that conveys your ability to turn out a well-written article and tells exactly what the scope of the article will be and whether photos are available." Length: 1,000-1,500 words. Pays $100-150.
Photos: State availability of photos. Payment negotiated. Captions preferred. Buys all rights. "No mug shots or people lined up against the wall shaking hands. We're always looking for good color photos relating to Opti-

mist activities that could be used on our front cover. Colors must be sharp and the composition must be suitable to fit an 8½x11 cover.''

Tips: ''We are mainly interested in seeing general-interest articles from freelancers because most club activities are better covered by club members. We're open to almost any idea; that's why all queries will be carefully considered. We don't want stories about a writer's Uncle Clem who 'had a rough life but always kept a smile on his face.' If you don't know about Optimist International, ask for our free sample magazine.''

PERSPECTIVE, Pioneer Clubs, Division of Pioneer Ministries, Inc., Box 788, Wheaton IL 60189. (312)293-1600. Editor: Lorraine G. Mulligan. 5% freelance written. ''All subscribers are volunteer leaders of clubs for girls and boys in grades 1-12. Clubs are sponsored by evangelical, conservative churches throughout North America.'' Quarterly magazine; 32 pages. Circ. 24,000. Pays on acceptance. Publishes ms an average of 6 weeks after acceptance. Buys first North American serial rights and second (reprint) rights to material originally published elsewhere. Submit seasonal/holiday material 9 months in advance. Simultaneous submissions OK. SASE. Reports in 6 weeks. Sample copy $1; writer's guidelines for SASE.

Nonfiction: How-to (projects for clubs, crafts, cooking, service), informational (relationships, human development, mission education, outdoor activities), inspirational (Bible studies, adult leading youths), interview (Christian education leaders), personal experience (of club leaders). Buys 4-10 mss/year; 3 unsolicited/year. Byline given. Query. Length: 200-1,500 words. Pays $10-60.

Columns/Departments: Storehouse (craft, game, activity, outdoor activity suggestions—all related to club projects for any age between grades 1-12). Buys 8-10 mss/year. Submit complete ms. Length: 150-250 words. Pays $8-10.

Tips: ''Submit articles directly related to club work, practical in nature, i.e., ideas for leader training in communication, Bible knowledge, teaching skills. They must have practical application. We want substance—not ephemeral ideas. In addition to a summary of the article idea and evidence that the writer has knowledge of the subject, we want evidence that the author understands our purpose and philosophy. We're doing more and more inhouse writing—less purchasing of any freelance.''

THE ROTARIAN, Official Magazine of Rotary International, 1600 Ridge Ave., Evanston IL 60201. (312)328-0100. Editor: Willmon L. White. 50% freelance written. For Rotarian business and professional men and their families; for schools, libraries, hospitals, etc. Monthly. Circ. 475,000. Usually buys all rights. Pays on acceptance. Free sample copy and editorial fact sheet. Query preferred. Reports in 1 month. SASE.

Nonfiction: ''The field for freelance articles is in the general interest category. These run the gamut from guidelines for daily living to such concerns as world hunger, the nuclear arms race, and preservation of environment. Recent articles have dealt with international illiteracy, energy, dehumanization of the elderly, and worldwide drug abuse and prevention. Articles should appeal to an international audience and should in some way help Rotarians help other people. An article may increase a reader's understanding of world affairs, thereby making him a better world citizen. It may educate him in civic matters, thus helping him improve his town. It may help him to become a better employer, or a better human being. We are interested in articles on unusual Rotary club projects or really unusual Rotarians. We carry debates and symposiums, but are careful to show more than one point of view. We present arguments for effective politics and business ethics, but avoid expose and muckraking. Controversy is welcome if it gets our readers to think but does not offend ethnic or religious groups. In short, the rationale of the organization is one of hope and encouragement and belief in the power of individuals talking and working together.'' Length: 1,000-2,000 words. Payment varies.

Photos: Purchased with mss or with captions only. Prefers 2¼x2¼ or larger color transparencies, but also uses 35mm. B&w prints and photo essays. Vertical shots preferred to horizontal. Scenes of international interest. Color cover.

THE SAMPLE CASE, The Order of United Commercial Travelers of America, 632 N. Park St., Box 159019, Columbus OH 43215. (614)228-3276. Editor: J. Jeffrey Rennie. Editorial Assistant: William J. Purpura. Bimonthly magazine covering news for members of the United Commercial Travelers. Emphasizes fraternalism for its officers and active membership. Circ. 180,000. Pays on publication. Buys one-time rights. Submit seasonal/holiday material 6 months in advance. Simultaneous queries and submissions OK. SASE. Reports in 3 months. Free sample copy and writer's guidelines.

Nonfiction: Articles on travel destination (cities and regions in the US and Canada); food/cuisine; health/fitness/safety; hobbies/entertainment; fraternal/civic activities; business finance/insurance. No fiction or personal experience written from first-person point of view. Submit complete ms. Length: 500-2,000 words. Pays 10¢/word.

Photos: David Knapp, art director. State availability of photos with ms. Pays minimum $20 for 5x7 b&w or larger prints; $30 for 35mm or larger color transparencies used inside (more for cover). Captions required.

Columns/Departments: Traveline (a regular column featuring information on certain travel topics—packing, train excursions, golf packages, etc.). Query with published clips. Length: 500-2,000 words. Pays 10¢/word.

THE TOASTMASTER, Box 10400, Santa Ana CA 92711. (714)542-6793. Editor-in-Chief: Tamara Nunn. 40-50% freelance written. Covers communication and leadership techniques; self-development for members of Toastmasters International, Inc. Monthly magazine; 32 pages. Circ. 100,000. Pays on acceptance. Buys all rights. Byline given. Photocopied submissions and previously published work OK. SASE. Reports in 3 weeks. Free sample copy and writer's guidelines.

Nonfiction: How-to (improve speaking, listening, thinking skills; on leadership or management techniques, etc., with realistic examples), humor (on leadership, communications or management techniques), interviews (with communications or management experts offering advice that members can directly apply to their self-development efforts; should contain "how to" information). No articles on fear of speaking, time management, meeting planning or basic speaking techniques. Buys 20-30 mss/year. Query. Length: 1,800-3,000 words. Pays $25-150.

Photos: Purchased with or without ms. Query. Pays $10-50 for 5x7 or 8x10 b&w glossy prints; $35-75 for color transparencies. Offers no additional payment for photos accepted with ms.

Tips: "The most annoying aspect of working with freelance writers is their insistence on calling to find out when we'll publish their work. Trends in magazine publishing that freelance writers should be aware of include a tendency toward specialization—stories that require a writer to have personal knowledge (indepth) of a topic. Also, word processing can make or break a freelancer. One freelancer said his income has *tripled* since he acquired a word processor."

‡VACATION TIMES AND BUSINESS TRAVEL, (formerly *Vacation Times*), Evening Star Inc. dba Airline Discount Club-International, Box 616, Parker CO 80134. (303)841-4337. Editor: Richard A. Bodner. A quarterly magazine available only to club members covering discounted accommodations, travel and other savings available through ADC-I. "We offer airline employee 'discount' prices to our members on a variety of accommodations, flights, car rentals and activities. We want to expand our format to feature money saving tips for vacation and destination feaures for the areas in which we have properties available. Readers are mature adults with above average income." Estab. 1982. Circ. 2000 +. Pays on acceptance. Byline given. Buys simultaneous rights and second serial (reprint) rights. Submit seasonal/holiday material 6 months in advance. Simultaneous, photocopied, and previously published submissions OK. SASE. Reports in 3 weeks. Sample copy $3; writer's guidelines 25¢.

Nonfiction: Historical/nostalgic, how-to, personal experience and travel. "Articles should relate to saving money while on vacation, features about destination activites, background/history of area(s), bargain purchases, how to plan a vacation, tips for the business traveler, and others of interest to the vacationer. Do not send articles that are unrelated to areas in which we have properties available. No articles about camping, hunting, fishing." Buys 12-16 mss/year. Send complete ms. Length: 300-1,200 words. Pays $35-100.

Photos: Brad Margritz, photo editor. State availability of photos. Pays $5-15 for b&w slides and 3x4 prints. Captions and model release required. Buys one-time rights.

Tips: "All articles should be geared to the vacationer or business traveller interested in saving money or pertain to areas in which we offer discounted accommodations. To expand our marketing horizons we will be adding a number of Hotels/Motels in the US and Europe that extend a direct discount to our members. The name of our magazine changed effective with the October 1984 issue to *Vacation Times and Business Travel*."

WOODMEN OF THE WORLD MAGAZINE, 1700 Farnam St., Omaha NE 68102. (402)342-1890, ext. 302. Editor: Leland A. Larson. 20% freelance written. Published by Woodmen of the World Life Insurance Society for "people of all ages in all walks of life. We have both adult and children readers from all types of American families." Monthly. Circ. 467,000. Not copyrighted. Buys 20 mss/year. Byline given. Pays on acceptance. Will send a sample copy to a writer on request. Will consider photocopied and simultaneous submissions. Submit complete ms. Submit seasonal material 3 months in advance. Reports in 5 weeks. SASE.

Nonfiction: "General interest articles which appeal to the American family—travel, history, art, new products, how-to, sports, hobbies, food, home decorating, family expenses, etc. Because we are a fraternal benefit society operating under a lodge system, we often carry stories on how a number of people can enjoy social or recreational activities as a group. No special approach required. We want more 'consumer type' articles, humor, historical articles, think pieces, nostalgia, photo articles." Buys 15-24 unsolicited mss/year. Length: 1,500 words or less. Pays $10 minimum, 5¢/word depending on count.

Photos: Purchased with or without mss; captions optional "but suggested." Uses 8x10 glossy prints, 4x5 transparencies ("and possibly down to 35mm"). Payment "depends on use." For b&w photos, pays $25 for cover, $10 for inside. Color prices vary according to use and quality with $100 maximum. Minimum of $25 for inside use; up to $100 for covers.

Fiction: Humorous and historical short stories. Length: 1,500 words or less. Pays "$10 minimum or 5¢/word, depending on count."

Astrology and Psychic

The person writing on these phenomena must rely on research—seeing a popular movie on the subjects in most cases won't suffice. The following publications regard astrology, psychic phenomena, ESP experiences, and related subjects as sciences or as objects of serious scientific research.

DOORWAYS TO THE MIND, Aries Productions, Inc., Box 24571, Creve Coeur MO 63141. (314)872-9127. Editor: Beverly C. Jaegers. Managing Editor: G. Weingart. 50-90% freelance written. Quarterly magazine covering mind development, PSI, practical ESP, stocks and Wall Street, and criminal detection with ESP, predictions. For a general audience interested in mental development and self-help/ESP using Russian/USA methods. Pays on publication. Publishes ms an average of 6 months after acceptance. Byline given. Not copyrighted. Buys one-time rights. Submit seasonal/holiday material 4 months in advance. Simultaneous queries, and simultaneous, photocopied, and previously published submissions OK. SASE. Reports in 6 weeks. Sample copy for $1, 9x12 SAE, and 3 first class stamps; writer's guidelines for business size SAE and 2 first class stamps.
Nonfiction: Michael Christopher, articles editor. Book excerpts, general interest, inspirational, interview/profile, opinion. Not interested in articles on witchcraft, the occult, UFOs, space creatures or space vehicles, etc. Buys 4-10 mss/year. Send complete ms. Length: 1,000-10,000 words. Pays $10 minimum.
Columns/Departments: Michael Christopher, column/department editor. News & Notes, Book Reviews. Buys 10-12 mss/year. Send complete ms. Length: 200-350 words. Pays $5 minimum.
Poetry: Light verse, traditional. Buys 3-4/year. Submit maximum 5 poems. Pays $5 minimum.
Fillers: Clippings, newsbreaks. Buys variable number/year. Length: 200-550 words. Pays $2 minimum.
Tips: "Write realistically. Research and include helpful data on ESP development, mind control and special studies such as grapho analysis, astrology, archeology, and crime detection with ESP."

FATE, Clark Publishing Co., 500 Hyacinth Place, Highland Park IL 60035. Editor: Mary Margaret Fuller. 70% freelance written. Monthly. Buys all rights; occasionally North American serial rights only. Byline given. Pays on publication. Query. Reports in 2 months. SASE.
Nonfiction and Fillers: Personal psychic experiences, 300-500 words. Pays $10. New frontiers of science, and ancient civilizations, 2,000-3,000 words; also parapsychology, occultism, witchcraft, magic, spiritual healing miracles, flying saucers, etc. Must include complete authenticating details. Prefers interesting accounts of single events rather than roundups. "We very frequently accept manuscripts from new writers; the majority are individuals' first-person accounts of their own psychic experience. We do need to have all details, where, when, why, who and what, included for complete documentation." Pays minimum of 5¢/word. Fillers should be fully authenticated. Length: 100-300 words.
Photos: Buys good glossy prints with mss. Pays $5-10.

HOROSCOPE, The World's Leading Astrological Magazine, Dell Publishing Co., Inc., 1 Dag Hammarskjold Plaza, 245 E. 47th St., New York NY 10017. (212)605-3439. Editor: Julia A. Wagner. Monthly magazine covering "mundane astrology, self-help, problem analysis. Audience is middle class in the age group 15-80." Circ. 240,000. Pays on acceptance. Byline given. Buys all rights. Submit seasonal/holiday material 6 months in advance. Simultaneous queries OK, but not submissions. SASE. Reports in 2 weeks on queries; 3 months on mss. Free sample copy and writer's guidelines.
Nonfiction: General interest, how-to, technical. Articles must be based on the tropical, not the sidereal, zodiac. No series, planets in the signs, planets in the houses. Buys 75 mss/year. Query. Length: 1,000-2,000 words. Pays 7¢/word.
Fillers: Anecdotes. Buys 240/year. Length: 30-100 words. Pays 7¢/word.
Tips: "You must be skilled as an astrologer and a writer. How-to and self-help articles are most open to freelancers."

HOROSCOPE GUIDE, Box 70, West Springfield MA 01090. Contact: Editor. 75% freelance written. For persons interested in astrology as it touches their daily lives; all ages. Monthly. Circ. 50,000. Buys all rights. Byline given. Buys 40 mss/year. Pays on publication. Publishes ms an average of 3 months after acceptance. Sample copy for $1.50. Photocopied submissions OK. Submit seasonal material 5 months in advance. Submit complete ms. SASE.
Nonfiction, Poetry and Fillers: Wants anything of good interest to the average astrology buff, preferably not so technical as to require more than basic knowledge of birth sign by reader. Mss should be light, readable, entertaining and sometimes humorous. Not as detailed and technical as other astrology magazines, "with the as-

tro-writer doing the interpreting without long-winded reference to his methods at every juncture. We are less reverent of astrological red tape." Wants mss about man-woman relationships, preferably in entertaining and occasionally humorous fashion. No textbook-type material. Does not want to see a teacher's type of approach to the subject. Length: 900-4,000 words. Pays 2-3¢/word. Buys traditional forms of poetry. Length: 4-16 lines. Pays $2-$8.
Tips: "Best way to break in with us is with some lively Sun-sign type piece involving some area of man-woman relationships—love, sex, marriage, divorce, differing views on money, religion, child-raising, in-laws, vacations, politics, lifestyles, etc."

‡**PREDICTION, The Magazine for Astrology and the Occult**, Link House Magazines (Croydon) Ltd., Link House, Dingwall Ave., Croydon, CR9 2TA, England. 01-686-2599. Editor: Jo Logan. Monthly magazine. Circ. 35,000. Pays on acceptance. Byline given. Buys first British serial rights. SAE and IRCs. Reports in 1 month. Free sample copy.
Nonfiction: New product (within confines of magazine); personal experience (of an occult nature only); and technical (astrology, tarot, palmistry, alternative medicine, etc.). Buys 50 mss/year. Send complete ms. Length: 1,000-2,000 words. Pays £20-80.
Columns/Departments: Astrology. Buys 12 mss/year. Length: 750 words. Pays £20.
Fillers: Clippings, anecdotes and newsbreaks.
Tips: "Feature articles with an occult slant and astrological profiles (with charts) of personalities living or dead are most open to freelancers."

Automotive and Motorcycle

Publications in this section detail the maintenance, operation, performance, racing and judging of automobiles, and recreational vehicles. Publications that treat vehicles as a means of transportation or shelter instead of as a hobby or sport are classified in the Travel, Camping, and Trailer category. Journals for teamsters, service station operators, and auto and motorcycle dealers will be found in the Auto and Truck classification of the Trade Journals section.

AMERICAN MOTORCYCLIST, American Motorcyclist Association, Box 141, Westerville OH 43081. (614)891-2425. Executive Editor: Greg Harrison. For "enthusiastic motorcyclists, investing considerable time and money in the sport. Unlike most motorcycle magazines, we never publish road tests or product evaluations unless they are related to safety or anti-theft. We emphasize the motorcyclist, not the vehicle." Monthly magazine. Circ. 127,000. Pays on publication. Rights purchased vary with author and material. Pays 25-50% kill fee. Byline given. Query. Submit seasonal/holiday material 4 months in advance. SASE. Reports in 1 month. Sample copy $1.25.
Nonfiction: How-to (different and/or unusual ways to use a motorcycle or have fun on one); historical (the heritage of motorcycling, particularly as it relates to the AMA); interviews (with interesting personalities in the world of motorcycling); photo feature (quality work on any aspect of motorcycling); and technical (well-researched articles on safe riding techniques). No product evaluations or stories on motorcycling events not sanctioned by the AMA. Buys 10-15 mss/year. Query. Length: 500 words minimum. Pays minimum $2/published column inch.
Photos: Purchased with or without accompanying ms, or on assignment. Captions required. Query. Pays $15 minimum per photo published.
Tips: "Accuracy and reliability are prime factors in our work with freelancers. We emphasize the rider, not the motorcycle itself. It's always best to query us first and the further in advance the better to allow for scheduling."

AUTOBUFF MAGAZINE, The Magazine for the Adult Automotive Enthusiast, Carnaby Communications Corp., Suite 100, 4480 N. Shallowford Rd., Atlanta, GA 30338. (404)394-0010. Executive Publisher: F. Fittanto. 35% freelance written. Monthly magazine covering high-performance automobiles for 18-34-year-old males with high discretionary incomes and an interest in beautiful women. Circ. 200,000. Pays on acceptance. Publishes ms an average of 4 months after acceptance. Byline given. Buys one-time rights. Simultaneous and photocopied submissions OK. SASE. Reports in 3 weeks. Sample copy for 9x12 SAE and $1.22 postage; writer's guidelines for SAE and 1 first class stamp.

Nonfiction: How-to (high performance automotive); humor (auto related); technical (high performance automotive). No women's lib, gay material. "Each issue features the finest 'street machines' the country has to offer along with the most attractive female models to be found anywhere." Buys 12 mss/year. Send complete ms. Length: 1,500-2,500 words. Pays $150-250.
Photos: Send photos with ms. Reviews 2¼ or 35mm color transparencies and 8x10 b&w prints. Captions and model release required. Buys all rights.
Fiction: Adventure, erotica, humorous. Buys 15 mss/year. Send complete ms. Length: 1,500-2,500 words. Pays $150-250.

AUTOMOBILE QUARTERLY, 221 Nassau St., Princeton NJ 08542. (609)924-7555. Editor-in-Chief: L. Scott Bailey. Emphasizes automobiles and automobile history. Quarterly hardbound magazine; 112 pages. Circ. 30,000. Pays on acceptance. Buys all rights. Pays expenses as kill fee. Byline given. SASE. Reports in 3 weeks. Sample copy $13.95.
Nonfiction: Authoritative articles relating to the automobile and automobile history. Historical, interview and nostalgia. Buys 5 mss/issue. Query. Length: 2,000-20,000 words. Pays $200-800.
Photos: Purchased on assignment. Captions required. Query. Uses 8x10 b&w glossy prints and 4x5 color transparencies. "Payment varies with assignment and is negotiated prior to assignment."
Tips: "Familiarity with the magazine a *must.*"

AUTOWEEK, Crain Consumer Group, Inc., 965 E. Jefferson, Detroit MI 48207. (313)567-9520. Managing Editor: Bill Lovell. 20% freelance written. Emphasizes automobile racing and the auto industry, domestic and international. Weekly tabloid. Circ. 150,000. Pays on publication. Byline "generally given." Buys first North American serial rights or by agreement with author. Submit seasonal material 2 months in advance. Computer printout submissions acceptable. SASE. Reports in 2-4 weeks. Publishes ms an average of 6 weeks after acceptance. Free sample copy and writer's guidelines.
Nonfiction: Wide variety of articles from nostalgia to news reports, driving impressions to technical analyses, personality profiles to 'sneak' previews of future products. "We maintain a fulltime staff in Detroit, with a group of regular correspondents around the country and overseas. We do, however, solicit manuscripts from literate, knowledgeable writers." Recent article example: Dutch Mandel's "In Search of the Van Culture" in the April 11, 1983 issue. Buys 24 mss/year. Length: 1,000-2,500 words. Query. Pays negotiable rates.
Photos: Pays $15/b&w; $35/color transparency.

BMX ACTION, Wizard Publications, 3162 Kashiwa, Torrance CA 90505. (213)539-9213. Editor: Steve Giberson. Publisher/Managing Editor: Bob Osborn. 5% freelance written. Monthly magazine covering bicycle motocross for "all young people (average reader: 14.5-year-old male) . . . whether they're actively racing or not." Circ. 230,000. Pays on publication. Byline given. Offers negotiable kill fee. Buys all rights. Publishes ms an average of 2 months after acceptance. Submit seasonal/holiday material 6 months in advance. Photocopied submissions OK. Computer printout submissions acceptable. SASE. Reports in 1 month on queries; 5 weeks on mss. Sample copy $2; writer's guidelines for business size SASE and 20¢ postage.
Nonfiction: General interest (impact of BMX, growth, etc.), how-to (BMX racing, bike repair, riding techniques, race preparation, nutrition, bike maintenance), humor ("doesn't hurt in any of our pieces"), interview/ profile (with established BMX stars, etc.), personal experience (only if tied to 'how-to'), photo feature ("will consider, but our photos are tops"), technical (product review and evaluation—query first), travel (BMX should be central theme . . . and how it's growing in other countries). No race coverage ("we do that ourselves!") and local track stories not of national interest. Query with clips of published work if available. Length: 1,500-2,500 words. Pays $25-250.
Photos: Bob Osborn, photo editor. Needs "good action shots." Pays $10-30 for 35mm color transparencies (more for cover shots). Pays $5-25 for 8x10 b&w prints. Captions and identification of subjects required.

BMX PLUS MAGAZINE, Daisy/Hi-Torque Publishing Co., Inc., 10600 Sepulveda Blvd., Mission Hills CA 91345. (714)545-6012. Editor: John Ker. Managing Editor: Dean Bradley. Monthly magazine covering the sport of bicycle motocross for a youthful readership (95% male, aged 8-25). 5% freelance written. Circ. 90,000. Pays on publication. Byline given. Buys one-time rights. Submit seasonal/holiday material 3 months in advance. Simultaneous queries and submissions OK. Computer printout submissions acceptable. SASE. Reports in 2 months. Publishes ms an average of 3 months after acceptance. Sample copy $2; writer's guidelines for business size SAE and 1 first class stamp.
Nonfiction: Historical/nostaglic, how-to, humor, interview/profile, new product, photo feature, technical, travel. "No articles for a general audience; our readers are BMX fanatics." Buys 20 mss/year. Send complete ms. Length: 500-1,500 words. Pays $30-250.
Photos: "Photography is the key to our magazine. Send us some exciting and/or unusual photos of hot riders in action." Send photos with ms. Pays $25 for color photo published; $10 for b&w photos. Reviews 35mm color transparencies and b&w negatives and 8x10 prints. Captions and identification of subjects required.
Tips: "The sport of BMX is very young. The opportunities for talented writers and photographers in this field

are wide open. Send us a good interview or race story with photos. Race coverage is the area that's easiest to break into. It must be a *big* race, preferably national or international in scope. Submit story within one week of completion of race."

CAR AND DRIVER, 2002 Hogback Rd., Ann Arbor MI 48104. (313)994-0055. Editor/Publisher: David E. Davis Jr. For auto enthusiasts; college-educated, professional, median 24-30 years of age. Monthly magazine; 120 pages. Circ. 825,000. Rights purchased vary with author and material. Buys all rights or first North American serial rights. Buys 10-12 unsolicited mss/year. Pays on acceptance. Submit seasonal material 4 months in advance. Query with clips of previously published work. Reports in 2 months. SASE.
Nonfiction: Non-anecdotal articles about the more sophisticated treatment of autos and motor racing. Exciting, interesting cars. Automotive road tests, informational articles on cars and equipment; some satire and humor. Personalities, past and present, in the automotive industry and automotive sports. "Treat readers as intellectual equals. Emphasis on people as well as hardware." Informational, how-to, humor, historical, think articles, and nostalgia. Length: 750-2,000 words. Pays $200-1,500. Also buys mini-features for FYI department. Length: about 500 words. Pays $100-500.
Photos: B&w photos purchased with accompanying mss with no additional payment.
Tips: "It is best to start off with an interesting query and to stay away from nuts-and-bolts stuff since that will be handled in-house or by an acknowledged expert. Our goal is to be absolutely without flaw in our presentation of automotive facts, but we strive to be every bit as entertaining as we are informative."

CAR COLLECTOR/CAR CLASSICS, Classic Publishing, Inc., Suite 144, 8601 Dunwoody Pl., Atlanta GA 30338. Editor: Donald R. Peterson. 75% freelance written. For people interested in all facets of collecting classic, milestone, antique, special interest and sports cars; also mascots, models, restoration, license plates and memorabilia. Monthly magazine; 76 pages. Circ. 55,000. Pays on publication. Publishes ms an average of 6 months after acceptance. Submit seasonal/holiday material 4 months in advance. Photocopied submissions OK. Computer printout submissions acceptable; prefers letter-quality to dot-matrix. SASE. Reports in 2 months. Sample copy for $2; free writer's guidelines.
Nonfiction: General interest, historical, how-to, humor, inspirational, interview, nostalgia, personal opinion, profile, photo feature, technical and travel. Buys 75-100 mss/year. Query with clips of published work. Buys 24-36 unsolicited mss/year. Length: 300-2,500 words. Pays 5¢/word minimum.
Photos: "We have a continuing need for high-quality color positives (e.g., 2¼ or 35mm) *with* copy." State availability of photos with ms. Offers additional payment for photos with accompanying mss. Uses b&w glossy prints; color transparencies. Pays a minimum of $75 for cover and centerfold color; $10 for inside color; $5 for inside b&w. Buys one-time rights. Captions and model release required.
Columns/Departments: "Rarely add a new columnist but we are open to suggestions." Buys 36/year. Query with clips of published work. Length: 2,000 maximum; prefer 1,000-2,000 words. Pays 5¢/word.
Recent Article Example: "The Secret Mercedes, the 1938-42" V12 (April 1984).

CAR CRAFT, Petersen Publishing Co., 8490 Sunset Blvd., Los Angeles CA 90069. (213)657-5100, ext. 345. Editor: Jeff Smith. For men and women, 18-34, "enthusiastic owners of 1949 and newer muscle cars." Monthly magazine; 132 pages. Circ. 400,000. Study past issues before making submissions or story suggestions. Buys all rights. Buys 2-10 mss/year. Computer printout submissions acceptable. Pays generally on publication, on acceptance under special circumstances. Query. SASE.
Nonfiction and Photos: How-to articles ranging from the basics to fairly sophisticated automotive modifications. Drag racing feature stories and some general car features on modified late model automobiles. Especially interested in do-it-yourself automotive tips, suspension modifications, mileage improvers and even shop tips and homemade tools. Stories about drag racing personalities are generally of more interest than stories about racing machinery. Length: open. Pays $100-200/page. Art director: Mike Austin. Photos purchased with or without accompanying text. Captions suggested, but optional. Reviews 8x10 b&w glossy prints; 35mm or 2¼x2¼ color negotiable. Pays $30 for b&w, color negotiable. "Pay rate higher for complete story, i.e., photos, captions, headline, subtitle: the works, ready to go."

CARMAG, Canadian Automobile Repair & Maintenance, CARM Publishing, Inc., 41 Mutual St., Toronto, Ontario, M58 2A7 Canada. (416)363-3013. Editor: Ed Belitsky. 60% freelance written. Bimonthly automotive magazine for the practical motorist. Circ. 72,000. Pays on publication. Publishes ms an average of 2 months after acceptance. Byline given. Offers $50-100 kill fee. Buys first rights. Computer printout submissions acceptable. Submit seasonal/holiday material 2 months in advance. SASE. Reports in 1 month. Free sample copy.
Nonfiction: How-to, interview/profile, photo feature, technical. Buys 30 mss/year. Query or send complete ms. Length: 600-1,200 words. Pays $100-250.
Photos: Send photos with ms. Reviews 35mm color transparencies; 5x7 or 4x5 color prints. Captions, model release, and identification of subjects required. "We do not buy manuscripts without photos if applicable. Only the very big publications can afford to send people to photograph an article individually. Today's freelancer has to be a photographer too."

Tips: "We emphasize quality of content, not quality of graphics. Our writers must research their subjects well. A brief note with an idea outline is probably the best way to begin. The editor may then offer a preferred angle of approach to the subject."

CORVETTE FEVER, Prospect Publishing Co., Inc., Box 55532, Ft. Washington MD 20744. (301)839-2221. Publisher: Patricia E. Stivers. 40% freelance written. Bimonthly magazine; 64-84 pages. Circ. 35,000. Pays on publication. Publishes ms an average of 4 months after acceptance. Buys first and reprint rights. Byline given. Phone queries OK. Submit seasonal/holiday material 4 months in advance. Photocopied submissions OK. SASE. Reports in 4 weeks. Sample copy and writer's guidelines $2.
Nonfiction: General interest (event coverage, personal experience); historical (special or unusual Corvette historical topics); how-to (technical and mechanical articles, photos are a must); humor (Corvette-related humor); interview (with important Corvette persons, race drivers, technical persons, club officials, etc.); nostalgia (relating to early Corvette car and development); personal experiences (related to Corvette car use and experiences); profile (prominent and well-known Corvette personalities wanted for interviews and articles); photo feature (centerspread in color of Corvette and female Vette owner; photo essays on renovation, customizing and show cars); technical (any aspect of Corvette improvement or custom articles); and travel (relating to Corvette use and adventure). Buys 4-6 mss/issue. Query or send complete ms. Length: 500-2,500 words. Pays $40-300.
Photos: Send photos with ms. Pays $5 for 5x7 b&w glossy prints; $10 for color contact sheets and transparencies. Captions preferred; model release required.
Columns/Departments: Innovative Ideas, In Print, Model Shop, Pit Stop, and Tech Vette. Buys 3 mss/issue. Send complete ms. Length: 300-800 words. Pays $24-200.
Fiction: "Any type of story as long as it is related to the Corvette." Buys 1-2 mss/issue. Send complete ms. Length: 500-2,500 words. Pays $40-200.
Fillers: Clippings, jokes, gags, anecdotes, short humor and newsbreaks. Buys 2-3/issue. Length: 25-150 words. Pays $2-15.

● **CORVETTE NEWS**, c/o GM Photographic, 3001 Van Dyke, Warren MI 48090. Managing Editor: David W. Barrett. 100% freelance written. For Corvette owners worldwide. Quarterly magazine. Circ. 150,000. Buys all rights. Pays on acceptance. Free sample copy and editorial guidelines. Query. Electronic submissions OK but requirements "need to be discussed with the writer;" requires hard copy also. Computer printout submissions acceptable. SASE.
Nonfiction: "Articles must be of interest to audience. Subjects considered include: (1) Technical articles dealing with restorations, engines, paint, body work, suspension, parts searches, etc. (2) Competition, 'Vettes vs. 'Vettes, or 'Vettes vs. others. (3) Profiles of Corvette owners/drivers. (4) General interest articles, such as the unusual history of a particular early model Corvette, and perhaps its restoration; one owner's do-it-yourself engine repair procedures, maintenance procedures; Corvettes in unusual service; hobbies involving Corvettes; sports involving Corvettes. (5) Celebrity owner profiles. (6) Special Corvette events such as races, drags, rallies, concourse, gymkhanas, slaloms. (7) Travel, in USA or abroad, via Corvette. We also encourage articles on Corvette owner lifestyles. This could include pieces not only about the mechanically-minded (who own Corvettes) but also about the fashion-conscious and people seeking the active good life. No articles negative to cars in general and Corvette in particular or articles not connected, in some way, to Corvette. Send an approximately 100-word query on the proposed article and add a statement about how you are prepared to supplement it with drawings or photographs." Length: 1,200-3,600 words. Pays $150 minimum.
Photos: Color transparencies are preferred when submitted with ms; 35mm smallest format accepted.
Tips: "We are always looking for new ideas, new writing approaches. But the writer must have a solid knowledge about Corvette—either owns one, has driven one, or comes in contact with people who do own the car. We need writers that have an ability to translate very technical subjects into readable prose."

CYCLE, Ziff-Davis Publishing, Co., 780-A Lakefield Rd., Westlake Village CA 91361. (213)889-4360. Editor: Phil Schilling. Managing Editor: Allyn Fleming. 5% freelance written. Monthly magazine covering motorcycles for motorcycle owners (mostly men). Circ. 450,000. Pays on publication. Publishes ms an average of 4 months after acceptance. Byline given. Buys first North American serial rights. Submit seasonal/holiday queries 4 months in advance. Simultaneous queries and photocopied submissions OK. Computer printout submissions acceptable. SASE. Reports in 1 month. Free sample copy.
Nonfiction: Investigative, historical, interview/profile (of racing personalities or others in the industry); photo feature; technical (theory or practice); travel (long-distance trips anywhere in the world); reports on racing; and investigative articles. Query "with references." Length: 2,000-4,000 words. Pays $400-700.
Photos: Pays $20-100 for b&w prints; $50-200 for 35mm color transparencies. Model release and identification of subjects required. Buys one-time rights.

CYCLE NEWS, WEST, 2201 Cherry Ave., Box 498, Long Beach CA 90801. (213)427-7433. Senior Editor: Dale Brown. Publisher: Sharon Clayton. Emphasizes motorcycle recreation for motorcycle racers and recreationists west of Mississippi River. Weekly tabloid; 48 pages. Circ. 50,000. Pays on 15th of month for work published in issues cover-dated the previous month. Buys all rights. SASE. Reports in 1 month. Free writer's guidelines.

Nonfiction: Expose; how-to; historical; humor; informational; interview (racers); personal experience (racing, nonracing with a point); personal opinion (land use, emission control, etc.); photo feature; profile (personality profiles); technical; and travel (off-road trips, "bikepacking"). Buys 1,000 mss/year. Submit complete ms. Pays $2/column inch.

Photos: Purchased with or without accompanying manuscript. Captions required. Submit contact sheet, prints, negatives or transparencies. Pays $5 minimum for 5x7 or 8x10 glossy prints; $10 minimum for 35mm slides or 2¼x2¼ color transparencies. Model release required. No additional payment for photos accepted with accompanying ms.

CYCLE WORLD, 1499 Monrovia Ave., Newport Beach CA 92663. Editor: Allan Girdler. 10% freelance written. For active motorcyclists, "young, affluent, educated, very perceptive." Subject matter includes "road tests (staff-written), features on special bikes, customs, racers, racing events; technical and how-to features involving mechanical modifications." Monthly. Circ. 375,000. Buys all rights. Buys 100 mss/year from freelancers. Pays on publication. Sample copy $2; free writer's guidelines. Submit seasonal material 2½ months in advance. Reports in 6 weeks. Publishes ms an average of 6 months after acceptance. Query. Computer printout submissions acceptable; prefers letter-quality to dot-matrix. SASE.

Nonfiction: Buys informative, well-researched, technical, theory and how-to articles; interviews; profiles; humor; and historical pieces. Taboos include articles about "wives learning to ride; 'my first motorcycle.' " Length: 800-5,000 words. Pays $100-150/published page. Columns include Competition, which contains short, local racing stories with photos. Column length: 300-400 words. Pays $75-100/published page.

Photos: Purchased with or without ms, or on assignment. "We need funny photos with a motorcycle theme." Captions optional. Pays $50 for 1-page; $25-35 for half page. 8x10 b&w glossy prints, 35mm color transparencies.

Fiction: Humorous stories. No racing fiction or "rhapsodic poetry." Length: 1,500-3,000 words. Pays $150 minimum/published page.

DUNE BUGGIES & HOT VWS, Wright Publishing Co., Inc., Box 2260, Costa Mesa CA 92626. Editor: Lane Evans. Monthly magazine. Circ. 85,000. Pays on publication. Buys one-time rights. Submit seasonal or holiday material 3 months in advance. Computer printout submissions acceptable; prefers letter-quality to dot-matrix. SASE. Free sample copy.

Nonfiction: Technical how-to and informational articles. No first person articles. Buys 6-8 mss/issue. Submit complete ms. Length: 500-2,000 words. Pays $60/published page.

Photos: Purchased with ms. Captions required. Send contact sheet. Pays $12.50 maximum for 8x10 b&w glossy prints; $15 minimum for color negs or slides.

EASYRIDERS MAGAZINE, Entertainment for Adult Bikers, Box 52, Malibu CA 90265. (213)889-8701. Editorial Director: Lou Kimzey. 60% freelance written. For "adult men—men who own, or desire to own, expensive custom motorcycles. The individualist—a rugged guy who enjoys riding a chopper and all the good times derived from it." Monthly. Circ. 488,000. Buys all rights. Buys 36-48 mss/year. Pays on acceptance. Publishes ms an average of 3 weeks after acceptance. Sample copy $2. Reports in 2-3 weeks. SASE.

Nonfiction, Fiction, and Fillers: Department Editor: Louis Bosque. "Masculine, candid material of interest to men. Must be bike-oriented, but can be anything of interest to any rugged man. It is suggested that everyone read a copy before submitting—it's not *Boy's Life*. Light, easy, conversational writing style wanted, like men would speak to each other without women being around. Gut level, friendly, man-to-man. Should be bike-oriented or of interest to a man who rides a motorcycle. *Easyriders* is entirely different from all other motorcycle magazines in that it stresses the lifestyle and good times surrounding the owning of a motorcycle—it's aimed at the rider and is nontechnical, while the others are nuts and bolts. Not interested in overly technical motorcycle articles. We carry no articles that preach or talk down to the reader, or attempt to tell him what he should or shouldn't do." Buys personal experience, interviews, especially humor, expose (of Big Brother, big government, red, white and blue, motorcycle-oriented) articles. Length: 1,000-3,000 words. Pays 10¢/word minimum, depending on length and use in magazine. "It's the subject matter and how well it's done—not length, that determines amount paid." Risque jokes, fillers, short humor. Length: open. Pays on acceptance.

Photos: Department Editor: Pete Chiodo. B&w glossy prints, 35mm color, 2¼x2¼ color transparencies purchased with mss. "We are only interested in *exclusive* photos of exclusive bikes that have never been published in, or photographed by, a national motorcycle or chopper publication. Bikes should be approved by editorial board before going to expense of shooting. Submit sample photos—Polaroids will do. Send enough samples for editorial board to get good idea of the bike's quality, originality, workmanship, interesting features, coloring." Payment is $50-$250 for cover, $100-350 for centerspread, $20 for b&w and $35 for color for "In the Wind," $25 up for arty, unusual shots, and $100-225 for a complete feature.

Fiction: "Gut level language okay. Any sex scenes, not to be too graphic in detail. Dope may be implied, but not graphically detailed. Must be biker male-oriented, but doesn't have to dwell on that fact. Only interested in hard-hitting, rugged fiction." Length: 2,000-3,500 words. Pays 10¢/word minimum, depending on quality, length and use in magazine.

Tips: "There is no mystery about breaking into our publication as long as the material is aimed directly at our macho, intelligent, male audience."

THE EJAG NEWS MAGAZINE, EJAG Publications, Box J, Carlisle MA 01741. (617)369-5531. Editor: Lori R. Toepel. Monthly magazine covering "everything about Jaguar and Daimler autos for readers ranging from corporate presidents to local car-fixers; Sunday mechanics—all Jaguar-Daimler fans." 25-50% freelance written. Circ. 30,000. Pays on acceptance. Byline given. Offers $10-25 kill fee. Buys all rights unless otherwise negotiated. Submit seasonal/holiday material 3 months in advance. Computer printout submissions acceptable "if easily readable"; prefers letter-quality to dot-matrix. SASE. Reports in 1 month. Publishes ms an average of 4 months after acceptance. Free sample copy and writer's guidelines.

Nonfiction: General interest (on auto field in general); historical/nostalgic (on Jaguars of previous eras, in USA and abroad); how-to (do it yourself pieces in depth for maintenance, repair, restoration); interview/profile (of Jag owners, racers, factory people, collectors); new product (anything applicable to Jaguars); personal experience; photo feature (on beautiful Jaguars, technical procedures, restorations); technical (do-it-yourself or general tech background). "No club news or club meets (we have direct lines to these). No technical articles that sound like manuals." Buys 25 or more unsolicited mss/year. Query. Length: 1,200-5,000 words. "Longer article accepted—for splitting into several months installments." Pays 5-8¢/word for general topics, 10-15¢/word for technical and do-it-yourself.

Photos: State availability of photos. Pays $5 maximum for 35mm, 3x3 color transparencies and 3x5 and 5x7 prints. Caption, model release and identification of subjects (if possible) required. Buys all rights unless otherwise negotiated.

Tips: "We welcome unpublished writers *but* you must know the subject. No non-Jaguar auto material. We meet too many freelancers who accept an assignment and never complete it or complete it months late. We don't like to chase after people. It would be nice to have a note saying the writer will be late or cannot do the work. The experienced writers we deal with take comments and suggestions with ease. We can have a real give and take over a topic. Inexperienced writers too often take personal offense at suggestions for change."

‡**ENTHUSIAST**, Harley-Davidson Motor Co., Inc., Box 653, Milwaukee WI 53202. (414)935-4524. Editor: Buzz Buzzelli. A quarterly magazine covering Harley-Davidson motorcycles and people. Circ. 239,000. Pays on acceptance. Byline given. Buys one-time rights. Submit seasonal/holiday material 3 months in advance. Simultaneous queries, and simultaneous, photocopied, and previously published submissions OK. Computer printout submissions acceptable. SASE. Reports in 2 months. Free sample copy and writer's guidelines.

Nonfiction: Historical/nostalgic; humor; personal experience; photo feature (color—touring, travel); and travel (with 4-color—must feature Harley Davidson product). No opinion articles. Buys 6 mss/year. Length: 1,500-3,000 words. Pays $100-300.

Photos: State availability or send photos with ms. Reviews 8x10 b&w prints. Buys one-time rights.

Fillers: Short humor. Length: 25-200 words. Pays $5-25.

Tips: "We want clear, concise, accurate information; light, up-beat style. Touring features with insightful themes are most open to freelancers. Avoid the 'Then We Woke Up, Then We Ate, Then We Brushed Our Teeth' stuff."

FOUR WHEELER MAGAZINE, 21216 Vanowen St., Canoga Park CA 91303. (213)992-4777. President/Publisher: Jon Pelzer. Senior Editor: Rich Johnson. Emphasizes four-wheel-drive vehicles competition, off-road adventure. Monthly magazine; 200 pages. Circ. 170,000. Pays on publication. Buys first rights. Written queries only. Submit seasonal/holiday material at least 4 months in advance. SASE. Sample copy $2 plus postage. Writer's guidelines for SASE.

Nonfiction: 4WD competition and adventure articles, technical ideas, how-to's, and vehicle features about a unique 4WD vehicle. "We like adventure: mud-running through treacherous timber trails, old desert ghost town four-wheeling trips, coverage of ice-racing jeeps; and unusual 4WD vehicles such as customized trucks, 4WD conversions. See features by Willie Worthy, Rich Johnson and Russ Leadabrand." Query or send complete ms. Length: 2,500 words maximum; average 2-4 pages when published. Pays variable rate.

Photos: Requires excellent quality photos, e.g., 10 b&w glossy 8x10s, 6 color transparencies. Captions required.

Tips: "Technical material is difficult to come by. A new writer has a better chance of success with us if he can offer new technical articles, maintenance and performance tips. Also, we like unique custom vehicle features."

● **FRIENDS MAGAZINE**, Ceco Communications, Inc., 30400 Van Dyke Blvd., Warren MI 48093. (313)575-9400. Editor: Bill Gray. Publishes ms an average of 6 months after acceptance. "The only common audience shares is they own Chevrolets." Monthly magazine; 32 pages. Circ. 1,000,000. Pays on acceptance. 75% freelance written. Rights vary. Submit seasonal/holiday material 6 months in advance. Simultaneous and photocopied submissions OK. SASE. Reports in 4 weeks. Free sample copy and writer's guidelines.

Nonfiction: Tom Morrisey, features editor. General interest (lifestyle); historical (when story has contemporary parallel); humor (any subject, but rarely accept first person); travel (only with a strong hook); and photo feature (strong photo essays that say something about American lifestyle). "We're looking for freelancers who can spot lifestyle trends with national impact. We're looking for fresh ideas. We'd like to break national feature stories." Address all queries and submissions to features editor. Query by mail only.

Photos: State availability of photos. Pays $200/page. Transparencies only. Captions and model releases required.

Tips: "Freelance writers should be aware of the need for top-quality, exciting illustrations or photography to accompany even the best writing; the need for more active—as opposed to pasive—stories, and the fact that we've seen most general queries 1,000 times before."

‡**HIGH PERFORMANCE PONTIAC**, JHS Publishing Co., 29 Grove St., South Hackensack NJ 07606. (201)440-2770. Editor: Cliff Gromer. Bimonthly magazine on Pontiac automobiles for Pontiac enthusiasts. Circ. 40,000. Pays on publication. Byline given. Offers 25% kill fee. Buys all rights. Submit seasonal/holiday material 3 months in advance. No simultaneous queries, or simultaneous, photocopied or previously published submissions. SASE. Reports in 2 weeks on queries; 3 weeks on mss. Sample copy for SAE.

Nonfiction: Historical/nostalgic; how-to (technical information on restoring and hopping up Pontiacs); interview/profile; new product; personal experience; photo feature; technical; travel; and "anything to do with high performance Pontiac automobiles." Buys 50 mss/year. Query. Length: 800-2,000 words. Pays $75-300.

Photos: State availability of photos or send photos with query. Reviews b&w and color transparencies and prints. Captions and identification of subjects required.

Tips: "Must have excellent photos with every article."

HOT ROD, Petersen Publishing Co., 8490 Sunset Blvd., Los Angeles CA 90069. (213)657-5100. Editor: Leonard Emanuelson. For readers 10 to 60 years old with automotive high performance, street rod, truck, drag racing and street machine interest. Monthly magazine; 120 pages. Circ. 900,000. Buys all rights. Byline given. Pays on acceptance. Free editorial guidelines. Submit seasonal material 4 months in advance. Reports on accepted and rejected material "as soon as possible." SASE.

Nonfiction and Photos: Wants how-to, photo, new product and technical pieces. Length: 2-12 ms pages. Pays $100-225/printed page. "Freelance quantity at *Hot Rod* will undoubtedly decline; staff will originate most material. Foresee more need for photo essays, less for the written word. We accept very little unsolicited (written) freelance or nontechnical material." Photos purchased with or without accompanying ms and on assignment. Sometimes offers no additional payment for photos accepted with ms. Captions required. Pays $25 for b&w prints and $25 minimum for color.

Tips: "Freelance approach should be tailored for specific type and subject matter writer is dealing with. If it is of a basic automotive technical nature, then story slant and info should be aimed at the backyard enthusiasts. What we do is attempt to entertain while educating and offering exceptional dollar value."

KEEPIN' TRACK OF VETTES, Box 48, Spring Valley NY 10977. (914)425-2649. Editor: Shelli Finkel. For Corvette owners and enthusiasts. Monthly magazine; 60-68 pages. Circ. 38,000. Pays on publication. Buys all rights. Byline given. Submit seasonal/holiday material 2-3 months in advance. SASE. Reports in 3-4 weeks. Free sample copy and writer's guidelines.

Nonfiction: Expose (telling of Corvette problems with parts, etc.); historical (any and all aspects of Corvette developments); how-to (restorations, engine work, suspension, race, swapmeets); humor; informational; interview (query); nostalgia; personal experience; personal opinion; photo feature; profile (query); technical; and travel. Buys 8-10 mss/issue. Query or submit complete ms. Pays $50-200.

Photos: Send photo with ms. Pays $10-35 for b&w contact sheets or negatives; $10-50 for 35mm color transparencies; offers no additional payment for photos with accompanying ms.

KIT CAR QUARTERLY, Box 9527, San Jose CA 95157. (408)295-2222. Editor: Philip B. Hood. Quarterly magazine on full-size, driveable automobiles in kit form for assembly at home. "*Kit Car Quarterly* aims to reach automotive do-it-yourselfers and anyone with a love for beautiful automobiles. We emphasize in-depth profiles of individual Kit Cars, good color photography, and how-to features." Circ. 87,500. Pays on publication. Byline given. Offers $25 kill fee. Buys one-time or all rights. Submit seasonal/holiday material 5 months in advance. Simultaneous queries and simultaneous, photocopied and previously published submissions OK. SASE. Reports in 1 month; sample copy $1; free writer's guidelines.

Nonfiction: How-to (build up articles on Kit Cars, hints for Kit Car assembly); interview/profile (designers/manufacturers with photos of cars and designs); new product (any products related to Kit Cars); personal experience (owner profiles of customized kits); photo feature (of unusual custom, hand-built autos). No articles knocking the entire industry. Buys 25 mss/year. Query or submit complete ms. Length: 500-2,500 words. Pays $35-250 (with photos).

Photos: Send photos with ms. Pays $5-25 for 35mm or larger color transparencies; $10 for 5x7 b&w prints. Model release and identification of subjects required.
Fiction: Would be interested in seeing automotive fiction. Do not currently buy any.
Tips: "Find a company with a photoworthy kit. Get all the facts, i.e., price of kit, contents, time to assemble, unique features, advantages and disadvantages of the particular car. Give the reader a 'hands on' feel for the car."

‡**THE MERCEDES BENZ STAR, Magazine of the Mercedes-Benz Club of America**, Toad Hall Motorbooks, Inc., 2275 Leyden St., Denver CO 80207. (303)320-0777. Editor: Frank Barrett. A bimonthly club magazine covering Mercedes-Benz automobiles. "Our readers are not just Mercedes-Benz owners but *enthusiasts* interested in the cars' history, how to maintain their cars properly, how to enjoy them more, and in knowing more about interesting Mercedes-Benz cars and people." Circ. 17,000. Pays on publication. Byline given. Buys first rights. Submit seasonal/holiday material 4-6 months in advance. Simultaneous queries, and simultaneous, photocopied and previously published submissions OK. Computer printout submissions acceptable; no dot-matrix. SASE. Reports in 2 weeks on queries; 1 month on mss. Sample copy $3.
Nonfiction: Book excerpts, historical, how-to, humor, interview/profile, personal experience, photo feature, technical and travel. "All must relate strongly to Mercedes-Benz and be of commensurate quality." Buys 6-10 mss/year. Query with published clips. Length: 1,000-7,000 words. Pays $50-300.
Photos: State availability of photos with query or ms. Reviews b&w contact sheets, 35mm up to 4x5 color transparencies, and 8x10 full-frame b&w prints. Pays negotiable rate. Buys one-time rights.
Columns/Departments: Buys 12 mss/year. Query with published clips. Length: 500-1,500 words. Pays variable rate; $150 maximum.
Tips: "We like factual articles on interesting cars and people. How-to technical articles are most appreciated, along with event coverage, but we could also use some good humor.

MOTOCROSS ACTION MAGAZINE, 10600 Sepulveda Blvd., Mission Hills CA 91345. (213)365-6831. Editor: Jody Weisel. For "primarily young and male, average age 12 to 30, though an increasing number of females is noticed. Education varies considerably. They are interested in off-road racing motorcycles, as either a profession or a hobby." Monthly magazine. Circ. 150,000. Buys all rights. Buys 20-25 mss/year. Pays on publication. Sample copy $1.50. Will consider photocopied but no simultaneous submissions. Reports in 1-6 months. Query. SASE.
Nonfiction and Photos: Wants "articles on important national and international motocross events, interviews with top professionals, technical pieces, and in-depth investigative reporting. Short stories and/or poetry will be greeted with a heartfelt yawn. It's best to obtain a copy of the magazine and read recent stories. Stories should be brief and to the point, though flair is appreciated. Top photography is a must. No blatant hero worship. For the coming year, we want to see articles on the evolution of Motocross from a backyard to a big-time, multi-million dollar sport and business." Takes informational, how-to, profile, humor and photo pieces. Length: 500-2,000 words. Pays $25-200. Photos purchased with accompanying ms with extra payment and on assignment. Captions optional. Pays $8-10 for 8x10 b&w glossy prints; $25-50 for 35mm or 2¼x2¼ color slides.

MOTOR TREND, Petersen Publishing Co., 8490 Sunset Blvd., Los Angeles CA 90069. (213)657-5100. Editor: Tony Swan. 15-20% freelance written. For automotive enthusiasts and general interest consumers. Monthly. Circ. 750,000. Buys all rights. "Fact-filled query suggested for all freelancers." Computer printout submissions acceptable; prefers letter-quality to dot-matrix. Reports in 30 days. SASE.
Nonfiction: Automotive and related subjects that have national appeal. Emphasis on domestic and imported cars, roadtests, driving impressions, auto classics, auto, travel, racing, and high-performance features for the enthusiast. Packed with facts. Freelancers should confine queries to feature material; road tests and related activity handled inhouse.
Photos: Buys photos, particularly of prototype cars and assorted automotive matter. Pays $25-250 for b&w glossy prints or 2¼x2¼ color transparencies.
Fillers: Automotive newsbreaks, humorous short takes, automotive cartoons, featurettes. 500 words maximum.

‡**MOTORCYCLE BUYERS' GUIDE**, CRV Publishing Canada Ltd., Suite 202, 2077 Dundas St. E., Mississauga, Ontario, L4X 1M2, Canada. Editorial Director: Reg Fife. An annual motorcycling magazine. Circ. 100,000. Pays on publication. Byline given. Buys first rights. Submit seasonal/holiday material 4 months in advance. SASE. Reports in 2 months. Free sample copy and writer's guidelines.
Nonfiction: Query. Length: 1,000-3,000 words. Pays variable rates.
Photos: State availability of photos. Reviews color transparencies and prints. Captions required. Buys one-time rights.

MOTORCYCLIST MAGAZINE, Petersen Publishing, 8490 Sunset Blvd., Los Angeles CA 90069. (213)657-5100. Editor-in-Chief: Art Friedman. Managing Editor: James Cowell. 10% freelance written. Emphasizes motorcycles or motorcycle enthusiasts. Monthly magazine; 100 pages. Circ. 250,000. Pays on publication. Publishes ms an average of 6 months after acceptance. Buys all rights. Byline given. Written queries preferred. SASE. Reports in 3 months. Free writer's guidelines.

Nonfiction: How-to, humor, informational, interview, new product, photo feature, profile and technical. Buys 12-25 mss/year. Length: 500-2,000 words. Pays $25-1,000.

Photos: Reviews contact sheets and negatives. Pays $25-100 for 8x10 b&w prints; $75-200 for 35mm color transparencies. Captions, model release and identification of subjects required.

Columns/Departments: Hotline (short news items); Last Page (humorous, bizarre, tip-type items); Sport (features on competitions, racers—timeliness is important). Buys 10/year. Send complete ms. Length: 50 words minimum.

Fiction: Adventure, fantasy, humorous. Buys 1-2 mss/year. Send complete ms.

Fillers: Short humor and newsbreaks. Buys 20/year. Length: 50-250 words. Pays $25-50.

‡**NISSAN DISCOVERY**, (formerly *Nissan's Datsun Discovery*), The Magazine for Datsun Owners, Donnelley Marketing, Box 4617, N. Hollywood CA 91607. (213)877-4406. Editor: Wayne Thoms. Bimonthly magazine for Datsun owners and their families. Circ. 500,000. Pays on acceptance. Byline given. Not copyrighted. Buys first North American serial rights. Submit seasonal/holiday material 5 months in advance. Photocopied and previously published submissions OK. SASE. Reports in 1 month. Sample copy $1.50 in cash or stamps, 9x12 SAE, and 80¢ postage; writer's guidelines for business-size SAE and 20¢ postage.

Nonfiction: Historical/nostalgic, humor, photo feature, travel. "We need general family interest material with heavy emphasis on outstanding color photos: travel, humor, food, lifestyle, sports, entertainment." No food articles. Buys 25 mss/year. Query. Length: 1,300-1,800 words. Pays $300-1,000.

Photos: State availability of photos. Reviews 2¼" and 35mm color transparencies. No b&w photos. "Payment usually is part of story package—all negotiated." Captions and identification of subjects required. Buys one-time rights.

Tips: "A freelancer can best break in to our publication by submitting a brief idea query with specific information on color slides available. Offer a package of copy and art."

‡**NORTHEAST RIDING**, Paul Essenfeld, 209 Whitney St., Hartford CT 06105. (203)236-6604. Editor: Paul Essenfeld. Monthly magazine "to entertain and inform the road and street motorcyclists of the Northeast, who ride for recreation and commuting. Area events, good roads to ride, and club activities are featured along with information on camping, service, safety, and political issues affecting riding in the area." Estab. 1983. Circ. 20,000. "Payment is negotiable prior to acceptance. Payment made on publication." Byline given. Buys first rights. Submit seasonal/holiday material 6 months in advance. Simultaneous queries, and simultaneous, photocopied, and previously published submissions OK. SASE. Reports in 2 weeks. Sample copy for 9x12 SAE and 88¢ postage.

Nonfiction: General interest (places to ride); historical/nostalgic (on vintage bikes); interview/profile (unusual biker); new product (accessories); opinion (legislation); personal experience (riding/touring); photo feature (motorcycles with people); technical (repair/service/testing); travel (mostly New England); and articles on safety. Buying very small amount of material; most is donated. No material on dirt bikes, enduros, or trials. Send complete ms. Length: 500-2,000 words. Payment is minimal.

Photos: Send photos with query or manuscript. Reviews 4x5 b&w prints. Captions required. Buys one-time rights.

Columns/Departments: Safety, Legal, Technical, Favorite ride. Send complete ms. Length 500-1,000 words. Payment is negotiable prior to acceptance. Payment made on publication.

Tips: "Submit ms and photos ready to use. Articles must be of interest to Northeastern motorcyclists, and photos should include motorcycles *and* people. The Favorite Ride department is most open to freelancers. Write about New England locations, specific description of route. Include at least one b&w photo of area *with* motorcycle."

OFF-ROAD MAG, Argus Publishing, Suite 316, 12301 Wilshire Blvd., Los Angeles CA 90025. (213)820-3601. Editor: Mike Parris. Monthly magazine covering off-pavement vehicles, particularly 4-wheel drive, utility, and pickup trucks; and off-road racing and rallying vehicles. Readers are owners and people who aspire to own off-road vehicles, as well as those who intend to modify engines and other components for off-road use. Circ. 120,000. Pays on publication. Byline given. Buys all rights, "but may reassign rights upon request. Submit seasonal/holiday material 4 months in advance. Computer printout submissions acceptable; prefers letter-quality to dot-matrix. SASE. Reports in 1 month. Writer's guidelines for business size SAE and 1 first class stamp.

Nonfiction: Technical (modification); travel (and adventure in the continental US); off-road groups; and land-closures. "The key to writing for us is technical expertise. You must be knowledgeable on the subject." Buys 50 mss/year. Send complete ms and photos or diagrams. Length: 2,000-3,000 words. Pays $125-400.

Photos: Send photos with ms. Reviews 35mm color transparenices and 8x10 b&w glossy prints.
Fillers: Fix it, How-to. Buys 25/year. Length: 750-1,000 words. Pays $50-100.
Tips: "Freelance writers should be aware that: 1. word processing is a must; 2. clean writing *isn't* enough; and 3. photographic skills should be polished."

ON TRACK MAGAZINE, The Auto Racing Newsmagazine, Paul Oxman Publishing, Unit M, 17165 Newhope St., Fountain Valley CA 92708. (714)966-1131. Editor: Art Michalik. Managing Editor: Cheryl Cooper. Bimonthly magazine covering auto racing. Circ. 25,000. Pays on publication. Byline given. Not copyrighted. Buys first North American serial rights. Simultaneous queries, and simultaneous and photocopied submissions OK. SASE. Reports in 6 weeks.
Nonfiction: General interest, how-to, interview/profile, opinion, personal experience, photo feature, technical—all related to auto racing. Query. Length: 250-3,000 words. Pays 50¢/column inch; some rates negotiable.
Photos: Anne Peyton, art director. State availability of photos. Pays $50 for 35mm color transparency, $7.50 for 5x7 or 8x10 b&w print. Buys one-time rights.

PETERSEN'S 4-WHEEL & OFF-ROAD, Petersen Publishing Company, 8490 Sunset Blvd., Los Angeles CA 90069. (213)657-5100. Editor: Michael Coates. Managing Editor: Elizabeth Jones. Monthly magazine covering automotive four-wheel drive vehicles. "We appeal to the off-road enthusiast who plays hard and likes to have fun with his or her 4x4. Our approach is slanted toward showing how to do-it-yourself when it comes to maintaining or modifying an off-road vehicle." Pays on acceptance. Byline given. Pays 50% kill fee. Buys all rights. Submit seasonal/holiday material 6 months in advance. Computer printout submissions acceptable; prefers letter-quality to dot-matrix. SASE. Reports in 3 weeks.
Nonfiction: How-to (modify a vehicle); interview/profile (of racers, engineers); photo feature (modified vehicles); and technical (modification of a vehicle). No first-person accounts of anything; no travel features. Buys 6-10 mss/year. Query or send complete ms. Length: 300-1,500 words. Pays $50-500.
Photos: Barry Wiggins, photo editor. Pays $10-75 for color transparencies; $5-25 for 8x10 b&w prints. Captions, model release, and identification of subjects required. Buys all rights.
Columns/Departments: Tailgate (miscellaneous automotive news). Buys 6 mss/year. Send complete ms. Length: 20-100 words. Pays $10-25.
Tips: "The best way to break in is with a well-photographed, action feature on a modified vehicle. Study our magazine for style and content. We do not deviate much from established editorial concept. Keep copy short, information accurate, and photos in focus."

PICKUPS & MINI-TRUCKS MAGAZINE, (formerly Pickup, Van & 4WD Magazine), Petersen Publishing Co., 8490 Sunset Blvd., Los Angeles CA 90069. (213)657-5100. Editor: John J. Jelinek. Managing Editor: Chriss Ohliger. 25% freelance written. Covers street pickups. Monthly magazine. Circ. 185,000. Pays on publication. Publishes ms an average of 3 months after acceptance. Buys all rights. Pays kill fee "depending on assignment." Byline given. Submit seasonal/holiday material 3-4 months in advance. Photocopied submissions OK "with guarantee of exclusivity." Computer printout submissions acceptable; prefers letter-quality to dot-matrix. Query and request writer's guidelines, "Contributor's Memo." SASE. Reports 1-2 months. Free writer's guidelines.
Nonfiction: How-to (modifications to light duty trucks, such as extra seats, tool storage, body and mechanical repairs, modifications, etc.), historical/nostalgic (restored trucks), technical and travel (2-wheel drive travel only, must show vehicle being used). Buys 2-3 mss/per issue. Submit complete ms. Length: 1,000-3,000 words. Pays $75/published page.
Photos: Purchased with accompanying manuscript or on assignment. Captions required. Query for photos. Pays $10-75 for 8x10 b&w glossy prints; $25-75 for 35mm or 2¼x2¼ color transparencies; offers no additional payment for photos accepted with ms. Model release required.

RIDER, 29901 Agoura Rd., Agoura CA 91301. Editor: Tash Matsuoka. 60% freelance written. For owners and prospective buyers of motorcycles to be used for touring, sport riding, and commuting. Monthly magazine; 100-160 pages. Buys all rights. Pays on publication. Sample copy $2. Free writer's guidelines. Query first. Submit seasonal material 3 months in advance. Photocopied submissions OK. Computer printout submissions acceptable; no dot-matrix. Reports in 1 month. SASE.
Nonfiction: Articles directly related to motorcycle touring, camping, commuting and sport riding including travel, human interest, safety, novelty, do-it-yourself and technical. "Articles which portray the unique thrill of motorcycling." Should be written in clean, contemporary style aimed at a sharp, knowledgeable reader. Buys informational how-to, personal experience, profile, historical, nostalgia, personal opinion, travel and technical. Length is flexible. Pays $100 for Favorite Ride feature and $150-450 for major articles.
Photos: Offers no additional payment for photos purchased with ms. Captions required. "Quality photographs are critical. Graphics are emphasized in *Rider*, and we must have photos with good visual impact."

ROAD & TRACK, 1499 Monrovia Avenue, Newport Beach CA 92663. Editor: John Dinkel. 10% freelance written. For knowledgeable car enthusiasts. Monthly magazine. Buys all rights. Query. Computer printout submissions acceptable. Reports in 6 weeks. Publishes ms up to 2 years after acceptance. SASE.
Nonfiction: "The editor welcomes freelance material, but if the writer is not thoroughly familiar with the kind of material used in the magazine, he is wasting both his time and the magazine's. *Road & Track* material is highly specialized and that old car story in the files has no chance of being accepted. We publish more serious, comprehensive and in-depth treatment of particular areas of automotive interest." Pays 12-25¢/word minimum depending upon subject covered and qualifications and experience of author.
Tips: "Freelancer must have intimate knowledge of the magazine. Unless he can quote chapter and verse for the last 20 years of publication he's probably wasting his time and mine."

ROAD KING MAGAZINE, Box 250, Park Forest IL 60466. Editor-in-Chief: George Friend. 10% freelance written. Truck driver leisure reading publication. Quarterly magazine; 48 pages. Circ. 226,515. Pays on acceptance. Publishes ms an average of 1 month after acceptance. Buys all rights. Byline given "always on fiction—if requested on nonfiction—copyright mentioned only if requested." Submit seasonal/holiday material 3 months in advance. Simultaneous and photocopied submissions OK. SASE. Sample copy for 7x10 SAE with 54¢ postage or get free sample copy at any Union 76 truck stop.
Nonfiction: Trucker slant or general interest, humor, and photo feature. No articles on violence or sex. Name and quote release required. Submit complete ms. Length: 500-2,500 words. Pays $50-150.
Photos: Submit photos with accompanying ms. No additional payment for b&w contact sheets or 2¼x2¼ color or transparencies. Captions preferred. Buys first rights. Model release required.
Fiction: Adventure, historical, humorous, mystery, suspense rescue-type and western. Especially about truckers. No stories on sex and violence. "We're looking for quality writing." Buys 4 mss/year. Submit complete ms. Length: approximately 1,200 words. Pays up to $400.
Fillers: Jokes, gags, anecdotes and short humor about truckers. Buys 20-25/year. Length: 50-500 words. Pays $5-100.
Tips: No collect phone calls or postcard requests. "We don't appreciate letters we have to answer." No certified, insured or registered mail. No queries. "Do not submit mss or art or photos using registered mail, certified mail or insured mail. Publisher will not accept such materials from the post office. Publisher will not discuss refusal with writer. Nothing personal, just legal. Do not write and ask if we would like such and such article or outline. We buy only from original and complete mss submitted on speculation. Do not ask for writer's guidelines. See above and/or get copy of magazine and be familiar with our format before submitting anything. Never phone for free copy as we will not have such phone calls."

ROAD RIDER, Box 678, South Laguna CA 92677. Editor: Bob Carpenter. 20% freelance written. Covers touring and camping on motorcycles for a family-oriented audience. Monthly magazine; 96 pages. Circ. 70,000. Pays on publication. Publishes ms an average of 2 months after acceptance. Buys all rights. Submit seasonal/holiday material 6 months in advance. Computer printout submissions acceptable; prefers letter-quality to dot-matrix. SASE. Reports in 1 month. Sample copy $3; free writer's guidelines with SASE.
Nonfiction: "We will consider any articles providing they are of sound base so far as motorcycling knowledge is concerned. Must be cycle-oriented. How-to's usually are of technical nature and require experience. We would love to see more humorous cycle experience type of material. Cycling personalities are also big here. We try to do three or four historical pieces per year. All evaluation/testing pieces are done in house. Travel pieces need good photos; same thing is true on historical or nostalgia material." No beginner articles. Buys 48 mss/year. Query or send complete ms. Length: 300-1,500 words. Pays $100-200.
Photos: Send photos with ms. Offers no additional payment for photos accepted with accompanying ms. Prefers 5x7 b&w glossy prints or 35mm color transparencies. Captions and model release required.
Fiction: Rarely accepts fiction.
Tips: "We are an enthusiast publication—as such, it is virtually impossible to sell here unless the writer is also an enthusiast and actively involved in the sport. A good, well-written, brief item dealing with a motorcycle trip, accompanied by top quality b&w and color photos receives prime time editorial attention. We are always on the lookout for good material from eastern seaboard or Midwest. Best way to hit this market is to buy and study a sample issue prior to submitting. Most of our contributors are Road Rider People. If you are unsure as to what Road Rider People refers, you will probably not be able to sell to this magazine. We continue to be overstocked on following: beginner articles (all ages, sexes, etc.), journal-format travel articles (not welcome) and travel articles from Southwestern US."

● **SMALL WORLD**, Volkswagen of America, 888 W. Big Beaver Rd., Box 3951, Troy MI 48099. Editor: Ed Rabinowitz. Magazine published 5 times/year for Volkswagen owners in the United States. Circ. 250,000. Buys all rights. Byline given. Buys 10-12 mss/year. Pays on acceptance. Free writer's guidelines. Computer printout submissions acceptable. Reports in 6 weeks. SASE.
Nonfiction: "Interesting stories on people using Volkswagens; useful owner modifications of the vehicle; travel pieces with the emphasis on people, not places; Volkswagenmania stories, personality pieces, inspira-

tional and true adventure articles. VW arts and crafts, etc. The style should be light. All stories must have a VW tie-in, preferably with a new generation VW model, i.e., Rabbit, Scirocco, Jetta, Vanagon or Quantum. Our approach is subtle, however, and we try to avoid obvious product puffery, since *Small World* is not an advertising medium. We prefer a first-person, people-oriented handling. No basic travelogues; articles on older VWs; stay away from Beetle stories. With all story ideas, please query first. All unsolicited manuscripts will be returned unopened. Though queries should be no longer than 2 pages, they ought to include a working title, a short, general summary of the article, and an outline of the specific points to be covered. We strongly advise writers to read at least 2 past issues before working on a story." Length: 1,500 words maximum; "shorter pieces, some as short as 450 words, often receive closer attention." Pays $100 per printed page for photographs and text; otherwise, a portion of that amount, depending on the space allotted. Most stories go 2 pages; some run 3 or 4.

Photos: Submit photo samples with query. Photos purchased with ms; captions required. "We prefer color transparencies, 35mm or larger. All photos should carry the photographer's name and address. If the photographer is not the author, both names should appear on the first page of the text. Where possible, we would like a selection of at least 40 transparencies. It is recommended that at least one show the principal character or author; another, all or a recognizable portion of a VW in the locale of the story. Quality photography can often sell a story that might be otherwise rejected. Every picture should be identified or explained." Model releases required. Pays $250 maximum for front cover photo.

Fillers: "Short, humorous anecdotes about Volkswagens." Pays $15.

Tips: "Style of the publication and its content are being structured toward more upscale, affluent buyer. VW drivers are not the same as those who used to drive the Beetle."

‡**SPORTS CAR GRAPHIC**, Petersen Publishing Co., 8490 Sunset Blvd., Los Angeles CA 90069. (213)657-5100. Editor: Craig Caldwell. 15% freelance written. Managing Editor: Debbie Feder. Monthly magazine on sports cars for the active, involved new or used sports car owner. Circ. 125,000. Pays on acceptance. Publishes ms an average of 4 months after acceptance. Byline given. Offers 50% kill fee. Buys all rights. Submit seasonal/holiday material 5 months in advance. Simultaneous queries OK. Computer submissions acceptable. SASE. Reports in 1 month. Free sample copy and writer's guidelines.

Nonfiction: Historical/nostalgic (retrospects on historic cars); how-to (maintenance/modification of sports cars); interview/profile (significant industry people); photo feature (events, vehicles); technical (modification of cars). No first-person accounts of life with a sports car. Buys 24-30 mss/year. Query. Length: 1,000-3,000 words. Pays $250 and up.

Photos: Randy Lorentzen, photo editor. State availability of photos. Reviews b&w contact sheets. Pays $10 minimum for 8x10 b&w prints; $15 minimum for color transparencies. Captions, model release, and identification of subjects required.

Columns/Departments: Interview; Sports Car Report (industry information); Competition Report (competition information). "See magazine for slant/use." Buys 30-50 mss/year. Query or send complete ms. Length: 50-2,000 words. Pays $25 and up.

Fillers: Clippings and photos. Length: 25-75 words. Pays $25 and up.

Tips: "Study magazine—what we print is highly representative of what we buy. Send concise query with samples of previous work. Look for the unusual, local sports car-related stories. Be creative, accurate. How-tos, photo features, and departments are most open to freelancers."

STOCK CAR RACING MAGAZINE, Box 715, Ipswich MA 01938. Editor: Dick Berggren. For stock car racing fans and competitors. Monthly magazine; 100 pages. Circ. 400,000. Pays on publication. Buys all rights. Byline given. SASE. Reports in 6 weeks.

Nonfiction: "Uses nonfiction on stock car drivers, cars, and races. We are interested in the story behind the story in stock car racing. We want interesting profiles and colorful, nationally interesting features." Query. Buys 50-60 mss/year. Length: 100-6,000 words. Pays $10-350.

Photos: State availability of photos. Pays $20 for 8x10 b&w photos; $50-250 for 35mm or larger color transparencies. Captions required.

Tips: "We get more queries than stories. We just don't get as much material as we want to buy. We have more room for stories than ever before. We are an excellent market with 12 issues per year."

SUPER CHEVY, Argus Publishing, Suite 316, 12301 Wilshire Blvd., Los Angeles CA 90025. (213)820-3601. Editor: Doug Marion. Feature Editor: Jeff Tann. Monthly magazine covering Chevrolet automobiles for anyone associated with Chevys—owners, mechanics, car builders and racing drivers. Circ. 160,000. Pays on acceptance. Byline given. Buys all rights. Submit seasonal/holiday material 4 months in advance. Simultaneous queries OK. Reports in 2 weeks on queries; 1 week on mss. Free sample copy.

Nonfiction: Historical (classic Chevy); interview; race coverage (drag, stock and sprint car). Buys 25 mss/year. Query by phone or letter. Length: 300-1,500 words. Pays $75-100/printed page.

Photos: State availability of photos. Pays $25-60/35mm color transparency; $10 minimum/5x7 or 8x10 b&w glossy print. Captions and model release required.

‡**VETTE MAGAZINE**, CSK Publishing Co., 29 Grove St., South Hackensack NJ 07606. (201)440-2770. Editor: Cliff Gromer. Bimonthly magazine on Corvette automobiles for Corvette enthusiasts. Circ. 85,000. Pays on publication. Byline given. Offers 25% kill fee. Buys all rights. Submit seasonal/holiday material 3 months in advance. SASE. Reports in 2 weeks on queries; 3 weeks on mss. Sample copy for SAE.
Nonfiction: Expose (auction frauds); general interest; historical/nostalgic; how-to (car modifications for more performance); interview/profile (Corvette people); new product; opinion; personal experience; photo feature; technical; travel or "anything that has to do with Corvette lifestyle." Buys 50 mss/year. Query. Length: 1,200-2,000 words. Pays $75-300.
Photos: State availability of photos or send photos with query. Reviews b&w and color transparencies and 5x7 prints. Captions and model release required.
Tips: "Must submit excellent photos with every article."

VW & PORSCHE, Argus Publishers, Suite 316, 12301 Wilshire Blvd., Los Angeles CA 90025. (213)820-3601. Editor: C. Van Tune. Bimonthly magazine covering VW and Porsche and Audi cars for owners. Circ. 65,000. Pays one month before publication. Byline given. Kill fee varies. Buys one-time rights. Submit seasonal/holiday material 4 months in advance. SASE. Reports in 2 weeks on queries. Free sample copy.
Nonfiction: How-to (restore, maintain or tune-up); Special, modified or restored VWs and Porsches. Buys 30-35 mss/year. Query. Length: 1,000-2,500 words. Pays $60-75/printed page. "More if color pictures are used."
Photos: State availability of photos. Reviews 8x10 glossy prints. Identification of subjects required. "Photo payment included in page price."
Tips: "Whoever writes for a 'nut' book should research their material extremely well. Our readers want straight, honest, new information. Errors are caught at once."

Aviation

Professional and private pilots, and aviation enthusiasts in general read the publications in this section. Magazines intended for passengers of commercial airlines are grouped in the In-Flight category. Technical aviation and space journals, and publications for airport operators, aircraft dealers and others in aviation businesses are listed under Aviation and Space in the Trade Journals section.

AERO, Fancy Publications, Box 4030, San Clemente CA 92572. (714)498-1600. Editor: Dennis Shattuck. 50% freelance written. For owners of private aircraft. "We take a unique, but limited view within our field." Circ. 75,000. Buys first North American serial rights. Buys about 20-30 mss/year. Pays after publication. Sample copy $3; writer's guidelines for SASE. Will consider photocopied submissions if guaranteed original. Reports in 2 months. Query. SASE.
Nonfiction: Material on aircraft products, developments in aviation, specific airplane test reports, travel by aircraft, development and use of airports. All must be related to general aviation field. Length: 1,000-4,000 words. Pays $75-250.
Photos: Pays $15 for 8x10 b&w glossy prints purchased with mss or on assignment. Pays $150 for color transparencies used on cover.
Columns/Departments: Weather flying, instrument flight refresher, new products.
Tips: "Freelancer must know the subject about which he is writing; use good grammar; know the publication for which he's writing; remember that we try to relate to the middle segment of the business/pleasure flying public. We see too many 'first flight' type of articles. Our market is more sophisticated than that. Most writers do not do enough research on their subject. Would like to see more material on business-related flying, more on people involved in flying."

AIR LINE PILOT, 1625 Massachussetts Ave. NW, Washington DC 20036. (202)797-4176. Editor-in-Chief: C.V. Glines. Managing Editor: Anne Kelleher. 20% freelance written. Covers commercial aviation issues for members of Air Line Pilots Association (ALPA). Monthly magazine; 48-64 pages. Circ. 45,000. Pays on acceptance. Publishes ms an average of 6 months after acceptance unless on assignment. Buys all rights. Computer printout submissions acceptable; no dot-matrix. Submit seasonal material 4 months in advance. SASE. Reports in 1 month. Free sample copy and writer's guidelines with SASE of correct size only.
Nonfiction: Historical (aviation/personal or equipment, aviation firsts); informational (aviation safety, related equipment or aircraft aids); interview (aviation personality); nostalgia (aviation history); photo feature; profile (airline pilots; must be ALPA members); and technical. No book reviews or advice on piloting techniques.

Buys 15 mss/year. Query. Length: 1,000-2,500 words. Pays $100-500.

Photos: State availability of photos with query. Purchased with or without accompanying ms. Captions required. Pays $10-25 for 8x10 b&w glossy prints; $20-250 for 35mm or 2¼x2¼ color transparencies. Covers: Pays $250.

Tips: "Unless a writer is experienced in the technical aspects of aviation, he is more likely to score with a pilot profile or aviation historical piece."

FLIGHT REPORTS, Peter Katz Productions, Inc., 1280 Saw Mill River Rd., Yonkers NY 10710. (914)423-6000. Editor: Mary Hunt. Managing Editor: Peter J. Katz. 50% freelance written. Monthly travel magazine for pilots and aircraft owners. Pays on publication. Byline given. Buys all rights. Submit seasonal/holiday material 2 months in advance. SASE. Reports in 2 weeks. Sample copy $1.

Nonfiction: Destination reports include what to do, where to stay, and airport facilities for domestic travel and Canada only. No foreign travel. Buys variable number of mss/year. Query. Length: 750-1,500 words. Pays $25-50.

Photos: State availability of photos. Pays $5 for 3½x5½ b&w and color prints. Captions required.

Tips: "Pilot's license and cross country flying experience is helpful. Some aviation background is required."

FLYING, Ziff-Davis Publishing Co., 1 Park Ave., New York NY 10016. (212)725-3500. Editor-in-Chief: Richard L. Collins. Editorial Coordinator: Linda Brown. 5% freelance written. For private and commercial pilots involved with, or interested in, the use of general-aviation aircraft (not airline or military) for business and pleasure. Monthly magazine; 116 pages. Circ. 370,000. Pays on acceptance. Buys one-time rights. Submit seasonal/holiday material 4 months in advance of issue date. SASE. Reports in 3 weeks.

Nonfiction: How-to (piloting and other aviation techniques); and technical (aviation-related). No articles on "My Trip" travel accounts, or historical features. Buys about 12 mss/year. Submit complete ms. Length: 750-3,500 words. Pays $50-1,000.

Columns/Departments: "I Learned About Flying From That" personal experience. Pays $100 minimum.

Tips: "New ideas and approaches are a must. Tone must be correct for knowledgeable pilots rather than the non-flying public. Facts must be absolutely accurate."

FREQUENT FLYER, Dun & Bradstreet, 888 7th Ave., New York NY 10106. Editor: Coleman A. Lollar. Monthly magazine covering business travel (airlines/airports/aviation) for mostly male high-level business executive readership. Circ. 300,000. Pays on acceptance. Byline given. Offers $75 kill fee. Buys all rights. Submit seasonal/holiday material 6 months in advance. SASE. Reports in 2 months on queries; 1 month on mss. Free sample copy and writer's guidelines.

Nonfiction: Book excerpts, expose, new product, technical, travel, news reporting, in particular on airports/aircraft/airlines/hotel/credit card/car rental. Not interested in queries on stress or anything written in the first person; no profiles, humor or interviews. "*FF* reports on travel as part of an executive's job. We do not assume that he enjoys travel, and neither should the freelancer." Buys 100 mss/year. Query with published clips. Length: 800-3,000 words. Pays $100-500.

Photos: Eve Cohen, articles editor. "We accept both b&w and color contact sheets, transparencies and prints; rates negotiable." Buys one-time rights.

Tips: "We publish very little destination material, preferring articles about how deregulation, airport developments, etc., have affected air services to a destination, rather than descriptive articles. We avoid all travel articles that sound promotional. We publish general business/economic features when they directly relate to the reader as a *mobile* businessman (portable computers, foreign banking, credit card/traveler's check development, etc.). We do not report on other business topics. We like service articles, but not in the usual 'how-to' format: our readers travel too much (average of almost 50 roundtrips a year) to be told how to pack a bag, or how to stay in touch with the office. In service articles, we prefer a review of how frequent travelers handle certain situations rather than how they *should* handle them. Unrequested mss will probably not be read. Give us a good, solid story idea. If accepted, expect a fairly detailed assignment from us. We rewrite heavily. Overly sensitive authors may want to avoid us."

GENERAL AVIATION NEWS, Box 110918, Carrollton TX 75006. (214)446-2502; 1-800-351-1372; (Texas), 1-800-592-4484. Editor: Dan Green. 20-40% freelance written. For pilots, aircraft owners, aviation buffs, aircraft dealers, and related business people. Weekly tabloid; 24-28 pages. Circ. 30,000. Pays on publication. Buys all rights. Byline on all features and most news stories. Phone queries OK. Submit seasonal/holiday material 1 month in advance. Original submissions only (no photocopies) unless prior arrangements made with editor. SASE. Sample copy $1; writer's guidelines for SASE. "*GAN* will verify manuscript arrival immediately. Proposal or rejection within 4 weeks."

Nonfiction: General aviation stories of interest to nationwide audience of persons connected to aviation. Articles on any aspect of aviation (including airline or military) will be accepted provided they are of interest to those in the general aviation community. Buys up to 80 mss/year. Buys 20-40 unsolicited mss/year. Length: 2,000 words maximum. Pays up to $2 per published inch if assigned by editor; 75¢ per published inch if unsolicited.

Photos: Send photo material with accompanying mss. Pays $3-5 for b&w or color prints. Captions required. Buys all rights.

Tips: "Writers should read *GAN* before sending mss; also recommend that writers read other aviation publications/periodicals, to have a grasp of current trends and attitudes in the general aviation world. Editor will personally contact all writers whose work is published in *GAN* and may assign those writers to produce other stories. *GAN* publishes approximately 30-40 stories per issue, most of which are no more than 3-5" in length. Newsworthiness of a story is far more important than length. I will be happy to discuss specifics of an assignment or story on phone. Follow the advice in the front of *Writer's Market*."

HOMEBUILT AIRCRAFT MAGAZINE, Werner & Werner Corp., Suite 201, 16200 Ventura Blvd., Encino CA 91436. (213)986-8400. Editorial Director: Steve Werner. Monthly magazine covering all aspects of homebuilding aircraft. Circ. 38,000. Pays on publication. Buys all rights. SASE. Reports in 1 month. Sample copy $2.50.

Nonfiction: How-to articles (construction methods from kits and scratch); informational (building techniques, materials); personal experiences (with building/flying; vintage homebuilts; homebuilt ultralights). Buys 75 mss/year. Query. Length: 1,000-3,000 words. Pays $100-300.

Photos: State availability of photos. Offers no additional payment for photos accepted with ms. Prefers 8x10, 2¼x2¼ or 35mm slides.

PLANE & PILOT MAGAZINE, Werner & Werner Corp., Suite 201, 16200 Ventura Blvd., Encino CA 91436. (213)986-8400. Editorial Director: Steve Werner. 75% freelance written. Emphasizes all aspects of general aviation—personal and business. Monthly magazine. Circ. 75,000. Pays on publication. Buys all rights. Query. Submit seasonal/holiday material 6 months in advance. SASE. Reports in 1 month. Sample copy $2.50.

Nonfiction: How-to articles (emergency procedures; weather); informational (proficiency; aircraft reports; jobs and schools; avionics); personal experience (regular features on "Flight I'll Never Forget;" travel). Buys 100 mss/year. Length: 1,000-3,000 words. Pays $100-300.

Photos: State availability of photos in query. Offers no additional payment for photos accepted with ms. Prefers 8x10 b&w prints and 2¼x2¼ or 35mm slides.

PRIVATE PILOT, Fancy Communications Corp., Box 4030, San Clemente CA 92672. (714)498-1600. Editor: Dennis Shattuck. 60% freelance written. For owner/pilots of private aircraft, for student pilots and others aspiring to attain additional ratings and experience. "We take a unique, but limited view within our field." Circ. 85,000. Buys first North American serial rights. Buys about 30-60 mss/year. Pays after publication. Sample copy $2; writer's guidelines for SASE. Will consider photocopied submissions if guaranteed original. No simultaneous submissions. Computer printout submissions acceptable "if double spaced and have upper and lower case letters." Reports in 2 months. Query. SASE.

Nonfiction: Material on techniques of flying, developments in aviation, product and specific airplane test reports, travel by aircraft, development and use of airports. All must be related to general aviation field. No personal experience articles. Length: 1,000-4,000 words. Pays $75-250.

Photos: Pays $15 for 8x10 b&w glossy prints purchased with mss or on assignment. Pays $150 for color transparencies used on cover.

Columns/Departments: Business flying, homebuilt/experimental aircraft, pilot's logbook. Length: 1,000 words. Pays $50-125.

Tips: "Freelancer must know the subject about which he is writing; use good grammar; know the publication for which he's writing; remember that we try to relate to the middle segment of the business/pleasure flying public. We see too many 'first flight' type of articles. Our market is more sophisticated than that. Most writers do not do enough research on their subject. Would like to see more material on business-related flying, more on people involved in flying."

ULTRALIGHT AIRCRAFT MAGAZINE, Werner & Werner Corp., Suite 201, 16200 Ventura Blvd., Encino CA 91436. (213)986-8400. Publisher: Steve Werner. Editor: James Lawrence. Monthly magazine covering all aspects of ultralight aircraft. Circ. 70,000. Pays on publication. Buys first North American serial rights. SASE. Reports in 2-4 weeks. Sample copy for $2 and 9x12 SAE; writer's guidelines for 9x12 SAE.

Nonfiction: How-to articles (building from kits and scratch); informational (building/flying techniques, aircraft reports, regulations, safety); personal experience (with building/flying, prototypes, new models). Also general interest (pilot profiles, ultralights in police work, farming, etc., adventure stories, technical, aerodynamic theory); historical/nostalgia (significant developments in ultralights, related flight history to ultralights); humor (anecdotal material related to ultralights); interview/profile (pilots, dealers, manufacturers, adventures, etc.); articles on ultralight training. Buys 50-80 mss/year. Query. Length: 1,000-4,000 words. Pays $150-400+.

Photos: State availability of photos. Offers no additional payment for photos accepted with ms. Prefers 8x10, 2½x2½ or 35mm slides. Captions and identification of subjects required. Buys one-time rights.

Columns/Departments: Ultralight book reviews. Buys 6 mss/year. Query. Length: 500-2,000 words. Pays $50/magazine page. "Hangar Flyins" personal experiences. Pays $25.

ULTRALIGHT FLYER, Ultralight Flyer, Inc., Box 98786, Tacoma WA 98499. (206)588-1743. Managing Editor: Dave Sclair. 30% freelance written. Monthly tabloid covering ultralight aviation nationwide. Provides upbeat coverage of ultralight news activities, and politics. Circ. 20,000. Pays on publication. Byline given. Buys first rights, first and second rights to the same material, and second (reprint) rights to material originally published elsewhere. Submit seasonal/holiday material 1 month in advance. Publishes ms an average of 1 month after acceptance. Simultaneous queries, and photocopied and previously published submissions (from non-competitive publications) OK. Computer printout submissions acceptable. Inquire about electronic submissions. SASE. Reports in 1 week on queries; 1 month on mss. Sample copy $2; writer's guidelines for business size SAE.
Nonfiction: General interest, historical/nostalgic, how-to (safety practices, maintenance), humor, inspirational, interview/profile, new product, opinion (letters to editor), personal experience, photo feature, technical, travel. "No 'gee whiz' type articles aimed at non-pilot audiences." Buys 100-200 mss/year. Query or send complete ms. Length: 250-1,500 words. Pays $20-150.
Photos: "Good pics a must." Send photos with ms. Pays negotiable rates for color transparencies; $10-20 for b&w contact sheet, negatives and 5x7 or larger prints. Identification of subjects required.
Tips: "We will have more special subject editions."

ULTRALIGHT PILOT, 421 Aviation Way, Frederick MD 21701. (301)695-2350. Editor: Thomas A. Horne. For ultralight owners, pilots and aviation industry. Official magazine of the Ultralight Division of the Aircraft Owners and Pilots Association. Bimonthly. Circ. 9,000. Pays on acceptance. Reports in 2 months. SASE. Queries preferred. Sample copy $3.
Nonfiction: Factual articles up to 2,500 words that will inform, educate and entertain ultralight pilots and owners. Pieces should be illustrated with good quality photos, diagrams or sketches. Quality and accuracy essential. Topics covered include maintenance, operating techniques, reports on aircraft and equipment, governmental policies (local, state and federal) relating to ultralight pilots and operations. Features on weather in relation to flying, legal aspects of aviation, flight education, aircraft and parts construction, pilot fitness and aviation history also are used occasionally. Pays $100 maximum.
Photos: Pays $25 minimum for each photo or sketch used. Original b&w negatives or color slides should be made available.

WESTERN FLYER, N.W. Flyer, Inc., Box 98786, Tacoma WA 98499. (206)588-1743. Managing Editor: Dave Sclair. 30% freelance written. Biweekly tabloid covering general aviation. Provides "upbeat coverage of aviation news, activities, and politics of general and sport aviation." Circ. 25,000. Pays on publication. Byline given. Buys one-time rights. Submit seasonal/holiday material 1 month in advance. Publishes ms an average of 1 month after acceptance. Simultaneous queries and photocopied and previously published submissions (from noncompetitive publications) OK. Computer printout submissions acceptable. Inquire about electronic submissions. SASE. Reports in 1 week on queries; 1 month on mss. Sample copy $2; writer's guidelines for business size SASE.
Nonfiction: General interest, historical/nostalgic, how-to (safety practices, maintenance), humor, inspirational, interview/profile, new product, opinion (letters to editor), personal experience, photo feature, technical, travel. "Every other issue is a special issue. Send for list. No 'gee-whiz' type articles aimed at non-pilot audiences." Buys 100 mss/year. Query or send complete ms. Length: 250-1,500 words. Pays $15-100.
Photos: "Good pics a must." Send photos with ms. Pays $10-20 for b&w contact sheet, negatives, and 5x7 or larger prints. Identification of subjects required.

WINGS MAGAZINE, Division of Corvus Publishing Group, Ltd., Suite 158, 1224 53rd Ave., NE, Calgary, Alberta T2E 7E2 Canada. (403)275-9457. Publisher: Paul Skinner. Covers private, commercial and military aviation. Readers are age 15-70 and are predominantly people employed in aviation or with a hobbyist's interest in the field. Bimonthly magazine. Circ. 10,500. Pays on publication. Buys first rights. Phone queries OK. SAE and IRCs. Sample copy $2.50.
Nonfiction: Historical (mainly Canadian history); how-to (technical); informational (technical aviation); interview (Canadian personalities in aviation circles); new product, photo feature; profile (Canadian individuals); technical; travel (flying-related); aircraft handling tests and technical evaluation of new products. No poetry or cartoons. Query; include phone number (with area code). Length: 500-2,000 words. Pays $50-200.
Photos: State availability of photos in query. Purchased with or without accompanying ms. Captions required. Offers no additional payment for photos accepted with ms. Pays $5-20 for 5x7 b&w glossy prints; $25-50 for 35mm color transparencies.
Tips: The writer must have a technical grounding in aviation, be employed in aviation, be a knowledgeable buff or a licensed pilot. Be sure story idea is unique and would be of interest to a Canadian audience. The audience has a high level of technical insight and needs reading material that is newsworthy and informative to the industry executive, aviation expert and worker.

Business and Finance

General interest business publications give executives information from different perspectives—from local reports to national overviews. The national and regional publications are listed below in separate categories. Those in the national grouping cover business trends nationwide, computers in business, and include some material on the general theory and practice of business and financial management for consumers and members of the business community. Those in the regional grouping report on the business climates of specific regions.

Magazines that use material on national business trends and the general theory and practice of business and financial management, but which have a technical slant, are classified in the Trade Journals section, under the Business Management, Finance, Industrial Operation and Management, or Management and Supervision categories.

National

BARRON'S NATIONAL BUSINESS AND FINANCIAL WEEKLY, 22 Cortlandt St., New York NY 10007. (212)285-5243. Editorial Director and Publisher: Robert M. Bleiberg. Editor: Alan Abelson. Managing Editor: Kate Welling. 25% freelance written. For business and investment people. Weekly. Free sample copy. Buys all rights. Pays on publication. Computer printout submissions acceptable; prefers letter-quality to dot-matrix. SASE. Publishes ms an average of 1 month after acceptance.
Nonfiction: Articles about various industries with investment point of view; shorter articles on particular companies, their past performance and future prospects. "Must be suitable for our specialized readership." Length: 1,000-2,500 words. Pays $500-1,000 for articles. Articles considered on speculation only.
Columns/Departments: News and Views, pays $200-400. Book Reviews, pays $150.

BETTER BUSINESS, National Minority Business Council, Inc., 235 E. 42nd St., New York NY 10017. (214)573-2385. Editor: John F. Robinson. 50% freelance written. Quarterly magazine covering small/minority business. Circ. 9,200. Pays on publication. Byline given. Buys first North American serial rights and all rights. Submit material 1 month in advance. Computer printout submissions acceptable; prefers letter-quality to dot-matrix. SASE. Publishes ms an average of 2 months after acceptance. Sample copy for $2 and 9x12 SAE with $1.20 postage; free writer's guidelines.
Nonfiction: Interview/profile, technical. Buys 10 mss/year. Query with clips. Length: 3,000-5,000 words. Pays $250-300.
Photos: State availability of photos. Reviews b&w prints. Captions required. Buys all rights.

BUSINESS COMPUTING, PennWell Publishing Co., 119 Russel St., Littleton MA 01460. (603)673-9544. Executive Editor: Chris Brown. Monthly business magazine covering uses and users of the IBM person computer. "Readers include middle managers, executive vice presidents, mom-'n'-pop entrepreneurs. We are a business publication first, computer magazine second, addressing the needs and interests of IBM Personal Computer users. We are totally independent; that is, not affiliated with IBM." Circ. 100,000. Pays on acceptance. Byline given. Buys first rights. Submit seasonal/holiday material 4 months in advance. No simultaneous, photocopied or previously published submissions. Reports in 1 month on queries; 3 weeks on mss. Free writer's guidelines.
Nonfiction: General interest (business computer); interview/profile (people finding success and/or new applications for personal computers); opinion (software or hardware reviews); "expertise" (an area of personal computing in which you have expertise, presented to readers in a nontechnical way). Special issues include Taxes and the PC; Integrated Software Packages; Working at Home; Creativity and the PC: The Business of Microcomputers. No fiction, jokes, lines and lines of computer programs, or overly simple writing. Buys 4-8 mss/issue. Query with clips of published work. Length: 1,500-5,000 words. Pays $500-1,000/feature article.
Tips: "We think of the PC as a business tool, liberator, and creativity enhancer. Our plain English editorial style is directed at the business reader who is a newcomer to the computer age, with little or no knowledge (*or interest!*) in the technical side. Thus our articles are concerned with those activities of personal computers and computerists that add to office or corporate productivity. Like most business publications, we also run corporate profiles, case histories and interviews as long as they relate to this field. The people who get published by *Business Computing* are those who can put a semi-technical subject into the kind of language that time-conscious business readers can understand and appreciate. We don't want 'too cute' or 'condescending tekkie.'

Write *Wall Street Journal* style. A different theme every issue calls for changing expertise in personal computing areas. However, we are always looking for new applications of personal computers, and the p.c. business itself.''

BUSINESS WEEK, 1221 Avenue of the Americas, New York NY 10020. Does not use freelance material.

COMMODITY JOURNAL, American Association of Commodity Traders, 10 Park St., Concord NH 03301. Editor: Arthur N. Economou. For investors interested in commodity trading based on cash, forward and option markets, alternative energy sources and foreign currencies. Bimonthly tabloid. Circ. 150,000. Pays on publication. Buys all rights. Byline given. Written queries OK. Photocopied and previously published submissions OK. SASE. Reports in 1 month. Free sample copy and writer's guidelines.
Nonfiction: Technical (alternative energy sources; commodity and foreign currency, trading, investing and hedging; commodity markets and foreign currency trends; written intelligibly for general public). "We are not interested in articles concerning the conventional futures market, except insofar as the spot or cash-based markets provide a better alternative." Buys 4 mss/issue. Query. Length: 1,000-2,500 words. Pays 10¢/word.

D&B REPORTS, Dun & Bradstreet, 99 Church St., New York NY 10007. (212)285-7683. Editor: Patricia W. Hamilton. 10% freelance written. Bimonthly magazine for owners and top managers of small businesses (average sales of $9 million annually.) Circ. 71,630. Pays on acceptance. Byline given. Buys all rights. Publishes ms an average of 2 months after acceptance. Simultaneous queries OK. Computer printout submissions acceptable; prefers letter-quality to dot-matrix. SASE. Reports in 2 weeks. Free sample copy and writer's guidelines.
Nonfiction: How-to (small business management, cash management, finance); interview/profile (of innovative managers); new product (how developed and marketed). "Articles provide concrete, hands-on information on how to manage more effectively. Articles on scientific developments or social change with implications for business are also of interest." Buys 8-12 mss/year. Query with clips of published work. Length: 2,000-3,000 words. Pays $500 minimum.
Tips: "The most rewarding aspect of working with freelance writers is discovering new talent, then being able to use it on a regular basis for article assignments.

DOLLARS & SENSE, National Taxpayers Union, 325 Pennsylvania Ave. SE, Washington DC 20003. Editor-in-Chief: M. Fiddes. 10% freelance written. Emphasizes taxes and government spending for a diverse readership. Monthly newspaper; 8-12 pages. Circ. 120,000. Pays on publication. Buys all rights. Submit seasonal/holiday material 1 month in advance. Previously published submissions OK. SASE. Free sample copy and writer's guidelines.
Nonfiction: Exposé dealing with wasteful government spending and excessive regulation of the economy. Buys 7 mss/year. Query. Length: 500-1,500 words. Pays $25-100.
Tips: "We look for original material on subjects overlooked by the national press and other political magazines. Probably the best approach is to take a little-known area of government mismanagement and examine it closely. The articles we like most are those that examine a federal program that is not only poorly managed and wasteful, but also self-defeating, hurting the very people it is designed to help. We are also interested in the long-term harm done by different kinds of taxation. Articles on IRS harassment and abuses are always needed and welcome. We have no use for financial or investment advice or broad philosophical pieces."

DONOGHUE'S MONEY FUND REPORT®, The Donoghue Organization, Inc., 360 Woodland St., Box 540, Holliston MA 01746. (617)429-5930. Senior Editor: James Henderson. Weekly newsletter covering the money market mutual fund industry. Pays "upon completion of assigned article." No byline given. Makes work-for-hire assignments. Simultaneous queries, and simultaneous and photocopied submissions OK. SASE. Reports in 8 weeks. Free sample copy and writer's guidelines.
Nonfiction: How-to, new product, technical; coverage of industry conferences and regulatory board meetings. "We use news updates in the money market mutual fund industry and news stories with focus on how news will affect participants in the money market." Buys variable number of mss/year. Query with published clips. Length: 100-500 words. Pays $75-100 for 400-500 words; "depends on article content."
Tips: Also publishes *Donoghue's Moneyletter* (for consumers interested in investment advice), *The Donoghue's Mutual Funds Almanac*, and *The Cash Manager* (for cash management professionals).

DUN'S BUSINESS MONTH, Technical Publications Co., A Division of Dun & Bradstreet Corp., 875 3rd Ave., New York NY 10022. (212)605-9400. Editor: Clem Morgello. Emphasizes business, management and finances for a readership "concentrated among senior executives of those companies that have a net worth of $1 million or more." Monthly magazine. Circ. 284,000. Pays on acceptance. Buys all rights. Submit seasonal/holiday material 3 months in advance. Photocopied submissions OK. Reports in 1 month. Sample copy $2.50.
Nonfiction: Business and government, historical (business; i.e., law or case history), management (new trends, composition), finance and accounting, informational, interview, personal opinion and company pro-

file. Buys 12 mss/year. Query first. Length: 1,200-2,500 words. Pays $200 minimum.

Photos: Art Director. Purchased with accompanying ms. Query first. Pays $75 for b&w photos; $150 for color.

Tips: "Make query short and clearly to the point. Also important—what distinguishes proposed story from others of its type."

THE EXECUTIVE FEMALE, NAFE, Suite 1440, 120 E. 56th St., New York NY 10022. (212)371-0740. Managing Editor: Susan Strecker. Assistant Managing Editor: Susan Kain. 30% freelance written. Emphasizes "upbeat and useful career and financial information for the upwardly mobile female." Bimonthly magazine; 60 pages. Circ. 120,000. Byline given. Pays on publication. Written queries only. Submit seasonal/holiday material 6 months in advance. Publishes ms an average of 4 months after acceptance. Buys first rights and second (reprint) rights to material originally published elsewhere. Simultaneous and photocopied submissions OK. Computer printout submissions acceptable. SASE. Reports in 3 months. Sample copy $1.50; free writer's guidelines.

Nonfiction: "Articles on any aspect of career advancement and financial planning are welcomed." Sample topics: managerial work issues, investment, coping with inflation, trends in the work place, money-saving ideas, financial planning, trouble shooting, business communication, time and stress management, and career goal setting and advancement. No negative or radical material. Article length: 1,000-2,500 words. Pays $50-$100 minimum.

Columns/Departments: Profiles (interviews with successful women in a wide range of fields, preferably nontraditional areas for women); Entrepreneur's Corner (successful female business owners with unique ideas); Horizons (career planning, personal and professional perspectives and goal-setting); More Money (specific financial issues, social security, tax planning); and Your Executive Style (tips on health and lifestyle). Department length: 800-1,200 words. Pays $25-50 minimum.

Tips: "Write with more depth. I have the feeling that most authors are just writing off the tops of their heads to have articles 'out there.' "

FACT, The Money Management Magazine, 711 3rd Ave., New York NY 10017. (212)687-3965. Editor-in-Chief: Daniel M. Kehrer. 50% freelance written. Monthly personal money management and investment magazine for sophisticated readers. Circ. 150,000. Pays on acceptance. Byline given. Offers 25% kill fee. Buys first rights and nonexclusive (reprint) rights. Simultaneous queries OK. Computer printout submissions acceptable; prefers letter-quality to dot-matrix. SASE. Reports in 6 weeks. Publishes ms an average of 2 months after acceptance. Free sample copy.

Nonfiction: General interest (specific money management topics); how-to (invest in specific areas); and new product. No business articles; no "how-to-balance your checkbook" articles. Writers must be knowledgeable and use lots of sidebars and tables. Buys 100 mss/year. Query with published clips. Length: 1,000-2,500 words. Pays $250-700.

Photos: Contact the art director. State availability of photos. Pays $25-120 for color transparencies. Captions, model release and identification of subjects required. Buys one-time rights.

Columns/Departments: Stocks, mutual funds, precious metals, bonds, real estate, collectibles, taxes, insurance, cash management and banking. Buys 50-60 mss/year. Query with published clips. Length: 1,500-1,800 words. Pays $250-600.

Tips: "Show writing credentials and expertise on a subject. Try something fresh, with photo possibilities. Read the magazine. Our readers are sophisticated about investments and money management."

FORBES, 60 5th Ave., New York NY 10011. "We occasionally buy freelance material. When a writer of some standing (or whose work is at least known to us) is going abroad or into an area where we don't have regular staff or bureau coverage, we have given assignments or sometimes helped on travel expenses." Pays negotiable kill fee. Byline usually given.

FORTUNE, 1271 Avenue of the Americas, New York NY 10020. Staff-written. Occasionally contract.

‡**INC MAGAZINE, The Magazine for Growing Companies**, INC Publishing Corp., 38 Commercial Wharf, Boston MA 02110. (617)227-4700. Editor: George Gendron. Managing Editor: Roberta W. Shell. A monthly business magazine for chief operating officers and managers of growing companies up to $100 million in sales. Circ. 550,000. Pays on acceptance. Byline given. Offers 33⅓% kill fee. Buys all rights. Submit seasonal/holiday material 3 months in advance. Computer printout submissions acceptable. Reports in 6 weeks on queries; 2 weeks on mss. Free sample copy and writer's guidelines.

Nonfiction: Interview/profile and opinion. Buys 25 mss/year. Query with published clips. Length: 350-4,000 words. Pays $150-2,500.

Columns/Departments: Financial Tactics, Capital Selling and Marketing, Managing People, and Technology. Buys 20 mss/year. Query with published clips. Length: 350-1,200 words. Pays $150-800.

Tips: "Features are most open to freelancers."

‡**INFO AGE MAGAZINE, Canada's Microsystems Magazine**, Plesman Publications, Suite 302, 211 Consumers Rd., Toronto, Ontario, M2J 4G8, Canada. (416)497-9562. Editor: Gord Campbell. Managing Editor: Bill Knapp. 95% freelance written. Monthly magazine on business microcomputers. "Our readers are mainly business people, professionals or corporate employees with microcomputers used for business purposes. Our editorial material is written in a down-to-earth style and in plain English as much as possible for novice- or intermediate-level computer users." Circ. 20,000. Pays on publication. Publishes ms an average of 2 months after acceptance. Byline given. Offers $50 kill fee. Buys first rights. Submit seasonal/holiday material 3 months in advance. No simultaneous queries, or simultaneous, photocopied or previously published submissions. Computer printout submissions acceptable. SASE. Reports in 1 week. Sample copy for $2.95; free writer's guidelines.
Nonfiction: Book excerpts; how-to (involving computers; usually assigned); interview/profile (outstanding companies or individuals in Canadian computer industry); new product (short pieces on new hardware or software); technical (computer-related; usually assigned). No personal experience, "humorous" pieces, highly technical pieces, jargon or program listings. Buys 120 mss/year. Query with published clips. Length: 1,500-2,500 words. Pays $150-350.
Photos: Pays $25 maximum for 8x10 b&w prints. Identification of subjects required. Buys one-time rights.
Tips: "It's not difficult to break into *InfoAge*—we are actively seeking writers. Send a letter indicating your availability, areas of expertise and samples. If you have a proposal for an article, it should be included in the form of a concise outline. Computer magazines used to be quite technical because readers were technically adept. As more people buy computers for what they can do as opposed to how they can be made to do them, magazines are adapting and have become less arcane."

INTERFACE AGE, Computing for Business, McPheters, Wolfe & Jones, 16704 Marquardt Ave., Cerritos CA 90701. (213)926-9544. Editorial Director: Les Spindle. Managing Editor: Frank Jones. 50% freelance written. Monthly magazine covering microcomputers in business. *IA*'s focus is toward the business computer user. Readers receive up-to-the-minute reports on new products, applications for business and programs they can apply to their own personal computer." Circ. 100,000. Pays on publication. Publishes ms an average of 6 months after acceptance. Byline given. Kill fee varies. Buys all rights. Submit seasonal/holiday material 4 months in advance. Simultaneous queries, and simultaneous and photocopied submissions OK. Computer printout and disk submissions acceptable "after phone-consulting with editors." Reports in 4-6 weeks on mss. Sample copy $3.75; free writer's guidelines.
Nonfiction: How-to, new product, opinion, personal experience, photo feature, technical. No agency- or company-written articles. "Articles should pertain to microcomputing applications in business, law, education, medicine, software, unique breakthroughs, future projections. We seek interviews/profiles of people well-known in the industry or making unusual use of microcomputers. Computer programs and sample listings must be printed with a new ribbon to get the best quality reproduction in the magazine." Buys 60 mss/year. Query with clips of published work or send complete ms. Length: 1,000-5,000 words. Pays $50 and more (negotiable)/printed page including photos, charts, programs and listings.
Photos: Send photos, charts, listings and programs with ms. Photos included in purchase price of article. Captions, model release and identification of subjects required.
Columns/Departments: Book reviews (brief appraisals of current computer titles. "We will send books to interested parties."). Buys 30 mss/year. Length: 300-1,000 words. Pays $20.
Tips: "Case study articles specifying how a particular type of business (law firm, retail store, office, etc.) implemented a computer to improve efficiency and not-yet-reviewed product reviews stand the best chance for acceptance. Hardware and software appraisals by qualified reviewers are desirable. Practical and business applications, rather than home/hobbyist pursuits, are encouraged. Focus tightly on 'Computing for Business' theme."

‡**LIST, The Business Magazine for Computer Users**, Redgate Publishing Co., Inc., 3381 Ocean Dr., Vero Beach FL 32963. (305)231-6904. Editor: Paul Kellam. Associate Editor: Thomas R. Kempf. 50% freelance written. Monthly magazine covering "business solution through computers." Circ. 125,000. Pays on acceptance. Publishes ms an average of 2 months after acceptance. Byline given. Offers 25% of agreed fee as kill fee. Buys first North American serial rights. Submit seasonal/holiday material 5 months in advance. Computer printout submissions acceptable. SASE. Reports in 2 weeks on queries; 1 month on mss. Sample copy for 9x12 SAE and $2 postage; free writer's guidelines.
Nonfiction: General interest (business solutions through software); how-to (how *he* solved his business problem with a computer); personal experience (how I solved my business problem with a computer). Special issues include January directory of business software. No technical, computer-programming, hardware-oriented, games, education. Avoid jargon or overdone subjects like "How to buy a computer." Buys 50-60 mss/year. Query with published clips. Length: 2,500-5,000 words. Pays $750 and up.
Photos: Accepts photos with articles only. Reviews b&w and color transparencies. Model releases and identification of subjects required. Buys one-time rights.
Columns/Departments: Buys 50 mss/year. Query with published clips. Length: 1,500-2,500 words. Pays $250-750.

Close-up

Daniel M. Kehrer
Editor-in-Chief, *Fact*

Photo by Mary Motley Kalergis

When Daniel Kehrer writes an article, he puts extensive research on paper quickly, but that doesn't mean he's done writing. He'll then add colorful details, subtract unnecessary words, personalize the piece for readers.

The former full-time freelancer uses a working lead for his first drafts. On the rewrites, he adds a lead with "punch" enough to get the reader to read on. "It's got to flow and have a ring to it like poetry," says the author of *Investing in Global Stocks* (Alexander Hamilton Institute) and *Pills and Potions* (Arco).

Kehrer describes himself as a writer who happens to be an editor. In fact, freelancing led to his involvement with *Fact.*

Employed on a month-to-month basis four years ago, he helped to develop the magazine. The work became *permanent*, and he became editor-in-chief. Kehrer, though, still writes articles for *Fact* and rewrites many of the freelance submissions.

He thought finding freelancers for the new magazine would be easy. "There's no shortage of people who want to write," he has found. "There's a shortage of people who know their topic."

Even some business writers have difficulty making a transition from finance writing for the corporation to finances *for the individual.* That slant is what makes *Fact* different, but also easily misunderstood by freelancers who don't thoroughly read the magazine. *Fact* is a consumer service magazine about personal money management and investing, *not* a business magazine, says Kehrer.

A sophisticated stock market investor, for example, may want to invest money in areas he knows little about. *Fact* includes monthly columns on investment possibilities such as precious metals and real estate. Readers want specific facts and statistics. "You have to put details in your articles"—the kind that only an insider will know to include.

"People don't read this magazine just for entertainment," he says. " . . . You have to give readers stories they can act upon."

What Kehrer wants from freelancers are queries with original ideas. Too much of his mail reiterates the same ideas. When an idea *looks* interesting or unusual, Kehrer asks himself: What new information will it provide to readers?

The writer must sometimes do most of the research *before* writing the query, he says. And once the writer gets an assignment, the follow-through is crucial. The writer must personalize his articles, addressing *Fact* readers as "you," citing examples, and writing tightly.

Kehrer also follows that advice as he continues to freelance in his spare time. Three specialties—business, personal finance, and medical writing—keep him at the personal computer.

He co-authors a syndicated column, Consumer Drug File. He is writing a book on precious metals. His bylines appear in *Science Digest*, *American Health*, *Islands*, and major U.S. newspapers.

Writers can benefit from developing a specialty, he says. Local and regional business periodicals enable the writer to research and write on business topics. Experience and clips will lead to more assignments and expertise.

The lazy writer, like the haphazard investor, doesn't research the market. Neither should expect dividends. As, Kehrer has found, it is the details that make the difference.

MONEY, Time-Life Bldg., Rockefeller Center, New York NY 10020. Managing Editor: Marshall Loeb. For the middle- to upper-income, sophisticated, well-educated reader. Major subjects: personal investing, financial planning, spending, saving and borrowing, careers, travel. Some freelance material.

‡**THE MONEYPAPER, A Financial Publication for Women**, Temper of the Times Communications, Inc., Rm. 209, 2 Madison Ave., Larchmont NY 10538. (914)833-0270. Editor: Vita Nelson. Executive Editor: Mary Ann Myers. A monthly newsletter covering financial issues, particularly as they relate to women. Complicated financial concepts are presented in straightforward language." Estab. 1982. Circ. 8,000. Pays on publication. Byline given. Offers $25 kill fee. Makes work-for-hire assignments. Submit seasonal/holiday material 1 month in advance. Simultaneous queries and photocopied submissions OK. Computer printout submissions acceptable. SASE. Reports in 2 weeks on queries; 1 month on mss. Sample copy for SAE and 2 first class stamps.
Nonfiction: How-to (personal finance); interview/profile (prominent women); and new product (investing, financial services). Buys 15 mss/year. Query with published clips. Pays 20¢/published word.
Columns/Departments: Taxes, Jobs, Investing, and Owning a Business. "Professionals in the field preferred as authors." Buys 36 mss/year. Length: 750/words. Pays $58 honorarium.
Tips: "We do respond to queries, but a telephone follow-up is good for the writer. We like to direct the focus of the articles, so a dialogue is often necessary. Feature articles are most open to freelancers. We look for thorough research and practical advice on ways to make and save more money."

PERSONAL AND PROFESSIONAL, The Independent Magazine For Digital Personal Computer Users, Personal Press, Inc., 921 Bethlehem Pike, Springhouse PA 19477. (215)542-7008. Managing Editor: James L. Trichon. 75-85% freelance written. Bimonthly magazine of personal computers for people who are DEC personal computer users. Estab. 1983. Circ. 50,000. Buys first rights. Pays on publication. Publishes ms an average of 2 months after acceptance. Byline given. Offers 50% kill fee. Simultaneous queries and photocopied and previously published submissions OK. Call for details on electronic submissions, but requires hard copy also. Computer printout submissions acceptable; prefers letter-quality to dot-matrix. Reports in 1 month on queries; 2 weeks on mss. Free sample copy and writer's guidelines,
Nonfiction: How-to (use a computer, software, etc.); interview/profile (of computer leaders); personal experience (user articles); technical (all aspects of hardware and software); all types of articles dealing with DEC PC market only. No opinion pieces. Buys 200-250 mss/year. Query. Length: 1,500-3,500 words. Pays $100-500+ "depending on the piece."
Tips: "The most annoying aspect of working with freelance writers is late copy, not getting what was promised and lack of computer knowledge."

SYLVIA PORTER'S PERSONAL FINANCE MAGAZINE, 380 Lexington Ave., New York NY 10017. (212)557-9100. Editor: Patricia Estess. Executive Editor: Elana Lore. 50% freelance written. Bimonthly magazine covering personal finance and consumer economics. Estab. 1983. Pays on acceptance. Publishes ms an average of 4 months after acceptance. Byline given. Offers 20% kill fee. Buys all rights. Submit seasonal/holiday material 4 months in advance. No simultaneous queries. No simultaneous, photocopied or previously published submissions. SASE. Reports in 2 months. Free sample copy; writer's guidelines are available.
Nonfiction: General interest (financial). Only articles dealing with personal finance; no financially technical articles. Query with published clips. Length: 1,000-1,500 words. Pays negotiable rates.
Columns/Departments: Funny Money (send mss to editor, Funny Money). "Funny Money is looking for personal stories of humorous observation or experience in the fields of saving, spending, borrowing, investing." Buys 50 mss/year. Send complete ms. Length: about 150 words. Pays $25.
Tips: "The magazine is grounded on the personal relationship between reader and writer. Writers and editors have the responsibility of giving the reader the impression that an article was written 'for me'—and, indeed, it will have been. Send a cover letter with original ideas or slants about personal finance articles you'd like to do for us, accompanied by clippings of your previously published work. The features section is most open to freelancers. We will be covering topics such as budgeting, saving, investing, real estate, taxes, in each issue. It's most important for us that our writers be familiar with the trends in their own special areas of personal finance so our magazine can be as up to date as possible. Features must be accurate, personal in tone, and must sparkle."

‡**SOFTWARE, To Increase Your Productivity, Optimize Time and Money**, Fast Access, Suite K, 2803 Ocean Park Blvd., Santa Monica CA 90405. (213)450-6646 or 450-8880. Editor: Michael White. Managing Editor: Earl Rand. Bimonthly magazine covering business and professional applications of microcomputers. Estab. 1983. Circ. 45,000. Pays on publication. Byline given. Offers $100 kill fee. Buys first North American serial rights, all rights, first rights, and makes work-for-hire assignments. Simultaneous queries and simultaneous submissions OK. Electronic submissions (Apple II 5¼" diskette only) OK. Computer printout submissions acceptable. SASE. Reports in 1 month. Sample copy for $2.50, 9x11 SAE and 85¢ postage; free writer's guidelines.

Nonfiction: How-tos (micros, software) and personal experience. No vague, general or reportorial-type articles. Query with published clips or send complete ms. Pays $50-400.
Columns/Departments: "We feature regular columns on small business, corporate, and government use of micros. We also have regular columns on word processing, spreadsheets, data base management, graphics and communications." Query with published clips or send complete ms. Pays $50-400.
Filler: Clippings, jokes, gags, anecdotes, short humor and newsbreaks. Pays $5-25.

TECHNICAL ANALYSIS OF STOCKS AND COMMODITIES, The Traders Magazine, Box 46518, Seattle WA 98146. (206)938-0570. Editor: Jack K. Hutson. 80% freelance written. Bimonthly magazine covering trading stocks and commodities. Circ. 1,000. Pays on publication. Publishes ms an average of 5-10 weeks after acceptance. Byline given. Offers 50% kill fee. Buys first rights and "both the author and *TA* have the right to reprint." Photocopied and previously published submissions OK. Electronic submissions via phone 300 baud or Apple II computer disk, but requires hard copy also. Computer printout submissions acceptable. SASE. Reports in 3 weeks on queries; 1 month on mss. Sample copy $5; detailed writer's guidelines for business size SAE and 2 first class stamps.
Nonfiction: Reviews (new software or hardware on the market that can make a trader's life easier; comparative reviews of books, articles, etc.); how-to (make a trade); technical (trading and software aids to trading); utilities (charting or computer programs, surveys, statistics, or information to help the trader study or interpret market movements); humor (unusual incidents of market occurrences, cartoons). No newsletter-type, buy-sell recommendations. The article subject must relate to a technical analysis charting or numerical technique used to trade securities or futures. Buys 60 mss/year. Query with published clips if available or send complete ms. Length: 1,500-4,000 words. Pays $100-500. (Applies base rate and premium rate—write for information).
Photos: Kevin O. Donohoe, photo editor. State availability of photos. Pays $15-50 for 8½x11 b&w glossy prints. Captions, model release and identification of subjects required. Buys one-time rights.
Columns/Departments: Buys 10 mss/year. Query. Length: 800-1,600 words. Pays $50-200.
Fillers: Kevin O. Donohoe, fillers editor. Jokes. Buys 20/year. Length: 100-500 words. Pays $10-50. Must relate to trading stocks or commodities.
Tips: "Describe how to use chart work and other technical analysis in day-to-day trading of stocks or commodities. A blow-by-blow account of how a trade was made, including the trader's thought processes, is, to our subscribers, the very best received story. One of our prime considerations is to instruct in a manner that the lay person can comprehend. We are not hyper-critical of writing style. The completeness and accuracy of submitted material is of the utmost consideration. Write for detailed writer's guidelines."

TRAVEL SMART FOR BUSINESS, Communications House, 40 Beechdale Rd., Dobbs Ferry NY 10522. (914)693-8300. Editor/Publisher: H.J. Teison. Executive Editor: Mary Hunt. Managing Editor: L.M. Lane. 20% freelance written. Monthly newsletter covering travel and information on keeping travel costs down for business travelers and business travel managers. Circ. 2,000. Pays on publication. Publishes ms an average of 6 weeks after acceptance. No byline given. "Writers are listed as contributors." Offers 25% kill fee. Buys first North American serial rights. Computer printout submissions acceptable; prefers letter-quality to dot-matrix. SASE. Reports in 6 weeks. Sample copy for business size SAE, and 2 first class stamps; writer's guidelines free for business size SAE and 1 first class stamp.
Nonfiction: Expose (of "inside" travel facts and companies dealing in travel); how-to (pick a meeting site, save money on travel); reviews of facilities and restaurants; analysis of specific trends in travel affecting business travelers. No general travel information, backgrounders, or non-business-oriented articles. "We're looking for value-oriented, concise, factual articles." Buys 20 mss/year. Query with clips of published work. Length: 250-1,500 words. Pays $20-150.
Tips: "We are primarily staff written, with a few regular writers. Contributions to 'Deal Alert' are welcome and can take the form of clips, etc. Know the travel business or have business travel experience. People with a specific area of experience or expertise have the inside track."

WEEKDAY, Enterprise Publications, Suite 3417, 20 N. Wacker Dr., Chicago IL 60606. For the average employee in business and industry. Circ. 30,000. Buys all rights. Byline given. Pays on acceptance. SASE.
Nonfiction and Photos: Uses articles slanted toward the average person, with the purpose of increasing his understanding of the business world and helping him be more successful in it. Also uses articles on "How to Get Along With Other People," and informative articles on meeting everyday problems—consumer buying, legal problems, community affairs, real estate, education, human relations, etc. Length: approximately 1,000 words maximum. Pays $15-40. Uses b&w human interest photos.

Regional

AUSTIN MAGAZINE, Austin Chamber of Commerce, Box 1967, Austin TX 78767. (512)478-9383. Editor: Hal Susskind. Managing Editor: Laura Tuma. A business and community magazine dedicated to telling the story of Austin and its people to Chamber of Commerce members and the community. Magazine published monthly by the Chamber; 72-128 pages. Circ. 12,000. Pays kill fee. Byline given "except if the story has to be completely rewritten; the author would be given credit for his input but he may not be given a byline." Sample copy for $1.75. Will consider original mss only. Computer printout submissions acceptable; prefers letter-quality to dot-matrix. Reports within 3 months. SASE.

Nonfiction: Articles should deal with interesting businesses or organizations, politics, events, people, or phenomena relating to the Austin community and in particular Chamber of Commerce members. Articles are also accepted on Austin's entertainment scene and the arts. Length: 750-3,000 words. Pays $75-300. B&w and color photos are purchased with mss.

‡**B.C. BUSINESS MAGAZINE**, Pacific Rim Publications, Ltd., 601-510 W. Hastings St., Vancouver, British Columbia, V6B 1L8, Canada. (604)689-2021. Editor: J. R. Martin. Managing Editor: Peter Morgan. Magazine covering British Columbia business through features on business conditions in pre-determined British Columbia industries for business executives. Circ. 20,000. Pays on acceptance. Byline given. Offers 50% kill fee. Buys second serial (reprint) rights or makes work-for-hire assignements. Simultaneous queries and photocopied submissions OK. Computer printout submissions acceptable. Reports in 2 weeks. Free sample copy and writer's guidelines.

Nonfiction: General interest, interview/profile and articles on business in British Columbia. No business product description. Buys 50 mss/year. Query with published clips. Length: 2,000-5,000 words. Pays $240-600.

Photos: State availability of photos. Captions, model releases and identification of subjects required. Buys one-time rights.

Tips: "A freelancer can best break into our publication by submitting detailed, factual, interesting reports on business conditions in a British Columbia industry."

‡**BOULDER BUSINESS REPORT, Our Readers Are Leaders**, Boulder Business Report, 2006 Broadway, Boulder CO 80302. (303)440-4952. Editor: Suzanne Gripman. Monthly newspaper covering Boulder area business issues. Offers "in-depth news tailored to a monthly theme and read by Boulder, Colorado businespeople and investors nationwide. Philosophy: Colorful, interesting prose designed to help the reader think. Draws pieces into 'big picture.' " Circ. 3,000. Pays on completion of assignment. Byline given. Offers 10% kill fee. Buys one-time rights and second serial (reprint) rights. Simultaneous queries and photocopied submissions OK. SASE. Reports in 1 month on queries; 2 weeks on mss. Sample copy $1.50; free writer's guidelines.

Nonfiction: Book excerpts, interview/profile, new product, photo feature of company, person or product. "All our issues are 'special issues' in that material is written around a monthly theme. No articles in which the subject has not been pursued in depth and no articles which cover an interesting subject but lack color and personality." Buys 24 mss/year. Query with published clips. Length: 250-3,000 words. Pays $25-300.

Photos: State availability of photos with query letter. Reviews b&w contact sheets; prefers "people portraits." Pays $10 maximum for b&w contact sheet. Identification of subjects required. Buys one-time rights and reprint rights.

Tips: "It would be difficult to write for this publication if a freelancer was unable to localize a subject. Business in Boulder is a bird of another color; those with entrepreneurial or high-tech background will have a good frame of reference in writing for this publication. In-depth articles are what we are looking for, written by assignment. The freelancer located in the Boulder, Colorado, area has an excellent chance here."

THE BUSINESS TIMES, The Business Times, Inc., 544 Tolland St., East Hartford CT 06108. (203)289-9341. Managing Editor: Deborah Hallberg. 20% freelance written. Monthly tabloid covering business and financial news within Connecticut for "the top executive or business owner in Connecticut." Circ. 25,000. Pays on publication. Byline given. Buys exclusive rights only within Connecticut. Phone queries OK. Submit seasonal/holiday material 1 month in advance. Publishes ms an average of 1 month after acceptance. Simultaneous queries and previously published submissions OK. Computer printout submissions acceptable; prefers letter-quality to dot matrix. SASE. Reports in 1 month. Sample copy $1.

Nonfiction: Interview/profile (of a Connecticut business person with a unique story); new product (pertaining to Connecticut only). "Features include legislative updates, state-of-the-economy analysis, industry profiles, etc. We use very little national news. It helps if out-of-state freelancers specialize in one area, e.g., real estate. Articles should be written with the business *owner*—not the office manager or secretary—in mind." Special monthly supplements include: computers, office design, word processing, copiers, real estate, tax shelters, transportation service, telecommunications, banking and finance. "We have a need for material for our monthly advertising supplements. These are usually nuts and bolts kind of articles—state-of-the-art, etc." No articles on improving sales techniques, time management, stress management, cash flow management or how to choose a computer. Buys 4-5 mss/year. Query with clips of published works. Length: 800-1,500 words. Pays $1/column inch.

Photos: State availability of photos. Reviews 8x10 b&w prints. Pays $15/first photo, $10 each additional photo. Captions required. Buys exclusive rights within Connecticut.

BUSINESS TO BUSINESS, Tallahassee's Business Magazine, Business to Business, Inc., Box 6085, Tallahassee FL 32314. (904)222-7072. Editor: Howard Libin. 70% freelance written. Monthly tabloid covering business in the North Florida-South Georgia Big Bend region. Circ. 16,000. Pays on acceptance. Byline given "generally." Offers 30% kill fee. Buys one-time rights. Submit seasonal/holiday material 4 months in advance. Publishes ms an average of 2 months after acceptance. Photocopied and previously published submissions OK. Computer printout submissions acceptable; prefers letter-quality to dot-matrix. SASE. Reports in 2 weeks on queries; 3 weeks on mss. Sample copy for 9x12 SAE and 4 first class stamps; writer's guidelines for SAE and 1 first class stamp.

Nonfiction: Book excerpts (reviews of business related books—Megatrends, Positioning); In Search of Excellence (topics of interest to business-minded people); historical/nostalgic (only pertaining to the Big Bend); how-to (select the right typewriter, adding machine, secretary, phone system, insurance plan); new products; technical (articles on finance marketing, investment, advertising and real estate as it applies to small business). Special "inserts" planned: advertising, office of the future, consulting, taxes. "No really basic material. Writers must assume that readers have some idea of business vocabulary. No new business profiles, or material without local handle." Have started an "After Work" section and can use a wide array of "lifestyle" pieces—health, food, hobbies, travel, recreation, etc. Buys 30-50 mss/year. Query with published clips if available. Length: 600-2,000 words. Pays $40-250.

Photos: Steve Bradley, Bob O'Lary, photo editors. State availability of photos. Pays $5-20 for b&w contact sheet and b&w prints. Identification of subjects required.

Columns/Departments: "Shorts accepted on all aspects of doing business. Each story should tackle one topic and guide reader from question to conclusion. General appeal for all trades and industries." Buys 50-70 mss/year. Query with published clips if available. Length: 600-1,000 words. Pays $40-90.

Tips: "Send a query with past writing sample included. If it seems that a writer is capable of putting together an interesting 500-800 word piece dealing with small business operation, we're willing to give him/her a try. Meeting deadlines determines writer's future with us. We're open to short department pieces on management, finance, marketing, investments, real estate. Must be tightly written—direct and to the point; yet keep it casual."

‡**BUSINESS VIEW OF SOUTHWEST FLORIDA**, Collier County Magazines, Inc., Box 1546, Naples FL 33939. (813)263-7525. Managing Editor: Karen Martin. Monthly magazine for business, financial, and investment community of southwest Florida. "The editorial material is factual, succinct and thought-provoking." Circ. 7,000. Pays on publication. Byline given. Offers $50 kill fee. Buys second serial (reprint) rights. Submit seasonal/holiday material 2 months in advance. Simultaneous queries, and simultaneous and previously published submissions OK "only if not locally simultaneously submitted." Computer printout submissions acceptable. SASE. Reports in 6 weeks. Sample copy $2; writer's guidelines for business-size SAE and 20¢ postage.

Nonfiction: How-to (business-related management), interview/profile (regional/Florida business leaders), opinion (business-related), personal experience (business-related), technical (business-related). "We like charts, graphs and statistics. We try to present the facts with an interesting format. Our topics have tie-in to southwest Florida." Query with published clips. Length: 1,750-3,500 words. Pays $125-250. "Special assignments can pay more."

Columns/Departments: Eleanor K. Springer, column/department editor. Columns of interest to the business, financial, retail, real estate, and investment community of Southwest Florida. Buys 24 mss/year. Send complete ms. Length: 750-1,500 words. Pays $25-150.

Fillers: Eleanor K. Springer, fillers editor. Short humor and newsbreaks (business-related). Buys 25-50 mss/year. Length: 200-600 words. Pays $5-25.

Tips: "We like tight, sophisticated writing that gets right to the point. It can be sprinkled with intelligent humor and puns. Our readers are busy business professionals in one of the fastest growing areas in the nation. Columns with management and legal tips for businesses, computer hints, equipment advances, etc., are open to freelancers."

‡**BUSINESSWOMAN**, THA, Inc., Box 23276, San Jose CA 95153-3276. (408)226-3311. Editor: Rachele Kanigel. A monthly magazine for Northern California businesswomen. "*BusinessWOMAN* is aimed at executive-level, upwardly mobile, businesswomen. It is first and foremost a business magazine, and secondly a woman's magazine." Circ. 6,000. Pays on publication. Byline given. Buys first North American serial rights. Submit seasonal/holiday material 7-8 months in advance. Simultaneous queries, and simultaneous, photocopied and previously published submissions OK. Computer printout submissions acceptable. SASE. Reports in 2 months. Free sample copy and writer's guidelines.

Nonfiction: Book excerpts; general interest (to businesswomen); how-to; interview/profile; new product; personal experience; technical; travel; and computers. Articles should be directed to Northern California businesswomen. Each issue focuses on a theme. Past themes include Communication, Travel, Art and Finance, and High Technology. Upcoming issues on Women and Law (Oct./Nov. 1984); Media/Marketing (Dec./Jan. 1984-85); and Balancing Career and Home (Feb./Mar. 1985). Most articles are assigned; send article ideas specific to certain issue 6-8 months before cover date. No fashion, make-up, sewing, cooking, reviews of arts, out-of-state focus. Buys 60-75 mss/year. Query with published clips, or send complete ms. Length: 500-2,500 words. Pays $10-25.

Columns/Departments: Rachele Kanigel, column/department editor. Travel-tips (for business travel); Computer (how-to, product surveys, new trends). Buys 12-20 mss/year. Query with published clips, send complete ms. Length: 500-1,000 words. Pays $10-25.

Tips: Write queries specific to theme of issue 6-8 months in advance of cover date, include clips and resumé or description of background and expertise. Profiles, features, how-to trends, and computer departments are most open to freelancers.

COLORADO BUSINESS MAGAZINE, Titsch and Associates, Box 5400 T.A., Denver CO 80217. (303)295-0900. Executive Editor: Ann Feeney. Editor: Sharon Almirall. Monthly magazine covering business. Circ. 20,634. Pays on publication. Byline given. Offers negotiable kill fee. Buys first North American serial rights. Submit seasonal/holiday material 4 months in advance. Simultaneous queries, and photocopied and previously published submissions (on occasion) OK. Computer printout submissions acceptable; prefers letter-quality to dot-matrix printouts. SASE. Reports in 2 weeks.

Nonfiction: Business-oriented articles only with Colorado "hook"; must be oriented to manager or executive. Buys 12 mss/year. Query. Length: 1,500-2,000 words. Pays $150-200.

COMMERCE MAGAZINE, 130 S. Michigan Ave., Chicago IL 60603. (312)786-0111. Editor: Carol Johnson. For top businessmen and industrial leaders in greater Chicago area. Also sent to chairmen and presidents of *Fortune* 1,000 firms throughout United States. Monthly magazine; varies from 100 to 300 pages, (8½x11½). Circ. 15,000. Buys all rights. Buys 30-40 mss/year. Pays on acceptance. Query. SASE.

Nonfiction: Business articles and pieces of general interest to top business executives. "We select our freelancers and assign topics. Many of our writers are from local newspapers. Considerable freelance material is used but almost exclusively on assignment from Chicago—area specialists within a particular business sector."

CORPORATE MONTHLY, 105 Chestnut St., Philadelphia PA 19106. Editor: Bruce Anthony. 80% freelance written. Emphasizes general business-oriented local material. Local writers preferred. Articles usually require some human interest angles, for anyone in business in the Delaware Valley. Monthly magazine. Pays on publication. Buys first North American serial rights or one-time rights. Publishes ms an average of 2 months after acceptance. Simultaneous queries OK. Computer printout submissions acceptable. Reports in 3 weeks. Free sample copy and writer's guidelines. SASE.

Nonfiction: "New trends in business; exclusive reports on subjects relating to the business of the Delaware Valley; health and quality of life articles; a fresh look or unique perspective on area problems. We don't want how-tos, puff, or pieces on accounting." Buys 100 mss/year. Query with published clips. Length: 1,000-3,000 words. Pays $75-125.

Tips: "We are in a fiercely competitive market. We are one of four publications trying to reach the business market here. So, knowing this publication is essential. Also, the freelancer should have a basic working knowledge of business if he hopes to do a business story. On the up side, we encourage, in fact need, more creativity in both writing and art than our competitors. We feel that being a business book is not a license to be boring."

EXECUTIVE, Airmedia, 2973 Weston Rd., Box 510, Weston, Ontario, M9N 3R3 Canada. (416)741-1112. Publisher: Donald Coote. Editor: Patricia Anderson. Monthly business magazine covering financial, political, company profiles for presidents and senior management. Circ. 53,000. Pays on acceptance. Byline given. Buys first rights. Reports as soon as possible. Free sample copy.

Nonfiction: Query with clips of published work.

Photos: Reviews photos. Identification of subjects required. Buys one-time rights.

EXECUTIVE REPORT, Riverview Publications, 213 S. Craig St., Pittsburgh PA 15213. (412)687-4803. Publisher: Charles W. Shane. 65% freelance written. Monthly magazine concentrating on the business, industry and finance of western Pennsylvania. Circ. 16,000. Pays within 30 days of publication. Byline given. Buys first and second rights to the same material. Submit seasonal/holiday material 3 months in advance. Simultaneous queries, and photocopied, simultaneous, and previously published submissions OK. Publishes ms an average of 4 months after acceptance. Computer printout submissions acceptable; prefers letter-quality to dot-matrix. SASE. Sample copy $2; free writer's guidelines.

Nonfiction: Deborah J. Ord, editor. Expose, interview/profile, new product, opinion, personal experience, travel. Buys 10-14 mss/year. Query with clips of published work. Length: 1,000-3,000 words. Pays $100-500.

THE FINANCIAL POST MAGAZINE, Maclean Hunter, Ltd., 777 Bay St., Toronto, Ontario M5W 1A7 Canada. (416)596-5658. Editor: Paul A. Rush. Monthly magazine covering Canadian business. Circ. 225,000. Pays on acceptance. Byline given. Offers 50% kill fee. Buys first North American serial rights. Sub-

mit seasonal/holiday material 3 months in advance. Simultaneous queries OK. SASE. Reports in 1 month. Free sample copy.
Nonfiction: Book excerpts, general interest, interview/profile, new product. No articles on women in management, stress, travel, U.S. politics and money, or fashion. Canadian angle required.

‡FLORIDA TREND, Magazine of Florida Business and Finance, Box 611, St. Petersburg FL 33731. (813)821-5800. Editor: Rick Edmonds. Managing Editor: Jeffrey Tucker. A monthly magazine covering business and economics for Florida business people or investors. Circ. 36,000. Pays on acceptance. Byline given. Offers 25% kill fee. Buys first North American serial rights. Computer printout submissions acceptable. Reports in 1 month. Sample copy $2.25.
Nonfiction: Business and finance. Buys 15-20 mss/year. Query with or without published clips. Length: 1,200-2,500 words. Pays $300-800.

INDIANA BUSINESS, Suite 248, 9302 N. Meridian, Indianapolis IN 46260. (317)844-8627. Editor: Joan S. Marie. Assistant Editor: Lee Lange. Monthly magazine. 35% freelance written. Pays 30 days after publication. Rights negotiable. Computer printout double-space submissions acceptable; prefers letter-quality to dot-matrix. SASE. Publishes ms an average of 4 months after acceptance. Free sample copy.
Nonfiction: "All articles must relate to Indiana business and must be of interest to a broad range of business and professional people." Especially interested in articles on agri-business, international affairs as they affect Indiana business, executive health issues, new science and technology projects happening in Indiana. "We would like to hear about business success stories but only as they pertain to current issues, trends, (i.e., a real estate company that has made it big because they got in on the Economic Development Bonds and invested in renovation property)." Buys 15-20 mss/year. Query or send complete ms. Pay negotiable.
Photos: State availability of photos. Pay negotiable for b&w or color photos. Captions and model release required.
Tips: "A query letter must show that the author is familiar with our publication. It should also be concise but catchy. Be willing to submit samples and/or articles on speculation. We are very interested in articles that flow well—business-like but not dry. Also, the more timely, the better. Be specific about a person, product, company, new program, etc. Stay away from generalizations. The magazine has 3 special sections: Agri-Business, International Affairs, New Technologies."

JEFFERSON BUSINESS, 3033 N. Causeway Blvd., Metairie LA 70002. (504)362-4310. Editor: Lan Sluder. Metro/regional business newsweekly tabloid covering business and professional news in the metro New Orleans area. Edited for upscale business executives, professionals and business owners. Pays on acceptance. Byline given. Buys available rights; at least exclusive in Louisiana. Submit seasonal/holiday material 1 month in advance. Simultaneous queries and simultaneous, photocopied and previously published submissions OK. Computer printout submissions acceptable; prefers letter-quality to dot-matrix. SASE. Reports in 2 weeks. Sample copy for 9x12 SAE and 8 first class stamps. Writer's guidelines for business size SAE and 1 first class stamp.
Nonfiction: Book excerpts (from quality business books); exposé (none about politics); general interest (about power, money, and winning and losing); how-to (well written for savvy business person); humor (only with a business slant); interview/profile (with people in New Orleans area or with a direct tie); new product (only in Louisiana); personal experience (in business); photo feature, technical (on energy, taxes, real estate, etc.). "We have special issues on real estate, finance, executive toys and dozens of other subjects of interest to executives." No "how-tos that are boring rehashes of common sense business practices." Buys 100+ mss/year. Send complete ms. Length: 500-1,800 words. Pays $35-200.
Photos: Send photos with ms. Pays $5-40 for 5x7 b&w prints. Captions, model release and identification of subjects required. Buys one-time rights.
Columns/Departments: "We occasionally buy mss to run in our rotating 'Leisure' column on executive lifestyles. Also, money management columns, of interest to top executives and professionals." Buys 50/year. Send complete ms. Length: 800-2,000 words. Pays $50-75.
Tips: "Write good, dense copy that makes business sound exciting. We look seriously at anything with a solid local connection—mainly Jefferson and Orleans Parishes—but we don't ignore other Louisiana business developments."

KANSAS BUSINESS NEWS, Kansas Business Publishing Co., Inc., Suite 124, 3601 S.W. 29th, Topeka KS 66614. (913)293-3010. Editor: Dan Bearth. 20% freelance written. Monthly magazine about Kansas business for the businessmen, executives and professionals who want to how what is going on in the state that will affect the way they do business, their profits, labor requirements, etc. All submissions must relate to local business conditions. Circ. 15,000. Pays on publication. Buys all rights. Phone queries OK. Submit seasonal material 3 months in advance. Simultaneous and previously published submissions OK. Publishes ms an average of 6 months after acceptance. Computer printout submissions acceptable. SASE. Free sample copy.
Nonfiction: How-to, humor, interview, profile, and technical. Query only. Pays $25-100.

Photos: Marsh Galloway, editor. State availability of photos or send photos with ms. Reviews b&w contact sheets and negatives. Offers no additional payment for photos accepted with ms. Captions preferred; model release required. Buys all rights.

Columns/Departments: Management, Finance, Government, Personnel Management, Taxes, Small Business, Computers and Technology, Insurance, Labor Relations and Investment. Query only. Pays $25 minimum.

KENTUCKY BUSINESS LEDGER, Box 3508, Louisville KY 40201. (502)589-5464. Editor: Rick Garr. Emphasizes Kentucky business and finance. Monthly tabloid. Circ. 14,500. Pays on publication. Buys all rights. Byline given at editor's option. Phone queries OK. Submit seasonal/holiday material 1 month in advance of issue date. Simultaneous, photocopied and previously published submissions OK. Computer printout submissions acceptable; prefers letter-quality to dot-matrix. SASE. Reports in 2 weeks. Sample copy $1.50; free writer's guidelines.

Nonfiction: How-to (tips for businesses on exporting, dealing with government, cutting costs, increasing profits—must have specific Kentucky angle); interview (government officials on issues important to Kentucky businesspersons); new product (new uses for coal;—"We are not interested in every company's new flange or gasket"); profile (of Kentucky businesspersons); and articles on the meanings of government laws and regulations to Kentucky businesses. "We get too many industry-wide trend stories, which we use hardly at all. We must have a strong Kentucky link to any story." No humor, book reviews or personal advice. Buys 25-30 mss/year. Query. Length: 2,000 words maximum. "We went from a 16" page to 13½"—so are running shorter articles." Pays $1.50/inch.

Photos: State availability of photos with query. Pays $10 up for b&w glossy prints.

Tips: "On technical subjects from unknown freelancers, we need a statement of expertise and/or previous work within the subject area."

LOS ANGELES BUSINESS JOURNAL, Cordovan Corp., Suite 506, 3727 W. 6th St., Los Angeles CA 90020. Editor: David A. Yochum. 10% freelance written. Weekly tabloid covering business developments within the Los Angeles area for business executives, managers and entrepreneurs. The publication is designed to help the decision-making process for businessmen in the areas of new trends and ideas important to commerce and industry. Circ. 15,000 guaranteed. Pays on publication. Buys all rights. Publishes ms an average of 2 weeks after acceptance. Computer printout submissions acceptable.

Nonfiction: "We are interested in Los Angeles area industry or business trend stories, as well as executive or company profiles. Illustrate trends with specific figures. Length: 800-3,000 words. No column material; hard news of business features only. Buys 24 mss/year. Query. Pays per column inch.

Tips: "Submit a story line query of two, three, or four sentences. List the specific points expected to be covered in the article."

‡**THE MANHATTAN COOPERATOR, The Co-Op & Condo Monthly**, 23 Leonard St., New York NY 10013. (212)226-0808. Editor: Vicki Chesler. A monthly tabloid covering real estate trends, taxation, legislation, interior design, management and maintenance for apartment owners. Circ. 100,000. Pays on publication. Byline given. Buys second serial (reprint) rights. Submit seasonal/holiday material 2 months in advance. Simultaneous queries, and simultaneous, photocopied, and previously published submissions OK. Computer printout submissions acceptable; prefers letter-quality to dot-matrix. Reports in 1 month. Free writer's guidelines.

Nonfiction: General interest (related to NYC metro area and within 200 miles); how-to (for apartment owners); interview/profile (on New Yorkers of interest preferably to apartment owners); new product (related to home ownership, security, energy conservation); technical (related to home improvement or real estate ownership); travel (within 300 miles of NYC or special areas); real estate; legal; taxation; and interior design. Special issues include Home Improvement/Vacation Condos (June); Interior Design (Oct.); Fuel Conservation (Nov.); and Financial Planning (Dec.). Query with or without published clips. Length: 750-1,500 words. Pays $50-150.

Photos: State availability of photos or send photos with query or ms. Pays $10-150 for 8x10 b&w prints. Identification of subjects required. Buys one-time and re-use rights.

Columns/Departments: Owner Profile (NYC apartment owner with interesting career); Insurance Advisor (related to apartment ownership); Maintenance (buildings over 30 units); Financial Finesse (investing); Building Management (over 30 units); Interior Design; Fuel Conservation; Letter of the Law; Tax Tips; Market Trends; and Security & Safety.

The double dagger (‡) before a listing indicates that the listing is new in this edition. New markets are often the most receptive to freelance contributions.

MEMPHIS BUSINESS JOURNAL, (formerly *Mid-South Business*), Mid-South Communications, Inc., Suite 322, 4515 Poplar St., Memphis TN 38117. (901)685-2411. Editor: Barney DuBois. 20% freelance written. Weekly tabloid covering industry, trade, agribusiness and finance in west Tennessee, north Mississippi, east Arkansas, and the Missouri Bootheel. "Articles should be timely and relevant to business in our region." Circ. 10,400. Pays on acceptance. Byline given. Pays $50 kill fee. Buys one-time rights, second serial (reprint) rights, and makes work-for-hire assignments. Submit seasonal/holiday material 2 months in advance. Publishes ms an average of 2 weeks after acceptance. Simultaneous queries and submissions OK. Computer printout submissions acceptable. SASE. Reports in 2 weeks. Free sample copy.
Nonfiction: Expose, historical/nostalgic, interview/profile, business features and trends. "All must relate to business in our area." Buys 130 mss/year. Query with or without clips of published work or send complete ms. Length: 750-2,000 words. Pays $80-200.
Photos: State availability of photos or send photos with ms. Pays $25-50 for 5x7 b&w prints. Identification of subjects required. Buys one-time rights.
Tips: "We welcome freelancers who can do features and articles on business in the smaller cities of our region. We are now a weekly, so our stories need to be more timely."

‡**MINNESOTA BUSINESS JOURNAL, For Decisionmakers of Growing Companies**, Dorn Communications, 7831 E. Bush Lake, Minneapolis MN 55435. (612)835-6855. Editor: Judith Yates Borger. Assistant Editor: Terry Fiedler. A monthly regional business magazine covering general business and Minnesota companies with revenue of less than $25 million per year for managers of small, growing, Minnesota-based companies. Circ. 26,000. Pays on publication. Byline given. Offers kill fee of 25% of agreed-upon price. Not copyrighted. Makes work-for-hire assignments. Simultaneous queries and simultaneous submissions OK. Computer printout submissions acceptable. Reports in 2 weeks on queries; 1 month on mss. Free sample copy.
Nonfiction: How-to (anything related to running a company efficiently, often written within the context of a company profile); and interview/profile (Minnesota business leaders, company profiles with how-to slant). "Articles all feature a how-to slant, how to manage people, how to cut costs, how to solve family business problems, etc." Buys 36 mss/year. Query with published clips. Length: 1,500-3,500 words. Pays $50-500.
Tips: Accepts queries and submissions only from Minnesota-based writers.

NEW MEXICO BUSINESS JOURNAL, New Mexico's Magazine of Management, Southwest Publications, Inc., Box 1788, Albuquerque NM 87103. (505)243-5581. Editor: George Hackler. 50% freelance written. Monthly magazine covering industry and management news. Circ. 14,000. Pays on publication. Byline given. Buys one-time rights. Submit seasonal/holiday material 3 months in advance. Simultaneous queries and simultaneous, photocopied and previously published submissions OK. Publishes ms an average of 3 months after acceptance. Computer printout submissions acceptable. SASE. Reports as soon as possible. Sample copy $2; free writer's guidelines.
Nonfiction: How-to (manage, invest); business interest; technical (accounting procedures, etc.). No consumer, travel, personal history or human interest articles. Query with clips of published work. Length: 500-1,500 words. Pays 5¢/word.
Photos: Send photos with query. Pays $5 for 5x7 b&w prints. Captions and identification of subjects required.

OHIO BUSINESS, Business Journal Publishing Co., 425 Hanna Bldg., Cleveland OH 44115. (216)621-1644. Editor: Robert W. Gardner. Managing Editor: Michael E. Moore. A monthly magazine covering general business topics. "*Ohio Business* serves the state of Ohio. Readers are business executives in the state engaged in manfacturing, agriculture, mining, construction, transportation, communications, utilities, retail and wholesale trade, services, and government." Circ. 35,000. Pays for features on acceptance; news on publication. Byline sometimes given. Kill fee can be negotiated. Buys one-time rights, and second serial (reprint) rights; depends on projects. Submit seasonal/holiday material 3-4 months in advance. Simultaneous queries, and simultaneous, photocopied, and previously published submissions OK. Computer printout submissions acceptable. SASE. Reports in 2 weeks on queries; 1 month on mss. Sample copy $2; free writer's guidelines.
Nonfiction: Book excerpts, general interest, how-to, interview/profile, opinion and personal experience. "In all cases, write with an Ohio executive in mind. Stories should give readers useful information on business within the state, trends in management, ways to manage better, or other developments which would affect them in their professional careers." No product news or personnel changes. Buys 14-20 mss/year. Query with published clips. Length: 100-2,500 words. Pays $25-50.
Photos: State availability of photos. Reviews b&w and color transparencies and prints. Captions and identification of subjects required. Buys variable rights.
Columns/Departments: News; People (features Ohio business execs); High-Tech (leading edge Ohio products and companies); Made in Ohio (unusual Ohio product/services). Query with published clips. Length 100-600 words. Pays $50 minimum.
Tips: "Features are most open to freelancers. Come up with new ideas or information for our readers: Ohio executives in manufacturing and service industries. Writers should be aware of the trend toward specialization in magazine publishing with strong emphasis on people in coverage.

OREGON BUSINESS, MIF Publications, Suite 500, 208 SW Stark, Portland OR 97204. (503)223-0304. Editor: Robert Hill. 40% freelance written. Monthly magazine covering business in Oregon. Circ. 20,000. Pays on publication. Byline given. Buys first rights and second serial (reprint) rights. Submit seasonal/holiday material 3 months in advance. Photocopied and previously published submissions OK. Computer printout submissions acceptable. SASE. Reports in 1 month. Publishes ms an average of 4 months after acceptance. Sample copy for business size SAE and $1.05 postage.
Nonfiction: General interest (real estate, business, investing, small business); interview/profile (business leaders); and new products. Special issues include tourism, world trade, finance. "We need articles on real estate or small businss in Oregon, outside the Portland area." Buys 24 mss/year. Query with clips of published work. Length: 900-2,000 words. Pays 10¢/word minimum; $200 maximum.

PHOENIX BUSINESS JOURNAL AND TUCSON BUSINESS CHRONICLE, Cordovan Corp., 1817 N. 3rd St., Phoenix AZ 85004. (602)271-4712. Editor: Tom Kuhn. 40% freelance written. Weekly tabloid covering business economics for CEOs and top corporate managers. Circ. 13,000. Pays on publication. Publishes ms an average of 3 weeks after acceptance. Byline given. Buys all rights. Submit seasonal/holiday material 1 month in advance. Computer printout submissions acceptable. SASE. Reports in 2 weeks. Sample copy free.
Nonfiction: How-to (solve management problems); interview/profile (of entrepreneurs); and "news affecting all types of Phoenix and Tucson area corporations, large and small. Our audience is all local." Buys 250 mss/year. Length: open. Pays average $2.75/column inch.

REGARDIES: THE MAGAZINE OF WASHINGTON BUSINESS, 1010 Wisconsin Ave., NW, Washington DC 20007. (202)342-0410. Editor: Henry Fortunato. 95% freelance written. Monthly magazine covering business in the Washington DC metropolitan area for Washington business executives. Circ. 30,000. Pays within 30 days after publication. Byline given. Pays variable kill fee. Buys all rights. Publishes ms an average of 6 weeks after acceptance. Computer printout submissions acceptable; no dot-matrix. Submit seasonal/holiday material 3 months in advance. Reports in 3 weeks. Sample copy free.
Nonfiction: Profiles (of business leaders), investigative reporting, real estate, advertising, politics, lifestyle, media, retailing, communications, labor issues, and financial issues—all on the Washington business scene. "If it isn't the kind of story that could just as easily run in a city magazine or a national magazine like *Harper's*, *Atlantic*, *Esquire*, etc., I don't want to see it." Buys 90 mss/year. Length: 4,000 words average. Buys 5-6/issue. Pays "generally 20¢/word."
Columns/Departments: Length: 1,500 words average. Buys 8-12/issue. Pays 20¢/word.

SEATTLE BUSINESS MAGAZINE, Seattle Chamber of Commerce, 1200 One Union Square, Seattle WA 98101. (206)447-7214. Editor-in-Chief: Ed Sullivan. 25% freelance written. Emphasizes regional socio-economic affairs. For business and government leaders, civic leaders, regional businessmen, educators, opinion makers, and the general public. Monthly magazine; 56 pages. Circ. 7,100. Pays on publication. Buys first rights. Submit seasonal/holiday material 2 months in advance. Previously published submissions OK. Publishes ms an average of 4 months after acceptance. SASE. Reports in 1 month. Free sample copy.
Nonfiction: Informational (socio-economic affairs) and technical. Buys 1-2 mss/issue. Query. Length: 500-2,500 words. Pays $50-300.
Photos: Purchased with accompanying ms or on assignment. Captions required. Pays $35-50 for b&w photos. Total purchase price for ms includes payment for photos. Model release required.
Tips: "The freelancer must be able to write—and have a basic awareness of and sympathy for—the interests and problems of the business community as these relate to the community at large. We can use person-to-person, human discussions about people in business."

TIDEWATER VIRGINIAN, Suite A, 711 W. 21st, Norfolk VA 23517. Executive Editor: Marilyn Goldman. 80% freelance written. Published by two Tidewater area chambers of commerce. Monthly magazine for business management people. Circ. 8,000. Buys first rights and second (reprint) rights to material originally published elsewhere. Byline given. Buys 60 mss/year. Pays on publication. Sample copy $1.50. Photocopied and simultaneous submissions OK. Reports in 3 weeks. Publishes ms an average of 2 months after acceptance. Query or submit complete ms. SASE.
Nonfiction: Articles dealing with business and industry in Virginia primarily; the surrounding area of southeastern Virginia (Tidewater area). Profiles, successful business operations, new product, merchandising techniques and business articles. Length: 500-2,500 words. Pays $25-150.
Tips: Recently published article: "The Year of the Efficient Office," (new supplies, machines and furniture available for offices).

‡**TUCSON BUSINESS DIGEST, The Business Quarterly**, Tucson Business Digest, #203, 2100 N. Wilmot, Tucson AZ 85712. (602)294-4376. Editor: Pam Prevost. Managing Editor: Ned Kalbfleish. A quarterly magazine for businessmen. Estab. 1983. Circ. 18,000. Pays on acceptance. Byline given. Offers $200 kill fee. Buys all rights. Submit seasonal/holiday material 6 months in advance. Photocpied and simultaneous

submissions OK. Electronic submissions OK; "Please query with SASE. We will forward access numbers and codes." Computer printout submissions acceptable. SASE. Reports in 1 month. Sample copy $2. Writer's guidelines for SAE and 1 first class stamp.

Nonfiction: How-to, interview/profile, photo feature and technical (computers). "Articles should be relative to business: trends, analysis, success, etc." Buys 18 mss/year. Send complete ms. Length: 700-6,000 words. Pays $100-1,500.

Photos: Send photos with ms. Reviews b&w and color contact sheets and color prints. Model release and identification of subjects required.

Fiction: Humorous, business related. Buys 3 mss/year. Send complete ms. Length: 1,500-2,500 words. Pays $150-300.

Fillers: Jokes. Buys 25/year. Pays $20-50.

Tips: Send complete ms with information on cost and b&w photo of writer to managing editor, or query with SASE.

WASHINGTON BUSINESS JOURNAL, Cordovan Corp., An E.W. Scripps subsidiary, Suite 430, 6862 Elm St., McLean VA 22101. (703)442-4900. Editor: Susan E. Currier. 20% freelance written. Weekly tabloid covering business in the District of Columbia, suburban Maryland and Northern Virginia areas for business persons in middle management as well as chief executive officers. Circ. 15,000. Pays on publication. Byline given. Not copyrighted. Buys all rights. SASE. Reports in 4 weeks on queries; 3 weeks on mss. Sample copy $1. Publishes ms an average of 1 month after acceptance. Computer printout submissions acceptable; prefers letter-quality to dot-matrix.

Nonfiction: Interview/profile (of a local figure—public or small entrepreneur); new product (inventions or patents from area people); business. Special issues are published frequently. Editorial calendar available on request. No generic or *national* business topics. Query with published clips or submit complete ms. Length: 600-1,800 words. Pays $3.50-$4.50/column inch.

Photos: State availability or send photos with ms. Pays negotiable rates for 8x10 b&w prints. Identification of subjects required.

Tips: "Queries should have decent writing samples attached. Manuscripts should be well researched, well written and thorough. Neatness and quality of presentation is a plus, as is accurate spelling and grammar. *WBJ* is interested in all business topics including: technology, real estate, accounting, associations, science, education, government, etc. Information sources should be high level and subject should be timely. Accompanying sidebars, photographs and graphs are also well received."

WESTERN INVESTOR, Northwest/Intermountain/Hawaii Investment Information, Willamette Publishing, Inc., Suite 1115, 400 SW 6th Ave., Portland OR 97204. (503)222-0577. Editor: S.P. Pratt. Managing Editor: Donna Walker. Quarterly magazine for the investment community of the Pacific Northwest, the Intermountain States and Hawaii. For stock brokers, corporate officers, financial analysts, trust officers, CPAs, investors, etc. Circ. 13,000. Pays on publication. Byline given. Buys one time and second serial (reprint) rights and makes work-for-hire assignments. Simultaneous queries and simultaneous, photocopied and previously published submissions OK. SASE. Reports in 6 weeks. Sample copy $1.50, SASE; writer's guidelines, SAE.

Nonfiction: General business interest ("trends, people, companies within our region"); new products. "Each issue carries a particular industry theme." Buys 8-12 mss/year. Query. Length: 200-5,000 words. Pays $50 minimum.

Photos: State availability of photos. Pays $10 minimum for 5x7 (or larger) b&w prints. Buys one-time rights.

Tips: "Send us a one-page introduction including your financial writing background, story ideas, availability for assignment work, credits, etc. What we want at this point is a good working file of authors to draw from; let us know your special areas of interest and expertise. Newspaper business page writers would be good candidates. If you live and work in the Northwest, so much the better."

WESTERN NEW YORK MAGAZINE, Buffalo Area Chamber of Commerce, 107 Delaware Ave., Buffalo NY 14202. (716)849-6689. Editor: J. Patrick Donlon. Monthly magazine of the Buffalo-Niagara Falls area. "Tells the story of Buffalo and western New York, with special emphasis on business and industry and secondary emphasis on quality of life subjects." Circ. 8,000. Pays on acceptance. Byline given. Offers $150 kill fee. Not copyrighted. Buys all rights. Submit seasonal/holiday material 3 months in advance. Simultaneous queries OK. SASE. Reports in 1 month. Sample copy for $2, 9x12 SAE and 3 first class stamps; writer's guidelines for business size SAE and 1 first class stamp.

Nonfiction: General interest (business, finance, commerce); historical/nostalgic (Buffalo, Niagara Falls); how-to (business management); interview/profile (community leader); western New York industry, quality of life. "Broad-based items preferred over single firm or organization. Submit articles that provide insight into business operations, marketing, finance, promotion, and nuts-and-bolts approach to small business management. No nationwide or even New York statewide articles or pieces on specific companies, products, services." Buys 30 mss/year. Query with clips of published work. Length: 1,000-2,500 words. Pays $150-300.

Photos: Amy R. Wopperer, art director. State availability of photos. Pays $10-25 for 5x7 b&w prints; reviews contact sheet.

Career, College, and Alumni

These publications prompt readers to look back or ahead in their lives, particularly toward college and career planning. Three types of magazines are listed in this section: university publications written for students, alumni, and friends of a specific institution; publications about college life, careers, and job hunting in general; and publications on career and job opportunities.

ALCALDE, Box 7278, Austin TX 78712. (512)476-6271. Editor: Ernestine Wheelock. Editorial Assistant: Leigh Sander. 50% freelance written. Bimonthly magazine. Circ. 39,000. Pays on publication. Buys all rights. Submit seasonal/holiday material 5 months in advance. Publishes ms an average of 6 months after acceptance. Computer printout submissions acceptable; prefers letter-quality to dot-matrix. SASE. Reports in 2 weeks.
Nonfiction: General interest; historical (University of Texas, research, and faculty profile); humor (humorous University of Texas incidents or profiles that include background data); interviews (University of Texas subjects); nostalgia (University of Texas traditions); profile (students, faculty or alumni); and technical (University of Texas research on a subject or product). No subjects lacking taste or quality, or not connected with the University of Texas. Buys 18 mss/year. Query. Length: 1,000-2,400 words. Pays according to importance of article.

THE BLACK COLLEGIAN, The National Magazine of Black College Students, Black Collegiate Services, Inc., 1240 S. Broad St., New Orleans LA 70125. (504)821-5694. Editor: James Borders. 40% freelance written. Magazine for black college students and recent graduates with an interest in black cultural awareness, sports, news, personalities, history, trends, current events and job opportunities. Published bimonthly during school year; (4 times/year). 160 pages. Circ. 190,000. Buys one-time rights. Byline given. Buys 6 unsolicited mss/year. Pays on publication. Offers ⅓ kill fee. Sample copy for 9x12 SAE and 3 first class stamps; writer's guidelines for #10 SAE and 1 first class stamp. Photocopied, previously published and simultaneous submissions OK. Computer printout submissions acceptable. Submit seasonal and special material 2 months in advance of issue date (Careers in Sciences, August; Computers/Grad School, November; Engineering and Travel/Summer Programs, January; Finance and Jobs, March; Medicine, May). SASE. Reports in 3 weeks on queries; 4 weeks on mss.
Nonfiction: Material on careers, sports, black history, news analysis. Articles on problems and opportunities confronting black college students and recent graduates. Book excerpts, exposé, general interest, historical/nostalgic, how-to (develop employability), opinion, personal experience, profile, inspirational, humor. Buys 40 mss/year. Query with published clips or send complete ms. Length: 500-2,500 words. Pays $25-350.
Photos: State availability of photos with query or ms, or send photos with query or ms. B&w photos or color transparencies purchased with or without mss. 8x10 b&w prints preferred. Captions, model releases and identification of subjects required. Pays $35/b&w; $50/color.
Tips: "Career features area is most open to freelancers."

CARNEGIE-MELLON MAGAZINE, Carnegie-Mellon University, Pittsburgh PA 15213. (412)578-2900. Editor: Ann Curran. Alumni publication issued fall, winter, spring covering university activities, alumni profiles, etc. Circ. 41,000. Pays on acceptance. Byline given. Not copyrighted. Submit seasonal/holiday material 4 months in advance. Simultaneous queries OK. SASE. Reports in 1 month.
Nonfiction: Book excerpts (faculty alumni); general interest; humor; interview/profile; photo feature. "We use general interest stories linked to CMU activities and research." No unsolicited mss. Buys 5 features and 5-10 alumni profiles/year. Query with published clips. Length: 2,500-6,000 words. Pays $250 or negotiable rate.
Poetry: Avant-garde or traditional. No previously published poetry. No payment.
Tips: "Consideration is given to professional writers among alumni."

‡**COLLEGE OUTLOOK AND CAREER OPPORTUNITIES**, Special distributions include *Art*, *High Tech*, *Christian Outlook* and *Minority Outlook*, etc., Townsend-Kraft Publishing Co., Box 239, Liberty MO 64068. (816)781-4941. Editor: Ellen Parker. Student information publication on subjects of interest to college or college-bound students. "*College Outlook* attempts to inform students on college admissions, financial aid, career opportunities, housing, clothing, and other subjects of interest to college-bound students." Circ. 2.5 million regular, plus special editions. Pays on publication. Byline given. Buys all rights and second (reprint) rights. Reports as soon as possible. Writer's guidelines for business size SAE.
Photos: State availability of photos. "We prefer to see photos with focus on students." Model release required. Buys all rights.
Fillers: Clippings, jokes, gags, anecdotes, short humor, newsbriefs. Buys up to 4 mss/year. Length: 100-500 words. Pays 10¢/word.

COLLEGIATE CAREER WOMAN, For Career Minded Women, Equal Opportunity Publications, Inc., 44 Broadway, Greenlawn NY 11740. (516)261-8899. Editor: James Schneider. Magazine published 3 times/ year (fall, winter, spring) covering career-guidance for college women. Strives "to aid women in developing career abilities to the fullest potential; improve job hunting skills; present career opportunities; provide personal resources; help cope with discrimination." Audience is 92% college juniors and seniors; 8% working graduates. Circ. 10,500. "Controlled circulation, distributed through college guidance and placement offices." Pays on publication. Byline given. Buys all rights. "Deadline dates: fall, August 5; winter, November 3; spring, February 8. Simultaneous queries, and simultaneous, photocopied and previously published submissions OK. Computer printout submissions acceptable; prefers typed mss. SASE. Free sample copy and writer's guidelines available on request.

Nonfiction: Book excerpts (on job search techniques, role models, success stories, employment helps); general interest (on special concerns of women); historical/nostalgic (on women's achievements, progress, and hopes for the future); how-to (on self-evaluation, job-finding skills, adjustment, coping with the real world); humor (student or career related); interview/profile (of successful career women, outstanding students); new product (new career opportunities); opinion (on women's progress, male attitudes, discrimination); personal experience (student and career experiences); technical (on career fields offering opportunities for women); travel (on overseas job opportunities); and contributions to the development of the whole person. Prefers not to see general stories about women's issues, but those specifically related to careers. Wants more profiles of successful career women. Special issues include career opportunities for women in industry and government in fields such as nursing and health care, communication, sales, marketing, banking, insurance, finance, engineering and computers, as well as opportunities in the government, military, and defense. Query or send complete ms. Length: 1,250-3,000 words.

Photos: Sheri Arbital, photo editor. Prefers 35mm color slides, but will accept b&w. Captions, model release and identification of subjects required. Buys all rights. More pictures needed.

Tips: Articles should focus on career-guidance, role model, and industry prospects for women.

‡THE COMPUTER & ELECTRONICS GRADUATE, The Entry-Level Career & Information Technology Magazine for CS Systems and EE Graduates, Equal Opportunity Publications, Inc., 44 Broadway, Greenlawn NY 11740. (516)261-8899. Editor: James Schneider. A quarterly career-guidance magazine for computer science/systems and electrical/electronics engineering students and professionals. "We strive to aid our readers in developing career abilities to the fullest potential; improve job-hunting skills; present career opportunities; provide personal resources." Estab. 1983. Circ. 26,000 (controlled circulation, distributed through college guidance and placement offices). Pays on publication. Byline given. Buys all rights. Deadline: fall, July 1; winter, Oct. 5; spring, Jan. 15; summer, May 3. Simultaneous queries and simultaneous, photocopied, and previously published submissions OK. Computer printout submissions acceptable; no dot-matrix. SASE. Reports in 1 month. Sample copy and writer's guidelines for 8½x11 SAE and 60¢ postage.

Nonfiction: Book excerpts (on job search techniques, role models, success stories, employment helps); general interest (on special concerns to computer science/systems, and electrical/electronics engineering students and professionals); how-to (on self-evaluation, job-finding skills, adjustment, coping with the real world); humor (student or career related); interview/profile (of successful computer science/systems and electrical/electronics engineering students and professionals); new product (new career opportunities); personal experience (student and career experiences); technical (on career fields offering opportunities); travel on overseas job opportunities; and coverage of other reader interests. Special issues inlcude careers in industry and government in computer science, computer systems, electrical engineering, software systems, robotics, artificial intelligence, as well as opportunities in the military and in defense. "We are planning to devote one issue to professionals." No sensitive or highly technical material. Buys 20-25 mss/year. Query. Length: 1,250-3,000 words. Pays 10¢/word.

Photos: Sheri Arbital, photo editor. State availability of photos or send photos with query or mss. Prefers 35mm color slides, but will accept b&w. Captions, model releases, and identification of subjects required.

Tips: "Articles should focus on career-guidance, role model, and industry prospects for computer science, computer systems and electrical and electronics engineering students and professionals."

EQUAL OPPORTUNITY, The Nation's Only Multi-Ethnic Recruitment Magazine for Black, Hispanic, Native American & Asian College Grads, Equal Opportunity Publications, Inc., 44 Broadway, Greenlawn NY 11740. (516)261-8899. Editor: James Schneider. Magazine published 3 times/year (fall, winter, spring) covering career-guidance for minorities. "Our audience is 90% college juniors and seniors, 10% working graduates. An understanding of educational and career problems of minorities is essential." Circ. 15,000. "Controlled circulation, distributed through college guidance and placement offices." Pays on publication. Byline given. Buys all rights. Deadline dates: fall, August 5; winter, November 3; spring, February 8. Simultaneous queries, and simultaneous, photocopied and previously published submissions OK. Computer printout submissions acceptable; prefers typed mss. SASE. Free sample copy and writer's guidelines.

Nonfiction: Book excerpts and articles (on job search techniques, role models); general interest (on specific minority concerns); how-to (on job-hunting skills, personal finance, better living, coping with discrimination);

humor (student or career related); interview/profile (minority role models); new product (new career opportunities); opinion (problems of minorities); personal experience (professional and student study and career experiences); technical (on career fields offering opportunities for minorities); travel (on overseas job opportunities); and coverage of Black, Hispanic, American Indian and Asian interests. Special issues include career opportunities for minorities in industry and government in fields such as banking, insurance, finance, communications, sales, marketing, engineering and computers, as well as careers in the government, military, and defense. "Prefers not to see politically or socially sensitive subjects." Query or send complete ms. Length: 1,250-3,000 words.

Photos: Prefers 35mm color slides and b&w. Captions, model release and identification of subjects required. Buys all rights.

Tips: Articles should focus on career-guidance, role model, and industry prospects for minorities.

‡**HELP WANTED, The Job Seeker's Monthly**, Limited Ventures, Inc., Box 515, Menominee MI 49858. (906)863-2644. Editor: John Hofer. Monthly tabloid. "*Help Wanted* is targeted at unemployed persons and persons already working who are seeking a better job. Our specific market is the blue collar worker and the low-to-middle level white collar worker in the North Central states. We strive both to motivate the unemployed person or career changer to take personal action to improve his or her situation and to show the readers how they can find a job or improve their job. We accentuate the positive, focusing on those sectors of the job market which offer most promise, job seeking techniques which pay off." Estab. 1983. Circ. 16,000. Pays on acceptance. Byline given. Not copyrighted. Buys second serial (reprint) rights. Submit seasonal/holiday material 2 months in advance. Simultaneous queries and photocopied submissions OK. SASE. Reports in 3 weeks. Sample copy for 9x12 SASE and 85¢ postage.

Nonfiction: Tom Torinus, articles editor. General interest (industries, geographic areas or occupations which hold most promise for job seekers); how-to (on successful techniques for finding a job, improving one's career status); interview/profile (people who have successfully found a job or improved their careers using a proven or novel technique); personal experience (first-person accounts of people who have experienced unemployment or unhappiness in career and have found ways to solve these problems). Buys 75 mss/year. Query with published clips. Length: 400-1,000 words. Pays $50-150.

Photos: Tom Torinus, photo editor. Pays $10-25 for b&w negatives. Model release and identification of subjects required. Buys all rights.

Tips: "Our style is simple, direct, and upbeat. We avoid bureaucratic and institutional jargon. We like to see stories about programs, trends and issues told through eyes of people involved in them or affected by them."

HIS, Box 1450, Downers Grove IL 60515. (312)964-5700. Editor: David Neff. 90% freelance written. Issued monthly from October-June for collegiate students, faculty, administrators and graduate students interested in the evangelical Christian persuasion. "It is an interdenominational, Biblical presentation, combining insights on Scripture and everyday life on campus. We need sophisticated humor, outstanding fiction with a Christian base, articles of interest to non-Christian readers." Buys first rights and second (reprint) rights to material originally published elsewhere. Pays on acceptance. Reports in 3 months. Publishes ms an average of 2 years after acceptance. Computer printout submissions acceptable; prefers letter-quality to dot-matrix. SASE.

Nonfiction and Fiction: "Articles dealing with practical aspects of Christian living on campus, relating contemporary issues to Biblical principles. Should show relationship between Christianity and various fields of study, Christian doctrine, or missions." Submit complete ms. Buys 55 unsolicited mss/year. Recent article example "Look at Me, Not My Wheelchair!" (January 1984). Length: 2,000 words maximum. Pays $35-70.

Poetry: Pays $10-20.

Tips: "Direct your principles and illustrations at the college milieu. Avoid preachiness and attacks on various Christian ministries or groups; share your insights on a peer basis."

‡**JOB CORPS IN ACTION**, Meridian Publishing Co. Inc., 1720 Washington Blvd., Ogden UT 84404. Editor: Caroll McKanna Halley. A monthly magazine covering Job Corps Centers throughout the United States. "We publish *upbeat* stories about successful individuals and programs that benefit our communities. Job Corps people and program stories only." Estab. 1984. Pays on acceptance. Byline given. Buys first North American serial rights. Submit seasonal/holiday material 6 months in advance. Simultaneous queries, and photocopied and previously published submissions OK. SASE. Reports in 3 weeks. Sample copy for $1 and 9x12 SAE; writer's guidelines for business size SAE and 1 first class stamp.

Nonfiction: Book excerpts (if applicable to labor, job, vocational training); historical/nostalgic (only in regard to Job Corps); inspirational (only in the sense of Job Corps success stories or help to communities); interview/profile; personal experience; photo feature; and technical. No expose, nothing depressing, no non-labor, non-education, non-job corps pieces. Buys 30 mss/year. Query with or without published clips or send complete ms. "All considered seriously." Length: 800-1,200 words. Pays 15¢/word.

Photos: State availability of photos, or send photos with query or ms. Pays $35 minimum for color slides to 8x10 transparencies and prints; negotiates payment for covers. Captions required. Buys one-time rights.

Fillers: Newsbreaks in related area. Length: 300-800 words. Pays 15¢/word.

Tips: "Make a *clear* query about Job Corps individuals or programs; make a good presentation—good spelling, grammer and logic. Be sincere, informed on your topic and sure that you have illustration/ideas or photos—color only. There's enough bad press about disadvantaged youth—we want our readers to hear success stories about people who have made a change in their lives for the better through Job Corps training. If you have an idea for a story, write immediately. This is a new publication and we're eager for freelancers. If your idea is sound we'll work with you."

‡**THE JOHNS HOPKINS MAGAZINE**, The Johns Hopkins University, Greenhouse Annex, Baltimore MD 21218. (301)338-7645. Editor: Elise Hancock. Assistant Editor: Edward C. Ernst. A bimonthly alumni general interest magazine with features on those subjects interesting Hopkins grads, i.e., medicine, literature, etc. Circ. 85,000. Pays on acceptance. Byline given. Offers $200 kill fee usually. Buys one-time rights and first rights. Submit seasonal/holiday material 4 months in advance. Simultaneous queries, and simultaneous and photocopied submissions OK. Electronic submissions OK if compatible with DEC Mate (Digital) word processors. Computer printout submissions acceptable. SASE preferred. Reports in 3 months. Sample copy for $1.50, 9x12 SAE, and 90¢ postage; free guideline letter.
Nonfiction: General interest, how-to, humor, and photo feature, all *Hopkins related stories*—medical, music, physics, arts and sciences, engineering, continuing education, astronomy. Also interview/profile (alumni of Hopkins), and personal experience (if related to Hopkins). Buys approximately 9 mss/year. Query with published clips or send complete ms. Length: 5,000 words maximum. Pays $25-1,000.
Photos: State availability of photos. Reviews b&w contact sheets. Model release and identification of subjects required. Buys one-time rights.
Fillers: Cartoons.
Tips: Contributions must be general enough (non-technical) to appeal to wide audience, yet at a level which is apropos for a university graduate. (Humor and personal facts help too). The whole magazine is most open to freelancers. Features and cartoons are most welcomed. Trends in alumni magazines are towards color, so promise of exciting color spreads lends the article to publication. Many general feature stories are people-oriented, with personal insights by writer. Most welcome, of course, are articles by or about Hopkins people. A careful study of what schools are at Hopkins reveals what the readership will be interested in. They like brain twisters or thought provoking ethical issues or articles on new techniques in their field."

‡**MAGALLATI (ARABIC MONTHLY)**, Middle East Media, Box 3324, Tulsa OK 74101. (918)587-9911. Editor: Dr. Tome R. Hayes. A monthly youth magazine published in Arabic (80% of material is adapted or translated from English language materials) and distributed in Middle East, Europe and North America. *Magallati* publishes general interest articles with a Christian perspective for an audience of 19.3 mean age, 60% male/40% female, upper income, college student population and career oriented. Circ. 40,000. Pays on publication. Byline given. Buys other translation—one-time rights. Submit seasonal/holiday material 3 months in advance. Simultaneous and previously published submissions OK. Computer printout submissions acceptable. SASE. Reports in 1 month on queries; 3 months on mss. Free sample copy.
Nonfiction: General interest, health/exercise, inspirational, interview/profile, personal experience, sports and travel. Special issues include annual edition with *strong* religious content. No political (Middle East conflict) nor religious criticism in content. Buys 12-15 mss/year. Query or send complete ms. Length: 1,200-1,500 words. Pays $25.
Fiction: Humorous (religious) and religious (mild evangelistic thrust). No articles comparing or criticizing other religions, nor any political material. Buys 12 mss/year. Send complete ms. Length: 1,200-1,500 words. Pays $25.
Tips: "We use a wide variety of material for college-age Arab youth. We have great interest in personal experience, inspirational, and general interest materials. We concentrate on and use an uplifting and challenging content."

MAKING IT!, Careers Newsmagazine, Rm. 4155, 2109 Broadway, New York NY 10023. (212)575-9018. Editor: Karen Rubin. Magazine published 4 times/year covering career opportunities for professionals and managers; specifically entry-level opportunities for college and graduate school students and strategic moves for employed professionals. "We are a newsmagazine with a news-feature format; we discourage generalized 'how-to' articles in favor of in-depth profiles of companies, agencies and industries. We will be looking for writers who have specialty in a particular area or interest and can become regular contributors." Circ. 30,000. Pays on publication (in most cases). Byline given. Offers 20% kill fee. Copyrighted. Makes work-for-hire assignments. Submit seasonal/holiday material 2 months in advance. Simultaneous queries OK. SASE. Reports in 2 months. Sample copy $1.50; writer's guidelines for business size SAE and 2 first class stamps.
Nonfiction: How-to ("we accept only a few, but these should relate to resume, interview, strategies for getting jobs); interview/profile (success stories and profiles about people who have "made it"); personal experience (strategies for getting the job you want). No superficial or general articles about careers or getting jobs. Buys variable number mss/year. Query with or without clips of published work. Length: 1,000-2,000 words. Pays $50-250.

Photos: "Photos that show young people in the work environment." State availability of photos. Pays $5-50 for contact sheets and 8x10 b&w prints. Captions and identification of subjects required. Buys one-time rights.

MISSISSIPPI STATE UNIVERSITY ALUMNUS, Mississippi State University, Alumni Association, Editorial Office, Box 5328, Mississippi State MS 39762. (601)325-3442. Editor-in-Chief: Linsey H. Wright. 10% freelance written ("but welcome more"). Emphasizes articles about Mississippi State graduates and former students. For well-educated and affluent audience. Quarterly magazine; 36 pages. Circ. 16,443. Pays on publication. Buys one-time rights. Pays 25% kill fee. Byline given. Phone queries OK. Submit seasonal/holiday material 3 months in advance. Simultaneous, photocopied and previously published submissions OK. Publishes ms an average of 6 months after acceptance. Computer printout submissions acceptable; prefers letter-quality to dot-matrix. SASE. Reports in 1 month. Free sample copy.
Nonfiction: Historical, humor (with strong MSU flavor; nothing risque), informational, inspirational, interview (with MSU grads), nostalgia (early days at MSU), personal experience, profile and travel (by MSU grads, but must be of wide interest to other grads). Recent article example: "The River's Not Too Wide for Morrison." "The story dealt with an MSU graduate in nuclear engineering who is now a country-western song writer in Nashville." Buys 2-3 mss/year ("but welcome more submissions.") Send complete ms. Length: 500-2,500 words. Pays $50-150 (including photos, if used).
Photos: Offers no additional payment for photos purchased with accompanying ms. Captions required. Uses 5x7 and 8x10 b&w photos and color transparencies of any size.
Columns/Departments: Statesmen, "a section of the *Alumnus* that features briefs about alumni achievements and professional or business advancement. We do not use engagements, marriages or births. There is no payment for Statesmen briefs."
Tips: "We welcome articles about MSU grads in interesting occupations and have used stories on off-shore drillers, miners, horse trainers, etc. We also want profiles on prominent MSU alumni and have carried pieces on Senator John C. Stennis, comedian Jerry Clower, professional football players and coaches, and Eugene Butler, editor-in-chief of *Progressive Farmer* magazine. We feature three alumni in each issue, alumni who have risen to prominence in their fields or who are engaged in unusual occupations or who are involved in unusual hobbies. We're using more short features (500-700 words) to vary the length of our articles in each issue. We pay $50-75 for these."

NATIONAL FORUM: THE PHI KAPPA PHI JOURNAL, The Honor Society of Phi Kappa Phi, East Tennessee State University, Box 19420A, Johnson City TN 37614. (615)929-5347. Editor: Stephen W. White. Managing Editor: Elaine M. Smoot. Quarterly interdisciplinary, scholarly journal. "We are an interdisciplinary journal that publishes crisp, nontechnical analyses of issues of social and scientific concern as well as scholarly treatments of different aspects of culture." Circ. 104,000. Pays on publication. Byline given. Buys all rights. Submit seasonal/holiday material 6 months in advance. Computer printout submissions acceptable; can accept 5¼" diskettes compatible with Lanier No-Problem Word Processor. Telecommunications capabilities if author has compatible equipment/software. SASE. Reports in 6 weeks on queries; 2 months on mss. Sample copy 65¢; free writer's guidelines.
Nonfiction: General interest, interview/profile and opinion. No how-to or biographical articles. Each issue is devoted to the exploration of a particular theme. Upcoming theme issues: "Why Celebrate the Constitution? Toward the Bicentennial of the Constitution," Liberal Education, the Decline of Writing and Trends Analysis. Recent article example: "The Next Industrial Revolution." Query with clips of published work. Buys 15 unsolicited mss/year. Length: 1,500-2,000 words. Pays $50-200.
Photos: State availability of photos. Identification of subjects required. Buys one-time rights.
Columns/Departments: Educational Dilemmas in the 80s and Book Review Section. Buys 8 mss/year for Educational Dilemmas, 40 book reviews. Length: Book reviews—400-800 words. Educational Dilemmas—1,500-1,800 words. Pays $15-25 for book reviews; $50/printed page, Educational Dilemmas.
Fiction: Humorous and short stories. Buys 2-4 mss/year. Length: 1,500-1,800 words. Pays $50/printed page.
Poetry: Professor Daniel Fogel, poetry editor. Avant garde, free verse, haiku, light verse, traditional. No love poetry. Buys 20 mss/year. Submit 5 poems maximum. Prefers shorter poems.

NOTRE DAME MAGAZINE, University of Notre Dame, Room 415, Administration Bldg., Notre Dame IN 46556. (219)239-5335. Editor: Walton R. Collins. Managing Editor: James Winters. Magazine published 5 times/year (February, May, July, October, December) covering news of Notre Dame and education and issues affecting the Roman Catholic Church. "We are interested in the moral, ethical and spiritual issues of the day and how Christians live in today's world. We are universal in scope and Catholic in viewpoint and serve Notre Dame students, alumni, friends an constituencies." Circ. 92,000. Pays on acceptance. Byline given. Kill fee negotiable. Buys first rights. Simultaneous queries OK. SASE. Reports in 3 weeks. Free sample copy.
Nonfiction: Opinion, personal experience, religion. "All articles must be of interest to Christian/Catholic readers who are well educated and active in their communities." Buys 35 mss/year. Query with clips of published work. Length: 600-2,000 words. Pays $500-1,500.
Photos: State availability of photos. Reviews b&w contact sheets, color transparencies, and 8x10 prints. Model release and identification of subjects required. Buys one-time rights.

OSU OUTREACH, Room 313A, Public Information Bldg., Oklahoma State University, Stillwater OK 74078. (405)624-6009. Editor: Doug Dollar. 5% freelance written. Quarterly magazine for OSU alumni. Circ. 12,500. Pays on acceptance. Byline given. Buys one-time rights. Submit seasonal/holiday material 3 months in advance. Simultaneous, photocopied and previously published submissions OK. Publishes ms an average of 4 months after acceptance. Computer printout submissions acceptable. SASE. Reports in 2 weeks. Free sample copy for 9x12 SASE.
Nonfiction: General interest; humor (with strong OSU tie); interview (with OSU grads); historical/nostalgic (OSU traditions, early days events, people, the campus); interview/profile (OSU subjects); personal experience; and photo feature. "Subjects must have strong connection to OSU, and must be of interest to alumni." Buys 5 mss/year. Query with clips of published work or send complete ms. Length: 500-2,000 words. Pays $15-25 (including photos, if used).
Photos: State availability of photos. Pays $5-15 for 5x7 b&w prints; reviews b&w contact sheets. Captions required. Buys one-time rights.
Columns/Departments: Campus, sports, alumni. Buys 30 mss/year. Send complete ms. Length: 100-300 words. Pays $5-10.
Tips: "Items on alumni personalities are of great value if they have strong human-interest appeal. We prefer a tight style."

PRINCETON ALUMNI WEEKLY, Princeton University Press, 41 William St., Princeton NJ 08540. (609)452-4885. Editor: Charles L. Creesy. Managing Editor: Margaret M. Keenan. 50% freelance written. Biweekly (during the academic year) magazine covering Princeton University and higher education for Princeton alumni, students, faculty, staff and friends. "We assume familiarity with and interest in the university." Circ. 50,000. Pays on publication. Byline given. Offers $100 kill fee. Buys one-time rights. Submit seasonal/holiday material 2 months in advance. Simultaneous queries or photocopied submissions OK. Electronic submissions OK but requirements must be clarified with publisher—"too complex to summarize here." Computer printout submissions acceptable; prefers letter-quality to dot-matrix. Reports "as soon as possible." Publishes ms an average of 3 months after acceptance. Sample copy for 9x12 SAE and 71¢ postage.
Nonfiction: Book excerpts, general interest, historical/nostalgic, interview/profile, opinion, personal experience, photo feature. "Connection to Princeton essential. Remember, it's for an upscale educated audience." Special issue on education and economics (February). Buys 20 mss/year. Query with clips of published work. Length: 1,000-6,000 words. Pays $75-450.
Photos: State availability of photos. Pays $25-50 for 8x10 b&w prints; $50-100 for color transparencies. Reviews (for ordering purposes) b&w contact sheet. Captions and identification of subjects required.
Columns/Departments: "Columnists must have a Princeton connection (alumnus, student, etc.)." Buys 50 mss/year. Query with clips of published work. Length: 750-1,500 words. Pays $50-150.

THE PURDUE ALUMNUS, Purdue Alumni Association, Purdue Memorial Union 160, West Lafayette IN 47907. (317)494-5184. Editor: Gay L. Totten. 10% freelance written. Magazine published 9 times/year (except February, June, August) covering subjects of interest to Purdue University alumni. Circ. 60,000. Pays on publication. Byline given. Buys first rights and makes work-for-hire assignments. Submit seasonal/holiday material 3 months in advance. Simultaneous queries, and simultaneous, photocopied, and previously published submissions OK. Publishes ms an average of 2 months after acceptance. Computer printout submissions acceptable; no dot-matrix. SASE. Reports in 1 week on queries; 2 weeks on mss. Free sample copy.
Nonfiction: Book excerpts, general interest, historical/nostalgic, humor, interview/profile, personal experience. Focus is on campus news, issues, opinions of interest to 60,000 members of the Alumni Association. Feature style, primarily university-oriented. Issues relevant to education. Buys 12 mss/year. Length: 3,000 words maximum. Pays $25 minimum.
Photos: State availability of photos. Reviews b&w contact sheet or 5x7 prints.
Tips: "We're always anxious for new material, and depend rather heavily on freelancers. We don't pay much, but we do credit and have a well-educated, worldwide audience."

‡**SCORECARD**, Falsoft, Inc., 9529 US Highway 42, Box 209, Prospect KY 40059. (502)228-4492. Editor: John Crawley. Assistant Editor: Wayne Fowler. A weekly tabloid sports fan magazine covering University of Louisville sports only. Estab. 1983. Circ. 3,000. Pays on publication. Byline given. Buys first rights. Submit seasonal/holiday material 1 month in advance. Previously published submissions OK "rarely." Reports in 2 weeks. Sample copy for $1 and SAE.
Nonfiction: Assigned to contributing editors. Buys 100 mss/year. Query with published clips. Length: 750-1,500 words. Pays $20-50.
Photos: State availability of photos.
Columns/Departments: Notes Page (tidbits relevant to University of Louisville sports program or former players or teams). Buys 25 mss/year. Length: Approximately 100 words. Pay undetermined.
Tips: "Be very familiar with history and tradition of University of Louisville sports program. Contact us with story ideas. Know subject."

THE STUDENT, 127 9th Ave. N., Nashville TN 37234. Editor: W. Howard Bramlette. 20% freelance written. Publication of National Student Ministries of the Southern Baptist Convention. For college students; focusing on freshman and sophomore levels. Published 12 times during the school year. Circ. 25,000. Buys all rights. Payment on acceptance. Mss should be double spaced on white paper with 50-space line, 25 lines/page. Prefers complete ms rather than query. Reports usually in 6 weeks. Publishes ms an average of 6 weeks after acceptance. Computer printout submissions acceptable; no dot-matrix. SASE. Free sample copy.
Nonfiction: Contemporary questions, problems, and issues facing college students viewed from a Christian perspective to develop high moral and ethical values. The struggle for integrity in self-concept and the need to cultivate interpersonal relationships directed by Christian love. Length: 750 words maximum. Pays 4¢/word after editing with reserved right to edit accepted material.
Fiction: Satire and parody on college life, humorous episodes; emphasize clean fun and the ability to grow and be uplifted through humor. Contemporary fiction involving student life, on campus as well as off. Length: 750 words. Pays 4¢/word.

‡**WPI JOURNAL**, Worcester Polytechnic Institute, 100 Institute Rd., Worcester MA 01609. Editor: Kenneth McDonnell. A quarterly alumni magazine covering science and engineering/education/business personalities for 15,500 alumni, primarily engineers, scientists, managers; parents of students, national media. Circ. 21,000. Pays on publication. Byline given. Buys one-time rights. Submit seasonal/holiday material 3 months in advance. Simultaneous queries, and simultaneous, photocopied and previously published submissions OK. Computer printout submissions acceptable. Reports in 2 weeks on queries; 1 month on mss.
Nonfiction: Book excerpts; expose (education, engineering, science); general interest; historical/nostalgic; how-to (financial, business-oriented); humor; interview/profile (people in engineering, science); personal experience; photo feature; and technical (with personal orientation). Query with published clips Length: 1,000-4,000 words. Pays negotiable rate.
Photos: State availability of photos with query or ms. Reviews b&w contact sheets. Pays negotiable rate. Captions required.
Fillers: Cartoons. Buys 4/year. Pays $75-100.
Tips: "Submit outline of story and/or ms of story idea or published work. Features are most open to freelancers."

Cartoon and Comic Books

Cartoonists and comic book artists can "draw" the latest information on their craft from these publications. Comic book firms looking for writers are also listed in this section. For publications specifically on humor, see the Humor category. Cartoonists and syndicates that buy gaglines can be found in the Gag Writing section near the back of the book.

‡**CARTOON WORLD**, Hartman Publishing Co., Box 30367, Lincoln NE 68503. (402)435-3191. Editor: George Hartman. Monthly newsletter on freelance cartooning, gag writing, art advertising, etc., with cartoon market news, tips, instruction, new markets. 100% freelance written. Circ. 150-300. Pays on acceptance. Byline given. Buys second (reprint) rights to material originally published elsewhere. Not copyrighted. Submit seasonal/holiday material 3 months in advance. Simultaneous submissions OK. Publishes ms an average of 1 month after acceptance. Computer printout submissions acceptable; no dot-matrix. SASE. Reports in 1 month. Sample copy $4.
Nonfiction: How-to, inspirational, new product. "We will accept only material about cartooning and gag writing; nothing negative." Buys 10 mss/year. Query. Length: 1,000 words. Pays $5/page minimum.
Fillers: Clippings and short humor. Buys 10/year. Pays $5 minimum/8½x11 page.

‡**ECLIPSE COMICS**, Box 199, Guerneville CA 95446. (707)869-9401. Editor: Dean Mullaney. Managing Editor: Catherine Yronwode. Publishers of various four-color comic books. *Eclipse* publishes comic books with high-quality paper and color reproduction, geared toward the discriminating comic book fan; sold through the "direct sales" specialty store market. Circ. varies (35,000-85,000). Pays on acceptance. Byline given. Buys first North American serial rights, second serial (reprint) rights with additional payment, and first option on collection. Simultaneous queries, and simultaneous and photocopied submissions OK. SASE. Reports in 1 month. Sample copy $1.50, writer's guidelines for business-size SAE.
Fiction: "All of our comics are fictional." Adventure, fantasy, mystery, romance, science fiction, suspense,

western. "We do not buy overly violent or sexually explicit material." Buys approximately 100 mss/year (mostly from established comics writers). Send complete ms (sample script and plot synopsis). Length: 8-28 pages. Pays $35 minimum/page.

Tips: "Look at the comics we publish, and submit a continuing series proposal that does not duplicate any existing series. Send character designs, model sheets, sample script, plot synopsis for first installment and general direction of future stories in series. Short, 8-10 page self-contained story introducing a character who could possibly continue in ongoing feature is the area most open to freelancers. While superheroes are the traditional mainstay in the field, comics are opening up to noncostumed, but still adventure-oriented series. Because all of our comics are copyrighted by the creators, we do not have need of 'fill-in' writers on existing series. It is difficult to 'break in' with a new full-book series in its own title without an artist in tow. However, it has been done."

FUNNYWORLD, THE MAGAZINE OF ANIMATION & COMIC ART, Box 1633, New York NY 10001. For animation and comic art collectors and others in the field. Quarterly magazine; 56 pages. Circ. 7,000. Pays on publication. Buys all rights. Photocopied and previously published submissions OK. Computer printout submissions acceptable. SASE. Reports in 1 month. Sample copy $3.50.

Nonfiction: Historical (history of animation and its creators; history of comic books, characters and creators); interview (with creators of comics and animated cartoons); and reviews (of materials in this field). Buys 6 unsolicited mss/year. Query. Pays $50 minimum.

Photos: "Photos of creators, film stills, comic strips and art used extensively." State availability of photos. Pay varies for 8x10 b&w and color glossy prints. Offers no additional payment for photos accepted with ms. Captions preferred.

‡**MARVEL COMICS**, 387 Park Ave. S., New York NY 10016. (212)576-9200. Editor: James Shooter. Publishes 30-40 comics and magazines per month, 6-12 graphic novels per year, and specials, storybooks, industrials, and paperbacks for all ages. 7 million copies sold/month. Pays a flat fee for most projects, an advance and incentive, or royalty. Pays on acceptance. Byline given. Rights purchased depend upon format and material. Submit seasonal/holiday material 6 months in advance. SASE.

Fiction: Adventure, fantasy, horror, humorous, romance, science fiction, western. No "non-comics." Buys 600-800 mss/year. Submit brief plot synopses *only*. Do not send scripts, short stories, or long outlines. A plot synopsis should be less than two typed pages. Send two synopses at most.

Tips: "Marvel Comics wants new talent. We want to maintain our leadership of the graphic storytelling medium, and grow."

Child Care and Parental Guidance

Just as children reach for something new every day, so do readers and editors of child care and parental guidance magazines. They want information on new research—on pregnancy, infancy, childhood, and the family—written *for* people who care for children. "Do not submit general topics, such as teaching kids to read or getting ready for school," says one editor. "Submit fresh topics or at least fresh angles." The publications below cover these subjects. Other markets that buy material about child care and the family are included in Education, Religious, and Women's sections of this book.

AMERICAN BABY MAGAZINE, For Expectant and New Parents, 575 Lexington Ave., New York NY 10022. (212)752-0775. Editor-in-Chief: Judith Nolte. Managing Editor: Phyllis Evans. A monthly magazine covering pregnancy, infant health/care, early childhood. "Readership is composed of women in late pregnancy (6-9 months) and early new motherhood (baby age 1-6 months). Most readers are first-time parents; some have older children (2-4 years). Many fathers also read the magazine." Circ. 1,000,000. Pays on acceptance. Publishes ms an average of 4 months after acceptance. Byline given. Submit seasonal/holiday material 4 months in advance. Simultaneous queries, and simultaneous, photocopied, and previously published submissions OK. Computer printout submissions acceptable; prefers letter-quality to dot-matrix. SASE. Reports in 3 weeks on queries; 2 months on mss. Sample copy for 9x12 SAE and 85¢ postage; writer's guidelines for business size SAE and 1 first class stamp.

Nonfiction: F. Holland George, articles editor. Book excerpts, how-to (some aspect of pregnancy or child care); interview/profile (expert in maternal/infant health, child-care expert); and personal experience (should give advice to new parents or parents to be). No "hearts & flowers," or fantasy pieces. Buys 90 mss/year. Query with or without published clips or send complete ms. Length: 500-2,000 words. Pays $100-400.

Photos: Reviews 8x10 b&w photos. Identification of subjects required. Buys one-time rights.

Columns/Departments: F. Holland George, columns/departments editor. My Own Experience (covers common problem of child raising/pregnancy with solutions). "Discuss personal experience (not diary style)—give advice on practical/psychological subject." Buys 12 mss/year. Send complete ms. Length: 1,000-2,000 words. Pays $100-150.

Fillers: Chuckles from Cherubs (kid's quotes); Tricks of the Trade (helpful hints). Buys 100/year. Length: 50-250 words. Pays $5-100.

Tips: "Send very brief biography with submissions. My Own Experience column and articles giving good advice are areas most open to freelancers."

BABY TALK, 185 Madison Ave., New York NY 10016. Editor: Patricia Irons. 50% freelance written. For new and expectant parents. Monthly. Circ. 925,000. Buys one-time rights. Publishes ms an average of 6 months after acceptance. Pays on acceptance. Submit complete ms. Computer printout submissions acceptable if letter-quality. SASE.

Nonfiction and Photos: Articles on all phases of baby care. Also true, unpublished accounts of pregnancy, life with baby or young children. B&w and color photos are sometimes purchased with or without ms. Buys 50-60 unsolicited mss/year. Payment varies.

‡BEST WISHES MAGAZINE, Family Communications, Inc., 37 Hanna Ave., Toronto, Ontario M6K 1X4, Canada. (416)530-4220. Managing Editor: D. Swinburne. 100% freelance written. Quarterly magazine on new baby and new mother topics. Circ. 285,000. Pays on publication. Byline given. Buys all rights. Submit material 3 months in advance. Simultaneous submissions OK. Publishes ms an average of 4 months after acceptance. Computer printout submissions acceptable; no dot-matrix. Reports in 3 weeks on mss. Sample copy and writer's guidelines $1.

Nonfiction: Book excerpts, how-to, some humor with practical tips. "All material must deal with topics of interest for first year with a new baby. The editorial content of *Best Wishes* is primarily designed to meet the immediate needs of the new baby and parents. Special detail is given to the areas of nutrition, baby care, and post-natal recuperation for the mother. Material must be of interest to the majority of new mothers; no personal tragedies." Send complete ms. Length: 700-1,400 words. Pays $125 (Canadian)/magazine page.

Photos: "Only professional photographs will be used." Send photos with ms. Pays $150 (Canadian) for transparencies and prints if published in the magazine."

Tips: "A freelancer can best break into our publication with a practical 'cookbook' approach to dealing with babies."

EXPECTING, 685 3rd Ave., New York NY 10017. (212)878-8700. Editor: Evelyn A. Podsiadlo. Assistant Editor: Grace Lang. Issued quarterly for expectant mothers. Circ. 1,150,000. Buys all rights. Pays 100% kill fee. Byline given. Pays on acceptance. Reports in 2-4 weeks. Free writer's guidelines. SASE.

Nonfiction: Prenatal development, layette and nursery planning, budgeting, health, fashion, husband-wife relationships, naming the baby, minor discomforts, childbirth, expectant fathers, working while pregnant, etc. Length: 800-1,600 words. Pays $200-300 for feature articles.

Fillers: Short humor and interesting or unusual happenings during pregnancy or at the hospital; maximum 100 words, $10 on publication; submissions to "Happenings" are not returned.

Poetry: Occasionally buys subject-related poetry; all forms. Length: 12-64 lines. Pays $10-30.

FAMILY JOURNAL, 1205 University Ave., Columbia MO 65201. (314)875-3003. Editor: Debra McAlear Gluck. Managing Editor: Kathleen Horrigan. 90% freelance written. Bimonthly magazine covering families with children up to about 8 years of age, for "the educated parent, aged 25-45, who desires sensible, useful information and advice. The reading audience is assumed to be sophisticated. Fathers are also readers of *Family Journal*, and are active in all decisions affecting the welfare of the child." Pays 30 days after publication. Byline given. Buys all rights. Submit seasonal/holiday material 6 months in advance. Simultaneous queries, and simultaneous, photocopied, and previously published submissions OK. Publishes ms an average of 2 months after acceptance. Computer printout submissions acceptable (if double-spaced with wide margins); no dot-matrix. SASE. Reports in 6-8 weeks. Writer's guidelines for SASE. Sample copy for $2.50.

Nonfiction: General interest, how-to, humor, interview/profile, personal experience, pregnancy, childbirth, and childrearing through preadolescence. "We look for articles that deal with the above subject areas in a lucid style. The magazine is pro-family, and it addresses such topics as single parents, parents who adopt, infertility, and the many cultural influences on families. The magazine does not take a political or religious stand." Buys 70 mss/year. Send complete ms. Length: 1,000-2,500 words. Pays $50.

Photos: Pays $25 for the first photo of an assignment, $10 each for subsequent photos on the same assignment.

Columns/Departments: Other Families (personal account, humor); Books for Parents, Family Album (photo); Books for Children. Buys 10 mss/year. Send complete ms. Length: 800-1,000 words. Pays $20-50.

Tips: "Writing ability and the magazine's editorial needs are taken into consideration in deciding payment. One's professional background is of less importance than the actual writing. *Family Journal* looks for writers who can articulate an experiential viewpoint as a parent. Send fresh topics or at least a fresh angle for best results. We always look for articles on pregnancy." No telephone queries accepted.

FAMILY LEARNING, For Parents Who Want to Help Their Children Learn, 19 Davis Dr., Belmont CA 94002. Editor: Buff Bradley. 75% freelance written. Bimonthly magazine "addressing the concerns parents have about their children's education, both formal and informal." Circ. 150,000. Pays on acceptance. Buys all rights. Submit seasonal/holiday material 6 months in advance. Photocopied submissions OK. Computer printout submissions acceptable; prefers letter-quality to dot-matrix. SASE. Reports in 2 months. Free writer's guidelines.
Nonfiction: "We publish articles that explain how parents can be involved with activities that help develop necessary skills; articles that give 'inside' information about what goes on in the classroom; articles that explore controversial issues, such as censorship, school prayer, discipline." Types of articles include: how-to, interview, personal experience, profile, essay, opinion, review. Recent article example: "Parents and Schools Form a New, Powerful Partnership" (March/April 1984). Buys 250 mss/year. Query. Length: 1,000-3,500 words. Pays $100-$500.
Photos: State availability of photos with query. Model release required. "Also interested in photos for posters that take families to high-adventure destinations, or behind the scenes at interesting events."

GIFTED CHILDREN NEWSLETTER, For the Parents of Children with Great Promise, Box 115, Sewell NJ 08080. (609)582-0277. Editor: Dr. James Alvino. Managing Editor: Jeanette Moss. Monthly newsletter covering parenting and education of gifted children for parents. Circ. 40,000. Pays on acceptance. Buys all rights and first rights. Submit seasonal/holiday material 4 months in advance. Simultaneous queries, and simultaneous, photocopied, and previously published submissions OK. SASE. Reports in 1 month on queries; 2 months on mss. Sample copy and writer's guidelines for 9x12 SASE.
Nonfiction: Book excerpts; personal accounts; how-to (on parenting of gifted kids); research into practice; outstanding programs; interview/profile; and opinion. Also puzzles, brainteasers and ideas for children's Spin-Off section. "Our Special Reports and Idea Place sections are most accessible to freelancers." Query with clips of published work or send complete ms. Buys 36 unsolicited mss/year. Length: Idea Place 500-750 words; Special Reports 1,000-2,500 words. Pays $10-200.
Tips: "It is helpful if freelancers provide copies of research papers to back up the article."

‡GROWING PARENT, Dunn & Hargitt, Inc., 22 N. 2nd St., Box 1100, Lafayette IN 47902. (317)423-2624. Managing Editor: Nancy Kleckner. 90% freelance written. Monthly newsletter on subjects of concern to parents of young children. "Audience: parents of children under 6 years old, highly educated, financially secure. Slant: be positive, be helpful, be enthusiastic, be realistic." Circ. 250,000. Pays on acceptance. Byline given. Buys all rights and second serial (reprint) rights. Submit seasonal/holiday material 6 months in advance. Simultaneous queries, and photocopied and previously published submissions OK. Publishes ms an average of 5 months after acceptance. Computer printout submissions acceptable. SASE. Reports in 4 weeks. Sample copy and writer's guidelines for 6x9 SAE and 1 first class stamp.
Nonfiction: General interest; how-to (anything on being a better parent/adult/spouse. Include lists of positive, practical, specific suggestions); and personal experience. "We do not want personal testimonials or anything disclaiming the wonders of parenthood, but often personal experience teaches a lesson worth sharing. Almost any subject of interest to adults/parents/couples/singles, but as the subject relates to being a parent. Recent general-interest topics have included guilt, tips for a happy marriage, relating to aged parents, sleep habits of babies and children, how to select guardians for minor children, teaching children traffic safety, fire safety in the home, tips on traveling with children, intimacy after parenthood, understanding the opposite sex, single parenthood, coping with death and dying and the emotions they bring, child abuse, sexual abuse. No first-time birth experience, nothing sugary on how wonderful parenthood is." Buys 20 mss/year. Query. Length: 500-2,000 words. Pays 15¢/word.
Fillers: Newsbreaks. "Fillers having to do with children: new products, etc." Length: 250 words maximum. No pay.
Tips: "Come up with a fresh, new angle on parental concerns. Have lists of suggestions of how to do things, how to change things, how to develop self-confidence in parenting skills. Major feature story is most open to freelancers. Look at your own experience as parent/adult/spouse. Pieces don't have to be 'researched' but should be realistic and common-sensical. For example, a mother wrote an article for us on hearing loss after discovering her son had a loss. The article described her experience, the treatment and result, and included a list of things to watch for if you suspect a hearing loss in a child."

HOME LIFE, Sunday School Board, 127 9th Ave. N., Nashville TN 37234. (615)251-2271. Editor-in-Chief: Reuben Herring. 40% freelance written. Emphasizes Christian family life. For married adults of all ages, but especially newlyweds and middle-aged marrieds. Monthly magazine; 64 pages. Circ. 800,000. Pays on acceptance. Buys all rights. Byline given. Phone queries OK, but written queries preferred. Submit seasonal/holiday material 1 year in advance. Publishes ms an average of 1 year after acceptance. Computer printout submissions acceptable. SASE. Reports in 6 weeks. Free sample copy and writer's guidelines.

Nonfiction: How-to (good articles on marriage and child care); informational (about some current family-related issue of national significance such as "Television and the Christian Family" or "Whatever Happened to Good Nutrition?"); personal experience (informed articles by people who have solved family problems in healthy, constructive ways). "No column material. We are not interested in material that will not in some way enrich Christian marriage or family life." Buys 150-200 mss/year. Submit complete ms. Length: 1,200-2,400 words. Pays 4¢/word.

Fiction: "Fiction should be family-related and should show a strong moral about how families face and solve problems constructively." Buys 12-18 mss/year. Submit complete ms. Length: 1,600-2,400 words. Pays 4¢/word.

Tips: "Study the magazine to see our unique slant on Christian family life. We prefer a life-centered case study approach, rather than theoretical essays on family life. Our top priority is marriage enrichment material."

L.A. PARENT, The Magazine for Parents in Southern California, (formerly *L.A. Parent/Pony Ride Magazine*), Pony Publications, Box 65795, Los Angeles CA 90065. (213)240-PONY. Editor: Jack Bierman. Managing Editor: Greg Doyle. 80% freelance written. Monthly tabloid covering parenting. Circ. 73,000. Pays on publication. Byline given. Buys all rights. Submit seasonal/holiday material 3 months in advance. Simultaneous queries and previously published submissions OK. Publishes ms an average of 4 months after acceptance. SASE. Reports in 1 month. Sample copy $1; free writer's guidelines.

Nonfiction: Steve Linder, articles editor. General interest, how-to. "We focus on southern California activities for families, and do round-up pieces, i.e., a guide to private schools, fishing spots." Buys 10-15 mss/year. Query with clips of published work. Length: 700-1,200 words. Pays $75.

‡**LIVING WITH CHILDREN**, Baptist Sunday School Board, 127 9th Ave. N., Nashville TN 37234. (615)251-2229. Editor: SuAnne Bottoms. 50% freelance written. Quarterly magazine covering parenting issues for parents of elementary-age children (ages 6 through 11). "Written and designed from a Christian perspective." Circ. 47,500. Pays on acceptance. Byline given. "We generally buy all rights to mss. First and reprint rights may be negotiated at a lower rate of pay." Submit seasonal/holiday material 1 year in advance. Previously published submissions (on limited basis) OK. Computer printout submissions acceptable; no dot-matrix. SASE. Reports in 1 month on queries; 2 months on mss. Publishes ms an average of 2 months after acceptance. Free sample copy and writer's guidelines.

Nonfiction: How-to (parent), humor, inspirational, personal experience, and articles on child development. No highly technical material or articles containing more than 15-20 lines quoted material. Buys 60 mss/year. Query or send complete ms (queries preferred). Length: 800-1,800 words (1,450 words preferred). Pays 4¢/word minimum.

Photos: "Submission of photos with mss is strongly discouraged."

Fiction: Humorous (parent/child relationships); and religious. "We have very limited need for fiction." Buys maximum of 4 mss/year. Length: 800-1,450 words. Pays 4¢/word.

Poetry: Light verse and inspirational. "We have limited need for poetry and buy only all rights." Buys 15 poems/year. Submit maximum 3 poems. Length: 4-30 lines. Pays $1.75 (for 1-7 lines) plus $1 for each additional line; pays $4.50 for 8 lines and more plus 65¢ each additional line.

Fillers: Jokes, anecdotes and short humor. Buys 15/year. Length: 100-400 words. Pays $5 minimum, 4¢/word maximum.

Tips: "Articles must deal with an issue of interest to parents. Material should be 800, 1,450, or 1,800 words in length. All sections, particularly articles, are open to freelance writers. Only regular features are assigned."

‡**LIVING WITH PRESCHOOLERS**, Baptist Sunday School Board, 127 9th Ave. N., Nashville TN 37234. (615)251-2229. Editor: SuAnne Bottoms. 50% freelance written. Quarterly magazine covering parenting issues for parents of preschoolers (infants through 5-year-olds). The magazine is "written and designed from a Christian perspective." Circ. 146,000. Pays on acceptance. Byline given. "We generally buy all rights to mss. First and reprint rights may be negotiated at a lower rate of pay." Submit seasonal/holiday material 1 year in advance. Previously published submissions (on limited basis) OK. Computer printout submissions acceptable; no dot-matrix. SASE. Reports in 1 month on queries; 2 months on mss. Publishes ms an average of 2 months after acceptance. Free sample copy and writer's guidelines.

Nonfiction: How-to (parent), humor, inspirational, personal experience, and articles on child development. No highly technical material or articles containing more than 15-20 lines quoted material. Buys 60 mss/year. Query or send complete ms (queries preferred). Length: 800-1,800 words (1,450 words preferred). Pays 4¢/word minimum.

Photos: "Submission of photos with mss is strongly discouraged."

Fiction: Humorous (parent/child relationships); and religious. "We have very limited need for fiction." Buys maximum of 4 mss/year. Length: 800-1,450 words. Pays 4¢/word.

Poetry: Light verse and inspirational. "We have limited need for poetry and buy only all rights." Buys 15 poems/year. Submit maximum 3 poems. Length: 4-30 lines. Pays $1.75 (for 1-7 lines) plus $1 for each additional line; pays $4.50 for 8 lines and more plus 65¢ each additional line.

Fillers: Jokes, anecdotes and short humor. Buys 15/year. Length: 100-400 words. Pays $5 minimum, 4¢/word maximum.

Tips: "Articles must deal with an issue of interest to parents. Material should be 800, 1,450, or 1,800 words in length. All sections, particularly articles, are open to freelance writers. Only regular features are assigned."

‡MOTHERING MAGAZINE, Mothering Publications Inc., Box 2208, Albuquerque NM 87103. (505)897-3131. Editor: Peggy O'Mara McMahon. Managing Editor: Ashisha. Quarterly magazine on birth, parenting, full-time mothering. Circ. 35,000. Pays on acceptance. Byline given. Offers negotiable kill fee. Buys all rights. Submit seasonal/holiday material 3 months in advance. Simultaneous queries and photocopied submissions OK. Computer printout submissions acceptable; prefers letter-quality to dot-matrix. Reports in 1 month on mss. Sample copy $3.75; free writer's guidelines.

Nonfiction: Pacia Sallomi, articles editor. General interest, humor, inspirational, interview/profile, personal experience on pregnancy, birth, parenting. Buys 30-50 mss/year. Query or send complete ms. Length: 1,000-3,000 words. Pays negotiable rates.

Photos: State availability of photos or send photos with query or ms. Reviews b&w contact sheets and 8x10 b&w prints. Pays negotiable rates. Model release required.

Poetry: "We want poetry pertaining to the mothering and fathering experience."

MOTHERS TODAY, 441 Lexington Ave., New York NY 10017. Editor-in-Chief: Janet Spencer King. Emphasizes pregnancy, and parenting of young children. Bimonthly magazine; 60-72 pages. Circ. 900,000. Pays on publication. Buys all rights. Pays 20% kill fee. SASE required. Reports in 6 weeks. Sample copy $1.25.

Nonfiction: Well-researched, and well-documented how-to, humor, informational, inspirational, personal experience and opinion stories. Read the magazine before submitting complete ms. Length: 500-2,000 words. Pays $50-650.

Poetry: Lyn Roessler, poetry editor. Free verse, light verse and traditional. "We are looking for good humor; short, crisp poetry, upbeat, amusing poetry as well as narrative." Pays $10-30.

Tips: "Send a short finished piece written in the first person. Follow with a query for a second piece on a different subject. We like to cultivate good writers."

NETWORK, The Paper for Parents, National Committee for Citizens in Education, 410 Wilde Lake Village Green, Columbia MD 21044. (301)997-9300. Editor: Chrissie Bamber. 10% freelance written. Tabloid published 8 times during the school year covering parent/citizen involvement in public schools. Circ. 6,000. Pays on publication. Byline given. Buys one-time rights, all rights and makes work-for-hire assignments. Submit seasonal/holiday material 3 months in advance. Simultaneous queries and photocopied submissions OK. Publishes ms an average of 1 year after acceptance. Computer printout submissions acceptable. SASE. Reports in 2 weeks. Free sample copy; writer's guidelines for #10 SAE and 20¢ postage.

Nonfiction: Book excerpts (elementary and secondary public education); exposé (of school systems which attempt to reduce public access); how-to (improve schools through parent/citizen participation); humor (related to public school issues); opinion (school-related issues); personal experience (school-related issues). "It is our intention to provide balanced coverage of current developments and continuing issues and to place the facts about schools in a perspective useful to parents. No highly technical or scholarly articles about education; no child rearing articles or personal opinion not backed by research or concrete examples." Buys 4-6 mss/year. Query with clips of published work or send complete ms. Length: 1,000-1,500 words. Pays $25-100.

Tips: "Readers want articles of substance with information they can use and act on, not headlines which promise much but deliver only the most shallow analysis of the subject. Information first, style second. A high personal commitment to public schools and preferably first-hand experience is the greatest asset. A clear and simple writing style, easily understood by a wide range of lay readers is a must."

PARENT'S CHOICE, Parents' Choice Foundation, Box 185, Waban MA 02168. (617)332-1298. Editor: Diana Huss Green. 100% freelance written. Emphasizes reviews of children's media, designed to alert parents to trends and events in books, TV, records, films, toys, educational issues, and computer software. Pays on publication. Buys all rights. Phone queries OK. Computer printout submissions acceptable; prefers letter-quality to dot-matrix. SASE. Reports in 2 months. Publishes ms an average of 8 months after acceptance. Sample copy and writer's guidelines $2.

Nonfiction: General interest (to parents interested in uses of the media); how-to (use books, films, TV, toys, games and records); humor; essays (on social and political issues related to media); interview (with writers of fiction for young adults and children, and directors, producers of films and TV); personal experience; photo feature (of parents and children, grandparents and children); and profile. Query. Pays $25 minimum.

Photos: State availability of photos. Offers no additional payment for photos accompanying ms. Uses b&w prints. Captions preferred.

Columns/Departments: A Parent's Essay and Choice Books; computer software reviews. Send complete ms. Length: 1,200-1,500 words.

PARENTS MAGAZINE, 685 3rd Ave., New York NY 10017. Editor: Elizabeth Crow. 25% freelance written. Monthly. Circ. 1,670,000. Usually buys first North American serial rights; sometimes buys all rights. Pays $100-350 kill fee. Byline given "except for 'Parents Report' or short items for which we pay only $20-75 and purchase all rights." Pays on acceptance. Reports in approximately 3 weeks. Query. SASE.
Nonfiction: "We are interested in well-documented articles on the development and behavior of preschool, school-age, and adolescent children and their parents; good, practical guides to the routines of baby care; articles which offer professional insights into family and marriage relationships; reports of new trends and significant research findings in education and in mental and physical health; articles encouraging informed citizen action on matters of social concern. Especially need articles on women's issues, pregnancy, birth, baby care and early childhood. We prefer a warm, colloquial style of writing, one which avoids the extremes of either slang or technical jargon. Anecdotes and examples should be used to illustrate points which can then be summed up by straight exposition." Length: 2,500 words maximum. Payment varies; pays $300 minimum.
Fillers: Anecdotes for "Parents Exchange," illustrative of parental problem-solving with children and teenagers. Pays $20 on publication.

PEDIATRICS FOR PARENTS, The Newsletter for Caring Parents, Pediatrics for Parents, Inc., 181 Broadway, Bangor ME 04401: (207)947-0221. Editor: Richard J. Sagall, M.D. Managing Editor: Judith Frost. 20% freelance written. Monthly newsletter covering medical aspects of raising children and educating parents about children's health. Circ. 2,800. Pays on publication. Byline given. Buys first North American serial rights, first and second rights to the same material, and second (reprint) rights to material originally published elsewhere. Rights always include right to publish article in our books on "Best of . . ." series. Submit seasonal/holiday material 6 months in advance. Simultaneous queries, and simultaneous, photocopied and previously published submissions OK. SASE. Reports in 1 month on queries; 6 weeks on mss. Sample copy for $1, 9x12 SAE and 2 first class stamps; writer's guidelines for business size SAE and 1 first class stamp.
Nonfiction: Book reviews; how-to (feed healthy kids, exercise, practice wellness, etc.); new product; technical (explaining medical concepts in shirtsleeve language). No general parenting articles. Buys 24 mss/year. Query with published clips or submit complete ms. Length: 25-1,000 words. Pays 2-5¢/edited word.
Columns/Departments: Book reviews; Please Send Me (material available to parents for free or at nominal cost); Pedia-Tricks (medically-oriented parenting tips that work). Buys 12 mss/year. Send complete ms. Pays $15-250. Pays 2¢/edited word.
Poetry: Light verse. No poetry extolling parenting and/or children. Pays $5-10.
Fillers: Clippings, anecdotes, short humor. Buys more than 10/year. Length: 25-150 words. Pays 2¢/edited word.
Tips: "We are dedicated to taking the mystery out of medicine for young parents. Therefore, we write in clear and understandable language (but not simplistic language) to help people understand and deal intelligently with complex disease processes, treatments, prevention, wellness, etc. Our articles must be well researched and documented. Detailed references must always be attached to any article for documentation, but not for publication. We strongly urge freelancers to read one or two issues before writing."

‡**PRE-PARENT ADVISOR and NEW PARENT ADVISOR, A Guide to Getting Ready for Birth/A Guide to Life With A New Baby**, 13-30 Corporation, 505 Market St., Knoxville TN 37902. (615)521-0600. Editor: Wayne Christensen. "The New Parent Series of annual magazines provides information about the physical, psychological, and emotional concerns to expectant parents (*PPA*), and parents with an infant from one-week to three-months of age (*NPA*), which is done in a manner that suggests the magazines are *for* parents rather than *about* babies." Circ. 1.2 million (each). Pays on acceptance. Byline given. Offers 25% kill fee. Buys first North American serial rights. Simultaneous queries OK. SASE. Reports in 3 weeks. Sample copy for 3x11 SAE and $1.10 postage; free writer's guidelines.
Nonfiction: How-to (many pieces service-oriented such as "how-to breastfeed"); interview/profile (with exceptionally well known baby authorities); and personal experience ("This adds a great deal to our magazine."). "To assure the consistent delivery of the concept from year to year, the following blend of articles appear in each issue: *PPA*: physical concerns, prenatal emotions, practical preparations, finances, labor and delivery, parent's roles and siblings, *NPA*: parents' roles, baby care, mother care, infant health and development, second-time concerns, unexpected outcomes and day care. Buys 30 full-length features/year. Query with published clips. Length: 1,000-3,000 words. Pays $500-1,500.
Columns/Departments: Pregnancy Today (a collection of short news, items on latest trends in pregnancy). Buys 5 mss/year. Query with published clips. Length: 150-400 words. Pays $75-200.
Tips: "We look for very experienced writers—if you're a beginner your cover letter will have to show a great deal of polish. Our stories rely heavily on letting our readers talk. Any articles must have extensive quotes from readers and experts."

THE SINGLE PARENT, Parents Without Partners, Inc., 7910 Woodmont Ave., Bethesda MD 20814. (301)654-8850. Editor-in-Chief: Kathryn C. Gerwig. Emphasizes marriage, family, divorce, widowhood and children. Distributed to members of Parents Without Partners, plus libraries, universities, psychologists, psychiatrists, etc. Magazine, published 10 times/year; 48 pages. Circ. 220,000. Pays on publication. Rights purchased vary. Written queries only. Submit seasonal/holiday material 3 months in advance of issue date. Simultaneous, photocopied and previously published submissions OK. SASE. Reports in 6-8 weeks. Free sample copy and writer's guidelines for SASE.

Nonfiction: Informational (parenting, career development, money management, day care); interview (with professionals in the field, with people who have successfully survived the trauma of divorce); how-to (raise children alone, travel, take up a new career, home/auto fix-up). No first-hand accounts of bitter legal battles with former spouses. Buys 20 unsolicited mss/year. Query. Length: 1,000-2,000 words. Pay is negotiable.

Photos: Purchased with accompanying ms. Query. Pays negotiable rates. Model release required.

Consumer Service and Business Opportunity

Readers turn to these publications to learn how to get the most for their money. Some magazines are geared to persons wanting to invest earnings or start a new business; others show readers how to make economical purchases. "Important trends in the coming year will continue to focus on computers and software," says an editor at *Entrepreneur Magazine*. For some publications, entrepreneurship is an important international topic. Publications for business executives and the informed public are listed under Business and Finance. Those on how to run specific businesses are classified in Trade, Technical and Professional Journals.

‡**BC REPORTS**, BC Studio Publications, Box 5908, Huntington Beach CA 92615. Editor: Shirleen Kaye. Managing Editor: Bill Camp. Short softbound reports (similar to newsletter) on any subject or problem that consumer, hobbyist or small business person needs to have solved, e.g., how-to, hobby, self-help, mailorder. "We publish on speculation. Pay if sells 500 + ; then we have recovered cost and will probably earn for both us and author." Byline not usually given. Prefers all rights, but might consider simultaneous and second serial (reprint) rights; also makes work-for-hire assignments. Prefers photocopied submissions; simultaneous and previously published submissions OK. SASE. Reports in 1 month on queries; 6 weeks on mss. Several samples and guidelines for $2, business size SAE and 2 loose first class stamps.

Nonfiction: Expose (consumer, health, money schemes, business); how-to (home, business, hobby, inventions, etc.); inspirational (not religious but self-help); new product (formulas wanted for new and old products); personal experience (if started a business, sideline or solved a problem in ways others could); and technical (how-to for home, business, hobby, inventions, etc.). All are one-shot type reports and booklets. No sex, religion, partisan politics, or extremely controversial material. Buys approximately 50 mss/year. Query or send complete ms. Length: 2-28 typed pages, single or double spaced. Pays $500 maximum for large report (10-28 pages); 8% begins when over 500 copies sold, to 10%.

Photos: B&w if illustrates how to use or build. Pays $10-25 for 3½x5 b&w prints. Captions, model release and identification of subjects required. Buys one-time rights.

Fillers: Clippings. "We might buy news or magazine clips that could be expanded into a report or folio. How-to, recipe (unusual only), diets, business and mailorder sales tips, etc." Buys up to 50/year. Length: open. Pays $7-25.

Tips: "Send us short reports of 2-28 pages on any subject for which a person might pay to find out answers, learn techniques, solve business or home problems. We want simple writing, and everything suggested must be actually workable."

BEST BUYS, the Magazine for Smart Shoppers, 150 5th Ave., New York NY 10011. (212)675-4777. Editor: Carol J. Richards. Publisher: Jon J. Bloomberg. Monthly magazine covering various products/goods for consumers. Circ. 100,000. Pays on publication. Byline given for original stories. Buys all rights. Submit consumer-oriented material 4 months in advance on speculation. Photocopied submissions OK. Does not return manuscripts. Notification upon acceptance. Writer's guidelines for business-size SAE and 1 first class stamp.

Nonfiction: General interest (educational articles for consumers), and how-to (bargain, find good buys). Buys 10-20 mss/year. Query with brief biography plus b&w photos. Length: 850-1,200 words. Pays $50 per 850-word printed page. No fiction or humor.
Photos: State availability of photos. Reviews 5x7 b&w glossy prints. Captions, model releases, and identification of subjects required.
Tips: "We look for research-oriented people who can write with an unbiased slant, correctly and with meticulous care to accuracy of copy."

‡**BEST BUYS MAGAZINE**, 1440 Willamet Rd., Kettering OH 45429. (513)298-4226. Editor/Publisher: Gary D. Bogan. A quarterly magazine circulated in state of Ohio covering price comparisons of all services/products withing a certain area. "Consumer section publishes complaints, how they were settled, and information consumers can use in the everyday marketplace. Our readers are interested in knowing how to protect themselves in the marketplace which covers medical, insurance, mail order, home improvement (and contractors), cars, loss of job, etc." Estab. 1983. Circ. 80,000. Pays on acceptance. Byline given. Buys one-time rights. Submit seasonal/holiday material 2 months in advance. Simultaneous quries, and simultaneous, photocopied, and previously published submissions OK. SASE. Reports in 1 month. Sample copy $3; writer's guidelines for business size SAE and 1 first class stamp.
Nonfiction: Expose (all type of consumer rip-off: transmission shops, mail order, etc); general interest (anything of interest to consumer); how-to (solve unusual consumer problems—"tell others how you did it"); humor (will consider consumer related); and interview/profile (unusual interview and/or information for consumers not normally available). Special issues include Annual Rating Guide, possible Yearbook. Buys 12 + mss/year. Length: 2,000 words maximum. Pays $25-100.
Photos: State availability of photos. Reviews any size b&w prints. "We haven't used photos except for cover, but if exceptional, we will consider."
Columns/Departments: "We want to have regular columns on insurance, mail order schemes/offers, medical, auto. We have many facts on file on these subjects, but need someone in these areas who can research/write. Any level writer has chance." Buys 12 mss/year. Send complete ms. Length: 500 words maximum. Pays $10 minimum. "Depends if writer is an expert or beginner in his field, how well written and how useful to readers."
Fillers: Clippings, anecdotes, newsbreaks. "If exceptional, will consider all areas related to consumerism." Length: 50 words maximum. Pays $5-15.
Tips: "All areas are open to freelancers. With our format we can 'experiment' with different writers/material. We would like 'harder' articles on consumerism than are usually found in major women's/supermarket magazines. We are constantly researching ideas that will be of practical use to our readers. We are open to all ideas."

‡**BUSINESS TODAY**, (formerly *Business Monthly*), Meridian Publishing, 1720 Washington Blvd., Ogden UT 84404. Editor: Wayne DeWald. 80% freelance written. Monthly magazine covering all aspects of business. "*Business Today* is geared toward small- and medium-size businesses with articles on all aspects of commerce. How to hire and how to fire, how to get the most from your sales staff or your secretary, and advertising ideas are at home here." Estab. 1984. Pays on acceptance. Publishes ms an average of 6 months after acceptance. Byline given. Buys first North American serial rights. Submit seasonal/holiday material six months in advance. Simultaneous queries and photocopied and previously published submissions OK. Computer printout submissions acceptable. SASE. Reports in 2 weeks. Sample copy for $1 and 9x12 SAE; writer's guidelines for legal-size SAE and 1 first class stamp.
Nonfiction: How-to, humor, interview/profile, and personal experience. Buys 40-50 mss/year. Query. Length: 600-1,200 words. Pays 15¢/word.
Photos: State availability of photos or send photos with query. "Photos should illustrate, not merely accompany, articles." Pays $35 for 35mm color transparencies. Identification of subjects required. Buys one-time rights.
Fillers: Anecdotes, short humor and newsbreaks. Buys 6/year. Length: 100-250 words. Pays 15¢/word.
Tips: "A freelancer can best break in to our publication by sending a tantalizing query, followed by a tightly written article within our word limits."

‡**CATALOG SHOPPER MAGAZINE**, EGW International Corp., #8, 1300 Galaxy Way, Concord CA 94520. (415)671-9852. Editor: Ellen DasGupta. Quarterly magazine covering mail-order catalogs in over 40 categories. "Our magazine provides a unique way to shop at home for catalogs in over 40 categories. Included are many hard-to-find items. It is designed to help our readers by satisfying their hobby needs and making their lives more interesting through knowledge of the variety of specialty catalogs available to them." Circ. 50,000. Pays on publication. Buys first North American serial rights. Submit seasonal/holiday material 6 months in advance. Simultaneous queries, and simultaneous, photocopied, and previously published submissions OK. SASE. Reports in 2 weeks on queries; 8 weeks on mss. Sample copy $1.50; writer's guidelines for SAE.
Nonfiction: Book excerpts, general interest, how-to, humor, inspirational, travel. Buys 40 mss/year. Query with or without published clips. Length: 25-300 words. Pays 4¢/word.

Photos: State availability of photos. Reviews b&w prints. Identification of subjects required.
Columns/Departments: Buys 8 mss/year. Query with or without published clips. Length: 100-300 words. Pays 4¢/word.
Fillers: Jokes, gags, anecdotes, short humor, newsbreaks. Buys 8 mss/year. Length: 25-250 words. Pays 4¢/word.

‡**CONSUMER ACTION NEWS**, V&V Enterprises, 1579 Lexington Ave., Springfield OH 45505. (513)256-0109. Editor: Victor Pence. A monthly newsletter circulated in state of Ohio for readers who are interested in knowing how to handle consumer complaints: everything from electricity bills to mail order. "We handle consumer complaints and publish results in newsletter." Circ. 500. Pays on acceptance. Byline given. Not copyrighted. Buys one-time rights. Submit seasonal/holiday material minimum two months in advance. Simultaneous queries, and simultaneous, photocopied, and previously published submissions OK. SASE. Reports in 3 weeks. Sample copy for 9x12 SAE and $1.05 postage.
Nonfiction: Exposé (material has to be documented or supported with some type of evidence that is legally sound); personal experience (how the writer was able to solve an unusual problem with a company—it might be funny, serious, etc.); general interest (could include experiences with a company—must name company, etc.); interviews ("We do not endorse any company, product or service, nor do we accept money from any company. But, in order to let consumers see the human side of the business people they deal with we will run profiles on interesting people. When we run a story about a company/person we obtain an agreement that our story is not meant to be advertising, an endorsement of him or his company and that our relationship as a consumer protection service continues if we have complaints against him or the company. So far this requirement has been no problem."); and how-to (anything that could help consumers get better use form the products they buy. For example: a new slant on car care, repairing washer/drier, etc. Has to be very different, not the type of thing found in *Popular Mechanics*, etc.). No material that is not consumer "protection" oriented. "Our Annual Rating Guide lists all of the companies we have dealt with during the year. It is like the movie or restaurant rating some papers publish. Ratings are based on the number of complaints a company receives, how they are handled, etc." Send complete ms. Length: 2,000 words maximum. Pays $10-100; $25 minimum for exposé (500-1,000 words).
Columns/Departments: "Will consider ideas." Send complete ms. Pays $10-100.
Tips: "Every area is open to freelancers. Our type of publication is new in that we print complaints of consumers and name names of the companies involved. We give credit where it is due—good or bad. When we write something bad about a company we give them every chance to correct the problem. We also want interviews of business people. These articles are printed with the understanding that we are not promoting the company or endorsing it."

CONSUMER REPORTS, 256 Washington St., Mt. Vernon NY 10553. Editor: Irwin Landau. Staff-written.

CONSUMERS DIGEST MAGAZINE, Consumers Digest, Inc., 5705 N. Lincoln Ave., Chicago IL 60659. (312)275-3590. Editor: Frank Bowers. Emphasizes anything of consumer interest. Bimonthly magazine. Circ. 1,000,000. Pays on publication. Buys first North American serial rights. SASE. Reports in 1 month. Free guidelines to published writers only.
Nonfiction: Exposé; general interest (on advice to consumers and consumer buying products, service, health, business, investments, insurance and money management); new products and travel. Query. Length: 1,200-3,000 words. Also buys shorter, more topical pieces (400-800 words) for Consumer Scope. Fees negotiable. First-time contributors usually are paid 25¢/word. Expenses paid.
Tips: "Send short query with samples of published work. Assignments are made upon acceptance of comprehensive outline."

CONSUMERS' RESEARCH, (formerly *Consumers' Research Magazine*), 517 2nd St. NE, Washington DC 20002. Executive Editor: Maureen Bozell. 25% freelance written. Monthly. Byline given "except when the article as written requires extensive editing, improvement or amplification. Limited amount of freelance material used. Buys first rights. Query. Publishes ms an average of 4 months after acceptance. Computer printout submissions acceptable; no dot-matrix. SASE.
Nonfiction: Articles of practical interest to consumers concerned with tests and expert judgment of goods and services they buy. Must be accurate and well-supported by professional knowledge of subject matter of articles, for instance, consumer economic problems, investments and finance. Recent article example: "What Kind of Telescope Should I Buy?" (December 1983). Pays approximately $100/page.

‡**COUPONING MAGAZINE**, AGH Publishing, 2929 Industrial Rd., Las Vegas NV 89109. (702)733-8080. Editor: John Snytsheuvel. Managing Editor: Suzanne Esau Regich. A monthly magazine covering couponing and refunding for "today's active consumer." Circ. 700,000. Pays on publication. Byline given. Buys first rights. Submit seasonal/holiday material 4 months in advance. Simultaneous and photocopied submissions OK. Computer printout submissions acceptable. SASE. Reports in 2 months. Free sample copy; writer's guidelines for SAE and 2 first class stamps.

Nonfiction: General interest, humor, interview/profile, personal experience and travel. Send complete ms. Length: 700-1,000 words. Pays $100 maximum.

Columns/Departments: Buys 6 mss/year. Query with clips of published work. Length: 700-1,000 words. Pays $100 maximum.

Fillers: Clippings, jokes, anecdotes, short humor and newsbreaks. Length: 25-100 words. Pays variable rate.

Tips: "It is our goal to be as consumer-oriented as possible for our readers; therefore, any writing submitted should be in that area, i.e., interviews with store managers, consumers, and any consumer news of the day."

ECONOMIC FACTS, The National Research Bureau, Inc., 424 N. 3rd St., Burlington IA 52601. Editor-in-Chief: Doris Ruschill. Magazine for industrial workers of all ages. 25% freelance written. Published 4 times/year. Circ. 30,000. Pays on publication. Buys all rights. Byline given. Submit seasonal/holiday material 6-7 months in advance of issue date. Previously published submissions OK. Publishes ms an average of 1 year after acceptance. Computer printout submissions acceptable; prefers letter-quality to dot-matrix. SASE. Reports in 1 week. Free sample copy and writer's guidelines.

Nonfiction: Rhonda Wilson, articles editor. General interest (private enterprise, government data, graphs, taxes and health care). Buys 3-5 mss/year. Query with outline of article. Length: 400-600 words. Pays 4¢/word.

ENTREPRENEUR MAGAZINE, 2311 Pontius, Los Angeles CA 90064. (213)473-0838. Publisher: Ron Smith. 50% freelance written. For a readership looking for highly profitable opportunities in small businesses, as owners, investors or franchisees. Monthly magazine. Circ. 200,000. Pays 60 days after acceptance. Buys all rights. Byline given. Submit seasonal/holiday material 4 months in advance of issue date. Photocopied submissions OK. Computer printout submissions acceptable; no dot-matrix. SASE. Reports in 1 month. Publishes ms an average of 45 days after acceptance. Sample copy $3; free writer's guidelines.

Nonfiction: How-to (in-depth start-up details on 'hot' business opportunities like tanning parlors or computer stores). Buys 50 mss/year. Query with clips of published work. Length: 1,200-2,000 words. Payment varies.

Photos: "We need good b&w glossy prints or color transparencies to illustrate articles." Offers additional payment for photos accepted with ms. Uses 8x10 b&w glossy prints or standard color transparencies. Captions preferred. Buys all rights. Model release required.

Columns/Departments: New Products; New Ideas; Promo Gimmicks. Query. Length: 200-500 words. Pays $25-100.

Tips: "It's rewarding to find a freelancer who reads the magazine *before* he/she submits a query—and who turns in a piece that's exactly what you've told him/her you want—especially if it doesn't have to be rewritten several times. We get so many queries with the wrong 'angle.' I can't stress enough the importance of reading and understanding our magazine and who our audience is before you write. We're looking for writers who can perceive the difference between *Entrepreneur* and 'other' business magazines."

FDA CONSUMER, 5600 Fishers Lane, Rockville MD 20857. (301)443-3220. Editor: Roger W. Miller. For "all consumers of products regulated by the Food and Drug Administration." A federal government publication. Monthly magazine. December/January and July/August issues combined. Circ. 16,000. Not copyrighted. Pays 50% kill fee. Byline given. "All purchases automatically become part of public domain." Buys 4-5 freelance mss a year. Pays after acceptance. Query. "We cannot be responsible for any work by writer not agreed upon by prior contract." Computer printout submissions acceptable. SASE.

Nonfiction: "Articles of an educational nature concerning purchase and use of FDA regulated products and specific FDA programs and actions to protect the consumer's health and pocketbook. Authoritative and official agency viewpoints emanating from agency policy and actions in administrating the Food, Drug and Cosmetic Act and a number of other statutes. All articles subject to clearance by the appropriate FDA experts as well as acceptance by the editor. The magazine speaks for the federal government only. Articles based on facts and FDA policy only; however, the publication has become more of a health magazine with the proviso that the subjects be connected to food, drugs, medicine, etc. All articles based on prior arrangement by contract." Length: average, 2,000 words. Pays $1,200.

Photos: B&w photos are purchased on assignment only.

INCOME OPPORTUNITIES, 380 Lexington Ave., New York NY 10017. Editor: Joseph V. Daffron. Managing Editor: Stephen Wagner. For all who are seeking business opportunities, full- or part-time. Monthly magazine. Buys all rights. Buys 50-60 mss/year. Two special directory issues contain articles on selling techniques, mail order, import/export, franchising and business ideas. Reports in 2 weeks. Query with outline of article development. SASE.

Nonfiction and Photos: Regularly covered are such subjects as mail order, direct selling, franchising, party plans, selling techniques and the marketing of handcrafted or homecrafted products. Wanted are ideas for the aspiring entrepreneur; examples of successful business methods that might be duplicated. No material that is purely inspirational. Length: 800 words for a short; 2,000-3,000 words for a major article. "Payment rates vary according to length and quality of the submission."

Tips: "Study recent issues of the magazine. Best bets for newcomers: Interview-based report on a successful small business venture."

INDEPENDENCE, A Digest for the Self-Employed, Agora Publishing, 2201 St. Paul St., Baltimore MD 21218. (301)235-7961. Editor-in-Chief: Elizabeth W. Philip. Monthly newsletter covering time-saving, money-saving information for the self-employed person who believes in being independent—philosophically, financially and personally. Circ. 5,000. Pays on acceptance. Byline given. Buys first North American and second serial rights. Simultaneous queries and photocopied and previously published submissions OK. SASE. Reports in 1 month on queries; 6 weeks on mss. Sample copy $2; writer's guidelines for business size SASE.
Columns/Departments: Legal; Investment Notes; New Business Opportunities; Personal Motivation. Length: 1,000-2,000 words; prefers 1,000 words. Pays $5-100.

LOTTERY PLAYER'S MAGAZINE, National Lottery List, Intergalactic Publishing Company, Box 188, Clementon NJ 08021. (609)783-0910. Editor: Samuel W. Valenza Jr. 60% freelance written. Monthly tabloid covering lottery players in 18 lottery and all non-lottery states, lottery games, gaming, travel, recreation associated with the lottery. Circ. 125,000. Pays on publication. Publishes ms an average of 10 weeks after acceptance. Byline given. Offers 10% kill fee. Buys simultaneous, first, and second serial (reprint) rights; also makes work-for-hire assignments. Submit seasonal/holiday material 2-3 months in advance. Simultaneous queries, and simultaneous, photocopied, and previously published submissions OK. Electronic submissions OK, but query for equipment compatibility. Computer printout submissions acceptable; prefers letter-quality to dot-matrix. SASE. Reports in 1 month on queries; 2 months on mss. Free sample copy.
Nonfiction: Book excerpts, expose, general interest, historical/nostalgic, how-to, humor, interview/profile, new product, opinion, personal experience, travel. All mss must pertain to lotteries, games of chance, lottery operations and their directors, popular gaming places (Las Vegas, Atlantic City, Monte Carlo, etc.), and lottery winners and losers. Special issues include Annual Traveler's Guide to the Lotteries, a list of winning numbers and relevant analysis for previous year. Buys 6-10 mss/year. Query with clips of published work or send complete ms. Length: 200-1,500 words. Pays $60-250.
Photos: Send photos with ms. Pays $10-25 for b&w prints; reviews contact sheet. Captions, model release and identification of subjects required. Buys one-time rights.
Columns/Departments: Numerology column (discussing relationship of numbers to everyday life—lucky numbers, etc.); reviews of books on gaming, games of chance." Buys variable number mss/year. Query with clips of published work or send complete ms. Length: 200-400 words. Pays $60-100.
Fiction: T.K. Fos, fiction editor. Adventure, fantasy, historical, humorous, and romance—associated with lottery. Buys 1-2 mss/year. Query with clips of published work. Length: 1,000-2,500 words. Pays $200-500.
Fillers: Clippings, jokes, gags, and anecdotes. Buys 20-40 fillers/year. Length: 25-100 lines. Pays $20-50.
Tips: "We would like to establish contact with photojournalists in the states with lotteries for the express purpose of covering millionaire and other big chance drawings on a regular basis. We will pay regular rates and agreed upon expenses. States are: New Hampshire, New York, Nevada, Connecticut, Pennsylvania, Massachusetts, Michigan, Maryland, Rhode Island, Maine, Illinois, Ohio, Delaware, Vermont, Colorado, Arizona."

MONEY MAKER, Your Guide to Financial Security & Wealth, Consumers Digest, Inc., 5705 N. Lincoln Ave., Chicago IL 60659. (312)275-3590. Editor: John Manos. Bimonthly magazine covering investment markets for unsophisticated investors. "Instructions for neophyte investors to increase their capital." Circ. 450,000. Pays on publication. Byline given. Offers 25% kill fee. Buys all rights. Simultaneous queries and photocopied submissions OK. Reports in 3-6 weeks on queries; 3 months on mss. Free sample copy and writer's guidelines.
Nonfiction: How-to (on investment areas); analysis of specific markets. "Indicate your areas of financial expertise." Buys 60 mss/year. Query with clips of published work if available. Length: 1,000-3,000 words. Pays $200-600 + .

THE NATIONAL SUPERMARKET SHOPPER, American Coupon Club, Inc., 500 Franklin Square, New York NY 11010. President: Martin Sloane. Editor-in-Chief: Ruth Brooks. 35% freelance written. Emphasizes smart supermarket shopping and the use of cents-off coupons and refund offers for "a wide audience of supermarket shoppers who want to save money. The editorial slant is definitely consumer-oriented." Monthly; 52 pages. Circ. 100,000. Pays on publication. Buys all rights. Byline given. Simultaneous, photocopied and previously published submissions OK. Computer printout submissions acceptable; prefers letter-quality to dot-matrix. SASE. Reports in 10 weeks. Publishes ms an average of 3 months after acceptance. Free sample copy; writer's guidelines for SASE.
Nonfiction: Lee Shore, managing editor. General interest; exposé (of supermarket operations, management, coupon misredemption); how-to (save money at the supermarket, tips, dollar stretchers; etc.); humor; interview (of top management, food manufacturers or supermarkets); new product (food, household products); and personal experience (couponing and refunding). Buys 2-3 mss/issue. Send complete ms. Length: 750-2,500 words. Pays 5¢/published word.
Fiction: "We use fiction occasionally if the events are in context of supermarket shopping." Query. Length: 750-2,500 words. Pays 5¢/published word.

Fillers: Jokes, short humor and newsbreaks. Buys 1-2/issue. Length: 50-200 words. Pays $5-10.
Tips: "The best way to break in is to read a copy of our magazine and get an idea of the type of material we publish. The consumer viewpoint is utmost in our minds."

PRIVILEGE, Associated BankCard Holders, #2 Executive Campus, Cherry Hill NJ 08002. (609)665-3332. Editor: Monique Whitaker. 100% freelance written. Bimonthly magazine covering consumer finance, consumer services and consumer interests for bank credit card holders. Circ. 200,000. Pays on publication. Publishes ms an average of 3 months after acceptance. Byline given. Buys first and second rights to the same material, and one-time rights. Submit seasonal/holiday material 3 months in advance. Simultaneous queries and simultaneous, photocopied and previously published submissions OK. Computer printout submissions acceptable; no dot-matrix. SASE. Reports in 2 weeks on queries; 1 month on mss. Sample copy for 9x12 SASE (with 6 first class stamps); free writer's guidelines.
Nonfiction: General interest (product background, e.g., how chocolate is made, packaged); how-to (buy any consumer product or service); humor (as it applies to consumers); interview/profile (of business people); new product (background, availability); travel. No "political, cause-oriented, sexual or product-biased material." Buys 35 mss/year. Query with clips. Length: 400-3,000 words. Pays $100-1,000.
Columns/Departments: Insurance; Legal; Leisuretime; Quest for the Best (buying the best consumer product of any kind); You Won't Believe It (humor with a consumer slant); Dollars and Sense (financial advice on investment). Buys 60 mss/year. Query with clips. Length: 500-1,000 words. Pays $100-200.
Tips: "We do read all submitted material, but it will save the author time and effort if he submits specifically requested material. We answer promptly. Feature and subfeature material should be current and mainstream."

PUBLIC CITIZEN, Public Citizen, Inc., Box 19404, Washington DC 20036. Editor: David Bollier. Quarterly magazine covering consumer issues for "contributors to Public Citizen, a consortium of five consumer groups established by Ralph Nader in the public interest: Congress Watch, the Health Research Group, the Critical Mass Energy Project, the Litigation Group, and the Tax Reform Group. Our readers have joined Public Citizen because they believe the consumer should have a voice in the products he or she buys, the quality of our environment, good government, and citizen rights in our democracy." 5% freelance written. Circ. 45,000. Pays on publication. Byline given. Buys first rights. Submit seasonal/holiday material 4 months in advance. Computer printout submissions acceptable. SASE. Reports in 1 month on queries; 2 months on mss. Publishes ms an average of 3 months after acceptance. Sample copy available. "Freelance material rarely used because Public Citizen is a public interest group with a modest budget."
Nonfiction: Exposé (of government waste and inaction and corporate wrongdoing); general interest (features on how consumer groups are helping themselves); how-to (start consumer groups such as co-ops, etc.); interview/profile (of business or consumer leaders, or of government officials in positions that affect consumers); and photo feature (dealing with consumer power). "We are looking for stories that go to the heart of an issue and explain how it affects individuals. Articles must be in-depth investigations that expose poor business practices or bad government or that call attention to positive accomplishments. Send us stories that consumers will feel they learned something important from or that they can gain inspiration from to continue the fight for consumer rights. All facts are double checked by our fact-checkers." No "fillers, jokes or puzzles." Query or send complete ms. Length: 500-2,500 words. Pays $125 maximum/article.
Photos: State availability of photos. Reviews 5x7 b&w prints. "Photos are paid for with payment for ms." Captions required. Buys one-time rights.
Columns/Departments: Reliable Sources ("book reviews"). Query or send complete ms—"no clips please." Length: 500-1,000 words. Pays $125 maximum/article.
Tips: No first-person articles, political rhetoric, or "mood" pieces; *Public Citizen* is a highly factual advocacy magazine. Knowledge of the public interest movement, consumer issues, and Washington politics is a plus.

‡**SWEEPSTAKES MAGAZINE**, AGH Publishing, 2929 Industrial Rd., Las Vegas NV 89109. (702)733-8080. Managing Editor: J.L. Phillips. A monthly magazine devoted to the hobby of entering sweepstakes and contests. Audience age group 16-90. Circ. 700,000. Pays on publication. Byline given. Buys first rights. Submit seasonal/holiday material 4 months in advance. Simultaneous and photocopied submissions OK. Computer printout submissions acceptable. SASE. Reports in 2 months. Free sample copy; writer's guidelines for SAE and 2 first class stamps.
Nonfiction: How-to, humor, interview/profile and personal experience. "All should lean toward winning! Our readers are looking for the quickest, easiest and most 'sure fire' way to win that 'Big One.' We are looking for information concerning shortcuts to entering, tips on winning, interviews with large prize winners, profiles on large winners, kinds of contests to avoid, best chance contests and sweepstakes and the like." Buys 6 mss/year. Send complete ms. Length: 700-1,000 words. Pays $100 maximum.
Columns/Departments: Buys 4 mss/year. Query with clips of published work. Length: 700-1,000 words. Pays 100 maximum.
Fillers: Clippings, jokes, anecdotes, short humor and newsbreaks. Length: 25-100 words. Pays variable rate.
Tips: Feature stories or fillers pertaining to the winning of contests and sweepstakes are most open to freelancers.

VENTURE, The Magazine for Entrepreneurs, Venture Magazine, Inc., 35 W. 45th St., New York NY 10036. Editor: Carl Burgen. Monthly magazine about entrepreneurs for people owning their own businesses, starting new businesses or wanting to do so.
Nonfiction: "We use stories on new startups of companies and current news on venture capital and entrepreneurs by assignment only." No unsolicited material. Query.

WINNING!, National Reporter Publications, Inc., 15115 S. 76th E. Ave., Bixby OK 74008. (918)366-4441. Managing Editor: Andre Hinds. Monthly tabloid covering "winning in all its aspects to help you cash in on the best things in life." 50% freelance written. Circ. 200,000. Pays on publication. Byline given. Buys first North American serial rights. Submit seasonal/holiday material 4 months in advance. Simultaneous queries and submissions OK. Publishes ms an average of 3 months after acceptance. Computer printout submissions acceptable. SASE. Reports in 6-8 weeks. Free sample copy and writer's guidelines.
Nonfiction: How-to (succeed/win); money making/saving ideas for the homemaker; and articles on winning/winners. Buys 36 mss/year. Length: 100-500 words. Pays 5¢/word.
Photos: State availability of photos. Pays $10 maximum for 5x7 b&w prints.

Detective and Crime

These magazines publish nonfiction accounts of espionage and crime. Markets for criminal fiction (mysteries) are listed in Mystery publications.

DETECTIVE CASES, Detective Files Group, 1440 St. Catherine St. W., Montreal, Quebec H3G 1S2 Canada. Editor-in-Chief: Dominick A. Merle. Art Director: Art Ball. Bimonthly magazine. See *Detective Files*.

DETECTIVE DRAGNET, Detective Files Group, 1440 St. Catherine St. W., Montreal, Quebec H3G 1S2 Canada. Editor-in-Chief: Dominick A. Merle. Art Director: Art Ball. Bimonthly magazine; 72 pages. See *Detective Files*.

DETECTIVE FILES, Detective Files Group, 1440 St. Catherine St. W., Montreal, Quebec H3G 1S2 Canada. Editor-in-Chief: Dominick A. Merle. Art Director: Art Ball. 100% freelance written. Bimonthly magazine; 72 pages. Pays on acceptance. Publishes ms an average of 3 months after acceptance. Buys all rights. Photocopied submissions OK. SASE. Reports in 4 weeks. Free sample copy and writer's guidelines.
Nonfiction: True crime stories. "Do a thorough job; don't double-sell (sell the same article to more than one market); and deliver, and you can have a steady market. Neatness, clarity and pace will help you make the sale." Query. Length: 3,500-6,000 words. Pays $175-300.
Photos: Purchased with accompanying ms; no additional payment.

THE DOSSIER, English Department, SUNY, Oneonta NY 13820. (607)431-3514. Editor: Richard L. Knudson. 90% freelance written. Quarterly magazine covering the world of espionage—real and fictional spies. Circ. 800. Payment method negotiable. Publishes ms an average of 1 month after acceptance. Byline given. Buys negotiable rights. Simultaneous queries, and photocopied and previously published submissions OK. Computer printout submissions acceptable. SASE. Reports in 2 weeks. Sample copy $3.
Nonfiction: Historical, how-to, interview/profile, new product, personal experience, photo feature and technical. No "fanzine" articles. Buys 20-30 mss/year. Query. Length: 500-2,000 words. Pays $30 minimum.
Photos: Send photos with ms. Pays $5 minimum for b&w prints. Captions, model release and identification of subjects required. Buys one-time rights.
Columns/Departments: "Book and film reviews should run about 500 words and aim at a sophisticated spy enthusiast." Buys 20-30 mss/year. Query. Length: 400-700 words. Pays $30 minimum.
Tips: "A writer should know his subject thoroughly; articles must be well-researched and documented (in the text). We're looking for writers willing to give us a break dollar-wise to become regulars later on when we can afford higher fees. No fiction or poetry."

‡**ESPIONAGE MAGAZINE**, Leo 11 Publications, Ltd., Box 1184, Teaneck NJ 07666. (201)569-4072. Editor: Jackie Lewis. A bimonthly magazine "totally devoted to spy stories of international intrigue, suspense, blackmail, confused loyalties, deception, and other things immoral. Fiction and non-fiction stories by top writers in the world of espionage." Estab. 1984. Pays on publication. Byline given. Buys one-time rights, all

rights, first rights, and second serial (reprint) rights. "Since we are a new publication, we have not restricted ourselves as to specific rights; we are open to many types." Simultaneous queries, and photocopied and previously published submissions OK. Computer printout submissions acceptable; no dot-matrix. SASE. Reports in 1 month. Sample copy for $2, 6x9 SAE, and 2 first class stamps; writer's guidelines for business size SAE and 1 first class stamp.

Nonfiction: Book excerpts, expose, historical/nostalgic, humor, interview/profile and personal experience. Anything relating to spy stories. Buys approximately 10 mss/year. Query with published clips or send complete ms. Length: 1,000-6,000 words. Pays 3-8¢/word.

Columns/Departments: Query with published clips. Length: 500-2,000 words. Pays 3-8¢/word.

Fiction: Adventure, condensed novels, confession, fantasy, historical, humorous, mystery, novel excerpts, romance, science fiction, serialized novels, suspense and western. Anything relating to intrigue, international suspense about spies. Buys 100 mss/year. Query with or without published clips, or send complete ms. Length: 1,000-6,000 words. Pays 3-8¢/word.

Fillers: Clippings, anecdotes, newsbreaks, cartoons, games, crossword puzzles, but only about spies. Length: 20-50 words. Pays $5.

Tips: "We are interested in any writer of fiction or nonfiction who writes spy stories. We will not accept explicit sex or gratuitous gore. Fiction short stories are most open to freelancers."

FRONT PAGE DETECTIVE, INSIDE DETECTIVE, Official Detective Group, R.G.H. Publishing Corp., 20th Floor, 460 W. 34th St., New York NY 10001. (212)947-6500. Editor-in-Chief: Art Crockett. Editor of Front Page and Inside: Rose Mandelsberg.

Nonfiction: The focus of these two publications is similar to the others in the Official Detective Group. "We now use post-trial stories; rarely are pre-trial ones published." Byline given. For further details, see *Official Detective*.

HEADQUARTERS DETECTIVE, Detective Files Group, 1440 St. Catherine St. W., Montreal, Quebec H3G 1S2 Canada. Editor-in-Chief: Dominick A. Merle. Art Director: Art Ball. Bimonthly magazine; 72 pages. See *Detective Files*.

MASTER DETECTIVE, Official Detective Group, R.G.H. Publishing Corp., 460 W. 34th St., New York NY 10001. Editor-in-Chief: Art Crockett. Managing Editor: Christos K. Ziros. Monthly. Circ. 350,000. Buys 9-10 mss/issue. See *Official Detective*.

OFFICIAL DETECTIVE, Official Detective Group, R.G.H. Publishing Corp., 460 W. 34th St., New York NY 10001. Editor-in-Chief: Art Crockett. Managing Editor: Christos Mirtsopoulos. "For detective story or police buffs whose tastes run to *true*, rather than fictional crime/mysteries." Monthly magazine. Circ. 500,000. Pays on acceptance. Buys all rights. Byline given. SASE. Reports in 2 weeks.

Nonfiction: "Only *fact* detective stories. We are actively trying to develop new writers, and we'll work closely with those who show promise and can take the discipline required by our material. It's not difficult to write, but it demands meticulous attention to facts, truth, clarity, detail. Queries are essential with us, but I'd say the quickest rejection goes to the writer who sends in a story on a case that should never have been written for us because it lacks the most important ingredient, namely solid, superlative detective work. We also dislike pieces with multiple defendants, unless all have been convicted." Buys 150 mss/year. Query. Length: 5,000-6,000 words. Pays $250.

Photos: Purchased with accompanying mss. Captions required. Send prints for inside use; transparencies for covers. Pays $12.50 minimum for b&w glossy prints, 4x5 minimum. Pays $200 minimum for 2¼x2¼ or 35mm transparencies. Model release required for color photos used on cover.

Tips: Send a detailed query on the case to be submitted. Include: locale; victim's name; type of crime; suspect's name; status of the case (indictment, trial concluded, disposition, etc.); amount and quality of detective work; dates; and availability and number of pictures. "We're always impressed by details of the writer's credentials."

STARTLING DETECTIVE, Detective Files Group, 1440 St. Catherine St. W., Montreal, Quebec H3G 1S2 Canada. Editor-in-Chief: Dominick A. Merle. Art Director: Art Ball. Bimonthly magazine; 72 pages. See *Detective Files*.

TRUE DETECTIVE, Official Detective Group, R.G.H. Publishing Corp., 460 W. 34th St., New York NY 10001. Editor-in-Chief: Art Crockett. Managing Editor: Christos Mirtsopoulos. Monthly. Circ. 500,000. Buys 11-12 mss/issue. Byline given. See *Official Detective*.

TRUE POLICE CASES, Detective Files Group, 1440 St. Catherine St. W., Montreal, Quebec H3G 1S2 Canada. Editor-in-Chief: Dominick A. Merle. Art Director: Art Ball. Bimonthly magazine; 72 pages. See *Detective Files*.

Ethnic/Minority

Ideas, interests and concerns of different nationalities and religions are voiced by publications in this category. General interest lifestyle magazines for these groups are also included. Additional markets for writing with an ethnic orientation are located in the following sections: Book Publishers; Career, College, and Alumni; Juvenile; Men's; and Women's.

ABOUT. . .TIME MAGAZINE, 30 Genesee St., Rochester NY 14611. (716)235-7150. Editor: Carolyne S. Blount. Monthly magazine for blacks and minorities. Circ. 20,000. Pays 30 days after publication. Byline given. Offers 20% kill fee. Buys negotiable rights. Submit seasonal/holiday material 3 months in advance. Simultaneous queries and previously published submissions OK. SASE. Reports in 6 weeks on queries; 6 weeks on mss. Sample copy for $1 and 9x12 SAE.
Nonfiction: General interest; how-to (save money, repair and make things, improve health); humor; interview/profile; opinion; photo feature; travel; health; and sports. Special issues include black/hispanic women, business, health, education, and entertainment. No erotica. Buys 60 mss/year. Query. Length: 500-5,000 words. Pays $30-100.
Photos: Send photos with query. Pays $3 for 3x5 b&w prints. Captions, model release and identification of subjects required. Buys all rights.
Columns/Departments: Fiction, book/film/record/theatrical reviews, Hobnobbing (PSAs, etc.), how-to, poetry, and health. Buys 80 mss/year. Query. Length: 75-5,000 words. Pays $20-50.
Poetry: Free verse, haiku, light verse, traditional. No avant-garde, erotica. Submit maximum 12 poems. Length: 60-150 lines. No payment for poetry.
Fillers: Short humor. Buys 15/year. Length: open. Pays $10-30.
Tips: "Information should be presented in a factual, positive and uplifting manner. *About . . .Time* documents the struggle by individuals, groups and organizations to keep a positive momentum going in the black communities. It deals with philosophy as well as strategy and presents numerous real-to-life examples of what is being done. Even local stories should reflect a national theme. Examine a copy of our publication. We feature one major topic (business, entertainment, women, etc.) in a single issue. Our cover story is usually an interview with a leader or influencing force in the subject area we cover."

‡**AIM MAGAZINE**, AIM Publishing Company, 7308 S. Eberhart Ave., Chicago IL 60619. (312)874-6184. Editor: Ruth Apilado. Managing Editor: Dr. Myron Apilado. 50% freelance written. Quarterly magazine on social betterment that promotes racial harmony and peace for high school, college and general audience. Circ. 10,000. Pays on publication. Offers 60% of contract as kill fee. Not copyrighted. Buys one-time rights. Submit seasonal/holiday material 6 months in advance. Simultaneous queries, and simultaneous and photocopied submissions OK. SASE. Reports in 6 weeks on queries. Publishes ms an average of 3 months after acceptance. Writer's guidelines for $2.50, 8½x11 SAE and 65¢ postage.
Nonfiction: Expose (education); general interest (social significance); historical/nostalgic (black or Indian); how-to (help create a more equitable society); and new product (one who is making social contributions to community). No religious material. Buys 16 mss/year. Send complete ms. Length: 500-800 words. Pays $25-35.
Photos: Reviews b&w prints. Captions and identification of subjects required.
Fiction: Ethnic, historical, mainstream, and suspense. Fiction that teaches the brotherhood of man. Buys 20 mss/year. Send complete ms. Length: 1,000-1,500 words. Pays $25-35.
Poetry: Avant-garde, free verse, light verse. No "preachy" poetry. Buys 20 poems/year. Submit maximum 5 poems. Length: 15-30 lines. Pays $3-5.
Fillers: Jokes, anecdotes, and newsbreaks. Buys 30/year. Length: 50-100 words. Pays $5.
Tips: "Interview anyone of any age who unselfishly is making an unusual contribution to the lives of less fortunate individuals. Include photo and background of person. We look at the nation of the world as part of one family. Short stories and historical pieces about blacks and Indians are the areas most open to freelancers. Articles and stories showing the similarity in the lives of people with different racial backgrounds are trends that writers should be aware of."

AMERICAN DANE MAGAZINE, Danish Brotherhood in America, Box 31748, Omaha NE 68131. (402)341-5049. Administrative Editor: Howard Christensen. Submit only material with Danish ethnic flavor. Monthly magazine. Circ. 11,000. Pays on publication. Buys all rights. Submit seasonal/holiday material 12 months in advance (particularly Christmas). Photocopied or previously published submissions OK. SASE. Byline given. Reports in 2 months. Sample copy $1. Free writer's guidelines.
Nonfiction: Historical; humor (satirical, dry wit notoriously Danish); informational (Danish items, Denmark

or Danish-American involvements); inspirational (honest inter-relationships); interview; nostalgia; personal experience; photo feature and travel. Buys 10-15 unsolicited mss/year. Length: 1,500 words maximum. Pays $25-50.
Photos: Purchased on assignment. Pays $10-25 for b&w. Total purchase price for ms includes payment for photos. Model release required.
Fiction: Danish adventure, historical, humorous, mystery, romance and suspense. Must have Danish appeal. Buys 12 mss/year. Query. Length: 500–1,500 words. Pays $25-50.
Fillers: Puzzles (crossword, anagrams, etc.) and short humor. Query. Length: 50-300 words.

ARARAT, The Armenian General Benevolent Union, 585 Saddle River Rd., Saddle Brook NJ 07662. Editor-in-Chief: Leo Hamalian. 100% freelance written. Emphasizes Armenian life and culture for Americans of Armenian descent and Armenian immigrants. "Most are well-educated; some are Old World." Quarterly magazine. Circ. 2,400. Pays on publication. Buys first North American serial rights and second (reprint) rights to material originally published elsewhere. Submit seasonal/holiday material at least 3 months in advance. Photocopied and previously published submissions OK. Computer printout submissions acceptable; no dot-matrix. SASE. Reports in 6 weeks. Publishes ms an average of 4 months after acceptance. Sample copy $3.
Nonfiction: Historical (history of Armenian people, of leaders, etc.); interviews (with prominent or interesting Armenians in any field, but articles are preferred); profile (on subjects relating to Armenian life and culture); personal experience (revealing aspects of typical Armenian life); and travel (in Armenia and Armenian communities throughout the world and the US). Buys 3 mss/issue. Query. Length: 1,000-6,000 words. Pays $25-100.
Columns/Departments: Reviews of books by Armenians or relating to Armenians. Buys 6/issue. Query. Pays $25. Open to suggestions for new columns/departments.
Fiction: Any stories dealing with Armenian life in America or in the old country. Buys 4 mss/year. Query. Length: 2,000-5,000 words. Pays $35-75.
Poetry: Any verse that is Armenian in theme. Buys 6/issue. Pays $10.
Tips: "Read the magazine, and write about the kind of subjects we are obviously interested in, e.g., Kirlian photography, Aram Avakian's films, etc. Remember that we have become almost totally ethnic in subject matter, but we want articles that present (to the rest of the world) the Armenian in an interesting way."

ATTENZIONE, Adam Publications, Inc., 152 Madison Ave., New York NY 10016. Senior: Lois Spritzer. Senior Editor: Mary Ann Castronovo. 80% freelance written. Monthly magazine emphasizing Italian-Americans for people who have an interest "in Italy and Italian-Americans, in their political, social and economic endeavors. We are a general interest magazine for a special interest group." Circ. 165,000. Pays 60 days after publication. Buys first North American serial rights. Submit seasonal material 5 months in advance. SASE. Reports in 2 months on queries. Publishes ms an average of 3 months after acceptance.
Nonfiction: Expose; general interest; historical (relating to something of current interest); humor; interview; profile; and travel (1 issue/year devoted extensively to travel in Italy). Buys 6 mss/issue. Query. Length: 1,500-2,500 words. Pays $350-600.

BALTIMORE JEWISH TIMES, 2104 N. Charles St., Baltimore MD 21218. (301)752-3504. Editor: Gary Rosenblatt. 25% freelance written. Weekly magazine covering subjects of interest to Jewish readers. "*Baltimore Jewish Times* reaches 20,000 Baltimore-area Jewish homes, as well as several thousand elsewhere in the US and Canada; almost anything of interest to that audience is of interest to us. This includes reportage, general interest articles, personal opinion, and personal experience pieces about every kind of Jewish subject from narrowly religious issues to popular sociology; from the Mideast to the streets of Brooklyn, to the suburbs of Baltimore. We run articles of special interest to purely secular Jews as well as to highly observant ones. We are Orthodox, Conservative, and Reform all at once. We are spiritual and mundane. We are establishment and we are alternative culture." Circ. 20,000. Pays on publication. Byline given. Buys one-time rights. Submit seasonal/holiday material 2 months in advance. Simultaneous queries, and photocopied and previously published submissions OK. Computer printout submissions acceptable; prefers letter-quality to dot-matrix. "We will not return submissions without SASE." Reports in 6 weeks. Publishes ms an average of 2 months after acceptance. Sample copy $2.
Nonfiction: Barbara Pash, editorial assistant. Book excerpts, expose, general interest, historical/nostalgic, humor, interview/profile, opinion, personal experience and photo feature. "We are inundated with Israel personal experience and Holocaust-related articles, so submissions on these subjects must be of particularly high-quality." Buys 100 mss/year. "Established writers query; others send complete ms." Length: 1,200-6,000 words. Pays $25-150.
Photos: Kim Muller-Thym, graphics editor. Send photos with ms. Pays $10-35 for 8x10 b&w prints.
Fiction: Barbara Pash, editorial assistant. "We'll occasionally run a high-quality short story with a Jewish theme." Buys 6 mss/year. Send complete ms. Length: 1,200-6,000 words. Pays $25-150.

BLACK ENTERPRISE MAGAZINE, For Black Men and Women Who Want to Get Ahead, Earl G. Graves Publishing Co., 130 5th Ave., New York NY 10011. (212)242-8000. Editor: Earl G. Graves. Managing Editor: S. Lee Hilliard. Monthly magazine covering black economic development and business for a high-ly-educated, affluent, black, middle-class audience interested in business, politics, careers and international issues. Circ. 260,000. Pays on acceptance. Byline given. Offers 25% kill fee. Buys all rights. Submit seasonal/ holiday material 4 months in advance. Simultaneous queries OK. No unsolicited mss. Reports in 4 weeks on queries; 1 month on mss. Sample copy and writer's guidelines free.

Nonfiction: Expose, general interest, how-to, interview/profile, technical, travel, and short, hard-news items of black interest. "We emphasize the how-to aspect." Special issues include: Careers, February; Black Business, June; and Money Management, October. "No fiction or poetry; no 'rags-to-riches,' ordinary-guy stories, please." Buys 30-40 feature length mss/year. Query with clips of published work. Send "a short, succinct letter that lets us know the point of the piece, the elements involved, and *why* our readers would want to read it." Length: 600-3,000 words. Buys 40 mss/year. Pays $100-800/article.

Columns/Departments: Derek Dingle, associate editor. In the News (short, hard-news pieces on issues of black interest); and Verve (lifestyle and leisure articles. Francis Ruffin, Verve editor). Query with clips of published work. Length: 300-1,000 words. Pays $75-300/article.

Tips: "We have stayed away from trivia and first-person pieces on the belief that our readers want hard-nosed reporting and innovative analysis of issues that concern them. *Black Enterprise* has a mission of informing, educating and entertaining an upscale, affluent audience that wants issues addressed from its unique perspective. We are most open to 'In the News,' an expression of a sensitivity to issues/events/trends that have an impact on black people."

‡**BLACK FAMILY MAGAZINE**, Black Family Publications, Suite 818, 360 N. Michigan Ave., Chicago IL 60601. (312)855-0200. Editor: Carolyn E. Shadd. Quarterly magazine covering black families. Pays on publication. Byline given. Makes work-for-hire assignments. Submit seasonal/holiday material 4 months in advance. Simultaneous queries, and simultaneous and photocopied submissions OK. SASE. Reports in 6 weeks. Sample copy $1.50; free writer's guidelines.

Nonfiction: General interest; historical/nostalgic; how-to (educational home repairs); inspirational; interview/ profile; personal experience; travel; and articles on careers and senior citizens. "We seek articles that fall into the following categories: family profiles (black families, not necessarily famous, but who are excelling in business, politics, religion or entertainment. We do not highlight interracial marriages or people of questionable integrity); articles with a black slant (addressing or explaining a problem or concern common to black families— whether it be in education, finance, or in the society in general); how-to articles (that explain points to consider when going about a purchase, choice or decision); senior citizen profiles (features on blacks who are 65 and older, and still making valuable contributions to society through their tireless efforts); and fine arts (profiles of black artists in the arts such as opera, dance, theatre, sculpture, etc.)." Special Anniversary Issue (highlighting the fourth anniversary of the magazine) is planned for Oct. or Nov. 1984. Buys 6-8 mss/year. Query with published clips. Length: 500 words and up. Pays $20-250.

Photos: "We do not buy photos."

Columns/Departments: Animal News, Cultural Offerings, Fix Its, Super Seniors, and Finance-Legal. Buys 3 mss/year. Query with published clips. Length: 500 words and up. Pays $20-50.

Tips: "Make sure articles are not too 'technical', and they should have a black slant. Super Seniors, Religion, Cultural Offerings, and Finance-Legal are the areas most open to freelancers. Our goal is to improve the family structure through informative, how-to articles, and by providing positive role models."

CANADIAN ZIONIST, Suite 800, 1310 Greene Ave., Montreal, Quebec H3Z 2B2 Canada. Editor: Dr. Leon Kronitz. Assistant to Editor: Susan Brodwin. 40% freelance written; emphasizes Zionism. Published by The Canadian Zionist Federation 6-7 times/year. Circ. 35,189. Byline given. Pays on publication. Submit seasonal/holiday material 2 months in advance. Photocopied submissions accepted.

Nonfiction: General interest (Jewish or Zionist current events); historical (Jewish or Zionist history); interview (with prominent figures in Israeli politics, art or science); profile (on Israeli political figures); and technical (Zionism, Jewish interest, Middle East politics). No stories on personal experiences or travel to Israel. Buys 10 mss/year. Query with clips of published work. Length: 1,500-2,500. Pays $75 minimum.

Photos: State availability of photos with query. No additional payment for b&w prints.

COLORADO BLACK LIFESTYLE, Downing Publishing, Inc., 3501 W. 38th Ave., Denver CO 80211. (303)480-9325. Editor: John W. Hoffman. Managing Editor: Betty Rudy. Monthly magazine for blacks in Colorado. Circ. 20,000. Pays on publication. Byline given. Buys all rights. Submit seasonal/holiday material 3 months in advance. SASE. Reports in 2 weeks on queries; 1 month on mss. Sample copy $2.

Nonfiction: Expose (all types), general interest, historical/nostalgic, humor, inspirational, interview/profile, personal experience, and photo feature. No essays. Buys 24 mss/year. Length: 3,000 words maximum. Pays $50-150.

Photos: Send photos with ms. Pays $10-30 for color transparencies and 8x10 b&w prints. Captions, model release (if needed) and identification of subjects required. Buys one-time rights.

Fiction: Adventure, erotica, ethnic, historical, humorous, mystery, romance, science fiction, and western.

"Fiction needs to have black slant." Buys 12 mss/year. Send complete ms. Length: 4,000 words maximum. Pays $75-150.
Poetry: Buys 75/year. Submit maximum 10 poems. Pays $5-25.

CONGRESS MONTHLY, American Jewish Congress, 15 E. 84th St., New York NY 10028. (212)879-4500. Editor: Nancy Miller. 90% freelance written. Magazine published 7 times/year covering topics of concern to the American Jewish community representing a wide range of views. Distributed mainly to the members of the American Jewish Congress; readers are intellectual, Jewish, involved. Circ. 30,000. Pays on publication. Byline given. Not copyrighted. Buys one-time rights. Submit seasonal/holiday material 2 months in advance. No photocopied and previously published submissions. Computer printout submissions acceptable; prefers letter-quality to dot-matrix. Reports in 2 months. Publishes ms an average of 3 months after acceptance.
Nonfiction: General interest ("current topical issues geared toward our audience"). No technical material. Buys 6 unsolicited mss/year. Recent article example: "Behind the Scenes With the Press in Lebanon" (February/March 1983). Send complete ms. Length: 2,000 words maximum. Pays $50-100/article.
Photos: State availability of photos. Reviews b&w prints. "Photos are paid for with payment for ms."
Columns/Departments: Book, film, art and music reviews. Buys 12 mss/year. Send complete ms. Length: 1,000 words maximum. Pays $50-75/article.
Tips: "I am looking for terser, punchier writing. I think my readers are looking for reporters who get to the heart of the matter without bringing their (the reporters') biases into the story. I also think readers are looking for more accurate and deeper investigative reporting and analysis."

‡**DINERO, in Spanish**, Pimienta Publishing Corp., 6360 NE 4th Court, Miami FL 33138. (305)751-1181. Managing Editor: W. Allan Sandler. Bimonthly magazine in the Spanish language covering business opportunities. "Editorial content is designed to advise middle-income men and women on all aspects of improving their standard of living and is not tailored for the 'high finance' audience. *Dinero* is the only domestic Spanish-language magazine with the unique format that informs the US Hispanic on such topics as how to earn more money, start and operate a business successfully, obtain a better job, invest more profitably, and spend money more sensibly." Estab. 1983. Pays on acceptance. Byline given. Buys one-time rights. SASE. Computer printout submissions acceptable; no dot-matrix. Sample copy for $1 and 8x11 SAE.
Nonfiction: Expose (money, jobs, etc.); how-to (save or spend); new product; and articles on business. "All copy is in Spanish." Buys 50-100 mss/year. Send complete ms. Length: 3,000-20,000 words. Pays $25-100.

EBONY MAGAZINE, 820 S. Michigan Ave., Chicago IL 60605. Editor: John H. Johnson. Managing Editor: Charles L. Sanders. For black readers of the US, Africa, and the Caribbean. Monthly. Circ. 1,600,000. Buys all rights. Buys about 10 mss/year. "We are now fully staffed, buying few mss." Pays on publication. Submit seasonal material 2 months in advance. Query. Reports in 1 month. SASE.
Nonfiction: Achievement and human interest stories about, or of concern to, black readers. Interviews, profiles and humor pieces are bought. Length: 1,500 words maximum. "Study magazine and needs carefully. Perhaps one out of 50 submissions interests us. Most are totally irrelevant to our needs and are simply returned." Pays $200 minimum.
Photos: Purchased with mss, and with captions only. Buys 8x10 glossy prints, color transparencies, 35mm color. Submit negatives and contact sheets when possible. Offers no additional payment for photos accepted with mss.

‡**ELANCEE MAGAZINE, The Magazine for Career Direction and Successful Living**, Renée House of Publishing, Box 8257, Chicago IL 60680. (312)939-7000. Managing Editor: Gloria Jean Royster. A bimonthly magazine covering career direction and success for upwardly mobile, professionally skilled women. Estab. 1983. Circ. 150,000. Pays on publication. Byline given. Offers kill fee of no less than 1/3 of the article fee. Buys first North American serial rights, one-time rights, all rights and simultaneous rights, and makes work-for-hire assignments. Submit seasonal/holiday material 3-4 months in advance. Simultaneous queries and simultaneous and previously published submissions OK. Computer printout submissions acceptable; no dot-matrix. SASE. Reports in 6 weeks. Free sample copy; writer's guidelines for 9x12 SAE and 1 first class stamp.
Nonfiction: Book excerpts; general interest; historical/nostalgic; how-to (self-esteem, discipline, motivation, time management, goal setting); humor; inspiration; interview/profile; opinion; personal experience; photo feature; and technical. "We have a regular pull-out section reflecting new ideas, discoveries, personalities, etc." Buys 30 mss/year. Query (1 page) with clips of published work. Length: 400-3,000 words maximum. Pays $75-450.
Photos: Darnell E. Pulphus, photo editor. State availability or send photos with query or ms. Reviews contact sheets. Rates for 8½x11 b&w prints and 35mm color prints vary. Model release and identification of subjects required. Buys one-time rights and all rights.
Columns/Departments: How-to (achieve self-esteem, motivation, discipline, time management, goal-setting); Mind Your Own (on women who own their own businesses; will also sometimes give advice on how to start a business); In Review (quality book, film, music, theatre reviews on commercial, foreign or independent

media, business and career-oriented topics); Bodyshop (department on physical fitness); Investment Entertaining (information on entertaining, at home or away, may sometimes include recipes); Inner Ways Acknowledgment (focusing on spiritual and emotional needs); Career Power (focuses on career development—how to restructure your career, how to gain better education, changing careers, etc.); She esSay (a personal view by an outstanding writer); Consumer Savvy (how to be a better consumer); Career Facts (a run-down of data and information on industry needs and trends); Assembly (women who do volunteer work); and In House (home and office interior design, how-tos for decorating, furnishing). Buys 90 mss/year. Query with clips of published work. Length: 800-1,000 words. Pays $150.

Tips: The columns/departments listed are open to freelancers. Looks for "simplicity and directedness in terms of style and content. Our readers thrive on information to *enhance* their *careers* and *lifestyles*. The word *elan* means 'style, flair, and enthusiasm' but it has no gender. By adding *cée* to the end of this work, we have feminized a highly appropriate concept."

ESSENCE, 1500 Broadway, New York NY 10036. (212)730-4260. Editor-in-Chief: Susan L. Taylor. Executive Editor: Audrey Edwards. Executive Editor: Cheryll Greene. Managing Editor: John Stoltenberg. Articles Editor: Cheryl Everette. Emphasizes black women. Monthly magazine; 150 pages. Circ. 750,000. Pays on acceptance. Makes assignments on work-for-hire basis. 3 month lead time. Pays 25% kill fee. Byline given. Submit seasonal/holiday material 6 months in advance. Computer printout submissions acceptable. SASE. Reports in 2 months. Sample copy $1.50; free writer's guidelines.

Features: "We're looking for articles that inspire and inform black women. Our readers are interested and aware; the topics we include in each issue are provocative. Every article should move the *Essence* woman emotionally and intellectually. We welcome queries from good writers on a wide range of topics: general interest, historical, how-to, humor, self-help, relationships, work, personality interview, personal experience, political issues, and personal opinion." Buys 200 mss/year. Query. Length: 1,500-3,000 words. Pays $500 minimum.

Photos: Folayemi Debra Wilson, art director. State availability of photos with query. Pays $75-200 for b&w prints; $100-300 for color transparencies. Captions and model release required.

Columns/Departments: Query department editors: Contemporary Living (home, food, lifestyle, consumer information): Stephanie Stokes Oliver, senior editor; Arts & Entertainment: Suzanne Kay; Health & Fitness: Jean Perry; Careers & Travel: Elaine C. Ray. Query. Length: About 1,000 words. Pays $100 minimum. No unsolicited poetry.

Tips: "We're looking for quality fiction; more self-improvement pieces, 'relationship' articles, career information and issues important to black women."

GREATER PHOENIX JEWISH NEWS, (formerly *Phoenix Jewish News*), Phoenix Jewish News, Inc., Box 26590, Phoenix AZ 85068. (602)264-0536. Executive Editor: Flo Eckstein. Managing Editor: Leni Reiss. 80% freelance written. Biweekly tabloid covering subjects of interest to Jewish readers. Circ. 5,500. Pays on publication. Byline given. Submit seasonal/holiday material 3 months in advance. Simultaneous queries, and simultaneous, photocopied, and previously published submissions OK. Computer printout submissions acceptable; prefers letter-quality to dot-matrix. ("Must be easy to read, with upper and lower case.') SASE. Reports in 4 weeks. Publishes ms an average of 6 weeks after acceptance. Sample copy for SAE and $1 postage.

Nonfiction: General interest, issue analysis, interview/profile, opinion, personal experience, photo feature and travel. Special issues include Fashion and Health, House and Home, Back to School; Summer Camps; Party Planning; Bridal; and Jewish Holidays. Buys 25 mss/year. Query with published clips or send complete ms. Length: 1,000-2,500 words. Pays $15-100; first rights pays $1.50/column inch.

Photos: Send photos with query or ms. Pays $10 for 8x10 b&w prints. Captions required.

Tips: "Our newspaper reaches across the religious, political, social and economic spectrum of Jewish residents in this burgeoning southwestern metropolitan area. We look for fairly short (maximum 1,500 words) pieces of a serious nature, written with clarity and balance. We stay away from cute stories as well as ponderous submissions."

GREEK ACCENT, Greek Accent Publishing Corp., 41-17 Crescent St., Long Island City NY 11101. (212)784-2960. Executive Editor: Steven Phillips. Bimonthly magazine. "We are a publication for and about Greek-Americans and philhellenes." Circ. 20,000. Pays on publication. Byline given. Offers 20% kill fee. Buys first North American serial rights. Submit seasonal/holiday material 1 year in advance. Photocopied submissions OK. Computer printout submissions acceptable; prefers letter-quality to dot-matrix. SASE. Reports in 1 month on queries; 3 months on mss. Sample copy $2.50 for 9x12 SAE and 83¢ postage.

Nonfiction: Michael Richard, articles editor. Book excerpts; expose; historical/nostalgic (historical more than nostalgic); how-to (only with a Greek slant, about Greece or Greeks); humor; interview/profile; new product (made or manufactured by Greeks or Greek-Americans); and travel. No " 'My Trip to Samothraki,' articles or 'Greece Through the Eyes of a Non-Greek.' We publish articles on Greeks and Greece, on Greek-Americans who have succeeded at their work in some important way or who are doing unusual things, and on general interest subjects that might specifically interest our audience, such as the role of Greek Orthodox priests' wives, the crisis in Greek-US political relations, the Cyprus problem, Greek school education in the US, and large Greek-

American communities like Astoria, New York." Query with clips of published work. "We buy almost no unsolicited articles—we work exclusively from queries." Length: 3,000-5,000 words. Pays $200-300.

Photos: Anna Lascari, art director. State availability of photos. Pays $10 for 8x10 prints or contact sheets; $15 for color transparencies. Model release and identification of subjects required. Buys one-time rights.

Fiction: Ethnic, fantasy, historical, humorous, mainstream, and mystery. No novels, Greek or Greek-American stereotyping. All fiction must in some way have a Greek theme. Send complete ms. Length: 1,500-3,000 words. Pays $100-200.

Tips: "Try to deal with problems and concerns peculiar to or of specific interest to Greek-Americans, rather than concentrating solely on Greece. With regard to Greece, heritage-historical-genealogical articles are of interest. We'd rather have investigative, informative articles than paeans to the glory that was Greece. Probably the easiest way to get published here is to do a good, in-depth piece on a large, active Greek-American community in the Midwest, West, or South, and back it up with pictures. The more we get from outside the tri-state area, the happier we'll be."

THE HIGHLANDER, Angus J. Ray Associates, Inc., Box 397, Barrington IL 60010. (312)382-1035. Editor: Angus J. Ray. Managing Editor: Ethyl Kennedy Ray. 20% freelance written. Bimonthly magazine covering Scottish history, clans, genealogy, travel/history, and Scottish/American activities. Circ. 32,000. Pays on acceptance. Byline given. Buys first North American serial rights and second (reprint) rights to material originally published elsewhere. Submit seasonal/holiday material 6 months in advance. Photocopied and previously published submissions OK. Computer printout submissions acceptable; no dot-matrix. SASE. Reports in 1 month. Publishes ms an average of 6 months after acceptance. Sample copy and writer's guidelines free.

Nonfiction: Historical/nostalgic. "No fiction; no articles unrelated to Scotland." Buys 20 mss/year. Query. Length: 750-2,000 words. Pays $50-100.

Photos: State availability of photos. Pays $5-10 for 8x10 b&w prints. Reviews b&w contact sheets. Identification of subjects required. Buys one-time rights.

Tips: "Submit something that has appeared elsewhere."

INSIDE, The Jewish Exponent Magazine, Federation of Jewish Agencies of Greater Philadelphia, 226 S. 16th St., Philadelphia PA 19102. (215)895-5700. Editor: Jane Biberman. Managing Editor: Robert Leiter. 80% freelance written (by assignment). Quarterly Jewish community magazine—for a 25 years and older general interest Jewish readership. Circ. 75,000. Pays on acceptance. Byline given. Offers 20% kill fee. Buys one-time rights. Submit seasonal/holiday material 3 months in advance. Simultaneous queries OK. Computer printout submissions acceptable. SASE. Reports in 3 weeks on queries; 3 weeks on mss. Publishes ms an average of 6 months after acceptance. Sample copy $1.50; free writer's guidelines.

Nonfiction: Book excerpts, general interest, historical/nostalgic, humor, interview/profile, and travel. Philadelphia angle desirable. No personal religious experiences or trips to Israel. Buys 50 mss/year. Query. Length: 1,500-3,500 words. Pays $200-500.

Photos: State availability of photos. Reviews color and b&w transparencies. Identification of subjects required.

Tips: "Personalities—very well known—and serious issues of concern to Jewish community needed."

JADE, The Asian American Magazine, 842 S. Citrus, Los Angeles CA 90036. (213)937-8659. Editor/Publisher: Gerald Jann. Managing Editor: Edward T. Foster. 50% freelance written. Quarterly magazine covering Asian-American people and events for Asian-Americans. Circ. 30,000. Pays on publication. Byline given. Offers 25% kill fee. Buys first North American serial rights only. Submit seasonal/holiday material 6 months in advance. Simultaneous queries and photocopied submissions acceptable. Computer printout submissions acceptable; prefers letter-quality to dot-matrix. SASE. Reports in 3 weeks. Publishes ms an average of 3 months after acceptance. Sample copy $1; writer's guidelines for business size SAE and 1 first class stamp.

Nonfiction: Interview/profile (Asian-Americans in unusual situations or occupations, especially successful people active in communities). Buys 15 unsolicited mss/year. Send complete ms. Length: 4,000 words maximum. Pays $25-200.

Photos: Photos are a *must* with all stories. Send photos with ms. Reviews 35mm color transparencies and 5x7 color and b&w glossy prints. Model release and identification of subjects required. Buys one-time rights.

Columns/Departments: Open to new suggestions for columns/departments.

Fillers: Newsbreaks. Pays $10-25.

Tips: "We're especially interested in hearing from writers who are not on the West Coast."

JET, 820 S. Michigan Ave., Chicago IL 60605. Executive Editor/Associate Publisher: Robert E. Johnson. For black readers interested in current news and trends. Weekly. Circ. 800,000. Primarily staff-written.

Nonfiction: Articles on topics of current, timely interest to black readers. News items and features: religion, education, African affairs, civil rights, politics and entertainment. Length: varies. Payment negotiated.

Photos: S.P. Flanagan, photo editor. Photo essays. Payment negotiable. Prefers b&w photos.

THE JEWISH MONTHLY, 1640 Rhode Island Ave. NW, Washington DC 20036. (202)857-6645. Editor: Marc Silver. Published by B'nai B'rith. 75% freelance written. Monthly magazine. Buys North American serial rights only. Pays on publication. Computer printout submissions acceptable. SASE.
Nonfiction: Articles of interest to the Jewish community: economic, demographic, political, social, biographical, cultural, and travel. No immigrant reminiscences. Queries (with clips of published work) should be direct, well-organized and map out the story. Buys 5-10 unsolicited mss/year. Length: 4,000 words maximum. Pays up to 15¢/word.
Tips: "The most annoying aspect of working with freelance writers is the discrepancy between the quality of clips and quality of writing."

‡**JEWISH NEWS**, 17515 W. 9 Mile Rd., Southfield MI 48075. (313)424-8833. Editor: Gary Rosenblatt. News Editor: Alan Hitsky. A weekly tabloid covering news and features of Jewish interest. Circ. 16,500. Pays on publication. Byline given. No kill fee "unless stipulated beforehand." Buys first North American serial rights. Simultaneous queries and photocopied submissions OK. Computer printout submissions acceptable; prefers letter-quality to dot-matrix. SASE. Reports in 2 weeks on queries; 1 month on mss. Sample copy for $1 and SASE.
Nonfiction: Book excerpts, humor, and interview/profile. Buys 10-20 mss/year. Query with or without published clips, or send complete ms. Length: 500-2,500 words. Pays $20-75.
Fiction: Ethnic. Buys 1-2 mss/year. Send complete ms. Length: 500-2,500 words. Pays $20-75.

JEWISH POST AND OPINION, National Jewish Post, Inc., Box 444097, Indianapolis IN 46202. (317)927-7800. Editor: Gabriel Cohen. Weekly tabloid covering only news of Jewish interest. Circ. 116,000. Pays on publication. Byline given.
Nonfiction: "Straight reporting of hard news and human interest feature stories involving Jews." Length: 500-750 words for features. Pays 4¢/word. "No articles now, please, but we can use stringers (correspondents) all throughout North America at 4¢ a word for news published." Information to involve Jewish person or incident.

‡**LECTOR, The Review Journal for Spanish Language and Bilingual Materials**, California Spanish Language Data Base, Box 4273, Berkeley CA 94704. (415)893-8702. Editor: Roberto Cabello-Argandona. Managing Editor: Vivian M. Pisano. A bimonthly magazine covering reviews of Spanish language and bilingual materials. "For people who work with Hispanic communities in the US or those interested in knowing what the current concerns are among US Hispanics, mainly professionals: librarians, bilingual educators, Spanish teachers and professors, and administrators who are directly involved or concerned with US Hispanics." Circ. 500. Pays on publication. Byline given. Offers kill fee. Buys all rights. Submit seasonal/holiday material 3 months in advance. Simultaneous queries, and simultaneous, photocopied, and previously published submissions "on occasion" OK. Computer printout submissions acceptable. SASE. Reports in 2 weeks on queries; 1 month on mss. Free sample copy and writer's guidelines.
Nonfiction: Claire Splan, articles editor. General interest (related to Hispanic culture), interview/profile (of authors, publishers, and other professionals); new product (new books, etc.); opinion (related to serving US Hispanic community); personal experience (related to US Hispanics). "Articles related to the Hispanic culture are always welcome. Articles of professional interest are also sought as long as they are not so technical that they would be boring to anyone not directly related to that field. Particularly of interest are stories about publishers and writers of Spanish language or bilingual materials." No very scholarly articles. Buys 12-18 mss/year. Query with published clips. Length: 1,500-2,500 words. Pays $50-100.
Photos: Claire Splan, photo editor. State availability of photos with query or mss. Reviews b&w snapshots. Identification of subjects required. Buys one-time rights.
Columns/Departments: Claire Splan, column/department editor. Publishers Corner (articles or interviews about publishers, writers, etc.); Perspective (interviews or first person articles about serving Hispanic community); and Events in Profile (current events related to Hispanic community). Buys 12-18 mss/year. Query with published clips. Length: 1,500-2,500 words. Pays $50-100.
Tips: "*Lector* is very open to freelancers. The best way to break in is to present a well-written, well-researched article written at a general reading level that will not insult our readers' intelligence. Our readers are professionals, but they want lively, interesting reading material that is related to their field without being overly-technical."

‡**MAINSTREAM AMERICA MAGAZINE**, Urban Improvement Corp., 2714 W. Vernon Ave., Los Angeles CA 90008. (213)290-1322. Editor: Diane Clark. Managing Editor: Adriene Diane L. Corbin. A monthly Black magazine for upward mobile professionals, businessmen, etc. Circ. 50,000. Pays on publication. Byline given. Buys all rights. Submit seasonal/holiday material 3 months in advance. Simultaneous queries and submissions OK. SASE. Reports in 1 month on queries; 2 months on mss. Free writer's guidelines.
Nonfiction: Expose (government, education, business as it impacts on Black Americans); general interest; historical/nostalgic; how-to (succeed in business, career, how to become a successful entrepreneur); inspirational; interview/profile; personal experience (in business, corporate, career). "Features should be upbeat as an ex-

ample for those striving toward success: political, Black enterprise, positive self image, education, etc." Buys 200 mss/year. Query with or without published clips, or send complete ms. Length: 500-3,000 words. Pays 6-8¢/word.

Photos: State availability of photos or send photos with query or ms. Pays $10-15 for 8x10 b&w prints. Captions, model releases, and identification of subjects required. Buys one-time rights.

Tips: "Read the magazine, follow format, and note subjects of interest. We're receptive to all well written material from known and unknown writers."

MALINI, Pan-Asian Journal for the Literati, Box 195, Claremont CA 91711. (714)625-2914. Editor: Chitra Chakraborty. Bimonthly ethnic literary magazine covering Pan-Asian (India to Japan including some Pacific islands) literature and culture. 30% freelance written; 10-25% of material published is poetry. Byline given. Buys all rights. Publishes ms an average of 1-4 months after acceptance. Submit seasonal/holiday material 4 months in advance. Computer printout submissions acceptable; no dot-matrix. SASE. Reports in 1 month. Sample copy $1.37; writer's guidelines for legal-size SAE and 1 first class stamp.

Nonfiction: Book excerpts, expose, general interest, historical/nostalgic, humor and personal experience. Does not want to see anything that does not concern Pan-Asian group. Buys 6-10 mss/year. Query. Length: 750-1,200 words. Pays $35-100 (on acceptance).

Fiction: Ethnic. Buys 2-3 mss/year. Query. Length: 750-1,200 words. Pays $25-100 (on acceptance).

Poetry: Avant-garde, free verse, haiku, light verse, traditional and translations. No monologues or profanity. First-time typed, original submissions only. Buys 18-20 poems/year. Submit maximum 6 poems. Poetry submissions should be single-spaced within stanzas, double-spaced between stanzas. Length: 3-33 lines. Pays $10-100 (on acceptance). Buys all rights.

Tips: "Anybody with ethnic awareness or sensitivity and literary talent can write for us. Ordering a sample copy will be of tremendous help to prospective contributors since there is no other magazine like *Malini* in the United States."

MIDSTREAM, A Monthly Jewish Review, 515 Park Ave., New York NY 10022. Editor: Joel Carmichael. 90% freelance written. Monthly. Circ. 14,000. Buys first rights. Byline given. Pays after publication. Publishes ms an average of 6 months after acceptance. Reports in 2 months. SASE.

Nonfiction: "Articles offering a critical interpretation of the present, searching examination of the past, and affording a medium for independent opinion and creative cultural expression. Articles on the political and social scene in Israel, on Jews in Russia and the US; generally it helps to have a Zionist orientation. If you're going abroad, we would like to see what you might have to report on a Jewish community abroad." Buys historical and think pieces, primarily of Jewish and related content. Pays 5¢/word.

Fiction: Primarily of Jewish and related content. Pays 5¢/word.

Tips: "A book review would be the best way to start. Send us a sample review or a clip, let us know your area of interest, suggest books you would like to review. The author should briefly outline the subject and theme of his article and give a brief account of his background or credentials in this field. Since we are a monthly, we look for critical analysis rather than a 'journalistic' approach."

MOMENT MAGAZINE, 462 Boylston St., Boston MA 02116. (617)536-6252. Editor: Leonard Fein. 20% freelance written. Emphasizes Jewish affairs. Monthly magazine. Circ. 25,000. Pays on publication. Buys all rights. Pays 25% kill fee on commissioned articles. Byline given. Phone queries OK. Computer printout submissions acceptable. Submit seasonal/holiday material 6 months in advance. Reports in 6 weeks. Publishes ms an average of 4 months after acceptance. Sample copy $3.50.

Nonfiction: Expose, informational, historical, political, humor, nostalgia, cultural, social action, profile and personal experience. Must have Jewish content. "We have a heavy backlog of poetry. A very high percentage of the material we receive deals with the Holocaust; we also get a large number of articles and stories focusing on grandparents. It's not that we don't want to see them, but we accept very few." Top literary quality only. Buys 100 mss/year. Query or submit complete ms. Length: 1,000-5,000 words. Pays $50 minimum.

Fiction: "We use only the highest quality fiction. Stories should have high Jewish content." Buys 3 mss/year. Submit complete ms. Length: 1,000-5,000 words. Pays $100-400.

Tips: "Read the magazine. Submit relevant material. Send a comprehensive letter that will outline elements to be covered as well as overall thrust of the article. It is helpful to include sources that will be used and a brief summary of your experience (other publications, relevant credentials)."

‡NEW BREED JOURNAL, Saskatchewan's Native Communication Corporation, Suite 210, 2505 11th Ave., Regina, Saskatchewan S4P 0K6 Canada. (306)525-9501. Editor: Joan Beatty. A monthly tabloid covering Native issues. "We provide information and feedback to the native people of Saskatchewan and across Canada." Circ. 5,000. Pays on publication. Byline given. Buys all rights. Submit seasonal/holiday material 2 months in advance. Simultaneous queries and submissions OK. SAE, IRC. Free sample copy and writer's guidelines.

Nonfiction: Book excerpts (reviews); interview/profile (Native people); opinion; photo feature (traditional

lifestyle); and traditional recipes. Special issues include First Ministers Conference, health, alcoholism, justice, human rights, and youth. Buys 1 mss/year. Query. Length: 300 words maximum. Pays $2.50/column inch.
Photos: Send photos with query. Reviews b&w contact sheets. Pays $5 for 5x7 b&w prints. Identification of subjects required. Buys one-time rights.
Columns/Departments: Reviews of films and books on Native-related subjects. Buys 5-10 mss/year. Query. Length: 150 words minimum.
Poetry: Any kind/style. Buys 12 poems/year. Length: 5-15 lines.
Fillers: Jokes, short humor, and newsbreaks. Buys 5/year. Length: 75 words minimum.

‡**PALM BEACH JEWISH WORLD**, Jewish World Publishing, Box 3343, West Palm Beach FL 33402. (305)833-8331. Editor: Tina Hersh. Weekly tabloid for the Jewish community. Pays on acceptance. Byline given. Not copyrighted. Buys first North American serial rights, one-time rights, and second (reprint) rights to material originally published elsewhere. Submit seasonal/holiday material 1½ months in advance. Simultaneous submissions OK. SASE. Reports in 1 month. Sample copy $1.
Nonfiction: "We staff-write news items, and prefer a creative style for features in keeping with the content. Profiles of individuals, for example, should reflect the reason the person is important to the Jewish community and particularly the south Florida region, whether positive or negative, and give the reader enough background to make a judgment for himself." Query with writing sample. Length: 750-1,200 words. Pays $45-100.
Photos: Photos of the subject, or his or her work, should accompany story." Pays $15 minimum for b&w 35mm negatives and 5x7 prints. Captions and identification of subjects required. Buys one-time rights.

PRESENT TENSE: The Magazine of World Jewish Affairs, 165 E. 56th St., New York NY 10022. (212)751-4000. Editor: Murray Polner. For college-educated, Jewish-oriented audience interested in Jewish life throughout the world. Quarterly magazine. Circ. 45,000. Buys all rights. Byline given. Buys 60 mss/year. Pays on publication. Computer printout submissions acceptable. Sample copy $3. Reports in 6-8 weeks. Query. SASE.
Nonfiction: Quality reportage of contemporary events (a la *Harper's*, *New Yorker*, etc.). Personal journalism, reportage, profiles and photo essays. Length: 3,000 words maximum. Pays $100-250.

RECONSTRUCTIONIST, 2521 Broadway, New York NY 10025. (212)361-3011. Editor: Dr. Jacob Staub. A general Jewish religious and cultural magazine. Monthly. Circ. 8,100. Buys all rights. Buys 35 mss/year. Pays on publication. Query. SASE. Free sample copy.
Nonfiction: Publishes literary criticism, reports from Israel and other lands where Jews live, and material of educational or communal interest. Preferred length is 2,000-3,000 words. Pays $25.
Fiction: Uses a small amount of fiction as fillers.
Poetry: Used as fillers.

SCANDINAVIAN REVIEW, American-Scandinavian Foundation, 127 E. 73rd St., New York NY 10021. (212)879-9779. Editor: Patricia McFate. "The majority of our readership is over 30, well educated, and in the middle income bracket. Most similar to readers of *Smithsonian* and *Saturday Review*. Have interest in Scandinavia by birth or education." Quarterly magazine. Circ. 6,000. Pays on publication. Buys all rights. Byline given. Previously published material (if published abroad) OK. SASE. Reports in 2 months. Sample copy $4.
Nonfiction: Historical, informational, interview, photo feature and travel. "Modern life and culture in Scandinavia." No American-Scandinavian memoirs. Recent article example: "The Economic Crises, Local Authority, and The Scandinavian Citizen" (December 1983). Send complete ms. Length: maximum 3,500 words. Pays $50-200.
Photos: Purchased with accompanying ms. Captions required. Submit prints or transparencies. Prefers sharp, high contrast b&w enlargements. Total purchase price for ms includes payment for photos.
Fiction: Literature. Only work translated from the Scandinavian. Buys 4-10 mss/year. Send complete ms. Length: 3,000 words maximum. Pays $75-125.
Poetry: Translations of contemporary Scandinavian poetry. Buys 5-20 poems/year. Pays $10.
Tips: "We will be using more Scandinavian authors and American translators and commissioning more articles, so that we are even less open to freelancers."

SOUTHERN JEWISH WEEKLY, Box 3297, Jacksonville FL 32206. (904)355-3459. Editor: Isadore Moscovitz. For a Jewish audience. General subject matter is human interest and short stories. Weekly. Circ. 28,500. Pays on acceptance. Not copyrighted. Buys all rights. Submit seasonal/holiday material 1 month in advance. SASE. Reports in 1 week. Free sample copy and writer's guidelines.
Nonfiction: "Any type of article as long as it is of Southern Jewish interest." Buys 15 mss/year. Length: 250-500 words. Pays $10-100.
Photos: State availability of photos. Pays $5-15 for b&w prints.

‡SPANISH TODAY, The National Magazine for the Hispanic Family, Cruzada Spanish Publications, Box 650909, Miami FL 33265. (305)386-5480. Editor: Andres Rivero. Managing Editor: Pilar E. Rivero. Bimonthly magazine covering Hispanic/Spanish market in the USA. "We reach professional Hispanics, businesspeople, professors, teachers, leaders and prominent Hispanics." Circ. 10,000. Pays on publication. Byline given. Buys all rights. Submit holiday/seasonal material 2 months in advance. Simultaneous submissions OK. SASE. Reports in 3 weeks on queries; 5 weeks on mss. Sample copy for $3; free writer's guidelines.
Nonfiction: Expose, general interest, historical/nostalgic, inspirational, interview/profile, personal experience, photo feature and travel. "We buy anything of interest and concern to Hispanics in the US." Buys 20 mss/year. Query. Word length and pay open for discussion.
Photos: State availability of photos. Reviews 8x10 prints.
Tips: "We buy articles written in either Spanish or English languages. Only well-written articles in Spanish are considered. No translations."

‡THE SPOT, Ve-ga Japan New York Publishing Corp., Room 605, 141 E. 44th St., New York NY 10017. (212)883-1215. Editor/Publisher: Michi Nakao. English Editor: David Galef. Weekly newspaper covering Japanese-American interests. "As New York's only Japanese-English newspaper, *The Spot* focuses on American culture with a Japanese slant. We feature articles on Japanese food and restaurants, informative pieces on Japanese economics and politics, columns on film, music, and culture—usually with some Japanese connection, though we also report on the New York cultural scene in general for our Japanese readers. Articles appear in both Japanese and English, our usual practice being to print a summary in the other language alongside the original." Estab. 1983. Circ. 10,000. Pays on publication. Byline given. Buys one-time rights. Submit seasonal/holiday material at least a month in advance. Photocopied submissions OK. Computer printout submissions acceptable. SASE. Reports in 2 weeks on queries; 1 month on mss.
Nonfiction: Expose, general interest, historical/nostalgic, interview/profile, opinion, personal experience, technical and travel—all items may be developed along a Japanese slant (what's happening in Japan), an American-Japanese bias, or even an American view (an American curious to know more about things Japanese). "We'd particularly like some interviews and profiles of famous Japanese-Americans, items on Japanese business in the U.S., and American business in Japan. We don't need more book reviewers—at least, not on a regular basis—or freelancers who are sure they could write a piece for us if we give them an idea." Special edition includes New Year's issue with Japanese seasonal food, festivities, and so on. No "just visited Japan and thought the people were lovely and polite" reminiscences. Buys 50-75 mss/year. Send complete ms. Length: 300-1,500 words. Pays $25 (higher for special articles).
Columns/Departments: " 'What I Want to Know about Japan, is a 1,000-1,500 words piece on almost any aspect of Japan in America or vice-versa. Recent articles have included teaching Japanese in the New York public school system and Japanese and American comics. 'In and Around' is more of a column space, generally 650-800 words, focusing on happenings in New York—exhibits, concerts, shows, and so on, though opinion pieces are also possible here." Buys 25 mss/year. Query or send complete ms (if writer knows paper). Length: 650-1,500 words. Pays $25 minimum.
WM **Editor's Note:** At press time, *The Spot* had suspended publication.

‡WEEKLY REVIEW, PRIONI, (formerly Prioni Greek-American Newspaper), Petallides Publishing Co. Inc., 9-11 E. 37th St., New York NY 10016. (212)578-4480. Editor: Dody Tsiantar. Weekly tabloid newspaper covering national and world news, Greek and Greek-American issues, problems, people. "We cover Greek-American communities, success stories, celebrities, leaders in the arts, business, and academia, human-interest stories relating to Greeks, travel to Greece and Cyprus, seasonal articles relating to Greek religious or national holidays or events (e.g., Christmas, Easter, March 25, October 28, the Turkish invasion of Cyprus)." Circ. 25,000. Pays on publication. Byline given. Offers 10% kill fee. Buys first North American serial rights. Submit seasonal/holiday material 2 months in advance. Simultaneous queries OK. SASE. Reports in 4 weeks on queries; 4 weeks on mss. Sample copy $1.
Nonfiction: Expose, historical/nostalgic, interview/profile, new product, photo feature, travel, art, culture, business. All must be Greek or Greek-American related. No pseudo-philosophical ramblings. Buys 25 mss/year. Query with clips. Length: 1,000-1,500 words. Pays $50-250.
Photos: John Haronides, photo editor. "We look for first-rate b&w glossy prints." Send photos with query or ms. Pays $5-15 for b&w prints, bought with ms, singly, or as series. Uses 5-10 photos for picture stories; pays $50-80 for double spread without ms. Captions, model release, and identification of subjects required. Buys one-time rights.
Columns/Departments: Book and film reviews (on Greek subjects or by Greek writers, directors, composers); Community (about Greek-American organizations, parishes, enclaves). Send complete ms. Length: 500-1,000 words. Pays $25-50.
Fiction: Ethnic-Greek. "Avoid Greek stereotyping, excessive violence, graphic sex, obscene language. The paper is read by the entire family. We are interested in young writers of merit." Send complete ms. Length: 500-1,500 words. Pays $50-75.
Fillers: Newsbreaks about Greeks and Greek-Americans. Length: 100-200 words. Pays $10-15 with b&w photos.

Tips: "We want original, informative, lively pieces that illuminate an aspect of Greek culture or life in America. Travel articles on Greece must be well researched, factual, sophisticated. Investigative pieces and personality profiles are more apt to be published than historical/nostalgic. Follow *Writer's Market* guidelines on submissions."

Food and Drink

Magazines appealing to readers' appreciation of fine wines and fine foods are classified here. Journals aimed at food processing, manufacturing, and retailing will be found in Trade Journals. Magazines covering nutrition for the general public are listed in the Health and Fitness category.

BON APPETIT, Knapp Communications, 5900 Wilshire Blvd., Los Angeles CA 90036. Editor-in-Chief: Paige Rense. Editor: Marilou Vaughan. Emphasizes food, cooking and wine "for affluent young, active men and women, interested in the good things of life." Monthly magazine. Circ. 1.3 million. Pays on acceptance for first rights. Submit seasonal/holiday material 6 months in advance. Reports in 6 weeks.
Nonfiction: William J. Garry, managing editor. How-to cook, and food articles with recipes. No historical food pieces. "We use only highly skilled food and wine writers." Query. Length: 2,000 words. Pay varies.

‡**THE COOK'S MAGAZINE, The Magazine of Cooking in America**, Pennington Publishing, 1698 Post Road E., Westport CT 06880. (203)255-8594. Editor: Judith Hill. A bimonthly magazine on cooking and food. "We take a direct approach to the subject of cooking in America and appeal to professionals and knowledgable cooks." Circ. 130,000. Pays on publication. Byline given. Offers 50% kill fee. Buys all rights. Computer printout submissions acceptable. SASE.
Nonfiction: Cooking and food. No travel pieces; nothing on European cooking. Buys 30 mss/year. Query with published clips. Length: 600-1,200 words plus recipes. Pays $150-300.
Columns/Departments: Major food articles, Science of Cooking. Buys 30 mss/year. Query with published clips. Length: 600-1,200 words plus recipes. Pays $150-300.

CUISINE, 1515 Broadway, New York NY 10036. (212)719-6201. Editor-in-Chief: Corey Winfrey. 95% freelance written. Monthly. Study several issues of the publication and query first. Buys first rights only. Computer printout submissions acceptable. SASE.

FOOD & WINE, Int. Review of Food & Wine Associates, an affiliate of American Express Publishing Corp., 1120 Avenue of the Americas, New York NY 10036. (212)386-5600. Editor: William Rice. Managing Editor: Warren Picower. Monthly magazine covering food and wine for "an upscale audience who cook, entertain, dine out and travel stylishly." 40-60% freelance written (varies from issue to issue). Circ. 400,000. Pays on acceptance. Byline or "signer" at the end is given. Pays 25% kill fee. Buys one-time world rights, first rights, and on occasion, second (reprint) rights to material originally published elsewhere. Submit seasonal/holiday material 6 months in advance. Computer printout submissions acceptable, "if completely legible"; prefers letter-quality to dot-matrix. SASE. Reports in 1 month; "letters of agreement are issued on every assignment.' Publishing time after acceptance "varies enormously because so much is seasonal."
Nonfiction: Contact: Catherine Bigwood, senior editor. How-to entertain, prepare and present food, or equip a kitchen; service/tips-oriented interviews (of chefs, restaurateurs, or persons who entertain well and are especially knowledgeable in food and wine); and "very specialized articles on food and wine worldwide." Contact John and Elin Walker on all beverage queries. Buys 75 mss/year. Query, "detailing an idea with a special slant for our magazine." Length: 1,000-2,200 words; "2,200-word maximum with or without recipes." Pays $800-1,800, "depending on length, amount of work involved, and quality."
Columns/Departments: Contact: Restaurants: Stanley Dry; Wine & Beverages: John and Elin Walker. Query. Length: 200-500 words. Pays $200. What's New (people, products, places, events): Warren Picower. Query. Length 100-200 words. Pays $100.
Tips: "In response to well-thought out proposals, quite a few assignments are made to writers we were not previously familiar with."

‡**THE GARDEN GOURMET, A Cooking and Gardening Journal**, Opportunity Press, Inc., Suite 1405, 6 N. Michigan Ave., Chicago IL 60602. (312)346-4790. Editor: Mary Ann Hickey. 80% freelance written. Monthly tabloid on cooking and gardening aimed at people interested in cooking with fresh produce and spices. Circ. 15,000. Pays on acceptance. Byline given. Offers 50% kill fee. Buys first North American serial rights and second (reprint) rights to material originally published elsewhere. Submit seasonal/holiday material 4 months in advance. Simultaneous queries and photocopied submissions OK. Computer printout submissions acceptable. Reports in 2 weeks on queries; 1 month on mss. Publishes ms an average of 2 months after accept-

ance. Sample copy for $2.50, 9x12 SAE, and 5 first class stamps.

Nonfiction: How-to, interview/profile, and new product. Query with published clips. Length: 800-3,500 words. Pays $75-300.

Photos: State availability of photos. Reviews b&w contact sheets and color transparencies. Model release and identification of subjects required. Buys one-time rights.

Tips: "We report on regional cuisine, i.e., local chefs, restaurants, unique cooking methods, people who grow, produce and cook. Interview/profile of chefs and unique individuals growing and cooking their own food are the areas most open to freelancers."

THE WINE SPECTATOR, M. Shanken Communications, Inc., Opera Plaza Suite 2040, 601 Van Ness Ave., San Francisco CA 94102. (415)673-2040. Editor/Publisher: Marvin R. Shanken. 35-40% freelance written. Twice monthly consumer newspaper covering wine. Circ. 32,000. Byline given. Buys first rights. Query. Submit seasonal/holiday material 3 months in advance. Computer printout submissions acceptable "as long as they are legible." SASE. Reports in 3 weeks. Publishes ms an average of 2 months after acceptance. Sample copy $1; free writer's guidelines.

Nonfiction: General interest (about wine or wine events); historical (on wine); how-to (build a wine cellar, taste wine, decant, etc.); humor; interview/profile (of wine; vintners, wineries); opinion; and photo feature. No "winery promotional pieces or articles by writers who lack sufficient knowledge to write below just surface data." Query with clips of published work. Length: 800-900 words average. Pays $100/base.

Photos: Send photos with ms. Pays $25 minimum for b&w contact sheets and 5x7 prints. Identification of subjects required. Buys one-time rights.

Tips: "A solid knowledge of wine is a must. Query letters help, detailing the story idea; many freelance writers do not understand what a query letter is and how important it is to selling an article. New, refreshing ideas which have not been covered before stand a good chance of acceptance. *The Wine Spectator* is a consumer-oriented *newspaper* but we are interested in some trade stories; brevity is essential."

WINE TIDINGS, Kylix International, Ltd., 5165 Sherbrooke St. W., 414, Montreal, Quebec H4A 1T6 Canada. (514)481-5892. Managing Editor: Judy Rochester. Magazine published 8 times/year primarily for men with incomes of over $40,000. "Covers anything happening on the wine scene in Canada." Circ. 28,000. Pays on publication. Byline given. Buys all rights. Submit seasonal/holiday material 3 months in advance. Computer printout submissions acceptable; prefers letter-quality to dot-matrix. Reports in 1 month.

Nonfiction: J. Rochester, articles editor. General interest; historical; humor; interview/profile; new product (and developments in the Canadian and US wine industries); opinion; personal experience; photo feature; and travel (to wine-producing countries). "All must pertain to wine or wine-related topics and should reflect author's basic knowledge of and interest in wine." Buys 20-30 mss/year. Send complete ms. Length: 500-2,000 words. Pays $25-200.

Photos: State availability of photos. Pays $10-100 for color prints; $10 for b&w prints. Identification of subjects required. Buys one-time rights.

WINE WORLD MAGAZINE, Suite 115, 6308 Woodman Ave., Van Nuys CA 91401. (213)785-6050. Editor-Publisher: Dee Sindt. For the wine-loving public (adults of all ages) who wish to learn more about wine. Bimonthly magazine; 48 pages. Buys first North American serial rights. Buys about 50 mss/year. Pays on publication. Send $1 for sample copy and writer's guidelines. No photocopied submissions. Simultaneous submissions OK "if spelled out." Query. SASE.

Nonfiction: "Wine-oriented material written with an in-depth knowledge of the subject, designed to meet the needs of the novice and connoisseur alike. Wine technology advancements, wine history, profiles of vintners the world over. Educational articles only. No first-person accounts. Must be objective, informative reporting on economic trends, new technological developments in vinification, vine hybridizing, and vineyard care. New wineries and new marketing trends. We restrict our editorial content to wine, and wine-oriented material. Will accept restaurant articles—good wine lists. No more basic wine information. No articles from instant wine experts. Authors must be qualified in this highly technical field." Length: 750-2,000 words. Pays $50-100.

WOMEN'S CIRCLE HOME COOKING, Box 1952, Brooksville FL 33512. Editor: Barbara Hall Pedersen. 95% freelance written. For women (and some men) of all ages who really enjoy cooking. "Our readers collect and exchange recipes. They are neither food faddists nor gourmets, but practical women and men trying to serve attractive and nutritious meals. Many work fulltime, and most are on limited budgets." Monthly magazine; 72 pages. Circ. 225,000. Pays on publication. Buys all rights. Submit seasonal/holiday material 6 months in advance. Computer printout submissions acceptable; prefers letter-quality to dot-matrix. SASE. Reports in 2-8 weeks. Publishes ms an average of 6 months after acceptance. Sample copy for large SASE.

Nonfiction: Expose, historical, how-to, informational, inspirational, nostalgia, photo feature and travel. "We like a little humor with our food, for the sake of digestion. Keep articles light. Stress economy and efficiency. Remember that at least half our readers must cook after working a fulltime job. Draw on personal experience to write an informative article on some aspect of cooking. We're a reader participation magazine. We don't go in for fad diets, or strange combinations of food which claim to cure anything." No medical advice or sick or gross humor. Buys 24 mss/year. Query. Length: 50-1,000 words. Pays 2-5¢/word.

Photos: State availability of photos. Pays $5 for 4x5 b&w or color sharp glossy prints; $35 minimum for 35 mm, 2¼x2¼ and 4x5 transparencies used on cover.

Fiction: Humorous fiction related to cooking and foods. Length: 1,200 words maximum. Pays 2-5¢/word.

Poetry: Light verse related to cooking and foods. Length: 30 lines. Pays $5/verse.

Fillers: Short humorous fillers. Length: 100 words. Pays 2-5¢/word.

Tips: Good articles discuss some aspect of cooking and provide several recipes.

‡**ZYMURGY, Journal of the American Homebrewers Association**, American Homebrewers Association, Box 287, Boulder CO 80306. (303)447-0816. Editor: Charles N. Papazian. Managing Editor: Kathy McClurg. 10% freelance written. Quarterly magazine on homebrewing. Circ. 7,000. Pays on publication. Buys one-time rights. Submit seasonal/holiday material 5 months in advance. Simultaneous queries, and simultaneous, photocopied, and previously published submissions OK. Computer printout submissions acceptable. Publishes ms an average of 6 months after acceptance. SASE. Sample copy $3; free writer's guidelines.

Nonfiction: General interest (beer), historical (breweries), interview/profile (brewers), photo feature, and travel (breweries). Query. Length: 750-2,000 words. Pays $25-75.

Photos: Reviews b&w contact sheets and 8x10 b&w prints. Captions, model releases, and identification of subjects required.

Fiction: Erotica and beer brewing. Buys 1-2 mss/year. Query. Length: 750-2,000 words. Pays negotiable rates.

Games and Puzzles

Playing games and solving puzzles can be serious business or an evening of enjoyment for readers of these publications. They are written by and for game enthusiasts—people interested both in traditional games and word puzzles and newer role-playing adventure and computer and video games. Additional home video game publications are listed in the Theatre, Movie, TV, and Entertainment section. Other puzzle markets may be found in the Juvenile section.

‡**ABYSS**, 1402 21st St. NW, Washington DC 20036. (512)477-1704. Editor: David F. Nalle. Managing Editor: Jon Schuller. 25% freelance written. Bimonthly magazine covering games (fantasy, science fiction, historical). "*Abyss* provides game background and theory articles for adult game players interested in expanding their sources and ideas, particularly in the area of interactive role-playing games. Our orientation is toward college-age gamers who take the hobby seriously as an educational and enlightening pursuit. We ask only for an open mind and an active imagination." Circ. 1,200-1,500. Pays on publication. Byline given. Buys one-time rights and first rights. Submit seasonal/holiday material 8 months in advance. Electronic submissions OK, but requires hard copy also. Computer printout submissions acceptable; prefers letter-quality to dot-matrix. SASE. Reports in 2 weeks on queries; 6 weeks on mss. Publishes ms an average of 4 months after acceptance. Sample copy for $1.50; free writer's guidelines.

Nonfiction: Expose (concentrate on major game companies like TSR, FGU, SJG, etc.); historical (preferably pre-20th century game-oriented); humor (preferably short game or fantasy related); new product reviews (games and small press items only); opinion (any gaming topic); technical (game design, game publishing, game variants); and articles on any gaming-related topic from a range of approaches. "Also bibliographical fantasy." No "why my campaign is wonderful" articles too closely wedded to only one game system." Buys 30 mss/year. Send complete ms. Length: 1,000-5,000 words. Pays $5-100.

Columns/Departments: John R. Davies, column/department editor. Berserkgang (opinion/expose); Worlds of . . . (fantasy or science fiction bibliographical relevant to gaming); In the Pentacle (demonscopy, send for sample); and In the Speculum (reviews of games, magazines and books). Buys 18 mss/year. Query. Length: 400-3,000 words. Pays $5-40.

Fiction: Adventure, fantasy, historical, horror and science fiction. "No derivative, pastiche or game-based fiction." Buys 8 mss/year. Send complete ms. Length: 1,000-5,000 words. Pays $5-100.

Tips: "The best way to break into *Abyss* is by writing good, short commentary or opinion articles with new information or perspectives. The areas most open to freelancers are In the Speculum (reviews must include copy of product or be assigned) and Worlds of . . . Query first to avoid duplication."

CHESS LIFE, United States Chess Federation, 186 Route 9W, New Windsor NY 12550. (914)562-8350. Editor: Frank Elley. 15% freelance written. Monthly magazine covering the chess world. Circ. 60,000. Pays variable fee. Byline given. Offers kill fee. Buys first or negotiable rights. Submit seasonal/holiday material 8 months in advance. Simultaneous queries, and simultaneous, photocopied and previously published submissions OK. Computer printout submissions acceptable. SASE. Reports in 1 month. Publishes ms an average of 6 months after acceptance. Free sample copy and writer's guidelines.
Nonfiction: General interest, historical, interview/profile, and technical—all must have some relation to chess. No "stories about personal experiences with chess. Buys 30-40 mss/year. Query with samples "if new to publication." Length: 3,000 words maximum.
Photos: Reviews b&w contact sheet and prints, and color prints and slides. Captions, model release and identification of subjects required. Buys all or negotiable rights.
Fiction: "Chess-related, high quality." Buys 1-2 mss/year. Pays variable fee.
Tips: "Articles must be written from an informed point of view—not from view of the curious amateur. Most of our writers are specialized in that they have sound credentials as chessplayers. Freelancers in major population areas (except New York and Los Angeles, which we already have covered) who are interested in short personality profiles and perhaps news reporting have the best opportunities. We're looking for more personality pieces on chessplayers around the country; not just the stars, but local masters, talented youths, and dedicated volunteers. Freelancers interested in such pieces might let us know of their interest and their range. Could be we know of an interesting story in their territory that needs covering."

‡**CHESS 'N STUFF**, Jeroyan Enterprises, 7210 Timothy Place, Longmont CO 80501. (303)652-3143. Editor: Raymond C. Alexis. Bimonthly magazine promoting the growth and enjoyment of chess (for the most part in a *nontechnical* way). Circ. 450. Pays on publication. Byline given. Submit seasonal/holiday material 2 months in advance. Electronic submissions on floppy disk (only) OK; must be compatible with TRS-80 Model III. Computer printout submissions acceptable. Sample copy $1.50.
Nonfiction: Historical/nostalgic; humor; interview/profile; opinion; personal experience (chess philately); photo feature (computer chess); and computer chess software reviews. Send complete ms. Length: 350-1,000 words. Payment negotiated on an individual basis.
Fiction: Humorous, science fiction on "fairy chess." Length: 350-1,000 words. Payment negotiable.
Poetry: Haiku on chess.
Fillers: Jokes, gags, anecdotes, and short humor. Length: 350 words maximum (generally).
Tips: "Contact us with questions. Art and cartoons must be camera-ready (either 1:1 or 2:1). Science fiction, fairy chess, chess art, chess cartoons, fillers and chess philately are the areas most open to freelancers."

‡**COMPUTER FUN**, Fun & Games Publishing, 902 Broadway, New York NY 10010. Editor: George Kopp. Managing Editor: Ms. Randi Hacker. Monthly magazine on recreational computing. "*Computer Fun* reaches an audience with a mean age of 17. While we aren't as technical as *Computer*, *Byte* or *Creative Computing*, we do recognize the sophistication of our audience and therefore require that writers not submit anything juvenile or condescending in style." Estab. 1982. Circ. 125,000. Pays on acceptance. Byline given. Offers 50% kill fee. Buys all rights and second (reprint) rights to material originally published elsewhere. Submit seasonal/holiday material 4 months in advance. Photocopied submissions OK. Computer printout submissions acceptable. SASE. Reports in 6 weeks on queries; 2 months on mss. Free sample copy; writer's guidelines for business-size SAE and 20¢ postage.
Nonfiction: How-to (computer hardware and software); technical (computer hardware and software); and articles on future technology in computing and software reviews. No humor, poetry, fiction, interviews or personal experience. "We try to limit our coverage to those computers that offer users a good deal of recreational software, i.e., the Apple, Commodore, Atari, Texas Instruments, TRS-80, Timex and IBM. While we don't do extensive reviewing of educational programs per se, we are an educational magazine in that we run articles on how to enhance home computer systems, on learning different computer languages, and on how to write programs." Buys 12 mss/year. Query with published clips. Length: up to 2,000 words. Pays $250-450.
Columns/Departments: "We run a monthly column called First Screening in which we publish game programs that have been written by our readers." Submit disk or cassette of game, complete computer printout, brief description, color picture of author and SASE. Pays $100.
Tips: "The best way to break in is to send us sample game reviews. Most of our freelancers started out in the game review section. Our reviews are short, pithy and strategy-oriented. Hits & Missiles, the game review section, is the area most open to freelancers."

‡**COMPUTER GAMES**, (formerly *Video Games Player*), Carnegie Publications, 888 7th Ave., New York NY 10106. Editor: Dan Gutman. Bimonthly magazine covering video and computer games for a "15-45-year-old audience." 50% freelance written. Circ. 135,000. Pays on publication. Byline given. Offers 25% kill fee. Buys all rights. Submit seasonal/holiday material 4 months in advance. Simultaneous queries and photocopied submissions OK. Computer printout submissions acceptable. SASE. Reports in 2 weeks. Publishes ms an average of 3 months after acceptance.

Nonfiction: General interest, how-to, humor, interview/profile, personal experience, photo feature and technical. No game reviews. Buys 48 mss/year. Query with published clips. Length: 1,000-2,500 words. Pays $200-400.

Photos: State availability of photos. Pays $15-50 for color transparencies. Captions and model release required. Buys all rights.

Columns/Departments: Feedback—column of reader opinion. Buys 6 mss/year. Send complete ms. Length: 1,000 words. Pays $50.

Fiction: Stories about computer games. Buys 3-4 mss/year. Send complete ms. Length: 2,000-2,500 words. Pays $300-400.

Tips: "Send me a query with an incredible idea nobody has done before, along with published samples of work."

‡**COMPUTER GAMING WORLD**, Golden Empire Publications, Box 4566, Anaheim CA 92803-4566. (714)776-4979. Editor: Russell Sipe. 50% freelance written. Bimonthly magazine on computer games (Apple, Atari, C-64). "*CGW* deals with commercially available computer games for the above listed machines; reviews, strategy and tactics, contest, game design articles, etc." Circ. 25,000. Pays on publication. Byline given. Buys first rights only. Submit seasonal/holiday material 2 months in advance. Photocopied submissions OK. Electronic submissions OK if compatible with CompuServe, The Source, or Applesoft text file. Computer printout submissions acceptable. SASE. Reports in 6 weeks. Sample copy $1.50; free writer's guidelines.

Nonfiction: How-to (design computer games), interview/profile, new product, game reviews and strategy articles. Buys 30-40 mss/year. Query. Length: 500-1,500 words. Pays 2-3¢/word.

Columns/Departments: "Other regular columns will be considered if subject is needed." Query with published clips or send complete ms. Length: 1,000-1,500 words. Pays $50 per installment of column.

Fiction: "We use *very little* fiction."

‡**DELL CHAMPION CROSSWORD PUZZLES, DELL CHAMPION VARIETY PUZZLES, and DELL CHAMPION WORDPLAY AND PUZZLE FUN**, Dell Publishing Co., Inc., 1 Dag Hammarskjold Plaza, New York NY 10017. (212)605-3460. Editor: Wayne Robert Williams. Senior Editor: Sandra Silbermintz. Bimonthly magazines for adults. "Although the majority of each of the magazines is devoted to puzzles, we feature editorial material that is of interest to puzzle solvers: contests; book, game and film reviews; interviews with puzzle and game personalities; puzzle related fiction or poetry; articles on events or trends in puzzles and games, and how-to articles." Estab. 1983. Pays on acceptance. Byline given. Offers variable kill fee. Buys all rights, second serial (reprint) rights, and makes work-for-hire assignments. Submit seasonal/holiday material 8 months in advance—seasonal material is not encouraged. Simultaneous queries, and photocopied and previously published submissions OK. Computer printout submissions acceptable. SASE. Reports in 1 month. Sample copy $2; writer's guidelines for 9x12 SAE.

Nonfiction: Book excerpts, how-to, humor, interview/profile, new product, opinion, personal experience, photo feature and technical. "Writers should keep in mind they are writing for puzzle solvers." Query with or without published clips, or send complete ms. Length: varies. Pays variable rate.

Photos: Send photos with query or ms. Reviews b&w contact sheets. Captions, model release, and identification of subjects required. Buys all rights.

Columns/Departments: Book/Game/Film Reviews; Puzzle News; Solve-It-Yourself Mysteries. Query with or without published clips, or send complete ms. Length: varies. Pays variable rate.

Fiction: Adventure, condensed novels, fantasy, humorous, mainstream, mystery, novel excerpts, science fiction and suspense. "Material must be of interest to puzzle solvers." Query with or without published clips, or send complete ms. Length: varies. Pays variable rate.

Poetry: Avant-garde, free verse, haiku, light verse, traditional. Length: varies. Pays variable rate.

Fillers: Jokes, gags, anecdotes, short humor. Length: varies. Pays variable rate.

Tips: "We are particularly interested in seeing: mysteries (especially solve-it-yourself mysteries) and material related to video, humor, trivia, wordplay and language. We are not interested in scholarly presentations. Writers should keep in mind that they are writing for an audience of puzzle solvers, and that our aim is entertainment, rather than education. In recent issues, we publish a history of jigsaw puzzles, a humorous 3-page poem on the theft of the English language, an article on the National Puzzlers League, reviews of board and video word games, and a behind-the-scenes look at crossword construction."

DRAGON® MAGAZINE, Monthly Adventure Role-Playing Aid, TSR, Inc., Box 110, Lake Geneva WI 53147. (414)248-3625. Editor: Kim Mohan. Monthly magazine of role-playing and adventure games and new trends in the gaming industry for adolescents and up. 95% freelance written. Circ. 120,000. Pays on publication. Byline given. Buys first North American serial rights for fiction; all rights for most articles. Submit seasonal/holiday material 6 months in advance. Simultaneous queries and photocopied submissions OK. Computer printout submissions acceptable. SASE. Reports in 2 weeks on queries; 5 weeks on submissions. Publishes ms an average of 4 months after acceptance. Sample copy $3; writer's guidelines for business size SAE and 2 first class stamps.

Nonfiction: Articles on the hobby of gaming and fantasy role-playing. No general articles on gaming hobby; "our article needs are *very* specialized. Writers should be experienced in gaming hobby and role-playing." Buys 100 mss/year. Query. Length: 1,000-10,000 words. Pays 3½-5¢/word.

Fiction: Patrick Price, fiction editor. Adventure, fantasy, science fiction, and pieces which deal with gaming hobby. No fiction based on a religious, metaphysical or philosophical theme; no rehashes of other authors' work or ideas. Buys 10 mss/year. Query. Length: 3,000-10,000 words. Pays 4-6¢/word.

Tips: "*Dragon Magazine* and the related publications of Dragon Publishing are *not* periodicals that the 'average reader' appreciates or understands. A writer must *be* a reader, and must share the serious interest in gaming our readers possess. It's particularly rewarding helping new writers break in."

‡**FTL, The Magazine of Science Fiction, Fantasy, and Gaming**, West End Games, Suite 4FE, 251 W. 30th St., New York NY 10001. (212)947-4828. Editor: Greg Costikyan. A quarterly trade paperback anthology series. Each issue contains a complete game; original science fiction, fantasy, and horror stories; and articles about games and gaming. Estab. 1984. Pays on acceptance. Byline given. Offers 100% kill fee. Buys first worldwide anthologization rights (nonexclusive). Submit seasonal/holiday material 6 months in advance. Photocopied and previously published submissions (if not previously published in North America) OK. Electronic submission OK if compatible with Apple II, text files. Computer printout submissions acceptable. SASE. Reports in 2 weeks on queries; 6 weeks on mss. Writer's guidelines for legal size SAE and 1 first class stamp.

Nonfiction: Book excerpts (from novels on which we base games); historical/nostalgic (life and society in pre-industrial societies); humor (science fiction, fantasy or horror-oriented); interview/profile (with authors and game designers); new product (book and game criticism); science articles; articles about games and gaming. No pseudo-science or dungeons. Buys 10 mss/year. Send complete ms. Length: 2,000-10,000 words. Pays 3-6¢/word.

Columns/Departments: Better Swords & Starships (discussions of the art of games mastering and how to do it better); Critical Mass (intelligent critical analysis of books [SF/F, horror] and games). Buys 8 mss/year. Query with published clips, send complete ms. Length: 1,000-4,000 words. Pays 3-6¢/word.

Fiction: Fantasy, horror, and science fiction. Buys 20 mss/year. Query or send complete ms. Length: 12,000 words maximum. Pays 5-10¢/word.

Poetry: Avant-garde, light verse, traditional. "No *Paris Review* level pretentions." Buys 6 poems/year. Submit maximum 3 poems. Length: open. Pays 25-50¢/line.

Tips: "Write stories with unusual ideas and approaches which nonetheless have recognizable characters and plots. If we feel a story can be made into an interesting game, we will pay an extra $50 upon acceptance as an option on the boardgame and role-playing game rights to the story. If we do publish a game based on the story, the author will receive an additional payment of as much as he was paid for the story alone for magazine publication of the game. If, for whatever reason, you cannot or do not wish to sell game rights to a story you submit to *FTL*, write 'first North American serial rights only; no game rights' across the first page of the manuscript."

GAMES, Playboy Enterprises, Inc., 515 Madison Ave., New York NY 10022. Editor: Jacqueline Damian. Monthly magazine featuring games, puzzles, mazes and brainteasers for people 18-49 years interested in verbal and visual puzzles, trivia quizzes, and original games. 50% freelance written. Circ. 650,000. Average issue includes 5-7 feature puzzles, paper and pencil games and fillers, bylined columns and 1-2 contests. Pays on publication. Byline given. Offers 25% kill fee. Buys all rights, first rights, first and second rights to the same material, and second (reprint) rights to material orgininally published elsewhere. Submit seasonal material 6 months in advance. Book reprints considered. Computer printout submissions acceptable; no dot-matrix. Reports in 6 weeks. Publishes ms an average of 6 months after acceptance. Free writer's guidelines with SASE.

Nonfiction: "We are looking for visual puzzles, rebuses, brainteasers and logic puzzles. We also want newsbreaks, new games, inventions, and news items of interest to game players." Buys 4-6 mss/issue. Query. Length: 500-2,000 words. Usually pays $110/published page.

Columns/Departments: Wild Cards (25-200 words, short brainteasers, 25-100 wordplay, number games, anecdotes and quotes on games). Buys 6-10 mss/issue. Send complete ms. Length: 25-200 words. Pays $10-100.

Fillers: Will Shortz, editor. Crosswords, cryptograms and word games. Pays $25-100.

‡**GIANT CROSSWORDS**, Scrambl-Gram, Inc., Puzzle Buffs International, 1772 State Road, Cuyahoga Falls OH 44223. (216)923-2397. Editors: C.J. Elum and C.R. Elum. Managing Editor: Carol L. Elum. 50% freelance written. Crossword puzzle and word game magazines issued quarterly. Pays on acceptance. No byline given. Buys all rights. Simultaneous queries OK. Computer printout submissions acceptable; no dot-matrix. SASE. Reports in several weeks. Publishes ms an average of 10 days after acceptance. "We furnish master grids and clue sheets and offer a 'how-to-make-crosswords' book for $6.

Nonfiction: Crosswords only. Query. Pays according to size of puzzle and/or clues.

‡**THE GRENADIER MAGAZINE, The Independent War Game Review**, J. Tibbetts & Son, Purveyers, 3833 Lake Shore Ave., Oakland CA 94610. (415)763-0928. Editor: Jeffry Tibbetts. Managing Editor: S.A. Jefferis-Tibbetts. 50% freelance written. Bimonthly magazine covering military simulation and history. Circ.

2,500. Pays on publication. Byline given. Buys all rights. Submit seasonal/holiday material 4 months in advance. Computer printout submissions acceptable. SASE. Reports in 1-2 weeks. Publishes ms an average of 4 months after acceptance. Sample copy for $3; writer's guidelines for legal-size SAE and 1 first class stamp.
Nonfiction: Historical/nostalgic, how-to, new product, opinion and technical. Buys 36 mss/year. Query. Length: 5,000-12,500 words. Pays $25-100.
Photos: John T. Lamont, photo editor. Send photos with query. pays $15 minimum for b&w contact sheets and for 8x10 b&w prints. Captions, model releases and identiciation of subjects required.
Columns/Departments: Donald Harrison, column/department editor. Solitaire Gaming, Short Reviews of new products, Book Reviews, Computer Reviews. Buys 108 mss/year. Send complete ms. Length: 150-500 words. Pays $5-15.

THE JOURNAL OF 20TH CENTURY WARGAMING, 1002 Warrington Dr., Austin TX 78753. (512)475-6719. Editor: Nick Schuessler. 15% freelance written. Hobby gaming magazine published 4-6 times/year covering twentieth century wargaming and military history aimed for a mature, adult wargaming audience. Circ. 1,200. Pays on publication. Buys first rights only. Byline given. Simultaneous queries and simultaneous, photocopied and previously published submissions OK. Computer printout submissions acceptable. SASE. Reports in 1 month. Publishes ms an average of 3 months after acceptance. Sample copy $2.50; free writer's guidelines.
Nonfiction: Historical, new product, and opinion. "All articles about games must deal with both the game itself and with the history that directs the game. Straight game review pieces, with simple descriptions of components and mechanics, are not accepted. Reviews or feature articles must compare the title under consideration to other titles previously published, as well as discuss both the history behind the game and how that history is (or is not) incorporated into the game design. Book reviews must provide a tie-in with either a game already published or a possible game topic." Query. Length: open. Pays negotiable rates "on a case-by-case" basis.

OFFICIAL CROSSWORD PUZZLES, DELL CROSSWORD PUZZLES, POCKET CROSSWORD PUZZLES, DELL WORD SEARCH PUZZLES, OFFICIAL WORD SEARCH PUZZLES, DELL PENCIL PUZZLES AND WORD GAMES, OFFICIAL PENCIL PUZZLES & WORD GAMES, DELL CROSSWORD SPECIALS, DELL CROSSWORDS AND VARIETY PUZZLES, DELL CROSSWORD YEARBOOK, and OFFICIAL CROSSWORD YEARBOOK, Dell Puzzle Publications, 245 E. 47th St., New York NY 10017. Editor: Rosalind Moore. For "all ages from 8 to 80—people whose interests are puzzles, both crosswords and variety features." 95% freelance written. Buys all rights. Computer printout submissions acceptable; prefers letter-quality to dot-matrix. SASE.
Puzzles: "We publish puzzles of all kinds, but the market here is limited to those who are able to construct quality pieces that can compete with the real professionals. See our magazines; they are the best guide to our needs. We publish quality puzzles which are well-conceived and well-edited, with appeal to solvers of all ages and in almost every walk of life. We are the world's leading name in puzzle publications and are distributed in many countries around the world in addition to the continental US. However, no foreign language puzzles, please! Our market for crosswords and anacrostics is very small, since long time contributors supply most of the needs in those areas. However, we are always willing to see material of unusual quality, or with a new or original approach. Since most of our publications feature variety puzzles in addition to the usual features, we are especially interested in seeing quizzes, picture features, and new and unusual puzzle features of all kinds. Please do not send us remakes of features we are now using. Send only one sample, please, and make sure name and address are in the upper left-hand corner. Nothing without an answer will be considered. Do not expect an immediate reply. Prices vary with the feature, but ours are comparable with the highest in the general puzzle field."

POWER/PLAY, Home Computing, Commodore Business Machines, 1200 Wilson Dr., West Chester PA 19380. (215)436-4211. Editor: Diane Lebold. Publisher: Neil Harris. Bimonthly magazine covering games and home computing for new computer owners interested in recreational computing. Circ. 165,000. Pays on publication. Byline given. Buys all rights; makes work-for-hire assignments. Submit seasonal/holiday material 6 months in advance. Simultaneous queries and previously published submissions OK. SASE. Reports in 1 month on queries; 2 months on mss. Free sample copy; writer's guidelines for legal-size SAE and 1 first class stamp.
Nonfiction: Book reviews; how-to (beat games); humor; new product (reviews); personal experience (learning from computers); photo feature; and computers for kids. "No highly technical material. Send that to *Commodore Microcomputers* instead." Buys 20 mss/issue. Query or send complete ms. Length: 1,000-8,000 words. Pays $50-100/page.
Photos: Send photos with ms. Reviews 5x7 b&w and color prints. Captions and identification of subjects required. Buys all rights.
Tips: "We're open to game reviews and advice and game programs. Find an interesting slant on computing at home!"

‡**VIDEO GAMES MAGAZINE**, Pumpkin Press, 350 5th Ave., New York NY 10118. (212)947-4322. Editor: Roger C. Sharpe. Managing Editor: Patricia Canole. Monthly magazine covering home and arcade video games and computers. Circ. 100,000. Pays on publication. Byline given. Offers 20% kill fee. Buys first North American serial rights. Submit seasonal/holiday material 3 months in advance. Simultaneous queries and photocopied submissions OK. SASE. Reports in 2 weeks. Free sample copy and writer's guidelines.

Nonfiction: Book excerpts; general interest; historical/nostalgic; how-to (game tips and playing strategies); interview/profile; new product; and personal experience. "We look for editorial coverage of the game, toy and computer industries—interviews, game reviews, product reviews and general business trend overviews." Special issues include Special End-of-the-Year Celebration of Games. No poetry. Buys 120 mss/year. Query with published clips. Length: 1,500-2,500 words. Pays $200-400.

Photos: State availability of photos. Pays $10-25 for b&w contact sheet and b&w transparencies; $50-100 for color transparencies. Captions, model release and identification of subjects required. Buys one-time rights.

Columns/Departments: Blips (short news items and mini-features on latest breaking developments); Game Efforts (product reviews); Hard Sell (system reviews); Soft Touch (computer game software reviews); and Book Beat (book reviews). Buys 80 mss/year. Query with published clips. Length: 1,000-3,000 words. Pays $200-450.

Fiction: "Looking for pieces with an obvious video or computer game slant." Buys 12 mss/year. Query with published clips. Length: 1,500-3,000 words. Pays $300-500.

Tips: "Look at back issues to familiarize yourself with our editorial content and style; then submit ideas which we will respond to. Part of the problem is finding individuals who understand the uniqueness of our publication in terms of subject matter; however, everything is open for those writers who can cover the material."

General Interest

General interest magazines, though edited for national, general audiences, can be as diverse as the families in a neighborhood. And each magazine develops a "personality"—one that a writer should study before sending *general* material to an editor. General interest magazines carry articles on subjects appealing to a broad spectrum of people. Other markets for general interest material will be found in these Consumer categories: Ethnic/Minority, In-Flight, Lifestyles, Men's, Regional, and Women's. Some company publications also cover general interest topics.

THE AMERICAN LEGION MAGAZINE, Box 1055, Indianapolis IN 46206. (317)635-8411. Editor: Daniel S. Wheeler. Monthly. 95% freelance written. Circ. 2,500,000. Buys first North American serial rights. Computer printout submissions acceptable; prefers letter-quality to dot-matrix. Reports on submissions "promptly." Publishes ms an average of 6 months after acceptance. Byline given. Pays on acceptance. SASE.

Nonfiction: Query first, but will consider unsolicited mss. "Prefer an outline query. Relate your article's thesis or purpose, tell why you are qualified to write it, the approach you will take and any authorities you intend to interview. War remembrance pieces of a personal nature (vs. historic in perspective) should be in ms form." Uses current world affairs, topics of contemporary interest, little-known happenings in American history and 20th century war-remembrance pieces, and 750-word commentaries or contemporary problems and points of view. No personality profiles, travel or regional topics. Buys 60 mss/year. Length: 2,000 words maximum. Pays $100-2000.

Photos: Chiefly on assignment.

Poetry: Short, humorous verse. Pays $4.50/line, minimum $10.

Fillers: Short, tasteful jokes, humorous anecdotes and epigrams. Pays $10-20.

Tips: Query should include author's qualifications for writing a technical or complex article. Also include: thesis, length, outline and conclusion. "Send a thorough query. Submit material that is suitable for us, showing that you have read several issues. Attach a few clips of previously published material. *The American Legion Magazine* considers itself '*the* magazine for a strong America.' Any query reflective of this theme (which includes strong economy, educational system, moral fiber, infrastructure and armed forces) will be given priority."

THE ATLANTIC MONTHLY, 8 Arlington St., Boston MA 02116. (617)536-9500. Editor-in-Chief: William Whitworth. For a professional, academic audience interested in politics, science, arts and general culture. Monthly magazine. Circ. 440,000. Pays soon after acceptance. Buys first North American serial rights. Pays negotiable kill fee "though chiefly to established writers." Byline given. Phone queries OK though written queries preferred. Submit seasonal/holiday material 3-5 months in advance. Simultaneous and photocopied submissions OK, if so indicated. SASE. Reports in 2-8 weeks. Sample copy $2.

Nonfiction: General interest, historical, humor, interview, nostalgia, personal experience, personal opinion, profile and travel. Query with clips of published work or send complete ms. Length: 1,000-6,000 words. Pays $1,500 and up/article.

Fiction: Mainstream. Buys 2 mss/issue. Send complete ms. Length: 2,000-6,000 words. Pays $2,000 and up/story.

Poetry: Avant-garde, free verse, light verse and traditional. "No concrete or haiku poetry." Buys 2-4 poems/issue. Submit in batches of 2-6. Length: 100 lines maximum. Pays $3 and up/line.

‡**THE BEST REPORT, "Exploring the World of Quality,"** Best Publications, Inc., Suite 4210, 350 Fifth Ave., New York NY 10118. (212)239-4400. Publisher: Norman Aronson. Monthly newsletter that "establishes qualitative hierarchies in goods, services, experiences." Circ. over 70,000. Pays on publication. No byline given. Offers negotiable kill fee; usually 25%. Buys all rights and second (reprint) rights to material originally published elsewhere, and makes work-for-hire assignments. Submit seasonal/holiday material 3 months in advance. Simultaneous queries. Computer printout submissions acceptable. SASE. Reports in 3 weeks on queries. Free sample copy and writer's guidelines.

Nonfiction: Book excerpts, how-to (buying guides, travel guides), new product, and travel. Buys 100 + mss/year. Query. Features length: 1,000 words (generally). Pays average 30¢/word.

Tips: "We want authoritative, documented reporting on 'bests' in any field of consumer-oriented quality. Short (250-500 words) items on goods, services of interest to high-income ($100,000-plus) audience are most open to freelancers."

A BETTER LIFE FOR YOU, The National Research Bureau, Inc., 424 N. 3rd St., Burlington IA 52601. (319)752-5415. Editor: Rhonda Wilson. Editorial Supervisor: Doris J. Ruschill. 75% freelance written. For industrial workers of all ages. Quarterly magazine. Pays on publication. Buys all rights. Previously published submissions OK. Computer printout submissions acceptable; prefers letter-quality to dot-matrix. SASE. Reports in 3 weeks. Publishes ms an average of 1 year after acceptance. Free writer's guidelines.

Nonfiction: General interest (steps to better health, on-the-job attitudes); and how-to (perform better on the job, do home repair jobs, and keep up maintenance on a car). Buys 10-12 mss/year. Query or send outline. Length: 400-600 words. Pays 4¢/word.

CAPPER'S WEEKLY, Stauffer Communications, Inc., 616 Jefferson St., Topeka KS 66607. (913)295-1108. Editor: Dorothy Harvey. 15% freelance written. Emphasizes home and family for readers who live in small towns and on farms. Biweekly tabloid. Circ. 400,000. Pays for poetry on acceptance; articles on publication. Buys first North American serial rights only. Submit seasonal/holiday material 2 months in advance. Computer printout submissions acceptable; prefers letter-quality to dot-matrix. SASE. Reports in 3 weeks; 8 months for serialized novels. Publishes ms an average of 1 year after acceptance. Sample copy 50¢.

Nonfiction: Historical (local museums, etc.), inspirational, nostalgia, travel (local slants) and people stories (accomplishments, collections, etc.). Buys 25 mss/year. Submit complete ms. Length: 700 words maximum. Pays $1/inch.

Photos: Purchased with accompanying ms. Submit prints. Pays $5 for 8x10 b&w glossy prints. Total purchase price for ms includes payment for photos. Limited market for color photos (35mm color slides, please).

Columns/Departments: Heart of the Home (homemakers' letters, recipes, hints), and Hometown Heartbeat (descriptive). Submit complete ms. Length: 300 words maximum. Pays $2-10.

Fiction: Novel-length mystery and romance mss. No explicit sex, violence or profanity. Buys 2-3 mss/year. Query. Pays $150-200.

Poetry: Free verse, haiku, light verse, and traditional. Buys 4-5/issue. Limit submissions to batches of 5-6. Length: 4-16 lines. Pays $3-5.

Tips: "Study a few issues of publication. Most rejections are for material that is 1) too long, 2) unsuitable (as short stories which we never use), or 3) out of character for our paper (too sexy, too much profanity, etc.). On occasion we must cut material to fit column space."

CHANGING TIMES, The Kiplinger Magazine, 1729 H St. NW, Washington DC 20006. Editor: Marjorie White. 5% freelance written. For general, adult audience interested in consumer information. Monthly. Circ. 1,350,000. Buys all rights. Reports in 1 month. Computer printout submissions acceptable. SASE. Pays on acceptance. Thorough documentation required.

Nonfiction: "Most material is staff-written but we accept some freelance." Query with clips of published work. No bylines.

THE CHRISTIAN SCIENCE MONITOR, 1 Norway St., Boston MA 02115. (617)262-2300, ext. 2303. Editor: Katherine W. Fanning. International newspaper issued daily except Saturdays, Sundays and holidays in

North America; weekly international edition. Special issues: travel, winter vacation and international travel, summer vacation, autumn vacation, and others. March and September: fashion. Circ. 160,000. Buys all newspaper rights for 3 months following publication. Buys limited number of mss, "top quality only." Publishes original (exclusive) material only. Pays on acceptance or publication, "depending on department." Submit seasonal material 2 months in advance. Reports in 4 weeks. Submit complete original ms or letter of inquiry. SASE. Writer's guidelines are available.

Nonfiction: Rushworth M. Kidder, feature editor. In-depth features and essays. Please query by mail before sending mss. "Style should be bright but not cute, concise but thoroughly researched. Try to humanize news or feature writing so reader identifies with it. Avoid sensationalism, crime and disaster. Accent constructive, solution-oriented treatment of subjects. Home Forum page buys essays of 400-900 words. Pays $70-140. Buys poetry of high quality in a wide variety (traditional, blank and free verse). Pays $25 average. Education, arts, real estate, travel, living, garden, books, sports, food, furnishings, and science pages will consider articles not usually more than 800 words appropriate to respective subjects." Pays $75-100.

COMMENTARY, 165 E. 56th St., New York NY 10022. (212)751-4000. Editor: Norman Podhoretz. Monthly magazine. Circ. 50,000. Byline given. "All of our material is done freelance, though much of it is commissioned." Pays on publication. Query, or submit complete ms. Reports in 1 month. SASE.

Nonfiction: Brenda Brown, editor. Thoughtful essays on political, social and cultural themes; general, as well as with special Jewish content. Length: 3,000 to 7,000 words. Pays approximately $100/printed page.

Fiction: Marion Magid, editor. Uses some mainstream fiction. Length: varies. Pays $100/printed page.

‡**COMMUTER DIGEST**, Marshall Douglas Publishing, 392 Quebec Ave., Toronto, Ontario M6P 2V4 Canada. (416)763-2591. Managing Editor: Jeff Paul. Monthly magazine. Estab. 1983. Circ. 80,000. Pays on publication. Byline given. Offers "half the word length payment" as kill fee. Buys first North American serial rights. Submit 3 months in advance. Simultaneous queries, and simultaneous and photocopied submissions OK. Computer printout submissions acceptable. "Only submissions with correct Canadian postage, IRCs, or $1 for postage and handling will be returned; no US postage." Reports in 1 month. Writer's guidelines for SAE (Canadian postage, IRCs, or $1 only). Envelopes with US postage will not be returned.

Nonfiction: Expose; general interest; historical/nostalgic (Canadian or international); how-to (light-hearted or humorous); humor; inspirational; interview/profile; new product (humorous in nature); personal experience (humorous); and travel (general). "Nothing of a pronographic or distasteful nature." Send complete ms. Length: 1,000-3,000 words. Pays 20¢-35¢/word.

Photos: Send photos with mss. Pays $15-25 for b&w prints and transparencies; $20-35 for color transparencies and prints. Model release required. Buys one-time rights.

Columns/Departments: Film Reviews, Travel, Consumer News, Secondary Sports (tennis, squash, etc.), Crossword Puzzles, Record Reviews (classical and jazz), Small Business, Photography, Television, and Interior Decorating Items. Send complete ms. Length: 1,500-2,000 words. Pays $300-600.

Fiction: Adventure, erotica (only of a humorous nature), historical, humorous, mainstream, mystery, romance, and science fiction. "Nothing distasteful or pornographic." Buys 35-40 mss/year. Send complete ms. Length: 1,500-2,000 words. Pays $300-450.

Poetry: No surrealism. Buys 30 poems/year. Submit maximum 5 poems. Length: 6-25 lines. Pays $15-35.

Fillers: Jokes, gags, anecdotes, and short humor. Buys 200/year. Length: 15-100 words. Pays $15-25. "Persons supplying very good short fillers on a continuous basis will have the opportunity to negotiate rates."

Tips: "Present easy-to-read, well laid out and researched mss. Humorous articles keep our magazine alive. Marshall Douglas has just purchased *Commuter Digest* and is making many changes to the content and format of the magazine."

DIALOGUE, The Magazine for the Visually Impaired, Dialogue Publications, Inc., 3100 Oak Park Ave., Berwyn IL 60402. (312)749-1908. Editor: Nolan Crabb. 50% freelance written. Quarterly magazine of issues, topics and opportunities related to the visually impaired. Pays on acceptance. Byline given. Buys all rights "with generous reprint rights." Submit seasonal/holiday material 6 months in advance. Photocopied submissions OK. Computer printout submissions acceptable; prefers letter-quality to dot-matrix. SASE. Reports in 2 weeks on queries; 1 month on mss. Publishes ms an average of 6 weeks after acceptance. Free sample copy to visually impaired writers; writer's guidelines for business-size SAE and 1 first class stamp.

Nonfiction: "Writers should indicate nature and severity of visual handicap." How-to (cope with various aspects of blindness); humor; interview/profile; new product (of interest to visually impaired); opinion; personal experience; technical (adaptations for use without sight); travel (personal experiences of visually impaired travelers); and first person articles about careers in which individual blind persons have succeeded. No "Aren't blind people wonderful" articles; articles that are slanted towards sighted general audience. Buys 60 mss/year. Query with published clips or submit complete ms. Length: 3,000 words maximum. Prefers shorter lengths but will use longer articles if subject warrants. Pays $10-50.

Photos: Stephen Flanagan, photo editor. Photographs of paintings, sculpture and pottery by visually handicapped artists; and photos taken by visually impaired persons. State availability or send photos with ms. Pays

Close-up

Rushworth M. Kidder
Feature Editor
The Christian Science Monitor

"I have a story and I'm going to do it for somebody—there's no question about that. It's a good story. It's going to find a home. I'm interested in knowing whether the *Monitor* might be the home."

That's the kind of attitude feature editor Rushworth Kidder looks for in professional writers.

He wants original—exclusive—material for *The Christian Science Monitor* sections he edits: Ideas, Arts and Leisure, and Home and Family. "We're very interested in getting specific feature stories from all parts of the country," he says. "One of the things I've always loved in my own writing and in editing other people's writing is a sense of a story of great significance from some tiny dateline that captures the flavor of the place yet has a significant enough story in it that the reader is going to want to follow it."

Writers with such a story to tell should send Kidder a one-page query. He can then discuss a length, an approach, and the direction for the article.

The poet and essayist also may find a home for their work in the *Monitor*. The daily Home Forum page uses more essays and poetry than most periodicals. Here, Kidder looks for personal introspective essays that depend on the quality of writing.

"One of the most valuable things we can do is to provide excellent writing in a fairly compact form on things that really do matter," says the author and former Wichita State University English professor, who joined the *Monitor* as its London correspondent in 1979. "The quality and finesse of the writing is what allows the reader to stay with the story so the real detail and educational part can come through."

The *Monitor* typically does not assign a writer to spend two or three months on a story. "In our own editing and selection of material, we really are a daily newspaper; we are not a magazine that happens to appear daily," says Kidder, who writes *TCSM*'s "Perspectives" column.

Kidder demands lively leads and quotes that compel the reader to finish a story. "Simply quoting because somebody said it is not enough. Is it a good quote; is it interesting in itself?" writers should ask themselves, he says. "Do you have a sense that the individual by the end of the story has stood up on the page the way a novelist would make him do, not by great excesses, but just with a few telling words. All of those things really allow the reader to make sense of the news and be interested in it."

The writer who doesn't read beyond the word, Christian, in the masthead might infer that the newspaper is committed to religion; it's purpose, actually is *education*—"to injure no man and bless all mankind." Though owned by the Christian Science Church, the *Monitor* is not a forum for the church's or Christian viewpoints. "We see ourselves as a solution-oriented paper," points out Kidder whose work with the *Monitor* began as a contributor. "We're not only interested in calling attention to some of the abysmal situations in the world, although that is crucial, but also insist that our own staff and contributors dig deep to find the people who are thinking about solutions to the problems."

Those kinds of stories will always find a home on Kidder's desk—and in *The Christian Science Monitor*.

$10-20 for 3½x4¾ b&w prints. Identification of subjects required. Buys one-time rights.

Columns/Departments: ABAPITA ("Ain't Blindness a Pain in the Anatomy")—short anecdotes relating to blindness; Recipe Round-UP, Around the House (household hints); Vox Pop (see magazine); Puzzle Box (see magazine and guidelines); book reviews of books written by visually impaired authors; Beyond the Armchair (travel personal experience); and Backscratcher (a column of questions, answers, hints). Buys 80 mss/year. Send complete ms. Payment varies.

Fiction: "Writers should state nature and severity of visual handicap." Annette Victorin, fiction editor. Adventure, fantasy, historical, humorous, mainstream, mystery, science fiction, suspense, and western. No plotless fiction or stories with unbelievable characters; no horror; no explicit sex and no vulgar language. Buys 12 mss/year. Send complete ms. Length: 3,000 words maximum; shorter lengths preferred. Pays $10-50.

Poetry: "Writers should indicate nature and severity of visual impairment." Annette Victorin, poetry editor. Free verse, haiku, light verse, and traditional. No religious poetry or any poetry with more than 20 lines. Buys 30 poems/year. Submit maximum 3 poems. Length: 20 lines maximum. Pays $5-20.

Fillers: Jokes, anecdotes, and short humor. Buys few mss/year. Length: 100 words maximum. Payment varies.

Tips: "*Dialogue* cannot consider manuscripts from authors with 20/20 vision or those who can read regular print with ordinary glasses. Any person unable to read ordinary print who has helpful information to share with others in this category will find a ready market. We believe that blind people are capable, competent, responsible citizens, and the material we publish reflects this view. This is not to say we never sound a negative note but criticism should be constructive."

EASY LIVING MAGAZINE, The Webb Co., 1999 Shepard Rd., St. Paul MN 55116. (612)690-7228. Editor: Peggy Brown Black. 90% freelance written. Emphasizes financial topics—personal finance, career, money management, consumer; and some foreign travel and food articles for a high-income audience 30-60 years of age. Published by Webb Company for financial institutions. Quarterly magazine. Circ. 250,000. Pays on acceptance. Buys one-time rights and nonexclusive reprint rights. Submit seasonal/holiday material 1 year in advance. Photocopied submissions OK. Computer printout submissions acceptable. SASE. Reports on queries and mss in 3-6 weeks. Publishes ms an average of 4 months after acceptance. Free sample copy and writer's guidelines. Nonfiction only. No first person or personal experience. Query. Length: 1,000-2,000 words. Pays $200-600.

Photos: Contact Rudy Schnasse at (612)690-7396 for current rates.

EQUINOX: THE MAGAZINE OF CANADIAN DISCOVERY, Equinox Publishing, 7 Queen Victoria Dr., Camden East, Ontario K0K 1J0 Canada. (613)378-6651. Editor: James Lawrence. Managing Editor: Bart Robinson. Executive Editor: Frank B. Edwards. Bimonthly magazine. "We publish in-depth profiles of people, places and wildlife to show readers the real stories behind subjects of general interest in the fields of science and geography." Circ. 150,000. Pays on acceptance. Byline given. Offers 50% kill fee. Buys first North American serial rights only. Submit seasonal/holiday material 1 year in advance. SAE and IRCs. Computer printout submissions acceptable; prefers letter-quality to dot-matrix. Reports in 6 weeks. Sample copy $5; free writer's guidelines.

Nonfiction: Book excerpts (occasionally), geography, science and art. No travel articles. Buys 40 mss/year. Query. "Our biggest need is for science stories. We do not touch unsolicited feature manuscripts." Length: 5,000-10,000 words. Pays $1,500-negotiated.

Photos: Send photos with ms. Reviews color transparencies—must be of professional quality; no prints or negatives. Captions and identification of subjects required.

Columns/Departments: Nexus, current science that isn't covered by daily media. "Our most urgent need." Buys 80/year. Query with clips of published work. Length: 500-1,000 words. Pays $250-350.

Tips: Submit 'Nexus' ideas to us—the 'only' route to a feature is through the 'Nexus' department if writers are untried."

FAMILY WEEKLY, The Newspaper Magazine, CBS, Inc., 1515 Broadway, New York NY 10036. (212)719-6976. Editor: Thomas Plate. Executive Editor: Kate White. Managing Editor: Tim Mulligan. Sunday newspaper supplement. Weekly magazine. Circ. 12.5 million. Pays on acceptance. Byline given. Kill fee varies (usually about 20%). Buys first North American serial rights. Submit seasonal/holiday material at least two months in advance. No simultaneous, photocopied or previously published submissions. SASE. Reports in 1 month on queries. Sample copy and writer's guidelines for SAE.

Nonfiction: "A writer's best bet is to simply read the magazine." Query with clips of published work. Length: 600-2,500 words. Pay varies.

Tips: "A freelancer can best break into our publication with good ideas and clips."

FORD TIMES, Ford Motor Co., Box 1899, The American Rd., Rm. 765, Dearborn MI 48121-1899. Editor: Arnold S. Hirsch. 75% freelance written. "General-interest magazine designed to attract all ages." Monthly magazine. Circ. 1,200,000. Buys first rights only. Pays kill fee. Byline given. Buys about 100 mss/year. Pays on acceptance. Submit seasonal material 6 months in advance. Computer printout submissions acceptable. Reports in 1 month. Publishes ms an average of 1 year after acceptance. Free sample copy and writer's guidelines. SASE.

Nonfiction: "Almost anything relating to contemporary American life that is upbeat and positive. Topics include lifestyle trends, vacation ideas, profiles, insights into big cities and small towns, the arts, the outdoors, and sports. We are especially interested in subjects that appeal to readers in the 18-35 age group. We also are beginning to use stories with international settings. We strive to be colorful, lively and, above all, interesting. We try to avoid subjects that have appeared in other publications or in our own." Length: 1,500 words maximum. Query required unless previous contributor. Pays $450 minimum for full-length articles.

Photos: "Speculative submission of high-quality color transparencies and b&w photos with mss is welcomed. We need bright, graphically strong photos showing people. We need releases for people whose identity is readily apparent in photos."

FRIENDLY EXCHANGE, Webb Company, 1999 Shepard Rd., St. Paul MN 55116. (612)690-7383. Editor: Adele Malott. 85% freelance written. Quarterly magazine "designed to encourage the sharing or exchange of ideas, information and fun among its readers, for young, traditional families between the ages of 19 and 39 who live in the western half of the United States." Circ. 4.5 million. Pays on acceptance. Offers 25% kill fee. Buys first North American serial rights and non-exclusive reprint rights for use in other Webb publications. Submit seasonal/holiday material 9 months in advance. Simultaneous queries and photocopied submissions OK. Computer printout submissions acceptable. SASE. Reports in 8 weeks. Publishes ms an average of 5 months after acceptance. Sample copy free for 9x12 SASE and postage; writer's guidelines free for business-size SAE and 1 first class stamp.

Nonfiction: General interest (family activities, sports and outdoors, consumer topics); historical/nostalgic (heritage and culture); how-to (decorate and garden); travel (domestic); and family lifestyle. "Whenever possible, a story should be told through the experiences of actual people or families in such a way that our readers will want to share experiences they have had with similar activities or interests. No product publicity material." Buys 10 unsolicited mss/year. Query. Length: 1,000-2,500 words. Pays $300-700/article.

Photos: Contact: Webb Company, art director. Send photos with ms. Pays $150-400 for 35mm color transparencies; and $75 for 8x10 b&w prints. Pays on publication.

Columns/Departments: All columns and departments rely on reader-generated ideas, recipes, household hints, etc. Study articles from Summer 1983 and Winter 1983 "Ice Cream" and "Does Your Neighborhood Do Anything?"

FUTURIFIC MAGAZINE, 280 Madison Ave., New York NY 10016. (212)684-4913. Editor: Balint Szent-Miklosy. 100% freelance written. Monthly. *FUTURIFIC* is a nonprofit research organization set up in 1976 to study the future. "We report on what is coming in all areas of life from international affairs to the arts and sciences. Mostly read by high income, well-educated government and corporate people." Circ. 10,000. Pays on publication. Byline given. Buys first rights, first and second rights to the same material and second (reprint) rights to material originally published elsewhere. Simultaneous, photocopied and previously published submissions OK. Computer printout submissions acceptable. SASE. Reports in 1 week. Publishes ms an average of 1 month after acceptance. Sample copy for 9x12 SAE and 37¢ postage.

Nonfiction: All subjects must deal with the future: book excerpts, expose, general interest, how to forecast the future—seriously, humor, interview/profile, new product, photo feature, and technical. No historical, opinion or gloom and doom. Send complete ms. Length: 5,000 words maximum. "The writer tells us the price. We either accept or reject."

Photos: Send photos with ms. Reviews b&w prints. "The photographer lets us know how much he/she wants." Identification of subjects required.

Columns/Departments: Medical breakthroughs, new products, inventions, etc. "Anything that is new or about to be new." Send complete ms. Length: 5,000 words maximum.

Poetry: Avant-garde, free verse, haiku, light verse, and traditional. "Must deal with the future." No gloom and doom or sad poetry. Buys 12/year. Submit unlimited number of poems. Length: open. Pay is "up to the poet."

Fillers: Clippings, jokes, gags, anecdotes, short humor, and newsbreaks. "Must deal with the future." Length: open. Pay is "up to the person submitting."

Tips: "We seek to maintain a light-hearted, professional look at forecasting. Be upbeat and show a loving expectation for the marvels of the future. Take any subject or concern you find in regular news magazines and extrapolate as to what the future will be. Use imagination. Get involved in the excitement of the international developments, social interaction, etc."

GEO, Knapp Communications Corp., 140 E. 45th St., New York NY 10017. (212)687-8666. Managing Editor: Kevin Buckly. Monthly magazine giving "a new view of our world in terms of science, environment, places and issues for sophisticated people with wide ranging international interests." Circ. 250,000. Pays on acceptance. Buys first North American serial rights. Submit seasonal material 4 months in advance. Simultaneous and photocopied submissions OK. SASE. Reports in 2 months. Sample copy $5.

Nonfiction: Historical (natural history); interview (of authorities in fields of *Geo*'s interest); opinion (essays); personal experience; photo feature (of recent topics, such as the tops of New York skyscrapers or machine parts as art); technical (frontiers of technology, science and medicine); and new scientific thinking, top level scientific research, such as studying the squid to learn about the human nervous system. "No pure travel pieces." Buys 8-10 mss/issue. "It is relatively rare that we use an unsolicited manuscript, and we do not encourage their submission. We prefer concise, clearly stated queries, explaining the story idea, the proposed approach and the photographic possibilities. Short clips from other publications are helpful. *Geo* stories often require a hefty investment, so it is unusual that we send an inexperienced writer on assignment." Query with clips of published work. Length: 3,000 words maximum. Pays $2,500 average. "The writer does not need to be an authority but must get to the top people in science, the environment and current issues."

Photos: Elizabeth Biondi, editor. State availability of photos. Reviews all sizes color prints and transparencies. Gives guarantee upon acceptance against $250/page upon publication. Captions and model release required. Buys one-time rights.

Tips: "All story ideas must have a very strong photo tie-in. You need not take photos. *Geo* will provide the photographer."

GLOBE, Cedar Square, 2112 S. Congress Ave., West Palm Beach FL 33406. Associate Editor: Robert Taylor. "For everyone in the family. *Globe* readers are the same people you meet on the street and in supermarket lines, average hard-working Americans who prefer easily digested tabloid news." Weekly national tabloid newspaper. Circ. 2,000,000. Byline given. SASE.

Nonfiction and Fillers: We want features on well-known personalities, offbeat people, places, events and activities. No personal essays. Current issue is best guide. Stories are best that don't grow stale quickly. No padding. Remember—we are serving a family audience. All material must be in good taste. If it's been written up in a major newspaper or magazine, we already know about it." Buys informational, how-to, interview, profile, inspirational, humor, historical, exposé, photo, and spot news. Length: 1,000 words maximum; average 500-800 words. Pays $250 maximum (special rates for "blockbuster" material).

Photos: Alistair Duncan, photo editor. Photos are purchased with or without ms, and on assignment. Captions are required. Pays $50 minimum for 8x10 b&w glossy prints. "Competitive payment on exclusives."

Tips: "*Globe* is constantly looking for human interest subject material from throughout the United States, and much of the best comes from America's smaller cities and villages, not necessarily from the larger urban areas. Therefore, we are likely to be more responsive to an article from a new writer than many other publications. This, of course, is equally true of photographs. A major mistake of new writers is that they have failed to determine the type and style of our content, and in the ever-changing tabloid field this is a most important consideration. It is also wise to keep in mind that what is of interest to you or to the people in your area may not be of equal interest to a national readership. Determine the limits of interest first. And, importantly, the material you send us must be such that it won't be 'stale' by the time it reaches the readers."

GOOD READING, Henry F. Henrichs Publications, Litchfield IL 62056. (217)324-2322. 95% freelance written. Monthly magazine. Circ. 8,000. Buys 30-50 unsolicited mss/year. Computer printout submissions acceptable. Buys first North American serial rights. Pays on acceptance. Publishes ms an average of 8 months after acceptance. SASE.

Nonfiction: Accurate articles on current or factual subjects, adventure or important places or successful people. Material based on incidents related to business or personal experiences that reveal the elements of success in human relationships. Humorous material welcome. Uses one quiz a month. All published material is wholesome and noncontroversial. No "over emphasized or common topics; no how-to articles or expositions." Length: 500-900 words. Pays $20-100.

Photos: Good quality b&w glossy prints illustrating an article are desirable and should be submitted with the article.

Fillers: 200-500 words. Pays $10-20.

Poetry: Does not pay for poetry, but publishes 4-5/month. Prefers pleasantly rhythmic humorous or uplifting material of 4-16 lines.

Tips: "In our magazines the trend is toward better-written, more professional-looking manuscripts. We no longer have time to tighten up manuscripts to make them acceptable for publication."

‡**GOODWIN'S**, Goodwin's Foundation Inc., Box 1043, Station B, Ottawa, Ontario K1P 5R1 Canada. (613)234-8928. Editor: Ron Verzuh. 75% freelance written. Quarterly magazine on social affairs and issues. "*Goodwin's* puts issues (workplace democracy, sexism, racism, energy, new technology, housing, health care, day care) into a broad alternative perspective by reporting on people's common problems, analyzing the roots of those problems, and showing how they are being tackled across the country." Estab. 1983. Circ. 4,500. Pays negotiable rates. Byline given. Offers negotiable kill fee. Buys first North American serial rights only. No photocopied or previously published submissions. Computer printout submissions acceptable if double-spaced. Reports in 1 month. Publishes ms an average of 4 months after acceptance. Sample copy $2.50; writer's guidelines for business-size SAE and 37¢ postage.

Nonfiction: Book excerpts (investigative), and expose (social or economic issue). No fiction, poetry, strident tracts or unjournalist writing. Buys 12 mss/year. Query with published clips. Length: 300-3,000 words. Pays in copies and up to $500.
Photos: State availability of photos. Pays $5-100 for 35mm color transparencies; $5-100 for 8x10 b&w prints. Captions, model release and identification of subjects required. Buys one-time rights.
Columns/Departments: Buys 12 mss/year. Query with published clips. Length: 750-1,000 words. Pays in copies and up to $100.
Tips: "Query first with clips; be prepared to rewrite. Organizing section (short items on unique organizing efforts by labor, students, women, poor people, natives, and other social movements) is most open to freelancers. Watch for the investigative element when developing story queries and outlines."

GRIT, Stauffer Communications, Inc., 208 W. 3rd St., Williamsport PA 17701. (717)326-1771. Editor: Naomi L. Woolever. 33% freelance written. For a general readership of all ages in small town and rural America. Tabloid newspaper. Weekly. Circ. 776,000. Buys first and second rights to the same material. Byline given. Buys 1,000-1,500 mss/year. Pays on acceptance for freelance material; on publication for reader participation feature material. Computer printout submissions acceptable; no dot-matrix. Publishes ms an average of 2 months after acceptance. Sample copy $1; free writer's guidelines. Reports in 2-4 weeks. Query or submit complete ms. SASE.
Nonfiction: Contact Joanne Decker, assignment editor. "Want mss about six basic areas of interest: people, religion, jobs (how individuals feel about their work), recreation, spirit of community (tradition or nostalgia that binds residents of a town together), and necessities (stories about people and how they cope—food, shelter, etc.) Also want sociological pieces about rural transportation and health problems or how a town deals effectively with vandalism or crime. Also first-person articles of 300 words or less about a person's narrowest escape, funniest moment, a turning point in life, or recollections of something from the past, i.e., a flood, a fire, or some other dramatic happening that the person experienced." Want good Easter, Christmas and holiday material. Mss should show some person or group involved in an unusual and/or uplifting way. "We lean heavily toward human interest, whatever the subject. Writing should be simple and down-to-earth." No "articles promoting alcoholic beverages, immoral behavior, narcotics, or unpatriotic acts." Length: 500 words maximum. Pays 12¢/word for first or exclusive rights; 6¢/word for second or reprint rights.
Photos: Photos purchased with or without ms. Captions required. No "deep shadows on (photo) subjects." Size: prefers 8x10 for b&w, but will consider 5x7. Transparencies only for color. Pays $25 for b&w photos accompanying ms; $100 for front cover color photos.
Poetry: Contact Joanne Decker. Buys traditional forms of poetry and light verse. Length: preferably 20 lines maximum. Pays $6 for 4 lines and under, plus 50¢/line for each additional line.
Tips: "The most rewarding aspect of working with freelance writers is coming across a writer whose prose one admires or whose photographs are outstanding in composition and technical quality. The freelancer would do well to write for a copy of our Guidelines for Freelancers. Everything is spelled out there about how-tos, submission methods, etc. All manuscripts should include in upper right-hand corner of first page the number of words and whether it's first or second rights."

HARPER'S MAGAZINE, 2 Park Ave., Room 1809, New York NY 10016. (212)481-5220. Managing Editor: Robert Karl Manoff. 40% freelance written. For well-educated, socially concerned, widely read men and women who value ideas and good writing. Monthly. Circ. 140,000. Rights purchased vary with author and material. Pays negotiable kill fee. Pays on acceptance. Computer printout submissions acceptable. Reports in 2 weeks. Publishes ms an average of 3 months after acceptance. SASE. Sample copy $2.50.
Nonfiction: "For writers working with agents or who will query first only, our requirements are: public affairs, literary, international and local reporting, and humor." No interviews. Complete mss and queries must include SASEs. No unsolicited fiction or poems will be accepted. Publishes one major article per issue. Length: 4,000-6,000 words. Publishes one major essay per issue. Length: 4,000-6,000 words. "These should be construed as topical essays on all manner of subjects (politics, the arts, crime, business, etc.) to which the author can bring the force of passionately informed statements." Generally pays 50¢-$1/word.
Photos: Deborah Rust, art director. Occasionally purchased with mss; others by assignment. Pays $50-500.

THE HUMAN, A Magazine of Life Issues, The Uncertified Human Publishing Co., Ltd., 1295 Gerrard St., E., Toronto, Ontario M4L 1Y8 Canada. Editor: Jessica M. Pegis. Managing Editor: Denyse Handler. Monthly magazine covering life and death issues and social concerns in a technological society for college-educated readers whose concern is "the enhancement of human life before and after birth. They like analysis—no lectures or movement rhetoric." Circ. 10,000. Pays on publication. Byline given. Not copyrighted. Buys first North American serial rights and second serial (reprint) rights. Submit seasonal/holiday material 6 months in advance. Simultaneous queries, and simultaneous, photocopied and previously published submissions "OK as long as identified as such." SASE. Reports in 6 weeks. Publishes ms an average of 4 months after acceptance. Sample copy $1; writer's guidelines $1. "Please send International Postage Coupons for manuscripts. US stamps end up in our 'Stamps Around the World Album.' "

Nonfiction: Expose (on medical racketeering); general interest ("we're happy to look at medium length articles on death and dying, suicide, child abuse, adoption, food and population concerns in developing countries; will consider articles on TV violence, capital punishment or the psychology of war."); humor (coping with a handicap, growing old); interview/profile (of people active in field of human rights); new product (for the retarded or physically handicapped); opinion (500 words on any subject relative to our concerns); technical (prenatal surgery, fetal alcohol syndrome and drug addiction; premature baby survival; biological aspects of aging; enhancing the potential of the mentally retarded through special education; new family planning methods, excluding abortion). "No religious tracts, unresearched opinions, term essays, anything that would offend any reasonable minority or oppose the legal right to life of any group including children before birth. No population doomsday or anti-people rhetoric." Buys 30 mss/year. Query with published clips. Length: 1,000-2,800 words. Pays 3¢/word (Canadian funds).
Poetry: Free verse, light verse, limericks. "We use only good quality verse and subjects dealt with in magazine." Buys 2-3 poems/year. Submit maximum 3 poems. Length: 2-12 lines. Pays 25¢/line (Canadian funds).
Tips: "Keep writing fresh, pungent and jargon free. We welcome new writers and are happy to see them develop, but our standards are high. A sample of your work, published or not, is essential. We are interested in reviews of books, plays and movies pertaining to science or medicine and human rights. Avoid stories like, 'When my mother died,' 'How I stopped drinking,' etc. *The Human* is seeking researched material, not confessions."

IDEALS MAGAZINE, 11315 Watertown Plank Rd., Milwaukee WI 53226. Publisher: Patricia Pingry. Editor: Kathy Pohl. 50% freelance written. Family-oriented magazine published 8 times/year: Christmas, Thanksgiving, Easter, and five other seasonal issues. Pays on publication. Byline given. Buys first rights only. Submit seasonal material 6 months in advance. Send copy, not original ms. "We do not assume responsibility for loss of mss." Previously published submissions OK. Although a ms may be retained for further consideration, there is no guarantee it will be used. Computer printout submissions acceptable; no dot-matrix. Publishes ms an average of 6 months after acceptance. Sample copy for $1 postage and handling; writer's guidelines for SASE.
Nonfiction: General interest (holidays, seasons, family, nature, crafts); nostalgia (family oriented); profile (notable people); and travel. Buys 2-3 mss/issue. Length: 650-800 words. Query or send complete ms. Pays $50-75.
Photos: State availability of photos with ms. Buys first rights only.
Fiction: Limited use. Length: 650-800 words. Pays $50-75.
Poetry: Short to medium length. Pays $10.
Tips: "Most of our readers are women, age 35-70, living in non-urban areas. Nostalgia, reminiscences of childhood, and humorous anecdotes appeal. Material must be wholesome, inspirational, and uplifting, in the tradition of the Ideals world."

KNOWLEDGE, Official Publication of the World Olympiads of Knowledge, RSC Publishers, 3863 Southwest Loop 820, Drawer 16489, Ft. Worth TX 76133. (817)292-4272. Editor: Dr. O.A. Battista. Managing Editor: N.L. Matous. 90% freelance written. For lay and professional audiences of all occupations. Quarterly magazine; 60 pages. Circ. 1,000. Pays on publication. Buys all rights. Byline given. Submit seasonal/holiday material 6 months in advance. Computer printout submissions acceptable; no dot-matrix. SASE. Reports in 2 weeks. Publishes ms an average of 6 months after acceptance. Sample copy $4.
Nonfiction: Informational—original new knowledge that will prove mentally or physically beneficial to all lay readers. Buys 30 unsolicited mss/year. Query. Length: 1,500 words maximum. Pays $50 minimum.
Columns/Departments: Journal section uses maverick and speculative ideas that other magazines will not publish and reference.

LIFE, Time & Life Bldg., Rockefeller Center, New York NY 10020. (212)841-3871. Managing Editor: Richard B. Stolley. Monthly general interest picture magazine for people of all ages, backgrounds and interests. Circ. 1.4 million. Average issue includes one short and one long text piece. Pays on acceptance. Byline given. Offers $500 kill fee. Buys first North American serial rights. Submit seasonal material 3-4 months in advance. Simultaneous and photocopied submissions OK. Computer printout submissions acceptable; prefers letter-quality to dot-matrix. SASE. Reports in 6 weeks on queries; immediately on mss.
Nonfiction: "We've done articles on anything in the world of interest to the general reader and on people of importance. It's extremely difficult to break in since we buy so few articles. Most of the magazine is pictures. We're looking for very high quality writing. We select writers who we think match the subject they are writing about." Buys 1-2 mss/issue. Query with clips of previously published work. Length: 2,000-6,000 words. Pays $3,000 minimum.

Columns/Departments: Portrait (1,800-2,500 word essay on a well-known person). "We like to do these on people in the news." Buys 1 ms/issue. Query with clips of previously published work. Length: 1,800-2,500 words. Pays $2,000.

MACLEAN'S, Maclean Hunter Bldg., 777 Bay St., 7th, Toronto, Ontario M5W 1A7 Canada. (416)596-5386. Contact: Section Editors (listed in masthead). For news-oriented audience. Weekly newsmagazine; 90 pages. Circ. 650,000. Frequently buys first North American serial rights. Pays on acceptance. "Query with 200- or 300-word outline before sending material." Reports in 2 weeks. Electronic submissions OK if MO-PASS. Computer printout submissions acceptable. SAE and IRCs.
Nonfiction: "We have the conventional newsmagazine departments (Canada, world, business, people, plus science, medicine, law, art, music, etc.) with roughly the same treatment as other newsmagazines. We specialize in subjects that are primarily of Canadian interest, and there is now more emphasis on international—particularly US—news. Most material is now written by staffers or retainer freelancers, but we are open to suggestions from abroad, especially in world, business and departments (like medicine, lifestyles, etc.). Freelancers should write for a free copy of the magazine and study the approach." Length: 400-3,500 words. Pays $300-1,500.

‡**MEDIA SIGHT MAGAZINE, The magazine of popular culture nostalgia**, Media Sight Publications, Box 2630, Athens OH 45701. (614)594-4993. Editor: Geoffrey Schutt. Quarterly magazine about popular culture and entertainment nostalgia covering film, television, literature and comic books. "*Media Sight* is geared toward the person who enjoys and misses the old Saturday afternoon matinee. The articles are written in this entertaining style." Circ. 3,000. Pays on publication. Byline given. Buys first rights only. Submit seasonal/holiday material 6 months in advance. Computer printout submissions acceptable. SASE. Reports in 2 weeks on queries; 2 months on mss. Free sample copy and writer's guidelines.
Nonfiction: Expose, general interest, historical/nostalgic, interview/profile, and personal experience. "We will look at everything sent, as one person's article is usually vastly different from another's on the same subject. We can't rule out anything until we see it." Buys 20 mss/year. Send complete ms. Length: 7,500 words maximum. Pays $10-75.
Tips: "Enthusiasm for what the freelancer is writing about, and a true love for entertainment and nostalgia are all that we require of freelancers. All departments are open to freelancers."

NATIONAL ENQUIRER, Lantana FL 33464. Editor: Iain Calder. Weekly tabloid. Circ. 5,250,000. Pays on acceptance at executive level, or negotiable kill fee. Query. "Story idea must be accepted first. We're no longer accepting unsolicited mss and all spec material will be returned unread." SASE.
Nonfiction: Any subject appealing to a mass audience. Requires fresh slant on topical news stories, waste of taxpayers' money by government, the entire field of the occult, how-to articles, rags to riches success stories, medical firsts, scientific breakthroughs, human drama, adventure and personality profiles. "The best way to understand our requirements is to study the paper." Pays $375-600 for most completed features, plus separate lead fees; more with photos. "Payments in excess of $2,000 are not unusual; we will pay more for really top, circulation-boosting blockbusters."
Photos: Uses single or series b&w and color photos that must be attention-grabbing. Wide range; anything from animal photos to great action photos. "We'll bid against any other magazine for once-in-lifetime pictures."

NATIONAL GEOGRAPHIC MAGAZINE, 17th and M Sts. NW, Washington DC 20036. Editor: Wilbur E. Garrett. For members of the National Geographic Society. Monthly. Circ. more than 10,000,000. Query.
Nonfiction: *National Geographic* publishes first-person, general interest, heavy illustrated articles on science, natural history, exploration and geographical regions. Almost half the articles are staff-written. Of the freelance writers assigned, most are experts in their fields; the remainder are established professionals. Fewer than one percent of unsolicited queries result in assignments. Query (500 words) by letter, not by phone, to Senior Assistant Editor (Contract Writers). SASE. Do not send manuscripts. Before querying, study recent issues and check a *Geographic Index* at a library since the magazine seldom returns to regions or subjects covered within the past ten years.
Photos: Photographers should query in care of the Illustration Division.

THE NEW YORK ANTIQUE ALMANAC, The New York Eye Publishing Co., Inc., Box 335, Lawrence NY 11559. (516)371-3300. Editor-in-Chief: Carol Nadel. Tabloid published 10 times/year. Emphasizes antiques, art, investments and nostalgia. 30% freelance written. Circ. 42,000. Pays on publication. Buys all rights. Byline given. Phone queries OK. Submit seasonal/holiday material "whenever available." Previously published submissions OK but must advise. SASE. Computer printout submissions acceptable; no dot-matrix. Reports in 6 weeks. Publishes ms an average of 6 months after acceptance. Free sample copy.
Nonfiction: Expose (fraudulent practices); historical (museums, exhibitions, folklore, background of events); how-to (clean, restore, travel, shop, invest); humor (jokes, cartoons, satire); informational; inspirational (es-

says); interviews (authors, shopkeepers, show managers, appraisers); nostalgia ("The Good Old Days" remembered various ways); personal experience (anything dealing with antiques, art, investments, nostalgia); opinion; photo feature (antique shows, art shows, fairs, crafts markets, restorations); profile; technical (repairing, purchasing, restoring); travel (shopping guides and tips); and investment (economics, and financial reviews). Also purchases puzzles and quizzes related to antiques or nostalgia. Pays $25. Buys 9 mss/issue. Query or submit complete ms. Length: 3,000 words maximum. Pays $15-70. "Expenses for accompanying photos will be reimbursed."

Photos: "Occasionally, we have photo essays (auctions, shows, street fairs, human interest) and pay $5/photo with caption."

Fillers: Personal experiences, commentaries, anecdotes. "Limited only by author's imagination." Buys 45 mss/year. Pays $5-15.

Tips: "Articles on shows or antique coverage accompanied by photos are definitely preferred." We enjoy "discovering exciting and exhilarating new talent; but we dislike rudeness and impatience when publication time is delayed."

THE NEW YORKER, 25 W. 43rd St., New York NY 10036. Editor: William Shawn. Weekly. Circ. 500,000. Reports in 2 months. Pays on acceptance. SASE.

Nonfiction, Fiction and Fillers: Long fact pieces are usually staff-written. So is "Talk of the Town," although ideas for this department are bought. Pays good rates. Uses fiction, both serious and light. About 90% of the fillers come from contributors with or without taglines (extra pay if the tagline is used).

THE OLD FARMER'S ALMANAC, Yankee Publishing, Inc., Dublin, NH 03444. (603)563-8111. Editor: Judson D. Hale Sr. Annual magazine; "a traditional collection of astronomical information, weather forecasts, and feature articles related to country living, for a general audience." Circ. 3.5 million. Pays on acceptance. Byline given. Rights purchased are negotiable. Submit material for the next year's issue by February. Photocopied submissions acceptable. Computer printout submissions acceptable. SASE. Reports in 1 month.

Nonfiction: Historical, humor, biography, gardening, science and philosophy. "We want fresh and unusual material. This is a national magazine with a nationwide readership." Buys 5-10 mss/year. Query with clips of published work. Length: 1,500 words average. Pays $300 minimum.

Columns/Departments: Anecdotes and Pleasantries (short, self-contained items); and Rainy Day Amusements (puzzles, word games, quizzes). Buys 10 mss/year. Send complete ms. Length: 250-500 words. Pays $50 and up.

Fillers: Anecdotes. Length: 300 words minimum.

OPENERS, America's Library Newspaper, American Library Association, 50 E. Huron St., Chicago IL 60611. (312)944-6780. Editor: Ann M. Cunniff. Managing Editor: Sandra Lieb. 80% freelance written. Quarterly tabloid covering "what's great to read: books, fitness and sports, art, music, TV and radio, movies, health, etc., as they relate/tie into the library. Avoid first-person articles. Avoid pompous tomes on the importance of reading and libraries. *Openers* is *fun* to read." Distributed free to library patrons. *Openers* is designed to be used outside the library to encourage library use and inside as a bonus to library patrons to help broaden their reading interests. Circ. 250,000. Pays on publication. Byline given. Buys all rights. Submit seasonal/holiday material 3 months in advance. Simultaneous queries, and simultaneous and photocopied submissions OK. Computer printout submissions acceptable; prefers letter-quality to dot-matrix. SASE. Reports in 2 months. Publishes ms an average of 6 months after acceptance. Sample copy for 9x12 SAE.

Nonfiction: General interest, how-to and humor as they tie-in to reading or books. "Send us an outline first." Buys 25+ mss/year. Query with published clips. Length: 200-1,000 words. Pays $25-100.

PARADE, Parade Publications, Inc., 750 3rd Ave., New York NY 10017. (212)573-7000. Editor: Walter Anderson. Weekly magazine for a general interest audience. 90% freelance written. Circ. 24 million. Pays on acceptance. Kill fee varies in amount. Buys first North American serial rights. Computer printout submissions acceptable; no dot-matrix. SASE. Reports in 2 weeks on queries. Publishes ms an average of 2 months after acceptance. Writer's guidelines free for 4x9 SAE and 1 first class stamp.

Nonfiction: General interest (on health, business or anything of interest to a broad general audience); interview/profile (of news figures, celebrities and people of national significance); and "provocative topical pieces of news value." Spot news events are not accepted, as *Parade* has a 6-week lead time. No fiction, fashion, travel, poetry, quizzes, or fillers. Buys 25 unsolicited mss/year. Address queries to Articles Editor. Length: 800-1,500 words. Pays $1,000 minimum.

Photos: Send photos with ms.

Tips: "Send a well-researched, well-written query targeted to our market. Please, no phone queries. We're interested in well-written exclusive manuscripts on topics of news interest. It's annoying having to explain and re-explain what kinds of stories we are looking for to writers, especially those who call up ill-advised and ill-prepared."

PEOPLE IN ACTION, Meridian Publishing Company, 1720 Washington Blvd., Ogden UT 84404. Editor: Caroll McKanna Halley. 95% freelance written. A monthly company magazine featuring "people doing something . . . overcoming, winning, enjoying life, helping others." Readers are upscale, mainstream, family oriented. Pays on acceptance. Byline given. Buys first North American serial rights. Simultaneous queries, and photocopied and previously published submissions OK; no simultaneous submissions. Computer printout submissions acceptable. SASE. Reports in 3 weeks. Publishes ms an average of 6 months after acceptance. Sample copy for $1 and 9x12 SAE; writer's guidelines for SAE and 20¢ postage.

Nonfiction: Historical/nostalgic (if person oriented); interview/profile (illustrated); and personal experience (occasionally, "but must be terrific"). "Our readers want to be pleasantly diverted with upbeat, positive stories about people with whom they can identify. Bring your subjects to life with their human qualities and show them in action with your words and your photos. If you're writing about someone else—leave yourself out of it unless you do it well and it is vital to the story line. We don't want anything depressing; the risque is out, so is the religious when it's preachy or confessional. Articles *must* have color photography of good quality or the story will not be used. All material must focus on a specific person or group of people." Buys 50 mss/year. Query with or without published clips or send complete ms. Length: 800-1,200 words. Pays 15¢/word.

Photos: State availability of photos or send photos with query or ms. Pays $35 inside photo, $50 cover photo; uses glossy color prints and transparencies (slide to 8x10). Captions required. Buys one-time rights.

Columns/Departments: Regular features: Celebrity Chef (an 800-word profile of anyone who likes to cook; a recipe and 1-2 good color transparencies are essential); Wit Stop (humor; 800-1,000 words); and The Arts (fine artists, dancers, musicians, 800-1,200 words). Wit Stop is most open to freelancers. Query with or without published clips or send complete ms. Pays 15¢/word.

Tips: "Every month we buy almost every article and photo from freelance contributors."

PEOPLE WEEKLY, Time, Inc., Time & Life Bldg., Rockefeller Center, New York NY 10020. Editor: Patricia Ryan. For a general audience. Weekly. Circ. 2.75 million. Rights purchased vary with author and material. Usually buys first North American serial rights with right to syndicate, splitting net proceeds with author 50/50. Pays on acceptance. Query. SASE.

Nonfiction: "Nearly all material is staff-produced, but we do consider specific story suggestions (not manuscripts) from freelancers. Every story must have a strong personality focus. Payment varies from $200 for Lookouts to $1,000 for Bios.

Photos: Photo payment is $300/page for b&w, minimum $100. Prefer minimum size of 8x10 from original negatives."

READER'S DIGEST, Pleasantville NY 10570. Monthly. Circ. 18 million. Includes general interest features for the broadest possible spectrum of readership. Items intended for a particular feature should be directed to the editor in charge of that feature, although the contribution may later be referred to another section of the magazine as seeming more suitable. Original contributions—which become the property of *Reader's Digest* upon acceptance and payment by *Reader's Digest*—should be typewritten if possible. When material is from a published source, please give the name and date of publication and the page number. Contributions cannot be acknowledged or returned. Please address contributions to the appropriate department editor, *Reader's Digest*, Pleasantville NY 10570.

Columns/Departments: "Life in These United States contributions must be true, unpublished stories from one's own experience, revelatory of adult human nature, and providing appealing or humorous sidelights on the American scene. Maximum length: 300 words. Contact Editor, Life in U.S. Payment rate on publication: $300. True and unpublished stories are also solicited for Humor in Uniform, Campus Comedy, and All in a Day's Work. Maximum length: 300 words. Payment rate on publication: $300. Contact Editor, Humor in Uniform, Campus Comedy or All in a Day's Work. Toward More Picturesque Speech: The first contributor of each item used in this department is paid $40 ($35 for reprints). Contributions should be dated, and the sources must be given. Contact Editor, Picturesque Speech. For items used in Laughter, the Best Medicine, Personal Glimpses, Quotable Quotes, and elsewhere in the magazine, payment is made at the following rates: to the *first* contributor of each item from a published source, $35. For original material, $20 per *Digest* two-column line, with a minimum payment of $50. Contact Excerpts Editor."

READERS NUTSHELL, Allied Publications, Drawer 189, Palm Beach FL 33480. Editor: Constance Dorval-Bernal. Bimonthly magazine for customers of insurance agents. 15% insurance-related material; 85% general interest. Circ. 69,000. Buys first rights only. Phone queries OK. Submit seasonal material 6 months in advance. Simultaneous, photocopied and previously published submissions OK. SASE. Reports in 2 weeks on queries; in 2 months on mss. Sample copy $1; free writer's guidelines.

Nonfiction: Insurance-related, general interest (non-controversial home, family, and safety articles); humor; and interview (of famous people). Buys 2 mss/issue. Send complete ms. Length: 400-800 words. Pays 5¢/published word. "Freelancers should limit submissions to 600 words, with good black and white photos."

Fiction: Prefers humor. 300-700 words. Pays 5¢/word.

Photos: Send photos with ms. Pays $5 for 8x10 b&w glossy prints. Captions preferred; model release required.

Fillers: Puzzles. Pays $10.

READERS REVIEW, The National Research Bureau, Inc., 424 N. 3rd St., Burlington IA 52601. Editor: Rhonda Wilson. Editorial Supervisor: Doris J. Ruschill. 75% freelance written. "For industrial workers of all ages." Quarterly magazine. Pays on publication. Buys all rights. Previously published submissions OK. Computer printout submissions acceptable; prefers letter-quality to dot-matrix. SASE. Reports in 3 weeks. Publishes ms an average of 1 year after acceptance. Free writer's guidelines.
Nonfiction: General interest (steps to better health, attitudes on the job); how-to (perform better on the job, do home repairs, car maintenance); and travel. No articles on car repair, stress and tension. Buys 10-12 mss/year. Query with outline. Length: 400-600 words. Pays 4¢/word.

THE SATURDAY EVENING POST, The Saturday Evening Post Society, 1100 Waterway Blvd., Indianapolis, IN 46202. (317)634-1100. Editor-in-Chief: Cory SerVaas M.D. Executive Editor: Ted Kreiter. 65% freelance written. For general readership. Magazine published 9 times/year; 112 pages. Circ. 735,000. Pays on publication. Buys all rights; one-time reprint and first serial rights. Simultaneous and photocopied submissions OK. Computer printout submissions acceptable; prefers letter-quality to dot-matrix. SASE. Reports in 2 months. Publishes ms an average of 3 months after acceptance. Free writer's guidelines for SASE.
Nonfiction: Angela Smith, editorial assistant. How-to (health, general living); humor; informational; people (celebrities and ordinary but interesting personalities); inspirational (for religious columns); interview; personal experience (especially travel, yachting, etc.); personal opinion; photo feature; profile; travel and small magazine "pick-ups." Buys 5 mss/issue. Query. Length: 1,500-3,000 words. Pays $100-1,000.
Photos: Patrick Perry, photo editor. Photos purchased with or without accompanying ms. Pays $25 minimum for b&w photos; $50 minimum for color photos. Offers no additional payment for photos accepted with mss. Model release required.
Columns/Departments: Editorials ($100 each); Food ($150-450); Medical Mailbox ($50-250); Religion Column ($100-250); and Travel ($150-300).
Fiction: Jack Gramling, fiction editor. Adventure, fantasy, humorous, mainstream, mystery, romance, science fiction, suspense, and western. Pays on publication. Query. Length: 1,500-5,000 words. Pays $150-750.
Fillers: Jack Gramling, Post Scripts. Jokes, gags, anecdotes, postscripts and short humor. Buys 10-15 Post Scripts/issue; pays $15.
Tips: "Interested in topics related to science, medicine, the arts, personalities with inspirational careers, and humor. We read unsolicited material."

SATURDAY REVIEW, Saturday Review Publishing Co., Suite 460, 214 Massachusetts Ave. NE, Washington DC 20002. (202)547-1106. Managing Editor: Frank Gannon. Senior Editor: DuPre Jones. Bimonthly magazine covering literature and the arts for a highly literate audience. Circ. 250,000. Pays on publication. Byline given. Submit seasonal/holiday material 6 months in advance. SASE. Reports in 3 weeks. Sample copy for $2.50, 9x12 SAE, and 2 first class stamps.
Nonfiction: Book excerpts; interview/profile (with artists and writers); and coverage of a cultural or an artistic event. Buys 30 mss/year. Send complete ms. Length: 800-2,500 words. Pays $350-1,500.
Photos: Send photos with ms. Pays $50-500 for color transparencies; $25-100 for 5x7 b&w prints. Model release and identification of subjects required.
Tips: "We'll have more and shorter reviews of books and films and other departments as appropriate. Features should involve a profile of an important artist or writer—preferably one who has just produced or is about to produce an important work. Avoid the obvious and the overdone; we don't want to do the same people everyone else is doing."

SELECTED READING, The National Research Bureau, Inc., 424 N. 3rd St., Burlington IA 52601. Editor: Rhonda Wilson. Editorial Supervisor: Doris J. Ruschill. 75% freelance written. For industrial workers of all ages. Quarterly magazine. Pays on publication. Buys all rights. Previously published submissions OK. Computer printout submissions acceptable; prefers letter-quality to dot-matrix. SASE. Reports in 3 weeks. Publishes ms an average of 1 year after acceptance. Free writer's guidelines.
Nonfiction: General interest (economics, health, safety, working relationships); how-to; and travel (out-of-the way places). No material on car repair. Buys 10-12 mss/year. Query. A short outline or synopsis is best. Lists of titles are no help. Length: 400-600 words. Pays 4¢/word.

SIGNATURE—The Citicorp Diners Club Magazine, 641 Lexington Ave., New York NY 10022. Editor: Horace Sutton. 95% freelance written. Basically for Diners Club members (but subscriptions open to all)— "businesspersons, urban, affluent and traveled." Monthly. Circ. 750,000. Pays on acceptance. Buys first rights only. Buys 175 mss/year. Submit seasonal material at least 5 months in advance. Computer printout submissions acceptable; prefers letter-quality to dot-matrix. Publishes ms an average of 4 months after acceptance. Query. SASE. Free writer's guidelines.
Nonfiction: Buys virtually all nonfiction from freelance writers. Front-of-the-book pieces deal with photography, sport, fitness, arts, and acquisitions. Length: Generally 1,200-1,500 words. Pays $700-900. "While travel and travel-related pieces are the major portion of the so-called 'well' or central part of the book, we will en-

tertain any feature-length piece that relates to the art of living well or at least living interestingly. That could include such pieces as 'In Search of the Ultimate Deli' to 'Traveling in the State Department plane with the Secretary of State.' Writing is of high quality and while celebrated bylines are sought and used, the market is open to any writer of talent and style. Writers who join the 'stable' are used with frequency." Feature length: 2,000-3,000 words. Pays $1,200 and up.

Photos: "Photographers are assigned to major pieces and often accompany the writer on assignment. In almost no cases are writers expected to take their own photographs. Quality standard in pictures is high and highly selective. Photography rates on request to the art director."

Tips: "While we are heavy on travel in all its phases—that is, far out Ladakh and Yemen and near at hand, e.g., Hemingway's Venice—we do try to embrace the many facets that make up the art of living well. So we are involved with good food, cuisine trends, sport in all forms, the arts, the stage and films and such concomitant subjects as fitness and finance."

SMITHSONIAN MAGAZINE, 900 Jefferson Drive, Washington DC 20560. Articles Editor: Marlane A. Liddell. 90% freelance written. For "associate members of the Smithsonian Institution; 85% with college education." Monthly. Circ. 2 million. Buys first rights only. Payment for each article to be negotiated depending on our needs and the article's length and excellence. Pays on acceptance. Submit seasonal material 3 months in advance. Computer printout submissions acceptable; prefers letter-quality to dot-matrix. Reports in 6 weeks. Publishes ms an average of 6 months after acceptance. Query. SASE.

Nonfiction: "Our mandate from the Smithsonian Institution says we are to be interested in the same things which now interest or should interest the Institution: cultural and fine arts, history, natural sciences, hard sciences, etc." Length: 750-4,500 words; pay negotiable. No fiction or poetry.

Photos: Purchased with or without ms and on assignment. Captions required. Pays $350/full color page.

THE STAR, 660 White Plains Rd., Tarrytown NY 10591. (914)332-5000. Editor/Publisher: Ian G. Rae. Executive Editor: Phil Bunton. 40% freelance written. "For every family; all the family—kids, teenagers, young parents and grandparents." Weekly tabloid; 48 pages. Circ. 3.5 million. Buys second serial (reprint) rights, and first North American serial rights. SASE. Free sample copy and writer's guidelines.

Nonfiction: Malcolm Abrams, managing editor. Exposé (government waste, consumer, education, anything affecting family); general interest (human interest, consumerism, informational, family and women's interest); how-to (psychological, practical on all subjects affecting readers); interview (celebrity or human interest); new product; photo feature; profile (celebrity or national figure); travel (how-to cheaply); health; medical; and diet. No first-person articles. Query or submit complete ms. Length: 500-1,000 words. Pays $50-1,500.

Photos: State availability of photos with query or ms. Pays $25-100 for 8x10 b&w glossy prints, contact sheets or negatives; $125-1,000 for 35mm color transparencies. Captions required. Buys one-time, or all rights.

Fillers: Statistical-informational. Length: 50-400 words. Pays $25-100.

SUNSHINE MAGAZINE, Henry F. Henrichs Publications, Litchfield IL 62056. (217)324-2322. 75% freelance written. For general audience of all ages. Monthly magazine. Circ. 90,000. Buys 120-140 unsolicited mss/year. Buys first North American serial rights. Pays on acceptance. Submit seasonal material 7 months in advance. Computer printout submissions acceptable. Reports in 1-2 months. Publishes ms an average of 8 months after acceptance. Complimentary copy sent to included authors on publication. Submit complete ms. SASE. Sample copy 50¢; free writer's guidelines.

Nonfiction: "We accept some short articles, but they must be especially interesting or inspirational. *Sunshine Magazine* is not a religious publication, and purely religious material is rarely used. We desire carefully written features about persons or events that have real human interest—that give a 'lift.' " Length: 100-300 words. Pays $10-50.

Columns/Departments: My Most Extraordinary Experience—Yes, It Happened to Me. Must be in first person, deal with a very unusual or surprising situation and have a positive approach. Length: 350-500 words. Payment: $25. Favorite Meditation and Gem of the Month, inspirational essays not exceeding 200 words. Payment: $20.

Fiction: "Stories must be wholesome, well-written, with clearly defined plots. There should be a purpose for each story, but any moral or lesson should be well-concealed in the plot development. Humorous stories are welcome. Avoid trite plots. A surprising climax is most desirable. Material should be uplifting, and noncontroversial." Length: 600-1,200 words. Youth story: 400-700 words. Pays $20-100.

Poetry: Buys one poem for special feature each month. Payment: $15. Uses several other poems each month but does not purchase these. Prefers pleasantly rhythmic, humorous or uplifting material. Length: 4-16 lines.

Fillers: 100-200 words. Payment: $10.

Tips: "We prefer not to receive queries. Enclose a SASE, be neat, accurate and surprising, but wholesome. Do not send anything dealing with alcohol, violence, divorce, death or depression."

TOWN AND COUNTRY, 1700 Broadway, New York NY 10019. (212)903-5000. Managing Editor: Jean Barkhorn. For upper-income Americans. Monthly. Not a large market for freelancers. Always query first. SASE.

Nonfiction: Frank Zachary, department editor. "We're always trying to find ideas that can be developed into good articles that will make appealing cover lines." Wants provocative and controversial pieces. Length: 1,500-2,000 words. Pay varies. Also buys shorter pieces for which pay varies.

Us, MacFadden Holdings, Inc., 215 Lexington Ave., New York NY 10016. (212)340-7577. Editor-in-Chief: Richard Kaplan. Biweekly magazine featuring personalities for readers from ages 18-34. Circ. 1.1 million. Computer printout submissions acceptable. Pays on publication. Buys all rights. Reports in 2 weeks.
Nonfiction: Richard Sanders, senior articles editor. General interest (human interest pieces with political, sports and religious tie-ins, fashion, entertainment, science, medicine); interview (of Hollywood figures); profile (of trend and style setters, political personalities, sports figures) and photo feature (personalities, not necessarily celebrities). No humor or essays. "We are looking for the odd story, the unusual story, featuring colorful and unusual people." Buys 5 mss/issue. Query with clips of previously published work. Length: 750-800 words. Pays $350-400.
Photos: State availability of photos. Reviews b&w prints. "Color is OK, but we will convert to black and white. We've got to have stories with pictures."
Tips: "We do what we call anticipatory journalism. That means you should peg the story to a specific date. For example, a story about an unusual track star would work best if published close to the date of the star's most important race. The editors work 5-6 weeks ahead on stories. Query with a one-paragraph description of the proposed subject."

‡**VANITY FAIR**, 350 Madison Ave., New York NY 10017. Publishes nonfiction and fiction and accepts unsolicited manuscripts for consideration.

WHAT MAKES PEOPLE SUCCESSFUL, The National Research Bureau, Inc., 424 N. 3rd St., Burlington IA 52601. Editor: Rhonda Wilson. Editorial Supervisor: Doris J. Ruschill. 75% freelance written. For industrial workers of all ages. Published quarterly. Pays on publication. Buys all rights. Previously published submissions OK. Computer printout submissions acceptable; prefers letter-quality to dot-matrix. SASE. Reports in 3 weeks. Publishes ms an average of 1 year after acceptance. Free writer's guidelines.
Nonfiction: How-to (be successful); general interest (personality, employee morale, guides to successful living, biographies of successful persons, etc.); experience; and opinion. No material on health. Buys 3-4 mss/issue. Query with outline. Length: 400-600 words. Pays 4¢/word.

Health and Fitness

The term, *health and fitness*, continuously takes on new connotations as people and publishers interpret the subjects in different ways. Consumers are learning that *they* (not only their doctors) are responsible for their own health; publishers are creating publications to cater to this awareness. For some, health and fitness mean living in "hot water" (the soothing kind). For others, they mean running, exercising or walking. In this section, you'll see people's preferences in keeping fit are as diverse as the publications that communicate those choices. The magazines listed here specialize in covering health- and fitness-related topics for a general audience. Magazines covering health topics from a medical perspective are listed in Trade Journals/Medical. Also see the Sports/Miscellaneous section where publications dealing with health and particular sports may be listed. And remember, nearly every general interest publication is a potential market for a health article.

ACCENT ON LIVING, Box 700, Bloomington IL 61701. (309)378-2961. Editor: Raymond C. Cheever. 80% freelance written. For physically disabled persons and rehabilitation professionals. Quarterly magazine; 128 pages. Circ. 19,000. Buys first rights and second (reprint) rights to material originally published elsewhere. Byline usually given. Buys 50-60 unsolicited mss/year. Pays on publication. Photocopied submissions OK. Computer printout submissions acceptable. Reports in 2 weeks. SASE. Sample copy $1.50; free writer's guidelines.
Nonfiction: Betty Garee, assistant editor. Articles about new devices that would make a disabled person with limited physical mobility more independent; should include description, availability, and photos. Medical

breakthroughs for disabled people. Intelligent discussion articles on acceptance of physically disabled persons in normal living situations; topics may be architectural barriers, housing, transportation, educational or job opportunities, organizations, or other areas. How-to articles concerning everyday living giving specific, helpful information so the reader can carry out the idea himself. News articles about active disabled persons or groups. Good strong interviews. Vacations, accessible places to go, sports, organizations, humorous incidents, self improvement, and sexual or personal adjustment—all related to physically handicapped persons. No religious-type articles. Length: 250-1,000 words. Pays 10¢/word for article as it appears in magazine (after editing and/or condensing by staff). Query.

Photos: Pays $5 minimum for b&w photos purchased with accompanying captions. Amount will depend on quality of photos and subject matter.

Tips: "We read all manuscripts so one writer won't get preferred treatment over another. Make sure that you are writing to disabled people, not a general audience. We are looking for upbeat material. Hint to writers: Ask a friend who is disabled to read your article before sending it to *Accent*. Make sure that he understands your major points, and the sequence or procedure."

ALCOHOLISM, The National Magazine, Alcom, Inc., Box C19051, Queen Anne Station, Seattle WA 98109. (206)362-8162. Editor: Elton Wclk. 50% freelance written. Bimonthly magazine covering alcoholism, treatment, and recovery. Circ. 30,000. Pays on publication. Byline given. Buys first rights only. Submit seasonal/holiday material 6 months in advance. Simultaneous queries, and simultaneous and photocopied submissions OK. SASE. Reports in 1 month. Publishes ms an average of 2 months after acceptance. Sample copy $5; writer's guidelines for business-size SAE and 1 first class stamp.

Nonfiction: How-to, humor, interview/profile, opinion, and "popularizations of research." New interest in business success through recovery. Special issues include Research Focus and Intervention Focus. No "this is how bad I was"; "this is how bad my parents (brother, etc.) were." Stress "the adventure of recovery" instead of the agony of the disease. No fiction. Especially interested in humor. Buys 20 major features/year. Query with clips of published work or send complete ms. Length: 300-2,000 words. Pays 10¢/word; $100/published page.

Photos: State availability of photos. Captions, model release, and identification of subjects required. Buys one-time rights.

Columns/Departments: "Road to Recovery": tips on ways of enhancing recovery. Buys 12-24 items/year. Send complete ms. Length: 500-750 words. Pays 10¢/word; $100/published page.

Poetry: Free verse, light verse, and traditional (lucid). Wants recovery-oriented material only. No "surrealism; alcoholics are rotten; ain't it terrible on skid road. No grim poetry, please." Buys 1-2/ issue. Submit maximum 5 poems. Length: 2-20 lines. Pays $5-25.

Fillers: Short humor and newsbreaks. Pays $5 minimum; 10¢/word "on longer items."

Tips: "We need writers who know something about alcoholism—something more than personal experience and superficial acquaintance—writers who make tough material readable and palatable for a popular and professional audience. We are always on the lookout for well-researched popularizations of research. We try to run one personal experience per issue dealing with recovery—how the alcoholic finds ways to make sobriety worth being sober for." Editors also interested in working with writers outside the US.

AMERICAN HEALTH MAGAZINE, Fitness of Body and Mind, American Health Partners, 80 Fifth Ave., New York NY 10011. (212)242-2460. Editor-in-Chief: T George Harris. Editor: Joel Gurin. Executive Editor: Hara Marano. 10 issues/year. General interest magazine that covers both scientific and "lifestyle" aspects of health, including laboratory research, clinical advances, fitness, holistic healing and nutrition. Circ. 800,000. Pays on acceptance. Byline given. Offers 25% kill fee. Buys all rights; "negotiable, in some cases." Computer printout submissions acceptable. SASE. Reports in 6 weeks. Sample copy for $2 and $1.75 first class postage and handling; writer's guidelines for 4x9 SAE and 1 first class stamp.

Nonfiction: Mail to Editorial/Features. Book excerpts; how-to; humor (if anyone can be funny, yes); interview/profile (health or fitness related); photo feature (any solid feature or news item relating to health); and technical. No first-person narratives, mechanical research reports, weight loss plans or recipes. "Stories should be written clearly, without jargon. Information should be new, authoritative and helpful to the readers. No first-person narrative about illness or recovery from an illness or accident." Buys 60-70 mss/year. Query with 2 clips of published work. "Absolutely *no* complete mss." Length: 1,000-3,000 words. Pays $600-2,000.

Photos: Mail to Editorial/Photo. Send photos with query. Pays $100-600 for 35mm transparencies and 8x10 prints "depending on use." Captions and identification of subjects required. Buys one-time rights.

Columns/Departments: Mail to Editorial/News. Consumer Alert, Medical News (technological update), Fitness Report, Life Styles, Nutrition Report, Tooth Report, and Skin, Scent and Hair. Other news sections included from time to time. Buys 500-600 mss/year. Query with clips of published work. Prefers 2 pages-500 words. Pays $125-375.

Fillers: Mail to Editorial/Fillers. Anecdotes and newsbreaks. Buys 30/year. Length: 20-50 words. Pays $10-25.

Tips: "Queries should be short (no longer than a page), snappy and to the point. Think short; think news. Give us a good angle and a paragraph of background. Queries only. We do not take responsibility for materials not accompanied by SASE."

BESTWAYS MAGAZINE, Box 2028, Carson City NV 89702. Editor/Publisher: Barbara Bassett. Emphasizes health, diet and nutrition. Monthly magazine; 120 pages. Circ. 300,000. Pays on publication. Buys all rights. Byline given. Submit seasonal/holiday material 6 months in advance. SASE. Reports in 6 weeks. Writer's guidelines for SASE.

Nonfiction: General interest (nutrition, physical fitness, preventive medicine, supplements, natural foods); how-to (diet and exercise); and technical (vitamins, minerals, weight control and nutrition). "No direct or implied endorsements of refined flours, grains or sugar, tobacco, alcohol, caffeine, drugs or patent medicines." Buys 4 mss/issue. Query. Length: 1,500 words. Pays 10¢/word.

Photos: State availability of photos with query. Pays $7.50 for 4x5 b&w glossy prints; $15 for 2¼x2¼ color transparencies. Captions preferred. Buys all rights. Model release required.

‡CELEBRATE HEALTH, (formerly *Celebrate Health Digest*), Bergan Mercy, Inc., 7500 Mercy Rd., Omaha NB 68124. (402)398-6303. Editor: David DeButts. 65% freelance written. Quarterly consumer-oriented magazine focusing on positive, upbeat news and features in the health/medical field. Circ. 25,000. Pays on acceptance. Byline given. Offers 25% kill fee. Buys variable rights "depending on author and material." Submit seasonal/holiday material 6 months in advance. Simultaneous queries, and simultaneous and photocopied submissions OK. Computer printout submissions acceptable; prefers letter-quality to dot-matrix. SASE. Reports in 6 weeks. Publishes ms an average of 6 months after acceptance. Sample copy $1 and a 9x12 envelope with 88¢ postage; writer's guidelines for business-size SAE and 1 first class stamp.

Nonfiction: General interest (family health); historical/nostalgic (medical); how-to (exercise, diet, keep fit); interview/profile (of doctors, health experts); and new product (exercise equipment, sports clothing). "Nothing on pro-abortion, sex, sterilization, or artificial birth control; and please, nothing about how awful doctors are or how corrupt the medical establishment is." Buys 6-12 mss/year. "We'd rather see completed articles rather than queries." Length: 500-2,500 words. Pays $50-500.

Photos: Send photos with query or ms. Pays $25-50 for b&w contact sheets and negatives; $50-100 for 2¼ or 4x5 color transparencies used inside; $100 for color covers. "35mm is OK for color, too, but must be Kodachrome." Captions, model release and identification of subjects required. Buys variable rights.

Columns/Departments: Medical, Living, World of Work, Childhood, Nutrition, and Prime Time (elderly). Buys 10 mss/year. Send complete ms. Length: 500-2,500 words. Pays $50-500.

Tips: "We use first person *rarely*; only when really substantiated with lots of facts. Every day's mail brings another: "My Experience with Cataracts" or "My Experience with Gout." Only put yourself in the article if there's a reason for you to be there. Writing should be crisp, snappy. The publication is edited according to the Associated Press stylebook. Interested in latest developments in health care facilities; all aspects of physical, mental and emotional health. Use authoritative sources. No medical jargon."

‡DIABETES SELF MANAGEMENT, Pharmaceutical Communications, 42-15 Crescent St., Long Island City NY 11101. (212)937-4283. Editor: James Hazlett. Quarterly magazine. "We publish how-to information dealing with all aspects of diabetes self-care for people whose needs are not satisfied by the other publications in this field." Estab. 1983. Circ. 256,000. Pays on publication. Byline given. Offers 50% kill fee. Makes work-for-hire assignments. Reports in 2 weeks on queries. Sample copy $2 with 9x13 SAE and 4 first class stamps.

Nonfiction: How-to (diabetes self-care); new product (diabetes care); and technical (diabetes self-care). "The writing of our articles requires on the writer's part a familiarity with the disorder. Most patients have blatantly insufficient knowledge of how to manage the disorder." Buys 12-15 mss/year. Query with published clips related to the subject. Length: 2,000-3,000 words. Pays $500-800.

Tips: "We have a definite style; read our magazine. Write as if the person is intelligent and had no information on the subject. What we want to avoid at all costs is to talk down to the reader."

‡ELAINE POWERS FEELING GREAT, Haymarket Group Ltd., Suite 407, 45 W. 34th St., New York NY 10001. (212)239-0855. Editor: Tim Moriarity. Managing Editor: Jane Collins. A monthly magazine covering women's health and fitness. Estab. 1984. Pays on acceptance. Byline given. Submit seasonal/holiday material 4 months in advance. Computer printout submissions acceptable. SASE. Reports in 1 month. Sample copy $1.95 and SAE; writer's guidelines for SAE and 1 first class stamp.

Nonfiction: Book excerpts, how-to, humor, inspirational, interview/profile, new product, opinion and personal experience. Subjects include exercise, nutrition, diet, medical news, self-help, sexuality, mental health, personal relationships and emotional wellbeing. Topics should be fairly specific. "We also have a need for short articles on food, interior design and decoration, crafts and on the humorous side of all the topics previously mentioned." Query with published clips. Length: 500-3,000 words. Pays $125-750.

Photos: State availability of photos. Reviews negatives and transparencies. Payment varies. Model release and identification of subjects required. Buys one-time rights.

Fillers: Clippings, jokes, anecdotes, short humor, and newsbreaks. Length: 25-200 words. Pays $10-100.

Tips: "We like articles to be written in an upbeat, personalized style that is friendly to the reader. All articles should be informative and preferably offer the reader some kind of inspiration or encouragement."

FRUITFUL YIELD NEWSLETTER, The Fruitful Yield, Inc., 721 N. Yale, Villa Park IL 60181. (312)833-8288. Editor: Doug Murguia. 90% freelance written. Biannual national newsletter covering natural foods, vitamins and herbs. Features subjects ranging from prenatal care to health and nutrition for all age groups. Circ. 15,000. Pays on publication. Buys first rights only. Phone queries OK. Submit seasonal material 2 months in advance. Photocopied submissions OK. Computer printout submissions acceptable; no dot-matrix. Reports in 6 months. Publishes ms an average of 6 months after acceptance. Free sample copy and writer's guidelines only for SASEs enclosed with request.

Nonfiction: "We are interested in three main types of articles: 1) detailed, documented articles written for the layman telling of the latest research findings in the field of nutrition; 2) personal experience articles telling how natural foods, vitamins or herbs help you or a friend overcome or relieve an ailment (should be detailed and describe your program); and 3) recipes using natural foods and/or giving cooking hints." Length: 250-500 words. Send complete ms. Buys 30 mss/yr. Pays $10-20.

Tips: "Be familiar with our content. We're looking for specific detailed, documented articles that make no assumptions. Use direct quotes from authorities."

FRUITION, The Plan, Box 872-WM, Santa Cruz CA 95061. (408)429-3020. Biannual newsletter covering healthful living/creation of public food tree nurseries and relative social and horticultural matters. 10% freelance written. Circ. 300. Payment method negotiable. Byline given. Offers negotiable kill fee. Buys all rights. Simultaneous queries, and simultaneous and photocopied, previously published submissions OK. Computer printout submissions acceptable. SASE. Reports in 2-4 weeks. Publishes ms an average of 6 months after acceptance. Sample copy $2; writer's guidelines for SASE.

Nonfiction: General interest, historical/nostalgic, how-to, inspirational, interview/profile, personal experience, photo feature—all must relate to public access—food trees, foraging fruit and nuts, and related social and horticultural matters. No articles "involving gardening with chemicals, or cloning plants. No articles on health with references to using therapies or medicines." Buys 4-6 mss/year. Length: 750-5,000 words. Pays negotiable fee.

Photos: Sunshine Nelson, photo editor. State availability of photos. Pays negotiable fee for b&w contact sheet and 5x5 or larger prints. Identification of subjects required. Buys one-time rights.

Poetry: E. Eagle, poetry editor. Avant-garde, free verse, haiku, light verse, and traditional. Buys 4-6/year. Submit maximum 6 poems. Length: 2 lines-750 words. Pays negotiable fee.

Fillers: Clippings, short humor, and newsbreaks. Buys 6-10/year. Length: 125-400 words. Pays negotiable fee.

Tips: "More humanistic stuff is needed to counter balance the militaristic promotion."

HEALTH, 149 5th Ave., New York NY 10010. Editor: Hank Herman. For health-minded men and women. 65% freelance written. Monthly magazine; 66 pages. Monthly. Circ. 1 million. Rights purchased vary with author and material. Pays 20% kill fee. Byline given. Pays within 8 weeks of acceptance. Query with fresh, new approaches; strongly angled. Submit complete ms for first-person articles. Computer printout submissions OK. SASE. Sample copy $2. Reports in 6 weeks. Publishes ms an average of 3 months after acceptance.

Nonfiction: Articles on all aspects of health: physical, sexual, mental, emotional advocacy articles, and medical breakthroughs. No "all about" articles (e.g., "All About Mental Health"). Informational (nutrition, fitness, diet and beauty), interview, profile, think articles, and expose. Length: 1,000-3,000 words. Pays $400-1,100. Also needed are brief (200-600 word) items on medical advances for the "Breakthrough" section (query optional).

Tips: For major articles, query with one-page sample of style intended for the whole story, and include an outline and author's background. "We don't often buy an unsolicited story or idea, but we often get back to a freelancer who has queried us when we get an idea that he or she might be qualified to write."

‡**HEALTHLINE**, McNeil Foundation, 2855 Campus Dr., San Mateo CA 94403. (415)570-4213. Editor: Jay Cornish. A monthly magazine of preventive health care information. Circ. 10,000. Pays on acceptance. Byline given. Submit seasonal/holiday material 2 months in advance. Computer printout submissions acceptable. Sample copy $2.

Nonfiction: Buys 20 mss/year. Length: 800 words minimum. Pays $100-200.

‡**HOLISTIC LIVING NEWS**, Association for Holistic Living, Box 16346, San Diego CA 92116. (619)280-0317. Editor: Judith Horton. 50% freelance written. Bimonthly newspaper covering the holistic field from a holistic perspective. Circ. 60,000. Pays on publication. Byline given. Not copyrighted. Buys first rights and second (reprint) rights to material originally published elsewhere. Submit seasonal/holiday material 6 months in advance. Simultaneous queries, and simultaneous, photocopied, and previously published submissions OK. Computer printout submissions acceptable. SASE. Reports in 1 month on queries; 2 months on mss. Publishes ms an average of 4 months after acceptance. Sample copy $1.50; free writer's guidelines.
Nonfiction: General interest (holistic or new age overviews of a general topic); and how-to (taking responsibility for yourself—healthwise). No profiles or personal experience. Buys 100 mss/year. Query with published clips. Length: 200-750 words. Pays $5-10.
Photos: Send photos with query. Pays $7.50 for 5x7 b&w prints. Model release and identification of subjects required.
Tips: "Study the newspaper—the style is different from a daily. The articles generally provide helpful information on how to feel your best (mentally, spiritually, physically). Any of the sections are open to freelancers: Creative Living, Health & Fitness, Arts, Nutrition and Network (recent events and upcoming ones). One of the main aspects of the paper is to promote the concept of a holistic lifestyle and help people integrate it into their lives by taking simple steps on a daily basis."

‡**HOT WATER LIVING, A Consumer's Guide To Hot Water Enjoyment**, Hester Communications, 1700 E. Dyer Rd., Santa Ana CA 92705. (714)549-4834. Editor: Stan Chambers. A semiannual magazine covering spas, hot tub, saunas and their use and maintenance; also, fitness products. "We educate consumers about benefits of hot water products and maintenance and how spas, etc. tie in with fitness and health." Estab. 1983. Pays on acceptance. Byline given. Buys first North American serial rights. Submit seasonal/holiday material 3 months in adance. Simultaneous queries and photocopied submissions OK. Computer printout submissions acceptable. SASE. Reports in 2 weeks on queries; 1 month on mss. Free sample copy and writer's guidelines.
Nonfiction: How-to (landscape around spa, build decks, maintain equipment); humor; personal experience; and photo feature (beautiful installations). Buys 6 mss/year. Query with published clips. Length: 250-2,000 words. Pays $100-250.
Photos: Reviews color transparencies. Model releases required. Buys one-time rights.

LET'S LIVE MAGAZINE, Oxford Industries, Inc., 4444 N. Larchmont Blvd., Box 74908, Los Angeles CA 90004. (213)469-3901. Managing Editor: Keith Stepro. Associate Publisher: Peggy MacDonald. Emphasizes nutrition. Monthly magazine; 160 pages. Circ. 140,000. Pays on publication. Buys all rights. Byline given unless: "it is a pen name and author fails to furnish legal name; vast amount of editing is required (byline is then shared with the editors of *Let's Live*); it is an interview by assignment in which 'questioner' is *LL* (*Let's Live*)." Submit seasonal/holiday material 4 months in advance. SASE. Reports in 3 weeks for queries; 6 weeks for mss. Sample copy $2; free writer's guidelines.
Nonfiction: General interest (effects of vitamins, minerals and nutrients in improvement of health or afflictions); historical (documentation of experiments or treatment establishing value of nutrients as boon to health); how-to (acquire strength and vitality, improve health of children and prepare tasty health-food meals); inspirational (first-person accounts of triumph over disease through substitution of natural foods and nutritional supplements for drugs and surgery); interview (benefits of research in establishing prevention as key to good health); advertised new product (120-180 words plus 5x7 or glossy of product); personal opinion (views of orthomolecular doctors or their patients on value of health foods toward maintaining good health); profile (background and/or medical history of preventive medicine, MDs or PhDs, in advancement of nutrition); and health food recipes ($5 on publication). "We do not want kookie first-person accounts of experiences with drugs or junk foods, faddist healers or unorthodox treatments." Buys 10-15 mss/issue. Query with clips of published work. Length: 750-2,000 words. Pays $50-150.
Photos: State availability of photos with ms. Pays $17.50 for 8x10 b&w glossy prints; $35 for 8x10 color prints and 35mm color transparencies. $150 for good cover shot. Captions and model releases required.
Columns/Departments: My Story and Interviews. Buys 1-2/issue. Query. Length: 750-1,200 words. Pays $50-250.
Tips: "We want writers with experience in researching nonsurgical medical subjects, interviewing authoritative MDs and hospital administrators, with the ability to simplify technical and clinical information for the layman. A captivating lead and structural flow are essential."

LISTEN MAGAZINE, 6830 Laurel St. NW, Washington DC 20012. (202)722-6726. Editor: Francis A. Soper. 50% freelance written. Specializes in drug prevention, presenting positive alternatives to various drug dependencies. "*Listen* is used in many high school classes, in addition to use by professionals: medical personnel, counselors, law enforcement officers, educators, youth workers, etc." Monthly magazine, 32 pages. Circ. 150,000. Buys all rights unless otherwise arranged with the author. Byline given. Buys 100-200 mss/year. Pays on acceptance. Computer printout submissions acceptable; prefers letter-quality to dot-matrix. Sample copy $1; send large manila SASE; free writer's guidelines. Reports in 4 weeks. Publishes ms an average of 5 months after acceptance. Query. SASE.

Nonfiction: Seeks articles that deal with causes of drug use such as poor self-concept, family relations, social skills or peer pressure. Especially interested in youth-slanted articles or personality interviews encouraging nonalcoholic and nondrug ways of life. Teenage point of view is essential. Popularized medical, legal and educational articles. Also seeks narratives which portray teens dealing with youth conflicts, especially those related to the use of or temptation to use harmful substances. Growth of the main character should be shown. "We don't want typical alcoholic story/skid-row bum, AA stories. We are also being inundated with drunk-driving accident stories. Unless yours is unique, consider another topic." Buys 75-100 unsolicited mss/year. Length: 500-1,500 words. Pays 4-7¢/word.

Photos: Purchased with accompanying ms. Captions required. Pays $5-15 per b&w print (5x7, but 8x10 preferred). Color preferred, but b&w acceptable.

Poetry: Blank verse and free verse only. Seeks image-invoking, easily illustrated poems of 5-15 lines to combine with photo or illustration to make a poster. Pays $15 maximum.

Fillers: Word square/general puzzles are also considered. Pays $15.

Tips: "True stories are good, especially if they have a unique angle. Other authoritative articles need a fresh approach. In query, briefly summarize article idea and logic of why you feel it's good." Recent article examples: "Inhalants—High Way to a Big Fall" (April 1983) and "How to Face a Crisis" (February 1983).

MUSCLE & FITNESS, Weider Health & Fitness, 21100 Erwin St., Woodland Hills CA 91367. (818)884-6800. Editor: Bill Reynolds. Executive Editor: Tim Conaway. 10% freelance written. Monthly magazine covering bodybuilding/physical fitness for fitness-minded men/women. Circ. 350,000 + . Pays 45 business days after acceptance. Byline given. Buys all rights. Photocopied and, occasionally, previously published submissions (such as excerpts) OK. Computer printout submissions acceptable. SASE. Reports in 6 weeks.

Nonfiction: Book excerpts (occasionally, if within our philosophy); how-to (only within our philosophy); inspirational; and interview/profile. No article on unknown bodybuilders; unauthoritative pieces. No humor, astrology or erotica. Buys 100 + mss/year. Query with clips or send outline proposal. Length: 2,500 words. Pays $150-negotiable/major feature.

Photos: Mandy Tanny, photo editor. Send proof sheets or transparencies. Pays negotiable rate for contact sheets, 60mm and 35mm transparencies, 8x10 prints. Captions, model release and identification of subjects required. Buys all rights. "We seldom use black and white and are interested only in photos of top bodybuilders or well-known athletes."

Columns/Departments: See an issue of the magazine. Buys 100 + /year. Query with clips of published work or send outline proposal. Length: 500-700 words. Pays $50-100.

Tips: "The specialized nature of our coverage requires authoritative scientific knowledge for nonpersonality articles. Personality articles require prior approval and photo access. We prefer to base assignments on detailed outline proposals."

‡**MUSCLE MAG INTERNATIONAL**, 52 Bramsteele Rd., Unit 2, Brampton, Ontario L6W 3M5 Canada. Editor: Robert Kennedy. 80% freelance written. For 16-30-year-old men interested in physical fitness and overall body improvement. Bimonthly magazine; 84 pages. Circ. 120,000. Buys all rights. Byline given. Buys 80 mss/year. Pays on acceptance. Sample copy $3. Reports in 4 weeks. Submit complete ms. IRCs.

Nonfiction: Articles on ideal physical proportions and importance of protein in the diet, training for muscle size. Should be helpful and instructional and appeal to young men who want to live life in a vigorous and healthy style. "We would like to see articles for the physical culturist on muscle building or an article on fitness testing." Informational, how-to, personal experience, interview, profile, inspirational, humor, historical, expose, nostalgia, personal opinion, photo, spot news, new product, and merchandising technique articles. Length: 1,200-1,600 words. Pays 6¢/word.

Columns/Departments: Nutrition Talk (eating for top results) and Shaping Up (improving fitness and stamina). Length: 1,300 words. Pays 6¢/word.

Photos: B&w and color photos are purchased with or without ms. Pays $10 for 8x10 glossy exercise photos; $10 for 8x10 b&w posing shots. Pays $100-200 for color cover and $15 for color used inside magazine (transparencies).

Fillers: Newsbreaks, puzzles, jokes, and short humor. Length: open. Pays $5 minimum.

Tips: "The best way to break in is to seek out the muscle-building 'stars' and do in-depth interviews with biography in mind. Picture support essential."

PATIENT MAGAZINE, American Health Publications, 500 3rd St., Wausau WI 54401. (715)845-2112. Editor: Judith C. Patterson. Annual magazine for hospitalized patients covering equipment, care, treatment and facilities. Circ. 500,000. Pays on acceptance. No byline given. Submit seasonal/holiday material 6 months in advance. Simultaneous queries OK. SASE. Reports in 3 months. Free sample copy.

Nonfiction: "Besides informing, educating and entertaining the patient/consumer, we are also a marketing tool for hospitals." No controversial issues or general consumer pieces. Buys 20-40 mss/year. Query with clips of published work. Length: 500-700 words. Pays negotiable rates.

Photos: Reviews 8x10 prints.

‡**RUNNING AND FITNESS**, American Running and Fitness Association, 2420 K St. NW, Washington DC 20037. (202)965-3430. Editor: Greg Merhar. A bimonthly membership tabloid covering running and aerobic exercise. "Our members are well educated and enjoy reading fresh material on all phases of running and general fitness care." Circ. 35,000. Pays on publication. Byline given. Buys first North American serial rights. Submit seasonal/holiday material 3 months in advance. Simultaneous queries, and simultaneous and photocopied submissions OK. SASE. Reports in 1 month. Sample copy $1; writer's guidelines for SAE and 1 first class stamp.

Nonfiction: Expose, general interest, how-to, interview/profile, photo feature and travel. Buys 20 mss/year. Query with or without published clips or send complete ms. Length 1,000-4,000 words. Pays 5-10¢/word.

Photos: Reviews contact sheets, negatives, 35mm transparencies, and 5x7 and 8x10 prints. Pays negotiable rates. Captions, model release, and identification of subjects required. Buys one-time rights.

Columns/Departments: Running Body (causes, treatment and prevention of specific injury); Travel (unique places to run, e.g., China; preparations; where to run); Features (must be fresh material pertaining to running and/or other aerobic activities. Buys 20 mss/year. Query with or without published clips or send complete ms. Length: 1,000-4,000 words. Pays 5-10¢/word.

Poetry: Buys 2 poems/year. Pays negotiable rate.

Fillers: Anecdotes and short humor. Buys 10 mss/year. Pays negotiable rate.

Tips: "Writing should be geared to general audience. No medical jargon. Interested in all phases of aerobic sports, new developments in health care, nutrition and injury treatment and prevention. All areas are open to freelancers. Our audience is made up mainly of upper/middle class professionals who keep up with developments in running."

‡**RUNNING THROUGH TEXAS**, Running Through Texas Inc., 409 W. 29th, Austin TX 78705. (512)472-4479. Editor: Robert M. McCorkle. 25% freelance written. Bimonthly magazine on running, jogging, physical fitness, and health. "Our magazine is designed primarily for runners, for beginning joggers to marathoners although our slant is geared more toward the serious runner than the novice." Circ. 4,000. Pays on publication. Byline given. Offers $25 kill fee. Buys first North American serial rights only. Submit seasonal/holiday material 3 months in advance. No simultaneous queries, or simultaneous, photocopied or previously published submissions. Computer printout submissions acceptable. SASE. Reports in 3 weeks on queries; 1 month on mss. Publishes ms an average of 6 months after acceptance. Sample copy $2.50; writer's guidelines for 9x12 SAE and 20¢ postage.

Nonfiction: Expose; general interest; historical/nostalgic; how-to (how to train less but run better, run faster, keep from getting bored with running, etc.); inspirational; interview/profile (with noted running stars, top Texas runners, and/or interesting runners); personal experience (only if relevant to other runners and a fresh approach to a topic, i.e., "How I Trained for My First Race," etc. or Pitfalls to Avoid When Racing); technical (must have plenty of supportive data and first-hand experience with product and should not read like an advertisement for product); and travel (only in regard to travels to race in Texas or to border states, also running races in Texas cities, towns). No "How I got started running" articles. Buys 10 mss/year. Query by phone or letter. Length: 500-2,000 words. Pays $25-100.

Photos: Send photos with query. Prefers unusual running-related, *in-focus* shots (pre-race, post-race). No "Start of race" lineup pics. Pays $10-15 for b&w contact sheets; $15-25 for 35mm or 2¼x2¼ color transparencies. Captions and identification of subjects required. Buys one-time rights.

Columns/Departments: The Starting Line (editor's column) and Letters to Editor; On Track (focus on top high school, college tracksters and cross country meets); Running Club News (features a Texas running club—size, when founded, membership information, top runners); Newsprints (brief newsy items pertaining to running, weird happenings); and The Finish Line (results of Texas races). Buys 20 mss/year. Query. Length: 100-200 words. Pays $5-15.

Tips: "A freelancer can best break in to our publication by informing us of any relatively unknown or new road races in his/her area for our 2-month race calendar—our most popular feature. We need to know several months in advance; date, name, distance, starting time, number of runners, where, and who to contact for more information. News sprints (short items about running, runners, new races, running trails in their town) and On the Road Again (1,000-word piece on favorite places to run; unusual trails) are most open to freelancers. We run a professional regional magazine with high standards that requires thorough, tight writing. Being small with limited advertising places space at a premium, writers should look for unique story angles, use proper grammar, and research their articles well. There are too many graduating from college nowadays who can't spell, organize thoughts, or write, yet consider themselves journalists and writers. Pay attention to detail; don't exchange thoroughness for flashiness."

SAN DIEGO AND IMPERIAL COUNTY'S HEALTH AND RESOURCE GUIDE, (formerly *San Diego County's Health and Resource Guide*), Community Resource Group, Box 81702, San Diego CA 92138-1702. (619)299-3718. Editor: Patricia F. Doering. 20% freelance written. Annual 225-page guide published in July or August containing sections on health and health-related subjects with listings of local community resources following editorial material. For public and health professionals. Circ. 5,000. Pays on publication. Submit all material in advance. Previously published submissions preferred due to deadlines. SASE required. Reports in 3 weeks on queries; in 3-6 months on mss. Publishes ms an average of 6 months after acceptance. If available, sample copy $5; $1.50 with SASE for writer's guidelines.

Nonfiction: General interest (cancer, heart disease, exercise); how-to (enter a nursing home, prepare for old age, avoid catastrophic illness, etc.); interviews; new products; books; and photo features (b&w only—drugs, alcohol, mental health and aging, etc.). "Nothing offbeat. No first-person stories. We are particularly in need of current statistical data which keeps the public informed of current trends and advances within both traditional medicine and holistic medicine. We are not a 'borderline' or 'off-beat' medical publication, but one wishing to keep abreast of changes nationwide." Editorial space limited—early January submissions helpful. Query with clips of previously published work. "We will *not* return manuscripts without SASE." Buys 3-8 unsolicited mss/year. Length: 300-1,500 words. Pays $25-500.

Tips: "Query early. Stories of wide and general interest preferred. Best *time* to submit is January-May, annually. Best *way* to submit is 1-2 pages of ms to give us idea of story and style, with cover letter and/or samples of previously published material. We retain ms longer than usual due to funding. We prefer writers to simultaneously submit elsewhere to allow the writer to sell his/her ms—rather than our exclusively holding onto materials.

SHAPE, Merging Mind and Body Fitness, Weider Enterprises, 21100 Erwin St., Woodland Hills CA 91367. (818)884-6800. Editor: Christine MacIntyre. Managing Editor: Pat Ryan. 25% freelance written. Monthly magazine covering women's health and fitness. Circ. 515,000. Pays on acceptance. Offers ⅓ kill fee. Buys all rights and reprint rights. Submit seasonal/holiday material 8 months in advance. Reports in 1 month on queries; 3 weeks on mss. Publishes ms an average of 3 months after acceptance.

Nonfiction: Judie Lewellen, articles editor. Book excerpts; expose (health, fitness related); how-to (get fit); interview/profile (of fit women); travel (spas). "We use health and fitness articles written by professionals in their specific fields. No articles which haven't been queried first." Query with or without clips of published work. Length: 500-2,000 words. Pays negotiable fee.

SLIMMER, Health and Beauty for the Total Woman, Suite 3000, 3420 Ocean Park Blvd., Santa Monica CA 90405. (213)450-0900. Editor: Angela Hynes. Bimonthly magazine covering health and beauty for "college-educated single or married women, ages 18-34, interested in physical fitness and weight loss." Circ. 250,000. Pays 30 days after acceptance. Byline given. Buys all rights. Submit seasonal/holiday queries 6 months in advance. SASE. Reports in 1 month.

Nonfiction: Fitness and nutrition. "We look for well-researched material—the newer the better—by expert writers." No fad diets, celebrity interviews/round-ups, fashion or first-person articles. Buys 7-9 unsolicited mss/year. Query with clips of published work. Length: 2,500-3,000 words. Pays $300.

Photos: State availability of photos.

‡**TLC, The Magazine for Recuperation and Relaxation**, TLC Publications, Inc., 1933 Chestnut St., Philadelphia PA 19103. (215)569-3574. Editor: Rebecca Stefoff. Bimonthly magazine with personality profiles, games, puzzles, humor, sports, food, travel, personal finance, grooming, art, book excerpts, etc. "*TLC* features articles and artwork (mostly reprints) chosen to entertain and divert our audience—hospital patients. Patients receive the magazine free during overnight hospital stays. We avoid health-related material and concentrate on offering general-interest items which will appeal to a demographically diverse readership." Estab. 1983. Circ. 250,000. Pays on publication. Byline given. Buys first rights and second (reprint) rights to material originally published elsewhere. Previously published submissions preferred. Computer printout submissions acceptable. SASE. Reports in 3 weeks on queries; 8 weeks on mss. Sample copy for 9x12 SAE and $2 postage.

Nonfiction: Book excerpts, general interest, historical/nostaglic, Americana, humor, interview/profile, lifestyle (food, the arts, etc.), photo feature, and travel. No health-related, medical, inspirational or religious articles. "We use mostly reprints." Buys approximately 3 original mss/year. Query with published clips. Length: 1,000-3,000 words. Payment negotiated on an individual basis.

Photos: State availability of photos. Model release and identification of subjects required. Buys one-time rights.

Tips: "We're most interested in brief (2-8 typed pages) items or excerpts for a diverse audience. Material too timely for a long shelf life, or too controversial to appeal to a majority of readers, is inappropriate for our publication."

TOTAL FITNESS, National Reporter Publications, Inc., 15115 S. 76th E. Ave., Bixby OK 74008. (918)366-4441. Editor: Anne H. Thomas. 95% freelance written. Magazine covers fitness and health topics of interest to men and women between the ages of 25-55 who are serious about their physical well-being. Magazine published 6-8 times times per year. Circ. 100,000. Pays on acceptance. Byline given. Computer printout submissions acceptable. SASE. Reports in 2 months or less. Publishes ms an average of 4 months after acceptance. Free sample copy and writer's guidelines.

Nonfiction: General interest health topics (adult onset epilepsy, how to avoid back pain); nutrition, diets and recipes (low-sodium, carob, vegetarian); special emphasis on exercise pieces (running, rowing, firming and conditioning arms, hips, calves, etc.); and personal experiences (almost anything can be written from the personal angle, but it must be well written). No fluff pieces or unsubstantiated health articles. "Articles are meant to inspire and/or instruct readers in the area of fitness." Buys 150 mss/year. Two or three paragraph query with clips of published work preferred. Length: 1,500-3,000 words. Pays $75-300.

TOTAL HEALTH, Trio Publications, Suite 300, 6001 Topanga Cyn. Bl., Woodland Hills CA 91367. (213)887-6484. Editor: Robert L. Smith. Bimonthly magazine devoted to holistic health for a family-oriented readership. Circ. 60,000. Pays on publication. Buys first rights only. Submit seasonal material 2½ months in advance. Photocopied submissions OK. SASE. Reports on queries in 3 weeks; on mss in 1 month. Sample copy $1.

Nonfiction: Expose; general interest (family health, nutrition and mental health); how-to (exercise, diet, meditate, prepare natural food); inspirational (meditation); new product (exercise equipment, sports clothing, solar energy, natural foods); and personal experience. No articles on Eastern religions. Buys 25 unsolicited mss/year. Length: 1,800-2,600 words. Pays $50-75.

Photos: Pays $15 maximum/5x7 and 8x10 b&w glossy print. Pays $25 maximum/5x7 and 8x10 color print. Offers no additional payment for photos accepted with ms. Captions and model release required. Buys one-time rights.

Columns/Departments: Buys 18 mss/year. Send complete ms. Length: 1,000-1,500 words. Pays $50-75.

‡**WALKING JOURNAL, The Art, Science and Sport of Walking**, Orenda Media, Box 454, Athens GA 30603. (404)546-1353. Editor: Kevin Kelly. Managing Editor: JoAnn Pulliam. 95% freelance written. Quarterly magazine with practical, useful, helpful and well-written information on walking in the 1980s. Estab. 1983. Circ. 4,000. Pays on publication. Byline given. Buys first North American serial rights only. Submit seasonal/holiday material 3 months in advance. Simultaneous queries, and simultaneous, photocopied, and previously published submissions OK. Electronic submissions OK if compatible with Applewriter II. Computer printout submissions acceptable. SASE. Reports in 1 month. Publishes ms an average of 3 months after acceptance. Sample copy $1; writer's guidelines for business-size SAE and 1 first class stamp.

Nonfiction: General interest (about walking); how-to (walk better, more quickly, less stressfully, etc.); interview/profile (famous/well-known people who are serious walkers); personal experience (what the author has done to make walking more common or more enjoyable); and travel (occasionally a walking guide of a particular place). No romantic reminiscences or unresearched articles. Buys 10 mss/year. Query with published clips or send complete ms. Length: 500-2,000 words. Pays $50-200.

Photos: State availability of photos. Reviews contact sheets. Pays $20-40 for small b&w prints. Captions required. Buys one-time rights.

Tips: "We prefer new freelancers because they have fresh ideas. Because walking is so ordinary, stories must be extremely well written or with an unusual idea. We are not impressed with previous credits. A thoroughly researched article that is lively and upbeat is the best way to break in. Features are also open to freelancers."

WEIGHT WATCHERS MAGAZINE, 360 Lexington Ave., New York NY 10017. (212)370-0644. Editor-in-Chief: Linda Konner. Managing Editor: Fred Levine. 50% freelance written. Monthly publication for those interested in weight loss and weight maintenance through sensible eating and health/nutrition guidance. Circ. 775,000. Buys first rights only. Buys 18-30 unsolicited mss/year. Pays on acceptance. Computer printout submissions acceptable; prefers letter-quality to dot-matrix. Reports in 4 weeks. Publishes ms an average of 3 months after acceptance. Sample copy and writer's guidelines $1.50.

Nonfiction: Subject matter should be related to food, fitness, health or weight loss, but not specific diets. Would like to see researched articles related to the psychological aspects of weight loss and control and suggestions for making the battle easier. Inspirational success stories of weight loss following the Weight Watchers Program also accepted. Send queries with SASE. No full-length mss. Feature ideas should be addressed to: Fred Levine, managing editor. "Before-and-after weight loss story ideas dealing either with celebrities or 'real people' should be sent to: Trisha Thompson, associate editor." Length: 1,500 words maximum. Pays $200-600.

Tips: "It's rewarding giving freelancers the rough shape of how an article should look and seeing where they go with it. It's frustrating working with writers who don't pay enough attention to revisions that have been requested and who send back second drafts with a few changes."

‡**WHOLE LIFE TIMES, Journal for Personal and Planetary Health**, Whole Life Co., 18 Shepard St., Brighton MA 02135. (617)783-8030. Editor: Shelly Kellman. Managing Editor: Kimberly French. Tabloid covering holistic health, environment, and including some material on world peace. Circ. 160,000. Pays 40-60 days after publication. Byline given. Offers 25% kill fee. Buys first North American serial rights, all rights, and second serial (reprint) rights, and makes work-for-hire assignments; depends on topic and author. Submit seasonal/holiday material 4 months in advance. Simultaneous queries, and simultaneous, photocopied, and

previously published submissions OK. SASE. Reports in 2 months. Free sample copy and writer's guidelines.
Nonfiction: Book excerpts (health, environment, community activism); general interest (health-sciences, holistic health, environment, alternative economics and politics); how-to (exercise, relaxation, fitness, appropriate technology, outdoors); interview/profile (on assignment); and new product (health, music, spiritual, psychological, natural diet). No undocumented opinion or narrative. Buys 36-40 mss/year. Query with published clips. Length: 1,150-3,000 words. Pays $50-300.
Photos: Richard Eivers, photo editor. Reviews b&w contact sheets, any size b&w and color transparencies and any size prints. Model release and identification of subjects required. Buys one-time rights.
Columns/Departments: Kimberly French and Barbara Bialick, column/department editors. Films, Books, Recipes, Herbs & Health, Nutrition, Whole Health Network, Living Lightly (appropriate technology), Peacefronts, News Views, Whole Life Person, Music, In the Market. Buys 45-55 mss/year. Query with published clips. Length: 150-1,000 words. Pays $25-80.

THE YOGA JOURNAL, California Yoga Teachers Association, 2054 University Ave., Berkeley CA 94704. (415)841-9200. Editor: Stephan Bodian. 75% freelance written. Bimonthly magazine covering yoga, holistic health, conscious living, spiritual practices, and nutrition. "We reach a middle-class, educated audience interested in self-improvement and higher consciousness." Circ. 25,000. Pays on publication. Byline given. Offers $35 kill fee. Buys first North American serial rights only. Submit seasonal/holiday material 4 months in advance. Simultaneous queries and photocopied submissions OK. SASE. Reports in 6 weeks on queries; 2 months on mss. Publishes ms an average of 6 months after acceptance. Sample copy $2.50; free writer's guidelines.
Nonfiction: Book excerpts; how-to (exercise, yoga, massage, etc.); inspirational (yoga or related); interview/profile; opinion; personal experience; photo feature; and travel (if about yoga). "Yoga is our main concern, but our principal features in each issue highlight other new age personalities and endeavors. Nothing too far-out and mystical. Prefer stories about Americans incorporating yoga, meditation, etc., into their normal lives." Buys 40 mss/year. Query. Length: 750-3,500 words. Pays $35-150.
Photos: Diane McCarney, art director. Send photos with ms. Pays $100-150 for color transparencies; $10-15 for 8x10 b&w prints. Model release (for cover only) and identification of subjects required. Buys one-time rights.
Columns/Departments: Forum; Food (vegetarian, text and recipes); Health; Music (reviews of new age music); and Book Reviews. Buys 12-15 mss/year. Pays $10-25.
Tips: "We always read submissions. We are very open to freelance material and want to encourage writers to submit to our magazine. We're looking for out-of-state contributors, particularly Midwest and east coast."

YOUR LIFE AND HEALTH, 55 W. Oak Ridge Dr., Hagerstown MD 21740. Editor: Ralph Blodgett. 95% freelance written. Buys first rights and sometimes second (reprint) rights to materials originally published elsewhere. Byline given. Buys 90-100 unsolicited mss/year. Pays on acceptance. Computer printout submissions acceptable; prefers letter-quality to dot-matrix. Sample copy $1.25. Free writer's guidelines. No disk submissions. Reports on material generally in 2 months. SASE necessary.
Nonfiction: The editors are looking for practical articles promoting a happier home, better health, and a more fulfilled life. We especially like articles on the family, features on breakthroughs in medicine, all aspects of health (physical, mental, emotional, and spiritual—well researched, with references to authorities or experts), interviews with personalities on health or the home, informational (home safety, etc.), how-to (get out of debt, save time, have a more rewarding life), marriage-improvement, and seasonal (submit 6 months in advance). *Your Life and Health* is written for the typical man/woman on the street. Therefore, articles must be written in an interesting, easy-to-read style. Manuscript length should range from 750 to 2,800 words. Pay ranges from $50-175.
Photos: Only considers color slides (or 5x7 or larger b&w prints) submitted with a ms.
Poetry: This is not a market for poetry.
Tips: "Information should be reliable, no faddism. Clear photocopy articles OK. We generally prefer seeing a finished manuscript rather than query. We are more conservative than other magazines in our field."

History

The history of an era or region becomes *present* in history publications. Listed here are these magazines and others written for historical collectors, genealogy enthusiasts, historic preservationists and researchers. The Hobby and Craft category lists antique and other history markets.

AMERICAN HERITAGE, 10 Rockefeller Plaza, New York NY 10020. Editor: Byron Dobell. Bimonthly. Circ. 125,000. Usually buys all rights. Byline given. Buys 20 uncommissioned mss/year. Pays on acceptance. Before submitting, "check our 28-year index to see whether we have already treated the subject." Submit seasonal material 12 months in advance. Computer printout submissions acceptable; prefers letter-quality to dot-matrix. Reports in 1 month. Query. SASE.
Nonfiction: Wants "historical articles intended for intelligent lay readers rather than professional historians." Emphasis is on authenticity, accuracy and verve. "Interesting documents, photographs and drawings are always welcome." Style should stress "readability and accuracy." Length: 1,500-5,000 words.
Tips: "We have over the years published quite a few 'firsts' from young writers whose historical knowledge, research methods and writing skills met our standards. Everything depends on the quality of the material. We don't really care whether the author is 20 and unknown, or 80 and famous."

AMERICAN HISTORY ILLUSTRATED, Box 8200, Harrisburg PA 17105. (717)657-9555. Editor: Ed Holm. 75% freelance written. "A magazine of cultural, social, military and political history published for a general audience." Monthly except July/August. Pays on acceptance. Byline given. Buys all rights. Computer printout submissions acceptable; no dot-matrix. SASE. Reports in 5 weeks on queries; 9 weeks on mss. Publishes ms an average of 1 year after acceptance. Writer's guidelines on request; sample copy $2.
Nonfiction: Regular features include: Pages from an American Album (brief profiles of interesting personalities); Artifacts (stories behind historical objects); Portfolio (pictorial features on artists, photographers and graphic subjects); Digging Up History (coverage of recent archaeological and historical discoveries); and Testaments to the Past (living history articles on restored historical sites). "Material is presented on a popular rather than a scholarly level." Writers are encouraged to query before submitting ms. "Query letters should be limited to a concise 1-2 page proposal defining your article with an emphasis on its qualities." Buys 60 mss/year. Length: 1,000-4,000 words depending on type of article. Pays $100-400.
Photos: Occasionally buys 8x10 glossy prints with mss; welcomes suggestions for illustrations.
Tips: "Key prerequisites for publication are thorough research and accurate presentation, precise English usage and sound organization, a lively style, and a high level of human interest."

AMERICAN WEST, 3033 N. Campbell Ave., Tucson AZ 85719. Managing Editor: Mae Reid-Bills. Editor: Thomas W. Pew Jr. Published by the Buffalo Bill Memorial Association, Cody WY. Sponsored by the Western History Association. Bimonthly magazine covering all aspects of the American West, past and present. 80 pages. Mostly freelance written. Circ. 150,000. Pays within 2-4 weeks of acceptance. Buys first North American periodical rights, plus anthology rights. Byline given. Submit seasonal/holiday material 6 months in advance. Computer printout submissions acceptable; no dot-matrix. SASE. Reports in 6-8 weeks. Query first.
Nonfiction: Lively, nonacademic, but carefully researched and accurate articles of interest to the intelligent general reader, linking the present with the past of the American West; pictorial features (presenting the life and works of an outstanding Old Western painter or photographer). Length: approx. 3,000 words.
Columns/Departments: Shorter regular features range from 850-1,000 words (best bets for unsolicited mss): Gourmet & Grub (historical background of a Western recipe); Shelters & Households (history behind a Western architectural form); Hidden Inns and Lost Trails (history behind Western landmarks and places to stay—no commercial promotion). Pays $200-800.
Photos: Submit with ms. Also Western Snapshots and Yesterday and Today (submissions from readers of interesting old and contemporary photos "that tell a story of a bygone day"). Payment on acceptance.
Tips: "We strive to connect what the West was with what it is today and what it is likely to become. We seek dynamic, absorbing articles that reflect good research and thoughtful organization of details around a strong central story line. We define 'the West' as the United States west of the Mississippi River, and, in proper context, Canada and Mexico."

‡**BACKWOODSMAN MAGAZINE, The Publication for 20th Century Frontiersmen**, Route 8, Box 579, Livingston TX 77351. Editor: Charlie Richie. 75% freelance written. Bimonthly magazine covering buckskinning, 19th century crafts, muzzleloading, homesteading and trapping. Circ. 5,000. Pays on publication. Byline given. Buys first North American serial rights. Reports in 2 weeks on queries. Publishes ms an average of 4 months after acceptance. Sample copy for $2.
Nonfiction: Historical/nostalgic (1780 to 1900); how-to (19th Century crafts); inspirational (wilderness survival); interview/profile (real-life backwoodsmen); new product (buckskinning field); and travel (American historical). "We want 19th century craft how-tos—mostly the simple kinds of everyday woodslore-type crafts." Buys 30-40 mss/year. Send complete ms. Length: 3-4 double-spaced pages. Pays $25 maximum.
Photos: "We prefer that at least one b&w photo or illustration be submitted with ms."
Fiction: Adventure (old time stories or wilderness camping) and historical (1780 to 1900). Busy 10-5 mss/year. Length: 3-4 double-spaced pages.
Tips: "We publish articles by real backwoodsmen and prefer that the writer just be himself and not Hemingway."

‡BLUE & GRAY MAGAZINE, "For Those Who Still Hear the Guns," Blue & Gray Enterprises, Inc., 5212 W. Broad St., Columbus OH 43228. (614)870-1861. Editor: David E. Roth. Assistant Editor: Tedd M. Trimbath. 65% freelance written. Bimonthly magazine on the Civil War period and current Civil War-related activities. "Our philosophy is color, quality and broad-based reporting. Included in this 'broad-based' reporting is the full range of Civil War-related topics, such as pure history articles, living history, relic hunting, collectibles, wargaming, book reviews, new discoveries, and tour guides of historical sites. Our distribution is international in scope and appeals to both a popular and scholarly market." Estab. 1983. Circ. 13,000 (with a 5% growth per issue). Pays on acceptance. Publishes ms an average of 6 months after acceptance. Byline given. Buys all rights. Submit seasonal/holiday material 6 months in advance. Return postage required. SASE. Reporting time varies with query/manuscripts. Sample copy for 9x12 SAE and 63¢ postage (4th class); free writer's guidelines.
Nonfiction: Book excerpts (history); expose (history); historical/nostalgic; how-to (history, living history, relic hunting, etc.); interview/profile (Civil War descendant); opinion (history); personal experience (history, re-enacting, relic hunting, etc.); photo feature (history); technical (history, re-enacting, relic hunting, etc.); travel (Civil War sites); or article on Civil War history. Query with or without published clips or send complete ms. Length: 1,000-6,000 words. Pays $25-350.
Photos: State availability of photos, or send photos with query or mss. Captions and identification of subjects required. Buys non-exclusive rights for continued use.
Columns/Departments: Book Reviews, Living History, Wargaming, Relic Hunting, Controversy, Profile, etc. Query with or without published clips, or send complete ms. Length: 1,000-4,000 words. Pays $25-250.
Fiction: Historical fiction only. Query with or without published clips, or send complete ms. Length: 1,000-6,000 words. Pays $25-250.
Poetry: Robin P. Roth, poetry editor. Free verse, light verse and traditional. Length: up to 100 lines. Pays $10-25.
Tips: "Submit an appropriate Civil War-related ms with sources listed (footnotes preferred), and photos or photo suggestions. All areas of our publication are open to freelancers except Tour Guides which is somewhat restricted because of already firm commitments."

BRITISH HERITAGE, Incorporating British History Illustrated, Historical Times, Inc., 2245 Kohn Rd., Box 8200, Harrisburg PA 17105. (717)657-9555. Executive Editor: Gail Huganir. 30% freelance written. Bimonthly magazine covering British history and travel in the British Isles, Commonwealth countries and old Empire. "*British Heritage* aims to present aspects of Britain's history and culture in an entertaining and informative manner." Circ. 60,000. Pays on acceptance. Buys first rights only. Byline given. Makes work-for-hire assignments. Simultaneous queries OK. Computer printout submissions acceptable; no dot-matrix. SASE. Reports in 3 weeks on queries; 14 weeks on mss. Publishes ms an average of 1 year after acceptance. Sample copy $4. Free writer's guidelines for SAE and 1 first class stamp before submitting work.
Nonfiction: Historical (British history) and travel. "We insist on sound research for both historical and general interest articles and need information for the "For the Visitor" section, such as houses, museums, exhibitions, etc., associated with the main topic. We prefer a popular (but no cliches) to a scholarly style and advocate simplicity and clarity in articles. Because of the great range of subject matter in Britain's history, we cover significant rather than trivial aspects of people, issues, events and places. We have, however, no bias against the little-known or controversial subject *per se* as long as it is interesting." No fiction, personal experience articles or poetry. Buys 30 unsolicited mss/year. Query with clips of published work. Length: 1,000-3,000 words. Pays $65/1,000 words; $400 maximum.
Photos: State availability of photos or send photocopies. "We will consider fine quality photos only." Pays $20 maximum for color transparencies; $10 maximum for b&w prints. Captions and identification of subjects required. Buys one-time rights.
Tips: "No footnotes needed but sources are required. English style and spelling only. Please read the magazine for hints on style and subject matter. Grab the reader's attention as early as possible, and don't be afraid to use humor. We look for accurate research written in a flowing, interesting style with excellent opportunities for illustration. Provide a list of further reading. There will be increased emphasis in the year ahead on shops, stately homes and old buildings, museums, old customs, inns and other areas of tourist interest."

CIVIL WAR TIMES ILLUSTRATED, 2245 Kohn Rd., Box 8200, Harrisburg PA 17105. (717)657-9555. Editor: John E. Stanchak. Magazine published monthly except July and August. Circ. 120,000. Pays on acceptance. Buys all rights, first rights or one-time rights, or makes work-for-hire assignments. Submit seasonal/holiday material 1 year in advance. SASE. Reports in 2 weeks on queries; 3 months on mss. Sample copy $2; free writer's guidelines.
Nonfiction: Profile, photo feature, and Civil War historical material. "Positively no fiction or poetry." Buys 20 mss/year. Recent article example: "Stonewall Jackson—The Wrath of God" (March 1984). Length: 2,500-5,000 words. Query. Pays $75-450.
Photos: Jeanne Collins, art director. State availability. Pays $5-50 for 8x10 b&w glossy prints and copies of Civil War photos; $400-500 for 4-color cover photos; and $150-250 for color photos for interior use.

Tips: "We're very open to new submissions. Querying us after reading several back issues, then submitting illustration and art possibilities along with the query letter is the best 'in.' Never base the narrative solely on family stories or accounts. Submissions must be written in a popular style but based on solid academic research. Manuscripts are required to have marginal source annotations."

GORHAM GENEALOGY AND HISTORY, 800 South Euclid St., Fullerton CA 92632. (714)526-2131. Publisher/Editor: Daniel J. Gorham. Quarterly magazine covering all branches of history and genealogy of Gorham family. 90% freelance written. Circ. 3,499. Pays on acceptance. Byline given. Offers 50% kill fee. Buys all rights. Submit seasonal/holiday material 8 months in advance. Previously published work OK. SASE. Reports in 3 weeks on queries; 2 months on mss. Publishes ms an average of 4 months after acceptance. Sample copy $2.
Nonfiction: Book excerpts; expose; general interest; historical/nostaglic; humor; interview/profile; new product (about innovations in capturing, storing and retrieving data); personal experience; photo feature; and travel. Query or send complete ms. Length: 500-3,000 words. Pays $75-300; or 2¢/word.
Photos: Send photos with ms. Pays $10-50 for 5x7 or larger b&w prints. Buys one-time rights.
Tips: "We need historical articles: places named after the Gorhams; Gorham pioneers, soldiers, horse thiefs; present day Gorhams, various Gorham family trees; how to trace your family tree; and interviews of persons involved in genealogy."

HISTORIC PRESERVATION, National Trust for Historic Preservation, 1785 Massachusetts Ave. NW, Washington DC 20036. Editor: Thomas J. Colin. A benefit of membership in the National Trust for Historic Preservation. Read by well-educated people with a strong interest in preserving America's architectural and cultural heritage. Bimonthly magazine. Circ. 140,000. Pays on acceptance. Buys one-time rights. SASE. Reports in 1 month. Free writer's guidelines.
Nonfiction: "We are willing to review queries from professional writers on subjects directly and indirectly related to historic preservation, including efforts to save buildings, structures and rural and urban neighborhoods of historical, architectural and cultural significance. No local history; must relate to sites, objects, buildings, people involved in preservation, and neighborhoods specifically. Also interested in maritime and archeological subjects relating to heritage preservation. Indirectly related subjects OK, such as old-style regional foods, cultural traditions. Interesting, well-written feature stories with a preservation angle are sought. Most material is prepared on a commissioned basis. Writer must be very familiar with our subject matter, which deals with a specialized field, in order to present a unique publication idea." Length: 1,000-2,500 words. Pays $800 maximum.
Photos: Query or send contact sheet. Pays for 8x10 b&w glossy prints purchased without mss or on assignment; $50-200 for color.

‡**THE MUZZLELOADING ARTILLERYMAN**, Century Publications, Inc., 3 Church St., Winchester MA 01890. (617)729-8100. Editor: C. Peter Jorgensen. Quarterly magazine covering antique artillery, fortifications, and crew-served weapons up to 1900 for competition shooters, collectors and living history reenactors using muzzleloading artillery; "emphasis on Revolutionary War and Civil War but includes everyone interested in pre-1900 artillery and fortifications, preservation, construction of replicas, etc." Circ. 3,100. Pays on publication. Byline given. Not copyrighted. Buys one-time rights. Simultaneous queries, and simultaneous, photocopied and previously published submissions OK. SASE. Reports in 3 weeks. Free sample copy and writer's guidelines.
Nonfiction: Historical/nostalgic; how-to (reproduce ordnance equipment/sights/implements tools/accessories, etc.); interview/profile; new product; opinion (must be accompanied by detailed background of writer and include references); personal experience; photo feature; technical (must have footnotes); and travel (where to find interesting antique cannon). Buys 24-30 mss/year. Send complete ms. Length: 300 words minimum. Pays $20-60.
Photos: Send photos with ms. Pays $5 for 5x7 and larger b&w prints. Captions and identification of subjects required.
Tips: "We regularly use freelance contributions for Places-to-Visit, Cannon Safety, The Workshop and Unit Profiles departments. Also need pieces on unusual cannon or cannon with a known and unique history."

NORTH CAROLINA HISTORICAL REVIEW, Historical Publications Section, Archives and History, 109 E. Jones St., Raleigh NC 27611. (919)733-7442. Editor: Marie D. Moore. 100% freelance written. Emphasizes scholarly historical subjects for historians and others interested in history, with emphasis on the history of North Carolina. Quarterly magazine; 100 pages. Circ. 2,000. Buys all rights. Phone queries OK. Computer printout submissions acceptable; prefers letter-quality to dot-matrix. SASE. Reports in 3 months. Publishes ms an average of up to 2 years after acceptance. Free writer's guidelines.
Nonfiction: Articles relating to North Carolina history in particular, Southern history in general. Topics about which relatively little is known or are new interpretations of familiar subjects. All articles must be based on primary sources and footnoted. Buys 10 unsolicited mss/year. Recent article example: "Neighbor against Neigh-

bor: The Inner Civil War in the Randolph County Area of Confederate North Carolina" (January, 1984). Length: 15-25 typed pages. Pays $25/article.

NORTH SOUTH TRADER, 8020 New Hampshire Ave., Langley Park MD 20783. (301)434-4080. Editor: Wm. S. Mussenden. Covers all aspects of American Civil War history with special attention to artifacts of the period for Civil War historians, collectors, relic hunters, libraries and museums. Bimonthly magazine; 52 to 68 (8½x11) pages. Circ. 10,000. Rights purchased vary with author and material; usually buys all rights. Buys 60 mss/year. Pays on publication. Photocopied and simultaneous submissions OK. Reports in 3 weeks. Query first or submit complete ms. Sample copy and writer's guidelines $1. SASE.
Nonfiction and Photos: General subject matter deals with famous, and/or unusual people/events of the Civil War, military artifacts (weapons, accoutrements, uniforms, etc.), battlefield preservation, relic restoration, and historical information on battles, politics, and commerce. Prefers a factual or documentary approach to subject matter. Also concerned with current events such as battle reenactments, living history and relic show coverage. Emphasis on current findings (archaeology) and research related to these artifacts. Not interested in treasure magazine type articles. Length: 500-3,000 words. Pays 2¢/word. B&w photos are purchased with or without ms. Captions required. Pays $2.

OLD WEST, Western Publications, Box 665, Perkins OK 74059. (405)547-2882. Editor: Jim Dullenty. Byline given. See *True West*.

PERSIMMON HILL, 1700 NE 63rd St., Oklahoma City OK 73111. Editor: Dean Krakel. Senior Editor: Sara Dobberteen. For an audience interested in Western art, Western history, ranching and rodeo, historians, artists, ranchers, art galleries, schools, and libraries. Publication of the National Cowboy Hall of Fame and Western Heritage Center. Quarterly. Circ. 25,000. Buys all rights. Byline given. Buys 12-14 mss/year. Pays on publication. Sample copy $3. Reporting time on mss accepted for publication varies. Returns rejected material immediately. Query. SASE.
Nonfiction: Historical and contemporary articles on famous Western figures connected with pioneering the American West, Western art, rodeo, cowboys, etc. (or biographies of such people), stories of Western flora and animal life, and environmental subjects. Only thoroughly researched and historically authentic material is considered. May have a humorous approach to subject. Not interested in articles that reappraise, or in any way put the West and its personalities in an unfavorable light. No "broad, sweeping, superficial pieces; i.e., the California Gold Rush or rehashed pieces on Billy the Kid, etc." Length: 2,000-3,000 words. Pays $150 minimum.
Photos: B&w glossy prints or color transparencies purchased with or without ms, or on assignment. Pays according to quality and importance for b&w and color. Suggested captions appreciated.

‡PRESERVATION NEWS, National Trust for Historic Preservation, 1785 Massachusetts Ave. NW, Washington DC 20016. (202)673-4072. Editor: Michael Leccese. Managing Editor: Arnold M. Berke. A monthly tabloid covering preservation of historic buildings in the US. "We cover effort and controversies involving historic buildings and districts. Most entries are news stories, features or essays. Our audience of 250,000 tends to be wealthy and middle-aged." Circ. 135,000. Pays on acceptance. Byline given. Offers variable kill fee. Not copyrighted. Buys one-time rights. Simultaneous queries, and photocopied and previously published submissions OK. SASE. Reports in 1 month on queries. Sample copy 25¢ and 40% postage; free writer's guidelines.
Nonfiction: Historical/nostalgic, humor, interview/profile, opinion, personal experience, photo feature, and travel. Buys 12 mss/year. Query with published clips. Length: 500-1,000 words. Pays $75-200.
Photos: State availability of photos with query or ms. Reviews b&w contact sheet. Pays $25-100. Identification of subjects required.
Columns/Departments: "We seek an urban affairs reporter who can give a new slant on development conflict throughout US." Buys 6 mss/year. Query with published clips. Length: 600-1,000 words. Pays $75-200.

TRUE WEST, Western Publications, Box 665, Perkins OK 74059. (405)547-2882. Editor: Jim Dullenty. 90% freelance written. Monthly magazine. Circ. 90,000. Pays on acceptance. Buys first North American serial rights. Byline given. "Magazine is distributed nationally, but if not on the newsstands in a particular location will send sample copy for $1. Queries should give proposed length of article, what rights are offered, whether pix are available, and enough information for us to check our file for material covered or on hand. Example: an ageless query, " 'Would you like an article on a mountain man?' Without his name we simply can't say." Computer printout submissions acceptable but discouraged. Publishes ms an average of 7 months after acceptance. SASE.
Nonfiction: "Factual accounts regarding people, places and events of the Frontier West (1830-1910). Sources are required. Fast-paced action, adventure, gun fights, Indian raids, and those things which contribute to an exciting story. We want stories about outlaws, lawmen and the major personalities of the Old West. If based on family papers, records, memoirs, etc., reminiscenses must be accurate as to dates and events. Unless the author is telling of his/her own experiences, please use third person whenever possible; that is, give the people names: 'James Brown,' instead of 'Grandfather,' etc. Family relationships can be stated at end. We also receive con-

siderable material which is good local history, but would have limited appeal for a national readership." Length: 500-3,000 words; "rarely will anything longer be accepted." Pays 5¢/word and up.
Photos: "All mss must be accompanied by usable b&w photos. We want at least two photos per 1,000 words. Photos are returned after publication." Pays $10/photo for one-time use.

VIRGINIA CAVALCADE, Virginia State Library, Richmond VA 23219. Primarily for readers with an interest in Virginia history. Quarterly magazine; 48 pages. Circ. 12,000. Buys all rights. Byline given. Buys 12-15 mss/year. Pays on acceptance. Rarely considers simultaneous submissions. Submit seasonal material 15-18 months in advance. Reports in 4 weeks to 1 year. Query. SASE. Sample copy $2; free writer's guidelines.
Nonfiction: "We welcome readable and factually accurate articles that are relevant to some phase of Virginia history. Art, architecture, literature, education, business, technology and transportation are all acceptable subjects, as well as political and military affairs. Articles must be based on thorough, scholarly research. We require footnotes but do not publish them. Any period from the age of exploration to the mid-20th century, and any geographical section or area of the state may be represented. Must deal with subjects that will appeal to a broad readership, rather than to a very restricted group or locality. Articles must be suitable for illustration, although it is not necessary that the author provide the pictures. If the author does have pertinent illustrations or knows their location, the editor appreciates information concerning them." Length: approximately 3,500 words. Pays $100.
Photos: Uses 8x10 b&w glossy prints; color transparencies should be at least 4x5.

‡**YE OLDE NEWES**, Stapleton Investments, Box 1508, Lufkin TX 75902-1508. (409)639-1314. Editor: Libby Stapleton. Managing Editor: C. Stapleton. 90+% freelance written. Historical/hysterical semiannual magazine about the Renaissance (1300 AD-1650 AD). "The prime purpose of *Ye Olde Newes* is to entertain. Its secondary purpose is to generate interest in the Renaissance period. Its market is the general public who might have some interest in the period 1300 AD through 1650 AD, or one of the Renaissance Festival theme parks across the country." Estab. 1983. Circ. 45,000. Pays on publication. Byline given. Offers $20 kill fee. Buys first North American serial rights, simultaneous rights, and second (reprint) rights to material originally published elsewhere, and makes work-for-hire assignments. Simultaneous queries, and simultaneous, photocopied, and previously published submissions OK. Computer printout submissions acceptable. Reports in 2 weeks on queries; 4 weeks on mss. Sample copy $2; writer's guidelines for business-size SAE and 20¢ postage.
Nonfiction: Historical/nostalgic (historical as well as "tongue in cheek" of the period); humor (bawdy, but good taste, of a medieval nature); and interview/profile (interviews of a funny nature with little-known characters of the 1300 AD-1650 AD period). All material must be appropriate to the medieval or Renaissance period. Query with or without published clips. Send complete ms. Length: 500-3,000 words. Pays 3¢/word.
Fiction: Fantasy (medieval); historical (tongue in cheek or humorous historical); and humorous (medieval). All material must be appropriate to the Renaissance period (1300 AD-1650 AD). Looks at 40-50 mss/year. Query with or without published clips or send complete ms. Length: 500-3,000 words. Pays 3¢/word.
Poetry: "A limited number of poems of a bawdy nature, but in good taste (not lewd) about the Renaissance period will be considered." Submit maximum 5 poems. Length: open. Pays $15 maximum.
Tips: "Query only on material relevant to the Renaissance. We prefer light and funny material about the period. All queries and mss are given prompt attention. Having been published previously is not considered. We are interested in articles about artists and craftspeople who perform medieval crafts or entertainment and how-to articles about the period (recipes, crafts, etc.). We don't receive enough submissions."

Hobby and Craft

Collectors, do-it-yourselfers, and craftsmen look to these magazines for inspiration and information. Publications covering antiques and miniatures are also listed here. Publications for electronics and radio hobbyists are included in the Science classification.

AMERICAN BOOK COLLECTOR, 274 Madison Ave., New York NY 10016. (212)685-2250. Consulting Editor: Anthony Fair. Bimonthly magazine on book collecting from the 15th century to the present for individuals, rare book dealers, librarians, and others interested in books and bibliomania. Circ. 3,500. Pays on publication. Submit seasonal material 3 months in advance. Photocopied and previously published submissions OK. Electronic submissions OK if IBM PC, "others by special arrangement." Computer printout submissions acceptable; prefers letter-quality to dot-matrix. SASE. Reports in 4-6 weeks. Sample copy and writer's guidelines for $3.50.

Nonfiction: General interest (some facet of book collecting: category of books; taste and technique; artist; printer; binder); interview (prominent book collectors; producers of contemporary fine and limited editions; scholars; librarians); and reviews of exhibitions. Buys 5-10 unsolicited mss/year. "We absolutely require queries with clips of previously published work." Length: 1,500-4,500 words. Pays 5¢/word.

Photos: State availability of photos. Prefers b&w glossy prints of any size. Offers no additional payment for photos accompanying ms. Captions and model release required. Buys one-time rights.

Columns/Departments: Contact editor. Book reviews of books on book collecting, and gallery exhibitions.

Tips: "Query should include precise description of proposed article accompanied by description of author's background plus indication of extent of illustrations."

‡**AMERICAN CERAMICS, The Ceramic Art Quarterly**, 14 W. 44th St., New York NY 10036. (212)944-2180. Editor: Michael McTwigan. Magazine covering ceramic art. Circ. 3,200. Pays on publication. Byline given. Buys one-time rights. Simultaneous queries OK. Computer printout submissions acceptable. SASE. Reports in 1 month on queries; 3 months on mss. Sample copy $5; free writer's guidelines.

Nonfiction: Book excerpts, historical, interview/profile and opinion. Buys 24 articles, 40 reviews/year. Query with published clips. Length: 1,000-3,000 words. Pays $150-250.

AMERICAN CLAY EXCHANGE, Page One Publications, Box 2674, La Mesa CA 92041. (619)697-5922. Editor: Susan N. Cox. Biweekly newsletter on any subjects relating to American made pottery—old or new—with an emphasis on antiques and collectibles for collectors, buyers and sellers of American made pottery, earthenware, china, etc. Pays on publication. "We sometimes pay on acceptance if we want the manuscript badly. If article has not been printed within 3 months, we will pay for it anyway." Byline given. Buys all rights or first rights "if stated when manuscript submitted." Submit seasonal/holiday material 4 months in advance. Computer printout submissions acceptable; no dot-matrix. SASE. Reports in 1 month on queries; 2 months on mss. Sample copy $1.50; free writer's guidelines.

Nonfiction: Book reviews (on books pertaining to American made pottery, china, earthenware); historical/nostalgic (on museums and historical societies in the US if they handle pottery, etc.); how-to (identify pieces, clean, find them); and interview/profile (if artist is up-and-coming). No "I found a piece of pottery for 10¢ at a flea market" types. Buys 30 mss/year. Query or send complete ms. Length: 1,000 words maximum. Pays $125 maximum.

Photos: Janet Culver, photo editor. Send photos with ms. Pays $5 for b&w prints. Captions required. Buys all rights; "will consider one-time rights."

Tips: "Know the subject being written about, including marks and values of pieces found. Telling a reader what 'marks' are on pieces is most essential. The best bet is to write a short (200-300 word) article with a few photos and marks. We are a small company willing to work with writers who have good, salable ideas and know our product. Any article that deals effectively with a little-known company or artist during the 1900-1950 era is most sought after. We will be adding a section devoted to dinnerware, mostly from the 1900-1950 era—same guidelines."

AMERICANA, 29 W. 38th St., New York NY 10018. (212)398-1550. Editor: Michael Durham. 90% freelance written. Bimonthly magazine featuring contemporary uses of the American past for "people who like to adapt historical ways to modern living." Circ. 365,000. Pays on acceptance. Byline given. Buys all rights. Submit seasonal material 6 months in advance. Computer printout submissions acceptable; prefers letter-quality to dot-matrix. SASE. Reports in 6 weeks. Publishes ms an average of 9 months after acceptance. Sample copy $1.95; SASE *required* for writer's guidelines.

Nonfiction: General interest (crafts, architecture, cooking, gardening, restorations, antiques, preservation, decorating, collecting, people who are active in these fields and museums); and travel (to historic sites, restored villages, hotels, inns, and events celebrating the past). "Familiarize yourself with the magazine. You must write from first-hand knowledge, not just historical research. Send a well thought out idea. Send a few snapshots of a home restoration or whatever you are writing about." Especially needs material for Christmas and Thanksgiving issues. Buys 10 mss/issue. Query with clips of previously published work. Length: 2,000 words minimum. Pays $400 minimum.

Columns/Departments: On Exhibit (short piece on an upcoming exhibit, $75-500); How-to (usually restoration or preservation of an historical object, 2,000 words, $400); Sampler (newsy items to fit the whole magazine, 500 words, $75); In the Days Ahead (text and calendar of events such as antique shows or craft shows, 1,000 words plus listing, $400).

Tips: "It's rewarding to discover an able writer with whom we can establish an on-going relationship."

THE ANTIQUARIAN, Box 798, Huntington NY 11743. (516)271-8990. Editor-in-Chief: Marguerite Cantine. Managing Editor: Elizabeth Kilpatrick. Emphasizes antiques and 19th-century or earlier art. Monthly tabloid. 10% freelance written. Circ. 15,000. Pays on publication. Buys all rights. Pays 10% kill fee. Byline given. Submit seasonal/holiday material 3 months in advance. Computer printout submissions acceptable; prefers letter-quality to dot-matrix. SASE with proper postage. Reports in 6 weeks. Publishes ms an average of 2 months after acceptance. Sample copy for 12x15½ SASE with $1.25 postage attached.

Nonfiction: How-to (refinish furniture, repair glass, restore old houses, paintings, rebind books, resilver glass, etc.); general interest (relations of buyers and dealers at antique shows/sales, auction reports); historical (data, personal and otherwise, on famous people in the arts and antiques field); interview; photo feature (auctions, must have caption on item including selling price); profile (wants articles around movie stars and actors who collect antiques; query); and travel (historical sites of interest in New York, New Jersey, Connecticut, Pennsylvania and Delaware). Wants concise articles, accurate research; no material on art deco, collectibles, anything made after 1900, cutesy things to 'remake' from antiques, or flea markets and crafts shows. Buys 6 mss/year. Submit complete ms. Length: 200-2,000 words. Pays 3¢/word.

Photos: Pays 50¢-$1 for 3½x5 glossy b&w prints. Captions required. Buys all rights. Model release required.

Tips: "Don't write an article unless you *love* this field. Write as though you were carrying on a nice conversation with your mother. No pretentions. No superiority. It's frustrating when freelancers don't read, follow instructions, or send an SASE, call the office and *demand* answers to questions, or act unprofessionally. But once in a blue moon they do get a totally fresh idea."

ANTIQUE MONTHLY, Boone, Inc., Drawer 2, Tuscaloosa AL 35402. (205)345-0272. Editor/Publisher: Gray D. Boone. Associate Publisher: Anita G. Mason. Senior Editor: Cindy Hobson. 20% freelance written. Monthly tabloid covering art, antiques, and major museum shows. "More than half are college graduates, over 27% have post-graduate degrees. Fifty-nine percent are in $35,000 and over income bracket. Average number of years readers have been collecting art/antiques is 20.5/years." Circ. 65,100. Pays on publication. Buys all rights. Submit seasonal/holiday material 2 months in advance. Photocopied submissions OK. SASE. Reports in 1 month on queries and mss. Free sample copy.

Nonfiction: Historical (pertaining to art, furniture, glass, etc. styles); travel (historic sites, restorations); museum exhibitions; and book reviews. Recent article example: "Americana at Auction: A Lot to Admire" (March 1984). No personal material. Buys 6-10 unsolicited mss/year. Length: 1,000-1,500 words. Pays $125 minimum/article.

Photos: "Black and whites stand a better chance of being used than color." State availability of photos. Prefers color transparencies and 5x7 b&w prints. "We rarely pay for photos; usually we pay only for costs incurred by the writer, and this must be on prior agreement." Captions required.

Tips: "Freelancers are important because they offer the ability to cover stories that regular staff and correspondents cannot cover."

THE ANTIQUE TRADER WEEKLY, Box 1050, Dubuque IA 52001. (319)588-2073. Editor: Kyle D. Husfloen. 25% freelance written. For collectors and dealers in antiques and collectibles. Weekly newspaper; 90-120 pages. Circ. 90,000. Buys all rights. Buys about 60 mss/year. Payment at beginning of month following publication. Photocopied and simultaneous submissions OK. Computer printout submissions acceptable; no dot-matrix. Submit seasonal material (holidays) 4 months in advance. Query or submit complete ms. Publishes ms an average of 1 year after acceptance. SASE. Sample copy 50¢; free writer's guidelines.

Nonfiction: "We invite authoritative and well-researched articles on all types of antiques and collectors' items and in-depth stories on specific types of antiques and collectibles. No human interest stories. We do not pay for brief information on new shops opening or other material printed as service to the antiques hobby." Pays $5-50 for feature articles; $50-150 for feature cover stories.

Photos: Submit a liberal number of good b&w photos to accompany article. Uses 35mm or larger color transparencies for cover. Offers no additional payment for photos accompanying mss.

Tips: "Send concise, polite letter stating the topic to be covered in the story and the writer's qualifications. No 'cute' letters rambling on about some 'imaginative' story idea. Writers who have a concise yet readable style and know their topic are always appreciated. I am most interested in those who have personal collecting experience or can put together a knowledgeable and informative feature after interviewing a serious collector/authority."

BANK NOTE REPORTER, Krause Publications, 700 E. State St., Iola WI 54990. (715)445-2214. Editor: Russ Rulau. 30% freelance written. Monthly tabloid for advanced collectors of US and world paper money. Circ. 4,250. Pays on acceptance. Byline given. Buys first and second rights to the same material. Photocopied submissions acceptable. Computer printout submissions OK; prefers letter-quality to dot-matrix. SASE. Reports in 2 weeks. Publishes ms an average of 4 months after acceptance. Free sample copy.

Nonfiction: "We review articles covering any phase of paper money collecting including investing, display, storage, history, art, story behind a particular piece of paper money and the business of paper money." No news items. "Our staff covers the hard news." Buys 4 mss/issue. Send complete ms. Length: 500-3,000 words. Pays 3¢/word to first-time contributors; negotiates fee for later articles.

Photos: Pays $5 minimum for 5x7 b&w glossy prints. Captions and model release required.

THE BLADE MAGAZINE, Stonewall Bldg., Suite 104, 112 Lee Parkway Dr., Chattanooga TN 37421. Editor: J. Bruce Voyles. 90% freelance written. For knife enthusiasts who want to know as much as possible about quality knives and edged weapons. Bimonthly magazine. Pays on publication. Buys all rights. Submit seasonal/holiday material 6 months in advance. Previously published submissions OK. Computer printout submissions acceptable; no dot-matrix. SASE. Reports in 6 weeks. Publishes ms an average of 1 year after acceptance. Sample copy $2.25.

Nonfiction: Historical (on knives and weapons); how-to; interview (knifemakers); new product; nostalgia; personal experience; photo feature; profile and technical. No poetry. Buys 75 unsolicited mss/year. Query with "short letter describing subject to be covered. We will respond as to our interest in the subject. We do not contract on the basis of a letter. We evaluate manuscripts and make our decision on that basis." Length: 1,000-2,000 words. Pays 5¢/word minimum.

Photos: Send photos with ms. Pays $5 for 8x10 b&w glossy prints, $25-75 for 35mm color transparencies. Captions required.

Tips: "The ideal article for us concerns a knife maker or a historical article on an old factory—full of well-researched long lost facts with entertaining anecdotes. Read the publication beforehand and save us both a lot of wasted time!"

THE BOOK-MART, Box 72, Lake Wales FL 33853. Editor: Robert Pohle. Publisher: Mae Pohle McKinley. 90% freelance written. Emphasizes book collecting and the used book trade. Bimonthly half-tabloid; 36 pages. Circ. 2,000. Pays on publication. Buys one-time rights. Submit seasonal/holiday material 6 weeks in advance. Simultaneous, photocopied and previously published submissions OK. Computer printout submissions acceptable. SASE. Reports in 6 weeks. Publishes ms an average of 3 months after acceptance. Sample copy for 40¢ in postage.

Nonfiction: "Especially need articles of interest to book dealers and collectors containing bibliographical and pricing data." Expose (literary forgeries); general interest (articles about regional authors, especially those highly collected); historical (about books, authors, publishers, printers, booksellers); how-to (book conservation and restoration techniques, no amateur binding); interview (if in field of interest); nostalgia (articles about paper collectibles, especially those with pricing information); personal experience; and travel (literary landmarks). "No rambling accounts with no specific focus or articles about an unknown poet who has published his/her first book." Buys 48 unsolicited mss/year. Query. Length: 1,000-2,500 words. Pays 50¢/column inch.

Photos: State availability of photos with query. Pays $5 minimum for 5x7 or larger b&w glossy or matte finish prints. Buys one-time rights.

Columns/Departments: Profiles of dealers and collectors, and I Collect. Query "unless of a timely nature." Pays 50¢/column inch.

‡CHRISTMAS ALMANAC/CHRISTMAS CROCHET, Harris Publication, 1115 Broadway, New York NY 10010. (212)434-4239. Editor: Barbara Jacksier. An annual holiday crafts magazine covering home-style, country ideas plus instructions on how to do them. Circ. 500,000. Pays on publication. Byline given. Buys one-time rights. Submit seasonal/holiday material 10 months in advance. Computer printout submissions acceptable. SASE. Reports in 2 months.

Nonfiction: How-to (holiday craft or decorating ideas). Buys 30-40 craft projects/year. Send complete ms. Pays $25-150.

Photos: Send photos with accompanying query or ms. Pays $20 for 5x7 b&w prints and color transparencies. Buys one-time rights.

COINS, Krause Publications, 700 E. State St., Iola WI 54990. (715)445-2214. Assistant to the Publisher: Bob Lemke. Monthly magazine about US and foreign coins for all levels of collectors, investors and dealers. Circ. 130,000. Average issue includes 8 features.

Nonfiction: "We'd like to see articles on any phase of the coin hobby; collection, investing, displaying, history, art, the story behind the coin, unusual collections, profiles on dealers and the business of coins." No news items. "Our staff covers the hard news." Buys 8 mss/issue. Send complete ms. Computer printout submissions acceptable; prefers letter-quality to dot-matrix. Length: 500-5,000 words. Pays 3¢/word to first-time contributors; fee negotiated for later articles.

Photos: Pays $5 minimum for b&w prints. Pays $25 minimum for 35mm color transparencies used. Captions and model release required. Buys first rights.

COLLECTIBLES ILLUSTRATED, Yankee Publishing Inc., Main St., Dublin NH 03444. (603)563-8111. Editor: Charles J. Jordan. 80% freelance written. Bimonthly magazine for people interested in collectibles. "Our editorial emphasis is on the new fields of collecting which are sweeping the country, items which have largely gained collecting status over the past quarter of a century and often date back no farther than 100 years (although we are flexible on this)." Circ. 85,000. Pays on acceptance. Byline given. Offers variable kill fee to assigned stories only. Buys all rights preferably, but will negotiate. Submit seasonal/holiday material 4-5 months in advance. SASE. Computer printout submissions acceptable. Reports in 2 weeks on queries; 3 weeks

on mss. Publishes ms an average of 8 months after acceptance. Free sample copy and writer's guidelines.
Nonfiction: General interest; historical/nostalgic (with collectibles slant); how-to (preserve, restore and display collectibles); interview/profile (on celebrity collectors and collectors-profiles); and travel (trips collectors can take to see public collectors/museums. "We are always in need of stories about unusual collectors, people with "the world's biggest collection" of anything, and 'Collector's Trip' features." No "canned" material, stories on antiques or non-American collectibles. Buys 50 mss/year. Query with clips. Length: 500-2,500 words. Pays $300-400 average.
Photos: State availability of photos. Pays $50 average for b&w contact sheets and 35mm color transparencies. Identification of subjects required. Buys all rights preferably, but will negotiate.
Columns/Departments: Display Case (newsy wrap-up of latest events of the collecting world—new exhibits, auctions, etc.). Buys 6-10/year. Query with clips of published work. Length: 200-700 words. Pays $25-100.
Tips: "We welcome writers and are interested in developing new first-time writers with promise. Areas most open to freelancers are: Collector Profiles ('lively stories about collectors with plenty of good quotes'); and Features (no writing 'off the top of your head'; quote experts, facts, information)."

COLLECTOR EDITIONS QUARTERLY, Collector Communications Corp., 170 5th Ave., New York NY 10010. Editor: R. C. Rowe. 35% freelance written. For collectors, mostly aged 30-65 in any rural or suburban, affluent area; reasonably well-educated. Quarterly. Circ. 80,000. Rights purchased vary with author and material. Buys all rights, first North American serial rights, first serial rights, second serial (reprint) rights, and simultaneous rights. Buys 15-30 mss/year. "First assignments are always done on a speculative basis." Pays on publication. Photocopied submissions OK. Computer printout submissions acceptable; no dot-matrix. Query with outline. Reports in 6-8 weeks. Publishes ms an average of 6 months after acceptance. SASE. Will send sample copy to writer for $1.
Nonfiction: "Short features about collecting, written in tight, newsy style. We specialize in contemporary (postwar) collectibles. Particularly interested in items affected by scarcity; focus on glass and ceramics. Values for pieces being written about should be included." Informational, how-to, interview, profile, expose, and nostalgia. Length: 500-2,500 words. Pays $50-150. Columns cover stamps, porcelains, glass, Western art and graphics. Length: 750 words. Pays $75.
Photos: B&w and color photos purchased with accompanying ms with no additional payment. Captions are required. "Wants clear, distinct, full-frame image that says something."

COLLECTORS NEWS & THE ANTIQUE REPORTER, 606 8th St., Box 156, Grundy Center IA 50638. (319)824-5456. Editor: Linda Kruger. 20% freelance written. A monthly tabloid covering antiques, collectibles and nostalgic memorabilia. Circ. 22,000. Buys 100 mss/year. Byline given. Pays on publication. Buys first rights and makes work-for-hire assignments. Submit seasonal material (holidays) 3 months in advance. Computer printout submissions acceptable; no dot-matrix. SASE. Reports in 2 weeks on queries; 6 weeks on mss. Publishes ms an average of 1 year after acceptance. Sample copy for $1.50 and 9x12 SAE; free writer's guidelines.
Nonfiction: General interest (any subject re: collectibles, antique to modern); historical/nostalgic (relating to collections or collectors); how-to (display your collection, care for, restore; appraise, locate, add to, etc.); interview/profile (covering individual collectors and their hobbies, unique or extensive; celebrity collectors, and limited edition artists); technical (in-depth analysis of a particular antique, collectible or collecting field); and travel (coverage of special interest or regional shows, seminars, conventions—or major antique shows, flea markets; places collectors can visit, tours they can take, museums, etc.). Special issues include January and June show/flea market issues; and usual seasonal emphasis. Buys 100-150 mss/year. Query with sample of writing. Length: 1,200-1,600 words. Pays 75¢/ column inch; $1/column inch for color features.
Photos: Reviews b&w prints and 35mm color slides. Payment for photos included in payment for ms. Captions required. Buys first rights.
Tips: Articles most open to freelancers are on celebrity collectors; collectors with unique and/or extensive collections; transportation collectibles; advertising collectibles; bottles; glass, china & silver; primitives; furniture; toys; political collectibles; and movie memorabilia.

CRAFTS 'N THINGS, 14 Main St., Park Ridge IL 60068. (312)825-2161. Editor: Nancy Tosh. Assistant Editor: Jackie Thielen. Bimonthly magazine covering crafts for "mostly women, around age 40." Circ. 250,000. Pays on publication. Byline, photo and brief bio given. Buys one-time rights. Submit seasonal/holiday material 6 months in advance. Simultaneous queries, and photocopied and previously published submissions OK ("if so indicated"). SASE. Reports in 1 month. Free sample copy.
Nonfiction: How-to (do a craft project). Buys 7-14 mss/issue. "Send in a photo of the item and complete directions. We will consider it and return if not accepted. Length: 1-4 magazine pages. Pays $50-200, "depending on how much staff work is required."
Photos: "Generally, we will ask that you send the item so we can photograph it ourselves."
Tips: "We're looking harder for people who can craft than people who can write."

CRAFTSWOMAN, Daedalus Publications, Inc., 1153 Oxford Rd., Deerfield IL 60015. (312)945-1769. Editor: Anne Patterson Dee. 95% freelance written. Bimonthly magazine covering craftswomen and their work. Pays on publication. Byline given. Buys first and second rights to the same material and second (reprint) rights to material originally published elsewhere. Submit seasonal/holiday material 2 months in advance. Photocopied, simultaneous and previously published submissions OK. Computer printout submissions acceptable. SASE. Reports in 1 month. Publishes ms an average of 6 months after acceptance. Sample copy $3.
Nonfiction: General interest (on craftswomen and their work); historical/nostalgic (quilting, stained glass, pottery, weaving, wood, etc.); how-to (run a shop, sell wholesale, do a trade show, promote shows, work with a sales rep, etc.); interview/profile (with successful craftswomen, shop owners, etc.); personal experience ("how I make money selling my designs," etc.) and travel. No "how-to-make-it articles." Buys 30 mss/year. Query or send complete ms if reprint. Length: 500-1,500 words. Pays $10-50.
Photos: "Especially need cover photos." Send photos with ms. Reviews 5x6 or 8x10 b&w glossy prints. Buys one-time rights.
Tips: "We need concise, well-written articles with lots of specifics, quotes and accompanying b&w photos."

‡**CREATIVE CRAFTS AND MINIATURES**, (incorporating *Creative Crafts* and *The Miniature Magazine*), Carstens Publications, Inc., Box 700, Newtown NJ 07860. Editor: Walter C. Lankenau. Bimonthly magazine covering crafts and miniatures for the serious adult hobbyist. "Quality how-to articles, biographical profiles, book and product reviews, events, question and answer columns, product testing and articles requested by readers." Circ. 50,000 + . Pays on publication. Buys all rights. Byline given. Submit seasonal/holiday material 7 months in advance. SASE. Reports in one month. Sample copy and writer's guidelines $1.75.
Nonfiction: How-to (step-by-step of specific projects or general techniques; instructions must be clearly written and accompanied by b&w procedural photos and/or drawings); and articles dealing with the crafting and collecting aspects of craft projects and miniatures (dollhouses, etc.). Query. Length: 1,200 words average. Pays $50/magazine page.
Photos: Purchased with accompanying ms.
Columns/Departments: Query. Length: 1,200 words average. Pays $50/magazine page.
Tips: "We desire articles written by craftsmen (or collectors) knowledgeable about hobbies/miniatures. We need quality crafts that offer some challenge to the hobbyist. When photographing miniatures, be sure to include some photos that have a scale relationship, i.e., a coin or hand next to the miniature to give an idea of proportion."

DOLLS, The Collector's Magazine, Collector Communications Corp., 170 5th Ave., New York NY 10010. (212)989-8700. Editor: Robert Campbell Rowe. Managing Editor: Krystyna Poray Goddu. Quarterly magazine covering doll collecting "for collectors of antique, contemporary and reproduction dolls. We publish well-researched, professionally written articles that are illustrated with photographs of high quality, color or black-and-white." Circ. 55,000. Pays on publication. Byline given. "Almost all first mss are on speculation. We rarely kill assigned stories, but fee would be about 33% of article fee." Buys first North American serial rights ("almost always"). Submit seasonal/holiday material 6 months in advance. Photocopied submissions considered (not preferred); previously published submissions OK. Computer printout submissions acceptable; no dot-matrix. Reports in 2 months. Publishes ms an average of 6 months after acceptance. Sample copy $2; free writer's guidelines.
Nonfiction: Krystyna Poray Goddu, managing editor. Book excerpts; historical (with collecting angle); how-to (make doll clothes with clear instructions, diagrams, etc.); interview/profile (on collectors with outstanding collections); new product (just photos and captions; "we do not pay for these, but regard them as publicity"); opinion ("A Personal Definition of Dolls"); technical (doll restoration advice by experts only); and travel (museums, collections and artists around the world). "No sentimental, uninformed 'my doll collection' or 'my grandma's doll collection' stories or trade magazine-type stories on shops, etc. Our readers are knowledgeable collectors." Query with clips. Length: 500-2,500 words. Pays $100-350.
Photos: Managing editor. Send photos with accompanying query or ms. Review 4x5 color transparencies; 4x5 or 8x10 b&w prints. "We do not buy photographs submitted without mss or unless we have assigned them; we pay for the manuscript/photos package in one fee." Captions required. Buys one-time rights.
Columns/Departments: Managing editor. Dolls Views—a miscellany of news and views of the doll world includes reports on upcoming or recently held events; possibly reviews of new books. "*Not* the place for new dolls, auction prices or dates; we have regular contributors or staff assigned to those columns." Query with clips if available or send complete ms. Length: 200-500 words. Pays $25-75. Dolls Views items are not bylined.
Fillers: "We don't really use fillers but would consider if we got something very good. Hints on restoring, for example, or a nice illustration." Length: 500 words maximum. Pays $25-75.
Tips: "We need experts in the field who are also good writers. Freelancers who are not experts should know their particular story thoroughly and do background research to get the facts correct. Well-written queries from writers outside NYC area especially welcome. Non-experts should stay away from technical or specific subjects (restoration, price trends). Short profiles of unusual collectors or a story of a local museum collection,

with good photos, might catch our interest. Editors want to know they are getting something from a writer they cannot get from anyone else. Good writing should be a given, a starting point. After that, it's what you know."

EARLY AMERICAN LIFE, Historical Times, Inc., Box 8200, Harrisburg PA 17105. Editor: Frances Carnahan. 70% freelance written. For "people who are interested in capturing the warmth and beauty of the 1600 to 1900 period and using it in their homes and lives today. They are interested in arts, crafts, travel, restoration, and collecting." Bimonthly magazine, 100 pages. Circ. 350,000. Buys all rights. Buys 50 mss/year. Pays on acceptance. Photocopied submissions OK. Free sample copy and writer's guidelines. Reports in 1 month. Query or submit complete ms. SASE.
Nonfiction: "Social history (the story of the people, not epic heroes and battles), crafts such as woodworking and needlepoint, travel to historic sites, country inns, antiques and reproductions, refinishing and restoration, architecture and decorating. We try to entertain as we inform and always attempt to give the reader something he can do. While we're always on the lookout for good pieces on any of our subjects, the 'travel to historic sites' theme is most frequently submitted. Would like to see more how-to-do-it (well-illustrated) on how real people did something great to their homes." Length: 750-3,000 words. Pays $50-400.
Photos: Pays $10 for 5x7 (and up) b&w photos used with mss, minimum of $25 for color. Prefers 2¼x2¼ and up, but can work from 35mm.
Tips: "Get a feeling for today's early Americans, the folks who are visiting flea markets, auctions, junkyards, the antique shops. They are our readers and they hunger for ideas on how to bring the warmth and beauty of early America into their lives. Then, conceive a new approach to satisfying their related interests in arts, crafts, travel to historic sites especially in houses decorated in the early American style. Write to entertain and inform at the same time, and be prepared to help us with illustrations, or sources for them."

EDGES, The Official Publication of the American Blade Collectors, American Blade, Inc., Stonewall Bldg., Suite 104, 212 Lee Parkway Dr., Chattanooga TN 37421. Editor: J. Bruce Voyles. Bimonthly tabloid covering the knife business. Circ. 20,000. Pays on publication. Byline given. Buys all rights. Submit seasonal/holiday material 6 months in advance. Simultaneous queries, and photocopied and previously published submissions OK "as long as they are exclusive to our market." SASE. Reports in 5 months. Acknowledges receipt of queries and ms in 6 weeks. Sample copy $1.
Nonfiction: Book excerpts, expose, general interest, historical (well-researched), how-to, humor, new product, opinion, personal experience, photo feature, and technical. "We look for articles on all aspects of the knife business, including technological advances, profiles, knife shows, and well-researched history. Ours is not a hard market to break into if the writer is willing to do a little research. To have a copy is almost a requirement." Buys 150 mss/year. Send complete ms. Length: 50-3,000 words "or more if material warrants additional length." Pays 5¢/word.
Photos: Pays $5 for 5x7 b&w prints. Captions and model release required (if persons are identifiable).
Fillers: Clippings, jokes, gags, anecdotes, short humor, and newsbreaks.
Tips: "If writers haven't studied the publication, don't bother to submit an article. If they have studied it, we're an easy market to sell to." Buys 80% of the articles geared to "the knife business."

FIBERARTS, The Magazine of Textiles, 50 College St., Asheville NC 28801. (704)253-0467. Editor: Christine Timmons. Bimonthly magazine covering textiles as art and craft (weaving, quilting, surface design, stitchery, knitting, crochet, etc.) for textile artists, craftspeople, hobbyists, teachers, museum and gallery staffs, collectors and enthusiasts. Circ. 26,000. Pays on publication. Byline given. Rights purchased are negotiable. Submit seasonal/holiday material 8 months in advance. Editorial guidelines and style sheet available. SASE. Reporting time varies. Sample copy $3.
Nonfiction: Book excerpts; historical/nostalgic; how-to; humor; interview/profile; opinion; personal experience; photo feature; technical; travel (for the textile enthusiast, e.g., collecting rugs in Turkey); and education, trends, exhibition reviews and textile news. Buys 25-50 mss/year. Recent example: "Give your baskets a long, healthy life: A basic guide to basketry conservation." Query. "Please be very specific about your proposal. Also an important consideration in accepting an article is the kind of photos—35mm slides and/or b&w glossies—that you can provide as illustration. We like to see photos in advance." Length: 250-1,200 words. Pays $25-180/article.
Tips: "Our writers are very familiar with the textile field, and this is what we look for in a new writer. The writer should also be familiar with *Fiberarts*, the magazine. We outline our upcoming issue in a column called '50 College St.' far enough in advance for a prospective writer to be aware of our future needs in proposing an article. (Also refer to January/February issue each year.)"

FINESCALE MODELER, Kalmbach Publishing Co., 1027 N. 7th St., Milwaukee WI 53233. (414)272-2060. Editor: Bob Hayden. 65% freelance written. Bimonthly magazine "devoted to how-to-do-it modeling information for scale modelbuilders who build non-operating aircraft, tanks, boats, automobiles, figures, dioramas, and science fiction and fantasy models." Circ. 30,000. Buys first and second rights to the same material. Electronic submissions OK, but requires hard copy also. Computer printout submissions acceptable.

Pays on acceptance. Byline given. SASE. Reports in 1 month on queries; 8 weeks on mss. Publishes ms an average of 1 year after acceptance. Sample copy for 9x12 SAE and 3 first class stamps; free writer's guidelines.
Nonfiction: How-to (build scale models); and technical (research information for building models). Query or send complete ms. Length: 750-3,000 words. Pays $30/published page minimum.
Photos: Send photos with ms. Pays $7.50 minimum for color transparencies and 5x7 b&w prints. Captions and identification of subjects required. Buys one-time rights.
Columns/Departments: FSM Showcase (photos plus description of model); and FSM Tips and Techniques (modelbuilding hints and tips). Buys 25-50/year. Query or send complete ms. Length: 100-1,000 words. Pays $10-75.
Tips: "A freelancer can best break in first through hints and tips, then through feature articles. Most people who write for FSM are modelers first, writers second. This is a specialty magazine for a special, quite expert audience. Essentially, 99% of our writers will come from that audience."

THE FRANKLIN MINT ALMANAC, Franklin Center PA 19091. (215)459-7016. Editor: Samuel H. Young. Associate Editor: Rosemary Rennicke. 85% freelance written. Bimonthly magazine covering collecting, emphasizing numismatics, philatelics, porcelain, crystal, books, records and graphics for members of Franklin Mint Collectors Society who are regular customers and others who request. Circ. 1,200,000. Pays on acceptance. Byline given. Pays negotiable kill fee. Buys one-time rights. Submit seasonal/holiday material 9 months in advance. Simultaneous queries, and simultaneous, photocopied, and previously published submissions OK. Computer printout submissions acceptable. Reports in 1 week on queries. Publishes ms an average of 5 months after acceptance.
Nonfiction: General interest (topics related to products offered by the Franklin Mint); interview/profile (with well-known people who collect or Franklin Mint collectors); and types of collections. Buys 8 mss/year. Query. Length: 1,500-2,000 words. Pays $500 average/article.
Photos: State availability of photos.
Fillers: Newsbreaks related to collecting. Pays negotiable fee.
Tips: Expanding audiences in Europe and Asia. "Solid writing credentials and a knowledge of collecting are a plus."

GEMS AND MINERALS, Box 687, Mentone CA 92359. (714)794-1173. Editor: Jack R. Cox. Monthly for the professional and amateur gem cutter, jewelry maker, mineral collector and rockhound. Buys first North American serial rights. Byline given. Pays on publication. Query. Reports in 4 weeks. SASE. Free sample copy and writer's guidelines.
Nonfiction: Material must have how-to slant. No personality stories. Field trips to mineral or gem collecting localities used; must be accurate and give details so they can be found. Instructions on how to cut gems; design and creation of jewelry. 4-8 typed pages plus illustrations preferred, but do not limit if subject is important. Frequently good articles are serialized if too long for one issue. Buys 75-120 unsolicited mss/year. Pays 50¢/inch for text.
Photos: Pays for b&w prints as part of text. Pays $1 inch for color photos as published.
Tips: "Because we are a specialty magazine, it is difficult for a writer to prepare a suitable story for us unless he is familiar with the subject matter: jewelry making, gem cutting, mineral collecting and display, and fossil collecting. Our readers want accurate instructions on how to do it and where they can collect gemstones and minerals in the field. The majority of our articles are purchased from freelance writers, most of whom are hobbyists (rockhounds) or have technical knowledge of one of the subjects. Infrequently, a freelancer with no knowledge of the subject interviews an expert (gem cutter, jewelry maker, etc.) and gets what this expert tells him down on paper for a good how-to article. However, the problem here is that if the expert neglects to mention all the steps in his process, the writer does not realize it. Then, there is a delay while we check it out. My best advice to a freelance writer is to send for a sample copy of our magazine and author's specification sheet which will tell him what we need. We are interested in helping new writers and try to answer them personally, giving any pointers that we think will be of value to them. Let us emphasize that our readers want how-to and where-to stories. They are not at all interested in personality sketches about one of their fellow hobbyists."

HANDMADE, Lark Communications, 50 College St., Asheville NC 28801. (704)253-0468. Inquiries to: NB/CL Editor. Editor: Rob Pulleyn. 20% freelance written. Bimonthly how-to crafts magazine featuring projects in all crafts (needlework, knitting, sewing, weaving, crafts, woodworking, etc.). Circ. 300,000. Pays on acceptance. Byline given. Offers negotiable kill fee. We make work-for-hire assignments. Buys first rights only. Submit seasonal/holiday material 6 months in advance. Photocopied submissions acceptable. Computer printout submissions OK; prefers letter-quality to dot-matrix. SASE. Reports in 3 weeks. Publishes ms an average of 4 months after acceptance. Sample copy $2; writer's guidelines for business-size SAE and 20¢ postage.
Nonfiction: Historical/nostalgic (crafts-related—traditional crafts, foreign crafts, etc.); how-to (crafts, all kinds with specific information); humor (crafts related); interview/profile (of craftspeople); photo feature (portfolio-type showing items in related, similar or identical media); technical; and travel (visit to foreign

places, crafts related). Buys 50-100 mss/year. Query with clips. Length: 100-1,000 words. Pays $25-400.
Photos: Send photos with ms (if possible). Reviews 35mm transparencies. Payment included in total fee. Captions and identification of subjects required. Buys all rights.

HANDS ON, Shopsmith Inc., 6640 Poe Ave., Dayton OH 45414. (513)898-6070. Contact: Editor. 10% freelance written, "but growing rapidly." Bimonthly magazine for woodworkers and do-it-yourselfers. Circ. 750,000. Pays on acceptance. Byline given. Buys rights by agreement. Computer printout submissions acceptable. Query. SASE. Reports in 3-6 weeks. Publishes ms an average of 6 months after acceptance. Free sample copy.
Nonfiction: Craftspersons' profiles must focus on creative use of Shopsmith tools, specific projects, and how to duplicate the project at home. "How-to research is crucial, and techniques should be tied to specific projects. Rough sketches OK; we supply professional drafting." General woodworking articles must focus on well-slanted fresh information: wood joinery, turning, choosing and using material, working efficiently, alternative techniques with power tools, safety, finishing, the therapy of woodworking, and joys and economy of doing it yourself. How-to projects: large or small, must feature use of Shopsmith tools. "Our nonprofessional woodworkers are looking to be 'heroes' to their loved ones, respected by their friends and affirmed in their choice of an avocation. We offer an authoritative variety of original simple to intermediate project plans and tips in each issue, as well as freshly-slanted general woodworking information." Query. Length: 1500 words maximum.
Photos: Send with ms. Likes photos with captions. Buys one-time rights or as agreed.
Tips: "Aim to make the joys of woodworking and DIY accessible to many. Present information clearly, with authority, and in a non-intimidating manner. Find a 'you can do it' slant. Get to know our tools. There is very little 'new' information in woodworking, but plenty of information that needs fresh presentation. Find a woodworker who has something to say about planning, constructing, finishing. Present project plans following our format (ask for latest issues)."

HANDWOVEN, from Interweave Press, 306 N. Washington, Loveland CO 80537. (303)669-7672. Editor: Linda C. Ligon. Bimonthly magazine (except July) covering handweaving, spinning and dyeing. Audience includes "practicing textile craftsmen. Article should show considerable depth of knowledge of subject, though tone should be informal and accessible." Circ. 25,000. Pays on publication. Byline given. Pays 50% kill fee. Buys first North American serial rights only. Simultaneous queries and photocopied submissions OK. Computer printout submissions acceptable; prefers letter-quality to dot-matrix. SASE. Sample copy for $3.50 and 8½x11 SAE; free writer's guidelines.
Nonfiction: Historical and how-to (on weaving and other craft techniques; specific items with instructions); and technical (on handweaving, spinning and dyeing technology). "All articles must contain a high level of in-depth information. Our readers are very knowledgeable about these subjects." Query. Length: 2,000 words. Pays $35-100.
Photos: State availability of photos. Identification of subjects required.
Tips: "We're particularly interested in articles about new weaving and spinning techniques as well as applying these techniques to finished products."

THE HOME SHOP MACHINIST, The Home Shop Machinist, Inc., 2779 Aero Park Dr., Box 1810, Traverse City MI 49685. (616)946-3712. Editor: Joe D. Rice. 95% freelance written. Bimonthly magazine covering machining and metalworking for the hobbyist. Circ. 19,000. Pays on publication. Byline given. Buys first North American serial rights only. Simultaneous submissions OK. Computer printout submissions acceptable; prefers letter-quality to dot-matrix. SASE. Reports in 3 weeks. Publishes ms an average of 10 months after acceptance. Free sample copy and writer's guidelines.
Nonfiction: How-to (projects designed to upgrade present shop equipment or hobby model projects that require machining); and technical (should pertain to metalworking, machining, drafting, layout, welding or foundry work for the hobbyist). No fiction. Buys 50 mss/year. Query or send complete ms. Length: open; "whatever it takes to do a thorough job." Pays $30/published page, plus $8/published photo; $50/page for camera-ready art; and $40 for b&w cover photo.
Photos: Send photos with ms. Pays $8-40 for 5x7 b&w prints. Captions and identification of subjects required.
Columns/Departments: Welding; Sheetmetal; Book Reviews; New Product Reviews; Micro-Machining; and Foundry. "Writer should become familiar with our magazine before submitting. Query first." Buys 8 mss/year. Length: 600-1,500 words. Pays $30-50.
Fillers: Machining tips/shortcuts. Buys 12-15/year. Length: 100-300 words. Pays $20-38.
Tips: "The writer should be experienced in the area of metalworking and machining; should be extremely thorough in explanations of methods, processes—always with an eye to safety; and should provide good quality b&w photos and/or clear drawings to aid in description. Visuals are of increasing importance to our readers. Carefully planned photos, drawings and charts will carry a submission to our magazine much farther along the path to publication."

LAPIDARY JOURNAL, Box 80937, San Diego CA 92138. Editor: Pansy D. Kraus. For "all ages interested in the lapidary hobby." Monthly. Rights purchased vary with author and material. Buys all rights or first serial rights. Byline given. Pays on publication. Photocopied submissions OK. Free sample copy and writer's guidelines. Query. SASE.
Nonfiction: Publishes "articles pertaining to gem cutting, gem collecting and jewelry making for the hobbyist." Buys informational, how-to, personal experience, historical, travel and technical articles. Pays 1¢/word.
Photos: Buys good contrast b&w photos. Contact editor for color. Payment varies according to size.

LIVE STEAM, Live Steam, Inc., 2779 Aero Park Dr., Box 629, Traverse City MI 49685. (616)941-7160. Editor: Joe D. Rice. 60% freelance written. Monthly magazine covering steam-powered models and full-size engines (i.e., locomotives, traction, cars, boats, stationary, etc.) "Our readers are hobbyists, many of whom are building their engines from scratch. We are interested in anything that has to do with the world of live steam-powered machinery." Circ. 12,800. Pays on publication. Byline given. Buys first North American serial rights only. Simultaneous submissions OK. Computer printout submissions acceptable. SASE. Reports in 3 weeks. Publishes ms an average of 10 months after acceptance. Free sample copy and writer's guidelines.
Nonfiction: Historical/nostalgic; how-to (build projects powered by steam); new product; personal experience; photo feature; and technical (must be within the context of steam-powered machinery or on machining techniques). No fiction. Buys 50 mss/year. Query or send complete ms. Length: 500-3,000 words. Pays $20/published page—$500 maximum.
Photos: Send photos with ms. Pays $40/page of finished art. Pays $6-40 for 5x7 b&w prints. Captions and identification of subjects required.
Columns/Departments: Steam traction engines, steamboats, stationary steam, and steam autos. Buys 6-8 mss/year. Query. Length: 1,000-3,000 words. Pays $20-50.
Tips: "At least half of all our material is from the freelancer. Requesting a sample copy and author's guide will be a good place to start. The writer must be well-versed in the nature of live steam equipment and the hobby of scale modeling such equipment. Technical and historical accuracy is an absolute must. Often, good articles are weakened or spoiled by mediocre to poor quality photos. Freelancers must learn to take a *good* photograph."

LONG ISLAND HERITAGE, A Journal of and Guide to the History, Art, Antiques and Crafts of Long Island, Community Newspapers, Inc., 29 Continental Pl., Glen Cove NY 11542. (516)676-1200. Editor: Tim O'Brien. 65% freelance written. Monthly tabloid covering history, art, antiques, crafts with emphasis on Long Island and New York state "written for the 'old' loving lifestyle." Circ. 18,000. Byline given. Offers 10% kill fee. Buys one-time and simultaneous rights and makes work-for-hire assignments. "We negotiate for payment to freelancer on acceptance." Submit seasonal/holiday material 4 months in advance. Simultaneous queries, and simultaneous, photocopied and previously published submissions OK. Computer printout submissions acceptable "only if printout is readable, workable size and in upper and lower case"; prefers letter-quality to dot-matrix. SASE. Reports in 1 week on queries; 3 weeks on mss. Publishes ms an average of 3 months after acceptance. Sample copy for 9x12 SAE and $1.05 postage; writer's guidelines for business size SAE and 1 first class stamp.
Nonfiction: General interest (antiques: explain one particular area of collecting); historical/nostalgic (Long Island histories, collecting old things, etc.); how-to (start a collection, find specific antiques, insure your collection, see your collection, etc.); humor ("we'd love to have some antique humor"); and photo feature (on antiques, Long Island historical events, etc). "We especially need stories and photos on doll, toy and miniature collecting." Special issues include Americana (October), and Dolls & Toys (April and November). Buys 36-50 mss/year. Query with clips of published work or send complete ms. Length: 400-1,200 words. Pays $15-25.
Photos: State availability of photos. Pays $5-7.50 for 5x7 and 8x10 b&w prints. Captions and identification of subjects required. "We print a 4-color cover and need seasonal photos/transparencies." Pays $50.
Tips: "Freelance writers should be aware of a less rigid and formal writing style, so there is more need to communicate than to write correctly. Also, I'm noticing (and buying) more packages (photos and story) from freelancers."

LOOSE CHANGE, Mead Publishing Corp., 21176 Alameda St., Long Beach CA 90810. (213)549-0730. Publisher: Daniel R. Mead. Monthly magazine covering collecting and investing in antique coin-operated machines. "Our audience is predominantly male. Readers are all collectors or enthusiasts of antique coin-operated machines, particularly antique slot machines. Subscribers are, in general, not heavy readers." Circ. 3,000. Pays on acceptance. Byline given. Prefers to buy all rights, but also buys first and reprint rights. "We may allow author to reprint upon request in noncompetitive publications." Photocopied submissions OK. Previously published submissions must be accompanied by complete list of previous sales, including sale dates. SASE. Reports in 1 month on queries; 6 weeks on mss. Sample copy $1; free writer's guidelines.
Nonfiction: Historical/nostalgic, how-to, interview/profile, opinion, personal experience, photo feature and technical. "Articles illustrated with clear, black and white photos are always considered much more favorably than articles without photos (we have a picture-oriented audience). The writer must be knowledgeable about his subject because our readers are knowledgeable and will spot inaccuracies." Buys up to 50 mss/year.

Length: 900-6,000 words; 3,500-12,000, cover stories. Pays $100 maximum, inside stories; $200 maximum, cover stories.

Photos: "Captions should tell a complete story without reference to the body text." Send photos with ms. Reviews 8x10 b&w glossy prints. Captions required. "Purchase price for articles includes payment for photos."

Fiction: "All fiction must have a gambling/coin-operated-machine angle. Very low emphasis is placed on fiction. Fiction must be exceptional to be acceptable to our readers." Buys maximum 6 mss/year. Send complete ms. Length: 800-2,500 words. Pays $60 maximum.

LOST TREASURE, 15115 S. 76th E. Ave., Bixby OK 74008. Managing Editor: Andre Hinds. 95% freelance written. For treasure hunting hobbyists, bottle and relic collectors, amateur prospectors and miners. Monthly magazine; 72 pages. Circ. 55,000. Buys first rights only. Byline given. Buys 100 mss/year. Pays on publication. Will consider photocopied submissions. No simultaneous submissions. Electronic submissions OK, but requires hard copy also. Computer printout submissions acceptable. Reports in 6-8 weeks. Submit complete ms. Publishes ms an average of 3 months after acceptance. SASE. Free sample copy and writer's guidelines.

Nonfiction: How-to articles about treasure hunting, coinshooting, personal, profiles, and stories about actual hunts. *Avoid* writing about the more famous treasures and lost mines. Length: 1,000-3,000 words. Pays 3¢/word.

Photos: Pays $5-10 for b&w glossy prints purchased with mss. Captions required. Pays $150 for color transparencies used on cover; 35mm minimum size.

Tips: Manuscripts submitted with good photos, maps and graphs will have a better chance of being included than manuscripts sent without art.

McCALL'S NEEDLEWORK & CRAFTS MAGAZINE, 825 7th Ave. (7th fl.), New York NY 10019. Editor: Margaret Gilman. Bimonthly. All rights bought for original needlework and handicraft designs. SASE.

Nonfiction: Submit preliminary color photos for editorial consideration. Accepted made-up items must be accompanied by directions, diagrams and charts. Payment ranges from a few dollars to a few hundred dollars.

MAKE IT WITH LEATHER, Box 1386, Fort Worth TX 76101. (817)335-4161. Editor: Earl F. Warren. 90% freelance written. Bimonthly. Circ. 60,000. Buys all rights. Byline given except for news releases or if ghosted or written on assignment with predetermined no byline. Buys 60 or more mss/year. Pays on publication. Computer printout submissions acceptable. Reports in 6-8 weeks. Publishes ms an average of 1 year after acceptance. SASE. Free sample copy and writer's guidelines.

Nonfiction: "How-to-do-it leathercraft stories illustrated with cutting patterns and carving patterns. First-person approach even though article may be ghosted. Story can be for professional or novice. Strong on details, logical progression in steps, easy to follow how-to-do-it." Length: 2,000 words or less suggested. Payment normally starts at $50 plus $10 per illustration. "All articles judged on merit and may range to '$250 plus' per ms. Depends on project and work involved by author."

Photos: 5x7, or larger, b&w photos of reproduction quality purchased with mss. Captions required. Color of professional quality is used on cover at $50/accepted photo. Ektachrome transparencies or sheet film stock. Negatives needed with all print film stock. All photos are used to illustrate project on step-by-step basis and finished item. "We can do photos in our studio if product sample is sent. No charge, but no payment for photos to writer. Letting us 'do it our way' does help on some marginal story ideas and mss since we can add such things as artist's sketches or drawings to improve the presentation."

Fillers: "Tips and Hints." Short practical hints for doing leathercraft or protecting tools, new ways of doing things, etc. Length: 100 words maximum. Pays $10 minimum.

Tips: "There are plenty of leathercraftsmen around who don't feel qualified to write up a project or who don't have the time to do it. Put their ideas and projects down on paper for them and share the payment. We need plenty of small, quick, easy-to-do ideas; things that we can do in one page are in short supply."

MINIATURE COLLECTOR, Acquire Publishing Co., Inc., 170 5th Ave., New York NY 10010. (212)989-8700. Editor: Robert Campbell Rowe. Managing Editor: Krystyna Poray Goddu. 50% freelance written. Bimonthly magazine; 72 pages. Circ. 60,000. Byline given. Buys first rights and occasionally second (reprint) rights to material originally published elsewhere. Pays on publication. Submit seasonal/holiday material 4 months in advance. Photocopied and previously published submissions OK. Computer printout submissions acceptable; no dot-matrix. SASE. Reports in 6-8 weeks. Publishes ms an average of 4 months after acceptance. Sample copy $1.

Nonfiction: How-to (detailed furniture and accessories projects in 1/12th scale with accurate patterns and illustrations); interview (with miniaturists, well-established collectors, museum curators, with pictures); new product (very short-caption type pieces—no payment); photo feature (show reports, heavily photographic, with captions stressing pieces and availability of new and unusual pieces); and profile (of collectors, with photos). Buys 3-6 mss/issue. Query. Length: 600-1,200 words. Pays $100-200. First manuscripts usually on speculation.

Photos: Send photos with ms; usually buys photo/manuscript package. Buys one-time rights. Captions required.

MODEL RAILROADER, 1027 N. 7th St., Milwaukee WI 53233. Editor: Russell G. Larson. For hobbyists interested in scale model railroading. Monthly. Buys exclusive rights. Study publication before submitting material. Reports on submissions within 4 weeks. Query. SASE.
Nonfiction: Wants construction articles on specific model railroad projects (structures, cars, locomotives, scenery, benchwork, etc.). Also photo stories showing model railroads. First-hand knowledge of subject almost always necessary for acceptable slant. Pays base rate of $54/page.
Photos: Buys photos with detailed descriptive captions only. Pays $7.50 and up, depending on size and use. Color: double b&w rate. Full color cover: $210.

NATIONAL KNIFE MAGAZINE, Official Journal of the National Knife Collectors Association, Box 21070, Chattanooga TN 37421. (615)899-9456. Editor/Publisher: James V. Allday. Monthly magazine covering knife collection, manufacturing, hand crafting, selling, buying, trading; stresses "integrity in all dealings involving knives and bladed tools/weapons." Circ. 15,000. Pays on publication. Byline given. Buys all rights. Submit seasonal/holiday material 3 months in advance. Simultaneous queries OK. Electronic submissions OK on TRS-80 Mod III Scripsit. Computer printout submissions acceptable. SASE. Reports in 4 weeks on queries; 2 weeks on mss. Sample copy for 9x12 SAE and 6 first class stamps; writer's guidelines for business-size SAE and 1 first class stamp.
Nonfiction: Analytical pieces, book reviews, general interest, historical, how-to, humor, interview/profile, new product, personal experience, photo feature, technical, and excerpts. Buys 50+ mss/year. Query with clips of published work. Length: 500-1,500 words. Pays 7¢ or more (negotiable)/word. No kill fee.
Photos: State availability of photos. Pays $7 for 5x7 prints. Captions and identification of subjects required.
Fiction: Adventure, fantasy, historical, humorous, and mainstream. No "non-knife-related stuff." Buys 6 mss/year. Query with clips of published work. Length: open. Pays 5-7¢/word.
Fillers: Anecdotes. Buys 10/year. Length: open. Pays $25.
Tips: "Get acquainted with the knife world and knife specialists by attending a knife show or the National Knife Museum in Chattanooga. We're a feature magazine aimed at knife collectors/investors."

NEEDLE & THREAD, Happy Hands Publishing, 4949 Byers, Ft. Worth TX 76107. (817)732-7494. Editor: Margaret Dittman. Bimonthly how-to magazine covering home sewing of all types for people interested in sewing fashions, home decorations and gifts. Circ. 750,000. Pays on acceptance. Byline given. Buys negotiable rights. Simultaneous queries and simultaneous and previously published submissions OK (if indicated where else they were submitted). Computer printout submissions acceptable "so long as quality is not compromised." Reports in 6 weeks. Sample copy $3.
Nonfiction: How-to (with completed sewing projects); and interview/profile (of outstanding seamstresses and designers). Buys 120 mss/year. Query with snapshots of projects or clips of published work. Pays negotiable fee depending on the project.
Tips: "All projects must be original designs. On garments a manufactured pattern may be used with original decorative techniques."

NEEDLECRAFT FOR TODAY, Happy Hands Publishing, 4949 Byers, Ft. Worth TX 76107. (817)732-7494. Editor: Charlie Davis. Editorial Director: Joyce Bennett. Bimonthly magazine for needlecraft enthusiasts. Circ. 1,200,000. Pays on acceptance "of total project." Designer credit given. Buys negotiable rights. Submit seasonal/holiday material 1 year in advance. Computer printout submissions acceptable "so long as it's black and clear enough for a typesetter to read"; prefers letter-quality to dot-matrix. SASE. Reports in 6 weeks. Sample copy $3; free writer's guidelines with SASE.
Nonfiction: "Crochet, needlepoint, quilting, counted cross-stitch, knitting and dollmaking are used in basically every issue. Any fiber project is of interest to us, including fashions, wall hangings, home decorative items and toys—but of the highest quality and workmanship. How-to must be originally designed project. Provide a finished sample, chart, pattern, list of material and instructions." Buys 240 mss/year. Length: average 1,500 words. Pays "by arrangement, depending on the project."
Photos: "We photograph most finished projects ourselves." Send color photos with query.
Columns/Departments: Forum, guest speaker on any subject of interest to needlecrafters; Needlecraft Principles, explains a craft to a beginner. Send complete ms. Pays $100-200.
Tips: "Writer must be able to write very clear step-by-step instructions for original projects submitted. We seek small bazaar items to advanced projects made from commercially available materials. Be an experienced needlecrafter."

‡**THE NEEDLEWORK TIMES**, Opportunity Press, Inc., Suite 1405, 6 N. Michigan Ave., Chicago IL 60602. (312)346-4790. Editor: Mary Ann Hickey. 80% freelance written. Bimonthly tabloid covering all forms of needlework arts (knitting, crocheting, embroidery, etc.) for a primarily female audience. Circ. 66,000. Pays on acceptance. Byline given. Offers 50% kill fee. Buys first North American serial rights and

second (reprint) rights to material originally published elsewhere. Submit seasonal/holiday material 6 months in advance. Simultaneous queries and photocopied submissions OK. Computer printout submissions acceptable. Reports in 2 weeks on queries; 1 month on mss. Publishes ms an average of 2 months after acceptance. Sample copy for $2.50, 9x12 SAE, and 5 first class stamps.

Nonfiction: How-to, interview/profile, and new product. Query with published clips. Length: 800-3,500 words. Pays $75-300.

Photos: State availability of photos. Reviews b&w contact sheets and color transparencies. Model release and identification of subjects required. Buys one-time rights.

Tips: "Cover a particular type of needleworking with an interview/profile on a person well versed in the field who can offer instructive information."

NOSTALGIAWORLD, for Collectors and Fans, Box 231, North Haven CT 06473. (203)239-4891. Editor: Bonnie Roth. Managing Editor: Stanley N. Lozowski. 50% freelance written. Bimonthly tabloid covering entertainment collectibles. "Our readership is interested in articles on all eras—everything from early Hollywood, the big bands, country/Western, rock n' roll to jazz, pop, and rhythm and blues. Many of our readers belong to fan clubs." Circ. 5,000-10,000. Pays on publication. Byline given. Buys all rights. Submit seasonal/holiday material 6 months in advance. Simultaneous queries, and simultaneous, photocopied, and previously published submissions OK. Computer printout submissions acceptable. SASE. Reports in 4 weeks on queries; 6 weeks on mss. Publishes ms an average of 4 months after acceptance. Sample copy $2; writer's guidelines for legal size SAE and 1 first class stamp.

Nonfiction: Historical/nostalgic; how-to (get started in collecting); and interview/profile (of movie, recording, or sport stars). "Articles must be aimed toward the collector and provide insight into a specific area of collecting. *Nostalgiaworld* readers collect records, gum cards, toys, sheet music, movie magazines, posters and memorabilia, personality items, comics, baseball, and sports memorabilia. We do *not* cater to antiques, glass, or other nonentertainment collectibles. Buys 20-30 unsolicited mss/year. All submissions must be double-spaced and typewritten."

Photos: Send photos with ms. Pays $10-25 for 5x7 b&w prints; reviews b&w contact sheets. Captions and identification of subjects required. Buys all rights.

Columns/Departments: Video Memories (early TV); and 78 RPM-For Collectors Only (advice and tips for the collector of 78 RPM recordings; prices, values, outstanding rarities). Buys varying number of mss/year. Query or send complete ms. Length: 500-1,500 words. Pays $10-25.

Tips: "Most readers are curious to find out what their collectibles are worth. With inflation running at such a high rate, people are investing in nostalgia items more than ever. *Nostalgiaworld* provides a place to buy and sell and also lists conventions and collectors' meets across the country. Our publication is interested in the entertainment field as it evolved in the twentieth century. Our readers collect anything and everything related to this field."

NUMISMATIC NEWS, Krause Publications, 700 E. State St., Iola WI 54990. (715)445-2214. Editor: Arlyn G. Sieber. 30% freelance written. Weekly magazine about US coins, medals, tokens, and collecting for beginning and advanced collectors. Circ. 55,000. Pays on acceptance. Byline given. Buys first North American serial rights. Photocopied submissions OK. Computer printout submissions acceptable; prefers letter-quality to dot-matrix. SASE. Reports in 2 weeks. Publishes ms an average of 3 months after acceptance. Free sample copy.

Nonfiction: "We're seeking features on any phase of coin collecting and investing." No news items. "Our staff covers the hard news." Buys 3-4 mss/issue. Send complete ms. Length: 500-3,000 words. Pays first time contributors 3¢/word; negotiates fees for others.

Photos: Send photos with ms. Pays $5 minimum for 5x7 b&w glossy prints. Captions and model release required.

NUTSHELL NEWS, Boynton and Associates, Clifton House, Clifton VA 22024. (703)830-1000. Editor: Ann Ruble. 75% freelance written. Monthly magazine about miniatures for miniatures enthusiasts, collectors, craftspeople and hobbyists. "*Nutshell News* is the only magazine in the miniatures field which offers readers comprehensive coverage of all facets of miniature collecting and crafting." Circ. 35,000. Pays on publication. Buys all rights in the field. Phone queries OK, "but would prefer letters and photos." Submit seasonal material 4 months in advance. Previously published submissions OK ("if they did not appear in a competing magazine"). Electronic submissions OK but requires hard copy also. Computer printout submissions acceptable; prefers letter-quality to dot-matrix. Reports in 2 months. Publishes ms an average of 10 months after acceptance. Sample copy $3; free writer's guidelines for SASE.

Nonfiction: Interview/profile of craftspeople specializing in miniatures. Research articles on design periods and styles. Articles on private and museum collections of miniatures. How-to articles on decorating, building miniature furniture, dollhouses, rooms, and accessories. Show reports, book reviews, and new product information. "We need stringers nationwide to work on an assignment basis, preferably freelancers with knowledge in the miniatures field to cover interviews with craftspeople and report on miniature shows." Buys 15 mss/issue. Query with "photos of the work to be written about. We're looking for craftspeople doing fine quality work, or collectors with top notch collections. Photos give us an idea of this quality." Length: 1,200-1,500 words. Pays 10¢/published word.

Photos: Pays $7.50 minimum for 5x7 b&w glossy prints. Pays $10 maximum for 35mm or larger color transparencies. Captions required.

OHIO ANTIQUE REVIEW, Box 538, Worthington OH 43085. Managing Editor: Charles Muller. (614)885-9757. 60% freelance written. For an antique-oriented readership, "generally well-educated, interested in folk art and other early American items." Monthly tabloid. Circ. 10,000. Pays on publication date assigned at time of purchase. Buys first North American serial rights, and second (reprint) rights to material originally published elsewhere. Byline given. Phone queries OK. Submit seasonal/holiday material 3 months in advance. Simultaneous, photocopied and previously published submissions OK. Computer printout submissions acceptable. SASE. Reports in 1 month. Publishes ms an average of 4 months after acceptance. Free sample copy and writer's guidelines.

Nonfiction: "The articles we desire concern history and production of furniture, pottery, china, and other antiques of the period prior to the 1880s. In some cases, contemporary folk art items are acceptable. We are also interested in reporting on antique shows and auctions with statements on conditions and prices. We do not want articles on contemporary collectibles." Buys 5-8 mss/issue. Query with clips of published work. Query should show "author's familiarity with antiques and an interest in the historical development of artifacts relating to early America." Length: 200-2,000 words. Pays $75-100.

Photos: State availability of photos with query. Payment included in ms price. Uses 5x7 or larger glossy b&w prints. Captions required. Articles with photographs receive preference.

Tips: "Give us a call and let us know of specific interests. We are more concerned with the background in antiques than in writing abilities. The writing can be edited, but the knowledge imparted is of primary interest."

THE OLD BOTTLE MAGAZINE, Box 243, Bend OR 97709. (503)382-6978. Editor: Shirley Asher. For collectors of old bottles, insulators, and relics. Monthly. Circ. 3,500. Buys all rights. Byline given. Buys 35 mss/year. Pays on acceptance. Current issue sample $2 sent ppd. No query required. Reports in 1 month. SASE.

Nonfiction, Photos and Fillers: "We are soliciting factual accounts on specific old bottles, canning jars, insulators and relics." Stories of a general nature on these subjects not wanted. "Interviews of collectors are usually not suitable when written by noncollectors. A knowledge of the subject is imperative. Would highly recommend potential contributors study an issue before making submissions. Articles that tie certain old bottles to a historical background are desired." Length: 250-2,500 words. Pays $10/published page. B&w glossy prints and clippings purchased separately. Pays $5.

OLD CARS NEWSPAPER, Krause Publications, 700 E. State St., Iola WI 54990. (715)445-2214. Editor: John Gunnell. 40% freelance written. "Our readers collect, drive and restore everything from 1899 locomobiles to 1976 Cadillac convertibles. They cover all age and income groups." Weekly tabloid; 60 pages. Circ. 95,000. Pays on acceptance. Buys all rights. Phone queries OK. Byline given. SASE. Reports in 2 days. Sample copy 50¢.

Nonfiction: Short (2-3 pages) timely articles on old cars and old car hobby with 1 photo. Buys 20 mss/issue. Query. Pays 3¢/word.

Photos: State availability of photos with query. Pays $5 for 5x7 b&w glossy prints. Captions required. Buys all rights.

Columns/Departments: Book reviews (new releases for hobbyists). Buys 1 ms/issue. Query. Pays 3¢/word.

Fillers: Newsbreaks. Buys 50/year. Pays 3¢/word. Pays $10 bonus for usable news tips.

Tips: "Must know automotive hobby well. One writer caught the editor's eye by submitting excellent drawings with his manuscript."

OLD CARS PRICE GUIDE, Krause Publications, 700 E. State St., Iola WI 54990. (715)445-2214. Editor: Dennis Schrimpf. Quarterly magazine of old car prices for old car hobbyists and investors. Circ. 85,000. Pays on acceptance. Byline given. Buys first North American serial rights. Submit seasonal/holiday material 3 months in advance. Computer printout submissions acceptable. Reports in 1 week. Sample copy $2.25 and 8x10 SASE.

Nonfiction: How-to (buy, sell, collector cars); opinion (on car values market); technical (how to fix a car to increase value); and investment angles. "All articles should be car-value related and include information or actual price lists on recent sales (of more than one car). Articles about brands or types of cars *not* covered in regular price lists are preferred. Plenty of research and knowledge of the old car marketplace is usually essential. Photos required with all articles. No historic or nostalgic pieces." Buys 8-12 mss/year. Send complete ms. Length: 600-1,000 words. Pays $75-150.

Photos: Send photos with ms. Pays $50 minimum for 4x4 color transparencies used on cover; $5 for b&w prints; "undetermined for color." Captions and identification of subjects required. Buys one-time rights.

Columns/Departments: Book Review (books on car values or investments). Buys 4 mss/year. Send complete ms. Length: 100-300 words. Pays 3¢/word; $5/photo.
Fillers: Jokes, gags, anecdotes, short humor, and newsbreaks (related to old car values). Pays 3¢/word.

POPULAR WOODWORKER, (formerly *Pacific Woodworker*), 1300 Galaxy Way, Concord CA 94520. (415)671-9852. Editor: Ellen DasGupta. Bimonthly magazine covering woodworking, woodcarving, cabinet-making for the small cabinet shop owner, wood craftsperson, advanced hobbyist or wood carver. Circ. 10,000. Pays on publication. Byline given. Buys first North American serial rights. Submit seasonal/holiday material 4 months in advance. Simultaneous queries, and simultaneous and photocopied submissions OK if identified as such. "Computer printout submissions acceptable from someone whose published or unpublished work I have already seen." SASE. Reports in 1 month on queries; 6 weeks on mss. Sample copy for $1, 9x12 SAE, and 88¢ postage; writer's guidelines for SAE and 1 first class stamp.
Nonfiction: Historical (on woodworking techniques); how-to (skills of interest to small business craftsmen); humor (woodcraft related); inspirational; interview/profile (of successful small wood crafters); new product (of interest to woodworkers); personal experience (related to running a small shop/selling/designing woodcraft products); technical (woodcraft related). "Specific topics we would like to see include: finishing techniques, workshop organization, workshop efficiency and shortcut hints, workshop safety, characteristics of specific woods, successful marketing techniques for the small shop owner, how to start a woodworking business, interviews with prominent woodworkers (especially if accompanied by quality photos of them and their work), new products and their use. No beginner level/hobby shop woodworking projects. Buys 100 mss/year. Query with or without published clips, or send complete ms. Length: 100-1,500 words maximum. Pays $3-5/published page.
Photos: Wayne Lin, photo editor. "We especially like articles accompanied by top quality, black-and-white glossy photos. Also need cover photos." State availability or send photos with query or mss. Prefers 5x7 glossy photos. Pays $5-25. Captions and identification of subjects required. Buys one-time rights. Photos returned if requested.
Columns/Departments: Marketing Techniques, New Ideas and Products, Show Reviews, Shortcuts That Work, Restortation and Architectural Woodworking. Buys 20 mss/year. Query or send complete ms. Length: 250-500 words. Pays $50 maximum.
Tips: "Knowledge of the subject matter through personal experience is most essential for our writers. Good ideas and solid know-how are more important than authors' previous publications. We will work with less experienced writers to develop and express workable ideas."

QUILTER'S NEWSLETTER MAGAZINE, Box 394, Wheatridge CO 80033. Editor: Bonnie Leman. Monthly. Circ. 150,000. Buys first North American serial rights or second rights. Buys 15 mss/year. Pays on acceptance. Free sample copy. Reports in 4-5 weeks. Submit complete ms. SASE.
Nonfiction: "We are interested in articles on the subject of quilts and quiltmakers *only*. We are not interested in anything relating to 'Grandma's Scrap Quilts', but could use material about contemporary quilting." Pays 3¢/word minimum.
Photos: Additional payment for photos depends on quality.
Fillers: Related to quilts and quiltmakers only.
Tips: "Be specific, brief, and professional in tone. Study our magazine to learn the kind of thing we like. Send us material which fits into our format but which is different enough to be interesting. Realize that we think we're the best quilt magazine on the market and that we're aspiring to be even better, then send us the cream off the top of your quilt material."

RAILROAD MODEL CRAFTSMAN, Box 700, Newton NJ 07860. (201)383-3355. Editor: William C. Schaumburg. 75% freelance written. For model railroad hobbyists, in all scales and gauges. Monthly. Circ. 97,000. Buys all rights. Buys 50-100 mss/year. Pays on publication. Sample copy $1.75. Submit seasonal material 6 months in advance. SASE requested for writer's and photographer's information.
Nonfiction: "How-to and descriptive model railroad features written by persons who did the work are preferred. Almost all our features and articles are written by active model railroaders familiar with the hobby. It is difficult for non-modelers to know how to approach writing for this field." Minimum payment: $1.75/column inch of copy ($50/page).
Photos: Purchased with or without mss. Buys sharp 8x10 glossy prints and 35mm or larger color transparencies. Minimum payments: $10 for photos or $2/diagonal inch of published b&w photos, $3 for color transparencies and $100 for covers which must tie in with article in that issue. Caption information required.

ROCKY MOUNTAIN MINIATURE JOURNAL, Box 3315, Littleton CO 80161. (303)978-1355. Editor: Norm Nielsen. 75% freelance written. Bimonthly magazine covering dollhouses and miniatures for collectors and crafters in the miniature hobby. Circ. 1,200. Pays on publication. Byline given. Buys one-time rights. Submit seasonal/holiday material 2 months in advance. Computer printout submissions acceptable. Publishes ms an average of 2 months after acceptance. Sample copy $2.25; SASE for writer's guidelines.

Nonfiction: Only articles and how-to's on miniatures, dollhouses and related miniatures topics. Query first. Pays 3¢/word.
Photos: Send photos with ms. 5x7 or 8x10 b&w glossies. Identification of subjects required. Photos returned only if requested.
Tips: "How-to pieces on subjects such as making furniture and crafts that can be adapted to dollhouses or miniatures are in great demand. We are constantly seeking articles about people anywhere in the world who make miniatures. The most rewarding aspect of working with freelance writers is receiving articles from unexpected new sources who write in good style and present fresh or different approaches and making contacts that may result in several articles from the same new person. The most frustrating aspect of working with freelance writers is that if their first article turns out to be too similar to one recently run and is not used, I don't like to discourage them—rather, I encourage them to try again. This can be avoided by sending a query first. In our experience, we often receive articles that are too short. We much prefer to receive longer articles—they could be split into a series, or shortened if space is a problem, but it's better to have too much than too little. We would like to receive more and better quality pictures. We emphasize the importance of photos to accompany articles."

JOEL SATER'S ANTIQUES & AUCTION NEWS, 225 W. Market St., Marietta PA 17547. (717)426-1956. Managing Editor: Joel Sater. Editor: Denise Murphy. For dealers and buyers of antiques, nostalgics and collectibles, and those who follow antique shows and shops. Biweekly tabloid; 24-32 pages. Circ. 80,000. Pays on publication. Buys all rights. Phone queries OK. Submit seasonal/holiday material 3 months in advance. Simultaneous (if so notified), photocopied and previously published submissions OK. SASE. Reports in 6 weeks. Free sample copy (must identify *Writer's Market*).
Nonfiction: Historical (related to American artifacts or material culture); how-to (restoring and preserving antiques and collectibles); informational (research on antiques or collectibles; "news about activities in our field"); interview; nostalgia; personal experience; photo feature; profile; and travel. Buys 100-150 mss/year. Query or submit complete ms. Length: 500-2,500 words. Pays $5-25.
Photos: Purchased with or without accompanying ms. Captions required. Send prints. Pays $2-10 for b&w photos. Offers no additional payment for photos purchased with mss.

SCOTT STAMP MONTHLY, 3 E. 57th St., New York NY 10022. (212)371-5700. Editor: Ira S. Zweifach. 40% freelance written. For stamp collectors, from the beginner to the sophisticated philatelist. Monthly magazine; 132 pages. Circ. 30,000. Rights purchased vary with author and material; usually buys all rights. Byline given. Buys 8-9 unsolicited mss/year. Pays within 1 month after acceptance. Submit seasonal or holiday material 3 months in advance. Computer printout submissions acceptable; no dot-matrix. Reports in 4 weeks. Publishes ms an average of 1 month after acceptance. SASE.
Nonfiction: "We want articles of a serious philatelic nature, ranging in length from 1,500-2,500 words. We are also in the market for articles, written in an engaging fashion, concerning the remote byways and often-overlooked aspects of the hobby. Writing should be clear and concise, and subjects should be well-researched and documented. Illustrative material should also accompany articles whenever possible." Query. Pays $200-250.
Photos: State availability of photos. Offers no additional payment for b&w photos used with mss.
Tips: "*Scott Stamp Monthly* is undergoing a complete change. Although most material deals with stamps, new writers are invited to seek assignments. It's rewarding to find a good new writer with good new material. Because our emphasis is on lively, interesting articles about stamps, including historical perspectives and human interest slants, we are open to writers who can produce the same. Of course, if you are an experienced philatelist, so much the better. We do not want stories about the picture on a stamp taken from a history book or an encyclopedia and dressed up to look like research. We want articles written from a philatelic standpoint. If idea is good and not a basic rehash, we are interested."

‡**SHUTTLE SPINDLE & DYEPOT**, Handweavers Guild of America, Inc., 65 La Salle Road, West Hartford CT 06107. (203)233-5124. Editor: Jane Bradley Sitko. Quarterly crafts magazine covering handweaving, handspinning and dyeing. "Our audience is handcrafts-oriented (many professional fiber artists)." Circ. 16,800. Pays on publication. Byline given. Offer negotiable kill fee. Buys one-time rights. Submit seasonal/holiday material 6 months in advance. Simultaneous queries, and photocopied and previously published submissions OK. SASE. Reports in 4 weeks on queries; 3 months on mss. Free sample copy and writer's guidelines.
Nonfiction: How-to (weaving, sewing) and technical (handweaving, handspinning). Buys 30 mss/year. Query. Length: 1,000-3,000 words. Pays $25-100 (award honorarium).
Photos: Send photos with query. Pays variable rates for 4x5 color transparencies. Model releases and identification of subjects required.
Tips: "We are seeking technical mss about weaving, but also need reviews on fiber or weaving exhibits and shows which do not require that the writer be familiar with handweaving. A freelancer can best break in by submitting interviews with famous fiber artists; national or international exhibit reviews; and personality pieces."

SPIN-OFF, Interweave Press, 306 N. Washington, Loveland CO 80537. (303)669-7672. Editors: Lee Raven, Anne Bliss. Quarterly magazine covering handspinning, dyeing, techniques and projects for using handspun fibers. Audience includes "practicing textile/fiber craftsmen. Article should show considerable depth of knowledge of subject, though the tone should be informal and accessible." Circ. 6,000. Pays on publication. Byline given. Pays 50% kill fee. Buys first North American serial rights. Simultaneous queries and photocopied submissions OK. SASE. Sample copy $2.50 and 8½x11 SAE; free writer's guidelines.
Nonfiction: Historical and how-to (on spinning; knitted, crocheted, woven projects from handspun fibers with instructions); interview/profile (of successful and/or interesting fiber craftsmen); and technical (on spinning, dyeing or fiber technology, use, properties). "All articles must contain a high level of in-depth information. Our readers are very knowledgeable about these subjects." Query. Length: 2,000 words. Pays $25-100.
Photos: State availability of photos. Identification of subjects required.

SPORTS COLLECTORS DIGEST, Krause Publications, 700 E. State St., Iola WI 54990. (715)445-2214. Editor: Steve Ellingboe. Sports memorabilia magazine published 26 times/year. "We serve collectors of sports memorabilia—baseball cards, yearbooks, programs, autographs, jerseys, bats, balls, books, magazines, ticket stubs, etc." Circ. 16,000. Pays on acceptance. Byline given. Buys first North American serial rights only. Submit seasonal/holiday material 3 months in advance. Simultaneous queries and photocopied submissions OK. SASE. Reports in 5 weeks on queries; 2 months on mss. Free sample copy and writer's guidelines.
Nonfiction: General interest (new card issues, research on older sets); historical/nostalgic (old stadiums, old collectibles, etc.); how-to (buy cards, sell cards and other collectibles, display collectibles, ways to get autographs, jerseys, and other memorabilia); interview/profile (or well-known collectors, ball players—but must focus on collectibles); new product (new card sets) and personal experience ("what I collect and why"-type stories). No sports stories. "We are not competing with *The Sporting News*, *Sports Illustrated* or your daily paper. Sports collectibles only!" Buys 40-60 mss/year. Query. Length: 300-3,000 words; prefers 1,000 words. Pays $10-50.
Photos: Unusual collectibles. State availability of photos. Pays $5-15 for b&w prints. Identification of subjects required. Buys all rights.
Columns/Departments: "We have all the columnists we need but welcome ideas for new columns." Buys 100-150 mss/year. Query. Length: 600-3,000 words. Pays $15-60.
Tips: "If you are a collector, you know what collectors are interested in. Write about it. No shallow, puff pieces; our readers are too smart for that. Only well-researched articles about sports memorabilia and collecting. Some sports nostalgia pieces are OK. Write only about the areas you know about. Many of our writers do not receive payment; they submit articles for satisfaction and prestige and to help their fellow hobbyists. It's that kind of hobby and that kind of magazine."

STANDARD CATALOG OF AMERICAN CARS 1899-1942, Krause Publications, 700 E. State St., Iola WI 54990. (715)445-2214. Editor: John A. Gunnell. 60% freelance written. We cover the collector car field from the turn-of-the-century to late-model specialty cars. Weekly tabloid; averages 52 pages. Circulation: 100,000. Pays on acceptance. Byline given. Buys all rights. Phone queries preferred. Reports in 4 days. Free sample copies (through Circulation Dept.—do not request samples from editors).
Nonfiction: For 1984 we are heavily over-stocked with lengthy feature material. We are interested mainly in purchasing hobby news stories, national news about antique cars, and short, detailed articles about *specific* models. (For example, 1940 Ford DeLuxe convertible or 1955 Chevrolet Bel Air 2-door sport coupe.) Short articles should include technical specifications. Also interested in features about cars owned by famous people, with old photos of the car and owner. Buys 12 mss/issue. Query. Pays 3¢/word.
Photos: State availability of photos with query. Pays $5 for 5x7 b&w glossy prints. Captions required. Buys all rights.
Columns/Departments: Book reviews (new releases for hobbyists). Buys 1 ms/issue. Query. Pays 3¢/word.
Fillers: Newsbreaks. Buys 50/year. Pays 3¢/word.
Tips: "Must know automotive hobby well."

TRI-STATE TRADER, Mayhill Publishing, Box 90, Knightstown IN 46148. Editor: Robert M. Reed. 90% freelance written. Weekly newspaper covering antiques, auctions, collectibles, genealogy for collectors nationwide interested in history and past lifestyles. Circ. 38,000. Pays on publication. Byline given. Buys first and second rights to the same material. Submit seasonal/holiday material 3 months in advance. Simultaneous queries and photocopied and previously published submissions OK. Computer printout submissions acceptable; no dot-matrix. SASE. Reports in 3 weeks on queries; 1 month on mss. Publishes ms an average of 4 weeks after acceptance. Sample copy for SAE and 60¢ postage; free writer's guidelines.
Nonfiction: Historical/nostalgic (of interest to collectors). "We're always interested in brief background articles on specific antiques and collectibles, and how today's antiques are used." Buys 175 mss/year. Query. Length: 300-1,100 words. Pays variable rates.
Fillers: History, places, dates, etc. Length: 30-150 words.
Tips: "We're interested in general news relating to collectibles and history. Read the *TST* and know this mar-

ket. We are open to most any writer, but our readers are most knowledgeable on our topics and expect the same from writers."

WESTERN & EASTERN TREASURES, People's Publishing, Inc., Box Z, Arcata CA 95521. Editor: Rosemary Anderson. Emphasizes treasure hunting for all ages, entire range in education, coast-to-coast readership. Monthly magazine. Circ. 70,000. Computer printout submissions acceptable; prefers letter-quality to dot-matrix. Pays on publication. Buys all rights. SASE. Reports in 8 weeks. Sample copy and writer's guidelines for 50¢.
Nonfiction: How-to (use of equipment, how to look for rocks, gems, prospect for gold, where to look for treasures, rocks, etc., "first-person" experiences). "No purely historical manuscripts or manuscripts that require two-part segments or more." Buys 200 unsolicited mss/year. Submit complete ms. Length: maximum 1,500 words. Pays 2¢/word maximum.
Photos: Purchased with accompanying ms. Captions required. Submit prints or transparencies. Pays $5 maximum for 3x5 and up b&w glossy prints; $35 and up for 35mm and cover slides. Model release required.
Columns/Departments: Detector Clinic, and Tip of the Month. Buys 50/year. Send complete ms. Length: 800-1,500 words. Pays 2¢/word maximum.

THE WOODWORKER'S JOURNAL, Madrigal Publishing Co., Inc., 517 Lichfield Rd., Box 1629, New Milford CT 06776. (203)355-2694. Editor: James J. McQuillan. Managing Editor: Thomas G. Begnal. Bimonthly magazine covering woodworking for woodworking hobbyists of all levels of skill. Circ. 100,000. Pays on acceptance. Byline given. Buys all rights. Submit seasonal/holiday material 3 months in advance. SASE. Reports in 6 weeks. Free sample copy and writer's guidelines.
Nonfiction: "In each issue, we try to offer a variety of plans—some selected with the novice in mind, others for the more experienced cabinetmaker. We also like to offer a variety of furniture styles, i.e., contemporary, colonial, Spanish, etc. We are always in the market for original plans for all types of furniture, wood accessories, jigs, and other shop equipment. We are also interested in seeing carving and marquetry projects." Buys 20-30 mss/year. Send complete ms. Length "varies with project." Pays $80-120/page. "Payment rate is for a complete project submission, consisting of dimensioned sketches, a write-up explaining how the project was built, and at least one high-quality b&w photo."
Photos: Send photos with ms. Reviews 5x7 b&w prints. "Photo payment is included in our basic payment rate of $80-120/page for a complete project submission." Captions required. Buys all rights.

THE WORKBASKET, 4251 Pennsylvania Ave., Kansas City MO 64111. Editor: Roma Jean Rice. Issued monthly except bimonthly June-July and November-December. Buys first rights. Pays on acceptance. Query. Reports in 6 weeks. SASE.
Nonfiction: Interested in articles of 400-500 words of step-by-step directions for craft projects and gardening articles of 200-500 words. Pays 7¢/word.
Photos: Pays $7-10 for 8x10 glossies with ms.
Columns/Departments: Readers' Recipes (original recipes from readers); and Making Cents (short how-to section featuring ideas for pin money from readers).

WORKBENCH, 4251 Pennsylvania Ave., Kansas City MO 64111. (816)531-5730. Editor: Jay W. Hedden. 95% freelance written. For woodworkers. Circ. 825,000. Pays on acceptance. Buys all rights then return all but first rights upon request, after publication. Byline given if requested. Computer printout submissions acceptable. SASE. Reports in 2-4 weeks. Query. Publishes ms an average of 1 year after acceptance. Free sample copy and writer's guidelines.
Nonfiction: "In the last couple of years, we have increased our emphasis on home improvement and home maintenance, and now we are getting into alternate energy projects. Ours is a nuts-and-bolts approach, rather than telling how someone has done it. Because most of our readers own their own homes, we stress 'retrofitting' of energy-saving devices, rather than saying they should rush out and buy or build a solar home. Energy conservation is another subject we cover thoroughly; insulation, weatherstripping, making your own storm windows. We still are very strong in woodworking, cabinetmaking and furniture construction. Projects range from simple toys to complicated reproductions of furniture now in museums." Pays $125/published page, up or down depending on quality of submission.
Columns/Departments: Shop tips bring $20 maximum with drawing and/or photo.
Tips: "If you can consistently provide good material, including photos, your rates will go up and you will get assignments. The field is wide open but only if you produce quality material and clear, sharp b&w photos. If we pay less than the rate, it's because we have to supply photos, information, drawings or details the contributor has overlooked. Contributors should look over the published story to see what they should include next time. Our editors are skilled woodworkers, do-it-yourselfers and photographers. We have a complete woodworking shop at the office, and we use it often to check out construction details of projects submitted to us."

WORLD COIN NEWS, Krause Publications, 700 E. State, Iola WI 54990. (715)445-2214. Editor-in-Chief: Russ Rulau. 30% freelance written. Weekly newspaper about non-US coin collecting for novices and advanced collectors of foreign coins, medals, and paper money. Circ. 15,000. Pays on acceptance. Byline given. Buys first North American serial rights only. Submit seasonal material 1 month in advance. Simultaneous and photocopied submissions OK. Computer printout submissions acceptable; no dot-matrix. Reports in 2 weeks. Publishes ms an average of 3 weeks after acceptance. Free sample copy.
Nonfiction: "Send us timely news stories related to collecting foreign coins and current information on coin values and markets." Send complete ms. Buys 30 mss/year. Length: 500-2,000 words. Pays 3¢/word to first-time contributors; fees negotiated for later articles.
Photos: Send photos with ms. Pays $5 minimum for b&w prints. Captions and model release required. Buys first rights and first reprint rights.

YESTERYEAR, Yesteryear Publications, Box 2, Princeton WI 54968. (414)295-3969. Editor: Michael Jacobi. 25% freelance written. For antique dealers and collectors, people interested in collecting just about anything, and nostalgia buffs. Monthly tabloid. Circ. 7,000. Pays on publication. Buys all rights. Byline given. Submit seasonal/holiday material 3 months in advance. Simultaneous, photocopied and previously published submissions OK. SASE. Reports in 1 month for queries; 1 month for mss. Publishes ms an average of 2 months after acceptance. Sample copy $1.
Nonfiction: General interest (basically, anything pertaining to antiques, collectible items or nostalgia in general); historical (again, pertaining to the above categories); and how-to (refinishing antiques, how to collect). The more specific and detailed, the better. "We do not want personal experience or opinion articles." Buys 36 mss/year. Send complete ms. Pays $5-25.
Photos: Send photos with ms. Pays $5 for 5x7 b&w glossy or matte prints; $5 for 5x7 color prints. Captions preferred.
Columns/Departments: "We will consider new column concepts as long as they fit into the general areas of antiques and collectibles and nostalgia." Buys 3 mss/issue. Send complete ms. Pays $5-25.

Home and Garden

"Home and garden" readers may live in log houses or penthouses but have one concern in common—to make the most of where they live. Some magazines here concentrate on gardens; others on the how-to of interior design. Still others focus upon homes and/or gardens in specific regions.

AUSTIN HOMES & GARDENS, Duena Development Corp., Box 5950, Austin TX 78763. (512)441-1980. Editor: Marsia Hart Reese. 50% freelance written. Monthly magazine emphasizing Austin, Texas homes, people, events, and gardens for current, former, and prospective residents. Circ. 11,000. Average issue includes 16 articles. Pays on publication. Byline given. "The material that we buy becomes the sole property of AH&G and cannot be reproduced in any form without written permission. Local phone queries OK. Photocopied submissions OK. Computer printout submissions acceptable "as long as there are margins on the paper without holes in them"; prefers letter-quality to dot-matrix. SASE. Reports in 1 month. Publishes ms an average of 2 months after acceptance "if assigned." Sample copy $1.
Nonfiction: General interest (interior design and architecture; trends in home furnishings and landscaping; arts and crafts); historical (local); how-to (on home or garden); and fashion feature. Buys 8 mss/issue. Query and samples of published articles. Length: 700-1,500 words. Pays $75 minimum.
Columns/Departments: Departments include Discoveries (unusual local business or services); The Errant Epicure (outstanding local restaurants); Breakaway (travel); and Profile (interesting Austin people). Query. Length: 500-1,000 words. Pays $75 minimum.
Tips: "Always looking for good freelancers, but can only work with writers who live in our area and are familiar with our publication."

BETTER HOMES AND GARDENS, 1716 Locust St., Des Moines IA 50336. (515)284-3000. Editor: David Jordan. For "middle-and-up income, homeowning and community-concerned families." Monthly. Circ. 8,000,000. Buys all rights. Pays on acceptance. Query preferred. Submit seasonal material 1 year in advance. Mss should be directed to the department where the story line is strongest. SASE.
Nonfiction: "Freelance material is used in areas of travel, health, cars, money management, and home enter-

tainment. Reading the magazine will give the writer the best idea of our style. We do not deal with political subjects or areas not connected with the home, community and family." Length: 500-2,000 words. Pays top rates based on estimated length of published article; $100-2,000.
Photos: Shot under the direction of the editors. Purchased with mss.
Tips: "Follow and study the magazine to see what we do and how we do it. There are no secrets, after all; it's all there on the printed page. Having studied several issues, the writer should come up with one or several ideas that interest him, and, hopefully, us. The next step is to write a good query letter. It needn't be more than a page in length (for each idea), and should include a good stab at a title, a specific angle, and a couple of paragraphs devoted to the main points of the article. This method is not guaranteed to produce a sale, of course; there is no magic formula. But it's still the best way I know to have an idea considered."

CANADIAN DO IT YOURSELF MAGAZINE, Centre Publications Ltd., Suite 1, 2000 Ellesmere Rd., Scarborough, Ontario M1H 2W4 Canada. (416)438-1153. Editor: Jo Ann Stevenson. Publications Director: G.S. Werlick. Magazine published 10 times/year for home do-it-yourselfers. Circ. 85,000. Pays on publication. Byline given. Buys all rights. Submit seasonal/holiday material 6 months in advance. SASE. Reports in 1 month on queries. Free sample copy.
Nonfiction: How-to (home improvement, woodworking, crafts, etc.). Buys variable number mss/year. Length: 500-3,000 words. Pays $200-600.
Photos: Send photos with ms.

CANADIAN WORKSHOP, The How-to Magazine, Chrimak Enterprises, Ltd., 100 Steelcase Rd. E., Markham, Ontario L3R 1E8 Canada. (416)475-8440. Editor: Bob Pennycook. 90% freelance written. Monthly magazine covering the "do-it-yourself market including projects, renovation and restoration, gardening, maintenance and decoration. Canadian writers only, please." Circ. 70,000. Pays on publication. Byline given. Offers 75% kill fee. Buys first rights only. Submit seasonal/holiday material 6 months in advance. Simultaneous queries OK. Computer printout submissions acceptable; no dot-matrix. SASE. Reports in 3 weeks. Publishes ms an average of 5 months after acceptance. Sample copy $2; free writer's guidelines.
Nonfiction: How-to (gardening, home and home machinery maintenance, renovation projects, and woodworking projects). Buys 20-40 mss/year. Query with clips of published work. Length: 1,500-4,000 words. Pays $225-600.
Photos: Send photos with ms. Pays $20-150 for 2¼x2¼ color transparencies; covers higher; $10-50 for b&w contact sheets. Captions, model release, and identification of subjects required.
Tips: "Freelancers must be aware of our magazine format. Product-types used in how-to articles must be readily available across Canada. Deadlines for articles are 5 months in advance of cover date. How-tos should be detailed enough for the amateur but appealing to the experienced."

COLORADO HOMES & LIFESTYLES, Suite 154, 2550 31st St., Denver CO 80216. (303)433-6533. Editor: Mary McCall. 50% freelance written. Bimonthly magazine covering Colorado homes and lifestyles for designers and upper-middle-class and high income households. Circ. 33,000. Pays on publication. Byline given. Buys all rights. Submit seasonal/holiday material 6 months in advance. Simultaneous queries and photocopied submissions OK. Computer printout submissions acceptable: prefers letter-quality to dot matrix. SASE. Reports in 1 month. Publishes ms an average of 4 months after acceptance.
Nonfiction: Fine furnishings in the home, gardening and plants, decorating and design, and fine food and entertaining. Buys 24 mss/year. Send complete ms. Length: 800-1,500 words. "For celebrity features (Colorado celebrity and home) pay is $300-1500. For unique, well-researched pieces on Colorado people, places, etc., pay is 15-50¢/word. For regular articles, 10-20¢/word. The more specialized and Colorado-oriented your article is, the more generous we are."
Photos: Send photos with ms. Reviews 35mm color transparencies and b&w glossy prints. Identification of subjects required.

‡**COLUMBUS HOME & LIFESTYLES**, Columbus Lifestyles, Inc., 2144 Riverside Dr., Columbus OH 43221. (614)486-2483. Editor: Eugenia Synder Morgan. Managing Editor: Gerald F. Kolly. A bimonthly magazine covering homes and lifestyles. "Our editorial mission is to portray Columbus and Columbus people in an exciting, upbeat manner. Estab. 1984. Circ. 15,000. Pays on publication. Byline given. Offers 25% kill fee. Buys all rights. Submit seasonal/holiday material 5-6 months in advance. Simultaneous queries, and simultaneous, photocopied, and previously published submissions OK. Computer printout submissions acceptable. SASE. Reports in 1 month on queries; 6 weeks on mss. Sample copy for $3, 9x12 SAE and postage ($1.90 first class, $1.15 third class); writer's guidelines for business size SAE and 1 first class stamp.
Nonfiction: General interest, historical/nostalgic, interview/profile and photo feature. "Stories need to lend themselves to color photography or other visual accompaniment." No how-to articles, or investigative journalism/exposes. Buys 4-6 mss/issue. Query with published clips. Length: 800-3,000 words. Pays $35-200.
Photos: State availability of photos. Pays negotiable rate for 4x5 color transparencies. Captions, model release, and identification of subjects required. Buys negotiable rights.

Columns/Departments: Homes and interiors, fashion and related subjects, historical perspectives, food and entertaining (no restaurant reviews), sports and outdoor activities, business, collectibles and nostalgia, performing arts and artists, visual arts and artists, interesting people, and general interest. Buys 2-4 mss/issue. Query with published clips. Length: 500-1,500 words. Pays $35-125.

Fiction: Stories by Central Ohio writers, or fiction about Central Ohio area. Buys 1-3 mss/year. Query with published clips. Length 1,000-3,000 words. Pays $75-200.

Poetry: Avant-garde, free verse, light verse, traditional. Buys 1-6 poems/year. Submit maximum 3 poems. Length: 10-50 lines. Pays $10-75.

Tips: "All sections of magazine are open to freelancers."

‡**COUNTRY LIVING**, Hearst Corporation, 224 W. 57th Ave., New York NY 10019. (212)262-3621. Editor: Rachel Newman. Managing Editor: Mary Roby. 10% freelance written. Monthly magazine on country homes/living. Circ. 1,425,000. Pays on acceptance. Byline given. Usually buys all rights; sometimes first rights only. Makes work-for-hire assignments. Submit seasonal/holiday material 1 year in advance. Photocopied submissions OK. Computer printout submissions acceptable. SASE. Reports in 2 weeks on queries; 1 month on mss.

Nonfiction: Mary Seehafer, articles editor. General interest, historical/nostalgic, interview/profile, and any article about living "country-style." No fiction or poetry. Buys 20 mss/year (excluding regular columnists). Query with published clips. Length: 300-1,200 words. Pays $100-350.

Photos: Julio Vega, photo editor. State availability of photos. Reviews b&w contact sheets, color transparencies, and 8x10 b&w and color prints. Captions required. Buys one-time rights.

Columns/Departments: Mary Seehafer, column/department editor. Buys 12 mss/year. Query with published clips. Length: 300-1,200 words. Pays $100-350.

Tips: "Send short typed piece with cover letter—it must relate to country living. Short informative essay on country furniture, pottery, quilts, textiles, or other specialty is the area most open to freelancers."

‡**EARTH SHELTER LIVING**, Webco Publishing Inc., 110 S. Greeley St., Stillwater MN 55082. (612)430-1113. Editor: Doug Seitz. 60% freelance written. Bimonthly magazine on earth sheltering aimed at knowledgable consumers and some professionals (architects, builders). Circ. 10,000. Pays on acceptance. Byline given. Offers 10% kill fee. Buys first rights only. Submit seasonal/holiday material 4 months in advance. Simultaneous queries and simultaneous, photocopied and previously published submissions OK. Computer printout submissions acceptable. Reports in 3 weeks. Publishes ms an average of 3 months after acceptance. Sample copy $3; free writer's guidelines.

Nonfiction: Book excerpts; how-to (earth shelter construction, passive solar or related areas); humor; interview/profile; new product; opinion; personal experience; photo feature and technical. "Present queries or ms on new methods or new angles on old methods. Earth shelterers are interested in anything different. No articles like those we've already used." Buys 20 mss/year. Query. Length: 1,000-2,500. Pays $50-125.

‡**THE FAMILY FOOD GARDEN**, F.F.G., Inc., 464 Commonwealth Ave., Boston MA 02215. (617)262-7170. Editor: Robert Fibkins. Managing Editor: Paula Lovejoy. 60% freelance written. Magazine published 8 times/year on food gardening. "Emphasis is on family participation in food gardening and self-sufficiency. Our readers are chemical and organic gardeners, practical-minded and inquisitive." Circ. 400,000. Pays on publication. Byline given. Buys all rights. Submit seasonal/holiday material 6 months in advance. Simultaneous queries, and simultaneous and photocopied submissions OK. SASE. Reports in 2 weeks. Publishes ms an average of 6 months after acceptance. Sample copy for 8½x11 SAE and $1.05 postage; writer's guidelines for SAE with 1 first class stamp.

Nonfiction: General interest (relating to food gardening and techniques); how-to (projects for garden); and personal experience (with gardening or gardening techniques). No humor, cartoons, poetry or fiction. Buys 15 mss/year. Query or send complete ms. Length: 400-1,500 words. Pays $75 and up (negotiable).

Photos: John Harold, photo editor. Send photos with query or ms. Reviews color transparencies and 8x10 b&w and color prints. Pays negotiable rates. Captions, model release, and identification of subjects required. Buys one-time rights.

Columns/Departments: "We do all departments in-house and do not accept freelance columns."

Tips: "Topics of interest include new gardening techniques, growing specific fruits/vegetables with a new twist, coping with unusual growing conditions, new and unusual food crops, and families with unusual gardens. The area most open to freelancers is features with plenty of good, useful information which would help our readers in their gardening efforts. In each case, the criteria for selection will include novelty, authenticity and meaty content. No gimmicks, please. Stories should be written more concisely and get to the point quickly."

FAMILY HANDYMAN, Webb Co., 1999 Shepard Rd., St. Paul MN 55116. Editor: Gary Havens. Emphasizes do-it-yourself home maintenance, repair and improvement. Publishes 10 issues yearly. Magazine; 100 plus pages. Circ. 1,200,000. Pays on acceptance. Submit seasonal material 6 months in advance. Computer printout submissions acceptable. SASE. Reports in 4-6 weeks. Free sample copy and writer's guidelines.

Nonfiction: How to do home, lawn and garden maintenance, repairs, remodeling, and shop projects. Recent article example: "Build Stronger with Adhesives" (May/June 1984). Buys 10 unsolicited mss/issue. Query or send complete ms. Length: 700-1,200 words. Pays $50-1,500 depending on length, whether color or b&w photos used, and quality of entire piece.

Photos: Send photos with ms. Uses 5x7 or 8x10 b&w glossy or 35mm or larger color transparencies. Offers additional payment for photos purchased with mss. Captions and model releases required.

Tips: Especially needs small-scale home remodeling, maintenance and repair projects and material on improving mobile homes.

‡**FARMING UNCLE®**, Box 91, Liberty NY 12754. Editor: Louis Toro. 25% freelance written. Quarterly magazine on nature, small stock, and gardening. Pays on acceptance. Publishes ms an average of 3 months after acceptance. Byline given. Buys all rights. SASE. Reports in 1 week on queries. Sample copy for $2 and $1.50 postage (first class).

Nonfiction: How-to (poultry, small stock, gardening, shelter building, etc.). Buys 12 mss/year. Send complete ms. Length: 500-750 words. Pays $7.50-10.

Photos: Send photos with ms. Pays $3-4 for b&w prints. Captions and identification of subjects required.

Poetry: "We publish poetry but do not pay for it."

FLOWER AND GARDEN MAGAZINE, 4251 Pennsylvania, Kansas City MO 64111. Editor-in-Chief: Rachel Snyder. 50% freelance written. For home gardeners. Bimonthly. Picture magazine. Circ. 600,000. Buys first rights only. Byline given. Pays on acceptance. Computer printout submissions acceptable; no dot-matrix. Free writer's guidelines. Query. Reports in 6 weeks. Publishes ms an average of 1 year after acceptance. SASE.

Nonfiction: Interested in illustrated articles on how to do certain types of gardening and descriptive articles about individual plants. Flower arranging, landscape design, house plants, patio gardening are other aspects covered. "The approach we stress is practical (how-to-do-it, what-to-do-it-with). We try to stress plain talk, clarity, and economy of words. An article should be tailored for a national audience." Buys 20-30 mss/year. Length: 500-1,500 words. Pays 7¢/word or more, depending on quality and kind of material.

Photos: Pays up to $12.50/5x7 or 8x10 b&w prints, depending on quality, suitability. Also buys color transparencies, 35mm and larger. "We are using more 4 color illustrations." Pays $30-125 for these, depending on size and use.

Tips: "Prospective author needs good grounding in gardening practice and literature. Then offer well-researched and well-written material appropriate to the experience level of our audience. Use botanical names as well as common. Illustrations help sell the story. Describe special qualifications for writing the particular proposed subject." Recent published article: "Flowering Holiday Cacti."

GARDEN DESIGN, The Fine Art of Residential Landscape Architecture, Publication Board of the American Society of Landscape Architects, 1190 E. Broadway, Louisville KY 40204. (502)589-1167. Editor: Linda B. Handmaker. Editor-in-chief: Susan Rademacher Frey. Quarterly magazine covering garden making, garden history, garden design emphasizing the *design* aspects of gardening rather than horticulture. "Design elements and considerations are presented in clear, simple language for both laymen and professionals." Circ. 19,000. Pays on publication. Byline given. Offers negotiable kill fee. Buys one-time rights and makes work-for-hire assignments. Submit seasonal/holiday material 1 year in advance. Previously published submissions OK. SASE. Reports in 2 weeks on queries; 5 weeks on mss. Sample copy $5.

Nonfiction: Historical/nostalgic, interview/profile, opinion, personal experience, photo feature, and travel. Photographic and editorial content addresses specific seasons—spring, summer, autumn, winter. No detailed horticultural or technical articles. Buys 20-30 mss/year. Query with published clips. Length: 500-3,000 words. Pays $50-250.

Photos: Send photos with query or ms. Pays $50-100 for 35mm color transparencies and 8x10 b&w prints. Captions, model release and identification of subjects required.

Columns/Departments: The Garden Life (personality profiles); Plant Page (design applications of plants); Seasonal Specifics; The Garden Traveler (public gardens outside U.S.); Focal Point (personal perspectives); Bookshelf (book reviews); and Eclectic (items/events of interest). Buys 10-15 mss/year. Query with published clips. Length: 100-1,500 words. Pays $50-250.

Tips: "We emphasize the experience of gardening over technique. Our editorial core covers an array of subjects—historical, contemporary, large and small gardens. Departments follow specific subjects—travel, plants, people, etc. Samples of previously published work are welcomed. Outlines or brief article descriptions of specific subjects are helpful. We are willing to work with authors in tailoring specific subjects and style with them."

GARDEN MAGAZINE, The Garden Society, A Division of the New York Botanical Garden, Bronx Park, Bronx NY 10458. Editor: Ann Botshon. 40% freelance written. Emphasizes horticulture, environment and botany for a diverse readership, largely college graduates and professionals united by a common interest in plants and the environment. Most are members of botanical gardens and arboreta. Bimonthly magazine. Circ. 29,000. Buys all rights. Submit seasonal/holiday material 4 months in advance. Photocopied submissions OK. Computer printout submissions acceptable; prefers letter-quality to dot-matrix. SASE. Reports in 2 months. Publishes ms an average of 18 months after acceptance. Sample copy $2.50.

Nonfiction: Ann Botshon, editor. "All articles must be of high quality, meticulously researched and botanically accurate." Expose (environmental subjects); how-to (horticultural techniques, must be unusual and verifiable); general interest (plants of interest, botanical information, ecology); humor (pertaining to botany and horticulture); photo feature (pertaining to plants and the environment); and travel (great gardens of the world). Buys 15-20 unsolicited mss/year. Recent article example: "Irises for the Windowsill" (January/February 1984). Query with clips of published work. Length: 500-2,500 words. Pays $50-300.

Photos: Tim Metevier, designer. Pays $35-50/5x7 b&w glossy print; $40-150/4x5 or 35mm color transparency. Captions preferred. Buys one-time rights.

Tips: "We appreciate some evidence that the freelancer has studied our magazine and understands our special requirements."

GARDENS FOR ALL NEWS, Newsmagazine of the National Association for Gardening, Gardens for All, 180 Flynn Ave., Burlington VT 05401. (802)863-1308. Editor: Ruth W. Page. 65% freelance written. Monthly tabloid covering food gardening and food trees. "We publish not only how-to-garden techniques, but also news that affects gardeners, like science advances. Specific, experienced-based articles with carefully worked-out techniques for planting, growing, harvesting, using garden fruits and vegetables sought. Most of our material is for gardeners with several years' experience." Circ. 225,000. Pays on acceptance. Byline given. Buys first rights only and occasionally second (reprint) rights to material originally published elsewhere. Submit seasonal/holiday material 4 months in advance. Photocopied and previously published submissions OK. Computer printout submissions acceptable; prefers letter-quality to dot-matrix. SASE. Reports in 2 weeks on queries; 1 month on mss. Sample copy and writer's guidelines for $1.

Nonfiction: How-to, humor, inspirational, interview/profile, new product, personal experience, photo feature, and technical. "All articles must be connected with food/gardening." Buys 80-100 mss/year. Query. Length: 300-3,500 words. Pays $15-200/article.

Photos: Kit Anderson, photo editor. Send photos with ms. Pays $5-15 for b&w photos; $15-35 for color photos. Captions, model releases and identification of subjects required.

GURNEY'S GARDENING NEWS, A Family Newsmagazine for Gurney Gardeners, Gurney Seed and Nursery Co., 2nd and Capitol, Yankton SD 57079. (605)665-4451. Editor: Janet H. Schoniger. Bimonthly newsmagazine covering gardening, horticulture and related subjects for home gardeners. Circ. 30,000. Pays on acceptance. Byline given. Buys first North American serial rights, but will consider second serial (reprint) rights to material originally published elsewhere. Submit seasonal/holiday material 6 months in advance. Computer printout submissions acceptable. SASE. Reports in 1 month on queries; 2 months on mss. Sample copy for 9x12 SAE; writer's guidelines for business-size SAE.

Nonfiction: "We are interested in well-researched, well-written and illustrated articles on all aspects of home gardening. We prefer articles that stress the practical approach to gardening and are easy to understand. We don't want articles which sound like a rehash of material from a horticultural encyclopedia or how-to-garden guide. We rarely buy articles without accompanying photos or illustrations. We look for a unique slant, a fresh approach, new gardening techniques that work and interesting anecdotes. Especially need short (300-500 words) articles on practical gardening tips, hints, and methods. We are interested in: how-to (raise vegetables, flowers, bulbs, trees); interview/profile (of gardeners); photo feature (of garden activities); and technical (horticultural-related)." Buys 70 unsolicited mss/year. Query. Length: 700-1,250 words. Pays $50-125. Also buys articles on gardening projects and activities for children. Length: 500-1,000 words. Pays $30-100.

Photos: Purchases photos with ms. Also buys photo features, essays. Pays $10-85 for 5x7 or 8x10 b&w prints or contact sheets. Caption, model release and identification of subjects required. Buys one-time rights.

Tips: "Please time articles to coincide with the proper season. Read Gurney's Seed and Nursery catalogs and be familiar with Gurney's varieties before you submit an article on vegetables, fruits, flowers, trees, etc. We prefer that it be Gurney's. Our readers know gardening. If you don't, don't write for us."

HERB QUARTERLY, Box 275, Newfane VT 05345. Editor: Sally Ballantine. 90% freelance written. Quarterly magazine for herb enthusiasts. Circ. 22,000. Pays $25 on publication. Buys North American serial rights and second (reprint) rights to manuscripts originally published elsewhere. Computer printout submissions acceptable. Prospective writers should check back issues or obtain sample copy ($5). Query letters recommended. SASE. Reports in 1 month. Publishes ms an average of 1 year after acceptance. Free writer's guidelines.

Nonfiction: Gardening (landscaping, herb garden design, propagation, harvesting); how-to (herb businesses, medicinal and cosmetic use of herbs, crafts); cooking; historical (folklore, focused piece on particular period—not general survey); interview of a famous person involved with herbs or folksy herbalist; personal experience; and photo essay ("cover quality" 8x10 b&w prints). "We are particularly interested in herb garden design,

contemporary or historical.'' No fiction or poetry. Send double-spaced ms. Length: 1,500-3,000 words. Reports in one month.
Tips: ''All too often we receive pieces that are totally inappropriate for the magazine.''

HOME BUYERS GUIDE, Bryan Publications, Inc., 1550 Bristol St. N., Newport Beach CA 92660. Editor: Janie Murphy. Emphasizes new homes available for homebuyers and homebuilders. Monthly tabloid. Circ. 115,000. Pays on publication. Buys first North American serial rights. Photocopied submissions OK. Previously published work OK, but state where and when it appeared. SASE. Reports in 2 months.
Nonfiction: General interest (taxes, insurance, home safety, mortgages); and opinion (by experts in a field, e.g., a CPA on taxes). ''Gear all material to the California homeowner and consumer. Write in an informative yet entertaining style. Give examples the reader can identify with.'' Buys 2 mss/issue. Send complete ms. Length: 500-1,500 words. Pays $75-200.
Photos: Send photos with ms. Uses b&w 8x10 glossy prints. Offers no additional payment for photos accepted with ms. Captions preferred, model release required. Buys one-time rights.
Columns/Departments: Energy, taxes, finance, community planning, home safety, architecture and design, new products; and Personalizing Your Home (how homeowners have customized development homes). Buys 2 mss/issue. Send complete ms. Length: 500-1,200 words. Pays $75-200.

HOME MAGAZINE, Home Magazine, Ltd., 690 Kinderkamack Rd., Oradell NJ 07649. (201)967-7520. Editor: Olivia Buehl. Executive Editor: Louise I. Driben. 80% freelance written. Monthly magazine covering home remodeling, home improving and home building. *Home* tells homeowners how to remodel, improve, or redecorate an existing home, build a new home, and deal effectively with architects, designers, contractors, and building supply dealers.'' Circ. 550,000. Pays on acceptance. Byline given. Pays negotiable kill fee. Buys all rights to copy and photocopy. Submit seasonal material 6 months in advance. Computer printout submissions acceptable. SASE. Reports in 3 weeks on queries; 6 weeks on mss. Publishes ms an average of 5 months after acceptance. Sample copy $2.
Nonfiction: How-to (homeowner-oriented, do-it-yourself projects); and financial subjects of interest to homeowners, (taxes, insurance, etc.). Buys 50-60 mss/year. Query with clips of published work. Length: 200-2,500 words. Pays $150-1,500.

THE HOMEOWNER, America's How-to Magazine, 149 5th Ave., New York NY 10010. Editor: Jim Liston. A publication of Family Media, Inc. Published 10 times/year. Circ. 600,000. Buys first rights only. Pays 50% kill fee. Byline given. Pays on acceptance. Sample copy $1.50; address request to Circulation Department. Submit seasonal material 7 months in advance. Reports in 3 weeks. SASE.
Nonfiction: Wants how-to information based on facts and experience—not theory. No material on gardening or decorating. ''Design ideas should be original and uncomplicated. They should be directed at young homeowners working with simple tools, and if possible, the kind of project that can be completed on a weekend. Likes articles on good before-and-after remodelings. All articles should contain a list of necessary materials and tools.'' Length: 1,200 words maximum. Pays $150/published page maximum.
Photos: Offers no additional payment for b&w photos used with mss. ''Photos are as important as words. B&w preferred. 4x5's are OK, but 8x10's are better.''
Fillers: It Worked for Me, a regular filler feature, pays $35 per captioned photo or drawing that contains a work-saving hint or solves a problem.
Tips: ''Send snapshots or even pencil sketches or plans of remodeling projects with query. To break in a writer should show a willingness to submit the proposed article on speculation. (Once a writer has proved himself to us, this is not required.)''

HORTICULTURE, The Magazine of American Gardening, 755 Boylston St., Boston MA 02116. Published by the Horticulture Associates. Editor: Thomas C. Cooper. 90% freelance written. Monthly. Buys first North American serial rights. Byline given. Pays on acceptance. Pays on acceptance. Query. Reports in 6 weeks. Publishes ms an average of 7 months after acceptance. SASE.
Nonfiction: Uses articles from 2,000-5,000 words on all aspects of gardening. ''We cover indoors and outdoors, edibles and ornamentals, noteworthy gardens and gardeners.'' Study publication.
Photos: Color transparencies and top quality b&w prints, preferably 8x10 only; ''accurately identified.'' Buys one-time rights.

HOUSE BEAUTIFUL, The Hearst Corp., 1700 Broadway, New York NY 10019. (212)903-5000. Editor: JoAnn Barwick. Executive Editor: Margaret Kennedy. Editorial Director: Mervyn Kaufman. Senior Editor/ Copy/Features: Carol Cooper Garey. Emphasizes design, architecture and building. Monthly magazine; 200 pages. Circ. 840,000. Pays on acceptance. Byline given. Submit seasonal/holiday material 4 months in advance of issue date. SASE. Reports in 5 weeks.
Nonfiction: Historical (landmark buildings and restorations); how-to (kitchen, bath remodeling service); humor; interview; new product; and profile. Submit query with detailed outline or complete ms. Length: 300-1,000 words. Pays varying rates.
Photos: State availability of photos with ms.

LOG HOME GUIDE FOR BUILDERS & BUYERS, Muir Publishing Company Ltd., 1 Pacific Ave., Gardenvale, Quebec H9X 1B0 Canada. (514)457-2045. Editor: Doris Muir. (705)754-2201. Quarterly magazine covering the buying and building of log homes. "We publish for persons who want to buy or build their own log home. The writer should always keep in mind that this is a special type of person—usually a back-to-the-land, back-to-tradition type of individual who is looking for practical information on how to buy or build a log home." Circ. 125,000. Pays on publication. Byline given. Buys one-time rights. Submit seasonal/holiday material 4 months in advance. Simultaneous queries, and simultaneous ("writer should explain"), photocopied, and previously published submissions OK. Reports in 2 weeks. Sample copy $2.75 (postage included).
Nonfiction: General interest; historical/nostalgic (log home historic sites, restoration of old log structures); how-to (anything to do with building log homes); inspirational (sweat equity—encouraging people that they can build their own home for less cost); interview/profile (with persons who have built their own log homes); new product (or new company manufacturing log homes—check with us first); personal experience (authors own experience with building his own log home, with photos is ideal); photo feature (on author or on anyone else building his own log home); and technical (for "Techno-log" section; specific construction details, i.e., new log buiding details, joining systems). Also, "would like photo/interview/profile stories on famous persons and their log homes—how they did it, where they got their logs, etc." Interested in log commercial structures. "Please no exaggeration—this is a truthful, back-to-basics type of magazine trying to help the person interested in log homes." Buys 25 mss/year. Query with clips of published work or send complete ms. "Prefer queries first with photo of subject house" Length: open. Pays $50 minimum.
Photos: State availability of photos. Send photos with query "if possible. It would help us to get a real idea of what's involved." Pays $5-25 for b&w or color prints. "All payments are arranged with individual author/submitter." Captions and identification of subjects required. Buys one-time rights.
Columns/Departments: Pro-Log (short news pieces of interest to the log-building world); Techno-Log (technical articles, i.e., solar energy systems; any illustrations welcome); and Book-Log (book reviews only, on books related to log building and alternate energy; "check with us first"). Buys "possible 50-75 mss/year. Query with clips of published work or send complete ms. Length: 100-1,000 words or more. All payments are arranged with individual author/submitter." No need to enclose SASE.

MECHANIX ILLUSTRATED, 1515 Broadway, New York NY 10036. (212)719-6630. Editor: Joseph R. Provey. Executive Editor: Harry Wicks. Special Feature Editor: Michael Morris. Monthly magazine for the home and car manager. "Articles on maintenance, repair, and renovation to the home and family car. Information on how to buy, how to select products useful to homeowners/carowners. Emphasis in home-oriented articles is on good design, inventive solutions to styling and space problems, and useful home-workshop projects." Circ. 1.6 million. Buys first North American serial rights. Byline given. Pays on acceptance. SASE. Query.
Nonfiction: Feature articles relating to homeowner/carowner, 1,500-2,500 words. "This may include personal home-renovation projects, professional advice on interior design, reports on different or unusual construction methods, and energy-related subjects; and outdoor/backyard project, etc. We are no longer interested in high-tech subjects such as aerospace, electronics, photography or military hardware. Most of our automotive features are written by experts in the field, but fillers, tips, how-to repair, or modification articles on the family car are welcome. Workshop articles on furniture, construction, tool use, refinishing techniques, etc., are also sought. Pays $300 minimum for features; fees based on number of printed pages, photos accompanying mss., etc."
Photos: Photos should accompany mss. Pays $600 and up for transparencies for cover. Inside color: $300/1 page, $500/2, $700/3, etc. Home and Shop Hints illustrated with 1 photo, $25. Captions and model release required.
Fillers: Tips and fillers useful to tool users or for general home maintenance. Pays $35 and up for illustrated and captioned fillers. Pays $75 for half-page fillers.
Tips: "If you're planning some kind of home improvement and can write, you might consider doing a piece on it for us. Good how-to articles on home improvement are always difficult to come by. Aside from that, no particular part of the book is easier to break into than another because we simply don't care whether you've been around or been published here before. We don't care who you are or whether you have any credentials—we're in the market for good journalism, and if it's convincing, we buy it."

METROPOLITAN HOME, 750 3rd Ave., New York NY 10017. Editor-in-Chief: Dorothy Kalins. For city dwellers. Monthly magazine; 110 pages. Circ. 750,000. Buys all rights. Buys 60-100 mss/year. Pays on acceptance. Submit seasonal material 6 months in advance. Computer printout submissions acceptable "as long as they are readable." Reports in 2 months. Query. SASE.
Nonfiction: Joanna Krotz, article editor. "Service material specifically for people who live in cities on interior designs, collectibles, equity, wines, liquor and real estate. Thorough, factual, informative articles." Buys 60-100 mss/year. Query. Length: 300-1,000 words. Pays $600-800.
Photos: B&w photos and color are purchased only on assignment.
Columns/Departments: Wanderlusting, High Spirits (wine and liquor), Equity and Real Estate. Length: 300-1,000 words. Pays $600-800.

N.Y. HABITAT MAGAZINE, For Co-op, Condominium and Loft Living, The Carol Group, Ltd., 928 Broadway, New York NY 10010. (212)505-2030. Editor: Carol J. Ott. Managing Editor: Tom Soter. 75% freelance written. Bimonthly magazine covering co-op, condo and loft living in metropolitan New York for "sophisticated, affluent and educated readers interested in maintaining the value of their homes and buying new homes." Circ. 10,000. Pays on publication. Byline given. Offers negotiable kill fee. Buys first North American serial rights. Submit seasonal/holiday material 3 months in advance. Computer printout submissions acceptable. SASE. Reports in 3 weeks. Publishes ms an average of 10 weeks after acceptance. Sample copy for $3, 9x12 SAE and 5 first class stamps; writer's guidelines for business-size SAE and 1 first class stamp.
Nonfiction: Only material relating to co-op and condominium living in New York metropolitan area. Buys 20 mss/year. Query with published clips. Length: 750-1,500 words. Pays $25-250.

NEW SHELTER, Rodale Press, 33 E. Minor St., Emmaus PA 18049. Articles Editor: David Bumke and Joe Carter. Magazine published 9 times/year about energy-efficient homes. Circ. 650,000. Pays on acceptance. Buys all rights. Submit seasonal material at least 6 months in advance. Computer printout submissions acceptable; prefers letter-quality to dot-matrix. SASE. Reports in 6 weeks.
Nonfiction: "We are the magazine of innovative home designs and projects of use to our audience of advanced do-it-yourselfers. We are looking for the work of innovators who are at the cutting edge of affordable housing, alternate energy, water and resource conservation, etc. Our subtitle is, "Innovative Answers For Today's Homeowners," and that really says it all. We don't want run-of-the-mill, wooden how-to prose. We want lively writing about what real people have done with their homes, telling how and why our readers should do the same." Query with clips of previously published work. Length: 1,000-5,000 words. Rate of payment depends on quality of ms.
Photos: Submit to Art Director. State availability of photos. Pays $15-25 for b&w contact sheets with negatives and 8x10 glossy prints with ms. Pays $25 minimum for 2x2 or 35mm color transparencies. Captions and model release required.
Tips: No hobby/craft or overly general, simplistic articles.

1001 HOME IDEAS, Family Media, 3 Park Ave., New York NY 10016. Editor-in-Chief: Anne Anderson. Executive Editor: Kathryn Larson. 50% freelance written. "We're primarily an interior design magazine for mainstream America." Monthly. Circ. 1.5 million. Buys variable rights. Pays on acceptance. Computer printout submissions acceptable. SASE. Publishes ms an average of 6 months after acceptance. Sample copy and writer's guidelines for $2 and SASE. Query first. SASE.
Nonfiction: Interior design material and home service articles on food, gardening, and money-saving tips. Length: 2,000 words maximum.
Photos: "Freelance photographs rarely accepted." Interior design queries should include snapshots of room and clear descriptions of the room and its contents. Professional photographers may contact Robert Thornton, art director, about possible assignments. Send SASE with sufficient postage.
Tips: "Our readers are looking for easy, attractive, and cost-effective ideas in a step-by-step format. Persons who want to suggest a room for possible inclusion in the magazine may do so by sending a query with detailed descriptions of the room and snapshots. Don't hire a professional photographer just to show us what the room looks like."

ORGANIC GARDENING, Rodale Press Publications, 33 E. Minor St., Emmaus PA 18049. (215)967-5171. Planning Editor: Jack Ruttle. For a readership "interested in health and conservation, in growing plants, vegetables and fruits without chemicals, and in protecting the environment." Monthly magazine; 160-240 pages. Circ. 1,200,000. Buys all rights and the right to reuse in other Rodale Press Publications with agreed additional payment. Pays 25% kill fee, "if we agree to one." Byline given. Buys 400-500 mss/year. Pays on acceptance. Computer printout submissions acceptable; no dot-matrix. Reports in 4-6 weeks. Query or submit complete ms. "Query with full details, no hype." SASE. Free sample copy and writer's guidelines.
Nonfiction: "Factual and informative articles or fillers, especially on food gardening and family self-sufficiency, stressing organic methods. Interested in all crops, soil topics, indoor gardening, greenhouses; natural foods preparation, storage, etc.; biological pest control; variety breeding, nutrition, recycling, energy conservation; and community and club gardening. Strong on specific details, step-by-step how-to, thorough research. We do not want to see generalized garden success stories; we print detailed stories on growing food. We would like to see material on garden techniques, raising fruit organically, grains, new and old vegetables, effective composting, soil building, waste recycling, food preparation, and insect control. Emphasis is on interesting, practical information, presented accurately." Length: 1,000-2,000 words for features. Pays $200-600.
Photos: B&w and color purchased with mss or on assignment. Enlarged b&w glossy print and/or negative preferred. Pays $15-25. 2¼x2¼ (or larger) color transparencies.
Fillers: Fillers on above topics are also used. Length: 150-500 words. Pays $50-100.
Tips: "Read the magazine regularly, like a hawk."

PHOENIX HOME/GARDEN, Arizona Home Garden, Inc., 3136 N. 3rd Ave., Phoenix AZ 85013. (602)234-0840. Editor: Manya Winsted. Managing Editor: Nora Burba. Assistant Editor; Stephanie Scott. 50% freelance written. Monthly magazine covering homes, furnishings, entertainment and gardening for Phoenix area residents interested in better living. Circ. 32,000. Pays on publication. Byline given. Buys all rights. Submit seasonal/holiday material 6 months in advance. Queries *only*. Simultaneous queries OK. SASE. Reports in 6 weeks on queries. Publishes ms an average of 3 months after acceptance. Sample copy $1.95.
Nonfiction: General interest (on interior decorating, architecture, gardening, entertainment, food); historical (on furnishings related to homes); some how-to (on home improvement or decorating); health, beauty, fashion; and travel (of interest to Phoenix residents). Buys 100 or more mss/year. Query with clips of published work. Length: 1,200 words maximum. Pays $75-300/article.
Tips: "It's not a closed shop. I want the brightest, freshest, most accurate material available. Study the magazine to see our format and style."

SAN DIEGO HOME/GARDEN, Westward Press, Box 1471, San Diego CA 92101. (714)233-4567. Editor: Peter Jensen. Managing Editor: Dirk Sutro. 85% freelance written. Monthly magazine covering homes and gardens and nearby travel for 30 to 40 year-old residents of San Diego city and county. Circ. 36,000. Pays on publication. Byline given. Buys first rights only. Submit seasonal material 3 months in advance. Photocopied submissions OK. Computer printout submissions acceptable. Reports in 1 month. Publishes ms an average of 6 months after acceptance. Free writer's guidelines for SASE.
Nonfiction: General interest (service articles with plenty of factual information, prices and "where to buy" on home needs); how-to (save energy, garden, cook); new product (for the house); photo feature (on houses and gardens) and architecture; home improvement; remodeling; and real estate. Articles must have local slant. Buys 10-15 unsolicited mss/year. Query with clips of previously published work. Length: 500-2,000 words. Pays $50-200.
Tips: "No out-of-town, out-of-state material. Most freelance work is accepted from local writers."

SELECT HOMES MAGAZINE, (incorporating *1001 Decorating Ideas*), 382 W. Broadway, Vancouver, British Columbia V5Y 1R2 Canada. (604)879-4144. Editor: Ralph Westbrook. Bimonthly. "We are a 4-color consumer publication, intended for the middle- and upper-income homeowning and community-oriented family. We cover every aspect of the shelter industry, including a selection of home plans in every issue for which working blueprints can be purchased. We emphasize help for the homeowner." Circ. 150,000. Pays half on acceptance, half on publication. Buys 60 or more text/photo packages/year. Byline and photo credits given. Buys first Canadian serial rights. Simultaneous, photocopied and previously published US submissions OK. Computer printout submissions acceptable. Reports in 1 month on queries, 6 weeks on mss. Sample copy and guidelines for $1 postage and handling.
Nonfiction: Every aspect of residential and recreational housing under many categories, such as: renovation, new home profiles, interior design, energy, how-to, money, decorating, maintenance/repairs, building science, real estate, and landscaping. Length: 100-2,000 words. "We prefer economy of words, in a step-by-step format wherever possible, with lengthier cut-lines for photos. Articles should be written for illustration with line-drawings, charts, graphs, etc., as we heavily emphasize the visual and pictorial. Will consider humorous and/or cartoon pieces if they apply to readership, i.e., the home and homeowning as central focus." Buys 60 or more mss/year. Pays top rates.
Columns/Departments: "We have informative columns on new products, techniques, housing information, government programs affecting housing, handyman hints, etc. Always open to other suggestions and contributions, especially practical tips." Pays $50-2,500.
Photos: "We prefer the photographer to employ negative film and submit contact sheets for consideration, from which we can request either negatives or finished, sized prints for layout." Prefers 2¼x2¼ or larger format. 35mm OK for article illustrations only. Pictures should not be sent alone unless intended for cover use. Model release required. Captions, credit lines required, or notes so that captions may be staff-written. Pays $10 minimum for b&w print, $20 minimum for color negative, print or transparency.
Tips: "Submissions should be fast-paced, hard-hitting and informative. Above all, the objective is to show the reader how to do it, or how to get it done, in an effort to get more enjoyment from home living."

THE SPROUTLETTER, Sprouting Publications, Box 62, Ashland OR 97520. (503)482-5627. Editor: Jeff Breakey. 50% freelance written. Bimonthly newsletter covering sprouting, live foods and indoor food gardening. "We emphasize growing foods (especially sprouts) indoors for health, economy, nutrition and food self-sufficiency. We also cover topics related to sprouting, live foods and holistic health." Circ. 2,200. Pays on publication. Byline given. Offers 50% kill fee. Buys first North American serial rights and second (reprint) rights to material originally published elsewhere. Submit seasonal/holiday material 2 months in advance. Previously published submissions OK. Computer printout submissions acceptable; prefers letter-quality to dot-matrix. SASE. Reports in 2 weeks on queries; 3 weeks on mss. Publishes ms an average of 3 months after acceptance. Sample copy $1.50; writer's guidelines for business size SAE and 1 first class stamp.
Nonfiction: General interest (raw foods, sprouting, holistic health); how-to (grow sprouts, all kinds of foods

indoors; build devices for sprouting or indoor gardening); personal experience (in sprouting or related areas); and technical (experiments with growing sprouts). No common health food/vitamin articles or growing ornamental plants indoors (as opposed to food producing plants). Buys 4-6 mss/year. Query. Length: 500-2,400 words. Pays $10-40. "We give twice as much if payment is accepted in the form of subscriptions or advertising in *The Sproutletter* or in books or merchandise which we sell."

Columns/Departments: Book Reviews (books oriented toward sprouts or holistic health). Reviews are short and informative. News Items (interesting news items relating to sprouts or live foods); Recipes (mostly raw foods). Buys 4-8 mss/year. Query. Length: 120-400 words. Pays $2-8.

Poetry: Buys 1-3 poems/year. Submit maximum 3 poems. Length: 15-70 lines. Payment for poems is a half-year subscription.

Fillers: Short humor and newsbreaks. Buys 2-4/year. Length: 50-150 words. Pays $1-5.

Tips: "Writers should have a sincere interest in holistic health and in natural whole foods. We like writing which is optimistic, interesting and very informative. Consumers are demanding more thorough and accurate information. Articles should cover any given subject in depth in an enjoyable and inspiring manner."

TEXAS GARDENER, The Magazine for Texas Gardeners, by Texas Gardeners, Suntex Communications, Inc., Box 9005, Waco TX 76714. (817)772-1270. Editor: Chris S. Corby. Managing Editor: Betsy A. Ritz. Bimonthly magazine covering vegetable and fruit production, ornamentals and home landscape information for home gardeners in Texas. Circ. 35,000. Pays on publication. Byline given. Buys all rights. Submit seasonal/holiday material 6 months in advance. SASE. Reports in 6 weeks. Sample copy $2.75; writer's guidelines for business-size SAE and 1 first class stamp.

Nonfiction: How-to, humor, interview/profile and photo feature. "We use feature articles that relate to Texas gardeners. We also like personality profiles on hobby gardeners and professional horticulturists who are doing something unique." Buys 50-100 mss/year. Query with clips of published work. Length: 800-2,400 words. Pays $50-200.

Photos: "We prefer superb color and b&w photos; 90% of photos used are color." State availability of photos. Pays negotiable rates for 2¼ color transparencies and 8x10 b&w prints and contact sheets. Model release and identification of subjects required.

Tips: "First, be a Texan. Then come up with a good idea of interest to home gardeners in this state. Be specific. Stick to feature topics like "How Alley Gardening Became a Texas Tradition." Leave topics like "How to Control Fire Blight" to the experts. High quality photos could make the difference. We would like to add several writers to our group of regular contributors and would make assignments on a regular basis."

YOUR HOME, Meridian Publishing Co., Inc., 1720 Washington, Box 10010, Ogden UT 84409. Editor: Peggie Bingham. A monthly company magazine (for approximately 200 companies) covering home/garden subjects for homeowners and renters of all ages. Circ. 90,000. Pays on acceptance. Byline given. Buys first North American serial rights only. Six-month lead time. Previously published submissions OK. SASE. Sample copy for $1 and 9x12 SAE; writer's guidelines for SAE and 20¢ postage.

Nonfiction: Historical/nostalgic (homes); how-to (home/garden); humor (home/garden); and photo feature (remodeling with some copy). "We're in need of good decorating/remodeling/gardening ideas, with super-quality *color* transparencies, for beginning homeowners, renters, trailer house owners, and *some* well-to-do homes described in photo feature. Also, we are just starting a 4-page bridal insert, and we're looking for bridal stories about fashion, showers, cooking for two, decorating a first home or apartment, wedding etiquette, honeymoon travel, family finance, historical pieces about wedding traditions, how to entertain, etc. Buys 50 mss/year. Query with or without published clips or send complete ms. Length: 800-1,000 words. Pays 15¢/word.

Photos: State availability of photos or send photos with query or ms. Pays $35 for color transparencies (slides to 8x10). "We also need color transparency covers of brides; pay is negotiable." Captions required. Buys one-time rights.

Fiction: Humorous (home/garden). Buys 5-10 mss/year. Send complete ms. Pays 15¢/word.

Fillers: Short humor. Buys 5-10/year. Length: 500-800 words. Pays 15¢/word.

Tips: "Send good decorating/remodeling/how-to's around the house and garden. Super sharp, clear color transparencies are essential—no snap shots."

Humor

"In a world where Life As We Know It is constantly being pulled from under us and replaced by new realities, humor is—and will continue to be—one of the few 'dependables'," says one humor magazine editor. ". . . Treat humor as an art, and not as a frivolity." Publications listed here specialize in gaglines or prose humor. Other publications that use humor can be found in nearly every category in this book. Some of these have special needs for major humor pieces; some use humor as fillers; many others are simply interested in material that meets their ordinary fiction or nonfiction requirements but has a humorous slant. Other markets for humorous material can be found in the Cartoon and Comic Books and Gag Writing sections. For a closer look at writing humor, consult *How to Write and Sell (Your Sense of) Humor*, by Gene Perret (Writer's Digest Books).

‡HUMOR MAGAZINE, Edward Savaria & Co., 144 Gay St., Philadelphia PA 19127. (215)482-7673. Editor: Edward Savaria, Jr. Managing Editor: Suzanne Tschanz. Monthly. Estab. 1984. Circ. 40,000. Pays on acceptance. Byline given. Buys one-time rights. Submit seasonal/holiday material minimum 3 months in advance. Simultaneous queries, and simultaneous, photocopied, and previously published submissions OK. Computer printout submissions acceptable. SASE. Reports in 2 weeks on queries. Sample copy for 9x12 SAE and 5 first class stamps; writer's guidelines for SAE and 1 first class stamp.
Nonfiction: Book excerpts; exposé (satire); general interest; historical/nostalgic; how-to (parody); humor; interview/profile (on comedians, directors of comedy); new product (if funny); opinion (humor angle); personal experience (humor); photo feature (humor); and travel. "Everything must be funny or have to do with humor-comedy. No porn (hard), no silly humor, no excess violence." Buys 15 mss/year. Query or send complete ms. Length: 50-1,000 words. Pays $25-300.
Photos: Humor angle. Send photos wth query or ms. Pays $10-25 + for 8x10 b&w prints.
Columns/Departments: T.V. Reviews and Movie Reviews (reviews of good, funny shows and movies, old and new); General National/World (any tibits or opinions, humor angle). Query or send complete ms. Length 50-300 words. Pays $25-200.
Fiction: Humorous. Any type of fiction with a humorous angle. Buys 15/mss year. Query or send complete ms. Length; 300-1,000 words. Pays $25-300.
Poetry: Light verse. Buys maximum 10 poems/year. Submit maximum 5 long, 20 short poems. Prefers short poems. Pays $5-50.
Fillers: Clippings, jokes, gags, anecdotes, short humor, newsbreaks—humorous. Buys 100/year. Length: 10-100 words. Pays $5-50.
WM **Editor's Note:** At *WM* press time, *Humor*'s editorial needs were being finalized. Send for guidelines and read the magazine.

‡LAUGH FACTORY MAGAZINE, Warner Publisher Services, #214, 400 S. Beverly Dr., Beverly Hills CA 90212. (213)656-1336. Editor: Jamie Masada. Managing Editor: Vic Dunlop. A monthly humor magazine. Circ. 225,000. Pays on publication. Byline given. Buys one-time rights. Submit seasonal/holiday material 3 months in advance. Simultaneous queries, and simultaneous, photocopied, and previously published submissions OK. Computer printout submissions acceptable; no dot-matrix. SASE. Reports in 6 weeks. Sample copy $2.50; writer's guidelines for SAE and 1 first class stamp.
Nonfiction: Humor. "We don't want 'humor' articles as such, we want material that makes people laugh out loud." Query. Length: 3,000 words. Pay rates are negotiable depending on length and quality of the piece."
Photos: State availability of photos with query or mss. Reviews prints. Also uses photos with captions, without accompanying ms.
Fillers: Jokes, gags, cartoons, short humor.
Tips: "The only restrictions we have are no four-letter words and nothing too gross."

LONE STAR: A Magazine of Humor, Lone Star Publications of Humor, Suite 103, Box 29000, San Antonio TX 78229. Editor: Lauren I. Barnett Scharf. 50% freelance written. Bimonthly humor magazine for "the general public and 'comedy connoisseur' as well as the professional humorist." Circ. 1,000. Pays on publication, "but we try to pay before that." Buys first North American serial rights, first rights and occasionally second serial (reprint) rights. Submit seasonal/holiday material 3 months in advance. Photocopied submissions and "sometimes" previously published work OK. SASE. Reports in 2 months on queries; 5 weeks on mss. Publishes ms an average of 8 weeks after acceptance. Sample copy $3.50; writer's guidelines for business-size SAE and 1 first class stamp.
Nonfiction: Humor (on anything topical/timeless); interview/profile (of anyone professionally involved in humor); and opinion (reviews of stand-up comedians, comedy plays, cartoonists, humorous books, *anything* concerned with comedy). "Inquire about possible theme issues." Buys 6 mss/year. Query with clips of published work if available. Length: 500-1,000 words; average is 700-800 words. Pays $5-20 and contributor's copy.
Fiction: Humorous. Buys variable mss/year. Query with clips if available or send complete ms. Length: 500-1,000 words. Pays $5-20 and contributor's copy.

Poetry: Free verse, light verse, traditional, clerihews and limericks. "Nothing too 'artsy' to be funny." Buys 10-20/year. Submit maximum 5 poems. Length: 4-16 lines. Pays $2-10.

Fillers: Clippings, jokes, gags, anecdotes, short humor and newsbreaks—"must be humorous or humor-related." Buys 20-30 mss/year. Length: 450 words maximum. Pays $1-5.

Tips: "We *do* like to know a writer's professional background. However, telling us that you've sold material to Phyllis Diller or that you're a personal friend of Isaac Asimov will not convince us to buy anything we don't find funny. Conversely, those with no background sales in humor should feel free to submit their material. The only real criteria are that it be original and *funny!* We recommend that those who are unfamiliar with *Lone Star* purchase a sample issue before submitting their work. However, this is *not* a requirement. We are also seeking funny/interesting letters for our "Letters to LONE STAR" column. Letters may be on any subject covered in the magazine or any aspect of humor. There is no payment for a letter—unless it contains short verse—but the writer receives a contributor's copy on publication."

MAD MAGAZINE, 485 Madison Ave., New York NY 10022. Editor: Al Feldstein. Buys all rights. Byline given.

Humor and Satire: "You know you're almost a *Mad* writer when: You include a self-addressed, stamped envelope with each submission. You realize we are a visual magazine, and we don't print prose, text or first/second/third-person narratives. You don't send us stuff like the above saying, 'I'm sure one of your great artists can do wonders with this!' You first submit a 'premise' for an article, and show us how you're going to treat it with three or four examples, describing the visuals (sketches not necessary). You don't send in 'timely' material, knowing it takes about 6 months between typewriter and on-the-stands. You don't send poems, song parodies, fold-ins, movie and/or TV show satires, Lighter Sides or other standard features. You understand that individual criticism of art or script is impossible due to the enormous amount of submissions we receive. You don't ask for assignments or staff jobs since *Mad* is strictly a freelance operation. You concentrate on new ideas and concepts other than things we've done (and over-done), like 'You Know You're a . . . when. . . .' " Buys 200-300 unsolicited mss/year.

‡**MOLE MAGAZINE**, Box 43403, Washington DC 20010. (202)667-1949. Editor: Gary Wasserman. Managing Editor: Mary W. Matthews. A bimonthly magazine of political satire and humor. "*Mole* is an eclectic humor magazine aimed at college-educated poeple who have outgrown the *National Lampoon*." Estab. 1983. Circ. 30,000. Pays on publication. Byline given. Buys first North American serial rights. Submit seasonal/holiday material 4 months in advnce. Simultaneous queries, and simultaneous, photocopied, and previously published submissions OK, "but we're not crazy about any of them." Electronic submissions OK on diskettes, 5¼", Kaypro format or Osborne 1, Xerox 820,-II, Superbrain, NEC PC-8001A, Micro Decision, Health w/ Magnolia Zenith Z-100, DEC VT180TI Professional Access Matrix. "Be sure to label which format!" Computer printout submissions acceptable. SASE. Reports in 2 months. Sample copy for $3 and 11x14 SAE; writer's guidelines for business-size SAE, and 1 first class stamp.

Nonfiction: Humor. Does not want "anything the writer thinks is witty instead of funny; deep, or important. Think frivolous!" Send complete ms. Length: 1,000 words maximum. Pays 20¢/word.

Photos: Mr. Pat Walsh, photo editor. State availability of photos with ms. Pays $25-100 for 8½x11 b&w prints. "Identification of subjects not required but strongly urged." Buys all rights.

Columns/Departments: Declassified (fake classifieds); Dearest Paula (advice to the politically forlorn), "by" Paula Parkinson; Good Reads/Sees/Hears (fake reviews); Hot Flashes (tomorrow's "news" today); Inside Word (fake news items); Blue Smoke & Mirrors (real, funny, news). Send complete ms. Length: 10-150 words. Pays 20¢/word.

Fiction: Humorous. "Nothing profound, sensitive, sweet, or spaced out. Think P.G. Wodehouse or Woody Allen." Send complete ms. Length: 1,000 words maximum. Pays 20¢/word.

Poetry: Light verse. "It *has* to be *boffo*, roll-on-the-floor funny, or don't bother." Buys 0-1 poems/year. Pays $10 maximum.

Tips: "We also publish fake ads, usually full-page, for products (e.g., "Diet Agent Orange") or services (e.g., "Guns for Nuns") etc. Send idea or complete layout. We buy most of our stuff from freelancers. They should read the magazine to get a sense of our style; and not be *too* topical—we've a 3-month lead time. (Let's-all-hate-the-President articles and anything about nuclear war are yawns.) *We'll print anything that makes us laugh out loud the first time we read it.*"

ORBEN'S CURRENT COMEDY, 1200 N. Nash St., #1122, Arlington VA 22209. (703)522-3666. Editor: Robert Orben. For "speakers, toastmasters, businessmen, public relations people, communications profes-

---

Market conditions are constantly changing! If this is 1986 or later, buy the newest edition of *Writer's Market* at your favorite bookstore or order directly from Writer's Digest Books.

sionals." Biweekly. Buys all rights. Pays at the end of the month for material used in issues published that month. "Material should be typed and submitted on standard size paper. Please leave 3 spaces between each item. Computer printout submissions acceptable. Unused material will be returned to the writer within a few days if SASE is enclosed. We do not send rejection slips. If SASE is not enclosed, all material will be destroyed after being considered except for items purchased."

Fillers: "We are looking for funny, performable one-liners, short jokes and stories that are related to happenings in the news, fads, trends and topical subjects. The accent is on laugh-out-loud comedy. Ask yourself, 'Will this line get a laugh if performed in public?' Material should be written in a conversational style, and if the joke permits it, the inclusion of dialogue is a plus. We are particularly interested in material that can be used by speakers and toastmasters: lines for beginning a speech, ending a speech, acknowledging an introduction, specific occasions, anything that would be of use to a person making a speech. We can use lines to be used at roasts, sales meetings, presentations, conventions, seminars and conferences. Short, sharp comment on business trends, fads and events is also desirable. Please do not send us material that's primarily written to be read rather than spoken. We have little use for definitions, epigrams, puns, etc. The submissions must be original. If material is sent to us that we find to be copied or rewritten from some other source, we will no longer consider material from the contributor." Pays $5.

Tips: "Follow the instructions in our guidelines. Although they are quite specific, we have received everything from epic poems to serious novels."

In-Flight

With the exception of one rail passenger magazine, publications in this category are read by airline passengers. Editors of these magazines use general interest material in addition to travel and popular aviation articles.

ABOARD, North-South Net, Inc., 135 Madeira, Coral Gables FL 33134. (305)442-0752. Editor: Camilo Delgado. Quarterly magazine covering destinations for the Peruvian, Panamanian, Paraguayan, Bolivian, Chilean, Salvadoran and Venezuelan national airlines. Entertaining, upbeat stories for the passengers. Circ. 120,000. Pays on publication. Byline given. Buys one-time rights. Simultaneous queries, and simultaneous, photocopied and previously published submissions OK. Computer printout submissions acceptable. SASE. Reports in 2 weeks on queries and mss. Sample copy for 11x14 SAE and $1.05 postage; writer's guidelines for #10 SAE and 1 first class stamp.

Nonfiction: General interest, how-to, interview/profile, new product, technical, travel, sports, business, science, technology and topical pieces. Nothing "controversial, political, downbeat or in any way offensive to Latin American sensibilities." Buys 20 mss/year. Query. Length: 1,500-3,000 words. Pays $50-150 (with photos).

Photos: State availability of photos with query letter. Prefers prints (b&w or color) and color transparencies. Pays $10-50 for 35mm color transparencies; $5-20 for 5x7 b&w prints. Captions required. Buys one-time rights."

Tips: "Study *Aboard* and other inflights, write exciting, succinct stories with an upbeat slant and enclose photos with captions. Break in with destination pieces for the individual airline or those shared by all seven. Writers must be accurate. Photos are almost always indispensable. Manuscripts are accepted either in English or Spanish. Translation rights must be granted. All manuscripts are subject to editing and condensation."

‡**ALASKA AERONAUTICAL, FLIGHT AND TIME (Wien Air Alaska), FLIGHT CRAFT, GOLDEN PACIFIC, GREAT AMERICAN AIRWAYS, HORIZON AIR, PACIFIC COAST AIRLINES, SAN JUAN AIRWAYS, SCENIC AIRWAYS, and WEST AIR**, Skies West Publishing Co., 0612 SW Idaho St., Portland OR 97201. (503)244-2299. Editor: Robert E. Patterson. Bimonthly inflight magazines for regional airlines in the western United States. "Our readers are affluent (median income is $40,159; 72% own property in excess of $100,000), well-educated (49% engaged in postgraduate study), businessmen/executives (78% are in professional/technical and managerial/administration fields), with a wide variety of interests and activities." Circ. 95,000. Pays on publication. Byline given. Offers 50% kill fee. Buys one-time rights. Submit seasonal/holiday material 3 months in advance. Simultaneous queries, and simultaneous, photocopied, and previously published submissions OK. Computer printout submissions acceptable. SASE. Reports in 2 weeks. Sample copy for 8½x11 SAE and $1.75 postage; writer's guidelines for business-size SAE and 1 first class stamp.

Nonfiction: Attractions in the the West, business, city features, general interest, health/medicine, historical/

nostalgic, investing, humor, inspirational, interview/profile, new product, photo feature, sports, technical and travel. Buys 60 mss/year. Query. Length: 500-1,500 words. Pays $100-300.
Photos: Prefers that photography accompany articles. State availability of photos. Reviews 35mm transparencies. Pays $25-50 for b&w and color photos. Captions and identification of subjects required.
Tips: "We also publish *Room Mate*, a quarterly in-room magazine for Thunderbird/Red Lion Inns."

ALASKAFEST, Seattle Northwest Publishing Co., Suite 503, 1932 1st Ave., Seattle WA 98101. (206)682-5871. Editor: Ed Reading. 90% freelance written. For travelers on Alaska Airlines. Monthly magazine; 80 pages. Circ. 25,000-35,000 (depending on season). Pays within 2 weeks of publication. Buys first right and second (reprint) rights to material originally published elsewhere. Byline given. Submit seasonal/holiday material 4 months in advance. Computer printout submissions acceptable. No OCR." SASE. Query with clips of published work. "A smart query is written in the style of the story. We don't get many like that." Publishes ms an average of 4 months after acceptance. Free sample copy and writer's guidelines.
Nonfiction: The audience is predominantly male, business travelers. We cover not only Alaska but the whole West Coast. Editorial content includes general-interest, adventure travel, business, life-style, and think pieces. We continue to look for humor and fiction. Buys 40 unsolicited mss/year. Length: 800-2,500 words. Pays $75-400.
Photos: State availability of photos with mss or send photos with ms. Pays $25-300 for photos. Captions required.
Tips: "Read a copy of the magazine. Then send something I would publish. Show, don't tell. Do not send anything that could appear in a newspaper supplement or travel section."

AMTRAK EXPRESS, East/West Network, Inc., 34 E. 51st St., New York NY 10022. (212)888-5900. Editor: James A. Frank. 90% freelance written. Monthly magazine for Amtrak riders who are upscale and discriminating. Circ. 160,000. Pays on acceptance. Byline given. Offers ¼ kill fee. Buys first North American serial rights. Submit seasonal/holiday material 6 months in advance. Simultaneous queries OK. SASE. Reports in 4 weeks on queries; 3 weeks on mss. Publishes ms an average of 4 months after acceptance. Sample copy for $2, 9x12 SAE and 3 first class stamps. Writer's guidelines for business size SAE and 1 first class stamp.
Nonfiction: General interest; interview/profile; photo feature; travel (limited amount and only within Amtrak territory); business; and science/technology. No poetry, personal experiences, train trip experiences. "We have moved away from mostly business articles to cover lifestyle, 'the good life,' personalities, consumer items and travel (limited amounts)." Buys 75 mss/year. Query with published clips. Length: 1,800-2,200 words. Pays $500-750.
Photos: State availability of photos. Pays $75-175 for 5x7 or 8x10 b&w prints; $125-400 for 35mm color transparencies. Identification of subjects required. Buys one-time rights.
Columns/Departments: Health, Books, Sports, Business, and Money ("should be a specific topic, well explained, informational and useful to readers"). Buys 35 mss/year. Query with published clips. Length: 1,200-1,800 words. Pays $350-500.
Tips: "Send a good idea, well explained with a detailed query that also tells something about you and your credits. We like to use new people, but we need some proof of competence."

CONTINENTAL MAGAZINE, East/West Network, Suite 800, 5900 Wilshire Blvd., Los Angeles CA 90036. (213)937-5810. Editor: Ellen Alperstein. Art Director: Frans Evenhuis. 90% freelance written. Monthly magazine offering general interest articles whose subjects represent individualism and a sense of place. Business, sports, trends and travel. Pays on acceptance. Byline given. Offers ⅓ to ¼ kill fee. Buys first North American serial rights. Submit seasonal/holiday material 4 months in advance. Simultaneous queries OK "provided writer informs us that it's submitted simultaneously." Computer printout submissions acceptable; no dot-matrix. SASE a must. Reports in 3 weeks on queries. Publishes ms an average of 3 months after acceptance. Sample copy $2 (requests to Diane Johnson); writer's guidelines and editorial outline for SAE and 1 first class stamp.
Nonfiction: Fast Track (a substantial profile of an individual with a demonstrable record of success); Closeup (solid pieces of reporting on trends; f-Stops (photo essay); Singular Sources (a color spread on "a person, place, product or service that is, without a doubt, unique"); Style & Substance (service feature to advise the traveling executive in the consumer marketplace); humor; any subject (sports, science, fashion, leisure, architecture and design) as long as it has a sense of individualism and geographic rooting; and Going Places (a major travel story with color photos offering "substantial service information to the Continental traveler"). Buys 130 features and department material/year. Length: 800-2,500 words. Pays $250-650 "plus some expenses." Query.
Columns/Departments: Creative Thinking (profiles of inventive people); Grapevine (tips from readers only on restaurants, hotels, business services geared to the business traveler—a reader's forum); Adventures (notable travel options for people who like a challange); and Last Laugh (monthly anecdote detailing in first person a resounding failure of an otherwise notable, successful person). Buys 75 mss/year. Length 800-2,000 words. Pays $250-350. Query.

DELTA SKY, Halsey Publishing, 12955 Biscayne Blvd., N. Miami FL 33181. (305)893-1520. Editor: Lidia de Leon. 90% freelance written. Readers are Delta Air Lines passengers. Monthly magazine. Circ. over 3 million monthly. "Unsolicited materials are rarely used, and only text/photo packages are considered." Computer printout submissions acceptable. Details and guidelines for SASE. Publishes ms an average of up to 6 months after acceptance.

Tips: "Freelance writers should be aware of heavier emphasis on graphics, necessitating "tighter" stories, via conveying idea, facts, etc. in a quicker, more provocative manner."

EAST/WEST NETWORK, INC., 34 E. 51st St., New York NY 10022. Publisher: Fred R. Smith. 80% freelance written. Publishes monthly inflight publications: *Continental* (Continental Airlines), *Republic* (Republic Airlines), *Ozark Magazine* (Ozark Airlines), *United* (United Airlines), *PSA Magazine* (Pacific Southwest Airlines), *ReView* (Eastern Airlines), *Texas Flyer*, (Texas International), *USAir* (US Air), *PanAm Clipper* (Pan-Am), *Western's World* (Western Airlines) and *Express* (Amtrak). Combined circ. 1.5 million. Pays within 60 days of acceptance. Buys first rights only; author retains other rights. Pays 50% kill fee. Byline given. Computer printout submissions acceptable; prefers letter-quality to dot-matrix. SASE. No telephone queries. Reports in 1 month. Publishes ms an average of 3 months after acceptance.

Nonfiction: "Magazines publish articles that are timely and have national significance to consumer magazine audience." No first person stories, airline stories, politics or downbeat material. Queries with published work for *United*, *PanAm*, *USAir*, *Express* and *ReView* should be sent to the individual magazine editor in the New York office. Queries for all other publications should be sent to the West Coast office to the Editor and name of publication at 5900 Wilshire Blvd., Los Angeles CA 90036. Length: 1,000-2,500 words. Pays $300-800. See individual listings for more information.

Photos: Wants no photos sent by writers.

‡GOLDEN FALCON, The Inflight Magazine for Gulf Air, Bryan Richardson & Associates, Parkway House, Sheen Lane, London SW14 8LS England. Editor: Joanna Donaldson. A monthly inflight magazine covering travel. Byline given. Buys first Mideast serial rights. Submit seasonal/holiday material at least 3 months in advance. Simultaneous queries, and simultaneous, photocopied, and previously published submissions OK "providing it has not been/will not be published in the Mideast before we publish it." Computer printout submissions acceptable; no dot-matrix. Reports in 4 weeks.

Nonfiction: General interest, historical/nostalgic, humor, personal experience, photo feature, technical and travel. No "material containing references to religion, sex, or politics which would offend the Muslim world." Buys approximately 100 mss/year. Send complete ms. Length: 1,000-2,000 words. Pays $100-130; £65-90 Sterling (per 1,000 words).

Photos: Pays $22-30 for "35mm + " color transparencies. Buys first Mideast serial rights.

Tips: "The travel section is most open to freelancers. When writing travel articles, avoid the first-person singular and stay away from brochure style."

OZARK MAGAZINE, East/West Network, 5900 Wilshire Blvd., Los Angeles CA 90036. Editor: Laura Doss. 99% freelance written. Monthly general interest inflight magazine slanted for a Midwest audience. Pays on acceptance. Offers 10% kill fee. Byline given. Buys first North American serial rights. Submit seasonal/holiday material at least 6 months in advance, other queries at least 4 months in advance. Simultaneous queries OK but not "masses of xeroxes." Computer printout submissions acceptable; prefers letter-quality to dot-matrix. SASE. Reports in 3 weeks on queries; 2 weeks on mss. Publishes ms an average of 2 months after acceptance. Sample copy $2.

Nonfiction: General interest, historical/nostalgic, humor, interview/profile, personal experience, photo feature, travel, food, fashion and sports. All articles must somehow relate to the Midwest. Buys 150-175 mss/year. Query with published clips or send complete ms. Length: 2,000-2,500 words. Pays $400-600.

Photos: State availability of photos, or send photos with ms. Prefers original 35mm transparencies. Identification of subjects and captions required. Buys one-time rights.

Columns/Departments: Hometown; Sports; Business; Lifestyle; The Right Stuff; Media; Outdoors. Buys 35-45 mss/year. Query with published clips or send complete ms. Length: 1,700 words maximum. Pays $250-300.

Tips: "Freelance writers should be aware of the habit of finding a stable of writers and sticking with them rather than chancing it on new talent . . . an understandable proclivity when you consider what garbage some inexperienced or lazy writers will palm off as professional quality work."

PACE MAGAZINE, Piedmont Airlines Inflight Magazine, Fisher-Harrison Publications Inc., 338 N. Elm St., Greensboro NC 27401. (919)378-6065. Managing Editor: Leslie P. Daisy. 100% freelance written. Bimonthly magazine covering travel, trends in business for the present and the future and other business-related articles. Circ. 2 million. Pays on publication. Byline given. Buys first North American serial rights. Submit holiday/seasonal material 6 months in advance. SASE. Reports in 1 month. Sample copy for $3 and SAE; free writer's guidelines with SASE.

Nonfiction: Travel (within the Piedmont flight route), trends in business, business management, employee re-

lations, business psychology and self-improvement as related to business and other business-related articles. No personal, religious, historical, nostalgic, humor, or interview/profile pieces. No cartoons. Buys 60 mss/year. Send query or complete ms. Length: 1,000-2,000 words. Pays $75-200.
Photos: Send photos with accompanying ms. Captions required.

PAN-AM CLIPPER, East/West Network, 34 E. 51st St., New York NY 10022. (212)888-5900. Editor: Richard Kagan. Senior Editor: Martha Lorini. Monthly magazine for passengers of Pan Am Airways (50% US, 50% foreign persons travelling on business or pleasure). Circ. 300,000. Pays on acceptance. Buys first world serial rights. Submit seasonal material 4 months in advance. Photocopied submissions OK. SASE. Reports in 1 month.
Nonfiction: General interest; interview (internationally important); profile; travel (destination pieces on unusual people and events of interest); humor (of worldwide appeal); technical (science and technology); and other (great stories of sports of international interest). Length: 1,500 words maximum. Query with clips of previously published work.
Photos: John Hair, art editor. State availability of photos. Reviews 8x10 b&w glossy prints and 35mm color transparencies. Captions and model release required. Buys one-time rights.

PSA MAGAZINE, East/West Network, Inc., Suite 800, 5900 Wilshire Blvd., Los Angeles CA 90036. (213)937-5810. Editor: Al Austin. 90% freelance written. Monthly magazine; 160 pages. Pays within 60 days after acceptance. Buys first rights only. Pays 25% kill fee. Byline given. Submit seasonal/holiday material 4 months in advance of issue date. Simultaneous and photocopied submissions OK. Computer printout submissions acceptable; prefers letter-quality to dot-matrix. SASE. Publishes ms an average of 3 months after acceptance. Sample copy $2.
Nonfiction: Prefers California/West Coast slant. General interest; interview (top-level government, entertainment, sports figures); new product (trends, survey field); profile and business (with California and West Coast orientation). Buys 10 mss/issue. Query. Length: 500-2,000 words. Pays $150-700.
Photos: State availability of photos with query. Pays ASMP rates for b&w contact sheets or negatives and 35mm or 2¼x2¼ color transparencies. Captions required. Buys one-time rights. Model release required.
Columns/Departments: Business Trends. Buys 1 ms/issue. Query. Length: 700-1,500 words. Pays $250-500.

REPUBLIC, (formerly *Republic Scene*), East/West Network, Inc., 5900 Wilshire Blvd., Los Angeles CA 90036. (213)937-5810. Editor: Jerry Lazar. 90% freelance written. Monthly in-flight magazine of Republic Airlines covering American popular culture for predominantly business travelers. Circ. 170,000 copies. Pays on acceptance. Byline given. Pays ⅓ kill fee. Buys first North American serial rights and second (reprint) rights to material originally published elsewhere. Submit seasonal/holiday material at least 3 months in advance. Computer printout submissions acceptable; prefers letter-quality to dot-matrix. SASE. Reports in 2 weeks on queries; 1 month on mss. Publishes ms an average of 3 months after acceptance. Sample copy and writer's guidelines for $2.
Nonfiction: General interest, humor, interview/profile, photo feature and travel. "Material must be of national interest—topical but noncontroversial." No reviews. Buys 96 mss/year. Query with clips of published work. Length: 2,000-3,000 words. Pays $250-600.
Photos: Sandi Silbert, art director. State availability of photos. Pays $75 minimum for color transparenices; $25 minimum for 8x10 b&w glossy prints. Captions preferred. Model releases required "where applicable." Buys one-time rights.
Columns/Departments: "Columns cover business, media, technology, health, law, Americana, sports and fitness. No reviews, but subjects vary widely. We mostly use writers whose work we know." Buys 24 mss/year. Length: 750-1,500 words. Pays $200-400.
Tips: "Freelance writers should be aware of the need for writers to think visually—an awareness of how words will look on the page and what kinds of graphics will accompany them."

‡**REVIEW MAGAZINE, Eastern Airline's Inflight Magazine**, East/West Network, 34 E. 51st St., New York NY 10022. (212)888-5900. Editor: Don Dewey. Associate Editor: Karen Kreps. Monthly magazine featuring reprints of articles previously published in leading consumer magazines, plus book excerpts and original articles. Circ. 1 million. Pays on acceptance. Byline given. Buys one-time rights. Photocopied and previously published submissions should be submitted by original publication, not by individuals. Computer printout submissions acceptable; prefers letter-quality to dot-matrix. SASE. Reports in 2 weeks on queries; 3 weeks on mss. Sample copy $2.
Nonfiction: General interest, historical/nostalgic, humor, interview/profile and photo feature. No how-to, travel, poetry or violence-related material. Buys 40 mss/year. Query. Length: 2,000-3,000 words. Pays $500-750 for original articles.
Photos: Nina Ovryn, photo editor. State availability of photos. Pays $75-600 for color transparencies; $75-500 for b&w prints. Identification of subjects required.

Tips: "We are always on the lookout for 2,000-word service and essay pieces on New York, Boston, and Washington subjects of interest to passengers on Eastern Air-Shuttle."

SKYLITE, Butler Aviation's Corporate Inflight Magazine, Halsey Publishing Co., 12955 Biscayne Blvd., North Miami FL 33181. (305)893-1520. Editor: Julio C. Zangroniz. Monthly magazine for corporate executives. Circ. 20,000. Pays on publication. Byline given. Offers 50% kill fee. Buys first North American serial rights. Submit seasonal/holiday material 6 months in advance. Simultaneous queries OK. Computer printout submissions acceptable. SASE. Reports in 3 months. Sample copy for $3; writer's guidelines for 4x9 SAE with 1 first class stamp.
Nonfiction: General interest; historical/nostalgic; how-to; inspirational; interview/profile (of corporate executives); travel (domestic and overseas); sports; science and consumer. No first person; anything dealing with politics, sex, drugs or violent crime. Buys 84-96 mss/year. Query. Length: 1,500-2,000 words. Pays $300-500.
Photos: State availability of photos. Reviews 35mm color transparencies. Captions required. Buys one-time rights. Pays for text/photo packages.
Tips: "Your query is your personal representative and *only* spokesman with an editor—make sure it is spotless, errorless and concise, a document that says 'I am a professional'. Queries not accompanied by SASE are not likely to get an answer due to manpower/economic limitations."

‡**SUNRISE, The Inflight Magazine for Kuwait Airways Corporation**, Bryan Richardson & Associates, Parkway House, Sheen Lane, London SW14 8L5 England. Editor: Joanna Donaldson. A monthly inflight magazine covering "mostly travel." Circ. 20,000. Pays on publication. Byline given. Buys first Mideast serial rights. Submit seasonal/holiday material at least 3 months in advance. Simultaneous queries, and simultaneous, photocopied, and previously published submissions OK, "provided it has not been/will not be published in the Mideast before we use it." Reports in 4 weeks.
Nonfiction: General interest, historical/nostalgic, humor, personal experience, photo feature, technical and travel. No "material containing references to religion, sex, or politics which would offend the Muslim world." Buys approximately 100 mss/year. Send complete ms. Length: 1,000-2,000 words. Pays $100-130; £65-90 Sterling (per 1,000 words).
Photos: State-availability of photos. Pays $22-30 for "35mm + " color transparencies. Buys first Mideast rights.
Tips: "The travel section is most open to freelancers. When writing travel articles, avoid the first-person singular and stay away from brochure style."

USAIR MAGAZINE, East/West Network, 34 E. 51st St., New York NY 10022. Editor: Richard Busch. Senior Editor: John Atwood. 90% freelance written. A monthly general interest magazine published for airline passengers, many of whom are business travelers, male, with high incomes and college educations. Circ. 190,000. Pays on acceptance. Buys first rights only. Submit seasonal material 6 months in advance. Photocopied submissions OK. Computer printout submissions acceptable; prefers letter-quality to dot-matrix. SASE. Reports in 2 weeks. Publishes ms an average of 4 months after acceptance. Sample copy $2; free writer's guidelines with SASE.
Nonfiction: Travel, business, sports, health, food, personal finance, nature, the arts, science and photography. "No downbeat stories or controversial articles." Buys 100 mss/year. Query with clips of previously published work. Length: 1,000-2,500 words. Pays $400-1,000.
Photos: Send photos with ms. Pays $75-150/b&w print, depending on size; color from $100-250/print or slide. Captions preferred; model release required. Buys one-time rights.
Columns/Departments: Sports, food, money, health, business, living, science and photography. Buys 3-4 mss/issue. Query. Length: 1,200-1,800 words.
Tips: "Send irresistible ideas and proof that you can write. It's great to get a clean manuscript from a good writer who has given me exactly what I asked for."

‡**WESTERN'S WORLD**, East-West Network, 5900 Wilshire Blvd., Los Angeles CA 90036. Editor: Ed Dwyer. 100% freelance written. Monthly magazine for Western Airlines with newsmakers, entrepreneurs, and "movers and shakers" of the West. "*WW* is a regional magazine with the West as its purview." Circ. 110,000. Pays on acceptance. Byline given. Offers 20% kill fee. Buys first North American serial rights. Submit seasonal/holiday material 3 months in advance. Computer printout submissions acceptable; no dot-matrix. SASE. Reports in 6 weeks on queries; 3 weeks on mss. Publishes ms an average of 2 months after acceptance. Sample copy $2.
Nonfiction: General interest (Western focus, a la city magazine formula); interview/profile (no celebrities or Q&A format); and travel (specific new trends or services in a Western city for Datelines). "Monthly 'Datelines' from around Western's system (e.g., 'Dateline: Hawaii') keep readers posted on valuable insiders' tips on where to go and what to see. Subjects include technology, business, sports, media, fashion and food." No personal travel accounts, financial writing, or bed and breakfast hotel articles. Buys 50 mss/year. Query with

published clips. Length: 1,700-2,000 words. Pays $200-800.
Photos: "A dramatic photo 'portfolio' introduces the readers to the natural marvels of the West." Captions required. Buys one-time rights. Please query. Do not send originals.
Columns/Departments: Buys 72 mss/year. Query with published clips. Length: 1,750 words. Pays $300-350.
Fiction: Western (excerpts of classics, e.g., Mark Twain, Zane Grey).
Tips: "Send brief, informative query with clips of previous work. Know the market—we are not a travel magazine."

Juvenile

"Vague memories from childhood may lead an author to wrong conclusions," says one children's magazine editor. Just as kids change (and grow), so do magazines. Children's editors stress that writers must read *recent* issues.

This section of *Writer's Market* includes publications for children aged 2-12. Magazines for young people 12-18 appear in the Teen and Young Adult category. *Writing for Children and Teenagers*, by Lee Wyndham (revised by Arnold Madison, Writer's Digest Books) offers information and advice on writing for both age groups.

Most of the following publications are produced by religious groups, and wherever possible, the specific denomination is given. For the writer with a story or article slanted to a specific age group, the following sub-index is a quick reference to markets for his story in that age group.

Editors who are willing to receive simultaneous submissions are indicated. (This is the technique of mailing the same story at the same time to a number of low-paying religious markets of nonoverlapping circulation. In each case, the writer, when making a simultaneous submission, should inform the editor. In fact, some editors prefer a query over a complete manuscript when the writer is considering making a simultaneous submission.) Mass circulation, nondenominational publications included in this section that have good pay rates are not interested in simultaneous submissions and should not be approached with this technique. Magazines that pay good rates expect, and deserve, the exclusive use of material.

Writers will also note in some of the listings that editors will buy "second rights" to stories. This refers to a story which has been previously published in a magazine and to which the writer has already sold "first rights." Payment is usually less for the re-use of a story than for first-time publication.

Juvenile Publications Classified by Age

Two- to Five-Year-Olds: *Chickadee, Children's Playmate, The Friend, Highlights for Children, Happy Times, Humpty Dumpty, Odyssey, Our Little Friend, Primary Treasure, Ranger Rick, Story Friends, Turtle Magazine for Preschool Kids, Wee Wisdom, Young American.*

Six- to Eight-Year-Olds: *Chickadee, Child Life, Children's Digest, Children's Playmate, Cobblestone, Dash, The Dolphin Log, Ebony Jr!, The Friend, Happy Times, Highlights for Children, Humpty Dumpty, Jack and Jill, Nautica, Odyssey, Our Little Friend, Pockets, Primary Treasure, R-A-D-A-R, Ranger Rick, Stickers, Story Friends, 3-2-1 Contact, Touch, Trails, Wee Wisdom, Wonder Time, The Young Crusader, Young American, Young Judean.*

Nine- to Twelve-Year-Olds: *Action, Ahoy, Bible-in-Life Pix, Chickadee, Child's Life, Children's Digest, Clubhouse, Cobblestone, Crusader Magazine, Dash, Digit, Discoveries, The Dolphin Log, Ebony Jr!, The Friend, Happy Times, Health Explorer, Highlights for Children, Jack and Jill, Junior Trails, K-Power, Medical Detective, Nautica, Odyssey, On the Line, Pockets, Primary Treasure, R-A-D-A-R, Ranger Rick, Stickers, Story Friends, 3-2-1 Contact, Touch, Trails, Wee Wisdom, The Young Crusader, Young American, Young Judean.*

ACTION, Dept. of Christian Education, Free Methodist Headquarters, 901 College Ave., Winona Lake IN 46590. (219)267-7656. Editor: Vera Bethel. 100% freelance written. For "57% girls, 43% boys, age 9-11; 48% city, 23% small towns." Weekly magazine. Circ. 25,000. Pays on publication. Rights purchased vary; may buy simultaneous rights, second rights or first North American serial rights. Submit seasonal/holiday material 3 months in advance. Simultaneous and previously published submissions OK. Computer printout submissions acceptable; no dot-matrix. Reports in 1 month. Free sample copy and writer's guidelines.
Nonfiction: How-to (make gifts and craft articles); informational (nature articles with pix); and personal experience (my favorite vacation, my pet, my hobby, etc.). Buys 50 mss/year. Submit complete ms with photos. Length: 200-500 words. Pays $15. SASE must be enclosed; no return without it.
Fiction: Adventure, humorous, mystery and religious. Buys 50 mss/year. Submit complete ms. Length: 1,000 words. Pays $25. SASE must be enclosed; no return without it.
Poetry: Free verse, haiku, light verse, traditional, devotional and nature. Buys 20/year. Limit submissions to batches of 5-6. Length: 4-16 lines. Pays $5.
Tips: "Send interview articles with children about their pets, their hobbies, a recent or special vacation—all with pix if possible. Kids like to read about other kids."

AHOY, A Children's Magazine, Box 5174, Armsdale, Nova Scotia B3L 4M7 Canada. (902)423-0415. Editor: (Mr.) Dana P. Doiron. 50% freelance written. Bimonthly magazine designed to "encourage children to read, enjoy learning and have fun—all at the same time." Circ. 9,000. Pays on acceptance. Byline given. Buys first North American serial rights. Submit seasonal/holiday material 6 months in advance. Simultaneous queries and photocopied submissions OK. Electronic submissions OK, but requires hard copy also. Computer printout submissions acceptable; prefers letter-quality to dot-matrix. SASE. Reports in 3 weeks on queries; 2 months on mss. Publishes ms an average of 6 months after acceptance. Sample copy $2 (Canadian funds) and 8x11 SAE and 2 first class stamps (Canadian postage); writer's guidelines for SAE and 1 first class stamp (Canadian postage) or IRC.
Nonfiction: General interest (to children); how-to; and of children with a particular interest i.e., skating, acting). Buys 16-24 mss/year. Send complete ms. Length: 300-1,000 words. Pays $15-50.
Photos: "We will accept b&w photos with a manuscript, but we do not buy photos."
Columns/Departments: Pays $50.
Fiction: Adventure, fantasy, historical, humorous and mystery. "We're always looking for good fiction—particularly adventure." No patronizing or sexist stories; no fiction aimed at children aged 8 and under. Buys 8-10 mss/year. Send complete ms. Length: 500-1,200 words. Pays $15-65.
Poetry: Light verse. Buys 10-15/year. Length: no restriction. Pays $15-30.
Fillers: "Jokes—usually from children."
Tips: "We are very open to contributions. The most successful stories are those which an adult might enjoy also. Too often the material we receive is quite condescending to children. Writers often expect personal attention in the review process. We receive over 10,000 submissions each year. Don't phone to ask about *your* submission. It's also aggravating to receive US submissions with US postage (return) followed by nasty letters with US postage."

BOYS' LIFE, Boy Scouts of America, Magazine Division, 1325 Walnut Hill Lane, Irving TX 75062. (214)659-2000. Editor: Robert Hood. Monthly magazine covering Boy Scout activities for "ages 8-18—Boy Scouts, Cub Scouts, and others of that age group." Circ. 1.5 million. Length: 1,000-3,000 words. Reports in 2 weeks. Pays on publication. Pays $350 minimum. Buys one-time rights.
Nonfiction: "Almost all articles are assigned. We do not encourage unsolicited material."
Columns/Departments: How How's (1-2 paragraphs on hobby tips). Buys 60 mss/year. Send complete ms. Pays $5 minimum.
Fillers: Jokes (Think and Grin—1-3 sentences). Pays $1 minimum.

CHICKADEE MAGAZINE, The Magazine for Young Children, The Young Naturalist Foundation, 59 Front Street East, Toronto, Ontario M5E 1B3 Canada. (416)364-3333. Editor: Janis Nostbakken. 25% freelance written. Magazine published 10 times/year (except July and August) for 4-9 year-olds. "Aim to interest (in an entertaining and lively way) children nine and under in the world around them." Circ. 84,000. Pays on publication. Byline given. Buys all rights. Submit seasonal/holiday material up to 12 months in advance. Reports in 2½ months. Sample copy for $1.25 and IRCs; writer's guidelines for IRC.
Nonfiction: How-to (arts and crafts for children); personal experience (real children in real situations); and photo feature (wildlife features). No articles for older children; no religious or moralistic features.
Photos: Send photos with ms. Reviews 35mm transparencies. Identification of subjects required.
Fiction: Adventure (relating to the 4-9 year old). No science fiction, fantasy, talking animal stories, or religious articles. Send complete ms. Pays $100-300.

CHILD LIFE, Benjamin Franklin Literary & Medical Society, Inc., 1100 Waterway Blvd., Box 567, Indianapolis IN 46206. Editor: Steve Charles. For youngsters ages 7-11. Monthly (except bimonthly issues in February/March, April/May, June/July and August/September) magazine. Pays on publication. Buys all rights. Byline given. Submit seasonal/holiday material 8 months in advance. Photocopied submissions OK. SASE. Reports in 10 weeks. Sample copy 75¢; writer's guidelines for SASE.

Nonfiction: Specifically needs articles dealing with health, safety, nutrition and exercise (including group sports). Also articles that stimulate a child's sense of wonder about the world. "We prefer not to sound encyclopedic in our presentation and therefore are always on the lookout for innovative ways to present our material. Articles on sports and sports figures are welcome, but they should try to influence youngsters to participate and learn the benefits of participation, both from a social and a physical point of view." In addition to health, seasonal articles are needed. Buys about 6 mss/issue. Submit complete ms; query not necessary. Length: 1,200 words maximum. Give word count on ms. Pays approximately 4¢/word.

Photos: Purchased only with accompanying ms. Captions and model release required. B&w glossies. Pays $5/photo used in publication. Buys one-time rights on most photos.

Fiction: Half of the stories accepted emphasize some aspect of health, but not necessarily as a main theme. Seasonal stories also accepted. Adventure, mystery, fantasy and humorous stories are favorites. Buys about 2 mss/issue. Submit complete ms; query not necessary. Length: 500-1,500 words. Give word count on ms. Pays approximately 4¢/word.

Tips: "We would prefer *not* to see blatantly religious materials (as this is not our thrust, and we would rather leave this subject to those publications that specialize in that area); talking inanimate objects; or recipes that contain sugar, salt, or fatty meat products."

CHILDREN'S DIGEST, Children's Better Health Institute, Box 567, Indianapolis IN 46206. (317)636-8881. Editor: Kathleen B. Mosher. Magazine published 8 times/year covering children's health for children ages 8-10. Pays on publication. Byline given. Buys all rights. Submit seasonal/holiday material 8 months in advance. Submit *only* complete manuscripts. "No queries, please." Photocopied submissions acceptable (if clear). SASE. Reports in 2 months. Sample copy 75¢; writer's guidelines for business-size SASE.

Nonfiction: Historical, interview/profile (biographical), craft ideas, health, nutrition, hygiene, exercise and safety. "We're especially interested in factual features that teach readers about the human body or encourage them to develop better health habits. We are *not* interested in material that is simply rewritten from encyclopedias. We try to present our health material in a way that instructs *and* entertains the reader." Buys 15-20 mss/year. Send complete ms. Length: 500-1,200 words. Pays 4¢/word.

Photos: State availability of photos. Pays $5-10 for 5x7 b&w glossy prints. Model release and identification of subjects required. Buys one-time rights.

Fiction: Adventure, humorous, mainstream and mystery. Stories should appeal to both boys and girls. "We need some stories that incorporate a health theme. However, we don't want stories that preach, preferring instead stories with implied morals. We like a light or humorous approach." Buys 15-20 mss/year. Length: 500-1,800 words. Pays 4¢/word.

Poetry: Pays $5 minimum.

CHILDREN'S PLAYMATE, 1100 Waterway Blvd., Box 567, Indianapolis IN 46206. (317)636-8881, ext. 247. Editor: Kathleen B. Mosher. 75% freelance written. "We are looking for articles, stories, and activities with a health, safety, exercise, or nutritionally oriented theme. Primarily we are concerned with preventative medicine. We try to present our material in a positive—not a negative—light, and we try to incorporate humor and a light approach wherever possible without minimizing the seriousness of what we are saying." For children ages 5-7. Magazine published 8 times/year. Buys all rights. Byline given. Pays on publication. "We do not consider outlines. Reading the whole ms is the only way to give fair consideration. The editors cannot criticize, offer suggestions, or review unsolicited material that is not accepted." Submit seasonal material 8 months in advance. Computer printout submissions acceptable; prefers letter-quality to dot-matrix. Reports in 2 months. Publishes ms an average of 8 months after acceptance. Sometimes may hold mss for up to 1 year, with author's permission. Write for guidelines. "Material will not be returned unless accompanied by a self-addressed envelope and sufficient postage." Sample copy 75¢; free writer's guidelines with SASE. No query.

Nonfiction: Beginning science, 600 words maximum. Monthly "All about . . ." feature, 300-500 words, may be an interesting presentation on animals, people, events, objects or places, especially about good health, exercise, proper nutrition and safety. "Include number of words in articles." Buys 30 mss/year. Pays about 4¢/word.

Fiction: Short stories words for beginning readers, not over 700. Seasonal stories with holiday themes. Humorous stories, unusual plots. Vocabulary suitable for ages 5-7. Pays about 4¢/word. "Include number of words in stories."

Fillers: Puzzles, dot-to-dots, color-ins, hidden pictures and mazes. Buys 30 fillers/year. Payment varies.

Tips: Especially interested in stories, poems and articles about special holidays, customs and events.

CLUBHOUSE, Your Story Hour, Box 15, Berrien Springs MI 49103. (616)471-3701. Editor: Elaine Meseraull. 33% freelance written. Magazine published 10 times/year covering many subjects with Christian approach. "Stories and features for fun for 9-13-year-olds. Main objectives: Let kids know that God loves them and provide a psychologically 'up' magazine that lets kids know that they are acceptable, 'neat' people.'' Circ. 15,000. Pays on acceptance. Byline given. Buys first North American serial rights, simultaneous and second serial (reprint) rights to material originally published elsewhere. Simultaneous queries, and simultaneous, photocopied and previously published submissions OK. Computer printout submissions acceptable. SASE. Reports in 3 weeks. Publishes ms an average of 1 year after acceptance. Sample copy for business- or larger size SAE and 3 first class stamps; writer's guidelines for business-size SAE and 1 first class stamp.

Nonfiction: How-to (crafts); personal experience; and recipes (without sugar or artificial flavors and colors). "No stories in which kids start out 'bad' and by peer or adult pressure or circumstances are changed into 'good.' " Send complete ms. Length: 750-800 words (\$30); 1,000-1,200 words (\$35).

Photos: Send photos with ms. Pays on publication according to published size. Buys first rights.

Columns/Departments: Body Shop (short stories or "ad" type material that is anti-smoking, drugs and alcohol and pro-good nutrition, etc.); and Jr. Detective (secret codes, word search, deduction problems, hidden pictures, etc.). Buys 10/year. Send complete ms. Length: 400 words maximum. Pays \$10-30.

Fiction: Adventure, historical, humorous and mainstream. "Stories should depict bravery, kindness, etc., without overt or preachy attitude." No science fiction, romance, confession or mystery. Buys 30-40 mss/year. Send complete ms. Length: 750-800 words (\$30); 1,000-1,200 words (\$35).

Poetry: Free verse, light verse and traditional. Buys 2-4/year. Submit 5 poems maximum. Length: 4-24 lines. Pays \$5-20.

Fillers: Short humor and cartoons. Buys 10-20/year. Pay \$10 maximum.

Tips: "All material for any given year is accepted April-May the year previous. Think from a kid's point of view and ask, 'Would this story make me glad to be a kid?' Keep the stories moving, exciting, bright and tense. Stay within length guidelines."

COBBLESTONE, Cobblestone Publishing, Inc., 28 Main St., Peterborough NH 03458. (603)924-7209. Editor: Carolyn P. Yoder. 100% freelance written; (approximately 2 issues/year are by "assignment only"). Monthly magazine covering American history for children 8-13 years old. "Each issue presents a particular theme, approaching it from different angles, making it exciting as well as informative." Circ. 44,000. Pays on publication. Byline given. Buys all rights. Makes some assignments on a work-for-hire basis. All material must relate to monthly theme. Simultaneous and previously published submissions OK. Computer printout submissions acceptable; prefers letter-quality to dot-matrix. SASE. Publishes ms an average of 4 months after acceptance. Sample copy \$2.75; writer's guidelines for SASE.

Nonfiction: Historical/nostalgic, how-to, interview and personal experience. "Request a copy of the writer's guidelines to find out specific issue themes in upcoming months." Include SASE. No Revolutionary War memorabilia, particularly hometown guides to monuments. No material that editorializes rather than reports. Buys 5-8 mss/issue. Length: 500-1,200 words. Query with clips of previously published work. Pays up to 15¢/word.

Fiction: Adventure, historical, humorous and biographical fiction. Buys 1-2 mss/issue. Length: 800-1,200 words. Request free editorial guidelines that explain upcoming issue themes and give query deadlines. "Message" must be smoothly integrated with the story. Pays up to 15¢/word.

Poetry: Free verse, light verse and traditional. Buys 6 mss/year. Submit maximum 2 poems. Length: 5-100 lines. Pays \$1.50/line.

Fillers: Word puzzles and mazes. Buys 1/issue. Pays \$75 maximum.

Tips: "All material is considered on the basis of merit and appropriateness to theme. Query should state idea for material simply, with rationale for why material is applicable to theme. Request writer's guidelines (includes themes and query deadlines) before submitting a query. Include SASE."

CRUSADER MAGAZINE, Box 7244, Grand Rapids MI 49510. Editor: G. Richard Broene. 30% freelance written. "*Crusader Magazine* shows boys (9-14) how God is at work in their lives and in the world around them." Magazine published 7 times/year. Circ. 13,000. Rights purchased vary with author and material. Byline given. Buys 20-25 mss/year. Pays on acceptance. Photocopied and simultaneous submissions OK. Computer printout submissions acceptable; no dot-matrix. Submit seasonal material (Christmas, Easter) at least 5 months in advance. Reports in 1 month. Publishes ms an average of 7 months after acceptance. Query or submit complete ms. Publishes ms an average of 7 months after acceptance. SASE. Free sample copy and writer's guidelines.

Nonfiction: Articles about young boys' interests: sports, outdoor activities, bike riding, science, crafts, etc., and problems. Emphasis is on a Christian multi-racial perspective, but no simplistic moralisms. Informational, how-to, personal experience, interview, profile, inspirational and humor. Length: 500-1,500 words. Pays 2-5¢/word.

Photos: Pays \$4-25 for b&w photos purchased with mss.

Fiction: "Considerable fiction is used. Fast-moving stories that appeal to a boy's sense of adventure or sense of humor are welcome. Avoid 'preachiness.' Avoid simplistic answers to complicated problems. Avoid long dialogue and little action." Length: 750-1,500 words. Pays 3¢/word minimum.

Fillers: Uses short humor and any type of puzzles as fillers.

DASH, Box 150, Wheaton IL 60189. Editor: David Leigh. For boys 8-11 years of age. Most subscribers are in a Christian Service Brigade program. Monthly magazine except for combined issues in April-May, July-August, October-November, January-February. Circ. 32,000. Rights purchased vary with author and material. Buys 8-10 mss/year. Pays on publication. Submit seasonal material 6 months in advance. Query. SASE. Sample copy $1.50 plus large SASE.
Nonfiction: "Our emphasis is on boys and how their belief in Jesus Christ affects their everyday lives." Uses short articles about boys of this age, problems they encounter. Interview and profile. Length: 1,000-1,500 words. Pays $30-70.
Photos: Pays $25 for 8x10 b&w photos for inside use.
Fiction: Avoid trite, condescending tone. Needs adventure, mystery action. A Christian truth should be worked into the storyline (not tacked on as a "moral of the story"). Length: 1,000-1,500 words. Pays $60-90.
Tips: "Queries must be succinct, well-written, and exciting to draw my interest. Send for sample copies, get a feel for our publication, query with ideas tailored specifically for us."

‡**DIGIT MAGAZINE, The Video/Computing Connection for Young People**, Beckwith/Benton Communications, Inc., 2342 North Point, San Francisco CA 94123. (415)931-1885. Editor: Lassie Benton. Managing Editor: Kendra Bonnett. Bimonthly magazine covering computers/high technology for use as an education/classroom tool. "*Digit* is written for young people between the ages of 10 and 16. Much of the information is edited and written by adults, but the material is generated by youngsters." Estab. 1983. Circ. 50,000. Pays on publication. Byline given. Photocopied submissions OK. SASE. Reports in 1 month on queries. Sample copy $3; free writer's guidelines.
Nonfiction: Book excerpts (computers for young people); how-to (dealing with technology interesting to young people); humor (for young people); interview/profile (dealing with youngsters and computers); new product (reviews); personal experience (dealing with technology); photo feature (dealing with youngsters); technical (only in a way that can be explained in layman language); and contests (educational). Query with clips of published work. Length: 1,000-2,500 words. Pays $50-500.
Photos: State availability of photos. Buys one-time rights.

DISCOVERIES, 6401 The Paseo, Kansas City MO 64131. Editor: Libby Huffman. 100% freelance written. For boys and girls ages 9-12 in the Church of the Nazarene. Weekly. Buys first and second (reprint) rights to material originally published elsewhere. "We process only letter-quality manuscripts; word processing with letter-quality printers acceptable. Minimal comments on pre-printed form are made on rejected material." SASE. Reports in 2-4 weeks. Publishes ms an average of 1 year after acceptance. SASE.
Fiction: Stories with Christian emphasis on high ideals, wholesome social relationships and activities, right choices, Sabbath observance, church loyalty, and missions. Informal style. Submit complete ms. Length: 800-1,000 words. Pays 3.5¢/word for first rights and 2¢/word for second rights.
Photos: Sometimes buys photos submitted with mss with captions only if subject has appeal. Send quality 8x10 photos.
Tips: "The freelancer needs an understanding of the doctrine of the Church of the Nazarene and the Sunday School material for 3rd-6th graders."

‡**THE DOLPHIN LOG**, The Cousteau Society, 8430 Santa Monica Blvd., Los Angeles CA 90069. (213)656-4422. Editor: Pamela Stacey. 25% freelance written. Quarterly magazine covering marine biology, ecology, environment, natural history, and water-related stories. "*The Dolphin Log* is an educational publication for children ages 7-15 offered by The Costeau Society. Subject matter encompasses all areas of science, history, and the arts which can be related to our global water system. Philosophy of the magazine is to delight, instruct, and instill an environmental ethic and understanding of the interconnectedness of living organisms, including people." Circ. 35,000. Pays on publication. Byline given. "We do not make assignments and therefore have no kill fee." Buys one-time rights and translation rights. Submit seasonal/holiday material 4 months in advance. Simultaneous queries OK. Computer submissions acceptable. SASE. Reports in 4 weeks on queries; 2 months on mss. Publishes ms an average of 6 months after acceptance. Sample copy for $2 with SAE and 54¢ postage; writer's guidelines for SAE.
Nonfiction: general interest (per guidelines); how-to (water-related crafts or science); interview/profile (of young person involved with aspect of ocean); personal experience (ocean-related); and photo feature (per guidelines). "Of special interest are games involving an ocean-water-related theme which develop math, reading and comprehension skills. Humorous articles and short jokes based on scientific fact are also welcome. Experiments that can be conducted at home and demonstrate a phenomenon or principle of science are wanted as are clever crafts or art projects which also can be tied to any ocean theme. Try to incorporate such activities into any articles submitted." No "talking" animals. Buys 4-12 mss/year. Query or send complete ms. Pays $25-150.
Photos: Send photos with query or ms (duplicates only). Prefers underwater animals, water photos with children, photos which explain text. Pays $25 for b&w; $25-100 for 35mm color transparencies. Captions, model release and identification of subjects required. Buys one-time and translation rights.

Columns/Departments: Discovery (science experiments or crafts a young person can easily do at home). Buys 4 mss/year. Send complete ms. Length: 200-750. Pays $25-50.

Fiction: Adventure (with ecological message); historical (how early cultures interacted with environment and/or animals); humorous (personal experiences with animals, ocean or environment); and science fiction (new ideas on future relationship with ocean, animals, environment). No anthropomorphism or "talking" animals. Buys "very few ms' but would like to find good ones." Length: 500-1,200 words. Pays $25-150.

Poetry: No "talking" animals. Buys 2 poems/year. Pays $25-100.

Fillers: Jokes, anecdotes, short humor and newsbreaks. Buys 8/year. Length: 100 lines maximum. Pays $25-50.

Tips: "A freelancer can best break in to our publication by researching a topic and writing good, scientifically sound articles. We are delighted with articles which offer new insights into a particular species or relationship in nature, or principle of ecology. Feature sections use clear, simple, factual writing style combined with sound, verifiable information."

EBONY JR!, Johnson Publishing Co., 820 S. Michigan Ave., Chicago IL 60605. (312)322-9272. Managing Editor: Marcia V. Roebuck-Hoard. 50% freelance written. For all children, but geared toward black children ages 6-12. Monthly magazine (except bimonthly issues in June/July and August/September). Circ. 200,000. Pays on acceptance. Buys all rights, second serial (reprint) rights or first North American serial rights. Byline given. Submit seasonal/holiday material 4 months in advance. Previously published work OK. SASE. Acknowledges receipt of material in 4 weeks. Reports in 6 weeks. Sample copy $1; free writer's guidelines.

Nonfiction: How-to (make things, gifts and crafts; cooking articles); informational (science experiments or articles explaining how things are made or where things come from); historical (events or people in black history); inspirational (career articles showing children they can become whatever they want); interviews; personal experience (taken from child's point of view); and profiles (of black Americans who have done great things—especially need articles on those who have not been recognized). Buys 25 unsolicited mss/year. Query or submit complete ms. Length: 500-1,500 words. Pays $75-200.

Photos: Purchased with or without mss. Must be clear photos; no Instamatic prints. Pays $10-15/b&w; $25 maximum/color. Send prints and transparencies. Model release required.

Columns/Departments: *Ebony Jr!* News uses news of outstanding black children and reviews of books, movies, TV shows, of interest to children. Pays $25-40.

Fiction: Must be believable and include experiences black children can relate to. Adventure, fantasy and historical (stories on black musicians, singers, actors, astronomers, scientists, inventors, writers, politicians, leaders; any historical figures who can give black children positive images). No violence. Buys 2 mss/issue. Query or submit complete ms. Length: 300-1,500 words. Pays $75-200.

Poetry: Free verse, haiku, light verse and traditional forms of poetry. Buys 2/issue. No specific limit on number of submissions, but usually purchases no more than two at a time. Length: 5-50 lines; longer for stories in poetry form. Pays $15-100.

Fillers: Jokes, gags, anecdotes, newsbreaks and current events written at a child's level. Brain teasers, word games, crossword puzzles, guessing games, dot-to-dot games; games that are fun, yet educational. Pays $15-85.

Tips: "Those freelancers who have submitted material featuring an event or person who is/was relatively unknown to the general public, yet is the type of material that would have great relevance and interest to children in their everyday lives, are usually the successful writers."

THE FRIEND, 50 East North Temple, Salt Lake City UT 84150. Managing Editor: Vivian Paulsen. 75% freelance written. Appeals to children ages 4-12. Publication of The Church of Jesus Christ of Latter-Day Saints. Issues feature different countries of the world, their cultures and children. Special issues: Christmas and Easter. Monthly. Circ. 200,000. Buys first and second rights to the same material. Pays on acceptance. "Submit only complete ms—no queries, please." Submit seasonal material 6 months in advance. Computer printout submissions acceptable. SASE. Publishes ms an average of 1 year after acceptance. Free sample copy and guidelines for writers.

Nonfiction: Subjects of current interest, science, nature, pets, sports, foreign countries, and things to make and do. Length: 1,000 words maximum. Pays 7¢/word minimum.

Fiction: Seasonal and holiday stories and stories about other countries and their children. Wholesome and optimistic; high motive, plot, and action. Also, simple but suspense-filled mysteries. Character-building stories preferred. Length: 1,200 words maximum. Stories for younger children should not exceed 700 words. Pays 7¢/word minimum.

Poetry: Serious, humorous and holiday. Any form with child appeal. Pays $15.

Tips: "Do you remember how it feels to be a child? Can you write stories that appeal to children ages 4-12 in today's world? We're interested in stories with an international flavor and those that focus on present-day problems. Send material of high literary quality slanted to our editorial requirements. Let the child solve the problem—not some helpful, all-wise adult. No overt moralizing. Nonfiction should be creatively presented—not an array of facts strung together. Beware of being cutesy."

‡**HAPPY TIMES, The Magazine That Builds Character and Confidence**, Eagle Systems International, 5600 N. University Ave., Provo UT 84604. (801)225-9000. Editor: Colleen Hinkley. Managing Editor: Jerold C. Johnson. 50% freelance written. Published 10 times/year for children ages 3-10 with emphasis on educational and moral content. "Each concept presented needs to teach or promote a moral value or educational concept." Estab. 1983. Circ. 30,000. Pays on publication. Byline given. Buys all rights and makes work-for-hire assignments. Submit seasonal/holiday material 5 months in advance. Simultaneous queries, and simultaneous, photocopied, and previously published submissions OK. Computer printout submissions acceptable. SASE. Report in 2 weeks on queries; 1 month on mss. Publishes ms an average of 3 months after acceptance. Writer's guidelines for SASE; sample copy for 5 first class stamps.

Nonfiction: Quint Randle, articles editor. General interest, historical/nostalgic, how-to, travel and unique puzzles that instruct children. "Writers must see our publication *before* submitting, or they'll be out in left field. Most 'articles' are less than 150 words long. The concept is more important than the copy; yet the copy must be super, super tight. Each issue has a theme. Themes include working, adventure (the world), courage, mystery, understanding, thanks, light, determination, cheerfulness and creativity. Query. "Submit several short ideas for articles or activities. We'll let you know what we want and give you further guidelines." Query. Length: 50-300 words. Pays $10-50.

Photos: State availability of photos. Pays negotiable rates for 35mm transparencies. Captions, model release and identification of subjects required. Rights negotiated.

Columns/Departments: Bedtime Story (a monthly column that teachs something of value—not just a fun story; prefers nonfiction biographical sketch or story). Buys 10 mss/year. Query with clips of published work. Length: 500-1,250 words. Pays $50-100.

HEALTH EXPLORER, Children's Better Health Institute, Box 567, Indianapolis IN 46206. (317)636-8881. Editor: Steve Charles. Quarterly health-oriented magazine for 5th and 6th grade readers. Pays on publication. Byline given. Buys variable rights. Submit seasonal/holiday material 8 months in advance. SASE. Reports in 10 weeks. Sample copy 75¢; writer's guidelines for business-size SAE and 1 first class stamp.

Nonfiction: Health (diet, nutrition, exercise, environment, health trends). "No dogmatic or 'preachy' articles." Will consider historical articles and stories. Buys variable number mss/year. Send complete ms. Length: 500-1,000 words. Pays approximately 4¢/word.

Photos: Send photos with ms. Pays $5 minimum for 8x10 b&w prints. Model release and identification of subjects required. Buys one-time rights.

Fiction: Health (nutrition, diet, exercise, environment, health trends). "Setting and characters may be fictional but keep information factual." Buys variable number mss/year. Send complete ms. Length: 500-1,000 words. Pays approximately 4¢/word.

Tips: "Take a close look at the area of preventive health for children ages 9-11. Write something (nonfiction, fiction) that readers can use to increase their knowledge in the area of health and safety and to improve and maintain health, and make it *entertaining*. Include list of sources or references used in manuscript."

HIGHLIGHTS FOR CHILDREN, 803 Church St., Honesdale PA 18431. Editor: Kent L. Brown Jr. 80% + freelance written. For children ages 2-12. Magazine published 11 times/year. Circ. 1,500,000. Buys all rights. Pays on acceptance. Computer printout submissions acceptable. Free writer's guidelines. Reports in about 2 months. Publishes ms an average of 18 months after acceptance. SASE.

Nonfiction: "We prefer factual features, including history and science, written by persons with rich background and mastery in their respective fields. Contributions always welcomed from new writers, especially engineers, scientists, historians, etc., who can interpret to children useful, interesting and authentic facts, but not of the bizarre type; also writers who have lived abroad and can interpret the ways of life, especially of children, in other countries, and who don't leave the impression that US ways are always the best. Sports material, biographies and articles of interest to children. Direct, simple style, interesting content, without word embellishment; not rewritten from encyclopedias. State background and qualifications for writing factual articles submitted. Include references or sources of information. Recent article example: "When African Lions Came Visiting" (April 1984). Length: 900 words maximum. Pays $65 minimum. Also buys original party plans for children ages 7-12, clearly described in 400-700 words, including drawings or sample of items to be illustrated. Also, novel but tested ideas in crafts, with clear directions and made-up models. Projects must require only free or inexpensive, easy-to-obtain materials. Especially desirable if easy enough for early primary grades. Also, fingerplays with lots of action, easy for very young children to grasp and parents to dramatize. Avoid wordiness. Pays minimum $30 for party plans; $15 for crafts ideas; $25 for fingerplays.

Fiction: Unusual, wholesome stories appealing to both girls and boys. Vivid, full of action. "Engaging plot, strong characterization, lively language." Seeks stories that the child aged 8-12 will eagerly read, and the child aged 2-6 will like to hear when read aloud. "We print no stories just to be read aloud. We encourage authors not to hold themselves to controlled word lists. Avoid suggestion of material reward for upward striving. The main character should preferably overcome difficulties and frustrations through her or his own efforts. The story should leave a good moral and emotional residue. We especially need stories in the suspense/adventure/mystery category, and short (200 words and under) stories for the beginning reader, with an interesting plot and a number of picturable words. Also need rebuses, stories with urban settings, stories for beginning readers (500 words), humorous and horse stories. We also need more material of one-page length (300-500 words), both fiction and factual. We need creative-thinking puzzles that can be illustrated, optical illusions, body teasers, and other 'fun' activities. War, crime and violence are taboo. Some fanciful stories wanted." Length: 400-900 words. Pays $65/minimum.

Tips: "We are pleased that many authors of children's literature report that their first published work was in the pages of *Highlights*. It is not our policy to consider fiction on the strength of the reputation of the author. We judge each submission on its own merits. With factual material, however, we do prefer either authorities in their field or people with first-hand experience. In this manner we can avoid the encyclopedic article that merely restates information readily available elsewhere. Query with simple letter to establish whether the nonfiction *subject* is likely to be of interest. A beginning writer should first become familiar with the type of material which *Highlights* publishes. We are most eager for easy stories for very young readers, but realize that this is probably the most difficult kind of writing. Include special qualifications, if any, of author. Write for the child, not the editor."

HUMPTY DUMPTY'S MAGAZINE, Children's Health Publications, 1100 Waterway Blvd., Box 567, Indianapolis IN 46206. Editor: Christine French Clark. Magazine published 8 times/year stressing health, nutrition, hygiene, exercise and safety for children ages 4-6. Combined issues: February/March, April/May, June/July, and August/September. Pays on publication. Buys all rights. Submit seasonal material 8 months in advance. Sample copy 75¢; writer's guidelines for SASE. Reports in 10 weeks.
Nonfiction: "Material with a health theme—nutrition, safety, exercise, hygiene—that encourages readers to develop better health habits without preaching. Very simple factual articles that creatively teach readers about their bodies. Simple crafts, some with emphasis on health. We also use several puzzles and activities in each issue—dot-to-dot, hidden pictures, *simple* crosswords, and easy-to-play "board" games. Keep in mind that most our readers are just *beginning* to learn to read and write, so word puzzles must be very basic." Submit complete ms. "Include number of words in manuscript and Social Security number." Length: 600 words maximum. Pays 4¢/word.
Fiction: "We're primarily interested in stories in rhyme and easy-to-read stories for the beginning reader. Currently we are needing seasonal stories with holiday themes. We use realistic stories and fantasy, some employing a health theme. We try to present our health material in a positive light, incorporating humor and a light approach wherever possible. Avoid sexual stereotyping. Characters in realistic stories should be modern and up-to-date. Remember, many of our readers have working mothers and/or come from single-parent homes. We need more stories that reflect these changing times but at the same time communicate good, wholesome values." Submit complete ms. "Include number of words in manuscript and Social Security number." Length: 600 words maximum. Pays 4¢/word.
Poetry: Short, simple poems. Pays $5 minimum.

JACK AND JILL, 1100 Waterway Blvd., Box 567, Indianapolis IN 46206. (317)636-8881. Editor: Christine French Clark. 85% freelance written. For children ages 6-8. Magazine published 8 times/year. Buys all rights. Byline given. Pays on publication. Submit seasonal material 8 months in advance. Computer printout submissions acceptable. Reports in 10 weeks. Publishes ms an average of 8 months after acceptance. May hold material seriously being considered for up to 6 months. "Material will not be returned unless accompanied by self-addressed envelope with sufficient postage." Sample copy 75¢; writer's guidelines for SASE.
Nonfiction: "*Jack and Jill*'s primary purpose is to encourage children to read for pleasure. The editors are actively interested in material that will inform and instruct the young reader and challenge his intelligence, but it must first of all be enjoyable reading. Submissions should appeal to both boys and girls." Current needs are for articles, stories, and activities with a health, safety, exercise, or nutritionally oriented theme. "We try to present our material in a positive—not a negative—light, and we try to incorporate humor and a light approach wherever possible without minimizing the seriousness of what we are saying. Fiction stories that deal with a health theme need not have health as the primary subject but should include it in some way in the course of events. Activities should be enjoyable to youngsters and encourage them to practice better health habits or teach them scientific facts about the body or nutrition. Articles should try not to be 'preachy,' but should be informative and appealing to young readers." Buys 95 mss/year. Length 500-1,200 words. Pays approximately 4¢/word.
Photos: When appropriate, should accompany mss. Sharp, contrasting b&w glossy prints. Pays $5 for each b&w photo.
Fiction: "May include, but is not limited to, realistic stories, fantasy, adventure—set in the past, present or future. All stories need plot structure, action and incident. Humor is highly desirable. Currently we need stories with holiday themes." Length: 500-1,500 words, short stories; 1,500 words/installment, serials of 2 parts. Pays approximately 4¢/word.
Fillers: "Short plays, puzzles (including various kinds of word and crossword puzzles), poems, games, science projects and creative construction projects. Instructions for activities should be clearly and simply written and accompanied by models or diagram sketches. Payment varies for fillers. Pays approximately 4¢/word for drama.

Tips: "We have been accused of using the same authors over and over again, not keeping an open mind when it comes to giving new authors a chance. To some extent, perhaps we do lean a little heavier toward veteran authors, but there is a good reason for this. Authors who have been published in *Jack and Jill* over and over again have shown us that they can write the kind of material we are looking for. They obtain *current* issues of the magazine and *study* them to find out our present needs, and they write in a style that is compatible with our current editorial policies. We would reject a story by the world's best-known author if it didn't fit our needs. After all, our young readers are more interested in reading a good story than they are in reading a good byline. We are constantly looking for new writers who have told a good story with an interesting slant—a story that is not full of outdated and time-worn expressions. If an author's material meets these requirements, then he or she stands as good a chance of getting published as anyone."

JUNIOR TRAILS, Gospel Publishing House, 1445 Boonville Ave., Springfield MO 65802. (417)862-2781. Editor: John Maempa. 100% freelance written. Weekly tabloid covering religious fiction; and biographical, historical, and scientific articles with a spiritual emphasis for boys and girls ages 10-11. Circ. 75,000. Pays on acceptance. Byline given. Not copyrighted. Buys simultaneous rights, first rights, or second (reprint) rights to material originally published elsewhere. Submit seasonal/holiday material 1 year in advance. Simultaneous and previously published submissions OK. Computer printout submissions acceptable. SASE. Reports in 6 weeks on queries; 2 months on mss. Publishes ms an average of 1 year after acceptance. Sample copy for 9x12 SAE and 2 first class stamps; writer's guidelines for 9x12 SAE and 2 first class stamps.
Nonfiction: Biographical, historical and scientific (with spiritual lesson or emphasis). Buys 30-40 mss/year. Send complete ms. Length: 500-1,000 words. Pays 2-3¢/word.
Fiction: Adventure (with spiritual lesson or application); and religious. "We're looking for fiction that presents believable characters working out their problems according to Biblical principles. No fictionalized accounts of Bible stories or events." Buys 50-70 mss/year. Send complete ms. Length: 1,000-1,800 words. Pays 2-3¢/word.
Poetry: Free verse and light verse. Buys 6-8 mss/year. Pays 20¢/line.
Fillers: Anecdotes (with spiritual emphasis). Buys 15-20/year. Length: 200 words maximum. Pays 2-3¢/word.
Tips: "Junior-age children need to be alerted to the dangers of drugs, alcohol, smoking, etc. They need positive guidelines and believable examples relating to living a Christian life in an ever-changing world. The most annoying aspect of working with freelance writers is failure to list Social Security number and number of words in mss; threadbare plots that indicate a lack of age-level understanding and creativity/originality."

‡**K-POWER, Magazine for the Computer Generation**, Scholastic, Inc., 730 Broadway, New York NY 10003. (212)505-3000. Editor: Anne Krueger. Managing Editor: June Rogoznicav. 75% freelance written. A monthly magazine for computer-proficient teens and pre-teens. Estab. 1984. Circ. 200,000. Pays on acceptance. Byline given. Offers variable kill fee. Buys world serial rights and makes work-for-hire assignments. Submit seasonal/holiday material 6 months in advance. Simultaneous queries, and simultaneous and previously published submissions OK. Electronic submissions OK if advance arrangements are made with editor. Computer printout submissions acceptable. SASE. Reports in 2 months on queries. Publishes ms an average of 4 months after acceptance. Free sample copy and writer's guidelines.
Nonfiction: How-to (programming information); humor (computer/kid related—hackers); interview/profile (computer pros, computing kids); new product; opinion (on today's technology); personal experience (computer related); technical (how-to's, future of technology); computers and celebrities, media—anything to do with kids and computers. "Writers must know how to write *about* and *for* young adults. Computer knowledge is necessary." Query with clips of published work.
Photos: Peter Aguanno, photo editor. State availability of photos. Reviews color slides or transparencies. Captions and identification of subjects required.
Columns/Departments: John Holmstrom, editor, Compuzine (short computing news) and Scrolling in Dough (kid-written money-making computer experience); Bernadette Grey, editor, K-NET (networking); Michael Tuomey, editor Screening Room (software, book reviews written by kids); John Wallace, editor, Rising Stars (new products, novelties, hardware); and John Jainschigg, editor, Hacker Heaven (programming). Buys 30 mss/year. Query with published clips if available. Length: 200-800 words. Pays $50-500; $25/reviews.
Fiction: Humorous. Buys 12-15 mss/year including humor. Query with published clips if available. Length: 250-1,000 words. Pays $200-350.
Fillers: John Holmstrom, editor. Jokes, gags, anecdotes, short humor and newsbreaks. Buys 25/year. Length: 50-150. pays $25-100.
Tips: "Know what kids like to read and how to write for the computer generation. Don't condenscend. Remember *K-Power* is a computer user's magazine. All articles should tie in something kids can do/use/try on the computer. Find a kid who's doing something new with computers. Know the market. Keep features user-oriented but go for the glitz."

MEDICAL DETECTIVE, (formerly *Jr. Medical Detective*), Children's Better Health Institute, Box 567, Indianapolis IN 46206. (317)636-8881. Editor: Steve Charles. Quarterly medical "mystery" magazine for 6th grade readers. Pays on publication. Byline given. Buys variable rights. Submit seasonal/holiday material 8 months in advance. SASE. Reports in 10 weeks. Sample copy 75¢; writer's guidelines for business-size SAE and 1 first class stamp.

Nonfiction: Medical "mysteries". Problems and solutions in area of diseases and illnesses. Buys variable number mss/year. Will consider historical material. Looking for articles on current medical research and technology. Send complete ms. Length: 500-1,000 words. Pays approximately 4¢/word.

Photos: Send photos with ms. Pays $5 minimum for 8x10 b&w prints. Model release and identification of subjects required. Buys one-time rights.

Fiction: Medical "mysteries." Stories in fictional setting which present factual problems or medical conditions and factual solutions. No hardboiled detectives or trite solutions to "unreal" problems. Buys variable number mss/year. Send complete ms. Length: 500-1,000 words. Pays approximately 4¢/word.

Tips: "Look around and find a medical health problem resulting from a condition or a disease. Lead the reader through the problem (investigation), and provide separate answer or include resolution in story. Include list of sources or references used in manuscript."

‡NAUTICA, The Magazine of the Sea for Young People, Spinnaker Press, Inc., Pickering Wharf, Salem MA 01970. (617)745-6905. Editor: Wayne C. Wendel. Managing Editor: Nancy L. Kells. 55% freelance written. Bimonthly children's magazine covering all aspects of the nautical and water world. Written for children 8 years and older. Reading grade level is between 6th and 7th grade. Estab. 1983. Pays on publication. Byline given. Offers 25% kill fee. Buys first North American serial rights. Submit seasonal/holiday material 3 months in advance. Photocopied and previously published submissions OK. Computer printout submissions acceptable. SASE. Reports in 6 weeks. Free writer's guidelines; sample copy $1.50.

Nonfiction: Nancy L. Kells, articles editor. Historical/nostalgic (nautical history); how-to (knot tying/rafting/skiing etc.); interview/profile (nautical character); personal experience (adventure); and photo feature (sea animals etc.). Buys 40 mss/year. Query or send complete ms. Length: 1,500-3,000 words. Pays 10-25¢/word.

Photos: John Kittredge, photo editor. Send photos with accompanying query or manuscript. Pays $25 maximum for b&w contact sheets; $50 maximum for color transparencies. Captions and model release required.

Columns/Departments: Nancy L. Kells, column/department editor. Departments/columns include Living Abroad (the daily life of people and children who live aboard naval ships, cruising sailboats, canal boats, etc.); Port-of-Call (reports the history, romance, daily life, special interests of ports all over the world); Folklore (the lore and legends of the sea); What is it? (a one-page photo/test educational feature of an interesting or unusual aspect of the sea, sea life, or sailing); Boat-of-the-Month (focuses on a particular boat with a brief history, explanation of design, and uses); Navigation (lessons and the basic how-tos of navigation such as reading a chart, using a compass, etc.); Nautica Lines (news clips and stories); and Book Review (a short review of children's books on the sea, lakes and rivers). Buys 40 items/year. Query. Length: 800-1,500 words. Pays 10-25¢/word.

Fiction: Nancy L. Kells, fiction editor. Adventure (nautical and oceanographic); historical; and humorous. Buys 40 mss/year. Length: 1,500-3,000 words. Pays 10-25¢/word.

Fillers: Nancy L. Kells, fillers editor. Cartoons. Buys 20 fillers/year.

Tips: "All areas of *Nautica* are opened to freelancers. The use of shorter sentences and a somewhat controlled vocabulary is advised."

ODYSSEY, AstroMedia Corp., 625 E. St. Paul Ave., Milwaukee WI 53202. (414)276-2689. Editor: Nancy Mack. 50% freelance written. Emphasizes astronomy and outer space for children ages 8-12. Monthly magazine. Circ. 100,000. Pays on publication. Buys all or first North American serial rights. Submit seasonal/holiday material 3-4 months in advance. Photocopied and published submissions OK. Computer printout submissions acceptable; prefers letter-quality to dot-matrix. SASE. Reports in 6-8 weeks. "Material with little news connection may be held up to 1 year." Free sample copy.

Nonfiction: General interest (astronomy, outer space, spacecraft, planets, stars, etc.); how-to (astronomy projects, experiments, etc.); and photo feature (spacecraft, planets, stars, etc.). "No general overview articles; for example, a general article on the Space Shuttle, or a general article on stars. We do not want science fiction articles." Buys about 12 mss/year. Query with clips of previously published work. Length: 750-2,000 words. Pays $100.

Photos: State availability of photos. Pays $10 for all photos. Buys one-time rights. Captions preferred; model release required.

Tips: "Since I am overstocked and have a stable of regular writers, a query is very important. I often get several mss on the same subject and must reject them. Write a very specific proposal and indicate why it will interest kids. If the subject is very technical, indicate your qualifications to write about it."

ON THE LINE, Mennonite Publishing House, 616 Walnut Ave., Scottdale PA 15683. (412)887-8500. Editor: Levi Miller. For children 10-14. Weekly magazine. Circ. 17,650. Pays on acceptance. Buys one-time rights. Byline given. Submit seasonal/holiday material 6 months in advance. Simultaneous, photocopied and previously published submissions OK. SASE. Reports in 2 weeks.

Nonfiction: How-to (things to make with easy-to-get materials); and informational (500-word articles on wonders of nature, people who have made outstanding contributions). Buys 95 unsolicited mss/year. Length: 500-1,200 words. Pays $10-24.

Photos: Photos purchased with or without accompanying ms. Pays $10-25 for 8x10 b&w photos. Total purchase price for ms includes payment for photos.

Columns/Departments: Fiction, adventure, humorous and religious. Buys 52 mss/year. Send complete ms. Length: 800-1,200 words. Pays $15-24.

Poetry: Light verse and religious. Length: 3-12 lines. Pays $5-15.

Tips: "Study the publication first. State theme and length of material in query."

OUR LITTLE FRIEND, PRIMARY TREASURE, Pacific Press Publishing Association, 1350 Villa St., Mountain View CA 94042. (415)961-2323, ext. 335. Editor: Louis Schutter. 99% freelance written. Published weekly for youngsters of the Seventh-Day Adventist church. *Our Little Friend* is for children ages 2-6; *Primary Treasure*, 7-9. Buys first serial rights (international). Byline given. "The payment we make is for one magazine right. In most cases, it is for the first one. But we make payment for second and third rights also." Simultaneous submissions OK. Computer printout submissions acceptable; prefers letter-quality to dot-matrix. "We do not purchase material during June, July and August." SASE. Publishes ms an average of 1 year after acceptance.

Nonfiction: All stories must be based on fact, written in story form. True-to-life, character-building stories; written from viewpoint of child and giving emphasis to lessons of life needed for Christian living. True to life is emphasized here more than plot. Nature or science articles, but no fantasy; science must be very simple. All material should be educational or informative and stress moral attitude and religious principle. Buys 300 unsolicited mss/year.

Photos: 8x10 glossy prints for cover. "Photo payment: sliding scale according to quality."

Fiction: Should emphasize honesty, truthfulness, courtesy, health, and temperance, along with stories of heroism, adventure, nature and safety. 700-1,000 words for *Our Little Friend*, 600 or 1,200 words for *Primary Treasure*. Fictionalized Bible stories are not used. Pays 1¢/word.

Poetry: Juvenile poetry. Up to 12 lines.

Fillers: Uses puzzles as fillers.

Tips: "We are in need of 1,200 word mss for the cover of *Primary Treasure*—an adventure story that has a premise or lesson embroidered into the plot. The cover story must have a scene that our illustrator can put his teeth into."

OWL MAGAZINE, The Discovery Magazine for Children, The Young Naturalist Foundation, 59 Front St. E., Toronto, Ontario M5E 1B3 Canada. (416)364-3333. Editor: Sylvia S. Funston. 25% freelance written. Magazine published 10 times/year (no July or August issues) covering natural science. Aims to interest children in their environment through accurate, factual information about the world around them presented in an easy, lively style. Circ. 105,000. Pays on publication. Byline given. Buys all rights and makes work-for-hire assignments. Submit seasonal/holiday material 1 year in advance. Computer printout submissions acceptable; no dot-matrix. SASE. Reports in 10 weeks. Publishes ms an average of 3 months after acceptance. Sample copy $1.50 and IRC; free writer's guidelines.

Nonfiction: How-to (activities, crafts); personal experience (real life children in real situations); photo feature (natural science, international wildlife, and outdoor features); science and environmental features. "Write for editorial guidelines first; know your topic. Our magazine never talks down to children." No folk tales, problem stories with drugs, sex or moralistic views, fantasy or talking animal stories. Query with clips of published work.

Photos: State availability of photos. Reviews 35mm transparencies. Identification of subjects required.

‡PENNYWHISTLE PRESS, Gannett Co., Inc., Box 500-P, Washington DC 20044. (703)276-3796. Editor: Anita Sama. A weekly tabloid newspaper supplement with stories and features for children 6-12 years old. Circ. 2,600,000. Pays on acceptance. Byline given. Buys all rights. Submit seasonal/holiday material 3-6 months in advance. Computer printout submissions acceptable. Photocopied submissions OK. SASE. Reports in 2 months. Sample copy for 50¢, SAE and 2 first class stamps; writer's guidelines for SAE and 1 first class stamp.

Nonfiction: General interest; how-to (sports, crafts); and photo feature (children). Buys 5 mss/year. Length: 500 words maximum. Pays $50 maximum.

Fiction: For children. Buys 25 mss/year. Send complete ms. Length: 250-850 words. Pays variable rate.

Poetry: Traditional poetry for children. Buys 5-10 poems/year. Submit maximum 1 poem. Pays variable rate.

Tips: Fiction is most open to freelancers.

POCKETS, Devotional Magazine for Children, The Upper Room, 1908 Grand Ave., Box 189, Nashville TN 37202. (615)327-2700. Editor: Judith E. Smith. 50% freelance written. Monthly magazine (except for January) for children ages 6-12, with articles specifically geared for ages 8-11. "The magazine offers stories, activities, prayers, poems—all geared to giving children a better understanding of themselves as children of God. Some of the material is not overtly religious but deals with situations, special seasons and holidays, ecological concerns from a Christian perspective. The overall goal is to build into a child's daily life a need for a devotional aspect." Circ. 70,000. Pays on acceptance. Byline given. Offers negotiable kill fee, when applicable. "We will attempt to publish every ms we formally accept." Buys newspaper and periodical rights. Submit seasonal/ holiday material 1 year in advance. Previously published submissions OK. Computer printout submissions acceptable; prefers letter-quality to dot-matrix. SASE. Reports in 3 weeks on queries; 3 months on mss. Publishes ms an average of 1 year after acceptance. Sample copy for 7x9 SAE and 3 first class stamps; writer's guidelines for business-size SAE and 1 first class stamp.

Nonfiction: Historical/nostalgic, how-to, inspirational, interview/profile, opinion, personal experience, photo feature and retelling of Scripture. All articles on children's level. Special issues with Easter, Lent, Thanksgiving, Christmas and All Saints themes. No "stories or articles dwelling on violence, containing sexual or racial stereotyping, relying on heavy moralizing to get a point across." Buys approximately 30 mss/year. Send complete ms. Length: 750-1,600 words. Pays 5¢/word and up. Honorarium for especially well written articles.

Photos: State availability of photos with query letter or ms. Pays $50 minimum for color transparencies; $15-25 for b&w prints. Buys one-time rights.

Columns/Departments: Loaves and Fishes, deals with ecology, world hunger, nutrition, alternative celebrations, more responsible life styles; Pocketsful of Prayer, prayer activities; The Refrigerator Door, meaningful posters, sayings, poems, etc., to be torn out and hung on refrigerator door to share with the family; Pocketsful of Love, activities to share with the family, for example, a family activity around the dinner table; Role Model Story, true-life story based on well-known person or a significant person in the author's own life. Buys 11-25/ year. Send complete ms. Length: 700-1,200 words, Role Model; others, 250 words. Pays 5¢/word and up. "All material must be documented through standard footnote material for verification. Writer should obtain permissions for use of previously copyrighted material which is quoted."

Fiction: Ethnic, fantasy, historical, mainstream and religious. All stories on children's level. No "violence, horror, sexual or racial stereotyping, or heavy moralizing." Buys 25 mss/year. Send complete ms. Length: 450-1,300 words. Pays 5¢/word and up.

Poetry: Cinquain, free verse, haiku and traditional. Nothing lengthy. Buys "perhaps 10"/year. Submit maximum 5 poems. Pays 50¢/line, $5-20 maximum.

Fillers: "Fillers should be in the form of children's games and activities—hidden word games, hidden picture games, crossword puzzles, maze, rebus and cartoons." Buys 24/year. Pays $5-25/activity.

Tips: "Send a well-written manuscript that does not 'write down' to children." All areas are open. "We are going to use more re-told Scripture stories and are seeking good writers."

PRIMARY TREASURE, Pacific Press Publishing Association, 1350 Villa St., Mountain View CA 94042. See *Our Little Friend*.

R-A-D-A-R, 8121 Hamilton Ave., Cincinnati OH 45231. (513)931-4050. Editor: Margaret Williams. 75% freelance written. For children grades 3-6 in Christian Sunday schools. Weekly. Rights purchased vary with author and material. Prefers buying first rights, but will buy first and second rights to same material and will buy second (reprint) rights to material published elsewhere. Occasionally overstocked. Pays on acceptance. Submit seasonal material 1 year in advance. Computer printout submissions acceptable; prefers letter-quality to dot-matrix. Reports in 4-6 weeks. Publishes ms an average of 1 year after acceptance. SASE. Free sample copy.

Nonfiction: Articles on hobbies and handicrafts, nature, famous people, seasonal subjects, etc., written from a Christian viewpoint. No articles about historical figures with an absence of religious implication. Length: 500-1,000 words. Pays 2¢/word maximum.

Fiction: Short stories of heroism, adventure, travel, mystery, animals and biography. True or possible plots stressing clean, wholesome, Christian character-building ideas, but not preachy. Make prayer, church attendance, Christian living a natural part of the story. "We correlate our fiction and other features with a definite Bible lesson. Writers who want to meet our needs should send for a theme list." No talking animal stories, science fiction, Halloween stories or first-person stories from an adult's viewpoint. Length: up to 1,000 words. Pays 2¢/word maximum.

RANGER RICK, National Wildlife Federation, 1412 16th St. NW, Washington DC 20036. (703)790-4270. Editorial Director: Trudy D. Farrand. 60% freelance written. For "children from ages 6-12, with the greatest concentration in the 7-10 age bracket." Monthly. Buys all world rights. Byline given "but occasionally, for very brief pieces, we will identify author by name at the end. Contributions to regular departments usually are not bylined." Pays on acceptance from $10-350, depending on length and content (maximum length, 900 words). Query. Computer printout submissions acceptable; no dot-matrix. Reports in 2 weeks. "Anything written with a specific month in mind should be in our hands at least 10 months before that issue date." Publishes ms an average of 18 months after acceptance. SASE.

Nonfiction: "Articles may be written on anything related to nature, conservation, environmental problems or natural science." Buys 20-25 unsolicited mss/year.

Fiction: "Same categories as nonfiction plus fantasy and science fiction. The attributing of human qualities to animals is limited to our regular feature, 'The Adventures of Ranger Rick' so please do not humanize wildlife. The publisher, The National Wildlife Federation, discourages keeping wildlife as pets."

Photos: "Photographs, when used, are paid for separately. It is not necessary that illustrations accompany material."

Tips: "Include in query details of what manuscript will cover; sample lead; evidence that you can write playfully and with great enthusiasm, conviction and excitement (formal, serious, dull queries indicate otherwise). Think of an exciting subject we haven't done recently, sell it effectively with query and produce manuscript of highest quality. Read past issues to learn successful styles and unique approaches to subjects. If your submission is commonplace in any way we won't want it."

STICKERS! MAGAZINE, For Kids Stuck on Stickers, Ira Friedman, Inc., 8th Floor, 16 W. 61st St., New York NY 10023. (212)541-7300. Editor: Bob Woods. A quarterly magazine covering all kinds of adhesive-backed stickers, related products, and activities. "Readers are children, generally girls, ages 6-14, who are wild about collecting, trading, and making things with stickers. We try to point out humor, education, friendship, sharing, benefits, and other positive aspects of using stickers." Estab. 1983. Circ. 200,000. Pays on acceptance. Byline given. Buys first North American serial rights. Submit seasonal/holiday material 3 months in advance. Photocopied submissions OK. Computer printout submissions acceptable; no dot-matrix. SASE. Reports in 3 weeks on queries; 2 weeks on mss. Sample copy and writer's guidelines for SAE.

Nonfiction: Historical/nostalgic; how-to; humor; interview/profile (with collectors, manufacturers, sticker stores); new product; personal experience; and photo feature. Query with published clips. Length: 250-2,000 words. Pays $50 minimum.

Fillers: Games, puzzles employing stickers.

Tips: "Send a letter that details your idea and lets us know you have more than a casual interest in the subject. We need more than just stories about collectors. Areas most open to freelancers: 'Stickerama,' all sorts of sticker stuff; 'Best Sticker Ideas' generated by readers; and 'Sticker People' short profiles."

STORY FRIENDS, Mennonite Publishing House, 616 Walnut Ave., Scottdale PA 15683. (412)887-8500. Editor: Marjorie Waybill. For children 4-9 years of age. Published monthly in weekly parts. Not copyrighted. Byline given. Pays on acceptance. Submit seasonal/holiday material 6 months in advance. SASE. Free sample copy.

Nonfiction: "The over-arching purpose of this publication is to portray Jesus as a friend and helper—a friend who cares about each happy and sad experience in the child's life. Persons who know Jesus have values which affect every area of their lives."

Fiction: "Stories of everyday experiences at home, at church, in school or at play can provide models of these values. Of special importance are relationships, patterns of forgiveness, respect, honesty, trust and caring. Prefers short stories that offer a wide variety of settings, acquaint children with a wide range of friends, and mirror the joys, fears, temptations and successes of the readers. *Story Friends* needs stories that speak to the needs and interests of children of a variety of ethnic backgrounds. Stories should provide patterns of forgiveness, respect, integrity, understanding, caring, sharing; increase the children's sense of self-worth through growing confidence in God's love for them as they are; help answer the children's questions about God, Jesus, the Bible, prayer, death, heaven; develop awe and reverence for God the Creator and for all of His creation; avoid preachiness, but have well-defined spiritual values as an integral part of each story; be plausible in plot; introduce children to followers of Jesus Christ; and develop appreciation for our Mennonite heritage." Length: 300-800 words. Pays 2½-3¢/word.

Poetry: Traditional and free verse. Length: 3-12 lines. Pays $5.

3-2-1 CONTACT, Children's Television Workshop, One Lincoln Plaza, New York NY 10023. (212)595-3456. Editor: Jonathan Rosenbloom. Associate Editor: Joanna Foley. 40-50% freelance written. Magazine published 10 times/year covering science for children 8-12. Circ. 320,000. Pays on acceptance. Publishes ms 6 months after acceptance. Submit seasonal material 6 months in advance. Simultaneous, photocopied, and previously published submissions OK if so indicated. Computer printout submissions acceptable. Reports in 1 month. Buys all rights "with some exceptions." Free writer's guidelines. SASE. Sample copy $1.25.

Nonfiction: General interest (space exploration, the human body, animals, the new technology, current science issues); profile (of interesting scientists or children involved in science or with computers); photo feature (centered around a science theme); and role models of women and minority scientists. No articles on travel not related to science. Buys 5 unsolicited mss/year. Query with clips of previously published work. Length: 700-1,000 words. Pays $150-400.

Photos: Reviews 8x10 b&w prints and 35mm color transparencies. Model release preferred.

Tips: "I prefer a short query, without manuscript, that makes it clear that an article is interesting. When sending an article, include your telephone number. Don't call us, we'll call you. Many submissions we receive are more like college research papers than feature stories. We like articles in which writers have interviewed kids or scientists, or discovered exciting events with a scientific angle. Library research is necessary; but if that's all you're doing, you aren't giving us anything we can't get ourselves. If your story needs a bibliography, chances are, it's not right for us."

TOUCH, Box 7244, Grand Rapids MI 49510. Editor: Joanne Ilbrink. 50-60% freelance written. Purpose of publication is to show girls ages 8-15 how God is at work in their lives and in the world around them. Monthly magazine. Circ. 14,000. Pays on acceptance. Buys simultaneous, second serial (reprint) rights and first North American serial rights. Byline given. Submit seasonal/holiday material 5 months in advance. Simultaneous, photocopied or previously published submissions OK. SASE. Reports in 3 weeks. Free sample copy and writer's guidelines.
Nonfiction: How-to (crafts girls can make easily and inexpensively); informational (write for issue themes); humor (needs much more); inspirational (seasonal and holiday); interview; travel; personal experience (avoid the testimony approach); and photo feature (query first). "Because our magazine is published around a monthly theme, requesting the letter we send out twice a year to our established freelancers would be most helpful. We do not want easy solutions or quick character changes from bad to good. No pietistic characters. Constant mention of God is not necessary if the moral tone of the story is positive. We do not want stories that always have a good ending." Buys 36-45 unsolicited mss/year. Submit complete ms. Length: 100-1,000 words. Pays 2¢/word, depending on the amount of editing.
Photos: Purchased with or without ms. Submit 3x5 clear glossy prints. B&w only. Pays $5-25 on publication.
Fiction: Adventure (that girls could experience in their hometowns or places they might realistically visit); humorous; mystery (believable only); romance (stories that deal with awakening awareness of boys are appreciated); suspense (can be serialized) and religious (nothing preachy). Buys 20 mss/year. Submit complete ms. Length: 300-1,500 words. Pays 2¢/word.
Poetry: Free verse, haiku, light verse and traditional. Buys 10/year. Length: 50 lines maximum. Pays $5 minimum.
Fillers: Puzzles, short humor and cartoons. Buys 3/issue. Pays $2.50-7.
Tips: "Prefers not to see anything on the adult level, secular material, or violence."

TRAILS, Pioneer Clubs, Box 788, Wheaton IL 60189. Editor: LoraBeth Norton. Asscociate Editor: Lorraine Mulligan. 40% freelance written. Emphasizes the development of a Christian lifestyle for girls and boys ages 6-12, most of whom are enrolled in the Pioneer Clubs program. It is kept general in content so it will appeal to a wider audience. Magazine published 5 times/year. Circ. 50,000. Pays on acceptance. Buys first, second (reprint) or simultaneous rights. Byline given. Submit seasonal/holiday material 6 months in advance. Computer printout submissions acceptable. SASE. Reports in 4-8 weeks. Publishes ms an average of 10 months after acceptance. Sample copy and writer's guidelines $1.50.
Nonfiction: How-to (crafts and puzzles); humor; informational; inspirational; and biography. Submit complete ms. Length: 800-1,500 words. Pays $25-50.
Fiction: Adventure, fantasy, historical, humorous, mainstream, mystery and religious. Buys 6 mss/issue. Submit complete ms. Length: 800-1,500 words. Pays $25-40.
Fillers: Puzzles. Pays $5-15.
Tips: "*Trails* buys only 15-20% unsolicited manuscripts."

TURTLE MAGAZINE FOR PRESCHOOL KIDS, Children's Better Health Institute, Benjamin Franklin Literary & Medical Society, Inc., 1100 Waterway Blvd., Box 567, Indianapolis IN 46206. (317)636-8881. Editor: Beth Wood Thomas. 95% freelance written. Monthly magazine (bimonthly February/March, April/May, June/July, August/September) for preschoolers—emphasizing health, safety, exercise and good nutrition. Pays on publication. Byline given. Buys all rights. Submit seasonal/holiday material 8 months in advance. SASE. Reports in 10 weeks. Publishes ms an average of 1 year after acceptance. Sample copy 75¢; writer's guidelines for business-size SAE.
Fiction: Fantasy, humorous and health-related stories. "Stories that deal with a health theme need not have health as the primary subject but should include it in some way in the course of events." No controversial material. Buys about 30 mss/year. Submit complete ms. Length: 700 words maximum. Pays approximately 4¢/word.
Poetry: "We use many stories in rhyme—vocabularly should be geared to a 3- to 5-year-old. Anthropomorphic animal stories and rhymes are especially effective for this age group to emphasize a moral or lesson without 'lecturing.' " Pays variable rates.
Tips: "We are primarily concerned with preventive medicine. We try to present our material in a positive—not a negative—light and to incorporate humor and a light approach wherever possible without minimizing the seriousness of what we are saying. We would like to see more stories, articles, craft ideas and activities with the following holiday themes: New Years Day, Valentine's Day, President's Day, St. Patrick's Day, Easter, Independence Day, Thanksgiving, Christmas and Hannukah. We like new ideas that will entertain as well as teach preschoolers. Publishing a writer's first work is very gratifying to us. It is a great pleasure to receive new, fresh material"

WEE WISDOM, Unity Village MO 64065. Editor: Colleen Zuck. 90% freelance written. Magazine published 10 times/year. "For children aged 13 and under dedicated to the truth that each person is a child of God and has an inner source of wisdom, power, love and health from the Father that can be applied in a practical manner to everyday life." Submit seasonal/holiday material 8 months in advance. Wants only completed mss. Buys first North American serial rights. Byline given. Pays on acceptance. Computer printout submissions acceptable; prefers letter-quality to dot-matrix. Publishes ms an average of 8 months after acceptance. SASE. Free sample copy, editorial policy on request.

Nonfiction: Entertaining nature articles or projects/activities to encourage appreciation of all life. Pays 3¢/word minimum.

Fiction: "Character-building stories that encourage a positive self-image. Although entertaining enough to hold the interest of the older child, they should be readable by the third grader. Characters should be appealing but realistic; plots should be plausible, and all stories should be told in a forthright manner but without preaching. Life itself combines fun and humor with its more serious lessons, and our most interesting and helpful stories do the same thing. Language should be universal, avoiding the Sunday school image." Length: 500-800 words. Pay 3¢/word minimum.

Poetry: Very limited. Pays 50¢/line. Prefers short, seasonal or humorous poems. Also buys rhymed prose for "read alouds" and pays $15 minimum.

Fillers: Pays $3 minimum for puzzles and games.

WONDER TIME, 6401 The Paseo, Kansas City MO 64131. (816)333-7000. Editor: Evelyn Beals. 75% freelance written. Published weekly by Church of the Nazarene for children ages 6-8. Buys first rights or second (reprint) rights to material originally published elsewhere. Byline given. Pays on acceptance. Publishes ms an average of 2 years after acceptance. Free sample copy. Computer printout submissions acceptable; prefers letter-quality to dot-matrix. SASE.

Fiction: Buys stories portraying Christian attitudes without being preachy. Uses stories for special days—stories teaching honesty, truthfulness, kindness, helpfulness or other important spiritual truths, and avoiding symbolism. "God should be spoken of as our Father who loves and cares for us; Jesus, as our Lord and Savior." Buys 150/mss year. Length: 400-600 words. Pays 3½¢/word on acceptance.

Poetry: Uses verse which has seasonal or Christian emphasis. Length: 4-12 lines. Pays 25¢/line minimum-$2.50.

Tips: "Any stories that allude to church doctrine must be in keeping with Nazarene beliefs. Any type of fantasy must be in good taste and easily recognizable. Overstocked now with poetry and stories with general theme. Brochure with specific needs available with free sample." Recently published "a story of a little boy whose grandfather dies, showing how his faith in God and belief in heaven helps his grief"; and "a story about a boy talking to his dad about income taxes; relating it to the biblical command to give to God and to Caesar."

‡YOUNG AMERICAN, Student News, Young American Publishing Co., Inc., Box 12409, Portland OR 97212. (503)230-1895. Editor: Karen Zurich. Managing Editor: Kris Forzley. A biweekly 16-24 page tabloid inserted in 9 surburan newspapers for students, ages 9-16, and the developing reader to whom two pages are devoted. "Subjects vary from world politics to children making headlines, and material is easy to digest as well as timely and pertinent." Estab. 1983. Circ. 108,000. Pays on publication. Byline given. Buys first North American serial rights. Submit seasonal/holiday material at least 3 months in advance. Simultaneous queries, and simultaneous and photocopied submissions OK. Computer printout submissions acceptable; no dot-matrix. SASE. Reports in 2 months. Sample copy for 9x12 SAE and 37¢ postage; writer's guidelines for SAE and 1 first class stamp.

Nonfiction: Exposé (pertaining to children); how-to (make money for kids, 150 words); interview/profile; technical (science). No violence or any articles which are not written for children under 16. Buys 48 mss/year. Send complete ms. Length: 150-300 words. Pays 5¢/word minimum ("only if a total rewrite has been done by editor"); 7¢/word maximum.

Photos: Send photos with ms. Pays $5-10 for 5x3½" b&w prints. Identification of subjects required. Buys one-time rights.

Columns/Departments: World News, You & the News (stories about newsworthy children, schools, or legistature pertaining to children); entertainment (book reviews); Science/Health; Sports; Fun of it; (poetry 300, maximum). Buys 5-15 mss/year. Length: 150-300 words. Pays 7¢/word.

Fiction: Adventure, fantasy, humorous, mystery, science fiction, suspense and western. Also Christmas story (700-950 words). "No condescending material, stories that are poorly written which tend to tell the reader instead of showing; no didactic material." Buys 12 mss/year. Send complete mss. Length: 500-950 words. Pays 7¢/word.

Poetry: Free verse, haiku, light verse, traditional. No long poems. Buys 10/year. Submit maximum 12 poems. Length 12-40 lines. Pays 7¢/word.

Fillers: Jokes, gags, newsbreaks. Buys 8/year. Length: 40-100 lines. Pays 7¢/word.

Tips: "Our manuscripts are short, 4½ pages maximum, so its best to send complete manuscript with cover letter and clips—except for cover stories which are written by editor on assignment. Fiction and cover stories are most open to freelancers. Cover story must be about real children who are involved with various subjects that would be of interest to readers: sports, computers, animals, making money, etc. Cover story should be queried. We are seeking superior writers who can hold a child's interest without violence or sensationalism."

YOUNG JUDAEAN, 50 W. 58th St., New York NY 10019. (212)355-7900, ext. 464, 465. Editor: Mordecai Newman. For Jewish children ages 8-13, and members of Young Judaea. Publication of Hadassah Zionist Youth Commission. All material must be on some Jewish theme. Special issues for Jewish/Israeli holidays, or particular Jewish themes which vary from year to year; for example, Hassidim, Holocaust, etc. Monthly (November through June). Circ. 8,000. Buys all rights or first North American serial rights. Byline given. Buys 3-6 mss/year. Payment in contributor's copies or small token payment. Sample copy and annual list of themes for 75¢. Prefers complete ms. Will consider photocopied and simultaneous submissions. Submit seasonal material 4 months in advance. Reports in 3 months. SASE.
Nonfiction: "Articles about Jewish-American life, Jewish historical and international interest. Israel and Zionist-oriented material. Try to awaken kids' Jewish consciousness by creative approach to Jewish history and religion, ethics and culture, politics and current events. Style can be didactic but not patronizing." Informational (300-1,000 words), how-to (300-500 words), personal experience, interview, humor, historical, think articles, photo, travel, and reviews (books, theater and movies). Length: 500-1,200 words. Pays $20-40. "Token payments only, due to miniscule budget."
Photos: Photos purchased with accompanying mss. Captions required. 5x7 maximum. B&w preferred. Payment included with fee for article. Illustrations also accepted.
Fiction: Experimental, mainstream, mystery, suspense, adventure, science fiction, fantasy, humorous, religious and historical fiction. Length: 500-1,000 words. Pays $5-25. Must be of specific Jewish interest.
Poetry: Traditional forms, blank verse, free verse, avant-garde forms and light verse. Poetry themes must relate to subject matter of magazine. Length: 25-100 lines. Pays $5-15.
Fillers: Newsbreaks, jokes and short humor purchased for $5.
Tips: "Think of an aspect of Jewish history/religion/culture which can be handled in a fresh, imaginative way, fictionally or factually. Don't preach; inform and entertain." Prefers not to get material with no Jewish relevance or material that deals with Jewish subject matter but from a Christian perspective.

Lifestyles

Individual philosophies and special interests merit front-page coverage in the following publications. They offer writers a forum for unconventional views or serve as a voice for a particular audience or cause. Here are magazines for single and widowed people, vegetarians, homosexuals, atheists, survivalists, back-to-the-land advocates, and others interested in alternative outlooks and lifestyles. Also included are "free press" publications that do not pay, except in copies.

THE ADVOCATE, Liberation Publications, Inc., Suite 200, 1800 N. Highland Ave., Los Angeles CA 90028. Editor-in-Chief: Robert I. McQueen. For gay men and women, ages 21-40; middle-class, college-educated, urban. Biweekly tabloid. Circ. 83,000. Pays on publication. Rights purchased vary with author and material. Byline given. SASE. Reports in 6 weeks.
Nonfiction: "Basically, the emphasis is on the dignity and joy of the gay lifestyle." News articles, interviews and lifestyle features. "Major interest in interviews or profiles of gay people whose names can be used." Informational, personal experience, humor, historical, photo feature and spot news. Query with "concrete description and writing sample." Length: open.
Photos: "Payment for b&w photos purchased without ms or on assignment depends on size of the reproduction."

AMERICAN ATHEIST, American Atheist Press, Box 2117, Austin TX 78768. (512)458-1244. Editor: R. Murray-O'Hair. Managing Editor: Jon Garth Murray. 40% freelance written. Monthly magazine covering atheism and topics related to it and separation of Church and State. Circ. 50,000. Pays in free subscription or 15 copies for first-time authors. Repeat authors paid $10 per 1000 words. Byline given. Buys one-time and all rights. Submit seasonal/holiday material 3 months in advance. Simultaneous queries and simultaneous, photocopied and previously published submissions OK. Computer printout submissions acceptable. SASE. Reports in 1 week on queries; 6 weeks on mss. Publishes ms an average of 4 months after acceptance. Free sample copy and writer's guidelines.

Nonfiction: Book excerpts, expose, general interest, historical, how-to, humor, interview/profile, opinion, personal experience and photo feature, but only as related to State/Church or atheism. No "religious or off-the-cuff, incoherent pieces which don't make a point." Buys 40 mss/year. Send complete ms. Length: 400-10,000 words. Pays $10 per thousand words.
Photos: Gerald Tholen, photo editor. Send photos with ms. Pays $15 maximum for 2x3 or 4x5 b&w prints. $100 for four-color cover photos. Identification of subjects required.
Columns/Departments: Atheism, Church/State separation and humor. Send complete ms. Length: 400-10,000 words.
Poetry: Avant-garde, free verse, haiku, light verse and traditional. Submit unlimited poems. Length: open. Pays $10 per thousand words maximum.
Fillers: Clippings, jokes, short humor and newsbreaks. Length: 300 words maximum, only as related to State/Church separation or atheism.

ASCENSION FROM THE ASHES, The Alternative Magazine, AFTA Press, Suite 2, 153 George St., New Brunswick NJ 08901. (201)828-5467. Editor: Bill-Dale Marcinko. Quarterly magazine covering popular culture (TV, film, books and music) political and sexual issues for young adults (ages 18-30) who are interested in rock music, films, literature and political and sexual issues. Circ. 25,000. Pays in copies. Buys one-time rights. Phone queries OK. Submit seasonal material 1 month in advance. Simultaneous, photocopied and previously published submissions OK. SASE. Reports in 2 weeks. Sample copy $3.50.
Nonfiction: Humor (satires on popular books, TV, films, records and social issues); interview (of authors, TV/film writers or directors, rock musicians and political movement leaders); opinion (reviews and reactions); profile; personal experience; and photo feature (on the making of a movie or TV program, coverage of a rock concert or political demonstration). *AFTA* also buys investigative articles on political, consumer and religious fraud. Buys 75 unsolicited mss/year. Query with clips of previously published work. Pays in copies.
Photos: State availability of photos. Reviews b&w prints. Pays in copies.
Columns/Departments: Books, Etc. (book reviews, fiction and nonfiction of interest to a young counterculture audience); Demons in Dustjackets (horror and science fiction book reviews); Medium Banal (TV reviews); Sprockets (film reviews); and Slipped Discs (record reviews). "We use short (3-4 paragraphs) reviews of comic books, underground comics, alternative magazines, recent books, television programs, films and rock albums, especially on gay, lesbian and politically controversial small press magazines and books. Buys 50 mss/year. Query with clips of previously published work. Length: 100-1,000 words. Pays in copies.
Fiction: Short stories. Experimental, erotic, humorous, science fiction, suspense and mainstream. Buys 10 mss/year. Query with clips of previously published work. Length: 1,000 words maximum. Pays in copies.
Poetry: Political; survival, humorous and erotic subjects. Pays in copies.
Fillers: "We print folk/rock songs on social issues with music. Buys 8 mss/year. Pays in copies. We also have a section in which readers describe their first-time sexual experiences (gay or straight)."
Tips: "Sending for a sample copy is probably the best way to familiarize yourself with the kind of writing in *AFTA*. Write with humor, simplicity, and intensity, first person if possible. Avoid being formal or academic in criticism. Write for a young adult audience. The short stories accepted generally have a style similar to the works of Vonnegut or Tom Robbins, very loose, playful and humorous. *AFTA* doesn't censor language in any submissions, and is known for printing material other magazines consider sexually and politically controversial."

THE BOSTON PHOENIX, 100 Massachusetts Ave., Boston MA 02115. (617)536-5390. Editor: Richard M. Gaines. 40% freelance written. For 18-40 age group, educated post-counterculture. Weekly alternative newspaper; 140+ pages. Circ. 139,000. Buys all rights. Pays kill fee for assignments only. Byline given. Pays on publication. Photocopied submissions OK. Computer printout submissions acceptable; no dot-matrix. Reports in 6 weeks. Query letter preferable to ms. SASE. Sample copy $1.50.
Nonfiction: News (local coverage, national, some international affairs, features, think pieces and profiles); Lifestyle (features, service pieces, consumer-oriented tips, medical, food, some humor if topical, etc.); Arts (reviews, essays, interviews); and Supplements (coverage of special-interest areas, e.g., stereo, skiing, automotive, computers, pro sound, education, home furnishings with local angle). Query Section Editor. "Liveliness, accuracy, and great literacy are absolutely required." No fiction or poetry. Pays 4¢/word and up.

THE CELIBATE WOMAN, A Journal for Women Who Are Celibate or Considering This Liberating Way of Relating to Others, 3306 Ross Place NW, Washington DC 20008. (202)966-7783. Editor: Martha Allen. 95% freelance written. Biannual special interest magazine on celibacy and women. Estab. 1982. Byline given. Not copyrighted. SASE. Reports in weeks. Publishes ms an average of 6 months after acceptance. Sample copy $4.
Nonfiction: Reflections on celibacy and sexuality. "The journal is a forum for presenting another view of sexuality—an opening up of alternatives in a sex-oriented society." Articles, artwork, letters, experiences, ideas and theory are welcome.

‡**COMMON LIVES/LESBIAN LIVES, A lesbian quarterly**, The CL/LL Collective, Box 1553, Iowa City IA 52244. Collective Contacts: Tess Catalano and Tracy Moore. A quarterly journal of contemporary lesbian culture. Circ. 2,000. Byline given. Rights revert to author. Submit seasonal/holiday material 3-6 months in advance. Photocopied submissions OK. Computer printout submissions acceptable; prefers letter-quality to dot-matrix. SASE. Reports in 1 month on queries; 6 months on mss. Sample copy $4; writer's guidelines for SAE and 1 first class stamp.

Nonfiction: Book excerpts, expose, general interest, historical/nostalgic, humor, inspirational, interview/profile, opinion, oral history and history, political analysis, personal experience, photo feature, travel and first source material such as journal, diary and correspondence. Buys 25 mss/year. Query or send complete ms. Length: 5,000 words. Pays in copies.

Photos: Send photos with query or ms. Reviews 3x5 b&w prints. Captions and model release required.

Columns/Departments: One paragraph book reviews. Query or send complete ms. Pays in copies.

Fiction: Adventure, condensed novels, confession, erotica, ethnic, experimental, fantasy, historical, horror, humorous, mainstream, mystery, novel excerpts, religious, romance, science fiction, suspense, western and political. No serialized novels. Buys 200 mss/year. Send complete ms. Length: 6,000 words maximum. Pays in copies.

Poetry: Free verse, haiku, light verse, traditional and narrative. No esoteric or abstract poetry. Buys 25 poems/year. Length: 400 lines maximum. Pays in copies.

Fillers: Jokes, anecdotes and short humor. Acquires 10/year. Length: 100-300 words. Pays in copies.

Tips: "Most lesbians we publish are very new writers or have been published only in a few places. We want original work in women's own voices, especially work from points of view new to our pages."

‡**CONTACT**, Boumain Publishing Co., Inc., Box 9248, Berkeley CA 94709. Editor: Elliott Leighton. 40% freelance written. Monthly magazine on relationships and singles activities. Circ. 45,000. Pays on acceptance. Byline given. Buys first and second rights to the same material and one-time rights. Submit seasonal/holiday material 6 months in advance. Simultaneous, photocopied, and previously published submissions OK. Computer printout submissions acceptable. SASE. No queries. Reports in 3 months on mss. Publishes ms an average of 2 months after acceptance. Sample copy $3; free writer's guidelines.

Nonfiction: Book excerpts (within subject area of relationships); expose; general interest; humor; interview/profile; opinion; personal experience; photo feature; and travel. "We prefer short pieces (1,000 to 2,500 words) on subjects of interest to our unmarried readership. We'd like to see more works grounded in personal experience and dealing with one or more of the following subjects: single lifestyles, divorce and custody, coping with loneliness, consciousness-raising, the dating game, traveling solo, making contact, body talk, communication, single parenting, surrogate parenting, recovering from difficult relationships, sex roles, dating services and matchmakers, cooking for one, overcoming shyness, the bar scene and alternatives, and health, nutrition and single living." No political, religious, erotic, non-realistic or philosophical material. Buys 10-15 mss/year. Send complete ms. Length: 1,000-4,000 words. Pays $10-100.

Photos: Sean Sprague, photo editor. Send photos with ms. Pays $50 maximum for 8½x11 prints. Model release and identification of subjects required. Buys one-time rights.

Columns/Departments: Book Reviews (books dealing with sexuality, relationships, etc. only); and Gazette (news items of interest to single). Buys 4-6 mss/year. Send complete ms. Length: 100-2,000 words. Pays $5-50.

Fiction: Adventure, confession, humorous, mainstream and romance "as they relate to subject of relationships, single lifestyle, etc." No erotic, religious, fantasy and science fiction, crime or sexist material. Buys 6-12 mss/year. Send complete ms. Length: 2,500-5,000 words. Pays $25-100.

Poetry: Jess River, poetry editor. Avant-garde, free verse, haiku, light verse and traditional. No epic (anything over 50 lines) poems. Buys 25 poems/year. Length: 2-50 lines. Pays 0-$10.

Tips: "A freelancer can best break into our publication by following our guidelines on subject areas and mss preparation; by reading what we publish; and by staying close to his/her own personal experience. The straight prose nonfiction article, somewhat confessional leading to insight in ways of relating to others, is the easiest way for a freelancer to break in."

COSMOPOLITAN CONTACT, Pantheon Press, Box 1566, Fontana CA 92335. Editor-in-Chief: Romulus Rexner. Managing Editor: Nina Norvid. Assistant Editor: Irene Anders. 40% freelance written. Magazine irregularly published 2 or 3 times a year. "It is the publication's object to have as universal appeal as possible to students, graduates and others interested in international affairs, cooperation, contacts, travel, friendships, trade, exchanges, self-improvement and widening of mental horizons through multicultural interaction. This polyglot publication has worldwide distribution and participation, including the Communist countries. Writers participate in its distribution, editing and publishing." Circ. 1,500. Buys first and second rights to the same material. Pays on publication in copies. Byline given. Simultaneous, photocopied and previously published submissions OK. Computer printout submissions acceptable; no dot-matrix. SASE. Reports in 6 weeks. Publishes ms an average of 3 months after acceptance. Sample copy $2.

Nonfiction: Expose (should concentrate on government, education, etc.); how-to; informational; inspiration-

al; personal experience; personal opinion and travel. Submit complete ms. Buys 15-30 mss/year. Maximum 500 words. "Material designed to promote across all frontiers bonds of spiritual unity, intellectual understanding and sincere friendship among people by means of correspondence, meetings, publishing activities, tapes, records, exchange of hospitality, books, periodicals in various languages, hobbies and other contacts."
Poetry: Traditional. Length: Maximum 40 lines.
Tips: "Most of the material is not written by experts to enlighten or to amuse the readers, but it is written by the readers who also are freelance writers. The material is didactic, provocative, pragmatic—not art-for-art's sake—and tries to answer the reader's question, 'What can I do about it?' The addresses of all contributors are published in order to facilitate global contacts among our contributors, editors and readers/members. Instead of writing, e.g., about Lincoln or history, it is better to be an emancipator and to make history by promoting high ideals of mankind. Consequently, the material submitted to us should not be only descriptive, but it should be analytical, creative, action- and future-oriented. We are not interested in any contribution containing vulgar language, extreme, intolerant, pro-Soviet or anti-American opinions." Recent article example: "Mastery of Life" (Vol. XX, No. 34).

‡**D.I.N. NEWSERVICE,** D.I.N. Publications, Box 5115, Phoenix AZ 85010. (602)257-0764. Editor: Jim Parker. 25% freelance written. An innovative, alternative newsmagazine covering behavior and health; published by the Do It Now Foundation. Estab. 1983. Circ. 10,000. Pays on publication. Byline given. Offers 30% kill fee. Buys first North American serial rights and second (reprint) rights to material originally published elsewhere. Simultaneous queries and photocopied submissions OK. Computer printout submissions acceptable. SASE. Reports in 1 month. Publishes ms an average of 3 months after acceptance. Sample copy $2.
Nonfiction: "News and features exploring breaking or nonmainstream developments in human health and behavior, and the constellation of issues and events impacting health and behavior." Buys features, profiles, interviews and opinions. Buys 5 mss/issue. Length: 500-3,500 words. Pays $50-400. Also buys news shorts. Length: 50-300 words. Pays $5-25.
Photos: Pays $10-50 for each b&w or color photo purchased with ms. More for assigned photos.
Columns/Departments: Newsfronts (shorts on current developments in health, behavior, substance abuse, consciousness, media, technology, etc.); Informat (specialized information on various behavioral health topics); Backwords (unusual or off-beat shorts and mini-features); Guestcolumn (guest opinion and commentary); and Postscripts (personal commentary on current news and events).
Tips: "Be authoritative but readable. Don't be afraid to be provocative if you have something to say. Study a sample copy for our viewpoint and style. If a topic interests you, chances are that it will interest us, too—unless it's already been run into the ground by major media. Query first. We'll turn down an interview with God if we ran an interview with God in our last issue."

EARTH'S DAUGHTERS MAGAZINE, Box 41, Central Park Station, Buffalo NY 14215. Collective editorship. For people interested in literature and feminism. Publication schedule varies from 2-4 times a year. Circ. 1,000. Acquires first North American serial rights; copyright reverts to author after publication. Byline given. Pays in contributor's copies. Clear photocopied submissions and clear carbons OK. Computer printout submissions acceptable; prefers letter-quality to dot-matrix. Reports "very slowly. Please be patient." Submit 3 or 4 poems maximum at a time; one short story/submission. "If part of larger work, please mention this." SASE. Sample copy $3.
Fiction: Feminist fiction of any and all modes. "Our subject is the experience and creative expression of women. We require a high level of technical skill and artistic intensity, and we are concerned with creative expression rather than propaganda. On occasion we publish feminist work by men." No anti-feminist material; no "hard-line, but shoddy, feminist work." Length: 1,500 words maximum. Pays in copies only.
Poetry: All modern, contemporary, and avant-garde forms. Length: 40 lines maximum preferred with occasional exceptions.
Tips: "We're doing smaller issues, one of which will be by invitation only to past contributors."

EARTHTONE, For People Tuned to the Earth, Publication Development, Inc., Box 23383, Portland OR 97223. (503)620-3917. Editor: Mary Bisceglia. Bimonthly publication for a western US readership interested in developing a self-sufficient lifestyle. "Editorial often deals with a back-to-the-land lifestyle but does not exclude those urban dwellers interested in becoming more independent and self-sufficient in their current residence." Circ. 50,000. Pays on publication. Byline given. Buys first North American serial rights. Submit seasonal/holiday material 6 months in advance. Simultaneous queries and simultaneous and photocopied submissions OK. SASE. Reports in 1 month. Free sample copy; writer's guidelines for SAE and 1 first class stamp.
Nonfiction: General interest (on country living, food, folk art); historical/nostalgic; how-to (crafts, home projects, small-scale low-cost building); humor; interview/profile (on people living this sort of lifestyle); new product (only if very unusual or revolutionary); personal experience (only if informative on various aspects of homesteading or country living and self-sufficient lifestyle); animal husbandry; health; energy; organic gardening and recreation. How-to articles should be accompanied by photos or illustrations. All articles should have a western US angle. Buys 6-10 mss/issue. Query with published clips if available. Length: 500-3,000 words. Pays $50-300.

Tips: "Break in with a clearly written how-to on crafts, gardening, small-scale low-cost building. Also, interesting personality sketches."

EAST WEST JOURNAL, East West Journal, Inc., 17 Station St., Box 1200, Brookline Village MA 02147. (617)232-1000. Editor: Mark Mayell. 40% freelance written. Emphasizes natural living for "people of all ages seeking balance in a world of change." Monthly magazine. Circ. 70,000. Pays on publication. Buys first rights or second (reprint) rights to material originally published elsewhere. Byline given. Submit seasonal/holiday material 5 months in advance. Simultaneous, photocopied and previously published submissions OK. Computer printout submissions acceptable; prefers letter-quality to dot-matrix. SASE. Reports in 1 month. Publishes ms an average of 4 months after acceptance.
Nonfiction: Expose (of agribusiness, modern medicine, the oil and nuclear industries); interviews and features (on solar and alternative energies, natural foods and organic farming and gardening, ecological and energy-efficient modes of transportation, natural healing, human-potential movement, whole food and technology). No negative, politically-oriented, or new-age material. "We're looking for original, first-person articles without jargon or opinions of any particular teachings; articles should reflect an intuitive approach." Buys 15-20 mss/year. Query. Length: 1,500-2,500 words. Pays 5-10¢/word.
Photos: Send photos with ms. Pays $15-40 for b&w prints; $15-175 for 35mm color transparencies (cover only). Captions preferred; model release required.
Columns/Departments: Body, Food, Healing, Gardening, Alternative Energy and Spirit. Buys 15 mss/year. Submit complete ms. Length: 1,500-2,000 words. Pays 5-10¢/word.

‡**THE EVENER**, The Evener Corporation, 29th and College, Cedar Falls IA 50613. (319)277-3599. Managing Editor: Susan Salterberg. 40% freelance written. Quarterly magazine on draft horses and other draft animals. *The Evener* is published primarily for draft horse, mule and oxen enthusiasts. It also reaches individuals who are interested in back-to-basics and rural life." Circ. 6,500. Pays on acceptance. Byline given. Prefers to buy all rights, but will make exceptions. Submit seasonal/holiday material 4 months in advance. Photocopied and previously published submissions OK. Computer printout submissions acceptable; prefers letter-quality to dot-matrix. Reports in 4 weeks on queries; 3 months on mss. Publishes ms an average of 6 months after acceptance. Sample copy for 9x12 SAE and $1.05 postage; writer's guidelines for business-size SAE and 37¢ postage; both $1.40.
Nonfiction: Susan Salterberg, articles editor. Book excerpts (from horse, mule, oxen or small farm-related books); historical/nostalgic (farming in the past, feature on a heartwarming event or situation related to draft animals, agricultural history of an area); how-to (making or repairing farm equipment, training a draft animal, breeding, making horse shoes, show decorations, around-home outdoors equipment); humor (draft animal or country life related); interview/profile (people using innovative farming/training/living methods or who are specialists as breeders, trainers, farmers, judges; people living unique country lifestyles; old-timers' philosophies and recollections); personal experience (draft horse, mule or oxen related, or a country living or farming angle); experience caring for draft horses on the farm); photo feature (draft horse, mule or oxen or country life related); and technical (horse health and economics of large vs. small farming). No vague how-to articles and those not relating to subject matter. Buys 15 mss/year. Send complete ms. Length: 300-3,000 words. Pays 3-10¢/word.
Photos: Send photos with ms. Pays $5-25 for b&w prints. Welcomes contact sheets. Captions and identification of subjects (if applicable or pertinent) required.
Columns/Departments: Yearlings & Colts (children's page); Spoons 'N Ladles (recipes); and Bits 'n Pieces (helpful hints); and Product Profile (horse products). "We are particularly interested in articles about children's activities with their draft horses or other draft animals. (Club projects, farm chores and activities, etc., will fit well in Yearlings & Colts.) Buys 10 mss/year. Send complete ms. Length: 75-400 words. Pays 3-10¢/word or free subscription.
Poetry: All types of poetry relating to draft animals. Buys 2 poems/year. Submit maximum 5 poems. Pays $5-20 or free subscription.
Fillers: Anecdotes and newsbreaks. Buys 10/year. Length: 100-750 words. Pays 3-10¢/word or free subscription.
Tips: "Thoroughly peruse the freelance guidelines and the magazine, taking note of our readers' personalities. Possibly attend draft horse and mule shows, horse pulls, sales and other related events. These events give you an excellent opportunity to interact with our audience so you understand our focus and aim. Then send us a 1,500-word manuscript with photographs or illustrations. We want articles that teach, evoke emotions, and/or challenge our readers. Freelancers can best break into our publication with nonfiction, especially how-to, interview/profile and technical and historical/nostalgic. Be creative, search for a unique angle and be credible."

FARMSTEAD MAGAZINE, Box 111, Freedom ME 04941. (207)382-6200. Editor-in-Chief: George Frangoulis. 45% freelance written. Magazine published 6 times/year covering gardening, small farming, homesteading, energy and home construction, and self-sufficiency. "We combine a practical, how-to approach with an appeal to aesthetic sense and taste." Circ. 150,000. Pays on publication. Buys first and second rights to the same material. Phone queries OK. Submit seasonal/holiday material 3 months in advance. Computer printout submissions acceptable; no dot-matrix. SASE. Reports in 3 months. Publishes ms an average of 1 year after acceptance. Free sample copy and writer's guidelines.

Nonfiction: General interest (related to rural living, gardening and farm life); how-to (gardening, farming, shelter, energy, construction, conservation, wildlife, livestock, crafts, and rural living); interview (with interesting and/or inspirational people involved with agriculture, farm life or self-sufficiency); new product (reviews of new books); traditional methods (of rural living; farm life self-sufficiency); and occasionally travel (agriculture in other lands). No sentimentality or nostalgia. Buys 60 mss/year. Submit complete ms. Length: 1,000-5,000 words maximum. Pays $50-250.

Photos: State availability of photos with ms. Pay starts at $10 for each 5x7 b&w print used; starts at $25 for color; $50-100 for each color transparency used on cover.

Tips: "Contribute a thorough well-researched or first-hand experience type article. B&w photos of good quality, 35mm color transparencies or careful diagrams or sketches are a boon. We look for an unusual but practical how-to article. An article sent in a folder is helpful. Presentation is important. We appreciate material from those who have lived and done what they are writing about. We like the how-to, hands-on approach; no theorizing." Send short factual pieces with good photos.

FIRST HAND, Experiences For Loving Men, Firsthand, Ltd., 310 Cedar Lane, Teaneck NJ 07666. (201)836-9177. Editor: Brandon Judell. Managing Editor: Jackie Lewis. 50% freelance written. Monthly magazine of homosexual erotica. Circ. 60,000. Pays 1 month after acceptance. Byline given. Buys all rights (exceptions made), and second (reprint) rights to material originally published elsewhere. Submit seasonal/holiday material 6 months in advance. Simultaneous queries and photocopied submissions OK. Computer printout submissions acceptable. SASE. Reports in 3 weeks. Publishes ms an average of 5 months after acceptance. Sample copy $3; free writer's guidelines.

Nonfiction: Book excerpts (should be erotic or offer advice); historical/nostalgic (gay life in the past); how-to (advice for homosexuals coming out); interview/profile (gay figure heads); personal experience ("this is our premise"); travel (where gays go); and erotica. No violent or negative articles about gay life. No bestiality or child abuse. Buys 96 mss/year. Query with or without published clips or send complete ms. Length: 1,500-3,000 words. Pays $25-150.

Columns/Departments: Survival Kit (short nonfiction pieces about all aspects of gay life). Buys 48 mss/year. Query with or without published clips or send complete ms. Length: 400-800 words. Pays $25-75.

Fiction: Novel excerpts.

Poetry: Free verse and light verse. Buys 12/year. Submit maximum 5 poems. Length: 10-30 lines. Pays $25.

Fillers: Jokes, gags and anecdotes. Buys 30 mss/year. Length: 24-400 words. Pays $15-25.

Tips: "Half of each issue is written by our readers. In their letters, they share their lusts, hopes, loves and fears stemming from their homosexuality. The main articles which are bought from freelancers should display the same candor and honesty. *First Hand* is more than a magazine to get off on. It offers a support system to many homosexuals who feel isolated in the heterosexual community. Many of our readers are married. A few have never had gay sex. Most are very loyal and save every issue."

FLORIDA SINGLES MAGAZINE AND DATE BOOK, Box 83, Palm Beach FL 33480. Editor: Harold Alan. Monthly magazine covering "singles' problems with life, dating, children, etc., for single, divorced, widowed and separated persons who compose over 50% of the adult population over 18." Circ. 12,000. Pays on publication. Buys second serial rights and one-time rights. Simultaneous, photocopied and previously published submissions OK. SASE. Reports in 4 months.

Nonfiction: "We want any article that is general in nature dealing with any aspect of single life, dating, problems, etc." Buys 1-3 mss/issue. Send complete ms. Length: 800-1,400 words. Pays $10-30. "We are associated with 2 other singles magazines: the East Coast and Louisville KY *Singles Magazine*. We pay up to $30 for the first-time use of an article in the first publication and $15 each for each time reprinted in the other magazines."

Photos: Offers no additional payment for photos accepted with ms. Model release required.

Fiction: "We will look at any ms that is general in nature dealing with any aspect of single life, dating, problems, etc."

THE FUTURIST, A Journal of Forecasts, Trends, and Ideas about the Future, World Future Society, 4916 St. Elmo Ave., Bethesda MD 20814. (301)656-8274. Editor: Edward S. Cornish. 80% freelance written. Bimonthly magazine on all aspects of the future for a general audience. *The Futurist* focuses on trends and developments that are likely to have a major impact on the way we live in the years ahead. It explores how changes in all areas—lifestyles, values, technology, government, economics, environmental affairs, etc.— will affect individuals and society in the next five to fifty years. We cover a very broad spectrum of topics— from assessing how a new technology like computers will affect the way people work to how the institution of marriage may change." Circ. 30,000. Byline given. Acquires variable rights "according to the article." Submit seasonal/holiday material 6 months in advance. Simultaneous queries and simultaneous (if so advised), photocopied and previously published submissions OK. Electronic submissions OK if approved of in advance. Computer printout submissions acceptable; prefers letter-quality to dot-matrix. SASE. Reports in 6 weeks on queries; 7 weeks on mss. Publishes ms an average of 3 months after acceptance. Free sample copy and writer's guidelines.

Nonfiction: Tim Willard, assistant editor. Book excerpts, general interest, how-to, interview/profile, new product and opinion. "We are especially looking for articles on the social areas of the future of human values, relationships, lifestyles, etc. These 'soft' subjects seem to be much more difficult for informed speculation and projection than the "hard" area of technology and its effects." No "vague articles that say, 'Wouldn't it be nice if the future were like this,' or 'If that happened in the future?' or articles lacking a future orientation." Acquires 45-50 mss/year. Query with clips or send complete ms. Length: 500-5,000 words. Pays in copies.

Tips: "Feature articles in *The Futurist* are almost entirely freelance written. The Tomorrow in Brief page and the World Trends and Forecasts section are primarily staff written."

‡**GAY CHICAGO MAGAZINE**, Ultra Ink, Inc., 1529 N. Wells St., Chicago IL 606-1305. (312)751-0130. Editor: Dan Di Leo. Weekly magazine published for the gay community of metropolitan Chicago. Circ. 15,000. Pays on publication. Byline given. Buys one-time rights. Submit seasonal/holiday material 2 months in advance. Photocopied submissions OK. Computer printout submissions acceptable. Reports in 1 month. SASE. Free sample copy.

Nonfiction: General interest and personal experience. "Since our magazine is available in many public places, such as restaurants, clothing stores, record stores, etc., the tone of the articles can be erotic but not X-rated pornographic." Buys 2-3 mss/year. Send complete ms. Length: 1,200 words maximum. Pays $10-50.

Photos: Send photos with ms. Pays $5-15 for 5x7 b&w prints. Captions, model release, and identification of subjects required.

Columns/Departments: Buys 2-3 mss/year. Send complete ms. Length: 500-1,000 words. Pays $10-40.

Fiction: Erotica, fantasy, historical, humorous, mystery and science fiction. "We seek any type of fiction that would appeal to the male gay reader, though we do accept pieces that would also appeal to the female gay reader." Buys 2-3 mss/year. Send complete ms. Length: 1,200 words maximum. Pays $10-50.

GAY NEWS, Masco Communications, 1108 Spruce, Philadelphia PA 19107. (215)625-8501. Managing Editor: Stan Ward. Publisher: Mark Segal. 50% freelance written. Weekly tabloid covering news and features of interest to the lesbian and gay community. Circ. 15,000. Pays on publication. Byline given. Offers ⅓ kill fee. Buys one-time rights. Submit seasonal/holiday material 2 months in advance. Photocopied and previously published submissions OK. Computer printout submissions acceptable. SASE. Reports in 4 weeks on queries; 6 weeks on mss. Publishes ms an average of 6 weeks after acceptance. Sample copy $1.

Nonfiction: Stan Ward, managing editor. Book excerpts (with lesbian/gay themes or characters); expose (of enemies to lesbian/gay community); historical/nostalgic (gay history, 'herstory'); humor (satire welcome); interview/profile (of entertainment or activist personalities); opinion (about direction of gay movement and how to achieve gay rights); and travel (resorts that welcome gay tourists, i.e., Key West, San Francisco). "Reflect a constructive attitude toward gay issues. Our emphasis is news and investigative reporting, but we also include entertainment, opinion and personality profiles." Feature articles include gay press, gay health problems, S&M. No personal sexual experiences. Buys 40-50 mss/year. Query with clips of published work. Length: 750-2,500 words. Pays $20-75.

Photos: "Illustrations of the person, place or subject." State availability of photos. Pays $5 maximum for 5x7 b&w prints. Identification of subjects required. Buys one-time rights.

Columns/Departments: Book reviews of books with lesbian/gay themes or characters. Buys 20 mss/year. Query. Length: 750-1,000 words maximum. Pays $20 maximum.

Tips: "It's rewarding to see a variety of viewpoints from freelancers."

HARROWSMITH MAGAZINE, Camden House Publishing, Ltd., Camden East, Ontario K0K 1J0 Canada. (613)378-6661. Editor/Publisher: James M. Lawrence. 75% freelance written. Published 6 times/year "for those interested in country life, nonchemical gardening, energy, self-sufficiency, folk arts, small-stock husbandry, owner-builder architecture and alternative styles of life." Circ. 154,000. Pays on acceptance. Buys first North American serial rights. Byline given. Submit seasonal/holiday material 6 months in advance. Computer printout submissions acceptable; prefers letter-quality to dot-matrix. SAE and IRCs. Reports in 6 weeks. Publishes ms an average of 4 months after acceptance. Sample copy $5; free writer's guidelines.

Nonfiction: Expose, how-to, general interest, humor, interview, photo feature, and profile. "We are always in need of quality gardening articles geared to northern conditions. No articles whose style feigns 'folksiness.' No how-to articles written by people who are not totally familiar with their subject. We feel that in this field simple research does not compensate for lack of long-time personal experience." Buys 10 mss/issue. Query. Length: 500-4,000 words. Pays $75-750 but will consider higher rates for major stories.

Photos: State availability of photos with query. Pays $50-250 for 8x10 b&w glossy prints and 35mm or larger color transparencies. Captions required. Buys one-time rights. "We regularly run photo essays for which we pay $250-750."

Tips: "We have standards of excellence as high as any publication in the country. However, we are by no means a closed market. Much of our material comes from unknown writers. We welcome and give thorough consideration to all freelance submissions. Our magazine is read by Canadians who live in rural areas or who hope to make the urban to rural transition. They want to know as much about the realities of country life as the dreams. They expect quality writing, not folksy cliches."

HIGH TIMES, Trans-High Corp., 17 W. 60th St., New York NY 10023. (212)974-1990. Editor: Larry Sloman. 50% freelance written. Monthly magazine for persons under 35 interested in lifestyle changes, cultural trends, personal freedom, sex and drugs. "Our readers are independent, adventurous free-thinkers who want to control their own consciousness." Circ. 250,000. Pays on publication. Buys all rights, second serial (reprint) rights or first North American serial rights. Submit seasonal/holiday material 5 months in advance. Computer printout submissions acceptable. SASE. Reports in 3 months. Publishes ms an average of 3 months after acceptance. Sample copy $2.95.

Nonfiction: Expose (on political, government or biographical behind the scenes); general interest (political or cultural activities); historical (cultural, literary, dope history, political movements); how-to (that aids the enhancement of one's lifestyle); interview (of writers, scientists, musicians, entertainers and public figures); new product (on dope-related or lifestyle enhancing); nostalgia (cultural or dope-related); opinion (only from public figures); photo feature (on dope- or travel-related topics); profile; technical (explorations of technological breakthroughs related to personal lifestyle); and travel (guides to places of interest to a young hip audience). "We want no material on 'My drug bust.' " Buys 5 mss/issue. Query with clips of published work. Length: 2,000-4,000 words. Pays $300-750.

Photos: Send photos with ms. Pays $25-150 for 8x10 glossy print per page; and $50-250 for 35mm color transparencies per page. Captions preferred; model releases required. Buys one-time rights.

Tips: "Think of article ideas that are too outrageous, visionary, radical or adventurous for any other magazine."

INTERNATIONAL LIVING, Agora Publishing, 2201 St. Paul St., Baltimore MD 21218. (301)235-7961. Editor: Elizabeth Philip. 25% freelance written. Monthly newsletter covering international lifestyles, travel and investment for Americans. Aimed at affluent and not-so-affluent dreamers to whom the romance of living overseas has a strong appeal, especially when it involves money-saving angles. Circ. 28,000. Pays on acceptance. Byline given. Buys first North American and second serial rights. Submit seasonal/holiday material 2 months in advance. Simultaneous queries, and photocopied and previously published work OK. Computer printout submissions acceptable. SASE. Reports in 1 month on queries; 6 weeks on mss. Publishes ms an average of 3 months after acceptance. Sample copy $2.50; writer's guidelines for business-size SAE and 1 first class stamp.

Nonfiction: Book excerpts (overseas, travel, retirement investment, save money overseas); historical/nostalgic (travel, lifestyle abroad); how-to (save money, find a job overseas); interview/profile (famous people and other Americans living abroad); personal experience; travel (unusual, imaginative destinations, give how-to's and costs); and other (financial aspects of overseas investment). "We want pithy, fact-packed articles. No vague, long-winded travel articles on well-trodden destinations." Buys 20 mss/year. Query with clips of published work or send complete ms. Length: 200-2,000 words. Pays $15 minimum.

Tips: "We are looking for writers who can combine original valuable information with a style that suggests the romance of life abroad. Break in with highly-specific, well-researched material combining subjective impressions of living in a foreign country or city with information on taxes, cost of living, residency requirements, employment and entertainment possibilities."

‡JOINT ENDEAVOR, Texas Department of Corrections, Box 32, Huntsville TX 77340. (713)295-6371, ext 655. Editor: Michael F. Vines. Associate Editor: Lonnie Griggs. 30% freelance written. Published bimonthly by inmates of Texas Department of Corrections. Covers criminal justice, offender programs, prison legislation and court actions. "Our readers are professionals, inmates, and anyone with an interest in criminal justice. Subject matter deals with crime, corrections and alternatives to corrections." Circ. 3,000 (national). Pays in copies and a 1-year subscription. Buys first rights and second (serial) rights to material originally published elsewhere. Rights reassigned upon publication. Submit seasonal/holiday material 2 months in advance. Simultaneous and photocopied submissions OK. Computer printout submissions acceptable; prefers letter-quality to dot-matrix. Reports in 3 weeks. For sample copy and writer's guidelines, send SASE (80¢).

Nonfiction: Articles on corrections, law or alternative programs; historical/nostalgic; prison humor; interview/profile (relating to crime and/or corrections); opinion on crime and corrections; personal experience (must be authentic); and biography. Wants material on rehabilitation, crime, prisons, probation, youth offenders, criminal psychology and re-entry programs. Special issues include "Parole Laws," "Prisons: Crisis and Alternatives"; "Diet and Crime" and "Minorities in Prison." Send complete ms. Length: open. Uses approximately 4 mss per issue.

Photos: Send photos with ms. Subjects must be identified. Prefers b&w prints.
Fiction: Larry Strifley, fiction editor. Partial to prison writers, but quality is the main concern. Should be criminal-justice-related. Humorous, mainstream and mystery. Send complete ms. Length: 5,000 or less.
Poetry: Uses mostly free verse with strong imagery. Needs approximately 20 poems/year.
Tips: "We deal with criminal-justice issues, so our eye is toward work in that area; nonfiction, especially, must pertain to some aspect of criminal justice. Poetry is open, but must be good."

‡**LETTERS FAMILY AFFAIRS**, Letters Magazine Inc., 310 Cedar Lane, Teaneck NJ 07666. (201)836-9177. Editor: Jackie Lewis. A "bimonthly erotic magazine" covering incest. "We are seeking first person sexual adventures that are erotic without being obscene and that sound real." Pays 1 month following month of acceptance. Byline given. Buys all rights. Submit seasonal/holiday material 6 months in advance. Computer printout submissions acceptable; no dot-matrix. SASE. Reports in 3 weeks. Sample copy $3; writer's guidelines free for SAE and 1 first class stamp.
Nonfiction: Book excerpts, historical/nostalgic and personal experience. First-person accounts only; no coercive sex. "No rape, adult/child in the present (incest), adult/child other or bestiality." Buys 40 mss/year. Send complete ms. Length: 1,800-2,200 words. Pays $100.

‡**LIVING ABROAD, A Publication for—and by—the World's Expatriate Population**, Living Abroad, 201 E. 36th St., New York NY 10016. (212)685-4023. Editor: Alison R. Lanier. Managing Editor: Robert F. Buck. Monthly newsletter with information relevant to Americans living and working outside the USA. "This is a working newsletter. We need facts, resources, addresses, and ideas that will help people stationed all over the world. We are not looking for descriptive, personal or 'inspirational' material." Estab. 1983. Pays on acceptance. Byline given. Buys one-time rights. "We don't want seasonal material." Previously published submissions OK. No queries. SASE. Reports in 2 months on mss. Sample copy for $1, business-size SAE, and 2 first class stamps; writer's guidelines for business-size SAE, and 1 first class stamp.
Nonfiction: "We only want material from expatriates or former expatriates covering information related to living or doing business abroad. No travel articles." Buys 12 mss/year. Send complete ms. Length: 100-300 words. Pays $25-50.
Columns/Departments: Living in Another Country (concrete advice about matters of relevance to expatriates—not country-specific, although such material may be used to illustrate points). Material should be of interest to anyone in any country (but ouside his/her own country). Send complete ms. Length: 200-300 words. Pays $25-50.
Tips: "We are looking for only 'experienced' information of real relevance to expatriates—solid, factual but readable and interesting."

LIVING SINGLE MAGAZINE, The Dispatch Printing Co., 40 S. 3rd St., Columbus OH 43215. (614)461-5575. Editor: Jim O'Connor. Managing Editor: Esther Fisher. 99% freelance written. Monthly magazine on all aspects of single life. Circ. 8,000. Pays on publication. Byline given. Buys one-time rights. Submit seasonal/holiday material 4 months in advance. Simultaneous queries, and photocopied and previously published submissions OK. Computer printout submissions acceptable; prefers letter-quality to dot-matrix. SASE. Reports in 2 months. Publishes ms an average of 2 months after acceptance. Sample copy $2; writer's guidelines for SAE and 1 first class stamp.
Nonfiction: General interest (all aspects of single life); how-to (home repair/decorating); interview/profile (single celebrity profiles); and travel (single travel). "No fiction, poetry, personal experience or non-researched articles." Buys 70 mss/year. Query with clips or send complete ms. Length: 2,000 words minimum. Pays $100 minimum.

‡**LOST GENERATION JOURNAL**, Lost Generation Journal Inc., Dept. of Journalism, Temple University, Route 1, Box 167D, St. James MO (314)265-8594. Editor: Dr. Thomas W. Wood Jr. Managing Editor: Deloris Wood. Magazine published 3 times/year covering American expatriates in Paris during the '20s. "We have just resumed publication with Vol. VII." Pays on publication. Byline given plus a 200-word biography and 1-column photo of author. Acquires first North American serial rights. Submit seasonal holiday material 6 months in advance. Simultaneous queries, and simultaneous and photocopied submissions OK "if we have first rights to material." SASE. Reports in 6 weeks on queries; 2 months on mss. Sample copy $4 (subscription, back issue and sample copy address: *LGJ*, Route 5, Box 134, Salem MO 65560); writer's guidelines for business-size envelope and 1 first class stamp.
Nonfiction: Expose (if research reveals what really happened to some aspect of the expatriate); historical/nostalgic (documentation for the historical presentation of the Paris expatriate—why he went, etc. "A nostalgic article about the life of an expatriate is great."); humor (if it relates to our young Americans in Paris during the '20s); interview/profile ("a well done indepth article on a survivor of the Paris '20s is our priority"); personal issues (if it relates/if the person was in Paris in the '20s); photo feature (old photos of expatriates); travel ("travel articles are welcome if they are about the means of travel used by the American to get to Paris and travel there in the 1920s"). Special issues include American artists in Paris during the '20s (Stephen Longstreet, Man Ray,

etc.); poets in Paris during the '20s (Ezra Pound, etc.); The Correspondent in Paris during the '20s (Ernest Hemingway, William L. Shirer, etc.); The Expatriate Musician, Student and Businesses in Paris during the '20s. We do not want boring pedantic lectures talking down to our readers or articles that assume that the readers have read all the works done, say, by Hemingway. We consider *LGJ* to be a place where a writer can start so prior publication is not necessary, but documentation of material is very important." Accepts 10-20 mss/year. Query or send complete ms. Length: 1,500-3,000 words. Pays in 3 contributor's copies (of issue in which article appears).

Photos: Send photos with query or ms if possible. Reviews b&w contact sheets, and 3x5, 4x6, 5x7 and 8x10 (cover) b&w prints. Captions, model release and identification of subjects required. Acquires one-time rights.

Columns/Departments: Between the Book Ends (books about or by Americans who started their careers in Paris between 1919 and 1939 and about places where they worked, like an American newspaper there or the embassy or American hospital). This will resume with Vol. VIII. Send complete ms. Length: 250-500 words. Pays in 2 contributor's copies.

Fiction: "Only fiction written by a survivor of the Paris '20s is used in *LGJ*. The reason *LGJ* was started was to capture and publish the works of the 'Lost Generation.' This section on fiction we hope would be nostalgic with the Paris they knew when they were there." Send complete ms. Length: varies (usually 3-5 double-spaced pages). Pays in 3 contributor's copies.

Poetry: Light verse and traditional. "We do not want to see poetry that does not have a theme of the American in Paris in the '20s." Submit maximum 12 poems. Length: 10-24 lines. Pays in 2 contributor's copies.

Fillers: Clippings. "We usually add drawings, but good fillers would be used if they related to the American in Paris in the '20s." Length: 4-12 lines. Pays in 1 contributor copy.

Tips: "Freelancers can best break in to our publication by telling a story about an American in Paris between 1919-1939 who started his/her career there. Tape record interview and keep a record of your research. Write clearly and make your expatriate come alive without using fiction. Query your idea to the editor and give enough information that he can be assured that you have a good character or topic. Nonfiction is most open to freelancers: features, historical/nostalgic, interview/profile and specials. We have three issues to put out this year and we are looking for interesting mss. We will do the artist in Paris first but the flow of material will determine what issue will be next. We are not interested in dull research papers. All research must be footnoted MLA style. Hemingway is always something our readers are interested in reading about if they read it in *LGJ* first."

‡**MODERN SINGLES, Canada's Magazine for Single People**, Modern Singles, Box 213, Station W, Toronto, Ontario M6M 4Z2 Canada. Editor: O. Slembeck. 90% freelance written. Bimonthly magazine. Estab. 1984. Pays on acceptance. No byline given. Buys first North American serial rights and second rights to the same material. Submit seasonal/holiday material 2 months in advance. Photocopied submissions OK. Computer submissions acceptable; prefers letter-quality to dot-matrix. SAE and IRC. Publishes ms an average of 3 months after acceptance. Sample copy for $3.50 and SAE; free writer's guidelines.

Nonfiction: General interest; how-to (e.g., overcome loneliness, establish new relationships, develop new interests and hobbies); humor; personal experience; travel; and articles on finance management and singles life from psychological point of view. Buys 60 mss/year. Send complete ms. Length: 1,000-2,000 words. Pays $100-400.

Fiction: Adventure, erotica, ethnic, experimental, humorous and romance. Buys 30 mss/year. Send complete ms. Length: 1,000-2,000 words. Pays $50-200.

Fillers: Anecdotes and short humor. Buys 20/year. Length: 300-600 words. Pays $30-60.

Tips: "All areas of our publication are open for freelancers."

THE MOTHER EARTH NEWS, Box 70, Hendersonville NC 28791. (704)693-0211. Editor: Bruce Woods. Bimonthly magazine. Emphasizes "back-to-the-land self-sufficiency for the growing number of individuals who seek a more rational self-directed way of life." Circ. 1,000,000. Pays on acceptance. "We buy all rights. However, after publication of our edited version, the rights to your original material may be reassigned to you. Then you may resell the unedited version as many times as you like." Byline given. Submit seasonal/holiday material 5 months in advance. Simultaneous, photocopied and previously published submissions OK if so indicated. Computer printout submissions acceptable; no dot-matrix. No handwritten manuscripts. SASE. Reports within 3 months. Publishes ms an average of 1 year after acceptance. Sample copy $3; free writer's guidelines.

Nonfiction: Roselyn Edwards, submissions editor. How-to, home business, alternative energy systems, low cost—$100 and up—housing, energy-efficient structures, seasonal cooking, gardening and crafts. Buys 300-350 mss/year. Query or send complete ms. "A short, to-the-point paragraph is often enough. If it's a subject we don't need at all, we can answer immediately. If it tickles our imagination, we'll ask to take a look at the whole piece. No phone queries, please." Length: 300-3,000 words. Pays $100/minimum/published page.

Photos: Purchased with accompanying ms. Captions and credits required. Send prints or transparencies. Uses 8x10 b&w glossies; any size color transparencies. Include type of film, speed and lighting used. Total purchase price for ms includes payment for photos.

Columns/Departments: "Contributions to Mother's Down-Home Country Lore and Barters and Bootstraps are paid by subscription. Profiles pays $25-50."

Fillers: Short how-to's on any subject normally covered by the magazine. Query. Length: 150-300 words. Pays $7.50-25.

Tips: "Probably the best way to break in is to study our magazine, digest our writer's guidelines, and send us a concise article illustrated with color transparencies that we can't resist. We want articles that tell what real people are doing to take charge of their own lives. Articles should be well-documented and tightly written treatments of topics we haven't already covered. We're not set up to handle queries by phone."

‡**THE MOUNTAIN LAUREL, Monthly Journal of Mountain Life,** Laurel Publications, Rt. 1, Meadows of Dan VA 24120. (703)593-3613. Editor: Susan Thigpen. Managing Editor: Bob Heafner. Tabloid devoted to an "appreciation of mountain heritage. We tell of the everyday life history, traditions and tales of the Blue Ridge Mountains. Half of our readers are in Virginia; the other half are in all remaining states (including Alaska, Hawaii, Puerto Rico), and Canada." Estab. 1983. Circ. 25,000. Pays in copies. Byline given. Acquires one-time rights. Submit seasonal/holiday material 4 months in advance. Simultaneous, photocopied, and previously published submissions "at times, not often" OK. Computer printout submissions acceptable; no dot-matrix. SASE. Reports in 3 weeks. Free sample copy.

Nonfiction: Book excerpts (about the Blue Ridge); historical/nostalgic; humor; interview/profile; personal experience (especially of older persons). "We like stories on a personal slant covering a specific aspect, not broad, general stories." Send complete ms. Length: 2,000 words maximum. "As we are still a new publication, we aren't at a point of paying our contributors. We hope to be able to do so within a year. We do give a full byline and will list books by the contributor and where they may be purchased."

Photos: Send photos with accompanying ms; photos will be returned. Reviews b&w prints. Model release and identification of subjects required. Also uses captioned old photos.

Fiction: Adventure, historical, humorous, and novel excerpts. "*No* erotica or horror; no stereotyped 'Hillbilly' stuff—real mountain people are smart." Send complete ms. Length: 2,000 words maximum.

Poetry: Traditional "down to earth." Accepts 0-1 poem/issue. Submit maximum 10 poems. Length: 20 words maximum.

Fillers: Short humor.

Tips: "Write in a down-to-earth (but no bad language, please) way, as if you were telling a story verbally. Shorter articles usually stand a better chance. We print many first articles by new writers. We like stories with honest sentiment in them."

NEW AGE JOURNAL, Rising Star Associates, Ltd., Parnership, 342 Western Ave., Brighten MA 02135. (617)787-2005. Editor: Marc Barasch. Managing Editor: Dee Allen. Monthly magazine covering alternative ideas and focusing on "what individuals can do to help solve the problems of the modern world." Circ. 68,000. Pays on publication. Byline given. Offers 25% kill fee. Buys one-time rights, first rights and second serial (reprint) rights, and makes work-for-hire assignments. Submit seasonal/holiday material 3 months in advance. Photocopied and previously published submissions OK. Computer printout submission acceptable; no dot-matrix. SASE. Reports in 6 weeks. Sample copy $2; writer's guidelines for business-size SAE and 1 first class stamp.

Nonfiction: Address queries to Articles Editor. "Interested in creative alternatives, solid investigative journalism, how-to; interview/profile (of people doing positive things in the world); personal experience; and some photo essays. Special issues include biannual book supplements and quarterly seasonal guides. Buys 60 mss/year. Query with clips of published work or send complete ms. Length: 500-7,000 words. Pays 15¢/word for items, $100-$300 for columns, up to $1,000 for cover stories.

Photos: Hans Teensma, design director. Send photos with ms. Pays $25-75 for 8x10 b&w prints and contact sheets; $75-200 for 35mm color transparencies. Captions and identification of subjects required.

Columns/Departments: Address inquiries: columns editor. Book and film reviews (100-500 words), energy, politics, spirituality, family, humor, profiles, opinion, personal experience. Buys 60 mss/year. Query with clips of published work or send complete ms. Length: 500-1,500 words. Pays $25-300.

Fiction: Address inquiries: fiction editor. Experimental, fantasy, humorous, novel excerpts and "new age" slant. Buys 6 mss/year. Send complete ms. Length: 1,200-4,000 words. Pays 10¢/word.

Poetry: Address inquiries: poetry editor. Avant-garde, free verse, and haiku. Buys 12/year. Submit maximum 4 poems. Length: 6-15 lines. Pays $15-30.

‡**NORTH DAKOTA REC,** North Dakota Association of Rural Electric Cooperatives, Box 727, Mandan ND 58554. (701)663-6501. Editor: Leland Ulmer. Managing Editor: Dennis Hill. Monthly magazine. "We cover the rural electric program, primarily funded through the Rural Electrification Administration, and the changes the REA program brought to rural North Dakota. Our focus is on the member/owners of North Dakota's 21 rural electric cooperatives, and we try to report each subject through the eyes of our members." Circ. 75,000. Pays on acceptance. Byline given. Offers one-third of agreed price as kill fee. Buys first North American serial rights. Submit seasonal/holiday material 3-5 months in advance. Simultaneous queries and photocopied submissions OK. Computer printout submissions acceptable; prefers letter-quality to dot-matrix. SASE. Reports in 2 weeks on queries; 2 months on mss. Sample copy for 9x12 SAE and $1.39 postage; free writer's guidelines.

Nonfiction: General interest (changes in ND agriculture); historical/nostalgic (on changes REA brought to country); how-to (on efficient use of electricity); and interview/profile (on notable North Dakota rural leaders). Special issues include 50th anniversary issue of REA in May/June 1985. No articles that do not show inpact/benefit/applicability to rural North Dakotans. Buys 12-15 mss/year. Query. Length: 400-2,000 words. Pays $35-200.

Photos: State availability of photos with query letter or ms. Pays $2.50-5 for b&w contact sheet; $25 maximum for 35mm color transparencies. Captions required. Buys one-time rights.

Fiction: Historical. Buys 2-3 mss/year. Query. Length: 400-1,200 words. Pays $35-150.

Poetry: JoAnn Wimstorfer, family editor. Buys 2-4 poems/year. Submit maximum 8 poems. Pays $5-50.

Tips: "Write about a North Dakotan—one of our members who has done something notable in the ag/energy/rural electric/rural lifestyle areas. Also needs energy efficiency articles on North Dakotans who make wise use of rural electric power."

THE PYRAMID, The national Newsletter for the National Association for Widowed People, Inc., Box 3564, Springfield IL 62708. (217)522-4300. Editor/Publisher: D.L. Doering. Quarterly National newsletter for members of the N.A.W.P., widowed people, professional corporations, colleges, universities and persons that service the widowed person, as well as interested community groups or organizations. Circ. 70,000. Pays on publication. Byline given. Buys second serial (reprint) rights. Submit seasonal/holiday material 2 months in advance. Photocopied and previously published submissions OK. SASE. Reports in 2 months. Sample copy $1; free writer's guidelines.

Columns/Departments: Health, insurance, investments, social security, Veterans Administration, Government, personal glimpse, cooking, inspiration and psychic. Buys 9 mss/year. Send complete ms. Length: 500-1,500 words. Pays $30-300.

Poetry: Nothing on married persons or twos; we are dealing with widowed people. Buys 9 poems/year. Submit maximum 2 poems. Length: 100 lines maximum. Pays $5-75.

Fillers: Anecdotes, short humor, newsbreaks and cartoons. Buys 9 mss/year. Length: 50-1,000 words. Pays $5-50.

RADICAL AMERICA, Alternative Education Project, Inc., #14, 38 Union Square, Somerville MA 02143. (617)628-6585. Editor: John P. Demeter. Managing Editor: Donna Penn. 35% freelance written. Bimonthly political journal of radical history, socialism, feminism, and community and workplace organizing; cultural analysis and commentary. "*RA* is a popularly written, nonacademic journal aimed at feminists, political activists and left academics written from socialist (independent) and feminist perspectives." Circ. 5,000. Pays in copies. Byline given. Buys all rights. Submit seasonal/holiday material 3 months in advance. Simultaneous queries and simultaneous, photocopied and previously published submissions OK. Computer printout submissions acceptable; no dot-matrix. SASE. Reports in 2 weeks on queries; 1 month on mss. Publishes ms an average of 6 months after acceptance. Sample copy $2; free writer's guidelines.

Nonfiction: James Stark, articles editor. Political opinion and history. No strictly journalistic accounts without analysis or commentary. Query with published clips. Length: 2,000-7,000 words. Pays in copies.

Photos: Phyllis Ewen, photo editor. State availability of photos. Pays $5-10 for b&w contact sheet. Captions and identification of subjects required. Buys one-time rights.

Poetry: J.S. Smutt, poetry editor. Avant-garde and free verse. No poetry without political or social theme. Length: 10-50 lines.

REINCARNATION REPORT, Sutphen Corp., Box 2010, Malibu CA 90265. (213)456-3934. Editor: Alan Vaughan. Associate Editor: Sharon Boyd. Monthly magazine dealing with reincarnation, and life-after-death studies. Circ. 25,000. Pays on publication. Byline given. Buys first North American serial rights. Simultaneous queries and photocopied submissions OK. Computer printout submissions acceptable. SASE. Reports in 4 weeks on queries and mss. Sample copy for 8½x11 SAE and 5 first class stamps; writer's guidelines for SASE.

Nonfiction: Book excerpts (on reincarnation and life after death); and personal experience (verifiable experiences of reincarnation). "We are looking for personal experiences that change your viewpoint or have a karmic lesson. Keep the story simple. If some facts are boring, leave them out. Give the evidence that what you say is true. Don't be literary—be direct. Either charm the readers with your warm, personal and fast-paced story or shock them. Give them something to think about. If your story changed you, communicate that emotional experience so that readers can join in the excitement. We draw material from personal experiences, scientific experiments, hypnotic regression research, or anything that convinces us that you have a good point and can back it up." No esoteric, technical or theoretical material: "Tell us your stories, not your theories." No material on other psychic subjects. Buys 48 mss/year. Query. Length: 1,000-3,000 words. Pays $75-150.

Photos: State availability of photos. Pays $5-25 for 5x7 b&w prints. Captions and identification of subjects required. Buys one-time rights; all rights if assigned.

Columns/Departments: Why I Believe. "We want personal accounts of experiences that led a person to believe in reincarnation or other after-life states." Buys 24 mss/year. Send complete ms. Length: 500-800 words. Writers receive a T-shirt or tape.

Tips: "Start with your personal story of reincarnation, or someone you know. We're looking for facts, controversy and scientific authority. Try a story on a past-life researcher in your town. Don't tell us why you think you were Joan of Arc. We're eager to print new writers with good stories and facts to back them. But there *must* be a tie-in with reincarnation or survival."

‡**THE ROBB REPORT**, Box 4071, Acton MA 01720. (617)263-7711. Editor: M.M. Winthrop. 100% freelance written. Monthly magazine covering leisure interests of the wealthy. Circ. 50,000. Pays 45 days after acceptance. Byline given. Buys all rights. Submit seasonal/holiday material 6 months in advance. Simultaneous queries and previously published submissions OK. Computer printout submissions acceptable. SASE. Reports in 1 week on queries; 2 weeks on mss. Publishes ms an average of 4 months after acceptance. Sample copy $5; writer's guidelines for business-size SAE.
Nonfiction: Book excerpts, expose, interview/profile, personal experience (travel), and travel. "Articles are usually focused in the following areas: automobiles, interiors/living, collectibles, travel, investments, fashion, wine and liquors, food and dining, and boating. These articles must be useful and informative to the reader, enabling him to make intelligent action choices with his high level of disposable income." Buys 84 mss/year. Query. Length: 2,500-3,500 words. Pays $600-750.
Tips: "The magazine requires sprightly writing—writing which grabs and holds the attention of the reader throughout the length of the piece. This sprightliness will derive not so much from adjectives as from verbs and from turns of the phrase."

ROOM OF ONE'S OWN, A Feminist Journal of Literature & Criticism, Growing Room Collective, Box 46160, Station G, Vancouver, British Columbia V6R 4G5 Canada. Editors: Gayla Reid, Pat Robertson, Mary Schendlinger, Eleanor Wachtel, Jeannie Wexler, Jean Wilson. 100% freelance written. Quarterly magazine of original fiction, poetry, literary criticism, and reviews of feminist concern. Circ 1,200. Pays on publication. Byline given. Buys first rights only. Photocopied submissions OK. Computer printout submissions acceptable "if readable and not in all caps"; prefers letter-quality to dot-matrix. SASE. Reports in 2 months. Publishes ms an average of 6 weeks after acceptance. Sample copy $2.75.
Nonfiction: Interview/profile (of authors) and literary criticism. Buys 8 mss/year. Send complete ms. Length: 1,500-6,000 words. Pays $25.
Fiction: "Quality short stories by women with a feminist outlook. Not interested in fiction written by men." Buys 12 mss/year. Send complete ms. Length: 1,500-6,000 words. Pays $25.
Poetry: Avant-garde, eclectic free verse and haiku. "Not interested in poetry from men." Buys 32/year. Submit maximum 10 poems. Length: open. Pays $10-25.

‡**SIMPLY LIVING**, Otter Publications Pty/Ltd., 53 Sydney Road, Manly, N.S.W. 2095, Australia. (02)977-8566. Editor: Robert Swan. Managing Editor: Verna Simpson. Quarterly magazine covering the environment and anti-nuclear, spiritual and natural health topics. Circ. 50,000. Pays on publication. Byline given. Buys first rights. Submit seasonal/holiday material 4 months in advance. Simultaneous queries, and previously published submissions OK. Computer printout submissions acceptable. SASE. Reports in 1 month. Sample copy and writer's guidelines for $3.95 (Australian) and 8½x11½ SAE.
Nonfiction: Expose (environmental); how-to (environmental, spiritual); humor; interview/profile; new product (energy conservation) and photo feature (natural portrait). No "hippy mysticism." Buys 20 mss/year. Query with published clips. Length: 1,000-5,000 words. Pays $100/1,000 words.
Photos: Jo Gange, photo editor. Send photos with query. Pays $80-200/page for color transparencies. Captions, model release and identification of subjects required. Buys one-time rights.
Fiction: Chris Mooney and Rob Swan, fiction editors. Adventure, fantasy, humorous, religious/spiritual, and fiction on environmental, animal and anti-nuclear issues. Buys 4 mss/year. Length: 1,500-2,000 words. Pays $100/1,000 words.
Poetry: Avant-garde, free-verse, haiku, light verse and traditional. Buys 8 poems/year. Submit maximum 1 poem. Pays $30-50.
Tips: "A freelancer can break in to our publication with a soft approach, new angle and commitment to philosophy."

SINGLELIFE (MILWAUKEE) MAGAZINE, SingleLife Enterprises, Inc., 3846 W. Wisconsin Ave., Milwaukee WI 53208. (414)933-9700. Editor: Gail Rose. 70% freelance written. Bimonthly magazine covering singles lifestyles. Circ. 15,000. Pays on publication. Byline given. Buys all rights. Submit seasonal/holiday material 3 months in advance. Simultaneous queries, and photocopied and previously published submissions OK. Computer printout submissions acceptable. SASE. Reports in 3 months. Publishes ms an average of 4 months after acceptance. Sample copy $2; writer's guidelines for business-size SAE and 1 first class stamp.
Nonfiction: Leifa Butrick, articles editor. Book excerpts, general interest, how-to, humor, opinion, photo feature and travel. Buys 25 mss/year. Query with published clips or send complete ms. Length: 1,000-2,500 words. Pays $25-100.
Photos: Art director. Send photos with query or ms. Pays $10-100 for b&w contact sheet, 2¼" transparencies

and 8x10 prints; pays $20-200 for 2¼" color transparencies and 8x10 prints. Captions, model release and identification of subjects required.

Columns/Departments: Leifa Butrick, column/department editor. Film and record reviews; book reviews; humor (situational with singles emphasis); single parenting column; travel; Quips & Quotes (news briefs); legal and health. Buys 30 mss/year. Send complete ms. Length: 800-2,000 words. Pays $25-100.

Poetry: Leifa Butrick, poetry editor. Avant-garde, free verse, haiku, light verse and traditional. Buys 10/year. Submit any number of poems. Length: open. Pays $10-100.

Fillers: Clippings and cartoons. Buys 10/year. Length: 100 words minimum. Pays $10.

Tips: Currently looking for someone to write a single parents column. "We are expanding in the Chicago area and are looking for writers familiar with Chicago nightlife and the singles scene."

‡**STALLION MAGAZINE, The Magazine of the Alternate Lifestyle**, Charlton Publications, 351 W. 54th St., New York NY 10019. (212)586-4432. Editor: Jerry Douglas. 75% freelance written. A monthly magazine for the gay community. Text includes articles and fiction for gay males; pictorially, male nudes. Circ. 80,000. Pays on publication. Byline given. Buys first North American serial rights. Submit seasonal/holiday material 6 months in advance. Simultaneous queries and simultaneous and photocopied submissions OK; rarely accepts previously published submissions. Computer printout submissions acceptable; no dot-matrix. SASE. Reports in 3-4 months on mss. Publishes ms an average of 4 months after acceptance. Free writer's guidelines.

Nonfiction: Book excerpts, expose, general interest, historical/nostalgic, inspirational, interview/profile, opinion, personal experience and photo feature. "We publish one piece of fiction in each issue, and while we certainly do not avoid erotic content in the stories, the work must have some other quality besides sexual heat. In other words, we are not looking for 'stroke pose' per se. We have accepted a wide range of fiction pieces, the only common denominator being that the work deal with some aspect of the gay experience." Buys 12 fiction/ 36 nonfiction mss/year. Send complete ms. Length: 2,000-3,000 words. Pays $200.

Tips: "Although the visual content of the magazine is strictly erotic, the textual content is not, and we seek articles and fiction of interest to the gay community, beyond the strictly erotic. We are more interested in articles than fiction."

SURVIVAL GUIDE, McMullen Publishing, Inc., 2145 W. La Palma Ave., Anaheim CA 92801. (714)635-9040. Editor: Dave Epperson. Associate Editor: Christine Miller. 50% freelance written. Monthly magazine covering "self-reliance, defense, meeting day-to-day threats—survivalism for survivalists." Circ. 92,000. Pays on publication. Byline given. Offers 50% kill fee. Not copyrighted. Buys first North American serial rights. Submit seasonal/holiday material 5 months in advance. Computer printout submissions acceptable; prefers letter-quality to dot-matrix. SASE. Reports in 3 weeks. Publishes ms an average of up to 2 years after acceptance. Sample copy $2.50; writer's guidelines for SAE.

Nonfiction: Expose (political); how-to; interview/profile; personal experience (how I survived); photo feature (equipment and techniques related to survival in all possible situations); emergency medical; food preservation; water purification; stealth tactics; self-defense; nutrition; tools; shelter; etc. "No general articles about how to survive. We want specifics and single subjects." Buys 60-100 mss/year. Query or send complete ms. Length: 1,500-4,000 words. Pays $125-400.

Photos: Send photos with ms. Pays $5-75 for b&w contact sheet or negatives; $20-100 for 35mm color transparencies or 8x10 b&w prints. Captions, model release and identification of subjects required. Buys all rights.

Tips: "We will be dealing more with weaponry, tactics, urban survival and nuclear considerations than with food preservation, food storage, water purification and like matters. Know and appreciate the survivalist movement. Prepare material of relevant value to individuals who wish to sustain human life no matter what the circumstance. This magazine is a text and reference."

SURVIVE, Survive Publications, Inc., Box 693, Boulder CO 80306. (303)449-2064. Editor/Publisher: Robert K. Brown. Executive Editor: John Metzger. Monthly magazine presenting material that is essential to survivalists. *Survive* informs and instructs readers in the survival arts and prepares them for "The Day After." Circ. 80,000. Pays on publication. Byline given. Offers 25% of word count kill fee. Buys first North American serial rights and makes work-for-hire assignments. Submit seasonal/holiday material 5 months in advance. Electronic submissions OK on Telex 450129, answer back on Omega News, BDR. Computer printout submissions acceptable. SASE. Reports in 2 months. Publishes ms an average of 4 months after acceptance. Sample copy $2.50; writer's guidelines for business-size SAE and 20¢ postage.

Nonfiction: How-to (self-reliance, survival); weapons; new product; and technical. Features include nuclear survival, survival weapons and survival foods. Buys 50 or more mss/year. Query. Length: 2,000-2,500 words. Pays $175-1,000.

Photos: State availability of photos. Captions, model release and identification of subjects required. Buys one-time rights.

Tips: "Feature articles should have highly technical data, charts and graphs boxed as sidebars. Informative articles should be lively, interesting and relevant. Freelance writers should be aware of heavier competition in special interest publications. Freelancers should write a story that will help an editor sell magazines."

‡**TAT JOURNAL**, Box 236, Bellaire OH 43906. Editor: Mark Jaqua. 75% freelance written. Annual magazine for all interested in esoteric philosophy, parapsychology, poetry, astrology, esoteric psychology and holistic health. Circ. 3,000. Pays in copies. Publishes ms an average of 9 months after acceptance. Returns copyright to author after publication. Simultaneous, photocopied and previously published submissions OK. Computer printout submissions acceptable. SASE. Reports in 2 weeks. Sample copy $3; free writer's guidelines.
Nonfiction: Expose (occult rip-offs, cults and spiritual gimmicks); how-to (psychological self-change techniques); opinion; personal experience (new insights into the unsolved mysteries of the universe); and Forum (short philosophic pieces from a personal viewpoint). "No articles that proselytize a fanatical belief." Accepts 15 mss/issue. Send complete ms. Length: 300-10,000 words. Pays in copies.
Tips: "We want material that stimulates the reader's curiosity, allowing him to come to his own conclusions; a more psychological bent as opposed to 'New Age' or occult."

TELEWOMAN, A Women's Newsletter, Telewoman, Inc., Box 2306, Pleasant Hill CA 94523. Editor: Anne J. D'Arcy. 100% freelance written. Monthly networking newsletter covering women's networking resources, literary/art/photography resources and connections for a lesbian and "woman-identified" readership. Circ. 500. Pays in copies. Not copyrighted. Simultaneous queries and simultaneous, photocopied and previously published submissions OK. Computer printout submissions acceptable. SASE. Reports in 2 weeks on queries; 1 month on mss. Publishes ms an average of 2 months after acceptance. Sample copy for $1, business-size SAE and 2 first class stamps.
Nonfiction: Book excerpts, interview/profile, personal experience, photo feature and reviews. No erotic material, political material or separatist slant. Send complete ms. Length: 500 words on reviews; 3,000 on spotlights, novel excerpts.
Photos: Reviews b&w prints.
Fiction: Novel excerpts; religious (women's spirituality); lesbian romance; and serialized lesbian novels. No erotic material.
Poetry: Avant-garde, free verse, haiku, light verse and traditional. No separatist, political, erotic content. Buys 60 poems/year. Submit unlimited poems with SASE. Length: 25 lines maximum. Pays in contributor's copies.
Tips: Most open to poetry, book reviews and music reviews. "We provide books and records for book and record reviews."

TORSO, Varsity Communications, 225 Lafayette St., New York NY 10012. (212)966-3656. Editor: Chris Volker. A monthly magazine for gay men. "Divergent viewpoints are expressed in both feature articles and fiction, which examine values and behavior patterns characteristic of a gay lifestyle. *Torso* has a continuing commitment to well-documented investigative journalism in areas pertaining to the lives and well-being of homosexuals." Estab. 1982. Circ. 60,000. Pays on publication. Byline given. Offers $50 kill fee. Buys first North American serial rights. Submit seasonal/holiday material 3 months in advance. Simultaneous queries, and simultaneous and photocopied submissions OK. SASE. Reports in 2 weeks on queries; 1 month on mss. Sample copy $5; writer's guidelines for business-size SAE.
Nonfiction: Expose, general interest, humor, interview/profile, opinion, personal experience, photo feature, and travel. "The tone must be positive regarding the gay experience." Buys 12 mss/year. Query with or without published clips, or send complete ms (typewritten and double-spaced). Length: 2,000-4,000 words. Pays $100-200.
Fiction: Adventure, erotica, fantasy, humorous, novel excerpts, and romance. No long, drawn out fiction with no form, etc. Buys 35 mss/year. Query with or without published clips, or send complete ms. Length: 2,000-4,000 words. Pays $100-150.
Tips: "Write about what is happening—what, you as a gay male (if you are) would care to read."

THE UNSPEAKABLE VISIONS OF THE INDIVIDUAL INC., Box 439, California PA 15419. Editors-in-Chief: Arthur Winfield Knight, Kit Knight. 50% freelance written. For "an adult audience, generally college-educated (or substantial self-education) with an interest in Beat (generation) writing." Annual magazine/book. Circ. 2,000. Payment (if made) on acceptance. Buys first North American serial rights. Computer printout submissions acceptable; no dot-matrix. Reports in 2 months. Publishes ms an average of 6 months after acceptance. Sample copy $3.
Nonfiction: Interviews (with Beat writers), personal experience and photo feature. "Know who the Beat writers are—Jack Keronac, Allen Ginserg, William S. Burroughs, etc." Uses 20 mss/year. Query or submit complete ms. Length: 300-15,000 words. Pays 2 copies, "sometimes a small cash payment, i.e., $10."
Photos: Used with or without ms or on assignment. Captions required. Send prints. Pays 2 copies to $10 for 8x10 b&w glossies. Uses 40-50/year.
Fiction: Uses 10 mss/year. Submit complete ms. Pays 2 copies to $10.
Poetry: Avant-garde, free verse and traditional. Uses 10/year. Limit submissions to batches of 10. Length: 100 lines maximum. Pays 2 copies to $10.

USA Singles, Inc. National Network System, Suite 101, 4100 Southern Blvd. NWS, Rio Rancho NM 87124. (505)892-5212. Editor: Jean Jordan. 90% freelance written. "The USA Singles, Inc. National Network System consists of monthly tabloid-type magazines published in various cities throughout the country. Each magazine is locally owned but published under the USA Single trade name using the USA Singles National Network System's general layout and format design plus a required number of nonfiction and fiction articles that are furnished by the national office. Our magazines are aimed at the entire single adult marketplace of each city. Readers are generally of above-average intelligence, income and education. Circulation varies from city to city; usually 20,000-60,000. Pays 8¢/word about 3-4 weeks following publication. Byline and photo credits given. Buys first North American serial rights. Submit seasonal/holiday material 4 months in advance. No simultaneous queries or previously published submissions. Computer printout submissions acceptable "if done in upper and lower case (*not* all caps) and in dark print"; prefers letter-quality to dot-matrix. Query or send complete ms with SASE. Prefers typed query letter outlining article and estimating word count. Reports in 1 month. Publishes ms an average of 6 months after acceptance. Writer's guidelines available with business-size SASE; sample copy of magazine with large, clasp SASE ($1 postage).

Nonfiction and Fiction: "We're looking for articles and fiction with a national approach that deal with every aspect of single living. We are NOT a 'swingers' magazine and will not accept articles of that nature. Subject matter may include interpersonal relationships, coping (with divorce, widowhood, a broken affair, loneliness, jealousy, etc.), self-improvement, real estate, financial matters, health and fitness, single parenting, romance, human sexuality, nutrition, sports, travel, senior singles, New Age topics, etc. Other possible topics are legal aspects of singlehood (such as laws governing sex, cohabitation, taxes, insurance needs, etc.); the social aspects of being single (dating, communication, changes in men's and women's roles and attitudes, getting along in a world still geared toward couples, etc.); career management; tips on how to manage 'on your own'; and general upbeat articles on positive attitudes (the science of happiness, humorous anecdotes on the life of a single, etc.). We use some articles written from a strictly personal point of view, but in general we prefer material that combines personal experience/observation with quotes/anecdotes from knowledgeable sources/experts and facts/research." Length: ½ page (650-900 words); ¾ page (950-1,200); full page (1,350-1,600); special 1½-page feature (1,600-2,500). Note size/word length of story in upper right-hand corner of first page when submitting manuscript.

Photos: State availability of photos. Photos purchased with or without ms. Cover shots must be color transparencies. " We want expressive-looking, story related or seasonal, innovative shots." Pays $15 minimum for 5x7 or 8x10 b&w prints and contact sheet; $100-125 for cover photo. Model release and identification of subjects required.

Tips: "We're rapidly expanding our network system to publish *USA Singles* in cities all over the country. We need 'national' stories that could be used in any of the *USA Singles* magazines. Material with a local slant should be queried through individual city publication (i.e., *Houston Singles Magazine*, *El Paso Singles Magazine*, etc.)."

VEGETARIAN TIMES, Box 570, Oak Park IL 60303. (312)848-8120. Editor: Paul Barrett Obis Jr. 50% freelance written. Monthly magazine. Circ. 150,000. Rights purchased vary with author and material. Buys first serial or all rights ("always includes right to use article in our books or 'Best of' series"). Byline given unless extensive revisions are required or material is incorporated into a larger article. Buys 120 mss/year. Pays on publication. Photocopied and simultaneous submissions OK. Computer printout submissions acceptable. Submit seasonal material 6 months in advance. Reports in 1 month. Publishes ms an average of 4 months after acceptance. Query. SASE. Sample copy $2.

Nonfiction: Features concise articles related to vegetarian cooking, health foods and articles about vegetarians. "All material should be well documented and researched. It would probably be best to see a sample copy." Informational, how-to, experience, interview, profile, historical, successful health food business operations and restaurant reviews. Length: average 1,500 words. Pays 5¢/word minimum. Will also use 500- to 1,000-word items for regular columns.

Photos: Pays $15 for b&w photos; $50 for color; b&w ferrotype preferred.

Tips: "The worst thing about freelance writers is that everybody who can type thinks they are a writer. And the less experience a writer has the more he/she hates editing. Some novices scream bloody murder when you delete their paragraphs or add words to make the copy flow better. They also think we editors have nothing to do all day but critique their article. Many writers have broken into print in our magazine." Write query with "brevity and clarity."

‡**WARRIORS, Self Defense and Survival Today**, Condor Books, Inc., 351 E. 54th St., New York NY 10019. (212)586-4432. Editor: Al Weiss. Managing Editor: Alan Paul. A bimonthly magazine covering self defense, survival, weaponry, mercenary activity, martial arts, and police and anti-crime subjects. Circ. 35,000. Pays a few weeks before publication. Byline given. Offers negotiable kill fee. Buys one-time rights. Submit seasonal/holiday material 4 months in advance. Previously published submissions OK. Computer printout submissions acceptable. SASE. Reports in 1 month. Sample copy for $2 and 85¢ postage, writer's guidelines for SAE and 1 first class stamp.

Nonfiction: Herman Petras, articles editor and David Weiss, assistant editor. Book excerpts, exposé, historical, how-to, interview/profile, new product, personal experience, photo feature and technical. Special issues include NINJA (assassins of Japan) and Survival Guide. Buys 40-50 mss/year. Send complete ms. Pays $125-200.

Photos: Bob Weiss, photo editor. Send photos with accompanying query or mss. Pays $5-50 for 8x10 b&w prints; $50-150 for 35mm color slides. Captions, model release and identification of subjects required.

Columns/Departments: David Weiss, column/department editor. Warriors, World (news, unusual items, humorous items); and Tools of the Trade (new products). Buys 50 mss/year. Send complete ms. Length: 50-250 words. Pays $10-50.

Tips: "Submit well-written pieces on subjects of interest to our readers, and include exciting, professional photos. Or submit a query letter on a proposed piece. Be exciting, make a point, don't overembellish! About 90% of all articles in *Warriors* are freelance."

THE WASHINGTON BLADE, Washington Blade, Inc., Suite 315, 930 F St. NW, Washington DC 20004. (202)347-2038. Managing Editor: Lisa M. Keen. 10% freelance written. Weekly tabloid covering the gay/lesbian community. Articles (subjects) should be written from or directed to a gay perspective." Circ. 20,000. Pays in 30 days. Byline given. Pays $15 kill fee. Buys first North American serial rights. Submit seasonal/holiday material 1 month in advance. Photocopied submissions OK. SASE. Reports in 1 month. Publishes ms an average of 1 month after acceptance. Free sample copy and writer's guidelines.

Nonfiction: Expose (of government, private agency, church, etc., handling of gay-related issues); historical/nostalgic; interview/profile (of gay community/political leaders; persons, gay or non-gay, in positions to affect gay issues; outstanding achievers who happen to be gay; those who incorporate the gay lifestyle into their professions); photo feature (on a nationally or internationally historic gay event); and travel (on locales that welcome or cater to the gay traveler). *The Washington Blade* basically covers two areas: news and lifestyle. News coverage of DC area gay community, local and federal government actions relating to gays, some national news of interest to gays. Section also includes features on current events. Greatest opportunity for freelancers resides in current events, features, interviews and book reviews. Special issues include: Annual gay pride issue (early June). No sexually explicit material. Buys 30 mss/year, average. Query with clips of published work. Length: 500-1,500 words. Pays 5-10¢/word.

Photos: "A photo or graphic with feature/lifestyle articles is particularly important. Photos with news stories are appreciated." State availability of photos. Reviews b&w contact sheets. Pays $15 minimum for 5x7 b&w glossy prints. Captions preferred. Model releases required. On assignment, photographer paid mutually agreed upon fee, with expenses reimbursed. Publication retains all rights.

Tips: "The most annoying aspect of working with freelance writers is getting freelancers to accept and become motivated by story ideas other than their own."

WOMEN'S RIGHTS LAW REPORTER, 15 Washington St., Newark NJ 07102. (201)648-5320. Legal journal emphasizing law and feminism for lawyers, students and feminists. Quarterly magazine. Circ. 1,300. No payment. Acquires all rights. SASE. Sample copy $5 individuals; $9 institutions.

Nonfiction: Historical and legal articles. Query or submit complete ms with published clips and education data. Length: 20-100 pages plus footnotes.

WOODSMOKE, Highland Publishing Co., Box 474, Centerville UT 84014. Editor: Richard Jamison. 60% freelance written. Quarterly magazine covering survival, aboriginal lifestyles, and primitive living for people of all ages who have an outdoor interest. Circ. 1,500. Pays on publication. Buys one-time and second rights to the same material. Byline given. Submit seasonal/holiday material 2 months in advance. Photocopied and previously published submissions OK. Computer printout submissions acceptable. SASE. Reports in 2 months. Publishes ms an average of 8 months after acceptance. Sample copy $1.

Nonfiction: Historical (on pioneer and Indian historical trips and hardships); how-to (on self-sufficiency theme, primitive skills, etc.); and personal experience (how-to and interesting experiences in the outdoors, true survival experiences). "We do not want any *researched* articles on edible plants or herbal medicines. Actual experiences OK. No cute stories on animals, cooking dandelions or stupid jokes." Buys 10-14 unsolicited mss/year. Send complete ms or query with SASE. Length: 500-2,000 words. Pays 2¢/word.

Photos: State availability of photos with ms. Offers no additional payment for photos accepted with ms. Uses only b&w prints. Captions preferred.

Columns/Departments: Wild and Free (wild edible plants and herbs); Recipe Box (natural and outdoor recipes); Survival Journal (true life survival experiences); and Who's Who (people with expertise in survival education or outdoor experience). Buys 6 columns/year. Send complete ms. Length: 500-1,000 words. Pays 2¢/word.

Poetry: Light verse and traditional. "We are open to verse that will fit our outdoor format." Submit in batches of 3. Pays $3 each.

Fillers: Appropriate jokes, gags, anecdotes, and short humor. Buys 2/issue. Length: 50-100 words.

Tips: "Send a brief but thorough outline of the subject matter. We need qualifications—a biography or references. Please send for a sample before submitting. We get a lot of mss that just don't fit our format."

Literary and "Little"

Literary magazines launch many writers into print for the first time. In some cases, the writer's career outlasts the magazine. "A lot of 'little' magazines and small presses are folding because the publishers had relied too much on grants which are much scarcer now," says one editor. Literary editors wish writers would "support" the magazines they want to write for—by just subscribing. Writers who want to get a story into print in a few months might have to wait a few years. Literary magazines, especially semiannuals, will buy good material and save it for a 1987 edition, for example. Submitting work to a "literary," the writer may encounter frequent address changes or unbusinesslike responses. On the other hand, many editors read submissions several times and send personal notes to writers.

Magazines that specialize in publishing poetry or poetry criticism are found in the Poetry category. Several of the poetry markets also buy short stories and nonfiction related to the poetic arts.

For more information about fiction technique—and some specialized markets—see *Fiction Writer's Market*, published by Writer's Digest Books.

‡**ACCENT**, American Institute of Discussion, Box 103, Oklahoma City OK 73101. (405)235-9681. Editor: John J. Corbin. Associate Editor: Barbara J. Williams. 25% freelance written. Monthly magazine covering (nonpolitical, educational) reading-discussion courses. "Our readers are interested in new ideas, literature, philosophy." Circ. 400. Pays on publication. Byline given. Buys one-time rights. Submit seasonal/holiday material 2 months in advance. Photocopied submissions OK. Computer printout submissions acceptable; no dot-matrix. SASE. Reports in 1 month on queries; 2 months on mss. Publishes ms an average of 1 month after acceptance.

Nonfiction: General interest; humor (tasteful, nonpolitical or religious); interview/profile (education, arts and humanities); personal experience (general interest, nonpolitical); and travel. Buys 12 mss/year. Send complete ms and cover letter. Length: 1,500 words maximum. Pays 1¢/word maximum.

Fiction: Adventure, fantasy, historical, humorous, mainstream, mystery, science fiction, suspense, and western. No material "heavy on sex," violence, religion or politics. Length: 3,500 words maximum. Pays 1¢/word maximum.

Tips: "A freelancer can best break in to our publication by submitting fiction dealing with ideas, philosophy, ethics, the human condition."

‡**AMELIA MAGAZINE**, Amelia Press, 329 E St., Bakersfield CA 93304. (805)323-4064. Editor: Frederick A. Raborg Jr. "*Amelia* is a semiannual (April and October) international magazine publishing the finest poetry and fiction available, along with expert criticism and reviews intended for all interested in contemporary literature." Estab. 1983. Circ. 1,000. Pays on publication. Byline given. Offers 50% kill fee. Buys first North American serial rights. Submit seasonal/holiday material 2 months in advance. Computer printout submissions acceptable. SASE. Reports in 2 months on mss. Sample copy $3; writer's guidelines for business size SAE and 1 first class stamp.

Nonfiction: Historical/nostalgic (in the form of belles lettres); humor (in fiction or belles lettres); interview/profile (poets and fiction writers); opinion (on poetry and fiction only); personal experience (as it pertains to poetry or fiction in the form of belles lettres); travel (in the form of belles lettres only); and criticism and book reviews of poetry and small press fiction titles. "Nothing overtly slick in approach. Criticism pieces must have depth; belles lettres must offer important insights into the human scene." Buys 4 mss/year. Send complete ms. Length: 1,000-2,000 words. Pays $25 or by arrangement. "Ordinarily payment for all prose is a flat rate of $25/piece, more for exceptional work."

Fiction: Adventure; book excerpts (original novel excerpts only); erotica (of a quality seen in Anais Nin or Henry Miller only); ethnic; experimental; fantasy; historical; horror; humorous; mainstream; mystery; novel excerpts; science fiction; suspense; and western. "We would consider slick fiction of the quality seen in *Redbook*." No pornography ("good erotica is not the same thing"). Buys 8-10 mss/year. Send complete ms. Length: 1,000-3,000 words. Pays $25 or by arrangement for exceptional work.

Poetry: Avant-garde, free verse, haiku, light verse, traditional. "No patently religious or stereotypical newspaper poetry." Buys 40-60 poems/year depending on lengths. Prefers submission of at least 3 poems. Length: 3-100 lines. Pays $2-10; additional payment for exceptional work, usually by established professionals.

Tips: "We are planning a series of poetry chapbooks at the rate of 2 per year commencing in 1985 (manuscripts will be reviewed after January 1, 1985)." Fiction and poetry are most open to freelancers. "*Have something to* *say* and say it well. If you insist on waving flags or pushing your religion, then do it with subtlety and class. We enjoy a good cry from time to time, too, but sentimentality does not mean we want to see mush. As in the firs issue of *Amelia*, 'name' writers are used, but newcomers who have done their homework suffer no disadvantage here."

THE AMERICAN SCHOLAR, 1811 Q St. NW, Washington DC 20009. (202)265-3808. Editor: Joseph Epstein. 5% freelance written. "For college-educated, mid-20s and older, rather intellectual in orientation and interests." Quarterly magazine. Circ. 32,000. Buys first rights only; rights stay in author's possession. Byline given. Buys 20-30 mss/year. Pays on acceptance. No simultaneous submissions. Computer printout submissions acceptable; prefers letter-quality to dot-matrix. Reports in 1 month. Publishes ms an average of 9 months after acceptance. Query, with samples, if possible. SASE. Sample copy $4; free writer's guidelines.
Nonfiction: "The aim of *The Scholar* is to fill the gap between the learned journals and the good magazines for a popular audience. We are interested not so much in the definitive analysis as in the lucid and creative exploration of what is going on in the fields of science, art, religion, politics, and national and foreign affairs. Advances in science particularly interest us." Informational, interview, profile, historical, think articles, and book reviews. Length: 3,500-4,000 words. Pays $350/article and $100 for reviews.
Poetry: Pays $50 for poetry on any theme. Approximately 5 poems published per issue. "We would like to see poetry that develops an image, a thought or event, without the use of a single cliche or contrived archaism. The most hackneyed subject matter is self-conscious love; the most tired verse is iambic pentameter with rhyming endings. The usual length of our poems is 30 lines. From 1-4 poems may be submitted at one time; *no more* for a careful reading. We urge prospective contributors to familiarize themselves with the type of poetry we have published by looking at the magazine."
Tips: "See our magazine in your public library before submitting material to us. Know what we publish and the quality of our articles."

‡**ANTAEUS**, The Ecco Press, 18 W. 30th St., New York NY 10001. (212)685-8240. Editor: Daniel Halpern. Managing Editor: Megan Ratner. Semiannual magazine with fiction and poetry. Circ. 5,000. Pays on publication. Byline given. Buys first North American serial rights. Photocopied submissions OK. SASE. Reports in 1 week on queries; 6 weeks on mss. Sample copy $5; free writer's guidelines.
Fiction: Experimental and novel excerpts. Buys 10-15 mss/year. Send complete ms. Length: no minimum or maximum. Pays $5/printed page.
Poetry: Avant-garde, free verse, light verse and traditional. Buys 30-35 poems/year. Submit maximum 8 poems. Pays $5.

ANTIOCH REVIEW, Box 148, Yellow Springs OH 45387. Editor: Robert S. Fogarty. 80% freelance written. For general, literary and academic audience. Quarterly. Buys all rights. Byline given. Pays on publication. Publishes ms an average of 10 months after acceptance. Computer printout submissions acceptable; prefers letter-quality to dot-matrix. Reports in 4-6 weeks. SASE.
Nonfiction: "Contemporary articles in the humanities and social sciences, politics, economics, literature and all areas of broad intellectual concern. Somewhat scholarly, but never pedantic in style, eschewing all professional jargon. Lively, distinctive prose insisted upon." Length: 2,000-8,000 words. Pays $10/published page.
Fiction: Quality fiction only, distinctive in style with fresh insights into the human condition. No science fiction, fantasy or confessions. Pays $10/published page.
Poetry: Concrete visual imagery. No light or inspirational verse. Contributors should be familiar with the magazine before submitting.

BLOOMSBURY REVIEW, Box 8928, Denver CO 80201. (303)455-0593. Editor: Tom Auer. 95% freelance written. Bimonthly magazine covering book reviews and essays of interest to book readers. Circ. 8,000. Pays 2 months after publication. Byline and one-line biography given. Buys one-time rights; rights revert back to writer on publication. Simultaneous queries OK. Computer printout submissions acceptable; prefers letter-quality to dot-matrix. SASE. Reports in 3 months on queries and mss. Publishes ms an average of 3 months after acceptance. Sample copy $2; free writer's guidelines with SASE.
Nonfiction: Historical/nostalgic (related to books and publishing); interview/profile (of prominent people in the book business such as authors and publishers); essays; and book reviews. "Submitting a book review is the best way to break into *Bloomsbury Review*." Query with clips of published work. Length: average 750 words. Pays $10 minimum."
Poetry: Original and unpublished. Buys 24/year. Pays $5 average.
Tips: "You've got to be a good writer and a better thinker to get in print."

BOOK FORUM, Hudson River Press, 38 E. 76th St., New York NY 10021. (212)861-8328. Editor: Marshall Hayes. Editorial Director: Marilyn Wood. Emphasizes contemporary literature, the arts, and foreign affairs for "intellectually sophisticated and knowledgeable professionals: university-level academics, writers, people in government, and the professions." Quarterly magazine; 192 pages. Circ. 5,200. Pays on publication. Buys all rights. Pays 33⅓% kill fee. Byline given. Phone queries OK. Photocopied submissions OK. SASE. Reports in 2 weeks. Sample copy $3.

Nonfiction: "We seek highly literate essays that would appeal to the same readership as, say, the *London Times Literary Supplement* or *Encounter.* Our readers are interested in professionally written, highly literate and informative essays, profiles and reviews in literature, the arts, behavior, and foreign and public affairs. We cannot use material designed for a mass readership, nor for the counterculture. Think of us as an Eastern establishment, somewhat snobbish literary and public affairs journal and you will have it right." General interest, interview (with select contemporary writers), profiles, and essays about contemporary writers. Buys 15-20 unsolicited mss/year. Query. Length: 1,400-3,000 words. Pays $25-100.

Tips: "To break in send with the query letter a sample of writing in an area relevant to our interests. If the writer wants to contribute book reviews, send a book review sample, published or not, of the kind of title we are likely to review—literary, social, biographical, art."

BOSTON REVIEW, 991 Massachusetts Ave., Cambridge MA 02138. (617)492-5478. Editor: Nicholas Bromell. 90% freelance written. Bimonthly magazine of the arts, politics and culture. Circ. 10,000. Pays on publication. Buys first rights, second serial (reprint) rights, and one-time rights; makes work-for-hire assignments. Acquires all rights, unless author requests otherwise. Byline given. Photocopied and simultaneous submissions OK. Computer printout submissions acceptable; no dot-matrix. SASE. Reports in 2 months. Publishes ms an average of 2 months after acceptance. Sample copy $3.

Nonfiction: Critical essays and reviews, natural and social sciences, literature, music, painting, film, photography, dance and theatre. Buys 20 unsolicited mss/year. Length: 1,000-3,000 words.

Fiction: Length: 2,000-4,000 words. Pays according to length and author, ranging from $50-200.

Poetry: Pays according to length and author.

‡**C.S.P. WORLD NEWS**, Editions Stencil, Box 2608, Station D, Ottawa, Ontario K1P 5W7 Canada. Editor-in-Chief: Guy F. Claude Hamel. Monthly literary journal. Emphasizes book reviews. Buys first rights. Photocopied submissions OK. SAE and IRCs. Reports in 2 months. Sample copy $2.

Nonfiction: Sociology and criminology. Buys 13 mss/year. Send complete ms. Length: 2,600-5,000 words. Typewritten, double-spaced page.

Columns/Departments: Writer's Workshop material. Buys 12 items/year. Send complete ms. Length: 20-50 words.

Poetry: Publishes avant-garde forms. Submit complete ms; no more than 2 at a time. Length: 6-12 lines.

Fillers: Jokes, gags and anecdotes. Payment negotiated.

THE CALIFORNIA QUARTERLY, 100 Sproul, University of California, Davis CA 95616. Editor: Elliot Gilbert. 95% freelance written. "Addressed to an audience of educated, literary, and general readers, interested in good writing on a variety of subjects, but emphasis is on poetry and fiction." Quarterly. Usually buys first North American serial rights. Computer printout submissions acceptable; prefers letter-quality to dot-matrix. Reports in 2 months but the editorial office is closed from July 1 to October 1. SASE.

Nonfiction: Original, critical articles and interviews. Length: 8,000 words maximum. Pays $3/published page for fiction; $4 for poetry and graphics.

Fiction: "Short fiction of quality with emphasis on stylistic distinction; contemporary themes, any subject." Experimental and mainstream. Buys 12 unsolicited mss/year. Length: 8,000 words maximum. Pays $3/published page.

Poetry: "Original, all types; any subject appropriate for genuine poetic expression; any length suitable to subject." Buys 150 unsolicited poems/year. Pays $4/published page.

CANADIAN FICTION MAGAZINE, Box 946, Station F, Toronto, Ontario M4Y 2N9 Canada. Editor: Geoffrey Hancock. Emphasizes Canadian fiction, short stories and novel excerpts. Quarterly magazine; 148 pages. Circ. 1,800. Pays on publication. Buys first North American serial rights. Byline given. SASE (Canadian stamps). Reports in 6 weeks. Back issue $4.00 (in Canadian funds). Current issue $5.50 (in Canadian funds).

Nonfiction: Interview (must have a definite purpose, both as biography and as a critical tool focusing on problems and techniques) and book reviews (Canadian fiction only). Buys 35 mss/year. Query. Length: 1,000-3,000 words. Pays $10/printed page plus 1-year subscription.

Photos: Purchased on assignment. Send prints. Pays $10 for 5x7 b&w glossy prints; $50 for cover. Model release required.

Fiction: "No restrictions on subject matter or theme. We are open to experimental and speculative fiction as well as traditional forms. Style, content and form are the author's prerogative. We also publish self-contained sections of novel-in-progress and French-Canadian fiction in translation, as well as an annual special issue on a single author such as Mavis Gallant, Leon Rooke, Robert Harlow or Jane Rule. Please note that *CFM* is an anthology devoted exclusively to Canadian fiction. We publish only the works of writers and artists residing in Canada and Canadians living abroad." Pays $10/printed page.

Tips: "Prospective contributors must study several recent issues carefully. *CFM* is a serious professional literary magazine whose contributors include the finest writers in Canada."

CANADIAN LITERATURE, University of British Columbia, Vancouver, British Columbia V6T 1W5 Canada. Editor: W.H. New. 90% freelance written. Quarterly. Circ. 2,000. Not copyrighted. Buys first Canadian rights only. Pays on publication. Computer printout submissions acceptable. Query "with a clear description of the project." Publishes ms an average of 2 years after acceptance. SAE and IRCs.
Nonfiction: Articles of high quality on Canadian books and writers only. Articles should be scholarly and readable. No fiction or fillers. Length: 2,000-5,500 words. Pays $5/printed page.

CAROLINA QUARTERLY, University of North Carolina, Greenlaw Hall 066A, Chapel Hill NC 27514. (919)933-0244. Editor: Mary Titus. Managing Editor: Jane Duke. 100% freelance written. Literary journal published 3 times/year. Circ. 1,000. Pays on publication. Byline given. Buys first North American serial rights. Photocopied submissions OK. Computer printout submissions acceptable; prefers letter-quality to dot-matrix. SASE. Reports in 4 months. Publishes ms an average of 2 months after acceptance. Sample copy $4 (includes postage); writer's guidelines for SASE and 1 first class stamp.
Nonfiction: Book reviews and photo feature. Publishes 6 reviews/year, 12 photographs/year.
Fiction: "We are interested in maturity: control over language; command of structure and technique; understanding of the possibilities and demands of prose narrative, with respect to stylistics, characterization, and point of view. We publish a good many unsolicited stories; *CQ* is a market for newcomer and professional alike." No pornography. Buys 12-18 mss/year. Send complete ms. Length: 7,000 words maximum. Pays $3/printed page.
Poetry: "*CQ* places no specific restrictions on the length, form or substance of poems considered for publication." Submit 2-6 poems. Buys 60 mss/year. Pays $5/printed poem.
Tips: "*One* fiction ms at a time; no cover letter is necessary. Address to appropriate editor, not to general editor. Look at the magazine, a recent number if possible."

‡**CHAPMAN**, 35 E. Claremont St., Edinburgh EH7 4HT Scotland. (031)556-5863. Editor: Joy M. Hendry. 50% freelance written. Triannual magazine of Scottish literature and culture. Circ. 2,000. Pays on publication. No byline given. Buys first rights. Not interested in seasonal/holiday material. Simultaneous submissions OK. SASE. Reports in 2 weeks on queries; 1 month on mss. Publishes ms an average of 1 year after acceptance. Sample copy $2.50.
Nonfiction: Literary criticism and linguistic material (Scottish or Gaelic). Buys 15 mss/year. Length: 1,000-4,000 words. Pays $10-50.
Fiction: Buys 15 mss/year. Send complete ms. Length: 1,500-4,000 words. Pays $10-50.
Poetry: Buys 150 poems/year. Pays $5-50.

THE CHARITON REVIEW, Northeast Missouri State University, Kirksville MO 63501. (816)785-4499. Editor: Jim Barnes. 100% freelance written. Semi-annual (fall and spring) magazine covering contemporary fiction, poetry, translation and book reviews. Circ. 600. Pays on publication. Byline given. Buys first North American serial rights. Computer printout submissions acceptable; no dot-matrix. SASE. Reports in 1 week on queries; 2 weeks on mss. Sample copy for $2 and 7x10 SAE and 63¢ postage.
Nonfiction: Book reviews. Buys 2-5 mss/year. Query or send complete ms. Length: 1,000-5,000. Pays $15.
Fiction: Ethnic, experimental, mainstream, novel excerpts and traditional. "We are not interested in slick material." Buys 6-8 mss/year. Send complete ms. Length: 1,000-5,000 words. Pays $5/page.
Poetry: Avant-garde, free verse and traditional. Buys 50-55 poems/year. Submit maximum 10 poems. Length: open. Pays $5/page.
Tips: "Read *Chariton* and similar magazines. Know the difference between good literature and bad. Know what magazine might be interested in your work. We are not a trendy magazine. We publish only the best." All sections are open to freelancers, all material is freelance. "Know your market or you are wasting your time—and mine."

CHICAGO SUN-TIMES SHOW/BOOK WEEK, *Chicago Sun-Times*, 401 N. Wabash Ave., Chicago IL 60611. (312)321-2131. Editor: Steven S. Duke. Emphasizes entertainment, arts and books. Weekly newspaper section. Circ. 750,000. Pays on publication. Buys all rights. Pays negotiable kill fee, except on speculative articles. Submit seasonal/holiday material at least 2 months in advance. Photocopied and previously published work OK. Computer printout submissions acceptable "if readable"; prefers letter-quality to dot-matrix. SASE. Reports in 3 weeks.
Nonfiction: "Articles and essays dealing with all the serious and lively arts—movies; theater (pro, semipro, amateur, foreign); filmmakers; painting; sculpture; and music (all fields, from classical to rock—we have regular columnists in these fields). Our Book Week column has from 6-8 reviews, mostly assigned. Material has to be very good because we have our own regular staffers who write almost every week. Writing must be tight. No warmed-over stuff of fan magazine type. No high-schoolish literary themes." Query. Length: 800-1,000 words. Pays $75-100.

CONFRONTATION, C.W. Post College of Long Island University, Greenvale NY 11548. (576)299-2391. Editor: Martin Tucker. 90% freelance written. Emphasizes creative writing for a "literate, educated, college-graduate audience." Semiannual magazine; 190 pages. Circ. 2,000. Pays on publication. Buys all rights. Pays 50% kill fee. Byline given. Phone queries, simultaneous and photocopied submissions OK. Computer printout submissions acceptable; prefers letter-quality to dot-matrix. SASE. Reports in 2 months. Publishes ms an average of 9 months after acceptance. Sample copy $2.
Nonfiction: "Articles are, basically, commissioned essays on a specific subject." Memoirs wanted. Buys 6 mss/year. Query. Length: 1,000-3,000 words. Pays $10-100.
Fiction: Martin Tucker, fiction editor. Experimental, humorous and mainstream. Buys 20 mss/year. Submit complete ms. Length: "completely open." Pays $15-100.
Poetry: W. Palmer, poetry editor. Avant-garde, free verse, haiku, light verse, traditional. Buys 60/year. Limit submissions to batches of 10. No length requirement. Pays $5-50.
Tips: "At this time we discourage fantasy and light verse. We do, however, read all mss. It's rewarding discovering a good manuscript that comes in unsolicited."

CROSSCURRENTS, 2200 Glastonbury Rd., Westlake Village CA 91361. Editor: Linda Brown Michelson. 40% freelance written. Quarterly magazine featuring fiction and poetry for an educated audience. Circ. 3,000. Uses limited amount of unsolicited material. Average issue includes 6-10 pieces of short fiction, 10-15 pieces of poetry and 1-2 pieces of nonfiction. Pays on acceptance. Byline given. Offers 50% kill fee. Buys first North American serial rights. Submit seasonal material 6 months in advance. Photocopied submissions OK. Computer printout submissions acceptable. SASE. Reports in 2 weeks on queries; in 6 weeks on mss. Publishes ms an average of 6 months after acceptance. Sample copy $4; free writer's guidelines for SASE.
Fiction: "We review unsolicited manuscripts between June 1 and November 30 each year; during that time we try to remain open to all types of fiction." Buys 30-40 mss/year. Send complete ms. Length: 6,000 words maximum. Pays $35 minimum. Also pays in copies.
Poetry: Elizabeth Bartlett, poetry editor. "We review unsolicited manuscripts between June 1 and November 30 each year. We want quality literary poetry."
Tips: "Study a sample issue of our publication, then send us something terrifically appropriate. We receive quite a bit of material that is well done, but just not quite right for us."

‡**ENCOUNTER**, Encounter, Ltd., 59 St. Martin's Lane, London WC2N 4JS England. Editors: Melvin J. Lasky and Anthony Thwaite. Monthly magazine (except August and September) covering current affairs and the arts. Circ. 16,000. Pays on publication. Buys one-time rights. SASE or IRC. Reports in 2 weeks on queries; 6 weeks on mss. Sample copy $4.50 including surface mail cost.
Nonfiction: Mainly articles on current affairs. Length: 1,500-5,000 words. Pays variable fee, but "averages £20/1,000 words."
Fiction: "Just good up-market stories." Length: 1,500-5,000 words. Pays variable fee, averages £20/1,000 words.
Poetry: "Just good up-market poetry." Submit maximum 6 poems. Length: 12-100 lines. Pays variable fee.
Tips: "Study the magazine first. A straight submission will be carefully considered." Stories and poems most open to freelancers.

‡**EPOCH**, Cornell University, 251 Goldwin Smith, Ithaca NY 14853. (607)256-3385. Editor: C.S. Griscombe. Literary magazine of original fiction and poetry published 3 times/year. Circ. 1,000. Pays on publication. Byline given. Buys first North American serial rights. SASE.
Fiction: "Potential contributors should *read* a copy or two. There is *no other way* for them to ascertain what we need or like." Buys 15-20 mss/year. Send complete ms. Pays $10/page.
Poetry: "Potential contributors should read magazine to see what type of poetry is used." Buys 20-30 poems/year. Pays $1/line.

EROTIC FICTION QUARTERLY, EFQ Publications, Box 4958, San Francisco CA 94101. Editor: Richard Hiller. Small literary magazine for thoughtful people interested in a variety of highly original and creative short fiction with sexual themes. Estab. 1983. Pays on acceptance. Byline given. Buys all rights. Photocopied submissions OK. Computer printout submissions acceptable; prefers letter-quality to dot-matrix. SASE. Writer's guidelines for SASE.
Fiction: Heartful, intelligent erotica, any style. Also, stories—not necessarily erotic—about some aspect of authentic sexual experience. No standard pornography or men's magazine-type stories; no contrived or formula plots or gimmicks; no broad satire or parody; no poetry. Send complete ms. Length: 500-5,000 words, average 1,500 words. Pays $35 minimum.
Tips: "I specifically encourage beginners who have something to say regarding sexual attitudes, emotions, roles, etc. Story ideas should come from real life, not media; characters should be real people. There are essentially no restrictions on content, style, explicitness, etc.; *originality*, *clarity*, and *integrity* are most important."

EVENT, c/o Kwantlen College, Box 9030, Surrey, British Columbia V3T 5H8 Canada. Managing Editor: Vye Flindall. 100% freelance written. For "those interested in literature and writing." Biannual magazine. Circ. 1,000. Uses 80-100 mss/year. Small payment and contributor's copy only. Buys first rights. Byline given. Photocopied and simultaneous submissions OK. Computer printout submissions acceptable; prefers letter-quality to dot-matrix. Reports in 4 months. Publishes ms an average of 6 months after acceptance. Submit complete ms. SAE and IRCs.
Nonfiction: "High-quality work." Reviews of Canadian books and essays.
Fiction: Short stories and drama.
Poetry: Submit complete ms. "We are looking for high quality modern poetry."

FICTION INTERNATIONAL, English Dept., San Diego State University, San Diego CA 92182. Editors: Harold Jaffe and Larry McCaffery. For "readers interested in the best writing by talented writers working in new forms or working in old forms in especially fruitful new ways; readers interested in contemporary literary developments and possibilities." Published annually in mid-winter. Pays on publication. Copyrighted; rights revert to author. Reports in 1-3 months. SASE. Mss considered only from September through December of each year.
Fiction: Study publication. Previous contributors include: Asa Baber, Russell Banks, Jonathan Baumbach, T. Coraghessan Boyle, Rosellen Brown, Jerry Bumpus, David Madden, Joyce Carol Oates, Ronald Sukenick, Gordon Weaver and Robley Wilson Jr. Highly selective. Not an easy market for unsophisticated writers. No length limitations but "rarely use short-shorts or mss over 30 pages." Portions of novels acceptable if self-contained enough for independent publication.
Interviews: Seeking interviews with well-known or innovative fiction writers "able to discuss their ideas and aesthetic predilections intelligently."
Reviews: G. E. Murray, review editor. By assignment only. No payment. *Fiction International* also sponsors the annual $1,000 St. Lawrence Award for Fiction for an outstanding first collection of short fiction published in North America.

‡**FICTION NETWORK MAGAZINE**, Fiction Network, Box 5651, San Francisco CA 94101. (415)552-3223. Editor: Jay Schaefer. 100% freelance written. Magazine of short stories. Fiction Network distributes short stories to newspapers, regional magazines, and other periodicals and also publishes *Fiction Network Magazine* (for agents, editors and writers). Estab. 1982. Circ. 6,000. Pays on publication. Byline given. Buys first rights, second serial (reprint) rights, and multi-publication rights for period of time. Fiction Network (which includes Fiction Supplement and Fiction Syndicate) buys non-book print rights for 1 to 3 years. Each story accepted may appear in several newspapers and magazines. Payments from publications that carry the story are divided 50/50 with the author. Simultaneous and photocopied submissions OK. Computer printout submissions acceptable. SASE. Reports in 3 months. Publishes ms an average of 3 months after acceptance. Does not return foreign submissions—notification only. Sample copy $4 USA and Canada; $6.50 elsewhere. Writer's guidelines for business-size SAE, and 1 first class stamp.
Fiction: All types of stories and subjects are acceptable; novel excerpts will be considered only if they stand alone as stories. No poetry, essays, reviews or interviews. No children's or young adult material. Buys 100 mss/year. Send complete ms. "Do not submit a second ms until you receive a response on the first ms." Length: 5,000 words maximum (2,500 words preferred). Pays $25 minimum.
Tips: "Our goal is to promote the reading and writing of fiction. We offer both known and unknown writers excellent exposure and reasonable fees while we open up new markets for stories." Contributors include Alice Adams, Max Apple, Ann Beattie, Andre Dubus, Lynne Sharon Schwartz and Marian Thurm.

THE FIDDLEHEAD, University of New Brunswick, The Observatory, Box 4400, Fredericton, New Brunswick E3B 5A3 Canada. (506)454-3591. Editor: Don Conway. 90% freelance written. Quarterly magazine covering poetry, short fiction, photographs and book reviews. Circ. 1,100. Pays on publication. Not copyrighted. Buys first North American serial rights. Submit seasonal/holiday material 6 months in advance. Simultaneous queries, and photocopied submissions (if legible) OK. Computer printout submissions acceptable; no dot-matrix. SAE and IRCs. Reports in 3 weeks on queries; 2 months on mss. Publishes ms an average of 6 months after acceptance. Sample copy $4, Canada; $4.25, US.
Fiction: Kent Thompson, Bill Davey and Ann Boyles. "Stories may be on any subject—acceptance is based on quality alone. Because the journal is heavily subsidized by the Canadian government, strong preference is given to Canadian writers." Buys 20 mss/year. Pays $20/page; $100/article.
Poetry: Robert Hawkes and Eric Trethewey. "Poetry may be on any subject—acceptance is based on quality alone. Because the journal is heavily subsidized by the Canadian government, strong preference is given to Canadian writers." Buys average of 60/year. Submit maximum 10 poems. Pays $20/page; $100 maximum.
Tips: "Quality alone is the criterion for publication. Return postage (Canadian, or IRCs) should accompany all mss."

‡FOUR QUARTERS, La Salle College, 20th St. and Olney Ave., Philadelphia PA 19141-1191. (215)951-1171. Editor: John Christopher Kleis. 100% freelance written. Quarterly magazine covering literature. "We publish poetry, essays, and fiction, largely (but not exclusively) directed toward and written by academics." Circ. 500. Pays on publication. Byline given. Buys all rights. Submit seasonal/holiday material 4 months in advance. SASE. Reports in 2 weeks on queries; 4 weeks on mss. Publishes ms an average of 6 months after acceptance. Sample copy $2; free writer's guidelines.

Nonfiction: Historical, interview, personal experience and literary. Buys 1 ms/year. Send complete ms. Length: 2,500-4,000 words. Pays $25 minimum.

Fiction: Experimental, mainstream and religious. Buys 15 mss/year. Send complete ms. Length: 2,500-4,000 words. Pays $25 minimum.

Poetry: Richard Lautz, poetry editor. Avant-garde, free verse and traditional. Buys 20 poems/year. Submit maximum 5 poems. Length: 3 lines minimum. Pays $5 minimum.

Tips: "We are getting more and more mss that have moved away from traditional forms toward a more fragmentary, impressionistic form."

‡THE GAMUT, A Journal of Ideas and Information, Cleveland State University, 1216 Rhodes Tower, Cleveland OH 44115. (216)687-4679. Editor: Louis T. Milic. 15% freelance written. Triannual magazine with sharply focused, well-documented articles developing a thesis or explaining a problem, process, or discovery of current interest in any field or profession—one of the sciences, arts, or social sciences, business, or industry. Circ. 1,000. Pays on publication. Byline given. Buys first North American serial rights. Simultaneous queries and photocopied submissions OK. Computer printout submissions acceptable. SASE. Reports in 2 weeks on queries; 6 weeks on mss. Publishes ms an average of 3 months after acceptance. Sample copy $2.50; writer's guidelines for business-size SASE and 1 first class stamp.

Nonfiction: Leonard M. Trawick, articles editor. General interest, humor, personal experience, and technical (provided it is understandable by the lay reader). "All material must be by Ohio authors or emphasize the *region*." Buys 25 mss/year. Query or send complete ms. Length: 2,000-8,000 words. Pays $25-250.

Photos: State availability of photos or send photos with ms. Reviews 8x10 b&w prints. Captions, model release, and identification of subjects (if applicable) required. Buys one-time rights.

Tips: "Authors should assume that *The Gamut* readers are well educated but not necessarily expert in the particular field of the article."

THE GENEVA REVIEW, 19 rue Centrale, 1580 Avenches, Switzerland. Editor-in-Chief: Jed Curtis. Executive Editor: Collin Gonze. 70% freelance written. Literary magazine "serving much the same function that *The Paris Review* did before it relocated to the US." For intelligent English-speakers in Europe. Pays on acceptance. Simultaneous queries, and simultaneous and previously published submissions OK "if other submissions are made outside Europe." Reports in 2-3 months.

Nonfiction: Contact: Michael O'Regan. "Though mss of any genre are considered, there are two requirements: excellence in writing; and a European slant." Science developments, writer's life, essays, how-to-get-by-in-Europe (especially Switzerland), historical, the arts, politics, profiles/interviews (especially prominent English-language literary figures living in Europe), and 'the undefinable'. Query with published clips. Reports in 2-3 months. Length: open; but under 2,500 words preferred. Pays variable rates.

Fiction: Contact: S.F. Stromberg. Mainstream, historical, humorous, adventure and some experimental. One science fiction story/issue. "This is typically set somewhere in continental Europe with at least one native English-speaker among the protagonists. For science fiction, 'European slant' might only mean the absence of an exclusively American viewpoint." Length: 2,000 words or less. Pays variable rates.

Poetry: Contact: Dorothy Oliveau. Any style OK. Submit maximum 5 poems. Length: 5-50 lines. Use of non-English words or sentences acceptable in giving flavor of some European nation.

Fillers: Jokes and anecdotes "always needed." Length: 250 words maximum.

Tips: "TGR draws primarily on the talents of English-language writers living anywhere in continental Europe (in conjunction with EWE, the English-Language Writers in Europe)."

‡GRAIN, Saskatchewan Writers' Guild, Box 1154, Regina, Saskatchewan S4P 3B4 Canada. (306)522-0811 (evenings). Editor: Brenda Riches. 100% freelance written. "A literary quarterly magazine that seeks to extend the boundaries of convention and challenge readers and writers." Circ. 850. Pays on acceptance. No byline given. Not copyrighted. Buys one-time rights. Photocopied submissions OK; no simultaneous queries, simultaneous or previously published submissions. Computer printout submissions; prefers letter-quality to dot-matrix. SAE and IRC. Reports in 1 month on queries; 3 months on mss. Publishes ms an average of 3 months after acceptance. Sample copy for $3, 5x8 SAE, and 65¢ postage.

Nonfiction: Literary essays. Buys up to 4 mss/year. Query. Pays $45-150.

Fiction: Brenda Riches and Bonnie Burnard, fiction editors. "Literary art only. No fiction of a popular nature." Buys 12-15 mss/year. Send complete ms. Length: 300-8,000 words. Pays 45-150.

Poetry: Brenda Riches and Allan Barr, poetry editors. Anne Szumigalski, poetry consultant. No poetry "that has no substance." Buys 40-60/year. Submit maximum 8 poems. Length: 3-200 lines. Pays $30.

Tips: "Only work of the highest literary quality is accepted. Read several back issues. Get advice from a practicing writer to make sure the work is ready to send. Then send it."

GREAT RIVER REVIEW, 211 W. 7th, Winona MN 55987. Editors: Orval Lund, Fiction; Paul Wadden, Poetry; Susan Williams, Reviews. Published 2 times/year. Magazine; 145 pages. Photocopied submissions OK. SASE. Reports in 3 months. Sample copy (back issues) $3; current issue $3.50.
Nonfiction: Essays on the region and articles on Midwestern writers. Query first on articles.
Fiction: Experimental and mainstream, but not mass circulation style. Buys 6-7 prose mss/issue, up to 30 poems. Length: 2,000-9,000 words.
Tips: Recent story examples: "The Round" (Vol. 3, No. 2) and "Going Home" (Vol. 4, No. 1).

GREEN FEATHER MAGAZINE, Box 2633, Lakewood OH 44107. Editor: Gary S. Skeens. Assistant Editor: Robin S. Moser. Annual magazine covering poetry and fiction. Circ. 150. Pays on publication. Byline given. Buys first North American serial rights. Submit seasonal/holiday material 6 months in advance. Simultaneous queries, and simultaneous, photocopied and previously published submissions OK. Computer printout acceptable; prefers letter-quality to dot-matrix. SASE. Reports in 1 week on queries; 1 month on mss. Sample copy $1; writer's guidelines for business-size SAE and 1 first class stamp.
Photos: "Photos are used primarily for the magazine's cover. Open subject matter or query as to our needs at a particular time." Send photos with ms. Reviews 8x10 b&w prints. Model release and identification of subjects required. Buys one-time rights.
Fiction: Adventure, erotica, experimental, mainstream and mystery. "No pornography or anything lacking strong sense of plot and character development." Buys 3 mss/year. Query. Length: 750-2,000 words. Pays $5-25.
Poetry: Free verse and light verse. Buys 25/year. Submit maximum 10 poems. Length: 5-30 lines. Pays $1-10.
Tips: "Prefers not to see anything of a pornographic, low-quality nature; poor plotting, dialogue, character development." Material must "grab the gut. Dishonesty will definitely be tossed back in the mail."

THE HUDSON REVIEW, 684 Park Ave., New York NY 10021. Managing Editor: Sharon Newton-Pritchett. Quarterly. Pays on publication. Reports in 6-8 weeks. SASE for return of submissions.
Nonfiction: Articles, translations and reviews. Length: 8,000 words maximum.
Fiction: Uses "quality fiction". Length: 10,000 words maximum. Pays 2½¢/word.
Poetry: 50¢/line for poetry.
Tips: Unsolicited mss are not read during the months of June, July, August and September.

IMAGE MAGAZINE, A Magazine of the Arts, Cornerstone Press, Box 28048, St. Louis MO 63119. (314)752-3704. Managing Editor: Anthony J. Summers. General Editor: James J. Finnegan. 100% freelance written. Triannual literary journal "for the educated, open-minded, thinking person." Circ. 600. Pays on publication. Byline given. Offers negotiable kill fee. Buys one-time and negotiable rights. Simultaneous queries OK. Computer printout submissions acceptable. SASE. Reports in 3 weeks on queries; 5 weeks on mss. Publishes ms an average of 3 months after acceptance. Sample copy for $3 and 50¢ postage; free writer's guidelines.
Fiction: Erotica, ethnic, experimental, fantasy, horror, humorous, novel excerpts and science fiction. No "cutesy, self-congratulating material." Buys variable number mss/year. Query or send complete ms. Length: open. Pays $1-100.
Poetry: Avant-garde, free verse, haiku, light verse and traditional. No "overly religious, Elvis poetry, 'The world is neat and happy' type, etc." Buys 20-100/year. Submit maximum 10 poems. Length: open. Pays $1-100.
Tips: "We receive very few reviews, interviews, interesting articles on the literary world, as well as plays and experimental material. Try these for a better shot."

THE IOWA REVIEW, 308 EPB, The University of Iowa, Iowa City IA 52242. (319)353-6048. Editor: David Hamilton, with the help of colleagues, graduate assistants, and occasional guest editors. Magazine. Published 3 times/year. Buys first rights. Photocopied submissions OK. SASE. Reports in 3 months.
Nonfiction: "We publish essays, stories and poems and would like for our essays not always to be works of academic criticism." Buys 65-85 unsolicited mss/year. Submit complete ms. Pays $1/line for verse; $10/page for prose.

JAM TO-DAY, Box 249, Northfield VT 05663. Editors: Judith Stanford and Don Stanford. 90% freelance written. Annual literary magazine featuring high-quality poetry, fiction and reviews. Especially interested in unknown or little-known authors. Circ. 300. Pays on publication. Byline given. Buys first rights and nonexclusive anthology rights. Photocopied submissions OK. Computer printout submissions acceptable. SASE. Reports in 6 weeks. Publishes ms an average of 6 months after acceptance. Sample copy $3.
Fiction: "We will consider quality fiction of almost any style or genre. However, we prefer not to receive ma-

terial that is highly allegorical, abstruse, or heavily dependent on word play for its effect." Buys 1-2 mss/year. Send complete ms. Length: 1,500-7,500 words. Pays $5/page.
Poetry: Avant-garde, free verse, haiku and traditional. No light verse. Buys 30-50/year. Submit 5 poems maximum. Length: open. Pays $5/poem; higher payment for poems more than 3 pages in length.

JAPANOPHILE, Box 223, Okemos MI 48864. Editor: Earl Snodgrass. 40% freelance written. For literate people who are interested in Japanese culture anywhere in the world. Quarterly magazine. Pays on publication. Buys first North American serial rights. Previously published submissions OK. SASE. Reports in 4 weeks. Publishes ms an average of 6 months after acceptance. Sample copy $3.
Nonfiction: "We want material on Japanese culture in *North America or anywhere in the world*, even Japan. We want articles, preferably with pictures, about persons engaged in arts of Japanese origin: a Michigan naturalist who is a haiku poet, a potter who learned raku in Japan, a vivid 'I was there' account of a Go tournament in California. We use some travel articles if exceptionally well-written, but we are *not* a regional magazine about Japan. We are a little magazine, a literary magazine. Our particular slant is a certain kind of culture wherever it is in the world: Canada, the US, Europe, Japan. The culture includes flower arranging, haiku, religion, art, photography and fiction. It is important to study the magazine." Buys 8 mss/issue. Query preferred but not required. Length: 1,200 words maximum. Pays $8-15.
Photos: State availability of photos. Pays $10-20 for 8x10 b&w glossy prints.
Fiction: Experimental, mainstream, mystery, adventure, science fiction, humorous, romance and historical. Themes should relate to Japan or Japanese culture. Length: 1,000-10,000 words. Pays $20. Contest each year pays $100 to best short story.
Columns/Departments: Regular columns and features are Tokyo Scene and Profile of Artists. "We also need columns of Japanese culture in other cities." Query. Length: 1,000 words. Pays $20 maximum.
Poetry: Traditional, avant-garde and light verse related to Japanese culture or in a Japanese form such as haiku. Length: 3-50 lines. Pays $1-100.
Fillers: Newsbreaks, puzzles, clippings and short humor of up to 200 words. Pays $1-50.
Tips: "We prefer to see more articles about Japanese culture in the US, Canada and Europe."

JOURNAL OF MODERN LITERATURE, Temple University, 921 Humanities Bldg., Philadelphia PA 19122. (215)787-8505. Editor-in-Chief: Maurice Beebe. Managing Editor: Kathleen Zsamar. 100% freelance written. Emphasizes scholarly studies for academics interested in literature of the past 100 years. Quarterly magazine. Circ. 2,000. Buys all rights. Phone queries OK. Photocopied submissions OK. Computer printout submissions acceptable. SASE. Reports in 8 weeks. Publishes ms an average of 2 months after acceptance. Free sample copy.
Nonfiction: Historical (20th-century literature); informational (20th-century literature); and photo feature on art and literature. Buys 30 mss/year. Query or send complete ms. Pays 2 issues and offprints.
Photos: Purchased only with accompanying nonfiction manuscript. Total purchase price for ms includes payment for photos.
Tips: Prefers not to see material on "How I started being a writer."

KALEIDOSCOPE, International Literary/Art Magazine by Persons with Disabilities, Kaleidoscope Press, 326 Locust St., Akron OH 44302. (216)762-9755, ext. 474. Editor: Carson W. Heiner Jr. 75% freelance written. Semiannual magazine with international collection of literature and art by disabled people for writers, artists, and anyone interested in fine art and literature. Present disability in factual way, but not maudlin." Circ. 3,000. Pays on publication. Byline given. Buys first North American serial rights. Simultaneous queries, and photocopied and previously published submissions OK. Computer printout submissions acceptable. SASE. Reports in 6 months. Publishes ms an average of 6 months after acceptance. Sample copy $2.75; writer's guidelines for SAE and 1 first class stamp.
Nonfiction: Book excerpts, reviews, historical/nostalgic, humor, inspirational, articles spotlighting arts/disability, interview/profile (on prominent disabled people in the arts), opinion, the craft of fiction, personal experience, photo feature and travel. Publishes 14 mss/year; purchases 2 mss/year. Query with clips if available or send complete ms. Length: 10,000 words maximum. Pays in contributor's copies or cash awards for top submissions.
Photos: No pay for photos except annual cash award for top submission and contributor's copies. Photographic art done by disabled artists. Reviews 3x5, 5x7 8x10 b&w and color prints. Captions and identification of subjects required.
Fiction: Experimental, fantasy, historical, horror, humorous, mainstream, mystery, religious, romance, science fiction, suspense. Short stories, plays, novellas and excerpts. Publishes 16 mss/year; purchases 4/year. Query with clips if available or send complete ms. Length: 10,000 words maximum.
Poetry: Avant-garde, free verse, haiku, light verse and traditional. Publishes 30 poems/year; purchases 4 poems/year. Submit maximum 6 poems. Length: open. Pays in contributor's copies or cash award for top submissions.
Fillers: Anecdotes and short humor. Length: open.

Tips: "Study the magazine and know the editorial requirements. Avoid triteness and stereotypes in all writing. Articles about arts programs for disabled people sought. Fiction and poetry are most open to freelancers. For fiction, have strong, believable characterizations. Poetry should be vivid and free of cliches." Magazine will add a children's literature section and a column about the theatre scene.

LOS ANGELES TIMES BOOK REVIEW, Times Mirror, Times Mirror Sq., Los Angeles CA 90053. (213)972-7777. Editor: Art Seidenbaum. 70% freelance written. Weekly tabloid reviewing current books. Circ. 1.3 million. Pays on publication. Byline given. Offers variable kill fee. Buys first North American serial rights. Simultaneous queries OK. Computer printout submissions acceptable; prefers letter-quality to dot-matrix. SASE. Reports in 2 weeks. Publishes ms an average of 3 weeks after acceptance.
Nonfiction: No unsolicited book reviews. No requests for specific titles to review. "Query with published samples—book reviews or literary features." Buys 500 mss/year. Length: 150-1,500 words. Pays $50-250.

THE MASSACHUSETTS REVIEW, Memorial Hall, University of Massachusetts, Amherst MA 01003. (413)545-0111. Editors: John Hicks and Mary Heath. Quarterly. Buys first North American serial rights. Pays on publication. Computer printout submissions acceptable; prefers letter-quality to dot-matrix. Reports in 3 months. Mss will not be returned unless accompanied by SASE. Sample copy for $4 plus 50¢ postage.
Nonfiction: Articles on literary criticism, women, public affairs, art, philosophy, music and dance. Average length: 6,500 words. Pays $50.
Fiction: Short stories or chapters from novels when suitable for independent publication. Length: 15-22 typed pages. Pays $50.
Poetry: 35¢/line or $10 minimum.

‡**METROSPHERE, Literary Journal**, Metropolitan State College, Dept. of English, Campus Box 32, Denver CO 80204. (303)629-2494/2495. Editor: Professor Robert J. Pugel. A semiannual literary magazine of original poetry, fiction and nonfiction "for the 35,000 students and faculty at the Auraria Higher Education Center, and the literate readers in the Denver Metro community." Estab. 1983. Circ. 10,000. Byline given. Acquires first North American serial rights. Submit seasonal/holiday material 4 months in advance. Simultaneous queries, and simultaneous, photocopied and previously published submissions OK. Computer printout submissions acceptable. SASE. Reports in 2 weeks on queries; 2 months on mss. Sample copy $1; writer's guidelines for SAE and 1 first class stamp.
Nonfiction: General interest; historical/nostalgic; how-to (arts/humanities slant); humor; inspirational; interview/profile; personal experience; feature articles on Colorado and Rocky Mountain West (past, present, future). Accepts 30 mss/year. Query. Length: 750-1,200 words. Pays in copies.
Photos: State availability of photos with query letter or ms. Reviews 5x7 b&w prints. Captions required. Acquires one-time rights.
Fiction: Adventure, condensed novels, confession, ethnic, experimental, fantasy, historical, horror, humorous, mainstream, mystery, novel excerpts, religious, romance, science fiction, suspense and western. Accepts 30 mss/year. Send complete ms. Length: short stories to 1,500 words; will use 2 5,000-word pieces. Pays in copies.
Poetry: Avant-garde, free verse, haiku, light verse and traditional. Accepts 100 poems/year. Submit maximum 10 poems. Length: open. Pays in copies.
Fillers: Anecdotes and short humor. Accepts 10/year. Length: 500 words maximum. Pays in copies.
Tips: "We provide a showcase for the literary and artistic talents of our writers. We are interested in discovering new writers of quality work. Send us your best poetry and fiction. We're wide open for profiles and interviews of important, or soon-to-be-important, writers, artists, actors, musicians, or anyone involved with the arts."

‡**MICHIGAN QUARTERLY REVIEW**, 3032 Rackham Bldg., University of Michigan, Ann Arbor MI 48109. Editor: Laurence Goldstein. 75% freelance written. Quarterly. Circ. 2,000. Pays on acceptance. Buys first rights only. Computer printout submissions acceptable; no dot-matrix. SASE. Reports in 4 weeks for mss submitted in September-May; in summer, 8 weeks. Publishes ms an average of 1 year after acceptance. Sample copy $2.
Nonfiction: "*MQR* is open to general articles directed at an intellectual audience. Essays ought to have a personal voice and engage a significant subject. Scholarship must be present as a foundation, but we are not interested in specialized essays directed only at professionals in the field. We prefer ruminative essays, written in a fresh style and which reach interesting conclusions." Length: 2,000-5,000 words. Pays $80-150, sometimes more.
Fiction and Poetry: No restrictions on subject matter or language. "We publish about 10 stories a year and are very selective. We like stories which are comic, unusual in tone and structure, and innovative in language." Send complete ms. Pays $8-10/published page.
Tips: "Read the journal and assess the range of contents and the level of writing. We have no guidelines to offer or set expectations; every ms is judged on its unique qualities. On essays—query with a very thorough descrip-

tion of the argument and a copy of the first page. Watch for announcements of special issues, which are usually expanded issues and draw upon a lot of freelance writing. Be aware that this is a university quarterly that publishes a limited amount of fiction and poetry; that it is directed at an educated audience, one that has done a great deal of reading in all types of literature."

THE MICROPSYCHOLOGY NEWSLETTER, Microsphere Enterprises, 234 Fifth Ave., New York NY 10001. (212)462-8573. Editor: Joan Virzera. Quarterly literary and psychological newsletter for laypeople and professionals. Circ. 3,000. Pays on publication. Byline given. Offers 100% kill fee. Buys first North American serial rights and second serial rights. Submit seasonal/holiday material 3 months in advance. Simultaneous queries, and simultaneous, photocopied, and previously published submissions OK. Computer printout submissions acceptable. SASE. Reports in 1 month. Sample copy $3; writer's guidelines for SASE.
Nonfiction: General interest, humor, inspirational, opinion and personal experience. "Nothing that does not conform to the theme—the importance of the seemingly trivial." Buys 25-50 mss/year. Send complete ms. Length: 1,200 words maximum. Pays variable rates and in contributor copies.
Fiction: Experimental, humorous, mainstream, novel excerpts and psychological fiction. "High quality, literary with an emphasis on the theme of the newsletter—the importance of the seemingly trivial." Buys 25-50 mss/year. Send complete ms. Length: 2,000 words maximum. Pays variable rates and in contributor copies.
Poetry: Avant-garde, free verse, haiku, light verse and traditional. Light verse and didactic poetry preferred. Buys 25-50 poems/year. No limit on number of poems submitted. Length: "short poems preferred."
Fillers: Short humor. Buys 25-50/year. Length: 500 words maximum. Pays variable rates and in contributor copies.
Tips: "Micropsychology is an area dealing with the importance of the seemingly trivial, such as minor irritations and daily frustrations that affect people on a level beyond awareness. A significant aspect of micropsychology is humor therapy—seeing problems with humor alleviates associated stress. I am looking for any well-written material conforming to this theme. Will not hesitate to publish never-published writers whose material is of high quality and applicable." No political or vulgar material. Buys art and photography, psychologically-oriented photos, illustrations and cartoons (10-20/year).

MID-AMERICAN REVIEW, Dept. of English, Bowling Green State University, Bowling Green OH 43403. (419)372-2725. Editor: Robert Early. 100% freelance written. Semiannual literary magazine of "the highest quality fiction and poetry." Also publishes critical articles and book reviews of contemporary literature. Pays on publication. Byline given. Buys one-time rights. Do not query. Photocopied submissions OK. Computer printout submissions acceptable; prefers letter-quality to dot-matrix. SASE. Reports in 2 months or less. Publishes ms an average of 6 months after acceptance. Sample copy $4.50.
Fiction: Character-oriented, literary. Buys 12 mss/year. Send complete ms. Pays $5/page up to $75.
Poetry: Strong imagery, strong sense of vision. Buys 60/year. Pays $5/page. Annual prize for best fiction, best poem.

‡MIDWAY REVIEW, Southwest Area Cultural Arts Council (Chgo), Suite 134, 3400 W. 11th St., Chicago IL 60655. (312)436-4442. Editor: Peter S. Cooper. Managing Editor: Linda Steger and Grace Kuikman. 90% freelance written. Semiannual fiction/poetry and visual arts magazine "where artists of different life, career or geographic experience can meet, be met, and see the integration of their best or most ambitious literary and visual ideas." Circ. 1,000 (autumn issue 2,000). Pays on publication. Byline given. Buys first rights and one-time rights. Simultaneous queries, and photocopied and previously published submissions (established writers) OK. Computer printout submissions acceptable. SASE. Reports in 3 weeks on queries; 6 weeks on mss. Publishes ms an average of 6 months after acceptance. Sample copy for $3.50 and 50¢ postage.
Nonfiction: Book excerpts, interview/profile, opinion, photo feature and technical (literary). Contest issue in Summer/1984 includes winners and best from Little Sister Awards. No hard news or soft pornography. Buys 2 mss/year. Send complete ms. Length: 300-3,000 words. Pays $5-25.
Photos: Pays $5-5 for 5x7 and 8x10 b&w prints. "Since photos are an integral part of the magazine, I included this information, which is the same for those interested in submitting graphic arts (b&w illustrations). Buys 20 each/year.
Fiction: Ethnic, experimental, fantasy, historical, horror, humorous, mainstream, mystery, short novel excerpts, religious, romance, science fiction, suspense and western. Buys 4-8 mss/year. Send complete ms. Length: 300-4,000 words. Pays $10-25.
Poetry: Avant-garde and free verse. "We use very little rhyme, never traditional verse." Buys 40-60 poems/year. Submit maximum 6 poems. Length: open; rarely uses over 60 lines. Pays $5-25 (mostly $5-10).
Tips: "We are very open to writers, poets, graphic artists and photographers. A sample issue will guide them as to our prejudices. We answer all submissions personally and look to establish a relationship with writers, artists and readers. Every department is open to freelancers, with the exception of the editors, and we are open to *positive* suggestions there. We feel there is a gap forming between 'literary' magazines and general-interest magazines (which pay more). We are looking to fill that gap, and feel that 'literary' writers might pay more attention to their audience and be more successful by doing so. *Midway Review* can be a valuable tool (experience) for

writers who are not established, as well as a medium for established writers to communicate with their beginnings."

‡**MISSISSIPPI ARTS & LETTERS**, Persons Publishing, Box 3510, Hattiesburg MS 39403-3510. (601)545-2949. Editor: Alec Clayton. Managing Editor: Gabi Clayton. 75% freelance written. Quarterly magazine on the arts in Mississippi. Estab. 1983. Circ. 5,000. Pays on publication. Byline given. Buys first rights and second (reprint) rights to material originally published elsewhere. Submit seasonal/holiday material 6 months in advance. Simultaneous queries, photocopied and previously published submissions OK. Computer printout submissions acceptable; no dot-matrix. SASE. Reports in 4 weeks on queries; 2 months on mss. Publishes ms an average of 3 months after acceptance. Sample copy for 8x10 SAE and 3 first class stamps; writer's guidelines for business-size SAE and 1 first class stamp.
Nonfiction: Historical/nostalgic; how-to (relative to arts, crafts, photos, etc.); humor; interview/profile; and photo feature. Buys 18-20 mss/year. Query with published clips. Length: 500-3,000 words (once in a while longer). Pays average ½¢/word (from copies to $50 maximum).
Photos: State availibility of photos. Reviews 5x7 or 8x10 b&w prints. Captions and identification of subjects required. Buys one-time rights.
Columns/Departments: "All columns done by staff except reviews." Book Reviews and In a Nutshell (short news items on arts). June/July issue is "a special fiction issue featuring writers from the deep South." Buys 5-10 mss/year. Send complete ms. Length: 100-500 words. Pays approximately ½¢/word for Book Reviews; pays in copies for news items.
Fiction: Experimental, fantasy, historical, horror, humorous, mainstream, mystery, novel excerpts, science fiction and suspense. No genre submissions. June/July issue is "a special fiction issue featuring writers from the deep South." Buys 12 mss/year. Send complete ms with cover letter. Length: 500-8,000 words. Pays $5-100.
Poetry: Avant-garde, free verse, haiku, light verse and traditional. No "mushy love poems." Buys 20 poems/year. Submit maximum 10 poems. Pays in copies for minimal amount.
Fillers: Clippings and short humor. "We do not have a policy of buying fillers, but you never know."
Tips: "A freelancer can break in to our publication with a good personality profile/interview with someone important in the arts with strong connections to the state of Mississippi (i.e., Leontyne Price or Willie Morris). Fiction is a freelancer's best bet at *Mississippi Arts & Letters*. We want good writing with a Southern setting."

‡**MISSOURI REVIEW**, University of Missouri, 231 Arts & Science, Columbia MO 65211. (314)882-6066. Editor: Speer Morgan. Managing Editor: Greg Michalson. Triannual magazine. Circ. 2,000. Pays on publication. Byline given. Offers negotiable kill fee. Buys first North American serial rights. Simultaneous queries and simultaneous submissions (when indicated by cover letter), and photocopied submissions OK. Reports in 4 weeks on queries; 10 weeks on mss. Sample copy $3.50.
Nonfiction: "Informed/informal essays of literary interest" and criticism. Buys 20-30 mss/year. Query with published clips or send complete ms. Pays $10/page minimum to $200 maximum.
Fiction: Bob Shacochis and Bill Peden, fiction editors. "We want fiction with a distinctly contemporary orientation." No young adult material. Buys 20-30 mss/year. Send complete ms. Pays $10/page minimum to $300 maximum.
Poetry: Sherod Santos, poetry editor. Buys 100 poems/year. Submit maximum 6 poems. Pays $10 minimum.

MSS MAGAZINE, founded by John Gardner, SUNY Binghamton, Binghamton NY 13901. Editors: L.M. Rosenberg and Joanna Higgins. Literary magazine covering fiction, poetry, essays and illustrations. "We are looking for fiction, poetry and essays that are beautiful, thoughtful, and in some way moving. We especially want to support young and/or unpublished writers." Circ. 1,000. Pays on publication. Please do not submit without reading a copy of *MSS* first. Closed to submissions May-Sept. SASE. Reports in 1-2 months. Sample copy free; writer's guidelines for SASE.
Fiction: "We want wonderful fiction, not merely acceptable, 'slick,' publishable fiction." Buys 25 mss/year. Send complete ms. Length: open. Pays $75-400.
Poetry: "Open to all magnificent possibilities. Nothing cheap, shoddy, sentimental, ill-made or commercial." Buys 60-100 poems/year. Submit maximum 6 poems. Length: open. Pays $25-100.

‡**NEW DAY**, (formerly *The Magic Aura*), "the unique little magazine for artists of society," Dmitrovic Publications, 56 Carlingwood Court, Agincourt, Ontario M1R 3Y1 Canada. (416)755-9318. Editor: Lorraine Dmitrovic. 75% freelance written. Quarterly magazine covering "the world of the fantastic in art forms: film, literary, art, etc. We are unique in the way we do not publish what everybody else does; the creative, the tasteful, the visionary view is what we project. Writers should keep foremost in mind that even the 'usual' and 'ordinary' can be fascinating through examining old aspects in a new way." Estab. 1983. Circ. 1,000. Pays on acceptance. Publishes ms an average of 3 weeks after acceptance. Byline given. Offers 100% kill fee. Not copyrighted. Buys first and second rights to the same material and second (reprint) rights to material originally published elsewhere. Submit seasonal/holiday material 4 months in advance. Simultaneous queries, and si-

multaneous, photocopied, and previously published submissions OK. Computer printout submissions acceptable; no dot-matrix. SASE with 2 IRCs or sufficient postage. Reports in 2 weeks on queries; 3 weeks on mss.
Sample copy $2; writer's guidelines for SAE and 1 first class stamp.
Nonfiction: Expose; general interest; historical/nostalgic; interview/profile (film stars, authors, scientists, old
and new); opinion; and personal experience (must be able to be substantiated upon request). No material on
topics which have been written to "death." No discussions of sex; no unimaginative relatings on any topic; no
pretentious or vain-glorious ego pieces. Buys 100+ mss/year. Send complete ms. Length: 300-15,000 words.
Pays $2-5 (plans to increase rates with press-run issues in the near future).
Photos: State availability of photos or send photos with ms. Prefers photos that pertain to ms. Pays $1 for 5x7
b&w prints. Captions, model release and identification of subjects required (unless from a film studio, e.g.,
Warner Bros.).
Columns/Departments: The Editorial (generally issue-related, i.e., survival, nuclear holocaust, corporation
or government cover-up, etc.); Film Reviews; The News; and Trivia. Buys 100 mss/year. Send complete ms.
Length: 300-2,000 words. Pays $2-5.
Poetry: Avant-garde, free verse, haiku, light verse and traditional. No "Jack and Jill went up the hill" poetry.
Buys 25 poems/year. Submit maximum 10 poems. Length: 1-35 lines. Pays $1.
Fillers: Anecdotes, short humor and newsbreaks. Length: 300-1,000 words. Pays $2.
Tips: "A freelancer can break in to our publication with anything unusual, fascinating and different; new looks
at old ideas; things imaginatively and creatively written; things which inspire high intellect; things artfully,
tastefully accomplished; and things which appeal to the soul. Write from the heart, earnestly, zestily, bring the
fantastic of imagination down to paper. Informative articles are always welcome. Try the new, break the
ground in an area; be logical. Articles for example, could cover 'the rumored is true,' health, anything which
motivates or inspires. Write intelligently and with clarity. There seems to be an old school returning—readers
are now seeking honesty and integrity in literary endeavors. Our readers, especially, would not appreciate
'light fluff entertainment, empty excursions, or informative pieces geared to a naive set."

‡**NEW OREGON REVIEW,** Transition Publications (a nonprofit corporation), 537 NE Lincoln St., Hillsboro OR 97124. (503)640-1375. Editor: Steven Dimeo, Ph.D. 80% freelance written. Semiannual magazine
with short stories and poetry. "We seek to publish fiction of lasting literary merit from both unacknowledged
and well established artists who recognize the time-honored values of literary excellence. Our magazine is for
the literate and learned who prefer strong, interesting narratives of substance rather than dry academic fiction."
Circ. 200. Pays on publication. Byline given. Buys first North American serial rights. Submit seasonal/holiday
material 6 months in advance. Photocopied submissions OK, "but only if they're clear, legible and neat."
Computer printout submissions acceptable; no dot-matrix. "Submissions must include short bio/bibliographi-
cal statement and should be neat and professional." SASE. Reports in 2 months on mss. Publishes ms an average of 1 year after acceptance. Sample copy $2.50; writer's guidelines for business size SAE and 1 first class
stamp.
Photos: Send photos with ms. Prefers "imaginative, moody b&w glossies or line drawings, especially nudes,
landscapes and portraits." Reviews negatives and prints. Pays $10/photo; $25/cover photo. Model release required. Buys one-time rights.
Fiction: Fantasy, horror, humorous, mainstream, mystery, science fiction, suspense and erotica. "In fiction
we're looking primarily for the well developed tale with thematic depth, skillful characterization, wit, dramatic
change, subtle foreshadowing and imaginative symbolism. We want nothing unduly experimental and nothing
moralistic or trite." Buys 4-6 mss/year. Send complete ms. Length: 3,000-5,000 words (occasionally longer).
Pays $25 flat fee. Annual contest for subscribers only.
Poetry: Free verse and traditional. "In poetry, we're almost *always* overstocked and consider only poems of
exceptional merit, usually from well established writers, that demonstrate careful attention to rhyme, rhythm,
internal tonal integrity, and progressive development from beginning to end. Contributors should write in the
tradition of Emily Dickinson, W.B. Yeats, Robert Frost, W.H. Auden, Theodore Roethke, etc. We automatically reject poems encumbered with Cummingsesque affectations (lower-case letters, little or no punctuation,
etc.) that do not in some way echo the sense." Buys 6-10 poems/year. Submit maximum 5 poems. Length: 12-
40 lines. Pays $10/flat fee.
Tips: "A freelancer can best break in to our publication with fiction. Authors we admire include John Collier,
Roald Dahl, Kurt Vonnegut, Franz Kafka and Mark Twain. We're always in the market for realistic narratives
laced with horror or the fantastic in the manner of William Faulkner's 'A Rose for Emily' or John Cheever's
'The Enormous Radio'. We prefer stories that focus on relationships."

**The double dagger (‡) before a listing indicates that the listing is
new in this edition. New markets are often the most receptive to
freelance contributions.**

the new renaissance, An International Magazine of Ideas and Opinions, Emphasizing Literature and the Arts, 9 Heath Road, Arlington MA 02174. Editor: Louise T. Reynolds. 92% freelance written. International biannual literary magazine covering literature, visual arts, ideas, opinions for general literate, sophisticated public. Circ. 1,300. Pays after publication. Buys all rights. Simultaneous queries and photocopied submissions OK if so notified. SASE. Computer printout submissions acceptable; prefers letter-quality to dot-matrix. Reports in 4 weeks on queries; 5-7 months on mss. Sample copy $2.10 back issue; $4.25 recent issue.

Nonfiction: Interview/profile (literary/performing artists); opinion and literary/artistic essays. "We prefer expert opinion and/or documented nonfiction written in a style suitable for a literary magazine (i.e., *not* journalistic). Because we are biannual, we prefer to have writers query us, with outlines, etc, on articles of a political/sociological nature and give a sample of their (published) writing." Buys 2-4 mss/year. Query with clips. SASE. Length: 14-35 pages. Pays $24-95. Publishes ms an average of 15 months after acceptance.

Photos: State availability of photos with query letter or ms or send photos with accompanying query or ms. Pays $5-7 for 5x7 b&w prints. Captions, model release and identification of subjects required, if applicable. Buys one-time rights.

Fiction: Quality fiction, well-crafted, serious; occasionally, experimental. No "formula or plotted stories; no pulp and no woman's magazine fiction. We looking for writing with a personal voice." Buys 4-10 mss/year. Send complete ms. Length: 2-35 pages. Pays $20-60.

Poetry: Stanwood Bolton, poetry editor. Avant-garde, free verse, light verse and traditional translations (with originals). No heavily academic poetry; we publish only occasional light verse but we do not want to see 'Hallmark Card writing.' " Submit maximum 6 average; 8 short, 3-4 long poems. Reports in 2-4 months. Buys 16-45 poems/year. Pays $10-27.

Tips: "Know your markets. We are bogged down with manuscripts that, had the writer any understanding of our publication, would have been directed elsewhere. *tnr* is a unique litmag and should be *carefully* perused. Close reading of 1-2 issues will reveal that we have a classicist philosophy. Fiction and poetry open to freelancers. Writers most likely to break in to *tnr* are serious writers, poets, those who feel 'compelled' to write. We don't want to see 'pop' writing, trendy writing or formula writing. We do not want to use writing where the 'statement' is imposed on the story, nor do we want writing where the author shows off his superior knowledge or sensibility."

THE NEW SOUTHERN LITERARY MESSENGER, The Airplane Press, 400 S. Laurel St., Richmond VA 23220. (804)780-1244. Editor: Charles Lohmann. 100% freelance written. Quarterly literary tabloid featuring short stories and political satire. Circ. 500. Pays on publication. Byline given. Buys first rights and second (reprint) rights to material originally published elsewhere. Queries and previously published submissions OK. Computer printout submissions acceptable; no dot-matrix. SASE. Reports in 1 week on queries; 3 months on mss. Publishes ms an average of 3 months after acceptance. Sample copy for $1; writer's guidelines for 4x9 SASE.

Fiction: Short prose and political satire. Avoid fantasy and science fiction. No formula short stories. Buys 16-20 mss/year. Query. Length: 500-2,500 words. Pays $5.

Tips: "Reading computer printout manuscripts an editor is often troubled by the thought that perhaps the author spent less time writing than the editor does reading."

NIMROD, 2210 S. Main, Tulsa OK 74114. (918)584-3333. Editor: Francine Ringold. 100% freelance written. For readers and writers interested in good literature and art. Semiannual magazine; 120 (6x9) pages. Circ. 1,000. Buys first rights only. Byline given. Payment in contributor's copies and $5/page when funds are available. Photocopied submissions OK, but they must be very clear. No simultaneous submissions. Computer printout submissions acceptable; no dot-matrix. Reports in 3 months. Publishes ms an average of 5 months after acceptance. Query or submit complete ms. SASE.

Nonfiction: Interviews and essays. Buys 150 unsolicited mss/year. Length: open.

Fiction and Poetry: Experimental and mainstream fiction. Traditional forms of poetry, blank verse, free verse and avant-garde forms. "We are interested in quality and vigor. We often do special issues. Writers should watch for announced themes and/or query."

Tips: "The most rewarding aspect of working with freelance writers is the possibility of discovering a new and dynamic voice."

THE NORTH AMERICAN REVIEW, University of Northern Iowa, Cedar Falls IA 50614. (319)273-2681. Editor: Robley Wilson Jr. 50% freelance written. Quarterly. Circ. 4,000. Buys all rights for nonfiction and North American serial rights for fiction and poetry. Pays on publication. Computer printout submissions acceptable; prefers letter-quality to dot-matrix. Familiarity with magazine helpful. Reports in 8-10 weeks. Publishes ms an average of 1 year after acceptance. Sample copy $2. Query for nonfiction. SASE.

Nonfiction: No restrictions, but most nonfiction is commissioned by magazine. Rate of payment arranged.

Fiction: No restrictions; highest quality only. Length: open. Pays minimum $10/page. Fiction department closed (no manuscripts read) from April 1 to October 1.

Poetry: Peter Cooley, department editor. No restrictions; highest quality only. Length: open. Pays 50¢/line minimum.

THE OHIO REVIEW, Ellis Hall, Ohio University, Athens OH 45701. (614)594-5889. Editor: Wayne Dodd. "A balanced, informed engagement of contemporary American letters, special emphasis on poetics." Published 3 times/year. Circ. 2,000. Rights acquired vary with author and material; usually buys all rights or first North American serial rights. Submit complete ms. Unsolicited material will be read only September-May. Computer printout submissions acceptable. SASE. Reports in 6 to 8 weeks.
Nonfiction, Fiction and Poetry: Buys essays of general intellectual and special literary appeal. Not interested in narrowly focused scholarly articles. Seeks writing that is marked by clarity, liveliness, and perspective. Interested in the best fiction and poetry. Buys 75 unsolicited mss/year. Pays minimum $5/page, plus copies.
Tips: "Make your query very brief, not gabby, one that describes some publishing history, but no extensive bibliographies."

ORBIS, The International Literary Magazine, 199 The Long Shoot, Nuneaton, Warwickshire CV11 6JQ England. Tel. (0203)327440. Editor: Mike Shields. 50-75% freelance written. Quarterly magazine covering literature in English and other languages. Circ. 500 (in 30 countries). Pays on publication. Extra prizes totaling 50 pounds in each issue. Byline given. Buys first rights only. Photocopied submissions OK. Computer printout submissions acceptable. SAE and IRCs. Reports in 6 weeks. Publishes ms an average of 9 months after acceptance. Sample copy $2.
Nonfiction: Literary criticism, how to write poetry, and how to develop a literary work. "No excessively literary or academically pretentious work; keep it practical. Wild avant-garde or ultra-traditional work unlikely to be used." Buys few mss/year. "We reject more than 98% of work received for simple lack of space, so don't be disappointed." Send complete ms. Length: 1,200 words maximum. Pays 2 pounds.
Columns/Departments: Letters (not paid for); Past Master (not paid for) "poem from the past accompanied by about 100 words on 'why' "; and Poem in Progress (description of how a favorite poem was developed). Pays 2 pounds.
Fiction: "We are looking for short (1,200 words) pieces of original and interesting work; prose poems, mood pieces, short stories, etc. No 'magazine' or 'formula' fiction." Buys few mss/year. Send complete ms. Length: 1,200 words maximum. Pays 2 pounds.
Poetry: Free verse, light verse and traditional. "We do not specifically exclude any type of poetry, but we feel that there are far too many undistinguished haiku around, and will not publish the meaningless gobbledegook which has featured in many magazines recently. No unoriginal rhymed poetry. We are looking for original poems which communicate modern thought and expression and show an excellence of language. Length is not a major factor, but we cannot handle *very* long poems. We need American poetry, long poems, English dialect poems and translated poetry." Buys 250/year. Submit maximum 6 poems. Length: "over 100 lines may be difficult." Pays 2 pounds. US stamps cannot be used to return material from the UK; IRCs should be enclosed.

‡THE PACIFIC QUARTERLY, 626 Coate Rd., Orange CA 92669. Editor-in-Chief: Mark D. Stancl. 90% freelance written. Quarterly anthology of fiction and nonfiction. "This magazine is for a highly sophisticated, intelligent audience. People who are well versed in academic and world affairs and events find that our publication meets their needs. We do not educate or teach our readers; we inform them and build upon previous knowledge and background." Estab. 1983. Circ. 800. Pays on acceptance. Byline given. Offers 50% kill fee. Buys first and second rights to the same material. Submit seasonal/holiday material 4 months in advance. Simultaneous queries, and simultaneous and photocopied submissions OK. Computer printout submissions acceptable. SASE. Reports in 4 weeks on queries; 6 weeks on mss. Publishes ms an average of 3-4 months after acceptance. Writer's guidelines for business-size SAE and 1 first class stamp.
Nonfiction: Book excerpts, expose, general interest, historical/nostalgic, humor, interview/profile, opinion, personal experience, photo feature and travel. Special issues include Ramifications of the Equal Rights Amendment, Nuclear Armament/Disarmament Issues, World Trade, Guerilla Uprisings, etc. No religious or inspiration material. Buys 40 mss/year. Query or send complete ms. Length: no limit. Pays variable "good" rates.
Columns/Departments: "We accept film and book reviews of only current releases and look for opinion articles on any current national/world issue (such as nuclear build-ups, embargoes, etc.)." Buys 10 mss/year. Query or send complete ms. Length: no limit. Pays variable "good" rates.
Fiction: Adventure, ethnic, experimental, fantasy, humorous, mainstream, mystery, novel excerpts, suspense and western. "We don't want a story with no point to be made or those that remain 'so what' in solution." Buys 50 mss/year. Query or send complete ms. Length: no limit. Pays variable "good" rates.
Poetry: Avant-garde, free verse, light verse and traditional. Buys 15 poems/year. Submit maximum 5 poems. Length: 15-50 lines. Pays variable "good" rates.
Fillers: Jokes, gags and short humor. Buys 15/year. Length: no limit. Pays variable "good" rates.
Tips: "Since this is a new publication, our staff is very receptive to all materials. Each ms will be carefully read, and all promising material will be commented upon. We want to emphasize that 90% of our magazine is freelance written. The fiction and poetry sections are not staff-written; we are always looking for new, unestablished writers with fresh insights about life. Make the mss sharp, witty, crisp; we abhor long, drawn-out sentences. Your point should be made quickly and effortlessly."

PARABOLA, 150 5th Ave., New York NY 10011. (212)924-0004. Editor: Lorraine Kisly. Executive Editor: Philip Zaleski. "Audience shares an interest in exploring the wisdom transmitted through myth and the great religious traditions." Quarterly magazine; 128 pages. Circ. 15,000. Buys all rights. Byline given. Pays on publication. Photocopied submissions OK. Manuscripts should be sent to the attention of the editors. SASE. Writer's guidelines for SASE.
Nonfiction: "We handle work from a wide range of perspectives, mostly related to myth or comparative religion. Don't be scholarly, don't footnote, don't be dry. We want fresh approaches to timeless subjects." Length: 3,500 words maximum. Buys 25 mss/year. Query. Pays $25-150.
Photos: Purchased with or without accompanying ms. No color. Pays $25.
Fiction: Prefers retellings of traditional stories, legends and myths. Length: 1,500 words maximum. Pays "negotiable rates."
Poetry: "Very little and only when theme-related."

THE PARIS REVIEW, 45-39 171st Place, Flushing NY 11358. Editor: George A. Plimpton. Quarterly. Buys all rights. Pays on publication. Address submissions to proper department and address. Computer printout submissions acceptable; no dot-matrix. SASE.
Fiction: Study publication. No length limit. Pays up to $250. Makes award of $500 in annual fiction contest. Submit to 541 E. 72nd St., New York NY 10021.
Poetry: Study publication. Pays $10 to 25 lines; $15 to 50 lines; $25 to 100 lines; $50 thereafter. Poetry mss must be submitted to Jonathan Galassi at 541 E. 72nd St., New York NY 10021. SASE. Sample copy $6.

PARTISAN REVIEW, 121 Bay State Rd., Boston MA 02215. (617)353-4260. Editor: William Phillips. Executive Editor: Edith Kurzweil. 90% freelance written. Quarterly literary journal covering world literature, politics and contemporary culture for an intelligent public with emphasis on the arts and political/social commentary. Circ. 8,200. Pays on publication. Buys first rights only. Byline given. Photocopied submissions OK. No previously published submissions. SASE. Reports in 6 months. Publishes ms an average of 9 months after acceptance. Sample copy $4; free writer's guidelines.
Nonfiction: Essays and book reviews. Buys 30-40 mss/year. Send complete ms. Pays $50-150.
Fiction: High quality, serious and contemporary fiction. No science fiction, mystery, confession, romantic or religious material. Buys 8-10 mss/year. Send complete ms. Pays $50-150.
Poetry: Buys 20/year. Submit maximum 6 poems. Pays $25.

PHANTASM, Literary Magazine, Heidelberg Graphics, Box 3606W, Chico CA 95927. (916)342-6582. Editor: Larry S. Jackson. Magazine published infrequently (usually 2 times/year) covering literature/creative writing. "*Phantasm* is a multi-cultural literary magazine breaking the staid formats of traditional journals with a dash of Western flavor and the dynamics of eclecticism. Its audience is primarily educators, poets, writers and others interested in contemporary literature." Circ. 1,100. Pays on publication. Byline given. Buys one-time rights. Submit seasonal/holiday material 6 months in advance. SASE. Reports in 1 month on queries; 4 months on mss. Sample copy $3; writer's guidelines published in magazine.
Nonfiction: Interview/profile (poets and writers), current literary events and literary feature articles. Buys 8 mss/year. Send complete ms. Length: 500-1,500 words. Pays $2.
Photos: Send photos with accompanying query or ms. Reviews 5x7 b&w prints. Captions required.
Columns/Departments: Guest columnist—regarding contemporary literature movement or appealing to writers, book reviews and interviews. Buys 4/year. Send complete ms. Length: 800-1,500 words. Pays $2.
Fiction: Adventure, erotica, ethnic, fantasy, historical, humorous, mainstream, mystery, suspense, western. Buys 4 mss/year. Send complete ms. Length: 600-1,500 words. Pays $2.
Poetry: Phillip Hemenway, poetry editor. Avant-garde, free verse, traditional and translations. Buys 24/year. Submit maximum 5 poems. Pays $2.
Tips: Break in "by sending us your best work in congruence with the magazine's format." Feature articles, poetry and reviews open to freelancers.

PIG IRON MAGAZINE, Pig Iron Press, Box 237, Youngstown OH 44501. (216)744-2258. Editors-in-Chief: Jim Villani and Rose Sayre. 90% freelance written. Emphasizes literature/art for writers, artists and intelligent lay audience with bias towards popular culture. Semiannual magazine. Circ. 1,500. Pays on publication. Buys one-time rights. Byline given. Submit seasonal/holiday material 4 months in advance. Photocopied and previously published submissions OK. Computer printout submissions acceptable. SASE. Reports in 3 months. Publishes ms an average of 18 months after acceptance. Sample copy $2.50; free writer's guidelines with SASE.
Nonfiction: General interest, interview, personal opinion, profile, political or alternative lifestyle/systems. Buys 3 mss/year. Query. Length: 8,000 words maximum. Pays $2/page minimum.
Photos: Submit photo material with accompanying query. Pays $2 minimum for 5x7 or 8x10 b&w glossy prints. Buys one-time rights.
Fiction: Rose Sayre, fiction editor. Fantasy, avant-garde, experimental, psychological fiction and science fic-

tion, humor, western and frontier. Buys 4-12 mss/issue. Submit complete ms. Length: 8,000 words maximum. Pays $2 minimum.

Poetry: Terry Murcko and George Peffer, poetry editors. Avant-garde and free verse. Buys 25-50/issue. Submit in batches of 10 or less. Length: open. Pays $2 minimum.

Tips: "Send modest batches of material at frequent intervals (3-4 times per year). Let us see the range of your talent and interests by mixing up styles, subject matter. We are interested in modernistic, surreal, satirical, futuristic and political subjects. Upcoming thematic issues include pyschological, humor, and The Wild West."

PLOUGHSHARES, Box 529, Dept. M, Cambridge MA 02139. Editor: DeWitt Henry. For "readers of serious contemporary literature: students, educators, adult public." Quarterly magazine. Circ. 3,400. Rights purchased vary with author and material; usually buys all rights or may buy first North American serial rights. Buys 25-50 unsolicited mss/year. Pays on publication. Photocopied submissions OK. No simultaneous submissions. Reports in 6 months. SASE. Sample copy $5.

Nonfiction, Poetry and Fiction: "Highest quality poetry, fiction and criticism." Interview and literary essays. Length: 5,000 words maximum. Pays $50. Reviews (assigned). Length: 500 words maximum. Pays $15. Fiction: experimental and mainstream. Length: 300-6,000 words. Pays $5-50. Poetry: buys traditional forms, blank verse, free verse and avant-garde. Length: open. Pays $10/poem.

PRAIRIE SCHOONER, Andrews Hall, University of Nebraska, Lincoln NE 68588. Editor: Hugh Luke. Poetry Editor: Hilda Raz. Quarterly. Usually acquires all rights unless author specifies first serial rights only. Computer printout submissions acceptable. Pays in copies of the magazine, offprints and prizes. Reports usually in 2-3 months. Publishes ms an average of 1 year after acceptance. SASE.

Nonfiction: Uses 1-2 articles per issue. Subjects of literary or general interest. Does not print academic articles. Length: 5,000 words maximum.

Fiction: Uses several stories per issue.

Poetry: Uses 20-30 poems in each issue of the magazine. These may be on any subject, in any style. Occasional long poems are used, but the preference is for the shorter length. High quality necessary.

PRISM INTERNATIONAL, Department of Creative Writing, University of British Columbia, Vancouver, British Columbia V6T 1W5 Canada. Editor-in-Chief: Michael Pacey. Managing Editor: Lasha Seniuk. Emphasizes contemporary literature, including translations. For university and public libraries, and private subscribers. Quarterly magazine. Circ. 1,000. Pays on publication. Buys first North American serial rights. Photocopied submissions OK. SAE and IRCs. Reports in 10 weeks. Sample copy $4.

Fiction: Experimental and traditional. Buys 3 mss/issue. Send complete ms. Length: 5,000 words maximum. Pays $15/printed page and one-year subscription.

Poetry: Avant-garde and traditional. Buys 30 poems/issue. Limit submissions to batches of 6. Pays $15/printed page and one-year subscription.

Drama: One-acts preferred. Pays $15/printed page and one-year subscription.

QUARRY, Quarry Press, Box 1061, Kingston, Ontario K7L 4Y5 Canada. (613)544-5400, ext. 165. Editor: David John Schleich. 99% freelance written. Quarterly magazine covering poetry, prose, reviews. "We seek high quality new writers who are aware of their genre and who are committed to their art." Circ. 1,500. Pays on publication. Byline given. Buys first North American serial rights. Simultaneous queries and photocopied submissions OK. Computer printout submission acceptable. SASE. Reports in 3 weeks on queries; 3 months on mss. Publishes ms an average of 6 months after publication. Sample copy $3; writer's guidelines for business-size SAE and 34¢ postage.

Nonfiction: Short stories, poetry and book reviews. "We need book reviews of Canadian work. Not interested in reviews of American or UK books. No literary criticism." Buys 100 mss/year. Send complete ms. Length: open. Pays $5-$10 per page plus one year subscription.

Fiction: Any short fiction of high quality. "No nonliterary fiction." Send complete ms. Length: 10-15 pages maximum. Pays $5-10/page.

Poetry: Avant-garde, free verse, haiku, light verse and traditional. "No amateur, derivative poetry." Buys 200/year. Submit maximum 10 poems. Length: open. Pays $5-10/page.

Tips: "The most annoying aspect of working with freelance writers is Americans who send SASE with US postage, forgetting that Canada is a foreign country."

QUEEN'S QUARTERLY, A Canadian Review, Queen's University, Kingston, Ontario K7L 3N6 Canada. (613)547-6968. Editor: Dr. Michael Fox. Quarterly magazine covering a wide variety of subjects, including: science, humanities, arts and letters, politics, and history for the educated reader. 10-15% freelance written. Circ. 1,900. Pays on publication. Byline given. Buys first North American serial rights. Photocopied submissions OK. Computer printout submissions acceptable; prefers letter-quality to dot-matrix. SASE. Reports in 2 weeks on queries; 2-3 months on mss. Publishes ms an average of 1 year after acceptance. Sample copy $4; free writer's guidelines.

Fiction: Fantasy, historical, humorous, mainstream and science fiction. Buys 4-6 mss/year. Send complete ms. Length: 5,000 words maximum. Pays $25-100.

Poetry: Avant-garde, free verse, haiku, light verse, traditional. No "sentimental, religious, or first efforts by unpublished writers." Buys 25/year. Submit maximum 6 poems. Length: open. Pays $10-25.

Tips: "Poetry and fiction are most open to freelancers. Include curriculum vita and brief description of what's unique about the submission. Don't send less than the best." No multiple submissions. No more than 6 poems or 1 story per submission. We buy just a few freelance submissions."

‡**RAMPIKE MAGAZINE, An Arts & Writing Journal**, Coach House Press, 95 Rivercrest Rd., Toronto, Ontario M6S 4H7 Canada. (416)767-6713. Editor: Karl E. Jirgens. Managing Editor: Eddy Nova. 100% freelance written. Triannual magazine covering post-modern (contemporary) art and writing. "*Rampike* is interested in artists and writers who are pioneers in their field. We have a different theme with each issue, and potential collaborators should contact the editors in advance." Circ. 2,000. Pays on publication and as per mutual agreement. Byline given. Buys first rights; "all rights remain with contributor." Submit seasonal/holiday material 1 month in advance. No simultaneous queries, simultaneous submissions, or previously published submissions. Photocopied submissions OK. Electronic submissions OK, but requires hard copy also. Computer printout submissions acceptable. SASE. Reports in 1 month. Publishes ms an average of 9 months after acceptance. Sample copy $2; writer's guidelines for 4x9½ SAE.

Nonfiction: Book excerpts, expose, humor, interview/profile, photo feature, technical, scientific and academic. No material that doesn't fit the theme or does not show awareness of post-modern editorial bias. Buys 50 mss/year. Query with or without published clips or send complete ms (photocopy only). Length: 2,000-6,000 words. Pays 0-$100.

Photos: Fausto Bedoya, photo editor. State availability of photos or send photos with query or ms. Pays 0-$100 for 6x16 b&w prints on theme. Captions, model release, and identification of subjects required. Buys one-time rights.

Fiction: Adventure, confession, erotica, experimental, fantasy, historical, horror, humorous, mystery, novel excerpts, romance, science fiction, serialized novels, suspense, academic and scientific. No material that is not post-modern or not on theme. Buys 50 mss/year. Query with or without published clips or send complete ms (photocopy only). Length: 2,000-6,000 words. Pays 0-$100.

Poetry: Fausto Bedoya, poetry editor. Avant-garde and free verse. No off-theme or non-postmodern poetry. Buys 50 poems/year. Submit maximum 12 poems. Length: 5-120 lines. Pays 0-$100.

Tips: "Contact editors, have strong interest in post-modern developments, and be aware of other artists and writers working in contemporary field. We are most interested in experimental or avant-garde fiction."

RIVER STYX MAGAZINE, Big River Association, 7420 Cornell, St. Louis MO 63130. Editor: Jan Garden Castro. Biannual, multicultural literary magazine of contemporary prose, poetry, photography and art. Circ. 1,500. Pays on publication. Byline given. Buys first rights to publication. Submit only in October 1985 and annually in October thereafter. Reports in November. SASE. Sample copy $3.50; writer's guidelines for SASE.

Photos: "We use photos without manuscripts." Send photos and SASE in October. Pays $10 for 8x10 b&w prints. Buys one-time rights.

Fiction: Ethnic, experimental. Buys 3-4 mss/year. Query. Pays $8/page, $100 maximum.

Poetry: Avant-garde, free verse, traditional. Submit only in October 1985 and annually in October thereafter, poems international in scope. Buys 20-50 poems/year. Submit maximum 5 poems. Length: open. Pays $8/page, $100 maximum.

Tips: "Read issue #14 and #15; submit only if your work is compatible with contents and exceptional on its own terms."

SECOND COMING, Box 31249, San Francisco CA 94131. Editor-in-Chief: A.D. Winans. 75% freelance written. Semiannual magazine. Circ. 1,000. Pays in copies. Acquires one-time rights. Query first with an "honest statement of credits." Computer printout submissions acceptable; prefers letter-quality to dot-matrix. SASE. Reports in 1-4 weeks. Publishes ms an average of 9 months after acceptance. Sample copy $3.

Fiction: Experimental (avant-garde) and humorous. Uses 6-12 mss/year. Submit complete ms. Recent example: Article on fiction in the US (Vol. 10, No. 122). Length: 1,000-3,000 words. Pays in copies.

Poetry: Avant-garde, free verse and surrealism. Uses 100-150/year. Limit submissions to batches of 6. No length requirement. Pays in copies.

Photos: Pays $5 token plus copies for b&w photos.

Tips: "We publish mostly veterans of the small press scene. Read at least 1 back issue."

SEWANEE REVIEW, University of the South, Sewanee TN 37375. (615)598-5931. Editor: George Core. 60% freelance written. For audience of "variable ages and locations, mostly college-educated and with interest in literature." Quarterly. Circ. 3,400. Buys all serial rights. Pays on publication. Computer printout submissions acceptable; prefers letter-quality to dot-matrix. Reports in 1 month. SASE. Publishes ms an average of 9 months after acceptance. Sample copy $4.75.

Nonfiction and Fiction: Short fiction (but not drama); essays of critical nature on literary subjects (especially modern British and American literature); and essay-reviews and reviews (books and reviewers selected by the editors). Length: 6,000-7,500 words. Payment varies: averages $10 per printed page.
Poetry: Selections of 4 to 6 poems preferred. In general, light verse and translations are not acceptable. Maximum payment is 60¢ per line.

THE SOUTHERN REVIEW, 43 Allen Hall, Louisiana State University, Baton Rouge LA 70803. (504)388-5108. Editors: James Olney and Lewis Simpson. For academic, professional, literary, intellectual audience. Quarterly. Circ. 3,000. Buys first rights only. Byline given. Pays on publication. Sample copy $2.50. No queries. Reports in 2 to 3 months. SASE.
Nonfiction: Essays with careful attention to craftsmanship and technique and to seriousness of subject matter. "Willing to publish experimental writing if it has a valid artistic purpose. Avoid extremism and sensationalism. Essays exhibit thoughtful and sometimes severe awareness of the necessity of literary standards in our time." Emphasis on contemporary literature, especially Southern culture and history. Minimum number of footnotes. Buys 80-100 mss/year. Length: 4,000-10,000 words. Pays $12/page for prose.
Fiction and Poetry: Short stories of lasting literary merit, with emphasis on style and technique. Length: 4,000-8,000 words. Pays $12/page for prose; $20/page for poetry.

SOUTHWEST REVIEW, Southern Methodist University, Dallas TX 75275. (214)692-3736. Editor: Willard Spiegelman. For adults and college graduates with literary interests and some interest in the Southwest, but subscribers are from all over America and some foreign countries. Quarterly magazine. Circ. 1,400. Buys all rights. Byline given. Buys 65 mss/year. Pays on publication. Sample copy $2.50. Query for nonfiction. Submit only complete ms for fiction and poetry. Reports in 3 months. SASE.
Nonfiction and Photos: "Articles, literary criticism, social and political problems, history (especially Southwestern), folklore (especially Southwestern), the arts, etc. Articles should be appropriate for a literary quarterly; no feature stories. Critical articles should consider a writer's whole body of work, not just one book. History should use new primary sources or a new perspective, not syntheses of old material. We're regional but not provincial." Interviews with writers, historical articles, and book reviews of scholarly nonfiction. Length: 1,500-5,000 words. Regular columns are Regional Sketchbook (Southwestern) and Points of View (personal essays). Uses b&w photos for cover and occasional photo essays.
Fiction: No limitations on subject matter for fiction. Prefer stories of character development, of psychological penetration, rather than those depending chiefly on plot. Some experimental fiction and mainstream fiction. Length: 1,500-5,000 words. The John H. McGinnis Memorial Award of $1,000 is made in alternate years for fiction and nonfiction pieces published in *SWR*.
Poetry: No limitations on subject matter. Not particularly interested in broadly humorous, religious or sentimental poetry. Free verse, some avant-garde forms, and open to all serious forms of poetry. "There are no arbitrary limits on length, but we find shorter poems are easier to fit into our format." The Elizabeth Matchett Stover Memorial Award of $100 is made annually for a poem published in *SWR*.

THE SPIRIT THAT MOVES US, The Spirit That Moves Us Press, Inc., Box 1585-W, Iowa City IA 52244. (319)338-5569. Editor: Morty Sklar. 99% freelance written. Semiannual literary magazine of poetry, fiction, artwork. "We prefer work which is concerned with life and living. We don't like sensational or academic writing." Circ. 800-1,500. Pays on publication. Byline given. Buys first North American serial rights and second (reprint) rights to material published elsewhere for anthologies. Simultaneous queries and photocopied submissions OK. Computer printout submissions acceptable; no dot-matrix. SASE. Reports in 1 week on queries; 1 month on mss. Publishes ms an average of 10 months after acceptance. Sample copy for $3; writer's guidelines for SASE.
Photos: Morty Sklar, photo editor. "Photographs which capture a sense of life, either in mood or energy." Send photos with ms. Pays $5-10 for 4x5 and larger b&w prints. Also pays in copies. Buys one-time rights. Write first to find out what our current themes are. Include SASE.
Fiction: "Anything goes as long as it shows concern for life and living and is well-written. No sensational or academic material (work which is skillfully written but has little human involvement)." Buys 4-20 mss/year. Send complete ms. Length: open. Pays $10-25 and copies.
Poetry: Any style or "school"; send what you like best. Buys 25-50 poems/year. Submit maximum 5 poems. Length: open. Pays $5-10; also pays in copies.
Tips: "Send the work *you* like best, not what you think we'll like."

‡**THE SQUATCHBERRY JOURNAL**, Box 205, Geraldton, Ontario P0T 1M0 Canada. (807)854-1184. Editor: Edgar J. Lavoie. 100% freelance written. Annual little arts and letters magazine that features writers and artists who portray Northern Ontario in fact, fiction, prose or poetry. Circ. 1,000. Pays on publication. Byline given. Buys one-time rights. Photocopied and simultaneous submissions OK. Computer printout submissions acceptpable. SASE. Publishes ms an average of 6 months after acceptance. Sample copy for $2.50, 9x12 SAE and $1 postage.

Nonfiction: Historical/nostalgic, humor, inspirational, interview/profile, personal experience, photo feature and travel. No articles not localized or set in Northern Ontario. Buys 20-25 mss/year. Send complete ms. Length: 2,500 words maximum. Pays $2-12.

Photos: State availability of photos or send photos with ms. Pays $1-2 for b&w prints. Identification of subjects required. Buys one-time rights.

Fiction: Adventure, ethnic, historical, humorous, novel excerpts and suspense. No erotica, confession, experimental or science fiction. Buys 20-25 mss/year.

Poetry: Free verse, haiku, light verse and traditional. Buys 50-60 poems/year. Submit minimum 3 poems. Pays $1-4.

Fillers: Anecdotes and short humor. Buys 12/year. Pays $1-2.

Tips: "A freelancer can best break into our publication by having a deep interest in Northern Ontario or wilderness/frontier areas."

‡**"STARR" WORLD JOURNAL**, J&A Enterprises, 5522 W. Acoma Rd., Glendale AZ 85306. (602)978-4740. Editor: Anna Trotta. A semiannual magazine. "We publish only *quality* poetry, fiction and general literature reaching readers of all ages." Estab. 1984. Circ. 300. Byline given. Acquires first North American serial rights. Submit seasonal/holiday material in January for Spring issue; July for Fall issue. Photocopied and previously published submissions OK. Computer printout submissions acceptable; no dot-matrix. SASE. Reports in 2 weeks. Sample copy for $2.50, 6x9 SAE and 20¢ postage; writer's guidelines for business-size SAE and 1 first class stamp.

Nonfiction: General interest, humor, inspirational, opinion, and personal experience. No articles on erotica. Send complete ms. Length: 100-300 words. Pays in copy.

Fiction: Adventure, confession, fantasy, historical, horror, humorous, mainstream, mystery, religious, romance, science fiction, suspense, and western. *No erotica!* Send complete ms. Length: 100-300 words. Pays in copy.

Poetry: Avant-garde, free verse, haiku, light verse, traditional. No erotica. Submit maximum 5 poems. Length: 20 lines maximum. Pays in copy.

Fillers: Anecdotes, short humor, newsbreaks. Length: 50-300 words. Pays in copy.

‡**STORIES**, 14 Beacon St., Boston MA 02108. Editor: Amy R. Kaufman. Bimonthly magazine publishing short fiction. "It is designed to encourage the writing of a particular kind of story—described most accurately by the term 'affective fiction'—for which, the editor believes, there is a demand." Circ. 2,000. Pays on publication. Byline given. Buys first North American serial rights. Photocopied submissions and simultaneous submissions OK (if so marked). Computer printout submissions acceptable; prefers letter-quality to dot-matrix. No queries. SASE. Reports in 10 weeks on mss. Sample copy $4 (including postage); writer's guidelines for business-size SAE and 1 first class stamp.

Fiction: Contemporary, ethnic, historical (general), humor/satire, literary, serialized/excerpted novel and translations. "We wish to promote literature that is capable of eliciting emotional response, not the type whose exclusive purpose is to entertain, inform, horrify or impress. We appreciate humor that is sharply perceptive, not merely amusing; political or moral pieces that make a point, not merely hint at one, and that do not proselytize. Ordinarily, romance, mystery, fantasy, political pieces and science fiction do not suit our purposes, but we will not exclude any story on the basis of genre; we wish only that the piece be the best of its genre." Buys 36-48 mss/year. Send complete ms. Length: 750-15,000 words; 4,000-7,000 words average. Pays $150 minimum.

Tips: "We look for characters identifiable not by name, age, profession, or appearance, but by symbolic qualities; timeless themes and styles that are sophisticated but not affected, straightforward but not artless, descriptive but not nearsighted."

‡**SWALLOW'S TALE MAGAZINE**, Swallow's Tale Press, Box 4328, Tallahassee FL 32315. (904)224-8859. Editor: Joe Taylor. Managing Editor: Patricia Willey. 100% freelance written. Semiannual magazine focusing on literature that entertains. Circ. 1,000. Pays on publication. Byline given. Offers 15% kill fee. Buys first North American serial rights. Photocopied submissions OK. Computer printout submissions acceptable. SASE. Reports in 2 weeks on queries; 10 weeks on mss. Publishes ms an average of 6 months after acceptance. Sample copy $4; writer's guidelines for business-size SAE and 1 first class stamp.

Nonfiction: Interview/profile. "We publish only a very few nonfiction articles: book reviews, critical assessments of literary trends, or a contemporary author's work. Buys 15 mss/year. Send complete ms. Length: 750-5,000 words. Pays $15-50.

Fiction: Experimental, fantasy, horror, humorous, literary and mainstream. Buys 25-30 mss/year. Send complete ms. Length: 750-7,500 words. Pays $25-100.

Poetry: Avant-garde, free verse, light verse and traditional. "We look for poetry that extends the personal moment to the universal, resolves well, and, of course, shows an awareness of language and rhythm." Buys 75-100 poems/year. Submit maximum 5 poems. Length: 8 lines minimum. Pays $10-50.

Tips: "We prefer fiction with plot and action, though we have and will continue to publish experimental fiction and minimalist work with an emphasis on language or theme, if well-crafted."

Close-up

Betsey Mills McDougall
Managing Editor
Southwest Review

When *Southwest Review* managing editor Betsey Mills McDougall finds a few stories that look especially promising, she takes them home. "It allows me to decide if this is really good or good only in the context of the office," she says. "It allows me to be more critical but also more sympathetic."

She asks herself: "How is this manuscript going to stand out to readers in the comfort of their living rooms?"

SWR stories, of course, travel farther than McDougall's living room before being cast in hot type. As with many university and literary magazines, each manuscript gets two to three readings by different editors. "Every editor wants to discover the diamond in the rough, and that's what we're looking for," says McDougall, who previously worked for the Wesleyan University Press.

The Southern Methodist University quarterly receives 1,700 manuscripts a year, many of them quite good. "What used to be published by the commercial presses is now falling to the university presses," an advantage that university press editors relish. "There's a lot of good material to be had," says McDougall. "It's a question of putting out a magazine to attract talent."

In its 70th year, *SWR* has given many bylines, some to well-known writers, Maxim Gorky, Robert Graves, and Robert Penn Warren. The magazine publishes articles on fiction, poetry, the history of the Southwest, contemporary affairs, the arts, and folklore, in addition to fiction, poetry, and interviews with writers. "We really want to make it a lively forum of life and letters for the Southwest," she says. "Everything has been done in big magazines. . . . You can experiment in a little magazine."

McDougall values the freedoms of a university lit mag. "You can publish works of literary excellence rather than things that need to make money," she points out.

"What we're looking for is good writing. The subject doesn't matter," says McDougall, *SWR*'s only full-time staffer since the journal and SMU Press became separate entities last year.

"We like work that is more psychologically interesting or that shows character development and psychological penetration," she points out. "We're not looking for work that relies on plot for interest. The design has to be strong; the grammar and syntax have to be impeccable."

What bothers McDougall are the manuscripts from writers who obviously don't read literary magazines. "Some stories I read are television-inspired," she believes. "The language is right from a TV script, the setting, the kind of plot that is set up."

In reading each piece of mail, she looks for writers with a knowledge of language, imagination, a sense of humor, and, above all, a resilience and belief in one's self. The last two qualities will keep an *undiscovered* writer writing, she says. "If you want to be a writer, it's good to find work that can nurture it and complement who you are and what you want to do."

The writer (wanting to work for or write for a lit mag) must do what McDougall does—read. And, like McDougall, he must ask himself: *how* does each story stand out?

‡**TABOO MAGAZINE**, Bottom Line Design, Inc., 429 E. Vermont, Indianapolis IN 46202. (317)636-8227. Editor: Don Berry. 60% freelance written. Monthly magazine. "The goal of *Taboo* is to make available the unheard of and too-little-heard-of; words and images which are original, creative and worth experiencing." Circ. 25,000. Pays on publication. Byline given. Buys first North American serial rights. Submit seasonal/holiday material 3 months in advance. Simultaneous queries, and simultaneous, photocopied, and previously published submissions OK. Computer printout submissions acceptable; prefers letter-quality to dot-matrix. SASE. Reports in 2 weeks on queries; 4 weeks on mss. Publishes ms an average of 4 months after acceptance. Sample copy for 50¢, 9x12 SAE, and 3 first class stamps; free writer's guidelines.
Nonfiction: Humor (satire); interview/profile (Indiana personalities only); and opinion (*Last Word* feature—significant issues only). Annual April Fool's Day paper has been published for 6 years. Buys 25-50 mss/year. Query with published clips. Length: 250-2,000 words. Pays 35¢/column inch.
Photos: Send photos with query. Reviews b&w contact sheets. Pays $5 for 5x7 or 8x10 b&w prints. Captions, model release, and identification of subjects required. Buys one-time rights.
Columns/Departments: Book Reviews, Film Reviews and Jurisprudence (commentary on judicial and legal system). Buys 20-30 mss/year. Query with published clips. Length: 750-1,250 words. Pays 35¢/column inch.
Fiction: Erotica, experimental, fantasy, humorous, mainstream and science fiction. "No pornography or sappy romance stories." Buys 12 mss/year. Send complete ms. Length: 1,000-2,500 words. Pays $10-25.
Poetry: Avant-garde, free verse and haiku. "No sappy romance poetry." Buys 20-40 poems/year. Pays 35¢/column inch.
Tips: "Be original, creative and experimental. There are more writers than ever—quality is more important. Fiction is the area most open to freelancers in our publication."

‡**TALES AS LIKE AS NOT . . .**, Second Unit Productions, Word Studies Division, 623 Laird Lane, Lafayette CA 94549. Editor: Dale Hoover. 100% freelance written. Quarterly magazine of science fiction, fantasy and horror. "Our philosophy is to provide entertainment that is fresh, original and personal. We are designed specifically for writers of short stories and poetry who are strictly amateur. Professionals need not contribute. If you already have a name, you don't need us." Estab. 1983. Pays on publication. Buys one-time rights. No seasonal material, except for Halloween; submit material 3 months in advance. Computer printout submissions acceptable. Reports in 1 month on mss. SASE. Publishes ms an average of 4 months after acceptance. Writer's guidelines for 9x12 SAE and 1 first class stamp.
Photos: "No photos, but we are looking for b&w camera-ready illustrations."
Fiction: Fantasy, horror and science fiction. "No sex, experimental, mainstream, ethnic or romance. No stories that teach the reader a lesson, and nothing more." Buys 36 mss/year. send complete ms. Length: 2,000-10,000 words. Pays $5 maximum plus contributor's copy.
Poetry: Free verse, light verse and traditional. "No avant-garde. No hashed-over Poe. Poetry must pertain to science fiction, fantasy or horror." Buys 6-12 poems/year. Submit maximum 3 poems. Length: 6-20 lines. Pays in contributor's copy only.
Tips: "Keep story lines and character development tight and to the point. Don't waste time. Write about what you know and how you feel, but remember that your job as a writer is to entertain and touch the heart of your reader. Don't cry on his shoulder; don't hash over old stories. One thing a reader hates to do after reading a story is say, 'It's been done before.' Don't rely on blood and gore to tell your story. Leave it to the reader's imagination. *T.A.L.A.N.* is designed to develop talent. It isn't the end of the road for a short story; it is the beginning."

TELESCOPE, The Galileo Press, Box 16129, Baltimore MD 21218. (301)366-7326. Editors: Jack Stephens and Julia Wendell. Triannual literary journal of poetry, fiction, essays, book reviews, interviews and graphics. Circ. 500. Pays on acceptance. No byline given. Makes work-for-hire assignments. Photocopied submissions OK. SASE. Reports in 1 week on queries; 2 months on mss. Sample copy $2; writer's guidelines for SAE and 20¢ postage.
Nonfiction: Interview/profile, personal experience and literary criticism. Special issues include Art in the Atomic Age and Cinema's Influence on Literature. Buys 10 mss/year. Send complete ms. Length: open. Pays $3/page.
Graphics: Jill Francis, art editor. Send graphics with ms. Reviews transparencies.
Fiction: "Sensitive and intelligent fiction" and novel excerpts.
Poetry: Buys 75/year. Submit maximum 10 poems. Length: open. Pays 50¢/line.
Tips: The editors strongly suggest that writers familiarize themselves with *Telescope* before submitting. They also suggest that writers query before submitting.

TRI-QUARTERLY, 1735 Benson Ave., Northwestern University, Evanston IL 60201. (312)492-3490. Editor: Reginald Gibbons. Published 3 times/year. Publishes fiction, poetry, and essays, as well as artwork. Computer printout submissions acceptable; prefers letter-quality to dot-matrix. Buys first serial rights and nonexclusive reprint rights. Pays on publication. Reports in 6 weeks. Study magazine before submitting; enclose SASE. Sample copy $3.

Nonfiction: Query before sending essays (no scholarly or critical essays except in special issues).
Fiction and Poetry: No prejudice against style or length of work; only seriousness and excellence are required. Buys 20-50 unsolicited mss/year. Pays $12/page.

‡**UNIVERSITY OF TORONTO QUARTERLY**, University of Toronto Press, 63 A St. George Street, Toronto, Ontario M5S 1A6 Canada. Editor-in-Chief: W.J. Keith. Emphasizes literature and the humanities for the university community. Quarterly magazine. Pays on publication. Buys all rights. Byline given. Photocopied submissions OK. SAE and IRCs. Sample copy $6.50.
Nonfiction: Scholarly articles on the humanities; literary criticism and intellectual discussion. Buys 12 unsolicited mss/year. Pays $50 maximum.

UNIVERSITY OF WINDSOR REVIEW, Windsor, Ontario N9B 3P4 Canada. (519)253-4232. Editor: Eugene McNamara. For "the literate layman, the old common reader." Biannual. Circ. 300 + . Acquires first North American serial rights. Accepts 50 mss/year. Sample copy $5 plus postage. Follow *MLA Style Sheet*. Reports in 4-6 weeks. Enclose SAE and IRCs.
Nonfiction: "We publish some articles on literature, history, social science, etc. I think we reflect competently the Canadian intellectual scene and are equally receptive to contributions from outside the country; I think we are good and are trying to get better." Length: about 6,000 words. Pays $25.
Photos: Contact: Evelyn McLean.
Fiction: Alistair MacLeod, department editor. Publishes mainstream prose with open attitude toward themes. Length: 2,000-6,000 words. Pays $25.
Poetry: John Ditsky, department editor. Accepts traditional forms, blank verse, free verse and avant-garde forms. No epics. Pays $10.

THE VIRGINIA QUARTERLY REVIEW, 1 W. Range, Charlottesville VA 22903. (804)924-3124. Editor: Staige Blackford. 50% freelance written. Quarterly. Pays on publication. Buys first rights only. Reports in 4 weeks. Publishes ms an average of 2 years after acceptance. SASE. Sample copy $3.
Nonfiction: Articles on current problems, economic, historical; and literary essays. Length: 3,000-6,000 words. Byline given. Pays $10/345-word page.
Fiction: Good short stories, conventional or experimental. Length: 2,000-7,000 words. Pays $10/350-word page. Prizes offered for best short stories and poems published in a calendar year.
Poetry: Generally publishes 15 pages of poetry in each issue. No length or subject restrictions. Pays $1/line.
Tips: Prefers not to see pornography, science fiction or fantasy.

WASCANA REVIEW, University of Regina, Saskatchewan, Canada. Editor-in-Chief: J. Chamberlain. Emphasizes literature and the arts for readers interested in serious poetry, fiction and scholarship. Semiannual magazine. Circ. 300. Pays on publication. Buys all rights. Photocopied submissions OK. SAE and IRCs. Reports in 6-8 weeks.
Nonfiction: Literary criticism and scholarship in the field of English, American, Canadian, French or German literature and drama; and reviews of current books (2,000-6,000 words). Buys 65-70 unsolicited mss/year. Send complete ms. Pays $3-4/page.
Fiction: Quality fiction with an honest, meaningful grasp of human experience. Any form. Buys 2-5 mss/issue. Send complete ms. Length: 2,000-6,000 words. Pays $3/page.
Poetry: Avant-garde, free verse, haiku, light verse and traditional. Buys 10-15 poems/issue. Length: 2-100 lines. Pays $10/page.

WESTERN HUMANITIES REVIEW, University of Utah, Salt Lake City UT 84112. (801)581-7438. Editor-in-Chief: Jack Garlington. 60% freelance written. For educated readers. Quarterly magazine. Circ. 1,000. Pays on acceptance. Buys all rights. Phone queries OK. Simultaneous and photocopied submissions OK. Computer printout submissions acceptable. SASE. Reports in 4 weeks.
Nonfiction: Authoritative, readable articles on literature, art, philosophy, current events, history, religion and anything in the humanities. Interdisciplinary articles encouraged. Departments on film and books. "We commission book reviews." Buys 40 unsolicited mss/year. Recent article example: "The Presence of the Past: The Value of Humanism and the Humanities" (spring 1983). Pays $50-150.
Fiction: Any type or theme. Recent short story example: "Why We Cry," (autumn 1983). Buys 2 mss/issue. Send complete ms. Pays $25-150.
Poetry: Avant-garde, free verse and traditional. "We seek freshness and significance." Buys 5-10 poems/issue. Pays $50.
Tips: Do not send poetry without having a look at the magazine first.

‡**WINEWOOD JOURNAL**, Winewood Publishing, Box 339, Black Hawk CO 80422. (303)582-5867. Editor: Kate Aiello. 100% freelance written. Semiannual magazine of poetry, essays, short stories and artwork for readers with an open-minded philosophy. Estab. 1983. Circ. 500. Byline given. Acquires one-time rights.

Submit seasonal/holiday material 4 months in advance. Photocopied and previously published submissions OK. Computer printout submissions acceptable. SASE. Reports in 1 week on queries; 1-2 weeks on mss. Publishes ms an average of 8 months after acceptance. Sample copy $2; writer's guidelines for 2 first class stamps.

Nonfiction: Send material to articles editor. Expose (government); humor (any subject); interview/profile (of poets, writers); and opinion (political). "No over-used subjects." Send complete ms. Length: 500-3,000 words. Pays in contributor copy.

Fiction: Erotica, ethnic, experimental and humorous. No religious material or condensed novels. Accepts 6-7 mss/year. Send complete ms. Length: 500-3,000 words. Pays in contributor copy.

Poetry: Avant-garde, free verse, haiku, light verse and traditional. No religious poems. Accepts 150 poems/year. Submit maximum 5 poems. Length: 3-60 lines. Pays in contributor copy.

Tips: "Winewood publishing also does chapbooks. Query first."

WOMEN ARTISTS NEWS, Midmarch Associates, Box 3304 Grand Central Station, New York NY 10163. Editor: Rena Hansen. 70% freelance written. For "artists and art historians, museum and gallery personnel, students, teachers, crafts personnel, art critics and writers." Buys first rights only when funds are available. Bimonthly magazine. Circ. 5,000. "Token payment as funding permits." Byline given. Submit seasonal material 1-2 months in advance. SASE. Reports in 1 month. Publishes ms an average of 2 months after acceptance. $2.50 for sample copy.

Nonfiction: Features, informational, historical, interview, opinion, personal experience, photo feature and technical. Query or submit complete ms. Length: 500-2,500 words.

Photos: Used with or without accompanying ms. Captions required. Query or submit contact sheet or prints. Pays $5 for 5x7 b&w prints when money is available.

‡WORDS AND VISIONS, Arts Showcase, Words & Visions Publications, Box 545, Norwood, Adelaide 5067 South Australia. Editor: Adam Dutkiewicz. 100% freelance written. A quarterly magazine covering arts and popular culture with focus on Australian content and some overseas material. Circ. 1,000. Pays on publication. Byline given. Buys first rights. Submit seasonal/holiday material 3 months in advance. Simultaneous, photocopied, and previously published submissions OK. Computer printout submissions acceptable; no dot-matrix, SAE and IRC. Reports in 3 months. Publishes ms an average of 3 months after acceptance. Sample copy $4 plus postage, writer's guidelines for SAE.

Nonfiction: Interview/profile. Buys 6 mss/year. Query. Length: 1,200-1,500 words. Pays $20-25.

Fiction: Span Hanna, fiction editor. Erotica, experimental, fantasy, humorous, mainstream, mystery, science fiction and suspense. No pornography. Buys 10 mss/year. Send complete ms. Length: 1,200-3,000 words. Pays $25-50.

Poetry: Martin Brakmanis, poetry editor. Avant-garde, free verse, haiku and traditional. Buys 40 poems/year. Length: 3-130 lines. Pays $15-30.

Tips: "Covering letter appreciated with some background on writing skills."

THE YALE REVIEW, 1902A Yale Station, New Haven CT 06520. Editor: Kai T. Erikson. Associate Editor: Penelope Laurans. 20% freelance written. Buys first North American serial rights. Pays on publication. Publishes ms an average of 1 year after acceptance. Computer printout submissions acceptable; no dot-matrix. SASE.

Nonfiction and Fiction: Authoritative discussions of politics, literature and the arts. Pays $75-100. Buys quality fiction. Length: 3,000-5,000 words. Pays $75-100.

Men's

Some men's magazines emphasize fashions and service features for men; others focus on features where clothing isn't important. "The men's magazine industry is becoming more specialized, not general in theme as *Playboy* and *Penthouse*," says one men's magazine editor. "More and more of us are specializing in a particular aspect of sexuality." *Cavalier*, for example, is becoming more directed toward female wrestling and weightlifting; *Gent* focuses only on large breasted women. Magazines that also use material slanted toward men can be found in Business and Finance, Lifestyles, Military, and Sports sections.

ADAM, Publishers Service, Inc., 8060 Melrose Ave., Los Angeles CA 90046. For the adult male. General subject: "Human sexuality in contemporary society." Monthly. Circ. 500,000. Buys first North American serial rights. Occasionally overstocked. Pays on publication. Writer's guidelines for SASE. Reports in 6 weeks, but occasionally may take longer. SASE.
Nonfiction: "On articles, please query first. We like hard sex articles, but research must be thorough." Length: 2,500 words. Pays $100-250.
Photos: All submissions must contain model release including parent's signature if under 21; fact sheet giving information about the model, place or activity being photographed, including all information of help in writing a photo story, and SASE. Photo payment varies, depending upon amount of space used by photo set.

CAVALIER, Suite 204, 2355 Salzedo St., Coral Gables FL 33134. (305)443-2370. Editor: Douglas Allen. 50% freelance written. For "young males, ages 18-29, 80% college graduates, affluent, intelligent, interested in current events, sex, sports, adventure, travel and good fiction." Monthly. Circ. 250,000. Buys first and second rights to same material and second (reprint) rights to material originally published elsewhere. Byline given. Buys 44 or more mss/year. Pays on publication. See past issues for general approach to take. Submit seasonal material at least 3 months in advance. Computer printout submissions acceptable (but no multiple submissions); no dot-matrix. SASE. Reports in 3 weeks. Publishes ms an average of 3 months after acceptance.
Nonfiction: Personal experience, interviews, humor, think pieces, expose and new product. "Frank—open to dealing with controversial issues." No material on Women's Lib, water sports, hunting, homosexuality or travel, "unless it's something spectacular or special." Query. Length: 2,800-3,500 words. Pays maximum $500 with photos.
Photos: Photos purchased with mss or with captions. No cheesecake.
Fiction: Nye Willden, department editor. Mystery, science fiction, humorous, adventure, contemporary problems "with at least one explicit sex scene per story. Very interested in female fighting." Send complete ms. Length: 2,500-3,500 words. Pays $250 maximum, "higher for special."
Tips: "Our greatest interest is in originality—new ideas, new approaches; no tired, overdone stories—both feature and fiction. We do not deal in 'hack' sensationalism but in high quality pieces. Keep in mind the intelligent 18- to 29-year-old male reader. We will be putting more emphasis in articles and fiction on sexual themes. Serious articles, not hack sexual pornography—fiction can be very imaginative and sensational."

CHERI MAGAZINE, The All-True Sex News Magazine, 215 Lexington Ave., New York NY 10016. (212)686-9866. Editor: C.B. Lucci. 10% freelance written. Monthly erotic men's magazine for predominantly blue-collar audience ages 18-40. Circ. 750,000. Pays on publication. Byline given. Offers variable kill fee. Buys first North American serial rights and second serial (reprint) rights; makes work-for-hire assignments. Submit seasonal/holiday material 6 months in advance. Simultaneous queries, and simultaneous, photocopied and previously published submissions OK. SASE. Reports in 5 weeks on queries; 7 weeks on mss. Publishes ms an average of 1 month after acceptance. Sample copy $3.75; writer's guidelines for business-size SASE.
Nonfiction: Carol Scott, articles editor. Book excerpts, sports, adventure, expose, general interest, how-to, humor, interview/profile, new product, personal experience, and photo feature. "We can't use any political expose-type stories, nor are we interested in heavily sexual features." Buys 10 mss/year. Query or send complete ms. Length: 1,800-2,400 words. Pays $300-500.
Photos: Peter Hurd, photo editor. Send photos with ms. Pays variable rates for 35mm color transparencies. Model release and identification of subjects required. Buys one-time rights.
Tips: "In our magazine we're moving toward more offbeat approaches, new angles on subjects, and more investigative on-the-scene reporting of stories and events. We like getting fresh ideas to add spice to our magazine, but it's frustrating when freelancers promise to deliver an article after we okay the query and then never send it to us."

CHIC MAGAZINE, Larry Flynt Publications, Suite 3800, 2029 Century Park E., Los Angeles CA 90067. Articles Editor: Richard Warren Lewis. For men, 20-35 years old, college-educated and interested in current affairs, entertainment and sports. Monthly magazine. Circ. 250,000. Pays 1 month after acceptance. Buys exclusive English and English translation world-wide magazine rights. Pays 20% kill fee. Byline given unless writer requests otherwise. SASE. Reports in 2 months.
Nonfiction: Expose (national interest only); interview (personalities in news and entertainment); and celebrity profiles. Buys 36 mss/year. Query. Length: 5,000 words. Pays $750.
Columns/Departments: Dope, Sex Life. Pays $300. Odds and Ends (front of the book shorts; study the publication first). Pays $50. Length: 100-300 words. Close Up (short Q&As) columns. Length: 1,000 words. Pays $200.
Tips: Prefers not to get humorous material.

ESQUIRE, 2 Park Ave., New York NY 10016. Senior Executive Editor: Betsy Carter. Editor: Phillip Moffitt. Monthly. Usually buys first serial rights. Pays on acceptance. Reports in 3 weeks. "We depend chiefly on solicited contributions and material from literary agencies. Unable to accept responsibility for unsolicited material." Query. SASE.

Nonfiction: Articles vary in length, but features usually average 3,000-7,000 words. Articles should be slanted for sophisticated, intelligent readers; however, not highbrow in the restrictive sense. Wide range of subject matter. Rates run roughly between $300 and $3,000, depending on length, quality, etc. Expenses are allowed, depending on the assignment.

Photos: April Silver, art director. Buys first periodical publication rights. Payment depends on how photo is used, but rates are roughly $300 for b&w; $500-750 for color. Guarantee on acceptance. Gives assignments and pays expenses.

Fiction: Rust Hills, fiction editor. "Literary excellence is our only criterion." Length: about 1,000-6,000 words. Payment: $350-1,500.

GALLERY, Montcalm Publishing Corp., 800 2nd Ave., New York NY 10017. (212)986-9600. Publisher: Milton J. Cueras. Editor-in-Chief: John Bensink. Managing Editor: Marc Lichter. Design Director: Michael Monte. 30% freelance written. Monthly magazine "focusing on features of interest to the young American man." Circ. 700,000. Pays 50% on acceptance, 50% on publication. Buys first North American serial rights; makes assignments on a work-for-hire basis. Pays 25% kill fee. Byline given. Submit seasonal/holiday material 6 months in advance. Photocopied submissions OK. SASE. Reports in 1 month on queries; 8 weeks on mss. Publishes ms an average of 3 months after acceptance. Sample copy $3.25 plus $1.75 postage and handling. Writer's guidelines available on request.

Nonfiction: Investigative pieces, general interest, how-to, humor, interview, new products and profile. "We *do not* want to see articles on pornography." Buys 6-8 mss/issue. Query or send complete mss. Length: 1,000-5,000 words. Pays $200-1,500. "Special prices negotiated."

Photos: Send photos with accompanying mss. Pay varies for b&w contact sheets or color contact sheets and negatives. Buys one-time rights. Captions preferred; model release required.

Fiction: Adventure, erotica, experimental, humorous, mainstream, mystery and suspense. Buys 2 mss/issue. Send complete ms. Length: 500-3,000 words. Pays $250-1,000.

GENESIS MAGAZINE, 770 Lexington Ave., New York NY 10021. Editor: Joseph J. Kelleher. Monthly magazine. Circ. 600,000. Query. Reports in 2 months. SASE.

Nonfiction: Articles about serious contemporary isssues, how-to-live-better service features, humor, celebrity interviews, features about young successful men on the rise, and comment on contemporary relationships.

Photos: Photo essays of beautiful women.

GENT, Suite 204, 2355 Salzedo St., Coral Gables FL 33134. (305)443-2378. Editor: John C. Fox. Monthly magazine "for men from every strata of society." Circ. 200,000. Buys first North American serial rights. Byline given. Pays on publication. Submit complete fiction ms. Query first on nonfiction. Reports in 3-6 weeks. SASE.

Nonfiction: Looking for traditional men's subjects (cars, racing, outdoor adventure, science, gambling, etc.) as well as sex-related topics. Length: 1,500-2,500 words. Buys 70 mss/year. Pays $100-200.

Photos: B&w and color photos purchased with mss. Captions (preferred). Length: 100 words.

Fiction: Erotic. "Stories should contain a huge-breasted female character as this type of model is *Gent*'s main focus. And this character's endowments should be described in detail in the course of the story. Some of our stories also emphasize sexy, chubby women, pregnant women and their male admirers." Length: 1,500-3,000 words. Pays $100-200.

GENTLEMEN'S QUARTERLY, Condé Nast, 350 Madison Ave., New York NY 10017. Editor-in-Chief: Arthur Cooper. Executive Editor: Peter Carlsen. Circ. 525,000. Emphasizes fashion and service features for men ages 25-39 with a large discretionary income. Monthly magazine. Pays $200 kill fee. Byline given. Pays on acceptance. Submit seasonal/holiday material 4-6 months in advance. Photocopied submissions OK. Computer printout submissions acceptable; prefers letter-quality to dot-matrix. SASE. Reports in 3 weeks.

Nonfiction: "Content is mostly geared toward self-help and service areas. Subject should cover physical fitness, national affairs, lifestyles, grooming, nutrition, psychological matters (different types of therapy, etc.), health, travel, personality profiles, money and investment and business matters—all geared to our audience and fitting our format." Buys 2-4 mss/issue. Query with outline of story content. No unsolicited mss. Length: 2,500-4,000 words. Pays $500-2,500.

Columns/Departments: Philip Smith, managing editor. Looking Good (physical fitness, diet, nutrition and grooming); Money (investments); Lifelines (self-help); World Wise, Destinations and Adventure (travel); Health; Westwords (West Coast matters); Home Tech (consumer electronics); Distinctively Black (black men's grooming); At Your Service and More Dash than Cash (fashion); Well Read (books); Viewpoints (the arts); Living (catchall for various stories that fit magazine format); and Pulse (details of the world at large). Buys 5-8/

issue. Query with outline of story content. Length: 1,000-2,500 words. Pays $350-400 and $100 for item used in Pulse.

Tips: "The best procedure to break in is really the outline and formulating a proposal structurally in terms of content and information."

HUSTLER MAGAZINE, 2029 Century Park E., Floor 38, Los Angeles CA 90067. (213)556-9200. Articles Editor: Richard Warren Lewis. Monthly magazine. Circ. 3 million. Rights purchased vary with author and material; usually buys exclusive English and English translation world-wide magazine rights. Buys 36 full-length mss/year. Pays on acceptance. Write for editorial guidelines. Photocopied submissions (although original is preferred) OK. Reports in 2 months. Query for nonfiction. Query or submit complete ms for other material. SASE.

Nonfiction: Will consider expose, profiles and interviews. Should be hard-hitting, probing, behind-the-scenes material. "We do not want fluff pieces or PR releases. Writing should be sophisticated and contemporary, devoid of any pretensions, aggressive and down-to-earth, exhibiting no-nonsense attitude. We try to mirror the reality of our times." The publication is "sexually explicit but no pornography." Wants expose material, particularly exposes in political/celebrity/business world. Buys 1 unsolicited ms/year. Length: 5,000 words. Pays $1,200 minimum. Material also needed for regular columns, Kinky Korner and Sex Play. Length: 1,500 words for Korner; 1,500-1,800 words for Play. Pays $100 for Korner; $350 for Play.

Photos: Photos used with mss; additional payment at usual space rates. Size: 35mm Kodachrome. Buys "total exclusive rights." Pays $300/page for color. "Check a recent copy to see our style. Slides should be sent in plastic pages. Soft-focus and diffusion are not acceptable."

Tips: "We prefer not to get humorous material."

NUGGET, Suite 204, 2355 Salzedo St., Coral Gables FL 33134. (305)443-2378. Editor: John Fox. Magazine "primarily devoted to fetishism." Buys first North American serial rights only. Byline given. Pays on publication. Submit complete ms. Reports in 6 weeks. SASE.

Nonfiction: Articles on fetishism—every aspect. Length: 2,000-3,000 words maximum. Buys 20-30 mss/year. Pays $100-200.

Photos: Erotic pictorials of women—essay types in fetish clothing (leather, rubber, underwear, etc.) or women wrestling or boxing other women or men, preferably semi- or nude. Captions or short accompanying manuscript desirable. Color or b&w photos acceptable.

Fiction: Erotic and fetishistic. Should be oriented to *Nugget's* subject matter. Length. 2,000-3,000 words. Pays $100-200.

Tips: "We require queries on articles only and the letter should be a brief synopsis of what the article is about. Originality in handling of subject is very helpful. It is almost a necessity for a freelancer to study our magazine first, be knowledgeable about the subject matter we deal with and able to write explicit and erotic fetish material."

OUI MAGAZINE, Laurent Publications, 300 W. 43rd St., New York NY 10036. (212)397-5889. Editor: Jeffrey Goodman. Managing Editor: Barry Janoff. A monthly magazine for men 18-40, college educated; "audience seeks mental as well as physical stimulation." Circ. 800,000+. Pays on publication. Byline given. Offers variable kill fee. Buys variable rights. Submit seasonal/holiday material 5 months in advance. Computer printout submissions acceptable; prefers letter-quality to dot-matrix. SASE. Reports in 1 month on queries; 7 weeks on mss. Sample copy $5; writer's guidelines for business-size SAE and 1 first class stamp.

Nonfiction: Expose (political); how-to (make money, survive, protect yourself from fraud, etc.); humor; interview/profile (top or upcoming actresses); technical; and travel (exotic locales with sexual overtones). "*No* articles on hookers, bordellos, massage parlors, porn stars or porn movies." Buys 18-25 mss/year. Query with published clips. Length: 2,000-3,000 words. Payment varies with author.

Photos: Send photos with query or ms. Reviews 35mm transparencies. Model release and identification of subjects required.

Fiction: Adventure, erotica, experimental, fantasy, horror, humorous, mystery, science fiction and suspense. Erotic/sexual slant preferred. "Avoid 'typical' situations: hookers, bordellos, massage parlors; writers are encouraged to explore new areas, create and invent new situations." Send complete ms. Length: 1,500-2,500 words. Payment is negotiable.

Fillers: Contact: Openers Editor. Sexually oriented situations, erotic happenings in everyday situations. Query or send news clipping.

Tips: "Nonfiction is an area *Oui* always needs to fill, in particular, hard-hitting exposes or documented undercover work. Query first with some background information, i.e., newspapers/magazine credits, etc. *Oui* gets too many pieces of fiction that are dull, boring, uninteresting, out of step with current trends, etc. Writers should not only be as current as possible but—and here's the trick—be ahead of their time. Set trends instead of copying."

PENTHOUSE, 1965 Broadway, New York NY 10023. Editor-in-Chief: Bob Guccione. 95% freelance written. For male (ages 18-34) audience; upper-income bracket, college-educated. Monthly. Circ. 5,350,000. Buys all rights. Pays 25% kill fee. Byline given. Buys 70-80 mss/year. Pays on acceptance. Photocopied submissions OK. Computer printout submissions acceptable; no dot-matrix. Reports in 1 month. Publishes ms an average of 8 months after acceptance. Query. SASE.
Nonfiction: Peter Bloch, department executive editor. Peter McCabe, senior editor, political features. Articles on general themes: money, sex, humor, politics, health, crime, etc. Male viewpoint only. Length: 5,000 words. General rates: $2,000 minimum.
Photos: Purchased without mss and on assignment. Pays $200 minimum for b&w; $350 for color. Spec sheet available from Richard Bleiweiss, art director.
Fiction: Kathryn Green, editor. Quality fiction. Experimental, mainstream, mystery, suspense and adventure, erotica, and science fiction. Action-oriented, central male character. Length: 3,500-6,000 words. Pays $1,500 minimum.

PENTHOUSE VARIATIONS, Penthouse International, Ltd., 1965 Broadway, New York NY 10023. 496-6100. Editor: Victoria McCarty. 100% freelance written. Monthly magazine. *Variations* is a pleasure guide for everyone who wants to expand his horizons of enjoyment. All forms of sensuality and eroticism appear in its pages, from monogamy to menaging, from bondage to relaxation, from foreplay to romance." Circ. 400,000. Pays on acceptance. No byline given. Buys total rights "to publish and republish the whole or part edited or unedited, internationally." Simultaneous queries OK. Computer printout submissions acceptable; prefers letter-quality to dot-matrix. Reports in 1 month on queries; 2 months on mss. Publishes ms an average of 6 months after acceptance. Free writer's guidelines.
Nonfiction: Personal experience. "We are looking for 2,500-3,000 word, first-person, true accounts of erotic experiences, squarely focused within *one* of the pleasure variations. No fiction, articles or short stories. No porno, favorite erotica; we are not a dirty-story clearing house." Buys 60 mss/year. Query. Length: 2,500-3,000 words. Pays $400.
Tips: "I am easily swayed by professionally neat mss style: clean ribbon, nonerasable paper, double-spacing, margins. I look for complete sentences and an electrically erotic mind sold in a business-like manner."

PLAYBOY, 919 N. Michigan, Chicago IL 60611. Managing Editor: Don Gold. Monthly. Buys first rights and others. Computer printout submissions acceptable; prefers letter-quality to dot-matrix. Reports in 1 month. SASE.
Nonfiction: James Morgan, articles editor. "We're looking for timely, topical pieces. Articles should be carefully researched and written with wit and insight. Little true adventure or how-to material. Check magazine for subject matter. Pieces on outstanding contemporary men, sports, politics, sociology, business and finance, music, science and technology, games, all areas of interest to the urban male." Query. Length: 3,000-5,000 words. On acceptance, pays $3,000 minimum. If a commissioned article does not meet standards, will pay a turn-down price of 20%. The *Playboy* interviews run between 10,000 and 15,000 words. After getting an assignment, the freelancer outlines the questions, conducts and edits the interview, and writes the introduction. Pays $4,000 minimum on acceptance. For interviews contact G. Barry Golson, Executive Editor, 747 3rd Ave., New York NY 10017.
Photos: Gary Cole, photography director, suggests that all photographers interested in contributing make a thorough study of the photography currently appearing in the magazine. Generally all photography is done on assignment. While much of this is assigned to *Playboy*'s staff photographers, approximately 50% of the photography is done by freelancers, and *Playboy* is in constant search of creative new talent. Qualified freelancers are encouraged to submit samples of their work and ideas. All assignments made on an all rights basis with payments scaled from $600/color page for miscellaneous features such as fashion, food and drink, etc.; $300/b&w page; $800/color page for girl features; cover, $1,500. Playmate photography for entire project: $15,000. Assignments and submissions handled by associate editors: Jeff Cohen, Janice Moses, and James Larson, Chicago; Marilyn Grabowski, Los Angeles. Assignments made on a minimum guarantee basis. Film, processing, and other expenses necessitated by assignment honored.
Fiction: Alice Turner, fiction editor. Both light and serious fiction. Entertainment pieces are clever, smoothly written stories. Serious fiction must come up to the best contemporary standards in substance, idea and style. Both, however, should be designed to appeal to the educated, well-informed male reader. General types include comedy, mystery, fantasy, horror, science fiction, adventure, social-realism, "problem" and psychological stories. Fiction lengths are 3,000-6,000 words; short-shorts of 1,000 to 1,500 words are used. Pays $2,000; $1,000 short-short. Rates rise for additional acceptances. Rate for Ribald Classics is $200.
Fillers: Party Jokes are always welcome. Pays $50 each on acceptance. Also interesting items for Playboy After Hours, front section (best check it carefully before submission). The After Hours front section pays anywhere from $50 for humorous or unusual news items (submissions not returned) to $500 for original reportage. Subject matter should be new trends, fads, personalities and cultural developments. Has movie, book, record reviewers but solicits queries for short (1,000 words or less) pieces on art, places, people, trips, adventures, experiences, erotica, television—in short, open-ended. Book and record reviews are on assignment basis only.

Ideas for Playboy Potpourri pay $75 on publication. Query. Games, puzzles and travel articles should be addressed to New York office.

PLAYERS MAGAZINE, Players International Publications, 8060 Melrose Ave., Los Angeles CA 90046. (213)653-8060. Editor: Joseph Nazel Jr. Associate Editor: Leslie Gersicoff. For the black male but "we have a high female readership—perhaps as high as 40%." Monthly magazine. Circ. 200,000. Pays on publication. Buys all rights. Submit seasonal/holiday material 6 months in advance. Photocopied submissions OK. SASE. Reports in 3 weeks minimum.
Nonfiction: "*Players* is *Playboy* in basic black." Expose; historical; humor; inspirational; sports; travel; reviews of movies, books and records; profile/interview on assignment. Length: 1,000-5,000 words. Pays 10¢/word. Photos purchased on assignment (pays $25 minimum for b&w; $250 maximum per layout). Model release required.
Fiction: Adventure, erotica, fantasy, historical (black), humorous, science fiction and experimental. Length: 1,000-4,000 words. Pays 6¢/word.
Tips: "Follow current style with novel theme in query or article. Looking for: city, night life of cities other than New York, Chicago, Los Angeles; interviews with black political leaders; and black history."

SCREW, Box 432, Old Chelsea Station, New York NY 10011. Managing Editor: Manny Neuhaus. 95% freelance written. For a predominantly male, college-educated audience; ages 21 through mid-40s. Tabloid newspaper. Weekly. Circ. 125,000. Buys all rights. Byline given. Buys 150-200 mss/year. Pays on publication. Computer printout submissions acceptable. Query on all other material. Free sample copy and writer's guidelines. Reports in 3 months. Publishes ms an average of 3 months after acceptance. Submit complete ms for first-person, true confessions.
Nonfiction: "Sexually related news, humor, how-to articles, first-person and true confessions. Frank and explicit treatment of all areas of sex; outrageous and irreverent attitudes combined with hard information, news and consumer reports. Our style is unique. Writers should check several recent issues." Length: 1,000-3,000 words. Pays $100-200. Will also consider material for "Letter From . . .," a consumer-oriented wrap-up of commercial sex scene in cities around the country; and "My Scene," a sexual true confession. Length: 1,000-2,500 words. Pays about $40. Recent feature article example: "Sex in Manila—A Tour of the City's Bars and Brothels."
Photos: B&w glossy prints (8x10 or 11x14) purchased with or without mss or on assignment. Pays $10-50.
Tips: "All mss get careful attention. Those written in *Screw* style on sexual topics have the best chance."

STAG, Swank Corp., 888 7th Ave., New York NY 10106. Editor: Susan Netter. Monthly magazine covering men's entertainment with an emphasis on sex for men ages 18-35. Circ. 170,000. Pays on publication. Byline given. Buys all rights. Submit seasonal/holiday material 6 months in advance. SASE. Reports in 1 month. Sample copy $5.
Nonfiction: Photo Features: "Subject matter of any article should lend itself to 4-6 pages of photos." Buys 8-10 noncommissioned mss/year. Query with clips of published work. Length: 2,500-3,000 words. Pays $350 minimum/article.
Photos: State availability of photos. Reviews 35mm Kodachrome transparencies. Payment varies according to usage rights.
Fiction: Buys 12 mss/year. Send complete ms. Length: 2,000 words average. Pays $300 minimum. "We prefer sexy, light-hearted or humorous subject matter."
Tips: "We like a query that tips us off to a new sex club, strip joint, love commune etc., that would cooperate with the writer and our photographers for a feature story. For all our articles, photographs or illustrations are essential. Prefers not to see anything not dealing with sex." Read the magazine.

‡**TURN-ONS**, AJA Publishing Corp., 313 W. 53rd St., New York NY 10019. (212)541-7351. Editor: Cheri Blake. Managing Editor: John Velvel. 100% freelance written. "A monthly, digest-sized magazine for people who like to read about erotica." Audience is predominantly well-educated, male. Circ. 150,000. Pays on publication (10 days after shipping). Byline given. Buys all rights. Submit seasonal/holiday material 6 months in advance. Simultaneous queries and photocopied submissions OK. Computer printout submissions acceptable; no dot-matrix. SASE. Reports in 6 weeks on queries. Publishes ms an average of 3 months after acceptance. Sample copy for SAE and 63¢ postage; writer's guidelines for SAE and 1 first class stamp.
Nonfiction: Book excerpts, interview/profile and personal experience. "We buy how-to articles on sex that range form 'How to Make Your Own Home Porn Videos' to 'How to Seduce a Woman' to 'The Sex Life of a Porn Star.' All how-to articles should include graphic case histories or examples." Publishes Special Edition 6 times/year. Buys 100 mss/year. Query with or without published clips or send complete ms. Length: 2,000-10,000 words. Pays $150 or negotiable rates.
Photos: State availability of photos. Reviews 2¼x2¼ b&w and color transparencies. Model release and identification of subjects required. Buys one-time rights.
Fiction: Erotica. "We buy first-person erotic stories of the kind 'Here is an experience I had . . .' We are open

to stories about unusual experiences, first-time experiences, sex fantasies, threesomes, costumed sex, woman-to-woman sex, etc." Buys 100 mss/year. Query with or without published clips, or send complete ms. Length: 2,000-10,000 words. Pays $150 or negotiable rates.

Fillers: Jokes and short humor. Buys "as many good ones as we can get." Length: 50-200 words.

Tips: "Essentially, we will consider any well-written piece of sexually oriented material for publication. There are no limits except the boundaries of good taste."

‡**TUX**, (formerly *Gentleman's Companion*), Modernismo Communications, Inc., 155 Avenue of the Americas, New York NY 10013. (212)691-7700. Articles Editor: Eve Ziegler. 30% freelance written. Monthly men's magazine. Estab. 1984. Pays within 30 days of acceptance. Byline given. Buys all rights. Submit seasonal/holiday material 3 months in advance. SASE. Reports in 1 month on queries. Publishes ms an average of 3 months after acceptance.

Nonfiction: "We are looking for hard-hitting, investigative reports on a wide variety of topics. Articles should be sexual in orientation, but not necessarily. Exposes most desired. We want short flashy service pieces on 'adult' toys—videos, cameras and home games. A 2-5 page proposal detailing the sources, style and direction of the article should be submitted for approval before the finished manuscript. Writers are responsible for providing all research and back-up for articles." Length: 3,000 words. Pays $300-500.

Columns/Departments: Finance, Travel and High-Tech Consumer Goods. Pays $75-250.

Fiction: "We will consider fiction with well-defined characters and at least one erotic episode. Plot and characterization should not be subordinated to sexual activities. The latter must grow logically from the story, rather than be forced or contrived. Science fiction with some erotica all right. Sexual stories about rape, childhood sex or bestiality are not appropriate." Length: 2,000-3,000 words. Pays $250.

Tips: "Innovative ways of presenting sexual or provocative material is desperately needed."

‡**WILDMAN, Today's Issues from the Male Viewpoint**, SLB Enterprises, Inc., #3342, John Hancock Center, Chicago IL 60611. (312)664-6446. Editor: Gale Ahrens. Managing Editor/Publisher: Robert Warren. The monthly magazine is a "forum for men's issues—upbeat, positive, stressing strong masculine behavior." Estab. 1983. Pays on publication. Byline given. Offers $50 kill fee. Buys first North American serial, one-time, first, second serial (reprint), and all rights. Submit seasonal/holiday material 4 months in advance. Simultaneous queries, and photocopied and previously published submissions OK. Computer printout submissions acceptable; no dot-matrix. No material is returned. Reports in 3 weeks.

Nonfiction: Book excerpts, expose (today's issues, how they affect men, what men can do); humor; interview/profile (strong male role models a la David Letterman); and personal experience (with today's women at work, divorce, child custody, abortion). No general interest, fashion or pornography. Buys 30 mss/year. Query. Length: 5,000 words maximum. Pays $100 minimum.

Columns/Departments: Mark Byers, column/department editor. Movie (book reviews revealing pro or anti-male sentiments); Newly Separated and Divorced, and Relationships (both of these columns biased toward men). Buys 30 mss/year. Query. Length: 1,000 words maximum. Pays $100 minimum.

Tips: "We look at all writers. We want to see strong, male writing—writing that's clear, easy to read and honest. Hemingwayesque. Slanted positively toward men. *Wildman* is a publication for men much like a *Ms.* or *Savvy* is for women."

‡**XL MAGAZINE, Dedicated to Excellence in a Man's World**, Power Publishing Co., Suite 100, 3000 Turtle Creek Plaza, Dallas TX 75219. (214)528-1020. Editor: Julie J. Bain. A monthly magazine of upbeat, fun coverage of average all-American men's general interest subjects (sports, automotive, science, outdoor adventure, interviews); *not* a highly sophisticated or affluent market." Estab. 1983. Circ. 700,000. Pays on acceptance. Byline given. Offers 25% kill fee. Buys first North American serial rights. Submit seasonal/holiday material 3 months in advance. SASE. Reports in 1 month. Sample copy for 8½x11 SAE with $1.05 postage; free writer's guidelines.

Nonfiction: General interest (sports, auto, science, adventure); how-to (men's general interest); inspirational (stories of men who excel); interview/profile (sports, entertainment, personality); new product (consumer electronics); and photo feature (funny, unusual, upbeat). "Heaviest coverage is in sports, automotive features, science, hunting and fishing, adventure and interviews. Our style is easy, conversational." No heavy, depressing investigative pieces, pornography, or travel articles. Buys 120 mss/year. Query. Length: 2,000-5,000 words. Pays $500-1,000.

Photos: State availability of photos. Pays $25-200 for variable size color transparencies; $10-100 for 8x10 b&w prints. Identification of subjects required. Buys one-time rights.

Columns/Departments: Achievers (brief stories about nonfamous people who excel) and New Products. Query. Length: 200-1,000 words. Pays $50-200.

Fillers: Anecdotes and short humor. Length: 50-250 words. Pays $50-100.

Tips: "We like lively, upbeat, conversational writing. Humor is great. Send a letter (with a great idea) that is lively, exciting and doesn't have any misspelled words. Provide photos with a story (with scintillating cutlines), and turn it all in *before* deadline.

Military

Technical and semitechnical publications for military commanders, personnel and planners, as well as those for military families and civilians interested in Armed Forces activities are listed here. All of these publications emphasize military or paramilitary subjects or aspects of military life.

AIR UNIVERSITY REVIEW, United States Air Force, Air University, Bldg. 1211, Maxwell Air Force Base AL 36112. (205)293-2773. Editor: Lt. Col. Donald R. Baucom, USAF. Professional military journal for military supervisory staff, command leadership personnel and top level civilians. Circ. 27,000. Not copyrighted. Byline given. Reports in 6 weeks. Query.
Nonfiction: "Serves as an open forum for exploratory discussion. Purpose is to present innovative thinking and stimulate dialogue concerning Air Force doctrine, strategy, tactics, and related national defense matters. Footnotes as needed. Prefers the author to be the expert. Reviews of defense-related books. Expository style. Only military and defense related matter, please; no announcements of meetings." Length: 1,500-3,500 words.
Photos: B&w glossy prints or charts to supplement articles are desired.
Tips: "We look for clear, concise writing."

ARMED FORCES JOURNAL, 1414 22nd St. NW, Washington DC 20037. Editor: Benjamin F. Schemmer. 30% freelance written. For "senior career officers of the US military, defense industry, Congressmen and government officials interested in defense matters, international military and defense industry." Monthly. Circ. 25,000. Buys all rights. Buys 10 unsolicited mss/year. Pays on publication. Photocopied submissions OK. Reports in 1 month. Publishes ms an average of 1 month after acceptance. Submit complete ms. SASE. Sample copy $2.75.
Nonfiction: Publishes "national and international defense issues: weapons programs, research, personnel programs and international relations (with emphasis on defense aspect). We do not want broad overviews of a general subject; more interested in detailed analysis of a specific program or international defense issue. Our readers are decision-makers in defense matters—hence, subject should not be treated too simplistically. Be provocative. We are not afraid to take issue with our own constituency when an independent voice needs to be heard." Buys informational, profile and think pieces. No poetry, biographies, or non-defense topics. Length: 1,000-3,000 words. Pays $100/page.

ARMY MAGAZINE, 2425 Wilson Blvd., Arlington VA 22201. (703)841-4300. Editor-in-Chief: L. James Binder. Managing Editor: Poppy Walker. 75% freelance written. Emphasizes military interests. Monthly magazine. Circ. 155,000. Pays on publication. Buys all magazine rights. Byline given except for back-up research. Submit seasonal/holiday material 3 months in advance. Photocopied submissions OK. Computer printout submissions acceptable; prefers letter-quality to dot-matrix. SASE. Publishes ms an average of 6 months after acceptance. Free sample copy and writer's guidelines.
Nonfiction: Historical (military and original); humor (military feature-length articles and anecdotes); interview; new product; nostalgia; personal experience; photo feature; profile; and technical. No rehashed history. "We would like to see more pieces about interesting military personalities. We especially want material lending itself to heavy, contributor-supplied photographic treatment. The first thing a contributor should recognize is that our readership is very savvy militarily. 'Gee-whiz' personal reminiscences get short shrift, unless they hold their own in a company in which long military service, heroism and unusual experiences are commonplace. At the same time, Army readers like a well written story with a fresh slant, whether it is about an experience in a foxhole or the fortunes of a corps in battle." Buys 12 mss/issue. Submit complete ms. Length: 4,500 words. Pays 8-12¢/word.
Photos: Submit photo material with accompanying ms. Pays $15-50 for 8x10 b&w glossy prints; $25-150 for 8x10 color glossy prints or 2¼x2¼ color transparencies, but will accept 35mm. Captions preferred. Buys all rights.
Columns/Departments: Military news, books, comment (*New Yorker*-type "Talk of the Town" items). Buys 8/issue. Submit complete ms. Length: 1,000 words. Pays $30-100.

ASIA-PACIFIC DEFENSE FORUM, Commander-in-Chief, US Pacific Command, Box 13, Camp H.M. Smith HI 96861. (808)477-5070/6663. Executive Editor: Lt. Col. Paul R. Stankiewicz. Editor: Phillip P. Katz. 100% (maximum) freelance written. For foreign military officers in 40 Asian-Pacific and Indian Ocean countries; all services—Army, Navy, Air Force and Marines. Secondary audience—government officials, media and academicians concerned with defense issues. "We seek to keep readers abreast of current status of US forces and of US national security policies, and to enhance international professional dialogue on military subjects." Quarterly magazine. Circ. 30,000. Pays on acceptance. Buys simultaneous, second serial (reprint) or one-time rights. Byline given. Phone queries OK. Simultaneous, photocopied and previously published submissions OK. Computer printout submissions OK; prefers letter-quality to dot-matrix. SASE. Reports in 3 weeks on queries; 10 weeks on mss. Publishes ms an average of 4 months after acceptance. Free sample copy and writer's guidelines.

Nonfiction: General interest (strategy and tactics, current type forces and weapons systems, strategic balance and security issues and Asian-Pacific armed forces); historical (occasionally used, if relation to present-day defense issues is apparent); how-to (training, leadership, force employment procedures, organization); interview and personal experience (rarely used, and only in terms of developing professional military skills). "We do not want overly technical weapons/equipment descriptions, overly scholarly articles, controversial policy, and budget matters; nor do we seek discussion of in-house problem areas. We do not deal with military social life, base activities or PR-type personalities/job descriptions." Buys 2-4 mss/year. Query or send complete ms. Length: 1,000-3,000 words. Pays $100-200.

Photos: State availability of photos with ms. "We provide nearly all photos; however, will consider good quality photos with mss." Uses 5x7 or 8x10 b&w glossy prints or 35mm color transparencies. Offers no additional payment for photos accompanying mss. Buys one-time rights. Captions required.

Tips: "Develop a 'feel' for our foreign audience orientation. Provide material that is truly audience-oriented in our view and easily illustrated with photos."

AT EASE, Division of Home Missions, Assemblies of God, 1445 Boonville Ave., Springfield MO 65802. Editor: Lemuel D. McElyea. Managing Editor: Ruby M. Enyart. 40% freelance written. For military personnel. Bimonthly magazine. Circ. 15,000. Buys all rights. "We are quite limited in what we would accept from freelance writers. Everything has to be slanted to the military." Pays on publication. Publishes ms an average of 4 months after acceptance. Free sample copy and writer's guidelines. "If we can't use a submission and we think another department can, we usually let them see it before replying. Otherwise, as soon as we reject it, we return it." Query first. SASE.

Nonfiction: Materials that will interest military men and women. Must have religious value. Buys 15 unsolicited mss/year. Length: 500 to 800 words. Pays minimum of 1½¢/word.

Tips: "Give a clear statement of background faith in your query. Military experience helpful."

‡**FOR YOUR EYES ONLY, Military Intelligence Summary**, Tiger Publications, Box 8759, Amarillo TX 79114. (806)655-2009. Editor: Stephen V. Cole. 5% freelance written. A biweekly newsletter covering military intelligence (post 1980). Circ. 1,200. Pays on publication. Byline given. Offers variable kill fee. Buys all rights. Simultaneous queries, and simultaneous, photocopied, and previously published submissions OK. Inquire about electronic submissions. Computer printout submissions acceptable. SASE. Reports in 2 weeks on queries; 1 month on mss. Publishes ms an average of 10 days after acceptance. Sample copy $2; writer's guidelines for SAE with 1 first class stamp.

Nonfiction: Expose, interview/profile, personal experience, technical, how to, arms sales, tests, current research, wars, battles and military data. "We're looking for technical material presented for nontechnical people, but our readership is highly intelligent/sophisticated, so do not talk down to them. Our emphasis is on how and why things work (and don't work)." No superficial or humorous material; nothing before 1981. Buys 20 mss/year. Query. Length: 50-2,000 words. Pays 3¢/word.

Photos: State availability of photos or send photos with ms. Pays $5-35 for b&w prints. Captions required. Buys one-time rights or negotiable rights.

Fillers: Newsbreaks. Buys 50-100/year. Length: 30-150 words. Pays $1-5.

Tips: "Read publication and author's guide; be aware of how much we generate internally. Briefings (100-300 words) and Newsnotes (30-150 words) are most open to freelancers."

INFANTRY, Box 2005, Fort Benning GA 31905. (404)545-2350. Editor: Albert N. Garland. 80% freelance written. Published primarily for combat arms officers and noncommissioned officers. Bimonthly magazine. Circ. 20,000. Not copyrighted. Buys first rights only. Pays on publication. Payment cannot be made to US government employees. Computer printout submissions acceptable. Reports in 1 month. Publishes ms an average of 9 months after acceptance. Free sample copy and writer's guidelines.

Nonfiction: Interested in current information on US military organization, weapons, equipment, tactics and techniques; foreign armies and their equipment; lessons learned from combat experience, both past and present; and solutions to problems encountered in the active Army and the Reserve components. Departments include Letters, Features and Forum, Training Notes, and Book Reviews. Uses 70 unsolicited mss/year. Recent article example: "The Other Side of the Hill" (January-February) 1984). Length of articles: 1,500-3,500 words. Length for Book Reviews: 500-1,000 words. Query. Accepts 75 mss/year.

Photos: Used with mss.

Tips: Start with letters to editor, book reviews to break in.

LEATHERNECK, Box 1775, Quantico VA 22134. (703)640-3171. Editor: Ronald D. Lyons. Managing Editor: Tom Bartlett. Emphasizes all phases of Marine Corps activities. Monthly magazine. Circ. 70,000. Pays on acceptance. Buys all rights. Phone queries OK. Submit seasonal/holiday material 3 months in advance of issue date. SASE. Reports in 2 weeks. Free sample copy and writer's guidelines.

Nonfiction: "All material submitted to *Leatherneck* must pertain to the US Marine Corps and its members." General interest, how-to, humor, historical, interview, nostalgia, personal experience, profile, and travel. No articles on politics, subjects not pertaining to the Marine Corps, and subjects that are not in good taste. Buys 24 mss/year. Query. Length: 1,500-3,000 words. Pays $50 and up per magazine page.

Photos: "We like to receive a complete package when we consider a manuscript for publication." State availability of photos with query. No additional payment for 4x5 or 8x10 b&w glossy prints. Captions required. Buys all rights. Model release required.

Fiction: Adventure, historical, and humorous. All material must pertain to the US Marine Corps and its members. Buys 3 mss/year. Query. Length: 1,000-3,000 words. Pays $50 and up per magazine page.

Poetry: Light verse and traditional. No poetry that does not pertain to the US Marine Corps. Buys 40 mss/year. Length: 16-20 lines. Pays $10-20.

THE MILITARY ENGINEER, 607 Prince St., Alexandria VA 22314. (703)549-3800. Editor: John J. Kern. 80% freelance written. Bimonthly magazine. Circ. 27,000. Pays on publication. Buys all rights. Byline given. Phone queries OK. Computer printout submissions acceptable. SASE. Reports in 1 month. Publishes ms an average of 9 months after acceptance. Sample copy and writer's guidelines $4.

Nonfiction: Well written and illustrated semitechnical articles by experts and practitioners of civil and military engineering, constructors, equipment manufacturers, defense contract suppliers and architect/engineers on these subjects and on subjects of military biography and history. "Subject matter should represent a contribution to the fund of knowledge, concern a new project or method, be on R&D in these fields; investigate planning and management techniques or problems in these fields, or be of militarily strategic nature." Buys 40-50 unsolicited mss/year. Length: 1,000-2,000 words. Query.

Photos: Mss must be accompanied by 6-10 well-captioned photos, maps or illustrations; b&w, generally. Pays approximately $25/page.

MILITARY LIVING R&R REPORT, Box 4010, Arlington VA 22204. (703)237-0203. Publisher: Ann Crawford. For "military consumers worldwide:" Bimonthly newsletter. "Please state when sending submission that it is for the *R&R Report Newsletter* so as not to confuse it with our monthly magazine which has different requirements." Buys first rights but will consider other rights. Pays on publication. Sample copy $1. SASE.

Nonfiction: "We use information on little-known military facilities and privileges, discounts around the world and travel information. Items must be short and concise. Stringers wanted around the world. Payment is on an honorarium basis. 1-1½¢/word."

MILITARY REVIEW, US Army Command and General Staff College, Fort Leavenworth KS 66027. (913)684-5642. Editor-in-Chief: Col. John D. Bloom. Managing Editor: Lt. Col. Dallas Van Hoose Jr. Features Editor: Major James L. Narel. Business Manager: Lt. Charles R. Rayhorn. 65% freelance written. Emphasizes the military for senior military officers, students and scholars. Monthly magazine. Circ. 27,000. Pays on publication. Buys one-time rights. Byline given. Phone queries OK. Photocopied submissions OK. Computer printout submissions acceptable; prefers letter-quality to dot-matrix. SASE. Reports in 1 month. Publishes ms an average of 8 months after acceptance. Free writer's guidelines.

Nonfiction: Military history, international affairs, tactics, new military equipment, strategy and book reviews. Prefers not to get material unrelated to defense subjects, poetry, or cartoons. Recently published "The Soviet Conventional Offensive in Europe". Buys 100-120 mss/year. Query. Length: 2,000-4,000 words. Pays $25-100.

Tips: "We need more articles from military personnel experienced in particular specialties. Examples: Tactics from a tactician, military engineering from an engineer, etc. We would appreciate receiving good quality, double-spaced letter-quality computer printout submissions."

NATIONAL GUARD, 1 Massachusetts Ave. NW, Washington DC 20001. (202)789-0031. Editor: Major Reid K. Beveridge. For officers of the Army and Air National Guard. Monthly. Circ. 69,000. Rights negotiable. Byline given. Buys 10-12 mss/year. Pays on publication. Query. SASE.

Nonfiction: Military policy, strategy, training, equipment, logistics, personnel policies: tactics, combat lessons learned as they pertain to the Army and Air Force (and impact on Army National Guard and Air National Guard). Material must be strictly accurate from a technical standpoint. Does not publish exposes, cartoons or jokes. Recent article example: "Reserve Retirement; A Bumpy Road Ahead" (April 1984). Length: 2,000-3,000 words. Payment ($75-500/article) depends on originality, amount of research involved, etc.

Photos: Photography pertinent to subject matter should accompany ms.

OFF DUTY, US: Suite C-2, 3303 Harbor Blvd., Costa Mesa CA 92626. Editor: Bruce Thorstad. Europe: Eschersheimer Landstrasse 69, Frankfurt/M, West Germany. Editor: J.C. Hixenbaugh. Pacific: Box 9869, Hong Kong. Editor: Jim Shaw. 50% freelance written. Monthly magazine for US military personnel and their families stationed around the world. Most readers 18-35 years old. Combined circ. 653,000. Buys first serial or second serial (reprint) rights. Pays on acceptance. Computer printout submissions acceptable. Publishes ms an average of 6 months after acceptance. Free sample copy and writer's guidelines.
Nonfiction: Three editions—American, Pacific and European. "Emphasis is on off duty travel, leisure, military shopping, wining and dining, sports, hobbies, music, and getting the most out of military life. Overseas editions lean toward foreign travel and living in foreign cultures. Also emphasize what's going on back home. In travel articles we like anecdotes, lots of description, color and dialogue. American edition uses more American trends and how-to/service material. Material with special US, Pacific or European slant should be sent to appropriate address above; material useful in all editions may be sent to US address and will be forwarded as necessary." Buys 30-50 mss/year for each of three editions. Query. Length: 1,500 words average. Also needs 500-word shorties. Pays 13¢/word for use in one edition; 16¢/word for use in 2 or more.
Photos: Bought with or without accompanying ms. Pays $25 for b&w glossy prints; $50 for color transparencies; $100 for full page color; $200 for covers. "Covers must be vertical format 35mm; larger format transparencies preferred."
Tips: "All material should take into account to some extent our special audience—the US military and their dependents. Our publication is subtitled 'The Military Leisuretime Magazine,' and the stories we like best are about how to get more out of the military experience. That 'more' could range from more fun to more satisfaction to more material benefits such as military privileges. Magazine will be adding pages and buying more articles in the year ahead."

OVERSEAS!, Military Consumer Today, Inc., BismarckstraBe 17, D-6900 Heidelburg, West Germany. Editor: Kent Olinger. General entertainment magazine serving American and Canadian military personnel stationed throughout Europe. Specifically directed to males ages 18-35. Monthly magazine. Circ. 83,000. Pays on publication. Buys rights to military communities in Europe. Submit seasonal/holiday material 4 months in advance of issue date. Simultaneous and previously published submissions OK. Computer printout submissions acceptable. SAE and IRCs (not US postage). Sample copy for 1 IRC.
Nonfiction: "We are a slick commercial giveaway magazine looking for flashy, sexy, young male-interest writing and photography. In the past we've bought how-to (travel by bike, van, foot, motorcycle; how to photograph women, rock stars, traveling subjects); interview and profile articles on music and sport celebrities; and do-it-yourself-sports (skiing, kayaking, sailing, soccer, tennis). Also need some music features—rock, soul, C&W, especially on musicians soon coming to Europe. We're looking for a new kind of travel article: the 'in scenes' of Europe written up especially for our young GIs. Should include nightlife, discos, bars, informal eating out, good music scenes, rather than fancy restaurants, cathedrals, or museums. Above all, tell our servicemen where the girls are. Query with a good idea that has not been worked to death, and give a lead paragraph that indicates the style and angle to be adopted, backed by a brief outline of where the article will go. All articles must be pertinent to someone living and working in Europe, or with a slant that is neutral—i.e., profile on celebrity." Buys 5-6 unsolicited mss/year. "Writer should be able to deliver a complete package (which means he or she has a means to find photos and any other additional info pertinent to the article) on time." Length: 800-1,500 words. DM4/column centimeter.
Photos: Purchased with accompanying ms. Captions required. Pays DM80 for b&w; DM100 minimum for color and DM400 for covers.
Tips: "Interesting travel stories with anecdotes are a good vehicle to break in, as are profiles of Americans making their mark in Europe. We are willing to consider any material that puts a premium on good, brisk and whenever possible, humorous writing that is written with our audience in mind."

PARAMETERS: JOURNAL OF THE US ARMY WAR COLLEGE, US Army War College, Carlisle Barracks PA 17013. (717)245-4943. Editor: LTC(P) William R. Calhoun Jr., US Army. Readership consists of senior leadership of US defense establishment, both uniformed and civilian, plus members of the media, government, industry and academia interested in scholarly articles devoted to national and international security affairs, military strategy, military leadership and management, art and science of warfare, and military history (provided it has contemporary relevance). Most readers possess a graduate degree. Quarterly. Circ. 9,000. Not copyrighted; unless copyrighted by author, articles may be reprinted with appropriate credits. Buys first rights only. Byline given. Pays on publication. Computer printout submissions acceptable; prefers letter-quality to dot-matrix. Reports in 6 weeks. Publishes ms an average of 6 months after acceptance.
Nonfiction: Articles preferred that deal with current security issues, employ critical analysis, and provide solutions or recommendations. Liveliness and verve, consistent with scholarly integrity, appreciated. Theses, studies and academic course papers should be adapted to article form prior to submission. Documentation in endnotes. Submit complete ms. Length: 5,000 words or less, preferably less. Pays $50 minimum; $100 average (including visuals).
Tips: "Research should be thorough; documentation should be complete."

PERIODICAL, Council on America's Military Past, 4970 N. Camino Antonio, Tucson AZ 85718. Editor-in-Chief: Dan L. Thrapp. Emphasizes old and abandoned forts, posts and military installations; military subjects for a professional, knowledgeable readership interested in one-time defense sites or other military installations. Quarterly magazine. Circ. 1,500. Pays on publication. Buys one-time rights. Simultaneous, photocopied and previously published (if published a long time ago) submissions OK. SASE. Reports in 3 weeks.
Nonfiction: Historical, personal experience, photo feature and technical (relating to posts, their construction/operation and military matters). Buys 4-6 mss/issue. Query or send complete ms. Length: 300-4,000 words. Pays minimum $2/page.
Photos: Purchased with or without accompanying ms. Captions required. Query. Glossy, single-weight, b&w up to 8x10. Offers no additional payment for photos accepted with accompanying ms.

THE RETIRED OFFICER MAGAZINE, 201 N. Washington St., Alexandria VA 22314. (703)549-2311. Editor: Colonel Minter L. Wilson Jr., USA-Ret. 90% freelance written. For officers of 7 uniformed services and their families. Monthly. Circ. 325,000. May buy all rights or first serial rights. Byline given. Pays on acceptance. Submit seasonal material (holiday stories with a military theme) at least 6 months in advance. Electronic submissions OK, but requires hard copy also. Computer printout submissions acceptable; prefers letter-quality to dot-matrix. Reports on material accepted for publication within 6 weeks. Publishes ms an average of 6 months after acceptance. Submit complete ms with SASE. Free sample copy and editorial requirements sheet.
Nonfiction: Recent military history, humor, hobbies, travel, second-career job opportunities and current affairs. Also, upbeat articles on aging, human interest and features pertinent to a retired military officer's milieu. True military experiences are also useful. "We tend to use articles less technical than a single-service publication might publish. We do not publish poetry of fillers." Buys 48 unsolicited mss/year. Length: 1,000-2,500 words. Pays $100-400.
Photos: Marjorie J. Seng, associate editor. 8x10 b&w photos (normal halftone). Pays $15. Original slides or transparencies for magazine cover must be suitable for color separation. Pays $75.
Tips: "We're concerned with publishing upbeat articles on aging and on running more recent (Korea and Vietnam) articles dealing with history."

SEA POWER, 2300 Wilson Blvd., Arlington VA 22201. Editor: James D. Hessman. Issued monthly by the Navy League of the US for naval personnel and civilians interested in naval maritime and defense matters. Buys all rights. Pays on publication. Will send free sample copy to a writer on request. Reports in 6 weeks. Query first. SASE.
Nonfiction: Factual articles on sea power in general, US industrial base, mineral resources, and the US Navy, the US Marine Corps, US Coast Guard, US Merchant Marine and naval services and other navies of the world in particular. Should illustrate and expound the importance of the seas and sea power to the US and its allies. Wants timely, clear, nontechnical, lively writing. Length: 500-2,500 words. No historical articles, commentaries, critiques, abstract theories, poetry or editorials. Pays $100-500 depending upon length and research involved.
Photos: Purchased with ms.

SERGEANTS, Air Force Sergeants Association, Box 31050, Temple Hills MD 20748. (301)899-3500. Editor: Belinda Reilly. 50% freelance written. Monthly magazine for the "air force enlisted (retired, active duty, reserve and guard). Features on all aspects of the Air Force and legislation affecting it." Circ. 125,000. Buys first rights only. Pays on publication. Byline given. Makes work-for-hire assignments. Submit seasonal/holiday material 3 months in advance. Simultaneous queries, and simultaneous, photocopied, and previously published submissions OK. Computer printouts acceptable. Reports in 1 week on queries; 1 month on mss. Publishes ms an average of 5 months after acceptance. Free sample copy and writer's guidelines.
Nonfiction: Historical/nostalgic (war stories in Air Force involvement enlisted Air Force personnel); interview/profile (of Air Force enlisted people in high positions); personal experience (accounts of interesting Air Force experiences); technical (advances in Air Force technology); and travel (what to see and do in and around Air Force bases). No "opinion pieces on legislation or government." Buys 12 mss/year. Query with clips of published work. Length: 500-1,500 words. Pays $50/printed page.

SOLDIER OF FORTUNE, The Journal of Professional Adventurers, Omega Group, Ltd., Box 693, Boulder CO 80306. (303)449-3750. Editor/Publisher: Robert K. Brown. Executive Editor: Dale Dye. 80% freelance written. Monthly magazine covering the military, police and the outdoors. "We take a strong stand on political issues such as maintenance of a strong national defense, the dangers of communism, and the right to keep and bear arms." Circ. 225,000. Buys first world rights only. Pays on publication. Byline given. Offers 25% kill fee "for proven freelancers." Makes work-for-hire assignments. Submit seasonal/holiday material 6 months in advance. Computer printout submissions acceptable if compatible with North Star Horizon CPM. Computer printout submissions acceptable; prefers letter-quality to dot-matrix. SASE. Reports in 1 month. Publishes ms an average of 4 months after acceptance. Sample copy $4; writer's guidelines for SAE.

Nonfiction: Expose (in-depth reporting from the world's hot spots—Afghanistan, Angola, etc.); general interest (critical focus on national issues—gun control, national defense); historical (soldiers of fortune, adventurers of past, history of elite units, Vietnam); how-to (outdoor equipment, weaponry, self-defense); humor (military, police); interview/profile (leaders or representatives of issues); new product (usually staff-assigned; outdoor equipment, weapons); personal experience ("I was there" focus); photo feature and technical (weapons, weapons systems, military tactics). Buys 75-100 mss/year. Query. Length: 1,000-3,500 words. Pays $175-1,000.
Photos: Photos with ms are integral to package. Separate submissions negotiable. Captions and identification of weapons and military equipment required. Buys first world rights.
Columns/Departments: I Was There/It Happened to Me (adventure and combat stories). Buys 12 mss/year. Send complete ms. Length: 500 words maximum. Pays $50.
Tips: "All authors should have professional background in the military or police work."

THE TIMES MAGAZINE, Army Times Publishing Company, Springfield, VA 22159. (703)750-8672. Editor: Marianne Lester. Managing Editor: Barry Robinson. Monthly magazine covering current lifestyles and problems of career military families around the world. Circ. 330,000. Pays on acceptance. Byline given. Offers negotiable kill fee. Buys all rights. Submit seasonal/holiday material 6 months in advance. Double- or triple-spaced computer printout submissions acceptable; no dot-matrix. SASE. Reports in 1 month. Free sample copy and writer's guidelines for 9x12 SAE.
Nonfiction: Expose (current military); how-to (military wives); interview/profile (military); opinion (military topic); personal experience (military only) and travel (of military interest). No poetry, cartoons or historical articles. Buys 100 mss/year. Query with clips of published work. Length: 1,000-3,000 words. Pays $50-600.
Photos: State availability of photos or send photos with ms. Reviews 35mm color contact sheets and prints. Caption, model releases, and identification of subjects required. Buys all rights.
Tips: "In query write a detailed description of story and how it will be told. A tentative lead is nice. Just one good story 'breaks in' a freelancer."

US NAVAL INSTITUTE PROCEEDINGS, Annapolis MD 21402. (301)268-6110. Editor-in-Chief: Clayton R. Barrow Jr. Managing Editor: Fred Rainbow. 95% freelance written. Emphasizes sea services (Navy, Marine Corps, Coast Guard, Merchant Marine) for sea services officers and enlisted personnel, other military services in the US and abroad, and civilians interested in naval/maritime affairs. Monthly magazine. Circ. 90,000. Pays on acceptance. Buys all rights. Byline given. Phone queries OK, but all material must be submitted on speculation. Submit seasonal/anniversary material at least 6 months in advance. Photocopied submissions OK. Computer printout submissions acceptable; prefers letter-quality to dot-matrix. "Prefers typed, double-spaced mss." SASE. Reports in 2 weeks on queries; 2 months on mss. Publishes ms an average of 1 year after acceptance. Free sample copy.
Nonfiction: Informational; analytical; historical (based on primary sources, unpublished and/or first-hand experience); humor; personal opinion; photo feature; technical; professional notes; and book reviews. No poetry. Query. Length: 4,000 words maximum. Pays $200-400.
Photos: Purchased with or without accompanying ms or on assignment. Captions required. Query. Pays $15 maximum for b&w 8x10 glossy prints. "We pay $2 for each photo submitted with articles by people other than the photographer."
Columns/Departments: Comment and Discussion (comments 500-700 words on new subjects or ones previously covered in magazine); Professional Notes; Nobody Asked Me, But . . . (700-1,000 words, strong opinion on naval/maritime topic); and Book Reviews. Buys 35 Book Reviews; 35 Professional Notes; 100 Comment and Discussion and 10 Nobody Asked Me, But columns a year. Pays $25-150.
Fillers: Miss Laraine Missory, assistant editor. Anecdotes should be humorous actual occurrences not previously published. Buys 25 fillers/year. Length: maximum 200 words. Pays $25 flat rate.
Tips: "The Comment and Discussion section is our bread and butter. It is a glorified letters to the editor section and exemplifies the concept of the *Proceedings* as a forum. We particularly welcome comments on material published in previous issues of the magazine. This offers the writer of the comment an opportunity to expand the discussion of a particular topic and to bring his own viewpoint into it. This feature does not pay particularly well, but it is an excellent opportunity to get one's work into print."

Music

Music fans follow the latest music industry news in these publications. Musicians and different types of music (such as jazz, opera, rock and bluegrass) are the sole focus of some magazines. Publications geared to music industry professionals can be found in the music section of Trade Journals. Additional music- and dance-related markets are included in the Theatre, Movie, TV, and Entertainment section.

‡**THE ABSOLUTE SOUND, The High End Journal**, Harry Pearson Jr., Box 115, Sea Cliff NY 11579. (516)676-2830. Editor: Harry Pearson Jr. Managing Editor: Brian Gallant. A quarterly magazine covering the music reproduction business, audio equipment and records for "up-scale, high tech men between 20 and 40, toy freaks." Pays on publication. Byline given. Buys all rights. Computer printout submissions acceptable; prefers letter-quality to dot-matrix. Sample copy $5.

Nonfiction: Exposé (of bad commercial audio practices); interview/profile (famous engineers, famous conductors); new product (audio); opinion (audio and record reviews); technical (how to improve your stereo system). Special issues include Canada Audio Products (July). No puff pieces about industry. Query with published clips. Length: 250-5,000 words. Pays $125-1,000.

Columns/Departments: Audio Musings (satires); Reports from Overseas (audio fairs, celebrities, record companies). Buys 12 mss/year. Query with published clips. Length: 250-750 words. Pays $125-200.

Fillers: Clippings, newsbreaks; "They Say" approach like *The New Yorker*, but audio or recording related. Buys 30/year. Length: 50-200 words. Pays $10-40.

Tips: "Writers should know about audio recordings and the engineering of same—as well as live music. The approach is *literate*, witty, investigative—good journalism."

‡**BAM, The California Music Magazine**, BAM Publications, 5951 Canning St., Oakland CA 94609. (415)652-3810. Editor: Dennis Zimmer. Editorial Assistant: Sally Engelfried. A biweekly contemporary music tabloid. Circ. 110,000. Pays on publication. Byline given. Offers negotiable kill fee. Submit seasonal/holiday material at least 6 weeks in advance. Computer printout submissions acceptable; no dot-matrix. submissions acceptable; no dot-matrix.

Nonfiction: Book excerpts, interview/profile, new product, photo feature, and live reviews and record reviews of musicians. "Most of *BAM*'s articles deal with rock and roll, slanted towards the 18-35 years of age market with frequent promusician features and some coverage of pop, jazz, country and blues." No self-indulgent, personal experience material. Buys 100-150 mss/year. Query with clips of published work. Pays $35-200.

Photos: Richard McCaffrey, photo editor. State availability of photos. Reviews b&w contact sheets. Pays $15-30 for 5x7 or 8x10 b&w prints; $50-150 for 5x7 or 8x10 color prints. Identification of subjects required. Buys one-time rights.

Columns/Departments: Industry News, Radio and Media News, Video, and Film. Buys 20 mss/year. Query with published clips. Length: 1,000-3,000 words. Pays variable rates.

Tips: "A good selection of clips and a crisply written cover letter always gets a response. Most our major profiles are freelance. They are *assigned* however; so query first. Avoid first person journalism when writing about another individual or group."

BEATLEFAN, The Goody Press, Box 33515, Decatur GA 30033. Editor: E.L. King. Managing Editor: Justin Stonehouse. 15% freelance written. Bimonthly magazine about the Beatles, John Lennon, Paul McCartney, George Harrison and Ringo Starr for a readership averaging 24 years of age, 53% males and 47% females. Circ. 2,500. Average issue includes 6 articles and 13 departments. Pays on publication. Byline given. Buys all rights. Submit seasonal material 4 months in advance. Simultaneous, photocopied and previously published submissions OK. Computer printout submissions acceptable; prefers letter-quality to dot-matrix. SASE. Reports in 10 weeks. Publishes ms an average of 4 months after acceptance. Sample copy $2.

Nonfiction: Historical (factual articles concerning the early Beatles tours in the US and anything to do with the band's early career); interview (with Beatles and any associates); nostalgia (articles on collecting Beatles memorabilia and trivia); personal experience (stories of meetings with the Beatles and associates); and photo feature (current photos of McCartney, Harrison and Starr and latterday photos of Lennon). Buys 8-10 unsolicited mss/year. Send complete ms. Length: 350-2,000 words. Pays $15-50. "We are looking for regular correspondents and columnists. We also need articles with tips on memorabilia collecting, record collecting, current book and record reviews. We have an anniversary issue each December (accounts of the days of the Beatlemania 1964-1966 especially needed) and in event of tours or appearances by any of the Beatles, reports from each city visited will be needed." No essays on the death of John Lennon; no poems of any type, fiction, non-Beatle material, or reviews of *old* records or books.

Photos: Send photos with ms. Pays $10-35/5x7 b&w glossy print. Offers no additional payment for photos accepted with ms. Captions required identifying subjects, places, date and photographer's name.

Columns/Departments: Book Review (any books published concerning the Beatles, foreign or domestic); Record Reviews (the Beatles together or individually; domestic or foreign; official or bootleg); Those Were the Days (articles about the Beatles that deal with generally unknown aspects or details of career together or personal lives); Collecting (articles with tips for collectors of rare records and memorabilia); Thingumybob (columns of opinion); Glass Onion (articles dealing with The Beatles' music and lyrics); Beatles Video (news and reviews of video releases); and Meeting The Beatles (stories of personal encounters). Buys 2 ms/issue. Send complete ms. Length: 500 words maximum. Pays $5-25.

Fillers: Clippings (not wire service stories) and puzzles having to do with the Beatles. Buys 3 mss/issue. Pays 50¢-$5.

Tips: "We get too many submissions that are general in nature and aimed at a general audience, repeating well-worn facts and events our readers already know by heart. We need articles that are specific, detailed and authoritative and that will tell confirmed Beatlemaniacs something they don't know. Articles should not be simple rewrites of reference book chapters. Opinion pieces should lean toward analysis backed by facts and examples. Among our contributing editors are noted Beatles authors Nicholas Schaffner and Wally Podrazik and former *Mersey Beat* editor Bill Harry. This shows the level of familiarity with the subject we expect. The year 1984 will mark the 20th anniversary of Beatlemania in the USA—a natural peg for stories."

BLUEGRASS UNLIMITED, Box 111, Broad Run VA 22014. (703)361-8992. Editor-in-Chief: Peter V. Kuykendall. 80% freelance written. Emphasizes old-time traditional country music for musicians and devotees of bluegrass, ages from teens through the elderly. Monthly magazine. Circ. 17,500. Pays on publication. Buys all rights. Pays variable kill fee. Byline given. Phone queries OK. Submit seasonal/holiday material 3 months in advance. Photocopied and previously published submissions OK. Computer printout submissions acceptable. SASE. Reports in 1 month. Publishes ms an average of 4 months after acceptance. Free sample copy and writer's guidelines.
Nonfiction: Historical, how-to, humor, informational, interview, nostalgia, personal experience, opinion, photo feature, profile and technical. Buys 20-40 mss/year. Query. Length: 500-5,000 words. Pays 4-5¢/word.
Photos: Purchased with or without accompanying ms. Query for photos. Pays $15-20/page for 5x7 or 8x10 b&w glossy prints, 35mm or 2¼x2¼ color transparencies; $125 for covers.
Columns/Departments: Record and book reviews. Buys 5-10/year. Query. Length: 100-500 words. Pays 4-5¢/word.
Fiction: Adventure and humorous. Buys 5-7 mss/year. Length: 500-2,500 words. Pays 4-5¢/word.
Tips: Prefers not to see "generalized material vaguely relating to music, e.g., a fictional piece (love story) in which the hero plays guitar."

‡**CONTINENTAL COUNTRY MUSIC NEWS**, Guerriero Music Inc. (BMI), Suite 206, 1425 Key Highway, Baltimore MD 21230. (301)837-5570. Editor: Ernest Cash. A monthly tabloid covering country music business for country music industry executives and fans. Reaches radio stations, record and song publishers, agencies, etc. Estab. 1984. Circ. 25,000. Pays on acceptance. No byline given. Buys all rights. Submit seasonal/holiday material 1 month in adance. SASE. Reports in several weeks. Sample copy $1; free writer's guidelines.
Nonfiction: General interest, humor and photo feature. "Most freelancers really not into country music." Query with published clips. Length: ⅓-1 full printed page. Pays negotiable rate.
Columns/Departments: Newcomers Corner (shorts about new artists or artists with first records just released). Send complete ms. Length: ⅓ page with picture space. Pays negotiable rate.
Tips: "Send sample works. Writer has to know country music industry as a whole. (Artists to agencies, songs, producers, etc.)."

CREEM, Suite 209, 210 S. Woodward Ave., Birmingham MI 48011. (313)642-8833. Editor: Dave DiMartino. Buys all rights. Pays on publication. Query. Reports in 6 weeks. SASE.
Nonfiction: Short articles, mostly music-oriented. "Feature-length stories are mostly staff-written, but we're open for newcomers to break in with short pieces. Freelancers are used a lot in the Beat Goes On section. Please send queries and sample articles to Bill Holdship, submissions editor. We bill ourselves as America's Only Rock 'n' Roll Magazine." Pays $50 minimum for reviews, $300 minimum for full-length features.
Photos: Freelance photos.
Tips: "You can't study the magazine too much—our stable of writers have all come from the ranks of our readers. The writer can save his time and ours by studying what we do print—and producing similar copy that we can use immediately. Short stuff—no epics on the first try. We really aren't a good market for the professional writer looking for another outlet—a writer has to be pretty obsessed with music and/or pop culture in order to be published in our book. We get people writing in for assignments who obviously have never even read the magazine, and that's totally useless to us."

FRETS MAGAZINE, GPI Publications, 20085 Stevens Creek Blvd., Cupertino CA 95014. (408)446-1105. Editor: Jim Hatlo. 30-60% freelance written. "For amateur and professional acoustic string music enthusiasts; for players, makers, listeners and fans. Country, jazz, classical, blues, pop and bluegrass. For instrumentalists interested in banjo, mandolin, guitar, violin, upright bass, dobro, dulcimer and others." Monthly magazine. Circ. open. Pays on acceptance. Buys first rights only. Prefers written queries. Submit material 4 months in advance. Computer printout submissions on 8½x11 sheets with legible type acceptable if not a photocopy or multiple submission. "All-caps printout unacceptable." SASE. Reports in 6 weeks. Free sample copy and writer's guidelines.
Nonfiction: General interest (artist-oriented); historical (instrument making or manufacture); how-to (instrument craft and repair); interview (with artists or historically important individuals); profile (music performer); and technical (instrument making, acoustics, instrument repair). "Prefers not to see humor; poetry; general-in-

terest articles that really belong in a less-specialized publication; articles (about performers) that only touch on biographical or human interest angles, without getting into the 'how-to' nuts and bolts of musicianship." Buys 14 mss/year. Query with clips of published work or sample lead paragraph. Length: 1,000-2,500 words. Pays $75-150. Experimental (instrument design, acoustics). Pays $75-150.

Photos: State availability of photos. Pays $25 minimum for b&w prints (reviews contact sheets); $100 for cover shot color transparencies. Captions and credits required. Buys one-time rights.

Columns/Departments: Repair Shop (instrument craft and repair); and *FRETS* Visits (on-location visit to manufacturer or major music festival). Buys 10 mss/year. Query. Length: 1,200-1,700 words. Pays $75-125, including photos.

Fillers: Newsbreaks, upcoming events and music-related news.

Tips: "Our focus also includes ancillary areas of string music—such as sound reinforcement for acoustic musicians, using personal computers in booking and management, recording techniques for acoustic music, and so on. We enjoy giving exposure (and encouragement) to talented new writers. We do not like to receive submissions or queries from writers who have only a vague notion of our scope and interest."

GUITAR PLAYER MAGAZINE, GPI Publications, 20085 Stevens Creek, Cupertino CA 95014. (408)446-1105. Editor: Tom Wheeler. For persons "interested in guitars; guitarists, manufacturers, guitar builders, bass players, equipment, careers, etc." Monthly magazine. Circ. 170,000. Buys first time and reprint rights. Byline given. Buys 30-40 mss/year. Pays on acceptance. Computer printout submissions acceptable; prefers letter-quality to dot-matrix. Free sample copy to a writer on request. Reports in 6 weeks. Query. SASE.

Nonfiction: Publishes "wide variety of articles pertaining to guitars and guitarists: interviews, guitar craftsmen profiles, how-to features—anything amateur and professional guitarists would find fascinating and/or helpful. On interviews with 'name' performers, be as technical as possible regarding strings, guitars, techniques, etc. We're not a pop culture magazine, but a magazine for musicians." Also buys features on such subjects as a guitar museum, the role of the guitar in elementary education, personal reminiscences of past greats, technical gadgets and how to work them, analysis of flamenco, etc." Recent article example: "Eddie Van Halen" (July 1984). Length: open. Pays $100-300.

Photos: Photos purchased. B&w glossy prints. Pays $35-50. Buys 35mm color transparencies. Pays $150 (for cover only). Buys one time rights.

HIGH FIDELITY/MUSICAL AMERICA, 825 7th Ave., New York NY 10019. Editor: Shirley Fleming. Monthly. Circ. 20,000. Buys all rights. Pays on publication. SASE.

Nonfiction: Articles, musical and audio, are generally prepared by acknowledged writers and authorities in the field, but does use freelance material. Query with clips of published work. Length: 1,200 words maximum. Pays $150 minimum.

Photos: New b&w photos of musical personalities, events, etc.

ILLINOIS ENTERTAINER, Box 356, Mount Prospect IL 60056. (312)298-9333. Editor: Guy C. Arnston. 95% freelance written. Monthly tabloid covering music and entertainment for consumers within 100-mile radius of Chicago interested in music. Circ. 75,000. Pays on publication. Byline given. Offers 100% kill fee. Buys one-time rights. Submit seasonal/holiday material 2 months in advance. Simultaneous queries OK. Computer printout submissions acceptable "if letters are clear"; no dot-matrix. SASE. Reports in 1 week on queries; 1 month on mss. Publishes ms an average of 6 weeks after acceptance. Sample copy $2; free writer's guidelines.

Nonfiction: Interview/profile (of entertainment figures). Recently published "Ebert & Siskel Sneak into the Movies." No Q&A interviews. Buys 200 mss/year. Query with clips of published work. Length: 500-2,000 words. Pays $15-100.

Photos: State availability of photos. Pays $10-20 for 5x7 or 8x10 b&w prints; $100 for color cover photo. Captions and identification of subjects required.

Columns/Departments: Software (record reviews stress record over band or genre); film reviews; and book reviews. Buys 500 mss/year. Query with clips of published work. Length: 150-250 words. Pays $6-20.

Tips: "Send samples in mail (published or unpublished) with phone number, and be patient."

INTERNATIONAL MUSICIAN, American Federation of Musicians, 1500 Broadway, New York NY 10036. (212)869-1330. Editor: J. Martin Emerson. For professional musicians. Monthly. Byline given. Pays on acceptance. Reports in 2 months. SASE.

Nonfiction: Articles on prominent instrumental musicians (classical, jazz, rock or country). Send complete ms. Length: 1,500-2,000 words.

IT WILL STAND, Dedicated to the Preservation of Beach Music, It Will Stand Prod., 1505 Elizabeth Ave., Charlotte NC 28204. (704)377-0700. Editor: Chris Beachley. Irregular monthly magazine covering beach music (especially soul 1940-present). Circ. 1,700. Pays on acceptance. Byline given. Offers negotiable kill fee. Buys all rights. Submit seasonal/holiday material 2 months in advance. Sample copy $2.

Nonfiction: Historical/nostalgic, interview/profile, opinion, personal experience and photo feature. Buys 5

and more mss/year. Query with clips of published work or send complete ms. Length: open. Pays variable fee.
Photos: State availability of photos. Reviews color and b&w contact sheets and prints.
Tips: "Contact us for direction. We even have artists' phone numbers ready for interviews." Magazine will buy more mss as it becomes a regular monthly publication in the year ahead.

KEYBOARD MAGAZINE, GPI Publications, 20085 Stevens Creek Blvd., Cupertino CA 95014. (408)446-1105. Editor: Tom Darter. For those who play piano, organ, synthesizer, accordion, harpsichord, or any other keyboard instrument. All styles of music; all levels of ability. Monthly magazine. Circ. 75,000. Pays on acceptance. Buys first and reprint rights. Byline given. Phone queries OK. SASE. Reports in 2 weeks. Free sample copy and writer's guidelines.
Nonfiction: "We publish articles on a wide variety of topics pertaining to keyboard players and their instruments. In addition to interviews with keyboard artists in all styles of music, we are interested in historical and analytical pieces, how-to articles dealing either with music or with equipment, profiles on well-known instrument makers and their products. In general, anything that amateur and professional keyboardists would find interesting and/or useful." Buys 20 unsolicited mss/year. Recent article example: "Oscar Peterson" (October 1983). Query; letter should mention topic and length of article and describe basic approach. "It's nice (not necessary) to have a sample first paragraph." Length: approximately 2,000-5,000 words. Pays $100-300.
Tips: "Query first (just a few ideas at at time, rather than twenty). A musical background helps, and a knowledge of keyboard instruments is valuable."

MODERN DRUMMER, 1000 Clifton Ave., Clifton NJ 07013. (201)778-1700. Editor-in-Chief: Ronald Spagnardi. Features Editor: Rick Mattingly. Managing Editor: Rick Van Horn. For "student, semi-pro and professional drummers at all ages and levels of playing ability, with varied specialized interests within the field." Monthly. Circ. 47,000. Pays on publication. Buys all rights. Phone queries OK. Photocopied and previously published submissions OK. SASE. Reports in 1 month. Sample copy $2.25; free writer's guidelines.
Nonfiction: How-to, informational, interview, personal opinion, new product, personal experience and technical. "All submissions must appeal to the specialized interests of drummers." Buys 5-10 mss/issue. Query or submit complete ms. Length: 3,000-6,000 words. Pays $200-500.
Photos: Purchased with accompanying ms. Considers 8x10 b&w and color transparencies. Submit prints or negatives.
Columns/Departments: Jazz Drummers Workshop, Rock Perspectives, In The Studio, Show Drummes Seminar, Teachers Forum, Drum Soloist, The Jobbing Drummer, Strictly Technique, Book Reviews and Shop Talk. "Technical knowledge of area required for most columns." Buys 10-15 mss/issue. Query or submit complete ms. Length: 500-1,500 words. Pays $25-150.

MODERN RECORDING & MUSIC, MR&M Publishing Corp., 1120 Old Country Rd., Plainview NY 11803. (516)433-6530. Editor: Jeff Tamarkin. Managing Editor: Ricki Zide. Monthly magazine covering semi-pro and professional recording of music for musicians, soundmen and recording engineers. Circ. 50,000. Pays second week of publication month. Buys all rights. Submit all material at least 3 months in advance. Photocopied submissions OK. SASE. Reports in 1 week. Provides sample copy "after assignment."
Nonfiction: Historical/nostalgic (recording industry); how-to (basic construction of a device using readily available parts to duplicate an expensive device in a small budget studio or at home); humor; and interview/profile (musician, engineer, producer or someone in an affiliated field). Buys 40 mss/year. Query with clips of published work and an outline. Length: 2,000 words minimum. Pays $150-200/article.
Photos: Reviews 2¼x2¼ or 35mm color transparencies; 8x10 glossy prints or contact sheets. Pays $25 inside color; $15 inside b&w; $75 for color cover; or package payment of $150.

MUSIC & SOUND OUTPUT, Testa Communications, 220 Westbury Ave., Carle Place NY 11514. (516)334-7880. Editor: Bill Stephen. 85% freelance written. Monthly magazine covering the business of making music for musicians and soundmen. Circ. 93,000. Pays on publication. Byline given. Offers 25% kill fee. Buys first North American serial rights. Photocopied submissions OK. Computer printout submissions acceptable. SASE. Reports in 3 weeks. Publishes ms an average of 6 weeks after acceptance. Sample copy $2.50; free writer's guidelines.
Nonfiction: Book excerpts; how-to (items that aid people in surviving in the music business); humor (cartoons and satire); interview/profile (music-related); new product (instruments); and opinion (reviews). Buys 75 mss/year. Query with clips. Length: 500-2,500 words. Pays $50-250.
Photos: State availability of photos. Pays $25-100 for 35mm b&w transparencies; $50-125 for 35mm color transparencies. Captions and identification of subjects required. Buys one-time rights.
Fiction: Story content must be music-related; all fiction forms are otherwise acceptable. Buys 8 mss/year. Query with clips. Length: 2,500-3,500 words. Pays $250-350.
Tips: "We're open to profiles/interviews. Look for the obscure or overlooked story."

MUSIC CITY NEWS, Suite 601, 50 Music Square W., Nashville TN 37203. (615)329-2200. Editor: Barry Bronson. 20% freelance written. Emphasizes country music. Monthly tabloid. Circ. 100,000. Buys all rights. Phone queries OK. Submit seasonal or holiday material 2 months in advance. Photocopied submissions OK. Computer printout submissions acceptable. SASE. Reports in 10 weeks. Free sample copy on request.
Nonfiction: "Interview type articles with country music personalities: question/answer, narrative/quote, etc. focusing on new and fresh angles about the entertainer rather than biographical histories." Buys 18-24 unsolicited mss/year. Query. Length: 500-1,250 words. Pays $100-125/feature, $75/junior feature, and $50/vignettes.
Photos: Purchased on acceptance by assignment. Query. Pays $10 maximum for 8x10 b&w glossy prints.

MUSIC MAGAZINE, Barrett & Colgrass Inc., Suite 202, 56 The Esplanade, Toronto, Ontario M5E 1A7 Canada. (416)364-5938. Editor: Ulla Colgrass. 90% freelance written. Emphasizes classical music. Bimonthly magazine. Circ. 11,000. Pays on publication. Buys all rights. Byline given. Phone queries OK. Submit seasonal/holiday material 4 months in advance. Photocopied and previously published submissions (book excerpts) OK. Computer printout submissions (double-spaced) acceptable. SAE and IRCs. Publishes ms an average of 4 months after acceptance. Reports in 3 weeks. Sample copy and writer's guidelines $2.
Nonfiction: Interview, historical articles, photo feature and profile. "All articles should pertain to classical music and people in that world. We do not want any academic analysis or short pieces of family experiences in classical music." Query with clips of published work. Unsolicited articles will not be returned. Length: 1,500-3,500 words. Pays $100-250.
Photos: State availability of photos. Pays $15-25 for 8x10 b&w glossy prints or contact sheets; $100 for color transparencies. No posed promotion photos. "Candid lively material only." Buys one-time rights. Captions required.
Tips: Send sample of your writing, suggested subjects. Off-beat subjects are welcome, but must be thoroughly interesting to be considered. A famous person or major subject in music are your best bets.

NOT JUST JAZZ, The Arts—Seen through the Eyes of the Artist, Not Just Jazz, Inc., 314 W. 52nd St., New York NY 10019. (212)664-1915. Editor: Randy Fordyce. Quarterly magazine covering music (particularly jazz)—all aspects with some emphasis on education; and other arts (visual, dance, etc.). "Enlightening information and entertainment by and about the people who make music and art happen." Estab. 1983. Circ. 30,000. Pays on publication. Byline given. Buys one-time rights. Submit seasonal/holiday material 5 months in advance. Simultaneous queries, and photocopied and simultaneous submissions OK. SASE. Reports in 2 weeks on queries; 1 month on mss. Sample copy for $1; free writer's guidelines.
Nonfiction: General interest (general for our area); humor; and interview/profile. No reviews, exposes, or "downers" of any kind. Buys 8-10 mss/year. Send complete ms. Length: 500-2,500 words. Pays $5-75.
Fiction: Fantasy, humorous, mainstream and science fiction, all related to the arts. Buys 1-6 mss/year. Send complete ms. Length: 1,000-3,000 words. Pays $25-100.
Tips: "We are not 'artsy' and communicate in plain language. A thorough reading of a sample issue should give a reality here. If it doesn't . . . that writer could probably not write for us." Personality interviews and profiles open to freelancers. The writer should *never* come between the subject and the reader. As the business becomes more and more vertical, it becomes more important for writers to write about what they know. Research is a poor substitute for experience."

OPERA CANADA, Suite 433, 366 Adelaide St. E., Toronto, Ontario M5A 3X9 Canada. (416)363-0395. Contact: Editor. For readers who are interested in serious music; specifically, opera. Quarterly magazine. Circ. 6,000. Not copyrighted. Byline given. Buys 10 mss/year. Pays on publication. Buys first rights only. Photocopied and simultaneous submissions OK. Computer printout submissions acceptable; no dot-matrix. Reports on material accepted for publication within 1 year. Returns rejected material in 1 month. Publishes ms an average of 1 year after acceptance. Query or submit complete ms. SAE and IRCs. Sample copy $3.50.
Nonfiction: "Because we are Canada's only opera magazine, we like to keep 75% of our content Canadian, i.e., by Canadians or about Canadian personalities/events. We prefer informative and/or humorous articles about any aspect of music theater, with an emphasis on opera. The relationship of the actual subject matter to opera can be direct or at least related. We accept record reviews (*only* operatic recordings); book reviews (books covering any aspect of music theater); and interviews with major operatic personalities. Please, no reviews of performances. We have staff reviewers." Length (for all articles except reviews of books and records): 1,000-3,000 words. Pays $50-150. Length for reviews: 100-500 words. Pays $10.
Photos: No additional payment for photos used with mss. Captions required.

OVATION, 320 W. 57th St., New York NY 10019. Editor: Sam Chase. Monthly magazine for classical music listeners covering classical music and the equipment on which to hear it. Average issue includes 4 features plus departments. Pays on publication. Byline given. Buys all rights. Submit seasonal material 4 months in advance. SASE. Reports in 1 month. Sample copy $2.79.
Nonfiction: "We are primarily interested in interviews with and articles about the foremost classical music art-

ists. Historical pieces will also be considered." Buys 5 unsolicited mss/year. Query with clips of previously published work. Length: 800-4,500 words. Pays $5/inch.
Photos: State availability of photos. May offer additional payment for photos accepted with ms. Captions required. Buys one-time rights.

POLYPHONY MAGAZINE, 1020 W. Wilshire, Box 20305, Oklahoma City OK 73156. (405)842-5480. 80% freelance written. Bimonthly magazine about electronic music and home recording for readers who are interested in building and using electronic music instruments to perform in bands or to make recordings in their studios. Circ. 4,000. Pays on publication. Buys all rights or by arrangement. Phone queries OK. Submit seasonal material 3 months in advance. Simultaneous, photocopied and previously published submissions OK. Computer printout submissions acceptable. SASE. Reports in 2 weeks on queries; in 3 weeks on mss. Publishes ms an average of 6 months after acceptance. Free sample copy.
Nonfiction: General interest (music theory, electronics theory, acoustics); how-to (design and build electronic music devices, record music); interview (with progressive musicians using electronic techniques or designers of electronic music equipment); new product; and technical. No mainstream type music and artist review articles. Buys 8 mss/issue. Query with clips of previously published work. "The feature stories we use are the best area for freelancers. We need construction projects, modifications for commercial equipment, computer software for music use, and tutorials dealing with electronic music and recording studio techniques, performance, design and theory. Freelancers should write in a conversational manner; provide enough details in project articles to allow novices to complete the project; provide informative charts, graphs, drawings or photos; present material which is practical to someone working in this medium." Length: 1,000-5,000 words. Pays $35/printed page.
Photos: State availability of photos or send photos with ms. Pays $25 minimum/5x7 b&w glossy print. Captions preferred; model release required. Buys all rights or by arrangement.

RELIX MAGAZINE, Music for the Mind, Relix Magazine, Inc., Box 94, Brooklyn NY 11229. (212)645-0818. Editor: Toni A. Brown. 90% freelance written. Bimonthly magazine covering rock 'n' roll music and "specializing in Grateful Dead, Springsteen, Stones, and other top groups for readers ages 13-35." Circ. 20,000. Pays on publication. Byline given. Buys all rights. Photocopied submissions OK. SASE. Publishes ms an average of 6 months after acceptance. Sample copy $2.
Nonfiction: Historical/nostalgic, interview/profile, new product, personal experience, photo feature and technical. Special issues include November photo special. Query with clips of published work if available or send complete ms. Length: open. Pays variable rates.
Columns/Departments: Query with clips of published work, if available, or send complete ms. Length: open. Pays variable rates.
Fiction: Query with clips of published work, if available, or send complete ms. Length: open. Pays variable rates.
Fillers: Clippings, jokes, gags, anecdotes, short humor and newsbreaks. Length: open. Pays variable rates.
Tips: "The most rewarding aspects of working with freelance writers are fresh writing and new outlooks."

ROCKBILL, Rave Communications, Suite 1201, 850 7th Ave., New York NY 10019. (212)977-7745. Editor: Stuart Matranga. Direct all music and column queries to Robert Edelstein, managing editor. Direct all fiction and more esoteric ideas to Robert O'Brian, executive editor. Direct all nonmusic general features to Robert Blau, senior editor. Direct all photo and illustration queries to Cliff Sloan, art director. 50% freelance written. Monthly magazine focusing on rock music and related topics for distribution at rock music clubs. Circ. 530,000. Pays on publication. Byline given. Buys one-time rights. Simultaneous queries OK. Computer printout submissions acceptable; no dot-matrix. No guarantee on return of submissions. Publishes ms an average of 2 months after acceptance. Free sample.
Nonfiction: Interview/profile, lifestyle and new music articles. "We're primarily interested in new artists on the verge." Buys 150 mss/year. Length: 150-800 words. Pays $25-75.
Photos: "We use color transparencies only. Identification of subjects required. No guarantee of returns."
Columns/Departments: Fashion, electronics, movies, jazz, country music, classical music, international music, classic album reviews, essays on cities, science and technology, new age-related topics, mysteries and the occult, video, radio, essays on youth, brief interviews with notables, satire, travel, etc. Length: 500-800 words.
Fiction: "Each issue we print four short fiction pieces in a section called Ficciones. We describe it as such: 'Magical realism, dangerous, imaginings, spontaneous history.' We're not sure what that means, but we admire Borges, Calvino, Marquez and that ilk." Length: under 150 words.
Tips: "We try to publish at least one new writer per issue. Our best advice is to keep trying to be as brilliant as possible; to think in terms of the big as well as the small, the apparent as well as the hidden, the molecular as well as the universal. The best way into our hearts is to write with integrity about something important to you and to everyone. And, remember, we're a small magazine in page size only. Our motto is 'More with Less.' "

ROLLING STONE, 745 5th Ave., New York NY 10151. Editor: Jann S. Wenner. 25-50% freelance written. "We seldom accept freelance material. All our work is assigned or done by our staff." Offers 25% kill fee. Buys first rights only. Byline given.

THE $ENSIBLE SOUND, 403 Darwin Dr., Snyder NY 14226. Editor/Publisher: John A. Horan. "All readers are high fidelity enthusiasts, and many have a high fidelity industry-related job." Quarterly magazine. Circ. 5,200. Pays on acceptance. Buys all rights. Byline given. Simultaneous, photocopied and previously published submissions OK. SASE. Reports in 2 weeks. Sample copy $2.
Nonfiction: Expose; how-to; general interest; humor; historical; interview (people in hi-fi business, manufacturers or retail); new product (all types of new audio equipment); nostalgia (articles and opinion on older equipment); personal experience (with various types of audio equipment); photo feature (on installation, or how-to tips); profile (of hi-fi equipment); and technical (pertaining to audio). "Subjective evaluations of hi-fi equipment make up 70% of our publication. Will accept 10/issue." Buys 2 mss/issue. Submit outline. Pays $25 maximum.
Columns/Departments: Bits & Pieces (short items of interest to hi-fi hobbyists); Ramblings (do-it-yourself tips on bettering existing systems); Record Reviews (of records which would be of interest to audiophiles). Query. Length: 25-400 words. Pays $10/page.

‡**SONGWRITER CONNECTION MAGAZINE**, Dynasty Media, Suite 106, 6640 Sunset Blvd., Hollywood CA 90028. (213)464-8942. Managing Editor: Marion Deegan. A monthly magazine covering songwriting for composers, artists, musicians and music industry personnel throughout the US and Canada. Circ. 40,000. Pays on publication. Byline given. Makes work-for-hire assignments. Submit seasonal/holiday material 3 months in advance. Simultaneous queries and photocopied submissions OK. Computer printout submissions acceptable. SASE. Reports in 2 weeks on queries; 1 month on mss. Sample copy for $2, 9x12 SAE, and 2 first class stamps; writer's guidelines for $1, 9x12 SAE, and 2 first class stamps.
Nonfiction: Bud Scoppa, articles editor. Expose (concentration on songwriting associations); general interest; historical/nostalgic (history of songwriting, popular music); how-to (technical music composition articles); humor; interview/profile (celebrities and personalities in the songwriting world); personal experience (dealing with the business of songwriting); technical (music composition); and items of interest to the songwriting community. "Articles must deal with songwriting and timely occurences in the popular music industry." Buys 80 mss/year. Query with published clips. Length: 750-3,500 words. Pays $40-250.
Photos: Send photos with accompanying query or ms. Pays $2-30 for 8x10 b&w prints; $5-50 for 35mm color slides. Identification of subjects required. Buys all rights.
Columns/Departments: Lawrence Payne, column/department editor. Technical music columns (lyrics, music, songcraft, demos); interviews (inside connections, business personalities); and reviews (LP records of interest to songwriters). Buys 150/year. Query with published clips. Length: 300-1,200 words. Pays $10-60.
Fiction: Lawrence Payne, fiction editor. Historical (only pertaining to the history of pop music) and mainstream (dealing with the business of songwriting). No fiction not oriented to popular music. Buys 1-2 mss/year. Query with published clips. Length: 1,000-4,000 words. Pays $40-200.
Fillers: Lawrence Payne, fillers editor. Clippings, anecdotes and newsbreaks. Buys 10/year. Length: 40-400 words. Pays $5-30.
Tips: "It is important to demonstrate an in-depth knowledge of songwriting, both in its business and artistic aspects. A good understanding of the people and companies involved in songwriting, the technical limitations and details, and a comprehension of popular music are all required. Feature stories and interviews are most open to freelancers. Write about interesting personalities who have made a significant contribution to songwriting over the years, or who are particularly popular right now."

TOWER RECORDS' PULSE!, 900 Enterprise Dr., Sacramento CA 95825. (916)920-4500. Editor: Mike Farrace. Monthly tabloid covering recorded music. Estab. 1983. Circ. 75,000. Pays on publication. Byline given. Buys first rights. Simultaneous and photocopied submissions OK. Computer printout submissions acceptable. SASE. Reports in 3 weeks. Free sample copy: writer's guidelines for SAE.
Nonfiction: Feature stories and interview/profile (angled toward artist's taste in music. Specifics: "Song and album titles, anecdotes about early record buying experiences. No 'influences', please! Always looking for good hardware reviews, concise news items and commentary about nonpopular musical genres." Buys 200-250 mss/year. Query or send complete ms. Length: 200-2,500 words. Pays $20-350.
Photos: State availability of photos. Reviews b&w prints. Caption and identification of subjects required. Buys one-time rights.
Fillers: Newsbreaks.
Tips: "Break in with 500-1,000 word news-oriented featurettes on recording artists or on record-product-related news: List price reductions, bonus discs, special packaging, great liner notes, etc."

TRADITION, Prairie Press, 106 Navajo, Council Bluffs IA 51501. (712)366-1136. Editor: Robert Everhard. 20¢ freelance written. Emphasizes traditional country music and other aspects of pioneer living. Quarterly magazine. Circ. 2,500. Pays on publication. Buys one-time rights. Byline given. Submit seasonal/holiday material 6 months in advance. Not copyrighted. Simultaneous queries, and simultaneous, photocopied and previously published submissions OK. Computer printout submissions acceptable. SASE. Reports in 1 month. Free sample copy.

Nonfiction: Historical (relating to country music); how-to (play, write, or perform country music); inspirational (on country gospel); interview (with country performers, both traditional and contemporary); nostalgia (pioneer living); personal experience (country music); and travel (in connection with country music contests or festivals). "Will probably buy 10-15 manuscripts in 1984-85." Query. Length: 800-1,200 words. Pays $25-50.

Photos: State availability of photos with query. Payment is included in ms price. Uses 5x7 b&w prints. Captions and model release required. Buys one-time rights.

Poetry: Free verse and traditional. Buys 4/year. Length: 5-20 lines. Submit maximum 2 poems. Pays $2-5.

Fillers: Clippings, jokes and anecdotes. Buys 5/year. Length: 15-50 words. Pays $5-10.

Tips: "Material must be concerned with what we term 'real' country music as opposed to today's 'pop' country music. Freelancer must be knowledgeable of the subject; many writers don't even know who the father of country music is, let alone write about him."

Mystery

Some readers like "mysteries" in their lives—the kind that only writers can create. Consult the Literary and "Little" category for additional mystery markets. For information on writing mysteries see the *Mystery Writer's Handbook*, by the Mystery Writers of America (revised by Lawrence Treat, Writer's Digest Books).

ALFRED HITCHCOCK'S MYSTERY MAGAZINE, Davis Publications, Inc., 380 Lexington Ave., New York NY 10017. Editor: Cathleen Jordan. Emphasizes mystery fiction. Magazine published 13 times a year. Circ. 200,000. Buys 115 mss/year. Pays on acceptance. Buys first and second and foreign rights. Byline given. Submit seasonal/holiday material 7 months in advance. Photocopied submissions OK. SASE. Reports in 2 months or less. Writer's guidelines for SASE.

Fiction: Original and well-written mystery and crime fiction. Length: 1,000-14,000 words.

ELLERY QUEEN'S MYSTERY MAGAZINE, Davis Publications, Inc., 380 Lexington Ave., New York NY 10017. Editor: Eleanor Sullivan. 100% freelance written. Magazine published 13 times/year. Circ. 375,000. Pays on acceptance. Buys first and second rights to the same material or second (reprint) rights to material originally published elsewhere. Byline given. Submit seasonal/holiday material 7 months in advance. Simultaneous, photocopied and previously published submissions OK. Computer printout submissions acceptable. SASE. Reports in 1 month. Publishes ms an average of 1 year after acceptance. Free writer's guidelines.

Fiction: Special consideration will be given to "anything timely and original. We publish every type of mystery: the suspense story, the psychological study, the deductive puzzle—the gamut of crime and detection from the realistic (including the policeman's lot and stories of police procedure) to the more imaginative (including 'locked rooms' and impossible crimes). We need private-eye stories, but do not want sex, sadism or sensationalism-for-the-sake-of-sensationalism." No gore or horror; seldom publishes parodies or pastiches. Buys 13 mss/issue. Length: 6,000 words maximum; occasionally higher but not often. Pays 3-8¢/word.

Tips: "We have a department of First Stories to encourage writers whose fiction has never before been in print. We publish an average of 20 first stories a year."

MIKE SHAYNE MYSTERY MAGAZINE, Renown Publications, Inc., Box 178, Reseda CA 91335. Editor: Charles E. Fritch. Monthly magazine. Buys nonexclusive world magazine serial rights. Photocopied submissions OK. Reports within 3 months.

Fiction: All kinds of mystery/suspense stories; prefers the offbeat and unusual rather than the conventional and cliched; horror is OK. Length: 10,000 words maximum. Pays 1½¢/word after publication.

Tips: "Avoid the cliches—the hard boiled private eye, the spouse-killer, the little old lady being threatened, the standard hit person, the investigator miraculously solving the case by making unverified conclusions, the criminal confessing at the last minute when there's no reason for him to do so, the culprit caught by some last minute revelation no one but the author knew about, and the poor sap who gets clobbered for no reason. Make it short and unusual, something we can't get any place else. *MSMM* frequently publishes first stories."

Nature, Conservation, and Ecology

The publications in this section promote reader awareness of the natural environment, wildlife, nature preserves and ecobalance. They do not publish recreation or travel articles except as they relate to conservation or nature. Other markets for this kind of material will be found in the Regional, Sports, and Travel, Camping, and Trailer categories, although the magazines listed there require that nature or conservation articles be slanted to their specialized subject matter and audience. Energy conservation topics for professionals are covered in the Trade Energy category.

AMERICAN FORESTS, American Forestry Association, 1319 18th St. NW, Washington DC 20036. (202)467-5810. Editor: Bill Rooney. 70% freelance written. "We are an organization for the advancement of intelligent management and use of our forests, soil, water, wildlife, and all other natural resources necessary for an environment of high quality and the well-being of all citizens." Monthly magazine. Circ. 50,000. Pays on acceptance. Buys one-time rights. Byline given. Phone queries OK but written queries preferred. Submit seasonal/holiday material 5 months in advance. Computer printout submissions acceptable. SASE. Reports in 6 weeks. Publishes mss an average of 8 months after acceptance. Free writer's guidelines.
Nonfiction: General interest, historical, how-to, humor and inspirational. "All articles should emphasize trees, forests, wildlife or land use." Buys 5 mss/issue. Query. Length: 2,000 words. Pays $200-400.
Photos: State availability of photos. Offers no additional payment for photos accompanying mss. Uses 8x10 b&w glossy prints; 35mm or larger color transparencies, originals only. Buys one-time rights. Captions required.
Tips: "Query should have honesty and information on photo support."

‡**THE AMICUS JOURNAL**, Natural Resources Defense Council, 45th Floor, 122 E. 42nd St., New York NY 10168. (212)949-0049. Editor: Peter Borrelli. Assistant Editor: Helena Von Rosenberg. A quarterly magazine covering environmental interests and education. Circ. 40,000. Pays on acceptance. Byline given. Offers ⅓ kill fee. Buys one-time rights. SASE. Free sample copy; writer's guidelines for SAE.
Nonfiction: Articles on environmental policy only. Query with published clips. Buys 15-20 mss/year. Length: 2,500 words maximum. Pays $350-1,500.
Photos: Send photos with query or mss. Captions, model release, and identification of subjects required.

‡**THE ATLANTIC SALMON JOURNAL**, The Atlantic Salmon Federation, Suite 1030, 1435 St. Alexandre, Montreal, Quebec H3A 2G4 Canada. (514)842-8059. Editor: Joanne Eidinger. A quarterly magazine covering conservation efforts for the Atlantic salmon for an "affluent and responsive audience—the dedicated angler and conservationist of the Atlantic salmon." Circ. 20,000. Pays on publication. Byline given. Buys one-time rights. Submit seasonal/holiday material 2 months in advance. Simultaneous queries, and simultaneous and photocopied submissions OK. Computer printout submissions acceptable; prefers letter-quality to dot-matrix. SASE. Reports in 3-6 weeks. Sample copy for SAE; free writer's guidelines.
Nonfiction: Expose, historical/nostalgic, how-to, humor, interview/profile, new product, opinion, personal experience, photo feature, technical, travel, conservation, cuisine, science and management. "We don't want to see anything that is not pertinent to the focus and purpose of our magazine, which is to inform and entertain our membership on all aspects of the Atlantic salmon's world." Buys 12-15 mss/year. Query with clips of published work. Length: 1,500-3,000 words. Pays $100-325.
Photos: State availability of photos with query letter or ms. Pays $35-50 for 3x5 or 5x7 b&w prints; $35-150 for 2¼x3¼ or 16mm color slides. Captions and identification of subjects required.
Columns/Departments: *Perspective* (opinion piece on any subject relating to the Atlantic salmon); *First Person* (nonfiction, anecdotal, from first person viewpoint, can be humorous). Buys about 12 mss/year. Length: 1,000-1,500 words. Pays $175-275.
Fiction: Adventure, fantasy, historical, humorous and mainstream. "We don't want to see anything that does not deal with Atlantic salmon directly or indirectly. Wilderness adventures are acceptable as long as they deal with Atlantic salmon." Buys 3 mm/year. Query with published clips. Length: 3,000 words maximum. Pays $150-250.
Fillers: Clippings, jokes, anecdotes and short humor. Length: 100-300 words average. Does not pay.
Tips: "Articles must reflect informed and up-to-date knowledge of Atlantic salmon. Writers need not be authorities, but research must be impeccable. Clear, concise writing is a plus, and submissions must be typed. Anecdote, River Log and photo essays are most open to freelancers."

AUDUBON MAGAZINE, 950 3rd Ave., New York NY 10022. "Not soliciting freelance material; practically all articles done on assignment only. We have a backlog of articles from known writers and contributors. Our issues are planned well in advance of publication and follow a theme." Pays negotiable kill fee. Byline given.

BIRD WATCHER'S DIGEST, Pardson Corp., Box 110, Marietta OH 45750. Editor: Mary B. Bowers. 65% freelance written. Focuses on birds and bird watching. Bimonthly magazine. Circ. 40,000. Pays on publication. Buys first North American serial rights and second (reprint) rights to material originally published elsewhere. Photocopied and previously published submissions OK. SASE. Reports in 6 weeks. Publishes ms an average of 9 months after acceptance. Sample copy $2; writer's guidelines for SASE.
Nonfiction: General interest (features on species, environmental issues involving birds, endangered and threatened species); historical; how-to; humor (essays); interview (and reports on research); nostalgia; opinion; profile (outstanding or unusual bird watchers); travel (where to go to see birds); personal experience (rare sightings; observations of displays and behavior); photo feature; technical (individual species); and accompanying artwork. Buys 60-65 unsolicited mss/year. Send complete ms or send clips of previously published work with query. Length: 600-3,000 words. Pays $25/reprint and up to $50/original.
Photos: State availability of photos. Reviews 5x7 and up b&w glossy prints and 35mm and up color transparencies. Pays $10 for each b&w photo used (returnable) and $25 for full color.
Poetry: Avant-garde, free verse, light verse, and traditional. Buys 12-20 mss/year. Maximum of 4. Pays $10 minimum.
Fillers: Anecdotes. Buys 3-6 mss/issue. Length: 50-225 words. Pays $5.
Tips: "We want good ornithology, good writing. Articles on birds suited for a general interest magazine may be too basic for us. Our audience is quite knowledgeable about birds. Writers must be at least as knowledgable."

‡**ECOLOGY DIGEST**, Box 60961, Sacramento CA 95860. (916)961-2942, ext. 22. Editor: Max Peters. Managing Editor: Ken Lastufka. 25-40% freelance written. A quarterly magazine covering environmental/political issues. "We try to present most sides of enviromental issues. Our readers are mainly people interested in the topic. We format the magazine so that it covers many topic areas, such as national and international issues; a special section devoted to one particular topic (which will be mentioned in the previous issue), and book and film reviews." Circ. 2,000. Pays on publication. Byline given. Buys one-time rights, and second (reprint) rights to material originally published elsewhere. Submit seasonal/holiday material 2 months in advance. Simultaneous queries, and photocopied and previously published submissions OK. Computer printout submissions acceptable. SASE. Reports in 2 months. Publishes ms an average of 3 months after acceptance. Sample copy for $1, 9x12 SAE and 5 first class stamps.
Nonfiction: Expose, general interest, historical/nostalgic, interview/profile and photo feature. No articles with only local interest. Buys 5-10 mss/year. Query. Length: 500-2,000 words. Pays $25-50.
Columns/Departments: Letters, Special Section, Books, The Nation, and The World.
Tips: "Write articles that are informative and easy to understand. Style your writing toward a magazine or newspaper article."

ENVIRONMENT, 4000 Albemarle St. NW., Washington DC 20016. Managing Editor: Jane Scully. For citizens, scientists, business and government executives, teachers, high school and college students interested in environment or effects of technology and science in public affairs. Magazine published 10 times/year. Circ. 17,000. Buys all rights. Byline given. Pays on publication to professional writers. Photocopied submissions OK. Computer printout submissions acceptable. Reports in 6-8 weeks. Query or submit 3 double-spaced copies of complete ms. SASE. Sample copy $3.50.
Nonfiction: Scientific and environmental material, and effects of technology on society. Preferred length: 2,500-4,500 words for full-length article. Pays $100-300, depending on material. Also accepts shorter articles (1,100-1,700 words) for "Overview" section. Pays $75. "All full-length articles must be annotated (referenced), and all conclusions must follow logically from the facts and arguments presented." Prefers articles centering around policy-oriented, public decision-making, scientific and technological issues.

ENVIRONMENTAL ACTION, 1346 Connecticut Ave., Washington DC 20036. Editors: Francesca Lyman, Richard Asinof and Kathleen Hughes. 20% freelance written. Emphasizes grass roots citizen action and congressional/governmental activity affecting the environment for a well-educated, sophisticated, politically oriented readership. Monthly magazine. Circ. 25,000. Pays on publication. Buys all rights. Byline given. SASE. Reports in 6 weeks. Publishes ms an average of 2 months after acceptance. Sample copy $2.50.
Nonfiction: Exposé; human interest feature; news feature; and political analysis (on such issues as the urban environment, chemical pollution, public health, alternative energy, and the public interest movement). Less interested in wilderness and wildlife issues. Prefers not to see material on nature appreciation, animal rights/cruelty, or photo essays. Buys 15-20 mss/year. Query with clips of published work. Length: 1,000-2,500 words. Pays according to length.
Photos: State availability of photos. Pays $15-50 for 8x10 b&w glossy prints. Buys all rights.
Tips: "We are frequently in the market for local stories that have national significance. Because we have virtually no travel budget, we are most receptive to articles that the editors cannot do from Washington."

FORESTS & PEOPLE, Official Publication of the Louisiana Forestry Association, Louisiana Forestry Association, Drawer 5067, Alexandria LA 71301. (318)443-2558. Editor: Kathryn T. Johnston. 50% freelance written. Quarterly magazine covering forests, forest industry, wood-related stories, wildlife for general readers, both in and out of the forest industry. Circ. 8,500. Pays on aecceptance. Byline given. Not copyrighted. Submit seasonal/holiday material 2 months in advance. Simultaneous queries, and simultaneous, photocopied, and previously published submissions OK. Reports in 2 weeks on queries; 3 weeks on mss. Publishes ms an average of 6 months after acceptance. Sample copy $1.75; free writer's guidelines.
Nonfiction: General interest (recreation, wildlife, crafts with wood, festivals); historical/nostalgic (logging towns, historical wooden buildings, forestry legends); interview/profile (of forest industry execs, foresters, loggers, wildlife managers, tree farmers); photo feature (of scenic forest, wetlands, logging operations); and technical (innovative equipment, chemicals, operations, forestland studies, or industry profiles). No research papers. Articles may cover a technical subject but must be understandable to the general public." Buys 12 mss/year. Query with clips of published work. Length: open. Pays $50.
Photos: State availability of photos. Reviews b&w and color contact sheets. Identification of subjects required.

HIGH COUNTRY NEWS, High Country News Foundation, Box V, Paonia CO 81428. (303)527-4898. Editor: Betsy Marston. 50% freelance written. Biweekly tabloid covering environment and natural resource issues in the Rocky Mountain states for environmentalists, politicians, companies, etc. Circ. 4,200. Pays on publication. Byline given. Buys one-time rights. Computer printout submissions acceptable if "double spaced (at least) and legible"; prefers letter-quality to dot-matrix. Submit seasonal/holiday material 6 weeks in advance. SASE. Reports in 1 month. Free sample copy and writer's guidelines.
Nonfiction: Expose (government, corporate); historical/nostalgic; how-to (appropriate technology); humor; interview/profile; opinion; personal experience; and photo feature. Special issues include those on states in the region. Buys 100 mss/year. Query. Length: 3,000 word maximum. Pays 5¢/word.
Photos: Send photos with ms. Reviews b&w contact sheets and prints. Captions and identification of subjects required.
Poetry: Chip Rawlins, poetry editor, Box 51, Boulder WY 82923. Avant-garde, free verse, haiku, light verse and traditional. Pays in contributor copies.
Tips: "We use a lot of freelance material, though very little from outside the Rockies. Start by writing short, 500-word news items of timely, regional interest."

INTERNATIONAL WILDLIFE, National Wildlife Federation, 1412 16th St. NW, Washington DC 20036. Managing Editor: Jonathan Fisher. 85% freelance written. For persons interested in natural history, outdoor adventure and the environment. Bimonthly. Circ. 500,000. Buys all rights to text; usually one-time rights to photos and art. Pays on acceptance. Query. "Now assigning most articles but will consider detailed proposals for quality feature material of interest to broad audience." Computer printout submissions acceptable; prefers letter-quality to dot-matrix. Reports in 3 weeks. Publishes ms an average of 4 months after acceptance. SASE.
Nonfiction: Focus on world wildlife, environmental problems and man's relationship to the natural world as reflected in such issues as population control, pollution, resource utilization, food production, etc. Especially interested in articles on animal behavior and other natural history, first-person experiences by scientists in the field and timely issues. Length: 2,000-3,000 words. Pays $750 minimum.
Photos: Purchases top quality color and b&w photos; prefers 'packages' of related photos and text, but single shots of exceptional interest and sequences also considered. Prefers Kodachrome transparencies for color, 8x10 prints for b&w."

JOURNAL OF FRESHWATER, Freshwater Society, 2500 Shadywood Rd., Box 90, Navarre MN 55392. (612)471-7467. Editor: Linda Schroeder. 10% freelance written. Always emphasizes freshwater issues. Annual (November) magazine; 64 pages. Pays on publication. Buys one-time rights, all rights and second (reprint) rights to material originally published elsewhere. Byline given. Phone queries OK. Reports in 6 weeks. Publishes ms an average of 6 months after acceptance. Sample copy $6; free writer's and photographer's guidelines. SASE.
Nonfiction: Scientific, yet easy to read how-to, general interest, humor, interview, nostalgia, photo feature and technical. "We will consider virtually any material dealing with freshwater environment as long as it is well-written and interesting. Entries must clearly and quickly answer the reader's question 'So what's that got to do with me, my pocketbook, or my relatives?'." No "bumper-sticker" philosophies, encyclopedia articles or unresearched material, please. No articles about dam controversies, personal travelogs, fish-catching stories, or long pieces of poetry. Buys 2-3 mss/year. Submit complete ms. Length: "2,500 words or less works best." Pays $100 (more with photos or art), per 800 words used.
Photos: Submit photos with accompanying ms. Payment for photos can be included in purchase price of article. Uses 5x7 minimum b&w glossy photos or 35mm, 2¼x2¼ or larger color transparencies. Captions preferred. Buys all rights for cover photos and all or one-time rights for others. Model release required.
Fiction: "We purchase very little fiction, but we're open to considering it as long as it's very water-related." Pays $100 (more with photos or art)/800 words used.

Poetry: Very short; free verse, haiku, or light verse. "We prefer poetry illustrated with *excellent* photos." Limit submissions to batches of 5. "Again, we use very little." Pays $20-50.

Tips: "Study at least 2 past issues of the journal. Query us before you write the article, to save your time and ours. Introduce yourself, state story idea and why we should be interested. Give a few key facts, state main sources you expect to use, propose a deadline you can meet, and offer to round up excellent photos to illustrate."

MICHIGAN NATURAL RESOURCES MAGAZINE, State of Michigan Department of Natural Resources, Box 30034, Lansing MI 48909. (517)373-9267. Editor: Russell McKee. Managing Editor: Richard Morscheck. Bimonthly magazine covering natural resources in the Great Lakes area. Circ. 140,000. Pays on acceptance. Byline given. Offers 100% kill fee. Buys first rights only. Submit seasonal/holiday material 1 year in advance. Simultaneous queries and simultaneous and photocopied submissions OK. SASE. Reports in 1 month. Sample copy for $2 and 9x12 SAE; writer's guidelines for business-size SAE and 1 first class stamp.

Nonfiction: Historical/nostalgic, how-to, humor, technical and travel. "All material must pertain to this region's natural resources; lakes, rivers, wildlife, flora, special features, energy and industry as it relates to natural resources. No personal experience, domestic animal stories or animal rehabilitation." Buys 24 mss/year. Query with clips of published work or send complete ms. Length: 1,000-4,000 words. Pays $150-400.

Photos: Gijsbert (Nick) vanFrankenhuyzen, photo editor. "Photos submitted with an article can help sell it, but they must be razor sharp in focus." Send photos with ms. Pays $50-200 for 35mm color transparencies. Model release and identification of subjects required. Buys one-time rights.

NATIONAL PARKS, 1701 18th St. NW, Washington DC 20009. (202)265-2717. Editors: Marjorie Corbett and Michele Strutin. 75% freelance written. For a highly educated audience interested in preservation of National Park System Units, natural areas and protection of wildlife habitat. Bimonthly magazine. Circ. 40,000. Pays on acceptance. Buys first North American serial rights and second (reprint) rights to material originally published elsewhere. Submit seasonal/holiday material 5 months in advance. Computer printout submissions acceptable if legible; prefers letter-quality to dot-matrix. SASE. Reports in 6-10 weeks. Sample copy $3; free writer's guidelines with SASE.

Nonfiction: Expose (on threats, wildlife problems to national parks); descriptive articles about new or proposed national parks and wilderness parks; brief natural history pieces describing park geology, wildlife, or plants; "adventures" in national parks (crosscountry skiing, bouldering, mountain climbing, kayaking, canoeing, backpacking); and travel tips to national parks. All material must relate to national parks. No poetry or philosophical essays. Buys 6-10 unsolicited mss/year. Query or send complete ms. Length: 1,000-1,500 words. Pays $75-200.

Photos: State availability of photos or send photos with ms. Pays $25-50 for 8x10 b&w glossy prints; $35-100 for color transparencies; offers no additional payment for photos accompanying ms. Buys one-time rights. Captions required.

NATIONAL WILDLIFE, 8925 Leesburg Pike, Vienna VA 22180. Managing Editor: Mark Wexler. Emphasizes wildlife. Bimonthly magazine; 64 pages. Circ. 770,000. Pays on acceptance. Buys all rights. Submit seasonal/holiday material 6 months in advance. Previously published submissions OK. SASE. Reports in 1 month. Free writer's guidelines.

Nonfiction: How-to, humor, informational, interview, personal experience, photo feature and profile. Buys 8 mss/issue. Query. Length: 2,000-3,000 words. Pays $750 minimum.

Photos: John Nuhn, photo editor. Photos purchased with or without accompanying ms or on assignment. Pays $75 and up for 8x10 b&w glossy prints; $125 minimum for 35mm color Kodachromes.

NATURAL HISTORY, Natural History Magazine, 79th and Central Park W., New York NY 10024. Editor: Alan Ternes. Over 75% freelance written. For "well-educated, ecologically aware audience: professional people, scientists and scholars." Monthly. Circ. 460,000. Buys first and second rights to same material. Buys 50 mss/year. Byline given. Pays on publication. Submit seasonal material 6 months in advance. Query or submit complete ms. Computer printout submissions acceptable; no dot-matrix. Publishes ms an average of 1 year after acceptance. SASE. Sample copy $3.

Nonfiction: Uses all types of scientific articles except chemistry and physics—emphasis is on the biological sciences and anthropology. Prefers professional scientists as authors. "We always want to see new research findings in almost all the branches of the natural sciences—anthropology, archeology, zoology and ornithology. We find that it is particularly difficult to get something new in herpetology (amphibians and reptiles) or entomology (insects), and we would like to see material in those fields. We lean heavily toward writers who are scientists or professional science writers. High standards of writing and research. Favor ecological slant in most of our pieces, but do not generally lobby for causes, environmental or other. Writer should have a deep knowledge of his subject; then submit original ideas either in query or by manuscript. Should be able to supply high-quality illustrations." Length: 2,000-4,000 words. Pays $400-750, plus additional payment for photos used.

Photos: Uses some 8x10 b&w glossy photographs; pays $125/page maximum. Much color is used; pays $250 for inside and up to $350 for cover. Photos are purchased for one-time use.
Tips: "Learn about something in depth before you bother writing about it."

OCEANS, 315 Fort Mason, San Francisco CA 94123. Editor-in-Chief: Keith K. Howell. 100% freelance written. Publication of The Oceanic Society. For people who love in the sea. Bimonthly magazine; 72 pages. Circ. 65,000. Pays on publication. Buys first rights; rarely second (reprint) rights to material published elsewhere. Byline given. Submit seasonal/holiday material 4 months in advance. Simultaneous and photocopied submissions OK. Computer printout submissions acceptable. SASE. Reports in 8 weeks. Publishes ms an average of 1 year after acceptance. Sample copy $2; free writer's guidelines.
Nonfiction: "We want articles on the worldwide realm of salt water; marine life (biology and ecology), oceanography, maritime history, marine painting and other arts, geography, undersea exploration and study, voyages, ships, coastal areas including environmental problems, seaports and shipping, islands, food-fishing and aquaculture (mariculture), peoples of the sea, including anthropological materials. Writing should be simple, direct, factual, very readable (avoid dullness and pedantry, make it lively and interesting but not cute, flippant or tongue-in-cheek; avoid purple prose). Careful research, good structuring, no padding. Factual information in good, narrative style. *Oceans* is authoritative but less technical than *Scientific American*. First person accounts of adventure and scuba tend to be overworked. Diving OK if unusual in results or story angle. We want articles on rarely visited islands, ports or shores that have great intrinsic interest, but not treated in purely travelogue style. Can use more on environmental concerns." Length: 500-4,000 words. Pays $100/page.

‡**OCEANUS, The Magazine of Marine Science and Policy**, Woods Hole Oceanographic Institution, Woods Hole MA 02543. (617)548-1400, ext. 2386. Editor: Paul R. Ryan. Associate Editor: Michael B. Downing. "*Oceanus* is an international quarterly magazine that monitors significant trends in ocean research, technology and marine policy. Its basic purpose is to encourage wise, environmentally responsible use of the oceans. In addition, two of the magazine's main tasks are to explain the significance of present marine research to readers and to expose them to the substance of vital public policy questions." Circ. 15,000. Pays on publication. Byline given. Buys all rights. Simultaneous queries OK. SASE. Reports in 2 months.
Nonfiction: Interview/profile and technical. *Oceanus* publishes 3 thematic issues a year and one general issue. Most articles are commissioned. Themes for 1984 included industry and the oceans, El Nino, hot vents, and underwater archaeology. Length: 2,700-3,500 words. Pays $300 minimum.
Photos: State availability of photos. Reviews b&w and color contact sheets and 8x10 prints. Pays variable rates depending on size; $125 full-page b&w print. Captions required. Buys one-time rights.

PACIFIC DISCOVERY, California Academy of Sciences, Golden Gate Park, San Francisco CA 94118. (415)221-5100. Editor: Sheridan Warrick. 100% freelance written. "A journal of nature and culture around the world read by scientists, naturalists, teachers, students, and others having a keen interest in knowing the natural world more thoroughly." Published quarterly by the California Academy of Sciences. Circ. 25,000. Buys first North American serial rights on articles; one-time rights on photos. Pays on publication. Query with 100-word summary of projected article for review before preparing finished ms. Computer printout submissions acceptable; prefers letter-quality to dot-matrix. SASE. Usually reports within 3 months. Publishes ms an average of 1 year after acceptance.
Nonfiction: "Subjects of articles include behavior and natural history of animals and plants, ecology, evolution, anthropology, geology, paleontology, biogeography, taxonomy, and related topics in the natural sciences. Occasional articles are published on the history of natural science, exploration, astronomy and archeology. Emphasis is on current research findings. Authors need not be scientists; however, all articles must be based, at least in part, on firsthand fieldwork." Length: 1,000-3,000 words. Pays 12¢/word.
Photos: Color transparencies and/or b&w 8x10 prints must accompany all mss or they will not be reviewed. Send 15-30 with each ms. Photos should have both scientific and aesthetic interest, be captioned in a few sentences on a separate caption list keyed to the photos and numbered in story sequence. Half of all photos in an issue are printed in color. Some photo stories are used. Pays $30/photo. All transparencies and prints are returned soon after publication.

SEA FRONTIERS, 3979 Rickenbacker Causeway, Virginia Key, Miami FL 33149. (305)361-5786. Editor: Jean Bradfisch. 95% freelance written. "For anyone with an interest in any aspect of the sea; its conservation, and the life it contains. Our audience is professional people for the most part; people in executive positions and students." Bimonthly. Circ. 50,000. Buys all rights. Byline given. Buys 45-50 mss/year. Pays on publication. Query. Will consider photocopied submissions "if very clear." Computer printout submissions acceptable; prefers letter-quality to dot-matrix. Reports on material within 2 months. SASE. Sample copy $2.50; free writer's guidelines with SASE.
Nonfiction: "Articles (with illustrations) covering interesting and little known facts about the sea, marine life, chemistry, geology, physics, fisheries, mining, engineering, navigation, influences on weather and climate, ecology, conservation, explorations, discoveries or advances in our knowledge of the marine sciences, or

describing the activities of oceanographic laboratories or expeditions to any part of the world. Emphasis should be on research and discoveries rather than personalities involved." Length: 500-3,000 words. Pays $20-30/page.

Photos: 8x10 b&w glossy prints and 35mm (or larger) color transparencies purchased with ms. Pays $50 for color used on front and $35 for the back cover. Pays $25 for color used on inside covers.

Tips: "Query to include a paragraph or two that tells the subject, the angle or approach to be taken, and the writer's qualifications for covering this subject or the authorities with whom the facts will be checked."

SIERRA, The Sierra Club Bulletin, 530 Bush Street, San Francisco CA 94108. (415)981-8634. Editor-in-Chief: James Keough. Associate Editor: Annie Stine. 75% freelance written. Emphasizes conservation and environmental politics for people who are well educated, activist, outdoor-oriented, and politically well informed with a dedication to conservation. Magazine published 6 times/year; 96 pages. Circ. 340,000. Buys first rights and second (reprint) rights to material originally published elsewhere. Pays on acceptance. Byline given. Photocopied submissions OK. Computer printout submissions acceptable; prefers letter-quality to dot-matrix. SASE. Reports in 6 weeks. Publishes ms an average of 4 months after acceptance. Writer's guidelines available.

Nonfiction: Expose (well-documented on environmental issues of national importance such as energy, wilderness, forests, etc.); general interest (well-researched pieces on areas of particular environmental concern); historical (relevant to environmental concerns); how-to (on camping, climbing, outdoor photography, etc.); interview (with very prominent figures in the field); personal experience (by or about children and wilderness); photo feature (photo essays on threatened areas); and technical (on energy sources, wildlife management land use, solid waste management, etc.). No "My trip to . . . " or why we must save wildlife/nature articles; no poetry or general superficial essays on environmentalism and local environmental issues. Buys 5-6 mss/issue. Query with clips of published work. Length: 800-2,500 words. Pays $200-400.

Photos: Linda Smith, art and production manager. State availability of photos. Pays $100 maximum for color transparencies; $200 for cover photos. Buys one-time rights.

Columns/Departments: Book reviews. Buys 15-18 mss/year. Length: 800-1,500 words. Pays $100. Query. For Younger Readers, natural history and conservation topics presented for children 8 to 13 years old. Pays $200-400. Submit queries to Jonathan King, associate editor.

Tips: "Queries should include an outline of how the topic would be covered and a mention of the political appropriateness and timeliness of the article. Familiarity with Sierra Club positions and policies is recommended. Statements of the writer's qualifications should be included."

SNOWY EGRET, 205 S. 9th St., Williamsburg KY 40769. (606)549-0850. Editor: Humphrey A. Olsen. 75% freelance written. For "persons of at least high school age interested in literary, artistic, philosophical and historical natural history." Semiannual. Circ. less than 500. Buys first North American serial rights. Byline given. Buys 40-50 mss/year. Pays on publication. Computer printout submissions acceptable; prefers letter-quality to dot-matrix. Usually reports in 2 months. Publishes ms an average of 3 months after acceptance. SASE. Sample copy $2.

Nonfiction: Subject matter limited to material related to natural history (preferably living organisms), especially literary, artistic, philosophical and historical aspects. Criticism, book reviews, essays and biographies. No columns. Pays $2/printed page. Send nonfiction prose mss and books for review to Humphrey A. Olsen.

Photos: No photos, but drawings acceptable.

Fiction: "We are interested in considering stories or self-contained portions of novels. All fiction must be natural history or man and nature. The scope is broad enough to include such stories as Hemingway's 'Big Two-Hearted River' and Warren's 'Blackberry Winter.' " Length: maximum 10,000 words. Pays $2/printed page. Send mss for consideration and poetry and fiction books for review to Alan Seaburg, poetry and fiction editor, 17 Century St., West Medford MA 02155. "It is preferable to query first."

Poetry: No length limits. Pays $4/printed page, minimum $2.

Personal Computing

Owners of personal computers rely on these magazines to learn more about their PC. Business applications for home computers are covered in the Consumer Business and Finance section. Magazines on computer games and recreational computing are in the Games and Puzzles category. Publications for data processing personnel are listed in the Data Processing section of Trade Journals. Uses of computers in specific professions are covered in the appropriate Trade Journals sections. Writer's Digest Books also publishes the *1985 Programmer's Market*, a book directed to the writing and marketing of freelance computer programs, and *The Complete Guide to Writing Software User Manuals*, by Brad M. McGehee.

A.N.A.L.O.G. COMPUTING, The Magazine for ATARI Computer Owners, A.N.A.L.O.G. Magazine Corp., Box 23, Worcester MA 01603. (617)892-9230. Editors: Michael DesChenes/Lee H. Pappas. Managing Editor: Jon A. Bell. Monthly magazine covering the Atari home computer. Pays on publication. Byline given. Buys all rights. Submit seasonal/holiday material 2 months in advance. Photocopied submissions OK. Electronic submissions OK "as long as the disk is prepared with one of the more common Atari word processing programs. Computer printout submissions acceptable." Reports in 2 weeks. Sample copy $3; writer's guidelines for business-size SASE.
Nonfiction: How-to and technical. "We publish beginner's articles, educational programs, utilities, multi-function tutorials, do-it-yourself hardware articles (such as how-to build your own 400 keyboard), and games (preferably arcade-style in BASIC and/or ASSEMBLY language). We also publish reviews of Atari software and hardware." Buys 150 mss/year. Send complete ms. Length: open. Pays $60/typeset magazine page.
Photos: Send photos with ms. Reviews 5x7 b&w prints. Captions required; "clipped to the photo or taped to the back." Buys all rights.
Columns/Departments: Atari software and hardware reviews. Buys 30 mss/year. Send complete ms. Length: open.
Tips: "Almost all submissions are from people who read the magazine regularly and use the Atari home computers. We have published many first-time authors. We have published programs written in BASIC, ASSEMBLY, PILOT, FORTH, LISP, and some information on PASCAL. When submitting any program over 30 lines, authors must send a copy of the program on magnetic media, either cassette or disk. We strive to publish personable, down-to-earth articles as long as the style does not impair the technical aspects of the article. Authors should avoid sterile, lifeless prose. Occasional humor (detailing how the author uses his or her computer or tackles a programming problem) is welcome."

‡AHOY!, Ion International Inc., Suite 407, 45 W. 34th St., New York NY 10001. (212)239-0855. Editor: Steve Springer. Managing Editor: Robert J. Sodaro. A monthly magazine for users of Commodore 64 and VIC 20 home computers. Estab. 1983. Pays on acceptance. Byline given. Offers variable kill fee. Buys first rights. Submit seasonal/holiday material 3 months in advance. Simultaneous queries and simultaneous, photocopied and previously published submissions OK. Electronic submissions OK on disk or cassette for Commodore 64 or VIC 20. Computer printout submissions acceptable. SASE. Sample copy $2.50; free writer's guidelines.
Nonfiction: Book excerpts (Commodore-related books); general interest (modern technology); how-to (programming, maintaining, repairing, and customizing Commodore computers); humor (computer-related); interview/profile (computer industry leaders); new product (new Commodore-64 and Vic-20 software and peripherals); and technical (how-to programming articles, mechanics of computers and peripherals). Buys 60 mss/year. Query with clips of published work. Length: 250-5,000 words. Pays $500 maximum.
Fillers: Gags for cartoons. Pays $15/cartoon gag.
Tips: "We are building an inventory of articles and programs. Our needs are high!"

‡A+, THE INDEPENDENT GUIDE TO APPLE COMPUTING, Ziff-Davis, 1 Davis Dr., Belmont CA 94002. (415)594-2290. Editor: Maggie Canon. Managing Editor: Leslie Steere. Staff editor: Jane Willson. Technical Editor: Fred Davis. 95% freelance written. Monthly magazine covering the Apple Computer product line and related products. "A+ aims to educate the Apple II, IIe, III, Lisa and Macintosh owner on professional uses of the various products." Estab. 1983. Circ. 125,000. Pays 6 weeks after acceptance. Byline given. Offers $50-100 kill fee. Buys first world-wide rights. Submit (all) seasonal/holiday material 4 months in advance. Computer printout submissions acceptable. SASE. Publishes ms an average of 6 months after acceptance. Sample copy for 9x12 SAE and 3 first class stamps; free writer's guidelines.
Nonfiction: How-to, new product and technical. Buys 200 mss/year. Query with published clips. Length: 1,000-4,000 words. pays negotiable rates.
Photos: Candy De Santis, photo editor. Send photos with query. Pays negotiable rates for color and b&w contact sheets. Captions, model release and identification of subjects required. Buys one-time and world-wide rights.
Columns/Departments: Jane Willson, features editor. "We are interested in features on computer topics from word processing to operating systems." Query with published clips. Length: 1,000-2,500 words. Pays negotiable rates.
Tips: "If you know about Apple computers and their uses and have some writing experience, we will consider you for a freelance assignment."

ANTIC MAGAZINE, The Atari Resource, Antic Publishing Co., 524 2nd St., San Francisco CA 94107. (415)957-0886. Editor: James Capparell. Monthly magazine for Atari 400/800, 1200XL, 600XL, 800XL, and

1450LXD computer users and owners of Atari game machines, compatible equipment and software. Circ. 100,000. Pays partial on acceptance; balance on publication. Byline given. Offers $60 kill fee. Buys all rights. Submit seasonal/holiday material 3 months in advance. Simultaneous queries and photocopied submissions OK. SASE. Reports in 2 weeks on queries; 4 weeks on mss. Sample copy $3; free writer's guidelines. Request text files or disks.

Nonfiction: How-to, interview/profile, new product, photo feature, and technical. Special issues include Education (Oct.) and Buyer's Guide (Dec.). No generalized, nontechnical articles. Buys 250 mss/year. Query or send complete ms. Length: 500-2,500 words. Pays $20-180.

Photos: State availability of photos or send photos with ms. Reviews color transparencies and b&w prints; b&w should accompany article. Identification of subjects required.

Columns/Departments: Starting Line (beginner's column); Assembly Language (for advanced programmers); Profiles (personalities in the business); and Product Reviews (software/hardware products). Buys 36 mss/year. Query or send complete ms. Length: 1,500-2,500 words. Pays $120-180.

Tips: "Write for the Product Reviews section. Contact David Duberman, editor. 400-600 words on a new software or hardware product for the Atari 400/800 computers. Give a clear description; personal experience with product; comparison with other available product; or product survey with charts."

‡**CHRISTIAN COMPUTING**, 72 Valley Hill Rd., Stockbridge GA 30281. (404)474-0007. Editor: Dr. Nancy White Kelly. A bimonthly magazine "for Christians who own a computer or plan to own one in the near future." Estab. 1984. Circ. 20,000. Pays on publication. Usually gives byline. Offers 50% kill fee. Buys all rights. Submit seasonal/holiday material in adance. Simultaneous queries, and simultaneous, photocopied, and previously published submissions OK. Electronic submissions OK after hard copy is accepted; prefers Apple transmission, possibly Compu-Serve. Computer printout submissions acceptable "if good quality." SASE. Reports in 6 weeks on queries; 2 months on mss. Sample copy $2; writer's guidelines for business size SAE and 1 first class stamp.

Nonfiction: Book excerpts, how-to (e.g., "How We Translated the Bible into Yawee language using computers"); inspirational; interview/profile (of pastor, church, or missionary successfully using computers); new product; opinion; personal experience; photo feature; and technical (not-too technical). "All submissions must have a tie between Christians and computers." Buys 20 mss/year. Query with published clips, or send complete ms. Length: 500-1,500 words. Pays 3¢/word minimum.

Photos: H.E. Kelly, photo editor. Pays $25-125 for 35mm and larger color transparencies; $20-100 for 8x10 b&w prints. Captions, model release on identifiable subjects and identification of subjects required.

Columns/Departments: C.E. Kelly, column/department editor. In The News; Telecommunications Crosstalk; and Missionary Bits and Bytes. Buys 12 mss/year. Query (preferred), or send complete ms. Length 200-500 words. Pays 3¢/word minimum.

Poetry: C.E. Kelly, poetry editor. Light verse. No serious poetry. Buys 2 poems/year. Submit maximum 3 poems. Length 6-12 lines. Pays $10-25.

Fillers: C.E. Kelly, fillers editor. Clippings, jokes, anecdotes, short humor and newsbreaks. Buys 20/year. Length: 100-500 lines. Pays $10-25.

Tips: "Don't be over technical. We like an "easy-reading" style. Don't presume prior knowledge—explain. Photos are a plus. How-to articles and success stories are most open to freelancers."

‡**CLOSING THE GAP**, Random Graphics, Box 68, Henderson MN 56044. (612)665-6573. Editor: Budd Hagen. Managing Editor: Bill Davey. 25% freelance written. Bimonthly tabloid covering microcomputers for handicapped readers. "We focus on currently available products and procedures written for the layman that incorporate microcomputers to enhance the educational opportunities and quality of life for the handicapped." Circ. 10,000. Pays on publication. Bylines given. Buys first rights only. Simultaneous queries, and simultaneous, photocopied, and previously published submissions OK. Electronic submissions via modem (ASCII text file, Apple II compatible if sent on disk) OK. Computer printout submissions acceptable (dot-matrix if printout has descenders). SASE. Reports in 2 weeks. Publishes ms an average of 2 months after acceptance. Free sample copy and writer's guidelines.

Nonfiction: How-to (simple modifications to computers or programs to aid handicapped); interview/profile (users or developers of computers to aid handicapped); new product (computer products to aid handicapped); personal experience (use of microcomputer to aid, or by, a handicapped person); and articles on current research on projects on microcomputers to aid the handicapped. No highly technical "computer hobbyist" pieces. Buys 25 mss/year. Query. Length: 500-2,000 words. Pays $25 and up (negotiable). "Many authors' material runs without financial compensation."

Tips: "Knowledge of the subject is vital, but freelancers do not need to be computer geniuses. Clarity is essential; articles must be able to be understood by a layman. Avoid computer, educator and rehabilitation jargon. All departments are open to freelancers. We are looking for new ideas. If you saw it in some other computer publication, don't bother submitting."

THE COLOR COMPUTER MAGAZINE for TRS-80 Color Computer users, Ziff-Davis Publishing Co., Highland Mill, Camden ME 04843. (207)236-9621. Editor: Debra Marshall. 90% freelance written. Monthly magazine covering "new ways for readers to use their TRS-80 Color Computers. Articles are aimed at the novice and expert and speak with enthusiasm and authority." Estab. 1983. Circ. 65,000. Pays on acceptance. Byline given. Buys all rights to solicited manuscripts, first rights to most unsolicited material. Submit seasonal/holiday material 7 months in advance. Simultaneous queries OK. Electronic submissions OK, but requires hard copy also. Programs must be on magnetic media; directions, source code and operating system must be included or identified. Computer printout submissions acceptable; no dot-matrix. SASE. Reports in 4 weeks on queries; 6 weeks on mss. Publishes ms an average of 7 months after acceptance. Sample copy for $2.95 and 9x12 SASE; free writer's guidelines.

Nonfiction: How-to ("main editorial focus is describing how to use your computer"); interview/profile; new product; technical; and reviews. Reviews: a crucial part of our magazine. We look for tough but fair reviewers. Payment depends on a number of factors and ranges from $25 to hundreds of dollars. Review guidelines available. No "I am a computer widow" articles. No "good golly, I own my very own computer" material. Buys 150+ mss/year. Query with tape of program. Pays $50/published page (average article pays $100-250).

Photos: State availability of photos with query letter and send photos with manuscript. Pays $5 for 35mm color transparencies; $5 for 8x10 b&w prints. Captions required.

Fiction: Adventure, humorous, and science fiction. Number of mss bought each year "will depend on quality of submissions." Send complete ms. Length: 1,000-3,000 words. Pays $65-250.

Fillers: Quick Tips. Number of items/year "open." Length: 500 words. Pays $50.

Tips: "Read the magazine. If an article doesn't give readers another program to use, or deeper insight into their Color Computer, we don't want it. Otherwise breaking in is as easy as a trip to the post office. Writers should replace their typewriters with microcomputers. Not only will word processing capabilities help them, but articles about computer's uses are in heavy demand. People who write well are badly needed. You don't have to be a 'technical whiz' to break into this field—just curious and creative."

COMMODORE MICROCOMPUTERS, (formerly *Commodore, The Microcomputer Magazine*), Commodore Business Machines, 1200 Wilson Dr., West Chester PA 19380. (215)436-4211. Editor: Diane LeBold. Publisher: Neil Harris. 75% freelance written. Bimonthly magazine for owners of Commodore computers, using them for business, programming, education, communications, art, etc. Circ. 150,000. Pays on publication. Byline given. Buys first North American serial rights, all rights, second serial rights, and makes work-for-hire assignments. Submit seasonal/holiday material 5 months in advance. Simultaneous queries and previously published submissions OK. Electronic submissions OK if CBM 8032/8050 Format, Wordcraft or Word Pro files with hard copy. Computer printout submissions acceptable. SASE. Reports in 1 month on queries; 2 months on mss. Publishes ms an average of 3 months after submission. Free sample copy; writer's guidelines for legal-size SAE and 1 first class stamp.

Nonfiction: Book reviews; how-to (write programs, use software); humor; new product (reviews); personal experience; photo feature; and technical. "Write for guidelines." Buys 120 mss/year. Query or send complete ms. Length: 750-2,500 words. Pays $50-100/page.

Photos: Send photos with ms. Reviews 5x7 b&w and color prints. Captions required. Buys all rights.

Tips: "Write or phone the editor. Talk about several specific ideas. Use Commodore computers. We're open to programming techniques and product reviews."

COMPUTE! The Leading Magazine of Home, Educational, and Recreational Computing, ABC Publishing, 324 W. Wendover Ave., Greensboro NC 27408. (919)275-9809. Editor: Robert Lock. Managing Editor: Kathleen Martinek. 50% freelance written. Monthly magazine covering consumer and personal computing. Circ. 420,000. Pays on acceptance. Byline given. Buys all rights. Submit seasonal/holiday material 6 months in advance. Simultaneous queries OK. Electronic submissions OK, but requires hard copy also. Computer printout submissions acceptable. SASE. Reports in 2 weeks on queries; 6 weeks on mss. Publishes ms an average of 3 months after acceptance. Sample copy $2.95; free writer's guidelines.

Nonfiction: How-to (compute) and technical (programs, games, utility programs for computers). No reviews. Send complete ms. Length: 500 words minimum. Pays $75-600.

Photos: Reviews 5x7 b&w glossy prints.

Tips: "We stress clarity and a tutorial approach and publish computer programs for many popular computers. Write for guidelines."

‡COMPUTER USER, For the Tandy/Radio Shack System, McPheters, Wolfe & Jones, 16704 Marquardt Ave., Cerritos CA 90701. (213)926-9544. Editorial Director: Les Spindle. Managing Editor: Catherine Semar. 95% freelance written. Monthly magazine covering the entire Radio Shack computer line and compatible equipment. "Our readers are mainly hobbyists, but the magazine will devote a section for the businessperson and the novice. We prefer technical articles." Estab. 1983. Circ. 300,000. Pays on publication. Byline given. Offers $25 kill fee. Buys all rights. Submit seasonal/holiday material 6 months in advance. Photocopied submissions OK. Computer printout submissions acceptable; prefers letter-quality to dot-matrix. Reports in 4 weeks on queries; 6 weeks on mss. Publishes ms an average of 3-6 months after acceptance. Sample copy $3.75; free writer's guidelines.

Nonfiction: Book excerpts, expose, general interest, how-to, interview/profile, new product, opinion, personal experience, technical, hardware and software review, and articles on application and implementation. No articles not dealing with the TRS-80 or compatible computer/equipment and no agency- or company-written articles. Buys 200 mss/year. Query with or without published clips or send complete ms. Length: 2,000-5,000 words. Pays $50/published page minimum or negotiable maximum.

Photos: Send photo with article to managing editor. Reviews contact sheets, color transparencies, and 8x10 b&w prints. "Payment included with purchase price of articles." Identification of subjects required.

Columns/Departments: Catherine Semar, column/department editor. Letters to the Editor; User Tips (short tips to aid readers in better understanding/use of their equipment); Crosswire (bulletin board for computerists); and Book Reviews. "We will send books to interested parties." Buys 50-75 mss/year. Query with published clips or send complete ms. Length: 300-1,000 words. Pays $20.

Tips: "Query about products that we have not yet reviewed or useful program listings. Our agenda calls for articles on such topics as computer art and graphics, educational programs, games, word processing, communications and networks, and hardware/software reviews. We also publish tutorials, and utility and language features. Good quality program listings, accompanied by articles explaining the programs, are sure bets for serious consideration during our screening process."

COMPUTERS AND ELECTRONICS, For Computer Enthusiasts, (formerly *Popular Electronics*), 1 Park Ave., New York NY 10016. (212)725-3566. Editor-in-Chief: Seth R. Alpert. 75% freelance written. Monthly. Circ. 600,000. Buys all rights. Pays 50% kill fee. Byline given. Buys about 75 mss/year. Pays on acceptance. No photocopied or simultaneous submissions. Electronic submissions not accepted unless arrangements agreed upon. Computer printout submissions acceptable. SASE. Reports in 2-4 weeks. Publishes ms an average of 3 months after acceptance. Query. Free writer's guidelines.

Nonfiction: "State-of-the-art" reports, how-to and tutorial articles, construction projects, etc. The writer must know what he's talking about and not depend on 'hand-out' literature from a few manufacturers or research laboratories. The writer must always bear in mind that the reader has some knowledge of computers and electronics." Informational, how-to, and technical articles. "No humor stories or superficial general-public material." Query. Length: 500-3,000 words. Pays $90-150/published page with photo, illustration, rough diagrams.

Photos: B&w glossy prints preferred, though color transparencies are sometimes used.

Tips: "Focus on personal computers for home and small-business applications will affect writers in the year ahead."

COMPUTE!'s GAZETTE, ABC Publishing, Suite 200, 324 W. Wendover Ave., Greensboro NC 27408. (919)275-9809. Editor: Robert Lock. Managing Editor: Kathleen Martinek. 50% freelance edited. Monthly magazine of consumer and personal computing for owners/users of VIC and Commodore 64 computer systems. "Our audience is mostly beginning and novice computer users." Estab. 1983. Circ. 240,000. Pays on acceptance. Byline given. Buys all rights. Submit seasonal/holiday material 6 months in advance. Simultaneous queries OK. Electronic submissions OK, but requires hard copy also. Computer printout submissions acceptable. SASE. Reports in 2 weeks on queries; 6 weeks on mss. Publishes ms an average of 3 months after acceptance. Sample copy $2.50; free writer's guidelines.

Nonfiction: How-to (compute); personal experience (with programming/computers); and technical (programs, games, utility programs for computers). No reviews. "We stress clarity and a tutorial approach, and publish quality computer programs for VIC and Commodore 64 computers. Follow the suggestions in our author's guide. Send complete ms. Length: 500 words minimum. Pays $70 minimum.

CREATIVE COMPUTING, 39 E. Hanover Ave., Morris Plains NJ 07950. Editor: Elizabeth Staples. Managing Editor: Peter J. Fee. Monthly magazine covering the use of computers in homes, businesses and schools for students, faculty, hobbyists—everyone interested in the effects of computers on society and the use of computers in school, at home or at work. Circ. 305,000. Pays on acceptance. "Buys first rights and usually first reprint rights so as to publish in 'Best of' volumes; then rights automatically revert to author." Byline given. Submit all material at least 4 months in advance. Computer printout submissions acceptable; dot-matrix acceptable but dot matrix print should have descenders. SASE. Reports in 2 weeks. Sample copy $2.95.

Nonfiction: Reviews of new hardware and software; how-to (building a computer at home, personal computer applications and software); informational (computer careers; simulations on computers; problem-solving techniques; use in a particular institution or discipline such as medicine, education, music, animation, space exploration, business or home use); historical articles (history of computers, or of a certain discipline, like computers and animation); interviews (with personalities in the hobbyist field, old-timers in the computer industry or someone doing innovative work); personal experience (first-person accounts of using hardware or software); and technical (programs, games and simulations with printouts). Buys 200 mss/year. Length: 500-3,000 words. Pays $50-100/printed page.

Photos: Usually purchased with mss, with no additional payment, but sometimes pays $3-50 for b&w glossy prints or $10-150 for any size color.

‡**DIGITAL REVIEW, The Magazine for DEC Microcomputing**, Ziff-Davis Publishing, 160 State St., Boston MA 02109. (617)367-7190. Editor: Patrick Kenealy. Managing Editor: Jane Silks. Monthly magazine covering personal computers. Circ. 55,000. Pays on acceptance. Byline given. Offers 15% kill fee. Buys first North American serial rights, one-time rights, all rights and makes work-for-hire assignements. Simultaneous queries OK. Electronic submissions OK via 300/1200 band async ASC II modem transmissions, DEC Rainbow or IBM-PC single-sided diskettes. Computer printout submissions acceptable. Reports in 2 weeks. Free sample copy and writer's guidelines.
Nonfiction: Book excerpts, expose, how-to, interview/profile, new product, personal experience and technical. Buys 100 mss/year. Query with published clips. Length: 2,000-4,000 words. Pays $500-2,500.

80 MICRO, (formerly *80 Microcomputing*), 80 Pine St., Peterborough NH 03458. (603)924-9471. Publisher: Wayne Green. Editor: Eric Maloney. 85% freelance written. Monthly magazine about microcomputing for "owners and users of TRS-80 by Radio Shack." Circ. 191,000. Payment on acceptance. Buys all rights. Written queries preferred. Photocopied submissions OK. "Require hard copy of articles and disk or tape of programs. Computer printout submissions acceptable." SASE. Reports in 2 months. Publishes ms an average of 6 months after acceptance. Sample copy $4.00; writer's guidelines for SASE.
Nonfiction: Applications programs for business, education, science, home and hobby; utilities; programming techniques; and tutorials. "We're looking for articles that will help the beginning, intermediate, and advanced TRS-80 microcomputer user become a better programmer. We also publish hardware construction projects. We buy about 15 manuscripts per issue. Query first; we are glutted!" Length: 1,000 words average. Pays $60/printed page.
Reviews: Writers interested in reviewing current available software are asked to query the review editor, stating areas of interest and equipment owned. Buys 8-15 reviews per issue.
Photos: Offers no additional payment for photos accepted with ms. Buys all rights.

‡**HOME COMPUTER MAGAZINE**, Emerald Valley Publishing Co., Suite 250, 1500 Valley River Dr., Eugene OR 97401. (503)485-8796. Features Editor: Greg Roberts. Managing Editor: Robert Ackerman. 40% freelance written. Monthly magazine for users of Texas Insturments and other home computers. "The magazine's purpose is to help home computer enthusiasts get the most from their machines." Circ. 250,000. Pays on acceptance. Byline given. Buys all rights. Submit seasonal/holiday material 4 months in advance. Simultaneous queries and photocopied submissions OK. Electronic submissions via IT-Writer, Pie-Writer, and Homeword OK. Computer printout submissions acceptable. SASE. Reports in 8 weeks on queries. Publishes ms an average of 4 months after acceptance. Sample copy $3.95; free writer's guidelines.
Nonfiction: General interest, how-to, humor, new product, personal experience, photo feature, and technical. "The 99'er HCM is omnivorous. We will take anything relevant to home computing on TI, Apple, Commodore and IBM PCjr machines." No politics or religion. Buys 50 mss/year. Send complete ms.
Photos: Send photos with ms.
Columns/Departments: Logo Times (informative, useful material on the LOGO language). Send complete ms.
Fillers: Anecdotes, short humor, and newsbreaks. "We are having a hard time getting good ones." Pays $25.
Tips: "If a piece has something valuable to say about home computing, we'll buy it, no matter how badly it's written. We completely rewrite many of our freelance articles. We buy computer programs for publication in the magazine. We are constantly looking for useful and entertaining programs for the TI 99/4A, Apple, Commodore and IBM PCjr computers. Well-researched, useful articles will always sell. Nonfiction opportunities have never been better."

HOT COCO, The magazine for TRS-80 Color Computer, and MC-10 users, Wayne Green Inc., Pine St., Peterborough NH 03458. (603)924-9471. Editor: Michael E. Nadeau. Managing Editor: Janet Fiderio. 98% freelance written. Monthly magazine covering TRS-80 Color Computers "to teach Color Computer owners new ways to use their machines, to provide working programs of practical or entertainment value, and to evaluate commercial products related to the Color Computer." Estab. 1983. Circ. 100,000. Pays on acceptance. Byline given. Offers 25% kill fee. Buys all rights. Submit seasonal/holiday material 5 months in advance. Computer printout submissions acceptable. Reports in 2 weeks on queries; 3 weeks on mss. Publishes ms an average of 8 months after acceptance. Sample copy $2.95; writer's guidelines for SAE and 20¢ postage.
Nonfiction: How-to (programming techniques, hardware projects). No "How I convinced my wife that my CoCo is really wonderful" articles. Buys 150-200 mss/year. Query. Length: 2,500 words maximum. Pays $50-500.

INFOWORLD, The Newsweekly for Microcomputer Users, Popular Computing, Inc., (subsidiary of CW Communications, Inc.), 1060 Marsh Rd., Menlo Park CA 94025. (415)328-4602. Editor: Stewart Alsop II

News Editor: David Needle. Technical Editor: Rory O'Connor. Applications Editor: Jacqueline Rae. Photo Editor: Gypsy Zaboroskie. 20% freelance written. "InfoWorld is the only weekly magazine that covers personal computers, personal computing, and the personal computer industry exclusively and comprehensively. We specialize in news and reviews. Writers interested in reporting for us have to know the industry and the products well and must be able to work fast; those interested in reviewing must understand one or two product categories extremely well." Circ. 125,000. Pays on acceptance. Byline given. Offers negotiable kill fee. Buys all rights. Submit seasonal/holiday material 6 weeks in advance of cover date. Electronic submissions OK; first contact Bob Hoskins, systems manager. Computer printout submissions acceptable; prefers letter-quality to dot-matrix. SASE. Sample copy with 8½x11 SAE and free writer's guidelines (specify news or reviews).
Nonfiction: General interest, interview/profile, new product, opinion, photo feature, technical, and application. Hardware, software, on-line services, product reviews commissioned according to strict standards and guidelines. Special issues include show coverage, biannual "In Review" retrospective, quarterly Special Reports, etc. No program listings, short stories, poetry or personal vendettas. "We don't buy very many news stories; usually specialized stories or coverage of overseas events or trends. Most of our freelance work is reviewing products, but you have to know what you're doing in order to review products for us." Buys 100 news mss and 350 review mss per year. Query with resume and clips of published work. Articles can be submitted in either typed hard copy or (preferably) uploaded to Atex system through a modem. Pays $100 to $300 per article.
Photos: "InfoWorld is very interested in finding photojournalists who know personal computer industry personalities and can supply us with timely photos for our People department and for regular news pages." Query photo editor with resume and sample photos. Reviews 8½x11 prints. Captions, model releases, and identification of subjects required. Buys one-time rights. Pays $25-150. Buys 150 photos per year.
Columns: "We have five weekly columns and are not interested in reviewing new columns ideas."

‡**JR MAGAZINE, for IBM's Home Computer**, Wayne Green Publications Group. 80 Pine St., Peterborough NH 03458. (603)924-9471. Editor: Daniel Sullivan. Managing Editor: Michael Thompson. 60% freelance written. Monthly magazine covering home computing in general and use of the IBM PCjr in particular. Estab. 1984. Circ. 100,000. Pays on acceptance. Byline given. Offers 50% kill fee. Buys all rights. Submit seasonal/holiday material 3½ months in advance. Simultaneous queries, and simultaneous and photocopied submissions OK. Electronic submissions OK if prior arrangements made with editorial staff, but requires hard copy alos. Computer printout submissions acceptable. SASE. Reports in 3 weeks on queries; 4 weeks on mss. Publishes ms an average of 3 months after acceptance. Sample copy for $2.95; free writer's guidelines.
Nonfiction: Eileen Terrill, articles editor. General interest (home computing); how-to (applications of using home computers and programs for specific tasks or for making money, etc.); interview/profile; new product (relating to IBM PCjr); photo feature and technical (relatively uncomplicated and practical programming tips and equipment use or modification relevant to IBM PCjr). Buys 100 mss/year. Length: 1,500-4,000 words. Pays $100-500.
Columns/Departments: Patricia Graham, column/department editor. Software Program Review, Computer Accessories/Peripheral Reviews, Computer Game Reviews, Computer Educational Program Reviews, and Book Reviews. Buys 50 mss/year. Query or send complete ms. Length: 300-750 words.
Tips: "A freelancer can best break into our publication with straight-to-the-point query letters and clear, concise writing that is neither overly technical nor condescendingly simplified. Reviews and practical and/or interesting applications-oriented stories are the areas most open to the freelancer in our publication."

‡**LINK-UP, Communications and the Small Computer**, On-Line Communications, Inc., 6531 Cambridge St., Minneapolis MN 55426. (612)927-4916. Managing Editor: Richard Hughes. 50% freelance written. Monthly magazine on small-computer communications. "Our purpose is to keep readers up to date on the fast growing field of small-computer communications—home and business." Estab. 1983. Pays on acceptance. Byline given. Offers negotiable kill fee. Submit seasonal/holiday material 4 months in advance. Simultaneous queries, and simultaneous and photocopied submissions OK. Electronic submissions OK on 4.25" diskette with ASCII files/MS DOS or IBM EasyWriter1.1. Computer printout submissions acceptable. SASE. Reports in 2 weeks on queries; 4-6 weeks on mss. Publishes ms an average of 2-3 months after acceptance. Sample copy for $3, 10x12 SAE and $1.25 postage; writer's guidelines for business-size SAE and 20¢ postage.
Nonfiction: Book excerpts; how-to (computer/communications); humor; interview/profile; new product; opinion; photo feature; and technical. Buys 50-60 mss/year. Query with published clips or send complete ms. Length: 1,000-3,000 words. Pays $200-400.
Photos: Send photos with query or ms. Reviews 35mm and larger color transparencies and (minimum) 5x7 prints. Pays variable/negotiable rates. Captions, model release and identification of subjects required. Buys one-time rights.
Fillers: Anecdotes, short humor, and newsbreaks. Buys "few" fillers. Length: 50-200 words. Pays $25-100.
Tips: "Study an issue or two; we're dealing with a lot of technical material, but we're *not* a tech-only magazine. Feature articles on small-computer communications for home and business—data bases, information networks, person-to-person-via-computer, etc.—are the areas most open to freelancers."

‡**MACWORLD, The Macintosh Magazine**, PC World Communications, Inc., 555 DeHaro St., San Francisco CA 94107. (415)861-3861. Editor: Kearney Rietmann. A monthly magazine covering use of Apple's Macintosh computer; also covers the Lisa II. Estab. 1984. Circ. 200,000. Pays on acceptance. Byline given. Offers negotiable kill fee. Buys all rights. Submit seasonal/holiday material 6 months in advance. Electronic submissions for ASCii file and/or WordStar OK. Computer printout submissions acceptable. SASE. Reports in 6 weeks. Free sample copy and writer's guidelines.

Nonfiction: Book excerpts, general interest, historical/nostalgic, how-to, humor, interview/profile, new product, opinion, personal experience, photo feature, technical and travel. Buys 50 mss/year. Query with published clips. Length: 1,500-3,500 words. Pays $350-650.

Photos: State availability of photos or send photos with query or ms. Pays $25-50 for color slides and 5x7 or 8x10 b&w prints. Captions, model release and identification of subjects required. Buys one-time rights.

Columns/Departments: Daniel Farber, column/department editor. Buys 50 mss/year. Send complete ms. Length: 1,200-2,000 words. Pays $250-500.

Tips: "We seek clearly written, useful articles."

MICRO MOONLIGHTER NEWSLETTER, 4121 Buckthorn Ct., Lewisville TX 75028. (214)539-1115. Editor: J. Norman Goode. Managing Editor: Mary K. Goode. 25% freelance written. Monthly newsletter covering personal computing. "Hard hitting techniques for establishing, building and maintaining a home-based business using a personal computer." Pays on acceptance. Byline given. Buys all rights. Electronic submissions OK if compatible with any 5¼" diskettes under CP/M or TRSDOS formats. Computer printout submissions acceptable. SASE. Reports in 1 month. Publishes ms an average of 1 month after acceptance. Sample copy $3.

Nonfiction: Book excerpts, expose, general interest, how-to, interview/profile, new product, opinion, personal experience, technical, and business case studies. Buys 24 mss/year. Query or send complete ms. Length: 500-6,000 words. Pays 3-5¢/word.

Columns/Departments: Business Case Studies. Buys 12/year. Query or send complete ms. Length: 500-6,000 words. Pays 3-5¢/word.

Tips: "Writers should submit articles of interest to personal computer owners, those who are interested in starting a home business using the personal computer, and/or articles on products associated with personal computers." Especially open to material on "cottage industry and entrepreneurship." Business Case Studies is most open to freelancers.

MICROCOMPUTING, 80 Pine St., Peterborough NH 03458. (603)924-9471. Publisher: Wayne Green. Editor-in-Chief: Keith Thompson. 30% freelance written. Monthly magazine about microcomputing for microcomputer users, businessmen interested in computer systems and students who want to learn about computers. Circ. 125,000. Pays on acceptance. Buys all rights. Photocopied submissions OK. SASE. Electronic submissions OK on IBM PC or Apple disks, but requires hard copy also. Computer printout submissions acceptable. Reports in 3 weeks. Publishes ms an average of 3 months after acceptance. Sample copy $2.95; writer's guidelines for SASE.

Nonfiction: General interest (the how and why of design, programs, algorithms, program modules, and experimental work in advanced fields); how-to (use for a hobby, in educational programs, business, etc.); new product (evaluations); and technical (all related to microcomputers, with diagrams included on a separate sheet). Buys 25-35 mss/issue. Query. Length: 3,000 words minimum. Pays $75-100/printed page.

Photos: Reviews 5x7 and 8x10 b&w glossy prints. Pays $150 minimum for 8x10 color glossy prints and transparencies. Especially needs microcomputer with a person in the picture (vertical). Offers no additional payment for photos accepted with ms. Captions and model release required.

Tips: *"Mircrocomputing* is a general interest magazine for the advanced to intermediate user."

‡**MICROSYSTEMS, The Journal for Advanced Microcomputing**, Ziff Davis Publishing Co., 1 Park Ave., New York NY 10016. (212)725-6856. Editor: Mark Rollins. Technical Editor: Chris Terry. A monthly magazine covering microcomputers ("practical help at the operation systems level") for technically knowledgeable readers. Circ. 75,000. Pays percentage on acceptance, balance on publication. Byline given. Offers kill fee. Buys North American serial and book rights. Simultaneous queries and photocopied submissions OK. Electronic submissions OK if 8" SSSD (IBM 3740 standard format) disk; or modem: 103/212A compatible up to 600 baud—maybe 1,200 baud in future. Computer printout sbumssions acceptable (dot-matrix OK for text, unacceptable for program listings). SASE. Reports in 3 weeks on queries; 1 month on mss. Free writer's guidelines.

Nonfiction: Highly technical articles or CP/M (all versions), MS-DOS, UNIX, and the hardware that supports these operating systems; hardware reviews; and system software reviews. No articles on computer games, reviews of application programs, or material on TRS-80, Atari, Commodore, or Apple. Query or send complete ms. Length: 1,000-5,000 words. Pays $75-120/printed page.

Tips: "Call Chris Terry with your ideas."

NIBBLE, The Reference for Apple Computing, Micro-SPARC Inc., 10 Lewis St., Lincoln MA 01773. (617)259-9039. Editor: Mike Harvey. Managing Editor: David Szetela. 90% freelance written. Magazine published 12 times/year covering personal computing for Apple computers. Readership is middle/upper-middle income professionals who own Apple or Apple-compatible computers. Circ. 80,000. Pays on acceptance. Byline given. Buys all rights. Submit seasonal/holiday material 6-8 months in advance. Electronic submission OK if Apple compatible 5¼'' disk; preferred format is a DOS 3.3 textfile without control codes. Requires hard copy also. Computer printout submissions acceptable. Reports in 1 week on queries; 4 weeks on mss. Publishes ms an average of 1 year after acceptance. Sample copy $3.50. Free writer's guidelines.
Nonfiction: David Krathwohl, programs editor. Apple programs in the areas of business, home, education, games, and programmers' utilities. Buys 400 mss/year. Send complete hardcopy ms and textfile of ms on diskette if possible. Length: 300-15,000 words. Pays $50-500.
Columns/Departments: David Krathwohl, programs editor. Beginning BASIC programming, VisiCalc, Graphics, and Assembly Language Programming, Legal. Buys 100 mss/year. Send complete hardcopy ms and textfile of ms on diskette if possible. Length: 300-2,000 words. Pays $100-300.
Tips: "Submit original personal computer programs for Apple computers—explain what they do, how to use them, how they work, and how the techniques can be used in the reader's own programs. Write or call for writer's guidelines."

‡**ONLINE TODAY, The Computer Communications Magazine**, (formerly *Today, The Videotex/Computer Magazine*), CompuServe Inc., 5000 Arlington Centre Blvd., Columbus OH 43220. (614)457-8600. Editor: Douglas G. Branstetter. Monthly magazine covering the computer communications/information industry. "*Today* is the videotex/microcomputer magazine that covers all topics of interest and concern to videotex and personal computer users, businesses, professionals and supporting industries." Circ. 160,000. Pays on acceptance. Byline given. Offers full agreed-upon price for completed projects and minimum 50% on works in progress as kill fees. Buys first North American serial and all rights. Submit seasonal/holiday material 4 months in advance. Simultaneous queries and photocopied submissions OK. Computer printout submissions acceptable. SASE. Reports in 8 weeks. Free sample copy and writer's guidelines.
Nonfiction: How-to (personal computing, using computer networks and information services); interview/profile; new product (computer-related); technical (microcomputer-related) and software, hardware and computer book reviews. "*Today* helps readers realize the maximum potential of their personal computing equipment by examining in clear, nontechnical terms how videotex and microcomputers can increase productivity, manage financial resources, communicate, inform and educate. *Today* also investigates the social and political implications that have arisen with the introduction of videotex and microcomputers to our society. No tutorials or programs with listings." Buys 500 mss/year. Query with published clips. Length: 500-8,000 words. Pays $50-1,500.
Photos: Thom Misiak, photo editor. State availability of photos. Payment maximum is standard day rate of $400-800 depending upon project. Reviews b&w contact sheets and 5x7 b&w prints. Model release and identification of subjects required. Buys all rights.
Columns/Departments: Ernest E. Mau, software/hardware reviews editor. Reviews (microcomputer software and hardware with special emphasis on micro-based computer communication and support devices). Mail reviews to 3108 S. Granby Way, Aurora CO 80014. Buys 200 mss/year. Query with published clips. Length: 300-1,500 words. Pays $50-750.
Tips: "Any writer who owns a computer equipped to communicate with our network will gain a definite advantage. Most of our editorial material is sent via modem and processed on the network. We want writers who have a good grasp of micro-based communications without being overly technical. Our magazine is 100% freelance material."

PC, The Independent Guide to IBM Personal Computers, Ziff-Davis Publishing Co., 1 Park Ave., New York NY 10016. (212)725-4328. Editor: Bill Machrone. Executive Editor/Features: Mike Edelhart. Executive Editor/Departments & News: Connie Winkler. Fortnightly magazine for users/owners of IBM Personal Computers and compatible systems. Pays on acceptance. Byline given. Buys all rights. Submit seasonal/holiday material 5 months in advance to executive editor. Photocopied submissions OK. SASE. Reports in 4 weeks. Sample copy $5.
Nonfiction: How-to (software and hardware); interview/profile; technical; product evaluations; and programs Query first for fiction. Buys 800 mss/year. Send complete ms. Length: 1,000-8,000 words.

PCjr. MAGAZINE, The Independent Guide to the IBM PCjr in Education, Home & Business, Ziff-Davis Publishing, 1 Park Ave., New York NY 10016. (212)725-7054. Editor: Corey Sandler. Managing Editor: Larry Frascella. Monthly magazine covering the IBM PCjr computer. Estab. 1984. Circ. 120,000 (est.). Pays on acceptance. Byline given. Offers negotiable kill fee. Buys all rights and makes work-for-hire assignments. No simultaneous queries, or simultaneous, photocopied and previously published submissions. Electronic submissions OK via disks compatible with IBM PC format and using Wordstar. Computer printout submissions acceptable.

Nonfiction: Don Kennedy, articles editor. How-to, interview/profile, new product, technical and product reviews. "We do not want entry-level or beginner pieces; no 'me and my computer' stories; and no highly technical pieces." Buys 300 mss/year. Query with published clips. Length: 1,500-3,000 words (special topics may warrant more words). Pays $600-negotiable rates for those who have written for PCjr.

Fillers: Anecdotes, newsbreaks and helpful hints. Length: 250-500 words. Pays negotiable rates.

Tips: "To break into our publication a writer should have a new idea of interest to PCjr owners—either a program, company or use which will expand the abilities of the Junior owner to get greater or better use out of the machine."

PC WORLD, The Comprehensive Guide to IBM Personal Computers and Compatibles, PC World Communications, Inc., 555 De Haro St., San Francisco CA 94107. (415)861-3861. Editor: Harry Miller. 80% freelance written. Monthly magazine plus two special issues covering IBM Personal Computers and compatibles. Circ. 300,000. Pays on acceptance. Byline given. Kill fee negotiable. Buys all rights to material originally published elsewhere. Submit seasonal/holiday material at least 6 months in advance. No simultaneous queries and submissions, previously published or photocopied submissions. Electronic submissions compatible with ASC II files and WordStar OK, but requires hard copy also. Computer printout submissions acceptable. SASE. Reports in 6 weeks on queries; 6 weeks on mss. Free sample copy and writer's guidelines.

Nonfiction: Book excerpts, general interest, historic/nostalgic, humor, opinion, personal experience, photo feature, travel, how-to, interview/profile, new product and technical. "*PC World* is composed of 5 sections: State of the Art, Getting Started, Review, Hands On, and Community. In State of the Art, articles cover developing technologies in the computer industry. The Getting Started section is specifically aimed at the growing number of new computer users. In Review, new hardware and software are critically and objectively analyzed by experienced users. Hands On offers 'how-to' articles, giving readers instructions on patching WordStar, setting up VisiCalc worksheets, inserting memory boards, developing programming skills and other related topics. Community covers a wide range of subjects, focusing on how society is being shaped by the influx of microcomputers in work places, schools and homes." No articles not related to the IBM PC or compatibles. Query with or without published clips or send complete ms. Buys 50 mss/year. Length: 1,500-3,500 words. Pays $35-650.

Photos: State availability of photos or send with query or ms. Reviews color slide transparencies and 8x10 b&w prints. Pays $25-50. Captions, model release and identification of subjects required. Buys one-time rights.

Columns/Departments: REMark (personal opinions about microcomputer-related issues); Compatible News (hardware, software, business and legal developments related to IBM and PC compatible market); and User Group Dispatch (IBM PC User Group topics). Buys 50 mss/year. Query with or without published clips or send complete ms. Length: 1,000-2,000 words. Pays $250-500.

Tips: "Familiarity with the IBM PC or technical knowledge about its operations often determines whether we accept a query. Send all queries to the attention of Proposals—Editorial Department. The Hands On section is especially open to freelancers with practical applications to offer."

‡**PCM, The Magazine for Professional Computer Management,** Falsoft, Inc., 9529 U.S. Highway 42, Box 209, Prospect KY 40059. (502)228-4492. Editor: Lawrence C. Falk. Managing Editor: Courtney Noe. 75% freelance written. A monthly ("brand specific") magazine for owners of the TRS-80 Model 100 portable computer and the TRS-80 Model 2000. Estab. 1983. Circ. 10,000. Pays on publication. Byline given. Buys first rights only. Submit seasonal/holiday material 4 months in advance. Photocopied submissions OK; no simultaneous or previously published submissions. Electronic submissions OK, but requires hard copy also. Computer printout submissions acceptable. Reports in 2 months. Publishes ms an average of 3 months after acceptance. Sample copy for SASE. Free writer's guidelines.

Nonfiction: Jutta Kapfhammer, submissions editor. How-to. "We prefer articles with programs." No general interest material. Buys 80 mss/year. Send complete ms. "Do not query." Length: 300 words minimum. Pays $40-50/page.

Photos: State availability of photos. Rarely uses photos.

Tips: "At this time we are only interested in submissions for the TRS-80 Model 100 and the TRS-80 Model 2000. Strong preference given those submissions accompanied by brief program listings. All listings must be submitted on tape or disk as well as in hardcopy form."

PERSONAL COMPUTER AGE, The Definitive Journal for the IBM Personal Computer User, Personal Computer Age, 8138 Foothill Blvd., Sunland CA 91040. (818)352-7811. Editor: Jack Crone. Managing Editor: Phil Hopkins. 80% freelance written. Monthly magazine covering the IBM Personal Computer. "Practical how-to guidance and technical education for the IBM PC user. The magazine is directed to the experienced computerist who is serious about utilizing the full capabilities of his machine, and the content of the articles reflects this focus." Circ. 50,000. Pays on acceptance. Byline given. Offers negotiable kill fee. Buys first North American serial rights only. Submit holiday/seasonal material 3 months in advance. Simultaneous queries and photocopied submissions OK. Electronic submissions OK; contact Sharon Gooding at *PC Age* first. Computer printout submissions acceptable. Reports in 1 month on queries; 3 months on mss. Publishes ms an average of 6 months after acceptance. Sample copy $2.50; free writer's guidelines.

Nonfiction: How-to (use IBM PC, etc.); humor (rarely); new product; technical (IBM PC only); and tutorials on computer technology oriented to the IBM PC. No "history or industry overviews." Buys 200 mss/year. Query with clips. Length: 1,000-6,000 words maximum. Pays $100-600.

Photos: Chris August, art director. State availability of photos with query letter or manuscript "only if pro-quality photographer." Reviews 35mm and larger color transparencies and 8x10 b&w prints. Captions, model release and identification of subjects required. Buys North American serial rights.

Tips: "Orient your thinking and writing to what the IBM PC user really needs to know to get the most out of his computer. Open with a concise tutorial, then go to specifics. Almost all articles are freelance written. Don't assume the reader has your technical background—spell it out for him. Clear, sequential story organization is important. Don't ramble and philosophize—get to the point and stick to it. We need fewer traditional, dry technical writing pieces and more stylish popular treatments, but with the same technical competence."

PERSONAL COMPUTING, Hayden Publishing Company, Inc., 10 Mulholland Dr., Hasbrouck Heights NJ 07604. (201)393-6000. Managing Editor: Ernie Baxter. Monthly magazine covering small business, office, home and school computing. Monthly magazine. Circ. 35,000. Pays on publication. Buys all rights. Byline given. Submit seasonal/holiday material 4 months in advance. Photocopied submissions OK, but state if material is not multiple submission. SASE. Sample copy $3; free writer's guidelines.

Nonfiction: Business applications articles, issues concerning computer users and the experience of computing; general interest (related to microcomputers); how-to (use computers); humor (fiction relating to computers and personal stories concerning computers); interview (with prominent figures in the field); new product (review, but not puff piece, must be objective); nostalgia (only if related to computing); personal experience (someone who has worked with a specific system and has learned something readers can benefit from); opinion (editorials, or opinion of someone in field); photo feature (only if accompanied by article); profile (of prominent person in field); and technical (program writing, debugging; especially good are applications for business, education, or home use). No articles on product hype or personal experiences that don't pass anything on to the reader. Buys 2 mss/issue. Query with outline preferred. Buys 6 unsolicited mss/year. Length: 1,000 words minimum. Pay varies.

Photos: State availability of photos with query or ms. Offers no additional payment for b&w or color pictures. Captions preferred. Buys all rights.

Columns/Departments: Editorials (on any topic in the field); Future Computing (a detailed look at one or more aspects of what's going on in the field and what's projected); *PC* Interview (of prominent figures in the field); Outlook (unusual applications, goings on, or stories about computers); and Products (product reviews, comments on, criticism of, and comparison). Does not accept unsolicited reviews.

POPULAR COMPUTING MAGAZINE, 70 Main St., Peterborough, NH 03458. (603)924-9281. Executive Editor: Richard L. Friedman. 60% freelance written. McGraw-Hill monthly magazine covering personal computers directed particularly at beginners and professional people such as educators, attorneys, doctors, etc. Circ. 350,000. Pays on acceptance. Buys first North American serial rights only. Photocopied submissions OK. Electronic submissions OK via the Source or CompuServe. SASE. Reports in 2 months. Publishes ms an average of 4 months after acceptance. Sample copy $2.75.

Nonfiction: "Articles should contain information about buying personal computers plus reviews of computers and other material related to personal computers." Buys 200 mss/year. Send detailed query letter to executive editor.

Tips: "Visit personal computer stores or read any of the books on the market pertaining to personal computers. The ideal *Popular Computing Magazine* article popularizes personal computer concepts without talking down to the reader. Articles should be free as much as possible of computer jargon. Send query letter before submitting manuscript."

‡**PORTABLE 100, The Magazine for TRS-80 Model 100 Users**, Computer Communications, Inc., 15 Elm St., Camden ME 04843. (207)236-4365. Editor: John P. Mello Jr. 90% freelance written. Monthly magazine covering TRS-80 Model 100 portable computers. "Material must be about Model 100." Estab. 1983. Circ. 22,000. Pays on publication. Byline given. Offers $100 kill fee. Buys first North American serial rights. Submit seasonal/holiday material 3 months in advance. No simultaneous queries, or simultaneous, photocopied, or previously published submissions. Electronic submissions OK if disk: TRS-80 Model IV, DOSPLUS 3.4; tape: saved in ASC II format from Model 100. Modem: CompuServe Source MCI-MAIL. Computer printout submissions acceptable. SASE. Reports on queries within 3 weeks; mss within 2 months. Publishes ms an average of 4 months after acceptance. Free sample copy and writer's guidelines.

Nonfiction: How-to (computer hardware projects); technical (tutorials in Basic computer language); travel (where and how Model 100 used on road); and other (computer programs). No fiction. Query with published clips. Length: 600-4,000 words. Pays $100-1,000.

Tips: "A freelancer must be a user of TRS-80 Model 100 portable computer. The best way to break in is to "write a good practical business application program.""

‡**RAINBOW MAGAZINE**, Falsoft, Inc., 9529 US Highway 42, Prospect KY 40059. (502)228-4492. Editor: Lawrence C. Falk. Managing Editor: James E. Reed. 60% freelance written. Monthly magazine covering the TRS-80 Color Computer and Dragon 32 computer. Circ. 75,000. Pays on publication. Byline given. Buys one-time rights and rights for "tape" service reprint as compilation only. Submit seasonal/holiday material 6 months in advance. No simultaneous queries, or simultaneous, photocopied and previously published submissions. Electronic submissions via disk or on magnetic tape OK, but requires hard copy also. Computer printout submissions acceptable. Reports in 3 months. Publishes ms an average of 4 months after acceptance. Sample copy $3.95; free writer's guidelines.

Nonfiction: Jutta Kapfhammer, submissions editor. Technical (computer programs and articles for Rainbow TRS-80 Color Computer or TRS-80 Model 100 Portable Computer. No general "overview" articles. "We want articles *with* programs or tutorials." Buys 300+ mss/year. Send complete ms. Pays $25-50/page.

Fillers: Cartoons (must be Color Computer-related).

‡**soft sector**, Falsoft, Inc., 9529 U.S. Highway 42, Box 209, Prospect KY 40059. (502)228-4492. Editor: Lawrence C. Falk. Managing Editor: Jim Reed. "A monthly bound specific magazine for the Sanyo MS-DOSS-based, IBM PC data compatible computer." Estab. 1984. Pays on publication. Byline given. Buys first rights. Submit seasonal/holiday material 4 months in advance. Simultaneous and photocopied submissions OK. Reports in 2 months. Free sample copy; writer's guidlines for SAE.

Nonfiction: Interested only in articles and programs specifically for the Sanyo 550-555 computer. "No general interest or computer commentary." Buys 120 mss/year. Send complete ms. Length: 200 words minimum. Pays $50 maximum/printed magazine page.

Tips: "Know specific computer or don't submit."

SOFTALK FOR THE IBM PERSONAL COMPUTER, Softalk Publishing Inc., 11160 McCormick St., North Hollywood CA 91601. (213)980-5074. Editor: Craig Stinson. Managing Editor: Mike Tighe. Monthly consumer and trade publication for novice to expert readers involved with the IBM Personal Computer. Pays on publication; on acceptance for material received by deadline. Byline given. Buys all rights. Simultaneous queries OK "if presented as such"; photocopied submissions OK "if neat and legible." Electronic submissions OK, but requires hard copy also. Computer printout submissions acceptable. SASE. Reports in 2 weeks on queries; 1 month on mss. Sample copy $3.

Nonfiction: How-to, humor, interview/profile (query), new product (query), personal experience, photo feature, and technical. All must be Personal Computer related. "Writers should emphasize news and personal interest, but avoid the words 'I' and 'me.' " Query. Pays 10-12¢/word.

Photos: Kurt A. Wahlner, photo editor. State availability of photos. Reviews b&w contact sheet, 6x6, 6x7 or 35mm color transparencies and 8x10 b&w prints. Captions and identification of subjects required. Buys one-time rights.

SOFTSIDE MAGAZINE, SoftSide Publications, Inc., 10 Northern Blvd., Amherst NH 03031. (603)882-2555. Editor: Roger Robitaille. Managing Editor: Carolyn Nolan. Monthly magazine of home and hobby microcomputing and related technologies for the home user of Apple, Atari, IBM-PC and TRS-80 microcomputers. Circ. 75,000 #. Pays on publication. Byline given. Offers 30% kill fee. Buys mostly one-time rights; also all rights, seond serial (reprint) rights, and makes work-for-hire assignments "depending on the article." Submit seasonal/holiday material 4 months in advance. Simultaneous queries, and photocopied and previously published submissions OK. "We encourage submissions on disk and pay a premium for them." SASE. Reports in 4 weeks on queries; 6 weeks on mss. Sample copy for 9x12 SAE and 9 first class stamps; writer's guidelines for business-size SAE and 2 first class stamps.

Nonfiction: Book excerpts, expose, general interest, historical/nostalgic, how-to (hardware and software tutorials), humor, interview/profile, new product, photo feature and technical (geared to the home/hobbyist/user computer market). Special issues include Microcomputer Graphics, Microcomputer Music, Computers in Education, Computer Telecommunications, Personal Finance and the Computer (see "SoftSide Schedule 84"). "Social comment articles should deal with some aspect of computers' effects on society." No articles on business computing. Send all material to Managing Editor. Buys 150 mss/year. Query with clips if available or send complete ms. Length: 1,000-5,000 words. Pays $75-500.

Photos: Send photos with ms. Pays $10-50 for 35mm color transparencies; $5-40 for 5x7 b&w prints. Captions, model release and identification of subjects required. Buys one-time rights.

Columns/Departments: Microcomputer software reviews, related book reviews, and hardware reviews. "Reviews should be complete with recommendations for improvement in product and use reports." Buys 50 mss/year. Query with clips or send complete ms. Length: 1,000-3,000 words. Pays $75-200.

Fiction: Experimental, fantasy, humorous and science fiction. Buys 10 mss/year. Send complete ms. Length: 500-2,000 words. Pays $40-125

Poetry: Avant-garde, free verse and haiku. No poetry of "the kind found in traditional collections of 'best loved' poems." Buys 10 poems/year. Submit maximum 5 poems. Length: 25-75 lines. Pays $25-65.

Fillers: Short humor and newsbreaks. Buys 15-20/year. Length: 200-1,000 words. Pays $10-50.

Tips: "A freelancer can best break in with a clear, concise cover letter stating purpose and thrust of the submission or query. Fiction, reviews, and social comment articles (computer-related) are the areas most open to freelancers. Extra consideration is given to text submitted on computer diskette for TRS-80, Apple, Atari or IBM-PC computers. Call for details."

SYNTAX, Syntax ZX80, Inc., Rd. 2 Box 457, Bolton Rd., Harvard MA 01451. (617)456-3661. Editor: Erick K. Olson. 50% freelance written. Monthly newsletter covering Timex Sinclair and ZX81 microcomputers for owners of all levels of expertise. Circ. 10,000. Pays on acceptance; 7¢ every 6 characters including punctuation. Token fee for programs. Byline given. Buys all rights; "nonexclusive." Submit seasonal/holiday material 2 months in advance. Electronic submissions OK if WordStar disks or Sinclair tapes. Computer printout submissions acceptable. SASE.

Nonfiction: How-to (hardware projects, software tutorials); new product (Timex Sinclair-related peripherals); and technical (programs: business, educational, home, utility, math or game programs written in BASIC or Z80 machine language; explanations of machine technical workings). "We need clearly written stories and reviews to both interest experts and educate beginners. An extremely tight style is especially important to our newsletter format. No long, chatty stories. We are a newsletter whose main purpose is to give readers as much information as possible in a minimum space. Set them to thinking rather than drowning them in explanation." Buys 48 mss/year. Length: 100-900 words.

Columns/Departments: "We need reviews of Timex Sinclair-related books on hardware and programming and reviews of software and hardware. Again, the piece must be user-oriented, but objective. Please include company or manufacturer's name, address and telephone number." Query. Length: 100-900 words.

Fillers: Newsbreaks (short-short information, such as 1-2 line commands to access computer memory). "Mostly staff-written but would buy 30/year if available." Length: 15-100 words.

Tips: "Demonstrate knowledge of Timex Sinclair computer, electronics, or programming and be able to express technical concepts clearly and simply. We have no strict submission requirements but prefer typed copy double-spaced and programs on cassette. For hardware projects and software stories make sure instructions are specific and clear, and writing should be super-tight. Of course, all projects and programs must work. The most rewarding aspect of working with freelance writers is high school kids who write well and also write good programs."

Photography

These publications give readers an additional view of photography—whether they carry a camera for fun or for weekend assignments. Magazines geared to the professional photographer can be found in Trade Journals.

‡**DARKROOM PHOTOGRAPHY MAGAZINE**, Sheptow Publishing Co., 1 Hallidie Plaza, San Francisco CA 94102. (415)989-4360. Editor: Richard Senti. Associate Editor: Kim Torgerson. A photography magazine with darkroom emphasis, published 8 times/year for both professional and amateur photographers "interested in what goes on *after* the picture's been taken: processing, printing, manipulating, etc." Circ. 100,000. Pays on publication; pays regular writers on acceptance. Byline given. Offers 50% kill fee. Buys all rights, but negotiable. Photocopied submissions OK. Computer printout submissions acceptable. SASE. Reports in 1 month. Sample copy and writer's guidelines for SASE.

Nonfiction: Historical/nostalgic (some photo-history pieces); how-to (darkroom equipment build-ins); interview/profile (famous photographers); and technical (articles on darkroom techniques, tools, and tricks). No stories on shooting techniques, strobes, lighting, or in-camera image manipulation. Query or send complete ms. Length: varies. Pays $35-500.

Photos: State availability or send photos with query or ms. Reviews transparencies and 8x10 prints. "Supporting photographs are considered part of the manuscript package."

Columns/Departments: Tools & Tricks, Special Effects, Making Money and Larger Formats. Query or send complete ms. Length: 800-1,200 words. Pays $100-150.

Tips: "Published darkroom-related "tips" receive free one-year subscriptions. Length: 100-150 words.

‡**DARKROOM TECHNIQUES**, Preston Publications, Inc., Box 48312, 6366 Gross Point Rd., Niles IL 60648. (312)965-0566. Publisher: Seaton Preston. Editor: Alfred DeBat. 75% freelance written. Bimonthly magazine focusing mainly on darkroom techniques, photochemistry, and photographic experimentation and innovation—particularly in the areas of photographic processing, printing and reproduction—plus general user-oriented photography articles aimed at advanced workers and hobbyists. Circ. 45,000. Pays on publication

within 1 week. Byline given. Buys first North American serial rights. Submit seasonal/holiday material 6 months in advance. Photocopied submissions OK. Computer printout submissions acceptable (but discouraged); prefers letter-quality to dot-matrix. SASE. Sample copy $3; free writer's guidelines with SASE.

Nonfiction: General interest articles within above topics; how-to, technical product reviews and photo features. Query or send complete ms. Length open, but most features run approximately 2,500 words or 4-5 magazine pages. Pays $100/published page for well-researched technical articles.

Photos: Send photos with ms. Ms payment includes photo payment. Prefers color transparencies and 8x10 b&w prints. Captions, model release (where appropriate), and identification of subjects required. Buys one-time rights.

Tips: "Successful writers for our magazine are doing what they write about. They have tried the photo technique and write detailed how-to articles—new twists for use with existing materials, etc. We have a list of nearly one hundred subjects our audience has told us they'd like to read about. Ask for this idea-jogger with the writer's guidelines."

PETERSEN'S PHOTOGRAPHIC MAGAZINE, Petersen Publishing Co., 8490 Sunset Blvd., Los Angeles CA 90069. (213)657-5100. Publisher: Paul R. Farber. Editor: Karen Geller-Shinn. 35% freelance written. Emphasizes how-to photography. Monthly magazine; 100 pages. Circ. 295,000. Pays on publication. Buys all rights. Submit seasonal/holiday material 5 months in advance. Photocopied submissions OK. Computer printout submissions acceptable. SASE. Reports in 2 months. Publishes ms an average of 9 months after acceptance. Sample copy $2.

Nonfiction: Karen Geller-Shinn, editor. How-to (darkroom, lighting, special effects, and studio photography). "We don't cover personalities. Buys 24-50 unsolicited mss/year. Recent article example: "Ingenius Images" (March 1984). Send story, photos and captions. Pays $60/printed page.

Photos: With coupon to Gallery Editor. Photos purchased with or without accompanying ms. Pays $25-35 for b&w and color photos. Model release and technical details required.

Tips: "We will be moving more into electronics/video uses and computers for photographers."

PHOTO INSIGHT, Suite 2, 169-15 Jamaica Ave., Jamaica NY 11432. Managing Editor: Conrad Lovelo Jr. 82% freelance written. Emphasizes up-to-date photography contests. For amateur and professional photographers. Bimonthly newsletter; 12 pages. Circ. 5,036. Pays on publication. Buys one-time rights. Submit seasonal or holiday material 3 months in advance. Simultaneous and previously published submissions OK. SASE. Reports in 2 months. Sample copy $2.

Nonfiction: How-to on winning contests, humor, inspirational and new products (related to photography). No material on the copyright law for photographers. Buys 1 mss/issue. Length: features-2,000 words. Pays $50 for photo-text package. Captions required.

Photos: Portfolios accepted for publication based on themes. One photographer's portfolio/issue: 6-10 photos.

Columns/Departments: Gallery Insight (photo show reviews) and In The News (new products or seminars). Buys 2 mss/issue. Query. Length: 100-300 words. Pays $25. Open to suggestions for new columns/departments.

Poetry: Contact: Poetry Editor. Traditional. Length: 4-12 lines. Pays $5.

Fillers: Jokes, gags and anecdotes. Length: 300 words maximum. Pays $5.

‡PHOTO LIFE, Camar Publications, 100 Steelcase Rd. E, Markham, Ontario L3R 1E8 Canada. (416)475-8440. Editor: Norm Rosen. A monthly photography magazine. "Articles help avid photographers develop their skills and expand their enjoyment of photography." Circ. 85,000. Pays on publication. Byline given. Offers negotiable kill fee. Buys first North American serial rights. Submit seasonal/holiday material 4-6 months in advance. Computer printout submissions acceptable. SASE. Reports in 2 months. Sample copy $2; free writer's guidelines.

Nonfiction: How-to, photo feature and travel. Accepts material with Canadian content only. Buys 120 mss/year. Query with published clips. "Do not send complete articles. Assignments made from query, ideas and clips." Length: 1,000-2,500 words. "Articles written on assignment only and paid nothing less than $100 Canadian money."

Photos: State availability of photos. Captions, model release, and identification of subjects required.

Tips: "Submit a sample, with outline of fresh, new idea." Entire publication is open to freelancers. Prefers Canadian material and if from US writers, it should have a Canadian slant. Should have high caliber illustrations (sharp picture, properly exposed).

PHOTOGRAPHER'S FORUM, 25 W. Anapamu, Santa Barbara CA 93101. (805)966-9392. Editor-in-Chief: Glen Serbin. 50% freelance written. Emphasizes college photographic work. Quarterly magazine; 64 pages. Pays on publication. Buys all rights. Byline given. Simultaneous and previously published submissions OK. SASE. Reports in 3 weeks.
Nonfiction: Expose, interview, general interest, and historical. "Articles must deal with some aspect of photography or student photography." Interviews (how one got started, views on the different schools); profile (of schools); and photo feature. "No technical articles." Submit complete ms. Length: 1,000-3,000 words. Pays $50-100.
Photos: State availability of photos with ms. 5x7 or 8x10 b&w matte prints. Buys one-time rights. Model release is recommended.
Columns/Departments: Book Review, Historical Analysis, Interview, School Profile, Photo Profile and Portfolio. Buys 6 mss/issue. Submit complete ms. Length: 1,000-3,000 words. Pays $50-100. Open to suggestions for new columns/departments.

PHOTOMETHODS, Ziff-Davis Publishing Co., 1 Park Ave., New York NY 10016. (212)725-3942. Editorial Director: Fred Schmidt. Managing Editor: Robert Kneller. 85% freelance written. Emphasizes photography (still, cine, video) as a tool; most readers are college or technical school graduates, many readers are in science, engineering or education. Monthly magazine; 80-96 pages. Circ. 53,000. Pays on publication. Buys first and one-time rights. Pays 100% kill fee. Byline given. Phone queries OK. Computer printout submissions acceptable. SASE. Reports in 6 weeks. Publishes ms an average of 5 months after acceptance. Free sample copy and writer's guidelines; mention *Writer's Market* in request.
Nonfiction: How-to (application stories to help readers in his/her work); interview (emphasis on technical management); personal experience (that will benefit the reader in his/her work); photo feature (rare, but will consider); profile (emphasis on technical management); and technical (always interested in 'popularizing' highly technical applications). No material dealing with amateur photography or snapshooters. Buys 60-70 mss/year. Query. Length: 1,500-3,000 words. Pays $75-300.
Photos: Steven Karl Weininger, art director. State availability of photos with query. Offers no additional payment for photos accepted with ms. Uses 5x7 and up matte-dried or glossy b&w prints and 35mm and up color transparencies. Captions required. Buys one-time rights. Model release required.
Tips: "Our subject matter is highly specialized. An extensive background in industrial/commercial photography is preferred."

POPULAR PHOTOGRAPHY, 1 Park Ave., New York NY 10016. Editorial Director: Arthur Goldsmith. 25% freelance written. "The magazine is designed for advanced amateur and professional photographers." Monthly. Circ. 925,000. Also publishes a picture annual and a photography buyer's guide. "Rights purchased vary occasionally but are usually one-time." Byline given. Buys 35-50 mss/year, "mostly from technical types already known to us." Pays on acceptance. Computer printout submissions acceptable; prefers letter-quality to dot-matrix. Submit material 4 months in advance. Reports in 1 month. Publishes ms an average of 4 months after acceptance. Query. SASE.
Nonfiction: This magazine is mainly interested in instructional articles on photography that will help photographers improve their work. This includes all aspects of photography, from theory to camera use and darkroom procedures. Utter familiarity with the subject is a prerequisite to acceptance here. It is best to submit article ideas in outline form since features are set up to fit the magazine's visual policies. "Style should be easily readable but with plenty of factual data when a technique story is involved. We're not quite as 'hardware'-oriented as some magazines. We use many equipment stories, but we often give more space to cultural and aesthetic aspects of the hobby than our competition does." Buys how-to, interviews, profiles, historical articles and photo essays. Length: 500-2,000 words. Pays $125/b&w display page; $200/color page.
Photos: Monica Cipnic, picture editor. Interested in seeing portfolios in b&w and color of highest quality in terms of creativity, imagination, and technique.

Poetry

"It is sobering for most freelancers to discover that the circulation of a literary magazine (the large ones included) is much smaller than the size of your typical football stadium audience," says one editor. Yet, while the number of fans cheering over a magazine's poetry may be small, another editor believes that "most important literary reputations are nowadays established through noncommercial magazines and small presses."

Publications in this category publish poetry and articles about poetry for an audience that includes poets, students and fans of the form. Many publications in the

Literary and "Little" category are also interested in poetry submissions. Various other poetry markets are listed in other categories throughout the Consumer sections. The Greeting Card Publishers section is another source for poets' material.

Some of these markets are also open to submissions of short stories and nonfiction related to the poetic arts.

Many of the markets that follow pay in contributor's copies, prizes or some form of remuneration other than money. Some publications may even require that you pay for the copy which features your poetry. We have included such markets because there are limited commercial outlets for poetry and these at least offer the poet some visibility.

Poetry manuscripts should have the poet's name and address typed in the upper left-hand corner. Total number of lines in the poem should appear in the upper right-hand corner. Center the title of the poem 8 to 10 lines from the top of the page. The poem should be typed, single spaced; double spaced between stanzas, unless noted otherwise in the listing. The poet's name should again appear at the end of the poem. In the case where the poet submits more than one poem to the editor, each poem should always be typed on a separate sheet of paper. Always enclose SASE with poetry submissions. For more information on poetry writing, consult Judson Jerome's *The Poet's Handbook* (Writer's Digest Books).

ANOTHER SEASON, A Quarterly Journal, Willowwood Publishing, Box 148, Cologne MN 55322. Editor: John M. Becknell. "A journal of the Midwest that strives for an integration of ideas and interests, mainly through the use of the personal essay. The aim of *Another Season* is to better understand life through the creative, personal honesty of the essay." 90% freelance written; 5% of material published is poetry. Circ. 500. Pays on publication. Publishes ms an average of 4 months after acceptance. Byline given. Buys first North American serial rights. Submit seasonal/holiday material 3 months in advance. Photocopied and previously published submissions OK. Computer printout submissions acceptable. SASE. Reports in 1 month. Writer's guidelines on request. Sample copy $1.50.
Poetry: Free verse and traditional. "We are very selective; poetry is not our emphasis." Acquires 8 poems/year. Submit maximum 4 poems. Poetry submissions should be double-spaced. Pays in published copies.

THE ANTIGONISH REVIEW, St. Francis Xavier University, Antigonish, Nova Scotia B2G 1C0 Canada. Editor: George Sanderson. For "those with literary interests." Quarterly magazine. 20% freelance written; 30% of material published is poetry. Circ. 700. Pays in copies only. Publishes ms an average of 1 year after acceptance. Not copyrighted. Photocopied submissions OK. Computer printout submissions acceptable. SASE. Reports in 6 weeks.
Poetry: Avant-garde and traditional. No erotic or political. Uses 30/issue. Poetry submissions should be single-spaced.
Fiction: 1,000-10,000 words.
Nonfiction: Light critical articles 3,000-4,000 words.

APALACHEE QUARTERLY, Box 20106, Tallahassee FL 32316. Collective Editorship. For an artistic/critical audience over 16 years of age. Quarterly magazine; 44-60 pages. Circ. 450. Acquires first rights. Uses 80 mss/year. Pays in copies. No simultaneous submissions. Reports in 3-8 weeks. Submit complete ms. Computer printout submissions acceptable; prefers letter-quality to dot-matrix. SASE. Sample copy for $2.
Poetry: Traditional forms of poetry, blank verse, free verse and avant garde forms. "No poetry told by rustic prepubescents in the vernacular, dead grandmother stories or poems, or stories about angst-ridden faculty members." Length: 8-100 lines. Send 3-5 poems.
Fiction: "We are looking for short short stories (1-5 pages long) as well as longer stories. Experiments in style and form are also encouraged."
Tips: "Our publication can be enjoyed by anyone with even a basic background in literature but is not for the barely literate. We publish things that our editors would take pride in having written. Therefore, take pride in what you submit. No queries please. If it's good, send it; if it is not, don't."

ARCHER, Camas Press, Box 41, Camas Valley OR 97416. (503)445-2327. Editor: Wilfred Brown. Quarterly magazine for people who enjoy reading and/or writing poetry. There is no special slant or philosophy. 90+% freelance written; 100% of material published is poetry. Circ. 500. Pays in copies. Average length of time between acceptance and publication varies. "We are too often tempted and admit that we have held some manuscripts for two or more years." Frequent prize contests (no entry fees). Buys one-time rights. Submit seasonal material 6 months in advance. Simultaneous and photocopied submissions OK. Computer printout submissions acceptable. SASE. Reports in 2 weeks. Sample copy $1.

Poetry: Avant-garde, free verse, haiku, light verse and traditional. "We're looking for imaginative and colorful verse that is relatively brief, with intended meaning not so obscure as to be unintelligible to the average reader. Brevity is usually an asset, but we do not like lines of only one or two words or only a punctuation mark, which we think detracts from what the poet is trying to say." No long poems. "We normally leave poems relating to sex, gay or lesbian attractions to other publications less conservative than *The Archer*. We do not use poems containing words long considered vulgar, even though they now are seen frequently in print." Buys about 300 poems/year. Submit maximum 4 poems. Poetry submissions should be double-spaced. Length: 2 lines minimum.

Tips: "Read thoroughly at least one copy of *The Archer*, and re-study each poem to be submitted to see if improvements might be made. Re-check carefully the typing, grammar, structure of sentences, and historic, literary or other allusions to be certain that they are accurate. Do not be adverse to using punctuation marks if they add to the clarity of what is being said."

ART AND LITERARY DIGEST, Summer address: Madoc-Tweed Art Centre, Tweed, Ontario, Canada. Winter address: 1109 N. Betty Lane, Clearwater FL 33515. Editor: Roy Cadwell. "Our readers are the public and former students of the Art and Writing Centre. As an educational publication we welcome new writers who have something to say and want to see their name in print and get paid for it." Small percentage of magazine freelance written; 50% of material published is poetry. No salacious material unsuitable for family audience. Quarterly. Circ. 1,000. Not copyrighted. Byline given. Pays on publication. "Photocopied mss are accepted, but not returned. You may submit elsewhere after one month. Original manuscripts must be accompanied by return envelope and unattached postage." Publishes ms an average of 1 month after acceptance. SASE. "We are no longer accepting unsolicited material other than poetry." Poetry submissions should be double-spaced. Sample copy $1.

THE ATAVIST, Box 5643, Berkeley CA 94705. Editors: Robert Dorsett and Loretta Ko. Semiannual magazine covering poetry and translation of poetry. 100% freelance written; 100% of material published is poetry. Circ. 400. Pays on publication. Publishes ms an average of 6 months after acceptance. Byline given. Buys all rights. Computer printout submissions acceptable. SASE. Reports in 4 months. Sample copy $2.25.

Poetry: "We prefer not to advocate 'types' of poetry because it often leads to confusion. We do not wish to see off-handed poems but expect to see serious poets who take us as seriously as we take them. Translations should include the original and the source of the original." Buys 40-60/year. No limit as to number of poems submitted. Length: open. Poetry submissions should be double-spaced. Pays in copies and subscription.

BEATNIKS FROM SPACE, The Neither/Nor Press, Box 8043, Ann Arbor MI 48107. Editor: Denis McBee. A semiannual magazine tabloid. 60% freelance written; 50% of material published is poetry. Circ. 1,000. Pays on publication. Publishes ms an average of 1 year after acceptance. Byline given. Acquires one-time rights. Photocopied submissions OK. Computer printout submissions acceptable; prefers letter-quality to dot-matrix. SASE. Send complete ms. Reports in 3 months. Sample copy $2.50.

Poetry: Avant-garde and free verse. Buys 8/year. Submit maximum 10 poems. Poetry submissions should be single-spaced within stanzas, double-spaced between stanzas. Length: 1-1,000 lines. Pays in 1-3 copies.

Tips: "We are Jackass Outlaw Publishers. Before the schools and parents and courts can say, 'You can't think like that, write like that. You can't draw that way.' We want to get in there and say, 'Yes you can' and 'Here it is.' The literature of the Apocalypse is in your hands now."

BELOIT POETRY JOURNAL, RFD 2, Box 154, Ellsworth ME 04605. Editors: David Stocking and Marion Stocking. "Our readers are people of all ages and occupations who are interested in the growing tip of poetry." Quarterly magazine; 40 pages. 100% of poems freelance written; 100% of material published is poetry. Circ. 1,100. Pays in copies of publication. Publishes ms an average of 1 month after acceptance. Acquires all rights. Byline given. Photocopied submissions OK. Computer printout submissions acceptable; prefers letter-quality to dot-matrix. SASE. Reports in 4 months; "actually most rejections are within a week; four months would be the maximum for a poem under serious consideration." Sample copy $1; SASE for writer's guidelines.

Poetry: Avant-garde, free verse and traditional. Uses 60/year. Limit submissions to batches of 6. Poetry submissions should be single-spaced within stanzas, double-spaced between stanzas. "We publish the best contemporary poetry submitted, without bias as to length, form, school or subject. We are particularly interested in discovering new poets, with strong imagination and intense, accurate language."

Tips: "Most of the unsatisfactory submissions show no acquaintance with the high quality of the poems we publish."

BITTERROOT, International Poetry Magazine, Spring Glen, NY 12483. Editor: Menke Katz. Magazine published 3 times/year. 100% freelance written; 100% of material published is poetry. Uses about 200 unsolicited mss/year. Pays in contributor copy. Publishes ms an average of 6 weeks after acceptance. Computer print-out submissions acceptable; no dot-matrix. SASE. Regular letter-size envelopes. Please notify of change of address immediately.

Poetry: "We need good poetry of all kinds. If we think a poem is very good, we will publish a two-page poem; mostly however, we prefer shorter poems, not longer than one page. We always discourage cliches and stereotyped forms which imitate fixed patterns and leave no individual mark. We inspire all poets who seek their own identity; it may be realistic or fantastic, close to earth and cabalistic. We have two annual contests with awards amounting to $325. December 31 of each year is the deadline for the William Kushner award and Heershe-Dovid Badanna awards. We do not return contest entries. The winners are published." Poetry submissions should be double-spaced. Submit 3-4 poems at one time.

Tips: "We want to see all subjects—it is *how* the poem is written which is more important than *what* the poem says. Avoid overused rhymes. Do not send changes after poem has been accepted."

THE BLACK WARRIOR REVIEW, The University of Alabama, Box 2936, University AL 35486. (205)348-7839. Editor: Will Blythe. Fiction and poetry—serious, literary work only. Semiannual magazine; 128 pages. 100% freelance written; 60% of material published is poetry. Circ. 1,500. Pays in copies, prizes. Publishes ms an average of 3 months after acceptance. Acquires all rights. Phone queries OK. Submit material for fall by Oct. 1; for spring by Feb. 1. SASE. Reports in 2 months. Sample copy $3. Suggests looking at copy of magazine before submitting.

Poetry: John Morrison, poetry editor. Buys 20/issue.

BLUE UNICORN, 22 Avon Rd., Kensington CA 94707. Editors: Ruth G. Iodice, B. Jo Kinnick and Harold Witt. "We appeal especially to the discriminating lover of poetry, whatever his/her taste runs to." Published 3 times/year. Magazine; 48-60 pages. 100% freelance written; 100% of material published is poetry. Circ. 500. Pays in copies on publication. Publishes ms an average of 3 months after acceptance. Acquires one-time rights. Photocopied submissions OK. Computer printout submissions acceptable; no dot-matrix. SASE. Reports in 3-4 months. Sample copy $3.

Poetry: "The main criterion is excellence. We like poems which communicate in a memorable way whatever is deeply felt by the poet—ones which delight with a lasting image, a unique twist of thought, and a haunting music. We don't want the hackneyed, the trite or the banal." Uses 150 poems/year. Limit submissions to batches of 3-4. "We will accept either double or single spacing, but manuscript must be clear." Prefers shorter verse; "rarely uses poetry over one page in length." Pays in contributor copy.

CACHE REVIEW, Cache Press, 4805 E. 29th St., Tucson AZ 85711. (602)748-0600. Editor: Steve Brady. Semiannual literary magazine of poetry, fiction, reviews, plays and interviews for "those interested in the best contemporary writing." 100% freelance written; 50% of material published is poetry. Circ. 250-500. Pays on publication. Publishes ms an average of 9 months after acceptance. Byline given. Buys one-time rights. Submit seasonal/holiday material 6 months in advance. Simultaneous queries and photocopied submissions OK. Computer printout submissions acceptable. SASE. Reports in 1 month. Sample copy $2; writer's guidelines for letter-size SAE and 1 first class stamp.

Nonfiction: Interviews with writers, editors and publishers; reviews of books—poetry, fiction—mostly small presses. Buys 10 mss/year. Send complete ms. Length: 50-3,000 words. Book reviews: 50-500 words. Pays in 2 copies.

Fiction: Adventure, experimental, fantasy, horror, mainstream, mystery, novel excerpts, science fiction and western. "We will consider almost anything of quality." Buys 6-8 mss/year. Length: 6,000 words maximum. Pays in 2 copies.

Poetry: Avant-garde, free verse, haiku and traditional. Buys 75 poems/year. Poetry submissions should be single-spaced within stanzas, double-spaced between stanzas. Submit 5-10 poems. Length: 30 pages maximum. Pays in 2 copies.

CALIFORNIA STATE POETRY SOCIETY QUARTERLY, California State Poetry Society, 20350 Stanford Ave., Riverside CA 92507. (714)686-4417. Editor: James E. MacWhinney. Journal published 3 times/year "slanted to give a forum to good poetry of all types." 100% freelance written; 100% of material published is poetry. Circ. 400. Byline given. Acquires one-time rights. Publishes ms an average of 3 months after acceptance. Put name and address on each sheet and enclose usual SASE. Computer printout submissions acceptable; no dot-matrix. Reports in 3 months. Sample copy $3; free writer's guidelines with SASE.

Poetry: Avant-garde, free verse, haiku, light verse and traditional. "No overly sentimental, self-serving poems, obscene poems for obscenity's sake or poems carelessly proofread." Publishes 180/year. Submit maximum 5 poems. Poetry submissions should be single-spaced within stanzas, double-spaced between stanzas. Length: 40 lines maximum "may go over if poem exceptionally fine." Pays in contributor copy.

CALYX, INC., A Journal of Art & Literature by Women, Calyx, Inc., Box B, Corvallis OR 97339. (503)753-9384. Editor: Margarita Donnelly. Triannual magazine publishing women artists and writers, fine art and literature by women. 100% freelance written; 50% of material published is poetry. Circ. 8,000. Pays in copies. Publishes ms an average of 8 months after acceptance. Computer printout submissions acceptable; prefers letter-quality to dot-matrix. SASE. Reports in 1 month on queries; up to 6 months on mss. Sample copy $4 and 75¢ postage; writer's guidelines for SAE and 1 first class stamp.

Poetry: "We publish serious and well-written poetry." Publishes 150 pages of poetry/year. Submit maximum 5 poems. Poetry submissions should be single-spaced within stanzas, double-spaced between stanzas. Length: open. Pays in contributor copies.

Fiction: Up to 5,000 words.

Reviews: Up to 800 words.

THE CAPE ROCK, Southeast Missouri State University Press, English Department, Cape Girardeau MO 63701. (314)651-2158. Editor: Harvey Hecht. For libraries and persons interested in poetry. Semiannual. Circ. 1,000. Uses 100 mss/year. Pays in contributor copies. Photocopied submissions OK. No simultaneous submissions. Sample copy $2; writer's guidelines for SASE. Reports in 1-4 months. SASE.

Poetry: "We publish poetry—any style, subject. Avoid cuteness, sentimentality, didacticism. We have summer and winter issues and try to place poetry in the appropriate issue, but do not offer strictly seasonal issues." Length: 70 lines maximum.

Tips: "We like to feature a single photographer each issue—usually about 12 photos with 'a sense of place.' "

CEDAR ROCK, 1121 Madeline, New Braunfels TX 78130. (512)625-6002. Editor-in-Chief: David C. Yates. For "persons with an active interest in stories, poems and ideas." Quarterly tabloid; 24-32 pages. Circ. 2,000. Pays on acceptance. Buys all rights. Byline given. Phone queries OK. Photocopied submissions OK. SASE. Reports in 4 weeks. Sample copy $2.50; writer's guidelines for SASE.

Poetry: Avant-garde, free verse, haiku, light verse and traditional. "No deliberately obscure or nature poems." Buys 200 poems/year. Limit submissions to 6 at one time. Length: 3-75 lines. Pays $2-200.

Fiction: John O'Keefe, fiction editor, 732 W. Coll, New Braunfels TX 78130. Buys 2-4/issue. Length: 1,000-3,500 words maximum. Pays $2-100.

Tips: "We like stories and poems that are 'deep' (i.e., mean something important) but at the same time are readable. No 'cute' nature poems or religious stories."

‡CLOCKWATCH REVIEW, A Waiting-room Journal of the Arts, Driftwood Publications, 737 Penbrook Way, Hartland WI 53029. (414)367-8315. Editor: James Plath. A semiannual magazine of fiction, poetry, music and art. 70% freelance written; 50% of material published is poetry. Estab. 1983. Circ. 1,500. Byline given. Publishes ms an average of 10 months after acceptance. Acquires first rights; rights revert to authors on publication. No simultaneous queries, or simultaneous, photocopied, or previously published submissions. Computer printout submissions acceptable; no dot-matrix. SASE. Reports in 2 weeks on queries; 2 months on mss. Sample copy $3.

Nonfiction: Interview/profile on well-known artists and musicians. Presently staff-written. Query. Length: 1,000-4,000 words. Pays in copies.

Fiction: Experimental, mainstream and literary. No slick genre types. "We *will* consider a genre piece if it goes beyond the mold in a literary way." Accepts 4 mss/year. Length: 1,200-4,000 words. Pays in copies. "We are working on a cash incentive plan for future issues."

Poetry: Avant-garde, free verse and traditional. No verse, morose poems or poems longer than 32 lines. Accepts 20 poems/year. Submit maximum 6 poems. Poetry submissions should be "as they would appear on the printed page." Length: 6-32 lines. Pays in copies.

Tips: "We like to feature unknown writers along side established ones; however, we are not an 'easy' market. We publish only work of exceptional literary quality which also has a strong voice and something which speaks as well to a more general, less literary audience. Too many authors seem to think 'accessible' means 'easy' or 'shallow', or somehow lacking literary complexity."

CONNECTIONS MAGAZINE, Bell Hollow Rd., Putnam Valley NY 10579. Editor-in-Chief: Toni Ortner-Zimmerman. Annual magazine; 70 pages. Covers fine quality modern poetry, especially by women. 100% freelance written; 100% of material published is poetry. Circ. 600. Pays in copies. Publishes ms an average of 1 week after acceptance. Computer printout submissions acceptable; no dot-matrix. SASE. Reports in 2 weeks. Sample copy for $3.50 and 75¢ postage.

Poetry: Avant-garde, free verse and traditional. Limit submissions to batches of 5. Poetry submissions should be single-spaced within stanzas, double-spaced between stanzas. Length: 50 lines maximum.

Tips: "We do not accept cliche verse, sexist poetry, or 'cute' poems (overly sentimental)."

‡THE COUNTRY POET, Wake-Brook House, 990 NW 53rd St., Fort Lauderdale FL 33309. (305)776-5884. Editor: Edna Meudt. A quarterly poetry magazine. Circ. 329. Pays on publication. Byline given. Buys first North American serial rights. Computer printout submissions acceptable; no dot-matrix. SASE. Sample copy $2.21.

Poetry: Edna Meudt, poetry editor, R.D. #3, Dodgeville WI 53533. Do not send poetry submissions to publication office. Good poetry about the seasons and country life. Nothing "cheap, profane, smart-alecky." Buys 200 poems/year. Length: open. Pays 1¢ for each paid subscriber; $3.29 at present.

CROTON REVIEW, Croton Council on the Arts, Inc., Box 277, Croton-on-Hudson NY 10520. (914)271-3144. Editors: Ruth Lisa Schechter and Dan B. Thomas. Annual literary and art tabloid-size magazine. 100% freelance written; 70% of material published is poetry. Circ. 2,000. Byline given. Pays on acceptance "if grants permit." Publishes ms an average of 3 months after acceptance. Photocopied submissions OK. Computer printout submissions acceptable. SASE. Reports in 3 months or sooner. Sample copy for $3; previous issues $2 plus 80¢ postage for single copies. Free writer's guidelines.
Poetry: Contemporary, free verse or traditional. "No cliches; we prefer poems showing craft, substance, originality and evidence of language. Our emphasis is quality literature." Annual *Croton Review* Awards in poetry. Send SASE for rules. Submit maximum 5-6 poems (length: 75 lines each, maximum); essays and short/short stories (8-16 pages). Poetry submissions should be single spaced within stanzas, double spaced between stanzas. Pays in contributor copies.
Tips: "We read new material only from September to February each year. We are not a glossy-slick, commercial magazine, rather a quality, literary journal."

DEROS, 6009 Edgewood Lane, Alexandria VA 22310. (703)971-2219. Editors: Lee-Lee Schlegel and Kenneth Rose. Quarterly poetry magazine devoted to those who served in Viet Nam. 100% freelance written; 100% of material published is poetry. Circ. 200. Byline given. Publishes ms an average of 4 months after acceptance. Acquires one-time rights. Previously published submissions OK. Computer printout submissions acceptable. SASE. Reports in 1 week. Sample copy $3.
Poetry: Avant-garde, free verse, haiku and traditional. Prefers not to see anything that does not deal with Viet Nam in the form of poetry. Submit maximum 1-10 poems. Length: 35 lines. No payment.
Tips: "The most rewarding aspect of working with freelance writers is the sincere appreciation that someone is doing something for the Viet Nam vets."

THE DEVIL'S MILLHOPPER, Route 3, Box 29, Elgin SC 29045. Editor: Jim Peterson. Semiannual poetry magazine. 100% freelance written; 100% of material published is poetry. Circ. 500. Pays on publication. Publishes ms an average of 4 months after acceptance. Byline given. Buys first North American serial rights. Simultaneous queries and photocopied submissions OK. Computer printout submissions acceptable "if they are very clean and readable." SASE. Reports in 2 weeks on queries; 1 month on mss. Sample copy $2.50; writer's guidelines for business-size SAE and 1 first class stamp.
Poetry: All types considered. Buys 50 poems/year. Submit maximum 8 poems. Length: open. Pays in 3 copies.

DREAM INTERNATIONAL QUARTERLY, 333-B Autumn Dr., San Marcos CA 92069. US Editor: Chuck Jones. Japan Editor: Les Jones. Japan address for Les Jones: 10-11-1 Ushita Waseda, Higashi-Ku, Hiroshima, 730 Japan. Quarterly magazine covering dreams, sleep and "daydreams" for laypersons "to explore their mysteries." Circ. 200. Pays on publication, plus annual prizes. Byline given. Buys one-time rights and second serial (reprint) rights for previously published mss. Submit seasonal/holiday material 6 months in advance. Photocopied and previously published submissions OK. SASE. Reports in 1 month on queries; 3 months on mss. Sample copy $3; writer's guidelines $1.
Nonfiction: Book excerpts; expose; historical/nostalgic; how-to (use dreams to help self, enjoy dreaming); interviews/profiles (of researchers); opinion (on all aspects of sleep and dreams); research and experiments. Must be dream, sleep-related. Buys 20 mss/year. Send complete ms. Length: 50-2,000 words. Pays in copies.
Columns/Departments: Dreamlets (column describing dream fragments); and Dreamlines (column summarizing "news" of research, experiments, etc). Buys variable number of mss. Send complete ms. Length: 10-100 words. Pays in copies.
Fiction: Dreams must be central to the story. Adventure, condensed novel, erotica, ethnic, experimental, fantasy, historical, horror, humorous, mainstream, mystery, novel excerpts, religious, romance, science fiction, serialized novels, western, parables and legends. Buys 5 mss/year. Send complete ms. Length: 100-1,500 words. Pays in copies.
Poetry: Avant-garde, free verse, haiku, light verse and traditional. Buys 20 poems/year. Length: 2-40 lines. Pays in copies.
Fillers: Clippings, jokes, gags, anecdotes, short humor and newsbreaks. Length: 20-100 words. Pays in copies.

EARTHWISE: A JOURNAL OF POETRY, Earthwise Publishing Co., Box 680-536, Miami FL 33168. (305)688-8558. Editor: Barbara Holley. Co-editor: Herman Gold. Quarterly magazine covering eclectic poetry for writers and poets. 80% freelance written; 50% of material published is poetry. Circ. 550. Pays on publication. Buys first North American serial rights. Phone queries OK. Submit seasonal material 3 months in advance. Photocopied and previously published submissions OK. Computer printout submissions acceptable; prefers letter-quality to dot-matrix. SASE. Reports in 1 month on queries; in 3 months on mss. Publishes ms an average of 9 months after acceptance. Sample copy $3; free writer's guidelines.

Nonfiction: Contact: Tere Hesin, (305)532-4100. Interviews (of poets, artists and writers); profile; travel (places pertaining to the media); and how-to (pertinent to poetry). Buys 20-30 mss/year. Query with SASE. "We like to have a letter that gets to the point immediately, tells what the writer has to offer, and what he expects in return. We can deal with a person like that. Also, always enclose SASE or don't expect a reply!" Length: 1,000 words maximum. Pays $20 minimum; pays $15 minimum for interviews without picture or poetry, $25 minimum with both. "We especially need brevity, uniqueness. Avoid didacticism, use good taste. Good English and punctuation a must. Our *Earthwise Newsletter* is a good place to break in." (No submissions read from June 15 to September 15.)

Fiction: Kaye Carter, editor. "We like short stories and will be doing an issue on fables this coming fall." Buys 6 mss/year. Query with clips of previously published work. Length: 500-1,000 words. Pays $10 minimum.

Poetry: Avant-garde, free verse, haiku, light verse, traditional and eclectic. "No porno, religious, depressive or downbeat poetry; no poems about love." Buys 200-250 mss/year. Submit maximum 6 poems. Pays $3 minimum/poem on publication. Poetry submissions should be double-spaced.

Fillers: Anecdotes, newsbreaks, short articles and translations of a specific locale (for newsletter). Buys 50 mss/year. Length: 250 words maximum. Pays $1 minimum.

Tips: "Again, send SASE and *be sure* your name and address appear on *each* sheet of work. Right now we are holding some lovely poetry which we cannot publish as we don't know its author! We accept only quality work, well structured."

‡**ELECTRUM**, Medina Press, 1435 Louise St., Santa Ana CA 92706. (714)543-5800. Editor: Bart Yoder. Managing Editor: Roger Suva. A quarterly poetry magazine. 90% freelance written; 95% of material published is poetry. Circ. 500. Byline given. Acquires first North American serial rights and second serial (reprint) rights. Publishes ms an average of 2 months after acceptance. Photocopied submissions OK. Computer printout submissions acceptable. SASE. Reports in 3 weeks on queries; 3 months on mss. Sample copy $2; writer's guidelines for SAE and 20¢ postage.

Poetry: Avant-garde, free verse, haiku and traditional. Accepts 120 poems/year. Submit maximum 5 poems. Poetry submissions should be single-spaced within stanzas, double-spaced between stanzas. Length: 40 lines maximum. Pays in copies.

ENCORE, A Quarterly of Verse and Poetic Arts, 1121 Major Ave. NW, Albuquerque NM 87107. (505)344-5615. Editor: Alice Briley. Quarterly. For "anyone interested in poetry from young people in school to established poets. Good poetry on any theme." Nearly 100% freelance written; 75% of material published is poetry. Circ. 500. Acquires first North American rights. Byline given. Uses 300 mss/year. Pays in contributor copies. Publishes ms an average of 1 month after acceptance. Photocopied submissions OK, "provided the author is free to assign rights to *Encore*. Will require assurance if poem is accepted." Submit seasonal material 9-12 months in advance. Reports on material within a month. Submit complete poetry ms. Query, for short reviews. SASE. Sample copy $1.

Nonfiction and Poetry: "Particularly likes poetry which illustrates the magazine's theme that poetry is a performing art. Fresh approach greatly desired." Traditional forms, blank verse, free verse, avant-garde and light verse. Limit submissions to batches of 3. Poetry submissions should be single-spaced within stanzas, double-spaced between stanzas. Some articles on poetry-related subjects. Profiles of poets, poetry reviews and technical verse writing. Length: open, but "very long articles rarely used." Also has poetry contests. "My poetry contests have grown considerably. Continuous contests have November 1 and May 1 deadlines. In addition, there are often very good special contests, including a student contest."

Photos: Prefers no larger than 5x8 b&w glossy prints with good contrast. Pays in contributor copies.

Tips: "No manuscripts will be considered unless accompanied by SASE with sufficient postage for return."

‡**FROGPOND, A Haiku Quarterly**, Haiku Society of America, 970 Acequia Madre, Santa Fe NM 87501. Editor: Elizabeth Searle Lamb. A magazine featuring haiku, renga, haiku related articles, Japanese poetry forms and occasional Zen poetry. 100% freelance written; 80% of material published is poetry. Circ. 500. Publishes ms an average of 3 months after acceptance. Byline given. Acquires first North American serial rights. No previously published work. Computer printout submissions acceptable; no-dot matrix. SASE. Reports in 1 month. Sample copy for $5 and SAE; writer's guidelines for SAE.

Nonfiction: How-to (articles on haiku and related forms); haiku poets; and photo feature (haiga). "No regular poetry articles; we're a *haiku* journal." Query. Length: 1,500 words maximum. Pays in copies.

Poetry: Haiku, senryu and renga. No poetry not related to haiku. Submit maximum 20 poems. Length: haiku—3 lines; 1 line; 2 lines. Poetry submissions should be double-spaced.

Tips: "In the case of *Frogpond*, freelance writers should know how English-language haiku is developing. It is not a static genre of literature."

GAMUT, Multidisciplinary Journal, Arts Corp., Suite 171, 238 Davenport Rd., Toronto, Ontario M5R 1J6 Canada. (416)929-3928. Editors: Haygo Demir and Alfredo Romano. Managing Editor: James McBain. Quarterly magazine covering the arts and humanities and "dedicated to bringing various disciplines into a single forum. Our intellectual pursuit is to break through the over-specialization in the arts, academics and humanities." 90% freelance written; 100% of material published is poetry. Circ. 3,000. Pays on publication. Publishes ms an average of 3 months or less after acceptance. Byline given. Buys one-time rights. Submit seasonal/holiday material 2 months in advance. Simultaneous queries, and simultaneous and photocopied submissions OK. Computer printout submissions acceptable. SASE or IRCs. Reports in 2 weeks on queries; 1 month on mss. Sample copy $3.

Nonfiction: Book excerpts, general interest, humor, interview/profile, opinion, photo feature and political and philosophical reviews. No articles with jargon; "the language must be able to communicate to all readers." Buys 12 mss/year. Send complete ms. Length: 800-3,000 words. Pays in copies.

Photos: Roger P. Handling, photo editor. Send photos with ms. Pays in copies for b&w contact sheet and 6x9 b&w prints.

Columns/Departments: Book reviews; film reviews; theatre; dance, etc. "Articles, however, should review with depth. The artist's career should be taken into account. These are essays more so than reviews. Interviews with key figures." Buys 10-12 mss/year. Send complete ms. Length: 1,000-3,000 words; "interviews can be longer." Pays in copies.

Fiction: Ethnic, experimental, humorous, mainstream and novel excerpts. Buys 8 mss/year. Send complete ms. Length: 3,000 words maximum; "longer will be considered." Pays in copies.

Poetry: Avant-garde, free verse, haiku, light verse and traditional. Buys 15-20 poems/year. Submit maximum 7 poems. Poetry submissions should be single-spaced within stanzas, double-spaced between stanzas. Length: open. Pays in copies.

Tips: "All departments are open; we strictly use freelancers. Music, dance and political essays are particularly needed."

GARGOYLE, Paycock Press, Box 3567, Washington DC 20007. (202)333-1544. Editor: Richard Peabody Jr. Biannual literary arts journal for a literate audience generally between ages 17 and 45. 95% freelance written; 10% of material published is poetry. Circ. 1,250 + . Pays on publication. Publishes ms an average of 1 year after acceptance. Byline given. Buys first North American serial rights. Photocopied and previously published submissions OK. Computer printout submissions acceptable. SASE. Reports in 1 week. Sample copy $4.

Columns/Departments: Book reviews, essays and interviews. Send complete ms. Length: 1-10 pages. Pays in contributor copy.

Fiction: Erotica, experimental, mainstream and novel excerpts. "We're not geared toward a genre market. We don't want to see romances or derivative work." Buys 30 mss/year (out of 3,000-4,000 received). Submit complete ms. Length: 700 words minimum. Pays in contributor copy.

Poetry: Gretchen Johnsen, poetry editor. Avant-garde and free verse. "We don't print traditional rhymed verse. In fact, we're not real big on the narrative poem that is currently in vogue either." Buys 30 poems/year. Submit maximum 5 poems. Poetry submissions should be single-spaced within stanzas, double-spaced between stanzas. Length: 1-50 lines, 2 pages. Pays in contributor copy. "We accept one out of every 1,000 poems we read."

Tips: "Freelancers often turn out reviews for the magazine. We provide the books on spec. We publish many young voices and are always interested in reading the poems or stories produced by writers under 30 years of age. We have a very broad range of interests and a very idiosyncratic and personalized way of approaching them."

GREEN'S MAGAZINE, Green's Educational Publishing, Box 3236, Regina, Saskatchewan S4P 3H1 Canada. Editor: David Green. For a general audience; "the more sentient, literate levels." Quarterly magazine. 100% freelance written; 100% of material published is poetry. Circ. 500. Buys first North American serial rights. Byline given. Buys 48 mss/year. Pays on publication. Publishes ms an average of 3 months after acceptance. Reports in 2 months. Submit complete ms. Computer printout submissions acceptable; prefers letter-quality to dot-matrix. SAE and IRCs. Sample copy $3.

Fiction: Mainstream, suspense and humorous; must have a realistic range in conflict areas. Slice-of-life situations enriched with deep characterization and more than superficial conflict. Avoid housewife, student, businessmen problems that remain "so what" in solution. Open on themes as long as writers recognize the family nature of the magazine. Length: 1,000-3,000 words.

Poetry: Haiku, blank verse and free verse. Poetry submissions should be single-spaced within stanzas, double-spaced between stanzas. Length: about 36 to 40 lines. Pays $2 to $3. (Payment temporarily suspended in 1983-84.)

‡**GRINNING IDIOT, A Magazine of the Arts**, Grinning Idiot Press, Box 1577, Brooklyn NY 11202. (212)522-4961. Editors: Jerome Weinberger and Barry Levy. A semiannual magazine. Estab. 1983. Circ. 500. Pays on publication. Byline given. Acquires one-time rights. Submit seasonal/holiday material 1 season in ad-

vance. Simultaneous queries, and simultaneous and photocopied submissions OK. Computer printout submissions acceptable. SASE. Reports in 1 month.

Nonfiction: Book excerpts (10 pages or less); expose (offbeat); humor (black); interview/profile (literary/jazz); personal experience (unusual); and photo feature (quality). Nothing "cute or sappy." Accepts 3 mss/year. Send complete mss. Length: 1-10 pages. Pays in copies (but hopes to pay writers, depending on business).

Photos: Send photos with accompanying ms. Reviews b&w prints.

Columns/Departments: In the works. Acquires approximately 3 mss/year. Length: 300-3,000 words.

Fiction: Confession (lurid); erotica (offbeat); experimental (all types); and humorous (black). Acquires 3 mss/year. Send complete ms. Length: 300-3,000 words.

Poetry: Avant-garde, free verse, haiku, light verse, traditional. Nothing "cute or sappy." Accepts 3 poems/year. Length: open.

Fillers: Clippings, short humor, newsbreaks. Acquires 3/year. Length: open.

Tips: Magazine is 100% freelance written.

HANGING LOOSE, 231 Wyckoff St., Brooklyn NY 11217. Editors: Robert Hershon, Dick Lourie, Mark Pawlak and Ron Schreiber. Quarterly. Acquires first serial rights. Pays in copies. Reports in 2-3 months. SASE. Sample copy $3.

Poetry: Fresh, energetic poems of any length. Excellent quality. Recent work by Jack Anderson, Michael Lally, Cathy Cockrell, Carol Cox, Frances Phillips, Donna Brook and Denise Levertov.

Tips: "We strongly suggest that writers read the magazine before sending work, to save our time and theirs. Also note that artwork and book manuscripts are by invitation only."

INDIANA REVIEW, 316 N. Jordan Ave., Bloomington IN 47405. (812)335-3439. Editor: Jane Hilberry. Associate Editor: Erin McGraw. Triannual literary magazine of contemporary poetry and fiction for a national audience. 100% freelance written; 25% of material published is poetry. Circ. 1,000. Pays on publication. Publishes ms an average of 18 months after acceptance. Byline given. Buys all rights. Photocopied submissions OK. Computer printout submissions acceptable. SASE. Reports in 3 months. Sample copy $4.

Fiction: Any type of fiction with literary interest, including experimental fiction. Buys 30 mss/year. Submit complete ms. Pays in copies: 2 copies of issue in which work appears and the rest of a year's subscription.

Poetry: Avant-garde, free verse and traditional. Buys 60 poems/year. Submit maximum 8 poems. Poetry submissions should be double-spaced. Length: open.

Tips: "We are interested in work that demonstrates skill in the craft of writing, as well as scope or import in content. We consider variety desirable in the magazine, given that work meets our qualitative standards. Editors invariably have tastes, but we prefer to let these operate on individual works, rather than as prejudices against particular types of material. For this reason, we place few restrictions on manuscripts submitted."

JUMP RIVER REVIEW, Jump River Press, Inc., 801 Oak, Medina OH 44256. Editor: Mark Bruner. Quarterly magazine covering a literary review of the basics, behavior and human culture. Circ. 400. Pays on publication in copies. Acquires one-time rights. Phone queries OK. Submit seasonal material 3½ months in advance. Photocopied submissions OK if not submitted elsewhere. SASE. Reports in 1-2 weeks. Query first. Sample copy $2.50; free writer's guidelines.

Nonfiction: Historical ("articles relating either historical or contemporary events to the nature of our cultural fabric"); how-to (article should be related to writing and publishing); interview (of literary figures); nostalgia (but no overly sentimental approaches); photo feature (query); and essays on the spiritual aspects of culture, ("not religious, spiritual"). Especially in need of opinion (in essay form and related to culture, literature and human behavior). Buys 2-3 mss/issue. Send complete ms. Length: approx. 900 words preferred. Pays in copies.

Poetry: Avant-garde, free verse, traditional and concrete. "Poetry is most open to freelancers because we publish so much of it. We don't want driveling sentiment, confessions or pretense. Feel free to experiment. We would like to see some more forms of concrete poetry and poetry related to myth, folklife, enchantment and primalism." Buys 90 mss/year. Pays in copies.

Tips: "Read *Jump River Review*. We devote a portion of each issue to young writers. If you're a high school or elementary aged writer, tell us. Right now the best chance of getting accepted is with essays, drama, criticism and short prose. If there is anyone out there who can produce a 5-6 page short drama, you have a good chance of getting our interest. Letting me know if you're young or unpublished sometimes makes me more apt to spend time with your work. And read the magazine—not only does that help us keep solvent, but it also saves everyone much time in correspondence."

KANSAS QUARTERLY, Dept. of English, Kansas State University, Manhattan KS 66506. (913)532-6716. Editors: Harold W. Schneider, Ben Nyberg, John Rees and W.R. Moses. Quarterly. For "adults interested in creative writing, literary criticism, Midwestern history, and art." 90% freelance written; 30-50% of material published is poetry. Circ. 1,200. Acquires all rights. Pays in contributor copies and the chance for annual

awards. Publishes ms an average of 18 months after acceptance. Query for nonfiction. Computer printout submissions acceptable; no dot-matrix. "Follow *MLA Style Sheet* and write for a sophisticated audience." Reports in 2-4 months. SASE. Sample copy $4.
Poetry: Traditional and avant-garde forms of poetry, blank verse and free verse. Poetry themes open. Poetry submissions should be double-spaced.
Tips: Yearly prizes (KQ/KAC) for poetry and fiction: $25 to $300; Seaton Awards annually to Kansas writers published: $25 to $250 each.

KARAMU, English Department, Eastern Illinois University, Charleston IL 61920. (217)345-5013. Editor: John Z. Guzlowski. 100% freelance written; 35% of material published in poetry. For literate, university-educated audience. Annually. Circ. 500. Acquires first North American serial rights. Uses 24 mss/year. Pays in 1 contributor copy. Submit complete ms. Computer printout submissions acceptable. Reports on poetry within 6 weeks; fiction within 2 months. Publishes ms an average of 2 months after acceptance. SASE. Sample copy $1.50.
Poetry: Traditional forms, free verse and avant-garde. Poetry submissions should be single-spaced within stanzas, double-spaced between stanzas.
Fiction: "We are interested in fresh material presented in either a traditional or experimental way. If the voice heard in the fiction is original, we are interested in it."

THE KINDRED SPIRIT, Groovy Gray Cat Publications, Route 2, Box 111, St. John KS 67576. (316)549-3933. Editor: Michael Hathaway. Semiannual creative writing journal of poetry, short stories, photos and b&w drawings. 100% freelance written; 70% of material published is poetry. Circ. 1,000. Pays on publication. Publishes ms an average of 3 weeks after acceptance. Byline given. Buys one-time rights. Simultaneous queries, and simultaneous, photocopied, and previously published submissions OK. Computer printout submissions acceptable. SASE. Reports in 1 month. Sample copy for $1; writer's guidelines for business-size SAE and 1 first class stamp.
Fiction: Experimental, fantasy, horror, humorous, mainstream, mystery, science fiction and suspense. Buys 4 mss/year. Submit complete ms. Length: 5,000-7,000 words. Pays in copies.
Poetry: Free verse, haiku, light verse, traditional and experimental. Buys 100-150 poems/year. Poetry submissions should be single-spaced within stanzas, double-spaced between stanzas. Length: open. Pays in copies.

THE LAKE STREET REVIEW, The Lake Street Review Press, Box 7188, Powderhorn Station, Minneapolis MN 55407. Editor: Kevin FitzPatrick. Semiannual Minneapolis/St. Paul literary magazine. No special slant or philosophy. 100% freelance written; 50% of material published is poetry. Circ. 550. Pays on acceptance. Publishes ms an average of 6 months after acceptance. Byline given. Buys first rights. Deadlines: March 1 and Oct. 1 of each year. Photocopied and previously published submissions OK. SASE. Reports in 2 weeks on queries; 2 months on mss. Sample copy $2; writer's guidelines for legal-size SAE and 1 first class stamp.
Fiction: Experimental, fantasy, humorous, mainstream, novel excerpts and science fiction. Buys 10 mss/year. Submit complete ms. Length: 400-4,500 words. Length: open. Pays in 2 copies.
Poetry: Avant-garde, free verse and traditional. Buys 50 poems/year. Submit maximum 4 poems. Poetry submissions should be single-spaced. Length: open. Pays in 2 copies.
Tips: "We're looking for writing that uses language vividly and imaginatively to explore both ordinary and extraordinary characters and situations in new ways."

LIGHT YEAR, Bits Press, Department of English, Case Western Reserve University, Cleveland OH 44106. (216)795-2810. Editor: Robert Wallace. Annual publication of light verse. 100% freelance written; 100% of material published is poetry. Circ. 2,600. Pays on publication. Publishes ms an average of 6 months after acceptance. Byline given. Buys one-time rights. Photocopied and previously published submissions OK. Computer printout submissions acceptable; prefers letter-quality to dot-matrix. SASE. Reports in 2 weeks on queries; within 2 months on mss. Sample copy $9.75 (hardbound).
Poetry: Light verse. "Poems funny, witty or just delicious. The range is from free verse to villanelles, from epigrams to ballads. We want high quality, tight, well-crafted poems. Good models would be the light verse of Ogden Nash, Richard Armour and John Updike. Zippy and up-to-date." Buys 200-250/year. Submit any number of poems. Poetry submissions should be single-spaced within stanzas, double-spaced between stanzas. Length: "No restrictions, but we prefer poems 2-40 lines." Pays in copies with small cash payment for longer poems.
Tips: "Submit typed poems; one poem/page. *Quality* is the only criterion for acceptance. The most rewarding aspect of working with freelance writers is finding a new, unexpected poet of excellence."

LITERARY REVIEW, Fairleigh Dickinson University, 285 Madison Ave., Madison NJ 07940. (201)377-4050. Editors: Martin Green, Harry Keyishian and Walter Cummins. Quarterly magazine; 128 pages. For international literary audience, largely libraries, academic readers and other poets and writers. 90% freelance written; 60% of material published is poetry. Circ. 1,000. Pays in copies. Publishes ms an average of 1 year after acceptance. Acquires first North American serial rights. Photocopied submissions OK. Computer printout submissions acceptable. Reports in 2-3 months. Sample copy $4.50.

Poetry: Avant-garde, free verse and traditional. Uses 40-50/issue. Poetry submissions should be single-spaced within stanzas, double-spaced between stanzas.

Fiction: Uses 4-5/issue. Translations from contemporary non-English literature.

Tips: "We are generally open to newcomers. Quality will tell."

LITTLE BALKANS REVIEW, A Southeast Kansas Literary and Graphics Quarterly, Little Balkans Press, Inc., 601 Grandview Heights Terrace, Pittsburg KS 66762. (316)231-1589 (after 5). Regional magazine of national interest for a general and academic audience. 98% freelance written; 30% of material published is poetry. Circ. 1,200. Pays on publication. Publishes ms an average of 6 months after acceptance. Buys one-time rights. Submit seasonal/holiday material 8 months in advance. Simultaneous queries OK. Computer printout submissions acceptable; prefers letter-quality to dot-matrix. SASE. Reports in 2 weeks on queries; 6 weeks on mss. Sample copy $2.50; writer's guidelines for business size SAE and 1 first class stamp.

Poetry: Gene DeGruson, poetry editor. Avant-garde, free verse, haiku, light verse and traditional. Buys 30/year. Submit maximum 5 poems. Poetry submissions should be single-spaced within stanzas, double-spaced between stanzas. Length: 1-500 lines. Pays in copies.

LOONFEATHER: MINNESOTA NORTH COUNTRY ART, Bemidji Arts Center, 5th and Bemidji, Bemidji MN 56601. Editor: Betty Rossi. Poetry Editor: William Elliott. Literary magazine published spring/summer/fall. Includes poetry, short prose, and graphics. Uses "occasional themes or special emphasis." Emphasis on northern Minnesota, though some work from outside the region accepted. Circ. 450. Pays in copies. Acquires one-time rights. Phone queries OK. Submit seasonal material 4 months in advance. Simultaneous, photocopied and previously published submissions OK. SASE. Reports in 2 months on mss.

Poetry: Free verse and some traditional verse. No inspirational poems. Length: 40 lines or less. Uses 12 poems/issue. Prose: 3,000 words or less. No science fiction. Uses 1 ms/issue.

‡**LUCKY STAR**, The Erie Street Press, 642 S. Clarence Ave., Oak Park IL 60304. (312)848-5716. Editor: Henry Kranz. Managing Editor: Harry Stephenson. A semiannual contemporary poetry magazine. 90% freelance written; 100% of material published is poetry. Circ. 350. Byline given. Buys one-time rights. Publishes ms an average of 6 months after acceptance. Submit seasonal/holiday material 2 months in advance. Simultaneous queries, and simultaneous, photocopied, and previously published submissions OK. Computer printout submissions acceptable; no dot-matrix. SASE. Reports in 2 months. Sample copy $3.50; writer's guidelines for SAE and 20¢ postage.

Poetry: Avant-garde, free verse and translations. "We like clear, nonacademic poetry that is more than a psychological exercise for the writer. No religious or political poems unless they are in the context of other themes." Accepts up to 100 poems/year. Poetry submissions should be single-spaced within stanzas, double-spaced between stanzas. Length: 1-100 lines. Pays in copies.

Tips: "From our very narrow perch, we'd like to see more freelance cartooning and poetry magazine, reading or book reviews."

THE LYRIC, 307 Dunton Dr. SW, Blacksburg VA 24060. Editor: Leslie Mellichamp. Quarterly magazine; 26 pages. 100% freelance written; 100% of material published is poetry. Circ. 1,000. Pays in prizes only: $25-100. Acquires first North American serial rights. Submit seasonal/holiday material 3-6 months in advance. Photocopied submissions OK. Computer printout submissions acceptable; prefers letter-quality to dot-matrix. SASE. Sample issue $2.

Poetry: Traditional, preferably rhymed, several light pieces/issue. "Poor market for social criticism/quarrels with the cosmos." Uses 45 poems/issue. Limit submissions to batches of 5. Length: 35 lines maximum.

MANNA, Prose-Poetry, Route 8, Box 368, Sanford NC 27330. Managing Editor: Nina A. Wicker. Semiannual poetry magazine. 50% freelance written; 100% of material published is poetry. Circ. varies. Pays in 3 small prizes awarded each issue. Byline given. Rights revert to author on publication. Publishes ms an average of 1 year after acceptance. Computer printout submissions acceptable; prefers letter-quality to dot-matrix. SASE. Reports in 3 weeks. Sample copy $2.50 (order a copy before submitting).

Poetry: Country humor, free verse, light verse and traditional. "No pornography or gutter language." Submit maximum 5 poems. Poetry submissions should be single-spaced within stanzas, double-spaced between stanzas. Length: 1-30 lines.

MIDWEST POETRY REVIEW, A Family of Poets, River City Publishers, Box 776, Rock Island IL 61202. (319)391-1874. Editor: Hugh Ferguson. Quarterly poetry magazine. 95% freelance written; 90% of material published is poetry. Pays on publication. Publishes ms an average of 3 months after acceptance. Byline given. Offers 100% kill fee. Buys first North American serial rights and one-time rights; makes work-for-hire assignments. Submit seasonal/holiday material 3 months in advance. Photocopied submissions OK. Computer print-out submissions acceptable. SASE. Reports in 2 weeks. Sample copy for $2 postage; writer's guidelines for business-size SAE and 1 first class stamp.

Nonfiction: Tom Tilford, articles editor. How-to (especially interested in aiding the working poet to sell his work); humor (about poetry only); interview/profile (of well-known poets); and technical (skills used in writing poetry). Special issue: Sixth Annual Contest. Deadline: May 25. Buys 4 mss/year. Query. Length: 250-750 words. Pays $25-100.

Poetry: Avant-garde, free verse, haiku, light verse and traditional. Any style; nothing blatantly erotic. Buys 300/year. Submit maximum 5 poems. Poetry submissions should be single-spaced within stanzas, double-spaced between stanzas. Length: 3 lines minimum. Pays $5-500.

Tips: "We accept submissions only from subscribers ($15 yearly; Canadians send in $15 US funds). Enter annual contest (March) or enter any one of three quarterly contests ($200 awards each quarterly contest; $1,300 annual awards). We are particularly interested in assisting the young or unpublished poet in breaking into print. We would like first chance to purchase your work; no simultaneous submissions."

MILKWEED CHRONICLE, Box 24303, Minneapolis MN 55424. (612)332-3192. Editor: Emilie Buchwald. Art Director: R.W. Scholes. Tabloid published 3 times/year featuring poetry, essays and graphics. 80% freelance written; 70% of material published is poetry. Circ. 5,000. Pays on publication. Buys first North American serial rights. Publishes ms an average of 2 months after acceptance. Simultaneous and photocopied submissions OK. SASE. Reports in 1 month on queries; in 2 months on mss. Sample copy $3.50.

Nonfiction: Photo feature (in collaboration with poetry), also first person essays by writers and artists.

Photos: Reviews contact sheets. Pays $25 for double-page graphic designs. Pays $5-$10 photo.

Poetry: Avant-garde, free verse, haiku, traditional and concrete. No religious, inspirational or poems for children. Buys 60 mss/issue. Submit 5 poems maximum. Poetry submissions should be double-spaced. Pays $5.

Tips: "Poetry will be presented in a visually advantageous format. We are interested in seeing collaborative projects. We are looking for an individual voice, for poems of high quality." No religious, overtly political, or humorous material.

‡**MINOTAUR**, Minotaur Press, Box 4094, Burlingame CA 94010. Editor: Jim Gove. A quarterly literary magazine of poetry, plays, experimental fiction and reviews. Circ. 500. Byline given. Acquires one-time rights. Submit seasonal/holiday material 6 months in advance. Simultaneous queries, and simultaneous, photocopied, and previously published submissions OK. SASE. Reports in 2 weeks. Sample copy for 8½x5½ SAE and 71¢ postage; free writer's guidelines.

Nonfiction: Interview/profile and literary scene. "Our bias is toward the experimental and the contemporary." Articles must be involved with literary scene. Acquires 2 mss/year. Send complete ms. Length: 500-3,000 words. Pays in copies.

Fiction: Chris Leddy, fiction editor. Ethnic, experimental, historical, humorous, mainstream and novel excerpts. "Fiction that is a bit too experimental for mainstream has the best chance. Also, we favor the 500-word short shorts." Acquires 6-8 mss/year. Send complete ms. Length: 500 words minimum. Pays in copies.

Poetry: Avant-garde, free verse and haiku. "No rhyming poems from poets who do not read poetry." Acquires 200-300 poems/year. Length: open. Pays in copies.

Tips: "Submit poetry that has its roots in real life."

MISSISSIPPI REVIEW, Center for Writers, University of Southern Mississippi, Southern Station, Box 5144, Hattiesburg MS 39406. (601)266-4321. Editor: Frederick Barthelme. For general literary audiences, including students, libraries and writers. Published 2 times/year; 120 pages. Buys all rights. Byline given. Pays in copies. SASE. Reports in 3 months. No submissions in June-August. Sample copy $4.50.

Fiction & Poetry: All types considered.

MISSISSIPPI VALLEY REVIEW, Department of English, Western Illinois University, Macomb IL 61455. Editor: Forrest Robinson. Magazine; 64 pages. For persons active in creating, teaching or reading poetry and fiction. Published twice a year. 100% freelance written; 100% of material published is poetry. Circ. 400. "Permission to reprint must be gained from individual authors." Accepts 80-100 mss/year. Payment in 2 contributor copies, plus a copy of the next 2 issues. Publishes ms an average of 1 year after acceptance. "Only excellent" photocopied submissions OK. Will consider simultaneous submissions only if the author "notifies us immediately upon receipt of an acceptance elsewhere. We try to return manuscripts within 3 months. We do not mind writers asking for progress reports if we are a bit late. Allow for no manuscript reading during summer." Computer printout submissions acceptable; no dot-matrix. Submit complete manuscript. SASE. Sample copy $2 plus postage.

Poetry and Fiction: John Mann, poetry editor. Loren Logsdon, fiction editor. Tries to provide a range and variety of style and subject matter. "*Writer's Market* guidelines for ms submission suggested. We publish no articles. We usually solicit our reviews." Poetry submissions should be double-spaced.

Tips: "Our contributors are experienced writers, usually—though not always—previously published. After acceptance, we ask the contributor for credits—not before."

MODERN HAIKU, Modern Haiku, Box 1752, Madison WI 53701. Editor: Robert Spiess. Triannual magazine featuring haiku poetry and related articles and book reviews for poets and appreciators of haiku. 90% freelance written; 80% of material published is poetry. Circ. 525. Buys first North American serial rights. Computer printout submissions acceptable; prefers letter-quality to dot-matrix. Publishes ms an average of 2½ months after acceptance. SASE. Reports in 1 week on queries; in 3 weeks on mss. Sample copy $3; free writer's guidelines.
Nonfiction: General interest (articles of a reasonably scholarly nature related to haiku). Uses 1-3 mss/issue. Send complete ms. Pays $5/page.
Poetry: Haiku and senryu. No tanka or nonhaiku poetry. Uses 145-165 mss/issue. Poetry submissions should be double-spaced. Pays $1/haiku upon acceptance. "Keep in mind: A haiku is not just a mere image, it must express the thing-in-itself and have insight into the nature of the event/experience being expressed."
Tips: "Study what the haiku is from authoritative books on the subject, read *Modern Haiku*, and don't write sentimental, pretty, ego-centered, or superficial little poems under the impression that these are haiku. Submit poems on ½ sheet of paper, with one haiku on each, with name and address on each sheet. Contributors should have a basic knowledge of the inner aspects of haiku beyond the mere knowledge of its form. Simply learn what a haiku really is before submitting material. The magazine has received three consecutive award/grants for excellence from the National Endowment for the Arts."

MOVING OUT, Feminist Literary and Arts Journal, Box 21249, Detroit MI 48221. Editors: M. Kaminski, J. Gartland, A. Cherry and Deborah Montwart. Annual literary magazine covering "poetry, fiction and art by women about women." 80% freelance written; 50% of material published is poetry. Circ. 1,000. Pays on publication. Publishes ms an average of 1 year after acceptance. Byline given. Buys first North American serial rights. Photocopied submissions OK. Computer printout submissions acceptable. SASE. Reports in 2 months on queries; 6 months on mss. Sample copy for $3, or $6 for current double issue, with 9x12 SAE and 60¢ postage; writer's guidelines for SAE and 1 first class stamp.
Poetry: Avant-garde and free verse. Buys 40/year. Submit maximum 5 poems. Poetry submissions should be double-spaced. Length: open. Pays in contributor copy.
Tips: No sexist work or work which exploits women; pornography. We publish few male writers, especially their creative work (poetry, fiction, etc.). Freelance writers should be aware of diary/journal writing, illustrated work, concrete poetry, feminist aesthetic, first and foremost for our journal."

‡NANTUCKET REVIEW, Box 1234, Nantucket MA 02554. Editors: Richard Cumbie and Richard Burns. A literary magazine of fiction, poetry and criticism published 3 times/year. Circ. 1,000. Byline given. Acquires first North American serial rights. Submit seasonal/holiday material 2 months in advance. Photocopied submissions OK. Computer printout submissions acceptable; no dot-matrix. Sample copy for $1.50, 6x9 SAE, and 42¢ postage.
Fiction: Translations, satire and novel excerpts. Accepts 15 mss/year. Length: 1,000-4,500 words. Pays in copies, and occasionally in cash.
Poetry: Jeffrey Faude, poetry editor. Avant-garde and traditional. Accepts 20 poems/year. Submit maximum 4 poems. Pays in copies, and occasionally in cash.

NEGATIVE CAPABILITY, Negative Capability, Inc., 6116 Timberly Rd. N., Mobile AL 36609. (205)661-9114. Editor: Sue Brannan Walker. Literary quarterly covering literature, art, music, essays, reviews and photography. 99% freelance written; 60% of material published is poetry. "We seek excellence in the arts and wish to promote new artists as well as those who are already established." Circ. 800. Pays in contributor copy. Publishes ms an average of 8 months after acceptance. Byline given. Buys first North American serial rights. Submit seasonal/holiday material 6 months in advance. Photocopied submissions OK. Computer printout submissions acceptable. SASE. Reports in 2 weeks on queries; 6 weeks on mss. Sample copy $3.50.
Nonfiction: General interest, humor, interview/profile and personal experience. "Seeking poetry and fiction for a special anthology of Southern writers." Buys 8 mss/year. Query or send complete ms. Length: 500-6,000 words. Pays in contributor copy.
Fiction: Humorous, mainstream and science fiction. Buys 16 mss/year. Submit complete ms. Length: 1,000-6,000 words. Pays in contributor copy.
Poetry: Avant-garde, free verse, haiku, light verse and traditional. Buys 1,500 poems/year. Submit maximum 5 poems. Poetry submissions should be single-spaced within stanzas, double-spaced between stanzas. Length: open. Pays in contributor copy.
Fillers: Short humor. Buys 5-10 mss/year. Length: open. Pays in contributor copy.
Tips: "Small press is the exciting avenue to diversity and professionalism in freelance work."

NEW COLLAGE MAGAZINE, 5700 N. Trail, Sarasota FL 33580. (813)355-7671, ext. 203. Editor: A. McA. Miller. Co-Editor: Carol Mahler. For poetry readers. Triquarterly magazine; 24 pages minimum. 100% freelance written; 90% of material published is poetry. Circ. 2,000. Acquires first rights. Uses 80 poems per year. No long fiction. Token payment or 3 contributor copies. Publishes ms an average of 6 months after ac-

ceptance. Photocopied submissions OK. Computer printout submissions acceptable; no dot-matrix. No simultaneous submissions. Reports in 3 weeks. SASE. Sample copy $2, together with editorial guidelines sheet.
Poetry: "We want poetry as a fresh act of language. No tick-tock effusions about everyday sentiments, please. First, read a sample copy. Then, and only then, send us poems. We especially want strong poems, more in Yeats' vein than in W.C. Williams, but we are open to any poem that sustains clear imagery and an expressive voice." Length: 150 lines maximum. Poetry submissions should be typed.
Tips: "Issues are often thematic; query before sending."

NEW ORLEANS REVIEW, Box 195, Loyola University, New Orleans LA 70118. (504)865-2152. Editor: John Mosier. Emphasizes art, film and literature. Magazine published 4 times/year. Approximately 90% freelance written; 35% of material published is poetry. Circ. 1,500. Pays honorarium. Publishes ms an average of 8 months after acceptance. Buys first North American serial rights. Byline given. Computer printout submissions acceptable. SASE. Reports in 2 months. Sample copy $6.
Poetry: Uses 20/year.

NEW VOICES, A Selection of Poetry, Astra Publications, 24 Edgewood Terrace, Methuen MA 01844. (617)686-5381. Editor: Lorraine Moreau-Laverriere. Annual small press poetry magazine. Circ. 300. Simultaneous, photocopied, and previously published submissions OK. SASE. Reports in 3 weeks or ASAP. Sample copy for $1 postage or five 20¢ stamps; free writer's guidelines.
Poetry: Avant-garde, free verse, haiku, light verse and traditional. No "rhymed poetry, moralizing or unclear messages." Submit maximum 6 poems. Length: 3-90 lines. Pays in contributor copy.

NEW WORLDS UNLIMITED, Box 556-WM, Saddle Brook NJ 07662. Editor-in-Chief: Sal St. John Buttaci. Managing Editor: Susan Linda Gerstle. For "professional and aspiring poets of all ages from here and abroad. We've published high school students, college students, graduates and people from all walks of life who write good poetry." Annual hardcover anthology; 140 pages. Circ. 500-900. No payment. Obtains all rights, but may reassign following publication. Photocopied submissions OK. Computer printout submissions acceptable; prefers letter-quality to dot-matrix. SASE. Reports immediately—up to 6 months. Writer's guidelines and contest rules for annual poetry contest for SASE.
Poetry: "We want previously unpublished poems rich in imagery, poems that show intelligent treatment of universal themes and reveal the poet's understanding, even limited, of the poetry craft." Avant-garde, free verse, haiku, light verse and traditional. No "overly sentimental poems or contrived rhymes." Uses 400/issue. Limit submissions to batches of 5. Length: 2-14 lines.
Tips: "Make sure sufficient postage is placed on enclosed SASE. Poets from other countries must enclose either US postage or IRCs."

‡**NIT&WIT, Chicago's Arts Magazine**, Nit&Wit Publications, Box 14685, Chicago IL 60614. (312)248-1183, ext. 977. Editor: Leonard J. Dominguez. Art Director: Shlomo Krudo. Publisher: Kathleen J. Cummings. A bimonthly literary arts magazine. "Nit&Wit is a magazine of creative perspectives publishing the best of fiction, humor, poetry, art, photography and social commentary from worldwide submissions as well as features on art, music, theatre, film and dance. We invite freelance work." 90% freelance written; 8% of material published is poetry. Circ. 7,000. Byline given. Publishes ms an average of 1 year after acceptance. Acquires first North American serial rights. Submit seasonal/holiday material 4 months in advance. Simultaneous queries and photocopied submissions OK. Computer printout submissions acceptable. SASE. Reports in 6 weeks on queries; 2 months on mss. Sample copy $2; writer's guidelines with SASE. Sponsors annual poetry, short fiction and photography contests.
Nonfiction: Humor; interview/profile; photo feature; criticism; essays; features on music, art, dance, film; and reviews. "Send query for special issues." No how-to articles. Accepts approximately 36 mss/year. Query. Length: 1,500 word maximum. Pays in copies.
Photos: Julie D. Taylor, photo editor. B&w photos. Acquires one-time rights.
Columns/Departments: Poetry; Bookworks (book reviews); Small Press Notebook (small press news and reviews); Art (art reviews and events); and Dance (dance reviews and events). Query. Length: 500-800 words. Pays in copies.
Fiction: Cherly Kent, fiction editor. Experimental, humorous, mainstream, literary and translations. No confession, erotica, romance, western or condensed novels. Accepts 24 mss/year. Send complete ms. Length: 1,500 words maximum. Pays in copies.
Poetry: Larry Hunt, poetry editor. Free verse, traditional and translation (include original). No light verse, haiku or incoherent poetry. Accepts 40-50 poems/year. Submit maximum 6 poems. Poetry submissions should be single-spaced within stanzas, double-spaced between stanzas. Length: 5-50 lines. Pays in copies.
Tips: "We accept work from new as well as prominent writers. Include a short letter with your manuscript to let us know who you are. It's best to avoid *deluging* us with your work. Submissions should be of manageable size. Poetry, short fiction and features are most open to freelancers."

NORTH AMERICAN MENTOR MAGAZINE, 1745 Madison St., Fennimore WI 53809. (608)822-6237. Editors: John Westburg and Mildred Westburg. 95% freelance written; 60% of material published is poetry. For "largely mature readers, above average in education, most being fairly well-to-do; many being retired persons over 60 years of age; college personnel and professional writers or aspirants to being professional." Quarterly. A small press noncommercial publication, primarily supported by the editors, other contributors and donors. Also sponsors annual poetry contest with cash awards. Acquires all rights. Byline given. Pays in contributor copies. Publishes ms an average of 6 months after acceptance. Photocopied and simultaneous submissions OK. Reports in 1 week to 6 months. SASE. Sample copy $2.
Poetry: Accepts traditional, blank and free verse, avant-garde forms and light verse. "Poetry from many cultures. We would like to see more poetry by new writers." Length: 50 lines maximum preferred.
Tips: "We are prejudiced against poems that are nasty, whiney, self-pitying, vulgar, vicious or pornographic, but view favorably those that are lofty in thought, show strength of character, reveal human values, deal with the commonplace, show wonder and awe and appreciation, and might even touch upon the erotic (lightly) and the political. We are now bored with 'free verse', for out of many hundreds of free verse poems we read, only a handful are interesting. The poet who aspires to elevate his poems above those of the common herd should avoid free verse whenever possible. We like to see poetry that is carefully literate, well-structured, that concludes with some significant thought. The poem should itself be a great metaphor that reveals human qualities and insights but should contain within itself minor metaphors that are interesting, exciting, meaningful but not so gaudy as to detract from the virtue of the whole poem."

NORTHWEST REVIEW, 369 P.L.C., University of Oregon, Dept. of English, Eugene OR 97403. (503)686-3957. Editor-in-Chief: John Witte. 100% freelance written; 20% of material published is poetry. For literate readership. "We have one issue per year with Northwest emphasis; the other two are of general interest to those who follow American/world poetry and fiction." Published 3 times/year. Circ. 2,000. Pays on publication in copies. Publishes ms an average of 4 months after acceptance. Buys first periodical rights. Phone queries OK. Photocopied submissions OK. Computer printout submissions acceptable "if perfectly legible"; prefers letter-quality to dot-matrix. SASE. Reports in 6-8 weeks. Sample copy $2.50; free writer's guidelines.
Poetry: Maxine Scates, poetry editor. Uses 20-30 poems/issue. Limit submissions to batches of 6-10. Poetry submissions should be single-spaced.
Fiction: Deb Casey, fiction editor. Uses 5-8 stories/issue. Stories in excess of 40 pages at a disadvantage.
Tips: "Persist: the more we can see of an author's work, the better we're able to assess it. Magazines are harder pressed than ever financially and exist at all by virtue of financial miracles. Editors, often volunteers, usually donate their time and are deluged with material to read carefully. Make it as pleasant and easy for them to accept your work as you possible can. Help by *subscribing*."

THE OHIO JOURNAL, A Magazine of Literature and the Visual Arts, Department of English, Ohio State University, 164 W. 17th Ave., Columbus OH 43210. Editor: William Allen. Magazine; 2 times a year. 90% freelance written; 50% of material published is poetry. Circ. 1,000. Pays in contributor copies. Publishes ms an average of 6 months after acceptance. Acquires all rights. Byline given. Photocopied and simultaneous submissions OK. Computer printout submissions acceptable. SASE. Reports in 6 weeks. Does not accept mss during the summer months.
Poetry: David Citino. No restrictions as to category or type. Poetry submissions should be single-spaced within stanzas, double-spaced between stanzas. Maximum length for fiction: 6,000 words. No critical studies.
Tips: "Freelance writers should be aware of the story that invites reader participation—minimal 'clues' to subtext of story—strong submerged plot."

ORPHEUS, The Magazine of Poems, Suite 203, 8812 W. Pico Blvd., Los Angeles CA 90035. (213)271-1460. Editor: P. Schneidre. Magazine published 3 times/year. Poems in English; no translations or articles. Circ. 1,800. Pays on publication. Byline given. Buys first rights. Photocopied submissions OK. SASE. Reports in 1 week. Sample copy for $4 from Grolier, 6 Plympton St., Cambridge MA 02138.
Poetry: Free verse and traditional. "Nothing with the words 'crystal,' 'energy' or 'consciousness.' We don't use political or surrealistic poems." Buys 50/year. Submit maximum 10 poems. Pays $5-100.

ORPHIC LUTE, Box 2815, Newport News VA 23602. Editor: Patricia Doherty Hinnebusch. Quarterly. 100% freelance written; 100% of material published is poetry. Circ. 200. Rights revert to author. Publishes ms an average of 2 months after acceptance. SASE.
Nonfiction: Short articles on subjects germane to poetry. Length: 400-800 words. Pays in one copy.
Poetry: Free, blank, light and traditional verse. Personal/lyrical rather than historical/political. New metaphors, sustained metaphors; involvement of all senses; concreteness; conciseness. Editor will comment if desired. No porn; no preaching. Uses 50-70/issue. Submit 3-4 poems. Preferred length: 3-40 lines; 80 lines maximum. Poetry submissions should be single-spaced.

PASSAGES NORTH, William Bonifas Fine Arts Center, 7th St. and 1st Ave. S., Escanaba MI 49829. (906)786-3833. Editor: Elinor Benedict. Managing Editor: Carol R. Hackenbruch. Semiannual literary tabloid (spring and fall) featuring high quality poetry, short fiction and graphics. 95% freelance written; 75% of material published is poetry. Circ. 1,000. Pays on publication. Publishes ms an average of 3 months after acceptance. Byline given. Rights revert to author. Photocopied submissions OK. Computer printout submissions acceptable; prefers letter-quality to dot-matrix. SASE. Reports in 2 weeks on queries; 3 months on ms. Sample copy for $1 and 50¢ postage; writer's guidelines for SAE and 1 first class stamp.
Poetry: "High quality contemporary poetry." No "greeting card, heavily-rhymed, sentimental, highly traditional" poetry. Buys 60/year. Submit maximum 4 poems. Poetry submissions should be single-spaced within stanzas, double-spaced between stanzas. Length: 40 lines maximum. Pays in 3 copies.
Fiction: High quality short stories, 3,000-word maximum preferred. Pays in 3 copies.

PHOEBE, The George Mason Review, George Mason University, 4400 University Dr., Fairfax VA 22030. (703)323-3730. Editor-in-Chief: Karenne Brown. Quarterly magazine; 44-120 pages. For the literary community. 100% freelance written; 50% of material published is poetry. Circ. 5,000. Pays in 4 contributor copies on publication. Publishes ms an average of 2 months after acceptance. Byline given. Computer printout submissions acceptable; no dot-matrix. SASE. Reports in 6 weeks. Sample copy $3.
Poetry: Avant-garde, free verse, haiku and traditional. Accepts 20-30 poems/issue. Poetry submissions should be double-spaced. Length: no more than 2 pages. Pays in contributor copies.
Tips: "*Phoebe* is devoted to publishing works of literary excellence. Works of poetry and fiction must meet our requirements of creativity, skill and insight. We only consider the serious and creative writer; all others not meeting these criteria will be rejected outright. Those beginning writers seeking publication should be aware of our high standards; we will not settle for less. All submitted work must reflect clear and perceptive writing; cliches must be avoided; old ideas must be presented in a new and refreshing manner; all works must generate strong emotions for the reader. Read the works of contemporary poets and fiction writers to see how they meet the requirements of lucid and imagistic writing."

PIEDMONT LITERARY REVIEW, Piedmont Literary Society, Box 3656, Danville VA 24541. Editor: David Craig. Quarterly magazine featuring poetry, short fiction and reviews. 100% freelance written; 90% of material published is poetry. "We also publish a 4-6 page newsletter with market listings, information, etc." Circ. 400. Pays in copies. Computer printout submissions acceptable; prefers letter-quality to dot-matrix. Publishes ms an average of 6 months after acceptance. Acquires one-time rights. Photocopied submissions OK. SASE. Reports in 2 weeks on queries; in 3 months on mss. Sample copy $2.50; writer's guidelines for SASE.
Nonfiction: "All submissions are given equal consideration, quality being the key factor in judging submissions. General interest; how-to (articles related to poetry and poetry analysis); and interview (with poets or writers). Buys 1-3 prose pieces/issue. Send complete ms. Length: 1,000 words maximum. Pays in copies.
Poetry: Barbara McCoy, haiku editor. Gail White, poetry editor. Avant-garde, free verse, haiku, light verse and traditional. "We will consider any type of poetry. Poetry submissions should be double-spaced. Lengthy poems do not stand a good chance of being published." Buys 160-200 poems/year. Submit maximum 5 poems. Length: 40 lines maximum. Pays in 1 contributor copy.
Tips: "We publish the best from the material submitted. We try to give special attention to works of students and previously unpublished poets. Writers should indicate if they are students or previously unpublished. Our tastes are eclectic but exacting, like avant-garde surrealistic poems. We still like nature poems—it's all right to mention a tree. We will always give special attention to short humorous pieces, especially satire. If it rhymes it had better be good. Lyric and sonnets can find a home here."

PLAINS POETRY JOURNAL (PPJ), Box 2337, Bismarck ND 58502. Editor: Jane Greer. Quarterly magazine. "A forum for poems and criticism demonstrating the importance of poetic form. We explore the relationship between form and content in poetry." 100% freelance written; 95% of material published is poetry. Circ. 200. Pays on publication. Publishes ms an average of 3 months after acceptance. Byline given. Acquires one-time rights. Photocopied and previously published submissions OK. Computer printout submissions acceptable. SASE. Reports in 1 week. Sample copy $3.50; writer's guidelines for business-size SAE and 1 first class stamp.
Poetry: Traditional. "No conversational, broken-prose free verse or 'Hallmark' verse. No subjects are taboo; the *poet's skill* at expression is what counts." Wants nothing but poetry and essays on poetry and poetic theory, methods and techniques. Buys 160/year. Submit maximum 10 poems. Poetry submissions should be double-spaced. "We prefer shorter poems; exceptional long poems will be considered." Pays in 2 copies.
Tips: "We are open to poetry and criticism or theory, but will probably publish only one piece of criticism per issue and many poems. Queries aren't necessary but will be answered immediately. Criticism should agree with the magazine's commitment to form in poetry; if it doesn't, it had better be brilliant. We believe *how* a thing is said (using poetic tools such as meter, rhyme, alliteration, assonance, etc.) is just as important as *what* is said. Otherwise, it's mere philosophy, not poetry."

POEM, c/o U.A.H., Huntsville AL 35899. Editor: Robert L. Welker. For adults; well-educated, interested in good poetry. Published 3 times/year; magazine, 65 pages. 100% freelance written; 100% of material published is poetry. Circ. 500. Acquires all rights. Byline given. Payment in contributor's copies. Publishes ms an average of 8 months after acceptance. Reports in 2 months. Submit complete ms only. Computer printout submissions acceptable. SASE.

Poetry: "We use nothing but superior quality poetry. Good taste (no pornography for its own sake) and technical proficiency. We give special attention to young and less well-known poets. Do not like poems about poems, poets, and other works of art." Traditional forms, blank verse, free verse, and avant-garde forms. Uses 200 unsolicited poems/year. Poetry submissions should be single-spaced within stanzas, double-spaced between stanzas. Length and theme: open.

Tips: "All our contributors are unsolicited. We welcome all submissions and always hope to find an unknown who deserves publication."

‡**A POET**, Realities Library, #76, 2745 Monterey Hwy., San Jose CA 95111. Editor: Ric Soos. A weekly poetry magazine. 100% freelance written; 100% of material published is poetry. Estab. 1983. Byline given. Acquires first North American serial rights. Publishes ms an average of 3 months after acceptance. Submit seasonal/holiday material 3 months in advance. Simultaneous queries and photocopied submissions OK. Computer printout submissions acceptable; prefers letter-quality to dot-matrix. SASE. Reports in 1 week. Sample copy for $1/5 issues or SAE and 20¢ postage; writer's guidelines for SAE and 20¢ postage.

Poetry: Avant-garde, free verse, haiku, light verse and translations. Accepts 150 poems/year. Submit maximum 15 poems. Poetry submissions should be single-spaced within stanzas, double-spaced between stanzas. Length: 20 lines maximum. Pays in copies.

Tips: "It doesn't hurt to be familiar with the format, but the biggest mistake writers make is in not sending poetry for consideration. We have published established poets, such as Robert Bly and Bukowski, but have concentrated on newer poets, such as M. Olcott. We are very open to varied offerings."

‡**POET LORE**, Heldref Publications, 4000 Albemarle St. NW, Washington DC 20016. (202)362-6445. Managing Editor: Susan Davis. A quarterly literary magazine publishing original poems of all kinds. Circ. 425. Byline given. Acquires one-time rights. Submit seasonal/holiday material 6 months in advance. Photocopied submissions OK. Computer printout submissions acceptable. SASE. Reports in 4 months. Sample copy $2.50; free writer's guidelines.

Nonfiction: Reviews of poetry collections. Send complete ms. No payment.

Poetry: Avant-garde, free verse, haiku, light verse and traditional. "We publish original poems of all kinds. We continue to welcome narrative poetry and original translations of works by contemporary world poets." Length: open. No payment.

‡**THE POET, Publisher of New American Poetry**, OakWoods Publishing House, Ltd., Box 44021, Shreveport LA 71134-4021. (318)424-8036. Editor: Peggy Cooper. Managing Editor: Robert Cooper. A quarterly magazine "to further the art of poetry and give new American poets more exposure." Estab. 1984. "Premiere issue will go to colleges and universities; subscriptions now being advertised." Pays on publication. Byline given. Acquires one-time rights; poets retain full rights/ownership. Submit seasonal/holiday material 3 months or more in adance. Simultaneous queries, and simultaneous, photocopied, and previously published submissions OK. Computer printout submissions acceptable; no dot-matrix. Reports in 6 months. Sample copy $3.75; writer's guidelines for business-size SAE and 1 first class stamp.

Nonfiction: Book excerpts; poetry book reviews; historical/nostalgic; how-to (write, publish, submit, and read/understand poetry); humor; inspirational; new product (publishing); opinion; photo feature (poetry, poets, publishing). "We do not accept any articles that do not deal with poets, poetry or the publishing industry." Accepts 25-100 mss/year. Send complete ms. Length: open. Pays in copies.

Photos: Send photos with ms. Reviews 5x7 or smaller b&w prints of adults/children/nature. Model release and identification of subjects required. Acquires one-time rights.

Columns/Departments: Books Reviews (Poetry), Poetry Critiques, Interviews with Poets with photo(s), Helpful Hints from writing and critiquing poetry, Poetry Markets, Poetry Grants, Poets of the Past, The Sonnet Syndrome, Musical Poems, Poetical Holidays (anything dealing with poetry). Accepts 100 mss/year. Send complete ms. Length: open. Pays in copies.

Poetry: Avant-garde, free verse, haiku, light verse, traditional, experimental. Accepts 200-1,000 poems/year. Submit maximum 25 poems. Length: open. Pays in contributor copies.

Fillers: Fillers regarding poetry, publishing of poetry, poets, poetry humor. Accepts 25-100/year. Pays in contributor copies.

Tips: "Acceptable work will be used as space permits in each issue. Acceptable work not used in one edition will be held for next edition. This publication will give exposure to new poets/writers/artists/photographers."

POETRY, The Modern Poetry Association, Box 4348, 601 S. Morgan St., Chicago IL 60680. Editor: Joseph Parisi. Monthly magazine; 64 pages. 100% freelance written; 75% of material published is poetry. Circ. 6,700.

Pays on publication. Publishes ms an average of 9 months after acceptance. Buys all rights. Byline given. Submit seasonal/holiday material 9 months in advance. Computer printout submissions acceptable; prefers letter-quality to dot-matrix. SASE. Reports in 4-6 weeks. Sample copy $2.60; writer's guidelines for SASE.
Poetry: "We consistently publish the best poetry being written in English. All forms may be acceptable." Buys 500/year. Limit submissions to batches of 6-8. Poetry submissions should be single-spaced within stanzas; double-spaced between stanzas. Pays $1/line.

POETRY AUSTRALIA, South Head Press, The Market Place, Berrima, NCW Australia 2577. (048)911407. Editor: Grace Perry. Managing Editor: John Millett. Quarterly magazine emphasizing poetry. 100% freelance written; 100% of material published is poetry. Circ. 2,000. Pays on publication. Publishes ms an average of 1 month after acceptance. No byline given. Buys Australian rights. Submit seasonal/holiday material 3 months in advance. Simultaneous queries, and simultaneous and photocopied submissions OK. Computer printout submissions acceptable. SASE. Reports in 1 month.
Poetry: Avant-garde, free verse, haiku, light verse and traditional. Buys "200 and more" mss/year. Submit maximum 4 poems. Poetry submissions should be double-spaced. Length: 3-200 lines. Pays $5-10 or overseas, in copies of magazine.

POETRY CANADA REVIEW, Poetry Canada Poesie Review, Inc., Box 1280, Station A, Toronto, Ontario M5W 1G7 Canada. Editor: Clifton Whiten. Quarterly literary tabloid featuring Canadian poetry; some international. 25% freelance written; 95% of material published is poetry. Publishes ms an average of 2 months after acceptance. SAE and IRCs. Computer printout submissions acceptable; prefers letter-quality to dot-matrix.
Poetry: Avant-garde, free verse, haiku, light verse and traditional. Buys 120/year. Submit maximum 12 poems. Pays $5 maximum.
Tips: Using 1 International page/issue.

POETRY/LA, Peggor Press, Box 84271, Los Angeles CA 90073. (213)472-6171. Editor: Helen Friedland. Semiannual anthology in paperback format "devoted exclusively to the best poetry offered by well-known and new poets living in the Los Angeles area." 100% freelance written; 100% of material published is poetry. Circ. 700. Byline given. Acquires first rights. Publishes ms an average of 6 months after acceptance. Photocopied submissions OK. Computer printout submissions acceptable; prefers letter-quality to dot-matrix. SASE. Reports in 2 weeks on queries; 2 months on mss. Sample copy $3.50; writer's guidelines for SAE and 1 first class stamp.
Poetry: Avant-garde, free verse and traditional. "No constraint as to subject matter or form." Buys 150/year. "Prefers about four to six poems or pages, but will consider larger submissions." Poetry submissions should be single-spaced within stanzas, double-spaced between stanzas. Length: open. Pays in minimum of 1 copy.

POETRY TODAY, The Magazine for Poets, (formerly *Poetry Magazine*), Spectrum Publishing, Box 20822, Portland OR 97220. (503)231-7628. Managing Editor: Greg Butkus. Consulting Editor: Mark Worden. Quarterly poetry magazine. 80% freelance written; 50% of material published is poetry. Circ. 5,000. Pays on publication. Publishes ms an average of 6 months after acceptance. Byline given. Acquires one-time rights. Submit seasonal/holiday material 4 months in advance. Simultaneous and photocopied submissions OK. Electronic submissions OK on floppy disk for TRS-80; requires hard copy also. Computer printout submissions acceptable. SASE. Reports in 2 months. Sample copy $1; free writer's guidelines with sample copy.
Nonfiction: How-to (tips for our readers on getting poems published). Buys 30-40 mss/year. Send complete ms. Length: 400-2,000 words. Pays 1/2¢/word, "unless otherwise arranged."
Poetry: Keith Van Vliet, editor. All types, but "we are tired of seeing love poems." Buys 300-400/year. Submit maximum 8 poems. Poetry submissions should be single-spaced within stanzas, double-spaced between stanzas. Length: 40 lines maximum; "4-16 line poems get published more often." Pays in copies.
Tips: "Always send sample poems with any other articles you may submit. We like to see photos of our authors as we sometimes use them in *PT*. In *Poetry Profile* we use articles by published poets who are passing along tricks of the trade. We need more 'how-to' submissions."

POETRY TORONTO, 217 Northwood Dr., Willowdale, Ontario M2M 2K5 Canada. Editors: Maria Jacobs and Robert Billings. Monthly magazine. 100% freelance written; 60% of material published is poetry. Circ. 700. Pays in subscription. Byline given. Not copyrighted. Acquires first North American serial rights. Publishes ms an average of 4 months after acceptance. Computer printout submissions acceptable; no dot-matrix. SAE and IRCs. Reports in 6 weeks. Back issues $2.
Poetry: Mary di Michele, poetry editor. Avant-garde, free verse, haiku and traditional. Submit maximum 8 poems. Poetry submissions should be single-spaced within stanzas, double-spaced between stanzas.

‡**POOR MAN'S PRESS**, Poor Man's Press, Box 1291, Station B, Ottawa, Ontario K1P 5R3 Canada. (613)722-0620. Editors: Bruce and Joan Brown. A quarterly magazine of the arts (short stories/poetry) based on themes. "We try to provide readers with a low cost publication." 100% freelance written; 40% of material

published is poetry. Estab. 1983. Circ. 500. Byline given. Acquires one-time rights; rights revert to author. Publishes ms an average of 4 months after acceptance. Submit seasonal/holiday material 1 month in advance. Simultaneous queries and photocopied submissions OK. Computer printout submissions acceptable. SAE and IRCs. Reports in 2 weeks on queries; 5 weeks on mss. Sample copy for $1.65, 9x6 SAE, and 2 Canadian first class stamps; writer's guidelines for SAE and 1 first class stamp.

Nonfiction: Book excerpts, expose, general interest, historical/nostalgic, how-to, humor, inspirational, new product, opinion and personal experience. "All material needed depends on upcoming theme. It's best to query." Accepts 4 mss/year. Query. Length: 500-3,000 words. Pays in copies.

Columns/Departments: Soap Box (any *opinionated* article). Accepts 6 mss/year. Send complete ms. Length: 500-3,000 words. Pays in copies.

Fiction: Adventure, experimental, fantasy, horrorm humorous, mainstream, mystery, religious, science fiction and suspense. "Any form of fiction that loosely ties into themes. Upcoming themes: animals, war, peace, children, love, politics, hate and horror." Accepts 31 mss/year. Send complete ms. Length: 500-4,500 words. Pays in copies.

Poetry: Joan Brown, poetry editor. Avant-garde, free verse, haiku, light verse and traditional. Accepts 40 poems/year. Submit maximum 10 poems. Poetry submissions should be double-spaced. Length: 1-30 lines. Pays in copies.

Tips: "We are very open to new writers. Part of our philosophy is to encourage new writers to write. We need tight, well-written stories. We are not large enough to pay but we can give exposure."

PORTLAND REVIEW, Portland State University, Box 751, Portland OR 97207. (503)229-4468. Editor: Nancy L. Moeller. Tri or biyearly magazine covering literature. 90% freelance written; 65% of material published is poetry. Circ. 1,800. Pays on publication. Byline given. Acquires first North American serial rights. Publishes ms an average of 6 weeks after acceptance. Simultaneous queries and photocopied submissions OK. Computer printout submissions acceptable; prefers letter-quality to dot-matrix. SASE. Reports in 3 weeks on queries; 4 months on mss. Sample copy $2; free writer's guidelines.

Nonfiction: Book excerpts (fiction, poetry, literary criticism); general interest; humor; interview/profile; and photo feature. Buys 30 mss/year. Send complete ms. Length: 5,000 words maximum. Pays in copies.

Fiction: Erotica, ethnic, experimental, fantasy, historical, horror, humorous, mainstream, mystery, novel excerpts, science fiction, suspense and prose poems. No formula fiction. Buys 8-15 mss/year. Send complete ms. Length: 4,000 words maximum. Pays in copies.

Poetry: Avant-garde, free verse, haiku, light verse and traditional prose. Buys 50-70/year. Submit maximum 5 poems. Poetry submissions should be double-spaced. Length: 90 lines maximum. Pays in copies.

Fillers: Aphorisms. Length: 20 words maximum. Pays in copies.

POSTPOETRY, Realities Library, #76, 2745 Monterey Hwy., San Jose CA 95111. Editor: Ric Soos. A weekly poetry magazine. Estab. 1983. Byline given. Acquires first North American serial rights. Submit seasonal/holiday material 3 months in advance. Simultaneous queries and photocopied submissions OK. SASE. Reports in 1 week. Sample copy for $1/5 issues or 4x6 SAE and 20¢ postage; writer's guidelines for SAE and 20¢ postage.

Poetry: Avant-garde, free verse, haiku, light verse, translations. Accepts 150 poems/year. Submit maximum 5 poems. Length: 20 lines. Pays in copies.

Tips: "It doesn't hurt to be familiar with the format, but the biggest mistake writers make is in not sending poetry for consideration. We have published established poets, such as Robert Bly and Bukowski, but have concentrated on newer poets, such as M. Olcott. We are very open to varied offerings."

‡POULTRY, A Magazine of Voice, Poultry, Inc., Box 727, Truro MA 02666. Editors: Brendan Galvin and George Garrett. A semiannual tabloid for writers with parodies of current poetry, fiction, and other literary business. "We try to lampoon some of the pretensions and foibles of the current literary scene." Circ. 1,000. Byline given. Not copyrighted. Acquires one-time rights. Computer printout submissions acceptable. Photocopied submissions OK. SASE. Reports in 1 month. Sample copy for $1, 8x11 SAE, and 2 first class stamps.

Nonfiction: Parodies of reviews, interviews, awards, etc. No serious material. Send complete ms. Length: open. Pays in 10 copies.

Photos: Send photos with ms. Must be parody of literary scene. Reviews b&w prints. Acquires one-time rights.

Fiction: Parodies of fictional types and styles. "Nothing serious, nothing funny that's *not* related to literary matters." Send complete ms. Length: open. Pays in 10 copies.

Poetry: Light verse, parodies of contemporary poems and famous poems. No serious poems. Length: open. Pays in 10 copies.

Fillers: Must relate to current literature. Length: open. Pays in 10 copies.

Tips: "We want pieces that lampoon current literary interests and pretensions. No personal attacks on writers, but parodies of their styles are always welcome. All areas are open to freelancers."

PRIMAVERA, University of Chicago, 1212 E. 59th St., Chicago IL 60637. (312)684-2742. Contact: Editorial Board. Annual magazine covering literature and art by women for readers high school age and up interested in contemporary literature and art. 100% freelance written; 80% of material published is poetry. Circ. 800. Average issue includes 6 short stories and 45 poems. Pays on publication. Byline given. Acquires first North American serial rights. Phone queries OK. Computer printout submissions acceptable; prefers letter-quality to dot-matrix. SASE. Reports in 2 months on queries; in 6 months on mss. Sample copy $4; free writer's guidelines.
Poetry: Ann Gearen, editor. Avant-garde, free verse and haiku. Buys 45 mss/year. Submit maximum 6 poems. Poetry submissions should be single-spaced within stanzas, double-spaced between stanzas. Length: 10 page maximum. Pays in 2 free copies.
Tips: "Read a recent issue. We publish a wide range of material, all by women. We're looking for new ideas and interesting styles. We do not publish scholarly articles or formula type fiction."

‡**PROOF ROCK, Literary Arts Journal**, Proof Rock Press, Box 607, Halifax VA 24558. Editor: Don R. Conner. A semiannual magazine of poetry and short stories. 95% freelance written; 75% of material published is poetry. Estab. 1983. Circ. 400. Pays on publication. Byline given. Acquires one-time rights. Publishes ms an average of 3 months after acceptance. Submit seasonal/holiday material 3 months in advance. Simultaneous, photocopied, and previously published submissions OK. Computer printout submissions acceptable. SASE. Reports in 1 week on queries; 3 months on mss. Sample copy $2.50; writer's guidelines for SAE and 1 first class stamp.
Nonfiction: Interview/profile of writers. Query or send complete ms. Length: 2,500 words maximum. Pays in copies.
Fiction: Adventure, erotica, experimental, fantasy, humorous, mainstream, romance and suspense. Accepts 3-6 mss/year. Send complete ms. Length: 2,500 words maximum. Pays in copies.
Poetry: Avant-garde, free verse, haiku, light verse and traditional. Accepts 200 poems/year. Submit maximum 6 poems. Poetry submissions should be single-spaced within stanzas, double-spaced between stanzas. Length: 2-32 lines. Pays in copies.
Tips: "No subject is considered taboo if treated in a civilized manner. The most annoying aspect of working with freelance writers is their failure to understand the myriad of differences between the small press and the commercial press."

‡**PROPHETIC VOICES, An International Literary Journal**, Heritage Trails Press, 94 Santa Maria Dr., Novato CA 94947. (415)897-5679. Editors: Ruth Wildes Schuler, Goldie L. Morales and Jeanne Leigh Schuler. A biannual poetry magazine. 90% freelance written; 90% of material published is poetry. Circ. 200. Byline given. Acquires one-time rights. Photocopied and previously published submissions OK. SASE. Reports in 1 month. Sample copy $3.50.
Nonfiction: "We are interested in some short essays on the poet philosopher." Send complete ms. Pays in copy.
Poetry: Mainly free verse, also avant-garde, haiku, light verse and traditional. "No portrait types of poems that just paint a picture but do not say anything of substance. We are interested in work that deals with the important issues in our society. Social and enivronmental issues are increasing in importance." Accepts 180 poems/year. Submit maximum 5 poems. Poetry submissions should be single-spaced within stanzas, double-spaced between stanzas. Length: open "but shorter poems have a better chance due to the shortage of space." Pays in copy.
Tips: "We see the poet in the role of philosopher and lean toward poems of social commentary, although any good poem has a chance here. We especially want to encourage foreign writers to submit. There are so few outlets that magazines quickly become overstocked, and writers should be patient when it takes a long period of time to be published after acceptance."

PUB, Ansuda Publications, Box 158-J, Harris IA 51345. Editor: Daniel Betz. Magazine of poetry and fiction allowing writers to express their gut feelings and concerns. 100% freelance written; 30% of material published is poetry. Circ. 300. Buys 20-30 unsolicited mss/year. Pays in copies. Publishes ms an average of 9 months. Acquires first North American serial rights. Simultaneous, photocopied and previously published submissions OK if so indicated. Computer printout submissions acceptable. SASE. Reports in 1 day on queries; 2 months on mss. Sample copy $1.50; free writer's guidelines with SASE.
Poetry: Free verse, traditional and blank verse. "No haiku and senseless rhyming." Submit maximum 6 poems. Poetry submissions should be single-spaced within stanzas, double-spaced between stanzas. Pays in copies.
Tips: "We are especially interested in new writers and other writers who cannot get published anywhere else. Let us know about you; you may have what we want. The poets are the ones we have trouble with. We would like to have more poetry in each issue, but many poetry submissions are just 'beautiful words' that leave no image in our minds; we'd like more concrete poetry."

PUDDING, In cooperation with Ohio Poetry Therapy Center and Library, 2384 Hardesty Drive South, Columbus OH 43204. (614)279-4188. Editor: Jennifer Groce Welch. Magazine of poetry and the creative arts in therapy, self-help and the human services. Published 3 times/year. 99% freelance written; 80% of material published is poetry. Subscribers are poets, psychologists, psychiatrists, nurses, doctors, mental health professionals, teachers, members of the clergy and those interested in self-help. Poetry of high quality (or, for a special section of the magazine, interesting/revealing writing by students/patients/clients/inmates). Articles on poetry and creative writing as discovery and therapy and poems that could evoke strong response for the reader are solicited. Also sponsors three annual poetry competitions. Authors are paid one copy/piece accepted and the Featured Poet is paid $10 plus 4 author copies. Circ. 2,000. Pays on publication. Byline given. Buys one-time rights or first rights. Publishes ms an average of 1 year after acceptance. Submit seasonal/holiday material 1 year in advance. Photocopied and previously published submissions OK if properly credited. Electronic submissions OK (video VHS and audio cassette chapbooks); requires hard copy also. Computer printout submissions acceptable; prefers letter-quality to dot-matrix. SASE. Reports in 2 weeks on queries; 3 weeks on mss. Sample copy $3.50; writer's guidelines for business-size SAE and 1 first class stamp.
Nonfiction: Book excerpts; general interest; how-to (conduct/facilitate creative writing groups); inspirational; interview/profile; opinion; personal experience; technical; creative writing/the writing process, etc. Looking for poetry about intense human situations, e.g., disasters, employment, hunger, parenting, counseling or being counseled, teaching, topical issues, mental and physical illness, specific problems or/and solutions; and poems by professionals and their clients from the human services. Appreciates query with letter indicating "your thought on poetry as therapy, your own poems, and/or your experience with poetry as a discovery tool." Buys up to 30 unsolicited mss/year. Send complete ms. Length: 100-2,000 words.
Photos: Need photos (5x7 screened b&w) that "evoke a poetic response."
Poetry: Avant-garde, free verse, light verse and freewriting. No sentimental, religious or trite themes. Buys 200 mss/year. Submit maximum 25 poems. Pays in copies.
Fillers: Anecdotes, short humor and newsbreaks. Buys a varying number/year. Length: 200 words maximum.

REBIRTH OF ARTEMIS, Astra Publications, 24 Edgewood Terrace, Methuen MA 01844. (617)686-5381. Editor: Lorraine Moreau-Laverriere. Annual poetry magazine for women by women. Circ. 500. Pays in contributor copy. Byline given. Rights revert to author on publication. Simultaneous, photocopied and previously published submissions OK. SASE. Reports in 3 weeks. Sample copy for $1 postage or five 20¢ stamps; writer's guidelines for SASE.
Poetry: Avant-garde, free verse and haiku. No rhymed poetry. Submit maximum 6 poems/year. Length: 3 lines-2 pages. Pays in contributor copy.

REVISTA/REVIEW INTERAMERICANA, Inter American University Press, GPO Box 3255, San Juan, Puerto Rico 00936. (809)754-8415/754-8370. Publication of the Inter American University of Puerto Rico. Editor: Gerard P. Marin. A bilingual scholarly journal oriented to Puerto Rican, Caribbean and Hispanic subjects. Poetry, short stories and reviews. Literary, contemporary, ethnic (Puerto Rican, Hispanic, Caribbean) translations, scholarly and experimental mss in either English or Spanish. Quarterly. Circ. 2,000. Acquires all rights, "but will pay 50% of money received if reprinted or quoted." Byline given. Uses about 75 mss/year. Payment in reprints (15) mailed to author. Query or submit complete ms (typed, double-spaced, clear copies) and brief bio with SASE. No simultaneous submissions. Submit seasonal material at least 6 months in advance. Reports in 6 months.
Nonfiction: "Articles on the level of educated laymen, bilingual. Book reviews. Preference to Puerto Rican, Caribbean and Latin American themes from multidisciplinary approach." Length: maximum 10,000 words.
Photos: B&w glossy prints, 4x5 minimum. Captions required. No color.
Fiction and Poetry: Bilingual; Spanish or English. Blank verse, free verse, experimental, traditional and avant-garde forms of poetry.

‡RHODE ISLAND REVIEW QUARTERLY, Rhode Island Review, Inc., Box 3028, Wayland Square, Providence RI 02906. (401)331-1034. Editor: Roy Collins. Managing Editor: James Anderson. Anthology magazine of literature and the arts; an "artistic, avant garde journal that promotes progressive writing and thought." 100% freelance written; 25% of material published is poetry. Circ. 1,000. Byline given. Acquires one-time rights. Publishes ms an average of 1 month after acceptance. Simultaneous queries, and simultaneous and photocopied submissions OK. Computer printout submissions acceptable; no dot-matrix. SASE. Reports in 2 weeks on queries; 2 months on mss. Sample copy for $1.75, SAE and 37¢ postage; writer's guidelines for SAE and 37¢ postage.
Nonfiction: Fred Fullerton, books editor. Book excerpts (no longer than 6 months on trade market); interview (artists and writers of international acclaim, question and answer format); and photo feature (submit 2-6 b&w 5x7's). "The interview format (i.e., questions and answers) is now reaching the level of highly readable literature." Query with clips of analytical work. Length: interviews, 300-1,250 words (1d½-5 pages); book excerpts, 1½-2½ pages. Pays in copies.
Photos: Bob Eggleton, photo/art director. Reviews 5x7 prints for "Portfolio" section and covers only. Captions and model release required. Pays in copies.

Fiction: Joel Hanan, fiction editor. Adventure, erotica, experimental, fantasy, humorous, science fiction and avante garde prose. No romance, historical, religious, self confessional stories; no hard-core pornography. Accepts about 20 mss/year. Query with clips of published work. Length: 250-2,500 words. Pays in copies.
Poetry: Bob Oberg, poetry editor. Avant-garde, free verse, American-flavored haiku, light verse and traditional. Especially wants free verse, progressive style. No self-confessional narratives; no "lovey-dovey" or blatant sex themes. Accepts 30 poems/year. Submit maximum 6 poems. Poetry submissions should be double-spaced. Length: 5-40 lines. Pays in copies.
Tips: New England-relevant articles are given priority in most cases, as well as New England writers. A short biography must accompany manuscript."

THE ROSE'S HOPE, 394 Lakeside Rd., Ardmore PA 19003. Editor: Peter Langman. Semiannual. Pays in copies. Authors retain all rights. Simultaneous, photocopied and previously published submissions OK. SASE. "Due to the volume of material received, no responses are given or manuscripts returned. If accepted, you'll know when you receive your free copy."
Poetry: "We are looking for poetry with the eloquence, poignance and originality of Harper and Spectre."

RUNESTONE, Asatru Free Assembly, Box 1832, Grass Valley CA 95945. Editor: Stephen A. McNallen. Quarterly newsletter about the religion and culture of pre-Christian Scandinavia and the Germanic lands generally, for people who follow the religion of the Vikings and related peoples, or are interested in neopaganism. 15% freelance written; 50% of material published is poetry. Circ. 400. Pays on publication. Publishes ms an average of 3 months after acceptance. Acquires all rights. Submit seasonal material 3 months in advance. Photocopied and previously published submissions OK. Computer printout submissions acceptable. SASE. Reports in 2 weeks. Sample copy $1.
Poetry: Free verse and traditional. "We are especially interested in skaldic poetry in the Old Norse style. Nothing too esoteric; nothing on general psychic/occult/metaphysical subjects." Buys 3 mss/year. Submit maximum 5 poems. Poetry submissions should be single-spaced within stanzas, double-spaced between stanzas. Length: 10-20 lines. Pays in copies.
Tips: "More emphasis on 'how-to-live' matters. Study a sample copy carefully to gain an understanding of our rather unorthodox views."

SALT LICK PRESS, 1804 E. 38½ St., Austin TX 78722. Editor-in-Chief: James Haining. Emphasizes literature. Magazine published irregularly; 68 pages. 50% freelance written; 80% of material published is poetry. Circ. 1,500. Pays in copies. Photocopied and previously published submissions OK. Computer printout submissions acceptable; prefers letter-quality to dot-matrix. SASE. Reports in 2 weeks. Sample copy $3.
Poetry: Open to all types. Poetry submissions should be single-spaced within stanzas, double-spaced between stanzas.

SAN FERNANDO POETRY JOURNAL, Kent Publications, 18301 Halsted St., Northridge CA 91325. Editor: Richard Cloke. Managing Editors: Lori C. Smith and Shirley J. Rodecker. Quarterly poetry magazine devoted to encouraging and promoting the literary arts. 100% freelance written; 100% of material published is poetry. Interested in social content and current technical and scientific advances, or regressions, in poetic form. "Interested in space age Zeitgeist: contemporary problems of peace, poverty, environment, alienation and minority rights. We focus on the outer world, seen from within, but not inwardly directed. This is a general preference; we will not reject quality poetry of any form or genre. But our crystal ball warns of trouble ahead." Prefers not to see subjectivist, surrealist, existentialist, internalist or ultratraditionalist material. Circ. 500. Pays on publication. Publishes ms an average of 1 year after acceptance. Acquires one-time rights. Photocopied and previously published submissions OK. Computer printout submissions acceptable "if legible." SASE. Reports in 3 weeks on queries; in 3 weeks on mss. Sample copy, our choice, $2.50 (20% off to libraries and poets who offer for publication); writer's guidelines for SASE.
Poetry: Social protest-free verse; and of meter, however. Buys 300 unsolicited poems/year. Submit maximum 5 poems. Poetry submissions should be single-spaced (short lines) and double-spaced (long lines). Length: 10-50 lines preferred. Will print up to 300 lines if exceptional. Pays in copies of magazine for each entry published.
Tips: "Our poetry is keyed to our space in time. No bias against meter and rhyme, if not forced or intrusive. To us, the 'me' generation is passe. The 'we' generation is emerging. We are now a tax exempt public corporation—welcome more diversity than before."

‡**SANCTUM QUARTERLY, "For the Poetic Mind,"** Sanctum Press, Box 29752, Richmond VA 23229. (804)740-7861. Editor: Forest Blake. Quarterly magazine. "We are the magazine of the short lyric. We eschew symbolism and present the clear, easily read, and memorable. We believe our readers are interested in reading the Emily Dickenson or Yvor Winters of today." Estab. 1984. Circ. 400. Pays on acceptance. Byline given. Buys all rights. Submit seasonal/holiday material 3 months in advance. Photocopied submissions OK. SASE. Reports in 2 weeks on queries; 1 month on mss. Sample copy $1.95; writer's guidelines for business-size SAE and 1 first class stamp.

Nonfiction: Dagny Taggart, articles editor. Technical. "We want to see only articles about the pleasures and techniques of writing poetry, slanted toward the short lyric." Buys 4 mss/year. Query. Length: 250-1,000 words. Pays 2.5¢/word.

Poetry: Dagny Taggart, poetry editor. Haiku, light verse, traditional. "We are not interested in poems that are merely cute. Poetry should express a timeless interest." Buys 30-40 poems/year. Submit maximum poems. Length: 3-50 lines; 3-20 lines preferred. Pays $1/line.

Tips: "Buy a sample copy of our magazine! That puts you on our mailing list and shows you are ready to deliver our quality of poetry. We check your submissions that way. Contributors usually subscribe for inspiration, as our quality and standard are very high. We publish three categories: Poetic Features, Light Verse Page, and Envoie. A feature should stand on its own merit; Light Verse should be light but not jokey; Envoie should have an epiphany. We feature monometer, dimeter, trimeter, tetrameter verse with pentameter of very high quality a sideline. Of these, tetrameter is the hardest, and you should submit tetrameter only after ironing out the 'sing-song.' "

SCRIVENER, A Semiannual Literary Magazine, McGill University, 853 Sherbrooke St. W., Montreal, Quebec H3A 2T6 Canada. (514)392-4483. Editor: Jill Palmer. Semiannual literary journal of poetry, fiction and book reviews. 70% freelance written; 50% of material published is poetry. Published in December and April. Accepts ms preferably September to March 1. Circ. 1,250. Pays on publication. Byline given. Writers retain copyrights of their work. Photocopied submissions OK. Computer printout submissions acceptable. Send short biographical sketch. SASE with Canadian postage or IRC. Reports in 2 months. Sample copy $2.

Columns/Departments: Book reviews of Canadian books only. "We accept recent Canadian fiction reviews only." Buys 20 mss/year. Send complete ms. Length: 500-1,000 words. Pays in 2 copies.

Fiction: Experimental. Any serious literary fiction whether the style be traditional or experimental. No forms of mainstream entertainment, such as romance, westerns, etc. Buys 15-20 mss/year. Send complete ms. Length: 500-6,000 words. Pays in 2 copies.

Poetry: Avant-garde, free verse, haiku and traditional. Open to all styles of well-written poetry. Buys 50 mss/year. Submit maximum 10 poems. Poetry submissions should be single-spaced within stanzas, double-spaced between stanzas. Length: 1-100 lines. Pays in 2 copies.

Tips: "Our only criterion for judgment is the literary and artistic quality of the piece. We tend towards writing that is fresh and imaginative—innovative, too. We change editors every year, so style changes slightly."

SERENADE, The Sylvan Quarterly Magazine, Sylvan Press Publishers, Box 15125, Richmond VA 23227. Editor: Sylvia Manolatos. Managing Editor: Annette Hohman. Quarterly literary magazine featuring a collection of well-written poems for adults with an appreciation for craftsmanship in the poetic arts. "We prefer a tolerant, nonbiased outlook in our subject matter." Estab. 1983. Circ. 120. Pays on publication. Byline given. Buys first North American serial rights. Submit seasonal/holiday material 3 months in advance. Photocopied submissions OK. SASE. No phone calls. Reports in 1 week on queries; 1 month on mss. Sample copy for $1, 5x7 SAE and 2 first class stamps; writer's guidelines for business-size SAE and 2 first class stamps.

Nonfiction: Lelia Koplin and Daphne Manolatos, articles editors. Opinion (short poetic criticism); and poet's biographies (short articles). No long, rhetorical articles, religious articles or pedantic viewpoints. Buys 4-6 mss/year. Send complete ms. Pays in 3 copies.

Poetry: Avant-garde, free verse, haiku and traditional. No religious or overly sentimental verse or "categorical" verse (such as verse for every species of bird, flower, musical instrument, etc.). No pornographic material. Buys 100 poems/year. Submit maximum 4 poems. Length: 50 lines maximum. Pays in 3 copies.

Tips: "We prefer shorter poems of a serious nature with no style restrictions. Avoid hackneyed phrases and overworked subject matter such as children, religion and self-pitying confessions."

SEVEN, 3630 NW 22, Oklahoma City OK 73107. Editor: James Neill Northe. Published 4 numbers to a volume on an irregular basis. Pays on acceptance $5/poem. Sample copy $2. *Please* no amateur verse. Study your market. Universal approach, no cataloging, but definite expression in finely written lines. Not impressed by the 'chopped prose' school or 'stream of consciousness' effusions.

‡SIDEWINDER, College of the Mainland, 8001 Palmer Highway, Texas City TX 77591. (409)938-1211. Editor: Thomas Poole. A biannual literary magazine. 100% freelance written; 50% of material published is poetry. Estab. 1983. Byline given. Acquires first North American serial rights. Publishes ms an average of 3 months after acceptance. Simultaneous queries, and simultaneous and photocopied submissions OK. Computer printout submissions acceptable; prefers letter-quality to dot-matrix. SASE. Reports in 2 months. Sample copy $3.

Fiction: Tom Carter, fiction editor. Experimental, nongenre (literary) short fiction. Accepts 8-10 mss/year. Send complete ms. Pays in copies.

Poetry: Brett Jarrett, poetry editor. Avant-garde and free verse. Accepts 50-70 poems/year. Poetry submissions should be single-spaced within stanzas, double-spaced between stanzas. Pays in copies.

Tips: "Quality is the ultimate standard. Any style or subject matter is acceptable as long as the writer demonstrates exceptional skill with his chosen form. Some preference is given to more daring, risky approaches if they are successful. The search for fresh approaches is constant. Considering the massive numbers of submissions received yearly, there is a discouraging sameness."

THE SMALL POND MAGAZINE OF LITERATURE, Box 664, Stratford CT 06497. (203)378-4066. Editor: Napoleon St. Cyr. For "some high school students, the rest college and college grad students who read us in college libraries, or, in general, the literati." 95% freelance written; 80% of material published is poetry. Published 3 times a year. 40 pages. Circ. 300. Acquires all rights. Payment in contributor copies. Will consider photocopied submissions. No simultaneous submissions. Computer printout submissions acceptable. Reports in 10-30 days. SASE. Sample copy $2.50.
Nonfiction and Fiction: All subjects except the Vietnam War, women's lib or science fiction. Fiction, articles, essays. 2,500 word maximum.
Poetry: Traditional and avant-garde forms of poetry, blank, free and light verse. Length: 100 lines maximum.

SOUTH DAKOTA REVIEW, Box 111, University Exchange, Vermillion SD 57069. (605)677-5229. Editor: John R. Milton. For a university audience and the college educated, although reaches others as well. Quarterly. Acquires North American serial rights and reprint rights. Byline given. Pays in contributor copies. Reports in 1 month or less, except in summer. SASE.
Nonfiction: Literary criticism, with first choice going to studies of Western American literature. Occasionally uses articles on aspects of American culture or history.
Fiction: Literary, serious, very well written. Not interested in stories about sports, hunting, fishing or juvenile characters "unless very well done and original in treatment." Prefers third person stories about adults.
Poetry: Prefers poetry which is disciplined and controlled, though open to any form (tends to prefer traditional free verse). Any length considered, but prefers 10-30 lines.
Tips: "Although most of our material is unsolicited, it generally comes from writers who like to write, or from college and university professors, not from people who try to make a living from writing. Therefore, in the technical sense, we do not cater to freelancers as such. We often find thematic numbers of the journal taking shape and will then select material supporting the general theme. We thrive on flexibility, which may cause some consternation among writers who expect a journal to publish the same kinds of material all the time."

SOU'WESTER, Department of English, Southern Illinois University, Edwardsville IL 62026. Editor: Dickie Spurgeon. "We publish fiction and poetry." Magazine published 3 times/year. 100% freelance written; 30% of material published is poetry. Circ. 300. Acquires all rights. Uses about 70 mss/year. Payment in contributor copies. Publishes ms an average of 4 months after acceptance. Will consider simultaneous and photocopied submissions. Reports in 4 to 6 weeks. Submit complete ms. Computer printout submissions acceptable; prefers letter-quality to dot-matrix. SASE. Sample copy $1.50.
Poetry: Traditional and avant-garde forms of poetry. Poetry submissions should be single-spaced within stanzas, double-spaced between stanzas. Length: no maximum.
Fiction: Up to 10,000 words.

SPARROW POVERTY PAMPHLETS, Sparrow Press, 103 Waldron St., West Lafayette, IN 47906. Editor-in-Chief: Felix Stefanile. Triannual magazine; 32 pages, one poet an issue. 100% freelance written; 100% of material published is poetry. Circ. 910. Pays on publication. Buys first North American serial rights. "We share anthology rights. Some previously published submissions OK, but major portion of manuscript should be first-time original." Computer printout submissions acceptable; no dot-matrix. SASE. "We read only in April and May of each year. Do not send at other times." Publishes ms an average of 8 months after acceptance. Reports in 6 weeks. Sample copy $2.
Poetry: "No form bias. Mature, serious work in the modern manner. Poetry must be human and relevant. Only interested in manuscripts typescript of from 20-32 pages." Poetry submissions should be single-spaced within stanzas, double-spaced between stanzas. Buys 20-30 poems/issue, each issue devoted to one poet. Pays $25 plus royalties; 20% after cost.
Tips: "We are read by poets of standing. We emphasize the modernist tradition of clarity, intellectual vigor and experiment with language. We are not faddist, not ideological, not NEA-funded. We are simply not a market for novices. Our authors are now in all anthologies—Untermeyer, Norton, Meridian, etc. The would-be contributor should get to know our taste and study past issues. Only 5% of people who send bother to buy and inspect issues. This, we understand, is a better record than for most poetry journals. Poets don't seem to study markets, as prose writers learn to do."

STAR*LINE, Newsletter of the Science Fiction Poetry Association, Box 491, Nantucket MA 02554. Editor: Robert Frazier. Managing Editor: Karen Jollie. Bimonthly newsletter covering science fiction, fantasy and horror poetry for association members. 80% freelance written; 75% of material published is poetry. Circ. 200. Pays on acceptance. Publishes ms an average of 3 months after acceptance. Byline given. Buys one-time rights. Submit seasonal/holiday material 3 months in advance. Simultaneous and photocopied submissions

OK. Computer printout submissions acceptable. SASE. Reports in 6 weeks. Sample copy $1; writer's guidelines for business-size SAE and 1 first class stamp.

Nonfiction: How-to (write a poem); interview/profile (of science fiction, fantasy and horror poets); and opinion (science fiction and poetics). "Articles must display familiarity with the genre." Buys 4-6 mss/year. Send complete ms. Length: 500-2,000 words. Pays $1-5/printed page and 2 complimentary copies.

Columns/Departments: Reviews (of books, chapbooks, collections of science fiction, fantasy or horror poetry); and Markets (current markets for science fiction, fantasy or horror poetry). Buys 40-60 mss/year. Send complete ms. Length: 200-500 words/reviews; 20-100 words/markets. Pays $.50-2.

Poetry: Avant-garde, free verse, haiku, light verse and traditional. "Must be related to speculative fiction subjects." Buys 60-80/year. Submit maximum 3 poems. Poetry submissions should be double-spaced. Length: 1-100 lines. Pays $1-10 and 2 complimentary copies.

Fillers: Speculative-oriented quotations, prose or poetic. Length: 10-50 words. Pays in copy.

Tips: "Send us good speculative poetry. Our latitude is very broad here. Serious free verse is most often accepted, but all other forms have appeared and still do. New writers are always needed. We also accept black-and-white illustrations, spot and cover, which are sharp, reproducible and speculative (science fiction/fantasy/horror) in nature." Query with SASE for specifics to Karen Jollie, 8350 Poole Ave., Sun Valley CA 91352.

STONE COUNTRY, Box 132, Menemsha MA 02552. (617)693-5832. Editor: Judith Neeld. Magazine published 2 times/year. 90% freelance written; 100% of material published is poetry. Acquires first North American serial rights. Byline given. Accepts 100-150 poems/year. Payment in contributor copy plus Phillips Award ($25) for best poem published in each issue. $15 for reviews and essays. Publishes ms an average of 6 months after acceptance. Reports in 2 months. Submit complete ms. "SASE, required, or we will destroy ms." Sample copy $3.50.

Poetry and Reviews: Robert Blake, reviews editor. Truscott. "We publish poetry, poetry criticism and commentaries. No thematic or stylistic limitations, but we are unable to publish long narrative poems in full. We look for the immediacy of language; concrete, uncommon imagery; the undisclosed; poetry as exploration, not statement." Free verse, traditional forms, blank verse and avant-garde forms. Uses 100+ unsolicited poems/year. Length: 40 lines maximum. Limit submissions to 5 poems at a time. Poetry submissions should be single-spaced.

Tips: "If you are just beginning to write poetry, do not submit to us. Read the magazine carefully before submitting; it is our only accurate guideline."

TAR RIVER POETRY, East Carolina University, Department of English, Greenville NC 27834. Editor: Peter Makuck. Biannual magazine "with mix of established poets and newcomers. Quality poetry, paper, layout, drawings and in-depth reviews." 52 pages. Circ. 1,000. Pays in contributor copies. No fee. SASE. Reports in 6-8 weeks. Sample copy $2.50.

Poetry: Free verse and fixed forms. "We do not want sentimental or flat statement poetry. We look for skillful use of figurative language." Uses 40 poems/issue. Submit in batches of 6. Length: 50 lines maximum. "We do not read manuscripts during May-August."

TAURUS, Box 28, Gladstone OR 97027. Editor: Bruce Combs. Quarterly magazine. Circ. 400. Pays on publication. Byline given. Acquires one-time and first North American serial rights. "Clear" photocopied submissions OK. Computer printout submissions acceptable if legible; prefers letter-quality to dot-matrix. SASE. Reports in 1 week. Sample copy $2.

Poetry: Avant-garde and free verse. "Fresh, earnest, virile use of language is more important than the topic." No conservative, rhymed, religious or sewing-circle poetry." Buys 200/year. Length: open; "but the shorter, the better." Pays 1 copy/poem page.

13TH MOON, Box 309, Cathedral Station, New York, NY 10025. Editor-in-Chief: Marilyn Hacker. A feminist literary magazine. Emphasizes quality work by women for a well-read audience. Semiannual magazine. 100% freelance written; 50% of material published is poetry. Pays in copies. Publishes ms an average of 1 year after acceptance. Acquires first North American serial rights. SASE. Reports in 2 months. Sample copy $5.95 plus 75¢ postage and handling. Reading a sample copy before submitting ms is strongly recommended.

Nonfiction: Book reviews of women authors, particularly of poetry and of books by Third World women.

Fiction: No predictable "slick" fiction, mawkish or sentimental writing, or themes based on "automatic" feminist responses. Does not accept handwritten mss or work submitted by men. "We would like more submissions from women of color."

Poetry: Open to all styles. Prefers poetry written by women who *read* contemporary poetry. Poetry submissions should be double-spaced with extra space between stanzas.

Tips: "Independent literary magazines cannot continue to exist unless those people so eager to send their manuscripts and be read and criticized, if not published, by editors, are equally eager to purchase, subscribe to and read such periodicals."

TIGHTROPE, Swamp Press, 323 Pelham Rd., Amherst MA 01002.(413)253-2270. Editors: Ed Rayher, Steve Ruhl, Gillian Conolcy, Domenic Stansberry and Francis Driscoll. Magazine published 2 times/year for readers interested in poetry and short fiction. 90% freelance written; 60% of material published is poetry. Circ. 250. Pays on publication. Publishes ms an average of 6 months after acceptance. Buys one-time rights. Phone queries OK. Photocopied submissions OK. Computer printout submissions acceptable. SASE. Reports in 6 weeks on queries; in 8 weeks on mss. Sample copy $3.
Nonfiction: Historical (poetry and writing in fiction); interview (with creative writers and artists); and opinion (reviews of poetry). Send complete ms. Pays $5/page.
Photos: Send photos with ms. Pays $5 minimum for b&w prints.
Columns/Departments: Reviews (of poetry books and prose-poetry). Send complete ms. Pays $5/page.
Fiction: Experimental, historical and mainstream. Query. Pays negotiable rate.
Poetry: Avant-garde, free verse, haiku, traditional and imagist. "No prolix abstractivism." Poetry submissions should be single-spaced within stanzas, double-spaced between stanzas. Buys 20 mss/issue. Pays $5/page.
Tips: "We take the liberty of writing comments upon any material submitted (except art work), unless otherwise instructed. No religious material."

TOUCHSTONE, New Age Journal, Houston Writer's Guild, Box 42331, Houston TX 77042. Fiction Editor: Frances Wegner. Poetry Editor: William Laufer. Quarterly literary magazine "for a liberal, well-educated, eclectic audience." 95% freelance written; 50% of material published is poetry. Circ. 1,000. Pays on publication. Byline given. Buys first rights. No simultaneous submissions. Photocopied submissions OK. Computer printout submissions acceptable; no dot-matrix. SASE. Reports in 2 weeks on queries; 6 weeks on mss. "We try to publish manuscripts within 6 months depending upon backlog." Sample copy for $1.95, 6x9 SAE, and 2 first class stamps.
Poetry: Free verse, haiku and traditional. "We seek clarity and skill, the experimental and the imaginative." Prefers not to get "the inspirational, saccharine or the sentimental." Buys 80/year. Submit maximum 12 poems. Poetry submissions should be single-spaced within stanzas, double-spaced between stanzas. Length: up to 50 lines. Pays in copies.
Tips: "We are actively seeking short essays, quality fiction and poetry. Minority viewpoints and translations are welcome. We will work with our writers, and we offer a free critique to new subscribers who are seeking help."

UP AGAINST THE WALL, MOTHER . . . , 6009 Edgewood Ln., Alexandria VA 22310. (703)971-2219. Editor: Lee-lee Schlegel. Art Director: Sibyl Lowen. Quarterly poetry magazine covering "women's thoughts and feelings, especially during crisis." 100% freelance written; 100% of material published is poetry. Circ. 250. Buys 400 unsolicited mss/year. Publishes ms an average of 6 months after acceptance. Byline given. Acquires one-time rights. Previously published submissions OK. Computer printout submissions acceptable. SASE. Reports in 1 week. Sample copy $3.
Poetry: Avant-garde, free verse, haiku and traditional. Submit maximum 1-10 poems. Length: 30 lines. Pay: "none yet." All submissions must be poetry that deals with women in crisis.

THE VILLAGER, 135 Midland Ave., Bronxville NY 10708. (914)337-3252. Editor: Amy Murphy. Publication of the Bronxville Women's Club. For club members and families; professional people and advertisers. Monthly, October through June. Circ. 750. Acquires all rights. Pays in copies only. Submit seasonal material (Thanksgiving, Christmas, Easter) 3 months in advance. Submit only complete ms. Reports in 2 weeks. SASE. "We will accept mss from US *only*; no foreign mail." Sample copy $1.
Poetry: Traditional forms of poetry, blank verse, free verse, avant-garde forms and light verse. Length: 20 lines.

VISIONS, The International Magazine of Illustrated Poetry, Black Buzzard Press, 4705 S. 8th Rd., Arlington VA 22204. (703)521-0142. Editor: Bradley R. Strahan. Associate Editor: Shirley G. Sullivan. Art Editor: Ursula Gill. Review Editor: Harold Black. Magazine published 3 times/year covering poetry, helpful information on "how to get published," the art and craft of poetry and reviews of poetry. 90% freelance written; 85% of material published is poetry. "Send us only your best. We showcase strong, open, imagistic poetry; vibrant work that draws the reader in, work that can be enjoyed by all people. We don't care if you're a 'big name' but poetry must be well crafted." Circ. 550. Pays on publication. Publishes ms an average of 8 months after acceptance. Byline given. Buys one-time rights. Submit seasonal/holiday material 3 months in advance. Photocopied submissions OK. Computer printout submissions acceptable. SASE required. Reports in 3 weeks. Latest issue $3. Sample copy $2; writer's guidelines available with the purchase of an issue of magazine only.
Poetry: Avant-garde, free verse and traditional. "There will be an issue featuring poems on American images a la Sandburg, Whitman and James Wright, early in 1985." No "God's in His Heaven and all's right with the world" poems. Nothing dry or obscure. No children's type poetry. Buys 9/year. Submit 3-9 poems. Poetry

submissions should be single-spaced within stanzas, double-spaced between stanzas, "but not important which way it's done." Length: 2-200 lines. Pays in copies or $5 maximum. "Cash payment *only* when we have a grant."

Tips: "We are striving to publish even a higher quality of poetry than previously. Trends in magazine publishing that freelance writers should be aware of include the decrease in places to get poetry published, due to over-commercialization and the failure of poets to support noncommercial presses."

VOICES INTERNATIONAL, 1115 Gillette Dr., Little Rock AR 72207. Editor-in-Chief: Clovita Rice. Quarterly magazine; 32-40 pages. 100% freelance written; 100% of material published is poetry except for reviews of books. Pays in copies on publication. Publishes ms an average of 18 months after acceptance. Acquires all rights. Submit seasonal/holiday material 1 year in advance. Computer printout submissions acceptable; prefers letter-quality to dot-matrix. SASE. Reports in 3 weeks. Sample copy $2.

Poetry: Free verse. Uses 200-300 unsolicited poems/year. Limit submissions to batches of 5. Poetry submissions should be double-spaced. Length: 3-40 lines. Will consider longer ones if good.

Tips: "We accept poetry with a new approach, haunting word pictures and significant ideas. Language should be used like watercolors to achieve depth, to highlight one focal point, to be pleasing to the viewer, and to be transparent, leaving space for the reader to project his own view. Our own trend is toward shorter poems—30 lines or less. Space is vital to us and it's harder to sustain interest and impact in a longer poem."

‡VOL. NO. MAGAZINE, Los Angeles Poets Press, 24721 Newhall Ave., Newhall CA 91321. (805)254-0851. Editors: Luis Campos, Richard Weekley, Jerry Davidson and Tina Megali. Quarterly literary/visual magazine of contemporary poetry for "open minded, literary, alert audience." Estab. 1983. Circ. 300. 100% freelance written; 100% of material published is poetry. Pays on publication. Byline given. Not copyrighted. Buys one-time rights. Simultaneous queries and simultaneous and photocopied submissions OK. Computer printout submissions acceptable. SASE. Reports in 3 months. Sample copy $2; writer's guidelines $2.

Poetry: Each issue of the magazine is subtitled. Future themes include fuerza de la stanza and cause and effect. Avant-garde, free verse, haiku, light verse and traditional. "No sentimental, loose, unimaginative work." Buys 80 poems/year. Submit maximum 6 poems. Poetry submissions should be single-spaced within stanzas, double-spaced between stanzas. Length: 1-70 lines. Pays in 2 copies.

Tips: "Query for theme specifics. Submit fresh and concise works on the theme. We're seeking progressive and adventuresome poets who connect with reality. Black and white visuals are desired in addition to poetry."

WAVES, 79 Denham Dr., Thornhill, Ontario L4J 1P2 Canada. (416)889-6703. Editor: Bernice Lever. For university and high school English teachers and readers of literary magazines. "Our main focus is publishing poetry and fiction from writers worldwide." Magazine published 3 times/year. 90% freelance written; 35% of material published is poetry. Circ. 1,000 plus. Acquires first North American serial rights. Publishes ms an average of 4 months after acceptance. Byline given. Pays $5/page. Photocopied submissions OK. Computer printout submissions acceptable "if clear"; prefers letter-quality to dot-matrix. No simultaneous submissions. Reports in 3-6 weeks. Submit complete ms. SAE and IRCs. Sample copy $1 cash or $2 check.

Poetry: Formal and free verse. Poetry submissions should be single-spaced within stanzas, double-spaced between stanzas. Length: 5-150 lines.

Tips: "Read a few back issues to see the level of language—intelligent without academic dryness—in reviews. Reviews Canadian authors only. In poetry, we look for subtle control of technique, with emotion and thought input. *Waves* aims to print manuscripts of the quality one reads in *The Atlantic* or *Paris Review*."

WEBSTER REVIEW, Webster University, Webster Groves MO 63119. (314)432-2657. Editor: Nancy Schapiro. For "academics, students, all persons interested in contemporary international literature." Semiannual magazine. 100% freelance written; 60% of material published is poetry. Circ. 1,000. Byline given. Uses 200 mss/year. Pays in copies. Photocopied and simultaneous submissions OK. Computer printout submissions acceptable; no dot-matrix. Reports in 1 month. SASE. Free sample copy.

Fiction and Poetry: Stories, poems, excerpts from novels, essays and English translations of foreign contemporary literature. "Subject matter is not important, but quality is. Our emphasis is on international as well as American contemporary quality writing." No restrictions on length. Poetry submissions should be double-spaced.

WELLSPRING, 321 O'Connor St., Menlo Park CA 94025. (415)326-7310. Editor: Tim Chown. Quarterly magazine featuring poetry written from a Christian perspective; a forum for Christian poets and artists. 100% freelance written; 100% of material published is poetry. Circ. 300. Pays on publication. Publishes ms an average of 6 months after acceptance. Acquires one-time rights. Submit seasonal material 6 months in advance. Simultaneous, photocopied and previously published submissions OK. Computer printout submissions acceptable. SASE. Reports in 2 months. Sample copy $2.50; free writer's guidelines with SASE.

Poetry: All forms and lengths. "No poetry with jokes, silly play on words, meaningless cliches, stale imagery or language, or greeting card homilies." Buys 100-125 mss/year. Submit maximum 6 poems. Poetry submis-

sions should be single-spaced within stanzas, double-spaced between stanzas. Pays in copy.
Tips: "Seek to write and to submit poetry that is powerful both in its communication to the spirit and artistic beauty. Use fresh imagery, language and sound that works on more than one level; the emotional as well as the spiritual. Send 4 to 6 poems. Learn to carefully critique your own work before submitting."

WHISKEY ISLAND MAGAZINE, University Center 7, Cleveland State University, Cleveland OH 44115. (216)687-2000. Editor: Mary Schmid. Annual literary magazine of poetry and short stories. 100% freelance written; 50% of material published is poetry. Byline given. Buys all rights and second serial (reprint) rights. Publishes ms an average of 4 months after acceptance. Simultaneous queries, and simultaneous and previously published submissions OK. SASE. Reports in 3 months. Free sample copy and writer's guidelines.
Poetry: Free verse, light verse and traditional. Length: 5-40 lines.
Fiction: 2,500 words or less.

WIND/LITERARY JOURNAL, R.F.D. 1, Box 809K, Pikeville KY 41501. (606)631-1129. Editor: Quentin R. Howard. For literary people. Triannual magazine. 100% freelance written; 65% of material published is poetry. Circ. 500. Uses 400 mss/year. Payment in contributor copies. Publishes ms an average of 1 year after acceptance. No photocopied or simultaneous submissions. Reports in 10-20 days. Submit complete ms. SASE. Sample copy $1.50.
Poetry: Blank verse, traditional and avant-garde forms of poetry, free verse and haiku.

WISCONSIN REVIEW, Box 276, Dempsey Hall, University of Wisconsin-Oshkosh, Oshkosh WI 54901. (414)424-2267. Editor: Tom Caylor. Tri-quarterly magazine; 32 pages. Circ. 2,000. Acquires first rights. Pays in contributor copies. Sample copy $1.50. Reports in 6 months. Submit complete ms. SASE.
Poetry: All forms and styles. "We are primarily interested in material that, in one way or another, attempts to elucidate, explain, discover or otherwise untangle the manifestly complex circumstances in which we find ourselves as Americans in the 1980s."
Fiction: Short stories.

THE WORMWOOD REVIEW, Box 8840, Stockton CA 95208-0840. Editor: Marvin Malone. Quarterly. 100% freelance written; 100% of material published is poetry. Circ. 700. Acquires all rights; reassigns rights to author upon request. Pays in copies or cash equivalent. Pays on publication. Publishes ms an average of 1 year after acceptance. Computer printout submissions acceptable; prefers letter-quality to dot-matrix. Reports in 2-8 weeks. SASE. Sample copy $3.
Poetry: Modern poetry and prose poems that communicate the temper and depth of the human scene. All styles and schools from ultra avant-garde to classical; no taboos. Especially interested in prose poems or fables. Length: 3-500 lines. Poetry submissions should be single-spaced within stanzas, double-spaced between stanzas.
Tips: "Be original. Be yourself. Have something to say. Say it as economically and effectively as possible. Don't be afraid of wit and intelligence."

WRIT MAGAZINE, 2 Sussex Ave., Toronto, Ontario M5S 1J5 Canada. Editor: Roger Greenwald. Associate Editor: Richard M. Lush. Annual literary magazine covering high quality fiction, poetry, and translations. 100% freelance written; 40% of material published is poetry. Circ. 700. Computer printout submissions acceptable; no dot-matrix. Pays in copies only. Publishes ms an average of 6 months after acceptance. SAE with IRCs or Canadian postage, brief biography, phone number.
Poetry and Fiction: Send complete typed ms or clear photocopy. Poetry submissions should be double-spaced. Translators: Enclose copy of original for our reference. See magazine for detailed instructions.

WRITERS FORUM, University of Colorado, Colorado Springs CO 80907. (303)593-3155 or (303)599-4023. Editor: Alex Blackburn. Annual book; 200 pages. Emphasizes quality fiction and poetry. For people of all ages interested in excellence in creative writing and in contemporary American literature, especially from regions west of the Mississippi. 100% freelance written; 25% of material published is poetry. Circ. 1,000. Authors retain rights. Publishes ms an average of 6 months after acceptance. Byline given. Simultaneous, photocopied, and previously published submissions OK. Computer printout submissions acceptable; prefers letter-quality to dot-matrix. "Send 2 copies of all submissions, brief biography in cover letter, and SASE." Reports in 3-6 weeks. Sample copy discounted 33% to $5.95 for *Writer's Market* readers; free writer's guidelines. SASE with request.
Fiction: Mainstream and experimental. Length: 1,000-15,000 words.
Poetry: Avant-garde, free verse and traditional, including poetic drama. Publishes 40/year. Submit in batches of 5. Poetry submissions should be double-spaced. Length: 10-2,000 words. Payment with free copy.
Tips: "We look for originality, verbal excitement, knowledge of forms, avoidance of 'commercial' themes and approaches, also acquaintance with *Writer's Forum* itself. We give special attention to work submitted on a writer's behalf by a professional writer, teacher of writers, agent or publisher."

XANADU, Box 773, Huntington NY 11743. Editors: Virginia Barmen, Mildred Jeffrey, Lois Walker, Anne-Ruth Baehr, Anibal Yaryura-Tobias and Barbara Lucas. Annual magazine; 64 pages. "For an audience interested in reading the best new poetry being written." 100% freelance writen; 100% of material published is poetry. Circ. 600. Copyright, first rights and first anthology rights. Uses about 60 poems/year. Pays in contributor copies. Publishes ms an average of 5 months after acceptance. No photocopied or simultaneous submissions. Computer printout submissions acceptable; prefers letter-quality to dot-matrix. Reports in 3 months. Submit no more than 5 poems. SASE. Sample copy $2.50.
Poetry: "Our main criteria for poetry are excellence of craft and clarity and force of vision. Only the highest quality contemporary poetry. We like to see up to 5 poems by a contributor at one time. Strongly realized poems rooted in human experience have an edge." Poetry submissions should be single-spaced within stanzas, double-spaced between stanzas.

‡**THE YELLOW BUTTERFLY**, The Yellow Butterfly Press, 835 W. Carolina St., Lebanon OR 97355. Editor: Joan M. Sherer. Quarterly magazine of poetry "primarily for poets and others in the literary world although I'm trying to reach people who think they don't like poetry. I want sad, haunting work that will be remembered, perhaps make the reader cry . . . at least make him think." 100% freelance written; 100% of material published is poetry. Estab. 1983. Circ. 250. Pays on publication. Publishes ms an average of 2 months after acceptance. Byline given. Buys one-time rights. Submit seasonal/holiday material 3 months in advance. Simultaneous queries, simultaneous, photocopied and previously published submissions OK. Computer printout submissions acceptable. SASE. Reports in 1 week. Writer's guidelines for business-size SAE and 1 first class stamp. Sample copy for $2.50.
Poetry: Avant-garde, free verse, haiku, light verse and traditional. No pornography or rhyme. Buys 600 mss/year. Poetry submissions should be single-spaced within stanzas, double-spaced between stanzas. Length: open. Pays in 1 copy.
Tips: "Poetry is reaching out—no longer limited to the very literary minded."

YELLOW SILK, Journal of Erotic Arts, verygraphics, Box 6374, Albany CA 94706. Editor: Lily Pond. Alternative, nonpornographic quarterly of written and visual erotica. "All persuasions; no brutality." 90% freelance written; 40% of material published is poetry. Circ. 5,000. Pays in copies on publication. Publishes ms an average of 6 months after acceptance. Byline given. Buys one-year rights plus possible inclusion in any anthology. Submit seasonal/holiday material 6 months in advance. Simultaneous queries and photocopied submissions OK. Computer printout submissions acceptable; prefers letter-quality to dot-matrix. SASE. Reports in 6 weeks on queries/mss. Sample copy $3.
Poetry: Avant-garde, free verse, haiku and traditional. Fiction and essays also considered. Buys 100/year (including foreign language poems with translation). Poetry submissions should be single-spaced within stanzas, double-spaced between stanzas. Length and number of submissions open.
Tips: Entirely freelance-written. Needs more fiction. Featured in past: W.S. Merwin, Ntozake Shange, Susan Griffin and Robert Silverberg. "Writing strength is the final consideration, along with appropriateness of material. Passion, subtlety, humor and beauty are the voices of the erotic. No 'blow-by-blow' descriptions; no salacious fantasies; nothing involving brutality in any form."

Politics and World Affairs

These publications cover politics for the general reader interested in current events. Other categories in *Writer's Market* include publications that will consider articles about politics and world affairs. Some of these categories are Business and Finance, Regional and General Interest. For listings of publications geared toward the professional, see Trade Journals/Government and Public Service *and* Trade Journals/International Affairs.

AFRICA REPORT, 833 United Nations Plaza, New York NY 10017. (212)949-5731. Editor: Margaret A. Novicki. 60% freelance written. For US citizens, residents with a special interest in African affairs for professional, business, academic or personal reasons. Not tourist-related. Bimonthly. Circ. 10,500. Rights purchased vary with author and material. Usually buys all rights. Negotiable kill fee. Byline given unless otherwise requested. Buys 15 unsolicited mss/year. Pays on publication. Publishes ms an average of 2 months after acceptance. Sample copy for $4; free editorial guidelines sheet. SASE.
Nonfiction: Interested in mss on "African political, economic and cultural affairs, especially in relation to US

foreign policy and business objectives. Style should be journalistic but not academic or light. Articles should not be polemical or long on rhetoric but may be committed to a strong viewpoint. I do not want tourism articles." Would like to see in-depth topical analyses of lesser known African countries, based on residence or several months' stay in the country. Pays $150-250 for nonfiction.

Photos: Photos purchased with or without accompanying mss with extra payment. B&w only. Pays $25. Submit 12x8 "half-plate."

Tips: "Read *Africa Report* and other international journals regularly. Become an expert on an African or Africa-related topic. Make sure your submissions fit the style, length, and level of *Africa Report*."

AMERICAN OPINION MAGAZINE, Belmont MA 02178. Managing Editor: Scott Stanley Jr. "A conservative, anti-communist journal of political affairs." Monthly except August. Circ. 35,000. Buys all rights. Kill fee varies. Byline given. Pays on publication. Sample copy $2. SASE.

Nonfiction: Articles on matters of political affairs of a conservative, anti-communist nature. "We favor highly researched, definitive studies of social, economic, political and international problems that are written with verve and originality of style." Length: 3,000-4,000 words. Pays $25/published page.

AMERICAS, Organization of American States, Editorial Offices, Administration Bldg., 19th St. and Constitution Ave., Washington DC 20006. Managing Editor: A.R. Williams. 70% freelance written. Official cultural organ of Organization of American States. Audience is persons interested in inter-American topics. Editions published in English and Spanish. Bimonthly. Circ. 100,000. Buys first publication and reprint rights. Byline given. Pays on publication. Publishes ms an average of 3 months after acceptance. Computer printout submissions acceptable. Free sample copy. Articles received on speculation only. Include cover letter with writer's background. Reports in 3 months. Not necessary to enclose SASE.

Nonfiction: Articles of general New World interest on travel, history, art, literature, theater, development, archeology, travel, etc. Emphasis on modern, up-to-date Latin America. Taboos are religious and political themes or articles with noninternational slant. Photos required. Recent article example: "The Wiz-dom of Geoffrey Holder" (May/June 1984). Buys 36 unsolicited mss/year. Length: 2,500 words maximum. Pays about $200 minimum.

Tips: "Send excellent photographs in both color and b&w, keep the article short and address an international readership, not a local or national one."

‡C.L.A.S.S. MAGAZINE, C.L.A.S.S. Promotions, Inc., 15 E. 40th St., New York NY 10016. (212)685-1404. Editor: W. Franklyn Joseph. 70% freelance written. Monthly magazine covering Caribbean/American Third World news and views. Circ. 200,000. Pays on acceptance. Byline given. Buys first rights and second (reprint) rights to material originally published elsewhere. Submit seasonal/holiday material 4 months in advance. Simultaneous queries and previously published submissions OK. SASE. Computer printout submissions acceptable; prefers letter-quality to dot-matrix. Reports in 1 month on queries; 6 weeks on mss. Free sample copy and writer's guidelines.

Nonfiction: Features, book excerpts, general interest, historical/nostalgic, inspirational, interview/profile, travel and international news, views and lifestyles in Third World countries. 90% of each issue is freelance written. Query or send complete ms. Length: 150-2,500 words. Articles over 700 words must be of international flavor in content.

Poetry: Avant-garde, free verse, haiku, light verse and traditional. Buys 10-20 poems/year. Submit maximum 10 poems. Length: 22-30 lines. Pays $10 minimum.

Tips: "Submit written queries; stick to Afro American/Third World interests and relate to an international audience."

CALIFORNIA JOURNAL, The California Center, 1714 Capitol Ave., Sacramento CA 95814. (916)444-2840. Editor-in-Chief: Robert Fairbanks. Managing Editor: A.G. Block. 50% freelance written. Emphasizes analysis of California politics and government. Monthly magazine; 40 pages. Circ. 20,000. Pays on publication. Buys all rights. Byline given. Publishes ms an average of 2 months after acceptance. Computer printout submissions acceptable. SASE.

Nonfiction: Profiles of state and local government and political analysis. No outright advocacy pieces. Buys 25 unsolicited mss/year. Query. Length: 900-3,000 words. Pays $75/printed page.

CONSERVATIVE DIGEST, Viguerie Communications, 7777 Leesburg Pike, Falls Church VA 22043. (703)893-1411. Editor: Lee Edwards. 10% freelance written. Monthly magazine; 48 pages. Circ. 40,000. Pays on publication. Buys second serial (reprint) and one-time rights. Pays 10% kill fee. Byline given. Simultaneous and previously published submissions OK. SASE. Reports in 3 weeks. Sample copy $2.

Nonfiction: Expose (government); how-to (political ideas); and interview. Buys 1 ms/issue. Submit complete ms. Length: 750-1,200 words.

Fillers: Susan Longyear, managing editor. Clippings and bureaucratic blunders. Pays $15-25.

CONSERVATIVE REGISTER, Proud Eagle Press, Box 8453, Riverside CA 92515. (714)785-5180. Publisher/Editor-in-Chief: Paul Birchard. Editor: Alana Cross. Bimonthly Christian newspaper covering politics from a conservative viewpoint. Audience includes activist readers. Circ. 3,500. Pays on acceptance. Byline given. Buys all rights. Submit seasonal/holiday material 2 months in advance. Photocopied and previously published submissions OK. SASE. Reports in 1 month. Sample copy $1; writer's guidelines for business-size SAE and 1 first class stamp. No material returned without SASE.
Nonfiction: Jay Sulsenbir, assignments. Expose (of government from a conservative viewpoint); general interest; inspirational (from a Christian viewpoint); interview/profile (of religious, government or business leaders); new product (on energy or consumer-related); and opinion. "We prefer material which cites a governmental action or law and then projects its impact for Christians and/or conservatives in future years." No racist, bigoted or immoral material. Buys 12 unsolicited mss/year. Submit ms. Length: 100-1,000 words. Pays $5-25.
Photos: State availability of photos. Pays $5-15 for b&w 8x10 prints. Captions, model release, and identification of subjects required.
Columns/Departments: Alana Cross, column/department editor. Buys 8 mss/year. Query. Length: 1,000 maximum. Pays $25. "We will feature a Christian book review in every issue. Also, any political 'thought' piece which fits our format is carefully considered."
Fiction: J. Sulsenbir, assignments. Political satire. Limited market but will consider. No racist or immoral fiction. Buys 2 mss/year. Query. Length: 300 words maximum. Pays $5-25.
Fillers: Alana Cross, fillers editor. Anecdotes, short humor and newsbreaks. Buys 3 mss/issue. Length: 25-100 words. Pays $5-10. "Interesting factual pieces are most desired. Local religious material with national interest especially welcome."
Tips: "We are slanting our material more heavily toward a Christian publication. The emphasis is still political but it is crucial to consider impact on Christians, home life, etc. We are an excellent publication for unpublished writers. We want circulation-boosting pieces. Please document material and avoid sensationalism. We look first at material that has photos—but photos are not mandatory. Please, no phone queries. We are somewhat general in format but specific in viewpoint. Steady income can be had for writing to meet our needs—even for new writers whom we encourage. We will not use any material over 1,000 words. Writers will have more success submitting material between 300-500 words."

CRITIQUE: A JOURNAL OF CONSPIRACIES & METAPHYSICS, Critique, Box 11451, Santa Rosa CA 95406. (707)525-9401. Editor: Bob Banner. Managing Editor: M. Banovitch. 90% freelance written. Quarterly journal "that explores conspiracy scenarios, behind-the-scenes news, exposes, and unusual news that frequently creates debacles within the ordinary mind set. *Critique* also explores assumptions, beliefs and hypotheses that we use to understand ourselves, our 'world' and the metaphysical crisis of our time." Circ. 2,000. Pays on publication. Byline given. Submit seasonal/holiday material 4 months in advance. Simultaneous queries, and simultaneous, photocopied and previously published submissions OK. Electronic submissions OK if compatible with Text Files operable in DOS for Apple IIe, but requires hard copy also. Computer printout submissions acceptable. SASE. Reports in 4 months. Publishes ms an average of 5 months after acceptance. Sample copy $3; free writer's guidelines.
Nonfiction: Book excerpts; book reviews; expose (political, metaphysical, cultural); interview/profile (those in the specified area); and personal experience (as it relates to cultural ideology). Not interested in "anything that gets published in ordinary, established media." Buys 8-25 mss/year. Send complete ms with bio/resume. Length: 200-3,000 words. Pays $30 maximum.
Tips: "We have published articles, reviews and essays that are difficult to categorize in the simplistic, dualistic Left or Right ideological camps. The material's purpose has been, and will be, to provoke critical thinking; to discriminate between valuable and manipulative information; to incite an awareness of events, trends, phases and our roles/lives within the global psyche that no ordinary consumer of ordinary media could even begin to conceive let alone use such an awareness to affect his/her life."

EUROPE, 2100 M St. NW, 707, Washington DC 20037. Editor: Webster Martin. For anyone with a professional or personal interest in Western Europe and European/US relations. Bimonthly magazine; 60 pages. Circ. 60,000. Buys about 100 mss/year. Pays on acceptance. Free sample copy. Submit seasonal material 3 months in advance. Reports in 1 month. Query or submit complete ms. Include resume of author's background and qualifications with query or ms. SASE.
Nonfiction: Interested in current affairs (with emphasis on economics and politics), the Common Market and Europe's relations with the rest of the world. Publishes occasional cultural pieces, with European angle. High quality writing a must. "We publish anything that might be useful to people with a professional interest in Europe." Length: 500-2,000 words. Average payment is $100-325.
Photos: Photos purchased with or without accompanying mss. Also purchased on assignment. Buys b&w and color. Average payment is $25-35 per b&w print, any size; $50 for inside use of color transparencies; $200-300 for color used on cover.

THE FREEMAN, 30 S. Broadway, Irvington-on-Hudson NY 10533. (914)591-7230. Editor: Paul L. Poirot. 60% freelance written. For "fairly advanced students of liberty and the layman." Monthly. Buys all rights, including reprint rights. Byline given. Buys 44 mss/year. Pays on publication. Computer printout submissions acceptable; prefers letter-quality to dot-maxtrix. SASE.
Nonfiction: "We want nonfiction clearly analyzing and explaining various aspects of the free market, private enterprise, limited government philosophy, especially as pertains to conditions in the United States. Though a necessary part of the literature of freedom is the exposure of collectivistic cliches and fallacies, our aim is to emphasize and explain the positive case for individual responsibility and choice in a free economy. Especially important, we believe, is the methodology of freedom; self-improvement, offered to others who are interested. We try to avoid name-calling and personality clashes and find satire of little use as an educational device. Ours is a scholarly analysis of the principles underlying a free market economy. No political strategy or tactics." Length: 3,500 words maximum. Pays 5¢/word.
Tips: "It's most rewarding to find freelancers with new insights, fresh points of view. Facts, figures, and quotations cited should be fully documented, to their original source, if possible."

GUARDIAN, Independent Radical Newsweekly, Institute for Independent Social Journalism, 33 W. 17th St., New York NY 10011. (212)691-0404. Editor: William A. Ryan. Weekly newspaper covering US and international news and politics for a broad left and progressive audience. Circ. 25,000. Pays on publication. Byline given. Simultaneous queries, and simultaneous and photocopied submissions OK if indicated. SASE. Reports in 3 weeks on queries; 1 month on mss. Sample copy for $1, 9x12 SAE and 5 first class stamps; writer's guidelines for business-size SAE and 1 first class stamp.
Nonfiction: Ellen Davidson, articles editor. Expose (of government, corporations, etc.). "About 90% of our publication is hard news and features on current events." Buys 200 mss/year. Query with published clips. Length: 200-1,800 words. Pays $10-90.
Photos: Jill Benderly, photo editor. State availability of photos. Pays $15 for b&w prints. Captions required.
Columns/Departments: Women, Labor, The Left, Blacks. Buys 30 mss/year. Query with published clips. Length: 200-700 words. Pays $10-30.

INQUIRY, 1320 G. St. SE, Washington DC 20003. (202)547-2770. Editor: Doug Bandow. 90% freelance written. Monthly magazine for "thinking people, people dissatisfied with conventional left/right analysis. Our philosophy is a deep belief in the rights and abilities of the individual, coupled with overriding skepticism about the government's ability to solve problems." Circ. 25,000. Pays on publication. Publishes ms an average of 3 months after acceptance. Byline given. Offers "usual" 25% kill fee. Buys negotiable rights. Simultaneous and photocopied submissions OK. Computer printout submissions acceptable. SASE. Reports in 3 weeks on queries; 1 month on mss. Free sample copy and writer's guidelines.
Nonfiction: Critical analysis (of current issues); expose (of government corruption or ineptitude); political humor; and profile (of political figures); "we want a blend of reporting and analysis." Special issues include winter book issue with 8-12 book reviews. No history or Erma Bombeck humor. Also no how-to material or general nonfiction without a current events/issue angle. Buys 5-10 unsolicited mss/year. Query with clips of published work. Length: 1,000-4,500 words. Pays 10¢/word.
Columns/Departments: Law, Education, Politics, Media, Corporate State and Therapeutic State. Buys 2-3 mss/issue. Query with clips of published work. Length: 1,000-2,500 words. Pays 10¢/word.
Tips: "Getting quality work or a unique perspective from someone previously unknown to us is the most rewarding aspect of working with freelance writers."

INTRIGUE, The International Journal of Reportage, Air Crafts Limited, Inc., Box 68, Woodbridge NJ 07095. Editor: Ted Pastuszak Jr. 20% freelance written. Fortnightly newsletter and special occasional papers covering unusual aspects of world affairs and developments compiled from foreign broadcasts and other diverse sources. For "a sophisticated readership consisting of executives, journalists and international investors." Circ. 2,000. Pays on publication. Byline given. Offers 20% kill fee. Buys first rights only. Simultaneous queries OK. Computer printout submissions acceptable; prefers letter-quality to dot-matrix. SASE. Reports in 1 month on queries. Publishes ms an average of 6 weeks after acceptance. Sample copy $1; free writer's guidelines. An update book list of source and reference titles that *Intrigue* distributes is also available free on request.
Nonfiction: Contact: "In Cold Type" Department. Book excerpts and reviews, expose, interview/profile and personal experience. All subjects should pertain to or concern political, social or economic events or developments. "Special issues include 'Islands of Intrigue', 'Espionage Special', and a 'Diplomatic Edition'. With regard to our coverage of foreign affairs, we would prefer *not* to receive material that takes a specific political stand without including proper documentation and research. In short, we prefer reporting to editorializing." Buys less than 50 mss/year. Query with clips. Length: 600-750 words. Pays $60-150.
Columns/Departments: Border Lines (background notes on current developments in countries and regions around the world) and The World of Intrigue (a compilation of pressing political situations both at home and abroad in a unique diary format). Buys less than 50 mss/year. Query with clips of published work. Length: 700-750 words. Pays 10-20¢/word.

Fillers: Contact: "Inside Information" Section. Clippings and newsbreaks. "We're looking for interesting asides to news stories not covered by the major press." Individual department include: Air Waves (notes on international radio); Provoca Touring (travel tips to unusual places currently in the news); Capital Ideas (business and financial items of interest); Arms & Ammunition (news pertaining to arms trade and development). Length: 40-80 words. Pays 10-20¢/word.

Tips: "News and information concerning the following subjects can also be found in our departments when applicable: covert action, foreign trade, oilfield development, international security issues, submarine technology, polar region affairs, reportage/journalism, subliminal research and devices. Since *Intrigue* is designed to be a professional fortnighty briefing on important international matters, writing must be concise and to the point. Freelance writers who submit unsolicited material should consider submitting outlines or concepts for articles before committing themselves to writing and sending out completed mss."

THE NATION, 72 5th Ave., New York NY 10011. Editor: Victor Navasky. Weekly. Buys first rights only. Query. SASE.

Nonfiction: "We welcome all articles dealing with the social scene, particularly if they examine it with a new point of view or expose conditions the rest of the media overlooks." Queries encouraged. Computer printout submissions acceptable; prefers letter-quality to dot-matrix. Length: 2,500 words maximum. Buys 100 mss/ year. Payment to be negotiated. Modest rates.

Tips: "We are firmly committed to reporting on the issues of labor, national politics, consumer affairs, environmental politics, civil liberties and foreign affairs. Those issues can never be over-reported."

NATIONAL DEVELOPMENT (DESAROLLO NACIONAL), Intercontinental Publications, Inc., Box 5017, Westport CT 06880. (203)226-7463. Editor-in-Chief: Virginia Fairweather. 80% freelance written. Emphasizes Third World infrastructure. For government officials in Third World—technocrats, planners, engineers and ministers. Published 9 times/year; 120 pages. Circ. 60,000. Pays on acceptance. Publishes ms an average of 6 months after acceptance. Buys all rights. Byline given. Phone queries OK. Previously published submissions OK. Computer printout submissions acceptable; prefers letter-quality to dot-matrix. SASE. Reports in 4 weeks. Free sample copy and writer's guidelines.

Nonfiction: Technical (construction, government management, planning, power, telecommunications); informational (agriculture, economics, public works, construction management); interview; photo feature and technical. Buys 6-10 mss/issue. Query with "inclusion of suggestions for specific article topics; point out your area of expertise." Length: 1,800 words. Pays $250.

Photos: B&w and color. Captions required. Query. Total price for ms includes payment for photos.

Columns/Departments: Power technology, telecommunications, computer technology (as applied to infrastructure and development projects), water treatment, financial technology (finances as they might affect Third World governments). Buys 4 mss/issue. Query. Length: 750-1,500 words. Pays $250. Open to suggestions for new columns/departments.

NATIONAL JOURNAL, 1730 M St. NW, Washington DC 20036. (202)857-1400. Executive Director: Julia M. Romero. Editor: Richard Frank. "No freelance material accepted because fulltime staff produces virtually all of our material." Byline given.

NEW GUARD, Young Americans for Freedom, Woodland Rd., Sterling VA 22170. (703)450-5162. Editor-in-Chief: R. Cort Kirkwood. 50% freelance written. Emphasizes conservative political ideas for readership of mostly young people with a large number of college students. Age range 14-39. Virtually all are politically conservative with interests in politics, economics, philosophy and current affairs. Mostly students or college graduates. Quarterly magazine; 48 pages. Circ. 7,000. Pays on publication. Publishes ms an average of 2 months after acceptance. Buys all rights. Byline given. Phone queries OK. Submit seasonal/holiday material 2-3 months in advance. SASE. Reports in 1 month. Free sample copy.

Nonfiction: Expose (government waste, failure, mismanagement, problems with education or media); historical (illustrating political or economic points); interview (politicians, academics, people with conservative viewpoint or something to say to conservatives); personal opinion; and profile. Buys 40 mss/year. Submit complete ms. Length: 1,500 words maximum. Pays $40-100.

Photos: Purchased with accompanying manuscript.

THE NEW REPUBLIC, A Weekly Journal of Opinion, 1220 19th St. NW, Washington DC 20036. Contact: Editor. 30% freelance written. Circ. 100,000. Buys all rights. Byline given. Pays on publication. Publishes ms an average of 1 month after acceptance. Computer printout submissions acceptable. SASE.

Nonfiction: This liberal, intellectual publication uses 1,000-2,500 word comments on public affairs and arts. Pays 10¢/published word.

NEWSWEEK, 444 Madison Ave., New York NY 10022. Staff-written. Unsolicited mss accepted for My Turn, a column of opinion. Copy must be original to *Newsweek*. Length: 1,100 words maximum. Computer printout submissions acceptable; no dot-matrix. Include SASE for answer. Reports in 1 month.

POLITICAL PROFILES, 209 C St. NE, Washington DC 20002. Publisher: Robert J. Guttman. Managing Editor: Susan Whitmore. Publishing company featuring a newsletter and magazine-style monographs on current political issues, election and campaign information. Newsletter published biweekly. Magazine varies. Pays on acceptance. Byline given. Buys all rights.
Nonfiction: Expose (investigative pieces); historical (current history); and profile (political). Query. "We are interested in assigning stories to well established political reporters. Write a letter outlining your credentials and your availability for assignments."

THE PROGRESSIVE, 409 E. Main St., Madison WI 53703. (608)257-4626. Editor: Erwin Knoll. 75% freelance written. Monthly. Buys all rights. Byline given. Pays on publication. Computer printout submissions acceptable "if legible and double-spaced"; prefers letter-quality to dot-matrix. SASE. Reports in 2 weeks. Publishes ms an average of 6 weeks after acceptance. Query.
Nonfiction: Primarily interested in articles which interpret, from a progressive point of view, domestic and world affairs. Occasional lighter features. "*The Progressive* is a *political* publication. General-interest material is inappropriate." Length: 3,000 words maximum. Pays $50-200.
Tips: "Display some familiarity with our magazine, its interests and concerns, its format and style. We want query letters that fully describe the proposed article without attempting to sell it—and that give an indication of the writer's competence to deal with the subject."

REASON MAGAZINE, Box 40105, Santa Barbara CA 93103. (805)963-5993. Editor: Mary Zupan. 50% freelance written. For a readership interested in individual liberty, economic freedom, private enterprise alternatives to government services, individualist cultural and social perspectives. Monthly. Circ. 37,000. Rights purchased vary with author and material. May buy all rights, first North American serial rights, or first serial rights. Pays kill fee sometimes. Byline given. Buys 50-70 mss/year. Pays on publication. Publishes ms an average of 2 months after acceptance. Double- or triple-spaced, typed mss only. Photocopied submissions OK. Reports in 2 months. Query. SASE. Sample copy $2.
Nonfiction: "*Reason* deals with social, economic and political issues, supporting both individual liberty and economic freedom. The following kinds of articles are desired: investigative articles exposing government wrongdoing and bungling; investigative articles revealing examples of private (individual, business, or group) ways of meeting needs; individualist analysis of policy issues (e.g., education, victimless crimes, regulation); think pieces exploring implications of individual freedom in economic, political, cultural, and social areas." Length: 1,000-5,000 words.

REVIEW OF THE NEWS, 395 Concord Ave., Belmont MA 02178. (617)489-0605. Editor: Scott Stanley Jr. Weekly magazine covering the news with a conservative and free market orientation. Circ. 60,000. Average issue includes capsulated news items, bylined sports, films, economic advice and overseas and congressional activities. Pays on acceptance or on publication. Byline given. Kill fee negotiated. Buys all rights. Photocopied submissions OK. SASE. Reports in 3 weeks on queries; in 6 weeks on mss. Sample copy $1.
Nonfiction: Expose (of government bungling); general interest (current events and politics); interview (with leading conservatives and newsmakers, heads of state, congressmen, economists and politicians); humor (satire on the news); and commentary on the news. Buys 3-4 mss/year. Query with clips of previously published work. Length: 1,500-3,000 words. Pays $150-250.

ROLL CALL, The Newspaper of the US Congress, 201 Massachusetts Ave. NE, Washington DC 20002. (202)546-3080. Editor: Sidney Yudain. Weekly tabloid covering national politics for Congress, congressional aides, the White House, political writers, newspeople, etc. Circ. 7,500. Pays on publication. Byline given. Buys first rights only. Submit seasonal/holiday material 1 month in advance. Simultaneous queries OK. Computer printout submissions acceptable; prefers letter-quality to dot-matrix. SASE. Reports in 2 weeks on queries; 1 month on mss. Sample copy for 9x12 SAE and 3 first class stamps.
Nonfiction: Historical/nostalgic, humor, interview/profile, personal experience and photo feature. Special issues include Anniversary Issue (June); and Welcome Congress Issue (January). "No material *not* pertaining to Congress except topical satire on a national political event such as Watergate, the election, major cabinet reshuffle, etc." Buys 6 mss/year. "We will be more liberal in use of submitted material if guidelines are followed." Send complete ms. Length: 1,800 words maximum. Pays $5-25.
Photos: Send photos with ms. Pays $5 maximum for 8x10 b&w prints. Identification of subjects required.
Poetry: Light verse. No heavy, serious verse about nonpolitical or non-Congressional subjects. Buys 12/year. Length: open. Pays $2-10.
Fillers: Jokes, gags, anecdotes and short humor. Pays $2 maximum.
Tips: "Submit well-researched original Congressional articles (oddities, statistical compilations, historical retrospectives), topical verse or topical satirical pieces and one-liners. No serious material far removed from the Congressional political world—material on national or international issues—we have all the 'experts' at our doorstep."

TEXAS OBSERVER, A Journal of Free Voices, 600 W. 7th, Austin TX 78701. (512)477-0746. Publisher: Ronnie Dugger. Editor: Geoffrey Rips. 50% freelance written. Bimonthly magazine covering Texas politics and culture for a small influential audience. Circ. 12,000. Byline given. Publishes ms an average of 3 months after acceptance. Buys first rights only. Submit seasonal/holiday material 1 month in advance. Simultaneous queries, and simultaneous and photocopied submissions OK. SASE. Reports in 3 weeks. Free sample copy and writer's guidelines.

Nonfiction: Expose, interview/profile, opinion, personal experience and political analysis. Buys 100 mss/year. Query with clips of published work. Length: 200-2,000 words. Pays $10-75.

Photos: State availability of photos. Pays $10 for b&w prints. Captions, model release and identification of subjects required. Buys one-time rights.

Poetry: Avant-garde, free verse, haiku and traditional. Buys 10/year. Length: open. Pays $10-35.

Tips: "We're interested in Texas literature, politics, and social issues; not interested in other topics."

WASHINGTON MONTHLY, 1711 Connecticut Ave., Washington DC 20009. (202)462-0128. Editor: Charles Peters. 35% freelance written. For "well-educated, well-read people interested in politics, the press and government." Monthly. Circ. 35,000. Rights purchased depend on author and material; buys all rights or first rights. Buys 20-30 mss/year. Pays on publication. Sometimes does special topical issues. Query or submit complete ms. Computer printout submissions acceptable. Tries to report in 2-4 weeks. Publishes ms an average of 6 weeks after acceptance. SASE. Sample copy $2.25.

Nonfiction: Responsible investigative or evaluative reporting about the US government, business, society, the press and politics. "No editorial comment/essays, please." Also no poetry, fiction or humor. Length: "average 2,000-6,000 words." Pays 5-10¢/word.

Photos: Buys b&w glossy prints.

Tips: "Best route to break in is to send 1-2 page proposal describing article and angle. The most rewarding aspect of working with freelance writers is getting a solid piece of reporting with fresh ideas that challenge the conventional wisdom."

‡**WORLD POLICY JOURNAL**, World Policy Institute, 777 UN Plaza, New York NY 10017. (212)490-0010. Editor: Sherle Schwenninger. A quarterly magazine covering international politics, economics and security issues. "We hope to bring a new sense of imagination, principle and proportion, as well as a restored sense of reality and direction to America's discussion of its role in the world." Estab. 1983. Circ. 12,000. Pays on acceptance. Byline given. Offers variable kill fee. Buys all rights. Photocopied submissions OK. Computer printout submissions acceptable. SASE. Reports in 1 month. Sample copy for $4.75 and SAE; free writer's guidelines.

Nonfiction: Articles that "define policies that reflect the shared needs and interests of all nations of the world." Query. Length: 30-40 pages (8,500 words maximum). Pays variable commissioned rate.

Tips: "By providing a forum for many younger or previously unheard voices, including those from Europe, Asia, Africa, and Latin America, we hope to replace lingering illusions and fears with new priorities and aspirations."

Regional

Editors welcome the writer who knows the charms and quirks of a region—realizing that regional magazines are as diverse as the regions they cover. Some regionals rely on staff-written material; others on freelance writers who live in or know the region. The *best* regional publication sometimes is the one nearest the writer's doorstep. It can be a city or state magazine or a Sunday magazine in a newspaper. Listed below are general interest magazines slanted toward residents of and visitors to a particular region. Next, regional publications are categorized alphabetically by state (including the District of Columbia), followed by a Puerto Rico, a Canada, and a foreign category. Many regional publications buy manuscripts on conservation and the natural wonders of their area; additional markets for such material will be found under the Nature, Conservation, and Ecology, and Sports headings. Publications that report on the business climate of a region are grouped in the regional division of the Business and Finance category. Recreation and travel publications specific to a geographical area are listed in the Consumer Travel section.

General

COASTAL JOURNAL, Box 84 Lanesville Sta., Gloucester MA 01930. Publisher: Joe Kaknes. 100% freelance written. Bimonthly magazine primarily focusing on coastal New England from Maine to Connecticut. Buys first rights only. Pays within 1 month of publication. Submit seasonal material 6 months in advance. Electronic submissions OK via hard copy. Computer printout submissions acceptable. SASE. Reports in 1 month. Publishes ms an average of 6 months after acceptance. Sample copy $5; free writer's guidelines.

Nonfiction: Social, political and natural history; biography and people profiles; environmental and other pertinent public policy issues; boating, commercial fishing, and other maritime-related businesses; travel; art; education; and lifestyles. Query. Length: 1,500-2,000 words. Pays approximately $100/article.

Photos: Prefers b&w glossy prints and 35mm color transparencies. Pays on publication; negotiable fee. Captions and credit lines required.

Fiction: "This magazine occasionally runs short fiction up to 3,000 words. Such manuscripts should have some connection to the sea, to the coast, or to New England's history or character. No restrictions on style; the main criterion is quality." Query or send complete ms.

Tips: "We look for the unusual story or angle, the fresh approach, and the review/assessment of coastal New England related issues. Avoid overwriting and turgid style; stories should be crisp, well-researched, lively and concise. We'd like to see more contemporary pieces about events, issues or people with whom readers can identify."

COUNTRY MAGAZINE, A Guide—From the Appalachians to the Atlantic, Country Sun, Inc., Box 246, Alexandria VA 22313. (703)548-6177. Publisher: Walter Nicklin. Managing Editor: Philip Hayward. Monthly magazine of country living in the mid-Atlantic region. "Our coverage aims at promoting an appreciation of the region, especially through writing about travel, history, outdoor sports, food, nature, the environment, gardening, the arts, and people in these states: Virginia, Maryland, Delaware, West Virginia, North Carolina, Pennsylvania and New Jersey." Circ. 75,000. Pays on publication. Byline given. Buys one-time rights. Submit seasonal/holiday material 6 months in advance. Photocopied submissions OK. SASE. Reports in 4 weeks. Sample copy for $1, 9x12 SAE, and $1.22 postage; writer's guidelines for business-size SAE and 1 first class stamp.

Nonfiction: Book excerpts (of regional interest); historical (mid-Atlantic history with current news peg); how-to (deal with country living: how to buy country property, how to tap a sugar maple, etc.); interview/profile (of mid-Atlantic residents); photo feature (regional); travel (mid-Atlantic—off the beaten path). Buys 120 mss/ year. Query with published clips if available. Length: 1,000-2,000 words. Pays $3.50/column inch.

Photos: State availability of photos. Pays $15-25 for 35mm color transparencies and 5x7 b&w prints. Captions, model release and identification of subjects required.

Columns/Departments: The Land, The Rivers, and The Bay (Chesapeake)—all deal with the natural features of the region. Buys 36 mss/year. Query with published clips if available. Length: 500-600 words. Pays $3.50/ column inch.

Fiction: Historical, mainstream and novel excerpts. No nonregional, noncountry oriented fiction; "we seldom run fiction." Buys 1 ms/year. Query with published clips if available. Length: 1,200-2,000 words. Pays $3.50/ column inch.

Poetry: "We seldom publish poetry." Buys 2 poems/year. Submit maximum 3 poems. Length: 50 lines maximum. Pays $25 maximum.

Tips: "Especially open to how-to, gardening and issue-oriented stories pegged to the mid-Atlantic region."

‡**GUEST INFORMANT**, 201 N. Robertson Blvd., Beverly Hills CA 90211. (213)274-8165. Editor: Carey Simon. Associate Editor: Maryanne Larson. 60-75% freelance written, on assignment. An annual hardcover, 4-color in-hotel-room city guidebook for sophisticated travelers who are interested in what the city has to offer: retail establishments, restaurants, sightseeing activities, sports information, arts events, etc. Publishes 31 editions: Los Angeles; Orange County, CA; San Diego; San Francisco; Sacramento; Phoenix; Tucson; Seattle; San Antonio; Dallas; Houston; Twin Cities (Mpls./St. Paul); Milwaukee; Kansas City; Cincinnati; St. Louis; Philadelphia; Pittsburgh; New York; New Orleans; Tampa/St. Petersburg; Miami; Palm Beach/Gold Coast; Orlando area; Puerto Rico; Detroit; Boston; Atlanta; Chicago; Denver; and Washington, D.C. Some editions are published under the name *Leisureguide*. Circ. (combined for 31 editions) over 97 million. Pays 60 days after receipt of copy. Byline given. Offers 50% kill free. Buys all rights. Previously published submissions OK. SASE. Reports in 1 month. Sample copy $2.50; free writer's guidelines.

Nonfiction: "Each annual edition is individualized for a particular city, and each has a lead article (usually an overview of the city), visual arts, lively arts, sports and sightseeing. Some of the books have lengthy articles on shopping, sometimes related to the suburbs, sometimes a shopping center section." No dining or destination travel pieces; no articles about foreign cities, or cities not covered by the *Guest Informant* network. Buys 75 mss/year. Query with published clips. Length: Depends on article and edition. Leads approx. 1,200 words; articles on the arts or sports, about 800 words. Pays $150-500; varies by article and edition.

Fillers: "Interesting sight or historical information, etc. on a particular city we cover." Buys 1-4 mss/year. Length: 420-825 words. Pays $100-200.

Tips: "It is rare that we would ever accept an unsolicited manuscript. Instead, we work on assignment. We are looking for freelancers who have imaginative writing skills and an indepth knowledge of their city. It helps if they have background in a particular aspect of the city (i.e., the museums and galleries, sports, the fashion scene, etc). We are always looking for good writers who have an extensive background in fashion and/or retail as applies to our individual cities. We do not send writers to other cities. Once we find a good writer in a city we tend to use him/her for two-to-three-years' worth of books."

● **INLAND, The Magazine of the Middle West**, Inland Steel Co., 30 W. Monroe St., Chicago IL 60603. (312)346-0300. Managing Editor: Sheldon A. Mix. 50% freelance written. Emphasizes steel products, services and company personnel. Quarterly magazine; 24 pages. Circ. 12,000. Pays on acceptance. Buys first rights only. Kill fee: "We have always paid the full fee on articles that have been killed." Byline given. Submit seasonal/holiday material at least 1 year in advance. Simultaneous submissions OK. Computer printout submissions acceptable. SASE. Reports in 6-8 weeks. Publishes ms an average of 1 year after acceptance. Free sample copy.

Nonfiction: Articles, essays, humorous commentaries and pictorial essays. "We encourage individuality. Half of each issue deals with staff-written steel subjects; half with widely ranging nonsteel matter. Articles and essays related somehow to the Midwest (Illinois, Wisconsin, Minnesota, Michigan, Missouri, Iowa, Nebraska, Kansas, North Dakota, South Dakota, Indiana and Ohio) in such subject areas as history, folklore, sports, humor, the seasons, current scene generally; nostalgia and reminiscence if well done and appeal are broad enough. But subject is less important than treatment. We like perceptive, thoughtful writing, and fresh ideas and approaches. Please don't send slight, rehashed historical pieces or any articles of purely local interest." Personal experience, profile, humor, historical, think articles, personal opinion and photo essays. No "nostalgia that is merely sentimental and superficial and that doesn't move the reader, or rehashes of historical personalities and highlights." Buys 10-15 unsolicited mss/year. Length: 1,200-5,000 words. Payment depends on individual assignment or unsolicited submission.

Photos: Purchased with or without mss. Captions required. "Payment for pictorial essay same as for text feature."

Tips: "Our publication particularly needs humor that is neither threadbare nor in questionable taste, and shorter pieces (800-1,500 words) in which word-choice and wit are especially important. A writer who knows our needs and believes in himself should keep trying." Recent published material: "The Emancipation of Mary Todd Lincoln" (history, No. 1, 1983).

‡**ISLANDS, An International Magazine**, Islands Publishing Company, 3886 State St., Santa Barbara CA 93105. Editor: Connie Bourassa-Shaw. 100% freelance written. Bimonthly magazine covering islands throughout the world. "We invite articles from many different perspectives: scientific, historical, exploratory, cultural, etc. We ask our authors to avoid the typical travel magazine style and concentrate on stimulating and informative pieces that tell the reader something he or she might not know about a particular island." Circ. 110,000. Pays 50% on acceptance and 50% within 30 days after publication. Byline given. Buys all rights. Simultaneous queries, and simultaneous, photocopied and previously published submissions OK. Computer printout submissions acceptable; prefers letter-quality to dot-matrix. SASE. Reports in 4 weeks on queries; 6 weeks on ms. Publishes ms an average of 4 months after acceptance. Sample copy for $4.65; writer's guidelines free.

Nonfiction: General interest, historical/nostalgic, how-to, interview/profile, personal experience, photo feature, technical, travel and any island-related material. "Each issue contains a major centerpiece of 7,000 words, 5 or 6 feature articles of roughly 3,000 words, and 2 or 3 topical articles for departments, each of which runs approximately 500 words. Any authors who wished to be commissioned should send a detailed proposal for an article, an estimate of costs (if applicable), and samples of previously published work." No "I went here and did this/I went there and ate that" travel articles. Buys 100 mss/year. "The majority of our mss are commissioned." Query with published clips or send complete ms. Length: 500-4,000 words. Pays $200-2,000.

Photos: State availability or send photos with query or ms. Pays $50-300 for 35mm color transparencies. "Fine color photography is a special attraction of *Islands*, and we look for superb composition, image quality and editorial applicability." Label slides with name and address, include abbreviated captions, and submit in protective plastic sleeves. Identification of subjects required. Buys one-time rights.

Columns/Departments: "Columns and departments are generally assigned, but we have accepted short features (500-2,000 words) for our Island Hopping department. These should be highly focused on some travel-oriented aspect of islands." Buys 10-20 mss/year. Query with published clips. Length: 250-1,500 words. Pays $125-750.

Tips: "A freelancer can best break in to our publication with short (1,000-2,000 word) features that are highly focused on some aspect of island life, history, people, etc. Stay away from general, sweeping articles."

‡**NEW ENGLAND MONTHLY**, New England Monthly Inc., Box 446, Haydenville MA 01039. (413)268-7262. Editor: Daniel Okrent. Managing Editor: Chris Jerome. A monthly magazine covering such topics as

recreation, politics, the arts, the outdoors, business and economics, food, people, gardening and sports and education for residents of Maine, New Hampshire, Massachusetts, Vermont, Rhode Island and Connecticut. Estab. 1984. Circ. 45,000. Pays on acceptance. Byline given. Offers 20% kill fee on commissioned work. Buys first North American serial rights and nonexclusive other rights. Submit seasonal/holiday material 4 months in advance. Simultaneous queries OK. Electronic submissions OK "only on commissioned articles, and only in CP/M-compatible forms." Computer printout submissions acceptable. SASE. Reports in 4 weeks. Sample copy $1.75; writer's guidelines for #10 SAE and 1 first class stamp.

Nonfiction: Lee Aitken, associate editor. Book excerpts, expose, general interest, photo feature, travel and general reportage. No nostalgic, reminiscence or inspirational articles. Buys 100 mss/year. Query with published clips. Length: 300-4,000 words. Pays $75-1,500.

Photos: Hans Teensma, photo editor.

Columns/Departments: Julie Michaels, column/department editor. "Column subjects purchased from freelancers include sports, outdoors, gardening, education, science, business, politics, performing arts, visual arts, and literature." Buys 40 mss/year. Length: 1,000-1,800 words. Pays $400-700.

Tips: "We always need a peg—it is not sufficient, for instance, to suggest a profile of, say, Paul Newman, simply because he lives in New England. The Region, which includes short (400-1,000 words) reportorial pieces on specific aspects of New England life and society, is the department that's most open to freelancers."

NORTHWEST MAGAZINE, *The Sunday Oregonian*, 1320 SW Broadway, Portland OR 97201. Editor: Paul Pintarich. For an upscale, 25-49-year-old audience distributed throughout the Pacific Northwest. Weekly newspaper Sunday supplement magazine; 24-40 pages. Circ. 420,000. Buys first rights for Oregon and Washington state. Buys 400 mss/year and pays mid-month in the month following acceptance. All mss on speculation. Simultaneous submissions considered. Reports in 2 weeks. Query much preferred, but complete ms considered. Computer printout submissions acceptable; prefers letter-quality to dot-matrix. SASE. Free writer's guidelines.

Nonfiction: "Contemporary, regional articles with a strong hook to concerns of the Pacific Northwest. Cover stories usually deal with regional issues and feature professional-level reporting and writing. Personality profiles focus on young, Pacific Northwest movers and shakers. Short humor, personal essays, regional destination travel, entertainment, the arts and lifestyle stories also are appropriate. No history without a contemporary angle, boilerplate features of the type that are mailed out en masse with no specific hook to our local audience, poorly documented and highly opinionated issue stories that lack solid journalistic underpinnings, routine holiday features, or gushy essays that rhapsodize about daisies and rainbows. We expect top-quality writing and thorough, careful reporting. Contemporary writing style that features involving literary techniques like scenic construction stands the best chance." Length: 800-3,000 words. Pays $75-500/mss. Pays $25-50.

Photos: Photographs should be professional quality b&w prints, contact sheets with negatives or Kodachrome slides. Pays $25-50.

Poetry: Short poetry of distinctive quality. "Due to space limitations we are now only accepting work from Northwest poets although themes may be universal. All material must be original and not published elsewhere." Send at least 3 poems for consideration; pays $5 each on acceptance. Length: 23 lines maximum.

Tips: "Pay rates and editing standards are up, and this market will become far more competitive. However, new writers with talent and good basic language skills still are encouraged to try us. Printing quality and flexibility should improve, increasing the magazine's potential for good color photographers and illustrators."

THE ORIGINAL NEW ENGLAND GUIDE, New England Publications, Inc., 60 Elm St., Camden ME 04843. (207)236-4393. Editor: Mimi E.B. Steadman. 90% freelance written. Travel/vacation guide to New England. Annual magazine published in the spring. Circ. 200,000. Pays on publication. Buys first rights only. Deadline for queries is September 30. Computer printout submissions acceptable; prefers letter-quality to dot-matrix. Reports in 2-3 weeks. Sample copy $4. Free writer's guidelines.

Nonfiction: "We look for pieces on New England's many leisure-time choices: sports, including some of the newer interests such as rafting, hang gliding, wind surfing, orienteering; antique shows; craft, music and art fairs; auctions; festivals and special celebrations; historical attractions; and personal-experience accounts only when they offer advice on how readers may enjoy similar experiences. Our major features include information on how a certain activity may be enjoyed in all six New England states. We also buy shorter pieces that pertain to only one state." No personal—How I Spent My Vacation—material. Buys up to 28 mss/issue. Pays approximately 10¢/word. Query first with writing sample (letter, not phone). Length: 500-1,500 words.

Photos: "Writers should feel free to include photographs (b&w prints or contact sheets or color transparencies) with their submissions. Even if they are not of publishable quality, they are helpful in giving a visual introduction to the subject of the article and may be used in making assignments to photographers."

Fillers: Rarely used.

Tips: Prefers "service-oriented pieces that help New England travelers and vacationers get more from their trip."

‡**PACIFIC CLIPPER**, Box 6398, Albany CA 94706. 50% freelance written. Free magazine mailed monthly (except January) to upscale East Bay homes. It covers travel and adventure, cooking and home improvement for readers who are sophisticated, well-educated and well-traveled." Estab. 1983. Circ. 50,000. Buys first or second (reprint) rights. Pays on publication. Byline given sometimes. Offers negotiable kill fee. Submit seasonal/holiday material 3 months in advance. Simultaneous queries and simultaneous, photocopied and previously published submissions OK. Computer printout submissions acceptable; prefers letter-quality to dot-matrix. SASE. Reports in 1 month on queries; 6 weeks on mss. Publishes ms an average of 2 months after acceptance. Sample copy and writer's guidelines $1.
Nonfiction: Book excerpts, general interest, historical/nostalgic, humor, interview/profile, personal experience and travel. Special issues include seasonal outdoor activities (skiing, backpacking, river running, etc.) and seasonal destinations. "In every issue we need a lead article with accompanying color transparencies on travel, nonfiction adventure or popular history in our areas of interest (greater San Francisco Bay area, northern California, the Pacific West, the Pacific East, and everything in between). We are looking for a writing style that is condensed, upbeat, practical and information-oriented. All of our lead articles have a 'sources' appendix at the end of the article. Humor is *not* taboo, politics and sex are. We welcome 'off the beaten trail' type information . . . not your standard Sunday travel section article." Buys 30-60 mss/year. Query with or without published clips or send complete ms. Length: 300-750 words; lead article, 1,000-1,500 words. Pays $25-200; lead article, $100-200.
Photos: Raye Santos, photo editor. Send photos with query or ms. Pays $20-70 for 35mm color transparencies; $20-40 each for transparencies with lead article; $10-25 for 5x7 b&w prints. Captions and identification of subjects required.
Tips: "It's rewarding finding something better than we could have or would have come up with on our own material. But it is sad to see someone who is obviously sincere in his/her strong desire to become a successful freelancer who can't punctiate or spell and probably doesn't even know it."

PACIFIC NORTHWEST, 222 Dexter Ave. N., Seattle WA 98109. Editor: Peter Potterfield. Emphasizes the arts, culture, recreation, service and urban and rural lifestyle in the Pacific Northwest. Monthly magazine (except January and August). Buys first rights only. Simultaneous and previously published submissions OK. SASE. Reports in 6 weeks. Will send writer's guidelines.
Nonfiction: Editorial material should entertain, inform or contribute to an understanding of the Pacific Northwest, including BC and Alaska. Subject matter includes travel and exploration, outdoor activities, issues in the region's development, science and the environment, arts, history, profiles of places and people, and current issues, ideas and events that concern the Northwest. Buys 4 mss/issue. Query with clips of published work. Length: 600-3,000 words. Pay starts at 10¢/word.
Photos: Send photos with or without ms. Pays $15-50 for b&w prints; $50-200 for color transparencies, 35mm or larger. Buys one-time rights. Captions preferred.
Columns/Departments: Scannings (news items); Books; Closer Look (regional issues and profiles); Travel; Food and Lodging; Back Page (photo); Calendar of Events; and Letters. Query.
Tips: "Query should have clear description of topic and relevance to Northwest with clips if writer is new to us. We look for entertaining as well as informative style and format plus original or unusual information and research. Many native, outdoors or history submissions assume a more narrowly interested audience than we are aiming for."

‡**POSH, (Profiles on the Southern Horizon)**, Box 221269, Charlotte NC 28222. (704)375-8034. Editor: Judy Coffin. A bimonthly southern fashion/lifestyle magazine for an upscale audience. Circ. 35,000. Pays 30 days after publication. Buys first rights. SASE. Reports in 3 weeks. Sample copy $2.
Nonfiction: Southern Profiles (spotlighting successful businesses and people); Fashion Accessories; Beauty; Health; Fitness. "We are seeking articles of interest throughout the southern region. Our readers are well educated and stylish, at home and in the workplace." Query or send complete ms. Length: 750-1,500 words. Pays $150-250 for feature articles.
Photos: "We are very interested in photos. All features are accompanied by photos; suggest sources if not including pictures." Buys b&w prints and color transparencies. Pays negotiable rate.
Columns/Departments: "We will consider all types of articles; however, the magazine is a fashion/lifestyle magazine. Length: 750-1,500 words. Pays $75-100.
Fillers: Anecdotes, newsbreaks, humor, preview of events and personalities. Send complete ms. Length: 250-500 words. Pays 5¢/word.

● **RURALITE**, Box 557, Forest Grove OR 97116. (503)357-2105. Editor: Ken Dollinger. Monthly magazine primarily slanted toward small town and rural families, served by consumer-owned electric utilities in Washington, Oregon, Idaho, Nevada and Alaska. "Ours is an old-fashioned down-home publication, with something for all members of the family." Circ. 203,000. Buys first North American serial rights and occasionally second (reprint) rights to material originally published elsewhere. Byline given. Pays on acceptance. Publishes ms an average of 6 months after acceptance. Submit seasonal material at least 3 months in advance. Computer

Close-up

Judson D. Hale, Sr.
Editor-in-Chief
Yankee

It's Judson Hale's turn this week to read the over-the-transom mail. At *Yankee*, editors rotate this responsibility each week.

"Would you like a manuscript on old houses?" asks a writer's query letter.

"No," thinks Hale.

A similar—but very different—query is in the same mail stack: "I propose to do an article on the eight most commonly made errors in restoring old houses."

"Yes," says Hale.

It happens every day—the well-focused idea from someone with know-how on the subject gets the assignment.

Out of the 2,500 over-the-transom submissions each year, only eight or nine articles become major pieces in the magazine. (Sixty to seventy percent of *Yankee*'s articles are done on freelance assignment.) Still, Hale, editor of *Yankee* since 1970, values the mail as a source for spotting trends, talent, and what's on people's minds.

As part owner of *Yankee* and also editor/part owner of *The Old Farmer's Almanac*, Hale has watched regional magazines evolve from PR and kitchen-table products to magazines with national distributions and staff members who could work on any national magazine.

Writers who judge *Yankee* by its 6x9 size, regional format, or by traditional attributes of New England won't get a "yes" from Hale. "The main thing is to throw out this idea of *Yankee* being quaint and that we're only looking for covered bridges and foliage. . . .," says Hale, also author of *Inside New England* (Harper & Row). "Discard all those preconceived notions, then read two or three recent issues of *Yankee* carefully.

"What I value the most in terms of writing is the idea. . . . The ideal writer knows exactly what to write about for a monthly magazine, implements and writes it beautifully, so you can take sentences out and run them in large bold type at the top of the page," he says. "Whenever there's an article that you can do that with, you know it's a dynamite article."

Puffery can make an article less than dynamite. If the writer's awe of his subject shows in an article, it ruins the piece, he points out. "Instead of making general descriptions about how so-and-so is dedicated and hard-working, it is much more effective to describe the reactions of that person and let the reader make the overall summary of impression.

"Anybody with an obsession is potentially [the subject for] a good article; anybody who is 'running against the current' is potentially a good article; and anybody who is extremely creative and I don't mean oil painting; or somebody who has a specialized way of life," says Hale.

He goes back to his stack of mail.

"How about a biography of Benedict Arnold?" asks a writer.

"No," thinks Hale.

"How about an account of Arnold's marriage to a devout Tory and his growing disillusionment with the Patriot cause," writes another writer in sentences worth printing in bold letters.

"Yes," says Hale.

printout submissions acceptable. Query. SASE. Sample copies $1; guidelines for SASE.

Nonfiction: Walter J. Wentz, nonfiction editor. Primarily human-interest stories about rural or small-town folk, preferably living in areas (Northwest states and Alaska) served by Rural Electric Cooperatives. Articles emphasize self-reliance, overcoming of obstacles, cooperative effort, hard or interesting work, unusual or interesting avocations, odd or unusual hobbies or histories, public spirit or service and humor. Will also consider how-to, advice for rural folk, little-known and interesting Northwest history, people or events. "Looking specifically for energy (sources, use, conservation) slant and items relating to rural electric cooperatives." No "sentimental nostalgia or subjects outside the Pacific Northwest; nothing racy." Buys 15-20 mss/year. Length: 500-1,500 words. Pays $30-100, depending upon length, quality, appropriateness and interest, number and quality of photos.

Photos: Reviews b&w negatives with contact sheets. Offers no additional payment for photos accepted with ms.

YANKEE, Dublin NH 03444. (603)563-8111. Editor-in-Chief: Judson D. Hale. Managing Editor: John Pierce. Emphasizes the New England region. Monthly magazine. Circ. 950,000. Pays on acceptance. Buys all, first North American serial or one-time rights. Byline given. Submit seasonal/holiday material at least 4 months in advance. SASE. Reports in 4-6 weeks. Free sample copy and writer's guidelines.

Nonfiction: Historical (New England history, especially with present-day tie-in); how-to (especially for Forgotten Arts series of New England arts, crafts, etc.); humor; interview (especially with New Englanders who have not received a great deal of coverage); nostalgia (personal reminiscence of New England life); photo feature (prefers color, captions essential); profile; travel (to the Northeast only, with specifics on places, prices, etc.); current issues; antiques to look for; and food. Buys 50 mss/year. Query with brief description of how article will be structured (its focus, etc.); articles must include a New England "hook." Length: 1,500-3,000 words. Pays $50-700.

Photos: Purchased with accompanying ms or on assignment; (without accompanying ms for "This New England" feature only; color only). Captions required. Send prints or transparencies. Pays $25 minimum for 8x10 b&w glossy prints. $125/page for 2¼x2¼ or 35mm transparencies; 4x5 for cover or centerspread. Total purchase price for ms usually includes payment for photos.

Columns/Departments: Traveler's Journal (with specifics on places, prices, etc.); Antiques to Look For (how to find, prices, other specifics); and At Home in New England (recipes, gardening, crafts). Buys 10-12 mss/year. Query. Length: 1,000-2,500 words. Pays $150-400.

Fiction: Deborah Naras, fiction editor. "Emphasis is on character development." Buys 12 mss/year. Send complete ms. Length: 2,000-4,000 words. Pays $750.

Poetry: Jean Burden, poetry editor. Free verse and modern. Buys 3-4 poems/issue. Send poems. Length: 32 lines maximum. Pays $35 for all rights, $25 for first magazine rights. Annual poetry contest with awards of $150, $100 and $50 for 1st, 2nd and 3rd prizes.

YANKEE MAGAZINE'S TRAVEL GUIDE TO NEW ENGLAND, Main St., Dublin NH 03444. (603)563-8111. Editor: Sharon W. Smith. Emphasizes travel and leisure for a readership from New England area and from all states in the union. Annual magazine. Circ. 175,000. Pays on acceptance. Buys first North American serial rights. Pays 25% kill fee. Byline given. Submit seasonal/holiday material 6-12 months in advance. Simultaneous and photocopied submissions OK. Electronic submissions OK on floppy disks compatible with IBM, PC, DD and DS. Computer printout submissions acceptable. SASE. Reports in 3 weeks. Sample copy $2.50; free writer's guidelines.

Nonfiction: "Unusual activities, places to stay, restaurants, shops, the arts, annual events, water activities, adventure travel, festivals, day trips, the outdoors, and towns or areas to visit. Strict emphasis on travel discoveries within New England. Since the *Guide* is set up on a state-by-state basis, each story must be confined to activities or attractions within a single state." Buys 15-25 mss/issue. Query. Length: 500-2,500 words. Pays $50-300.

Photos: Picture editor. Purchased with or without accompanying ms or on assignment. Send contact sheet or transparencies plus list of stock photos on file. Pays $25-75 for b&w 8x10 glossy prints; $50-150 for 35mm or 2¼x2¼ color transparencies.

Tips: "Send a query letter for your ideas and explain why you are qualified to write about a given subject. Include samples. Ask for a copy of our writer's guidelines."

Alabama

‡**BIRMINGHAM**, Birmingham Area Chamber of Commerce, 2027 First Ave. N., Birmingham AL 35203. (205)323-5461. Editor: Ray Martin. A monthly magazine for primarily residents of the Birmingham area, including area Chamber of Commerce members. Circ. 8,500. Pays on publication. Byline given. Buys first North American serial rights. Submit seasonal/holiday material 4 months in advance. Photocopied submissions OK. Computer printout submissions acceptable; prefers letter-quality to dot-matrix. SASE. Reports in 2 weeks on queries; 1 month on mss. Sample copy $1.25.

Nonfiction: General interest (subject and its relationship to Birmingham, including local individuals who are involved with a particular hobby, business, sport, organization or occupation); historical/nostalgic (focus on the Birmingham of the past, often comparing an area's past history and appearance with its current characteristics); interview/profile (individual's personality in addition to mentioning the person's accomplishments and how the accomplishments were attained; individuals with interesting or unusual occupations are often the subjects of profiles); personal experience (usually relating the unique experiences of Birmingham residents, often humorous; another type is one which presents the writer's reflections on a specific event or experience, such as a feature published recently about a writer's trip on AMTRAK). No stories that have no direct connection with Birmingham. Buys 144 mss/year. Query with published clips. Length: 4-15 double-spaced typed pages. Pays $50-150.

Tips: "We present Birmingham and its people in an informative, entertaining and positive manner. Rather than reshaping current events and competing with other media on stories having current news value, *Birmingham* prefers to take a deeper look at local individuals who are exceptional in some way. The emphasis of *Birmingham* is always on people rather than things. These people might have an unusual career, hobby or business, but their story always has a tangible connection to our area. *Birmingham* strives for a 50-50 mix of quotes and narrative material. Writers are encouraged to present the atmosphere surrounding their subject as well as descriptions of the individual's physical characteristics."

Alaska

ALASKA MAGAZINE, Box 4-EEE, Anchorage AK 99509. Editor: Tom Gresham. 90% freelance written. Monthly magazine. Buys first rights only. Byline given. Computer printout submissions acceptable "but some standards apply as to typewriters: new ribbon, easily readable type"; prefers letter-quality to dot-matrix. Pays on acceptance. Publishes ms an average of 1 year after acceptance. SASE.

Nonfiction: *"Alaska Magazine's* subtitle is 'The Magazine of Life on the Last Frontier,' and, as implied, our interests are broad. Feature subjects include backpacking, resource management, sport fishing, wildlife encounters, kayaking and canoeing, trapping, cross-country skiing, snowshoeing, hunting, travel in Alaska, commercial fisheries, native affairs, mining, arts and crafts, mountaineering, bush-country life, profiles of Alaskans, history, town profiles, and wilderness photo essays. Manuscripts may run up to about 4,000 words, but we prefer shorter photo-illustrated pieces in the 1,000-2,000-word range. Rates for illustrated material range from $50-400, depending on length."

Photos: "We're heavy on sharp color photographs of Alaska and northwestern Canada, buying about 1,000 transparencies each year. Photos should ideally be Kodachrome slides—no duplicates, please. One-time rates are $200 for covers, $150 for 2-page spreads, $100 for full-page; and $50 for half-page.

Columns/Departments: "Regular monthly features include full-page color photos, letters, book reviews, personality profiles, bush-living tips, and short factual stories on Alaskan creatures."

NEW ALASKAN, Rt. 1, Box 677, Ketchikan AK 99901. Publisher: R.W. Pickrell. 75% freelance written. For residents of southeast Alaska. Tabloid magazine; 28 pages. Monthly. Circ. 5,500. Rights purchased vary with author and material. May buy all rights or second serial (reprint) rights. Byline given. Buys 30 mss/year. Pays on publication. Photocopied submissions OK. Submit complete ms. SASE. Sample copy $1.

Nonfiction: Bob Pickrell, articles editor. Feature material about southeast Alaska. Emphasis is on full photo or art coverage of subject. Informational, how-to, personal experience, interview, profile, inspirational, humor, historical, nostalgia, personal opinion, travel, successful business operations and new product. Length: 1,000 words minimum. Pays 1½¢/word.

Photos: B&w photos purchased with or without mss. Minimum size: 5x7. Pays $5 per glossy used. Pays $2.50 per negative. Negatives are returned. Captions required.

Fiction: Bob Pickrell, articles editor. Historical fiction related to southeast Alaska. Length: open. Pays 1½¢/word.

Arizona

ARIZONA HIGHWAYS, 2039 W. Lewis Ave., Phoenix AZ 85009. (602)258-6641. Editor: Don Dedera. 80% freelance written. State-owned publication designed to help attract tourists into and through the state. Magazine. Computer printout submissions acceptable; prefers letter-quality to dot-matrix. Pays on acceptance. Publishes ms an average of 8 months after acceptance.

Nonfiction: Managing editor. "Article categories include first and third-person narratives dealing with contemporary events, history, anthropology, nature, special things to see and do, outstanding arts and crafts, travel, profiles, etc.; all must be Arizona oriented." Buys 6 mss/issue. Buys first rights only. Query with "a lead paragraph and brief outline of story. We deal with professionals only, so include list of current credits." Length: 1,500-2,000 words. Pays 20-30¢/word.

Photos: Picture editor. Pays $80-300 for b&w print or color transparencies. Buys one-time rights. "We will use 2¼), 4x5 or larger, and 35 mm when it displays exceptional quality or content. We prefer Kodachrome in 35mm. Each transparency *must* be accompanied by information attached to each photograph: where, when, what. No photography will be reviewed by the editors unless the photographer's name appears on *each* and *every* transparency."

Tips: "Writing must be professional quality, warm, sincere, in-depth and well-peopled. Romance of the Old West feeling is important. Avoid themes that describe first trips to Arizona, Grand Canyon, the desert, etc. Emphasis to be on romance and themes that can be photographed."

ARIZONA MAGAZINE, Box 1950, Phoenix AZ 85001. (602)271-8291. Editor: Paul Schatt. For "everyone who reads a Sunday newspaper." Weekly; 60 pages. Circ. 440,000. Kill fee only on assigned articles. Byline given. Buys 250 mss/year. Pays when article is scheduled for publication. Photocopied submissions OK; simultaneous submissions OK if exclusive regionally. Reports in 2 weeks. Query or submit complete ms. SASE. For sample copy and guidelines for writers send 50¢.

Nonfiction: "General subjects that have an Arizona connection, are of interest to the West or are of universal interest. We're looking for good writing above all and writer mastery of the subject. Should have an abundance of quotes and anecdotes. Some regional travel and entertainment. Outstanding profiles. We are interested in Arizona, the West and universal subjects, not always in that order. We want to be topical and lively. We want stories that show some creativity in their approach. If story reads like a cliche Sunday Magazine story, redo it. Historical subjects are being overworked. No routine historical pieces; willing to see *the* dynamite story of how it really happened, but not any more routine stuff." Length: 1,000-3,000 words. "There is a trend to slightly shorter lead pieces which likely will make room for more inside articles. Articles of 800-1,500 words will get fair hearings."

Photos: State availability of photos. Pays $50-350. B&w and color photos purchased with or without mss or on assignment. Pays $15-25 for 8x10 b&w glossy prints; $25-80 for color (35mm or larger).

Tips: "Find a good personal subject and write about him so the reader will feel he is with the subject. Know the subject well enough to react to the material. Describe the subject in anecdotes and let him reveal himself by his quotes. Please include social security and telephone numbers."

‡**ELITE MAGAZINE, The Southwest Features/Society Magazine**, Elite Publishing Inc., Suite 2, 54 W. Main St., Box 1685, Mesa AZ. (602)890-1778. Editor: Ellie Schultz. A quarterly magazine covering the interests of the affluent and jet setter. Circ. 1,900. Pays on publication. Byline given. Offers kill fee if work is assigned. Buys first rights only. Submit seasonal/holiday material 4 months in advance. Simultaneous queries OK. Computer printout submissions acceptable; prefers letter-quality to dot-matrix. SASE. Reports in 2 weeks. Sample copy $1.15; free writer's guidelines.

Nonfiction: General interest; historical/nostalgic (from and about anywhere); inspirational (sometimes, but mostly as mind development); and travel (off beaten path type of story). Buys approximately 12 mss/year. Length: 1,500-2,500 words. Inquire about pay rates. Pays $75-100 for some articles.

Photos: State availability of photos. Pays $15 maximum for color transparencies; $10 maximum for 5x7 or 8x10 b&w prints. Identification of subjects required. Buys one-time rights.

PHOENIX MAGAZINE, 4707 N. 12th St., Phoenix AZ 85014. (602)248-8900. Editor: Jeff Burger. 50% freelance written. For professional, general audience. Monthly magazine. Circ. 40,000. Usually buys all rights. Occasionally pays kill fee. Byline given in most cases. Buys 120 mss/year. Pays within 2 weeks of publication. January issue: Superguide to what to see and do in area; February issue: Gardening Guide, March issue: Arizona Lifestyle; June issue: Summer SuperGuide; July issue: The Phoenix Lists; August issue: Valley Progress Report; November issue: Home Decorating. Submit special issue material 3 months in advance. Computer printout submissions acceptable; prefers letter-quality to dot-matrix. Sample copy $1.95 plus $1.25 for postage. Reports in 1 month. Publishes ms an average of 2 months after acceptance. Query or submit complete ms. SASE.

Nonfiction: Predominantly features subjects unique to Phoenix life: urban affairs, arts, lifestyle, etc. Subject should be locally oriented. Informational, how-to, interview, profile and historical. Each issue also embraces 1 or 2 in-depth reports on crucial, frequently controversial issues that confront the community. Length: 1,000-3,000 words. Payment is negotiable. Payment for features averages $100-150.

Photos: Photos are purchased with ms with no additional payment, or on assignment.

Tips: "Write for a copy of our 'Guidelines for Writers' (enclose SASE), then study our magazine and send us some ideas along with samples of your work."

Arkansas

ARKANSAS TIMES, Arkansas Writers' Project, Inc., Box 34010, Little Rock AR 72203. (501)375-2985. Editor: Bob Lancaster. 25% freelance written. Monthly magazine. "We are an Arkansas magazine. We seek to appreciate, enliven and, where necessary, improve the quality of life in the state." Circ. 28,000. Pays on publication, "but with exceptions." Byline given. Pays negotiable kill fee. Not copyrighted. Buys first North American serial rights. Submit seasonal/holiday material 3 months in advance. Simultaneous, photocopied, and previously published submissions OK. SASE. Reports in 2 weeks on queries; 1 month on mss. Publishes ms an average of 3 months after acceptance. Sample copy $3.

Nonfiction: Mel White, articles editor. Book excerpts; expose (in investigative reporting vein); general interest; historical/nostalgic; humor; interview/profile; opinion; recreation; and entertainment, all relating to Arkansas. "The Arkansas angle is all-important." Buys 24 mss/year. Query. Length: 250-6,000 words. Pays $100-400.

Photos: Mary Jo Meade, photo editor. State availability of photos. Pays $25-75 for 8x10 b&w or color prints. Identification of subjects required. Buys one-time rights.

Columns/Departments: Paul Williams, column editor. Arkansas Reporter ("articles on people, places and things in Arkansas or with special interest to Arkansans). This is the department that is most open to freelancers." Buys 25 mss/year. Query. Length: 250-750 words. Pays $100.

Fiction: Adventure, historical, humorous, mainstream and romance. "All fiction must have an Arkansas angle." Buys 4 mss/year. Send complete ms. Length: 1,250-5,000 words. Pays $200-300.

Poetry: Paul Williams, poetry editor. Avant-garde, free verse, haiku, light verse, traditional and ballad. Buys 30-40 mss/year. Submit maximum 5 poems. Pays $50 maximum; "poems are generally without payment."

Tips: "The most annoying aspect of working with freelance writers is receiving well written manuscripts about unanticipated topics."

California

‡ANDERSON VALLEY ADVERTISER, Box 459, Boonville CA 95415. (707)895-3536. Editor: Bruce Anderson. Country weekly (liberal) with "democratic socialistic" slant. Pays on acceptance. Byline given. Not copyrighted. Buys one-time rights. Submit seasonal/holiday material 2 months in advance. Simultaneous, photocopied and previously published submissions OK. Reports in 2 weeks.

Nonfiction: Expose (education, rural, agriculture); humor (sophisticated); and opinion (unusual, off-beat). Buys 10 mss/year. Send complete ms. Length: 3,000 words maximum. Pays $25-200.

Poetry: Avant-garde, free verse, haiku. Buys 25-40 poems/year. Submit maximum 25. Pays $10-15.

Tips: "Unpublished, quality writers will be given a change, even preference, here."

‡BAJA TIMES, Editorial Playas De Rosarito, S.A., Box 755, San Ysidro CA 92073. Publisher: Hugo Torres. General Manager: Carlos Chabert. Editorial Consultant: John Utley. 65% freelance written. Current Baja information for Americans visiting or living in northern Baja California, Mexico. Monthly tabloid. Circ. 600,000. Byline given. Pays on publication. Makes work-for-hire assignments. Submit seasonal/holiday material 3 months in advance. Photocopied and previously published submissions OK. Computer printout submissions acceptable. Reports in 4-6 weeks. Publishes ms an average of 6 months after acceptance. Free sample copy.

Nonfiction: Historical (Baja); sports and fishing; travel (in Baja); money-saving Baja advice; Baja cooking; Baja book reviews; Baja gardening; unusual events, people and animals; customs, etc.; and personal experience (of those familiar with Baja). "We are interested in all ideas and new slants on old topics. Photo essays welcome." Buys 4 mss/issue. Send complete ms. SASE. Length: 700-1,500 words. Pays $25-50; longer ms somewhat higher.

Photos: Send photos with ms. Pays $5 for b&w. Captions required. Buys one-time rights. Please do NOT send color.

Tips: "All over the US are descendants of men who explored or invested in Baja during the 19th century and the first 35 years of the 20th. Deeds, photographs, maps, any memorabilia their heirs can assemble would be valuable subject matter for us."

BAKERSFIELD LIFESTYLE, 123 Truxtun Ave., Bakersfield CA 93301. (805)325-7124. Editor and Publisher: Steve Walsh. Monthly magazine covering local lifestyles for college educated males/females ages 25-49 in a balanced community of industrial, agricultural and residential areas. Circ. 10,000. Byline and brief bio given. Buys first North American serial rights. Simultaneous queries and simultaneous and photocopied submissions OK. Computer printout submissions acceptable. SASE. Reports in 6 month. Sample copy $2.50.

Nonfiction: General interest (topical issues); travel (up to 1,500 words); and articles on former residents who are now successful elsewhere. No investigative reporting, politics or negative editorial. Buys 12-15 mss/year. Length: 2,500 words maximum. Pays $15.

Photos: Send photos with ms. Pays $1/photo used.

Fiction: "Anything in good taste." Buys 20 mss/year. Length: 3,000 words maximum. Pays $15 maximum.

‡THE BERKELEY MONTHLY, Klaber Publishing Co., 910 Parker St., Berkeley CA 94710. (415)848-7900. Editor: Margaretta Kamiya. A monthly local, general interest tabloid focusing on East Bay issues and

personalities. Circ. 75,000. Pays 30 days after publication. Byline given. Offers $25 kill fee for features. Buys first North American serial rights. Submit seasonal/holiday material 6 months in advance. Simultaneous queries, and photocopied and previously published work "outside our market" OK. SASE. Reports in 2 months on queries; 5 months on mss. Sample copy for $2, 9x12 SAE and 2 first class stamps.
Nonfiction: Book excerpts; expose (local political issues; Berkeley, Oakland); humor; and interview/profile (local personalities). No religious material, war stories or anthing outside local area. Buys 50 mss/year. Query with published clips. Length: 800-4,000 words. Pays $25-200.

‡**CALIFORNIA LIVING**, *San Francisco Examiner*, 110 Fifth St., San Francisco CA 94103. (415)777-7905. Editor: Hal Silverman. Managing Editor: Wendy Thomas. Magazine of the Sunday *Examiner and Chronicle* covering lifestyle, leisure, service and untold stories with a Bay area and/or regional focus, for newspaper readers. Circ. 750,000. Pays on publication. Byline given. Buys first North American rights, first rights, and one-time rights. Submit seasonal/holiday material 6 months in advance. Photocopied submissions OK. Computer printout submissions acceptable; prefers letter-quality to dot-matrix. SASE. Reports in 3 weeks. Sample copy "available on newsstands."
Nonfiction: Lifestyle, leisure and service articles, untold stories, and behind-the-scenes news stories; must have a Bay area and/or regional focus. Buys 150 unsolicited mss/year. Query. Length: 1,200-2,500 words. Pays $150-250.
Photos: Jack Atkinson and Jon Lombardi, photo editors. State availability or send photos with query or ms. Reviews 35mm color transparencies and 8x10 glossy prints. Pays "open fee." Captions, model release and identification of subjects required. Buys one-time rights.
Fiction: Novel excerpts (relating to the Bay area).

CALIFORNIA MAGAZINE, 1601 Wilshire Blvd., 18th Floor, Los Angeles CA 90025. (213)273-7516. Executive Editor: Tom Bates. Editor: Harold Hayes. Publishes 12 issues/year. Buys first rights only. Offers 20% kill fee. Byline given. SASE. Reports in 6 weeks. Sample copy $3.50.
Nonfiction: Fresh, original, well-written pieces with a California focus—good, solid sports articles; service pieces with a statewide appeal; political, environmental, and business issues, ambitious profiles; in addition to well-researched investigative pieces. No fiction. Query with clips of published work. No phone queries. Length: 4,000-10,000 words. Pay varies.
Photos: State availability of photos. "We assign almost all photos." Buys first rights. Captions preferred; model releases required.
Columns/Departments: "Departments are written regularly by contributing editors, with the exception of Westword, an opinion page (ideas not often generated in-house, writers assigned), and California Reporter. Reporter items are timely, newsworthy close-ups which run up to 1,000 words and pay up to $250." Buys up to 30 unsolicited mss/year.

HUMBOLDT COUNTY MAGAZINE, Box 3150, Eureka CA 95501. (707)445-9038. Editor/Publisher: Craig J. Beardsley. Annual magazine covering travel and tourism in Humboldt County, Northern California. This county, roughly the size of Delaware and Rhode Island combined, encompasses more than half of all the world's redwoods. Circ. 150,000. Pays on acceptance. Buys first rights only. Submit material 3 months in advance. SASE. Usually reports the same day. Sample copy $2.
Nonfiction: Reason for the publication's existence: "To educate, entertain and inform the 2.5 million visitors who travel through Humboldt County each year. Freelancers welcomed with open arms . . . if they know their subject matter." Recent article includes "Where to Go for Gifts". Query. Buys 3-5 unsolicited mss/year. Length: 1,500-3,000 words. Pays $200-500.
Photos: Pays $50 minimum for b&w and color.
Tips: "It's the subject matter that catches an editor's eye rather than the approach."

LOS ANGELES MAGAZINE, Suite 920, 1888 Century Park E., Los Angeles CA 90067. Executive Editor: Lew Harris. Editor: Geoff Miller. Monthly. Circ. 165,000. Buys first North American serial rights. Pays 30% kill fee. Byline given. Query. SASE.
Nonfiction: Uses articles on how best to live (i.e., the quality of life) in the "changing, growing, diverse Los Angeles urban-suburban area; ideas, trends, people, and occasionally places. Writer must have an understanding of contemporary living and doing in Southern California; material must appeal to an upper-income, better-educated group of people. Fields of interest include urban problems, pleasures, personalities, careers and cultural opportunities, candid, irreverent interviews of topical interest; the arts. Solid research and reportage required. No essays." Length: 1,000-3,500 words. Also uses some topical satire and humor. Pays $50-1,200.
Photos: Most photos assigned to local photographers. Occasionally buys photographs with mss. B&w should be 8x10. Pays $25-50 for single article photos.

LOS ANGELES READER, 8471 Melrose Ave., Second Floor, Los Angeles CA 90069. (213)655-8810. Editor: James Vowell. Arts Editor: Richard Gehr. Assistant Editor: Nancy Gottesman. Weekly tabloid of features, reviews and fiction for "affluent young Los Angelenos interested in the arts and popular culture." Circ. 75,000. Pays on publication. Byline given. Buys one-time rights. Submit seasonal/holiday material 2 months in advance. Simultaneous queries and photocopied submissions OK. Computer printout submissions acceptable; prefers letter-quality to dot-matrix. SASE. Reports in 2 months. Sample copy $1; free writer's guidelines.

Nonfiction: Expose, general interest, historical/nostalgic, interview/profile, personal experience and photo features. "No aimless satire." Buys "hundreds" of mss/year. Send complete ms. Length: 200-4,000 words. Pays $10-300.

Fiction: Adventure, confession, experimental, historical, mainstream and novel excerpts. Interested in serious fiction. Buys 4-5 mss/year. Send complete ms. Length: 1,000-4,000 words. Pays $50-200.

Tips: "Break in with submission for our Cityside page: short news items on Los Angeles happenings/semi-hard news. We are nearly entirely a local publication and want only writing about local themes, topics, people by local writers."

MONTEREY LIFE, The Magazine of California's Spectacular Central Coast, Box 2107, Monterey CA 93942. (408)372-9200. Editor: William Morem. Monthly magazine covering art, photography, regional affairs, music, sports, environment and lifestyles for "a sophisticated readership in the central California coast area." Circ. 20,000. Pays on publication. Byline given. Offers variable kill fee. Buys first North American serial rights. Submit seasonal/holiday material 4 months in advance. Simultaneous queries and simultaneous and photocopied submissions OK. Computer printout submissions acceptable. SASE. Reports in 3 weeks on queries; 6 weeks on mss. Sample copy for $1.75, SAE and $1.92 postage.

Nonfiction: Historical/nostalgic, humor, interview/profile, photo feature and travel—no poetry. "All articles apply to this region except Getaway which covers travel within one day's drive." Buys 75 mss/year. Query with clips if available. Length: 175-2,500 words. Pays $25-200.

Photos: State availability of photos. Pays $20-100 for color transparencies; $15-25 for 5x7 and 8x10 b&w prints. Captions, model release, and identification of subjects required. Buys one-time rights.

Columns/Departments: Community Focus. Query with clips of published work. Length: 250-1,000 words. Pays $25-40.

‡**NORTHCOAST VIEW**, Blarney Publishing, Box 1374, Eureka CA 95502. (707)443-4887. Publishers/Editors: Scott K. Ryan and Damon Maguire. A monthly magazine covering entertainment, recreation, the arts, consumer news, in-depth news, fiction and poetry for Humboldt County audience, mostly 18-50 year olds. Circ. 20,000. Pays on publication. Byline given. Generally buys all rights, but will reassign. Submit seasonal/holiday material 4-6 months in advance. Simultaneous queries, and simultaneous (so long as not in our area), photocopied, and previously published (so long as rights available) submissions OK. Computer printout submissions acceptable. SASE. Reports in 2 weeks on queries; 2 months on mss. Sample copy $1; free writer's guidelines.

Nonfiction: Book excerpts (locally written); expose (consumer, government); historical/nostalgic (local); humor; interview/profile (entertainment, recreation, arts or political people planning to visit county); new product (for arts); photo feature (local for art section); and travel (weekend and short retreats accessible from Humboldt County). "Most features need a Humboldt County slant." Special issues include Kinetic Sculpture Race (May), Christmas (Dec.), and St. Patrick's Day (March). Buys 30-40 mss/year. Query with published clips or send complete ms. Length: 1,250-2,500 words. Pays $25-75.

Photos: State availability of photos with query letter or ms and send proof sheet, if available. Pays $5-15 for 5x7 b&w prints; $25-100 for 35mm Ecktachrome slides for color. Captions, model release and identification of subjects required. Buys all rights but will reassign.

Columns/Departments: Outdoors (outdoor activities in Humboldt County including crabbing, fishing, boating, skiing, etc.); A La Carte (restaurant reviews of county restaurants); Ex Libris (books); Reel Views (film); Vinyl Views (albums); Cornucopia (calendar); Poetry; Rearview (art). Buys 80-100 mss/year. Send complete ms. Length: 500-750 words. Pays $10-25.

Fiction: Adventure, condensed novels, erotica (light), experimental, fantasy, horror, humorous, mystery, novel excerpts (local), science fiction and suspense. "We are open to most ideas and like to publish new writers. Topic and length are all very flexible—quality reading the only criteria." No cliche, contrived or predictable fiction—"we like a twist to stories." Buys 10-15 mss/year. Send complete ms. Length: 600-4,500 words; "longer good piece may run 2-3 months consecutively, if it breaks well."

Poetry: Stephen Miller and Mary Johnson, poetry editors. Avant-garde, free verse, haiku, light verse and traditional. Open to all types. No "sappy, overdone or symbolic poetry." Buys work of 12-20 poets (3-4 poems each)/year. Submit maximum of 5 poems. Length: 12-48 lines. Pays $5-20.

Tips: "Our greatest need always seems to be for reviews—book, album and film. Films need to be fairly current, but remember that some films take awhile to get up to Humboldt County. Book and album—we're always looking for somewhat current but lesser known works that are exceptional to turn our readers onto. Now we are almost exclusively entertainment, recreation and the arts but look to expand to general, in-depth and consumer reporting—so we are looking for those kinds of stories, especially those that we may be able to put a local angle to or have a local side story accompany."

‡**ORANGE COAST MAGAZINE, The Magazine of Orange County**, O.C.N.L., Inc., 18200 W. McDurmott, Irvine CA 92714. (714)660-8622. Editor: Lou Schuler. Assistant Editor: Andrea Holm. 90% freelance written. *Orange Coast* is designed to inform and enlighten the educated, upscale residents of affluent Orange Country, California: It is the largest magazine in the county and is highly graphic and well researched. Monthly. Circ. 40,000. Pays on acceptance. Byline given. Buys first North American serial rights. Submit seasonal/ holiday material 6 months in advance. Simultaneous queries, and simultaneous and photocopied submissions OK. Computer printout submissions acceptable; prefers letter-quality to dot-matrix. SASE. Reports in 2 months. Publishes ms an average of 5 months after acceptance. Sample copy for $2.50, 10x12 SAE and $2.25 postage; writer's guidelines for SAE and 1 first class stamp.
Nonfiction: Expose (Orange Country government, refugees, politics, agencies, prisons); general interest (anything dealing with Orange County); historical/nostalgic; guides to activities and services; interview/profile (Orange County prominent citizens); local sports; and lifestyle features. Special issues include Dining (March); Health and Beauty (June); Finance (August); Home and Garden (September); and Holiday (December). No articles not dealing with Orange County at least peripherally. Buys 100 mss/year. Query or send complete ms. Length: 2,500-4,000 words. Pays $150 maximum.
Columns/Departments: Local Consumer, Investments, Sports, Profiles, Medicine, plus Local Reviews (music, art, theater, film, restaurants). Buys 100 mss/year. Query or send complete ms. Length: 1,500-2,000 words. Pays $100 maximum.
Fiction: Historical, humorous, mainstream, novel/excerpts, serialized novels and suspense. No fiction not set in Orange County or science fiction. Buys 3 Christmas-oriented mss/year, others under extremely rare circumstances. Send complete ms. Length: 1,000-5,000 words. Pays $150 maximum.
Tips: "Don't try to sell us 'generic' journalism. *Orange Coast* prefers well written stories with specific and unusual angles that in some way include Orange County. Entertaining and well researched lifestyle stories are bought fastest. Be professional and write manuscripts that present you as a stylized, creative and caring writer. All features and departments are open to freelancers except for the celebrity interview which is written in house. It's most rewarding seeing a really bright new talent emerge and being able to help him/her along. There's nothing more refreshing than a writer coming into my office with new ideas, new approaches to the medium and a no-restraints approach to his/her job."

‡**THE SACRAMENTO BEE**, Box 15779, Sacramento CA 95852. 5% freelance written. For a general readership; higher-than-average education; higher-than-average interest in politics and government; oriented toward outdoor activity. Newspaper; 60 pages. Daily. Circ. 219,000 daily; 254,000 Sunday. Not copyrighted. Buys first rights only. Buys 200 mss/year. Pays on publication. Will consider simultaneous submissions if they are not duplicated in Northern California. Computer printout submissions acceptable. Reports in 2 weeks. Publishes ms an average of 1 month after acceptance. Query or submit complete ms to features editor or scene editor.
Nonfiction: Human interest features, news background. Prefers narrative feature style. Does not want to see sophomoric humor. Will consider interviews, profiles, nostalgic articles; expose; and personal experience. Buys 5-10 unsolicited mss/year. Length: 100-1,500 words. Pays $20-100.
Photos: B&w glossy prints and color (negatives) purchased with or without mss. Pays $15-75 for b&w; $25-100 for color. Captions required.

SACRAMENTO MAGAZINE, Box 2424, Sacramento CA 95811. Editor: Cheryl Romo. 80% freelance written. Monthly magazine emphasizing a strong local angle on politics, local issues, human interest and consumer items for readers in the middle to high income brackets. Pays on acceptance within a 30-day billing period. Buys all rights. Original manuscripts only (no previously published work). Computer printout submissions acceptable; prefers letter-quality to dot-matrix. No phone calls; query by letter. Reports in 6 weeks. SASE. Writer's guidelines for SASE.
Nonfiction: Local issues vital to Sacramento quality of life. Past articles have included "Gasping at Straws" (rice straw burning and its resultant air pollution) and "Missing" (the disappearance of a young sailor). Buys 15 unsolicited feature mss/year. Query first. Length: 200-3,000 words, depending on author, subject matter and treatment.
Photos: State availability of photos. Payment varies depending on photographer, subject matter and treatment. Captions (including IDs, location and date) required.
Columns/Departments: Media, gourmet, profile, sports, city arts, and home and garden (850-1,250 words); City Lights (250 words).

SAN DIEGO MAGAZINE, Box 85409, San Diego CA 92138. (619)225-8953. Editor-in-Chief: Edwin F. Self. Emphasizes San Diego. Monthly magazine; 250 pages. Circ. 53,063. Pays on publication. Buys all rights. Pays negotiable kill fee. Byline given. Submit seasonal/holiday material 6 months in advance of issue date. Simultaneous and photocopied submissions OK. SASE. Reports in 2 months. Sample copy $3.
Nonfiction: Expose (serious, documented); general interest (to San Diego region); historical (San Diego region); interview (with notable San Diegans); nostalgia; photo essay; profile; service guides; and travel. Buys 7

mss/issue. Query with clips of published work or submit complete ms. Buys 12 unsolicited mss/year. Length: 2,000-3,000 words. Pays $500 maximum.

Photos: State availability of photos with query. Pays $25-75 b&w; $45-150 color; $250 for cover. Captions required. Buys all rights. Model release required.

Tips: "Write better lead paragraphs; write shorter, with greater clarity; wit and style appreciated; stick to basic magazine journalism principles."

‡**THE SAN DIEGO UNION**, Box 191, San Diego CA 92112. Associate Editor: Ed Nichols. "The bulk of the material we buy is for our Sunday section, Opinion. Optimum pieces are analytical essays on international, geo-political developments or commentary on domestic social, economic, scientific and political trends. We're looking for in-depth research, some original material in the article, and cogency of thought." Length: 1,200 words. Byline given. Pays $125 on publication. Op-ed page: interested in material on a broad range of topics related to current events and in-depth pieces on world events. Uses the whole spectrum of original writing—but piece must have a purpose (such as humor) or throw new light on an issue. Length: 750 words.

SAN FRANCISCO FOCUS, The KQED Magazine for the San Francisco Bay Area, KQED Inc., 500 8th St., San Francisco CA 94103. (415)553-2119. Editor: Mark K. Powelson. Managing Editor: Warren Sharpe. A monthly city/regional magazine. Circ. 160,000. Pays on publication. Byline given. Offers ⅓ of assigned rate for kill fee. Buys one-time rights. Submit seasonal/holiday material 2-3 months in advance. Simultaneous queries and previously published submissions OK. Computer printout submissions acceptable. SASE. Reports in 6 weeks. Sample copy $1.50; free writer's guidelines.

Nonfiction: Expose, humor, interview/profile and travel. All stories should relate in some way to the San Francisco Bay Area (travel excepted). Query with published clips or send complete ms. Length: 750-3,000 words. Pays $75-400.

SAN FRANCISCO MAGAZINE, 950 Battery St., San Francisco CA 94110. (415)777-5555. Editor: Michael Singer. Monthly magazine covering general interest topics for San Francisco and northern California residents. Circ. 50,000. Pays within 30 days of the issue's appearance on the newsstand. Byline and brief bio given. No kill fee. Buys first North American serial rights. Photocopied submissions OK. Reports in 3 weeks.

Nonfiction: General interest (lifestyles, fashion); humor; interview/profile (of person with a Northern California connection); personal experience (first person pieces); photo feature; consumer; and science. "Topics may be of national scope. We want well researched, well written articles with a northern California fix." Buys fewer than 10 unsolicited mss/year. Query with clips of published work or send complete ms. Length: 2,000-5,000 words. Pays $500 average.

Photos: State availability of photos. Reviews 35mm color transparencies and 8x10 b&w glossy prints. Negotiates pay separately for package of photos or ms/photo package.

THE SAN GABRIEL VALLEY MAGAZINE, Miller Books, 2908 W. Valley Blvd., Alhambra CA 91803. (213)284-7607. Editor-in-Chief: Joseph Miller. 75% freelance written. For upper to middle-income people who dine out often at better restaurants in Los Angeles County. Bimonthly magazine; 52 pages. Circ. 3,400. Pays on publication. Buys simultaneous, second serial (reprint) and one-time rights. Phone queries OK. Submit seasonal/holiday material 1 month in advance. Simultaneous, photocopied and previously published submissions OK. Computer printout submissions acceptable. SASE. Reports in 2 weeks. Publishes ms an average of 45 days after acceptance. Sample copy $1.

Nonfiction: Expose (political); informational (restaurants in the Valley); inspirational (success stories and positive thinking); interview (successful people and how they made it); profile (political leaders in the San Gabriel Valley); and travel (places in the Valley). Interested in 500-word humor articles. Buys 18 unsolicited mss/year. Length: 500-10,000 words. Pays 5¢/word.

Columns/Departments: Restaurants, Education, and Valley News and Valley Personality. Buys 2 mss/issue. Send complete ms. Length: 500-1,500 words. Pays 5¢/word.

Fiction: Historical (successful people) and western (articles about Los Angeles County). Buys 2 mss/issue. Send complete ms. Length: 500-10,000 words. Pays 5¢/word.

Tips: "Send us a good personal success story about a Valley or a California personality. We are also interested in articles on positive thinking and people who have made it."

‡**THE TRIBUNE**, (formerly *Oakland Tribune/Eastbay Today*), Box 24424, Oakland CA 94623. (415)645-2000. 1% freelance written. Daily newspaper for the greater San Francisco/Oakland Bay area. Circ. 150,000. Pays on publication. Byline given. Not copyrighted. Buys one-time rights. Submit seasonal/holiday material 6 weeks in advance. Simultaneous queries and simultaneous, photocopied, and previously published submissions OK. Electronic submissions OK if compatible with AP Datespeed. Computer printout submissions acceptable; prefers letter-quality to dot-matrix. SASE. Publishes ms an average of 3 weeks after acceptance.

Nonfiction: Diane L. Borden, assistant managing editor. Length: 800 words maximum. Pays $75 maximum.

VENTURA COUNTY & COAST REPORTER, The Reporter, VCR Inc., 4732 Telephone Rd. "B", Ventura CA 93003. (805)658-2244; (805)656-0707. Editor: Nancy Cloutier. Weekly tabloid covering local news. Circ. 25,000. Pays on publication. Byline given. Buys first North American serial rights. SASE. Reports in 3 weeks.
Nonfiction: General interest, humor, interview/profile and travel (local—within 500 miles). "Local (Ventura County) slant predominates." Length: 2-5 double-spaced typewritten pages. Pays $10-25.
Photos: State availability of photos with ms. Reviews b&w contact sheet.
Columns/Departments: Boating Experience (southern California). Send complete ms. Pays $10-25.

‡**VICTOR VALLEY MAGAZINE, The High Desert Illustrated**, Desert Alive Publishing Company, Box 618, Victorville CA 92392. Editor: Grace Spann. Managing Editor: David Stratton. 100% freelance written. A magazine covering regional events, personalities, issues, etc., published monthly except January/February and July/August combined. Circ. 9,700. Pays within 2 weeks of publication. Byline given. Offers 50% kill fee. Buys first North American serial rights. Submit seasonal/holiday material 3 months in advance. Simultaneous queries, and simultaneous, photocopied and previously published submissions OK. Computer printout submissions acceptable "if upper and lower case." SASE. Reports in 1 month. Publishes ms an average of 3 months after acceptance. Free sample copy; writer's guidelines for SAE and 1 first class stamp.
Nonfiction: General interest, historical/nostalgic, how-to, interview/profile, personal experience, photo feature and travel. No book reviews, film reviews, controversy, or political articles. Buys 50 mss/year. Send complete ms. Length: 600-1,000 words. Pays $20-75.
Photos: Send photos with ms. Pays $25-50 for color transparencies; $5-25 for 4x5 b&w prints. Captions, model release, and identification of subjects required. Buys one-time rights.
Columns/Departments: Desert Alive (stories about the animal and plant life in and around the high desert area: what nature enthusiasts can look for, how desert-dwellers can better live with the local wildlife, etc.); Growing in the High Desert (when to plant, what to plant, how to cultivate, interesting local personalities who have mastered the severe elements of the Mojave Desert); History and Lore (stories about the western development of the high desert area, from the fierce Mojave Indian tribe to the Mormon settlers; from historical landmarks to old Route 66; Family Living Today (dealing with family and social relationships, children, self-improvement, popular culture, etc.); and Desert Personalities (interesting locals, not necessarily of prominence. Avoid the typical biography or profile; focus on the day-to-day individuals and what makes them or what they do special. For example, in the Superior Court, the life of a bailiff or court reporter may be of more interest than the judge).
Tips: "Our readers have expressed a strong interest in local history (Mojave Desert), interesting personalities, and living better in the high desert. Start with *growing* in the desert, wildlife and desert-related activities (rock hounding, prospecting, 4-wheeling, etc."

WEST, (formerly *CalToday*), 750 Ridder Park Dr., San Jose CA 95190. (408)920-5602. Editor: Jeffrey Klein. For a general audience. Weekly rotogravure newspaper/magazine, published with the *San Jose Mercury News*. Circ. 300,000. Byline given. Buys 50 mss/year. Pays on acceptance. Will consider photocopied and simultaneous submissions if the simultaneous submission is out of their area. Submit seasonal material (skiing, wine, outdoor living) 3 months in advance. Reports in 4 weeks. Query. SASE. Free sample copy.
Nonfiction: A general newspaper-magazine requiring that most subjects be related to California (especially the Bay Area) and the interests of California. Will consider subjects outside California if subject is of broad or national appeal. Length: 1,000-4,000 words. Pays $250-600.
Photos: Payment varies for b&w and color photos purchased with or without mss. Captions required. Queries should be submitted to the attention of Carol Doup Muller.

WESTWAYS, Box 2890, Terminal Annex, Los Angeles CA 90051. (213)741-4760. Managing Editor: Mary Ann Cravens. 90% freelance written. For "fairly affluent, college-educated, mobile and active southern California families. Average age of head of household is 42. Monthly. Buys first rights only. Byline given. Pays prior to publication for mss; on publication for most photos. Computer printout submissions acceptable. Reports in 2 weeks. Publishes ms an average of 6 months after acceptance. Query. SASE.
Nonfiction: "Informative articles, well researched and written in fresh, literate, honest style." This publication "covers all states west of the Rockies, including Alaska and Hawaii, western Canada and Mexico. We're willing to consider anything that interprets and illuminates the American West—past or present—for the western American family. Employ imagination in treating subject. Avoid PR hand-out type style and format, and please know at least something about the magazine." Subjects include "travel, history and modern civic, cultural and sociological aspects of the West; camping, fishing, natural science, humor, first-person adventure and experience, nostalgia, profiles, occasional unusual and offbeat pieces and foreign travel." Buys 150-200 unsolicited mss/year. Length: 1,000 to 1,500 words. Pays 20¢/word minimum.
Photos: Buys color and b&w photos with mss. Prefers 35mm color. Pays $25 minimum "for each b&w used as illustration"; $50/transparency.

Colorado

BOULDER SUNDAY CAMERA MAGAZINE, (formerly *Boulder Daily Camera Focus Magazine*), Box 591, Boulder CO 80306. (303)442-1202. Editor-in-Chief: Vicki Groninger. 75% freelance written. Emphasizes subjects of particular interest to Boulder County residents. Weekly tabloid; 32 pages. Circ. 37,000. Pays on publication. Buys first rights and second (reprint) rights to material originally published elsewhere. Byline given. Phone queries OK. Submit seasonal/holiday material 6-8 weeks in advance. Photocopied submissions OK. Computer printout submissions acceptable; no dot-matrix. SASE. Reports in 6 weeks. Publishes ms an average of 1 month after acceptance.
Nonfiction: Expose (anything relevant to Boulder County that needs exposing); informational (emphasis on good writing, warmth and impact); historical (pertaining to Boulder County or Colorado in general); interview and profile (stress local angle); photo feature (featuring Boulder County or areas in Colorado and Rocky Mountain West where Boulder County residents are apt to go). Buys 100 mss/year. Query. Length: 700-2,000 words. Rates and guidelines available on request.
Photos: Purchased with or without mss or on assignment. Captions required. Query. Pays $10 for 8x10 b&w glossy prints; $20 for 35mm or 2¼x2¼ (or larger) color transparencies.
Tips: "We're demanding a more sophisticated style than we have in the past. Trends in magazine publishing that freelance writers should be aware of include use of more graphics—they should think visually."

‡**THIS WEEK IN DENVER**, Queen City Publishing, Inc. Box 22542, Denver CO 80222. (303)759-2977. Editor: Eileen Wigginton. Managing Editor: Liza Cabot. A monthly regional (Colorado) magazine covering entertainment, fine arts, music and sports for "readers who are well educated (23% have a Masters or higher graduate degree); earn upwards of $40,000 annually." Circ. 50,000. Pays on publication. Byline given. Buys all rights. Submit seasonal/holiday material 2 months in advance. Simultaneous queries, and photocopied and previously published submissions (with complete information and releases) OK. SASE. Reports in 1 month. Free sample copy and writer's guidelines.
Nonfiction: General interest, historical/nostalgic, how-to, humor, inspirational, interview/profile (by query only), personal experience (essay form) and travel. Special issues include seasonal sports. "We are very interested in reflective essays, historical essays and humorous essays. Generally we prefer essays that are of light subjects and not more than 1,100 words. Drawings and other illustrations are welcomed." No political or erotic articles. Buys 6 mss/year. Query with published clips. Length: 500-2,000 words. Pays 5-10¢/word.
Columns/Departments: Benefits (local), children, dance, film, fine arts, museums, music, nightlife, poetry, radio, shopping, sports, theatre and tours. Query with published clips or send complete ms. Length: 500-1,500 words. Pays 5-10¢/word.
Fiction: Adventure, historical, humorous, mainstream, mystery, suspense and western. Buys 11 mss/year. Send complete ms. Length: 1,100-2,000 words. Pays 5¢/word.
Poetry: Avant-garde, free verse, haiku, light verse, traditional. No erotic or political poetry. Buys 11 poems/year. Length: open. Pays $5 minimum.
Fillers: Jokes, short humor and serial game or mystery (see games in magazine sample). Pays negotiable rate.
Tips: "Fiction, humorous essay and historical short essays for our 'From Out of the West' section are most open to freelancers."

Connecticut

CONNECTICUT MAGAZINE, 636 Kings Hwy., Fairfield CT 06430. (203)576-1205. Managing Editor: Elizabeth H. O'Neil. Monthly magazine for an affluent, sophisticated suburban audience. Pays on publication. Buys all rights. Reports in 2 months. Sample copy $2.
Nonfiction: "We want only those features which pertain specifically to Connecticut, with emphasis on service, investigative and consumer articles." No fiction or poetry. Buys 50 mss/year. Query with clips of published work and "a full, intelligent, *neat* outline of the proposed piece. The more information offered, the better the chance of an assignment." Pays $100-600.
Photos: State availability of photos. Pays $35-75 for b&w prints; $75-200 for color transparencies. Captions and model releases required.
Columns/Departments: General features, business and politics pertaining to Connecticut. Buys 50 columns/year. Query. Length: 1,000 words minimum. Pays $100-450.

The double dagger (‡) before a listing indicates that the listing is new in this edition. New markets are often the most receptive to freelance contributions.

Tips: "Read past issues of the magazine and submit queries relevant to our state and style. Have good solid ideas and present them in a clear and interesting manner."

‡**CONNECTICUT TRAVELER, Official Publication of the Connecticut Motor Club/AAA,** Connecticut Motor Club/AAA, 2276 Whitney Ave., Hamden CT 06518. (203)288-7441. Director of Publications: Elke Martin. Monthly (beginning November 1984) tabloid covering anything of interest to the Connecticut motorist for Connecticut Motor Club members. Estab. 1983. Circ. 155,000. Pays on publication. Byline given. Buys first North American serial rights, first rights, and second serial (reprint) rights. Submit seasonal/holiday material 4 months in advance. Photocopied and previously published submissions OK. SASE. Reports in 2 weeks on queries; 1 month on mss. Sample copy for 8½x11 SAE; writer's guidelines for legal-size SAE and 1 first class stamp.
Nonfiction: How-to (variety, how to make traveling with children fun, etc.); humor (travel or auto related); and travel (regional economy or low-budget with specifics, i.e., what accommodations, restaurants, sights, recreation are available). "We are a regional publication and focus on events, traveling and other topics within the New England area. We do not want to see mechanical or highly complicated automotive how-tos or exotic travel stories that would be financially out of reach for the average traveler." Buys 20 mss/year. Query or send complete ms. Length: 500-1,500 words. Pays $25-75.
Photos: Send photos with accompanying query or ms. Pays $5-10 for 8x10 b&w prints. Captions, model releases and identification of subjects required. Buys one-time rights.
Tips: "If you can get us a story on a travel destination that's unusual and hasn't been beaten to death and cover the specifics in an interesting and fun-to-read manner, we'll definitely consider the story for publication. Stress regional slant, suitability (will senior citizen, children, etc., enjoy this trip?), and what makes the particular destination special."

NEW HAVEN INFO MAGAZINE, Box 1618, New Haven CT 06506. (203)562-3243. Editor: Sandra Brugos. For those interested in art, music, theatre, recreational activities, etc. Monthly magazine; 64 pages. Circ. 5,000. Not copyrighted. Byline given. Buys 20 mss/year. Pays on publication. Will consider photocopied and simultaneous submissions. Computer printout submissions acceptable. Reports in 1 month. Query. SASE. Sample copy 50¢.
Nonfiction: "Most of our material is on assignment. We publish articles dealing with New Haven area events and people." Personal experience, interview, profile, historical and nostalgia. No religious, scientific or political material. Buys 10 unsolicited mss/year. Length: 350-700 words. Pays $15/page (about 350 words).

NORTHEAST MAGAZINE, *The Hartford Courant*, 179 Allyn St., Hartford CT 06103. (203)241-3701. Editor: Lary Bloom. Weekly magazine for a Connecticut audience. Circ. 300,000. Pays on acceptance. Buys 100-150 mss/year. Byline given. Buys one-time rights. Previously published submissions OK. Unsolicted ms or queries accepted; reports in 3 weeks. SASE.
Nonfiction: General interest; in-depth investigation of stories behind news; historical/nostalgic; interview/profile (of famous or important people with Connecticut ties); and personal essays (humorous or anecdotal). No poetry. Length: 750-4,500 words. Pays $200-1,000.
Fiction: Well-written, original short stories. Length: 750-4,500 words.
Photos: Most assigned; state availability of photos. "Do not send originals."

Delaware

DELAWARE TODAY MAGAZINE, Box 3029, Wilmington DE 19804. (302)995-7146. Editor: Peter Mucha. 80 percent freelance written. Monthly magazine covering subjects of broad interest in Delaware. 100 pages. Circ. 15,000. Pays month of publication. SASE necessary. Reports in 6 weeks.
Nonfiction: Features: Human interest articles. "We want lively, vivid writing about people, organizations, communities, lifestyles and trends or events that are of special interest to people in Delaware." Service articles: "Each month we try to run an informative guide to goods or services or leisure activities. Except for travel articles, must have a Delaware tie-in." Short subjects: "When our budget permits, we will accept items that are brief but informative, perceptive or amusing. Must relate to Delaware." In all cases, query first with writing samples. Features pay $125-250; short subjects $15-50. Columns/Departments pays $50-100.
Photos: Uses monthly photo essays of people and places of interest in the state. Must express local color or let readers see themselves in the subject. Pays $100-150. All photography is freelance. Pays $15-25 for b&w photo; $100-150 for photos illustrating an entire article.
Tips: "Study the magazine first and then think big. The more people who might be interested in the subject, the more likely we are to be interested."

District of Columbia

THE WASHINGTON DOSSIER, Adler International Ltd., 3301 New Mexico Ave. NW, Washington DC 20016. (202)362-4040. Editor: Sonia Adler. Senior Editor: Don Oldenburg. 50% freelance written. Monthly general interest magazine covering the Washington social and cultural scene for politicians, business people, financiers, diplomats, jet-setters, socialites, "and people who would like to be any or all of these." Circ. 40,000. Pays on acceptance. Byline given. Offers 20% kill fee. Buys first rights and second (reprint) rights to material originally published elsewhere. Submit seasonal/holiday material 4 months in advance. Simultaneous queries and photocopied and previously published submissions OK "if mentioned as such in cover letter." Computer printout submissions acceptable; prefers letter-quality to dot-matrix. SASE. Reports in 2 months. Publishes ms an average of 3 months after acceptance. Sample copy $2.50; writers guidelines for SAE and 1 first class stamp.

Nonfiction: Book excerpts, general interest, how-to, humor, interview/profile, personal experience, photo feature and travel, all with a sophisticated Washington angle. Buys 45 mss/year. Query with clips or send complete ms. Length: 1,200-2,500 words. Pays 15¢ and up per assigned word.

Columns/Departments: Design for Living (focus on fashionable living, home interiors); Fashion (worked around a theme); and Annabell's File (Washington insider news and gossip in short takes). Query with clips of published work. Length: 1,200-2,500 words. Pays "standard fee, except for reviews and short takes."

Fiction: "We accept very little fiction and run about 3 or 4 pieces a year. Must be about sophisticated life in Washington. Please, no presidential assassinations, no protest marches or murder stories." Buys 3 mss/year. Query with clips of published work or send complete ms. Length: 1,000-2,500 words. Pays 15¢ and up per assigned word.

Poetry: Avant-garde, free verse, light verse and traditional. Favors poetry by Washingtonians. Buys 20/year. Submit maximum 5 poems. Length: open. Pays $25 maximum.

Tips: "The best bet is a solid query that gives me an idea of what the story is about and how you would handle it. Write the query's first graph as if it were the lead paragraph of the story. Also tell me who you are, show me some clips. Propose some ideas that suit the magazine. One difficulty writers outside of the Washington area have is trying to do a piece that requires their 'presence' here. If you can't be 'here' to do a piece like that, then consider a different kind of story that doesn't need that immediacy. If you are a thorough and stylish writer who can handle 2,000 words of a feature while both informing and entertaining the reader, you can break into the magazine in any of its sections. But remember: the flavor and slant here is the nation's capital and sophistication. We are trying to broaden our base without losing the edge our image currently gives us as an elitist magazine of Washington's cultural and social world. We're open to substantive, even controversial, articles."

THE WASHINGTON POST, 1150 15th St. NW, Washington DC 20071. (202)334-6000. Travel Editor: Morris D. Rosenberg. Weekly travel section (Sunday). Pays on publication. Byline given. "We are now emphasizing staff-written articles as well as quality writing from other sources. Stories are rarely assigned to freelance writers, all material comes in on spec; there is no fixed kill fee." Buys first publication rights anywhere. Query with clips of published work. Legible computer printout submissions acceptable; no dot-matrix. Usually reports in 3 weeks.

Nonfiction: Emphasis in on travel writing with a strong sense of place, color, anecdote and history. Length: 1,500-2,000 words.

Photos: State availability of photos with ms (b&w only). "Good travel photos that illustrate and complement the article, not fuzzy vacation snapshots." Captions and identification of subjects required ("when germane").

THE WASHINGTON POST MAGAZINE, *The Washington Post*, 1150 15th St., NW, Washington D.C. 20071. Managing Editor: Stephen Petranek. 50% freelance written. Weekly rotogravure featuring regional and national interest articles (Washington DC, southern Pennsylvania, Delaware, Maryland, West Virginia and northern Virginia) for people of all ages and all interests. Circ. 1 million (Sunday). Average issue includes 4-6 feature articles and 4-5 columns. Pays on acceptance. Byline given. Buys all rights or first North American serial rights depending on fee. Submit seasonal material 4 months in advance. Photocopied submissions OK. Computer printout submissions acceptable; prefers letter-quality to dot-matrix. SASE. Reports in 1 month on queries; in 3 weeks on mss. Publishes ms an average of 2 months after acceptance. Free sample copy.

Nonfiction: "Controversial and consequential articles of regional interest. Subject areas include children, science, politics, law and crime, media, money, arts, behavior, sport and society." Photo feature. Buys 2 ms/issue. Query with clips of previously published work. Length: 1,500-4,500 words. Pays $200-up.

Photos: Reviews 4x5 or larger b&w glossy prints and 35 mm or larger color transparencies. Offers no additional payment for photos accepted with ms. Model release required.

Fiction: Fantasy, humorous, mystery, historical, mainstream and science fiction. Buys 6 mss/year. Send complete ms. Length: 3,000 words maximum. Pays $200-$750.

THE WASHINGTONIAN MAGAZINE, 1828 L St. NW, Washington DC 20036. Editor: John A. Limpert. 33% freelance written. For active, affluent and well-educated audience. Monthly magazine; 250 pages. Circ. 130,000. Buys first rights only. Buys 75 mss/year. Pays on publication. Simultaneous and photocopied submissions OK. Computer printout submissions acceptable; prefers letter-quality to dot-matrix. Reports in 4-6 weeks. Query or submit complete ms. SASE.

Nonfiction: *"The Washingtonian* is written for Washingtonians. The subject matter is anything we feel might interest people interested in the mind and manners of the city. The style, as Wolcott Gibbs said, should be the author's—if he is an author, and if he has a style. The only thing we ask is thoughtfulness and that no subject be treated too reverently. Audience is literate. We assume considerable sophistication about the city, and a sense of humor." Buys how-to, personal experience, interview/profile, humor, coverage of successful business operations, think pieces and exposes. Length: 1,000-7,000 words; average feature 3,000 words. Pays 25¢/word.
Photos: Photos rarely purchased with mss.
Fiction and Poetry: Margaret Cheney, department editor. Must be Washington-oriented. No limitations on length. Pays 10¢/word for fiction. Payment is negotiable for poetry.

Florida

BOCA RATON MAGAZINE, JES Publishing Corp., Box 820, Boca Raton FL 33429. (305)392-3311. Editor: Gregg Fales. 85% freelance written. Published 6 times/year—October-May. *"Boca Raton* is directed toward residents of South Palm Beach County, Florida. It examines the area's elements of the land, the sea, the people, the culture and history; in short, the Florida experience—its industry, successes, lifestyle and beauty." Circ. 10,000. Pays on acceptance. Byline given. Offers 100% kill fee. Buys one-time rights and makes work-for-hire assignments. Submit seasonal/holiday material 4 months in advance. Simultaneous queries and previously published submissions OK. Electronic submissions OK via modem with query approval, or on 5¼" floppy disk in ASC II, WordStar or EasyWriter; requires hard copy also. Computer printout submissions acceptable. SASE. Reports in 2 months on queries; 5 weeks on mss. Publishes ms an average of 6 months after acceptance if not assigned; 3 months if assigned. Sample copy for $2.50, #11 SAE and $1.75 postage.
Nonfiction: General interest (upscale, sophisticated, classy); historical/nostalgic (preferably regional); interview/profile (by subject grouping, locally); photo feature (mostly on assignment); travel (usually within a day's drive); art; and lifestyle. No humor, opinion or how-to. Buys 35-45 mss/year. Query. Length: 2,000-4,000 words. Pays $100-350.
Photos: High density (or contrast), artfully composed. State availability of photos. Pays $45-150 for color transparencies; $25-50 for b&w contact sheet and 5x7 or larger b&w prints. Captions, model release and identification of subjects required.
Columns/Departments: Regional travel (not camping) to places of unusual beauty and/or imagination; food of elegance appropriate for Florida lifestyle. Buys 12 mss/year. Query. Length: 1,000-5,000 words. Pays $100-450.
Fiction: Fantasy, historical and mainstream. No horror, religious, western, erotica, ethnic or romance genre. Buys 2-4 mss/year. Query. Length: 2,000-10,000 words. Pays $200-500.
Poetry: Poetry editor. Free verse, light verse and traditional. Buys 12 poems/year. Submit maximum 3 poems. Length: 8 lines minimum. Pays in 2 copies.

FLORIDA GULF COAST LIVING MAGAZINE, Baker Publications Inc., Suite 109, 1311 N. Westshore Blvd., Tampa FL 33607. Publications Director: Tina Stacy. Managing Editor: Milana McLead Petty. Magazine published 7 times/year covering real estate and related subjects for "newcomers and local residents looking for new housing in the area we cover." Circ. 575,000 annually. Pays on acceptance. Buys all rights. Submit seasonal/holiday material 3 months in advance. Photocopied submissions OK. SASE. Reports in 2 months. Sample copy $2; free writer's guidelines.
Nonfiction: General interest (on housing-related subjects, interior decorating, retirement living, apartment living, plants, landscaping, moving tips); historical (area history); how-to (build a greenhouse, decks, etc.); and travel (interesting trips around Florida, particularly near the area we cover). No personal views. Buys 5-10 mss/year. Query with clips of published work or send complete ms. Length: 500-1,200 words. Pays $15-125.
Photos: State availability of photos or send photos with ms. "Your package will be more valuable to us if you provide the illustrations. For color work, 35mm is acceptable." Pays $3-10 for color transparencies; $3-5 for 8x10 glossy prints. "I prefer to include photos in the total package fee." Captions and model release required. Buys one-time rights or all rights, "depending on the subject."
Columns/Departments: Query with suggestions for new columns or departments.
Tips: "Housing features, Retirement Living, Interiors, Home Marketplace, Products and Services, and other ideas, are the departments most open to freelancers. Be sure the subject is pertinent to our magazine. Know our magazine's style and write for it."

FLORIDA KEYS MAGAZINE, FKM Publishing Co., Inc., Box 818, 6161 O/S Hwy., Marathon FL 33050. (305)743-3721. Editor: David Ethridge. 90% freelance written. Bimonthly general interest magazine covering the Florida Keys for residents and tourists. Circ. 10,000. Pays on publication. Byline given. Buys first rights only. Submit seasonal/holiday material 3 months in advance. Simultaneous queries and simultaneous and photocopied submissions OK. Computer printout submissions acceptable; prefers letter-quality to dot-matrix. SASE. Reports in 1 month. Publishes ms an average of 3 months after acceptance. Sample copy $2.

Nonfiction: General interest; historical/nostalgic; how-to (must be Florida Keys related: how to clean a conch; how to catch a lobster); interview/profile; new product; personal experience; photo feature and travel. Query with clips of published work. Length: 400-2,000 words. Pays $3/inch.

Photos: State availability of photos. Reviews 35mm transparencies, pays $5-20 for 5x7 b&w prints; $15-100 for 5x7 color prints. Identification of subjects required.

GULFSHORE LIFE, Gulfshore Publishing Co., Inc., 3620 Tamiami Trail N., Naples FL 33940. (813)262-6425. Editor: Molly J. Burns. For an upper-income audience of varied business and academic backgrounds; actively employed and retired; interested in travel, leisure, business, and sports, as well as local environmental issues. Monthly magazine. Circ. 18,000. Buys first rights, and requests permission for subsequent reprint rights in other publications published by the firm. Byline given. Buys 50 mss/year. Pays on publication, $75-300. Photocopied or simultaneous submissions OK. Submit seasonal material 2 months in advance. Query. SASE.

Nonfiction: Local personalities, sports, travel, nature, environment, business, boating and fishing and historical pieces. Everything must be localized to the southwest coast of Florida. No political or controversial articles. Length: 1,500-2,500 words. Buys 5-10 unsolicited mss/year.

Photos: Bought separately, b&w prints or color transparencies only. Annual contest deadline: April 1st. Each entry must convey the theme of "Life Along the Gulfshore". SASE. Cash awards and publication for winner. B&w only.

Fiction: Annual fiction contest deadline: March 1st. Entries must have a Florida locale; 3,500 words maximum. Cash awards and publication of winner. SASE.

Tips: "Familiarize yourself with the magazine and the location: Naples, Marco Island, Ft. Myers, Ft. Myers Beach, Sanibel-Captiva, Whiskey Creek, Punta Gorda Isles and Port Charlotte. Submissions accepted at any time."

ISLAND LIFE, The Enchanting Barrier Islands of Florida's Gulf Coast, Island Life Publications, Box X, Sanibel FL 33957. (813)472-4344. Editor: Joan Hooper. Editorial Associate: Susan Shores. 70-90% freelance written. Quarterly magazine of the Barrier Islands from Longboat Key to Marco Island for upper-income residents and vacationers of Florida's Gulf Coast area. Circ. 16,000. Pays on publication. Byline given. Buys first and second rights to the same material. Submit seasonal/holiday material 6 months in advance. Simultaneous queries and simultaneous and photocopied submissions OK. Computer printout submissions acceptable. SASE. Reports in 8 weeks on queries; 12 weeks on mss. Publishes ms an average of 6 months after acceptance. Sample copy for $3, 10x13 envelope and 63¢ postage; writer's guidelines for business-size SAE and 1 first class stamp.

Nonfiction: General interest, historical/nostalgic, inspirational, interview/profile and travel. No fiction or first person experiences. "Our editorial emphasis is on the history, culture, scenic, sports, social and leisure activities of the area." Buys 30-40 mss/year. Query with published clips. Length: 500-1,500 words. Pays 5¢/word.

Photos: Send photos with query or ms. Pays $5-10 for 2x3 b&w prints; $5-25 for 2x2 or 4x5 color transparencies. Captions, model release and identification of subjects required.

JACKSONVILLE MAGAZINE, Drawer 329, Jacksonville FL 32201. (904)353-0313. 90% freelance written. Bimonthly. Circ. 13,000. Buys all rights. Buys 40-45 mss/year. Pays on publication. Query. Submit seasonal material 3-6 months in advance. Computer printout submissions acceptable, prefers letter-quality to dot-matrix. Reports in 3 weeks. SASE.

Nonfiction: Buys historical, business and other feature articles pertaining specifically to Jacksonville. Length: usually 1,500-3,000 words. Pays $100-300.

Photos: "We accept b&w glossy prints, good contrast; color transparencies." Pays $30 minimum for b&w; color terms to be arranged.

Tips: "We are reducing the length of our articles."

‡**JACKSONVILLE MONTHLY**, Jacksonville Monthly, Inc., 555 Wharfside Way, Jacksonville FL 32207. (904)396-0555. Editor: Paul K. Harral. Managing Editor: Marie B. Speed. A monthly city magazine covering North Florida lifestyle. "We are an upscale publication dedicated to teaching our readers how to draw the best from their living experiences in Florida and Jacksonville." Estab. 1982. Circ. 25,000. Pays 30 days following publication. Byline given. Offers approximately 30% kill fee. Makes work-for-hire assignments. Submit seasonal/holiday material 3-4 months in advance. Simultaneous queries, and simultaneous, photocopied, and previously published submissions OK. Computer printout submissions acceptable. SASE. Reports in 1 month. Free sample copy.

Nonfiction: Expose (all subjects, especially drug, environmentally oriented); general interest (oriented to lifestyle); historical/nostalgic (Florida/North Florida); how-to (renovation, redecorating, cooking); humor (on life in Florida; specifically our area); photo feature (Florida, wildlife, lifestyle); hunting, fishing, boating, travel (from Jacksonville). Special issues include boating guide and gardening guide. Buys 50 mss/year. Query with published clips. Length: 750-2,000 words. Pays $150-500.

Photos: Mary Fisher, photo editor. State availability of photos with query or ms. Reviews contact sheets and 35mm slides. "We generally handle photos on a negotiated fee basis, processing excluded. We do not have a specific picture or page rate established; fees approximate the rates for writers." Buys all rights.

Columns/Departments: Datebook (the most complete listing of area events available); Escape (travel to exotic destinations and nearby hideaways); Fare (restaurant reviews, a guide to fine dining and even recipes); Fling (an informed guide to night life and entertainment); Muses (focusing on art, music and other cultural pursuits); Outdoors (Monroe Campbell's guide to fishing and hunting); Body (exercise, health, nutrition and medicine); Habitat (complete coverage of your home, inside and out); Greenbacks (an insight into understanding investments); Graffiti (a little of this, a little of that, news and gossip all in fun); Games (sports and the sports who play them); Dateline (knowledgeable coverage of our sister media); and Bazaar (an up-to-date look at shopping and fashion). Buys 40-50 mss/year. Query with published clips. Length: 750-1,000 words. Pays $150.

Tips: "First, we look for writing quality. Second, we are interested in articles of specific interest to our readers. We are highly local interest and it is difficult for those outside the area to publish. Travel, food and adventure-style of stories are most likely area for freelancers. Even here, there must be great attention to the North Florida area and mind set."

‡**THE LOCAL NEWS**, The Local News, Inc., Box 466, Windermere FL 32786-0466. (305)298-2401. Assicate Editor: Darrell R. Julian. A biweekly newsmagazine serving Central Florida. "Our readers tend to fall into two distinct groups: the age group 25-40 years, college educated, upper middle-class from all over the country and the world; and age group 55 years old or older; (perhaps 40% of our readership) most of whom are middle-class retirees from across the nation." Circ. 5,000. Pays on acceptance. Byline given. Buys one-time rights, first rights, and second serial (reprint) rights. Submit seasonal/holiday material 2 months in advance. Photocopied and previously published submissions OK; prefers previously unpublished material. SASE. Reports in 2 months minimum. Sample copy for 12x15½ SAE, and $1.40 postage, or send postage only; writer's guidelines for business size SAE and 1 first class stamp.

Nonfiction: General interest, humor, interview/profile, opinion and travel. "Although we serve Central Florida, we are not interested in regional material since we develop this work from our staff. All articles must be in good taste; no erotic or tasteless material would be suitable." Buys 30 mss/year. Send complete ms. Length: 750-3,000 words. Pays $20-25.

Photos: Send photos with accompanying ms. Buys one-time rights.

Columns/Departments: "We would like to develop a regular column with wit and humor and a political column with conservative orientation." Send complete ms. Pays $20-25.

Fillers: Jokes, anecdotes and short humor. Buys 10/year. Pays $10.

Tips: "The *Local News* plans to become a weekly publication. Articles suited to the Sunday magazine section of a daily newspaper would be desirable. We will consider most material submitted during this transition."

MIAMI/SOUTH FLORIDA MAGAZINE, (formerly *Miami Magazine*), Box 340008, Coral Gables FL 33134. (305)856-5011. Editor: Erica Rauzin. 30% freelance written. For involved citizens of south Florida; generally well educated. Monthly magazine. Circ. 30,000. Rights purchased vary with author and material; usually buys first publication rights "exclusive forever in our region. We split 50/50 with writer on anything we resell." Rarely buys second (reprint) rights to material originally published elsewhere. Buys about 30 unsolicited mss/year. Pays on publication. Sample copy $1.95; free writer's guidelines. Electronic submissions on Apple IIe compatible disk OK; "Apple writer is the only word processing program we can pick up." Computer printout submissions acceptable. Query preferred or submit complete ms. Reports in 2 months. SASE. Publishes ms an average of 6 months after acceptance.

Nonfiction: Investigative pieces on the area; thorough, general features; exciting, in-depth writing. Informational, how-to, interview, profile and expose. Strong local angle and fresh, opinionated and humorous approach. "No travel stories from freelancers, that's mostly staff generated. We do not like to get freelance mss that are thinly disguised press releases. We don't need film because we have a regular columnist. My main thing is that writers READ the magazine first—then they'll know what to send and what not to send." Length: 3,000 words maximum. Pays $100-800.

Columns/Departments: Humor, business, books, art (all kinds) and home design. Length: 1,500 words maximum. Payment ranges from $100-250.

Tips: "We are regional in our outlook, not just Miami, but also Key West and Ft. Lauderdale."

‡**MIAMI MENSUAL (MIAMI MONTHLY)**, **The International Magazine of South Florida**, Quintus Communications Group, 265 Sevilla, Coral Gables FL 33134. (305)444-5678. Editor: Frank Soler. 50% freelance written. "The only Spanish-language monthly city magazine in the US for a sophisticated, decidedly upscale multicultural, multilingual internationally-oriented audience." City/regional magazine format. Circ. 25,000. Pays on publication. Byline given. Offers 50% kill fee. Buys all rights. Submits seasonal/holiday material 3 months in advance. Simultaneous queries, and simultaneous, photocopied and previously published submissions OK. Computer printout submissions acceptable. SASE. Reports in 2 weeks. Free sample copy and writer's guidelines.

Nonfiction: Book excerpts, expose, general interest, humor, interview/profile, opinion, personal experience, photo feature and travel. Buys 50-70 mss/year. Query with published clips if available or send complete ms. Length: 1,500-3,000 words. Pays variable rates.

Photos: Maribel Moore, art director. Send photos with query or ms. Reviews b&w contact sheet, color transparencies and b&w prints. Captions, model release and identification of subjects required. Buys one-time or all rights.

Columns/Departments: Humor, Opinion, TV, Movies, Audio/Video, Books, Jet Set and Gastronomy/Wine. "All must be applicable to a highly sophisticated international audience." Buys 50-70 mss/year. Query with published clips if available or send complete ms. Length: 1,000-1,500 words. Pays variable rates.

Fiction: Adventure and condensed novels. Send complete ms. Length: open. Pays variable rates.

Tips: "We're open to feature stories about or of interest to prominent international figures in business and the arts. Our publication is equivalent to a combination of a glossy city magazine and *Vanity Fair*, *Connoisseur*, and *Town & Country* for Hispanics."

‡**MIAMI METRO GUIDE**, Pope and Associates, Inc., 1224 NW 72nd Ave., Miami FL 33126. (305)591-4332. Editor: Fred Pope. A monthly magazine guide to the city of Miami. Circ. 20,000. Pays on publication. Byline given. Buys all rights. Submit seasonal/holiday material 3 months in advance. Computer printout submissions acceptable; no dot-matrix. SASE. Reports in 2 months. Sample copy $1.50.

Nonfiction: Travel (tips in general), and other articles related to the city of Miami or Florida. "We do not need long articles." Query with published clips. Length: 1,000-1,400 words. Pays $30-100.

Fillers: Jokes.

Tips: "We now have a *cartoon* page."

‡**ON DESIGN**, P.D.A., Inc., 4510 NE 2nd Ave., Miami FL 33137. (305)576-1268. Editor-in-Chief: Gloria Blake. Executive Editor: Al Alschuler. A bimonthly tabloid covering design-related features (interiors, architecture, fashion, art, antiques, etc.) for an upscale, affluent South Florida audience. Estab. 1983. Circ. 30,000. Pays on publication. Byline depends upon subject and treatment. Buys first rights only. Submit seasonal/holiday material 4 months in advance. Simultaneous queries and photocopied submissions OK. Computer printout submissions acceptable; prefers letter-quality to dot-matrix. SASE. Reports in 2 weeks on queries; 1 month on mss. Sample copy for 9x12 SAE and 5 first class stamps.

Nonfiction: Humor (a possibility); new product (brief, with photo); travel (if near at hand to Floridians); and investment, etc. "No articles *not* relative to affluent South Floridians; *must* be generally local in nature or of suitable general interest." Query. Length: 100-1,000 words. Pays $15-200.

Photos: State availability of photos with query letter or mss. Reviews 4x5 and 8x10 b&w photos, and any size color transparencies. Payment for photos included in payment for ms. Buys one-time rights.

Columns/Departments: World Class (as relates to South Floridians; only outstanding resorts, restaurants, hotels, services, etc.). Query. Length: 100-250 words. Pays $20-50.

Tips: "No special section is especially open to freelancers, but we look for knowledge of a sort that would interest our readers and not likely be available elsewhere."

ORLANDO-LAND MAGAZINE, Box 2207, Orlando FL 32802. (305)644-3355. Editor-in-Chief: E.L. Prizer. Managing Editor: Carole De Pinto. Emphasizes central Florida information for "a readership made up primarily of people new to Florida—those here as visitors, traveling businessmen, new residents." Monthly magazine; 144 pages. Circ. 26,000. Pays on acceptance. Buys all rights or first North American serial rights. Byline given. Phone queries OK. Submit seasonal/holiday material 2 months in advance. Photocopied and previously published submissions OK. Computer printout submissions acceptable. SASE. Reports in 6 weeks. Sample copy $2.

Nonfiction: Historical, how-to and informational. "Things involved in living in Florida." Pay $25-75.

Photos: B&w glossy prints. Pays $5.

Tips: "Always in need of *useful* advice-type material presented as first person experience that relates to central Florida area. Also, travel (excursion) pieces to places open to general public within one day's (there and back) journey of Orlando or experience pieces (hobbies, sports, etc.) that would not be practical for staff writers—sky diving, delta kites, etc. Must be available in central Florida. Specialized topical columns are being added in health, environment, architecture and travel."

PALM BEACH LIFE, Box 1176, Palm Beach FL 33480. (305)837-4750. Managing Editor: Kathleen H. Moran. Mostly freelance written. "*Palm Beach Life* caters to a sophisticated, high-income readership and reflects its interests. Readers are affluent . . . usually over 40, well-educated." Monthly. Circ. 23,000. Buys first North American serial rights. Pays on acceptance. Computer printout submissions acceptable; prefers letter-quality to dot-matrix. Reports in 3 weeks. Publishes ms an average of 3 months after aceptance. Query with outline. SASE. Sample copy $3.50.

Nonfiction: Subject matter involves "articles on fashion, music, art and related fields; subjects that would be of interest to the sophisticated, well-informed reader. Buys informational, feature, photo and travel articles.

Length: 1,000-2,500 words. Payment varies depending on length and research.

Photos: Purchases photos with mss, or on assignment. "We feature color photos, but are looking for good b&w." Captions are required. Buys 8x10 b&w glossy prints. Also buys 35mm or 2¼x2¼ transparencies and photo stories. Pay is negotiable.

Tips: "Please consider our magazine format—send for a sample copy and peruse magazine. We like stories (including good, well-written features) that appeal to upper-income, sophisticated readers."

SOUTH FLORIDA LIVING, Baker Publications, Inc., Suite 102, Bldg. 3, 700 W. Hillsboro Blvd., Deerfield Beach FL 33441. (305)428-5602. Editor: Cynthia M. Marusarz. 70% freelance written. Bimonthly magazine covering real estate market in Dade, Broward, Martin, Palm Beach, St. Lucie and Indian River counties, for newcomers and home buyers. Circ. 80,000. Pays on acceptance. Byline given. Buy first rights and makes work-for-hire assignments. Submit seasonal/holiday material 4 months in advance. Photocopied and previously published submissions OK. SASE. Reports in 2 weeks. Publishes ms an average of 3 months after acceptance. Sample copy and writer's guidelines free.

Nonfiction: Real estate industry trends; home security; historical; how-to (finance, build, design); moving tips; landscaping and gardening; banking; interior decorating; retirement living; and apartment living. No personal stories or articles not related to South Florida. Buys 18-20 mss/year. Query letters, "no phone calls, please." Length: 1,500-2,000 words. Pays 10¢/word for local stories.

Photos: State availability of photos. Pays negotiable fee for 35mm color transparencies and 5x7 b&w prints. Captions and model releases required. Buys all rights.

Tips: "National assignments on decorating, financing, etc., for all of Baker's city magazines are made by Tina Stacy, publication director. Payment is 20¢/word. Query her at: *Living*, Suite 400, 5757 Alpha Rd., Dallas TX 75240."

‡**SUNSHINE MAGAZINE, The Magazine of the Fort Lauderdale News & Sun-Sentinel**, The News & Sun-Sentinel Co., Box 14430, Fort Lauderdale FL 33302. (305)761-4037. Editor: John Parkyn. A general interest Sunday magazine for the newspaper's 800,000 readers in south Florida. Estab. 1983. Circ. 300,000. Pays within 1 month of acceptance. Byline given. Offers 25% kill fee for assigned mss. Buys first or one-time rights in the state of Florida. Submit seasonal/holiday material 2 months in advance. Simultaneous queries, and simultaneous, photocopied and previously published submissions OK. SASE. Reports in 2 weeks on queries; 1 month on mss. Free sample copy and writer's guidelines.

Nonfiction: General interest, how-to, interview/profile and travel. "Articles must be relevant to the interests of adults living in south Florida." No personal experience or historical articles. Buys about 100 mss/year. Query with published clips. Length: 1,000-5,000 words; preferred length 2,000 words. Pays 15-25¢/word to $1,000 maximum.

Photos: State availability of photos. Pays negotiable rate for 35mm color slides and 8x10 b&w prints. Captions, model releases and identification of subjects required. Buys one-time rights for the state of Florida.

Tips: "Do NOT phone—we don't have the staff to handle calls of this type—but do include your phone number on query letter. Keep your writing tight and concise—readers don't have the time to wade through masses of 'pretty' prose. Be as sophisticated and stylish as you can—Sunday magazines have come a long way from the Sunday 'supps' of yesteryear."

TALLAHASSEE MAGAZINE, Homes & Land Publishing Corp., Box 12848, Tallahassee FL 32308. (904)222-5467. Editor: William L. Needham. Managing Editor: W.R. Lundquist. 80% freelance written. Quarterly magazine covering people, events and history in and around Florida's capital city. Circ. 15,000. Pays on publication. Buys first North American serial rights. Submit seasonal/holiday material 6 months in advance. Simultaneous queries and photocopied and previously published submissions OK. Computer printout submissions acceptable; prefers letter-quality to dot-matrix. SASE. Reports in 2 weeks on queries; 1 month on mss. Publishes ms an average of 3 months after acceptance. Sample copy for 9x12 SAE.

Nonfiction: General interest (relating to Florida or Southeast); historical/nostalgic (for Tallahassee, North Florida, South Georgia); and interview/profile (related to North Florida, South Georgia). No fiction, poetry or topics unrelated to area. Buys 12 mss/year. Query. Length: 500-1,400 words. Pays 10¢/word.

Photos: State availability of photos with query letter or ms. Pays $35 minimum for 35mm color transparencies; $20 minimum for b&w prints. Model release and identification of subjects required. Buys one-time rights.

Tips: "We seek to show positive aspects of life in and around Tallahassee. Know the area. Brief author biographic note should accompany mss."

TAMPA BAY MONTHLY, Florida City Magazines, Inc. 2502 Rocky Point Dr., Tampa FL 33607. Editor: Heidi A. Swanson. Associate Editor: Julia Benson Hughes. 60% freelance written. Monthly magazine for upscale Tampa Bay area readers. Circ. 25,000. Pays within 30 days of publication. Byline given. Buys all rights. Submit seasonal/holiday material 3 months in advance. Simultaneous queries OK. Computer printout submissions acceptable. SASE. Reports in 6 weeks. Publishes ms an average of 10 weeks after acceptance. Writer's guidelines available upon request.

Nonfiction: In-depth investigative, general interest, humor, historical/nostalgic, and interview/profile—pertaining to the Tampa Bay area reader. Occasionally needs get-away pieces for Bay Area residents, fashion pieces and food/drink articles. Buys 24-36 mss/year. Query with clips of published work. Length: 300-500 words for short articles; 3,000-5,000 words for feature articles. Pays $50-500. Will consider book or movie reviews.

Photos: Linda Titus, art director. State availability of photos. Reviews contact sheets. Captions, model releases, and identification of subjects required. Buys all rights.

‡**WEST FLORIDA LIFE MAGAZINE, The Magazine of Gulf Coast Living**, Good Florida Publications, 1487 2nd St., Sarasota FL 33581. (813)957-1511. Editor: Pam Daniel. A bimonthly city/regional magazine covering life along Florida's Gulf Coast aimed at a sophisticated, arts-oriented readership. Estab. 1983. Circ. 23,550. Pays on publication. Byline given. Buys negotiable rights. Submit seasonal/holiday material 4 months in advance. Simultaneous queries, and simultaneous, photocopied and previously published submissions OK. SASE. Reports in 1 month. Sample copy for SAE and $2 postage.

Nonfiction: Book excerpts (if strong regional interest); general interest; historical/nostalgic (about West Florida); humor; interview/profile; opinion (about arts, business, politics, media); photo feature; and travel (western Florida). Articles must have a strong regional focus. Buys 40 mss/year. Query with published clips or send complete ms. Length: open, generally 1,000-2,000 words. Pays $50-150.

WM Editor's Note: At press time we had a report that *West Florida Life* had ceased publication.

Georgia

ATLANTA MAGAZINE, 6255 Barfield Rd., Atlanta GA 30328. (404)256-9800. Editor: Neil Shister. Monthly city magazine covering the metro Atlanta area. Focuses on lifestyles, personalities, entertainment, culture and social concerns of local interest. Computer printout submissions acceptable.

ATLANTA WEEKLY, Atlanta Newspapers, Box 4689, Atlanta GA 30302. (404)526-5415. Editor: Lee Walburn. Sunday general interest magazine. Circ. 500,000. Pays on acceptance. Byline given. Offers 40% kill fee. Buys one-time rights. Submit seasonal/holiday material 6 months in advance. Simultaneous queries and previously published submissions OK. SASE. Reports in 6 weeks. Free sample copy and writer's guidelines.

Nonfiction: Andrew Sparks, articles editor. Book excerpts and general interest. "Articles should deal with topics of interest around Atlanta, the South and Southeast." Special issues include Home Decorating issue; Fashion issue; and Christmas Gift Guide. No first person or travel articles. Buys 100 mss/year. Query with clips if available. Length: 250-3,000 words. Pays $50-800.

Photos: Ike Hussey, photo editor. State availability of photos.

Fillers: Contact: ETC editor. Short humor and newsbreaks. Buys 20/year. Length: 100-200 words. Pays $15-50.

‡**GEORGIA JOURNAL**, Agee Publishers, Inc., Box 526, Athens GA 30603. (404)548-5269. Editor: Jane Agee. A bimonthly magazine covering the state of Georgia. Circ. 5,000. Pays on acceptance. Byline given. Buys one-time rights. Submit seasonal/holiday material 4-6 months in advance. Photocopied submissions OK. Reports in 1 month. Sample copy $3; writer's guidelines for SAE and 1 first class stamp.

Nonfiction: "We are interested in almost everything going on within the state. Although we specialize in an area, we maintain a general interest format. We do prefer to get pieces that are current that have a human interest slant. We are also very interested in natural science pieces. We do special focus issues and suggest that writers send for special focus schedule. We are always swamped with historical articles, and we are not interested in sentimental reminiscences, anything risque, specifically political or religious pieces. Buys 50-60 mss/year. Query. Length: 1,200-2,000 words. Pays $20-25.

Photos: State availability of photos or send photos with query or ms. Reviews sharp 8x10 b&w glossies. Captions, model release and identification of subjects required.

Fiction: Hugh Agee and Patti McWhorter, fiction editors. "Because we are in almost all school systems in the state, fiction must be suitable for all ages." Buys 3-4 mss/year. Send complete ms. Length: 1,200-2,000 words. Pays $25.

Poetry: Peggy Lyles, poetry editor. Free verse, haiku, light verse and traditional. No poetry specifically dealing with another part of the country (out of the South) or anything not suitable for school children. "Most of our school-age readers are middle school and older. Buys 20 poems/year. Submit maximum 4 poems. Length: 25 lines. Pays in copies.

Tips: "We have a section of short pieces (3-8 paragraphs) called Under the Chinaberry Tree where we always need good general interest submissions. These pieces are usually on topics not meriting feature article length. See a sample copy for 'Chinaberry Tree' pieces that have been used. Another area for freelancers is Georgia

Makers where we feature very short pieces on individuals in Georgia who have done something of merit or who have a human interest slant. Basically, though, it is merit-oriented."

Hawaii

HONOLULU, Honolulu Publishing Co., Ltd., 36 Merchant St., Honolulu HI 96813. (808)524-7400. Editor: Brian Nicol. Monthly magazine covering general interest topics relating to Hawaii. Circ. 35,000. Pays on acceptance. Byline given. Offers $50 kill fee. Buys one-time rights. Submit seasonal/holiday material 5 months in advance. Simultaneous queries and simultaneous and photocopied submissions OK. SASE. Sample copy for $2, 9x11 SAE and $1.50 postage.
Nonfiction: Marilyn Kim, articles editor. Expose, general interest, historical/nostalgic and photo feature (all Hawaii-related). "We run regular features on food, fashion, interior design, travel, etc., plus other timely, provocative articles. No personal experience articles." Buys 10 mss/year. Query with clips if available. Length: 2,500-5,000 words. Pays $250-400.
Photos: Teresa Black, photo editor. State availability of photos. Pays $15 maximum for b&w contact sheet; $25 maximum for 35mm color transparencies. Captions and identification of subjects required. Buys one-time rights.
Columns/Departments: Marilyn Kim, column/department editor. Calabash (a light, "newsy," timely, humorous column on any Hawaii-related subject). Buys 15 mss/year. Query with clips of published work or send complete ms. Length: 250-1,000 words. Pays $25-35.

Illinois

CHICAGO MAGAZINE, 3 Illinois Center, Chicago IL 60601. Editor-in-Chief: Allen H. Kelson. Editor: John Fink. 40% freelance written. For an audience which is "95% from Chicago area; 90% college-trained; upper income; overriding interests in the arts, dining, good life in the city and suburbs. Most are in 25-50 age bracket, well-read and articulate. Generally liberal inclination." Monthly. Circ. 217,000. Buys first and second rights for 90 days only. Buys about 50 mss/year. Pays on acceptance. Submit seasonal material 4 months in advance. Computer printout submissions acceptable "if legible"; prefers letter-quality to dot-matrix. Reports in 2 weeks. Publishes ms an average of 5 months after acceptance if unassigned; 3 months if assigned. Query; indicate "specifics, knowledge of city and market, and demonstrable access to sources." SASE. For sample copy, send $3 to Circulation Dept.
Nonfiction: "On themes relating to the quality of life in Chicago: past, present, future." Writers should have "a general awareness that the readers will be concerned, influential longtime Chicagoans reading what the writer has to say about their city. We generally publish material too comprehensive for daily newspapers or of too specialized interest for them." Buys personal experience and think pieces, interviews, profiles, humor, spot news, historical articles, travel and exposes. Length: 1,000-6,000 words. Pays $100-$2,500.
Photos: Photos purchased with mss. Uses b&w glossy prints, 35mm color transparencies or color prints.
Fiction: Christine Newman, articles editor. Mainstream, fantasy and humor. Preferably with Chicago orientation. No word-length limits, but "no novels, please." Pays $250-500.
Tips: "Submit plainly, be businesslike and avoid cliche ideas. We are depending more and more on staff written material."

CHICAGO READER, Box 11101, Chicago IL 60611. (312)828-0350. Editor: Robert A. Roth. 80% freelance written. "The *Reader* is distributed free in Chicago's lakefront neighborhoods. Generally speaking, these are Chicago's best educated, most affluent neighborhoods—and they have an unusually high concentration of young adults." Weekly tabloid; 128 pages. Circ. 117,000. Pays "by 15th of month following publication." Buys all rights. Byline given. Phone queries OK. Photocopied submissions OK. Computer printout submissions acceptable; prefers letter-quality to dot-matrix. SASE. Reports "very slow," up to 1 year or more.
Nonfiction: "We want magazine features on Chicago topics. Will also consider reviews." Buys 500 mss/year. Submit complete ms. Length: "Whatever's appropriate to the story." Pays $50-675.
Photos: By assignment only.
Columns/Departments: By assignment only.

‡ILLINOIS TIMES, Downstate Illinois' Weekly Newspaper, Illinois Times, Inc., Box 3524, Springfield IL 62708. (217)753-2226. Editor: Fletcher Farrar Jr. 50% freelance written. Weekly tabloid covering that part of the state outside of Chicago and its suburbs for a discerning, well-educated readership. Circ. 35,000. Pays on publication. Byline given. Buys first rights and second (reprint) rights to material originally published elsewhere. Submit seasonal/holiday material 1 month in advance. Simultaneous queries, and simultaneous, photocopied and previously published submissions OK. Computer printout submissions acceptable. SASE. Reports in 3 weeks on queries; 8 weeks on mss. Publishes ms an average of 2 months after acceptance. Sample copy 50¢.

Nonfiction: Book excerpts, expose, general interest, historical, how-to, interview/profile, opinion, personal experience, photo feature, travel "in our area," book reviews, politics, environment, energy, etc. "We are not likely to use a story that has no Illinois tie-in." Annual special issues: Lincoln (February); Health & Fitness (March); Gardening (April); Summer (June); Fall Home (September); and Christmas (Books). No articles filled with "bureaucratese or generalities; no articles naively glorifying public figures or celebrity stories for celebrity's sake." Buys 50 mss/year. Query or send complete ms. Length: From 1,500 to 2,500 words maximum. Pays 4¢/word; $100 maximum.

Photos: State availability of photos. Pays $15 for 8x10 prints. Identification of subjects required. Buys one-time rights.

Columns/Departments: Guestwork (opinion column, any subject of personal experience with an Illinois angle). Buys 25 mss/year. Send complete ms. Length: 1,500 words maximum. Pays 4¢/word; $60 maximum.

Tips: "The ideal *IT* story is one the reader hates to put down. Good writing, in our view, is not necessarily fancy writing. It is (in the words of a colleague) whatever 'will engage the disinterested reader.' In other words, nothing dull, please. But remember that any subject—even the investment policies of public pension funds—can be made 'engaging.' It's just that some subjects require more work than others. Good illustrations are a plus. As an alternative newspaper we prefer to treat subjects in depth or not at all. Please, no general articles that lack an Illinois angle."

Indiana

INDIANAPOLIS, 32 E. Washington St., Indianapolis IN 46204. (317)639-6600. Editor: Pegg Kennedy. 98% freelance written. Emphasizes Indianapolis-related problems/features or regional related topics. Monthly magazine. Circ. 20,000. Pays on publication. Buys first rights only. Byline given. Queries or manuscripts. Submit seasonal/holiday material 4 months in advance. Simultaneous, photocopied and previously published submissions OK. Computer printout submissions acceptable; prefers letter-quality to dot-matrix. SASE. Reports in 1 month. Publishes ms an average of 4 months after acceptance. Sample copy $1.75.

Nonfiction: Expose (interested, but have no specifics; "we're interested in any Indianapolis-related topic including government and education"); historical (Indianapolis-related only); how-to (buying tips); inspirational (not generally but will read submitted ms); interview (Indianapolis-related person, native sons and daughters); nostalgia (Indianapolis-related); photo feature (human interest, Indianapolis-related); profile (Indianapolis-related); and travel (within a day's drive of Indianapolis). "We only want articles with Indianapolis or central Indiana ties, no subjects outside of our region. No essays, opinions—unless they are qualified by professional credits for an opinion/essay. We aren't very interested in broad-based, national topics without a local angle. National issues can be broken into 'how does it affect Indianapolis?' or 'what does it mean for Indianapolis?' (We're big on sidebars.) Buys 150 unsolicited mss/year. Query. Length: 500-3,500 words. Pays $40-250.

Photos: State availability of photos. Pays $15 for b&w; $20-35 for color transparencies. Buys one-time rights. Captions required.

Columns/Departments: Business, life style, sports, marketplace, leisure, money, health and people.

Tips: "We are planning to expand our circulation area to include central Indiana so that we are more of a regional magazine rather than city."

INDIANAPOLIS MONTHLY, Mayhill Publications, Inc., Box 30071, Indianapolis IN 46230. (317)259-8222. Editor: Deborah Paul. Associate Editor: Steve Bell. 50% freelance written. Monthly magazine covering subject matter of interest to those in central Indiana. All material must be upbeat, written in a lively style, of interest to Indiana residents. Circ. 25,000. Pays on publication. Byline given. Usually buys first rights and occasionally second (reprint) rights to material originally published elsewhere. Submit seasonal/holiday material 4 months in advance. Photocopied submissions OK. Computer printout and disk submissions OK "if good, clear quality"; prefers letter-quality to dot-matrix. SASE. Reports in 1 month. Publishes ms an average of 2 months after acceptance. Sample copy $1.50.

Nonfiction: Expose (in-depth reporting on government, education, health, if it is fairly presented); general interest (sport, business, media, health); historical/nostalgic (pertaining to Indiana landmarks only; no first person); design (at-home features, maximum 1,000 words about a unique home with transparencies or slides with cutlines); interview/profile (of regional personalities, success stories about Indiana natives); color photo feature (seasonal material from Indiana); and travel (weekends in Indiana; no first person). Always looking for fresh angles on Indianapolis 500. No first person narratives, domestic humor or poetry. Query with clips of published work or send complete ms. Length: 500-3,000 words. Pays $50-250.

Photos: B&w glossies with good contrast. Photos to accompany ms are especially welcomed. Pays $20 for published b&w prints; variable rate for 2¼x2¼, 35mm color transparencies. Captions or identification of subjects required.

Columns/Departments: Business—success stories, unique regional business; sport—personalities or season-

al sport; media—personalities or trends in print or broadcast; health, new innovations or specialists. Query with clips of published work or send complete ms. Length: 600-1,000 words. Pays $50-150.
Fillers: Newsbreaks from or about regional personalites or institutions. Length: 300-1,000 words. Pays $50-100.
Tips: "Especially open to freelance specialized writer in areas of interior design, Indiana history, or architecture, health and sport. We discourage first person narratives and overdone topics."

MICHIANA, Sunday Magazine of *The South Bend Tribune*, Colfax at Lafayette, South Bend IN 46626. (219)233-6161. Editor: Bill Sonneborn. 90% freelance written. For "average daily newspaper readers; perhaps a little above average since we have more than a dozen colleges and universities in our area." Weekly. Circ. 125,000. May buy first North American serial rights or simultaneous rights providing material offered will be used outside of Indiana and Michigan. Byline given. Buys 100 unsolicited mss/year. Pays on publication. Will consider photocopied submissions if clearly legible. Computer printout submissions acceptable. Publishes ms an average of 5 weeks after acceptance. Submit special material for spring and fall travel sections at least 1 month in advance. Reports in 2 weeks. Submit complete ms. SASE.
Nonfiction: "Items of general and unusual interest written in good, clear, simple sentences with logical approach to subject. We like material oriented to the Midwest, especially Indiana, Michigan, Ohio and Illinois. We avoid all freelance material that supports movements of a political nature. We seldom use first person humor." Length: 800-3,000 words. Payment is $50-60 minimum, with increases as deemed suitable.
Photos: All mss must be accompanied by illustrations, b&w photos or 35mm or larger color transparencies.

Iowa

‡**THE IOWAN MAGAZINE**, Mid-America Publishing Corp., 214 9th St., Des Moines IA 50309. (515)282-8220. Editor: Charles W. Roberts. 65% freelance written. Quarterly magazine covering the "history, people, places and points of interest in Iowa." Circ. 22,000. Pays on publication. Byline given. Buys one-time rights. Submit seasonal/holiday material 5 months in advance. Photocopied and previously published submissions OK. Computer printout submissions acceptable. Reports in 1 month. Publishes ms an average of 1 year after acceptance. Sample copy for $3.50, 9x12 SAE and $1.75 postage; free writer's guidelines.
Nonfiction: General interest; historical (history as in American heritage, not personal reminiscence); interview/profile and travel. No "articles from non-Iowans who come for a visit and wish to give their impression of the state." Buys 32 mss/year. Query with clips. Length: 750-3,000 words. Pays $75-350.
Photos: Send photos with ms. Pays $10-25 for b&w; $35-50 for color transparency. Captions and identification of subjects required.
Tips: "If you are writing about Iowa, write on a specific topic. Dont be *too* general. Write a query letter with maybe two or three ideas."

Kansas

KANSAS!, Kansas Department of Economic Development, 503 Kansas Ave., 6th Floor, Topeka KS 66603. (913)296-3806. Editor: Andrea Glenn. Emphasizes Kansas "faces and places for all ages, occupations and interests." Quarterly magazine; 40 pages. Circ. 48,000. Pays on acceptance. Buys one-time rights. Byline given. Submit seasonal/holiday material 8 months in advance. Simultaneous or photocopied and previously published submissions OK. SASE. Reports in 2 months. Free sample copy and writer's guidelines.
Nonfiction: "Material must be Kansas-oriented and well written. We run stories about Kansas people, places and events that can be enjoyed by the general public. In other words, events must be open to the public, places also. People featured must have interesting crafts etc." General interest, interview, photo feature, profile and travel. No exposes. Query. "Query letter should clearly outline story in mind. I'm especially interested in Kansas freelancers who can supply their own photos." Length: 5-7 pages double-spaced, typewritten copy. Pays $75-125.
Photos: "We are a full-color photo/manuscript publication." State availability of photos with query. Pays $25-50 ("generally included in ms rate") for 35mm color transparencies. Captions required.
Tips: "History and nostalgia stories do not fit into our format because they can't be illustrated well with color photography."

Kentucky

‡**KENTUCKY HAPPY HUNTING GROUND**, Kentucky Dept. of Fish and Wildlife Resources, 1 Game Farm Rd., Frankfort KY 40601. (502)564-4336. Editor: John Wilson. A bimonthly state conservation magazine covering hunting, fishing, general outdoor recreation, conservation of wildlife and other natural re-

sources. Circ. 35,000. Pays on publication. Byline given. Buys one-time rights. Submit seasonal/holiday material at least 3 months in advance. Previously published submissions OK. Computer printout submissions acceptable. SASE. Reports in 3 weeks on queries; 2 months on mss. Free sample copy.

Nonfiction: General interst, historical/nostalgic, how-to, humor, interview/profile, personal experience and photo feature. "All articles should deal with some aspect of the natural world, with outdoor recreation or with natural resources conservation or management, and should relate to Kentucky. No "Me and Joe" stories (i.e., accounts of specific trips); nothing off-color or otherwise unsuitable for a state publication." Buys 6-12 mss/year. Query or send complete ms. Length: 500-2,000 words. Pays $50-150 (with photos).

Photos: State availability of photos with query; send photos with accompanying ms. Reviews color transparencies (2¼ preferred, 35mm acceptable) and b&w prints (5x7 minimum). No separate payment for photos, but amount paid for article will be determined by number of photos used.

Tips: "We would be much more kindly disposed toward articles accompanied by several good photographs (or other graphic material) than to those without."

Louisiana

NEW ORLEANS MAGAZINE, Box 26815, New Orleans LA 70186. (504)246-2700. Editor: Linda Matys. 50% freelance written. Monthly magazine; 125 pages. Circ. 37,000. Pays on publication. Buys first-time rights. Byline given. Submit seasonal/holiday material 4 months in advance. Computer printout submissions acceptable; prefers letter-quality to dot-matrix. SASE. Reports in 2 months. Publishes ms an average of 4 months after acceptance.

Nonfiction: General interest, interview and profile. Buys 3 mss/issue. Submit complete ms. Length: 1,200-3,000 words. Pays $100-500.

Photos: John Maher, art director. State availability of photos with ms. Captions required. Buys one-time rights. Model release required.

‡**SHREVEPORT**, Shreveport Chamber of Commerce, Box 20074, Shreveport LA 71120-9982. (318)226-8521. Editor: Mary L. Baldwin. 90% freelance written. *Shreveport* is a monthly city magazine reflecting life and interests of the people in the Ark-La-Tex area. "The magazine strives to offer its readership solid reporting on issues affecting the quality of life in the Ark-La-Tex and feature stories on interesting events, activities or people in the area. It is written for our well-educated, upper and middle income readership in the Ark-La-Tex. Circ. 5,200. Pays on acceptance. Byline given. Offers negotiable kill fee. Buys first North American serial rights. Submit seasonal/holiday material 3 months in advance. "Computer printout submissions, as long as they are legible, are fine"; prefers letter-quality to dot-matrix. SASE. Reports in 6 weeks on queries; 2 months on mss. Publishes ms an average of 2 months after acceptance. Sample copy $1.50 and $1.50 postage.

Nonfiction: General interest, historical/nostalgic, interview/profile, new product, photo feature and travel. Special issues include Housing Guide, Vistor's Guide, Media Section, Financial Section, Oil and Gas Industry Guide and Office Guide. Buys 60-72 mss/year. Query with clips or send mss for review. Length: 1,000-4000 words. Pays $50-125.

Photos: Send photos with ms. Pays $50-100 for color transparencies; $25-75 for 8x10 color prints. Captions, model release and identification of subjects required. Buys one-time rights.

Columns/Departments: Monthly departments include Potpourri, a listing of upcoming events in the area; Arts, stories of local theater, artists, opera, etc.; Commerce, a monthly economic report from the Center for Business Research at Louisiana State University in Shreveport and stories on business trends and timely developments; Cuisine, a review by food experts of an area restaurant; Diversions, places to go after work hours; History; Health; and Travel. Buys 72-96 mss/year. Query with clips of published work or send mss for review. Length: 500-2,000 words. Pays $50-125.

Maine

‡**BITTERSWEET, The Flavor of Northcountry Living**, Bittersweet, Inc., Box 266, Cornish ME 04020. (207)625-3975. Editor: Nancy Marcotte. 80% freelance written. Magazine published 10 times/year "for people who appreciate *good* news and views of life and living in the rural Northeast." Circ. 5,000. Pays on publication. Publishes ms an average of 6 months after acceptance. Byline given. Buys first North American serial rights, one-time rights and second serial (reprint) rights. Photocopied and previously published submissions OK. Computer printout submissions acceptable. SASE. Report in 1 month on queries. Publishes ms an average of 6 months after acceptance. Sample copy for 9x12 SAE and $1.05 postage.

Nonfiction: Book excerptsl general interest (people-centered); historical/nostalgic (specific to the Northeastern uplands); how-to (make the best of all four seasons); humor (dry); interview/profile (even celebrities are just plain folk); personal experience; and photo feature. No travelogues and "issues." Buys 25-30 mss/year.

Query or send complete ms. Length: 500-2,500 words. Pays $10-50/published page.

Photos: Send photos with query or ms. Pays $5-50 for color transparencies; $5-10 for b&w prints. Model releases and identification of subjects required. Buys one-time rights.

Columns/Departments: "We're developing columns now and are looking for good ideas." Query. Length: 500-800 words. Pays negotiable rates.

Fiction: Historical, humorous, mainstream and novel excerpts. "We're open to any 'good read' that bears on our part of the world. *Nothing* dreary or apocalyptic, however." Buys 20 mss/year. Send comples ms. Length: 800-3,000 words. Pays $10-30/published page.

Poetry: Free verse, light verse and traditional. Buys 50 poems/year. Submit maximum 5 poems. Pays $5-10.

Fillers: Anecdotes and short humor. Buys 20/year. Length: 50-200 words. pays $5-10.

Tips: "We're open to new writers/photographers/artists. You don't need credentials, just a positive attitude, craftsmanship and people-centered work. Our readers like to know about people—their neighbors—and what they're doing that's interesting and worthwhile (not necessarily unusual)."

‡**GREATER PORTLAND MAGAZINE,** Chamber of Commerce of the Greater Portland Region, 142 Free St., Portland ME 04101. (207)772-2811. Editor: Colin W. Sargent. A quarterly magazine covering metropolitan and island lifestyles of Greater Portland. "We cover the arts, night life, islands, people, and progressive business atmosphere in and around Greater Portland. Circ. 10,000. Pays on publication. Byline given. Buys first North American serial rights. Submit seasonal/holiday material 6 months in advance. No simultaneous queries, or simultaneous, photocopied or previously published submissions. Reports in 1 week on queries; 2 weeks on mss. Free sample copy.

Nonfiction: General interest, humor, interview/profile and personal experience. "*Greater Portland* is completely freelance written. We have a intown lifestyle slant and are looking for complete stories, not just verbal scenery. For example, if you write a story about our luxury ferry, "The Scotia Prince", stay overnight and take the readers aboard. We shy away from survey stories. Cover one subject deliciously instead. First person narratives are welcome." Buys 30 mss/year. Query with published clips or send complete ms. Length: 500-2,000 words. Pays $150 maximum.

Photos: Buys b&w and color slides with or without ms. Captions required.

Fiction: Short, mainstream fiction that takes place in Greater Portland; humorous; suspense; myster; and historical. Length: 1,000 words maximum.

Tips: "Send some clips with a cover letter or query. We're always looing for good Casco Bay island stories, with lots of anecdotes."

MAINE LIFE, Box 111, Freedom ME 04901. Editor: George Frangoulis. 80% freelance written. For readers of all ages in urban and rural settings. 50% of readers live in Maine; balance are readers in other states who have an interest in Maine. Published 6 times/year. Circ. 30,000. Pays on publication. Buys first and second rights to the same material. Submit seasonal/holiday material 4 months in advance. Computer printout submissions acceptable; no dot-matrix. Reports in 1 month. Publishes ms an average of 6 months after acceptance. SASE. Sample copy $1.50.

Nonfiction: Maine travel, home and garden, wildlife and recreation, arts and culture; Maine people, business, energy and environment and some poetry. Query. Length: 500-2,000 words. Pays 5¢/word.

Photos: B&w and color slides purchased with or without accompanying ms. Captions required.

Maryland

BALTIMORE MAGAZINE, 26 S. Calvert St., Baltimore MD 21202. (301)752-7375. Editor: Stan Heuisler. 50% freelance written. Monthly magazine; 150 pages. Circ. 50,000. Pays on publication. Byline given. Submit seasonal/holiday material 3 months in advance. Electronic submission information supplied on request. Computer printout submissions acceptable. SASE. Reports in 6 weeks. Publishes ms an average of 2 months after acceptance. Sample copy $2.34; free writer's notes with SASE.

Nonfiction: Consumer, profile, life-style, issues, narratives and advocacy. Must have local angle. "We do not want to see any soft, nonlocal features." Buys 4 mss/issue. Length: 1,000-5,000 words. Pays $100-500.

Photos: State availability of photos with ms. Uses color and b&w glossy prints. Captions preferred.

Columns/Departments: Hot Stuff (local news tips), Tips & Touts (local unusual retail opportunities), Class Cars and Tech Talk (high-tech product advice). Query.

CHESAPEAKE BAY MAGAZINE, Suite 200, 1819 Bay Ridge Ave., Annapolis MD 21403. (301)263-2662. Editor: Betty D. Rigoli. 45% freelance written. "*Chesapeake Bay Magazine* is a regional publication for those who enjoy reading about the Bay and its tributaries. Our readers are yachtsmen, boating families, fishermen, ecologists—anyone who is part of Chesapeake Bay life." Monthly magazine; 64-72 pages. Circ. 18,000. Pays either on acceptance or publication, depending on "type of article, timeliness and need." Buys first North American serial rights. Submit seasonal/holiday material 4 months in advance of issue date. Simultaneous (if not to magazines with overlapping circulations) and photocopied submissions OK. Computer printout submissions acceptable; prefers letter-quality to dot-matrix. SASE. Reports in 1 month. Publishes ms an average of 14 months after acceptance. Sample copy $1.50; writer's guidelines for SASE.

Nonfiction: "All material must be about the Chesapeake Bay area—land or water." How-to (fishing, hunting, and sports pertinent to Chesapeake Bay); general interest; humor (welcomed, but don't send any "dumb boater" stories where common safety is ignored); historical; interviews (with interesting people who have contributed in some way to Chesapeake Bay life: authors, historians, sailors, oystermen, etc.); and nostalgia (accurate, informative and well-paced. No maudlin ramblings about "the good old days"); personal experience (drawn from experiences in boating situations, adventures, events in our geographical area); photo feature (with accompanying ms); profile (on natives of Chesapeake Bay); technical (relating to boating, hunting, fishing); and Chesapeake Bay folklore. "We do not want material written by those unfamiliar with the Bay area, or general sea stories. No personal opinions on environmental issues or new column (monthly) material and no rehashing of familiar ports-of-call (e.g., Oxford, St. Michaels)." Recent article example: "Retriever Rapture" (March 1984). Buys 25-40 unsolicited mss/year. Query or submit complete ms. Length: 1,000-2,500 words. Pays $65-85.

Photos: Virginia Leonard, art director. Submit photo material with ms. Uses 8x10 b&w glossy prints; pays $100 for 35mm, 2¼x2¼ or 4x5 color transparencies used for cover photos; $15/color photo used inside. Captions required. Buys one-time rights with reprint permission. Model release required.

Fiction: "All fiction must deal with the Chesapeake Bay and be written by persons familiar with some facet of bay life." Adventure, fantasy, historical, humorous, mystery and suspense. "No general stories with Chesapeake Bay superimposed in an attempt to make a sale." Buys 8 mss/year. Query or submit complete ms. Length: 1,000-2,500 words. Pays $60-85.

Poetry: Attention: Poetry Editor. Free verse or traditional. Must be about Chesapeake Bay. "We want well crafted, serious poetry. Do not send in short, 'inspired' seasick poetry or 'sea-widow' poems." Buys 2/year. Limit submissions to batches of 4. Length: 5-30 lines. Pays $10-25. Poetry used on space available basis only.

Tips: "We are a regional publication entirely about the Chesapeake Bay and its tributaries. Our readers are true 'Bay' lovers, and look for stories written by others who obviously share this love. We are particularly interested in material from the Lower Bay (Virginia) area and the Upper Bay (Maryland/Delaware) area."

Massachusetts

BOSTON GLOBE MAGAZINE, *Boston Globe,* Boston MA 02107. Editor-in-Chief: Michael J. Larkin. 25% freelance written. Weekly magazine; 64 pages. Circ. 781,500. Pays on publication. Buys first rights only. Submit seasonal/holiday material 3 months in advance. Reports in 2-4 weeks. Computer printout submissions acceptable; no dot-matrix. Publishes ms an average of 6 weeks after acceptance. SASE must be included with ms or queries for return.

Nonfiction: Expose (variety of issues including political, economic, scientific, medicine and the arts); interview (not Q&A); profile; and book excerpts (first serial rights only). No travelogues or personal experience pieces. Buys 65 mss/year. Query. Length: 3,000-5,000 words. Pays $600-900.

Photos: Purchased with accompanying ms or on assignment. Captions required. Send contact sheet. "Pays standard rates according to size used."

BOSTON MAGAZINE, 1050 Park Square Bldg., Boston MA 02116. Editor-in-Chief: Donald H. Forst. Monthly magazine. For upscale readers eager to understand and participate in the best that New England has to offer; majority are professional, college-educated and affluent. Pays on publication. Buys one-time rights. Pays 20% kill fee. Written queries mandatory. Submit seasonal/holiday material 5 months in advance. SASE. Reports in 3 weeks.

Nonfiction: Investigative reporting (subject matter varies); profiles (of Bostonians or New Englanders); business stories; and first person accounts of personal experiences. Buys fewer than 10 unsolicited mss/year. Query Charles Matthews, articles editor. Length: 1,000-6,000 words. Pays $200-1,200; more for exceptional material. For short takes, brief items of interest in Boston or throughout New England to run in the Reporter section, query Ric Kahn. Pays 10-20¢/word.

Photos: Stan McCray, art director. B&w and color purchased on assignment only. Query. Specifications vary. Pays $25-150 for b&w; average $275 color.

Tips: "There are many freelance writers in the Boston area, and we have a large group of regular contributing writers, so our need for freelance material from writers based outside the New England area is very slight indeed. Most of all, we look for stories that no one else in our region is doing, either because the subject or the treatment of it hasn't occurred to them, or because the writer has expertise that gives her or him a special insight into the story. A *Boston* story must have a strong and specific focus on Boston or New England, be solidly reported, and be of interest to a wide variety of readers."

‡**CAPE COD LIFE, Including Martha's Vineyard and Nantucket,** Cape Cod Life, Inc., Box 222, Osterville MA 02655. (617)428-5706. Editor: Brian F. Shortsleeve. Managing Editor: Alison L. Sporborg. Maga-

zine published 6 times/year (weighted toward summer publication), focusing on "area lifestyle, history and culture, people and places, business and industry, and issues and answers." Readers are "year-round and summer residents of Cape Cod as well as non-residents who spend their leisure time on the Cape." Circ. 40,000. Pays on publication. Byline given. "Kill fees are paid at discretion of publisher." Buys first North American serial rights and makes work-for-hire assignments. Submit seasonal/holiday material 6 months in advance. Simultaneous queries and photocopied submissions OK. Computer printout submissions acceptable; no dot-matrix. Reports in 2 weeks on queries; 1 month on mss. Sample copy $3; writer's guidelines for SAE.

Nonfiction: General interest, historical/nostalgic, how-to, humor, interview/profile, photo feature, travel, marine, nautical, nature, arts and antiques. Buys 15 mss/year. Query with published clips. Length: 1,200-2,500 words. Pays $3/published column inch (1,000 words equals approximately 30").

Photos: James Canavan, art director. State availability of photos with query letter or ms. Pays $7.50-15 for 35mm b&w slides; $10-20 for 35mm color slides. Captions and identification of subjects required. Buys one-time rights.

Poetry: Traditional. "We only accept poetry that has a Cape Cod, Martha's Vineyard or Nantucket theme." Buys 3 poems/year. Length: 30 lines maximum. Pays $50 maximum.

Tips: "Those freelancers who submit *quality* spec articles generally have a good chance at publication. We do like to see a wide selection of writer's clips before giving assignments. We accept more spec work written about Cape and Islands history than any other area."

NEW BEDFORD, (formerly New Bedford/Fall River), 5 S. 6th St., New Bedford MA 02740. Editor: Ms. Dee Giles Forsythe. 100% freelance written. Bimonthly magazine primarily focusing on southeastern Massachusetts. Pays within period of publication. Buys first rights and second (reprint) rights to material originally published elsewhere. Submit seasonal material 6 months in advance. Computer printout submissions acceptable; prefers letter-quality to dot-matrix. SASE. Reports in 1 month. Publishes ms an average of 1 year after acceptance. Sample copy $1.50; free writer's guidelines.

Nonfiction: Social, political and natural history; biography and people profiles; environmental and other pertinent public policy issues; boating, commercial fishing, and other maritime-related businesses; the arts; education; and lifestyles. Query the Editor. Length: 1,500-2,500 words. Pays approximately $100.

Photos: Prefers b&w glossy prints; will consider 35mm color transparencies. Pays on publication; negotiable fee. Captions and credit lines required.

Fiction: "This magazine occasionally runs short fiction up to 3,000 words. Such manuscripts should have some connection to the sea, to the coast, or to southern New England's history or character. No restrictions on style; the main criterion is quality. Query or send complete ms.

Tips: "We look for the unusual story or angle, the fresh approach, pieces about events, issues or people in the southeastern Massachusetts and Rhode Island area with whom readers can identify. It's particularly rewarding to see the variety of writer's styles, approaches, their personalities; and their willingness to stay with an editor who treats them honestly."

WESTERN MASSACHUSETTS MAGAZINE, (formerly *Country Side*), The Benjamin Company, Box 76, Northampton MA 01061-0076. (413)586-7242. Editor: Paul A. Benjamin. Managing Editor: Michael R. Evans. Consulting Editor: Susan M. Benjamin. 80% freelance written. Bimonthly magazine covering western Massachusetts and surrounding areas. Cir. 20,000. Pays on acceptance. Byline given. Offers 20% kill fee. Buys first North American serial, one-time or all rights. Submit seasonal/holiday material 3 months in advance. Photocopied submissions OK; previously published submissions considered "on occasion." Electronic submissions OK if compatible with Apple IIe disk; requires hard copy also. Computer printout submissions acceptable; prefers letter-quality to dot-matrix. SASE. Reports in 1 month. Publishes ms an average of 3 months after acceptance. Free writer's guidelines; sample copy $2.75.

Nonfiction: Michael R. Evans, managing editor. How-to, historical, humor, investigative reporting, interview/profile, personal experience, agriculture, industry/business, recreation and art. Buys 2-5 mss/issue. Query or send complete ms. Length: 300-3,500 words. Pays 4-10¢/published word.

Photos: Neil F. Hammer, photo editor. Pays negotiable fees for 35mm color transparencies or 8x10 b&w glossy prints. Photos purchased with or without ms. Captions and credit lines required.

Columns/Departments: Michael R. Evans, managing editor. Notebook—short articles about the unusual and interesting in western Massachusetts. Length: 50-300 words. Pays $10-25.

Fiction: "Only well written material focusing on the western Massachusetts area will be considered. Humor welcome." Send complete ms. Length: 300-1,500 words. Pays 4-10¢/published word.

Tips: "All material must be of interest to readers in western Massachusetts. Find the hidden, intriguing piece we haven't heard about yet. Be concise, be sharp."

WORCESTER MAGAZINE, Box 1000, Worcester MA 01614. (617)799-0511. Editor: Dan Kaplan. 10% freelance written. Emphasizes the central Massachusetts region. Weekly tabloid; 48 pages. Circ. 50,000. Pays on acceptance. Buys all rights. Byline given. Submit seasonal/holiday material 2 months in advance. Simultaneous and photocopied submissions OK. Computer printout submissions acceptable. SASE. Reports in 2

weeks. Publishes ms an average of 3 weeks after acceptance. Sample copy $1; free writer's guidelines.
Nonfiction: Expose (area government, corporate); how-to (concerning the area, homes, vacations); interview (local); personal experience; opinion (local); and photo feature. No nonlocal stories. "We leave national and general topics to national and general publications." Buys 30 mss/year. Query with clips of published work. Length: 1,000-3,500 words. Pays $50-125.
Photos: State availability of photos with query. Pays $25-75 for b&w photos. Captions preferred. Buys all rights. Model release required.

Michigan

ANN ARBOR OBSERVER, Ann Arbor Observer Company, 206 S. Main, Ann Arbor MI 48104. Editors: Don and Mary Hunt. 75% freelance written. Monthly magazine featuring stories about people and events in Ann Arbor. Circ. 40,000. Pays on publication. Byline given. Buys one-time rights. Computer printout submissions acceptable. Reports in 3 weeks on queries; 4 weeks on mss. Publishes ms an average of 2 months after acceptance. Sample copy $1.
Nonfiction: Expose, historical/nostalgic, interview/profile, personal experience and photo feature. Buys 75 mss/year. Query. Length: 100-7,000 words. Pays up to $1,200/article.
Tips: "If you have an idea for a story, write us a 100-200 word description telling us why the story is interesting and what its major point is. We are most open to investigative features of up to 5,000 words. We are especially interested in well researched stories that uncover information about some interesting aspect of Ann Arbor."

DETROIT MAGAZINE, *The Detroit Free Press*, 321 W. Lafayette Blvd., Detroit MI 48231. (313)222-6446. Contact: Editor. 20% freelance written. For a general newspaper readership; urban and suburban. Weekly magazine. Circ. 771,000. Pays within 6 weeks of publication. Buys first rights. Kill fee varies. Byline given. Computer printout submissions acceptable. Reports in 3-4 weeks. Publishes ms an average of 6 months after acceptance. SASE.
Nonfiction: "Seeking quality magazine journalism on subjects of interest to Detroit and Michigan readers: lifestyles and better living, trends, behavior, health and body, business and political intrigue, crime and cops, money, success and failure, sports, fascinating people, arts and entertainment. *Detroit Magazine* is bright and cosmopolitan in tone. Most desired writing style is literate but casual—the kind you'd like to read—and reporting must be unimpeachable." Buys 50-60 mss/year. Query or submit complete ms. "If possible, the letter should be held to one page. It should present topic, organizational technique and writing angle. It should demonstrate writing style and give some indication as to why the story would be of interest to us. It should not, however, be an extended sales pitch." Length: 2,000 words maximum. Pays $125-300.
Photos: Purchased with or without accompanying ms. Pays $25 for b&w glossy prints or color transparencies used inside; $100 for color used as cover.
Tips: "Try to generate fresh ideas, or fresh approaches to older ideas. Always begin with a query letter and not a telephone call. If sending a complete ms, be very brief in your cover letter; we really are not interested in previous publication credits. If the story is good for us, we'll know, and if the most widely published writer sends us something lousy, we aren't going to take it."

GRAND RAPIDS MAGAZINE, Suite 1040, Trust Bldg., 40 Pearl St., NW, Grand Rapids MI 49503. (616)459-4545. Publisher: John H. Zwarensteyn. Editor: John J. Brosky Jr. Managing Editor: William Holm. 33% freelance written. Monthly general feature magazine serving western Michigan. Circ. 13,500. Pays 15th of month of publication. Buys first run exclusive rights. Phone queries OK. Submit seasonal material 3 months in advance. Photocopied and previously published submissions OK. Computer printout submissions acceptable; prefers letter-quality to dot-matrix. SASE. Reports in 2 months. Publishes ms an average of 4 months after acceptance.
Nonfiction: Western Michigan writers preferred. Western Michigan subjects only: government, labor, education, general interest, historical, interview/profile and nostalgia. Inspirational and personal experience pieces discouraged. No breezy, self-centered "human" pieces or "pieces not only light on style but light on hard info." Humor appreciated, but specific to region. Buys 5-8 unsolicited mss/year. "If you live here, see Bill Holm before you write. If you don't, send a query letter with clips or phone. Length: 500-4,000 words. Pays $15-150.
Photos: State availability of photos. Pays $10 + /5x7 glossy print and $22 + /35 or 120mm color transparencies. Captions and model release required.
Tips: "Television has forced city/regional magazines to be less provincial and more broad based in their approach. People's interests seem to be evening out from region to region. The subject matters should remain largely local, but national trends must be recognized in style and content. And we must *entertain* as well as inform."

MICHIGAN: The Magazine of the Detroit News, 615 Lafayette, Detroit MI 48231. (313)222-2620. Articles Editor: Susan Slobojan. 35% freelance written. Weekly rotogravure featuring the state of Michigan for general interest newspaper readers. Circ. 820,000. Average issue includes 3 feature articles, departments and staff written columns. Pays on publication. Byline given. Kill fee varies. Buys first Michigan serial rights. Phone queries OK. Submit seasonal material 2 months in advance. Simultaneous and previously published submissions OK, if other publication involved is outside of Michigan. Computer printout submissions acceptable; prefers letter-quality to dot-matrix. Reports in 3 weeks on queries; in 1 month on mss. Publishes ms an average of 2 months after acceptance.

Nonfiction: Profiles, places and topics with Michigan connections. Buys 18 unsolicited mss/year. Recent article example: "The Picasso of Newaygo County," (March 25, 1984). Query with clips of previously published work. Length: 750-3,000 words. Pays $100 minimum.

Photos: Pays $50 minimum/5x7 b&w glossy print. Pays $100-$350/35mm or larger color transparency. Captions required.

Tips: "Magazines are looking for more people-oriented stories now than ever before, in roto magazines, specifically. There's a great effort to run articles more in the vein of a city-oriented magazines and less of the old-style 'roto' (ala *Parade*)-type pieces."

WEST MICHIGAN MAGAZINE, West Michigan Telecommunications Foundation, 7 Ionia SW, Grand Rapids MI 49503. (616) 774-0204. Editor: Dotti Clune. 80% freelance written. Monthly magazine covering geographical region of West Michigan. Circ. 20,000. Pays on publication. Byline given. Buys first rights and second (reprint) rights to material originally published. Submit seasonal/holiday material 3 months in advance. Simultaneous queries, and photocopied and previously published submissions OK. Computer printout submissions acceptable. SASE. Reports in 2 weeks on queries; 1 month on mss. Publishes ms an average of 3 months after acceptance. Free sample copy and writer's guidelines.

Nonfiction: Arts, business, dining, entertainment, recreation, travel, expose (government/politics), interview/profile and photo features. Buys 36 mss/year. Query with published clips if available. Length: 500-2,000 words. Pays $25-200.

Photos: State availability of photos.

Tips: "We look for lively, thought-provoking articles ranging from serious examinations of important issues to humorous glimpses at the lighter side of life in West Michigan. We like articles offering taste, style, and compelling reading; articles capturing the personality of West Michigan—the quality of life in the region and the spirit of its people; and articles appealing to a discriminating audience. We accept only materials with a regional angle."

Minnesota

MPLS. ST. PAUL MAGAZINE, Suite 1030, 12 S. 6th St., Minneapolis MN 55402. (612)339-7571. Editor-in-Chief: Brian Anderson. Managing Editor: Marla J. Kinney. 90% freelance written. For "professional people of middle to upper income levels, college educated, interested in the arts, dining and the good life of Minnesota." Monthly magazine. Circ. 46,000. Pays on publication. Buys negotiable rights. Pays 25% maximum kill fee. Byline given except for extremely short pieces and stories that require considerable rewriting. Submit seasonal/holiday material 4 months in advance. Computer printout submissions acceptable; prefers double-spaced and letter-quality to dot-matrix. SASE. Reports in 1 month. Publishes ms an average of 3 months after acceptance.

Nonfiction: In-depth, informational, historical, local humor, interview, profile and photo feature. "We can use any of these as long as they are related to Minneapolis/St. Paul." Buys 10 unsolicited mss/year. Query. Length: 300-3,000 words. Pays $20-500.

Photos: William Bloedow, art director. Purchased on assignment. Query. Pays $25-200 for b&w; $40-400 for color.

Tips: "I like short, to-the-point, even informal queries; I hate cute, beat-around-the-bush, detailed queries. I often suggest that the writer develop a lead, followed by a couple graphs saying where the story would go. If I want to read more after the lead, then so might our readers. Don't try first person stories unless you are a good writer and have an exceptional story. Submission of a 300-500 word profile on spec. should be followed in a couple of weeks by a phone call. If I send a manuscript back I usually make suggestions for improving or scrapping the piece. If improvements are made and I see potential in the writer, then I'll make an appointment to discuss the writer's ideas for future stories. He/she may get a larger assignment on spec at this point."

‡**TWIN CITIES READER, News, Opinion & Entertainment Weekly,** MCP, Inc., 600 1st Ave. N, Minneapolis MN 55403. (612)338-2900. Editor: Deborah L. Hopp. "We are a general interest weekly tabloid serving the needs of the community via investigative features, local news and profiles, politics, consumer information, lifestyle trends, general arts and entertainment (with special emphasis on film, music and theatre) and food and dining features. We try to address the special needs and interests of our reader, leaving the daily press to cover topics or angles best suited to the general population of Minneapolis/St. Paul. Our readers are 25-44 years old and enjoy largely managerial/professional positions. They are well educated and active; they also participate

enthusiastically in the arts and entertainment opportunities of our community and are considered to be both well-read and well-informed." Circ. 140,000. Pays on publication. Byline given. Buys one-time rights. Submit seasonal/holiday material 1 month in advance. Simultaneous queries, and simultaneous and photocopied submissions OK. Computer printout submissions acceptable; no dot-matrix. SASE. Reports in 3 weeks. Sample copy for 10x13 SAE, and $1.22 postage; free writer's guidelines.

Nonfiction: Travel, fitness and health. Special issues include fitness/health, general real estate, and home interiors. Buys 100 mss/year. Send complete ms. Length: 750-1,500 words. Pays $25-100.

Photos: Greg Helgeson, photo editor. Send photos with accompanying ms. Reviews b&w contact sheets. Pays $10-100 for 5x7 or 8½x11 b&w prints; $50-300 for 5x7 color transparencies. Model release and identification of subjects required.

Columns/Departments: Books. Buys 20 mss/year. Send complete ms. Length: 500-1,250 words. Pays $25-60.

Tips: "Our readers are young (20-45), well-educated, savvy. Do not write for 'general' readers or the unsophisticated. Books, travel, and health and fitness are most open to freelancers. We like short, light style with sense of humor."

Mississippi

DELTA SCENE, Box B-3, Delta State University, Cleveland MS 38733. (601)846-1976. Editor-in-Chief: Dr. Curt Lamar. Business Manager: Ms. Sherry Van Liew. 100% freelance written. For an art-oriented or history-minded audience wanting more information (other than current events) on the Mississippi Delta region. Quarterly magazine; 32 pages. Circ. 1,500. Pays on publication. Buys first rights only. Byline given. Submit seasonal/holiday material at least 4 months in advance. Simultaneous, photocopied and previously published submissions OK. Computer printout submissions acceptable; prefers letter-quality to dot-matrix. SASE. Reports in 4 weeks. Publishes ms an average of 1 year after acceptance. Sample copy $1.50.

Nonfiction: Historical and informational articles; interviews, profiles and travel articles; and technical articles (particularly in reference to agriculture). "We have a list of articles available free to anyone requesting a copy." Buys 2-3 mss/issue. Query. Length: 1,000-2,000 words. Pays $5-20.

Photos: Purchased with or without ms, or on assignment. Pays $5-15 for 5x7 b&w glossy prints or any size color transparency.

Fiction: Humorous and mainstream. Buys 1/issue. Submit complete ms. Length: 1,000-2,000 words. Pays $10-20.

Poetry: Traditional forms, free verse and haiku. Buys 1/issue. Submit unlimited number. Pays $5-10.

Tips: "The freelancer should follow our magazine's purpose. We generally only accept articles about the Delta area of Mississippi, the state of Mississippi, and South in general. We are sponsored by a state university so no articles, poetry, etc. containing profanity or other questionable material. Nonfiction has a better chance of making it into our magazine than short stories or poetry."

Missouri

MISSOURI LIFE, The Magazine of Missouri, Missouri Life Publishing Co., Suite 500, 1205 University Ave., Columbia MO 65201. (314)449-2528. Editor: Bill Nunn. Bimonthly magazine covering Missouri people, places and history. Circ. 30,000. Pays on publication. Byline given. Buys all rights; makes work-for-hire assignments. Submit seasonal/holiday 3 months in advance. Simultaneous queries, and simultaneous, photocopied, and previously published submissions OK. SASE. Reports in 1 month. Sample copy $3.50; writer's guidelines for business-size SAE and 1 first class stamp.

Nonfiction: General interest, historical/nostalgic, interview/profile, personal experience, photo feature and travel. Special issues planned for St. Louis, Kansas City and Lake of the Ozarks. Buys 35-40 mss/year. Query. Length: 1,200-3,000 words. Pays $50-100.

Photos: State availability of photos. Pays $10-25 for 2x2 color transparencies and 5x7 and 8x10 b&w prints. Identification of subjects required.

Columns/Departments: Missouri Homes tours of interesting houses and neighborhoods around the state; Southland stories from the southern part of the state; Voices profiles of interesting Missourians; Eastside St. Louis area stories; Westside Kansas City area stories. Buys 25-30 mss/year. Query. Length: 1,000-2,500 words. Pays $50-100.

Tips: "All sections of the magazine are open to writers. If the material has anything to do with Missouri, we're interested. Keep the writing unaffected and personal."

Montana

MONTANA MAGAZINE, Box 5630, Helena MT 59604. (406)443-2842. Publisher: Rick Graetz. 75% freelance written. For residents of Montana and out-of-state residents with an interest in Montana. Bimonthly.

Pays on publication. Buys one-time rights. Byline given. Electronic submissions OK if IBM PC-compatible. Computer printout submissions acceptable. Reports in 2 months. Publishes ms an average of 6 months after acceptance. Query. SASE. Sample copy $2; free writer's guidelines.

Nonfiction: Articles on life in Montana; history and recreation. "How-to, where-to." Limited usage of material on Glacier and Yellowstone National Parks. Prefers articles on less publicized areas. Personalities, profile, think pieces, nostalgia, travel and history. Length varies.

Photos: Pays $40-75 for short articles with b&w photos; $75-150 for larger articles and accompanying b&w photos. Photo size: 5x7 or 8x10.

Tips: "Know Montana—especially little known recreational opportunities, resource issues and geographic areas within the state."

Nevada

NEVADA MAGAZINE, Carson City NV 89710-0005. (702)885-5416. Editor-in-Chief: Caroline J. Hadley. Managing Editor: David Moore. 50% freelance written. Bimonthly magazine published by the state of Nevada to promote tourism in the state. Circ. 62,000. Pays on publication. Buys first North American serial rights. Byline given. Phone queries OK. Submit seasonal/holiday material 6 months in advance. Computer printout submissions acceptable; prefers letter-quality to dot-matrix. SASE. Reports in 2 months. Publishes ms an average of 4 months after acceptance. Sample copy $1; free writer's guidelines.

Nonfiction: Nevada topics only. Historical, nostalgia, photo feature, people profile, recreational and travel. "We welcome stories and photos on speculation." Buys 40 unsolicited mss/year. Submit complete ms. Length: 500-2,000 words. Pays $75-300.

Photos: Send photo material with accompanying ms. Pays $10-50 for 8x10 glossy prints; $15-75 for color transparencies. Captions required and name and address labeled. Buys one-time rights.

Tips: "Keep in mind that the magazine's purpose is to promote tourism in Nevada. Keys to higher payments are quality and editing effort (more than length). Send cover letter, no photocopy."

THE NEVADAN, *The Las Vegas Review Journal,* Box 70, Las Vegas NV 89101. (702)385-4241. Editor-in-Chief: A.D. Hopkins. 15% freelance written. For Las Vegas and surrounding small town residents of all ages "who take our Sunday paper—affluent, outdoor-oriented." Weekly tabloid; 16 pages. Circ. 100,000. Pays on publication. Buys one-time rights. Byline given. Phone queries OK. Submit seasonal/holiday material 2 months in advance of issue date. Photocopied and previously published submissions OK. Computer printout submissions acceptable; prefers letter-quality to dot-matrix. SASE. Reports in 3 weeks. Publishes ms an average of 2 months after acceptance. Free sample copy and writer's guidelines; mention *Writer's Market* in request.

Nonfiction: Historical (more of these than anything else, always linked to Nevada, southern Utah, northern Arizona and Death Valley); personal experience (any with strong pioneer Nevada angle, pioneer can be 1948 in some parts of Nevada). "We buy a very few contemporary pieces of about 2,400 words with good photos. An advance query is absolutely essential for these. No articles on history that are based on doubtful sources; no current show business material; and no commercial plugs." Buys 52 mss/year. Query. Length: average 2,000 words (contemporary pieces are longer). Usually pays $60.

Photos: State availability of photos. Pays $10 for 5x7 or 8x10 b&w glossy prints; $15 for 35 or 120mm color transparencies. Captions required. Buys one-time rights.

Tips: "Offer us articles on little-known interesting incidents in Nevada history, and good historic photos. In queries come to the point. Tell me what sort of photos are available, whether historic or contemporary, black-and-white or color transparency. Be specific in talking about what you want to write."

New Hampshire

NEW HAMPSHIRE PROFILES, Profiles Publishing Co., 81 Hall St., Concord NH 03301. (603)224-5193. Editor: David Minnis. 50% freelance written. All articles are for and about 25-49 year-old, up-scale consumer-oriented reader who wants to know more about the quality of life in New Hampshire. Magazine published monthly. Approximately 96 pages. Circ. 25,000. Pays on publication. Buys first rights only. Computer printout submissions acceptable. SASE. Reports in 2 months. Publishes ms an average of 3 months after acceptance. Sample copy $2; free writer's guidelines with SASE.

Nonfiction: Interview, opinion, profile, photo feature and interesting activities. Publishes social, political, economic and cultural articles for and about the state of New Hampshire and people who live in it. "We are interested in informative, entertaining articles addressing the cost of living and the quality of life in New Hampshire." Buys 4-5 mss/issue. Query with clips of published work. Length varies from 1,000-3,000 words, depending on subject matter. Pays $125-350.

Photos: State availability of photos. Pays $15-25 for b&w 5x7 or 8x10 glossy prints; $50-150 for 2¼x2¼ or 35mm color transparencies.
Tips: "Query before submitting ms and don't send us your only copy of the ms—photocopy it."

New Jersey

‡**NEW JERSEY LIVING**, Central Jersey Monthly Inc., 8300 Raymond Road, R.D. #4, Princeton NJ 08540. (201)329-2100. Editor: John J. Turi. Managing Editor: Marie C. Turi. A monthly magazine covering New Jersey interests. Circ. 25,000. Pays on publication. Byline given. Buys one-time rights and all rights. Submit seasonal/holiday material 3 months in advance. Simultaneous queries, and simultaneous, photocopied and previously published submissions OK. Computer printout submissions acceptable; no dot-matrix. SASE. Reports in 6 weeks. Sample copy for SAE; writer's guidelines for SAE.
Nonfiction: Book excerpts, general interest, historical/nostalgic, how-to, humor, inspirational, interview/profile, new product, opinion, personal experience, photo feature, technical and travel. Query with published clips. Length: 2,000-3,000 words. Pays $50.
Photos: Send photos with query or ms. Captions, model release, and identification of subjects required.
Columns/Departments: Query with published clips. Length: 500-1,000 words.
Poetry: Avant-garde, free verse, light verse and traditional. Length: 10-60 lines. No payment.
Fillers: Clippings, jokes, gags, anecdotes and short humor. Length: 10-100 words. No payment.

NEW JERSEY MONTHLY, 7 Dumont Place, Morristown NJ 07960. Editor-in-Chief: Colleen Katz. Managing Editor: Larry Marscheck. 95% freelance written. Emphasizes New Jersey interests. Monthly magazine; 100-150 pages. Circ. 95,000. Pays on publication. Buys first North American serial rights. Submit seasonal/holiday material 4 months in advance. Prefers typed submissions but will accept computer printout if letter-quality. SASE. Reports in 6 weeks. Publishes ms an average of 2 months after acceptance.
Nonfiction: Politics (government or any institution in New Jersey); general interest (unusual or significant events, national trends with NJ implications, in-depth look at situations which define a community); how-to (service pieces must cover entire state; should concentrate on living the 'better' life at reasonable cost); profiles (people who are living and doing something in New Jersey—something that affects our readers, as opposed to someone who was born in New Jersey but hasn't lived here in years); and personal experience (only if it sheds light on something going on in the state). "We like articles that are well written and that tell a *story*." Buys 4-6 mss/issue. Query. Length: 1,000-3,500 words. Pays $250-1,250.
Columns/Departments: Departments run shorter than articles and include sports, media, health, travel, profile, books, politics, arts, history, travel (within NJ), people, and others. Buys 8-10 mss/issue. Query. Length: 1,000 words. Pays $250.
Tips: To break into *New Jersey Monthly*, "either write an impressive query letter or begin supplying good items to our gossip section *The New Jersey Informer*, or better still, promise a good, statewide service piece."

THE SANDPAPER, The Newsmagazine of Southern Ocean County, The SandPaper, Inc., 1816 Long Beach Blvd., Surf City NJ 08008. (609)494-2034. Publisher/Editor: Curt Travers. News Editor: Gerry Paul Little. 60% freelance written. Weekly tabloid (monthly in January and February) covering southern New Jersey shore life. "We aim our stories at the wide variety of residents and vacationers at the Jersey shore; we shoot for objectivity." Circ. 35,000. Pays on publication. Byline given. Buys all rights; makes work-for-hire assignments. Submit seasonal/holiday material 2 months in advance. Computer printout submissions acceptable. SASE. Reports in 2 weeks on queries; 6 weeks on mss. Publishes ms an average of 6 weeks after acceptance. Sample copy 50¢.
Nonfiction: Expose (local, county and state government, other area institutions, chemical companies, etc.); general interest (Shore, South Jersey, sports, entertainment, news); historical/nostalgic (relating to coverage area); humor; interview/profile (colorful people, also business and government leaders who have impact on our area); and opinion. "All must somehow relate to life in and around southern Ocean County/Jersey Shore." No first person. "Material must be focused. We don't need a story on fishing. We would use a story on how striped bass quotas have affected the Island's annual fishing tournament." Buys 50-75 mss/year. Query with published clips. Length: 1,200-2,000 words. Pays 2-5¢/word.
Photos: State availability of photos. Pays $4-50 for b&w negatives. Identification of subjects required. Buys one-time or all rights.
Columns/Departments: Currents (250-600 word news items, local looks at national events, discoveries, ironies and oddities). Can include fiction and poetry. "SpeakEasy—our guest column—is open to anyone and any subject (except erotica); views are the author's, not ours." Buys 40 mss/year. Send complete ms. Length: 500-2,000 words. Pays $15 maximum.
Fillers: Newsbreaks. Buys 10-20 mss/year. "Mostly staff-written." Length: 250-600 words. Pays 2-4¢/word.
Tips: "SpeakEasy is open to anyone. It's our version of an editorial page, so we like opinions (even if we don't agree). We also lean heavily toward humor in this section, especially if it relates to local or national news,

trends, etc. Include biographical information. While we prefer to work with published writers, and we won't give an assignment to someone who doesn't have a proven track record, we have given quite a few aspiring writers a start."

‡**THE WAVE**, The WAVE Press, 300 First Ave., Spring Lake NJ 07762. (201)449-8064. Editor: Michael Napoliello. Managing Editor: Jason Moskowitz. A weekly tabloid covering art/entertainment/science/social politics of local interest to people in New Jersey. Estab. 1982. Circ. 25,000. Pays on acceptance. Byline given. Offers 33% kill fee plus expenses. Buys simultaneous rights. Submit seasonal/holiday material 2 weeks in advance. Simultaneous queries and photocopied submissions OK. SASE. Reports in 2 weeks on queries; 1 week on mss. Sample copy for business size SAE and 3 first class stamps; writer's guidelines for SAE and 1 first class stamp.

Nonfiction: J.T.M. Templi, articles editor. Expose, general interest, humor, inspirational, interview/profile, opinion, art reviews, social commentary and satire. "We seek articles dealing with personal growth, like a New Age publication might. We appreciate comment and insight into popular as well as sub-culture entertainment, like the *Rolling Stone* or *Vanity Fair*. We want stories of local interest to people in the state of New Jersey—articles that take the uncommon, the deep, the revealing, the people's, etc., point of view. Stories that present the personal, or the little known side of national issues, philosophies, science, and general interest matter are also candidates for publication. All of this could be summed up simply—we want articles that reflect the essence of a conversation amongst good and concerned friends." Buys 80 mss/year. Send complete ms. Length: 100-6,500 words. No mss longer than 5 typed pages unless it can be printed in subsequent issues. Pays $10-150 plus expenses if applicable, must be certified by editor.

Photos: Marc Stuarts, photo editor. Send photos with accompanying query or ms. Prefers expressionistic, experimental, additive to story, etc. Reviews 4x5 b&w prints. Pays additional 10% of ms rate.

Columns/Departments: Michael Napoleillo, column/department editor. Send for writer guidelines. Query with published clips.

Fiction: Jean Valjean, fiction editor. Adventure, experimental, fantasy, horror, humorous, science fiction and philosophy. Buys 54 mss/year. Send complete ms. Length: 100-6,500 words. Pays $15-150.

Poetry: Michael Arroyo, poetry editor. Avant-garde, free verse, haiku, light verse, traditional. "All types are welcome." Buys 200 poems/year. Length: open. Most poems are submitted contributions. Pay can be discussed with poetry editor.

Tips: "It seems an inherent in newspaper styling to present the readers with a subject report in an objective format. The WAVE's philosophy is the antithesis of that; we want an objective report in any format the writer feels best embodies the truth of the particular subject. As far as an overall or general policy, we look for articles that have the characteristics of a popular song: catchy, bright, moving, to the point. Articles that have their source in New Jersey, or that appeal to general humanistic concerns (art, science, society, etc.) are considered first. Writing that is factual or imaginative in content, and unique in style is encouraged. Literally all sections of the paper are opened to freelancers. Short articles (600-1,200 words) dealing with art, entertainment, or New Jersey issues and social growth, are priority. Phone calls are appreciated and will be beneficial to the writer."

New Mexico

NEW MEXICO MAGAZINE, Bataan Memorial Bldg., Santa Fe NM 87503. (505)827-2642. Editor: Richard Sandoval. Managing Editor: Scottie King. 70% freelance written. Emphasizes New Mexico for a college educated readership, above average income, interested in the Southwest. Monthly magazine; 64-80 pages. Circ. 80,000. Pays on publication. Buys first North American serial or one-time rights for photos/compilation. Submit seasonal/holiday material 8 months in advance. Computer printout submissions acceptable; no dot-matrix. SASE. Reports in 10 days to 4 weeks. Publishes ms an average of 9 months after acceptance. Sample copy $1.75.

Nonfiction: "New Mexico subjects of interest to travelers. Historical, cultural, humorous, nostalgic and informational articles." No columns or cartoons, no non New Mexico subjects. Buys 5-7 mss/issue. Query. Length: 500-2,000 words. Pays $50-300.

Photos: Purchased with accompanying ms or on assignment. Captions required. Query, or send contact sheet or transparencies. Pays $30-50 for 8x10 b&w glossy prints; $30-75 for 35mm; prefers Kodachrome; (photos in plastic-pocketed viewing sheets). Model release required. SASE.

Tips: "Send a superb short (300 words) manuscript on a little-known event, aspect of history or place to see in New Mexico. Faulty research will immediately ruin a writer's chances for the future. Good style, good grammar, please! No generalized odes to the state or the Southwest. No sentimentalized, paternalistic views of Indians or Hispanics. No glib, gimmicky 'travel brochure' writing."

New York

ADIRONDACK LIFE, 420 E. Genesse St., Syracuse NY 13202. Editor: Laurie J. Storey. 95% freelance written. Emphasizes the Adirondack region of New York State for a readership ages 30-60 whose interests include outdoor activities, history and natural history directly related to the Adirondacks. Bimonthly magazine; 80 pages. Circ. 50,000. Pays on publication. Buys one-time rights. Pays 20% kill fee. Byline given. Submit seasonal/holiday material 1 year in advance. Previously published book excerpts OK. Computer printout submissions acceptable; no dot-matrix. SASE. Reports in 6 weeks. Publishes ms an average of 1 year after acceptance. Sample copy $2.50; free writer's guidelines.
Nonfiction: Outdoor recreation (Adirondack relevance only); how-to (should relate to activities and lifestyles of the region, e.g., managing the home woodlot); informational (natural history of the region); photo feature (Adirondack relevance required); profile (Adirondack personalities); and historical (Adirondacks only). Buys 24-28 unsolicited mss/year. Query. Length: 2,500-3,500 words. Pays $100-300.
Photos: Purchased with or without mss or on assignment. Captions required (Adirondacks locale must be identified). Submit contact sheet or transparencies. Pays $15 for 8x10 glossy, semi-glossy or matte photos; $40 for 35mm or larger color transparencies, $150 for covers (color only). Credit line given.
Tips: "Start with a good query that tells us what the article offers—its narrative line and, most importantly, its relevance to the Adirondacks, which is the essential ingredient in every article. It's rewarding to see writers display a variety of refreshing ideas about the Adirondack region."

AVENUE, 145 E. 57th St.; New York NY 10022. (212)758-9516. Editor: Michael Shnayerson. Managing Editor: Lisa Grunwald. Monthly magazine (except January, July and August) covering Manhattan's Upper East Side. Circ. 72,000. Pays on publication. Byline given. Offers 50% kill fee. Buys first North American serial rights. Submit seasonal/holiday material 10 weeks in advance. SASE. Reports in 1 month. Sample copy $5; free writer's guidelines.
Nonfiction: Interview/profile. "Our main need is for profiles of quietly influential Upper East Siders in business or the arts. Business profiles must be of major movers and shakers, corporate or entrepreneurial." Buys 90-100 mss/year. Query with clips. Length: 2,000-3,000 words. Pays $400 minimum.

COUNTY LIFE, Radius Magazines, Inc., 437 Ward Ave., Mamaroneck NY 10543. (914)698-8203. Editor: Cathy Urbach. Associate Editor: Nina Amir. Monthly leisure magazine about Westchester (NY) and Fairfield County (CT) lifestyles. "We reach an upscale, over 30, mostly married, highly educated readership. Our articles are geared to the needs and interests of an affluent, successful audience." Circ. 53,000. Pays on publication. Byline given. Offers 30% kill fee. Buys first North American serial rights. Submit seasonal/holiday material 4-6 months in advance. Simultaneous queries OK; previously published submissions OK "for travel, at times." SASE. Reports in 4 weeks. Sample copy for 9x12 SAE and $1.05 postage.
Nonfiction: Susan Bennett, articles editor. General interest, historical/nostalgic, interview/profile, opinion, photo feature, and travel (within 300 mile radius of metropolitan area). No international travel, fiction or poetry. Special issues include Dining Guide (Jan.), Boating (Feb.), Weddings, Interior/Exterior Decorating (March), Real Estate (April), Corporate (May), Home Entertaining (July), Education (Aug.), Corporate, Home Improvement (Oct.), and Holidays (Nov. and Dec.). Query with clips of published work. Length: 250-3,-000 words. Pays $25-500.
Photos: Tricia Nostrand, photo editor. State availability of photos. Pays $75-125 for 35mm color transparencies; $50-125 for 8x10 b&w prints. Identification of subjects required. Buys one-time rights.
Columns/Departments: Nina Amir, column/department editor. Health, Shopping, Education, Business Profiles and General Business, Celebrity Close-ups, Front Runner (250-word news and human-interest items), Promotions & Motions (new product and executive promotions), Calendar of Events, Inquisitive Shopper (unusual shops), Movies, Theatre. Buys 150 items/year. Query with clips. Length: 250-2,000 words. Pays $25-300.
Fillers: Anecdotes, crossword puzzles, cartoons, word jumbles, short humor and newsbreaks (*must* be about Westchester or Fairfield).
Tips: "The best way to break in is to submit queries for Front Runner (250 word news or human interest) articles; or to submit queries for columns such as Health, Business, or Celebrity profiles."

FOCUS, 375 Park Ave., New York NY 10022. (212)628-2000. Editor: Steven De Arakie. Managing Editor: Kristine B. Schein. Annual publication featuring a guide to New York City and to New York shops for hotel guests and New York residents. Circ. 250,000. Pays on acceptance. Buys one-time rights. Phone queries OK. Sample copy $1.50.
Nonfiction: "We want reviews of antique shops, art galleries, home furnishing stores, women's shops, men's shops and restaurants. The writer must interview an owner and write a description to be approved by the owner. This is all done on assignment." Buys 120 mss/issue. Query with clips of previously published work. Length: 110 words minimum. Pays $35 minimum.

HUDSON VALLEY MAGAZINE, Box 425, Woodstock NY 12498. (914)679-5100. Editor: Joanne Michaels. 100% freelance written. Monthly. Circ. 26,000. Pays on publication. Byline given. Buys first North American serial rights, one-time rights and second serial (reprint) rights. Submit seasonal/holiday material 3 months in advance. Simultaneous submissions OK. Computer printout submissions acceptable; no dot-matrix. SASE. Reports in 1 month on queries. Publishes ms an average of 6 months after acceptance.
Nonfiction: Joanne Michaels, articles editor. Book excerpts; general interest; historical/nostalgic (Hudson Valley); how-to (home improvement); interview/profile (of area personalities); photo feature; and travel. No fiction or personal stories. Length: 1,500-2,000 words. Query. Pays $20-50.
Photos: State availability of photos. Reviews 5x7 b&w prints. Captions required.

‡**LONG ISLAND LIFE, A New York Radius Magazine**, Radius Magazines, Inc., 437 Ward Ave., Mamaroneck NY 10543. (914)698-8203. Editor: Cathy Urbach. Associate Editor: Susan Bennett. A monthly magazine covering Nassau and Suffolk Counties, Long Island. Circ. 52,000. Pays on publication. Byline given. Offers 30% kill fee. Buys first North American serial rights. Submit seasonal/holiday material 4-6 months in advance. Simultaneous queries OK. Computer printout submissions acceptable; no dot-matrix. SASE. Reports in 1 month. Sample copy for 9x12 SAE and 95¢ postage; writer's guidelines for 4x9½ SAE and 20¢ postage.
Nonfiction: General interest (relating to LI—health, education, business, politcs, shopping); historical/nostalgic (town profiles, LI history); interview/profile (celebrity, executive, political); opinion (letters to editor, community issues); travel (with 300 mile radius of New York City); recipes; and calendar of events information. Special issues include Dining Guide (Jan.); Boating (Feb.); Weddings, Interior/Exterior Decorating (March); Real Estate (April); Corporate (May); Home Entertaining (July); Education (Aug.); Corporate, Home Improvement (Oct.); Holidays (Nov. and Dec.).
Columns/Departments: Health; Shopping, Education; Business Profiles and General Business; Celebrity Close-ups; Front Runner (250 word news and human interest items); Promotions & Motions (new product and executive promotions); Calendar of Events; Inquisitive Shopper (unusual shops); Movies; and Theatre. Buys 150 mss/year. Query with published clips. Length: 250-2,00 words. Pays $25-300.
Fillers: Crossword puzzles, word jumbles. Pays negotiable rate.
Tips: "The best way to break in is to submit queries for Front Runner (250-word, news or human interest) articles or to submit queries for columns such as health, business, or celebrity profiles. Front Runner pieces should be concise, light and witty. Business or celebrity profiles should be 1,500 words."

‡**LONG ISLAND'S NIGHTLIFE**, MJC Publications Inc., 1770 Deer Park Ave., Deer Park NY 11729. (516)242-7722. Publisher: Michael Cutino. Managing Editor: Bill Ervolino. A monthly entertainment magazine. Circ. 50,000. Pays on publication. Byline given. Offers $15 kill fee. Buys first North American serial rights and all rights. Submit seasonal/holiday material 10 weeks in advance. Simultaneous queries and photocopied submissions OK. SASE. Reports in 10 weeks. Free sample copy and writer's guidelines.
Nonfiction: General interest, humor, inspirational, interview/profile, new product, photo feature, travel and entertainment. Length: 500-1,000 words. Pays $25-75.
Photos: Send photos with ms. Reviews b&w and color contact sheets. Pays $10 for color transparencies and b&w prints. Captions and model releases required. Buys all rights.
Columns/Departments: Films, Movies, Albums, Sports, Fashion, Entertainment and Groups. Buys 150 mss/year. Send complete ms. Length: 400-600 words. Pays $25.
Fillers: Clippings, jokes, gags, anecdotes, short humor and newsbreaks. Buys 10/year. Length: 25-100 words. Pays $10.

‡**NEW YORK DAILY NEWS**, Travel Section, 220 E. 42 St., New York NY 10017. (212)949-3573. Travel Editor: Bert Shanas. 40% freelance written. Weekly tabloid. Circ. 2 million. "We are the largest circulating newspaper travel section in the country and take all types of articles ranging from experiences to service oriented pieces that tell readers how to make a certain trip." Pays on publication. Byline given. Makes work-for-hire assignments. Submit seasonal/holiday material 4 months in advance. Contact first before submitting electronic submissions; requires hard copy also. Computer printout submissions acceptable. SASE. Reports "as soon as possible."
Nonfiction: General interest, historical/nostalgic, humor, inspirational, personal experience and travel. "Most of our articles involve practical trips that the average family can afford—even if it's one you can't afford every year. We put heavy emphasis on budget saving trips and budget tips on all trips. We also run stories now and then for the Armchair Traveler, a person taking an exotic and usually expensive trip. We are looking for professional quality work from professional writers who know what they are doing. The pieces have to give information and be entertaining at the same time." No 'How I Spent My Summer Vacation' type articles. No PR hype. Buys 60 mss/year. Query with SASE. Length: 1,500 words maximum. Pays $75-125.
Photos: "Good pictures always help sell good stories." State availability of photos with ms. Reviews contact sheet and negatives. Captions and identification of subjects required. Buys one-time rights.
Columns/Departments: "Short Hops is based on trips to places within a 300 mile radius of New York City." Length: 800-1,000 words.

Tips: "A writer might have some luck gearing a specific destination to a news event or date: 'In Search of Irish Crafts' in March, for example."

NEW YORK MAGAZINE, News Group Publications, Inc. 755 2nd Ave., New York 10017. (212)880-0700. Editor: Edward Kosner. Managing Editor: Laurie Jones. Emphasizes the New York metropolitan area. Weekly magazine. Queries preferred. Pays on acceptance. Submit seasonal/holiday material 2 months in advance. Photocopied submissions OK. SASE. Reports in 1 month.
Nonfiction: Expose, general interest, interview, profile, behavior/lifestyle, health/medicine, local politics and entertainment. Pays $500-1,500.

OUR TOWN, East Side/West Side Communications Corp., Suite 202, 1751 2nd Ave., New York NY 10028. (212)289-8700. Editor: Kalev Pehme. Weekly tabloid covering neighborhood news of Manhattan (96th St.-14th St.). Circ. 110,000. Pays on publication. Byline given. Buys all rights. Submit seasonal/holiday material 1 month in advance. SASE.
Nonfiction: Expose (especially consumer ripoffs); historical/nostalgic (Manhattan, 14th St.-96th St.); interview/profile (of local personalities); photo feature (of local event); and animal rights. "We're looking for local news (Manhattan only, mainly 14th St.-96th St.). We need timely, lively coverage of local issues and events, focusing on people or exposing injustice and good deeds of local residents and business people. (Get *full names, spelled right!*)" Special issues include Education (January, March and August); and Summer Camps (March). Query with clips of published work. Length: 1,000 words maximum. Pays "70¢/20-pica column-inch as published."
Photos: Pays $2-5 for 8x10 b&w prints. Buys all rights.
Tips: "Come by the office and talk to the editor. (Call first.) Bring samples of writing."

UPSTATE MAGAZINE, *Democrat and Chronicle*, 55 Exchange St., Rochester NY 14614. (716)232-7100. Editor: Mary Rita Kurycki. Assistant Editor: Dierck Casselman. Art Director: Kate Weisskopf. 90% freelance written. A Sunday magazine appearing weekly in the Sunday *Democrat and Chronicle*. A regional magazine covering topics of local interest written for the most part by area writers. Circ. 230,000. Pays on publication. Byline given. Buys first North American serial rights and second (reprint) rights to material originally published elsewhere. Submit seasonal/holiday material 3 months in advance. Computer printout submissions acceptable. SASE. Reports in 6-8 weeks. Publishes ms an average of 6 months after acceptance.
Nonfiction: Investigative; general interest (places and events of local interest); historical/nostalgic; humor; interview/profile (of outstanding people in local area); personal experience; photo feature (with local angle); and travel (regional). Buys 150-200 mss/year. Query. Length: 1,000-3,000 words. Pays $60-325. Do not send fiction or fillers.

North Carolina

CHARLOTTE MAGAZINE, Box 221269, Charlotte NC 28222. (204)375-8034. Editor: Melinda Meschter. 95% freelance written. Emphasizes probing, researched and upbeat articles on local people, places and events. Monthly magazine. Circ. 10,000. Pays 1 month after publication. Buys first rights and second (reprint) rights to material originally published elsewhere. Computer printout submissions acceptable. SASE. Reports in 3 weeks. Publishes ms an average of 2 months after acceptance. Sample copy $2.25.
Nonfiction: Departments: lifestyles (alternative and typical); business (spotlight successful, interesting business and people); town talk (short, local articles of interest); theater, arts, book reviews and sports. No PR promos. "We are seeking articles indicating depth and research in original treatments of subjects. Our eagerness increases with articles that give our well-educated audience significant information through stylish, entertaining prose and uniqueness of perspective. Remember our local/regional emphasis." Query or send complete ms. Length: 1,000-2,000 words. Pays $150-250 for feature articles.
Photos: State availability of photos. Buys b&w and color prints; pay negotiable. Captions preferred; model releases required.
Columns/Departments: "Will consider all types of articles." Buys 6 columns/issue. Query. Length: 1,000-1,500 words. Pays $75-150.
Fillers: Anecdotes, newsbreaks, humor, preview of events and personalities. Buys 6-8/issue. Length: 250-750 words. Pays 5¢/word.

THE STATE, *Down Home in North Carolina*, Box 2169, Raleigh NC 27602. Editor: W.B. Wright. 70% freelance written. Monthly. Buys first rights only. Pays on acceptance. Deadlines 1 month in advance. Computer printout submissions acceptable; prefers letter-quality to dot-matrix. SASE. Sample copy $1 (for postage and handling).
Nonfiction: "General articles about places, people, events, history, nostalgic and general interest in North

Carolina. Emphasis on travel in North Carolina, (devote features regularly to resorts, travel goals, dining and stopping places)." Will use humor if related to region. Length: average of 1,000-2,000 words. Pays $15-50, including illustration.

Photos: B&w photos. Pays $3-20, "depending on use."

Ohio

BEND OF THE RIVER® MAGAZINE, 143 W. Third St., Box 239, Perrysburg OH 43551. (419)874-7534. Publishers: Christine Raizk Alexander and R. Lee Raizk. 50% freelance written. For readers interested in Ohio history, antiques, etc. Monthly magazine. Circ. 2,000. Buys first rights only. Byline given. Buys 50-60 mss/year. Pays on publication. No photocopied or simultaneous submissions. Submit seasonal material 2 months in advance; deadline for holiday issue is October 15. Reports in 1 month. Publishes ms an average of 6 months after acceptance. Submit complete ms. SASE. Sample copy 50¢.
Nonfiction: "We deal heavily in Ohio history. We are looking for well researched articles about local history and modern day pioneers, doing the unusual. We'd like to see interviews with historical (Ohio) authorities; travel sketches of little-known but interesting places in Ohio; grass roots farmers; and preservation. Our main interest is to give our readers happy thoughts and good reading. We strive for material that says 'yes' to life, past and present." No personal reflection or nostalgia. Buys 60 unsolicited mss/year. Length: 1,500 words. Pays $5-15.
Photos: Purchases b&w photos with accompanying mss. Pays $1 minimum. Captions required.
Tips: "Any Toledo area, well researched history will be put on top of the heap! Send us any unusual piece that is either cleverly humorous, divinely inspired or thought provoking. We like articles about historical topics treated in down-to-earth conversational tones. We pay a small amount (however, we're now paying more) but usually use our writers often and through the years. We're loyal." Recent article subject: the Apple Festival in Bryan, Ohio.

THE BLADE TOLEDO MAGAZINE, 541 Superior St., Toledo OH 43660. (419)245-6121. Editor: Sue Stankey. General readership. Weekly magazine; 32 pages. Circ. 210,000. Pays on publication. Buys one-time rights. Byline given. Submit seasonal/holiday material 6 months in advance. Simultaneous, photocopied and previously published submissions OK. SASE.
Nonfiction: Historical (about northwestern Ohio); informational; interview; and personal experience. Buys 1 ms/issue. Query. Length: 2,000-5,000 words. Pays $75-500.
Photos: Photos purchased with accompanying ms. Captions required. Pays $15-30 for 8x10 b&w glossy prints; $10-45 for 35mm, 2¼x2¼ or 8x10 color glossy prints. Total purchase price for ms includes payment for photos. Model release required.
Tips: "Stories should pertain to our circulation area: Toledo, Ohio and southern Michigan."

CINCINNATI MAGAZINE, Suite 900, 617 Vine St., Cincinnati OH 45202. (513)721-3300. Editor: Laura Pulfer. Emphasizes Cincinnati living. Monthly magazine; 88-120 pages. Circ. 28,000. Pays on acceptance. Buys all rights. Pays 33% kill fee. Byline given. Submit seasonal/holiday material 3 months in advance. Simultaneous, photocopied and previously published submissions OK. SASE. Reports in 3-5 weeks.
Nonfiction: How-to, informational, interview, photo feature, profile and travel. No humor. Buys 4-5 mss/issue. Query. Length: 2,000-4,000 words. Pays $150-400.
Photos: Kay Walker, art director. Photos purchased on assignment only. Model release required.
Columns/Departments: Travel, how-to, sports and consumer tips. Buys 5 mss/issue. Query. Length: 750-1,500 words. Pays $75-150.
Tips: "It helps to mention something you found particularly well done. It shows you've done your homework and sets you apart from the person who clearly is not tailoring his idea to our publication. Send article ideas that probe the whys and wherefores of major issues confronting the community, making candid and in-depth appraisals of the problems and honest attempts to seek solutions. Have a clear and well defined subject about the city (the arts, politics, business, sports, government, entertainment); include a rough outline with proposed length; a brief background of writing experience and sample writing if available. We are looking for critical pieces, smoothly written, that ask and answer questions that concern our readers. We do not run features that are 'about' places or businesses simply because they exist. There should be a thesis that guides the writer and the reader. We want balanced articles about the city—the arts, politics, business, etc."

‡**CLEVELAND MAGAZINE**, City Magazines, Inc., 1621 Euclid Ave., Cleveland OH 44120. (216)771-2833. Editor: Michael D. Roberts. Managing Editor: Frank Bentayou. 40% freelance written. Monthly magazine covering the Greater Cleveland area. Editorial material "ranges from soft lifestyle features (on food, travel, decor, the arts) to hard investigative articles about the city and its institutions. *Cleveland Magazine* tends toward the hard-hitting." Circ. 55,000. Pays on publication. Byline given. Offers negotiable kill fee. Submit seasonal/holiday material 3 months in advance. Simultaneous queries OK. Computer printout submissions ac-

ceptable. SASE. Reports in 6 weeks. Publishes ms an average of 3 months after acceptance.

Nonfiction: "*Cleveland Magazine* looks for depth and good reporting from its writers. We maintain a close relationship between writer and editor so that articles proceed in the direction that will best meet the needs of our upscale and literate readers." Buys 60 mss/year. Query with published clips. Length: 1,500-4,000 words. Pays $200-500.

Photos: Gary Sluzewski, art director. State availability of photos. Reviews contact sheets and transparencies. Model releases and identification of subjects required. Buys one-time rights.

Columns/Departments: Media; Personality (shorter in-depth profiles); Et Cetera (a back-page essay of 700-2,000 words); Personal Finance; and Epicure. Buys 30 mss/year. Query with published clips. Length: 1,000-2,000 words. Pays $150-250.

Fiction: "We run fiction only once a year (December) when we publish the winner of a fall fiction contest.

Tips: "The best bet for a freelancer is to aim for our Inside Cleveland section of short, upfront items (300-700 words). We look for bright, witty pieces for this section or for little 'zingers' about government or other institutions. Good reporting is very important in these shorts."

COLUMBUS MONTHLY, 171 E. Livingston Ave., Columbus OH 43215. (614)464-4567. Editorial Director: Lenore E. Brown. Emphasizes subjects of general interest primarily to Columbus and central Ohio. Monthly magazine. Pays on publication. Buys all rights. Byline given. SASE. Reports in 1 month. Sample copy $2.65.

Nonfiction: "We want general articles which relate specifically to Columbus or central Ohio area." No humor, essays or first person material. Buys 6 mss/issue. Query. "I like query letters which: 1. are well-written; 2. indicate the author has some familiarity with *Columbus Monthly*; 3. give me enough detail to make a decision; and 4. include at least a basic bio of the writer." Buys 4-5 unsolicited mss/year. Length: 100-4,500 words. Pays $15-400.

Photos: State availability of photos. Pay varies for b&w or color prints. Model releases required.

Columns/Departments: Art, business, food and drink, movies, politics, sports and theatre. Buys 2-3 columns/issue. Query. Length: 1,000-2,000 words. Pays $100-175.

Tips: "It makes sense to start small: something for our Around Columbus section, perhaps. Stories for that section run between 400-1,000 words."

DAYTON MAGAZINE, Dayton Area Chamber of Commerce, 1980 Kettering Tower, Dayton OH 45423. (513)226-1444. Editor: Linda Lombard. Bimonthly magazine covering the Dayton area and its people; "promotes the community through an honest editorial approach." Circ. 10,000. Pays on publication. Byline given. Buys first rights only. Submit seasonal/holiday material 4 months in advance. SASE. Reports in 2 months. Sample copy for SAE and $1.50 postage.

Nonfiction: General interest, historical/nostalgic, how-to, humor, interview/profile, opinion and photo feature. "Must relate to Dayton area." No articles lacking local appeal or slant. Buys 36 mss/year. Query with clips of published work. Length, 1,400-3,000 words.

Photos, Send photos with ms. Payment "depends on feature." Reviews b&w and color contact sheets and color transparencies. Captions, model release and identification of subjects required. Buys one-time rights.

Columns/Departments, Buys 60 mss/year. Query with clips of published work. Length, 750-1,000 words.

‡THE ENQUIRER MAGAZINE, The Cincinnati Enquirer (Gannett), 617 Vine St., Cincinnati OH 45201. (513)721-2700. Editor: Betsa Marsh. 60% freelance written. Newspaper Sunday magazine covering a wide range of topics. Circ. 300,000. Pays on publication. Byline given. Pays 40% kill fee. Buys first rights only. Submit seasonal/holiday material 3 months in advance. Simultaneous queries, and simultaneous, photocopied, and previously published submissions OK. Computer printout submissions acceptable. SASE. Reports in 2 weeks on queries. Publishes ms an average of 6 months after acceptance. Free sample copy and writer's guidelines.

Nonfiction: Book excerpts, expose, general interest, historical/nostalgic, humor, interview/profile, personal experience and travel (rarely). No editorials, how-to, new products, inspirational or technical material. Buys 48-60 mss/year. Send complete ms. Length: 1,000-2,400 words. Pays $85-250.

Photos: State availability of photos. Pays $15-20 for b&w contact sheets; $25-50 for color contact sheets. Reviews color transparencies. Identification of subjects required. Buys one-time rights.

Fiction: Adventure, mainstream, mystery and suspense. Buys 3-4 mss/year. Send complete ms. Length: 1,200-2,400 words. Pays $85-250.

Fillers: Short humor. Buys 6-12/year. Length: 500-700 words. Pays $50-85

THE MAGAZINE, 4th and Ludlow Sts., Dayton OH 45401. (513)225-2360. Editor: Ralph A. Morrow. 30% freelance written. Sunday supplement. Circ. 225,000. Byline given. Pays on publication. Buys first rights and second (reprint) rights to material originally published elsewhere. Computer printout submissions acceptable. SASE. Usually reports in 2 weeks. Publishes ms an average of 3 months after acceptance.

Nonfiction: Magazine focuses on people, places, trends. No first person or essays. Emphasis is on color trans-

parencies supplemented by stories. No travel. Length: open. *"The Daily News* will evaluate articles on their own merits. Average payment per article: $125." Payments vary depending on quality of writing.
Photos: Photos should be glossy. Evaluates photos on their own merit. Payment variable depending on quality.

OHIO MAGAZINE, Ohio Magazine, Inc., Subsidiary of Dispatch Printing Co., 40 S. 3rd St., Columbus OH 43215. Editor-in-Chief: Robert B. Smith. Managing Editor: Ellen Stein. 65% freelance written. Emphasizes news and feature material of Ohio for an educated, urban and urbane readership. Monthly magazine; 96-156 pages. Circ. 96,573. Pays on publication. Buys all rights, second serial (reprint) rights, or one-time rights. Pays 20% kill fee. Byline given "except on short articles appearing in sections." Submit seasonal/holiday material 5 months in advance. Simultaneous, photocopied and previously published submissions OK. Computer printout submissions acceptable; no dot-matrix. SASE. Reports in 8 weeks. Publishes ms an average of 4 months after acceptance. Free writer's guidelines.
Nonfiction: Features: 2,000-8,000 words. Pays $250-700. Cover pieces $600-850; Ohioana and Ohioans (should be offbeat with solid news interest; 50-250 words, pays $15-50); Short Cuts (on Ohio or Ohio-related products including mail ordering and goods or people that perform a service that are particularly amusing or offbeat; 100-300 words, pays $15-20); Ohioguide (pieces on upcoming Ohio events, must be offbeat and worth traveling for; 100-300 words, pays $10-15); Diner's Digest ("we are still looking for writers with extensive restaurant reviewing experience to do 5-10 short reviews each month in specific sections of the state on a specific topic. Fee is on a retainer basis and negotiable"); Money (covering business related news items, profiles of prominent people in business community, personal finance—all Ohio angle; 300-1,000 words, pays $50-250); and Living (embodies dining in, home furnishings, gardening and architecture; 300-1,000 words, pays $50-250). "Send submissions for features to Robert B. Smith, editor-in-chief, or Ellen Stein, managing editor; Ohioguide and Diner's Digest to services editor; and Money to Ellen Stein, managing editor. No political columns or articles of limited geographical interest (must be of interest to all of Ohio). Buys 40 unsolicited mss/year.
Columns & Departments: Contact Ellen Stein. Sports, Last Word, travel, fashion, and wine. Open to suggestions for new columns/departments.
Photos: Tom Hawley, art director. Rate negotiable.
Tips: "Freelancers should send a brief prospectus prior to submission of the complete article. All articles should have a definite Ohio application."

Oklahoma

‡**OKLAHOMA LIVING MAGAZINE**, Criss-Cross Numerical Directory, Inc.—Clyde Blyth, Box 75579, Oklahoma City OK 73147. (405)943-4289. Editor: Christy Nedbalek. 5% freelance written. A bimonthly magazine for home buyers in central Oklahoma. "We have three magazines within the cover of *Oklahoma Living* that are centered around the housing industry: Home Living, Apartment Living and Multi-Unit Living. We also have a City Living magazine that includes articles of general interest." Buys 10-15 mss/year. Query with published clips. Length: 4 pages typed, double-spaced. Computer printout submissions acceptable; no dot-matrix. Pays $100/published page (4 double-spaced typed pages). Buys first rights and second (reprint) rights to material originally published elsewhere. Publishes ms an average of 75 days after acceptance.
Photos: State availability of photos. Pays $15-20 for 5x7 b&w prints. Captions, model release and identification of subjects required.
Columns/Departments: "We have our own local columns but would consider columns on related subjects." Query with published clips.
Tips: "Each magazine has its own cover story. Past features in City Living have included subjects like pardon and parole in Oklahoma, bankruptcy, health and fitness, behind the scenes at an Oklahoma University football game, and passing down of family businesses, as well as fashion and how-to's. We also want and require localized stories and may want a story of national interest and add a side-bar on a local slant of our own."

OKLAHOMA TODAY, Oklahoma Department of Tourism and Recreation, Box 53384, Oklahoma City OK 73152. (405)521-2496. Editor: Sue Carter. Managing Editor: Kate Jones. 65% freelance written. Bimonthly magazine covering travel and recreation in the state of Oklahoma. "We are interested in showing off the best Oklahoma has to offer; we're pretty serious about our travel slant but will also consider history and personality profiles." Circ. 30,000. Pays on acceptance. Buys first rights only. Byline given. Offers 50% kill fee. Submit seasonal/holiday material 1 year in advance "depending on photographic requirements." Simultaneous queries and photocopied submissions OK. "We don't mind letter-quality computer printout submissions at all—provided they are presented in ms format; i.e., double spaced and on 8½x11 sheets, or a size close to that. No scrolls, please." Reports in 2 months. Publishes ms an average of 4 months after acceptance. SASE. Sample copy $2; free writer's guidelines.
Nonfiction: Book excerpts (pre-publication only, on Oklahoma topics); photo feature and travel (in Oklahoma). "We are a specialized market; no first person reminiscences or fashion, memoirs—though just about any

topic can be used if given a travel slant." Buys 35-40 mss/year. Query with clips; no phone queries. Length: 1,000-1,500 words. Pays $150-250.

Photos: High-quality color transparencies, b&w prints. "We are especially interested in developing contacts with photographers who either live in Oklahoma or have shot here. Send samples and price range." Free photo guidelines. Send photos with ms. Pays $50-100 for b&w and $50-250 for color; reviews 2¼ and 35mm color transparencies. Model release, identification of subjects and other information for captions required. Buys one-time rights plus right to use photos for promotional purposes.

Tips: "The best way to become a regular contributor to *Oklahoma Today* is to query us with one or more story ideas, each developed to give us an idea of your proposed slant. We're looking for *lively* writing—and writing that doesn't need to be heavily edited. We have a two-person editorial staff, and freelancers who can write and have done their homework get called again and again."

TULSA WORLD, Box 1770, Tulsa OK 74102. (918)581-8300. Executive Editor: Bob Haring. Sunday Magazine Editor: David Averill. 25% freelance written. Sunday magazine of daily newspaper, covering travel. Pays on publication. Buys first rights and second (reprint) rights to material originally published elsewhere. Simultaneous and previously published submissions OK. Inquire about electronic submissions. Computer printout submissions acceptable; prefers letter-quality to dot-matrix. SASE. Reports in 3 weeks "if rejected." Publishes ms an average of 3 months after acceptance.

Nonfiction: General interest (features); interview/profile (of Oklahoma people making good elsewhere); and travel ("lean toward locally produced material on exotic or nearby destinations"). No fiction or first person pieces. Buys 15 mss/year. Send complete ms. Length: 300-500 words; 600-1,200 words for general interest features and interview/profiles. Pays $75-225.

Photos: Pays $30 for any size b&w glossy prints; $50 for color transparencies or prints. Captions required.

Oregon

CASCADES EAST, 716 NE 4th St., Box 5784, Bend OR 97708. (503)382-0127. Editor: Geoff Hill. 100% freelance written. For "all ages as long as they are interested in outdoor recreation in central Oregon: fishing, hunting, sight-seeing, hiking, bicycling, mountain climbing, backpacking, rockhounding, skiing, snowmobiling, etc." Quarterly magazine; 48 pages. Circ. 7,000 (distributed throughout area resorts and motels and to subscribers). Pays on publication. Buys all rights. Byline given. Computer printout submissions acceptable; no dot-matrix. Submit seasonal/holiday material 6 months in advance. SASE. Reports in 6 weeks. Publishes ms an average of 6 months after acceptance. Sample copy $2.

Nonfiction: General interest (first person experiences in outdoor central Oregon—with photos, can be dramatic, humorous or factual); historical (for feature, "Little Known Tales from Oregon History", with b&w photos); and personal experience (needed on outdoor subjects: dramatic, humorous or factual). "No articles that are too general, sight-seeing articles that come from a travel folder, or outdoor articles without the first person approach." Buys 20-30 unsolicited mss/year. Query. Length: 1,000-3,000 words. Pays 3-10¢/word.

Photos: "Old photos will greatly enhance chances of selling a historical feature. First person articles need black and white photos, also." Pays $8-15 for b&w; $15-50 for color transparencies. Captions preferred. Buys one-time rights.

Tips: "Submit stories a year or so in advance of publication. We are seasonal and must plan editorial for summer '84 in the spring of '83, etc., in case seasonal photos are needed."

Pennsylvania

ERIE & CHAUTAUQUA MAGAZINE, Charles H. Strong Building, 1250 Tower Lane, Erie PA 16505. (814)452-6070. Editor: Gerry B. Wallerstein. 80% freelance written. Quarterly magazine covering Erie County, Pennsylvania and Chautauqua County, New York for upscale readers with above average education and incomes. Circ. 20,000. Pays $35/published page for all rights upon publication. Will reassign rights to author upon written request after publication. Computer printout submissions acceptable; prefers letter-quality to dot-matrix. SASE. Reports in 2-4 weeks. Publishes ms an average of 9 months after acceptance. Sample copy $2; free writer's guidelines for SASE.

Nonfiction: Feature articles (usually five per issue) on "key issues affecting our coverage area, lifestyle topics, major projects or events which are of importantance to our readership, area history with relevance to life today, preservation and restoration, arts and cultural subjects." Also profiles, humor and satire. Length: 2,500 words maximum for articles; 1500 words maximum for personality profiles; 750 words for humor and satire. "All material *must* have relevance to our coverage area."

Photos: Color photos for covers by assignment only to local photographer. Will consider 8x10 b&w glossies with stories. Pays $15 per b&w for all rights upon publication. Model release and captions required.

Columns/Departments: Business, education, social life, arts and culture, travel, food/wine/fashions and medicine items written by contributing editors. Will consider new departmets on the basis of a resume showing expertise and two sample columns. Length: 750 words maximum.

Tips: "It's rewarding to see a variety of ideas and styles in freelancers. We enjoy being able to give new writers a start and finding the person with special expertise for a special story. But we regret reviewing inappropriate material guidelines, WM listings, etc., and notice a lack of discipline in meeting deadlines, and inadequate research—stories without 'meat'."

THE INQUIRER MAGAZINE, *Philadelphia Inquirer*, Box 8263, Philadelphia PA 19101. Editor: David Boldt. Managing Editor: Charles Layton. Sunday magazine section for city and suburban readers. Weekly. Circ. 1,050,000. Pays on publication. Buys first North American serial rights. Submit seasonal/holiday material 3 months in advance of issue date. Photocopied submissions OK. Computer printout submissions acceptable. SASE. Reports in 2 months. Free sample copy.

Nonfiction: "About half of our material is written by freelance writers. Major feature articles generally run 3,000-6,000 words. Also buy some shorter articles (500-800 words) for the *Our Town* section, and, occasionally short humorous articles with local angle. We use mainly articles that consist of reporting on, and analysis of, local issues and personalities. Blatant bias in favor of local writers." Buys 20-30 mss/year. Query. Pays $400-500 for major articles from first-time contributors.

Tips: "Query should have high-impact idea, evidence of an effective writing style, clear concept of story structure and reporting plan, with good clips. We will be increasingly selective and will increase what we pay for what we want." Recently published examples: "The Day the H-Bomb Hit Philadelphia," by Michael Schwartz.

‡PENNSYLVANIA HERITAGE, Pennsylvania Historical and Museum Commission, Box 1026, Harrisburg PA 17108-1026. (717)787-1396. Editor: Douglas H. West. 90% freelance written. Quarterly magazine covering Pennsylvania history and culture. "*Pennsylvania Heritage* introduces readers to Pennsylvania's rich culture and historic legacy, educates and sensitizes them to the value of preserving that heritage and entertains and involves them in such as way as to ensure that Pennsylvania's past has a future. The magazine is intended for intelligent lay readers." Circ. 9,000. Pays on acceptance. Byline given. Buys all rights. Simultaneous queries, and simultaneous and photocopied submissions OK. Computer printout submissions acceptable; prefers letter-quality to dot-matrix. Reports in 3 weeks on queries; 6 weeks on mss. Publishes ms an average of 9 months after acceptance. Sample copy for $2.50; free writer's guidelines.

Nonfiction: Expose, general interest, historical/nostalgic, how-to, humor, interview/profile, new product, personal experience, photo feature, technical and travel. No articles which in no way relate to Pennsylvania history or culture. Buys 20-24 mss/year. Query. Length: 2,000-3,500 words. Pays $0-100.

Photos: State availability or send photos with query or ms. Pays $25-100 for color transparencies. Captions and identification of subjects required. Buys one-time rights.

Tips: "Because we've just begun to pay freelancers, the opportunity for acceptance is good. We are looking for well written, interesting material that pertains to any aspect of Pennsylvania history or culture. Our goal is to entertain readers while educating them. Authors should make history readable and entertaining."

PHILADELPHIA MAGAZINE, 1500 Walnut St., Philadelphia PA 19102. Editor: Ron Javers. For sophisticated middle and upper income people in the Greater Philadelphia/South Jersey area. Monthly magazine. Circ. 140,000. Buys first rights only. Pays 20% kill fee. Byline given. Buys 50 mss/year. Pays on publication or within 2 months. Free writer's guidelines for SASE. Reports in 4 weeks. Queries and mss should be sent to Ben Yagoda, articles editor. SASE.

Nonfiction: "Articles should have a strong Philadelphia focus but should avoid Philadelphia stereotypes—we've seen them all. Lifestyles, city survival, profiles of interesting people, business stories, music, the arts, sports and local politics, stressing the topical or unusual. No puff pieces. We offer lots of latitude for style, but before you make like Norman Mailer, make sure you have something to say." Length: 1,000-7,000 words. Pays $100-1,000.

PITTSBURGH MAGAZINE, Metropolitan Pittsburgh Public Broadcasting, Inc., 4802 5th Ave., Pittsburgh PA 15213. (412)622-1360. Editor-in-Chief: Martin Schultz. 50% freelance written. "The magazine is purchased on newsstands and by subscription and is given to those who contribute $25 or more a year to public TV in western Pennsylvania." Monthly magazine; 132 pages. Circ. 56,700. Pays on publication. Buys all rights. Pays kill fee. Byline given. Submit seasonal/holiday material 6 months in advance. Computer printout submissions acceptable; prefers letter-quality to dot-matrix. SASE. Reports in 2 month. Publishes ms an average of 4 months after acceptance. Sample copy $2; free writer's guidelines.

Nonfiction: Expose, lifestyle, sports, informational, service, interview, nostalgia and profile. No humorous or first person material. Query or send complete ms. Length: 2,500 words. Pays $50-500. Query for photos. Model release required.

Columns/Departments: Art, books, films, dining, health, sports and theatre. "All must relate to Pittsburgh or western Pennsylvania."

Tips: "Possible new columns coming. It's rewarding to see more varied information and experience in free-lancers than staff personnel."

THE PITTSBURGH PRESS, *Sunday* weekly magazine (formerly *Roto*), 34 Blvd. of Allies, Pittsburgh PA 15230. Editor: Ed Wintermantel. Circ. 625,000. Not copyrighted. Byline given. Buys 40-50 mss/year. Pays on publication. Computer printout submissions OK. Buys first rights in the Pittsburgh area. Reports in 1 month. **Nonfiction:** Local and regional interest material on issues, trends or personalities. "Articles should be provocative, controversial or simply interesting, and may be either serious or offbeat." No hobbies, how-tos or timely events pieces. Query. "When submitting manuscript, writer must include his or her Social Security number, this is a requirement of the Internal Revenue Service since payments for published stories must be reported." Length: 1,000-3,000 words. Pays $100-400.

‡**SUNDAY**, The Pittsburgh Press Co., 34 Boulevard of the Allies, Pittsburgh PA 15230. (412)263-1510. Editor: Ed Wintermantel. A weekly general interest newspaper magazine for a general audience. Circ. 625,000. Pays on publication. Byline given. Not copyrighted. Buys first rights in circulation area. Simultaneous queries OK. SASE. Reports in 1 month.
Nonfiction: Regional or local interest, humor and interview/profile. No articles on hobbies, how-to or timely events. Buys 25-50 mss/year. Query. Length: 1,000-3,000 words. Pays $100-400.

SUSQUEHANNA MONTHLY MAGAZINE, Susquehanna Times and Magazine, Inc., Box 75A, R.D.1, Marietta PA 17547. (717)426-2212. Editor: Richard S. Bromer. 25% freelance written. Monthly magazine about regional Lancaster County, Pennsylvania, for people in the upper middle socio-economic level who are college educated, ages 25-60, home and family and community oriented, and interested in local history and customs. Circ. 6,000. Pays on publication. Buys all rights. Phone queries OK. Submit seasonal material 2 months in advance. Simultaneous and photocopied submissions OK. Computer printout submissions acceptable; no dot-matrix. SASE. Reports in 2 months. Publishes ms an average of 3 months after acceptance. Sample copy $2 in advance.
Nonfiction: General interest (history, arts); and historical (local events and personalities). "This material must have a special relationship to the area we cover: Lancaster County and nearby areas in southeast Pennsylvania." Serious and scholarly material. Buys 60 mss/year. Send complete ms. Length: 750-2,500 words. Pays $35-75.
Photos: Offers no additional payment for photos accepted with ms. Captions preferred; model release required.
Tips: "Read several copies of *Susquehanna Magazine* to get a feel for our style and preferred material. Write up fresh material or fresh approach to old material, e.g., historical incidents. We accept 'class' material only (informative, intellectually stimulating, accurate)—nothing trite or 'term paper'."

South Carolina

‡**COLUMBIA REVIEW**, Publications South, Inc., Box 61079, Columbia SC 29260. Editor: Margaret-Ann Trimble. Monthly magazine edited for decision makers and consumers in the Columbia area. Estab. 1983. Circ. 17,000. Pays 1-2 months after publication. Byline given. Buys all rights; sometimes purchases limited rights. Submit seasonal/holiday material 2 months in advance. Photocopied submissions OK. SASE. Reports in 1 month. Sample copy $1.50; free writer's guidelines.
Nonfiction: Expose (investigative material); general interest; historical/nostalgic; interview/profile; photo feature; and travel (seasonal). "Emphasis is on local interest events, culture, history, business and people." Buys 100 mss/year. Query with clips. Length: open. Pays $15-50.
Photos: Send photos with ms. Pays $5 maximum for 5x7 b&w prints. Captions and identification of subjects required.
Columns/Departments: Film review, recipes, craft, financial and real estate (local slant). Buys 50 mss/year. Query with clips of published work. Length: open. Pays $15-50.
Fiction: Accepts limited amount of fiction; *must* have local slant or must be by local writer. Buys 10 mss/year. Query with clips of published work. Length: open. Pays $25-50.
Fillers: Length: open. Pays $5-25.

‡**GREENVILLE MAGAZINE**, Greenville Magazine, Inc., Box 8695, Greenville SC 29604. (803)232-2380. Editor: Margaret-Ann Trimble. 90% freelance written. Monthly magazine edited for decision makers and consumers in Greenville, Spartanburg and surrounding areas. Circ. 10,000. Pays on publication. Byline given. Buys all rights. Submit seasonal/holiday material 2 months in advance. Photocopied submissions OK. Computer printout submissions acceptable. SASE. Reports in 1 month. Publishes ms an average of 3 months after acceptance. Sample copy $1.50; free writer's guidelines.
Nonfiction: Expose (investigative material); general interest; historical/nostalgic; interview/profile; photo

feature; and travel (seasonal). "Emphasis is on local interest events, culture, history, business and people." Buys 100 mss/year. Query with clips. Length: open. Pays $15-75.

Photos: Send photos with ms. Pays $5 maximum for 5x7 b&w prints. Captions and identification of subjects required.

Columns/Departments: Film review, book review, recipes, craft, financial and real estate (local slant). Buys 50 mss/year. Query with clips of published work. Length: open. Pays $15-50.

Fiction: "We don't, as a general rule, accept fiction." Buys 1 mss/year. Query with clips of published work. Length: open. Pays $25-50.

Fillers: Length: open. Pays $5-25.

Tips: "The most rewarding aspect of working with freelance writers is that each writer brings to the magazine a unique style that keeps the articles from all sounding the same."

Tennessee

MEMPHIS, Towery Press, Box 370, Memphis TN 38101. (901)345-8000. Executive Editor: Kenneth Neill. Circ. 30,000. Pays on publication. Buys all rights. Pays $35 kill fee. Byline given. Phone queries OK. Simultaneous, photocopied and previously published submissions OK. SASE. Reports in 6 weeks. Sample copy $2.
Nonfiction: Expose, general interest, historical, how-to, humor and interview/profile. "Virtually all our material has strong Memphis connections." Buys 25 unsolicited mss/year. Query or submit complete mss or clips of published work. Length: 1,500-5,000 words. Pays $75-500.
Tips: "The kinds of manuscripts we most need have a sense of story (i.e., plot, suspense, character), an abundance of evocative images to bring that story alive, and a sensitivity to issues at work in Memphis. Tough investigative pieces would be especially welcomed."

MID SOUTH MAGAZINE, *Commercial Appeal*, 495 Union Ave., Memphis TN 38101. (901)529-2794. Editor: Karen Brehm. Sunday newspaper supplement. Circ. 300,000. Pays after publication. Byline given. Buys one-time rights. Simultaneous queries, and photocopied and previously published submissions (if so indicated) OK. SASE. Reports in 3 weeks.
Nonfiction: General interest (with regional tie-in). Buys 12 mss/year. Query with clips of published work. Length: 1,500-2,000 words. Pays $100.
Photos: State availability of photos. Reviews color transparencies and 5x7 b&w glossy prints. "Photos are paid for with payment for ms." Buys one-time rights.
Columns/Departments: Viewpoints (political background, economic commentary, psychological issues, social issues). Buys 50 mss/year. Send complete ms. Length: 1,500-2,000 words. Pays $100.

Texas

AUSTIN LIVING, Baker Publications, Suite 207, 1805 Rutherford Lane, Austin TX 78754. (512)837-3534. Publisher: Sandy Ellis. Bimonthly magazine for newcomers and prospective homebuyers in the Austin area. Circ. 40,000. Pays on acceptance. Byline given. Buys all rights. Submit seasonal/holiday material 4 months in advance. Simultaneous queries and photocopied and previously published submissions OK. SASE. Reports in 1 week. Free sample copy; writer's guidelines for 1 business-size SAE and 1 first class stamp.
Nonfiction: "Interior decorating, housing trends, financing, home building—anything of interest to home buyers or people relocating to Austin." Query. Length: 2,000 words maximum. Pays 20¢/word.
Photos: State availability of photos. Pays $6 for 5x7 or 8x10 b&w glossy prints. Captions and model release required.
Tips: "National assignments on decorating, financing, etc., for all of Baker's city magazines are made by Tina Stacy, publication director." Pays 20¢/word.

DALLAS/FORT WORTH LIVING, Baker Publications, Suite 400, 5757 Alpha Rd., Dallas TX 75240. (214)239-2399. Publication Director: Tina Stacy. Bimonthly magazine covering housing and relocation for persons in the market for houses, apartments, townhouses and condominiums. Circ. 80,000. Pays on publication. Byline given. Buys all rights. Submit seasonal/holiday material 4 months in advance. Simultaneous queries OK. SASE. Reports in 6 weeks. Free sample copy; writer's guidelines for business-size SAE and 1 first class stamp.
Nonfiction: How-to (decorate); new product (local "discoveries"); and technical (energy-saving devices/methods). Buys 30 mss/year. Query with clips of published work "that show flexibility of writing style." Length: 1,000-3,000 words. Pays 20¢/word.
Photos: State availability of photos. Pays negotiable fee for color transparencies and 8x10 b&w glossy prints. Identification of subjects required. Buys all rights.
Columns/Departments: Luxury Living (customizing a new or old home). Query with clips of published work. Length: 1,000 words minimum. Pays 10¢/word.

Tips: "National assignments on decorating, financing, etc. for all of Baker's city magazines are made by Tina Stacy, publication director. Query her at *Living*, Suite 400, 5757 Alpha Rd., Dallas TX 75240."

DALLAS LIFE MAGAZINE, Sunday Magazine of *The Dallas Morning News*, Belo Corporation, Communications Center, Dallas TX 75265. (214)745-8432. Editor: Melissa East. Weekly magazine. "We are a lively, topical, sometimes controversial city magazine devoted to informing, enlightening and entertaining our urban sunbelt readers with material which is specifically relevant to Dallas lifestyles and interests." Circ. 417,000. Pays on "scheduling". Byline given. Buys first North American serial rights or simultaneous rights. Submit seasonal/holiday material 3 months in advance. Simultaneous queries and simultaneous submissions OK ("if not competitive in our area"). Computer printout submissions OK; prefers letter-quality to dot-matrix. SASE. Reports in 1 month on queries; 6 weeks on mss. Sample copy $1.
Nonfiction: Expose ("anything Dallas-related that is fully substantiated"); general interest; how-to (home, shelter and garden); humor (short); interview/profile; and new product. "We look for an exciting style in short, lively, fresh material that is written to indulge the reader rather than the writer. All material must, repeat *must*, have a Dallas metropolitan area frame of reference." Special issues include: Spring and fall home furnishings theme issues. Buys 15-25 unsolicited mss/year. Query with clips of published work or send complete ms. Length: 750-2,000 words. Pays $100-600.
Photos: State availability of photos. Pays $15-25 for b&w contact sheets; and $25-150 for 35mm or larger color transparencies. Captions, model release and identification of subjects required. Buys one-time rights.
Tips: "We are focusing sharply on an upwardly mobile, achievement oriented readership in 25-45 age range."

DALLAS MAGAZINE, 1507 Pacific Ave., Dallas TX 75201. (214)954-1390. Editor: D. Ann Shiffler. Associate Editor: Jeff Hampton. 65% freelance written. Emphasizes business and other topics of interest to Dallas upper income business people. Monthly magazine; 100 pages. Circ. 30,000. Pays on acceptance. Buys all rights. Pays 100% kill fee "but kill fee is not offered on stories where quality is poor or editor's directions are not followed." Byline given. Submit seasonal/holiday material 3 months in advance. Photocopied submissions OK. Electronic (telecommunications) encouraged: ASKI II through modem. Computer printout submissions acceptable. SASE. Reports in 1 month. Publishes ms an average of 2 months after acceptance. Sample copy $1.50.
Nonfiction: General interest (of interest to successful work oriented men and women); historical (only on Dallas); humor (rarely accepted, but will use exceptional articles); interview (of Dallas executive or Dallas resident in an important government job or the like); profile (same as interview); and business features. "We do not want stories that underestimate our readers. Controversies involving technique or practices, not people, can be acceptable." Business issues are explored with solutions offered where appropriate. "We prefer not to see general information on such items as cooking, etc. unless the subject and/or article can be related to the Dallas business scene." Buys 3-5/mss issue. Query with "an outline that reflects preliminary research." Length: 1,000-3,000 words. Pays $100-500.
Photos: State availability of photos. Pays $75-200 for 8x10 b&w glossy prints; $75-500 for color transparencies. Captions required.
Columns/Departments: Portraits (see "interview" above); Enterprise (profile of a local company and its new product, new program, new approach, etc.); and Trends (how-to/self-help for business executives at work or at leisure).

EL PASO MAGAZINE, El Paso Chamber of Commerce, 10 Civic Center Plaza, El Paso TX 79901. (915)544-7880. Editor: Russell S. Autry. 100% freelance written. Monthly magazine "takes a positive look at El Paso people and area activities. Readers are owners and managers of El Paso businesses." Circ. 5,000. Pays on publication. Byline given. Buys first North American serial rights. Submit seasonal/holiday material 3 months in advance. Simultaneous queries and simultaneous and photocopied submissions OK. Computer printout submissions acceptable; prefers letter-quality to dot-matrix. SASE. Reports in 2 months. Publishes an average of 3 months after acceptance. Free sample copy and writer's guidelines.
Nonfiction: General interest, historical/nostalgic, interview/profile, photo feature. Buys 75 mss/year. Query with clips of published work. Length: 1,000-2,500 words. Pays $100-200.
Photos: Send photos with ms. Pays $10/photo; $300 for cover photo. Captions, model releases and identification of subjects required. Buys one-time rights.
Tips: "We are actively seeking feature writers."

‡**FORT WORTH Magazine**, Ft. Worth Chamber of Commerce, 700 Throckmorton, Ft. Worth TX 76102. (817)336-2491. Editor: Rose Tulecke. A monthly community magazine about people, places and happenings within Tarrant County for an "affluent well-educated readership including civic leaders, the chief executive officers of local corporations, and out-of-state FORTUNE 500 companies interested in a reflection of the Ft. Worth lifestyle." Circ. 10,000. Pays on acceptance. Byline given. Not copyrighted. Buys first North American serial rights. Computer printout submissions acceptable. SASE. Reports in 2 months. Sample copy $2.33; free writer's guidelines.

Nonfiction: Historical/nostalgic (Ft. Worth); business (local angle); photo feature (Ft. Worth link); and Ft. Worth and Tarrant County events. No personal experience. Buys 60 mss/year. Query with published clips. Length: 2,000 words. Pays $100.
Photos: Anthony Torres, photo editor. Send photos with accompanying query or ms. Reviews photos of Fort Worth, cover quality. Pays $75 for 35mm slides or transparencies; $15 for 8x10 b&w prints. Captions, model release and identification of subjects required. Buys one-time rights.
Tips: Feature articles are most open to freelancers. "Because of the Ft. Worth Chamber of Commerce's strong involvement in business, the quality of life and tourism, all of these issues are addressed in some way in the planning of the magazine."

HOUSTON CITY MAGAZINE, Southwest Media Corp., Suite 1450, 1800 W. Loop S., Houston TX 77027. (713)850-7600. Publisher: Lute Harmon. Managing Editor: Ann Powell. Monthly magazine for highly upscale audience. Circ. 60,000. Pays on acceptance. Byline given. Offers 25% kill fee. Buys first North American serial rights. Reports in 1 week. Sample copy $1.75; free writer's guidelines.
Nonfiction: Jan Short, articles editor. Book excerpts, interview/profile (Houston angle), photo feature—have Houston or Texas angle. No poetry, religion or fiction. Buys 35-40 mss/year. Query. Length: 1,200-5,000 words. Pays $500-2,000.
Photos: Elizabeth Robben, photo editor. State availability of photos. Captions, model release and identification of subjects required. Buys one-time rights.
Columns/Departments: Attention: Jan Short. Health, food, travel and books. Buys 36 mss/year. Query. Length: open. Pays $300-400.

HOUSTON LIVING, Baker Publications, Suite 450, 5444 Westheimer, Houston TX 77056. (713)626-2812. Publication Director: Tina Stacy. Bimonthly magazine covering housing for newcomers and other prospective home buyers in the Houston area. Circ. 80,000. Pays on acceptance. Byline and brief bio given. Buys all rights. Submit seasonal/holiday material 4 months in advance. Simultaneous queries, and photocopied and previously published submissions OK. SASE. Reports in 1 month. Free sample copy; writer's guidelines for business-size SAE and 1 first class stamp. *
Nonfiction: "Articles should be slanted toward buying a home. We want to run solid articles on trends, specifically slanted for the Houston area market." Buys 6 mss/year. Query with clips of published work. Length: 500-1,500 words. Pays 20¢/word (of 3 or more letters).
Photos: State availability of photos. Reviews any size b&w glossy prints.
Tips: "The writer should demonstrate lively, informative style and personal qualifications for writing on the subject. National assignments on decorating, financing, etc., for all of Baker's city magazines are made by Tina Stacy, publication director. Payment is 20¢/word. Query her at: Living, 5757 Alpha Rd., Suite 400, Dallas TX 75240."

‡**INNER-VIEW, The Newsmagazine of Houston's Innercity**, Inner-View Publishing Co., Inc., Box 66156, Houston TX 77266. (713)523-NEWS. Editor: Kit van Cleave. A monthly general tabloid "specifically for 'inside The Loop' in Houston—the artistic, affluent, trendy part of town." Circ. 35,000. Pays on publication. Byline given. Buys all rights. Submit seasonal/holiday material 3 months in advance. Simultaneous queries and simultaneous, photocopied, and previously published submissions OK. Computer printout submissions acceptable; prefers letter-quality to dot-matrix. SASE. Reports in 2 weeks. Sample copy for $1.05 postage and 9x12 SAE; writer's guidelines for SAE and 1 first class stamp.
Nonfiction: Historical/nostalgic (about Houston only), humor, interview/profile, opinion and travel. "No religious or broad-general articles—pieces need to be exceptional or about Texas or Houston." Buys 20 mss/year. Query with or without published clips or send complete ms. Length: 350-700 words. Pays $50-200.
Photos: Jim Caldwell, photo editor. State availability of photos with query letter or ms. Pays variable rate for 8x10 b&w prints; "we don't buy many photos." Captions and identification of subjects required. Buys one-time rights.
Columns/Departments: Humor. Buys 5-10 mss/year. Query or send complete ms. Length: 350-700 words. Pays $50-200.
Tips: "We would be happy to look at nonfiction and newsy pieces of short length, but we're a local consumer general-interest publication with content like *New York*, *New West*, *Chicago Reader*, *D Magazine* and *Texas Monthly*. Feature articles on people who live or work in the 'center-city' area of Houston are most open to freelancers."

‡**SAN ANTONIO HOMES & GARDENS**, Duena Development Corp., Box 5950, Austin TX 78763. (512)441-1980. Publisher: Hazel W. Gully. Monthly magazine emphasizing San Antonio homes, people, events and gardens for current, former and prospective residents. First issue September 1984. Anticipated circulation 10,000. See *Austin Homes & Gardens* for format, departments, rates and requirements.
Tips: "Since this is a new publication, we will be looking for steady freelancers in the San Antonio, Texas, area."

SAN ANTONIO MAGAZINE, Greater San Antonio Chamber of Commerce, Box 1628, San Antonio TX 78296. (512)229-2108. Editor: Alice Costello. Emphasizes business and quality of life articles about San Antonio. Monthly magazine; 88 pages. Pays on acceptance. Buys all rights. Photocopied submissions OK. SASE. Reports in 1 month. Free sample copy and writer's guidelines.

Nonfiction: "The magazine's purpose is to tell the story of San Antonio, its businesses and its people, primarily to the membership of the Greater San Antonio Chamber of Commerce to the San Antonio community and to prospective businesses and industries. No material about the Alamo, cowboys and Indians, or any non San Antonio topic." Buys 65 mss/year. Query or send complete ms, "query should be readable, typed and give me an element of the story, as well as some idea of the person's writing ability." Length: 800-3,000 words. Pays $75-300.

Photos: Purchased with mss or on assignment. Captions required. Query. Pays $10-25 for 8x10 b&w glossy prints. Prefers to pay according to the number of photos used in an article, a bulk rate.

Tips: "The best way to break in is to be a resident of San Antonio and, therefore, able to write on assignment or to query the editor personally. Again, we are looking for material which is related to the city of San Antonio, its people and the business community. We consider all possible angles and tie-ins. We like to see writers who can tie national economic or business events to San Antonio and support information with figures."

SAN ANTONIO MONTHLY, San Antonio Publishing Corp., Box 17554, San Antonio TX 78217. (512)732-6142. Editor: Tom Bell. Managing Editor: Elizabeth Boyd. 50% freelance written. Monthly city lifestyle magazine for San Antonio metropolitan area and surrounding vicinities. Circ. 10,000. Pays on publication. Byline given. Buys first rights only. Submit seasonal/holiday material 3 months in advance. Simultaneous queries, and simultaneous and previously published submissions OK. Computer printout submissions acceptable; no dot-matrix. SASE. Reports in 1 month. Publishes ms an average of 3 months after acceptance.

Nonfiction: Book excerpts (Texan); expose; general interest; historical/nostalgic; interview/profile (local politicians or personalities); photo feature; travel; business; sports (with local angle); and film reviews. Special issues include December, gift guide; February, spring fashion; March, annual restaurant guide; April, Fiesta guide; May, travel; August, fall fashion; and September, theater guide. No "personality profiles and business articles that are all fluff and no depth. Give us an opinion, *please*." Buys 24 mss/year. Query with published clips. Length: 500-3,500 words. Pays $40-300.

Photos: Coco Cates, art director. State availability of photos. Reviews b&w contact sheet, color transparencies and 8x10 b&w prints. Identification of subjects required. Buys one-time rights.

Columns/Departments: Sports (local only); Business (entrepreneurs, national companies based in San Antonio) and What's News (short news articles on political and city issues, comments on events and personalities). Buys 24 mss/year. Query with published clips or send complete ms. Length: 250-2,500 words. Pays $25 (What's News)-$150.

Tips: "Editorial features in *San Antonio Monthly* reflect a city of changing attitudes and lifestyles. As the city grows—both physically and population-wise—so does the market; our readers are middle to upper income, educated people, both 'new' and 'old' San Antonians. They turn to *San Antonio Monthly* to keep tap on what's changing in the city, where the city is headed, who's taking it there and why. The best way for a freelancer to start writing for us is to bring us an *idea*, or several ideas. Telling us that you'd 'love to write just anything' for us does not impress us. Instead, write us about a story idea for What's News or a department (Business or Sports are wide open) with some preliminary research. Then, follow up with a phone call, and if we like the idea, we'll have you in to talk about it. We welcome queries from freelancers, but they must be specific."

TEXAS WEEKLY MAGAZINE, *Pasadena Citizen*, Box 6192, Pasadena TX 77506. (713)477-0221. Editor: Dick Nichols. 25% freelance written. Sunday supplement to *Pasadena Citizen*. Circ. 11,000. Pays on publication. Byline given. Buys first rights only. Submit seasonal/holiday material 2 months in advance. Simultaneous queries, and simultaneous and photocopied submissions OK. Computer printout submissions acceptable; no dot-matrix. SASE. Reports in 2 weeks. Publishes ms an average of 2 months after acceptance. Sample copy for 8½x11 SASE.

Nonfiction: General interest, historical/nostalgic and interview/profile. "Stories on interesting people or places, mainly Texas based, greater Houston area." No poetry or fiction. Query with clips of published work, if available.

Photos: State availability of photos. "We like stories with photos. One, we like longer stories (up to 2,000 words), with at least two color prints, 8x10 or 5x7, one for the cover with main features plus 2-5 b&w prints, or can use good color shots as b&w halftones to accompany the article. We pay $100 flat fee for a turnkey story like this. Or, for our inside features, a shorter story with two or three b&w photos, we pay $50 flat." Captions and identification of subjects required.

ULTRA MAGAZINE, Farb Publications, Inc., Suite 200, 2000 Bering Dr., Houston TX 77057. (713)961-4132. Editor: David Bertugli. Managing Editor: Rhona Schwartz. Monthly magazine about Texas and Texans targeted to affluent Texans. Subjects covered include: people, fashion, travel, the arts, food and wine, design interiors, entertainment and social events, all of which must have a strong Texas slant. Circ. 95,000. Pays on acceptance. Byline given. 25% kill fee on assignments not used. Submit material 4 months in advance. Do not submit simultaneous queries. SASE. Reports in 2-3 weeks. Sample copy $4; writer's guidelines for business-size SAE and 1 first class stamp.

Nonfiction: General interest, interview/profile, photo features and fashion features. No fiction, poetry, investigative or political stories. "All stories must be of interest to upscale Texans." Buys 30-40 mss/year. Query with resume and clips of published works. Length 1,000-4,000 words. Pays $400-1,500. Travel stories must have photos or state availability of photos.

Photos: Veta Redmond, photo editor. Reviews color transparencies. Model release and identification of subjects required.

Columns: Gary McKay, column/department editor. Texas people and events, profiles, food and wine, the arts, homes, health, beauty, fashion, jewelry and real estate. Length: 500-1,500 words. Pays $200-500. Query with published clips.

WESTWARD, *Dallas Times-Herald*, 1101 Pacific, Dallas TX 75202. Editor: Janet Vitt. 33% freelance written. Weekly magazine. Circ. 400,000. Pays on publication. Byline given. Buys first North American serial rights or one-time rights. Submit seasonal/holiday material 3 months in advance. Simultaneous queries, and simultaneous (if outside circulation area) and previously published submissions OK. Computer printout submissions acceptable; no dot-matrix. SASE. Reports in 2 months. Publishes ms an average of 6 weeks after acceptance.

Nonfiction: Investigative (of Southwest interest); historical/nostalgic; interview/profile (outstanding people of regional interest); opinion (essays); photo feature (album style); and discovery pieces on out-of-the-way places. No service articles. Buys 25 unsolicited mss/year. Query. Length: 1,500-3,000 words. Pays $250-750.

Photos: State availability of photos. Reviews 35mm color transparencies and 8x10 b&w glossy prints. Pays negotiable fee. Captions required. Buys one-time rights.

Tips: "Our only criterion is that we find the material interesting and well written, although most accepted submissions have a Southwest slant." Recent article/story example: "An Encounter with Ultra-Orthodox Judaism."

Vermont

VERMONT LIFE MAGAZINE, 61 Elm St., Montpelier VT 05602. (802)828-3241. Contact: Editor. 95% freelance written. Quarterly magazine. Circ. 120,000. Buys first rights. Byline given. Buys 60 mss/year. "Query by letter is essential." Computer printout submissions acceptable; prefers letter-quality to dot-matrix. SASE. Publishes ms an average of 9 months after acceptance.

Nonfiction: Wants articles on today's Vermont, those which portray a typical or, if possible, unique aspect of the state or its people. Style should be literate, clear and concise. Subtle humor favored. No Vermont dialect attempts as in "Ayup", outsider's view on visiting Vermont or "Vermont cliches"—maple syrup, town meetings or stereotyped natives. Length: average 1,500 words. Pays 20¢/word.

Photos: Buys photographs with mss and with captions and seasonal photographs alone. Prefers b&w contact sheets to look at first on assigned material. Color submissions must be 4x5 or 35mm transparencies. Buys one-time rights, but often negotiates for re-use rights also. Rates on acceptance; color, $75 inside, $200 for cover. Gives assignments but only with experienced photographers. Query in writing.

Tips: "Writers who read our magazine are given more consideration because they understand we want Vermontish articles about Vermont."

‡**VERMONT VANGUARD PRESS, Statewide Weekly**, Vanguard Publishing, 87 College St., Burlington VT 05401. (802)864-0506. Editor: Joshua Mamis. Managing Editor: Gail E. Hudson. 70% freelance written. A weekly alternative newsppaer, locally oriented, covering Vermont politics, environment, arts, development, etc. Circ. 20,000. Pays on publication. Byline given. Offers 50% kill fee only after written acceptance. Not copyrighted. Buys first rights only. Submit seasonal/holiday material 1 month in advance. Simultaneous queries, and simultaneous, photocopied, and previously published submissions OK. SASE. Reports in 1 month. Publishes ms an average of 6 weeks after acceptance.

Nonfiction: Expose and humor. Articles should have a Vermont angle. Buys about 12 mss/year. Query with published clips. Length: 500-2,500 words. Pays $20-100.

Photos: Rob Swanson, photo editor. State availability of photos. Pays $10-20 for b&w contact sheets and negatives. Captions, model release and identification of subjects required. Buys one-time rights.

Tips: "Short news stories are most open to freelancers. Knowledge of Vermont politics is essential."

Virginia

COMMONWEALTH, Box 1710, Norfolk VA 23501. (804)625-4800. Editor: Deborah Marquardt. 30% freelance written. For urban adults interested in lifestyles and important issues in southeastern Virginia.

Monthly magazine; 96 pages. Circ. 48,000. Pays on publication. Buys all rights. Pays negotiable kill fee. By-line given. Phone queries OK. Submit seasonal/holiday material 6 months in advance. Photocopied and previously published submissions OK. SASE. Reports in 4-6 weeks. Publishes ms an average of 3 months after acceptance. Sample copy $1.95; free writer's guidelines.
Photos: State availability of photos. Pays $20-40 minimum/5x7 color and b&w glossy prints; offers no additional payment for photos accompanying ms. Captions preferred; model release required.
Columns/Departments: Arts/entertainment; business; outdoors; people; health; gourmet; lifestyle; and travel (prefers inside story on popular or unusual local or regional spots). Buys 4 columns/issue. Query. Length: 800-1,200 words. Pays $20-100.
Fiction: "Must be about Virginia or the South." Buys 4-6 mss/year. Submit complete ms. Length: open. Pays 10¢/word.
Fillers: "No limericks or humorous ditties, please. We use them but we generate them locally."
Tips: "Visit with the editor, establish a rapport, show genuine interest in and prior knowledge of the magazine, be prepared with good ideas, show an eagerness to dig for a good story, and keep in touch."

NORTHERN VIRGINIAN, 135 Park St., Box 1177, Vienna VA 22180. (703)938-0666. Contact: Editor. 80% freelance written. Buys first and second rights to the same material. Reports in 30 days. Computer printout submissions acceptable. Publishes ms an average of 3 months after acceptance. Sample copy $1 (to cover postage and handling); free writer's guidelines.
Nonfiction: "Freelance manuscripts welcomed on speculation. Particularly interested in articles about or related to northern Virginia."
Photos: "B&w photos, as appropriate, with mss enhance publication probability."
Tips: "Longer articles preferred, minimum 2,500 words."

‡**SHENANDOAH/VIRGINIA TOWN AND COUNTRY**, Shenandoah Valley Magazine Corp., Box 8, New Hope VA 24469. (703)885-0388. Editor: Hunter S. Pierce, IV. Bimonthly magazine. Circ. 20,000. Pays on publication. Byline given. Offers negotiable kill fee. Buys negotiable rights. Submit seasonal/holiday material 2 months in advance. Simultaneous queries, and simultaneous, photocopied, and previously published submissions OK. SASE. Reports in 1 month. Sample copy $3.
Nonfiction: Book excerpts, general interest, historical/nostalgic, how-to, humor, inspirational, interview/profile, personal experience, photo feature and travel. Buys 20 mss/year. Query with or without published clips, or send complete ms. Length: 1,000-1,500 words. Pays negotiable rate.
Photos: State availability of photos. Buys one-time rights.
Tips: "Be familiar enough with the magazine to know the tone and character of the feature articles."

Washington

COMPASS, *Tacoma News Tribune*, Box 11000, Tacoma WA 98411. (206)597-8649. Editor: Bill Smull. 30% freelance written. Sunday supplement. Circ. 112,000. Pays on publication. Buys first rights and second (reprint) rights to material originally published elsewhere. Byline given. Query. Reports "immediately." Computer printout submissions acceptable. SASE. Publishes ms an average of 3 months after acceptance.
Nonfiction: Articles and photos about Pacific Northwest, particularly the Puget Sound area. Historical, biographical, recreational, humor and home-related stories. No fiction. Length: 1,000 words maximum. Pays $60/printed tabloid page, whether pictures, text or both. Northwest subjects only.
Photos: Pays $60/printed tabloid page, whether pictures, text or both. Also occasionally buys a color cover transparency for $120.

THE SEATTLE WEEKLY, Sasquatch Publishing, 1921 2nd Ave., Seattle WA 98101. (206)623-3700. Editor: David Brewster. Managing Editor: Ann Senechal. 30-50% freelance written. Weekly tabloid covering arts, politics, food, business, sports and books with local and regional emphasis. Circ. 25,000. Pays 3 weeks after publication. Byline given. Offers variable kill fee. Buys first North American serial rights. Submit seasonal/holiday material 1 month in advance. Simultaneous queries OK. Computer printout submissions acceptable. SASE. Reports in 1 month. Publishes ms an average of 1 month after acceptance. Sample copy 75¢; free writer's guidelines.
Nonfiction: Book excerpts; expose; general interest; historical/nostalgic (Northwest); how-to (related to food and health); humor; interview/profile; opinion; travel; and arts-related essays. Buys 25 cover stories/year. Query with published clips. Length: 700-4,000 words. Pays $75-800.

‡**WASHINGTON, The Evergreen State Magazine**, Evergreen Publishing Co., #1, 13029 Northup Way NE, Bellevue WA 98005. Editor/Publisher: Kenneth A. Gouldthorpe. Managing Editor: Knute O. Berger. A bimonthly magazine covering all facets of life in Washington State for an in-state audience. Estab. 1984. Circ. 30,000. Pays on acceptance for assigned stories; on publication for "on spec" material. Byline given. Offers

20% kill fee on accepted stories. Submit seasonal/holiday material 6 months in advance. Electronic submissions OK on disks formatted for Kaypro II. Computer printout submissions acceptable. SASE. Reports in 2 weeks on queries; 1 month on mss. Sample copy for 10x13 SAE and $1.80 postage; free writer's guidelines.
Nonfiction: Book excerpts (unpublished Washington-related); general interest; historical/nostalgic; how-to (relating to the state); humor; interview/profile; new product; personal experience; photo feature; and travel. "Evergreen Publishing Company undertakes book and one-shot publication projects. Washington state ideas encouraged. No political, exposes, reviews, or anything not pertaining to Washington or Washingtonians." Query with or without published clips. Length: features, 2,000-3,500 words; sidebars, 300-1,000 words. Pays $350-750.
Photos: Large format. Carrie Seglin, photo editor. State availability of photos with query, send photos with accompanying query or ms. Pays $50-250 for 35mm b&w slides; $125-325 for 35mm color slides. Captions, model release and identification of subjects required. Buys one-time rights.
Columns/Departments: On Display (exhibits, museums, galleries and shows); Eyewitness (memories and reminiscences by people who were there); Landscapes (gardens, flora and the countryside itself); Interiors (homes, architecture, decorating, interiors); State of Mind (thoughts and perspectives on the Evergreen State); Washington Post (our letters column); Cityscape (urban lifestyle, activities and events); Backroads (at large on the byways and backroads); The Attic (our backpage potpourri of ads, pictures, curios etc.); Our Town (where we live, from backwoods to small towns and places you've never seen before); Centerstage (the performing arts); Journeys End (inns, lodges, bed and breakfast hideaways); Players (sports and athletes, games and gamesmen); statewatch (a round-up from all corners: people, quotes and anecdotes from the lighter side of life); Enterprise (business and commerce); Crafts (crafts and craftsmen); Home Cooking (a look at great food and recipes from here); Heritage (history and the past); Folklore (myths, legends and tall tales); The Wild Side (wildlife, nature); Anniversary (commentary on any event which falls within the cover dates); The Open air (outdoors and outdoor activities, from backpacking to picnics, from hang gliding to kite flying); Your Bid (fantasy items for sale: islands, boats, unique homes, etc.); Speaking Volumes (books, writers and wordsmithing); Repasts (great dining, from grand souffles to small cafes); Cheers (wines, bars and brews). Buys 75 mss/year. Query with published clips. Length: 1,200-1,500 words. Pays $150-250.
Fillers: Clippings, jokes, gags, anecdotes, short humor, newsbreaks. Length: 50-300 words. Pays $25-100.
Tips: "Query with clips of work. All areas are open to freelancers."

Wisconsin

MADISON MAGAZINE, Box 1604, Madison WI 53701. Editor: James Selk. General city magazine aimed at upscale audience. Magazine; 76-104 pages. Monthly. Circ. 18,500. Buys all rights. 100 mss/year. Pays on publication. Reports on material accepted for publication 10 days after publication. Returns rejected material immediately. Query. SASE. Sample copy $3.
Nonfiction: General human interest articles with strong local angles. Length: 1,000-5,000 words. Pays $25-500.
Photos: Offers no additional payment for b&w photos used with mss. Captions required.

‡**WISCONSIN,** *Milwaukee Journal*, Box 661, Milwaukee WI 53201. (414)224-2341. Editor: Beth Slocum. 50% freelance written. Emphasizes general interest reading for a cross section of Wisconsin and upper Michigan. "We are targeting the younger reader, consumer and family." Weekly magazine; 24-88 pages. Circ. 530,000. Pays on acceptance. Buys first rights. Byline given. Submit seasonal/holiday material at least 2 months in advance. Computer printout submissions acceptable; prefers letter-quality to dot-matrix. SASE. Reports in 2 months. Free sample copy.
Nonfiction: Humor, profiles, expose, opinion, travel, personal experience, provocative essays and nostalgia. Buys 50-150 mss/year. Query or send complete ms. Length: 1,000-3,000 words. Pays $200-500.
Columns/Departments: His & Hers (a point/counterpoint style pitting female vs. male writer); Shaping Up (diet and exercise); Fashionable People (Wisconsin stylists); Fine Living (good design); and Time Out (thoughtful essays). Query with published clips. Length: 750-1,000 words. Pays $100-200.
Tips: "Read the magazine and get a feel for its content. Then you might try a personal experience article, a thought provoking essay or a lively profile. We also need 750-1,000 word fillers—examples of which you'll find in the magazine. Much of our material comes from Wisconsin writers. Generally, we're not a good market for out-of-state writers, although we may buy originals or reprints from time to time from established writers. Query with specific outline of proposed story."

WISCONSIN TRAILS, Box 5650, Madison WI 53705. (608)241-5603. Managing Editor: Susan Pigorsch. 80% freelance written. For readers interested in Wisconsin; its natural beauty, history, recreation, contemporary issues and personalities; and the arts. Bimonthly magazine. Circ. 28,000. Rights purchased vary with author and material. Byline given. Buys 15 unsolicited mss/year. Pays on publication. Publishes ms an average of 3 months after acceptance. Photocopied submissions OK. Computer printout submissions acceptable. Submit seasonal material at least 1 year in advance. Reports in 1 month. Query or send outline. SASE. Writer's guidelines available.

Nonfiction: "Our articles focus on some aspect of Wisconsin life; an interesting site or event, a person or industry, history or the arts. We do not use first-person essays or biographies about people who were born in Wisconsin, but made their fortunes elsewhere. Poetry exclusively on assignment. No articles that are too local for our audience, or articles about obvious places to visit in Wisconsin. We need more articles about the new and little-known." Length: 1,000-3,000 words. Pays $100-300, depending on assignment length and quality.

Photos: Purchased with or without mss or on assignment. Captions preferred. Color photos usually illustrate an activity, event, region or striking scenery. B&w photos usually illustrate a given article. Pays $10-20 each for b&w on publication. Pays $50 for inside color; pays $100 for covers and center spreads. "Transparencies; 2¼x2¼ or larger are preferred, but 35mm is OK."

Tips: "We're looking for active articles about people, places, events, and outdoor adventures in Wisconsin. We want to publish one in-depth article of state-wide interest or concern per issue, and several short (1,000-word) articles about short trips, recreational opportunities, and cultural activities. We will be looking for more articles about out-of-the-way places in Wisconsin that are exceptional in some way."

Puerto Rico

WALKING TOURS OF SAN JUAN, Magazine/Guide, Caribbean World Communications, Inc., First Federal Building, Office 301, Santurce PR 00909. (809)722-1767. Editor: Al Dinhofer. Managing Editor: Julie Jewel. Magazine published 2 times/year (winter and summer). Circ. 22,000. Pays on publication. Byline given. Buys first rights only. SASE. Reports in 1 month. Sample copy $4 for 9x12 SAE and $2 postage.

Nonfiction: Historical/nostalgic. "We are seeking historically based articles on San Juan. Any aspect of Spanish colonial culture, art, architecture, etc. would probably satisfy our needs. We must have sources—in fact, we will publish source material at the end of each article for reader reference." Buys 3 mss/year. Query. Length: 2,000-3,000 words. Pays $150.

Canada

CANADIAN GEOGRAPHIC, 488 Wilbrod St., Ottawa, Ontario K1N 6M8 Canada. Publisher: J. Keith Fraser. Editor: Ross Smith. Managing Editor: Ian Darragh. 90% freelance written. Circ. 120,000. Bimonthly magazine. Pays on publication. Buys first Canadian rights; interested only in first time publication. Computer printout submissions acceptable; prefers letter-quality to dot-matrix. Publishes ms an average of 3 months after acceptance. Leaflet for guidance of contributor available on request.

Nonfiction: Buys authoritative geographical articles, in the broad geographical sense, written for the average person, not for a scientific audience. Predominantly Canadian subjects by Canadian authors. Buys 30-45 unsolicited mss/year. Length: 1,200-2,500 words. Pays 15¢ minimum/word. Usual payment for articles with illustrations, $350-800 and up. Higher fees reserved for commissioned articles on which copyright remains with publisher unless otherwise agreed.

Photos: 35mm slides, 2¼x2¼ transparencies or 8x10 glossies. Pays $35-125 for color shots, depending on published size; $20-40 for b&w.

Tips: "Refer to our leaflet for guidance of contributors, and pay attention to our requirements."

KEY TO TORONTO, Key Publishers Company, Ltd., 59 Front St. E., Toronto, Ontario M5E 1B3 Canada. (416)364-3333. Editor: Caren Pummell. 75% freelance written. Monthly magazine covering Toronto entertainment, dining and sightseeing. Circ. 80,000. Byline given. Offers 25-50% kill fee. Buys first North American serial rights, first rights and second (reprint) rights to material originally published elsewhere. Submit seasonal/holiday material 2 months in advance. Previously published work OK. Computer printout submissions acceptable; prefers letter-quality to dot-matrix. SASE. Reports in 2 weeks on queries; 1 month on mss. Publishes ms an average of 6 weeks after acceptance. Sample copy $2.50.

Nonfiction: Historical/nostalgic (pertaining to Toronto only); and interview/profile. "*Key* appears free in all hotel rooms in the city and provides an informed guide for visitors. Writers must know Toronto to supply an insider's tour of activities and entertainments." Buys 48 mss/year. Length: 1,200-2,500 words. Pays $300-500.

Photos: State availability of photos. Pays $20-50 for 8x10 b&w prints. Page rate: $50. Identification of subjects required. Buys one-time rights.

Tips: Be willing to "change direction or rewrite according to the editor's needs, and do additional research. All articles require color, mood, background, as well as lots of service detail. The articles are meant to give visitors an inside look at our city and urge them to explore it."

‡OTTAWA MAGAZINE, Ottawa Magazine Inc., 340 Maclaren St., Ottawa, Ontario K2P 0M6 Canada. (613)234-7751. Editor: Louis Valenzuela. 90% freelance written. Monthly magazine covering life in Ottawa and environs. "*Ottawa Magazine* reflects the interest and lifestyles of its readers who tend to be female ages

25-55, upwardly mobile and suburban.'' Circ. 42,500. Pays on acceptance. Byline given. ''Kill fee depends on agreed-upon fee. Kill fees are very seldom used.'' Buys first North American serial rights, and second (reprint) rights to material originally published elsewhere. Simultaneous queries, and photocopied and previously published submissions OK. Computer printout submissions acceptable. Reports in 6 weeks. Publishes ms an average of 3 months after acceptance. Free sample copy and writer's guidelines.

Nonfiction: Book excerpts (by local authors or about regional issues); expose (federal or regional government, education); general interest; interview/profile (on Ottawans who have established national or international reputations); photo feature (for recurring section called Freezeframe); and travel (recent examples are Bimini, Oxbridge, Mexico). ''No articles better suited to national or special-interest publication.'' Buys 50 mss/year. Query with published clips. Length: 2,000-4,500 words. Pays $350-750; payment under review.

Columns/Departments: James Hale, column/department editor. Lifelines (short editorial style glimpses at the city, including the best (Bull's-Eye) and worst (Bull) aspects of Ottawa. Buys 50 mss/year. Send complete ms. Length: 50-250 words. Pays $25-50.

Tips: ''A phone call to our assistant editor is the best way to assure that queries receive prompt attention. Once a query interests me the writer is assigned a detailed 'treatment' of the proposed piece which is used to determine viability of story. Our feature section is the most open. Writer should strive to inject personal style and avoid newspaper style reportage. We strive for originality. *Ottawa Magazine* doesn't stoop to boosterism and points out the bad along with the good.''

THORNHILL MONTH MAGAZINE, Your Community Magazine, Thornhill Publications, Ltd., Box 250, Thornhill, Ontario L3T 3N3 Canada. 60% freelance written. Monthly magazine ''of the people, for the people, by the people of the community of Thornhill.'' Circ. 18,000. Pays on publication. Byline given. Photocopied and previously published submissions acceptable. Computer printout submissions OK. SASE. Reports in 2 weeks.

Nonfiction: Expose, humor, interview/profile, new product and photo feature. Special issues include industrial and historical. No travel or personal experiences. Stories must have local angle. Buys 80 mss/year. Query with or without clips of published work. Length: 500-1,500 words. Pays $25-60.

Photos: Send photos with ms. Captions required. Buys one-time rights.

Fiction: 500-1,000 words by local writers only.

Tips: Also publishes *Markham Month Magazine*, a community magazine parallel to *Thornhill Month*. ''Any article published in one magazine may appear in our sister publication at editor's discretion.''

TORONTO LIFE, 59 Front St. E., Toronto, Ontario M5E 1B3 Canada. (416)364-3333. Editor: Marq de Villiers. 100% freelance written. Emphasizes local issues and social trends, short humor/satire, and service features for upper income, well educated and, for the most part, young Torontonians. Uses some fiction. Monthly magazine. Pays on acceptance. Buys first North American serial rights. Pays 50% kill fee ''for commissioned articles only.'' Byline given. Phone queries OK. Reports in 3 weeks. Publishes ms an average of 5 months after acceptance. SAE and IRCs. Sample copy $2.

Nonfiction: Uses most all types articles. Buys 17 mss/issue. Query with clips of published work. Buys about 40 unsolicited mss/year. Length: 1,000-5,000 words. Pays $400-1,500.

Photos: State availability of photos. Uses good color transparencies and clear, crisp black b&w prints. They seldom use submitted photos. Captions and model release required.

Columns/Departments: ''We run about five columns an issue. They are all freelanced, though most are from regular contributors. They are mostly local in concern and cover politics, money, fine art, performing arts, movies and sports.'' Length: 1,200 words. Pays $400-700.

‡**WATERSHED MAGAZINE**, Pump House Publishing, Ltd., Bag 5000, Fairview, Alberta T0H 1L0 Canada. Editor: Mark A. Craft. 80% freelance written. A bimonthly magazine covering the practices of western Canada with emphasis on ''unique aspects and qualities of the Prairies.'' Pays on publication. Byline given. Buys first North American serial rights. Submit seasonal/holiday material 6 months in advance. Previously published material considered. Computer printout submissions acceptable. Electronic submissions OK if 5¼'' diskettes which can be read by Uniform. SASE. Reports in 4-6 weeks. Publishes ms an average of 6 weeks after acceptance. Sample copy $2.50; writer's guidelines for SAE and IRC.

Nonfiction: How-to and outdoor recreation. Features on ''Famous People You Never Heard Of,'' community or small town in the area, agriculture techniques, food—using ingredients from the region, western wildlife; ''Past, Present and Future'' (oral history approach examining the progress and future of an idea, technique or institution). Query. Length: 1,200-4,500 words. Pays $100-300, main articles; others $35-150; shorts $15-48; fiction $100-200.

Photos: ''We buy both color and b&w.''

Columns/Departments: Book reviews (usually on assignment); music; energy; arts and culture; tools; education; and history. ''Most departments consist of 1-3 short pieces with a combined length of 2,200 words.'' Query. Pays $20/printed page.

Fiction: Write for guidelines.

Tips: "Query first with your idea in a clear, concise form. Include one page sample writing if available (preferably something we can retain). Always include SAE and IRC."

WESTERN LIVING, Comac Communications, Ltd., 303-2930 Arbutus St., Vancouver, British Columbia V6J 3Y9 Canada. (604)736-8121. Editor: Andrew Scott. 50% freelance written. Monthly general interest and home magazine for western Canadian readers interested in home design, cuisine, travel, people, etc. Circ. 280,000. Pays on acceptance. Byline given. Offers 50-100% kill fee. Buys first North American serial rights. Submit seasonal/holiday material 6 months in advance. Electronic submissions OK if 5¼" or 8" disks compatible with Xerox 820 system. Computer printout submissions acceptable; prefers letter-quality to dot-matrix. SASE. Reports in 1 month. Publishes ms an average of 2 months after acceptance. Free sample copy and writer's guidelines.

Nonfiction: Book excerpts (occasionally); general interest (western Canadian); historical (western Canadian); how-to (home oriented); new product (home oriented); travel; food; and profiles. Ideas must be geared to the western Canadian region. Buys 50-100 mss/year. Query with published clips. Length: 1,500-3,000 words. Pays $200-1,000.

Photos: Peter Manning, art director. Send photos with query. Pays $25-400 for color transparencies; b&w contact sheet and 8x10 b&w prints. Model release and identification of subjects required. Buys one-time rights.

WESTERN PEOPLE, Western Producer Publications, Box 2500, Saskatoon, Saskatchewan S7K 2C4 Canada. (306)665-3500. Editor: R.H.D. Phillips. Managing Editor: Mary Gilchrist. 90% freelance written. Weekly supplement to *The Western Producer*. "*Western People* is about people in western Canada, past and present. Its emphasis is rural but not necessarily agricultural." Circ. 140,000. Pays on acceptance. Byline given. Offers negotiable kill fee. Not copyrighted. Buys first North American serial rights; rarely buys second (reprint) rights to material originally published elsewhere. Submit seasonal/holiday material 2 months in advance. Computer printout submissions acceptable; prefers letter-quality to dot-matrix. SASE; IRCs outside Canada. Reports in 2 weeks on queries; 1 month on mss. Publishes ms an average of 9 months after acceptance. Sample copy and writer's guidelines for SAE with 37¢ Canadian postage or IRCs (48¢).

Nonfiction: Mary Gilchrist, managing editor. General interest, profiles of western Canadians, historical/nostalgic, humor, interview/profile, personal experience and photo feature. No opinion or book reviews. Buys 300 mss/year. Send complete ms. Photos increase chance of acceptance. Length: 600-2,500 words. Pays $40-200.

Photos: Mary Gilchrist, managing editor. Photos accompanying ms increase chance of acceptance. Send photos with ms. Pays $10-50/color transparency; $5-25/b&w print and $10-50/color print. Captions and identification of subjects required. Buys one-time rights.

Fiction: Mary Gilchrist, managing editor. Adventure, historical, humorous, mainstream, science fiction, serialized novels, suspense and western. No city stories. "Our readership is rural." Buys 100 mss/year. Send complete ms. Length: 1,000-2,500 words. Pays $50-175.

Poetry: Mary Gilchrist, managing editor. Free verse, light verse and traditional. Buys 50/year. Submit maximum of 6 poems. Pays $10-50.

Fillers: Mary Gilchrist, managing editor. Short humor. Buys 50/year. Length: 100-500 words. Pays $10-50.

Tips: "Subject matter must be western Canadian. Writing must be crisp because of format (16 pages, 8x11). Best to send manuscripts rather than queries until editor is familiar with your work." Most open to profiles and contemporary issues in western Canada. "Focus on people, avoid rambling, bring the reader close to the subject."

THE WESTERN PRODUCER, Box 2500, Saskatoon, Saskatchewan S7K 2C4 Canada. (306)665-3500. Publisher/Editor: R.H.D. Phillips. 6% freelance written. Emphasizes agriculture for western Canadian farm families. Weekly newspaper; 56-80 pages. Circ. 140,000. Pays on acceptance. Buys first North American serial rights. Byline given. Submit seasonal/holiday material 2 months in advance of issue date. Computer printout submissions acceptable; prefers letter-quality to dot-matrix. SAE, IRC. Reports in 2 weeks. Free writer's guidelines.

Nonfiction: General interest, historical (Western Canada), personal experience, photo feature and profile. "Urban living material not appreciated; nor is material patronizing farm people." Buys 1,200 mss/year. Submit complete ms. Pays $5-300.

Photos: Submit photos with ms. Pays $10-25 for 5x7 b&w prints. Captions and model release required. Buys one-time rights.

Fiction: Adventure, historical, humorous, mainstream, mystery, suspense and western Canadian subjects. Buys 40 mss/year. Length: 1,500 words maximum. Pays $25-100.

Poetry: Traditional. Buys 51/year. Pays $5-15.

Tips: "Write a story of interest to nonurban readers—and realize that 'nonurban' doesn't mean 'dodo'."

WINDSOR THIS MONTH MAGAZINE, Box 1029, Station A, Windsor, Ontario N9A 6P4 Canada. (519)966-7411. Editor: Laura Rosenthal. 75% freelance written. "*Windsor This Month* is mailed out in a system of controlled distribution to 19,000 households in the area. The average reader is a university graduate, middle income, and active in leisure areas." Circ. 22,000. Pays on publication. Buys first North American serial rights. Phone queries OK. Submit seasonal/holiday material 3-4 months in advance. "We will accept computer printout submissions or industry compatible magnetic media." SAE and IRCs. Reports in 4 weeks.

Nonfiction: "Windsor oriented editorial: issues, answers, interviews, lifestyles, profiles, photo essays and opinion. How-to accepted if applicable to readership. Special inserts: design and decor, gourmet and travel featured periodically through the year." Buys 5 mss/issue. Query. Buys 15 unsolicited mss/year. Length: 500-5,000 words. Pays $20-200.

Photos: State availability of photos with query. Pays $10 for first published and $5 thereafter for b&w prints. Captions preferred. Buys all rights.

Tips: "If experienced—arm yourself with published work and a list of ten topics that demonstrate knowledge of the Windsor market, and query the editor. Recent article example: "The Hospice" (3 part series).

Foreign

GLIMPSES OF MICRONESIA, Box 3191, Agana, Guam 96910. Editor: Dirk Anthony Ballendorf. 90% freelance written. "A regional publication for Micronesia lovers, travel buffs and readers interested in the United States' last frontier. Our audience covers all age levels and is best described as well educated and fascinated by our part of the world." Quarterly magazine; 100 pages. Circ. 25,000. Pays on publication. Buys first rights only. Pays 10% kill fee on assignments. Byline given. Submit seasonal/holiday material 8 months in advance. Computer printout submissions acceptable. SASE. Reports in 1 month. Sample copy $2; free writer's guidelines.

Nonfiction: "Range of subjects is broad, from political analysis of Micronesia's newly emerging governments to examination of traditional culture; historical (anything related to Micronesia that is lively and factual); personal experience (first person adventure, as in our recently published piece about a sailing expedition to the uninhabited islands of the northern Marianas); interviews/personality profiles of outstanding Micronesian or western Pacific individuals; scientific/natural history (in lay terms); photo features (we're very photo-oriented—query us on island or Pacific themes); and travel (we use 1/issue about destinations in Asia and the Pacific). No articles from fly-by-night (overnight) visitors to Micronesia." Buys 30 mss/year. Query. Length: 1,500-5,000 words. Pays 5-10¢/word.

Photos: Purchased with or without accompanying ms. Pays minimum $10 for 8x10 b&w prints or $15 for 4x5 color transparencies or 35mm slides. Pay $200-300 for photo essays; $100 for covers. Captions required.

Columns/Departments: Short think pieces on contemporary Micronesia are accepted for the Island Views section. Opinions are welcomed but must be well founded and must reflect the writer's familiarity with the subject. Length: 500-1,200 words. Pays $30.

Poetry: "We use very little but are willing to look at Pacific related themes to be used with photos." Only traditional forms. Pays minimum $10.

Tips: "Writers living in or having first hand experience with Micronesia and the western Pacific are scarce. If you have that experience, have made yourself familiar with *Glimpses*, and have a good story idea, then we're willing to work with you in developing a good article."

Religious

Like a church congregation, each religious magazine relishes certain styles and beliefs. Editors' views on current trends illustrate that the religious market is moving in different directions—depending on each magazine's slant. Such diversity makes reading *each* magazine essential for the writer hoping to break in. "Overall, there is a move away from a total focus on 'comforting' features and toward a more aggressive 'challenge the reader' stance," says one editor. A *Light and Life* editor believes the "religious market seems to be moving away from first-person accounts of triumph over tragedy (at least we are)." Still, another editor says "a great need exists for personal experience writing that is creative, relevant to these times, and written for a wide audience."

Educational and inspirational material of interest to church members, workers and leaders within a denomination or religion is needed by the publications in this category. Publications intended to assist lay and professional religious workers in teaching and managing church affairs are classified in Church Administration and

Ministry in the Trade Journals section. Religious magazines for children and teenagers will be found in the Juvenile, and Teen and Young Adult classifications.

Tips on writing for the religious market are available in *Writing to Inspire: A Guide to Writing and Publishing for the Expanding Religious Market*, by William Gentz, Lee Roddy, et al. (Writer's Digest Books).

AGLOW, Today's Publication for Christian Women, Women's Aglow Fellowship, Box I, Lynnwood WA 98046-1557. (206)775-7282. Editor: Gwen Weising. 85% freelance written. Bimonthly nondenominational Christian charismatic magazine for women. Pays on acceptance. Byline given. Buys first rights only. Submit seasonal/holiday material 6 months in advance. Simultaneous queries and simultaneous and photocopied submissions acceptable. Computer printout submissions OK. SASE. Reports in 2 months. Publishes ms an average of 6 months after acceptance. Writer's guidelines for business-size SAE and 1 first class stamp.
Nonfiction: Personal experience, inspiration and humor, only Christian oriented articles. "Each article should be either a testimony of or teaching about Jesus as Savior, as Baptizer in the Holy Spirit, or as Guide and Strength in everyday circumstances." Send complete ms. "We would like to see material about 'Women of Vision' who have made and are making an impact on their world for God. Query on these first." Length: 1,000-2,000 words. Pays $65-150.

ALIVE NOW!, The Upper Room, 1980 Grand Ave., Box 189, Nashville TN 37202. (615)327-2700. Editor: Mary Ruth Coffman. Bimonthly magazine including short prose pieces, poetry and essays relating to a theme concerned with Christian life and action, for a general Christian audience interested in reflection and meditation. Circ. 75,000. Pays on publication. Byline given. Pays "negotiated kill fee, when applicable." Rights purchased are negotiated ("may be one-time rights, or newspaper and periodical"). Submit seasonal/holiday material 8 months in advance. Previously published work OK. Computer printout submissions acceptable. SASE. Reports in 2 months on queries; 6 months on mss. Sample copy and writer's guidelines free, but must send SASE with request.
Nonfiction: Book excerpts, humor, inspirational and personal experience. "Send a typed, interesting story or poem that deals with personal faith journey, relations with other people and the world, questions of meaning, responsibility for the natural world, and/or thoughts on the meaning of existence. Writing should be for the young adult or mature adult, or the adult with a growing faith awareness." No polemic articles. Buys 120 unsolicited mss/year. Send complete ms. Length: 500 words maximum. Pays $5-40.
Photos: Pamela Watkins, photo editor. Send photos with ms. Pays $50-100 for 4x5 color transparencies; $15-25 for 8x10 b&w prints. Buys one-time rights.
Columns/Departments: Excerpts from devotional classics. Buys 4 mss/year. Query with clips of published work. Length: 350-800 words. Pays $25-40.
Fiction: Fantasy, humorous and religious. No confession, erotica, horror, romance or western. Buys 10 mss/year. Query with clips of published work. Length: 100-450 words. Pays $25-40.
Poetry: Avant garde and free verse. Buys 30 poems/year. Submit maximum 5 poems. Length: 10-45 lines. Pays $5-25.
Fillers: Anecdotes and short humor. Buys 6/year. Length: 25-150 words. Pays $5-15.
Tips: "We are seeing *too* many old chestnuts, clippings and plagiarized material now. There used to be very few."

ASPIRE, 1819 E. 14th Ave., Denver CO 80218. Editor: Jeanne Pomranka, 33% freelance written. For teens and adults; "Those who are looking for a way of life that is practical, logical, spiritual or inspirational." Monthly; 64 pages. Circ. 2,500. Buys all rights. Byline given. Buys 45-50 unsolicited mss/year. Pays following publication. Submit seasonal material 7 months in advance. Computer printout submissions acceptable; prefers letter-quality to dot-matrix. Sample copy 40¢ in stamps. Reports in 2 weeks. Publishes ms an average of 8 months after acceptance. No queries necessary before submitting.
Nonfiction: Uses inspirational articles that help to interpret the spiritual meaning of life. Needs are specialized since this is the organ of the Divine Science teaching. Personal experience, inspirational and reflection pieces. Also seeks material for God at Work, a department "written in the form of letters to the editor in which the writer describes how God has worked in his life or around him." Pays maximum 1¢/published word.
Fiction: "Anything illustrating spiritual law at work in life." Length: 250-1,000 words. Pays maximum 1¢/published word.
Poetry: Traditional, contemporary and light verse. "We use very little poetry." Length: average 8-16 lines. Pays $1-2/page.
Tips: "Avoid 'churchiness' as opposed to man's true relationship with God and his fellowmen. The latter is what we need—articles on prayer, consciousness building, faith at work, spiritual law, etc. We want good, simple, clear writing—no trite, overused phrases, no over emphasis of tragedy, but emphasis on positive, constructive attitudes that overcome such situations. Must be inspirationally written."

AXIOS, 800 S. Euclid St., Fullerton CA 92632. (714)526-2131. Editor: Daniel J. Gorham. 50% freelance written. Monthly journal seeking spiritual articles mostly on Orthodox Christian background, either Russian, Greek, Serbian, Syrian or American. Circ. 4,789. Pays on publication. Byline given. Offers 50% kill fee. Buys all rights. Submit seasonal/holiday material 4 months in advance. Simultaneous queries, and simultaneous, photocopied, and previously published submissions OK. SASE. Reports in 1 month. Publishes ms an average of 3 months after acceptance. Sample copy $2.

Nonfiction: Book excerpts; expose (of religious figures); general interest; historical/nostalgic; interview/profile; opinion; personal experience; photo feature; and travel (shrines, pilgrimages). Special issues include The Persecution of Christians in Iran, Russia, behind Iron Curtain or in Arab lands; Roman Catholic interest in the Orthodox Church. Nothing about the Pope or general "all-is-well-with-Christ" items. Buys 14 mss/year. Send complete ms. Length: 1,000-3,000 words. Pays 4¢/word minimum.

Columns/Departments: Reviews religious books and films. Buys 80 mss/year. Query.

Tips: "We need some hard hitting articles on the 'political' church—the why, how and where of it and why it lacks the timelessness of the spiritual!"

BRIGADE LEADER, Box 150, Wheaton IL 60189. Editor: David Leigh. 20% freelance written. For leaders in the Christian Service Brigade program throughout US and Canada. Quarterly magazine; 32 pages. Buys first rights or second serial (reprint) rights. Buys 6-8 mss/year. Pays on publication. Submit seasonal material 5 months in advance. Photocopied submissions OK. Computer printout submissions acceptable; prefers letter-quality to dot-matrix. Reports in 2 months. Publishes ms an average of 2 months after acceptance. Query. SASE. Sample copy for $1.50 and large SASE.

Nonfiction: "We are interested in articles about: problems in father-son/man-boy relationships, the holistic development of the Christian man, men as role models for boys, and helping boys to cope with their problems." Informational, personal experience and inspirational. Length: 900-1,500 words.

Photos: Photos purchased with or without ms. Pays $25 for b&w, inside; $50-75 for b&w, cover.

THE CATHEDRAL VOICE, St. Willibrord's Press, Box 98, Highlandville MO 65669. Editor: Karl Pruter. 20% freelance written. Bimonthly magazine of the World Peace Academy. Covers peace and peace making; "We take the commandment 'Thou Shalt Not Kill' literally. Estab. 1983. Circ. 1,200. Pays on acceptance. Byline given. Not copyrighted. Buys first North American serial rights. Submit seasonal/holiday material 2 months in advance. Simultaneous queries and photocopied submissions OK. SASE. Reports in 2 weeks. Publishes ms an average of 2 months after acceptance. Sample copy for SAE and 2 first class stamps.

Nonfiction: Expose, general interest, historical/nostalgic, inspirational and personal experience. Length: 1,000-4,000 words. Pays $20-40.

Fiction: Religious. Length: 1,000-4,000 words. Pays $20-40.

Poetry: Free verse, light verse and traditional. Length: 24 lines maximum. Pays $10.

CATHOLIC DIGEST, Box 43090, St. Paul MN 55164. Editor: Henry Lexau. Managing Editor: Richard Reece. 50% freelance written. Monthly magazine covering the daily living of Roman Catholics for an audience that is 60% female, 40% male; 37% is college educated. Circ. 600,000. Byline given. Buys first North American serial rights or one-time reprint rights. Submit seasonal material 6 months in advance. Previously published submissions OK, if so indicated. Computer printout submissions acceptable; prefers letter-quality to dot-matrix. SASE. Reports in 3 weeks. Publishes ms an average of 7 months after acceptance.

Nonfiction: General interest (daily living and family relationships); interview (of outstanding Catholics, celebrities and locals); nostalgia (the good old days of family living); profile; religion; travel (shrines); humor; inspirational (overcoming illness, role model people); and personal experience (adventures and daily living). Buys 25 articles/issue. No queries. Send complete ms. Length: 500-3,000 words, 2,000 average. Pays on acceptance $200-400 for originals, $100 for reprints.

Columns/Departments: "Check a copy of the magazine in the library for a description of column needs. Payment varies and is made upon publication. We buy about 5/issue."

Fillers: Jokes, anecdotes and short humor. Buys 10-15 mss/issue. Length: 10-300 words. Pays $3-50 on publication.

CATHOLIC LIFE, 35750 Moravian Dr., Fraser MI 48026. Editor-in-Chief: Robert C. Bayer. 40% freelance written. Emphasizes foreign missionary activities of the Catholic Church in Burma, India, Bangladesh, the Philippines, Hong Kong, Africa, etc., for middle-aged and older audience with either middle incomes or pensions. High school educated (on the average), conservative in both religion and politics. Monthly (except July or August) magazine; 32 pages. Circ. 16,500. Pays on publication. Buys all rights. Byline given. Submit seasonal/holiday material 3-4 months in advance. Simultaneous submissions OK. Computer printout submissions acceptable; no dot-matrix. SASE. Reports in 2 weeks. Publishes ms an average of 3 months after acceptance.

Nonfiction: Informational and inspirational foreign missionary activities of the Catholic Church. Buys 20-25 unsolicited mss/year. Query or send complete ms. Length: 1,000-1,500 words. Pays 4¢/word.

Tips: "Query with short, graphic details of what the material will cover or the personality involved in the biographical sketch. Also, we appreciate being advised on the availability of good b&w photos to illustrate the material."

CATHOLIC NEAR EAST MAGAZINE, Catholic Near East Welfare Association, 1011 1st Ave., New York NY 10022. (212)826-1480. Editor: Regina J. Clarkin. 90% freelance written. For a general audience with interest in the Near East, particularly its religious and cultural aspects. Quarterly magazine; 24 pages. Circ. 130,000. Buys first North American serial rights. Byline given. Buys 16 mss/year. Pays on publication. Submit seasonal material (Christmas and Easter in different Near Eastern lands or rites) 6 months in advance. Photocopied submissions OK if legible. Computer printout submissions acceptable; no dot-matrix. Reports in 3-4 weeks. Publishes ms an average of 4 months after acceptance. Free sample copy and writer's guidelines. Query or submit complete ms. SASE.
Nonfiction: "Cultural, territorial, devotional material on the Near East, its history, peoples and religions (especially the Eastern Rites of the Catholic Church). Style should be simple, factual, concise. Articles must stem from personal acquaintance with subject matter, or thorough up-to-date research. No preaching or speculations." Length: 1,200-1,800 words. Pays 10¢/word.
Photos: "Photographs to accompany ms are always welcome; they should illustrate the people, places, ceremonies, etc. which are described in the article. We prefer color but occasionally use b&w. Pay varies depending on the quality of the photos."
Tips: "Writers please heed: stick to the Near East. Send factual articles; concise, descriptive style preferred. Not too flowery. Pictures are a big plus; if you have photos to accompany your article, please send them at the same time."

CATHOLIC TWIN CIRCLE, (formerly *Twin Circle*), Twin Circle Publishing, Suite 900, 6404 Wilshire Blvd., Los Angeles CA 90048. (213)653-2200. Executive Editor: Mary Louise Frawley. Weekly tabloid covering Catholic personalities and Catholic interest topics for a mostly female Catholic readership. Circ. 76,000. Average issue includes 6-7 feature articles. Pays on publication. Byline given. Buys all rights. Submit seasonal material 2 months in advance. Simultaneous and photocopied submissions OK, if so indicated. Computer printout submissions acceptable; prefers letter-quality to dot-matrix. SASE. Reports in 2 months on queries; in 1 month on mss. Free writer's guidelines with SASE. Not responsible for unsolicited manuscripts.
Nonfiction: "We are looking for articles about prominent Catholic personalities in sports, entertainment, politics and business; ethnic stories about Catholics from other countries and topical issues of concern to Catholics. We are interested in writers who are experienced and write on an ongoing basis." No theological issues. Buys 3-4 mss/issue. Length: 250-1,000 words. Pays 8¢/word.
Photos: State availability of photos. Reviews 5x7 b&w glossy prints. Price negotiated. Captions required. Rights vary.

CHARISMA, The Magazine About Spirit-led Living, Strang Communications Inc., Box 2003, Winter Park FL 32790. (305)645-2022. Editor and Publisher: Stephen Strang. Senior Editor: Howard Earl. Editor-at-large: Jamie Buckingham. Managing Editor: Rob Kerby. 50% freelance written. Monthly magazine covering Christianity—especially the pentecostal/charismatic movement. Circ. 100,000. Pays on publication. Byline given. Buys first rights only. Submit seasonal/holiday material 6 months in advance. Electronic submissions acceptable on disks compatible with Apple IIe or TRS-80 III, but requires hard copy also. Computer printout submissions acceptable. SASE. Reports in 1 month. Publishes ms an average of 6 months after acceptance. Sample copy $1.95; writer's guidelines for 9x12 SASE and 2 first class stamps.
Nonfiction: Howard Earl, articles editor. How-to (overcome fear, how to be a better parent; how to be more loving); interview/profile (well-known Christian leaders, Christian musicians); personal experience (well-known Christian personality profiles); and photo feature (religious themes). Special issues include Christian music in July/August; missions in December; and Bible in January. Buys 40 mss/year. Query. Length: 2,000-3,000 words. Pays $150 for most over-the-transom articles; up to $500 for assigned special projects such as cover stories.
Tips: "We run almost no fiction and are very skeptical about fiction from unknowns."

CHICAGO STUDIES, Box 665, Mundelein IL 60060. (312)566-1462. Editor: Rev. George J. Dyer. 50% freelance written. For Roman Catholic priests and religious educators. Magazine; published 3 times/year; 112 pages. Circ. 10,000. Buys all rights. Buys 30 mss/year. Pays on acceptance. Photocopied submissions OK. Computer printout submissions acceptable. Submit complete ms. Reports in 2 months. SASE. Sample copy $3.
Nonfiction: Nontechnical discussion of theological, Biblical and ethical topics. Articles aimed at a nontechnical presentation of the contemporary scholarship in those fields. Length: 3,000-5,000 words. Pays $35-100.

CHRISTIAN HERALD, 40 Overlook Dr., Chappaqua NY 10514. (914)769-9000. Editor: David E. Kucharsky. 80% freelance written or commissioned. Emphasizes religious living in family and church. Monthly magazine; 64 pages. Circ. 200,000. Pays on acceptance. Buys all rights. Submit seasonal/holiday material 6 months in advance. Photocopied submissions OK. SASE. Sample copy $2; free writer's guidelines with SASE.

Nonfiction: How-to, informational, inspirational, interview, profile, and evangelical experience. Buys 10-20 mss/year. Query first. Length: 1,500 words. Pays $50 minimum.

Photos: Purchased with or without accompanying ms. Send transparencies. Pays $10 minimum for b&w; $25 minimum for 2¼x2¼ color transparencies.

Poetry: Meaningfully Biblical. Buys 30 poems/year. Length: 4-20 lines. Pays $10 minimum.

‡**CHRISTIAN HOME & SCHOOL**, Christian Schools International, 3350 East Paris Ave. SE, Box 8709, Grand Rapids MI 49508. (616)957-1070. Editor: Gordon L. Bordewyk. Assistant Editor: Kimberley D. Paxton. Magazine published 8 times/year covering family life and Christian education. "The magazine is designed for parents who support Christian education. We feature material on a wide range of topics of interest to parents." Pays on publication. Byline given. Buys first North American rights only. Submit seasonal/holiday material 4 months in advance. Simultaneous queries and photocopied submissions OK. Computer printout submissions acceptable; prefers letter-quality to dot-matrix. SASE. Reports in 3 weeks on queries; 1 month on mss. Sample copy for 9x21 SAE and 71¢ postage.

Nonfiction: Book excerpts, interview/profile, opinion, personal experience and articles on parenting and school life. "We publish features on issues which affect the home and school and profiles on interesting individuals, providing that the profile appeals to our readers and is not a tribute or eulogy of that person." Buys 40 mss/year. Send complete ms. Length: 500-2,000 words. Pays $25-60.

Photos: "If you have any photos appropriate for your article, send them along."

Tips: "Features are the area most open to freelancers. Since our recent format change, we are publishing articles that deal with contemporary issues which affect parents; keep that in mind. Use an informal easy-to-read style rather than a philosophical, academic tone. Try to incorporate vivid imagery and concrete, practical examples from real life."

CHRISTIAN LIFE MAGAZINE, 396 E. St. Charles Rd., Wheaton IL 60188. Editor-in-Chief: Robert Walker. Executive Editor: Janice Franzen. 75% freelance written. Monthly religious magazine with strong emphasis on spiritual renewal. Circ. 100,000. Pays on publication. Buys all rights. Submit seasonal/holiday material 8-12 months in advance. SASE. Free sample copy and writer's guidelines. Reports in 1 month.

Nonfiction: Adventure articles (usually in the first person, told in narrative style); devotional (include many anecdotes, preferably from the author's own experience); general features (wide variety of subjects, with special programs of unique benefit to the community); inspirational (showing the success of persons, ideas, events and organizations); personality profiles (bright, tightly written articles on what Christians are thinking); news (with human interest quality dealing with trends); news feature (providing interpretative analysis of person, trend, events and ideas); and trend (should be based on solid research). Pays $200 maximum.

Fiction: Short stories (with good characterization and mood); pays $125 maximum. Length: 1,500-2,500 words maximum.

CHRISTIAN SINGLE, Family Ministry Dept., Baptist Sunday School Board, 127 9th Ave. N., Nashville TN 37234. (615)251-2228. Editor: Cliff Allbritton. Monthly magazine covering items of special interest to Christian single adults. "*Christian Single* is a contemporary Christian magazine that seeks to give substantive information to singles for living the abundant life. It seeks to be constructive and creative in approach." Circ. 102,000. Pays on acceptance "for immediate needs"; on publication "for unsolicited manuscripts." Byline given. Buys all rights or makes work-for-hire assignments. Submit seasonal/holiday material 1 year in advance. SASE. Reports in 6 weeks. Free sample copy and writer's guidelines.

Nonfiction: Humor (good, clean humor that applies to Christian singles); how-to (specific subjects which apply to singles; query needed); inspirational (of the personal experience type); personal experience (of single adults); photo feature (on outstanding Christian singles; query needed); and travel to places (appropriate for Christian singles; query needed). No "shallow, uninformative mouthing off. This magazine says something, and people read it cover to cover." Buys 120-150 unsolicited mss/year. Query with clips of published work. Length: 300-1,200 words. Pays 4¢/word.

Tips: "We look for freshness and creativity, not duplication of what we have already done. We seek variety targeted to singles' needs. We give preference to Christian single adult writers but publish articles by *sensitive* and *informed* married writers also. Remember that you are talking to educated people who attend church."

CHRISTIANITY TODAY, 465 Gundersen Dr., Carol Stream IL 60188. Editor: V. Gilbert Beers. 25% freelance written. Emphasizes orthodox, evangelical religion. Semimonthly magazine; 55 pages. Circ. 180,000. Pays on acceptance. Usually buys first rights. Submit seasonal/holiday material at least 8 months in advance. Computer printout submissions acceptable. SASE. Reports in 1-2 months. Publishes ms up to a year after acceptance. Free sample copy and writer's guidelines.

Nonfiction: Theological, ethical and historical and informational (not merely inspirational). Buys 4 mss/issue.

Query only. Unsolicited mss not accepted and not returned. Length: 1,000-4,000 words. Pays $100 minimum.
Columns/Departments: Ministries (practical and specific, not elementary); and Refiner's Fire (Christian review of the arts). Buys 12 mss/year. Send complete ms. Length: 800-900 words. Pays $100.
Tips: "We are developing more of our own mss and requiring a much more professional quality of others."

CHURCH & STATE, Americans United for Separation of Church and State, 8120 Fenton St., Silver Spring MD 20910. (301)589-3707. Managing Editor: Joseph Conn. 15% freelance written. Emphasizes religious liberty and church/state relations matters. Readership "includes the whole religious spectrum, but is predominantly Protestant and well educated." Monthly magazine; 24 pages. Circ. 50,000. Pays on acceptance. Buys all rights. Simultaneous, photocopied and previously published submissions OK. Computer printout submissions acceptable; prefers letter-quality to dot-matrix. SASE. Reports in 1 month. Free sample copy and writer's guidelines.
Nonfiction: Expose, general interest, historical, and interview. Buys 11 mss/year. Query. Length: 3,000 words maximum. Pays negotiable fee.
Photos: State availability of photos with query. Pays negotiable fee for b&w prints. Captions preferred. Buys one-time rights.

THE CHURCH HERALD, 1324 Lake Dr. SE, Grand Rapids MI 49506. Editor: Dr. John Stapert. 10% freelance written. Publication of the Reformed Church in America. 22 times/year; 32 pages. Circ. 58,000. Buys all rights, first serial rights, or second serial (reprint) rights. Buys about 60 mss/year. Pays on acceptance. Photocopied and simultaneous submissions OK. Submit material for major Christian holidays 6 months in advance. Computer printout submissions acceptable. SASE. Reports in 4 weeks. Publishes ms an average of 1 year after acceptance. Query or submit complete ms. Sample copy 50¢; free writer's guidelines.
Nonfiction: "We expect all of our articles to be helpful and constructive, even when a point of view is vigorously presented. Articles on subjects such as Christianity and culture, government and politics, forms of worship, the media, ethics and business relations, responsible parenthood, marriage and divorce, death and dying, challenges on the campus, evangelism, church leadership, Christian education, Christian perspectives on current issues, spiritual growth, etc." Length: 400-1,500 words. Pays 4½¢/word.
Photos: Photos purchased with or without accompanying ms. Pays $20 minimum/8x10 b&w glossy print.
Fiction and Fillers: Religious fiction. Length: 400-1,500 words. Pays 4¢/word.
Poetry: Length: 30 lines maximum. Pays $15 minimum.

COLUMBIA, Drawer 1670, New Haven CT 06507. Editor: Elmer Von Feldt. For Catholic families; caters particularly to members of the Knights of Columbus. Monthly magazine. Circ. 1,360,958. Buys all rights. Buys 50 mss/year. Pays on acceptance. Submit seasonal material 6 months in advance. Reports in 4 weeks. Query or submit complete ms. SASE. Free sample copy and writer's guidelines.
Nonfiction: Fact articles directed to the Catholic layman and his family and dealing with current events, social problems, Catholic apostolic activities, education, ecumenism, rearing a family, literature, science, arts, sports and leisure. Length: 2,500-3,500 words. Color glossy prints, transparencies or contact prints with negatives are required for illustration. Articles without ample illustrative material are not given consideration. Pays $600 maximum, including photos. Photo stories are also wanted.
Photos: Pays $25/photo used. Pays 10¢/word.
Fiction: Humor or satire should be directed to current religious, social or cultural conditions. Length: 1,000 words. Pays $200.

COMBONI MISSIONS, 8108 Beechmont Ave., Cincinnati OH 45230. (513)474-4997. Editor: Todd Riebe, MCCJ. Quarterly magazine for those interested in Third World topics and mission efforts of the Comboni Missionaries and Comboni Missionary Sisters (formerly Verona Fathers and Sisters). Distribution 20,000. Buys all rights, first rights, or second serial (reprint) rights. Byline given. Pays on acceptance. Reports in 6 weeks. SASE. Free sample copy.
Nonfiction: Background information, human interest articles, interviews, profiles, personal experience articles and photo features on the work of Comboni Missionaries, especially in the developing countries of Africa and Latin America and among US minority groups. Should be written knowledgeably in a popular, conversational style, and reflect a positive outlook on efforts in social and religious fields. Length: 250-1,000 words, shorter features; 3,000 words maximum, major articles. Pays $25-200.
Photos: B&w (5x7 minimum) photos and color transparencies purchased with ms or on assignment. "We want grabbing 'people photos' with a good sense of place. We'd consider purchasing photos without ms if of a people or area (foreign) served by Comboni Missionaries. All the better if a Comboni missionary appears in the photo and is identified by his/her complete name, native country, and mission country." Captions required. Pays $8 minimum/b&w glossy print; $30/color transparency.
Tips: "We treat Third World subjects sympathetically and multi-dimensionally and always in a Christian context. We want good, solid handling of facts and balanced, realistic stuff. We're a good market for second rights if the article fits our needs and photos are available."

COMMUNICATE, Box 600, Beaverlodge, Alberta T0H 0C0 Canada. Editor: K. Neill Foster. 5% freelance written. Monthly tabloid covering family and church activities for "a Christian (Protestant) and generally quite conservative readership; average age is about 45." Circ. 18,000. Pays on publication. Buys first-time rights. Previously published submissions OK. Send Canadian postage or IRCs with return envelope. US postage is not acceptable. Publishes ms an average of 6 months after acceptance.

Nonfiction: News ("we're always open to short news items of international or Canadian interest"); inspirational/devotional articles, 1,500-2,000 words (on how to apply Biblical principles to daily living); and news features/human interest (on unusual religious events, activities, personalities). No material with no Christian/moral/ethical significance or features on American politicians, entertainers, etc. who are Christians." Query or send complete ms. Length: 200-2,000 words. Pays $40 maximum.

Photos: Reviews 5x7 b&w prints.

Fiction: "Any fiction we would use would illustrate the application of Christian values, or perhaps the lack thereof, in the life of an individual."

Poetry: "We're looking for poetry that is inspirational, short and understandable."

Tips: "We are very receptive to American writers. Your best bet is to write along lines of general interest to North Americans and to avoid making your 'Americanness' obvious."

THE COMPANION OF ST. FRANCIS AND ST. ANTHONY, Conventual Franciscan Friars, Box 535, Postal Station F, Toronto, Ontario M4Y 2L8 Canada. (416)924-6349. Editor-in-Chief: Friar Philip Kelly, OFM Conv. 75% freelance written. Emphasizes religious and human values and stresses Franciscan virtues—peace, simplicity, joy. Monthly magazine; 32 pages. Circ. 10,000. Pays on acceptance. Buys all rights. Phone queries OK. Submit seasonal/holiday material 6 months in advance. Computer printout submissions acceptable; prefers letter-quality to dot-matrix. SASE, Canadian postage. Reports in 3 weeks. Publishes ms an average of 2 months after acceptance. Writer's guidelines for SAE and IRCs.

Nonfiction: Historical; how-to (medical and psychological coping); informational; inspirational; interview; nostalgia; profile; and family. No old time religion, anti-Catholic or pro-abortion material. Buys 6 mss/issue. Send complete ms. Length: 800-1,000 words. Pays 6¢/word, Canadian funds.

Photos: Photos purchased with accompanying ms. Captions required. Pays $8/5x7 (but all sizes accepted) b&w glossy print or color photo. Send prints. Total purchase price for ms includes payment for photos.

Fiction: Adventure, humorous, mainstream, and religious. Canadian settings preferred. Buys 6 mss/year. Send complete ms. Length: 800-1,000 words. Pays 6¢/word, Canadian funds.

Tips: "Mss on human interest with photos are given immediate preference. In the year ahead we will be featuring shorter articles, more Canadian and Franciscan themes, and better photos." No poetry.

CONTEMPORARY CHRISTIAN MAGAZINE, CCM Publications, Inc., Box 6300, Laguna Hills CA 92654. (714)951-9106. Editor-in-Chief/Publisher: John W. Styll. Editor: Ted Ojarovsky. Assistant Editor: Carolyn A. Burns. Monthly magazine covering contemporary Christian lifestyle. "We are a Christian publication that presents in-depth profiles on vital contemporary Christians; reviews music and the arts from a Christian perspective; profiles people who support or, occasionally, challenge the Christian world view; and explores current issues to help readers better understand their faith and how it relates to the world around them. The magazine is read primarily by 18-34 year old Christians with a strong interest in music." Circ. 40,000. Pays on publication. Byline given. Buys first rights only. Submit seasonal/holiday material 4 months in advance. Simultaneous queries OK. Computer printout submissions acceptable; prefers letter-quality to dot-matrix. SASE. Reports in 3 months. Publishes ms an average of 5 months after acceptance. Sample copy $1.95; writer's guidelines for SASE. Address queries to editor.

Nonfiction: Book excerpts; expose (investigative religious topics and news); general interest (about Christian young adults); historical/nostalgic (seasonal, strong on Christian life and doctrine); how-to (live the Christian life in the world, but not of it); humor (with a moral or a religious allegory); inspirational; interview/profile (well-known Christians in entertainment, art, literary, sports & politics); opinion (guest editorials on subjects of interest to living an effective Christian life, opinions); personal experience (eye-witness accounts of events, and autobiographies); photo feature (young people practicing their faith); other (criticism of books, films, and records; reviews of media, secular or Christian). No traditional religious material—any manuscript or query from a writer who has never read *Contemporary Christian Magazine*. Buys 20 mss/year. Query with clips of published work. Length: 1,000-3,000 words. Pays 5-10¢/word.

Photos: John Sutton, art director. State availability of photos. Pays negotiable rate for b&w prints or color transparencies. Identification of subjects required. Buys one-time rights.

Columns/Departments: Needs information on events, persons and news of the contemporary Christian scene in the US and worldwide. Query. Length: 10-500 words. Pays $50 maximum.

Poetry: Avant-garde, free verse, haiku and light verse. Buys 16/year. Submit maximum of 3 poems at one time. Line length: 5-50. Pays $10-50.

Tips: "We look for a fresh, honest approach to people and events for a realistic reflection of religion in America."

‡**CORNERSTONE, The Voice of This Generation**, Jesus People USA, 4707 N. Malden, Chicago IL 60640. Editor: Dawn Herrin. A bimonthly magazine covering "contemporary issues in the light of Evangelical Christianity." Circ. 90,000. Pays on publication. Byline given. Buys first rights. Submit seasonal/holiday material 6 months in advance. Computer printout submissions acceptable; no dot-matrix.

Nonfiction: Buys 1-2 mss/year. Length: 2,700 words maximum. Pays negotiable rate.

Photos: Send photos with accompanying ms. Reviews 8x10 b&w and color prints and 35mm slides. Indentification of subjects required. Buys negotiable rights.

Columns/Departments: Music (interview with artists, mainly rock, focusing on artist's worldview and value system as expressed in his/her music); Current Events; Personalities; Film and Book Reviews (focus on meaning as compared and contrasted to biblical values). Buys 2-6 mss/year. Length: 100-2,500 words (negotiable). Pays negotiable rate.

Fiction: "May express Christian worldview but should not be unrealistic or "syrupy." Other than smut, the sky's the limit. We want fiction as creative as the Creator." Buys 1-4 mss/year. Send complete ms. Length: 250-2,500 words (negotiable). Pays negotiable rate.

Poetry: Avant-garde, free verse, haiku, light verse, traditional. No limits *except* for epic poetry ("We've not the room!"). Buys 10-50 poems/year. Submit maximum 10 poems. Payment negotiated.

Fillers: Anecdotes, short humor, newsbreaks. Buys 5-15 year. Length: 20-200 words (negotiable). Payment negotiable.

Tips: "A display of creativity which expresses a biblical worldview without cliches or cheap shots at non-Christians is the ideal. We are known as the most avant-garde magazine in the Christian market, yet attempt to express orthodox beliefs in language of the '80s. *Any* writer who does this may well be published by *Cornerstone*. Creative fiction is begging for more Christian participation. We anticipate such contributions gladly. Interviews where well-known personalities respond to the gospel are also strong publication possibilities. Much of our poetry and small feature content is published without payment to the writer. This does not mean we do not pay ever, but rather that many of our readers enjoy being published as payment in and of itself. Inform us of a desire for payment and we will contact you before any decision to publish."

THE COVENANT COMPANION, 5101 N. Francisco Ave., Chicago IL 60625. (312)784-3000. Editor-in-Chief: James R. Hawkinson. 25% freelance written. Emphasizes Christian life and faith. Monthly magazine; 48 pages. Circ. 26,500. Pays following publication. Submit seasonal/holiday material 3 months in advance. Simultaneous, photocopied and previously published submissions OK. Computer printout submissions acceptable. SASE. Reports in 2-3 months. Sample copy $1.

Nonfiction: Humor; informational; inspirational (especially evangelical Christian); interviews (Christian leaders and personalities); and personal experience. "No articles promoting organizations or people not in the church we serve (Evangelical Covenant Church)." Buys 20-30 mss/year. Length: 100-110 lines of typewritten material at 70 characters/line (double-spaced). Pays $15-35.

DAILY MEDITATION, Box 2710, San Antonio TX 78299. Editor: Ruth S. Paterson. Quarterly. Rights purchased vary. Byline given. Submit seasonal material six months in advance. Sample copy sent to writer on receipt of 50¢.

Nonfiction: Inspirational, self-improvement and nonsectarian religious articles, 500-1,600 words, showing path to greater spiritual growth.

Fillers: Length: 400 words maximum. Pays 1-1½¢/word for articles.

Poetry: Inspirational. Length: 16 lines maximum. Pays 14¢/line.

Tips: "All our material is freelance submission for consideration, and we buy approximately 250 mss/year."

DAUGHTERS OF SARAH, 2716 W. Cortland, Chicago IL 60647. (312)252-3344. Editorial Coordinator: Reta Finger. Managing Editor: Annette Huizenga. 50% freelance written. Bimonthly magazine covering Christian feminism. Circ. 3,200. Pays on publication. Byline given. Offers 33-50% kill fee. Buys first North American serial rights. Submit seasonal/holiday material 4 months in advance. Computer printout submissions acceptable. Reports in 2 weeks on queries; 2 months on mss. Publishes ms an average of 2 months to 1 year after acceptance. Sample copy $1.50; writer's guidelines for SASE.

Nonfiction: Book excerpts (book reviews on Christian feminist books); historical (on Christian women); humor (feminist); inspirational (biblical articles about women or feminist issues); interview/profile (of contemporary Christian women from feminist point of view); personal experience (women's—or men's—experiences from Christian feminist point of view); and issues of social justice relating to women. Special issues include the male experience, women in prison, raising feminist children, sexuality and whether feminists stay in the church. "No general, elementary aspects of Christian feminism; we've gone beyond that. We particularly do not want pieces about women or women's issues that are not written from a feminist and Christian point of view." Buys 10-15 mss/year. Query with or without clips of published work. Length: 500-2,000 words. (Book reviews on Christian feminist books, 100-500 words). Pays $15-60.

Fiction: Christian feminist. Buys 2-4 mss/year. Query with clips of published work. Length: 500-2,000 words. Pays $15-60.

DECISION MAGAZINE, 1300 Harmon Place, Minneapolis MN 55403. (612)338-0500. Editor: Roger C. Palms. 69% freelance written. Conservative evangelical monthly publication of the Billy Graham Evangelistic Association. Magazine; 16 pages. Circ. 2,000,000. Buys first rights only on unsolicited manuscripts. Byline given. Pays on publication. Computer printout submissions acceptable; no dot-matrix. SASE. Publishes ms an average of 1 year after acceptance. Reports in 2 months.

Nonfiction: Uses some freelance material. Buys 21 full length unsolicited mss/year. Best opportunity is in testimony area (1,800-2,200 words); buys 11 unsolicited short testimonies for Where Are They Now? column. Also uses short narratives, 400-400 words and original quotes; bought 25 unsolicited short narratives and quotes in 1983. "Our function is to present Christ as Savior and Lord to unbelievers and present articles on deeper Christian life and human interest articles on Christian growth for Christian readers. No tangents. Center on Christ in all material."

Poetry: Uses short poems (limit: 24 lines) in Quiet Heart column. Positive, Christ-centered. Uses limited number of poems; send only if considered appropriate for magazine.

Tips: "The purpose of *Decision* is: 1) To set forth the Good News of salvation with such vividness and clarity that the reader will feel drawn to make a commitment to Christ; 2)to strengthen the faith of believers and to offer them hope and encouragement; and 3)to report on the ministries of the Billy Graham Evangelical Association."

THE DISCIPLE, Box 179, St. Louis MO 63166. Editor: James L. Merrell. 10% freelance written. Published by Christian Board of Publication of the Christian Church (Disciples of Christ). For ministers and church members, both young and older adults. Monthly. Circ. 60,000. Buys all rights. Pays month after publication. Photocopied and simultaneous submissions OK. Computer printout submissions acceptable; prefers letter-quality to dot-matrix. Submit seasonal material at least 6 months in advance. Reports in 2 weeks to 3 months. Publishes ms an average of 9 months after acceptance. SASE. Sample copy $1; free writer's guidelines.

Nonfiction: Articles and meditations on religious themes, short pieces, and some humorous. No fiction. Buys 100 unsolicited mss/year. Length: 500-800 words. Pays $10-50.

Photos: B&w glossy prints, 8x10. Occasional b&w glossy prints, any size, used to illustrate articles. Pays $10-25. Pays $35-200/cover. Occasional color. "We are looking for b&w photos of church activities—worship, prayer, dinners, etc." Pays for photos at end of month after acceptance.

Poetry: Uses 3-5 poems/issue. Traditional forms, blank verse, free verse and light verse. Length: 16 lines limit. Themes may be seasonal, historical, religious and occasionally humorous. Pays $3-20.

Tips: "We're looking for personality features about lay disciples, churches. Give good summary of story idea in query. We use articles primarily from disciples, ministers and lay persons since our magazine is written to attract the denomination. We work with more secular poets than writers and the poets write in religious themes for us."

EPIPHANY JOURNAL, Epiphany Press, Box 14727, San Francisco CA 94114. (415)431-1917. Editor: Philip Tolbert. Quarterly magazine covering religious topics for the contemplative Christian. Circ. 3,000. Pays on publication. Byline given. Buys one-time rights and makes work-for-hire assignments. Submit seasonal/holiday material 6 months in advance. Simultaneous queries, and simultaneous and previously published submissions OK. Computer printout submissions OK; prefers letter-quality to dot-matrix. SASE. Reports in 2 weeks on queries; 2 months on mss. "Sample copy and writer's guidelines available for $4, which will be refunded with payment for your first article."

Nonfiction: Inspirational (examinations of aspects of the contemplative life, and of the Christian's role and responsibility in the modern world); interview/profile (interviews with current Christian figures; profiles of past and present figures in Christian life); and photo feature (series of artistic photos expressing a theme, e.g., "Transformation," "A Sense of the Divine," "The House of the Lord," and linked with poetry and prose). Buys 10-20 mss/year. Query or send complete ms. Length: 2,000-8,000 words. Pays 2¢/word ($100 maximum). Also book excerpts (from forthcoming or recently published spiritual or religious works).

Columns/Departments: Book reviews (any current literature of interest to the Christian thinker). Buys 10-15 mss/year. Query or send complete ms. Length: 1,000-2,500 words. Pays 2¢/word ($30 maximum).

Tips: "Get to know our magazine, then send us a query letter or ask for an assignment suggestion. We prefer not to see first person/anecdotal accounts."

THE EPISCOPALIAN, 1930 Chestnut St., Philadelphia PA 19103. (215)564-2010. Editor: Henry L. McCorkle. Managing Editor: Judy Mathe Foley. Monthly tabloid covering the Episcopal Church for Episcopalians. Circ. 285,000. Pays on publication. Byline given. Submit seasonal/holiday material 2 months in advance. Previously published submissions OK. SASE. Reports in 1 month. Sample copy for 2 first class stamps.

Nonfiction: Inspirational, and interview/profile (of Episcopalians participating in church or community activities). "I like action stories about people doing things and solving problems." No personal experience articles. Buys 24 mss/year. Send complete ms. Length: 1,000-1,500 words. Pays $25-200.

Photos: Pays $10 for b&w glossy prints. Identification of subjects required. Buys one-time rights.

‡**ETERNITY MAGAZINE, The Evangelical Monthly**, Evangelical Ministries, Inc. 1716 Spruce St., Philadelphia PA 19103. (215)546-3696. Editor: William J. Petersen. Managing Editor: Deborah H. Barackman. A monthly magazine intended "to help readers apply God's Word to all areas of life today." Circ. 42,000 + . Pays on acceptance. Byline given. Offers $25-50 kill fee; "this rarely happens." Buys one-time rights (poetry) or first rights (articles). Submit seasonal/holiday material 6 weeks in advance. Computer printout submissions acceptable; prefers letter-quality to dot-matrix. SASE. Reports in 6 weeks. Sample copy $2; writer's guidelines for SAE and 1 first class stamp.
Nonfiction: Ken Myers, executive editor. General interest (the Christian in the culture); how-to (apply Scripture to problems); inspirational (Biblical study); and interview/profile (well known evangelicals). No fiction; no short, devotional fillers. Buys 20 mss/year. Query. Length: 500-1,500 words. Pays $35-150.
Poetry: Lois Sibley, poetry editor. Free verse, haiku, light verse and traditional. "Must be short." Buys 10-12 poems/year. Submit maximum 3 poems. Length: 3-15 lines. Pays $20-40.
Tips: "For general articles, begin with illustration, apply Scriptural principles to current problems/topics and include an application that will help readers. In poetry, we are looking for a good use of imagery, effectively controlled emotion, and words that elicit a sensory response—a memorable poem. And, the poem must be a good expression of Biblical theology.

EVANGEL, Dept. of Christian Education, Free Methodist Headquarters, 901 College Ave., Winona Lake IN 46590. (219)267-7161. Editor: Vera Bethel. 100% freelance written. Audience is 65% female, 35% male; married, 25-31 years old, mostly city dwellers, high school graduates, mostly nonprofessional. Weekly magazine; 8 pages. Circ. 35,000. Pays on publication. Buys simultaneous, second serial (reprint) or one-time rights. Submit seasonal/holiday material 3 months in advance. Computer printout submissions acceptable; no dot-matrix. SASE. Reports in 4 weeks. Publishes ms an average of 1 year after acceptance. Free sample copy and writer's guidelines.
Nonfiction: Interview (with ordinary person who is doing something extraordinary in his community, in service to others); profile (of missionary or one from similar service profession who is contributing significantly to society); and personal experience (finding a solution to a problem common to young adults; coping with handicapped child, for instance, or with a neighborhood problem. Story of how God-given strength or insight saved a situation). Buys 100 mss/year. Submit complete ms. Length: 300-1,000 words. Pays $10-25.
Photos: Purchased with accompanying ms. Captions required. Send prints. Pays $5-10 for 8x10 b&w glossy prints; $2 for snapshots.
Fiction: Religious themes dealing with contemporary issues dealt with from a Christian frame of reference. Story must "go somewhere". Buys 50 mss/year. Submit complete ms. Length: 1,200-1,500 words. Pays $35-40. SASE required.
Poetry: Free verse, haiku, light verse, traditional and religious. Buys 50/year. Limit submissions to batches of 5-6. Length: 4-24 lines. Pays $5. SASE required.
Tips: "Seasonal material will get a second look (won't be rejected so easily) because we get so little. Write an attention grabbing lead followed by a body of article that says something worthwhile. Relate the lead to some of the universal needs of the reader—promise in that lead to help the reader in some way. Remember that everybody is interested most in himself. Lack of SASE brands author as a nonprofessional; I seldom even bother to read the script. If the writer doesn't want the script back, it probably has no value for me, either."

THE EVANGELICAL BEACON, 1515 E. 66th St., Minneapolis MN 55423. (612)866-3343. Editor: George Keck. 35% freelance written. Denominational magazine of the Evangelical Free Church of America— evangelical Protestant readership. Published twice monthly except monthly July, August and December. Rights purchased vary with author and material. Buys all or first rights, some reprints. Pays on publication. Computer printout submissions acceptable; prefers letter-quality to dot-matrix. Sample copy and writer's guidelines for 75¢. Reports on submissions in 6-8 weeks. Publishes ms an average of 3 months after acceptance. SASE must be included.
Nonfiction: Articles on the church, Christ-centered human interest and personal testimony articles, well researched on current issues of religious interest. Desire crisp, imaginative, original writing—not sermons on paper. Length: 250-2,000 words. Pays 3¢/word with extra payment on some articles, at discretion of editor.
Photos: Prefers 8x10 b&w photos. Pays $7.50 minimum.
Fiction: Not much fiction used, but will consider. Length: 100-1,500 words.
Poetry: Very little poetry used. Pays variable rate, $3.50 minimum.
Tips: "Articles need to be helpful to the average Christian—encouraging, challenging, instructive. Also needs material presenting reality of the Christian faith to non Christians. Some tie-in with the Evangelical Free Church of America is helpful but is not required."

EVANGELIZING TODAY'S CHILD, Child Evangelism Fellowship Inc., Warrenton MO 63383. (314)456-4321. Editor: Mrs. Elsie Lippy. 75% freelance written. Our purpose—to equip Christians to win the world's children to Christ and disciple them. Our readership—Sunday school teachers, Christian education leaders and children's workers in every phase of Christian ministry to children up to 12 years old. Computer printout submissions acceptable; prefers letter-quality to dot-matrix. Publishes ms an average of 6 months after acceptance.
Nonfiction: Unsolicited articles welcomed from writers with Christian education training or experience. Pays 4-7¢/word.
Photos: Submissions of photos on speculation accepted. Needs photos of children or related subjects. Please include SASE. Pays $20-25 for 8x10 b&w glossy prints; $50-150 for color transparencies.

‡FAITH FOR THE FAMILY, Bob Jones University, Greenville SC 29614. (803)242-5100, ext. 7200. Editor: Bob Jones. Managing Editor: Robert W. Franklin. 65% freelance written. Published 10 times/year. Magazine covering fundamental Christianity. Circ., 70,000. Pays on acceptance. Byline given. Buys all rights. Submit seasonal/holiday material 4 months in advance. Simultaneous queries submissions OK. Computer printout submissions acceptable. SASE. Report in 2 weeks on queries; 4 weeks on mss. Publishes ms an average of 4 months after acceptance. Free sample copy and writer's guidelines.
Nonfiction: Expose, general interest, historical/nostalgic, how-to and inspirational. Query or send complete ms. Length: 500-1,500 words. Pays 3¢/word minimum.
Photos: Pays $10 minimum for color transparencies and for 8x10 b&w prints. Captions, model release and identification of subjects required. Buys one-time rights.
Fiction: Religious and Christian. Query or send complete ms. Length: 1,000-1,500 words. Pays 3¢/word minumum.
Tips: "Fiction and practical how-to Christian nonfiction are the areas most open for freelancers."

FAMILY LIFE TODAY MAGAZINE, Box 93670, Pasadena CA 91109. (213)791-0039. Publisher/Editor-in-Chief: Clif Cartland. 90% freelance written. Emphasizes "building strong marriages and helping Christian families deal with the realities of contemporary life." Monthly magazine; 48 pages. Circ. 50,000. Pays on publication. Byline given. Buys first rights only. Submit seasonal/holiday material 6 months in advance of issue date. Previously published submissions OK, "but we're accepting few reprints these days. Computer printouts acceptable "if separated and in regular page order; prefers traditional form." SASE. Reports in 2 months. Publishes ms an average of 6 months after acceptance. Sample copy and writer's guidelines for $1 and 9x12 SASE.
Nonfiction: All articles need to reflect a Christian value system. How-to (any family related situation with narrow focus: how to help the hyperactive child, etc.); humor (if wholesome and family related); interview (with person who is recognized authority in area of marriage and family life); personal experience ("when my husband lost his job," etc.); and photo feature (family related). Buys 100 unsolicited mss/year. Query. Length: 300-1,500 words. Pays 10¢/word for original material; 5¢/word for reprints.
Tips: "We would like to see more manuscripts written by husbands and fathers."

FRIDAY (OF THE JEWISH EXPONENT), 226 S. 16th St., Philadelphia PA 19102. (215)893-5745. Editor: Jane Biberman. 98% freelance written. For the Jewish community of Greater Philadelphia. Monthly literary supplement. Circ. 100,000. Buys first rights only. Pays 25% kill fee. Byline given. Buys 25 unsolicited mss/year. Pays after publication. Free sample copy and writer's guidelines. Photocopied submissions OK. No simultaneous submissions. Computer printout submissions acceptable. Submit special material 3 months in advance. Reports in 3 weeks. Publishes ms an average of 6 months after acceptance. SASE.
Nonfiction: "We are interested only in articles on Jewish themes, whether they be historical, thought pieces, Jewish travel or photographic essays. Topical themes are appreciated." Length: 6-20 double-spaced pages. Pays $75 minimum.
Fiction: Short stories on Jewish themes. Length: 6-20 double-spaced pages. Pays $75 minimum.
Poetry: Traditional forms, blank verse, free verse, avant-garde forms and light verse; must relate to a Jewish theme. Length varies. Pays $15 minimum.
Tips: "Pieces on Jewish personalities—artists, musicians and authors—are most welcome." Include illustrative material.

‡FUNDAMENTALIST JOURNAL, Old-Time Gospel Hour, Langhorne Plaza, Lynchburg VA 24514. (804)528-4112. Editor: Jerry Falwell. Managing Editor: Nelson Keener. 40% freelance written. A Christian magazine (nonprofit organization) published monthly (July/August combined) covering "matters of interest to all Fundamentalists, providing discussion of divergent opinions on relevant issues; also human interest stories and news reports. Audience is 65% Baptist; 35% other denominations; 30% pastors, 70% other. Circ. 56,000. Pays on publication. Byline given. Offers negotiable kill fee. Buys all rights and makes work-for-hire assignments. Submit seasonal/holiday material 3 months in advance. Previously published submissions OK. Computer printout submissions acceptable. SASE. Reports in 3 months. Publishes ms an average of 6 months after acceptance. Free sample copy; writers guidelines for SAE and 1 first class stamp.

Nonfiction: Deborah Huff, articles editor. Book excerpts; expose (government, communism, education); general interest; historical/nostalgic (regarding the Bible, Christianity, great Christians of old); inspirational, interview/profile; opinion and personal experience. "Writing must be consistent with Fundamentalist doctrine. We do not want articles that are critical in naming leaders of churches or Christian organizations." Buys 77 mss/year. Send complete ms. Length: 800-2,500 words. Pays 10¢/printed word.

Columns/Departments: W. David Beck, book editor. Book/film reviews of interest to the Christian family or to pastors, profiles of churches/pastors, articles regarding missions, successful teaching ideas and Bible study. Buys 88 mss/year. Query or send complete ms. Length; 300-2,000 words. Pays 10¢/printed word; $25-50 for book reviews.

Tips: "News is usually by assignment; various articles of general interest to Fundamentalist Christian readers, perspective, profiles, missions articles, successful teaching ideas are most open to freelancers. Samples of previously published work would be helpful."

GOOD NEWS, The Forum for Scriptural Christianity, Inc., Box 165, Wilmore KY 40390. (606)858-4661. Editor: James V. Heidinger II. Associate Editor: James S. Robb. 25% freelance written. For United Methodist lay people and pastors, primarily middle income; conservative and Biblical religious beliefs; broad range of political, social and cultural values. "We are the only evangelical magazine with the purpose of working within the United Methodist Church for Biblical reform and evangelical renewal." Bimonthly magazine. Circ. 17,000. Pays on acceptance. Buys first rights. Byline given. Phone queries OK. Submit seasonal/holiday material 6 months in advance. Simultaneous submissions OK. Prefers original mss and not photocopies of reprinted material. Computer printout submissions acceptable. SASE. Reports in 2 months. Publishes ms an average of 1 year after acceptance. Sample copy $1; free writer's guidelines.

Nonfiction: Historical (prominent people or churches from the Methodist/Evangelical United Brethren tradition); how-to (build faith, work in local church); humor (good taste); inspirational (related to Christian faith); personal experience (case histories of God at work in individual lives); and any contemporary issues as they relate to the Christian faith and the United Methodist Church. No sermons or secular material. Buys 25 mss/year. Query with a "brief description of the article, perhaps a skeleton outline. Show some enthusiasm about the article and writing (and research). Tell us something about yourself (though not a list of credentials); whether you or the article has United Methodist tie-in." Pays $20-75.

Photos: Photos purchased with accompanying ms or on assignment. Captions required. Uses fine screen b&w glossy prints. Total purchase price for ms includes payment for photos. Payment negotiable.

Columns/Departments: Good News Book Forum. Query.

Fillers: Anecdotes, United Methodist newsbreaks and short humor. Buys 15 fillers/year. Pays $5-10.

Tips: "We are using more short articles (4-5 magazine pages), tighter writing, more visual writing and fewer reprints."

GOOD NEWS BROADCASTER, Box 82808, Lincoln NE 68501. (402)474-4567. Editor: Theodore H. Epp. 40% freelance written. Interdenominational magazine for adults from 17 years of age and up. Monthly. Circ. 160,000. Buys first rights only. Buys approximately 100 mss/year. Pays on acceptance. Sample copy and writer's guidelines for postage. Submit seasonal material at least 1 year in advance. Computer printout submissions acceptable; no dot-matrix. Reports in 5 weeks. SASE required.

Nonfiction: Norman A. Olson, managing editor. Articles which will help the reader learn and apply Christian Biblical principles to his life. From the writer's or the subject's own experience. "We are especially looking for true, personal experience 'salvation,' church, children's ages 4-10, missions, 'youth' (17 years and over), 'parents', 'how to live the Christian life' articles, reports and interviews regarding major and interesting happenings and people in fundamental, evangelical Christian circles." Nothing rambling or sugary sweet, or without Biblical basis. Details or statistics should be authentic and verifiable. Style should be conservative but concise. Prefers that Scripture references be from the *New American Standard Version* or the *Authorized Version* or the *New Scofield Reference Bible*. Length: 1,500 words maximum. Pays 4-10¢/word. "When you can get us to assign an article to you, we pay nearer the maximum. More ms are now rejected if unaccompanied by photos.

Photos: Pays $25 maximum for b&w glossies; $75 maximum for color transparencies. Photos paid on publication.

Tips: "The basic purpose of the magazine is to explain the Bible and how it is relevant to life because we believe this will accomplish one of two things—to present Christ as Saviour to the lost or to promote the spiritual growth of believers, so don't ignore our primary purposes when writing for us. Nonfiction should be Biblical and timely; at the least Biblical in principle. Use illustrations of your own experiences or of someone else's when God solved a problem similar to the reader's. Be so specific that the meanings and significance will be crystal clear to all readers."

GOSPEL CARRIER, Messenger Publishing House, Box 850, Joplin MO 64802. (417)624-7050. Editor-in-Chief: Roy M. Chappell, D.D. Denominational Sunday School take-home paper for adults, ages 20 through retirement. Quarterly publication in weekly parts; 104 pages. Circ. 3,500. Pays quarterly. Buys simultaneous, second serial and one-time rights. Byline given. Submit seasonal/holiday material 1 year in advance. Simultaneous, photocopied and previously published submissions OK. SASE. Reports in 3 months. Sample copy and writer's guidelines for 50¢.

Nonfiction: Historical (related to great events in the history of the church); informational (may explain the meaning of a Bible passage or a Christian concept); inspirational (must make a Christian point); nostalgia (religious significance); and personal experience (Christian concept). No puzzles, poems and filler material.

Fiction: Adventure, historical, romance, and religious. Must have Christian significance. Buys 13-20 mss/issue. Submit complete ms. Length: 1,500-1,800 words. Pays 1¢/word.

GUIDEPOSTS MAGAZINE, 747 3rd Ave., New York NY 10017. Editor: Van Varner. "*Guideposts* is an inspirational monthly magazine for all faiths in which men and women from all walks of life tell how they overcame obstacles, rose above failures, met sorrow, learned to master themselves, and became more effective people through the direct application of the religious principles by which they live." Buys all rights. Pays 25% kill fee for assigned articles. Buys 40-60 unsolicited mss/year. Byline given. "Most of our stories are first-person ghosted articles, so the author would not get a byline unless it was his/her story." SASE.

Nonfiction and Fillers: Articles and features should be written in simple, anecdotal style with an emphasis on human interest. Short mss of approximately 250-750 words ($25-100) would be considered for such features as "Quiet People" and general one-page stories. Full-length mss, 750-1,500 words ($200-300). All mss should be typed, double-spaced and accompanied by a stamped, self-addressed envelope. Annually awards scholarships to high school juniors and seniors in writing contest.

Tips: "The freelancer would have the best chance of breaking in by aiming for a 1-page or maybe 2-page article. That would be very short, say 2½ pages of typescript, but in a small magazine such things are very welcome. A sensitively written anecdote that could provide us with an additional title is extremely useful. And they are much easier to just sit down and write than to have to go through the process of preparing a query. They should be warm, well-written, intelligent and upbeat. We like personal narratives that are true and have some universal relevance, but the religious element does not have to be hammered home with a sledge hammer." Address short items to Nancy Schraffenberger.

INDIAN LIFE, Intertribal Christian Communications, Box 3765, Station B, Winnipeg, Manitoba R2W 3R6 Canada. (204)338-0311. Editor: George McPeek. Bimonthly magazine of Christian experience from a native American (Indian) point of view for readers in 30 different denominations and missions. Circ. 12,000. Pays on publication. Byline given. Buys first rights and second serial (reprint) rights. Submit seasonal/holiday material 4 months in advance. Photocopied and previously published submissions OK. Computer printout submissions acceptable; prefers letter-quality to dot-matrix. Canada: SAE and IRCs outside Canada. Reports in 3 weeks on queries; 6 weeks on mss. Publishes ms an average of 6 months after acceptance. Sample copy for 9x12 SAE and $1 Canadian postage; writer's guidelines for $1, business-size SAE and 37¢ Canadian postage.

Nonfiction: Historical/nostalgic (with a positive approach); inspirational; interview/profile (of Indian Christian personalities); personal experience; photo feature; general news (showing Indian achievements); and human interest (wholesome, but not necessarily religious). Special edition on the Indian and alcohol (statistics, self-help programs, personal experience, etc.). No political, sexually suggestive, or negative articles on personalities, groups or points of view. Buys 12 mss/year. Query with clips. Length: 500-1,500 words. Pays $20-45; less for news items.

Photos: State availability of photos. Pays $3-5 for b&w contact sheet; $10-20 for 35mm slides or other color transparencies; $5-10 for 5x7 b&w prints. Captions, model release and identification of subjects required. Buys one-time rights.

Fiction: Adventure, confession, historical, religious and legends with Christian applications. No explicit sex or negative themes. Buys 4-6 mss/year. Query with clips of published work. Length: 500-1,200 words. Pays $20-40.

Fillers: Clippings, jokes, anecdotes, short humor and newsbreaks. Buys 25-30/year. Length: 50-200 words. Pays $3-10.

Tips: "First person stories must be verifiable with references (including one from pastor or minister) attached. Most material is written by Indian people, but some articles by non Indians are accepted. Maintain an Indian point of view. We seek to build a positive self-image, provide culturally relevant material and serve as a voice for the Indian church."

INSIGHT, The Young Calvinist Federation, Box 7244, Grand Rapids MI 49510. (616)241-5616. Editor: John Knight. Assistant Editor: Martha Kalk. 10% freelance written. For young people ages 16-21, a Christian magazine. Monthly (except June and August) magazine; 28 pages. Circ. 18,500. Pays on publication. Buys simultaneous, second serial (reprint) and first North American serial rights. Byline given. Submit seasonal/holiday material 6 months in advance. Simultaneous, photocopied and previously published submissions OK. SASE. Sample copy and writer's guidelines for 9x12 SASE. Publishes ms an average of 3 months after acceptance.

Photos: Photos purchased without accompanying ms. Pays $15-25/8x10 b&w glossy print; $50-200 for 35mm or larger color transparencies. Total purchase price for ms includes payment for photos.

Close-up

Van Varner
Editor, *Guideposts*

Guideposts, for readers, is a sanctuary—filled with everyday problems and solutions. For the writer, it is a market *if*, in writing, he can convey human experience and apply faith in God to a situation. "Some of the very finest writers in the country cannot write for us," says *Guideposts* editor Van Varner.

More than 31,000 unsolicited manuscripts arrive at Varner's New York office annually. *Guideposts* also receives 10 million pieces of reader mail each year in the New York and California offices. "We're interested in receiving transom material; we live by it because we're looking for personal human experience," says Varner. "Our greatest problem is that we get too many stories that are similar."

Health problems and handicaps inspire readers to write to the magazine. *Writers* who can find the extraordinary story that readers will relate to may get a "yes" from Varner. "And we will always be reaching for the same thing in a *Guideposts* story, that is, identification with the reader, a certain story sense, and something that readers can use in their own lives."

Varner reads manuscripts looking for this reader-involving material; he buys an estimated 40-60 unsolicited manuscripts a year. "The writer has to know at the outset what it is in that story that is going to help the reader," he points out. "Once that is done, you get to the story itself and make it of dramatic interest. You can't just be telling a story because it is a good one."

Varner's stacks of mail tell him all writers don't understand what *Guideposts* publishes. "So many writers think we're interested in sermons and we're not; we're interested in living testimonials," he says. "They're more inclined to think if something is simply beautiful, that that's enough, but it isn't."

A common mistake that writers make in writing about health problems is to dwell on the hospital experience or problem. One *Guideposts* story, for example, told of a man whom doctors said would remain in a coma following a car accident; the man's brother spent two years at his side. "It was the sacrifice of the brother that was so important; it was *sacrifice* that became the essential part of the story; we really weren't dealing with coma."

Of course, Varner checks with ministers and sources in some cases to verify that the writer isn't writing fiction. He also meets some of those potential writers at the writing workshop the magazine sponsors every two years. The workshop helps to upgrade the quality of Christian writing. It was also this goal that prompted Varner and three *Guideposts* associates to create Chosen Books, a house dedicated to religious publishing.

Varner has since given up editorial ties with Chosen Books. Besides editing *Guideposts* now, he writes devotionals for the annual *Daily Guideposts*. Through his own writing experiences— he has written four books and hundreds of *Guideposts* pieces during his 31 years with the magazine—and by talking with writers, Varner has found there are very few "natural" writers. "You have to work at writing." And, for *Guideposts* writers, they must inspire worshippers of many denominations. "It's the value to the reader that's the important thing."

Fiction: Humorous, mainstream and religious. "Looks for short stories and nonfiction that lead readers to a better understanding of how the Christian faith is relevant to daily life, social issues and the arts. They must do more than entertain—must make the reader see things in a new light." No sentimental, moralistic guidance articles. Buys 1-2 mss/issue. Send complete ms. Length: 1,000-3,000 words. Pays $45-100.
Poetry: Free verse. Buys 10 poems/year. Length: 4-25 lines. Pays $20-25.
Fillers: Youth oriented cartoons, puzzles and short humor. Length: 50-300 words. Pays $10-35.
Tips: "We are looking for shorter contributions and short, short stories."

INTERLIT, David C. Cook Foundation, Cook Square, Elgin IL 60120. (312)741-2400, ext. 322. Editor-in-Chief: Gladys J. Peterson. 90% freelance on assignment. "Please study publication and query before submitting manuscripts." Emphasizes sharpening skills in Christian communications and journalism. Especially for editors, publishers, and writers in the Third World (developing countries). Also goes to missionaries, broadcasters and educational personnel in the US Quarterly journal; 24 pages. Circ. 9,000. Pays on acceptance. Buys all rights. Photocopied submissions OK. Computer printout submissions acceptable; prefers letter-quality to dot-matrix. SASE. Reports in 2 weeks. Publishes ms an average of 2 weeks after acceptance. Free sample copy.
Nonfiction: Technical and how-to articles about communications, media and literacy. Also photo features. Buys 7 mss/issue, mostly on assignment. Length: 500-1,500 words. Pays 6¢/word.
Photos: Purchased with accompanying ms only. Captions required. Query or send prints. Uses b&w.

LIGHT AND LIFE, Free Methodist Publishing House, 901 College Ave., Winona Lake IN 46590. Managing Editor: Lyn Cryderman. 35% freelance written. Emphasizes evangelical Christianity with Wesleyan slant for a cross section of adults. Published monthly. Magazine; 36 pages. Circ. 50,000. Pays on publication. Prefers first rights, sometimes buys second (reprint) rights to material originally published elsewhere. Byline given. Submit seasonal/holiday material 6 months in advance. Previously published submissions OK. Computer printout submissions acceptable; prefers letter-quality to dot-matrix. SASE. Reports in 6 weeks. Publishes ms an average of 6 months after acceptance. Sample copy $1.50; writer's guidelines for SASE.
Nonfiction: "Each issue includes a mini-theme (2 or 3 articles addressing contemporary topics such as death and dying, science and faith, Christians as citizens), so freelancers should request our schedule of mini-theme topics. We also need fresh, upbeat articles showing the average layperson how to be Christ-like at home, work and play. Never submit anything longer than 2,500 words." Submit complete ms. Buys 70-80 unsolicited ms/year. Pays 3¢/word.
Photos: Purchased without accompanying ms. Send prints. Pays $5-35 for b&w photos. Offers additional payment for photos accepted with accompanying ms.

LIGUORIAN, Liguori MO 63057. Editor: the Rev. Norman Muckerman. 50% freelance written. For families with Catholic religious convictions. Monthly. Circ. 570,000. Byline given "except on short fillers and jokes." Pays on acceptance. Buys all rights but will reassign rights to author *after* publication upon request. Submit seasonal material 5-6 months in advance. Electronic submissions OK on disk compatible with TRS80 Model III, "but we ask contributors to send printout first, disk upon acceptance. Computer printout submissions acceptable; prefers letter-quality to dot-matrix. Reports in 6-8 weeks. Publishes ms an average of 9 months after acceptance. SASE.
Nonfiction: "Pastoral, practical and personal approach to the problems and challenges of people today. No travelogue approach or unresearched ventures into controversial areas. Also, no material found in secular publications—fad subjects that already get enough press, pop psychology, negative or put-down articles." Recent article examples: "You Can Go Home Again" (March 1984). Buys 60 unsolicited mss/year. Length: 400-2,000 words. Pays 7-10¢/word. Photos purchased with mss; b&w glossy prints.

LILLENAS PROGRAM RESOURCES, Lillenas Publishing Company, Box 527, Kansas City MO 64141. Editor: Paul Miller. 99% freelance written. Booklets that include program scripts, outlines and ideas for the Sunday school and church. "We look for unique program ideas for use in Sunday schools and churches, large and small." Bookstore circulation. Pays on acceptance. Byline given. Buys first rights. Submit seasonal/holiday material 1 year in advance. Computer printout submissions acceptable; prefers letter-quality to dot-matrix. "Only original material, no previously published submissions." SASE. Reports in 1 month. Publishes ms an average of 1 year after acceptance. Free writer's guidelines and need sheet for SAE and 20¢ postage.
Nonfiction: "Some inspirational and devotional articles suitable for readings. Skits, devotional messages, emcee ideas and banquet plans. Christmas is overworked; Thanksgiving is wide open. Any program you might present in your own church would have a chance in this market." No "secular subjects, such as Santa Claus, Easter bunnies, etc." Send complete ms. Payment depends upon length and quality.
Poetry: "Recitations; poems suitable for reading before an audience. Sacred poetry only." Pays 25¢/line.
Tips: "We are introducing a new line of full length plays for the experienced director and cast. Will welcome submissions."

LIVE, 1445 Boonville Ave., Springfield MO 65802. (417)862-2781. Editor: Kenneth D. Barney. 100% freelance written. For adults in Assemblies of God Sunday schools. Weekly. Circ. 225,000. Not copyrighted. Buys about 100 mss/year. Pays on acceptance. Buys first rights only. Submit seasonal material 10 months in advance; do not mention Santa Claus, Halloween or Easter bunnies. Reports on material within 6 weeks. Publishes ms an average of 1 year after acceptance. SASE. Free sample copy and writer's guidelines for SASE.
Nonfiction: "Articles with reader appeal emphasizing some phase of Christian living presented in a down-to-earth manner. Biography or missionary material using fiction techniques. Historical, scientific or nature material with a spiritual lesson. Be accurate in detail and factual material. Writing for Christian publications is a ministry. The spiritual emphasis must be an integral part of your material." Prefers not to see material on highly controversial subjects. Length: 1,000-1,600 words. Pays 3¢/word for first rights; 2¢/word for second rights, according to the value of the material and the amount of editorial work necessary. "Please do not send large numbers of articles at one time."
Photos: Color photos or transparencies purchased with mss, or on assignment. Pay open.
Fiction: "Present believable characters working out their problems according to Bible principles; in other words, present Christianity in action without being preachy. We use very few serials, but we will consider 3-4 part stories if each part conforms to average word length for short stories. Each part must contain a spiritual emphasis and have enough suspense to carry the reader's interest from one week to the next. Stories should be true to life but not what we would feel is bad to set before the reader as a pattern for living. Stories should not put parents, teachers, ministers or other Christian workers in a bad light. Setting, plot and action should be realistic, with strong motivation. Characterize so that the people will live in your story. Construct your plot carefully so that each incident moves naturally and sensibly toward crisis and conclusion. An element of conflict is necessary in fiction. Short stories should be written from one viewpoint only. We do not accept fiction based on incidents in the Bible." Length: 1,200-1,600 words. Pays 3¢/word for first rights; 2¢/word for second rights. "Please do not send large numbers of articles at one time."
Poetry: Buys traditional, free and blank verse. Length: 12-20 lines. "Please do not send large numbers of poems at one time." Pays 20¢/line, for first rights.
Fillers: Brief and purposeful, usually containing an anecdote, and always with a strong evangelical emphasis. Length: 200-600 words.

‡**LIVING WITH HOPE, A Message of Encouragement for Today's Woman**, Encouragement Ministries, 911 E. Highland Ave., Box 428, Geneva AL 36340. (205)684-6159. Editor: Lura Zerick. 95% freelance written. A quarterly newsletter co-ordinated with radio/music ministry emphasizing "growing and overcoming problems in life; maturity in the Christian life." Circ. 1,000. Pays on publication. Byline given. Buys one-time rights. Submit seasonal/holiday material 4-5 months in advance. Photocopied and previously published submissions OK. Computer printout submissions acceptable. SASE. Reports in 2-3 weeks on queries; 4-6 weeks on mss. Sample copy for $1.50, SAE and 2 first class stamps; writer's guidelines for SAE and 1 first class stamp.
Nonfiction: Inspirational and personal experience. "Articles should be written from a woman's viewpoint, sharing how obstacles were overcome with victorious power of Jesus. They should strengthen and encourage others to walk closer to the Lord." No romantic articles (stories with no spiritual involvement). Buys 18 mss/year. Query with published clips or send complete ms. Length: 300-1,000 words. Pays 3¢/word.
Photos: "We seldom use photos."
Columns/Departments: Book reviews: uses 2/issue; 300 words maximum; pays $5 each. Puzzles: uses 1/issue; pays $10. Meditation: uses 1/issue; 200 words; pays $5. Buys 16 mss/year. Send complete ms.
Poetry: Free verse, haiku, light verse and traditional. No long poems and "please, no romantic poetry." Buys 35 poems/year. Submit maximum 6 poems. Length: 3-12 lines. Pays 50¢/line.
Fillers: Anecdotes and short humor. Must relate to Christian living. Buys 12/year. Length: 100-250 words. Pays 3¢/word.
Tips: "Since we are 95% freelance written, all departments are open, including articles, poetry, reviews and meditation."

LIVING WITH TEENAGERS, Baptist Sunday School Board, 127 9th Ave., Nashville TN 37234. (615)251-2273. Editor: E. Lee Sizemore. 50% freelance written. Quarterly magazine about teenagers for the Baptist parents of teenagers. Circ. 35,000. Pays within 2 months of acceptance. Buys all rights. Submit seasonal material 1 year in advance. Computer printout submissions acceptable. Reports in 2 months. Publishes ms an average of 15 months after acceptance. Send 30¢ postage for a sample copy.
Nonfiction: "We are looking for a unique Christian element. We want a genuine insight into the teen/parent relationships." General interest (on communication, emotional problems, growing up, drugs and alcohol, leisure, sex education, spiritual growth, working teens and parents, money, family relationships, and church relationships); inspirational; and personal experience. Buys 80 unsolicited mss/year. Query with clips of previously published work. Length: 600-2,000 words. Pays 4¢/published word.
Photos: Pays $15 minimum/5x7 b&w glossy print. Reviews b&w contact sheets and 2¼x2¼ and 35mm color transparencies. "We need cover transparencies of parents with youth." Captions preferred; model release required.

Fiction: Humorous and religious, but must relate to parent/teen relationship. "No stories from the teen's point of view." Buys 2 mss/issue. Query with clips of previously published work. Length: 600-2,000 words. Pays 4¢/published word.

Poetry: Free verse, light verse, traditional and devotional inspirational; all must relate to parent/teen relationship. Buys 3 mss/issue. Submit 5 poems maximum. Length: 33 characters maximum. Pays $1.50 plus 85¢/line for 1-7 lines; $4.30 plus 50¢/line for 8 lines minimum.

Tips: "Write in the first person. Make liberal use of illustrations and case studies. Write from the parent's point of view."

THE LOOKOUT, 8121 Hamilton Ave., Cincinnati OH 45231. (513)931-4050. Editor: Mark A. Taylor. 50% freelance written. For the adult and young adult of the Sunday morning Bible school. Weekly. Pays on acceptance. Byline given. Buys first or second (reprint) rights. Simultaneous submissions OK. Computer printout submissions acceptable; prefers letter-quality to dot-matrix. SASE. Reports in 2 months. Sample copy and writer's guidelines 50¢.

Nonfiction: "Seeks stories about real people or Sunday school classes; items that shed Biblical light on matters of contemporary controversy; and items that motivate, that lead the reader to ask, 'Why shouldn't I try that?' or 'Why couldn't our Sunday school class accomplish this?' Should tell how real people are involved for Christ. In choosing topics, *The Lookout* considers timeliness, the church and national calendar and the ability of the material to fit the above guidelines. Tell us about ideas that are working in your Sunday school and in the lives of its members. Remember to aim at laymen." Submit complete ms. Length: 1,200-1,800 words. Pays 4-6¢/word. We also use inspirational short pieces. "About 600-800 words is a good length for these. Relate an incident that illustrates a point without preaching." Pays 4-5¢/word.

Fiction: "A short story is printed in most issues; it is usually between 1,200-1,800 words long and should be as true to life as possible while remaining inspirational and helpful. Use familiar settings and situations. Most often we use stories with a Christian slant."

Photos: B&w prints, 4x6 or larger. Pays $5-25. Pays $50-150 for color transparencies for covers and inside use. Needs photos of people, especially adults in a variety of settings.

THE LUTHERAN, 2900 Queen Lane, Philadelphia PA 19129. (215)438-6580. Editor: Edgar R. Trexler. 50% freelance written. General interest magazine of the Lutheran Church in America. Twice monthly, except single issues in July, August and December. Buys one-time rights. Pays on acceptance. "We need informative, detailed query letters. We also accept manuscripts on speculation only, and we prefer not to encourage an abundance of query letters."Computer printout submissions acceptable; prefers letter-quality to dot-matrix. Publishes ms an average of 9 months after acceptance. Free sample copy and writer's guidelines. SASE.

Nonfiction: Popularly written material about human concerns with reference to the Christian faith. "We are especially interested in articles in 4 main fields: Christian ideology; personal religious life, social responsibilities; Church at work; and human interest stories about people in whom considerable numbers of other people are likely to be interested." Write "primarily to convey information rather than opinions. Every article should be based on a reasonable amount of research or should explore some source of information not readily available. Most readers are grateful for simplicity of style. Sentences should be straightforward with a minimum of dependent clauses and prepositional phrases." Length: 500-2,000 words. Pays $90-270.

Photos: Buys photos submitted with mss. Good 8x10 glossy prints. Pays $15-25. Also color for cover use. Pays up to $150.

Tips: "A great need exists for personal experience writing that is creative, relevant to these times and written for a wide audience."

LUTHERAN FORUM, 308 W. 46th St., New York NY 10036-3894. (212)757-1292. Editor: Glenn C. Stone. For church leadership, clerical and lay. Magazine; 40 pages. Quarterly. Circ. 5,400. Rights purchased vary with author and material. Buys all rights, first North American serial rights, second (reprint) rights and simultaneous rights. Byline given. Buys 12-15 mss/year. Pays on publication. Will consider photocopied and simultaneous submissions. Computer printout submissions acceptable; prefers letter-quality to dot-matrix. Reports in 4-6 weeks. Query or submit complete ms. SASE. Sample copy $1.25.

Nonfiction: Articles about important issues and developments in the church's institutional life and in its cultural/social setting. Special interest in articles on the Christian's life in secular vocations. No purely devotional/inspirational material. Payment varies; $20 minimum. Length: 1,000-3,000 words. Informational, how-to, interview, profile, think articles and expose. Length: 500-3,000 words. Pays $20-50.

Photos: Purchased with mss or with captions only. Prefers 4x5 prints. Pays $10 minimum.

THE LUTHERAN JOURNAL, 7317 Cahill Rd., Edina MN 55435. Editor: The Rev. Armin U. Deye. Family magazine for Lutheran Church members, middle age and older. Quarterly magazine; 32 pages. Circ. 130,000. Byline given. Buys 12-15 mss/year. Pays on publication. Will consider photocopied and simultaneous submissions. Reports in 2 months. Submit complete ms. SASE. Free sample copy.

Nonfiction: Inspirational, religious, human interest and historical articles. Interesting or unusual church projects. Informational, how-to, personal experience, interview, humor and think articles. Length: 1,500 words maximum; occasionally 2,000 words. Pays 1-3¢/word.

Photos: B&w and color photos purchased with accompanying ms. Captions required. Payment varies.

Fiction: Mainstream, religious and historical fiction. Must be suitable for church distribution. Length: 2,000 words maximum. Pays 1-1½¢/word.

Poetry: Traditional poetry, blank verse, free verse, related to subject matter.

THE LUTHERAN STANDARD, 426 S. 5th St., Box 1209, Minneapolis MN 55440. (612)330-3300. Editor: The Rev. Lowell G. Almen. 35% freelance written. For families in congregations of the American Lutheran Church. Semimonthly. Circ. 588,000. Usually buys one-time rights. Byline given. Buys 30-50 mss/year. Pays on acceptance. Computer printout submissions acceptable; no dot-matrix. SASE. Reports in 3 weeks. Publishes ms an average of 9 months after acceptance. Free sample copy. Query.

Nonfiction: Inspirational articles, especially about members of the American Lutheran Church who are practicing their faith in noteworthy ways, or congregations with unusual programs. "Should be written in language clearly understandable to persons with a mid high school reading ability." Also publishes articles that discuss current social issues and problems (crime, family life, divorce, etc.) in terms of Christian involvement and solutions. No poetry. Length: limit 1,200 words. Pays 10¢/word.

Tips: "We are interested in personal experience pieces with strong first person approach. The manuscript may be on a religious and social issue, but with evident human interest using personal anecdotes and illustrations. How has an individual faced a serious problem and overcome it? How has faith made a difference in a person's life? We prefer letters that clearly describe the proposed project. Excerpts from the project or other samples of the author's work are helpful in determining whether we are interested in dealing with an author. We would appreciate it if more freelance writers seemed to have a sense of who our readers are and an awareness of the kinds of manuscripts we in fact publish."

LUTHERAN WOMEN, 2900 Queen Lane, Philadelphia PA 19129. Editor: Terry Schutz. 40% freelance written. 10 times/year. Circ. 40,000. Decides about acceptance within 2 months. Prefers to see mss 6 months ahead of issue, at beginning of planning stage. Can consider up to 3 months before publication. Buys first rights only. Computer printout submissions acceptable; no dot-matrix. SASE. Sample copy 75¢.

Nonfiction: Anything of interest to mothers—young or old—professional or other working women related to the contemporary expression of Christian faith in daily life, community action and international concerns. Family publication standards. No recipes or housekeeping hints. Length: 1,500-2,000 words. Some shorter pieces accepted. Pays up to $50 for full length ms with photos.

Photos: Purchased mostly with mss. Should be clear, sharp b&w.

Fiction: Should show deepening of insight; story expressing new understanding in faith; story of human courage, self-giving and building up of community. Length: 2,000 words. Pays $30-40.

Poetry: Very little is used. "Biggest taboo for us is sentimentality. We are limited to family magazine type contributions regarding range of vocabulary, but we don't want almanac type poetry." No limit on number of lines. Pays $20-35/poem.

MARIAN HELPERS BULLETIN, Eden Hill, Stockbridge MA 01262. (413)298-3691. Editor: the Rev. Joseph J. Sielski, M.I.C. 90% freelance written. For average Catholics of varying ages with moderate religious views and general education. Quarterly. Circ. 1,000,000. Not copyrighted. Byline given. Buys 18-24 mss/ year. Pays on acceptance. Submit seasonal material 6 months in advance. Reports in 4-8 weeks. SASE. Free sample copy.

Nonfiction: "Subject matter is of general interest on devotional, spiritual, moral and social topics. Use a positive, practical and optimistic approach, without being sophisticated. We would like to see articles on the Blessed Virgin Mary." Buys informational and inspirational articles. Length: 300-900 words. Pays $25-35.

Photos: Photos are purchased with or without mss; captions optional. Pays $5-10 for b&w glossy prints.

MARRIAGE & FAMILY LIVING, St. Meinrad IN 47577. (812)357-8011. Managing Editor: Kass Dotterweich. 50% freelance written. Monthly magazine. Circ. 45,000. Pays on acceptance. Buys first North American serial rights, first book reprint option, and control of other reprint rights. Byline given. Query. Computer printout submissions acceptable; prefers letter-quality to dot-matrix. SASE. Reports in 4-6 weeks. Sample copy 50¢.

Nonfiction: Uses 1) Articles designed to enrich husband/wife and parent/child relationships by expanding religious and psychological and by deepening sensitivies. (Note: Ecumenically Judeo-Christian); 2) Practical informative articles aimed at helping couples cope with problems of modern living; and 3) Personal essays relating amusing, heartwarming or insightful incidents which refelct the rich human side of marriage and family life. Length: 2,500 words maximum. Pays 7¢/word.

Photos: Attention, art director. B&w glossy prints (5x7 or larger) and color transparencies or 35mm slides (vertical preferred). Pays $300/4-color cover or center spread photo; uses approximately 6-8 photos (b&w/col-

or) and illustrations inside. Pays variable rate on publication. Photos of couples, families and individuals especially desirable. Model releases required.
Poetry: Any style and length. Pays $15 on publication.
Tips: Query with a brief outline of article and opening paragraphs.

MENNONITE BRETHREN HERALD, 159 Henderson Hwy., Winnipeg, Manitoba R2L 1L4 Canada. Contact: Editor. Family publication "read mainly by people of the Mennonite faith, reaching a wide crosssection of professional and occupational groups, but also including many homemakers. Readership includes people from both urban and rural communities." Biweekly. Circ. 12,000. Pays on publication. Not copyrighted. Byline given. Sample copy 75¢. Reports in 1 month. SAE and IRCs.
Nonfiction: Articles with a Christian family orientation; youth directed, Christian faith and life, and current issues. Wants articles critiquing the values of a secular society, attempting to relate Christian living to the practical situations of daily living; showing how people have related their faith to their vocations. 1,500 words. Pays $25-40.
Photos: Photos purchased with mss; pays $5.

THE MESSENGER OF THE SACRED HEART, 661 Greenwood Ave., Toronto, Ontario M4J 4B3 Canada. Editor: the Rev. F.J. Power, S.J. 10% freelance written. For "adult Catholics in Canada and the US who are members of the Apostleship of Prayer." Monthly. Circ. 17,500. Buys first rights only. Byline given. Pays on acceptance. Submit seasonal material 3 months in advance. Computer printout submissions acceptable; prefers letter-quality to dot-matrix. Reports in 1 month. SAE and IRCs. Unsolicited manuscripts, unaccompanied by return postage, will not be returned. Sample copy $1.
Nonfiction: Mary Pujolas, department editor. "Articles on the Apostleship of Prayer and on all aspects of Christian living." Current events and social problems that have a bearing on Catholic life, family life, Catholic relations with nonCatholics, personal problems, the liturgy, prayer and devotion to the Sacred Heart. Material should be written in a popular, nonpious style. "We are not interested in column material." Buys 12 mss/year. Length: 1,800-2,000 words. Pays 2¢ word.
Fiction: Mary Pujolas, department editor. Wants fiction which reflects the lives, problems and preoccupations of reading audience. "Short stories that make their point through plot and characters." Length: 1,800-2,000 words. Pays 2¢/word.

‡**MESSENGER OF ST. ANTHONY**, Prov. Pad. F.M.C. Editore, Basilica del Santo, 35123 Padova, Italy. (049)664-322. Editor: G. Panteghini. Monthly magazine covering family, social and religious issues with a Christian outlook. Circ. 20,000. Pays on publication. Byline given. Offers 30% kill fee. Buys simultaneous rights. Submit seasonal/holiday material 4 months in advance. Simultaneous queries, and simultaneous and photocopied submissions OK. SASE. Reports in 1 month on queries; 6 weeks on mss. Free sample copy and writer's guidelines.
Nonfiction: Historical/nostalgic, humor, inspirational, personal experience, photo feature and travel. Special issue on the first five years of Pope John II. "No sexist articles." Buys 60 mss/year. Query. Length: 1,800-2,700 words. Pays $60-130.
Photos: "We prefer 10x14 or 13x18 cm photos." Send photos with ms. Pays $10-15 for color prints; $5-10 for b&w prints. Identification of subjects required. Buys one-time rights.
Columns/Departments: Religion, health, living together (social issues), religion and art, and science (human dimensions). Buys 40 mss/year. Query with or without clips of published work. Length: 1,800-2,700 words. Pays $60-130.
Fiction: Confession (religious witness); ethnic; historical; humorous; and religious. "Only fiction with human, social or religious value." Buys 12-15 mss/year. Query. Length: 1,800-2,700 words. Pays $60-130.

THE MIRACULOUS MEDAL, 475 E. Chelten Ave., Philadelphia PA 19144. Editorial Director: the Rev. Robert P. Cawley, C.M. 40% freelance written. Quarterly. Buys first North American serial rights. Buys articles only on special assignment. Pays on acceptance. SASE. Publishes ms an average of 2 years after acceptance. Free sample copy.
Fiction: Should not be pious or sermon-like. Wants good general fiction—not necessarily religious, but if religion is basic to the story, the writer should be sure of his facts. Only restriction is that subject matter and treatment must not conflict with Catholic teaching and practice. Can use seasonal material; Christmas stories. Length: 2,000 words maximum. Occasionally uses short-shorts from 750-1,250 words. Pays 2¢/word minimum.
Poetry: Maximum of 20 lines, preferably about the Virgin Mary or at least with religious slant. Pays 50¢/line minimum.

MODERN LITURGY, Suite 290, 160 E. Virginia St., San Jose CA 95112. Editor: Kenneth Guentert. For artists, musicians and creative individuals who plan group worship, services; teachers of religion. Magazine; 40-48 pages. Nine times/year. Circ. 15,000. Buys all rights. Byline given. Buys 10 mss/year. Pays three months after publication. Computer printout submissions acceptable. Reports in 6 weeks. Query. SASE. Sample copy $3; free writer's guidelines.

Nonfiction and Fiction: Articles (historical, theological and practical) which address special interest topics in the field of liturgy; example services; and liturgical art forms (music, poetry, stories, dances, dramatizations, etc.). Practical, creative ideas; and art forms for use in worship and/or religious education classrooms. "No material out of our field." Length: 750-2,000 words. Pays $5-30.

‡MOODY MONTHLY, The Christian Family Magazine, Moody Bible Institute, 2101 W. Howard St., Chicago IL 60645. (312)274-1879. Editor: Eric Fellman. Managing Editor: Michael Umlandt. 25% freelance written. Monthly magazine covering evangelical Christianity. "Believing the Bible to be God's word, *Moody Monthly* offers Bible-centered departments and articles to evangelical readers looking for help in living as Christians in today's world." Circ. 225,000. Pays on acceptance. Byline given. Buys first North American serial rights. Submit seasonal/holiday material 6 months in advance. Computer printout submissions acceptable. SASE. Reports in 1 month on queries; 2 months on mss. Publishes ms an average of 6 months after acceptance. Free sample copy and writer's guidelines.

Nonfiction: General interest (related to evangelical Christianity); how-to (living the Christian life); and personal experience (related to living the Christian life). No death or trauma stories. Buys 50 mss/year. Query. Length: 1,200-2,500 words. Pays 10¢/word.

Photos: Pays $35 minimum for color transparencies. Identification of subjects required. Buys one-time rights.

Columns/Departments: Parenting and First Person (testimony). Buys 20 mss/year. Query. Length: 900-1,500 words. Pays 10¢/word.

Tips: "First Person department is a good start for freelancers, but writer must study back issues."

THE NEW ERA, 50 E. North Temple, Salt Lake City UT 84150. (801)531-2951. Managing Editor: Brian K. Kelly. 60% freelance written. For young people of the Church of Jesus Christ of Latter-Day Saints (Mormon); their church leaders and teachers. Monthly magazine; 51 pages. Circ. 180,000. Buys all rights. Byline given. Buys 100 mss/year. Pays on acceptance. Submit seasonal material 1 year in advance. Computer printout submissions acceptable; prefers letter-quality to dot-matrix. Reports in 1 month. Publishes ms an average of 1 year after acceptance. Query preferred. SASE. Sample copy 75¢.

Nonfiction: "Material that shows how the Church of Jesus Christ of Latter-Day Saints is relevant in the lives of young people today. Must capture the excitement of being a young Latter-Day Saint. Special interest in the experiences of young Mormons in other countries. No general library research or formula pieces without the *New Era* slant and feel." Uses informational, how-to, personal experience, interview, profile, inspirational, humor, historical, think pieces, travel and spot news. Length: 150-3,000 words. Pays 3-6¢/word. *For Your Information* (news of young Mormons around the world).

Photos: Uses b&w photos and color transparencies with mss. Payment depends on use in magazine, but begins at $10.

Fiction: Experimental, adventure, science fiction and humorous. Must relate to young Mormon audience. Pays minimum 3¢/word.

Poetry: Traditional forms, blank verse, free verse, avant-garde forms, light verse and all other forms. Must relate to their editorial viewpoint. Pays minimum 25¢/line.

NEW WORLD OUTLOOK, Room 1351, 475 Riverside Dr., New York NY 10115. (212)870-3758. Editor: Arthur J. Moore. Executive Editor: George M. Daniels. 60% freelance written. For United Methodist lay people; not clergy generally. Monthly magazine; 48 pages. Circ. 40,000. Buys all rights and first North American serial rights. Buys 15-20 mss/year. Pays on publication. Publishes ms an average of 3 months after acceptance. Free sample copy and writer's guidelines. Query or submit complete ms. SASE.

Nonfiction: "Articles about the involvement of the church around the world, including the US in outreach and social concerns and Christian witness. Write with good magazine style. Facts, actualities important. Quotes. Relate what Christians are doing to meet problems. Specifics. We have too much on New York and other large urban areas. We need more good journalistic efforts from smaller places in US. Articles by freelancers in out-of-the-way places in the US are especially welcome." Length: 1,000-2,000 words. Usually pays $50-150. "Writers are encouraged to illustrate their articles photographically if possible.

Photos: "Generally use b&w but covers will be considered. They are always 4-color. Photos are purchased separately at standard rates."

Tips: "A freelancer should have some understanding of the United Methodist Church, or else know very well a local situation of human need or social problem which the churches and Christians have tried to face. Too much freelance material we get tries to paint with broad strokes about world or national issues. The local story of meaning to people elsewhere is still the best material. Avoid pontificating on the big issues. Write cleanly and interestingly on the 'small' ones."

NORTH AMERICAN VOICE OF FATIMA, Fatima Shrine, Youngstown NY 14174. Editor: Steven M. Grancini, C.R.S.P. 40% freelance written. For Roman Catholic readership. Circ. 3,000. Not copyrighted. Pays on acceptance. Reports in 6 weeks. SASE. Free sample copy.

Nonfiction and Fiction: Inspirational, personal experience, historical and think articles. Religious and historical fiction. Length: 700 words. All material must have religious slant. Pays 2¢/word.
Photos: B&w photos purchased with mss.

OBLATES MAGAZINE, Missionary Association of Mary Immaculate, 15 S. 59th St., Belleville IL 62222. (618)233-2238. Contact: Managing Editor. Bimonthly religious magazine for Christian families. Circ. 500,000. Pays on acceptance. Byline given. Buys one-time rights. Submit seasonal/holiday material 6 months in advance. SASE. Reports in 1 month. Free sample copy.
Nonfiction: Inspirational, personal experience and articles on Oblates around the world. Stories should be inspirational and present Gospel values. "Don't be preachy or pious. No 'How I found Jesus stories'." Buys 12 mss/year. Send complete ms. Length: 500 words. Pays $60.
Poetry: Light verse and traditional. "Nothing that takes too much effort to decipher. Emphasis should be on inspiration and relationship with God." Buys 6 poems/year. Submit 3 poems. Length: 8-16 lines. Pays $10-20.
Tips: "Our readership is made up mostly of mature Americans who are looking for comfort, encouragement and applicable Christian direction. They don't want to spend a lot of time wading through theology laden or personal spiritual journey pieces. But if you can take an incident from Christ's life, for example, and in a creative and clever way parallel that with everyday living or personal experience, all in about 500 words, we're holding a couple of pages for you. This formula will also work for any Gospel theme, e.g., forgiveness, selflessness, hope."

THE OTHER SIDE, Box 3948, Fredericksburg VA 22402. Co-Editors: Mark Olson and John Alexander. Assistant Editor: Kathleen Hayes. Publisher: Philip Harnden. 66% freelance written. "A magazine focusing on peace, justice and economic liberation from a radical Christian perspective." Monthly. Circ. 14,000. Pays on acceptance. Buys all rights. Byline given. Query about electronic submissions; requires hard copy also. Computer printout submissions acceptable. SASE. Reports in 1 month. Publishes ms an average of 4 months after acceptance. Sample copy $1.50. Writer's guidelines available.
Nonfiction: Eunice Amarantides Smith, articles editor. "Articles on current social, political and economic issues in the US and around the world: personality profiles, interpretative essays, interviews, how-to's, personal experiences and investigative reporting. Articles must be lively, vivid and down-to-earth, with a radical Christian perspective." Length: 300-4,000 words. Pays $25-250.
Photos: Dan Hamlett-Leisen, art director. "Photos or photo essays illustrating current social, political, or economic reality in the US and Third World." Pays $15-50 for b&w photos.
Fiction: Joseph Comanda, fiction editor. "Short stories, humor and satire conveying insights and situations that will be helpful to Christians with a radical commitment to peace and justice." Length: 300-4,000 words. Pays $25-250.
Poetry: Rosemary Camilleri, poetry editor. "Short, creative poetry that will be thought provoking and appealing to radical Christians who have a strong commitment to peace and justice." Length: 3-100 lines. Pays $15-20.

OUR FAMILY, Oblate Fathers of St. Mary's Province, Box 249, Battleford, Saskatchewan S0M 0E0 Canada. (306)937-2131, 937-7344. Editor-in-Chief: Albert Lalonde, O.M.I. 50% freelance written. For average family men and women of high school and early college education. Monthly magazine. Circ. 17,552. Pays on acceptance. Generally purchases first North American serial rights; also buys all rights, simultaneous, second serial (reprint) or one-time rights. Pays 100% kill fee. Byline given. Phone queries OK. Submit seasonal/holiday material 4 months in advance. Simultaneous, photocopied and previously published submissions OK. Computer printout submissions acceptable; no dot-matrix. "Writer should inquire with our office before sending letter-quality computer printout or disk submissions." SASE. Reports in 1 month. Publishes ms an average of 6 months after acceptance. Sample copy $1.50. Enclose SASE and 37¢ for writer's guidelines.
Nonfiction: Humor (related to family life or husband/wife relations); inspirational (anything that depicts people responding to adverse conditions with courage, hope and love); personal experience (with religious dimensions); and photo feature (particularly in search of photo essays on human/religious themes and on persons whose lives are an inspiration to others). Buys 72-88 unsolicited mss/year.
Photos: Photos purchased with or without accompanying ms. Pays $25 for 5x7 or larger b&w glossy prints and color photos (which are converted into b&w). Offers additional payment for photos accepted with ms (payment for these photos varies according to their quality). Free photo spec sheet with SASE.
Fiction: Humorous and religious. "Anything true to human nature. No romance, he-man adventure material, science fiction, moralizing or sentimentality." Buys 1-2 ms/issue. Send complete ms. Length: 700-3,000 words. Pays 7-10¢/word minimum for original material. Free fiction requirement guide with SASE.
Poetry: Avant-garde, free verse, haiku, light verse, and traditional. Buys 4-10 poems/issue. Length: 3-30 lines. Pays 75¢-$1/line.
Fillers: Jokes, gags, anecdotes and short humor. Buys 2-10 fillers/issue.
Tips: "Writers should be aware that if they write about nostalgia that not everything in the 'good old days' was

good; our readers do not mind a writer who shares, but the approach, 'now I the expert, will tell you, the ignorant one, what you must know," i.e.; talking down to the reader is a no-no; and simplicity in poetry is beautiful."

OUR SUNDAY VISITOR MAGAZINE, Noll Plaza, Huntington IN 46750. (219)356-8400. Executive Editor: Robert Lockwood. For general Catholic audience. Weekly. Circ. 300,000. Byline given. Buys 25 mss/year. Pays on acceptance. Submit seasonal material 2 months in advance. Reports in 3 weeks. Query. SASE. Free sample copy.
Nonfiction: Uses articles on Catholic related subjects. Should explain Catholic religious beliefs in articles of human interest; articles applying Catholic principles to current problems, Catholic profiles, etc. Payment varies depending on reputation of author, quality of work and amount of research required. Length: 1,000-1,200 words. Minimum payment for major features is $100 and a minimum payment for shorter features is $50-75.
Photos: Purchased with mss; with captions only. B&w glossy prints, color transparencies, 35mm color. Pays $125/cover photo story, $75/b&w story; $25/color photo. $10/b&w photo.

PARISH FAMILY DIGEST, Our Sunday Visitor, Inc., 200 Noll Plaza, Huntington IN 46750. (219)356-8400. Editor: Patrick R. Moran. 95% freelance written. *"Parish Family Digest* is geared to the Catholic family and to that family as a unit of the parish." Bimonthly magazine; 48 pages. Circ. 150,000. Pays on acceptance. Buys all rights on a work-for-hire basis. Byline given. Submit seasonal/holiday material 5 months in advance. Photocopied and previously published submissions OK; all manuscripts are retyped as edited. Computer printout submissions OK. SASE. Reports in 2 weeks for queries; 3 weeks for mss. Sample copy and writer's guidelines for postage.
Nonfiction: General interest, historical, inspirational, interview, nostalgia (if related to overall Parish involvement), and profile. No personal essays or preachy first person "Thou shalt's or shalt not's." Send complete ms. Recent article example: "That Special Sunday at Mission San Rafael" (March/April 1984). Buys 82 unsolicited mss/year. Length: 1,000 words maximum. Pays $5-50.
Photos: State availability of photos with ms. Pays $10 for 3x5 b&w prints. Buys all rights. Captions preferred. Model release required.
Fillers: Anecdotes and short humor. Buys 6/issue. Length: 100 words maximum.
Tips: "Know thy publication. Query with outline, title, approximate word length and possible photos. Read the magazine, get the feel of our parish family unit or involvement, and keep manuscripts to no more than 1,000 words maximum. Original ideas usually come through as winners for the beginning writer. Avoid reference book biographicals, and write of real persons."

‡**PARTNERSHIP, The Magazine for Wives in Ministry**, Christianity Today, Inc., 465 Gunderson Dr., Carol Stream IL 60188. (312)260-6200. Executive Editor: Terry C. Mack. Managing Editor: Ruth Senter. A bimonthly magazine for wives of Christian ministers. Estab. 1983. Circ. approximately 40,000. Pays on acceptance. Byline given. Offers variable kill fee. Buys first rights. Submit seasonal/holiday material 9 months in advance. Computer printout submissions acceptable. SASE. Reports in 2 weeks on queries; 1 month on mss. Sample copy for 8½x11 SAE and 2 first class stamps; free writer's guidelines.
Nonfiction: Book excerpts, humor, inspirational, interview/profile, opinion, and personal experience ("My Problem and How I Solved It"). "Articles must be narrowly slanted to interests and needs of the wives of ministers (Christian). If the article fits a general readership publication, it will *not* be suitable for *Partnership*." Buys 120 mss/year. Query. Length: 500-1,500 words. Pays $50-250.
Photos: State availability of photos with query letter or ms. Reviews b&w and color contact sheets and 5x7 prints. Pays variable rate. Identification of subjects required.
Columns/Departments: Reaching Out (ministry wives who serve outside their church); Partnership Counselor (answers from professionals to specific questions); In The Beginning (for seminary wives and those in early years of ministry); Perspective (opinion on current topics/thought pieces); Hospitality (advice or suggestion, or stories relating to wives of ministers). Buys 50 mss/year. Send complete ms. Length: 500-1,500 words. Pays $50-250.
Fiction: Buys 0-1 ms/year. Query with or without published clips or send complete ms.
Tips: "Writer needs to know and understand wives of ministers and their unique position. Articles by these wives are given preference. 'My Problem and How I Solved It' is a frequent theme. In the Beginning and Books are most open to freelancers. Query first, since this is a narrow market."

PENTECOSTAL EVANGEL, The General Council of the Assemblies of God, 1445 Boonville, Springfield MO 65802. (417)862-2781. Editor: Richard G. Champion. 33% freelance written. Emphasizes news of the Assemblies of God for members of the Assemblies and other Pentecostal and charismatic Christians. Weekly magazine; 32 pages. Circ. 290,000. Pays on publication. Buys first rights, simultaneous, second serial (reprint) or one-time rights. Byline given. Submit seasonal/holiday material 6 months in advance. Simultaneous, photocopied and previously published submissions OK. SASE. Reports in 3 months. Free sample copy and writer's guidelines.

Nonfiction: Informational (articles on home life that convey Christian teachings); inspirational; and personal experience. Buys 5 mss/issue. Send complete ms. Length: 500-2,000 words. Pays 3¢/word maximum.
Photos: Photos purchased without accompanying ms. Pays $7.50-15/8x10 b&w glossy prints; $10-35/35mm or larger color transparencies. Total purchase price for ms includes payment for photos.
Poetry: Religious and inspirational. Buys 1 poem/issue. Limit submissions to batches of 6. Pays 20-40¢/line.
Tips: "Break in by writing up a personal experience. We publish first person articles concerning spiritual experiences; that is, answers to prayer for help in a particular situation, of unusual conversions or healings through faith in Christ. All articles submitted to us should be related to religious life. We are Protestant, evangelical, Pentecostal, and any doctrines or practices portrayed should be in harmony with the official position of our denomination (Assemblies of God)."

PRAIRIE MESSENGER, Catholic Weekly, Benedictine Monks of St. Peter's Abbey, Box 190, Muenster, Saskatchewan S0K 2Y0 Canada. (306)682-5215. Editor: Andrew Britz. 8% freelance written. Saskatchewan and Manitoba Catholic weekly (48 issues/year). Covering religion, culture and social change, as well as local, national and international events. Circ. 16,500. Pays on publication. Byline given. Not copyrighted. Buys first and second rights to the same material, and makes work-for-hire assignments. Submit seasonal/holiday material 2 months in advance. Simultaneous queries and simultaneous, photocopied, and previously published submissions OK. Computer printout submissions acceptable; no dot-matrix. SASE. Reports in 3 weeks on queries; 3 months on mss. Publishes ms an average of 2 months after acceptance.
Nonfiction: General interest, humor, inspirational, interview/profile, opinion and personal experience. Buys less than 10 mss/year. Send complete ms. Length: 500-800 words. Pays $1.45/column inch.
Photos: Send photos with ms. Pays $1.50 maximum for b&w negatives; $5.50 maximum for b&w prints. Captions and identification of subjects required. Buys one-time rights.
Columns/Departments: Pastoral Perspectives; Politics Today; Theological Review; Social Action (on the religious scene); and Ecumenical Forum. Buys 20 mss/year. Send complete ms. Length: 750 words; 1,000 for center spreads. Pays $1.45/column inch or "$22.50 for comment and analysis columns which have been requested."

PRESBYTERIAN RECORD, 50 Wynford Dr., Don Mills, Ontario M3C 1J7 Canada. (416)444-1111. Editor: the Rev. James Dickey. 50% freelance written. For a church-oriented, family audience. Monthly magazine. Circ. 82,000. Buys 15 mss/year. Pays on publication. Submit seasonal material 3 months in advance. Publishes ms an average of 3 months after acceptance. Reports on manuscripts accepted for publication in 1 month. Computer printout submissions acceptable; prefers letter-quality to dot-matrix. Returns rejected material in 2 months. Query. SAE and Canadian stamps. Free sample copy.
Nonfiction: Material on religious themes. Check a copy of the magazine for style. Also, personal experience, interview, and inspirational material. No material solely American in context. Buys 10-15 unsolicited mss/year. Length: 1,000-2,000 words. Pays $45-55.
Photos: Pays $10-15 for b&w glossy photos. Captions required. Use positive color transparencies for the cover. Pays $50.
Tips: "There is a trend away from maudlin, first person pieces redolent with tragedy and dripping with simplistic pietistic conclusions."

PRESBYTERIAN SURVEY, Presbyterian Publishing House, 341 Ponce de Leon Ave. NE., Atlanta GA 30365. (404)873-1549. Editor: Vic Jameson. 65% freelance written. Monthly magazine covering religion, ethics and public issues for members of the Presbyterian Church (USA). Pays on acceptance. Byline given. Offers negotiable kill fee. Buys first North American serial rights. Query or submit complete ms. Submit seasonal/holiday material 3 months in advance. Simultaneous, photocopied and previously published submissions OK. Computer printout submissions acceptable; no dot-matrix. SASE. Reports in 3 weeks on queries; 1 month on mss. Publishes ms an average of 3 months after acceptance. Writer's guidelines for SASE.
Nonfiction: Book excerpts, general interest, inspirational, personal experience. "Columns are arranged at our initiative and invitation; queries about columnist opening will be pointless." Buys 50 mss/year. Query or send complete ms. Length: 1,000-2,500 words. Pays $50-150.
Tips: "A denominational merger has widened our audience from regional (17 states in the South and Southwest) to national. Therefore, we are looking for manuscripts from all parts of the country, and on subjects affecting all aspects of the life of the church. We want more substantive subjects and will not look with much favor on first person inspirational pieces."

PURPOSE, 616 Walnut Ave., Scottdale PA 15683. Editor: James E. Horsch. "For adults, young and old, general audience with interests as varied as there are persons. My particular readership is interested in seeing Christianity work in tough situations." Monthly magazine. Circ. 18,500. Buys one-time rights. Byline given. Buys 175-200 unsolicited mss/year. Pays on acceptance. Submit seasonal material 6 months in advance. Photocopied and simultaneous submissions OK. Reports in 6 weeks. Computer printout submissions acceptable if legible. Submit complete ms. SASE required. Free sample copy and writer's guidelines.

Nonfiction: Inspirational articles from a Christian perspective. "I want material that goes to the core of human problems in business, politics, religion, sex and many other areas—and shows how the Christian faith resolves them. Don't send superficial, sentimental or civil religion pieces. I want critical stuff that's upbeat. *Purpose* is a story paper which conveys truth either through quality fiction or through articles that use the best fiction techniques. Our magazine accents Christian discipleship. Christianity affects all of life, and we expect our material to demonstrate this. We're getting too much self-centered material. I would like to see story-type articles on how individuals, groups and organizations are intelligently and effectively working at some of the great human problems such as overpopulation, food shortages, international understanding, etc., motivated by their faith." Length: 200-1,200 words. Pays 1-4¢/word.

Photos: Photos purchased with ms. Captions desired. Pays $5-35/b&w, depending on quality. Normal range is $7.50-15. Must be sharp enough for reproduction; prefers prints in all cases. Can use color prints at the same rate of payment.

Fiction: Humorous, religious and historical fiction related to the theme of the magazine. "Produce the story with specificity so that it appears to take place somewhere and with real people. Should not be moralistic."

Poetry: Traditional poetry, blank verse, free verse and light verse. Length: 3-12 lines. Pays 50¢-$1/line.

Fillers: Jokes, short humor, and items up to 400 words. Pays 2¢ minimum/word.

Tips: "We are looking for articles which show that Christianity is working at issues where people hurt, but we want the stories told and presented professionally. Good photographs help place material with us."

QUEEN, Montfort Missionaries, 26 S. Saxon Ave., Bay Shore NY 11706. (516)665-0726. Editor: James McMillan, S.M.M. Managing Editor: Roger Charest, S.M.M. Emphasizes doctrine and devotion to Mary. Bimonthly magazine; 40 pages. Circ. 8,500. Pays on acceptance. Buys all rights. Phone queries OK. Submit seasonal/holiday material 4 months in advance. SASE. Reports in 1 month.

Nonfiction: Expose (doctrinal), historical, informational, inspirational and interview. Buys 5 mss/issue. Send complete ms. Length: 1,500-2,000 words. Pays $35-45.

Poetry: Free verse and traditional forms. Marian poetry only. Buys 2/issue. Limit submissions to batches of 2. Pays in free subscription for 2 years.

‡THE RAINBOW HERALD, Witnessing Stories Written by Everyday Christians for Everyday People, Rainbow's End Company, Box 173, Baden PA 15005. (412)266-7495. Editor/Publisher: Bettie Tucker. 100% freelance written. A quarterly nondenominational Christian witnessing magazine. Estab. 1983. Circ. 1,000. Pays on publication. Byline given. Buys first rights only. Submit seasonal/holiday material 6 months in advance. Simultaneous queries, and simultaneous and photocopied submissions OK. Previously published submissions at discretion of publisher. Computer printout submissions acceptable; prefers letter-quality to dot-matrix. SASE. Report in 3 weeks on queries; 6 weeks on mss. Sample copy for $1; writer's guidelines for SAE and 1 first class stamp.

Nonfiction: Judith Blanarik, articles editor. Let Me Tell You (first person accounts of divine intervention and miracles) 1,500-2,000 words; It Happened to Me (first person accounts of spiritual growth) 1,000-2,000 words; Everyday Heroes (stories written about a person who helps others through Christian ministering and concern) 500-1,000 words; and Interviews (query first). Buys 30 mss/year. Send complete ms. Pays $25-50.

Columns/Departments: "Do You Know" (awareness column) Christians speaking out on current critical issues which concern the church (examples: abortion, women in the ministry), must be thoroughly researched. Length: 1,000 words. Pays $25-50.

Poetry: Fawn Fulton, poetry editor. Free verse, light verse, traditional and spiritual poetry only. "We do not want poetry that is not inspirational." Buys 15-20 poems/year. Submit maximum 3 poems. Length: 12-24 lines; "This can vary with exceptional material." Pays $10.

Tips: Since we are a new publication, this is a ground opportunity for Christian writers. Witness to readers by conveying personal witnessing stories in which readers can easily identify with the writer. Include extensive dialogue and scripture references throughout stories—don't preach. Be honest with your writing—don't exaggerate. Christian readers easily spot this."

REVIEW FOR RELIGIOUS, 3601 Lindell Blvd., Room 428, St. Louis MO 63108. (314)535-3048. Editor: Daniel F.X. Meenan, S.J. 100% freelance written. Bimonthly. For Roman Catholic priests, brothers and sisters. Pays on publication. Buys first and second rights to the same material. Byline given. Computer printout submissions acceptable; prefers letter-quality to dot-matrix. Reports in about 8 weeks. Publishes ms an average of 9 months after acceptance. SASE.

Nonfiction: Articles on ascetical, liturgical and canonical matters only; not for general audience. Length: 2,000-8,000 words. Pays $6/page.

Tips: "The writer must know about religious life in the Catholic Church and be familiar with prayer, vows and problems related to them."

ST. ANTHONY MESSENGER, 1615 Republic St., Cincinnati OH 45210. Editor-in-Chief: Norman Perry. 55% freelance written. For a national readership of Catholic families, most of them have children in grade school, high school or college. Monthly magazine; 59 pages. Circ. 365,000. Pays on acceptance. Buys first North American serial rights. Byline given. Submit seasonal/holiday material 4 months in advance. Electronic submissions OK if compatible with CPT word processor, but requires hard copy also. Computer printout submissions acceptable; no dot-matrix. SASE. Publishes ms an average of 9 months after acceptance. Free sample copy and writer's guidelines.

Nonfiction: How-to (on psychological and spiritual growth; family problems); humor; informational; inspirational; interview; personal experience (if pertinent to our purpose); personal opinion (limited use; writer must have special qualifications for topic); and profile. Buys 12 mss/year. Length: 1,500-3,500 words. Pays 12¢/word.

Fiction: Mainstream and religious. Buys 12 mss/year. Submit complete ms. Length: 2,000-3,500 words. Pays 12¢/word.

Tips: "The freelancer should ask why his/her proposed article would be appropriate for us, rather than for *Redbook* or *Saturday Review*. We treat human problems of all kinds, but from a religious perspective. Get authoritative information (not merely library research; we want interviews with experts). Write in popular style."

ST. JOSEPH'S MESSENGER & ADVOCATE OF THE BLIND, Sisters of St. Joseph of Peace, St. Joseph's Home, Box 288, Jersey City NJ 07303. Editor-in-Chief: Sister Ursula Maphet. 25% freelance written. Quarterly magazine; 30 pages. Circ. 51,000. Pays on acceptance. Buys first and second rights to the same material, second (reprint) rights to material originally published elsewhere and all rights, but will reassign rights back to author after publication asking only that credit line be included in next publication. Submit seasonal/holiday material 3 months in advance (no Christmas issue). Simultaneous and previously published submissions OK. Reports in 3 weeks. Publishes ms an average of 6 months after acceptance. Free sample copy and writer's guidelines.

Nonfiction: Humor, inspirational, nostalgia, personal opinion, and personal experience. Buys 24 mss/year. Submit complete ms. Length: 300-1,500 words. Pays $3-15.

Fiction: "Fiction is our most needed area." Romance, suspense, mainstream, and religious. Buys 30 mss/year. Submit complete ms. Length: 600-1,600 words. Pays $6-25.

Poetry: Light verse and traditional. Buys 25/year. Limit submissions to batches of 10. Length: 50-300 words. Pays $5-20.

Tips: "It's rewarding to know that someone is waiting to see freelancers' efforts rewarded by 'print'. It's annoying, however, to receive poor copy, shallow material or inane submissions."

SCOPE, 426 S. 5th St., Box 1209, Minneapolis MN 55440. (612)330-3413. Editor: Constance Lovaas. 40% freelance written. For women of the American Lutheran Church. Monthly. Circ. 275,000. Buys first rights and occasionally second (reprint) rights to material originally published elsewhere. Byline given. Buys 200-300 mss/year. Occasionally overstocked. Pays on acceptance. Submit seasonal material 4-5 months in advance. Computer printout submissions acceptable; prefers letter-quality to dot-matrix. SASE. Reports in 4 weeks. Publishes ms an average of 6 months after acceptance. Free sample copy.

Nonfiction: "The magazine's primary purpose is to be an educational tool in that it transmits the monthly Bible study material which individual women use in preparation for their group meetings. It contains articles for inspiration and growth, as well as information about the mission and concerns of the church, and material that is geared to seasonal emphasis. We are interested in articles that relate to monthly Bible study subjects. We also want articles that tell how faith has affected, or can influence, the lives of women or their families; we are interested in articles by and about singles and working mothers. But we do not want preachy articles. We are interested in any subject that concerns women." No articles built around nonLutheran teaching and practices but may be written by nonLutherans. Submit complete ms. Length: 400-800 words. Pays $15-50.

Photos: Buys 3x5 or 8x10 b&w photos with mss or with captions only. Pays $10-30.

Poetry: "We use very little poetry and are very selective." Pays $5-15.

Fillers: "We can use interesting, brief, pithy, significant or clever filler items. We do not buy cute sayings of children." Pays $5-15.

Tips: "Writers should be aware of need for inclusive language to avoid discrimination among races, sexes or persons who are disabled or elderly; recognition of women active in all aspects of the marketplace; and recognition that women, too, are editors of magazines."

SEEK, Standard Publishing, 8121 Hamilton Ave., Cincinnati OH 45231. (513)931-4050, ext. 165. Editor: Leah Ann Crussell. 98% freelance written. For young and middle-aged adults who attend church and Bible classes. Sunday school paper; 8 pages. Quarterly, in weekly issues. Circ. 60,000. Byline given. Prefers first serial rights. Buys 100-150 mss/year. Pays on acceptance. Submit seasonal (Christmas, Easter, New Year's) material 1 year in advance. Query not necessary; submit complete ms. Computer printout submissions acceptable; prefers letter-quality to dot-matrix. Reports in 5-10 days. SASE. Publishes ms an average of 1 year after acceptance. Free sample copy and writer's guidelines.

Nonfiction: "We look for articles that are warm, inspirational, devotional, of personal or human interest; that deal with controversial matters, timely issues of religious, ethical or moral nature, or first person testimonies, true-to-life happenings, vignettes, emotional situations or problems; communication problems and examples of answered prayers. Article must deliver its point in a convincing manner but not be patronizing or preachy. Must appeal to either men or women. Must be alive, vibrant, sparkling and have a title that demands the article be read. Always need stories of families, marriages, problems on campus and life testimonies." No poetry. Length: 400-1,200 words. Pays 2½¢/word.

Photos: B&w photos purchased with or without manuscripts. Pays $10 minimum for good 8x10 glossy prints.

Fiction: Religious fiction and religiously slanted historical and humorous fiction. Length: 400-1,200 words. Pays 2½¢/word.

Tips: Submit mss which tell of faith in action or victorious Christian living as central theme. "We select manuscripts as far as one year in advance of publication. Complimentary copies are sent to our published writers immediately following printing."

‡**SHARING THE VICTORY, Publication of the Fellowship of Christian Athletes**, Fellowship of Christian Athletes (FCA), 8701 Leeds Road, Kansas City MO 64129. (816)921-0909. Editor: Skip Stogsdill. 10% freelance written. Managing Editor: Jack Roberts. A bimonthly magazine for Christian athletes and coaches "aimed at enabling high school and college athletes, male and female, to become stronger in their Christian faith." Circ. 43,000. Pays on publication. Byline given. Buys first rights only. Publishes ms an average of 6 months after acceptance. Submit seasonal/holiday material 3-4 months in advance. Computer printout submissions acceptable; no dot-matrix. SASE. Reports in 2 weeks. Sample copy for $1, SAE and 3 first class stamps; free writer's guidelines.

Nonfiction: Interview/profile and personal experience. Buys 6-10 mss/year. Query. Length; 500-1,000 words. Pays $25-50.

Photos: State availability of photos. Pays $15-35 for 5x7 or 8x10 b&w prints; $25-50 for 5x7 or 8x10 color prints and transparencies. Buys one-time rights.

Tips: "Profiles and interviews are most open to freelancers."

‡**SISTERS TODAY**, The Liturgical Press, St. John's Abbey, Collegeville MN 56321. Editor-in-Chief: Sister Mary Anthony Wagner, O.S.B. Associate Editor: Sister Barbara Ann Mayer, O.S.B. 90% freelance written. Magazine for religious women of the Roman Catholic Church, primarily. Published 10 times/year. Circ. 10,000. Pays on publication. Buys all rights. Byline given. Submit seasonal/holiday material 4 months in advance. Computer printout submissions acceptable; no dot-matrix. SASE. Reports in 2-3 months. Publishes ms an average of 1 year after acceptance. Sample copy, $1.50.

Nonfiction: How-to (pray, live in a religious community, exercise faith, hope, charity etc.); informational; and inspirational. Also articles concerning religious renewal, community life, worship and the role of Sisters in the world today. Buys 33-40 unsolicited mss/year. Recent article example: "I Believe in Community" (March 1984). Query. Length: 500-2,500 words. Pays $5/printed page.

Poetry: Free verse, haiku, light verse and traditional. Buys 3 poems/issue. Limit submissions to batches of 4. Pays $10.

SOCIAL JUSTICE REVIEW, 3835 Westminister Place, St. Louis MO 63108. (314)371-1653. Editor. Harvey J. Johnson. 25% freelance written. Issued bimonthly. Not copyrighted; "however special articles within the magazine may be copyrighted, or an occasional special issue has been copyrighted due to author's request." Buys first rights only. Query. Computer printout submissions acceptable. SASE.

Nonfiction: Wants scholarly articles on society's economic, religious, social, intellectual and political problems with the aim of bringing Catholic social thinking to bear upon these problems. 2,500-3,500 words. Pays about $6/column.

SOLO MAGAZINE, Solo Ministries, Inc., Box 1231, Sisters OR 97759. Editor: Jerry Jones. Assistant Editor: Ann Staatz. Bimonthly magazine about today's single adults who desire to live within the framework of Christ's teachings. Circ. 30,000. Pays on publication. Submit seasonal material 8 months in advance. Accepts queries only. No unsolicited mss. Reports in 3 months on queries. Sample copy and writer's guidelines $2.50 with large magazine-size SASE.

Nonfiction: General interest (articles on travel, adventure appealing to single adults); historical (outstanding single adults in history; views of or on single adults of the past); how-to (repair, cook, garden, etc.); humor (anything that helps us laugh with others and at ourselves); inspirational (outstanding single adults who have done something inspirational); nostalgia; opinion (from a wide range of people on any topics of interest to singles; divorce, sexual attitudes and habits, viewpoints, etc.); profile (Christain single adults who are giving of themselves to make a difference in their world); travel; new product; personal experience; and personal victory (*Guidepost* style stories about a single adult who has gone through a specific battle or crisis in life—and has won). "No articles that are not in harmony with Christian principles and Christ's teachings." Buys 20-30 mss/year. Length: 200-2,000 words. Pays 5¢/word.

Columns/Departments: Relationships (how to build healthy ones, how to argue, how to break up and how to start new ones); Devotional/Bible Study (anything that would assist in the single adult's spiritual growth and development); Single Parenting (anything helpful to the single parent); and Personal Motivation/Self-Help (anything that would help motivate and challenge people to reach for their maximum). Buys 20-30 mss/year. Query. Length: 200-600 words. Pays 5¢/word.

Poetry: Avant-garde, free verse, haiku, light verse and traditional. Buys 4 mss/year. Submit maximum 2 poems. Length: 5-40 lines. Pays $5-$25.

Fillers: Clippings on single adult news and newsbreaks. Buys 36 mss/year. Length: 10-100 words. Pays 5¢/word.

Tips: "Get a copy of our magazine to know our market *before* submitting query. Ask single friends what kinds of things they would most want to see in a magazine specifically for them, and write about it. Wherever their greatest needs and interests are, there are our stories."

SPIRITUAL LIFE, 2131 Lincoln Rd. NE, Washington DC 20002. (202)832-6622. Editor: the Rev. Christopher Latimer, O.C.D. 80% freelance written. "Largely Catholic, well educated, serious readers. High percentage are priests and religious, but also some laymen. A few are nonCatholic or nonChristian." Quarterly. Circ. 17,000. Buys first rights only. Buys 20 mss/year. Pays on acceptance. "Brief autobiographical information (present occupations, past occupations, books and articles published, etc.) should accompany article. Follow Chicago *Manual of Style*." Reports in 2 weeks. Publishes ms an average of 1 year after acceptance. SASE. Free sample copy and writer's guidelines.

Nonfiction: Serious articles of contemporary spirituality. Quality articles about man's encounter with God in the present day world. Language of articles should be college level. Technical terminology, if used, should be clearly explained. Material should be presented in a positive manner. Sentimental articles or those dealing with specific devotional practices not accepted. "*Spiritual Life* tries to avoid the 'popular,' sentimental approach to religion and to concentrate on a more intellectual approach. We do not want first person accounts of spiritual experiences (visions, revelations, etc.) nor sentimental treatments of religious devotions." Buys inspirational and think pieces. No fiction or poetry. Length: 3,000-5,000 words. Pays $50 minimum. "Five contributor's copies are sent to author on publication of article." Book reviews should be sent to Rev. Steven Payne, O.C.D., Carmelite Monastery, 514 Warren St., Brookline MA 02146.

SPIRITUALITY TODAY, Aquinas Institute, 3642 Lindell Blvd., St. Louis MO 63108. Editor: the Rev. Christopher Kiesling O.P. 25% freelance written. "For those interested in a more knowing and intense Christian life in the 20th century." Buys first North American serial rights. Byline given. Pays on publication. Submit complete ms. Computer printout submissions acceptable; no dot-matrix. SASE. Publishes ms an average of 1 year after acceptance. Sample copy $1; free writer's guidelines.

Nonfiction: "Articles that seriously examine important truths pertinent to the spiritual life, or Christian life, in the context of today's world. Scriptural, biographical, doctrinal, liturgical and ecumenical articles are acceptable." Recent article example: "Christian Spirituality for the Single Parent" (Spring 1984). Buys 15 unsolicited mss/year. Length: 4,000 words. Pays 1¢/word.

Tips: "Examine the journal. It is not a typical magazine. Given its characteristics, the style of writing required is not the sort that regular freelance writers usually employ."

SUNDAY DIGEST, 850 N. Grove Ave., Elgin IL 60120. Editor: Judy C. Couchman. 75% freelance written. Issued weekly for Christian adults, mainly Protestants. *Sunday Digest* provides a weekly combination of original articles and reprints, selected to help adult readers better understand the Christian faith, to keep them informed of issues and happenings within the Christian community, and to challenge them to a deeper personal commitment to Christ. Buys first rights only. Pays on acceptance. Computer printout submissions acceptable; prefers letter-quality to dot-matrix. SASE. Reports in 6 weeks. Publishes ms an average of 1 year after acceptance. Free sample copy and writer's guidelines for 6½x9½ SAE and 2 first class stamps.

Nonfiction: Needs articles applying the Christian faith to personal and social problems, articles of family interest and on church subjects, personality profiles, inspirational self-help articles, personal experience articles and anecdotes. Query or submit complete ms. Length: 500-1,800 words. Pays 7¢/word minimum.

Fiction: Uses true-to-life fiction that is hard-hitting, fast-moving, with a real woven-in, not "tacked on", Christian message. Also publishes allegory, fantasy, satire, and other fiction types. Length: 1,000-1,500 words. Pays 7¢/word minimum.

Poetry: Would like uplifting free verse poetry.

Tips: "It is crucial that the writer is committed to high quality Christian communication."

‡**THIS PEOPLE MAGAZINE, The LDS People Magazine**, This People Publishing, Division of Strata Tek Corp., Suite 200, 5505 S. 900 E., Salt Lake City UT 84117. (801)263-3577. Editor: Sheri L. Dew. 75% freelance written. A bimonthly human interest magazine profiling members of the LDS (Mormon) church. "Editorial slant appeals to an educated, progressive, family-oriented audience and promotes family solidarity, self-improvement, and high moral values, spotlighting individuals whose lives exemplify said traits." Circ. 45,000. Pays on publication for first-time writers, on acceptance for veterans. Publishes ms an average of 6 months after acceptance. Byline given. Offers 40% kill fee. Buys first rights. Submit seasonal/holiday materi-

al 6-8 months in advance. Computer printout submissions acceptable; prefers letter-quality to dot-matrix. SASE. Reports in 6 weeks on queries; 2 months on mss. Sample copy for SAE and $1.37 postage; free writer's guidelines.

Nonfiction: Inspirational, interview/profile, personal experience, photo feature, travel. No articles that are not LDS-oriented or people-oriented. Buys 55 mss/year. Query with published clips. Length: 800-2,800 words. Pays $100-450.

Photos: State availability of photos. Reviews b&w contact sheets and 35mm color slides. Buys all rights for commissioned photos; one-time rights for freelance photos.

Columns/Departments: Buys 35 mss/year. Query with published clips. Length: 350-750 words. Pays $75-200.

Fiction: Buys 5 mss/year. Query with published clips. Length: 1,000-3,000 words. Pays $100-450.

Tips: "Contact editor with specific suggestions as to possible profile subjects. Be willing to write initially on speculation while adapting to editorial style. Editor is willing to work with writers. Writer must be observant, creative, and have good use of language. Must be willing to emphasize the positive. Slant is conservative."

TODAY'S CHRISTIAN PARENT, 8121 Hamilton Ave., Cincinnati OH 45231. (513)931-4050. Editor: Mrs. Mildred Mast. 70% freelance written. Quarterly. Rights purchased vary with author and material. Buys first North American serial rights and occasionally second (reprint) rights to material originally published elsewhere. Pays on acceptance. No simultaneous submissions. Computer printout submissions acceptable; prefers letter-quality to dot-matrix. SASE. Publishes ms an average of 1 year after acceptance. Free sample copy and writer's guidelines for 7x9 or larger SASE.

Nonfiction: Devotional, inspirational and informational articles for the family. Also articles concerning the problems and pleasures of parents, grandparents and the entire family; Christian childrearing. Timely articles on moral issues, ethical and social situations, in depth as much as possible in limited space. Length: 600-1,200 words. Can use short items on Christian family living; and fillers serious or humorous. Very little poetry. Study magazine before submitting. Pays up to 2½¢/word.

Tips: "Write about familiar family situations in a refreshingly different way, so that help and inspiration shine through the problems and pleasures of parenthood. Ms should be crisp, tightly-written. Avoid wordiness, trite situations or formats. Slant: from a Christian perspective."

THE UNITED BRETHREN, United Brethren in Christ denomination, 302 Lake St., Huntington IN 46750. (219)356-2312. Editor: Steve Dennie. 40% freelance written. Denominational monthly for conservative evangelical Christians, ages 16 and up. Circ. 5,000. Pays on acceptance. Publishes ms an average of 6 months after acceptance. Byline given. Buys one-time rights. Send complete ms. Submit seasonal/holiday material 6 months in advance. Simultaneous, photocopied and previously published submissions OK. Computer printout submissions acceptable; prefers letter-quality to dot-matrix. SASE. Reports in 2 months. Sample copy $2; free writer's guidelines for SAE and 1 first class stamp.

Nonfiction: General interest, how-to, humor, inspirational, personal experience. Must have religious slant. No purely secular pieces. Buys 36 mss/year. Length: 500-3,000 words. Pays 1½¢/word.

Photos: Bought normally accompanying ms. Send photos with ms. Buys one-time rights. Pays $5 maximum for 8x10 b&w glossy prints. No color.

Fiction: All types, but religious slant necessary. Length: 500-2,000 words. Buys 5 mss/year. Pays 1½¢/word.

Poetry: Traditional. Buys "three poems, preferably rhyming." Pays $2-15.

THE UNITED CHURCH OBSERVER, 85 St. Clair Ave. E., Toronto, Ontario M4T 1M8 Canada. (416)960-8500. Editor: Hugh McCullum. Managing Editor: Muriel Duncan. 35% freelance written. A 60-page newsmagazine for persons associated with the United Church of Canada. Monthly. Deals primarily with events, trends, and policies having religious significance. Most coverage is Canadian, but reports on international or world concerns will be considered. Buys first rights. Byline usually given. Publishes ms an average of 3 months after acceptance. Computer printout submissions acceptable.

Nonfiction: Occasional opinion features only. Extended coverage of major issues usually assigned to known writers. Submissions should be written as news, no more than 900 words length, accurate and well researched. Queries preferred. Pays by publication. Rates depend on subject, author, and work involved.

Photos: Buys photographs with mss. B&w should be 5x7 minimum; color 35mm or larger format. Payment varies.

Tips: "Include samples of previous *news* writing with query. Indicate ability and willingness to do research, and to evaluate that research. No opinion pieces, or poetry."

UNITED EVANGELICAL ACTION, Box 28, Wheaton IL 60189. (312)665-0500. Editor: Donald Brown. 25% freelance written. Offers "an objective evangelical viewpoint and interpretive analysis" of specific issues of consequence and concern to the American Church and updates readers on ways evangelicals are confronting those issues on the grass-roots level. Bimonthly magazine; alternating 16-20 pages. Circ. 7,600. Pays on publication. Publishes ms an average of 2 months after acceptance. Buys all rights. Phone queries OK. Computer printout submissions acceptable. SASE. Reports in 4 weeks. Free sample copy and writer's guidelines.

Nonfiction: Christopher Lutes, managing editor. Issues and trends in the Church and society that affect the on-going witness and outreach of evangelical Christians. Content should be well thought through, and should provide practical suggestions for dealing with these issues and trends. Buys 8-10 mss/year. Query. Length: 900-1,000 words. Pays 5-8¢/word.

Tips: Editors would really like to see news (action) items that relate to the National Association of Evangelicals. "Keep writing terse, to the point, and stress practical over theoretical."

UNITED METHODIST REPORTER/NATIONAL CHRISTIAN REPORTER, Box 221076, Dallas TX 75222. (214)630-6495. Editor/General Manager: Spurgeon M. Dunnam III. The *United Methodist Reporter* is for a United Methodist national readership and *National Christian Reporter* is for a nondenominational national readership. Weekly newspaper. Circ. 487,000. Pays on acceptance. Not copyrighted. Byline given. SASE. Free sample copy and writer's guidelines.

Nonfiction: "We welcome short features, approximately 500 words. Articles need not be limited to a United Methodist angle. Write about a distinctly Christian response to human need or how a person's faith relates to a given situation." Send complete ms. Pays 4¢/word.

Photos: Purchased with accompanying ms. "We encourage the submission of good action photos (5x7 or 8x10 b&w glossy prints) of the persons or situations in the article." Pays $10.

Poetry: "Poetry welcome on a religious theme; blank verse or rhyme." Length: 2-20 lines. Pays $2.

Fillers: Crossword, other puzzles on religious or Biblical themes. Pays $5.

UNITY MAGAZINE, Unity Village MO 64065. Editor: Pamela Yearsley. 90% freelance written. Publication of Unity School of Christianity. Magazine; 64 pages. Monthly. Circ. 430,000. Buys first serial rights. Buys 200 mss/year. Pays on acceptance. Publishes ms an average of 7 months after acceptance. Computer printout submissions acceptable; prefers letter-quality to dot-matrix. Submit seasonal material 6-8 months in advance. Reports in 1 month. Submit complete ms. SASE. Free sample copy and writer's guidelines.

Nonfiction and Photos: "Inspirational articles, metaphysical in nature, about individuals who are using Christian principles in their living." Personal experience and interview. "We specialize in religious, inspirational material—anything else is rejected out of hand." Length: 3,000 words maximum. Pays minimum of 2¢/word. 4x5 or 8x10 color transparencies purchased without mss. "We are using more color photography inside." Pays $75-100.

Poetry: Traditional forms, blank verse and free verse. Pays 50¢-$1/line.

Tips: "Be innovative and use new twists on old truths."

THE UPPER ROOM, DAILY DEVOTIONAL GUIDE, The Upper Room, 1908 Grand Ave., Nashville TN 37202. (615)327-2700. Managing Editor: Mary Lou Redding. 97% freelance written. Bimonthly magazine "offering a daily inspirational message which includes a Bible reading, text, prayer, and 'Thought for the Day.' Each day's meditation is written by a different person and is usually a personal witness about discovering meaning and power for Christian living through some experience from daily life." Circ. 2,225,000 (US) +; 385,000 outside US. Pays on publication. Byline given. Offers negotiable kill fee. Buys first North American serial rights and translation rights. Submit seasonal/holiday material 1 year in advance. Computer printout submissions acceptable; prefers letter-quality to dot-matrix. SASE. Reports in 3 weeks on queries; 6 months on mss. Publishes ms an average of 1 year after acceptance. Free sample copy and writer's guidelines.

Nonfiction: Inspirational and personal experience. No poetry, lengthy "spiritual journey" stories. Buys 360 unsolicited mss/year. Send complete ms. Length: 250 words maximum. Pays $10 minimum.

Columns/Departments: Prayer Workshop—"a 2-page feature which suggests some meditation or prayer exercise. For 1985, we will feature reflection/meditation exercises about the special days of the Christian year (Epiphany, Pentecost, Ascension, All Saints' Day, etc.)." Buys 6 mss/year. Query with clips of published work. Length: 400-600 words. Pays $50-100. "All quoted material used must be documented through standard footnote material for verification. Writer should obtain permission for use of previously copyrighted material which is quoted."

Tips: "The best way to break into our magazine is to send a well-written manuscript that looks at the Christian faith in a fresh way. Standard stories and sermon illustrations are immediately rejected. We very much want to find new writers and welcome good material. Daily meditations are most open. 'Prayer Workshops' are usually assigned. Good repeat meditations can lead to work on longer assignments for our other publications, which pay more. We encourage theological diversity and especially welcome faith-perspective approaches to current social problems and controversial issues within the Christian faith."

VIRTUE, Box 850, Sisters OR 97759. (503)549-8261. Editor: Lee Zanon. 70% freelance written. Bimonthly Christian magazine for women. Circ. 95,000. Average issue includes 15 feature articles. Pays on publication. Publishes ms an average of 4 months after acceptance. Byline given. Buys first rights. Submit seasonal material 6 months in advance. Simultaneous and previously published submissions OK, if so indicated. Computer printout submissions acceptable; prefers letter-quality to dot-matrix. SASE. Reports in 3 weeks on queries; in 6 weeks on ms. Sample copy $2. Free writer's guidelines.

Nonfiction: Interviews with Christian women; *current issues*; how-to (upkeep and organizational tips for home); inspirational (spiritual enrichment); personal experience; and family information for husbands, wives and children. "No mystical, preachy articles and no more housewife vs. career woman articles." Recent article example: "Menopause & Male Mid-Life Crisis" (feature). Buys 20 mss/issue. Query or send complete ms. Length: 1,000-1,500 words. Pays 5-7¢/word.

Photos: Reviews 3x5 b&w glossy prints. Offers additional payment for photos accepted with ms. Captions required. Buys all rights or first rights.

Columns/Departments: Opinion piece (reader editorial); foods (recipes and entertaining); and crafts, decorating, gardening, fitness, health, creative projects. Buys 4-8 mss/issue. Send complete ms. Length: 500-1,000 words. Pays 5¢/word.

Fiction: Christian adventure, humor, and romance. Buys 1 ms/issue. Send complete ms. Length: 1,000-1,500 words. Pays 5-7¢/word.

Fillers: Anecdotes, short humor, newsbreaks and thought-provoking family stories. Buys 2 mss/issue. Pays 5-7¢/word.

Tips: "We may be increasing our standard magazine size, and will be needing more well-researched articles on current issues."

VISTA, Wesleyan Publishing House, Box 2000, Marion IN 46952. Address submissions to Editor of *Vista*. 80% freelance written. Publication of The Wesleyan Church. For adults. Weekly. Circ. 60,000. Not copyrighted. "Along with mss for first use, we also accept simultaneous submissions, second rights, and reprint rights. It is the writer's obligation to secure clearance from the original publisher for any reprint rights." Pays on publication. Publishes ms an average of 6 months after acceptance. Byline given. Submit material 9 months in advance. Reports in 2 months. Computer printout submissions acceptable; prefers letter-quality to dot-matrix. "SASE for sample copy and with all manuscripts." Not responsible for unsolicited mss.

Nonfiction: Devotional, biographical, and informational articles with inspirational, religious, moral or educational values. Favorable toward emphasis on: "New Testament standard of living as applied to our day; soul-winning (evangelism); proper Sunday observance; Christian youth in action; Christian education in the home, the church and the college; good will to others; worldwide missions; clean living, high ideals, and temperance; wholesome social relationships. Disapprove of liquor, tobacco, theaters, dancing. Mss are judged on the basis of human interest, ability to hold reader's attention, vivid characterizations, thoughtful analysis of problems, vital character message, expressive English, correct punctuation, proper diction. Know where you are going and get there." Length: 500-1,500 words. Pays 2½¢/word for quality material.

Photos: Pays $15-40/5x7 or 8x10 b&w glossy print portraying people in action, seasonal emphasis, or scenic value. Various reader age-groups should be considered.

Fiction: Stories should have definite Christian emphasis and character-building values, without being preachy. Setting, plot and action should be realistic. Length: 1,500 words; also short-shorts and vignettes. Pays 2½¢/word for quality material.

WAR CRY, The Official Organ of the Salvation Army, 799 Bloomfield Ave., Verona NJ 07044. Editor: Henry Gariepy. Weekly magazine for "persons with evangelical Christian background; members and friends of the Salvation Army, the 'man in the street.' " Circ. 280,000. Buys first rights and second (reprint) rights to material originally published elsewhere. Pays on acceptance. SASE. Reports in 2 months. Free sample copy.

Nonfiction: Inspirational and informational articles with a strong evangelical Christian slant, but not preachy. In addition to general articles, needs articles slanted toward most of the holidays including Easter, Christmas, Mother's Day, Father's Day, etc. Buys 100 mss/year. Length: approximately 1,000-1,400 words. Pays 4¢/word.

Photos: Occasionally buys photos submitted with mss, but seldom with captions only. Pays $15-35 for b&w glossy prints.

Fiction: Prefers complete-in-one-issue stories, with a strong Christian slant. Can have modern or Biblical setting, but must not run contrary to Scriptural account. Length: 1,100-1,400 words. Pays 4¢/word.

Poetry: Religious or nature poems. Length: 4-24 lines. Pays $5-25.

THE WITTENBERG DOOR, 1224 Greenfield Dr., El Cajon CA 92021. (714)440-2333. Contact: Mike Yaconelli. Bimonthly magazine for men and women, usually connected with the church. Circ. 19,000. Pays on publication. Buys all rights. Computer printout submissions acceptable; prefers letter-quality to dot-matrix. SASE. Reports in 3 months. Free sample copy.

Nonfiction: Satirical or humorous articles on church renewal, Christianity, organized religion. Few book reviews. Buys about 30 mss/year. Query or submit complete ms. Length: 1,000 words maximum, 500-750 preferred. Pays $25-100.

Tips: "We look for someone who is clever, on our wave length and has some savvy about the evangelical church. We are very picky and highly selective."

WORLD ENCOUNTER, 2900 Queen Lane, Philadelphia PA 19129. (215)438-6360. Editor: James Solheim. For persons who have more than average interest in, and understanding of, overseas missions and current human social concerns in other parts of the world. Quarterly magazine; 32 pages. Circ. 6,000. Buys all rights. Pays 35% kill fee. Byline given. Buys 10 mss/year. Pays on publication. Publishes ms an average of 3 months after acceptance. Sample copy $1. Photocopied, and simultaneous submissions OK, if information is supplied on other markets being approached. Computer printout submissions acceptable; no dot-matrix. Reports in 1 month. Query or submit complete ms. SASE.

Nonfiction and Photos: "This is a religious and educational publication using human interest features and think pieces related to the Christian world mission and world community. Race relations in southern Africa; human rights struggles with tyrannical regimes; social and political ferment in Latin America; resurgence of Eastern religions. Simple travelogues are not useful to us. Prospective writers should inquire as to the countries and topics of particular interest to our constituents. Material must be written in a popular style but the content must be more than superficial. It must be theologically, sociologically and anthropologically sound. We try to maintain a balance between gospel proclamation and concern for human and social development. We focus on what is happening in Lutheran groups. Our standards of content quality and writing are very high." No religious editorializing or moralizing. Length: 500-1,800 words. Pays $50-200. B&w photos are purchased with or without accompanying mss or on assignment. Pays $10-25. Captions required.

Tips: "Write the editor, outlining your background and areas of international knowledge and interest, asking at what points they converge with our magazine's interests. In our field writers should be aware of a radically different understanding of Christian missions in the Third World."

Retirement

These publications give people of retirement age specialized information. Some want service articles; others want material that helps readers see the advantages of more free time.

DYNAMIC YEARS, 215 Long Beach Blvd., Long Beach CA 90802. Executive Editor: Lorena F. Farrell. 90% freelance written. "*Dynamic Years* is an official publication of the American Association of Retired Persons emphasizing stories relating to the interests of midlife (ages 45-65) career people." Bimonthly. Circ. 200,000. Buys first-use or first North American rights. Pays negotiable kill fee. Byline given. Pays on acceptance. Submit seasonal material 6 months in advance. Reports in 2 months. Query or submit complete ms. "Submit only 1 ms at a time." SASE. Free sample copy.

Nonfiction: General subject matter is "financial planning/investment, lifestyle, preretirement planning, health/fitness, humor, the world of work and job-related pieces, second careers, personal adjustment, sports, fashion/beauty, entertaining, generational relationships, 'people in action' with unusual activities, exciting uses of leisure, and travel. No pieces about individuals long retired; no quizzes, poetry, jokes or inspirational preachments. Primary concern is superb writing style, depth and accuracy of information." Buys 100 mss/year. Length: 1,000-3,000 words. Pays $150 for items, $350 minimum for short pieces, $800-2,000 for full-length features.

Photos: State availability of photos with ms. Captions required. Pays $75 minimum for professional quality b&w. Pays $150 minimum for professional quality color slides or transparencies.

50 PLUS, 850 3rd Ave., New York NY 10022. Editor: Bard Lindeman. Managing Editor: Mark Reiter. "Current demands upon our editorial staff prohibit the reviewing of material that has not been assigned." No unsolicited mss, photographs or query letters.

MATURE LIVING, The Sunday School Board of the Southern Baptist Convention, 127 9th Ave. N., Nashville TN 37234. (615)251-2274. Editor: Jack Gulledge. Assistant Editor: Zada Malugen. 80% freelance written. A Christian magazine for retired senior adults 60+. Monthly magazine; 52 pages. Pays on acceptance. Publishes ms an average of 15 months after acceptance. Buys all rights. Byline given. Submit seasonal/holiday material at least 12-15 months in advance. Computer printout submissions acceptable. SASE. Reports in 6 weeks. Free sample copy and writer's guidelines.

Nonfiction: How-to (easy, inexpensive craft articles made from easily obtained materials); informational (safety, consumer fraud, labor-saving and money-saving for senior adults); inspirational (short paragraphs with subject matter appealing to older persons); nostalgia; unique personal experiences; and travel. Buys 7-8 mss/issue. Send complete ms. Length: 450-1,550 words; prefers articles of 925 words. Pays $14-49.

Photos: Some original photos purchased with accompanying ms. Pays about $5-15 for b&w glossy prints, depending on size. Model release required.

Fiction: Everyday living, humor and religious. "Must have suspense and character interaction." Buys 1 ms/issue. Send complete ms. Length: 925-1,550 words. Pays 4¢/word.

Fillers: Short humor, religious or grandparent/grandchild episodes. Length: 125 words maximum. Pays $5.
Tips: "We want warm, creative, unique manuscripts. Presentations don't have to be moralistic or religious, but must reflect Christian standards. Don't write *down* to target audience. Speak *to* senior adults on issues that interest them. They like contemporary, good-Samaritan, and nostalgia articles. We buy some light humor. We use 140-word profiles of interesting, unusual, senior adults worthy of recognition, when accompanied by a quality action b/w photo. Pays $25. Query should emphasize the uniqueness of proposed copy."

MATURE YEARS, 201 8th Ave., S., Nashville TN 37202. Editor: Daisy D. Warren. 15% freelance written. For retired persons and those facing retirement; persons seeking help on how to handle problems and privileges of retirement. Quarterly. Rights purchased vary with author and material; usually buys all rights. Buys 24 unsolicited mss/year. Pays on acceptance. Publishes ms an average of 3 months after acceptance. Submit seasonal material 14 months in advance. Computer printout submissions acceptable; no dot-matrix. Reports in 6 weeks. Submit complete ms. SASE. Free writer's guidelines.
Nonfiction: "*Mature Years* is different from the secular press in that we like material with Christian and church orientation. Usually we prefer materials that have a happy, healthy outlook regarding aging. Advocacy (for older adults) articles are at times used; some are freelance submissions. Articles dealing with many aspects of pre-retirement and retirement living. Short stories and leisure-time hobbies related to specific seasons. Give examples of how older persons, organizations, and institutions are helping others. Writing should be of interest to older adults, with Christian emphasis, though not preachy and moralizing. No poking fun or mushy, sentimental articles. We treat retirement from the religious viewpoint. How-to, humor and travel also considered." Length: 1,200-2,000 words.
Photos: 8x10 b&w glossy prints purchased with ms or on assignment.
Fiction: "We buy fiction for adults. Humor is preferred. Please, no children's stories and no stories about depressed situations of older adults." Length: 1,000-2,000 words. Payment varies, usually 4¢/word.
Tips: "The most rewarding aspect of working with freelance writers is getting articles on unusual topics."

MODERN MATURITY, American Association of Retired Persons, 215 Long Beach Blvd., Long Beach CA 90801. Editor-in-Chief: Ian Ledgerwood. 75% freelance written. For readership over 50 years of age. Bi-monthly magazine. Circ. 9.5 million. Pays on acceptance. Buys all rights. Byline given. Submit seasonal/holiday material 6 months in advance. SASE. Reports in 4 weeks. Free sample copy and writer's guidelines.
Nonfiction: Historical, how-to, humor, informational, inspirational, interview, new product, nostalgia, personal experience, opinion, photo feature, profile and travel. Query or send complete ms. Length: 1,000-2,500 words. Pays $1,000-3,000.
Photos: Photos purchased with or without accompanying ms. Pays $150 and up for color and $75 and up for b&w.
Poetry: All types. Length: 40 lines maximum. Pays $75.
Fillers: Clippings, jokes, gags, anecdotes, newsbreaks, puzzles (find-the-word, not crossword) and short humor. Pays $25 minimum.

NEW ENGLAND SENIOR CITIZEN/SENIOR AMERICAN NEWS, Prime National Publishing Corp., 470 Boston Post Rd., Weston MA 02193. Editor-in-Chief: Ira Alterman. 80% freelance written. For men and women aged 60 and over who are interested in travel, finances, retirement lifestyles, special legislation, nostalgia, etc. Monthly newspaper; 24-32 pages. Circ. 60,000. Pays on publication. Publishes ms an average of 9 months after acceptance. Buys all rights. Byline given. Submit seasonal/holiday material 3 months in advance. Previously published material OK. Computer printout submissions acceptable. SASE. Reports in 4 months. Sample copy 50¢.
Nonfiction: General interest; how-to (anything dealing with retirement years); inspirational; historical; humor; interview; nostalgia; profile; travel; personal experience; photo features; and articles about medicine relating to gerontology. Buys 10-15 mss/issue. Submit complete ms. Length: 500-1,500 words. Pays $25-50.
Photos: Purchased with ms. Captions required. Pays $5-15/5x7 or 8x10 b&w glossy print. Captions and model releases required.
Fiction: Adventure, historical, humorous, mystery, romance, suspense and religious. Buys 1 ms/issue. Submit complete ms. Length: 500-1,500 words. Pays $25-50.
Tips: "Submit clean, typed, top-quality copy aimed at older tastes, interests, lifestyles and memories."

‡**NEW HORIZONS**, Eastern Nebraska Office on Aging, 885 S. 72nd St., Omaha NE 68114. (402)444-6654. Editor: Andy Bradley. A monthly tabloid covering aging. Circ. 30,000. Pays on acceptance. Byline given. Not copyrighted. Buys one-time rights and second serial (reprint) rights. Submit seasonal/holiday material 60 days in advance. Simultaneous queries, and simultaneous, photocopied, and previously published submissions OK. SASE. Reports in 1 month. Free sample copy.
Nonfiction: Historical/nostalgic (20th Century); how-to (consumer guides for the aged); and new product (if senior citizen related). Special issues include corporate ownership of nursing homes; merchants providing discounts to seniors; divorce and the elderly; summer travel; and consumer guide to retirement homes. No person-

ality profiles or fashion. Send complete ms. Length: 500-2,500 words. Pays $25-50.

Photos: State availability of photos. Pays $5-15 for 5x7 b&w glossy prints. Captions required. Buys one-time rights.

Columns/Departments: Nutrition, Consumer Watchdog, Blindness, Employment, Volunteerism, Mental Health, Physical Health. Send complete ms. Length: 300-1,500 words. Pays $15-35.

Tips: Freelancer can best break in with "well-written nonfiction that can improve the quality of life for our readers, average age is 73. Please, no stories about 'My favorite person—My Grandmother' or 'Gee WOW, look at Grandma on her skateboard!' Health, consumer affairs, mental well-being areas are most open to free-lancers. There is a trend in senior publications to view the aging person as a fully competent, participating member of society—not to be written down to, patronized, made light of or otherwise dismissed."

PRIME TIMES, Grote Deutsch & Co., 2802 International Lane, Madison WI 53704. Executive Director: Steve Goldberg. Managing Editor: Glenn Deutsch. Associate Editor: Ana María M. Guzmán. 90% freelance written. Quarterly magazine for people who want to redefine retirement. The audience is primarily people over 50 who were or are credit union members and want to plan and manage their retirement. Circ. 75,000. Buys first rights (pays upon acceptance) and second serial (reprint) rights (pays upon publication). Submit seasonal material 6 months in advance. Previously published submissions OK as long as they were not in another national maturity-market magazine. Computer printout submissions acceptable; no dot-matrix. SASE. Reports in 1 month. Publishes ms an average of 4 months after acceptance. Free sample copy only with 9x12 SAE and 5 first-class stamps; free writer's guidelines for SASE. No exceptions.

Nonfiction: Expose and how-to (related to financial planning methods, consumer activism, health, travel, and working after retirement); interview (of people over 50 who are leading active or important retirements); opinion; profile; travel; popular arts; self-image; personal experience; and photo feature. "No rocking chair reminiscing." Buys 30-40 mss/year "of which 4-10 are from new talent. This, from well over 3,500 submissions a year." Query with clips of previously published work. Length: 500-2,500 words. Pays $50-500. SASE. "Be sure to keep a photocopy—just in case gremlins pinch the original."

Photos: Pays $25-50/8x10 b&w glossy high-contrast prints; $25-50/35mm color transparency or according to ASMP guidelines or negotiation. $7.50/cutline. Captions and model release required. Buys one-time rights. Will not reproduce color prints. SASE. "Do not send irreplaceable *anything*."

Tips: "Query should state qualifications (such as expertise or society memberships). Freelancers should submit copy—double-spaced and typed 60 characters/line with SASE. They should also send photos, copies of photos, or other art accompanying the articles with SASE. Special issues requiring freelance work include publications on mature friendship; comparative aging (cross-cultural); second careers; money management; minorities over 50; continuing education; and the young-old *vis-à-vis* the old-old. Whether urban or rural, male or female, if attempts at humor, lightness or tongue-in-cheek seem off-target to you, they will to us, too. And we don't gloss over important matters. If you identify a problem, try to identify a solution. Every word counts. And remember that there are at least two generations reading *Prime Times*—folks over 50, and folks over 70. Most are not retired (average age: 61) and about 55% of our readers are women."

SENIOR WORLD OF SAN DIEGO/SENIOR WORLD OF SANTA BARBARA, Californian Publishing Co., Box 1565, El Cajon CA 92022. (619)442-4404. Editor: Laura Impastato. Travel Editor: Leonard J. Hansen. 10% freelance written. Monthly tabloid newspaper for active older adults living in San Diego and Santa Barbara counties. Circ. 103,000 in San Diego; 17,000 in Santa Barbara. Pays on publication. Publishes ms an average of 4 months after acceptance. Buys all rights. Simultaneous and photocopied submissions OK. Computer printout submissions acceptable; no dot-matrix. SASE. Reports in 2 months. Sample copy $2; free writer's guidelines.

Nonfiction: "We are looking for stories on health stressing wellness and prevention; travel—international, domestic and how-to; profiles of senior celebrities and remarkable seniors; finance and investment tips for seniors; interesting hobbies; some food and cooking material geared to older persons." Send query or complete ms. Length: 200-1,000 words. Pays $25-75.

Photos: State availability of photos. Need b&w with model release. Will pay extra for photos. Buys all rights to photos selected to run with a story.

Columns/Departments: Most of our columns are local or staff-written. We will consider a query on a column idea accompanied by a sample column.

Tips: "No 'pity the poor seniors' material. Our readers are active, vital adults 55 years of age and older. *Senior World* coverage encompasses everything from Washington D.C. news to travel, lifestyle, health, remarkable seniors, celebrities and hobbies. No nostalgia about how grandma used to do things." No telephone queries.

Romance and Confession

More than "daytime drama" fans read today's romances and confession stories. Listed here are publications that need these stories and publications that help writers write better romances. Also to help you write better romances is Writer's Digest Books' *Writing Romance Fiction—For Love and Money*, by Helene Schellenberg Barnhart.

AFFAIRE DE COEUR, Leading Publication for Romance Readers and Writers, Affaire de Coeur, Inc., 5660 Roosevelt Place, Fremont CA 94538. (415)656-4804. Editor/Publisher: Barbara N. Keenan. Monthly magazine for romance readers and writers. Circ. 5,000. Pays on publication. Byline given. Buys all rights. Submit seasonal/holiday material 3-4 months in advance. Simultaneous queries; and photocopied and previously published submissions OK. SASE. Reports in 3 weeks. Sample copy $2; writer's guidelines for SAE and $5 postage and handling.
Nonfiction: Book excerpts (on romantic fiction); how-to (write romantic fiction); interview/profile (on romance authors). Nothing that doesn't pertain to romantic fiction. Buys 12 mss/year. Query. Length: varies. Pays $10-25.
Columns/Departments: Beth Rowe, Lovelore editor.
Fiction: Jane Bonander, senior editor. Novel excerpts, romance, serialized novels. Buys variable number mss/year. Query. Length: 1,000-1,500 words. Pays $25-50.
Fillers: Beth Rowe, fillers editor. Newsbreaks. Buys 50/year. Length: varies. Pays with credit line.

MODERN ROMANCES, Macfadden Women's Group, Inc., 215 Lexington Ave., New York NY 10016. Editor: Jean Sharbel. 100% freelance written. For blue-collar, family-oriented women, 18-35 years old. Monthly magazine; 88 pages. Circ. 200,000. Pays the last week of the month of the issue. Buys all rights. Submit seasonal/holiday material 6 months in advance. SASE. Reports in 12-16 weeks.
Nonfiction: General interest; baby and child care; how-to (homemaking subjects); humor; inspirational; and personal experience. Submit complete ms. Length: 200-1,500 words. Pay depends on merit. "Confession stories with reader identification and a strong emotional tone. No third person material." Buys 14 mss/issue. Submit complete ms. Length: 1,500-8,500 words. Pays 5¢/word.
Poetry: "Light, romantic poetry, to 24 lines." Buys 36/year. Pay "depends on merit."

‡THE ROMANTIC BOOK GUIDE, Reviews of Romance Books, R&B Creative Enterprises, Manchester Mall 811, Main St., Box 10, Manchester CT 06040. (203)647-9613. Editor: Bea Sheftel. Quarterly magazine covering romantic novels and contemporary-historical industry news. "We use a positive non-critical approach, reviewing past and present romance books." Estab. 1983. Circ. 2,000+. Pays on publication. Byline given. "Authors are paid only for accepted work." Buys one-time rights. Submit seasonal/holiday material 2 months in advance. Simultaneous queries OK. Computer printout submissions acceptable. SASE. Reports in 1 month. Sample copy for $2; writer's guidelines for business-size SAE.
Nonfiction: Book excerpts; inspirational (how I became a published romance novelist); "in-depth" interview/profile (on romance novelists or editors in field); personal experience (in the romance novel field); photo feature (camera-ready workshops, conferences, etc., in romance field); and travel (backgrounds used in romance novels). Special issues include a once-a-year souvenir edition (handed out at conferences). Nothing not related to romantic fiction. Buys 4-12 mss/year. Query. Length: 150-1,000 words. Pays 2¢ a word minimum. Payment varies according to type of article.
Photos: Robert Sheftel, photo editor. Send screened, camera-ready prints only with query. Pays $5 minimum for b&w prints no larger than 5x7. Captions and identification of subjects required. Buys one-time rights.
Columns/Departments: "The Open Door" (how to become a professional writer). "We are constantly improving, changing and growing and may add more types of items during the year."
Poetry: Free verse and traditional on romantic themes only (male-female idealized love). No erotica or nothing other than romantic poetry. Buys 3+ poems/year. Submit maximum 2 poems. Length: 35 lines maximum.
Tips: "We will do all we can to help freelancers submitting queries or suitable material to us. However, a letter asking 'tell me all you know about romantic writing' will get nowhere. We don't have the time. Read our magazines and be specific."

ROMANTIC TIMES, The Complete Newspaper for Readers of Romantic Fiction, Romantic Times, Inc., Suite 1234, 163 Joralemon St., Brooklyn Heights NY 11201. (212)875-5019. Managing Editor: Kathryn Falk. Bimonthly newspaper covering romantic fiction for readers and writers of romantic novels. Circ. 60,000. Pays on publication. Byline given. Pays $20 kill fee. Rights purchased vary. Submit seasonal/holiday material 6 months in advance. Simultaneous queries, and simultaneous, photocopied, and previously published submissions OK. SASE. Reports in 3 weeks. Sample copy $1.

Nonfiction: Book excerpts; historical/nostalgic (pertaining to historical novels); how-to (write romantic novels); interview/profile (with romance writers); and personal experience (How I Write Romantic Novels). "Submit an interesting, revealing interview with a long-time reader of those novels, explaining his enjoyment and recommendations. An interview with a famous author, present or past, would be most welcomed." Special issues include: Regency Issue and Romantic Suspense Issue. Buys "at least 12" mss/year. Query. Length: 1,000-2,500 words. Pays $50.
Fiction: Needs "short-stories, novels and serials for the historical, contemporary, regency and romantic suspense genres." Pays $50-200.
Photos: "We need photos of writers at work or at home." State availability of photos. Pays $10 for b&w prints. Captions, model release, and identification of subjects required. Buys one-time rights.
Columns/Departments: Book reviews, gossip and historical tidbits. Query. Length: 500-1,000 words. Pays $20-30.
Tips: "The best freelancer would be one who reads or writes romantic fiction, and has a feel for what the average romantic novel fan would like to read in a newspaper devoted to this subject. We like to see in-depth, but not academic-sounding, articles on the genre of romantic fiction."

‡**TELLER PUBLICATION**, Box 5480, Springfield VA 22150. (703)922-8562. Managing Editor: Robert Teller. 75% freelance written. Monthly publication in book form covering all categories of romance and mystery stories for a general audience. Estab. 1983. Circ. 1,000,000 estimated. Pays on acceptance or publication. Publishes ms an average of 4 months after acceptance. Buys variable rights. Computer printout submissions acceptable. Reports in 2 months.
Fiction: Linda Lee, fiction editor. "We will later be needing fiction mss in adventure, historical and other fictional realms." Send complete ms or first few chapters and outline. Length: average 25,000-30,000 words. Pays variable rates. "We pay top dollar for good work."

‡**TORCH AND TORCHLIGHT ROMANCES**, Quest Publications, 8353A Greensboro Dr., McLean VA 22102. (703)734-5700. Editor: Elizabeth Brandon-Brown. 80% freelance written. Two monthly romantic lifestyle magazines featuring articles and "provocative, contemporary romance novels." Estab. 1983. Circ. 150,000. Pays royalty on novels or buys outright; pays on acceptance for articles. Publishes ms an average of 3 months after acceptance. Byline given. Buys one-time rights for novels or buys outright; all rights for articles. Submit seasonal/holiday material 5 months in advance. Photocopied submissions OK. Computer printout submissions acceptable; prefers letter-quality to dot-matrix. SASE. Reports in 6 weeks on queries; 2 months on mss. Sample copy $1.75; writer's guidelines for SASE.
Nonfiction: How-to (relationships, self-improvement); diet, fitness, fashion, decorating, beauty, travel. Buys 50 mss/year. Query with published clips. Length: 600-1,500 words. Pays $75-150.
Fiction: "Novels that revolve around the developing relationship between a hero and heroine. Stories should contain a strong, well-plotted romance that results in a permanent commitment based on love and marriage. Tension, excitement and adventure are the watchwords. Stores should have an American setting or an exotic one as long as it doesn't overshadow the romance. Heroines should be mature, spirited, sensitive women between 24 and 36 who have a strong sense of identity. Their counterparts should be thoroughly modern men that any woman could imagine falling in love with." Write for detailed guidelines describing the treatment of sex, detail, and observation vital to the novel. Buys 24 mss/year. Query with first 3 chapters and an outline or send complete ms. Length: 54,000-56,000 words. Buys ms outright or pays royalty and advances.

TRUE CONFESSIONS, Macfadden Women's Group, 215 Lexington Ave., New York NY 10016. Editor: Barbara J. Brett. 90% freelance written. For high-school-educated, blue-collar women, teens through maturity. Monthly magazine. Circ. 250,000. Buys all rights. Byline given on poetry and some articles. Pays during the last week of month of issue. Publishes ms an average of 6 months after acceptance. Submit seasonal material 6 months in advance. Reports in 4 months. Submit complete ms. SASE.
Stories, Articles, and Fillers: Timely, exciting, emotional first-person stories on the problems that face today's young women. The narrators should be sympathetic, and the situations they find themselves in should be intriguing, yet realistic. Every story should have a strong romantic interest and a high moral tone, and every plot should reach an exciting climax. Careful study of a current issue is suggested. Length: 2,000-6,000 words; 5,000 word stories preferred; also book lengths of 8,000-10,000 words. Pays 5¢/word. Also, articles and short fillers.
Poetry: Romantic poetry, free verse and traditional, of interest to women. Submit maximum 4 poems. Length: 16 lines maximum. Pays $10 minimum.

TRUE LOVE, Macfadden Women's Group, 215 Lexington Ave., New York NY 10016. (212)340-7500. Editor: Marte Mestrovic. For young, blue-collar women. Monthly magazine; 80 pages. Circ. 225,000. Buys all rights. Byline given for nonfiction. Buys about 150 mss/year. Pays after publication. Submit seasonal material at least 6 months in advance. Reports in 2 months. Submit complete ms. SASE.
Nonfiction: Confessions, true love stories (especially young romance); problems and solutions; health prob-

lems; marital and child-rearing difficulties. Avoid graphic sex. Stories dealing with reality, current problems, everyday events, with emphasis on emotional impact. Length: 1,500-8,000 words. Pays 3¢/word. Informational and how-to articles. Length: 250-800 words. Pays 5¢/word minimum.
Tips: "The story must appeal to the average blue collar woman. It must deal with her problems and interests. Characters—especially the narrator—must be sympathetic."

TRUE STORY, Macfadden Women's Group, 215 Lexington Ave., New York NY 10016. Editor: Helen Vincent. 80% freelance written. For young married, blue-collar women, 20-35; high school education; increasingly broad interests; home-oriented, but looking beyond the home for personal fulfillment. Monthly magazine. Circ. 1,700,000. Buys all rights. Byline given "on articles only." Buys about 125 full-length mss/year. Pays on publication. Submit seasonal material 4 months in advance. Make notation on envelope that it is seasonal material. Query for fact articles. Submit only complete mss for stories. Reports in 3-4 months. SASE.
Fiction: "First-person stories covering all aspects of women's interests: love, marriage, family life, careers, social problems, etc. The best direction a new writer can be given is to carefully study several issues of the magazine; then submit a fresh, exciting, well-written true story. We have no taboos. It's the handling and believability that make the difference between a rejection and an acceptance." Length: 1,500-10,000 words. Pays 5¢/word; $150 minimum.
Nonfiction: Pays a flat rate for columns or departments, as announced in the magazine.
Photos: Gus Gazzola, art director. Query about all possible photo submissions.

Science

Publications here are edited for laymen interested in technical and scientific developments and discoveries, applied science, and technical or scientific hobbies. Publications of interest to the personal computer owner/user are listed in the Personal Computing category. Journals for scientists, engineers, repairmen, etc., are found in Trade Journals.

ALTERNATIVE SOURCES OF ENERGY MAGAZINE, 107 S. Central Ave., Milaca MN 56353. Executive Editor: Donald Marier. 10% freelance written. Emphasizes alternative energy sources and the exploration and innovative use of renewable energy sources. Audience is predominantly male, age 36, college educated and concerned about energy and environmental limitations. Bimonthly magazine. Circ. 23,000. Pays on acceptance. Buys first rights. Phone queries OK. Simultaneous, photocopied, and previously published submissions OK, "if specified at time of submission." SASE. Reports in 6 weeks. Sample copy $4.25.
Nonfiction: Larry Stoiaken, editor. How-to (plans, kits); informational (new sources of data, products); interview (any active person in field); and technical (plans, kits, designs). "We're especially interested in wind and hydro-power stories. A story (with photo support) detailing installation of low-head hydro or wind-generator with follow-up on the energy produced is higher on our readership survey than most topics." Submit an outline before complete ms. Buys 10-15 unsolicited mss/year. Recent article example: "Build Your Own Solar Electric Panel" (issue No. 53). Length: 500-3,000 words. Pays 5¢/word.
Photos: Pays $7.50, prefers b&w.
Tips: "We need well-researched articles emphasizing the practical application of alternative sources of energy: solar, water, wind, biofuels, etc. Always include addresses of all products and/or publications listed. Stay away from philosophical underpinnings; stick to how-to-do-it or rules of thumb."

‡BIOSCIENCE, American Institute of Biological Sciences, 1401 Wilson Blvd., Arlington VA 22209. (703)527-6776. Editor: Ellen Chu. Managing Editor: Penny Allen. A monthly magazine covering biology as well as science and environmental policy. "*BioScience* is written for professional biologists. It goes to them, their professional societies, and to libraries. Although most of the magazine consists of scientific papers, the "Features and News" section accepts freelance news and feature stories on revelant topics, ranging from reviews of current biological research to analyses of controversial science policy issues." Circ. 12,000. Pays on publication. Byline given. Offers 33% kill fee. Buys all rights. Submit seasonal/holiday material 3 months in advance. Simultaneous queries OK. Computer printout submissions acceptable. SASE. Reports in 1 month. Free sample copy.
Nonfiction: Laura Tangley, features and news editor. Interview/profile, photo feature (mostly b&w) and technical. "We accept stories *only* related somehow to biologists, biological research, or science and environmental policy." Buys 12 mss/year. Query with published clips. Length: 1,000-4,500 words. Pays $200/*BioScience* page.
Photos: State availability of photos. Captions required. Payment included in page rate.
Tips: "*BioScience* has only recently begun accepting freelance work, so good ideas that are also well written

have a good chance of being published. Ideas should be timely—something that is news, or at least unfamiliar, to most biologists. Stories about research have a better chance of acceptance because we follow policy closely here. Presently the *Feature-News* section is the *only* one open to freelancers . . . reading through past issues of *BioScience* in the library would give writers a good idea of what we are interested in and what we've already covered.''

CQ: THE RADIO AMATEUR'S JOURNAL, 76 N. Broadway, Hicksville NY 11801. (516)681-2922. Editor: Alan Dorhoffer. 50% freelance written. For the amateur radio community. Monthly journal. Circ. 100,000. Pays on publication. Buys first rights. Phone queries OK. Submit seasonal/holiday material 3 months in advance. Computer printout submissions acceptable. SASE. Reports in 2-3 weeks. Publishes ms an average of 1 year after acceptance. Free sample copy.
Nonfiction: "We are interested in articles that address all technical levels of amateur radio. Included would be basic material for newcomers and intermediate and advanced material for oldtimers. Articles may be of a theoretical, practical or anecdotal nature. They can be general interest pieces for all amateurs or they can focus in on specific topics. We would like historical articles, material on new developments, articles on projects you can do in a weekend, and pieces on long-range projects taking a month or so to complete." Length: 6-10 typewritten pages. Pays $35/published page.

‡**EQUILIBRIUM, The Science of All Sciences**, Agnostic Publishing Co., Box 162, Golden CO 80402. (303)231-6293. Editor: Gary A. Eagle. A magazine published in series written for "the average intelligent individual." Estab. 1983. Pays on acceptance or publication. Byline given. Offers 50% kill fee; varies for ghosts. Buys all rights. Computer printout submissions acceptable; no dot-matrix. Simultaneous queries, and simultaneous, photocopied, and previously published submissions OK. SASE. Reports in 1 month on queries; 6 weeks on mss. Sample copy for $3, 9x12 SAE, and 3 first class stamps; writer's guidelines for business-size SAE, and 1 first class stamp.
Nonfiction: Historical/nostalgic (history repeats itself); how-to (physics, psychology, political science, medical, evolution, economics, philosophical, religion); photo feature (any photo to show balance of something, with article or without); and technical. All should have equilibrium slant. Inquire about special issues. Modern events not accepted. No profanity, direct defamation or anything not of the common interest. "Much of our literature is controversial." Buys 20 mss/year. Query. Length: 50-1,000 words; more than 1,000 words if article series. Pays $50-500.
Photos: State availability or send photos with query or ms. Pays $20-40 for 1" b&w and color slides, and b&w and color prints. Captions required.
Columns/Departments: Especially wants editorials; must speak favorably for equilibrium theory. Length: 250 words. Pays $50-100.
Poetry: Light verse, traditional. "None will be accepted if not dealing with the balance of the universe." Submit maximum 10 poems. Length: 5-20 lines. Pays $10-50.
Fillers: Clippings, jokes, gags, short humor, cartoons. Buys 20/year. Length: 5-20 words. Pays $10-50.
Tips: "Article should be written simply even if you are a professional. State the structure in query." Encourages new writers. "We read everything that comes in. Though our program has been geared toward the philosophical, we are receptive to a variety of subjects . . . our needs are flexible." First-, second- *and* third-person approach OK; controversial material acceptable.

‡**MODERN ELECTRONICS, For electronics and computer enthusiasts**, Modern Electronics Publishing Co., 15 Range Dr., Merrick NY 11566. (516)378-4960. A monthly magazine covering consumer electronics, personal computers, electronic circuitry and technology for readers with a technical affinity. Estab. 1984. Circ. 105,000. Pays on acceptance. Byline given. Offers 25-50% kill fee. Buys first North American serial rights; and makes work-for-hire assignments. Submit seasonal/holiday material minimum 4 months in advance. Computer printout submissions acceptable. SASE. Reports in 1 week on queries; 3 weeks on mss. Writer's guidelines for business-size SAE, and 1 first class stamp.
Nonfiction: General interest (new technology, product buying guides); how-to (construction projects, applications); new product (reviews); opinion (experiences with electronic and computer products); technical (features and tutorials: circuits, applications); and stereo, video, communications equipment. "Articles must be technically accurate. Writing should be 'loose,' not textbookish." No long computer programs. Buys 75 mss/year. Query. Length: 500-4,000 words. Pays $100-150/published page.
Photos: Send photos with query or ms. Reviews color transparencies and 5x7 b&w prints. Captions, model release and identification of subjects required. Buys variable rights depending on mss.
Tips: "Writer must have technical or applications acumen; well-researched material. Articles should reflect latest products and technology. Sharp, interesting photos are helpful."

OMNI, 1965 Broadway, New York NY 10023-5965. Executive Editor: Gurney Williams, III. Monthly magazine of the future covering science fact, fiction, and fantasy for readers of all ages, backgrounds and interests. Circ. 850,000. Average issue includes 3-4 nonfiction feature articles and 1-2 fiction articles; also numerous columns and 2 pictorials. Pays on acceptance. Offers 25% kill fee. Buys exclusive worldwide and first English rights and rights for *Omni* Anthology. Submit seasonal material 4-6 months in advance. Photocopied submissions OK. Computer printout submissions acceptable; prefers letter-quality to dot-matrix. SASE. Reports in 6 weeks. Free writer's guidelines with SASE (request fiction or nonfiction).

Nonfiction: "Articles with a futuristic angle, offering readers alternatives in housing, energy, transportation, medicine and communications. Scientists can affect the public's perception of science and scientists by opening their minds to the new possibilities of science journalism. People want to know, want to understand what scientists are doing and how scientific research is affecting their lives and their future. *Omni* publishes articles about science in language that people can understand. We seek very knowledgeable science writers who are ready to work with scientists to produce articles that can inform and interest the general reader." Send query/proposal. Length: 2,500-3,500 words. Pays $1,500-1,750.

Photos: Frank DeVino, graphic director. State availability of photos. Reviews 35mm slides and 4x5 transparencies.

Columns/Departments: Explorations (unusual travel or locations on Earth); Breakthroughs (new products); Mind (by and about psychiatrists and psychologists); Earth (environment); Life (biomedicine); Space (technology); Arts (theatre, music, film, technology); Interview (of prominent person); Continuum (newsbreaks); Antimatter and UFO Update (unusual newsbreaks, paranormal); Stars (astronomy); First/Last Word (editorial/humor); Artificial Intelligence (computers); The Body (medical). Query with clips of previously published work. Length: 1,500 words maximum. Pays $750-850; $150 for Continuum and Antimatter items.

Fiction: Contact: Ellen Datlow. Fantasy and science fiction. Buys 3 mss/issue. Send complete ms. Length: 10,000 words maximum. Pays $1,250-2,000.

Tips: "Consider science fact and science fiction pictorials with a futuristic leaning. We're interested in thematic composites of excellent photos or art with exciting copy."

POPULAR MECHANICS, 224 W. 57th St., New York NY 10019. (212)262-4815. Editor: John A. Linkletter. Executive Editor: Joe Oldham. Managing Editor: Bill Hartford. 50% freelance written. Monthly magazine; 200 pages. Circ. 1,625,000. Computer printout submissions acceptable; prefers letter-quality to dot-matrix. Buys all rights. Byline given. Pays "promptly." Publishes ms an average of 6 months after acceptance. Query. SASE.

Nonfiction: Needs material on "ingenious ways readers are coping with growing energy shortages—both in their homes and in their automobiles. Principal subjects are automotive (new cars, car maintenance) and how-to (woodworking, metalworking, home improvement and home maintenance). In addition, we use features on new technology, sports, electronics, photography and hi-fi." Exciting male interest articles with strong science, exploration and adventure emphasis. Looking for reporting on new and unusual developments. The writer should be specific about what makes it new, different, better, cheaper, etc. "We are always looking for fresh ideas in home maintenance, shop technique and crafts for project pieces used in the back part of the book. The front of the book uses articles in technology and general science, but writers in that area should have background in science." Length: 300-2,000 words. Pays $300-1,500.

Photos: Dramatic photos are most important, and they should show people and things in action. Occasionally buys picture stories with short text block and picture captions. The photos must tell the story without much explanation. Topnotch photos are a must with Home and Shop Section articles. Can also use remodeling of homes, rooms and outdoor structures. Pays $25 minimum.

POPULAR SCIENCE MONTHLY, 380 Madison Ave., New York NY 10017. Editor-in-Chief: C.P. Gilmore. 40% freelance written. For the well-educated adult, interested in science, technology, new products. Monthly magazine; 180-200 pages. Circ. 1,850,000. Buys all rights. Pays negotiable kill fee. Byline given. Buys several hundred mss a year. Pays on acceptance. Free guidelines for writers. Computer printout submissions acceptable. Submit seasonal material 4 months in advance. Reports in 3 weeks. Publishes ms an average of 2 months after acceptance. Query. SASE.

Nonfiction: "*Popular Science Monthly* is devoted to exploring (and explaining) to a nontechnical but knowledgeable readership the technical world around us. We cover the physical sciences, engineering and technology, and above all, products. We are largely a 'thing'-oriented publication: things that fly or travel down a turnpike, or go on or under the sea, or cut wood, or reproduce music, or build buildings, or make pictures, or mow lawns. We are especially focused on the new, the ingenious and the useful. We are consumer-oriented and are interested in any product that adds to a man's enjoyment of his home, yard, car, boat, workshop, outdoor recreation. Some of our 'articles' are only a picture and caption long. Some are a page long. Some occupy 4 or more pages. Contributors should be as alert to the possibility of selling us pictures and short features as they are to major articles. Freelancers should study the magazine to see what we want and avoid irrelevant submissions. No biology or life sciences." Recent article example: "New Powerful Portables—Best Buy in a Personal Computer." Pays $200 a published page minimum. Use both color and b&w photos.

Tips: "Probably the easiest way to break in here is by covering a news story in science and technology that we haven't heard about yet. We need people to be acting as scouts for us out there and we are willing to give the most leeway on these performances. We are interested in good, sharply focused ideas in all areas we cover. Please query first."

RADIO-ELECTRONICS, 200 Park Ave. S., New York NY 10003. (212)777-6400. Editor: Art Kleiman. For electronics professionals and hobbyists. Monthly magazine, 128 pages. Circ. 211,000. Buys all rights. Byline given. Pays on acceptance. Submit seasonal/holiday material 6-8 months in advance. SASE. Reports in 3 weeks. Send for "Guide to Writing."
Nonfiction: Interesting technical stories on all aspects of electronics, including video, radio, computers, communications, and stereo written from viewpoint of the electronics professional, serious experimenter, or layman with technical interests. Construction (how-to-build-it) articles used heavily. Unique projects bring top dollars. Cost of project limited only by what item will do. Emphasis on "how it works, and why." Much of material illustrated with schematic diagrams and pictures provided by author. Also high interest in how-to articles. Length: 1,000-5,000 words. Pays about $50-500.
Photos: State availability of photos. Offers no additional payment for b&w prints or 35mm color transparencies. Model releases required.
Columns/Departments: Pays $50-200/column.
Fillers: Pays $15-35.
Tips: "The simplest way to come in would be with a short article on some specific construction project. Queries aren't necessary; just send the article, 5 or 6 typewritten pages."

SCIENCE DIGEST, Hearst Magazines Division, Hearst Corp., 888 7th Ave., New York NY 10106. (212)262-7990. Editor-in-Chief: Oliver Moore, III. Managing Editor: Barbara Brynko. Emphasizes sciences and technologies for all ages with a scientific bent. Monthly magazine; 140 pages. Circ. 600,000. Pays on acceptance. Buys all magazine and periodical rights worldwide but for use only in *Science Digest* in all of its editions worldwide. Pays 25% kill fee. Byline given. Reports on queries and mss in 1 month. Sample copy $2; free writer's guidelines with SASE.
Nonfiction: Informational (authentic, timely information in all areas of science). Book excerpts, expose, interview/profile, new product, opinion, photo feature and technical. Also seeking material on computers, innovation and inventors. Length: 500-2,000 words. Buys 200 mss/year. Query with or without clips or send complete ms.
Columns/Departments: Astronomy, Speculations, Human Nature and Viewpoint. Buys about 40/year. Query with or without clips of published work or send complete ms. Length: 500-1,000 words.
Photos: Purchased with or without accompanying ms or on assignment. Send photos with accompanying query or ms. Reviews contact sheets, negatives, color transparencies and prints. Captions, model releases, and identification of subjects required. Buys all magazine and periodical rights worldwide but for use only in *Science Digest* in all of its editions worldwide.
Fillers: Amazing scientific facts. Length: 50-250 words. Pays $25-50.
Tips: "Our goal is to help our readers appreciate the beauty of science and the adventure of technology. Articles are geared toward the alert, inquisitive layman, fascinated by all facets of science."

SCIENCE 85, American Association for the Advancement of Science, 10th Floor, 1101 Vermont Ave. NW, Washington DC 20005. (202)842-9500. Editor: Allen L. Hammond. Managing Editor: Eric Schrier. Mostly freelance written. Monthly magazine covering popular science. Circ. 725,000. Pays on acceptance. Publishes ms an average of 1 month after acceptance. Byline given. Offers 20% kill fee. Buys all rights, shares reprint royalties. Submit seasonal/holiday material 4 months in advance. Computer printout submissions acceptable. SASE. Reports in 1 month. Sample copy $2; free writer's guidelines.
Nonfiction: Susan Williams, articles editor. Book excerpts, expose, humor, profile, photo feature—"only if about science or related." Buys 80 mss/year. Query with clips. Length: 1,500-3,000 words. Pays $800-2,000.
Columns/Departments: Buys 200 mss/year. Query with clips. Length: 200-1,000 words. Pays $150-800.
Poetry: Bonnie Gordon, poetry editor. Free verse, traditional. "Science-related poetry only." Buys 10/year. Submit maximum 5 poems. Length: 50 lines maximum. Pays $400.
Tips: Wants well thought-out, well-researched, well-written, succinct query. Section most open to freelancers is Crosscurrent. Looks for grace, intelligence and wit.

SCIENTIFIC AMERICAN, 415 Madison Ave., New York NY 10017. Articles by professional scientists only.

‡**SPACE JOURNAL, The First Newspaper of Space**, Aerospace Communications, 350 Cabrini Blvd., New York NY 10040. (212)927-8919. Editor: Jeffrey Manber. A quarterly tabloid covering commercial exploration of space. "We provide commentary and articles on the evolution of business into space, and its impact on our society." Circ. 4,000. Pays on acceptance. Byline given. Buys first North American serial rights. Submit seasonal/holiday material 3 months in advance. Simultaneous queries OK. Computer printout submissions acceptable. SASE. Reports in 3 weeks on queries; 1 month on mss. Sample copy $1; free writer's guidelines.
Nonfiction: Book excerpts (on space and high-tech nonfiction); expose (government contracts with the space program); interview/profile (key members of the space community—the chairman of a new satellite venture, for instance); opinion (relating to space issues, funding for a space station, cooperation with Europe, etc.).

"All opinion and reporting must be based on facts; our audience is fascinated with the long range impact of this field. No 'I want to be an astronaut, and other pieces which are not of interest to a well-informed reader." Buys 15 mss/year. Query with or without published clips. Length: 1,000 words minimum. Pays $25-75.

Tips: "We are interest in all areas of space: satellite TV, using home computers to help in locating planets (though we are *not* an astronomy publication). Freelancers can best break in with reporting on local news in their area, a new company which supplies software for the shuttle, international news, or space projects being researched on a campus nearby."

TECHNOLOGY REVIEW, Alumni Association of the Massachusetts Institute of Technology, Room 10-140, Massachusetts Institute of Technology, Cambridge MA 02139. Editor-in-Chief: John I. Mattill. 30% freelance written. Emphasizes technology and its implications for scientists, engineers, managers and social scientists. Magazine published 8 times/year. Circ. 75,000. Pays on publication. Publishes ms an average of 2 months after acceptance. Buys all rights. Phone queries OK. Submit seasonal/holiday material 6 months in advance of issue date. Simultaneous and photocopied submissions OK. Computer printout submissions acceptable; prefers letter-quality to dot-matrix. SASE. Reports in 6 weeks. Sample copy $2.50.

Nonfiction: General interest, interview, photo feature and technical. Buys 5-10 mss/year. Query. Length: 1,000-10,000 words. Pays $50-750.

Columns/Departments: Book Reviews; Trend of Affairs; Technology and Economics; and "Prospects" (guest column). Also special reports on other appropriate subjects. Query. Length: 750-4,000 words. Pays $50-750.

UFO REVIEW, Global Communications, 316 5th Ave., New York NY 10001. (212)685-4080. Editor: Timothy Beckley. Emphasizes UFOs and space science. Published 4 times/year. Tabloid. Circ. 50,000. Pays on publication. "We syndicate material to European markets and split 50-50 with writer." Phone queries OK. Photocopied submissions OK. SASE. Reports in 3 weeks. Sample copy $1.

Nonfiction: Expose (on government secrecy about UFOs). "We also want articles detailing on-the-spot field investigations of UFO landings, contact with UFOs, and UFO abductions. No lights-in-the-sky stories." Buys 1-2 mss/issue. Query. Length: 1,200-2,000 words. Pays $25-75.

Photos: Send photos with ms. Pays $5-10 for 8x10 b&w prints. Captions required.

Fillers: Clippings. Pays $2-5.

Tips: "Read the tabloid first. We get a lot of material unrelated to our subject."

UMOJA SASA NEWS JOURNAL, Pre-Professional Publications, 512 E. State St., Ithaca NY 14850. (607)272-0995. Publisher: Tyrone Taborn. Editor: Grady Wells. Bimonthly magazine covering technical, science and engineering for black and minority students. Circ. 15,500. Pays on publication. Publishes ms an average of 2 months after acceptance. Byline given. Offers $25 kill fee. Buys first rights. Submit seasonal material 2 months in advance. Simultaneous queries OK. SASE. Reports in 1 month on queries; 2 months on mss. Sample copy and writer's guidelines $3.

Nonfiction: Send complete ms only if on science or engineering. Queries demanded on all other subjects. "We are moving to a complete technical science and engineering book. Always need computer articles, civil engineering, etc." Prefers articles with a technical slant. No travel, crime, sports, how-to, ethnic material, or nontechnical personal interviews. Buys 30 mss/year. Length: 750-2,000 words. Pays $25-200/article.

Photos: Send photos with ms. Pays $25-35 for b&w 8x10 prints. Buys one-time rights.

Fillers: Cartoons. Pays $20-40.

Tips: "We need articles on new developments in science and engineering. We buy for most of the entire year during late summer."

Science Fiction

Readers eager to experience distant times and places turn to publications in this category. Additional science fiction markets are found in the Literary and "Little" category. To learn the secrets of writing science fiction consult *Writing and Selling Science Fiction*, by the Science Fiction Writers of America (Writer's Digest Books).

AMAZING® **Science Fiction Stories**, (Combined with *Fantastic Stories*), Dragon Publishing, Box 110, Lake Geneva WI 53147-0110. Editor: George H. Scithers. Managing Editor: Patrick L. Price. Bimonthly magazine of science fiction and fantasy short stories. "Audience does not need to be scientifically literate, but the authors must be, where required. *AMAZING* is devoted to the best science fiction and fantasy by new and established writers. There is no formula. We require the writers using scientific concepts be scientifically convincing, and that every story contain believable and interesting characters and some overall point. Circ. 13,000. Pays on acceptance. Byline given. Buys first North American serial rights; "single, non-exclusive re-use option (with additional pay)." Photocopied submissions OK. SASE. Reports in 3 weeks. Sample copy for $2.25; writer's guidelines $2.

Nonfiction: Historical (about SF history and figures); interview/profile and science articles of interest to SF audiences; reviews and essays about major SF movies written by big names. No "pop pseudo-science trends: The Unified Field Theory Discovered; How I Spoke to the Flying Saucer People; Interpretations of Past Visits by Sentient Beings, as Read in Glacial Scratches on Granite, etc." Buys 4-8 mss/year. Query with or without published clips. Length: 300-10,000 words. Pays 6¢/word up to 7,500 words; 4¢/word for 12,000 or more words.

Fiction: Fantasy; novel excerpts (rarely—query); science fiction; serialized novels (query first). "No 'true' experiences, media-derived fiction featuring *Star Wars* (etc.) characters, stories based on UFO reports or standard occultism and modern-scene horror." Buys 50-60 mss/year. Send complete ms. Length: 200-20,000 words. "Anything longer, ask." Pays 6¢/word to 7,500 words; 4¢/word for 12,000 or more words.

Poetry: All types are OK. No prose arranged in columns. Buys 20 poems/year. Submit maximum 3 poems. Length: 45 lines maximum; ideal length, 30 lines or less. Pays 50¢-$1/line.

Tips: "Short fiction is the best way for freelancers to break in to our publication. We basically want good stories. Don't try to especially tailor one for our 'slant.' We want original concepts, good writing, and well-developed characters. Avoid certain obvious clichés: UFO landings in rural areas, video games which become real (or vice-versa), stories based on contemporary newspaper headlines. '*Hard*' science fiction, that is, SF which is based on a plausible extrapolation from real science, is increasingly rare and very much in demand. The standard pseudo-medieval fantasy is very easy to get, but dull because of its standardness. Exceptional originality is required in that area."

ANALOG SCIENCE FICTION/SCIENCE FACT, 380 Lexington Ave., New York NY 10017. Editor: Dr. Stanley Schmidt. 100% freelance written. For general future-minded audience. Monthly. Buys first North American serial rights and nonexclusive foreign serial rights. Byline given. Computer printout submissions (with dark ink) acceptable; prefers letter-quality to dot-matrix. SASE. Reports in 1 month. Publishes ms an average of 8 months after acceptance.

Nonfiction: Illustrated technical articles dealing with subjects of not only current but future interest, i.e., with topics at the present frontiers of research whose likely future developments have implications of wide interest. Buys about 12 mss/year. Query. Length: 5,000 words. Pays 5.75¢/word.

Fiction: "Basically, we publish science fiction stories. That is, stories in which some aspect of future science or technology is so integral to the plot that, if that aspect were removed, the story would collapse. The science can be physical, sociological or psychological. The technology can be anything from electronic engineering to biogenetic engineering. But the stories must be strong and realistic, with believable people doing believable things—no matter how fantastic the background might be." Buys 60-100 unsolicited mss/year. Send complete ms on short fiction; query about serials. Length: 2,000-60,000 words. Pays 3.5-4.6¢/word for novelettes and novels; 5.75-6.9¢/word for shorts under 7,500 words. $430-525 for intermediate lengths; on acceptance for first North American serial rights.

Tips: "In query give clear indication of central ideas and themes and general nature of story line—and what is distinctive or unusual about it. We have no hard-and-fast editorial guidelines, because science fiction is such a broad field that I don't want to inhibit a new writer's thinking by imposing 'Thou Shalt Not's.' Besides, a really good story can make an editor swallow his preconceived taboos. *Analog* will consider material submitted from any writer and consider it solely on the basis of merit. We are definitely anxious to find and develop new, capable writers. No occult or fantasy."

EERIE COUNTRY, Box 149, Amherst Branch, Buffalo NY 14226. Editor-in-Chief: W. Paul Ganley. "100% freelance written; however, there are certain 'pro' writers who appear often." Modern "pulp magazine" published randomly emphasizing weird fantasy (swords and sorcery, supernatural horror, pure fantasy) for educated, mature readers of all ages. Circ. 200. Pays on publication. Publishes ms an average of 3 years after acceptance. Buys first North American serial rights and right to reprint as part of entire issue. Photocopied submissions OK. Computer printout submissions acceptable; prefers letter-quality to dot-matrix. SASE. Sample copy $2.75 (make checks payable to Weirdbook Press); writer's guidelines for SASE.

Fiction: Adventure (with weird elements); experimental (maybe, if in fantasy or horror area); tightly-plotted traditional fantasy and supernatural. Buys 12 unsolicited mss/year. Submit complete ms. Length: 20,000 words maximum. Pays ¼¢/word.

Poetry: Length: 20 lines maximum. No payment.

FANTASY BOOK, Box 60126, Pasadena CA 91106. Executive Editor: Dennis Mallonee. Editor: Nick Smith. 100% freelance written. Quarterly magazine of illustrated fantasy fiction for all ages; "bulk of the readership is in the 17-35 range." Circ. 5,000. Pays on "approval of galleys." Publishes ms an average of 6 months after acceptance. Byline given. Buys first North American serial rights. Submit seasonal/holiday material 6 months in advance. Photocopied submissions OK. Computer printout submissions acceptable. SASE. Reports in 6 weeks on mss. Sample copy $3; writer's guidelines for legal size SAE and 1 first class stamp.

Fiction: "We will consider any story related to fantasy fiction. We look for stories with strong characterization and carefully developed plot." Buys 50 mss/year. Send complete ms. Length: 2,000-10,000 words. Pays 2½-4¢/word.

Poetry: Light verse, traditional. Buys 8/year. Submit maximum 4 poems. Length: open. Pays $5-20.

‡**FANTASY REVIEW**, (formerly *Fantasy Newsletter*), Florida Atlantic University, 500 NW 20th St., Boca Raton FL 33431. (305)393-3839. Editor: Robert A. Collins. Managing Editor: Catherine Fischer. A monthly genre literary magazine of fantasy/horror/science fiction for authors, fans, scholars, editors, publishers, dealers, book store owners and students. Circ. 3,500. Pays on publication. Byline given. Buys first North American serial rights. Submit seasonal/holiday material 4 months in advance. Simultaneous queries, and simultaneous and photocopied submissions OK. Electronic submissions 8" single side, single density CP/M system (sysgen) for disks; 300 baud, CP/M MODEM 9 handholding program for modems. SASE. Reports in 3 weeks on queries; 6 weeks on mss. Sample copy $2; free writer's guidelines.

Nonfiction: General interest (essays directed to fans); historical/nostalgic (about authors, publishers, artist in field); humor (concerning genre literature); interview/profile (of articles and authors in field); new product (new books, films, magazines, art in field); opinion (reviews of books, films, art); personal experience (by authors on getting published); photo feature (fantasy and science fiction events); and surveys of foreign fiction, foreign fandom. "We don't want breezy fluff. We need solid research and reasoning, knowledge of field, plus easy style. No 'little green men invade our city' stuff. Writers must know the field." Buys 36 mss/year. Query or send complete ms. length: 1,000-5,000 words. Pays $20-100.

Photos: State availability of photos with query letter, send photos with ms. Pays $5-25 for 5x7 or 8x10 b&w prints. Captions, model release, and identification of subjects required. Buys one-time rights.

Columns/Departments: Commentary Department: reviews of forthcoming books, films, magazines, art shows; Opinion: topics of fan interest. Other columns are assigned. Buys 50 mss/year. Length: 500-1,000 words. Pays $10-20.

Poetry: Free verse, haiku, light verse, traditional. "Poems must have a fantasy, horror, or science fiction twist. We don't want conventional topics." Buys 12 poems/year. Submit maximum 5 poems. Length: 3-30 lines. Pays $5-25.

Fillers. Clippings, jokes, gags, newsbreaks. Fillers must have genre interest. Length: 50-150 words. Pays $5.

Tips: "We especially need good articles (*solid thinking*, entertaining style) on odd or representative authors, trends, topics within the field; also interviews with up-and-coming authors and artists *with pictures*."

THE HORROR SHOW, Phantasm Press, Star Rte. 1, Box 151-T, Oak Run CA 96069. (916)472-3540. Editor: David B. Silva. 95% freelance written. Quarterly horror magazine. Circ. 500. Publishes ms an average of 4 months after acceptance. Buys first rights. Computer printout submissions acceptable; prefers letter-quality to dot-matrix. SASE. Reports in 3 weeks. Sample copy for $4 and $1 postage; writer's guidelines for SASE.

Columns/Departments: Curses (letters to the editor).

Fiction: Contemporary horror. "Should *not* splash over into sf or fantasy (sword and scorcery). We are specifically looking for material which contains a twist or shock at the end. Do not over-indulge in sex or violence." Send complete ms. Length: 3,500 words maximum. Pays ¼¢/word plus contributor's copy.

Tips: "We will work with anyone who has a good idea and is willing to adopt suggestions. This is a good opportunity for new writers to break into print."

‡**INTERZONE, Imaginative Fiction and Art**, Interzone Collective, 21 The Village St., Leeds LS4 2PR England. Editor: Collective Of 5. A quarterly magazine of science fiction, fantasy and related imaginative fiction. Circ. 2,500. Pays on publication. Byline given. Buys first English language serial rights. Photocopied submissions OK. SAE and IRCs. Computer printout submissions acceptable. Sample copy $3 from US agent, Apt. 5, 145 E. 18th St., Costa Mesa CA 92627—"do *not* send mss here."

Fiction: Fantasy (not sword and sorcery); mainstream (but must have some fantasy/surreal content); and science fiction. Buys 20 mss/year. Send complete ms—"1 story at a time, please." Length: 1,000-8,000 words. Pays £30-35/1,000 words.

Tips: "Please read *Interzone* before you submit. Optimun length is 5,000 words. Best to submit disposable double-spaced photocopies with IRCs for our letter of reply. We like to publish fiction which is topical; it should be innovative yet entertaining; SF stories should be aware of recent technological advances, not regurgitations of SF clichés from past decades."

ISAAC ASIMOV'S SCIENCE FICTION MAGAZINE, Davis Publications, Inc., 380 Lexington Ave. New York NY 10017. (212)557-9100. Editor-in-Chief: Shawna McCarthy. 100% freelance written. Emphasizes science fiction. 13 times a year magazine; 176 pages. Circ. 150,000. Pays on acceptance. Buys first North

American serial rights and nonexclusive foreign serial rights. "Clear and dark" photocopied submissions OK but no simultaneous submissions. Computer printout submissions acceptable; prefers letter-quality to dot-matrix. SASE. Reports in 2-6 weeks. Publishes ms an average of 6 months after acceptance. Writer's guidelines for SASE.

Nonfiction: Science. Query first.

Fiction: Science fiction primarily. Some fantasy and poetry. "It's best to read a great deal of material in the genre to avoid the use of some *very* old ideas." Buys 10 mss/issue. Submit complete ms. Length: 100-20,000 words. Pays 3½-5½¢/word.

Tips: Query letters not wanted, except for nonfiction. "Response time will be somewhat slower than in years past, and I'll be using a higher proportion of 'form' rejection slips."

THE MINNESOTAN SCIENCE FICTION READER, 3339 Noble Ave. N., Golden Valley MN 55422. (612)529-3243. Editor: Matthew E. Tabery. 85% freelance written. Bimonthly on science fiction and writing science fiction. Pays on acceptance. Publishes ms an average of 4 months after acceptance. Byline given. Buys first North American serial rights. Submit seasonal/holiday material 3 months in advance. Photocopied submissions OK. Computer printout submissions acceptable. SASE. Reports in 1½ weeks on queries; 3 weeks on mss. Sample copy $1.40; writer's guidelines for business-size SAE and 1 first class stamp.

Nonfiction: How-to (write science fiction); humor (on sf/sf writing); interview/profile; convention reports. Length: 1,000-1,800 words. Pays $5-9.

Fiction: Experimental, science fantasy, humorous, science fiction, avant-garde—all science fiction related. No mainstream sf, occult or metaphysics. Buys 12-20 mss/year. Send complete ms. Length: 4,000 words maximum. Pays ½¢/word. Buys first North American serial rights.

Tips: "Write what you know (don't try to write a Robert L. Forward story if you failed all your science classes in high school). If you know what you're writing, this should come through in your story."

‡**ORION'S CHILD, Science Fiction and Fantasy Magazine**, Orion Press, 8047 Drake Stateline NE, Burghill OH 44404. (216)772-4100. Executive Editor: Debra L. Whitmore-Cole. Managing Editor: Timothy Cole. 95% freelance written. Bimonthly magazine of classic science fiction and fantasy. Estab. 1984. Circ. 2,000 + . Pays immediately prior to publication. Byline given. Offers 20% kill fee. Buys first North American serial rights, one-time rights, first rights, and second serial (reprint) rights. Submit seasonal/holiday material 6 months in advance. Simultaneous queries, and photocopied and previously published submissions OK. SASE. Reports in 2 weeks on queries; 6 weeks on mss. Sample copy for $2.50, 9x12 SAE and $1.05 postage; writer's guidelines for business-size SAE and 1 first class stamp.

Nonfiction: Interview/profile. Buys 6 mss/year. Query. Length: 1,500-4,000 words. Pays ½¢/word-$20.

Photos: Fred Stahl, photo editor. For nonfiction only. State availability of photos. Pays $25 for 8x10 b&w prints. Captions, model release, and identification of subjects required. Buys one-time rights.

Columns/Departments: "Columns and departments are still in the planning stages and until we have a firm goal, we will be accepting nothing for this area."

Fiction: Adventure (science fiction or heroic fantasy); fantasy; historical (time travel); humorous (must relate to theme); science fiction. "Realism and believability are the keys to any successful story as long as there is a reason for the characters doing what they do." Buys 60 mss/year. Send complete ms. Length: 10,000 words maximum. Pays ½¢/word.

Poetry: Avant-garde, free verse, haiku, light verse and traditional. "Must relate to theme." Submit maximum 3 poems. Length: 2 pages maximum. Pays $25 maximum.

Fillers: Clippings, newsbreaks and cartoons. Length: 300 words maximum. Pays $5 maximum.

Tips: "*Orion's Child* is for adolescents on up, not necessarily a juvenile or teen market. None the less, we will reject all manuscripts that contain sexual innuendo, pornography, gratuitous violence, or foul or vulgar language. We are not a religious publication; but we will accept stories with religious themes so long as they relate to the genre of the magazine. The only criterion is that stories be *entertaining*."

PANDORA, Role-Expanding Science Fiction and Fantasy, Empire Books, Box 625, Murray KY 42071. Editors: Jean Lorrah and Lois Wickstrom. Send mss to Lois Wichstrom, 10612 Altman St., Tampa FL 33612. 95% freelance written. Magazine published 2 times/year covering science fiction and fantasy. Circ. 600. Pays on acceptance. Publishes ms an average of 6 months after acceptance. Byline given. Offers $10 kill fee. Buys first North American serial rights; one-time rights on some poems. Photocopied submissions OK. Readable computer printout submissions on white 8½x11 paper acceptable. SASE. Reports in 4 weeks. Sample copy $3.

Columns/Departments: Books briefly. "We buy 200-word reviews of science fiction and fantasy books that a reader truly loves and feels are being ignored by the regular reviewers. Small press titles as well as major press titles are welcome." Buys 3-4 mss/year. Query or send complete ms. Length: 200-250 words. Pays 1¢/word.

Fiction: Experimental, fantasy, science fiction. "No pun stories. Nothing x-rated. No inaccurate science." Buys 15 mss/year. Send complete ms. Length: 1,000-5,000 words "except for controversial stories which may go to 10,000 words." Pays 1¢/word.

Poetry: Steve Tem, poetry editor. "We're over bought for at least the next year." Buys 9/year. Length: open.

Tips: "Send us a complete short story. If we like it, we'll send you a critique with suggestions, if we don't want it just the way it is, but would want it with some more work. You don't have to do exactly what we've suggested, but you should fix weak spots in your story."

SPACE AND TIME, 138 W. 70th St., New York NY 10023. Editor: Gordon Linzner. Biannual magazine covering fantasy fiction, with a broad definition of fantasy that encompasses science fiction, horror, swords and sorcery, etc. Circ. 500. 100% freelance written. Pays on acceptance. Byline given. Buys first North American serial rights. Photocopied submissions OK. Computer printout submissions acceptable; prefers letter-quality to dot-matrix. SASE. Reports in 2 months. Publishes ms an average of 2 years after acceptance. Sample copy $4.

Fiction: Fantasy, horror and science fiction. "Submit skillful writing and original ideas. We lean toward strong plot and character. No fiction based on TV shows or movies (*Star Trek*, *Star Wars*, etc.) or popular established literary characters (e.g., Conan) except as satire or other special case. No UFO, gods from space, or material of that ilk, unless you've got a drastically new slant." Buys 24 unsolicited mss/year. Length: 15,000 words maximum. Pays ¼¢/word plus contributor's copies.

Poetry: Free verse, haiku, light verse, traditional and narrative. "No poetry without a definite fantastic theme or content." Buys 12 mss/year. Submit maximum 5 poems. Length: open. Pays in contributor's copies.

Tips: "All areas are open to freelancers, but we would particularly like to see more hard science fiction, and fantasies set in 'real' historical times. No nonfiction or no fiction that cannot be considered science fiction or fantasy. We particularly enjoy uncovering new talent and offbeat stories for which there are few (if any) markets otherwise; seeing *S&T* authors go on to better paying, wider circulating markets. We regret that we can't publish more material more often. A lot of good, interesting stories have to be passed over, and there are few other markets for genre fiction."

‡**STARLOG MAGAZINE, The Magazine of the Future**, Starlog Group, 8th Floor, 475 Park Ave. S., New York NY 10016. (212)689-2830. Editor: Howard Zimmerman. Managing Editor: David McDonnell. Monthly magazine covering "the science fiction-fantasy-adventure genre: its films, TV, books, art and personalities. We explore the fields of science fiction and fantasy with occasional forays into adventure (i.e., the James Bond films and *Raiders of the Lost Ark*) and horror. We concentrate on the personalities and behind-the-scenes angles of science fiction/fantasy films with comprehensive interviews with actors, directors, screenwriters, producers, special effects technicians and, on occasion, composers, stuntmen, cinematographers." 60% freelance written. Pays on publication or after 3 months from deadline date if article held and budget allows. Byline given, except on log entries/news item material—those contributors are credited in masthead. Offers $50 kill fee "only to mss *written* or interviews *done*." Buys first North American serial rights, one-time rights, first rights and second serial (reprint) rights. Submit seasonal/holiday material 5 months in advance. Simultaneous queries, and photocopied submissions OK. Computer printout submissions acceptable. SASE. Reports in 4 weeks on queries; 6 weeks on mss. Publishes ms an average of 3 months after acceptance. Free sample copy "if we like your clips" or $2.95 "if you don't enclose clips."

Nonfiction: Interview/profile (actors, directors, screenwriters who have made significant science fiction contributions or are now making them in a currently-filming movie, or science fiction novelists); photo features (occasionally on fun happenings); special effects how-tos (on filmmaking only); retrospectives of famous science fiction films and TV series; occasional pieces on science fiction fandom, conventions, etc., and aspects of that area of science fiction fans' lives. "We also cover animation (especially Disney and WB) and remain interested in video games, computers, science, etc." Two special issues are open to freelance submissions. "One is the anniversary issue, published in June, which includes interviews and other material in addition to the regular features. The summer film review issue, published in October, includes bylined reviews of the year's films, written by noted science fiction and fantasy authors such as Robert Bloch, Norman Spinrad, Ron Goulart and Alan Dean Foster. We are always looking for other noted 'name' authors to add to our reviewer roster." Otherwise, no personal opinion or views of *Star Wars*, *Star Trek* or memories of when the writer first saw some film. *No* first person. "We prefer article format as opposed to questions and answers." No reviews. Buys 70-75 mss/year. Query first with published clips. Length: 500-3,500 words. Pays $25-200.

Photos: State availability of photos. Pays $10-25 for color slide transparencies and 8x10 b&w prints depending on quality. Captions, model release, identification of subjects, and credit line on photos required. Buys all rights.

Columns/Department: L.A. Offbeat ("quirky" articles on science fiction/fantasy films/personalities based in California—not quite the normal slant); Fan Scene (articles on science fiction fandom and its aspects—basically staff written at this point); Log Entries (the *Starlog* news section which regularly includes the three following staff-written items: Booklog—the science fiction/fantasy/horror book news and mini-reviews; Medialog—news of upcoming science fiction films and TV projects; and Videolog—videocassette and disk releases of genre interest). "We also require science fiction news items of note, mini-interviews on new projects with science fiction authors (500 words, usually promoting a new book—almost entirely freelance written); Comics Scene items (profiles of upcoming comic books/strips), science items, items on fantasy, science fiction gaming, merchandising items of interest, toys, games and reunion photos/feature material." Buys 24-30 mss/

year (probably will increase this year). Query with published clips. Length: 500-1,000 words (most logs are 500 words maximum). No kill fee on logs.

Fiction: "We do *not* publish any fiction."

Tips: "The prospective writer can best break in through Log Entries with miniauthor interviews or news items which show initiative, or if they have very unusual interviews or articles that we can't get through normal channels (for example, an interview with Dino De Laurentiis; we'd like one). We are always looking for *new* angles on *Star Wars, Star Trek* and currently want a small number of features investigating aspects and personalities of series which remain very popular with a number of our readers: *Lost in Space, Space 1999, Battlestar Galactica, The Twilight Zone*. Know science fiction media before you try to write for us. We enjoy discovering new freelancers; seeing them get cover stories; assisting them in some way."

‡**STARWIND**, The Starwind Press, Box 98, Ripley OH 45167. (513)392-4549. Editor: David F. Powell. Managing Editor: Susannah C. West. A quarterly magazine "for the young adult (18-25 or thereabouts) who has an interest in science and technology, and who also enjoys reading well-crafted science fiction and fantasy." Circ. 2,500. Pays on publication. Byline given. Rights vary with author and material; negotiated with author. Photocopied submissions OK. Electronic submissions OK on disks, IBM PC format: SS, SD; SS, DD; DS, DD; DS, QD. Computer printout submissions acceptable. SASE. Reports in 2 months. Sample copy for $2.50; writer's guidelines for business-size SAE and 1 first class stamp.

Nonfiction: How-to (technological interest, e.g., how to build a robot eye, building your own radio receiver, etc.); interview/profile (of leaders in science and technology fields); and technical ("did you know" articles dealing with development of current technology). "No speculative articles, dealing with topics such as the Abominal Snowman, Bermuda Triangle, etc. At present, nonfiction is staff-written or reprinted from other sources. We hope to use more freelance written work in the future." Query. Length: 1,000-5,000 words. Pays 1-4¢/word.

Photos: Send photos with accompanying query or ms. Reviews b&w contact sheets and prints. Model release and identification of subjects required. "If photos are available, we prefer to purchase them as part of the written piece." Buys negotiable rights.

Fiction: Fantasy and science fiction. "No stories whose characters were created by others (e.g., *Lovecraft*, *Star Trek*, *Star Wars* characters, etc.)." Buys 15-20 mss/year. Send complete ms. Length: 2,000-10,000 words. Pays 1-4¢/word.

Tips: "We have changed *Starwind*'s format from that of a strictly literary magazine to one which includes more nonfiction."

‡**THRUST—SCIENCE FICTION IN REVIEW**, Thrust Publications, 8217 Langport Terrace, Gaithersburg MD 20877. (301)948-2514. Editor: D. Douglas Fratz. 30% freelance written. A semiannual literary review magazine covering science fiction and fantasy literature. "*Thrust—Science Fiction in Review* is the highly acclaimed, Hugo-Award-nominated magazine about science fiction and fantasy. Since 1972, *Thrust* has been featuring in-depth interviews with science fiction's best known authors and artists, articles and columns by the field's most outspoken writers, and reviews of current science fiction books. *Thrust* has built its reputation on never failing to take a close look at the most sensitive and controversial issues concerning science fiction, and continues to receive the highest praise and most heated comments from professionals and fans in the science fiction field." Circ. 1,500. Pays on publication. Publishes ms an average of 6 months after acceptance. Byline given. Buys first North American serial rights, one-time rights and second serial (reprint) rights. Submit seasonal/holiday material 3-6 months in advance. Simultaneous queries, and simultaneous, photocopied and previously published submissions OK. Computer printout submissions acceptable; prefers letter-quality to dot-matrix. SASE. Reports in 2 weeks on queries; 1-2 months on mss. Sample copy for $2.50; writer's guidelines for SAE and 1 first class stamp.

Nonfiction: Humor, interview/profile, opinion, personal experience and book reviews. Buys 5-10 mss/year. Query or send complete ms. Length: 2,000-5,000 words. Pays ½-2¢/word.

Photos: "We publish only photos of writers being interviewed." State availability of photos. Pays $1-10 for smaller than 8x10 b&w prints. Buys one-time rights.

Columns/Departments: Uses science fiction and fantasy book reviews and film reviews. Buys 25-30 mss/year. Send complete ms. Length: 100-1,000 words. Pays ½-1¢/word. (Reviews usually paid in subscriptions, not cash.)

‡**TWILIGHT ZONE**, Montcalm Publishing Co., 800 2nd Ave., New York NY 10017. (212)986-9600. Editor: T.E.D. Klein. Managing Editor: Robert Sabat. 60% freelance written. A bimonthly magazine of supernatural fiction with short stories in the Rod Serling tradition. Circ. 150,000. Pays 50% on acceptance, 50% on publication. Publishes ms an average of 4 months after acceptance. Byline given. Offers 25% kill fee. Buys first North American serial rights, first and second rights to the same material, and second (reprint) rights to material originally published elsewhere. Submit seasonal/holiday material 8 months in advance. Simultaneous and photocopied submissions OK. Computer printout submissions acceptable; prefers letter-quality to dot-matrix. SASE. Reports in 3 months. Sample copy $3.

Fiction: Fantasy, horror. No sword and sorcery; hardware-oriented science fiction; vampire, werewolf and deals-with-the-devil stories; sadistic stories; imaginary-world fantasy. Buys 35 mss/year. Send complete ms. Length: 5,000 words maximum. Pays 5¢/word; $150 minimum.

WEIRDBOOK, Box 149, Amherst Branch, Buffalo NY 14226. Editor-in-Chief: W. Paul Ganley. Emphasizes weird fantasy (swords and sorcery, supernatural horror, pure fantasy) for educated, mature readers of all ages. A modern "pulp magazine" published once or twice a year; 64 pages. Circ. 900. Pays on publication. Buys first North American serial rights and right to reprint as part of entire issue. Photocopied submissions OK. Electronic submissions OK on disk for Apple II or IIe. Computer printout submissions acceptable; prefers letter-quality to dot-matrix. SASE. Sample copy $5.75; writer's guidelines for SASE.
Fiction: Adventure (with weird elements); experimental (maybe, if in fantasy or horror area); tightly-plotted traditional fantasy and supernatural. Example of recently published fiction: "Gramma," by Stephen King. Buys 12 unsolicited mss/year. Submit complete ms. Length: 20,000 words maximum. Pays ½¢/word.
Poetry: Length: 20 lines maximum. No payment except contributor's copy.

WONDER MAGAZINE, The SF Magazine, (formerly *Novalis*), Wonder Press, Box 58367, Louisville KY 40258. Managing Editor: Walter Gammons. 100% freelance written. Bimonthly magazine of highly literate and entertaining short fiction for adults (18-45). Circ. 5,000. Pays on publication. Byline given. Offers 15% kill fee. Buys first North American serial rights and first anthology option. Submit seasonal/holiday material 4 months in advance. Photocopied submissions OK. Computer printout submissions acceptable. SASE. Reports in 1 month on queries; 3 months on mss. Publishes ms an average of 5 months after acceptance. Sample copy for $4, 9x12 SAE and 4 first class stamps; writer's guidelines for $2, 9x12 SAE and 2 first class stamps.
Nonfiction: Science-fiction, humor, interview/profile, new product, opinion, and photo feature. No political, religious or pornographic material. Buys 6 mss/year. Send complete ms. Length: 1,000-8,000 words. Pays 1-5¢/word.
Photos: Pays variable rates for 2¼, 4x5 color transparencies and 8x10 color prints. Captions, model release and identification of subjects required.
Columns/Departments: Buys 6 mss/year. Send complete ms. Length: 1,000-4,000 words. Pays 1-5¢/word.
Fiction: Adventure, sf-erotica, experimental, horror, humorous, science fiction, and suspense. Mainly interested in fantasy, myths, fables in the short story form. No pornography, cliches, religious, political, vignettes, scenarios. Buys 60 mss/year. Send complete ms. Length: 1,000-8,000 words. Pays 1-5¢/word.
Poetry: Avant-garde, free verse, light verse, traditional, science fiction, or fantasy. No depressing, overdramatic, political or religious poetry. Submit maximum 6 poems. Length: 8-50 lines. Pays $5-20.
Fillers: Harbinger Harris, fillers editor. Clippings, anecdotes, short humor. Buys 20/year. Length: 50-500 words. Pays $5-20.
Tips: "We look for a science fiction or fantasy story with a good, fast-moving plot, good characterization, and a magnetic beginning, middle and end."

Social Science and Self-Improvement

These publications cover a wide range of topics with each magazine slanted to a particular audience.

THE HUMANIST, American Humanist Association, 7 Harwood Dr., Box 146, Amherst NY 14226. (716)839-5080. Editor: Lloyd L. Morain. Managing Editor: William J. Harnack. 60% freelance written. Bimonthly magazine covering philosophy, psychology, religion, ethics. "Discusses social issues and personal concerns in the light of humanistic ideas and developments in philosophy and science." Circ. 14,000. Pays on publication. Publishes ms an average of 2 months after acceptance. Byline given. Buys all rights "unless arranged with author." Previously published submissions OK. SASE. Reports in 3 months on mss. Sample copy $2.50.
Nonfiction: General interest, opinion, personal experience, humanistic concerns, philosophy, controversial topics. "We like creative, upbeat articles." Buys 35 mss/year. Send complete ms. Length: 3,000-8,000 words. Pays variable rates from copies to $200 maximum.
Photos: "Does not buy photos; however, authors are encouraged to submit them with ms."
Columns/Departments: Humanism in Literature (humanistic slants on literature, especially contemporary). Buys 3 mss/year. Send complete ms. Length: 600-2,500 words. Pays variable rates from copies to $50 maximum.

JOURNAL OF GRAPHOANALYSIS, 111 N. Canal St., Chicago IL 60606. Editor: V. Peter Ferrara. For audience interested in self-improvement. Monthly. Buys all rights. Pays negotiable kill fee. Byline given. Pays on acceptance. Reports on submissions in 1 month. SASE.
Nonfiction: Self-improvement material helpful for ambitious, alert, mature people. Applied psychology and personality studies, techniques of effective living, etc.; all written from intellectual approach by qualified writers in psychology, counseling and teaching, preferably with degrees. Length: 2,000 words. Pays about 5¢/word.

PRACTICAL KNOWLEDGE, 111 N. Canal St., Chicago IL 60606. Editor: Lee Arnold. Bimonthly. A self-advancement magazine for active and involved men and women. Buys all rights, "but we are happy to cooperate with our authors." Pays on acceptance. Reports in 2-3 weeks. SASE.
Nonfiction and Photos: Uses success stories of famous people, past or present, applied psychology, articles on mental hygiene and personality by qualified writers with proper degrees to make subject matter authoritative. Also human interest stories with an optimistic tone. Up to 5,000 words. Photographs and drawings are used when helpful. Pays 5¢/word minimum; $20 each for illustrations.

PSYCHOLOGY TODAY, American Psychological Association, 1200 17th St. NW, Washington DC 20036. Editor: Patrice D. Horn. 75% freelance written. For intelligent laymen concerned with society and individual behavior. Monthly. Buys all rights. Pays 20% kill fee. Publishes ms an average of 1 month after acceptance. Byline given. Computer printout submissions acceptable; prefers letter-quality to dot-matrix. Each ms will be edited by staff and returned to author prior to publication for comments and approval. Author should retain a copy. Reports in 1 month. Address all queries to Articles Editor. SASE.
Nonfiction: Most mss are based on scientific research and written by scholars; freelancers are used very rarely. Primary purpose is to provide the nonspecialist with accurate, surprising and/or fresh readable information about society and behavior. Technical and specialized vocabularies should be avoided except in cases where familiar expressions cannot serve as adequate equivalents and technical expressions, when necessary, should be defined carefully for the nonexpert. References to technical literature should not be cited within article. One-page queries should usually be accompanied by one or more of the scholarly presentations or papers on which suggested story is based. Usual length of finished articles: 2,000 words. Usual payment is $1,000.
Tips: "Be a researcher with talent, imagination and a solid grasp of social science methodology—or a trained science journalist thoroughly knowledgeable in the field being reported."

ROSICRUCIAN DIGEST, Rosicrucian Order, AMORC, Rosicrucian Park, San Jose CA 95191. (408)287-9171, ext. 213. Editor-in-Chief: Robin M. Thompson. 50% freelance written. Emphasizes mysticism, science and the arts. For "men and women of all ages, seeking answers to life's questions." Monthly magazine. Circ. 70,000. Pays on acceptance. Publishes ms an average of 6 months after acceptance. Buys first rights and rights to reprint. Byline given. Submit seasonal or holiday material 5 months in advance. Photocopied and previously published submissions OK. Computer printout submissions acceptable; no dot-matrix. SASE. Reports in 1 month. Free sample copy and writer's guidelines.
Nonfiction: How to deal with life's problems and opportunities in a positive and constructive way. Informational articles—new ideas and developments in science, the arts, philosophy and thought. Historical sketches, biographies, human interest, psychology, philosophical and inspirational articles. No religious, astrological or political material or articles promoting a particular group or system of thought. Buys 20-30 mss/year. Query. Length: 1,000-1,500 words. Pays 6¢/word.
Photos: Purchased with accompanying ms. Send prints. Pays $10/8x10 b&w glossy print.
Fillers: Short inspirational or uplifting (not religious) anecdotes or experiences. Buys 6/year. Query. Length: 25-250 words. Pays 2¢/word.
Tips: "Be specific about what you want to write about—the subject you want to explore—and be willing to work with editor. Articles should appeal to worldwide circulation. The most rewarding aspect of working with freelance writers is to see an article 'grow' from the original 'seed' into something that will touch the lives of our readers."

Sports

With the enthusiasm of a sports fan and a knowledge of sports and language, the writer shouldn't have to play second string. The publications in this category buy material for sports fans and activists on how to practice and enjoy both team and individual sports, material on conservation of streams and forests, and articles reporting on and analyzing professional sports.

Writers will note that several editors mention that they do not wish to see "Me 'n Joe" stories. These are detailed accounts of one hunting/fishing trip taken by the author and a buddy—starting with the friends' awakening at dawn and ending with their return home, "tired but happy."

For the convenience of writers who specialize in one or two areas of sport and outdoor writing, the publications are subcategorized by the sport or subject matter they emphasize. Publications in related categories (for example, Hunting and Fishing; Archery and Bowhunting) often buy similar material (in this case articles on bow and arrow hunting). Consequently, writers should read through this entire Sports category to become familiar with the subcategories and note the ones that contain markets for their own type of writing.

Publications concerned with horse breeding, hunting dogs or the use of other animals in sport are classified in the Animal category, while horse racing is listed here. Publications dealing with automobile or motorcycle racing will be found in the Automotive and Motorcycle category. Markets interested in articles on exercise and fitness are offered in the Health and Fitness section. Outdoor publications that exist to further the preservation of nature, placing only secondary emphasis on preserving nature as a setting for sport, are listed in the Nature, Conservation, and Ecology category. Regional magazines are frequently interested in conservation or sports material with a local angle. Camping publications are classified in the Travel, Camping, and Trailer category.

Archery and Bowhunting

ARCHERY WORLD, Suite 306, 715 Florida Ave. S., Minneapolis MN 55426. Editor: Richard Sapp. 40-60% freelance written. For "archers of average education, hunters and target archers, experts to beginners." Subject matter is the "entire scope of archery—hunting, bowfishing, indoor target, outdoor target, field." Bimonthly. Circ. 125,000. Buys first serial rights. Buys 30-35 mss/year. Pays on publication. Publishes ms an average of 6 months after acceptance. Will send a free sample copy to a writer on request. Reports in 6 weeks. Query. Computer printout submissions acceptable; prefers letter-quality to dot-matrix. SASE.
Nonfiction: "Try, in ms, to entertain archer, show him how to enjoy his sport more and be better at it." Wants how-to, semitechnical, and hunting where-to and how-to articles. "Looking for more good technical stories and short how-to pieces." Buys 10 unsolicited mss/year. Also uses profiles and some humor. Length: 1,000-2,200 words. Payment is $75-225.
Photos: B&w glossies purchased with mss and with captions. "Like to see proofsheets and transparencies with submitted stories. We make own cropping and enlargements." Pays $150 for color transparencies used on cover; $25 minimum for b&w.
Tips: "Not enough serious, talented writers pay attention to the archery/bowhunting magazines. The field is growing and in need of more qualified writers."

BOW AND ARROW, Box HH/34249 Camino Capistrano, Capistrano Beach CA 92624. Managing Editor: Dan Bisher. 75% freelance written. For archery competitors and bowhunters. Bimonthly. Buys all rights, "but will relinquish all but first American serial rights on written request of author." Byline given. Pays on acceptance. Publishes ms an average of 5 months after acceptance. Reports on submissions in 6-8 weeks. Author must have some knowledge of archery terms. Computer printout submissions acceptable; prefers letter-quality to dot-matrix. SASE.
Nonfiction: Articles: bowhunting, major archery tournaments, techniques used by champs, how to make your own tackle, and off-trail hunting tales. Likes a touch of humor in articles. "No dead animals or 'my first hunt.' " Also uses one technical article per issue. Submit complete ms. Length: 1,500-2,500 words. Pays $50-200.
Photos: Purchased as package with mss; 5x7 minimum or submit contacts with negatives (returned to photographer). Pays $75-100 for cover chromes, 35mm or larger.
Tips: "Good b&w photos are of primary importance. Don't submit color prints."

BOWHUNTER MAGAZINE, 3150 Mallard Cove Lane, Fort Wayne IN 46804. (219)432-5772. Editor: M. R. James. 90% freelance written. For "readers of all ages, background and experience who share two common passions—hunting with the bow and arrow and a love of the great outdoors." Bimonthly magazine; 112 pages. Circ. 160,000. Buys first publication rights. Pays on acceptance. Publishes ms an average of 6 months after acceptance. Sample copy $1; free writer's guidelines. "Effective with 1984 we included our Bowhunting Annual as part of the subscription package. This means we have seven issues each year including the Annual (on sale in July) and a Special Deer Hunting Issue (on sale in August)." Submit seasonal material 6-8 months in advance.

Reports in 6 weeks. Query or submit complete ms. Computer printout submissions acceptable; prefers letter-quality to dot-matrix. SASE.

Nonfiction: "We want articles that inform as well as entertain readers. Writers should anticipate every question a reader may ask and answer questions in the article or accompanying sidebar. Most features deal with big or small game bowhunting (how-to, where-to-go, etc.) and the 'Me and Joe' article is not dead here. We do avoid most technical pieces. Also, we do not cover all aspects of archery—only bowhunting. Unusual experiences are welcome and freshness is demanded, especially when covering common ground. Readers demand accuracy and writers hoping to sell to us must have a thorough knowledge of bowhunting. No writer should attempt to sell material to us without first studying one or more issues of the magazine. We especially like articles that promote responsible bowhunting and combat anti-hunting attacks. Humor, personal experiences, interviews and personality profiles, nostaglia, personal opinions, and historical articles are good bets. No 'See what animal I bagged—ain't I great' articles." Buys approximately 100 mss/year. Length: 200-3,500 words. Pays $25-250 or more.

Photos: Photos purchased with or without accompanying ms. Captions optional. Pays $20-35 for 5x7 or 8x10 b&w prints; $50 minimum for 35mm or 2¼x2¼ color.

Tips: "Keep the reader foremost in mind. Write for him, not yourself. Know the sport and share your knowledge. Weave helpful information into the storyline (e.g., costs involved, services of guide or outfitter, hunting season dates, equipment preferred and why, tips on items to bring, where to write for information, etc.). We have no set formula per se, but most features are first person narratives and most published material will contain elements mentioned above. We enjoy working with promising newcomers who understand our magazine and our needs."

Bicycling

‡**BICYCLE SPORT**, Wizard Publications, 3162 Kashiwa St., Torrance CA 90505. (213)539-9213. Editor: Cheri Wolpert. 60% freelance written. A monthly magazine covering the cycling lifestyle. "We write to one intelligent reader who is interested in cycling." Estab. 1983. Circ. 110,000. Pays on publication. Publishes ms an average of 3 months after acceptance. Byline given. Offers negotiable kill fee. Buys first North American serial rights. Submit seasonal/holiday material 3-4 months in advance. Computer printout submissions acceptable; prefers letter-quality to dot-matrix. SASE. Reports in 1 month. Sample copy $2; free writer's guidelines.

Nonfiction: Book excerpts, historical/nostalgic, interview/profile, new product, personal experience, photo feature, travel. All articles must focus on cycling, fitness. "Write colorful copy that indicates a definite interest in people and the cycling, fitness lifestyle. Write to an intelligent reader who enjoys the freedom of hopping on his bike to go somewhere. We anticipate a special buyer's guide in the fall." Buys 75 mss/year. Query with published clips. Length; 1,000-2,500 words. Pays negotiable rate; usually starts at 10¢/word.

Photos: Reviews 35mm color slides and 8x10 b&w prints. Identification of subjects required. Buys one-time rights or negotiable rights.

Columns/Departments: Occasional guest editorial—all other departments are assigned. Buys 80 mss/year. Query with published clips. Length: 750-800 words. Pays $100-175.

Tips: "Touring and travel articles are most open to freelancers, as long as appropriate photography can be arranged; also personality profiles, interviews, race coverage. Our goal is to have the reader want to hop on his bike after he's finished reading our publication. Compelling stories will help accomplish that goal."

BICYCLING, Rodale Press, Inc., 33 E. Minor St., Emmaus PA 18049. Editor and Publisher: James C. McCullagh. 50% freelance written. 9 issues/year (6 monthly, 3 bimonthly); 180-200 pages. Circ. 240,000. Pays on publication. Buys all rights. Byline given. Submit seasonal/holiday material 5 months in advance. Computer printout submissions acceptable. SASE. Free writer's guidelines.

Nonfiction: How-to (on all phases of bicycle touring, bike repair, maintenance, commuting, riding technique, nutrition for cyclists, conditioning); travel (bicycling must be central here); photo feature (on cycling events of national significance); and technical (component review—query). "We are strictly a bicycling magazine. We seek readable, clear, well-informed pieces. We rarely run articles that are pure humor or inspiration but a little of either might flavor even our most technical pieces. No poetry or fiction." Buys 5-10 unsolicited mss/issue. Query. Length: 2,500 words maximum. Pays $25-300.

Photos: State availability of photos with query letter or send photo material with ms. Pays $10 minimum for b&w prints and $15 minimum for color transparencies. Captions preferred; model release required.

Fillers: Anecdotes and other items for "Open Road" section. Buys 1-2/issue. Length: 150-200 words. Pays $15-25.

Tips: "Fitness is becoming an increasingly important subject. Also, study some recent issues of our magazine. We continue to evolve."

‡**CYCLING U.S.A., The Official Publication of the U.S. Cycling Federation**, 1750 E. Boulder St., Colorado Springs CO 80909. (916)265-9334. Editor: Jim McFadden. A monthly tabloid covering reportage and

commentary on American bicycle racing, personalities, and sports physiology for USCF licensed cyclists. 50% freelance written. Circ. 17,000. Pays on publication. Byline given. Offers 30% kill fee. Buys first and second rights to the same material. Submit seasonal/holiday material 30 days in advance. Simultaneous queries; and photocopied and previously published submissions OK. Computer printout submissions accceptable; dot-matrix submissions OK if double-spaced. SASE. Reports in 2 weeks. Publishes ms an average of 4 months after acceptance. Sample copy for 10x12 SAE and 60¢ postage; writer's guidelines for SAE and 1 first class stamp.

Nonfiction: How-to (train, prepare for a bike race); interview/profile; opinion; personal experience; photo feature; technical; and race commentary on major cycling events. No comparative product evaluations. Buys 15 mss/year. Query with published clips. Length: 850-3,000 words. Pays $85-500.

Photos: State availability of photos. Pays $10-25 for 5x7 b&w prints; $125 for color transparencies used as cover. Captions required. Buys one-time rights.

Columns/Departments: Ask the Doctor, Racing Form—The Coach's Column. Buys 24 mss/year. Query with published clips. Length: 850-1,000 words. Pays $50-100.

Tips: "A background in bicycle racing is important because the sport is somewhat insular, technical and complex. Race reports are most open to freelancers. Be concise, informative and anecdotal."

VELO-NEWS, A Journal of Bicycle Racing, Box 1257, Brattleboro VT 05301. (802)254-2305. Editor: Ed Pavelka. 20% freelance written. Monthly tabloid, (October-March, biweekly April-September) covering bicycle racing. Circ. 15,000. Pays on publication. Publishes ms an average of 1 month after acceptance. Byline given. Buys all rights. Simultaneous queries, and simultaneous, photocopied and previously published submissions OK. Computer printout submissions acceptable; also phone transmissions of ASCII at 1200 baud (call for specs). SASE. Reports in 2 weeks. Sample copy for 9x12 SAE.

Nonfiction: How-to (on bicycle racing); interview/profile (of people important in bicycle racing); opinion; photo feature; and technical. Buys 50 mss/year. Query. Length: 300-3,000 words. Pays $2/column inch.

Photos: State availability of photos. Pays $15-30 for 8x10 b&w prints. Captions and identification of subjects required. Buys one-time rights.

Tips: "We would prefer electronic submissions."

Billiards

BILLIARDS DIGEST, National Bowlers Journal, Inc., Suite 1801, 875 N. Michigan Ave., Chicago IL 60611. (312)266-7179. Editor: Michael Panozzo. 40% freelance written. Emphasizes billiards/pool for "readers who are accomplished players and hard core fans—also a trade readership." Bimonthly magazine; 48-70 pages. Circ. 7,000. Pays on publication. Publishes ms an average of 2 months after acceptance. Buys all rights. Byline given. Phone queries OK. Submit seasonal/holiday material 2 months in advance of issue date. Simultaneous, photocopied and previously published submissions OK. Computer printout submissions acceptable; prefers letter quality to dot-matrix. SASE. Reports in 2 weeks. Sample copy $2; free writer's guidelines.

Nonfiction: General Interest (tournament results, features on top players); historical (features on greats of the game); how-to (how to improve your game, your billiard room, billiards table maintenance); humor (anecdotes, any humorous feature dealing with billiards); interview (former and current stars, industry leaders); new product (any new product dealing with billiards, short 'blip' or feature); and profile (former and current stars—prefer current stars). No basic news stories. "We want features that provide in-depth material, including anecdotes, atmosphere and facts." Buys 3 mss/issue. Query. Length: 1,000-1,500 words. Pays $75-150.

Photos: State availability of photos with query. Pays $10-25 for 8x10 b&w glossy prints; $15-25 for 35mm or 2¼x2¼ color transparencies. Cover negotiable. Captions preferred. Buys all rights.

Tips: "The best way to break in at *Billiards Digest* is a simple query with day and night phone numbers, so we can get in touch for suggestions. Worst way is to submit ms that starts with a cliche, 'The stranger walked into the pool room . . .' We are *very* interested in tips from stars (past and present). But query, first."

Boating

‡**BOAT PENNSYLVANIA**, Pennsylvania Fish Commission, Box 1673, Harrisburg PA 17105-1673. (717)657-4520. Editor: Art Michaels. A bimonthly magazine covering powerboating, canoeing, kayaking, sailing, rafting, and water skiing. Estab. 1984. Pays on acceptance. Byline given. Buys variable rights. Submit seasonal/holiday material 8 months in advance. Computer printout submissions acceptable; prefers letter-quality to dot-matrix. SASE. Reports in 2 weeks on queries; 2 months on mss. Writer's guidelines for SASE.

Nonfiction: How-to, interview/profile, technical, and travel (only in Pennsylvania for boating). No fishing or hunting articles. Buys 30 mss/year. Query or send complete ms. Length: 200-1,500 words. Pays $20-200.

Photos: State availability of photos with query; send photos with accompanying ms. Reviews 35mm or 2¼x2¼ color transparencies and 8x10 b&w prints. Caption, model release, and identification of subjects required. Buys variable rights.

Columns/Departments: Query or send complete ms.

Tips: "The best way to break into print here is to submit a technically detailed, accurate how-to article with professional-quality b&w 8x10 prints or color slides (35mm) on a powerboating, sailing, canoeing, kayaking, rafting, or water skiing subject. Material must be wholly appropriate to Pennsylvania waterways."

BOATING, 1 Park Ave., New York NY 10016. (212)725-3972. Publisher: J. Samuel Huey. Editor: Roy Attaway. For powerboat enthusiasts—informed boatmen, not beginners. Publishes special Boat Show issue in January; Fall show issue in September; New York National Boat Show issue in December. Monthly. Circ. 187,000. Buys first periodical rights. Buys 100 mss/year. Pays on acceptance. Submit seasonal material 6-8 months in advance. Reports in 2 months. Query. SASE.

Nonfiction: Uses articles about cruises in powerboats with color photos, that offer more than usual interest; how-to pieces illustrated with good b&w photos or drawings; piloting articles, seamanship, etc.; new developments in boating; profiles of well-known boating people; and lifestyle. "Don't talk down to the reader. Use little fantasy, emphasize the practical aspects of the subject." Length: 300-3,000 words. Pays $150-1,000, and varies according to subject and writer's skill.

Photos: Prefers Kodachrome 25 transparencies of happenings of interest to a national boating audience, for both cover and interior use. Pays $250/color page; $500/color cover for one-time use "but not for anything that has previously appeared in a boating publication."

Fillers: Uses short items pertaining to boating that have an unusual quality of historical interest, timeliness, or instruction. No "funky old boats" material. Pays $50-100.

‡CANADIAN YACHTING MAGAZINE, Maclean Hunter Bldg., 7th Floor, 777 Bay St., Toronto, Ontario M5W 1A7 Canada. Editor: Penny Caldwell. 80% freelance written. Monthly magazine aimed at owners of power and sail pleasure boats, both cruising and racing. Most but not all of the audience is Canadian. Circ. 30,000. Pays on acceptance. Buys first North American serial rights. Previously published submissions OK, but remember "our obligation not to duplicate material published in larger American magazines available in our reader area." Publishes ms an average of 6 months after acceptance. SAE and IRCs.

Nonfiction: "Much of our 'entertainment' coverage of important racing events must be handled by US freelancers. Cruise stories are welcome from anyone." Also uses technical pieces, especially on motor maintenance. Buys 40 unsolicited mss/year. Send complete ms. Length: 1,800-2,500 words. Pays $180-500.

Photos: Pays $15-40 for 8x10 b&w prints; $25-200 for 35mm color transparencies.

Tips: "Query should contain writer's experience and reassurance of photo quality (usually sample)."

CANOE MAGAZINE, New England Publications, Highland Mill, Camden ME 04843. Editor: John Viehman. Managing Editor: Dave Getchell. 90% freelance written. "*Canoe* represents the self-propelled water traveler." For an audience ranging from weekend canoe-camper to Olympic caliber flatwater/whitewater racing, marathon, poling, sailing, wilderness tripping or sea-cruising types. Six times/year; 72 pages. Circ. 55,000. Buys first time or all rights. Pays 25% kill fee. Byline given. Buys 50+ mss/year. Pays on publication or on acceptance by prior arrangement. Publishes ms an average of 2 months after acceptance. Free sample copy and writer's guidelines for $1 and 9x12 SASE. Electronic disks OK if compatible with TRS-80; but all disk submissions should be checked out with editor first. Computer printout submissions acceptable; no dot-matrix. Reports in 60 days. Query or submit complete ms. SASE.

Nonfiction and Photos: "We publish a variety of state of the art canoeing and kayaking articles, striving for a balanced mix of stories to reflect all interests in this outdoor activity, recreational or competitive. Also interested in any articles dealing with conservation issues which may adversely affect the sport. Writing should be readable rather than academic; clever rather than endlessly descriptive. Diary type first-person style not desirable. A good, provocative lead is considered a prime ingredient. We want stories about canoeing/kayaking activities in the 50 states and Canada with which canoeists/kayakers of average or better ability can identify. Also interested in articles discussing safety aspects or instructional items. Occasional call for outdoor photography feature as relates to water accessible subjects. Please pick up and study a recent issue before querying. Also study back issues and published index (each issue) to avoid duplication. No hunting/fishing articles with minimal emphasis on the canoes involved." Length: 1,500-3,000 words. Pays $100-500. Will consider relevant book reviews (pays $25 on publication); length, 200-350 words. Short news and other items of interest, pays $25-100; "payment increases with accompanying photos."

Tips: "We've started a number of regular departmental stories that offer freelancers a good chance to break into our publication. Look for 1984 issues for examples."

CRUISING WORLD, 524 Thames St., Newport RI 02840. (401)847-1588. Editor: George Day. 75% freelance written. For all those who cruise under sail. Monthly magazine; 220 pages. Circ. 120,000. Rights purchased vary with author and material. May buy first North American serial rights or first world serial rights. Pays on acceptance. Reports in about 8 weeks. Submit complete ms. Computer printout submissions acceptable. SASE.

Nonfiction and Photos: "We are interested in seeing informative articles on the technical and enjoyable aspects of cruising under sail. Also subjects of general interest to seafarers." Buys 135-140 unsolicited mss/year. Length: 500-3,500 words. Pays $50-500. B&w prints (5x7) and color transparencies purchased with accompanying ms.

CURRENTS, Voice of the National Organization for River Sports, 314 N. 20th St., Colorado Springs CO 80904. (303)473-2466. Editor: Eric Leaper. Managing Editor: Mary McCurdy. 40% freelance written. Bimonthly magazine covering river running (kayaking, rafting, river canoeing). Circ. 10,000. Pays on acceptance. Publishes ms an average of 4 months after acceptance. Byline given. Offers 25% kill fee. Buys first North American serial rights and first rights. Submit seasonal/holiday material 2 months in advance. Simultaneous queries, and simultaneous, photocopied, and previously published submissions OK. Computer printout submissions acceptable. SASE. Reports in 2 weeks on queries; in 1 month on mss. Writer's guidelines for #10 SAE and 1 first class stamp.
Nonfiction: How-to (run rivers and fix equipment); in-depth reporting on river conservation and access issues and problems; humor (related to rivers); interview/profile (any interesting river runner); new product; opinion; personal experience; technical; travel (rivers in other countries). "We tell river runners about river conservation, river access, river equipment, how to do it, when, where, etc." No trip accounts without originality; no stories about "my first river trip." Buys 20 mss/year. Query with or without clips of published work. Length: 500-2,500 words. Pays $12-75.
Photos: State availability of photos. Pays $10-35. Reviews b&w or color prints or slides; b&w preferred. Captions and identification of subjects (if racing) required. Buys one-time rights.
Columns/Departments: Book and film reviews (river-related). Buys 5 mss/year. Query with or without clips of published work or send complete ms. Length: 100-500 words. Pays $5-50.
Fiction: Adventure (river). Buys 2 mss/year. Query. Length: 1,000-2,500 words. Pays $25-75.
Fillers: Clippings, jokes, gags, anecdotes, short humor, newsbreaks. Buys 5/year. Length: 25-100 words. Pays $5-10.
Tips: "Go to a famous river and investigate it; find out something we don't know—especially about rivers that are *not* in Colorado or adjacent states—we already know about the ones near us."

LAKELAND BOATING, 106 W. Perry St., Port Clinton OH 43452. (419)734-5774. Editor: David G. Brown. 80% freelance written. Emphasizes pleasure boating on freshwater lakes; both sail and power, but more emphasis on power. Monthly magazine. Circulation 46,000. Pays on publication. Buys first rights. Computer printout submissions acceptable if legible. SASE. Reports in 1 month. Sample copy $1.75.
Nonfiction: 2-3 "Cruise" stories/issue. May be personal experiences, but reader must get enough details on ports, marinas, dangers, etc. to perform a similar cruise. Include sketches, maps, lists of marinas, access ramps, harbors of refuge. Length: 1,000 to 2,500 words. "We need 'people' stories about individuals living a water lifestyle on the Great Lakes or major inland rivers. Focus should be on the person who is the subject of the story and how boats and boating influence his/her life. We also need stories about waterfront developments such as new harbors, condominiums with dockage and tourist-type attractions which can be visited by boat." Query first.
Photos: Send photos with ms. 5x7 or 8x10 b&w can also be submitted separately. Send negatives if you cannot have professional quality prints made. Original 35mm or larger transparencies for color stories. Captions required or identification of all pictures, prints or transparencies. "Please stamp every transparency with name and address." Original photo materials are returned.
Tips: "We are a regional publication, so all stories must have a Great Lakes or Midwestern freshwater slant. Cruise stories must give details. We don't want a 'Me 'n Joe' narrative of every breakfast and fuel stop. The waters being cruised and ports being visited are always more important than the people doing the cruising. Biggest reason for stories being rejected is failure to meet our regional needs. We would rather spend time developing a story right from the beginning than reject an otherwise well-written manuscript."

MOTORBOATING AND SAILING, 224 W. 57th St., New York NY 10019. (212)262-8768. Editor: Peter A. Janssen. Monthly magazine covering powerboats and sailboats for people who own their own boats and are active in a yachting lifestyle. Circ. 140,000. Average issue includes 8-10 feature articles. Pays on acceptance. Byline given. Buys one-time rights. SASE. Reports in 3 months.
Nonfiction: General interest (navigation, adventure, cruising), and how-to (maintenance). Buys 5-6 mss/issue. Query. Length: 2,000 words.
Photos: Reviews 5x7 b&w glossy prints and 35mm or larger color transparencies. Offers no additional payment for photos accepted with ms. Captions and model release required.

NAUTICAL QUARTERLY, Nautical Quarterly Co., 373 Park Ave. S., New York NY 10016. (212)685-9114. Editor: Joseph Gribbins. Managing Editor: Michael Levitt. 75% freelance written. Quarterly hardcover magazine covering yachting, power and sail. "We are specifically a yachting publication—not a maritime or shipping publication—with special emphasis on the best in yachts and small boats, and nautical experience, power and sail, past and present." Circ. 20,000. Pays on acceptance. Publishes ms an average of 1 year after acceptance. Byline given. Buys first North American serial rights and all rights. Simultaneous queries, and simultaneous, photocopied, and previously published submissions OK. SASE. Reports in 2 months. Sample copy $16.

Nonfiction: Historical/nostalgic, interview/profile, opinion, personal experience, photo feature, technical. "No articles on maritime (i.e., non-yachting) subjects such as tugboats, commercial ships, lighthouses, clipper ships, etc." Buys 20-25 mss/year. Query with published clips. Length: 2,500-8,000 words. Pays $500-1,000.

Photos: Marilyn Rose, photo editor. State availability of photos or send photos with ms. Reviews 35mm color transparencies. Payment varies by arrangement with the photographer. Identification of subjects required. Buys one-time rights.

Tips: "A query, accompanied by writing samples, will succeed if both the idea and the samples suit our standards."

‡OFFSHORE, New England's Boating Magazine, Offshore Publications, Inc., Box 148, Waban MA 02168. (617)244-7520. Editor: Herbert Gliick. A monthly magazine (oversize) covering boating and the New England coast for New England boat owners. Circ. 17,000. Pays within 4 weeks of acceptance. Byline given. Offers negotiable kill fee. Buys first North American serial rights. Submit seasonal/holiday material 2 months in advance. Simultaneous queries, and simultaneous, photocopied and previously published submissions OK. Computer printout submissions acceptable. SASE. Reports in 1 week. Sample copy for 11x14 SAE and 88¢ postage.

Nonfiction: Articles on boating and New England coastal places and people. Buys 125 mss/year. Query with clips of published work or send complete ms. Length: 750-3,000 words. Pays $2-2.75/column inch.

Photos: Reviews photocopies of 5x7 b&w prints. Identification of subjects required. Buys one-time rights.

Tips: "Demonstrate familiarity with New England coast and ability to recognize subjects of interest to regional boat owners. Those subjects need not be boats. *Offshore* does not take itself as seriously as most national boating magazines."

PACIFIC YACHTING, Power and Sail in British Columbia, S.I.P. Division, Maclean Hunter, Ltd., 1132 Hamilton St., Vancouver, British Columbia V6B 2S2 Canada. (604)687-1581. Editor: Paul Burkhart. Monthly magazine of yachting and recreational boating. Circ. 20,000. 50% freelance written. Pays mostly on publication. Byline given. Buys first and second serial (reprint) rights and makes work-for-hire assignments. Submit seasonal/holiday material 4 months in advance. Simultaneous queries, and simultaneous, photocopied, and previously published submissions OK. Computer printout submissions acceptable; prefers letter-quality to dot-matrix. SAE and IRCs. Reports in 2 months on queries; 6 months on mss. Publishes ms an average of 6 months after acceptance. Sample copy $2.

Nonfiction: Book excerpts, how-to, humor, interview/profile, new product, opinion, personal experience, photo feature, technical, travel. "Freelancers can break in with first-person articles about yachting adventures on the west coast of Canada accompanied by good 35mm photos. We're open to 'how-to' pieces by writers with strong technical backgrounds in the marine recreation field." No "poetry, religious, or first sailing experiences." Buys 150 mss/year. Will buy fewer stories in the year ahead. Query. Length: 100-2,000 words. Pays 10¢/word.

Photos: Send photos with ms. Reviews b&w contact sheets, b&w and color negatives, 35mm color transparencies (preferred) and prints. Captions and identification of subjects required. Buys various rights.

Columns/Departments: Scuttlebutt (news and light items, new gear, book reviews) and Boat Care (how-to). Buys 80 mss/year. Send complete ms. Length: 100-400 words. Pays $10-40.

Fillers: Clippings, newsbreaks. Length: 100-200 words. Pays $10-25.

Tips: "In working with freelancers we enjoy discovering fresh new perspectives in our own backyard. We regret, however, their failure to inquire or check out our magazine style."

PLEASURE BOATING MAGAZINE, Graphcom Publishing, Inc., 1995 NE 150th St., North Miami FL 33181. (305)945-7403. Managing Editor: Joe Greene. 50% freelance written. Monthly magazine of recreational boating and fishing throughout the South including cruising, racing and diving subjects. Circ. 30,000. Pays on publication. Publishes ms an average of 2 months after acceptance. Buys all rights. Phone queries OK. Computer printout submissions acceptable. SASE. Reports in 1 month. Free sample copy.

Nonfiction: Technical, how-to departments on fishing, electronics, engines, etc. Features designed to entertain and inform readers in the areas of recreational boating and fishing. Pays $100 for department pieces (1,500 words) to $200 for feature-length articles (3,000 words) with color. Buys 15 unsolicited mss/year. Send complete ms. Length: 500-3,000 words. Pays 5-10¢/word.

Photos: Send photos with ms. Reviews photos suitable for cover. Pays $50-150. Color transparencies requested for use with features; b&w glossies for use with department material. Buys all rights. Captions and model releases required.

‡ROWING USA, U.S. Rowing Association, #4 Boathouse Row, Philadelphia PA 19130. (215)769-2068. Editor: Kathryn M. Reith. A bimonthly magazine for U.S. Rowing Association members, primarily competitive rowers, plus a substantial number of recreational rowers (mostly sliding seat boats). Circ. 11,500. Pays on publication. Byline given. Buys one time rights. Submit seasonal/holiday material 3 months in advance. Simultaneous queries, and simultaneous, photocopied, and previously published submissions OK. Electronic submissions OK via IBM Displaywriter disks only. Computer printout submissions acceptable; prefers letter-quality to dot-matrix. Reports in 2 weeks on queries; 1 month on mss.

Nonfiction: Historical/nostalgic; how-to (rowing, boat-building, rigging, coaching); interview/profile; opinion; personal experience; and photo feature. "Articles should have relevance to individual members or member organizations. Anticipates buying 4-7 mss/year. Query. Length: 350-3,500 words. Pays $150 maximum.

Photos: Send photos with accompanying query or ms. Pays $25 maximum for b&w prints. Captions and identification of subjects required. Buys one-time rights.

Columns/Departments: Rowing Shorts (humor) and Book/video/film reviews. Query. Length: 350-1,100 words. Pays $50 maximum.

Poetry: Free verse, haiku, light verse and traditional. Rowing-related only. Pays $50 maximum.

Fillers: Anecdotes and short humor. Pays $15 maximum.

SAIL, 34 Commercial Wharf, Boston MA 02110. (617)227-0888. Editor: Keith Taylor. 60% freelance written. For audience that is "strictly sailors, average age 35, above average education." Special issues: "Cruising issues, chartering issues, fitting-out issues, special race issues (e.g., America's Cup), boat show issues." Monthly magazine. Pays on publication. Publishes ms an average of 6 months after acceptance. Buys first North American serial rights. Submit seasonal or special material at least 3 months in advance. Reports in 6 weeks. Computer printout submissions acceptable; prefers letter-quality to dot-matrix. SASE. Free sample copy.

Nonfiction: Patience Wales, managing editor. Wants "articles on sailing: technical, techniques and feature stories." Interested in how-to, personal experience, profiles, historical and new products. "Generally emphasize the excitement of sail and the human, personal aspect. No logs." Buys 200 mss/year (freelance and commissioned). Length: 1,500-3,000 words. Pays $100-800.

Photos: Offers additional payment for photos. Uses b&w glossy prints or Kodachrome 64 color transparencies. Pays $500 if photo is used on the cover.

SEA, Petersen Publishing Co., Suite F, 419 Old Newport Blvd., Newport Beach CA 92663. (714)645-1611. Editor: David Speer. Managing Editor: Liz Cheston. 60% freelance written. Monthly magazine covering recreational boating, both power and sail. Circ. 50,000. Pays on publication. Publishes ms an average of 4 months after acceptance. Byline given. Offers 50% kill fee. Buys first North American serial rights. Submit seasonal/holiday material 6 months in advance. Simultaneous queries OK. Computer printout submissions acceptable; prefers letter-quality to dot-matrix. SASE. Reports in 6 weeks on queries; 3 months on mss. Free sample copy and writer's guidelines.

Nonfiction: Book excerpts; how-to (boating-oriented); humor; interview/profile; personal experience; photo feature; and technical. Buys 60 mss/year. Query or send complete ms. Length: 750-2,500 words. Pays $50-300.

Photos: Roger Morrison, art director. State availability of photos or send photos with ms. Pays $10-50 for 8x10 b&w prints; $50-200 for 35mm color transparencies. Model release and identification of subjects required. Buys one-time rights.

Tips: "We attempt to tell our readers how, when and where to use their boats for the most enjoyment and the greatest efficiency."

SOUNDINGS, The Nation's Boating Newspaper, Pratt St., Essex CT 06426. (203)767-0906. Editor: Christine Born. National monthly boating newspaper with nine regional editions. Features "news—hard and soft—for the recreational boating public." Circ. 80,000. Pays on "the 10th of the month of publication." Byline given. Buys one-time rights. Deadline 5th of month before issue. Simultaneous queries and simultaneous and photocopied submissions OK. SASE. Reports in 2 months on queries; 5 weeks on mss. Sample copy for 8½x11 SAE and 7 first class stamps; free writer's guidelines.

Nonfiction: General interest, historical/nostalgic, interview/profile, opinion and photo feature. Race coverage is also used; supply full names, home towns and the full scores for the top 10 winners in each division. No personal experiences. Send complete ms. Length: 250-1,000 words. Pays $10-100.

Photos: Send photos with ms. Pays $15 minimum for 8x10 b&w prints. Identification of subjects required. Buys one-time rights.

Fillers: Short humor, newsbreaks. Length: 50-100 words. Pays $10-20.

SOUTHERN BOATING MAGAZINE, Southern Boating & Yachting, Inc., 1975 NW South River Dr., Miami FL 33125. (305)642-5350. Publisher and Editor: Skip Allen. Managing Editor: Andree Conrad. 50% freelance written. Monthly magazine; 75 pages. Circ. 25,000. Pays on publication. Buys all rights. Byline given. Phone queries OK. Submit seasonal/holiday material 2 months in advance. Photocopied submissions OK. Computer printout submissions acceptable; prefers letter-quality to dot-matrix. SASE. Reports in 3 weeks.

Nonfiction: Historical, how-to, personal experience and travel, navigation. "All articles should be related to yachting. We do want technical articles." Buys approximately 4 mss/issue. Send complete ms. Length: 2,000-5,000 words. Pays $35-75.

Photos: State availability of photos or send photos with ms. Captions and model releases required.

Tips: "The best query device is to ask a question or series of questions that a boat owner/operator might ask, then explain how the proposed article answers those questions. Send cover letter with manuscript. Send accompanying artwork with ms. Include address and phone number where to be reached during the day. If possible, include name and address on back of photos or on slide covers. We are a boating magazine and do not publish poetry, unaccompanied cartoons, run-of-the-mill personal experiences, or cruising articles outside the magazine's region (Southern US, not California)."

TRAILER BOATS MAGAZINE, Poole Publications, Inc., Box 2307, Gardena CA 90248. (213)323-9040. Editor: Jim Youngs. Managing Editor: Jean Muckerheide. 30% freelance written. Emphasizes legally trailerable boats and related activities. Monthly magazine (Nov./Dec. issue combined); 80 pages. Circ. 80,000. Pays on publication. Publishes ms an average of 4 months after acceptance. Buys all rights. Byline given. Submit seasonal/holiday material 3 months in advance. Computer printout submissions acceptable; prefers letter-quality to dot-matrix. SASE. Reports in 4 weeks. Sample copy $1.25; free writer's guidelines with SASE.

Nonfiction: General interest (trailer boating activities); historical (places, events, boats); how-to (repair boats, installation, etc.); humor (almost any boating-related subject); nostalgia (same as historical); personal experience; photo feature; profile; technical; and travel (boating travel on water or highways). No "How I Spent My Summer Vacation" stories not even remotely connected to trailerable boats and related activities. Buys 18-30 unsolicited mss/year. Query or send complete ms. Length: 500-3,000 words. Pays $50 minimum.

Photos: Send photos with ms. Pays $7.50-50/5x7 or 8x10 b&w glossy print; $10-100/35mm color transparency. Captions required.

Columns & Departments: Boaters Bookshelf (boating book reviews); Over the Transom (funny or strange boating photos); and Patent Pending (an invention with drawings). Buys 2/issue. Query. Length: 100-500 words. Pays $15. Mini-Cruise (short enthusiastic approach to a favorite boating spot). Need map and photographs. Length: 500-750 words. Pays $50. Open to suggestions for new columns/departments.

Fiction: Adventure, experimental, historical, humorous and suspense. "We do not use too many fiction stories but we will consider them if they fit the general editorial guidelines." Query or send complete ms. Length: 500-1,500 words. Pays $50 minimum.

Tips: "Query should contain short general outline of the intended material; what kind of photos; how the photos illustrate the piece. Write with authority covering the subject like an expert. Use basic information rather than prose, particularly in travel stories. We've added a new magazine that is a bit more freelance written: *The Western Boatman*—a bimonthly Western regional boating lifestyle magazine—13 Western states."

WATERWAY GUIDE, 93 Main St., Annapolis MD 21401. (301)268-9546. Managing Editor: Jerri Anne Hopkins. A pleasure-boater's cruising guide to the Intracoastal Waterway, East Coast waters and the Great Lakes. Annual magazine. Four regional editions.

Nonfiction: "We occasionally have a need for a special, short article on some particular aspect of pleasure cruising—such as living aboard, sailing vs. powerboating, having children or pets on board—or a particular stretch of coast—a port off the beaten track, conditions peculiar to a certain area, a pleasant weekend cruise, anchorages and so on." Query with ms.

Photos: State availability of photos. "We have a need for good photographs, taken from the water, of ports, inlets and points of interest. Guidelines on request with SASE."

Tips: "Keep the query simple and friendly. Include a short bio and boating experience. Prefer to see manuscript sample attached. No personal experiences, i.e., we need information, not reminiscences."

YACHT RACING & CRUISING MAGAZINE, North American Publishing Co., 23 Leroy Ave., Box 1700, Darien CT 06820. Editor: John Burnham. 66% freelance written. Magazine published 11 times/year; 120 pages. Circ. 50,000. Pays on publication. Publishes ms an average of 4 months after acceptance. Buys first North American serial rights. Byline given. Computer printout submissions acceptable. SASE. Reports in 2 months. Sample copy $2.50.

Nonfiction: How-to for performance racing/cruising sailors, personal experience, photo feature, profile, regatta reports, and travel. No travelogs. Buys 5-10 unsolicited mss/year. Query. Length: 1,000-2,500 words. Pays $150 per equivalent of one magazine page.

Tips: "Send query with outline and include your experience."

YACHTING, Ziff-Davis Publishing Co., 5 River Rd., Box 1200, Cos Cob CT 06807. Executive Editor: Marcia Wiley. For yachtsmen interested in powerboats and sailboats. Monthly. Circ. 150,000. Buys first North American serial rights. SASE.

Nonfiction: Nuts-and-bolts articles on all phases of yachting; good technical pieces on engines, electronics, and sailing gear. Buys 50-100 unsolicited mss/year. Recent article example: "Return of the Motorsailer" (June

1984). Length: 2,500 words maximum. Article should be accompanied by 6-8 or more color transparencies. **Photos:** Pays $50 for b&w photos, "more for color when used." Will accept a story without photos, if story is outstanding. See magazine for style, content.

Bowling

BOWLERS JOURNAL, 875 N. Michigan, Chicago IL 60611. (312)266-7171. Editor-in-Chief: Mort Luby. Managing Editor: Jim Dressel. 30% freelance written. Emphasizes bowling. Monthly magazine; 100 pages. Circ. 19,000. Pays on acceptance. Buys all rights. Phone queries OK. Submit seasonal/holiday material 3 months in advance of issue date. Photocopied submissions OK. SASE. Reports in 6 weeks. Sample copy $2.
Nonfiction: General interest (stories on top pros); historical (stories of old-time bowlers or bowling alleys); interview (top pros, men and women); and profile (top pros). "We publish some controversial matter, seek out outspoken personalities. We reject material that is too general; that is, not written for high average bowlers and bowling proprietors who already know basics of playing the game and basics of operating a bowling alley." Buys 5-6 unsolicited mss/year. Query. Length: 1,200-3,500 words. Pays $75-175.
Photos: State availability of photos with query. Pays $5-15 for 8x10 b&w prints; and $15-25 for 35mm or 2¼x2¼ color transparencies. Buys one-time rights.

BOWLING, 5301 S. 76th St., Greendale WI 53129. (414)421-6400, ext. 230. Editor: Rory Gillespie. 15% freelance written. Official publication of the American Bowling Congress. Monthly. Rights purchased vary with author and material. Usually buys all rights. Byline given. Pays on acceptance. Publishes ms an average of 2 months after acceptance. Reports in 30 days. SASE. Computer printout submissions acceptable; prefers letter-quality to dot-matrix.
Nonfiction and Photos: "This is a specialized field and the average writer attempting the subject of bowling should be well-informed. However, anyone is free to submit material for approval." Wants articles about unusual ABC sanctioned leagues and tournaments, personalities, etc., featuring male bowlers. Nostalgia articles also considered. No first-person articles or material on history of bowling. Length: 500-1,200 words. Pays $25-150 per article; $10-15 per photo. No poems.
Tips: "Submit feature material on bowlers, generally amateurs competing in local leagues, or special events involving the game of bowling. Should have connection with ABC membership. Queries should be as detailed as possible so that we may get a clear idea of what the proposed story would be all about. It saves us time and the writer time. Samples of previously published material in the bowling or general sports field would help. Once we find a talented writer in a given area, we're likely to go back to him in the future. We're looking for good writers who can handle assignments professionally and promptly." No articles on professionals.

THE WOMAN BOWLER, 5301 S. 76th St., Greendale WI 53129. (414)421-9000. Editor: Paula McMartin. Emphasizes bowling for women bowlers, ages 8-90. Monthly (except for combined July/August) magazine; 64 pages. Circ. 155,000. Pays on acceptance. Buys all rights. Byline given "except on occasion, when freelance article is used as part of a regular magazine department. When this occurs, it is discussed first with the author." Submit seasonal/holiday material 2 months in advance. Photocopied and previously published submissions OK. SASE. Reports in 1 month. Free sample copy and writer's guidelines.
Nonfiction: Historical (about bowling and of national significance); interview; profile; and spot news. Buys 25 mss/year. Query. Length: 1,500 words maximum (unless by special assignment). Pays $25-100.
Photos: Purchased with accompanying ms. Identification required. Query. Pays $5-10 for b&w glossy prints. Model release required.

Football

‡**FOOTBALL FORECAST**, Baltimore Bulletin, 25 Walker Ave., Baltimore MD 21208. (301)653-3690. Editor: Rick Snider. 75% freelance written. A weekly seasonal sports tabloid covering professional and college football. Circ. 30,000 (seasonal). Pays on publication. Publishes ms an average of 1 month after acceptance. Byline given. Not copyrighted. Buys first and second serial (reprint) rights to the same material and makes work-for-hire assignments. Submit seasonal/holiday material 1 month in advance. Photocopied and previously published submissions OK. Computer printout submissions acceptable; no dot-matrix. SASE. Reports in 1 month. Free sample copy and writer's guidelines.
Nonfiction: Interview/profile (on coaches, players). "Audience likes backstage life of football." Buys 10 mss/year. Query. Length: 500-2,000 words. Pays $25-100.
Photos: State availability of photos. Needs "action, backstage, artsy" photos. Pays $10-50 for 5x7 b&w prints. Captions and identification of subjects required. Buys reprint rights.
Columns/Departments: Opinion. Buys 5 mss/year. Query. Length: 1,000-2,000 words. Pays $50-100.
Fiction: Sports. Buys 5 mss/year. Query. Length: 750-1,500 words. Pays $50-100.

Poetry: Must pertain to person, event of big-time sports. Buys 5 poems/year. Submit maximum 5 poems. Length: 20-40 lines. Pays $20-40.
Tips: "We're only interested in big-time football."

‡**THE JOHNNY UNITAS HUDDLE**, Baltimore Bulletin, 25 Walker Ave., Baltimore MD 21208. (301)653-3690. Editor: Rick Snider. 75% freelance written. A weekly seasonal sports tabloid covering professional and college football. Circ. 30,000 (seasonal). Pays on publication. Publishes ms an average of 1 month after acceptance. Byline given. Not copyrighted. Buys first and second serial (reprint) rights to the same material and makes work-for-hire assignments. Submit seasonal/holiday material 1 month in advance. Photocopied and previously published submissions OK. Computer printout submissions acceptable; no dot-matrix. SASE. Reports in 1 month. Free sample copy and writer's guidelines.
Nonfiction: Sports. "Audience is interested in behind-the-scenes sports look." Buys 10 mss/year. Query. Length: 500-2,000 words. Pays $25-100.
Photos: State availability of photos. Needs "action, artsy, backstage" photos. Pays $10-50 for 5x7 b&w prints. Captions and identification of subjects required. Buys reprint rights.
Columns/Departments: Opinion. Buys 5 mss/year. Query. Length: 500-2,000 words. Pays $25-100.
Fiction: Sports. Buys 5 mss/year. Query. Length: 500-2,000 words. Pays $50-100.
Poetry: Must pertain to person, event of big-time sports. Buys 5 poems/year. Submit maximum 5 poems. Length: 20-40 lines. Pays $20-40.
Tips: "Write tight, but descriptive material."

Gambling

CASINO & SPORTS, Gamblers Book Club Press, 630 S. 11th St., Las Vegas NV 89101. (702)382-7555. Editor: Howard Schwartz. Bimonthly gambling magazine geared to casino and sports betting. Offers "inside information on how to bet; how to find an informational edge; how to spot an angle; managing your bankroll, percentage of bankroll betting, etc." Circ. 3,000. Pays on publication. Byline given. Buys one-time rights. Submit seasonal/holiday material 2 months in advance. Simultaneous queries, and simultaneous, photocopied and previously published submissions OK, "but we wish to be notified about such." SASE. Reports in 1 month. Free sample copy; writer's guidelines for SASE.
Nonfiction: Expose (gambling, cheating, hustling, bar bets, scams); historical/nostalgic (history of black games, Chinese games); how-to (gamble on individual casino games, horses, greyhounds, poker, cock fighting, golf, tennis, sports wagering); interview/profile (with famous bettors, gamblers, law enforcement personnel, ex-cheats); new product (related to gambling); personal experience (how-to hints on winning, finding illegal games); travel (gambling in other countries, rules of games, "house edges," caveats). No beginner's how-to articles. Buys 4 mss/year. Query with or without published clips. Length: 500 words minimum. Pays $50-100.
Tips: "Writers should do their homework and do a survey of literature and see what's already been done; what the future holds; what the new 'hot' subjects are. Remember the goal, aim and thrust of the publication."

GAMBLING TIMES MAGAZINE, 1018 N. Cole Ave., Hollywood CA 90038. (213)463-4833. Editor: Len Miller. Address mss to Vanessa Jackson, Associate Editor. 50% freelance written. Monthly magazine; 100 pages. 50% freelance written. Circ. 70,000. Pays on publication. Buys first North American serial rights. Byline given. Submit seasonal/holiday material 5-6 months in advance of issue date. Computer printout submissions acceptable; prefers letter-quality to dot-matrix. Write for instructions on specific ms preparation for electronic typesetting equipment after query acceptance. SASE. Double-space all submissions, maximum 10 pp. Reports in 4-6 weeks. Publishes ms an average of 5 months after acceptance. Free writer's guidelines; mention *Writer's Market* in request.
Nonfiction: How-to (related to gambling systems, betting methods, etc.); humor; photo feature (racetracks, jai alai, casinos); and travel (gambling spas and resort areas). "Also interested in investigative reports focusing on the political, economical and legal issues surrounding gambling in the US and the world and new gambling developments. No cutesy stuff. Keep your style clean, hard-edged and sardonic (if appropriate). Writers may query on any subject which is germane to our format." Buys 100 mss/year; prefers pictures with mss. Query. Pays $50-150.
Fiction: "We only use heavily gambling-related material and prefer fast-paced, humorous stories. Please, no more 'man scores big and dies' stuff." Buys 12 mss/year. Submit complete ms double spaced, maximum 9 pp. Pays $50-100.
Tips: "Know gambling thoroughly. *Pictures with mss will add $50 to the payment.* Action shots—always people shots: Photographs must show something unique to the subject in article. We enjoy the feeling of accomplishment when we've helped an amateur or beginner to make it into print. But we dislike a writer to begin a series of phone inquiries the day after he's mailed a submission."

‡**MIKE WARREN'S BETTING SPORTS**, Baltimore Bulletin, 25 Walker Ave., Baltimore MD 21208. (301)653-3690. Editor: Rick Snider. 50% freelance written. A bimonthly tabloid covering professional sports. "We reach a public that likes to read about the big sports, and we have a gambling readership that likes issues related to pro sports." Circ. 20,000 (weekly). Pays on publication. Publishes ms an average of 1 month after acceptance. Byline given. Not copyrighted. Buys first and second serial (reprint) rights to the same material and makes work-for-hire assignments. Submit seasonal/holiday material 1 month in advance. Simultaneous queries and previously published submissions OK. Computer printout submissions acceptable; no dot-matrix. Reports in 1 month. Free sample copy and writer's guidelines.
Nonfiction: Book excerpts (sports books); expose (sports, drugs, gambling); interview/profile (on pro players and coaches). Special issue, Football Annual (July) with features on pro and college football. Buys variable number of mss/year. Query. Length: 500-2,000 words. Pays $25-125.
Photos: State availability of photos. Pays $10-50 for 5x7 b&w prints. Captions and identification of subjects required.
Columns/Departments: College and Pro Football, Basketball, Gambling. Buys 10 mss/year. Query. Length: 500-2,000 words. Pays $50-100.
Fiction: Sports. Buys variable number of mss/year. Query. Length: 500-1,000 words. Pays $25-100.
Poetry: Poems on sports figures and events. Buys very few poems/year. Submit maximum 5 poems. Length: 20-40 lines. Pays $20-40.
Tips: "Be natural and get to the point for news, write descriptively for features. Don't get hung up by the word gambling. Our readers like to read about sports too."

‡**POKER PLAYER**, Gambling Times Inc., 1018 N. Cole Ave., Hollywood CA 90038. (213)466-5261. Editor: Mike Caro. Managing Editor: Phil Hevener. A biweekly tabloid covering poker games. (This is the only poker publication in the US.) Circ. 25,000. Pays on acceptance. Byline given. Buys all rights. Computer printout submissions acceptable. SASE. Reports in 1 month. Sample copy $1; free writer's guidelines.
Nonfiction: Book excerpts; how-to; humor; interview/profile; personal experience; photo feature; technical (poker strategy). All articles must be poker related. 70% freelance written. Query. Length: 150-2,000 words. Pays $50 maximum.
Photos: State availability of photos. Reviews b&w prints.
Tips: "Especially interested in first-person accounts of poker games."

SYSTEMS & METHODS, Gamblers Book Club Press, 630 S. 11th St., Las Vegas NV 89101. (702)382-7555. Editor: Howard Schwartz. Bimonthly gambling magazine geared to pari-mutuel betting. Offers "inside information on how to bet; how to find an informational edge, etc." Circ. 3,000. Pays on publication. Byline given. Buys one-time rights. Simultaneous queries, and simultaneous, photocopied and previously published submissions OK, "but we wish to be notified about such." SASE. Reports in 1 month. Free sample copy; writer's guidelines for SASE.
Nonfiction: How-to (gamble on horses, greyhounds, cock fighting, jai alai); interview/profile (with famous bettors, gamblers, law enforcement personnel, ex-cheats); new product (related to gambling); personal experience; pari-mutuel gambling in other countries. No beginner's how-to articles. Query with or without published clips. Length: 500 words minimum. Pays $50-100.
Tips: "Writers should do their homework and do a survey of literature and see what's already been done; what the future holds; what the new 'hot' subjects are. Remember the goal, aim and thrust of the publication."

General Interest

‡**ATHLETES IN ACTION MAGAZINE**, Here's Life Publishers, Inc., Box 1576, San Bernardino CA 92402. (714)886-7981. Editor: John Carvalho. 10% freelance written. Quarterly magazine covering sports. "*Athletes in Action* magazine seeks to reach non-Christians with Christ's message and to help Christians grow in their faith by demonstrating how Jesus Christ is relevant to life today—using Christian athletes as role models." Audience is mainly men ages 18-30. Circ. 25,000. Pays on publication. Publishes ms an average of 9 months after acceptance. Byline given. Offers $25 kill fee. Buys first rights. Submit seasonal/holiday material 6 months in advance. Simultaneous queries OK. Computer printout submissions acceptable; prefers letter-quality to dot-matrix. Reports in 2 weeks on queries; 4 weeks on mss. Free sample copy and writer's guidelines.
Nonfiction: Sara Anderson, articles editor. Expose (on issues involving sports); historical/nostalgic (of prominent Christian athletes now retired); how-to (on participant sports skill); humor; and interview/profile (in-depth material on prominent Christian athletes). No personal experience articles. Buys 5 mss/year. Query with published clips. "We prefer to assign articles to reliable freelancers." Length: 1,200-2,000 words. Pays 10¢/word.
Tips: "Personality features are most open to freelancers. We don't just want to know that the athlete has strong Christian beliefs. We want to know how they help him."

CITY SPORTS MAGAZINE, Pier 5 South, Box 3693, San Francisco CA 94119. Editor: Maggie Cloherty in northern California, and 1120 Princeton Dr., Marina del Rey CA 90291. Editor: Will Balliel. 80% freelance written. Monthly controlled circulation tabloid covering participant sports for active sports participants. Circ. in California 195,000. Two editions published monthly—one covering sports in northern California and the other for southern California's participant sportsmarket. "For the most part, we use separate writers for each magazine." Pays on publication. Publishes ms an average of 2 months after acceptance. Byline and brief bio given. Pays negotiable kill fee. Buys one-time rights. Submit seasonal/holiday material 3 months in advance. Simultaneous queries OK; previously published submissions ("from outside readership area") OK. Computer printout submissions acceptable; no dot-matrix. SASE. Reports in 1 month on queries. Sample copy $2.
Nonfiction: Interview/profile (of athletes); travel; and instructional and service pieces on sports. Special issues include: April, Tennis; May, Running; June, Outdoors and Biking; July, Water Sports; November, Skiing; December, Cross Country Skiing and Indoor Sports. Buys 60 mss/year. Query with clips of published work. Length: 1,800-2,800 words. Pays $150-400.
Photos: Pays $50-300 for 35mm color; $25-35 for b&w 8x10 glossy prints. Model release and identification of subjects required.

COLORADO SPORTS MONTHLY, Colorado's Oldest and Largest Sports Publication, Colorado Springs Publishing, Box 6253, Colorado Springs CO 80934. (303)630-3330. Editor: Robert Erdmann. 90% freelance written. Monthly tabloid covering Colorado's individual participation sports. "We are a regionally focused sports magazine. *All* of our stories must have a Colorado 'hook'." Circ. 35,000. Pays 30 days after publication. Buys first North American serial rights. Submit seasonal/holiday material 3 months in advance. Photocopied submissions OK. Computer printout submissions acceptable. Reports in 1 month. Free sample copy.
Nonfiction: Expose (sports-related); general interest (but with a fresh slant); historical; how-to (must be written with clear expertise); humor ("we can always use a good laugh"); interview/profile (usually use at least 1/issue); new product (occasionally); opinion (only if it's strong, well thought out and cleverly presented); personal experience (if it is impressive); photo feature (1/issue); technical (sports-related); travel ("we publish an annual travel, i.e., sports vacations issue"); skiing; running; kayaking. No team, pro-sports, or hunting. Buys 60 mss/year. Query with clips of published work. Length: 900-2,000 words. Pays $50 minimum to "around $100, but is negotiable depending on length and difficulty of subject."
Photos: Robert Horton, photo editor. State availability of photos. Pays $5-75 for b&w contact sheet. Captions required. Buys one-time rights.
Columns/Departments: Bicycling; Running; Sports Medicine; Skiing; Outdoor/Backcountry Safety. Buys 48 mss/year. Query with clips of published work. Length: 900 words. Pays $50.
Fillers: Newsbreaks (Colorado sports—or with hook). Buys 30/year. Length: 150 words minimum. Pay $15 minimum.
Tips: "The best way to break in is not to set off any alarms. Send a query with clips of work or an extended query showing writing style. We like service pieces. We like adventure stories and we love writers who have a sense of drama, irony and humor."

‡IT'S SPORTS!, Fox & Fink Inc., 8610 Suwanee Ave., Box 8077, Tampa FL 33604. (813)932-4441. Editor: Ronald S. Combs. Assistant Editor: bj Altschul. Monthly magazine. "We present lively behind-the-scenes insight into all Tampa Bay area professional and amateur sports and personalities, including celebrity athletes competing or living in the area. Our audience is spirited and sports-conscious at any age. Each issue features a different 'Sport of the Month.' " Circ. 10,000. Pays on publication. Byline given. Buys first North American serial rights. Submit seasonal/holiday material 3-4 months in advance. Simultaneous queries and photocopied submissions OK. SASE. Reports in 1 month. Sample copy $2.
Nonfiction: How-to (specific query first will be appreciated); interview/profile; new product (usually PR material); opinion; personal experience; photo feature; travel (sports-oriented resorts in Florida). All must relate to sports in the Tampa Bay area/Florida. "Our typical schedule (but this is subject to change) goes like this: Year in Review/Preview (Jan.); Auto Racing (Feb.); Tampa Bay Bandits (Mar.); Baseball Spring Training (Apr.); Wrestling/Boxing/Physical Fitness/Martial Arts (May); Beach and Water Sports, Golf and Tennis (June); US Football League (July); Soccer (Aug.); Tampa Bay Buccaneers, football in general, youth football (Sept.-Oct.-Nov.); Basketball (Dec.). "No full-length features on sports personalities who don't even come to the Tampa Bay area—we must have some logical regional connection." Buys 50 mss/year. Query with published clips. Length: 300-1,200 words. Pays $20-75.
Photos: "We particularly need good strong action shots of sporting events and participation sports—beyond what we can get from publicity offices of major organizations. Again, we stress—must have local/regional connection." State availability of photos; send photos with query or ms. Pays $5-10 for 5x7 or 8x10 b&w prints. "The only color we currently use is on the cover and in the centerfold, strictly by assignment. Query first." Pays $50-100 for 2¼ or 35mm color transparencies. Captions, model releases and identification of subjects required. Buys one-ime rights.
Columns/Departments: Joe Doc (easy tips on exercise, nutrition, sports, medicine); Checkered Flag (area au-

to racing events, history, people); and Angler's Angles (fishing hints). Buys 10 mss/year. Query with published clips or send complete ms. Length: 500-800 words. Pays $15-25.

Tips: "We're a good market if you either love sports/love to write about sports, or if you are looking for a way to begin by getting a byline. Our rates are modest; our enthusiasm is a home run." All sections of the magazine are open to freelancers.

OUTDOOR CANADA MAGAZINE, 953A Eglinton Ave. E., Toronto, Ontario M4G 4B5 Canada. (416)429-5550. Editor-in-Chief: Sheila Kaighin. 50% freelance written. Emphasizes noncompetitive outdoor recreation in Canada *only*. Published 8 times/year; magazine; 72-104 pages. Circ. 130,000. Pays on publication. Publishes ms an average of 3 months after acceptance. Buys first rights. Submit seasonal/holiday material 5-6 months in advance of issue date. Byline given. Originals only. Computer printout submissions acceptable; no dot-matrix. *SASE or IRCs or material not returned.* Reports in 1 month. Sample copy $1.50; writer's guidelines 50¢; mention *Writer's Market* in request.

Nonfiction: Expose (only as it pertains to the outdoors, e.g. wildlife management); and how-to (in-depth, thorough pieces on how to select equipment for various subjects, or improve techniques only as they relate to outdoor subjects covered). Buys 35-40 mss/year. Submit complete ms. Length: 1,000-5,000 words. Pays $100-400.

Photos: Submit photo material with accompanying ms. Pays $5-35 for 8x10 b&w glossy prints and $35-100 for 35mm color transparencies; $200/cover. Captions preferred. Buys all rights. Model release required.

Fillers: Outdoor tips. Buys 20/year. Length: 350-500 words. Pays $25-50.

Tips: All submissions *must* include SASE or IRCs.

OUTSIDE, Mariah Publication Corp., 1165 N. Clark St., Chicago IL 60610. (312)951-0990. Editor: John Rasmus. 80% freelance written. Emphasizes outdoor subjects. Monthly. Circ. 220,000. Pays on publication or before. Publishes ms an average of 6 months after acceptance. Buys first North American serial rights. Submit seasonal/holiday material 4 months in advance. Computer printout submissions acceptable; no dot-matrix. SASE. Reports in 1 month (queries); 2 months (ms). Sample copy $3; free writer's guidelines.

Nonfiction: Investigative (environmental/political and consumer outdoor equipment); general interest (as pertains to the outdoors); expedition and adventure stories; historical (profiles of early pioneers and expeditions); how-to (photography, equipment, techniques used in outdoor sports); humor (as pertains to outdoor activities); profiles (leaders and major figures associated with sports, politics, ecology of the outdoors); new product (hardware/software, reviews of performance of products used in camping, backpacking, outdoor sports, etc.); personal experience (major and minor expeditions and adventures); photo feature (outdoor photography); technical (of outdoor equipment); and travel (to exotic regions and cultures rarely visited). Buys 150 mss/year. Query with clips of published work. Length: 1,000-4,000 words. Pays $350-1,200.

Photos: Send photos with ms. Pays $50-200 for 35mm color transparencies. Buys one-time rights. Captions required.

Columns/Departments: Dispatches (news items); Equipage (articles on broad categories of outdoor equipment); Hardware/Software (short equipment reviews, slant to new innovative products, must include evaluation); Natural Acts (natural sciences); Destinations (travel); Law of the Land (legal and political issues that affect the outdoors). Buys 3-4/issue. Query with clips of published work. Length: 200-1,500 words. Pays $150-400.

Fiction: Adventure, fantasy and humorous. Query with clips of published work or send finished manuscript. Length: 1,000-4,000 words. Pays $250-1,000.

REFEREE, Referee Enterprises, Inc., Box 161, Franksville WI 53126. (414)632-8855. Managing Editor: Tom Hammill. For well-educated, mostly 26- to 50-year-old male sports officials. Monthly magazine. Circ. 42,000. Pays on acceptance of completed manuscript. Publishes ms an average of 7 months after acceptance. Buys all rights. Submit seasonal/holiday material 6 months in advance. Photocopied and previously published submissions OK. Computer printout submissions acceptable. SASE. Reports in 2 weeks. Free sample copy.

Nonfiction: How-to, informational, humor, interview, profile, personal experience, photo feature and technical. Buys 54 mss/year. Query. Length: 700-2,000 words. Pays 4-10¢/word. "No general sports articles." Recent article example: "High school official who was unhappy with his assignments fought to implement a rating system within his local association." (Jan. 1984).

Photos: Purchased with or without accompanying ms or on assignment. Captions preferred. Send contact sheet, prints, negatives or transparencies. Pays $15-25 for each b&w used; $25-40 for each color used; $75-100 for color cover.

The double dagger (‡) before a listing indicates that the listing is new in this edition. New markets are often the most receptive to freelance contributions.

Columns/Departments: Arena (bios); Law (legal aspects); Take Care (fitness, medical). Buys 24 mss/year. Query. Length: 200-800 words. Pays 4¢/word up to $50 maximum for Law and Take Care. Arena pays about $15 each, regardless of length.

Fillers: Jokes, gags, anecdotes, puzzles and referee shorts. Query. Length: 50-200 words. Pays 4¢/word in some cases; others offer only author credit lines.

Tips: "Queries with a specific idea appeal most. It is helpful to obtain suitable photos to augment story. Don't send fluff—we need hard-hitting, incisive material tailored just for our audience. Anything smacking of PR is a no sale."

SPORT, Sports Media Corp., 119 W. 40th St., New York NY 10018. (212)869-4700. Senior Editor: Peter Griffin. Managing Editor: Neil Cohen. 95% freelance written. Monthly magazine covering primarily college and pro sports—baseball, football, basketball, hockey, boxing, tennis, others—for sports fans. Circ. 1.25 million. Pays on acceptance. Publishes ms an average of 2 months after acceptance. Byline given. Offers 25% kill fee. Buys first North American serial rights. Submit seasonal/holiday material 3 months in advance. SASE. Reports in 2 weeks.

Nonfiction: General interest; interview (sport interview in Q&A format); and investigative reports on the world of sports. Buys 75 mss/year. Query with clips of published work. No telephone queries. Length: 2,500-3,000 words. Pays $1,000 minimum.

Columns/Departments: Sport Talk (briefs on news or offbeat aspects of sport). Buys 48 mss/year. Length: 250-500 words. Pays $100-150, depending on length and type of piece. Contact: Barry Shapiro, associate editor.

Tips: "Writers should read the magazine to keep up with the broadening subjects we're dealing with."

SPORTING NEWS, 1212 N. Lindbergh Blvd., St. Louis MO 63132. "We do not actively solicit freelance material."

SPORTS ILLUSTRATED, Time & Life Bldg., Rockefeller Center, New York NY 10020. Articles Editor: Myra Gelband. Primarily staff-written, with small but steady amount of outside material. Weekly. Computer printout submissions acceptable. Reports in 1 month. Pays on acceptance. Buys all North American rights or first North American publication rights. Byline given "except for Scorecard department." SASE.

Nonfiction: "Material falls into two general categories: regional (text that runs in editorial space accompanying regional advertising pages) and national text. Runs a great deal of regional advertising and, as a result, considerable text in that section of the magazine. Regional text does not have a geographical connotation; it can be any sort of short feature: Shopwalk, Footloose, Viewpoint, Sideline, On Deck, Spotlight, Sports Rx, Replay, Update, and Stats (400 to 1,100 words); Yesterday, Nostalgia, Reminiscence, Perspective, First Person, On the Scene (1,200-2,000 words), but it must deal with some aspect of sports. National text (1,500-6,000 words) also must have a clear sporting connection; should be personality, personal reminiscence, knowing look into a significant aspect of a sporting subject, but national text should be written for broad appeal, so that readers without special knowledge will appreciate the piece." No how-to or instructional material. Pays $500-1,000 for regional pieces, $1,500 and up for national text. Smaller payments are made for material used in special sections or departments.

Photos: "Do not submit photos or artwork until story is purchased." No fiction, no poetry.

Tips: "Regional text is the best section for a newcomer. National text is difficult as most of the national sections are staff-written."

SPORTS PARADE, Meridian Publishing Co., Inc., 1720 Washington Blvd., Odgen UT 84404. Editor: Wayne DeWald. A monthly general interest sports magazine distributed by business and professional firms to employees, customers, clients, etc. Readers are predominantly upscale, mainstream, family oriented. Pays on acceptance. Byline given. Buys first North American serial rights. Submit seasonal/holiday material 6 months in advance. Simultaneous queries and previously published submissions OK. SASE. Reports in 2 weeks. Sample copy $1; writer's guidelines for SAE and 1 first class stamp.

Nonfiction: General interest, humor, and interview/profile. "Emphasis is about 2-to-1 in favor of spectator sports over participant." Buys 40-50 mss/year. Query. Length: 600-1,200 words. Pays 15¢/word.

Photos: State availability of photos or send with query or ms. Pays $35 for 35mm color transparencies. Identification of subjects required. Buys one-time rights.

Fillers: Anecdotes, short humor. Buys 6/year. Length: 100-250 words. Pays 15¢/word.

Tips: "Best area for freelancers is 'Yesterday's Heroes' 800-word profiles on past sports heroes. Query on an athlete with good name recognition. The article should give a brief summary of his or her accomplishments and bring us up to date."

SPORTSCAPE, The Boston Sports Journal, 1318 Beacon St., Brookline MA 02146. (617)277-3823. Editor: Todd Logan. Managing Editor: Marc Onigman. Monthly sports magazine for participants in running, racquet sports, bicycling, skiing, and outdoors activities. Must have New England angle. Circ. 70,000. Pays on acceptance. Byline given. Offers 33% kill fee. Buys all rights. Submit seasonal/holiday material 6 months in advance. Simultaneous queries and simultaneous and photocopied submissions OK. Computer printout submissions acceptable. SASE. Reports in 1 month on queries; 2 months on mss. Sample copy for $1 and 9x12 SAE.

Nonfiction: Must have New England angle. Humor; interview/profile (not the standard "gee-whiz" approach); new product; and travel (participant-sports related). Fiction OK. "Participant pieces must offer something new and genuine." Recent article example: "Solitary Cross Country Skiing." Buys 30 unsolicited mss/year. Query with clips of published work. Length: 1,800-3,500 words. Pays $150 minimum.

Photos: Meg Birnbaum, photo editor. State availability of photos. Pays $5-20 for b&w contact sheets. Captions, model release, and identification of subjects required.

Tips: "We are looking for more participant-sports stories about New England."

‡THE SPORTSMEN MAGAZINE, CRV Publications Canada Ltd., Suite 202, 2077 Dundas St. E, Mississauga, Ontario L4X 1M2 Canada. (416)624-8218. Editorial Director: Reg Fife. An annual magazine covering "the whole, broad outdoor recreation field, especially enjoyment of the outdoors." Circ. 320,000. Pays on publication. Byline given. Buys first rights. Submit seasonal/holiday material 4 months in advance. Computer printout submissions acceptable; no dot-matrix. SASE. Reports in 2 months. Free sample copy and writer's guidelines.

Nonfiction: General interest; historical/nostalgic (sometimes); how-to; new product; personal experience; photo feature; technical; and travel. No regional material; must deal with Canada in a coast-to-coast manner. Buys 12 mss/year. Query. Length: 1,500-2,000 words. Pays $300-500.

Photos: Send photos with query or ms. Reviews contact sheets, negatives, transparencies (send duplicates) and prints. Identification of subjects required. Buys first serial rights.

‡SPORTSNOW, The Magazine for Young America, The Sporting News Publishing Company, 1212 N. Lindbergh Blvd., St. Louis MO 63166. (314)997-7111. Editor: Dick Kaegel. A monthly sports tabloid aimed at active youth ages 12-19. Estab. 1983. Circ. 500,000. Pays on publication. Byline given. Buys all rights. Submit seasonal/holiday material 3 months in advance. Simultaneous queries and submissions OK. SASE. Reports in 2 weeks. Sample copy for 9x12 SAE and 5 first class stamps; writer's guidelines for business-size SAE and 1 first class stamp.

Nonfiction: Book excerpts (sports); historical/nostalgic (sports); how-to (physical fitness); humor (sports); interview/profile (young athlete); new product (sporting goods, apparel, video, nutrition); personal experience (pro athletes only); photo feature (sports); unusual hobbies; television; high school athlete. No personal reflections as a sports fan or player. Buys 120 mss/year. Query with published clips. Length: 1,000-1,500 words. Pays $35 minimum.

Photos: Melanie J. Webb, associate editor. State availability of photos or send photos with query or ms. Pays $35 for 5x7 b&w and color prints; $35 minimum, $200 maximum for cover for 1¾ color transparencies. Identification of subjects required. Buys one-time rights.

Columns/Departments: Humor; Training Table (nutrition, fitness); Word Games (sports puzzles); Tuning In (video, TV, records); Flashbacks (historical events); Other Stuff (video games, records, films). Buys 15 mss/year. Send complete ms. Length: 800-1,000 words. Pays $25 minimum.

Fiction: Tom Raber, associate editor. Historical (sports), humorous (sports); novel excerpts. No erotica or experimental. Buys 2 mss/year. Send complete ms. Length: 1,500 words maximum.

Fillers: Clippings, anecdotes, short humor, newsbreaks—all sports oriented. Length: 100 words maximum. Pays $5.

Tips: Feature articles are most open to freelancers. "We are basically a news magazine searching for stories on outstanding high school and college athletes and how young America stays in shape. Keep it simple. Be upbeat and enthusiastic. Remember the audience."

‡ULTRASPORT, Endurance Sports, Inc., 11 Beacon St., Boston MA 02108. (617)227-1988. Editor: Chris Bergonzi. Associate Editor: Seth Bauer. 90% freelance written. Bimonthly magazine covering endurance sports for participant athletes. Estab. 1983. Circ. 75,000. Pays on acceptance. Publishes ms an average of 6 weeks after acceptance. Offers up to ⅓ kill fee. Rights purchased vary. Submit seasonal/holiday material 3 months in advance. Photocopied submissions OK. Computer printout submissions acceptable; prefers letter-quality to dot-matrix. SASE. Reports in 3 weeks on queries; 1 month on mss. Sample copy for 9x12 SAE and $1.22 postage.

Nonfiction: Expose, general interest, interview/profile, and photo feature. Little how-to material. Buys 50 mss/year. Query with published clips or send complete ms. Length: 1,500-3,500 words. Pays $300-800.

Photos: State availability of photos. Pays $80-375 for color transparencies.

Columns/Departments: Face-to-Face (interview with prominent athlete) and Body and Soul (profile of athlete focusing on training). Buys 12 mss/year. Query with published clips. Length: 1,200-2,000 words. pays $300-600.

Fiction: Buys up to 6 mss/year. Send complete ms. Length: 1,500-3,500 words. Pays $300-800.

Poetry: "We've not yet published poetry but might if the right piece came in."

Tips: "A freelancer can best break in to our publication with a query on a profile or an issue which is sports-related but not overdone or circus-like. We publish adventure pieces if they have an athletic component."

WOMEN'S SPORTS MAGAZINE, Women's Sports Publications, Inc., 310 Town & Country Village, Palo Alto CA 94301. Editor: Amy Rennert. Query Editor: Mary Witherell. Emphasizes women's sports, fitness and health. Monthly magazine; 72 pages. Circ. 125,000. Pays on publication. Buys all rights. Submit seasonal/holiday material 3 months in advance. Computer printout submissions acceptable; no dot-matrix. SASE. Reports in 1 month (queries); 6 weeks (ms). Sample copy $2; SASE for writer's guidelines.

Nonfiction: Profile, service piece, interview, how-to, historic, personal experience, personal opinion, travel, new product, reviews. "All articles should pertain to women's sports and fitness or health. All must be of national interest." Buys 5 mss/issue. Length: 2,500-3,000 words. Pays $300-600 for features.

Photos: State availability of photos. Pays about $25 for b&w prints; about $50 for 35mm color transparencies. Buys one-time rights.

Columns/Departments: Buys 6-8/issue. Query with clips of published work. Length: 500-1,500 words. Pays $50 minimum.

Fillers: Clippings, newsbreaks and health and fitness information. Length: 100-250 words.

Tips: "We prefer queries to manuscripts. The best query letters often start with a first paragraph that could be the first paragraph of the article the writer wants to do. Queries should indicate that the writer has done the preliminary research for the article and has an ''angle'' or something to give the article personality. Published clips help too. Freelancers can best break into *Women's Sports* by submitting short items for the Sports Pages and Active Woman's Almanac sections or opinion pieces for End Zone. We are not looking for profiles of athletes that lack depth or a real understanding of the athlete; we are looking for items of concern to active women—and we interpret that broadly—from the water she drinks to women to watch or remember, from adventure/travel to event coverage."

Golf

‡AMATEUR GOLF REGISTER, Amateur Golf Association of America, Inc., 5555 Hollywood Blvd., Hollywood FL 33021. Managing Editor: Edward Foley. 30% freelance written. A monthly magazine for amateur golfers of all ages. Circ. 25,000+. Pays on acceptance. Publishes ms an average of 1 month after acceptance. Byline given. Buys all rights. Submit seasonal/holiday material 2 months in advance. Photocopied submissions OK. Computer printout submissions acceptable; no dot-matrix.

Nonfiction: Book excerpts, how-to, interview/profile, new product; photo feature, travel. Topics should be golf-related. Buys variable number of mss/year. Send complete ms. Length: 200-500 words. Pays $15-50.

Photos: K. Foley, photo editor. State availability of photos. Pays variable rate for 8x10 prints. Captions, model release, and identification of subjects required. Buys all rights.

Columns/Departments: D. Lundy, column/department editor. Buys variable number/year. Query. Length: 200-500 words. Pays $15-50.

Fillers: Jokes, short humor, newsbreaks. Length: 50-300 words. Pays $5-25.

‡GULF COAST GOLFER, Gulf Coast Golfer, Inc., 5715 NW Central Dr., Houston TX 77092. (713)460-9551. Editor: Bobby Gray. 60% freelance written. A monthly magazine convering results of major area competition, data on upcoming tournaments, reports of new and improved golf courses, and how-to tips for active, competitive golfers in the Texas Gulf Coast area. Estab. 1983. Circ. 30,000. Pays on publication. Publishes ms an average of 2 weeks after acceptance. Byline given. Buys one-time rights. Submit seasonal/holiday material 3 months in advance. Computer printout submissions acceptable; prefers letter-quality to dot-matrix. SASE. Reports in 3 weeks. Sample copy for 9x12 SAE; free writer's guidelines.

Nonfiction: How-to and personal experience golf articles. No routine coverage. Query. Length: by arrangement. Pays negotiable rates.

Tips: Especially wants articles on how-to subjects about golf in Gulf Coast area.

GOLF DIGEST, 495 Westport Ave., Norwalk CT 06856. (203)847-5811. Executive Editor: John R. McDermott. 30% freelance written. Emphasizes golfing. Monthly magazine; 160 pages. Circ. 1.2 million. Pays on acceptance. Publishes ms an average of 6 weeks after acceptance. Buys all rights. Byline given. Submit seasonal/holiday material 4 months in advance. Photocopied submissions OK. Computer printout submissions acceptable; prefers letter-quality to dot-matrix. SASE. Reports in 4-6 weeks.

Nonfiction: Expose, how-to, informational, historical, humor, inspirational, interview, nostalgia, opinion, profile, travel, new product, personal experience, photo feature and technical; "all on playing and otherwise enjoying the game of golf." Recent article example: "USGA Declares Open Season on Sandbaggers" (May 1984). Query. Length: 1,000-2,500 words. Pays 20¢/edited word minimum.

Photos: Nick DiDio, art director. Purchased without accompanying ms. Pays $10-150 for 5x7 or 8x10 b&w prints; $25-300/35mm color transparency. Model release required.

Poetry: Lois Hains, assistant editor. Light verse. Buys 1-2/issue. Length: 4-8 lines. Pays $25.
Fillers: Lois Hains, assistant editor. Jokes, gags, anecdotes, cut lines for cartoons. Buys 1-2/issue. Length: 2-6 lines. Pays $10-25.

GOLF MAGAZINE, Times Mirror Magazines, Inc., 380 Madison Ave., New York NY 10017. (212)687-3000. Editor: George Peper. 20% freelance written. Emphasizes golf for males, ages 15-80, college-educated, professionals. Monthly magazine; 150 pages. Circ. 770,000. Pays on acceptance. Buys all rights. Byline given. Submit seasonal/holiday material 4 months in advance. Photocopied submissions OK. SASE. Reports in 4 weeks. Sample copy $1.50.
Nonfiction: How-to (improve game, instructional tips); informational (news in golf); humor; profile (people in golf); travel (golf courses, resorts); new product (golf equipment, apparel, teaching aids); and photo feature (great moments in golf; must be special. Most photography on assignment only). Buys 4-6 unsolicited mss/ year. Query. Length: 1,200-2,500 words. Pays $350-500.
Photos: Purchased with accompanying ms or on assignment. Captions required. Query. Pays $50 for 8½x11 glossy prints (with contact sheet and negatives); $75 minimum for 3x5 color prints. Total purchase price for ms includes payment for photos. Model release required.
Columns/Departments: Golf Reports (interesting golf events, feats, etc.). Buys 5-10 mss/year. Query. Length: 250 words maximum. Pays $50. Open to suggestions for new columns/departments.
Fiction: Humorous, mystery. Must be golf-related. Buys 1-2 mss/year. Query. Length: 1,200-2,000 words. Pays $350-500.
Fillers: Short humor. Length: 20-35 words. Pays $25.
Tips: "Best chance is to aim for a light piece which is not too long and is focused on a personality. Anything very technical that would require a consummate knowledge of golf, we would rather assign ourselves. But if you are successful with something light and not too long, we might use you for something heavier later. Probably the best way to break in would be by our Golf Reports section in which we run short items on interesting golf feats, events and so forth. If you send us something like that, about an important event in your area, it is an easy way for us to get acquainted."

‡THE LINKS LETTER, The Newsletter for Golfers Who Travel, The Bartlett Group, Inc., 1483 Fairview Road NE, Atlanta GA 30306. Editor: James Y. Bartlett. 5% freelance written. Monthly newsletter covering golf travel, golf resorts and international travel with news of interest to traveling golfers: where to stay, where to play, what else to do and how much. Circ. 3,000. Pays on publication. Publishes ms an average of 2 months after acceptance. Byline given. Buys first North American serial rights. Submit seasonal/holiday material 3-4 months in advance. Computer printout submissions acceptable. SASE. Reports in 3 weeks on queries. Sample copy for $7.50, 5x7 SAE and 1 first class stamp.
Nonfiction: Travel (not just puffs). Annual issues include Florida, Scotland, Fall Foliage and Spring Azalea resorts. "We don't run any flowery travel pieces. Our readers want down and dirty, hard information, recommendations, places to visit and places to avoid." Buys 3-5 mss/year. Query. Length: 500 words maximum. Pays $25 maximum.
Tips: "Read the newsletter for style and content, then query with an idea for someplace we haven't been (and we've been almost everywhere)."

‡SCORE, Canada's Golf Magazine, Canadian Controlled Media Communications, 287 MacPherson Ave., Toronto, Ontario M4V 1A4 Canada. (416)961-5141. Managing Editor: Lisa A. Leighton. Magazine published 7 times/year covering golf. "*Score* magazine provides seasonal coverage of the Canadian golf scene, professional, amateur, senior and junior golf for men and women golfers in Canada, the US and Europe through profiles, history, editorial comment, instruction, photo features, and regular editorial contributions from the Royal Canadian Golf Association, the Canadian Ladies' Golf Association, and the Canadian Professional Golfers' Association (the three national governing bodies of the game in Canada)." Circ. 171,650. Pays on publication. Byline given. Offers negotiable kill free although kill fees are rarely required. Buys all rights and second serial (reprint) rights if applicable. Submit seasonal/holiday material 8 months in advance. SASE. Reports in 1 month. Sample copy for $2 (Canadian), 9x12 SAE and IRCs; writer's guidelines for business-size SAE and IRC.
Nonfiction: Book excerpts (golf); historical/nostalgic (golf and golf characters); humor (golf); interview/profile (prominent golf professionals); photo feature (golf); and travel (golf destinations only). The *1985 Golf Annual* (publication issue date March, 1985), will include 1984 tournament results from Canada, the US, Europe, Asia, Australia, etc., history, profile, and regular features. "No personal experience, technical, opinion or general-interest material. Most articles are by assignment only." Buys 25-30 mss/year. Query with published clips or send complete ms. Length: 700-3,500 words. Pays $125-600.
Photos: Send photos with query or ms. Pays $50-100 for 35mm color transparencies (positives) or $50 for 8x10 or 5x7 b&w prints. Captions, model release, and identification of subjects required. Buys one-time rights.
Columns/Departments: Interview (currently prominent PGA or LPGA professional golfer); Profile (histori-

cal or current golf personalities or characters); Great Moments ("Great Moments in Canadian Golf"—description of great single moments, usually game triumphs); New Equipment (annual review—Canadian availability only); Travel (golf destinations, including "hard" information such as greens fees, hotel accommodations, etc.); Instruction (by special assignment only; usually from teaching golf professionals); The Mental Game (psychology of the game; by special assignment only); humor (golf humor); and History (golf equipment collections and collectors, development of the game, legendary figures and events). Byys 17-20 mss/year. Query with published clips or send complete ms. Length: 800-1,700 words. Pays $125-300.

Fiction: Historical (golf only) and humorous (golf only). No science fiction or adventure. Buys 1-3 mss/year. Query with published clips or send complete ms. Length: 800-1,700 words. Pays $125-300.

Poetry: Light verse and traditional. No free verse (avant-garde). Buys 1-2 poems/year. Submit maximum 5 poems. Length: 4-20 lines. Pays $10-25.

Fillers: Clippings, jokes, anecdotes, short humor and newsbreaks. Buys 5/year. Length: 20-100 words. Pays $10-25.

Tips: "Only writers with an extensive knowledge of golf and familiarity with the Canadian and/or US golf scene(s) should query or submit in-depth work to *Score*. Golf-oriented humor and verse are the only exceptions to this rule. Many of our features are written by professional people who play the game for a living or work in the industry. All areas mentioned under Columns/Departments are most open to freelancers."

Guns

‡**AMERICAN HANDGUNNER**, Publishers Development Corp., 591 Camino De La Reina, San Diego CA 92108. Editor: J. Rakusan. 90% freelance written. A bimonthly magazine about combat shooting, metallic silhouette shooting, target shooting and big game shooting with handguns. Circ. 150,000 + . Pays on publication. Byline given. Offers 25% kill fee. Publishes ms an average of 6 months after acceptance. Buys first North American serial rights. Simultaneous queries and simultaneous, photocopied and previously published submissions OK. SASE. Computer printout submissions acceptable; prefers letter-quality to dot-matrix. Reports in 3 weeks. Free writer's guidelines.

Nonfiction: Historical (relating to guns and ammunition); how-to (conversions and alterations); interview (which gunsmiths or manufacturers); opinion (pros and cons of styles of combat shooting); new product (objective test reports); photo feature (of competitions); and technical. "This is a highly technical field. You must know what you're writing about. Nothing on periphery of shooting subjects." Buys 50-60 mss/year. Query. Length: 600-2,000 words. Pays $75-400.

Photos: State availability of photos with query letter; send photos with accompanying ms. Reviews b&w contact sheets and color transparencies. Payment for photos included in payment for ms. Buys one-time rights.

‡**THE AMERICAN MARKSMAN**, National Rifle Association, Publications Division, 1600 Rhode Island Ave. NW, Washington DC 20036. (202)828-6395. Editor: John Zent. 10% freelance written. A monthly association journal covering competition shooting. Circ. 8,000. Pays on acceptance. Publishes ms an average of 3 months after acceptance. Byline given. Buys first North American serial rights. Simultaneous queries OK. Computer printout submissions acceptable; no dot-matrix. SASE. Reports in 1 month. Sample copy and writer's guidelines free.

Nonfiction: General interest (on national/international competition); how-to (coaching, equipment modification); humor (experiences in practice, competition); interview/profile (of champion shooters, coaches); new product; and technical (equipment evaluation—request detailed requirements). Special issues include Olympics and World Shooting Championships. No political articles. Buys 15 mss/year. Send complete ms. Length: 1,500-3,000 words. Pays $50-250.

Photos: Send photos with ms. Reviews 8x12 prints. Identification of subjects required. Buys one-time rights.

THE AMERICAN SHOTGUNNER, Box 3351, Reno NV 89505. Publisher: Bob Thruston. Monthly. Circ. 120,000. Buys all rights. Buys 12-15 unsolicited mss/year. Pays on publication. Free sample copy and writer's guidelines. Submit special material (hunting) 3-4 months in advance. Reports on material accepted for publication in 30 days. Returns rejected material. Submit query. SASE.

Nonfiction and Photos: Sue Thruston, managing editor. All aspects of shotgunning—trap and skeet shooting and hunting, reloading, shooting clothing and shooting equipment. Emphasis is on the how-to and instructional approach. "We give the sportsman actual material that will help him to improve his game, fill his limit, or build that duck blind, etc. Hunting articles are used in all issues, year round." Length: open. Pays $75-250. No additional payment for photos used with mss. "We also purchase professional cover material. Send transparencies (originals)."

COMBAT HANDGUNS, Harris Publications Outdoor Group, 1115 Broadway, New York NY 10010. (212)807-7100. Editor: Harry Kane. Bimonthly magazine covering use of handguns in combat situations and in military, police and personal defense. Readers are persons in law enforcement and the military and those interested in the uses and the history of combat firearms. Circ. 80,000. 10% freelance written. Pays on acceptance. Byline given. Buys all rights. Submit seasonal/holiday material 4 months in advance. Simultaneous queries, and photocopied and previously published submissions OK. SASE. Reports in 2 months. Publishes ms an average of 6 months after acceptance.

Nonfiction: Book excerpts; general interest (modifications and uses in combat situations; also gun use in every area of personal defense); how-to; profile (of gunsmith schools); opinion; personal experience ("moment of truth"); photo feature and technical. Recent article examples: any gun test, any tactical scenario. Buys 20 unsolicited mss/year. Query. Length: 1,500-3,500 words. Pays $150-400.

Photos: B&w prints only. "What I really like is photos and plenty of good ones." State availability of photos or send photos with ms. Buys first rights.

Columns/Departments: Combat Course, Pistol Smithing, Taking Aim (opinion) and Cop Talk (about law enforcement). Buys 5 mss/issue. Query. Length: 400-800 words. Pays $150 minimum.

Tips: "It's most rewarding when freelancers meet deadlines. No phone calls, please."

‡**GUN DIGEST, HANDLOADER'S DIGEST**, DBI Books, Inc., Suite 315, 1 Northfield Plaza, Northfield IL 60093. (312)441-7010. Editor-in-Chief: Ken Warner. An annual journal/magazine covering guns and shooting. Pays on acceptance. Byline given. Buys all rights. Computer printout submissions acceptable. Reports in 1 month.

Nonfiction: Buys 50 mss/issue. Query. Length: 1,000-4,000 words. Pays $100-600; includes photos or illustration package from author.

Photos: State availability of photos with query letter or ms. Reviews 8x10 b&w prints. Payment for photos included in payment for ms. Captions required.

Tips: "Know a lot about guns and have something new to say about them." John T. Amber Award of $1,000 to author of best article (juried) in each issue.

GUNS & AMMO MAGAZINE, Petersen Publishing Co., 8490 Sunset Blvd., Los Angeles CA 90069. Editor-in-Chief: Howard E. French. Managing Editor: E.G. Bell. Emphasizes the firearms field. Monthly magazine; 108 pages. Circ. 475,000. Pays on publication. Buys all rights. Submit seasonal/holiday material 4 months in advance. Computer printout submissions acceptable; dot-matrix printouts must have descenders. SASE. Reports in 1 month. Free writer's guidelines.

Nonfiction: Informational and technical. Especially needs semi-technical articles on guns, shooting and reloading. Buys 7-10 mss/issue. Send complete ms. Length: 1,200-3,000 words. Pays $150-400.

Photos: Purchased with accompanying ms. Captions required. Uses 8x10 b&w glossy prints. Total purchase price for ms includes payment for photos. Model release required.

‡**GUNS MAGAZINE**, 591 Camino de la Reina, San Diego CA 92108. (714)297-5352. Editor: J. Rakusan. 90% freelance written. Monthly for firearms enthusiasts. Circ. 135,000. Buys all rights. Buys 100-150 mss/year. Pays on publication. Publishes ms an average of 6 months after acceptance. Computer printout submissions acceptable; prefers letter-quality to dot-matrix. Will send free sample copy to a writer on request. Reports in 2-3 weeks. SASE.

Nonfiction: Test reports on new firearms; how-to on gunsmithing, reloading; round-up articles on firearms types. Historical pieces. Does not want to see anything about "John and I went hunting" or rewrites of a general nature, or controversy for the sake of controversy, without new illumination. "More short, punchy articles will be used in the next year. Payments will not be as large as for full-length features, but the quantity used will give more writers a chance to get published." Length: 1,000-2,500 words. Pays $100-250.

Photos: Major emphasis is on good photos. No additional payment for b&w glossy prints purchased with mss. Pays $50-$100 for color; 2¼x2¼ minimum.

NEW BREED, The Magazine for Bold Adventurer, New Breed Publications, Inc., 30 Amarillo Dr., Nanuet NY 10954. (914)623-8426. Editor: Harry Belil. Managing Editor: Gary Parsons. 80% freelance written. Bimonthly magazine covering military adventures, new weapons, survival. For persons interested in "where the action is—hot spots on the globe where the voice of adventure calls." Circ. 250,000. Pays on publication. Publishes ms an average of 2 months after acceptance. Byline given. Offers 50% kill fee. Buys all rights. Photocopied and previously published submissions OK, if so indicated. Computer printout submissions acceptable. SASE. Reports in 2 weeks on queries; 3 weeks on mss. Sample copy for $2, 9x12 SAE, and first class postage; free writer's guidelines.

Nonfiction: "Give us the best possible information on state-of-the-art field weaponry, combat practice and survival techniques for the professional soldier. Material should be slightly right-wing, pro-weapons (including handguns), somewhat hawkish in diplomacy, pro-freedom, pro-constitution, thus, libertarian and capitalist (in the real sense of the term) and consequently anti-totalitarian. Submit mss on all units of the armed forces, as well as soldiers of fortune, police officers and individuals who can be classified as 'New Breed.' " Special annual "combat guns" issue. Buys 80 mss/year. Send complete ms. Length: 3,000-4,000 words. Pays $125-250 for articles with b&w and color photos.

Tips: "It would help sell the story if some visual material was included."

SHOTGUN SPORTS, Shotgun Sport, Inc., Box 5400, Reno NV 89513. (702)329-4519. Editor: Frank Kodl. Managing Editor: Fredi Kodl. 90% freelance written. Monthly magazine covering the sport of shotgunning. Circ. 105,000. Pays on publication. Publishes ms an average of 8 months after acceptance. Byline given. Buys one-time rights. Submit seasonal/holiday material 3 months in advance. Computer printout submissions acceptable. SASE. Reports in 1 month. Free sample copy and writer's guidelines.
Nonfiction: Book excerpts, expose, general interest, historical/nostalgic, how-to, humor, inspirational, interview/profile, new product, opinion, personal experience, photo feature, technical and travel; "all articles must be related directly to shotgunning to include trap, skeet or hunting." Buys 50-70 mss/year. Query or send complete mss. Length: open. Pays $50-200.
Photos: State availability of photos or send photos with ms. Reviews 5x7 b&w prints. "Photos included in payment for ms." Captions required.

Horse Racing

THE BACKSTRETCH, 19363 James Couzens Hwy., Detroit MI 48235. (313)342-6144. Editor: Ann Moss. Managing Editor: Ruth LeGrove. For thoroughbred horse trainers, owners, breeders, farm managers, track personnel, jockeys, grooms and racing fans who span the age range from very young to very old. Publication of United Thoroughbred Trainers of America, Inc. Quarterly magazine; 100 pages. Circ. 25,000.
Nonfiction: "*Backstretch* contains mostly general information. Articles deal with biographical material on trainers, owners, jockeys, horses and their careers on and off the track, historical track articles, etc. Unless writer's material is related to thoroughbreds and thoroughbred racing, it should not be submitted. Articles accepted on speculation basis—payment made after material is used. If not suitable, articles are returned immediately. Articles that do not require printing by a specified date are preferred. No special length requirement and amount paid depends on material. Advisable to include photos if possible. Articles should be original copies and should state whether presented to any other magazine, or whether previously printed in any other magazine. Submit complete ms. SASE. Sample copy $1. We do not buy crossword puzzles, cartoons, newspaper clippings, fiction or poetry."

HOOF BEATS, United States Trotting Association, 750 Michigan Ave., Columbus OH 43215. (614)224-2291. Editor: Dean A. Hoffman. Managing Editor: Edward Keys. 15% freelance written. Monthly magazine covering harness racing for the participants of the sport of harness racing. "We cover all aspects of the sport—racing, breeding, selling, etc." Circ. 26,000. Pays on publication. Publishes ms an average of 3 months after acceptance. Byline given. Buys negotiable rights. Submit seasonal/holiday material 2 months in advance. Computer printout submissions acceptable. Reports in 3 weeks.
Nonfiction: General interest, historical/nostalgic, humor, inspirational, interview/profile, new product, personal experience, photo feature. Buys 15-20 mss/year. Query. Length: open. Pays $75-200.
Photos: State availability of photos. Pays variable rates for 35mm transparencies and prints. Identification of subjects required. Buys one-time rights.
Fiction: Historical, humorous, interesting fiction with a harness racing theme. Buys 2-3 mss/year. Query. Length: open. Pays $75-200.

HUB RAIL, Hub Rail, Inc., 6320 Busch Blvd., Columbus OH 43229. (614)846-0770. Publisher and Editor: David M. Dolezal. Emphasizes harness horse racing or breeding. Bimonthly magazine; 120 pages. Circ. 10,000. Pays on publication. Buys all rights. Phone queries OK. Submit seasonal/holiday material 3 months in advance. Simultaneous and photocopied submissions OK. SASE. Reports in 4 weeks. Free sample copy and writer's guidelines.
Nonfiction: General interest, historical, humor and nostalgia. "Articles should pertain to harness racing." Buys 10 mss/year. Send clips of published work. Length: 1,000-5,000 words. Pays $50-200.
Fiction: "We use short stories pertaining to harness racing." Buys 2 mss/year. Send clips of published work. Length: 2,500-7,000 words. Pays $50-200.

RACING DIGEST, Racing Digest Publishing Co., Inc., Box 101, Dover PA 17315. (717)292-5608. Publisher: Cole Atwood. Editor: Robin Fidler. Weekly newspaper covering thoroughbred horse racing and breeding, primarily in eastern states. Circ. 58,000. Pays on publication. Byline given. Makes "very few" work-for-hire assignments. Submit seasonal/holiday material 2 months in advance. Simultaneous queries, and simultaneous and photocopied submissions OK. SASE. Reports in 2 weeks. Sample copy for $2 and 9x12 SAE.
Nonfiction: Query. Length: 500-2,000 words. Pay "depends on article, assignment, etc."
Photos: State availability of photos. Reviews b&w contact sheets and prints. Captions and identification of subjects required. Buys one-time rights.

‡**SPEEDHORSE MAGAZINE**, Speedhorse, Inc., Box 1000, Norman OK 73070. (405)288-2391. Editor: Margaret S. Jaffe. A monthly journal "devoted to those involved with breeding or racing quarter horses. It is

not a general circulation horse publication." Circ. 9,000. Pays on publication. Byline given. Offers negotiable kill fee. Buys negotiable rights. Simultaneous queries OK. Computer printout submissions acceptable. Reports in 1 month. Sample copy $3; free writer's guidelines.

Nonfiction: How-to (directed specifically at racing); interview/profile (of prominent horsemen); and photo feature (of racing). "Our articles address those topics which interest an experienced horseman. Articles dealing with ranch operations, racing bloodlines and race coverage are of special interest." No general interest stories. Special issues include Stallion articles (Nov., March); Stakes Winner Issue (Apr.); Service Issue, articles on various services offered horsemen, i.e., transportation, trainers, travel, etc. (May); Broodmare Issue (June); Horse sales and auctions (July, Aug.); Racing Wrap-up (Sept.); and Thoroughbred Issue (Oct.). Buys 3 mss/year. Query. Length: 1,000 words minimum. Pays $25-300.

Photos: Andrew Golden, photo editor. State availability of photos with query or ms. Reviews b&w and color contact sheets. Pays $5 for b&w and color. Identification of subjects required. Buys one-time rights.

Columns/Departments: Book Review and Vet Medicine, by assignment only. Buys 1-2 mss/year. Query. Length: 1,000 words. Pays $50-75.

Fiction: Adventure (race related); historical; humorous; and western. "All fiction must appeal to racing industry." Buys 3 mss/year. Query. Length: 1,000 words minimum. Pays $25-200.

Tips: "If the writer has a good working knowledge of the horse industry and access to people involved with the quarter horse racing industry, the writer should call the editor to discuss possible stories. Very few blind articles are accepted. Most stories are assigned with much editorial direction. Most feature stories are assigned to freelance writers who have been regular contributors to *Speedhorse*. They are located in areas of the country with active quarter horse racing. Many are track publicity directors or newspaper sports writers."

SPUR, Box 85, Middleburg VA 22117. (703)687-6314. Editor: Connie Coopersmith. 70% freelance written. Bimonthly magazine covering thoroughbred horses and the people who are involved in the business and sport of the thoroughbred industry. Circ. 10,000. Pays on publication. Publishes ms an average of 6 weeks after acceptance. Byline given. Buys all rights. Computer printout submissions acceptable; prefers letter-quality to dot-matrix. SASE. Reports in 2 weeks on queries; 1 month on mss. Sample copy $3; writer's guidelines for business size SAE and 1 first class stamp.

Nonfiction: Historical/nostalgic, thoroughbred care, personality profile, farm, special feature, regional, photo essay, steeplechasing and polo. Buys 30 mss/year. Query with clips of published work, "or we will consider complete mss." Length: 300-4,000 words. Payment negotiable.

Photos: State availability of photos. Reviews color and b&w contact sheets. Captions, model releases and identification of subjects required. Buys all rights "unless otherwise negotiated."

Columns/Departments: Query or send complete ms to Editorial Dept. Length: 100-500 words. Pays $50 and up.

Fillers: Anecdotes, short humor. Length: 50-100 words. Pays $25 and up.

Tips: "Writers must have a knowledge of horses, horse owners, breeding, training, racing, and riding—or the ability to obtain this knowledge from a subject and to turn out a good article."

THE THOROUGHBRED RECORD, Thoroughbred Publishers, Inc., Box 4240, Lexington KY 40544. (606)276-5311. Editor: Timothy T. Capps. Managing Editor: Robin Foster. 5% freelance written. Weekly magazine covering thoroughbred racing/breeding. Circ. 13,000. Pays on publication. Publishes ms an average of 2 months after acceptance. Byline given. Buys one-time rights. Simultaneous queries and photocopied submissions OK. Computer printout submissions acceptable; no dot-matrix. SASE. Reports in 1 week on queries; 1 month on mss. Sample copy $2.

Nonfiction: Book excerpts, historical/nostalgic, humor, interview/profile, photo feature, and technical. Special issues include several regional and international editions scattered throughout the year. "Best approached by query from author. No first-person-type articles on anything." Query with clips or send complete ms. Length: 500-3,000 words. Pays $25 minimum; 10¢/word maximum.

Photos: Send photos with ms. Pays $25 for b&w contact sheet if published; negatives OK for submission; $50 for color contact sheet, negatives and 35mm transparencies (preferred); $150 for color cover. Identification of subjects required.

TROT, 233 Evans Ave., Toronto, Ontario M8Z 1J6 Canada. Executive Editor: Michel Corbeil. Editor: Rolly Ethier. 75% freelance written. Official publication of the Canadian Trotting Association. "Quite a number of our readers derive all their income from harness racing." Circ. 20,000. Pays on acceptance. Publishes ms an average of 2 months after acceptance. Buys first North American serial rights. SAE and International Reply Coupons.

Nonfiction: "General material dealing with any aspect of harness racing or prominent figures in the sport. We would appreciate submissions of any general material on harness racing from anywhere in the US. Nothing dealing with strictly US subjects." Query. Length: 1,000-1,500 words. Pays $150-250.

Hunting and Fishing

ALABAMA GAME & FISH, Game & Fish Publications, Inc., Box 741, Marietta GA 30061. (404)953-9222. Editor: Priscilla Crumpler. Monthly how-to, where-to, when-to hunting and fishing magazine covering Alabama. Pays on publication. Byline given. Buys one-time rights. Submit seasonal material 8 months in advance. Simultaneous queries, and simultaneous and photocopied submissions OK. Computer printout submissions acceptable; no dot-matrix. SASE. Reports in 2 months. Sample copy for $2 and 10x12 SAE; writer's guidelines for SASE.
Nonfiction: How-to (hunting and fishing *only*); humor (on limited basis); interview/profile (of successful hunter/angler); personal experience (hunting or fishing adventure). No hiking, backpacking, camping. No fiction or poems. No "my first deer" articles. Buys 60 mss/year. Query with or without published clips. Length: 1,800-2,200 words. Pays $150.
Photos: State availability of photos. Pays $50-100 for full-page, color leads; $225 for covers; $10-45 for b&w photos not submitted as part of story package. Captions and identification of subjects required. Buys one-time rights.

ALASKA OUTDOORS, Swensen's Publishing, Box 8-3550, Fairbanks AK 99708. (907)276-2672. Editor: Christopher Batin. 80% freelance written. Bimonthly magazine covering hunting and fishing in Alaska. Circ. 73,000. Pays on publication. Publishes ms an average of 6 months after acceptance. Buys first rights. Byline given. Submit seasonal/holiday material 4 months in advance. Computer printout submissions acceptable; prefers letter-quality to dot-matrix. SASE. Reports in 2 weeks. Sample copy $2; writer's guidelines for 4x9½ SAE and 1 first class stamp.
Nonfiction: How-to, investigative reports on outdoor issues in Alaska, and articles on where to go to fish and hunt in Alaska. "Articles should include a sidebar that will aid the reader in duplicating your adventure. No survival-type articles or personal brushes with death." Buys 75 unsolicited mss/year. Query. Length: 800-1,800 words. Pays $50-300; "$250 minimum for article with photographic support."
Photos: Send photos with ms to the attention of photo editor. Pays $10-25 for b&w contact sheets; $50-200 for 2¼x2¼ or 35mm color transparencies. Captions required. Buys one-time rights.
Tips: "Include more information and more descriptive writing, and less storytelling and Me 'n Joe type articles. No first-person accounts. Most of our writers have visited or live in Alaska. We are more than just a regional publication; we're distributed nationally."

AMERICAN HUNTER, 1600 Rhode Island Ave. NW, Washington DC 20036. Editor: Tom Fulgham. 90% freelance written. For sport hunters who are members of the National Rifle Association. Circ. over 1,200,000. Buys first North American serial rights. Byline given. Free sample copy and writer's guidelines. Computer printout submissions acceptable; prefers letter quality to dot matrix. SASE.
Nonfiction: Factual material on all phases of sport hunting. Not interested in material on fishing or camping. Prefers queries. Length: 2,000-3,000 words. Pays $25-400.
Photos: No additional payment made for photos used with mss. Pays $25 for b&w photos purchased without accompanying mss. Pays $40-275 for color.

ARKANSAS SPORTSMAN, Game & Fish Publication, Inc., Box 741, Marietta GA 30061. (404)953-9222. Editor: Keith Brooks. Monthly how-to, where-to, when-to hunting and fishing magazine covering Arkansas. Pays on publication. Byline given. Buys one-time rights. Submit seasonal material 8 months in advance. Simultaneous queries, and simultaneous and photocopied submissions OK. Computer printout submissions acceptable; no dot-matrix. SASE. Reports in 2 months. Sample copy for $2 and 10x12 SAE; writer's guidelines for SASE.
Nonfiction: How-to (hunting and fishing *only*); humor (on limited basis); interview/profile (of successful hunter/angler); personal experience (hunting or fishing adventure). No hiking, backpacking, camping. No "my first deer" articles. Buys 60 mss/year. Query with or without published clips. Length: 1,800-2,200. Pays $150.
Photos: State availability of photos. Pays $50-100 for full-page, color leads; $225 for covers; $10-45 for b&w photos not submitted as part of story package. Captions and identification of subjects required. Buys one-time rights.

‡BADGER SPORTSMAN, Vercauteren Publishing, Inc., 19 E. Main, Chilton WI 53014. (414)849-4651. Editor: Mike Goc. Managing Editor: Gary Vercauteren. A monthly tabloid covering Wisconsin outdoors. Circ. 12,800. Pays on publication. Byline given. Buys one-time rights. Submit seasonal/holiday material 2 months in advance. Previously published submissions OK. Computer printout submissions acceptable; no dot-matrix. SASE. Reports in 2 weeks. Sample copy for 9x13 SAE; free writer's guidelines.
Nonfiction: General interest; how-to (fishing, hunting, etc., in the Midwest outdoors); humor; interview/profile; personal experience; technical; and travel. Buys 400-500 mss/year. Query. Length: open. Pays 35¢/column inch ($15-40).

Photos: Send photos with accompanying query or ms. Reviews 3x5 or larger b&w and color prints. Pays by column inch. Identification of subjects required.
Tips: "We publish stories about Wisconsin fishing, hunting, camping; outdoor cooking; and general animal stories."

BASSMASTER MAGAZINE, B.A.S.S. Publications, Box 17900, Montgomery AL 36141. (205)272-9530. Editor: Bob Cobb. 50% freelance written. Bimonthly magazine (monthly January-April) about large-mouth, smallmouth, spotted bass and striped bass for dedicated beginning and advanced bass fishermen. Circ. 400,000. Pays on acceptance. Byline given. Buys all rights. Submit seasonal material 6 months in advance. Simultaneous and photocopied submissions OK, if so indicated. Letter-quality computer printout submissions acceptable, "but still prefer typewritten material." SASE. Reports in 1 week. Sample copy $2; free writer's guidelines with SASE.
Nonfiction: Historical; interview (of knowledgeable people in the sport); profile (outstanding fishermen); travel (where to go to fish for bass); how-to (catch bass and enjoy the outdoors); new product (reels, rods and bass boats); and conservation related to bass fishing; "Short Cast/News & Views" (upfront regular feature covering news-related events such as new state bass records, unusual bass fishing happenings, etc.; conservation, new products and editorial viewpoints; 250-400 words). "No 'Me and Joe Go Fishing' type articles." Query. Length: 400-2,100 words. Pays $100-300.
Photos: "We want a mixture of black and white and color photos." Pays $15 minimum for b&w prints. Pays $100-150 for color cover transparencies. Captions required; model release preferred. Buys all rights.
Fillers: Anecdotes, short humor and newsbreaks. Buys 4-5 mss/issue. Length: 250-500 words. Pays $50-100.
Tips: "Editorial direction continues in the short, more direct how-to article. Compact, easy-to-read information is our objective. Shorter articles with good graphics, such as how-to diagrams, step-by-step instruction, etc., will enhance a writer's articles submitted to *Bassmaster Magazine*."

CAROLINA GAME & FISH, Game & Fish Publications, Inc., Box 741, Marietta GA 30061. (404)953-9222. Editor: Aaron Pass. Monthly how-to, where-to, when-to hunting and fishing magazine covering North and South Carolina. Pays on publication. Byline given. Buys one-time rights. Submit seasonal material 8 months in advance. Simultaneous queries, and simultaneous and photocopied submissions OK. SASE. Reports in 1-2 months. Sample copy for $2 and 10x12 envelope; writer's guidelines for SASE.
Nonfiction: How-to (hunting and fishing *only*); humor (on limited basis); interview/profile (of successful hunter/angler); personal experience (hunting or fishing adventure). No hiking, backpacking or camping. No "my first deer" articles. Buys 60 mss/year. Query with or without published clips. Length: 1,800-2,200 words. Pays $150.
Photos: State availability of photos. Pays $50-100 for full-page, color leads; $225 for covers; $10-45 for b&w photos not submitted as part of story package. Captions and identification of subjects required. Buys one-time rights.

DEER AND DEER HUNTING, The Stump Sitters, Inc., Box 1117, Appleton WI 54912. (414)734-0009. Editors: Al Hofacker and Dr. Rob Wegner. Bimonthly magazine covering deer hunting for individuals who hunt with bow, gun, or camera. 75% freelance written. Circ. 40,000. Pays on publication. Byline given. Offers $50 kill fee. Buys first North American serial rights and second (reprint) rights to material originally published elsewhere. Submit seasonal/holiday material 2 months in advance. Computer printout submissions acceptable; prefers letter-quality to dot-matrix. SASE. Reports in 1 week on queries; 2 weeks on mss. Publishes ms an average of 6 months after acceptance. Free sample copy and writer's guidelines.
Nonfiction: Historical/nostalgic; how-to (hunting techniques); interview/profile; opinion; personal experience; photo feature; technical; book review. "Our readers desire factual articles of a technical nature, that relate deer behavior and habits to hunting methodology. We focus on deer biology, management principles and practices, habitat requirements, natural history of deer, hunting techniques, and hunting ethics." No hunting "Hot Spot" or "local" articles. Buys 40 mss/year. Query with clips of published work. Length: 1,000-4,000 words. Pays $40-250.
Photos: State availability of photos. Pays $100 for 35mm color transparencies; $350 for front cover; $30 for 8x10 b&w prints. Captions and identification of subjects required. Buys one-time rights.
Columns/Departments: Review Stand (reviews of books of interest to deer hunters); Deer Browse (unusual observations of deer behavior). Buys 20 mss/year. Query. Length: 200-800 words. Pays $10-50.
Fillers: Clippings, anecdotes, newsbreaks. Buys 20/year. Length: 200-800 words. Pays $10-40.
Tips: "Break in by providing material of a technical nature, backed by scientific research, and written in a style understandable to the average deer hunter. We focus primarily on white-tailed deer but periodically use material on mule deer."

FIELD AND STREAM, 1515 Broadway, New York NY 10036. Editor: Duncan Barnes. 50% freelance written. Monthly. Buys first rights. Byline given. Reports in 4 weeks. Query. SASE. Writer's guidelines for SASE.

Nonfiction and Photos: "This is a broad-based outdoor service magazine. Editorial content ranges from very basic how-to stories that tell either in pictures or words how an outdoor technique is accomplished or a device is made to articles of penetrating depth about national hunting, fishing, camping, equipment, and other activities allied to the outdoors. The 'me and Joe' story is about dead, with some exceptions. Prefers color photos to b&w. Submit outline first with photos. Length: 2,000-2,500 words. Payment varies depending on the name of the author, quality of work, importance of the article. Pays $500 and up for features. *Field & Stream* also publishes regional sections with feature articles on hunting and fishing in specific areas of the country. The sections are geographically divided into Northeast, Midwest, Far West, West and South, and appear 12 months a year. Usually buys photos with mss. When purchased separately, pays $450 minimum for color. Buys first rights to photos.

Fillers: Buys "how it's done" fillers of 500-900 words. Must be unusual or helpful subjects. Pays $250 on acceptance.

FISHING WORLD, 51 Atlantic Ave., Floral Park NY 11001. Editor: Keith Gardner. 100% freelance written. Bimonthly. Circ. 285,000. Buys first North American serial rights. Byline given. Pays on acceptance. Free sample copy. Photocopied submissions OK. Computer printout submissions acceptable; no dot-matrix. Reports in 2 weeks. Query. SASE.

Nonfiction and Photos: "Feature articles range from 1,000-2,000 words with the shorter preferred. A good selection of color transparencies and b&w glossy prints should accompany each submission. Subject matter can range from a hot fishing site to tackle and techniques, from tips on taking individual species to a story on one lake or an entire region, either freshwater or salt. However, how-to is definitely preferred over where-to, and a strong biological/scientific slant is best of all. Where-to articles, especially if they describe foreign fishing, should be accompanied by sidebars covering how to make reservations and arrange transportation, how to get there, where to stay. Angling methods should be developed in clear detail, with accurate and useful information about tackle and boats. Depending on article length, suitability of photographs and other factors, payment is up to $300 for feature articles accompanied by suitable photography. Color transparencies selected for cover use pay an additional $250. B&w or unillustrated featurettes are also considered. These can be on anything remotely connected with fishing. Length: 1,000 words. Pays $25-100 depending on length and photos. Detailed queries accompanied by photos are preferred. Cover shots are purchased separately, rather than selected from those accompanying mss. The editor favors drama rather than serenity in selecting cover shots."

THE FLYFISHER, 1387 Cambridge, Idaho Falls ID 83401. (208)523-7300. Editor: Dennis G. Bitton. 60% freelance written. "*The Flyfisher* is the official publication of the Federation of Fly Fishers, a nonprofit organization of member clubs and individuals in the US, Canada, United Kingdom, France, New Zealand, Chile, Argentina, Japan and other nations. It serves an audience of conservation-minded fly fishermen." Quarterly magazine; 64-72 pages. Circ. 10,000. Pays after publication. Buys first North American serial rights. Byline given. Submit seasonal/holiday material 60 days in advance of issue date. Computer printout submissions acceptable. SASE. Reports in 2 weeks. Publishes ms an average of 3 months after acceptance. Sample copy $3, available from FFF, Box 1088, West Yellowstone MT 59758. Writer's guidelines for SASE; write to 1387 Cambridge, Idaho Falls ID 83401.

Nonfiction: How-to (fly fishing techniques, fly tying, tackle, etc.); general interest (any type including where to go, conservation); historical (places, people, events that have significance to fly fishing); inspirational (looking for articles dealing with Federation clubs on conservation projects); interview (articles of famous fly fishermen, fly tiers, teachers, etc.); nostalgia (articles of reminiscences on flies, fishing personalities, equipment and places); and technical (about techniques of fly fishing in salt and fresh waters). Buys 6-8 mss/issue. Query. Length: 500-2,500 words. Pays $50-200.

Photos: Pays $15-50 for 8x10 b&w glossy prints; $20-80 for 35mm or larger color transparencies for inside use. $100-150 for covers. Captions required. Buys one-time rights. Prefers a selection of transparencies and glossies when illustrating with a manuscript, which are purchased as a package.

Fiction: (Must be related to fly fishing). Adventure, conservation, fantasy, historical, humorous, and suspense. Buys 2 mss/issue. Query. Length, 500-2,000 words. Pays $75-200.

Tips, "We make every effort to assist a writer with visuals if the idea is strong enough to develop. We will deal with freelancers breaking into the field. Our only concern is that the material be in keeping with the quality established. We prefer articles submitted by members of FFF, but do not limit our selection of good articles."

FUR-FISH-GAME, 2878 E. Main, Columbus OH 43209. Editor: Ken Dunwoody. For outdoorsmen of all ages who are interested in hunting, fishing, trapping, camping, conservation and related topics. Monthly magazine; 64-88 pages. 65% freelance written. Circ. 190,000. Buys 150 unsolicited mss/year. Pays on acceptance. Byline given. Usually buys first rights or all rights but considers reassignment to author. Prefers nonsimultaneous submissions. Computer printout submissions acceptable; prefers letter-quality to dot-matrix. Reports in 3-5 weeks. Publishes ms an average of 7 months after acceptance. Submit complete ms with photos and SASE. Free writer's guidelines with SASE; sample copy 60¢.

Nonfiction: "We are looking for informative, down-to-earth stories about hunting, fishing, trapping, camping, boating, conservation and related subjects. Nostalgic articles are also used. Many of our stories are 'how to' and should appeal to small-town and rural readers who are true outdoorsmen. Some recent articles have told how to train a gun dog, catch big-water catfish, outfit a bowhunter and trap late-season muskrat. We also use personal experience stories and an occasional profile, such as an article about an old-time trapper. 'Where to' stories are used occasionally if they have broad appeal and include a map and sidebar giving information on travel, lodging, etc. Length: 1,500-3,000 words. Pays $80-225 depending upon quality, photo support, and importance to magazine. Short filler stories pay $35-80. We are increasing our payment scale to writers and photographers and improving the graphics and layout of the magazine."

Photos: Send photos with ms. Photos are part of ms package and receive no additional payment. Prefer b&w but color prints or transparencies OK. Prints can be 5x7 or 8x10. Caption information required. Photos are also purchased without accompanying ms and usually pay $10-35.

Tips: "We are always looking for quality articles that tell how to hunt or fish for game animals or birds that are popular with everyday outdoorsmen but often overlooked in other publications, such as catfish, bluegill, crappie, squirrel, rabbit, crows, etc. We also use articles on standard seasonal subjects such as deer and pheasant, but like to see a fresh approach or new technique. Trapping articles, especially instructional ones based on personal experience, are useful all year. Articles on gun dogs, ginseng and do-it-yourself projects are also popular with our readers. An assortment of photos and/or sketches greatly enhances any ms and sidebars, where applicable, can also help."

GEORGIA SPORTSMAN, Game & Fish Publications, Box 741, Marietta GA 30061. (404)953-9222. Editor: Priscilla Crumpler. Monthly how-to, where-to, when-to hunting and fishing magazine covering Georgia. Pays on publication. Byline given. Buys one-time rights. Submit seasonal material 8 months in advance. Simultaneous queries, and simultaneous and photocopied submissions OK. Computer printout submissions acceptable; no dot-matrix. SASE. Reports in 1-2 months. Sample copy for $2 and 10x12 SAE; writer's guidelines for SASE.

Nonfiction: How-to (hunting and fishing *only*); humor (on limited basis); interview/profile (of successful hunter/angler); personal experience (hunting or fishing adventure). No hiking, backpacking or camping. No "my first deer" articles. Buys 60 mss/year. Query with or without published clips. Length: 1,800-2,200 words. Pays $150.

Photos: State availability of photos. Pays $50-100 for full-page, color leads; $225 for covers; $10-45 for b&w photos not submitted as part of story package. Captions and identification of subjects required. Buys one-time rights.

GRAY'S SPORTING JOURNAL, 42 Bay Road, So. Hamilton MA 01982. Editor/Publisher: Ed Gray. 95% freelance written. Emphasizes hunting, fishing and conservation for sportsmen. Published 4 times/year. Magazine; 128 pages. Circ. 60,000. Buys first North American serial rights. Byline given. Computer printout submissions acceptable. SASE. Reports in 6 months. Sample copy $5; writer's guidelines for SASE.

Nonfiction: Articles on hunting and fishing experiences. Humor, historical, personal experience, opinion, and photo feature. Buys 7 mss/issue. Submit complete ms. Length: 500-5,000 words. Pays $500-1,000 on publication.

Photos: Submit photo material with accompanying ms. Pays $50-300 for any size color transparencies. Captions preferred. Buys one-time rights.

Fiction: Mostly thoughtful and low-key, and humor. Submit complete ms. Length: 500-5,000 words. Pays $500-1000.

Poetry: Free verse, light verse, and traditional. Buys 1 poem/issue. Pays $50-75.

Tips: Show that you are "someone who knows his material but is not a self-acclaimed expert; someone who can write well and with a sense of humor; someone who can share his experiences without talking down to the readers; someone who can prepare an article with focus and a creative approach to his prose." No how-to or where-to-go articles.

GREAT LAKES FISHERMAN, Great Lakes Fisherman Publishing Co., 1570 Fishinger Rd., Columbus OH 43221. (614)451-9307. Editor: Woody Earnheart. Managing Editor: Ottie M. Snyder, Jr. Monthly magazine covering how, when and where to fish in the Great Lakes region. 90% freelance written. Circ. 68,000. Pays on acceptance. Byline given. Offers $40 kill fee. Buys first North American serial rights. Submit seasonal/holiday material 3 months in advance. Computer printout submissions acceptable; prefers letter-quality to dot-matrix. SASE. Reports in 5 weeks. Free sample copy and writer's guidelines.

Nonfiction: How-to (where to and when to freshwater fish). "No humor, me and Joe or subject matter outside the Great Lakes region." Buys 84 mss/year. Query with clips of published work. "Letters should be tightly written, but descriptive enough to present no surprises when the ms is received. Prefer b&w photos to be used to illustrate ms with query." Length: 1,500-2,500 words. Pays $125-200.

Photos: Send photos with ms. "Black and white photos are considered part of manuscript package and as such receive no additional payment. We consider b&w photos to be a vital part of a ms package and return more packages because of poor quality photos than any other reason. We look for four types of illustration with each article: scene (a backed off shot of fisherman); result (not the typical meat shot of angler grinning at camera with big stringer but in most cases just a single nice fish with the angler admiring the fish); method (a lure shot or illustration of special rigs mentioned in the text); and action (angler landing a fish, fighting a fish, etc.). Illustrations (line drawings) need not be finished art but should be good enough for our artist to get the idea of what the author is trying to depict." Prefers cover shots to be verticals with fish and fisherman action shots. Pays $100 minimum for 35mm color transparencies; reviews 8x10 b&w prints. Captions, model release and identification of subjects required. Buys one-time rights.

Tips: "Our feature articles are 99.9 percent freelance material. The magazine is circulated in the eight states bordering the Great Lakes, an area where one-third of the nation's licensed anglers reside. All of our feature content is how, when or where, or a combination of all three covering the species common to the region. Fishing is an age-old sport with countless words printed on the subject each year. A fresh new slant that indicates a desire to share with the reader the author's knowledge is a sale. We expect the freelancer to answer any anticipated questions the reader might have (on accommodations, launch sites, equipment needed, etc.) within the ms. We publish an equal mix each month of both warm- and cold-water articles."

GUN DOG, The Magazine of Upland Bird and Waterfowl Dogs, Gun Dog Publications, Inc., Box 68, Adel IA 50003. Publisher: Dave Meisner. Managing Editor: Dough Lidster. Bimonthly magazine covering hunting with upland and waterfowl dogs for "gentlemen-sportsmen." 40% freelance written. Circ. 55,000. Pays on acceptance. Byline given. Does not give assignments. Buys first North American serial rights and one-time rights. Submit seasonal/holiday material 6 months in advance. SASE. Reports in 2 weeks on queries; 1 month on mss. Publishes ms an average of 1 year after acceptance. Sample copy $2.95; writer's guidelines for business size SAE and 1 first class stamp.

Nonfiction: Needs "how-to," "where-to," "when-to" articles on upland bird and waterfowl hunting—pieces that entertain, inform, and instruct. Good selection of photos important. Pays $150-300. Length: 1,500-3,000 words. Always in need of short (1,000-1,500 word) tips on dog training and shotgunning, as well as humor. Pays $50-150. Little need for fiction.

Photos: State availability of photos. Reviews b&w contact sheet; no extra pay for photos submitted with mss. Pays $150 for covers. Captions and identification of subjects required.

Tips: "Sixty percent of our publication is written by assigned columnists—the best in the business. Freelance material must meet the standards set by our columnists. Because we are so specialized, it is an absolute 'must' to have seen the magazine before trying to write for it."

LOUISIANA GAME & FISH, Game & Fish Publications, Inc., Box 741, Marietta GA 30061. (404)953-9222. Editor: Aaron Pass. Monthly how-to, where-to, when-to hunting and fishing magazine covering Louisiana. Pays on publication. Byline given. Buys one-time rights. Submit seasonal material 8 months in advance. Simultaneous queries, and simultaneous and photocopied submissions OK. Computer printout submissions acceptable; prefers letter-quality to dot-matrix. SASE. Reports in 1-2 months. Sample copy for $2 and 10x12 SAE; writer's guidelines for SASE.

Nonfiction: How-to (hunting and fishing *only*); humor (on limited basis); interview/profile (of successful hunter/angler); personal experience (hunting or fishing adventure). No hiking, backpacking or camping. No "my first deer" articles. Buys 60 mss/year. Query with or without published clips. Length: 1,800-2,200 words. Pays $150.

Photos: State availability of photos. Pays $50-100 for full-page, color leads; $225 for covers; $10-45 for b&w photos not submitted as part of story package. Captions and identification of subjects required. Buys one-time rights.

‡TOM MANN'S JUNIOR FISHERMAN MAGAZINE, Rt. 2, Box 84C, Eufaula AL 36027. (205)687-7044. Editor: Suzanne Newsom. Magazine published February, March, April, May, July and November on outdoor-related topics for youth audience. Estab. 1983. Circ. 50,000. Pays on publication. Byline given. Kill fee to be determined. Buys first rights. Submit seasonal/holiday material 6 months in advance. Simultaneous queries, and some previously published submissions OK. Electronic submissions via diskette compatible with IBM Displaywriter Textpack 4 OK. Computer printout submissions acceptable; no dot-matrix. SASE. Sample copy for SAE and $1.40 postage; free writer's guidelines.

Nonfiction: How-to (on fishing, camping, canoeing, and other outdoor activities); humor (some); and Indian lore. Buys 40 mss/year. Query with published clips. Length: 500-1,000 words. Pays $75-100/printed page.

Photos: John D. Andrews, photo editor. Pays $25 for color transparencies; $15 maximum for b&w prints. Captions and identification of subjects required. Buys one-time rights.

Fiction: Adventure, and humorous (some). Buys 6 mss/year. Query with published clips. Length: 500-1,000 words.

Fillers: Newsbreaks. "We will be adding a new section featuring interesting information and tips on all phases of the outdoors experience. Pay is yet to be determined."

Tips: "We are looking for writers who can relate to young people and the great outdoors in an intelligent manner. Material must be presented in a wholesome, healthy and positive attitude. Fishing equipment and good methods and techniques are the areas most open to freelancers."

MICHIGAN OUT-OF-DOORS, Box 30235, Lansing MI 48909. (517)371-1041. Editor: Kenneth S. Lowe. 50% freelance written. Emphasizes outdoor recreation, especially hunting and fishing, conservation and environmental affairs. Monthly magazine; 116 pages. 50% freelance written. Circ. 110,000. Pays on acceptance. Buys first North American serial rights. Byline given. Phone queries OK. Submit seasonal/holiday material 6 months in advance. SASE. Reports in 1 month. Publishes ms an average of 6 months after acceptance. Sample copy $1; free writer's guidelines.

Nonfiction: Expose, historical, how-to, informational, interview, nostalgia, personal experience, personal opinion, photo feature and profile. No humor. "Stories *must* have a Michigan slant unless they treat a subject of universal interest to our readers." Buys 8 mss/issue. Send complete ms. Length: 1,000-3,000 words. Pays $60 minimum for feature stories.

Photos: Purchased with or without accompanying ms. Pays $15 minimum for any size b&w glossy prints; $60 maximum for color (for cover). Offers no additional payment for photos accepted with accompanying ms. Buys one-time rights. Captions preferred.

Tips: "Top priority is placed on true accounts of personal adventures in the out-of-doors—well-written tales of very unusual incidents encountered while hunting, fishing, camping, hiking, etc. The most rewarding aspect of working with freelancers is realizing we had a part in their development. But it's annoying to respond to queries that never produce a manuscript."

MID WEST OUTDOORS, Mid West Outdoors, Ltd., 111 Shore Drive, Hinsdale (Burr Ridge) IL 60521. (312)887-7722. Editor: Gene Laulunen. Emphasizes fishing, hunting, camping and boating. Monthly tabloid. 100% freelance written. Circ. 55,000. Pays on publication. Buys simultaneous rights. Byline given. Submit seasonal material 2 months in advance. Simultaneous, photocopied and previously published submissions OK. SASE. Reports in 3 weeks. Publishes ms an average of 3 months after acceptance. Sample copy $1; free writer's guidelines.

Nonfiction: How-to (fishing, hunting, camping in the Midwest) and where-to-go (fishing, hunting, camping within 500 miles of Chicago). "We do not want to see any articles on 'my first fishing, hunting or camping experiences,' 'Cleaning My Tackle Box,' 'Tackle Tune-up,' or 'Catch and Release.' " Buys 840 unsolicited mss/year. Send complete ms. Length: 1,000-1,500 words. Pays $15-25.

Photos: Offers no additional payment for photos accompanying ms; uses b&w prints. Buys all rights. Captions required.

Columns/Departments: Archery, Camping, Dogs, Fishing and Hunting. Open to suggestions for columns/departments. Send complete ms. Pays $20.

Tips: "Break in with a great unknown fishing hole within 500 miles of Chicago. Where, how, when and why. Know the type of publication you are sending material to."

MISSISSIPPI GAME & FISH, Game & Fish Publications, Box 741, Marietta GA 30061. (404)953-9222. Editor: Priscilla Crumpler. Monthly how-to, where-to, when-to hunting and fishing magazine covering Mississippi. Pays on publication. Byline given. Buys one-time rights. Submit seasonal material 8 months in advance. Simultaneous queries, and simultaneous and photocopied submissions OK. SASE. Reports in 2 months. Sample copy for $2 and 10x12 SAE; writer's guidelines for SASE.

Nonfiction: How-to (hunting and fishing *only*); humor (on limited basis); interview/profile (of successful hunter/angler); personal experience (hunting or fishing adventure). No hiking, backpacking, camping. No fiction or poems. No "my first deer" articles. Buys 60 mss/year. Query with or without published clips. Length: 1,800-2,200 words. Pays $150.

Photos: State availability of photos. Pays $50-100 for full-page, color leads; $225 for covers; $10-45 for b&w photos not submitted as part of story package. Captions and identification of subjects required. Buys one-time rights.

OHIO FISHERMAN, Ohio Fisherman Publishing Co., 1570 Fishinger Rd., Columbus OH 43221. (614)451-5769. Editor: Woody Earnheart. Managing Editor: Ottie M. Snyder, Jr. Monthly magazine covering the how, when and where of Ohio fishing. Circ. 45,000. Pays on publication. Byline given. Offers $40 kill fee. Buys first rights. Submit seasonal/holiday material 3 months in advance. Computer printout submissions acceptable; prefers letter-quality to dot-matrix. SASE. Reports in 5 weeks. Free sample copy and writer's guidelines.

Nonfiction: How-to (also where to and when to fresh water fish). "Our feature articles are 99% freelance material, and all have the same basic theme—sharing fishing knowledge. No humorous or 'me and Joe' articles." Buys 84 mss/year. Query with clips of published work. Letters should be "tightly written, but descriptive enough to present no surprises when the ms is received. Prefer b&w photos to be used to illustrate ms with query." Length: 1,500-2,500 words. Pays $100-150.

Photos: 99% of covers purchased are verticals involving fishermen and fish—action preferred." Send photos with query. "We consider b&w photos to be a vital part of a ms package and return more mss because of poor quality photos than any other reason. We look for four types of illustration with each article: scene (a backed off shot of fisherman); result (not the typical meat shot of angler grinning at camera with big stringer, but in most cases just a single nice fish with the angler admiring the fish); method (a lure or illustration of special rigs mentioned in the text); and action (angler landing a fish, fighting a fish, etc.). Illustrations (line drawings) need not be finished art but should be good enough for our artist to get the idea of what the author is trying to depict." Pays $100 minimum for 35mm color transparencies (cover use); also buys 8x10 b&w prints as part of ms package—"no additional payments." Captions and identification of subjects required. Buys one-time rights.

Tips: "The specialist and regional markets are here to stay. They both offer the freelancer the opportunity for steady income. Fishing is an age-old sport with countless words printed on the subject each year. A fresh new slant that indicates a desire to share with the reader the author's knowledge is a sale. We expect the freelancer to answer any anticipated questions the reader might have (on accommodations, launch sites, equipment needed, etc.) within the ms."

‡OKLAHOMA GAME & FISH, Game & Fish Publications, Box 741, Marietta GA 30061. (404)953-9222. Editor: Keith Brooks. A monthly how-to, where-to, when-to hunting and fishing magazine covering Oklahoma. Pays on publication. Byline given. Buys one-time rights. Submit seasonal material 8 months in advance. Simultaneous queries, and simultaneous and photocopied submissions OK. SASE. Reports in 2 months. Sample copy for $2 and 10x12 SAE; writer's guidelines for SASE.

Nonfiction: How-to (hunting and fishing *only*); humor (on limited basis); interview/profile (of successful hunter/angler); personal experience (hunting or fishing adventure). No hiking, backpacking or camping. No "my first deer" articles. Buys 60 mss/year. Query with or without published clips. Length: 1,800-2,200 words. Pays $150.

Photos: State availability of photos. Pays $50-100 for full-page, color leads; $225 for covers; $10-45 for b&w photos not submitted as part of story package. Captions and identification of subjects required. Buys one-time rights.

ONTARIO OUT OF DOORS, 3 Church St., Toronto, Ontario M5E 1M2 Canada. (416)368-3011. Editor-in-Chief: Burton J. Myers. 90% freelance written. Emphasizes hunting, fishing, camping, and conservation. Monthly magazine; 72 pages. Circ. 55,000. Pays on acceptance. Buys first rights. Phone queries OK. Computer printout submissions acceptable. Submit seasonal/holiday material 5 months in advance of issue date. Reports in 6 weeks. Publishes ms an average of 4 months after acceptance. Free sample copy and writer's guidelines; mention *Writer's Market* in request.

Nonfiction: Expose of conservation practices; how-to (improve your fishing and hunting skills); humor; photo feature (on wildlife); travel (where to find good fishing and hunting); and any news on Ontario. "Avoid 'Me and Joe' articles or funny family camping anecdotes." Buys 20-30 unsolicited mss/year. Query. Length: 150-3,500 words. Pays $35-350.

Photos: Submit photo material with accompanying query. No additional payment for b&w contact sheets and 35mm color transparencies. "Should a photo be used on the cover, an additional payment of $250-350 is made."

Fillers: Outdoor tips. Buys 24 mss/year. Length: 20-50 words. Pays $20.

Tips: "We expect our rates to climb and our expectations on quality of submissions to become more demanding. It's rewarding for us to find a freelancer who reads and understands a set of writer's guidelines, but it is annoying when writers fail to submit supporting photography."

OUTDOOR AMERICA, Suite 1100, 1701 N. Ft. Myer Dr., Arlington VA 22209. (703)528-1818. Editor: Carol Dana. Quarterly magazine about natural resource conservation and outdoor recreation for 50,000 members of the Izaak Walton League. Circ. 50,000. Pays on publication. Byline given. Buys all or first North American serial rights, depending on arrangements with author. Submit seasonal material 6 months in advance. Simultaneous and photocopied submissions OK, if so indicated. Computer printout submissions acceptable; prefers letter-quality to dot-matrix. SASE. Reports in 2 months. Publishes ms an average of 4 months after acceptance. Sample copy $1.50; free writer's guidelines with SASE.

Nonfiction: "We are interested in current, issue-oriented articles on resource topics, conservation, government activities that hurt or improve the land, air, water and forests, and articles about outdoor recreation such as hunting, fishing, canoeing, wilderness activities." Query with clips of previously published work. Length 1,500-2,500 words. Pays minimum 10¢/word for major features; 5-10¢/word for shorter pieces.

Photos: Reviews 5x7 b&w glossy prints and 35mm and larger color transparencies. Generally offers no additional payment for photos accepted with ms. Pays $100 for covers. Caption and model release required. Buys one-time rights.

Tips: "The most rewarding aspect of working with freelance writers is that rare occasion when we receive a manuscript that needs little editing or revising."

PENNSYLVANIA ANGLER, Pennsylvania Fish Commission, Box 1673, Harrisburg PA 17105-1673. (717)787-2411. Editor: Art Michaels. Monthly magazine of fishing, boating and conservation topics. 75% freelance written. Circ. 65,000. Pays on acceptance. Byline given. Buys all rights. Submit seasonal/holiday material 8 months in advance. Computer printout submissions acceptable; prefers letter-quality to dot-matrix. SASE. Reports in 1 week on queries; 2 months on mss. Publishes ms an average of 6 months after acceptance. Free writer's guidelines for SASE. Sample copy for 9x12 SAE and 71¢ postage.

Nonfiction: How-to and where-to in Pennsylvania fishing and boating. Technical and the latest trends in fishing. No "Me 'n' Joe" fishing articles and no hunting material. Query for articles over 1,000 words. Length: 200-1,200 words. Pays $50-200.

Photos: Pays $15 minimum for inside color; $5-25 for b&w prints. Pays $100-150 for color cover photos; $50 for back cover photos.

Columns/Departments: Short subjects (with photos) related to fishing. Length: 200-250 words. Pays $50.

Tips: "Timeliness and fresh, sharply focused subjects are important for short fishing pieces, and these are the best way new writers can break in to print. Any technical fishing subject appropriate to Pennsylvania waterways is useful, and material should not exceed 200 words. Another way to break in to print here is to know Pennsylvania angling and write a detailed account of fishing a specific waterway."

PENNSYLVANIA GAME NEWS, Box 1567, Harrisburg PA 17105-1567. (717)787-3745. Editor-in-Chief: Bob Bell. 85% freelance written. Emphasizes hunting in Pennsylvania. Monthly magazine; 64 pages. Circ. 210,000. Pays on acceptance. Buys all rights. Byline given. Phone queries OK. Submit seasonal/holiday material 6 months in advance. Photocopied submissions OK. Computer printout submissions acceptable; prefers letter-quality to dot-matrix. SASE. Reports in 1 month. Free sample copy and writer's guidelines.

Nonfiction: Historical, how-to, informational, personal experience, photo feature and technical. "Must be related to outdoors in Pennsylvania." No fishing or boating material. Buys 4-8 unsolicited mss/issue. Query. Length: 2,500 words maximum. Pays $250 maximum.

Photos: Purchased with accompanying ms. Pays $5-20 for 8x10 b&w glossy prints. Model release required.

PETERSEN'S HUNTING, Petersen Publishing Co., 8490 Sunset Blvd., Los Angeles CA 90069. (213)657-5100. Editor-in-Chief: Craig Boddington. Emphasizes sport hunting. Monthly magazine; 84 pages. 20% freelance written. Circ. 265,000. Pays on acceptance. Buys all rights. Submit seasonal/holiday material 6 months in advance. Computer printout submissions acceptable. SASE. Reports in 2 months. Publishes ms an average of 8 months after acceptance. Sample copy $1.75. Free writer's guidelines.

Nonfiction: How-to (how to be a better hunter, how to make hunting-related items); personal experience (use a hunting trip as an anecdote to illustrate how-to contents). Buys 15 unsolicited mss/year. Recent article example: "How to Hunt Pressured Whitetails," (June, 1984). Query. Length: 1,500-2,500 words. Pays $250-350.

Photos: Photos purchased with or without accompanying ms. Captions required. Pays $25 minimum for 8x10 b&w glossy prints; $50-150 for 2¼x2¼ or 35mm color transparencies. Total purchase price for ms includes payment for photos. Model release required. Ms should include a selection of 8x10 b&w prints and color slides. Ms without photo support will not normally be considered.

Tips: "Write an unusual hunting story that is not often covered in other publications. We enjoy that rare occasion when a complete package with good, clean well-written copy accompanied by good photos appears."

PRO BASS, The Weekend Anglers Guide to Better Fishing, National Reporter Publishing Co., 15115 S. 76th E. Ave., Bixby OK 74008. (918)366-4441. Editor: Bob Bledsoe. Magazine published 8 times/year covering freshwater fishing with emphasis on black bass. 80% freelance written. Circ. 100,000+. Pays on acceptance. Byline given. Buys first serial rights. Submit seasonal/holiday material 6 months in advance. Computer printout submissions acceptable. Reports in 4-6 weeks. Publishes ms an average of 4 months after acceptance. Sample copy for $1, 11x14 SAE and 3 first class stamps; writer's guidelines for business-size SAE and 1 first class stamp.

Nonfiction: How-to and where to stories on bass fishing. Profiles famous or successful anglers. Prefers queries. Length: 1,000-3,000 words. Pays $150-250.

Photos: Send photos with ms. Pays $25-100 for inside photos, color and b/w. More for outstanding color. Pays $200 for color cover. Send b/w prints or color transparencies. Buys one time rights

Columns/Departments: Send complete ms. Length: 500-1,000 words. Pays $100 minimum.

SALT WATER SPORTSMAN, 186 Lincoln St., Boston MA 02111. (617)426-4074. Editor-in-Chief: Barry Gibson. 85% freelance written. Emphasizes saltwater fishing. Monthly magazine; 120 pages. 85% freelance written. Circ. 105,000. Pays on acceptance. Buys first North American serial rights. Pays 100% kill fee. Byline given. Submit seasonal material 8 months in advance. SASE. Reports in 1 month. Publishes ms an average of 6 months after acceptance. Free sample copy and writer's guidelines.

Nonfiction: How-to, personal experience, technical and travel (to fishing areas). "Readers want solid how-to, where-to information written in an enjoyable, easy-to-read style. Personal anecdotes help the reader identify with the writer." Prefers new slants and "specific" information. Query. "It is helpful if the writer states experience in salt water fishing and any previous related articles. We want 1, possibly 2 well-explained ideas per query letter—not merely a listing." Buys 100 unsolicited mss/year. Length: 1,500-2,000 words. Pays $200 and up.

Photos: Purchased with or without accompanying ms. Captions required. Uses 5x7 or 8x10 b&w prints and color slides. Pays $300 minimum for 35mm, 2¼x2¼ or 8x10 color transparencies for cover. Offers additional payment for photos accepted with accompanying ms.

Tips: "There are a lot of knowledgeable fishermen/budding writers out there who could be valuable to us with a little coaching. Many don't think they can write a story for us, but they'd be surprised. We work with writers. Shorter articles that get to the point which are accompanied by good, sharp photos are hard for us to turn down. Having to delete unnecessary wordage—conversation, cliches, etc.—that writers feel is mandatory is annoying."

SOUTH CAROLINA WILDLIFE, Box 167, Rembert Dennis Bldg., Columbia SC 29202. (803)758-0001. Editor: John Davis. Managing Editor: Tom Poland. For South Carolinians interested in wildlife and outdoor activities. Bimonthly magazine; 64 pages. Circ. 60,000. Byline given. Pays on publication. Buys first rights. Free sample copy. Reports in 1 month. Submit 1-page outline and 1-page explanation. Computer printout submissions acceptable.

Nonfiction and Photos: Articles on outdoor South Carolina with an emphasis on preserving and protecting our natural resources. "Realize that the topic must be of interest to South Carolinians and that we must be able to justify using it in a publication published by the state wildlife department—so if it isn't directly about hunting, fishing, a certain plant or animal, it must be somehow related to the environment and conservation. Readers prefer a broad mix of outdoor related topics (articles that illustrate the beauty of South Carolina's outdoors and those that help the reader get more for his/her time, effort, and money spent in outdoor recreation). These two general areas are the ones we most need. Subjects vary a great deal in topic, area and style, but must all have a common ground in the outdoor resources and heritage of South Carolina. Review back issues for articles by writers such as George Reiger, Joel Vance, Scott Derks, and Nancy Coleman." Query with "a one-page outline citing sources, giving ideas for graphic design, explaining justification and giving an example of the first two paragraphs." Does not need any column material. Manuscripts or photographs submitted to *South Carolina Wildlife* should be addressed to: The Editor, Box 167, Columbia SC 29202, accompanied by SASE. The publisher assumes no responsibility for unsolicited material. Buys 9-14 unsolicited mss/year. Length: 1,000-3,000 words. Pays 10¢/word. Pays $25 for b&w glossy prints purchased with or without ms, or on assignment. Pays $50 for color.

Tips: "While our pay rates are not 'inspirational,' we need more writers in the outdoor field who take pride in the craft of writing and put a real effort toward originality and preciseness in their work. Very restricted budgeting may cause us to turn away even good material."

SPORTS AFIELD, 250 W. 55th St., New York NY 10019. Editor: Tom Paugh. Managing Editor: Fred Kesting. 33% freelance written. For people of all ages whose interests are centered around the out-of-doors (hunting and fishing) and related subjects. Monthly magazine. Circ. 525,000. Buys first North American serial rights and all rights for SA Almanac. Byline given. Pays on acceptance. Publishes ms an average of 6 months after acceptance. "Our magazine is seasonal and material submitted should be in accordance. Fishing in spring and summer; hunting in the fall; camping in summer and fall." Submit seasonal material 6 months in advance. Computer printout submissions acceptable. Reports in 1 month. Query or submit complete ms. SASE.

Nonfiction and Photos: "Informative articles and personal experiences with good photos on hunting, fishing, camping, boating and subjects such as conservation and travel related to hunting and fishing. We want first-class writing and reporting." Buys 15-17 unsolicited mss/year. Recent article example: "Hog Wild" (April 1984). Length: 500-2,500 words. Pays $750 minimum, depending on length and quality. Photos purchased with or without ms. Pays $50 minimum for 8x10 b&w glossy prints. Pays $50 minimum for 35mm or larger transparencies.

Fiction: Adventure, humor (if related to hunting and fishing).

Fillers: Send to Almanac editor. Almanac pays $25 and up depending on length, for newsworthy, unusual, how-to and nature items.

TENNESSEE SPORTSMAN, Game & Fish Publications, Box 741, Marietta GA 30061. (404)953-9222. Editor: Keith Brooks. Monthly how-to, where-to, when-to hunting and fishing magazine covering Tennessee. Pays on publication. Byline given. Buys one-time rights. Submit seasonal material 8 months in advance. Simultaneous queries, and simultaneous and photocopied submissions OK. Computer printout submissions acceptable; no dot-matrix. SASE. Reports in 2 months. Sample copy for $2 and 10x12 SAE; writer's guidelines for SASE.

Nonfiction: How-to (hunting and fishing *only*); humor (on limited basis); interview/profile (of successful hunter/angler); personal experience (hunting or fishing adventure). No hiking, backpacking, camping. No "my first deer" articles. Buys 60 mss/year. Query with or without published clips. Length: 1,800-2,200 words. Pays $150.

Photos: State availability of photos. Pays $50 for full-page, color leads; $225 for covers; $10-45 for b&w photos not submitted as part of story package. Captions and identification of subjects required. Buys one-time rights.

THE TEXAS FISHERMAN, Voice of the Lone Star Angler, Cordovan Corp., 5314 Bingle Rd., Houston TX 77092. Editor: Larry Bozka. For freshwater and saltwater fishermen in Texas. Monthly tabloid. 80% freelance written. Circ. 55,899. Rights purchased vary with author and material. Byline given. Usually buys second serial (reprint) rights. Buys 5-8 mss/month. Pays on publication. Publishes ms an average of 3 months after acceptance. Free sample copy and writer's guidelines. Will consider simultaneous submissions. Reports in 1 month. Query. SASE.
Nonfiction and Photos: General how-to, where-to, features on all phases of fishing in Texas. Strong slant on informative pieces. Strong writing. Good saltwater stories (Texas only). Length: 1,500-2,000 words. Pays $75-200, depending on length and quality of writing and photos. Mss must include 4-7 good action b&w photos or illustrations.
Tips: "Query should be a short, but complete description of the story that emphasizes a specific angle. When possible, send black and white photos with manuscripts. Good art will sell us a story that is mediocre, but even a great story can't replace bad photographs, and better than half submit poor quality photos. How-to stories are preferred."

TEXAS SPORTSMAN, Game & Fish Publications, Box 741, Marietta GA 30061. (404)953-9222. Editor: Steve Burch. Monthly how-to, where-to, when-to hunting and fishing magazine covering Texas. Pays on publication. Byline given. Buys one-time rights. Submit seasonal material 8 months in advance. Simultaneous queries, and simultaneous and photocopied submissions OK. SASE. Reports in 2 months. Sample copy for $2 and 10x12 SAE; writer's guidelines for SASE.
Nonfiction: How-to (hunting and fishing *only*); humor (on limited basis); interview/profile (of successful hunter/angler); personal experience (hunting or fishing adventure). No hiking, backpacking or camping. No "my first deer' articles. Buys 60 mss/year. Query with or without published clips. Length: 1,800-2,200 words. Pays $150.
Photos: State availability of photos. Pays $50-100 for full-page, color leads; $225 for covers; $10-45 for b&w photos not submitted as part of story package. Captions and identification of subjects required. Buys one-time rights.

‡THE TRAPPER, Spearman Publishing & Printing, Inc., 213 N. Saunders, Box 550, Sutton NE 68979. (402)773-4343. Editor: Don Shumaker. A monthly tabloid covering trapping, outdoor occupations, fur farming, medicinal roots and herbs, calling predators and fur markets for both novice and pro audience, male and female, all ages. Circ. 51,000. Pays on publication. Byline given. Buys first North American serial rights, one-time rights, and all rights, and makes work-for-hire assignments. Submit seasonal/holiday material 4 months in advance. Simultaneous queries, and simultaneous and previously published submissions OK. Computer printout submissions acceptable; no dot-matrix. SASE. Reports in 2 weeks on queries; 3 weeks on mss. Sample copy for SAE; writer's guidelines for SAE and 1 first class stamp.
Nonfiction: Book excerpts (trapping or related); how-to (trapping, raising fur, etc.); and personal experience (trapping, outdoor-related experiences). "We do not want to see anything that refers to or condones overharvesting, bragging, etc." Buys 24 mss/year. Query. Length: 500-3,000 words. Pays $20-200.
Photos: Send photos with accompanying query or ms. Pays $5-25 for 8x10 b&w, and color prints. Captions required. Buys one-time rights and all rights.
Tips: "We stress good outdoor ethics, conservation and public relations. How-to articles are always needed; look for fresh ideas or different slant."

‡TURKEY, Spearman Publishing & Printing, Inc., 213 N. Saunders, Box 550, Sutton NE 68979. (402)773-4343. Editor: Don Shumaker. A monthly magazine covering turkey hunting, biology and conservation of the wild turkey, gear for turkey hunters, where to go, etc. for both novice and experienced wild turkey enthusiasts. "We stress wildlife conservation, ethics, and management of the resource." Estab. 1984. Circ. 30,000. Pays on publication. Byline given.
Nonfiction: Book excerpts (turkey related); how-to (turkey-related); and personal experience (turkey hunting). Buys 75-100 mss/year. Query. Length: 500-3,000 words. Pays $20-200.
Photos: Send photos with accompanying query or ms. Pays $5-25 for 8x10 b&w, and color prints; $100 for color slides for cover.
Columns/Departments: "Nearly all columns are done inhouse, but freelancers often do our 'state of the month' column." Buys 12 mss/year. Query. Pays $25-100.
Fillers: Clippings and newsbreaks that relate to or could affect turkey hunting or management. Length: 50-200 words. Pays $10-40.
Tips: "How-to articles, using fresh ideas, are most open to freelancers. We also need more short articles on turkey management programs in all states, and especially need articles on western turkey hunting."

TURKEY CALL, Wild Turkey Bldg., Box 530, Edgefield SC 29824. (803)637-3106. Editor: Gene Smith. 50% freelance written. An educational publication for members of the National Wild Turkey Federation. Bimonthly magazine. Circ. 28,000. Buys one-time rights. Byline given. Normally pays upon publication. Sample copy $2 when supplies permit. Reports in 4 weeks. No queries necessary. Submit complete package. Wants original ms only (no carbons or other copies). Publishes ms an average of 6 months after acceptance. Computer printout submissions acceptable. SASE.

Nonfiction and Photos: Feature articles dealing with the history, management, restoration, distribution and hunting of the American wild turkey. Must be accurate information and must appeal to national readership of sportsmen and wildlife management experts. No poetry or first person accounts of unremarkable hunting trips. May use some fiction that educates or entertains in a special way. Length: 1,200-1,500 words. Pays $25 for items, $50 for short fillers of 400-500 words, $200-500 for illustrated features. "We want quality photos submitted with features." Art illustrations also acceptable. "We are using more and more inside color illustrations." Prefers b&w 8x10 glossies. Color transparencies of any size are acceptable. Wants no typical hunter-holding-dead-turkey photos or poorly staged setups using mounted birds or domestic turkeys. Photos with how-to stories must make the techniques clear (example: how to make a turkey call; how to sculpt or carve a bird in wood). Pays $10 minimum for one-time rights on b&w photos and simple art illustrations; up to $75 for inside color, reproduced any size. Covers: Most are donated. Any purchased are negotiated.

VIRGINIA WILDLIFE, Box 11104, Richmond VA 23230. (804)257-1000. Editor: Harry L. Gillam. Send manuscripts to managing editor, Sarah Bartenstein. 50% freelance written. For sportsmen and outdoor enthusiasts. Pays on acceptance. Buys first North American serial rights and reprint rights. Publishes ms an average of 1 year after acceptance. Byline given. Computer printout submissions acceptable; prefers letter-quality to dot-matrix. Free sample copy and writer's guidelines. SASE (8½x11).

Nonfiction: Uses factual outdoor stories, set in Virginia. "Currently need boating subjects, women and youth in the outdoors, wildlife and nature in urban areas. Always need good fishing and hunting stories—not of the 'Me and Joe' genre, however. Slant should be to enjoy the outdoors and what you can do to improve it. Material must be applicable to Virginia, sound from a scientific basis, accurate and easily readable. No subjects which are too controversial for a state agency magazine to address; poetry and cartoons; sentimental or humorous pieces (not because they're inherently bad, but because so few writers are good at either); 'how I nursed an abandoned _____ back to health' or stories about wildlife the author has become 'pals' with." Submit photos with ms. Length: prefers approximately 1,200 words. Pays 5¢/word.

Photos: Buys photos with mss; "and occasionally buys unaccompanied good photos." Prefers color transparencies, but also has limited need for 8x10 b&w glossy prints. Captions required. Pays $10/b&w photo; $10-15 for color.

Tips: "We are currently receiving too many anecdotes and too few articles with an educational bent—we want instructional, 'how-to' articles on hunting, fishing and outdoor sports, and also want semi-technical articles on wildlife. We are not receiving enough articles with high-quality photographs accompanying them; also, photos are inadequately labeled and protected. Catering to these needs will greatly enhance chances for acceptance of manuscripts. We have more 'backyard bird' articles than we could ever hope to use, and not enough good submissions on trapping or bird hunting. We are cutting back substantially on number of freelance, over-the-transom submissions we purchase, in favor of making assignments to writers with whom we have established relationships and articles written by our own staff. The trend in our magazine is to pay more for fewer, longer, more in-depth, higher-quality stories. As always, a fresh angle sells, especially since we are basically publishing the same topics year after year."

WASHINGTON FISHING HOLES, Box 499, Snohomish WA 98290. (206)631-4962. Editor: Terry Sheely. 65-75% freelance written. For Washington anglers from 8-80, whether beginner or expert, interested in the where-to and how-to of Washington fishing. Magazine published monthly; 80 pages. Circ. 10,000. Pays on publication. Buys first and second North American serial rights. Submit material 90-120 days in advance. Computer printout submissions acceptable. Reports in 3 weeks. Free sample copy and writer's guidelines. SASE. Query essential.

Nonfiction: How-to (angling only); and informational (how-to). "Articles and illustrations *must* be local, Washington angling or readily available within short distance for Washington anglers." Buys 120 mss/year. Query. Length: 1,000-1,500 words. Pays approximately $90-120.

Photos and Line Art: Purchased with accompanying ms at $10 each extra. Captions required. Buys color and b&w glossy prints or 35mm color transparencies with article. Model release required. Covers $50. Color transparency, ASA 64 film.

WATERFOWLER'S WORLD, Waterfowl Publications, Ltd., Box 38306, Germantown TN 38183. (901)754-7484. Editor: Cindy Dixon. Bimonthly magazine covering duck and goose hunting for the serious hunter and experienced waterfowler, with an emphasis on improvement of skills. 60% freelance written. Circ. 35,000. Pays on publication. Buys first North American serial rights. SASE. Reports in 2 months. Publishes ms an average of 1 year after acceptance. Computer printout submissions acceptable. Sample copy $2.50; writer's guidelines for $1.

Nonfiction: General interest (where to hunt); how-to written for the serious duck hunter. Query. Length: 1,500 words. Pays $75-200.

Photos: Reviews 8x10 b&w prints and 35mm color transparencies. Pays $50/cover.
Columns/Departments: Fowlweather Gear (outdoor clothes and supplies).

WESTERN OUTDOORS, 3197-E Airport Loop, Costa Mesa CA 92626. (714)546-4370. Editor-in-Chief: Burt Twilegar. Emphasizes hunting, fishing, camping, boating for 11 Western states only, Baja California, Canada, Hawaii and Alaska. Monthly magazine; 88 pages. 75% freelance written. Circ. 150,000. Pays on acceptance. Buys one-time rights. Query (in writing). Submit seasonal material 4-6 months in advance. Photocopied submissions OK. Computer printout submissions are acceptable if double-spaced; prefers letter-quality to dot-matrix. SASE. Reports in 4-6 weeks. Sample copy $1.50; free writer's guidelines for SASE.
Nonfiction: Where-to (catch more fish, bag more game, improve equipment, etc.); informational; photo feature. "We do not accept fiction, poetry, cartoons." Buys 70 unsolicited mss/year. Query or send complete ms. Length: 1,000-2,000 words maximum. Pays $200-300.
Photos: Purchased with accompanying ms. Captions required. Uses 8x10 b&w glossy prints; prefers Kodachrome II 35mm slides. Offers no additional payment for photos accepted with accompanying ms. Pays $150 for covers.
Tips: "Provide a complete package of photos, map, trip facts and manuscript written according to our news feature format. Stick with where-to type articles. Both b&w and color photo selections make a sale more likely. We are beginning new section, 'Best In The West.' Write for details."

WESTERN SALTWATER FISHERMAN, Dyna Graphics, Inc., 6200 Yarrow Dr., Carlsbad CA 92008. (619)438-2511. Editor: Carl Calvert. 90% freelance written. Monthly magazine covering saltwater fishing on the West Coast. Circ. 20,000. Pays on acceptance. Byline given. Buys all rights. Submit seasonal/holiday material 4 months in advance. Computer printout submissions acceptable. SASE. Reports in 2 weeks. Publishes ms an average of 3 months after acceptance. Sample copy $2; writer's guidelines for legal-size SAE and 1 first class stamp.
Nonfiction: General interest (fishing); how-to (fishing techniques); personal experience (angler's adventures); technical (tackle); travel (fishing in the West). Write for theme issue schedule. "We use material on techniques, species, hot spot locations, etc., for saltwater fishing on the West Coast, including South Pacific and Mexico. Informative and entertaining pieces on West Coast fishing, geared more toward the *experienced* angler than the beginner." Buys 100 mss/year. Query with or without published clips. Length: 1,500-4,000 words. Pays $75-300.
Photos: Photos are a *must* with all submitted articles. State availability of photos. Pays $15-150 (cover photos) for color transparencies and 5x7 color prints. Captions, model release and identification of subjects required.
Columns/Departments: Shorelines (shore fishing); Angler's Adventure (experiences); Tackle Topics (equipment); Charter Trips & Tips. Buys 48 mss/year. Query with or without published clips. Length: 1,000-2,000 words. Pays $100-200.
Tips: "It helps to be 'fishing wise.' We're looking for something different in West Coast fishing—not standard fishing stories. Angler's Adventure is very open to freelancers—any battle with a large fish, rare occurrence while fishing, spectacular catches, etc. Quality says it all."

WESTERN SPORTSMAN, Box 737, Regina, Saskatchewan, S4P 3A8 Canada. (306)352-8384. Editor: J.B. (Red) Wilkinson. 90% freelance written. For fishermen, hunters, campers and others interested in outdoor recreation. "Please note that our coverage area is Alberta and Saskatchewan." Quarterly magazine; 64-112 pages. Circ. 25,000. Rights purchased vary with author and material. May buy first North American serial rights or second serial (reprint) rights. Byline given. Pays on publication. Sample copy $3; free writer's guidelines. "We try to include as much information as possible on all subjects in each edition. Therefore, we usually publish fishing articles in our winter magazine along with a variety of winter stories. If material is dated, we would like to receive articles 2 months in advance of our publication date." Will consider photocopied submissions. Reports in 4 weeks. SAE and IRCs.
Nonfiction: "It is necessary that all articles can identify with our coverage area of Alberta and Saskatchewan. We are interested in mss from writers who have experienced an interesting fishing, hunting, camping or other outdoor experience. We also publish how-to and other informational pieces as long as they can relate to our coverage area. Our editors are experienced people who have spent many hours afield fishing, hunting, camping, etc., and we simply cannot accept information which borders on the ridiculous. We are more interested in articles which tell about the average guy living on beans, guiding his own boat, stalking his game and generally doing his own thing in our part of Western Canada than a story describing a well-to-do outdoorsman traveling by motorhome, staying at an expensive lodge with guides doing everything for him except catching the fish, or shooting the big game animal. The articles that are submitted to us need to be prepared in a knowledgable way and include more information than the actual fish catch or animal or bird kill. Discuss the terrain, the people involved on the trip, the water or weather conditions, the costs, the planning that went into the trip, the equipment and other data closely associated with the particular event in a factual manner. We're always looking for new writers. I would be very interested in hearing from writers who are experienced campers and snowmobilers." Buys 80 mss/year. Submit complete ms. Length: 1,500-3,000 words. Pays $100-225.

Photos: Photos purchased with ms with no additional payment. Also purchased without ms. Pays $10-15/5x7 or 8x10 b&w print; $100-150/35mm or larger transparency for front cover.

WISCONSIN SPORTSMAN MAGAZINE, Wisconsin Sportsman Inc., Box 2266, Oshkosh WI 54903. (414)233-1327. Editor: Tom Petrie. Hunting and fishing magazine published 7 times/year serving the active sportsman in Wisconsin. "Our readers require solid information on fishing and hunting in their home state." 40% freelance written. Circ. 75,000. Pays on acceptance. Byline given. Buys first North American serial rights. Submit seasonal/holiday material 6 months in advance. Simultaneous queries, and simultaneous, photocopied, and previously published submissions OK (very rarely). Computer printout submissions acceptable. SASE. Reports in 3-6 weeks. Publishes ms an average of 4 months after acceptance. Sample copy $1.
Nonfiction: Expose (Dept. of Natural Resources, poachers, etc.); historical/nostalgic (pertaining to Wisconsin); how-to (fishing and hunting); interview/profile; photo feature (wildlife of Wisconsin, etc.); technical (hunting and fishing). Buys 25-35 mss/year. Query. Length: 300-2,000 words. Pays $50-300. As a member of Great Lake Sportsman group network, *Wisconsin Sportsman* also buys some materials in combination with its sister publications in Minnesota, Michigan and Pennsylvania.
Photos: Janet Wissink, photo editor. State availability of photos. Reviews transparencies and prints (8x10 glossy).
Columns/Departments: Afield in WI (little notes about what is happening in the Wisconsin outdoors). Buys 20-30 mss/year. Send complete ms. Length: 100-300 words. Pays $25-75.
Tips: "It's rewarding working with freelance writers and finding the rare pearl in a pile of oysters. It's annoying receiving hackneyed writing techniques regarding hackneyed subjects (a problem perhaps unique to outdoor writing)."

Martial Arts

‡**ATA MAGAZINE, Martial Arts and Fitness**, ATA Magazine Co., Inc., 4180 Elvis Presley Blvd., Memphis TN 38116. (901)396-2893. Editor: Milo Dailey. Managing Editor: Carla Dailey. *ATA Magazine* is the official publication of the American Taekwondo Association and ATA Fitness Centers, Inc. covering general health and fitness with emphasis on martial arts (Taekwondo), aerobics, and Nautilus strength training equipment. Estab. 1983. Circ. 10,000. Pays on publication. "Most of publication copyrighted." Buys all rights unless otherwise arranged. Submit seasonal/holiday material at least 6 months in advance. Sometimes accepts previously published submissions. Computer printout submissions acceptable; dot-matrix submissions OK "if on non-heat-sensitive paper." Reports in 3 weeks. Sample copy $2; writer's guidelines for SAE.
Nonfiction: Interview/profile (on persons notable in other fields who train under ATA programs). "Special slant is that martial arts are primarily for fitness and personal development. Defense and sports aspects are to reinforce primary aims. Freelancers who are not ATA members should concentrate on non-martial arts aspects of fitness or on ATA martial artists' personalities. We're not interested in fads, non-ATA martial arts or overt 'sex' orientation." Currently articles are staff-written, assigned to ATA experts or ATA member freelancers; would possibly buy 4-6 outside freelance mss. Query. Length: depends on material. Pays $25-150.
Photos: Payment for photos included in payment for ms. Prefers b&w prints of size appropriate to quality reproduction. Model release and identification of subjects "with enough information for a caption" required.
Fiction: "We would take a look at fiction—but becuase of the overall magazine subject matter, would be very, very, very leery. It would almost take a writer who is an ATA martial arts member to get the right outlook."
Tips: "So far *ATA Magazine* has served as a developmental organ for ATA members who are or wish to be writers. We're willing to work with writers on nontechnical coverage of subjects of interest to our readership— which is mostly 'adult' in its approach to martial arts and fitness in general. The 'ATA Slant," except in areas of diet, is virtually mandatory. Most ATA centers have a good story. Most martial arts and strength-training articles are staff-written or assigned to association experts. This leaves nutrition and special personality pieces most open to freelancers, along possibly with fiction. But to get the right slant, proximity to ATA sources (which are currently in about 200 communities coast to coast) is almost mandatory. It seems a major problem in writing for most magazines today is to have expert knowledge with ability to communicate at the non-expert level. A middle ground is the 'special interest' magazine such as ours which allows presumption of both interest and a basic knowledge of the subject. Still, it's easy to become too technical and forget that emotion retains readers—not just facts."

BLACK BELT, Rainbow Publications, Inc., 1813 Victory Place, Burbank CA 91504. (213)843-4444. Publisher: Michael James. Emphasizes martial arts for both practitioner and layman. Monthly magazine; 116 pages. Circ. 90,000. Pays on publication. Buys all rights. Submit seasonal/holiday material 6 months in advance. Photocopied submissions OK. Computer printout submissions acceptable. SASE. Reports in 1 month. Free sample copy.
Nonfiction: Expose, how-to, informational, interview, new product, personal experience, profile, technical and travel. No biography, material on teachers or on new or Americanized styles. Buys 6 mss/issue. Query or

send complete ms. Length: 1,200 words minimum. Pays $10-15/page of manuscript.

Photos: Very seldom buys photos without accompanying mss. Captions required. Pays $4-7 for 5x7 or 8x10 b&w or color transparencies. Total purchase price for ms includes payment for photos. Model release required.

Fiction: Historical. Buys 1 ms/issue. Query. Pays $35-100.

Fillers: Pays $5 minimum.

Tips: "Our payment will rise, in step with the continuation of growth during the past year."

FIGHTING STARS, Rainbow Publications, 1813 Victory Place, Box 7728, Burbank CA 91510-7728. (818)843-4444. Executive Editor: Kurt Seemann. Bimonthly magazine about the training and fighting techniques of the top martial artists in the world. Circ. 80,000. Pays on publication. Buys first North American serial rights. Submit seasonal material 4 months in advance. Simultaneous and photocopied submissions OK. Computer printout submissions acceptable. SASE. Reports in 3-6 weeks. Free sample copy; free writer's guidelines with SASE.

Nonfiction and Photos: General interest or training articles (with standout martial artists); profiles (on championship or superior martial artists); how-to (featuring, again, top-quality martial artists). Buys 25 unsolicited mss/year. Send query or complete ms. Length: 1,200-2,000 words. Pays $50-200. State availability of photos. Most ms should be accompanied by photos. Reviews 5x7 and 8x10 b&w and color glossy prints. Can reproduce prints from negatives. Offers no additional payment for photos accepted with ms. Model releases required. Buys all rights.

Fiction: General interest (keeping with theme of fighting stars).

Tips: "We are specifically concerned with training, technical, and personality pieces involving the top martial artists in all realms, be it tournament karate, full-contact karate, judo, kendo, or any other martial arts style. We welcome articles on self-defense training, fitness, nutrition, or conditioning, as long as they deal with at least one standout martial artist."

‡**FIGHTING WOMAN NEWS, Martial Arts, Self-Defense, Combative Sports Quarterly**, Box 1459, Grand Central Station, New York NY 10163. (212)228-0900. Editor: Valerie Eads. Quarterly magazine. "*FWN* combines sweat and philosophy, the deadly reality of street violence and the other worldliness of such eastern disciplines as Zen. Our audience is composed of adult women actually practicing martial arts with an average experience of 4 + years. Since our audience is also 80 + % college grads and 40% holders of advanced degrees we are an action magazine with footnotes. Our material is quite different from what is found in newsstand martial arts publications." Circ. 6,734. Pays on publication. Byline given. Buys one-time rights. Submit seasonal/holiday material 6 months in advance. Simultaneous queries, and simultaneous, photocopied and previously published submissions OK. "For simultaneous and previously published we *must* be told about it!" Computer printout submissions acceptable, prefers letter-quality to dot-matrix. SASE. Reports as soon as possible. Sample copy $3; writer's guidelines for business-size SAE and 37¢ postage.

Nonfiction: Book excerpts, Expose (discrimination against women in martial arts govering bodies); historical/ nostalgic; how-to (martial arts, self-defense techniques); humor; inspirational (e.g., self-defense success stories); interview/profile ("we have assignments waiting for writers in this field); new product; opinion; personal experience; photo feature; technical; travel. "All materials *must* be related to our subject matter. No tabloid sensationalism, no 'sweat is sexy too' items, no fantasy presented as fact, no puff pieces for an instructor or school with a woman champion in house." Buys 12 mss/year. Query. Length: 1,000-5,000 words. Pays in copies or $10 maximum. Expenses negotiated in some cases.

Photos: Muskat Buckby, photo editor. State availability of photos with query or ms. Reviews "technically competent" b&w contact sheets and 8x10 b&w prints. "We negotiate photos and articles as a package. Sometimes expenses are negotiated. Captions and identification of subjects required. The need for releases depends on the situation."

Columns/Departments: Notes & News (short items relevant to our subject matter); Letters (substantive comment regarding previous issues); Sports Reports; and Reviews (of relevant materials in any medium). Query or send complete ms. Length: 100-1,000 words. Pays in copies or negotiates payment.

Fiction: Muskat Buckby, fiction editor. Adventure, fantasy, historical and science fiction. "Any fiction must feature a woman skilled in martial arts." Buys 0-1 mss/year. Query. Length: 1,000-5,000 words. "We will consider serializing longer stories." Pays in copies or negotiates payment.

Poetry: Muskat Buckby, poetry editor. "We'll look at all types. Must appeal to an audience of martial artists." Buys 3-4 poems/year. Length: open. Pays in copy or negotiates payment.

Tips: "Our greatest need is for solid martial arts material. Non-martial-artist writers can be given interview assignments."

INSIDE KARATE, The Magazine for Today's Total Martial Artist, (formerly *Kick Illustrated*), Unique Publications, 4201 Vanowen Pl., Burbank CA 91505. (213)467-1300. Editor: Mark Shuper. Assistant Editor: Rhonda Wilson. 75% freelance written. Monthly magazine covering the martial arts. Circ. 120,000. Byline given. Offers $25 kill fee. Buys first North American serial rights. Submit seasonal/holiday material 4 months in advance. Simultaneous queries, and simultaneous and photocopied submissions OK. SASE. Reports in 3 weeks on queries; in 6 weeks on mss. Publishes ms an average of 3 months after acceptance. Sample copy for $2 and 9x12 SAE and 5 first class stamps; free writer's guidelines.

Nonfiction: Book excerpts; expose (of martial arts); historical/nostalgic; humor; interview/profile (with approval only); opinion; personal experience; photo feature; and technical (with approval only). *Kick Illustrated* deals specifically with all aspects of the gi disciplines of the martial arts, and on occasion with the Chinese arts or the lesser known esoteric practices which are slanted more toward *Inside Karate's* sister publication, *Inside Kung Fu. Inside Karate* seeks a balance of the following in each issue: tradition, history, glamour, profiles and/ or interviews (both by assignment only), technical, philosophical and think pieces. To date, most "how to" pieces have been done in-house. Buys 70 mss/year. Query. Length: 1,000-2,500 words; "preferred—10-12 page ms." Pays $25-125.

Photos: Send photos with ms. Reviews b&w contact sheets, negatives and 8x10 prints. Captions and identification of subjects required. Buys one-time rights.

Tips: "Trends in magazine publishing that freelance writers should be aware of include the use of less body copy, better (and interesting) photos to be run large with 'story' caps. If the photos are poor and the reader can't grasp the whole story by looking at photos and copy, forget it."

INSIDE KUNG-FU, The Ultimate In Martial Arts Coverage!, Unique Publication, 7011 Sunset Blvd., Hollywood CA 90028. (213)467-1300. Editor: Sandra Segal. Monthly magazine covering martial arts for those with "traditional, modern, athletic and intellectual tastes. The magazine slants toward little-known martial arts, and little-known aspects of established martial arts." Circ. 100,000. Pays on publication. Byline given. Offers $35 kill fee. Buys first North American serial rights. Submit seasonal/holiday material 4 months in advance. Simultaneous queries, and simultaneous and photocopied submissions OK. Computer printout submissions acceptable; no dot-matrix. SASE. Reports in 3 weeks on queries; 6 weeks on mss. Publishes ms an average of 6 months after acceptance. Sample copy $1.75 with 9x12 SAE and 5 first class stamps; free writer's guidelines.

Nonfiction: Expose (topics relating to the martial arts); historical/nostalgic; how-to (primarily technical materials); cultural/philosophical; interview/profile; personal experience; photo feature; and technical. "Articles must be technically or historically accurate." No "sports coverage, first-person articles, or articles which constitute personal aggrandizement." Buys 100 mss/year. Query or send complete ms. Length: 10-15 pages, typewritten. Pays $75-100.

Photos: Send photos with accompanying ms. Reviews b&w contact sheets, b&w negatives and 8x10 b&w prints. "Photos are paid for with payment for ms." Captions and model release required. Buys one-time rights.

Fiction: Adventure, historical, humorous, mystery and suspense. "Fiction must be short (500-2,000 words) and relate to the martial arts. We buy very few fiction pieces." Buys 2-3 mss/year. Length: 500-2,000 words. Pays $75.

KARATE ILLUSTRATED, Rainbow Publications, Inc., 1813 Victory Place, Burbank CA 91504. (213)843-4444. Publisher: Michael James. Emphasizes karate and kung fu from the traditional and tournament standpoint and training techniques. Monthly magazine. Circ. 80,000. Pays on publication. Buys all rights. Submit seasonal/holiday material 6 months in advance. Simultaneous and photocopied submissions OK. SASE. Reports in 4-6 weeks. Free sample copy.

Nonfiction: Expose, historical, how-to, informational, interview, new product, personal experience, opinion, photo feature, profile, technical and travel. Buys 6 mss/issue. Query or submit complete ms. Pays $35-150.

Photos: Purchased with or without accompanying ms. Submit 5x7 or 8x10 b&w or color photos. Total purchase price for ms includes payment for photos.

Fiction: Historical. Query. Pays $35-150.

Fillers: Newsbreaks. Query. Pays $5.

‡OFFICIAL KARATE, 351 W. 54th St., New York NY 10019. Editor: Al Weiss. For karatemen or those interested in the martial arts. Monthly. Circ. 100,000. Rights purchased vary with author and material; generally, first publication rights. Pays 50% kill fee. Byline given. Buys 60-70 mss/year. Pays on publication. Will consider photocopied submissions. Reports in 1 month. Query or submit complete ms. SASE.

Nonfiction and Photos: "Biographical material on leading and upcoming karateka, tournament coverage, controversial subjects on the art ('Does Karate Teach Hate?', 'Should the Government Control Karate?', etc.). We cover the 'little man' in the arts rather than devote all space to established leaders or champions; people and happenings in out-of-the-way areas along with our regular material." Informational, how-to, interview, profile, spot news. Length: 1,000-3,000 words. Pays $50-200. B&w contacts or prints. Pays $10-15.

Miscellaneous

THE AMATEUR BOXER, Taylor Publishing Corp., Box 249, Cobalt CT 06414. (203)342-4730. Editor: Bob Taylor. Bimonthly magazine for boxers, coaches and officials. Circ. 2,000. Pays on publication. Byline given. Buys first rights. Submit seasonal/holiday material 2 months in advance. Simultaneous queries, and simultaneous, photocopied and previously published submissions OK. SASE. Reports in 2 weeks on queries; 1 month on mss. Sample copy for 9x12 SAE and 54¢ postage.

Nonfiction: Interview/profile (of boxers, coaches, officials); results; tournament coverage; any stories connected with amateur boxing; photo feature; and technical. Buys 35 mss/year. Query. Length: 500-2,500 words. Pays $15-40.

Photos: State availability of photos. Pays $7-25 for b&w prints. Captions and identification of subjects required. Buys one-time rights.

Tips: "We're very receptive to new writers."

AMERICAN COWBOY, The Magazine of Ranch & Rodeo, Longhorn Publishing Co., Box 311, Walsenburg CO 81089. (303)738-1803. Associate Publisher: Shelley Searle. Managing Editor: Charles Searle. Quarterly magazine covering all aspects of the cowboy's life for "cowboys and cowgirls who average 25 years of age and are generally conservative, independent thinkers." 15% freelance written. Circ. 25,000. Pays on publication. Byline given. Buys first North American serial rights or second (reprint) rights to material originally published elsewhere. Submit seasonal/holiday material 4 months in advance. Photocopied and previously published submissions OK. Computer printout submissions acceptable; prefers letter-quality to dot-matrix. SASE. Reports in 3 weeks. Publishes ms an average of 4 months after acceptance. Sample copy $1; free writer's guidelines.

Nonfiction: Expose (politics behind rodeo, ranching, western horse competition); general interest (with a western tie-in); historical/nostalgic (old-time cowboy heroes); how-to (tips from pros on road life, competition, fitness); interview/profile (of rodeo contestants as people, not just athletes); photo feature (on rodeo, rodeo contestants) and travel (to towns or areas with strong rodeo tie-in). Special issues include youth rodeo, women in rodeo, ranch cowboys, horse care and training, history of rodeo, commercial ranching. "Features/photos of current or past rodeo contestants, particularly PRCA, WPRA, CPRA, INFR, NOTRA, NIRA, NHSRA, LBRA. Primary focus is on the personality of rodeo; statistics and records are secondary. Especially interested in rodeo-related topics like cowboys/cowgirls involved in motion pictures, entertainment, charities, off-beat rodeo news, foreign rodeo contestants. Also interested in stories on ranch cowboys and the side-ventures of rodeo contestants." Buys 8 mss/year. Query with clips or send complete ms. Length: 700-2,000 words. Pays $35-150.

Photos: State availability of photos. Pays $6-10 for 5x7 b&w prints; $50-75 for color photos or transparencies used on magazine cover. Identification of subjects required. Buys one-time rights.

Columns/Departments: Book or record reviews with western themes; pro, women's, Canadian and youth rodeo; guest editorials on the positives/negatives and current politics; tips on ranching. Buys 1-2 mss/year. Send complete ms. Length: 100-500 words. Pays $10-50.

Poetry: Light verse and traditional. "Nothing too corny. Our readers are down-to-earth but they are not without sophistication." Buys 1-2 poems/year. Submit maximum 3 poems. Length: open.

Fillers: Newsbreaks. Buys 5/year. Length: 45-150 words. Pays $5-10.

Tips: "Make sure all pieces are written from an insider's point of view—our readers don't need an explanation of a cowboy's equipment; rather, they want a peek into his *specific*, *personal* lifestyle and thoughts. Writing profiles of students in rodeo is the easiest way to get accepted. We are usually desperate for youth news, especially from the NIRA, AJRA, NTHSRA, NLBRA, WSJRA, LSHSRA."

BALLS AND STRIKES, Amateur Softball Association, 2801 NE 50th St., Oklahoma City OK 73111. (405)424-5266. Editor: Bill Plummer III. Monthly tabloid covering amateur softball. 20% freelance written. Circ. 245,000. Pays on publication. Buys first rights. Byline given. SASE. Reports in 3 weeks. Publishes ms an average of 2 weeks after acceptance. Free sample copy.

Nonfiction: General interest, historical/nostalgic, interview/profile and technical. Query. Length: 2-3 pages. Pays $50-150.

THE BOSTON MARATHON, The Official Magazine of the B.A.A. Marathon, Boston Phoenix, Inc., 100 Massachusetts Ave., Boston MA 02115. (617)536-5390. Editor: Tory Carlson. Managing Editor: Clif Garboden. Magazine published annually covering the Boston Marathon. 60%+ freelance written. Circ. 135,000. Pays on publication. Byline given. Buys first North American serial rights and one-time rights. SASE. Reports in January/February. Publishes ms an average of 3 weeks after acceptance. Sample copy $2.50.

Nonfiction: Articles pertaining to marathon running and the Boston Marathon. "No unsolicited manuscripts." Query with clips of published work. Length: 800-1,200 words. Pays negotiable fee.

Photos: State availability of photos. Pays negotiable fee for 35mm color transparencies. Caption and identification of subjects required. Buys one-time rights and all rights.

Tips: This is the official race guide to the Boston Marathon. Articles, etc. must deal with the Boston Marathon. "We like to develop good writers; but missed deadlines are annoying."

FLORIDA RACQUET JOURNAL, Racquetball-Sports, Florida Racquet Journal, Inc., Box 11657, Jacksonville FL 32239. (904)721-3660. Editor: Norm Blum. Managing Editor: Kathy Blum. Monthly tabloid covering racquetball in the Southeast. 50% freelance written. Circ. 20,000. Pays on acceptance. Byline given. Makes work-for-hire assignments and buys second (reprint) rights to material originally published elsewhere. Offers $25 kill fee. Submit seasonal/holiday material 3 months in advance. Simultaneous queries, and simultaneous and photocopied and previously published submissions OK. Computer printout submissions acceptable. SASE. Reports in 2 weeks. Sample copy for $1, SAE, and 2 first class stamps.
Nonfiction: Book excerpts (from racquetball books); expose (of racquetball clubs); historical/nostalgic; humor; new product; personal experience. "No how-to or instructional articles." Buys 12-15 mss/year. Query. Length: 400-900 words. Pays $10-40.
Columns/Departments: Horoscope, crossword puzzle, and health items—all for racquetball players. Buys 36 mss/year. Query. Length: 400-800 words. Pays $10-30.
Fiction: Humorous. Buys variable number mss/year. Query. Length: 500-1,500 words. Pays $10-30.
Poetry: Free verse. Buys variable number/year. Length: 30-60 lines. Pays $5-10.
Fillers: Clippings, jokes, gags, anecdotes, short humor, newsbreaks. Length: 30-50 words. Pays $1-5.
Tips: "We don't want your opinion—let the subject tell the story. If we like your first article we'll keep using you."

HANG GLIDING, United States Hang Gliding Association, Box 66306, Los Angeles CA 90066. (213)390-3065. Editor: Gilbert Dodgen. Monthly magazine; 56 pages. Circ. 10,000. Buys all rights. Phone queries OK. Submit seasonal/holiday material 6 weeks in advance. SASE. Reports in 2 months. Free sample copy.
Nonfiction: Technical articles on non-powered hang gliders, instruments, aerodynamics, expose, general interest, historical, how-to, humor, inspirational, interview, nostalgia, new product, experience, opinion, photo feature, profile, and travel. Buys 1-2 mss/issue. Query with detailed description of subject, type of treatment, and clips of published work or send complete ms. Length: 500-2,000 words. Payment negotiable.
Photos: State availability of photos or send photos with ms. Pays variable rates for b&w negatives. Buys one-time rights. Captions and model releases required.
Fiction: Adventure, fantasy, experimental, historical, humorous, mystery and suspense. "We prefer short, to-the-point articles. We do not want anything other than articles about hang gliding." Query with clips of published work or send complete ms. Payment negotiable.
Poetry: "Anything that pertains to hang gliding." Submit in batches of 4 or 5. Length: 25 lines maximum. No pay.
Fillers: Clippings, jokes, gags, anecdotes, newsbreaks, short humor, comic strips, photos and letters to the editor.

INDIANA RACQUET SPORTS, Suite 303, 630 N. College Ave., Indianapolis IN 46204. (317)637-5683. Editor: Don Nixon. Monthly tabloid newspaper. 10% freelance written. Circ. 8,000. Pays on publication. Byline given. Buys first and second rights to the same material. Submit seasonal/holiday material 2 months in advance. Simultaneous, photocopied and previously published submissions OK. Computer printout submissions acceptable. SASE. Reports in 2 weeks. Publishes ms an average of 1 month after acceptance. Sample copy for 9x12 SAE and 2 first class stamps; writer's guidelines for business-size SAE and 1 first class stamp.
Nonfiction: Health/nutrition; any racquet sport with Indiana connection—tennis, platform tennis, squash, table tennis, badminton, racquetball. Length: open. Pays $20.
Photos: Send photos with ms. Pays $5-10 for 5x7 b&w prints. Buys one-time rights.
Columns/Departments: Buys 12 mss/year. Query. Length: open. Pays $20.
Fillers: Buys 50/year. Length: 75 words maximum.

INSIDE RUNNING, 8100 Bellaire Blvd., No. 1318, Houston TX 77036. Editor/Publisher: Joanne Schmidt. 40% freelance written. Monthly tabloid covering "news and features of interest to runners and joggers. We are a *Texas* magazine and our focus is on runners and running in the state." Circ. 12,000. Buys all rights. Pays on acceptance. Publishes ms an average of 2 months after acceptance. SASE. Reports "within six weeks." Sample copy $1; writer's guidelines for SASE.
Nonfiction: "Strongly researched service pieces, profiles, race reports, and coverage of developments in the sport. We would like to discover correspondents and writers in Texas who run or have a familiarity with the sport and are looking for assignments in their area. Coverage in north and east Texas badly needed. Running opportunities and scenery throughout state would be very helpful. We want very much to include capsule accounts of races from around the state for our Texas Round-up section. No personal 'How I Ran the Marathon' pieces, please." Recent article example: "Millie Cooper: First Lady of Aerobics" (March 1984). Buys 24 unsolicited mss/year. Query, and explain background and photographic experience; include writing samples, if possible. Pays $35-100. "We may pay more if the writer has worked with us before and demonstrated a knowledge of our needs. We will negotiate with established writers as well."
Photos: "Strong photos earn extra payment." Pays $10 for b&w 5x7 prints.
Fiction: Pays $35-100, "depending on length, quality and originality."

Tips: "Report on races in your area, profile a local runner doing something unusual, focus on ways to make running more fun or exciting. Emphasize a Texas locale with running as part of a 'lifestyle.' We will work with writers and offer concrete, specific suggestions if they will follow through. Quotes and good b&w photos will give you the edge."

INTERNATIONAL OLYMPIC LIFTER, IOL Publications, 3916 Eagle Rock, Box 65855, Los Angeles CA 90065. (213)257-8762. Editor: Bob Hise. Managing Editor: Herb Glossbrenner. 20% freelance written. Bimonthly magazine covering the Olympic sport of weight lifting. Circ. 10,000. Pays on publication. Publishes ms an average of 3 months after acceptance. Byline given. Offers $25 kill fee. Buys one-time rights or negotiable rights. Submit seasonal/holiday material 5 months in advance. Photocopied submissions OK. Computer printout submissions acceptable; no dot-matrix. SASE. Reports in 6 weeks. Sample copy $1.50; writer's guidelines for SAE and 4 first class stamps.
Nonfiction: Training articles, contest reports, diet—all related to Olympic weight lifting. Buys 20-30 mss/ year. Query. Length: 250-2,000 words. Pays $25-100.
Photos: Action (competition and training). State availability of photos. Pays $1-5 for 5x7 b&w prints. Identification of subjects required.
Columns/Departments: Buys 10 mss/year. Query. Length: 150-250 words. Pays $10-20.
Poetry: Keith Cain, poetry editor. Light verse, traditional—related to Olympic lifting. Buys 6-10 poems/year. Submit maximum 3 poems. Length: 12-24 lines. Pays $10-20.
Fillers: Gags, anecdotes related to weight lifting. Buys 6 mss/year. Length: 100-150 words. Pays $10-15.

THE MAINE SPORTSMAN, Box 365, Augusta ME 04330. Editor: Harry Vanderweide. 70% freelance written. Monthly tabloid. Circ. 20,000. Pays "shortly after publication." Buys first rights. Byline given. Computer printout submissions acceptable. SASE. Reports in 2-4 weeks. Publishes ms an average of 3 months after acceptance.
Nonfiction: "We publish only articles about Maine outdoor activities. Any well-written, researched, knowledgable article about that subject area is likely to be accepted by us." Expose, how-to, general interest, interview, nostalgia, personal experience, opinion, profile, and technical. Buys 25-30 mss/issue. Submit complete ms. Length: 200-2,000 words. Pays $20-80.
Photos: "We can have illustrations drawn, but prefer 1-3 b&w photos." Submit photos with accompanying ms. Pays $5-50 for b&w print.
Tips: "It's rewarding finding a writer who has a fresh way of looking at ordinary events."

NATIONAL RACQUETBALL, Publication Management, Inc., 1800 Pickwick Ave., Glenview IL 60025. Publisher: Hugh Morgan. Associate Publisher/Editor: Chuck Leve. For racquetball players of all ages. Monthly magazine. 40% freelance written. Circ. 32,500. Pays on publication. Buys all rights. Byline given. Submit seasonal/holiday material 2-3 months in advance. SASE. Publishes ms an average of 2 months after acceptance. Sample copy $2.
Nonfiction: How-to (play better racquetball or train for racquetball); interview (with players or others connected with racquetball business); opinion (usually used in letters but sometimes fullblown opinion features on issues confronting the game); photo feature (on any subject mentioned); profile (short pieces with photos on women or men players interesting in other ways or on older players); health (as it relates to racquetball players—food, rest, eye protection, etc.); and fashion. No material on tournament results. Buys 4 mss/issue. Query with clips of published work. Length: 500-2,500 words. Pays $25-150.
Photos: State availability of photos or send photos with ms. Offers no additional payment for photos accompanying ms. Uses b&w prints or color transparencies. Buys one-time rights. Captions and model releases required.
Fiction: Adventure, humorous, mystery, romance, science fiction and suspense. "Whatever an inventive mind can do with racquetball." Buys 3 mss/year. Send complete ms. Pays $25-150.
Tips: "Break into *National Racquetball* by writing for monthly features—short pieces about racquetball players you know. We need more contributions from all over the country. Our object is national and international coverage of the sport of racquetball."

‡**PRIME TIME SPORTS & FITNESS**, GND Prime Time Publishing, Box 6091, Evanston IL 60204. (312)864-8113/276-2143. Editor: Dennis A. Dorner. Managing Editor: Nicholas J. Schmitz. A monthly magazine covering racquet and health club sports and fitness. Estab. 1983. 80% freelance written. Circ. 35,000. Pays on publication. Byline given. Buys all rights; will assign back to author in 85% of cases. Submit seasonal/ holiday material 3 months in advance. Photocopied and previously published submissions OK. No simultaneous submissions. Computer printout submissions acceptable; prefers letter-quality to dot-matrix. SASE. Reports in 6 weeks. Publishes ms an average of 3 months after acceptance. Sample copy for SAE and 3 first class stamps; writer's guidelines for business size SAE and 1 first class stamp.
Nonfiction: Book excerpts (fitness and health); expose (in tennis, fitness, racquetball, health clubs, diets); adult (slightly risque and racy fitness); historical/nostalgic (history of exercise and fitness movements); how-to

(expert instructional pieces on any area of coverage); humor (large market for funny pieces on health clubs and fitness); inspirational (on how diet and exercise combine to bring you a better body, self); interview/profile; new product; opinion (only from recognized sources that know what they are talking about); personal experience (definitely—humor); photo feature (on related subjects); technical (on exercise and sport); travel (related to fitness, tennis camps, etc.); news reports (on racquetball, handball, tennis, running events). Special issues: Swimsuit and Resort Issue (March); Summer Fashion (July); Fall Fashion (October); Christmas Gifts and related articles (December). '' We love short articles that get to the point. No articles on local only tennis and racquetball tournaments without national appeal except when from Chicago/Milwaukee area." Buys 50 mss/year. Length: 2,000+ words maximum. Pays $20-150.

Photos: Eric Matye, photo editor. Send photos with ms. Pays $5-75 for b&w prints. Captions, model release and identification of subjects required. Buys all rights, "but returns 75% of photos to submitter."

Columns/Departments: Linda Jefferson, column/department editor. New Products; Fitness Newsletter; Handball Newsletter; Racquetball Newsletter; Tennis Newsletter; News & Capsule Summaries; Fashion Spot (photos of new fitness and bathing suits); related subjects. Buys 100 mss/year. Send complete ms. Length: 50-250 words ("more if author has good handle to cover complete columns"). Pays $5-25.

Fiction: Joy Kiefer, fiction editor. Erotica (if related to fitness club); fantasy (related to subjects); humorous (definite market); religious ("no God-is-my shepherd, but Body-is-God's-temple OK"); romance (related subjects). "No raunchy or talking down exercise stories, Upbeat is what we want." Buys 10 mss/year. Send complete ms. Length: 500-2,500 words maximum. Pays $20-150.

Poetry: Free verse, haiku, light verse, traditional on related subjects. Length: up to 150 words. Pays $10-25.

Fillers: Linda Jefferson, fillers editor. Clippings, jokes, gags, anecdotes, short humor, newsbreaks. Buys 400/year. Length: 25-200 words. Pays $5-15.

Tips: "Send us articles dealing with court club sports, exercise and nutrition that exemplify an upbeat 'you can do it' attitude. Good short fiction or humorous articles can break in. Expert knowledge of any related subject can bring assignments. Any area is open. A humorous/knowledgable columnist in weight lifting, aerobics, running is presently needed. We review the author's work on a nonpartial basis. We consider everything as a potential article, but are turned off by credits, past work and degrees."

PRORODEO SPORTS NEWS, 101 Prorodeo Dr., Colorado Springs CO 80919. (303)593-8840. Professional Rodeo Cowboys Association. Editor: Bill Crawford. 70% freelance written. Tabloid for rodeo contestants, contract members, committeemen and rodeo fans. Published every other Wednesday (1 issue in January; 1 in December). Circ. 30,000. Publishes the Annual Championship Edition, a 120-page slick paper magazine, following the National Finals Rodeo each December. Buys all rights; "on request we usually return rights." Clear and sharply printed computer printout submissions acceptable; no dot-matrix. SASE. Reports in 2 weeks. Sample copy $1; contributor's guidelines for SASE.

Nonfiction: News of professional rodeo, columns, interviews, features about PRCA contestants, rodeo animals, contract members and committeemen; appropriate photographs. Material must focus on a single issue; emphasis on professionalism. All material must be accurate and attributable. Avoid countrified dialect. All material must relate directly to PRCA rodeos. "We will not buy fiction based upon the old myths: rodeo cowboys are drunken, womanizing barroom brawlers; anything of any kind that proves the writer knows nothing about professional rodeo as it exists today: a multi-million dollar, international professional sport which outdraws NFL pro football." Length: 18 column inches maximum, 800 words. Query or send complete ms.

Photos: Pays $10 for b&w 8x10 glossy prints. Rodeo action, wrecks, PRCA members involved in other activities, such as competing in other sports, receiving awards, working with disabled persons, etc. Should have complete information written on the front in the white borders. Action photos should give name and hometown of rider, score made on the ride, name or number and owner of the animal, date and place photo taken. Wreck photos should contain information as to outcome. Continuous need for mugshots, candid, unposed. Particular needs are rodeo action in all events. Pays $50 for color transparencies; $130 for color transparency used on front cover of annual.

Fiction: "Professionally written and plotted authentic rodeo fiction." Length: 40 column inches maximum, approximately 1800 words.

Tips: "We're one of the best potential markets in the business. We buy over 100 manuscripts a year, but we only buy from writers who have studied and learned to write the kind of material we publish. One year one knowledgeable and dependable freelancer got over 30 assignments, did them well and won the outstanding contributor buckle award: a gold and silver trophy buckle worth over $500 and was paid $1500+ as well."

RACING PIGEON PICTORIAL, The Racing Pigeon Publishing Co. Ltd., 19 Doughty St., London WCIN 2PT, England. Editor-in-Chief: Colin Osman. 50% freelance written. Emphasizes racing pigeons for "all ages and occupations; generally 'working class' backgrounds, both sexes." Monthly magazine. Circ. 13,000. Pays on publication. Publishes ms an average of 3 months after acceptance. Buys first rights, first and second rights to the same material, and second (reprint) rights to material originally published elsewhere. Submit seasonal/holiday material 3 months in advance. Photocopied and previously published submissions OK. SAE and IRCs. Reports in 5 weeks. Sample copy $2.

Nonfiction: Michael Shepherd, Articles Editor. How-to (methods of famous fanciers, treatment of diseases, building lofts, etc.); historical (histories of pigeon breeds); informational (practical information for pigeon fanciers); interview (with winning fanciers); and technical (where applicable to pigeons). "Don't bother, if you're not a specialist!" Buys 4 mss/issue. Submit complete ms. Length: 6,000 words minimum. Pays $30/page minimum.

Photos: Rick Osman, photo editor. Purchased with or without accompanying ms or on assignment. Captions required. Send 8x10 b&w glossy prints or 2¼x2¼ or 35mm color transparencies.

RACQUETBALL ILLUSTRATED, 4201 Vanowen Place, Burbank CA 91505. (818)845-2656. Executive Editor: Rhonda Wilson. 40% freelance written. Monthly magazine about racquetball for an audience that is 18-65 years old. 55% male, upper middle class, members of private clubs. Circ. 100,000. Pays on publication. Publishes ms an average of 10 weeks after acceptance. Buys first rights. Submit seasonal material 3 months in advance. Photocopied submissions OK. Computer printout submissions acceptable; no dot-matrix. Reports in 1 month. Sample copy $1.50.

Nonfiction: Expose (politics of the racquetball industry); general interest; historical; how-to (turn a loser into a winner, psych out an opponent); humor; interview (of pros, unusual characters, celebrities); profile; travel; photo feature (kids in racquetball; racquetball in interesting cities). No first person or puff pieces. Instruction done only by touring pros or qualified instructors. "Find a player interesting on a national level and query. Also, we have annual special issues on shoes, racquets, balls, accessories, travel, health and instruction." No " 'first time on the court' stories." Buys 5 mss/issue. Query explaining subject matter in detail and giving background information on persons. Length: 1,500-3,000 words. Pays $100-125.

Photos: Editor: Ed Ikuta. State availability of photos. Pays $15-30 for 8x10 b&w prints. Reviews color transparencies. Offers $25-50 additional payment for photos accepted with ms. Captions preferred; model release required. Buys one-time rights.

Fiction: "We are interested in general fiction with racquetball as the theme." Buys 6 mss/year. Send complete ms. Length: 2,500 words minimum. Pays $100-300.

Fillers: Short humor. Pays $15 minimum.

Tips: "I want a variety of articles to appeal to beginners as well as advanced players, the general player as well as the hard-core player. I'm not afraid to run a controversial article. Almost sure sellers are medical or psychological stories for 'Rx for winning' column."

THE RUNNER, 1 Park Ave., New York NY 10016. Editor-in-Chief: Marc Bloom. Emphasizes the world of running in the broadest scope with its main thrust in jogging, roadrunning and marathoning/fitness and health. Monthly magazine. Circ. 265,000. Pays on acceptance. Buys most first North American serial rights. Pays 20% kill fee. Byline given. Submit seasonal/holiday material 3 months in advance. SASE. Reports in 2-3 weeks. Free sample copy.

Nonfiction: Profiles, body science, historical, event coverage, training, lifestyle, sports medicine, phenomena and humor. Buys 5-6 mss/issue. Query with clips of published work. Length: 2,000-4,000 words. Pays usually $500-1,000.

Photos: State availability of photos. Pay is negotiable for b&w contact sheets and 35mm color transparencies. Buys one-time rights. Captions required.

Columns/Departments: Training, statistical listings, humor, food, medicine, and physiology. Regular columnists used. Buys 3-4/issue. Length: 900-1,200 words. Pays $200 and up.

Warmups: Short news items, whimsical items, and advice on improving running. Length: 100-500 words. Pays $75.

RUNNING TIMES, Running Times, Inc., Suite 20, 14416 Jefferson Davis Highway, Woodbridge VA 22191. (703)643-1646. Editor: Edward Ayres. Emphasizes running, jogging, holistic health and fitness. Monthly magazine; 72 pages. Circ. 100,000. Pays on publication. Buys all rights. Byline given. Submit seasonal/holiday material 3 months in advance. Simultaneous and photocopied submissions OK. SASE. Reports in 1 month. Sample copy $2.

Nonfiction: How-to (training techniques, racing techniques, self-treatment of injuries, etc.); humor; interview; photo feature; profile; and technical (written for an educated readership). "We do not want opinions or ideas which are not backed up by solid research." Buys 1-2 mss/issue. Query or send complete ms. Length: 500-2,500 words. Pays $25-400.

Photos: State availability of photos. Pays $15-40 for 5x7 or 8x10 b&w glossy prints; $30-250 for color transparencies. Captions preferred.

Fiction: Adventure, erotica, fantasy and humorous. "Subjects must involve runners or running." Buys 10 mss/year. Send complete ms or clips of published work. Length: 700-2,500 words. Pays $50-200.

SIGNPOST MAGAZINE, 16812 36th Ave. W., Lynnwood WA 98037. Publisher: Louise B. Marshall. Editor: Ann L. Marshall. About hiking, backpacking and similar trail-related activities, mostly from a Pacific Northwest viewpoint. Monthly. 10% freelance written. Will consider any rights offered by author. Buys 6 mss/

year. Pays on publication. Publishes ms an average of 6 months after acceptance. Sample copy $1. Will consider photocopied submissions. Reports in 3 weeks. Query or submit complete ms. Electronic submissions OK on Perfect Writer Software series; computer printout submissions acceptable. SASE.

Nonfiction and Photos: "Most material is donated by subscribers or is staff-written. Payment for purchased material is low, but a good way to break into print or spread a particular point of view."

Tips: "We cover only *self-propelled* outdoor sports; won't consider mss about trail bikes, snowmobiles, power boats."

‡**SKEET SHOOTING REVIEW**, National Skeet Shooting Association, Box 28188, San Antonio TX 78228. (512)688-3371. Editor: Laura Brzezinski. The official magazine of the National Skeet Shooting Association; a monthly covering skeet shooting, shotguns (safety, etc.) and reloading. Circ. 16,000. Pays on publication. Byline given. Buys one-time rights. Submit seasonal/holiday material 4 months in advance. Simultaneous queries, and simultaneous, photocopied, and previously published submissions OK. Computer printout submissions acceptable. SASE. Reports in 1 week. Sample copy $1.

Nonfiction: How-to, humor, interview/profile, new product, personal experience, photo feature and technical. Buys 12-15 mss/year. Query with published clips. Pays $50-200.

Photos: State availability of photos. Pays negotiable rates for 5x7 or 3x5 b&w or color prints. Captions required. Buys one-time rights.

SKYDIVING, Box 189, Deltona FL 32728. (904)736-9779. Editor: Michael Truffer. Monthly tabloid featuring skydiving for sport parachutists, worldwide dealers and equipment manufacturers. Circ. 6,000. Average issue includes 3 feature articles and 3 columns of technical information. Pays on publication. Byline given. Buys one-time rights. Simultaneous, photocopied and previously published submissions OK, if so indicated. SASE. Reports in 1 month. Sample copy $2; free writer's guidelines with SASE.

Nonfiction: "Send us news and information on equipment, techniques, events and outstanding personalities who skydive. We want articles written by people who have a solid knowledge of parachuting." No personal experience or human-interest articles. Query. Length: 500-1,000 words. Pays $25-100.

Photos: State availability of photos. Reviews 5x7 and larger b&w glossy prints. Offers no additional payment for photos accepted with ms. Captions required.

Fillers: Newsbreaks. Length: 100-200 words. Pays $25 minimum.

SPORTSWISE, The Magazine for the Active Lifestyle, S/W Magazine Inc., 1633 Broadway, New York NY 10019. (212)940-3900. Editor: Richard O'Connor. Managing Editor: Bob Condor. A bimonthly magazine with issues in 6 distinct markets: New York, Boston, Philadelphia, Atlanta, Chicago and D.C., covering participant sports. Readers are affluent, active people; generally 18-about 45. Circ. 125,000 New York City; varies in other 5 markets. Pays 1 month before publication. Byline given. Offers 25% kill fee. Buys first North American serial rights. Submit seasonal/holiday material minimum 6 months in advance. Simultaneous queries, and simultaneous and photocopied submissions OK. Computer printout submissions acceptable. SASE. Reports in 1 month. Sample copy for SAE; writer's guidelines for SAE and 1 first class stamp.

Nonfiction: Book excerpts; exposé (issues of participant sports); humor; interview/profile; new product (short pieces); sports medicine and nutrition. No historical accounts, or hard-core how-to technique pieces. Buys 30-50 mss/year. Length: 1,800-2,500 words. Pays $400-800.

Columns/Departments: Mary Brady, column/department editor. Warmups (about equipment, trends, people, events; particular interest in regional material; 200-400 words); Sports Medicine and Nutrition (1,000 words). Buys 15-30 Warmups mss/year, pays $50; 10-12 Sports Medicine and Nutrition mss/year, pays $300-400.

Fiction: Bob Condor and Mary Brady, fiction editors. Participant sports related of any type. Buys 1-3 mss/year. Length: open. Pays variable rate.

Poetry: Sports related. Buys a few poems/year. Submit maximum 10 poems. Length: open. Pays variable rate.

Tips: "Write an item for our Warmup department or humorous first person account of a sporting experience. Write short, informative queries. Area most open to freelancers is Warmup. Study our style here; it's conversational, lively, to-the-point."

‡**TRI-ATHLETE**, 6660 Banning Dr., Oakland CA 94611. (415)530-4580. Editor-in-chief: William R. Katovsky. Associate Editor: Theresa S. Taylor. A monthly magazine providing coverage of multisport events, primarily triathlons. "The magazine is directed toward serious triathletes, whether beginning or experienced, and features articles on training, diet and nutrition, major races, equipment and topics of general interest to triathletes. It also includes extensive interviews/profiles of top triathletes and a full race calendar." Estab. 1983. Circ. 105,000. Pays on publication. Byline given. Offers negotiable kill fee. Buys first North American serial rights. Submit seasonal/holiday material 3 months in advance. Computer printout submissions acceptable. Reports in 1 month on queries; 2 months on mss. Sample copy $2; free writer's guidelines.

Nonfiction: Book reviews; general interest; historical; training; humor; inspirational; interviews; new product; opinion; personal experience (but not "Why I did my first triathlon"); photo feature; technical and equipment reviews; and diet and nutrition. "We prefer writing that is insightful, analytical, thoughtful and comprehensive. A cynical or skeptical perspective is also welcome. We will not accept writing on a wide-eyed, naive, 'how do those guys do it' level, or writing that has not been well researched or thought out." Buys 50 mss/year. Query with clips of published or unpublished work, or send complete ms. Length: 1,500-3,500 words. Pays 5-20¢/published word.

Columns/Departments: At the Races (short race reports nationwide); Tri-Athlete Talk (general interest, humor, gossip); Bio Feedback (letters to the editor and short commentary). Send complete ms. Length: 500-1,500 words. Pays 5-10¢/published word.

Fillers: Clippings or newsbreaks, jokes, anecdotes, short humor. Length: 100-1,000 words. Pays 5-10¢/published word.

Tips: "Freelancers should have a specific subject in mind; those who submit complete manuscripts have a better chance of being published in *Tri-Athlete* than those who merely inquire. Features and race section are most open to freelancers. Feature stories on training or racing should not be written on a beginner, or elementary level—assume the reader already knows the basics, but needs more detailed, comprehensive information. All possible features should be well organized, interesting and analytical. The race section includes short (500-1,000 words) stories on races that are held across the country. These accounts should be concise, include race results of top finishers and give lively reports. Color slides should accompany race reports. Writers with a background on the subject on which they are writing are preferred."

Skiing and Snow Sports

POWDER MAGAZINE, Box 1028, Dana Point CA 92629. (714)496-5922. Executive Publisher: Steve Pezman. Creative Editor: Neil Stebbins. Managing Editor: Pat Cochran. 90% freelance written. 7/year, including two special issues: pre-season equipment review and photo annual. Circ. 100,000. Rights purchased vary with author and material. May buy all rights, but will reassign rights to author after publication; or first North American serial rights; or simultaneous rights. Buys 10-15 unsolicited mss/year. Pays on publication. Publishes ms an average of 5 months after acceptance. Sample copy for $1. Submit material late spring, early summer for publication the following season. Computer printout submissions acceptable. Reports on material accepted for publication in 2 months. Phone query preferred.

Nonfiction and Photos: "We want material by or about people who reach out for the limits of the ski experience. Avoid classical ski-teaching technique problems, travelogue features, or beginner-oriented articles. We try to emphasize the quality and enjoyment of the ski experience rather than its mechanics, logistics, or purely commercial aspects." Length: 500-2,500 words. Pays approximately 10¢/word. *Top quality* b&w and color transparencies purchased with or without mss or on assignment. Pays approximately $25-75 for b&w, full or partial page, $40-150 for color, full or partial page; $300 cover.

Fiction: Humorous, mainstream adventure and experimental fiction. Must relate to subject matter. Length: open. Pays 7-10¢/word.

Tips: "Be creative in approaches to articles. We look for quality, writing, imagination, personality and humor. Review our magazine thoroughly . . . back at least 6 issues . . . before querying."

SKATING, United States Figure Skating Association, 20 First St., Colorado Springs CO 80906. (303)635-5200. Editor-in-Chief: Ian A. Anderson. Monthly magazine; 64 pages. Circ. 31,000. Pays on publication. Buys all rights. Byline given. Phone queries OK. Submit seasonal/holiday material 3 months in advance. Photocopied and previously published submissions OK. SASE. Reports in 1 month. Writer's guidelines for SASE.

Nonfiction: Historical; how-to (photograph skaters, training, exercise); humor; informational; interview; personal experience; personal opinion; photo feature; profile (background and interests of national-caliber amateur skaters); technical; and competition reports. Buys 4 mss/issue. Query or send complete ms. Length: 500-1,000 words. Pays $50.

Photos: Ian Anderson, editor. Photos purchased with or without accompanying ms. Pays $15 for 8x10 or 5x7 b&w glossy prints and $35 for color transparencies. Query.

Columns/Departments: European Letter (skating news from Europe); Ice Abroad (competition results and report from outside the US); Book Reviews; People; Club News (what individual clubs are doing); and Music column (what's new and used for music for skating). Buys 4 mss/issue. Query or send complete ms. Length: 100-500 words. Pays $35. Open to suggestions for new columns/departments.

Fillers: Newsbreaks and short humor. Buys 2 fillers/issue. Query. Length: 50-250 words. Pays $20.

SKI, 380 Madison Ave., New York NY 10017. (212)687-3000. Editor: Dick Needham. 15% freelance written. 8 times/year, September through April. Buys first rights in most cases. Pays 50% kill fee. Byline given "except when report is incorporated in 'Ski Life' department." Pays on publication. Computer printout submissions acceptable; no dot-matrix. Reports in 1 month. SASE.

Nonfiction: Prefers articles of general interest to skiers, travel, adventure, how-to, budget savers, unusual people, places or events that reader can identify with. Must be authoritative, knowledgeably written, in easy, informative language and have a professional flair. Cater to middle to upper income bracket readers who are college graduates, wide travelers. No fiction or poetry. Length: 1,500-2,000 words. Pays $150-300.

Photos: Buys photos submitted with manuscripts and with captions only. Good action shots (slides only) in color for covers; pays minimum $300. B&w photos, pays $40 each; minimum $150 for photo stories. (Query on these.) Color slides. Pays $50 each; $200/page.

Tips: "Another possibility is our monthly column, Ski People, which runs 300-400-word items on unusual people who ski and have made some unique contribution to the sport. We want to see outline of how author proposes to develop story for *Ski*, sample opening page or paragraph; include previous clippings or published writing samples. Humor is welcome."

SKI RACING MAGAZINE, International Journal of Skiing, Ski Racing Inc., Box 70, Fair Haven VT 05743. (802)468-5666. Editor: Don A. Metivier. Tabloid covering major ski competition events worldwide for the serious skier and ski industry person. Published 20 times during the ski season (September-April). 70% freelance written. Circ. 30,000. Pays on publication. Byline given. Buys one-time rights. Reports "at once, because of the time frame of events we cover." Publishes ms an average of 3 days after acceptance. Free sample copy.

Nonfiction: "We cover only news and interviews with those making it. Prefer not to get opinion from writers." Buys 200 mss/year. Query with clips of published work. Length: "depends on the story; from minimum of a paragraph and list of top 5 finishers to maximum of 500-750 words." Pays $1/inch for news stories; $50-100 for longer assignments; negotiates fees prior to assignment on interviews.

Photos: Pays $10-25 for photos; $50 for covers, action photos, and candids for picture pages and interviews. $50 and up for photos (b&w only) used by advertisers.

Tips: "It's frustrating working with freelance writers who miss deadlines. We publish 3 times a month—old news isn't news."

‡SKI SOUTH, The Magazine of Southern Skiers, Leisure Publishing Co., 3424 Brambleton Ave., Box 12567, Roanoke VA 24026. (703)989-6138. Managing Editor: Richard Wells. Magazine published twice/year covering skiing in the south. "*Ski South* reaches an affluent, young adult audience of recreational skiing enthusiasts. Emphasis on Southern ski resorts, technique, equipment, fashion, etc." Circ. 18,000. Pays on publication. Byline given. Makes work-for-hire assignments. Simultaneous queries OK. SASE. Reports in 6 weeks. Free sample copy.

Nonfiction: Interview/profile, opinion, personal experience, photo feature and travel. Buys 6-8 mss/year. Send complete ms. Length: 500-1,500 words. Pays $35-150.

Photos: Send photos with ms. Pays $50-100 for 35mm color transparencies. Captions required. Buys one-time rights.

SKIING MAGAZINE, Ziff-Davis Publishing Co., 1 Park Ave., New York NY 10016. Editor-in-Chief: Alfred H. Greenberg. Executive Editor: Dinah B. Witchel. 50% freelance written. Published 7 times/year (September-March). Magazine; 175 pages. Circ. 430,000. Pays on acceptance. Buys first rights. Byline given. Submit seasonal/holiday material 4 months in advance. SASE. Publishes ms an average of 1 year after acceptance. Sample copy $2.

Nonfiction: "This magazine is in the market for any material of interest to skiers. Material must appeal to and please the confirmed skier. Much of the copy is staff-prepared, but many freelance features are purchased provided the writing is fast-paced, concise and knowledgeable." Buys 10 unsolicited mss/year. Submit complete ms. Length: 1,500-3,000 words.

Photos: Erin Kenney, art director. Purchased with or without accompanying ms or on assignment. Send contact sheet or transparencies. Pays $125/full page for 8x10 b&w glossy or matte photos; $300 minimum/full page for 35mm transparencies, pro-rated for partial pages. Model release required.

SNOW GOER, The Webb Co., 1999 Shephard Rd., St. Paul MN 55116. (612)690-7200. Editor: Jerry Bassett. Managing Editor: Bill Monn. Magazine published 4 times seasonally for snowmobilers. Circ. 2,200,000. Buys all rights. Byline given. Pays on acceptance. Submit special issue material 1 year in advance. Simultaneous queries OK. Reports in 2 months. Query. "High-quality" computer printout submissions acceptable; prefers letter-quality to dot-matrix. SASE.

Nonfiction: General interest; historical/nostalgic; how-to (mechanical); interview/profile; personal experience; photo feature; technical; and travel. Features on snowmobiling with strong secondary story angle, such as ice fishing, mountain climbing, snow camping, conservation, rescue. Also uses features relating to man outdoors in winter. " 'Me and Joe' articles have to be unique for this audience." Buys 1 unsolicited ms/issue. Query. Length: 1,000-1,500 words. Pays $100-300.

Photos: State availability of photos; send photos with ms. Pays $5-25 for 5x7 or 8x10 b&w glossy contact sheets; $15-50 for 35mm color transparencies. Offers no additional payment for photos with accompanying ms. Captions, model releases, and identification of subjects required. Buys all rights.

SNOWMOBILE CANADA, Suite 202, 2077 Dundas St. E., Mississauga, Ontario L4X 1M2 Canada. (416)624-8218. Editor: Reg Fife. Snowmobiling magazine published in September, October and November "to satisfy the needs of Canada's snowmobilers from coast to coast." Circ. 60,000. Pays on publication. Byline given. Buys first rights. Submit seasonal/holiday material "by July for fall publication." Simultaneous queries acceptable. Computer printout submissions acceptable. Reports in 1 month on queries; 2 months on mss. Free sample copy.

Nonfiction: Personal experience (on snowmobiling in Canada); photo feature (nature in winter); technical (new snowmobile developments); travel (snowmobile type). "We look for articles on nature as it relates to snowmobile use; trail systems in Canada; wilderness tips; the racing scene; ice fishing using snowmobiles, maintenance tips and new model designs." Buys 12 mss/year. Query or send complete ms. Length: 800-2,000 words. Pays $75-150.

Photos: Captions required. Buys one-time rights.

SNOWMOBILE MAGAZINE, Winter Sports Publishing, Inc., Suite 306, 715 Florida Ave. S., Minneapolis MN 55426. (612)545-2662. Editor: C.J. Ramstad. Managing Editor: Dick Hendricks. Magazine published 4 times/year covering snowmobiling for snowmobilers throughout North America. Circ. 500,000. Pays on publication. Byline given. Buys all rights, but "author may request return." Simultaneous and previously published submissions OK ("if publication and date are indicated"). SASE. Reports in 1 month on mss. Free sample copy and writer's guidelines.

Nonfiction: "We want articles on travel, adventure, technology, personality and history involving snowmobiling or winter recreation." Humor; interview/profile; first person. No material on accidents. Buys 2-3 mss/year. Send complete ms. Length: 1,800-3,000 words. Pays $175-350.

Photos: Send photos with or without accompanying ms. Reviews 35mm color transparencies.

Columns/Departments: Newsreal (short items pertaining to snowmobiling). Send complete ms. Length: 200-500 words. Pays $25-50 with b&w photo.

SNOWMOBILE WEST, 520 Park Ave., Box 981, Idaho Falls ID 83402. Editor: Steve Janes. For recreational snowmobile riders and owners of all ages. Magazine; 48 pages. 5% freelance written. Publishes 4 issues each winter. Circ. 200,000. Buys first North American serial rights. Pays kill fee if previously negotiated at time of assignment. Byline given on substantive articles of two pages or more. Buys 5 mss/year. Pays on publication. Publishes ms an average of 3 months after acceptance. Free sample copy and writer's guidelines. Reports in 2 months. Articles for one season are generally photographed and written the previous season. Query. Computer printout submissions acceptable. SASE.

Nonfiction and Photos: Articles about snowtrail riding in the Western US; issues affecting snowmobilers; and maps of trail areas with good color photos and b&w. Pays 3¢/word; $5/b&w; $10/color. B&w should be 5x7 or 8x10 glossy print; color should be 35mm transparencies or larger, furnished with mss. With a story of 1,000 words, typically a selection of 5 b&w and 5 color photos should accompany. Longer stories in proportion. Length: 500-2,000 words.

Tips: "It's rewarding finding a freelance writer who understands the nature and personality of our publication. It's annoying when writers say they have the story that we *really need* to use."

Soccer

SOCCER AMERICA, Box 23704, Oakland CA 94623. (415)549-1414. Editor-in-Chief: Ms. Lynn Berling-Manuel. For a wide range of soccer enthusiasts. Weekly tabloid. 10% freelance written. Circ. 10,000. Pays on publication. Buys all rights. Byline given. Submit seasonal/holiday material 30 days in advance. SASE. Reports in 2 months. Publishes ms an average of 2 months after acceptance. Sample copy and writer's guidelines $1.

Nonfiction: Expose (why a pro franchise isn't working right, etc.); historical; how-to; informational (news features); inspirational; interview; photo feature; profile; and technical. "No 'Why I Like Soccer' articles in 1000 words or less. It's been done!" Buys 1-2 mss/issue. Query. Length: 200-1,500 words. Pays 50¢/inch minimum.

Photos: Photos purchased with or without accompanying ms or on assignment. Captions required. Pays $12 for 5x7 or larger b&w glossy prints. Query.

Tips: "Freelancers mean the addition of editorial vitality. New approaches and new minds can make a world of difference. But if they haven't gotten themselves familiar with the publication . . . total waste of my time and theirs."

Tennis

TENNIS, 495 Westport Ave., Box 5350, Norwalk CT 06856. Publisher: Howard R. Gill. Editor: Shepherd Campbell. For persons who play tennis and want to play it better. Monthly magazine. Circ. 500,000. Buys all rights. Byline given. Pays on publication. SASE.

Nonfiction and Photos: Emphasis on instructional and reader service articles, but also seeks lively, well-researched features on personalities and other aspects of the game, as well as humor. Query. Length varies. Pays $200 minimum/article, considerably more for major features. Pays $50-150/8x10 b&w glossies; $75-350/color transparencies.

WORLD TENNIS MAGAZINE, CBS Consumer Publishing, a Division of CBS Inc., 1515 Broadway, New York NY 10036. Publisher: Francis X. Dealy, Jr. Editor-in-Chief: Neil Amdur.

Water Sports

DIVER, Seagraphic Publications, Ltd., Suite 210, 1807 Maritime Mews, Granville Island, Vancouver, British Columbia V6H 3W7 Canada. (604)681-3166. Publisher: Peter Vassilopoulos. Editor: Neil McDaniel. 75% freelance written. Emphasizes scuba diving, ocean science and technology (commercial and military diving) for a well-educated, outdoor-oriented readership. Published 9 times/year. Magazine; 48-56 pages. Circ. 25,000. Payment "follows publication." Buys first North American serial rights. Byline given. Query (by mail only). Submit seasonal/holiday material 3 months in advance of issue date. Computer printout submissions acceptable; prefers letter-quality to dot-matrix. SAE and IRCs. Reports in 6 weeks. Publishes ms an average of 2 months after acceptance.
Nonfiction: How-to (underwater activities such as photography, etc.); general interest (underwater oriented); humor; historical (shipwrecks, treasure artifacts, archeological); interview (underwater personalities in all spheres—military, sports, scientific or commercial); personal experience (related to diving); photo feature (marine life); technical (related to oceanography, commercial/military diving, etc.); and travel (dive resorts). No subjective product reports. Buys 40 mss/year. Submit complete ms. Length: 800-2,000 words. Pays $2.50/column inch.
Photos: "Features are mostly those describing dive sites, experiences, etc. Photo features are reserved more as specials, while almost all articles must be well illustrated with b&w prints supplemented by color transparencies." Submit photo material with accompanying ms. Pays $7 minimum for 5x7 or 8x10 glossy b&w prints; $15 minimum for 35mm color transparencies. Captions and model releases required. Buys one-time rights.
Columns/Departments: Book reviews. Submit complete ms. Length: 200 words maximum. Pays $2.50/column inch.
Fillers: Anecdotes, newsbreaks and short humor. Buys 8-10/year. Length: 50-150 words. Pays $2.50/column inch.
Tips: "It's rewarding finding a talented writer who can make ordinary topics come alive. But dealing with unsolicited manuscripts that don't even come close to being suitable for *Diver* is the most frustrating aspect of working with freelancers."

OCEAN REALM MAGAZINE, Ocean Realm Publishing, 2333 Brickell Ave., Miami FL 33129. (305)285-0252. Editor-in-Chief: Richard H. Stewart. Editor: Patricia Reilly. Quarterly magazine covering all aspects of sport diving, and the ocean environment. 30% freelance written. Circ. 50,000. Pays on publication. Byline given. Buys one-time rights. Submit seasonal/holiday material 6 months in advance. Simultaneous queries OK. Computer printout submissions acceptable; prefers letter-quality to dot-matrix. SASE. Reports in 3 months. Publishes ms an average of 1 year after acceptance. Sample copy for $3.50 and 9x12 SAE; free writer's guidelines.
Nonfiction: Book reviews, general interest, historical/nostalgic, how-to, humor, interview/profile, new product, opinion, personal experience, technical and creative photo features, technology, marine life, travel. Prefers not to see sailing, boating, destinations or marine maintenance material. Buys 48 mss/year. Send complete ms. Length: 1,500-2,500 words. Pays $200-300.
Photos: State availability of "clear, sharp, colorful photos." Pays $20-50 for 35mm color transparencies; $20-50 for 8x10 b&w prints. Captions, model release and identification of subjects required.

SAILBOARD NEWS, The International Journal of Boardsailing, Sports Ink Magazines, Inc., Box 159, Fair Haven VT 05743. (802)265-8153. Editor: Mark Gabriel. 50% freelance written. Monthly boardsailing tabloid. Circ. 19,000. Pays 30 days after publication. Publishes ms an average of 2 weeks after acceptance. Byline given. Buys one-time rights. Submit seasonal/holiday material 3 weeks in advance. Simultaneous queries OK. Computer printout submissions acceptable. SASE. Reports in 3 weeks. Free sample copy and writer's guidelines.
Nonfiction: Book excerpts, expose, general interest, historical/nostalgic, how-to, humor, inspirational, interview/profile, new product, opinion, photo feature, technical, travel. Buys 50 mss/year. Send complete ms. Length: 750 words minimum. Pays $50-200.
Photos: Send photos with ms. Reviews b&w negatives and 8x10 prints. Identification of subjects required.
Columns/Departments: Buys 12 mss/year. Query with published clips or send complete ms.

SAILORS' GAZETTE, Coastal Communicators of St. Petersburg, Inc., 5580 4th St. N., St. Petersburg FL 33703. (813)525-5647. Editor: John Weber. 70% freelance written. Monthly tabloid covering sailing in the southeastern states for sailboat owners. Circ. 10,000. Pays on publication. Publishes ms an average of 45 days after acceptance. Byline given. Offers 50% kill fee. Buys one-time rights. Submit seasonal/holiday material 3 months in advance. Computer printout submissions acceptable. SASE. Reports in 2 weeks on queries; 3 weeks on mss. Sample copy $2; free writer's guidelines.

Nonfiction: Historical/nostalgic (sailboats with direct ties to SE states); interview/profile (with sailboat owners); personal experience (sailboat cruising in SE); photo feature (b&w on sailing or waterfront scenes in SE states); technical (sailboat maintenance, not general boat maintenance). No poetry; articles about sailboats with no connection to Southeastern states; articles about first-time sailors. Buys 125 mss/year. Query with published clips. Length: 500-2,000 words. Pays $50-250.
Photos: State availability of photos. Pays $10-25 for high contrast 8x10 b&w prints. Captions and identification of subjects required. Buys one-time rights.
Tips: "The manuscripts that we turn down are usually too general and far removed from the Southeastern themes. We're open to where-to and how-to, as it pertains to the Southeast; also interviews with cruising and racing sailors.

SCUBA TIMES, The Active Diver's Magazine, Poseidon Publishing Co., Box 6268, Pensacola FL 32503. (904)478-5288. Managing Editor: Lisa Novak. Publisher: M. Wallace Poole. 80% freelance written. Bimonthly magazine covering scuba diving. "Our reader is the young, reasonably affluent scuba diver looking for a more exciting approach to diving than he could find in the other diving magazines." Circ. 50,000. Pays 6 weeks after publication. Publishes ms an average of 6 months after acceptance. Byline given. Buys first world serial rights. Simultaneous queries OK. Computer printout submissions acceptable. SASE. Reports in 2 months. Sample copy $3. Writer's guidelines for business size SAE and 1 first class stamp.
Nonfiction: General interest; how-to; interview/profile ("of 'name' people in the sport, especially if they're currently doing something radical"); new product (how to more effectively use them); personal experience (good underwater photography pieces); and travel (pertaining to diving). Especially want illustrated articles on avant-garde diving and diving travel, such as nude diving, singles only dive clubs, deep diving, new advances in diving technology, etc. No articles without a specific theme. Buys 25 mss/year. Query with clips of published work. Length: 500-1,200 words. Pays $50-250.
Photos: Art Dept. "Underwater photography must be of the *highest* quality in order to catch our interest. We can't be responsible for unsolicited photo submissions." Pays $25-250 for 35mm color transparencies; reviews 8x10 b&w prints. Captions, model release, and identification of subjects required. Buys first world rights.
Tips: "Our current contributors are among the top writers in the diving field. A newcomer must have a style that draws the reader into the article, leaves him satisfied at the end of it, and makes him want to see something else by this same author soon! Writing for diving magazines has become a fairly sophisticated venture. Writers must be able to compete with the best in order to get published. We only use contributors grounded in underwater photojournalism."

SURFER, Box 1028, Dana Point CA 92629. (714)496-5922. Editor: Paul Holmes. For teens and young adults. Slant is toward the contemporary, fast-moving and hard core enthusiasts in the sport of surfing. Monthly. Circ. 91,000. Rights purchased vary with author and material. Pays on publication. Sample copy $3. Computer printout submissions acceptable; prefers letter-quality to dot-matrix. SASE.
Nonfiction: "We use anything about surfing if interesting and authoritative. Must be written from an expert's viewpoint. We're looking for good comprehensive articles on any surfing spot—especially surfing in faraway foreign lands." Length: preferably not more than 5 pages typewritten. No poetry. Pays 10-15¢/word.
Photos: Buys photos with mss or with captions only. Likes 8x10 glossy b&w proofsheets with negatives. Also uses expert color 35mm and 2¼x2¼ transparencies carefully wrapped. Pays $10-100 b&w; $25-350/35mm color transparencies.

SURFING MAGAZINE, Western Empire, 2720 Camino Capistrano, San Clemente CA 92672. (714)492-7873. Editor: David Gilovich. Monthly magazine covering all aspects of the sport of surfing. "*Surfing Magazine* is a contemporary, beach lifestyle/surfing publication. We reach the entire spectrum of surfing enthusiasts." Circ. 80,000. Pays on publication. Byline given. Buys all rights. Submit seasonal/holiday material 4 months in advance. Photocopied submissions OK. SASE. Reports in 2 weeks. Free sample copy and writer's guidelines for SAE.
Nonfiction: Book excerpts (on surfing, beach lifestyle, ocean-related); how-to (surfing-related); interview/profile (of top surfing personality); new product; photo feature (of ocean, beach lifestyle, surfing); travel (to surfing locations only). Buys 50 mss/year. Query with clips of published work or send complete ms. Length: 3,000 words maximum. Pays 10-15¢/word.
Photos: Larry Moore, photo editor. State availability of photos or send photos with ms. Pays $35-500 for 35mm color transparencies; $20-75 for b&w contact sheet and negatives. Identification of subjects required. Buys one-time rights.
Columns/Departments: Bill Sharp, column/department editor. "Currents"—mini-features of current topical interest about surfing. This department includes reviews of books, films, etc. Buys 36 mss/year. Query with clips of published work, if available, or send complete ms. Length: 100-500 words. Pays $75-100.
Fiction: Adventure, humorous. No fantasy fiction. Buys 3 mss/year. Send complete ms. Length: 1,000-4,000 words. Pays 10-15¢/word.
Tips: "Begin by contributing small, mini-news features for our 'Currents' department. New editorial policy suggests that we will be more receptive than ever to bringing in new writers."

SWIMMING WORLD, 1130 W. Florence Ave., Inglewood CA 90301. (213)641-2727. Editor: Robert Ingram. 2% freelance written. For "competitors (10-24), plus their coaches, parents, and those who are involved in the enjoyment of the sport." Monthly. Circ. 40,000. Buys all rights. Byline given. Buys 10-12 mss/year. Pays on publication. Reports in 1-2 months. Query. SASE.
Nonfiction: Articles of interest to competitive swimmers, divers and water poloists, their parents and coaches. Can deal with diet, body conditioning or medicine, as applicable to competitive swimming. Nutrition and stroke and diving techniques. Psychology and profiles of athletes. Must be authoritative. Length: 1,500 words maximum. Pays $50 maximum.
Photos: Photos purchased with mss. Does not pay extra for photos with mss. 8x10 b&w only. Also photos with captions. Pays $20 maximum for b&w.

UNDERCURRENT, Box 1658, Sausalito CA 94965. (415)332-3684. Managing Editor: Ben Davison. 20-50% freelance written. Monthly consumer-oriented scuba diving newsletter; 12 pages. Circ. 13,000. Pays on publication. Buys first rights. Pays $50 kill fee. Byline given. Simultaneous (if to other than diving publisher), photocopied and previously published submissions OK. Computer printout submissions acceptable. SASE. Reports in 4-6 weeks. Free sample copy and writer's guidelines; mention *Writer's Market* in request.
Nonfiction: Equipment evaluation, how-to, general interest, new product, and travel review. Buys 2 mss/issue. Query. Length: 2,000 words maximum. Pays $50-250.
Fillers: Buys clippings and newsbreaks. Buys 20/year. Length: 25-500 words. Pays $5-20.

THE WATER SKIER, Box 191, Winter Haven FL 33882. (813)324-4341. Editor: Duke Cullimore. Official publication of the American Water Ski Association. 15% freelance written. Published 7 times/year. Circ. 17,500. Buys North American serial rights only. Byline given. Buys limited amount of freelance material. Query. Pays on acceptance. Publishes ms an average of 3 months after acceptance. Free sample copy. Reports on submissions within 10 days. Computer printout submissions acceptable "if double-spaced and standard ms requirements are followed"; prefers letter-quality to dot-matrix. SASE.
Nonfiction and Photos: Occasionally buys exceptionally offbeat, unusual text/photo features on the sport of water skiing. Will put more emphasis on technique, methods, etc., in the year ahead.
Tips: "Freelance writers should be aware of specializations of subject matter in magazine publishing; need for more expertise in topic; more professional writing ability."

‡**WINDRIDER, The Magazine of Boardsailing**, World Publications, Inc., Box 2456, Winter Park FL 32790. (305)628-4802. Editor: Nancy K. Crowell. Magazine published 6 times/year (monthly June, July) on boardsailing/a.k.a. "windsurfing" for boardsailors around the world of all skill levels. "Writers absolutely must be skilled boardsailors with extensive knowledge about the sport." Circ. 40,000. Pays 30 days after publication. Byline given. Buys first rights. Submit seasonal/holiday material 3 months in advance. Computer printout submissions acceptable. SASE. Reports in 6 weeks on queries; 3 weeks on ms. Sample copy $2.50; writer's guidelines for business-size SAE and 1 first class stamp.
Nonfiction: How-to ("we use established boardsailors for this type of article") and technical (must have technical background in the sport). No fiction, poetry, cartoons or "first time on a sailboard" material. Buys 18 mss/year. Query with published clips. Length: 750-2,500 words. Pays $75-250.
Tips: "You must be involved in the boardsailing world to write for our publication—as competitor, manufacturer or engineer, instructor, etc. We occasionally use freelancers for travel on specific areas, but this is only in the event we can't get there ourselves. Probably the best area for freelancers is our Equipment Tip section."

WORLD WATERSKIING MAGAZINE, World Publications, Box 2456, Winter Park FL 32790. (305)628-4802. Editor: Terry L. Snow. Managing Editor: Theresa T. Temple. Magazine published 7 times/year. Covers various levels of water skiing. Circ. 57,000. Pays on publication. Byline given. Buys variable rights. Submit seasonal/holiday material 6 months in advance. Simultaneous queries, and simultaneous, photocopied, and previously published submissions OK. SASE. Reports in 3 weeks.
Nonfiction: Historical/nostalgic (anything dealing with water skiing); how-to (tips on equipment and repair of skis, bindings, etc.); humor ("always looking for a good laugh about water skiing); inspirational (someone who beat the odds—handicapped skier, for example); interview/profile (only on assignment); photo feature (action or special effects); technical (on assignment only); travel (picturesque water skiing sites); sports medicine. No first-person accounts or fiction. Buys 10-30 mss/year. Query with or without clips of published work. Pays $150-200/feature story; $75/medical, sports medicine; $40/tips.
Photos: Tom King, senior photographer. "We need lots of sharp photos for our annual issue in October. Send photos with ms. Prefers b&w prints or contact sheet, 35mm or 2 ¼ color slides/transparencies. Model release and identification of subjects required. Buys negotiable rights. Buys 5-15 mss/year. Query with clips of published work. Length: 250-300 words. Pays $40-75.
Fillers: Buys 5/year. Length: 100-150 words. Pays $5-15.
Tips: "We would love to hear from good sportswriters with a lively interest in water skiing. We're especially open to features and sports medicine articles. Medical writing would require background in specialized area and proof with resume, etc."

Teen and Young Adult

Today's young readers won't read "lectures" or stories about yesterday's problems. The publications in this category are for young people aged 12 to 18. Publications aimed at 2- to 12-year-olds are classified in the Juvenile category. Publications for college students are listed in Career, College, and Alumni.

ALIVE FOR YOUNG TEENS, Christian Board of Publication, Box 179, St. Louis MO 63166. Editor: Mike Dixon. 95% freelance written. Ecumenical, mainline publication with a Protestant slant; aimed at young teens. "We especially appreciate submissions of useable quality from 12- to 15-year-olds. Those in this age range should include their age with the submission. We appreciate use of humor that early adolescents would appreciate. Please keep the age group in mind." Publishes ms an average of 1 year after acceptance. Buys first rights. Computer printout submissions acceptable; prefers letter-quality to dot-matrix. SASE required with all submissions. Sample copy 50¢.
Nonfiction: "Articles should concern interesting youth, church youth groups, projects and activities. There is little chance of our taking an article not accompanied by at least 3-4 captioned b&w photos." Length: 800-1,000 words. Pays 2¢/word; photos $3-5.
Fiction: "Give us fiction concerning characters in the *Alive for Young Teens* readers' age group (12-15), dealing with problems and situations peculiar to that group." Length: 100-1,200 words. Pays 2¢/word. Uses 6-10 photo features/issue. Pays $5/photo maximum.
Photos: Send photos with ms. Submit in batches. Pays $10-20 for b&w prints.
Poetry: Length: 20 lines maximum. Pays 25¢/line.
Fillers: Puzzles, riddles and daffy definitions. Pays $10 maximum.

AMERICAN NEWSPAPER CARRIER, American Newspaper Boy Press, Box 15300, Winston-Salem NC 27103. Editor: Marilyn H. Rollins. 10% freelance written. Buys all rights. Pays on acceptance. Publishes ms an average of 3 months after acceptance. Queries not required. Computer printout submissions acceptable. Reports in 10 days. SASE.
Fiction: Uses a limited amount of short fiction written for teen-age newspaper carriers, male and female. It is preferable that stories be written around newspaper carrier characters. Humor, mystery and adventure plots are commonly used. No material not related to teen-age interests or stories featuring newspaper carrier contests, prizes, etc. Length: 1,000-2,000 words. "Stories are purchased with the understanding that they are original and that the *American Newspaper Carrier* purchases all rights thereto." Pays $15 minimum.

‡**BOP**, Laufer Publishing Company, #720, 7060 Hollywood Blvd., Hollywood CA 90028. (213)469-3551. Editor: Kerry Laufer. Managing Editor: Linda Benjamin. A monthly entertainment magazine covering music, TV and film personalities of interest to young people, specifically teenage girls—average age 14. Estab. 1983. Circ. 300,000. Pays on acceptance. No byline given. Submit seasonal/holiday material 2-3 months in advance. Photocopied and previously published submissions OK. SASE. Reports in 2 weeks on queries; 1 month on mss. Sample copy for $1.50, 9x12 SAE, and 2 first class stamps; writer's guidelines for legal-size SAE and 1 first class stamp.
Nonfiction: Interview/profile (stars/celebrities popular with teens); personal experience (meeting stars/celebrities popular with teens); photo feature (stars/celebrities popular with teens). Buys 0-6 mss/year. Query with published clips. Length: 500-1,000 words. Payment varies.
Photos: Send photos with query or ms. Reviews b&w contact sheets. Pays $15-25 for b&w prints; $35-150 for color transparencies. Captions and identification of subjects required. Buys all rights.
Tips: "Query first with samples of work. Accepted work is dependent upon newsworthiness. It's important that contributor be aware of trends in teenage entertainment world."

BOYS' LIFE, Boy Scouts of America, Magazine Division, 1325 Walnut Hill Lane, Irving TX 75062. (214)659-2000. Editor: Robert Hood. Monthly magazine covering Boy Scout activities for "ages 8-18—Boy Scouts, Cub Scouts, and others of that age group." Circ. 1.5 million. Pays on publication. Byline given.
Nonfiction: "Almost all articles are assigned. We do not encourage unsolicited material."
Columns/Departments: Hobby How's (1-2 paragraphs on hobby tips). Buys 60 mss/year. Send complete ms. Pays $5 minimum.
Fillers: Jokes (Think and Grin—1-3 sentences). Pays $1 minimum.

BREAD, 6401 The Paseo, Kansas City MO 64131. (816)333-7000, ext. 214. Editor: Gary Sivewright. 10% freelance written. Christian leisure reading magazine for junior and senior high students, published by the Church of the Nazarene. Monthly. Pays on acceptance. Publishes ms an average of 8 months after acceptance. Accepts simultaneous submissions. Computer printout submissions acceptable. Buys first rights, sometimes second rights. Byline given. Free sample copy and editorial specifications sheet for SASE.

Nonfiction: Helpful articles in the area of developing the Christian life; first-person, "this is how I did it" stories about Christian witness. Length: up to 1,500 words. Articles must be theologically acceptable. Looking for fresh approach to basic themes. Also needs articles dealing with doctrinal subjects such as the Holy Spirit, written for the teen reader. Pays 3½¢/word for first rights and 3¢/word for second rights. Works 6 months ahead of publication.

Photos: 8x10 b&w glossy prints of teens in action. Payment is $15 and up. Uses 1 color transparency/month for cover.

Fiction: "Adventure, school, and church-oriented. No sermonizing." Send us fresh, innovative fiction stories. Avoid the same old formula kinds of pieces. We buy more fiction than anything. Make sure dialogue and situations are up to date." Length: 1,500 words maximum. Pays 3-3.5¢/word for first rights and 3¢/word for second rights.

Poetry: Free verse, light verse and traditional. Buys 10 poems/year. Length: 25 lines maximun. Submit poems in batches of 3. Pays 25¢ a line.

Tips: Send complete ms by mail for consideration. Reports in 6-8 weeks. SASE.

CAMPUS LIFE MAGAZINE, Christianity Today, Inc., 465 Gundersen Dr., Carol Stream IL 60188. Executive Editor: Scott Bolinder. Editor: Gregg Lewis. Managing Editor: Jim Long. Associate Editor: Verne Becker. 20% freelance written. For a readership of young adults, high school and college age. "Though our readership is largely Christian, *Campus Life* reflects the interests of all young people—music, bicycling, photography, media and sports." Largely staff-written. "*Campus Life* is a Christian magazine that is *not* overtly religious. The indirect style is intended to create a safety zone with our readers and to reflect our philosophy that God is interested in all of life. Therefore, we publish message stories side by side with general interest, humor, etc." Monthly magazine. Circ. 150,000. Pays on acceptance. Publishes ms an average of 6 months after acceptance. Buys one-time rights. Byline given. Submit seasonal/holiday material 6 months in advance. Simultaneous, photocopied and previously published submissions OK. Computer printout submissions acceptable. SASE. Reports in 2 months. Sample copy $2; writer's guidelines for SASE.

Nonfiction: Contact: Gregg Lewis. Personal experiences, photo features, unusual sports, humor, short items—how-to, college or career, travel, etc. Query or submit complete manuscript. Length: 500-3,000 words. Pays $100-250.

Photos: Verne Becker, photo editor. Pays $50 minimum/8x10 b&w glossy print; $90 minimum/color transparency; $250/cover photo. Buys one-time rights.

Fiction: Contact: Gregg Lewis. Stories about problems and experiences kids face. Trite, simplistic religious stories are not acceptable.

Tips: "The best ms for a freelancer to try to sell us would be a well-written first person story (fiction or nonfiction) focusing on a common struggle young people face in any area of life—intellectual, emotional, social, physical or spiritual. Most manuscripts that miss us fail in quality or style. Since our style is distinctive, it is one of the biggest criteria in buying an article, so interested writers must study *Campus Life* to get an understanding of our audience and style. Don't submit unless you have *at least* read the magazine."

CHRISTIAN ADVENTURER, Messenger Publishing House, Box 850, Joplin MO 64802. (417)624-7050. Editor-in-Chief: Roy M. Chappell, D.D. Managing Editor: Mrs. Rosmarie Foreman. A denominational Sunday School take-home paper for teens, 13-19. Quarterly; 104 pages. Circ. 3,500. Pays quarterly. Buys simultaneous, second serial (reprint) or one-time rights. Byline given. Submit seasonal/holiday material 1 year in advance. Photocopied and previously published submissions OK. SASE. Reports in 4-6 weeks. Sample copy 50¢. Free writer's guidelines with sample copy.

Nonfiction: Historical (related to great events in the history of the church); informational (explaining the meaning of a Bible passage or a Christian concept); inspirational; nostalgia; and personal experience. Send complete ms. Length: 1,500-1,800 words. Pays 1¢/word.

Fiction: Adventure, historical, religious and romance. Length: 1,500-1,800 words. Pays 1¢/word.

CHRISTIAN LIVING FOR SENIOR HIGHS, David C. Cook Publishing Co., 850 N. Grove, Elgin IL 60120. (312)741-2400. Associate Editor: Anne E. Dinnan. "A take-home paper used in senior high Sunday School classes. We encourage Christian teens to write to us." Quarterly magazine; 4 pages. Pays on acceptance. Publishes ms an average of 1 year after acceptance. Buys all rights. Byline given. Phone queries OK. Computer printout submissions acceptable; prefers letter-quality to dot-matrix. Reports in 3-5 weeks. SASE. Free sample copy and writer's guidelines.

Nonfiction: How-to (Sunday School youth projects); historical (with religious base); humor (from Christian perspective); inspirational and personality (nonpreachy); personal teen experience (Christian); poetry written by teens and photo feature (Christian subject). "Nothing not compatible with a Christian lifestyle. Since this is difficult to define, author should query doubtful topics." Buys 6 mss/issue. Submit complete ms. Length: 900-1,200 words. Pays $80; $40 for short pieces.

Fiction: Adventure (with religious theme); historical (with Christian perspective); humorous; mystery; and religious. Buys 2 mss/issue. Submit complete ms. Length: 900-1,200 words. Pays $80-100. "No preachy experiences."

Photos: Cindy Carter, photo editor. Photos purchased with or without accompanying ms or on assignment. Send contact sheet, prints or transparencies. Pays $20-35 for 8½x11 b&w photos; $50 minimum for color transparencies.

Tips: "Our demand for manuscripts should increase, but most of these will probably be assigned rather than bought over-the-transom. Authors should query us, sending samples of their work. That way we can keep them on file for specific writing assignments."

CIRCLE K MAGAZINE, 3636 Woodview Trace, Indianapolis IN 46268. Executive Editor: Chuck Jonak. 60% freelance written. "Our readership consists almost entirely of college students interested in the concept of voluntary service. They are politically and socially aware and have a wide range of interests." Published 5 times/year. Magazine; 16 pages. Circ. 14,500. Pays on acceptance. Publishes ms an average of 3 months after acceptance. Normally buys first North American serial rights. Byline given. Submit seasonal/holiday material 6 months in advance. Computer printout submissions acceptable; no dot-matrix. SASE. Reports in 4 weeks. Free sample copy and writer's guidelines.

Nonfiction: Informational (general interest articles on any area pertinent to concerned college students); community concerns (voluntarism, youth, medical, handicapped, elderly, underprivileged). No "first-person confessions, family history or travel." Recent article example: "Runaways: Victims of Society?" (Jan./Feb. 1984). Query or submit complete ms. Length: 1,500-2,500 words. Pays $175-250.

Photos: Purchased with accompanying ms. Captions required. Query. Total purchase price for ms includes payment for photos.

Tips: "The new organizational theme, 'Achieve Unity Through Service,' will open the magazine to family-related features. Feature ideas about family concerns—in touch, in turmoil, in transition—will be needed. Query must be typed, and should indicate familiarity with the field and sources."

‡**DOLLY MAGAZINE,** Magazine Promotions, 57 Regent St., Chippendale, New South Wales, Australia 2008. (02)699-3622. Editor: Lisa Wilkinson. 25% freelance written. Monthly magazine. Informed entertainment for girls 14-20. Fashion, beauty, personalities, general interest. Circ. 200,000. Pays on acceptance. Publishes ms an average of 4 months after acceptance. Byline given. Offers 50% kill fee. Buys first, all, or second serial reprint rights (depends on story). Submit seasonal/holiday material 4 months in advance. Simultaneous and previously published submissions OK. Computer printout submissions acceptable; prefers letter-quality to dot-matrix. SASE. Reports in 2 weeks on queries; 1 month on mss. Sample copy for 37x27 cms SAE and $1 postage; writer's guidelines for 23x10 cms SAE and 50¢ postage.

Nonfiction: General interest (aimed at teenage girls); interview/profile (of pop stars, actors, etc.); photo feature (cover, beauty shots). No heavy sex mss. Buys 50 mss/year. Query with clips of published work or send complete ms. Length: 1,000-2,500 words. Pay "decided on sight."

Photos: Send photos with ms. Pay "depends on sighting" for 2¼x2¼ color transparencies. Captions, model release and identification of subjects required. Buys one-time rights.

Columns/Departments: Decor—ideas for teenage rooms, flats, etc. Buys 150 mss/year. Query with clips of published work. Length: 100-1,000 words. Pay "depends on sighting."

Fiction: Lisa Wilkinson, fiction editor. Adventure (with a touch of romance); very condensed novels; confession; fantasy (not kinky); historical (romance); humor/satire; juvenile; romance (contemporary); suspense/mystery; women's; young adult. "Characters to be between 17 and 20 and unmarried. We like element of romance." Buys 2 mss/issue. Query with clips of published work and IRCs. Length: 1,000-25,000 words; 2,500 words average. Payment "depends on story and content."

‡**ENTER MAGAZINE, The World of Computers & Electronic Games,** Children's Television Workshop, 1 Lincoln Place, New York NY 10023. (212)595-3456. Editor: Ira Wolfman. Senior Editor: Jim Lewis. A computer, new technology and electronic games magazine for kids 10-16 years old, published 10 times/year. Estab. 1983. Circ. 200,000. Pays on acceptance. Byline given. Offers 33-50% kill fee. Buys all rights and makes work-for-hire assignments. Submit seasonal/holiday material 4-6 months in advance. Electronic submissions OK for programming only on Apple IIe disks, Commodore, Atari, TRS 80 Color Computer, Cassette: T.I., Timex-Sinclaiir. Computer printout submissions acceptable; prefers letter-quality to dot-matrix. SASE. Reports in 3 weeks on queries; 1 month on mss. Sample copy $2; writer's guidelines for business-size SAE and 1 first class stamp.

Nonfiction: Book excerpts; general interest (computers); how-to (computers); humor; interview/profile; new product; personal experience (by kids 10-18 only); and photo feature. No company profiles or very technical articles. Buys 80 mss/year. Query with published clips. Length: 900-2,500 words. Pays $300-750.

Photos: Liz Heltich, photo editor. State availability of photos with query or ms. Model release and identification of subjects required. "Rights negotiated on a case-by-case basis."

Columns/Departments: Richard Cherat, basic training (programming) editor. Basic Training—programming. "We buy short original programs for any of 9 computers (Adam, Apple, Atari, Commodore VIC and 64,

IBM, T.I., TRS 80, Timex-Sinclair)." Buys 20 mss/year. Query with published clips. Pays $50-300.
Fiction: Mystery. "We only accept computer-related fiction." Buys 3-5 mss/year. Query with published clips. Length: 1,500-5,000 words. Pays $300-800.
Fillers: Clippings and newsbreaks. Length: 100-500 words. Pays $25-100.
Tips: "Send a query (with clips) that is about a teenager doing something interesting with computers or high technology. Bring to our attention an offbeat human interest piece about computers. Remember timeliness! We are a news/feature magazine. Areas most open for freelancers: personality profiles; for programmers: BASIC Training; for teenagers: Random Access. All Children's Television Workshop publications (*Enter* is one) are nonsexist, nonviolent, and committed to presenting strong minority and female role models."

‡**EQ MAGAZINE, Equal, A Magazine for Today's Youth**, Vision Communications, #7, 2428 Newport Blvd., Costa Mesa CA 92627. (714)645-5979. Editor: Lori Bassett. A monthly magazine for teens. Estab. 1983. Circ. 75,000. Pays on publication. Byline given. Buys first North American serial, one-time, first, and second serial (reprint) rights, and makes work-for-hire assignments. Submit seasonal/holiday material 6 months in advance. Simultaneous queries, and simultaneous, photocopied, and previously published submissions OK. Electronic submissions OK "if 5¼" disk compatible with Commodore 64 or IBM P.C. Computer printout submissions acceptable. SASE. Reports in 1 month. Free sample copy.
Nonfiction: Historical/nostalgic, humor; interview/profile (about teenagers); personal experience (from teenagers only); photo feature. No negative articles about teenagers, or those not applicable to youth. Buys 10 mss/year. Query with or without published clips. Length: 500-2,500 words. Pays 5¢/word.
Photos: State availability of photos or send photos with query or ms. Pays $10 for 5x7 b&w prints. Captions and identification of subjects required. Buys one-time rights.
Fiction: Adventure, condensed novels, ethnic, fantasy, historical, mystery, science fiction, suspense. Buys 10 mss/year. Query or send complete ms. Length: 1,000-4,000 words. Pays 5¢/word.

EXPLORING MAGAZINE, The Journal for Explorers, Boy Scouts of America, 1325 Walnut Hill Ln., Irving TX 75062. (214)659-2365. Editor: Robert E. Hood. Executive Editor: Scott Daniels. 85% freelance written. Magazine published 4 times/year—January, March, May, September. Covers the Exploring program of the BSA. Circ. 480,000. Pays on acceptance. Publishes ms an average of 6 months after acceptance. Byline given. Buys one-time and first rights. Submit seasonal/holiday material 6 months in advance. Simultaneous queries OK. Computer printout submissions acceptable; prefers letter-quality to dot-matrix. SASE. Reports in 2 weeks. Sample copy for 8½x10 SAE and 85¢ postage; writer's guidelines for business-size SAE and 1 first class stamp.
Nonfiction: General interest, how-to (achieve outdoor skills, organize trips, meetings, etc.); interview/profile (of outstanding Explorer); travel (backpacking or canoeing with Explorers). "Nothing dealing with sex, drugs, or violence." Buys 3 mss/year. Query with clips. Length: 800-2,000 words. Pays $300-450.
Photos: Gene Daniels, photo editor. State availability of photos with query letter or ms. Reviews b&w contact sheets. Captions required. Buys one-time rights.
Tips: "Contact the local Exploring Director in your area (listed in phone book white pages under Boy Scouts of America). Find out if there are some outstanding post activities going on and then query magazine editor in Irving TX. Strive for shorter texts, faster starts and stories that lend themselves to dramatic photographs." Write for guidelines and "What is Exploring?" fact sheet.

FREEWAY, Box 632, Glen Ellyn IL 60138. Editor: Cindy Atoji. 90% freelance written. For "young Christian adults of high school and college age." Weekly. Circ. 70,000. Prefers first rights but buys some reprints. Purchases 100 mss/year. Byline given. Reports on material accepted for publication in 5-6 weeks. Publishes ms an average of 1 year after acceptance. Returns rejected material in 4-5 weeks. Computer printout submissions acceptable.
Nonfiction: *FreeWay*'s greatest need is for personal experience stories showing how God has worked in teens' lives. Stories are best written in first person, 'as told to' author. Incorporate specific details, ancedotes, and dialogue. Show, don't tell, how the subject thought and felt. Weave spiritual conflicts and prayers into entire manuscript; avoid tacked-on sermons and morals. Stories should show how God has helped the person resolve a problem or how God helped save a person from trying circumstances (1,000 words or less). Short-short stories are also needed as fillers. We also need self-help or how-to articles with practical Christian advice on daily living, and trend articles addressing secular fads from a Christian perspective." Pays 4-7¢/word.
Photos: Whenever possible, provide clear 8x10 or 5x7 b&w photos to accompany mss (or any other available photos). Payment is $5-30.
Fiction: "We use little fiction, unless it is allegory, parables, or humor."
Tips: "Write to us for our 'Tips to Writers' pamphlet and free sample copy. Study them, then query or send complete mss. In your cover letter include information about who you are, writing qualifications and experience working with teens. Include SASE. Trends in magazine publishing that freelance writers should be aware of include planning issues around one topic, and assignment rather than freelance."

GROUP, Thom Schultz Publications, Box 481, Loveland CO 80539. (303)669-3836. Editor-in-Chief: Thom Schultz. 60% freelance written. For members and leaders of high-school-age Christian youth groups; average age 16. Magazine published 8 times/year. Circ. 60,000. Pays on publication. Buys all rights. Byline given. Phone queries OK. Submit seasonal/holiday material 5 months in advance. Special Easter, Thanksgiving and Christmas issues and college issues. Simultaneous, photocopied and previously published submissions OK. SASE. Reports in 3-4 weeks. Sample copy $1; writer's guidelines for SASE.
Nonfiction: How-to (fund-raising, membership-building, worship, games, discussions, activities, crowd breakers, simulation games); informational; (drama, worship, service projects); inspirational (issues facing young people today); interview and photo feature (group activities). Buys 3 mss/issue. Query. Length: 500-1,500 words. Pays $50-150.
Photos: Photos purchased with or without accompanying ms or on assignment. Captions required. Pays $20 minimum for 8x10 b&w glossy prints, $50 minimum for 35mm color transparencies.
Columns/Departments: Try This One (short ideas for games; crowd breakers, discussions, worships, fund raisers, service projects, etc.). Buys 6 mss/issue. Send complete ms. Length: 500 words maximum. Pays $15.

GUIDE, 55 W. Oak Ridge Dr., Hagerstown MD 21740. Editor: Penny Estes Wheeler. 90% freelance written. A Seventh-Day Adventist journal for junior youth and early teens. "Its content reflects Seventh-Day Adventist beliefs and standards. Another characteristic which probably distinguishes it from many other magazines is the fact that all its stories are nonfiction." Weekly magazine; 32 pages. Circ. 60,000. Buys first serial rights, and second (reprint) rights to material originally published elsewhere. Byline given. Buys about 350 mss/year. Pays on acceptance. Publishes ms an average of 6 months after acceptance; "depends on season." Reports in 6 weeks. Computer printout submissions acceptable; prefers letter-quality to dot-matrix. SASE.
Nonfiction: Wants articles and nonfiction stories of character-building and spiritual value. All stories must be true and include dialogue. Should emphasize the positive aspects of living—faithfulness, obedience to parents, perseverance, kindness, gratitude, courtesy, etc. "We need stories relevant to the needs and problems of today's Christian youth. We do not use stories of hunting, fishing, trapping or spiritualism." Send complete ms (include word count). Length: 1,500-2,500 words. Pays 2-4¢/word. Also buys serialized true stories. Length: 10 chapters.
Poetry: Buys traditional forms of poetry; also some free verse. Length: 4-16 lines. Pays 50¢-$1/line.

IN TOUCH, Wesleyan Publishing House, Box 2000, Marion IN 46952. Editor: Jim Watkins. Published to reinforce Sunday school curriculum. Most writing on assignment basis, but constantly looking for new writers. Best way to "break in" is to send unsolicited ms that shows you're "in touch" with our 13-19 year old readers. Weekly, not copyrighted. Byline given. Pays on acceptance. No queries. Submit holiday/seasonal material 9 months in advance. Computer printout submissions acceptable; prefers letter-quality to dot-matrix. SASE. Reports in 6 weeks. Free sample copy for SASE.
Nonfiction: Testimonies, observations on contemporary issues, self-help articles, humor, and interviews with famous Christians. Length: 1,200-1,500 words. Pays 2-3¢/word.
Fiction: Looking for "good honest fiction." Must be third person. "No Sunday school soap opera with easy out, pat answers." Length: 1,200-1,500 words. Pays 2-3¢/word.
Photos: Need b&w glossies of teens in variety of situations. *Seventeen, Campus Life* type cover shots, candid closeups of faces. Pays $15-25.

‡JUST ABOUT ME (JAM), A Magazine for Kids 10-15, Suite 202, 56 The Esplanade, Toronto, Canada M5E 1A7. (416)364-5938. Editor: Ulla Colgrass. 95% freelance written. Bimonthly magazine providing information and entertainment for boys and girls 10-15. Circ. 15,000. Readership and conent are Canadian. Pays on publication. Publishes ms an average of 4 months after acceptance. Byline given. Buys first North American serial or first rights. Simultaneous queries, and simultaneous, photocopied, and previously published submissions OK. Computer printout submissions acceptable if double spaced. SASE. Sample copy $2.60; writer's guidelines for SAE and 32¢ Canadian postage.
Nonfiction: Book excerpts (subject: children's 10-15); general interest; historical/nostalgic; how-to (teens project); humor; inspirational; interview/profile (of people who have had an effect on youths or who are young); new product; opinion (avoid preaching); personal experience (from a youthful perspective); technical (simple); travel (that would be of interest to 10-15 year-olds); sports. Buys 4-8 mss/year. Query with clips of publishd work. Length: 500-1,500 words. Pays $100-200.
Fiction: Anne Barrett, publisher. Adventure, condensed novels, ethnic, fantasy, historical, horror (mild), humorous, mainstream, mystery, novel excerpts, science fiction, suspense. "Material should appeal to boys and girls 10-15." Buys 6 mss/year. Send complete ms. Length: 15-20 typed pages. Pays $50 maximum.
Poetry: Avant-garde, free verse, haiku, light verse, traditional. Buys varied number of poems/year. Pays $10 maximum.

‡KEYNOTER, Key Club International, 3636 Woodview Trace, Indianapolis IN 46268. (317)875-8755, ext. 432. Executive Editor: David Brill. A youth magazine published monthly Oct.-May (Dec./Jan. combine/issue), distributed to members of Key Club International, a high school service organization for young men and women. Circ. 100,000. Pays on acceptance. Byline given. Buys first North American serial rights. Submit seasonal/holiday material 7 months in advance. Simultaneous queries and simultaneous (if advised), photocopied and previously published submissions OK. Computer printout submissions acceptable; prefers letter-quality to dot-matrix. SASE. Reports in 1 month. Sample copy for 9x12 SAE and 3 first class stamps; writer's guidelines for 9½x4 SAE and 1 first class stamp.

Nonfiction: Book excerpts (may be included in articles but are not accepted alone); general interest (must be geared for intelligent teen audience); historical/nostalgic (generally not accepted); how-to (if it offers advice on how teens can enhance the quality of lives or communities); humor (accepted very infrequently; if adds to story, OK); interview/profile (rarely purchased, "would have to be on/with an irresistible subject"); new product (only if affects teens); photo feature (if subject is right, might consider); technical (if understandable and interesting to teen audience); travel (sometimes OK, but must apply to club travel schedule); subjects that entertain and inform teens on topics that relate directly to their lives. "Please, no first-person confessions, no articles that are written down to our teen readers." Buys 5-10 mss/year. Query. Length: 1,500-2,500 words. Pays $125-250.

Photos: State availability of photos. Reviews b&w contact sheets and negatives. Identification of subjects required. Buys one-time rights. Payment for photos included in payment for ms.

Tips: "We want to see articles written with attention to style and detail that will enrich the world of teens. Articles must be thoroughly researched and should draw on nationally and internationally respected sources. Our readers are 13-15, mature and dedicated to community service. We are very committed to working with good writers, and if we see something we like in a well written query, we'll try to work it through to publication."

‡**LIGHTED PATHWAY**, Church of God, 922 Montgomery Ave., Cleveland TN 37311. (615)476-4512. Editor: Hoyt E. Stone. 25% freelance written. A monthly magazine emphasizing Christian living for youth and young marrieds ages 13-25. Circ. 22,000. Pays on acceptance. Publishes ms an average of 3 months after acceptance. Byline given. Buys first North American serial rights and one-time rights. Submit seasonal/holiday material 4 months in advance. Simultaneous queries, and simultaneous, photocopied, and previously published submissions OK. Computer printout submissions acceptable. SASE. Reports in 2 weeks on queries; 1 month on mss. Free sample copy and writer's guidelines.

Nonfiction: Inspirational, interview/profile, personal experience, photo feature and travel. "Our primary objective is inspiration, to portray happy, victorious living through faith in God." No westerns, gothics, mysteries, animal. Buys 40 mss/year. Query or send complete ms. Length: 1,000-2,000 words. Pay 2-4¢/word.

Photos: State availability of photos or send photos with query or ms. Pays $10-20 for 8x10 b&w prints. Buys one-time rights and all rights.

Fiction: Adventure, historical and religious. Buys 24 mss/year. Query or send complete ms. Length: 1,000-2,000 words. Pays 2-4¢/word.

Tips: "Write to evangelical, conservative audience, about current subjects involving young people today." Fiction and human interest stories are most open to freelancers.

THE MODERN WOODMEN, 1701 1st Ave., Rock Island IL 61201. (309)786-6481. Editor: Gloria J. Bergh. 10% freelance written. For members of Modern Woodmen of America, a fraternal insurance society. Quarterly magazine; 24 pages. Circ. 325,000. Not copyrighted. Pays on acceptance. Sample copy and writer's guidelines for SASE. Photocopied and simultaneous submissions OK. Reports in 1 month. SASE.

Nonfiction: "Nonfiction may be either for children or adults with an emphasis on community involvement and family life. Our audience is broad and diverse. We want clear, educational, inspirational articles for children and young people. We don't want religious material, teen romances, teen adventure stories." Buys informational, how-to and historical articles. Buys 8-10 unsolicited mss/year. Submit complete ms. Length: 1,500-2,000 words. Also buys shorter articles of 200-500 words. Pays $40 minimum.

Photos: B&w and color photos purchased with ms. Captions optional. Payment varies with quality and need.

Fiction: Mainstream and historical fiction. Length: 1,500-2,500 words. Pays $40.

Tips: "We seek more articles with a human interest angle."

PROBE, Baptist Brotherhood Commission, 1548 Poplar Ave., Memphis TN 38104. (901)272-2461. Editor-in-Chief: Timothy C. Seanor. 10% freelance written. For "boys age 12-17 who are members of a missions organization in Southern Baptist churches." Monthly magazine; 32 pages. Circ. 48,000. Byline given. Pays on acceptance. Publishes ms an average of 8 months after acceptance. Buys one-time rights. Submit seasonal/holiday material 6 months in advance. Simultaneous submissions OK. Computer printout submissions acceptable. SASE. Reports in 1 month. Free sample copy and writer's guidelines with 9x12 SASE ($1.18 postage).

Nonfiction: How-to (crafts, hobbies); informational (youth, religious especially); inspirational (personalities); personal experience (any first-person by teenagers—especially religious); photo feature (sports, teen subjects). No "preachy" articles, fiction or excessive dialogue. Submit complete ms. Length: 500-1,500 words. Pays $15-45.

Photos: Purchased with accompanying ms or on assignment. Captions required. Query. Pays $10 for 8x10 b&w glossy prints.
Tips: Editorial changes include aiming for the mid-teen instead of younger teen. Will affect writers in the year ahead.

PURPLE COW, Atlanta's Newsmagazine for Teens, Purple Cow, Inc., 315 Cates Center, 110 E. Andrews Dr. NW, Atlanta GA 30305. (404)233-7618/7654. Editor: Pam Perry. Monthly tabloid (10 issues) covering any subject of interest to the 12-18-year-old. Distributed free to high school and middle school students in metro Atlanta. Circ. 41,000. Pays on acceptance. Byline given. Buys one-time rights. Submit seasonal/holiday material 2 months in advance. Simultaneous queries, and simultaneous, photocopied, and previously published submissions OK. Computer printout submissions acceptable. SASE. Reports in 1 month. Sample copy $1; no SASE for sample copy. Writer's guidelines for SASE.
Nonfiction: Book excerpts; general interest; how-to (do anything—from dress fashionably to survive exams); humor; interview/profile (of people of interest to teens); personal experience (teen-related); sports (general, anecdotal—no "How to Play Soccer"); coping (different slants on drugs, sex, school, parents, peer pressure, dating, entertainment, money, etc.). Special issues include junion-senior proms and Christmas. No puzzles, games, fiction or first-person nonfiction. Buys 50 mss/year. Query with clips of published work or send complete ms. Length: 500-3,000 words. Pays $10.
Photos: Send photos with ms. Pays $5 for b&w transparencies and contact sheet.
Columns/Departments: Buys 5 mss/year. Length: 150-500 words. Pays $10 maximum.
Fillers: Buys 10-20/year. Length: 150 words maximum. Pays $5.
Tips: "We are written about 80% by high school students. Adult writers must have unique slant to be considered. Know what you're talking about. Don't talk down. Write in a style that is neither cynical nor preachy. Have something new to say."

SCHOLASTIC SCOPE, Scholastic Magazines, Inc., 730 Broadway, New York NY 10003. Editor: Katherine Robinson. Circ. 1,100,000. Buys all rights. Byline given. Issued weekly. 4-6th grade reading level; 15-18 age level. Reports in 4-6 weeks. SASE.
Nonfiction and Photos: Articles with photos about teenagers who have accomplished something against great odds, overcome obstacles, performed heroically, or simply done something out of the ordinary. Prefers articles about people outside New York area. Length: 400-1,200 words. Pays $125 and up.
Fiction and Drama: Problems of contemporary teenagers (drugs, prejudice, runaways, failure in school, family problems, etc.); relationships between people (interracial, adult-teenage, employer-employee, etc.) in family, job, and school situations. Strive for directness, realism, and action, perhaps carried through dialogue rather than exposition. Try for depth of characterization in at least one character. Avoid too many coincidences and random happenings. Although action stories are wanted, it's not a market for crime fiction. Occasionally uses mysteries and science fiction. Length: 400-1,200 words. Uses plays up to 15,000 words. Pays $150 minimum.

SEVENTEEN, 850 3rd Ave., New York NY 10022. Executive Editor: Ray Robinson. Monthly. Circ. 1,500,000. Buys first rights for nonfiction, features and poetry. Buys first rights on fiction. Pays 25% kill fee. Byline given. Pays on acceptance. Computer printout submissions acceptable; prefers letter-quality to dot-matrix. SASE. Reports in 3 weeks.
Nonfiction: Articles and features of general interest to women who are concerned with the development of their own lives and the problems of the world around them; strong emphasis on topicality and helpfulness. Send brief outline and query, including a typical lead paragraph, summing up basic idea of article. Also like to receive articles and features on speculation. Length: 2,000-3,000 words. Pays $50-500 for articles written by teenagers but more to established adult freelancers. Articles are commissioned after outlines are submitted and approved. Fees for commissioned articles generally range from $350-1,500.
Photos: Photos usually by assignment only. Vicky Peslak, art director.
Fiction: Bonni Price, fiction editor. Top-quality stories featuring teenagers—the problems, concerns and preoccupations of adolescence, which will have recognition and identification value for readers. Does not want "typical teenage" stories, but high literary quality. Avoid oversophisticated material; unhappy endings acceptable if emotional impact is sufficient. Humorous stories that do not condescend to or caricature young people are welcome. Best lengths are 2,500-3,000 words. Pays $700-1,000. "We publish a novelette every July (not to exceed 30 doubled-spaced manuscript pages)—sometimes with a suspenseful plot." Conducts an annual short story contest.
Poetry: By teenagers only. Pays $15. Submissions are nonreturnable unless accompanied by SASE.
Tips: "The best way for beginning teenage writers to crack the *Seventeen* lineup is for them to contribute suggestions and short pieces to the Free-For-All column, a literary format which lends itself to just about every kind of writing: profiles, puzzles, essays, exposes, reportage, and book reviews."

SPRINT, 850 N. Grove, Elgin IL 60120. (312)741-2400. Editor: Kristine Miller Tomasik. For junior high school age students who attend Sunday School. Weekly. Buys all rights. Buys 20-30 mss/year. Pays on acceptance. Free sample copy and writer's guidelines. SASE. Rarely con. lers photocopied or simultaneous submissions. Submit seasonal material for Christmas, Easter and Thanksgiving issues 1 year in advance. Reports in 3 months.

Nonfiction: Wants "very short, catchy articles (600-800 words) reporting on teen involvement in church/community projects; interviewing outstanding teens or personalities of interest to teens; dealing with difficult situations and emotional needs of teens; etc. We are using the photo feature format increasingly to treat these topics." All mss should present a Christian approach to life. Query first for nonfiction. Pays $65-75.

Fiction: "Fiction must be believable, with realistic characters and dialogue. If your sole purpose in writing is to preach, please don't send your story to us." Stories should be 1,000-2,000 words. Pays $65-75. Submit only complete mss for fiction and poetry. SASE.

Photos: Photo editor: Barbra Sheperd. Photos purchased with or without mss on assignment. Captions optional. Pays $20 for b&w glossy prints. Pays $50 for color transparencies. Color photos rarely used.

STRAIGHT, Standard Publishing Co., 8121 Hamilton Ave., Cincinnati OH 45231. (513)931-4050. Editor: Dawn Brettschneider. 90% freelance written. "Teens, age 13-19, from Christian backgrounds generally receive this publication in their Sunday School classes or through subscriptions." Weekly (published quarterly) magazine; 12 pages. Pays on acceptance. Buys first rights, or second serial (reprint) rights. Byline given. Submit seasonal/holiday material 1 year in advance. Reports in 3-6 weeks. Free sample copy; writer's guidelines with SASE. Computer printout submissions acceptable. Include Social Security number on ms. SASE.

Nonfiction: Religious-oriented topics, teen interest (school, church, family, dating, sports, part-time jobs), humor, inspirational, personal experience. "We want articles that promote Christian values and ideals." No puzzles. Query or submit complete ms. Length: 800-1,500 words. Pays 2¢/word.

Fiction: Adventure, historical, humorous, religious and suspense. "All fiction should have some message for the modern Christian teen." Fiction should deal with all subjects in a forthright manner, without being preachy and without talking down to teens. No tasteless manuscripts that promote anything adverse to Bible's teachings. Submit complete ms. Length: 1,000-1,500 words. Pays 2¢-2½¢/word; less for reprints.

Photos: May submit photos with ms. Pays $20-25 for 8x10 b&w glossy prints. Model release should be available. Buys one-time rights.

Tips: "Don't be trite. Use unusual settings or problems. Use a lot of illustrations, a good balance of conversation, narration, and action. Style must be clear, fresh—no sermonettes or sicky-sweet fiction. Take a realistic approach to problems. Be willing to submit to editorial policies on doctrine; knowledge of the *Bible* a must. Also, be aware of teens today, and what they do. Language, clothing, and activities included in mss should be contemporary. We are becoming more and more selective about freelance material and the competition seems to be stiffer all the time."

'TEEN MAGAZINE, 8490 Sunset Blvd., Hollywood CA 90069. Editor: Roxanne Camron. For teenage girls. Monthly magazine; 100 pages. Circ. 1,000,000. Buys all rights. Predominantly staff-written. Freelance purchases are limited. Reports in 2-4 months. Computer printout submissions acceptable; prefers letter-quality to dot-matrix. SASE.

Fiction: Dealing specifically with teenagers and contemporary teen issues. More fiction on emerging alternatives for young women. Suspense, humorous and romance. No prom or cheerleader stories. "Young love is all right, but teens want to read about it in more relevant settings." Length: 2,500-4,000 words. Pays $100.

Tips: "No nonfiction; no fiction with explicit language, casual references to drugs, alcohol, sex, or smoking; no fiction with too depressing outcome."

TEEN POWER, Box 632, Glen Ellyn IL 60138. (312)668-6000. Editor: Christopher Grant. Eight-page weekly magazine for junior and senior high Christian teens. Circ. 115,000. Pays on acceptance. Byline given. Buys first rights. Submit seasonal/holiday material 9 months in advance. Photocopied and previously published submissions OK. Computer printout submissions acceptable; prefers letter-quality to dot-matrix. SASE. Reports in 1 month on queries; 6 weeks on mss. Sample copy and writer's guidelines for business-size SAE and one first class stamp.

Nonfiction: How-to (issues of Christian maturity); inspirational (young teen); interview/profile (Christian personality); personal experience (God's interaction). No reviews or non-Christian-oriented material. "Need evidence of mature, Christian integration with life; no tacked-on morals; creative presentation." Buys 40 mss/year. Send complete ms. Length: 800-1,100 words. Pays $40-90.

Photos: "Simple, bold photos illustrating the ms." Send photos with true story ms only. Pays $5-20 for 3x5 b&w prints. Buys one-time rights.

Columns/Departments: Any mss dealing with application of Bible to everyday teen life—personal experience, expository. Buys 40 mss/year. Send complete ms. Length: 250-400 words. Pays $20-60.

Fiction: Adventure; confession (Christian insight); ethnic; fantasy; humorous; religious; and suspense. Only fiction with teen Christian slant. Buys 40 mss/year. Send complete ms. Length: 800-1,100 words. Pays $60-90.

Tips: Shorter word length and search for more varied, contemporary subjects/issues will affect writers in the year ahead. No poetry; filler material.

Close-up

Ray Robinson
Executive Editor, *Seventeen*

At the ballpark, old ballplayers get Ray Robinson's attention; at home he enjoys political and sports books and reviews on *Willa* (his wife's book). But in the offices of *Seventeen*, the writer with "a strong empathy for the audience, a lively intelligence, and a good wit" gets his attention.

Robinson looks for articles with information that 12- to 20-year-old teen women can rely on. "In many respects, we're a surrogate parent for many of the teens who find they can get reliable answers from us that they often times can't pry loose from their parents, their peers, or their friends," says the magazine's executive editor.

When Robinson moved from *Good Housekeeping* to *Seventeen* 15 years ago, his three children were teenagers. He draws upon their experiences, letters from readers, talks with today's teens, his own reading, and the ideas of a youthful staff to know what concerns teens. "We try not to exhort them or deliver constant pep talks; we simply try to reason with them," he says.

Today's teenagers are more sophisticated than his earlier readers. Three years ago, *Seventeen* added a column, Sex and Your Body. "You wouldn't have found this column in this magazine 20 years ago."

That's why writers must read recent *Seventeen* issues rather than *remembering* the magazine from their teenage years.

Spending time with and appreciating teenagers help writers relate to *Seventeen* readers. "No writers are ever asked to write down to our audience," says Robinson, a magazine editor for 35 years. "That would be an insult to our audience and to the writer."

Seventeen writers can be 17 or 67. Article assignments go to professional writers. Teens often write material in the magazine but not on assignment. The annual fiction contest helps Robinson discover young talent. "This is probably one of the few magazines in the world that publishes the efforts of teen writers—boys and girls."

Robinson weighs the concerns and mercurial interests of his readers in selecting articles. "What marks us as a magazine for 40 years is our enormous credibility with our audience," he says. "We have an unmatched track record for prudence, fairness and quality."

Robinson's own freelancing makes him an empathetic *listener* to writers' mail and phone queries. At the same time, he expects writers to research a subject thoroughly, recognize the facts, observe deadlines, and follow his recommendations on assignments.

As a freelancer, he has published more than 300 articles. He often writes baseball articles for *TV Guide* and *The New York Times*. His credits include twenty sports paperbacks and six hardcover titles.

"The writer has to overcome the capriciousness of many editors," he points out. "The business of being a freelance writer is a misnomer; there is nothing free about it.

"The only way that one can achieve ultimately (provided he has the basic skills) is to give total attention to his work, do the appropriate homework, and be able to have enough zeal and wit to avoid the negatives involved in the publishing field," Robinson says. And, like *Seventeen* readers and the baseball players he writes about in his free time, "you have to have a tremendous amount of vitality."

TEENAGE MAGAZINE, (formerly *Highwire Magazine*), Box 948, Lowell MA 01853. (617)458-6416. Editor-in-Chief: Bill Weber. 30% freelance written. Monthly magazine covering news, lifestyles, opinion, and entertainment of interest to older, college-bound students. Circ. 100,000. Pays on publication. Byline given. Offers 25% kill fee. Buys first rights, and second (reprint) rights to material originally published elsewhere. Submit seasonal/holiday material 6 months in advance. Simultaneous queries, and simultaneous, photocopied and previously published submissions OK. Computer printout submissions acceptable. SASE. Reports in 1 month. Free writer's guidelines.

Nonfiction: Book excerpts, expose, general interest, sports, music, how-to, humor, interview/profile (of outstanding high school students), opinion, personal experience, photo feature, travel. "All categories must relate in some way to teenagers' concerns. No moralistic or cautionary tales intended to warn impressionable youngsters about the evils of the world. Direct, realistic accounts of the evils of the world are okay." Buys 100 mss/year. Query. Length: 200-2,000 words. Pays $20-500.

Photos: Emilie McCormick, art director. State availability of photos. Pays $25-150 for color transparencies and b&w or color prints. Model release and identification of subjects required. Buys one-time rights.

Columns/Departments: Nancy Rutter, senior editor. Travel: cheap ways to travel, jobs or programs with international slant; areas of interest to young people; Arts/Entertainment: reviews of music, movies, TVs; Computers: new technology, educational applications, profiles of young, successful computer users; Profiles: of outstanding teenagers; College: information on applications, financial aid, preparing for college; tips on unusual or good colleges; Jobs: for young people, entrepreneurs, etc. News: short news items. Buys 40 mss/year. Query. Length: 100-750 words. Pays $10-250.

Fiction: Amy MacDonald, fiction editor. Experimental, fantasy, humorous, mainstream, romance. "We buy *only* student-written work of high quality. Adult freelancers should not submit fiction." Buys 4-8 mss/year. Send complete ms. Length: 4,000 words maximum. Pays $50-250. No poetry.

Fillers: Betsy Basch, fillers editor. Clippings, anecdotes, short humor, newsbreaks. Specific categories: "A" for Effort (funny answers to real exam questions); classroom humor; funny excuses (for being late for school, absent, etc.). Buys 60-100/year. Length: 150 words maximum. Pays $25.

Tips: "Always identify yourself as a student, if you are one, because preference is given to student writers. We are not looking for articles written by adults that 'talk down' to students, give advice, preach, etc. *TeenAge* will be paying more attention to music, video, the arts in general, television, sports, student lifestyles, fashion, dating, sex and relationships. *TeenAge* takes young people as they really are and offers them straightforward, sensitive and entertaining articles that will help them understand and deal with their problems and special concerns in a positive and realistic manner."

TEENS TODAY, Church of the Nazarene, 6401 The Paseo, Kansas City MO 64131. (816)333-7000. Editor: Gary Sivewright. 25% freelance written. For junior and senior high teens, to age 18, attending Church of the Nazarene Sunday School. Weekly magazine; 8 pages. Circ. 70,000. Pays on acceptance. Publishes ms an average of 8 months after acceptance. Buys first rights and second rights. Byline given. Submit seasonal/holiday material 10 months in advance. Simultaneous, photocopied and previously published submissions OK. Computer printout submissions acceptable. SASE. Reports in 6-8 weeks. Free sample copy and writer's guidelines for SASE.

Photos: Photos purchased with or without accompanying ms or on assignment. Pays $10-30 for 8x10 b&w glossy prints. Additional payment for photos accepted with accompanying ms. Model release required.

Fiction: Adventure (if Christian principles are apparent); humorous; religious; and romance (keep it clean). Buys 1 ms/issue. Send complete ms. Length: 1,200-1,500 words. Pays 3½¢/word, first rights; 3¢/word, second rights.

Poetry: Free verse; haiku; light verse; and traditional. Buys 15 poems/year. Pays 25¢/line.

Tips: "We're looking for quality nonfiction dealing with teen issues: peers, self, parents, vocation, Christian truths related to life, etc."

TIGER BEAT MAGAZINE, D.S. Magazines, Inc., 105 Union Ave., Cresskill NJ 07626. (201)569-5055. Editorial Director: Sharon Lee. Editor: Nancie Martin. 15% freelance written. For teenage girls ages 14 to 18. Monthly magazine; 80 pages. Circ. 400,000. Electronic submissions OK on single-sided CP/M or MS/DOS disks, but requires hard copy also. Computer printout submissions acceptable. Buys all rights. Buys 25 mss/year. Pays on acceptance. Publishes ms an average of 5 months after acceptance.

Nonfiction: Stories about young entertainers; their lives, what they do, their interests. Also service-type, self-help articles. Quality writing expected, but must be written with the 14-18 age group in mind. Length: 100-750 words depending on the topic. Pays $50-100. Send query. SASE.

Photos: Pays $25 for b&w photos used with mss; captions optional. Pays $50-75 for color used inside; $75 for cover. 35mm transparencies preferred.

Tips: "A freelancer's best bet is to come up with something original and exclusive that the staff couldn't do or get. Writing should be aimed at a 17- or 18-year-old intelligence level. Trends in magazine publishing that freelance writers should be aware of include shorter articles, segmenting of markets, and much less 'I' journalism."

TIGER BEAT STAR, D.S. Magazines, Inc., 105 Union Ave., Cresskill NJ 07626. (201)569-5055. Editor: Anne Raso. Associate Editor: Nancie S. Martin. 50% freelance written. Monthly teenage fan magazine for young adults interested in movie, TV and recording stars. "It differs from other teenage fan magazines in that we feature many soap opera stars as well as the regular teenage TV, movie and music stars." Circ. 400,000. Average issue includes 20 feature interviews, and 2 or 3 gossip columns. Pays upon publication. Publishes ms an average of 1 month after acceptance. No byline given. Buys first North American serial rights. Submit seasonal material 10 weeks in advance. Previously published submissions discouraged. Electronic submissions OK on disk for Victor 9000 system, but requires hard copy also. Computer printout submissions acceptable; no dot-matrix. Reports in 2 weeks.

Nonfiction: Interview (of movie, TV and recording stars). Buys 1-2 mss/issue. Query with clips of previously published work. "Write a good query indicating your contact with the star. Investigative pieces are preferred." Length: 200-400 words. Pays $50-125.

Photos: State availability of photos. Pays $25 minimum for 5x7 and 8x10 b&w glossy prints. Pays $50 minimum for 35mm and 2¼ color transparencies. Captions and model release required. Buys all rights.

Tips: "Be aware of our readership (teenage girls, generally ages 9-17); be 'up' on the current TV, movie and music stars; and be aware of our magazine's unique writing style (it's not geared down *too* far for the young readers or we lose attention of older girls)."

VENTURE MAGAZINE, Box 150, Wheaton IL 60189. Editor: David Leigh. 10% freelance written. Publication of Christian Service Brigade. For young men 12-18 years of age. Most participate in a Christian Service Brigade program. Monthly magazine except for combined issues in April/May, July/August, October/November, January/February. Circ. 22,000. Published 8 times/year. Buys first rights on unsolicited material. Buys 1-3 mss/issue. Pays on publication. Publishes ms an average of 2 months after acceptance. Submit seasonal material 6 months in advance. Usually reports in 2-3 weeks. Query. Computer printout submissions acceptable; prefers letter-quality to dot-matrix. SASE. Sample copy $1.50 plus large SASE; writer's guidelines for SASE.

Nonfiction: "Religious articles from boys' perspective; teen-age problems, possible solutions. Interested in photo features on innovative teenage boys who do unusual things, also true-story adventures. Assigned articles deal with specific monthly themes decided by the editorial staff. Most material has an emphasis on boys in a Christian or Brigade setting. No trite 'Sunday school' mss." Length: 400-1,200 words. Pays $50-100.

Photos: No additional payment is made for 8x10 b&w photos used with mss. Pays $25 for those purchased on assignment; $50-75 for b&w cover photos of boys.

Fiction: "Action-packed adventures with Christian theme or lesson. No far-fetched, contrived plots or trite themes/settings." Length 1,000-1,800 words. Pays $50-100.

Tips: "Queries must be succinct, well written, and exciting to draw my interest. Send for sample copy; get a feel for our publication; then query with ideas tailored specifically for us."

‡**VOICE FOR YOUTH, Church of God Youth Magazine**, 10830 Sharondale Rd., Cincinnati OH 45241. (513)769-4848. Editor: Nancy M. Weaver. Managing Editor: Paul J. Weaver, Jr. 50% freelance written. A monthly church magazine for Fundamental youth readers. Circ. approximately 2,000. Pays on acceptance. Byline given. Copyright presently being researched.Buys one-time rights. Submit seasonal/holiday material 4 months in advance. Simultaneous and photocopied submissions OK. SASE. Reports in 5 weeks. Free sample copy.

Nonfiction: Historical/nostalgic (Christian perspective of history); how-to (be a better Christian, be more loving, overcome temptations); humor (wholesome, youth or family oriented); inspirational (from a fundamental view; "Holy Spirit", tongues, is unacceptable); personal experience ("when I put my character to work"); photo feature (religious themes, youth or family related). No articles dealing with "tongues" (Holy Spirit); Christian feminism; theological or doctrinal issues. Buys 12-20 mss/year. Send complete ms. Length: 500-2,000 words. Pays $10-50.

Photos: Send photos with ms. Pays $10-25 for 5x7 b&w prints. Identification of subjects required. Buy all rights.

Fiction: Adventure (Christian youth, "Danny Orlis" type); condensed novels (religious); historical (with religious slant); humorous; religious (Fundamental); romance (Christian youth, dating, etc.); suspense (religious message); western (religious message). No science fiction, horror, ethnic. Buys 12-25 mss/year. Send complete ms. Length: 100-2,000 words. Pays $10-50.

Poetry: Light verse, traditional. Buys 5-10 poems/year. Submit maximum 10 poems. Length: 5 lines minimum. Pays 50¢-$1/line.

WORKING FOR BOYS, Box A, Danvers MA 01923. Editor: Brother Alphonsus Dwyer, C.F.X. 37% freelance written. For junior high, parents, grandparents (the latter because the magazine goes back to 1884). Quarterly magazine; 28 pages. Circ. 16,000. Not copyrighted. Buys 30 mss/year. Pays on acceptance. Submit special material (Christmas, Easter, sports, vacation time) 6 months in advance. Reports in 1 week. Submit only complete ms. Address all mss to the Associate Editor, Brother Alois, CFX, St. John's High School, Main St., Shrewsbury MA 01545. SASE. Free sample copy.

Nonfiction: "Conservative, not necessarily religious, articles. Seasonal mostly (Christmas, Easter, etc.). Cheerful, successful outlook suitable for early teenagers. Maybe we are on the 'square' side, favoring the traditional regarding youth manners: generosity to others, respect for older people, patriotism, etc. Animal articles and tales are numerous, but an occasional good dog or horse story is okay. We like to cover seasonal sports." Buys informational, how-to, personal experience, historical and travel. Length: 800-1,200 words. Pays 4¢/word.

Photos: 6x6 b&w glossy prints purchased with ms for $10 each.

Fiction: "Fiction should be wholesome and conservative." Mainstream, adventure, religious, and historical fiction. Theme: open. Length: 500-1,000 words. Pays 4¢/word.

Poetry: Length: 24 lines maximum. Pays 40¢/line.

YOUNG AMBASSADOR, The Good News Broadcasting Association, Inc., Box 82808, Lincoln NE 68501. (402)474-4567. Editor-in-Chief: Melvin A. Jones. Managing Editor: David Lambert. 50% freelance written. Emphasizes Christian living for church-oriented teens, 12-17. Monthly magazine. Circ. 80,000. Buys first North American serial rights and second (reprint) rights to material originally published elsewhere. Publishes ms an average of 15 months after acceptance. Byline given. Phone queries OK. Submit seasonal/holiday material a year in advance. Previously published submissions OK. SASE. Reports in 8 weeks. Free sample copy and writer's guidelines.

Nonfiction: David Lambert, managing editor. How-to (church youth group activities); interview; personal experience; photo features; inspirational and informational features on spiritual topics. Buys 3-5 mss/issue. Query or send complete ms. Length: 500-1,800 words. Pays 4-7¢/word for unsolicited mss; 7-10¢ for assigned articles. "Material that covers social, spiritual and emotional needs of teenagers and well-researched articles on current trends and issues, science and technology, sports personalities. Interviews with teens who are demonstrating their faith in Christ in some noteworthy way. Biographical articles about teens who have overcome obstacles in their lives."

Fiction: David Lambert, managing editor. "Needs stories involving problems common to teens in which the resolution (or lack of it) is true to our readers' experiences. Needs more stories set in unusual or exotic times and places. Spiritual interest a must, but no preaching. If the story was written just to make a point, we don't want it. Most of our stories feature a protagonist 14-17 years old." Buys 35 mss/year. Query or send complete ms. Length: 800-2,500 words. Pays 4-7¢/word for unsolicited mss; 7-10¢/word for assigned fiction.

Fillers: Puzzles on biblical themes. Send complete mss. Pays $3-10.

Tips: "Each issue follows a theme. Write for our list of themes for upcoming issues."

YOUNG AND ALIVE, Christian Record Braille Foundation, Inc., Editorial Dept., 4444 S. 52nd St., Lincoln NE 68506. Editor: Richard Kaiser. 90% freelance written. Monthly magazine for blind and visually impaired young adults (16-20) published in braille and large print for an interdenominational Christian audience. Pays on acceptance. Publishes ms an average of 10 months after acceptance. Computer printout submissions acceptable; must be letter-quality. SASE. Free writer's guidelines.

Nonfiction: Adventure, biography, camping, health, history, hobbies, nature, practical Christianity, sports and travel. "From a Christian point of view, *Young and Alive* seeks to encourage the thinking, feelings, and activities of people afflicted with sight impairment. While it's true that many blind and visually impaired young adults have the same interests as their sighted counterparts, the material should meet the needs for the sight-impaired, specifically." Length: 800-1,400 words. Query. Pays 3¢-5¢/word.

Fiction: "All forms of stories (such as serials, parables, satire) are used. Their content, however, must be absolutely credible." Length: 800-1,400 words. Query. Pays 3¢-5¢/word.

Photos: Pays $3-4 for b&w glossy prints.

Tips: "From my experience, I would like to see more colorful descriptions, more forceful verbs, and more intense feelings presented in the manuscripts."

YOUNG MISS, 685 3rd Ave., New York NY 10017. Editor-in-Chief: Phyllis Schneider. 85% freelance written. Published 10 times/year for teen girls, aged 12-17. Buys first rights. Byline given. Pays on acceptance. Editorial requirement sheet for SASE. Query on nonfiction. Reports on submissions in 6 weeks. Publishes mss an average of 1 year after acceptance. All mss must be typed, double-spaced. Computer printout submissions acceptable. SASE. Sample copy $2.

Nonfiction: Deborah Purcell, features/fiction editor. Personal growth and self-improvement; all aspects of boy-girl relationships; first-person humor; quizzes; and profiles of sports, TV, film and music figures appealing to teens. Buys 10-20 unsolicited mss/year. Length: 1,500-2,500 words. Pays $75 and up for fillers (1,000 words maximum); $250 and up for articles. No illustrations.

Fiction: Deborah Purcell, features/fiction editor. "All fiction should be aimed at young adults, not children; when in doubt, develop older rather than younger characters. Stories may be set in any locale or time, and stories about romance and personal dilemmas are particularly welcomed. The protagonist may be either male or female. Length: 2,500-3,500 words. Pays $350 and up.

Tips: "Queries for nonfiction should express original thought; desire and ability to do thorough research where applicable; clear understanding of the interests and needs of 12-17 year olds; fresh angles. We are not interested in lightweight nonfiction material or style except where applicable (e.g., humor). Fitness and health, fashion and beauty, food and lifestyles articles are all done in-house.''

‡YOUNG SALVATIONIST, A Christian Living Magazine, The Salvation Army, 799 Bloomfield Ave., Verona NJ 07044. (201)239-0606. Editor: Capt. Dorothy Hitzka. Managing Editor: Major Henry Gariepy. Monthly magazine for high school teens. "Only material with a definite Christian message will be considered.'' Circ. 43,000. Pays on acceptance. Byline given. Submit seasonal/holiday material 6 months in advance. SASE. Reports in 1 month on queries; 3 weeks on mss. Sample copy for 8½x11 SASE; writer's guidelines for business-size SASE.
Nonfiction: Inspirational. "Lead articles should carry Christian truth but not in a 'preachy' manner; should deal with 'real life' issues facing teens today; must be factual; and any references to The Salvation Army must be authentic. Articles must have a logical progression of thoughts with a definite conclusion or solution but no tacked-on morals. The lesson or point should be inherent in the article itself.'' Buys 36 mss/year. Send complete ms. "State whether your submission is for the Young Salvationist or the Young Soldier section.'' Length: 800-1,200 words. Pays 3-5¢/word.
Columns/Departments: Magazine includes a Young Soldier "pull-out'' section for children ages 6-12 with 600-800 word stories (fiction) relating to children rather than teens. "Two-page spreads of activities that relate to the story will be used in each issue. These should emphasize the truth taught but be an activity that the child can complete.'' Puzzles and related items are also used in each issue. Buys 24 mss/year. Send complete ms. Length: 250-300 words. Pays 3-5¢/word.
Fiction: "Story must have logical and convincing plot with good characterization and should deal with issues facing today's teens. Dialogue must be natural. No 'put on' teen jargon or Biblical fiction. Fiction must carry a strong Christian truth which is to be inherent in the story itself.'' Length: 1,000-1,200 words.
Fillers: "We have several columns which deal with self-image, marriage, teen leadership in the church, and other related teen topics. These fillers should meet the same criteria for content as nonfiction.'' Length: 250-300 words.

Theatre, Movie, TV, and Entertainment

This category features publications covering live, filmed, or videotaped entertainment, including home video, TV, dance, theatre, and adult entertainment. For those publications whose emphasis is on music and musicians, see the Music section. For markets covering video games, see Games and Puzzles.

AFTER DARK, Box 1693, Burbank CA 91507. Editor: Lee Swanson. 70% freelance written. For a sophisticated audience 20-55 years old, "visually oriented, who wants to know what's news and who's making the news in the world of entertainment.'' Monthly. Circ. 74,000. Buys first rights. Buys about 10 mss/year. Pays on publication. Publishes ms an average of 2 months after acceptance. Submit seasonal material 2 months in advance. Computer printout submissions acceptable; prefers letter-quality to dot-matrix. Reports in 3-4 weeks. Query, including copies of previously published work; some mention of access to illustrative materials is imperative. A SASE *must* accompany work if return is desired. Sample copy $5.
Nonfiction: Articles on "every area of entertainment and entertainer—films, TV, theater, nightclubs, books, video, music, records. No 'think' or survey pieces about the social or psychological implications to be gleaned from some entertainment trend. The fastest approach would be to offer access to some hard-to-reach entertainment celebrity who customarily has not given interviews. However, we do not want lurid, tasteless accounts laced with sexual anecdote, but do like provocative and titillating copy and visuals.'' Length: 500-1,000 words. Pays $75-150 (negotiable).
Photos: Photos a must with captions only. B&w glossy prints, color transparencies. Pays $20-75.
Tips: "The best way to crack *After Dark* is by doing a piece on some new trend in the entertainment world. We have people in most of the important cities, but we rely on freelancers to send us material from out-of-the-way places where new things are developing. Some of our contributing editors started out that way. Query.''

AFTERNOON TV, Television Publications, 529 W. 42nd St., New York NY 10036. (212)947-8531. Editor: Diane Masters. Managing Editor: Bonnie Scheffer. Monthly magazine of soap opera and daytime TV. Publications: *Afternoon TV*, *Daytime Stars*, *Soap Opera*, *Nightime TV Stars*, and four romance magazines bimonthly. Circ. 240,000. Pays on publication. Byline given. Buys all rights. Submit seasonal/holiday material 5 months in advance. Photocopied submissions OK. SASE. Reports in 1 month.

Nonfiction: Interview/profile (of daytime celebrities); behind-the-scenes with producers/directors. Buys 145 mss/year. Query. Length: 2,500 words. Pays $125-150.
Photos: State availability of photos. Reviews b&w and color contact sheets. Captions, model release and identification of subjects required.
Tips: "We are looking for 5,000-word romance stories; can be sexy but no pornography please."

AMERICAN FILM, American Film Institute, Kennedy Center, Washington DC 20566. (202)828-4060. Editor: Peter Biskind. 80% freelance written. For film professionals, students, teachers, film enthusiasts, culturally oriented readers. Monthly magazine. Circ. 140,000. Buys first North American serial rights, and first and second rights to the same material. Pays kill fee. Byline given. Pays 90 days after acceptance. Sample copy $2.50. Will consider photocopied submissions. Submit material 3 months in advance. Reports in 1 month. Query. Computer printout submissions acceptable. SASE.
Nonfiction: In-depth articles on film and television-related subjects. "Our articles require expertise and first-rate writing ability." Buys informational, profile, historical and "think" pieces. No film reviews. Buys 10 unsolicited mss/year. Length: 500-4,000 words. Pays $100-1,000.
Tips: "No 'my favorite moments in films' or other 'fanzine' type pieces."

AMERICAN SQUAREDANCE, Burdick Enterprises, Box 488, Huron OH 44839. (419)433-2188. Editors: Stan and Cathie Burdick. 10% freelance written. Monthly magazine of interviews, reviews, topics of interest to the modern square dancer. Circ. 13,000. Pays on publication. Publishes ms an average of 6 months after acceptance. Byline given. Buys all rights. Submit seasonal/holiday material 3 months in advance. Computer printout submissions acceptable. Reports in 2 weeks on queries. Sample copy for 6x9 SAE; free writer's guidelines.
Nonfiction: General interest, historical/nostalgic, humor, inspirational, interview/profile, new product, opinion, personal experience, photo feature, travel. Must deal with square dance. Buys 6 mss/year. Send complete ms. Length: 1,000-1,500 words. Pays $10-35.
Photos: Send photos with ms. Reviews b&w prints. Captions and identification of subjects required.
Fiction: Subject related to square dancing only. Buys 1-2 mss/year. Send complete ms. Length: 2,000-2,500 words. Pays $25-35.
Poetry: Avant-garde, free verse, haiku, light verse, traditional. Square dancing subjects only. Buys 6 poems/year. Submit maximum 3 poems. Pays $1 for 1st 4 lines; $1/verse thereafter.

‡**ARTSLINE**, Creative Publications, Inc., Box 24287, Seattle WA 98124. (206)325-4400. Executive Editor: Sonia Grunberg. Editor: Alice Copp Smith. 80% freelance written. Monthly arts magazine serving as program magazine for six Seattle theatres and dance presenters. "We feature performing and visual arts, nationwide but with an emphasis on the Pacific Northwest. *ArtsLine* is a magazine of information and opinion, a showcase for fine artists' work (each cover offers an original piece of fine art, usually by a local artist). It also affords local writers, designers, and photographers an opportunity to be published." Estab. 1983. Circ. 73,000. Pays on acceptance. Publishes ms an average of 3 months after acceptance. Byline given. Offers 50% kill fee. Buys first North American serial rights. Submit seasonal/holiday material 3 months in advance. Simultaneous queries, and photocopied submissions OK. Computer printout submissions acceptable; prefers letter-quality to dot-matrix. SASE. Reports in 3 weeks. Sample copy for 9x12 SAE and 3 first class stamps; writer's guidelines for SAE and 1 first class stamp.
Nonfiction: Book excerpts; humor; interview/profile (arts-related only); opinion (arts-related only); photo feature (arts-related only); and performing or visual arts features. No crafts; no arts pieces of regional interest only, when region is not Pacific Northwest. Buys 24 features, 48 columns/year. Query with or without published clips or send complete ms. Length: 750-2,000 words. Pays $75-200.
Photos: Send photos with query or ms. Reviews b&w contact sheets. Pays $25-50 for 35mm or 4x5 color transparencies; $25-50 for 8x10 b&w prints. Captions and identification of subjects required. Buys one-time rights. Photo credit given.
Columns/Departments: On Wine; On Food (staff writer); On Broadway (staff writer); On Film; On Record (staff writer); On Dance; On Music. Buys 48 mss/year. Query with or without published clips or send complete ms. Length: 750-1,000 words. Pays $75-100.
Fillers: Jokes, anecdotes, short humor (arts-related only). Length: 150 words maximum.
Tips: "A freelancer can best break in to our publication by sending well-written material that fits our format. Feature articles are most open to freelancers. First submission from a writer new to us has to be on speculation; thereafter, we're willing to assign. Know your subject and the Northwest arts scene; write with clarity and grace; know our audience (we'll help). Trends in magazine publishing that freelance writers should be aware of include increasing sophistication of Pacific Northwest readers and their strong support of the arts. Also the proliferation of new publishing ventures in the region (not all of which have survived)."

AUSTRALIAN VIDEO AND COMMUNICATIONS, Incorporating *Australian Video Review*, General Magazine Company Pty., Ltd., 9 Paran Place, Glen Iris, Victoria 3146 Australia. (03)25-6456. 50% freelance written. Editor: Geoffrey M. Gold. Monthly magazine covering home video and telecommunications. Circ. 29,000. Pays on publication. Byline given. Offers 25% kill fee. Buys all Australian rights. Submit seasonal/ holiday material 4 months in advance. Simultaneous queries, and photocopied and previously published submissions OK. SASE. Reports in 2 weeks. Sample copy $2.
Nonfiction: Book excerpts, historical/nostalgic, humor, interview/profile, new products and services. Special issues include Australian Video and Computer Games Annual; Australian Video Trade Reference Book; Australian Video Annual (movies); Video-X monthly. No specifically North American material. "We require 'internationalized' material suitable for Australian readers." Buys 100 mss/year. Query with published clips. Length: 500-3,000 words. Pays $25-350.
Photos: State availability of photos. Pays $25-50 for color transparencies; $15-35 for b&w prints. Captions, model release and identification of subjects required.
Columns/Departments: New Products; Network (humorous round-up); video games. Buys 20 mss/year. Query. Length 50-600 words. Pays $25-75.
Fiction: Buys 3 mss/year. Query.
Tips: "Contact us with suggestions and copy of previously published work. All sections are open. North American writers should become more aware of the wider international market for their material. Our Australian, New Zealand and Pacific region readers insist on locally relevant articles. At the same time, they are highly literate and wise to the international scene and appreciate foreign articles that bridge the 'national' gap. Our publications need to reflect US 'hard news' bias, British 'whimsy' and European 'flair' with Australian/New Zealand information."

BALLET NEWS, The Metropolitan Opera Guild, Inc., 1865 Broadway, New York NY 10023. (212)582-3285. Editor: Robert Jacobson. Managing Editor: Karl F. Reuling. 75% freelance written. Monthly magazine covering dance and the related fields of films, video and records. Circ. 40,000. Average issue includes 4-5 feature articles. "All are accompanied by many photos and graphics. We are writing for a dance audience who wants to better appreciate the art form. We include reviews, calendar, TV previews, and book reviews." Pays on publication. Byline given. Kill fee negotiable. Buys first rights. Photocopied submissions OK. Computer printout submissions acceptable; prefers letter-quality to dot-matrix. SASE. Reports in 1 month. Sample copy $2.50.
Nonfiction: General interest (critical analysis, theatres); historical; interview (dancers, choreographers, entrepreneurs, costumers, stage designers); profile; travel (dance in any location); and technical (staging, practice). Query, send complete ms, or send clips of previously published work. Length: 2,500 words. Pays 10¢/word.
Photos: State availability of photos or send photos with ms. Payment negotiable for b&w contact sheets.

‡**BEAUX ARTS, A Regional Cultural Arts Quarterly**, Arts Forum, 506 W. Chestnut St., Louisville KY 40202. (502)584-3126. Editor: Frederick Smock. Quarterly magazine covering regional cultural arts for an upscale, literate audience interested in the arts as they pertain to the Ohio Valley. Circ. 10,000. Pays on publication. Byline given. Offers 50% kill fee. Buys first North American serial rights. Submit seasonal/holiday material 3 months in advance. Simultaneous queries OK. SASE. Reports in 3 weeks on queries; 2 weeks on mss. Sample copy for business-size envelope and 2 first class stamps; free writer's guidelines.
Nonfiction: Interview/profile, photo feature and regional arts. Buys 12 mss/year. Query with published clips. Length: 750-2,000 words. Pays $150-300.

‡**CINEFANTASTIQUE MAGAZINE, The review of horror, fantasy and science fiction films**, Box 270, Oak Park IL 60303. (312)366-5566. Editor: Frederick S. Clarke. Managing Editor: Michael Kaplan. A bimonthly magazine covering horror, fantasy and science fiction films. Circ. 25,000. Pays on publication. Byline given. Buys all magazine rights. Simultaneous queries and photocopied submissions OK. Computer printout submissions acceptable. SASE. Reports in 6 weeks.
Nonfiction: Historical/nostalgic (retrospects of film classics); interview/profile (film personalities); new product (new film projects); opinion (film reviews, critical essays); technical (how films are made). Buys 100-125 mss/year. Query with published clips. Length: 1,000-10,000 words. Pays variable rate depending on article length.
Photos: State availability of photos with query letter or ms.
Tips: "Develop original story suggestions; develop access to film industry personnel; submit reviews that show a perceptive point-of-view."

Market conditions are constantly changing! If this is 1986 or later, buy the newest edition of *Writer's Market* at your favorite bookstore or order directly from Writer's Digest Books.

‡**DALLAS OBSERVER**, Observer Publications, 4216 Herschel, Dallas TX 75219. (214)521-9450. Editor: Bob Walton. Biweekly tabloid covering arts and entertainment. Circ. 50,000. Pays on publication. Byline given. Offers 50% kill fee. Buys one-time rights. Submit seasonal/holiday material 2 months in advance. Simultaneous queries and photocopied submissions OK. SASE. Reports in 1 month. Sample copy for $1.50, 8x10 SAE and 4 first class stamps.

Nonfiction: Interview/profile (Dallas only) and arts features. "Write intelligently about local Dallas arts and entertainment subjects." No articles written in the first person or in inverted-pyramid style. Buys 400 mss/year. Query with published clips. Length: 500-5,000 words. Pays $20-200.

Columns/Departments: Local Dallas arts and entertainment news. Buys 100 mss/year. Query with published clips. Length: 500-1,000 words. Pays $20-75.

Tips: "Freelancers can best break in to our publication with thought-provoking essays."

DANCE IN CANADA, 38 Charles St. E, Toronto, Ontario, M4Y 1T1 Canada. (416)921-5169. Editor: Michael Crabb. 75% freelance written. Quarterly magazine covering dance (ballet and modern) in Canada plus limited foreign dance coverage. "A serious dance magazine providing news, analysis, opinion and criticism of dance events, films and books. Circ. 3,000. Pays within 30 days of publication. Publishes ms an average of 3 months after acceptance. Byline given. Offers 75% kill fee. Buys first Canadian serial rights. Submit seasonal/holiday material 3 months in advance. Photocopied and previously published submissions (under special circumstances) OK. Computer printout submissions acceptable "if there's space to copyedit"; prefers letter-quality to dot-matrix. SASE. Reports in 2 weeks on queries; 1 month on mss. Sample copy $3; free writer's guidelines.

Nonfiction: General interest (current professional dance company news, etc.); historical/nostalgic (Canadian dance history); how-to (related to helping professional dancers in all areas); interview/profile (of leading Canadian dance people); opinion (interesting dance issues where writer has authority); personal experience (dance-related experience of interest to broad readership); photo feature ("Photo-Gallery" for Canadian dance photographers); technical (specialized aspects of dance technique with educational slant). "Nothing puffy. Prefer work from writers with broad, sound knowledge." Buys 15 mss/year. Query with clips of published work. Length: 1,000-2,500 words. Pays $75-125.

Photos: Holly Small, photo editor. State availability of photos. Pays $15-25 for 8x10 b&w prints; $25-50 for color transparencies. Captions, model release and identification of subjects required. Buys one-time rights.

Fillers: Holly Small, fillers editor. Newsbreaks. Buys 5-20/year. Length: 50-200 words. Pays $5-20.

Tips: "Provide lucid, accurate information in an engaging style likely to appeal to a broad readership, some of whom may only have a basic knowledge of dance but who love the art and want their passion fed. Dance reviewers need to have ability to give clear idea of what happened plus their own comments on the artistic worth of the performance."

DANCE MAGAZINE, 33 W. 60th St., New York NY 10023. (212)921-9300. Editor: William Como. Managing Editor: Richard Philp. 10% freelance written. Monthly. For the dance profession and members of the public interested in the art of dance, all areas of the performing art—stage performances, concerts, history, teaching, personalities—while retaining the format of an art publication. "Freelancer must have knowledge of dance; experience, technical or dance critic background. We do not encourage non-dance writers to submit articles and please . . . no poetry." Buys all rights. Pays on publication. Sample copy $3. Query with outline of knowledge of dance. Publishes ms an average of 6 months after acceptance. SASE.

Nonfiction: Personalities, knowledgable comment, news. No personality profiles or personal interviews. Length: 2,000-2,500 words. Pays $300 maximum.

Photos: Purchased with articles or with captions only. Pays $5-15.

Tips: "Query first, preferably by mail. Do a piece about a local company that's not too well known but growing; or a particular school that is doing well which we may not have heard about; or a local dancer who you feel will be gaining national recognition."

DANCE TEACHER NOW, SMW Communications, Inc., 1333 Notre Dame Dr., Davis CA 95616. (916)756-6222. Editor: Susan Wershing. 100% freelance written. For professional teachers of stage, ballroom, and fitness dance in private studios, fitness centers, etc. Bimonthly magazine. Circ. 5,000. Average issue includes 6-8 feature articles, departments, and calendar sections. Pays on acceptance. Publishes ms an average of 2 months after acceptance. Computer printout submissions acceptable; "as long as the covering letter assures us the author is not shotgunning the article to a dozen publications at once." Byline given. Buys all rights. Submit seasonal material 6 months in advance. Reports in 2 months. Sample copy $2; free writer's guidelines.

Nonfiction: "Dance techniques, legal issues, health and dance injuries, business, advertising, taxes and insurance, curricula, student/teacher relations, government grants, studio equipment, concerts and recitals, competitions, departmental budgets, etc. The writer must choose subject matter suitable to the knowledgable, professional people our readers are." Buys 4-6 mss/issue. Query with clips of previously published work. Length: 1,000-3,000 words. Pays $100-300.

Photos: Photos to accompany articles only. Pays $20 minimum for 5x7 b&w glossy prints. Model release required. Buys all rights.

Columns/Departments: Practical Tips (3-4 paragraphs, short items of immediate practical use to the teacher), Building Your Library, and Spotlight on Successful Teachers (one per issue).

Tips: "We like complete reportage of the material with all the specifics, but personalized with direct quotes and anecdotes. The writer should speak one-to-one to the reader, but keep the national character of the magazine in mind. To achieve the practical quality in each article, the most important question in any interview is 'How?' We do not want personality profiles. Articles must include material of practical value to reader. We do not want philosophical or 'artsy' articles; straightforward reporting only."

‡**DIAL, The Magazine for Public Television**, 304 W. 58th St., New York NY 10019. (212)664-7000. Editor: Jane Ciabattari. Managing Editor: David Doty. Monthly magazine covering public television. "*Dial* goes to 1.3 million subscribers to public television in 15 cities, including New York, Boston, Chicago, Washington DC, Los Angeles, Dallas, Detroit, Seattle, St. Louis, Portland, Miami, Salt Lake City, Indianapolis, New Orleans and Rochester NY." Pays on acceptance. Byline given. Offers 25% kill fee. Buys first North American serial rights and promotional rights. Submit seasonal/holiday material 6 months in advance. SASE. Reports in 1 month. Direct queries to editor-in-chief.

Nonfiction: "All material must have some connection with public television programming." Interview/profile; new product (new technology column); technical and travel. "A freelancer can best break in to our publication by being aware of upcoming public television programming." Query with published clips. Length: 750-3,000 words. Pays $750-1,000.

Columns/Departments: Contact editor-in-chief. Business (personal finance); New Tech (television innovations, personal computing, other electronic wizardry); Good Taste (food and drink); and Locations (programming—related essays). Buys 40+ mss/year. Query with published clips. Length: 750-1,000 words. Pays $750-1,000.

THE DRAMA REVIEW, New York University, 300 South Bldg., 51 W. 4th St., New York NY 10003. (212)598-2597. Editor: Michael Kirby. 70% freelance written. Emphasizes avant-garde performance art for professors, students and the general theater and dance-going public as well as professional practitioners in the performing arts. Quarterly magazine; 144 pages. Circ. 10,000. Pays on publication. Query by letter only. Submit material 4 months in advance. Photocopied and previously published (if published in another language) submissions OK. SASE. Reports in 3 months. Publishes ms an average of 6 months after acceptance. Sample copy $5; free writer's guidelines.

Nonfiction: Jill Dolan, managing editor. Historical (the historical avant-garde in any performance art, translations of previously unpublished plays, etc.) and informational (documentation of a particular performance). Buys 10-20 mss/issue. Query. Pays 2¢/word for translations and other material.

Photos: Jill Dolan, managing editor. Photos purchased with accompanying ms on assignment. Captions required. Pays $10 for b&w photos. No additional payment for photos accepted with accompanying ms.

Tips: "No criticism in the sense of value judgments—we are not interested in the author's opinions. We are only interested in documentation theory and analysis. No criticism or scholarly, footnoted work."

DRAMATICS MAGAZINE, International Thespian Society, 3368 Central Pkwy., Cincinnati OH 45225. (513)559-1996. Editor-in-Chief: S. Ezra Goldstein. Associate Editor: Donald Corathers. 25-30% freelance written. For theatre arts students, teachers and others interested in theatre arts education. Magazine published monthly, September through May; 44-52 pages. Circ. 40,000. Pays on acceptance. Publishes ms an average of 3 months after acceptance. Buys first North American serial rights. Byline given. Submit seasonal/holiday material 3 months in advance. Simultaneous, photocopied and previously published submissions OK. Computer printout submissions acceptable; prefers letter-quality to dot-matrix. SASE. Reports in 3 weeks. Sample copy $2; free writer's guidelines.

Nonfiction: How-to (technical theatre); informational; interview; photo feature; humorous; profile; and technical. Buys 30 mss/year. Submit complete ms. Length: 1,000-3,000 words. Pays $30-150.

Photos: Purchased with accompanying ms. Uses b&w photos and color transparencies. Query. Total purchase price for ms includes payment for photos.

Fiction: Drama (one-act plays). No "plays for children, Christmas plays, or plays written with no attention paid to the playwriting form." Buys 5-9 mss/year. Send complete ms. Pays $50-200.

Tips: "The best way to break in is to know our audience—drama students and teachers and others interested in theatre—and to write for them. Writers who have some practical experience in theatre, especially in technical areas, have a leg-up here, but we'll work with anybody who has a good idea. Some freelancers have become regular contributors. Others ignore style suggestions included in our writer's guidelines."

DRAMATIKA, 429 Hope St., Tarpon Springs FL 33589. Editors: John and Andrea Pyros. Magazine; 40 pages. For persons interested in the theater arts. Published 2 times/year. Circ. 500-1,000. Buys all rights. Pays on publication. Sample copy $2. Query. SASE. Reports in 1 month.

Fiction: Wants "performable pieces—plays, songs, scripts, etc." Will consider plays on various and open themes. Query first. Length: 20 pages maximum. Pays about $25/piece; $5-10 for smaller pieces.
Photos: B&w photos purchased with ms with extra payment. Captions required. Pays $5. Size: 8x11.

‡**FANGORIA**, Starlog Press/O'Quinn Studios, 475 Park Ave. S, New York NY 10016. (212)689-2830. Editors: R. H. Martin/David Everitt. 35% freelance written. Published 8 times/year. Magazine covering horror films. Circ. 100,000. Pays on publication. Byline given. Offers 15% kill fee. Buys first North American serial rights with option for second rights to same material. Submit seasonal/holiday material 5 months in advance. Simultaneous queries OK. Computer printout submissions acceptable. SASE. Reports in 6 weeks. Publishes ms an average of 6 weeks after acceptance. Sample copy $3.
Nonfiction: Book excerpts, interview/profile. No 'think' pieces, opinion pieces, reviews, or sub-theme overviews (i.e., vampire in the cinema). Buys 40 mss/year. Query with published clips. Length: 1,000-8,000 words (multipart run in consecutive issues, up to 3). Pays $100-600.
Photos: State availability of photos. Reviews b&w and color transparencies and prints. "No separate payment for photos provided by film studios." Captions or identification of subjects required. Buys one-time rights.
Columns/Departments: Monster Invasion (news about new productions; must be exclusive, early information). Query with published clips. Length: 100-500 words. Pays $15-35.
Tips: "Other than recommending that you examine one or several copies of *Fangoria*, we only describe it as a horror film magazine consisting primarily of interviews with technicians and filmmakers in the field. Study the magazine and be sure to stress the interview subjects' words—not your own opinions. We are very interested in small, independent filmmakers working outside of Hollywood. These people are usually more accessible to writers, and more cooperative. Because much of our magazine is written in-house, the little independents are sometimes hard for us to contact from New York, whereas outside writers may find a local group mounting an independent production."

FILM QUARTERLY, University of California Press, Berkeley CA 94720. (415)642-6333. Editor: Ernest Callenbach. 100% freelance written. Quarterly. Buys all rights. Byline given. Pays on publication. Publishes ms an average of 3 months after acceptance. Query; "sample pages are very helpful from unknown writers. We must have hard-copy printout and don't care how it is produced, but we cannot use dot-matrix printouts unless done on one of the new printers that gives type-quality letters." SASE.
Nonfiction: Articles on style and structure in films, articles analyzing the work of important directors, historical articles on development of the film as art, reviews of current films and detailed analyses of classics, book reviews of film books. Must be familiar with the past and present of the art; must be competently, although not necessarily breezily, written; must deal with important problems of the art. "We write for people who like to think and talk seriously about films, as well as simply view them and enjoy them. We use no personality pieces or reportage pieces. Interviews usually work for us only when conducted by someone familiar with most of a filmmaker's work. (We don't use performer interviews.)" Length: 6,000 words maximum. Pay is about 2¢/word.
Tips: "*Film Quarterly* is a specialized academic journal of film criticism, though it is also a magazine (with pictures) sold in bookstores. It is read by film teachers, students, and die-hard movie buffs, so unless you fall into one of those categories, it is very hard to write for us. Currently, we are especially looking for material on independent, documentary, etc. films not written about in the national film reviewing columns."

MEDIA HISTORY DIGEST, Media Digest History Corp., c/o Editor & Publisher, 11 W. 19th St., New York NY 10011. Editor: Hiley H. Ward. Magazine published quarterly covering media history—newspapers, books, film, radio-TV and magazines—for "both a specialized (history, journalism) and a general market. Articles must have high popular interest." Circ. 2,000. Buys first rights. Submit seasonal/holiday material 6 months in advance. Prefers typed mss. SASE. Reports in 2 months. Sample copy $3.
Nonfiction: Historical/nostalgic—media; emphasis on people and human interest; humor (related to the media, present or historical); and interview/profile (older people's oral history). No "unreadable academic articles of narrow interest." Uses 50 mss/year. Query. Length: 500-1,500 words. Pays $50-100.
Photos: "Most of our photos would come from historical files." State availability of photos.
Fillers: Puzzles (media history quizzes, crosswords on specific topics). Pays $25.
Tips: "We will publish regularly and expand; return to color, etc., as result of magazine being acquired by *Editor and Publisher* magazine."

PERFORMING ARTS IN CANADA, 2nd Fl., 52 Avenue Rd., Toronto, Ontario M5R 2G3 Canada. (416)921-2601. Editor: Deborah Burrett. For professional performers and general readers with an interest in Canadian theatre, dance and music. Covers "all three major fields of the performing arts (music, theatre and dance), modern and classical, plus articles on related subjects (technical topics, government arts policy, etc.)." Quarterly magazine. Circ. 80,550. Pays 1 month following publication. Buys first rights. Pays 30-50% kill fee. Byline given. Reports in 3-6 weeks. Computer printout submissions acceptable; prefers letter-quality to dot-matrix. SAE and IRCs. Sample copy $1.

Nonfiction: "Lively, stimulating, well-researched articles on Canadian performing artists or groups. We tend to be overstocked with theatre pieces; most often in need of good classical music articles." No non-Canadian, non-performing arts material. Buys 30-35 mss/year. Query. Length: 1,500-2,000 words. Pays $150.
Tips: "Query preferably with an outline. Writers new to this publication should include clippings."

PHILADELPHIA/NEW YORK SOPHISTICATED ACTION NEWSPAPER, (formerly *Philadelphia/ New York Action Newspaper*), PNS Research, Inc., Box 733, Fort Washington PA 19034. (800)523-6600, or (215)628-3030. Editor: Bob Rose. Managing Editor: George Finster. 10% freelance written. Entertainment tabloid covering sex and the commercial sex business. "We are an entertainment newspaper for sophisticated adults. Our editorial philosophy is that sex, in all of its wonderful variations, between consenting adults, is more fun than anything." Circ. 10,000. Pays on publication "with definite publication date and check issuing date." Publishes ms an average of 2 months after acceptance. Byline given; pen names are also acceptable. Buys first North American serial rights and "rights to reprint only in our own publications." Submit seasonal/holiday material 6 months in advance (specify seasonal material on outside of envelope). Photocopied submissions OK. Electronic submissions OK on 8" floppy disk compatible with AM Varity per COM/SET 3500. Requires hard copy on initial submission only. Computer printout submissions acceptable. SASE. Reports in 6 weeks on queries; 3 months on mss. Sample copy $1; writer's guidelines for business size SAE and 1 first class stamp.
Nonfiction: Personal experience (unusual sexual experience). Buys 6-8 mss/year. Query. Length: 2,500-3,000 words. Pays $50-200.
Fiction: Erotica (unusual with the emphasis on enjoyment); humorous (emphasis on sex); science fiction (emphasis on sex). "Nothing with children or rape stories or stories in which one or more of the sexual participants are not enjoying themselves." Buys 12 mss/year. Query or send complete ms. Length: 2,500-3,000 words. Pays $50-200.
Tips: "Send only professionally done manuscripts, which are erotic, unusual and fun. We expect to buy mostly fiction manuscripts in the coming year. We currently have a considerable backlog of manuscripts. Writers, especially those submitting for the first time, should be patient with our response. Please inquire about the status of your manuscript in writing, not by phone."

PLAYBILL MAGAZINE, 100 Avenue of the Americas, New York NY 10013. Editor-in-Chief: Ms. Joan Alleman. Monthly; free to theatregoers. "It is the only magazine in Manhattan that focuses entirely on the New York theatre." Buys first and second US magazine rights. Pays 25% kill fee. Byline given. Computer printout submissions acceptable. SASE.
Nonfiction: "The major emphasis is on current theatre and theatre people. Wants sophisticated, informative prose that makes judgments and shows style. Uses unusual interviews, although most of these are staff written. Article proposal must be about a current Broadway show or star, or playwright, director, composer, etc. We do not use parody or satire. We occasionally publish 'round-up' articles—stars who play tennis, or who cook, etc. Style should be worldly and literate without being pretentious or arch; runs closer to *New Yorker* than to *Partisan Review*. Wants interesting information, written in a genuine, personal style. Humor is also welcome. Between 1,000 and 2,500 words for articles." Pays $100-400.
Tips: "We're difficult to break into and most of our pieces are assigned. We don't take any theatre pieces relating to theatre outside New York. The best way for a newcomer to break in is with a 750-word article for *A View From The Audience* describing how a Broadway play or musical deeply affected the writer." Pays $100.

PRE-VUE, Box 31255, Billings MT 59107. Publisher: Virginia Hansen. Editor: Valerie Hansen. "We are the cable-TV guide for Montana, and also for satellite 'dish' owners and members of the industry nationwide." Weekly magazine; 32-48 pages. Circ. 22,000. Pays on acceptance. Publishes ms an average of 2 months after acceptance. Byline given. Not copyrighted. Buys first and second rights to the same material. Query. Electronic submissions OK if Editwriter 7500; prefers standard ms form. Computer printout submissions acceptable; prefers letter-quality to dot-matrix. SASE. Reports in 2 months.
Nonfiction: "Subject matter is general, but must relate in some way to television or our reading area (Montana). For the national satellite edition, we would like articles which tell of the newest advances in the industry or what is happening with the satellites, including legislation concerning them. We would like articles to have a beginning, middle and end; in other words, popular magazine style, heavy on the hooker lead." Informational, how-to, interview, profile, humor and historical. Feature length: 500-750 words. Pays 2¢/word minimum.
Photos: 8x10 (sometimes smaller) b&w photos purchased with mss or on assignment. Pays $3-6. Captions required.
Tips: "We're looking for work from experienced writers. We prefer writing that is short and peppy, or very informative or humorous."

‡PREVUE, Today's Personalities and Tomorrow's Entertainment, Prevue Entertainment, Box 974, Reading PA 19603. (215)374-7477. Editor: Jim Steranko. Bimonthly magazine covering entertainment, film, TV, music and books. "We want factual information on film and TV productions and their stars. Readership is pre-

dominantly young and male. We prefer to use opinions of the subjects covered rather than the writer's. Heavy visuals accompany all features. Manly features cover entertainment *in advance* of the event." Circ. 250,000. Pays on acceptance. Byline given. Offers negotiable kill fee. Makes work-for-hire assignments. Photocopied submissions OK. Computer printout submissions acceptable. SASE. Reports in 2 weeks. Sample copy for $2.95, 8½x11 SAE, and $1 postage; writer's guidelines with initial assignment.
Nonfiction: Interview/profile (film and TV stars, musicians, personalities). Buys 50-100 mss/year. Query with published clips or send complete ms. Length: 750-6,000 words. Pays negotiable rates.
Columns/Departments: Film news. Buys 10-20 mss/year.
Tips: "We gravitate toward writers who know grammar, punctuation, syntax, etc.—and *use* them. We like tight, lean copy, a maximum amount of information in a minimum amount of space. A freelancer can best break in to our publication by listing his/her connections to film and TV personalities."

PROLOG, 104 N. St. Mary, Dallas TX 75204. (214)827-7734. Editor: Mike Firth. 10% freelance written. For "playwrights and teachers of playwriting." Quarterly newsletter; 8 pages. Circ. 300. Buys 4 mss/year. Pays on acceptance; "may hold pending final approval." Publishes ms an average of 4 months after acceptance. Sample copy $2. Photocopied and simultaneous submissions OK. Reports in "over 3 months." Electronic submissions OK—Apple disk preferred; others possible. Computer printout submissions acceptable; prefers letter-quality "for direct pasteup, otherwise dot-matrix OK." SASE.
Nonfiction: Wants "articles and anecdotes about writing, sales and production of play scripts. Style should be direct to reader (as opposed to third-person observational)." No general attacks on theatre, personal problems, problems without solutions, or general interest. Pays 1¢/word.

R&R ENTERTAINMENT DIGEST, R&R Werbe GmbH, Bismarckstrasse 17, 6900 Heidelberg, West Germany. Editor: Tory Billard. 60% freelance written. Monthly entertainment magazine (*TV Guide* size) for Americans based in Europe (military/DoD market). "We publish 3 separate magazines—all include a common 32-page section of interest to Americans and Canadians based throughout Europe; then we have regionalized editorial for Germany, Britain and Med plus the areas encompassed by them (i.e., Med includes Spain, Greece, Italy, etc.). Covers travel, music, audio/video/photo, homemaker scene. "Our audience ranges from 19-year-olds, to the over-30 married couple to retirees." Circ. 185,000. Pays on publication. Byline given. Offers 50% kill fee. Buys first and second rights to the same material in US military market in Europe only. Submit seasonal/holiday material 3 months in advance. Simultaneous queries, and simultaneous, photocopied and previously published submissions OK as long as outside the military European market. Computer printout submissions acceptable; text must be printed in both upper and lower case letters. SASE. Reports in 1 month on queries; 2 weeks on mss. Publishes ms an average of 6 months after acceptance. Writer's guidelines for legal-size SAE and postage.
Nonfiction: Humor (travel through Europe); personal experience (travel through Europe); technical (audio/video/photo, geared to market for military in Europe); travel (throughout Europe); and homemaker stories. "Only deal with entertainment that readers can readily do. We normally don't deal in stories that have already happened, i.e., interviews of rock stars, historical pieces, etc." Buys 20 mss/year. Query with published clips. Length: 600-1,500 words. Pays $25-40/page of text "depending on the edition it is in."
Photos: State availability of photos. Pays $30 for 35mm color transparency; $20 for 5x7 or 8x10 b&w print. Buys variable rights.
Columns/Departments: Regular columns consist of European and German events occurring that month; general sports stories (how-to-oriented—not on personalities—or a big European event like Wimbledon); and homemaker/shopping in Europe. Buys 5-8 mss/year. Query with published clips. Length: 600-1,200 words. Pays $25-40/page text in magazine.
Fiction: Humorous (dealing with travel experiences). "We use very little fiction—mainly dealing with travel." Buys 5-6 mss/year. Query with published clips. Length: 600-800 words. Pays $25-40/page of text in magazine.
Tips: "I favor freelancers who are clever, snappy writers who send in clean, easy-to-read copy, and who accompany their manuscript with a good selection of *color slides* (and sometimes black/white prints)."

‡**SATELLITE DISH MAGAZINE, Your Complete Satellite TV Entertainment Guide**, Satellite America Publications, Inc., 460 Tennessee Ave., Box 8, Memphis TN 38101. (901)521-1580/9000. Editor: Kathy Ferguson. 90% freelance written. Biweekly national magazine with TV/movie entertainment news, features, reviews and personality profiles. "We are looking for two basic styles: the lively entertainment feature on current or upcoming TV (satellite/pay/cable/network) programming; and the in-depth, informative article, usually written in first person, about an issue and its relation to the satellite TV or movie/film industry." Estab. 1983. Circ. 10,000 + . Pays on publication. Publishes ms an average of 2 months after acceptance. Byline given. Offers negotiable kill fee. Buys first North American serial and second serial (reprint) rights. Submit seasonal/holiday material 2 months in advance. Previously published submissions "sometimes" OK. Computer printout submissions acceptable; prefers letter-quality to dot-matrix. SASE. Reports in 1 month. Free sample copy and writer's guidelines.

Nonfiction: General interest; historical/nostalgic; interview/profile; opinion (as it relates to a topic or issue); personal experience (as it relates to a topic or issue); technical (satellite TV news, issues). "We also recommend specialized writing on any of the satellite TV programming categories: Adult Programming, Business News, Children's Programming, Consumer Events, Cultural Information, Education, Entertainment Specials, Ethnic Programming, Family Programming, Health, Movies, Music, News, Public Affairs, Public Broadcasting, Religion, Science, Sports, Unique Variety Programmings and Women's Programming. This could be a piece on an upcoming program, or a specific category or subject and how it relates to satellite television." Query with published clips or send complete ms. Length: 800-2,000 words. Pays $100-1,000.

Photos: State availability of photos and/or send photos with query or mss. Pays $50 minimum for color transparencies; $25 minimum for 8x10 b&w prints; $50 minimum for 8x10 color prints. Captions required. Buys one-time rights.

Columns/Departments: Film/Movie Reviews (on movies premiering on the pay/cable/satellite networks); Books (as they relate to TV/movies); Celebrity/People (on people as they relate to TV/movies). Buys 50-100 mss/year. Query with published clips or send complete ms. Length: 1,000-1,500 words. Pays $300-750.

Tips: "Personality profiles and movie reviews are most open to freelancers."

SATELLITE ORBIT, The Magazine of Satellite Entertainment & Electronics, CommTek Publishing Company, 418 N. River, Box 1048, Hailey ID 83333. (208)788-4936. Publisher: David G. Wolford. Executive Editor: Bruce Kinnaird. 90% freelance written. Monthly magazine covering satellite television for "an audience that is affluent, educated, and interested in reaching beyond the ordinary. Our readers are interested—and knowledgeable—in electronics of all types related to entertainment." Circ. 175,000. Pays on publication. Publishes ms an average of 2 months after acceptance. Byline given. Offers 33% of payment for kill fee. Buys first North American serial rights, one-time rights, all rights, first rights, or makes work-for-hire assignments. Submit seasonal/holiday material 2 months in advance. Electronic submissions OK on 1,200 baud modem. Computer printout submissions acceptable; prefers letter-quality to dot-matrix. SASE. Reports in 2 weeks. Sample copy $5 (includes 1st class mailing); writer's guidelines free for business-sized SAE and 1 first class stamp.

Nonfiction: Humor (if there is an angle); interview/profile (satellite entertainment figure); new product (in field of electronics); opinion (satellite and entertainment related); technical (innovations). Query. "Unsolicited material will receive *no* consideration. No material about how satellite television is booming—we know that. No nostalgia." Buys 50-60 mss/year. Length: 1,000-1,700 words. Pays $75-650.

Photos: State availability of photos with query letter or ms. Reviews 35mm color transparencies and 8x10 b&w prints. Pays negotiable fee. Captions required. Rights negotiable.

Columns/Departments: *Profiles* of name figures who own a satellite antenna for TV reception: 750-1,000 words; short, lively piece on owner, why he bought antenna and what benefits he derives from it. *Celebrities*: 1,000-1,500 word pieces about entertainment newsmakers. Buys 24-30 items/year. Query. Pays $75-500.

Tips: "Do not make phone queries. Learn the terms of the satellite entertainment field and use those terms in a query letter. Keep track of the industry: What's new in programming? What new satellite networks are going up? Who's making news in the field? The field of satellite entertainment is relatively new, but the market for articles of this nature is going to rocket in a year or two. Initial research into the field might be a bit laborious at first, but freelancers looking for a lucrative new market would be well advised to learn the ropes of this one. Also, freelancers should become more versed in libel law. Plaintiffs are currently winning about 80% of their cases."

SOAP OPERA DIGEST, 254 W. 31st St., New York NY 10001. Executive Editor: Meredith Brown. 25% freelance written. Biweekly magazine; 144 pages. Circ. 750,000. Pays on acceptance. Buys all rights. Submit seasonal/holiday material 4 months in advance of issue date. Computer printout submissions acceptable. SASE. Reports in 1 month.

Nonfiction: Ellen Howard, managing editor, freelance material. "Articles only directly about daytime and nighttime personalities or soap operas." Interview (no telephone interviews); nostalgia; photo features (must be recent); profiles; special interest features: health, beauty, with soap opera personalities and industry news, with a strong interest in nighttime soaps. "We are a 'newsy' magazine—not gossipy, and are highly interested in very interesting news stories. No poorly written material that talks down to the audience." Buys 2-3 mss/issue. Query with clips of previously published work. Length: 1,000-2,000 words. Pays $200 and up.

Photos: State availability of photos with query. Captions preferred. Buys all rights. "Writers must be good at in-depth, personality profiles. Pack as much info as possible into a compact length. Also want humor pieces."

STARWEEK MAGAZINE, Toronto Star Newspapers, Ltd., 1 Yonge St., Toronto, Ontario M5E 1E6 Canada. (416)367-2425. Editor: Robert Crew. Weekly television newspaper supplement covering personalities, issues, technology, etc., relating to all aspects of video programming. Circ. 800,000. Pays by arrangement. Byline given. Offers 50% kill fee. Not copyrighted. Buys first rights. Submit seasonal/holiday material 6 weeks in advance. Computer printout submissions acceptable; prefers letter-quality to dot-matrix. SASE. Reports "as soon as possible." Sample copy for 8x11 SAE.

Nonfiction: Interview/profile (of TV personalities); technical. Buys 750 mss/year. Query with clips of published work. Length: 500-1,000 words. Pays $200-400.
Photos: Send photos with ms. Pays $50-100 for 8x10 b&w prints; $75-250 for 2x5 or 35mm color transparencies. Identification of subjects required. Buys one-time rights.
Tips: "I prefer to commission 'comment' or analysis pieces from writers whose credentials I know."

TUNED IN MAGAZINE, Tuned In, Corp., Suite A, 6867 Nancy Ridge Dr., San Diego CA 92121. (619)450-1630. Editor: Christina F. Paolini. 15% freelance written. Weekly magazine covering TV, including cable, radio and entertainment for "entertainment-oriented San Diegans, usually between the ages of 18 and 50, of a middle-income background." Circ. 55,000. Pays on publication. Publishes ms an average of 1 month after acceptance. Byline given. Buys one-time rights. Submit seasonal/holiday material 6 weeks in advance. Simultaneous and photocopied submissions OK. Computer printout submissions acceptable; prefers letter-quality to dot-matrix. SASE. Reports in 2 weeks on queries; 1 month on mss. San Diego writers only.
Nonfiction: General interest (personality stories, TV/radio articles, entertainment); how-to (get involved in the media; to interact and be a part of it); humor (lighthearted looks at the media and entertainment technology, etc.); interview/profile (of San Diegans who made good; visiting celebrities); and new product (technological updates; services such as radio for the blind). "We're looking for sharp, snappy articles that deal with some aspect of the San Diego entertainment field, or entertainment (TV, radio, film) as it *impacts* San Diego. We run 1 freelance article per issue, and 8 columns (staff-written). Query. Length: 2,000-2,500 words. Pays $125.
Photos: Send photos with accompanying ms. Captions required.
Tips: "Think in terms of national trends as they affect the local community, entertainment options that don't get much coverage, public-service articles, and guides."

TV GUIDE, Radnor PA 19088. Editor (National Section): David Sendler. Editor (Local Sections): Roger Youman. Managing Editor: R.C. Smith. Weekly. Circ. 17.2 million. Study publication. Query to Andrew Mills, assistant managing editor. SASE.
Nonfiction: Wants offbeat articles about TV people and shows. This magazine is not interested in fan material. Also wants stories on the newest trends of television, but they must be written in clear, lively English. Length: 1,000-2,000 words.
Photos: Uses professional high-quality photos, normally shot on assignment, by photographers chosen by *TV Guide*. Prefers color. Pays $250 day rate against page rates—$350 for 2 pages or less.

TV PICTURE LIFE, 355 Lexington Ave., New York NY 10017. (212)391-1400. Creative Director: Robert Schartoff. Executive Editor: Gerri Miller. Bimonthly magazine; 80 pages. Rights purchased vary with author and material. Usually buys all rights. Pays negotiable kill fee. Byline given. Pays on acceptance. Reports "immediately." Query. SASE.
Nonfiction: Celebrity interviews, profiles and angles that are provocative, enticing and truthful. Length: 1,000 words. Pays $100 minimum.
Photos: Photos of celebrities purchased without ms or on assignment. Pays $25-35 minimum for photos.

‡**VIDEO MOVIES MAGAZINE, For Home Viewing on Tape and Disc,** Publications International, Ltd., 3841 W. Oakton St., Skokie IL 60076. (312)676-3470. Editor: Matthew White. Managing Editor: Rita Vano. 75% freelance written. Monthly magazine covering all software available for videotape and videodisc players. "We explore the movies and other aspects of entertainment available for video. Our audience watches a lot of pre-recorded tape. We provide both information (what's new) and ideas. We specialize in movie themes and in creating film festivals." Estab. 1984. Circ. 150,000. Pays on acceptance. Publishes ms an average of 4 months after acceptance. Byline given. Rights bought depend on material. Submit seasonal/holiday material 4 months in advance. Photocopied submissions OK. Computer printout submissions acceptable. SASE. Reports in 4 weeks. Sample copy for $2.95; free writer's guidelines.
Nonfiction: Book excerpts; historical/nostalgic (old movies); interview/profile (no question and answer worked into overview of movies); photo feature; and articles on themes, festivals, or anything from a performer's career to the most ingenious theme possible. "Writers will be judged on their ability to produce genuinely stimulating articles about watching movies. We intend to publish writers who can engage the reader throughout and who can knowingly expand a reader's awareness of film." Limit articles to those movies available on videotape or disc. No articles on theatrical-only movies. Buys 50 mss/year. Query with published clips. Length: 1,000-3,500 words. Pays 20¢/word.
Photos: State availability of photos. Wants color transparencies and b&w prints "as big as possible." Identification of subjects required. "We only buy photo stills from movies."
Columns/Departments: Darrell Moore, column/department editor. Movie Reviews (minimum 25 freelance 500-word reviews per issue); and Alternative Programming Reviews (exercise, music, etc.). Buys 400 mss/year. Query with published clips. Length: 100-1,000 words. Pays 20¢/word.
Fillers: Anecdotes and "stories behind the movies: casting, problems, script changes, etc." Length: 50-500 words. Pays $35 per anecdote.

Tips: "We need people who can accurately critique material being made specifically for video. We especially want people who watch a lot of videotape/disc—and think about it as its own medium. All areas, except signed columns, are open to freelancers. To write features, a freelancer must have a strong and proven grasp of film, or subject matter. Anecdotes are basically strong research. Reviews most often are assigned to those who appreciate a certain type of movie (horror, etc.)."

‡**X-IT, A general arts and entertainment magazine**, Offshore Promotions, Box 102, St. John's, Newfoundland A1C 5H5 Canada. (709)753-8802. Editor: Ken J. Harvey. Managing Editor: Beth Fiander. A triannual entertainment magazine concentrating on new ideas and thoughts in arts and literature (written and visual) for the general public. Estab. 1983. Circ. 3,000. Pays on publication. Byline given. Buys one-time rights. Submit seasonal/holiday material 2 months in advance. Simultaneous, photocopied, and previously published submissions OK. SASE. Reports in 3 weeks on queries; 1 month on mss. Sample copy $3.
Nonfiction: All nonfiction is assigned by the editor. Query.
Fiction: Adventure, erotica, experimental, fantasy, horror, humorous, mystery, science fiction and suspense. "We are open to practically all areas of literature. Our only demand is quality." Buys 12 mss/year. Send complete ms. Length: 1,500-4,800 words. Pays $10-150.
Poetry: Allela English, poetry editor. Avant-garde, free verse, light verse and traditional. Buys 30 poems/year. Submit maximum 10 poems. Length: open. Pays $10-50.
Fillers: Jokes and short humor. Buys 12/year. Length: "preferably short." Pays $5-25.
Tips: "Send along a short bio with submissions and a covering letter describing how work would fit in with the publication. Fiction and poetry are most open to freelancers."

Travel, Camping, and Trailer

"A good travel writer reads other travel writers voraciously and studies their styles to figure out why their articles moved them so much," says one editor. Freelance writers should also work as a team with photographers "where pictures are so important," says another editor. Publications in this category tell campers and tourists the where-tos and how-tos of travel. Publications that buy how-to camping and travel material with a conservation angle are listed in the Nature, Conservation, and Ecology classification. Regional publications are frequently interested in travel and camping material with a local angle. Hunting and fishing and outdoor publications that buy camping how-to material will be found in the Sports category. Those dealing with automobiles or other vehicles maintained for sport or as a hobby will be found in the Automotive and Motorcycle category. Many magazines in the In-Flight category are also in the market for travel articles and photos.

AAA-WORLD, The Webb Co., 1999 Shepard Rd., St. Paul MN 55116. (612)690-7304. Editor: Dick Schaaf. Managing Editor: Jim Carney. 80% freelance written. Bimonthly national magazine of the American Automobile Association covering driving safety and general travel (as opposed to destination travel) topics for readers in their 50s. Eleven AAA clubs in 13 states may add regional copy to their editions of the national magazine. Queries relating to regional interests will be forwarded to the appropriate region. Circ. 1.6 million. Pays on acceptance. Publishes ms an average of 4 months after acceptance. Byline given. Offers 25% kill fee. Buys one-time rights and nonexclusive reprint rights. Submit seasonal/holiday material 6 months in advance. Simultaneous queries and photocopied submissions OK. Computer printout submissions acceptable. SASE. Reports in 2 weeks on queries; 4 weeks on mss. Sample copy for 9x12 SAE and 71¢ postage; free writer's guidelines.
Nonfiction: General interest; how-to (driving safety, driving techniques); travel (1 travel piece/issue). No long destination pieces; first person stories; highly technical automotive maintenance features; stories aimed at younger audience. Buys 18 mss/year. Query. Length: 500-1,500 words. Pays $250-500, "except for occasional special longer pieces."

ACCENT, Meridian Publishing Company, 1720 Washington, Box 10010, Ogden UT 84409. Editor: Peggie Bingham. A monthly inhouse travel magazine distributed by various companies to employees, customers, stockholders, etc. "Readers are predominantly upscale, mainstream, family oriented." Circ. 88,000. Pays on acceptance. Byline given. Buys first North American serial rights. Previously published submissions OK. SASE. Reports in 2 weeks. Sample copy $1 and 9x12 SAE; writer's guidelines for legal size SAE and first class stamp.
Nonfiction: Historical/nostalgic (on places); humor (travel); travel. "We want travel articles—destinations, new resorts, advice to travelers, travel humor. We want upbeat pieces slanted toward the average traveler, but

we also welcome some exotic travel." Buys 48-50 mss/year. Query with or without published clips or send complete ms. Length: 800-1,000 words. Pays 15¢/word.

Photos: State availability of photos or send photos with query or ms. Pays $35 for color transparencies (slides to 8x10) and 8x10 color prints. Captions required. Buys one-time rights.

Fiction: Humorous (on travel). Buys 5-10 mss/year. Send complete ms. Pays 15¢/word.

Fillers: Short humor. Length: 500-800 words. Pays 15¢/word.

Tips: "Write about interesting places. Super color transparencies are essential."

‡**ADVENTURE ROAD**, Diners Club Media Services, 641 Lexington Ave., New York NY 10022. (212)663-3923. Editor: Susan Ochshorn. A bimonthly magazine for members of the Amoco Motor Club, the majority of whom are white-collar workers, college-educated, moderately affluent, middle-aged and enthusiastic about travel. "*Adventure Road* conveys information on car care and club benefits as well as vacation planning." Circ. 1.5 million. Pays on acceptance. Byline given. Offers 25% kill fee. Buys first rights. Submit seasonal/holiday material at least 6 months in advance. SASE. Reports in 1 month on queries; 3 weeks on mss. Sample copy for 8½x10 SAE and 7 first class stamps; writer's guidelines for business size SAE and 1 first class stamp.

Nonfiction: Book excerpts; how-to (travel-related); photo feature; and travel (restricted to domestic destinations). Buys 35 mss/year ("commissioned; rarely, if ever unsolicited"). Query with published clips. Length: 1,500-2,200 words. Pays $300-500.

Tips: "Freelancers can best break in to our publication by writing a literate, well conceived query letter and providing exciting clips. We are looking for an angle and for destinations or kinds of trips that are unusual in some way. Major features are most open to freelancers. Although our articles tend to be seasonal, we do like to provide our readers with material that they will be able to use in making plans for future trips. We are also interested in pieces about the experience of car travel. Features along these lines have included games people play in their cars and a guide to rare on-the-road radio."

ASU TRAVEL GUIDE, ASU Travel Guide, Inc., 1325 Columbus Ave., San Francisco CA 94133. (415)441-5200. Managing Editor: Howard Baldwin. 20% freelance written. Quarterly guidebook covering international travel features and travel discounts for well-traveled airline employees. Circ. 37,000. Pays on acceptance. Byline given. Offers kill fee. Buys first North American serial rights, first and second rights to the same material, and second serial (reprint) rights to material originally published elsewhere. Makes work-for-hire assignments. Submit seasonal/holiday material 6 months in advance. Simultaneous queries and simultaneous, photocopied and previously published submissions OK. Computer printout submissions acceptable. SASE. Reports in 1 month. Publishes ms an average of 6 months after acceptance. Send SASE for writer's guidelines. No telephone queries.

Nonfiction: International travel articles "similar to those run in consumer magazines." Not interested in amateur efforts from inexperienced travelers or personal experience articles that don't give useful information to other travelers. Buys 16-20 mss/year. Destination pieces only; no "Tips On Luggage" articles. "We will be accepting fewer manuscripts and relying more on our established group of freelance contributors." Length: 1,200-1,500 words. Pays $200.

Photos: "Interested in clear, high-contrast photos; we prefer not to receive material without photos." Reviews 5x7 and 8x10 b&w prints. "Payment for photos is included in article price; photos from tourist offices are acceptable."

Tips: "Query with samples of travel writing and a list of places you've recently visited. We appreciate clean and simple style. Keep verbs in the active tense and involve the reader in what you write. Avoid 'cute' writing, excess punctuation (especially dashes and ellipses), coined words and stale cliches. Any article that starts with the name of a country followed by an exclamation point is immediately rejected."

AWAY, 888 Worcester St., Wellesley MA 02181. (617)237-5200. Editor: Gerard J. Gagnon. For "members of the ALA Auto & Travel Club, interested in their autos and in travel. Ages range from approximately 20-65. They live primarily in New England." Slanted to seasons. Quarterly. Circ. 170,000. Buys first serial rights. Pays on acceptance. Submit seasonal material 6 months in advance. Reports "as soon as possible." Although a query is not mandatory, it may be advisable for many articles. SASE. Free sample copy.

Nonfiction: Articles on "travel, tourist attractions, safety, history, etc., preferably with a New England angle. Also, car care tips and related subjects." Would like a "positive feel to all pieces, but not the chamber of commerce approach." Buys both general seasonal travel and specific travel articles, for example, travel-related articles (photo hints, etc.); outdoor activities, for example, gravestone rubbing, snow sculpturing; historical articles linked to places to visit; humor with a point; photo essays. "Would like to see more nonseasonally oriented material. Most material now submitted seems suitable only for our summer issue. Avoid pieces on hunting and about New England's most publicized attractions, such as Old Sturbridge Village and Mystic Seaport." Length: 800-1,500 words, "preferably 1,000-1,200." Pays approximately 10¢/word.

Photos: Photos purchased with mss. Captions required. B&w glossy prints. Pays $5-10/b&w photo, payment on publication based upon which photos are used. Not buying color at this time.

Tips: "We have decided to sharply limit purchases of articles and photographs from outside sources; we will now publish more staff-produced material."

BACKPACKER, Ziff-Davis, 1 Park Ave., New York NY 10016. (212)725-7080. Editor: J. Delves. 40% freelance written. Bimonthly magazine for backpackers who want "hard information" on equipment, skills and places to go. Circ. 180,000. Pays on acceptance. Byline given. Buys first North American serial rights, all rights and second (reprint) rights to material published elsewhere. Submit seasonal/holiday material 4 months in advance. Simultaneous queries, and simultaneous and photocopied submissions OK. Computer printout submissions acceptable. SASE. Reports in 1 month. Publishes ms an average of 6 months after acceptance. Free writer's guidelines.

Nonfiction: How-to (outdoor skills); humor; interview/profile; opinion (chiefly regarding government policies and regulations); personal experience; photo feature; technical; travel. Special issue includes October/November on ski packing, December/January on mountaineering. No fiction or exotic destinations. Buys 50 mss/year. Query with published clips. Length: 1,000-4,000 words. Pays variable rates.

Photos: Stan Green, art director. Send photos with query or ms. Reviews 35mm color transparencies. Captions and identification of subjects required. Buys one-time rights.

Columns/Departments: Body Language; Geosphere; Forum; First Exposure; Materiel; and Weekend Wilderness. Buys 75 mss/year. Query with published clips. Length: 1,500-2,500 words. Pays variable rates.

Fillers: Tips and Techniques. Buys 12/year. Length: 250-500 words. Pays $100 maximum.

BIKEREPORT, Bikecentennial, Inc., Box 8308, Missoula MT 59807. (406)721-1776. Editor: Daniel D'Ambrosio. 75% freelance written. Bimonthly bicycle touring magazine for Bikecentennial members—all bicycle tourists. Circ. 18,000. Pays on publication. Byline given. Buys first rights. Submit seasonal/holiday material 3 months in advance. Simultaneous queries and photocopied submissions OK. Computer printout submissions acceptable. SASE. Reports in 2 weeks on queries; 4 weeks on mss. Publishes ms an average of 8 months after acceptance. Free sample copy and guidelines. Include short bio with manuscript.

Nonfiction: Historical/nostalgic (interesting spots along bike trails); how-to (bicycle); humor (touring); interview/profile (bicycle industry people); personal experience ("my favorite tour"); photo feature (bicycle); technical (bicycle); travel ("my favorite tour"). No articles on activism—biker's rights. Buys 20-25 mss/year. Query with published clips or send complete ms. Length: 800-1,500 words. Pays $10-50 per published page.

Photos: Bicycle, scenery, portraits. State availability of photos. Pays $5-25 for b&w and color. Model release and identification of subjects required. Buys one-time rights.

Fiction: Adventure, experimental, historical, humorous. Not interested in anything that doesn't involve bicycles. Query with published clips or send complete ms. Length: 800-1,200 words. Pays $10-50 per published page.

CAMPERWAYS, 1108 N. Bethlehem Pike, Box 460, Spring House PA 19477. (215)643-2058. Editor-in-Chief: Charles E. Myers. 60% freelance written. Emphasis on recreation vehicle camping and travel. Monthly (except Dec. and Jan.) tabloid. Circ. 33,000. Pays on publication. Buys first, simultaneous, second serial (reprint) or regional rights. Byline given. Submit seasonal/holiday material 3-4 months in advance. Simultaneous, photocopied and previously published submissions OK. Self-addressed envelope and loose postage. Reports in 1 month. Publishes ms an average of 6 months after acceptance. Sample copy $1 and free writer's guidelines.

Nonfiction: Historical (when tied in with camping trip to historical attraction or area); how-to (selection, care, maintenance of RVs, accessories and camping equipment); humor; personal experience; and travel (camping destinations within 200 miles of New York-DC metro corridor). No "material on camping trips to destinations outside stated coverage area." Buys 60-70 unsolicited mss/year. Query. Length: 800-2,000 words. Pays $40-85.

Photos: "Good photos greatly increase likelihood of acceptance. Don't send snapshots, polaroids. We can't use them." Photos purchased with accompanying ms. Captions required. Uses 5x7 or 8x10 b&w glossy prints. Total purchase price for ms includes payment for photos.

Columns/Departments: Camp Cookery (ideas for cooking in RV galleys and over campfires. Should include recipes). Buys 10 mss/year. Query. Length: 500-1,500 words. Pays $25-50.

Tips: "Articles should focus on single attraction or activity or on closely clustered attractions within reach on the same weekend camping trip rather than on types of attractions or activities in general. We're looking for little-known or offbeat items. Emphasize positive aspects of camping: fun, economy, etc. We want feature items, not shorts and fillers."

‡CAMPING CANADA, CRV Publishing Canada Ltd., Suite 202, 2077 Dundas St. East, Mississauga, Ontario L4X 1M2 Canada. (416)624-8218. A magazine published six times/year, covering camping and RVing. Circ. 100,000. Pays on publication. Byline given. Buys first rights. Submit seasonal/holiday material 3 months in advance. Computer printout submissions acceptable; no dot-matrix. SASE. Reports in 2 months. Free sample copy and writer's guidelines.

Nonfiction: General interest; historical/nostalgic (sometimes); how-to; new product; personal experience; and photo feature; technical; and travel. No material unrelated to Canada and RVing. Buys 50 mss/year. Query. Length: 1,000-2,000 words. Pays $150-300.

Photos: Send photos with query or manuscript. Reviews contact sheets, negatives, transparencies (send duplicates) and prints. Identification of subjects required. Buys first serial rights.

‡**CAMPING TODAY, Official Publication of National Campers & Hikers Association**, T-A-W Publishing Co., 1219 Bracy, Greenville MI 48838. (616)754-9179. Editors: Dave and Martha Higbie. The monthly official membership publication (tabloid) of the NCHA, "the largest nonprofit camping organization in the United States and Canada. Members are heavily oriented toward RV travel, both weekend and extended vacations. A small segment is interested in backpacking. Concentration is on activities of members within chapters, conservation, wildlife, etc." Estab. 1983. Circ. 30,000. Pays on publication. Byline given. Buys one-time rights. Submit seasonal/holiday material 3 months in advance. Simultaneous, photocopied, and previously published submissions OK. Computer printout submissions acceptable; prefers letter-quality to dot-matrix. SASE. Reports in 1 month. Sample copy and writer's guidelines for SAE.
Nonfiction: Humor (camping or travel related); interview/profile (interesting campers); new product (RV's and related equipment); technical (RV's); and travel (camping, hiking and RV travel). Buys 12-24 mss/year. Send complete ms. Length: 750 1,000 words. Pays $75-100.
Photos: Send photos with accompanying query or ms. Reviews color transparencies and 5x7 b&w prints. Pays $25 maximum for color transparencies. Captions required.
Tips: "Freelance material on RV travel, RV technical subjects and items of general camping and hiking interest throughout the United States and Canada will receive special attention. Color cover every month."

‡**CAPE COD GUIDE, What to do, where to go, things to see while on Cape Cod**, MPG Communications, Specialty Publications, Box 959, Plymouth MA 02360. (617)746-5555, ext. 241. Editor/Publisher: Walter Brooks. Office Manager: D. Sellon. 20% freelance written. A tourist magazine digest covering tourism on Cape Cod. Weekly May-Oct.; monthly Nov.-Apr. Circ. 50,000 weekly. Pays on publication. Byline given. Buys first and second rights to the same material and second (reprint) rights to material originally published elsewhere. Photocopied and previously published submissions OK. Computer printout submissions acceptable. SASE. Reports in 2 months. Publishes material an average of 6 months after acceptance. Free sample copy.
Nonfiction: General interest, historical/nostalgic, humor, interview/profile, personal experience. "Articles must be Cape Cod appropriate." Buys 30 mss/year. Send complete ms. Pays $25-40.
Photos: State availability of photos. Reviews b&w contact sheet, and 3x5 and 5x7 b&w prints. Payment negotiated with ms. Captions, model release, and identification of subjects required. Buys reprint rights with ms.
Columns/Departments: Art; Antiques; Hidden Cape (places not heavily publicized by tourist media); and Seafood Recipes; Nite Life. Buys 20-50 mss/year. Query. Length: 500-750 words. Pays $25-40.
Fiction: Adventure, fantasy, historical, horror, humorous. "All must be Cape Cod oriented!" Buys 30 mss/year. Send complete ms. Length: 500-750 words. Pays $25-40.
Tips: "Submit humorous, tongue-in-cheek, anecdotal copy specifically tied to Cape Cod or of interest to Cape Cod tourists. Our features are primarily freelanced each year. Historical based fiction, unique happenings on Cape are of special interest."

CHEVRON USA, Box 6227, San Jose CA 95150. (408)296-1060. Editor: Mark Williams. For members of the Chevron Travel Club. 75% freelance written. Quarterly. Buys first North American serial rights. Publishes ms an average of 7 months after acceptance. Pays for articles on acceptance. Pays for photos on publication. Computer printout submissions acceptable; no dot-matrix. SASE. Free sample copy, writer's and photographer's guidelines. Tables of contents planned approximately 1 year in advance. Reports in 6 to 8 weeks.
Nonfiction: "We need lively, well-organized articles with sense of place and history, yet packed with see-and-do information geared toward families. Enthusiasm for, and knowledge of, subject should show. In addition to destination articles, and round-up stories, we carry general interest (circuses, ballet), photo essays and pieces on sports and the outdoors. No public relations, brochure approach; no historical treatises, personality profiles or travelogues." Buys 10 mss/issue. Recent article example: "Portland: The City of Roses." Length: 700-1,500 words. Pays 25¢/word average.
Photos: Subject matter to illustrate copy. "Sharp, bright, original transparencies in 35mm or larger. Color only. Majority of photos must show people, but no models or setups." Pays $100-175 for inside photos; $350 for article-related front cover; $250 for non-article-related back cover.
Columns/Departments: Family Activities (600 words on craft or activity families can enjoy together); Humor (75-100 word original anecdotes on personal travel experiences). Pays $25.

‡**COAST MAGAZINE, The Weekly Vacationers Guide**, Resort Publications, Ltd., 5000 N. Kings Highway, Box 2448, Myrtle Beach SC 29577. (803)449-5415. Editor: Valerie M. Coyne. Published 38 times/year covering tourism. "We reach more than one million readers/tourists. Our slant is vacation articles, beach, North/South Carolina orientation with coastal information, fiction." Circ. 18,000. Pays on acceptance. Byline given. Buys one-time rights (regional). Submit seasonal/holiday material at least 2 months in advance. Simultaneous queries, and simultaneous, photocopied, and previously published submissions OK. SASE. Reports

in 2 weeks on queries; 1-2 months on mss. Free sample copy and writer's guidelines.

Nonfiction: Expose (airlines); historical/nostalgic (low country, South); new product (beach, tourist-related); and personal experience (tourist). Special issues include "Movers and Shakers in South Carolina." Buys 10 mss/year. Send complete ms. Length: 400-1,000 words. Pays $30 minimum.

Photos: John Pinson, photo editor. Send photos with ms. Pays $50-100 for b&w or 4-color (cover photos) transparencies; $50 minimum for b&w and color prints. Model release and identification of subjects required. Buys one-time rights (regional).

Fiction: Mary Miller, fiction editor. Adventure (ocean, lake, hunting); fantasy (resort, tourist); fantasy (resort, tourist); historical (low country history, South Carolina and North Carolina); humorous (fishing, beach, tourist); romance (Southern-oriented); and articles on music and beach music. No religious, ethnic or erotic material. Buys 2-3 mss/year. Send complete ms. Length: 1,000 words maximum.

Fillers: Bill Marjenhoff, fillers editor. Clippings, jokes, gags, anecdotes and short humor.

Tips: "Freelancer can best break in to our publication by submitting resort-oriented, and Southern historical material."

ENDLESS VACATION, Endless Vacation Publications, Inc., Box 80260, Indianapolis IN 46280-0260. (317)848-0500. Editor-in-Chief: Betsy Sheldon. Freelance Editor: Kathy Hannon. Bimonthly travel magazine for an "audience whose interest and involvement with travel and vacationing is inherent. The readership is almost entirely made up of vacation timeshare owners and those who seek variety and quality from their vacation experiences—affluent executives and professionals." Circ. 355,000. Pays on acceptance. Byline given. Offers 25% kill fee. Buys variable rights; "mostly first North American and one-time rights." Submit seasonal/holiday material at least 4 months in advance. Simultaneous queries and simultaneous and previously published submissions OK. Computer printout submissions acceptable. SASE. Reports in 2 months. Sample copy $1 and free writer's guidelines.

Nonfiction: Book excerpts (on subject of travel only); photo feature; and travel. "Feature stories may focus on a specific travel location or an interesting vacation activity, but must be based on a unique or unexpected angle. Rather than a story on vacationing in the Poconos, treatment might be the Poconos as a relaxing travel base for day trips to New York City or Philadelphia. We also encourage sidebars along with the article, covering specifics such as a close-up profile of a "real" cowboy for a story on Montana, or a list of the five best-known white water tour companies as a sidebar for a story on rafting in the Rockies. We buy primarily short features and featurettes from 800-1,200 words. Stories should have a specific focus—'souvenir' shopping in San Francisco's incredible warehouse of international bargains, Cost Plus on Fisherman's Wharf; the foreign flavor of Texas—a German Wurstfest in the heart of cowboy country. Articles should avoid environmentalist stance; also, no straight recitations of dry facts." Buys 6-10 mss/year. Query with published clips. Pays $300 and up "according to importance of story, its length, and the author's credentials."

Photos: Joyce Hadley, art director. "Most of the photography in *Endless Vacation* is supplied by professional photographers. We do not require photographs from the writers, but we will consider them if submitted. Images should be included with the original query and must be accompanied by photographer's name, model releases and full identification and/or captions. They must be 35mm, 2¼x2¼ or 4x5 transparencies. No more than 12 images should be sent." Pays negotiable rates. "We reserve the right to keep photos up to 3 or 4 months, and we will return them via registered mail." Buys one-time, exclusive rights in the industry.

Tips: "We are looking for *specific* information that we can't get out of a guidebook or a library—*firsthand* facts presented in a colorful, readable fashion. A good, thorough query—preferably with one or two sample introductory paragraphs—and published clips are a must to show your writing skills."

FAMILY MOTOR COACHING, 8291 Clough Pike, Cincinnati OH 45244-2796. (513)474-3622. Editor: Terry Duschinski. Managing Editor: Pamela Wisby. 75% freelance written. Emphasizes travel by motorhome, and motorhome mechanics, maintenance and other technical information. Monthly magazine; 190-260 pages. Circ. 36,000. Pays on acceptance. Buys first-time, 12 months exclusive rights. Byline given. Phone queries discouraged. Submit seasonal/holiday material 5 months in advance. Computer printout submissions acceptable; prefers letter-quality to dot-matrix. SASE. Reports in 2 months. Sample copy $2; free writer's guidelines.

Nonfiction: Motorhome travel and living on the road; travel (various areas of country accessible by motor coach); how-to (modify motor coach features); bus conversions; and nostalgia. Buys 20 mss/issue. Query. Length: 1,000-2,000 words. Pays $50-200.

Photos: State availability of photos with query. Offers no additional payment for b&w contact sheet(s) 35mm or 2¼x2¼ color transparencies. Captions required. B&w glossy photos should accompany nontravel articles. Buys first rights.

Tips: "Keep in mind, stories must have motorhome angle or connection; inclusion of information about FMCA members enhances any travel article. Stories about an event somewhere should allude to nearby campgrounds, etc. The stories should be written assuming that someone going there would be doing it by motorhome. We need more articles from which to select for publication. We need geographic balance and a blend of travel, technical and incidental stories. No first-person accounts of vacations."

‡**FAR EAST TRAVELER, Largest Hotel Magazine in the Far East**, Far East Reporters, Inc., 4-28, 1-chome, Moto-Azabu, Minato-ku 106, Tokyo, Japan. (03)452-0705. Editor: Beth Reiber. Managing Editor: Masa Hirukawa. A monthly English-language travel magazine distributed free to guest rooms in 35 first-class hotels in 7 Asian countries. Readership consists primarily of English-speaking tourists and business travelers interested in travel articles on destinations throughout Asia and the Pacific. Circ. 25,000. Pays 1 month following publication. Byline given. Buys one-time rights, simultaneous rights, and second serial (reprint) rights. Submit seasonal/holiday material 3 months in advance. Simultaneous, photocopied, and previously published submissions OK. Computer printout submissions acceptable. Reports in 1 month. Sample copy for 5 IRCs for surface post; writer's guidelines for 1 IRC.

Nonfiction: Historical/nostalgic (on interesting or unusual things of Asia's past); how-to (tips on traveling, especially for businessmen); humor (on traveling, customs in Asia, etc.); personal experience (unusual traveling experience); photo feature (photo essays or any Asian subject); and travel (on any destination in Asia except mainland China). "Although most of our readers are businessmen, we work under the assumption that businessmen are people just like everyone else. We therefore like to see articles with a broad base of appeal written for anyone who enjoys traveling. Articles can range from adventure stories to destination pieces, from trekking in Thailand to shopping in Tokyo. Writers should keep in mind that because of our monthly turnover of readership, we are constantly looking for articles on all major and offbeat destinations in Asia. Just because we published an article on Seoul last year doesn't mean we can't use another one this year. Because of the magazine's close ties to Taiwan, we cannot use any articles on mainland China. Also, no boring, encyclopedia-like articles." Buys 60 mss/year. Complete mss preferred, or send query with published clips. Length: 500-1,600 words. Pays US 10¢/word.

Photos: Color only, no b&w. State availability of photos or send photos with ms. Pays $25-40 for color transparencies; $70-100 for cover. Captions required. Buys one-time rights.

Columns/Departments: Oriental Oddities (unique things in the Orient, such as unusual, exotic or interesting customs, habits, historicals events, etc.); Business Beat (business-related subjects about any country of the Orient, such as travel hints for businessmen or how to conduct business in specific Asian countries); Asia in Focus (photo essays, generally a two-page spread, on any destination or subject in Asia); Festivities (an article focusing on any festival in Asia, such as the Sapporo Snow Festival in Japan). Buys 30-40 mss/year. Send complete ms. Length: 500-1,000 words. Pays US 10¢/word.

Tips: "Well-written articles accompanied by good color photography stand a much better chance of being accepted. Specifically, we are looking for travel articles that entertain as well as inform, for articles that have a natural balance of anecdotes, description and information. Traveling itself can be very exciting—yet it's amazing how many writers fail to convey this excitement in their writing. We want writers to tell what it *feels* like to be there, to give our readers smells and sounds and descriptive imagery. To insure up-to-date material, writers must inform us *when* they visited the place they're writing about. The easiest way to break in is to write for the Business Beat department—we *always* need material."

GREAT EXPEDITIONS, Canada's Adventure and Travel Magazine, Box 46499, Station G, Vancouver, British Columbia V6R 4G7 Canada. (604)734-4948. Editor: Marilyn Marshall. 100% freelance written. Bimonthly magazine covering adventure and travel "for people who want to discover the world around them (archaeology to climbing volcanoes); basically a how-to *National Geographic*. We focus on travel (not tourism) and adventure—a mix of Canadian and world content. We are much like a society or club—we provide services besides the basic magazine—and encourage articles and information from our readers." Circ. 4,000. Pays on publication. Byline given. Buys first rights or second (reprint) rights to material originally published elsewhere. Submit seasonal/holiday material 6 months in advance. Simultaneous queries, and simultaneous, photocopied and previously published submissions OK. Computer printout submissions acceptable; prefers letter-quality to dot-matrix. SASE; IRCs outside of Canada. Reports in 1 month. Publishes ms an average of 6 months after acceptance. Sample copy $2; free writer's guidelines.

Nonfiction: Book reviews (travel and adventure); how-to (travel economically, do adventure trips); humor (on travel or adventure); interview/profile (travel or adventure-related); personal experience (travel or adventure); travel (economy and budget, exotic-*not* touristic!). No tourism articles. Buys 30 mss/year. Query or send complete ms. Length: 1,000-3,000 words. Pays $35 maximum. "We have limited funds and generally prefer barter instead of cash (we'll make exceptions, though, providing a free subscription for material.)"

Photos: "It is important to send photos with the manuscript. Otherwise we are reluctant to accept pieces (humor, how-to's and book reviews excepted)." Pays $10 for 35mm color transparencies and 5x7 color and b&w prints for color photo. "Color reproduced in b&w for magazine." Captions required. Buys one-time rights.

Columns/Departments: Viewpoint—opinion on travel, adventure, outdoor recreation, environment. Photography—for the traveler, adventurer: equipment techniques. Health—for travelers and adventurers: how to keep healthy, be healthy. Money—best buys, best countries to visit. Length: 400-800 words. Pays $25 maximum.

Tips: "Best to send for a copy—we are rather different from most magazines because we are a network of travelers and adventurers and rely on this network for our information. We have a yearly article and photo contest. Prizes are $50 for best article and $25 for best photo."

JOURNAL OF CHRISTIAN CAMPING, Christian Camping International, Box 646, Wheaton IL 60187. Editor: Gary L. Wall. Managing Editor: Charlyene Wall. 75% freelance written. Emphasizes the broad scope of organized camping with emphasis on Christian camping. "Leaders of youth camps and adult conferences read our magazine to get practical help in ways to run their camps." Bimonthly magazine; 32-48 pages. Circ. 6,000. Pays on acceptance. Buys all rights. Pays 25% kill fee. Byline given. SASE. Reports in 6 weeks. Publishes ms an average of 6 months after acceptance. Sample copy $2; writer's guidelines for SASE.

Nonfiction: General interest (trends in organized camping in general and Christian camping in particular); how-to (anything involved with organized camping from motivating staff, to programming, to record keeping, to camper follow-up); inspirational (limited use, but might be interested in practical applications of Scriptural principles to everyday situations in camping, no preaching); interview (with movers and shakers in camping and Christian camping in particular; submit a list of basic questions first); and opinion (write a letter to the editor). Buys 30-50 mss/year. Query desired, but accepts unsolicited mss. Length: 600-2,500 words. Pays 5¢/word.

Photos: Send photos with ms. Pays $10/5x7 b&w contact sheet or print; price negotiable for 35mm color transparencies. Buys all rights. Captions required.

MICHIGAN LIVING, Automobile Club of Michigan, 1700 Executive Plaza Drive, Dearborn MI 48126. (313)336-1211. Editor: Len Barnes. 50% freelance written. Emphasizes travel and auto use. Monthly magazine; 48 pages. Circ. 820,000. Pays on acceptance. Publishes ms an average of 4 months after acceptance. Buys first North American serial rights. Pays 100% kill fee. Byline given. Submit seasonal/holiday material 3 months in advance. SASE. Reports in 4-6 weeks. Buys 50-60 unsolicited mss/year. Free sample copy and writer's guidelines.

Nonfiction: Travel articles on US and Canadian topics, but not on California, Florida or Arizona. Send complete ms. Length: 200-1,000 words. Pays $75-300.

Photos: Photos purchased with accompanying ms. Captions required. Pays $25-150 for color transparencies; total purchase price for ms includes payment for b&w photos.

Tips: "In addition to descriptions of things to see and do, articles should contain accurate, current information on costs the traveler would encounter on his trip. Items such as lodging, meal and entertainment expenses should be included, not in the form of a balance sheet but as an integral part of the piece. We want the sounds, sights, tastes, smells of a place or experience so one will feel he has been there and knows if he wants to go back."

THE MIDWEST MOTORIST, The Auto Club of Missouri, 12901 North Forty Dr., St. Louis MO 63141. Editor: Michael J. Right. Managing Editor: Tim Sitek. Associate Editor: Jean Kennedy. 70% freelance written. For the motoring public. Bimonthly magazine; 32 pages. Circ. 320,000. Pays on acceptance or publication depending on the situation. Not copyrighted. Buys first rights and second (reprint) rights to material originally published elsewhere. Pays kill fee as agreed. Byline given. Submit seasonal/holiday material 3-4 months in advance. Simultaneous, photocopied and previously published submissions OK. Computer printout submissions acceptable; prefers letter-quality to dot-matrix. SASE. Reports in 1 month. Sample copy and writer's guidelines for 9x12 SASE.

Nonfiction: General interest; historical (of Midwest regional interest); humor (motoring slant); interview, profile, travel and photo feature. No technical auto or safety stories. Buys 4-5 mss/issue. Query with list of credits or clips of published work. Avoid the "laundry list" approach ("are you interested in 1-50 different articles or ideas?"); prefers 1-2 specific queries on a particular place (and idea). No phone queries. Buys 15 unsolicited mss/year. Length: 1,000-1,800 words. Pays $50-200.

Photos: Send photos with ms. Uses b&w contact sheets or prints, color transparencies for inside and cover. Offers no additional payment for photos accepted with ms. Captions requested.

Tips: "We are tired of cliche-ridden travel stories and articles on the well-known vacation spots. We are moving more into big illustrations versus copy."

‡**NATIONAL GEOGRAPHIC TRAVELER**, National Geographic Society, 17th and M St. NW, Washington DC 20036. Editor: Joan Tapper. A quarterly magazine covering primarily United States and Canadian subjects with about 10% of articles on foreign destinations—most often Europe, Mexico, and the Caribbean, and occasionally the Pacific. Estab. 1984. Pays on acceptance. Offers 50% kill fee. Buys all rights. Reports in 1 month on queries. Free writer's guidelines.

Nonfiction: Articles on national parks, historic places, cities and parts of cities, sport-and resort-oriented travel, regional crafts and cooking, and places of archeological interest. Submit 1-2 page proposal saying why the destination is of interest; include relevant published clips, a resume, and some indication of areas of expertise. Length: 1,500-4,000 words. Pays $1,500-5,000, depending on length, importance, and the writer's experience.

Tips: "In general, *Traveler* articles avoid a guidebook approach. The places are brought to life through the writer's eyes, and his or her experiences are used to deepen those of the reader. We look for a strong sense of the author's personality and experiences, and a high literary quality."

NATIONAL MOTORIST, National Automobile Club, Suite 300, 1 Market Plaza, San Francisco CA 94105. (415)777-4000. Editor: Jane M. Offers. 75% freelance written. Emphasizes motor travel in the West. Bimonthly magazine; 32 pages. Circ. 233,000. Pays on acceptance for article, layout stage for pix. Buys first publication rights. Byline given. Submit seasonal/holiday material 3 months in advance SASE. Reports in 2 weeks.
Nonfiction: Well-researched articles on care of car, travel by car. Profile/interview (of someone in transportation/energy field); and travel (interesting places and areas to visit in the 11 Western states). Buys 2-3 mss/issue. Query. Length: "around 1,100 words." Pays 10¢/word and up.
Photos: "Suggestions welcome. May accompany ms, but considered separately. Payment either with ms or separately, depending on source. Often procured from source other than author." Captions optional, "but must have caption info for pix." Send prints or transparencies. Pays $20 maximum/8x10 b&w glossy print; $30 minimum/35mm, 2¼x2¼ or 4x5 color transparency. Model release required.

NORTHEAST OUTDOORS, Box 2180, Waterbury CT 06722. (203)755-0158. Editor: Howard Fielding. 80% freelance written. Monthly. Circ. 14,000. Buys first serial or one-time rights. Byline given. Pays on publication. "Queries not required, but are useful for our planning and to avoid possible duplication of subject matter. If you have any questions, contact the editor." No "unannounced simultaneous submissions." Deadlines are on the 1st of the month preceding publication. Electronic disk submissions OK if compatible with Kaypro II (single-sided), with Perfect Writer. Computer printout submissions acceptable; prefers letter-quality to dot-matrix. Reports in 15-30 days. Publishes ms an average of 5 months after acceptance. SASE. Sample copy for 9x12 SASE (75¢).
Nonfiction and Photos: Interested in articles and photos that pertain to outdoor activities in the Northeast. Recreational vehicle tips and campgrounds are prime topics, along with first-person travel experiences in the Northeast while camping. No articles on pets, product reviews or endorsements; or features on destinations outside the northeast US. Buys 50-60 unsolicited mss/year. "While the primary focus is on camping, we carry some related articles on outdoor topics like skiing, nature, hiking, fishing, canoeing, etc. One reader-written feature is 'My Favorite Campground'. Payment for this is $10 and writing quality need not be professional. Our pay rate for features is flexible, but generally runs from $30-50 for features without photos, and up to $80 for features accompanied by 2 or more photos. Features should be from 300-1,000 words. Premium rates are paid on the basis of quality, not length. Pays $10/8x10 b&w print."
Tips: "We're growing in advertising, as a result of more ambitious marketing and of an upturn in the economy (and hence the RV industry). This will mean increased space and an increased market for writers."

ODYSSEY, H.M. Gousha Publications, Box 6227, San Jose CA 95150. (408)296-1060. Editor: Bruce Todd. 90% freelance written. Quarterly magazine devoted to travel and leisure with national and international coverage. Pays on acceptance. Publishes ms an average of 1 year after acceptance. Buys first North American serial rights. Submit seasonal material 1 year in advance. Computer printout submissions acceptable. SASE. Reports in 1 month. "If no response to query within 6 weeks, writer should feel free to offer idea elsewhere." Free sample copy and writer's guidelines.
Nonfiction: Travel and travel-related features; how-to (get started in a new sport, hobby or recreation). "*Odyssey* seeks lively, well-researched articles packed with helpful information, combining historical and cultural highlights with information on where to go and what to see and do including off-the-beaten path points of interest. Descriptive detail should give a strong sense of place. We want readers to see and feel a place. The style should be friendly and not too informal. Personalization and anecdotes, if skillfully done, are helpful. Please study magazine before sending submission." Query with clips of previously published work or send completed ms. Length, major feature: 1,200-1,600 words. Pays $240-320 (first-time contributors) for major features.
Photos: Nancy Brazil, photo editor. State availability of color slides. Pays $100-175 for 2¼, 4x5 or 35mm color transparencies. Pays $350 for a front cover that is article related and $250 for a back cover. Buys one-time rights; payment on publication. Does not assign photos.
Columns/Departments: Cities and Sights (500-600 words about US towns, museums, zoos, marketplaces, historic sights or scenic attractions); People in Travel (500-600 words about someone who travels a great deal in pursuit of career or hobby; must have color vertical photo); and Driver's Seat (about driving safety, auto maintenance). Buys 3 mss/issue. Send complete ms on spec or query with clips of previously published work. Length: 500-600 words. Pays $120 (first-time contributors) for Cities and Sights and People In Travel; $150 for solid, informative Driver's Seat articles and/or auto/safety quizzes.
Tips: "New editor is initiating a few new departments, dropping others."

PACIFIC BOATING ALMANAC, Box Q, Ventura CA 93002. (805)644-6043. Editor: William Berssen. For "Western boat owners." Published in 3 editions to cover the Pacific Coastal area. Circ. 25,000. Buys all rights. Buys 12 mss/year. Pays on publication. Sample copy $9.95. Submit seasonal material 3 to 6 months in advance. Reports in 4 weeks. Query. SASE.
Nonfiction: "This is a cruising guide, published annually in 3 editions, covering all the navigable waters in the Pacific coast. Though we are almost entirely staff-produced, we would be interested in well-written articles on

cruising and trailer-boating along the Pacific coast and in the navigable lakes and rivers of the Western states from Baja, California to Alaska inclusive." Pays $50 minimum.
Photos: Pays $10/8x10 b&w glossy print.
Tips: "We are also publishers of boating books that fall within the classification of 'where-to' and 'how-to.' Authors are advised not to send mss until requested after we've reviewed a 2-4 page outline of the projected books."

ROMANTIC DINING & TRAVEL LETTER, James Dines & Co., Inc., Box 837, Belvedere CA 94920. Editor: James Dines. Monthly newsletter covering food, wine and travel. "In-depth reviews of 'special places' around the world; hotels, restaurants with detailed wine list commentary. Appeals to a very affluent audience." Pays on publication. Buys all rights. Submit seasonal/holiday material 4 months in advance. Simultaneous queries and simultaneous and photocopied submissions OK. Computer printout submissions acceptable; prefers letter-quality to dot-matrix. Reports in 3 weeks. Sample copy $3; free writer's guidelines.
Nonfiction: Travel and dining (special places only, not tourist traps or student hangouts). No budget tips or human interest articles. Buys 10-20 mss/year. Query with clips. Pays $100-1,000 ("according to quality, not length.")
Photos: State availability of photos with query letter or ms. Photos with query preferred. Reviews any size b&w or color prints. Pays negotiable fee. Identification of subjects required. Buys one-time rights.
Tips: "We are very specialized; if a writer makes a special 'discovery' of a place—a secluded hideaway, romantic restaurant, or a particularly romantic and elegant hotel—we'll want it. We want our articles to be very detailed and useful in their description. If the quality is there we will see it." Major travel features are most open to freelancers.

RV'N ON, 10417 Chandler Blvd., North Hollywood CA 91601. (213)763-4515. Editor/Publisher: Kim Ouimet. Teen Editor: Guy Ouimet. 40% freelance written. Monthly international mini-newspaper, 16-30 pages, about recreational vehicles (motorhomes, campers and trailers, etc.) Official publication of the International Travel and Trailer Club, Inc. Circ. 5,500. "Payments are made 60 days after publication." Buys first rights. Submit seasonal material 3 months in advance. SASE. Reports in 6 weeks. Sample copy $1 plus SASE. Query first on *all* submissions except Rolling Kitchen column.
Nonfiction: General interest; historical; how-to; humor; interview; nostalgia; opinion; travel; new product; personal experience; and technical. Must be geared to RVs or boats. Buys 30 mss/year. Send complete ms. Length: 100-300 words. Pays 2¢ per word.
Columns/Departments: Campfire Tales (fiction or humorous, anecdotes or short bedtime stories for children); Roadwise Driving Tips; Rolling Kitchen; An Unusual Place (places off the road worth visiting); A Most Unusual Person (release required if name used); and "Teen Talk." Buys 12 mss/year. Query first. Length: 100-500 words. Pays in copies.
Fiction: Adventure, fantasy, historical, humorous, and suspense. Must be geared to RVs or boats. No lengthy items. No poetry or children's tales. Buys 6 mss/year. Query. Length: 200-400 words. Pays in copies.
Fillers: Jokes, anecdotes, short humor and newsbreaks, geared to RVs or boats. Buys 12 mss/year. Length: 25-50 words. Pays in copies.
Tips: "Know motorhomes, campers, etc. and what will be of interest to owners, such as storage tips, repairs, tips of traveling with animals and children. We are anxious to have actual RVers submit material. We keep receiving general material which is scanned and returned immediately. We cannot send particular or individual replies on returns. We always know when someone is not familiar with RVs. We do not need how-to on photography and keep receiving poorly written photography articles. Our policy of query first must be followed. This will help us and the writers."

‡**TEXAS HIGHWAYS MAGAZINE, Official Travel Magazine for the State of Texas**, State Dept. of Highways and Public Transportation, 11th and Brazos, Austin TX 78701. (512)475-6068. Editor: Franklin T. Lively. Managing Editor: Ms. Tommie Pinkard. 80% freelance written. A monthly tourist magazine covering travel and history for Texas only. Pays on acceptance. Publishes ms an average of 6 months after acceptance. Byline given. Offers $50 kill fee. Not copyrighted. Buys one-time rights. Submit seasonal/holiday material 6 months in advance. Simultaneous queries and submissions OK. Computer printout submissions acceptable; prefers letter-quality to dot-matrix. Reports in 1 week on queries; 1 month on mss. Free sample copy and writer's guidelines.
Nonfiction: Historical/nostalgic, photo feature, travel. Must be concerned with travel in Texas. "No disaster features, please." Buys 75 mss/year. Query with published clips. Length: 1,200-1,600 words. Pays $400-600.
Photos: Randy Green, photo editor. Send photos with query or ms. Pays $75-250 for 4x5, 35mm color transparencies. Captions, model releases, and identification of subjects required. Buys one-time rights.
Tips: Send material on "what to see, what to do, where to go in *Texas*." Material must be tourist-oriented. "Freelance writers should be aware standards of quality are becoming higher."

TOURING TIMES, RFD, Inc., Box 7324, Overland Park KS 66211. (913)383-1600. Editor: Norman F. Rowland. Quarterly magazine covering group travel. Many tours have either agricultural or horticultural emphasis. Publishes 2 editions quarterly—one for people who have traveled with Rural Route Tours International (foreign) or American Group Travel (domestic) of Kansas City; one for Southland Travel Service of Birmingham, Alabama. Circ. 50,000. Pays on acceptance. Byline given. Offers ⅓ kill fee. Buys one-time, simultaneous, second serial reprint and variable rights. Submit seasonal/holiday material 6 months in advance. Simultaneous queries, and simultaneous, photocopied and previously published submissions OK "if other markets are specified." Reports in 6 weeks. Free sample copy and writer's guidelines.

Nonfiction: Travel. "All material must be travel related to some degree and present group touring in a positive light." No "restaurant reviews or overly sophisticated off-the-beaten-track pieces." Buys 8 or more mss/year. Query with or without published clips. Length: 1,000-2,500 words. Pays $350-500.

Photos: State availability of photos. Do not send unsolicited transparencies. Pays $60-125 for 2¼ or 35mm color transparencies. Captions, model release and identification of subjects required. Buys one-time rights.

Tips: "Send for sample copies in order to study style and tour destinations. Areas we're presently serving include Alaska, Hawaii, Australia, New Zealand, Pacific Northwest, West Coast, Rockies, Canada-New England, Old South, Carolinas-Florida, American Heritage (Washington to Williamsburg), British Isles, Western Europe, Southern Europe, Scandinavia and South America. China, Spain and Caribbean (cruise) go from time to time. We're particularly interested in developing working relationships with writers who have excellent photo skills."

‡**TRAILBLAZER MAGAZINE**, Thousand Trails, Inc., 4800 S. 188th Way, Seattle WA 98188. (206)246-5406. Editor: Gregg Olsen. 60% freelance written. A monthly company magazine of Thousand Trails, Inc., a developer/operator of membership campgrounds, for members, who are outdoor-oriented recreational vehicle owners and campers. Circ. 55,000. Pays on publication. Byline given. Buys first and second rights to the same material. Submit seasonal/holiday material 6 months in advance. Simultaneous queries, and simultaneous and photocopied submissions OK. Computer printout submissions acceptable. SASE. Reports in 1 month on queries; 6 weeks on mss. Sample copy for SAE and 3 first class stamps; writer's guidelines for SAE and 1 first class stamp.

Nonfiction: General interest; historical/nostalgic; how-to (relating to RV owner); humor; interview/profile; new product; personal experience; technical; and travel. Write for editorial calendar. No articles on religion. Buys 30 mss/year. Query. Length: 500-3,000 words. Pays 10¢/word.

Photos: Karen Palmer, photo editor. State availability of photos. Reviews b&w contact sheet, and 35mm and 2¼ color slides. Pays variable rate depending on size and use. Captions required.

Tips: Best areas for freelancers are "RV-related articles, subjects in close proximity to our report/campgrounds. Writing should be bright, lively. We believe that an RV/outdoor publication need not be stodgy or old-fashioned in its editorial approach."

TRAILER LIFE, TL Enterprises, Inc., 29901 Agoura Rd., Agoura CA 90301. (213)991-4980. Associate Publisher: Don E. Brown. Editor: Bill Estes. Monthly magazine for owners and potential buyers of travel trailers, campers and motorhomes. Circ. 324,906. Pays on publication. Buys first rights. Phone queries acceptable. Submit seasonal material 4 months in advance. Computer printout submissions acceptable. SASE. Reports in 2 weeks on queries; in 3 weeks on mss. Free writer's guidelines.

Nonfiction: Art of using a trailer, camper or motorhome and the problems involved. Length: 2,000 words maximum. How-to articles with step-by-step photos a necessity. Length: 800 words maximum. Combine as many operations in each photo or drawing as possible. Personal experience stories must be truly interesting. Merely living in or traveling by RV is not enough. Uses travel articles with color transparencies about trips that are inexpensive or unusual, into areas which are accessible by a travel trailer or motorhome. Photos must be top quality. Length: 1,000-2,000 words. Also uses short travel pieces, with a couple of photos of interesting places off the established routes. Length: 100-250 words. Allied interest articles are one of main interests, things that RV owners do, like boating, hiking, fishing and spelunking hobbies. A definite tie-in with travel trailers, motorhomes or pickup campers is essential. Tell the reader how RVs fit into the sport and where they can park while there. All travel articles should include basic information on RV parking facilities in the areas, costs, location, and time of year, etc. Payment varies "from $100 to $400 based on the quality of the material submitted and how it's used."

Photos: "We seek scenic photographs suitable for use on our cover. Payment for cover photos ranges up to $300. An RV must appear in the photo, but it need not dominate the photo. We normally work with 35mm Kodachrome film but will consider larger transparencies on other types of film. In most cases we do not have use for photographs unaccompanied by an article (except for the cover). Black and white photos should be 8x10 glossy. Prints should be numbered and identified on an accompanying caption sheet."

TRAILS-A-WAY, 1219 Bracy Ave., Greenville MI 48838. (616)754-9179. Editor: Martha Higbie. 25% freelance written. Newspaper published 8 times/year on camping in the Midwest (Michigan, Ohio, Indiana and Illinois). "Fun and information for campers who own recreational vehicles." Circ. 50,000. Pays on publication. Byline given. Buys first and second rights to the same material, and second (reprint) rights to material originally published elsewhere. Submit seasonal/holiday material 3 months in advance. Simultaneous queries and submissions OK. Computer printout submissions acceptable; no dot-matrix. SASE. Reports in 1 month. Sample copy 75¢; writer's guidelines for business size SAE and 1 first class stamp.

Nonfiction: How-to (use, maintain recreational vehicles—5th wheels, travel and camping trailers, pop-up trailers, motorhomes); humor; inspirational; interview/profile; new product (camp products); personal experience; photo feature; technical (on RVs); travel. March/April issue: spring camping; September/October: fall camping. Winter issues feature southern hot spots. "All articles should relate to RV camping in Michigan, Ohio, Indiana and Illinois—or south in winter. No tenting or backpacking articles." Buys 16-24 mss/year. Send complete ms. Length: 1,000-1,500 words. Pays $50-100.

Photos: Send photos with ms. Pays $5-10 for b&w and color prints. No slides. Captions required. Buys one-time rights.

Tips: "Recently made the 50,000 circulation into four editions—Ohio edition, Michigan edition, Indiana edition and Illinois edition. Editorial thrust will be closer to state requirements as far as travel stories are concerned. Otherwise same general camping material will be used in all four. Payment is based on total circulation so that articles may appear in all four."

TRAVEL & STUDY ABROAD, (formerly *Transitions*), 18 Hulst Rd., Amherst MA 01002. (413)256-0373. Editor and Publisher: Prof. Clayton A. Hubbs. 80% freelance written. A resource guide to work, study, and special interest travel abroad, for low budget, independent travelers. Bound magazine. Circ. 15,000. Pays on publication. Buys first rights and second (reprint) rights to material originally published elsewhere. Byline given. Written queries only. SASE. Reports in 4 weeks. Publishes ms an average of 4 months after acceptance. Sample copy $2.50; writer's guidelines for SASE.

Nonfiction: How-to (find courses, inexpensive lodging and travel); interview (information on specific areas and people); personal experience (evaluation of courses, special interest and study tours, economy travel); and travel (what to see and do in specific areas of the world, new learning and travel ideas). Foreign travel only. No travel pieces for businessmen. Few destination pieces. Buys 40 unsolicited mss/issue. Query with credentials. Length: 500-1,500 words. Pays $25-75.

Photos: Send photos with ms. Pays $10-15 for 8x10 b&w glossy prints, higher for covers. No color. Offers no additional payment for photos accompanying ms, but photos increase likelihood of acceptance. Buys one-time rights. Captions required.

Columns/Departments: Studynotes (evaluation of courses or programs); Travelnotes (new ideas for offbeat independent travel); and Jobnotes (how to find it and what to expect). Buys 8/issue. Send complete ms. Length: 1,000 words maximum. Pays $10-50.

Fillers: Newsbreaks (having to do with travel, particularly offbeat educational travel and work or study abroad). Buys 5/issue. Length: 100 words maximum. Pays $5-20.

Tips: "We like nuts and bolts stuff. Real practical information, especially on how to work and cut costs abroad. Be specific: names, addresses, current costs. We are particularly interested in educational (offbeat, low-budget) travel and study abroad for adults and senior citizens—a rapidly growing audience."

TRAVEL AND LEISURE, 1120 Avenue of the Americas, New York NY 10036. (212)382-5600. Editor-in-Chief: Pamela Fiori. Monthly. Circ. 925,000. Buys first worldwide serial rights. Pays 25% kill fee. Byline given unless material is assigned as research. Pays on acceptance. Reports in 2 weeks. Query. SASE.

Nonfiction: Uses articles on travel and vacation places, food, wine, shopping, sports. Nearly all articles are assigned. Length: 2,000-3,000 words. Pays $750-2,000.

Photos: Makes assignments mainly to established photographers. Pays expenses.

Tips: "New writers might try to get something in one of our regional editions (East, West, South and Midwest). They don't pay as much as our national articles ($600), but it is a good way to start. We have a need for pieces that run no more than 800-1,200 words. Regionals cover any number of possibilities from a profile of an interesting town in a certain state to unusual new attractions."

TRAVEL SMART, Communications House, Inc., Dobbs Ferry NY 10522. (914)693-4208. Editor/Publisher: H.J. Teison. Managing Editor/Publisher: Mary L. Hunt. Covers information on "budget, good-value travel." Monthly newsletter. Pays on publication. Buys all rights. Photocopied submissions OK. Computer printout submissions acceptable. SASE. Reports in 6 weeks. Free sample copy and writer's guidelines for #10 SASE with 37¢ postage.

Nonfiction: Mary L. Hunt, managing editor. "Interested primarily in great bargains or little-known deals on transportation, lodging, food, unusual destinations that won't break the bank. Please, no destination stories on major Caribbean islands, London, New York, no travelogues, my vacation, poetry, fillers. No photos or illustrations. Just hard facts. We are not part of 'Rosy fingers of dawn . . .' School. More like letter from knowledgeable friend who has been there." Query first. Length: 100-1,000 words. Pays "under $100.".

Tips: "Send clippings of ads for bargain airfares, package tours, hotel deals in your area (outside New York only). When you travel, check out small hotels offering good prices, little known restaurants, and send us brief rundown (with prices, phone numbers, addresses) of at least 4 at one location. Information must be current and backed up with literature, etc. Include your phone number with submission, because we sometimes make immediate assignments."

TRAVEL-HOLIDAY MAGAZINE, Travel Magazine, Inc., 51 Atlantic Ave., Floral Park NY 11001. (516)352-9700. Executive Editor: Scott Shane. For the active traveler with time and money to travel several times a year. Monthly magazine; 100 pages. Circ. 816,000. Pays on acceptance. Buys first North American serial rights. Byline given. Submit seasonal/holiday material 6 months in advance. Computer printout submissions acceptable; prefers letter-quality to dot-matrix. SASE. Reports in 2 months. Sample copy $1; free writer's guidelines. No phone queries.

Nonfiction: Interested in travel destination articles. Send query letter/outline; clips of previously published work *must* accompany queries. Only the highest quality writing and photography are considered by the new staff. "Don't ask if we'd like to see any articles on San Francisco, France or China. Develop a specific story idea and explain why the destination is so special that we should devote space to it. Are there interesting museums, superb restaurants, spectacular vistas, etc.? Tell us how you plan to handle the piece—convey to us the mood of the city, the charm of the area, the uniqueness of the museums, etc. No food and wine, medical, photo tips, poetry or boring travelogues." Length: featurettes (800-1,300 words), $250 and up; features (1,600-1,800), $400; "Here and There" column (575 words), $150. For "Here and There" column use "any upbeat topic that can be covered succinctly (with 1 piece of b&w art) that's travel related and deserves special recognition. When querying, please send suggested lead and indicate "Here and There" in the cover letter."

Photos: B&w prints $25; color converted to b&w will be paid at $25 rate; color transparencies (35mm and larger) pays $75-400 depending upon use. Pays on publication.

Tips: "Feature stories should be about major destinations: large cities, regions, etc. Featurettes can be about individual attractions, smaller cities, side trips, etc. We welcome sidebar service information. Stimulate reader interest in the subject as a travel destination through lively, entertaining and accurate writing. A good way to break in—if we're not familiar with your writing—is to send us a good idea for a featurette (a walking tour of Milan, a trip to Saba, a famous castle, etc., are featurettes we've run recently). Convey the mood of a place without being verbose; although we like good anecdotal material, our primary interest is in the destination itself, not the author's adventures. The format of the magazine has changed—do not query without having first read several recent issues. Style of the magazine has changed—we no longer use any broadbased travel pieces. Each article must have a specific angle. We are assigning articles to the best writers we can find and those writers who develop and produce good material and will continue to work with us on a regular basis. We have also become much more service-oriented in our articles."

TRAVELORE REPORT, 225 S. 15th St., Philadelphia PA 19102. (215)545-0616. Editor: Ted Barkus. For affluent travelers; businessmen, retirees, well-educated; interested in specific tips, tours, and bargain opportunities in travel. Monthly newsletter; 6 pages. Buys all rights. Buys 10-20 mss/year. Pays on publication. Sample copy $2. Submit seasonal material 2 months in advance. Computer printout and disk submissions acceptable.

Nonfiction: "Brief insights (25-200 words) with facts, prices, names of hotels and restaurants, etc., on offbeat subjects of interest to people going places. What to do, what not to do. Supply information. We will rewrite if acceptable. We're candid—we tell it like it is with no sugar coating. Avoid telling us about places in United States or abroad without specific recommendations (hotel name, costs, rip-offs, why, how long, etc.). No destination pieces which are general with no specific 'story angle' in mind, or generally available through PR departments." Pays $5-20.

VISTA/USA, Box 161, Convent Station NJ 07961. (201)538-7600. Editor: Patrick Sarver. Managing Editor: Barbara OByrne. 90% freelance written. Quarterly magazine of the Exxon Travel Club. "Our publication uses articles on North American areas without overtly encouraging travel. We strive to use as literate a writing as we can in our articles, helping our readers to gain an in-depth understanding of cities, towns and areas as well as other aspects of American culture that affect the character of the nation." Circ. 900,000. Pays on acceptance. Buys first North American serial rights. Query about seasonal subjects 18 months in advance. Computer printout submissions acceptable. SASE. Reports in 1 month. Publishes ms an average of 12 months after acceptance. Free sample copy (enclose a 9x12 or larger SASE) and writer's guidelines.

Nonfiction: General interest (geographically-oriented articles on North America focused on the character of an area; also general articles related to travel and places); humor (related to travel or places); photo features (photo essays on subjects such as autumn, winter, highly photogenic travel subjects; and special interest areas) and some articles dealing with Americana, crafts and collecting. "We buy feature articles on North America, Hawaii, Mexico and the Caribbean that appeal to a national audience." No articles that mention driving or follow routes on a map or articles about hotels, restaurants or annual events. Uses 7-10 mss/issue. Query with outline and clips of previously published work. Length: 1,500-2,500 words. Pays $600 minimum.

Photos: Henry M. Pedersen, art director. Send photos with ms. Pays $100 minimum for color transparencies. Captions preferred. Buys one-time rights.

Tips: "We are looking for readable pieces with good writing that will interest armchair travelers as much as readers who may want to visit the areas you write about. Articles should have definite themes and should give our readers an insight into the character and flavor of an area or topic. Stories about personal experiences must impart a sense of drama and excitement or have a strong human-interest angle. Stories about areas should communicate a strong sense of what it feels like to be there. Good use of anecdotes and quotes should be included. Study the articles in the magazine to understand how they are organized, how they present their subjects, the range of writing styles, and the specific types of subjects used. Then query and enclose samples of your best writing."

WORLD TRAVELING, Midwest News Service, Inc., 30943 Club House Lane, Farmington Hills MI 48018. Editor: Theresa Mitan. 90% freelance written. Bimonthly magazine. Circ. 50,000. Pays on publication. Buys all rights. Byline given. Submit seasonal/holiday material 6 months in advance. Simultaneous submissions OK. SASE. Reports in 3 months or longer. Publishes ms an average of about 3 months after acceptance. Sample copy $2 plus postage.
Nonfiction: General interest; adventure travel (such as hang-gliding); humor; photo feature; and travel. Buys 6 mss/issue. Send complete ms. Length: 1,000 words. Pays $100 for 1,000 words.
Photos: Send photos with ms. Pays $10 for b&w prints; $10 for color transparencies or prints. Buys one-time rights.
Columns & Departments: Good Restaurant Guide and Question and Answers about travel. Query or send complete ms. Length: 500 words.

Union

Union members learn more about their union and field of work in the following publications.

BROTHERHOOD OF MAINTENANCE OF WAY EMPLOYES JOURNAL, 12050 Woodward Ave., Detroit MI 48203. (313)868-0490. Editor: O.M. Berge. Associate Editor: R.J. Williamson. 1% freelance written. Monthly trade union magazine for railroad track workers. "Our readers are members of our union, and their work is on the railroad where they build and maintain the tracks, bridges and buildings." Circ. 110,000. Pays on publication. Byline given. Buys one-time, non-exclusive rights and second (reprint) rights to material originally published elsewhere. Submit seasonal/holiday material 4 months in advance. Simultaneous queries, and simultaneous, photocopied and previously published submissions OK. SASE. Reports in 1 month. Publishes ms an average of 1 month after acceptance. Free sample copy.
Nonfiction: Historical/nostalgic and anecdotal pieces. "All material must relate to railroad/track work." Buys 2-3 mss/year. Length: averages 2 typewritten pages. Pays average $40. No additional fee for photos with ms.
Photos: "Photos must be dynamic and sharp." Send photos with query or ms. Pays $10 for 4x5 b&w print used inside. Pays $100-200 for 4x5 or larger color transparencies used as cover. Must be vertical format. Identification of subjects required; caption preferred.

OCAW UNION NEWS, Box 2812, Denver CO 80201. (303)987-2229. Editor: Jerry Archuleta. 5% freelance written. Official publication of Oil, Chemical and Atomic Workers International Union. For union members. Bimonthly tabloid newspaper; 16-24 pages. Circ. 130,000. Not copyrighted. Buys first rights. Byline given. Pays on acceptance. Computer printout submissions acceptable; prefers letter-quality to dot-matrix. Reports in 30 days. Publishes ms an average of up to 1 year after acceptance. Query. SASE. Free sample copy.
Nonfiction: Labor union materials, political subjects and consumer interest articles, slanted toward workers and consumers, with liberal political view. Interview, profile, think pieces and exposes. Most material is done on assignment. "We have severe space limitations." Length: 1,500-1,800 words. Pays $50-75.
Photos: No additional payment is made for 8x10 b&w glossy photos used with mss. Captions required.

Women's

Today's readers of women's magazines have more options but less time. "They are looking for stories and articles that deliver something substantial in a relatively short space," says one *Redbook* editor. Readers seek women's publications as diverse as their own daily schedules. Magazines that also use material slanted to women's interests can be found in the following categories: Business and Finance; Child Care and Parental Guidance; Food and Drink; Hobby and Craft; Home and Garden; Lifestyles; Religious; Romance and Confession; and Sports.

AMIT, (formerly *The American Mizrachi Woman*), AMIT Women, 817 Broadway, New York NY 10003. (212)477-4720. Editor: Micheline Ratzersdorfer. 10% freelance written. Magazine published 6 times/year "concerned with Jewish and Israeli themes, i.e., Jewish art, Jewish sociology, Jewish communities around the world to an audience with an above average educational level, a commitment to Jewish tradition and Zionism and a concern for the future of the Jewish community the world over." Circ. 50,000. Pays on publication. Buys all rights. Submit seasonal material 6 months in advance. Computer printout submissions acceptable "as long as it can be read by the human eye and has adequate leading and margins for editing." Prefers letter-quality to dot-matrix. SASE. Reports in 1 month. Publishes ms an average of 3 months after acceptance. Free sample copy and writer's guidelines.
Nonfiction: General interest; historical; interview (with notable figures in Jewish and Israeli life); nostalgia; travel; and photo feature (particularly Jewish holiday photos). "We do special holiday features for all Jewish holidays." No fiction, no memoirs about "Momma's Chicken Soup" and things of that ilk; no political analyses of the Middle East unless they can stand a six-month delay until publication; no travelogues lauding non-kosher restaurants. Buys 10 unsolicited mss/year. Query. Length: 1,000-2,000 words. Pays $50 maximum.
Photos: State availability of photos. Reviews 5x7 b&w glossy prints. Offers no additional payment for photos accepted with ms. Captions preferred. Buys one-time rights.
Columns/Departments: Jews Around the World (1,000-2,000 words); Life in Israel (1,000-2,000 words). Buys 5 mss/year. Query. Length: 1,000-2,000 words. Pays $50 maximum.
Poetry: Publishes rarely. Submit 3 maximum. Length: 10-50 lines. Pays $10 minimum.
Tips: "We are interested in adding to our stable of freelance writers. The best way to break in is to send a detailed query about a subject you would like to handle for the magazine. All queries will be carefully considered and answered. We've been cut from 8 to 6 issues per year for budgetary reasons, so we're buying less material. But we're still reading whatever comes in. How-to articles in our magazine fall in the categories of Jewish-oriented travel and performance of rituals or religious observance. Humorous treatments of 'coping with life in Israel' are also enjoyed by our readers."

BRIDE'S, Conde Nast Bldg., 350 Madison Ave., New York NY 10017. (212)880-8800. Editor-in-Chief: Barbara D. Tober. For the first- or second-time bride, her family and friends, the groom and his family and friends. Magazine published 6 times/year. Circ. 400,000. Buys all rights. Offers 20% kill fee, depending on circumstances. Byline given. Buys 40 unsolicited mss/year. Pays on acceptance. Reports in 8 weeks. Query or submit complete ms. Article outline preferred. Address mss to Features Department. Free writer's guidelines.
Nonfiction: "We want warm, personal articles, optimistic in tone, with help offered in a clear, specific way. All issues should be handled within the context of marriage. How-to features on all aspects of marriage: communications, in-laws, careers, money, sex, housework, family planning, religion, step-parenting, second marriage, reaffirmation of vows; informational articles on the realities of marriage, the changing roles of men and women, the kinds of troubles in engagement that are likely to become big issues in marriage; stories from couples or marriage authorities that illustrate marital problems and solutions to men and women both; and how-to features on wedding planning that offer expert advice. Also success stories of marriages of long duration. We're using less of the first-person piece and requiring more that articles be well researched, relying on quotes from authorities in the field." Length: 1,000-3,000 words. Pays $300-600.
Poetry: See the "Love" column.
Tips: "Send us a query or a well-written article that is both easy to read and offers real help for the bride as she adjusts to her new role. We're interested in unusual ideas, experiences, and life styles. No 'I used baby pink rose buds' articles. For example of the kinds of features we want, study any issue; read articles listed in table of contents under 'Planning for Marriage.' "

CHATELAINE, 777 Bay St., Toronto, Ontario M5W 1A7 Canada. Editor-in-Chief: Mildred Istona. Monthly general-interest magazine for Canadian women, from age 20 and up. *Chatelaine* is read by one women in three across Canada, a readership that spans almost every age group but is concentrated among those 25 to 45 including homemakers and working women in all walks of life. Circ. over 1 million. Pays on acceptance. Byline given. Free writer's guidelines. "Writers new to us should query us with ideas for upfront columns on nutrition, fitness, relationships, feelings, and parents and kids." Pays $350 for about 1,000 words. Prefers queries for nonfiction subjects on initial contact plus a resume and writing samples. Reports within 2 weeks. All mss must be accompanied by a SASE (IRCs in lieu of stamps if sent from outside Canada). Sample copy $1.50 and postage.
Nonfiction: Elizabeth Parr, senior editor, articles. Submit a page or two outline/query first. Full-length major pieces run from 2,000 to 3,500 words. Pays minimum $1,000 for acceptable major article. Buys first North American serial rights in English and French (the latter to cover possible use in *Chatelaine*'s sister French-language edition, edited in Montreal for French Canada). "We look for important national Canadian subjects, examining any and all facets of Canadian life, especially as they concern or interest Canadian women. For all serious articles deep, accurate, thorough research and rich detail are required." Also seeks full-length personal experience stories with deep emotional impact. Pays $750. Features on beauty, food, fashion and home decorating are supplied by staff writers and editors, and unsolicited material is not considered.

Fiction: Barbara West, fiction editor. Mainstream fiction of 3,500 words. Pays $1,500 minimum. "Upbeat stories about man/woman relationships are the ones most likely to appeal. The central character should be a woman in the 25-45 age range, and the story should deal with and resolve contemporary problems and conflicts our readers relate to. We look for strong human interest, pace, emotional impact, believable characters, romance, humor. Avoid violence, too-explicit sex, science fiction, avant-garde experiments, short-shorts. Canadian settings and characters are a plus. No query necessary for fiction."

‡CONSUMING PASSIONS, Newsletter Devoted to the Strange Relationship between Women and Food, 771 Union St., Brooklyn NY 11215. Editor: Lisa Rogak. 50% freelance written. A bimonthly newsletter about women and eating problems. Pays on publication. Byline given. Buys one-time rights. Submit seasonal/holiday material 6 months in advance. Computer printout submissions acceptable; prefers letter-quality to dot-matrix. SASE. Reports in 3 weeks. Publishes ms an average of 6 months after acceptance. Sample copy for $1, SAE, and 1 first class stamp; writer's guidelines for SASE.

Nonfiction: Humor (if handled very carefully); inspirational; interview/profile; opinion; and personal experience. No "Ha-Ha, my latest stab at the Scarsdale Diet really was something!"; *No diet material* or "I love chocolate" odes. "We provide a heartening and often tongue-in-cheek view of the way women deal with food. We feel diets cause women to be obsessed with food, so any material on this subject we receive *will not be returned*, out of disgust. Anyone who's actually suffered from anorexia or bulimia will be our best kind of writer. In-depth, sometimes ugly pictures of destructive eating, *with* viable solutions are in need." Buys 18 mss/year. Query with published clips or send complete ms. Length: 50-1,000 words. Pays negotiable rate.

Fillers: Short humor, newsbreaks. Pays negotiable rate.

Tips: Best opportunity for freelancers is personal experience article. "Give your brief (750-word) story a beginning, middle, and end and let our readers know there is hope."

COSMOPOLITAN, Hearst Corp., 224 W. 57th St., New York NY 10019. Editor: Helen Gurley Brown. Managing Editor: Guy Flatley. For career women, ages 18-34. Monthly. Circ. 2,500,000. Buys all rights. Pays on acceptance. Not interested in receiving unsolicited manuscripts. Most material is assigned to established, known professional writers who sell regularly to top national markets, or is commissioned through literary agents. Reports in 2-6 weeks.

Nonfiction: Not interested in unsolicited manuscripts; for agents and top professional writers, requirements are as follows: "We want pieces that tell an attractive, 18-34-year-old, intelligent, good-citizen girl how to have a more rewarding life—'how-to' pieces, self-improvement pieces as well as articles which deal with more serious matters. We'd be interested in articles on careers, part-time jobs, diets, food, fashion, men, the entertainment world, emotions, money, medicine and psychology and fabulous characters." Uses some first-person stories. Logical, interesting, authoritative writing is a must, as is a feminist consciousness. Length: 1,000-3,000 words. Pays approx. $750 for short pieces, $1,500 for longer articles (4,500 words).

Photos: Photos purchased on assignment only.

Fiction: Betty Kelly, department editor. Not interested in unsolicited manuscripts; for agents and top professional writers, requirements are as follows: "Good plotting and excellent writing are important. We want short stories dealing with adult subject matter which would interest a sophisticated audience, primarily female, 18-34. We prefer serious quality fiction or light tongue-in-cheek stories on any subject, done in good taste. Stories must have solid upbeat plots, sharp characterizations, and focus on contemporary issues such as man/woman relationships. Sophisticated handling and a sensitive approach are a must. Female protagonists preferred since readers most easily identify with them. Short-shorts are okay but we prefer them to have snap or 'trick' endings. The formula story, the soap opera, skimpy mood pieces or character sketches are not for us." Length: short-shorts, 1,500-3,000 words; pays $300-600. Short stories, 4,000-6,000 words; condensed novels and novel excerpts; pays $1,000. "We occasionally use murder or suspense stories of about 25,000-30,000 words dealing with the upper class stratum of American living. A foreign background is acceptable, but the chief characters should be American." Has published the work of Agatha Christie, Joyce Carol Oates, Evan Hunter, and other established writers.

‡DARLING, It's Fun to be Young, Republican Press, Box 2595, Johannesburg 2000 South Africa. (011)337-1300. Editor: Sue Anne Brenner. A bimonthly magazine for 16-25 year-olds covering fashion, beauty and subjects concerning young women. Circ. 60,000. Pays on publication. Byline given. Buys one-time rights and first rights. Submit seasonal/holiday material 3 months in advance. Simultaneous submissions OK. SAE, IRCs. Reports in 3 months.

Nonfiction: Humor, inspirational and interview/profile. No articles on mother/child, homelife or unrealistic romance. Buys about 50 mss/year. Send complete ms. Length: 1,200-3,000 words. Pays $100-350.

Fiction: Horror; humorous; romance (contemporary, not "soppy"). No traditional boy-meets-girl, or mid-life-crisis stories. Buys about 30 mss/year. Send complete ms. Length: 2,000-5,000 words. Pays $100-180.

‡FAIRFIELD COUNTY WOMAN, Gamer Publishing Group, 15 Bank St., Stamford CT 06901. (203)323-3105. Editor: Dorothy Whitcomb. Monthly tabloid for women who are out in the business world, running their

own business, and the professional woman. Estab. 1982. Circ. 40,000. Pays on publication. Byline given. Buys first North American serial rights. Submit seasonal/holiday material 6 months in advance. Simultaneous queries, and simultaneous and previously published submissions OK. SASE. Reports in 2 months. Free sample copy and writer's guidelines.

Nonfiction: How-to, interview/profile, photo feature and travel. All should relate to the woman in the business world. Buys 36-50 mss/year. Query with published clips. Length: 500-1,500 words. Pays $25-250.

Photos: State availability of photos. Reviews b&w contact sheets. Pays $5-50. Captions required. Buys one-time rights.

Tips: "Feature articles are most open to freelancers. Articles that help working women simplify their lives are increasingly in demand."

FAMILY CIRCLE GREAT IDEAS, Family Circle Magazine, 488 Madison Ave., New York NY 10022. (212)593-8181. Editor: Marie T. Walsh. Managing Editor: Shari E. Hartford. 20-95% freelance written. Published 9 times/year; 128 pages. Circ. 1,000,000. Pays on publication. Publishes ms an average of 3 months after acceptance. Buys all rights. Submit seasonal/holiday material 9 months in advance. Computer printout submissions acceptable; no dot-matrix. Writer's guidelines upon request with SASE. Reports in 4 weeks. Sample copy $1.95.

Nonfiction: How-to (fashion, decorating, crafts, food and beauty) and new product (for home and family). Article queries should be directed to managing editor; must be accompanied by SASE. Buys 2 mss/issue. Query. Pays $150-350.

FAMILY CIRCLE MAGAZINE, 488 Madison Ave., New York NY 10022. (212)593-8000. Editor-in-Chief: Arthur Hettich. 60% freelance written. For women. Published 17 times/year. Usually buys all rights. Pays 25% kill fee. Byline given. Pays on acceptance. Reports in 6-8 weeks. Query. "We like to see a strong query on unique or problem-solving aspects of family life, and are especially interested in writers who have a solid background in the areas they suggest." SASE.

Nonfiction: Margaret Jaworski, articles editor. Women's interest subjects such as family and social relationships, children, humor, physical and mental health, leisure-time activities, self-improvement, popular culture, travel. Service articles. For travel, interested mainly in local material. "We look for service stories told in terms of people. We want well-researched service journalism on all subjects." Length: 1,000-2,500 words. Pays $250-2,500.

Fiction: Contact: Nicole Gregory, book editor. Occasionally uses fiction related to women. Buys short stories, short-shorts, vignettes. Length: 2,000-2,500 words. Payment negotiable. Minimum payment for full-length story is $250. Reports in 6 weeks.

Tips: Query letters should be "concise and to the point. We get some with 10 different suggestions—by the time they're passed on to all possible editors involved, weeks may go by." Also, writers should "keep close tabs on *Family Circle* and other women's magazines to avoid submitting recently run subject matter."

FARM WIFE NEWS, Box 643, Milwaukee WI 53201. (414)423-0100. Managing Editor: Ruth Benedict. 70% freelance written. For farm and ranch women of all ages; nationwide and Canada. "We are the one and only completely-dedicated-to-farm/ranch-women's magazine. Unlike some farm magazines, which only dedicate a few pages to rural women's interests, we try to make each and every issue appropriate to a farm woman's busy, unique and important life. The farm and ranch woman feels a great deal of pride in her role as farmer, partner, and key assistant in the operation." Circ. 350,000. Byline given. Buys 300 unsolicited mss/year. Buys first rights and second (reprint) rights to material originally published elsewhere. Pays on acceptance. Sample copy $2.50; free writer's, photographers's guidelines. Submit seasonal material 6 months in advance. *No photocopied or simultaneous submissions.* Computer printout submissions acceptable; prefers letter-quality to dot-matrix. Reports in 6 weeks. Publishes ms an average of 1 year after acceptance. Query, also stating availability of photos, if any, or, submit complete ms. SASE.

Nonfiction: "We are always looking for good freelance material. Our prime consideration is that it is farm-oriented, focusing on a farm woman or a subject that would appeal especially to her. Our readers are very interested in lifestyle, health, child care and family issues. So much about rural living has been said before—'it's the best place to raise children, work together with the family, etc.'—FWM is quite interested in hearing from people with a new point of view." Uses a wide variety of material: daily life, sewing, gardening, humor, crafts, women in careers, nostalgia, decorating, outstanding farm women, etc. *Topic should always be approached from a rural woman's point of view.* Also, informational, how-to, personal experience, interview, profile, inspirational, think pieces, nostalgia, opinion, successful sideline business operations from farm and/or ranches. Length: 1,000-1,500 words maximum. Departments and columns which also use material are: A Day in Our Lives, Besides Farming, Country Crafts, Why Farm Wives Age Fast (humor), Gardening, Country Decorating, and I Remember When. Pays $45-300.

Photos: Color transparencies, color prints and b&w photos are purchased with or without accompanying mss. "We look for scenic, seasonal color photos and shots of farm women at work and at play on the farm." Caption information required. Payment depends on use, but begins at $40 for b&w photos; at $50 and up for color slides or transparencies. Photo credits given for photos purchased to accompany an article.

Fiction: Mainstream, humorous. Themes should relate to subject matter. Length: 1,500 words maximum. Pays $60-200.

Poetry: Rural themes only. Pays $40-60. "Please limit your submissions to 6 or less. As a rule, the poems we publish run 16-24 lines maximum with very few exceptions."

Fillers: Word puzzles and short humor. Pays $20-45.

FIFTY UPWARD NETWORK Newsletter, F.U.N.,, Network Publications, Box 4714, Cleveland OH 44126. Editor/Publisher: Nancy C. Meyer. Approximately 20% freelance written. Bimonthly newsletter covering the 50 + single (divorced, widowed, or never married) woman. "Nonprofit national organization offers newsletter as one of membership benefits. Our newsletter is an enthusiastic 'up' publication which details the many advantages of being free, female, mature and gutsy. We are a practical, down-to-earth, supportive publication and this is the slant we would require in submissions." Circ. 800-1,000. Pays on publication. Byline given. Buys first rights and second (reprint) rights to material originally published elsewhere. Topics may include financial planning, retirement for career women, and mid-life dating and re-marriage; solo travel entrepreneurial enterprises, current Washington scene with regard to seniors, etc. Health & fitness. Also pertinent cartoons and short inserts. Simultaneous queries, and simultaneous, photocopied and previously published submissions OK "if pertinent." Computer printout submissions acceptable. SASE. Reports in 2-3 weeks. Publishes ms an average of 4 months after acceptance. Sample copy for $2 and business-size SAE with 37¢ postage; writer's guidelines only for SAE and 20¢ postage.

Nonfiction: Interview/profile ("we cameo 50 + nationally-known women with power, talent, charm and brains"); and travel (solo jaunting column). "We are open to submissions for our columns on career alternatives, You & Your Money, and Y.O.U. Inc. (sideline business). No hard-core feminist, or 'swinging single' type articles or expose or nostalgia pieces. 'Please read sample issue carefully first.' " Query with clips if available with 37¢ postage. "We do not require that writer has been published." Length: 1,000-1,500 words. Pays $20-30. "This will increase. Even though we do not pay top fees, the writer can feel certain that he/she *will* be paid."

Columns/Department: Power, Talent Charm & Brains at 50 + ; Your Battered Buck; Marry Go Round; You Inc.; Climbing Out; and "When a Woman's Work Is Done (retirement). Length: 1,000-1,500 words.

Tips: "We suspect (although this is *not* a must) that a 50 + woman writer could lend a very pertinent and personal slant to anything submitted. Submissions should be down-to-earth, practical, believable without a definite negative slant. We are willing to give a *nonpublished writer* a chance so long as article is appropriate. Our newsletter has a standard column format (which could change as time passes). We are open to submissions in any of the columns previously mentioned. And also might consider a column idea not at present covered. Newsletter is in development stage. I would think it should get longer with more columns, subjects."

FLARE, 777 Bay St., Toronto, Ontario M5W 1A7 Canada. (416)596-5453. Editor: Bonnie Hurowitz. Associate Editor: Jane Hess. Fashion magazine published 12 times/year for 18-34-year-old Canadian working women. Covers fashion, beauty, health, careers, lifestyle features. Circ. 201,000. Pays on acceptance. Byline given. Buys first North American serial rights; buys all rights for career page material. Submit seasonal material 3 months in advance. Simultaneous, photocopied and previously published submissions OK. Reports in 1 month. Sample copy $1.

Nonfiction: General interest and profile articles no more than 3,500 words on (up-and-coming Canadians in arts, sports, politics and sciences, etc.). "All material must be for a Canadian market using Canadian research." Buys 2 mss/issue. Do not send complete mss. Query with resume and clips of previously published work. Unsolicited mss returned only if accompanied by SASE. US stamps not valid in Canada. Length: 3,500 words maximum.

Columns/Departments: Career News: 100-word Canadian clippings, ideas, and news items for working women. Courses, conferences, solutions to problems, research findings, breakthroughs.

Tips: "Usually start with small items, e.g., Career News, etc."

GLAMOUR, Conde Nast, 350 Madison Ave., New York NY 10017. (212)880-8800. Editor-in-Chief: Ruth Whitney. For college-educated women, 18-35-years old. Monthly. Circ. 1.9 million; 6.5 million readers. Computer printout submissions acceptable "if the material is easy to read." Prefers letter-quality to dot-matrix printouts. SASE. Pays on acceptance. Pays 20% kill fee. Byline given. Reports within 5 weeks. Writer's guidelines available for SASE.

Nonfiction: Janet Chan, articles editor. "Editorial approach is 'how-to' with articles that are relevant in the areas of careers, health, psychology, interpersonal relationships, etc. We look for queries that are fresh and include a contemporary, timely angle. Fashion, beauty, decorating, travel, food and entertainment are all staff-written. We use 1,000-1,200 word opinion essays for our Viewpoint section. Pays $400. Our His/Hers column features generally stylish essays on relationships or comments on current mores by male and female writers in alternate months. Pays $800 for His/Hers mss. Buys first North American serial rights." Buys 10-12 mss/issue. Query "with letter that is detailed, well-focused, well-organized, and documented with surveys, statistics and research, personal essays excepted." Reports in 5 weeks. Short articles and essays (1,500-2,000 words) pay $800 and up; longer mss (2,500-3,000 words) pay $1,000 minimum on acceptance.

Tips: "We're looking for sharply focused ideas by strong writers and constantly raising our standards. We are very interested in getting new writers; and we are approachable, mainly because our range of topics is so broad."

GOOD HOUSEKEEPING, Hearst Corp., 959 8th Ave., New York NY 10019. Editor-in-Chief: John Mack Carter. Executive Editor: Mina Mulvey. Managing Editor: Mary Fiore. Mass women's magazine. Monthly; 250 pages. Circ. 5,000,000. Pays on acceptance. Buys all rights. Pays 25% kill fee. Byline given. Submit seasonal/holiday material 8 months in advance. SASE. Reports in 1 month. Sample copy $1.95. Free writer's guidelines with SASE.

Nonfiction: Joan Thursh, articles editor. How-to-informational; investigative stories; inspirational; interview; nostalgia; personal experience; and profile. Buys 8-10 mss/issue. Query. Length: 1,500-3,000 words. Pays $1,500 on acceptance for full articles from new writers. Regional Editor: Shirley Howard. Pays $250-350 for local interest and travel pieces of 2,000 words.

Photos: Herbert Bleiweiss, art director. Photos purchased on assignment mostly. Some short photo features with captions. Pays $50-350 for b&w; $50-400 for color photos. Query. Model release required.

Columns/Departments: Light Housekeeping & Fillers, edited by Mary Ann Littell. Humorous short-short prose and verse. Jokes, gags, anecdotes. Pays $25-100. The Better Way, edited by Erika Mark. Ideas and in-depth research. Query. Pays $500. "Only outstanding material has a chance here."

Fiction: Naome Lewis, fiction editor. Uses romance fiction and condensations of novels that can appear in one issue. Looks for reader identification. "Presently overstocked." Buys 3 mss/issue. "We get 1,500 short stories a month; a freelancer's odds are overwhelming—but we do look at all submissions." Send complete mss. Length: 1,500 words (short-shorts); 20,000 words (novels); average 4,000 words. Pays $1,000 minimum for fiction short-shorts; $1,250 for short stories.

Poetry: Arleen Quarfoot, poetry editor. Light verse and traditional. "Presently overstocked." Buys 3 poems/issue. Pays $5/line for poetry on acceptance.

HADASSAH MAGAZINE, 50 W. 58th St., New York NY 10019. Executive Editor: Alan M. Tigay. Monthly, except combined issues (June-July and August-September). Circ. 370,000. Buys 10 unsolicited mss/year. Buys first rights. Reports in 6 weeks. SASE.

Nonfiction: Primarily concerned with Israel, Jewish communities around the world, and American civic affairs. Length: 1,500-2,000 words. Pays $200-400, less for reviews.

Photos: "We buy photos only to illustrate articles, with the exception of outstanding color from Israel which we use on our covers. We pay $175 and up for a suitable cover photo. Offers $50 for inside b&w/photo."

Fiction: Contact: Roselyn Bell. Short stories with strong plots and positive Jewish values. No personal memoirs, "schmaltzy" fiction, or women's magazine fiction. Length: 3,000 words maximum. Pays $300 minimum.

Tips: Of special interest are "strong fiction with a Jewish orientation; unusual experiences with Jewish communities around the world—or specifically Israel."

HARPER'S BAZAAR, 1700 Broadway, New York NY 10019. Editor-in-Chief: Anthony Mazzola. For "women, late 20s and above, middle income and above, sophisticated and aware, with at least 2 years of college. Most combine families, professions, travel, often more than one home. They are active and concerned with what's happening in the arts, their communities, the world." Monthly. Circ. 720,000. All rights purchased. Query first. SASE.

Nonfiction: "We publish whatever is important to an intelligent, modern woman. Fashion questions plus beauty and health—how the changing world affects her family and herself; how she can affect it; how others are trying to do so; changing life patterns and so forth. Query us first."

‡**THE HOMEMAKER**, General Communications Corp., 929 Kansas City St., Box 8283, Rapid City SD 57709. (605)348-9090. Managing Editor: Jane Wilson Ritter. A bimonthly magazine covering homemaking—food, nutrition, health, gardening, management of family and personal resources, decorating, gardening, and travel. Audience is 99% women. "Over half of our readers live in small towns and rural areas. They are slightly ahead of national averages in income and education. A large percentage are employed outside the home." Circ. 150,000. Pays on publication. Byline given. Buys all rights. Submit seasonal/holiday material 6-8 months in advance. Computer printout submissions acceptable. SASE. Reports in 1 month. Sample copy for $2, 9x12 SAE, and 50¢ postage; writer's guidelines for 9x12 SAE and 1 first class stamp.

Nonfiction: Humor (women's experiences); inspirational (non-sectarian, non-denominational); and personal experience (homemaking in unusual locations). Does not want anything derogatory of women or anything political. Buys 20 mss/year. Query. Length: 800-2,000 words. Pays 10¢/word minimum.

Photos: Pays $15 for 8x10 b&w prints; $25 minimum for 2x2 color slides. Captions, model release, and identification of subjects required.

Fiction: Buys 2 mss/year. Query. Length: 500-1,500 words. Pays 10¢/word minimum.
Poetry: Light verse. Buys 45 poems/year. Length: 4-50 lines. Pays $15-25.

IT'S ME, Your Large-Size Fashion Magazine, Happy Hands Publishing Co., 4949 Byers, Ft. Worth TX 76107. (817)732-7494. Editor: Marilyn Thelen. 80% freelance written. Bimonthly magazine covering fashion and lifestyles for women size 16 and over. "Designed to speak to women who are larger sized, giving them information on lifestyle subjects and fashion to build their sense of self-esteem and encourage them to live a life that is both satisfying and creative. Editorially, we support the thesis that people are the size that they are by choice and that everyone should consider all the choices that life presents . . . we do not take a position that size is at issue . . . but we do stress ways to feel good about oneself by positive thinking, having a healthy body and dressing in a fashionable way." Circ. 200,000. Pays on acceptance. Byline given. Buys first rights and second (reprint) rights to material originally published elsewhere. Submit seasonal/holiday material 6 months in advance. Simultaneous queries and photocopied submissions OK. Computer printout submissions acceptable; no dot-matrix. SASE. Reports in 3 weeks on queries; 1 month on mss. Publishes ms an average of 6 months after acceptance. Writer's guidelines for SASE with 1 first class stamp. Sample copy—send $3.
Nonfiction: Humor; inspirational; celebrity; interview/profile; opinion; personal experience; exercise; health; fitness (information about activities that will stimulate wellness); self discovery features emphasizing self-worth and commitment to a better life; and beauty articles (focusing on hands, feet, skin, makeup and face). "All must be slanted to our readers." Buys 75 mss/year. Query with or without published clips. Length: 1,000-2,000 words. Pays $50-300.
Photos: State availability of photos. Buys only photos to support copy submission. Reviews b&w and color contact sheets; 35mm transparencies and 3x5 b&w and color prints. Captions, model release and identification of subjects required.
Columns/Departments: Entertaining at Home, New Products, Book Reviews, Sewing, and Careers/Jobs. "All must be slanted to our readers." Buys 6-8 mss/year. Query with published clips. Length: 750-2,000 words. Pays $100-250.
Fiction: Short romantic stories. Mini-romances detailing a larger woman facing a lifestyle experience. "We like happy endings." Length: 1,500 words.
Tips: "To write for *It's Me*, it is necessary to be comfortable with people and issues dealing with larger sizes and positive attitudes."

• **LADIES' HOME JOURNAL**, 3 Park Ave., New York NY 10016. Editor: Myrna Blyth. 50% freelance written. Monthly magazine. Pays on acceptance. Prefers story proposals, not completed ms, and does not like multiple submissions. Submit seasonal/holiday material at least 6 months in advance.
Nonfiction: Jan Goodwin, executive editor: investigations/exposés, reportage, celebrity, major medical and human interest. Sondra Forsyth Enos, executive editor: psychological, relationships, child care, education, health, first person stories, "Women Today" column.
Fiction: Constance Leisure, book and fiction editor. Short stories are only accepted through literary agents.

LADYCOM, Downey Communications, Inc., 1732 Wisconsin Ave. NW, Washington DC 20007. Editor: Sheila Gibbons. 90% freelance written. For wives of military men who live in the US or overseas. Published 10 times a year. Magazine. Circ. 500,000. Pays on publication. Buys first North American serial rights and second (reprint) rights to material originally published elsewhere. Submit seasonal/holiday material 6 months in advance. Computer printout submissions acceptable; prefers letter-quality to dot-matrix. SASE. Reports in 4 weeks. Publishes ms an average of 6 months after acceptance. Sample copy $1. Free writer's guidelines.
Nonfiction: "All articles must have special interest for military wives. General interest articles are OK if they reflect situations our readers can relate to." How-to (crafts, food), humor, interview, personal experience, personal opinion, health, profile and travel. Buys 50 unsolicited mss/year. "Query letter should name sources, describe focus of article, use a few sample quotes from sources, indicate length, and should describe writer's own qualifications for doing the piece." Length: 800-2,000 words. Pays $475-600/article.
Photos: Purchased with accompanying ms and on assignment. Uses 5x7 or 8x10 b&w glossy prints; 35mm or larger color transparencies; stock photo fee payment for photo with accompanying ms. Captions and model releases are required. Query art director.
Columns/Departments: It Seems to Me—personal experience pieces by military wives. Your Travels—highlights of life at various bases and posts and nearby cities. Also, Your Pet, and Babycom. Query. Length: 1,100-1,800 words. Rates vary.
Fiction: Mystery, romance and suspense. "Military family life or relationship themes only, please!" Buys 6-8 mss/year. Query. Length: 1,500-2,500 words. Pays $150-250.
Tips: "Our ideal contributor is a military wife who can write. However, I'm always impressed by a writer who has analyzed the market and can suggest some possible new angles for us. Sensitivity to military issues is a must for our contributors, as is the ability to write good personality profiles and/or do thorough research about military family life. We don't purchase gothic fiction; hints from Heloise-type material (no one does it better than she does, anyway); Erma Bombeck imitations; Vietnam War-era fiction; and parenting advice that is too personal and limited to the writer's own experience."

LADY'S CIRCLE MAGAZINE, Lopez Publications, Inc., 23 W. 26th St., New York NY 10010. Editor: Mary E. Terzella. For homemakers. Monthly. Buys all rights. Byline given. Pays on publication. Submit seasonal/holiday material 6 months in advance. Reports in 3 months. Query with brief outline. SASE. Free writer's guidelines for SASE.

Nonfiction: "Particularly likes first-person or as-told-to inspirational stories about people coping with or overcoming illnesses/handicaps; pieces about individuals or nonprofit organizations doing good works or helping others. Also how homemakers and mothers make money at home; ways to save time and/or money. Articles on child rearing, home management, dieting, gardening, and problems of the homemaker. Each issue features how-to crafts, needlework and hobbies. Articles must be written on specific subjects and must be thoroughly researched and based on sound authority. We don't feature travel, investments, pet care, car care or decorating pieces." Length: 2,500 words maximum. Pays $125 minimum for 2,500 words.

Photos: Pays $10 each for quality b&w and color photos accompanying articles.

Fiction: Emotional stories of 2,000-2,500 words. "We're looking for stories that touch the heartstrings of the readers whether the emotion be happiness, sadness, grief or triumph. These are stories that homemakers can relate to." Pays $125 minimum for 2,500 words.

McCALL'S, 230 Park Ave., New York NY 10169. Editor: Robert Stein. Managing Editor: Don McKinney. 90% freelance written. "Study recent issues." Our publication "carefully and conscientiously services the needs of the woman reader—concentrating on matters that directly affect her life and offering information and understanding on subjects of personal importance to her." Monthly. Circ. 6,200,000. Pays on acceptance. Pays 20% kill fee. Buys first rights only. Byline given. Computer printout submissions acceptable; no dot-matrix. Reports in 2 months. SASE.

Nonfiction: Don McKinney, managing editor. No subject of wide public or personal interest is out of bounds for *McCall's* so long as it is appropriately treated. The editors are seeking meaningful stories of personal experience. They are on the lookout for new research that will provide the basis for penetrating articles on the ethical, physical, material and social problems concerning readers. They are most receptive to humor. *McCall's* buys 200-300 articles/year, many in the 1,000- to 1,500-word length. Pays variable rates for nonfiction. Mrs. Helen Del Monte and Andrea Thompson are editors of nonfiction books, from which *McCall's* frequently publishes excerpts. These are on subjects of interest to women: biography, memoirs, reportage, etc. Almost all features on food, household equipment and management, fashion, beauty, building and decorating are staff-written. Query. "All manuscripts must be submitted on speculation, and *McCall's* accepts no responsibility for unsolicited manuscripts."

Columns/Departments: "The Mother's Page (edited by Maryann Brinley); short items that may be humorous, helpful, inspiring and reassuring. Pays $100 and up. Vital Signs (edited by Judith Stone); short items on health and medical news. Pay varies. Back Talk (edited by Barbara Blakemore); 1,000-word essay in which the writer makes a firm statement of opinion, often taking an unexpected or unpopular point of view. Whether humorous or serious in tone, the piece must reflect the writer's strong feelings on the subject. Pays $1,000. VIP-ZIP (edited by Annette Canby & Anne Cassidy); high-demography regional section. Largely service-oriented, it covers travel, decorating and home entertainment. The editors are also interested in short essays (humorous or serious) and in profiles for the Singular Woman feature. The woman spotlighted here has accomplished something not expected of her and is someone our readers can admire." Pay varies.

Fiction: Department Editor: Helen DelMonte. "Again the editors would remind writers of the contemporary woman's taste and intelligence. Most of all, fiction can awaken a reader's sense of identity, deepen her understanding of herself and others, refresh her with a laugh at herself, etc. *McCall's* looks for stories which will have meaning for an adult reader of some literary sensitivity. *No* stories that are grim, depressing, fragmentary or concerned with themes of abnormality or violence. *McCall's* principal interest is in short stories; but fiction of all lengths is considered." Length: about 3,000 words average. Length for short-shorts: about 2,000 words. Payment begins at $1,500; $2,000 for full length stories.

Tips: "Except for humor, query first. Material is running shorter than few years ago. We are much more open to very short pieces, 750 words up."

MADEMOISELLE, 350 Madison Ave., New York NY 10017.

Nonfiction: Contact: Articles Editor. 90% assigned to writers whose work is known to the magazine. Directed to college-educated, unmarried working women 18-34. Circ. 1,100,000. Reports in 3-4 weeks. Buys first North American serial rights. Pays on acceptance; rates vary. Prefers written query plus samples of published work. SASE. Particular concentration on articles of interst to the intelligent young woman, including personal relationships, health, careers, and current social problems. Articles should be well-researched and of good quality. Length: 1,500-3,000 words.

Art: Kati Korpijaakko, art director. Commissioned work assigned according to needs. Photos of fashion, beauty, travel. Payment ranges from no-charge to an agreed rate of payment per shot, job series or page rate. Buys all rights. Pays on publication for photos.

Fiction: Eileen Schnurr, fiction editor. Quality fiction by both established and unknown writers. "We are interested in encouraging and publishing new writers and welcome unsolicited fiction manuscripts. However we are not a market for formula stories, genre fiction, unforgettable character portraits, surprise endings or oblique stream of consciousness sketches. We are looking for well-told stories that speak in fresh and individual voices and help us to understand ourselves and the world we live in. Stories of particular relevance to young women have an especially good chance, but stories need not be by or from the point of view of a woman—we are interested in good fiction on any theme from any point of view." Buys first North American serial rights. Pays $1,500 for short stories (10-25 pages); $1,000 for short shorts (7-10 pages). Allow 8-10 weeks for reply. SASE required. In addition to year-round unqualified acceptance of unsolicited fiction manuscripts, *Mademoiselle* conducts a once-a-year fiction contest open to unpublished writers, male and female, 18-30 years old. First prize is $1,000 plus publication in *Mademoiselle*; second prize, $500 with option to publish. Watch magazine for announcement, usually in January issue.

MODERN BRIDE, 1 Park Ave., New York NY 10016. Editor-in-Chief: Cele G. Lalli. Managing Editor: Mary Ann Cavlin. Bimonthly. Buys first periodical publishing rights. Byline given. Pays on acceptance. Reports in 2 weeks. SASE.
Nonfiction: Uses articles of interest to brides-to-be. "We prefer articles on etiquette, marriage and planning a home. Travel is staff written or specially assigned. We edit everything, but don't rewrite without permission." Length: about 2,000 words. Payment averages 25¢/word.
Poetry: Occasionally buys poetry pertaining to love and marriage. Pays $20-30 for average short poem.

MS. MAGAZINE, 119 W. 40th St., New York NY 10018. (212)719-9800. Editor-in-Chief and Publisher: Patricia Carbine. Editor: Gloria Steinem. 50% freelance written. For "women and men; varying ages, backgrounds, but committed to exploring new lifestyles and changes in their roles and society." Monthly. Circ. 450,000. "We do read unsolicited manuscripts: poetry, fiction, and nonfiction articles or profiles. Manuscripts are considered for body-of-the-book articles (3,000 word limit) or for front-of-the-book features (1,500 word limit), and are purchased at competitive magazine prices." Send mss to Manuscript Reader and indicate on envelope what type of piece is being submitted. No mss will be read unless accompanied by SASE. Accepts only 1 in 1,000 unsolicited manuscripts. Rights purchased vary with author and material. Pays on acceptance. Will consider photocopied submissions. Submit seasonal material at least 3 months in advance. Reports in 6-8 weeks. Publishes ms an average of 4 months after acceptance.
Photos: Purchased with mss, without mss, or on assignment. Payment "depends on usage." Address to Art Department.
Tips: "The Gazette section which features short news items is the easiest way to get published here and is especially receptive to regional material from New York; but much has to be rejected because of space limitations and lack of professional standards. We use a lot of material from all over the country on politics, the women's movement and human interest features. It is possible to move from the Gazette to do other work for *Ms*."

MY WEEKLY, The Magazine for Women Everywhere, D.C. Thomson & Co., Ltd., 80 Kingsway E., Dundee DD4 8SL Scotland. Editor: Stewart D. Brown. Weekly entertainment magazine for women. "Entertainment means we do not lecture or try to educate our readers." Circ. 756,512. Pays on acceptance. Byline given. Buys first British serial rights. Submit seasonal/holiday material 3 months in advance. Previously published submissions OK. SASE. Reports in 1 month. Free sample copy.
Nonfiction: General interest; humor (feminine, domestic); interview/profile; personal experience; and photo feature. No political articles, explicit sex or anything that "attempts to lecture" the reader. Buys over 300 mss/year. Send complete ms. Length: 800-3,000 words. Pays variable rates.
Photos: Send photos with ms. Reviews 2¼x2¼ transparencies. Captions, model release and identification of subjects required. Buys one-time rights.
Fiction: Humorous; romance; serialized novels; suspense (with feminine interest); and stories dealing with *real* emotional, domestic problems. No material dealing explicitly with sex, violence or politics. Buys 150 mss/year. Send complete ms. Length: 1,500-6,000 words. Pays variable rates.
Fillers: Short humor (feminine). Length: 800-1,200 words. Pays variable rates.
Tips: "We invite our readers to meet and share the lives and experiences of interesting people—through both first person articles and the interviews our writers supply. Much of this applies to our fiction, too. If our readers read *My Weekly* to 'escape,' it's to escape not into a glossy, unreal world of actresses, millionaires, politicians, but into the 'real' world of other people dealing with the problems of 'ordinary' life with dignity, warmth and humour."

NEW CLEVELAND WOMAN JOURNAL, 106 E. Bridge St., Cleveland OH 44017. (216)243-3740. Editor: Linda Kinsey. Monthly tabloid for women who work outside of the home—either for pay or as volunteers. Geared toward the managerial-level, upwardly-mobile woman. Circ. 30,000. Pays on publication. Byline given. Offers 10% kill fee. Buys negotiable rights. Submit seasonal/holiday material 3 months in advance. Previously published submissions OK "if it didn't appear in the Cleveland area or another women's magazine." SASE. Reports in 5 weeks. Writer's guidelines for business-size SAE and 1 first class stamp. Queries welcome. Not responsible for unsolicited mss improperly sent.

Nonfiction: General interest (only as relates to working women specifically); how-to (succeed in business, manage career and family); humor (relating to working women); interview/profile (of successful women); personal experience (OK in some cases); and travel (as relates to working women). No "general interest that you'd find in any newspaper. Articles must be geared toward our specific market, and must offer the reader information she will benefit from." Buys 60 mss/year. Query with published clips or send complete ms. Length: 1,500 words maximum. Pays 80¢/column inch.

Photos: State availability of photos or send photos with ms. Pays $5 minimum for 8x10 b&w and color prints. Buys negotiable rights.

Columns/Departments: Buys 36 mss/year. Query with published clips or send complete ms. Length: 750-1,000 words. Pays 40¢/column inch.

Tips: "We are mostly interested in stories that appeal to the Cleveland woman or stories based on national trends."

NEW WOMAN, New Woman, Inc., Drawer 189, Palm Beach FL 33480. (305)833-4583. Editor/Publisher: Margaret Harold Whitehead. Associate Editor/Publisher: Wendy Danforth. Query first *in writing*. "It is essential to familiarize yourself with *New Woman*'s editorial format." SASE. Pays variable rates.

PIONEER WOMAN, Magazine of Pioneer Women/Na'amat, the Women's Labor Zionist Organization of America, Pioneer Women/Na'amat, 200 Madison Ave., New York NY 10016. (212)725-8010. Editor: Judith A. Sokoloff. 80% freelance written. Magazine published 5 times/year covering Jewish themes and issues; Israel; women's issues; Labor Zionism; and occasional pieces dealing with social, political and economic issues. Circ. 30,000. Pays on publication. Byline given. Not copyrighted. Buys first North American serial, one-time and first rights; second serial (reprint) rights to book excerpts; and makes work-for-hire assignments. SASE. Reports in 1 month on queries, 2 months on mss. Free sample copy and writer's guidelines.

Nonfiction: Book excerpts; expose; general interest (Jewish); historical/nostalgic; humor; inspirational; interview/profile; opinion; personal experience; photo feature; travel (Israel); art; and music. "All articles must be of interest to the Jewish community." Buys 35 mss/year. Query with clips of published work or send complete ms. Length: 1,000-3,000 words. Pays 5¢/word.

Photos: State availability of photos. Pays $10-30 for b&w contact sheet and 4x5 or 5x7 prints. Captions and identification of subjects required. Buys one-time rights.

Columns/Departments: Film and book reviews with Jewish themes. Buys 20-25 mss/year. Query with clips of published work or send complete ms. Length: 500-1,000 words. Pays 5¢/word.

Fiction: Historical/nostalgic, humorous, women-oriented, and novel excerpts. "Good intelligent fiction with Jewish slant. No maudlin nostalgia or trite humor." Buys 3 mss/year. Send complete ms. Length 1,200-3,000 words. Pays 5¢/word.

PLAYGIRL, 3420 Ocean Park Blvd., Santa Monica CA 90405. (213)450-0900. Editor: Dianne Grosskopf. Senior Editor: Vanda Krefft. 30% freelance written. Monthly entertainment magazine for 20-29 year old females. Circ. 850,000. Average issue includes 4 articles and 1 interview. Pays 1 month after acceptance. Byline given. Offers 15% kill fee. Buys all rights. Submit seasonal material 4 months in advance. Simultaneous and photocopied submissions OK, if so indicated. SASE. Reports in 1 month on queries; in 2 months on mss. Publishes ms an average of 3 months after acceptance. Free writer's guidelines with SASE. Sample copy $5.

Nonfiction: Vanda Krefft, articles editor. Travel pieces; "humor for the modern woman"; exposes (related to women's issues); interview (Q&A format with major show business celebrities); articles on sexuality; hard information on credit and finances; medical breakthroughs; relationships; coping; and careers. Buys 4 mss/issue. Query with clips of previously published work. Length: 2,500 words. Pays $500-850.

Fiction: Mary Ellen Strote, fiction editor. Contemporary romance stories of 2,500 words. Send complete fiction ms. "The important thing to remember is we don't want graphic sex, and no adventure, suspense, science fiction, murder or mystery stories. We want something emotional." Pays $300 and up for fiction.

Tips: "We are not a beginner's nonfiction market. We're looking for major clips and don't really consider nonpublished writers."

REDBOOK MAGAZINE, 224 W. 57th St., New York NY 10019. (212)262-8284. Editor-in-Chief: Annette Capone. Managing Editor: Jennifer Johnson. Health Editor: Jean Maguire. Monthly magazine; 200 pages. Circ. 3,800,000. Rights purchased vary with author and material. Computer printout submissions acceptable; prefers letter-quality to dot-matrix. Pays on acceptance. SASE. Reports in 6-8 weeks. Publishes ms an average of 5 months after acceptance. Free writer's guidelines on writing fiction for *Redbook* for SASE.

Nonfiction: Karen Larson, articles editor. Articles relevant to the magazine's readers, who are women 18-34 years old. Also interested in submissions for Young Mother's Story. "We are interested in stories for the Young Mother series offering the dramatic retelling of an experience involving you, your husband and child. Possible topics might include: how you have handled a child's health or school problem, or conflicts within the family.. For each 1,500-2,000 words accepted for publication, we pay $750. Mss accompanied by a large, stamped, self-addressed envelope, must be signed, and mailed to: Young Mother's Story, c/o *Redbook Maga-*

zine. Length: articles, 2,500-3,000 words; short articles, 1,000-1,500 words. Young Mother's reports in 3-4 months."

Fiction: Kathyrne Sagan, associate fiction editor. "Out of the 35,000 unsolicited manuscripts that we receive annually, we buy about 50 stories/year. We find many more stories that, for one reason or another, are not suited to our needs but are good enough to warrant our encouraging the author to send others. Sometimes such an author's subsequent submission turns out to be something we can use. *Redbook* looks for stories by and about men and women, realistic stories and fantasies, funny and sad stories, stories of people together and people alone, stories with familiar and exotic settings, love stories and work stories. But there are a few things common to all of them, that make them stand out from the crowd. The high quality of their writing, for one thing. The distinctiveness of their characters and plots; stock characters and sitcom stories are not for us. We look for stories with a definite resolution or emotional resonance. Cool stylistic or intellectual experiments are of greater interest, we feel, to readers of literary magazines than of a magazine like *Redbook* that tries to offer insights into the hows and whys of day-to-day living. And all the stories reflect some aspect of the experience, the interests, or the dreams of *Redbook*'s particular readership." Short-short stories (7-9 pages, 1,400-1,600 words) are always in demand; but short stories of 10-15 pages, (3,000-5,000 words) are also acceptable. Stories 20 pages and over have a "hard fight, given our tight space limits, but we have bought longer stories that we loved. *Redbook* no longer reads unsolicited novels." Manuscripts must be typewritten, double-spaced, and accompanied by SASE the size of the manuscript. Payment begins at $850 for short shorts; $1,000 for short stories.

Tips: "It is very difficult to break into the nonfiction section, although the Young Mother's story, which publishes short personal experience pieces (1,500-2,000 words), does depend on freelancers."

SAVVY, The Magazine for Executive Women, 111 8th Ave., New York NY 10011. (212)255-0990. Editor: Wendy Reid Crisp. 75% freelance written. Monthly magazine covering the business and personal aspects of life for highly educated, professional career women. Circ. 300,000. Average issue includes 4-6 features. Pays on publication. Byline given. Buys first North American serial rights. SASE. Reports in 1-2 months. Publishes ms an average of 6 months after acceptance.

Nonfiction: General interest. Articles should be slanted toward high level executive women who have a wide range of interests with an emphasis on their professional concerns. No "food, home, decorating or 'helpful hint' articles. Send in one or two well-developed ideas and some previously published work to show how you carry out your ideas." Recent article example: "Boot Camp For Business," by Amanda Segal (March 84). "We require articles on speculation before we make an assignment to a writer not known to us." Query with clips of previously published work; letters should be "concise and to the point, with the angle of the proposed article made very specific and should include SASE." Length: 1,500-3,500 words. Pays $400-850.

Photos: Wendy Palitz, art director.

Columns/Departments: Tools of the Trade (ideas and strategies for doing business better, 500-1,500 words); and 1,000 Words (essays on anything of general interest to executive women based on personal experience, 750 words). Departments: Professional Connections (women's business networks), Health, Executive Etiquette, Consuming Passions, Frontlines (short news items), Brief Encounters (personal essays), and others.

Tips: "We commission at least 75% of the articles we publish. Unsolicited manuscripts that come to us are generally inappropriate. It is essential that writers have a solid familiarity with the magazine before submitting material."

SELF, Conde-Nast, 350 Madison Ave., New York NY 10017. (212)880-8834. Editor: Phyllis Starr Wilson. Managing Editor: Valorie Weaver. 50% freelance written. Monthly magazine emphasizing self improvement of emotional and physical well-being for women of all ages. Circ. 1,029,315. Average issue includes 12-20 feature articles and 3-4 columns. Pays on acceptance. Byline given. Offers 20% kill fee. Buys first North American serial rights. Submit seasonal material 4 months in advance. Simultaneous and photocopied submissions OK. Computer printout submissions acceptable; prefers letter-quality to dot-matrix. SASE. Reports in 1 month. Free (but minimal) writer's guidelines.

Nonfiction: Well-researched service articles on self improvement, mind, the psychological angle of daily activities, health, careers, nutrition, male/female relationships and money. "We try to translate major developments and complex information in these areas into practical, personalized articles." Buys 6-10 mss/issue. Query with clips of previously published work. Length: 1,000-2,500 words. Pays $700-1,500. "We are always looking for any piece that has a psychological or behavioral side. We rely heavily on freelancers who can take an article on interior decorating, for example, and add a psychological aspect to it. Everything should relate to the whole person."

Photos: Submit to art director. State availability of photos. Reviews 5x7 b&w glossy prints.

Columns/Departments: Self issues (800-1,000 words on current topics of interest to women such as nutrition and diet scams, finding time for yourself, personal decision making and political issues); Health Watch (800-1,000 words on health topics); and Your Money (800-1,000 words on finance topics). Buys 1-2 mss/issue. Query. Pays $700-1,200.

Tips: "Original ideas backed up by research, not personal experiences and anecdotes, open our doors."

SUNDAY WOMAN, The King Features Syndicate, 235 E. 45th, New York NY 10017. Editor: Merry Clark. 90% freelance written. A weekly newspaper supplement which runs in more than 50 markets in the US and Canada with circulation of more than 3 million. Buys first rights, and second (reprint) rights to material originally published elsewhere. Sample issue and writer's guidelines for SASE (8x10).
Nonfiction: Solid, reportorial articles on topics affecting women, their families, lifestyles, relationships, careers, health, money, and business. "We often run a fascinating success story about women in business or about women entrepreneurs." Also uses celebrity cover stories. No food, fashion or pet stories. 1,500-2,000 words. National focus. No poetry, fiction or essays. Pays $50-500 upon acceptance. "We are happy to consider first person stories-reprints only—for Outlook column." Reports in 2 weeks. "Submit previously published pieces for second serial publication by us." Include cover letter with address, phone number, and Social Security number; not responsible for mss submitted without SASE. Manuscripts should be typed and double-spaced. Computer printout submissions acceptable; no dot-matrix. "Query, short and to the point, with clips of published material." No phone calls.
Tips: "Women and women's roles are changing dramatically. *Sunday Woman* is reflecting this. I don't want the same old service piece or 'First Woman' stories. We're moving on from that. Writers must come up with story ideas that also reflect these changes."

‡**TODAY'S CHRISTIAN WOMAN**, 184 Central Ave., Old Tappan NJ 07675. Editor: Dale Hanson Bourke. Senior Editor: Evelyn Bence. A bimonthly magazine for Christian women of all ages, single and married, homemakers and career women. Circ. 150,000. Pays on acceptance. Byline given. Buys first rights only. Submit seasonal/holiday material 6 months in advance. Simultaneous queries OK. Computer printout submissions acceptable; prefers letter-quality to dot-matrix. SASE. Sample copy $3.50; free writer's guidelines.
Nonfiction: Book excerpts, how-to and inspirational (a woman's "turning point"). Query. "The query should include experience, a brief description of the article, a short excerpt and an explanation of its value to our readers. Each issue we publish an article on a woman's turning point. It is based on a change in attitude." Pays 10¢/ word.
Fiction: Historical, humorous, mystery, religious, romance and suspense. Query.

VOGUE, 350 Madison Ave., New York NY 10017. (212)880-8800. Editor: Grace Mirabella. Monthly magazine for highly intelligent women. Pays variable rates on acceptance "depending on the material, our needs, and the specialization of the writer." Buys variable rights. Byline given. Computer printouts acceptable; prefers letter-quality to dot-matrix. SASE.
Nonfiction: Contact: Features Editor. Uses articles and ideas for features. Fashion articles are staff-written. Material must be of high literary quality, contain good information. Query a must. Length: 500-2,500 words. "Our readers are interested not only in their appearance, but in what goes on inside them both intellectually and physically. They are contemporary American women who have deep and varied interests." Short reviews of theatre, art, books, movies, TV, music and restaurants. Ideal article length is 1,000-1,500 words. "Read Vogue and you'll see the enormous range of subjects we cover."

WOMAN MAGAZINE, Harris Publishing, 1115 Broadway, New York NY 10010. (212)807-7100. Editor: Sherry Amatenstein. 35% freelance written. Magazine published 6 times/year covering "every aspect of a woman's life. Offers self-help orientation, guidelines on lifestyles, careers, relationships, finances, health, etc." Circ. 395,000. Pays on acceptance. Publishes ms an average of 4 months after acceptance. Byline given. Buys all rights or first rights "if requested." Photocopied and previously published submissions OK. Computer printout submissions acceptable; no dot-matrix. SASE. Reports in 2 weeks on queries; 3 weeks on mss. Sample copy $1.75; writer's guidelines for letter-size SAE and 1 first class stamp.
Nonfiction: Book excerpts (most of magazine is book reprints); how-to; humor; inspirational (how I solved a specific problem); interview/profile (short, 200-1,000 words with successful or gutsy women); and personal experience (primary freelance need: how a woman took action and helped herself—emotional punch, but not "trapped housewife" material). No articles on "10 ways to pep up your marriage"—looking for unique angle. Buys 100 mss/year. Query with published clips or send complete ms. Length: 200-1,500 words. Pays $25-125.
Columns/Departments: Bravo Woman (1,000 word interviews with women who overcame numerous obstacles to start their own business); Woman in News (200 word pieces on successful women); and Woman Forum (controversial issues regarding women). Query with published clips or send complete ms. Length: 200-1,000 words. Pays $20-100.
Tips: "We're for all women—ones in and out of the home. We don't condescend, neither should you. Personal experience pieces are your best bet."

WOMAN'S DAY, 1515 Broadway, New York NY 10036. Contact: Editor. 95% freelance written. 15 issues/ year. Circ. over 7,000,000. Buys first and second rights to the same material. Pays negotiable kill fee. Byline given. Pays on acceptance. Computer printout submissions acceptable; no dot-matrix. Reports in 2-4 weeks on queries; longer on mss. Publishes ms an average of 1 year after acceptance. Submit detailed queries first to Rebecca Greer, articles editor. SASE.

Nonfiction: Uses articles on all subjects of interest to women—marriage, family life, child rearing, education, homemaking, money management, careers, family health, work and leisure activities. Also interested in fresh, dramatic narratives of women's lives and concerns. "These must be lively and fascinating to read." Length: 500-3,500 words, depending on material. Payment varies depending on length, type, writer, and whether it's for regional or national use, etc. *Woman's Day* has started a new page called Reflections, a full-page essay running 1,000 words. "We're looking for both tough, strong pieces and softer essays on matters of great and real concern to women. We're looking for strong points of view, impassioned opinions. The topics can be controversial, but they have to be convincing. We look for significant issues—medical ethics and honesty in marriage—rather than the slight and the trivial issues."

Fiction: Contact Eileen Jordan, department editor. Uses high quality, genuine human interest, romance and humor, in lengths between 1,500 and 3,000 words. Payment varies. "We pay any writer's established rate, however."

Fillers: Neighbors and Tips to Share columns also pay $50/each for brief practical suggestions on homemaking, child rearing and relationships. Address to the editor of the appropriate section.

Tips: "We are publishing more articles and devoting more pages to textual material. We're departing from the service format once in a while to print 'some good reads.' We're more interested in investigative journalism."

WOMAN'S WORLD, The Woman's Weekly, Heinrich Bauer North American, Inc., 177 N. Dean St., Box 671, Englewood NJ 07631. (201)569-0006. Editor-in-Chief: Dennis Neeld. Weekly magazine covering "controversial, dramatic, and human interest women's issues" for women across the nation. Pays on acceptance. Byline given. Offers kill fee. Buys first North American serial rights. Submit seasonal/holiday material 4 months in advance. Simultaneous queries, and simultaneous, photocopied and previously published submissions OK. SASE. Reports in 6 weeks on queries; 1-2 months on mss. Sample copy $1 and self-addressed mailing label; writer's guidelines for business-size SAE and 1 first class stamp.

Nonfiction: Well-researched material with "a hard-news edge and topics of national scope." Reports of 1,000 words on vital trends and major issues such as women and alcohol or teen suicide; dramatic, personal women's stories; articles on self-improvement, medicine and health topics; and the economics of home, career and daily life. Features include In Real Life (true stories); Turning Point (in a woman's life); Families (highlighting strength of family or how unusual families deal with problems). Other regular features are Report (1,500-word investigative news features with national scope, statistics, etc.); Women and Crime (true stories of 1,000-1,200 on female criminals "if possible, presented with sympathetic" attitude); Between You and Me (600-word humorous and/or poignant slice-of-life essays); and Living Together (800 words on pop psychology or coping). Queries should be addressed to Jane Bladow, articles editor.

Fiction: Elinor Nauen, fiction editor. Short story, romance and mainstream of 4,500 words and mini-mysteries of 1,200-2,000 words. "Each of our stories has a light romantic theme with a protagonist no older than forty. Each can be written from either a masculine or feminine point of view. Women characters may be single, married or divorced. Plots must be fast moving with vivid dialogue and action. The problems and dilemmas, inherent in them should be contemporary and realistic, handled with warmth and feeling. The stories must have a positive resolution." Not interested in science fiction, fantasy or historical romance. No explicit sex, graphic language or seamy settings. Humor meets with enthusiasm. Pays $1,200 on acceptance for North American serial rights for 6 months. "The mini-mysteries, at a length of 1,700 words, may feature either a 'whodunnit' or 'howdunnit' theme. The mystery may revolve around anything from a theft to a murder. However, we are not interested in sordid or grotesque crimes. Emphasis should be on intricacies of plot rather than gratuitous violence. The story must include a resolution that clearly states the villain is getting his or her come-uppance." Pays $500 on acceptance. Pays approximately 50¢ a published word on acceptance. Buys first North American serial rights. Queries with clips of published work are preferred; accepts complete mss.

Photos: State availability of photos. "State photo leads. Photos are assigned to freelance photographers." Buys one-time rights.

Tips: "Come up with good queries. Short queries are best. We have a strong emphasis on well-researched material. Writers must send research with manuscript including book references and phone numbers for double checking."

WOMEN IN BUSINESS, Box 8728, Kansas City MO 64114. (816)361-6621. Editor: Sharon K. Tiley. 20% freelance written. Bimonthly magazine for working women in all fields and at all levels; ages 26-55; primarily members of the American Women's Association; national coverage. Circ. 110,000. Pays on acceptance. Buys all rights. Phone queries OK. Computer printout submissions acceptable; prefers letter-quality to dot-matrix. SASE. Reports in 2 months. Publishes ms an average of 6 months after acceptance. Free sample copy and writer's guidelines for 9x12 SAE with 88¢ postage.

Nonfiction: General interest, self-improvement, business trends, and personal finance. Articles should be slanted toward the average working woman. No articles on women who have made it to the top or "slice of life opinions/editorials. We also avoid articles based on first-hand experiences (the 'I' stories)." Buys 25 mss/year. Query or submit complete ms. Length: 1,000-1,500 words. Pays $100-200.

Photos: State availability of photos with query or submit with accompanying ms. Pays $50-100 for 8x10 b&w

glossy contact sheet; $150-250 for cover color transparency. Captions preferred. Buys all rights. Model release required.

WOMEN'S CIRCLE, Box 428, Seabrook NH 03874. Editor: Marjorie Pearl. 100% freelance written. Monthly magazine for women of all ages. Buys all rights. Byline given. Pays on acceptance. Submit seasonal material 7 months in advance. Reports in 3 months. Publishes ms an average of 1 year after acceptance. SASE. Sample copy $1. Writer's guidelines for SASE.
Nonfiction: How-to articles of 1,000-2,000 words on handicrafts, all kinds of needlework and dolls. Also articles with b&w photos about female entrepreneurs and hobbyists. Informational approach. Needs Christmas crafts for Christmas annual. Buys 200 mss/year. Query or submit complete ms. Length: open. Pays minimum of 3¢/word, extra for photos.
Tips: "We welcome crafts and how-to directions for any media—crochet, fabric, etc."

WOMEN'S WEAR DAILY, 7 E. 12th St., New York NY 10003. Completely staff-written newspaper.

WOMEN'S WORLD, B'nai B'rith Women, Inc., 1640 Rhode Island Ave. NW, Washington DC 20036. (202)857-6640. Editor: Susan Tomchin. Tabloid published 6 times/year for Jewish women concerned about Israel, Judaism, community affairs, women's issues, public affairs, the elderly, and youth. Circ. 125,000. Pays on acceptance. Byline given. Offers 15% kill fee. Buys first rights only. Submit seasonal/holiday material 4 months in advance. SASE. Reports in 1 month on queries; 2 months on mss. Sample copy for 9x12 SAE and 3 first class stamps.
Nonfiction: Book excerpts (on women and Judaism); general interest (on women and Judaism, social issues); Jewish historical/nostalgic; interview/profile (of interesting women or Jews); and photo feature (on Judaism). Buys 4 mss/year. Query with clips of published work or send complete ms. Length: 500-1,000 words. Pays $25-100.
Photos: State availability of photos. Pays $10-25 for 5x7 b&w prints. Identification of subjects required. Buys one-time rights.

WORKING MOTHER MAGAZINE, McCall's Publishing Co., 230 Park Ave., New York NY 10169. (212)551-9412. Editor: Vivian Cadden. Managing Editor: Mary McLaughlin. For the working mothers in this country whose problems and concerns are determined by the fact that they have children under 18 living at home. Monthly magazine; 140 pages. Circ. 500,000. Pays on acceptance. Buys all rights. Pays 20% kill fee. Byline given. Submit seasonal/holiday material 6 months in advance. SASE. Reports in 1 month. Sample copy $1.95.
Nonfiction: Service humor (material pertinent to the working mother's predicament). "Don't just go out and find some mother who holds a job and describe how she runs her home, manages her children and feels fulfilled. Find a working mother whose story is inherently dramatic." Buys 9-10 mss/issue. Query. Length: 750-2,000 words. Pays $300-500.
Fiction: "Stories that are relevant to working mothers' lives. We are interested in fiction if the right piece comes along, but we're still more interested in nonfiction pieces." Length: 2,000 words (average). Pays an average of $500/story.

WORKING WOMAN, Hal Publications, Inc., 342 Madison Ave., New York NY 10173. (213)309-9800. Executive Editor: Jacqueline Giambanco. Editor: Anne Mollegen Smith. Monthly magazine for executive, professional and entrepreneur women. "Readers are ambitious, educated, affluent managers, executives, and business owners. Median age is 33. Material should be sophisticated, witty, not entry-level, and focus on work-related issues." Circ. 635,000. Pays on acceptance. Byline given. Offers 20% kill fee after attempt at rewrite to make ms acceptable. Buys all rights, first rights for books, and second serial (reprint) rights. Submit seasonal/holiday material 6 months in advance. Computer printout submissions acceptable; prefers letter-quality to dot-matrix. SASE. Sample copy for $2.50 and 8½x12 SAE.
Nonfiction: Julia Kagan, articles editor. Book excerpts; how-to (management skills, small business); humor; interview/profile (high level executive, political figure or entrepreneur preferred); new product (office products, computer/high tech); opinion (issues of interest to managerial, professional entrepreneur women); personal experience; technical (in management or small business field); travel (businesswomen's guide); and other (business). No child-related pieces that don't involve work issues; no entry-level topics; no fiction/poetry. Buys roughly 200 mss/year. Query with clips of published work. Length: 250-3,000 words. Pays $50-750.
Photos: State availability of photos with ms.
Columns: Management/Enterprise, Basia Hellwig; Career/Consumer, Jacqueline Paris-Chitanvis; Auto/Education/Ethics, Donna Brown; Law, Technology, Paula Gottlieb. Query with clips of published work. Length: 1,200-1,500 words. Pays $400.
Tips: "Be sure to include clips with queries and to make the queries detailed (including writer's expertise in the area, if any). Columns are more open than features. We do not accept phone submissions."

Close-up

Kate Rand Lloyd
Editor-at-Large
Working Woman

When Kate Rand Lloyd joined *Working Woman* as editor-in-chief, she outlawed the words, "busy schedule" and "hectic day." True, the words describe her own and her readers' schedules. But, in articles from writers, she wants more than clichés.

Now addressing groups across the country, Lloyd tells writers and readers to avoid the easy, boring communication brought on by clichés.

"I have learned so much more about everything since I went on the road for *Working Woman* than I knew when I sat behind a desk," she says.

It was from behind a desk, in fact, that Lloyd watched and worked for women's magazines as they evolved. The former managing editor for *Vogue* and *Glamour* has spent 40 years writing and editing for women. "The trap for any writer or editor is cutting off lines of communication," she says, suggesting that aspiring *WW* writers join as many organizations as possible—and read the magazine. Also listen to what working women are talking about.

"You have to just take that extra ounce of energy to develop a story line that is not only appropriate but irresistible," said Lloyd after giving a lively talk at a YWCA luncheon. (She had a plane to catch, a call to make to the office, and a reader who politely interrupted this interview to ask for an autograph. Lloyd apologized that there is so little time.)

WW editors always collect information about work areas and social change. "What we don't have time to do is to see how to take that body of material and turn it into the appropriate story slanted for our audience," she says. "When you find a writer who can do that for you, she or he is going to get a lot of work."

Lloyd whose career began as a staff writer for *Vogue* looks for writers with the "gift of words." This gift, she admits, is hard to describe: "You know it when you see it."

When Joan Didion wrote promotion copy for *Vogue*, editors knew Didion had the gift of words. "The words go together in a way that produces not only information but an image or an emotion, or a quality of place or community atmosphere, an atmosphere beyond the information provided by the words," points out Lloyd.

But gifted words—without research—can't convey sophisticated business and financial information. "Our audience is becoming more sophisticated every day," she says. "We will see some broadening of the issues that we discuss, as women become more concerned about political, social, and economic trends in this country and take charge themselves."

Lloyd's on-the-road research keeps *WW* a step ahead of trends. In one week, for example, she heard women in Chicago, Houston, and Philadelphia talking about owning their own businesses. As a result, the magazine discussed entrepreneurship two years before most media noticed, she says. *WW* now has a column devoted to the subject.

"It's that kind of scavenging in the minds of women that we have to do in order to stay on top," stresses Lloyd.

That's why women learn about more than *hectic* schedules in the magazine.

Trade, Technical, and Professional Journals

"Knowledge is the only instrument of production that is not subject to diminishing returns."

—J.M. Clark,
Journal of Political Economy (1927)

From accounting to veterinary medicine, trade journals supply the latest knowledge to colleagues in a particular field. They show the field's experts how to earn more, learn more, and do more—more efficiently.

Some journals are *the voice* of an industry; others contribute to the industry's total *voice*. And that's why any writer who thinks small circulations signal an easy market should avoid this specialized group of magazines.

"I'm not going to pay full price for an article that a writer has done for another industry and thinks would be just great for me with a few editing changes," says one editor.

Thumbing through trade journals is like going to a trade convention—people talk *shop* and everyone understands. If you can't converse with such a crowd, query a consumer magazine in that field instead. The exception, of course, is for stories where research and an objective eye can uncover useful trade information.

Finding trade-knowledgable writers can be a problem for editors who, themselves, are sometimes experts in a field. They can immediately spot inaccuracies in an article.

Most trade journal editors prefer queries to complete manuscripts. Including your credentials and evidence of your experience in the field (in the query) is essential to landing an assignment. If you work (by day) in a particular trade, you have an immediate advantage. Try writing for that trade audience.

In addition to technical trade journals, company publications are another option for the writer. This year's *Writer's Market* lists the trade-oriented company publications in the Trade Journals section. The symbol (●) will enable you to spot these company publications at a glance. Company publications that feature general interest material for a firm's employees and friends are listed in the consumer section of the book.

Like consumer magazine editors, trade editors encounter deadlines and space limitations and also editorial problems characteristic of their fields. "The rapid pace of change in technical fields places greater emphasis on timeliness," says one trade editor. "We seldom have the luxury of working with an author over a period of several months to bring a story to perfection."

As at consumer magazine offices, trade journal editors fear that computer printouts are simultaneous submissions. (See the Consumer Magazine introduction for more on this subject.) "I hate getting mass-produced queries from 'experts' in accounting and promising stories 'tailored' to the gourmet industry," says another editor. "It's so obviously one of one hundred similar queries sent to a hundred different trade magazines."

Trade journals are highly competitive with one another. Reading copies of the magazine you hope to query and its competition gives you an insider's edge. Such knowledge can lead to increasing returns (perhaps a byline and check) for you—and future assignments.

Accounting

The accountant doesn't subscribe to a trade journal to read about what he already knows. He wants to learn more efficient ways to do his job—and trends that might affect his job. Some accountants are wondering what impact the microcomputer will have in cutting auditing costs. It is this and other trends that accounting trade journals explore. If you want to write for an accounting magazine, first find out about its readers. Are they accountants in a small firm or corporate treasurers? Reading the magazine will generally give you answers to this question. Also don't assume that an accounting practice in the United States will thrill editors of Canadian trade journals. As one magazine editor points out, "All submissions must be relevant to *Canadian* accounting."

CA MAGAZINE, 150 Bloor St., W., Toronto, Ontario M5S 2Y2 Canada. Editor: Nelson Luscombe. 10% freelance written. Monthly magazine for accountants and financial managers. Circ. 55,000. Pays on publication for the article's copyright. Buys first rights only. Computer printout submissions acceptable; prefers letter-quality to dot-matrix. Publishes ms an average of 4 months after acceptance.
Nonfiction: Accounting, business, management and taxation. "We accept whatever is relevant to our readership, no matter the origin as long as it meets our standards. No inflation accounting articles or nonbusiness, nonaccounting articles." Length: 3,000-5,000 words. Pays $100 for feature articles, $75 for departments and 10¢/word for acceptable news items.

CASHFLOW, Coordinated Capital Resources, Inc., 1807 Glenview Rd., Glenview IL 60025. (312)998-6688. Editor: Vince DiPaolo. 50% freelance written. Magazine published 10 times/year, covering treasury professionals in organizations or "professionals who are called upon to fulfill corporate treasury functions." Almost half hold the 'Treasurer' title and the remainder are either directly or peripherally involved in treasury activities. A good number hold CPAs or other professional designations. Circ. 13,000. Pays on publication. Byline sometimes given. Buys all rights. Electronic submissions OK if compatible with Apple WordStar. Computer printout submissions acceptable. SASE. Reports in 1 month. Publishes ms an average of 75 days after acceptance. Sample copy $6; free writer's guidelines.
Nonfiction: Material must specifically relate to the interests of treasury managers. Accepts no material "without a query first." Buys 10 mss/year. Send query and outline with clips of published work. Length: 1,000-2,500 words ("set by editor when assigning article"). Pays $7/published inch.
Photos: Reviews b&w and color contact sheets, negatives, transparencies and prints. Model release and identification of subjects required.
Tips: "Opportunities are also available to cover news beats on a monthly basis. Contact editor for details."

CGA MAGAZINE, Suite 740, 1176 W. Georgia St., Vancouver, British Columbia V6E 4A2 Canada. (604)669-3555. 50% freelance written. For accountants and financial managers. Magazine published 12 times/year; 48 pages. Circ. 33,000. Pays on acceptance. Buys first rights. Byline given. Phone queries OK. Simultaneous and photocopied submissions OK. Computer printout submissions acceptable; prefers letter-quality to dot-matrix. SASE. Reports in 2-4 weeks. Publishes ms an average of 3 months after acceptance. Free sample copy and writer's guidelines.
Nonfiction: "Accounting and financial subjects of interest to highly qualified professional accountants. All submissions must be relevant to Canadian accounting. All material must be of top professional quality, but at the same time written simply and interestingly." How-to, informational, academic, research, and technical. Buys 36 mss/year. Query with outline and estimate of word count. Length: 1,500-5,000 words. Pays $150-500.
Illustrations: State availability of photos, tables, charts or graphs with query. Offers no additional payment for illustrations.

● Bullet preceding a listing indicates a company publication.

Advertising, Marketing, and PR

Trade journals for professional advertising executives, copywriters and marketing and public relations professionals are listed in this category. Those whose main interests are the advertising and marketing of specific products (such as Beverages and Bottling and Hardware) are classified under individual product categories. Journals for sales personnel and general merchandisers are found in the Selling and Merchandising category.

ADVERTISING AGE, 740 N. Rush, Chicago IL 60611. (312)649-5200. Managing Editor: Richard L. Gordon. Currently staff-produced. Includes weekly sections devoted to one topic (i.e., marketing in southern California, agribusiness/advertising, TV syndication trends). Much of this material is done freelance—on assignment only. Pays kill fee "based on hours spent plus expenses." Byline given "except short articles or contributions to a roundup."

ADVERTISING TECHNIQUES, ADA Publishing Co., 10 E. 39th St., New York NY 10616. (212)889-6500. Managing Editor: Lauren Bernstein. 30% freelance written. For advertising executives. Monthly magazine; 50 pages. Circ. 4,500. Pays on acceptance. Not copyrighted. Buys first and second rights to the same material. Reports in 1 month. Publishes ms an average of 2 months after acceptance. Sample copy $1.75.
Nonfiction: Articles on advertising techniques. Buys 10 mss/year. Query. Pays $25-50.

ADVERTISING WORLD, The Magazine For Multi-National Advertising, Directories International, Inc., Suite 610, 150 5th Ave., New York NY 10011. (212)807-1660. Editor: Caroline W. Krebs. Managing Editor: Jack A. Smith. Bimonthly magazine for advertising executives (both in advertising companies and agencies) and media executives (publishers, representatives). "*AW* talks about multinational advertising from a US base: how to select media, how to plan a campaign." Circ. 5,050. Pays on publication. Byline given. Makes work-for-hire assignments. Submit seasonal/holiday material 2 months in advance. Simultaneous queries OK. SASE. Reports in 2 weeks. Free sample copy.
Nonfiction: Technical (international advertising and marketing). No articles not specifically pertaining to international advertising and/or marketing. Buys 20 mss/year. Query. Length: 3-5 pages. Pays 50¢/column line.
Columns/Departments: Media Notes & Quotes (new developments on the international media front); Other Notes & Quotes (developments on international advertising front not specifically about the media). Buys few items; material usually compiled from press releases. Query. Length: short. Pays 50¢/column line.
Tips: "This is not really a freelancer's publication; our writers tend to be practitioners of international advertising who don't rely on us for income (we pay very little and not until publication), just for prestige in the industry."

AMERICAN DEMOGRAPHICS, American Demographics, Inc., Box 68, Ithaca NY 14851. (607)273-6343. Editor: Bryant Robey. Managing Editor: Caroline Eckstrom. 50% freelance written. For business executives, market researchers, media and communications people, public policymakers and those in academic world. Monthly magazine; 52 pages. Circ. 7,000. Pays on publication. Publishes ms an average of 5 months after acceptance. Buys all rights. Submit seasonal/holiday material 5-6 months in advance. Simultaneous, photocopied and previously published submissions OK. Electronic submissions OK if 5" disk, text file. Computer printout submissions acceptable; prefers letter-quality to dot-matrix. SASE. Reports in 1 month on queries; in 2 months on mss. Include self-addressed stamped postcard for return word that ms arrived safely. Sample copy $5.
Nonfiction: General interest (on demographic trends, implications of changing demographics, profile of business using demographic data); and how-to (on the use of demographic techniques, psychographics, understand projections, data, apply demography to business and planning). No anecdotal material or humor.
Tips: "Writer should have clear understanding of specific population trends and their implications for business and planning."

ART DIRECTION, Advertising Trade Publications, Inc., 10 E. 39th St., New York NY 10016. (212)889-6500. Managing Editor: Lauren Bernstein. 15% freelance written. Emphasis on advertising design for art directors of ad agencies (corporate, in-plant, editorial, freelance, etc.). Monthly magazine; 100 pages. Circ. 12,000. Pays on publication. Buys one-time rights. SASE. Reports in 3 months. Sample copy $3.
Nonfiction: How-to articles on advertising campaigns. Pays $25 minimum.

‡● **BARTER COMMUNIQUE**, Full Circle Marketing Corp., Box 2527, Sarasota FL 33578. (813)349-3300. Editor-in-Chief: Robert J. Murely. 100% freelance written. Emphasizes bartering for radio and TV sta-

tion owners, cable TV, newspaper and magazine publishers and select travel and advertising agency presidents. Semiannual tabloid; 48 pages. Circ. 50,000. Pays on publication. Publishes ms an average of 3 months after acceptance. Rights purchased vary with author and material. Phone queries OK. Simultaneous, photocopied and previously published submissions OK. Computer printout submissions acceptable. SASE. Reports in 4 weeks. Free sample copy and writer's guidelines.

Nonfiction: Articles on "barter" (trading products, goods and services, primarily travel and advertising). Length: 1,000 words. "Would like to see travel mss on southeast US and the Bahamas, and unique articles on media of all kinds. Include photos where applicable. No manuscripts on barter for products, goods and services—primarily travel and media—but also excess inventory of business to business." Pays $30-50.

Tips: "Computer installation will improve our ability to communicate."

‡**BEST MEDIA**, EGW International Corp., #8, 1300 Galaxy Way, Concord CA 94520. (415)671-9852. Editor: Ellen DasGupta. A quarterly magazine covering mail order advertising. Estab. 1983. Circ. 10,000. Pays on publication. Buys all and second serial (reprint) rights. Submit seasonal/holiday material 6 months in advance. Simultaneous queries, and simultaneous, photocopied and previously published submissions OK. SASE. Reports in 2 weeks on queries; 2 months on mss. Sample copy $1; free writer's guidelines.

Nonfiction: How-to and other articles related to mail order advertising. Buys 16 mss/year. Query. Length: 1,000-1,500 words. Pays $25-100.

Columns/Departments: Buys 4 mss/year. Query. Length: 250-1,000 words. Pays $10-50.

Fillers: Jokes, anecdotes, short humor and newsbreaks. Buys 10/year. Length: 100-500 words. Pays $2-20.

BUSINESS MARKETING, Crain Communications, Inc., 740 N. Rush St., Chicago IL 60611. (312)649-5260. Editor: Bob Donath. Managing Editor: Dan Brown. Monthly magazine covering the advertising, sales and promotion of business and industrial products and services for an audience in marketing/sales middle management and corporate top management. Circ. 35,000. Rights reserved. Send queries first. Submit seasonal material 3 months in advance; 1½ months in advance for spot news. SASE. Computer printout submissions without format coding acceptable. Reports in 1 month on queries. Sample copy $3.

Nonfiction: Expose (of marketing industry); how-to (advertise, do sales management promotion, do strategy development); interview (of industrial marketing executives); opinion (on industry practices); profile; and technical (advertising/marketing practice). "No self promotion or puff pieces." No material aimed at the general interest reader. Buys 10 mss/year. Query. Length: 1,000-2,000 words.

Photos: State availability of photos. Reviews 8x10 b&w glossy prints and color transparencies. Offers no additional payment for photos accepted with ms. Captions preferred; model release required.

Columns/Departments: Query. Length: 500-1,000 words. "Column ideas should be queried, but generally we have no need for paid freelance columnists."

Fillers: Newsbreaks. Buys 2 mss/issue. Length: 100-500 words.

THE COUNSELOR MAGAZINE, Advertising Specialty Institute, NBS Bldg., 1120 Wheeler Way, Langhorne PA 19047. (215)752-4200. Editor: Theresa Crown. For executives, both distributors and suppliers, in the ad specialty industry. Monthly magazine; 250 pages. Circ. 5,000. Pays on acceptance. Buys first rights only. No phone queries. Submit seasonal/holiday material 3 months in advance. Simultaneous, photocopied and previously published submissions OK. Reports in two months.

Nonfiction: Contact: Managing Editor. How-to (promotional case histories); interview (with executives and government figures); profile (of executives); and articles on specific product categories. Articles almost always have a specialty advertising slant and quotes from specialty advertising practitioners." Buys 30 mss/year. Length: 1,000 words minimum. Query with samples. Pays $150-190.

Photos: State availability of photos. B&w photos only. Prefers contact sheet(s) and 5x7 prints. Offers no additional payment for photos accepted with ms. Captions and model releases required. Buys one-time rights.

Tips: "If a writer shows promise, we can modify his suggestions to suit our publication and provide leads. Writers must be willing to adapt or rewrite their material for a specific audience. If an article is suitable for 5 or 6 other publications, it's probably not suitable for us. The best way to break in is to write for *Imprint*, a quarterly publication we produce for the clients of ad specialty counselors. *Imprint* covers promotional campaigns, safety programs, trade show exhibits, traffic builders and sales incentives—all with a specialty advertising tie-in."

‡**DIRECT RESPONSE PROFIT-LETTER**®, "Your Private Post-Graduate Course in Target Marketing", PMG Publications/An Operating Division of Pacific Marketing Group, Suite 3-627, 1750 Kalakaua Ave., Honolulu HI 96286. (808)942-3786. Editor: Thom Reiss. 40% freelance written. A monthly newsletter covering direct response marketing/direct mail/mail order for business executives, entrepreneurs, consultants and those involved in the marketing of goods or services by direct marketing. Estab. 1983. Pays on acceptance. Byline given. Offers 10% kill fee. Buys all rights and makes work-for-hire assignments. Simultaneous and photocopied submissions OK. Computer printout submissions acceptable. SASE. Reports in 2 weeks on queries; 1 month on mss. Publishes ms an average of 3 months after acceptance. Sample copy for $8, SAE and 1 first

class stamp; writer's guidelines for SAE and 1 first class stamp.

Nonfiction: How-to (advertising copy, graphic design, mail-order, marketing, list management, etc.); and new product (suitable for mail order selling). "We publish 4 Special Research Reports annually. All are freelance written. Query for subject suitability." Buys 4-20 mss/year. Query. Length: 5,000-10,000 words. Pays $500-1,000.

Columns/Departments: Direct Response Copywriting, Direct Mail/Mail Order Graphic Design, Telemarketing, Publicity and Promotion (as they related to direct marketing). Buys 80-100 mss/year. Send complete ms. Length: 50-400 words. Pays $50-100.

Fillers: Clippings, newsbreaks. Buys 25-50/year. Length: 25-100 words. Pays $10-25.

Tips: "We need material for our Special Research Reports. We are also very open now for interview pieces with very successful mail-order entrepreneurs, stressing 'How they did it'."

DM NEWS, THE NEWSPAPER OF DIRECT MARKETING, DM News Corp., 19 W. 21st St., New York NY 10010. (212)741-2095. Editor: Joe Fitz-Morris. 90% freelance written. Twice-a-month tabloid about direct response marketing for users and producers of direct response marketing throughout the nation. Circ. 27,163. Pays on acceptance. Byline given. Buys first rights and makes work-for-hire assignments. Computer printout submissions acceptable; no dot-matrix. Phone queries OK. Publishes ms an average of 2 weeks after acceptance. SASE.

Nonfiction: "Come up with a newsbeat scoop and check it out with the editor." Query. Pays $50-100.

Photos: Send photos with ms. Reviews 8x10 b&w glossy prints. Offers no additional payment for photos accepted with ms. Captions and model release required. Buys one-time rights.

● **THE FLYING A**, Aeroquip Corp., 300 S. East Ave., Jackson MI 49203. (517)787-8121. Editor-in-Chief: Wayne D. Thomas. 10% freelance written. Emphasizes Aeroquip customers and products. Quarterly magazine; 24 pages. Circ. 30,000. Pays on acceptance. Buys first or second rights, depending upon circumstances. Simultaneous submissions OK. Reports in 1 month.

Nonfiction: General interest (feature stories with emphasis on free enterprise, business-related or historical articles with broad appeal, human interest.) "An Aeroquip tie-in in a human interest story is helpful." No jokes, no sample copies; no cartoons, no short fillers. Buys 1-2 mss/issue. Query with biographic sketch and clips of published work. Length: not to exceed five typewritten pages. Pays $50 minimum.

Photos: Accompanying photos are helpful.

Fillers: Human interest nonfiction. Pays $50 minimum for a two-page article. No personal anecdotes, recipes or fiction. "Suggest the writer contact editor by letter with proposed story outline."

Tips: "We publish a marketing-oriented magazine as opposed to an employee publication. Despite our title, we are *not* an aviation magazine, although we do produce aerospace products."

‡**HIGH-TECH MARKETING**℠, Technical Marketing Corporation, 163 Main St., Westport CT 06880. (203)222-0935. Editor: Patrick J. O'Connor. 45% freelance written. A monthly magazine covering the marketing of high technology products for senior marketing executives in high technology industries. Estab. 1983 (first issue, 3/84). Circ. 10,000. Pays on acceptance. Publishes ms an average of 6 weeks after acceptance. Byline given. Offers negotiable kill fee. Buys first North American serial rights. Submit seasonal/holiday material 6 months in advance. Simultaneous queries and photocopied submissions OK; previously published submissions OK (only if author has rights). Electronic submissions OK; must be IBM PC (MS-DOS) format. Computer printout submissions acceptable. SASE. Reports in 2 weeks on queries; 4 weeks on mss. Sample copy $3; free writer's guidelines.

Nonfiction: Book excerpts (must be on marketing; no texts); how-to (use of techniques; must be aimed at upper level management); interview/profile (of significant individual in marketing); opinion (from practicing marketers *only*); and analyses of marketing strategies based on interviews; and overviews of industry trends. No new product, historical, or academically oriented material; articles must address current problems of marketing strategy and implementation. Buys 50 mss/year. Query with published clips. Length: 2,000-4,000 words. Pays $300-600; "bonuses possible for excellent articles."

Columns/Departments: Normally staff-written.

Tips: "Since we have a strong concept of what we want to do and an editorial calendar planned six months or more in advance, the best way is to call and find out what we're working on, then explain why you're the writer to do a particular piece or contribute a complementary piece. Best possibilities for feature coverage would be single company stories on marketing strategy and interviews with marketing executives. We're looking for people who want to do a first rate job on every article, with a writers willingness to do detailed, extensive research, then craft it into good articles."

IMPRINT, The Magazine of Specialty Advertising Ideas, Advertising Specialty Institute, 1120 Wheeler Way, Langhorne PA 19047. (215)752-4200. Editor: Theresa Crown. Quarterly magazine covering specialty advertising. Circ. 50,000 + . Pays on acceptance. Byline given. Pays $25 kill fee. Buys one-time rights. Submit seasonal/holiday material 6 months in advance. Simultaneous queries OK. Reports in 1 month. Free sample copy.

Nonfiction: How-to (case histories of specialty advertising campaigns); and features (how ad specialties are distributed in promotions). "Emphasize effective use of specialty advertising. Avoid direct-buy situations. Stress the distributor's role in promotions. No generalized pieces on print, broadcast or outdoor advertising." Buys 10-12 mss/year. Query with clips of published work. Length: 750-1,500 words. Pays $50-150.

Photos: State availability of photos. Pays $10-25 for 5x7 b&w prints. Captions, model release and identification of subjects required.

Tips: "Query with a case history suggestion and writing samples. We can provide additional leads. All articles must be specifically geared to specialty advertising (and sometimes, premium) promotions."

INCENTIVE MARKETING, Bill Communications, Inc., 633 3rd Ave., New York NY 10017. (212)986-4800. Editor: Bruce Bolger. For buyers of merchandise and travel used in motivational promotions. Monthly magazine; 100 pages. Circ. 37,000. Pays on acceptance. Buys all rights. Byline given. SASE. Reports in 2 weeks. Sample copy and writer's guidelines $3.

Nonfiction: Informational and case histories. "No bank premium stories, please!" Buys 50 mss/year. Query. Length: 1,000-3,000 words. Pays $125-200.

Tips: "We need coverage in the West, the South and Chicago."

‡THE INFORMATION AGE LETTER, A direct marketing tool for information merchants, Towers Club Press, Box 2038, Vancouver WA 98668. (206)699-4428. Editor: Jerry Buchanan. A monthly newsletter (except Aug. and Dec.) covering advertising and marketing tips for those who deal in information of any type." Estab. 1984. Circ. 250. Pays on publication. No byline given. Buys one-time rights. Submit seasonal/holiday material 6 weeks in advance. Simultaneous, photocopied, and previously published submissions OK. Computer printout submissions acceptable. SASE. Reports in 2 weeks. Sample copy $3.

Nonfiction: How-to (advertise or market information, press releases, etc); mail order tips, postal tips, directories available, cottage industry success stories, etc., newsletters; and new product (software, word processors). No long dissertations or editorials; only "short, pithy, impact news, tips and sources." Buys 50-100 mss/year (estimated). Send complete ms. Length: 50-150 words. Pays $25-75.

Columns/Departments: New books department: Short reviews on books pertaining to main theme, including those on word processing, advertising techniques, salesmanship, information industry, work-at-home themes, consulting, seminars, etc. Buys 10-25 mss/year. Send complete ms. Length: 50-150 words. Pays $15-25.

Fillers: Clippings and newsbreaks. Buys 10-15/year. Length: 35-75 words. Pays $5.

MAGAZINE AGE, 225 Park Ave., New York NY 10169. (212)986-7366. Editor: Wallis Wood. 30% freelance written. Monthly magazine for advertisers and advertising agencies designed to examine how they use a wide range of publications, including consumer, business, trade, farm, etc. Circ. 32,000. Pays on acceptance. Publishes ms an average of 2 months after acceptance. Buys all rights. Computer printout submissions acceptable; prefers letter-quality to dot-matrix. Reports in 2 weeks. Sample copy $3; free writer's guidelines for SASE.

Nonfiction: "We are interested in magazine advertising success and failure stories. We want marketing pieces, case histories, effective use of magazine advertising and current trends." Buys 4 mss/issue. Query first. Will not respond to handwritten inquiries. Length: 3,000 words maximum. Pays $500 maximum.

Tips: "Find an unusual aspect of print advertising."

‡● MORE BUSINESS, 11 Wimbledon Court, Jerico NY 11753. Editor: Trudy Settel. 50% freelance written. "We sell publications material to business for consumer use (incentives, communication, public relations)— look for book ideas and manuscripts." Monthly magazine. Circ. 10,000. Pays on acceptance. Publishes ms an average of 1 month after acceptance. Buys all rights. Computer printout submissions acceptable; no dot-matrix. SASE. Reports in 1 month.

Nonfiction: General interest, how-to, vocational techniques, nostalgia, photo feature, profile and travel. Buys 10-20 mss/year. Word length varies with article. Payment negotiable. Query. Pays $4,000-7,000 for book mss.

‡● THE PRESS, The Greater Buffalo Press, Inc., 302 Grote St., Buffalo NY 14207. Managing Editor: Mary Lou Vogt. Quarterly tabloid for advertising executives at Sunday newspapers, ad agencies, retail chains and cartoonists who create the Sunday funnies. Circ. 4,000. Pays on acceptance. Buys all rights. Photocopied submissions and previously published submissions OK. SASE. Reports in 1 month. Sample copy 50¢; free writer's guidelines.

Nonfiction: Short biographies of people in advertising, retailing, business or unusual occupations. No travel/leisure or personal experience articles. Back issues sent upon written request. Buys 4-6 mss/issue. Query. Length: 800-1,500 words. Pays $100-125.

Photos: State availability of photos (with ms only). Uses 35mm transparencies or larger (color preferred). Offers no additional payment for photos accepted with ms. Captions optional. Photos are usually returned after publication. "We do not accept photographs or artwork unless they accompany a ms."

SALES & MARKETING MANAGEMENT IN CANADA, Ingmar Communications, Ltd., Suite 303, 416 Moore Ave., Toronto, Ontario M4G 1C9 Canada. (416)424-4441. Editor: Ernie Spear. Monthly magazine. Circ. 13,000. Pays on publication. Byline given. Buys first North American serial rights. Simultaneous queries and photocopied submissions OK. Reports in 2 weeks.
Nonfiction: How-to (case histories of successful marketing campaigns). "Canadian articles only." Buys 3 mss/year. Query. Length: 800-1,500 words. Pays $200 maximum.

SIGNS OF THE TIMES, The Industry Journal since 1906, ST Publications, 407 Gilbert Ave., Cincinnati OH 45202. (513)421-2050. Editor: Tod Swormstedt. Managing Editor: Bill Dorsey. 5% freelance written. Magazine published 13 times/year; special buyer's guide between November and December issue. Circ. 16,000. Pays on publication. Publishes ms an average of 3 months after acceptance. Byline given. Buys variable rights. Simultaneous queries, and simultaneous, photocopied and previously published submissions OK. Computer printout submissions acceptable; prefers letter-quality to dot-matrix. SASE. Reports in 2 weeks. Free sample copy. Writer's guidelines flexible.
Nonfiction: Historical/nostalgic (regarding the sign industry); how-to (carved signs, goldleaf, etc.); interview/profile (usually on assignment but interested to hear proposed topics); photo feature (query first); and technical (sign engineering, etc.). Nothing "nonspecific on signs, an example being a photo essay on 'signs I've seen.' We are a trade journal with specific audience interests." Buys 10-12 mss/year. Query with clips. Pays $150-250.
Photos: Send photos with ms. "Sign industry-related photos only. We sometimes accept photos with funny twists or misspellings."

VISUAL MERCHANDISING & STORE DESIGN, ST Publications, 407 Gilbert Ave., Cincinnati OH 45202. Associate Publisher: Pamela Gramke. Editor: Ms. P.K. Anderson. 30% freelance written. Emphasizes store design and merchandise presentation. Monthly magazine; 72 pages. Circ. 10,000. Pays on publication. Buys first and second rights to the same material. Simultaneous and previously published submissions OK. Computer printout submissions acceptable. SASE. Reports in 1 month. Publishes ms an average of 3 months after acceptance.
Nonfiction: Expose; how-to (display); informational (store design, construction, merchandise presentation); interview (display directors and shop owners); profile (new and remodeled stores); new product; photo feature (window display); and technical (store lighting, carpet, wallcoverings, fixtures). No "advertorials" that tout a single company's product or product line. Buys 24 mss a year. Query or submit complete ms. Length: 500-3,000 words. Pays $50-200.
Photos: Purchased with accompanying ms or on assignment.
Tips: "Be fashion and design conscious and reflect that in the article. Submit finished manuscripts with photos or slides always. Look for stories on department and specialty store visual merchandisers and store designers (profiles, methods, views on the industry, sales promotions and new store design or remodels). The size of the publication could very well begin to increase in the year ahead. And with a greater page count, we will need to rely on an increasing number of freelancers."

ZIP MAGAZINE, North American Publishing, 401 N. Broad St., Philadelphia PA 19108. (212)371-4100. Editorial Director: Ray Lewis. Emphasizes marketing, list selection and testing, circulation, communications, and direct mail/mailing systems for mail-oriented professionals in business, industry and direct marketing. Typical articles published recently were on marketing to rural buyers, improved business-to-business communications, and justifying mailroom equipment purchases in a tight economy. Some ideas they would be interested in are "Future of Communications in General," mail-order, telephone marketing, fund raising, publication mail programs, and articles dealing with mail handling/processing. Interested in freelance stories on equipment and methods used to mail, process mail, transfer names onto and out of computers, labeling and packaging. "No clever or cute opinion or overview pieces." Published 12 times/year. Circ. 37,500. Pays on publication in some cases, acceptance in others. Rights purchased vary. No phone queries. Simultaneous, photocopied and previously published submissions OK. Reports in 2 weeks. Free sample copy.
Nonfiction: General interest (about magazine circulation or direct mail stories); how-to (improve mailroom operation, direct marketing case histories); interview, profile and photo features should be about mail-oriented executives and professionals. "We are not interested in personal opinion or experience articles." Buys 10-15 unsolicited mss/year. Query or send complete ms. Length: 500-1,000 words. Pays $100-200.
Photos: State availability of photos or send with ms. Accepts only b&w photos and prefers contact sheet and 4x5 glossy prints. Pays $20-100. Captions preferred. Buys one-time rights.

Agricultural Equipment and Supplies

CUSTOM APPLICATOR, Little Publications, Suite 540, 6263 Poplar Ave., Memphis TN 38119. Editor: Tom Griffin. Managing Editor: Rob Wiley. For "firms that sell and custom apply agricultural chemicals." Circ. 17,000. Buys all rights. Pays on publication. "Query is best. The editor can help you develop the story line regarding our specific needs." SASE.
Nonfiction: "We are looking for articles on custom application firms telling others how to better perform jobs of chemical application, develop new customers, handle credit, etc. Lack of a good idea or usable information will bring a rejection." Length: 1,000-1,200 words "with 3 or 4 b&w glossy prints." Pays 20¢/word.
Photos: Accepts b&w glossy prints.

FARM SUPPLIER, Watt Publishing Co., Sandstone Bldg., Mount Morris IL 61054. (815)734-4171. Editorial Director: Dr. Charles Olentine. For retail farm supply dealers and managers over the US. Monthly magazine; 64 pages. Circ. 30,000. Pays on acceptance. Buys all rights in competitive farm supply fields. Byline given. Phone queries OK. Submit seasonal material or query 2 months in advance. SASE. Computer printout submissions acceptable. Reports in 2 weeks.
Nonfiction: How-to, informational, interview, new product and photo feature. "Articles emphasizing product news and how new product developments have been profitably resold or successfully used. We use material on successful farm dealers, particularly involving custom application, fertilizer, herbicides, etc." No "general how-to articles that some writers blanket the industry with, inserting a word change here or there to 'customize.' " Buys 12 unsolicited mss/year. Recent article example: Feature on North Carolina fertilizer dealer (April 1984). Query. Length: 600-2,000 words. Pays $75-400. "Longer articles must include photos, charts, etc."
Photos: Purchased with accompanying ms. Submit 5x7 or 8x10 b&w prints; 35mm or larger color transparencies. Total purchase price for a ms includes payment for photos.
Tips: "Because of a constantly changing industry, *FS* attempts to work only two months in advance. Freelancers should slant stories to each season in the farm industry—examples: herbicides in January-March, feed and grain in May, application equipment in September—and should provide vertical color photos whenever possible with longer features."

Art, Design, and Collectibles

"It's not necessary to be sloppy to exhibit creativity; a neat manuscript is just as respected . . .," says one editor. The business of art, art administration, architecture, environmental/package design and antique collectibles is covered in these listings. Art-related topics for the general public are located in the Consumer Art category. Antiques magazines are listed in Consumer Hobby and Craft.

ANTIQUES DEALER, 1115 Clifton Ave., Clifton NJ 07013. (201)779-1600. Editor: Nancy Adams. 90% freelance written. For antiques dealers. Monthly magazine. Circ. 7,500. Average issue includes 5 features, 4 columns. Rights purchased vary with author and material; buys all rights. Byline given. Buys 40 mss a year. Pays on publication. Submit seasonal/holiday material 4 months in advance. Will send free sample copy to writer on request. Query first. No photocopied material. Indent paragraphs/type double-space. Reports in 3 weeks. SASE.
Nonfiction: "Remember that we are a trade publication and all material must be slanted to the needs and interests of antiques dealers. Only articles of national interest to dealers; may be tutorial if by authority in one specific field (how to restore antiques, open a dealership, locate a specific antique); otherwise of broad general interest to all dealers and news of the international antique trade. Emphasis is currently on collectibles (20-50 years old), heirlooms (50-100 years old), as well as antiques (over 100 years old). Buys 2 mss/issue. Length: minimum 500 words (2 pages double-spaced); maximum 1,500 words (6 pages double-spaced). Pays $50 full page for features; $1.50/column inch thereafter.
Photos: Should always accompany mss. Pays $10 per b&w photo no smaller than 5x7 (glossy). Professional quality only; no slides, color prints or Polaroids.
Fillers: How-to-run-your-shop-better and humor. Length: 500 words. Pays $50 full page.
Tips: "It is more important that the writer know the subject well, as a specialist, or one interviewing a special-

ist, than demonstrating writing excellence. But I am also looking for good business journalists who can cover shows and interviews well. Send outline of ideas, resume and writing samples."

ART BUSINESS NEWS, Myers Publishing Co., 2135 Summer St., Stamford CT 06905. (203)356-1745. Editor: Jo Yanow. Managing Editor: Caroline Myers Just. Monthly tabloid covering news relating to the art and picture framing industry. Circ. 19,000. Pays on publication. Byline given. Buys all rights. Submit seasonal/holiday material 2 months in advance. Photocopied and simultaneous submissions OK. Computer printout submissions acceptable; prefers letter-quality to dot-matrix. Reports in 2 months. Sample copy $1.50.
Nonfiction: General interest; interview/profile (of persons in the art industry); new product; articles focusing on small business people—framers, art gallery management, art trends; and how-to (occasional articles on "how-to-frame" accepted). Buys 8-20 mss/year. Length: 1,000 words maximum. Query first. Pays $75-250.

ARTS MANAGEMENT, 408 W. 57th St., New York NY 10019. (212)245-3850. Editor: A.H. Reiss. For cultural institutions. Published five times/year. 2% freelance written. Circ. 6,000. Buys all rights. Byline given. Pays on publication. Mostly staff-written. Computer printout submissions acceptable; no dot-matrix. Query. Reports in "several weeks." SASE.
Nonfiction: Short articles, 400-900 words, tightly written, expository, explaining how art administrators solved problems in publicity, fund raising and general administration; actual case histories emphasizing the how-to. Also short articles on the economics and sociology of the arts and important trends in the nonprofit cultural field. Must be fact-filled, well-organized and without rhetoric. Payment is 2-4¢/word. No photographs or pictures.

INDUSTRIAL DESIGN, Design Publications, Inc., 330 W. 42nd St., 11th Fl., New York NY 10036. (212)695-4955. Managing Editor: Steven Holt. 60% freelance written. Subject of this publication is design (of products, packaging, graphics and environments). Bimonthly magazine. Circ. 12,000. Pays on publication. Buys all rights. Byline given. Phone queries OK. Computer printout submissions acceptable; prefers letter-quality to dot-matrix. SASE. Publishes ms an average of 3 months after acceptance. Sample copy $5.
Nonfiction: Expose (design related); how-to (all aspects of design), interview (of important people in design); profile (corporate, showing value of design and/or how design is managed); design history; and new product. "The writer gets top pay and a bonus for hard work, extensive research, a 'how-to' sidebar, and a humorous example or two." Buys 6 unsolicited mss/year. Length: 1,800 words. Query with point-by-point outline and clips of published work. Pays $100-500.
Photos: State availability of photos. Wants very good quality b&w glossy prints and contact sheets. Offers no additional payment for photos accepted with ms. Captions required.
Departments: Portfolio (new products); Visual Communications (graphics, packaging); Environments; and News. Query with clips of published work.
Tips: "Show that you are thoroughly backgrounded on the general aspects of your topic, as well as specifics. Read the magazine."

PROGRESSIVE ARCHITECTURE, 600 Summer St., Box 1361, Stamford CT 06904. Editor: John M. Dixon. Monthly. Buys first-time rights for use in architectural press. Pays on publication. SASE.
Nonfiction: "Articles of technical professional interest devoted to architecture, interior design, and urban design and planning and illustrated by photographs and architectural drawings. We also use technical articles which are prepared by technical authorities and would be beyond the scope of the lay writer. Practically all the material is professional, and most of it is prepared by writers in the field who are approached by the magazine for material." Pays $50-250.
Photos: Buys one-time reproduction rights to b&w and color photos.

Auto and Truck

The journals below aim at automobile, motorcycle, and truck dealers; service department personnel; or fleet operators. Publications for highway planners and traffic control experts are classified in the Government and Public Service category.

AMERICAN CLEAN CAR, Serving the Car & Truck Cleaning Industries, American Trade Magazines, 500 N. Dearborn, Chicago IL 60610. (312)337-7700. Editor: Renald Rooney. Associate Editor: Paul Partyka. Bimonthly magazine of the professional car washing industry for owners and operators of car washes. Circ. 20,000. Pays on publication. Offers negotiable kill fee. Buys first rights and second serial (reprint) rights. Submit seasonal/holiday material 3 months in advance. SASE. Reports in 2 weeks. Free sample copy and writer's guidelines.

Nonfiction: How-to (develop, maintain, improve, etc. car washes); interview/profile (industry leaders); new product (concerned with industry—no payment here); and technical (maintenance of car wash equipment). "We emphasize car wash operation and use features on industry topics: Utility use and conservation, maintenance, management, customer service and advertising. A case study should emphasize how the operator accomplished whatever he or she did—in a way that the reader can apply to his or her own operation. Manuscripts should have no-nonsense, businesslike approach." Buys 18 mss/year. Query. Length: 500-3,000 words. Pays 6-8¢/word.

Photos: State availability of photos. Pays $6-8 for each photo used. Supply b&w contact sheet. Captions required. Buys all rights.

Columns/Departments: "Most of our columnists are from the industry or somehow related." Buys 18 mss/year. Query. Length: 500-1,000 words. Pays $50-55.

Fillers: Clippings and newsbreaks. Buys 6-12/year. Length: 200-300 words. Pays 6-8¢/word.

Tips: "Query about subjects of current interest. Be observant of car wash operations—how they are designed and equipped; how they serve customers; and how (if) they advertise and promote their services. Most general articles are turned down because they are not aimed specifically to audience. Most case histories are turned down because of lack of practical purpose (nothing new or worth reporting)."

AMERICAN TRUCKER MAGAZINE, American Trucker Marketing, Box 6366, San Bernardino CA 92412. (714)889-1167. Publisher: Steve Krieger. Editor: Steve Sturgess. 10% freelance written. Monthly magazine for professional truck drivers, owners, management and other trucking personnel. Articles, fillers and other materials should be generally conservative and of particular interest to the readership, of an informative or entertaining nature relating to the trucking industry. Circ. 46,700. Pays on publication. Publishes ms an average of 3 months-1 year after acceptance. First-time rights requested. Submit seasonal/holiday material 3 months in advance. Computer printout submissions acceptable; prefers letter-quality to dot-matrix. SASE. Reports in 3 weeks. Phone queries OK. Free sample copy and writer's guidelines.

Nonfiction: Realistic articles directed to trucking professionals which promote a positive image of the industry. Photo and features of outstanding rigs, truck maintenance and repair, and business aspects of trucking. 450-2,500 words. Buys 60 articles/year. Pays standard column inch rate. Buys six/year.

Photos: State availability of photos or send captioned photos with ms. Model release required.

Fiction: Realistic, "slice of life" for truckers, adventure and humor. Query. Length: 1,200-2,500 words. Buys 6/year. Pays standard column inch rate.

Tips: Freelance writers offer a balance of writing style throughout the magazine.

AUTO LAUNDRY NEWS, Columbia Communications, 370 Lexington Ave., New York NY 10017. (212)532-9290. Publisher/Editor: Ralph Monti. For sophisticated carwash operators. Monthly magazine; 45-100 pages. Circ. 15,000+. Pays on publication. Buys all rights. Phone queries OK. Submit seasonal/holiday material 2 months in advance. Computer printout submissions acceptable; no dot-matrix. SASE. Reports in 1 month. Free sample copy.

Nonfiction: How-to, historical, humor, informational, new product, nostalgia, personal experience, technical, interviews, photo features and profiles. Buys 15 mss/year. Query. Length: 1,000-2,000 words. Pays $75-175.

Tips: "Read the magazine; notice its style and come up with something interesting to the industry. Foremost, the writer has to know the industry."

AUTO TRIM NEWS, National Association of Auto Trim Shops (NAATS), 1623 N. Grand Ave., Box 86, Baldwin NY 11510. (516)223-4334. Editor: Nat Danas. Associate Editor: Dani Ben-Ari. 25% freelance written. Monthly magazine for auto trim shops, installation specialists, customizers and restylers, marine and furniture upholsterers as well as manufacturers, wholesalers, jobbers and distributors serving them. Circ. 7,900. Pays on publication. Byline given. Buys first rights only. Simultaneous and previously published submissions OK. SASE. Reports in 1 month. Sample copy $1.50; free writer's guidelines for SAE and 2 first class stamps.

Nonfiction: How-to, interview/profile, photo feature on customizing, restoration, convertible conversions, and restyling of motor vehicles (cars, vans, trucks, motorcycles, boats and aircraft). Query or send complete ms. Length: 500-1,000 words. Pays $50-100.

Photos: State availability of photos. Pays $5 maximum for b&w print. Reviews b&w contact sheet. Captions and identification of subjects required. Buys one-time rights.

Tips: "No material dealing with engines and engine repairs. We are an aftermarket publication."

‡**AUTOBODY AND THE RECONDITIONED CAR**, Spokesman Publishing Co., Suite 300, 431 Ohio Pike, Cincinnati OH 45230. (513)528-5530. Editor: Richard Broshar. Associate Editor: Fran Cummins. A monthly magazine covering autobody repair, reconditioning and refinishing. Audience includes independent body shops; new and used car dealers and fleet operators with body shops; paint, glass and trim shops; radiator

shops; jobbers and manufacturers of automobile straightening equipment and refinishing supplies. Circ. 20,000. Pays on publication. Byline given. Buys first North American serial rights and one-time rights. Submit seasonal/holiday material 3 months in advance. Simultaneous queries, and simultaneous, photocopied, and previously published (if so indicated) submissions OK. Computer printout submissions acceptable; prefers letter-quality to dot-matrix. Reports in 1 month. Writer's guidelines for business-size SAE and 1 first class stamp.

Nonfiction: Book excerpts (autobody repair, small business management); how-to (manage an autobody shop, do a specific autobody repair); inspirational (bodyshop owner); photo feature (manufacturer of equipment or supplier); and technical (equipment, supplies and processes in an autobody shop). Editorial calendar will be provided with writer's guidelines. No personal experience as a customer of an autobody shop, or how *not* to run a shop. Buys 36 mss/year. Query with published clips or send complete ms. Length: 500-2,500 words. Pays $150-200 with photos.

Photos: State availability of photos and send one sample, or send photos with ms. Reviews color negatives and 4x5 transparencies, and 3½x5 b&w and color prints. Payment for photos included in payment for ms. Captions required. Buys one-time rights.

Tips: "Visit 10 autobody shops and ask the owners what they want to read about; find sources, then send in a query; or send in a letter with 10 article topics that you know you can cover and wait for an assignment. Experience in trade publication writing helps. Area most open to freelancers is technical and management how-tos. We want technical, technical, technical articles. Autobody people work with everything from laser beam measuring benches to catalytic thermoreactors. Be willing to learn about such subjects."

AUTOMOTIVE BOOSTER OF CALIFORNIA, Box 765, LaCanada CA 91011. (213)790-6554. Editor: Don McAnally. 2% freelance written. For members of Automotive Booster clubs, automotive warehouse distributors and automotive parts jobbers in California. Monthly. Circ. 3,500. Not copyrighted. Byline given. Pays on publication. Buys first rights only. Submit complete ms. SASE. Publishes ms an average of 1 month after acceptance.

Nonfiction: Will look at short articles and pictures about successes of automotive parts outlets in California. Also can use personnel assignments for automotive parts people in California. Query first. Pays $1.25/column inch (about 2½¢/word).

Photos: Pays $5 for b&w photos used with mss.

AUTOMOTIVE REBUILDER MAGAZINE, Babcox Publications, Inc., 11 S. Forge St., Akron OH 44304. (216)535-6117. Editor-in-Chief: Andrew J. Doherty. Managing Editor: John F. Davisson. Assistant Editor: Linda Sample. Emphasizes the automotive and heavy duty mechanical/parts rebuilding industry and jobber machine shops. Monthly magazine; 108 pages. Circ. 21,000. Pays on publication. Buys all rights. Phone queries OK. Submit seasonal/holiday material 6 weeks in advance. Simultaneous, photocopied and previously published submissions OK. SASE. Reports in 2 weeks. Free sample copy.

Nonfiction: "How-to (technical writing); humor (we particularly like humor, must be relevant to rebuilders); historical (historical automotive); inspirational (concentrate on how a rebuilder overcomes disaster or personal handicap); interview (concentrate on growth or success stories); nostalgia (only if it applies to rebuilding); personal experience (experiences with rebuilding); personal opinion (comment on legislation affecting rebuilders); photo feature (on machine shops; try to get people in photos, we want photojournalism, not photo illustration); profile (about individual rebuilder; perhaps the small rebuilder); technical (you must know what you're talking about, rebuilders don't just fall off Christmas trees); and articles on regulation at the state and local level (conservation of resources, air and water pollution)." Buys 8 mss/year. Query. Length: 500-1,500 words. Pays 4-6¢/word.

Columns & Departments: People (profile or close-up of industry figures welcome); Tech Notes (this entails technical how-to writing); New Product ("we generally do this ourselves"); and The Forum Guest (opinions on current events relevant to rebuilders). Buys 1 ms/year. Query. Length: 200-1,500 words. Pays 4-6¢/word. Open to suggestions for columns/departments.

AUTOMOTIVE VOLUME DISTRIBUTION, 7300 N. Cicero Ave., Lincolnwood IL 60646. (312)588-7300. Editor: Larry Moore. For "specialists in the auto parts and hardware distribution field who are doing above one million dollars business per year." Published 10 times/year. Circ. 30,000. Buys all rights. Pays on publication. Most material is staff-written. Reports "within a reasonable amount of time." Computer printout submissions acceptable; prefers letter-quality to dot-matrix. SASE.

Nonfiction: "Business management subjects limited to the automotive parts distribution field." No specific product stories or seasonal subjects. Query. Length: 1,500-2,000 words. Pays $200-300 "based on value to industry and the quality of the article."

Photos: Photos purchased with and without mss; captions required. Wants "sharp 5x7 prints." Pays maximum $6.

Tips: Addition of hardware distributors adds new dimensions to coverage and editorial features.

THE BATTERY MAN, Independent Battery Manufacturers Association, Inc., 100 Larchwood Dr., Largo FL 33540. (813)586-1409. Editor: Celwyn E. Hopkins. Emphasizes SLI battery manufacture, applications and new developments. For battery manufacturers and retailers (garage owners, servicemen, fleet owners, etc.). Monthly magazine. Circ. 6,200. Pays on acceptance. Buys all rights. Byline given. Submit seasonal/holiday material 3 months in advance. Simultaneous, photocopied and previously published submissions OK. SASE. Reports in 6 weeks. Sample copy $2.50.
Nonfiction: Technical articles. Submit complete ms. Buys 19-24 unsolicited mss/year. Recent article example: "Separators for the 80s" (April 84). Length: 750-1,200 words. Pays 6¢/word.

BRAKE & FRONT END, 11 S. Forge St., Akron OH 44304. (216)535-6117. Editor: Jeffrey S. Davis. 10% freelance written. For owners of automotive repair shops engaged in brake, wheel, suspension, chassis and frame repair, including: specialty shops, general repair shops, new car and truck dealers, gas stations, mass merchandisers and tire stores. Monthly magazine; 68 pages. Circ. 28,000. Pays on publication. Buys exclusive rights in field. Byline given. Computer printout submissions acceptable; prefers letter-quality to dot-matrix. SASE. Reports immediately. Publishes ms an average of 3 months after acceptance. Sample copy and editorial schedule $3.
Nonfiction: Specialty shops taking on new ideas using new merchandising techniques; growth of business, volume; reasons for growth and success. Expansions and unusual brake shops. Prefers no product-oriented material. Query. Length: about 800-1,500 words. Pays 7-9¢/word.
Photos: Pays $8.50 for b&w glossy prints purchased with mss.

CANADIAN TRANSPORTATION & DISTRIBUTION MANAGEMENT, Southam Communications, Ltd., 1450 Don Mills Rd., Don Mills, Ontario M3B 2X7 Canada. (416)445-6641. Editor: Lou Volpintesta. 35% freelance written. Monthly magazine covering physical distribution and freight transportation. Circ. 12,177. Pays on publication. Byline given. Buys first and second rights to the same material, and second serial (reprint) rights to material originally published elsewhere: Simultaneous queries OK. SASE or SAE and IRCs. Reports in 3 weeks on queries; 2 weeks on mss. Publishes ms an average of 2 months after acceptance. Free sample copy and reader profile.
Nonfiction: How-to (save distribution costs, fuel or evaluate distribution services); interview/profile; photo feature; and news feature based on legislation trends, disruptions, etc. in physical distribution. Special needs include president's issue (Nov.): educational material on physical distribution for chief executives. No product descriptions or work without Canadian slant unless has international implication. No product news, literature/brochure announcements, transport company profiles—unless strong shipper slant. Buys 25 mss/year. Query with clips of published work. Length: 750-2,000 words. Pays $100-300.
Photos: State availability of photos. Reviews contact sheets; pays $10-30 for 5x7 b&w prints. Identification of subjects required. Buys all rights.
Columns/Departments: News columns: new distribution services; legislation; industry/association reaction; plant/office expansions; and rates and tariffs. Buys 50 mss/year. Query. Length: 250-750 words. Pays $4/column inch (columns 13 picas wide).
Tips: "News columns and feature bank—items must be topical and timely. Writing should be terse and to the point—more interested in logical progression and tight writing than flowery prose. News stories for our columns are due the 25th of each month. The economy has affected the number of editorial pages available. That, plus cost cutting programs we are pursuing, will mean fewer articles needed and fewer articles purchased from freelancers."

THE CHEK-CHART SERVICE BULLETIN, Box 6227, San Jose CA 95150. Associate Editor: Jo L. Phelps. 20% freelance written. Emphasizes trade news and how-to articles on automobile service for professional mechanics. Monthly newsletter; 8 pages. Circ. 20,000. Pays on acceptance. Buys all rights. No byline. Submit seasonal/holiday material 3-4 months in advance. SASE. Reports in 2 weeks. Publishes ms an average of 2 months after acceptance. Free sample copy and writer's guidelines; mention *Writer's Market* in request.
Nonfiction: "The *Service Bulletin* is a trade newsletter, *not* a consumer magazine. How-to articles and service trade news for professional auto mechanics, also articles on merchandising automobile service. No 'do-it-yourself' articles." Also no material unrelated to car service. Buys 6 unsolicited mss/year. Query with samples. Length: 700-1,100 words. Pays $75-125.
Photos: State availability of photos with query. Offers no additional payment for photos accepted with ms. Uses 8x10 b&w glossy photos. Captions and model release required. Buys all rights.
Tips: "Be willing to work in our style. Ask about subjects we would like to have covered in the future."

COLLISION, Kruzakaleidoscopix, Inc., Box 389, Franklin MA 02038. Editor: Jay Kruza. For auto dealers, auto body repairmen and managers, and tow truck operators. Magazine published every 6 weeks; 66 pages. Pays on acceptance. Buys all rights. Submit seasonal/holiday material 4 months in advance. Simultaneous, photocopied and previously published submissions OK. SASE. Reports in 2-3 weeks. Sample copy $2; free writer's guidelines.

Nonfiction: Expose (on government intervention in private enterprise via rule making; also how any business skims the cream of profitable business but fails to satisfy needs of motorist); and how-to (fix a dent, a frame, repair plastics, run your business better). No general business articles such as how to sell more, do better bookkeeping, etc. Query before submitting interview, personal opinion or technical articles. "Journalism of newsworthy material in local areas pertaining to auto body is of interest." Buys 20 or more articles/year. Length: 100-1,500 words. Pays $25-125.

Photos: "Our readers work with their hands and are more likely to be stopped by photo with story." Send photos with ms. Pays $25/first, $5/each additional for 5x7 b&w prints. Captions preferred. Model release required if not news material.

Columns & Departments: Stars and Their Cars, Personalities in Auto Dealership, Auto Body Repair Shops, Association News and Lifestyle (dealing with general human interest hobbies or past times). Almost anything that would attract readership interest. "Photos are very important. Stories that we have purchased are: 'Clearing the Farm . . . of Rattlesnakes'; 'Annual Mule Convention in Bishop, California'; and 'Cochise's Hidden Treasure.' " Buys 10/year. Query. Length: 200-500 words. Pays $40-100.

‡**COMMERCIAL CARRIER JOURNAL, for Private Fleets & For Hire Trucking**, Chilton Co., Division of American Broadcasting Co., Chilton Way, Radnor PA 19089. (215)964-4513. Editor-in-Chief: Gerald F. Standley. Executive Editor: Carl R. Glines. 2% freelance written. Monthly magazine that provides news and features on trends, technology, legislation and management techniques for management, operations and maintenance executives of the nation's private and for hire truck and bus fleets. Circ. 77,000. Pays on acceptance. Offers negotiable kill fee. Buys all rights. Submit seasonal/holiday material 6 months in advance. No simultaneous queries, or simultaneous, photocopied and previously published submissions. SASE. Reports in 1 month on queries. Publishes ms an average of 6 months after acceptance.

Nonfiction: How-to, interview/profile, photo feature and technical. No "superficial garbage. A writer *must* know something about the industry and/or topic." Buys 2 mss/year. Query or send complete ms. Pays $50-600.

Photos: Send photos with query or ms. Reviews color transparencies and prints. Captions, model releases, and identification of subjects required.

Tips: Call the Editor-in-Chief "if you are already an expert on the topic that you want to write about. Concentrate more on content and less on style."

FARM-TO-MARKET TRUCKERS' NEWS, h.e.r. Publications, Ink., 2123 4th St., Sioux City IA 51101. (712)258-0782. Co-Editors: Dianne Rose and Jane Hunwardsen. 20% freelance written. Monthly trucking newspaper for company drivers, owner/operators, owners of large and small trucking firms and persons in allied industries in the Midwest. Circ. 8,000. Pays on publication. Byline given. Not copyrighted. Buys first rights and second (reprint) rights to material originally published elsewhere. Submit seasonal/holiday material 2 months in advance. Simultaneous queries, and simultaneous, photocopied and previously published submissions OK. Computer printout submissions acceptable; no dot-matrix. SASE. Reports in 1 month. Publishes ms an average of 2 months after acceptance. Sample copy $1; free writer's guidelines.

Nonfiction: Expose, general interest, historical/nostalgic, how-to, humor, interview/profile, new product, personal experience, photo feature and technical. "Our special May Truckers' Day issue is the largest. Material should be submitted by March 15." Send complete ms. Length: 375-1,250 words. Pays $25-50.

Photos: Send photos with ms. Pays $10-25 for 5x7 prints. Captions, model release and identification of subjects required.

Tips: "Good, bright features about people in transportation are always welcome, especially when accompanied by a photo."

GO WEST MAGAZINE, 1240 Bayshore Hwy., Burlingame CA 94010. Editor: Bill Fitzgerald. 20% freelance written. Emphasizes truck transport for the truck operator who is concerned with operation, maintenance and purchase of trucks and related equipment, and running a profitable business. Monthly magazine; 80 pages. Circ. 51,000. Pays on acceptance. Buys all rights. Pays full kill fee. Byline given except "series using same format but different locations and subjects." Phone queries OK. Submit seasonal/holiday material 6 months in advance of issue date. SASE. Reports in 2 weeks. Free sample copy; mention *Writer's Market* in request.

Nonfiction: Expose, general interest, how-to, interview, and new product. No fiction. Buys 2 mss/issue. Query. Length: 500-3,500 words. Pays $200-600.

Photos: State availability of photos with query. Pays $5-15 for b&w photos; $100 for 2¼x2¼ color transparencies. Captions required. Buys all rights.

HEAVYDUTY MARKETING, Babcox Publications, 11 S. Forge St., Akron OH 44304. (216)535-6117. Editor: Jeffrey S. Davis. 20% freelance written. Publishes 9 issues/year. Magazine about heavy duty truck parts and service. Circ. 18,000. Pays on publication. Byline given. Buys first North American serial rights. Submit seasonal material 2 months in advance. Simultaneous and photocopied submissions OK. Computer printout submissions acceptable; prefers lette-quality to dot-matrix. SASE. Reports in 1 week. Publishes ms an average of 3 months after acceptance. Sample copy $2.50.

Nonfiction: Interview (related to heavy duty truck parts and service); profile; and technical. No stories about truck fleets. Buys 12 mss/year. Query. Length: 750-3,000 words. Pays 7¢-9¢/word. "We need feature stories on established businesses in heavy duty aftermarket, including truck dealers and factory branches, trailer dealers, parts distributors and repair facilities. We also need interviews with high level executives in heavy duty parts and service."

Photos: State availability of photos. Pays $8.50 maximum for b&w negatives and contact sheets. Reviews color negatives and contact sheets. Payment negotiated. Captions required. Buys all rights.

IMPORT AUTOMOTIVE PARTS & ACCESSORIES, Import Automotive Publishers, 7637 Fulton St., North Hollywood CA 91605. (213)764-0611. Editor: John Rettie. Managing Editor: Jacquie Kreiman. 10% freelance written. Monthly magazine covering import automotive aftermarket. "We take a business editorial approach to automotive trade." Circ. 33,000. Pays on publication. Byline given. Offers negotiable kill fee. Buys all rights. Submit seasonal/holiday material 3 months in advance. Simultaneous queries OK. Computer printout submissions acceptable. SASE. Publishes ms an average of 3 months after acceptance. Sample copy and writer's guidelines for $2.

Nonfiction: Jacquie Kreiman, articles editor. How-to (service on autos); interview/profile (of automotive corporation); and technical (hard parts). No nonautomotive mss. Searches for "the most in-depth and up-to-date information for our industry." Buys 24 mss/year. Query with clips of published work. Length: 1,000-5,000 words. Pays $100-500.

Tips: "We do not generally consider manuscripts not written specifically for our publication. We solicit from field specialists for the vast majority of our pieces. If a writer were interested and qualified, we might use for nontechnical pieces."

JOBBER/RETAILER, Bill Communications, Box 5417, Akron OH 44313. Managing Editor: Sandie Stambaugh. 10% freelance written. "Readership is the automotive parts jobber who has entered the world of retailing to the automotive do-it-yourselfer and also wholesales to dealer trade. Editorial slant is business, merchandising/marketing-oriented with news secondary." Monthly tabloid; 56 pages. Circ. 31,750. Pays on publication. Buys all rights. Submit seasonal/holiday material 2-3 months in advance. Simultaneous, photocopied and previously published submissions in noncompetitive publications OK. Computer printout submissions acceptable; no dot-matrix. SASE. Publishes ms an average of 6 months after acceptance. Free sample copy and writer's guidelines; mention *Writer's Market* in request.

Nonfiction: How-to (merchandising do-it-yourself auto parts, store layout and design, transforming traditional jobber facilities to retail operations as well); computer usage; financial information; and technical (on do-it-yourself repairs). Buys 24 mss/year. Recent article examples: What a POS computer can do for you" (February 1984). Submit complete ms. Length: 500-1,500 words maximum. Pays $100-200.

JOBBER TOPICS, 7300 N. Cicero Ave., Lincolnwood IL 60646. (312)588-7300. Articles Editor: Jack Creighton. 1% freelance written. "A digest-sized magazine dedicated to helping its readers—auto parts jobbers and warehouse distributors—succeed in their business via better management and merchandising techniques; and a better knowledge of industry trends, activities and local or federal legislation that may influence their business activities." Monthly. Buys all rights. No byline given. Pays on acceptance. Query with outline. SASE.

Nonfiction: Most editorial material is staff-written. "Articles with unusual or outstanding automotive jobber procedures, with special emphasis on sales and merchandising; any phase of automotive parts and equipment distribution. Especially interested in merchandising practices and machine shop operations. Most independent businesses usually have a strong point or two. We like to see a writer zero in on that strong point(s) and submit an outline (or query), advising us of those points and what he intends to include in a feature. We will give him, or her, a prompt reply." Length: 2,500 words maximum. Pay based on quality and timeliness of feature.

Photos: 5x7 b&w glossies or 4-color transparencies purchased with mss.

‡MIDWEST FLEET MANAGEMENT, Construction Digest Publications, Box 603, Indianapolis IN 46206. (317)634-7374. Editor: Thomas F. Hayes. A monthly magazine covering new products, government regulations, safety, manufacturers' news and features dealing with maintenance, fleet operations, and industry trends for Midwest trucking industry management. Estab. 1983. Circ. 27,000. Pays on publication. Byline given. Makes work-for-hire assignments. Submit seasonal/holiday material 2 months in advance. Simultaneous queries, and simultaneous and photocopied submissions OK. Computer printout submissions acceptable. Reports in 2 weeks on queries; 1 month on mss. Free sample copy and writer's guidelines.

Nonfiction: Expose (on trucking trends); general interest (trucking); how-to (maintenance and safety facets of trucking); interview/profile (trucking management); new product; photo feature; and technical (aspects of trucking). Summer Safety issue (June); Winter Preparation issue (Sept.). Prefers articles with quotes. Buys 6-10 mss/year. Query. Length: 350-1,500 words. Pays $100-350.

Photos: State availability of photos. Reviews 35mm color slides and 5x7 b&w prints. Captions and identification of subjects required. Buys one-time rights.
Columns/Departments: Query.
Fillers: Newsbreaks.
Tips: "Features are most open to freelancers. Provide timely stories on industry trends and legislative news with quotes from industry leaders."

MILK AND LIQUID FOOD TRANSPORTER, Dairy Marketing Communications, N80 W12878 Fond du Lac Ave., Box 878, Menomonee Falls WI 53051. (414)255-0108. Editor: Karl F. Ohm III. 60% freelance written. Monthly magazine for owner/operators, trucking firms and management people involved in transporting bulk milk and other liquid food products in the US and Canada. Circ. 16,600. "We need more feature stories (with b&w photos and color slide cover shots) about owner/operators and large fleets, especially in California, the Midwest, Central South (i.e., Kentucky and Tennessee), the Northeast and Canada which haul bulk milk from farms to dairy plants. We also need stories on major liquid food hauling firms. We also welcome feature stories involving dairy plants, cheese factories and other processing firms who haul finished food products in refrigerated trailers." Pays on acceptance. Byline given. Buys all rights. Submit seasonal material 3 months in advance. No duplicate submissions. Computer printout submissions OK; no dot-matrix. SASE. Reports in 2 weeks on queries; 2-3 weeks on mss. Publishes ms an average of 3 months after acceptance. "We encourage freelance writers to send for free sample copies, sources for story leads, and writer's and photographer's guidelines."
Nonfiction: Expose (government regulation, state and federal); historical; interview; profile; how-to (maintenance); new product (staff written); and technical (truck maintenance). No personal opinion, humor, first person nostalgia, travel or inspirational. "We do interpretative reporting and features on timely issues affecting the business of transporting milk and other liquid food products i.e., vegetable oils, corn sweeteners, liquid sugars and apple and orange juice concentrates. We prefer articles that cover topics unique to haulers in a particular state. Well-written and well-organized articles about innovative milk and liquid food transporters stand a better chance of being accepted." Buys 8-10 mss/year. Query. "I like to know why the writer thinks his/her story is pertinent to my publication. I also would like to know why the writer chose a particular slant." Length: 3,500-3,700 words. Pays $200-400.
Photos: State availability of photos. Pays for b&w contact sheets and usable photos. Pays extra for color cover shot. Detailed captions and model release required. Photo release forms are available upon request. Buys all rights.
Tips: "If freelancers take the time to study our magazine and develop a good story, they will find out that the *Milk and Liquid Food Transporter* is not a tough market to crack. If any freelancer produces a good feature (with photos) for the magazine, I will usually give him/her good contacts for generating additional, local stories or a story assignment."

MODERN TIRE DEALER, 77 N. Miller Rd., Box 5417, Akron OH 44313. (216)867-4401. Editor: Greg Smith. 25% freelance written. For independent tire dealers. Monthly tabloid, plus 2 special emphasis issue magazines; 50-page tabloid, 80-page special issues. Published 14 times annually. Buys all rights. Photocopied submissions OK. Computer printout submissions acceptable; no dot-matrix. Query. Reports in 1 month. Publishes ms an average of 2 months after acceptance. SASE. Free writer's guidelines.
Nonfiction: "How independent tire dealers sell tires, accessories and allied services such as brakes, wheel alignment, shocks and mufflers. The emphasis is on merchandising and management. We prefer the writer to zero in on some specific area of interest; avoid shotgun approach." Length: 1,500 words. Pays $100-250.
Photos: 8x10, 4x5, 5x7 b&w glossy prints purchased with mss.

MOTOR MAGAZINE, Hearst Corp., 555 W. 57th St., New York NY 10019. (212)262-8616. Editor: Kenneth Zino. Emphasizes auto repair. "Readers are professional auto repairmen or people who own auto repair facilities." Monthly magazine; 80-90 pages. Circ. 135,000. Pays on acceptance. Buys all rights. Pays a kill fee. Byline given. SASE. Reports in 1 month. Query first.
Nonfiction: How-to. "Writers should be able to relate their own hands-on experience to handling specific repair and technical articles." Buys 6 mss/issue. Recent article examples: "How to Fix Cadillac's V8-6-4 Engine"; "Servicing the Split-Diagonal Brake System of the Escort"; "How to Perform an Accurate Wheel Alignment"; "Diagnosing GM's THM 125 Transaxle"; and "Chevy Valve Guide Restoration". Query. Length: 700-2,000 words. Pays $150-1,000.
Photos: "Photos and/or rough artwork must accompany how-to articles." State availability of photos. Uses 5x7 glossy prints. Offers no additional payment for photos accepted with ms. Captions and model releases required.

MOTOR SERVICE, Hunter Publishing Co., 950 Lee, Des Plaines IL 60016. Editor: Larry W. Carley. 75% freelance written. Monthly magazine for professional auto mechanics and the owners and service managers of repair shops, garages and fleets. Circ. 131,000. Pays on acceptance. Buys all rights. Pays 100% kill fee. Byline given. Computer printout submissions acceptable. Publishes ms an average of 2 months after acceptance. Free sample copy.

Nonfiction: Technical how-to features in language a mechanic can enjoy and understand; management articles to help shop owners and service managers operate a better business; technical theory pieces on how something works; new technology roundups, etc. No "generic business pieces on management tips, increasing sales, employee motivation, etc." Recent article includes "Meet GM's Self-diagnosing Computer Command Control System." Length: 1,500-2,500 words. Pays $75 for departmental material, $375-$500 for feature articles. Buys 35-40 mss/year, mostly from regular contributing editors. Query first. "Writers must know our market."

Photos: Photos and/or diagrams must accompany technical articles. Uses 5x7 b&w prints or 35mm transparencies. Offers no additional payment for photos accepted with ms. Captions and model releases required. Also buys color transparencies for cover use. Pays $125-200.

Tips: "We're always looking for new faces but finding someone who is technically knowledgeable in our field who can also write is extremely difficult. Good tech writers are hard to find."

O AND A MARKETING NEWS, Box 765, LaCanada CA 91011. (213)790-6554. Editor: Don McAnally. For "service station dealers, garagemen, TBA (tires, batteries, accessories) people and oil company marketing management." Bimonthly. 5% freelance written. Circ. 1,500. Not copyrighted. Pays on publication. Buys first rights only. Reports in 1 week. SASE.

Nonfiction: "Straight news material; management, service and merchandising applications; emphasis on news about or affecting markets and marketers *within the publication's geographic area of the 11 Western states.* No restrictions on style or slant. We could use straight news of our industry from some Western cities, notably Las Vegas, Phoenix, and Salt Lake City. Query with a letter that gives a capsule treatment of what the story is about." Buys 25 mss/year. Length: maximum 1,000 words. Pays $1.25/column inch (about 2½¢ a word).

Photos: Photos purchased with or without mss; captions required. No cartoons. Pays $5.

REFRIGERATED TRANSPORTER, Tunnell Publications, 1602 Harold St., Houston TX 77006. (713)523-8124. Editor: Gary Macklin. 5% freelance written. Monthly. Not copyrighted. Byline given. Pays on publication. Reports in 1 month. Computer printout submissions acceptable; prefers letter-quality to dot-matrix. SASE.

Nonfiction: "Articles on fleet management and maintenance of vehicles, especially the refrigerated van and the refrigerating unit; shop tips; loading or handling systems, especially for frozen or refrigerated cargo; new equipment specifications; conversions of equipment for better handling or more efficient operations. Prefers articles with illustrations obtained from fleets operating refrigerated trucks or trailers." Pays variable rate, approximately $100 per printed page.

Fillers: Buys newspaper clippings. "Do not rewrite."

SOUTHERN MOTOR CARGO, Box 4169, Memphis TN 38104. Editor: Mike Pennington. 10% freelance written. For "trucking management and maintenance personnel of private, contract, and for-hire carriers in 16 Southern states (Ala., Ark., Del., Fla., Ga., Ky., La., Md., Miss., N.C., Okla., S.C., Tenn., Tex., Va., and W. Va.) and the District of Columbia." Special issues include "ATA Convention," October; "Transportation Graduate Directory," January; "Mid-America Truck Show," February; "Leasing or Buying?", June; and "Annual Industry Forecast, and Winterization," October. Monthly. Circ. 53,000. Buys first rights within circulation area. Pays on publication (or on acceptance in certain cases). Publishes ms an average of 2 months after acceptance. Free sample copy to sincere, interested contributors. SASE.

Nonfiction: "How a Southern trucker builds a better mousetrap. Factual newspaper style with punch in lead. Don't get flowery. No success stories. Pick one item, i.e., tire maintenance, billing procedure, etc., and show how such-and-such carrier has developed or modified it to better fit his organization. Bring in problems solved by the way he adapted this or that and what way he plans to better his present layout. Find a segment of the business that has been altered or modified due to economics or new information, such as 'due to information gathered by a new IBM process, it has been discovered that an XYZ transmission needs overhauling every 60,000 miles instead of every 35,000 miles, thereby resulting in savings of $$$ over the normal life of this transmission.' Or, 'by incorporating a new method of record keeping, claims on damaged freight have been expedited with a resultant savings in time and money.' Compare the old method with the new, itemize savings, and get quotes from personnel involved. Articles must be built around an outstanding phase of the operation and must be documented and approved by the firm's management prior to publication." Length: 1,000-3,000 words. Pays minimum 8¢ a word for "feature material."

Photos: Purchased with cutlines; glossy prints. Pays $10.

SPECIALTY & CUSTOM DEALER, Babcox Publications, 11 S. Forge St., Akron OH 44304. (216)535-6117. Publisher: Gary Gardner. Editor: Linda Prochazka. "Audience is primarily jobbers and retailers of specialty automotive parts and accessories, warehouse distributors and manufacturers. Average reader has been in business for 10 years and is store owner or manager. Educational background varies, with most readers in the high school graduate with some college category." Monthly magazine. Circ. 22,000. Pays on publication. Buys all rights. Submit seasonal or holiday material 4 months in advance. SASE. Reports in 6 weeks. Sample copy $3.

Nonfiction: Publishes informational (business techniques), interview, new product, profile and technical articles. "No broad generalizations concerning a 'great product' without technical data behind the information. Lack of detail concerning business operations." Buys 3-5 unsolicited mss/year. Query. Length: 1,000-2,000 words. Pays $100-250.

Tips: "For the most part, an understanding of automotive products particularly in the high performance and specialty automotive market and business practices is essential. Features on a specific retailer, his merchandising techniques and unique business methods are most often used. Such a feature might include inventory control, display methods, lines carried, handling obsolete products, etc."

THE SUCCESSFUL DEALER, Kona-Cal, Inc., 707 Lake Cook Rd., Deerfield IL 60015. (312)498-3180. Editor: Denise L. Rondini. Managing Editor: R. Patricia Herron. 30% freelance written. Magazine published 6 times/year covering dealership management of medium and heavy duty trucks, construction equipment, forklift trucks, diesel engines and truck trailers. Circ. 19,000. Pays on publication. Byline sometimes given. Buys first rights only. Simultaneous queries, and simultaneous and photocopied submissions OK. Computer printout submissions acceptable. SASE. Reports in 2 weeks. Publication date "depends on the article; some are contracted for a specific issue, others on an as need basis."

Nonfiction: How-to (solve problems within the dealership); interview/profile (concentrating on business, not personality); new product (exceptional only); opinion (by readers—those in industry); personal experience (of readers); photo feature (of major events); and technical (vehicle componentry). Special issues include: March-April: American Truck Dealer Convention; September-October: Parts and Service. Query. Length: open. Pays $100-150/page.

Tips: "Phone first, then follow up with a detailed explanation of the proposed article. Allow two weeks for our response. Know dealers and dealerships, their problems and opportunities; heavy equipment industry."

‡**TIRE REVIEW**, Babcox Publications, 11 S. Forge St., Akron OH 44034. (216)535-6117. Editor: Tom Cooney. A monthly magazine covering tire and auto service and wholesaling. "*Tire Review* is edited primarily to help tire dealers make money." Circ. 30,500. Pays on publication. Byline given. Buys all rights. Simultaneous queries OK. Computer printout submissions acceptable. SASE. Reports in 2 weeks on queries; 1 month on mss. Sample copy $1.

Nonfiction: "Articles should cover one of the following areas: sales motivation, retail marketing strategies, merchandising techniques, advertising inventory procedures, tax tips, cash flow or employee relations. We are currently seeking automotive service articles covering front-end alignment, brake repair, muffler repair and tune-ups. Special attention will be given to those articles offering service merchandising ideas." Buys 50 mss/year. Query with published clips. Length: 1,500-4,500 words. Pays 100 maximum.

Photos: State availability of photos with query letter or ms. Reviews b&w contact sheets. Identification of subjects required.

TOW-AGE, Kruzka Kaleidoscopix, Inc., Box 389, Franklin MA 02038. Editor: J. Kruza. For readers who run their own towing service business. Published every 6 weeks. Circ. 12,000. Buys all rights; usually reassigns rights. Buys about 12 mss/year. Pays on acceptance. Photocopied and simultaneous submissions OK. Reports in 1-4 weeks. SASE. Sample copy $1; free writer's guidelines.

Nonfiction: Articles on business, legal and technical information for the towing industry. "Light reading material; short, with punch." Informational, how-to, personal, interview and profile. Query or submit complete ms. Length: 200-800 words. Pays $40-80. Spot news and successful business operations. Length: 100-500 words. Technical articles. Length: 100-1,000 words.

Photos: Pays up to 8x10 b&w photos purchased with or without mss, or on assignment. Pays $25 for first photo; $5 for each additional photo in series. Captions required.

WARD'S AUTO WORLD, 28 W. Adams, Detroit MI 48226. (313)962-4433. Editor-in-Chief: David C. Smith. Managing Editor: James W. Bush. Senior Editor: Richard L. Waddell. Associate Editors: Drew Winter and Jeffrey Zygmoni. New Copy Editor: Barbara A. Koch. 10% freelance written. For top and middle management in all phases of auto industry. Also adding heavy-duty vehicle coverage. Monthly magazine; 72 pages. Circ. 75,000. Pays on publication. Buys all rights. Pay varies for kill fee. Byline given. Phone queries OK. Submit seasonal/holiday material 1 month in advance. Computer printout submissions acceptable. SASE. Reports in 2 weeks. Publishes ms an average of 1 month after acceptance. Free sample copy and writer's guidelines.

Nonfiction: Expose, general interest, historical, humor, interview, new product, nostalgia, personal experience, photo feature and technical. Few consumer type articles. No "nostalgia or personal history type stories (like 'My Favorite Car')." Buys 4-8 mss/year. Query. Length: 700-5,000 words. Pay $100-600.

Photos: "We're heavy on graphics." Submit photo material with query. Pay varies for 8x10 b&w prints or color transparencies. Captions required. Buys one-time rights.

Tips: "Don't send poetry, how-to and 'My Favorite Car' stuff. It doesn't stand a chance. This is a business newsmagazine and operates on a news basis just like any other newsmagazine."

WAREHOUSE DISTRIBUTOR NEWS, 11 S. Forge St., Akron OH 44304. Editor: Larry Silvey. 10% freelance written. For warehouse distributors and redistributing jobbers of automotive parts and accessories, tools and equipment and supplies (all upper management personnel). Magazine; 40 pages. Bimonthly. Circ. 12,000. Rights purchased vary with author and material. May buy exclusive rights in field. Byline given. Buys about 12 mss/year. Pays on publication. Photocopied and simultaneous submissions OK. Reports at once. SASE. Sample copy $3 plus postage.

Nonfiction: Automotive aftermarket distribution management articles and those on general management, success stories, etc., of interest to the industry. Articles on manufacturers and their distributors. Must be aftermarket-oriented. Each issue centers around a theme such as rebuilt parts issue, import issue, materials handling issue, etc. Schedule changes yearly based on developments in the industry. Does not want to see freelance material on materials handling or product information. Would be interested in merchandising articles; those on EDP startup, and interviews with prominent industry figures. Query. Length: open. Pay varies.

Photos: B&w (5x7) photos purchased with or without ms. Captions required.

Aviation and Space

In this category are journals for aviation business executives, airport operators and aviation technicians. Publications for professional and private pilots are classified with the Aviation magazines in the Consumer Publications section.

AG-PILOT INTERNATIONAL MAGAZINE, Bio-Aeronautic Publishers, Inc. 10 N.E. Sixth, Milton-Freewater OR 97862. (503)938-5502. Editor: Tom J. Wood. Executive Editor: Rocky Kemp. Emphasizes agricultural aerial application (crop dusting). "This is intended to be a fun-to-read, technical, as well as humorous and serious publication for the ag pilot and operator. They are our primary target." Monthly magazine; 48 pages. Circ. 10,200. Pays on publication. Buys all rights. Byline given unless writer requested holding name. Phone queries OK. Simultaneous, photocopied and previously published (if not very recent) submissions OK. SASE. Reports in 2 weeks. Sample copy $2.

Nonfiction: Expose (of EPA, OSHA, FAA or any government function concerned with this industry); general interest; historical; interview (of well-known ag/aviation person); nostalgia; personal opinion; new product; personal experience; and photo feature. "If we receive an article, in any area we have solicited, it is quite possible this person could contribute intermittently. The international input is what we desire. Industry related material is a must. No newspaper clippings." Send complete ms. Length: 300-1,500 words. Pays $20-100.

Photos: "We would like one b&w 5x7 (or smaller) with the manuscript, if applicable—it will help the chance of utilization." Four color. Offers no additional payment for photos accepted with ms. Captions preferred, model release required.

Columns/Departments: International (of prime interest, as they need to cultivate this area—aviation/crop dusting-related); Embryo Birdman (should be written, or appear to be written, by a first year spray pilot); The Chopper Hopper (by anyone in the helicopter industry); Trouble Shooter (ag aircraft maintenance tips); Bio-Graphical Interview Type (of well-known person in aviation related position); and Catchin' The Corner (written by a person obviously skilled in the crop dusting field of experience or other interest-capturing material related to the industry). Send complete ms. Length: 700-1,500 words. Pays $20-100.

Poetry: Interested in all agri-aviation related poetry. Buys 1/issue. Submit no more than 2 at one time. Maximum length: one 10 inch x 24 picas maximum. Pays $5-25.

Fillers: Short jokes, short humor and industry-related newsbreaks. Length: 10-100 words. Pays $5-20.

Tips: "Writers should be witty and knowledgeable about the crop dusting aviation world. Material *must* be agricultural/aviation-oriented. Crop dusting or nothing! We plan a Spanish language edition to all Spanish-speaking countries."

‡AGRICULTURAL AVIATION, National Agricultural Aviation Association, #103, 115 D St. SE, Washington DC 20003. (202)546-5722. Editor: Harold C. Collins. A monthly magazine covering improved technology, legislative issues, product information, articles of small business interests and special events in agricultural aviation. Circ. 8,500. Byline given. Buys variable rights by individual arrangement. Photocopied submissions OK. SASE. Reporting time "depends on nature of the piece." Free sample copy and writer's guidelines.

Nonfiction: How-to (plane maintenance). Special convention issue (Nov.) Send complete ms. Word length varies. "Most articles are provided by the industry gratis."

AIRPORT PRESS, J.A.J. Publishing Co., 161-15 Rockaway Blvd., Jamaica NY 11434. (212)528-8600. Editor-in-Chief: Gary Stoller. 25% freelance written. Monthly business tabloid presenting US airports' viewpoint of the airline industry for airline management, employees, unions, the air freight industry, airline-related businesses, travel agents and government officials. Circ. 22,000. Pays on publication. Byline given. Offers 100% kill fee. Not copyrighted. Buys first rights only. Submit seasonal/holiday material 3 months in advance. Computer printout submissions acceptable; no dot-matrix. SASE. Reports in 3 weeks on queries; 1 week on mss. Publishes ms an average of 1 month after acceptance. Sample copy $1.
Nonfiction: Expose, general interest, interview/profile, financial, technical, travel and hard news. "Articles most desired: business and government issues affecting the airlines and the industry on a national basis; new airline industry developments; and industry trends." Query with clips of published work or send complete ms. Length: 1,000-2,000 words. Pays $125 minimum.
Columns/Departments: General news, business, air cargo, commuter airlines, labor, government, marketing, finance, US and NY airports. Query with clips of published work or send complete ms. Length: 750-1,000 words. Pays $125 minimum.

AIRPORT SERVICES MANAGEMENT, Lakewood Publications, 731 Hennepin Ave., Minneapolis MN 55403. (612)333-0471. Editor: Sher Jasperse. 33% freelance written. Emphasizes management of airports, airlines and airport-based businesses. Monthly magazine. Circ. 20,000. Pays on acceptance. Buys all rights. Byline given. Phone queries OK. Submit seasonal/holiday material 3 months in advance. Photocopied submissions OK but must be industry-exclusive. Computer printout submissions acceptable; prefers letter-quality to dot-matrix. SASE. Reports in 1 month. Publishes ms an average of 2 months after acceptance. Free sample copy and writer's guidelines.
Nonfiction: How-to (manage an airport, aviation service company or airline; work with local governments, etc.); interview (with a successful operator); and technical (how to manage a maintenance shop, snow removal operations, bird control, security operations). "No flying, no airport nostalgia or product puff pieces. We don't want pieces on how one company's product solved everyone's problem. (How one airport or aviation business solved its problem with a certain type of product is okay.) No descriptions of airport construction projects (down to the square footage in the new restrooms) that don't discuss applications for other airports. All articles that begin with anything like, 'She's cute, petite and dresses like a lady, but by golly she runs the Shangrila Airport with a firm hand' are burned on the spot. Just plain 'how-to' story lines, please." Buys 40-50 mss/year, "but at least half are short (250-750 words) items for inclusion in one of our monthly departments." Query. Length: 250-2,500 words. Pays $100/published page.
Photos: State availability of photos with query. Payment for photos is included in total purchase price. Uses b&w photos, charts and line drawings.
Tips: "We're using more shorter feature articles (average 2,000 words) because I find that the longer, in-depth, issue-oriented articles are better when they are staff researched and written. No 'gee-whiz' approaches. Writing style should be lively, informal and straightforward, but the *subject matter* must be as functional and as down-to-earth as possible. Trade magazines are *business* magazines that must help readers do their jobs better."

AVIATION EQUIPMENT MAINTENANCE, The Irving-Cloud Publishing Co., 7300 N. Cicero Ave., Lincolnwood IL 60646. (312)588-7300. Editor: Paul Berner. Bimonthly magazine covering aircraft maintenance for mechanics and their managers. Circ. 22,000. Pays on acceptance. Byline given. Buys all rights. Submit seasonal/holiday material 1½ months in advance. Simultaneous queries and simultaneous submissions OK. SASE. Reports in 2 weeks. Sample copy for 9x12 SAE.
Nonfiction: How-to, photo feature and technical. Uses technical, hands-on maintenance and management articles. Buys 15-20 mss/year. Send complete ms. Length: 2,000-4,000 words. Pays $200-400.
Photos: State availability of photos or send photos with ms. Payment for photos is included in payment for ms. Reviews 2¼ color transparencies and 8x10 color prints. Captions required. Buys one-time rights.
Columns/Departments: Products and Literature. Buys few mss/year. Query.

INTERLINE REPORTER, 2 W. 46th St., New York NY 10036. (212)575-9000. Editor/Publisher: Eric Friedheim. Managing Editor: Ed Sullivan. An inspirational and interesting magazine for airline employees. Buys first serial rights. Query. SASE.
Nonfiction: Wants nontechnical articles on airline activities; stories should be slanted to the sales, reservations and counter personnel. Articles on offbeat airlines and, most of all, on airline employees—those who lead an adventurous life, have a unique hobby, or have acted above and beyond the call of duty. Personality stories showing how a job has been well done are particularly welcome. Length: up to 1,200 words. Pays $50-75 for articles with photographic illustrations.

INTERNATIONAL AVIATION MECHANICS JOURNAL, Box 4102, Winston-Salem NC 27115. (919)767-0241. Publisher: Richard Siuniak. 50% freelance written. For aviation maintenance professionals, including licensed airframe and powerplant mechanics involved in maintaining fixed and rotary wing aircraft, and students. Monthly magazine; 80 pages. Circ. 12,319. Buys all rights. Pays within 1 month of publication. Photocopied submissions OK. Computer printout submissions acceptable; no dot-matrix. Reports in 1 month. Publishes ms an average of 1 month after acceptance. SASE. Free sample copy.
Nonfiction: Technical articles on aircraft maintenance procedures and articles helping the mechanics to be more efficient and productive. All material should be written from the point of view of an aircraft mechanic, helping him solve common field problems. Buys 30-40 mss/year. Query or submit complete ms. Informational (length: 500-2,000 words; pays $100-250); how-to (length: 100-500 words; pays $25); photo articles (length: 50-100 words; pays $20); and technical (length: 500-4,000 words; pays $100-250).

JET CARGO NEWS, The Management Journal for Air Marketing, 5314 Bingle Rd., Houston TX 77092. (713)688-8811. Editor: Art Eddy. Designed to serve international industry concerned with moving goods by air. "It brings to shippers and manufacturers spot news of airline and aircraft development, air routes, CAB ruling, shipping techniques, innovations and rates." Monthly. Circ. 30,500. Buys all rights. Buys up to 50 mss/year. Pays on publication. Will not consider photocopied or simultaneous submissions. Submit seasonal material 1 month in advance. Reports in 1 month if postage is included. Submit complete ms. SASE. Will send a sample copy and writer's guidelines on request.
Nonfiction: "Direct efforts to the shipper. Tell him about airline service, freight forwarder operations, innovations within the industry, new products, aircraft, and pertinent news to the industry. Use a tight magazine style. The writer must know marketing." Buys informational articles, how-to's, interviews and coverage of successful business operations. Length: 1,500 words maximum. Pays $4/inch.
Photos: 8x10 b&w glossy prints purchased with and without mss; captions required. Pays $10.

ROTOR & WING INTERNATIONAL, PJS Publications Inc., Box 1790, Peoria IL 61656. (309)682-6626. Editor: Don Toler. Managing Editor: David Jensen. Monthly magazine covering the international civil and military helicopter industry. "Prime audience: civil and military helicopter owners and operators; secondary audience: manufacturers. Covers all phases of the helicopter industry with special interest in military, civil government, and commerical offshore operations; and corporate/business use of rotorcraft." Circ. 40,000 (approximately). Pays on acceptance. Byline given. Buys all rights. Computer printout submissions acceptable; prefers letter-quality to dot-matrix. Reports in 2 weeks. Free sample copy and writer's guidelines.
Nonfiction: Interview/profile (key figures of importance to rotorcraft); and technical (rotorcraft piloting and operations). No articles "pertaining to homebuilt rotorcraft or run-of-the mill rescues . . ." Buys 60 mss/year ("however, 98% come from regular freelance staff"). Query with clips. L ength: 1,500-2,000 words. Pays $250-550.
Photos: State availability of photos. "Photos are considered part of manuscript and not purchased separately." Reviews b&w prints. Identification of subjects required.
Tips: "Convince the editors you have a understanding of the civil helicopter industry and have experience with technical/business writing." General features and some news stringing are most open to freelancers.

Beverages and Bottling

Manufacturers, distributors and retailers of soft drinks and alcoholic beverages read these publications. Publications for bar and tavern operators and managers of restaurants are classified in the Hotels, Motels, Clubs, Resorts and Restaurants category.

BEER WHOLESALER, Dogan Enterprises, Inc., 75 SE 4th Ave., Delray Beach FL 33444. (305)272-1223. Editor: Kenneth Breslauer. Bimonthly magazine about the beer industry for beer wholesalers, importers and brewers. Circ. 5,000. Pays on publication. Byline given. Buys all rights. Reports in 3 weeks on queries; in 2 months on mss. Sample copy $5.
Nonfiction: General interest, interview, profile, how-to and technical. "Submit articles that are business-oriented and presented in an organized manner. Dig for the unusual; what makes this beer wholesaler different? What new ideas can be used? No consumer-oriented articles such as stories on beer can collecting." Query. Length: 1,200-5,000 words. Pays $70-150.
Photos: Send photos with ms. Offers no additional payment for photos accepted with ms. Captions required. Buys all rights.
Tips: Doesn't normally accept freelance material but will read queries.

‡**BEVERAGE WORLD**, Keller International Publishing, 150 Great Neck Rd., Great Neck NY 11021. (800)645-3580, (516)829-9210. Editor: Larry Jabbonsky. Managing Editor: Tim Davis. A monthly magazine covering the soft drink, beer, wine, spirits, juices and bottled water industry. Circ. 22,000. Pays on acceptance. Byline given. Offers 50% kill fee. Buys one-time rights. Submit seasonal/holiday material 6 weeks in advance. Simultaneous queries OK. Computer printout submissions acceptable; no dot-matrix. SASE. Reports in 1 month. Sample copy $3.50.
Nonfiction: Jeanne Lukasick, senior editor. Interview/profile (leaders in the soft drink/spirits industry), and case histories (on new equipment and companies). "All articles are assigned." Buys 10 mss/year. Query with published clips. Length: 1-3 typewritten pages. Pays $250-350.
Tips: "We need material about specific companies and people in the industry."

MID-CONTINENT BOTTLER, 10741 El Monte, Overland Park KS 66207. (913)341-0020. Publisher: Floyd E. Sageser. 5% freelance written. For "soft drink bottlers in the 20-state Midwestern area." Bimonthly. Not copyrighted. Pays on acceptance. Buys first rights only. Reports "immediately." SASE. Publishes ms an average of 2 months after acceptance. Free sample copy.
Nonfiction: "Items of specific soft drink bottler interest with special emphasis on sales and merchandising techniques. Feature style desired." Buys 2-3 mss/year. Length: 2,000 words. Pays $15-$100.
Photos: Photos purchased with mss.

WINES & VINES, 1800 Lincoln Ave., San Rafael CA 94901. Editor: Philip E. Hiaring. 10% freelance written. For everyone concerned with the grape and wine industry including winemakers, wine merchants, growers, suppliers, consumers, etc. Monthly magazine. Circ. 5,500. Buy first North American serial rights or simultaneous rights. Pays on acceptance. Submit special material (brandy, January; vineyard, February; Man-of-the-Year, March; water, April; export-import, May; enological, June; statistical, July; marketing, September; equipment and supplies, November; champagne, December) 3 months in advance. Reports in 2 weeks. Publishes ms an average of 3 months after acceptance. SASE. Free sample copy.
Nonfiction: Articles of interest to the trade. "These could be on grape growing in unusual areas; new wine-making techniques; wine marketing, retailing, etc." Interview, historical, spot news, merchandising techniques and technical. No stories with a strong consumer orientation as against trade orientation. Author should know the subject matter, i.e., know proper grape growing/winemaking terminology. Buys 3-4 ms/year. Query. Length: 1,000-2,500 words. Pays $25-50.
Photos: Pays $15 for 4x5 or 8x10 b&w photos purchased with mss. Captions required.

Book and Bookstore Trade

AB BOOKMAN'S WEEKLY, Box AB, Clifton NJ 07015. (201)772-0020. Editor-in-Chief: Jacob L. Chernofsky. For professional and specialist booksellers, acquisitions and academic librarians, book publishers, book collectors, bibliographers, historians, etc. Weekly magazine; 200 pages. Circ. 8,500. Pays on publication. Buys all rights. Byline given. Phone queries OK. Submit seasonal or holiday material 2-3 months in advance. Simultaneous and photocopied submissions OK. SASE. Reports in 1 month. Sample copy $5.
Nonfiction: How-to (for professional booksellers); and historical (related to books or book trade or printing or publishing). Personal experiences, nostalgia, interviews and profiles. Query. Length: 2,500 words minimum. Pays $60 minimum.
Photos: Photos used with mss.

AMERICAN BOOKSELLER, Booksellers Publishing, Inc., 122 E. 42nd St., New York NY 10168. (212)867-9060. Editor: Ginger Curwen. This publication emphasizes the business of retail bookselling and goes to the 5,700 members of the American Booksellers Association and to more than 2,400 other readers nationwide, most of whom are involved in publishing. Monthly magazine; 48 pages. Circ. 8,700. Pays on publication. Buys all rights. Pays 25% kill fee. Byline given "except on small news stories." Submit seasonal/holiday material 3 months in advance. Computer printout submissions acceptable. SASE. Reports in 2 months. Sample copy $3.
Nonfiction: General interest (on bookselling); how-to (run a bookstore, work with publishers); interview (on authors and booksellers); photo feature (on book-related events); and solutions to the problems of small businesses. Buys 2 mss/issue. Query with clips of published work and background knowledge of bookselling. Length: 750-2,000 words. Pays $50-200.
Photos: State availability of photos. Uses b&w 5x7 matte prints and contact sheets. Pays $10-20. Uses 35mm color transparencies. Pays $10-50. Captions and model releases required.

Tips: "While we buy a number of articles for each issue, very few come from freelance writers. Since the focus of the magazine is on the business of bookselling, most of our contributors are booksellers who share their *firsthand* experience with our readers. 85% of these articles are assigned; the rest are unsolicited—but those come mainly from booksellers as well."

CHRISTIAN BOOKSELLER, (formerly *Christian Booksellers & Librarian*), 396 E. St. Charles Rd., Wheaton IL 60188. (312)653-4200. Editor: Karen M. Ball. 80% freelance written. Emphasizes "all aspects of Christian bookselling and religious library management." Monthly magazine; 68 pages. Circ. 10,000. Pays on publication. Buys all rights. Phone queries OK. Submit seasonal/holiday material 6 months in advance. Computer printout submissions acceptable. SASE. Reports in 4-6 weeks. Publishes ms an average of 3 months after acceptance. Writer's guidelines available.

Nonfiction: "*Christian Bookseller* is a trade magazine serving religious bookstores. Needs articles on bookstore management, marketing, merchandising, personnel, finance, ministry, advertising, profiles of successful and unique bookstores and libraries, in-depth interviews with authors and publishers and interviews with musicians." Buys 36-48 mss/year. No fiction. Query. Length: 1,000-2,500 words. Pays $25-100.

Photos: "Photos are to accompany all articles." State availability of photos with query. Reviews 5x7 b&w glossy prints and contact sheets. Offers no additional payment for photos accompanying ms. Uses 2-3 b&w photos/story. Captions preferred. Buys all rights.

Fillers: Short, filler-type articles dealing with the publishing, bookseller or librarian fields.

Tips: "In queries get to the point; cut the hype; state credentials factually—tell me what you're going to write. All manuscripts must be substantial in content, authoritatively written, and well documented where called for. Writers must exhibit knowledge and understanding of the religious retailing business and industry."

COLLEGE STORE EXECUTIVE, Box 1500, Westbury NY 11590. (516)334-3030. Editor: Stephanie Wood. 5% freelance written. Emphasizes merchandising and marketing in the college store market. Publishes 10 issues/year. Tabloid; 40 pages. Circ. 8,500. Pays on publication. Buys all rights. Byline given. Submit seasonal/holiday material 2-3 months in advance. Photocopied submissions OK. SASE. Reports in 3 weeks. Publishes ms an average of 3 months after acceptance. Must include SASE for writer's guidelines. For sample copy, use large manilla envelope only.

Nonfiction: Expose (problems in college market); general interest (to managers); how-to (advertise, manage a college store); store profile of new or remodeled location; personal experience (someone who worked for a publisher selling to bookstores); personal opinion (from those who know about the market); photo feature (on specific college bookstores in the country or outside); and technical (how to display products). No articles on the typical college student or general "how-to" articles. Buys 8-10 mss/year. Query. Length: 1,000 words. Pays $2/column inch.

Photos: State availability of photos with query. Pays $5 for b&w prints. Captions preferred. Buys all rights.

Tips: "No general business advice that could apply to all retail establishments—articles must deal directly with college stores. This is a good place for someone to start—but they have to understand the market." No interviews with managers on their theories of life or public relations pieces on specific products.

‡COMPUTER BOOKBASE, McPheters, Wolfe & Jones, 16704 Marquardt Ave., Cerritos CA 90701. (213)926-9544. Editorial Director: Les Spindle. Managing Editor: Sandra Kent. 80% freelance written. A monthly magazine covering new titles and featuring articles on the computer book and software publishing industry for publishers, sellers and consumers. Estab. 1983. Circ. 5,000. Pays on publication. Publishes ms an average of 6 months after acceptance. Byline given. Offers variable kill fee. Buys all rights. Submit seasonal/holiday material 4 months in advance. Simultaneous queries, and simultaneous and photocopied submissions OK. Electronic submissions OK; call for requirements. Computer printout submissions acceptable; prefers letter-quality to dot-matrix. SASE. Reports in 6 weeks. Sample copy $4.95; free writer's guidelines.

Nonfiction: Book excerpts; general interest; humor; interview/profile (with author, publisher, other industry figures); opinion; personal experience; photo feature; and technical. "Articles must be articulate and well researched on subjects of concern to our audience." Editorial calendar available. Buys 60 mss/year. Query; telephone queries OK. Length: 2,000-5,000 words. Pays $50/published page; negotiable maximum.

Photos: Send photos with query or ms. Reviews b&w prints and color transparencies. Payment for photos included in payment for ms. Captions, model release, and identification of subjects required. Buys all rights.

Columns/Departments: Book reviews (introductory and children's books to business applications and advanced programming; fiction with a computer theme may be included). Buys 50/year. Query detailing fields of interest and what systems are owned or accessible (if any). Length: 300-1,000 words. Pays $20 minimum.

Tips: "Seek out and query us about interesting developments in the computer book publishing industry."

FINE PRINT, A Review for the Arts of the Book, Fine Print Publishing Co., Box 3394, San Francisco CA 94119. (415)776-1530. Editor: Sandra D. Kirshenbaum. Quarterly magazine covering the arts of the book plus history of books and publishing, including printing, typography, type design, graphic design, calligraphy, bookbinding and papermaking. "We seek to cover contemporary fine book making and all related arts for printers, librarians, graphic artists, book collectors, publishers, booksellers, bookbinders, typographers, etc." Circ. 3,000. Pays on publication. Byline given. Buys first North American serial rights and "rights to publish in collections." Submit seasonal/holiday material 9 months in advance. Simultaneous queries, and simultaneous and photocopied submissions OK. SASE. Reports in 3 months on queries; 6 months on mss. Sample copy $9; free writer's guidelines.

Nonfiction: Interview/profile (of contemporary book artists and printers); new product (relating to printing, bookbinding, etc.); personal experience ("Book Arts Reporter" covering book events, conferences, workshops, lectures, etc.); technical (related to books, printing, typography, etc.); and exhibit reviews (of book-related exhibits in libraries, museums, galleries). Buys 4-5 mss/year. Query. Length: 2,000-4,000 for lead articles. Pays $150 for lead articles only; pays in copies for other articles.

Photos: State availability of photos with ms. Identification of subjects required. Buys one-time rights.

Columns/Departments: On Type (essays on typography and type design, contemporary and historical); Book Arts Profile; The Featured Book Binding; Exhibit Reviews; and Recent Press Books (reviews of fine limited edition books). Query. Length: 500-1,300 words. No payment "except review copies of fine books."

Fillers: Newsbreaks. Shoulder Notes—In Brief (short notices and descriptions of events, personalities and publications dictating to book arts).

‡INTERNATIONAL BOOK COLLECTORS ALMANAC/NEWSLETTER, A Cornucopia for Booklovers, Pegasus Publishers, Inc., Box 602, Vashon WA 98070. (206)567-5224. Managing Editor: J.H. Raymond. A monthly newsletter of useful and interesting facts related to authors, books and book collecting for libraries, book collectors and booksellers. Estab. 1984. Circ. 2,000. Pays on acceptance. Byline given. Buys one-time rights and second serial (reprint) rights. Simultaneous queries, and simultaneous, photocopied, and previously published submissions OK. Reports in 2 weeks on queries; 3 weeks on mss. Sample copy for 2 first class stamps.

Nonfiction: Historical/nostalgic, how-to, interview/profile, opinion and personal experience. Buys 40+ mss/year. Query with or without published clips, or send complete ms. Length: 500-2,500 words. Pays $25-100.

Columns/Departments: "We will consider unsolicited book reviews if the subject is appropriate. We have need for qualified book reviewers in all collectible book fields." Buys 40-50 mss/year. Query with published clips. Length: 250-500 words. Pays $15-30 plus the book reviewed.

Tips: Book reviews and short articles are most open to freelancers.

‡INTERRACIAL BOOKS FOR CHILDREN BULLETIN, Council on Interracial Books for Children, Inc., 1841 Broadway, New York NY 10023. (212)757-5339. Editor: Bradford Chambers. Managing Editor: Ruth Charnes. A magazine published 8 times/year covering children's literature/school materials. "Our publication reaches teachers, librarians, editors, authors and parents. It focuses on issues on bias/equity in children's literature and school materials." Circ. 5,000. Pays on publication. Byline given. Offers variable kill fee. Buys first North American serial rights and one-time rights. Submit seasonal/holiday material 6 months in advance. Computer printout submissions acceptable; prefers letter-quality to dot-matrix. Simultaneous queries, and photocopied submissions OK. SASE. Reports in 1 month on queries; 3 months on mss. Sample copy $2.50; writer's guidelines for SAE and 1 first class stamp.

Nonfiction: Personal experience (strategies for teaching/encouraging equity); interview/profile (of authors/illustrators/teachers/others seeking bias-free children's materials); and analysis of children's materials (textbooks, literature, etc.). Buys 25 mss/year. Query. Length: 1,500-2,500 words. Pays 50-200.

Columns/Departments: Review of children's books and AV materials, resources for adults. "Our policy is that books about various groups, e.g., feminists, Third World people, older people, disabled people, etc., be reviewed by members of that group." Buys 100 mss/year. Query with or without published clips. Length: 250-350 words. Pays $10-25.

Tips: "Our goal is a society that is pluralistic and bias-free. We seek the perspectives of groups that have been oppressed by a society dominated by upper class white males. We seek documentation of that oppression in the world of children's books and school learning materials and positive ways to develop awareness of that oppression and ways to conteract it. The primary consideration in writing for the *Bulletin* is sensitivity to racism, sexism, ageism, homophobia, handicapism and other forms of injustice."

NEW PAGES: News & Reviews of the Progressive Book Trade, New Pages Press, 4426 S. Belsay Rd., Grand Blanc MI 48439. (313)742-9583. Editors: Grant Burns and Casey Hill. Quarterly tabloid covering independent publishing, libraries and bookstores. Pays on publication. Byline given. Buys first North American serial rights. SASE. Reports in 1 month. Sample copy $3.

Nonfiction: Interview, opinion and book reviews. "We cover the alternative press with articles, news, reviews, listings and useful information for publishers, librarians and booksellers." Query with published clips. Length: (for book reviews) 25-250 words. Pays $5.

PUBLISHERS WEEKLY, 205 E. 42nd Ave., New York NY 10017. (212)916-1877. Editor-in-Chief: John F. Baker. Weekly. Buys first North American serial rights only. Pays on publication. Reports "in several weeks." Computer printout submissions acceptable; prefers letter-quality to dot-matrix. SASE.
Nonfiction: "We rarely use unsolicited manuscripts because of our highly specialized audience and their professional interests, but we can sometimes use news items about publishers, publishing projects, bookstores and other subjects relating to books. We will be paying increasing attention to electronic publishing." No pieces about writers or word processors. Payment negotiable; generally $150/printed page.
Photos: Photos purchased with and without mss "occasionally."

‡**SMALL PRESS, The Magazine of Independent Book Publishing**, R.R. Bowker Co.-Xerox Corp., 205 E. 42nd St., New York NY 10017. (212)916-1887. Editor-in-Chief: John F. Baker. Executive Editor: Marlene Charnizon. A bimonthly magazine covering small presses and independent publishers for publishers, librarians, bookstores and "dreamers." Estab. 1983. Circ. 7,000. Pays on publication. Byline given. Offers kill fee. Buys first North American serial rights. Submit seasonal/holiday material 4 months in advance. Computer printout submissions acceptable; no dot-matrix. Reports in 1 month. Publishes ms an average of 4 months after acceptance. Free sample copy.
Nonfiction: Book excerpts (on occasion); how-to; humor; interview/profile; new product; personal experience; photo feature (perhaps); and technical. Buys 36 mss/year. Query with or without published clips or send complete ms. Length: 2,000-3,000 words. Pays $100/printed page.
Photos: State availability of photos. Pays minimum $25 for 5x7 b&w prints. Identification of subjects required. Buys one-time rights.
Columns/Departments: "Columns treat the how-tos of such subjects as printing, paper, distribution, contracts, etc." Buys 36 mss/year. Query with or without published clips or send complete ms. Length: 1,800 words approximately. Pays $100/printed page.
Tips: "Someone really knowledgeable about small presses who writes well, has been published and respects deadlines is ideal."

Brick, Glass, and Ceramics

BRICK AND CLAY RECORD, Cahners Plaza, 1350 E. Touhy Ave., Box 5080, Des Plaines IL 60018. (312)635-8800. Editor-in-Chief: Wayne A. Endicott. For "the heavy clay products industry." Monthly. Buys all rights. Pays on publication. Query first. Reports in 15 days. SASE.
Nonfiction: "News concerning personnel changes within companies; news concerning new plants for manufacture of brick, clay pipe, refractories, drain tile, face brick, glazed tile, lightweight clay aggregate products and abrasives; and news of new products, expansion and new building." Length: 1,500-2,000 words. Pays minimum $75/published page.
Photos: No additional payment for photos used with mss.
Fillers: "Items should concern only news of brick, clay pipe, refractory or abrasives plant operations. If news of personnel, should be only of top-level plant personnel. Not interested in items such as patio, motel, or home construction using brick; consumer oriented items; weddings or engagements of clay products people, unless major executives; obituaries, unless of major personnel; or items concerning floor or wall tile (only structural tile); of plastics, metal, concrete, bakelite, or similar products; items concerning people not directly involved in clay plant operation." Pays minimum $6 for "full-length published news item, depending on value of item and editor's discretion. Payment is only for items published in the magazine. No items sent in can be returned."

CERAMIC INDUSTRY, Cahners Plaza, 1350 E. Touhy Ave., Box 5080, Des Plaines IL 60018. (312)635-8800. Editor: Patricia A. Janeway. For the ceramic industry; manufacturers of glass, porcelain enamel, whiteware and advanced ceramics (electronic, industrial and high tech). Magazine; 50-60 pages. Monthly. Circ. 7,500. Buys all rights. Byline given. Buys 10-12 mss/year (on assignment only). Pays on publication. Will send free sample copy to writer on request. Reports immediately. Query first. SASE.
Nonfiction: Semitechnical, informational and how-to material purchased on assignment only. Length: 500-1,500 words. Pays $75/published page.
Photos: No additional payment for photos used with mss. Captions required.

CERAMIC SCOPE, Box 48497, Los Angeles CA 90048. (213)935-1122. Editor: Mel Fiske. Associate Editor: Nancy J. Lee. Monthly magazine covering hobby ceramics business. For "ceramic studio owners and teachers operating out of homes as well as storefronts, who have a love for ceramics but meager business education." Also read by distributors, dealers and supervisors of ceramic programs in institutions. Circ. 8,000. Pays on acceptance. Buys all rights. Pays $100-200. Byline given unless it is a round-up story with any number of sources. Phone queries OK. Submit seasonal/holiday material 5 months in advance. Computer printout submissions acceptable. SASE. Reports in 2 weeks. Sample copy $1.

Nonfiction: "Articles on operating a small business specifically tailored to the ceramic hobby field; photo feature stories with in-depth information about business practices and methods that contribute to successful studio operation. We don't need articles dealing primarily with biographical material or how owner started in business."

Photos: State availability of photos or send photos with ms. Pays $5/4x5 or 5x7 glossy b&w print; $25-50/color contact sheets. Captions required.

‡**GLASS, For the Architectural and Automotive Glass Industries**, (formerly *Glass Dealer*), National Glass Association, #302, 8200 Greensboro Drive, McLean VA 22102. (703)442-4890. Editor: Debbie Levy. 50% freelance written. A monthly magazine covering the architectural and automotive glass industries for members of the glass and architectural trades. Circ. 17,000. Pays on acceptance. Byline given. Offers varying kill fee. Not copyrighted. Buys first rights only. Computer printut submissions acceptable; prefers letter-quality to dot-matrix. SASE. Reports in 1 week. Publishes ms an average of 3 months after acceptance. Sample copy $4; writer's guidelines free.

Nonfiction: Interview/profile (of various glass businesses; profiles of industry people or glass business owners); and technical (about glazing processes). Buys 50 mss/year. Query with published clips. Length: 800 words minimum. Pays $200-1,000.

Photos: State availability of photos. Reviews b&w and color contact sheets. Pays $20-50 for b&w; $50-100 for color. Identification of subjects required. Buys one-time rights.

Tips: "We are looking to set up a network of freelancers who can cover assigned stories."

GLASS DIGEST, 310 Madison Ave., New York NY 10017. (212)682-7681. Editor: Charles R. Cumpston. Monthly. Buys first rights only. Byline given "only industry people—not freelancers." Pays on publication "or before, if ms held too long." Will send a sample copy to a writer on request. Reports "as soon as possible." Enclose SASE for return of submissions.

Nonfiction: "Items about firms in glass distribution, personnel, plants, etc. Stories about outstanding jobs accomplished—volume of flat glass, storefronts, curtainwalls, auto glass, mirrors, windows (metal), glass doors; special uses and values; and who installed it. Stories about successful glass/metal distributors, dealers and glazing contractors—their methods, promotion work done, advertising and results." Length: 1,000-1,500 words. Pays 7¢/word, "usually more. No interest in bottles, glassware, containers, etc., but leaded and stained glass good."

Photos: B&w photos purchased with mss; "8x10 preferred." Pays $7.50, "usually more."

Tips: "Find a typical dealer case history about a firm operating in such a successful way that its methods can be duplicated by readers everywhere."

Building Interiors

‡**KITCHEN & BATH DESIGN NEWS**, KBC Publications, Box 1719, Fort Lee NJ 07024. (201)585-0551. Editor: Eliot Sefrin. Managing Editor: Nancy Furstinger. Monthly magazine covering kitchen and bath industry for kitchen and bath dealers, designers, remodelers, distributors and manufacturers of kitchen cabinets, countertops, bath vanities and built-in kitchen and bathroom products. Estab. 1983. Circ. 36,500. Pays on acceptance. Byline given. Buys first North American serial rights or makes work-for-hire assignments. Computer printout submissions acceptable. Reports in 2 weeks. Free sample copy.

Nonfiction: How-to (outstanding installations, innovative design, application of new technologies); interview/profile (noteworthy industry figures); new product; and personal experience (business-oriented success stories). "We do not seek articles geared to consumers. Articles must be written from the perspective that our readership is knowledgeable and sophisticated, yet still in need of sound business information." Buys 24 mss/year. Query with published clips. Length: 1,200-3,500 words. Pays $150-400.

Photos: State availability of photos. "Specifications for photos are worked out on a case-to-case basis." Identification of subjects required.

Columns/Departments: "Columnists are regular contributors. No freelance submissions are sought. However, departments include Design Update (the latest trends in design) and Consumer Buying Trends (what the public is purchasing in kitchens and baths)." Buys 10 mss/year. Query with published clips. Length: 1,000-1,200 words. Pays $150-350.

Tips: "Our readers are interested in the latest innovations in the kitchen and bath industry, and in down-to-earth practical advice on how to operate their businesses more productively. Freelancers should know our industry, the current market and current applications of new products, etc. Trade publishing background is generally desired."

LIGHTING DIMENSIONS MAGAZINE, Suite 8, 1590 S. Coast Hwy., Laguna Beach CA 92651. (714)499-2233. Managing Editor: Barbara Hall. Magazine published seven times/year featuring entertainment lighting (for theaters, films, TV, disco, touring and laser shows) for lighting designers in all areas of entertainment, production managers, technical directors, technicians, instructors, laser specialists, holographers and manufacturers and suppliers. Circ. 10,000. Byline given. Buys first North American serial rights. Phone queries OK. Submit seasonal material 2 months in advance. Simultaneous, photocopied and previously published submissions OK. SASE. Reports in 2 weeks. Free sample copy and writer's guidelines.
Nonfiction: Interview (with well-known lighting designers); profile; how-to; photo feature; and technical. "Articles may be technical, describing new equipment or techniques. They can also be on lighting in a specific play, opera, dance production, film, TV show or nightclub installation. We also like interviews with designers and cinematographers." Buys 3 mss/issue. Send complete ms. Pays $25-150.
Photos: State availability of photos or send photos with ms. Reviews b&w glossy prints and 8x10 color glossy prints. Offers no additional payment for photos accepted with ms. Model release required. Buys one-time rights.
Tips: "It would be tremendously helpful if the writer had some theater background, knowledge of film production, etc."

MODERN FLOOR COVERINGS, US Business Press, Inc., 11 W. 19th St., New York NY 10011. (212)953-0940. Editor: Michael Karol. 20% freelance written. Monthly tabloid featuring profit-making ideas on floor coverings, for the retail community. Circ. 28,000. Pays on acceptance. Buys first rights only. Byline given. Makes work-for-hire assignments. Computer printout submissions acceptable; no dot-matrix. Publishes ms an average of 1 month after acceptance. SASE.
Nonfiction: Interview and features/profiles. Send complete ms. Length: 1,000-10,000 words. Pays $50-250.
Tips: "It's rewarding working with freelancers and getting different points of view on a familiar subject.

PAINTING AND WALLCOVERING CONTRACTOR, Painting and Decorating Contractors of America, 7223 Lee Hwy., Falls Church VA 22046. (703)534-1201. Editor: Gerald L. Wykoff. 25% freelance written. Emphasizes the application, maintenance, restoration and removal of paint, wallcoverings, special coatings and sealants for professional painting and decorating contractors. Monthly magazine. Circ. 16,000. Pays on publication. Publishes ms an average of 3 months after acceptance. Buys first North American serial rights. Queries preferred. Reports in 3 weeks. Free sample copy for SASE.
Nonfiction: Publishes how-to and informational articles. Buys 17-20 mss/year. Query. Length: 1,500 words. Pays 5-15¢.
Photos: Purchased with accompanying ms. Captions required. Pays $7.50 for professional quality 8x10 or 5x7 glossy b&w prints. Model release required.
Tips: "Gear your writing to our specializations. Query us first with precis."

Business Management

The publications here are geared toward owners of businesses and top-level business executives. They cover business trends and general theory and practice of management. Publications that use similar material but have a less technical slant are listed in Business and Finance in the Consumer Publications section. Journals dealing with banking, investment, and financial management are classified in the Trade Finance category.

Journals for middle management (including supervisors and office managers) are found in Management and Supervision. Those for industrial plant managers are listed under Industrial Operation and Management and under the names of specific industries such as Machinery and Metal Trade. Publications for office supply store operators are included with the Office Environment and Equipment journals.

‡**ASSOCIATION & SOCIETY MANAGER**, Brentwood Publishing Corp., 825 S. Barrington Ave., Los Angeles CA 90049. (213)826-8388. Editor: Nancy Zimmerman. 90% freelance written. Bimonthly magazine on management of nonprofit organizations. "Our magazine goes to association and society managers and covers convention and meeting planning, including site selection, price negotiation, program content and 'how-to'—running an association, member benefits, computers, insurance, legislation and finance." Circ. 24,000. Pays on acceptance. Publishes ms an average of 6 months after acceptance. Byline given. Buys all rights. Sub-

mit seasonal/holiday material 6 months in advance. Computer printout submissions acceptable; prefers letter-quality to dot-matrix. SASE. Reports in 1 month. Free sample copy and writer's guidelines.

Nonfiction: How-to (plan conventions and meetings, run an association); interview/profile (of association managers); technical (automation for association management functions); and travel (convention site evaluations). No "typical travelogue-type destination pieces or articles plugging a specific product." Buys 50 mss/year. Query with published clips. Length: 1,000-2,200 words. Pays 10-12¢/word.

Columns/Departments: Automation (computer information for association management) and Insurance (specific types to offer members; liability). Buys 20 mss/year. Query with published clips. Length: 1,000-2,000 words. Pays 10-12¢/word.

Tips: "Remember that trade journals are designed to help the professional do his/her job better. Writing must be concise and easy to read; article content must be specific rather than general. We don't entertain our readers; we educate them. Study the publication for format. Follow 'how to' approach, keep to generic approach when discussing services."

‡**BOARDROOM REPORTS**, 500 5th Ave., New York NY 10110. (212)354-0005. Managing Editor: Donald Ediger. Biweekly magazine covering business advice for business executives at the managerial level. Pays on acceptance. Byline sometimes given "if writer is also expert in the field." Buys one-time rights. Submit seasonal/holiday material 3 months in advance. Previously published work OK. Reports in 1 week on queries. Free sample copy and writer's guidelines.

Nonfiction: Needs articles giving "advice to business executives on such subjects as taxes, investments, management, management psychology, personnel and law." Also personal executive advice on health, travel, etc. Query. Length: 400 words maximum. Pays "competitive rates."

EXECUTIVE REVIEW, Suite 700, 100 N. LaSalle St., Chicago IL 60602. (312)346-3822. Editor-in-Chief: Franklin E. Sabes. 5% freelance written. For management of small and middle class companies, middle management in larger companies and enterprises. Monthly magazine; 32 pages. Circ. 20,000. Pays on publication. Buys one-time rights and second (reprint) rights to material originally published elsewhere. Publishes ms an average of 5 months after acceptance. Byline given. Submit seasonal/holiday material 6 months in advance. Simultaneous, photocopied and previously published submissions OK. Computer printout submissions acceptable. SASE. Reports in 3 months. Free sample copy and writer's guidelines; mention *Writer's Market* in request.

Nonfiction: How-to (articles that will be of interest to businessmen in the operation of their companies, and ideas that can be adapted and successfully used by others); interview; personal experience (business); profile; and travel. Buys 7 mss/issue. Submit complete ms. Length: 1,000-1,500 words. Pays $15-50.

‡**COMMUNICATION BRIEFINGS**, Encoders, Inc., 806 Westminster Blvd., Blackwood NJ 08012. (609)589-3503, 227-7371. Editor: Frank Grazian. Managing Editor: Anthony Fulginiti. A monthly newsletter covering business communication and business management. "Most readers are in middle and upper management. They comprise public relations professionals, editors of company publications, marketing and advertising managers, fund raisers, directors of associations and foundations, school and college administrators, human resources professionals, and other middle managers who want to communicate better on the job." Circ. 10,000. Pays on acceptance. Byline given sometimes on Bonus Items and on other items if idea originates with the writer. Offers 25% kill fee. Buys one-time rights. Submit seasonal/holiday material 2 months in advance. Previously published submissions OK, "but must be rewritten to conform to our style." Computer printout submissions acceptable; prefers letter-quality to dot-matrix. SASE. Reports in 3 weeks on queries; 1 month on mss. Sample copy and writer's guidelines for #10 SAE and 2 first class stamps.

Nonfiction: "Most articles we buy are of the 'how-to' type. They consist of practical ideas, techniques and advice that readers can use to improve business communication and management. Areas covered: writing, speaking, listening, employee communication, human relations, public relations, interpersonal communication, persuasion, conducting meetings, advertising, marketing, fund raising, telephone techniques, teleconferencing, selling, improving publications, handling conflicts, negotiating, etc. Because half of our subscribers are in the nonprofit sector, articles that appeal to both profit and nonprofit organizations are given top priority." *Short Items*: Articles consisting of one or two brief tips that can stand alone. Length: 40-70 words. *Articles*: A collection of tips or ideas that offer a solution to a communication or management problem or that show a better way to communicate or manage. Examples: 'How to produce slogans that work,' 'The wrong ways to criticize employees,' 'Mistakes to avoid when leading a group discussion,' and '5 ways to overcome writer's block.' Length: 150-250 words. *Bonus Items*: In-depth pieces that probe one area of communication or management and cover it as thoroughly as possible. Examples: 'Producing successful special events,' 'How to evaluate your newsletter,' 'How to write to be understood.' Length: 1,000 words. Buys 30-50 mss/year. Pays $15-35; Bonus Items, $200.

Tips: "Our readers are looking for specific and practical ideas and tips that will help them communicate better both within their organizations and with outside publics. Most ideas are rejected because they are too general or too elementary for our audience. Our style is down-to-earth and terse. We pack a lot of useful information into short articles. Our readers are busy executives and managers who want information dispatched quickly and without embroidery. We omit anecdotes, lengthy quotes and long-winded exposition."

HARVARD BUSINESS REVIEW, Soldiers Field, Boston MA 02163. (617)495-6800. Editor: Kenneth R. Andrews. For top management in business and industry; younger managers who aspire to top management responsibilities; policymaking executives in government, policymakers in nonprofit organizations; and professional people interested in the viewpoint of business management. Published 6 times/year. Buys all rights. Byline given. Pays on publication. Reports in 4 to 6 weeks. SASE.
Nonfiction: Articles on business trends, techniques and problems. *"Harvard Business Review* seeks to inform executives about what is taking place in management, but it also wants to challenge them and stretch their thinking about the policies they make, how they make them and how they administer them. It does this by presenting articles that provide in-depth analyses of issues and problems in management and, wherever possible, guidelines for thinking out and working toward resolutions of these issues and problems." Length: 3,000-6,000 words. Pays $500 for full article.

IN BUSINESS, JG Press, Inc., Box 323, Emmaus PA 18049. (215)967-4135. Editor: Jerome Goldstein. Managing Editor: Ina Pincus. Bimonthly magazine covering small businesses, their management and new developments for small business owners or people thinking about starting out. Circ. 60,000. Pays on publication. Buys first North American serial rights. Submit seasonal material 3 months in advance. SASE. Reports in 6 weeks. Sample copy $2; free writer's guidelines.
Nonfiction: Expose (related to small business, trends and economic climate); how-to (advertise, market, handle publicity, finance, take inventory); profile (of an innovative small scale business); and new product (inventions and R&D by small businesses). "Keep how-tos in mind for feature articles; capture the personality of the business owner and the effect of that on the business operations." Buys 5 unsolicited mss/year. Recent article example: "Great Business Ideas That Work" (March 1984). Query with clips of published work. Length: 1,000-2,000 words. Pays $75-200.
Photos: State availability of photos. Pays $25-75. Reviews contact sheets. Captions preferred; model release required.
Tips: "Get a copy of the magazine and read it carefully so you can better understand the editorial focus. Send several specific article ideas on one topic, so we can sharpen the focus. Keep in mind that the reader will be looking for specifics and transferable information."

MANAGING, Graduate School of Business, University of Pittsburgh, 326 Mervis Hall, Pittsburgh PA 15260. (412)624-6667. Editor-in-Chief: Karen Hoy. Art Director: Barbara U. Dinsmore. 85% freelance written. Emphasizes business and management issues. Many of the readers are Graduate School of Business alumni; others are upper and middle level managers and executives in the city, tristate region and country. Magazine published two times/year (June and December); 48 pages. Circ. 5,000. Pays on acceptance. Publishes ms an average of 6 months after acceptance. Buys all rights and one-time rights. Submit seasonal/holiday material 3 months in advance. Photocopied submissions OK; previously published submissions OK, but not for full-length features. Computer printout submissions acceptable; prefers letter-quality to dot-matrix. SASE. Reports in 2 months. Free sample copy and writer's guidelines.
Nonfiction: Profile (on corporate executive to give full picture of man and his work); and business or management oriented features which stem from a regional base, but the story should have national impact. No "articles on personnel, sales or creativity." Buys 3-4 mss/issue. Length: 1,500-4,000 words. Query with samples. "Queries should include information about the author's previously published works and why he/she is qualified to handle the assignment. Prefer information on angle (direction) article will take, persons to be interviewed and subjects explored." Pays $100-400.
Photos: State availability of photos. Pays $10-40 for b&w contact sheets.
Columns/Departments: Your Turn (a column on personal views toward a business or management issue written with a background in the area); Management (medium length article dealing with a particular management problem and how to solve it); and Brief Cases (short synopses of interesting management research topics with humorous twist). Buys 1/issue. Send complete ms. Length: 500-1,500 words. Pays $25 if used.
Tips: "Our magazine is not written for the average business person. It is published twice a year so articles are in-depth and are meant to be referred to by our readers. Articles *must* have an unusual slant and contain a lot of information—information our readers can't get from the popular business publications."

MAY TRENDS, 111 S. Washington St., Park Ridge IL 60068. (312)825-8806. Editor: John E. McArdle. 20% freelance written. For owners and managers of medium- and small-sized businesses, hospitals and nursing homes, trade associations, Better Business Bureaus, educational institutions and newspapers. Publication of George S. May International Company. Magazine published without charge 3 times a year; 28-30 pages. Circulation: 30,000. Buys all rights. Byline given. Buys 10-15 mss/year. Pays on acceptance. Publishes ms an average of 6 months after acceptance. Returns rejected material immediately. Query or submit complete ms.

Computer printout submissions acceptable. SASE. Reports in 2 weeks. Will send free sample copy to writer on request.

Nonfiction: "We prefer articles dealing with problems of specific industries (manufacturers, wholesalers, retailers, service businesses, small hospitals and nursing homes) where contact has been made with key executives whose comments regarding their problems may be quoted. We like problem solving articles, *not* success stories that laud an individual company." Focus is on marketing, economic and technological trends that have an impact on medium- and small-sized businesses, not on the "giants"; automobile dealers coping with existing dull markets; and contractors solving cost—inventory problems. Will consider material on successful business operations and merchandising techniques. Length: 2,000-3,000 words. Pays $150-250.

Tips: Query letter should tell "type of business and problems the article will deal with. We specialize in the problems of small (20-500 employees, $500,000-2,500,000 volume) businesses (manufacturing, wholesale, retail and service), plus medium and small health care facilities. We are now including nationally known writers in each issue—writers like the Vice Chairman of the Federal Reserve Bank, the US Secretary of the Treasury; names like Walter Mondale and Murray Wiedenbaum; titles like the Chairman of the Joint Chiefs of Staff. This places extra pressure on freelance writers to submit very good articles."

‡**MEETING NEWS, Facts, News, Ideas For Convention and Meeting Planners Everywhere**, Gralla Publications, 1515 Broadway, New York NY 10010. (212)869-1300. Editor/Co-Publisher: Peter Shure. Executive Editor: Jane Edelstein. A monthly tabloid covering news, facts, ideas and methods in meeting planning; industry developments, legislation, new labor contracts, business practices and costs for meeting planners. Circ. 70,400. Pays on acceptance. Byline given. Buys all rights. Computer printout submissions acceptable; prefers letter-quality to dot-matrix. SASE. Reports in 1 month on queries; 2 weeks on mss. Free sample copy.

Nonfiction: Travel; and specifics on how a group improved its meetings or shows, saved money or drew more attendees. "Stress is on business articles—facts and figures." Four special issues covering specific states as meeting destination—Florida/Colorado/Texas/California. No general or philosophical pieces. Buys 25-50 mss/year. Query with published clips. Length: varies. Pays variable rates.

Tips: "Special issues focusing on certain states as meeting sites are most open. Best suggestion—query in writing, with clips, on any area of expertise about these states that would be of interest to people planning meetings there. Example: food/entertainment, specific sports, group activities, etc."

‡**MEETING PLANNERS' NEWS, New York/New England**, McKenzie Communications Inc., 96 N. Pleasant St., Amherst MA 01002. (413)253-9441. Editor/Publisher: Paul McKenzie. A monthly tabloid of mostly features on business meeting facilities in New England and New York, ranging from country inns to big hotels and resorts, for meeting planners at companies throughout New England and New York. Estab. 1984. Circ. 2,400. Pays on publication. Byline given. Offers negotiable kill fee. Buys first North American serial rights. Submit seasonal/holiday material 4 months in advance. Photocopied submissions OK. SASE. Reports in 2 weeks. Sample copy for 9x12 SAE, and 5 first class stamps.

Nonfiction: Interview/profile (on meeting planners and conference managers); and travel (business meeting destinations). Query. Length: 200-2,000 words. Pays negotiable rate.

Photos: Send photos with query or ms. Pays negotiable rate for 5x7 and 8x10 b&w prints. Captions, model release and identification of subjects required. Buys one-time rights.

Columns/Departments: Query. Length: 100-400 words. Pays negotiable rate.

Fillers: Jokes, newsbreaks. Pays negotiable rate.

NATION'S BUSINESS, Chamber of Commerce of the United States, 1615 H St., NW, Washington DC 20062. (202)463-5650. Editor: Robert P. Gray. Monthly magazine covering business as related to government for business owners and executives. Circ. 850,000+. Pays on acceptance. Byline given. Buys all rights. Reports in 2 months.

Nonfiction: "Trends in business and business relations with the federal government." Articles on improving different business procedures. Recent article example: "Learning to Work Overseas" (March 1984). Buys 10 unsolicited mss/year. Query by mail; include phone number. Length: 1,500 words average. "Payment is subject to agreement."

Photos: State availability of photos.

NPO RESOURCE REVIEW, The Nonprofit Manager's Guide to Information Resources, NPO Management Services, Inc., Caller Box A-6, Cathedral Station, New York NY 10025. (212)678-7077. Editor: Godwyn Morris. 100% freelance written. Bimonthly newsletter covering management resources for nonprofit organizations. Pays on acceptance. Publishes ms an average of 3 months after acceptance. Byline given. Offers $10 kill fee. Buys all rights. Computer printout submissions acceptable. SASE. Reports in 3 weeks. Sample copy for $2.75, business-size SAE and 37¢ postage; writer's guidelines for business-size SAE and 1 first class stamp.

Nonfiction: Book excerpts (management and business); how-to (find and use information resources); and interview/profile. Query with clips. Length: 250-1,200 words. Pays $10-100.

Tips: "We will consider anyone familiar with the workings of nonprofit organizations. Writers are free to call us for more information or to discuss ideas."

‡● **PERSPECTIVE, Issues and Ideas in the business of Borg-Warner**, Borg-Warner Corp., 200 S. Michigan Ave., Chicago IL 60604. (312)322-8500. Director: Barry Nelson. *"Perspective* is a quarterly tabloid magazine that uses strong, lively feature writing and vivid black and white photography to report on ideas and issues of interest to Borg-Warner managers in a variety of businesses world-wide." Circ. 3,500. Pays on acceptance. Byline given. Offers $400 kill fee. Buys all rights. Submit seasonal/holiday material 4 months in advance. Computer printout submissions acceptable. Reports in 2 weeks on queries; 3 weeks on mss. Free sample copy and writer's guidelines.

Nonfiction: Interview/profile (Borg-Warner manager); new product (Borg-Warner product); Opinion (business issues that affect Borg-Warner); and Borg-Warner businesses. No general, generic business stories; "we assign all stories with very specific story objectives in mind." Buys 6-12 mss/year. Query with published clips. Length: 800-1,500 words. Pays $1,000.

Tips: "Contact communications director Barry Nelson, (312)322-8666; or send samples of writing, business features preferred." Area most open to freelancers is At Issue (a critique of Borg-Warner management practices in a specific technique or discipline). "Writing needs to be tight, lively, well-organized, captivating."

‡**TOP LINE, An Executive Briefing Service**, 13-30 Corporation, 505 Market St., Knoxville TN 37902. (615)521-0600. Group Editor: Tom Lombardo. Executive Editor: Frank Finn. 33% freelance written. A quarterly magazine covering business management information for owners and CEOs of small and medium sized firms (under $100 million). Circ. 150,000. Pays on acceptance. Publishes ms an average of 2 months after acceptance. Byline given. Offers $250 kill fee. Buys first North American serial rights. Simultaneous queries OK. Computer printout submissions acceptable. Reports in 1 week. Sample copy for 9x12 SAE and 5 first class stamps.

Nonfiction: Topics include human resources, finance and taxes, law and government, marketing strategy, trends, strictly personal. *"Top Line* offers how-to, actionable management information." No unsolicited material. Buys 4 mss/year. Query with published clips. Length: 4,000 words. Pays $1,500 minimum.

Tips: "Experience in business writing is a must. Each issue contains one feature article; past topics have included exporting for small companies, planning for profit, new-product development, and doing business with the government."

Church Administration and Ministry

‡**CHRISTIAN LEADERSHIP**, Board of Christian Education of the Church of God, Box 2458, Anderson IN 46018-2458. (317)642-0257. Editor: Donald A. Courtney. 30% freelance written. A monthly magazine (except July and August) covering local church school Sunday school teachers, administrators, youth workers, choir leaders and other local church workers. Circ. 4,160. Pays on publication. Byline given. Buys first rights and second (reprint) rights to material originally published elsewhere. Submit seasonal/holiday material 4 months in advance. Simultaneous queries OK. Computer printout submissions acceptable. SASE. Reports in 4 months. Publishes ms an average of 5 months after acceptance. Free sample copy and writer's guidelines.

Nonfiction: General interest, how-to, inspirational, personal experience, guidance for carrying out programs for special days, and continuing ministries. No articles that are not specifically related to local church leadership. Buys about 90 mss/year. Send complete ms, a brief description of persent interest in writing for church leaders, background and experience. Length: 300-1,800 words. Pays $5-30.

Photos: Send photos with ms. Pays $10 for 5x7 b&w prints.

Tips: "How-to articles related to Sunday school teaching, program development and personal teacher enrichment or growth, with illustrations of personal experience of the authors, are most open to freelancers."

THE CHRISTIAN MINISTRY, 407 S. Dearborn St., Chicago IL 60605. (312)427-5380. Editorial Director: James M. Wall. 10% freelance written. For the professional clergy (primarily liberal Protestant). Bimonthly magazine; 40 pages. Circ. 12,000. Buys all rights. Buys 50 mss/year. Pays on publication. Reports in 2 weeks. SASE. Free sample copy.

Nonfiction: "We want articles by clergy—theologians who know the clergy audience. We are interested in articles on local church problems and in helpful how-to as well as 'think' pieces." Query. Length: 1,200-1,800 words. Pay varies, $10/page minimum.

CHURCH ADMINISTRATION, 127 9th Ave. N., Nashville TN 37234. (615)251-2060. Editor: George Clark. For Southern Baptist pastors, staff and volunteer church leaders. 15% freelance written. Monthly. Buys all rights. Byline given. Uses limited amount of freelance material. Pays on acceptance. Publishes ms an average of 8 months after acceptance. Computer printout submissions acceptable; prefers letter-quality to dot-matrix. Free sample copy and writer's guidelines upon request. SASE.

Nonfiction: "Ours is a journal for effectiveness in ministry, including church programming, organizing, and staffing; administrative skills; church financing; church food services; church facilities; communication; and pastoral ministries and community needs." Length: 1,200-1,500 words. Pays 4¢/word.

Tips: "A beginning writer should first be acquainted with organization and policy of Baptist churches and with the administrative needs of Southern Baptist churches. He should perhaps interview one or several SBC pastors or staff members, find out how they are handling a certain administrative problem such as 'enlisting volunteer workers' or 'sharing the administrative load with church staff or volunteer workers.' I suggest writers compile an article showing how *several* different administrators (or churches) handled the problem, perhaps giving meaningful quotes. Submit the completed manuscript, typed 54 characters to the line, for consideration. Freelancers must meet the need of a target audience, with a style and format in compliance."

CHURCH MANAGEMENT—THE CLERGY JOURNAL, Box 1625, Austin TX 78767. (512)327-8501. Editor: Manfred Holck Jr. 100% freelance written. For professional clergy and church business administrators. Monthly (except June and December) magazine; 44 pages. Circ. 15,000. Pays on publication. Buys all rights. Pays 50% kill fee. Byline given. Submit seasonal/holiday material 6 months in advance. Photocopied submissions OK. SASE. Reports in 2 months. Sample copy $2.50.

Nonfiction: How-to (be a more effective minister or administrator); and inspirational (seasonal sermons). No poetry or personal experiences. Buys 4 mss/issue. Submit complete ms. Length: 1,000-1,500 words. Pays $25-35.

Columns/Departments: Stewardship; Church Administration; Sermons; Tax Planning for Clergy; and Problem Solving. Buys 2/issue. Send complete ms. Length: 1,000-1,500 words. Pays $20-35. Open to suggestions for new columns/departments.

Tips: "Send completed mss. Avoid devotional, personal stories, and interviews. Readers want to know how to be more effective ministers."

CHURCH PROGRAMS FOR PRIMARIES, 1445 Boonville Ave., Springfield MO 65807. Editor: Sinda S. Zinn. Assistant Editor: Diana Ansley. 1% freelance written. "For teachers of primary age children in a children's church, extended session, story hour, or Bible club setting." Quarterly magazine. Circ. 4,500. Pays on acceptance. Publishes ms an average of 6 months after acceptance. Buys one-time rights or first North American serial rights. Phone queries OK. Submit seasonal/holiday material 12-15 months in advance. Previously published submissions OK "if you tell us." Computer printout submissions acceptable. Reports in 6 weeks. SASE. Free sample copy and writer's guidelines.

Nonfiction: How-to ("Get Seven Helpers Out of an Old Sock," worship through music, etc.); inspirational; and practical help for the teacher. The spiritual must be an integral part of your material and articles should reflect actual experience or observations related to working with 6-to-7 year olds. "Articles and stories should be oriented both to children and to a church programs setting. Some how-to articles are helpful." Buys 10-12 mss/year. Submit complete ms. Length: 500-1,200 words. Pays $15-36.

Photos: Purchased with mss about handcrafted items. Offers no additional payment for photos accepted with ms.

Fiction: Most religious stories done on assignment. Buys 13 mss/issue. Query. Length: 2,000-2,200 words.

Tips: "Write, requesting a sample of our publication and a copy of our writer's guidelines."

CHURCH TRAINING, 127 9th Ave. N., Nashville TN 37234. (615)251-2843. Publisher: The Sunday School Board of the Southern Baptist Convention. Editor: Richard B. Sims. 5% freelance written. For all workers and leaders in the Church Training program of the Southern Baptist Convention. Monthly. Circ. 30,000. Buys all rights. Byline given. Buys 25 mss/year. Pays on acceptance. No photocopied or simultaneous submissions. Computer printout submissions acceptable. Reports in 6 weeks. Query with rough outline. SASE. Will send sample copy to writer on request. Write for copy of guidelines for writers.

Nonfiction: "Articles that pertain to leadership training in the church. Success stories that pertain to Church Training. Associational articles. Informational, how-to's that pertain to Church Training." Buys 15 unsolicited mss/year. Length: 500-1,500 words. Pays 4¢/word.

Tips: "Write an article that reflects the writer's experience of personal growth through church training. Keep in mind the target audience: workers and leaders of Church Training organizations in churches of the Southern Baptist Convention."

‡**CIRCUIT RIDER, A Journal for United Methodist Ministers**, United Methodist Publishing House, Box 801, Nashville TN 37202. (615)749-6488. Editor: J. Richard Peck. Managing Editor: Bette Prestwood. 70% freelance written. A monthly magazine covering professional concerns of clergy. Circ. 48,000. Pays on ac-

ceptance. Publishes ms an average of 1 year after acceptance. Byline given. Buys all rights. Submit seasonal/holiday material 6 months in advance. Photocopied submissions OK. Computer printout submissions acceptable. Reports in 3 weeks.
Nonfiction: How-to (improve pastoral calling, preaching, counseling, administration, etc.). No personal experience articles; no interviews. Buys 50 mss/year. Send complete ms. Length: 600-2,000 words. Pays $30-100.
Photos: State availability of photos. Pays $25-50 for 8x10 b&w prints. Model release required. Buys one-time rights.
Tips: "Know the concerns of a United Methodist pastor. Be specific. Think of how you can help pastors."

KEY TO CHRISTIAN EDUCATION, Standard Publishing, 8121 Hamilton Ave., Cincinnati OH 45231. (513)931-4050. Editor-in-Chief: Virginia Beddow. 50% freelance written. For "church leaders of all ages, Sunday school teachers and superintendents, ministers, Christian education professors and youth workers." Quarterly magazine; 48 pages. Circ. 70,000. Pays on acceptance. Publishes ms an average of 2 years after acceptance. Buys first North American serial rights. Byline given. Submit seasonal/holiday material 15 months in advance. Photocopied and previously published submissions OK. Computer printout submissions acceptable; prefers letter-quality to dot-matrix. SASE. Reports in 1 month. Free sample copy and writer's guidelines.
Nonfiction: How-to (programs and projects for Christian education); informational; interview; opinion; and personal experience. Buys 10 mss/issue. Query or submit complete ms. Length: 700-2,000 words. Pays $20-60.
Photos: Purchased with accompanying ms. Submit prints. Pays $5-25 for any size glossy finish b&w prints. Total price for ms includes payment for photos. Model release required.
Fillers: Purchases short ideas on "this is how we did it" articles. Buys 10 mss/issue. Submit complete ms. Length: 50-250 words. Pays $5-10.
Tips: "Write for guidelines, sample issue and themes. Then write an article that fits one of the themes following the guidelines. Be practical. If the article pertains to a specific age group, address the article to that department editor."

PASTORAL LIFE, Society of St. Paul, Route 224, Canfield OH 44406. Editor: Ignatius W. Staniszewski, SSP. 66% freelance written. Emphasizes priests and those interested in pastoral ministry. Magazine; 64 pages. Monthly. Circ. 8,800. Buys first rights only. Byline given. Pays on acceptance. Publishes ms an average of 3 months after acceptance. Will send sample copy to writer on request. Query with a outline before submitting ms. "New contributors are expected to include, in addition, a few lines of personal data that indicate academic and professional background." Computer printout submissions acceptable; prefers letter-quality to dot-matrix. Reports in 7-10 days. SASE.
Nonfiction: "*Pastoral Life* is a professional review, principally designed to focus attention on current problems, needs, issues and all important activities related to all phases of pastoral work and life." Buys 30 unsolicited mss/year. Length: 2,000-3,400 words. Pays 3¢/word minimum.

THE PRIEST, Our Sunday Visitor, Inc., 200 Noll Plaza, Huntington IN 46750. (219)356 8400. Editor: Father Vincent J. Giese. Associate Editor: Robert A. Willems. Monthly magazine (July-August combined issue) covering the priesthood. "Our magazine is basically for priests, by priests, although much is now being accepted from laypeople." Circ. 10,050. Pays on acceptance. Byline given. Not copyrighted. Buys one-time rights. Submit seasonal/holiday material 5 months in advance. SASE. Reports in 1 week on queries; 2 weeks on mss. Free sample copy.
Nonfiction: How-to, inspirational, interview/profile, opinion, personal experience and technical. "Material must deal with the day-to-day problems of the priest in his work in the parish. Don't pad articles." Recent article includes: "Disabled People: Your Parish's Hidden Minority" (April 1984). Buys 60 mss/year. Send complete ms. Length: 500-3,000 words. Pays $25-150.

SUCCESS, Christian Education Today, (formerly *Success: A Christian Education Magazine*), Box 15337, Denver CO 80215. Editor: Edith Quinlan. Research Editor: Charles Luckenbill. 90% freelance written. Quarterly magazine. Byline given. Reports in 2-3 weeks. SASE. Free sample copy and writer's guidelines sent on request.
Nonfiction: Invites articles from Christian education directors in local churches as well as professors in Christian education. Articles should provide ideas helpful to Christian education workers and may be slanted to the general areas or to specific age groups such as preschool, elementary, youth or adult. Payment commensurate with length and value of article to total magazine. Articles should be from 500-2,000 words.

YOUR CHURCH, Religious Publishing Co., 198 Allendale Rd., King of Prussia PA 19406. Editor: Phyllis Mather Rice. Bimonthly magazine; 56 pages. Circ. 188,000. Pays on publication. Buys first rights only. Pays 50% kill fee. Photocopied submissions OK. Computer printout submissions acceptable; no dot-matrix. SASE. Reports in 2-3 months.

Nonfiction: "Articles for pastors, informative and cogently related to some aspect of being a pastor (counseling, personal finance, administration, building, etc.). No poems, sermons or devotional material." Buys 66 mss/year. Length: 5-15 typewritten pages. Pays $5/page, not to exceed $75.

Tips: "Always send a covering letter with some information about the article and the author."

Clothing

APPAREL INDUSTRY MAGAZINE, Shore Publishing, Suite 110, 6255 Barfield Rd., Atlanta GA 30328. Editor: Karen Schaffner. Managing Editor: Ray Henderson. 30% freelance written. For executive management in apparel companies with interests in equipment, government intervention in the garment industry, finance, management and training in industry. Monthly magazine; 64-125 pages. Circ. 18,600. Byline given. Buys 30 mss/year. Buys first rights only. Pays on publication. Publishes ms an average of 3 months after acceptance. Will consider legible photocopied submissions. Computer printout submissions acceptable. Reports in 1 month. Query. SASE. Sample copy $3.

Nonfiction: Articles dealing with equipment, manufacturing techniques, training, finance; state and federal government, quality control, etc., related to the industry. "Use concise, precise language that is easy to read and understand. In other words, because the subjects are often technical, keep the language comprehensible. Material must be precisely related to the apparel industry. We are not a retail oriented magazine." Informational, interview, profile, successful business operations and technical articles. Length: 3,000 words maximum. Pays 15¢/word.

Photos: Pays $5/photo with ms.

APPAREL NEWS SOUTH, Apparel News Group, 945 S. Wall St., Los Angeles CA 90015. (800)421-8867. Editor: Stephen Siciliano. Tabloid published 5 times/year about the women's and children's apparel industry for retailers in 11 states of the Southeast. Average issue includes 6-10 features. Pays on publication. Byline given. Buys all rights. Submit seasonal material 2 months in advance. Simultaneous and previously published submissions OK if so indicated. Reports in 1 month.

Nonfiction: General interest (trends in fashion retailing and textile, fiber and fabrics industries); profile (of individuals and stores); and how-to (run an apparel retail store, display, manage personnel, energy, accounting and buying). Buys 2-3 mss/issue. Query with clips of previously published work and synopsis. Length: 750-1,000 words. Pays negotiable rates.

Photos: State availability of photos. Pays negotiable rate for 5x7 b&w glossy prints. Captions and model release required. Buys one-time rights.

Tips: "Query should be a brief description of the article proposed and why the writer feels it should interest me. State availability of photos with a brief explanation of why the writer is capable of doing the article. Must know the fashion retail field."

BODY FASHIONS/INTIMATE APPAREL, Harcourt Brace Jovanovich Publications, 545 5th Ave., New York NY 10017. (212)888-4364. Editor-in-Chief: Jill Gerson. Emphasizes information about men's and women's hosiery: women's undergarments, lingerie, sleepwear, robes, hosiery and leisurewear. For merchandise managers and buyers of store products, manufacturers and suppliers to the trade. Monthly tabloid insert, plus 10 regional market issues called *Market Maker*; 24 pages minimum. Circ. 13,500. Pays on publication. Buys all rights. Phone queries OK. Submit seasonal/holiday material 2 months in advance. Previously published submissions not accepted. SASE. Reports in 1 month.

Columns/Departments: New Image (discussions of renovations of *Body Fashions/Intimate Apparel* department); Creative Retailing (deals with successful retail promotions); and Ad Ideas (descriptions of successful advertising campaigns). Buys 6 features/year. Query. Length: 500-2,500 words. Pays 15¢/word as edited. Open to suggestions for new columns and departments.

Photos: B&w (5x7) photos purchased without mss. Captions required. Send contact sheet, prints or negatives. Pays $5-25. Model release required.

FOOTWEAR FOCUS, National Shoe Retailers Association, 200 Madison Ave., Room 1409, New York NY 10016. (212)686-7520. Managing Editor: Anisa Mycak. Magazine published 4 times/year about shoes for shoe store owners, buyers and managers from all over the US. The publication features articles pertaining to new methods, creative ideas and reliable information to help them better operate their businesses. Circ. 20,000. Average issue includes 5 articles/4 departments. Pays on acceptance. Byline given. Makes work-for-hire assignments. SASE. Reports in 1 month. Free sample copy and writer's guidelines.

Nonfiction: Contact: Editor, *Footwear Focus*. Interview (with buyers and store owners); how-to (advertise, display, create interiors, do inventory accounting, and manage data processing systems); new product (shoes and accessories); and technical (new methods of shoe manufacturing). "No generic-type articles that can be applied to any industry. No articles on salesmanship, management training, generic items or computers." Buys 5 mss/year. Query with resume and clips of previously published work. "We do not accept mss." Length: 900-1,500 words. Pays $100-200. "We want feature articles that are personality interviews or how-to articles. They must be closely related to the shoe industry. All how-tos must pertain to some aspect of shoe retailing such as developing advertising plans, interior displays, setting up an open-to-buy or fashion merchandising."
Tips: "Freelancers must have knowledge, experience or background in fashion merchandising and retailing, preferably in shoes. Other areas open are advertising and promotion, customer services, and buying and inventory control. We prefer article suggestions to actual manuscripts, as most freelance writing is assigned according to the editor's choice of subject and topic areas. Those writers interested in doing personal interviews and covering regional events in the shoe industry have the best opportunity, since NYC staff writers can cover only local events."

IMPRESSIONS, Gralla Publications, Inc., Suite 112, 15400 Knoll Trail Dr., Dallas TX 75248. (214)239-3060. Editor: Carl Piazza. 5% freelance written. Monthly magazine about the imprinted sportswear industry for retailers, printers, wholesalers, manufacturers and suppliers. Circ. 25,000. Pays on publication. Publishes ms an average of 2 months after acceptance. Buys first rights. Submit seasonal material 3 months in advance. Increased rates when photos or illustrations available. Phone queries OK. Buys 12 or more mss/year. Pays $100-300.
Nonfiction: Technical or general interest related to imprinted sportswear industry. Examples: screen printing of textiles (techniques, materials, etc.), direct or heat transfers printing (methods, mediums, etc.); manufacturing of equipment, imprintables (T-shirts, caps, uniforms, etc.), supplies; business management (employee management, accounting and credit, inventory control, computers, etc.); legal materials (copyright and trademark rulings, sales contracts, etc.); art (preparation for transfers, screen printing, advertising, etc.); sales techniques; retailing; and merchandising.
Tips: "Freelancers offer us the flexibility of subject material. We dislike, however, getting early demands for payment."

KIDS FASHIONS, Larkin-Pluznick-Larkin, 210 Boylston St., Chestnut Hill MA 02167. (617)964-5100. Editor: Elizabeth Cridland. Managing Editor: Mary Ann Wood. Monthly magazine covering children's wear. Circ. 15,000. Pays on acceptance. Byline given. Buys all rights. Submit seasonal/holiday material 9 months in advance. SASE. Reports in 2 weeks. Free sample copy.
Nonfiction: Mary Ann Wood, articles editor. How-to (on business); retailer/store profiles (of successful merchants); and technical. "Knowledge of retail and/or business practices and procedures necessary." No articles previously published in apparel trade books. Buys 24 mss/year. Query with or without clips of published work. Length: 750-6,000 words. Pays $150-250.
Photos: State availability of photos. Reviews b&w contact sheet. Captions and identification of subjects required. Buys one-time rights.
Fillers: Mary Ann Wood, fillers editor. Jokes, gags, short humor and newsbreaks. Buys 20/year. Length: 50-200 words. Pays variable rate.

KNITTING TIMES, National Knitted Outerwear Association, 386 Park Ave., S., New York NY 10016. (212)683-7520. Editor: David Gross. 10% freelance written. For the knitting industry, from the knitter to the cutter and sewer to the machinery manufacturer, to the fiber and yarn producer, chemical manufacturer, and various other suppliers to the industry. Monthly magazine; 80 pages. Circ: 6,100. Pays on publication. Publishes ms an average of 2 months after acceptance. Buys all rights. Submit seasonal or holiday material 1 month in advance. SASE. Reports in 1 month. Free sample copy and writer's guidelines.
Nonfiction: Historical (various parts of the knitting industry; development of machines, here and abroad); how-to (cut and sew various outer garments; knit, dye and finish; needle set-outs for various knit constructions); informational (market or show reports, trends, new fabrics, machine, fiber, yarn, chemical developments); interviews (with leading figures in the industry; may be knitter, head of fiber company, etc. Must say something significant such as new market development, import situation, projections and the like); new product (on anything in the industry such as machines, fibers, yarns, dyeing and finishing equipment, etc.); photo features (on plants or plant layouts, how to cut and sew sweaters, skirts, etc.); profiles (can be on industry leaders, or on operation of a company; specifically plant stories and photos); and technical (on machines, chemical processes, finishing, dyeing, spinning, texturing, etc.). Length: 750 words minimum. Query first. Pays $125 for 1,000 words.
Photos: B&w glossies (8x10) purchased with mss. Query first. Pays $3 for glossies; $5/diagram.
Tips: "With freelancers we are able to cover a broader market."

TACK 'N TOGS MERCHANDISING, Box 67, Minneapolis MN 55440. (612)374-5200. Editor: Dan De-Wese. For "retailers of products for horse and rider and Western and English fashion apparel." Monthly. Circ. 18,000. Rights purchased vary with author and material; may buy all rights. Byline given "except on simultaneous submissions, or nonexclusive articles that may appear in slightly edited form in other publications." Buys 10-12 mss/year. Pays on acceptance. Query; "style isn't important, but substance has to be something I need—suggest angle from which writer will cover the story." Computer printout submissions acceptable; prefers letter-quality to dot-matrix. SASE. Will send a sample copy to a writer on request. Write for copy of guidelines for writers.
Nonfiction: "Case histories and trends of industry." Buys informational articles, how-tos, interviews, profiles, coverage of successful business operations and articles on merchandising techniques. No boiler-plate articles. Length: open. Pays "up to $150."
Photos: B&w glossies and color transparencies purchased with mss.
Tips: "Write a letter describing a geographic area you can cover. Show some expertise in a particular phase of retail management."

TEENS & BOYS, 71 W. 35th St., New York NY 10001. 10% freelance written. For retailers, manufacturers and resident buying offices in male apparel trade. Monthly magazine; 48-100 pages. Pays on publication. Buys one-time rights. Byline given. Submit seasonal/holiday material 6 months in advance. SASE.
Nonfiction: *Teens & Boys* is edited for large and small retailers of apparel for boys and male teenage students ages 4-18. It forecasts style trends and reports on all aspects of retailing. All factual, carefully researched, pertinent articles presented in a lively style will be considered. No tax articles." Buys 2 mss/issue. Query with "well-detailed outline and writing samples to corporate headquarters: Attn: Mary Ann Wood, Teens & Boys, 210 Boylston St., Chestnut Hill MA 02167. Retail related stories most appreciated." Length: 1,000-2,000 words. Pays $100-250.
Photos: Photos necessary with article. Payment included in article. Will accept contact sheets and negatives or 5x7, 8x10 b&w glossy prints. Captions required. Buys one-time rights.
Tips: "Phone inquiries followed up in writing are most successful. We strive for regional representation of retailers, so geographic distribution is good."

TEXTILE WORLD, Suite 420, 4170 Ashford, Dunwoody Rd. NE, Atlanta GA 30319. Editor-in-Chief: Laurence A. Christiansen. Monthly. Buys all rights. Pays on acceptance. SASE.
Nonfiction: Uses articles covering textile management methods, manufacturing and marketing techniques, new equipment, details about new and modernized mills, etc., but avoids elementary, historical or generally well-known material. Pays $25 minimum/page.
Photos: Photos purchased with accompanying ms with no additional payment, or purchased on assignment.

WESTERN & ENGLISH FASHIONS, (formerly *Western Wear and Equipment*), Bell Publishing, 2403 Champa, Denver CO 80205. (303)572-1777. Editor: Larry Bell. Managing Editor: Lee Darrigrand. For "Western and English apparel and equipment retailers, manufacturers and distributors. The magazine features retailing practices such as marketing, merchandising, display techniques, buying and selling to help business grow or improve, etc. Every issue carries feature stories on Western/English/square dance apparel stores throughout the US." Monthly magazine; 50 pages. Circ. 13,000. Pays on publication. Not copyrighted. Byline given unless extensive rewriting is required. Phone queries OK. Submit seasonal/holiday material 3 months in advance. Simultaneous (to noncompeting publications), photocopied and previously published submissions OK. Computer printout submissions acceptable. No fiction or foreign material. SASE. Free sample copy and writer's guidelines.
Nonfiction: Expose (of government as related to industry or people in industry); general interest (pertaining to Western lifestyle); interview (with Western/English store owners); new product (of interest to Western/English clothing retailers—send photo); and photo feature. "We will be doing much more fashion oriented articles and layouts." Buys 20-25/year. Query with outline. Length: 800-3,600 words. Pays $50-150.
Photos: "We buy photos with manuscripts. Occasionally we purchase photos that illustrate a unique display or store with only a cutline." State availability of photos. Captions required with "names of people or products and locations." Buys one-time rights.

WESTERN OUTFITTER, 5314 Bingle Rd., Houston TX 77092. (713)688-8811. Editor: Anne DeRuyter. For "owners and managers of retail stores in all 50 states and Canada. These stores sell clothing for riders and equipment for horses, both Western and English style." Monthly. Buys all rights. Pays on publication. Query. SASE.
Nonfiction: Method stories: "in-depth treatment of subjects each merchant wrestles with daily. We want stories that first describe the problem, then give details on methods used in eliminating the problem. Be factual and specific." Subjects include all aspects of retailing. "To merit feature coverage, this merchant has to be a winner. It is the uniqueness of the winner's operation that will benefit other store owners who read this magazine." Length: 1,000-1,500 words for full length feature; 500-600 words for featurette. Pays 8-10¢/word.

"Send us copies of stories you have done for other trade magazines. Send us queries based on visits to Western dealers in your territory."

Photos: "Excellent photos make excellent copy much better. Plan photos that bring to life the key points in your text. Avoid shots of store fixtures without people. Submit contact prints or 5x7 glossies. Sharp focus is a must." Captions required. "Cover photos: We will pay $50 for a color transparency if used for a cover (2¼x2¼ or 35mm). Your 35mm shots are fine for interior b&w art." Pays $10/b&w photo used with ms. Also uses "single photos, or pairs of photos that show display ideas, tricks and promotional devices that are different and that bring more business." Pays $10.

Tips: "The queries that have thought out the subject, advance some angles on which the story is built, and show that the writer has digested our detailed guidelines statement are a real pleasure to respond to."

Coin-Operated Machines

AMERICAN COIN-OP, 500 N. Dearborn St., Chicago IL 60610. (312)337-7700. Editor: Ben Russell. For owners of coin-operated laundry and dry cleaning stores. Monthly magazine; 42 pages. Circ. 19,000. Rights purchased vary with author and material but are exclusive to the field. No byline. Buys 25 mss/year. Pays two weeks prior to publication. Reports as soon as possible; usually in 2 weeks. Computer printout submissions acceptable; prefers letter-quality to dot-matrix. SASE. Free sample copy.

Nonfiction: "We emphasize store operation and use features on industry topics: utility use and conservation, maintenance, store management, customer service and advertising. A case study should emphasize how the store operator accomplished whatever he did—in a way that the reader can apply to his own operation. Mss should have no-nonsense, business-like approach." Uses informational, how-to, interview, profile, think pieces and successful business operations articles. Length: 500-3,000 words.

Photos: Pays 6¢/word minimum. Pays $6 minimum for 8x10 b&w glossy photos purchased with mss. (Contact sheets with negatives preferred.)

Fillers: Newsbreaks and clippings. Length: open. Pays $5 minimum.

Tips: "Query about subjects of current interest. Be observant of coin-operated laundries—how they are designed and equipped, how they serve customers and how (if) they advertise and promote their services. Most general articles are turned down because they are not aimed well enough at audience. Most case histories turned down because of lack of practical purpose (nothing new or worth reporting)."

ELECTRONIC SERVICING & TECHNOLOGY, Intertec Publishing Corp., Box 12901, Overland Park KS 66212. (913)888-4664. Editor: Conrad Persson. Managing Editor: Rhonda Wickham. Monthly magazine for electronic enthusiasts who are interested in buying, building, installing and repairing home entertainment electronic equipment (audio, video, microcomputers, electronic games, etc.) Circ. 60,000. Pays on publication. Byline given. Buys all rights. Submit seasonal/holiday material 4 months in advance. Simultaneous queries OK. Computer printout submissions acceptable. Reports in 2 weeks on queries; 1 month on mss. Free sample copy and writer's guidelines.

Nonfiction: How-to (service, build, install and repair home entertainment electronic equipment); personal experience (troubleshooting); and technical (home entertainment electronic equipment; electronic testing and servicing equipment). "Explain the techniques used carefully so that even hobbyists can understand a how-to article." Buys 36 mss/year. Send complete ms. Length: 10,000 words minimum. Pays $100-200.

Photos: "Included in payment for ms." Send photos with ms. Reviews color and b&w transparencies and b&w prints. Captions and identification of subjects required. Buys all rights.

Columns/Departments: Jane Cigard, column/department editor. Troubleshooting Tips. Buys 12 mss/year. Send complete ms. Length: open. Pays $30-40.

LEISURE TIME ELECTRONICS, US Business Press, Inc., 124 E. 40th St., New York NY 10016. (212)953-0230. Editor: Dan Shannon. Tabloid published monthly covering electronic games and toys, personal computers and software, audio and video hardware and software, auto electronics and personal electronics for retailers of leisure electronics. Circ. 51,000. Pays on acceptance. Byline and brief bio given. Buys "all rights in the trade." Queries requested. Reports "promptly." Free sample copy.

Nonfiction: Technical (state-of-the-art explaining technology); and merchandising (all aspects). Buys 20 mss/year. Query with clips of published work and resume. Length: 1,000 words average. Pays rates "competitive with any national magazine."

Photos: "We ask writers to request photos from storeowners. Product photos come from manufacturers." Reviews color transparencies and 8x10 b&w glossy prints. Identification of subjects required.

PLAY METER MAGAZINE, Skybird Publishing Co., Inc., Box 24170. New Orleans LA 70184. Publisher: Ralph Lally. Managing Editor: Laura Braddock. 25% freelance written. Trade publication for owners/operators of coin-operated amusement machine companies, e.g., pinball machines, video games, arcade pieces, jukeboxes, etc. Semimonthly magazine; 100 pages. Circ. 13,000. Pays on publication. Buys all rights. Byline given. Submit seasonal/holiday material 2 months in advance of issue date. Photocopied and previously published submissions OK. Computer printouts acceptable "as long as they are clear and readable." SASE. Query answered in 2 months. Sample copy $2; free writer's guidelines.

Nonfiction: How-to (get better locations for machines, promote tournaments, evaluate profitability of route, etc.); interview (with industry leaders); new product (if practical for industry, not interested in vending machines); unusual arcades (game rooms); and photo features (with some copy). "No 'puff' or 'plug' pieces about new manufacturers. Our readers want to read about how they can make more money from their machines, how they can get better tax breaks, commissions, etc. Also no stories about *playing* pinball. Our readers don't play the games per se; they buy the machines and make money from them." Recent article example: "The Jukebox: Operators search for stability" (April 1984). Buys 48 mss/year. Submit complete ms. Length: 250-3,000 words. Pays $30-215.

Photos: "The photography should have news value. We don't want 'stand 'em up-shoot 'em down' group shots." Pays $15 minimum for 5x7 or 8x10 b&w prints. Captions preferred. Buys all rights. Art returned on request.

Tips: "*Do not* submit ms on erasable bond paper."

VENDING TIMES, 211 E. 43rd St., New York NY 10017. Editor: Arthur E. Yohalem. For operators of vending machines. Monthly. Circ. 14,700. Buys all rights. Pays on publication. Query. "We will discuss in detail the story requirements with the writer." SASE.

Nonfiction: Feature articles and news stories about vending operations; practical and important aspects of the business. "We are always willing to pay for good material."

Confectionery and Snack Foods

CANDY INDUSTRY, HBJ Publications, 7500 Old Oak Blvd., Cleveland OH 44130. (216)243-8100. Editor: Pat Magee. 5% freelance written. For confectionery manufacturers. Monthly. Publishes ms an average of 4 months after acceptance. Buys all rights. Computer printout submissions acceptable; prefers letter-quality to dot-matrix. SASE. Reports in 2 weeks.

Nonfiction: "Feature articles of interest to large scale candy manufacturers that deal with activities in the fields of production, packaging (including package design), merchandising; and financial news (sales figures, profits, earnings), advertising campaigns in all media, and promotional methods used to increase the sale or distribution of candy." Length: 1,000-1,250 words. Pays 15¢/word; "special rates on assignments."

Photos: "Good quality glossies with complete and accurate captions, in sizes not smaller than 5x7." Pays $5; $20 for color.

Fillers: "Short news stories about the trade and anything related to candy and snacks." Pays 5¢/word; $1 for clippings.

PACIFIC BAKERS NEWS, NE 4791 North Shore Rd., Belfair WA 98528. (206)275-6421. Publisher: Leo Livingston. 50% freelance written. Business newsletter for commercial bakeries in the Western states. Monthly. Pays on publication. No byline given; uses only one-paragraph news items.

Nonfiction: Uses bakery business reports and news about bakers. Buys only brief "boiled-down news items about bakers and bakeries operating only in Alaska, Hawaii, Pacific Coast and Rocky Mountain states. Welcome clippings. Need monthly news reports and clippings about the baking industry and the donut business. No pictures, jokes, poetry or cartoons." Length: 10-200 words. Pays 6¢/word for clips and news used.

Construction and Contracting

Builders, architects, and contractors learn the latest news of their trade in these publications. Journals aimed at architects are included in the Art, Design, and Collectibles section. Those for specialists in the interior aspects of construction are listed under Building Interiors. Also of interest would be the markets in the Brick, Glass, and Ceramics section.

ARCHITECTURAL METALS, National Association of Architectural Metal Manufacturers, 221 N. LaSalle St., Chicago IL 60601. (312)346-1600. Editor: James Mruk. Editorial Director: August L. Sisco. 10% freelance written. Published winter, spring and fall. Magazine covers architectural metal applications for architects, specifiers and other engineers involved in using architectural metal products. Circ. 15,000. Pays on acceptance. Publishes ms an average of 3 months after acceptance. Byline given. Buys first North American serial rights and simultaneous rights on work-for-hire assignments. Simultaneous queries, and simultaneous, photocopied and previously published submissions OK. Computer printout submissions acceptable; no dot-matrix. Reports in 2 weeks on queries; 1 month on mss. Free sample copy and writer's guidelines.
Nonfiction: "No articles that are too general." Number of mss bought/year "depends on need." Query with clips of published work or send complete ms. Phone queries preferred. Length: 1,000 words minimum. Pays $150-400/article.
Photos: Send photos with ms. Payment negotiable for quality b&w prints. Captions required.
Tips: "Have a knowledge of architectural metals and write clearly. Applications of hollow metal doors and frames/metal flagpoles/metal bar grating/architectural metal products are all open. Technical details are a must. We enjoy obtaining new sources of quality material from freelancers, but it's difficult to find writers knowledgeable about our industry."

AUTOMATION IN HOUSING & MANUFACTURED HOME DEALER, (formerly *Automation in Housing & Systems Building News*), CMN Associates, Inc., Box 120, Carpinteria CA 93013. (805)684-7659. Editor-in-Chief: Don Carlson. Specializes in management for industrialized (manufactured) housing and volume home builders. Monthly magazine; 88 pages. Circ. 25,000. Pays on acceptance. Buys first North American serial or one-time rights. Phone queries OK. Computer printout submissions acceptable; no dot-matrix. SASE. Reports in 2 weeks. Free sample copy and writer's guidelines.
Nonfiction: Case history articles on successful home building companies which may be 1) production (big volume) home builders; 2) mobile home manufacturers; 3) modular home manufacturers; 4) prefabricated home manufacturers; or 5) house component manufacturers. Also uses interviews, photo features and technical articles. "No architect or plan 'dreams'. Housing projects must be built or under construction." Buys 6 mss/year. Query. Length: 500-1,000 words maximum. Pays $250 minimum.
Photos: Purchased with accompanying ms. Captions required. Query. No additional payment for 4x5, 5x7 or 8x10 b&w glossies or 35mm or larger color transparencies (35mm preferred).

BUILDER, The Magazine of the National Association of Home Builders, Hanley-Wood, Inc., National Housing Center, 15th and M Sts. NW, Washington DC 20005. (202)822-0390. Editor: Frank Anton. Executive Editor: Wendy Jordan. 10% freelance written. Monthly magazine of the home building and light commercial industry for those involved with the industry. Circ. 175,000. Pays "60 days after invoice." Publishes ms an average of 2 months after acceptance. Byline given. Offers negotiable kill fee. Buys first North American serial rights. Submit seasonal/holiday material 3 months in advance. Simultaneous queries and photocopied submissions OK. Computer printout submissions acceptable. Reports in 2 weeks on queries; 1 month on mss. Free sample copy and writer's guidelines.
Nonfiction: New product, technical and business needs. No consumer oriented material. Buys 10 mss/year. Query with published clips. Length: 500-1,200 words. Pays $100-400.
Photos: Send photos with query or ms. Reviews 4x5 color transparencies and 8x10 color prints. Identification of subjects required. Buys one-time rights.

BUILDER INSIDER, Box 191125, Dallas TX 75219-1125. (214)651-9994. Editor: Mike Anderson. Monthly; covering the entire north Texas building industry for builders, architects, contractors, remodelers and homeowners. Circ. 8,000. Photocopied submissions OK. SASE. Free sample copy.
Nonfiction: "What is current in the building industry" is the approach. Wants "advertising, business builders, new building products, building projects being developed and helpful building hints localized to the Southwest and particularly to north Texas." Submit complete ms. Length: 100-900 words. Pays $30-50.

CALIFORNIA BUILDER & ENGINEER, 4110 Transport St., Palo Alto CA 94303. Associate Editor: Linda A. Adreveno. "For contractors, engineers, and machinery distributors in the heavy construction industry, and civic officials concerned with public works. Our coverage is limited to California, Hawaii, Nevada and western Arizona." Published twice a month. Circ. 12,500. Pays on publication. Not copyrighted. Buys first rights only. Computer printout submissions acceptable; prefers letter-quality to dot-matrix. SASE. Reports in 3 weeks. Publishes ms an average of 2 months after acceptance. Free sample copy.
Nonfiction: "We are particularly interested in knowledgeable articles on nonconstruction issues that affect

both the large and small contractor in our region. For example: accounting for the contractor, labor issues, pending legislation or office automation. These articles must be written with rigid accuracy, often requiring specialized knowledge. We are also interested in job stories from Hawaii on heavy public construction. We are not interested in residential construction. Field experience or in-depth knowledge of the industry are essential in writing for us." Buys 4-5 unsolicited mss/year. Query. Length: 1,500-2,200 words. Pays $50/page.
Photos: Send photos with ms. Reviews 5x7 b&w glossy prints. Offers no additional payment for photos accompanying ms. Captions and model release required. Buys one-time rights.

CANADIAN BUILDING, The Business Magazine of the Building Development Industry, Maclean Hunter Ltd., 481 University Ave., Toronto, Ontario M5W 1A7 Canada. (416)596-5760. Editor: John A. Fennell. 40% freelance written. Monthly magazine covering "all building development: housing, office, shopping centers, industrial, etc." Circ. 18,500. Pays on acceptance. Publishes ms an average of 2 months after acceptance. Byline given. Buys first publication rights. Simultaneous queries OK. Computer printout submissions acceptable; no dot-matrix. Reports in 1 month. Sample copy $4.
Nonfiction: Interview/profile (of major building developer); new product; opinion; and photo feature. Buys 36 mss/year. Query. Length: 800-4,000 words. Pays $200-600.
Photos: State availability of photos. Reviews 8x10 b&w prints and contact sheets and 3x5 color transparencies. Captions, model release and identification of subjects required.

● **CATERPILLAR WORLD**, Caterpillar Tractor Co., 100 NE Adams AB1D, Peoria IL 61629. (309)675-5829. Editor: Tom Biederbeck. 10% freelance written. Emphasizes "anything of interest about Caterpillar people, plants or products. The magazine is distributed to 100,000 Caterpillar people and friends worldwide. It's printed in French and English. Readers' ages, interests and education vary all over the map." Quarterly magazine; 24-32 pages. Pays on acceptance. Publishes ms an average of 6 months after acceptance. Buys first and second rights to the same material and second (reprint) rights to material originally published elsewhere. Computer printout submissions acceptable. First submission is always on speculation. Free sample copy.
Nonfiction: "Everything should have a Caterpillar tie. It doesn't have to be strong but it has to be there. How-to (buy one piece of equipment and become a millionaire, etc.); general interest (anything that may be of interest to Cat people worldwide); humor (it's hard to find something humorous yet interesting to an international audience; we'd like to see it, however); interview (with any appropriate person: contractor, operator, legislator, etc.); products (large projects using Cat equipment; must have human interest); personal experience (would be interesting to hear from an equipment operator/writer); photo feature (on anything of interest to Cat people; should feature people as well as product); and profile (of Cat equipment users, etc.). Prints occasional lifestyle and health articles (but must apply to international audience). Written approval by the subjects of the article is a must." Query. Length: "What ever the story is worth."
Photos: "The only articles we accept without photos are those obviously illustrated by artwork." State availability of photos in query. Captions and model release required.
Tips: "The best way to get story ideas is to stop in at local Cat dealers and ask about big sales, events, etc."

CONSTRUCTION DIGEST, Construction Digest, Inc., Box 603, Indianapolis IN 46206. (317)634-7374. Senior Editor: Art Graham. Editor: Michael Brown. 10% freelance written. Magazine. "*CD* serves the engineered construction and public works industries in Illinois, Indiana, Ohio, Kentucky and eastern Missouri. It features bids asked, awards, planned work, job photo feature articles, industry trends, legislation, etc." Circ. 14,087. Pays on publication. Publishes ms an average of 2 months after acceptance. Byline "depends on nature of article." Not copyrighted. Makes work-for-hire assignments. Computer printout submissions acceptable; prefers letter-quality to dot-matrix. Reports in 2 weeks. Free sample copy and writer's guidelines.
Nonfiction: How-to, new product, photo feature, technical, and "nuts and bolts" construction jobsite features. No personality/company profiles. Buys 4 mss/year. Send complete ms. Length: 175 typewritten lines, 35 character count, no maximum. Pays $75/published page.
Tips: "We are putting more emphasis on topical features—market trends, technology applied to construction, legislation, etc.—rather than traditional 'nuts & bolts' articles."

CONSTRUCTION EQUIPMENT OPERATION AND MAINTENANCE, Box 1689, Cedar Rapids IA 52406. (319)366-1597. Editor: C.K. Parks. 15% freelance written. For users of heavy construction equipment. Bimonthly. Buys all rights. Pays on acceptance. Query. Reports in 1 month. SASE.
Nonfiction: "Articles on selection, use, operation or maintenance of construction equipment; articles and features on the construction industry in general; and job safety articles." Length: 1,000-2,000 words. Also buys a limited number of job stories with photos and feature articles on individual contractors in certain areas of US and Canada. Length varies. Pays $50-200.

CONSTRUCTION SPECIFIER, 601 Madison St., Alexandria VA 22314. (703)684-0200. Editor: Jack Reeder. Professional society magazine for architects, engineers, specification writers and project managers. 50% freelance written. Monthly. Circ. 16,000. Buys one-time North American serial rights. Pays on publication. Deadline: 60 days preceding publication on the 1st of each month. Electronic submissions OK; "ask first." Computer printout submissions acceptable; prefers letter-quality to dot-matrix. "Call or write first." SASE. Model releases, author copyright transferral requested. Reports in 2-3 weeks. Free sample copy.

Nonfiction: "Articles on selection and specification of products, materials, practices and methods used in commercial (nonresidential) construction projects, specifications as related to construction design, plus legal and management subjects." Query. Length: 5,000 words maximum. Pays 10¢/published word, plus art.

Photos: Photos desirable in consideration for publication; line art, sketches, diagrams, charts and graphs also desired. Full color transparencies may be used. Prices negotiable. 8x10 glossies, 3¼ slides preferred.

Tips: "We will get bigger and thus need good technical articles."

CONSTRUCTOR MAGAZINE (The Management Magazine for the Construction Industry), 1957 E St. NW, Washington DC 20006. Editor: Diane B. Snow. Publication of the Associated General Contractors of America for "men and women in the age range of approximately 25-70 years (predominantly 40s and 50s), most with a college education. Most own or are officers in their own corporations." Monthly. Circ. 40,000. Buys all rights. Buys 5 mss/year. Pays on publication. Query or submit complete ms. "Often telephone query first is best." Reports in 2 months. SASE. Sample copy $2; free writer's guidelines.

Nonfiction: "Feature material dealing with labor, legal, technical and professional material pertinent to the construction industry. We deal only with the management aspect of the construction industry." Buys informational articles, interviews, think pieces, exposes, photo features, coverage of successful business operations and technical articles. "Please no new product plugs, technical articles, or AGC construction project stories where the contractor wasn't an AGC member." Length: "no minimum or maximum; subject much more important than length." Pays $150 minimum.

Photos: State availability of photos. Reviews 8x10 b&w semiglossy prints and 35mm color transparencies. Offers no additional payment for photos accompanying ms. Captions required with "action description, date, location, names of persons, general contractor's firm's name, location and AGC chapter affiliation, if applicable." Model release required. Buys all rights.

DIXIE CONTRACTOR, Box 280, Decatur GA 30031. (404)377-2683. 10% freelance written. For contractors, public officials, architects, engineers, and construction equipment manufacturers and dealers. Biweekly magazine; 125 pages. Circ. 10,000. Pays on publication. Buys all rights. Phone queries OK. Submit seasonal/holiday material 2 months in advance of issue date. Photocopied submissions OK. SASE. Reports in 2 weeks. Free sample copy.

Nonfiction: How-to (articles on new construction techniques and innovations); and interview (with government officials influencing construction, or prominent contractors). Buys 7 mss/year. Query or submit complete ms. Length: 1,500-2,000 words. Pays $50 minimum/published page. "Articles usually run two pages."

Photos: State availability of photos with query or ms. Captions and model release required. Buys all rights.

Columns/Departments: Labor/Management Relations in Construction. Submit complete ms. Length: 1,000-1,500 words. Pays $50 minimum.

Tips: "We are interested only in freelancers who have a business writing background. We won't reply to people who write about the West Coast, Midwest or upper Northeast. It's a waste of our time."

‡EQUIPMENT GUIDE NEWS, Equipment, Products and Services for the Construction Industry, Dataquest, Inc., a subsidiary of A.C. Nielsen, 1290 Ridder Park Dr., San Jose CA 95131. (408)971-9000. Editor: James N. Harrah. Features Editor: Doug Canfield. A monthly tabloid covering construction equipment for contractors. Circ. 60,323. Pays on acceptance. Byline given for features, not for departments. Offers 30% kill fee. Not copyrighted. Buys one-time rights. Submit seasonal/holiday material 2 months in advance. Simultaneous queries, and simultaneous, photocopied and previously published submissions OK (if not published by direct competitor). SASE. Reports in 2 weeks. Free sample copy and writer's guidelines.

Nonfiction: Historical/nostalgic (evolution of a type of equipment); how-to (how a contractor can improve his business operation, profits, etc.); humor; interview/profile (of successful contractors); new product (unusual or prototype equipment products); personal experience ("How I get the most from my equipment"); and technical (discussions of equipment components). "We're less interested in telling contractors how to use equipment than we are in telling him about it—how it is made, new technology trends, how much it costs, what's available, how machines can increase profits, etc. We don't use how-to job stories." Buys about 12 mss/year. Query with published clips or send complete ms. Length: 400-1,200 words. Pays $30-300.

Photos: State availability of photos or send photos with query or ms. Reviews b&w and color contact sheets. Pays $15 for first b&w or color print; $5 for additionals. Model release and identification of subjects required. Buys one-time rights.

Columns/Departments: Tech Talk (electronic technology update relating to computers or microprocessor driven equipment); and Business Talk (how to market, improve, or cut the cost of a contractor's business). Buys 6+ mss/yeear. Query with published clips or send complete ms. Length: 400-600 words. Pays $30-100.

Tips: "If you know the construction business, there's a good chance that we can develop an ongoing relationship. Phone call queries or introductions are acceptable, as are submissions by starting writers. We're beginning a major new emphasis on feature editorial so almost all areas are wide open. We're especially receptive to unusual or prototype equipment articles (short) and to technical discussions of equipment components (the ins-and-outs of crawler undercarriages or ground engaging parts, for example).

FENCE INDUSTRY, 6255 Barfield Rd., Atlanta GA 30328. (404)256-9800. Editor/Associate Publisher: Bill Coker. 60% freelance written. For retailers and installers of fencing materials. Monthly magazine; 54-80 pages. Circ. 15,000. Buys all rights. Buys 25-35 mss/year. Pays on publication. Publishes ms an average of 2 months after acceptance. Electronic submissions OK if floppy disks compatible with Rainbow or Digital Delmate. Computer printout submissions acceptable. Reports in 3 months. Free sample copy. Query.
Nonfiction: Case histories, as well as articles on fencing for highways, pools, farms, playgrounds, homes and industries. Surveys and management and sales reports. Interview, profile, historical, successful business operations and articles on merchandising techniques. No how-to articles. "They generally don't apply to installers in our industry." Buys 15-20 unsolicited mss/year. Length: open. Pays 10¢/word.
Photos: Pays $10 for 5x7 b&w photos purchased with mss. Captions required.

FINE HOMEBUILDING, The Taunton Press, Inc., 52 Church Hill Rd., Box 355, Newtown CT 06470. (203)426-8171. Editor: John Lively. Bimonthly magazine covering house building, construction, design for builders, architects and serious amateurs. Circ. 170,000. Pays on publication. Byline given. Offers negotiable kill fee. Buys first rights and "use in books to be published." Computer printout submissions acceptable. Reports as soon as possible. Sample copy $3.50; free writer's guidelines.
Nonfiction: Technical (unusual techniques in design or construction process). Query. Length: 2,000-3,000 words. Pays $150-900.
Columns/Departments: Reports (conferences, workshops, products or techniques that are new or unusual); Great Moments in Building History (humorous, embarrassing, or otherwise noteworthy anecdotes); Reviews (short reviews on books of building or design). Query. Length: 300-1,000 words. Pays $75-150.

‡THE HOUSING INSIDER, 8282 S. Memorial Dr., Tulsa OK 94133. (619)628-0202. Editor: Merle Tyler. 15% freelance written. A quarterly magazine covering new trends and successful ventures in marketing, financing and design in the real estate/building industry for builders, developers and any services connected with the housing industry in the sunbelt. Circ. 25,000. Pays on acceptance. Publishes ms an average of 45 days after acceptance. Byline given. Buys first rights only. Submit seasonal/holiday material 2 months in advance. Simultaneous queries, and simultaneous, photocopied and previously published submissions OK. Computer printout submissions acceptable. SASE. Reports in 2 weeks. Free sample copy.
Nonfiction: Book excerpts, general interest, historical/nostalgic, how-to, humor, interview/profile, new product, opinion, personal experience, photo feature and technical (not too). All articles must be related to housing industry. Buys 12 mss/year. Query or send complete ms. Length: 750-2,500 words. Pays $50-150.
Photos: State availability of photos or send photos with query or ms. Reviews b&w contact sheets. Pays $15-25 for 8x10 b&w prints; $25-50 for color transparencies. Captions and identification of subjects required. Buys one-time rights.
Columns/Departments: Inside Look (interior decorating); Uncommon Grounds (landscaping); Housing Hearsay (news briefs); and Advantages (marketing). Buys 6 mss/year. Query or send complete ms. Length: 100-2,000 words. Pays $20-100.
Fillers: Short humor and newsbreaks. Buys 6/year. Length: 50-300 words. pays $15-50.
Tips: "A writer must know the housing industry and be able to communicate his ideas without being too stiff, formal or dreary. We're very open to all sorts of submissions related to the housing industry."

‡INSULATION GUIDE, Insulation International, 1145 19th St. NW, Washington DC 20036. (202)483-2552. A magazine covering industrial, utility, commercial and marine insulation published 8 times/year for contractors, buyers, specifiers, architects, designers, engineers, plant maintenance personnel and end users. Estab. 1983. Circ. 6,000. Pays on publication. Byline given. Buys variable rights. Submit seasonal/holiday material 4 months in advance. Photocopied and previously published submissions OK. SASE. Reports by return mail on queries. Sample copy for $2.50 and free writer's guidelines.
Nonfiction: Interview/profile, new product, photo feature and technical. No humor. Buys 30 mss/year. Query. Length: negotiable. Pays negotiable rates.
Columns/Departments: Conservation Concepts, Industry Issues, Enterprise, Washington Report, Buyer's Guide, Employment Trends, Safety, Effective Management and Contracts and Claims. Query with published clips. Length: varies. Pays variable rate.

LOG HOME AND ALTERNATIVE HOUSING BUILDER, 16 First Ave., Corry PA 16407. (814)664-8624. Editor: M.J. Potocki. 15% freelance written. Bimonthly magazine covering alternative housing including log, dome, solar and underground homes. Circ. 10,000. Pays on publication. Publishes ms an average of 6 months after acceptance. Byline given. Buys all rights. Computer printout submissions acceptable; no dot-matrix. Reports in 2 weeks on queries; 3 weeks on mss. Free sample copy.

Nonfiction: Energy saving devices and techniques; and unique applications for alternative types of homes and commercial buildings. Restaurants are no longer unique. More efficient business management techniques and sales and marketing ideas. "We do not buy articles on how a husband and wife erected their home, or the trials and tribulations of the first-time log or dome home buyer." Buys 6 mss/year. Length: 2,000-4,000 words. Pays $50-200. Buys 6 mss/year.
Photos: Send photos with ms. Pays $15-30 for 8x10 color prints; $10-25 for 8x10 b&w prints. Captions and identification of subjects required.

LOUISIANA CONTRACTOR, Rhodes Publishing Co., Inc., 18271 Old Jefferson Hwy., Baton Rouge LA 70817. (504)292-8980. Editor: Dianne Sins. Monthly magazine comprehensive covering heavy commercial, industrial and highway construction in Louisiana, the 6th largest construction market in the US. Circ. 6,500. Pays on publication. Offers negotiable kill fee. Not copyrighted. Buys all rights. Reports in 2 weeks on queries; 2½ months on mss. Sample copy $1.50.
Nonfiction: "We are particularly interested in writers who can get clearance into a chemical plant or refinery and detail unusual maintenance jobs. Our feature articles are semitechnical to technical, balanced by a lot of name dropping of subcontractors, suppliers and key job personnel. We want quotes, and we never run a story without lots of photos either taken or procured by the writer. Stories on new methods of construction and unusual projects in the state are always wanted. Nothing from anyone unfamiliar with the construction industry in Louisiana." Recent article example: "Harmony Corp. Handles Mechanical Work at Air Products' New Convent Plant" (March 1984). Buys 8-12 mss/year. Query. Length: 1,000-3,500 words. Pays negotiable rate.
Photos: State availability of photos. Reviews 5x7 or 8x10 b&w glossy prints. Captions and identification of subjects required.

METAL BUILDING REVIEW, Nickerson & Collins, 1800 Oakton, Des Plaines IL 60018. (312)298-6210. Editor: Gene Adams. Monthly magazine for contractors, dealers, erectors, architects, designers and manufacturers in the metal building industry. Circ. 22,000. Pays on acceptance. Buys first North American serial rights or all rights. Submit seasonal/holiday material 6 months in advance. Simultaneous queries, and simultaneous, photocopied and previously published submissions OK. Reports in 3 weeks. Free sample copy.
Nonfiction: How-to, interview/profile, photo feature and technical. "Freelancers can break in with on-the-job-site interviews." Query with or without clips of published work or send complete ms. Length: 1,000-3,000 words. Pays 3-6¢/word.
Photos: State availability of photos. Pays $5-10 for 5x7 b&w prints; $20-75 for 5x7 color prints. Captions, model release and identification of subjects required. Buys one-time or all rights.

P.O.B., Point of Beginning, P.O.B. Publishing Co., Box 810, Wayne MI 48184. (313)729-8400. Editor: Edwin W. Miller. 50% freelance written. Bimonthly magazine featuring articles of a technical, business, professional and general nature for the professionals and technicians of the surveying and mapping community. Circ. 60,000. Pays on publication. Byline given "with short biography, if appropriate." Offers 50% kill fee. Buys all rights or makes work-for-hire assignments. Submit seasonal/holiday material 3 months in advance. Simultaneous queries and photocopied submissions OK. Computer printout submissions acceptable; prefers letter-quality (with no right margin justification) to dot-matrix. SASE. Reports in 1 month. Publication date after acceptance "varies with backlog." For free sample copy sned 10x13 SAE. Free author's guidelines.
Nonfiction: Phil Roman, associate editor. Historical/nostalgic; how-to; interview/profile; photo feature; technical (only related to surveying, mapping, construction—profession and business of); and travel (only sites of professional society meetings). Buys 12 mss/year. Submit complete ms. Length: 1,000-4,000 words. Pays $100-400.
Photos: Send captioned photos with ms. Pays $10-50 for color transparencies and prints; $5-25 for 5x7 b&w prints. Model release and identification of subjects required.
Columns/Departments: A Conversation With (interview of people in the field about their professional involvement, point of view); and Picture Profile (profile of people in the field slanted toward their special interest, talent, involvement that is unusual to the profession). Buys 6 mss/year. Query associate editor. Length: 1,000-2,500 words. Payment varies.

RESTAURANT AND HOTEL DESIGN MAGAZINE, Bill Communications, 633 3rd Ave., New York NY 10017. (212)986-4800, ext. 438, 440. Editor: Barbara Knox. Managing Editor: Jerry Cooper. 30% freelance written. Magazine about restaurant/hotel industries for architects, designers and restaurant and hotel executives; published eight times/year. Circ. 33,000. Pays on acceptance. Publishes ms an average of 3 months after acceptance. Byline given. Buys first North American serial rights. Phone queries OK. Photocopied and previously published submissions OK. SASE. Reports in 1 month on queries; 2 months on mss. Free sample copy.
Nonfiction: Profile. Buys 4-10 mss/year. Query with clips of previously published work. Length: 1,500-2,500 words.
Tips: "We generally work very closely with a writer, directing research and focusing articles. We ask for rewriting frequently. As a result, unsolicited works seldom suit our format. Query should have clarity, brevity,

knowledge of the magazine and design language. Submit quality photography with any project query so that we can determine whether or not we can use the story."

‡ROOFER MAGAZINE, D&H Publications, Box 06253, Ft. Myers FL 33906. (813)275-7663. Editor: Karen S. Parker. A monthly magazine covering the roofing industry for roofing contractors. Circ. 16,000. Pays on publication. Byline given. Buys first North American serial rights, first rights, and second serial (reprint) rights. Submit seasonal/holiday material 2 months in advance. Simultaneous queries and simultaneous and previously published submissions OK. Computer printout submissions acceptable. SASE. Reports in 2 weeks on queries; 1 month on mss. Free sample copy and writer's guidelines.
Nonfiction: Eileen Dezotell, articles editor. Historical/nostalgic; how-to (solve application problems, overcome trying environmental conditions); interview/profile; new product and technical. "Write articles directed toward areas of specific interest; don't generalize too much. We do not want to see tax, small business articles; how to hire and fire; management programs; tax evasions and shelters; accounting articles, etc." Buys 7 mss/year. Query. Length: 3,000-7,000 words. Pays $125-250.
Photos: Send photos with accompanying query or ms. Reviews 8x10 b&w prints and standard size transparencies. Identification of subjects required. Buys all rights.
Columns/Departments: Legal column (contract agreements, litigations, warranties, etc.); technology and application problems; and safety. Buys 30-50 mss/year. Query with published clips. Length: 3,000-7,000 words. Pays $125-250.
Tips: "Articles about unusual projects, application problems, new technology and business trends in roofing are most open to freelancers."

ST. LOUIS CONSTRUCTION NEWS & REVIEW, The Voice for the St. Louis Area Construction Industry, Finan Publishing Co., Inc., 130 W. Lockwood, St. Louis MO 63119. (314)961-6644. Editor: Thomas J. Finan. Monthly tabloid covering all aspects of St. Louis area building design and construction tailored to the management end of the industry. Circ. 11,000. Pays on publication. Byline given. Buys first rights only. Makes work-for-hire assignments. SASE. Reports in 1 month. Sample copy $2.
Nonfiction: Expose (of local, construction related practices); interview/profile (by assignment only); photo feature (with local construction emphasis); and technical. "No material unrelated to design and construction industries." Buys 2-5 mss/year. Query with clips of published work. Length: open. Pays $40-300.
Photos: Send photos with ms. Pays variable rates for 8x10 b&w glossy prints and contact sheets. Captions and identification of subjects required. Buys one-time rights.
Tips: "Break in with some story ideas and samples of expertise and experience in a specific area. Follow professional writers' general practices."

WORLD CONSTRUCTION, 875 3rd Ave., New York NY 10022. (212)605-9755. Editorial Director: Ruth W. Stidger. 20% freelance written. For "English speaking engineers, contractors and government officials everywhere except the US and Canada." Monthly. Buys all rights. Byline given unless "the article is less than one page long." Pays on publication. Publishes ms an average of 3 months after acceptance. Computer printout submissions acceptable; prefers letter-quality to dot-matrix. SASE. Query. Reports in 1 month. Free sample copy.
Nonfiction: "How-to articles that stress how contractors can do their jobs faster, better or more economically. Articles are rejected when they tell only what was constructed, but not how it was constructed and why it was constructed in that way. No clippings from newspapers telling of construction projects." Length: 1,000-6,000 words. Pays $100-200/magazine page, or 5 typed ms pages, depending on content and quality.
Photos: State availability of photos. Photos purchased with mss; uses 4x5 or larger b&w glossy prints.
Tips: "At present time we would prefer buying articles dealing with construction projects in overseas locations."

Dairy Products

THE NATIONAL DAIRY NEWS, National Dairy News, Inc., Box 951, Madison WI 53701. (608)257-9577. Publisher: Gerald Dryer. 5% freelance written. Weekly tabloid newspaper, covering dairy processing and marketing. Circ. 4,000. Pays on publication. Publishes ms an average of 2 months after acceptance. Byline given. Offers negotiable kill fee. Buys one-time rights. Submit seasonal holiday material 1 month in advance. Simultaneous queries and simultaneous, photocopied and previously published submissions OK. Computer printout submissions acceptable; no dot-matrix. SASE. Reports in 1 week on queries; 1 month on mss. Free sample copy and writer's guidelines.
Nonfiction: Margaret Patterson, articles editor. How-to (improve dairy processing and marketing ventures);

humor; interview/profile; new product; photo feature; and technical. "No material that has no connection at all with dairy processing, food broking, etc.—that is, not general information." Buys 10-40 mss/year. Send complete ms. Length: 50-2,500 words. Pays $25-300.

Photos: Margaret Patterson, photo editor. Send photos with ms. Pays $10-50 for 8x10 b&w prints. Model release and identification of subjects required.

Fillers: Margaret Patterson, fillers editor. Clippings, jokes, gags, anecdotes, short humor and newsbreaks. Length: 25-150 words. Pays $5-25. Avoid general fillers.

Tips: "We are a newspaper. Submit material on innovative dairies (in your region of the country) that are of interest nationally. We'll be needing more freelance material as we're growing but can't afford more staff for a while. We are not read by dairy farmers; thus, we do not need dairy farmer material."

Data Processing

BUSINESS SOFTWARE MAGAZINE, 2464 Embarcadeo Way, Palo Alto CA 94303. Editor: Jeffrey Brown. Managing Editor: Kenis Dunne. Monthly magazine covering computer software applications in business for corporate decision makers, high level professionals, managers and business owners seeking a better understanding of the business software available to them. Circ. 50,000+. Pays on publication. Byline given. Buys first rights only. Photocopied and previously published submissions OK "in some cases." SASE. Reports in 1 month. Sample copy for 9x12 SAE; writer's guidelines for legal-size SAE.

Nonfiction: Corporate case studies of Fortune 500-like companies detailing their successful (and unsuccessful) business software applications; tutorials on widely used business oriented software programs. Send query to editor. The magazine is written to expand the decision making process and usage of business software including database, telecommunications, electronic spreadsheet applications, word processing, graphics and more. All editorial material should be written for a business audience. No articles on computer or arcade games. Buys 36-40 mss/year. Query. Length: 1,500-2,000 words. "There are exceptions, and treatments exceeding 2,000 words may be submitted. A definite query is a must. Writers of longer articles should be made aware that editing may be needed." Pays $250-450 "with additional consideration given to longer articles."

Photos: State availability of photos. Photos purchased with ms package. Model release and identification of subjects required. Buys one-time rights.

COMPUTER DEALER, Gordon Publications, Inc., Box 1952, Dover NJ 07801-0952. (201)361-9060. Editor: David Shadovitz. Business management ideas for dealers, computer stores, systems houses, consultants, consumer electronics outlets and business equipment dealers. Monthly magazine. Circ. 25,000. Pays on publication. Buys all rights. Phone queries OK. Submit seasonal/holiday material 6 months in advance. Previously published submissions OK. Computer printout submissions acceptable; prefers letter-quality to dot-matrix. SASE. Reports in 1 month. Free sample copy.

Nonfiction: How-to (sell, market, etc.); interview (with computer notables and/or where market information is revealed); and articles on capital formation, etc. Writers "must have a knowledge of marketing and the computer industry, and the ability to ferret information or restate information known in other fields in a usable, interesting and particularly applicable way to those persons engaged in selling computers and peripheral products. Prefers not to see general marketing articles." Buys 3-6 mss/issue. Query. Length: 1,000-4,000 words. Pays 8-14¢/word.

Photos: "Photos (artwork) provide and spark greater reader interest and are most times necessary to explicate text." Send photos with ms. Uses b&w 8½x11 glossy prints. Offers no additional payment for photos accepted with ms. Captions and model releases required.

Columns/Departments: "Columns are solicited by editor. If writers have suggestions, please query."

COMPUTER DESIGN, 119 Russell St., Littleton MA 01460. Editor-in-Chief: Michael Elphick. Managing Editor: Sydney F. Shapiro. 35% freelance written. For digital electronic design engineers and engineering managers. Monthly with greater frequency in 1985. Buys all rights. Pays on publication. Byline given. Reports in 3 months. Electronic submissions OK if IBM PC compatible floppy disk; requires hard copy also. Computer printout submissions acceptable; no dot-matrix. SASE. Free sample copy.

Nonfiction: Engineering articles on the design and application of digital equipment and systems used in computing, data processing, control, automation, instrumentation and communications. "We do not accept column material from nonstaff writers. All accepted material need be of value and interest to practicing design engineers." Query. Pays $40-50/page.

Tips: "Send query letter before outline or manuscript. Know the subject intimately before attempting to write an article. List suggested title, scope and length of article and why *CD* readers would be interested."

COMPUTER GRAPHICS WORLD, 1714 Stockton St., San Francisco CA 94133. (415)398-7151. Publisher/Editor: Randall Stickrod. Monthly magazine covering computer graphics for managers in business, industry, government and institutions; readers are interested in computer graphic application and technology. Circ. 17,000. Pays on publication. Byline and brief bio given. Buys first North American serial rights; "reprints should give us credit." Simultaneous queries and photocopied submissions OK. Reports immediately. Free sample copy; Editorial Highlights available.
Nonfiction: Case studies, success stories in using computer graphics to solve problems. "Articles must be relevant to the needs of persons interested in applying computer graphics." Buys 25 mss/year. Query by phone or brief letter. Length: 1,500 words typical. Pays $50/printed page.
Photos: Prefers negative transparencies and 8x10 b&w glossy prints. State availability of photos or graphics. Captions required. Buys all rights.

COMPUTER MERCHANDISING, The Magazine for High Technology Retailers, Eastman Publishing, Suite 222, 15720 Ventura Blvd., Encino CA 91436. (818)995-0436. Editor: Mike Hogan. Managing Editor: Larry Tuck. 30% freelance written. Monthly magazine covering retailing of computers for home and small business use. "The emphasis of the magazine is to aid the growing number of computer retailers." Circ. 25,000. Pays on acceptance. Publishes ms an average of 3 months after acceptance. Buys first rights only. Byline given. Submit seasonal/holiday material 3 months in advance. Computer printout submissions acceptable. SASE. Reports in 2 weeks. Sample copy for 9x12 SAE.
Nonfiction: Interview/profile (of industry figures); technical (simple explanation of computers, related products); merchandising suggestions; sales training promotion tips; and case histories. No articles on general topics with no relation to the retailing of computers. Buys 60 mss/year. Query. Length: 1,000-2,000 words. Pays $150-350.
Tips: Submit "query which shows research of the specifics of retailing computer products—good grasp of key issues, major names, etc. It's rewarding finding someone who listens to us when we explain what we want and who consistently gives us what we ask for."

COMPUTER RETAILING, W.R.C. Smith Publishing, 1760 Peachtree Rd., Atlanta GA 30357. (404)874-4462. Editor: Greg Landers. Emphasizes retailing microcomputers. Monthly tabloid. Circ. 30,000. Pays on acceptance. Buys first rights only. Pays 50% kill fee. Byline given. Phone queries OK. Submit seasonal/holiday material 2 months in advance. Computer printout submissions acceptable. SASE. Reports in 2 weeks.
Nonfiction: Interested in interviews with local computer/software stores for miniprofile editorial. Guidelines provided. Query. Length: 750 words. Pays $100.
Photos: $50 for color slides of interior/exterior computer store (interesting, colorful, arty). Buys one-time rights. Captions required.

COMPUTERWORLD, 375 Cochituate Rd., Box 880, Framingham MA 01701. (617)879-0700. Editor: John C. Whitmarsh. 10% freelance written. For management level computer users chiefly in the business community, but also in government and education. Weekly. Circ. 120,000. Buys all rights. Pays negotiable kill fee; "we have to initiate the assignment in order to pay a kill fee." Pays on publication. Photocopied submissions OK, if exclusive for stated period. Submit special issue material 2 months in advance. Reports in 2-4 weeks. SASE. Free sample copy, if request is accompanied by story idea or specific query; free writer's guidelines.
Nonfiction: Articles on problems in using computers; educating computer people; trends in the industry; new, innovative and interesting uses of computers. "We stress impact on users and need a practical approach. What does a development mean for other computer users? Most important facts first, then in decreasing order of significance. We would be interested in material on factory automation and other areas of computer usage that will impact society in general and not just businesses. We prefer *not* to see executive appointments or financial results. We occasionally accept innovative material that is oriented to unique seasonal or geographical issues." Buys 100 mss/year. Query, "or call specific editor to ask what's needed at a particular time, establish phone rapport with individual editor." Length: 250-1,200 words. Pays 10¢/word, "except In Depth articles and feature articles for special CW publications, which pay a nominal honorarium. Consult individual editor."
Photos: B&w (5x7) glossy prints purchased with ms or on assignment. Captions required. Pays $10 minimum.
Fillers: Newsbreaks and clippings. Query. Length: 50-250 words. Pays 10¢/word.

COMPUTING CANADA, Canada's Bi-Weekly Data Processing Newspaper, Plesman Publications, Ltd., 2 Lansing Square, Willowdale, Ontario M2J 4P8 Canada. (416)497-9562. Editor: Gordon A. Campbell. Managing Editor: David Paddon. 30% freelance written. Biweekly tabloid covering data processing, the computer industry and telecommunications for data processing management and professionals. Circ. 30,000. Pays on publication. Publishes ms an average of 6 weeks after acceptance. Byline given. Buys one-time rights. Submit seasonal/holiday material 1 month in advance. Simultaneous queries and submissions OK. Electronic submissions OK if 300 baud ASCII. Computer printout submissions acceptable; prefers letter-quality to dot-matrix. SASE. Reports in 1 month. Free sample copy and writer's guidelines.
Nonfiction: How-to, interview/profile and current industry news. Special features (software report, office au-

tomation, computers in education, etc.) in each issue. Length: 250-1,500 words. Pays $25-100.

Tips: "Suggest a story on an industry event or trend we haven't picked up on. More use of freelance material and more coverage of the microcomputer and office automation markets will affect writers in the year ahead."

DATA MANAGEMENT MAGAZINE, The Magazine for Information Processing Professionals, Data Processing Management Association (DPMA), 505 Busse Hwy., Park Ridge IL 60068. (312)825-8124. Editor: Bill Zalud. Monthly magazine covering information processing management for professionals with corporate level responsibility for information resource and consulting services, DP service organizations and businesses with emphasis on information processing. Circ. 51,010. Pays on publication or on a negotiable basis. Byline given. Buys one-time rights. Submit seasonal/holiday material 3 months in advance. Simultaneous queries OK. Reports in 2 weeks on queries; 3 weeks on mss. Free sample copy and writer's guidelines.

Nonfiction: Interview/profile and technical. "Editorial calendar available upon request. Nothing out-dated— material must be timely." Buys 10-25 mss/year. Send complete ms. Length: 1,500-3,000 words. Pays negotiable fee.

Photos: State availability of photos with query letter or ms. Reviews 35mm color transparencies and b&w 5x7 prints. Pays negotiable fee. Captions and identification of subjects required.

Fiction: Humorous. Buys 5-10 mss/year. Send complete ms. Length: 500-1,500 words. Pays negotiable fee.

Tips: "All articles submitted to *Data Management* must contain the point of view of the information processing manager. Authors should keep in mind that our readers are professionals."

DATAMATION, Technical Publishing D & B, 875 3rd Ave., New York NY 10022. Executive Editor: John Kirkley. Monthly magazine for scientific, engineering and commercial data processing professionals. Circ. 150,000. Pays on publication. Byline given. Pays negotiable kill fee. Buys all rights. Submit seasonal/holiday material 3 months in advance. Photocopied submissions and previously published submissions ("if indicated where") OK. SASE. Reports as soon as possible on queries. Free sample copy and writer's guidelines. "Request our list of themes for the coming year."

Nonfiction: "Horizontal publication covering all aspects of computer industry technical, managerial and sociological concerns, as well as computer industry news analysis." No general articles on computers. Buys 30 mss/year. Query with clips of published work. Length: 2,000-4,000 words. Pays $300-1,000/article.

Photos: Reviews 35mm color transparencies and 8x10 b&w prints. "No extra payment for photos—included in payment for manuscript."

THE DEC PROFESSIONAL, Professional Press, Inc., Box 362, Ambler PA 19002. (215)542-7008. Publishers: Carl B. Marbach and R.D. Mallery. 95% freelance written. Bimonthly magazine covering Digital Equipment Corp. computers. "We publish highly technical, user-written articles concerning DEC equipment. We are a forum for DEC users worldwide." Circ. 80,000. Publishes ms an average of 10 weeks after acceptance. Byline given. Buys all rights. Simultaneous queries, and simultaneous, photocopied and previously published submissions OK. Electronic submissions OK (contact office first), but requires hard copy also. Computer printout submissions acceptable (prefers 800 or 1600 BPI mag tape); prefers letter-quality to dot-matrix. Free sample copy and writer's guidelines.

Nonfiction: Technical (computer related). No articles "not highly technical concerning DEC computers and related topics." Send complete ms. Length: 1,500-5,000 words. Pays $100-300.

Tips: "Please send articles of approximately 1,500-5,000 words, preferably on an 800/1600 BPI mag tape in PIP format, or in WORD-11. We also accept 5¼" RX50 floppy disks—Rainbow 100, Professional 300 series, or DECmate II compatible. In addition, we can read RT-11 (only), RX01 or RX02 8" floppies. If not available, a letter-quality hardcopy may be forwarded to the editors at Professional Press."

HARDCOPY, The Magazine of Digital Equipment, Seldin Publishing Co., Suite D, 1061 S. Melrose, Placentia CA 92670. (714)632-6924. Editor: Larry McClain. 50% freelance written. Monthly magazine covering Digital Equipment Corporation (DEC)-related computer equipment, software, peripherals and compatibles primarily for computer-sophisticated users and equipment manufacturers looking for more information on how to sell, distribute or improve their computer products. Circ. 60,000. Pays on publication. Publishes ms an average of 4 months after acceptance. Byline given. Buys all rights to new material. "Will negotiate to all North American rights if author is located abroad." Occasionally buys second (reprint) rights to material originally published elsewhere. Submit seasonal/holiday material 4 months in advance. Computer printout submissions acceptable if double-spaced. SASE. Reports in 2 weeks on queries; 2 months on mss. Sample copy for 9x12 SAE and $1.90 postage; writer's guidelines for business-size SAE and 1 first class stamp.

Nonfiction: How-to (sell product; computer-oriented management and business); interview/profile (DEC or DEC-compatible manufacturers); and technical (DEC computer-oriented). No noncomputer related features or computer-oriented features that do not relate in any way to Digital Equipment Corporation. Buys 24 mss/year. Query with clips. Length: 2,000-3,500 words. Pays $200-500.

Photos: Pays $10-25 for 5x7 b&w prints; $25 for 35mm color transparencies. Indentification of subjects required.

Tips: "We need solid technical and how-to features from contributors. Research must be thorough and the article's main point must somehow relate to DEC. For example, a market trend article should explain how DEC's market will be affected. We suggest you query to receive direction, since our needs are very specific."

ICP SERIES & BUSINESS SOFTWARE REVIEW, (formerly *ICP Interface Series*), International Computer Programs, Inc., 9000 Keystone Crossing, Indianapolis IN 46240. (317)844-7461. Editor-in-Chief: Dennis Hamilton. Editors: Paul Pinella and Sheila Cunningham. Managing Editor: Louis W. Harm. Five quarterly magazines and one bimonthly magazine covering computer software applications and program use in the business and scientific community. Circ. 198,000. Pays on acceptance. Byline given. Buys all rights. Phone queries OK. Submit seasonal material 3 months in advance. Simultaneous and photocopied submissions OK. Computer printout submissions acceptable; prefers letter-quality to dot-matrix. Reports in 3 weeks. Free sample copy and writer's guidelines.
Nonfiction: Expose (waste, corruption, misuse of computers); interview (of major computer industry figures); opinion (of computer applications); how-to (computer solutions); humor (computer related); new product; personal experience (case studies); and technical (application). Recent article example: "Ten Data Base Management Systems for IBM Main Frames" (April 1984). No articles discussing the merits of a single product. Buys 5-10 unsolicited mss/year. Length: 1,000-3,000 words. Pays $100-500.

INFORMATION SYSTEMS NEWS for Information Systems Management, CMP Publications, 111 E. Shore Rd., Manhasset NY 11030. (516)365-4600. Editor: James Moran. 15% freelance written. Biweekly tabloid covering hardware, software, computer communication and office automation for managers and staff of major computer installations at US corporations. Circ. over 100,000. Pays within 30 days of acceptance. Publishes ms an average of 1 month after acceptance. Byline given. Buys all rights. Computer printout submissions acceptable; prefers letter-quality to dot-matrix. SASE. Reports in 1 month.
Nonfiction: "We're looking for articles of business-oriented news for managers of information systems." Buys 50 mss/year. Query by phone or mail. Length: 500 words minimum. Pays $150 minimum/article.
Photos: State availability of photos.
Tips: "Unsolicited manuscripts are discouraged, but clippings, queries and resumes are considered carefully. Be sure to include a phone number."

JOURNAL OF SYSTEMS MANAGEMENT, 24587 Bagley Road, Cleveland OH 44138. (216)243-6900. Publisher: James Andrews. 100% freelance written. For systems and procedures and management people. Monthly. Buys all serial rights. Byline given. Pays on publication. Publishes ms an average of 3 months after acceptance. Reports "as soon as possible." Computer printout submissions acceptable. SASE. Free sample copy.
Nonfiction: Articles on case histories, projects on systems, forms control, administrative practices and computer operations. No computer applications articles, humor or articles promoting a specific product. Query or submit ms in triplicate. Length: 3,000-5,000 words. Pays $25 maximum.
Tips: "We expect to receive articles over hard lines direct to our electronic terminals soon. We like freelancers because they work harder at digging out stories than company PR types because they have to sell to eat. But sometimes they have a prima donna attitude toward copy changes."

MINI-MICRO SYSTEMS, Cahners Publishing Co., 221 Columbus Ave., Boston MA 02116. (617)536-7780. Editor-in-Chief: Georg Kotelly. 45% freelance written. Monthly magazine covering minicomputer and microcomputer industries for manufacturers and users of computers, peripherals and software. Circ. 120,000. Pays on publication. Byline given. Buys all rights. Simultaneous queries and photocopied submissions OK. Computer printout submissions acceptable; prefers letter-quality to dot-matrix. SASE. Reports in 1 month on queries. Publishes ms an average of 3 months after acceptance. Free sample copy; free writer's guidelines for 4x9 SAE and 1 first class stamp.
Nonfiction: "Articles about highly innovative applications of computer hardware and software 'firsts'." Buys 60-100 mss/year. Query with clips of published work. Length: 500-2,500 words. Pays $70-100/printed page, including illustrations.
Photos: Send line art, diagrams, photos or color transparencies.
Tips: "The best way to break in is to be affiliated with a manufacturer or user of computers or peripherals."

‡NEWS/34-38, For Users of IBM Systems 34/36/38, Duke Corporation, Suite 210, 295 E. 29th St., Loveland CO 80537. (303)667-4132. Editor: David A. Duke. Managing Editor: Robert S. Skowron. A technically-oriented monthly magazine for data processing uses of IBM Systems 34/36/38. Circ. 18,000. Pays on publication. Byline given. Buys all rights. Submit seasonal/holiday material 3 months in advance. Simultaneous queries. Electronic submissions OK if compatible with WordStar and IBM PC. Computer printout submissions acceptable. Reports in 1 month. Free sample copy.
Nonfiction: How-to (use Systems 34/36/38); interviews (with users); new product (review); opinion; personal experience (as a DP manager); and technical (tips and techniques). No fluff. Buys 50-100 mss/year. Query

Close-up

Joyce Schelling, Editor
TeleSystems Journal

Writers—who envy Voltaire and Twain for living during colorful times—can write about a world that neither author experienced. "It's just the most fantastic time to be a writer," says *TeleSystems Journal* editor Joyce Schelling.

Data processing trade publications need articles. Companies want freelancers to write computer guides. "We have the technicians but now we need people to translate this very technical material into language that the ordinary person can understand," she says.

Schelling advises writers bent on *creative* writing to at least try technical writing. "All day long, technical writers are working with language. You put something on paper, you go over it, and say, 'have I gotten my message across'," she points out. "I think the sharp distinction that you make between creative writing and technical or expository writing is an illusion because it's all language."

The writer willing to take computer courses can find a niche in computer trade magazines. That's what Schelling did (before quitting her job as a writing instructor at New York University). She doesn't regret the move.

Computer technicians now write the articles best suited for *TSJ*. But this will change, she predicts, as (nontechnician) writers learn computer language.

The estimated six months it takes to develop a specialty could lead to writing assignments. "It might not be as fulfilling as writing the 'great American novel,' but it pays," she says. "I know people who do technical writing and then they write the 'great American novel' at night."

As a freelancer, Schelling had submitted articles, children's stories, and poems to magazines. She knows how writers long to sell their work. Now as an editor, she *receives* manuscripts; some

of them need to be entirely rewritten. "Writing is just coming of age in this industry," says Schelling (whose free time is spent working on her Ph.D. dissertation on stylistics). "If there's something in a manuscript that I can salvage, I will do that."

In evaluating writers, Schelling looks for "receptivity to editorial change." She sometimes sees "arrogant writers who have fallen in love with their writing." Her main concern, though, is pleasing *TSJ*'s 1,400 subscribers, 95 percent of whom use IBM's CICS software product.

She is developing a department in the magazine on CICS documentation for technical writing—to expand *TSJ*'s readership. "That to me is creativity and it's in the field of writing and providing a service to writers," she says. "That's where I get my joy in this job."

Schelling works on four issues in different stages without a six-month lead time, but she'll still discuss story ideas with writers over the telephone. The image of an editor red-penning a writer's manuscript bothers her. "You can teach a writer that in any piece of writing you have the opportunity to make it better, and that's editing."

Schelling predicts it will take five years to bridge the gap between the data processing industry and people who know little about computers. "We are in the golden age of writing right now," she says.

It's no time to cruise the Mississippi.

with or without published clips. Length: 1,000-5,000 words. Pays $100-500.

Photos: State availability of photos, send photos with query or ms. Pays $5-10 for b&w prints; $5-20 for color transparencies. Captions, model release and identification of subjects required. Buys all rights.

Columns/Departments: Technical Tips. Buys 12 mss/year. Query. Length: 50-500 words. Pays $10-100.

Fillers: Newsbreaks. Buys 25/year. Length; 50-500 words. Pays $10-100.

Tips: "We are a very targeted magazine going to a technically-oriented audience. Our writers *must* have a working knowledge of the IBM Systems 34/36/38 computers. Tutorial topics, user stories and management topics are most open to freelancers."

SMALL SYSTEMS WORLD, Hunter Publishing, 950 Lee St., Des Plaines IL 60016. (312)296-0770. Editor: Hellena Smejda. Monthly magazine covering applications of small computer systems in business. Circ. 40,000. Pays on acceptance. Byline given. Buys all rights. Submit seasonal/holiday material 4 months in advance. Reports in 2 weeks on queries. Sample copy $5.

Nonfiction: How-to (use the computer in business); and technical (organization of a data base or file system). "A writer who submits material to us should be an expert in computer applications. No material on large scale computer equipment." No poetry. Buys 4 mss/year. Query. Length: 3,000-4,000 words.

TELESYSTEMS JOURNAL, OSI Publications, Ltd., Fort Lee Executive Park, Two Executive Dr., Fort Lee NJ 07024. (201)592-0009, (800)526-0272. Editor: Joyce Schelling. 95% freelance written. Bimonthly trade journal covering large scale IBM main frame computers and the associated on-line software. "A forum for the exchange of technological information among computer professionals." Circ. 1,400. Pays on publication. Publishes ms an average of 6 months after acceptance. Byline given. Buys all rights. Submit seasonal/holiday material 6 months in advance. Photocopied submissions OK. Computer printout submissions acceptable; prefers letter-quality to dot-matrix. Reports in 6 weeks. Free sample copy and writer's guidelines.

Nonfiction: General interest (computer security, auditing and privacy controls—all areas of project planning, such as project life cycle, feasibility, design, and implementation); personal computers (articles dealing with direct hook-up to a large main frame, and personal computers in the business world); new products (articles about IBM releases); personal experience (case studies, such as the technical story behind a major programming effort; use of a new product, including features of the product and what it accomplished for the installation; problems and/or methodology of installing or generating a system such as NCP); telecommunications (networking; philosophy and actual case implementation; latest in hardware, such as a description of, or innovative use of, 3270 and 8775 terminals and 3705 controllers); and interview/profile (profile of the hardware and software used by an IBM shop). Special issues include computer security for on-line systems; IBM/DB/DC; VTAM; data processing training and education, and others. Write for details. "We don't want to see articles about non IBM or non IBM compatible equipment; theory articles such as '37 Formulae to Use When Designing Data Structures'. We'd rather have 'How to use bi-directional pointers in your IMS data base'; articles such as 'How to program your TRS-80'. We'd rather have 'Personal computers and business graphics'. Query or send complete ms. Length: 2,000-15,000 words. Pays $100-600.

Photos: "Send photos, diagrams and charts with manuscripts. No extra payment for photos."

Columns/Departments: Linkage Editor ("We seek questions about IBM on-line software that we answer in the first available issue") and book reviews (of high tech books). Query or send complete ms. Length: 25-100 words for Linkage Editor; 300-1,000 words for Book Reviews. Pays $25 for Linkage Editor; $25-100 for Book Reviews.

Tips: "We stress the technological side of the major IBM software packages. We are interested in all aspects of computer training for these software packages; for their innovative use; for how-to's, how does it work, and for reviews of software announcements. Some examples of articles that would interest us are: 'How to Design Efficient BMS Screens for the 3270 Terminal' and 'How to Tune Your CICS/MVS System'. We also seek articles on computer security, pricing, law and auditing. Finally, we balance our journal with articles on management topics, such as project management, capacity planning and management strategies. All sections are open to freelancers. Our freelancers are generally computer technicians with some writing ability or writers who are comfortable in the esoteric world of high technology. Query by telephone and establish rapport with the editor."

‡**two/sixteen magazine, The journal for business, professional & scientific members of the TRS-80 community**, 131 E. Orange St., Lancaster PA 17602. (717)397-3364. Publisher: Richard H. Young. Managing Editor: Barbara S. Albert. A bimonthly magazine covering TRS-80 models II, 12 and 16 microcomputers from Radio Shack for people in business, professional and scientific pursuits who use their microcomputers as part of the way they make their living. Circ. 5,000. Pays on publication. Byline given. Buys all rights. Simultaneous queries, and simultaneous and photocopied submissions OK. Electronic submissions OK if single-sided, single- or double-density 8" diskette. WordStar, ASCII or SCRIPSIT format acceptable. Computer printout submissions acceptable except for program listings. SASE. Reports in 1 week on queries; 1 month on mss. Free sample copy and writer's guidelines.

Nonfiction: How-to, new product, personal experience and technical. "We use only hardware specific articles that can be of direct benefit to TRS-80 Model II, 12 and 16 microcomputer users. No general or theoretical or essay type articles—they must be user-oriented." Query. Buys 120 mss/year. Length: open. Pays $30/ published page (7,000 characters/1 page).

Columns/Departments: "We have a Special User Report section where we publish reviews of products that we have not supplied. Be concise, be specific. Don't be too formal. We go for a conversational style. Address readers as 'you' and refer to yourself as 'I.' Buys 120 mss/year. pays $30/published page (7,000 characters/1 page).

Tips: "Our readers are getting more and more sophisticated. No one wants to read about 'my first word processing experience' because they've all been through that by now. They want to learn how to up-grade their computers and their knowledge to get the full capacity from their machines. They want to get their money's worth as well as make some money using the computer."

‡**UNIX/WORLD, Your Complete Guide to the Frontiers of the Unix System**, Tech Valley Publishing Inc., 289 S. San Antonio Rd., Los Altos CA 94022. (415)949-3737. Editor: Dr. Rebecca Thomas. 40% freelance written. A monthly magazine covering the UNIX operating system (computers) for data processing professionals. Estab. 1983. Circ. 45,000. Pays on publication. Publishes ms an average of 2 months after acceptance. Byline given. Offers 25% kill fee. Buys first North American serial rights and second (reprint) rights to material originally published elsewhere. Submit seasonal/holiday material 6 months in advance. Simultaneous queries, and photocopied and previously published submissions OK. Electronic submissions OK if compatible with 300 baud ASC II format, UUCP (UNIX). Computer printout submissions acceptable. SASE. Reports in 2 weeks. Sample copy $3; free writer's guidelines.

Nonfiction: David Coleman, articles editor. Book excerpts; how-to (technical articles on the UNIX system or the C language); interview/profile; new product; technical (see how-to); and product reviews. "All articles should be written for data processing professionals who are encountering the UNIX system for the first time. We are not interested in articles written by marketing departments that push one product line." Buys 100 mss/ year. Query with published clips. Length: 2,500-7,000 words. Pays $50-500.

Photos: Send photos with query or ms. Reviews b&w contact sheets. Identification of subjects required. Buys one-time rights.

Columns/Departments: Wizard's Grabbag (tips and techniques that ease the programmer's burden). Buys 100 mss/year. Send complete ms. Length: 100-1,000 words. Pays $25-50.

Tips: "UNIX is trademark of AT&T Bell Labs. *UNIX/WORLD* is not affiliated with AT&T Bell Labs."

Dental

The semiannual visit to the dentist won't make the writer an expert in writing for dental trade publications. "Many freelancers send us manuscripts better suited for the consumer press," says one dental magazine editor. "Articles must contain some specific tools a dentist can utilize in his/her practice."

CONTACTS, Box 407, North Chatham NY 12132. Editor: Joseph Strack. 80% freelance written. For laboratory owners, managers, and dental technician staffs. Bimonthly. Circ. 1,200. Pays on acceptance. Publishes ms an average of 5 months after acceptance. Buys first and second rights to the same material. Byline given. Reports in 1-2 weeks. SASE. Free sample copy.

Nonfiction: Writer should know the dental laboratory field or have good contacts there to provide technical articles, how-to, and successful business operation articles. Query. Length: 1,500 words maximum. Pays 3-5¢/ word. Willing to receive suggestions for columns and departments for material of 400-1,200 words. Payment for these negotiable.

DENTAL ECONOMICS, Box 3408, Tulsa OK 74101. Editor: Dick Hale. 60% freelance written. Emphasizes "practice management for dentists." Monthly magazine; 90 pages. Circ. 103,000. Pays on acceptance. Buys all rights. Byline given. "Occasionally no byline is given when it's an article combining talents of several authors, but credit is always acknowledged." Submit seasonal/holiday material 4 months in advance of issue date. Computer printout submissions acceptable, "but we question 'exclusivity'—we must have exclusives in our field." SASE. Reports in 4 weeks. Free sample copy and writer's guidelines.

Nonfiction: Expose (closed panels, NHI); how-to (hire personnel, bookkeeping, improve production); humor (in-office type); investments (all kinds); interview (doctors in the news, health officials); personal experience (of dentists, but only if related to business side of practice); profile (a few on doctors who made dramatic lifestyle changes); and travel (only if dentist is involved). Buys 100-120 unsolicited mss/year. Query or submit complete ms. Length: 600-3,500 words. Pays $50-500.

Photos: State availability of photos with query or submit photos with ms. Pays $10 minimum for 8x10 glossy photos; $25 minimum for 35mm color transparencies. Captions and model release required. Buys all North American rights.

Columns/Departments: Viewpoint (issues of dentistry are aired here). Buys 1 ms/issue. Submit complete ms. Length: 600-1,500 words.

Tips: *DE's* advice to freelancers is: "Talk to dentists about their problems and find an answer to one or more of them. Know the field. Read several copies of *DE* to determine slant, style and length. Write for one dentist, not 100,000. We're growing—need more submissions—need *objective* look at computers—both hardware and software."

DENTAL MANAGEMENT, The National Business Magazine for Dentists, HBJ Publications, 7500 Old Oak Blvd., Cleveland OH 44130. (216)243-8100. Editor: Belinda Wilson. Managing Editor: John Sabol. Monthly magazine covering business and financial aspects of dental practice, practice management, malpractice, insurance, investments and psychological aspects of dentistry for dentists in clinical practice. Circ. 104,000. Pays on publication. Buys all rights. Byline given. SASE. Reports in 3 weeks. Writer's guidelines for SASE.

Nonfiction: Expose (bad investments, tax shelters, poor insurance deals); general interest; how-to (investments, advertising, getting new patients); interview; opinion; and personal experience. No clinical mss, fiction, cartoons, poetry. Buys 100 mss/year. Query. Length: 3,000 words maximum. Pays $125/published page.

Columns/Departments: "Office Innovations column most open to freelancers. Interview dentist or staff on tips for dentists on the business/financial aspects of dentistry. Should be innovations actually used by dental office." Buys 60/year. Send complete ms. Length: 250-500 words. Pays $25/published item.

PROOFS, The Magazine of Dental Sales and Marketing, Box 3408, Tulsa OK 74101. (918)835-3161. Publisher: Joe Bessette. Editor: Mary Elizabeth Good. Magazine published 10 times/year; combined issues July/August, November/December. Pays on publication. Byline given. Will send free sample copy on request. Query. Reports in 2 weeks. SASE.

Nonfiction: Uses short articles, chiefly on selling to dentists. Must have understanding of dental trade industry and problems of marketing and selling to dentists and dental laboratories. Pays about $75.

TIC MAGAZINE, Box 407, North Chatham NY 12132. (518)766-3047. Editor: Joseph Strack. For dentists, dental assistants, and oral hygienists. 80% freelance written. Monthly. Buys first and second rights to the same material. Byline given. Pays on acceptance. Publishes ms an average of 5 months after acceptance. Reports in 2 weeks. SASE.

Nonfiction: Uses articles (with illustrations, if possible) as follows: 1) lead feature: dealing with major developments in dentistry of direct, vital interest to all dentists, 2) how-to pieces: ways and means of building dental practices, improving professional techniques, managing patients, increasing office efficiency, etc., 3) special articles: ways and means of improving dentist-laboratory relations for mutual advantage, of developing auxiliary dental personnel into an efficient office team, of helping the individual dentist to play a more effective role in alleviating the burden of dental needs in the nation and in his community, etc., and 4) general articles: concerning any phase of dentistry or dentistry-related subjects of high interest to the average dentist. "Especially interested in profile pieces (with b&w photographs) on dentists who have achieved recognition/success in nondental fields—business, art, sport or whatever. Interesting, well-written pieces a sure bet." No material written for patients instead of dentists or "humorous" pieces about pain. Query. Length: 800-3,200 words. Pays 5¢ minimum/word.

Photos: Photo stories: 4-10 pictures of interesting developments and novel ideas in dentistry. B&w only. Pays $10 minimum/photo.

Tips: "We can use fillers of about 500 words or so. They should be pieces of substance on just about anything of interest to dentists. A psychoanalyst broke in with us recently with pieces relating to interpretations of patients' problems and attitudes in dentistry."

Drugs, Health Care and Medical Products

THE APOTHECARY, HealthCare Marketing Services, 334 State St., Box AP, Los Altos CA 94022. (415)941-3955. Editor: Jerold Karabensh. Managing Editor: Janet Goodman. 100% freelance written. Magazine published 6 times/year covering pharmacy. "*The Apothecary* aims to provide practical information to community retail pharmacists." Circ. 65,000. Pays on acceptance. Publishes ms an average of 5 months after acceptance. Byline given. Buys all rights. Submit seasonal/holiday material 6-8 months in advance. Simultaneous queries and photocopied submissions OK. Computer printout submissions acceptable; prefers letter-quality to dot-matrix. SASE. Reports in 6 weeks on queries; 5 months on mss. Free sample copy and writer's guidelines.

Nonfiction: Janet Goodman, articles editor. How-to (e.g., manage a pharmacy); opinion (of registered pharmacists); technical (related to drug therapy); and health-related feature stories. "We publish only those general health articles with some practical application for the pharmacist as businessman. No general articles not geared to our pharmacy readership; no fiction." Buys 10 mss/year. Query with clips of published work. Length: 750-3,000 words. Pays $100-350.

Columns/Departments: Janet Goodman, column/department editor. Commentary (views or issues relevant to the subject of pharmacy or to pharmacists). Send complete ms. Length: 750-1,000 words. "This section unpaid; will take submissions with byline."

Tips: "Write according to our policy, i.e., business articles with emphasis on practical information for a community pharmacist. Suggest reading several back issues and following general feature story tone, depth, etc. Stay away from condescending use of language. Though our articles are written in simple style, they must reflect knowledge of subject and reasonable respect for the readers' professionalism and intelligence."

● **BRISTOL-MYERS NEW YORK**, 345 Park Ave., New York NY 10154. (212)546-4000. Editor: Madeleine Dreyfack. Emphasizes consumer and pharmaceutical products for employees. Monthly magazine. Circ. 2,000. Pays on publication. Buys first rights only. Simultaneous and photocopied submissions OK. SASE. Reports in 3 weeks. Free sample copy.

Nonfiction: Company news, employee news, job safety, new products, photo features and profiles. "Company tie-in essential. We emphasize stories that help employees understand the company and its operations better." Buys less than 1 ms/issue. Query. Length: 350-750 words. Pays $100-300.

CANADIAN PHARMACEUTICAL JOURNAL, 101-1815 Alta Vista Dr., Ottawa, Ontario K1G 3Y6 Canada. (613)523-7877. Editor: Jean-Guy Cyr. Assistant Editors: Mary MacDonald and Catherine Partington. 5% freelance written. For pharmacists. Monthly journal; 48 pages. Circ. 13,000. Pays on acceptance. Publishes ms an average of 3 months after acceptance. Buys first rights only. Computer printout submissions acceptable; prefers letter-quality to dot-matrix. Reports in 2 months. Free sample copy and writer's guidelines.

Nonfiction: Relevant to Canadian pharmacy. Publishes exposes (pharmacy practice, education and legislation); how-to (pharmacy business operations); historical (pharmacy practice, Canadian legislation, education); and interviews with and profiles on Canadian and international pharmacy figures. Length: 200-400 words (for news notices); 800-1,200 words (for articles). Query. Payment is contingent on value; usually 15¢/word.

Photos: B&w (5x7) glossies purchased with mss. Captions required. Pays $5/photo. Model release required.

Tips: "Query with complete description of proposed article, including topic, sources (in general), length, payment requested, suggested submission date, and whether photographs will be included. It is helpful if the writer has read a *recent* (1984) copy of the journal; we are glad to send one if required. The letter should describe the proposed article thoroughly. References should be included where appropriate (this is vital where medical and scientific information is included). Send 2 copies of each ms. Author's degree and affiliations (if any) should be listed; author's writing background should be included (in brief form)."

DRUG TOPICS, 680 Kinderkamack Rd., Oradell NJ 07649. (201)262-3030. Editor: Valentine Cardinale. Executive Editor: Ralph M. Thurlow. For retail drug stores and wholesalers and manufacturers. Semimonthly. Circ. over 80,000. Buys all rights. Pay varies. Byline given "only for features." Pays on acceptance. Computer printout submissions acceptable. SASE.

Nonfiction: News of local, regional, state pharmaceutical associations, legislation affecting operation of drug stores, news of pharmacists and store managers in civic and professional activities, etc. No stories about manufacturers. Query on drug store success stories which deal with displays, advertising, promotions and selling techniques. Query. Length: 1,500 words maximum. Pays $5 and up for leads, $25 and up for short articles, $100-300 for feature articles, "depending on length and depth."

Photos: May buy photos submitted with mss. May buy news photos with captions only. Pays $10-20.

HOME HEALTH CARE BUSINESS, Cassak Publications, 454 Morris Ave., Springfield NJ 07081. (201)564-9400. Editor: Laurie Cassak. For pharmacists, home health care managers and manufacturers of patient aid products. Bimonthly. Circ. 8,000. Buys all rights. Pays on publication. Photocopied and simultaneous submissions OK. SASE. Free sample copy and writer's guidelines.

The double dagger (‡) before a listing indicates that the listing is new in this edition. New markets are often the most receptive to freelance contributions.

Nonfiction: "Articles about existing home health care centers or opportunities for proprietors; articles about new technologies in the home care field; helpful hints for the pharmacist engaged in serving the booming consumer/home health care field. It is essential to understand your reading audience. Articles must be informative but not extremely technical." No human interest stories. Buys informational, how-to, interview and photo articles. Query. Length: 1,000-1,500 words.
Photos: Photos purchased with accompanying ms with no additional payment. Captions optional.

RX HOME CARE, The Journal of Home Health Care and Rehabilitation, Brentwood Publishing Corp., 825 S. Barrington Ave., Los Angeles CA 90049. (213)826-8388. Managing Editor: Nancy Greengold. 85% freelance written. Monthly magazine of the home health care marketplace for medical equipment supply dealers. Circ. 22,000. Pays on acceptance. Byline given. Buys all rights. Submit seasonal/holiday material 4 months in advance. SASE. Reports in 1 month. Sample copy $5; free writer's guidelines.
Nonfiction: Equipment-oriented articles on assignment only. "Therapists, nurses and freelancers may contribute to this journal. Articles are of an educational or marketing/business nature." No write-ups of specific products or general interest stories. Buys 60 mss/year. Query with resume and published clips. Length: 1,000-2,500 words. Pays $100-300.
Columns/Departments: Management Matters (tips on running a medical equipment supply business); and Sidelights (1,000-word descriptions of specific dealerships). "All mss must be assigned." Buys 20 mss/year. Query with published clips. Length: 750-1,000 words. Pays $75-100.
Tips: "Submit resume with clips of published work. We will contact you if we are interested. We are continually on the lookout for new freelancers and often keep resumes on file for months before we get back to you. Writers skilled in marketing or business writing are most successful."

WHOLESALE DRUGS, 1111 E. 54th St., Indianapolis IN 46220. Editor: William F. Funkhouser. Bimonthly. Buys first rights only. Query. SASE.
Nonfiction: Wants features on presidents and salesmen of full line wholesale drug houses throughout the country. No set style, but article should tell about both the subject and his/her company—history, type of operation, etc. Pays $50 for text and pictures. Primarily staff-written.

Education

Professional educators, teachers, coaches and school personnel—as well as other people involved with training and education—read the journals classified here. Education-related publications for students are included in the Career, College, and Alumni and Teen and Young Adult sections of Consumer Publications.

THE AMERICAN SCHOOL BOARD JOURNAL, National School Boards Association, 1055 Thomas Jefferson St. NW, Washington DC 20007. (202)337-7666. Features Editor: Jerome Cramer. Emphasizes public school administration and policymaking. For elected members of public boards of education throughout the US and Canada, and high-level administrators of same. Monthly magazine; 64 pages. Circ. 50,000. Pays on acceptance. Buys all rights. Phone queries OK. Photocopied submissions OK. Computer printout submissions acceptable. SASE. Reports in 2 months. Free sample copy and guidelines.
Nonfiction: Publishes how-to articles (solutions to problems of public school operation including political problems); and interviews with notable figures in public education. "No material on how public schools are in trouble. We all know that; what we need are *answers*." Buys 20 mss/year. Query. Length: 400-2,000 words. Payment for feature articles varies, "but never less than $75."
Photos: B&w glossies (any size) and color purchased on assignment. Captions required. Pays $10-50. Model release required.

‡ARTS & ACTIVITIES, Publishers' Development Corporation, Suite 200, 591 Camino de la Reina, San Diego CA 92108. (619)297-5352. Editor: Dr. Leven C. Leatherburg. Managing Editor: Maryellen Bridge. Monthly (except July and August) art education magazine covering art education at levels from preschool through college for educators and therapists engaged in arts and crafts education and training. Circ. 22,042. Pays on publication. Byline given. Not copyrighted. Buys one-time rights. Submit seasonal/holiday material 4 months in advance. Photocopied submissions OK. Computer printout submissions acceptable; prefers letter-quality to dot-matrix. SASE. Reports in 6-8 weeks. Sample copy for 9x12 envelope and $2 postage; writer's guidelines for business-size SAE and 1 first class stamp.

Nonfiction: Historical/nostalgic (arts activities history); how-to (classroom art experiences, artists' techniques); interview/profile (of artists); opinion (on arts activities curriculum, ideas on how to do things better); personal experience ("this ties in with the how-to—we like it to be *personal*, no recipe style"); and articles on exceptional art programs. Buys 50-80 mss/year. Length: 200-2,000 words. Pays $35-150.

● **CALLIGRANEWS, The Calligrafree Company's Newsletter**, Box 96, Brookville OH 45309. (513)833-5677. Editor: A. Lincoln. 25% freelance written. Bimonthly newsletter covering calligraphy for teachers and professionals. "We introduce new books and tools and announce important events. We also use the 4-page insert to deal with one specific 'how to' theme in calligraphy. The insert is '. . . Talk,' i.e., Brushtalk, Pentalk, Papertalk, etc. The series is planned for 26 individual issues (or inserts), but will be expanded." Circ. 5,000 + . Pays on acceptance. Publishes ms an average of 1 month after acceptance. Byline given. Buys all rights. Submit seasonal/holiday material 3 months in advance. Simultaneous queries and photocopied submissions OK. Electronic submissions OK on Apple II Plus but requires hard copy also. Computer printout submissions acceptable. SASE. Reports in 1 month. Sample copy for SAE and 54¢ postage; free writer's guidelines.
Nonfiction: How-to, inspirational, interview/profile, new product, opinion, personal experience and photo feature—all related to calligraphy. Also needs b&w catalog cover ideas. "No personal write-ups slanted toward free advertising for author." Buys 6-12 mss/year. Query with clips. Length: 500-2,500 words. Pays $50-150.
Photos: Send photos with ms. Pays $5-25/5x7 b&w prints. Captions, model release and identification of subjects required. Buys all rights.
Tips: "Study the subject thoroughly—research in library titles helps. The readers are teachers and professionals and know their trade. Best area for freelancers is in coverage of the numerous exhibits and shows each year in most cities. Also, reports on successful teachers of calligraphy. How to do it is needed, especially in high tech areas—as in computer calligraphy. Will probably expand size and scope to include handwriting in elementary schools. The most rewarding aspect of working with freelance writers is that some terrific ideas come in on occasion."

CATECHIST, Peter Li, Inc., 2451 E. River Rd., Dayton OH 45439. Editor: Patricia Fischer. Emphasizes religious education for professional and volunteer religious educators working in Catholic schools and parish programs. Monthly (July/August—April) magazine; 70 pages. Circ. 50,000. Pays on publication. Buys all rights. Submit seasonal/holiday material 3 months in advance. Computer printout submissions acceptable. SASE. Reports in 2 months. Sample copy $2; free writer's guidelines.
Nonfiction: Publishes how-to articles (methods for teaching a particular topic or concept); informational (theology and church-related subjects, insights into current trends and developments); and personal experience (in the religious classroom). Buys 45 mss/year. Query. Length: 1,500 words maximum. Pays $30-75.
Photos: Pays $15-25 for b&w 8x10 glossy prints purchased without mss. Send contact sheet.
Tips: "We like to see articles that would be of practical use for the teacher of religion or an article that results from personal experience and expertise in the field."

‡**CLASSROOM COMPUTER LEARNING**, 19 Davis Dr., Belmont CA 94002. Editor: Holly Brady. 50% freelance written. Emphasizes elementary through high school educational computing topics. Monthly magazine published during school year. Circ. 80,000. Pays on acceptance. Buys all rights. Submit seasonal/holiday material 6 months in advance. Photocopied submissions OK. Computer printout submissions acceptable; prefers letter-quality to dot-matrix. SASE. Reports in 2 months. Free writer's guidelines.
Nonfiction: "We publish manuscripts that describe innovative ways of using computers in the classroom as well as articles that discuss controversial issues in computer education." How-to (specific computer-related activities for children in one of three segments of the school population: K-5, 6-9, or 10-12); interview; featurettes describing fully developed and tested classroom ideas. Recent article example: "Science Software in High-Button Shoes" (March 1984). Buys 50 mss/year. Query. Length: 600 words or less for classroom activities; 1,000-1,500 words for classroom activity featurettes; 1,500-2,500 words for major articles. Pays $25 for activities; $75 for featurettes; varying rates for longer articles. Educational Software Reviews: Assigned through editorial offices. "If interested, send a letter telling us of your areas of interest and expertise as well as the microcomputer(s) you have available to you." Pays $50 per review.
Photos: State availability of photos with query. Also interested in series of photos for posters showing real-world use of computers and innovative computer art.

COACHING REVIEW, Coaching Association of Canada, 333 River Rd., Ottawa, Ontario K1L 8B9 Canada. (613)741-0036. Editor: Vic MacKenzie. For volunteer, community and paid coaches, high school and university sports personnel. Bimonthly magazine in separate English and French issues; 64 pages. Circ. 15,000. Pays on acceptance. Buys first North American serial rights. Pays 50-75% kill fee. Byline given unless author requests otherwise. Phone queries OK. Submit seasonal/holiday material 3 months in advance. Computer printout submissions acceptable. Reports in 3 weeks. Free sample copy.
Nonfiction: How-to (coach-related of a general interest to all sports); humor (in coaching situations); inspira-

tional (coaching success stories); interview (with top successful coaches); and new product (new ideas and ways of coaching). Wants "authoritative original material on coaching topics." Does not want sports stories with little or no relevance to coaching. Buys 20-30 unsolicited mss/year. Query with complete ms. Length: 1,500-2,500 words. Pays up to $300.

Photos: State availability of photos. Pays $5-25 for b&w contact sheets; $15-30 for slide size color transparencies. Captions required. Buys one-time rights.

COLLEGE UNION MAGAZINE, 825 Old Country Rd., Box 1500, Westbury NY 11590. Managing Editor: Stephanie Wood. 5% freelance written. Emphasizes campus activity and service professionals. Published 6 times/year. Circ. 10,000. Pays on publication. Buys all rights. Queries suggested. Photocopied submissions OK. Reports in 3 weeks on queries. Publishes ms an average of 3 months after acceptance. Must include SASE for writer's guidelines. Include large manilla envelope for sample copy.

Nonfiction: General interest (food service, computers, vending, refurbishing building); historical (history of a particular school's union); how-to (run or operate any aspect of student activities); profiles (of particular union operation); personal experience (within college union work); and photo feature (operations, game room, cultural program, whole building, lobby, theater, ballroom). No fillers. Wants "good quotes, well-rounded treatment of the topic." No articles about students in college or anything *not* pertaining to the union, student activities, food service, housing, programming, etc. Buys 3-5 mss/year. Query. Length: 1,500 words maximum. Pays $2/column inch.

Photos: Pays $5 for 5x7 b&w prints and contact sheets.

Columns/Departments: Pinpoint (trends in campus life). Query. Length: 50-200 words.

Tips: "Submit articles aimed at professional employees who operate college unions, not students. Tightened budgets will force me to become more selective. Writers should include samples of other articles written for publication—just so I can get a feel for their abilities. Saves me time—saves them time."

COMPUTERS IN EDUCATION, (formerly *Teaching Electronics & Computing*), Unit 6, 25 Overlea Blvd., Toronto, Ontario M4H 1B1 Canada. (416)423-3262. Editor: William Markwick. 50% freelance written. Articles of interest to those in the educational field. Some features are presented as (limited) copyright free teachers' notes. Magazine published 10 times/year; 32-48 pages. Circ. 18,000. Pays on publication. Buys all rights. Byline given. Phone queries OK. Photocopied submissions OK. Free sample copy and writer's guidelines.

Nonfiction: Use of computers in education and techniques of teaching. Buys 3 unsolicited mss/year (but want many more). Length: 700-2,000 words. Pays 10¢/word.

Photos: Author should supply photos if necessary and applicable. Pays extra for photos. Captions required. Buys all rights.

CURRICULUM REVIEW, (formerly *Curriculum Review and Curriculum Review Subject Reports*), Curriculum Advisory Service, 517 S. Jefferson St., Chicago IL 60607. (312)939-3010. Editor-in-Chief: Irene M. Goldman. Managing Editor: Charlotte H. Cox. 80% freelance written. A multidisciplinary magazine for K-12 principals, department heads, teachers, curriculum planners and superintendents; published 5 times/year (bimonthly through school year). Circ. 10,000. Each issue includes articles in the areas of language arts/reading, mathematics, science, social studies, and the educational uses of computers. A separate feature section varies from issue to issue. Pays on publication. Byline given. Buys all rights. Photocopies and multiple queries OK, but no multiple submissions. Computer printout submissions acceptable only if legible. SASE. Reports in 3-6 weeks on queries; 4 months on mss. Publishes ms an average of 4 months after acceptance. Free sample copy and writer's guidelines.

Nonfiction: Barbara Berndt, articles editor. How-to articles should consider primarily an audience of secondary educators and describe successful teaching units or courses which might be implemented elsewhere. Other articles should focus on innovative or practical programs, teaching units, new curriculum trends, and controversial or stimulating ideas in education. "While we need articles in all 4 areas (language arts/reading, math, science, social studies), math and science are especially welcome." Buys 45 mss/year. Length: 1,000-2,000 words. Query. Pays $25-100.

Photos: State availability of photos with query or ms. Prefers 35mm color transparencies or 8x10 b&w or color prints. Model release required. Buys all rights with ms; no additional payment.

Columns/Departments: 600 book reviews/year on an assigned basis with educational vita; textbook, supplements, media, and computer software selection in language arts/reading, mathematics, science and social studies. Emphasizes secondary level. "We are looking for new treatments of educational topics. Description of specific teaching units or courses are welcome if they have broad implications for other schools. Use fresh, descriptive, plain language—no educationalese." Length: 300-600 words. Pays $20-50.

Tips: "In 1985 we will feature science and societal issues, human rights in a participatory democracy, comprehension skills, and computers. Schedule available upon request."

FORECAST FOR HOME ECONOMICS, 730 Broadway, New York NY 10003. Editorial Director: Kathy Gogick. Senior Editor: Cheryl Mead. 10% freelance written. Monthly (September-May/June) magazine; 80

pages. Circ. 78,000. Pays on publication. Buys first rights only. Pays negotiable kill fee. Byline given. Submit seasonal/holiday material 6-8 months in advance. SASE. Free writer's guidelines.

Nonfiction: Current consumer/home economics-related issues, especially energy, careers, family relations/ child development, teaching techniques, health, nutrition, metrics, mainstreaming the handicapped, appealing to both boys and girls in the classroom, money management, housing, crafts, bulletin board and game ideas. Buys 3 mss/issue. Query first; do not send full length mss. Length: 1,000-3,000 words. Pays $100 minimum.

Photos: State availability of photos with query. No additional payment for b&w glossy prints. Captions required. Model release required.

Tips: "Contributors to *Forecast* should be professional home economists and *should* query editorial director before submitting an article. Be sure to include in your query letter "some information about your background and a list of potential articles with a 2-3 line descriptive blurb about what will be included in each article."

INSTRUCTOR MAGAZINE, 345 5th Ave., New York NY 10017. (212)503-2888. Editor-in-Chief: Leanna Landsmann. 30% freelance written. Emphasizes elementary education. Monthly magazine; 180 pages. Circ. 269,281. Pays on acceptance. Buys all rights. Phone queries OK. Submit seasonal/holiday material 6 months in advance. Photocopied submissions OK. SASE. Reports in 6 weeks. Free writer's guidelines; mention *Writer's Market* in request.

Nonfiction: How-to articles on elementary classroom practice—practical suggestions as well as project reports. Query. Length: 750-2,500 words. No poetry.

LEARNING, The Magazine for Creative Teaching, 19 Davis Dr., Belmont CA 94002. Editor: Buff Bradley. 45% freelance written. Emphasizes elementary and junior high school education topics. Monthly during school year. Magazine; 150 pages. Circ. 200,000. Pays on acceptance. Publishes ms an average of 1 year after acceptance. Buys all rights. Submit seasonal/holiday material 6 months in advance. Photocopied submissions OK. Computer printout submissions acceptable. SASE. Reports in 2 months. Writer's guidelines sent upon request.

Nonfiction: "We publish manuscripts that describe innovative teaching strategies or probe controversial and significant social/political issues related to the professional and classroom interest of preschool to 8th grade teachers." How-to (classroom management, specific lessons or units or activities for children—all at the elementary and junior high level, and hints for teaching in all curriculum areas): interview; new product; personal experience (from teachers in elementary and junior high schools); and profile (with teachers who are in unusual or innovative teaching situations). Strong interest in articles that deal with discipline, teaching strategy, motivation and working with parents. Recent article example: "The Holocaust and Today's Kids" (Nov. 1983). Buys 250 mss/year. Query. Length: 1,000-3,500 words. Pays $50-350.

Photos: State availability of photos with query. Model release required. "Also interested in series of photos for teaching posters that present a topic or tell a story that will be of interest to children."

MEDIA & METHODS, 1511 Walnut St., Philadelphia PA 19102. Editor: Ann Caputo. 80% freelance written. For teachers who have an abiding interest in humanistic and media-oriented education, plus a core of librarians, media specialists, filmmakers, and educational computer specialists. Magazine. Monthly (September through May). Circ. 32,000. Normally buys all rights. About half of each issue is freelance material. Pays on publication. Free writer's guidelines with SASE. Will consider photocopied submissions. Computer printout submissions acceptable. Reports in 3-4 months. Publishes ms an average of 5 months after acceptance. Submit complete ms or query. SASE.

Nonfiction: "We are looking for the educator who has something vital and interesting to say. Subjects include practical how-to articles with broad applicability to our readers, new electronic educational technologies, and innovative, challenging, conceptual stories that deal with educational change. Our style is breezy and conversational, occasionally offbeat. We make a concentrated effort to be nonsexist. Photos welcome." Recent article example: "Robots in the Classroom" (Jan. 1984). Material must have an educational focus and include specific, useful information readers can use. Buys 15-25 unsolicited mss/year. Length: 2,000 words maximum. Pays $25-100.

Tips: "We look for articles that talk to educators about the media and the methods that they can put to work in the classroom. In the year ahead there will be more emphasis on newer technologies and an expansion of editorial focus to encompass more computer-related material."

MEDIA PROFILES: The Career Development Edition, Olympic Media Information, 70 Hudson St., Hoboken NJ 07030. (201)963-1600. Editor: Walt Carroll. For colleges, community colleges, libraries, corporate training directors, manpower specialists, education and training services, career development centers, audiovisual specialists and administrators. Serial in magazine format, published every 2 months. Circ. 1,000. Buys all rights. Pays on publication. "Send resume of your experience in human resource development to introduce yourself." Enclose $5 for writer's guidelines and sample issue (refunded with first payment upon publication). Electronic submissions OK if WordStar. Reports in 2 months.

Nonfiction: "Reviews of instructional films, filmstrips, videotapes, sound/slide programs and the like. We have a highly specialized, rigid format that must be followed without exception. Besides job training areas, we are also interested in the areas of values and personal self-development, upward mobility in the world of work, social change, futuristics, management training, problem solving and adult education. Tell us, above all, about your experience with audiovisuals, and what audiovisual hardware you have access to." Buys 200-240 mss/ year. Query. Pays $10-15/review.

MEDIA PROFILES: The Health Sciences Edition, Olympic Media Information, 70 Hudson St., Hoboken NJ 07030. (201)963-1600. Publisher: Walt Carroll. 100% freelance written. For hospital education departments, nursing schools, schools of allied health, paramedical training units, colleges, community colleges, local health organizations. Serial, in magazine format, published every 2 months. Circ. 1,000 + . Buys all rights. Buys 240 mss/year. Electronic submissions OK on WordStar only. Computer printout submissions acceptable. Pays on publication. "Sample copies and writer's guidelines sent on receipt of resume, background, and mention of audiovisual hardware you have access to. Enclose $5 for writer's guidelines and sample issue. (Refunded with first payment upon publication)." Reports in 1 month. Query.
Nonfiction: "Reviews of all kinds of audiovisual media. We are the only review publication devoted exclusively to evaluation of audiovisual aids for hospital and health training. We have a highly specialized, definite format that must be followed in all cases. Samples should be seen by all means. Our writers should first have a background in health sciences; second, have some experience with audiovisuals; and third, follow our format precisely. Writers with advanced degrees and teaching affiliations with colleges and hospital education departments given preference. We are interested in reviews of media materials for nursing education, in-service education, continuing education, personnel training, patient education, patient care and medical problems. We will assign audiovisual aids to qualified writers and send them these to review for us. Unsolicited mss not welcome." Pays $15/review.

MOMENTUM, National Catholic Educational Association, 1077 30th St., NW, Washington DC 20007. Editor: Patricia Feistritzer. 10% freelance written. For Catholic administrators and teachers, some parents and students, in all levels of education (preschool, elementary, secondary, higher). Quarterly magazine; 56-64 pages. Circ. 14,500. Buys first rights only. Buys 28-36 mss/year. Pays on publication. Submit material 3 months in advance. Query with outline of article. SASE. Reports in 1 month. Free sample copy.
Nonfiction: "Articles concerned with educational philosophy, psychology, methodology, innovative programs, teacher training, research, financial and public relations programs and management systems—all applicable to nonpublic schools. Book reviews on educational/religious topics. Avoid general topics or topics applicable *only* to public education. We look for a straightforward, journalistic style with emphasis on practical examples, as well as scholarly writing and statistics. All references must be footnoted, fully documented. Emphasis on professionalism." Length: 1,500-2,000 words. Pays 2¢/word.
Photos: Pays $7 for b&w glossy photos purchased with mss. Captions required.

‡**NEA TODAY, A Newspaper for Members of the National Education Association**, National Education Association, 1201 16th St. NW, Washington DC 20036. (202)822-7200. Editor: Ann Kurzius. Association tabloid published monthly during school year (8 issues) covering public education: news and short features of interest to classroom teachers and other public school staff (*not* school administrators). Emphasis is on activities of NEA members and NEA local affiliates. Estab. 1982. Circ. 1,600,000. Pays on acceptance. Byline given. Makes work-for-hire assignments. Submit seasonal/holiday material 3 months in advance. Photocopied and previously published submissions OK. Computer printout submissions acceptable; prefers letter-quality to dot-matrix. SASE. Reports in 1 month. Free sample copy and writer's guidelines.
Nonfiction: How-to (improve classroom learning, motivate students, make instruction come alive, etc. "Prefer that writer *be* a classroom teacher!"); humor (must deal with public education); and photo feature (on public education). "No dissertations, reminiscences about the 'old days,' research reports, statements of personal philosophy, articles geared to parents, articles about higher education, or articles about private schools." Buys 6 mss/year. Query with published clips, or send complete ms. Length: 400-4,000 words. Pays $100-500.
Photos: Bill Fischer, photo editor. State availability of photos with query or ms.
Fillers: Cartoons. Must relate to life in public schools. Buys 4/year. Pays $20-75.
Tips: "Be a classroom teacher before you start freelancing. Keep your submission short, punchy, and free of education jargon. Use lots of quotes and concrete details to bring the article to life. Area most open to freelancers is In the Classroom—half-page or full-page features spotlighting teaching techniques, topics teachers can relate to. Advice must be practical and based on *experience*. Good photos are a real plus that often tip the balance in our decision to publish an article."

PHI DELTA KAPPAN, Box 789, Bloomington IN 47402. Editor: Robert W. Cole Jr. 2% freelance written. For educators—teachers, K-12 administrators and college professors. All hold BA degrees; one-third hold doctorates. Monthly magazine; 72 pages. Circ. 140,000. Buys all rights. Pays on publication. Publishes ms an average of 6 months after acceptance. SASE. Reports in 1-2 months. Free sample copy.
Nonfiction: Feature articles on education—emphasizing policy, trends, both sides of issues, controversial de-

velopments. Also informational, how-to, personal experience, inspirational, humor, think articles and expose. "Our audience is scholarly but hard-headed." Buys 5 mss/year. Submit complete ms. Length: 500-4,000 words. Pays $50-500. "We pay a fee only occasionally, and then it is usually to an author whom *we* seek out. We do welcome inquiries from freelancers, but it is misleading to suggest that we buy very much from them."
Photos: Pays average photographer's rates for b&w photos purchased with mss, but captions are required. Will purchase photos on assignment. Sizes: 8x10 or 5x7 preferred.

SCHOOL ARTS MAGAZINE, 50 Portland St., Worcester MA 01608. Editor: David W. Baker. 85% freelance written. Serves arts and craft education profession, K-12, higher education and museum education programs. Written by and for art teachers. Monthly, except June, July and August. Publishes ms an average of 2 months "if timely; if less pressing, can be 1 year or more" after acceptance. Buys first and second rights to same material. Pays on publication. Computer printout submissions acceptable; prefers letter-quality to dot-matrix. Reports in 3 months. SASE. Will send a sample copy to potential writers on request.
Nonfiction: Articles, with photos, on art and craft activities in schools. Should include description and photos of activity in progress as well as examples of finished art work. Query or send complete ms. Length: 600-1,400 words. Pays $20-100.
Tips: "We prefer articles on actual art projects or techniques done by students in actual classroom situations. Philosophical and theoretical aspects of art and art education are usually handled by our contributing editors. Keep in mind that art teachers want practical tips, above all. Our readers are visually, not verbally, oriented. Write your article with the accompanying photographs in hand."

SCHOOL SHOP, Prakken Publications, Inc., Box 8623, Ann Arbor MI 48107. Editor: Lawrence W. Prakken. A monthly (except June and July) magazine covering issues, trends and projects of interest to industrial, vocational and technical educators at the secondary and post secondary school levels. Special issue in April deals with varying topics for which mss are solicited. Circ. 45,000. Buys all rights. Pays on publication. Byline given. Prefers authors who have "direct connection with the field of industrial and/or technical education." Submit seasonal material 3 months in advance. Simultaneous queries, and simultaneous, photocopied and previously published submissions OK. Computer printout submissions acceptable. Reports in 6 weeks. SASE. Free sample copy and writer's guidelines.
Nonfiction: Alan H. Jones, managing editor. Uses articles pertinent to the various teaching areas in industrial education (woodwork, electronics, drafting, machine shop, graphic arts, computer training, etc.). "Outlook should be on innovation in educational programs, processes or projects which directly apply to the industrial/ technical education area." Buys general interest, how-to, opinion, personal experience, technical and think pieces, interviews, humor and coverage of new products. Buys 135 unsolicited mss/year. Length: 200-2,000 words. Pays $20-100.
Photos: Alan H. Jones, managing editor. Send photos with accompanying query or ms. Reviews b&w and color prints. Payment for photos included in payment for ms.
Columns/Departments: Alan H. Jones, managing editor. Shop Kinks (brief items which describe short-cuts or special procedures relevant to the industrial arts classroom). Buys 30 mss/year. Send complete ms. Length: 20-100 words. Pays $10 minimum.
Tips: "We are most interested in articles written by industrial, vocational and technical educators about their class projects and their ideas about the field."

SIGHTLINES, Educational Film Library Association, Inc., 45 John St., New York NY 10038. (212)227-5599. Editor-in-Chief: Marilyn Levin. 80% freelance written. Emphasizes the nontheatrical film and video world for librarians in university and public libraries, independent filmmakers and video makers, film teachers on the high school and college level, film programmers in the community, university, religious organizations and film curators in museums. Quarterly magazine; 44 pages. Circ. 3,000. Pays on publication. Buys all rights. Byline given. Phone queries OK. SASE. Reports in 2 months. Free sample copy.
Nonfiction: Informational (on the production, distribution and programming of nontheatrical films); interview (with filmmakers who work in 16mm, video; who make documentary, avant-garde, children's, and personal films); new product; and personal opinion (for regular Freedom To View column). No fanzine or feature film material. Buys 4 mss/issue. Query. Length: 4,000-6,000 words. Pay 2½¢/word.
Photos: Purchased with accompanying ms. Captions required. Offers no additional payment for photos accepted with accompanying ms. Model release required.
Columns/Departments: Who's Who in Filmmaking (interview or profile of filmmaker or video artist who works in the nontheatrical field); Members Reports (open to those library or museum personnel, film teachers, who are members of the Educational Film Library Association and who have creative ideas for programming films or media in institutions, have solved censorship problems, or other nuts-and-bolts thoughts on using film/ media in libraries/schools). Buys 1-3 mss/issue. Query. Pays 2½¢/word. Open to suggestions for new columns or departments.

SPECIAL EDUCATION: FORWARD TRENDS, 12 Hollycroft Ave., London NW3 7QL England. Editor: Margaret Peter. 40% freelance written. Quarterly. Circ. 6,000. Pays token fee for commissioned articles. Buys first British rights. Publishes ms an average of 9 months after acceptance. Electronic submissions OK, but requires hard copy also. SAE and IRCs.
Nonfiction: Articles on the education of all types of handicapped children. "The aim of this journal of the National Council for Special Education is to provide articles on special education and handicapped children that will keep readers informed of practical and theoretical developments not only in education but in the many other aspects of the education and welfare of the handicapped. While we hope that articles will lead students and others to further related reading, their main function is to give readers an adequate introduction to a topic which they may not have an opportunity to pursue further. References should therefore be selective and mainly easily accessible ones. It is important, therefore, that articles of a more technical nature (e.g., psychology, medical, research reviews) should, whenever possible, avoid unnecessary technicalities or ensure that necessary technical terms or expressions are made clear to nonspecialists by the context or by the provision of brief additional explanations or examples. No jargon-filled articles with insubstanital content. Send query that summarizes the proposed content of the article in some detail, i.e., up to 500 words." No material not related to education. Length: 2,200-3,300 words. Payment by arrangement for commissioned articles only.
Tips: "It's not easy for freelancers to break in unless they are practitioners and specialists in special education. If they have the appropriate specialized knowledge and experience, then articles in easily understood, jargon-free language are welcome, provided the depth of analysis and description are also there."

‡**TEACHING AND COMPUTERS, The Magazine for Elementary Teachers**, Scholastic Inc., 730 Broadway, New York NY 10003. (212)505-3051. Editor: Mary Dalheim. 80% freelance written. Monthly magazine covering computers and education, especially how to incorporate the computer into the teacher's everyday curriculum. Estab. 1983. Circ. 38,000. Pays on acceptance. Publishes ms an average of 5 months after acceptance. Byline given. Offers varying kill fee. Buys all rights. Submit seasonal/holiday material 7 months in advance. Simultaneous queries OK. Computer printout submissions acceptable. SASE. Reports in 3 weeks. Sample copy for SAE and 8½x11 envelope; writer's guidelines for #10 envelope and 1 first class stamp.
Nonfiction: How-to (use computers in the classroom); new product; opinion (on computers); and photo feature. No book reviews. Buys 40 mss/year. Send complete ms. Length: 500-2,000 words. Pays $50-300.
Fiction: Short stories and plays about computers for children in grades K-8. Buys 4 mss/year. Send complete ms. Length: 2,000 words maximum. Pays $50-300.

TODAY'S CATHOLIC TEACHER, 26 Reynolds Ave., Ormond Beach FL 32074. (904)672-9974. Editor-in-Chief: Ruth A. Matheny. 25% freelance written. For administrators, teachers and parents concerned with Catholic schools, both parochial and CCD. Circ. 45,000. Pays on publication. Publishes ms an average of 3 months after acceptance. Buys all rights. Byline given. Phone queries OK. Submit seasonal/holiday material 3 months in advance. Computer printout submissions acceptable; no dot-matrix. SASE. Sample copy $2; free writer's guidelines for SASE; mention *Writer's Market* in request.
Nonfiction: How-to (based on experience, particularly in Catholic situations, philosophy with practical applications); interview (of practicing educators, educational leaders); personal experience (classroom happenings); and profile (of educational leader). Buys 40-50 mss/year. Submit complete ms. Length: 800-2,000 words. Pays $15-75.
Photos: State availability of photos with ms. Offers no additional payment for 8x10 b&w glossy prints. Captions preferred. Buys one-time rights. Model release required.

Electricity

Publications classified here are edited for electrical engineers; electrical contractors; and others who build, design, and maintain systems connecting and supplying homes, businesses, and industries with power. Publications for appliance servicemen and dealers will be found in the Home Furnishings and Household Goods classification.

ELECTRIC LIGHT & POWER, Technical Publishing Co., 1301 S. Grove Ave., Barrington IL 60010. (312)381-1840. Editor: Robert A. Lincicome. Managing Editor: Robert W. Smock. Monthly tabloid covering engineering and operations for electric utility executives, managers and engineers. Circ. 42,500. Pays on publication. Byline given. Buys first rights only. Submit seasonal/holiday material 4 months in advance. Simultaneous queries OK. SASE. Reports in 3 weeks.

Nonfiction: Technical. "No general electricity articles or pieces discussing benefits of electrification, lighting, industrial, commercial or residential uses of electricity." Buys 12-15 mss/year. Query. Length: 4,000 words maximum. Pays $25-200/published page.
Photos: Send photos or copies of photos with ms.
Tips: "Writers must be familiar with electric utility technology and engineering, finance, regulation and operations."

ELECTRICAL BUSINESS, Kerrwil Publications, Ltd., 443 Mt. Pleasant Rd., Toronto, Ontario, Canada M4S 2L8. (416)482-6603. Editor-in-Chief: Randolph W. Hurst. 25% freelance written. For "marketing and operating personnel in electrical manufacturing, maintenance and construction as well as distributors." Monthly magazine. Circ. 22,000. Pays on acceptance. Buys first North American serial rights. Pays 10% kill fee. Byline given. Phone queries OK. Submit seasonal/holiday material 4 months in advance. Previously published submissions "sometimes considered." SAE and IRCs. Reports in 2 weeks. Free sample copy.
Nonfiction: Canadian electrical industry content only. How-to (problem solving, wiring, electrical construction and maintenance); general interest (to the electrical industry); interview (with electrical distributors and maintenance men); new product ("from manufacturers—we don't pay for news releases"); and technical. Query. Length: 500-1,500 words. Pays 10¢/word.
Photos: State availability of photos with query. Pays $5 for b&w photos; "negotiable" payment for color transparencies. Captions required. Buys one-time rights.

ELECTRICAL CONTRACTOR, 7315 Wisconsin Ave., Bethesda MD 20814. (301)657-3110. Editor: Larry C. Osius. 10% freelance written. For electrical contractors. Monthly. Circ. 51,000. Publishes ms an average of 2 months after acceptance. Buys first rights, reprint rights or simultaneous rights. Byline given. Computer printout submissions acceptable; prefers letter-quality to dot-matrix. Will send free sample copy on request. Usually reports in 1 month. SASE.
Nonfiction: Installation articles showing informative application of new techniques and products. Slant is product and method contributing to better, faster and more economical construction process. Query. Length: 800-2,500 words. Pays $85/printed page, including photos and illustrative material.
Photos: Photos should be sharp, reproducible glossies, 5x7 and up.

IEEE SPECTRUM, Institute of Electrical and Electronics Engineers, Inc., 345 E. 47th St., New York NY 10017. (212)705-7555. Editor/Publisher: Donald Christiansen. Administrative Editor: Ronald K. Jurgen. Monthly magazine covering electrical/electronics engineering for executive and staff electrical and electronics engineers in design, development, research, production, operations, maintenance in the field of electronic and allied product manufacturing, commercial users of electronic equipment, independent research development firms, government and military departments and service/installation establishments. Circ. 240,000. Pays on acceptance. Buys all rights. Phone queries OK. Submit material 4 months in advance. Photocopied submissions OK. Computer printout submissions acceptable; prefers letter-quality to dot-matrix. Reports in 2 weeks. Free sample copy and writer's guidelines.
Nonfiction: Interview (about socio-technical subjects and energy); technical overviews; historical; and opinion (about careers and management). No elementary business, accounting or management topics. Buys 1 ms/issue. Query. Length: 4,000-5,000 words. Pays $400-$1,500.
Columns/Departments: Relate to meetings; industrial developments and publications in the electrical or electronics engineering field. Most departmental material is staff written.
Tips: "Contact the senior editor with story ideas. Be able to exhibit a working knowledge of the magazine's charter."

PUBLIC POWER, 2301 M St. NW, Washington DC 20037. (202)775-8300. Editor: Vic Reinemer. 20% freelance written. Bimonthly. Not copyrighted. Byline given. Pays on publication. Publishes ms an average of 6 months after acceptance. Buys first rights only. Query. Electronic submissions OK if compatible with IBM PC; requires hard copy also. Computer printout submissions acceptable. "Tips for Authors" sent on request.
Nonfiction: Features on municipal and other local publicly-owned electric systems. Payment negotiable.
Photos: Uses b&w and glossy color prints.

● **SUNSHINE SERVICE NEWS**, Florida Power & Light Co., Box 029100, Miami FL 33102. (305)552-3523. Editor: Tom Veenstra. 5% freelance written. Monthly employee newspaper for the electrical utility industry. Circ. 14,500. Pays on publication. Publishes ms an average of 3 months after acceptance. Buys first rights only. Not copyrighted. Computer printout submissions acceptable. Free sample copy.
Nonfiction: Company news, employee news, general interest, historical, how-to, humor and job safety. Company tie-in preferred. Query. Pays $25-100.

Electronics and Communication

The reorganization of the AT&T system and developments on cable television service theft affect the electronics and communication magazine market, as do other trends. It is a fast-as-the-speed-of-sound market. Listed here are publications for electronics engineers, radio and TV broadcasting managers, electronic equipment operators, and builders of electronic communications systems and equipment (including stereos, television sets, radio-TV, and cable broadcasting systems). Journals for professional announcers or communicators are found under Journalism and Entertainment and the Arts; those for electric appliance retailers are in Home Furnishings and Household Goods; publications on computer design and data processing systems are listed in Data Processing. Magazines on personal computers appear in the Consumer/Personal Computing section. Publications for electronics enthusiasts or stereo hobbyists will be found in Science or Music in the Consumer Publications section.

ANSWER LINE, On Page Enterprises, Box 439, Sudbury MA 01776. Editor: Stanley J. Kaplan. Managing Editor: Bette Sidlo. 10% freelance written. Bimonthly newsletter focusing on telephone answering services for professional and medical offices, sales and service centers as well as small business people who need telephones monitored when they are not in. Circ. 50,000 initially. Pays on acceptance. Publishes ms an average of 4 months after acceptance. Buys all rights. Phone queries OK. Submit seasonal material 3 months in advance. No simultaneous, photocopied or previously published submissions. SASE. Reports in 2 weeks. Free sample copy and writers' guidelines.
Fillers: Clippings, jokes, gags, anecdotes, short humor and newsbreaks. "We are particularly interested in anecdotes in the first person narrative, stories of people and their *positive* answering service experiences and newsbreaks on various developments in business communications as they relate to telephone answering service applications. We particularly seek seasonal material." Buys 10-20 mss/year. Length: 75-150 words. Pays $25-40 minimum.
Tips: Submissions should be geared to telephone answering service clients with emphasis on the advantages of retaining such service. "Nothing on answering machines—they compete with our customers' services."

AV VIDEO, (formerly *Audio Visual Directions*), Montage Publishing, Inc., Suite 314, 25550 Hawthorne Blvd., Torrance CA 90505. (213)373-9993. Publisher: Joy McGrath. Associate Publisher: Lloyd McGrath. 100% freelance written. Magazine published 12 times/year about the uses of audiovisuals and video for readers who use audiovisuals, video and computer graphics in their professional capacities in business, industry, government, health care, financial and educational institutions and civil and community service organizations, such as police, fire, museums, libraries and churches. Circ. 37,500. Pays on publication. Byline given. Buys first rights only. Letter queries OK. Submit seasonal material 4 months in advance. Photocopied submissions OK. Electronic submissions OK, but requires hard copy also. "We are fairly receptive to computer printout submissions as long as the lines are at least double spaced with one inch margins." Prefers letter-quality to dot-matrix. Publishes ms an average of 3 months after acceptance. Free sample copy and writer's guidelines.
Nonfiction: Sam Stalos, editor. How-to. "In every issue we attempt to publish a wide variety of articles relating to all aspects of audiovisual productions as well as developments in video and computer graphics. We welcome all informed, well-written articles pertaining to slides, sound, video, audio, overheads, multi-image, computer graphics and all attendant applications." Nothing related to company profile, personnel or promotion material.
Columns/Departments: Showbill (write-ups on schools, seminars, shows, courses and conferences dedicated to educating the AV user); Software Solutions (showcase for professionally made software programs for training, education and internal communications); Products on Parade (news articles on "what's new" in equipment, materials and services); Anatomy of a Show (descriptive information on a current audiovisual show, what went into producing it, equipment used and a biography on the producer); and monthly columns of the uses and applications of audio, video, computers, computer graphics and multi-image. Send complete ms. Pays $100 minimum.
Tips: "We would like to receive more audio related articles by professionals in the field and more articles on interactive video/videodisc applications. Freelancers should have some direct involvement or experience with audiovisuals—creating or producing AV productions, scripting, using audiovisual equipment, teaching AV courses, running programs, etc. They should have some relevant information which they want to share with readers, to teach to readers, relating to audiovisuals."

BROADCAST ENGINEERING, Box 12901, Overland Park KS 66212. Editorial Director: Bill Rhodes. 30% freelance written. For "owners, managers, and top technical people at AM, FM, TV stations, cable TV operators, as well as recording studios." Monthly. Circ. 35,000. Buys all rights. Buys 50 mss/year. Pays on acceptance; "for a series, we pay for each part on publication." Publishes ms an average of 3 months after acceptance. Free sample copy and writer's guidelines. Computer printout submissions acceptable. Reports in 6 weeks. SASE.
Nonfiction: Wants technical features dealing with design, installation, modification and maintenance of radio and TV broadcast equipment; interested in features of interest to communications engineers and technicians as well as broadcast management, and features on self-designed and constructed equipment for use in broadcast and communications field. "We use a technical, but not textbook, style. Our publication is mostly how-to, and it operates as a forum. We reject material that is far too general, not on target, not backed by evidence of proof, or is a sales pitch. Our Station-to-Station column provides a forum for equipment improvement and build-it-yourself tips. We pay up to $30. We're especially interested in articles on recording studios and improving facilities and techniques." Buys 10-20 unsolicited mss/year. Query. Length: 1,500-2,000 words for features. Pays $75-200.
Photos: Photos purchased with or without mss; captions required. Pays $5-10 for b&w prints; $10-100 for 2¼x2¼ or larger color transparencies.

BROADCAST MANAGEMENT/ENGINEERING, 295 Madison Ave., New York NY 10017. (212)685-5320. Editor: Robert Rivlin. 10% freelance written. For broadcast executives, general managers, chief engineers and program directors of radio and TV stations. Monthly. Circ. 33,372. Buys all rights. Byline given unless "article is used as backup for staff-written piece, which happens rarely." Buys 15-20 mss/year. Pays on publication. Reports in 1 month. Query. Electronic submissions OK if compatible with Televideo Systems CPM. Computer printout submissions acceptable; prefers letter-quality to dot-matrix. SASE.
Nonfiction: Articles on technical trends and business trends affecting broadcasting. Particularly interested in equipment applications by broadcasters in the production of radio and television programs. Emphasis on "competitive advantage. No product puff pieces. No general management pieces or general information stories. Our readers are interested in details." Length: 1,200-3,000 words. Pays $200-300.
Tips: "To break in demonstrate a knowledge of the industry we serve. Send for an editorial schedule and sample copy of the magazine; then suggest an idea which demonstrates an understanding of our needs. Pictures, graphs, charts, schematics and other graphic material a must."

BROADCAST TECHNOLOGY, Box 420, Bolton, Ontario L0P 1A0 Canada. (416)857-6076. Editor-in-Chief: Doug Loney. 50% freelance written. Emphasizes broadcast engineering. Bimonthly magazine; 72 pages. Circ. 7,000. Pays on publication. Buys all rights. Byline given. Phone queries OK.
Nonfiction: Technical articles on developments in broadcast engineering, especially pertaining to Canada. Query. Length: 500-1,500 words. Pays $100-300.
Photos: Purchased with accompanying ms. Captions required. B&w or color. Total purchase price for a ms includes payment for photos.
Tips: "Most of our outside writing is by regular contributors, usually employed fulltime in broadcast engineering. Specialized nature of magazine requires specialized knowledge on part of writer, as a rule."

BROADCASTER, 7 Labatt Ave., Toronto, Ontario M5A 3P2 Canada. (416)363-6111. Editor: Barbara Moes. For the Canadian "communications industry—radio, television, cable, ETV, advertisers and their agencies." Monthly. Circ. 7,200. Buys all rights. Byline given. Buys 50-60 mss/year. Pays on publication. Writers should submit outlines and samples of published work; sample issue will be sent for style. Not responsible for unsolicited mss. SAE and IRCs.
Nonfiction: Technical and general articles about the broadcasting industry, almost exclusively Canadian. Length: 1,000-2,000 words. Pays $125-350.
Photos: Rarely purchased.

CABLE COMMUNICATIONS MAGAZINE, Canada's Authoritative International Cable Television Publication, Ter-Sat Media Publications Ltd., 4 Smetana Dr., Kitchener, Ontario N2B 3B8 Canada. (519)744-4111. Editor: Udo Salewsky. 33% freelance written. Monthly magazine covering the cable television industry. Circ. 6,016. Pays on acceptance. Publishes ms an average of 6 weeks after acceptance. Byline given. Buys all rights. Submit seasonal/holiday material 1 month in advance. Photocopied submissions OK. Computer printout submissions acceptable; prefers letter-quality to dot-matrix. Reports in 2 weeks on queries; 1 month on mss. Free sample copy and writer's guidelines.
Nonfiction: Expose, how-to, interview/profile, opinion, technical articles and informed views and comments on topical, industry related issues. No fiction. Buys 50 mss/year. Query with clips or send complete ms. Length: 1,000-4,000 words. Pays $200-800.
Columns/Departments: Buys 48 items/year. Query with clips of published work or send complete ms. Length: 1,000-1,500 words. Pays $200-300.

Tips: "Forward manuscript and personal resume. Break in with articles related to industry issues, events and new developments; analysis of current issues and events. Be able to interpret the meaning of new developments relative to the cable television industry and their potential impact on the industry from a growth opportunity as well as a competitive point of view. Material should be well supported by facts and data."

CABLE MARKETING, The Marketing/Management Magazine for Cable Television Executives, Jobson Publishing, 352 Park Ave. South, New York NY 10010. (212)685-4848. Executive Editor: Nicolas Furlotte. 20% freelance written. Monthly magazine for cable industry executives dealing with marketing and management topics, new trends and developments and their impact. Circ. 15,000. Pays on publication. Publishes ms an average of 2 months after acceptance. Byline given. Buys all rights. Simultaneous queries and photocopied submissions OK. Computer printout submissions acceptable; no dot-matrix. Reports in 1 month on queries and mss. Free sample copy.
Nonfiction: How-to, interview/profile, new product and technical. "Subject areas include advertising, promotion, direct marketing, direct sales, programming, engineering/technology, cable system case histories and profiles." No consumer-oriented, general press stories. Buys 20 mss/year. Query with clips of published work. Length: 1,000-2,500. Pays $250-600.
Columns/Departments: Cable Tech (technology, engineering and new products); Fine Tuning (programming items with emphasis on stand-alone products and alternative forms of programming, also Hollywood/movie studio items); and Cable Scan (news items and marketing featurettes mostly about cable system activities and developments). Buys 20 mss/year. Query with clips of published work. Length: 200-1,000 words. Pays $50-200.
Tips: "Learn something about the cable TV business before you try to write about it. Have specific story ideas. Have some field of expertise that you can draw upon (e.g., marketing or advertising)." Not interested in "reviews" of programming. Editorial focus is on the *business* of cable television.

COMMUNICATOR'S JOURNAL, The Magazine of Applied Communications, Communicator's Journal, Inc., Downtown Station, Box 602, Omaha NB 68101. (402)551-0444. Editor: James D. Fogarty. Publisher: James H. Beck. 70% freelance written. Bimonthly magazine of organizational communication for executives in public relations and advertising, marketing, training, audiovisual, design and graphics; senior business executives; and editors and writers. "We stress practical articles and columns (advice)." Circ. 20,000. Pays on acceptance. Publishes ms an average of 4 months after acceptance. Byline given. Submit seasonal/holiday material 3 months in advance. Simultaneous queries OK. Computer printout submissions acceptable. SASE. Reports in 6 weeks on queries; 8 weeks on mss. Sample copy $6.
Nonfiction: How-to, new product and technical. Special issues include Video Teleconferencing; Computer Graphics; State-of-the-Art Disaster Communications. No fiction. Buys 40 mss/year. Query with published clips or send complete ms. Length: 2,000-4,000 words. Pays $100-350.
Photos: Steve Kline, photo editor. Will buy to match specific features.
Columns/Departments: People in the Business; Digest (news briefs); Hi-Tech (shorts on technological developments); Reviews (viewing and reading); Non-Verbal Communication; and Word Shop (language commentary). Buys 20 mss/year. Query with published clips or send complete ms. Length: 1,000 words maximum. Pays negotiable rates.
Fillers: For column material. Clippings, jokes, anecdotes and newsbreaks. Pays $15 maximum on publication only.

DEALERSCOPE, (formerly *Home Entertaining Marketing*), 115 2nd Ave., Waltham MA 02154. (617)890-5124. Editorial Director: James Barry. Monthly magazine covering consumer electronics, home entertainment and major appliances for retailers and manufacturers. Circ. 25,000. Pays on publication. Byline given. Offers 50% kill fee. Submit seasonal material 3 months in advance. Electronic submissions OK but "should call us before sending disk to ensure compatibility with our system." Computer printout submissions acceptable; prefers letter-quality to dot-matrix. SASE. Reports in 1 month. Sample copy for SAE.
Nonfiction: How-to and marketing information for retailers; profiles and interviews of retailers and industry leaders; new product; personal experience in home electronics retailing; technical information relating to new products and sales; and marketing analysis. No hobbyist pieces. Query with clips. Length: 750-3,000 words. Pays $100-450.
Columns/Departments: Legal, finance, satellite TV, computers and videogames, audio, video (hardware and software), telephones, retailing, electronics accessories and major appliances.

EE'S ELECTRONICS DISTRIBUTOR, Sutton Publishing Company, Inc., 707 Westchester Ave., White Plains NY 10604. (914)949-8500. Editor-in-Chief: Edward J. Walter. Monthly tabloid for distributors of electronic parts and equipment (not hi-fi, television or computer). Circ. 15,000. Pays on publication. Byline given. Buys first North American serial rights. Photocopied submissions OK. SASE. Reports in 2 weeks. Free sample copy.
Nonfiction: Stories about specific areas of a distributor's operation such as sales, purchasing, inventory con-

trol, etc. No general columns on tax tips, government issues or inventory control. Buys 10 mss/year. Query. Length: 1,250 words typical. Pays $2/column inch, negotiable.

Photos: Send photos with ms. Pays $10-15 for b&w contact sheets. Also reviews 5x7 prints. Captions required.

Tips: "We'll be more feature- and less news-oriented in the year ahead."

ELECTRONIC BUYERS' NEWS, The High Technology Purchasing Newsweekly, 111 E. Shore Rd., Manhasset NY 11030. Editor: Paul Hyman. 2% freelance written. For purchasers in the electronics industry. Newspaper; 96 pages. Circ. 50,000. Pays on publication. Publishes ms an average of 2 months after acceptance. Usually buys first rights. Byline given. Computer printout submissions acceptable. SASE. Reports in 2 months. Rejected material not returned unless requested. Accepts very little freelance material; query first. Prefer telephone queries. Free sample copy.

Nonfiction: "Each issue features a specific theme or electronic component. Occasionally stories are accepted from authors knowledgeable in the field." All material is aimed directly at the purchasing profession. Length: open. Pays negotiable rates.

Tips: "Writers should have a working knowledge of the electronics marketplace and/or electronics purchasing. We are always interested in ideas for news features or columns that are new, timely and informative in our field."

ELECTRONIC PACKAGING AND PRODUCTION, Cahners Publishing Co., 1350 E. Touhy Ave., Box 5080, Des Plaines IL 60018. (312)635-8800. Editor: Nikita Andreiev. Emphasizes electronic equipment fabrication for engineering and production personnel, including product testing. Monthly magazine; 150-300 pages. Circ. 45,000. Pays on publication. Publishes ms an average of 3 months after acceptance. Buys all rights. Byline given. Phone queries OK. Photocopied submissions OK. Computer printout submissions acceptable. SASE. Reports in 3 weeks. Free sample copy and writer's guidelines.

Nonfiction: How-to (innovative packaging, production or testing technique); interview (new features about technological trends in electronics); and technical (articles pertaining to the electronic packaging, production and testing of electronic systems and hybrids). "No single product-oriented articles of a commercial sales pitch nature." Buys 40 or more mss/year. Query or submit complete ms. Length: 1,000-2,500 words.

Photos: State availability of photos with query or submit photos with ms. Offers no additional payment for 4x5 or larger b&w or color prints. Captions preferred. Buys all rights.

Tips: "Freelancers tend to be very punctual, but often they lack technical knowledge."

ELECTRONICS WEST, Concept Publishing, Inc., 2250 N. 16th St., Phoenix AZ 85006. (602)253-9086. Editor/Publisher: Walter J. Schuch. Monthly magazine covering a "broad spectrum of electronics for middle managers and above associated with the Southwest electronics industry (manufacturing, wholesaling and retailing)." Circ. 20,000. Pays on publication. Byline given. Submit seasonal/holiday material 3 months in advance. Simultaneous queries and photocopied submissions OK. Computer printout submissions acceptable. SASE. Reports in 3 weeks on queries.

Nonfiction: Historical/nostalgic (electronics related), how-to (manage business); humor (unique applications of electronic technology); interview/profile (of businesses and business leaders); personal experience (of managers); photo feature; and technical (written in a nontechnical manner and in a marketing style). Buys 4-5 unsolicited mss/year. Query with clips of published work. Length: 1,000-2,000 words. Pays 10¢/word maximum.

Photos: State availability of photos; $10 for 8x10 b&w glossy prints. Captions and model releases required. Rights purchased are negotiable.

Tips: No articles dealing with consumer products—i.e., radio, TV, CB radios, etc., or articles dealing with electricity rather than electronics.

‡**THE INDEPENDENT, Film & Video Monthly,** Foundation for Independent Video & Film, 9th Floor, 625 Broadway, New York NY 10012. (212)473-3400. Editor: Kathleen Hulser. 60% freelance written. A monthly magazine of practical information for producers of independent film and video with focus on low budget, art and documentary work from nonprofit sector. Circ. 5,000. Pays on acceptance. Byline given. Buys one-time rights. Submit seasonal/holiday material 4 months in advance. Simultaneous queries OK. SASE. Reports in 1 month on queries; 2 weeks on mss. Publishes ms an average of 3 months after acceptance. Sample copy for 9x12 SAE and 4 first class stamps.

Nonfiction: Book excerpts ("in our area"); how-to; and technical (low tech only). No reviews or critical pieces. Buys 60 mss/year. Query with published clips. Length: 1,200-2,500 words. Pays $30-75.

‡**INTERNATIONAL TELEVISION, The Journal of the International Television Association,** Ziff-Davis Publishing Co., One Park Ave., New York NY 10016. (212)725-5742. Editor: Shonan Noronha. Managing Editor: Robert Kneller. A bimonthly magazine covering all aspects of private, nonbroadcast teleproduction for comunications managers, television producers and engineers in business, government, law enforcement, cable and other noncommercial fields. Estab. 1983. Circ. 26,000. Pays on publication. Byline given.

Buys one-time rights. SASE. Reports in 1 month on queries; 2 months on mss. Free sample copy and writer's guidelines.
Nonfiction: How-to, interview/profile, opinion, personal experience and technical. No consumer television topics. Buys 40 mss/year. Query. Length: 1,500-3,000 words. Pays $75/printed page of copy.
Columns/Departments: Your Business (career and career path). Buys 25 mss/year. Query. Length: 1,000-1,500 words.

LASERS & APPLICATIONS, High Tech Publications, Inc., 23717 Hawthorne Blvd., Torrance CA 90505. (213)534-3700. Editor: James Cavuoto. 20% freelance written. Monthly magazine of the laser and optical industry for engineers and designers. Circ. 20,600. Pays on acceptance. Publishes ms an average of 3 months after acceptance. No byline given. Offers 25% kill fee. Buys all rights. Electronic submissions OK but call first. Computer printout submissions acceptable. SASE. Reports in 1 month. Sample copy $4.
Nonfiction: "We stress new applications of lasers and laser processes in medical, electronics, metalworking, communication, printing, military and other fields. Articles describe how a laser was used to perform a task better or cheaper; what kind of laser and operating conditions used; and what the prognosis is for selling lasers based on this process. Particularly interested in applications of lasers in foreign countries." Query with published clips. Length: 250-1,500 words. Pays $50-200.

MASS HIGH TECH, Mass Tech Times, Inc., 113 Terrace Hall Ave., Burlington MA 01830. (617)229-2768. Editor: Joeth S. Barlas. Associate Editor: Alan R. Earls. 15% freelance written. Bimonthly trade tabloid covering feature news of electronics, computers, biotech, systems analysis, for high-tech professionals. Circ. 30,000. Pays on publication. Publishes ms an average of 2 weeks after acceptance. Byline given. Not copyrighted. Buys first North American serial rights. Submit seasonal/holiday material 1 month in advance. Simultaneous queries, and simultaneous, photocopied and previously published submissions OK "if not in our immediate market." Computer printout submissions acceptable. SASE. Reports in 1 month. Sample copy for 9x12 SAE and 2 first class stamps; writer's guidelines for business-size SAE and 1 first class stamp.
Nonfiction: Book excerpts; historical (technology); humor; interview/profile; new product; opinion (qualified scientist); personal experience; and photo feature (needs technical orientation and strong Boston area orientation). "Material should inform without over simplifying. Light, amusing approach is OK." Buys 50 mss/year. Send complete ms. Length: 400-1,200 words. Pays $50-250.
Photos: Send photos with ms. Pays $25 for 5x7 b&w prints. Captions and identification of subjects required (if appropriate). Buys one-time rights.
Columns/Departments: Buys 50 mss/year. Query "with idea" or send one sample ms. Length: 300-900 words. Pays $50 and up.
Fillers: Anecdotes, short humor and newsbreaks. Buys 100 mss/year. Length: 25-100 words. Pays $10 and up.
Tips: "Know the Boston high-tech scene or have knowledgeable contacts. Material should be plausible to trained professionals. Trends in magazine publishing that freelance writers should be aware of include the need for more sophisticated graphics—photos or drawings are often available free from their corporate subjects (in our market)."

MEDIA PROFILES: The AV Marketing Newsletter, Olympic Media Information, 70 Hudson St., Hoboken NJ 07030. (201)963-1600. Editor: Hariet Lundgaard. Managing Editor: Walt Carroll. Quarterly newsletter covering the marketing, production and distribution of nontheatrical and educational films and video. Estab. 1983. Circ. 500. Pays on publication. Byline given. Buys all rights. Submit seasonal/holiday material 4 months in advance. Simultaneous queries, and simultaneous, photocopied, and previously published submissions OK. Electronic submissions OK if WordStar. SASE. Reports in 1 month. Writer's guidelines for $5 (refunded with first payment upon publication), 9x12 SAE and 4 first class stamps (includes sample issue).
Nonfiction: How-to distribute/market films, video, and other audiovisual software. "We're not interested in 'how I made' but in 'how I sell.' " Buys 50 mss/year. Query. Length: 400-2,000 words. Pays. $5-50.
Tips: "Perhaps you are working for an audiovisual distribution company or are marketing your films and video on your own. Your experiences, good and bad, will interest our readers who are just like you. How did you make money (or lose it) marketing your products? We want factual reports from people who are making and selling nontheatrical films and video or slides or cassettes (pre-packaged, off-the-shelf products, not 'sponsored' or 'client-paid' ones). We're interested in those just starting out as well as those experienced in audiovisual marketing."

MEDIA PROFILES: The Whole Earth Edition, Olympic Media Information, 70 Hudson St., Hoboken NJ 07030. (201)963-1600. Editor: Walt Carroll. Managing Editor: John Githens. Quarterly magazine covering "nontheatrical films, video, slides and tapes—(news of and reviews of) in new age, alternative, futurism and social ecology subjects for people to use for personal and group self-education." Estab. 1983. Circ. 1,000. Pays on publication. Byline given. Buys all rights. Submit seasonal/holiday material 4 months in advance. Simultaneous queries, and simultaneous, photocopied and previously published submissions OK. Electronic

submissions OK if WordStar. SASE. Reports in 1 month. Writer's guidelines for $5 (refunded with first payment upon publication), 9x12 SAE and 4 first class stamps (includes sample issue).
Nonfiction: How-to (get access to and get the most out of "alternative" media programs); interview/profile (film and video makers); new products (films, video, etc.); and reviews and reports on films and video. Buys 50 mss/year. Query. Length: 400-2,000 words. Pays $5-50.
Tips: "By all means see a sample issue (available from us or perhaps at your local university library or public library). Though our editorial style differs markedly from most magazines, it is not difficult to follow. If you're an interesting 'head' with access to audiovisual equipment and software, we have plenty for you to do. People who can tip us (and our readers) off to unusual, out-of-the ordinary films, video, etc. in whole earth or new age areas shouldn't fail to get in touch with us."

MICROELECTRONICS JOURNAL, Benn Electronics Publications Ltd., Box 28, Luton L72 0ED England. 0582-417438. Publishing Director: Philip Rathkey. 90% freelance written. For electronics engineers engaged in research design, production, applications, sales in commercial or government organizations, academics (teaching, research) and higher degree students. "Writer must be active in the microelectronics industry (including academics or higher degree students) and have either an original observation to make or be able to inform/update readers on the state-of-the-art in a specialty area, or on the activities of an organization." Bimonthly magazine; 84 pages. Circ. 1,500. Pays on publication. Buys all rights. Phone queries OK. Submit seasonal/holiday material 3 months in advance. Photocopied submissions OK. Accepts previously published work only if first English translation of foreign language paper. Computer printout submissions acceptable. SAE and IRCs. Reports in 3 weeks to US. Free sample copy and writer's guidelines.
Nonfiction: Expose (technical critique of manufacturers' products, of government, commercial, trade); general interest (state-of-the-art technical/marketing articles); how-to (on new designs, applications, production, materials, technology/techniques); interview (of eminent captain of industry or government politician); nostalgia (concerning how microelectronics companies got started or techniques were invented); personal opinion (on any relevant technical/commercial subject); profile and short notes (of company research activities, university research activities); new product (assessment and evidence of product's importance); photo feature (must include write-up explaining its technical/commercial significance); and technical (on integrated circuit technology and systems, memories, microprocessors, optoelectronics, infra-red, hybrid integrated circuits, microwave solid state devices, CCD and SAW techniques, semiconductor materials and chemicals, semiconductor production equipment and processing techniques, and automatic test techniques and equipment). Buys 10-30 mss/year. Query or submit complete ms. Length: 4,000-6,000 words. Pays $25/published page including diagrams, photos, etc.
Photos: Prefers b&w 6½x4½ prints unless color is technically essential. Offers no additional payment for photos accepted with ms. Captions required.
Tips: "Nonspecialist staff increasingly involved in typesetting. It is important that manuscripts be submitted without ambiguities and with correct punctuation, layout, explanation of abbreviations, acronyms, etc."

MICROWAVES & RF, 10 Mulholland Dr., Hasbrouck Height NJ 07604. (201)393-6285. Editor: Walter J. Bojsza. 50% freelance written. Emphasizes radio frequency design. "Qualified recipients are those individuals actively engaged in microwave and RF research, design, development, production and application engineering, engineering management, administration or purchasing departments in organizations and facilities where application and use of devices, systems and techniques involve frequencies from HF through visible light." Monthly magazine; 200 pages. Circ. 55,000. Pays on publication. Buys all rights. Phone queries OK. Photocopied submissions OK. Electronic submissions OK if DEC Mate or Apple II (Pie Writer or compatible word processing software). Computer printouts acceptable "if legible." SASE. Reports in 6 weeks. Free sample copy and writer's guidelines; mention *Writer's Market* in request.
Nonfiction: "Interested in material on research and development in microwave and RF technology and economic news that affects the industry." How-to (circuit design); new product; opinion; and technical. Buys 40 mss/year. Query. Pays $30-50/published page.
Fillers: Newsbreaks. Pays $10 (minimum).

‡**MSN (Microwave Systems News),** EW Communications, Inc., 1170 E. Meadow Dr., Palo Alto CA 94303. (415)494-2800. Editor: Alexander E. Braun. Managing Edigor: Cedric R. Braun. A monthly magazine covering developments in the microwave industry: communications, radar, avionics, monolithic integration, testing, etc. "*MSN* reaches an audience composed primarily of electrical engineers, who are interested in solving design problems and in the latest developments in the microwave industry." Circ. 48,000 +. Pays on publication. Byline given. Buys all rights. Submit seasonal/holiday material 3 months in advance. Computer printout submissions acceptable; prefers letter-quality to dot-matrix. SASE. Reports in 2 weeks. Sample copy for legal size SAE and $3 postage; free writer's guidelines.
Nonfiction: Technical. "No PR-hype articles or marketing articles." Buys 96 mss/year. Query. Length: 3,500-4,000 words. Pays $200 minimum.
Photos: Send photos with query or ms. Reviews 8x10 b&w and color prints. Payment for photos included in

payment for ms. Captions and indentification of subjects required.

Tips: "Since our publication goes to a very specialized audience, prospective authors should have a solid technical writing background and possibly an engineering degree. Query first—always. We are always looking for the latest technical developments in the microwave industry. If the proposed article is solid, it'll sell itself."

‡**MULTICHANNEL NEWS, A Fairchild Business Publication**, Fairchild Publications, #450, 300 S. Jackson St., Denver CO 80209. (303)393-6397. Editor: Thomas P. Southwick. Managing Editor: Debbie Narrod. 10% freelance written. Weekly newspaper/tabloid covering cable and pay television with hard news only. "We invite stringer queries for markets outside New York, Los Angeles, Washington, Atlanta and Denver." Circ. 15,000. Pays on publication. Publishes ms an average of 1 week after acceptance. Byline given. Buys one-time rights. Photocopied and electronic submissions OK. Computer printout submissions acceptable; no dot-matrix. Reports in 2 weeks on queries. Sample copy for $1.

Nonfiction: New product and technical on local cable system news or involvement. Articles are by assignment only. Wants news articles; no features. Query, then follow up your letter with a phone call. Length: 1,000 words maximum. Pays by column inch.

Tips: "Freelancer can break in to our publication with hard, breaking news about cable and/or pay TV. Use AP and UPI news style."

ON PAGE, On Page Enterprises, Box 439, Sudbury MA 01776. Editor: Stanley J. Kaplan. Managing Editor: Bette Sidlo. Monthly newsletter about the beeper industry (radio pocket paging) for professionals, medical people, sales people, small businessmen, municipal employees and any person whose job takes him/her away from the telephone and who must maintain communications. Circ. 100,000. Pays on acceptance. Buys all rights. Phone queries OK. Submit seasonal material 3 months in advance. No simultaneous, photocopied or previously published submissions. SASE. Reports in 2 weeks. Free sample copy and writer's guidelines.

Fillers: Clippings, jokes, gags, anecdotes, short humor and newsbreaks. "We are particularly interested in anecdotes for our On Page Forum column in the first person narrative, stories of people and their beeper experiences, and newsbreaks on a variety of communication subjects of interest to people who use beepers. We especially look for seasonal freelance contributions." Buys 10-20 mss/year. Length: 75-150 words. Pays $25-40.

Tips: "Submissions should be geared to beeper users (e.g., subject matter must be related to communications or mobility). No sarcasm or comments insulting those who carry/use a beeper."

‡**PERSONAL COMMUNICATIONS MAGAZINE**, Future Comm Publications, Inc., Suite 304, 4041 University Dr., Fairfax VA 22030. (703)352-1200. Editor: Stuart Crump, Jr. Assistant Editor: Benn Kobb. A monthly magazine covering telecommunications developments with an emphasis on the individual user of cellular radio, paging, voice mail, etc. *PEM* is directed toward telecommunication professionals, e.g., telephone companies, radio common carriers, interconnect companies, etc. Estab. 1983. Circ. 13,000+. Pays shortly after acceptance. Byline given. Offers 50% kill fee. Buys first rights. "We encourage reprints with the proper accreditation." Submit seasonal/holiday material 2-3 months in advance. Simultaneous queries and simultaneous, photocopied and previously published submissions OK. Computer printout submissions acceptable. SASE. Reports in 1 month. Free sample copy and writer's guidelines.

Nonfiction: General interest (telecommunications); historical/nostalgic (on telecommunications); how-to (select the best _____, get the most for your money, install a specific system); humor (personal communications devices and technology); interview/profile (on people or companies in the telecommunications area); new product (telecommunications); opinion (on telecommunications); personal experience (with communications devices, services, technolgoies). Also interested in high-tech stories, interpretative articles for laymen, and articles on marketing methods of new radio businesses. "No articles which are too general, even if they concern personel communications." Buys 60 mss/year. Query. Length: 1,000-2,000 words. Pays $200-400.

Photos: Reviews contact sheets, negatives, transparencies and prints. Identification of subjects required. Buys one-time rights.

Columns/Departments: Query. Length: 1,000-2,000 words. Pays $200-350.

Fiction: Experimental and humorous. Query with or without published clips. Length: 1,000-2,000 words. Pays $200-400.

Fillers: Short humor. Buys 6/year. Length: 500-2,000 words. Pays $150-300.

Tips: "Concentrate on various personal communications devices such as: cellular radio, 2-way radio, pagers, voice mail, mobile and portable phones and computer links." Interested in "solid telecommunications articles written with the industry generalist and informed amateur in mind."

PHOTONICS SPECTRA, Optical Publishing Co., The Berkshire Common, Box 1146, Pittsfield MA 01202. (413)499-0514. Publisher: Teddi C. Laurin. Editor-in-Chief: Diane Kelley. Executive Editor: Robert S. Clark. 10% freelance written. Monthly magazine. "*Photonics Spectra* circulates monthly among scientists, engineers and managers who work in the fields of optics, electro-optics, fiber optics, vacuum technology and lasers. The magazine's purpose is to keep its readers abreast of new developments in our specific fields and related ones." Circ. 45,000. Average issue includes 20 departments, 2 or 3 contributed pieces in addition to staff reports. Buys first and second rights to the same material. Photocopied submissions OK. Publishes ms an average of 3 months after acceptance. Reports in 2 weeks on queries; in 1 month on mss. SASE. Sample copy and writer's guidelines free for SASE.

Nonfiction: *"Photonics Spectra* is a technically and scientifically-oriented publication of optics, electro-optics, fiber-optics and lasers. We offer a combination of timely news reports and feature articles examining aspects of the industries and related industries." Interview (prominent figures in the industry); profile (prominent figures in the industry); other (trends in the field, specific developments). Buys 4 unsolicited mss/year. Length: 750-3,000 words.

Photos: State availability of photos.

Columns/Departments: Query with clips of previously published work.

Tips: "Query about topic; ask for sample copy of the magazine."

PRO SOUND NEWS, International News Magazine for the Professional Sound Production Industry, Testa Communications, 220 Westbury Ave., Carle Place NY 11514. (516)334-7880. Editor: Randolph P. Savicky. 50% freelance written. Monthly tabloid covering the recording, sound reinforcement, TV and film sound industry. Circ. 13,000. Pays on publication. Publishes ms an average of 1 month after acceptance. Byline given. Buys first rights only. Simultaneous queries and photocopied and previously published submissions OK. Computer printout submissions acceptable. SASE. Reports in 2 weeks.

Nonfiction: Query with clips of published work. Pays 10¢/word.

PROMOTION NEWSLETTER, Radio and TV, Drawer 50108, Lighthouse Point FL 33064. (305)426-4881. Editor: William N. Udell. 20% freelance written. Monthly newsletter covering promotional activities of radio and television stations. Circ. 580. Pays on acceptance. Byline may or may not be given. Not copyrighted. Buys one-time rights, nonexclusive reprints, and makes work-for-hire assignments. Submit seasonal/holiday material 3 months in advance. Simultaneous queries and simultaneous and photocopied submissions OK. Computer printout submissions acceptable; prefers letter-quality to dot-matrix. Reports in 2 weeks on queries; 1 month on mss. Publishes ms an average of 1 month after acceptance. Free sample copy (while available).

Nonfiction: How-to; interview/profile (of promotional director of a busy station); and photo feature. "Interested in all promotional activities of radio and TV stations; unusual examples of successful promotional events. Looking for special material for all holidays." No "fan" material. Query or send complete ms. Length: 100-500 words, sometimes more. Pays $15-150.

Photos: "Reprints of ads and other material acceptable." Send photos with ms. Pays $5 minimum for b&w contact sheets and prints. Identification of subjects required. Buys one-time rights.

Fillers: Clippings and newsbreaks. Length: 100-500 words. Pays $15-150.

RECORDING ENGINEER/PRODUCER, Box 2449, Hollywood CA 90078. (213)467-1111. Publisher: Martin Gallay. Editor: Mel Lambert. 100% freelance written, mainly specially commissioned. Emphasizes recording and production technology and live performance sound for "all levels of professionals within the recording and sound industry." Bimonthly magazine; 180 pages. Circ. over 22,000. Pays on publication. Buys first rights and reprint rights (for fee) for overseas magazines. Photocopied submissions OK. Electronic submissions OK if compatible with 300 baud ASCII; requires hard copy also. Computer printout submissions acceptable. SASE. Reports in 1 month. Publishes ms an average of 2 months after acceptance. Sample copy $3.

Nonfiction: Interview (known engineering and producing personalities from the recording industry); new product (as related to technological advances within the recording, film, video and concert sound industry); and technical (recording and concert sound information). Buys 8 mss/issue. Query with initial outline. Pays $200-300.

SATELLITE COMMUNICATIONS, Cardiff Publishing Corp., 6430 S. Yosemite St., Englewood CO 80111. (303)694-1522. Editor: Irl Marshall. Emphasizes satellite communications industry. Readership includes broadcast management and engineering management, satellite industry personnel, cable television operators, government, educators, medical personnel, common carriers, military and corporate telecommunications management, and spacecraft manufacturing companies. Monthly magazine. Circ. 12,500. Pays on publication. Buys all rights. Byline given. Phone queries OK. Computer printout submissions acceptable; prefers letter-quality to dot-matrix. SASE. Reports in 3 weeks. Free sample copy.

Nonfiction: Interviews (of industry figures); case studies; technical features; new satellite services, systems descriptions, and application articles; marketing articles; satellite future studies; descriptions of satellite experiments; corporate profiles, technological developments, business news; FCC policy analysis; video-teleconferencing; current issues in space communication; launches and industry conventions; demonstrations; and articles on new products. No items that do not pertain to the satellite communications industry. Buys 3-6 unsolicited mss/year. Query. Length: 750-2,000 words. Pays $50/published page.

Photos: Prefers b&w 5x7 glossy prints and color slides. Offers no additional payment for photos accepted with ms.

Tips: "We prefer a letter personally addressed, clear, concise, with an idea for a story in it, one page, informal but from a writer who is flexible on terms and prompt with copy. We regularly print articles by business leaders and engineers who can write, usually gratis with byline only."

‡**SATELLITE Dealer, The Magazine for the Home Satellite Systems Industry**, CommTek Publishing Co., Box 2700, Dept. D, Hailey ID 83333. (208)788-8522. Senior Editor: Ron Rudolph. Executive Editor: Bruce Kinnaird. Monthly magazine covering the satellite television industry. Estab. 1983. Circ. 15,000. Pays on publication. Byline given. Offers 33% kill fee. Buys first North American serial rights, one-time rights, all rights, first rights, and makes work-for-hire assignments. Submit seasonal/holiday material 4 months in advance. Previously published submissions OK. Electronic submissions, baud 1200 on modem OK. Computer printout submissions acceptable; prefers letter-quality to dot-matrix. SASE. Reports in 3 weeks on queries. Free sample copy and writer's guidelines.

Nonfiction: Book excerpts (possible from new releases in industry); expose (on government communications policy); how-to (on installation of dishes); humor (if there is an angle); interview/profile (on industry leaders and exceptional dealers); personal experience (from TVRO dealers); photo feature (of unusual dish installations); technical (on radio theory as it pertains to satellite TV); and marketing. Special issues include trade show editions. "We print articles concerning the home satellite television industry. We also touch on SMATV (private cable). Everything we print must in some way be valuable to the satellite television dealer's business. Marketing techniques, installation tips, legal explanations and how-to or technical articles are examples of material we often use. All articles should be analytical in nature. No introductory articles on how great this industry is." Buys 120 mss/year. Query with published clips. Length: 700-2,000 words. Pays $75-300.

Photos: State availability of photos with query or ms. Prefers unusual installations, interesting dishes, i.e., landscaped, painted. Reviews contact sheets, and 4x4 and 35mm color transparencies. Pays $10-50 for 8x10 b&w prints; $25-150 for 8x10 color prints. Captions and identification of subjects required. Buys negotiable rights.

Tips: "Exhibit knowledge of either satellite TV or retail sales, and a command of the English language. Everything we print must in some way be of value to the satellite systems retailer. No phone queries."

SAT-GUIDE, Cable's Satellite Magazine, CommTek Publishing Co., 419 N. River, Box 1048, Hailey ID 83333. (208)788-4936. Editor: Terrance Stanton. Direct queries to editor. Monthly magazine covering satellite-related communications technologies for cable operators, programmers and distributors and those in the field of MDS, SMATV, STV, LPTV and related areas. Circ. 13,000. Pays on publication. Byline given. Offers ⅓ kill fee. Buys one-time rights, all rights, first rights; makes work-for-hire assignments. Submit seasonal/holiday material 6 weeks in advance. Computer printout submissions acceptable. SASE. Reports in 2 weeks. Sample copy $5; writer's guidelines for business-size SAE and 1 first class stamp.

Nonfiction: How-to (upgrade business operations, break into new field, etc.); interview/profile (industry leaders); new product (hardware); opinion (of industry leaders); technical (hardware information and reviews); and new programming available to cable operators. No "fiction, nostalgia, poetry, clippings, news releases, old information, uninformed articles on 'the future of communications,' etc." Buys 20 mss/year. Query with clips. Length: 700-1,500 words. Pays $100-500.

Photos: Fran Fuller, photo editor. State availability of photos. Pays $25-150 for 8x10 b&w prints and 35mm color transparencies. Captions and identification of subjects required. Buys negotiable rights.

Columns/Departments: Industry profiles (interviews with programmers and cable operators). Buys 10 mss/year. Query with clips. Length: 700-1,200 words. Pays $100-250.

Tips: "This field is now a very lucrative one for writers and is likely to be more so in the future. The key to success: basic research into the technological terms and pertinent areas of concern in the field of satellite communications. The areas most open to freelancers are those dealing with new hardware applications, economic concerns of cable operators and new programming planned. These topics are not as 'dry' as they seem—interesting slants and styles are duly appreciated. The field is now monopolized by a small group of freelancers who can pick and choose their assignments. Though the terminology may seem intimidating to the uninitiated, the field itself is fascinating and should be investigated."

‡**TELECOMMUNICATIONS COUNSELOR**, Voice & Data Resources Inc., Room 2860, 420 Lexington Ave., New York NY 10017. (212)697-1361. Editor: Robert W. Ryley. A biweekly newsletter covering the telecommunications industry from the perspective of business telephone users for business people who purchase telephone equipment and services for their companies. Circ. 750. Pays on publication. Byline given. Buys all rights. Submit seasonal/holiday material 6 weeks in advance. Simultaneous queries and submissions OK. SASE. Reports in 2 weeks on queries; 3 weeks on mss. Free sample copy; writer's guidelines for SAE with 1 first class stamp.

Nonfiction: General interest (to communications personnel); how-to (cut long distance costs etc.); and interviews (with key telecommunications executives). "In March each year we publish an annual industry handbook which largely contains freelance work about telecommunications. Provide clear, concise and well researched material about business telecommunications. We are interested in 'how to cut cost' type articles as well as those that illustrate an innovative use of equipment. Articles about the merger of voice and data technologies are also welcome." No exposes or opinion articles. Buys 10-15 mss/year. Query or send complete ms. Length: 750-2,500 words. (Note: Handbook submission can be longer.) Pays $35-150.

Tips: "We are flexible in that we can literally build an issue around a good, timely piece. There is no specific column or department that someone should write for. In addition to our print edition, the newsletter—and all its contents—are published in an electronic edition via NewsNet. We will include bylines in this edition too."

TELEPHONE ANGLES, How to Manage an Efficient, Cost Effective, Business Telephone System, Box 633, W. Hartford CT 06107. (203)247-6355. Editor: Bob Frank. Monthly newsletter covering the voice telecommunications industry for telecommunications users interested in managing an efficient, cost effective business telephone system. Pays on publication. Byline given. Offers negotiable kill fee. Buys all rights. Simultaneous queries, and simultaneous, photocopied and previously published submissions OK. SASE. Reports in 1 week. Sample copy $1; writer's guidelines for SAE and 1 first class stamp.

Nonfiction: Book excerpts (telecommunications); general interest; how-to (use phone system equipment, services, etc.); interview/profile (industry leaders); new products and services; and case history/applications. Buys 60 mss/year. Query. Length: 250-2,000 words. Pays 10¢/word.

TELEVISION INTERNATIONAL MAGAZINE, Box 2430, Hollywood CA 90028. (213)876-2219. Publisher/Editor: Al Preiss. For management/creative members of the TV industry. Published every 2 months. Circ. 16,000 (USA); 6,000 (foreign). Rights purchased vary with author and material. Pays on publication. Will send sample copy to writer for $3. Will consider photocopied submissions. Reports in 1 month. Query. SASE.

Nonfiction: Articles on all aspects of TV programming. "This is not a house organ for the industry. We invite articles critical of TV." Length: 800-3,000 words. Pays $150-500. Column material of 600-800 words. Pays $75. Will consider suggestions for new columns and departments.

Photos: Pays $25 for b&w photos purchased with mss; $35 for color transparencies.

TWO-WAY RADIO DEALER, Titsch Communications, Box 5727 TA, Denver CO 80217. Editor: Phil Murray. Monthly magazine covering the sales and service of two-way radios for dealers, service people and technicians. Circ. 11,500. Average issue includes 2-3 feature articles. Pays on publication. Byline given. Buys first North American serial rights or one-time rights. Phone queries OK. Simultaneous, photocopied and previously published submissions OK. SASE. Reports in 2 weeks on queries; in 1 month on mss. Free sample copy with 9x12 SASE and 75¢ postage.

Nonfiction: "We need very technical articles which include schematics and problem solving, and business articles concerning marketing, finance and self employment. The writer must have special knowledge of land-mobile radio use or the business of running a dealership. We want to increase the amount of freelance material used." Buys 1-2 mss/issue. Send complete ms. Length: 1,500-3,000 words. Pays $50-$250.

Photos: Reviews 5x7 b&w glossy prints and 35mm and larger color transparencies. Offers no additional payment for photos accepted with ms. Captions and model release required. Buys one-time rights.

VIDEO SYSTEMS, Box 12901, Overland Park KS 66212. (913)888-4664. Publisher: Cameron Bishop. Editor: David Hodes. 80% freelance written. For qualified persons engaged in professional applications of non-broadcast audio and video who have operating responsibilities and purchasing authority for equipment and software in the video systems field. Monthly magazine. Circ. 20,500. Pays on acceptance. Buys all rights. Submit seasonal/holiday material 2 months in advance of issue date. Photocopied submissions OK. SASE. Reports in 2 months. Free sample copy and writer's guidelines.

Nonfiction: General interest (about professional video); how-to (use professional video equipment); historical (on professional video); new product; and technical. No consumer video articles. Buys 2-6 unsolicited mss/year. Submit complete ms. Length: 1,000-3,000 words. Pays $125.

Photos: State availability of photos with ms. Pay varies for 8x10 b&w glossy prints; $100 maximum for 35mm color transparencies. Model release required.

VIDEOGRAPHY, United Business Publications, 475 Park Ave. S., New York NY 10016. (212)725-2300. Editor: Marjorie Costello. Monthly magazine for professional users of video and executives in the videotape and videodisc industries. Circ. 25,000. Pays 1 month after publication. Buys all rights. Phone queries OK. SASE. Reports in 1 month. Sample copy $2.

Nonfiction: Any article about the use of video in business, education, medicine, etc. Especially interested in stories about the use of new video technology to solve production problems. Also stories about cable TV and pay TV services. Buys 2 mss/issue. Query with clips of previously published work. Length: 1,000-2,500 words. Pays $300.

Photos: Do not submit photo material with accompanying query. Offers no additional payment for 5x7 b&w glossy prints or color transparencies. Captions required. Buys all rights.

VIEW MAGAZINE, The Magazine of TV Programming, View Communications, 150 E. 58th St., New York NY 10022. (212)486-7111. Editor: Kathy Haley. Managing Editor: Charline Allen. Monthly magazine covering the TV program market place. Circ. 9,000. Pays 45 days after acceptance. Byline given. Buys all rights. Reports in 1 month. Free sample copy and writer's guidelines.
Nonfiction: General interest (issues facing the industry—pay-per-view programming, ratings and audience measurement, consumer attitudes toward cable and broadcast TV programming); and trends (in children's, sports, news and entertainment programming). "We will not consider any unsolicited mss or articles not directly related to the TV industry." Buys 50 mss/year. Query with clips of published work. Length: 2,500-5,000 words. Pays $300-350 for first-time contributors.
Fillers: Buys 25/year. Length: 250-500 words. Pays $75.
Tips: "Most of *View's* feature articles are written by freelancers who understand the cable TV business. Only writers with experience covering the entertainment industry need query."

Energy

Oil, gas, and solar energy topics are covered here as well as energy conservation for industry professionals. Electric energy publications are listed in the Electricity category.

‡**ALTERNATIVE ENERGY RETAILER**, Zackin Publications, Inc., Box 2180, Waterbury CT 06722. (203)755-0158. Editor: John Florian. Monthly magazine on selling alternative energy products—chiefly solid fuel burning appliances. "We seek detailed how-to tips for retailers to improve business. Most freelance material purchased is about retailers and how they succeed." Circ. 14,000. Pays on publication. Offers 10% kill fee. Buys first North American serial rights. Submit seasonal/holiday material 4 months in advance. SASE. Reports in 2 weeks on queries. Sample copy for 8½x11 SAE; writer's guidelines for business-size SAE.
Nonfiction: How-to (improve retail profits and business know-how); and interview/profile (of successful retailers in this field). No "general business articles not adapted to this industry." Buys 40 mss/year. Query. Length: 1,500-2,000 words. Pays $200-300.
Photos: State availability of photos. Pays $25 maximum for 5x7 b&w prints and $100 maximum for 5x7 color prints. Reviews color slide transparencies. Identification of subject required. Buys one-time rights.
Tips: "A freelancer can best break in to our publication with features about readers (retailers). Stick to details about what has made this person a success."

● **BAROID NEWS BULLETIN**, Box 1675, Houston TX 77251. Editor-in-Chief: Virginia Myers. 50% freelance written. Emphasizes the petroleum industry for a cross-section of ages, education and interests, although most readers are employed by the energy industries. Quarterly magazine; 36 pages. Circ. 20,000. Pays on acceptance. Publishes ms an average of 9 months after acceptance. Buys first North American serial rights. Byline given. Submit seasonal/holiday material 1 year in advance. Computer printout submissions acceptable; prefers letter-quality to dot-matrix. SASE. Reports in 5 weeks. Free sample copy and writer's guidelines.
Nonfiction: General interest and historical. No travel articles or poetry. Buys 12 mss/year. Complete ms preferred. Length: 1,000-3,000 words. Pays 8-10¢/word.
Photos: "Photos may be used in the publication, or as reference for illustration art." Submit b&w prints. No additional payment for photos accepted with ms. Captions preferred. Buys first North American serial rights.
Tips: Manuscripts accompanied by good quality photos or illustrations stand a much better chance of acceptance.

DIESEL PROGRESS/DIESEL & GAS TURBINE WORLDWIDE, 13555 Bishop's Court, Brookfield WI 53005. Editorial Director: Robert A. Wilson. Senior Editor: J. Kane. Managing Editor: Mike Osenga. 5% freelance written. Monthly magazine; 88 pages. Circ. 25,000. Pays on publication. Buys first rights only. Submit editorial material 6 weeks in advance. Previously published submissions OK. SASE. Reports in 1 month. Sample copy $2.
Nonfiction: "The articles we would consider from freelancers would be technical descriptions of diesel engine applications—including extensive technical descriptions of the installation, the method of operations and maintenance." Buys 10 mss/year. Query and submit clips of published work. Length: 1,600-2,400 words. Pay based on use.
Photos: "All stories are illustrated, and photos of the engine installation must accompany the text, or it is really of little value." State availability of photos with query. No additional payment for 8x10 b&w glossy prints and 8x10 color glossy prints (cover only). Captions preferred. Buys all rights.

ENERGY MANAGEMENT REPORT, Box 1589, Dallas TX 75221. (214)748-4403. Publisher: Jim Donnelly. Editor: Cindy Mays. Comment by Rich McNally. 20% freelance written. Emphasizes energy for operating management of oil/gas operating companies and supply/service companies. Monthly section in *Petroleum Engineer International* and *Pipeline & Gas Journal*; 16 pages. Circ. 66,433. Pays on publication. Buys all rights. Query. SASE. Free sample copy; mention *Writer's Market* in request.
Nonfiction: Uses energy briefs and concise analysis of energy situations. "Across-the-board interpretive reporting on current energy events." Publishes briefs about energy world news, offshore energy business, energy financing, and new products (price information on crude oil and gasoline). No nuclear or electric material. Pays 15¢/word.

ENERGY NEWS, Energy Publications—division of Harcourt Brace Jovanovich, Box 1589, Dallas TX 75221. (214)748-4403. Editor: Jim Watts. 5% freelance written. Emphasizes natural gas production, transmission, distribution, regulation and projects for executives or managers of energy, supply and financial companies or the government; particularly utilities. Biweekly newsletter; 4 pages. Circ. 500. Pays on publication. Publishes ms an average of 1 week after acceptance. Buys all rights. Phone queries OK. Simultaneous and photocopied submissions OK. Computer printout submissions acceptable; no dot matrix. SASE. Reports in 1 month. Free sample copy and writer's guidelines.
Nonfiction: Interviews with energy industry or government leaders keyed to recent news and technical articles on natural gas projects, trends, prices or new technologies. "We can't use anything not related to natural gas or utilities." Buys 1-2 mss/issue. Length: 250 words maximum. Pays 15¢/word.

FUEL OIL NEWS, Hunter Publishing Co., Box 360, Whitehouse NJ 08888. (201)534-4156. Editor: George Schultz. Monthly magazine about the home heating oil market. Circ. 17,000. Pays on publication. Byline given. Offers $75 kill fee. Makes work-for-hire assignments. Phone queries OK. Submit seasonal material 3 months in advance. Simultaneous, photocopied and previously published submissions OK. Computer printout submissions acceptable. Reports in 2 months. Free sample copy and writer's guidelines.
Nonfiction: Interview (industry); profile (of industry leaders); how-to (on industry methods of delivering fuel or servicing equipment); and technical. No general business articles or new product information. Buys 2 mss/issue. Query. Length: 1,000-3,000 words. Pays $70-200. "Articles should be geared to helping fuel oil dealers maintain viability in the marketplace or to some aspect of home heating or oil delivery."
Photos: State availability of photos. Pays $25 maximum for b&w contact sheets. Captions preferred; model release required. Buys all rights.

FUELOIL AND OIL HEAT, 200 Commerce Rd., Cedar Grove NJ 07009. (201)239-5800. Editor: Paul Geiger. 10% freelance written. For distributors of fuel oil, heating and air conditioning equipment dealers. Monthly. Buys first rights only. Pays on publication. Computer printout submissions acceptable; prefers letter-quality to dot-matrix. Reports in 2 weeks. Publishes ms an average of 3 months after acceptance. SASE.
Nonfiction: Management articles dealing with fuel oil distribution and oil heating equipment selling. Cannot use articles about oil production or refining. Length: up to 2,500 words. Pays $50/printed page. "Mostly staff written."

GAS DIGEST, Box 35819, Houston TX 77235. (713)723-7456. Editor: Ken Kridner. 30% freelance written. For operating personnel of the gas industry. Monthly magazine; 24 pages. Circ. 5,000. Rights may be retained by the author. Pays on publication. Photocopied submissions OK. Reports in 1 month. Query.
Nonfiction: Applications stories and new developments. All material must be gas operations-oriented and meaningful to one working in the gas industry. How-to and technical articles. Length: 500-1,000 words. Pays 2¢/word minimum.
Photos: B&w photos purchased with ms. Pays $5 minimum.

HYDROCARBON PROCESSING, Box 2608, Houston TX 77001. Editor: Harold L. Hoffman. 95% freelance written by industry authors. For personnel in oil refining, gas and petrochemical processing; or engineering contractors, including engineering, operation, maintenance and management phases. Special issues: January, Maintenance; April, Natural Gas Processing; July, Energy Management; September, Refining Processes; October, Environmental Management; and November, Petrochemical Processes. Monthly. Buys first rights only. Write for copy of writer's guidelines. SASE.
Nonfiction: Wants technical manuscripts on engineering and operations in the industry that will help personnel. Also nontechnical articles on management, safety and industrial relations that will help technical men become managers. Length: open, "but do not waste words." Pays about $25/printed page.
Tips: "Articles must all pass a rigid evaluation of their reader appeal, accuracy and overall merit. Reader interest determines an article's value. We covet articles that will be of real job value to subscribers. Before writing, ask to see our *Author's Handbook*. You may save time and effort by writing a letter, and outline briefly what you have in mind. If your article will or won't meet our needs, we will tell you promptly."

● **MARATHON WORLD**, Marathon Oil Co., 539 S. Main St., Findlay OH 45840. (419)422-2121. Editor-in-Chief: Norman V. Richards. 20% freelance written. Emphasizes petroleum/energy for educators, legislators, government officials, libraries, community leaders, students and employees. Quarterly magazine; 24 pages. Circ. 45,000. Pays on acceptance. Buys first North American serial rights. Pays 20% kill fee. Byline given on contents page, not with article. Photocopied submissions OK. SASE. Reports in 3 weeks. Free sample copy and writer's guidelines.
Nonfiction: Informational features. Especially needs "articles on subjects to help readers live better, handle problems (economic, social, personal, medical) more effectively, and generally get more out of life. We like articles on self-awareness, science, cultural events, outdoor sports and activities, and Americana in areas where Marathon operates (primarily Midwest). No articles promoting travel by car. No local sights or festivals; subjects should have broader geographic base. Freelancers should not attempt to sell articles on Marathon or oil industry operations; these are staff written." Buys one to two mss/issue. Query. Length: 800-1,500 words. Pays $1,000-1,200.
Photos: Photos generally not purchased with accompanying ms. Art director makes assignments to professional photographers. Pay negotiable.
Tips: "Because of the special nature of the *World* as a corporate external publication and the special limits imposed on content, the best approach is through initial query. Include as many details as possible in a one-two page letter."

NATIONAL PETROLEUM NEWS, 950 Lee St., Des Plaines IL 60016. (312)296-0770. Editor: Marvin Reid. For businessmen who make their living in the oil marketing industry, either as company employees or through their own business operations. Monthly magazine; 80 pages. Circ. 19,000. Rights purchased vary with author and material. Usually buys all rights. Buys 3-4 mss/year. Pays on acceptance if done on assignment. Pays on publication for unsolicited material. "The occasional freelance copy we use is done on assignment." Query. SASE.
Nonfiction: Thomas Olson, managing editor. Material related directly to developments and issues in the oil marketing industry and "how-to" and "what-with" case studies. Informational, and successful business operations. "No unsolicited copy, especially with limited attribution regarding information in story." Length: 2,000 words maximum.
Photos: Pays $150/printed page. Payment for b&w photos "depends upon advance understanding."

OCEAN INDUSTRY, Gulf Publishing Co., Box 2608, Houston TX 77001. (713)529-4301. Editor-in-Chief: Donald M. Taylor. Associate Editors: Maretta Tubb, Ken Edmiston and Charles McCabe. Department Editor: Teena Campbell. 15% freelance written. "Our readers are generally engineers and company executives in companies with business dealings with off-shore petroleum and deep sea mining interests." Monthly magazine. Circ. 33,000. Pays on publication. Buys all rights. Pays kill fee: "If we assign an article and it is not used, we pay full rate on estimated length." Byline given. Phone queries OK. Photocopied and previously published submissions OK. Computer printout submissions acceptable. SASE. Reports in 2 months. Publishes ms an average of 3 months after acceptance. Free sample copy and writer's guidelines.
Nonfiction: Technical articles relating to hydrocarbon exploration and development, diving and ROVs, deep sea mining, oil terminals, oil and LNG shipping, electronics, instruments and computers for oil field and off-shore applications. No oceanographic, fisheries, aquaculture or mariculture material. Buys 120-140 mss/year. Query. Length: 300-1,500 words. Pays $35-150/published page.
Photos: "Technical concepts are easier to understand when illustrated." State availability of photos with query. No additional payment for 5x7 or 8x10 glossy b&w or color prints. Captions required. Buys all rights.
Tips: "It's rewarding to have a freelancer bring an inchoate story with good potential to a state of clear, coherent readability."

‡**OFFSHORE RESOURCES**, Box 91760, West Vancouver, British Columbia V7V 4S1 Canada. (604)986-9501. Editor: Duncan Cumming. A bimonthly magazine covering offshore oil and gas industry in Canada and Alaska. Circ. 9,000. Pays on publication. Byline given. Pays 50% kill fee. Buys first rights or makes work-for-hire assignments. Simultaneous queries, and simultaneous, photocopied and some previously published submissons OK. SASE. Reports in 2 weeks on queries; 1 month on mss. Sample copy $2; free writer's guidelines.
Nonfiction: How-to (pertaining to energy and mineral exploration/development); interview/profile; new product; and technical (new technology). Buys 12 mss/year. Query. Length: 100-2,000 words. Pays $15-500.
Photos: State availability of photos. Pays $10-100 for 35mm and larger color transparencies; $5-20 for 5x7 and larger b&w prints. Captions required. Buys one-time rights.
Tips: "A high level of technical or engineering writing experience is required."

OIL & GAS DIGEST, The Magazine of Oil and Gas Industry Management, OGD Publishing Co., 915 Antoine, Houston TX 77024. (713)688-4429. 50% freelance written. Monthly magazine for "all phases of the petroleum industry from exploration and refining to financial news." Circ. 38,000. Pays on publication. Publishes ms an average of 3 months after acceptance. Byline given. Offers 100% kill fee. Buys all rights. Si-

multaneous queries and simultaneous, photocopied and previously published submissions OK. Computer printout submissions acceptable. SASE. Reports in 2 months. Free sample copy; call for writer's guidelines.
Nonfiction: General interest, interview/profile, new product, opinion and technical. "All articles should be petroleum industry specific and should apply to specific topics on the editorial calendar. No general interest articles that are not specifically related to oil and gas." Buys 40-60 mss/year. Query by phone. Length: 600-2,400 words. Pays $8/column inch.
Photos: State availability of photos or send photos with query. Pays $8/column inch for 35mm color transparencies and 3x5 or 8x10 color and b&w prints. Captions required. Buys one-time or all rights (whichever is specified).
Columns/Departments: Noelle Hawman, column/department editor. People and Companies.
Tips: "A freelancer can best break in to our publication with information on regional industry activities and industry trends."

PETROLEO INTERNACIONAL, PennWell Publishing Co., Box 1260, Tulsa OK 74101. (918)835-3161. Editor: Gustavo Pena. Monthly magazine about the Latin American petroleum industry for the management, engineering and technical operating personnel in the oil and gas industry of the Spanish speaking world. Circ. 9,000. Average issue includes 6-7 main articles and several shorter ones. Pays on publication. Byline given. Makes work-for-hire assignments. Phone queries OK. Submit seasonal material 1 month in advance. Simultaneous, photocopied and previously published submissions OK. SASE. Reports in 2 weeks. Free sample copy and writer's guidelines.
Nonfiction: Technical (oil and gas, petrochemical industry and equipment for the petroleum industry). Query. Pays $25 minimum.
Photos: Send photos with ms. Reviews b&w prints and color prints. Offers no additional payment for photos accepted with ms. Captions required. Buys one-time rights.
Columns/Departments: "We have a section on people involved in the industry; new literature out for the industry, business in the industry, and current happenings in the petroleum industry." Pays $25 minimum.
Fillers: Newsbreaks. Pays $25 minimum.

PETROLEUM INDEPENDENT, 1101 16th St. NW, Washington DC 20036. (202)857-4775. Editor: Joe W. Taylor. For "college educated men and women involved in high risk petroleum ventures. Our readers drill 90% of all the exploratory oil wells in this country. They pit themselves against the major oil companies, politicians, and a dry hole rate of 9 out of 10 to try to find enough petroleum to offset imports. They are in a highly competitive, extremely expensive business and look to this magazine to help them change the political landscape, read about their friends and the activities of the Independent Petroleum Association of America, and be entertained. Contrary to popular opinion, they are not all Texans. They live in almost every state and are politically motivated. They follow energy legislation closely and involve themselves in lobbying and electoral politics." Bimonthly magazine. Circ. 15,000. Pays on acceptance. Buys all rights. Byline given "except if part of a large report compiled in-house." SASE. Reports in 2 weeks. Sample copy $1.
Nonfiction: "Articles need not be limited to oil and natural gas—but must tie in nicely." Expose (bureaucratic blunder); informational; historical (energy-related; accurate; with a witty twist); humor (we look for good humor pieces and have found a few); and interview (with energy decision makers. Center with questions concerning independent petroleum industry. Send edited transcript plus tape); opinion; profile (of Independent Petroleum Association of America members); and photo feature. Buys 30 mss/year. Query with brief outline. SASE. Length: 750-3,000 words. Pays $100-500. Longer articles on assignment; pay negotiable.
Photos: Reviews color and b&w transparencies. Purchased with or without accompanying ms or on assignment.
Tips: "Call first, then send outline and query. Don't write with a particular slant. Write as if for a mainstream publication."

PIPELINE & GAS JOURNAL, Box 1589, Dallas TX 75221. (214)748-4403. Editor-in-Chief: Dean Hale. 5% freelance written. Emphasizes energy transportation (oil, natural gas, refined petroleum products and coal slurry) by pipeline. Monthly magazine; 100 pages. Circ. 28,000. Pays on publication. Buys all rights. Phone queries OK. Photocopied submissions OK. SASE. Reports in 6-10 weeks. Free sample copy.
Nonfiction: Technical. No articles on management. Buys 5-6 mss/year. Query. Length: 800-1,500 words. Pays minimum $50/printed page.
Photos: State availability of photos with query. No additional payment for 8x10 b&w glossy prints and 5x7 or 8x10 color glossy prints. Captions required. Buys all rights. Model release required.

PIPELINE & UNDERGROUND UTILITIES CONSTRUCTION, Oildom Publishing Co. of Texas, Inc., Box 22267, Houston TX 77027. Editor: Oliver Klinger. Managing Editor: Chris Horner. 10% freelance written. Monthly magazine covering oil, gas, water, and sewer pipeline construction for contractors and construction workers who build pipelines. Circ. 13,000. No byline given. Not copyrighted. Buys first North American serial rights. Simultaneous queries and photocopied submissions OK. SASE. Reports in 2 weeks on queries; 3

weeks on mss. Publishes ms an average of 2 months after acceptance. Sample copy for $1 and 9x12 SAE.
Nonfiction: How-to. Query with clips of published work. Length: 1,500-2,500 words. Pays $100/printed page "unless unusual expenses are incurred in getting the story."
Photos: Send photos with ms. Reviews 5x7 and 8x10 prints. Captions required. Buys one-time rights.
Tips: "We supply guidelines outlining information we need."

PIPELINE DIGEST, Universal News, Inc., Box 55225, Houston TX 77055. (713)468-2626. Publisher: H.M. Stemmer. Managing Editor: Thelma Marlowe. Semimonthly magazine of the worldwide pipeline construction industry for individuals and companies involved in construction and operation of pipelines (gas, oil, slurry, water) worldwide. Includes design and engineering projects and updated listings of projects proposed, awarded and under construction. Circ. 9,500. Pays on publication. Byline given. Previously published submissions OK. SASE. Reports in 2 weeks on queries; 2 months on mss.
Nonfiction: Interview/profile (of people in industry); and new product. All material must relate to the oil and gas industry. Query with clips of published work. Length: 250-1,000 words. Pays negotiable fee.

SAVING ENERGY, 5411 - 117 Ave. SE, Bellevue WA 98006. (206)643-4248. Editor/Publisher: Larry Liebman. 5% freelance written. Emphasizes energy conservation, ideas, and case histories aimed at business, industry and commerce. Monthly newsletter. Pays on acceptance. Publishes ms an average of 10 days after acceptance. Buys all rights. No byline given. Phone queries OK. Computer printout submissiosn acceptable; prefers letter-quality to dot-matrix. SASE. Reports in 2 weeks. Free writer's guidelines.
Nonfiction: "I need good, tightly written case histories on how industry and commerce are saving energy, listing problems and solutions. The item should present an original energy saving idea. No long stories with art. Include full name and address of business so readers can contact for follow-up." How-to (conserving energy, what the problem was, how it was resolved, cost, how fast the payback was, etc.); and technical (case histories). Buys 25 unsolicited mss/year. Submit complete ms. Length: 200-800 words. Pays $10-25.
Tips: "Take potluck with a well-written item that meets specs, since the item could be shorter than the query letter after editing."

‡**SOLAR ENGINEERING & CONTRACTING, The Independent Trade Magazine for the Solar Industry**, Business News Publishing Co., Box 3600, Troy MI 48007. (313)362-3700. Editor: Wayne Johnson. Managing Editor: Tim Fausch. A bimonthly magazine for people who design, manufacture, sell, install or maintain solar and other alternative energy systems for profit. Circ. 16,000. Pays on acceptance. Byline given. Offers negotiable kill fee. Buys first rights only. Computer printout submissions acceptable. SASE. Reports in 6 weeks on queries; 1 month on mss. Sample copy for $2.50.
Nonfiction: Interview/profile, new product, opinion, personal experience, photo feature and technical. No do-it-yourself or consumer-oriented articles. Buys 12 mss/year. Query with published clips. Length: 500-2,500 words. Pays $100-250.
Photos: Prefers stages of construction of solar or other alternative energy systems. State availability of photos with query letter or ms. Pays $10-25 for b&w and color prints; $25-300 for b&w and color prints and color transparencies used for covers.
Columns/Departments: National, regional news; stocks, financial information; passive solar; photovoltaics; and book reviews. Buys 10 mss/year. Send complete ms. Length: 50-250 words. Pays $25-100.
Fillers: Clippings and newsbreaks. Buys 10/year. Length: 50-250 words. Pays $5-25.
Tips: "Learn what makes a solar energy system/design unique before you try to pitch us on a story. Know the manufacturers of all equipment in a system and talk to the installers. It is difficult, but not impossible, for writers without a solar background to get published by *SE&C*."

● **TIME BREAK**, AMF Geo Space Corp., Box 36374, Houston TX 77036. (713)666-1611. Editor: Lee C. Dominey. 5% freelance written. Quarterly (March, June, September, December). "The purpose of *Time Break* is to inform 'friends and customers' about new products and applications plus trends and items of interest in the geophysical exploration field. It includes technical and semitechnical articles." Circ. 4,000. Pays on acceptance. Publishes ms an average of 3 months after acceptance. Buys all rights. Byline given. Submit seasonal/holiday material 3 months in advance of issue date. Simultaneous and previously published submissions OK. SASE. Reports in 1 month. Free sample copy.
Nonfiction: "All articles need to be related to seismic exploration." General interest (to people engaged in seismic exploration); historical; interview; and nostalgia. Query. Length: 500-5,000 words. Pays $50-250.
Photos: "Hopefully, *all* articles in the magazine have photos." State availability of photos. Pays $10-50 for b&w photos. Captions preferred. Buys all rights. Model release required.
Tips: "Some knowledge of the seismic exploration industry is a *must*. Magazine is now published quarterly, but is smaller in size than previously."

Engineering and Technology

Engineers and professionals with different specialties read the publications in this section. Publications for electrical engineers are classified under Electricity; journals for electronics engineers are classified under the Electronics and Communication heading. Magazines for computer professionals are listed in the Trade/Data Processing section; for magazines on personal computing, see the Consumer/Personal Computing section.

CONTROL ENGINEERING, Technical Publishing, 1301 S. Grove Ave., Barrington IL 60010. (312)381-1840. Editor: Edward Kompass. Monthly magazine for control engineers—horizontal to industry, product and system-oriented—highly technical. Circ. 85,000. Byline usually given.
Nonfiction: New product, photo feature and technical. "We need submissions from writers who are engineers." No commercial mss. Query or send complete ms. Length: open. Pays $25/page.

DIGITAL DESIGN, Morgan-Grampian Publishing Co., 1050 Commonwealth Ave., Boston MA 02215. (617)232-5470. Editor: Jerry Borrell. Managing Editor: Debra Lambert. Monthly magazine of computer electronics for designers and engineers of computer systems, peripherals and components. "Our readers are among the leaders in technical planning and management for computing technology." Circ. 85,000. Pays on publication. Byline given. Buys all rights "except by arrangement with editor." Reports in 2 weeks. Free sample copy and writer's guidelines.
Nonfiction: Debra Lambert, articles editor. How-to (design various types of systems); new product (exclusive articles on unannounced new computer products); and technical. Buys 10 mss/year. Query. Length: 1,500-3,000 words. Pays $35-75/page.
Photos: "Relevant photos and other art should be submitted with manuscript. There is no additional payment." State availability of photos. Reviews 35mm slides only. Captions and identification of subjects required.
Columns/Departments: Mary Rose Hanrahan, column/department editor. Applications Notebook (unique, useful circuit designs or microcomputer subroutines of interest to computer electronics engineers). Buys 10 mss/year. Query. Length: 500-1,500 words. Pays $70.
Tips: "Most of our material is written by engineers about their field of expertise. Nonengineers should at least be conversant in the field about which they are writing and should query an editor about their idea before proceeding. Freelancers should remember that *Digital Design* is a technical publication written specifically to help computer engineers do their job better."

‡**LASER FOCUS MAGAZINE**, Including *ELECTRO-OPTICS* magazine, (formerly *Laser Focus* with *Fiberoptic Technology* and *Electro-Optics*, formerly *Electro-Optical System Design*), 119 Russell St., Littleton MA 01460. (617)486-9501. Editor-in-Chief: Dr. Morris Levitt. Managing Editor: Richard Mack. 33% freelance written. A monthly magazine for physicists, scientists and engineers involved in the research and development, design, manufacturing and applications of lasers, laser systems and all other segments of electro-optical technologies. Circ. 38,000. Pays on publication. Byline given unless anonymity requested. Buys all rights. Computer printout submissions acceptable; prefers letter-quality to dot-matrix. Publishes ms an average of 6 months after acceptance. Sample copy on request.
Nonfiction: Lasers, laser systems, fiberoptics, optics and other electro-optical materials, components, instrumentation and systems. "Each article should serve our reader's need by either stimulating ideas, increasing technical competence or improving design capabilities in the following areas: natural light and radiation sources, artificial light and radiation sources, light modulators, optical materials and components, image detectors, energy detectors, information displays, image processing, information storage and processing, subsystem and system testing, support equipment and other related areas." No "flighty prose, material not written for our readership, or irrelevant material." Query first "with a clear statement and outline of why the article would be important to our readers." Pays $30/printed page.
Photos: Send photos with ms. Reviews 8x10 b&w glossies or 4x5 color transparencies.
Tips: "We use few freelancers that are independent professional writers. Most of our submitted materials come from technical experts in the areas we cover."

THE MINORITY ENGINEER, An Equal Opportunity Career Publication for Professional and Graduating Minority Engineers, (formerly *The Woman Engineer and The Minority Engineer*), Equal Opportunity Publications, Inc., 44 Broadway, Greenlawn NY 11740. (516)261-8899. Editor: James Schneider. 50% freelance written. Magazines published 4 times/year (fall, winter, spring, summer professional edition) covering career guidance for minority engineering students and professional minority engineers. Circ. 12,000. Pays on publication. Byline given. Buys all rights. "Deadline dates: fall, July 1; winter, September 1; spring, December 15; summer, April 1." Simultaneous, photocopied, and previously published submissions OK. Electronic submissions OK, but requires hard copy also. Computer printout submissions acceptable; prefers typed mss and no dot-matrix. Publishes ms an average of 3 months after acceptance. SASE. Sample copy and writer's guidelines available on request.

Nonfiction: Book excerpts; articles (on job search techniques, role models); general interest (on specific minority engineering concerns); how-to (land a job, keep a job, etc.); interview/profile (minority engineer role models); new product (new career opportunities); opinion (problems of ethnic minorities); personal experience (student and career experiences); and technical (on career fields offering opportunities for minority engineers). "We're interested in articles dealing with career guidance and job opportunities for minority engineers." Query or send complete ms. Length: 1,250-3,000 words.

Photos: Prefers 35mm color slides but will accept b&w. Captions, model release and identification of subjects required. Buys all rights.

Tips: "Articles should focus on career guidance, role model and industry prospects for minority engineers. Prefer articles related to careers, not politically or socially sensitive."

THE ONTARIO TECHNOLOGIST, Ontario Association of Certified Engineering Technicians and Technologists, Suite 253, 40 Orchard View Blvd., Toronto, Ontario M4R 2G1 Canada. (416)488-1175. Editor: Ruth M. Klein. Bimonthly professional association journal covering technical processes and developments in engineering for association members, educational institutions, government and industry. Circ. 13,342. Pays in membership dues or subscription fee. Byline given. Buys first rights only. Submit seasonal/holiday material 2 months in advance. Photocopied and previously published submissions OK. SASE. Reports in 1 month. Free sample copy and writer's guidelines.

Nonfiction: New product and technical (manpower news). Buys 4 mss/year. Query with clips of published work. Length: 500-1,500 words. Pays 25¢/word.

Photos: State availability of photos. Pays $25 maximum for 8x10 b&w prints. Captions and identification of subjects required. Buys one-time rights.

RESOURCE TECHNOLOGY, (formerly *Resource Development*), IBIS Holdings, Inc., Box 91760, West Vancouver, British Columbia V7V 4S1 Canada. (604)986-9501. Editor: Duncan Cumming. Bimonthly magazine covering Canadian energy and mineral exploration/development. Circ. 17,000. Pays on publication. Byline given. Pays 50% kill fee. Buys first rights or makes work-for-hire assignments. Simultaneous queries, and simultaneous, photocopied and some previously published submissions OK. SASE. Reports in 2 weeks on queries; 1 month on mss. Sample copy $2; free writer's guidelines.

Nonfiction: How-to (pertaining to energy and mineral exploration/development); interview/profile; new product; and technical (new technology). Buys 12 mss/year. Query. Length: 100-2,000 words. Pays $15-500.

Photos: State availability of photos. Pays $10-100 for 35mm and larger color transparencies; $5-20 for 5x7 and larger b&w prints. Captions required. Buys one-time rights.

Tips: "A high level of technical or engineering writing experience is required."

THE WOMAN ENGINEER, An Equal Opportunity Career Publication for Graduating Women and Experienced Professionals, (formerly *The Woman Engineer and The Minority Engineer*), Equal Opportunity Publications, Inc., 44 Broadway, Greenlawn NY 11740. (516)261-8899. Editor: James Schneider. 50% freelance written. Magazine published 4 times/year (fall, winter, spring, summer professional edition) covering career guidance for women engineering students and professional women engineers. Circ. 12,000. Pays on publication. Byline given. Buys all rights. Deadline dates: fall, July 1; winter, September 1; spring, December 15; summer, April 1. Simultaneous, photocopied, and previously published submissions OK. Computer printout submissions acceptable; prefers typed mss and no dot-matrix. Publishes ms an average of 3 months after acceptance. SASE. Sample copy and writer's guidelines available on request.

Nonfiction: Book excerpts and articles (on job search techniques, role models); general interest (on specific women engineering concerns); how-to (land a job, keep a job, etc.); interview/profile (women engineer role models); new product (new career opportunities); opinion (problems of women engineers); personal experience (student and career experiences); and technical (on career fields offering opportunities for women engineers). "We're interested in articles dealing with career guidance and job opportunities for women engineers." Query or send complete ms. Length: 1,250-3,000 words.

Photos: Prefers 35mm color slides but will accept b&w. Captions, model release and identification of subjects required. Buys all rights.

Tips: "Articles should focus on career guidance, role model and industry prospects for women engineers. Prefer articles related to careers, not politically or socially sensitive."

Entertainment and the Arts

The business of the entertainment/amusement industry (arts, film, dance, theatre, etc.) is covered by these publications. Journals that focus on the people and equipment of various music specialties are listed in the Trade Music section.

AMUSEMENT BUSINESS, Billboard Publications, Inc., Box 24970, Nashville TN 37202. (615)748-8120. Editor: Tom Powell. Executive Editor: Steve Rogers. Emphasizes hard news of the amusement and mass entertainment industry. Read by top management. Weekly tabloid; 24-48 pages. Circ. 15,000. Pays on publication. Buys all rights. Byline sometimes given; "it depends on the quality of the individual piece." Phone queries OK. SASE. Submit seasonal/holiday material 2-3 weeks in advance.
Nonfiction: How-to (case history of successful promotions); interview; new product; and technical (how "new" devices, shows or services work at parks, fairs, auditoriums and conventions). Likes lots of financial support data: grosses, profits, operating budgets and per-cap spending. No personality pieces or interviews with stage stars. Buys 500-1,000 mss/year. Query. Length: 400-700 words. Pays $1-2.50/published inch.
Photos: State availability of photos with query. Pays $3-5 for b&w 8x10 glossy prints. Captions required. Buys all rights. Model release required.
Columns/Departments: Auditorium Arenas; Fairs, Fun Parks; Food Concessions; Merchandise; Promotion; Shows (carnival and circus); Talent; Tourist Attractions; and Management Changes.

ARABESQUE, A Magazine of International Dance, Ibrahim Farrah, Inc., Suite 22F, 1 Sherman Square, New York NY 10023. (212)595-1677. Editor: Magda Baron. Bimonthly magazine of ethnic dance. "The magazine takes its name from the flowing lines and patterns of Islamic art, a fitting image for the interconnectedness of all dancing forms." Circ. 6,000. Pays on publication. Byline given. Makes work-for-hire assignments. Submit seasonal/holiday material 6 months in advance. Simultaneous queries OK. SASE. Reports in 1 month. Sample copy $2.50.
Nonfiction: How-to, interview/profile, personal experience and technical. Buys 18 mss/year. Query with published clips. Length: 1,000-1,500 words. Pays $35-50.

BILLBOARD, The International News Weekly of Music and Home Entertainment, 1515 Broadway, New York NY 10036. (212)764-7300. 9107 Wilshire Blvd., Beverly Hills CA 90210. (213)273-7040. Editor: Adam White. Publisher: Jerry Hobbs. Special Issues Editor: Ed Ochs. L.A. Bureau Chief: Sam Sutherland. Video Editor: Tony Seideman. Record Review—Singles/Campus Editor: Nancy Erlich. Albums: Sam Sutherland. (All Los Angeles.) Editor: Adam White. Managing Editor: George Finley. Pro Equipment: Steve Dupler. Deputy Editor: Irv Lichtman. Radio/TV Editor: Rollye Bornstein. Black Music: Nelson George. Executive/Classical Editor: Is Horowitz. (All New York.) Country Music Editor: Kip Kirby (Nashville). International Editor: Peter Jones (London). Weekly. Buys all rights. Pays on publication. SASE.
Nonfiction: "Correspondents are appointed to send in spot amusement news covering phonograph record programming by broadcasters and record merchandising by retail dealers." Concert reviews, interviews with artists, and stories on video software (both rental and merchandising).

BOXOFFICE MAGAZINE, RLD Publishing Corp., Suite 316, 1800 N. Highland Ave., Hollywood CA 90028. (213)465-1186. Editor: Alexander Auerbach. 10% freelance written. Monthly business magazine about the motion picture industry for members of the film industry: theater owners, film producers, directors, financiers and allied industries. Circ. 14,000. Pays on publication. Publishes ms an average of 2 months after acceptance. Byline given. Buys one-time rights. Phone queries OK. Submit seasonal material 2 months in advance. Simultaneous, photocopied and previously published submissions OK. Electronic submissions OK if Modem, Altos 5¼", but requires hard copy also. Computer printout submissions acceptable; "if dot-matrix, use descenders." SASE. Reports in 2 weeks.
Nonfiction: Expose, interview, nostalgia, profile, new product, photo feature and technical. "We are a general news magazine about the motion picture industry and are looking for stories about trends, developments, problems or opportunities facing the industry. Almost any story will be considered, including corporate profiles, but we don't want gossip or celebrity stuff." Buys 1-2 mss/issue. Query with clips of previously published work. Length: 1,500-2,500 words. Pays $75-150.
Photos: State availability of photos. Pays $10 minimum for 8x10 b&w prints. Captions required.
Tips: "Write a clear, comprehensive outline of the proposed story and enclose a resume and clip samples. We welcome new writers but don't want to be a classroom. Know how to write."

‡**CHRISTIAN MODELS U.S.A. NATIONAL SOURCE DIRECTORY**, CMUSA Source Directory, Dorsey Agency (Dorsey Advertising/Public Relations), Box 64951, Dallas TX 75206. (214)288-8900. Editor/

Publisher: Lon Dorsey. Annual 8½x11 hardback source directory and monthly newsletter. "The purpose of the *CMUSA Source Directory* is to offer to persons opportunities in modeling and talent without compromise of standards, beliefs, etc. Also has business services section. Audience: Film producers, creative directors, publishers, Christian organizations, manufacturers, corporations, editors, writers, photographers, production managers, etc." Estab. 1983. Circ. 10,000 (expected). Pays on acceptance or publication (depending if directory or newsletter). Byline given depending upon material. Buys one-time rights and all rights depending on material. Submit seasonal/holiday material 2 months in advance. Simultaneous queries and simultaneous submissions OK. SASE. Reports in 2 months on queries; 6 weeks on mss. Inquire about cost of *Source Directory*; sample copy of *Newsletter* for 9x12 SAE; writer's guidelness for $2, business-size SAE and 2 first class stamps.

Nonfiction: Contact Publisher, *CMUSA Newsletter*. (*Source Directory* is a September publication.) Book excerpts (achievements of great persons); expose; general interest (modeling, morals Christian slant); how-to (model with morals); humor (funny/comical items of models, religious); inspirational; interview/profile; new product; opinion ("What D'you Say," special briefs on what models think of morals in the field); personal experience (Christians in modeling—talent); photo feature; technical (film production, movies, etc); and "My Inner Desire" (short interview story of great persons with moral fiber). Special Issue Magazine: 1985 Models for Morals. No sexually oriented articles, no vulgarity, coy (blush) jokes, slander, nudity or otherwise immoral material; no compromising romance, etc." Send complete ms. Length: 250-5,000 words. Pays $25-500 or negotiated.

Photos: Contact Publisher, *CMUSA Newsletter*. Send photos with ms. Pays negotiable rate for b&w and color negatives and b&w prints. Indentification of subjects required. Buys one-time rights and all rights.

Poetry: Contact Publisher, *CMUSA Newsletter*. Nothing sexually oriented, vulgar, coy (blush), slanderous or otherwise immoral; no compromising romantic poetry. Length: 4-20 lines. Pays negotiable rate.

Fillers: Contact Publisher, *CMUSA Newsletter*. Clippings and newsbreaks on related subjects. Pays negotiable rates.

Tips: "The *Christian Models U.S.A. National Source Directory* and the *CMUSA Newsletter* both offer opportunities to writers from every area of the country who would like to show that they have 'the right stuff' which CMUSA is interested in. Most of all, CMUSA is interested in writers who will follow guidelines well."

THE ELECTRIC WEENIE, Box 25866, Honolulu HI 96825. (808)395-9600. Editor: Tom Adams. Monthly magazine covering "primarily radio, for 'personalities' world wide (however, mostly English speaking). We mail flyers mainly to radio people, but obviously no one is excepted if he/she wants a monthly supply of first-rate gags, one liners, zappers, etc." Circ. 1,000. Pays on publication. No byline given. Buys all rights. Submit seasonal/holiday material 6 months in advance. SASE. Sample copy for $1, business-size SAE and 1 first class stamp.

Fillers: Jokes, gags, short humor, one liners, etc. "SHORT is the bottom line." Uses 300/month. Pays $1/gag used.

Tips: "We like to receive in multiples of 100 if possible; not mandatory, just preferred."

ENTERTAINMENT INDUSTRY WEEKLY/ENTERTAINMENT DIGEST, Entertainment Industry Publications, Box 10804, Beverly Hills CA 90213. (213)275-6240. Editor: Lisa Galgon. Managing Editor: Steve Travis. 90% freelance written. Weekly newsletter magazine of the entertainment industry; provides total coverage of entertainment industry from performing to business. Circ. 50,000. Pays on publication. Byline given. Offers $25 kill fee. Buys all rights. Simultaneous queries, and simultaneous, photocopied and previously published submissions OK. Computer printout submissions acceptable. SASE. Reports in 1 month. Publishes ms an average of 3 months after acceptance.

Nonfiction: Steve Davis, articles editor. Uses any entertainment industry subject including unions, pay TV, cable, broadcast, film, music, home video, public TV, video tape/disc, advertising, commercials, casting. No fiction. Buys 60-100 mss/year. Send complete ms. Length: open. Pays variable rates.

THE HOLLYWOOD REPORTER, Verdugo Press, 6715 Sunset Blvd., Hollywood CA 90028. (213)464-7411. Publisher: Tichi Wilkerson. Editor: Eliot Tiegel. Emphasizes entertainment industry, film, TV and theatre and is interested in everything to do with financial news in these areas. Daily entertainment trade publication: 25-100 pages. Circ: 25,000. SASE. Reports in 1 month. Sample copy $1.

THE LONE STAR COMEDY MONTHLY, Lone Star Publications of Humor, Suite #103, Box 29000, San Antonio TX 78229. Editor: Lauren Barnett Scharf. Monthly comedy service newsletter for professional humorists—DJs, public speakers, comedians. Includes one-liners and jokes for oral expression. Estab. 1983. Pays on publication "or before." Publishes ms an average of 6 weeks after acceptance. Byline given if 2 or more jokes are used. Buys exclusive rights for 6 months from publication date. Submit seasonal/holiday material 1 month in advance. Photocopied submissions OK. Computer printout submissions acceptable; prefers letter-quality to dot-matrix. SASE. Reports in 1 month. Sample copy $3.50; writer's guidelines for business-size SAE and 1 first class stamp.

Fillers: Jokes, gags and short humor. Buys 20-60/year. Length: 100 words maximum. Pays $1-5. "Submit several (no more than 20) original gags on one or two subjects only."

‡**OPPORTUNITIES FOR ACTORS & MODELS, "A Guide to Working in Cable TV-Radio-Print Advertising,"** Copy Group, Suite 315, 1900 N. Vine St., Hollywood CA 90068. Editor: Len Miller. 60% freelance written. A monthly newsletter "serving the interests of those people who are (or would like to be) a part of the cable-TV, radio, and print advertising industries." Estab. 1983. Circ. 10,000. Pays on acceptance. Byline given. Buys all rights. Simultaneous queries OK. SASE. Reports in 3 weeks. Publishes ms an average of 2 weeks after acceptance. Free sample copy and writer's guidelines.
Nonfiction: How-to, humor, inspirational, interview/profile, local news, personal experience, photo feature and technical (within cable TV). Coverage should include the model scene, little theatre, drama groups, comedy workshops and other related events and places. "Detailed information about your local cable TV station should be an important part of your coverage. Get to know the station and its creative personnel." Buys 120 mss/year. Query. Length: 100-950 words. Pays $50 maximum.
Photos: State availability of photos. Model release and identification of subjects required. Buys one-time or all rights.
Columns/Departments: "We will consider using your material in a column format with your byline." Buys 60 mss/year. Query. Length: 150-450 words. Pays $50 maximum.
Tips: "Good first person experiences, interviews and articles, all related to modeling, acting, little theatre, photography (model shots) and other interesting items" are needed.

PERFORMANCE, 1020 Currie St., Fort Worth TX 76107. (817)338-9444. Editor: Don Waitt. 75% freelance written. The international trade weekly for the touring entertainment industry. "*Performance* publishes tour routing information, updated on a weekly basis. These itineraries, along with box office reports, street news, industry directories, live performance reviews and industry features are of interest to our readers." Weekly magazine; also publishes industry directories once a month. Circ. 20,000. Buys all rights. Phone queries OK. Submit seasonal/holiday material 2 months in advance. Publishes ms an average of 2 weeks after acceptance. Simultaneous submissions OK. Computer printout submissions acceptable. SASE. Reports in 1 month. Sample copy and writer's guidelines $3.
Nonfiction: "This is a trade publication, dealing basically with the ins and outs of booking live entertainment. We are interested in adding freelancers from major cities around the US to provide us with hard news and spot information on sound, lighting, clubs, ticketing, facilities, and college news relevant to the live entertainment industry. We also publish interviews and overviews from time to time." Interviews, opinion and profile. Pays 25¢/printed line.
Photos: State availability of photos with ms. B&w photos only. Captions preferred. Buys all rights.

‡**SUPER 8 NEWSLETTER,** Box 47, Ellijay GA 30540. Editor: M.F. Quarles. A bimonthly newsletter covering Super 8 filmmaking as a professional medium. "We tell our readers how to make quality films in Super 8 that can be shown on TV or blown up to 35mm for theatrical distribution." Circ. 500. Pays on acceptance. By line given. Buys first North American serial rights. Submit seasonal/holiday material 4 months in advance. Simultaneous queries, and simultaneous, photocopied and previously published submissions OK. Computer printout submissions acceptable. SASE. Reports in 1 month. Sample copy $1; writer's guidelines for SAE and 1 first class stamp.
Nonfiction: Historical/nostalgic (the early amateur filmmaking movement and early exploitation in filmmaking); how-to (any aspect of making films in Super 8); interview/profile; new product (cameras, projectors, new gadgets); personal experience ("writer should tell the full story of making a film, *everything* about it"); and technical. No video, unless it's a film-to-video transfer story. Buys 20 mss/year. Query or send complete ms. Length: 100-5,000 words. Pays 1¢/word.
Poetry: Light verse. "No poetry unless somebody who knows Super 8 could do something that was genuinely funny, and short." Pays $1 maximum.
Fillers: Newsbreaks. Length: 50-400 words. Pays 1¢/word.
Tips: "Be a filmmaker. Know Super 8 film, which is a medium different from any other. We believe Super 8 is the coming medium for low-budget filmmaking. Video hasn't 'taken over.' "

THEATRE CRAFTS MAGAZINE, Theatre Crafts Associates, 135 5th Ave., New York NY 10010. Editor: Patricia MacKay. Magazine of the performing arts, video and film, with an emphasis on production and design. Published 9 times/year. "The primary information source for working professionals." Circ. 27,500. Pays on acceptance. Byline given. Buys variable rights. Simultaneous queries and photocopied submissions OK. SASE. Reports in 1 month on queries; 2 months on mss. Sample copy $5; free writer's guidelines.
Nonfiction: How-to; new products (and new applications of old products); and technical (advances and developments in administration, design and technology). Buys 18 mss/year. Query. Pays $25-200.

VANTAGE POINT: ISSUES IN AMERICAN ARTS, (formerly *American Arts*), American Council for the Arts, 570 7th Ave., New York NY 10018. (212)354-6655. Editor: David Kuhn. Bimonthly magazine. Circ. 70,000. Pays on publication. Byline given. Buys first North American serial rights. Simultaneous queries and simultaneous and photocopied submissions OK. SASE. Reports in 6 weeks. Free sample copy, if interested in query or submission—otherwise available for $2.50 and 9x12 SAE and 88¢ postage; writer's guidelines for business-size SAE and 20¢ postage.
Nonfiction: Features, profiles, essays and interviews. Buys 24 mss/year. Length: 500-5,000 words. Pays $100-150.
Photos: Andrea Chapin, photo editor. Pays $50-500 for 8x10 b&w or color prints from contact sheets of photos or illustrations. Captions, model release, and identification of subjects required. Buys one-time rights.
Tips: *Vantage Point* focuses on contemporary issues (social, political, economics and artistic) as they affect the art community on all levels. Readers include high level art executives, trustees, patrons, members of the corporation, foundation and education communities, artists and elected government officials.''

VARIETY, 154 W. 46th St., New York NY 10036. Does not buy freelance material.

Farm

Today's farm publication editor wants more than rewrites of USDA and extension press releases. Farm magazines reflect this, and the successful freelance farm writer turns his attention to the business end of farming.

Do you need to be a farmer to write about farming? The general consensus is yes, and no, depending on the topic. For more technical articles, most editors feel that writers should have a farm background (and not just summer visits to Aunt Rhodie's farm, either) or some technical farm education. But there are plenty of writing opportunities for the general freelancer, too. Easier stories to undertake for farm publications include straight reporting of agricultural events; meetings of national agricultural organizations; or coverage of agricultural legislation. Other ideas might be articles on rural living, rural health care or transportation in small towns.

Always a commandment in any kind of writing, but possibly even more so in the farm field, is the tenet "*Study Thy Market*." The following listings for farm publications are broken down into five categories, each specializing in a different aspect of farm publishing: crops and soil management; dairy farming; general interest farming and rural life (both national and local); livestock; and miscellaneous.

The best bet for a freelancer without much farming background is probably the general interest, family-oriented magazines. These are the *Saturday Evening Posts* of the farm set. The other four categories are more specialized, dealing in only one aspect of farm production.

Where can a writer go for information about farming specialties? Go to a land-grant university; there's one in every state. Also try farming seminars or the county extension offices.

There's no room for hayseeds in the farm writing field. But for the freelance writer who is willing to plow into research, there's a good chance he'll find himself in the middle of a cash crop.

Crops and Soil Management

AVOCADO GROWER MAGAZINE, Rancher Publications, Box 2047, Vista CA 92083. Editor: Gregg A. Payne. Emphasizes avocado and subtropical fruit for growers and professionals (doctors, pilots, investors). Monthly magazine; 64 pages. Circ. 8,000. Pays on publication. Buys all rights. Byline given. Phone queries OK. Submit seasonal material at least 3 months in advance. Simultaneous, photocopied and previously published submissions OK. SASE. Reports in 2-3 weeks. Sample copy $2.
Nonfiction: General interest (relative to avocado industry); historical (on avocado industry); how-to (grow avocados, any interesting cultural aspects); interview (with avocado industry leader); and new product (briefs on-

ly). Open to suggestions for photo features. Buys 2-3 mss/issue. Query with clips of published work or submit complete ms. Pays $1-2/column inch.

Photos: "If it can be said more explicitly with photos, use them to supplement the manuscript." State availability of photos. Pays $3-4.50 for any size b&w prints. No color. Captions preferred and model releases required for minors.

Tips: "Be thorough in the outline. I must be convinced the article has facts, readability and punch. I'm most interested in quality, completeness and readability."

CRANBERRIES, Taylor Publishing Corp., Box 249, Cobalt CT 06414. (203)342-4730. Editor: Bob Taylor. Monthly magazine covering cranberry growing and processing—anything of interest to growers. Circ. 700. Pays on publication. Byline given. "No kill fee. If we accept a story, we'll work writer through. Also we'll pay for the story if events make it impossible to run." Buys first rights. Submit seasonal/holiday material 2 months in advance. Simultaneous queries, and simultaneous, photocopied and previously published submissions OK. Computer printout submissions acceptable; prefers letter-quality to dot-matrix. SASE. Reports in 1 month on queries; 2 months on mss. Sample copy for 8½x11 SAE and 54¢ postage.

Nonfiction: Humor, interview/profile, personal experience, photo feature and technical. Buys 50 mss/year. Query. Length: 500-2,500 words. Pays $15-40.

Photos: State availability of photos. Pays $7-25 for any size b&w print. Captions and identification of subjects required. Buys one-time rights. Pays $15-35 for illustrations.

Tips: "Either know your subject matter or produce material published before. However, we're very receptive to new writers." Profiles on growers are open to freelancers. "While we do not pay big bucks, payment is prompt and will increase as the fortunes of the magazine go up. I also like to feel that young or beginning writers get the benefit of patience and good editing."

THE MUSHROOM NEWS, The American Mushroom Institute, 907 E. Baltimore Pike, Kennett Square PA 19348. (215)388-7806. Editor: Charles R. Harris. Monthly magazine covering material of interest to mushroom growers, suppliers and buyers. Circ. 1,000. Pays on publication. Byline given. Offers 25% kill fee. Buys one-time or second serial (reprint) rights or makes work-for-hire assignments. Submit seasonal/holiday material 1 month in advance. Phone queries, and simultaneous photocopied and previously published submissions OK. Reports in 2 weeks. Sample copy $5; writer's guidelines for SASE.

Nonfiction: Historical/nostalgic (of mushrooms, the mushroom industry); how-to (grow better mushrooms, make better compost, etc.); humor (farmer-oriented); interview/profile (figures of pertinence to the mushroom industry—exceptional grower, etc.); new product (of interest to mushroom growers); opinion (on the state of the mushroom industry); photo feature; and technical. "Anything of interest to a mushroom grower." Buys 12 mss/year. Query. Length: 750 words minimum. Pays $2/printed column inch.

Photos: Send photos with ms. Pays $3-12 for 8x10 b&w prints. Captions and identification of subjects required. Buys one-time rights.

Columns/Departments: Buys variable number mss/year. Query. Length: 100-400 words. Pays $2/printed column inch.

Fillers: Clippings, jokes, gags, anecdotes, short humor and newsbreaks. Buys 20/year. Length: 100-400 words. Pays $2/printed column inch.

Tips: "Many of our stories are scientific, written by the scientist. An approved (by the scientist) recap of a technical article is especially desirable."

PECAN SOUTH, Publications South, Inc., 741 Piedmont Ave., Atlanta GA 30308. (404)892-6812. Editor: Ernest F. Jessee. Publisher: Rebecca H. Johnson. Bimonthly agribusiness magazine of the Southern pecan industry covering research and technology with some economic, marketing and human-interest stories of industrial interest. Circ. 11,000. Pays on publication. Byline given. Buys one-time and first rights. Submit seasonal/holiday material 4 months in advance. Simultaneous phone queries and simultaneous submissions OK. SASE. Reports in 1 month. Sample copy $3; free writer's guidelines.

Nonfiction: General interest (in the Southeast); how-to (grow, market, promote, handle problems in culture, etc.), interview/profile (of notables or recognized contributors to industries); opinion (of experts only); personal experience (of reputable growers or researchers); and technical (new tools, techniques, plant varieties, chemicals, equipment, etc.). Special issues: irrigation (May); marketing (September); equipment (November). No "home gardening material, commercially slanted stories, or information not of widespread industry interest in the Southeast." Buys variable number mss/year. Query. Length: 900-6,000 words. Pays $25-150.

Photos: Send photos with ms. Pays $10 maximum for b&w contact sheet and 8x10 prints; reviews 8x10 color prints. Captions required. Buys one-time rights.

Tips: "Discuss material with us by phone before writing; submit completed works well in advance of copy deadlines; include charts, photos and illustrations. We need more grower and related stories in both wholesale and retail categories. Marketing, shipping and economic features are also needed. Very long features (8-10 typed pages) are rarely welcome from freelancers."

POTATO GROWER OF IDAHO, Harris Publishing, Inc., Box 981, Idaho Falls ID 83402. (208)522-5187. Editor: Steve Janes. 25% freelance written. Emphasizes material slanted to the potato grower and the business of farming related to this subject—packing, shipping, processing, research, etc. Monthly magazine; 48-96 pages. Circ. 18,000. Pays on publication. Buys first North American serial rights. Byline given. Phone queries OK. Submit seasonal/holiday material 3 months in advance. Simultaneous queries, and photocopied and previously published submissions OK. Computer printout submissions acceptable. SASE. Reports in 1 month. Sample copy for $1, 8½x11 SAE, and 37¢ postage; writer's guidelines for 5½x7 SAE and 1 first class stamp.
Nonfiction: Expose (facts, not fiction or opinion, pertaining to the subject); how-to (do the job better, cheaper, faster, etc.); informational articles; interviews ("can use one of these a month, but must come from state of Idaho since this is a regional publication; on unique personalities in the potato industry, and telling the nation 'how Idaho grows potatoes' "); all types of new product articles pertaining to the subject; photo features (story can be mostly photos, but must have sufficient outlines to carry technical information); and technical articles (all aspects of the industry of growing, storage, processing, packing and research of potatoes in general, but must relate to the Idaho potato industry). Buys 5 mss/year. Query. Length: 1,000-2,000 words. Pays $15-100.
Photos: B&w glossies (any size) purchased with mss or on assignment; use of color limited. Query if photos are not to be accompanied by ms. Pays $5-15 for 5x7 b&w prints; $10-50 for 35mm color slides. Captions, model release, and identification of subjects required. Buys one-time rights.
Columns/Departments: Buys 2 mss/year. Query. Length: 750-1,000 words. Pays $20-35.
Fillers: Newsbreaks. Buys 5/year. Length: 50-500 words. Pays $5-15.
Tips: "Choose one vital, but small aspect of the industry; research that subject and slant it to fit the readership and/or goals of the magazine. All articles on research must have a valid source for foundation. Material must be general in nature about the subject or specific in nature about Idaho potato growers. Write a query letter, noting what you have in mind for an article; be specific." Articles on advancement in potato-growing methods or technology are most open to freelancers.

‡**THE RICE WORLD & SOYBEAN NEWS**, J.P. Gaines, Box 829, Folsom LA 70437. (504)796-3012. Publisher J.P. Gaines. 10% freelance written. Monthly tabloid covering rice, soybeans, wheat, sorghum, corn and fish farming with new developments, research, farm experience, new products and market information. Circ. 10,00. Pays on publication. Publishes ms an average of 1 month after acceptance. Buys first rights only. Byline given (if desired). Not copyrighted. Submit seasonal/holiday material 2 months in advance. Simultaneous queries, and photocopied and previously published submissions OK. Computer printout submissions acceptable; prefers letter-quality to dot-matrix. SASE. Reports in 3 weeks. Free sample copy and writer's guidelines.
Nonfiction: How-to, inspirational, interview/profile, new product, personal experience and technical. "All material must be applicable to Southern farming." No political material. Buys 15 mss/year. Query with published clips. Length: 400-600 words. Pays $50-100.
Photos: State availability of photos. Pays $5-10 for 3x5 b&w prints. Captions required. Buys one-time rights.
Tips: "A freelancer can best break in to our publication with creative stories on new farming methods and new products and new ideas. Be interesting. We give priority to exclusive material."

SINSEMILLA TIPS, Domestic Grower's Journal, New Moon Publishing, 217 SW 2nd, Box 2046, Corvallis OR 97339. (503)757-2532. Editor: Thomas Alexander. 50% freelance written. Quarterly magazine tabloid covering the domestic cultivation of marijuana. Circ. 5,000. Pays on publication. Publishes ms an average of 2 months after acceptance. Byline given. "Some writers desire to be anonymous for obvious reasons." Buys one-time rights. Submit seasonal/holiday material 2 months in advance. Computer printout submissions acceptable. SASE. Reports in 2 months. Sample copy $3.
Nonfiction: Book excerpts and reviews; expose (on political corruption); general interest; how-to; interview/profile; opinion; personal experience; and technical. Send complete ms. Length: 500-2,000 words. Pays $25-100.
Photos: Send photos with ms. Pays $10-20 for b&w prints. Captions optional. Model release required. Buys all rights.

SOYBEAN DIGEST, Box 27300, 777 Craig Rd., St. Louis MO 63141. (314)432-1600. Editor: Gregg Hillyer. 75% freelance written. Emphasizes soybean production and marketing. Monthly magazine. Circ. 180,000. Pays on acceptance. Buys all rights. Byline given. Phone queries OK. Submit seasonal material 2 months in advance. Reports in 3 weeks. Sample copy $2; mention *Writer's Market* in request.
Nonfiction: How-to (soybean production and marketing); and new product (soybean production and marketing). Buys over 100 mss/year. Query or submit complete ms. Length: 1,000 words. Pays $50-275.
Photos: State availability of photos with query. Pays $25-100 for 5x7 or 8x10 b&w prints and $50-275 for 35mm color transparencies and up to $350 for covers. Captions and/or manuscript required. Buys all rights.

TOBACCO REPORTER, Suite 300, 3000 Highwoods Blvd., Box 95075, Raleigh NC 27625. Editor: Anne Shelton. 5% (by those who *know* the industry) freelance written. International business journal for tobacco pro-

ducers, processors, warehousemen, exporters, importers, manufacturers and distributors of cigars, cigarettes and other tobacco products. Monthly. Buys all rights. Pays on publication. Computer printout submissions acceptable; no dot-matrix. Publishes ms an average of 2 months after acceptance. SASE.
Nonfiction: Uses exclusive original material on request only. Pays 10-15¢/word.
Photos: Pays $25 for photos purchased with mss.
Fillers: Wants clippings on new tobacco product brands, smoking and health, and the following relating to tobacco and tobacco products: job promotions, honors, equipment, etc. Pays $5-10/clipping on use only.

WINE WEST, Box 498, Geyserville CA 95441. (703)433-7306. Editor/Publisher: Mildred Howie. 95% freelance written. For entire West coast and for those who make, grow and enjoy wine. Circ. 2,500. Covers western Mexico through western Canada and as far as east Texas. Buys 35-45 mss/year. Byline given. Pays on publication. Buys first rights only. Prefers query before submitting ms. Computer printout submissions acceptable; no dot-matrix. SASE. Reports in 2-4 weeks. Publishes ms an average of 4 months after acceptance.
Nonfiction: Must be wine oriented. Technical articles on viticulturists and wine ecology. "Features and articles in *Wine West* are involved with Western wine districts, the people, the practices and the lifestyle." Length: 300-3,000 words. Pays $2.50/inch.
Photos: Pays $10 for b&w photos only purchased with mss.

Dairy Farming

Publications for dairy farmers are classified here. Publications for farmers who raise animals for meat, wool, or hides are included in the Livestock category. Other magazines that buy material on dairy herds are listed in the General Interest Farming and Rural Life classification. Journals for dairy products retailers are found under Dairy Products.

BUTTER-FAT, Fraser Valley Milk Producers' Cooperative Association, Box 9100, Vancouver, British Columbia V6B 4G4 Canada. (604)420-6611. Editor: C.A. Paulson. Managing Editor: T.W. Low. 20% freelance written. Bimonthly magazine emphasizing this dairy cooperative's processing and marketing operations for dairy farmers and dairy workers in British Columbia. Circ. 3,300. Pays on acceptance. Publishes ms an average of 4 months after acceptance. Byline given. Buys first rights and first and second rights to the same material. Makes work-for-hire assignments. Phone queries preferred. Submit seasonal material 4 months in advance. Simultaneous, photocopied and previously published submissions OK. Reports in 1 week on queries; in 1 month on mss. Free sample copy and writer's guidelines.
Nonfiction: Interview (character profile with industry leaders); local nostalgia; opinion (of industry leaders); and profile (of association members and employees).
Photos: Reviews 5x7 b&w negatives and contact sheets. Offers $10/published photo. Captions required. Buys all rights.
Columns/Departments: "We want articles on the people, products, business of producing, processing and marketing dairy foods in this province." Query first. Buys 3 mss/issue. Length: 500-1,500 words. Pays 7¢/word.
Fillers: Jokes, short humor and quotes. Buys 5 mss/issue. Pays $10.
Tips: "Make an appointment to come by and see us!"

DAIRY GOAT JOURNAL, Box 1808, Scottsdale AZ 85252. Editor: Kent Leach. 10% freelance written. Monthly for breeders and raisers of dairy goats. Pays on publication. Buys first rights. Computer printout submissions acceptable; prefers letter-quality to dot-matrix. SASE. Query. Reports in 1 month. Publishes ms an average of 8 months after acceptance. Free sample copy.
Nonfiction: Uses articles, items and photos that deal with dairy goats and the people who raise them; goat dairies and shows. How-to articles up to 1,000 words. Buys 12-25 unsolicited mss/year. Pays by arrangement.
Photos: Buys 5x7 or 8x10 b&w photos for $1-15.
Tips: "In query give the thrust or point of the article, what illustrations may be available, how soon it might be finished—and if payments are expected, state how much or if negotiable."

‡DAIRY HERD MANAGEMENT, Miller Publishing Co., Box 67, Minneapolis MN 55440. (612)374-5200. Editor: Sheila Widmer Vikla. Emphasizes dairy farming. Monthly magazine; 60 pages. Circ. 100,000. Pays on acceptance. Buys first North American serial rights. Submit seasonal/holiday material 2 months in advance. Photocopied and previously published submissions OK. SASE. Reports in 3-6 weeks. Free sample copy and writer's guidelines.

Nonfiction: How-to, informational and technical. Buys 6 mss/year. Query. Length: 1,000-3,000 words. Pays $75-200. "Articles should concentrate on useful management information. Be specific rather than general."

‡**DAIRY LIFE NORTHWEST**, Cottage Publications Inc., Box 98, Heisson WA 98622. (206)687-4476. Publisher/Editor: Dixie Ross. 50% freelance written. A bimonthly magazine covering commercial dairy farming in northwest region of the US. Circ. 7,000 +. Pays on publication. Publishes ms an average of 6 months after acceptance. Byline given. Not copyrighted. Buys one-time rights. Submit seasonal/holiday material 2 months in advance. Simultaneous queries, and simultaneous, photocopied and previously published submissions OK. SASE. Reports in 1 month. Free sample copy and writer's guidelines.
Nonfiction: Historical/nostalgic, how-to, humor, interview/profile, new products and technical. No articles that are not oriented to commercial dairy farmers in northwest region of US. Buys 12-24 mss/year. Query with or without published clips or send complete ms. Length: 1,000-1,500 words. Pays $1.50/column inch.
Photos: State availability of photos with query; send photos with ms. Pays $8 for b&w prints; $30 for color prints; size open. Captions and identification of subjects required.
Fiction: Humorous (northwest US farm-oriented). Buys 12 mss/year. Query with or without published clips or send complete ms. Length: 1,000-1,500 words. Pays $1.50/column inch.
Poetry: Light verse and traditional. Buys 4-6 poems/year. Submit maximum 1 poem. Pays $1.50/column inch.
Tips: "Contact local dairy farmer groups, college or county extension agents for tips on dairy farming activities in their local area of northwest region. On-the-farm type interviews and personal profile of Northwest commercial dairy farmers are most open to freelancers. We would be glad to suggest article topics and tips to any interested freelance writer; also open to first timers."

THE DAIRYMAN, Box 819, Corona CA 91720. Editor: Dennis J. Halladay. 10% freelance written. For large herd dairy owners. Monthly. Buys first rights and second (reprint rights) to material originally published elsewhere. Pays on publication. Publishes ms an average of 45 days after acceptance. Computer printout submissions acceptable. Reports in 3 weeks. SASE. Free sample copy.
Nonfiction: Uses articles on anything related to dairy farming, preferably anything new and different or substantially unique in operation, for US subjects. Acceptance of foreign dairy farming stories based on potential interest of readers. No politics, religion, food or cinema/arts. Buys 5-10 unsolicited mss/year; would possibly buy 20-25. Pays $2/printed inch.
Photos: Buys b&w photos with mss only, pays $10 each. Buys color with or without mss, pays $20-50 each. Also buys drawings, sketches and other art used to illustrate story. Greater use of freelance material and some use of 4 color art inside with stories in the year ahead.
Tips: "Break in by sending us something . . . we're very informal about freelancers. We enjoy receiving repeat submissions, articles which are better than their predecessors and continually improve as the writer learns the market. We only publish material concerning dairying—no pigs, horses, beef cattle or otherwise. We don't care about the upper Midwest, or upper Atlantic coast. Our readers are the best dairymen in the world; stories should reflect the modern times of the industry."

DAIRYMEN'S DIGEST (Southern Region Edition), Box 5040, Arlington TX 76005. Editor: Phil Porter. For commercial dairy farmers and their families throughout the central US with interests in dairy production and marketing. Magazine; 32 pages. Monthly. Circ. 9,000. Not copyrighted. Byline given. Buys 34 mss/year. Pays on publication. Reports in 3 weeks. Computer printout or disk submissions acceptable. SASE. Will send free sample copy to writer on request.
Nonfiction: Emphasis on dairy production and marketing. Buys articles of general interest to farm families, especially dairy-oriented. Seeks unusual accomplishments and satisfactions resulting from determination and persistence. Must be positive and credible. Needs fresh ideas, profile and personal experience articles. Buys some historical, inspirational or nostalgia. Also articles of interest to farm wives. "I don't want to see material that is not related to dairying or milk marketing." Length: 50-1,500 words. Pay varies from $10-125, plus additional amount for photos, depending on quality.
Photos: Pays according to quality.

General Interest Farming and Rural Life

The publications listed here are read by farm families or farmers in general and contain material on sophisticated agricultural and business techniques. Magazines that specialize in the raising of crops are in the Crops and Soil Management classification; publications that deal exclusively with livestock raising are classified in the

Livestock category. Magazines for farm suppliers are grouped under Agricultural Equipment and Supplies.

National

‡**ACRES U.S.A., A Voice for Eco-Agriculture**, Acres U.S.A., Box 9547, Kansas City MO 64133. (816)737-0064. Editor: Charles Walters Jr. Monthly tabloid covering biologically sound farming techniques. Circ. 16,000. Pays on acceptance. Byline given (sometimes). Not copyrighted. Buys all rights. Submit seasonal/holiday material 3 months in advance. Computer printout submissions acceptable. Reports in 1 month. Sample copy $2.
Nonfiction: Expose (farm-related); how-to; and case reports on farmers who have adopted eco-agriculture (organic). No philosophy on eco-farming or essays. Buys 80 mss/year. Query with published clips. Length: open. Pays 7¢/word.
Photos: State availability of photos. B&w photos only. Pays $6 for b&w contact sheets, negatives and 7x10 prints.
Tips: "We need on-scene reports of farmers who have adopted eco-farming—good case reports. We must have substance in articles and need details on systems developed."

AGRI NEWS, Rochester Post-Bulletin, 18 1st Ave. SE, Rochester MN 55901. (507)285-7707. Editor: Myron Williams. Managing Editor: William Boyne. Weekly newspaper for southeastern Minnesota and northeastern Iowa farmers interested in changes in agriculture, people in agriculture, and agriculture worldwide. Circ. 18,000. Pays on publication. Byline given. Not copyrighted. Buys first rights only. Submit seasonal/holiday material 1 month in advance. Simultaneous queries OK. "We prefer typed copy, although letter-quality computer printouts are acceptable." SASE. Reports in 3 weeks. Sample copy for 9x12 SAE and 5 first class stamps; writer's guidelines for 5x9 envelope and 2 first class stamps.
Nonfiction: Interview/profile (of anyone involved in agriculture); opinion (news analysis—ag related); technical; and features on agriculture. "Stories should be written in an objective but in-depth newspaper style which is hard-hitting, clear and interesting to read. We take the view that the farmer is sophisticated enough to read professionally written pieces and not rambling stories about life in the country." No homespun writing, articles written for urban readers or first person stories. Buys 150 mss/year. Query with clips of published work. Length: 800-1,000 words. Pays $1.50/printed inch.
Columns/Departments: "Our editorial page is in need of additional copy to keep it fresh, interesting and opinionated. We're always interested in viewing new column material about a variety of subjects as they pertain to agriculture. Queries will always be viewed closely and not just filed away." Buys 150 mss/year. Query with clips of published work. Length: 800-1,000 words. Pays $1.50/printed inch.
Tips: "We may buy less freelance material later in the year because of additions to our staff—more staff writers means less dependence on freelancers."

AGWAY COOPERATOR, Box 4933, Syracuse NY 13221. (315)477-7061. Editor: Jean Willis. For farmers. Published 9 times/year. Pays on acceptance. Usually reports in 1 week. SASE.
Nonfiction: Should deal with topics of farm or rural interest in the Northeastern US. Length: 1,200 words maximum. Pays $100, usually including photos.

BLAIR AND KETCHUM'S COUNTRY JOURNAL, Box 870, Manchester VT 05255. Publisher: William Blair. Editor: Richard M. Ketchum. Managing Editor: Thomas H. Rawls. Monthly magazine featuring country living for people who live in rural areas or who are thinking about moving there, small and part-time farmers. Circ. 300,000. Average issue includes 8-10 feature articles and 10 departments. Pays on acceptance. Byline given. Buys first North American serial and second (reprint) rights. Submit seasonal material 6 months in advance. Photocopied submissions OK. SASE. Reports in 1 month. Sample copy $2; free writer's guidelines.
Nonfiction: Book excerpts; general interest; opinion (essays); profile (people who are outstanding in terms of country living); how-to (2,000-2,500 words on practical gardening, energy and animal care); personal experience; photo feature; and technical (new developments in a certain category). No historical or reminiscence. Buys 8-10 mss/issue. Query with clips of previously published work. Length: 2,000-3,500 words. Pays $400-500.
Photos: John Wood, photo editor. State availability of photos. Reviews b&w contact sheets, 5x7 and 8x10 b&w glossy prints and 35mm or larger color transparencies. Captions, model release and identification of subjects required. Buys one-time rights.
Columns/Departments: John Barstow, column/department editor. Listener (brief articles on country topics, how-to's, current events and updates). Buys 10 mss/year. Query with published clips. Length: 200-400 words. Pays approx. $75.
Poetry: Donald Hall, poetry editor. Free verse, light verse and traditional. Buys 1 ms/issue. Pays $2/line.

Tips: "Be as specific in your query as possible and explain why you are qualified to write the piece (especially for how-to's and controversial subjects).

‡**BUYING FOR THE FARM**, Elmbrook Publishing, Inc., 21100 W. Capitol Dr., Pewaukee WI 53072. (414)783-5157. Editor: H. Lee Schwanz. A monthly farming and ranching magazine "concentrating on ways farmers can save money on inputs for crops and livestock production. Prices are compared for classes of inputs." Circ. 25,000. Pays on acceptance. Byline given. Offers negotiable kill fee. Buys all rights. Submit seasonal/holiday material 2 months in advance. Simultaneous queries OK. SASE. Reports in 2 weeks.
Nonfiction: Articles related to purchasing for the farm. Buys 50 mss/year. Query with farm writing credentials. Length: 400-800 words. Pays $100-300.
Photos: Reviews b&w contacts and negatives. Buys one-time rights.
Tips: "We do farmer experience articles and want wide geographical distribution."

‡**FARM & RANCH LIVING**, Reiman Publications, 5400 S. 60th St., Greendale WI 53129. (414)423-0100. Editor: Roy Reiman. Managing Editor: Bob Ottum. A bimonthly lifestyle magazine aimed at families engaged full time in farming or ranching. "*F&RL* is *not* a 'how-to' magazine—it deals with people rather than products and profits." Circ. 230,000. Pays on acceptance. Byline given. Offers 25% kill fee. Buys first North American serial rights. Submit seasonal/holiday material 3-6 months in advance. Previously published submissions OK. SASE. Reports in 2 weeks. Sample copy $2; writer's guidelines for business-size SAE and 1 first class stamp.
Nonfiction: Historical/nostalgic, humor, inspirational, interview/profile, personal experience and photo feature. No how-to articles or stories about 'hobby farmers' (doctors or lawyers with weekend farms), or 'hard-times' stories (farmers going broke or selling out). Buys 50 mss/year. Query with or without published clips. Length: 1,000-3,000 words. Pays $150-500.
Photos: State availability of photos with query or ms. Pays $20-40 for b&w photos; $75-200 for 35mm color slides. Captions required. Buys one-time rights.
Fillers: Clippings, jokes, anecdotes and short humor. Buys 150/year. Length: 50-150 words. Pays $20 minimum.
Tips: "A freelancer must see *F&RL* to fully appreciate how different it is from other farm publications . . . ordering a sample is strongly advised (not available on newsstands). Query first—we'll give plenty of help and encouragement if story looks promising, and we'll explain why if it doesn't. Most Interesting Farmer (or Rancher) I've Ever Met (human interest profile); Prettiest Place in the Country (tour in text and photos of an attractive farm or ranch); and photo features (about interesting farm or ranch families) are most open to freelancers."

‡**FARM FUTURES, The Business and Marketing Magazine of American Agriculture**, Agri Data Resources, 205 W. Highland, Milwaukee WI 53210. (414)273-0873. Editor: David Skoloda. Managing Editor: David Pelzer. 10% freelance written. A monthly magazine covering farm business and marketing. Circ. 210,000. Pays on publication. Publishes ms an average of 6 weeks after acceptance. Byline given. Offers negotiable kill fee. Buys first rights only. Simultaneous queries, and photocopied and previously published submissions OK; no simultaneous submissions. Electronic submissions OK; inquire about requirements. Computer printout submissions acceptable. SASE. Reports in 1 month on queries; 2 weeks on mss. Free sample copy.
Nonfiction: Expose (agriculturally oriented, national focus); how-to (e.g., manage farm labor, shop for computer software, market using options trading); and interview/profile. Buys 5-10 mss/year. Query with published clips. Length: 1,000-6,000 words. Pays $300-1,500.
Tips: Concise, to-the-point "profiles on farmers' management practices and articles on key farm policy issues on regional level (corn, soybean, cotton, wheat belts) are best areas for freelancers."

FARM INDUSTRY NEWS, Webb Publishing, 1999 Shepard Rd., St. Paul MN 55116. (612)690-7284. Editor: Den Gardner. Managing Editor: Joe Degnan. 10% freelance written. Magazine published 10 times/year in 16 midwest and mideast states. Covers product news, buying information. "We treat high volume farmers as purchasing agents rather than producers. Our stories provide farmers with in-depth information on new products they may consider buying." Circ. 305,000. Pays on acceptance. Publishes ms an average of 2 months after acceptance. Byline given. Buys one-time rights. Computer printout submissions acceptable. SASE. Reports in 3 weeks. Free sample copy and writer's guidelines.
Nonfiction: Interview/profile, new product and technical. No production stories, fiction or poetry. "Please study the publication before submitting stories." Query or send complete ms. Length: 500-1,500 words. Pays $50-400.
Photos: Reviews b&w contact sheets, 35mm color transparencies or 8x10 b&w prints. Payment depends on use and is included with ms. Captions and indentification of subjects required.
Tips: "Read the magazine, then query with specific idea and contacts. Good photographs showing a product and human involvement help in selling an article." Phone queries OK.

FARM JOURNAL, 230 W. Washington Square, Philadelphia PA 19105. Contact: Editor. "The business magazine of American agriculture" is published 14 times/year with many regional editions. Material bought for one or more editions depending upon where it fits. Buys all rights. Byline given "except when article is too short or too heavily rewritten to justify one." Payment made on acceptance and is the same regardless of editions in which the piece is used. SASE.
Nonfiction: Timeliness and seasonableness are very important. Material must be highly practical and should be helpful to as many farmers as possible. Farmers' experiences should apply to one or more of these 8 basic commodities: corn, wheat, milo, soybeans, cotton, dairy, beef and hogs. Technical material must be accurate. No farm nostalgia. Query to describe a new idea that farmers can use. Length: 500-1,500 words. Pays 10-20¢/word published.
Photos: Much in demand either separately or with short how-to material in picture stories and as illustrations for articles. Warm human interest pix for covers—activities on modern farms. For inside use, shots of homemade and handy ideas to get work done easier and faster, farm news photos, and pictures of farm people with interesting sidelines. In b&w, 8x10 glossies are preferred; color submissions should be 2¼x2¼ for the cover, and 35mm for inside use. Pays $50 and up for b&w shot; $75 and up for color.
Tips: *"Farm Journal* now publishes in hundreds of editions reflecting geographic, demographic, and economic sectors of the farm market."

FERTILIZER PROGRESS, The Fertilizer Institute, 1015 18th St. NW, Washington DC 20036. (202)861-4900. Publishing Director: Thomas E. Waldinger. Editor: Michael J. Fritz. Assistant to the Editor: Kathleen S. Bova. Bimonthly magazine covering fertilizer, farm chemical and allied industries for business and management, with emphasis on the retail market. Circ. 22,000. Pays on publication. Byline given. Offers 2½¢/word kill fee. Buys all rights. Submit seasonal/holiday material 2 months in advance. Photocopied submissions OK. SASE. Reports in 2 weeks on queries; 3 weeks on mss. Free sample copy.
Nonfiction: Articles on sales, services, credit, products, equipment, merchandising, production, regulation, research and environment. Also news about people, companies, trends and developments. No "highly technical or philosophic pieces; we want relevance—something the farm retail dealer can sink his teeth into." No material not related to fertilizer, farm chemical and allied industries, or to the retail market. Send complete ms. Length: 400-2,500 words. Pays $40-250.
Photos: Send photos with ms. Pays $5-20 for 5x7 b&w and color prints. Captions and identification of subjects required.
Columns/Departments: Elements of Success (productive agronomic advice for dealers to use in selling to farmers); Fit to be Tried (ideas that really work); and Worth Repeating (agricultural-related editorial commentary). Send complete ms. Length: 500-750 words. Pays $40-60.

‡HIGH PLAINS JOURNAL, "The Farmers Paper", High Plains Publishers, Inc., Box 760, Dodge City KS 67801. (316)227-7171. Editor: Galen Hubbs. Managing Editor: Bob Keating. Weekly tabloid with news, features and photos on all phases of farming and livestock production. Circ. 55,000. Pays on publication. Byline given. Not copyrighted. Buys first rights only. Submit seasonal/holiday material 1 month in advance. Simultaneous queries and photocopied submissions OK. Computer printout submissions acceptable; prefers letter-quality to dot-matrix. SASE. Reports in 3 weeks on queries; 4 weeks on mss. Sample copy for 75¢ and SAE with 3 first class stamps; writer's guidelines for SAE and 1 first class stamp.
Nonfiction: General interest (agriculture); how-to; interview/profile (farmers or stockmen within the High Plains area); and photo feature (agricultural). No rewrites of USDA, extension or marketing association releases. Buys 50-60 mss/year. Query with published clips. Length: 10-40 inches. Pays $1/column inch.
Photos: State availability of photos. Pays $5-10 for 4x5 b&w prints. Captions and "complete" identification of subjects required. Buys one-time rights.
Tips: "Limit submissions to agriculture. Stories should not have a critical time element. Stories should be informative with correct information. Use quotations and bring out the human aspects of the person featured in profiles."

THE NATIONAL FUTURE FARMER, Box 15130, Alexandria VA 22309. (703)360-3600. Editor-in-Chief: Wilson W. Carnes. Managing Editor: Michael Wilson. Bimonthly magazine for members of the Future Farmers of America who are students of vocational agriculture in high school, ranging in age from 14-21 years; major interest in careers in agriculture/agribusiness and other youth interest subjects. Circ. 475,073. Pays on acceptance. Buys all rights. Byline given. Submit seasonal/holiday material 3-4 months in advance. Computer printout submissions acceptable; prefers letter-quality to dot-matrix. SASE. Usually reports in 1 month. Free sample copy and writer's guidelines.
Nonfiction: Contact: Michael Wilson. How-to for youth (outdoor-type such as camping, hunting, fishing); informational (getting money for college, farming; and other help for youth). Informational, personal experience and interviews are used only if FFA members or former members are involved. Recent article example: "Growing Up with the Computer" (February/March 1984). Buys 15 unsolicited mss/year. Query or send complete ms. Length: 1,000 words maximum. Pays 4-6¢/word.

Photos: Purchased with mss.(5x7 or 8x10 b&w glossies; 35mm or larger color transparencies). Pays $7.50 for b&w; $30-40 for inside color; $100 for cover.

Tips: "Find an FFA member who has done something truly outstanding that will motivate and inspire others, or provide helpful information for a career in farming, ranching or agribusiness. We are also very interested in stories on the latest trends in agriculture and how those trends may affect our readers. As a result of cutbacks in money for pages, we're accepting manuscripts now that are tighter and more concise. Get straight to the point."

SUCCESSFUL FARMING, 1716 Locust St., Des Moines IA 50336. (515)284-2693. Editor: Richard Krumme. Magazine of farm management published for top farmers. 13 times/year. Circ. 650,000. Buys all rights. Pays on acceptance. Reports in 2 weeks. SASE.

Nonfiction: Semitechnical articles on the aspects of farming with emphasis on how to apply this information to one's own farm. "Most of our material is too limited and unfamiliar for freelance writers, except for the few who specialize in agriculture, have a farm background and a modern agricultural education." Recent article example: "Grass Roots Marketing: Meetings That Make Money!" (Dec. 1983). Buys 100 unsolicited mss/year. Query with outline. Length: about 1,500 words maximum. Pays $250-600.

Photos: Jim Galbraith, art director. Prefers 8x10 b&w glossies to contacts; color should be transparencies, not prints. Buys exclusive rights. Assignments are given, and sometimes a guarantee, provided the editors can be sure the photography will be acceptable. Pays expenses.

Local

AcreAGE, Malheur Publishing Co., Box 130, Ontario OR 97914. (503)889-5387. Editor: Rick Swart. 20% freelance written. Monthly tabloid covering anything and everything relating to farming and ranching for all rural boxholders in southern Idaho and eastern Oregon. Circ. 40,000. Pays on acceptance. Byline given. Buys first and second rights to the same material. Computer printout submissions acceptable; prefers letter-quality to dot-matrix. SASE. Reports in 3 weeks. Sample copy $1.

Nonfiction: General interest (on farming and ranching); how-to (install fence, irrigate, plant, harvest, etc.); interview/profile (of leaders in agriculture); and personal experience (better ways to farm and ranch). No nostalgic pieces. "About 50% of our articles are technical pieces about such things as ag chemicals, irrigation, etc. These pieces are difficult for writers lacking a good ag background and proximity to a university or research center specializing in such work. No mss on 'how nice (or bad) it is to be a farmer or rancher.' " Buys 24 mss/year. Query or send complete ms. Length: 9 typewritten pages maximum. Pays $1-1.25/inch.

Photos: Pays $7 minimum for 5x7 (minimum) b&w glossy prints. Identification of subjects required.

Tips: "Avoid telling the obvious, e.g., 'Holsteins are a breed of cow that gives lots of milk.' Writers will have better luck breaking in with human interest features (farm-ranch oriented). Past articles have included a power hang-glider (ultralight) pilot who used his machine to check irrigation lines; Landsat satellites for water and crop management; an old-time threshing bee; and a farmer who collects antique farm machinery. The majority of our articles deal with farming and ranching in the southern Idaho, eastern Oregon region."

ATLANTIC FARM & FOREST, (formerly *Farm & Forest*), Henley Publishing, Ltd., Box 130, Woodstock, New Brunswick E0J 2B0 Canada. (506)328-8863. Editor: Gordon F. Catt. Monthly tabloid for residents of Atlantic Canada engaged or interested in agriculture and forestry in the province. Circ. 5,000. Pays on publication. Byline given. Pays 50% kill fee. Not copyrighted. Buys one-time rights. Submit seasonal/holiday material 4 months in advance. Photocopied and previously published submissions OK. Computer printout submissions acceptable. SASE. Reports in 2 weeks on queries; 1 month on mss. Sample copy $1; writer's guidelines for business-size SAE and 32¢ Canadian postage.

Nonfiction: General interest; how-to (better ways to harvest, house cattle, adapt machinery); interview/profile (people in regional farming, forestry); and technical. No opinion pieces or inspirational material. "We are looking for freelancers living in our area who can write profiles of regional people in the agriculture and forestry industries. We will also contract with freelancers to cover specific events in our province. Submit articles on farm forestry outside our primary distribution areas as long as they tie in with what's happening here." Buys 12 mss/year. Query. Length: 500-1,200 words. Pays 5¢/word except for special advance contracts.

Photos: State availability of photos. Pays $5-10 for 5x7 b&w prints. Captions and identification of subjects required.

Poetry: Free verse, haiku, light verse and traditional. "No erotica." Buy 12/year. Submit maximum 2 poems. Length: 6-20 lines. Pays $3.

Tips: "Change to monthly publication means we'll purchase fewer manuscripts, and those we use will have to be tighter in length and of definite interest to our readers who are mostly in Canada's Atlantic Provinces region and its agricultural and forest industries. We absolutely will not reply or return material without SASE or SAE and return postage (Canadian or IRCs)."

‡**COASTAL PLAINS FARMER MAGAZINE**, Specialized Agricultural Publications, Inc., Suite 300, 3000 Highwoods Blvd., Raleigh NC 27625. (919)872-5040. Editor: Sid Reynolds. Managing Editor: Marilyn Burns. A monthly magazine covering agriculture and rural living. "Primarily, *Coastal Plains Farmer* is a business-of-farming magazine with 70 percent of its content devoted to concise how-to and bottom-line articles. Twenty percent of the content deals with the real, ever-present needs of rural communities, from state legislation and its impact on education, rural health, retirement, and the many topics that are as much a part of farming as field work. The remaining 10 percent of the *Coastal Plains Farmer* is devoted to the human aspects of farming and living in the rural Coastal Plains areas. Estab. 1983. Circ. 110,000 + . Pays on acceptance. Byline sometimes given; "depends on significance." Buys first North American serial rights. Submit seasonal/holiday material 3 months in advance. Simultaneous queries OK. Computer printout submissions acceptable. SASE. Reports in 2 weeks on queries; 2 months on mss. Sample copy and writer's guidelines free.
Nonfiction: How-to (specific money slant on farm techniques in sandy-textured soils); humor (on rural life in the Coastal Plains); and interview/profile (on farmers in the Coastal Plains). No one-source articles. Query with published clips. Length: 100-2,500 words. Pays $25-500.
Photos: Send photos with query or ms. Pays $15-500 for 5x7 color transparencies; $10-100 for 5x7 b&w prints. Captions, and identification of subjects required; model releases sometimes required.
Columns/Departments: Sid Reynolds, column/department editor. Machine Shop (farmers in the Coastal Plains who have adapted machinery for a specific function); Bottomline (farm financial management tips or legislative information). Buys 5 mss/year. Query. Length: 100-1,000 words. Pays $25-100.
Tips: "It helps to have practical experience in farming."

COUNTRY ESTATE, Northern Miner Press Ltd., RR1, Terra Cotta, Ontario L0P 1N0 Canada. (Editorial only). (416)838-2800. Editor: Michael Pembry. 30% freelance written. Quarterly magazine covering country living for upper income country homeowners. "Subjects must inform or entertain this specific audience." Circ. 52,000 (within 50 miles of Toronto). Pays on publication. Byline given. Buys first North American serial rights. Simultaneous queries and photocopied and simultaneous submissions OK. Computer printout submissions acceptable. SASE. Reports in 1 month. Sample copy for $2.50 and 9x11 SAE and 60¢ postage or IRC; writer's guidelines for 30¢ postage or IRC.
Nonfiction: Historical/nostalgic; how-to; humor (on country living); interview/profile (country personalities in southern Ontario); personal experience; and photo feature. "All subjects must relate to country living and people in Ontario, especially areas within 50 miles of Toronto." No "articles written for a very general audience." Buys 30 mss/year. Query. Length: 500-1,500 words. Pays $75-150.
Photos: State availability of photos with query letter or ms, or send photos with accompanying ms. Reviews transparencies and 5x7 prints. Payment included with article. Captions required. Buys one-time rights.
Tips: "Have a good grasp of our audience. Pick a subject which really relates specifically to country living in Ontario. Submit clean, edited material. Articles with good photos always preferred."

FLORIDA GROWER & RANCHER, 723 E. Colonial Dr., Orlando FL 32803. Editor: Frank Abrahamson. 10% freelance written. For citrus grove managers and production managers, vegetable growers and managers, and livestock raisers; all agricultural activities in state. Monthly magazine. Circ. 32,500. Buys all rights. Pays on publication. Computer printout submissions acceptable; no dot-matrix. Publishes ms an average of 6 months after acceptance. Reports in 1 month. Query. SASE.
Nonfiction: Articles on production and industry-related topics. In-depth and up-to-date. Writer must know the market and write specifically for it. Informational, how-to, personal experience, interview, profile, opinion and successful business operations. Buys a minimum of outside material due to fulltime staff additions. Length: 500-1,500 words for features; 100 words or less for short items. Pays "competitive rates."
Photos: B&w illustrations desirable with features. Color illustrations purchased only occasionally.

INDIANA PRAIRIE FARMER, a Farm Progress Publication, Box 41281, Indianapolis IN 46241. (317)248-0681. Editor: Paul Queck. Semimonthly magazine covering farm management, production technology and policy for owners of farms, farm workers and agribusiness people. Controlled circ. 89,500. Pays on acceptance. No byline given. Buys first North American serial rights. Submit seasonal/holiday material 6 months in advance. Reports in 2 weeks. SASE.
Nonfiction: "We are a farm business magazine using articles on farm management and production with emphasis on farmer interviews." Buys 20-25 mss/year. Length: 600-1,200 words. Pays $75-150.
Photos: Send photos with ms. Pays $100-150 for 35mm color transparencies; $15-25 for 8x10 b&w prints. B&w photo payment included in payment for ms. Captions and model release required. Buys first rights.

IOWA REC NEWS, Suite 48, 8525 Douglas, Urbandale IA 50322. (515)276-5350. Editor: Karen Tisinger. 15% freelance written. Emphasizes energy issues for residents of rural Iowa. Monthly magazine. Circ. 125,000. Pays on publication. Buys first rights and second (reprint) rights to material originally published elsewhere. Not copyrighted. Simultaneous, photocopied and previously published submissions OK. Computer printout submissions acceptable. Publishes ms an average of 4 months after acceptance. SASE.

Nonfiction: General interest, historical, humor, farm issues and trends, rural lifestyle trends, energy awareness features, and photo features. Recent article example: "What Will I Do With My Farm?" Buys approximately 18 unsolicited mss/year. Send complete ms. Pays $40-60.

Tips: "The easiest way to break into our magazine is: include a couple paragraphs about the author, research a particular subject well, and include appropriate attributions to establish credibility, authority. Reading and knowing about farm people is important. Stories that touch the senses or can improve the lives of the readers are highly considered, as are these with a strong Iowa angle. Freelancers have the advantage of offering subject matter that existing staff may not be able to cover. Often, however, many articles lack evidence of actual research—provide lots of information but do not include any sources to give the story any credibility. (Rarely is the author a renowned expert on the subject he's written about.)"

MICHIGAN FARMER, 3303 W. Saginaw St., Lansing MI 48901. (517)321-9393. Associate Editor: Dave Weinstock. 10% freelance written. Semimonthly. Buys first North American serial rights. Byline given. Pays on publication. Publishes ms an average of 3 months after acceptance. Reports in 1 month. Query. SASE.
Nonfiction: Uses problem solving articles of interest and value to Michigan farmers, which discuss Michigan agriculture and the people involved in it. Also articles for home section about Michigan farm housewives and what they are doing. Lucid, easy-to-understand writing is desired. Length depends on topic. Rates are $1/column inch minimum; special stories bring higher rates.
Photos: Buys some b&w singles; also a few color transparencies for cover use. Prefers subject matter to have either people or animals in it. Pays $5-10 each for b&w, depending on quality. Pays $60 for selected cover transparencies of identifiable Michigan farm or rural scenes; accepts only verticals.

MISSOURI RURALIST, Harvest Publishing, Suite 600, 2103 Burlington, Columbia MO 65202. Editor: Larry Harper. Managing Editor: Joe Link. Semimonthly magazine featuring Missouri farming for people who make their living at farming. Pays on acceptance. Byline given. Buys first North American serial rights and all rights in Missouri. Photocopied submissions OK. Computer printout submissions acceptable; prefers letter-quality to dot-matrix. SASE. Reports in 1 month. Sample copy $1.50.
Nonfiction: "We use articles valuable to the Missouri farmer, discussing Missouri agriculture and people involved in it, including homemakers. Technical articles must be written in an easy-to-read style. The length depends on the topic." No corny cartoons or poems on farmers. Query. Pays $60/published page.
Photos: State availability of photos. Pays $5-10 for 5x7 b&w glossy prints. Pays $60 maximum for 35mm transparencies for covers. Captions required.
Fillers: Newsbreaks. Length: 100-500 words. Pays $60/printed page.

N.D. REC MAGAZINE, N.D. Association of RECs, Box 727, Mandan ND 58554. (701)663-6501. Editor-in-Chief: Leland Ulmer. Managing Editor: Dennis Hill. Monthly magazine covering rural electric program and rural North Dakota lifestyle. "Our magazine goes to the 70,000 North Dakotans who get their electricity from rural electric cooperatives. We cover rural lifestyle, energy conservation, agriculture, farm family news and other features of importance to this predominantly agrarian state. Of course, we represent the views of our statewide association." Circ. 74,000. Pays on publication; "acceptance for assigned features." Byline given. Buys first North American serial rights. Submit seasonal/holiday material 6 months in advance. Simultaneous queries OK. Computer printout submissions acceptable; prefers letter-quality to dot-matrix. SASE. Reports in 2 weeks. Sample copy for 9x12 SAE with $1.37 postage.
Nonfiction: Dennis Hill, managing editor. Expose (subjects of ND interest dealing with rural electric, agriculture, rural lifestyle); historical/nostalgic (ND events or people only); how-to (save energy, weatherize homes, etc.); interview/profile (on great leaders of the rural electric program, agriculture); and opinion (why family farms should be saved, etc.). No fiction that does not relate to our editorial goals. Buys 10-12 mss/year. Length: open. Pays $35-300.
Photos: Dennis Hill, managing editor. "We need 5x7 b&w glossy prints for editorial material. Transparencies needed for cover, ag/rural scenes only—ND interest." Pays $25 maximum for 35mm color transparencies; $5 minimum for 5x7 b&w prints. Captions and identification of subjects required. Buys one-time rights.
Columns/Departments: Dennis Hill, managing editor. Guest Spot: Guest opinion page, preferably about 700-850 words, about issues dealing with agriculture, rural social issues and the rural electric program. Buys 12 mss/year. Length: 700-1,000 words. Pays $35-75.

NEW ENGLAND FARMER, NEF Publishing Co., Box 391, St. Johnsbury VT 05819. (802)748-8908. Editor: Dan Hurley. Managing Editor: Thomas Gilson. Monthly tabloid covering New England agriculture for farmers. Circ. 13,052. Pays on publication. Byline given. Buys all rights and makes-work-for-hire assignments. Submit seasonal/holiday material 2 months in advance. Previously published submissions OK. SASE. Reports in 3 months. Free sample copy.
Nonfiction: How-to, interview/profile, opinion and technical. No romantic views of farming. "We use on-the-farm interviews with good b&w photos that combine technical information with human interest. No poetics!" Buys 150 mss/year. Send complete ms. Pays $40-100.

Photos: Send photos with ms. Payment for photos is included in payment for articles. Reviews b&w contact sheet and 8x10 b&w prints.

Tips: "Good, accurate stories needing minimal editing, with art, of interest to commercial farmers in New England are welcome."

THE OHIO FARMER, 1350 W. 5th Ave., Columbus OH 43212. (614)486-9637. Editor: Andrew Stevens. For Ohio farmers and their families. Biweekly magazine; 50 pages. Circ. 103,000. Usually buys all rights. Buys 5-10 mss/year. Pays on publication. Will consider photocopied submissions. Reports in 2 weeks. Submit complete ms. SASE.Sample copy $1; free writer's guidelines.

Nonfiction: Technical and on-the-farm stories. Buys informational, how-to, and personal experience. Length: 600-700 words. Pays $15.

Photos: Photos purchased with ms with no additional payment, or without ms. Pays $5-25 for b&w; $35-100 for color. Size: 4x5 for b&w glossies; transparencies or 8x10 prints for color.

Tips: "We are now doing more staff-written stories. We buy very little freelance material."

RURAL KENTUCKIAN, Box 32170, Louisville KY 40232. (502)451-2430. Editor: Gary W. Luhr. 50% freelance written. Monthly feature magazine primarily for Kentucky residents. Circulation: 270,000. Pays on acceptance. Publishes ms an average of 8 months after acceptance. Byline given. Not copyrighted. Buys first rights for Kentucky. Submit seasonal/holiday material at least 4 months in advance. Will consider photocopied, previously published and simultaneous submissions if previously published and simultaneous submission is outside Kentucky. Computer printout submissions acceptable; prefers letter-quality to dot-matrix. SASE. Reports in 2 weeks. Free sample copy.

Nonfiction: Prefers Kentucky-related profiles (people, places or events), history, biography, recreation, travel, lesiure or lifestyle articles or book excerpts; articles on contemporary subjects of general public interest and general consumer-related features including service pieces. Publishes some humorous and first person articles of exceptional quality and opinion pieces from qualified authorities. No general nostalgia. Buys 24-36 mss/yr. Query or send complete ms. Length: 800-2000 words. Pays $50-$250.

Photos: State availability of photos. Reviews color slide transparencies and b&w prints. Identification of subjects required. Payment included in payment for ms. Pays extra if photo used on cover.

Tips: "The quality of writing and reporting (factual, objective, thorough) is considered in setting payment price. We prefer well-documented pieces filled with quotes and anecdotes. Avoid boosterism. Writers need not confine themselves to subjects suited only to a rural audience but should avoid subjects of a strictly metropolitan nature. Despite its name, *Rural Kentuckian* is not a farm publication."

‡WALLACES FARMER, Suite 501, 1501 42nd Street, W. Des Moines IA 50265. (515)224-6000. Editor: Monte N. Sesker. 4% freelance written. Semimonthly magazine for Iowa farmers and their families. Buys Midwest states rights (Nebraska, Minnesota, Wisconsin, Illinois, Missouri, South Dakota and Iowa). Pays on acceptance. Publishes ms an average of 2 weeeks after acceptance. Computer printout submissions acceptable; prefers letter-quality to dot-matrix. Reports in 2 weeks. SASE.

Nonfiction: Occasional short feature articles about Iowa farming accompanied by photos. Buys 10 unsolicited mss/year. Query. Length: 500-1,000 words. Pays about 4-5¢/word.

Photos: Photos purchased with or without mss. Should be taken on Iowa farms. Pays $7-15 for 5x7 b&w; $50-100 for 4x5, 2¼x2¼ color transparencies. See recent issue covers for examples.

Tips: "We are moving toward more staff-produced articles."

WYOMING RURAL ELECTRIC NEWS, 340 West B St., Casper WY 82601. (307)234-6152. Editor: Gale Eisenhauer. 10% freelance written. For audience of primarily farmers and ranchers. Monthly magazine; 16 pages. Circ. 35,000. Not copyrighted. Byline given. Buys 12-15 mss/year. Pays on publication. Publishes ms an average of 2 months after acceptance. Buys first rights. Will consider photocopied and simultaneous submissions. Submit seasonal material 2 months in advance. Computer printout submissions acceptable. Reports in 3-4 weeks. SASE. Free sample copy.

Nonfiction and Fiction: Wants energy-related material, "people" features, historical pieces about Wyoming and the West, and things of interest to Wyoming's rural people. Buys informational, humor, historical, nostalgia and photo mss. Submit complete ms. Length for nonfiction and fiction: 1,200-1,500 words. Pays $10-25. Buys some experimental, western, humorous and historical fiction. Pays $10-25.

Photos: Photos purchased with accompanying ms with no additional payment, or purchased without ms. Captions required. Pays $10 for cover photos. B&w preferred.

Tips: "Study an issue or two of the magazine to become familiar with our focus and the type of freelance material we're using. Submit entire manuscript. Don't submit a regionally set story from some other part of the country and merely change the place names to Wyoming. Photos and illustrations (if appropriate) are always welcomed."

Livestock

Farmers who raise cattle, sheep or hogs for meat, wool or hides are the audience for these journals. Publications for farmers who raise other animals are listed in the Miscellaneous category; many magazines in the General Interest Farming and Rural Life classification buy material on raising livestock. Magazines for dairy farmers are included under Dairy Farming. Publications dealing with raising horses, pets or other pleasure animals are found under Animal in the Consumer Publications section.

BEEF, The Webb Co., 1999 Shepard Rd., St. Paul MN 55116. (612)690-7374. Editor-in-Chief: Paul D. Andre. Senior Managing Editor: Warren Kester. Managing Editor: William Gnatzig. Monthly magazine. For readers who have the same basic interest—making a living feeding cattle or running a cow herd. Circ. 120,000. Pays on acceptance. Buys one-time rights. Byline given. Phone queries OK. Submit seasonal material 3 months in advance. Computer printout submissions acceptable. SASE. Reports in 2 months. Free sample copy and writer's guidelines.
Nonfiction: How-to and informational articles on doing a better job of producing feeding cattle, market building, managing and animal health practices. Material must deal with cattle beef only. Buys 8-10 mss/year. Query. Length: 500-2,000 words. Pays $25-300.
Photos: B&w glossies (8x10) and color transparencies (35mm or 2¼x2¼) purchased with or without mss. Captions required. Query or send contact sheet or transparencies. Pays $10-50 for b&w; $25-100 for color. Model release required.
Tips: "Be completely knowledgeable about cattle feeding and cowherd operations. Know what makes a story. We want specifics, not a general roundup of an operation. Pick one angle and develop it fully."

BLACKS UNLIMITED INC., Box 578, Webster City IA 50595. Editor: Greg Garwood. Monthly magazine published for North American cattlemen interested in Angus cattle or Angus cross cattle such as Brangus and Chiangus. The publication reaches purebred breeders as well as commercial cattlemen. Circ. 12,000. Pays on publication. Rights negotiable. Phone queries OK. Submit seasonal material 2 months in advance. Simultaneous, photocopied and previously published submissions OK. Reports in 2 weeks. Free sample copy and writer's guidelines.
Nonfiction: Expose, general interest, how-to, interview, opinion, profile, travel, new product, photo feature and research in breeding cattle. Buys 4 mss/issue. Query. Length: 2,000-2,500 words. Pays $25-500.
Photos: State availability of photos. Reviews b&w contact sheets. Payment negotiable.

‡THE CATTLEMAN MAGAZINE, Texas & Southwestern Cattle Raisers Association, 1301 W. 7th St., Ft. Worth TX 76102. (817)332-7155. Senior Editor: Larry M. Marshall. Editor: Dale Segraves. Managing Editor: Don C. King. Emphasizes beef cattle production and feeding. "Readership consists of commercial cattlemen, purebred seedstock producers, cattle feeders and horsemen in the Southwest." Monthly magazine; 170 pages. Circ. 22,500. Pays on acceptance. Byline given. Buys all rights. SASE. Reports in 3 weeks. Sample copy $1.50; writer's guidelines for business-size SAE and 1 first class stamp.
Nonfiction: Need informative, entertaining feature articles on specific commercial ranch operations, cattle breeding and feeding, range and pasture management, profit tips, and university research on beef industry. "We feature various beef cattle breeds most months." Will take a few historical western-lore pieces. Must be well-documented. No first-person narratives or fiction or articles pertaining to areas outside the Southwest or outside beef cattle ranching. Buys 24 mss/year. Query. Length 1,500-2,000 words. Pays $75-200.
Photos: Photos purchased with or without accompanying ms. State availability of photos with query or ms. Pays $15-25 for 5x7 b&w glossies; $100 for color transparencies used as cover. Total purchase price for ms includes payment for photos. Captions, model release, and identification of subjects required.
Fillers: Cartoons.
Tips: "Submit an article dealing with ranching in the Southwest. Too many writers submit stories out of our general readership area. Economics may force staff writers to produce more articles, leaving little room for unsoliticed articles."

‡LIMOUSIN WORLD, Limousin World Inc., 6408 S. College Ave., Fort Collins CO 80525. Editor: June A. Runnion. Managing Editor: Louise Kello. A monthly magazine on the Limousin breed of beef cattle for people who breed and raise them. Estab. 1983. Circ. 13,000. Pays on acceptance. Byline given. Buys negotiable rights. Submit seasonal/holiday material 2 months in advance. Simultaneous queries, and photocopied and previously published submissions OK. Computer printout submissions acceptable. SASE. Reports in 2 weeks. Free sample copy and writer's guidelines.

Nonfiction: How-to (beef herd management equipment); interview/profile (interesting Limousin breeders); new product (limited); and travel (Limousin oriented). "Write interesting, informative, entertaining articles on farm and ranch operations where Limousin breeding has an influence. Management, feeding, breeding, profit producing methods, university research and interesting people are all good topics. Queries should be made on subject for herd features before doing. Short human interest articles on well-known popular personalities who are also breeding Limousin are used." Special issue on Herd Reference. No inflammatory or controversial articles. Query. Length: open. Pays $25-200.

Photos: Send photos with query or ms. Pays $5-25 for 5x7 and 8x10 b&w prints; $25-100 for 5x7 and 8x10 color prints. Captions required. Buys first-time rights.

Tips: "Our readers are in the cattle breeding and raising business for a living so writing should be directed to an informed, mature audience."

POLLED HEREFORD WORLD, 4700 E. 63rd St., Kansas City MO 64130. (816)333-7731. Editor: Ed Bible. For "breeders of polled Hereford cattle—about 80% registered breeders, 5% commercial cattle breeders; remainder are agribusinessmen in related fields." Monthly. Circ. 15,000. Not copyrighted. Buys "no unsolicited mss at present." Pays on publication. Photocopied submissions OK. Computer printout submissions acceptable; prefers letter-quality to dot-matrix. Submit seasonal material "as early as possible: 2 months preferred." Reports in 1 month. Query first for reports of events and activities. Query first or submit complete ms for features. SASE. Free sample copy.

Nonfiction: "Features on registered or commercial polled Hereford breeders. Some on related agricultural subjects (pastures, fences, feeds, buildings, etc.). Mostly technical in nature; some human interest. Our readers make their living with cattle, so write for an informed, mature audience." Buys informational articles, how-to's, personal experience articles, interviews, profiles, historical and think pieces, nostalgia, photo features, coverage of successful business operations, articles on merchandising techniques, and technical articles. Length: "varies with subject and content of feature." Pays about 5¢/word ("usually about 50¢/column inch, but can vary with the value of material").

Photos: Purchased with mss, sometimes purchased without mss, or on assignment; captions required. "Only good quality b&w glossies accepted; any size. Good color prints or transparencies." Pays $2 for b&w, $2-25 for color. Pays $25 for color covers.

‡THE RECORD STOCKMAN, 102 Livestock Exchange Bldg., Denver CO 80216. (303)296-1073. Editor: T.J. Gilles. 10% freelance written. A weekly newspaper covering business news and trends in the beef cattle industry and related agriculture, emphasizing Western ranching and cattle feeding. Readers are purebreed and commercial cattlemen and feeders and other in fields related to the cattle and sheep industries. Circ. 15,000. Pays on publication. Publishes ms an average of 2 weeks after acceptance. Byline given. Offers payment of expenses as kill fee. Buys first rights only. Submit seasonal/holiday material 2 months in advance. Simultaneous queries OK. Computer printout submissions acceptable; prefers letter-quality to dot-matrix. SASE. Reports in 1 week on queries; 2 weeks on mss. Free sample copy; writer's guidelines for SAE with 20¢ postage.

Nonfiction: Expose (query); historical/nostalgic (particular old-time ranch or ranching district); humor/personal experience (related to cattle business); interview/profile (leaders with outstanding viewpoints on industry); opinion (informed conclusions about meat or ranching industries); photo feature; and technical/how-to (successful adaptations in ranching or feeding). "Rather than the soft feature about some ranch or valley, we're looking for articles and features which help describe the past and present while looking into the future. The 'megatrends' in the cattle business and in agriculture are the prime articles we're seeking." Special issues include Annual Magazine (Dec.); Cattle Feeders' Annual (July); and Feeder Cattle Tabloid (Aug.). No "broadbrush or general approach to any story. We like to deal in specifics." Buys 75-100 mss/year. Query or send complete ms. Length: 400-3,000 words. Pays $25-150 plus expenses.

Photos: Prefers livestock industry in action or livestock amongst scenery. State availability of photos or send photos with query or ms. Pays $10-30 for b&w prints; $30-75 for color prints; $30-75 for 35mm color slides. Captions and identification of subjects required. Buys one-time rights.

Tips: "Many have broken in by receiving assignments to cover one event or handle a feature in their area. We also could use some ideas about new trends in a freelancer's area that could be a hard news or feature topic. We are particularly in need of stringers in Nebraska, Wyoming and Kansas. Someone who can fill our needs in these areas could have stories in the *Record Stockman* on a regular basis."

SHEEP! MAGAZINE, Rt. 1, Box 78, Helenville WI 53137. (414)674-3029. Editor: Doris Thompson. 60% freelance written. Monthly magazine. "We're looking for clear, concise, useful information for sheep raisers who have a few sheep to a 1,000 ewe flock." Circ. 8,500. Pays on publication. Publishes ms an average of 1 month after acceptance. Byline given. Offers $30 kill fee. Buys first rights or makes work-for-hire assignments. Submit seasonal/holiday material 3 months in advance. Computer printout submissions acceptable. SASE. Reports in 1 month. Sample copy for 9x12 SAE with postage.

Nonfiction: Book excerpts; information (on personalities and/or political, legal or environmental issues affecting the sheep industry); how-to (on innovative lamb and wool marketing and promotion techniques, effi-

cient record-keeping systems or specific aspects of health and husbandry). "Health and husbandry articles should be written by someone with extensive experience or appropriate credentials—i.e., a veterinarian or animal scientist."); profiles (on experienced sheep producers who detail the economics and management of their operation); features (on small businesses that promote wool products and stories about local and regional sheep producer's groups and their activities); new products (of value to sheep producers; should be written by someone who has used them); and technical (on genetics, health and nutrition). First person narratives. Buys 80 mss/year. Query with clips of published work or send complete ms. Length: 750-2,500 words. Pays $35-115.
Photos: "Color—vertical compositions of sheep and/or people—for our cover. Use only b&w inside magazine. B&w, 35mm photos or other visuals improve your chances of a sale." Pays $50 maximum for 35mm color or transparencies; $5-30 for 5x7 b&w prints. Identification of subjects required. Buys all rights.
Tips: "Send us your best words and photos!"

SIMMENTAL SHIELD, Box 511, Lindsborg KS 67456. Publisher: Chester Peterson Jr. Associate Publisher/Editor: Jim Cotton. 5% freelance written. Official publication of American Simmental Association. Readers are purebred cattle breeders and/or commercial cattlemen. Monthly; 150 pages. 5% freelance written. Circ. 7,000. Buys all rights. Pays on publication. Publishes ms an average of 3 months after acceptance. Computer printout submissions acceptable. January is AI issue; July is herd sire issue; December is brood cow issue. Submit material 3-4 months in advance. Reports in 1 month. Query first or submit complete ms. SASE. Will send free sample copy to writer on request.
Nonfiction and Fillers: Farmer experience and management articles with emphasis on ideas used and successful management ideas based on cattleman who owns Simmental. Research: new twist to old ideas or application of new techniques to the Simmental or cattle business. Wants articles that detail to reader how to make or save money or pare labor needs. Buys informational, how-to, personal experience, interview, profile, humor and think articles. Rates vary.
Photos: Photos purchased with accompanying ms with no additional payment. Interest in cover photos; accepts 35mm if sharp, well exposed.
Tips: "Articles must involve Simmental and/or beef breeding cattle. Be conversant with our lingo and community."

Miscellaneous

AMERICAN BEE JOURNAL, Dadant and Sons, Inc., 51 S. 2nd St., Hamilton IL 62341. (217)847-3324. Editor: Joe Graham. Monthly magazine about beekeeping for hobbyist beekeepers, commercial beekeepers and researchers. Circ. 20,000. Average issue includes 8-10 nonscientific articles and 1-2 scientific articles by researchers. Pays on publication. Byline given. Buys all rights. Submit seasonal material 2 months in advance. Previously published submissions OK, if so indicated. SASE. Reports in 2 weeks. Free sample copy.
Nonfiction: General interest (articles that deal with beekeeping management; honey packing and handling; bee diseases; other products of the hive such as royal jelly, pollen and beeswax; pesticide hazards to honeybees; and occasional articles on beekeeping as a business). No general information about beekeeping. Buys 20-40 unsolicited mss/year. Send complete ms. Length: 1,200-1,500 words. Pays 2½¢/word minimum.
Photos: Send photos with ms. Pays $5 minimum for 5x7 b&w glossy prints. Captions and model release required.
Fillers: Newsbreaks. Buys 1-2 mss/issue. Pays 2½¢/word minimum.

‡**CANADA POULTRYMAN, Includes L'Aviculteur Canadien**, Farm Papers Ltd., 605 Royal Ave., New Westminster, British Columbia V3M 1J4 Canada. (604)526-8525. Editor: Anthony Greaves. A monthly magazine covering the egg/chicken/turkey production industry for commercial size producers in Canada plus the majority of the government departments and service industries. Circ. 11,500. Pays on publication. Byline given. Submit seasonal/holiday material 2 months in advance. Photocopied and previously published submissions (if mentioned nonexclusive) OK. Computer printout submissions acceptable. Submissions returned only if requested.
Nonfiction: General interest (poultry slant); historical/nostalgic (poultry); humor (agricultural slant); interview/profile (only after specific personality is assigned okayed); technical (applicable to poultry); and poultry in other countries. Special issue Who's Who of Canada's poultry industry (June) includes listings of companies and organizations. "We need profiles of provincial poultry people, but only after projects are specifically assigned." Buys 70 mss/year. Send complete ms or send proposal on specific project. Length: 1,500 words maximum. Pays $100/30 column inches.
Photos: Send photos with query or ms. Pays $4 for 3x5 b&w prints; $75 if usable for cover. Captions and identification of subjects required. Buys one-time rights.
Poetry: Satyrical—lampooning poultry industry participants, particularly government. Buys 3 poems/year. Submit maximum 1 poem. Length: 4 column inches. Pays $25 maximum.

GLEANINGS IN BEE CULTURE, Box 706, Medina OH 44258. Editor: Lawrence R. Goltz. For beekeepers. Monthly. Buys first North American serial rights. Pays on publication. Writer's guidelines available upon request/SASE. Reports in 15-90 days. SASE.
Nonfiction: Interested in articles giving new ideas on managing bees. Also uses success stories about commercial beekeepers. No "how I began beekeeping" articles. No highly advanced, technical and scientific abstracts or impractical advice. Length: 3,000 words maximum. "We'll be changing format to allow for approximately 35% more copy space for articles." Pays $23/published page.
Photos: Sharp b&w photos pertaining to honeybees purchased with mss. Can be any size, prints or enlargements, but 4x5 or larger preferred. Pays $3-5/picture.
Tips: "Do an interview story on commercial beekeepers who are cooperative enough to furnish accurate, factual information on their operations."

THE SUGAR PRODUCER, Harris Publishing, Inc., 520 Park, Box 981, Idaho Falls ID 83402. (208)522-5187. Editor: Steve Janes. 25% freelance written. Bimonthly magazine covering the growing, storage, use and by-products of the sugar beet. Circ. 19,000. Pays on publication. Publishes ms an average of 3 months after acceptance. Buys one-time rights. Byline given. Phone queries OK. Photocopied and previously published submissions OK. Computer printout submissions acceptable. SASE. Reports in 1 month. Free sample copy and writer's guidelines.
Nonfiction: "This is a trade magazine, not a farm magazine. It deals with the business of growing sugar beets, and the related industry. All articles must tell the grower how he can do his job better, or at least be of interest to him, such as historical, because he is vitally interested in the process of growing sugar beets, and the industries related to this." Expose (pertaining to the sugar industry or the beet grower); how-to (all aspects of growing, storing and marketing the sugar beet); interview; profile; personal experience; and technical (material source must accompany story—research and data must be from an accepted research institution). Query or send complete ms. Length: 750-2,000 words. Pays 3¢/word.
Photos: Purchased with mss. Captions required. Pays $5 for any convenient size b&w; $10 for color print or transparency; $25 for color shot used on cover. Model release required.

Finance

These magazines deal with banking, investment, and financial management. Publications that use similar material but have a less technical slant are listed in Consumer Publications under Business and Finance.

ABA BANKING JOURNAL, 345 Hudson St., New York NY 10014. (212)620-7200. Editor: Lyman B. Coddington. Managing Editor: William Streeter. Executive Editor: Joe W. Kizzia. 20% freelance written. Monthly magazine; 150 pages. Circ. 41,000. Pays on publication. Query. Photocopied submissions OK. SASE. Reports in 4-6 weeks. Sample copy sent to writer "only if a manuscript is commissioned."
Nonfiction: How-to, new product and articles dealing with banking. Buys 24-36 mss/year. Query. Average length: 2,000 words. Pays $100/magazine page, including headlines, photos and artwork.
Photos: State availability of photos with query. Uses 8x10 b&w glossy prints and 35mm color transparencies. Buys one-time rights.

AMERICAN BANKER, 1 State St. Plaza, New York NY 10004. (212)943-0400. Editor: William Zimmerman. Managing Editor: Robert Casey. Daily tabloid covering banking and finance for top management of banks, savings banks, savings and loans and other financial service institutions. Circ. 23,000. Pays on publication. Byline given. Buys all rights. Simultaneous and previously published ("depending on where published") submissions OK. Reports in 1 month.
Nonfiction: Patricia Stundza, features editor. Book excerpts and technical (relating to banking/finance). No "nonbanking or nonbusiness-oriented articles—must be specific." Query. Length: 1,500-3,000 words. Pays $75-200.
Photos: State availability of photos. Pays $100 minimum for 8x10 b&w prints. Captions and identification of subjects required. Buys one-time rights.

BANK DIRECTOR & STOCKHOLDER, Box 6847, Orlando FL 32853. Executive Editor: William P. Seaparke. 100% freelance written. Semiannual journal; 24 pages. Circ. 8,000. Pays on publication. Publishes ms an average of 3 months after acceptance. Buys all rights with loan back agreements sometimes. Pays 50% kill fee. Byline given. Electronic submissions OK if compatible with TRS 80 Model II. Computer printout submissions acceptable. SASE. Reports in 3 months.

Nonfiction: Case studies of financial problems which would be of interest to corporate directors and shareholders, particularly banking institutions or financial corporations. Recent article example: "Synergism: The Bank and the Bank Director" (Spring, 1984). Buys a few unsolicited mss/year. Query. Length: 500-3,000 words. Payment varies.

Photos: State availability of photos with query. Pays $10-100 for 5x7 b&w glossy prints; $20-200 for 35mm color transparencies. Captions and model release required. Buys all rights.

Columns/Departments: Economy, interview and energy. Query. Length: 600-3,000 words. Pays $20 minimum. Open to suggestions for new columns/departments.

BANK SYSTEMS & EQUIPMENT, 1515 Broadway, New York NY 10036. Editor: Joan Prevete Hyman. For bank, savings and loan association, mutual savings banks and credit union operations executives. Monthly. Circ. 22,000. Buys all rights. Byline given. Pays on publication. Query for style sheet and specific article assignment. Mss should be triple-spaced on one side of paper only with wide margin at left-hand side of the page. SASE.

Nonfiction: Third person case history articles and interviews as well as material related to systems, operations and automation. Charts, systems diagrams, artist's renderings of new buildings, etc. may accompany ms and must be suitable for reproduction. Prefers one color only. Length: open. Pays $100 for each published page.

Photos: 5x7 or 8x10 single-weight glossies. Candids of persons interviewed, views of bank, bank's data center, etc. Captions required. "We do not pay extra for photos."

Tips: "Writers can break in by covering telecommunications in banks and thrifts."

BENEFITS CANADA, Pension Fund Investment and Employee Benefit Management, Maclean Hunter Ltd., 777 Bay St., Toronto, Ontario M5W 1A7 Canada. (416)596-5958. Editor: Robin Schiele. Magazine published 10 times/year covering money management, investment management, pension fund administration and employee benefits industry for experts in the field. "However, there is a degree of overlap between the investment and benefits sides. Knowledge of each side should be assumed in the readership." Circ. 13,000. Pays on acceptance. Byline given. Buys first North American serial rights. Reports in 2 weeks on queries; 1 month on mss. Free sample copy.

Nonfiction: Interview/profile and opinion (of people in pension fund, investments or employee benefits); and technical (investment or employee benefit administration). Query with clips of published work or send complete ms. Length: 1,000-2,200 words. Pays $125-400.

BIOTECHNOLOGY INVESTMENT OPPORTUNITIES, High Tech Publishing Co., Box 266, Brattleboro VT 05301. (802)869-2833. Editor: Philip T. DiPeri. 10% freelance written. Monthly newsletter covering investment opportunities in high technology aimed at "sophisticated, well-informed investors seeking calculated-risk investments. Identifies and analyzes emerging investment opportunities in genetic engineering; follows trends and conditions having significant impact on the development and commercial application of leading-edge biotechnology research. Emphasis is on new enterprise formation, capital formation, emerging markets and applications." Circ. 1,000. Pays on publication. Byline given. Buys all rights. Simultaneous queries and simultaneous, photocopied and previously published submissions OK. Computer printout submissions acceptable. SASE. Reports in 2 weeks. Publishes ms an average of 1 month after acceptance. Sample copy for business-size SAE and 1 first class stamp.

Nonfiction: Interview/profile (high technology, capital providers, firms, idea/research/patent generators); new product (potential commercialization of research concepts and ideas); technical (new patents with commercial possibilities, related instrumentation); and current research efforts in various high technology areas. Special issues include bimonthly supplements providing in-depth reporting of important aspect of investing in genetic engineering and high technology. Buys 150 mss/year. Send complete ms. Length: 25-500 words. Pays 10-25¢/word.

Columns/Departments: New patents (in genetic engineering with commercial possibilities); new applications (of biotech processes and products); and people (briefs on the principal players in biotechnology). Buys 100 mss/year. Send complete ms. Length: 25-500 words. Pays 10-25¢/word.

Fillers: Newsbreaks. Buys 10/year. Length: 25-500 words. Pays 10-25¢/word.

Tips: "Submit completed manuscript or, if extensive investigation or research is needed, query first. We're looking for newsletter-style writing with a high proportion of nouns and verbs over adjectives and adverbs."

CANADIAN BANKER, The Canadian Bankers' Association, Box 282, T-D Centre, Toronto, Ontario M5K 1K2 Canada. Editor: Brian O'Brien. 90% freelance written. Emphasizes banking in Canada. Bimonthly magazine. Circ. 45,000. Buys first North American serial rights. Byline given. SAE and IRCs. Reports in 1 month.

Nonfiction: Informational articles on international banking and economics; interviews, nostalgic and opinion articles; and book reviews. Query. Length: 750-2,000 words. Pays $100-300. "Freelancer should be an authority on the subject. Most contributors are bankers, economists and university professors."

FLORIDA BANKER, Box 6847, Orlando FL 32853. Executive Editor: William P. Seaparke. 60% freelance written. Monthly magazine; 52 pages. Circ. 7,300. Pays on publication. Publishes ms an average of 3 months after acceptance. Buys all rights; loans usage back to writers on agreement. Pays 50% kill fee. Byline given. Electronic submissions OK if compatible with TRS 80, Model II. Computer printout submissions acceptable. SASE. Reports in 3 months. Sample copy and writer's guidelines $2 prepaid.

Nonfiction: General interest (banking-oriented); historical (on banking); how-to (anything in banking industry or trade); inspirational (occasionally, must deal with banking); interview; nostalgia; photo feature; profile; technical; and travel. Recent article example: "Priorities in Trust" (February 1984). Buys 12-25 unsolicited mss/year. Query. Length: 500-3,000 words. Pays $50-200.

Photos: State availability of photos with query. Pays $10-100 for 5x7 b&w glossy prints; $20-200 for 35mm color transparencies. Captions and model release required. Buys all rights. Loans usage back to photographers on agreement.

Columns/Departments: Economy, interviews and technology in banking. Query. Length: 600-3,000 words. Pays $25 minimum. Open to suggestions for new columns/departments.

FUTURES MAGAZINE, (formerly *Commodities Magazine*), 219 Parkade, Cedar Falls IA 50613. (319)677-6341. Publisher: Merrill Oster. Editor-in-Chief: Darrell Jobman. For private, individual traders, brokers, exchange members, agribusinessmen, bankers, anyone with an interest in futures or commodity options. Monthly magazine; 124-140 pages. Circ. 50,000. Buys all rights. Byline given. Pays on publication. Photocopied submissions OK. Computer printout submissions acceptable. Reports in 1 month. Query or submit complete ms. SASE. Free sample copy.

Nonfiction: Articles analyzing specific commodity futures and options trading strategies; fundamental and technical analysis of individual commodities and markets; interviews, book reviews, "success" stories; and news items. Material on new legislation affecting commodities, trading, any new trading strategy ("results must be able to be substantiated"); and personalities. No "homespun" rules for trading and simplistic approaches to the commodities market. Treatment is always in-depth and broad. Informational, how-to, interview, profile, technical. "Articles should be written for a reader who has traded commodities for one year or more; should not talk down or hypothesize. Relatively complex material is acceptable." No get-rich-quick gimmicks, astrology articles or general, broad topics. Buys 30-40 mss/year. Length: No maximum or minimum; 1,500 words optimum. Pays $50-1,000, depending upon author's research and writing quality.

Tips: "Writers must have a solid understanding and appreciation for futures or options trading. We will have more financial and stock index features as well as new options contracts that will require special knowledge and experience."

ILLINOIS BANKER, Illinois Bankers Association, Suite 1100, 205 W. Randolph, Chicago IL 60606. (312)984-1500. Editor: Cindy L. Altman. Editorial Assistant: Anetta Gauthier. 1% freelance written. Monthly magazine about banking for top decision makers and executives, bank officers, title and insurance company executives, elected officials and individual subscribers interested in banking products and services. Circ. 3,000. Pays on publication. Byline given. Buys first rights. Phone queries OK. Submit material by the 10th of the month prior to publication. Simultaneous submissions OK. Computer printout submissions acceptable; no dot-matrix. Reports in 2 weeks. Free sample copy and writer's guidelines.

Nonfiction: Interview (ranking government and banking leaders); personal experience (along the lines of customer relations); and technical (specific areas of banking). "The purpose of the publication is to educate, inform and guide its readers in the activities and projects of their banks and those of their fellow bankers, while keeping them aware of any developments within the banking industry and other related fields. Any clear, fresh approach geared to a specific area of banking, such as agricultural bank management, credit, lending, marketing and trust is what we want." Buys 4-5 unsolicited mss/year. Send complete ms. Length: 825-3,000 words. Pays $50-100.

Fillers: Jokes, anecdotes and financial puzzles. Buys 8 mss/year. Pays $15-50.

Tips: "Cutbacks in purchasing have made us more selective."

‡INDEPENDENT BANKER, Independent Bankers Association of America, Box 267, Sauk Centre MN 56378. (612)352-6546. Editor: Norman Douglas. 10% freelance written. Monthly magazine for the administrators of small, independent banks. Circ. 10,000. Pays on acceptance. Publishes ms an average of 3 months after acceptance. Byline given. Not copyrighted. Buys all rights. Computer printout submissions acceptable. Reports in 1 week. Free sample copy and writer's guidelines.

Nonfiction: How-to (banking practices and procedures); interview/profile (popular small bankers); technical (bank accounting, automation); and banking trends. "Factual case histories, banker profiles or research pieces of value to bankers in the daily administration of their banks." No material that ridicules banking and finance or puff pieces on products and services. Buys 12 mss/year. Query. Length: 2,000-2,500 words. Pays $300 maximum.

Tips: "The most rewarding aspect of working with freelance writers is that they are a valued extension of coverage for this one-man staff."

MONEYFAX, National Association of Financial Consultants, Ivy Publications, Box 1, Ischua NY 14746. (716)557-8900. Editor: Jeffrey Brisky. 5% freelance written. Monthly newsletter covering financing, loans, real estate, leasing and mortgages. Byline given. Buys all rights. Submit seasonal/holiday material 2 months in advance. Simultaneous queries, and simultaneous and previously published submissions OK. Computer printout submissions acceptable. SASE. Reports in 1 week on queries; 3 weeks on mss. Publishes ms an average of 2 months after acceptance. Sample copy and writer's guidelines free for business-size SAE and 28¢ postage.
Nonfiction: Expose (of loan frauds); how-to (get loans); and humor (money jokes). "No nonfinancial material." Query. Length: 300-1,000 words. Pay is negotiable.
Columns/Departments: "We're interested in anything regarding financing, real estate, leasing or loan brokerage." Query. Length: 300-1,000 words. Pay is negotiable.
Fillers: Clippings, news for immediate release, jokes and newsbreaks (anything about financing and money brokerage). Length: open. Pay is negotiable.

MOUNTAIN STATES BANKER, Mountain States Publishing Co., Suite 900, 912 Baltimore, Kansas City MO 64105. (816)421-7941. Editor: Sharon Smith. Monthly magazine for bankers and others interested in financial services. Features new techniques and developments for improving banking performance. Circ. 2,000. Pays on publication. Byline given. Buys all rights. Submit seasonal/holiday material 4 months in advance. Simultaneous queries and simultaneous, photocopied and previously published submissions OK. SASE. Reports in 2 weeks on queries; 1 month on mss. Sample copy $3; writer's guidelines for business-size SAE and 1 first class stamp.
Nonfiction: How-to, interview/profile, opinion and technical. Buys 10-20 mss/year. Send complete ms. Length: 500-2,500 words. Pays $50-200.
Photos: State availability of photos. Pays negotiable rate for b&w contact sheets and prints. Captions and identification of subjects required. Buys one-time rights.
Columns/Departments: "All columns and departments are written in-house."

THE NABW JOURNAL, Suite 1400, 500 N. Michigan Ave., Chicago IL 60611. (312)661-1700. Contact: Editor. Bimonthly magazine for members of the National Association of Bank Women. Circ. 30,000. Byline given. Buys all rights. Submit seasonal material 3 months in advance. Simultaneous queries and photocopied submissions OK. SASE. Reports in approximately 1 month. Sample copy $2.
Nonfiction: "We are looking for articles in the general areas of banking and finance, career advancement, businesswomen's issues and management. Because the financial services industry is in a state of flux at present, articles on how to adapt to and benefit from this fact, both personally and professionally, are particularly apt." Query with resume and clips of published work. Length: 1,000-4,000 words. Pays variable rates. Book reviews on related topics; 750-1,500 words.
Photos: "Photos and other graphic material can make an article more attractive to us." Captions and model release required.

‡**SAVINGS INSTITUTIONS**, US League of Savings Institutions, 111 E. Wacker Dr., Chicago IL 60601. (312)644-3100. Editor: Lee Crumbaugh. A monthly business magazine covering management of savings institutions. Circ. 30,000. Pays on acceptance. Byline given. Buys negotiable rights. Simultaneous queries and photocopied submissions OK. Computer printout submissions acceptable. SASE. Reports in 1 month. Free sample copy.
Nonfiction: How-to (manage or improve operations); new products (application stories at savings institutions); and technical (financial management). No opinion or 'puff' pieces. Buys 1-3 mss/year. Query with or without published clips. Length: 3,000-8,000. Pays $100/published page.
Columns/Departments: Maria Kulczycky, column/department editor. Operations, Marketing, Personnel, and Wholesale Funds. Buys 10 mss/year. Query with or without published clips. Length: 800-3,000 words. Pays $100/published page.
Tips: "Operations and Marketing departments are most open to freelancers."

Fishing

COMMERCIAL FISHERIES NEWS, Box 37, Stonington ME 04681. (207)367-2396. Managing Editor: Robin Alden Peters. 33% freelance written. Emphasizes commercial fisheries. Monthly newspaper with New England wide coverage; 52 pages. Circ. 8,500. Pays on publication. Publishes ms an average of 2 months after acceptance. Byline given. Buys first rights only. Computer printout submissions acceptable. SASE. Reports in 2 weeks. Sample copy $1.25.

Nonfiction: "Material strictly limited to coverage of commercial fishing, technical and general; occasional environment, business, etc. articles as they relate to commercial fishing in New England." Buys 10 unsolicited mss/year. Query. Pays $50-150.

NATIONAL FISHERMAN, Diversified Communications, 21 Elm St., Camden ME 04843. (207)236-4342. Editor-in-Chief: James W. Fullilove. Managing Editor: Linda S. Stanley. 70% freelance written. For amateur and professional boat builders, commercial fishermen, armchair sailors, bureaucrats and politicians. Monthly tabloid; 92 pages. Circ. 58,000. Pays in month of acceptance. Buys first rights only. Byline given. Phone or letter queries advised. Submit seasonal material 3 months in advance. Photocopied submissions OK. Computer printout submissions acceptable if double spaced; prefers letter-quality to dot-matrix. SASE. Reports in 1 month. Publishes ms an average of 2 months after acceptance. Free sample copy and writer's guidelines; mention *Writer's Market* in request.
Nonfiction: Expose, how-to, general interest, humor, historical, inspirational, interview, new product, nostalgia, personal experience, opinion, photo feature, profile and technical, but all must be related to commercial fishing in some way. Especially needs articles on commercial fishing techniques (problems, solutions, large catches, busts); gear development; and marine historical and offbeat articles. No articles about sailboat racing, cruising and sportfishing. Buys approximately 35 unsolicited mss/year. Submit complete ms. Length: 100-3,500 words.
Photos: State availability of photos with ms. "Photos improve chances of being used." Pays $5-15 for 5x7 or 8x10 b&w prints; color cover photo pays $250. Buys one-time rights.
Tips: "We are soliciting historical and human-interest articles in addition to business-related articles."

PACIFIC FISHING, Pacific Fishing Partnership, 1515 NW 51st St., Seattle WA 98107. (206)789-5333. Editors: Ken Talley, Doug McNair. 60% freelance written. Monthly business magazine for commercial fishermen and others in the West Coast commercial fishing industry. *Pacific Fishing* views the fisherman as a small businessman and covers all aspects of the industry, including harvesting, processing and marketing. Circ. 10,000. Pays on publication. Publishes ms an average of 2 months after acceptance. Byline given. Offers negotiable kill fee. Buys one-time rights or makes arrangements with publisher. Queries highly recommended. Computer printout submissions acceptable. Reports in 1 month. Free sample copy and writer's guidelines.
Nonfiction: Interview/profile and technical (usually with a business hook or slant). "Articles must be concerned specifically with *commercial* fishing." Buys 20 mss/year. Query. Length: 1,500-3,000 words. Pays 7-10¢/word.
Tips: "We enjoy finding a writer who understands our editorial needs and satisfies those needs, a writer willing to work with an editor to make the article just right."

Florists, Nurseries, and Landscaping

"Computers will become more of a force in this industry, but so many retailers are still too small to get very involved in computerization," observes one garden magazine editor. In either case, the writer should explore such businesses with an insider's perspective when writing for these publications. Magazines geared to consumers interested in gardening are listed in the Consumer Home and Garden section.

AMERICAN CHRISTMAS TREE JOURNAL, 611 E. Wells St., Milwaukee WI 53202. (414)276-6410. Editors: Phil Jones and Jane A Svinicki. 90% freelance written. Quarterly magazine. Circ. 2,000. Byline given. Pays on publication. Publishes ms an average of 6 months after acceptance. Simultaneous, photocopied and previously published submissions OK. Computer printout submissions acceptable; no dot-matrix. Reports in 1 month. Free sample copy and writer's guidelines.
Nonfiction: How-to; interview; job safety (any farm equipment); vocational techniques; new product (chemicals, equipment, tags, shearing knives and chain saws, etc.); personal experience; profile; and technical (foresters, researchers). Query. Length: 2,000 words minimum. Pays $50.

DESIGN FOR PROFIT, Florafax International, Inc., 4175 S. Memorial Dr., Box 470745, Tulsa OK 74145. (918)622-8415. Editor: Beth Schmidt. Quarterly magazine covering trends in the floral industry. "The publication is designed to be a creative sales tool for retail florists." Circ. 15,000. No byline given. Buys all rights. Submit seasonal/holiday material 4 months in advance. Simultaneous queries, and simultaneous and photocopied submissions OK. SASE. Reports in 2 weeks on queries; 3 months on mss. Free sample copy and writer's guidelines.

Nonfiction: Historical/nostalgic (themes tying into floral arranging); how-to (floral designs—how to carry through themes, innovative ideas); interview/profile (prominent individuals in the profession); new product; personal experience (unique, unusual, outstanding in industry); and photo feature. Features or news/features only. Buys variable number of mss/year. Query with published clips. Length: 300 words maximum. Pays negotiable rates.

Photos: Send photos with query or ms. Pays negotiable rates for 4x5 transparencies and prints. Captions, model release and identification of subjects required. Buys all rights.

Poetry: Avant-garde, free verse, haiku, light verse and traditional. Buys variable number of poems/year. Submit unlimited number of poems. Length: 30 lines maximum. Pays negotiable rates.

FLORIST, Florists' Transworld Delivery Association, 29200 Northwestern Hwy., Box 2227, Southfield MI 48037. (313)355-9300. Editor-in-Chief: William P. Golden. Managing Editor: Bill Gubbins. 5% freelance written. For retail florists, floriculture growers, wholesalers, researchers and teachers. Monthly magazine; 96 pages. Circ. 25,000. Pays on acceptance. Buys one-time rights. Pays 10-25% kill fee. Byline given "unless the story needs a substantial rewrite." Phone queries OK. Submit seasonal/holiday material 3-4 months in advance. Simultaneous, photocopied and previously published submissions OK. Computer printout submissions acceptable. SASE. Reports in 1 month.

Nonfiction: How-to (more profitably run a retail flower shop, grow and maintain better quality flowers, etc.); general interest (to floriculture and retail floristry); and technical (on flower and plant growing, breeding, etc.). Buys 5 unsolicited mss/year. Query with clips of published work. Length: 1,200-3,000 words. Pays 10¢/word.

Photos: "We do not like to run stories without photos." State availability of photos with query. Pays $10-25 for 5x7 b&w photos or color transparencies. Buys one-time rights.

Tips: "Send samples of published work with query. Suggest several ideas in query letter. We're now paying more for freelance material."

FLOWER NEWS, 549 W. Randolph St., Chicago IL 60606. (312)236-8648. Managing Editor: Lauren Oates. For retail, wholesale florists, floral suppliers, supply jobbers and growers. Weekly newspaper; 40 pages. Circ. 14,500. Pays on acceptance. Byline given. Submit seasonal/holiday material at least 2 months in advance. Photocopied and previously published submissions OK. SASE. Reports "immediately." Free sample copy and writer's guidelines.

Nonfiction: How-to articles (increase business, set up a new shop, etc.; anything floral related without being an individual shop story); informational (general articles of interest to industry); and technical (grower stories related to industry, but not individual grower stories). No articles on "protecting your business from crime; how to get past due accounts to pay; attitudes for salespeople." Submit complete ms. Length: 3-5 typed pages. Pays $10.

Photos: "We do not buy individual pictures. They may be enclosed with manuscript at regular manuscript rate (b&w only)."

FLOWERS &, Suite 260, 12233 W. Olympic Blvd., Los Angeles CA 90064. Publisher and Editor-in-Chief: Barbara Cady. 20% freelance written. Published by Teleflora Inc. for members of the floriculture industry. Positioned as "the magazine with a new approach to the floriculture industry." Monthly. Circ. 25,000w. Buys one-time rights in floral trade magazine field. Byline given unless "article is not thorough enough but portions are included in another article." Most articles are staff-written. Pays on acceptance. Publishes ms an average of 2 months after acceptance. Computer printout submissions acceptable; no dot-matrix. SASE. Reports in 3 weeks. Must send query letter with proposed, brief outline first.

Nonfiction: Articles dealing with floral retailing, merchandising of product, sales promotion, management, designing, shop remodeling, display techniques, etc. Also, allied interests such as floral wholesalers, growers, tradespeople, gift markets, etc. Covers general interest stories and news about retail business, finances and taxes. All articles must be thoroughly researched and professionally relevant. Buys 5 unsolicited mss/year. Length: 1,000-3,000 words. Pays approximately 14¢/published word.

Tips: "Queries should be brief and to the point, include author's qualifications and past published experience plus a brief outline detailing the proposed article. We prefer to see no unsolicited manuscripts without prior query."

Market conditions are constantly changing! If this is 1986 or later, buy the newest edition of *Writer's Market* at your favorite bookstore or order directly from Writer's Digest Books.

GARDEN SUPPLY RETAILER, Miller Publishing, Box 67, Minneapolis MN 55440. (612)374-5200. Managing Editor: Kay Melchisedcch Olson. 15% freelance written. Monthly magazine for lawn and garden retailers. Circ. 40,000w. Pays on acceptance in most cases. Buys first rights, and occasionally second (reprint) rights to material originally published elsewhere. Publishes ms an average of 3 months after acceptance. Previously published submissions "in different fields" OK as long as not in overlapping fields such as hardware, nursery growers, etc. Prefers double spaced, typewritten manuscripts. "We will not guarantee reading material submitted in other forms." SASE. Reports in 2 weeks on rejections, acceptance may take longer. Sample copy $2.

Nonfiction: "We aim to provide retailers with management, merchandising, tax planning and computer information. No technical advice on how to care for lawns, plants and lawn mowers. Articles should be of interest to *retailers* of garden supply products. Stories should tell retailers something about the industry that they don't already know; show them how to make more money by better merchandising or management techniques; address a concern or problem directly affecting retailers or the industry." Buys 15-20 mss/year. Send complete ms or rough draft plus clips of previously published work. Length: 800-1,000 words. Pays $150-200.

Photos: Send photos with ms. Reviews color negatives and transparencies, and 5x7 b&w prints. Captions and identification of subjects required.

Tips: Previously published submissions "in different fields" are considered only if references and examples apply specifically to the garden supply industry. "We will not consider manuscripts offered to 'overlapping' publications such as the hardware industry, nursery growers, etc. Query letters outlining an idea should include at least a partial rough draft; lists of titles are uninteresting."

THE LANDSCAPE CONTRACTOR, Official Publication of the Illinois Landscape Contractors Association, Better Business Communicators, 4A East Wilson St., Batavia IL 60510. (312)879-0765. Editor: Bonnie Zaruba. 20% freelance written. Monthly magazine covering landscaping, landscape architecture and horticulture—business articles as they pertain to the landscape contracting profession or allied fields. Circ. 2,000. Pays on publication. Byline given. Buys first and second serial rights to the same material. Submit seasonal/holiday material 4 months in advance. Simultaneous queries, and simultaneous, photocopied and previously published submissions OK. SASE. Reports in 2 weeks on queries; 6 weeks on mss. Publishes ms an average of 3 months after acceptance. Sample copy for 9x12 SAE and 5 first class stamps.

Nonfiction: Expose (government/landscaping); how-to (photos, trade shows); interview/profile (of business/owner in field); new product (or method of doing job); and technical (as related to horticulture/landscaping). "No light, general interest pieces; no 'how the businessman can save time' articles." Buys 10 mss/year. Send complete ms. Length: 1,250-3,750 words. Pays $60-180.

Photos: Send photos with ms. Pays $8-15 for 5x7 and 8x10 b&w prints. Captions and identification of subjects required. Buys one-time rights.

LAWN CARE INDUSTRY, Harcourt Brace Jovanovich, Inc., 7500 Old Oak Blvd., Cleveland OH 44130. (216)243-8100. Editor: Jerry Roche. 10% freelance written. For lawn care businessmen. Monthly tabloid; 40 pages. Circ. 12,000. Pays on acceptance. Publishes ms an average of 3 months after acceptance. Buys all rights. Phone queries OK. Submit seasonal/holiday material 3 months in advance. Simultaneous and photocopied submissions OK. Computer printout submissions acceptable. SASE. Reports in 2 weeks. Free sample copy.

Nonfiction: General interest (articles related to small business operation); how-to (run a lawn care business); interview (with lawn care operator or industry notable); new product (helping to better business practices); and profile (of lawn care businessmen). Buys 2 mss/issue. Query. Length: 500-1,000 words. Pays $50-250.

Photos: State availability of photos with query. Pays $10-100 for 5x7 glossy b&w prints; $50-250 for 35mm color transparencies. Captions required. Buys one-time rights.

WESTERN LANDSCAPING NEWS, Voice of the Landscaping Industry, Hester Communications, Inc., Suite 250, 1700 E. Dyer Rd., Santa Ana CA 92705. (714)549-4834. Editor: Jan Kingaard. Managing Editor: Jack Schember. A monthly magazine plus annual directory in December covering the exterior professional landscaping market for professional landscape architects, designers, contractors, and maintenance owners/managers. Circ. 17,500. Pays on acceptance. Byline given. Buys first North American serial rights and all rights. Submit seasonal/holiday material 3-6 months in advance. Photocopied submissions OK. Computer printout submissions acceptable, no dot-matrix. SASE. Reports in 2 months. Sample copy for $2 and SAE; writer's guidelines for SAE and 1 first class stamp.

Nonfiction: Business tie-ins with state of the economy, computerization, accounting, construction industry; also design, maintenance, and installation how-to's. "Familiarity with the Western landscaping industry is imperative." No general interest, consumer oriented, nonbusiness or nontechnical articles. Query with published clips or send complete ms. Length: 500-2,500 words. Pays $300 maximum.

Photos: Send photos with query or ms. Reviews 5x7 prints. "We can process from negatives." Captions, model release and identification of subjects required. Buys all rights or negotiates rights.

Columns/Departments: Latest news update/profile (500 words maximum); Plant Topics, Turf Topics, Chem-

ical Topics and Event Closeup (300-1,000 words). Query with published clips. Pays negotiable rate.
Fillers: Newsbreaks. Length: 25-300 words. Pays $50 maximum.
Tips: "Areas most open to freelancers are business, legislative, chemical/plant/topics, regulatory fillers, and network information impacting landscaping, in additon to features on successful or problem solving projects. We are always interested in a fresh approach, expertise, and well documented and illustrated articles."

Food Products, Processing, and Service

In this section are journals for food wholesalers, processors, warehouses, caterers, institutional managers, and suppliers of grocery store equipment. Publications for grocery store operators are classified under Groceries. Journals for food vending machine operators are found under Coin-Operated Machines.

‡**FOOD PEOPLE**, Olson, Inc., 6427 Roswell Rd., Atlanta GA 30328. (404)252-0732. Editor: Mark W. Pryor. Monthly tabloid covering the retail food industry. "We write news and 'news features' about food stores, wholesalers and brokers in the Sunbelt and food manufacturers nationwide." Circ. 19,000. Pays on publication. Byline given. Buys all rights. Submit seasonal/holiday material 6 weeks in advance. Photocopied submissions OK. Computer printout submissions acceptable; prefers letter-quality to dot-matrix. SASE. Reports in 1 month. Free sample copy.
Nonfiction: Interview/profile (of major food industry figures); photo feature (of food industry conventions, expos and meetings); and news of store/warehouse openings, ad campaigns, marketing strategies, important new products and services. "Articles should be informative, tone is upbeat. Do not send recipes or how-to shop articles; we cover food as a *business*." Buys 120-180 mss/year. Query or send complete ms. Length: 200-1,000 words. Pays $2/published inch.
Photos: "Photos of people. Photos of displays, or store layouts, etc., that illustrate points made in article are good, too. But stay away from store-front shots." State availability of photos with query or send photos with ms. Pays $10 plus expenses for b&w contact sheets and 5x7 b&w prints; and $30 plus expenses for color transparencies. Captions required. Buys one-time rights.
Columns/Departments: SunBelt News (1-2 paragraph newsbriefs from the South, West, and Pacific West). Send complete ms. Pays $10.
Tips: "Begin with an area news event—store openings, new promotions. Write that as news, then go further to examine the consequences. Talk with decision makers to get 'hows' and 'whys.' Because we are news-oriented, we have short deadlines for a monthly. We look for contributors who work well quickly and who *always* deliver. We understand that some stories just do not 'make,' but we hate excuses."

MEAT PLANT MAGAZINE, 9701 Gravois Ave., St. Louis MO 63123. (314)638-4050. Editor: Tony Nolan. For meat processors, locker plant operators, freezer provisioners, portion control packers, meat dealers and food service (food plan) operators. Monthly. Pays on publication. Reports in 2 weeks. SASE for return of submissions.
Nonfiction and Fillers: Buys feature-length articles and shorter subjects pertinent to the field. Length: 1,000-1,500 words for features. Pays 5¢/word.
Photos: Pays $5 for photos.

PRODUCE NEWS, 2185 Lemoine Ave., Fort Lee NJ 07024. Editor: Melvina Bauer. For commercial growers and shippers, receivers and distributors of fresh fruits and vegetables, including chain store produce buyers and merchandisers. Weekly. Circ. 5,300. Pays on publication. Deadline is Wednesday afternoon before Friday press day. SASE. Free sample copy.
Nonfiction: News stories (about the produce industry.) Buys profiles, spot news, coverage of successful business operations and articles on merchandising techniques. Query. Pays $1/column inch for original material, 40¢/column inch for clippings.
Photos: B&w glossies purchased with ms or caption.

QUICK FROZEN FOODS, Harcourt Brace Jovanovich, 7500 Old Oak Blvd., Cleveland OH 44130. (216)243-8100. Editor: John N. Saulnier. Senior Editor: C. Ross Chamberlain. 10% freelance written. For executives of processing plants, distributors, warehouses, transport companies, retailers and food service operators involved in frozen foods. Monthly magazine; 100 pages. Circ. 25,000. Pays on acceptance. Buys all rights. Pays kill fee up to full amount if reasons for kill are not fault of author. Byline given unless it is work-for-hire or ghostwriting. Submit seasonal/holiday material 3 months in advance of issue date. SASE. Reports in 1 week. Free sample copy; mention *Writer's Market* in request.

Nonfiction: Interview, new product, photo feature, profile and technical. Buys 12 mss/year. Query or submit complete ms. Length: 1,500-3,000 words. Pays 5¢/word. "For special circumstances will offer flat rate for package which may be higher than word rate."

Photos: State availability of photos with query or ms. Pays $5 for 4x5 b&w smooth prints. Captions required. Buys all rights.

QUICK FROZEN FOODS INTERNATIONAL, E.W. Williams Publishing Co., 80 8th Ave., New York NY 10011. (212)989-1101. Editor: Sam Martin. 20% freelance written. Quarterly magazine covering frozen foods outside US—"every phase of frozen food manufacture, retailing, food service, brokerage, transport, warehousing, merchandising, providing it is outside the US, though we will print stories about US firms that sell abroad, but that must be emphasis." Circ. 10,000. Pays on publication. Byline given. Offers kill fee; "if satisfactory, we will pay promised amount. If bungled, half." Buys all rights, but will relinquish any rights requested. Submit seasonal/holiday material 6 months in advance. Photocopied submissions OK ("if not under submission elsewhere"). Computer printout submissions acceptable; prefers letter-quality to dot-matrix. SASE. Sample copy for $1 and SAE.

Nonfiction: Book excerpts; general interest; historical/nostalgic; interview/profile; new product (from overseas); personal experience; photo feature; technical; and travel. No articles peripheral to frozen food industry such as taxes, insurance, government regulation, safety, etc. Buys 20-30 mss/year. Query or send complete ms. Length: 500-4,000 words. Pays 3¢/word or by arrangement. "We will reimburse postage on articles ordered from overseas."

Photos: "We prefer photos with all articles." State availability of photos or send photos with accompanying ms. Pays $7 for 5x7 b&w prints (contact sheet if many shots). Captions and identification of subject required. Buys all rights. "Release on request."

Columns/Departments: News or analysis of frozen foods abroad. Buys 20 columns/year. Query. Length: 500-1,500 words. Pays by arrangement.

Fillers: Newsbreaks. Length: 100-500 words. Pays $5-20.

Tips: "Always query (though we will buy unsolicited manuscripts if they are suitable). A recent freelancer visited Poland before the crackdown and reported on the state of frozen foods in stores—turned out to be a scoop. Same reporter did the same on recent trip to Israel. Another did the same for China; all queried in advance."

SNACK FOOD, HBJ Publications, Inc., 1 E. 1st St., Duluth MN 55802. (218)727-8511. Editor-in-Chief: Jerry L. Hess. 15% freelance written. For manufacturers and distributors of snack foods. Monthly magazine; 60 pages. Circ. 10,000. Pays on acceptance. Buys first North American serial rights. Occasional byline. Phone queries OK. Photocopied submissions OK. "Prefer manuscript to be scannable; instructions provided." SASE. Reports in 2-3 weeks. Free sample copy and writer's guidelines.

Nonfiction: Informational, interview, new product, nostalgia, photo feature, profile and technical articles. "We use an occasional mini news feature or personality sketch." Length: 300-600 words for mini features; 1,000-1,500 words for longer features. Pays 10-12¢/word.

Photos: Purchased with accompanying ms. Captions required. Pays $15 for 5x7 b&w photos; $15-20 for 4x5 color transparencies. Total purchase price for a ms includes payment for photos. Buys all rights.

Tips: "Query should contain specific lead and display more than a casual knowledge of our audience."

THE WISCONSIN RESTAURATEUR, Wisconsin Restaurant Association, 122 W. Washington, Madison WI 53703. (603)251-3663. Editor: Jan La Rue. Emphasizes restaurant industry for restaurateurs, hospitals, institutions, food service students, etc. Monthly magazine "except November/December combined." Circ. 3,600. Pays on acceptance. Buys all rights or one-time rights. Pays 10% kill fee. Byline given. Phone queries OK. Submit seasonal/holiday material 2-3 months in advance. Previously published work OK; "indicate where." SASE. Reports in 3 weeks. Free sample copy and writer's guidelines with large post paid envelope.

Nonfiction: Interested in expose, general interest, historical, how-to, humor, inspirational, interview, nostalgia, opinion, profile, travel, new product, personal experience, photo feature and technical articles pertaining to restaurant industry. "No features on nonmember restaurants." Buys 1 ms/issue. Query with "copyright clearance information and a note about the writer in general." Length: 700-1,500 words. Pays $10-20.

Photos: Fiction and how-to article mss stand a better chance for publication if photo is submitted. State availability of photos. Pays $15 for b&w 8x10 glossy prints. Model releases required, captions are not.

Columns/Departments: Spotlight column provides restaurant member profiles. Buys 6/year. Query. Length: 500-1,500 words. Pays $5-10.

Fiction: Likes experimental, historical and humorous stories related to food service only. Buys 12 mss/year. Query. Length: 1,000-3,000 words. Pays $10-20.

Poetry: Uses all types of poetry, but must have food service as subject. Buys 6-12/year. No more than 5 submissions at one time. Length: 10-50 lines. Pays $5-10.

Fillers: Uses clippings, jokes, gags, anecdotes, newsbreaks and short humor. No puzzles or games. Buys 12/year. Length: 50-500 words. Pays $2.50-7.50.

Funeral Services

C & S (Casket and Sunnyside), Funeral Services Publication, 274 Madison Ave., New York NY 10016. (212)685-8310. Editor: Howard Barnard. 10% freelance written. "This magazine is circulated to funeral directors of all ages, more and more who are becoming college educated." Published 10 times/year; 48 pages. Circ. 8,500. Pays on publication. Buys all rights. Byline given. Submit seasonal/holiday material 2 months in advance. SASE. Reports in 2 weeks.
Nonfiction: General interest (stories on mortuaries); historical (articles dealing with embalming, early funeral vehicles and ambulances, etc.); how-to (handle difficult or unusual restorative art or embalming cases); inspirational (public relations achievements); and "short items or new products in the funeral field." Buys 20 mss/year. Query. Length: 2,500-3,500 words. Pays $75.
Photos: State availability of photos with query. Pays $5 for 5x7 or 8x10 b&w prints. Captions required. Buys all rights.
Fillers: Clippings, obituaries and items concerning various activities of funeral directors. Buys 10-15/issue. Pays $3.
Tips: "We appreciate a straightforward inquiry, indicating concisely what the author proposes to write about. We are interested in receiving stories on new or remodeled mortuaries."

Government and Public Service

Below are journals for individuals who provide governmental services, either in the employ of local, state, or national governments or of franchised utilities. Included are journals for city managers, politicians, civil servants, firefighters, police officers, public administrators, urban transit managers, and utilities managers.

Journals for professionals in world affairs are found in the International Affairs section. Publications for lawyers are found in the Law category. Journals for teachers and school administrators are found in Education. Those for private citizens interested in politics, government, and public affairs are classified with the Politics and World Affairs magazines in the Consumer Publications section.

AMERICAN FIRE JOURNAL, Suite 7, 9072 E. Artesia Blvd., Bellflower CA 90706. (213)866-1664. Editor: Heidi M. Ziolkowski. 40% freelance written. For fire chiefs of paid and volunteer departments in metropolitan and small communities throughout the US. Also read by other fire department officers and personnel. Monthly magazine; 66 pages. Circ. 8,000. Pays on publication. Buys first North American serial rights. Will not purchase material already published in the fire service press. Absolutely *no* multiple submissions. Byline given. Computer printout submissions acceptable; prefers letter-quality to dot-matrix. SASE. Reports in 2 months. Publishes ms an average of 3 months after acceptance. Sample copy $2; free writer's guidelines.
Nonfiction: How-to (develop or build a new piece of fire protection equipment or facility) and technical (new ideas in fire protection techniques, management, training and prevention). Buys 15 unsolicited mss/year. Query. Pays $1.50-2/inch.
Photos: State availability of photos with query. Pays $6 for b&w and glossy prints or $30 for 35mm color transparencies, vertical format (for covers only). Captions preferred. Buys one-time rights.
Tips: "We are increasing focus on human factor aspects of fire service, such as community outreach efforts, bilingual skills for emergency personnel and fair employment practices, while retaining traditional topics such as apparatus, incident stories and fireground tactics."

FIRE ENGINEERING, 875 3rd Ave., New York NY 10022. Editor: Tom Brennan. For paid and volunteer firefighters and fire officers, members of military and industrial fire departments, fire protections, safety and prevention engineers and fire equipment manufacturers. Buys first rights. Byline given. Pays on publication. Electronic submissions OK if Apple. Computer printout submissions acceptable. Reports in 3 weeks.

Nonfiction: Wants articles on fire suppression, fire prevention, fire administration and any other subject that relates to fire service. Buys 115 unsolicited mss/year. Length: open. Payment varies.

Photos: Inside photos used only with articles. Particular need for color photos for cover; small print or slide satisfactory for submission, but must always be a vertical or capable of being cropped to vertical. Transparency required if accepted. Pays $125 for color shots used on cover.

Tips: "Some freelancers hesitate to write because they have never written an article. We encourage them to set down the facts as though they were talking to someone. We take care of putting the article into our style."

FOREIGN SERVICE JOURNAL, 2101 E St. NW, Washington DC 20037. (202)338-4045. Editor: Stephen R. Dujack. 90% freelance written. For Foreign Service personnel and others interested in foreign affairs and related subjects. Monthly (July/August combined). Buys first North American serial rights. Computer printout submissions acceptable. Byline given. Pays on publication. Publishes ms an average of 6 months after acceptance. SASE.

Nonfiction: Uses articles on "international relations, internal problems of the State Department and Foreign Service, diplomatic history and articles on Foreign Service experiences. Much of our material is contributed by those working in the fields we reach. Informed outside contributions are welcomed, however." Query. Buys 5-10 unsolicited mss/year. Length: 1,000-4,000 words. Pays 2-6¢/word.

FOUNDATION NEWS, The Magazine of Philanthropy, Council on Foundations, 1828 L St. NW, Washington DC 20036. (202)466-6512. Editor: Arlie Schardt. Managing Editor: Kathleen Hallahan. 36% freelance written. Bimonthly magazine covering the world of philanthropy, nonprofit organization and their relation to current events. Read by staff and executives of foundations, corporations, hospitals, colleges and universities and various nonprofit organizations. Circ. 16,000. Pays on acceptance. Publishes ms an average of 4 months after acceptance. Byline given. Offers negotiable kill fee. Not copyrighted. Buys all rights. Submit seasonal/holiday material 3 months in advance. Simultaneous queries and previously published submissions OK. Computer printout submissions acceptable; prefers letter-quality to dot-matrix. SASE. Reports in 1 month on queries; 3 weeks on mss.

Nonfiction: Book excerpts, expose, general interest, historical/nostalgic, how-to, humor, interview/profile and photo feature. Special issue on the role of religion in American life and how religious giving affects social welfare, culture, health conditions, etc. Buys 25 mss/year. Query. Length: 500-3,000 words. Pays $200-2,000.

Photos: State availability of photos. Pays negotiable rates for b&w contact sheet and prints. Captions and identification of subjects required. Buys one-time rights; "some rare requests for second use."

Columns/Departments: Buys 12 mss/year. Query. Length: 900-1,400 words. Pays $100-500.

Tips: "Writers should be able to put current events into the perspective of how nonprofits affect them and are affected by them."

THE GRANTSMANSHIP CENTER NEWS, The Grantsmanship Center, 1031 S. Grand Ave., Los Angeles CA 90015. (213)749-4721. Editor: Norton J. Kiritz. 10% freelance written. Emphasizes fundraising, philanthropy, grants process and nonprofit management for professionals in government, foundations and nonprofit organizations. Bimonthly magazine; 88 pages. Circ. 14,000. Pays on acceptance. Publishes ms an average of 4 months after acceptance. Makes assignments on a work-for-hire basis. Pays variable kill fee. Byline given. Simultaneous, photocopied and previously published submissions OK. SASE. Reports in 2 months. Sample copy $4.65.

Nonfiction: Expose, general interest, how-to and interview. "Familiarity with the field is an asset." Buys 1-2 mss/issue. Query with clips of published work. Length: 1,500-10,000 words. Pays $50-350.

Photos: State availability of photos. Uses b&w contact sheets and color transparencies. Offers no additional payment for photos accepted with ms. Captions preferred; model release required. Buys all rights.

‡**GRASSROOTS FUNDRAISING JOURNAL**, Klein & Honig, Partnership, Box 14754, San Francisco CA 94114. (415)669-1118. Editors: Kim Klein and Lisa Honig. A bimonthly newsletter covering grassroots fund raising for small social change and social service nonprofit organizations. Circ. 3,000. Pays on publication. Byline given. Buys simultaneous rights. Submit seasonal/holiday material 2 months in advance. Simultaneous queries, and simultaneous, photocopied and occasionally previously published submissions OK. SASE. Reports in 2 weeks on queries; 2 months on mss. Sample copy $3.

Nonfiction: Book excerpts; how-to (all fund raising strategies); and personal experience (doing fundraising). Buys 10 mss/year. Query. Length: 2,000-20,000 words. Pays $35 minimum.

LAW AND ORDER, Hendon Co., 1000 Skokie Blvd., Wilmette IL 60091. (312)792-1838. Editor: Bruce W. Cameron. 90% freelance written. Monthly magazine covering the administration and operation of law enforcement agencies, directed to police chiefs and supervisors. Circ. 26,000. Pays on publication. Publishes ms an average of 6 months after acceptance. Byline given. Buys first North American serial rights. Submit seasonal/holiday material 3 months in advance. Photocopied submissions OK. No simultaneous queries. Computer printout submissions acceptable; prefers letter-quality to dot-matrix. Reports in 1 month. Sample copy for 9x12 SAE.

Nonfiction: General police interest; how-to (do specific police assignments); new product (how applied in police operation); and technical (specific police operation). Special issues include Buyers Guide (January); Communications (February); Training (March); International (April); Administration (May); Small Departments (June); Police Science (July); Equipment (August); Weapons (September); Mobile Patrol (November); and Working with Youth (December). No articles dealing with courts (legal field) or convicted prisoners. No nostalgic, financial, travel or recreational material. Buys 20-30 mss/year. Length: 1,000-3,000 words. Pays $50-300.

Photos: Send photos with ms. Reviews transparencies and prints. Identification of subjects required. Buys all rights.

Tips: *"L&O* is a respected magazine that provides up-to-date information that chiefs can use. Writers must know their subject as it applies to this field. Case histories are well received. We are upgrading quality for editorial—stories *must* show some understanding of the law enforcement field."

‡MARINE CORPS GAZETTE, Professional Magazine for United States Marines, Marine Corps Association, Box 1775, Quantico VA 22134. (703)640-6161. Editor: Col. John E. Greenwood, USMC (Ret). Managing Editor: Joseph D. Dodd. Monthly magazine. *"Gazette* serves as a forum in which serving Marine officers exchange ideas and viewpoints on professional military matters." Circ. 31,000. Pays on publication. Byline given. Buys first North American serial rights; change to all rights under consideration. Computer printout submissions acceptable. Reports in 3 weeks on queries; 2 months on mss. Sample copy $1; free writer's guidelines.

Nonfiction: Historical/nostaglic (Marine Corps operations only); technical (Marine Corps related equipment). "The magazine is a professional journal oriented toward hard skills, factual treatment, technical detail—no market for lightweight puff pieces—analysis of doctrine. Lessons learned goes well. A very strong Marine Corps background and influence are normally prerequisites for publication." Buys 4-5 mss/year. Query or send complete ms. Length: 2,500-5,000 words. Pays $200-400; short features, $50-100.

Photos: "We welcome photos and charts." Payment for illustrative material included in payment for ms. Photos need not be original, nor have been taken by author, but they must support the article."

Columns/Departments: Book Reviews (of interest and importance to Marines), and Ideas & Issues (an assortment of topical articles, e.g., opinion or argument; ideas for better way to accomplish task; reports on weapons and equipment, strategies and tactics, etc.; also short vignettes on history of Corps). Buys 60 book reviews, 120 Ideas & Issues mss/year. Query. Length: 500-1,500 words. Pays $25-50 plus book for 750-word book review; $50-100 for Ideas & Issues.

Tips: "Book Reviews or short articles (500-1,500 words) on Marine Corps related hardware or technological development are best way to break in. Section/departments most open to freelancers are Book Reviews and Ideas & Issues section—query first. We are not much of a market for those outside US Marine Corps or who are not closely associated with current Marine activities."

‡THE NATIONAL CENTURION, A Police Lifestyle Magazine, Constable Press, Suite 230, 3180 University Ave., San Diego CA 92104. (619)282-6295. Managing Editor: Denny Fallon. A monthly lifestyle magazine for the law enforcement community covering national law enforcement issues, interesting people in the profession and the challenges that face them. Estab. 1983. Circ. 52,000. Pays on publication. Byline given. Offers 20% kill fee. Buys first North American serial rights. Submit seasonal/holiday material 3 months in advance. Simultaneous queries OK. SASE. Reports in 2 weeks. Free sample copy and writer's guidelines.

Nonfiction: Expose, historical/nostalgic, humor, interview/profile and photo feature. Buys 70 mss/year. Query with published clips. Length: 1,200-4,000 words. Pays $150-1,000.

Photos: Ken Arnone, photo editor. Send photos with query or ms. Reviews b&w prints and 35mm slides. Captions, model release and identification of subjects preferred. Buys one-time rights.

Columns/Departments: Buys 35 mss/year. Query with published clips. Length: 1,200-2,000 words. Pays $150-300.

Tips: "We prefer features be accompanied by both b&w prints and color slides. We place a strong emphasis on attractive design and layout, and we expect our contributors to assist us in making their stories look appealing and interesting in the magazine."

‡OSC CORPORATION, 46 Leo Birmingham Pkwy., Boston MA 02135. (617)787-0005. Managing Editor: Penny Deyoe. 50% freelance written. Several magazines covering law enforcement for law enforcement personnel, legislators, and local government leaders. Circ. 100,000. Pays on publication. Publishes ms an average of 2 months after acceptance. Byline given. Buys all rights. Submit seasonal/holiday material 4 months in advance. Simultaneous queries and photocopied submissions OK. Computer printout submissions acceptable. SASE.

Nonfiction: General interest (consumer, health, trends in law enforcement); historical/nostalgic (if it can be tied to something current); interview/profile (of interesting police and legendary criminals); offbeat crimes; and white collar crime. "We like to cover trends in the profession, such as the current trend toward using more civilians for inside work. Also, our readers like to read about the legendary criminals. No blood and gore." Buys 100 mss/year. Query. Length: 2,000 words minimum. Pays 5¢/word.

Photos: Pays $5 minimum for 5x7 or 8x10 b&w glossy prints. Captions and model release required.

Columns/Departments: Criminal justice (new laws, Supreme Court decisions) and Consumer Information (money stretching tips). Send complete ms. Length: 2,000 words minimum. Pays 5¢/word.

Tips: "Writers need to keep in mind that subject matter is in line with the times. Readers want *current* issues to be covered—not something that has been milked to death."

PLANNING, American Planning Association, 1313 E. 60th St., Chicago IL 60637. (312)955-9100. Editor: Sylvia Lewis. 25% freelance written. Emphasizes urban planning for adult, college-educated readers who are regional and urban planners in city, state or federal agencies or in private business or university faculty or students. Monthly. Circ. 25,000. Pays on publication. Publishes ms an average of 3 months after acceptance. Buys all rights or first rights. Byline given. Photocopied and previously published submissions OK. Computer printout submissions acceptable; prefers letter-quality to dot-matrix. SASE. Reports in 2 months. Free sample copy and writer's guidelines.

Nonfiction: Expose (on government or business, but on topics related to planning, housing, land use, zoning); general interest (trend stories on cities, land use, government); historical (historic preservation); how-to (successful government or citizen efforts in planning; innovations; concepts that have been applied); and technical (detailed articles on the nitty-gritty of planning, zoning, transportation but no footnotes or mathematical models). Also needs news stories up to 500 words. "It's best to query with a fairly detailed, one-page letter. We'll consider any article that's well written and relevant to our audience. Articles have a better chance if they are timely and related to planning and land use and if they appeal to a national audience. All articles should be written in magazine feature style." Buys 2 features and 1 news story/issue. Length: 500-2,000 words. Pays $50-400. "We pay freelance writers and photographers only, not planners."

Photos: "We prefer that authors supply their own photos, but we sometimes take our own or arrange for them in other ways." State availability of photos. Pays $25 minimum for 8x10 matte or glossy prints and $200 for 4-color cover photos. Captions preferred. Buys one-time rights.

‡**POLICE NET MAGAZINE, Personal Computing For Law Enforcement**, Educational Learning Systems, 5401 W. 23rd, Topeka KS 66614. (913)232-3086. Editor: Larry Gaines. Managing Editor: Gerald Griffin. A monthly magazine covering use of personal computers by law enforcement departments, officers and their families. Estab. 1983. Circ. 20,000. Pays on publication. Byline given. Buys first North American serial rights. Submit seasonal/holiday material 3 months in advance. Simultaneous queries, and simultaneous, photocopied and previously published submissions OK. Electronic submissions OK on 5¼" CPM (Epson). Computer printout submissions acceptable. SASE. Reports in 5 weeks. Free sample copy; writer's guidelines for SAE and 2 first class stamps.

Nonfiction: Book excerpts (computer); general interest (home use of computers); historical/nostalgic (police history); how-to (write software programs); humor (police stories); interview/profile (with police officers and police department using computers); new product (hardware and software); personal experience (police officer computer usage); photo feature (computer); technical (computer); and travel (vacation). Buys 100 mss/year. Send complete ms. Length: 100-2,000 words. Pays 10-25¢/word.

Photos: Phyllis Griggs, photo editor. Send photos with query or ms. Reviews b&w contact sheets. Pays $5-10 for 8x10 b&w prints; $15-25 for 8x10 color prints; $5-20 for 8x10 b&w cover shot; $20-200 for 8x10 color cover. Captions required. Buys all rights.

Columns/Departments: Computer News, and Computer Technical. Buys 10 mss/year. Send complete ms. Length: 100-500 words. Pays negotiable rate.

Fillers: Clippings, jokes, gags, anecdotes, short humor and newsbreaks.

POLICE PRODUCT NEWS, Dyna Graphics, Inc., Box 847, 6200 Yarrow Dr., Carlsbad CA 92008. (619)438-2511. Editor: James Daigh. For all law enforcement personnel. Monthly magazine. Circ. 50,000. Pays on publication. Buys all rights. Byline given. SASE. Reports in 1 week. Sample copy $2; free writer's guidelines.

Nonfiction: Expose; historical; how-to; humor; interview; profile (of police departments around the country); new product (testing/evaluation/opinion); and technical. "All material must be clearly related to law enforcement." Buys 54 unsolicited mss/year. Send query and clips of published work. Length: 1,500-3,000 words. Pays $100-400 (with color photo) for feature length article.

Photos: State availability of photos. Pays $10-25 for b&w 8x10 glossy prints; $25-100 for color transparencies; and $100-150 for color cover photo. Model release required.

Columns/Departments: Articles for departments. Length: 1,000-2,000 words. Pays $50-125 with b&w photos or without photos. Pays $100-225 with minimum of 3 color photos.

POLICE TIMES/COMMAND MAGAZINE, 1100 NE 125th St., North Miami FL 33161. (305)891-1700. Editor: Gerald Arenberg. 90% freelance written. For "law enforcement officers: federal, state, county, local and private security." Magazine published eight times/year. Circ. 87,000. Buys all rights. Buys 50-100 mss/year. Pays on acceptance. Computer printout submissions acceptable. SASE. Reports "at once." Sample copy for $1 postage.

Nonfiction: Interested in articles about local police departments all over the nation. In particular, short articles about what the police department is doing, any unusual arrests made, acts of valor of officers in the performance of duties, etc. Also articles on any police subject from prisons to reserve police. "We prefer newspaper style. Short and to the point. No fiction. Photos and drawings are a big help." Length: 300-1,200 words. Pays $5-15—up to $25 in some cases based on 1¢/word.

Photos: Uses b&w Polaroid and 8x10 b&w glossy prints, "if of particular value." Pays $5-15 for each photo used.

STATE LEGISLATURES, National Conference of State Legislatures, Suite 1500, 1125 17th St., Denver CO 80202. (303)292-6600. Editor: John Chaffee. Emphasizes current issues facing state legislatures for legislators, legislative staff members and close observers of state politics and government. Magazine published 10 times/year; 32 pages. Pays on acceptance. Buys all rights. Byline given. SASE. Reports in 1 month. Free sample copy.

Nonfiction: "We're interested in original reporting on the responses of states (particularly state legislatures) to current problems, e.g., tax reform, health care, energy and consumer protection. We seldom publish articles that deal exclusively with one state; our usual approach is to survey and compare the actions of states across the country." Query preferred, but will consider complete ms. Pays $300-500, depending on length.

SUPERINTENDENT'S PROFILE & POCKET EQUIPMENT DIRECTORY, Profile Publications, 220 Central Ave., Box 43, Dunkirk NY 14048. (716)366-4774. Editor: Robert Dyment. 60% freelance written. Monthly magazine covering "outstanding" town, village, county and city highway superintendents and Department of Public Works Directors throughout New York state only. Circ. 2,500. Publishes ms an average of 4 months after acceptance. Pays on publication. Byline given for excellent material. Buys one-time rights. Submit seasonal/holiday material 3 months in advance. Simultaneous queries OK. Computer printout submissions acceptable. SASE. Reports in 2 weeks on queries; 1 month on mss. Sample copy for 9x12 SAE and 2 first class stamps.

Nonfiction: John Powers, articles editor. Interview/profile (of a highway superintendent or DPW director in NY state who has improved department operations through unique methods or equipment); and technical. Special issues include winter maintenance profiles. No fiction. Buys 20 mss/year. Query. Length: 1,500-2,000 words. Pays $75 for a full-length ms. "Pays more for excellent material. All manuscripts will be edited to fit our format and space limitations."

Photos: John Powers, photo editor. State availability of photos. Pays $5-10 for b&w contact sheets; reviews 5x7 prints. Captions and identification of subjects required. Buys one-time rights.

Poetry: Buys poetry if it pertains to highway departments. Pays $5-15.

Tips: "We are a widely read and highly respected state-wide magazine, and although we can't pay high rates, we expect quality work. Too many freelance writers are going for the expose rather than the meat and potato type articles that will help readers. We will have a need for more manuscripts and photos because of two new publications being launched."

TRANSACTION/SOCIETY, Rutgers University, New Brunswick NJ 08903. (201)932-2280, ext. 83. Editor: Irving Louis Horowitz. 15% freelance written. For social scientists (policymakers with training in sociology, political issues and economics). Published every 2 months. Circ. 45,000. Buys all rights. Byline given. Pays on publication. Publishes ms an average of 6 months after acceptance. Will consider photocopied submissions. No simultaneous submissions. Reports in 4 weeks. Query. SASE. Free sample copy and writer's guidelines.

Nonfiction: Michele Teitelbaum, articles editor. "Articles of wide interest in areas of specific interest to the social science community. Must have an awareness of problems and issues in education, population and urbanization that are not widely reported. Articles on overpopulation, terrorism, international organizations. No general think pieces." Payment for articles is made only if done on assignment. *No payment for unsolicited articles.*

Photos: Joan DuFault, photo editor. Pays $200 for photographic essays done on assignment or accepted for publication.

Tips: "Submit an article on a thoroughly unique subject, written with good literary quality. Present new ideas and research findings in a readable and useful manner."

VICTIMOLOGY: An International Journal, Box 39045, Washington DC 20016. (703)528-8872. Editor-in-Chief: Emilio C. Viano. "We are the only magazine specifically focusing on the victim, on the dynamics of victimization; for social scientists, criminal justice professionals and practitioners, social workers and volunteer and professional groups engaged in prevention of victimization and in offering assistance to victims of rape, spouse abuse, child abuse, incest, abuse of the elderly, natural disasters, etc." Quarterly magazine. Circ. 2,500. Pays on publication. Buys all rights. Byline given. SASE. Reports in 6-8 weeks. Sample copy $5; free writer's guidelines.

Nonfiction: Expose, historical, how-to, informational, interview, personal experience, profile, research and technical. Buys 10 mss/issue. Query. Length: 500-5,000 words. Pays $50-150.

Photos: Purchased with accompanying ms. Captions required. Send contact sheet. Pays $15-50 for 5x7 or 8x10 b&w glossy prints.

Poetry: Avant-garde, free verse, light verse and traditional. Length: 30 lines maximum. Pays $10-25.

Tips: "Focus on what is being researched and discovered on the victim, the victim/offender relationship, treatment of the offender, the bystander/witness, preventive measures, and what is being done in the areas of service to the victims of rape, spouse abuse, neglect and occupational and environmental hazards and the elderly."

THE VOLUNTEER FIREMAN, A Fire Service Publication, Publico, Box 220783, Charlotte NC 28222. (704)535-8200. Editor: Pattie Toney. Managing Editor: Martha Tatum. 75% freelance written. Quarterly magazine for volunteer fire fighters nationwide covering fire safety/protection, news of saves and special fire ground situations. Circ. 20,000. Pays on publication. Publishes ms an average of 9 months after acceptance. Byline given. Buys first rights. Photocopied submissions OK. Computer printout submissions acceptable. SASE. Reports in 1 month. Sample copy for 9x12 SAE and 2 first class stamps; writer's guidelines for $1, 9x12 SAE, and 2 first class stamps.

Nonfiction: Expose; general interest; historical/nostalgic; how-to (raise funds for volunteer fire departments); humor; interview/profile; new product; opinion; personal experience; photo feature; and technical. "We want 'glamor' articles. We want good, exciting and honest news. No mom 'n' pop, picnic news, etc." Length: 200-1,500 words. Pays $10-105.

Photos: L.P. Coleman, photo editor. Send photos with ms. Pays $5-25 for 5x7 b&w prints. Captions, model release and identification of subjects required.

Columns/Departments: News, features and product reviews. Buys 8-10 ms/year. Length: 100-750 words. Pays $5-52.50.

Fillers: Clippings, anecdotes, short humor and newsbreaks. Buys 20/year. Length: 25-100 words. Pays $1.75-10.

Tips: "Writers should keep our readership in mind. Volunteer fire fighters are highly interested in ways to save other people's lives while not harming their own."

WISCONSIN SHERIFF & DEPUTY, Wisconsin Sheriffs & Deputy Sheriffs Association, Box 145, Chippewa Falls WI 54729. (715)723-7173. Contact: Editor. Quarterly magazine covering law enforcement in Wisconsin. Circ. 3,000. Pays on publication. Byline given. Offers 25% kill fee. Buys one-time, first, and second serial (reprint) rights. Submit seasonal/holiday material 2 months in advance. Photocopied and previously published submissions OK. Reports in 1 month. Writer's guidelines for business-size SAE with 20¢ postage.

Nonfiction: Articles about Wisconsin Sheriffs' Departments, professional matters that would be of interest to sheriffs and deputy sheriffs. "Tell our readers what sheriffs and deputy sheriffs are doing to improve law enforcement and crime prevention in Wisconsin's 72 counties." No general matter of interest to sheriffs and deputy sheriffs. Query with clips of published work. Length: 1,000-1,500. Pays $25-100.

Photos: State availability of photos. "Photos of Wisconsin sheriffs and/or deputy sheriffs in action, unless accompanied by article." Pays $5-15 for 8x10 b&w prints. Captions and identification of subjects required. Buys one-time rights.

YOUR VIRGINIA STATE TROOPER MAGAZINE, Box 2189, Springfield VA 22152. (703)451-2524. Editor: Kerian Bunch. 90% freelance written. Biannual magazine covering police topics for troopers, police, libraries, legislators and businesses. Circ. 10,000. Pays on acceptance. Publishes ms an average of 3 months after acceptance. Byline given. Buys first North American serial rights and all rights on assignments. Submit seasonal/holiday material 2 months in advance. Simultaneous and photocopied submissions OK. Computer printout submissions acceptable; prefers letter-quality to dot-matrix. Reports in 1 month.

Nonfiction: Book excerpts; expose (consumer or police-related); general interest; nutrition/health; historical/nostalgic; how-to (energy saving); humor; interview/profile (notable police figures); opinion; personal experience; technical (radar); and other (recreation). Buys 40-45 mss/year. Query with clips of published work or send complete ms. Length: 2,500 words. Pays $250 maximum/article (10¢/word).

Photos: Send photos with ms. Pays $25 maximum/5x7 b&w glossy print. Captions and model release required. Buys one-time rights.

Fiction: Adventure, humorous, mystery, novel excerpts and suspense. Buys 4 mss/year. Send complete ms. Length: 2,500 words minimum. Pays $250 maximum (10¢/word) on acceptance.

Groceries

These journals are for owners and operators of retail food stores. Journals for food wholesalers, packers, warehousers and caterers are classified with the Food Products, Processing, and Service journals. Publications for food vending machine operators are found in the Coin-Operated Machines category.

CANADIAN GROCER, Maclean-Hunter Ltd., Maclean Hunter Building, 777 Bay St., Toronto, Ontario M5W 1A7 Canada. (416)596-5772. Editor: George H. Condon. 8% freelance written. Monthly magazine about supermarketing and food retailing for Canadian chain and independent food store managers, owners, buyers, executives, food brokers, food processors and manufacturers. Circ 16,000. Pays on publication. Publishes ms an average of 2 months after acceptance. Byline given. Buys first Canadian rights. Phone queries OK. Submit seasonal material 2 months in advance. Previously published submissions OK. Computer printout submissions acceptable; prefers letter-quality to dot-matrix. SAE and IRCs. Reports in 2 weeks. Sample copy $4.
Nonfiction: Interview (national trendsetters in marketing, finance or food distribution); technical (store operations, equipment and finance); and news features on supermarkets. "Freelancers should be well versed on the supermarket industry. We don't want unsolicited material. Writers with business and/or finance expertise are preferred. Know the retail food industry and be able to write concisely and accurately on subjects relevant to our readers: food store managers, senior corporate executives, etc. A good example of an article would be 'How a Six Store Chain of Supermarkets Improved Profits 2% and Kept Customers Coming.' " Buys 14 mss/year. Query with clips of previously published work. Pays $25-175.
Photos: State availability of photos. Pays $5-15 for 8x10 b&w glossy prints. Captions preferred. Buys one-time rights.

ENTRÉE, Fairchild, 7 E. 12th St., New York NY 10003. (212)741-4009. Editor: Geri Brin. Managing Editor: Debra Kent. Monthly magazine covering "trends in cooking, housewares and food industry news, new products in the gourmet and lifestyle areas for specialty retailers and department store buyers of gourmet housewares and food, and executives and managers in the gourmet product industry." Circ. 15,000. Average issue includes 5-11 features, 5 columns, a calendar, news and 50% advertising. Pays on publication. Byline given. Kill fee varies. Buys all rights. Phone queries OK. Computer printout submissions acceptable; no dot-matrix. SASE. Reports in 6 weeks on queries; in 1 week on mss. Sample copy $2.
Nonfiction: Profile (of major retailers); new product ("hot product categories"); photo feature; and technical (cookware and specialty food in terms retailers can apply to their businesses). No first person, humor, cartoons and unsolicited stories on obscure retailers or general pieces of any kind such as accounting or computer stories. Buys 2-3 mss/issue. Query. Length: 1,500-3,000 words. Pays $250-400.
Photos: Julia Gorton, art director. Always looking for illustrations and photographs.
Tips: "We've expanded into specialty foods, in addition to gourmet housewares. We're much more interested in experienced *trade* writers rather than experienced consumer magazine writers. We've rejected stories from successful consumer writers because they simply don't meet the requirements of a *business* magazine. *Entrée* is actively searching for qualified, experienced trade writers. We use two to three freelancers every issue and now wish to establish a core of regular writers we can rely on. Our problem is that, while writers are in abundance, experienced *trade* writers are not. We need a writer who can thoroughly analyze a market, whether it be cutlery, cheese, pate or ice cream machines. We need someone who can do in-depth retail profiles with major retailers. Most important, we're not particularly interested in hearing queries. We'd rather interview qualified writers who can accept *our* assignments month after month. A typical feature pays $400."

FLORIDA FOOD DEALER, Retail Grocers Association of Florida, 2810 NE 14th St., Ocala FL 32670. (904)351-2300. Editor: Andy Williams. Assistant Editor: Tyler Ward. 1% freelance written. Monthly magazine covering the Florida retail supermarket and convenience store industry. Circ. 4,000. Byline given. Offers negotiable kill fee. Buys first North American serial rights. Submit seasonal/holiday material 2 months in advance. Simultaneous queries and photocopied and previously published submissions OK. Computer printout submissions acceptable; prefers letter-quality to dot-matrix. SASE. Reports in 1 week on queries, 2 weeks on mss. Sample copy $1.
Nonfiction: Historical/nostalgic; how-to; inspirational; interview/profile; new product; personal experience; technical—Florida angle. "Conservative business-oriented." Special issues include new equipment (July); dairy (May); security (June). No coupon handling, consumer tips, recipes. Buys 12 mss/year. Query. Length: 500-1,500 words. Pays $50-150.
Tips: "Know supermarket and convenience store industry from owner's standpoint."

HEALTH FOODS BUSINESS, Howmark Publishing Corp., 567 Morris Ave., Elizabeth NJ 07208 (201)353-7373. Editor-in-Chief: Alan Richman. 20% freelance written. For owners and managers of health food stores. Monthly magazine; 100 pages. Circ. over 8,000. Pays on publication. Byline given "if story quality warrants it." Phone queries OK. "Query us about a good health foods store in your area. We use many store profile stories." Simultaneous and photocopied submissions OK if exclusive to their field. Previously published work OK, but please indicate where and when material appeared previously. Computer printout submissions acceptable if double-spaced and in upper and lower case; prefers letter-quality to dot-matrix. SASE. Reports in 1 month. Sample copy $3; plus $2 for postage and handling.
Nonfiction: Expose (government hassling with health food industry); how-to (unique or successful retail operators); informational (how or why a product works; technical aspects must be clear to laymen); historical (natural food use); interviews (must be prominent person in industry or closely related to the health food industry); and photo features (any unusual subject related to the retailer's interests). Buys 1-2 mss/issue. Query for interviews and photo features. Will consider complete ms in other categories. Length: long enough to tell the whole story without padding. Pays $50 and up for feature stories, $75 and up for store profiles.
Photos: "Most articles must have photos included"; negatives and contact sheet OK. Captions required. No additional payment.

IGA GROCERGRAM, Fisher-Harrison Publications, 338 N. Elm St., Greensboro NC 27401. (919)378-6000. Managing Editor: Leslie P. Daisy. Monthly magazine for independent grocery retailers and wholesalers affiliated with IGA, Inc. Circ. 11,000. Pays on publication. Byline given. Buys first rights only. Submit seasonal/holiday material 3 months in advance. SASE. Reports in 2 weeks on queries; 1 month on mss. Free sample copy.
Nonfiction: Book excerpts, interview/profile, new product and technical. "All articles must concentrate on the independent grocery business." Buys 25-35 mss/year. Query with clips of published work. Pays $25-500.
Photos: Send photos with ms. Reviews b&w contact sheets and color transparencies. Buys one-time rights.

PENNSYLVANIA GROCER, 1355 Old York Rd., Abington PA 19001. (215)228-0808. Editor: John McNelis. 15% freelance written. For grocers, their families and employees, and store managers; food people in general. Monthly magazine; 16 pages. Circ. 3,000. Byline given. Pays on publication. Publishes ms an average of 3 months after acceptance. Buys first and second rights to the same material. Computer printout submissions acceptable; no dot-matrix. SASE. Reports in 1 month. Sample copy $1.
Nonfiction: Articles on food subjects in retail food outlets; mainly local, in Pennsylvania and surrounding areas. Informational, interviews, profiles, historical, successful business operations, new product, merchandising techniques and technical articles. Buys 12-15 unsolicited mss/year. Query or submit complete ms. Length: 500-900 words. Pays $25.
Photos: Pays $25 maximum for minimum of 2 b&w photos purchased with ms.
Tips "We need graphics and will use more color."

WHOLE FOODS, The Largest Circulation in the Natural Foods Industry, Whole Foods Communications, Inc., 195 Main St., Metuchen NJ 08840. Publisher: Howard Waines. Monthly magazine edited for health food wholesalers and manufacturers serving the community. Byline given on articles and columns; photocredits also. Pays on publication. Buys first North American serial rights. Submit seasonal material 3 months in advance. Photocopied submissions OK. Computer printout submissions acceptable "if highly readable." Prefers double-spaced letter-quality to dot-matrix. SASE. Reports in 1 month. Length: 500-2,000 words. Writer's guidelines and sample copy available with 9x12 SASE. "Good freelancers wanted."
Nonfiction: Editorial content targets product knowledge and aids retailers in making responsible and profitable inventory selection through nutritional education, market awareness and merchandising expertise. Feature articles explain products, including manufacturing procedures, proper storage and preparation, as well as nutritional benefits. Industry members speak out about the industry issues in the Debate department. Calendar, book reviews, industry news and product showcase are written in-house. No consumer-oriented pieces other than one-subject consumer tearouts (i.e., "Everything You Need To Know About Tofu . . . or Sprouts . . ."). Not interested in undocumented, unreferenced, experiential pieces unless company or store profile of success (or specifics about failure). Wants "higher quality, compact, documentable work." Testimonials/healing stories NOT wanted."
Photos: Photos desirable with ms. Provide captions and model release if appropriate.
Tips: "We are in the market for qualified freelancers who submit on-target pieces which do not require considerable editing, retyping, etc. Writer should read three issues of the magazine and have observed the operation of a health food store prior to beginning any work. Industry exclusive a must for all submissions. We will provide list of competitors' magazines."

Grooming Products and Services

AMERICAN SALON EIGHTY-FIVE, (formerly *American Hairdresser/Salon Owner*), Suite 1000, 100 Park Ave., New York NY 10017. (212)532-5588. Editor: Louise Cotter. For beauty salon owners and operators. Monthly. Buys all rights. Pays on publication. Computer printout submissions acceptable; prefers letter-quality to dot-matrix. SASE.
Nonfiction: Profiles, how-to and management. Technical material is mainly staff written. "We are not interested unless material is directly related to the needs of beauty salon professionals."

WOMAN BEAUTIFUL, Allied Publications, Inc., Drawer 189, Palm Beach FL 33480. (305)833-4593. Editor: Constance Dorval-Bernal. For "students at beauty schools and people who go to beauty salons." Used as a recruiting tool at cosmetology schools. Bimonthly magazine; 16 pages. Pays on publication. Buys one-time rights. Simultaneous submissions OK. Sample copy $1. Free writer's guidelines. Reports in 1 month. SASE.
Nonfiction: "Articles on hairstyling, beauty and women's fashion." Interested in some new product articles; interviews (with famous hairstylists) and anything related to celebrities and hairstyles. Occasionally uses a history piece such as an article on the history of wigs. Buys 2-4 mss/issue. Length: 400-800 words. Pays 5¢/published word. Send complete ms.
Columns/Departments: What's New. Pays 5¢/published word.

Hardware

Journals for general hardware wholesalers and retailers, locksmiths, and retailers of miscellaneous special hardware items are listed in this section. Journals specializing in the retailing of hardware for a certain trade, such as plumbing or automotive supplies, are classified with the other publications for that trade.

‡**CHAIN SAW AGE**, 3435 N.E. Broadway, Portland OR 97232. Editor: Ken Morrison. 1% freelance written. For "mostly chain saw dealers (retailers); small businesses—typically small town, typical ages, interests and education." Monthly. Circ. 18,000. Buys "very few" mss/year. Pays on acceptance or publication—"varies." Publishes ms an average of 4 months after acceptance. Will consider photocopied submissions. Query first. SASE. Free sample copy.
Nonfiction: "Must relate to chain saw use, merchandising, adaptation, repair, maintenance, manufacture or display." Buys informational articles, how-tos, personal experience articles, interviews, profiles, inspirational articles, personal opinion articles, photo features, coverage of successful business operations, and articles on merchandising techniques. Length: 500-1,000 words. Pays $20-50 ("2½¢/word plus photo fees").
Photos: Photos purchased with or without mss, or on assignment; captions required. For b&w glossies, pay "varies."

HARDWARE AGE, Chilton Co., Chilton Way, Radnor PA 19089. (215)964-4275. Editor: Jay Holtzman. Managing Editor: Wendy Ampolsk. 5% freelance written. Emphasizes retailing, distribution and merchandising of hardware and building materials. Monthly magazine; 180 pages. Circ. 71,000. Buys first North American serial rights. No guarantee of byline. Simultaneous, photocopied and previously published submissions OK, if exclusive in the field. SASE. Reports in 1-2 months. Sample copy and writer's guidelines $1; mention *Writer's Market* in request.
Nonfiction: Wendy Ampolsk, managing editor. How-to more profitably run a hardware store or a department within a store. "We particularly want stories on local hardware stores and home improvement centers, with photos. Stories should concentrate on one particular aspect of how the retailer in question has been successful." Also wants technical pieces (will consider stories on retail accounting, inventory management and business management by qualified writers). Buys 5-10 unsolicited mss/year. Submit complete ms. Length: 500-3,000 words. Pays $75-200.
Photos: "We like store features with b&w photos. Usually use b&w for small freelance features." Send photos with ms. Pays $25 for 4x5 glossy b&w prints. Captions preferred. Buys one-time rights.
Columns/Departments: Retailers' Business Tips; Wholesalers' Business Tips; and Moneysaving Tips. Query or submit complete ms. Length: 1,000-1,250 words. Pays $100-150. Open to suggestions for new columns/departments.

HARDWARE MERCHANDISER, The Irving-Cloud Publishing Co., 7300 N. Cicero, Lincolnwood IL 60646. (312)674-7300. Editor: James W. Stapleton. Managing Editor: Pamela Taylor. Monthly tabloid covering hardware, home center and hardlines market for owners and managers of hardware stores, home centers and executives of businesses serving them. Circ. 65,000. Pays on acceptance. Buys first North American serial rights. SASE. Reports in 1 month on queries. Free sample copy.
Nonfiction: Profile (of hardware business). Buys 10 mss/year. Query or send complete ms "on speculation; enough to tell the story."
Photos: Send photos with ms. Reviews 35mm or larger color transparencies. "Photos are paid for as part of article payment."

HARDWARE RETAILING, The Hardware Home Center Magazine, National Retail Hardware Association, 770 N. High School Rd., Indianapolis IN 46224. (317)248-1261. Editor: John Hammond. Executive Editor: Ellen Hackney. 5% freelance written. Monthly magazine covering hardware stores, home centers and consumer building material dealers. Circ. 65,000. Pays on acceptance. Publishes ms an average of 8 months after acceptance. Byline given. Buys one-time rights. Photocopied submissions OK. Computer printout submissions acceptable; prefers letter-quality to dot-matrix. Reports in 2 weeks on queries; 3 weeks on mss. Free sample copy.
Nonfiction: How-to (manage your retail hardware/home center business). "Expert articles on specific management problems and opportunities." No column material. "We have too many columns now and it seems we constantly receive suggested columns." Buys 10 mss/year. Send complete ms. Length: open. Pays $50-150.
Tips: "We have an increasing interest in management articles directed to the consumer-oriented lumber yard."

Home Furnishings and Household Goods

Readers rely on these publications to learn more about the home furnishings trade. Included in this section are magazines that focus on specific aspects of home furnishings such as glassware and water beds. Magazines geared to consumers interested in home furnishings are listed in the Consumer Home and Garden section.

APPLIANCE SERVICE NEWS, 110 W. Saint Charles Rd., Box 789, Lombard IL 60148. Editor: William Wingstedt. For professional service people whose main interest is repairing major and portable household appliances. Their jobs consist of either service shop owner, service manager or service technician. Monthly "newspaper style" publication. Circ. 41,000. Buys all rights. Byline given. Pays on publication. Will consider simultaneous submissions. Reports in about 1 month. SASE. Sample copy $1.50.
Nonfiction: James Hodl, associate editor. "Our main interest is in technical articles about appliances and their repair. Material should be written in a straightforward, easy-to-understand style. It should be crisp and interesting, with a high informational content. Our main interest is in the major and portable appliance repair field. We are not interested in retail sales." Query. Length: open. Pays $200-300/feature.
Photos: Pays $10 for b&w photos used with ms. Captions required.

CHINA GLASS & TABLEWARE, Ebel-Doctorow Publications, Inc., Box 2147, Clifton NJ 07015. (201)779-1600. Editor-in-Chief: Susan Grisham. 30% freelance written. Monthly magazine for buyers, merchandise managers and specialty store owners who deal in tableware, dinnerware, glassware, flatware and other tabletop accessories. Pays on publication. Buys one-time rights. Byline given. Phone queries OK. Submit seasonal/holiday material 3 months in advance. SASE. Reports in 2-3 weeks. Free sample copy and writer's guidelines; mention *Writer's Market* in request.
Nonfiction: General interest (on store successes, reasons for a store's business track record); interview (personalities of store owners; how they cope with industry problems; why they are in table ware); and technical (on the business aspects of retailing china, glassware and flatware). "Bridal registry material always welcomed." No articles on how-to or gift shops. Buys 2-3 mss/issue. Query. Length: 1,500-3,000 words. Pays $40-50/page.
Photos: State availability of photos with query. No additional payment for b&w contact sheets or color contact sheets. Captions required. Buys one-time rights.
Fillers: Clippings. Buys 2/issue. Pays $3-5.
Tips: "Show imagination in the query; have a good angle on a story—that makes it unique from the competition's coverage and requires less work on the editor's part for rewriting a snappy beginning."

‡**DRAPERIES & WINDOW COVERINGS, The Magazine for the American Window Coverings Industry**, L.C. Clark Publishing Co., Suite 209, 9112 Alt. A.1A., Lake Park FL 33403. (305)863-9551. Editor: Lynn Mohr. Publisher: John A. Clark. A bimonthly magazine, plus 2 special issues, on draperies and window coverings for retailers, wholesalers, designers and manufacturers. Circ. 25,000. Pays on publication. Byline given. Buys all rights. Submit seasonal/holiday material 3 months in advance. Simultaneous queries OK. SASE. Reports in 3 weeks on queries; 2 months on mss. Sample copy $3; writer's guidelines for SAE.
Nonfiction: How-to (make special window treatments, handle difficult treatments); and interview/profile (success stories). Query with published clips. Length: 1,000-2,000 words. Pays $150-250.
Photos: State availability of photos. Reviews 8x10 b&w and color prints. Pays negotiable rate. Captions, model release and identification of subjects required.

‡**FLOORING MAGAZINE**, 757 3rd Ave., New York NY 10017. Editor: Michael Korsonsky. 10% freelance written. For floor covering retailers, wholesalers, floor covering specifiers, architects, etc. Monthly. Circulation: 22,000. Buys all rights. No byline. Buys 5-6 mss/year. Pays on acceptance. Publishes ms an average of 1 month after acceptance. Query. Reports in 2-4 weeks. SASE. Free sample copy.
Nonfiction: "Merchandising articles, new industry developments, unusual installations of floor coverings, etc. Conversational approach; snappy, interesting leads; plenty of quotes." Informational, how-to, interview, successful business operations, merchandising techniques and technical. Recent article example: "D.F. Ferent by Design" (January, 1984). Length: 1,500-1,800 words. Pays $200-500/feature.
Photos: Photos *must* accompany feature. Captions required.
Tips: "It pays to talk to the subject before sending query letter."

‡**FLOTATION SLEEP INDUSTRY, The Journal for the Waterbed Trade**, Hester Communications, Inc., Suite 250, 1700 E. Dyer Rd., Santa Ana CA 92705. (714)549-4834. Editor: Kurt Indrik. Managing Editor: Leslie Holden. A monthly magazine covering the waterbed industry, geared towards the retailer. Circ. 7,500. Pays on acceptance. Byline given. Not copyrighted. Buys all rights. Submit seasonal/holiday material 3 months in advance. Simultaneous queries and photocopied submissions OK. Computer printout submissions acceptable. SASE. Reports in 1 month. Free sample copy and writer's guidelines.
Nonfiction: How-to, interview/profile, new product, personal experience and technical. Buys 6-12 mss/year. Query with published clips. Length: 300-1,500 words. Pays $100-300.
Photos: State availability of photos with query or ms.
Tips: "Writer should have a solid feel for retail business and story ideas that will help the retailer be more successful. Features are most open to freelancers."

FURNITURE WORLD, (formerly *Furniture World/South*), Towse Publishing Co., 127 E. 31st St., New York NY 10016. (212)686-3910. Editor: Phillip Mazzurco. Monthly magazine covering the furniture industry for retailers and manufacturers. Pays on publication. Byline given. Not copyrighted. Buys one-time rights. Submit seasonal/holiday material 1 month in advance. SASE. Reports in 1 month. Free sample copy and writer's guidelines.
Nonfiction: General interest (economics affecting furniture and housing industries); interview/profile (of successful retailers, manufacturers); and technical. Query. Pays $50/published page.
Photos: State availability of photos. Reviews b&w negatives and prints. Captions required. Buys one-time rights.
Columns/Departments: Interviews with top industry leaders about economic future of furniture industry.

GIFTS & DECORATIVE ACCESSORIES, 51 Madison Ave., New York NY 10010. (212)689-4411. Editor-in-Chief: Phyllis Sweed. Managing Editor: Susan Stashkevetch. 10% freelance written. Published primarily for quality gift retailers. Monthly magazine; 300 pages. Circ. 33,000. Pays on publication. No byline. Buys all rights. Submit seasonal/holiday material 6 months in advance. Photocopied submissions OK. SASE. Reports "as soon as possible." Free writer's guidelines.
Nonfiction: "Merchandising how-to stories of quality stores—how they have solved a particular merchandising problem or successfully displayed or promoted a particularly difficult area." Nothing about discount stores or mass merchants. No cartoons, poems or think pieces. Buys 6 unsolicited mss/year. Query or submit complete ms. Length: 500-1,500 words. Pays $75-200.
Photos: "Photos should illustrate merchandising points made in a story." Pays $7.50-10 for good 5x7 glossy b&w prints; $15-25 for 4x5 color transparencies or 35mm transparencies. Captions required. Buys all rights.
Tips: "We're always in the market for a good story from the West or Southwest."

GIFTWARE BUSINESS, 1515 Broadway, New York NY 10036. (212)869-1300. Editor: Rita Guarna. For "merchants (department store buyers, specialty shop owners) engaged in the resale of giftware, china and glass, and decorative accessories." Monthly. Circ. 37,500. Buys all rights. Byline given "by request only." Pays on publication. Will consider photocopied submissions. SASE. Query or submit complete ms.
Nonfiction: "Retail store success stories. Describe a single merchandising gimmick. We are a tabloid for-

mat—glossy stock. Descriptions of store interiors are less important than sales performance unless display is outstanding. We're interested in articles on aggressive selling tactics. We cannot use material written for the consumer." Buys coverage of successful business operations and merchandising techniques. Length: 750 words maximum.

Photos: Purchased with mss and on assignment; captions required. "Individuals are to be identified." Reviews b&w glossy prints (preferred) and color transparencies.

HOME FURNISHINGS, 4313 N. Central Expressway, Box 64545, Dallas TX 75206. (214)526-7757. Editor: Tina Berres Filipski. 20% freelance written. Biannual magazine for home furnishings retail dealers, manufacturers, their representatives and others in related fields. Circ. 15,000. Pays on acceptance. Publishes ms an average of 2 months after acceptance. Buys first rights. No simultaneous submissions. Computer printout submissions acceptable; no dot-matrix. SASE.

Nonfiction: Informational articles about retail selling; success and problem solving stories in the retail business; economic and legislative-related issues, etc. "No profiles of people out of our area or nonmembers of the association. No trite, over-used features on trends, lighthearted features." Query. Length: open; appropriate to subject and slant. Pays 15¢/word. "Extensive research projects done on assignment negotiated in addition to the per-word rate; particularly interested in articles related to the Southwest furniture retailing." Photos desirable.

HOME LIGHTING & ACCESSORIES, Box 2147, Clifton NJ 07015. (201)779-1600. Editor-in-Chief: Peter Wulff. 35% freelance written. For lighting stores/departments. Monthly magazine. Circ. 7,000. Pays on publication. Buys all rights. Phone queries OK. Submit seasonal/holiday material 6 months in advance. Publishes ms an average of 3 months after acceptance. Computer printout submissions acceptable; no dot-matrix. SASE. Free sample copy.

Nonfiction: How-to (run your lighting store/department, including all retail topics); interview (with lighting retailers); personal experience (as a businessperson involved with lighting); opinion (about business approaches and marketing); profile (of a successful lighting retailer/lamp buyer); and technical (concerning lighting or lighting design). Buys 30 mss/year. Query. Pays $60/published page.

Photos: State availability of photos with query. Offers no additional payment for 5x7 or 8x10 b&w glossy prints. Pays additional $90 for color transparencies used on cover. Captions required.

HOUSEHOLD AND PERSONAL PRODUCTS INDUSTRY, 26 Lake St., Ramsey NJ 07446. Editor: Hamilton C. Carson. 10% freelance written. For "manufacturers of soaps, detergents, cosmetics and toiletries, waxes and polishes, insecticides, and aerosols." Monthly. Circ. 14,000. Not copyrighted. Buys 3 to 4 mss a year, "but would buy more if slanted to our needs." Pays on publication. Will consider photocopied submissions. Submit seasonal material 2 months in advance. Query. SASE. Will send a sample copy to a writer on request.

Nonfiction: "Technical and semitechnical articles on manufacturing, distribution, marketing, new products, plant stories, etc., of the industries served. Some knowledge of the field is essential in writing for us." Buys informational articles, interviews, photo features, spot news, coverage of successful business operations, new product articles, coverage of merchandising techniques and technical articles. No articles slanted toward consumers. Query with clips of published work. Length: 500-2,000 words. Pays $10-200.

Photos: 5x7 or 8x10 b&w glossies purchased with mss. Pays $10.

LINENS, DOMESTICS AND BATH PRODUCTS, 370 Lexington Ave., New York NY 10017. (212)532-9290. Editor-in-Chief: Maddalena S. Vitriol. For department stores, mass merchandisers, specialty stores and bath boutiques. Published 6 times/year. Buys all rights. Pays on publication. Reports in 4-6 weeks. SASE.

Nonfiction: Merchandising articles that educate the buyer on sales and fashion trends, promotions, industry news, and styles; in-depth articles with photos on retail stores/departments for bath accessories, linens and sheets, tablecloths, napkins and place mats, towels, and comforters. Especially focusing on interesting promotions and creative displays within these departments. Buys 6-10 mss/year. Length: 700-1,500 words. Pays $150-250.

Photos: Photos purchased with mss.

NATIONAL HOME CENTER NEWS, Lebhar-Friedman, Inc., 425 Park Ave., New York NY 10022. (212)371-9400. Editor: Wyatt Kash. 6% freelance written. Biweekly tabloid covering "business news in the $60 billion retail building supply and do-it-yourself home improvement industry." Circ. 32,000. Pays on publication. Publishes ms an average of 1 month after acceptance. Byline given in some cases. Rights purchased are negotiable. Submit seasonal/holiday material 1 month in advance. Simultaneous queries, and simultaneous and photocopied submissions acceptable. Computer printout submissions acceptable, "as long as the copy is easily read and edited. We have no ability, however, to receive stories via computer, or wire. (We *do* use facsimile machines.)" Reports in 2 weeks.

Nonfiction: "We use very little freelance material. Please write first. Query editor on possible story ideas concerning specific retail building supply/home center companies, housing, home improvements and home improvement products.'' No how-to stories on running a business or on do-it-yourself projects. ''We're looking for business stories on actual companies or on trends regarding home improvement products sales and merchandising of interest to retailers and wholesalers of those products.''

Tips: ''In the past, we tended to survey only retailers about what was happening in the retail building supply/ home improvement market. We are now surveying wholesalers and manufacturers as well as retailers. Readers are responding increasingly to 'market intelligence' information in the business (trade) publishing field. They value news, analysis with a human interest twist far more now than 'how-to,' 'did you know?' articles. Their time is more valuable than ever. Articles must propel the reader quickly, and *deliver.*''

PROFESSIONAL FURNITURE MERCHANT MAGAZINE, The Business Magazine for Progressive Furniture Retailers, Vista Publications, 9600 W. Sample Rd., Coral Springs FL 33065. (305)753-7400. Editor: Julia McNair Docke. 35% freelance written. Monthly magazine covering the furniture industry from a retailer's perspective. In-depth features on direction, trends, certain retailers doing outstanding jobs, and analyses of areas affecting industry (housing, economy, etc.). Circ. 20,000. Pays on publication. Publishes ms an average of 1 month after acceptance. Byline given. Buys one-time rights. Submit seasonal/holiday material 3 months in advance. Simultaneous queries and submissions OK. SASE. Reports in 1 month. Sample copy and guidelines $6.

Nonfiction: Expose (relating to or affectng furniture industry); how-to (business oriented how-to control cash flow, inventory, market research, etc.); interview/profile (furniture retailers); and photo feature (special furniture category). No general articles, fiction or personal experience. Buys 24 mss/year. Send complete ms. Length: 1,000-2,400 words. Pays $150-350.

Photos: State availablity of photos. Pays $5 maximum for 4x5 color transparencies; $5 maximum for 3x5 b&w prints. Captions, model release and identification of subjects required.

Tips: ''Read the magazine. Send manuscript specifically geared to furniture retailers, with art (photos or drawings) specified.'' Break in with features. ''First, visit a furniture store, talk to the owner and discover what he's interested in.''

‡**THE PROFESSIONAL UPHOLSTERER, Official Publication of the National Association of Professional Upholsterers**, Cummunications/Today Publishing, Ltd., 200 S. Main St., Box 1808, High Point NC 27261. (919)889-0113. Editor: Keith Ferrell. Managing Editor: Joyce Earnhardt. A monthly magazine edited for the craftsman/businessman engaged in the making and reupholstering of furniture and home furnishings. The publication covers the basic how-to's of upholstering furniture, profiles of successful upholsterers, small business guidance advice, new products, calendar of events, etc. Estab. 1984. Circ. 26,000. Pays on publication. Byline given. Buys first rights. Submit seasonal/holiday material 2 months in advance. Simultaneous queries, and simultaneous, photocopied, and previously published submissions OK. Electronic submissions OK if compatible with an Itek system. Computer printout submissions acceptable. SASE. Reports in 2 weeks. Free sample copy.

Nonfiction: Book excerpts (small business guidance, upholstering); how-to (sewing, machine techniques, furniture upholstering); and new product (in the upholstering industry). Buys 36 mss/year. Query with published clips. Length: 1,000-2,500 words. Pays $50-100.

Columns/Departments: Small business guidance. Buys 24 mss/year. Query with published clips. Length: 750-1,500 words. Pays $75-100.

• **RAYTHEON MAGAZINE**, Raytheon Company, 141 Spring St., Lexington MA 02173. (617)862-6600, ext. 2415. Editor-in-Chief: Robert P. Suarez. Quarterly magazine for Raytheon stockholders, employees, customers, suppliers, plant city officials, libraries and interested persons. ''Ours is a company publication that strives to avoid sounding like a company publication. All stories must involve some aspect of Raytheon or its products.'' Circ. 200,000. Pays on acceptance. Byline given. Free sample copy.

Nonfiction: General interest, humor, interview/profile, new product, nostalgia, photo feature, technical and travel. ''This is a corporate publication designed to illustrate the breadth of Raytheon Company in a low key manner through six general-interest articles per issue. Photos are used liberally, top quality and exclusively color. Stories are by assignment only.'' Buys 5 mss/issue. Query with clips of published work, stating specialties, credentials and other publication credits. Length: 800-1,000 words. Pays $750-1,000/article.

Tips: ''Submit resume and magazine style writing samples. We are looking for established writers who are capable of crisp, interesting magazine journalism. We are not looking to promote Raytheon, but rather to inform our audience about the company, very subtly. Heavy marketing-style or house organ writing is of no interest to us.''

RETAILER AND MARKETING NEWS, Box 191105, Dallas TX 75219-1105. (214)651-9959. Editor: Michael J. Anderson. For ''retail dealers and wholesalers in appliances, TVs, furniture, consumer electronics, records, air conditioning, housewares, hardware, and all related businesses.'' Monthly. Circ. 10,000. Photocopied submissions OK. SASE. Free sample copy.

Nonfiction: "How a retail dealer can make more profit" is the approach. Wants "sales promotion ideas, advertising, sales tips, business builders and the like, localized to the Southwest and particularly to north Texas." Submit complete ms. Length: 100-900 words. Pays $30.

SEW BUSINESS, Box 1331, Ft. Lee NJ 07024. Editor: Christina Holmes. For retailers of home sewing, quilting and needlework merchandise. "We are the only glossy magazine format in the industry—including home sewing and the *Art Needlework* and *Quilt Quarterly* supplements." Monthly. Circ. 19,000. Not copyrighted. Pays on publication. Reports in 5 weeks on queries; in 6 weeks on ms. SASE. Free sample copy and writer's guidelines.
Nonfiction: Articles on department store or fabric, needlework, or quilt shop operations, including coverage of art needlework, piece goods, patterns, quilting and sewing notions. Interviews with buyers—retailers on their department or shop. "Stories must be oriented to provide interesting information from a *trade* point of view. Looking for retailers doing something different or offbeat, something that another retailer could put to good use in his own operation. Best to query editor first to find out if a particular article might be of interest to us." Buys 25 unsolicited mss/year. Query. Length: 750-1,500 words. Pays $100 minimum.
Photos: Photos purchased with mss. "Should illustrate important details of the story." Sharp 5x7 b&w glossies. Offers no additional payment for photos accompanying ms.

UNFINISHED FURNITURE MAGAZINE, United States Exposition Corp., 1850 Oak St., Northfield IL 60093. (312)446-8434. Editor: Lynda Utterback. Bimonthly magazine for unfinished furniture retailers, distributors and manufacturers throughout the US, Canada, England, Australia and Europe. Circ. 6,000. Pays on publication. Byline give. Buys all rights. Submit seasonal/holiday material 6 months in advance. Simultaneous queries and simultaneous and photocopied submissions OK. Computer printout submissions acceptable. Reports in 3 weeks on queries; 1 month on mss. Free sample copy and writer's guidelines.
Nonfiction: How-to, interview/profile, new product, personal experience and technical (as these relate to the furniture industry). Production distribution, marketing, advertising and promotion of unfinished furniture and current happenings in the industry. Buys 10 unsolicited mss/year. Send complete ms. Length: 2,000. Pays $50-100.
Photos: Pays $5 for b&w photos.

Hospitals, Nursing, and Nursing Homes

In this section are journals for nurses; medical and nonmedical nursing homes; clinical and hospital staffs; and laboratory technicians and managers. Journals publishing technical material on new discoveries in medicine and information for physicians in private practice are listed in the Medical category. Publications that report on medical trends for the consumer are in the Health and Science categories.

AMERICAN JOURNAL OF NURSING, 555 West 57th St., New York NY 10019. (212)582-8820. Editor: Mary B. Mallison, RN. Monthly magazine covering nursing and health care. Circ. 330,000. Pays on publication. Byline given. Simultaneous queries OK. Computer printout submissions acceptable; prefers letter-quality to dot-matrix. Reports in 3 weeks on queries, 4 months on mss. Sample copy $3; free writer's guidelines.
Nonfiction: How-to, satire, new product, opinion, personal experience, photo feature and technical. No material other than nursing care and nursing issues. "Nurse authors mostly accepted for publication." Query. Length: 1,000-1,500 words. Pays $20 minimum/published page.
Photos: Forbes Linkhorn, art editor. Reviews b&w and color transparencies and prints. Model release and identification of subjects required. Buys variable rights.
Columns/Departments: Buys 12 mss/year. Query with or without clips of published work.

DIMENSIONS IN HEALTH SERVICE, Canadian Hospital Association, Suite 100, 17 York St., Ottawa, Ontario K1N 9J6 Canada . (613)238-8005. Executive Editor: Jean-Claude Martin. Managing Editor: Ruta Siulys. 5% freelance written. Monthly magazine for health care administration. Circ. 11,500. Pays on publication. Publishes ms an average of 6 months after acceptance. Byline given. Buys first rights only. Submit seasonal/holiday material 3 months in advance. Simultaneous queries and previously published submissions OK. Computer printout submissions acceptable; no dot-matrix. SASE. Reports in 3 weeks on queries; 1 month on mss. Sample copy $2 (Canada); $3 (US); free writer's guidelines.

Nonfiction: How-to (improve patient care, manage health facilities); interview/profile (of figures in Canadian health field); and technical (health services). Recent editoral themes: manpower; emergency services, interconnection; finance/cost control; computers; I.C.U./C.C.U.; laundry/housekeeping; safety and security; design and construction; food services; community services, fundraising; technology; communications; infection control; conventions; purchasing; geriatrics; and rehabilitation. Buys 10 mss/year. Query. Length: 800-3,000 words. Pays $100-300.

Photos: State availability of photos. Pays $15 minimum for 2x2 color transparencies; $15-30 for prints; $15-30 for 2x2 b&w transparencies and prints. Captions required. Buys one-time rights.

Tips: "Emphasize Canadian or international aspects. Write with easy reading style, a bit of humor, and include *photos.*"

HOSPITAL SUPERVISOR'S BULLETIN, Bureau of Business Practice, 24 Rope Ferry Rd., Waterford CT 06386. Editor: Jill Wasserman. 50% freelance written. For non medical hospital supervisors. Semimonthly newsletter; 8 pages. Circ. 8,000. Pays on acceptance. Publishes ms an average of 5 months after acceptance. Buys all rights. No byline. Submit seasonal/holiday material 6 months in advance. Photocopied submissions OK. Computer printout submissions acceptable; no dot-matrix. SASE. Reports in 1 month. Free sample copy and writer's guidelines.

Nonfiction: Publishes interviews with non-medical hospital department heads. "You should ask supervisors to pinpoint current problems in supervision, tell how they are trying to solve these problems and what results they're getting—backed up by real examples from daily life." Also publishes interviews on people problems and good methods of management. People problems include the areas of training, planning, evaluating, counseling, discipline, motivation, supervising the undereducated, getting along with the medical staff, etc., with emphasis on good methods of management. No material on hospital volunteers. "We prefer 6- to 8-page typewritten articles, based on interviews." Pays 12¢/word after editing.

HOSPITALS, American Hospital Publishing, Inc., 211 E. Chicago Ave., Chicago IL 60611. (312)951-1100. Editor: Daniel Schechter. Managing Editor: Frank Sabatino. 5% freelance written. Bimonthly magazine featuring hospitals and health care systems. Circ. 95,000. Average issue includes 4-5 articles. Pays on acceptance. Byline given. Buys first North American serial rights. Phone queries OK. Submit seasonal material 4 months in advance. Photocopied submissions OK. Inquire about electronic submissions. Computer printout submissions acceptable. Reports in 2 weeks on queries; in 2 months on mss. Publishes ms an average of 6 months after acceptance. Free sample copy and writer's guidelines.

Nonfiction: How-to and new product. "Articles must address issues of the management of health care institutions." Buys 10-12 unsolicited mss/year. "Moving to staff-written magazine in the year ahead." Query with "reasonably detailed summary or outline of proposed article." Length: 3,000 words maximum. Pays $250-500.

Columns/Departments: "Columns are published on cost containment, architecture and design, and long-term care. Another column includes short features on innovative hospital programs."

‡**LICENSED PRACTICAL NURSE, Official Publication of the National Federation of LPN's**, Publico, Suite 100, 3553 N. Sharon Amity, Charlotte NC 28705. (704)535-8200. Editor: John Kerr. Managing Editor: Betty Jones. 70% freelance written. A quarterly magazine on nursing for members of the National Federation of LPN's. Estab. 1983. Circ. 10,000. Pays on publication. Byline given. Offers 100% kill fee. Buys first North American serial rights. Submit seasonal/holiday material 3 months in advance. Photocopied submissions OK. SASE. Reports in 1 month. Sample copy for 9x12 SAE and 2 first class stamps; free writer's guidelines.

Nonfiction: Book excerpts/reviews; historical/nostalgic; how-to (improve basic skills, new methods, etc.); humor/puzzles; new product/product reviews; opinion/topics of controversy (such as life support systems, unionization, etc.); personal experience; photo feature; non technical medical news; nurse/doctor and nurse/patient situations; legal liabilities of nurses; tax update for nurses; nursing ethics; and continuing education. Special Convention Issue mid-summer each year. No highly technical articles or articles devoted to RN situations that would have no bearing on LPN's. Buys 20 mss/year. Query. Length: 300-2,500 words. Pays $15-125.

Photos: State availability of photos, or send photos with query or ms if available. Reviews b&w and color contact sheets. Pays $10-25 for 5x7 b&w prints; $10-75 for 5x7 color prints and color transparencies. Captions, model release, and identification of subjects required. Buys one-time rights.

Fillers: Clippings, anecdotes, short humor and newsbreaks. Buys 25/year. Length: 50-200 words. Pays $2.50-$10.

Tips: "First choice is given to LPN writers, then nurse writers, then all others. Articles are chosen because of their value to LPNs in LPN work situations. Content must be invigorating and readable. Dull, technical material will not be accepted."

NURSINGWORLD JOURNAL, Prime National Publishing Corp., 470 Boston Post Rd., Weston MA 02193. Editor: Eileen DeVito. Contains reviews of all the pertinent nursing and healthcare articles plus news

and feature stories about nursing. Each issue also contains the latest career and employment opportunities in selected hospitals in specific states. "We accept feature articles dealing with the issues and concerns of the profession and manuscripts describing the problems and opportunities in specific types of nursing, for example, oncology nursing. Monthly journal, 24-72 pages. Circ. 40,000. Pays on publication. Buys one-time rights. Byline given. Phone queries OK. Submit seasonal/holiday material 1-3 months in advance. Previously published work OK. SASE. Reports in 4 months. Sample copy $2.
Nonfiction: General interest; how-to; interview (with nurses, students); opinion; profile; travel; personal experience; photo feature; employment; and issues or concerns. All articles must be related to nursing or hospitals. Buys 1 mss/issue. Send complete ms. Length: 1,500 words maximum. Pays $50 minimum.
Photos: Pays $5-15 each b&w 5x7 or 8x10 glossy print. Captions and model releases required.
Columns/Departments: Open to suggestions for new columns or departments.

RN, 680 Kinderkamack Rd., Oradell NJ 07649. (201)262-3030. Editor: James A. Reynolds. For registered nurses, mostly hospital-based but also in physicians' offices, public health, schools and industry. Monthly magazine; 120 pages. Circ. 325,000. Buys all rights. Pays 25% kill fee for specifically commissioned material. Byline given. Pays on publication. Submit seasonal/holiday material 8 months in advance. Reports in 6-8 weeks. SASE. Sample copy $3. Free writer's guidelines.
Nonfiction: "If you are a nurse who writes, we would like to see your work. Editorial content: diseases, clinical techniques, surgery, therapy, equipment, drugs, etc. These should be thoroughly researched and sources cited. Personal anecdotes, experiences, and observations based on your relations with doctors, hospitals, patients and nursing colleagues. Our style is simple and direct, not preachy. Do include examples and case histories that relate the reader to her own nursing experience. Talk mostly about people, rather than things. Dashes of humor or insight are always welcome. Include photos where feasible." Buys 100 mss/year. Query or submit complete ms. Length: 1,000-2,000 words. Pays $100-300.
Photos: "We want good clinical illustration." Send photos with ms. Pays $25 minimum/b&w contact sheet; $35 minimum/35mm color transparency. Captions required; model release required. Buys all rights.

TODAY'S OR NURSE, Slack, Inc., 6900 Grove Rd., Thorofare NJ 08086. (609)848-1000. Editor: Judith B. Paquet, RN. 4% freelance written. Monthly magazine covering general interest, features and scientific information for operating room nurses. Circ. 35,000. Pays on publication. Publishes ms an average of 9 months after acceptance. Byline given. Buys all rights. Submit seasonal material 5 months in advance. Computer printout submissions acceptable; prefers letter-quality to dot-matrix. Reports in 3 weeks on queries; 2 months on mss. Free sample copy and writer's guidelines.
Nonfiction: General interest, how-to, humor, personal experience and technical. Must be pertinent to operating room nurses. No travel material. Query with clips of published work or send complete ms. Length: 500-750 words. Pays 10¢/word.
Photos: Send photos with ms. Pays $5-25 for 35mm or 2¼x2¼ b&w transparencies and 8x10 b&w prints; $10-250 for color. Model release and identification of subjects required.
Columns/Departments: Humor, how-to, profiles, human interest and reviews—all about or pertaining to OR nurses. Buys 18 mss/year. Query with clips of published work or send complete ms. Length: 500-1,000 words. Pays 10¢/word.
Tips: "We're looking for timely, useful, original articles pertaining to operating room nurses. Illustrated material is best."

Hotels, Motels, Clubs, Resorts, Restaurants

Hotel and restaurant management obtains trade tips from these publications for owners, managers and operators of these establishments. Journals for manufacturers and distributors of bar and beverage supplies are classified in the Beverages and Bottling category. For publications slanted to food wholesalers, processors and caterers, see Food Products, Processing, and Service.

‡**COOKING FOR PROFIT**, Metanoia Corp., Box 267, Fond du Lac WI 54935. (414)923-3700. Editor: Karen Boehme. A monthly magazine covering foodservice operations for restaurants, hospitals and nursing homes, hotels/motels and others in foodservice industry. Circ. 35,000. Pays on publication. Byline given. Buys variable rights. Submit seasonal/holiday material 6 months in advance. Simultaneous submissions OK.

Computer printout submissions acceptable. SASE. Reports in 1 month. Sample copy for 9x12 SAE and 40¢ postage; free writer's guidelines.

Nonfiction: Book excerpts, new product, photo feature and technical. "Articles should always go beyond general trends, overviews and theory and offer practical advice and information." No articles on promotions or any front-of-the-house topics. Buys 60-70 mss/year. Query with clips of published work. Length: 500-1,500 words. Pays $100-350.

Photos: Send photos with accompanying query or ms. Pays $50-75 for 8x10 b&w prints; $50-150 for 4x5 color slides. Captions, model release and identification of subjects required. Buys one-time rights.

Columns/Departments: Foodservice equipment energy and maintenance. Query.

Fillers: Clippings, anecdotes and newsbreaks. Length: 75-200 words. Pays $10-25.

Tips: Writers should "send clips of their work; thoroughly describe and, preferably, outline their query and give an idea what kind of fee they are looking for. Features, particularly restaurant profiles, are most open to freelancers."

FLORIDA HOTEL & MOTEL NEWS, The Official Publication of the Florida Hotel & Motel Association, Accommodations, Inc., Box 1529, Tallahassee FL 32302. (904)224-2888. Editor: Mrs. Jayleen Woods. Monthly magazine for managers in the lodging industry (every licensed hotel, motel and resort in Florida). Circ. 6,500. Pays on publication. Byline given. Offers $50 kill fee. Buys all rights and makes work-for-hire assignments. Submit seasonal/holiday material 3 months in advance. Photocopied submissions OK. SASE. Reports in 1 month. Sample copy for 9x12 SAE and 3 first class stamps; writer's guidelines for business-size SAE and 1 first class stamp.

Nonfiction: General interest (business, finance, taxes); historical/nostalgic (old Florida hotel reminiscences); how-to (improve management, housekeeping procedures, guest services, security and coping with common hotel problems); humor (hotel-related anecdotes); inspirational (succeeding where others have failed); interview/profile (of unusual hotel personalities); new product (industry-related and non brand preferential); photo feature (queries only); technical (emerging patterns of hotel accounting, telephone systems, etc.); travel (transportation and tourism trends only—no scenics or site visits); and property renovations and maintenance techniques. Buys 10-12 mss/year. Query with clips of published work. Length: 750-2,500 words. Pays $75-250 "depending on type of article and amount of research."

Photos: Send photos with ms. Pays $25-100 for 4x5 color transparencies; $10-15 for 5x7 b&w prints. Captions, model release and identification of subjects required.

Tips: "We prefer feature stories on properties or personalities holding current membership in the Florida Hotel & Motel Association. Memberships and/or leadership brochures are available (SASE) on request. We're open to articles showing how Mom & Dad management copes with inflation and rising costs of energy systems, repairs, renovations, new guest needs and expectations."

INDEPENDENT RESTAURANTS, (formerly *Foodservice Marketing*, EIP, Inc., 2132 Fordem Ave., Madison WI 53704. (608)244-3528. Editor: Jeanette Riechers. Monthly magazine covering management and marketing of independently owned and operated restaurants. Circ. 106,000. Pays on acceptance. No byline given. Offers negotiable kill fee. Buys first North American serial rights. Submit seasonal/holiday material 6 months in advance. Photocopied submissions OK. Computer printout submissions acceptable; prefers letter-quality to dot-matrix. SASE. Reports in 2 months. Sample copy $2.50.

Nonfiction: How-to (improve management of independent restaurant; marketing techniques, promotions, etc.); and interview/profile (with independent restaurateur; needs a strong angle). "Send us a query on a successful independent restaurateur with an effective marketing program, unusual promotions, interesting design and decor, etc." No restaurant reviews, consumer-oriented material, non restaurant-oriented management articles. Buys variable number mss/year. Length: open. Pays variable fee.

Photos: State availability of photos. Captions, model release and identification of subjects required. Buys all rights.

INNKEEPING WORLD, Box 15480, Seattle WA 98115. Editor/Publisher: Charles Nolte. 50% freelance written. Emphasizes the hotel industry worldwide. Published 10 times a year; 12 pages. Circ. 2,000. Pays on acceptance. Buys all rights. No byline. Submit seasonal/holiday material 1 month in advance. SASE. Reports in 1 month. Free sample copy and writer's guidelines with SASE.

Nonfiction: Main topics: Managing—interview with successful hotel managers of large and/or famous hotels/resorts (length: 600-1,200 words); Marketing—interviews with hotel marketing executives on successful promotions/case histories (length: 300-1,000 words); Lodging Classics—stories of famous or highly-rated hotels/inns/resorts, domestice and overseas listing of hotels available from the publisher (length: 300-1,000 words); Bill of Fare—outstanding hotel restaurants, menus and merchandising concepts (length: 300-1,000 words); and The Concierge—interviews with the world's most experienced about their experience in guest relations (length: 300-1,000 words). Pays $100 minimum or 15¢/word (whichever is greater) for main topics. Other topics, advertising, creative packages, cutting expenses, guest comfort, guest relations, hospitality, ideas, interior design, public relations, sales promotion, special guestrooms, special reports, staff relations and trends. Length: 50-500 words. Pays 15¢/word.

MEETINGS & CONVENTIONS, Ziff-Davis Publishing Co., 1 Park Ave., New York NY 10016. Editor-in-Chief: Mel Hosansky. 15% freelance written. For association and corporate executives who plan sales meetings, training meetings, annual conventions, incentive travel trips and any other kind of off premises meeting. Monthly magazine; 150 pages. Circ. 74,500. Pays on acceptance. Publishes ms an average of 5 months after acceptance. Buys first rights. Photocopied submissions and previously published work (if not published in a competing publication) OK. Computer printout submissions acceptable; prefers letter-quality to dot-matrix. SASE. Reports in 1-2 months.
Nonfiction: "Publication is basically how-to. We tell how to run better meetings, where to hold them, etc. Must be case history, talking about specific meeting." No destination write-ups. Buys 7-10 unsolicited mss/year. Query. Length: 250-2,000 words. Pays $200-800.
Photos: Uses b&w slides. Query.

‡**RESORT MANAGEMENT MAGAZINE**, Western Specialty Publications, Inc., Suite 1E, 4501 Mission Bay Dr., San Diego CA 92109. (619)270-7710. Editor: James McVicar. A magazine published 8 times/year covering the hotel/resort and condo/timeshare industries. "We do not reach motels or motor lodges" Pays on publication. Byline given. Offers $50 kill fee. Buys all rights. Submit seasonal/holiday material 2 months in advance. Simultaneous queries and photocopied and previously published submissions OK. Computer printout submissions acceptable. SASE. Reports in 3 month. Sample copy $5.
Nonfiction: Book excerpts, expose, general interest, historical/nostalgic, how-to, humor, inspirational, interview/profile, new product, opinion, personal experience, photo feature, technical and travel. Especially interested in state-of-the-art technology and management methods, industry megatrends and instant cost saving devices. Buys 6 mss/year. Query with clips of published work. Length: 500-2,000 words. Pays $50-100.
Photos: Bella Silverstein, photo editor. Send photos with accompanying query or ms. "Won't return without SASE." Pays $5-10 for b&w and color prints; $10-20 for b&w transparencies; $10-25 for color transparencies. Buys all rights.

RESTAURANT HOSPITALITY, Penton IPC, Penton Plaza, 1111 Chester Ave., Cleveland OH 44114. (216)696-7000. Editor: Stephen Michaelides. Managing Editor: Michael DeLuca. 10% freelance written. Monthly magazine covering the foodservice industry for owners and operators of independent restaurants, hotel foodservices, executives of national and regional restaurant chains and foodservice executives of schools, hospitals, military installations and corporations. Circ. 85,000. Average issue includes 10-12 features. Pays on acceptance. Byline given. Buys exclusive rights. Query first. SASE. Reports in 1 week. Publishes ms an average of 3 months after acceptance. Free sample copy for 9x12 SASE.
Nonfiction: Michael DeLuca, managing editor. General interest (articles that advise operators how to run their operations profitably and efficiently); interview (with operators); and profile. No restaurant reviews. Buys 20 mss/year. Query with clips of previously published work and a short bio. Length: 500-1,500 words. Pays $100/published page.
Photos: Send color photos with manuscript. Captions required.
Tips: "We're accepting fewer queried stories but assigning more to our regular freelancers. We need new angles on old stories, and we like to see pieces on emerging trends and technologies in the restaurant industry. Stories on psychology, consumer behavior, managerial problems and solutions, how-to's on buying insurance, investing (our readers have a high degree of disposable income), design elements and computers in foodservice. Our readers don't want to read how to open a restaurant or why John Smith is so successful. We are accepting 100-150 word pieces with photos (slides preferred; will accept b&w) for our Restaurant People department. Should be light, humorous, anecdotal." Byline given. Pays $75.

TEXAS FOOD & SERVICE NEWS, Texas Restaurant Association, Box 1429, Austin TX 78767. (512)444-6543. Editor: Kate Fox. 15% freelance written. Magazine published 10 times/year about the Texas food service industry for restaurant owners and operators. Circ. 5,500. Pays on acceptance. Publishes ms an average of 3 months after acceptance. Byline given. Not copyrighted. Buys first and second rights to the same material, and second (reprint) rights to material originally published elsewhere. Written queries preferred. Submit seasonal material 2 months in advance. Simultaneous queries, and photocopied and previously published submissions OK. Computer printout submissions acceptable. SASE. Reports in 1 month. Free sample copy.
Nonfiction: Interview, profile, how-to, humor and personal experience. "The magazine spotlights many general categories (economy, energy, labor relations, new products and staff editorials) in short columns. Therefore, we appreciate getting good, terse articles with a how-to-improve-your-business slant. These we prefer with sharp, black and white photos. All articles should be substantiated with plenty of facts or specific examples. Avoid too much vocabulary. Opt for shorter sentences and shorter words." No restaurant critiques. Buys 10 mss/year. Query. Length: 1,000-1,500 words. Pays $15-50.

Photos: State availability of photos. Pays $10-20 for b&w contact sheet; $10-50 for b&w and color negatives. Buys one-time rights.

Columns/Departments: Send complete ms.

Tips: "All of our readers are business people seeking to improve their operations. We like to feature specific areas of food service, such as employee relations; serving health food, computers and eating out trends. The magazine adopts a professional approach to the food service industry. In other words, articles must contain ideas and information that will make money."

Industrial Operation and Management

Industrial plant managers, executives, distributors and buyers read the journals that follow. Subjects include equipment, supplies, quality control, and production engineering. Some industrial management journals are also listed under the names of specific industries, such as Machinery and Metal Trade. Publications for industrial supervisors are listed in Management and Supervision.

COMPRESSED AIR, 253 E. Washington Ave., Washington NJ 07882. Editor/Publications Manager: S.M. Parkhill. 75% freelance written. Emphasizes general industrial/technology subjects for engineers and managers. Monthly magazine; 48 pages. Circ. 150,000. Buys all rights. Computer printout submissions acceptable; no dot-matrix. SASE. Reports in 4-6 weeks. Free sample copy, editorial schedule and writer's guidelines; mention *Writer's Market* in request.

Nonfiction: "Articles must be reviewed by experts in the field." How-to (save costs with air power); and historical (engineering). Recent article example: "Geothermal Energy Generates Excitement" (April 1984). Buys 30 mss/year. Query with clips of previously published work. Pays negotiable fee.

Photos: State availability of photos in query. Payment for 8x10 glossy b&w photos is included in total purchase price. Captions required. Buys all rights.

Tips: "We are presently looking for freelancers with a track record in industrial/technology writing. Editorial schedule is developed well in advance and relies heavily on article ideas from contributors. Resume and samples help. Writers with access to authorities preferred; prefer interviews over library research. The magazine's name doesn't reflect its contents; suggest writers request sample copies."

INDUSTRIAL CHEMICAL NEWS, Bill Communications, 633 3rd Ave., New York NY 10025. (212)986-4800. Editor: Irvin Schwartz. Managing Editor: Susan Neale. Monthly magazine covering the scientific, business industrial aspects of chemistry for chemists working in industry. Circ. 40,000. Pays on publication. Byline given. Pays $100 kill fee. Buys all rights. SASE. Reports within weeks. Free sample copy and writer's guidelines.

Nonfiction: Expose (of government or industry matters); interview/profile (related to the chemical industry); personal experience (of a chemist's work life); photo feature (of a chemical development); and technical overviews (chemical or biological). "The features in *ICN* are written in an informative and fresh style. We do not intend to burden our readers with complex technical jargon when the facts can be told more simply, and other publications cover research articles. But neither do we want a basic story; we must tell them something new, something they must know. The features emphasize examples and details of how the research was actually accomplished (equipment used, dollars spent, etc.). Always, the emphasis is our readers: How will the industrial chemist learn from the information?" Buys 3-6 unsolicited mss/year. Query with clips of published work. Length: 1,000-3,000 words. Pays $200-500.

Photos: State availability of photos. "It would be helpful if the author could supply the artwork or recommend material that could be used to clearly portray points made in the written material." Buys one-time rights.

Columns/Departments: Book reviews (new books); employment briefs ("news items on chemical careers"); and news ("broad topic of interest to chemists"). Length: 300-3,000 words.

INDUSTRIAL FABRIC PRODUCTS REVIEW, Industrial Fabrics Assoc., Suite 450, 345 Cedar Bldg., St. Paul MN 55101. (612)222-2508. Editor: Brian Becker. Director of Publications: Carey Bohn. Monthly magazine covering industrial textiles for company owners, salespersons and researchers in a variety of industrial textile areas. Circ. 6,000. Pays on publication. Byline given. Buys all rights. Submit seasonal/holiday material 4 months in advance. Simultaneous queries, and photocopied and previously published submissions OK. SASE.

Reports in 2 weeks. Sample copy free "after query and phone conversation."
Nonfiction: Technical, marketing and other topics "related to any aspect of industrial fabric industry from fiber to finished fabric product." Special issues include new products, industrial products and equipment. No historical or apparel oriented articles. Buys 12 mss/year. Query with phone number. Length: 1,200-3,000 words. Pays $75/published page.
Photos: State availability of photos. Reviews 8x10 b&w glossy prints. Pay is negotiable. Model release and identification of subjects required. Buys one-time rights.

INDUSTRY WEEK, Penton/IPC, Inc., 1111 Chester Ave., Cleveland OH 44114, (216)696-7000. Editor-in-Chief: Stanley Modic. 10% freelance written. Emphasizes manufacturing and service industries for top or middle management (administrating, production, engineering, finance, purchasing or marketing) throughout industry. Biweekly magazine; 96 pages. Circ. 300,000. Pays on publication. Publishes ms an average of 3 months after acceptance. Buys all rights. Byline given depending on length of article. Phone queries OK. Submit seasonal or holiday material 3 months in advance. Simultaneous and photocopied submissions OK. Computer printout submissions acceptable. SASE. Reports in 1 month. Sample copy $2.
Nonfiction: Robert W. Gardner, managing editor. How-to and informational articles (should deal with areas of interest to executive audience, e.g., developing managerial skills or managing effectively). "No product news or case histories, please." Length: 1,000-4,000 words. Pays $300/first 1,000 words; $100/additional 1,000 words. Buys 5-10/year. Query. No product news or clippings.
Photos: Nick Dankovich, art director. B&w and color purchased with ms or on assignment. Query. Pays $35 minimum. Model release required.

INSULATION OUTLOOK, National Insulation Contractors Association, Suite 410, 1025 Vermont NW, Washington DC 20005. (202)783-6278. Editor: Dixie M. Lee. Monthly magazine about general business, commercial and industrial insulation for the insulation industry in the United States and abroad. Publication is read by engineers, specifiers, buyers, contractors and union members in the industrial and commercial insulation field. There is also representative distribution to public utilities, and energy-related industries. Pays on publication. Byline given. Buys first rights only. Phone queries OK. Written queries should be short and simple, with samples of writing attached. Submit seasonal material 6 months in advance. Simultaneous, photocopied and previously published submissions OK. SASE. Sample copy $2; free writer's guidelines. "Give us a call. If there seems to be compatibility, we will send a free issue sample so the writer can see directly the type of publication he or she is dealing with."
Columns/Departments: Query. Pays $50-300.

PLANT MANAGEMENT & ENGINEERING, MacLean Hunter Bldg; 777 Bay St., Toronto, Ontario M5W 1A7 Canada. Editor: Ron Richardson. 10% freelance written. For Canadian plant managers and engineers. Monthly magazine. Circ. 26,000. Pays on acceptance. Publishes ms an average of 6 months after acceptance. Buys first Canadian rights. SAE and IRCs. Computer printout submissions acceptable; prefers letter-quality to dot-matrix. Reports in 2-3 weeks. Free sample copy with SAE only.
Nonfiction: How-to, technical and management technique articles. Must have Canadian slant. No generic articles that appear to be rewritten from textbooks. Buys less than 20 unsolicited mss/year. Query. Pays 12¢/word minimum.
Photos: State availability of photos with query. Pays $25-50 for b&w prints; $50-100 for 2¼x2¼ or 35mm color transparencies. Captions preferred. Buys one-time rights.
Tips: Query first by letter. "Read the magazine. Know the Canadian readers' special needs. Case histories and interviews only—no theoretical pieces. Trends in magazine publishing that freelance writes should be aware of include computers, robotles and high tech."

PRODUCTION ENGINEERING, Penton Plaza, Cleveland OH 44114. (216)696-7000. Managing Editor: Donald E. Hegland. Executive Editor: John McRainey. 50% freelance written. For "men and women in production engineering—the engineers who plan, design and improve manufacturing operations." Monthly magazine; 100 pages. Circ. 95,000. Pays on publication. Buys exclusive first North American serial rights. Byline given; "if by prior arrangement, an author contributed a segment of a broader article, he might not be bylined." Phone queries OK. Photocopied submissions OK, if exclusive. Computer printout submissions acceptable. SASE. Reports in 2 weeks. Free sample copy and writer's guidelines.
Nonfiction: How-to (engineering, data for engineers); personal experience (from *very* senior production or manufacturing engineers only); and technical (technical news or how-to). "We're interested in solid, hard hitting technical articles on the gut issues of manufacturing. Not case histories, but no-fat treatments of manufacturing concepts, innovative manufacturing methods, and state-of-the-art procedures. Our readers also enjoy articles that detail a variety of practical solutions to some specific, everyday manufacturing headache." Buys 2 mss/issue. Query. Length: 800-3,000 words. Pays $25-150.

PURCHASING EXECUTIVE'S BULLETIN, Bureau of Business Practice, 24 Rope Ferry Rd., Waterford CT 06386. (203)442-4365. Editor: Claire Sherman. Managing Editor: Wayne Muller. For purchasing managers and purchasing agents. Semimonthly newsletter; 4 pages. Circ. 5,500. Pays on acceptance. Buys all rights. Submit seasonal/holiday material 3 months in advance. Reports in 2 weeks. Free sample copy and writer's guidelines.
Nonfiction: How-to (better cope with problems confronting purchasing executives); and direct interviews detailing how purchasing has overcome problems and found better ways of handling departments. No derogatory material about a company; no writer's opinions; no training or minority purchasing articles. "We don't want material that's too elementary (things any purchasing executive already knows)." Buys 2-3 mss/issue. Query. Length: 750-1,000 words.
Tips: "Make sure that a release is obtained and attached to a submitted article."

QUALITY CONTROL SUPERVISOR'S BULLETIN, Natonal Foremen's Institute, 24 Rope Ferry Rd., Waterford CT 06386. (800)243-0876. Editor: Steven J. Finn. 100% freelance written. Biweekly newsletter for quality control supervisors. Circ. 10,000. Pay on acceptance. No byline given. Buys all rights. Computer printout submissions acceptable. SASE. Reports in 2 weeks on queries; 1 month on mss. Free sample copy and writer's guidelines.
Nonfiction: Interview and "articles with a strong how-to slant that make use of direct quotes whenever possible." Buys 70 mss/year. Query. Length: 800-1,100 words. Pays 8-14¢/word.
Tips: "Write for our freelancer guidelines and follow them closely. We're looking for steady freelancers we can work with on a regular basis."

SEMICONDUCTOR INTERNATIONAL, Cahners Publishing Co., 1350 E. Touhy Ave., Box 5080, Des Plaines IL 60018. (312)635-8800. Editor: Donald E. Swanson. 5% freelance written. Monthly magazine covering semiconductor industry processing, assembly and testing technology subjects for semiconductor industry processing engineers and management. "Technology stories that cover all phases of semiconductor product manufacturing and testing are our prime interest." Circ. 32,005. Pays on publication. "News items are paid for upon acceptance." Byline given. Buys all rights and makes work-for-hire assignments. Computer printout submissions acceptable; no dot-matrix. Reports in 2-4 weeks. Publishes ms an average of 4 months after acceptance. Free sample copy and writer's guidelines.
Nonfiction: Technical and news pertaining to the semiconductor industry in the US and overseas. No "articles that are commercial in nature or product oriented." Buys 50 mss/year (including feature articles and news). Query with "your interest and capabilities" or send complete ms. Length: 2,500 words maximum.
Photos: State availability of photos or send photos with ms. Reviews 8x10 b&w prints. Captions and identification of subjects required.
Columns/Departments: "News of the semiconductor industry as it pertains to technology trends is of interest. Of special interest is news of the semiconductor industry in foreign countries such as Japan, England, Germany, France, and the Netherlands." Buys 30-40 mss/year. Query. Length: 200-1,500 words. Pays 15¢/word for accepted, edited copy.

WEIGHING & MEASUREMENT, Key Markets Publishing Co., Box 5867, Rockford IL 61125. (815)399-6970. Editor: David M. Mathieu. For users of industrial scales and meters. Bimonthly magazine; 32 pages. Circ. 15,000. Pays on acceptance. Buys all rights. Pays 20% kill fee. Byline given. Reports in 2 weeks. Free sample copy.
Nonfiction: Interview (with presidents of companies); personal opinion (guest editorials on government involvement in business, etc.); profile (about users of weighing and measurement equipment); and technical. Buys 25 mss/year. Query on technical articles; submit complete ms for general interest material. Length: 750-2,500 words. Pays $45-125.

Insurance

BUSINESS INSURANCE, 740 N. Rush Street, Chicago IL 60611. Editor: Kathryn J. McIntyre. For "corporate risk, employee benefit and financial executives, insurance brokers and agents, and insurance company executives interested in commercial insurance, risk and benefit financing, safety, security and employee benefits." Special issues on self insurance, safety, pensions, health and life benefits, brokers, reinsurance and international insurance. Weekly. Circ. 41,000. Buys all rights. Pays negotiable kill fee. Byline given. Buys 50 mss/year. Pays on publication. Submit seasonal or special material 2 months in advance. Reports in 2 weeks. Query. SASE.

Nonfiction: "We publish material on corporate insurance and employee benefit programs and related subjects. We take everything from the buyer's point of view, rather than that of the insurance company, broker or consultant who is selling something. Items on insurance companies, insurance brokers, property/liability insurance, union contract (benefit) settlements, group life/health/medical plans, of interest—provided the *commercial* insurance or benefits angle is clear. Special emphasis on corporate risk management and employee benefits administration requires that freelancers discuss with us their proposed articles. Length is subject to discussion with contributor." Pays $7/column inch or negotiated fee.

Tips: "Send a detailed proposal including story angle and description of sources."

● **COMPASS**, Marine Office of America Corporation (MOAC), 180 Maiden Lane, New York NY 10038. (212)440-7718. Editor: Patricia Phillips. Annual magazine of the Marine Office of America Corporation covering insurance. Magazine is distributed world wide to persons in marine (agents, brokers, risk managers) insurance and the media. Circ. 25,000. Pays half on acceptance, half on publication. Byline given. Offers $250 kill fee. Not copyrighted. Buys all rights and makes work-for-hire assignments. Simultaneous queries, and simultaneous, photocopied and previously published submissions OK. Reports in 2 weeks on queries; 1 month on mss. Free sample copy and writer's guidelines.

Nonfiction: Patricia Phillips, articles editor. General interest, historical/nostalgic and technical. "Historical/nostalgia should relate to ships, trains, airplanes, balloons, bridges, sea and land expeditions, seaports and transportation of all types. General interest includes marine and transportation subjects; fishing industry; and environmental events—improvements relating to inland waterways, space travel and satellites. Articles must have human interest. Technical articles may cover energy exploration and development—offshore oil and gas drilling, developing new sources of electric power and solar energy; usages of coal, water and wind to generate electric power; and special cargo handling such as containerization on land and sea. Articles must not be overly technical and should have reader interest." No book excerpts, exposes, how-to, humor or opinion. Buys 14 mss/year. Query with or without published clips. Length: 1,500-2,000 words. Pays $1,000 maximum.

Photos: Robert A. Cooney, photo editor. (212)838-6200. State availability of photos. Reviews b&w and color transparencies and prints. Captions and identification of subjects required. Buys one-time rights.

Tips: "Send a brief outline of the story idea to articles editor mentioning also the availability of photographs in b&w and color. All articles must be thoroughly researched and original. Articles should have human interest through the device of interviews."

● **CORRESPONDENT**, Aid Association for Lutherans, Appleton WI 54919. (414)734-5721. Editor: Linda J. Peterson. Emphasizes fraternal programs and benefits for Lutherans and their families. Bimonthly magazine. Circ. 800,000. Pays on publication. Buys one-time rights. Simultaneous and photocopied submissions OK. SASE. Reports in 1 month. Free sample copy.

Nonfiction: Profiles of Lutherans doing unusual jobs. Company tie-in essential. Buys 2-3 mss/year. Rarely uses submitted mss. Query. Length: 500-1,500 words. Pays 10¢/word.

Photos: Pays $10 for b&w glossy prints; $25 for color prints or slides.

PROFESSIONAL AGENT MAGAZINE, Professional Insurance Agents, 400 N. Washington St., Alexandria VA 22314. (703)836-9340. Editor/Publisher: Janice J. Artandi. 25% freelance written. Monthly magazine covering insurance/small business for independent insurance agents. Circ. 40,000. Pays on acceptance. Byline given. Buys exclusive rights in the industry. Submit seasonal/holiday material 3 months in advance. Simultaneous queries, and simultaneous, photocopied and previously published submissions OK. Computer printout submissions acceptable. SASE. Reports in 1 month. Sample copy for SAE.

Nonfiction: Expose, general interest, historical/nostalgic, how-to, inspirational, interview/profile, photo feature and technical. Special issues on life insurance and computer interface. Buys 24 mss/year. Query with published clips or send complete ms. Length: 1,000-3,000 words. Pays $100-300.

Photos: State availability of photos. Pays $35-200 for 5x7 b&w prints; $50-300 for 35mm color transparencies. Captions, model release and identification of subjects required. Buys one-time rights.

International Affairs

These publications cover global relations, international trade, economic analysis and philosophy for business executives and government officials involved in foreign affairs. Consumer publications on related subjects are listed in Politics and World Affairs.

‡**CHINA BUSINESS REVIEW**, National Council for US China Trade, Suite 350, 1050 17th St., NW, Washington DC 20036. (202)828-8300. Editor: Jim Stepanek. Bimonthly magazine covering "US/China trade de-

velopment, and China's economy and foreign trade policies for firms that engage in US/China trade—primarily members of the National Council for US/China Trade." Circ. 4,500. Pays on publication. Byline given. Buys all rights. SASE. Reports in 2 weeks. Sample copy $15.
Nonfiction: "Focus China trade developments." Buys 6 mss/year. Query "by phone or letter." Length: 8,000 words maximum. Pays negotiable fee.
Photos: State availability of photos. Pays negotiable fee for 35mm color transparencies and 8x10 b&w glossy prints. Captions required.

PROBLEMS OF COMMUNISM, US Information Agency, P/PMP, Room 402, 301 4th St., Washington DC 20547. (202)485-2230. Editor: Paul A. Smith Jr. For scholars and decision makers in all countries of the world with higher education and a serious interest in foreign area studies and international relations. Circ. 28,905 (English language); 5,400 (Spanish language). Not copyrighted. Pays 20% kill fee. Byline given. Buys 60-70 mss/year. Pays on acceptance. Photocopied submissions OK. Reports in 3 months. Free sample copy.
Nonfiction: "*Problems of Communism* is one of a very few journals devoted to objective, dispassionate discourse on a highly unobjective, passionately debated phenomenon: communism. It is maintained as a forum in which qualified observers can contribute to a clearer understanding of the sources, nature and direction of change in the areas of its interest. It has no special emphasis or outlook and represents no partisan point of view. Standards of style are those appropriate to the field of international scholarship and journalism. We use intellectually rigorous studies of East/West relations, and/or related political, economic, social and strategic trends in the USSR, China and their associated states and movements. Length is usually 5,000 words. Essay reviews of 1,500 words cover new books offering significant information and analysis. Emphasis throughout *Problems of Communism* is on original research, reliability of sources and perceptive insights. We do not publish political statements or other forms of advocacy or apologetics for particular forms of belief." Query or submit complete ms. Pays $600/article; $300/essay reviews.
Photos: Pays minimum $45 for b&w glossy prints.

Jewelry

Glittering products will attract customers to jewelry counters, but not jewelry trade editors. These editors want in-depth information for jewelers who read their magazines.

AMERICAN JEWELRY MANUFACTURER, 8th Floor, 825 7th Ave., New York NY 10019. (212)245-7555. Editor: Steffan Aletti. For jewelry manufacturers, as well as manufacturers of supplies and tools for the jewelry industry; their representatives, wholesalers and agencies. Monthly. Circ. 5,000. Buys all rights (with exceptions). Byline given. Will consider photocopied submissions. Computer printout submissions acceptable. Submit seasonal material 3 months in advance. Reports in 1 month. Query. SASE. Free sample copy and writer's guidelines.
Nonfiction: "Topical articles on manufacturing; company stories; economics (e.g., rising gold prices). Story must inform or educate the manufacturer. Occasional special issues on timely topics, e.g., gold; occasional issues on specific processes in casting and plating. We reject material that is not specifically pointed at our industry; e.g., articles geared to jewelry retailing or merchandising, not to manufacturers." Informational, how-to, interview, profile, historical, expose, successful business operations, new product, merchandising techniques and technical. Buys 5-10 unsolicited mss/year. Length: open. Payment "usually around $50/printed page."
Photos: B&w photos purchased with ms. 5x7 minimum.
Tips: "Query first; we have accepted some general business articles, but not many."

THE DIAMOND REGISTRY BULLETIN, 30 W. 47th St., New York NY 10036. Editor-in-Chief: Joseph Schlussel. 15% freelance written. Monthly newsletter. Pays on publication. Buys all rights. Submit seasonal/holiday material 1 month in advance. Simultaneous and previously published submissions OK. Computer printout submissions acceptable; prefers letter-quality to dot-matrix. SASE. Reports in 3 weeks. Sample copy $5.
Nonfiction: Prevention advice (on crimes against jewelers); how-to (ways to increase sales in diamonds, improve security, etc.); and interview (of interest to diamond dealers or jewelers). Submit complete ms. Length: 50-500 words. Pays $10-150.
Tips: "We seek ideas to increase sales of diamonds."

‡**SOUTHERN JEWELER**, 75 3rd St. NW, Atlanta GA 30365. (404)881-6442. Editor: Roy Conradi. 15% freelance written. For Southern retail jewelers and watchmakers. Monthly. Circ. 8,500. Not copyrighted. Buys first rights only. Pays on publication. Publishes ms an average of 2 months after acceptance. Submit seasonal material 2 months in advance. SASE.

Nonfiction: Articles related to Southern retail jewelers regarding advertising, management and merchandising. Buys spot news about Southern jewelers and coverage of successful business operations. Prefers *not* to see material concerning jewelers outside the 14 Southern states. No articles on general sales techniques. Recent article example: cover feature on a typical case history article on a retail jeweler in the South (March 1984). Buys 12 unsolicited mss/year. Length: open. Pays $50-150 for features; $2/clipping.

Photos: Buys b&w glossies. Pays $5.

Tips: "Query should describe specifically the type article proposed. Writer should be based in the South. Ideally, he/she should have retail jewelry trade background, but a good writer can pick up technical points from us. (Samples of features used in past will be sent upon request.) We get an unbiased view of the jewelry industry which is the most rewarding/exhilarating aspect of working with freelance writers. Send a sample of your work related to any trade or industry, along with a couple of b&w pictures of the subject character and the establishment."

WATCH AND CLOCK REVIEW, 2403 Champa St., Denver CO 80205. (303)296-1600. Managing Editor: Jayne L. Barrick. 20% freelance written. The magazine of watch/clock sales and service. Monthly magazine; 68 pages. Circ. 16,000. Pays on publication. Buys first rights only. Byline given. Submit seasonal/holiday material 3 months in advance. SASE. Reports in 2-3 weeks. Free sample copy.

Nonfiction: Articles on successful watch/clock manufacturers and retailers; merchandising and display; and profiles of industry leaders. Buys 15 mss/year. Query. Length: 1,000-2,000 words. Pays $100-250.

Photos: Submit photo material with accompanying ms. No additional payment for b&w glossy prints. Captions preferred. Buys first rights. Model release required.

Columns/Departments: Buys 7/issue. Pays $150-200. Open to suggestions for new columns/departments.

Tips: "Brevity is helpful in a query. Find the right subject—an interesting clock shop, a jewelry store with unique watch displays, a street clock of antiquarian interest, etc."

Journalism

Writers tell other writers how to write more effectively and to chart the latest trends affecting the journalism world in these publications. Both paying and non-paying markets of the writing trade are included here. Writers wishing to contribute material to these publications should query about requirements before submitting their work.

‡**THE AMERICAN SCREENWRITER**, Grasshopper Productions, Inc., Box 67, Manchaca TX 78652. (512)282-2749. Editor: Gerald J. LePage. A bimonthly newsletter covering scriptwriting for the screen and TV. "We address scriptwriters who ask for help through our script evaluation program. We aim at writers who are struggling to find their place in the market." Estab. 1984. Circ. 300 estimated. Pays by arrangement with author. Byline given. Buys one-time rights. Submit seasonal/holiday material 2 months in advance. Simultaneous queries, and simultaneous, photocopied, and previously published submissions OK. SASE. Reports in 1 month. Sample copy for $1 and SASE; writer's guidelines for SASE.

Nonfiction: Book excerpts, interview/profile, and personal experience related to scriptwriting. "No sophisticated material that oozes of past films which require reader having seen them." Query with published clips. Length: 200-400 words. Payment scale to be arranged.

Tips: "The Plight of the Screenwriter section and interviews with other writers are most open to freelancers. We want short, comprehensive articles that bring home a problematical point in less than one minute's reading."

BOOK ARTS REVIEW, The Center for Book Arts, 15 Bleecker St., New York NY 10012. (212)460-9768. Managing Editor: Bryan R. Johnson. Emphasizes bookbinding, printing and exploring the arts of the book. Quarterly newsletter; 6 pages. Circ. 1,000. Pays in copies. "Rights revert to artist." Byline given. Submit seasonal/holiday material 3 months in advance. Simultaneous, photocopied and previously published submissions OK. Computer printout submissions acceptable. Reports in 2 months. SASE.

Nonfiction: Reviews (exhibitions, lectures, conferences, shows, etc. dealing with printing, bookbinding, papermaking, calligraphy or preservation); and interview (with book artists). No censorship, fiction or material dealing with writing. Query. Pays in copies.

BOOK DEALERS WORLD, American Bookdealers Exchange, Box 2525, La Mesa CA 92041. (619)462-3297. Editorial Director: Al Galasso. Senior Editor: Cynthia Schuber. Consulting Editor: Lon Choate. 50% freelance written. Quarterly magazine covering writing, self-publishing and marketing books by mail. Circ. 20,000. Pays on publication. Publishes ms an average of 6 months after acceptance. Byline given. Buys first rights and second (reprint) rights to material originally published elsewhere. Simultaneous and previously published submissions OK. Computer printout submissions acceptable. SASE. Reports in 1 month. Sample copy $1.

Nonfiction: Book excerpts (how-to, mail order, direct mail, publishing); how-to (home business by mail, advertising); and interview/profile (of successful self-publishers). Positive articles on self-publishing, new writing angles, marketing, etc. Buys 10 mss/year. Send complete ms. Length: 1,000-1,500 words. Pays $25-50.

Columns/Departments: Print Perspective (about new magazines and newsletters); From The Source (items of interest to mail order entrepreneurs); Small Press Scene (news about small press activities); and Self-Publisher Profile (on successful self-publishers and their marketing stratgey). Buys 20 mss/year. Send complete ms. Length: 250-1,000 words. Pays $5-20.

Fillers: Clippings. "Fillers to do with writing, publishing or books." Buys 6/year. Length: 100-250 words. Pays $3-10.

Tips: "In the year ahead we'll be using more success-oriented pieces on self-publishing and marketing books along with more in-depth interviews."

‡**BYLINE**, McCarville Publications, Suite 204, 7901 N.E. 10th, Midwest City OK 73110. (405)733-1129. Editor: Mike McCarville. 100% freelance written. A monthly magazine covering poetry and writing. "We stress encouragement of beginning writers." Circ. 2,450. Pays on acceptance. Publishes ms an average of 1 year after acceptance. Byline given. Buys first North American serial rights. Submit seasonal/holiday material 6 months in advance. SASE. Reports in 2 months. Sample copy $2.75; writer's guidelines for SAE and 20¢ postage.

Nonfiction: How-to (write and sell); humor; inspirational; and personal experience. Buys 700 mss/year. Send complete ms. Length: 50-2,500 words. Pays $5-250.

Fiction: Mysteries with a literary setting or twist. No science fiction. Buys approximately 70 mss/year. Send complete ms. Length: 1,000-2,500 words. Pays $50 minimum.

Poetry: Free verse, light verse and traditional. Buys 200 poems/year. Submit maximum 5 poems. Length: 4-36 words. Pays $2 minimum.

CALIFORNIA PUBLISHER, Suite 1040, 1127 11th St., Sacramento CA 95814. (916)443-5991. Editor: Jackie Nava. 5% freelance written. Monthly tabloid read by publishers, journalism teachers, editors and managers in newspaper publishing in California. Byline given. Buys first and second rights to the same material. Computer printout submissions acceptable; prefers letter-quality to dot-matrix. Publishes ms an average of 2 months after acceptance.

Nonfiction: In-depth stories or articles designed to inform and amuse California newspaper publishers. Sample topics include: newsprint shortage, changing role of papers, historical profiles on California journalism greats, success stories, role of minorities in the newspaper field, profiles on California newspapers, and technological advances. No general "humorous" material. "If it isn't specific to *California* journalism, we don't want it." Query. Length: 2,000 words maximum. Pays $25-30.

Photos: Reviews b&w glossy prints.

Tips: "Go on; query us! Stories used will be read by all the newspaper publishers who count in the state of California. We'd like to showcase first effort, good writing talent."

CANADIAN AUTHOR & BOOKMAN, Canadian Authors Association, 24 Ryerson Ave., Toronto, Ontario M5T 2P3 Canada. Editor: Anne Osborne. 75% freelance written. "For writers—all ages, all levels of experience." Quarterly magazine; 32 pages. Circ. 5,000. Pays on publication. Buys first Canadian rights. Byline given. Written queries only. Computer printout submissions acceptable; prefers letter-quality to dot-matrix. SASE (Canadian stamps); sample copy $3.50.

Nonfiction: How-to (on writing, selling; the specifics of the different genres—what they are and how to write them); informational (the writing scene—who's who and what's what); interview (on writers, mainly leading ones, but also those with a story that can help others write and sell more often); and opinion. No personal, lightweight writing experiences; no fillers. Query with immediate pinpointing of topic, length (if ms is ready), and writer's background. Length: 800-1,500 words. Pays 1¢/word.

Photos: "We're after an interesting-looking magazine, and graphics are a decided help." State availability of photos with query. Offers $5/photo for b&w photos accepted with ms. Buys one-time rights.

Poetry: High quality. "Major poets publish with us—others need to be as good." Buys 40 poems/year. Pays $5.

Tips: "We dislike 1) material that condescends to its reader; and 2) articles that advocate on adversarial approach to writer/editor relationships. We agree that there is a time and place for such an approach, but good sense should prevail."

CHILDREN'S LITERATURE, The Children's Literature Foundation, Box 370, Windham Center CT 06280. (203)456-1900. Editor: Francelia Butler. Managing Editor: John C. Wandell. Annual; 250-300 pages. Circ. 3,500. Pays in reprints. Byline given. Phone queries OK. Submit seasonal/holiday material 1 year in advance. SASE. Reports in 1 month.
Nonfiction: Scholarly or critical articles *only*—not creative work. Manuscripts must conform to MLA Handbook. Uses 20 mss/issue. Query or send complete ms. Length: 7,500 words.
Photos: State availability of photos. Uses 4x5 or 8x10 b&w glossy prints. Captions and permission to publish required.
Columns/Departments: Book review articles (send to Prof. John Cech, University of Florida, Gainesville FL 32611). Uses 20/year. Query. Length: 3,000 words. Open to suggestions for new columns/departments.

THE CHRISTIAN WRITER, The Professional Writing Magazine for Christians, Box 5650, Lakeland FL 33807. (813)644-3548. Editor: Thomas A. Noton. Monthly writing magazine aimed at a Christian audience. "We reach Christians who desire to write or are writers. Our aim is to help create the professional approach to this craft." Circ. 15,000. Offers no payment. Byline given. Acquires first rights; no reprints. Submit seasonal/holiday material 4 months in advance. Simultaneous queries and photocopied submissions OK. SASE. Reports in 1 month on queries; 6 weeks on mss. Free sample copy and writer's guidelines. SASE.
Nonfiction: How-to (specifics on authoring, selling, related subjects); humor (rare); inspirational (limited); interview/profile (top Christian authors); new product (electronic writing); and personal experience (some). Material on conferences, workshops, clubs, etc. for annual Service Guide. We receive too many 'this is my life' articles. We want more specific articles helping others overcome specialized problems in authoring." Buys 36 mss/year. Query with published clips. Length: 800-2,500 words. Pays $10 minimum for fillers to $150 for feature articles. Payment depends on need and article.
Tips: "We're looking for freelancers who have answers for specific problems in writing, marketing, querying, rewriting, editing or self-publishing. We are only interested in professionalism as it applies to the craft of writing. Although we use the Christian influence, we do not deal with it directly. We deal with the craft, its problems and answers."

COLLEGE MEDIA REVIEW, School of Journalism, Louisiana State University, Baton Rouge LA 70803-7302. (504)388-2336. Editor: J. William Click. For members of College Media Advisers and staffs, editors and faculty advisers of college publications, journalism professors, and others interested in student communication media. Quarterly. Circ. 1,200. Acquires all rights. No payment. Photocopied submissions OK. Submit two copies of all articles. No simultaneous submissions. Reports in 5 months. Query or submit complete ms. SASE. Sample copy $2.50; free writer's guidelines.
Nonfiction: Articles by, about and of interest to college publications advisers, staffs and editors. Articles should focus on editing, advising and producing college newspapers, yearbooks and magazines and operating electronic media, including radio, television and cable. "We like to use articles reporting research in publications and journalistic skills and well-thought-out opinion and essays on issues in the student media. Legal research specifically is welcome. Articles should be in a readable style with adequate attribution but without overuse of footnotes." Topical subjects of interest include increasing income, reducing costs, promoting publications, use of new technology, censorship cases at private colleges, tips on purchasing new equipment, how-to articles, and advances in techniques and resources. Length: 3,000 words maximum.
Photos: B&w glossy photos used with ms. Captions required.

COLUMBIA JOURNALISM REVIEW, 700 Journalism Bldg., Columbia University, New York NY 10027. (212)280-5595. Managing Editor: Gloria Cooper. "We welcome queries concerning media issues and performance. *CJR* also publishes book reviews. We emphasize in-depth reporting, critical analysis and good writing. All queries are read by editors."

‡**COMPUTER BOOK REVIEW**, Comber Press, 735 Ekekela Pl., Honolulu HI 96817. (808)595-7337. Editor: Carlene Char. 30% freelance written. A bimonthly magazine that critically reviews and rates microcomputer books. Estab. 1983. Electronic edition on News Net. Circ. 2,000. Byline given. Buys all rights; "author may freely use work later, with written permission from CBR." Publishes ms an average of 1 month after acceptance. Simultaneous queries, and simultaneous and photocopied submissions OK. Electronic submissions OK on 5¼" floppy disks, IBM-PC DOS 2.0 format preferred, but prefers hard copy also. Computer printout submissions acceptable. SASE. Reports in 1 week. Sample copy $3; writer's guidelines for SASE.
Nonfiction: Book reviews only. Query with published clips or send complete ms. Length: 250 words. Pays in copies.

CREATIVE YEARS With Writer's Opportunities, Coronado Publishers, #40, 2490 SW 14th Dr., Gainesville FL 32608. (904)373-7445. Editor: Eloise Cozens Henderson. Associate Editors: Mary Onkka and Rose Mary Pleiman. Bimonthly magazine for new and unpublished writers. Circ. 2,000. Pays on publication. Buys one-time rights. Submit seasonal/holiday material 3 months in advance. Simultaneous submissions OK.

SASE. Reports in 3 weeks on queries; 3 months on mss. Sample copy $2; writer's guidelines for SASE.
Nonfiction: General interest, historical/nostalgic, interview, humor, inspirational, opinion and personal experience. "We feature regular tips on writing nostalgia, short stories, articles, recipes and poetry and are open to other subjects." No obscenity, profanity, or liquor/drug related articles. Buys 30 mss/year. Length: 450-500 words. Send complete ms. Pays presently in copies only.
Fiction: Humorous, historical and religious. No obscenity, profanity, liquor/drug related mss. Buys 30 mss/year. Length: 450-500 words. Send complete ms. Pays in copies only.
Poetry: Light verse, traditional. No far out, agnostic, atheist, etc. poetry. Buys 12/year. Pays in copies only.
Tips: "We especially need Biblical quiz and other puzzle material. We are also seeking short articles about old times in sports (Babe Ruth, Ty Cobb, etc.)."

‡**CROSS-CANADA WRITERS' QUARTERLY, The Canadian Writers Magazine**, Cross-Canada Writer's Inc., Box 277, Station F, Toronto, Ontario M4Y 2L7 Canada. (416)690-0917. Editor: Ted Plantos. Associate Editor: Susan Ioannou. 80% freelance written. A quarterly literary writer's magazine covering Canadian writing within an international context. Circ. 2,000. Pays on publication. Byline given. Buys first North American serial rights. Submit seasonal/holiday material 6 months in advance. Photocopied submissions OK. Computer printout submissions acceptable. SASE. Reports in 3 weeks on queries; 2 months on mss. Publishes ms an average of 1 year after acceptance. Sample copy $3.95, 9x12 SAE, and 39¢ Canadian postage or IRC.
Nonfiction: How-to (literary, slanted for poetry and fiction); and interview/profile (established authors, editors, publishers—in-depth with photos). "Articles and interviews must have depth, be thought-provoking and offer practical advice and background information." No how-to's on nonliterary kinds of writing. Buys 4-10 mss/year. Query or send complete ms. "Each case is different. With an interview, a query could save time and work. A straight article we would have to read." Payment on publication.
Photos: State availability of accompanying photos with query or send photos with ms, 5x7 b&w prints. Captions, model release and identification of subjects required. Buys one-time rights.
Columns/Departments: Contact Reference Shelf editor or WQ Forum editor. Reference Shelf (capsule reviews of reference books for writers, preferably Canadian, recent titles; buys 8 mss/year; query); and WQ Forum (opinion pieces on writing, aesthetic theories; buys 6-8 mss/year; send complete ms). Length: 200-300 words. Payment on publication.
Fiction: Contact fiction editor. Mainstream. No slight material—mere anecdotes rather than fully developed stories. Buys 4-8 mss/year. Send complete ms. Length: 1,000-3,000 words. Payment on publication.
Poetry: Poetry Editor. Free verse, haiku and traditional (if well-done). No concrete poetry, "diary excerpts" merely, highly obscure private poems or doggerel. Buys 40-50 poems/year. Submit maximum 10 poems. Length: 100 lines maximum "in exceptional cases." Pays in copies.

EDITOR & PUBLISHER, 11 W. 19th St., New York NY 10011. Editor: Robert U. Brown. 10% freelance written. For newspaper publishers, editors, executives, employees and others in communications, marketing, advertising, etc. Weekly magazine; 60 pages. Circ. 29,000. Pays on publication. Publishes ms an average of 2 weeks after acceptance. Buys first rights only. Computer printout submissions acceptable; prefers letter-quality to dot-matrix. Sample copy $1. SASE.
Nonfiction: John P. Consoli, department editor. Uses newspaper business articles and news items; also newspaper personality features and printing technology. Query.
Fillers: "Amusing typographical errors found in newspapers." Pays $2.

EMPIRE, for the SF Writer, c/o Unique Graphics, 1025 55th St., Oakland CA 94608. (415)655-3024. Editor: Millea Kenin. 100% freelance written. Quarterly magazine covering writing, editing and publishing science fiction and fantasy. "*Empire's* aim is to assist, entertain and inform science fiction and fantasy writers." Circ. 1,500. Pays on publication. Byline given. Buys first English language serial rights, and occasionally second (reprint) rights to material originally published elsewhere. Simultaneous queries and photocopied submissions OK. "We are completely receptive to computer printout submissions as long as they are NOT dot matrix. Dot matrix printouts will be returned unread." SASE. Reports in 1 month. Publishes ms an average of 6 months after acceptance. Sample copy $2, payable to Unique Graphics. Guidelines available for SASE.
Nonfiction: Expose (of publishing industry); how-to (on specific writing techniques and skills for science fiction & fantasy); humor (about the science fiction writer's life; "If you find any, send it to us."); inspirational (what to do after the electricity has been cut off; how to believe in yourself; how to learn from rejections); interview/profile (of writers, editors, agents, publishers, filmmakers involved in the SF genre); personal experience ("how I wrote and sold"); and technical (science fact with application to science fiction). "We use articles about writing, editing and publishing *science fiction and fantasy*; our material is written by professional SF writers for would-be professional SF writers. We are not interested in general articles for the beginning writer. We take a practical nuts-and-bolts approach." Buys 32 mss/year. Send complete ms. Length: 1,000-3,500 words. Pays in copies and a one-year subscription. Pay negotiable to regular contributors.
Fiction: Crazy Diamonds. "Each issue contains 1 story which has failed to sell elsewhere and three critiques of the story by professional SF writers. We use no other fiction." Buys 4 mss/year. Length: 3,500 words maxi-

mum, shorter preferred. Pays in copies and subscription.

Poetry: "Short humorous or serious verse about the act of writing or the writer's life."

Tips: "If you have not seen a copy of *Empire* and are not closely involved with the SF genre, it is better to query with a proposal rather than submitting an unsolicited article."

feed/back, THE CALIFORNIA JOURNALISM REVIEW, 1600 Holloway, San Francisco CA 94132. (415)469-2086. Editor: Shannon Bryony. 50% freelance written. For working journalists, journalism students, professors and news buffs. Magazine; 48 pages. Quarterly. Circ. 1,750. Byline given. Pays in subscriptions and copies. Publishes ms an average of 3 months after acceptance. Sample copy $2.50. Will consider photocopied and simultaneous submissions. Computer printout submissions acceptable "if good quality with ascenders/descenders." Reports in 2 months. Query. SASE mandatory.

Nonfiction: In-depth views of California journalism. Criticism of journalistic trends throughout the country, but with a local angle. Reviews of books concerning journalism. Informational, interview, profile, humor, historical, think pieces, expose, nostalgia, spot news, successful (or unsuccessful) business operations, new product, and technical; all must be related to California journalism. "Articles must focus on the state press and be of interest to professional journalists—they are our audience. We like articles that examine press performance—strengths and weaknesses; we also like personality articles on offbeat or little-known editors and journalists who escape national attention." Rejects articles that are not documented, or those in which the subject matter is not pertinent or those which show personal prejudice not supported by evidence. Length: 1,000-5,000 words.

Photos: B&w glossies (8x10 or 11x14) used with or without mss. Pays in subscriptions and/or copies.

FOLIO: The Magazine for Magazine Management, 125 Elm St., New Canaan CT 06840-4006. Editor-in-Chief: J. Hanson. Mostly staff written. Computer printout submissions acceptable; prefers letter-quality to dot-matrix.

Tips: "In the year ahead we will have more editorial pages and more *assigned* freelance work."

THE INKLING, Inkling Publications, Inc., Box 128, Alexandria MN 56308. (612)762-2020. Editor: Marilyn Bailey. Associate Editor: Betty Ulrich. Managing Editor: John Hall. Monthly journal covering advice, guidance and inspiration for writers and poets. "The *INKLING* is both informative and motivational, providing a forum for writers. Well-written articles and timely market news are the main criteria." Circ. 3,000. Pays on publication. Publishes ms an average of 2 months after acceptance. Byline given. Buys one-time rights. Submit seasonal/holiday material 3 months in advance. Simultaneous queries OK. Electronic submissions OK if compatible with TRS DOS or C/PM operative systems (TRS 80 Model III or IV). Computer printout submissions acceptable. SASE. Reports in 2 weeks on queries; 1 month on mss. Sample copy $2; writer's guidelines for business-size SAE and 1 first class stamp.

Nonfiction: How-to (on the business and approach to writing); inspirational; interview/profile; opinion; and personal experience. Buys 10-15 mss/year. Send complete ms. Length: 500-1,500 words. Pays $15-50.

Poetry: Avant-garde, free verse, haiku, light verse, traditional. "The *INKLING* runs two poetry contests each year—spring and fall: Winner and 2nd place cash prizes and two Honorable Mentions." Buys 8-10 poems/year. Submit maximum 3 poems. Length: 25 lines maximum. Pays $5-15.

Tips: "Query first with an outline. Articles must be *well* written and slanted toward the business (or commitment) of writing and/or being a writer." Break in with informative "interviews with established writers. In-depth, particularly reporting interviewee's philosophy on writing, how (s)he got started, how (s)he 'does it.' Tape interviews, transcribe, then edit!"

THE JOURNALISM EDUCATOR, School of Journalism, University of North Carolina, Chapel Hill NC 27514.(919)962-4084. Editor: Thomas A. Bowers. 100% freelance written. For journalism professors, administrators, and a growing number of professional journalists in the US and Canada. Published by the Association for Education in Journalism and Mass Communication. Founded by the American Society of Journalism School Administrators. Quarterly. Byline given. Publishes ms an average of 6 months after acceptance. Computer printout submissions acceptable. SASE.

Nonfiction: "We do accept some unsolicited manuscripts dealing with our publication's specialized area—problems of administration and teaching in journalism education. Because we receive more articles than we can use from persons working in this field, we do not need to encourage freelance materials, however. A writer, generally, would have to be in journalism/communications teaching or in some media work to have the background to write convincingly about the subjects this publication is interested in. The writer also should become familiar with the content of recent issues of this publication." Nothing not directly connected with journalism education at the four year college and university level. Maximum length: 2,500 words. Does not pay.

JOURNALISM QUARTERLY, School of Journalism, Ohio University, Athens OH 45701. (614)594-5013. Editor: Guido H. Stempel III. 100% freelance written. For members of the Association for Education in Journalism and Mass Communication and other academicians and journalists. Quarterly. Usually acquires all rights. Circ. 4,200. Photocopied submissions OK. Computer printout submissions acceptable. Publishes ms

an average of 6 months after acceptance. Reports in 4-6 months. Free writer's guidelines. SASE.
Nonfiction: Research in mass communication. Recent articles include "How Newspaper Editors Reacted To *Post's* Pulitzer Prize Hoax." No essays or opinion pieces. Length: 4,000 words maximum. Submit complete ms in triplicate. No payment.
Tips: "Query letters don't really help either the author or me very much. We can't make commitments on the basis of query letters, and we are not likely to reject or discourage the manuscript either unless it is clearly outside our scope. Do a good piece of research. Write a clear, well-organized manuscript."

MEDICAL COMMUNICATIONS, 4404 Sherwood Rd., Philadelphia PA 19131. (215)877-1137. Editor: Edith Schwager. 55% freelance written. For members of the American Medical Writers Association, physicians, medical libraries, journal and medical news editors, pharmaceutical writers, editors, advertising people, medical journalists, and other communicators in medical and allied fields. Quarterly. 32- to 48-page digest size magazine. Circ. 3,500. Acquires first North American serial rights, first and second rights to same material and second (reprint) rights to material originally published elsewhere. Byline. Uses 6-8 mss/issue. Pays 3 contributor copies. Computer printout submissions acceptable; no dot-matrix. Sample copies available. Reports in 6 weeks. Publishes ms an average of 3 months after acceptance. Query. SASE.
Nonfiction: Articles related to any aspect of medical communication. May be philosophic, scholarly or how-to. "We are more of a journal than a magazine but like to take a less formal approach." Uses fairly serious, simple, straightforward style. Special features accepted. Length: 1,500-3,000 words. Tables, figures and footnotes are used with mss, if needed.
Tips: "We're especially interested in articles on physician/patient and physician/public interaction and on subjects not usually covered in other journals aimed at medical writers/editors: translation, indexing and speaking. We accept few articles resting on a humorous base. Most of our members are experienced, literate and literary-minded writers and editors. Only the best writing holds their interest; the topic must be important to them, too."

‡**NSN, The Newsletter for Beginning and Not-So-Neophyte Writers**, Suite 7, 1735 S. Main, Pleasant Ridge MI 48069. Editor: Barbara K. Johnson. 99% freelance written. A bimonthly newsletter covering writing and marketing of writing. Circ. 1,000. Pays on publication. Byline given except for fillers and Did You Know?. Buys first rights and second (reprint) rights to material originally published elsewhere. Submit seasonal/holiday material 4 months in advance preferably, but 2 months OK. Simultaneous queries, and simultaneous, photocopied and previously published submissions OK. Computer printout submissions acceptable. SASE. Reports in 1 month on queries; 2 months on mss. Publishes ms an average of 2 months after acceptance. Sample copy for SAE and 1 first class stamp; one writer's guidelines for SAE and 1 first class stamp (or 37¢/envelope for both).
Nonfiction: Book excerpts (on writing and business of writing); general interest; historical/nostalgic (about writers and writing only); how-to (on writing, getting published, research, buying equipment, etc.); humor ("we don't get enough"); interview/profile (authors and field related persons, not necessarily famous); new product (ads, Did You Know?); technical (how to articles); and poetry (about writing and writers, and the writing experience). "We have a desperate need for short how-to articles on all kinds of poetry, verse, limericks, etc." Also interested in articles about cable, agents and scripts. "How-to articles are the most needed freelance manuscripts. They can be about any kind of writing or about equipment, sources, techniques, business practices, writing-related areas, markets, whatever might be of interest to other writers." Nothing "depressing or down without a positive/hopeful ending." Query or send complete ms. Length: 350-1,200 words. Pays in copies.
Columns/Departments: Personal Perspectives (a 300-word column about writing, for and by writers with special emphasis on the writer's feelings about the problems/joys of being, or trying to be a writer); Q&A (a column of questions from subscribers and other writers usually asking for how-to or where-to information); Bits & Tads (an occasional section of *brief*, bulleted tips picked up at writing/business conferences); and Mini Reviews (short reviews of how-to books, and/or articles, etc. of interst to a writer with information as to publisher, cost, and where to get the book). Buys variable number of mss/year. Query or send complete ms. Length: 300-500 words. Pays in copies.
Poetry: "Poetry is used only as part of how-to articles or as a statement about writing, writers and the writing experience." Buys 2-6 poems/year. Submit maximum 5-10 short poems. Length: 5-20 lines (50-75 words). Pays in copies.
Fillers: Clippings, anecdotes, short humor, newsbreaks, quotes by writers and writing-field related persons, crosswords, quizzes and games about writing subjects. Buys variable number/year. Length: 25-100 words. Pays in copies.
Tips: "How-to articles, Personal Perspectives, Q&A are all most open to freelancers. You do not have to be published to make it in *NSN*."

PHILATELIC JOURNALIST, 154 Laguna Court, St. Augustine Shores FL 32086. (904)797-3513. Editor: Gustav Detjen Jr. 25% freelance written. For "journalists, writers and columnists in the field of stamp collecting. *The Philatelic Journalist* is mainly read by philatelic writers, professionals and amateurs, including all of the members of the Society of Philaticians, an international group of philatelic journalists." Bimonthly. Circ. 1,000. Not copyrighted. Pays on publication. Publishes ms an average of 15 days after acceptance. Free sample copy. Will consider photocopied submissions. Computer printout submissions acceptable. Submit seasonal material 2 months in advance. Reports in 2 weeks. Query. SASE.

Nonfiction: "Articles concerned with the problems of the philatelic journalist, how to publicize and promote stamp collecting, how to improve relations between philatelic writers and publishers and postal administrations. Philatelic journalists many of them amateurs, are very much interested in receiving greater recognition as journalists, and in gaining greater recognition for the use of philatelic literature by stamp collectors. Any criticism should be coupled with suggestions for improvement." Buys profiles and opinion articles. Length: 250-500 words. Pays $15-30.

Photos: Photos purchased with ms; captions required.

PRO/COMM, The Professional Communicator, published by Women in Communications, Inc., Box 9561, Austin TX 78766. (512)345-8922. Managing Editor: Gene T. Krane. 95% freelance written, mostly by WICI members and without pay. Monthly January-August; combination September/October and November/December issues; 8-12 pages. Circ. more than 12,000. Byline given. Publishes ms an average of 6 weeks after acceptance. Photocopied and previously published submissions OK. SASE. Reports in 4 weeks. Sample copy $1.50.

Nonfiction: General interest (media, freedom of information, legislation related to communications); how-to (improve graphics, take better photos, write a better story, do investigative reporting, sell ideas, start a magazine or newspaper, improve journalism education, reach decision-making jobs, etc.); personal experience (self-improvement, steps to take to reach management level jobs); profile (people of interest because of their work in communications); and technical (advancements in print or electronic media). Query. Length: 1,000-1,500 words.

Photos: Offers no additional payment for photos accepted with mss. State availability of photos with query. Uses b&w photos. Captions required.

PUBLISHING TRADE, Serving Non-Consumer Publications, Northfield Publishing, 464 Central Ave., Northfield IL 60093. Editor: Rosanne Ullman. 30% freelance written. Bimonthly magazine covering nonconsumer magazine and tabloid publishing. Circulated to more than 5,000 publishers, editors, ad managers, circulation managers, production managers and art directors of nonconsumer magazines and tabloids." Circ. 5,000. Pays on publication. Byline given. Buys first North American serial rights and makes work-for-hire assignments. Submit seasonal/holiday material 6 months in advance. SASE. Reports in 2 months on queries. Publishes ms an average of 2 months after acceptance. "Do not send manuscript without prior query." Sample copy $4.

Nonfiction: How-to (write, sell advertising, manage production, manage creative and sales people, etc.); interview/profile (*only* after assignment—must be full of "secrets" of success and how-to detail); personal experiences (only after assignment); new product (no payment); and technical (aspects of magazine publishing). "Features deal with every aspect of publishing, including: creating an effective ad sales team; increasing ad revenue; writing effective direct-mail circulation promotion; improving 4-color reproduction quality; planning and implementing ad sales strategies; buying printing; gathering unique information; writing crisp, clear articles with impact; and designing publications with visual impact." No general interest. "Everything must be keyed directly to our typical reader—a 39-year-old publisher/editor producing a trade magazine for 30,000 special interest readers." Buys 12-18 mss/year. Query. Length: 900-3,000 words. Pays $100.

Photos: Send photos with ms. Reviews b&w contact sheets. Payment included in payment for ms. Captions, model release and identification of subjects required. Buys first rights.

Tips: "Articles must present practical, useful, new information in how-to detail, so readers can do what the articles discuss. Articles that present problems and discuss how they were successfully solved also are welcome. These must carry many specific examples to flesh out general statements."

THE REVIEW OF BOOKS AND RELIGION, Managing Editor's Office, Duke University Divinity School, Durham NC 27706. (606)255-9591. Publisher: Dennis Campbell. Managing editor: Christopher Walters-Bugbee. Editor: Kendig Brubaker Cully, Box 1460, Lexington KY 40591. Tabloid published monthly except August and December, reviewing religion—ecumenically conceived—and related fields. Circ. 10,000. "We do not pay for reviews. Reviewer keeps book." Byline given. Submit seasonal holiday material 3 months in advance. SASE. Reports in 1 month. Sample copy available from: *The Review of Books and Religion*, Business Office, Duke University Divinity School, Durham NC 27706.

Nonfiction: Book reviews. "Submit qualifications for reviewing serious works."

Fiction: Query. "Only religious thematic material, broadly understood and not longer than 1,000 words." No payment for fiction and articles.

Poetry: Avant-garde, free-verse, haiku, light verse and traditional (religious imagery only). "We do not pay for poetry." Submit maximum 2 poems.

THE ROMANTIST, F. Marion Crawford Memorial Society, Saracinesca House. 3610 Meadowbrook Ave., Nashville TN 37205. (615)292-9695 or 226-1890. Editor: John C. Moran. Associate Editors: Don Herron and Steve Eng. Emphasizes modern romanticism; especially fantastic literature and art. Annual magazine. 100% freelance written; 15% of material published is poetry. Circ. 300. Buys first rights. Publishes ms an average of 9 months after acceptance. Byline given. Photocopied poems and previously published submissions OK. No computer printout submissions. SASE. Reports in 1 month. Free writer's guidelines.
Nonfiction: No articles without querying first.
Poetry: Traditional and free verse. "We prefer rhymed and metered poems, but no homespun doggerel. Prefer the tradition of Swinburne, Poe, Noyes, de la Mare, Masefield, Clark Ashton Smith; especially weird or fantastic verse." Poetry submissions should be double-spaced. Uses 15 unsolicited poems/year.
Tips: Closed currently to poetry.

ST. LOUIS JOURNALISM REVIEW, 8606 Olive Blvd., St. Louis MO 63132. (314)991-1699. Editor/Publisher: Charles L. Klotzer. Monthly tabloid newspaper critiquing St. Louis media, print, broadcasting, TV and cable primarily by working journalists and others. Also covers advertising and public relations. Occasionally buys articles on national media criticism. No taboos. Circ. 12,000. Buys all rights. Byline given. SASE.
Nonfiction: "We buy material which analyzes, critically, St. Louis area and, less frequently, national media institutions, personalities or trends." Payment depends.

SAN FRANCISCO REVIEW OF BOOKS, Box 32-0090, San Francisco CA 94133. Editor: Ron Nowicki. 60% freelance written. For a college-educated audience interested in books and publishing. Bimonthly magazine; 40 pages. Circ. 20,000. Acquires all rights. Byline given. Uses about 180 mss/year. Payment in contributors copies and subscription. Publishes ms an average of 3 months after acceptance. Sample copy $1. No photocopied or simultaneous submissions. Reports on material accepted for publication in 4-6 weeks. Query for nonfiction; submit complete ms for book reviews. SASE.
Nonfiction: Book reviews, and articles about authors, books and their themes. Contains Western Publisher supplement. "No glib, slick writing. Primarily serious; humor occasionally acceptable. No restrictions on language provided it is germane to the book or article." Interviews, profiles, historical and think articles. Length: 1,000 words maximum for reviews; 2,000 words maximum for articles.

SCIENCE FICTION CHRONICLE, Algol Press, Box 4175, New York NY 10163. (212)643-9011. Editor: Andrew Porter. 5% freelance writen. Monthly magazine about science fiction publishing for science fiction readers, editors, writers, et al., who are interested in keeping up with the latest developments and news in science fiction. Publication also includes market reports and media news. Circ. 3,500. Buys first rights only. Pays on publication. Publishes ms an average of 3 months after acceptance. Makes work-for-hire assignments. Phone queries OK. Submit seasonal material 4 months in advance. Electronic submissions OK on MS-DOS 1-25. Computer printout submissions acceptable. SASE. Reports in 1 week. Sample copy $1.75.
Nonfiction: Interviews, articles, new product and photo feature. No articles about UFOs, or "news we reported six months ago." Buys 15 unsolicited mss/year. Send complete ms. Length: 200-2,000 words. Pays 1-3¢/word.
Photos: Send photos with ms. Pays $5-15 for 4x5 and 8x10 b&w prints. Captions preferred. Buys one-time rights.
Tips: "News of publishers, booksellers and software related to SF is most needed from freelancers."

SMALL PRESS REVIEW, Box 100, Paradise CA 95969. Editor: Len Fulton. Associate Editor: Ellen Ferber. For "people interested in small presses and magazines, current trends and data; many libraries." Monthly. Circ. 3,000. Accepts 50-200 mss/year. Byline given. "Query if you're unsure." Reports in 1 to 2 months. SASE. Free sample copy.
Nonfiction: "News, short reviews, photos, short articles on small magazines and presses. Get the facts and know your mind well enough to build your opinion into the article." Uses how-tos, personal experience articles, interviews, profiles, spot news, historical articles, think pieces, photo pieces, and coverage of merchandising techniques. Length: 100-200 words.
Photos: Uses b&w glossy photos.

● **WDS FORUM**, Writer's Digest School, 9933 Alliance Rd., Cincinnati OH 45242. (513)984-0717. Editor: Kirk Polking. 100% freelance written. Bimonthly magazine covering writing techniques and marketing for students of courses in fiction and nonfiction writing offered by Writer's Digest School. Circ. 7,500. Pays on acceptance. Buys first rights and second (reprint) rights to material originally published elsewhere. Pays 25% kill fee. Byline given. Phone queries OK. Submit seasonal/holiday material 3 months in advance. Simultaneous, photocopied and previously published submissions OK. Electronic submissions OK, but requires hard copy also. Computer printout submissions acceptable; no dot-matrix. SASE. Reports in 3 weeks. Publishes ms an average of 6 months after acceptance. Free sample copy.
Nonfiction: How-to (write or market short stories, articles, novels, poetry, etc.); and interviews (with well-

Close-up

Judith Arcana
Author

Writer Judith Arcana considers herself a beginner, but so do thousands of other writers. The surprising difference, though, is that she has written two books plus articles for *Redbook*, *Cosmopolitan*, and other magazines.

"I'm working on another style," says the author of *Our Mothers' Daughters* (Shameless Hussy Press) and *Every Mother's Son* (Doubleday). "So far what I've been doing is nonfiction—explanatory prose that tells what I think, tells what other people think, and explains and analyzes all the ideas under consideration; I'm not interested in doing that right now."

While continuing to do magazine nonfiction, she is learning (actually writing) poetry and short stories. "I'm interested in making art instead of making explanations."

Working on a Ph.D. in literature at Loyola University of Chicago and teaching there is another part of the transition. "To change from being the teacher to the student; from being the expert to the novice is very difficult emotionally," says Arcana, a teacher of 12 years. It is difficult to tell readers who ask about her next book that she is *learning* to write fiction.

"I want to use words the way a musician uses sound, not just the way someone speaking through a microphone uses sound. If you're playing the piano or clarinet, people are going to dance. Before I wanted people to think about what I was saying; now I want people to dance to what I'm saying," she says.

As an "expert" in nonfiction, Arcana advises writers to remember their readers. "Beginning writers are so worried about whether they're different and special that they can lose consciousness of the audience and they can lose that sense of interacting with the reader," she says.

With this in mind, Arcana formed an editorial panel to read her books chapter by chapter prior to their publication. She found five readers (not writers) for each panel who would honestly critique each chapter at meetings she held at her home.

In addition to forming editorial panels, writers should have distribution and publicity agreements and budgets written into their book contracts, she advises. The standard contract with a large publisher doesn't guarantee a book's continuous promotion. Sometimes the writer benefits most from a small publisher who takes pride in distributing the book.

"No one writes and doesn't care if it's read. Why write it then? Why not just think it as you walk along the lake?" she says. "Writing is about publicity. It's about performance."

One reality that writers must confront is that few writers make a full-time living from writing. The public thinks published authors are rich. Most writers, though, teach part time or have "money jobs," she says.

Arcana gives workshops and lectures and works in nonwriting-related office jobs. She writes at 5 a.m., evenings, weekends, and at other times she sets aside *for writing*.

Most artists lead double lives, says Arcana, unwilling to consider writing a hobby or to confine her writing to a diary. "What it is to be a writer is to touch the mind of the other person and hopefully the heart and the spirit."

known authors of short stories, novels and books). Buys 10 mss/year. Query. Length: 500-1,500 words. Pays $10-30.

Photos: Pays $5 for 8x10 b&w prints of well-known writers to accompany mss. Captions required. Buys one-time rights.

‡**WEEKLIES' IDEA SERVICE**, Berkley-Small, Inc., 1000 Hillcrest Rd., Box 91460, Mobile AL 36691. (205)343-1717. Editor: Helen M. Hendrick. A monthly magazine covering timely information pertaining to the nondaily newspaper—circulation, promotion, advertising, management, etc.—for publishers and editors of weekly newspapers. Circ. 338 weekly newspapers. Pays on publication. Publishes ms an average of 2 months after acceptance. Byline given. Buys all rights. Submit seasonal/holiday material 3 months in advance. Simultaneous queries, and simultaneous, photocopied and previously published submissions OK. Reports in 2 months. Free sample copy and writer's guidelines.

Nonfiction: Book excerpts; expose (the weekly newspaper); general interest; how-to (successfully operate a weekly newspaper: promotion, precedures, advertising, etc.); humor; inspirational; interview/profile; opinion; personal experience; and technical. Suggested topics: building advertising revenue, increasing market penetration, forming better advertiser/newspaper relations, designing better office procedures, creating greater public awareness, competing with a local daily newspaper, personnel turnover, developing reader contests and holding readership. Buys 12 mss/year. Query with published clips or send complete ms. Length: 1,000-2,000 words. Pays $35-50.

Columns/Departments: Staff Writers, Editors, Management Consultants, Publishers, Advertisers, Promotion Personnel. Query with published clips or send complete ms. Length: 1,000-2,000 words. Pays $35-50.

Fillers: Clippings, anecdotes, short humor and newsbreaks. Buys variable number/year. Length: 500-1,000 words. Pays $15-25.

Tips: "The writer is expected to show a certain expertise with subject matter because he is familiar with it, has researched it, or has consulted experts and uses their quotes (with permission)."

WEST COAST REVIEW OF BOOKS, Rapport Publishing Co., Inc., 5301 Sunset Blvd., Hollywood CA 90027. (213)464-2662. Editor: D. David Dreis. Bimonthly magazine for book consumers. "Provocative articles based on specific subject matter, books and author retrospectives." Circ. 80,000. Pays on publication. Byline given. Offers $50 kill fee. Buys all rights. SASE. Sample copy $2.

Nonfiction: General interest, historical/nostalgic and profile (author retrospectives). "No individual book reviews." Buys 12 mss/year. Query. Length: open.

Tips: "There must be a reason (current interest, news events, etc.) for any article here. Example: 'The Jew-Haters' was about anti-semitism which was written up in six books; all reviewed and analyzed under that umbrella title. Under no circumstances should articles be submitted unless query has been responded to." No phone calls.

WORD PROCESSING NEWS, Word of Mouth Enterprises, #210, 211 E. Olive Ave., Burbank CA 91502. (213)845-7809. Publisher/Executive Editor: Barbara Elman. Managing Editor: Glenn Schiffman. Associate Editor: Judith Lovejoy. 60% freelance written. Bimonthly newsletter covering writing on computers and general computer information. "Audience owns or is interested in writing on computers instead of typewriter." Circ. 3,000. Pays on publication. Publishes ms an average of 3 months after acceptance. Byline given. Buys first North American serial rights, one-time rights or second serial (reprint) rights. Simultaneous queries, and simultaneous, photocopied and previously published submissions OK. Computer printout submissions acceptable. Electronic submissions OK if query first. Reports ASAP. Sample copy $2; writer's guidelines available.

Nonfiction: Book excerpts and reviews; general interest; how-to (tips on using word processing for specific computer or type of writing); humor; interview/profile; new product; opinion; and personal experience ("all articles have personal slant"). "Each issue focuses on a different type of writing (script, freelance, self-publish). SASE for list of future and back issues." No "how to choose a computer/word processor—most readers already have one." Query with clips if available or send complete ms. Buys 24 mss/year. Length: 250-2,000 words. Pays 5¢/word minimum.

Columns/Departments: A Writer's Point of View (personal experiences); Choices (program and system comparisons); Another Writer's POV (interviews). Query with clips if available or send complete ms. Length: varies. Pays 5¢/word.

Fillers: Anecdotes and newsbreaks. Buys 20 fillers/year. Length: 25-100 words. Pays $15-20.

Tips: "Send for sample or subscribe and check out style. Send query and/or manuscript direct. Writers sending articles for reprint should include information on where it was published before. We're buying *more* articles from contributors and seeking reviewers for all brands of computer. Our readers include business and academic writers as well as screenwriters and novelists."

THE WRITER, 8 Arlington St., Boston MA 02116. Editor: Sylvia K. Burack. Monthly. Pays on acceptance. Buys first rights only. Uses little freelance material. Computer printout submissions acceptable; no dot-matrix. SASE. Sample copy $1.50.
Nonfiction: Articles of instruction for writers. Length: about 2,000 words. Pays good rates, on acceptance.

WRITER'S DIGEST, 9933 Alliance Rd., Cincinnati OH 45242. (513)984-0717. Editor: William Brohaugh. Asst. Editor: Sharon Rudd. 90% freelance written. Monthly magazine about writing and publishing. "Our readers write fiction, poetry, nonfiction, plays and all kinds of creative writing. They're interested in improving their writing skills, improving their sales ability, and finding new outlets for their talents." Circ. 200,000. Pays on acceptance. Publishes ms an average of 5 months after acceptance. Buys first North American serial rights for one-time editorial use, microfilm/microfiche use, and magazine promotional use. Pays 20% kill fee. Byline given. Submit seasonal/holiday material 8 months in advance. Previously published and photocopied submissions OK. "Electronic submissions are possible a few years down the line. We'll accept computer printout submissions, of course—but they *must* be readable. That's the rule behind any submission to any magazine. We strongly recommend letter-quality." SASE. "If you don't want your manuscript returned, indicate that on the first page of the manuscript or in a cover letter." Reports in 1 month. Sample copy $2; writer's guidelines for SASE.
Nonfiction: "Our mainstay is the how-to article—that is, an article telling how to write and sell more of what you write. For instance, how to write compelling leads and conclusions, how to improve your character descriptions, how to become more efficient and productive. Be alert in spotting the new opportunities for writers and be concise in letting the reader know how to write for that market, and how to market the article once it's written. We like plenty of examples, anecdotes and $$$ in our articles—so other writers can actually see what's been done successfully by the author of a particular piece. We like our articles to speak directly to the reader through the use of the first person voice. Don't submit an article on what five book editors say about writing mysteries. Instead, submit an article on how you cracked the mystery market and how our readers can do the same. But don't limit the article to your experiences; include the opinions of those five editors to give your article increased depth and authority." General interest (about writing); how-to (writing and marketing techniques that work); humor (short pieces); inspirational; interview and profile (query first); new product; and personal experience (marketing and freelancing experiences). "We can always use articles on fiction technique, and solid articles on poetry or poets are always welcome. No articles titled 'So You Want to Be a Writer'—first person pieces that ramble without giving a lesson or something readers can learn from in the sharing of the story." Buys 90-100 mss/year. "Queries are preferred, but complete mss are OK." Length: 500-3,000 words. Pays 10¢/word minimum.
Photos: "All things being equal, photos do make a difference, especially for interviews and profiles. State availability of photos or send contact sheet with ms." Pays $25 for 5x7 or larger b&w prints. Captions required.
Columns/Departments: And You Can Quote Me (uses authors' quotes; depending on length, pays $2-5/quote; include source); Chronicle (first-person narratives of writing adventures; length: 1,200-1,500 words; pays 10¢/word); The Writing Life (length: 50-800 words; pays 10¢/word); Trends/Topics (short, unbylined news items about topics and issues that affect writers; pays 10¢/word); and My First Sale (an "occasional" department; a first person account of how a writer broke into print; length: 1,000 words; pays 10¢/word). "For First Sale items, use a narrative, anecdotal style to tell a tale that is both inspirational and instructional. Before you submit a My First Sale item, make certain that your story contains a solid lesson that will benefit other writers." Buys approximately 200 articles/year for Writing Life section, Trends/Topics and shorter pieces. Send complete ms.
Poetry: Light verse about "the writing life"—joys and frustrations of writing. "We are also considering poetry other than short light verse—but related to writing, publishing, other poets and authors, etc." Buys 2/issue. Submit poems in batches of 1-8. Length: 2-20 lines. Pays $10-50/poem.
Fillers: Anecdotes and short humor, primarily for use in The Writing Life column. Uses 2/issue. Length: 50-200 words. Pays 10¢/word.

WRITER'S LIFELINE, Box 1641, Cornwall, Ontario K6H 5V6 Canada. Contact: Editor. Monthly magazine "aimed at freelance writers of all ages and interests." Acquires first rights. Previously published submissions OK. SAE and IRCs.
Nonfiction: "Articles on all aspects of writing and publishing." Send complete ms. Length: 500 words maximum. Payment: 3 free issues in which article appears.
Fiction: Must be tied in to writing and publishing. Poetry published. Payment: 3 free issues in which story or poem appears.
Tips: "Writer should show evidence of his qualification to write on subject. All articles should be pegged to current concerns of writers: self-publishing, hitting local markets, anecdotes of new writer breaking in, and preparing book reviews are among articles we have published recently."

‡**WRITERS WEST, For Working Writers**, Kriss Enterprise, Box 16097, San Diego CA 92116. (619)278-6108. Editor: Betty Dodds. Managing Editor: Doug Emry. 90% freelance written. A monthly magazine for the professional writer. "The editorial thrust is away from how-to articles and toward subjects of interest to working writers, whether they are working on a novel or producing short stories, poetry or nonfiction." Circ. 2,500. Pays on acceptance. Publishes ms an average of 2 months after acceptance. Byline given. Buys first North American serial rights, and second (reprint) rights to material originaly published elsewhere. Simultaneous queries, and simultaneous, photocopied and previously published submissions OK. Computer printout submissions acceptable. SASE. Reports in 2 weeks. Sample copy $2; writer's guidelines for SAE and 1 first class stamp.

Nonfiction: Expose (similar to "Vanity Schemes Exposed" (Oct. 83) and "Trauma of a First Novel" (Oct. 83); interview/profile (well-known authors, writing-related personalities); and opinion (writing related). "No elementary how-tos or how great it is being a writer." Buys 24 mss/year. Query or send complete ms. Length: 2,500 words maximum. "Token payment plus copies.

Photos: "Photos with articles are welcome—preferably with the subject in his/her working environment, or head shots. Include the photographer's credit line." State availability of photos. Reviews 5x7 and larger b&w prints. Payment included in payment for ms. Identification of subjects required. Buys one-time rights.

Columns/Departments: Betty Abell Jurus, Writing Connection columnist. Writing Connection (news about writers: book length works-in-progress, information on special events, groups, clubs, workshops and organizations). "Please provide dates, phone numbers and mailing addresses." Deadline: 35 days prior to publication date. Length: book descriptions, 2 paragraphs maximum; include mailing address. No payment.

Fiction: "Will consider anything of quality. See "In The Lion's Den" (Nov. '83) about a starlet in MGM's commissary. No trials and tribulations of being a writer." Buys 12 mss/year. Send complete ms; include short biography. Length: 2,500 words maximum.

Poetry: Prefers upbeat, positive poems. Buys 12 poems/year. Length: 50 lines maximum. "Token payment plus copies. No free verse."

Tips: "Most feature articles are assigned, but the quality of unsolicited submissions is encouraging, and we have printed some." Query or submit.

WRITER'S YEARBOOK, 9933 Alliance Rd., Cincinnati OH 45242. Editor: William Brohaugh. Asst. Editor: Sharon Rudd. 100% freelance written. Newsstand annual for freelance writers, journalists and teachers of creative writing. "We provide how-to features and information to help our readers become more skilled at writing and successful at selling their writing." Buys first North American serial rights and (occasionally) reprint rights. Pays 20% kill fee. Byline given. Buys 10-15 mss/year. Pays on acceptance. Publishes ms an average of 6 months after acceptance. "Writers should query in spring with ideas for the following year." Send detailed query or outline of what you have in mind. Previously published (book reprints) and high-quality photocopied submissions OK. Computer printout submissions acceptable; prefers letter-quality to dot-matrix. SASE. "If you don't want your manuscript returned, indicate that on the first page of the manuscript or in a cover letter."

Nonfiction: "We want articles that reflect the current state of writing in America. Trends, inside information and money-saving and money-making ideas for the freelance writer. We try to touch on the various facets of writing in each issue of the *Yearbook*—from fiction to poetry to playwriting, and any other endeavor a writer can pursue. How-to articles—that is, articles that explain in detail how to do something—are very important to us. For example, you could explain how to establish mood in fiction, how to improve interviewing techniques, how to write for and sell to specialty magazines, or how to construct and market a good poem. We are also interested in the writer's spare time—what she/he does to retreat occasionally from the writing wars; where and how to refuel and replenish the writing spirit. 'How Beats the Heart of a Writer' features interest us, if written warmly, in the first person, by a writer who has had considerable success. We also want interviews or profiles of well-known bestselling authors, always with good pictures. Articles on writing techniques that are effective today are always welcome." Recent article example: "Life in the Rabbit Hole: The Adventure of a Hollywood Screenwriter," by William F. Nolan (1984). Length: 750-4,500 words. Pays 10¢/word minimum.

Photos: Interviews and profiles must be accompanied by high quality photos. B&w only; depending on use, pays $20-50/published photo. Captions required.

WRITING!, Curriculum Innovations, Inc., 3500 Western Ave., Highland Park IL 60035. Editor: Bonnie Bekken. Monthly magazine (September through May) covering writing skills for junior and senior high school students. Pays on publication. Buys all rights. Byline given. Submit seasonal/holiday material 5 months in advance. Computer printout submissions acceptable; prefers letter-quality to dot-matrix. SASE. Reports in 6 weeks.

Nonfiction: Interviews wth professional writers. Should stress the writer's introduction into the craft and his/her own reading preferences as a student. Query with brief outline. Length 1,000-1,500 words. Pays 5¢/word minimum.

‡**WRITING UPDATE, News, Tips & Resources for Persons on the Rise**, #250, 4812 Folsom Blvd., Sacramento CA 95819. Editor/Publisher: Kimberly A. Edwards. 3% freelance written. A monthly newsletter covering writing, freelancing, teaching of writing, consulting, and business: digest of issues for persons who write for fun, profit or promotion of themselves/their careers. "We appeal largely to career-oriented communicators of the 80's who see writing as an integral part of their personal/professional lives, and at the same time are busy juggling writing, career and home. Readers want clean, simple, streamlined information they can read over a quick sandwich. They want solid tips they can apply to their lives. They don't want to wade through paragraphs to get to the good stuff." Estab. 1983. Mostly staff written. Sample copy $1.50.

Columns/Departments: Contact: Trade-Off editor. Trade-off (short tips from folks on any aspect of freelancing or writing for fun, profit or promotion of their career). "Just send us a note or short letter—a paragraph or two—describing something you've found helpful—a writing, marketing or organizational tip you'd like to share with others." Pays in 1 copy.

Laundry and Dry Cleaning

Some journals in the Coin-Operated Machines category are also in the market for material on laundries and dry cleaning establishments.

AMERICAN DRYCLEANER, 500 N. Dearborn St., Chicago IL 60610. (312)337-7700. Editor: Earl V. Fischer. 15% freelance written. For professional drycleaners. Monthly. Circ. 28,000. Buys all rights or industry-exclusive rights. Pays on publication. Publishes ms an average of 3 months after acceptance. Will send free sample copy to writers with specific queries. Reports "promptly." Computer printout submissions acceptable. SASE.

Nonfiction: Articles on all aspects of running a drycleaning business. "These can be narratives about individual drycleaners and how they are handling, say, advertising, counter service, customer relations, cleaning, spot removal, pressing, inspection, packaging, paperwork, or general business management; interpretive reports about outside developments, such as textile innovations or government reglations affecting drycleaners; or how-to articles offering practical help to cleaners on any facet of their business. The important thing is that the reader find practical benefit in the article, whichever type submitted." No basic advertising and public relations material. "We have regulars for this who know our industry." Pays a minimum of 6¢/published word. Recent article example: "8.50 a suit and all the business they can handle" (February 1984).

Photos: Photos purchased with mss; quality 8x10 or 5x7 b&w glossies. Photos should help tell story. No model releases required. Pays $6 minimum.

Tips: "I would like each query letter to state as specifically as possible the proposed subject matter. It would help to get a theme sentence or brief outline of the proposed article. Also helpful would be a statement of whether (and what sort of) photos or other illustrations are available. Anyone with the type of article that our readers would find helpful can break into the publication. Find a successful drycleaner—one with unusually satisfied customers, for example, or one that seems to be making a lot of money. Find out what makes that cleaner so successful. Tell us about it in specific, practical terms, so other cleaners will be able to follow suit. Articles should help our readers operate their drycleaning businesses more successfully; the appropriateness and practical value of information given are more important than writing style. We prefer *short* reports about *small* cleaning companies doing *one thing* well enough for others to want to know about it and how they might do the same. Reports can range from less than 250 words up to any length the writer can justify."

AMERICAN LAUNDRY DIGEST, American Trade Magazines, Inc., 500 N. Dearborn St., Chicago IL 60610. (312)337-7700. Editor: Larry Kai Ebert. 26% freelance written. For a professional laundering, linen supply, uniform rental audience (non coin-ops). Monthly magazine; 52 pages. Circ. 17,100. Pays 2 weeks prior to publication. Buys all rights. Phone queries OK. Photocopied submissions OK. SASE. Reports in 2 weeks. Free sample copy and writer's guidelines.

Nonfiction: Business oriented articles about how laundrymen have cut costs, increased production, improved safety, gained sales, etc. "Interviews with laundrymen about how they run a successful plant would be welcome." Query. Length: 300-3,000 words. Pays minimum of 5¢/word.

Photos: B&w glossies (8x10 preferred; 5x7 acceptable) purchased with mss. Send contact sheet. Pays minimum of $5.

INDUSTRIAL LAUNDERER, Suite 613, 1730 M St. NW, Washington DC 20036. (202)296-6744. Editor: David A. Ritchey. 10% freelance written. For decisionmakers in the industrial laundry industry. Publication of the Institute of Industrial Launderers, Inc. Magazine; 124 pages. Monthly. Circ. 2,500. Buys all rights. Pays on acceptance. Publishes ms an average of 3 months after acceptance. Computer printout submissions acceptable. Reports in 1 week. Query. SASE. Sample copies $1; limited sample copies available. Write for copy of guidelines for writers.

Nonfiction: General interest pieces for the industrial laundry industry; labor news, news from Washington; and book reviews on publications of interest to people in this industry. Technical advancements and "people" stories. Informational, personal experience, interview, profile, historical, successful business operations and merchandising techniques. No "general business articles or articles not specifically related to the industrial laundry industry." Buys 5-10 unsolicited mss/year. Length: 750 words minimum. Payment negotiable.

Photos: No additional payment for 8x10 b&w glossies used with ms. Pays $5 minimum for those purchased on assignment. Captions required.

‡**WESTERN CLEANER AND LAUNDERER**, Box 722, La Canada CA 91011. (213)247-8595. Editor: Monida Urquhart. 15% freelance written. For owner/managers and key employees of drycleaning, laundry, rug cleaning, drapery and cleaning plants. Monthly tabloid; 44 pages. Circ. 9,500. Pays on publication. Buys all rights. Phone queries OK. Submit seasonal/holiday material 2 months in advance. Computer printout submissions acceptable; no dot-matrix. SASE. Reports in 1 month. Free sample copy.

Nonfiction: General interest (successful operation of drycleaning or laundry business); how-to (operate a cleaning/laundry plant); new product; and profile. Buys 10-12 mss/year. Query. Length: 400-1,200 words. Pays 5¢/word.

Photos: State availability of photos with query. Pays $4 each for 4x5 b&w glossy prints for number used with story. Captions and model release required. Buys all rights.

Law

‡**ABA JOURNAL**, American Bar Association, 750 N. Lake Shore Dr., Chicago IL 60611. (312)988-5000. Editor: Richard Allen. Associate Editor: Larry Bodine. 50% freelance written. Monthly magazine covering law and lawyers. "The content of the *Journal* is designed to appeal to the association's diverse membership with emphasis on the general practitioner." Circ. 340,000. Pays on acceptance. Publishes ms an average of 2 months after acceptance. Byline given. "Editor works with writer until article is in acceptable form." Buys all rights. Submit seasonal/holiday material 3 months in advance. Simultaneous queries, and simultaneous and photocopied submissions OK. Computer printout submissions acceptable; no dot-matrix. Contact publisher about electronic submissions. Reports in 3 weeks. Free sample copy and writer's guidelines.

Nonfiction: Book excerpts; general interest (legal); how-to (law practice techniques); humor; interview/profile (law firms and prominent individuals); personal experience ("war stories"); and technical (legal trends). "The emphasis of the *Journal* is on the practical problems faced by lawyers in general practice and how those problems can be overcome. Articles should emphasize the practical rather than the theoretical or esoteric. Writers should avoid the style of law reviews, academic journals or legal briefs and should write in an informal, journalistic style. Short quotations from people and specific examples of your point will improve an article." Special issues have featured women and minorities in the legal profession. Buys 60 mss/year. Query with published clips or send complete ms. Length: 1,000-3,000 words. Pays $300-800.

Columns/Departments: War Stories (contains true, funny anecdotes about lawyers at work). Buys 30 mss/year. Send complete ms. Length: 100 words maximum. Pays $25 if published.

Tips: "Write to us with a specific idea in mind and spell out how the subject would be covered. Full length profiles and feature articles are always needed. We look for practical information. Don't send us theory, philosophy or wistful meanderings. Our readers want to know how to win cases and operate their practices more efficiently."

THE ALTMAN & WEIL REPORT TO LEGAL MANAGEMENT, Altman & Weil Publications, Inc., Box 472, Ardmore PA 19003. (215)649-4646. Editor: Robert I. Weil. Monthly newsletter covering law office purchases (equipment, insurance services, space, etc.). Circ. 2,200. Pays on publication. Byline given. Buys all rights; sometimes second serial (reprint) rights. Photocopied and previously published submissions OK. Reports in 1 month on queries; 6 weeks on mss. Sample copy for business-size SAE and 1 first class stamp.

Nonfiction: How-to (buy, use, repair); interview/profile; and new product. Buys 6 mss/year. Query. Length: 500-2,500 words. Pays $125/published page.

Photos: State availability of photos. Reviews b&w prints; payment is included in payment for ms. Captions and model release required. Buys one-time rights.

BARRISTER, American Bar Association Press, 1155 E. 60th St., Chicago IL 60637. (312)947-4072. Editor: Anthony Monahan. For young lawyers who are members of the American Bar Association concerned about practice of law, improvement of the profession and service to the public. Quarterly magazine; 64 pages. Circ.

155,000. Pays on acceptance. Buys all rights, first serial rights, second serial (reprint) rights, or simultaneous rights. Photocopied submissions OK. SASE. Reports in 4-6 weeks. Free sample copy.

Nonfiction: "As a magazine of ideas and opinion, we seek material that will help readers in their interrelated roles of attorney and citizen; major themes in legal and social affairs." Especially needs expository or advocacy articles; position should be defended clearly in good, crisp, journalistic prose. "We would like to see articles on issues such as the feasibility of energy alternatives to nuclear power, roles of women and minorities in law, the power and future of multinational corporations; national issues such as gun control; and aspects of the legal profession such as salary comparisons, use of computers in law practice." Recent article example: "Are You Meant to Be a Partner?" No humorous court reporter anecdote material or political opinion articles. Buys 20-25 unsolicited mss/year. Length: 3,000-4,000 words. Query with a working title and outline of topic. "Be specific." Pays $300-450.

Photos: Donna Tashjian, photo editor. B&w photos and color transparencies purchased without accompanying ms. Pays $35-150.

Tips: "We urge writers to think ahead about new areas of law and social issues: sexual habits, work habits, corporations, etc."

CALIFORNIA LAWYER, The State Bar of California, 555 Franklin St., San Francisco CA 94102. (415)561-8286. Editor: Jonathan R. Maslow. Associate Editor: Tom Brom. 80% freelance written. Monthly magazine. Law-related articles and general interest subjects of appeal to attorneys. Circ. 90,000. Pays on acceptance. Publishes ms an average of 3 months after acceptance. Byline given. Offers 1/3 kill fee. Buys all rights. Simultaneous queries, and simultaneous and photocopied submissions OK. Computer printout submissions acceptable. Reports in 2 weeks on queries; 3 weeks on mss. Sample copy for 8 1/2x11 SAE and $1.50 postage; writer's guidelines for SAE and 1 first class stamp.

Nonfiction: General interest, historical, humor, interview/profile, opinion, technical, travel, personal finance advice and personal effectiveness. "We are interested in concise, well-written and well-researched articles on recent trends in the legal profession, legal aspects of issues of current concern, as well as general interest articles of potential appeal and benefit to the state's lawyers. We would like to see a description or outline of your proposed idea, including a list of possible information sources."Buys 36 mss/year. Query with clips if available. Length: 2,000-3,000 words (features). Pays $300-550.

Photos: Jan Leonard, photo editor. State availability of photos with query letter or manuscript. Reviews prints. Identification of subjects required.

Columns/Departments: Business of Practice; After Hours; Profile; Money; Effectiveness. Buys 100/year. Query with clips if available. Length: 1,000-1,500 words. Pays $150-300.

Tips: "Trends in magazine publishing that freelance writers should be aware of include shorter articles, more emphasis on individual magazine styles; stricter guidelines for libel and fact checking."

LEGAL ECONOMICS, Box 11418, Columbia SC 29211. Managing Editor/Art Director: Delmar L. Roberts. 10% freelance written. For the practicing lawyer. Bimonthly magazine; 76-92 pages. Circ. 23,000. Rights purchased vary with author and material. Usually buys all rights. Byline given. Pays on publication. Publishes ms an average of 6 months after acceptance. Computer printout submissions acceptable. Query. SASE. Free writer's guidelines. Sample copy $2.50 (make check payable to American Bar Association). Returns rejected material in 90 days, if requested.

Nonfiction: "We assist the practicing lawyer in operating and managing his or her office by providing relevant articles and departments written in a readable and informative style. Editorial content is intended to aid the lawyer by conveying management methods that will allow him or her to provide legal services to clients in a prompt and efficient manner at reasonable cost. Typical topics of articles include timekeeping systems; word processing developments; microcomputer applications; client/lawyer relations; office equipment; computerized research; compensation of partners and associates; information retrieval; and use of paralegals." No elementary articles on a whole field of technology, such as, "why you need word processing in the law office." Pays $50-200.

Photos: Pays $25-40 for b&w photos purchased with mss; $45-50 for color; $75 up for cover transparencies.

Tips: "We normally do not publish thematic issues. However, we have published one issue exclusively on computer hardware and have a software issue in preparation."

‡**LEGAL TIMES**, Harcourt Brace Jovanovich, Publishers, 1666 Connecticut Ave. NW, Washington DC 20009. (202)797-9600. Editor: Larry Lempert. Managing Editor: Steve Nelson. Tabloid. 1 national weekly, 1 monthly for DC, and 1 monthly for New York covering the legal profession. "Weekly covers trends and news developments of interest to sophisticated legal audience, mostly business lawyers, as well as articles about the legal profession per se; monthly includes more feature material about lawyers and law firms." Circ. weekly 6,000; monthlies 30,000-50,000. Pays on publication. Byline given. Buys all rights. Simultaneous queries and photocopied submissions OK. Computer printout submissions acceptable. Free sample copy.

Nonfiction: Leslie Goodman-Malamuth, associate managing editor. General interest and interview/profile. "All must relate to lawyers, law firms, or trends in the law." Opinion, personal experience and travel "also accepted, but we do not pay for these." Occasional "special sections" on computer litigation support, law office management, and office use of technology. Buys 24 mss/year, but many are from "regulars." Query with published clips. Length: 6,000 words maximum. Pays sliding scale depending on experience.

‡**LOS ANGELES LAWYER**, Los Angeles County Bar Association, Box 55020, Los Angeles CA 90055. (213)627-2727, ext. 265. Editor: Rebecca Morrow. Monthly (except for combined July/August issue) magazine covering legal profession with "journalistic and scholarly articles of interest to the legal profession." Circ. 17,000. Pays on acceptance. Byline given. Buys first rights only. Submit seasonal/holiday material 4 months in advance. Simultaneous queries and photocopied submissions OK. Computer printout submissions acceptable; prefers letter-quality to dot-matrix. Reports in 2 months on queries; 3 months on mss. Sample copy for $1.50; free writer's guidelines.

Nonfiction: How-to (tips for legal practitioners); humor; interview (leading legal figures); opinion (on area of law, lawyer attitudes or group, court decisions, etc.); travel (very occasionally); and consumer-at-law feature articles on topics of interest to lawyers. Special issues include Law Office of the Future and Immigration issue. No first person, nonlegal material. Buys 22 mss/year. Query with published clips. Length: 4,000-4,500 words for feature (cover story); 2,000-2,750 words for consumer article. Pays $500-600 for cover story, $200-225 for consumer article.

Tips: "Feature (cover story) articles and consumer-at-law articles articles are the areas most open to freelancers in our publication."

THE NATIONAL LAW JOURNAL, New York Law Publishing Company, 111 8th Ave., New York NY 10011. (212)741-8300. Editor: Timothy Robinson. Managing Editor: Albert Robbins. 20% freelance written. Weekly newspaper for the legal profession. Circ. 37,000. Pays on publication. Publishes ms an average of 1 month after acceptance. Byline given. Offers $75 kill fee. Buys all rights. Simultaneous queries OK. Computer printout submissions acceptable; no dot-matrix. SASE. Reports in 3 weeks on queries; 5 weeks on mss. Sample copy $2.

Nonfiction: Expose (on subjects of interest to lawyers); and interview/profile (of lawyers or judges of note). "The bulk of our freelance articles are 2,000-2,500 word profiles of prominent lawyers, or trend stories relating to the legal profession. We also buy a steady stream of short, spot-news stories on local court decisions or lawsuits; often, these come from legal affairs writers on local newspapers. No articles without a legal angle." Buys 60 mss/year. Query with clips of published work or send complete ms. Length: 1,500-3,000 words. Pays $300-500.

Tips: "For those who are not covering legal affairs on a regular basis, the best way into *The National Law Journal* is probably through our On Trial feature. Every week we print a sort of reporter's notebook on some proceeding currently underway in a courtroom. These stories come from all around the country and range from gory murder trials to a night in small claims court. They usually run about 1,000 words and are stylistically quite flexible. We also use op-ed pieces on subjects of legal interest, many of which come from freelancers. Writers interested in doing an op-ed piece should query first."

‡**ONTARIO LAWYERS WEEKLY, The Newspaper for the Legal Profession in Ontario**, Butterworth (Canada) Inc., 2265 Midland Ave., Scarborough, Ontario M1P 4S1 Canada. (416)292-1421. Editor: D. Michael Fitz-James. A weekly tabloid covering law and legal affairs for a "sophisticated up-market readership of lawyers and accountants." Estab. 1983. Circ. 19,600. Pays on publication. Byline given. Offers negotiable kill fee. Usually buys all rights; sometimes second serial (reprint) rights or negotiable rights. Submit seasonal/holiday material 1 month in advance. Computer printout submissions acceptable. SASE. Reports in 1 month. Sample copy for 8½x11 SAE.

Nonfiction: Book reviews; expose; general interest (law); historical/nostalgic; how-to (professional); humor; interview/profile (lawyers and judges); opinion; technical; news; and case comments. "We try to wrap up the week's legal events and issues in a snappy informal package with lots of visual punch. We especially like news stories with photos or illustrations. We are always interested in feature or newsfeature articles involving current legal issues, but contributors should keep in mind our audience is trained in English/Canadian Common law— not US law. That means most US constitutional or criminal law stories will not be accepted. Contributors should also keep in mind they're writing for *lawyers* and they don't need to reduce legal stories to simple-minded babble often seen in the daily press." Special Christmas issue. No routine court reporting or fake news stories about commercial products. Buys 200-300 mss/year. Query or send complete ms. Length: 200-2,000 words. Pays $25 minimum, negotiable maximum (have paid up to $250 in the past). Payment in Canadian dollars.

Photos: State availability of photos with query letter or ms. Reviews b&w contact sheets, negatives, and 5x7 and 8x10 prints. Identification of subjects required. Buys negotiable rights.

Columns/Departments: Buys 30-40 mss/year. Send complete ms. Length: 500-1,000 words. Pays negotiable rate.

Fillers: Clippings, jokes, gags, anecdotes, short humor and newsbreaks. Length: 50-200 words. Pays $10 minimum.

Tips: "Freelancers can best break in to our publication by submitting news, features, and accounts of unusual or bizarre legal events." No unsolicited mss returned without SASE.

‡**THE PARALEGAL, The Publication for the Paralegal Profession**, Paralegal Publishing Corp./National Paralegal Association, 60 E. State St., Box 629, Doylestown PA 18901. (215)348-5575. Editor; William Cameron. Bimonthly magazine covering the paralegal profession for practicing paralegals, attorneys, paralegal educators, paralegal associations, law librarians and court personnel. Special and controlled circulation includes law libraries, colleges and schools educating paralegals, law schools, law firms and governmental agecies, etc. Estab. 1983. Circ. 4,000. Byline given. Buys all rights. Simultaneous queries, and simultaneous, photocopied and previously published submissions. SASE. Reports in 1 week on queries; 1 month on mss. Writer's guidelines for business-size SAE.
Nonfiction: Book excerpts, expose, general interest, historical/nostalgic, how-to, humor, interview/profile, new product, opinion, personal experience, photo feature, technical and travel. Suggested topics include the paralegal (where do they fit and how do they operate within the law firm in each specialty); the government; the corporation; the trade union; the banking institution; the law library; the legal clinic; the trade or professional association; the educational institution; the court system; the collection agency; the stock brokerage firm; and the insurance company. Articles also wanted on paralegals exploring "where have they been? Where are they now? Where are they going." Query or send complete ms. Length: 1,500-3,000 words. Pays variable rates.
Photos: Send photos with query or ms. Captions, model release and identification of subjects required.
Columns/Departments: Case at Issue (a feature on a current case from a state or federal court which either directly or indirectly affects paralegals and their work with attorneys, the public, private or governmental sector); Humor (cartoons, quips, short humorous stories, anecdotes and one liners in good taste and germain to the legal profession); and My Position (an actual presentation by a paralegal who wishes to share with others his/her job analysis). Query.
Fillers: Clippings, jokes, gags, anecdotes, short humor and newsbreaks.

THE PENNSYLVANIA LAWYER, Pennsylvania Bar Association, 100 South St., Box 186, Harrisburg PA 17108. (717)238-6715. Executive Editor: Francis J. Fanucci. Editor: Donald C. Sarvey. 20% freelance written. Magazine published 7 times/year as a service to the legal profession. Circ. 24,000. Pays on acceptance. Publishes ms an average of 3 months after acceptance. Byline given. Buys negotiable rights; generally first rights. Submit seasonal/holiday material 5 months in advance. Simultaneous queries OK. Reports in 2 weeks. Free sample copy.
Nonfiction: General interest, how-to, humor, interview/profile, new product, and personal experience. All features must relate in some way to Pennsylvania lawyers or the practice of law in Pennsylvania. Buys 12 mss/year. Query. Length: 800-2,500 words. Pays $75-350.

STUDENT LAWYER, American Bar Association, 750 N. Lake Shore Dr., Chicago IL 60611. (312)947-4087. Editor: Lizanne Poppens. Associate Editor: Sarah Hoban. 95% freelance written. Monthly (September-May) magazine; 56 pages. Circ. 45,000. Pays on publication. Buys first rights and second (reprint) rights to material originally published elsewhere. Pays negotiable kill fee. Byline given. Submit seasonal/holiday material 2 months in advance. Photocopied submissions OK. Computer printout submissions acceptable. Reports in 1 month. Publishes ms an average of 3 months after acceptance. Sample copy $2; free writer's guidelines.
Nonfiction: Expose (government, law, education and business); profiles (prominent persons in law-related fields); opinion (on matters of current legal interest); essays (on legal affairs); interviews; and photo features. Recent article example: "Kids Who Kill" (October 1983). Buys 5 mss/issue. Query. Length: 3,000-5,000 words. Pays $250-600.
Photos: State availability of photos with query. Pays $50-75 for 8x10 b&w prints; $50-250 for color. Model release required (please send copy along).
Columns/Departments: Briefly (short stories on unusual and interesting developments in the law); Legal Aids (unusual approaches and programs connected to teaching law students and lawyers); Esq. (brief profiles of people in the law); End Note (very short pieces on a variety of topics; can be humorous, educational, outrageous)); Pro Se (opinion slot for authors to wax eloquent on legal issues, civil rights conflicts, the state of the union); and Et Al. (column for short features that fit none of the above categories). Buys 4-8 mss/issue. Length: 250-1,000 words. Pays $75-250.
Fiction: "We buy fiction only when it is very good and deals with issues of law in the contemporary world or offers insights into the inner workings of lawyers. No mystery or science fiction accepted."
Tips: "*Student Lawyer* actively seeks good, new writers. Legal training definitely not essential; writing talent is. The writer should not think we are a law review; we are a features magazine with the law (in the broadest sense) as the common denominator. Past articles concerned gay rights, prison reform, the media, pornography, capital punishment, and space law. Find issues of national scope and interest to write about; be aware of subjects the magazine—and other media—have already covered and propose something new. Write clearly and well."

‡VERDICT MAGAZINE, American Lifestyle Communications Inc., 123 Truxtun Ave., Bakersfield CA 93301. (805)325-7124. Managing Editor: Steve Walsh. A quarterly magazine covering defense law (corporate). Estab. 1983. Circ. 5,000. Pays on publication. Byline given. Buys first North American serial rights. Submit seasonal/holiday material 4 months in advance. Photocopied submissions OK. Computer printout submissions acceptable. SASE. Reports in 2 months. Sample copy for $2.50, 9x12 SAE and $2 postage; free writer's guidelines.

Nonfiction: How-to (corporate defense law); interview/profile; personal experience; and technical. Buys 12 mss/year. Send complete ms. Length: 1,500-3,000 words. Pays $20-35.

Photos: Send photos with ms. Pays $5-10 for 3x5 b&w prints. Captions required. Buys all rights.

Columns/Departments: Buys 4 mss/year. Send complete ms. Length: 500-750 words. Pays $15-20.

Fiction: Historical and mystery. Buys 4 mss/year. Send complete ms. Length: 1,500-3,000 words. Pays $20-35.

Fillers: Jokes and short humor. Length: 25-100 words. Pays $2-5.

Leather Goods

LUGGAGE & TRAVELWARE, Business Journals, 22 S. Smith St., Norwalk CT 06855. (203)853-6015. Editor: Roger Zimmer. Monthly magazine covering luggage, leather goods and travel accessories for specialty and department store retailers and mass merchandisers. Circ. 9,000. Pays on publication. Byline given. Not copyrighted. Simultaneous queries and simultaneous and photocopied submissions OK. SASE. Reports in 2 weeks. Free sample copy.

Nonfiction: "We're looking for timely features and business-oriented articles on merchandising display and retailing." No material that is not tied in fairly closely to the industry. Length: 6-8 typewritten pages. Pays $200-300.

SHOE SERVICE, SSIA Service Corp., 154 W. Hubbard St., Chicago IL 60610. (312)670-3732. Editor: Lori Allen. 50% freelance written. Monthly magazine for business people who own and operate small shoe repair shops. Circ. 6,500. Pays on publication. Publishes ms an average of 3 months after acceptance. Byline given. Buys exclusive industry rights. Submit seasonal/holiday material 3 months in advance. Simultaneous queries, and photocopied and previously published submissions OK. Computer printout submissions acceptable; no dot-matrix. SASE. Reports in 6 weeks. Sample copy $1.

Nonfiction: How-to (run a profitable shop); interview/profile (of an outstanding or unusual person on shoe repair); and business articles (particulary about small business practices in a service/retail shop). Buys 12-24 mss/year. Query with clips of published work or send complete ms. Length: 500-2,000 words. Pays 5¢/word.

Photos: "Quality photos will help sell an article." State availability of photos. Pays $10-30 for 8x10 b&w prints. Uses some color photos, but mostly uses b&w glossies. Captions, model release and identification of subjects required.

Tips: "Visit some shoe repair shops to get an idea of the kind of person who reads *Shoe Service*. Profiles are the easiest to sell to us if you can find a repairer we think is unusual."

Library Science

AMERICAN LIBRARIES, 50 E. Huron St., Chicago IL 60611. (312)944-6780. Editor: Arthur Plotnik. 5% freelance written. For librarians. "A highly literate audience. They are for the most part practicing professionals with a down-to-earth interest in people and current trends." Published 11 times a year. Circ. 41,500. Buys first North American serial rights. Publishes ms an average of 4 months after acceptance. Pays negotiable kill fee. Byline given. Will consider photocopied submissions if not being considered elsewhere at time of submission. Computer printout submissions acceptable; no dot-matrix. Submit seasonal material 6 months in advance. Reports in 10 weeks. SASE.

Nonfiction: "Material reflecting the special and current interests of the library profession. Nonlibrarians should browse recent journals in the field, available on request in medium-sized and large libraries everywhere. Topic and/or approach must be fresh, vital, or highly entertaining. Library memoirs and stereotyped stories about old maids, overdue books, fines, etc., are unacceptable. Our first concern is with the American Library Association's activities, and how they relate to the 39,000 reader/members. Tough for an outsider to

write on this topic, but not to supplement it with short, offbeat or profoundly significant library stories and features." No fillers. Recent article example: "Online Encyclopedias: Are They Ready for Libraries?" (March 1983).
Photos: "Will look at all good b&w, well-lit photos of library situations, and at color transparencies for possible cover use." Buys 10-15 mss/year. Pays $25-200 for briefs and articles. Pays $25-75 for b&w photos.
Tips: "You can break in with a sparkling, 300-word report on a true, offbeat library event, use of new technology, or with an exciting photo and caption. Though stories on public libraries are always of interest, we especially need arresting material on academic and school libraries."

EMERGENCY LIBRARIAN, Dyad Services, Box 46258, Stn. G, Vancouver, British Columbia V6R 4G6 Canada. Co-Editors: Carol Ann Haycock and Ken Haycock. Bimonthly magazine. Circ. 3,500. Pays on publication. Photocopied submissions OK. No multiple submissions. SAE and IRCs. Reports in 4-6 weeks. Free writer's guidelines.
Nonfiction: Emphasis is on improvement of library service for children and young adults in school and public libraries. Also annotated bibliographies. Buys 3 mss/issue. Query. Length: 1,000-3,500 words. Pays $50.
Columns/Departments: Five regular columnists. Also Book Reviews (of professional materials in education, librarianship). Query. Length: 100-300 words. Payment consists of book reviewed.

LIBRARY JOURNAL, 205 E. 42nd St., New York NY 10017. Editor-in-Chief: John N. Berry III. For librarians (academic, public, special). 115-page magazine published every 2 weeks. Circ. 30,000. Buys all rights. Buys 50-100 mss/year (mostly from professionals in the field). Pays on publication. Submit complete ms. SASE.
Nonfiction: *"Library Journal* is a professional magazine for librarians. Freelancers are most often rejected because they submit one of the following types of article: 'A wonderful, warm, concerned, loving librarian who started me on the road to good reading and success'; 'How I became rich, famous, and successful by using my public library'; 'Libraries are the most wonderful and important institutions in our society, because they have all of the knowledge of mankind—praise them.' We need material of greater sophistication, dealing with issues related to the transfer of information, access to it, or related phenomena. (Current hot ones are copyright, censorship, the decline in funding for public institutions, the local politics of libraries, trusteeship, etc.)" Professional articles on criticism, censorship, professional concerns, library activities, historical articles, information technology, automation and management, and spot news. Outlook should be from librarian's point of view. Recent article example: "The Secret Garden Censorship: Ourselves" (Sept. 1, 1983). Buys 50-65 unsolicited mss/year. Length: 1,500-2,000 words. Pays $50-350.
Photos: Payment for b&w glossy photos purchased without accompanying mss is $30. Must be at least 5x7. Captions required.

MEDIA: LIBRARY SERVICES JOURNAL, 127 9th Ave. N., Nashville TN 37234. (615)251-2752. Editor: Floyd B. Simpson. For adult leaders in church organizations and people interested in library work (especially church library work). Quarterly magazine; 50 pages. Circ. 17,500. Pays on publication. Buys all rights. Byline given. Phone queries OK. Submit seasonal/holiday material 14 months in advance. Previously published submissions OK. SASE. Reports in 1 month. Free sample copy and writer's guidelines.
Nonfiction: "Primarily interested in articles that relate to the development of church libraries in providing media and services to support the total program of a church and in meeting individual needs. We publish personal experience accounts of services provided, promotional ideas, exciting things that have happened as a result of implementing an idea or service; human interest stories that are library-related; and media education (teaching and learning with a media mix). Articles should be practical for church library staffs and for teachers and other leaders of the church." Buys 15-20 mss/issue. Query. Pays 4¢/word.

‡**SCHOOL LIBRARY JOURNAL**, 1180 Avenue of the Americas, New York NY 10036. Editor: Lillian N. Gerhardt. For librarians in schools and public libraries. Magazine published 10 times/year; 88 pages. Circ. 43,000. Buys all rights. Pays on publication. Reports in 6 months. SASE.
Nonfiction: Articles on library services, local censorship problems, and how-to articles on programs that use books or films. Informational, personal experience, interview, expose, and successful business operations. "Interested in history articles on the establishment/development of children's and young adult services in schools and public libraries." Buys 24 mss/year. Length: 2,500-3,000 words. Pays $100.

WILSON LIBRARY BULLETIN, 950 University Ave., Bronx NY 10452. (212)588-8400. Editor: Milo Nelson. For professional librarians and those interested in the book and library worlds. Monthly (September-June). Circ. 30,000. Buys North American serial rights only. Pays on publication. Sample copies may be seen on request in most libraries. "Manuscript must be original copy, double-spaced; additional photocopy or carbon is appreciated." Computer printout submissions acceptable; prefers letter-quality to dot-matrix. Deadlines are a minimum 2 months before publication. Reports in 2-3 months. SASE.
Nonfiction: Uses articles "of interest to librarians throughout the nation and around the world. Style must be

lively, readable and sophisticated, with appeal to modern professionals; facts must be thoroughly researched. Subjects range from the political to the comic in the world of media and libraries, with an emphasis on the human as well as the technical aspects of any story. No condescension: no library stereotypes." Buys 30 mss/year. Send complete ms. Length: 2,500-6,000 words. Pays about $100-250, "depending on the substance of article and its importance to readers."

Tips: "The best way you can break in is with a first-rate b&w photo and caption information on a library, library service, or librarian that departs completely from all stereotypes and the commonplace. Note: Libraries have changed! You'd better first discover what is now commonplace."

Lumber and Woodworking

B.C. LUMBERMAN MAGAZINE, Box 34080, Station D, Vancouver British Columbia V6J 4M8 Canada. (403)731-1171. Editorial Director: Brian Martin. 60% freelance written. For the logging and saw milling industries of Western Canada and the Pacific Northwest of the United States. Monthly magazine; 75 pages. Circ. 8,500. Pays on acceptance. Buys first Canadian rights. Query first. Submit seasonal/holiday material 2 months in advance. Reports in 2 weeks. Publishes ms an average of 2 months after acceptance.
Nonfiction: How-to (technical articles on any aspect of the forest industry); general interest (anything of interest to persons in forest industries in western Canada or US Pacific Northwest); interview (occasionally related to leading forestry personnel); and technical (forestry). No fiction or history. Buys 8 mss/issue. Query with clips of published work. Average length: 1,500 words. Pays 15¢/word (Canadian).
Photos: State availability of photos with query. Pays $5-25 for b&w negatives and $50-80 for 8x10 glossy color prints. Captions required. Buys first Canadian rights.

NORTHERN LOGGER AND TIMBER PROCESSOR, Northeastern Loggers' Association, Box 69, Old Forge NY 13420. (315)369-3078. Editor: Eric A. Johnson. 60% freelance written. Monthly magazine of the forest industry in the northern US (Maine to Minnesota and south to Virginia and Missouri). We are not a purely technical journal, but are more information oriented." Circ. 11,500. Pays on publication. Byline given. Buys all rights. Submit seasonal/holiday material 3 months in advance. Photocopied and previously published submissions OK. "Any computer printout submission that can be easily read is acceptable." SASE. Reports in 2 weeks. Publishes ms an average of 3 months after acceptance. Free sample copy.
Nonfiction: Expose, general interest, historical/nostalgic, how-to, interview/profile, new product and opinion. "We only buy feature articles, and those should contain some technical or historical material relating to the forest products industry." Buys 12-15 mss/year. Query. Length: 500-2,500 words. Pays $25-125.
Photos: Send photos with ms. Pays $20-35 for 35mm color transparencies; $5-15 for 5x7 b&w prints. Captions and identification of subjects required.
Tips: "We accept most any subject dealing with this part of the country's forest industry, from historical to logging, firewood, and timber processing."

● **ROSEBURG WOODSMAN,** Roseburg Lumber Co., c/o Hugh Dwight Advertising, Suite 101, 4905 SW Griffith Dr., Beaverton OR 97005. Editor: Shirley P. Rogers. 99% (but most rewritten) freelance written. Monthly magazine for wholesale and retail lumber dealers and other buyers of forest products, such as furniture manufacturers. Emphasis on wood products, including company products. Publishes a special Christmas issue. Circ. 8,000. Buys first (or one-time) rights. No byline given. Buys approximately 15-20 mss/year. Pays on publication. Publishes ms an average of 9 months after acceptance. Submit seasonal material 6 months in advance. Computer printout submissions acceptable; prefers letter-quality to dot-matrix. Reports in 1 week. Free sample copy and writer's guidelines.
Nonfiction: Features on the "residential, commercial and industrial applications of wood products, such as lumber plywood, prefinished wall paneling, and particleboard, particularly Roseburg Lumber Co. products. We look for unique or unusual uses of wood and stories on hobbyists and craftsmen. No 'clever,' 'wise' or witty contributions unless they tell a fascinating story and are well-illustrated. No fillers, isolated photos or inadequately illustrated articles." Query or submit complete ms. Length: 250-500 words. Pays $50-$100.
Photos: "Photos are essential. Good pictures will sell us on a story." Rarely uses b&w photos. Will accept prints, but prefers 120 color transparencies or 35mm slides. Pays $25-$50/color transparency or color-corrected print; more for cover photo; less for b&w glossy print; purchased only with ms.
Tips: "I sometimes hire a freelancer 'on assignment' at a higher rate. Send letter specifying experience, publications, types of stories and geographic area covered. We have an absolute need for good, striking, interesting photos."

Machinery and Metal Trade

ASSEMBLY ENGINEERING, Hitchcock Publishing Co., Wheaton IL 60188. Editor: Wally Maczka. 5% freelance written. For design and manufacturing engineers and production personnel concerned with assembly problems in manufacturing plants. Monthly. Buys first rights only. Pays on publication. "Query on leads or ideas. We report on manuscript decision as soon as review is completed and provide edited proofs for checking by author, prior to publication." SASE. Sample copy will be sent on request.

Nonfiction: Wants features on design engineering and production practices for the assembly of manufactured products. Material should be submitted on "exclusive rights" basis. Subject areas include selection, specification, and application of fasteners, mounting hardware, electrical connectors, wiring, hydraulic and pneumatic fittings, seals and gaskets, adhesives, joining methods (soldering, welding, brazing, etc.) and assembly equipment; specification of fits and tolerances; joint design; design and shop assembly standards; time and motion study (assembly line); quality control in assembly; layout and balancing of assembly lines; assembly tool and jig design; programming assembly line operations; working conditions, incentives, labor costs, and union relations as they relate to assembly line operators; hiring and training of assembly line personnel; and supervisory practices for the assembly line. Also looking for news items on assembly-related subjects, and for unique or unusual "ideas" on assembly components, equipment, processes, practices and methods. "We want only technical articles, not PR releases." Requires good quality photos or sketches, usually close-ups of specific details. Pays $35 minimum/published page.

AUTOMATIC MACHINING, 228 N. Winton Rd., Rochester NY 14610. (716)654-8964. Editor: Donald E. Wood. For metalworking technical management. Buys all rights. Byline given. Query. Computer printout submissions acceptable. SASE.

Nonfiction: "This is not a market for the average freelancer. A personal knowledge of the trade is essential. Articles deal in depth with specific job operations on automatic screw machines, chucking machines, high production metal turning lathes and cold heading machines. Part prints, tooling layouts always required, plus written agreement of source to publish the material. Without personal background in operation of this type of equipment, freelancers are wasting time. No material researched from library sources." Length: "no limit." Pays $20/printed page.

Tips: "In the year ahead there will be more emphasis on plant and people news so less space will be available for conventional articles."

CANADIAN MACHINERY AND METALWORKING, 777 Bay St., Toronto, Ontario M5W 1A7 Canada. (416)596-5714. Editor: Nick Hancock. 33% freelance written. Monthly. Buys first Canadian rights. Pays on acceptance. Query. Publishes ms an average of 6 weeks after acceptance. SAE and IRCs.

Nonfiction: Technical and semitechnical articles dealing with metalworking operations in Canada and in the US, if of particular interest to Canadian readers. Accuracy and service appeal to readers is a must. Pays minimum 18¢/word.

Photos: Purchased with mss and with captions only. Pays $10 minimum for b&w features.

FOUNDRY MANAGEMENT AND TECHNOLOGY, Penton Plaza, Cleveland OH 44114. (216)696-7000. Editor: J.C. Miske. 5% freelance written. Monthly. Byline given. Buys first rights only. Publishes ms an average of 1 month after acceptance. Computer printout submissions acceptable; no dot-matrix. SASE. Reports in 2 weeks.

Nonfiction: Uses articles describing operating practice in foundries written to interest companies producing metal castings. Buys 7-10 unsolicited mss/year. Length: 3,000 words maximum. Pays $50/printed page.

Photos: Uses illustrative photographs with article; uses "a great deal of 4-color photos."

INDUSTRIAL MACHINERY NEWS, Hearst Business Media Corp., IMN Division, 29516 Southfield Rd., Box 5002, Southfield MI 48086. (313)557-0100. Editorial: M.M. Ecksel. Emphasizes metalworking for buyers, specifiers, manufacturing executives, engineers, management, plant managers, production managers, master mechanics, designers and machinery dealers. Monthly tabloid; 200 pages. Circ. 80,000. Pays on publication. Buys first North American serial rights. Submit seasonal/holiday material 3 months in advance. Simultaneous, photocopied and previously published submissions OK. SASE. Reports in 3-6 weeks. Sample copy $4.

Nonfiction: Articles on "metal removal, metal forming, assembly, finishing, inspection, application of new and used machine tools, technology, measuring, gauging equipment, small cutting tools, tooling accessories, materials handling in metalworking plants, and safety programs. We give our publication a newspaper feel— fast reading with lots of action or human interest photos." Buys how-tos. Pays $25 minimum. Length: open.

Photos: Photos purchased with mss; captions required. Pays $5 minimum.
Fillers: Puzzles, jokes and short humor. Pays $5 minimum.
Tips: "We're looking for stories on older machine tools—how they're holding up and how they're being used. We're also interested in metalworking machinery and equipment application articles that illustrate techniques geared to improving efficiency and productivity in the metalworking plant."

MODERN MACHINE SHOP, 6600 Clough Pike, Cincinnati OH 45244. Editor: Ken Gettelman. Monthly. Byline given. Pays 1 month following acceptance. Query. Reports in 5 days. SASE.
Nonfiction: Uses articles dealing with all phases of metal manufacturing and machine shop work, with photos. No general articles. "Ours is an industrial publication, and contributing authors should have a working knowledge of the metalworking industry." Buys 10 unsolicited mss/year. Length: 800-3,000 words. Pays current market rate.
Tips: "The use of articles relating to computers in manufacturing is growing."

PRODUCTS FINISHING, 6600 Clough Pike, Cincinnati OH 45244. Editor: G. Thomas Robison. 1% freelance written. Monthly. Buys all rights. Byline given "except on press releases from agencies." Pays within 1 month after acceptance. Publishes ms an average of 8 months after acceptance. Computer printout submissions acceptable; prefers letter-quality to dot-matrix. SASE. Reports in 1 week.
Nonfiction: Uses "material devoted to the finishing of metal and plastic products. This includes the cleaning, plating, polishing and painting of metal and plastic products of all kinds. Articles can be technical and must be practical. Technical articles should be on processes and methods. Particular attention given to articles describing novel approaches used by product finishers to control air and water pollution, and finishing techniques that reduce costs." Pay negotiable (approximately 10¢/word).

‡**SERVICE BUSINESS, Published Quarterly for the Self-Employed Professional Cleaner**, Service Business Magazine, Inc., Suite 345, 1916 Pike Place, Seattle WA 98101. (206)622-4241. Editor: Martha M. Ireland. 80% freelance written. Quarterly magazine covering technical and management information relating to cleaning and self-employment. "We cater to those who are self-employed in any facet of the cleaning and maintenance industry who seek to be top professionals in their field. Our readership is small but select. We seek concise, factual articles, realistic but definitely upbeat." Circ. 3,500. Pays between acceptance and publication. Publishes ms an average of 4 months after acceptance. Byline given. Buys first rights, second serial (reprint) rights, and makes work-for-hire assignments. Submit seasonal/holiday material 4 months in advance. Simultaneous queries and previously published work (rarely) OK. Computer printout submissions acceptable. SASE. Reports in 3 months. Sample copy for $3, 9x7½ SAE and 3 first class stamps; writer's guidelines for business-size SAE and 1 first class stamp.
Nonfiction: Expose (safety/health business practices); how-o (cleaning, maintenance, small business management); humor (clean jokes, cartoons); interview/profile; new product (must be unusual to rate full article—mostly obtained from manufacturers); opinion; personal experience; and technical. Special issues include "What's New?" (Feb. 10). No "wordy tomes written off the top of the head, obviously without research, and needing more editing time than was spent on writing." Buys 40 mss/year. Query with or without published clips. Length: 500-3,000 words. Pays $5-80. ("Pay depends on amount of work, research and polishing put into article much more than on length.")
Photos: State availability of photos or send photos with ms. Pays $5-25 for "smallish" b&w prints. Captions, model release and identification of subjects required. Buys one-time rights and reprint rights. "Magazine size is 8½x7—photos need to be proportionate."
Columns/Departments: "Ten regular columnists now sell 4 columns per year to us. We are interested in adding a Safety & Health column (related to cleaning and maintenance industry). We are also open to other suggestions—send query." Buys 36 columns/year; department information obtained at no cost. Query with or without published clips. Length: 500-1,500 words. Pays $15-45.
Fillers: Jokes, gags, anecdotes, short humor, newsbreaks and cartoons. Buys 40/year. Length: 3-200 words. Pays $1-20.
Tips: "A freelancer can best break in to our publication with fairly technical articles on how to do specific cleaning/maintenance jobs; interviews with top professionals covering this and how they manage their business; and personal experience. Our readers demand concise, accurate information. Don't ramble. Write only about what you know and/or have researched. Editors don't have time to rewrite your rough draft. Organize and polish before submitting."

33 METAL PRODUCING, McGraw-Hill Bldg., 36th Floor, 1221 Avenue of the Americas, New York NY 10020. (212)512-2000. Editor: John J. Dwyer Jr. For "operating managers (from turn foreman on up), engineers, metallurgical and chemical specialists, and corporate officials in the steelmaking industry. Work areas for these readers range from blast furnace and coke ovens into and through the steel works and rolling mills. *33*'s readers also work in nonferrous industries and foundries." Monthly. Buys all rights. Pays on publication. Query. Reports in 3 weeks. SASE. Free sample copy.

Nonfiction: Case histories of primary metals producing equipment in use, such as smelting, blast furnace, steelmaking and rolling. "Broadly speaking, *33 Metal Producing* concentrates its editorial efforts in the areas of technique (what's being done and how it's being done), technology (new developments), and equipment (what's being used). Your article should include a detailed explanation (who, what, why, where and how) and the significance (what it means to operating manager, engineer, or industry) of the techniques, technology or equipment being written about. In addition, your readers will want to know of the problems you experienced during the planning, developing, implementing and operating phases. And, it would be especially beneficial to tell of the steps you took to solve the problems or roadblocks encountered. You should also include all cost data relating to implementation, operation, maintenance, etc., wherever possible. Benefits (cost savings, improved manpower utilization, reduced cycle time, increased quality, etc.) should be cited to gauge the effectiveness of the subject being discussed. The highlight of any article is its illustrative material. This can take the form of photographs, drawings, tables, charts, graphs, etc. Your type of illustration should support and reinforce the text material. It should not just be an added, unrelated item. Each element of illustrative material should be identified and contain a short description of exactly what is being presented. We reject material that lacks in-depth knowledge of the technology on operations involved in metal producing." Pays $50/published page.
Photos: Minimum 5x7 b&w glossies purchased with mss.

Maintenance and Safety

EQUIPMENT MANAGEMENT, 7300 N. Cicero Ave., Lincolnwood IL 60646. (312)588-7300. Editor: Greg Sitek. 10% freelance written. Magazine; 76-110 pages. Monthly. Circ. 55,000. Rights purchased vary with author and material. Usually buys all rights. Buys 12 mss/year. Pays on publication. No photocopied or simultaneous submissions. Computer printout submissions acceptable; prefers letter-quality to dot-matrix. Reports in 1 month. Query with outline. SASE. Free sample copy.
Nonfiction: "Our focus is on the effective management of equipment through proper selection, careful specification, correct application and efficient maintenance. We use job stories, technical articles, safety features, basics and shop notes. No product stories or 'puff' pieces." Length: 2,000-5,000 words. Pays $25/printed page minimum, without photos.
Photos: Uses 35mm and 2¼x2¼ or larger color transparencies with mss. Pays $50/printed page when photos are furnished by author.
Tips: "Know the equipment, how to manage it and how to maintain/service/repair it."

‡**SANITARY MAINTENANCE**, Trade Press Publishing Co., 2100 W. Florist Ave., Milwaukee WI 53209. (414)228-7701. Managing Editor: Don Mulligan. Assistant Editor: Susan M. Netz. A monthly magazine for the sanitary supply industry covering "trends in the sanitary supply industry; offering information concerning the operations of janitor supply distributors and building service contractors; and helping distributors in the development of sales personnel." Circ. 13,756. Pays on publication. Byline given. Buys first North American serial rights. Photocopied submissions OK. Computer printout submissions acceptable. SASE. Free sample copy and writer's guidelines.
Nonfiction: How-to (improve sales, profitability as it applies to distributors, contractors); and technical. No product application stories. Buys 8-12 mss/year. Query with clips of published work. Length: 1,500-3,000 words. Pays $75-200.
Photos: State availability of photos with query letter or ms. Reviews 5x7 prints. Payment for photos included in payment for ms. Identification of subjects required.
Tips: Articles on sales and financial information for small businesses are open to freelancers.

Management and Supervision

This category includes trade journals for middle management business and industrial managers, including supervisors and office managers. Journals for business executives and owners are classified under Business Management. Those for industrial plant managers are listed in Industrial Operation and Management.

CONSTRUCTION SUPERVISION & SAFETY LETTER, CL Bureau of Business Practice, 24 Rope Ferry Rd., Waterford CT 06386. (203)442-4365. Editor: DeLoris Lidestri. Emphasizes all aspects of construction supervision. Semimonthly newsletter; 4 pages. Buys all rights. Phone queries OK. Submit seasonal material at least 4 months in advance. SASE. Reports in 4-6 weeks. Free sample copy and writer's guidelines.

Nonfiction: Publishes solid interviews with construction managers or supervisors on how to improve a single aspect of the supervisor's job. Buys 100 unsolicited mss/year. Length: 360-720 words. Pays 8-12¢/word.

Photos: B&w head and shoulders "mug shots" of person interviewed purchased with mss. Send prints. Pays $10.

EMPLOYEE RELATIONS AND HUMAN RESOURCES BULLETIN, Bureau of Business Practice, 24 Rope Ferry Rd., Waterford CT 06386. Supervisory Editor: Barbara Kelsey. For personnel, human resources and employee relations managers on the executive level. Semimonthly newsletter; 8 pages. Circ. 3,000. Pays on acceptance. Buys all rights. No byline. Phone queries OK. Submit seasonal/holiday material 6 months in advance. Photocopied submissions OK. Computer printout submissions acceptable; prefers letter-quality to dot-matrix. SASE. Reports in 1 month. Free sample copy and writer's guidelines.

Nonfiction: Interviews about all types of business and industry such as banks, insurance companies, public utilities, airlines, consulting firms, etc. Interviewee should be a high level company officer—general manager, president, industrial relations manager, etc. Writer must get signed release from person interviewed showing that article has been read and approved by him/her, before submission. Some subjects for interviews might be productivity improvement, communications, compensation, government regulations, safety and health, grievance handling, human relations techniques and problems, etc. No general opinions and/or philosophy of good employee relations or general good motivation/morale material. Buys 3 mss/issue. Query. Length: 700-2,000 words. Pays 10¢/word after editing.

THE FOREMAN'S LETTER, Bureau of Business Practice, 24 Rope Ferry Rd., Waterford CT 06386. (203)442-4365. Editor: Carl Thunberg. 50% freelance written. For industrial supervisors. Semimonthly. Buys all rights. Pays on acceptance. Interested in regular stringers (freelance). Computer printout submissions acceptable. Publishes ms an average of 2 months after acceptance. SASE. Comprehensive guidelines available.

Nonfiction: Interested primarily in direct in-depth interviews with industrial supervisors in the US and Canada. Subject matter would be the interviewee's techniques for becoming a more effective manager, bolstered by illustrations out of the interviewee's own job experiences. Slant would be toward informing readers how to solve a particular supervisory problem. "Our aim is to offer information which readers may apply to their own professional self improvement. No copy that focuses on the theme that 'happy workers are productive workers.' " Buys 15-20 unsolicited mss/year. Length: 600-1,200 words. Pays 8¢-14½¢/word "after editing for all rights."

Photos: Buys photos submitted with mss. "Captions needed for identification only." Head and shoulders, any size b&w glossy from 2x3 up. Pays $10.

Tips: "Study our editorial guidelines carefully. Emulate the style of sample issues. Write a how-to article focusing on one specific topic. A new freelancer should be willing to rewrite submissions if neccessary. Editor will offer suggestions. An effort will be made to cultivate freelancers who comply the *closest* to editorial guidelines."

HIGH-TECH MANAGER'S BULLETIN, TEM, Bureau of Business Practice, Inc. 24 Rope Ferry Rd., Waterford CT 06386. (203)442-4365. Editor: Sally Wagner. 100% freelance written. Bimonthly newsletter for technical supervisors wishing to improve their managerial skills in high technology fields. Pays on acceptance. No byline given. Buys all rights. Computer printout submissions acceptable. Reports in 2 weeks on queries, 6 weeks on mss. Free sample copy and writer's guidelines.

Nonfiction: How-to (solve a supervisory problem on the job); and interview (of top-notch supervisors and managers). "Sample topics could include: how-to increase productivity, cut costs, achieve better teamwork, and help employees adapt to change." No articles about company programs. Buys 72 mss/year. Query. "A resume and sample of work are helpful." Length: 750-1,000 words. Pays 8-14¢/word.

Tips: "We need interview-based articles that emphasize direct quotes. Each article should include a reference to the interviewee's company (location, size, products, function of the interviewee's department and number of employees under his control). Define a problem and show how the supervisor solved it. Write in a light, conversational style, talking directly to technical supervisors who can benefit from putting the interviewee's tips into practice."

LE BUREAU, Suite 1000, 1001 de Maisonneuve W., Montreal, Quebec H3A 3E1 Canada. (514)845-5141. Editor: Paul Saint-Pierre, C.Adm. For "office executives." Published 6 times/year. Circ. 10,600. Buys all rights. Byline given. Buys about 10 mss/year. Pays on acceptance. Query or submit complete ms. Submit seasonal material "between 1 and 2 months" in advance. SAE and IRCs.

Nonfiction: "Our publication is published in the French language. We use case histories on new office systems, applications of new equipment and articles on personnel problems. Material should be exclusive and above average quality." Buys personal experience articles, interviews, think pieces, coverage of successful

business operations and new product articles. Length: 500-1,000 words. Pays $100-200.
Photos: B&w glossies purchased with mss. Pays $25 each.

MANAGE, 2210 Arbor Blvd., Dayton OH 45439. (513)294-0421. Editor-in-Chief: Douglas E. Shaw. 60%
freelance written. For first-line and middle management and scientific/technical managers. Quarterly magazine; 36 pages. Circ. 72,000. Pays on acceptance. Buys North American magazine rights with reprint privileges; book rights remain with the author. Phone queries OK. SASE. Reports in 1 month. Free sample copy and
writer's guidelines.
Nonfiction: "All material published by *Manage* is in some way management oriented. Most articles concern
one or more of the following categories: communications, cost reduction, economics, executive abilities,
health and safety, human relations, job status, labor relations, leadership, motivation and productivity and professionalism. Articles should be specific and tell the manager how to apply the information to his job immediately. Be sure to include pertinent examples, and back up statements with facts and, where possible, charts and
illustrations. *Manage* does not want essays or academic reports, but interesting, well-written and practical articles for and about management." Buys 6 mss/issue. Submit complete ms. Length, 600-2,000 words. Pays 5¢/
word.
Tips: "Keep current on management subjects; submit timely work."

OFFICE ADMINISTRATION AND AUTOMATION, Geyer-McAllister Publications, Inc., 51 Madison
Ave., New York NY 10010. (212)689-4411. Editor: William A. Olcott. Executive Editor: Walter J. Presnick.
Monthly business publication covering office systems, equipment, personnel, and management for adminis-
trators and systems specialists in charge of office operations. Estab. 1983. Circ. 65,000. Pays on publication.
Byline given. Offers negotiable kill fee. Buys all rights. Photocopied submissions OK. SASE. Reports in 1
month. Sample copy $3.50; free writer's guidelines.
Nonfiction: Book excerpts, how-to, interview/profile, new product, opinion, photo feature and technical. No
"college thesis" articles. Buys 50 mss/year. Query. Length: 500-2,500 words. Pays $50-500.
Photos: Send photos with ms. Pays $50 maximum for 8x10 b&w prints; $75 maximum for 4x5 color transparencies. Captions, model release and identification of subjects required. Buys one-time rights.
Tips: "Analyze and interpret clearly, especially if subject is technical. Assume readers have years of experience in the field."

PERSONNEL ADVISORY BULLETIN, Bureau of Business Practice, 24 Rope Ferry Rd., Waterford CT
06386. (203)442-4365. Editor: John Fuller. 75% freelance written. Emphasizes all aspects of personnel management for personnel managers in all types and sizes of companies, both white collar and industrial. Semimonthly newsletter; 4 pages. Pays on acceptance. Buys all rights. Phone queries OK. Submit seasonal/holiday
material 4 months in advance. Computer printout submissions acceptable; no dot-matrix. SASE. Reports in 2
weeks. Free sample copy and writer's guidelines.
Nonfiction: Interviews with personnel managers or human resource executives on topics of current interest in
the personnel field. No articles on hiring and interviewing, discipline, or absenteeism/tardiness control. Buys
30 mss/year. Query with brief, specific outline. Length: 800-1,000 words. Pays 10¢/word after editing.
Tips: "It's very easy to break in. Just query by phone or letter (preferably phone) and we'll discuss the topic.
We especially need writers in the Midwest and West. Send for guidelines and sample first, though, so we can
have a coherent conversation."

‡**PERSONNEL JOURNAL**, A.C. Croft, Inc., Box 2440, Costa Mesa CA 92628. (714)646-5007. Editor:
Margaret Magnus. Monthly magazine covering human resource management and employee relations. Circ.
20,000. Pays on acceptance. Byline given. Offers $250 kill fee. Buys all rights. No seasonal material. SASE.
Simultaneous queries OK. Reports in 1 month on queries; 3 months on mss. Free sample copy and writer's
guidelines.
Nonfiction: Book excerpts, how-to, interview/profile, new product, opinion and personal experience. Buys 3
mss/year. Query with published clips. Length: 1,000-3,000 words. Pays negotiable rates.
Photos: Marcia Forsberg, photo editor. Reviews b&w contact sheets and prints. Model release and identification of subjects required. Buys one-time rights.

PRODUCTIVITY IMPROVEMENT BULLETIN, PIB, Bureau of Business Practice, 24 Rope Ferry Rd.,
Waterford CT 06386. (203)442-4365. Editor: Paula Brisco. Semimonthly newsletter covering productivity
improvement techniques of interest to middle and top management. Pays on acceptance. No byline given.

**The double dagger (‡) before a listing indicates that the listing is
new in this edition. New markets are often the most receptive to
freelance contributions.**

Buys all rights. Computer printout submissions acceptable. Reports in 2 weeks on queries; 1 month on mss. Free sample copy and writer's guidelines.

Nonfiction: Interviews with managers from business or industry discussing productivity innovations. No articles on general management theory. Buys 50 mss/year. Query. Length: 1,000-2,000 words. Pays 8-14¢/word "after editing."

Columns/Departments: "Personal Productivity column uses interview-based copy explaining specific measures our readers can take to increase their effectiveness." Buys 12 mss/year. Query. Length: 800-1,200 words. Pays 8-14¢/word.

Tips: "Lead story articles *must* cover a 'problem-process-solution-results' format as described in the writer's guidelines. Be willing to rewrite, if necessary. Topics should be well focused. (Check with us before doing the write-up. We like to talk to freelancers.) Writing should be conversational; use the 'you' approach. Use subheads and questions to guide the reader through your piece. Articles on activities of a specific company are subject to its approval."

SALES MANAGER'S BULLETIN, The Bureau of Business Practice, 24 Rope Ferry Rd., Waterford CT 06386. Editor: Paulette S. Withers. 25% freelance written. For sales managers and salespeople interested in getting into sales management. Newsletter published twice a month; 8 pages. Pays on acceptance. Publishes ms an average of 6 months after acceptance. Phone queries from regulars OK. Submit seasonal/holiday material 6 months in advance. Original submissions only. Computer printout submissions acceptable. SASE. Reports in 2 weeks. Free sample copy and writer's guidelines only when accompanied by SASE.

Nonfiction: How-to (motivate salespeople, cut costs, create territories, etc.); interview (with working sales managers who use innovative techniques); and technical (marketing stories based on interviews with experts). No articles on territory management, saving fuel in the field, or public speaking skills. Break into this publication by reading the guidelines and sample issue. Follow the directions closely and chances for acceptance go up dramatically. One easy way to start is with an interview article ("Here's what sales executives have to say about . . ."). Recent article example: "Training the 'Conceptional' Sales Force" (February 1984). Buys 5 unsolicited mss/year. Query is vital to acceptance; "send a simple postcard explaining briefly the subject matter, the interviewees (if any), slant, length, and date of expected completion, accompanied by a SASE." Length: 800-1,500. Pays 10-15¢/word.

Tips: "Freelancers should always request samples and writer's guidelines, accompanied by SASE. Requests without SASE are discarded immediately. Examine the sample, and don't try to improve on our style. Write as we write. Don't 'jump around' from point to point and don't submit articles that are too chatty and with not enough real information. The more time a writer can save the editors, the greater his or her chance of a sale and repeated sales, when queries may not be necessary any longer."

SECURITY MANAGEMENT, American Society for Industrial Security, Suite 1200, 1655 N. Fort Myers Dr., Arlington VA 22209. (703)522-5800. Editor: Shari Mendelson Gallery. Senior Editor: Mary Alice Crawford. Managing Editor: Pamela Blumgart. Monthly professional magazine of the security business (i.e., protecting assets from loss). Circ. 20,000. Pays on publication. Byline given. Buys all rights. Submit seasonal/holiday material 6 months in advance. Simultaneous queries and simultaneous, photocopied and previously published submissions to noncompetitive magazines OK. Computer printout submissions acceptable. SASE. Reports in 3 weeks on queries; 10 weeks on mss. Sample copy $3; writer's guidelines for business-size SAE and 1 first class stamp.

Nonfiction: Mary Alice Crawford, articles editor. Book excerpts, how-to, interview/profile, opinion, personal experience, photo feature and technical. Case studies, analytical pieces and new approaches to persistent security problems such as access control and computer security. No humor. "Send a coherent outline query." Buys 5-10 mss/year. Query with or without clips of published work. Length: 1,500-5,000 words. Pays 10¢/word; $250 maximum.

Photos: State availability of photos. Reviews b&w and color contact sheets and prints, and color transparencies.

Fillers: Cecily Roberts, fillers editor. Clippings, anecdotes and newsbreaks. Buys variable number/year. Length: 50-200 words. Pays $5-25.

Tips: "We need more substantive, technical articles, not cursory overviews."

SECURITY MANAGEMENT: PROTECTING PROPERTY, PEOPLE & ASSETS, Bureau of Business Practice, 24 Rope Ferry Rd., Waterford CT 06386. Editor: Alex Vaughn. Emphasizes security for industry. "All material should be slanted toward security directors, preferably industrial, but some retail and institutional as well." Semimonthly newsletter; 4 pages. Circ. 3,000. Pays on acceptance. Buys all rights. Phone queries OK. Photocopied submissions OK. SASE. Reports in 2 weeks. Free sample copy and writer's guidelines.

Nonfiction: Interview (with security professionals only). "Articles should be tight and specific. They should deal with new security techniques or new twists on old ones." Buys 2 mss/issue. Query. Length: 750-1,000 words. Pays 10¢/word.

SUPERVISION, 424 N. 3rd St., Burlington IA 52601. Publisher: Michael S. Darnall. Editorial Supervisor: Doris J. Ruschill. Editor: Barbara Boeding. 95% freelance written. For first-line foremen, supervisors and office managers. Monthly magazine; 24 pages. 8½x11 inches. Circ. 8,950. Pays on publication. Buys all rights. Reports in 3 weeks. Free sample copy and writer's guidelines; mention *Writer's Market* in request. SASE.
Nonfiction: How-to (cope with supervisory problems, discipline, absenteeism, safety, productivity, goal setting, etc.); and personal experience (unusual success story of foreman or supervisor). No sexist material written from only a male viewpoint. Buys 12 mss/issue. Query. Length: 1,500-1,800 words. Pays 4¢/word.
Tips: "Query to be brief, but long enough to give a clear picture of material and approach being used. We are particularly interested in writers with first-hand experience—current or former supervisors who are also good writers. Following AP stylebook would be helpful." Uses no photos or advertising.

TRAINING, The Magazine of Human Resources Development, 731 Hennepin Ave., Minneapolis MN 55403. (612)333-0471. Managing Editor: Jack Gordon. Monthly magazine for persons who train people in business, industry, government and health care. Circ. 46,000. Rights purchased vary with author and material. Usually buys all rights. Buys 10-20 mss/year; pays on acceptance. Will consider photocopied submissions. No simultaneous submissions. Computer printout submissions acceptable; prefers letter-quality to dot-matrix. Works three months in advance. Reports in 6 weeks. Query only. SASE. Sample copy and writers guidelines for 9x12 SAE and $1.25 postage.
Nonfiction: Articles on management and techniques of employee training. "Material should discuss a specific training problem or need; why the need existed, how it was met, alternatives considered, criteria for success, etc. Should furnish enough data for readers to make an independent judgment about the appropriateness of the solution and identify implications for their own situations. We want names and specific details on all techniques and programs used." Would like to see "articles relating general business concerns to specific training and development functions; interesting examples of successful training and management development programs; articles about why certain types of the above seem to fail; profiles of trainers who have moved into upper level executive positions; emerging trends in the training and development field." Informational, how-to. Recent article example: "Computer Literacy for Managers: Will Trainers Accept the Challenge?" (February 1983). No puff or "gee whiz" material. Buys 5 unsolicited mss/year. Length: 1,200-3,000 words. Training Today: Reports on research, opinions or events of significance to human resources development professionals; length; 300-700 words. No extra payment for photos. Prefers b&w or color transparencies, with captions. Pays negotiable rates.

UTILITY SUPERVISION AND SAFETY LETTER, US Bureau of Business Practice, 24 Rope Ferry Rd., Waterford CT 06386. (203)442-4365. Editor: DeLoris Lidestri. Emphasizes all aspects of utility supervision. Semimonthly newsletter; 4 pages. Pays on acceptance. Buys all rights. Phone queries OK. Submit seasonal material 4 months in advance. SASE. Reports in 4-6 weeks. Free sample copy and writer's guidelines.
Nonfiction: Publishes how-to (interview on a single aspect of supervision with utility manager/supervisor concentrating on how reader/supervisor can improve in that area). Buys 100 mss/year. Query. Length: 500-1,000 words. Pays 8-12¢/word.
Photos: Purchased with accompanying ms. Pays $10 for b&w prints of "head and shoulders 'mug shot' of person interviewed." Total purchase price for ms includes payment for photos.

WAREHOUSING SUPERVISOR'S BULLETIN, WSB, Bureau of Business Practice, Inc. 24 Rope Ferry Rd., Waterford CT 06386. (203)442-4365. Editor: Sally Wagner. Biweekly newsletter covering traffic, materials handling and distribution for warehouse supervisors "interested in becoming more effective on the job." Pays on acceptance. No byline given. Buys first rights only. Computer printout submissions acceptable. Reports in 2 weeks on queries; 6 weeks on mss. Free sample copy and writer's guidelines.
Nonfiction: How-to (increase efficiency, control or cut costs, cut absenteeism or tardiness, increase productivity, raise morale); interview (of warehouse supervisors who have solved problems on the job). No descriptions of company programs, noninterview articles, textbook-like descriptions or union references. Buys 50 mss/year. Query. "A resume and sample of work are helpful." Length: 800-1,200 words. Pays 8-14¢/word.
Tips: "Interview-based articles must emphasize direct quotes. They should also include a reference to the interviewee's company (location, size, products, function of the interviewee's department and number of employees under his control). Focus articles on one problem and get the interviewee to pinpoint the best way to solve it. Write in a light, conversational style, talking directly to warehouse supervisors who can benefit from putting the interviewee's tips into practice."

Marine Industries and Water Navigation

BOATING INDUSTRY, 850 3rd Ave., New York NY 10022. Editor/Publisher: Charles A. Jones. Editor: Olga Badillo. 15% freelance written. For "boating retailers and distributors." Monthly. Circ. 26,300. Buys all rights. Byline given. Buys 10-15 feature mss/year. "Interested in good column material, too." Pays on publication. Publishes ms an average of 3 months after acceptance. "Best practice is to check with editor first on story ideas for go-ahead." Submit seasonal material 3-4 months in advance. Reports in 2 months. SASE.

Nonfiction: Business-oriented pieces about marine management. Buys 70-80 mss/year. Query. Length: 1,500-4,000 words. No clippings. Pays 9-15¢/word.

Photos: B&w glossy photos purchased with mss.

CANADIAN SHIPPING AND MARINE ENGINEERING, Suite 204, 5200 Dixie Rd., Mississauga, Ontario L4W 1E4 Canada. Editor: Patrick Brophy. Monthly magazine covering ship building, repair and operation. Circ. 3,800. Pays on publication. Buys first Canadian rights. SAE and IRCs.

Nonfiction: "*Competent, authoritative*, technical or historical material dealing with maritime subjects of interest to Canadian readers." Query or send complete ms. Length: 1,000-2,000 words. Pays 10-12¢/word.

Photos: Uses 5x7 b&w prints and 35mm or larger color transparencies or prints with articles.

● **THE COMPASS**, Mobil Sales and Supply Corp., 150 E. 42nd St., New York NY 10017. Editor-in-Chief: R. Gordon MacKenzie. 90% freelance written. Emphasizes marine or maritime activities for the major international deep sea shipowners and ship operators who are Mobil's marine customers. 40 pages. Circ. 20,000. Pays on acceptance. Publishes ms an average of 18 months after acceptance. Buys one-time rights. Byline given. Simultaneous, photocopied and previously published submissions OK. SASE. Reports in 2 weeks. Free sample copy.

Nonfiction: Marine material only. General interest, historical, new product, personal experience and technical. No travelogues. Query or submit complete ms. Length: 2,000-4,000 words. Pays $175-250.

Photos: Purchased with accompanying ms. Submit 5x7 or larger b&w prints or 35mm color transparencies. Offers no additional payment for photos accepted with ms. Captions preferred. Buys one-time rights. Model release required.

SEAWAY REVIEW, The Business Magazine of the Great Lakes Seaway System, Harbor Island, Maple City Postal Station MI 49664. Production office: 8715 Parmater Rd., Elmira MI 49730. Publisher: Jacques LesStrang. Managing Editor: Michelle Cortright. 10% freelance written. For "the entire Great Lakes maritime community, executives of companies that ship via the Great Lakes, traffic managers, transportation executives, federal and state government officials and manufacturers of maritime equipment." Quarterly magazine. Circ. 16,000. Pays on publication. Buys first North American serial rights. Submit seasonal material 2 months in advance. Photocopied submissions OK. Computer printout submissions acceptable. SASE. Reports in 3 weeks. Sample copy $3.

Nonfiction: "Articles dealing with Great Lakes shipping, shipbuilding, marine technology, economics of 8 states in the Seaway region (Michigan, Minnesota, Illinois, Indiana, Ohio, New York, Pennsylvania and Wisconsin), and Canada (Ontario, Quebec), port operation, historical articles dealing with Great Lakes shipping, current events dealing with commercial shipping on lakes, etc." No subjects contrary to our editorial statement. Submit complete ms. Length: 1,000-4,000 words. Pay "varies with value of subject matter and knowledgeability of author, $50-300."

Photos: State availability of photos with query. Pays $10-50 for 8x10 glossy b&w prints; $10-100 for 8x10 glossy color prints or transparencies. Captions required. Buys one-time rights. Buys "hundreds" of freelance photos each year.

Fillers: Clippings and spot news relating to ports and the Great Lakes. Buys 3/issue. Length: 50-500 words. Pays $5-50.

THE WORK BOAT, H.L. Peace Publications, Box 2400, Covington LA 70434. (504)893-2930. Publisher/Editor: Harry L. Peace. Managing Editor: Rick Martin. Monthly. Buys all rights. Pays on acceptance. Query. Reports in 1 month. SASE. Sample copy $3; writer's guidelines for SASE.

Nonfiction: "Articles on waterways, river terminals, barge line operations, work boat construction and design, barges, offshore oil vessels and tugs. Best bet for freelancers: One-angle article showing in detail how a barge line, tug operator or dredging firm solves a problem of either mechanical or operational nature. This market is semitechnical and rather exacting. Such articles must be specific, containing firm name, location, officials of company, major equipment involved, by brand name, model, power, capacity and manufacturer; with color or b&w photos." Length: 1,000-2,000 words. Pays $150 minimum.

Photos: 5x5 or 5x7 b&w; 4x5 color prints only. No additional payment for photos accompanying ms. Captions and model release required. Buys one-time rights.

Medical

The writer with a manuscript criticizing a physician's office procedures or fees won't find a home for it in the following publications. Through these journals, private physicians and mental health professionals learn how other professionals help their patients—among other technical topics. Listed here are publications and journals for physicians and health professionals also reporting on new discoveries in medicine. Journals for nurses, laboratory technicians, and other medical workers are included with the Hospitals, Nursing, and Nursing Home journals. Publications for druggists and drug wholesalers and retailers are grouped with the Drugs and Health Care Products journals. Publications that report on medical trends for the consumer can be found in the Health and Science categories.

● **ADVANCES FOR MEDICINE**, Hewlett-Packard Medical Products Group, 3000 Minuteman Rd., Andover MA 01810-1085. (617)687-1501, ext. 2027. Editor: Ronna Borenstein. Magazine published 4 times/year for medical professionals—physicians, nurses, biotechnicians, hospital administrators covering Hewlett-Packard's wide range of products and services, with an international emphasis. Circ. 30,000. Pays on acceptance. Buys one-time rights or makes work-for-hire assignments. Simultaneous queries, and simultaneous, photocopied and previously published submissions OK. SASE. Reports in 5 weeks. Free sample copy.
Nonfiction: Book excerpts; expose; interview/profile; new product releases; personal experience (of medical professionals); and technical (application stories must feature Hewlett-Packard instrumentation). Buys 7 mss/year. Query with clips of published work or send complete ms. Length: 300-2,500 words. Pays $100 minimum.
Photos: Steve Cahill, photo editor. State availability of photos or send photos with ms. Reviews contact sheets. Captions, model release and identification of subjects required.
Tips: "Submit articles with a human tone on how a specific procedure/HP product has changed (made more efficient, accurate) medical care—stress *unique* applications. Start with a case study of a patient problem, introduce the potential solution, spice with quotations by physicians, and show how the problem is solved and an advancement has been realized—include technological information."

‡**AMERICAN FAMILY PHYSICIAN**, 1740 W. 92nd St., Kansas City MO 64114. (816)333-9700. Publisher: Walter H. Kemp. Monthly. Circ. 130,000. Buys all rights. Pays on publication. "Most articles are assigned and written by physicians." Query first "with a clear outline plus author's qualifications to write the article." Reports in 2 weeks. SASE.
Nonfiction: Interested only in clinical articles. Length: 2,500 words. Pays $100-250.

APA MONITOR, 1200 17th St. NW, Washington DC 20036. (202)955-7690. Editor: Jeffrey Mervis. Associate Editor: Kathleen Fisher. 5% freelance written. For psychologists and other social scientists and professionals interested in behaviorial sciences and mental health area. Monthly newspaper. Circ. 70,000. Pays on publication. Publishes ms an average of 3 months after acceptance. Buys first serial rights. Computer printout submissions acceptable. Free sample copy.
Nonfiction: News and feature articles about issues facing psychology both as a science and a mental health profession; political, social and economic developments in the behavioral sciences area. Interview, profile and historical pieces. No personal views, reminiscences or satire. Buys no mss without query. Length: 300-3,000 words.
Tips: "Our writers almost need to be longtime readers or science writers to strike the balance between some of the top PhDs in the country and graduate students at small colleges that we try to reach."

CANADIAN DOCTOR, 1450 Don Mills Rd., Don Mills, Ontario M3B 2X7 Canada. (416)445-6641. Editor-in-Chief: Kimberly Coffman. Assistant Editor: Ellen Gardner. 85% freelance written. Monthly magazine; 100 pages. Circ. 36,000. Pays on publication. Publishes ms an average of 3 months after acceptance. Buys all rights. Byline given. Computer printout submissions acceptable; prefers letter-quality to dot-matrix. Reports in 3 weeks. Free sample copy and writer's guidelines. SAE and IRCs are essential for return of material.
Nonfiction: How-to (run a physician's practice efficiently); interview (with Canadian doctors, perhaps those who have moved to US); socioethical concerns and social implications of some diseases; a humanistic approach (rather than clinical) to patients and their pathologies; personal opinion (from Canadian doctor about the profession); and profile (of Canadian doctor). No human interest or lifestyle pieces. Buys 20 unsolicited mss/

year. Query with outline of article, "preferably in point form so that editors can add/change to meet needs." Length: 1,000-2,500 words. Pays 20¢/word.

Photos: State availability of photos with query. Pays $15 for b&w glossy prints; $25 for color. Captions required. Buys one-time rights. Model release required.

Tips: "We are a Canadian magazine aimed at a Canadian audience, 36,000 + . We have different problems (a health insurance scheme for one, based on fee-for-service, and which varies from one province to another), but we can learn about medical business management from anywhere. In the year ahead there will be great emphasis on practice management and brass tacks of business procedures needed for an efficient and profitable medical practice."

‡**CME BULLETIN, The Journal of Continuing Medical Education for Primary Care Physicians**, American Medical Reports, Box 77552, San Francisco CA 94107. (415)541-0670. 60% freelance written. Quarterly magazine on continuing medical education "listing CME activities for primary care physicians as well as conference, travel and other articles of interest to our readers." Circ. 120,000. Pays on publication. Publishes ms an average of 2 months after acceptance. Byline given. Offers 50% kill fee. Buys all rights. Submit seasonal/holiday material 4 months in advance. Simultaneous queries, and photocopied submissions OK. SASE. Reports in 3 weeks. Sample copy for $2.50 and 6 first class stamps; writer's guidelines for business-size SAE and 1 first class stamp. "Writers are encouraged to call managing editor personally for writer's guidelines."

Nonfiction: Book excerpts (current medical texts); expose (CME activities); general interest (appealing to physicians); interview/profile (prominent medical leaders); personal experience (physician's experience); photo feature (travel- or conference-related); technical (relating to CME); and travel (articles by and about physicians, especially international and national CME conferences). Article topics include the medical conference industry, interactive video, medical data bases, teleconferencing and computer education. No "poorly researched points of view." Buys 24-30 mss/year. Query with published clips or send complete ms. Length: 2,000-4,500 words. Pays $300-1,000 + .

Photos: State availability of photos or send photos with query or ms. "We want travel and conference photos to accompany manuscripts." Pays $25 minimum for b&w negatives and 2¼ transparencies; $35 for color negatives; $45 for 2¼ color transparencies. Captions, model release and identification of subjects required. Buys all rights.

Columns/Departments: OP/ED, Book Reviews, Travel, Conferences, Interviews, Recreation for Physicians, and International Travel/Conferences. Buys 45 mss/year. Query with published clip or send complete ms. Length: 2,000 words minimum. Pays $300 minimum.

Tips: "A freelancer can best break in to our publication if he/she is an experienced travel/medical writer. You will be writing for an intelligent, upper income group of readers. Intelligent material, well-presented, is welcome. All sections of our publication except OP/ED are open to freelancers."

DIAGNOSTIC IMAGING, Miller Freeman, 500 Howard St., San Francisco CA 94105. Publisher: Thomas Kemp. Editor: Peter Ogle. 10% freelance written. Monthly news magazine covering radiology, nuclear medicine and ultrasound for physicians in diagnostic imaging professions. Circ. 24,000. Average issue includes 4-5 features. Pays on acceptance. Byline given. Buys all rights. No phone queries. "Written query should be well written, concise and contain a brief outline of proposed article and a description of the approach or perspective the author is taking." Submit seasonal material 1 month in advance. Simultaneous and photocopied submissions OK. SASE. Reports in 2 weeks. Publishes ms an average of 2 months after acceptance. Free sample copy.

Nonfiction: "We are interested in topical news features in the areas of radiology, nuclear medicine and ultrasound, especially news of state and federal legislation, new products, insurance, regulations, medical literature, professional meetings and symposia and continuing education." Buys 10-12 mss/year. Query with clips of previously published work. Length: 1,000-2,000 words. Pays 15¢/word minimum.

Photos: Reviews 5x7 b&w glossy prints and 35mm and larger color transparencies. Offers $20 for photos accepted with ms. Captions required. Buys one-time rights.

EMERGENCY, Box 159, Carlsbad CA 92008. Managing Editor: James Daigh. 60% freelance written. Emphasizes emergency medical services for anyone involved in emergency services, including ambulance personnel, paramedics, search and rescue personnel, emergency room personnel, law enforcement personnel and firefighters. Monthly magazine; 80 pages. Circ. 40,000. Pays on publication. Publishes ms an average of 3 months after acceptance. Buys all rights. Byline and biographical information given. Submit seasonal/holiday material 4 months in advance. SASE. Reports in 2 months. Free sample copy and writer's guidelines.

Nonfiction: How-to (better execute a certain emergency procedure, guidelines for emergency medical techniques). Buys 24 unsolicited mss/year. Query. Length: 800-3,000 words. Pays $50-175.

Photos: State availability of photos with query. Pays $15 minimum for 5x7 b&w glossy prints; $25-35 for

35mm color transparencies. Captions required. Buys all rights. Buys 2-5 cover color transparencies/year. Pays $100-150.

Columns/Departments: News Briefs (short items of interest to emergency personnel). Buys 30/year. Query. Length: 50-100 words. Pays $1/inch. Open to suggestions for new columns/departments.

Tips: "All articles are carefully reviewed; therefore, any well-written article, especially one including 35mm transparencies, has a good chance of being published."

GENETIC ENGINEERING NEWS, The Information Source of the Biotechnology Industry, Mary Ann Liebert, Inc., 157 E. 86th St., New York NY 10028. (212)289-2393. Editor: Peter Wesley Dorfman. 60% freelance written. Tabloid published 8 times/year featuring articles on industry and research in all areas of biotechnology such as recombinant DNA and hybridoma technology. Circ. 14,500. Pays on acceptance. Publishes ms an average of 6 weeks after acceptance. Byline given. Buys all rights. Computer printout submissions acceptable. SASE. Reports in 6 weeks on queries; 1 month on mss.

Nonfiction: Interview/profile (of corporate executives, academicians or researchers); new product; technical (any articles relating to biotechnology with emphasis on application); and financial (Wall Street analysis, etc.—of new companies). No company personnel changes or rewritten press releases. Buys 75 mss/year. Query with clips of published work. Length: 1,000-1,200 words. "All negotiable."

Photos: Send photos with ms. Pays negotiable fee for b&w contact sheets. Identification of subjects required.

Tips: "Writers submitting queries must be extremely knowledgeable in the field and have direct access to hard news."

‡**GERIATRIC CONSULTANT**, Medical Publishing Enterprises, Box 1548, Marco Island FL 33937. (813)394-0400. Editor: John H. Lavin. 70% freelance written. Bimonthly magazine covering medical care of the elderly. "We're a clinical magazine directed to doctors and physician assistants. All articles must *help* these health professionals to help their elderly patients. We're too tough a market for nonmedical beginners." Circ. 105,000. Pays on acceptance. Publishes ms an average of 3 months after acceptance. Byline given. Offers 20% kill fee. Buys North American serial rights. Simultaneous queries OK. Computer printout submissions acceptable; prefers letter-quality to dot-matrix. Reports in 1 month. Sample copy for $1; free writer's guidelines.

Nonfiction: How-to (diagnosis and treatment of health problems of the elderly) and technical/clinical. No fiction or no articles directed to a lay audience. Buys 20 mss/year. Query. Length: 750-3,000 words. Pays $100-300.

Photos: State availability of photos. (Photos are not required.) Model release and identification of subjects required. Buys one-time rights.

Fillers: Anecdotes. Buys 6-8/year. Length: 250 words. Pays $25 maximum.

Tips: "Many medical meetings are now held in the field of geriatric care. These offer potential sources and subjects for us."

HEALTH INDUSTRY TODAY, 454 Morris Ave., Springfield NJ 07081. Editor: David Cassak. For medical/surgical dealers and dealer/salesmen. Monthly magazine; 92 pages. Circ. 11,000. Buys exclusive industry rights. Byline given. Buys 5-10 mss/year. Pays on publication. Will consider photocopied and simultaneous submissions. Query or submit complete ms. SASE. Free sample copy and writer's guidelines.

Nonfiction: "We publish articles touching on all aspects of healthcare supply, from company and individual profiles to market studies, and from government regulatory action and its impact to coming trends. We are also interested in new technologies and products, but from a marketing perspective, not a technical one. Keep in mind that we deal with the marketing (or selling) of healthcare supplies to hospitals, doctors and the home healthcare trade, and that our readers are, for the most part, sophisticated businessmen. We insist that submitted articles demonstrate an understanding of the issues that affect the industry." No general articles on finances (especially around tax time) or selling that could apply to a variety of fields. Length: approximately 2,500 words. Pays 10¢/word or negotiable fee.

Photos: No additional payment for b&w photos used with mss.

Tips: "We are always eager to receive quality freelance submissions and would gladly enter into a long term arrangement with a freelancer whose work we like. Submitted articles can relieve a burden on our own staff and give our publication a wider perspective. The problem we encounter with most freelancers, however, quality of writing aside, is that they want to write general articles that they can submit to a number of publications and thus do not want to write articles of sufficient sophistication for our readers. Simply put, the articles are so general in approach, they rarely provide any real information at all for anyone even slightly exposed to the field. Know either the publication or the field. We encourage freelancers to write for a sample copy of our publication."

‡**HEALTH LITERATURE REVIEW, A Distinctive Health Journal**, True-To-Form Press, Box 8029, St. Paul MN 55119. (612)731-1816. Editor: Sheila Nauman-Haight. Managing Editor: Tammy Rognlie. A bimonthly journal that reviews health literature for health care professionals who are interested in consumer health education. Estab. 1983. Circ. 2,500. Pays on publication. Byline given. Buys all rights. Submit season-

al/holiday material 3-6 months in advance. Computer printout submissions acceptable. SASE. Reports in 2 weeks on queries; 2 months on mss. Sample copy $2.25; free writer's guidelines.

Nonfiction: Book excerpts, historical/nostalgic, how-to, humor, interview/profile, new product, opinion and personal experience. All should pertain to health care communications and health literature. Special issues include Men's Health Care Literature; Women's Health Care Literature; Pediatrics Health Literature; and Teenage Health Literature. Buys 12-18 mss/year. Query. Length: 1,500-,000 words. Pays 10¢/word.

Photos: State availability of photos or send photos with ms. Reviews b&w and color contact sheets. Captions, model release and identification of subjects required.

Columns/Departments: Book Reviews (on any health literature); Editorial column. Query. Length: 100-500 words.

Fillers: Anecdotes, short humor and newsbreaks. Length: 25-100 words.

Tips: "Writers *must* have health care *expertise*. Health book reviews are most open to freelancers."

‡**THE JOURNAL**, Addiction Research Foundation of Ontario, 33 Russell St., Toronto, Ontario M5S 2S1 Canada. (416)595-6053. Editor: Anne MacLennan. 50% freelance written. Monthly tabloid covering addictions and related fields around the world. "*The Journal* alerts professionals in the addictions and related fields or disciplines to news events, issues, opinions and developments of potential interest and/or significance to them in their work, and provides them an informed context in which to judge developments in their own specialty/geographical areas." Circ. 24,550. Pays on publication. Publishes ms an average of 3 months after acceptance. Byline given. Kill fee negotiable. Not copyrighted. Buys first and second rights to the same material. Computer printout submissions acceptable. SAE with Canadian postage. Reports in 2 months on queries; 3 months on mss. Free sample copy and writer's guidelines.

Nonfiction: Interview/profile and new product. Query with published clips or send complete ms. Length: 1,000 words maximum. Pays 18¢/word maximum.

Photos: Terri Etherington, production editor. State availability of photos. Pays $10-35 for 5x7 or 8x10 b&w prints. Captions, model releases and identification of subjects required. Buys one-time rights.

Columns/Departments: Query with published clips.

Tips: "A freelancer can best break in to our publication with six years reporting experience, preferably with medical/science writing background."

THE MAYO ALUMNUS, Mayo Clinic, 200 SW 1st St., Rochester MN 55905. (507)284-2511. Editor: Rosemary A. Klein. For physicians, scientists and medical educators who trained at the Mayo Clinic. Quarterly magazine; 48 pages. Circ. 10,000. Pays on acceptance. Buys all rights. Submit seasonal/holiday material 6 months in advance. Previously published submissions OK. SASE. Reports in 2 months. Free sample copy; mention *Writer's Market* in request. No writer's guidelines available at this time.

Nonfiction: "We're interested in seeing interviews with members of the Mayo Alumni Association—stories about Mayo-trained doctors/educators/scientists/researchers who are interesting people doing interesting things in medicine, surgery or hobbies of interest, etc." Query with clips of published work. Length: 1,000-3,000 words. Pays 15¢/word, first 1,500 words. Maximum payment is $275.

Photos: "We need art and must make arrangements if not provided with the story." Pays $10 for b&w photos. State availability of photos with query. Captions preferred. Buys all rights.

MD MAGAZINE, MD Publications, Inc., 30 E. 60th St., New York NY 10022. (212)355-5432. Editor: A.J. Vogl. Managing Editor: Barbara Guidos. Monthly magazine of information and culture for practicing physicians. Circ. 160,000. Pays on acceptance. Byline given. Offers 25% kill fee. Buys one-time rights. Submit seasonal/holiday material 5 months in advance. Simultaneous queries, and photocopied and previously published submissions OK. SASE. Reports in 6 weeks.

Nonfiction: Janet Wilson, articles editor. Book excerpts; general interest; historical/nostalgic; interview/profile (of physicians); photo feature; technical (medicine); and travel. Buys 120 mss/year. Query with clips of published work. Length: 750-3,000 words. Pays $250-700.

Photos: William Nabors, picture editor. State availability of photos. Pays ASMP rates for b&w contact sheet and 35mm color transparencies. Captions, model release and identification of subjects required.

Tips: "I'm especially looking for lively writing on contemporary subjects."

‡**MEDICAL ECONOMICS**, Medical Economics Co., Inc., 680 Kinderkamack Rd., Oradell NJ 07649. (201)262-3030. Editor: Don L. Berg. Managing Editor: Richard Service. Less than 5% freelance written. Bi-weekly magazine covering topics of nonclinical interest to office-based private physicians (MDs and DOs only). "We publish practice/management and personal/finance advice for office-based MDs and osteopaths." Circ. 167,000. Pays on acceptance. Publishes ms an average of 3 months after acceptance. Byline given. Offers 25% of full article fee as kill fee. Buys all rights and first rights. Computer printout submissions acceptable. SASE. Reports in 2 months on queries; 3 weeks on mss. Sample copy for $3 and 9x12 SASE.

Nonfiction: Contact Lilian Fine, chief of Outside Copy Division. How-to (office and personnel management, personal-money management); personal experience (only involving DMs or DOs in private practice); and travel (how-to articles). No clinical articles, hobby articles, personality profiles or office design articles. Buys 8-10 mss/year. Query with published clips. Length: 1,500-3,000 words. Pays $750-1,800. "The payment level is decided at the time go-ahead is given after query."

Photos: Contact Lilian Fine, chief of Outside Copy Division. State availability of photos. Pays negotiable rates for b&w contact sheets and for 35mm color slides. Model release and identification of subjects required. Buys one-time rights.

Tips: "How-to articles should fully describe techniques, goals, options and caveats—in terms that are clear and *realistic* for the average physician. Use of anecdotal examples to support major points is crucial. Our full-time staff is quite large, and therefore we buy only freelance articles that are not already assigned to staff writers. This puts a premium on unusual and appealing subjects."

THE MEDICAL POST, 481 University Ave., Toronto, Ontario M5W 1A7 Canada. Editor: Derek Cassels. For the medical profession. Biweekly. Will send sample copy to medical writers only. Buys first Canadian serial rights. Pays on publication. SAE and IRCs.
Nonfiction: Uses newsy, factual reports of medical developments. Must be aimed at professional audience and written in newspaper style. Length: 300-800 words. Pays 18¢/word.
Photos: Uses photos with mss or captions only, of medical interest; pays $10 up.

MEDICAL TIMES, Romaine Pierson Publishers, Inc. 80 Shore Rd., Port Washington NY 11050. (516)883-6350. Editors: A.J. Bollet, M.D., and A.H.Bruckheim, M.D. Managing Editor: Susan Carr Jenkins. Monthly magazine covering clinical medical subjects for primary care physicians in private practice. Circ. 105,000. Pays on acceptance. Byline given. Offers 100% kill fee. Buys all rights and makes work-for-hire assignments. Submit seasonal/holiday material 6 months in advance. Simultaneous queries OK. Reports in 1 month on queries; 2 months on mss. Sample copy $5; writer's guidelines for business-size SAE and 1 first class stamp.
Nonfiction: "We accept only clinical medical and medicolegal material. It is useless to send us any material that is not related directly to medicine." Buys 100 mss/year. Query. Length: 500-2,500 words. Pays $25-300.
Photos: State availability of photos. Pays variable rates for 2x2 b&w and color transparencies, and 4x5 or 8x10 b&w and color prints. Model release and identification of subjects required.
Fillers: Anecdotes. "Must be true, unpublished and medically oriented." Buys 25/year. Length: 25-200 words.
Tips: "A query letter is a must. 99% of our material is 'invited.' "

‡MEDICINE AND COMPUTER MAGAZINE, The Practical Medical Computer Magazine, 470 Mamaroneck Ave., White Plains NY 10605. (914)681-0040. Editor: Jeffrey Rothfeder. Managing Editor: Sally Ketchum. 25% freelance written. Monthly magazine covering computer applications in medicine with "a simple nontechnical approach to describing the ways computers are used in medicine by private practitioners." Estab. 1983. Circ. 125,000. Pays 1-2 months after acceptance. Offers 10% kill fee. Buys all rights. No simultaneous queries. Photocopied submissions OK. Electronic submissions via disk (IBM-compatible WordStar or Multimate Software) or via modem ("send to our mailbox at Compu-Serve or The Source") OK. Computer printout submissions acceptable. SASE. Reports in 1 month. Publishes ms an average of 2 months after acceptance. Sample copy for $4; free writer's guidelines.
Nonfiction: Book excerpts (on medical computing); how to (use software and hardware in the physician's office); interview/profile (with leading medical computing luminaries); new product (review of important computer hardware and software for physicians); opinion (essays on issues that affect physicians and their use of computers); personal experience (first person MD accounts of computerization); photo feature (breakthroughs in medical computing, e.g., DNA modeling—with color slides); and features describing how physicians are using computers from simple applications to more esoteric ones. Special issue includes Practice Management with Computers (feature accounts, application, how-to, etc.). Buys 12 mss/year. Query with published clips. Length: 2,000-3,000 words. Pays $300-1,000.
Photos: State availability of photos. Pays negotiable rates for 3x5 b&w and color transparencies. Model release and identification of subjects required.
Tips: "Find the most exciting uses of computers in medicine, interview the movers and shakers involved with it, and tell us about it. Do not overwhelm the physicians with your knowledge about the subject; overwhelm them with your ability to impart their knowledge."

THE NEW PHYSICIAN, 1910 Association Dr., Reston VA 22091. Editor: Renie Schapiro. 20% freelance written. For medical students, interns and residents. Published 9 times/year; 56 pages. Circ. 80,000. Buys all rights. Buys 6-12 mss/year. Pays on publication. Will consider simultaneous submissions. Computer printout submissions acceptable. Reports in 1-2 months. Publishes ms an average of 3 months after acceptance. Query or completed ms. SASE. Free sample copy.
Nonfiction: "Articles on social, political, economic issues in medicine/medical education. Our readers need more than a superficial, simplistic look into issues that affect them. We want skeptical, accurate, professional contributors to do well-researched, comprehensive, incisive reports and offer new perspectives on health care

problems." Not interested in material on "my operation," or encounters with physicians, or personal experiences as physician's patient, investment/business advice for physicians, or highly technical material. Occasionally publishes special topic issues, alternatives in medical training. Humorous articles and cartoons for physicians-in-training. Informational articles, interviews and exposes are sought. Length: 500-3,500 words. Pays $25-400.

Photos: Pays $10-35 for b&w photos used with mss. Captions required.

Tips: "Our magazine demands real sophistication on the issues we cover because we are a professional journal. Those freelancers we publish reveal in their queries and ultimately in their manuscripts a willingness and an ability to look deeply into the issues in question and not be satisfied with a cursory review of those issues."

NUCLEUS SCIENCE JOURNAL, 520 N. Genessee, Chicago IL 60085. Editor: Mark A. Young. Managing Editor: Lisa C. Bogdonoff. Annual scientific journal covering biology, chemistry, medicine and natural science. Circ. 7,000. Pays on publication. Byline given. Buys all rights. Submit seasonal material 3 months in advance. Simultaneous queries, and simultaneous, photocopied and previously published submissions OK. SASE. Reports in 2 weeks on queries; 1 month on mss. Sample copy $1; free writer's guidelines.

Nonfiction: Mark A. Young, articles editor. Book excerpts; interview/profile (with scientists who have made significant contributions to furthering an understanding of science); and photo feature. Buys 20 mss/year. Query with or without published clips. Length: open. Pays $50 minimum; sometimes pays in copies; sometimes commissions articles.

Photos: Louis Wenger, photo editor. Reviews b&w contact sheet. Payment depends on photo.

Fillers: Nat Soloman, fillers editor. Anecdotes and newsbreaks. Buys 10/year. Length: open.

Tips: "Well written scientific 'journal style' articles are what we seek. Articles should be slanted toward laymen and scientists alike. Articles on medical topics written by MDs are especially welcome."

ONCOLOGY TIMES, Herlitz Publications, Inc. 404 Park Ave. S., New York NY 10016. (212)532-9400. Editor: Jonathan S. Wood. Monthly tabloid covering cancer research with a clinical emphasis for oncologists and allied professionals. Circ. 25,000. Pays on publication. Byline given. Buys all rights. Reports in 2 weeks on queries; 1 week on mss. Free sample copy and writer's guidelines.

Nonfiction: Articles on cancer research—some basic, primarily clinical. News interviews and articles based on meetings and current literature reviews. No anecdotal stories. No unsolicited mss. Buys 240 mss/year. Query with resume and clips of published work. Length: 750-1,500 words. Pays $150 minimum. Medical/science writers only.

‡ORTHOPEDICS TODAY, Slack, Inc., 6900 Grove Rd., Thorofare NJ 08086. (609)848-1000. Managing Editor: Mario Cavallini. 5% freelance written. Twice-monthly newspaper covering the latest news on surgical practice, trends, products, etc. for orthopedic surgery, orthopedic surgeons and related specialists. Circ. 26,000. Pays on publication. Buys all rights. Submit seasonal/holiday material 3 months in advance. Simultaneous queries, and simultaneous and photocopied submissions OK. Computer printout submissions acceptable. Reports in 1 month. Publishes ms an average of 3 months after acceptance. Free sample copy and writer's guidelines.

Nonfiction: How-to, interview/profile, new product, opinion, photo feature and technical. Buys 12 mss/year. Query with clips of published work or send complete ms. Length: 500-2,500 words. Pays $50-300.

Photos: Send photos with ms. Pays $10-50 for 35mm or 2¼ b&w transparencies and 8x10 prints; $10-250 for 35mm or 2¼ color transparencies, 8x10 prints and contact sheets. Captions, model release and identification of subjects required. Buys one-time rights.

Columns/Departments: Book Reviews, Interviews, and Personal Profile. Buys 12 mss/year. Query with clips of published work. Length: 500-2,500 words. Pays $25-200.

Tips: "Be specific as to what you want to submit. Specify price. Timeliness, accuracy, need are important."

‡PEOPLE'S MEDICAL SOCIETY NEWSLETTER, People's Medical Society, 14 E. Minor St., Emmaus PA 18049. (215)967-2136. Editor: Ed Weiner. A bimonthly newsletter for members of PMS covering health/medical issues, grassroots health actions, and medical politics. "Our readers are interested in preventive medicine, alternatives to standard medical care, and a consumer activist way with the health/medical care system." Estab. 1983. Circ. 50,000. Pays on acceptance. Byline given. Offers 33% kill fee or as arranged. Not copyrighted. Buys rights by arrangement with author. Submit seasonal/holiday material 4-6 months in advance. Simultaneous queries, and simultaneous, photocopied and previously published submissions OK. Electronic submissions OK at present on 5¼" and 8" CPM 2.2 disks. Computer printout submissions acceptable; prefers letter-quality to dot-matrix. SASE. Reports in 1 month. Sample copy for $1, business-size SAE, and first class stamp.

Nonfiction: Book excerpts, expose, how-to, humor, inspirational, interview/profile, opinion, and personal experience. "All articles must be health related, from a consumer activist standpoint; experiences with the medical establishment, fighting, insensitivity of doctor/hospital-patient relationship." No articles on specific

nutritional therapies, or articles with a religious overtone. Query with published clips or send complete ms. Length: 500-1,500 words. Pays $35-125.
Fillers: Cartoons.
Tips: "First-person accounts, interviews, and cartoons are most open to freelancers."

‡**THE PHYSICIAN AND SPORTSMEDICINE**, McGraw-Hill, 4530 W. 77th St., Edina MN 55435. (612)835-3222. Editor: Allan J. Ryan, MD. Managing Editor: Frances Caldwell. Monthly magazine covering medical aspects of sports and exercise. "We look in our feature articles for subjects of practical interest to our physician audience." Circ. 130,000. Pays on acceptance. Byline given. Buys one-time rights. Submit seasonal/holiday material 6 months in advance. Simultaneous queries OK. Reports in 2 weeks. Sample copy for $3; free writer's guidelines.
Nonfiction: Interview/profile (persons active in this field); and technical (new developments in sports medicine). Buys 24 mss/year. Query. Length: 1,500-2,500 words. Pays $400-600.
Photos: Gary Legwold, photo editor. State availability of photos. Pays ASTM rates for color transparencies. Buys one-time rights.

PHYSICIAN'S MANAGEMENT, Harcourt Brace Jovanovich Health Care Publications, 7500 Old Oak Blvd., Cleveland OH 44130. (216)243-8100. Editor: Bob Feigenbaum. 90% freelance written. Emphasizes finances, investments, malpractice, socioeconomic issues, estate and retirement planning, small office administration, practice management, leisure time, computers, travel, automobiles, and taxes for primary care physicians in private practice. Monthly magazine. Circ. 110,000. Pays on acceptance. Publishes ms an average of 6 months after acceptance. Buys first rights only. Submit seasonal or holiday material 5 months in advance. Computer printout submissions acceptable; no dot-matrix. SASE. Reports in 2-4 weeks.
Nonfiction: "*Physician's Management* is a practice management/economic publication, not a clinical one." Publishes how-to articles (limited to medical practice management); informational (when relevant to audience); and personal experience articles (if written by a physician). No fiction, clinical material or satire that portrays MD in an unfavorable light; or soap opera, "real-life" articles. Length: 2,000-2,500 words. Buys 15-20 mss/issue. Query. Pays $125/3-column printed page. Use of charts, tables, graphs, sidebars and photos strongly encouraged.
Tips: "Talk to doctors first about their practices, financial interests, and day-to-day nonclinical problems and then query us. Also, the ability to write a concise, well-structured and well-researched magazine article is essential. Freelancers who think like patients fail with us. Those who can think like MDs are successful. Our magazine is growing significantly. The opportunities for good writers will, therefore, increase greatly."

PODIATRY MANAGEMENT, 401 N. Broad St., Philadephia PA 19108. (215)925-9744. Publisher: Scott C. Borowsky. Editor: Barry Block, D.P.M. Managing Editor: M.J. Goldberg. Business magazine published 7 times/year for practicing podiatrists. "Aims to help the doctor of podiatric medicine to build a bigger, more successful practice, to conserve and invest his money, to keep him posted on the economic, legal and sociological changes that affect him." Circ. 11,000. Pays on publication. Byline given. Buys first North American serial and second (reprint) rights. Submit seasonal/holiday material 4 months in advance. Simultaneous queries, and simultaneous, photocopied and previously published submissions OK. Send mss to Dr. Block, 225 E. 64th St., New York NY 10021. SASE. Reports in 2 weeks. Sample copy $2; free writer's guidelines.
Nonfiction: General interest (taxes, investments, estate planning, recreation hobbies); how-to (establish and collect fees, practice management, organize office routines, supervise office assistants, handle patient relations); interview/profile; and personal experience. "These subjects are the mainstay of the magazine, but offbeat articles and humor are always welcome." Buys 25 mss/year. Query. Length: 1,000-2,500 words. Pays $150-350.
Photos: State availability of photos. Pays $10 for b&w contact sheet. Buys one-time rights.

PRIVATE PRACTICE, Box 12489, Oklahoma City OK 73157. Executive Editor: Karen C. Murphy. 80% freelance written. For "medical doctors in private practice." Monthly. Buys first North American serial rights. "If an article is assigned, it is paid for in full, used or killed." Byline given "except if it was completely rewritten or a considerable amount of additional material is added to the article." Pays on acceptance. Publishes ms an average of 3 months after acceptance. Query. "Computer printout submissions acceptable; prefers letter-quality to dot-matrix. SASE.
Nonfiction: "Articles that indicate importance of maintaining freedom of medical practice or which detail outside interferences in the practice of medicine, including research, hospital operation, drug manufacture, etc. Straight reporting style. No cliches, no scare words, no flowery phrases to cover up poor reporting. Stories must be actual, factual, precise and correct. Copy should be lively and easy to read. We also publish travel and leisure." No general short humor, poetry or short stories. "Please, no first person humor or other type of personal experiences with your doctor—i.e., my account of when my doctor told me I needed my first operation, etc." Buys 50-60 unsolicited mss/year. Length: up to 2,500 words. Pays "usual minimum $150."

Photos: Photos purchased with mss only. B&w glossies, 8x10. Payment "depends on quality, relevancy of material, etc."
Tips: "The article we are most likely to buy will be a straight report on some situation where the freedom to practice medicine has been enhanced, or where it has been intruded on to the detriment of good health."

‡**RESIDENT & STAFF PHYSICIAN**, Romaine Pierson Publishers, Inc., 80 Shore Rd., Port Washington NY 11050. (516)883-6350. Editor: Alfred Jay Bollet, MD. Managing Editor: Anne Mattarella. 15% freelance written. Monthly journal covering clinical medicine and practice management for residents and staff physicians. "*Resident & Staff Physician* goes to hospital-based physicians throughout the country, including practically all residents and the full-time hospital staff responsible for their training." Circ. 100,000. Pays on acceptance. Byline given. Buys all rigths. Submit seasonal/holiday material 1 year in advance. Simultaneous queries and photocopied submissions OK. Reports in 3 weeks on queries; 4 months on mss. Publishes ms an average of 1 year after acceptance. Sample copy for $5; free writer's guidelines.
Nonfiction: Historical/nostalgic (medical); new product (medical); and clinical, review-type articles and those for practice management. No case reports. Buys 2 mss/year. Query. Length: 6-8 typewritten pages. Pays $200-300.
Photos: State availability of photos. "Payment is included in manuscript payment." Captions, model release and identification of subjects required. Buys all rights.
Columns/Departments: Medical Mixups (terms patients mix up, e.g., Cadillacs in the eyes instead of cataracts). Buys 5-10 mss/year. Send complete ms. Length: 50 words. Pays $25 maximum.
Fillers: Jokes, anecdotes, short humor and newsbreaks. Buys 5/year. Length: 25-500 words. Pays $25 to $100.
Tips: "A freelancer can best break in to our publication with filler items or humorous anecdotes. Keep the audience in mind. Jokes about high doctor fees are *not* funny to doctors. Freelancers frequently insult doctors."

SURGICAL ROUNDS, Romaine Pierson Publishers, Inc., 80 Shore Rd., Port Washington NY 11050. (516)883-6350. Editor: Mark M. Ravitch, MD. Managing Editor: Roxane Cafferata. Monthly magazine for surgeons and surgical specialists throughout the country, including all surgical interns, all surgical residents, all surgical faculty in medical schools, plus full-time hospital and private practice surgeons and operating room supervisors. Circ. 70,000. Pays on acceptance. Byline given. Buys all rights. Reports in 1 month. Sample copy $5; free writer's guidelines.
Nonfiction: How-to (practical, everyday clinical applications). "Articles for 'The Surgeon's Laboratory' should demonstrate a particular procedure step-by-step and be amply and clearly illustrated with intraoperative color photographs and anatomical drawings." Buys 80 mss/year. Query with clips of published work. Length: 1,500-2,000 words. Pays $150-400.
Poetry: Only poetry related to hospital, physician, or operative experience. Buys 6/year. Pays $25.

THE SURGICAL TECHNOLOGIST, Association of Surgical Technologists, Caller No. E, Littleton CO 80120. (303)978-9010. Editor: William Teatsch. Bimonthly magazine covering surgery, operating room issues, and legal, social and ethical implications. Makes available the total picture of advanced operating room techniques, health care issues, educational programs, new instruments, supplies and equipment. Circ. 11,000. Pays on acceptance. Byline given. Buys all rights. Submit seasonal/holiday material 6 months in advance. Simultaneous queries and simultaneous, photocopied and previously published submissions OK. Free sample copy and writer's guidelines.
Nonfiction: Book excerpts, expose, general interest, historical/nostalgic, how-to, humor, inspirational, interview/profile, new product, opinion, personal experience, photo feature and technical. All must relate to the hospital or operating room. Buys "unlimited" number mss/year. Query with clips if available or send complete ms. Length: 1,000-6,000 words. Pays $50-150.
Photos: State availability of photos or send photos with ms. Reviews all types of photos. Pays $25-100.

Mining and Minerals

AMERICAN GOLD NEWS, Box 457, Ione CA 95640. (209)274-2196. Editor: Cecil Helms. 25% freelance written. For anyone interested in gold, gold mining, gold companies, gold stocks, gold history, gold coins and the future of gold in our economy. Monthly tabloid newspaper; 20 pages. Circ. 3,500. Not copyrighted. Byline given. Pays on publication. Publishes ms an average of 6 months after acceptance. Buys first rights. No photocopied or simultaneous submissions. Submit seasonal material (relating to seasonal times in mining country) 2 months in advance. Computer printout submissions acceptable; prefers letter-quality to dot-matrix. Reports in

2-4 weeks. Query or submit complete ms. SASE. Sample copy and writer's guidelines for $1.
Nonfiction: "This is not a literary publication. We want information on any subject pertaining to gold told in the most simple, direct and interesting way." How to build gold mining equipment; history of mines (with pictures); history of gold throughout the US; financial articles on gold philosophy in money matters; picture stories of mines, mining towns and mining country. Would like to see more histories of mines, from any state. No fiction. Buys 12-24 unsolicited mss/year. Length: 500-2,000 words. Pays $10-50.
Photos: B&w photos purchased with or without ms. Must be sharp (if not old historical photos). Pays $2.50-25. Captions required.

COAL AGE, 1221 Avenue of the Americas, New York NY 10020. Editor: Joseph F. Wilkinson. For supervisors, engineers and executives in coal mining. Monthly. Circ. 20,000. Buys all rights. Pays on publication. Query. Reports in 2-3 weeks. SASE.
Nonfiction: Uses some technical (operating type) articles; some how-to pieces on equipment maintenance; and management articles. Pays $200/page.

COAL INDUSTRY NEWS, Coal's National Newspaper, Whitney Communications Corp., 850 3rd Ave., New York NY 10022. (212)715-2766. Editor: Gene Smith. Managing Editor: Nick Snow. Biweekly tabloid covering all coal-related news and companies "aimed at decision-makers and upper echelon of coal/energy industry and government officials who deal with the industry." Circ. 12,000. Pays on publication. Byline given. Offers negotiable kill fee. Buys one-time rights. Simultaneous queries, and simultaneous and previously published submissions OK. Computer printout submissions acceptable; prefers letter-quality to dot-matrix. Reports in 2 weeks. Free sample copy.
Nonfiction: General interest; how-to (case histories or reports on new technology); interview/profile; new product; and technical (not too technical). Write for schedule of special supplements. No material on heavy technology. Buys 20-30 mss/year. Query. Length: 500-1,500 words. Pays $71.25/column.
Photos: State availability of photos. Pays $5 for 8x10 b&w print. Captions and identification of subjects required.
Tips: "A simple query in writing or by phone will get immediate response. All areas are open. Stress is on newspaper format—we are not technically oriented."

KENTUCKY COAL JOURNAL, Box 573, Frankfort KY 40602. (502)223-1619. Editor: Mike Bennett. Monthly tabloid about coal mining; specifically, the constrictions placed on the industry by federal and state bureaus regulating it, and market conditions. Circ. 10,000. Pays on publication. Byline given. Buys one-time rights. Phone queries OK. Submit seasonal material 1 month in advance. Photocopied and previously published submissions OK. Reports in 1 week. Free sample copy.
Nonfiction: Expose (of government); historical (of old coal mines); opinion; profile (of Kentucky coal mines and miners); humor; new product (revolutionary); and photo feature. "We have been called an example of 'personal journalism,' meaning we inject comments, viewpoints, etc., into just about anything that's printed. We first took up for the small, independent operator; now we have become the unofficial spokesman for the entire Kentucky coal industry, although our circulation is national." No fictional or highly technical articles. Buys 2-3 mss/issue. Send complete ms. Length: 300 words minimum. Pays $25-300.
Photos: State availability of photos. Pay $15 minimum for any size b&w glossy prints. Captions required. Buys one-time rights.
Tips: "Tell us about a unique coal venture, mine or person. Tell us how to bust a particular bureaucracy. Or write a timely, factual story that fits into our editorial philosophy. We do not object to an adversary point of view, but no diatribes, please. If you have a valid and logical reason for opposing something, fine. Reading a copy of the *Coal Journal* will help. We don't want anything that does not relate directly to coal—preferably Kentucky coal."

‡**WORLD MINING EQUIPMENT**, Technical Publishing, 875 3rd Ave., New York NY 10022. (212)605-9400. Editorial Director: Ruth W. Stidger. 20% freelance written. Monthly magazine on mining, mineral processing and mineral exploration for mine managers and engineers worldwide. Circ. 23,000. Pays on publication. Publishes ms an average of 3 months after acceptance. Byline varies, depending on background. Buys first rights and makes work-for-hire assignments. Submit seasonal/holiday material 4 months in advance. Simultaneous queries, and simultaneous and previously published submissions OK (if not to direct competition). Computer printout submissions acceptable; prefers letter-quality to dot-matrix. Reports in 2 weeks. Free sample copy.
Nonfiction: Technical. Buys 40 mss/year. Send complete ms. Length: 1,500-8,000 words. Pays $100-800.
Photos: Send photos with ms. Pays 425-200 for 35mm and 2¼x2¼ color transparencies. Captions, model release and identification of subjects required. Buys one-time rights.

Music

ASCAP IN ACTION, A Publication of the American Society of Composers, Authors and Publishers, 1 Lincoln Plaza, New York NY 10023. (212)595-3050. Executive Editor: Karen Sherry. Magazine published 3 times/year covering music and its creators and publishers. Circ. 50,000 to ASCAP members, the music industry, college libraries, and foreign performing rights organizations. Pays on acceptance. Byline "generally given." Buys first North American serial rights. Photocopied submissions OK. Reports in 1 month. Free sample copy.
Nonfiction: Profile (of an individual or event); publishing trends; and performing rights issues. No articles on BMI members or music people who are not writers." Buys 10-15 mss/year. Query with clips of published work. Length: 3,000-3,500 words. Pays $350.
Photos: "Whenever possible we get free use of photos through publicity agents; otherwise we buy." State availability of photos. Reviews color transparencies and 8x10 glossy prints. Captions required. Buys one-time rights.

CADENCE, Cadence Jazz & Blues Magazine, Ltd., Cadence Building, Redwood NY 13679. (315)287-2852. Editor: Robert D. Rusch. Monthly jazz and blues trade magazine published for serious jazz and blues fans who are writers, performers, producers and record collectors. Pays on acceptance. Byline given. Buys all rights. Simultaneous queries, and simultaneous and photocopied submissions OK. SASE. Reports in weeks. Sample copy $2.
Nonfiction: Interview/profile. "We only use interviews (Q&A) and oral histories" related to jazz and blues. Query or send complete ms. Length: variable. Pays in credits for goods.
Photos: Reviews prints. Identification of subjects required.

THE CHURCH MUSICIAN, 127 9th Ave. N., Nashville TN 37234. (615)251-2961. Editor: William Anderson. 30% freelance written. Southern Baptist publication. For Southern Baptist church music leaders. Monthly. Circ. 20,000. Buys all rights. Pays on acceptance. No query required. Reports in 2 months. SASE. Free sample copy.
Nonfiction: Leadership and how-to features, success stories and articles on Protestant church music. "We reject material when the subject of an article doesn't meet our needs. And they are often poorly written, or contain too many 'glittering generalities' or lack creativity." Length: maximum 1,300 words. Pays up to 4¢/word.
Photos: Purchased with mss; related to mss content only. "We use only b&w glossy prints."
Fiction: Inspiration, guidance, motivation and morality with Protestant church music slant. Length: to 1,300 words. Pays up to 3½¢/word.
Poetry: Church music slant, inspirational. Length: 8-24 lines. Pays $5-15.
Fillers: Short humor. Church music slant. No clippings. Pays $5-15.
Tips: "I'd advise a beginning writer to write about his or her experience with some aspect of church music; the social, musical and spiritual benefits from singing in a choir; a success story about their instrumental group; a testimonial about how they were enlisted in a choir—especially if they were not inclined to be enlisted at first. A writer might speak to hymn singers—what turns them on and what doesn't. Some might include how music has helped them to talk about Jesus as well as sing about Him. We would prefer most of these experiences be related to the church, of course, although we include many articles by freelance writers whose affiliation is other than Baptist. A writer might relate his experience with a choir of blind or deaf members. Some people receive benefits from working with unusual children—retarded, or culturally deprived, emotionally unstable, and so forth. Photographs are valuable here."

CLAVIER, 200 Northfield Rd., Northfield IL 60093. (312)328-6000. Editor: Barbara Kreader. Magazine; 48 pages. Published 10 times/year. Buys all rights. Pays on publication. No simultaneous submissions. "Suggest query to avoid duplication." SASE. Free sample copy.
Nonfiction: Wants "articles aimed at teachers of piano and organ. Must be written from thoroughly professional point of view. Avoid, however, the thesis style subject matter and pedantic style generally found in scholarly journals. We like fresh writing, practical approach. We can use interviews with concert pianists and organists. An interview should not be solely a personality story but should focus on a subject of interest to musicians. Any word length. Photos may accompany ms." Buys 65 + unsolicited mss/year. Pays $35/printed page.
Photos: "We need color photos for cover, such as angle shots of details of instruments, other imaginative photos, with keyboard music themes."

THE INSTRUMENTALIST, 1418 Lake St., Evanston IL 60204. Editor: Kenneth L. Neidig. For instrumental music educators. Monthly. Circ. 22,527. Buys all rights. Byline given. Buys 200 mss/year. Pays on publication. Submit seasonal material 4 months in advance. New Products (February); Summer Camps, Clinics, Workshops (March); Marching Bands (June); Back to School (September); and Fundraising (October). Reports on material accepted for publication within 4 months. Returns rejected material within 3 months. Query. SASE. Sample copy $2.

Nonfiction: "Practical information of immediate use to instrumentalists. Not articles 'about music and musicians,' but articles by musicians who are sharing knowledge, techniques and experience. 'In-service education.' Professional help for instrumentalists in the form of instrumental clinics, how-to articles, new trends and practical philosophy. Most contributions are from professionals in the field." Interpretive photojournalism. "Query for manuscripts over 1,000 words." Length: 100-1,500 words. Pays according to length (approximately $25-45/printed page), plus 2 contributors copies.

Photos: Quality b&w prints. Pays $5-10. Color: 35mm and up. Pays $50-75 if used for cover.

‡**MUSIC CONNECTION MAGAZINE, The Alternative Music Trade Publication**, Connection Publications, Suite 201, 6640 Sunset Blvd., Hollywood CA 90028. (213)462-5772. Editor: J. Michael Dolan. Managing Editor: Bud Scoppa. A biweekly magazine covering the entire music industry for musicians and trade executives. Circ. 20,000. Pays on publication. Byline given. Makes work-for-hire assignments. Submit seasonal/holiday material 6 weeks in advance. Simultaneous queries and photocopied submissions OK. Computer printout submissions acceptable. SASE. Reports in 2 weeks on queries; 1 month on mss. Sample copy for $1.50; 9x12 SAE, and 2 class stamps; writer's guidelines for 9x12 SAE and 2 first class stamps.

Nonfiction: Bud Scoppa, articles editor. Expose (dealing with major music industry companies or organizations); interview/profile (pesonalities of interest in popular music); and (new technological developments in instruments and musical computers); and how-to (breaking in to the industry, cutting records, etc.). Special issues include: Recording Studios, Music Books, Clubs, and Year-End Review. "All articles must deal with factual and timely occurences and personalities in the music industry." Buys 120 mss/year. Query with resume and published clips. Length: 800-2,500 words. Pays $30-150.

Photos: Lawrence Payne, photo editor. Send photos with accompanying query or ms. Pays $2.20 for 8x10 b&w prints; $5.50 for 35mm color slides. Identification of subjects required. Buys all rights.

Columns/Departments: Lawrence Payne, column/department editor. Concert and Night Club Reviews (acts playing southern California); Record Reviews (recent release LPs, EPs, singles and cassettes); and News & Local Notes (noteworthy happenings in the popular music industry). Buys 500 mss/year. Query with resume and published clips. Length: 200-800 words. Pays $10-40.

Fiction: Bud Scoppa, fiction editor. Historical (dealing with the historical background of the music and record industry); humorous (dealing with the music business and the trials of getting accepted); and mainstream (pertaining to the record industry and the night club scene). "We do not want to see anything which is irrelevant to popular music." Buys 1-2 mss/year. Query with resume and published clips. Length: 750-2,500 words. Pays $25-100.

Fillers: Lawrence Payne, fillers editor. Clippings, gags, anecdotes and newsbreaks. Buys 5/year. Length 30-300 words. Pays $5-25.

Tips: "Previous experience in the music industry and proven background as a professional writer in related publications are very important. Send as complete a resume as possible, including samples of previously published work, and a cover letter disucssing your musical interests. Feature stories, interviews, and news-article writing are the areas where we most often use freelancers. It is important to take an authoritative and knowledgeable music industry slant when writing these articles. There is no substitute for intensive research when writing a piece for any publication. It becomes painfully obvious to the informed reader when the writer is unsure of his subject matter."

MUSIC EDUCATORS JOURNAL, 1902 Association Dr., Reston VA 22091. (703)860-4000. Editor: Rebecca Taylor. Less than 10% freelance written. For music educators in elementary and secondary schools and universities. Monthly (September-May) magazine. Circ. 56,000. Pays only for solicited articles by authors outside the music education field. Publishes ms an average of 6 months after acceptance. Byline given. "We prefer typed manuscripts, but will consider computer printouts." SASE. Reports in 6-8 weeks. Free author's guidesheet.

Nonfiction: "*MEJ* is the communications organ for the members of Music Educators National Conference. We publish articles on music education at all levels—not about individual schools, but about broad issues, trends and instructional techniques. Particularly interested in issue-oriented articles, pieces on individual aspects of American and nonWestern music, and up-beat interviews with musicians, composers and innovative teachers." No articles on personal awards or group tours. Length: 1,000-3,000 words. Query the editor.

Tips: "Our readers are experts in music education, so accuracy and complete familiarity with the subject is essential. A selection of appropriate professional quality 8x10 b&w glossy prints submitted with a manuscript greatly increases the chances of acceptance."

‡**MUSICLINE**, CCM Publications Inc., Suite 201, 25231 Paseo De Alicia, Laguna Hills CA 92653. (714)951-9106. Editor-in-Chief: John W. Styll. Editor: Thom Granger. Monthly magazine covering the gospel

music industry. "*MusicLine* is a newsmagazine for the gospel music industry. Our readers include record company executives, booking agents, artist managers, recording artists, songwriters, church music directors and fans. Our approach is similar to other music trades such as *Billboard*, *Cashbox*, etc., with information as current as possible about news and events as well as current product reviews." Estab. 1983. Circ. 5,000. Pays on publication. Byline given. Pays 5¢/word kill fee. Buys first North American serial rights. Submit seasonal/holiday material 4 months in advance. Photocopied submissions OK. Computer printout submissions acceptable. SASE. Report in 2 weeks on queries; 1 month on mss. Free sample copy and writer's guidelines.
Nonfiction: General interest (news stories); how-to (ideas for retailers); inspirational; interview/profile (with key industry people); new product; and opinion (guest editorials, book reviews, record reviews). No personality profiles or "human interest" pieces. Buys 15 mss/year. Query. Length: 300-1,200 words. Pays 8¢/word.
Columns/Departments: Reviews of current gospel albums and reviews of books related to the music industry. "Reviews (we will contact you by phone with assignments) and Bottom Line (inspiration pieces relating to gospel music—submit ms) are the areas most open to freelancers." Buys 200 mss/year. Send published clips. Length: 150-700 words. Pays 8¢/word.
Tips: "A freelancer can best break in to our publication with a specific query explaining the article and how and where the article will fit in, with a sample or proposal of ideas."

OPERA NEWS, 1865 Broadway, New York NY 10023. Editor: Robert Jacobson. 75% freelance written. For all people interested in opera; opera singers, opera management people, administrative people in opera, opera publicity people, and artists' agents; people in the trade and interested laymen. Monthly magazine (May-November); biweekly (December-April). Circ. 115,000. Buys first rights only. Pays negotiable kill fee. Byline given. Pays on publication. Query. No telephone inquiries. Computer printout submissions acceptable; prefers letter-quality to dot-matrix. SASE. Sample copy $2.50.
Nonfiction: Most articles are commissioned in advance. In summer, uses articles of various interests on opera; in the fall and winter, articles that relate to the weekly broadcasts. Emphasis is on high quality in writing and an intellectual interest in the opera-oriented public. Informational, how-to, personal experience, interview, profile, humor, historical, think pieces, and personal opinion; opera reviews. Length: 2,500 words maximum. Pays 11¢/word for features; 9¢/word for reviews.
Photos: Pays minimum of $25 for photos purchased on assignment. Captions required.

SONGS OF A SERVANT, Prime Composition, Box 20048, Jackson MS 39209. (601)922-5941. Editor: Patricia Jane Prime. Managing Editor: W. Davis Prime. 60% freelance written. Triquarterly magazine of Christian music "for musicians of small to mid-range memberships of churches. The musicians are volunteers and have a wide range of training." Circ. 5,000. Pays on acceptance. Publishes ms an average of 6 months after acceptance. Byline given. Offers $5 kill fee. Buys one-time rights. Submit seasonal/holiday material 6 months in advance. Simultaneous queries, and simultaneous and previously published submissions OK. Computer printout submissions acceptable. SASE. Reports in 3 months. Sample copy $3; writer's guidelines 30¢.
Nonfiction: General interest, historical/nostalgic, humor, inspirational, interview/profile, personal experience, photo feature and technical. "All articles should be written with the small to mid-range membership of churches in mind (volunteer leadership with no training to college degrees). Submit articles about small church choirs with successful or unique music ministries. We want articles of an entertaining nature about large church programs. Articles can be on choir organization and leadership (tied in with small churches). Send articles on choirs (large and small, Presbyterian and other denominations) and on performers. We will even consider articles of an inspirational nature. We are not interested in articles on 'how to start a bell choir on $2,000 or more,' or in other words, articles directed toward large church choir directors with unlimited budgets or pastors planning a service." Buys 6-12 mss/year. Send complete ms. Length: 500-2,000 words. Pays $20-100.
Photos: Send photos with ms. Pays $5-25 for 8x10 b&w prints. Captions, model release and identification of subjects required. Buys all rights.
Columns/Departments: Music Reviews, printed and records, for Christian performers and choirs. "The slant should be on listening or performance by a performer or small choir. Emphasis should be on how to obtain the reviewed materials." Buys 3 mss/year. Query. Length: 500-1,000 words. Pays $20-50.
Fillers: Short humor. Buys 9-12 mss/year. Length: 50-500 words. Pays $5.
Tips: "Find a small Presbyterian (or other protestant) church in your community and write about their music program. They do not have to have a spectular ministry but one where they are committed to the ministry despite the obstacles."

SYMPHONY MAGAZINE, American Symphony Orchestra League, 633 E St., NW, Washington DC 20004. (202)628-0099. Editor: Robin Perry Allen. Associate Editor: Chester Lane. 60% freelance written. Bimonthly magazine covering symphony orchestras in North America and the classical music industry for members of the association, including managers, conductors, board members, musicians, volunteer association members, music businesses, schools, libraries, etc. Circ. 14,500. Pays on publication. Publishes ms an average of 6 weeks after acceptance. Byline given. Pays negotiable kill fee. Buys all rights. Simultaneous queries, and photocopied and previously published submissions OK. Computer printout submissions acceptable; no dot-matrix. Reports in 1 month. Free sample copy.

Nonfiction: How-to (put together a symphony); interview/profile (conductors and personalities in the field); technical (budgeting, tour planning); and "thoughtful, reflective looks at the state of the classical music industry." Buys 20 mss/year. Query with clips of published work. Length: 2,500-3,000 words. Pays $50-400.

Photos: "We prefer action shots and informal shots." State availability of photos. Pays $25-50 for 8x10 glossy prints. Captions required.

UP BEAT MAGAZINE, Maher Publications, Inc., 222 W. Adams St., Chicago IL 60606. Editor: Herb Nolan. Managing Editor: Al DeGenova. Magazine published 10 times/year about the musical instrument and sound equipment industry for retailers of musical instruments and sound equipment. Circ. 11,200. Average issue includes 8 features and 3-4 columns. Pays on publication. Byline given. Buys all rights. Phone queries OK. Submit seasonal material 2½ months in advance. Simultaneous and photocopied submissions OK. SASE. Reports in 2 weeks. Sample copy $2.50.

Nonfiction: Interview, profile, how-to, new product and technical. "We want breezy how-to articles dealing with the musical instrument industry, slanted toward retailers. Articles are largely based on phone interviews with successful music industry people (retailers and manufacturers); some interpret trends in musical taste and how they affect the equipment industry. Articles should be clear and incisive, with depth and hard business advice." Buys 40 mss/year. Query with clips of previously published work. Length: 1,000-3,000 words. Pays $75-125.

Photos: Send photos with ms. Pays $15-25 for 8x10 b&w glossy prints. Buys one-time rights.

Columns/Departments: Money, Management, Clinics, Promotions, Education, and Selling. "Department articles should be based on interviews with knowlegeable music industry figures." Buys 4 mss/issue. Query with clips of previously published work. Length: 1,000-2,800 words. Pays $50-125.

Tips: "All articles should be well-researched, with quotes from successful retailers and manufacturers of musical instruments and sound equipment."

Office Environment and Equipment

GEYER'S OFFICE DEALER TOPICS, (formerly *Geyer's Dealer Topics*), 51 Madison Ave., New York NY 10010. (212)689-4411. Editor: C. Edwin Shade. 20% freelance written. For independent office equipment and stationery dealers, and special purchasers for store departments handling stationery and office equipment. Monthly. Buys all rights. Pays kill fee. Byline given. Pays on publication. Publishes ms an average of 3 months after acceptance. Computer printout submissions acceptable; prefers letter-quality to dot-matrix. Reports "immediately." SASE.

Nonfiction: Articles on dealer efforts in merchandising and sales promotion; programs of stationery and office equipment dealers. Problem-solving articles related to retailers of office supplies, social stationery items, office furniture and equipment and office machines. Must feature specified stores. Pays $125 minimum but quality of article is real determinant. Query. Length: 300-1,000 words.

Photos: B&w glossies are purchased with accompanying ms with no additional payment.

MARKING INDUSTRY MAGAZINE, Marking Devices Publishing Co., 2640 N. Halsted, Chicago IL 60614. (312)528-6600. Editor: David Hachmeister. Monthly magazine for manufacturers and dealers of marking products. Pays on acceptance. Byline given. Rights purchased vary. Simultaneous queries, and simultaneous, photocopied and previously published submissions OK. Reports in 2 weeks. Free sample copy and writer's guidelines.

Nonfiction: How-to, inspirational, interview/profile, new products and technical. "We publish a promotional quarterly for which we need cartoons, jokes and fillers. Nothing controversial." Buys 12-18 mss/year. Query with clips of published work. Length: 4,000 words maximum. Pays $25 minimum.

Photos: State availability of photos. Buys one-time rights.

Fillers: Jokes and short humor. Buys 20/year. Pays $30 minimum.

WESTERN OFFICE DEALER, 41 Sutter St., San Francisco CA 94104. Editor: Pactrick Totty. Monthly magazine; 60-70 pages. Circ. 9,000. Byline given. Buys 12 mss/year. Pays on acceptance. No photocopied or simultaneous submissions. Submit seasonal (merchandising) material 4 months in advance. Reports in 1 week. Query or submit complete ms. SASE. Sample copy $2.

Nonfiction: "Our main interest is in how Western retailers of stationery and office products can do a better selling job. We use how-to-do-it merchandising articles showing dealers how to sell more stationery and office products to more people at a greater profit. Seasonal merchandising articles always welcome, if acceptable." Informational, how-to, personal experience, interview and successful business operations. "We only want material pertaining to successful merchandising activities." Length: 1,000-1,500 words. Pays 2¢/word.

Photos: Pays $5 for b&w photos used with mss; 3x5 minimum. Captions required.

Packing, Canning, and Packaging

The journal in this category is for shippers, brokers, retailers and others concerned with methods of growing foods in general. Other publications that buy similar material are found under the Food Products, Processing and Service heading.

THE PACKER, Box 2939, Shawnee Mission KS 66201. (913)381-6310. Editor: Paul Campbell. 10% freelance written. For shippers, fruit and vegetable growers, wholesalers, brokers and retailers. Newspaper; 36 pages. Weekly. Circ. 16,000. Buys all rights. Buys about 10 mss/year. Pays on publication. Will send free sample copy to writer on request. Write for copy of guidelines for writers. Will consider simultaneous submissions. Reports in 2 weeks. Returns rejected material in 1 month. Query or submit complete ms. SASE.
Nonfiction: Articles on growing techniques, merchandising, marketing, transportation and refrigeration. Emphasis is on the "what's new" approach in these areas. Length: 1,000 words. Pays $40 minimum.
Tips: "It's important to be a good photographer, too. Have features on new growing, merchandising or shipping techniques."

Paint

AMERICAN PAINTING CONTRACTOR, American Paint Journal Co., 2911 Washington Ave., St. Louis MO 63103. (314)534-0301. Editor: Rick Hirsch. For painting and decorating contractors, in-plant maintenance painting department heads, architects and paint specifiers. Monthly magazine; 80 pages. Circ. 13,000. Buys all rights. Phone queries OK. Submit seasonal/holiday material 2 months in advance. Simultaneous and photocopied submissions OK. SASE. Reports in 3 weeks. Free sample copy.
Nonfiction: Historical, how-to, humor, informational, new product, personal experience, opinion and technical articles, interviews, photo features and profiles. Buys 10-15 unsolicited mss/year. "Freelancers should be able to write well and have some understanding of the painting and decorating industry. We do not want general theme articles such as 'How to Get More Work Out of Your Employee' unless they relate to a problem within the painting and decorating industry." Length: 1,000-2,500 words. Pays $150-225.
Photos: B&w and color purchased with mss or on assignment. Captions required. Send contact sheets, prints or transparencies.

DECORATIVE PRODUCTS WORLD, American Paint Journal Co., 2911 Washington, St. Louis MO 63103. (314)534-0301. Editor: Rick Hirsch. Bimonthly magazine about decorating outlets for retailers of paint, wallpaper and related items. Circ. 33,000. Pays on publication. Byline given. Submit seasonal material 3 months in advance. Reports in 1 month. Free sample copy and writer's guidelines.
Nonfiction: Profile (of stores). "Find stories that will give useful information for our readers. We are basically a service to our readers and our articles reflect that." Buys 1-2 mss/issue. Length: varies. Query. Pays $150.
Photos: "Photos must accompany a story in order to be published." State availability of photos. Pays $10 maximum for b&w prints. Pays $25 maximum for color transparencies. Captions required. Buys one-time rights.
Fillers: Short humor. Buys 3 mss/issue. Pays $4 maximum.

Paper

Writers for these publications know that *pulp* is more than magazine jargon.

FORET ET PAPIER, 1001 de Maisonneuve W., Montreal, Quebec H3A 3E1 Canada. (514)845-5141. Editor: Paul Saint-Pierre, C. Adm. For engineers and technicians engaged in the making of paper. Bimonthly magazine; 50 pages. Circ. 7,000. Rights purchased vary with author and material. Buys first North American serial rights, second (reprint) rights, and simultaneous rights. Buys about 12 mss/year. Pays on acceptance. Will consider photocopied submissions. Reports on mss accepted for publication in 1 week. Returns rejected material in 2 days. SASE. Free sample copy.

Nonfiction: Uses technical articles on papermaking. Buys informational, how-to, personal experience, interview, photo and technical. Length: 1,000 words maximum. Pays $25-150.

Photos: Photos purchased with accompanying ms with extra payment or purchased on assignment. Captions required. Pays $25 for b&w. Color shots must be vertical. Pays $150 maximum for color cover shots.

PAPERBOARD PACKAGING, 7500 Old Oak Blvd., Cleveland OH 44130. (216)243-8100. Editor: Mark Arzoumanian. 15% freelance written. 15% freelance written. For "managers, supervisors, and technical personnel who operate corrugated box manufacturing, folding cartons converting and rigid box companies and plants." Monthly. Circ. 15,000. Buys all rights. Pays on publication. Publishes ms an average of 3 months after acceptance. Will consider photocopied submissions. Submit seasonal material 3 months in advance. Query. Computer printout submissions acceptable; no dot-matrix. SASE. Will send a sample copy to a writer on request.

Nonfiction: "Application articles, installation stories, etc. Contact the editor first to establish the approach desired for the article. Especially interested in packaging systems using composite materials, including paper and other materials." Buys technical articles. Length: open. Pays "$75/printed page (about 1,000 words to a page), including photos. We do not pay for commercially oriented material. We do pay for material if it is not designed to generate business for someone in our field.

Photos: "Will not pay photography costs, but will pay cost of photo reproductions for article."

Tips: "Freelance writers should be aware that the 'jack of all trades" (in the writing sense) is out the window. The need to specialize is paramount today."

PULP & PAPER CANADA, Southam Communications, Ltd., Suite 201, 310 Victoria Ave., Montreal, Quebec H3Z 2M9 Canada. (514)487-2302. Editor: Peter N. Williamson. Managing Editor: Graeme Rodden. 5% freelance written. Monthly magazine. Circ. 8,266. Pays on publication. Publishes ms an average of 6 months after acceptance. Byline given. Offers kill fee according to prior agreement. Buys first North American serial rights. Submit seasonal/holiday material 2 months in advance. SASE. Reports in 2 weeks on queries; 3 weeks on mss. Sample copy $3 (Canada), $5 (other countries); free writer's guidelines.

Nonfiction: How-to (related to processes and procedures in the industry); interview/profile (of Canadian leaders in pulp and paper industry); and technical (relevant to modern pulp and/or paper industry). No fillers; short industry news items; product news items. Buys 10 mss/year. Query with or without clips of published work or send complete ms. Articles with photographs (b&w glossy) or other good quality illustrations will get priority review. Length: 1,500-2,000 words (with photos). Pays $130 (Canadian funds)/published page, including photos, graphics, charts, etc.

Pets

Listed here are publications for professionals in the pet industry, wholesalers, manufacturers, suppliers, retailers, owners of pet specialty stores, pet groomers, aquarium retailers, distributors, and those interested in the fish industry. Publications for pet owners are listed in the Animal section of Consumer Publications.

PET AGE, The Largest Circulation Pet Industry Trade Publication, H.H. Backer Associates, Inc., 207 S. Wabash Ave., Chicago IL 60604. (312)663-4040. Editor: Raymond Gudas. Monthly magazine about the pet industry for pet retailers and industry. Circ. 16,000. Pays on acceptance. Byline given. Buys all rights. Submit seasonal material 6 months in advance. Computer printout submissions acceptable; prefers letter-quality to dot-matrix. SASE. Reports in 6 weeks. Sample copy $2.50; free writer's guidelines.

Nonfiction: Profile (of a successful, well-run pet retail operation); how-to; interview; photo feature and technical—all trade-related. Query first with published clips. Buys 12 mss/year. "Query as to the name and location of a pet operation you wish to profile and why the operation is successful and why it would make a good feature. No general retailing articles or consumer-oriented pet articles." Length: 1,500-2,500 words. Pays $75-150.

Photos: State availability of photos. Reviews 5x7 b&w glossy prints, contact sheets and color transparencies. Offers no additional payment for photos accepted with ms. Captions and identification of subjects required. Buys all rights.

Columns/Departments: Fish Care, Retailing, Government Action, Tax & Finance, Bird Care, New Products and Industry News. Query with published clips. Length: 1,000-1,500 words. Pays $50-100.

Tips: "We are interested in profiling successful or otherwise imaginative and/or unique retailing operations. Focus should be on the aspects that make the business successful: history/background of business and owners;

description of service/products, sales and marketing strategies, advertising and promotional activities, etc. You must be able to provide 10-12 good b&w photos.''

PET BUSINESS, Pet Business, Inc., 7330 NW 66th, Miami FL 33166. Publisher: Robert L. Behme. 20% freelance written. For the complete pet industry—retailers, groomers, breeders, manufacturers, wholesalers and importers. Monthly magazine; 48 pages. Circ. 14,500. Pays on acceptance. Buys first rights only. Publishes ms an average of 4 months after acceptance. Not copyrighted. Previously published submissions acceptable. Computer printout submission acceptable "as long as it is readable, easy to edit and well written. But there are exceptions—we hate dot-matrix." SASE. Reports in 3 weeks. Sample copy $1; free writer's guidelines.
Nonfiction: General interest (to retailers—what a store is doing, etc.); historical (when there is a reason—death, sale, etc.); how-to (sell more, retailer ideas); interview (with successful stores and manufacturers); opinion (with background); photo feature (on occasion); and news of stores. Buys 15-30 mss/year. "We will consider anything if queried first." Length: 600-1,500 words. Pays $35-250.
Photos: State availability of photos. Pays $10 for 5x7 or larger b&w prints; and $30 for any size color prints. Captions required.
Columns/Departments: "We're interested in ideas that relate to retailing, e.g., dogs, cats, small animals—but it must be on a retail, not hobby, level." Open to suggestions for new columns/departments. Query. Pays $100.
Tips: "We are looking at international editions."

THE PET DEALER, Howmark Publishing Corp., 567 Morris Ave., Elizabeth NJ 07208. (201)353-7373. Editorial Director: Alan Richman. 15% freelance written. Emphasizes merchandising, marketing and management for owners and managers of pet specialty stores, departments, and pet groomers and their suppliers. Monthly magazine; 80 pages. Circ. 11,000. Byline given. Pays on publication. Publication "may be many months between acceptance of a manuscript and publication." Phone queries OK. Submit seasonal/holiday material 3 months in advance. Computer printout submissions acceptable; no dot-matrix. SASE. Reports in 1 week. Free sample copy and writer's guidelines.
Nonfiction: How-to (store operations, administration, merchandising, marketing, management, promotion and purchasing). Consumer pet articles—lost pets, best pets, humane themes—*not* welcome. Emphasis is on *trade* merchandising and marketing of pets and supplies. Buys 8 unsolicited mss/year. Recent article example: "Playful Puppies Are Star Attractions At California Petland" (March 1984). Length: 800-1,200 words. Pays $50-100.
Photos: Submit photo material with ms. No additional payment for 5x7 b&w glossy prints. "Six photos with captions required." Buys one-time rights.
Tips: "We're interested in store profiles outside the New York, New Jersey, Connecticut and Pennsylvania metro areas. Photos are of key importance. Articles focus on new techniques in merchandising or promotion. Submit query letter first, with writing background summarized; include samples. We seek one-to-one, interview-type features on retail pet store merchandising. Indicate the availability of the proposed article, your willingness to submit on exclusive or first-in-field basis, and whether you are patient enough to await payment on publication."

PETS/SUPPLIES/MARKETING, Harcourt Brace Jovanovich Publications, 1 E. 1st St., Duluth MN 55802. (218)727-8511. Editor: David Kowalski. For independent pet retailers, chain franchisers, livestock and pet supply wholesalers, and manufacturers of pet products. Monthly magazine. Circ. 14,200. Pays on publication. Buys first rights only. Phone queries OK. Submit seasonal/holiday material 4 months in advance. Photocopied submissions OK. SASE. Reports in 2 months. Free writer's guidelines. Sample copy $5.
Nonfiction: How-to (merchandise pet products, display, set up window displays, market pet product line); interviews (with pet store retailers); opinion (of pet industry members or problems facing the industry); photo features (of successful pet stores or effective merchandising techniques and in-store displays); profiles (of successful retail outlets engaged in the pet trade); and technical articles (on more effective pet retailing, e.g., building a central filtration unit, constructing custom aquariums or display areas). Business management articles must deal specifically with pet shops and their own unique merchandise and problems. Length: 1,000-2,000 words. Buys 1-2 mss/issue. Query. Pays 10¢/word.
Photos: Purchased with or without mss or on assignment. "We prefer 5x7 or 8x10 b&w glossies. But we will accept contact sheets and standard print sizes. For color, we prefer 35mm kodachrome transparencies or 2¼x2¼." Pays $10 for b&w; $25 for color. Captions and model release required.
Columns/Departments: Suggestions for new columns or departments should be addressed to the editor. No clippings, please.
Tips: "We want articles which stress professional retailing, provide insight into successful shops, and generally capture the excitement of an exciting and sometimes controversial industry. All submissions are read. However, an initial query could save time and energy and ensure a publishable article."

Photography

AMERICAN PREMIERE, Penthouse Suite, 8421 Wilshire Blvd., Beverly Hills CA 90211. Editor: Susan Royal. 80% freelance written. Quarterly trade magazine "for and about persons in the film industry—executives, producers, directors, actors, and all others associated." Circ. 25,000. Pays on publication. Byline given. Pays negotiable kill fee. Buys first North American serial rights. Submit seasonal/holiday material 2 months in advance. Sample copy $4 (address request to "Circulation"); writer's guidelines for business-size SAE and 1 first class stamp.
Nonfiction: Investigative; historical; how-to (incorporate yourself, read a contract, etc.); humor (satire); interview/profile (directors, producers, businesses, top persons in the industry); and other themes associated with the film industry. "Only business-oriented articles." No fan material or gossip. Buys 7-20 unsolicited mss/year. Query with "limited samples" of published work and resume. Length: 1,200-3,000 words. Pays $50-150.
Tips: "Writers should be well versed on the workings of the film industry. We're interested in people who can pen statistical, but not boring, articles."

ON LOCATION MAGAZINE, On Location Publishing, Inc., Suite 501, 6777 Hollywood Blvd., Hollywood CA 90028. (213)467-1268. Editor-in-Chief: Steven Bernard. 30% freelance written. Monthly trade magazine covering film, videotape production and music video production; for producers, directors, production managers, cinematographers and sound, lighting, motion picture and video equipment suppliers. Circ. 23,300. Pays on publication. Byline given. Buys all rights. Submit specialized and related material 4 months in advance. Simultaneous queries and photocopied submissions OK. Computer printout submissions acceptable. SASE. Reports in 3 weeks. Publishes ms an average of 2 months after acceptance. Free sample copy; editorial forecasts and writer's guidelines, send $4 in first class stamps to cover postage & shipping/handling.
Nonfiction: Location/production/equipment related editorial; how-to (use innovations and unusual techniques); and technical (semi technical articles, naming equipment brand names). No interviews with performers. Buys 10-12 mss/year. Query with clips of published work to managing editor. Length 3-5, 6-10, 10-14 typewritten, double-spaced 8½x11 pages.
Photos: If production related, writer must contact unit publicist for photo material.
Fillers: Columns and sidebars OK if facility related or unique "hands-on" personalities. "Must be right on target. Writer must know cinematography well and video also." Buys 5/year. Length: 3-5 pages, double-spaced, 8½x11. Pays $50-75.
Tips: "Query should include a strong hook and convince us that the filming location, production, facility, equipment, etc., is unique. We like to have a feeling that the writer has first hand communication, if possible, or the best re-creation thereof relating to editorial material regarding film and/or location production. The same applies to video production, music video, special effects and commercial shoots. Talk with a director, cinematographer and set designer to find out how they solved problems down to the finest details. We use many regional correspondents. Our most successful editorial develops with the direction or thrust toward the 'hands-on' person."

PHOTO LAB MANAGEMENT, PLM Publishing, Inc., 1312 Lincoln Blvd., Santa Monica CA 90406. (213)451-1344. Editor: Carolyn Ryan. Associate Editor: Patrice Apodaca. Bimonthly magazine covering process chemistries, process control, process equipment and marketing/administration for photo lab owners, managers and management personnel. Circ. 8,600. Pays on publication. Byline and brief bio given. Buys first North American serial rights. Submit seasonal/holiday material 6 months in advance. SASE. Reports on queries in 6 weeks. Free sample copy and writer's guidelines for business-size SAE and 1 first class stamp.
Nonfiction: Interview/profile (lab or lab managers); personal experience (lab manager); technical; and management or administration. Buys 12-15 mss/year. Query with brief biography. Length: 1,200-1,800 words. Pays $48/published page.
Photos: Reviews 35mm color transparencies and 4-color prints suitable for cover. "We're looking for outstanding cover shots of things to do with photo finishing."
Tips: "Send a query if you have some background in the industry or a willingness to dig out information and research for a top quality article that really speaks to our audience."

PHOTO WEEKLY, Billboard Publications, Inc., 1515 Broadway, New York NY 10036. (212)764-7415. Editor: Willard Clark. Weekly photography tabloid featuring industry news for photographic retailers and photofinishers. Circ. 15,000. Pays on acceptance. Byline given. Buys one-time rights.

PHOTOFLASH, Models & Photographers Newsletter, Box 7946, Colorado Springs CO 80933. Managing Editor: Ron Marshall. 20% freelance written. Quarterly newsletter of photographic modeling and glamour photography "for models, photographers, publishers, picture editors, modeling agents, advertising agencies, and others involved in the interrelated fields of modeling and photography." Pays on publication. Byline given. Buys one-time rights and second (reprint) rights to material originally published elsewhere. Submit seasonal/holiday material 6 months in advance. Simultaneous queries, and simultaneous, photocopied and previously published submissions OK. Computer printout submissions acceptable. SASE. Reports in 3 months on queries; 4 months on mss. Publishes ms an average of 3 months after acceptance. Sample copy $5.

Nonfiction: Interview/profile (of established and rising professionals in the field, especially models); photo feature; and technical (illustrating/explaining photographic and modeling "tricks"). Send complete ms. "We prefer photo illustrated text packages."

Photos: Send photos with ms. "Payment is for the complete photo-text package; it includes a credit line, contributor copies and up to $15-25 depending on quality, completeness, etc. of the submissions." Reviews 8x10 b&w prints. Captions and model release required.

PHOTOGRAPHER'S MARKET NEWSLETTER, F&W Publications, Inc., 9933 Alliance Rd., Cincinnati OH 45242. (513)984-0717. Editor: Robert D. Lutz. 25% freelance written. Monthly newsletter on freelance photography covering "markets and marketing techniques and strategies for amateur and professional photographers who want to begin selling or sell more of their work." Pays on publication. Publishes ms an average of 6 months after acceptance. Byline given. Buys one-time rights. Simultaneous and previously published submissions acceptable. Computer printout submissions acceptable. SASE. Reports in 2 weeks on queries; 1 month on mss. Sample copy $3.50.

Nonfiction: How-to (sell photos); interview/profile (photography professionals); personal experience (in photo to marketing); photo feature (previously published work); and technical (must relate to selling). No purely technical material on cameras, film and equipment. Buys 12 mss/year. Query. Length: 1,500-2,000 words plus photos. Pays $75-125.

Photos: State availability of photos. Reviews 8x10 b&w prints; payment included with purchase price. Captions required.

Tips: "We're especially interested in hearing from photographer/writers who employ computers in their freelance business. Query with article ideas based on your personal experience in photography-related computer applications."

PHOTOMETHODS, Ziff-Davis Publishing Co., 1 Park Ave., New York NY 10016. (212)725-3942. Editorial Director: Fred Schmidt. 85% freelance written. For professional and in-plant image makers (still, film, video, AV) and visual communications managers. Monthly magazine; 80-96 pages. Circ. 50,000. Pays on publication. Publishes ms an average of 6 weeks after acceptance. Buys first rights only. Pays 100% kill fee. Byline given. Phone queries OK. Computer printout submissions acceptable "as long as pages are ripped and collated." SASE. Reports in 6 weeks. Free sample copy and writer's guidelines.

Nonfiction: How-to and photo features (solve problems with image-making techniques: photography, etc.); technical management; informational (to help the reader use photography, cine and video); interviews (with working pros); personal experience (in solving problems with photography, cine and video); profiles (well-known personalities in imaging); and technical (on photography, cine and video). No material written for the amateur photographer. Buys 5 mss/issue. Length: 1,500-3,000 words. Pays $75 minimum.

Photos: Steven Karl Weininger, art director. B&w photos (5x7 up matte or dried glossy) and color (35mm transparencies minimum or 8x10 print) purchased with or without mss, or on assignment. Captions required. Query or submit contact sheet. Pays $35 for b&w; $50 for color; more for covers. Model release required.

Tips: "You can get my attention by knowing who we are and what we publish. Anything sent must be professionally packaged: neatly typed, well organized; and have patience. Don't come across as a writer we cannot live without. Don't contact us unless you know the magazine and the type of articles we publish. No unsolicited mss. Please query first."

THE RANGEFINDER, 1312 Lincoln Blvd., Santa Monica CA 90406. (213)451-8506. Editor: Patrice Apodaca. Associate Editor: Carolyn Ryan. Emphasizes professional photography. Monthly magazine; 100 pages. Circ. 48,500. Pays on publication. Buys first North American serial rights. Phone queries OK. Submit seasonal material 4 months in advance. Byline given. SASE. Reports in 6 weeks. Sample copy $2.50; free writer's guidelines.

Nonfiction: How-to (solve a photographic problem; such as new techniques in lighting, new poses or set-ups); interview; and technical. "Articles should contain practical, solid information. Issues should be covered in depth. Look thoroughly into the topic." No opinion, experience or biographical articles. Buys 5 mss/issue. Query with outline. Length: 800-1,200 words. Pays $60/published page.

Photos: State availability of photos with query. Captions preferred. Buys one-time rights. Model release required.

Tips: "Exhibit some knowledge of photography. Introduce yourself with a well-written letter and a great story idea."

‡**STUDIO PHOTOGRAPHY**, PTN Publishing Corp., 101 Crossways/Park West, Woodbury NY 11797. (516)496-8000. Editor: Louis P. Desiderio. 65% freelance written. Monthly magazine. Circ. 65,000. Pays on publication. Not copyrighted. Buys first rights only. Submit seasonal/holiday material 5 months in advance. SASE. Reports in 6 weeks. Publishes ms an average of 6 months after acceptance.

Nonfiction: Interview, personal experience, photo feature, communication-oriented, technical and travel. No business-oriented articles. Buys 2-3 mss/issue. Length: 1,700-3,000 words. Pays $75 minimum/published page.

Photos: State availability of photos with query. Photos and article in one package.

Columns/Departments: Point of View (any aspect of photography dealing with professionals only). Buys 1 ms/issue. Length: 1,700 words minimum. Pays $35 minimum.

Tips: "No handwritten queries will even be looked at. We look for professional quality in writing. No originals, only fine quality duplicates. Prefer layer format, though not essential. Submit b&w photos with all articles. Only people with definite ideas and a sense of who they are need apply for publication."

TECHNICAL PHOTOGRAPHY, PTN Publishing Corp., 101 Crossways Park West, Woodbury NY 11797. Editor-in-Chief: Don Garbera. 50% freelance written. Publication of the "on-staff (in-house) industrial, military and government still, cinema, video and AV professional who must produce (or know where to get) visuals of all kinds." Monthly magazine; 64 pages. Circ. 60,000. Pays on publication. Publishes ms an average of 2 months after acceptance. Buys first North American serial rights. Byline given "except when it needs complete rewrite or when supplied through public relations agency." Computer printout submissions acceptable. SASE. Reports in 1 month. Free sample copy.

Nonfiction: How-to; interview; photo feature; profile (detailed stories about in-house operations); and technical. "All manuscripts must relate to industrial, military or government production of visuals." Buys 75-110 mss/year. Query. Length: "as long as needed to get the information across." Pays $50-350 minimum/display page.

Photos: Offers no additional payment for photos purchased with ms. Captions required. Query.

Plumbing, Heating, Air Conditioning, and Refrigeration

Plumbers and repairmen—and how they can do a better job—get center-stage treatment in these publications. Publications for fuel oil dealers who also install heating equipment are classified with the Energy journals.

CONTRACTOR MAGAZINE, 1301 S. Grove Ave., Barrington FL 60010. Editor: John A. Schweizer. 15% freelance written. For mechanical contractors and wholesalers. Newspaper; 50 (11x15) pages. Twice monthly. Circ. 46,100. Buys 8 mss/year. Pays on publication. Buys first rights. Publishes ms an average of 2 months after acceptance. Photocopied submissions OK. No simultaneous submissions. Computer printout submissions acceptable. Reports in 1 month. Query first or submit complete ms. SASE. Sample copy for $3.

Nonfiction: Articles on materials, use, policies, and business methods of the air conditioning, heating, plumbing, piping, solar, energy management, contracting industry. Topics covered include interpretive reports, how-to, informational, interview, profile, think articles, expose, spot news, successful business operations, merchandising techniques and labor. Pays $300 maximum.

Photos: 5x7 b&w glossies purchased with or without ms. Pays $10. Captions required.

‡**DISTRIBUTOR, The Voice of Wholesaling**, Technical Reporting Corp., Box 479, Wheeling IL 60090. (312)537-6460. Editorial Director: Ed Schwenn. Managing Editor: Keith Kramer. Bimonthly magazine on heating, ventilating, air conditioning and refrigeration. Editorial material shows "executive wholesalers how they can run better businesses and cope with personal and business problems." Estab. 1983. Circ. 10,000. Pays on publication. Byline given. Buys one-time rights. Submit seasonal/holiday material 3 months in advance. "We want material exclusive to the field (industry)." Photocopied submissions OK. Computer printout submissions acceptable; prefers letter-quality to dot-matrix. SASE. Reports in 2 weeks. Sample copy $4; free writer's guidelines with purchased copy of magazine.

Nonfiction: How-to (run a better business, cope with problems); and interview/profile (the wholesalers). No flippant or general approaches. Buys 6 mss/year. Query with or without published clips or send complete ms. Length: 1,000-3,000 words. Pays $100-250.

Photos: State availability of photos or send photos with query or ms. Pays $10-25 for color contact sheets; $15-

30 for 35mm color transparencies; and $15-30 for 5x7 color prints. Captions and identification of subjects required.
Tips: "Know the industry—come up with a different angle on an industry subject (one we haven't dealt with in a long time). Wholesale ideas, profiles and interviews are most open to freelancers."

DOMESTIC ENGINEERING MAGAZINE, Construction Industry Press, 135 Addison Ave., Elmhurst IL 60126. Editor: Stephen J. Shafer. Managing Editor: David J. Hanks. Emphasizes plumbing, heating, air conditioning and piping for contractors, and for mechanical contractors in these specialties. Gives information on management, marketing and merchandising. Monthly magazine; 100 pages. Circ. 40,000. Pays on acceptance. Buys all rights, simultaneous rights, or first rights. Simultaneous, photocopied and previously published submissions OK. SASE. Reports in 1 month. Sample copy $4.
Nonfiction: How-to (some technical in industry areas). Expose, interview, profile, personal experience, photo feature and technical articles are written on assignment only and should be about management, marketing and merchandising for plumbing and mechanical contracting businesssmen. Buys 12 mss/year. Query. Pays $25 minimum.
Photos: State availability of photos. Pays $10 minimum for b&w prints (reviews contact sheets) and color transparencies.

‡**EXPORT**, 386 Park Ave. S., New York NY 10016. Editor: R. Weingarten. For importers and distributors in 167 countries who handle hardware, air conditioning and refrigeration equipment and related consumer hardlines. Bimonthly magazine; 60-80 pages in English and Spanish editions. Circ. 38,500. Buys first rights and second (reprint) rights to material originally published elsewhere. Byline given. Buys about 10 mss/year. Pays on acceptance. Publishes ms an average of 5 months after acceptance. Reports in 1 month. Query. SASE.
Nonfiction: News stories of products and merchandising of air conditioning and refrigeration equipment, hardware and related consumer hardlines. Informational, how-to, interview, profile and successful business operations. Length: 1,000-3,000 words. Pays $300 maximum.
Tips: "One of the best ways to break in here is with a story originating outside the US or Canada. Our major interest is in new products and new developments—but they must be available and valuable to overseas buyers. We also like company profile stories. Departments and news stories are staff-written."

FLORIDA FORUM, FRSA Services Corp., Drawer 4850, Winter Park FL 32793. (305)671-3772. Editor: Gerald Dykhuisen. 10% freelance written. Monthly magazine covering the roofing, sheet metal and air conditioning industries. Circ. 8,300. Pays on publication. Publishes ms an average of 2 months after acceptance. Byline given. Buys one-time rights. Submit seasonal/holiday material 2 months in advance. Simultaneous queries, and simultaneous, photocopied and previously published submissions OK. Electronic submissions OK "if compatible with Hewlett Packard 3000." Computer printout submissions acceptable. Reports in 2 weeks. Free sample copy.
Nonfiction: General interest, historical/nostalgic, humor, interview/profile, new product, opinion, personal experience and technical. Buys 25 mss/year. Send complete ms. Length: open. Pays variable rates.
Photos: Send photos with ms. Pays variable rates for b&w prints.
Columns/Departments: Buys 12 mss/year. Send complete ms. Length: open. Pays variable rates.

HEATING, PLUMBING, AIR CONDITIONING, 1450 Don Mills Rd., Don Mills, Ontario M3B 2X7 Canada. (416)445-6641. Editor: Ronald H. Shuker. For mechanical contractors; plumbers; warm air heating, refrigeration, ventilation, air conditioning and insulation contractors; wholesalers; architects; consulting and mechanical engineers who are in key management or specifying positions in the plumbing, heating, air conditioning and refrigeration industries in Canada. Monthly. Circ. 14,500. Pays on publication. Reports in 2 months. For a prompt reply, "enclose a sheet on which is typed a statement either approving or rejecting the suggested article which can either be checked off, or a quick answer written in and signed and returned." Free sample copy.
Nonfiction: News, technical, business management and "how-to" articles that will inform, educate and motivate readers who design, manufacture, install, sell, service, maintain or supply all mechanical components and systems in residential, commercial, institutional and industrial installations across Canada. Length: 1,000-1,500 words. Pays 10-20¢/word.
Photos: Photos purchased with mss. Prefers 5x7 or 8x10 glossies.
Tips: "Topics must relate directly to the day-to-day activities of *HPAC* readers in Canada. Must be detailed, with specific examples, quotes from specific people or authorities—show depth. We specifically want material from other parts of Canada besides southern Ontario. Not really interested in material from US unless specifically related to Canadian readers' concerns. We primarily want articles that show *HPAC* readers how they can increase their sales and business step-by-step based on specific examples of what others have done."

SNIPS MAGAZINE, 407 Mannheim Rd., Bellwood IL 60104. (312)544-3870. Editor: Nick Carter. 2% freelance written. For sheet metal, warm air heating, ventilating, air conditioning and roofing contractors.

Monthly. Buys all rights. "Write for detailed list of requirements before submitting any work." Publishes ms an average of 3 months after acceptance. SASE.

Nonfiction: Material should deal with information about contractors who do sheet metal, warm air heating, air conditioning, ventilation and roofing work; also about successful advertising campaigns conducted by these contractors and the results. Length: "prefers stories to run less than 1,000 words unless on special assignment." Pays 2¢ each for first 500 words, 1¢ each for additional word.

Photos: Pays $2 each for small snapshot pictures, $4 each for usable 8x10 pictures.

‡**WOOD 'N ENERGY**, Energy Publications Inc., Box 2008, Laconia NH 03261. (603)528-4285. Editor: Ken Daggett. Associate Editor: Steve Maviglio. Monthly magazine covering wood, coal and solar heating (residential). "*Wood 'n Energy* is mailed to retailers, distributors and manufacturers of wood, coal and solar heating equipment in the US and Canada. A majority of our readers are small businessmen who need help in running their businesses and want to learn secrets to prospering in a field that has seen better days when oil embargoes were daily happenings." Circ. 32,000. Pays on publication. Publishes ms an average of 2 months after acceptance. Byline given. Buys one-time rights and all rights. Submit seasonal/holiday material 4 months in advance. Simultaneous queries OK. Electronic submissions OK if compatible with TRS-80, Model III or IV. Computer printout submissions acceptable. SASE. Reports in 2 weeks. Sample copy $2.50.

Nonfiction: Interview/profile (of stove dealers, manufacturers, others); photo feature (of energy stores); and technical (nuts and bolts of stove design and operation). Special issue includes Buyers Guide/Retailers Handbook (annual issue with retail marketing articles, 'how to run your business,' accounting. "The best times of year for freelancers are in our fall issue (our largest) and also in February and March." No "how wonderful renewable energy is" and experiences with stoves. "This is a *trade* book." Buys 25 mss/year. Query with or without published clip or send complete ms. Pays $25-300.

Photos: State availability of photos or send photos with query or ms. Pays $35 minimum for b&w contact sheets; $125 maximum for color contact sheets. Identification of subjects required. Buys one-time rights.

Columns/Departments: Reports (energy news; potpourri of current incentives, happenings); Regulations (safety and standard news); and Retailers Corner (tips on running a retail shop). "We are also looking for freelancers who could serve in our 'network' around the country. If there's a law passed regulating wood-stove emissions in their town, for example, they could sent us a clip and/or rewrite the story. These pay $50 or so, depending on the clip. Contact editor on a individual basis (over the phone is OK) for a green light." Query with or without published clips. Length: 150-500 words. Pays $35-150.

Tips: "Short, hot articles on retailers (500 words and photographs) are desparately needed. We're looking for serious business articles. Freelancers who know the ins and outs of running a business have an excellent shot at being published."

‡**WOODHEAT '85: The Woodstove Directory**, Energy Publications Inc., Box 2008, Laconia NH 03247. (603)528-4285. Editor: Ken Daggett. An annual buyer's guide and sourcebook on wood heat, published in August. Circ. 125,000. Pays on variable schedule. Byline given. Offers variable kill fee. Buys variable rights. Simultaneous queries and submissions OK. SASE. Reports in 1 month.

Nonfiction: How-to (installation, etc.); interview/profile (of those in the field, retailers, consumers); new product (new wood energy products); photo feature (of stove installations and/or energy efficient homes); and technical (details on buying and installing). No personal experiences with wood stoves. Buys 5-8 mss/year. Query. Length: 100-2,550 words. Pays $50-500.

Photos: State availability of photos with query or ms. Uses all types. Pays $35-250. Captions, model release and identification of subjects required. Buys variable rights.

Columns/Departments: Reports (potpourri of energy news, wood heat news). Buys 0-10 mss/year. Query. Length: 150-400 words. Pays $35-100.

Tips: "Articles in the magazine must appeal to both current owners and buyers. Personality is a plus in any article; we'd like features on someone who has invented a better burning stove or someone who is handcrafting masonry fireplaces, for example. Article ideas are formulated by mid-March, so query letters should be on hand at that time. Be specific with story ideas. Shorter articles on a wide range of energy issues—in a section called Reports—can be accepted until May. These must be accompanied by a photo. Writing should be spicy, interesting and short. All areas are open to freelancers. We find that freelancers score better with articles with local slants. With 14 million households having wood stoves, there are bound to be many stories to tell."

Printing

"The influence of computer-aided design has changed our type of story, interest and readership," says one design/drafting/reprographics magazine editor. This and other trends will affect publications in this section. These magazines are geared for printers and publishers in various types of plants.

‡**AMERICAN INK MAKER**, 101 W. 31st St., New York NY 10001. (212)279-4455. Editor-in-Chief: Francine Del Vescovo. 10% freelance written. Monthly magazine; 70 pages. Circ. 4,000. Pays on publication. Buys one-time rights. Phone queries OK. Photocopied submissions OK. SASE. Reports in 2 weeks. Free sample copy.
Nonfiction: General interest, historical, humor, interview, new product, personal experience, opinion, profile and technical. Buys 4 mss/year. Submit complete ms. Length: 800-1,500 words. Pays $135-150.
Photos: No additional payment for photos with accompanying ms. Captions preferred. Buys all rights.

AMERICAN PRINTER, 300 W. Adams St., Chicago IL 60606. Editor: Elizabeth G. Berglund. 45% freelance written. For qualified personnel active in any phase of the graphic arts industry. Monthly. Circ. 88,000. Buys all rights, unless otherwise specified in writing at time of purchase. Byline given. Pays on publication. Submit seasonal material 2 months in advance. "Study publication before writing." SASE. Free sample copy.
Nonfiction: Management and technical subjects with illustrations pertinent to the graphic arts industry. Query. Length: 1,500-3,000 words. Pays $200-650.
Photos: Purchased with mss; also news shots of graphic arts occurrences. Uses 5x7 or 8x10 glossy prints. Pays $25-40.
Fillers: Clippings about product installations, plant openings, acquisitions and purchases, and business reorganization. Particularly interested in items on newspapers; not interested in personnel announcements. Pays $5-15.

‡**THE ENGRAVERS JOURNAL**, The Engravers Journal, Inc., 26 Summit St., Box 318, Brighton MI 48116. (313)229-5725. Managing Editor: Michael J. Davis. A bimonthly magazine covering engraving, marking, awards, jewelry, and signage industry. "We provide industry and/or small business related information for the education and advancement of our readers' trade/business." Pays on acceptance. Byline given "only if writer is recognized authority." Buys all rights (usually). Submit seasonal/holiday material 4-6 months in advance. Photocopied and previously published submissions OK. Computer printout submissions acceptable; prefers letter-quality to dot-matrix. SASE. Reports in 2 weeks. Free sample copy and writer's guidelines.
Nonfiction: General interest (industry related); how-to (e.g., small business subjects, increase sales, develop new markets, use new techniques, etc.); inspirational; interview/profile; new product; photo feature (e.g., a particularly outstanding signage system); and technical. No general overviews of the industry. Buys 12 mss/year. Query with published clips or send complete ms. Length: 1,000-5,000 words. Pays $50-300.
Photos: Send photos with query or ms. Reviews 8x10 prints. Pays variable rate. Captions, model release and identification of subjects required. Buys variable rights.
Tips: "Articles aimed at the small business person offering practical and useful information are most open to freelancers. Steer away from the 'textbook' writing approach."

‡**GRAPHIC ARTS MONTHLY**, Technical Publishing Co., 875 Third Ave., New York NY 10022. (212)605-9574. Editor: Roger Ynostroza. Managing Editor: Peter Johnston. A monthly magazine covering the printing industry. Circ. 80,000. Pays on publication. Byline given. Buys all rights. Submit seasonal/holiday material 3 months in advance. Simultaneous queries OK. Computer printout submissions acceptable. SASE. Reports in 1 month. Free sample copy and writer's guidelines.
Nonfiction: New product, photo feature and technical. Buys 15 mss/year. Query. Pays 10¢/word.
Photos: State availability of photos with query or ms. Captions required.
Fillers: Cartoons. Buys 50/year. Pays $15 minimum.

HIGH VOLUME PRINTING, Innes Publishing Co., Box 368, Northbrook IL 60062. (312)564-5940. Editor: Virgil J. Busto. Bimonthly magazine for book and magazine publishers, large commercial printing plants with 20 or more employees. Aimed at telling the reader what he needs to know to manage his company or department more efficiently and more profitably. Circ. 20,000. Pays on publication. Byline given. Buys one-time rights and makes work-for-hire assignments. Simultaneous queries OK. Reports in 2 weeks. Free sample copy and writer's guidelines.
Nonfiction: How-to (printing production techniques); interview/profile (of trade personalities); new product (printing, auxiliary equipment, plant equipment); photo feature (case histories featuring unique equipment); technical (printing product research and development); shipping; and publishing distribution methods. No product puff. Buys 12 mss/year. Query. Length: 700-3,000 words. Pays $50-200.
Photos: Send photos with ms. Pays $25-100 for 3x5 and larger b&w prints; $25-150 for any size color transparencies and prints. Captions, model release, and identification of subjects required.

Use an up-to-date Market Directory!

Don't let your Writer's Market turn old on you.

You may be reluctant to give up this copy of Writer's Market. After all, you would never discard an old friend.

But resist the urge to hold onto an old Writer's Market! Like your first typewriter or your favorite pair of jeans, the time will come when this copy of Writer's Market will have to be replaced.

In fact, if you're still using this 1985 Writer's Market when the calendar reads 1986, your old friend isn't your best friend anymore. Many of the editors listed here have moved or been promoted. Many of the addresses are now incorrect. Rates of pay have certainly changed, and even the editorial needs are changed from last year.

You can't afford to use an out-of-date book to plan your marketing efforts. But there's an easy way for you to stay current—order the 1986 Writer's Market. All you have to do is complete the attached post card and return it with your payment or charge card information. Best of all, we'll send you the 1986 edition at the 1985 price—just $19.95. The 1986 Writer's Market will be published and ready for shipment in October 1985.

Make sure you have the most current marketing information—order the new edition of Writer's Market now.

1440

Tips: "Feature articles covering actual installations and industry trends are most open to freelancers. Be familiar with the industry, spend time in the field, and attend industry meetings and trade shows where equipment is displayed."

IN-PLANT PRINTER, Innes Publishing, Box 368, Northbrook IL 60062. (312)564-5940. Editor: Bill Esler. Bimonthly magazine covering in-house print shops. Circ. 35,000. Pays on publication. Byline "usually" given. Buys first and second rights. Submit seasonal/holiday material 2 months in advance. Photocopied and previously published submissions OK. Computer printout submissions OK. Reports in 2 weeks. Free sample copy and writer's guidelines.
Nonfiction: Book excerpts, how-to and case history. "No nebulous management advice; undetailed stories lacking in concrete information. No human interest material." Buys 18 mss/year. Query or send complete ms. Length: 1,500-3,000 words. Pays $100-250.
Photos: Send photos with ms. "No additional payment is made for photos with ms, unless negotiated." Captions required. Buys all rights.

IN-PLANT REPRODUCTIONS, North American Publishing Co., 401 N. Broad St., Philadelphia PA 19108. (215)238-5300. Editor: Ida Crist. Assistant Editor: Stephanie Harris. Monthly magazine about in-plant printing management for printing departments in business, government, education and industry. These graphic arts facilities include art, composition, camera, platemaking, press, and finishing equipment, xerographic and other business communications systems. Circ. 40,000. Pays on publication. Byline given. Buys first North American serial rights or all rights. Phone queries OK. SASE. Reports in 1 month. Sample copy $5.
Nonfiction: Interview, profile, how-to and technical. Buys 4 mss/issue. Query. Length: 500-2,500 words. Pays $75-200.

INSTANT PRINTER, Innes Publishing, 425 Huehl Rd., Bldg. 11B, Northbrook IL 60062. (312)564-5940. Editor: Daniel Witte. Bimonthly magazine covering the instant/retail printing industry for owners/operators of instant print shops. "We are primarily concerned with ways to be successful, ways to avoid failure, ways to make lots of money, and what to do with the money. Basically we try to focus on the needs and concerns of the entrepreneurial type." Circ. 17,000. Pays on publication. Byline given. Buys first North American serial rights with option for future use. Submit seasonal/holiday material 6 months in advance. Photocopied and previously published submissions OK. SASE. Reports in 2 weeks on queries; 1 month on mss. Sample copy $3; free writer's guidelines.
Nonfiction: Book excerpts (primarily on small business-related or graphic arts-related topics); general interest (anything about taxing the small business, regulating small businesses); how-to (focus on more efficient ways to do everyday things instant printers do: and technical, business, financial); interview/profile (case histories of successful instant printers with angle on unique or special services); personal experience (any small printer who has tried marketing some new or unique service, successful or not); technical (any printing-related topic). Buys 18-25 mss/year. Query with or without clips of published work or send complete ms. Pays $200 maximum.
Photos: State availability of photos. Pays $50 maximum for b&w contact sheets, slides or 3x5 prints; $100 maximum for color contact sheets, slides or 3x5 prints. Captions, model release and identification of subjects required. Buys all rights.
Columns/Departments: Promotion—about advertising/promotion techniques used by instant printers (with samples); and Computers—information about computers and software for instant printers. Buys 6 mss/year. Query with or without clips or send complete ms. Length: 1,000 words maxmimum. Pays $75 maximum.
Fillers: Clippings, anecdotes, newsbreaks, and printing or marketing hints. Pays $10 maximum.
Tips: "I would suggest reading copies of our magazine, as well as related publications, e.g., *Inc.*, *Entrepreneur*, *Business Week*, any graphic arts magazine for style."

NEWSPAPER PRODUCTION, North American Publishing Co., 401 N. Broad St., Philadelphia PA 19108. (215)238-5300. Demographic edition of *Printing Impressions*. Editor-in-Chief: Fred G. Phillips. For the newspaper industry; production personnel through management to editor and publisher. Bimonthly demographic section magazine; 8-24 pages. Circ. 17,500. Pays on publication. Buys all rights. Phone queries OK. Photocopied submissions OK, "but please identify if simultaneous elsewhere." SASE. Reports in 3 weeks.
Nonfiction: Publishes production case histories and how-to articles (production techniques); nothing about the editorial side of newspapers. Length: 1,500 words minimum. Query or submit complete ms. Pays $50-175.
Photos: B&w and color purchased with or without mss, or on assignment. Captions required. Query or submit contact sheet or prints. Additional payment for those used with mss computed into article's length. Model release required.

PLAN AND PRINT, 9931 Franklin Ave., Box 879, Franklin Park IL 60131. (312)671-5356. Editor-in-Chief: James C. Vebeck. 50% freelance written. For computer-aided design users, commercial reproduction companies, in-plant reproduction, printing, drafting and design departments of business and industry and architects.

Monthly magazine. Circ. 23,000. Pays on publication. Buys all rights. Byline given. Submit seasonal/holiday material 4-6 months in advance. SASE. Reports in 2 weeks. Free sample copy and writer's guidelines.

Nonfiction: How-to (how certain problems may have been solved; new methods of doing certain kinds of reproduction and/or design/drafting/computer-aided design work); and technical (must relate to industry). "Strong interest in computer-aided design." Buys 50 mss/year. Query with clips of previously published work. Length: 250-5,000 words. Pays $25-300.

Photos: State availability of photos with query. Pays $5-10 for 8x10 b&w glossy prints. Captions required. Buys all rights. Model release required.

Columns/Departments: Open to suggestions for new columns/departments.

Poetry: Light verse related to the industry. Buys 6/year. Length: 4-12 lines. Pays $8 maximum.

PRINTING VIEWS, For the Midwest Printer, Midwest Publishing, 8328 N. Lincoln, Skokie IL 60077. (312)539-8540. Editor: Len Berman. Managing Editor: Mary Lou Parker. Monthly magazine about printing and graphic arts for commercial printers, typographers, platemakers, engravers and other trade people. Circ. 15,000. Average issue includes 3-4 articles. Pays on publication. Byline given. Buys one-time rights. Phone queries OK. Computer printout submissions acceptable; prefers letter-quality to dot-matrix. SASE. Reports in 2 weeks. Sample copy $1.

Nonfiction: Mary Lou Parker, nonfiction editor. Interview (possibly with graphic arts personnel); new product (in graphic arts in a Midwest plant); management/sales success in Midwest printing plant; and technical (printing equipment). Buys 8 mss/year. Query with clips of previously published work. "We will entertain query letters; no unsolicited manuscripts." Length: 2-9 typed pages. Pays $100-150.

Photos: State availability of photos. Reviews b&w contact sheets. Offers additional payment for photos accepted with ms. Captions preferred. Buys one-time rights.

SCREEN PRINTING, 407 Gilbert Ave., Cincinnati OH 45202. (513)421-2050. Editor: Tamas S. Frecska. 30% freelance written: For the screen printing industry, including screen printers (commercial, industrial and captive shops), suppliers and manufacturers, and ad agencies and allied professions. Monthly magazine; 120 pages. Circ. 11,000. Buys all rights. Byline given. Pays on publication. Electronic submissions OK, but requires hard copy also. Computer printout submissions acceptable. Reporting time varies. Publishes ms an average of 2 months after acceptance. SASE. Free writer's guidelines.

Nonfiction: "Since the screen printing industry covers a broad range of applications and overlaps other fields in the graphic arts, it's necessary that articles be of a significant contribution, preferably to a specific area of screen printing. Subject matter is fairly open, with preference given to articles on administration or technology; trends and developments. We try to give a good sampling of technical business and management articles; articles about unique operations. We also publish special features and issues on important subjects, such as material shortages, new markets and new technology breakthroughs. While most of our material is nitty-gritty, we appreciate a writer who can take an essentially dull subject and encourage the reader to read on through concise, factual, 'flairful' and creative, expressive writing. Interviews are published after consultation with and guidance from the editor." Interested in stories on unique approaches by some shops. No general, promotional treatment of individual companies. Buys 6-10 unsolicited mss/year. Length: 1,500-2,000 words. Pays minimum of $150 for major features; minimum of $75 for minor features; minimum of $50 for back of book articles.

Photos: Cover photos negotiable; b&w or color. Published material becomes the property of the magazine.

THE TYPOGRAPHER, Typographers International Association, Suite 101, 2262 Hall Pl. NW., Washington DC 20007. (202)965-3400. Editor: Geoff Lindsay. Bimonthly tabloid of the commercial typesetting industry for owners and executives of typesetting firms. Circ. 10,000. Pays on publication. Byline given. Buys one-time rights. Simultaneous queries, and simultaneous, photocopied and previously published submissions OK. Computer printout submissions acceptable. Reports in 1 week. Free sample copy.

Nonfiction: Book excerpts, historical/nostalgic, how-to, interview/profile, new product, opinion, personal experience, photo feature and technical. "All articles should relate to typesetting management." No opinion pieces. Buys 20 mss/year. Query with clips of published work. Length: 1,000-2,000 words. Pays $50-150.

Photos: State availability of photos. Pays $20-35 for 5x7 b&w prints. Captions and identification of subjects required.

Columns/Departments: Sales column (how to improve sales of typesetting). Buys 15 mss/year. Query with clips of published work. Length: 1,200 words minimum. Pays $50-100.

WORLD-WIDE PRINTER, North American Publishing Co., 401 N. Broad St., Philadelphia PA 19108. Editor: Jane Smith. Emphasizes printing and printing technology for printers, packagers and publishers of newspapers, books, magazines, any and all printed matter in all parts of the world. Distributed internationally. Semi-annual magazine; 110 pages. Circ. 14,000. Pays on publication. Buys all rights. Phone queries OK. Simultaneous, photocopied and previously published submissions OK, if identified as to other possible placement. Reports in 3 weeks. Sample copy $5.

Nonfiction: Technical material only. "Knowledge of printing technology is absolutely necessary in the writer, even if the subject is only an interview or plant story." Buys 2-3 mss/issue. Query. Length: 500-1,000 words. Pays $25-150.

Photos: State availability of photos. Wants 5x7 b&w prints.

Real Estate

‡**APARTMENT AGE, the voice of the industry**, Apartment Association of Greater Los Angeles, 551 S. Oxford Ave., Los Angeles CA 90020. (213)384-4131. Editor: Kevin B. Postema. A monthly magazine covering rental housing, geared toward apartment house owners/operators/managers/investors. Circ. 36,300. Pays on publication. Byline given. Buys all rights. Simultaneous queries OK. Computer printout submissions acceptable; prefers letter-quality to dot-matrix. SASE. Reports in 1 month. Free sample copy and writer's guidelines fpr business-size SAE and 1 first class stamp.

Nonfiction: Historical/nostaglic; how-to (apartment maintenance); humor; personal experience; and legal/political. Query. Length: 500-1,000 words. Pays $25-50.

AREA DEVELOPMENT MAGAZINE, 525 Northern Blvd., Great Neck NY 11021. (516)829-8990. Editor-in-Chief: Tom Bergeron. Emphasizes corporate facility planning and site selection for industrial chief executives worldwide. Monthly magazine; 110-190 pages. Circ. 33,000. Pays when edited. Buys first rights only. Byline given. Photocopied submissions OK. Computer printout submissions acceptable. Reports in 3 weeks. Free sample copy and writer's guidelines.

Nonfiction: How-to (case histories of companies; experiences in site selection and all other aspects of corporate facility planning); historical (if it deals with corporate facility planning); interview (corporate executives and industrial developers); and related areas of site selection and facility planning such as taxes, labor, government, energy, architecture and finance. Buys 8-10 mss/yr. Query. Pays $25-35/ms page; rates for illustrations depend on quality and printed size.

Photos: State availability of photos with query. Prefer 8x10 or 5x7 b&w glossy prints. Captions preferred.

Tips: "Articles must be accurate, objective (no puffery) and useful to our industrial executive readers. Avoid any discussion of the merits or disadvantages of any particular areas or communities."

BUSINESS FACILITIES, BUS FAC Publishing Co., 170 Broad St., Box 8729, Red Bank NJ 07701. (201)842-7433. Editor: Eric C. Peterson. 10% freelance written. Magazine published 10 times/year (March/April, July/August combined issues) covering economic development, industrial and commercial real estate. "Emphasis is on news and trends, including market conditions, economics, finance, legislation, innovations—anything that could affect the economic development practitioner on a national, regional or local level." Circ. 35,000. Pays on acceptance. Byline given. Buys all rights. Simultaneous queries, and simultaneous and photocopied submissions OK. Computer printout submissions acceptable; prefers letter-quality to dot-matrix. SASE. Reports in 1 month on queries, 2 weeks on mss. Publishes ms an average of 2 months after acceptance. Free sample copy and writer's guidelines.

Nonfiction: General interest (newsy case histories); how-to (innovations, construction features, operation of facilities); interview/profile (of top corporate real estate, development and government figures); and technical (construction and operation techniques). No mss that are too generic. Buys under 20 mss/year. Query. Length: 1,000-3,000 words. Pays $200-600.

Photos: Send photos with ms. Pays negotiable rate. Reviews b&w contact sheets with negatives and 5x7 or 8x10 prints, and color transparencies. Identification of subjects required. Buys one-time rights.

Tips: "We buy a limited amount of freelance material, so such material must be exceptional or should give us an 'in' with a top development or corporate or governmental official—an exclusive, in other words. Easiest way to turn us off is to telephone; please write. Know something about the field—any field. Don't submit material that your next door neighbor can understand. In this business, you're talking to established experts—and you should have solid expertise, too.

COMMUNITY DEVELOPMENT PUBLICATIONS, Suite 100, 8555 16th St., Silver Spring MD 20910. (301) 588-6380. Various newsletters for government officials and industry executives in community development; local growth; housing market; managing housing; community and economic development programs; neighborhoods; and infrastructure. Pays end of month after publication. SASE if return desired. Sample copy and writer's guidelines for SASE.

Fillers: Uses contributions of significant newspaper clippings on housing, community and economic development, and infrastructure; substantive actions and litigation of interest to housing and development professionals, state and local government, beyond immediate area. Particularly wants regular contributors for multistates, region, or at least a full state, especially state capitals. Buys 500-1,000 clippings. Normally pays $3 for each use of an accepted clipping.

FINANCIAL FREEDOM REPORT, National Institute of Financial Planning, Suite C, 1831 Fort Union Blvd., Salt Lake City UT 84121. (801)943-1280. Chairman of the Board: Mark O. Haroldsen. Managing Editor: Michael Hansen. 15% freelance written. For "professional and nonprofessional investors, and would-be investors in real estate—real estate brokers, insurance companies, investment planners, truck drivers, housewives, doctors, architects, contractors, etc. The magazine's content is presently expanding to interest and inform the readers about other ways to put their money to work for them." Monthly magazine; 72 pages. Circ. 50,000. Pays on publication. Buys all rights. Phone queries OK. Simultaneous submissions OK. Computer printout submissions acceptable; prefers letter-quality to dot-matrix. SASE. Reports in 2 weeks. Publishes ms an average of 2 months after acceptance. Sample copy $3; free writer's guidelines.
Nonfiction: How-to (find real estate bargains, finance property, use of leverage, managing property, developing market trends, goal setting, motivational); and interviews (success stories of those who have relied on own initiative and determination in real estate market or other business endeavors, e.g., Ray Kroc of McDonald's). Buys 10-15 unsolicited mss/year. Query with clips of published work or submit complete ms. Length: 1,500-4,500 words. "If the topic warranted a two- or three-parter, we would consider it." Pays 5-10¢/word.
Photos: Send photos with ms. Uses b&w 8x10 matte prints. Offers no additional payment for photos accepted with ms. Captions required.
Tips: "We would like to find several specialized writers in our field of real estate investments."

‡**FREP JOURNAL, Serving Florida's Real Estate Professionals**, Box 878, DeLeon Springs FL 32028. Editor: Evelyn Phillips Mantz. 70% freelance written. Bimonthly magazine covering real estate professionals in Florida. "We're looking for bright, succinct writing on almost any subject of interest to real estate professionals *as* real estate professionals. They need sales techniques, financial information, help in choosing modes of educational advancement and automobiles and insurance and employers. They need to psychologically probe buyers and sellers and learn to manage their commissions (feast or famine) and their time better. They want to expand their horizons and broaden their market base." Estab. 1983. Pays before publication. Byline given. Buys negotiable rights. Submit seasonal/holiday material 4 months in advance. Simultaneous queries, and photocopied (if good) and previously published submissions OK. Computer printout submissions acceptable; prefers letter-quality to dot-matrix. SASE. Reports in 2 weeks on queries; 1 month on mss. Publishes ms an average of 4 months after acceptance. Sample copy for $2; writer's guidelines for business-size SAE and 1 first class stamp.
Nonfiction: Book excerpts, expose, general interest, historical/nostalgic, how-to, humor, inspirational, interview/profile, new product, opinion, personal experience, photo feature, technical and travel. "Possible topics for writers serving the Florida real estate scene include: where are minority brokers; how are airplanes used in marketing real estate; haunted houses in the state; computer use in real estate offices; funny true experiences of Florida real estate people; writing the 'perfect' classified ad; unusual Florida architecture; information on condominiums, co-ops, time-share and PUDs; developers vs. homeowner associations; and spin-offs of the business. Keep in mind that articles must be helpful, amusing, etc., to real estate *professionals*." Buys 30-40 mss/year. Query with published clips (preferred) or send complete ms. Length 2-4 pages "But will consider longer pieces when the topic merits." Pays 8¢/word.
Photos: State availability of photos. Reviews b&w contact sheets and 5x7 prints. Captions and identification of subjects required. Pays negotiable rates.
Columns/Departments: Reviews of book, seminars, course, etc. Query first with or without published clips. Pays 8¢/word.
Fillers: Clipping, anecdotes, short humor and newsbreaks. Buys "lots (the more, the merrier)." Length: 30-300 words.
Tips: "People in the business should have a big advantage in breaking in to our publications. Stay away from flowery excess verbage. Use 'over the backyard fence' stories of individuals as specific examples. Quotes from experts are fine but they still need backing up with those specific anecdotes."

PROPERTIES MAGAZINE, 4900 Euclid Ave., Cleveland OH 44103. (216)431-7666. Editor: Gene Bluhm. Monthly. Buys all rights. Pays on publication. Query. SASE.
Nonfiction: Wants articles of real estate and construction news value. Interested primarily in articles relating to northeastern Ohio. Length: up to 900 words.
Photos: Buys photographs with mss, 5x7 preferred.

SOUTHWEST REAL ESTATE NEWS, Communication Channels, Inc., Suite 240, 18601 LBJ Freeway, Mesquite TX 75150. (214)270-6651. Associate Publisher/Editor: Jim Mitchell. Managing Editor: Sheryl Roberts. 30% freelance written. Monthly tabloid newspaper about commercial and industrial real estate for professional real estate people, including realtors, developers, mortgage bankers, corporate real estate executives,

architects, contractors and brokers. Circ. 17,000. Average issue includes 4 columns, 20-50 short news items, 2-5 special articles and 10 departments. Pays on publication. Publishes ms an average of 2 months after acceptance. Byline given. Buys all rights. Phone queries OK. Submit seasonal material 2 months in advance. Photocopied submissions OK. Computer printout submissions acceptable; dot-matrix only if it has ascenders and descenders. Prefers letter-quality." SASE. Reports in 4-6 weeks. Free sample copy and writer's guidelines.
Nonfiction: "We're interested in hearing from writers in major cities in the states that we cover, which are TX, OK, CO, NM, LA, AZ, AR, southern Nevada and southern California. We are particularly interested in writers with newspaper experience or real estate background. Assignments are made according to our editorial schedule which we will supply upon request. Most open to freelancers are city reviews and special articles. Contact the staff to discuss ideas first. No unsolicited material." Buys 3-5 mss/issue. Query. Pays $100-400.
Columns/Departments: Offices, Shopping Centers, Industrials, Multiplexes, Leases, Sales and Purchases, Mortgage and Financial, Realty Operations, Residentials, and People in the News. No newspaper clippings. Buys 3 mss/issue. Query. Length: 1,000-5,000 words. Pays $75-100.

TIME SHARING INDUSTRY REVIEW, Box 4301920, South Miami FL 33143. (305)667-0202. Managing Editor: Bob Kearney. Monthly magazine for professionals involved in the timesharing industry. Pays on acceptance. Publishes ms an average of 1 month after acceptance. Buys first rights only. Computer printout submissions acceptable; no dot-matrix. Reports in 1 month. Publishes ms an average of 1 month after acceptance. Sample copy and writer's guidelines $1.
Nonfiction: Well-researched news features about new developments, marketing trends, financing, sales strategies, consumer profiles, interviews with key industry personalities, etc. Query. Length: 1,000-5,000 words. Pays according to length.
Photos: Pays extra for photo used.
Tips: "We are an international publication covering every aspect of this dynamic, rapidly growing industry. We need freelance writers with solid feature writing experience in every location where timesharing is part of the vacation scene. Send three clips demonstrating your best work, along with a brief resume. If you're convincing, we'll send you our writer's guidelines and give you an assignment. We're also interested in story ideas you generate on your own."

Resources and Waste Reduction

‡**PUMPER PUBLICATIONS, Eastern Pumper, Midwest Pumper and Western Pumper**, COLE Inc., Drawer 220, Three Lakes WI 54562. (715)546-3347. Editors: Bob Kendall and Pete Lawonn. A monthly tabloid covering the liquid waste hauling industry (portable toilet renters, septic tank pumpers, industrial waste haulers, chemical waste haulers, oil field haulers, and hazardous waste haulers). "Our publication is read by companies that handle liquid waste and manufacturers of equipment." Circ. 15,000. Pays on publication. Byline given. Offers negotiable kill fee. Buys first rights. Submit seasonal/holiday material 3 months in advance. Simultaneous queries, and simultaneous, photocopied, and previously published submissions OK. Computer printout submissions acceptable. SASE. Reports in 1 month. Free sample copy.
Nonfiction: Expose (government regulations, industry problems, trends, public attitudes, etc.); general interest (state association meetings, conventions, etc.); how-to (related to industry, e.g., how to incorporate septage or municipal waste into farm fields, how to process waste, etc.); humor (related to industry, especially septic tank pumpers or portable toilet renters); interview/profile (including descriptions of business statistics, type of equipment, etc.); new product; personal experience; photo feature; and technical (especially reports on research projects related to disposal). "Studies on land application of sanitary waste are of great interest." Query or send complete ms. Pays 7.5¢/word.
Photos: Send photos with query or ms. Pays $10-15 for b&w and color prints. "We need good contrast." Captions "suggested" and model release "helpful." Buys one-time rights.
Tips: "We hope to expand the editorial content of our monthly publications."

‡**RESOURCE RECYCLING, Journal of Recycling, Reuse and Waste Reduction**, Resource Conservation Consultants, Inc., Box 10540, Portland OR 97210. (503)227-1319. Editor: Jerry Powell. Bimonthly magazine covering recycling of paper, metals, glass, etc. for recycling processors. "*Resource Recycling* provides thorough assessments of trends and developments in waste recovery." Circ. 3,000 in 20 countries. Pays on publication. Byline given. "We don't assign manuscripts." Buys first rights. "No seasonal material in our trade." Simultaneous queries, and simultaneous, photocopied and previously published submissions OK. Computer printout submissions acceptable. SASE. Reports in 1 month. Free sample copy and writer's guidelines.
Nonfiction: Historical/nostalgic, interview/profile, new product, photo feature and technical. No "nontechni-

cal or opinion articles." Buys 15-20 mss/year. Query with published clips. "Queries should include a step-by-step outline of the proposed manuscript." Length: 1,500-3,000 words. Pays $100-250.

Photos: State availability of photos. Pays $5-10 for b&w contact sheets, negatives and prints. Identification of subjects required. Buys one-time rights.

Tips: "A freelancer can best break in to our publication with overviews of one recycling aspect in one state (e.g., oil recycling in Alabama). We can supply lists of sources, data, etc."

Selling and Merchandising

In this category are journals for sales personnel and merchandisers interested in how to sell products successfully. Journals in nearly every other category of this Trade Journal section also buy sales-related material if it is slanted to the specialized product or industry they deal with, such as clothing or paint. Publications for advertising and marketing professionals will be found under Advertising, Marketing, and PR.

THE AMERICAN SALESMAN, 424 N. 3rd St., Burlington IA 52601. Publisher: Michael S. Darnall. Editorial Supervisor: Doris J. Ruschill. Editor: Barbara Boeding. 95% freelance written. For distribution through company sales representatives. Monthly magazine; 44 pages, (5x7). Circ. 3,012. Pays on publication. Buys all rights. SASE. Free sample copy and writer's guidelines; mention *Writer's Market* in request.

Nonfiction: Sales seminars, customer service and followup, closing sales, sales presentations, handling objections, competition, telephone usage and correspondence, managing your territory and new innovative sales concepts. No sexist material, illustration written from only a salesman's viewpoint. No mss dealing with supervisory problems. Query. Length: 900-1,200 words. Pays 3-5¢/word. Uses no photos or advertising. Follow AP Stylebook.

ARMY/NAVY STORE AND OUTDOOR MERCHANDISER, 567 Morris Ave., Elizabeth NJ 07208. (201)353-7373. Editor: Alan Richman. 20% freelance written. For the owners of army/navy surplus and outdoor goods stores. Circ. 5,400. Byline given. Buys 30 mss/year. Pays on publication. SASE. Reports in 1 month. Sample copy $2 plus $1.50 postage and handling.

Nonfiction: Articles on the methods stores use to promote items; especially on how army/navy items have become fashion items, and the problems attendant to catering to this new customer. Sources of supply, how they promote, including windows, newspapers, etc. Writer's guidelines are available. Length: 1,000-2,000 words. Pays $50-125. "Most articles—especially on stores—must have photos included."

Photos: Minimum 5x7 b&w glossies with captions.

Tips: "The best material always has a unique—but not forced—slant. Play up the special things a store does to succeed—whether it's display, pricing policy, emphasis on certain merchandise, advertising or whatever. Be specific."

‡**ART MATERIAL TRADE NEWS, The Journal of All Art, Craft, Engineering and Drafting Supplies**, Communication Channels Inc., 6255 Barfieldd Rd., Atlanta GA 3028. (404)256-9800. Editor: Nancy Celani. 30% freelance written. Monthly magazine on art materials. "Our editorial thrust is to bring art materials retailers, distributors and manufacturers information they can use in their everyday operations." Circ. 10,000. Pays on publication. "All assigned manuscripts are published." Buys first rights only. Submit seasonal/holiday material 3 months in advance. Photocopied submissions OK. Computer printout submissions acceptable; prefers letter-quality to dot-matrix. SASE. Reports in 6 weeks. Sample copy for 9x12 SAE and $1 postage; writer's guildeines for 4x9½ SAE and 1 first class stamp.

Nonfiction: How-to (sell, retail/wholesale employee management, advertising programs); interview/profile (within industry); and technical (commercial art drafting/engineering). "We encourage a strong narrative style where possible. We publish an editorial 'theme' calendar at the beginning of each year." Buys 36-40 mss/year. Query with published clips. Length: 2,500-3,000 words (prefers 2,500 words). Pays 10¢/word and expenses with prior approval.

Photos: State availability of photos. Pays $10 maximum for b&w contact sheets. Identification of subjects required.

Columns/Departments: Business Talk (the impact of current economic or political events on art materials

business). Buys 12-15 mss/year. Query with published clips. Length: 1,000-2,000 words. Pays $75-200.
Tips: "A current, solid background in any one of these areas helps—commercial art, retail selling, wholesale selling, business finance, employee management, interviewing or advertising. We appreciate clean, concise copy. We do a lot of dealer profiles throughout US. They must be written in good conversational tone with complete, accurate background information."

‡**CASUAL LIVING**, Columbia Communications, 370 Lexington Ave., New York NY 10164. (212)532-9290. Editor: Ralph Monti. A monthly magazine covering outdoor furniture for outdoor furniture specialists, including retailers, mass merchandiser and department store buyers. Circ. 11,000. Pays on publication. Tagline given. Buys first North American serial rights. Submit seasonal/holiday material 2 months in advance. Computer printout submissions acceptable. SASE. Reports in 1 month. Sample copy with writer's guidelines for 9x12 SAE, and 28¢ postage.
Nonfiction: Interview/profile (case histories of retailers in the industry); new product; opinion; and technical. Buys 12-13 mss/year. Query with or without published clips, then follow up with phone call. Length: 1,000 words average. Pays $200-400.
Photos: State availability of photos with query letter or ms. "Photos are essential with all articles." Reviews b&w contact sheet. Pays $75-100 for b&w prints. Buys all rights.
Tips: "Know the industry, trades and fashions and what makes a successful retailer."

CONVENIENCE STORE NEWS, BMT Publications, Inc., 254 W. 31st St., New York NY 10001. (212)594-4120. Editor: Barbara J. Bagley. 15% freelance written. For convenience store chain executives, middle management and owner/operators; franchisors and franchisees; convenience store managers, wholesalers, distributors, service merchandisers, food brokers and manufacturers involved in the food retailing and convenience store business. Tabloid published 16 times/year. Circ. 75,000. Pays on publication. Buys all rights. Phone queries OK. Query for submission of seasonal/holiday material. Reports on queries in 1-2 weeks. Publishes ms an average of 3 months after acceptance. Free sample copy and writer's guidelines.
Nonfiction: General interest, how-to, interview, profile and photo feature. Interested in news about convenience stores and chains and oil retailers who operate convenience stores, their personnel, operations and product mix trends, promotions and legislative activities on all levels of government that affect the operations of these businesses. Buys 90 unsolicited mss/year. Query. Pays $3/column inch.
Photos: Send photos with ms. Pays $5 for b&w glossy prints; $35 for contact sheet and negatives, "provided at least one photo is used." Captions required.
Columns/Departments: Store Managers section. Buys 16-20 mss/issue. Query. Length: 4 double-spaced ms pages maximum. Pays $3/column inch.
Fillers: Newsbreaks ("in our industry only"). Length: 1-2 pages, double-spaced.

• **GEMCO COURIER, A Publication for Members of America's Finest Membership Department Stores**, Lucky Stores, Inc. 6565 Knott Ave., Box 5001, Buena Park CA 90622. Articles Editor: Robyn McGee. 90% freelance written. Monthly advertising supplement used to promote Gemco merchandise. Circ. 5.5 million. Pays on acceptance. Buys first North America serial rights. Photocopied submissions OK. Electronic submissions OK, but requires hard copy also. Computer printout submissions acceptable. SASE. Reports in 6 weeks. Publishes ms an average of 4 months after acceptance. Sample copy for 9x12 SASE; writer's guidelines for business-size SASE.
Nonfiction: Articles that promote merchandise sold in our stores are the only ones being considered at the present time. No biography, humor, historical, personal experiences, anecdotes, trivia, poetry, fiction, first person narratives, or articles of a religious/political/controversial nature. Length: 225-1,000 words. Query. Pays $75-400.
Tips: "The best way a freelancer can begin writing for us is to familiarize himself/herself with our merchandise, either by 'shopping' our stores or through back issues of the *Courier*. Please send for back issues and writer's guidelines before sending a query."

INFO FRANCHISE NEWSLETTER, 11 Bond St., St. Catharines, Ontario L2R 4Z4 Canada or 728 Center St., Box 550, Lewiston NY 14092. (716)754-4669. Editor-in-Chief: E.L. Dixon Jr. Managing Editor: Jean Baird. Monthly newsletter; 8 pages. Circ. 5,000. Pays on publication. Buys all rights. Photocopied submissions OK. SASE. Reports in 1 month.
Nonfiction: "We are particularly interested in receiving articles regarding franchise legislation, franchise litigation, franchise success stories, and new franchises. Both American and Canadian items are of interest. We do not want to receive any information which is not fully documented or articles which could have appeared in any newspaper or magazine in North America. An author with a legal background who could comment upon such things as arbitration and franchising or class actions and franchising, would be of great interest to us." Expose, how-to, informational, interview, profile, new product, personal experience and technical. Buys 10-20 mss/year. Length: 25-1,000 words. Pays $10-300.

KEY NEWSLETTER, Voice Publications, 1016 S. Fly Ave., Goreville IL 62939-9720. (618)995-2027. Editor: Bernard Lyons. 5% freelance written, "but would like to see more." Emphasizes direct marketing/mail order, specifically for those using classified columns of national magazines. Quarterly newsletter; 16 pages. Pays on acceptance. Buys all rights. Submit seasonal/holiday material 4 months in advance. Photocopied submissions OK. SASE. Reports in 24 hours. One sample copy, $5; mention *Writer's Market* in request.
Nonfiction: Expose (fraud in mail order/direct marketing); historical (old classified ads); how-to (write classified ads, match markets, increase response to ads); humor (funny classifieds); inspirational (examples of successful classifieds, personal stories of successful mail order through classifieds); interview (with successful mail order/direct market persons using classifieds); new product (if of help to small business); personal experience (summary of test results); profile (successful users of classifieds, written in first person); and technical (math for mail order/direct marketing). Buys 10 mss/year. Submit complete ms. Length: 50-1,500 words. Pays $10-75.
Tips: "We do not cover want-ads, but only classified ads in the national publications, those that you find on the newsstand. To break in find a consistent mail order advertiser; write up his or her experiences, including start, problems, ad response, etc.; mail it to us today, without anything more than the clearest and simplest language describing the who, why, what, where, when and how."

NON-FOODS MERCHANDISING, US Business Press Inc., 124 E. 40th St., New York NY 10024. Editor: John Morse. 10% freelance written. For buyers, manufacturers and distributors of health and beauty aids and general merchandise (nonfoods) in the supermarket. Monthly tabloid; 85 pages. Circ. 22,000. Pays on publication. Buys all rights. Byline given on major features. Photocopied submissions OK. SASE.
Nonfiction: "Reports on aspects of our business. We want to be in on the news." Analytical trends, historical, interview, profile, how-to and new product. Buys 2 mss/issue. Query with clips of published work. Length: 2,000-6,000 words. Pays $150-350.
Photos: "No extra fee paid for photos included with ms." Uses color slides and b&w prints. Buys all rights. Expenses are covered.

ON THE UPBEAT, A Few Thoughts to Help People Who Sell for a Living Recharge Their Batteries, The Economics Press, Inc., 12 Daniel Rd., Fairfield NJ 07006. (201)227-1224. Editor: Robert Guder. 75% freelance written. Monthly magazine "serving as a refresher for veteran salespeople and a training tool for new salespeople." Circ. 36,851. Pays on acceptance. Offers 100% kill fee. Buys all rights. Submit seasonal/holiday material 3 months in advance. Photocopied submissions OK. Electronic submissions OK if 5¼" floppy, HP/125 compatible. Computer printout submissions acceptable. Reports in 6 weeks. Publishes ms an average of 3 months after acceptance. Free sample copy and writer's guidelines.
Nonfiction: Historical/nostalgic (incidents involving historical figures that highlight a positive personality trait); humor (wholesome jokes, cute stories—any subject); personal experience (anecdotes/stories about selling or about a helpful salesperson); and travel (anecdotes about traveling salespeople or helpful techniques to make the most of travel time, etc.). Original material only. Buys 60-100 mss/year. Send complete ms. Length: 50-300 words. Pays $20-50.
Fillers: Buys 60-100/year. Length: 50-300 words. Pays $20-50.
Tips: "True stories/anecdotes about sales experience, either from the salesperson's viewpoint or the buyer's, are always welcome. Story should be unusual and serve as an example of a technique salespeople should use or stay away from. *On the Upbeat* is a business publication. Please stay away from subjects unrelated to working/ business, etc. However, jokes and cute stories may be on any *wholesome* subject."

PHOTO MARKETING, 3000 Picture Place, Jackson MI 49201. Editor: Monica Smiley. Managing Editor: Therese Wood. 25% freelance written. For camera store dealers, photofinishers, manufacturers and distributors of photographic equipment. Publication of the Photo Marketing Association, International. Monthly magazine; 75 pages. Circ. 15,000. Buys all rights. Pays on publication. Reports in 21 days. Publishes ms an average of 1 month after acceptance. Query with outline and story line. SASE.
Nonfiction: Business features dealing with photographic retailing or photofinishing operations, highlighting unique aspects, promotional programs and special problems. Buys 12 unsolicited mss/year. Length: 300-500 typewritten lines. Pays 5-7¢/word minimum.
Photos: Pays $10-15/published 5x7 glossy photo.
Tips: Query should have: "indications that freelancer understands who our reader is—the businessperson who needs advice; intent by freelancer to tailor article to our market by talking to/interviewing people in the photo business. Writers should send us a list of articles they have prepared, with descriptions, and their qualifications/background. If they're doing an article on selling techniques, for example, I'd like to know who they talked with or if they've worked in retailing to get info. Generic articles that could run in a wide variety of publications no longer have the same appeal—specifically in trade publications. Writers must tailor work to the target audience, and this often does not require much work."

PRIVATE LABEL, The Magazine for House Brands and Generics, E.W. Williams Publishing Co., 80 8th Ave., New York NY 10011. (212)989-1101. Editor: Sam Martin. Managing Editor: Mark Edgar. Bimonthly magazine covering food and nonfood private label and generic products. Circ. 25,000. Pays on acceptance. Byline given. Offers 50-100% kill fee "depending on circumstances." Buys first rights and second serial (reprint) rights on material originally published elsewhere. Submit seasonal/holiday material 4 months in advance. Photocopied submissions OK "if not under submission elsewhere." Computer printout submissions acceptable; prefers letter-quality to dot-matrix. SASE. Reports in "weeks." Sample copy for $1 and SAE.
Nonfiction: Book excerpts (if segments are appropriate); general interest; historical/nostalgic; how-to; interview/profile; personal experience; photo feature; and travel. "We use feature articles showing how retailers promote, buy, display, sell, and feel about their store brands (private label and generic products). We're always interested in coverage of areas more than 300 miles from New York. No articles on peripheral topics such as taxes, insurance, safety, etc." Buys 30-40 mss/year. Query or send complete ms. Length: 500-4,000 words; Pays 3¢/word; "flat fee by special arrangement."
Photos: "We prefer articles with photos." Send photos with ms. Pays $7 minimum for 5x7 b&w prints; reviews contact sheets (if large selection). Captions and identification of subjects required. Buys all rights; "release on request."
Tips: "We are wide open to freelancers who can line up store permission (preferably headquarters) for feature articles on philosophy, purchase, consumer attitudes, retailer attitudes, display and promotion of private label and generic products."

PROFESSIONAL SELLING, 24 Rope Ferry Rd., Waterford CT 06386. (203)442-4365. Editor: Paulette S. Withers. 33% freelance written. Bimonthly newsletter for sales professionals covering industrial or wholesale sales. "Provides field sales personnel with both the basics and current information that can help them better perform the sales function." Pays on acceptance. No byline given. Buys all rights. Submit seasonal/holiday material 4 months in advance. Computer printout submissions acceptable. SASE. Reports in 2 weeks. Publishes ms an average of 6 months after acceptance. Sample copy for business-size SAE and 1 first class stamp; writer's guidelines available for same.
Nonfiction: How-to (successful sales techniques); and interview/profile (interview-based articles). "We buy only interview-based material." Buys 12-15 mss/year. Query. Length: 800-1,000 words.
Tips: "Only the lead article is open to freelancers. That must be based on an interview with an actual sales professional. Freelancers may occasionally interview sales managers, but the slant must be toward field sales *not* management."

SALESMAN'S OPPORTUNITY MAGAZINE, 6 N. Michigan Ave., Chicago IL 60602. Managing Editor: Jack Weissman. 30% freelance written. "For anyone who is interested in making money, full or spare time, in selling or in independent business program." Monthly magazine. Circ. 190,000. Pays on publication. Buys all rights. Byline given. Submit seasonal/holiday material 6 months in advance. Computer printout submissions acceptable; prefers letter-quality to dot-matrix. SASE. Free sample copy and writer's guidelines.
Nonfiction: "We use articles dealing with sales techniques, sales psychology or general self-improvement topics." How-to, inspirational, and interview (with successful salespeople who are selling products offered by direct selling firms, especially concerning firms which recruit salespeople through *Salesman's Opportunity Magazine*). Articles on self-improvement should deal with specifics rather than generalities. Would like to have more articles that deal with overcoming fear, building self-confidence, increasing personal effectiveness, and other psychological subjects. Submit complete ms. Buys 35-50 unsolicited mss/year. Length: 250-900 words. Pays $20-35.
Photos: State availability of photos with ms. Offers no additional payment for 8x10 b&w glossy prints. Captions required. Buys all rights. Model release required.
Tips: "Many articles are too academic for our audience. We look for free-and-easy style in simple language which is packed with useful information, drama and inspiration. Check the magazine before writing. We can't use general articles. The only articles we buy deal with material that is specifically directed to readers who are opportunity seekers—articles dealing with direct sales programs or successful ventures that others can emulate. Try to relate the article to the actual work in which the reader is engaged."

SELLING DIRECT, Communication Channels, Inc., 6255 Barfield Rd., Atlanta GA 30328. (404)256-9800. Publisher: William Hood. Editor: Susan Spann. 20% freelance written. For independent businessmen and women who sell door-to-door, store-to-store, office-to-office and by the party plan method as well as through direct mail and telephone solicitation; selling products and services. Monthly magazine; 50-100 pages. Circ. 500,000. Pays on publication. Buys all rights. Byline given. Submit seasonal/holiday material 3 months in advance. Electronic submissions OK if compatible with Decmate or Decmate II. Computer printout submissions acceptable. SASE. Reports in 3 months. Publishes ms an average of 1 year after acceptance. Free sample copy and writer's guidelines.
Nonfiction: How-to (sell better; increase profits); historical (related to the history of various kinds of sales pitches, anecdotes, etc.); and inspirational (success stories, "rags to riches" type of stories)—with no addi-

tional payment. Buys 30 unsolicited mss/year. Query or submit complete ms. Length: 500-1,500 words. Pays 10¢/word.
Photos: Photos purchased with accompanying ms.
Columns/Departments: Ideas Exchange (generated from our readers). Submit complete ms. Open to suggestions for new columns/departments.
Fillers: Jokes, gags, anecdotes and short humor. Buys 2/issue. Length: 150-500 words. Pays $10 for each published item.
Tips: No general articles on "How to be a Super Salesperson." Writers should concentrate on one specific aspect of selling and expand on that.

‡**SOFTWARE MERCHANDISING, Home Software, Computer Books, Accessories, Home Computers**, Eastman Publishing Company, Inc., Suite 222, 15720 Ventura Blvd., Encino CA 91436. (818)995-0436. Editor: Jim McCullaugh. Associate Editor: Wolf Schneider. 50% freelance written. Monthly magazine covering home computer software. "We are a marketing tool, targeted toward the buyers of home software at such retail outlets as computer specialty, software, department, mass merchant, book and record stores. We publish features and regular sections on how to successfully sell home software and computer products." Circ. 25,000. Pays 1 month after acceptance. Byline given. Offers 50% kill fee. Buys all rights. Submit seasonal/holiday material 3 months in advance. Photocopied submissions OK. Computer printout submissions acceptable. SASE. Reports in 1 week. Publishes ms an average of 2 months after acceptance. Free sample copy and writer's guidelines.
Nonfiction: How-to (market computer software and books for the home buyer); interview/profile (retailers); new product (computer software); and technical (softech feature). Buys 60 mss/year. Query with published clips and resume; follow up with phone call. Length: 2,000-3,000 words. Pays $200-350.
Photos: Photos are assigned. Captions and identification of subjects required.
Columns/Departments: Education, Entertainment, Productivity, Marketing and Merchandiser's Notebook.
Tips: "A freelancer can best break in to our publication with some knowledge of the home computer industry and some retail trade writing experience."

STORES, National Retail Merchants Association, 100 W. 31st St., New York NY 10001. (212)244-8780. Editor: Joan Bergmann. Managing Editor: Carol Ellen Messenger. Monthly magazine about retail issues for top retail management. Circ. 25,000. Pays on publication. Byline given. Buys all rights. Reports in 2 weeks on queries; in 2 months on mss. Free sample copy and writer's guidelines.
Nonfiction: Buys 8-10 mss/issue. Query with clips of previously published work. Length: 1,000 words minimum. Pays 12¢/word.
Photos: Send photos with ms on assigned story. Pays $5 for each b&w used. Buys all rights.
Tips: "Send writing samples and background; assignments sometimes are given on the basis of writing style."

VIDEO BUSINESS, CES Publishing, 135 W. 50th St., New York NY 10020. (212)957-8800. Editor: John HuBach. Managing Editor: Frank Moldstad. Associate Editor: Larry Henchey. Monthly magazine covering home video industry. Also covers video game and home computer industries. Circ. 26,000. Pays on publication. Byline given. Buys all rights in the industry. Simultaneous queries and previously published submissions OK ("indicate where and when published"). Computer printout submissions acceptable. SASE. Reports in 1 month. Free sample copy.
Nonfiction: Informational pieces (on marketing, merchandising and selling themes). No "technical articles or how-tos dealing with cutting costs, managing people, etc." Buys 10 mss/year. Query. Length: 1,500-2,000 words. Pays 12.5¢/word.
Photos: State availability of photos.
Tips: "Our style has become more upbeat. Writers should avoid 'dry' language."

WALLCOVERINGS MAGAZINE, Publishing Dynamics, Inc., 2 Selleck St., Stamford CT 06902. Publisher/Editor: Martin A. Johnson. Associate Publisher: Robert Johnson. Managing Editor: Dorianne Russo. Associate Editor: Kathleen Hand. Monthly trade journal of the flexible wallcoverings industry. Circ. 9,000. Submit query on all nonfiction article ideas. Computer printout submissions acceptable. Buys all rights. SASE. Sample copy $2.
Nonfiction: Articles about manufacturers, distributors and retailers who sell wallcoverings. Query with clips of previously published work.
Photos: On assignment. 8x10 b&w prints or contact sheets with negatives. Rates negotiable. Model release required.

Sport Trade

AMERICAN BICYCLIST AND MOTORCYCLIST, 80 8th Ave., New York NY 10011. (212)206-7230. Editor: Konstantin Doren. For bicycle sales and service shops. Monthly. Circ. 10,068. Buys all rights. "Only staff-written articles are bylined, except under special circumstances." Pays on publication.
Nonfiction: Typical story describes (very specifically) unique traffic-builder or merchandising ideas used with success by an actual dealer. Articles may also deal exclusively with moped sales and service operation within conventional bicycle shop. Emphasis is on showing other dealers how they can follow a similar pattern and increase their business. Articles may also be based entirely on repair shop operation, depicting efficient and profitable service systems and methods. Buys 8 mss/year. Query. Length: 1,000-2,800 words. Pays 5¢/word, plus "bonus for outstanding manuscript."
Photos: Relevant b&w photos illustrating principal points in article purchased with ms; 5x7 minimum. No transparencies. Pays $8 per photo. Captions required. Buys all rights.

AMERICAN FIREARMS INDUSTRY, American Press Media Association, Inc., 2801 E. Oakland Park Blvd., Ft. Lauderdale FL 33306. Specializes in the sporting arms trade. Monthly magazine. Circ. 30,000. Pays on publication. Buys all rights. Submit all material with SASE. Reports in 2 weeks.
Nonfiction: R.A. Lesmeister, articles editor. Publishes informational, technical and new product articles. No general firearms subjects. Query. Length: 900-1,500 words. Pays $100-150.
Photos: B&w 8x10 glossy prints. "Manuscript price includes payment for photos."

AMERICAN HOCKEY AND ARENA MAGAZINE, Amateur Hockey Association of the United States, 2997 Broadmoor Valley Rd., Colorado Springs CO 80906. (303)576-4990. Publisher: Hal Trumble. Managing Editor: Jeff Mordhorst. 80% freelance written. Monthly magazine covering hockey equipment and arena components for teams, coaches and referees of the Amateur Hockey Association of the United States, ice facilities in the US and Canada, buyers, schools, colleges, pro teams, and park and recreation departments. Circ. 35,000. Pays on publication. Publishes ms an average of 1 month after acceptance. Byline given. Buys first rights and makes work-for-hire assignments. Phone queries OK. Submit seasonal material 4 months in advance. Photocopied and previously published submissions OK. SASE. Reports in 1 month. Sample copy $2.
Nonfiction: General interest, profile, new product and technical. Query. Length: 500-3,000 words. Pays $50 minimum.
Photos: Reviews 5x7 b&w glossy prints and color slides. Offers no additional payment for photos accepted with ms. Captions preferred. Buys one-time rights.
Columns/Departments: Rebound Shots (editorial); Americans in the Pros (US players in the NHL); College Notes; Rinks and Arenas (arena news); Equipment/Sports Medicine; Referees Crease; Coaches Playbook; For the Record; and Features (miscellaneous). Query.

ARCHERY RETAILER, Suite 306, 715 Florida Ave., S., Minneapolis MN 55426. (612)545-2662. Editor: Richard Sapp. 10% freelance written. Emphasizes business of the archery industry. Magazine published 6 times/year. Circ. 16,200. Pays on publication. Buys first rights only. Byline given. Phone queries OK, "but we prefer mail queries." Submit seasonal/holiday material 4 months in advance. Computer printout submissions acceptable; prefers letter-quality to dot-matrix. SASE. Reports in 3 weeks. Free sample copy and writer's guidelines.
Nonfiction: How-to (better buying, selling, displaying, advertising, etc.); interview; and profile. Features on sporting goods retail and specifically the marketing of archery equipment and accessories. "No stories about basement bandits selling because they love archery but have no idea of profitability." Query. Length: 500-1,200 words. Pays $50-150.
Photos: Purchased with or without accompanying ms. Captions required. Pays $10-25 for 8x10 b&w glossies.
Tips: "Our primary purchases are shop features these days—stories on successful archery dealers. We're looking for writing that entertains as well as informs."

BICYCLE BUSINESS JOURNAL, 1904 Wenneca, Box 1570, Fort Worth TX 76101. Editor: Levy Joffrion. 10% freelance written. Monthly. Circ. 10,000. Pays on acceptance. Buys first rights only. Computer printout submissions acceptable. SASE. Publishes ms an average of 3 months after acceptance.
Nonfiction: Stories about dealers who service what they sell, emphasizing progressive, successful sales ideas in the face of rising costs and increased competition. Length: 3 double-spaced pages maximum. Also includes moped dealerships.
Photos: B&w glossy photo a must; vertical photo preferred. Query.
Tips: "We are requesting greater professionalism and more content and research in freelance material."

‡**BICYCLE DEALER SHOWCASE**, Hester Communications, Inc. Suite 250, 1700 E. Dyer Rd., Santa Ana CA 92705. (714)549-4834. Editor/Publisher: Walt Jarvis. Managing Editor: Molly Ingram. A monthly magazine covering the bicycle industry for bicycle/moped dealers and industry personnel. Circ. 12,000. Pays on publication. Byline given. Buys all rights. Submit seasonal/holiday material 2 months in advance. Computer printout submisions acceptable; prefers letter-quality to dot-matrix. SASE. Reports in 1 month on queries; 6 weeks on mss. Free sample copy and writer's guidelines for 9x12 SAE.
Nonfiction: How-to (design a store window, special clothing department, deal with security problems); humor; interview/profile; new product; personal experience; photo feature; and technical. "No self-serving articles if writing about a particular new product and company. Don't over simplify." Buys 6-12 mss/year. Query. Length: 500-1,500 words. Pays $100-300.
Photos: Send photos with query or ms. Pays $10-20 for b&w contact sheets with negatives; $10 for b&w negatives; $10-20 for b&w photos depending on size and number used; prefers 5x7. Captions and identification of subjects required. Buys one-time rights.
Columns/Departments: Salesmanship (question and answer on various retail problems and solutions, also management tips); Store Design (how to build a profitable store environment, merchandising and product display, store image, etc.); On the Road (personal interviews and bike retailers); and advertising and financial management. Query with published clips. Length: 250-1,000 words. Pays $100-300.
Fillers: Jokes, anecdotes and short humor. "We are also interested in good cartoons illustrated with one liners." Length: 50-250 words. Pays $25-100.
Tips: "Material must be fairly straightforward, with a slant toward economic factors or marketing techniques. Articles dealing with marketing bicycle products, and financing, better management techniques, and current trends, as related to bicycle equipment, are the best way for freelancers to break in. Areas most open to freelancers are articles on financial management of small retailer, and technical expertise in the area of bicycles (tips for bicycle mechanics on specific shop problems).

FISHING TACKLE RETAILER, B.A.S.S. Publications, 1 Bell Rd., Montgomery AL 36141. (205)272-9530. Editor: Dave Ellison. Quarterly magazine "designed to promote the economic health of retail sellers of freshwater and saltwater angling equipment." Circ. 22,000. Byline usually given. Buys all rights. Submit seasonal/holiday material 6 months in advance. SASE. Reports in 6 weeks. Sample copy $2; writer's guidelines for standard-size SAE and 1 first class stamp.
Nonfiction: How-to (merchandising and management techniques); technical (how readers can specifically benefit from individual technological advances); and success stories (how certain fishing tackle retailers have successfully overcome business difficulties and their advice to their fellow retailers). Articles must directly relate to the financial interests of the magazine's audience. Buys 100 mss/year. Query with clips of published work. Length: 50-3,000 words. Pays $10-600.
Photos: State availability of photos. Payment included with ms.
Columns/Departments: Retail Pointers (200-300 words) and Profit Strategy (750-900 words)—how-to tips, should be accompanied by illustration. Buys variable number mss/year.

FITNESS INDUSTRY, Industry Publishers, Inc., 1545 NE 123rd St., North Miami FL 33161. (305)893-8771. Executive Editor: Michael J. Keighley. Bimonthly magazine about the fitness industry. Includes racquetball, dancercize, running, physical therapy, swimming and aerobocize. For retailers and business people in the industry. Circ. 18,500. Pays on publication. Byline given. Buys all rights. Submit seasonal material 2 months in advance. SASE. Reports in 6 weeks. Sample copy $2.50; free writer's guidelines.
Nonfiction: "Content must be general, not featuring one specific manufacturing company or individual shop case-study. Articles can feature products, such as an examination of women's racquetball apparel, but must include industry-wide information, not pertaining specifically to the product of one manufacturer. Design, display, merchandising techniques, retailing procedures, shop layout and lighting are among those categories that would be of interest to our readers." Query. Length: 2,000-2,500 words. Pays 5¢/word.

GOLF COURSE MANAGEMENT, Golf Course Superintendents Association of America, 1617 St. Andrews, Lawrence KS 66044. (913)841-2240. Editor: Clay Loyd. Monthly magazine covering golf course and turf management. Circ. 15,000. Byline given. Buys all rights. Submit seasonal/holiday material 6 months in advance. Simultaneous queries and submissions OK. Reports in 2 weeks on queries; 1 month on mss. Free sample copy and writer's guidelines.
Nonfiction: Book excerpts, historical/nostalgic, interview/profile, personal experience and technical. "All areas that relate to the golf course superintendent—whether features or scholarly pieces related to turfgrass management. We prefer all submissions to be written *simply*." Special issues include January "conference issue"—features on convention cities used each year. Buys 20 mss/year. Query with clips of published work. Length: 1,500-3,000 words. Pays $100-300.
Photos: Send photos with ms. Pays $50-250 for color, 4x5 transparencies preferred. Captions, model release and identification of subjects required. Buys one-time rights.

Tips: "Call communications department (913)841-2240, offer idea, follow with outline and writing samples. Response from us is immediate."

GOLF INDUSTRY, Industry Publishers, Inc., 1545 NE 123rd St., North Miami FL 33161. (305)893-8771. Executive Editor: Michael J. Keighley. Emphasizes the golf industry for country clubs, pro-owned golf shops, real estate developments, municipal courses, military and schools. Bimonthly magazine; 75 pages. Circ. 17,000. Pays on publication. Buys all rights. Submit seasonal/holiday material 2-3 months in advance. SASE. Reports "usually in 6-8 weeks." Sample copy $2.50. Free writer's guidelines.
Nonfiction: Publishes informational articles "dealing with a specific facet of golf club or pro shop operations, e.g., design, merchandising, finances, etc." Buys 20 mss/year. Submit complete ms. Length: 2,500 words maximum. Pays 5¢/word.
Tips: "Since we don't make freelance assignments, a query is not particularly important. We would rather have a complete manuscript which conforms to our policy of general, but informative, articles about one specific facet of the business of golf merchandising, financing, retailing, etc. Well-written manuscripts, if not used immediately, are often held in our files for use in a future issue. We never publish articles concentrating on one specific manufacturer or extolling the virtues of one product over another. We seldom feature one club or retail outlet. We don't deal with the game itself, but with the business end of the game."

GOLF SHOP OPERATIONS, 495 Westport Ave., Norwalk CT 06856. (203)847-5811. Editor: Nick Romano. For golf professionals and shop operators at public and private courses, resorts, driving ranges and golf specialty stores. Magazine published 6 times/year. Circ. 12,500. Byline given. Pays on publication. Photocopied submissions OK. Computer printout submissions acceptable. Submit seasonal material (for Christmas and other holiday sales, or profiles of successful professionals with how-to angle emphasized) 3 months in advance. Reports in 1 month. Free sample copy.
Nonfiction: "We emphasize improving the golf retailer's knowledge of his profession. Articles should describe how pros are buying, promoting and merchandising and displaying wares in their shops that might be of practical value. Must be aimed only at the retailer." How-to, profile, successful business operation and merchandising techniques. Buys 6-8 mss/year. Phone queries preferred. Pays $165-200.
Photos: "Pictures are mandatory with all manuscript submissions." Captions required.
Tips: "I'm less inclined to assign anything unless the person can handle a camera. The profile pieces must have decent photos. We're really looking for the freelancers that understand the golf business. This helps us in that we won't have to rewrite a lot or have the writer go back and ask the obvious questions."

PGA MAGAZINE, Professional Golfer's Association of America, 100 Avenue of Champions, Palm Beach Gardens FL 33410. (305)626-3600. Editor: William A. Burbaum. Monthly magazine about golf for 14,000 club professionals and apprentices nationwide. Circ. 38,000. Average issue includes 8-10 articles and 6 departments. Pays on acceptance. Byline given. Phone queries OK. Submit seasonal material 3 months in advance. Photocopied and previously published submissions OK. Reports in 3 weeks. Free sample copy.
Nonfiction: Historical (great moments in golf revisited); personality profiles; off-beat (e.g., golf in stamps, unique collections); inspirational (personal success stories); and photo feature (great golf courses). Buys 15 mss/year. Query with outline and clips of previously published work. Length: 900-1,500 words. Pays 15¢/word minimum. "Exhibit knowledge and interest in the professional business and in other needs of today's club professional."
Photos: Pays $25/b&w contact sheets. Pays $75-100/35mm inside color transparencies; $150 for cover photos. Captions and model release required.

POOL & SPA NEWS, Leisure Publications, 3923 W. 6th St., Los Angeles CA 90020. (213)385-3926. Editor-in-Chief: J. Field. 40% freelance written. Emphasizes news of the swimming pool and spa industry for pool builders, pool retail stores and pool service firms. Semimonthly magazine. Circ. 12,000. Pays on publication. Buys all rights. Phone queries OK. Photocopied submissions OK. Computer printout submissions acceptable; no dot-matrix. SASE. Reports in 2 weeks. Publishes ms an average of 1 month after acceptance.
Nonfiction: Interview, new product, profile and technical. Length: 500-2,000 words. Pays 8¢/word.
Photos: Pays $8 per b&w photo used.

RODEO NEWS, Rodeo Publishing Corp., Box 5418, Norman OK 73070. (405)364-9444. Editor: G.D. Hollingsworth. A monthly special interest magazine devoted to the sport of rodeo and the West. Circ. 15,000. Pays on publication. Byline given. Offers 50% kill fee. Buys first North American serial rights. Submit seasonal/holiday material 3 months in advance. Photocopied submissions OK. Computer printout submissions acceptable. SASE. Reports in 1 month on queries; 2 weeks on mss. Sample copy $3; free writer's guidelines.
Nonfiction: Historical/nostalgic, how-to, humor, interview/profile, new product, personal experience, photo feature and technical. Buys 20 mss/year. Query with published clips. Length: 1,200-5,000 words. Pays $100-500.
Photos: State availability of photos. Pays $25 for 8x10 b&w photos; $75 for color transparencies. Captions and

identification of subjects required. Buys all rights.
Fillers: Newsbreaks. Buys 50/year. Length: 500 words. Pays $75 maximum.

RVB, RECREATIONAL VEHICLE BUSINESS, 29901 Agoura Rd., Agoura CA 91301. Editor: Michael Schneider. Managing Editor: Sheryl Davis. 50% freelance written. For men and women of the RV industry, primarily those involved in the sale of trailers, motorhomes, pickup campers and vans. Also, owners and operators of trailer supply stores, plus manufacturers and executives of the RV industry nationwide and in Canada. Monthly magazine; 100 pages. Circ. 25,000. Buys first North American serial rights. Pays on publication. Computer printout submissions acceptable. Free sample copy and writer's guidelines. Reports in 1 month. Publishes ms an average of 4 months after acceptance. SASE.
Nonfiction: "Stories that show trends in the industry; success stories of particular dealerships throughout the country; news stories on new products; accessories (news section); and how-to (sell, increase profits, be a better businessman). Interested in broad-based, general interest material of use to all RV retailers, rather than mere trade reporting." Informational, how-to, personal experience, interview, profile, humor, think articles, successful business operations and merchandising techniques. Buys 75 mss/year. Query. Length: 1,000-2,000 words. Pays $150-350. Shorter items for regular columns or departments run 800 words. Pays $50-125.
Photos: Photos purchased with accompanying ms with no additional payment. Captions required.
Columns/Departments: Dealer/industry items from over the country and newsbreaks. Length: 100-200 words; with photos, if possible. Payment based on length.
Tips: "A more broad-based approach will affect writers in the year ahead."

THE SHOOTING INDUSTRY, 591 Camino de la Reina, San Diego CA 92108. (619)297-8521. Editor: J. Rakusan. For manufacturers, dealers and sales representatives of archery and shooting equipment. Monthly. Buys all rights. Byline given. Pays on publication. Reports in 2-3 weeks. SASE. Free sample copy.
Nonfiction: Articles that tell "secrets of my success" based on experience of individual gun dealer; articles of advice to help dealers sell more guns and shooting equipment. Also, articles about and of interest to manufacturers and top manufacturers' executives. Buys about 135 mss/year. Query. Length: 3,000 words maximum. Pays $100-200.
Photos: Photos essential; b&w glossies purchased with ms.

SKI BUSINESS, 975 Post Rd., Darien CT 06820. Editor: Bob Gillen. 70% freelance written. Tabloid magazine published 11 times/year. For ski retailers, both alpine and cross-country markets; also covers sailboard industry. Circ. 18,000. Byline given, except on "press releases and round-up articles containing passages from articles submitted by several writers." Pays on publication. Buys first rights plus reprint rights for promotional use and republication in special editions. Submit seasonal material 3 weeks in advance. Computer printout submissions acceptable; prefers letter-quality to dot-matrix. Reports in 1 month. Publishes ms an average of 2 months after acceptance. Free sample copy available to qualified writers. SASE.
Nonfiction: Will consider ski shop case studies; mss about unique and successful merchandising ideas; and ski area equipment rental operations. "All material should be slanted toward usefulness to the ski shop operator. Always interested in interviews with successful retailers." Uses round-ups of preseason sales and Christmas buying across the country from September to December. Would like to see reports on what retailers in major markets are doing. Buys about 150 mss/year. Query first. Pays $50-200.
Photos: Photos purchased with accompanying mss. Buys b&w glossy 8x10 photos. Pays minimum of $25/photo; more for color and 35mm transparencies.

‡**SPA AND SAUNA TRADE JOURNAL, The Voice of the Hot Water Industry**, Hester Communications, Inc., Suite 250, 1700 E. Dyer Rd., Santa Ana CA 92705. Editor: Susan Kopicki. Monthly magazine. "Our publication is a trade magazine for people who make or sell spas, hot tubs and related items. Our primary focus is to provide retailers of these items with as much information as possible that will help increase their sales." Circ. 7,500. Pays on acceptance. Byline given. Buys first North American serial rights. Submit seasonal/holiday material 3 months in advance. Simultaneous queries and previously published submissions OK. Computer printout submissions acceptable. SASE. Reports in 2 weeks on queries; 1 month on mss. Free sample copy and writer's guidelines.
Nonfiction: How-to (almost all facets of running a spa retail operation); photo feature (possibly of spa, hot tub, sauna installations of merit); and technical (installing spas, hot tubs and saunas). Buys 15 mss/year. Query with published clips. Length: 750-2,000 words. Pays $50-200.
Photos: "No prices have been established; will negotiate individually."
Tips: "Write articles that are specific, showing nuts-and-bolts knowledge of what it takes to run a spa store." Features are most open to freelancers.

THE SPORTING GOODS DEALER, 1212 N. Lindbergh Blvd., St. Louis MO 63132. (314)997-7111. President/Chief Executive Officer: Richard Waters. Editor: Gary Goldman. 20% freelance written. For members of the sporting goods trade: retailers, manufacturers, wholesalers, and representatives. Monthly magazine. Circ. 27,000. Buys second serial (reprint) rights. Buys about 15 mss/year. Pays on publication. Computer printout submissions acceptable; no dot-matrix. Reports in 2 weeks. Publishes ms an average of 3 months after acceptance. Query. SASE. Sample copy $1 (refunded with first ms); free writer's guidelines.

Nonfiction: "Articles about specific sporting goods retail stores, their promotions, display techniques, sales ideas, merchandising, timely news of key personnel; expansions, new stores, deaths—all in the sporting goods trade. Specific details on how individual successful sporting goods stores operate. What specific retail sporting goods stores are doing that is new and different. We would also be interested in features dealing with stores doing an outstanding job in retailing of baseball, fishing, golf, tennis, camping, firearms/hunting and allied lines of equipment. Query on these." Successful business operations and merchandising techniques. Does not want to see announcements of doings and engagements. Length: open. Rates negotiated by assignment. Also looking for material for the following columns: Terse Tales of the Trade (store news); Selling Slants (store promotions); and Open for Business (new retail sporting goods stores or sporting goods departments). All material must relate to specific sporting goods stores by name, city, and state; general information is not accepted.

Photos: Pays minimum of $3.50 for sharp clear b&w photos; size not important. These are purchased with or without mss. Captions optional, but identification requested.

Fillers: Clippings. These must relate directly to the sporting goods industry. Pays 1-2¢/published word.

SPORTS MERCHANDISER, W.R.C. Smith Publishing Co., 1760 Peachtree Rd. NW, Atlanta GA 30357. (404)874-4462. Editor: Eugene R. Marnell. 5% freelance written. For retailers and wholesalers of sporting goods in all categories; independent stores, chains, specialty stores and department store departments. Monthly tabloid; 100 pages. Circ. 30,000. Pays on acceptance. Buys all rights. Submit seasonal/holiday material 4-6 months in advance. Computer printout submissions acceptable; prefers letter-quality to dot-matrix. SASE. Reports in 4 months. Publishes ms an average of 3 months after acceptance.

Nonfiction: "Articles telling how retailers are successful in selling a line of products, display ideas, successful merchandising programs, inventory operations, and advertising program successes. No articles on business history. Query to be one-page with card (reply) enclosed. Letters to state full name of contact, address, etc. and describe type of business relative to volume, inventory and positioning in local market. Tell particular slant author believes most interesting." Length: 1,000-2,000 words. Pays $75-175.

Photos: State availability of photos with query. Offers no additional payment for 5x7 or 8x10 b&w prints. Captions required. Buys all rights.

Tips: "The retail order season is almost six months opposite the retail buying season (i.e., consumer buying). Lead time for ordering is six months—sometimes more on hardgoods and softgoods. Other products have full-year ordering cycle. Hence, query will help everyone."

SPORTS TRADE CANADA, Page Communications, Ltd., 501 Oakdale Rd., Downsview, Toronto, Ontario M3N 1W7 Canada. (416)746-7360. Editor: Hugh McBride. For sporting goods retailers, manufacturers, wholesalers, jobbers, department and chain stores, camping equipment dealers, bicycle sales and service, etc. Magazine published 7 times/year. Circ. 9,800. Pays on publication. Buys first rights only. Reports in 2 months. SAE and IRCs.

Nonfiction: Technical and informational articles. Articles on successful Canadian business operations, new products, merchandising techniques and interviews. No US-oriented articles. Query. Length: 1,200-2,000 words. Pays 10¢/word or $60/published page.

Tips: Submit Canadian-oriented articles only; "new sales help techniques are best."

‡**SPORTSTYLE**, Fairchild Publications, Inc., 7 E. 12th St., New York NY 10003. (212)741-5995. Editor: Steven Lang. A bimonthly tabloid covering the sporting goods industry for sporting goods retailers and manufacturers of athletic footwear, apparel and equipment. Circ. 25,000. Pays on publication. Byline given. Offers negotiable kill fee. Computer printout submissions acceptable. Reports in 1 month. Free sample copy.

Nonfiction: "We run business stories only and use a lot of retailer profiles and occasionally manufacturer profiles." Buys 25 mss/year. Query. Length: 2,000 words. Pays $5/column inch.

SWIMMING POOL AGE & SPA MERCHANDISER, Communication Channels, Inc., 6255 Barfield Rd., Atlanta GA 30328. (404)256-9800. Editor: Bill Gregory. Emphasizes pool, spa and hot tub industry. Monthly tabloid. Circ. 15,000. Pays on publication. Buys all rights. Phone queries OK. Submit seasonal/holiday material 3 months in advance.

Nonfiction: Expose (if in industry, company frauds); how-to (do more business, installation techniques, service and repairs, tips, etc.); interview (with people and groups within the industry); photo feature (pool/spa/tub construction or special use); technical (should be prepared with expert within the industry); industry news; and market research reports. Buys 10-20 unsolicited mss/year. Query. Length: 250-1,500 words. Pays 10¢/word.

Photos: Purchased with accompanying ms or on assignment. Captions required. Query or send contact sheet. Will accept 35mm transparencies of good quality.

Columns/Departments: "Short news on personality items always welcome." Association News and Continuing Education.
Fiction: Humor about the industry. Length: 1,000 words maximum. Pays 10¢/word.

TENNIS INDUSTRY, Industry Publishers, Inc., 1545 NE 123 St., North Miami FL 33161. (305)893-8771. Editor: Michael J. Keighley. Emphasizes the tennis industry for department store divisionals, teaching pros, pro shop managers, specialty shop managers, country club managers, coaches, athletic directors, etc. Monthly magazine; 200 pages. Circ. 19,000. Pays on publication. Buys all rights. Submit seasonal/holiday material 2-3 months in advance. Previously published submissions OK. SASE. Reports "usually in 6-8 weeks." Sample copy $2.50; free writer's guidelines.
Nonfiction: Publishes informational articles dealing "with specific facets of the tennis club or pro shop operation, e.g., design, merchandising, finances, etc." Buys 20 mss/year. Submit complete ms. Length: 2,500 words maximum. Pays 5¢/word.
Tips: "Since we do not make freelance assignments, a query is not particularly important. We would rather have a complete manuscript which conforms to our policy of general but informative articles about one specific facet of the business of tennis merchandising, financing, retailing, etc. Well-done manuscripts, if not used immediately, are often held in our files for use in a future issue. We never publish articles concentrating on one specific manufacturer or extolling the virtues of one product over another. We seldom feature one club or retail outlet. We don't deal with the game itself, but with the business end of the game."

‡**WOODALL'S CAMPGROUND MANAGEMENT**, Woodall Publishing Co., 500 Hyacinth Pl., Highland Park Il 60035. (312)433-4550. Editor: Mike Byrnes. A monthly tabloid covering campground management and operation for managers of private and public campgrounds throughout the United States. Circ. 17,200. Pays after publication. Byline given. Buys all rights. Submit seasonal/holiday material 4 months in advance. Simultaneous queries OK. SASE. Reports in 2 weeks on queries; 6 weeks on mss. Free sample copy and writer's guidelines.
Nonfiction: How-to, interview/profile and technical. "Our articles tell our readers how to maintain their resources, manage personnel and guests, market, develop new campground areas and activities, and interrelate with the major tourism organizations within their areas. 'Improvement' and 'profit' are the two key words." Buys 48+ mss/year. Query. Length: 500 words minimum. Pays $50-200.
Photos: Send contact sheets and negatives. "We pay for each photo used."
Tips: "Contact us and give us an idea of your ability to travel and your travel range. We sometimes have assignments in certain areas. The best type of story to break in with is a case history type approach about how a campground improved its maintenance, physical plant or profitability."

Stone and Quarry Products

CONCRETE CONSTRUCTION MAGAZINE, 426 South Westgate, Addison IL 60101. Editor: Ward R. Malisch. For general and concrete contractors, architects, engineers, concrete producers, cement manufacturers, distributors and dealers in construction equipment and testing labs. Monthly magazine; 80 pages average. Circ. 82,000. Buys all rights. "Bylines are used only by prearrangement with the author." Pays on acceptance. Buys 8-10 mss/year. Photocopied submissions OK. Reports in 1-2 months. Submit query with topical outline. SASE. Free sample copy and writer's guidelines.
Nonfiction: "Our magazine has a major emphasis on cast-in-place (site cast) concrete. Precast and prestressed concrete is also covered. Our articles deal with tools, techniques and materials that result in better handling, better placing, and ultimately an improved final product. We are particularly firm about not using proprietary names in any of our articles. Manufacturer and product names are never mentioned; only the processes or techniques that might be of help to the concrete contractor, the architect or the engineer dealing with the material. We do use reader response cards to relay reader interest to manufacturers." Does not want to see job stories or promotional material. Pays $200/2-page article. Prefers 1,000-2,000 words with 2-3 illustrations.
Photos: Photos are used only as part of a complete ms.
Tips: "Condensed, totally factual presentations are preferred."

CONCRETE INTERNATIONAL: DESIGN AND CONSTRUCTION, American Concrete Institute, 22400 W. Seven Mile Rd., Detroit MI 48219. (313)532-2600. Advertising Coordinator: Lorette Edwards. 1% freelance written. Monthly magazine about concrete for design engineers, management and construction people. Circ. 17,000. Pays on publication. Publishes ms an average of 3 months after acceptance. Buys all rights, first rights, second serial rights, and makes assignments on a work-for-hire basis. Phone queries OK. Submit seasonal material 4 months in advance. Computer printout submissions acceptable. SASE. Reports in 2 weeks on queries; in 1 month on mss. Free sample copy and writer's guidelines.

Nonfiction: Historical (concrete structures); how-to (concrete construction, new methods, techniques); new product (concrete-related); and technical (concrete-related). Query. Length: 300-5,000 words. Pays $100/printed page.

Photos: State availability of photos or send photos with ms. Reviews b&w contact sheets and 5x7 and 8x10 prints. Offers no additional payment for photos accepted with ms. Captions and model release required. Buys one-time rights.

Columns/Departments: Legal (related to concrete construction); Problems, Solutions and Practices; and Management Techniques. Query. Length: 600-1,000 words.

MINE AND QUARRY, Ashire Publishing Ltd., 42 Gray's Inn Rd., London WC1X 8LR England. Editor: Cyril G. Middup. Monthly magazine; for senior management at mines and quarries. 80 pages. Circ. 4,600. Buys all rights. Phone queries OK. Submit seasonal/holiday material 2 months in advance. Simultaneous, photocopied and previously published submissions OK. Computer printout submissions acceptable. SAE and IRCs. Reports in 2 months. Free sample copy and writer's guidelines.

Nonfiction: Technical and new product articles related to the industry. Buys 10 mss/year. Submit complete ms. Length: 200-1,000 words. Pays $10-20.

Photos: B&w glossy prints and color transparencies purchased with or without mss. Captions required. Send contact sheet, prints or transparencies. Pays $3-6.

STONE IN AMERICA, American Monument Association, 6902 N. High St., Worthington OH 43085. (614)885-2713. Managing Editor: Bob Moon. Monthly magazine for the retailers of upright memorials in the US and Canada. Circ. 2,600. Pays on acceptance. Buys interment industry rights. Phone queries preferred. SASE. Reports in 1 month. Free sample copy and writer's guidelines.

Nonfiction: How-to (run a monument business); informational (major news within the industry, monuments as an art form); profile (successful retailers); and technical. Buys 30-40 mss/year. Length: 1,500-2,000 words. Query. Pays $100-400.

Photos: Pays $20-50 for 5x7 or 8x10 b&w glossy prints.

Columns/Departments: Businss Brief (small business practices); Retail Report (successful retailers); and Panorama (industry news and features). Length: 1,500 words minimum.

Toy, Novelty, and Hobby

CREATIVE PRODUCT NEWS, Box 584, Lake Forest IL 60045. (312)234-5052. Editor: Linda F. Lewis. Monthly tabloid for retailers of crafts, needlework and art materials for fine art, hobby art and doll house miniatures. Circ. 28,000. Pays on acceptance. Byline given. Buys first North American serial rights. Submit seasonal/holiday material 7 months in advance. Simultaneous queries and photocopied submissions OK. SASE. Reports in 1 month. Free sample copy.

Nonfiction: "We need only one thing: packages containing 4-6 photos and 200- to 500-word descriptions. Topic should be demonstration of a new art or craft technique; photos must show finished article, supplies used and procedure." Buys 12 mss/year. Query with clips of published work. Pays $50.

Tips: "Our total concern is what's new. Submit only ideas that are truly new."

MINIATURES & DOLL DEALER MAGAZINE, Boynton & Associates Inc., Clifton House, Clifton VA 22024. (703)830-1000. Assistant Editor: Geraldine Williams. 30% freelance written. For "retailers in the dollhouse/miniatures and collectible doll trade. Our readers are generally independent, small store owners who don't have time to read anything that does not pertain specifically to their own problems." Monthly magazine; 80 pages. Circ. 7,000. Pays on publication. Publishes ms an average of 3 months after acceptance. Buys all rights. Byline given. Phone queries OK. Submit seasonal/holiday material 4 months in advance. Photocopied, previously published and simultaneous submissions (if submitted to publications in different fields) OK. Computer printout submissions acceptable. SASE. Reports in 3 weeks. Sample copy $1.50; free writer's guidelines (SASE).

Nonfiction: How-to (unique articles—e.g., how to finish a dollhouse exterior—are acceptable if they introduce new techniques or ideas; show the retailer how learning this technique will help sell dollhouses); profiles of miniatures and/or doll shops; and business information pertaining to small store retailers. Buys 4-6 mss/issue. Query or send complete ms. "In query, writer should give clear description of intended article, when he could have it to me plus indication that he has studied the field, and is not making a 'blind' query. Availability of photos should be noted." Pay negotiable.

Photos: "Photos must tie in directly with articles." State availability of photos. Pays $7 for each photo used. Prefers 5x7 b&w glossy prints (reviews contact sheets). Captions and model release preferred.

Tips: "The best way for a freelancer to break in is to study several issues of our magazine, then try to visit a miniatures and/or doll shop and submit an *M&DD* Visits . . . article. This is a regular feature that can be written by a sharp freelancer who takes the time to study and follow the formula this feature uses. Also, basic business articles for retailers—inventory control, how to handle bad checks, etc., that are written with miniatures and doll dealers in mind, are always needed. *M&D* is extremely interested in good business articles."

MODEL RETAILER MAGAZINE, Clifton House, Clifton VA 22024. (703)830-1000. Editor: Geoffrey Wheeler. 70% freelance written. "For hobby store owners—generally well-established small business persons, fairly well educated, and very busy." Monthly magazine. Circ. 7,300. Pays on publication. Buys first-time rights. Byline given. Phone queries OK (no collect calls, please), but prefers written queries. Submit seasonal/holiday material 3 months in advance. Simultaneous, photocopied and previously published submissions OK. Computer printout submissions acceptable; prefers letter-quality to dot-matrix. SASE. Reports in 3 weeks. Sample copy $1.50; free writer's guidelines.

Nonfiction: Retailer profiles; articles on store management, marketing, merchandising, advertising; and photo feature (if photos tie in with marketing techniques or hobby store operation, etc.). "No company profiles, 'human interest' stories, self-publicity articles, or reports on trade shows. (We do those ourselves)." Buys 2-4 mss/issue. Query. Length: 1,200-2,500 words. Pays for complete article package of: main copy, side bars (if needed), working headline, and illustrative material (if needed). Range: $125-300, depending on length and degree of specialization.

Photos: "Photos that illustrate key points and are of good quality will help the article, particularly if it concerns business operation. Photos are paid for as part of total article package."

THE STAMP WHOLESALER, Box 706, Albany OR 97321. Editor/Publisher: Jim Magruder. 80% freelance written. For small-time independent businessmen; many are part-time and/or retired from other work. Published 26 times/year; 80 pages. Circ. 7,500. Buys all rights. Byline given. Buys 60 mss/year. Pays on publication. Will send free sample copy to writer on request. Reports in 10 weeks. Submit complete ms. SASE.

Nonfiction: How-to information on how to deal more profitably in postage stamps for collections. Emphasis on merchandising techniques and how to make money. Does not want to see any so-called "humor" items from nonprofessionals. Length: 1,000-1,500 words. Pays $50 and up per article.

Tips: "Send queries on business stories. Send manuscript on stamp dealer stories. We need stories to help dealers make and save money."

Travel

AIRFAIR INTERLINE MAGAZINE, The Authority On Interline Travel, Airline Marketing, Inc., 25 W. 39th St., New York NY 10018. (212)840-6714. Editor: Gayle Guynup. Assistant Editor: Nancy Mattia. Monthly magazine covering travel information for airline employees; describing travel packages by air, land or ship and including information on hotels and restaurants. Circ. 30,000. Pays on publication. Byline given. Buys first North American serial rights. Submit seasonal/holiday material 2 months in advance. Simultaneous queries, and simultaneous and photocopied submissions OK. SASE. Reports in 6 months on queries; 4 months on mss. Free sample copy and writer's guidelines.

Nonfiction: Travel (should concentrate on foreign destinations). Buys 20 mss/year. Query with clips of published work. Length: 2,000 words maximum. Pays $75 maximum.

ASTA TRAVEL NEWS, 488 Madison Ave., New York NY 10022. Editor: Patrick Arton. Managing Editor: Kathi Froio. 75% freelance written. Emphasizes travel, tourism and transportation. Monthly magazine; 120 pages. Circ. 19,500. Pays on acceptance. Buys all rights. Submit seasonal/holiday material 3 months in advance. Photocopied submissions OK. Reports in 1 month. Publishes ms an average of 3 months after acceptance.

Nonfiction: How-to, interview, new product, profile, technical and travel. No first person personal experience. Buys 75 mss/year. Query. Length: 500-1,500 words. Pays $50-250.

Photos: Submit photo material with accompanying query. No additional payment for b&w prints or color transparencies. Captions required.

BUS RIDE, Friendship Publications, Inc., Box 1472, Spokane WA 99210. (509)328-9181. Editor: William A. Luke. Magazine published 8 times/year covering bus transportation. Circ. 12,500. Byline given. Not copyrighted. SASE. Sample copy $3; free writer's guidelines.
Nonfiction: How-to (on bus maintenance, operations, marketing); new product; and technical. Only bus transportation material is acceptable. Query. Length: 500-1,500 words. No payment from publication; "writer may receive payment from company or organization featured."
Photos: State availability of photos. Reviews b&w 8x10 prints. Captions required.
Fillers: Newsbreaks. Length: 50-100 words.
Tips: "A freelancer can contact bus companies, transit authorities, suppliers and products for the bus industry to write articles which would be accepted by our publication."

BUS TOURS MAGAZINE, The Magazine of Bus Tours and Long Distance Charters, National Bus Trader, Inc., Rt. 3, Box 349B (Theater Rd.), Delavan WI 53115. (414)728-2691. Editor: Larry Plachno. Editorial Assistant: Dianna Woss. Bimonthly magazine for bus companies and tour brokers who design or sell bus tours. Circ. 9,306. Pays as arranged. Byline given. Not copyrighted. Buys rights as arranged. Submit seasonal/holiday material 9 months in advance. Simultaneous queries OK. Reports in 1 month. Free sample copy and writer's guidelines.
Nonfiction: Historical/nostalgic, how-to, humor, interview/profile, new product, personal experience, and travel; all on bus tours. Buys 10 mss/year. Query. Length: open. Pays negotiable fee.
Photos: State availability of photos. Reviews 35mm transparencies and 6x9 or 8x10 prints. Caption, model release and identification of subjects required.
Columns/Departments: Bus Tour Marketing; and Buses and the Law. Buys 15-20 mss/year. Query. Length: 1-1½ pages.
Tips: "Most of our feature articles are written by freelancers under contract from local convention and tourism bureaus. Specifications on request. Writers should query local bureaus regarding their interest. Must have extensive background and knowledge of bus tours."

BUS WORLD, Motor Coach Photo-Feature Magazine, Sunrise Enterprises, Box 39, Woodland Hills CA 91365. (818)710-0208. Editor: Ed Stauss. 75% freelance written. Quarterly trade journal covering the transit and intercity bus industries. "*Bus World* is edited to inform and entertain people who have an interest in buses—bus owners, managers, drivers, enthusiasts, and historians. With extensive photographic coverage, *Bus World* describes the function and lore of the bus industry including intercity, transit, tour, and charter." Circ. 5,000. Pays on publication. Byline given. Buys first North American serial rights. Submit seasonal/holiday material 6 months in advance. Electronic submissions OK if compatible with 300 baud or IBM-formatted disk. Computer printout submissions acceptable. SASE. Reports in 3 weeks. Publishes ms an average of 6 months after acceptance. Sample copy $1; writer's guidelines for SAE and 1 first class stamp.
Nonfiction: Historical/nostalgic, humor, interview/profile, new product, opinion, personal experience, photo feature and technical. "Author must show an understanding of the bus industry. Coverage includes descriptions of new vehicles, surveys of operating systems, first person experiences with transit and intercity operations, and reviews of historic equipment and systems. Primary coverage is North America." No tourist or travelog viewpoints. Buys 8-12 mss/year. Query. Length: 500-2,000 words. Pays $20-60.
Photos: "Photos should be sharp and clear." State availability of photos. "No separate payment for photos. We buy photos with manuscripts under one payment." Reviews 35mm color transparencies and 8x10 b&w prints. Captions required. Buys one-time rights.
Fillers: Cartoons. Buys 4-6/year. Pays $10-25.
Tips: "Be employed in or have a good understanding of the bus industry. Be enthusiastic about buses—their history and future—as well as current events. Acceptable material will be held until used and will not be returned unless requested by sender. Unacceptable and excess material will be returned only if accompanied by suitable SASE."

‡CANADIAN CAMPING & RV DEALER, Suite 202, 2077 Dundas St. E., Mississauga, Ontario L4X 1M2 Canada. (416)624-8218. Published 7 times/year "to better the development and growth of Canada's recreational vehicle and camping accessory dealers." Circ. 8,000. Pays on publication. Byline given. Buys first rights only. SASE. Reports in 2 months. Free sample copy and writer's guidelines.
Nonfiction: Personal experience, photo feature and technical. Recent articles have covered sanitation equipment for campers, distributor meetings and new models. Query.

● **GO GREYHOUND**, The Greyhound Corp., Greyhound Tower 1810, Phoenix AZ 85077. (602)248-5714. Editor: Donald L. Behnke. 10% freelance written. Quarterly in-house publication for Greyhound shareholders, employees and other interested individuals. Circ. 200,000. Pays on acceptance. No byline given. Buys one-time rights. Submit seasonal/holiday material 9 months in advance. Simultaneous queries and simultaneous and photocopied submissions OK. Computer printout submissions acceptable; no dot-matrix. Reports in 3 months. Publishes ms an average of 6 months after acceptance. Free sample copy and writer's guidelines.

Nonfiction: Mary Jo Orkild, publications assistant. Travel (to places reached by Greyhound bus). "We review features about historic, scenic or entertainment attractions that can be reached by Greyhound bus." No personal experience stories. Buys 4 mss/year. Query or send complete ms. Length: 500-800 words. Pays $350 maximum with color pictures.

Photos: Mary Jo Orkild, publications assistant. "Articles must be accompanied by a minimum of 12 good quality color transparencies from which we may choose to illustrate the story." Payment included with purchase of ms. Reviews 35mm and larger color transparencies and 5x7 color prints.

Tips: "Follow our writer's guidelines. We must see accompanying transparencies, and we require excellent color pictures to accompany travel stories. We will only review stories with pictures—professional quality. Articles submitted without required transparencies will not be considered. Do not send personal experience travel on bus."

INCENTIVE TRAVEL MANAGER, Brentwood Publishing Corp., 825 S. Barrington Ave., Los Angeles CA 90049. (213)826-8388. Editor: Nancy Zimmerman. 90% freelance written, mostly on assignment. Monthly magazine for corporate executives in charge of incentive travel. Circ. 40,000. Pays "by edited word count on acceptance." Byline given. Buys all rights. Computer printout submissions acceptable; prefers letter-quality to dot-matrix. SASE. Reports "when an assignment is available." Publishes ms an average of 6 months after acceptance.

Nonfiction: General interest (incentive travel, planning, promotion, selecting destinations, execution); interview/profile (of executives); and travel (destination updates). Buys 60-70 mss/year. Query with published clips. Length: 1,000-2,200 words. Pays 10-12¢/word.

Tips: "We are not interested in travel articles geared to the average tourist or travel agent. Ours is a very specific focus; you must familiarize yourself with our content and know something about the field."

NATIONAL BUS TRADER, The Magazine of Bus Equipment for the United States and Canada, Rt. 3, Box 349B (Theater Rd.), Delavan WI 53115. (414)728-2691. Editor: Larry Plachno. Monthly magazine for manufacturers, dealers and owners of buses and motor coaches. Circ. 7,354. Pays on either acceptance or publication. Byline given. Not copyrighted. Buys rights "as required by writer." Simultaneous queries and simultaneous, photocopied and previously published submissions OK. Computer printout submissions acceptable. Reports in 1 month. Free sample copy.

Nonfiction: Historical/nostalgic (on old buses); how-to (maintenance repair); new products; photo feature; and technical (aspects of mechanical operation of buses). "We are finding that more and more firms and agencies are hiring freelancers to write articles to our specifications. We are more likely to run them if someone else pays." No material that does NOT pertain to bus tours or bus equipment. Buys 3-5 unsolicited mss/year. Query. Length: varies. Pays variable rate.

Photos: State availability of photos. Reviews 5x7 or 8x10 prints and 35mm transparencies. Captions, model release and identification of subjects required.

Columns/Departments: Bus maintenance; Buses and the Law; Regulations; and Bus of the Month. Buys 20-30 mss/year. Query. Length: 1-1½ pages. Pays variable rate.

Tips: "We are a very technical publication. Writers should submit qualifications showing extensive background in bus vehicles. We're always looking for new column ideas. We probably will add more pages in the next year which will require more editorial."

RVBUSINESS, TL Enterprises, Inc., 29901 Agoura Rd., Agoura CA 91301. (818)991-4980. Editor: Michael Schneider. Managing Editor: Sheryl Davis. Monthly magazine covering the recreational vehicle and allied industries for "people of the RV industry—dealers, manufacturers, suppliers, park management, legislators and finance experts." Circ. 25,000. Pays on publication. Byline given. Offers 50% kill fee. Buys first North American serial rights. Submit seasonal/holiday material 6 months in advance. Photocopied submissions OK. SASE. Reports in 3 weeks on queries; 6 weeks on mss. Sample copy for 9x12 SAE and 3 first class stamps; writer's guidelines for business-size SAE and 1 first class stamp.

Nonfiction: Expose (carefully done and thoroughly researched); historical/nostalgic (companies, products or people pertaining to the RV industry itself); how-to (deal with any specific aspect of the RV business); interview/profile (persons or companies involved with the industry—legislative, finance, dealerships, park management, manufacturing, supplier); new product (no payment for company promo material—Product Spotlight usually requires interview with company spokesperson, firsthand experience with product; specifics and verification of statistics required—must be factual; opinion (controversy OK); personal experience (must be something of importance to readership—must have a point: it worked for me, it can for you; or this is why it didn't work for me); photo feature (4-color transparencies required with good captions; photo coverage of RV shows, conventions and meetings not appropriate topics for photo feature); and technical (photos required, 4-color preferred). General business articles may be considered. Buys 60 mss/year. Query with published clips.

Send complete ms—"but only read on speculation." Length: 1,000-2,000 words. Pays variable rate up to $400.

Photos: State availability of photos with query or send photos with ms. Reviews 35mm transparencies and 8x10 b&w prints. Captions, model release and identification of subjects required. Buys one-time or all rights; unused photos returned.

Columns/Departments: Guest editorial; News (50-500 words maximum, b&w photos appreciated); and RV People (color photos/4-color transparencies; this section lends itself to fun, upbeat copy). Buys 100-120 mss/year. Query or send complete ms. Pays $10-200 "depending on where used and importance."

Tips: "Query. Phone OK; letter preferable. Send one or several ideas and a few lines letting us know how you plan to treat it/them. We are always looking for good authors knowledgeable in the RV industry or related industries."

THE STAR SERVICE, Sloane Travel Agency Reports, Box 15610, Fort Lauderdale FL 33318. (305)472-8794. Editor: Robert D. Sloane. 100% freelance written. Editorial manual sold to travel agencies on subscription basis. Buys all rights. Buys about 4,000 reports/year. Pays 15 days prior to publication. "Write for instruction sheet and sample report form. Initial reports sent by a new correspondent will be examined for competence and criticized as necessary upon receipt; but once established, a correspondent's submissions will not usually be acknowledged until payment is forwarded, which can often be several months, depending on immediate editorial needs." Computer printout submissions acceptable. Query. SASE.

Nonfiction: "Objective, critical evaluations of worldwide hotels and cruise ships suitable for North Americans, based on inspections. Forms can be provided to correspondents so no special writing style is required, only perception, experience and judgment in travel. No commercial gimmick—no advertising or payment for listings in publication is accepted." With query, writer should "outline experience in travel and writing and specific forthcoming travel plans, and time available for inspections. Leading travel agents throughout the world subscribe to *Star Service*. No credit or byline is given correspondents due to delicate subject matter often involving negative criticism of hotels. We would like to emphasize the importance of reports being based on current experience and the importance of reporting on a substantial volume of hotels, not just isolated stops (since staying in a hotel is not a requisite) in order that work be profitable for both publisher and writer. Experience in travel writing and/or travel industry is desirable." Length: "up to 350 words, if submitted in paragraph form; varies if submitted on printed inspection form." Pays $15/report (higher for ships) used. "Guarantees of acceptance of set numbers of reports may be made on establishment of correspondent's ability and reliability, but always on prior arrangement. Higher rates of payment sometimes arranged, after correspondent's reliability is established."

THE TRAVEL AGENT, 2 W. 46th St., New York NY 10036. Editor/Publisher: Eric Friedheim. For "travel agencies and travel industry executives." Semiweekly. Circ. 35,000. Not copyrighted. Pays on acceptance. Query. Reports "immediately." SASE.

Nonfiction: Uses trade features slanted to travel agents, sales and marketing people, and executives of transportation companies such as airlines, ship lines, etc. No travelogues such as those appearing in newspapers and consumer publications. Articles should show how agent and carriers can sell more travel to the public. Length: up to 2,500 words. Pays $50-100.

Photos: Photos purchased with ms.

TRAVELAGE MIDAMERICA, Official Airlines Guide, Inc., A Dun & Bradstreet Co., Suite 2416 Prudential Plaza, Chicago IL 60601. (312)861-0432. Editor/Publisher: Martin Deutsch. Managing Editor: Linda Ball. 15% freelance written. "For travel agents in the 13 midAmerica states and in Ontario and Manitoba." Biweekly magazine. Circ. 15,000. Pays on publication. Buys one-time rights. Submit seasonal/holiday material 3 months in advance. Simultaneous, photocopied and previously published submissions OK. Computer printout submissions acceptable ("but not pleased with"); prefers letter-quality to dot-matrix. Query first. SASE. Reports in 2 weeks. Publishes ms an average of 2 months after acceptance. Free sample copy and writer's guidelines.

Nonfiction: "News on destinations, hotels, operators, rates and other developments in the travel business." Also runs human interest features on retail travel agents in the readership area. No stories that don't contain prices; no queries that don't give detailed story lines. No general destination stories, especially ones on "do-it-yourself" travel. Buys 12-15 mss/year. Query. Length: 400-1,500 words. Pays $1.50/column inch.

Photos: State availability of photos with query. Pays $1.50/column inch for glossy b&w prints.

TRAVELAGE WEST, Official Airline Guides, Inc., 582 Market St., San Francisco CA 94104. Executive Editor: Donald C. Langley. 5% freelance written. For travel agency sales counselors in the western US and Canada. Weekly magazine. Circ. 25,000. Pays on publication. Buys all rights. Pays kill fee. Byline given. Submit seasonal/holiday material 2 months in advance. Computer printout submissions acceptable. SASE. Reports in 1 month. Free writer's guidelines.

Nonfiction: Travel. Buys 40 mss/year. Query. Length: 1,000 words maximum. Pays $1.50/column inch. "No promotional approach or any hint of do-it-yourself travel. Emphasis is on news, not description. No static descriptions of places, particularly resort hotels."

Tips: "Query should be a straightforward description of the proposed story, including (1) an indication of the news angle, no matter how tenuous, and (2) a recognition by the author that we run a trade magazine for travel agents, not a consumer book. I am particularly turned off by letters that try to get me all worked up about the 'beauty' or excitement of some place. Authors planning to travel might discuss with us a proposed angle before they go; otherwise their chances of gathering the right information are slim."

Veterinary

MODERN VETERINARY PRACTICE, American Veterinary Publications, Inc., Drawer KK, 300 E. Canon Perdido, Santa Barbara CA 93101. For graduate veterinarians. Monthly magazine; 90 pages. Circ. 22,000. Pays on publication. Buys all rights. Phone queries OK. Submit seasonal/holiday material 3 months in advance. Computer printout submissions acceptable; prefers letter-quality to dot-matrix. SASE. Reports in 1 month. Sample copy $2.50.

Nonfiction: How-to (clinical medicine, new surgical procedures, business management); informational (business management, education, government projects affecting practicing veterinarians, special veterinary projects); interviews (only on subjects of interest to veterinarians; query first); and technical (clinical reports, technical advancements in veterinary medicine and surgery). Buys 12-15 unsolicited mss/year. Submit complete ms, but query first on ideas for pieces other than technical or business articles. Pays $50 for first published page; $25 for each additional page.

Photos: B&w glossies (5x7 or larger) and color transparencies (5x7) used with mss. No additional payment.

Tips: "Contact practicing veterinarians or veterinary colleges. Find out what interests the clinician and what new procedures and ideas might be useful in a veterinary practice. Better yet, collaborate with a veterinarian. Most of our authors are veterinarians or those working with veterinarians in a professional capacity. Knowledge of the interests and problems of practicing veterinarians is essential."

‡**NEW METHODS, The Journal of Animal Health Technology**, New Methods, Box 22605, San Francisco CA 94122. (415)664-3469. Editor: Ronald S. Lippert, A.H.T. Managing Editor: Charles Linebarger. 75% freelance written. Monthly magazine on animal care in the veterinary field with a veterinary slant; for employee-related audience of professionals. Circ. 5,400. Pays on publication. Byline given. Buys one-time rights and first rights. Contact editor first before submitting seasonal/holiday material. Computer printout submissions acceptable; prefers letter-quality to dot-matrix. SASE. Reports in 2 weeks on queries; 4 months on mss. Publishes ms an average of 6 months after acceptance. Sample copy for $3.60; 9x12 SAE, and $1.05 postage; writer's guidelines for business-size SAE and 1 first class stamp.

Nonfiction: Book excerpts, expose, general interest, historical/nostalgic, how-to, humor, inspirational, interview/profile, new product, opinion, personal experience, photo feature, technical and travel. "We advise writer to communicate with staff editor before writing for *New Methods*." Special issues include August: Index, October: Convention Special, and February: Convention Special. English speaking and writing requested. Buys 40+ mss/year. Query with published clips or send complete ms. Length: 800-3,200 words. Pays $8-35.

Photos: Larry Rosenberg, photo editor. State availability of photos or send photos with query or ms. "We prefer b&w photos depicting segments of the article." Call or write for details. Reviews b&w contact sheets, negatives, and 5x7 prints. Captions, model release and identification of subjects required. Buys one-time rights.

Columns/Departments: "We are open to suggestions. Writers should contact Charles Linebarger before submitting material to *New Methods*." Buys 40+ mss/year. Query with or without published clips or send complete ms. Length: 800 words minimum. Pays is determined by publisher, generally $35.

Fiction: Historical and humorous. Buys 12 mss/year. Query with or without published clips or send complete ms. Length: 800 words minimum. Pays $35 maximum.

Poetry: "We are open to all styles as long as content is acceptable." No unrelated themes that are not suitable for *New Methods*. Buys 6 poems/year. Length: varies. Pays $35 maximum.

Fillers: Jokes, short humor and newsbreaks. "We use many but buy few." Length: open. Pays $35 maximum.

Tips: "A simple, straightforward, clean approach is requested. Make every word count. Focus on the reality, humor, and/or gratification of working in the animal health technology field."

‡**VETERINARY COMPUTING**, American Veterinary Publications, Inc., Drawer KK (300 E. Canon Perdido St.) Santa Barbara CA 93102 (street-93101). (800)235-6947 CA, AK or HI (805)963-6561. Editors: Steve Beale and Paul Pratt, VMD. 50% freelance written. Monthly newsletter covering computer applications in veterinary medicine and practice management. "Our readers are veterinary practitioners who have computers or

are thinking about buying them. They are looking for information on the best and most cost-effective ways to purchase and use computers in their practices." Estab. 1983. Pays on publication. Byline given. Buys all rights. Submit seasonal/holiday material 3 months in advance. Simultaneous queries and photocopied submissions OK. Electronic submissions OK if 5¼" single- or double-sided disks with an Osborne 1 CP/M WordStar; requires hard copy also. Computer printout submissions acceptable. SASE. Reports in 3 weeks on queries; 1 month on mss. Publishes ms an average of 4 months after acceptance. Sample copy for 9x12 SAE and 3 first class stamps; free writer's guidelines.

Nonfiction: How-to, new product, book and software reviews, and computer-user tips. No profiles or overly philosophical articles. "We want concrete, practical, usable pieces about how veterinarians can most effectively use computers." Buys 12-24 mss/year. Query or send complete ms (on short articles). Length: 150-2,000 words. Pays $10 (for short tips; $25/printed page for longer articles; printed page equals 1¾ typed double-spaced pages).

Columns/Departments: Book reviews, software reviews, computing tips, new product and news briefs. Buys 12 mss/year. Query or send complete ms (for short articles). Length: 150-500 words. Pays $10-50.

Tips: "Make submissions concise, practical, and usable in plain, nontechnical language. We are especially interested in material on how to use canned software such as VisiCalc, dBase II and WordStar in veterinary practice. Reviews/articles about canned software and money saving computer tips are the areas most open to freelancers in our publication."

VETERINARY ECONOMICS MAGAZINE, Box 13265, Edwardsville KS 66113. (913)422-5010. Editor: Mike Sollars. 50% freelance written. For all practicing veterinarians in the US. Monthly. Buys exclusive rights in the field. Pays on publication. Computer printout submissions acceptable. SASE. Publishes ms an average of 3 months after acceptance.

Nonfiction: Uses case histories telling about good business practices on the part of veterinarians. Also, articles about financial problems, investments, insurance and similar subjects of particular interest to professionals. "We reject articles with superficial information about a subject instead of carefully researched and specifically directed articles for our field." Pays negotiable rates.

VETERINARY MEDICINE/SMALL ANIMAL CLINICIAN, Box 13265, Edwardsville KS 66113. Executive Editor: Ray Ottinger. 5% freelance written. For graduate veterinarians, student veterinarians, animal health technicians, libraries, representatives of drug companies and research personnel. Monthly magazine; 160 pages. Circ. 19,400. Pays on publication. Buys first North American serial rights. Byline given. Phone queries OK. Submit seasonal/holiday material 5-6 months in advance. Previously published submissions OK. Prefers typewritten rather than computer printout submissions. SASE. Reports in 2-3 weeks. Free writer's guidelines.

Nonfiction: Accepts only articles dealing with medical case histories, surgery, diagnosis, treatments, and practice management. No "cutesy" stories about animals. Buys 3 mss/issue. Submit complete ms. Length: 1,500-5,000 words. Pays $50-200.

Photos: State availability of photos with ms. Reviews b&w and color glossy prints, and 35mm color transparencies. Captions required. Buys one-time US and reprint rights. Model release required.

‡**VETERINARY PRACTICE MANAGEMENT**, 13-30 Corporation, 505 Market St., Knoxville TN 37919. (615)521-0759. Group Editor: Thomas Lombardo. 90% freelance written. Semiannual magazine—"a business guide to small animal practitioners." Estab. 1983. Circ. 27,000. Pays on acceptance. Byline given. Offers $250 kill fee. Buys first and second rights to the same material. Simultaneous queries OK. Publishes ms an average of 3 months after acceptance. Free sample copy to experienced business writers.

Nonfiction: David M. Freedman, associate editor. How-to, profile, and successful business (practice) management techniques. No "how to milk more dollars out of your clients" articles. Buys 16 mss/year. Query with published clips. Pays $1,000-2,000.

Columns/Departments: Management Briefs, and In the Know. "Most items are written in-house, but we will consider ideas." Query with published clips.

Market conditions are constantly changing! If this is 1986 or later, buy the newest edition of *Writer's Market* at your favorite bookstore or order directly from Writer's Digest Books.

Scriptwriting

Scriptwriters, in a way, should imitate their most memorable characters—the ones taking risks regardless of the consequences. Writing for theatregoers, students, and the business community is a risk. Venturing beyond the keyboard or notepad to work in the field will give you an edge. Your involvement in the production, management, or business end of these visual forms will help you write scripts that please producers, clients, and audiences. Writing for local theatre or TV and radio stations tells producers you're willing to work. Writers at times must track down industrial and theatre companies to commission their work. Screenwriters also must pursue routes to get their work in front of the camera. For tips and techniques on TV, radio, film and theatre writing, consult *The Complete Book of Scriptwriting*, by J. Michael Straczynski (Writer's Digest Books).

Business and Educational Writing

"Your script must meet customer needs more than ever before," points out one educational film producer. The advice certainly isn't new, but with increased competition among media and media firms, those which please the customer get "top billing."

"Clients want choices," says another producer. With the options of film, video, and multi-image becoming more affordable, business and education representatives want to choose which medium will best serve their audiences and organization's goals.

To be more competitive in the marketplace, some companies are expanding the media services they offer. Scriptwriters must likewise broaden the range of assignments they handle.

"Scriptwriters should be aware of interactive video with tape and videodisks for training purposes," says one producer. Other producers say video tape is becoming increasingly popular among clients.

With companies entering the software and cable markets, there is an additional need for freelancers. The software subheading has been added to the listings of firms needing software. A square (□) to the left of a listing denotes firms interested in cable TV scripts. Reading each *Writer's Market* listing will tell you what companies want and don't want in scripts.

Companies, for example, need technical scriptwriters to develop training and industrial films and videotape presentations for employees and customers. Educational firms that produce video cassettes for the school market also need scripts.

Whether you write for businesses or schools, producers want "visual" scripts. Avoid cliché scenes and unrealistic, condescending dialogue. Careful research will give you a wide range of images and ideas to choose from.

Above all, become familiar with the particular firm you plan to query. What else have they produced? Arrange for a screening that will help you define their audiences, formats and style. Contact local producers directly. Write to out-of-town firms for a list of their clients in your area. If they are interested in your writing, you may be able to view their AV material at a local company or school that uses it. Be sure that your script idea fits with a company's established image. A résumé that establishes you as a writer and writing samples that prove it are very important in this business. Read carefully the market listings detailing how to make initial contact with a production company.

Meeting deadlines and doing quality work are essential. And in helping companies and schools communicate important messages to their audiences, you (like them) will have more choices (at assignments).

A.V. MEDIA CRAFTSMAN, INC., Suite 600, 110 E. 23rd St., New York NY 10010. (212)228-6644. President: Carolyn Clark. Produces training material for corporations and educational material for publishers. Works with New York area writers only. Contracts scripts for 10-15 projects per year. Query with samples and resume. Reports immediately. Buys all rights.
Needs: "Most of our projects are 10-15 minute training scripts with related study materials for corporations and educational publishers. We create multi-screen presentations for conferences as well." Produces slide shows, sound filmstrips, multiscreen shows, multimedia kits, overhead transparencies, tapes and cassettes, films in many formats, and teaching machine programs. Pays in outright purchase of $350-500, for scripts.
Tips: "Accept changes, do accurate research, and enjoy the subject matter. Write—do *not* call."

‡□ **ABS MULTI-IMAGE**, 705 Hinman, Evanston IL 60202. (312)328-8697. President: Alan Soell. "We produce material for all levels of corporate, medical, cable, and educational institutions for the purposes of training and development, marketing, and meeting presentations. We also are developing programming for the broadcast areas. 75% freelance written. We work with a core of 3-5 freelance writers from development to final drafts." All scripts published are unagented submissions. Buys all rights. Previously produced material OK. Computer printout submissions acceptable. SASE. Reports in 2 weeks on queries.
Needs: Charts, 16mm films, silent and sound filmstrips, multimedia kits, overhead transparencies, realia, slides, tapes and cassettes, television shows/series, videotape presentations. Currently interested in "sports instructional series that could be produced for the consumer market on tennis, gymnastics, bowling, golf, aerobics, health and fitness, cross-country skiing, cycling. Also home improvement programs for the novice—for around the house—in a series format. These two areas should be 30 minutes and be timeless in approach for long shelf life." Sports audience, age 25-45; home improvement, 25-65. "Cable TV needs include the two groups of programming detailed here. We are also looking for documentary work on current issues, nuclear power, solar power, urban development, senior citizens—but with a new approach." Query or submit synopsis/outline and resume. Pays by contractual agreement.
Tips: "I am looking for innovative approaches to old problems that just don't go away. The approach should be simple and direct so there is immediate audience identification with the presentation. I also like to see a sense of humor used. Trends in the audiovisual field include interactive video with tape and video disk—for training purposes."

DOM ALBI ASSOCIATES, INC., Suite 1C, 251 W. 92nd St., New York NY 10025. (212)799-2202. President: Dom Albi. Produces material for corporate and business audiences. Buys 20-30 scripts/year. Query or submit resume listing types of clients. Buys all rights.
Needs: Produces 16mm films, multimedia programs and videotape slide presentations. Payment negotiable.
Tips: "We expect our writers to spend as much time on concept and purpose, as they do on finished script."

ALLEGRO FILM PRODUCTIONS, INC., 10915 Boca Woods Rd., Boca Raton FL 33433. President: Mr. J. Forman. Produces for the general and school markets. Buys 3-20 scripts/year. Submit resume. Computer printout submissions acceptable. Buys all rights.
Needs: Science films for education, films for industry and government, and documentaries. Produces 16mm and 35mm films. Pays negotiable fee.

ANCO/BOSTON, INC., 441 Stuart St., Boston MA 02116. (617)267-9700. Director, Instructional Systems: R. Hoyt. Produces manuals and AV programs for the industrial and business communities. 15% freelance written. Buys 2-3 scripts/year from unpublished/unproduced writers. All scripts produced are unagented submissions. Submit resume. Computer printout submissions acceptable. SASE. Buys all rights.
Needs: "Technical or business-oriented material on specific subjects for specific customized needs." Produces charts, sound filmstrips, multimedia kits, overhead transparencies and cassettes and slides.

‡**KEN ANDERSON FILMS**, Box 618, Winona Lake IN 46590. (219)267-5774. President: Ken Anderson. Produces material for church-related libraries with evangelical bias; films for all ages, with particular interest in children and teenagers. Previously published submissions OK. Considers brief, 1-page story synopses only. "We try to maintain a very warm attitude toward writers and will try to give careful consideration to queries. Unsolicited mss will be returned unread. We only produce 4-6 films/year, so our quantity needs are limited." Free catalog.
Needs: Religious material only. "We are constantly looking for good material that is positively Christian and relates realistically to today's life-style. We want true stories for young people and adults; fiction for children." Pays "as low as $100 for basic story idea, which the author could then market elsewhere. But general payment

---

□ *Open box preceding a listing indicates a cable TV market.*

runs more between $250-1,000, depending upon story quality and adaptability for audiovisual production." **Tips:** "We are currently looking for filmstrip material appealing to Third World audiences."

ANIMATION ARTS ASSOCIATES, INC., 1100 E. Hector St., Conshohocken PA 19428. (215)563-2520. Contact: Harry E. Ziegler Jr. For "government, industry, engineers, doctors, scientists, dentists, general public, military." 100% freelance written. Send resume of credits for motion picture and filmstrip productions and software. Buys average 12 scripts/year. "The writer should have scriptwriting credits for training, sales, promotion, public relations." SASE.
Needs: Produces 3½-minute 8mm and 16mm film loops; 16mm and 35mm films (ranging from 5-40 minutes); 2¼x2¼ or 4x5 slides; and teaching machine programs for training, sales, industry and public relations. Pay dependent on client's budget.
Software: Michael Levanios, general manager. Motion picture scripts for training, sales promotion; recruitment films.
Tips: "Send us a resume listing writing and directing credits for films and sound/slide programs."

‡□ **APPALSHOP INC.**, Box 743, Whitesburg KY 41858. (606)633-0108. President: Katharine Pearson. "Most audiovisuals are educational, thus geared to educational TV, etc. A good part, however, are documentary and of interest to a diversified audience." Currently works with approximately 15 writers, scriptwriters, etc. Buys first rights. Previously produced material OK. Computer printout submissions acceptable; no dot-matrix. SASE. Reports in several months. Catalog for SASE. Writer's guidelines available.
Needs: 16mm films, sound filmstrips, phonograph records, slides, study prints, tapes and cassettes, television shows/series, videotape presentations. Query with or without samples or submit synopsis/outline and resume. Pays in outright purchase.

ARZTCO PICTURES, INC., 15 E. 61st St., New York NY 10021. (212)753-1050. President/Producer: Tony Arzt. Produces material for industrial, education, and home viewing audiences (TV specials and documentaries). 80% freelance written. 75% of scripts produced are unagented submissions. Buys 8-10 scripts/year. Buys all rights. Previously produced material OK ("as sample of work only"). Computer printout submissions acceptable; prefers letter-quality to dot-matrix. SASE, "however, we will only comment in writing on work that interests us." Reports in 3 weeks.
Needs: Business films, sales, training, promotional, educational. "Also interested in low-budget feature film scripts." 16mm and 35mm films and videotapes and cassettes. Submit synopsis/outline or completed script and resume. Pays in accordance with Writers Guild standards.
Software: Needs feature scriptwriters of high caliber.
Tips: "We would like writers to understand that we cannot find time to deal with each individual submission in great detail. If we feel your work is right for us, you will definitely hear from us. We're looking for writers with originality, skill in turning out words, and a sense of humor when appropriate. We prefer to work with writers available in the New York metropolitan area."

ASSOCIATED AUDIO VISUAL, 2821 Central, Evanston IL 60201. (312)866-6780. President/Creative Director: Ken Solomon. Vice President Sales & Marketing: Norman Lindquist. Produces material for corporate/industrial/TV commercials and programs. 75% freelance written. Buys 6-12 scripts/year. Buys all rights. Electronic submissions OK on 8" diskette straight ASCII File or IBM PC File 5¼". Computer printout submissions acceptable; prefers letter-quality to dot-matrix printouts. SASE. Reports in 1 month. Catalog for 8x10 SAE and 1 first class stamp.
Needs: Open. Produces 16mm films, slides, tapes and cassettes. "Call first; then send samples." Pays in negotiable outright purchase.
Tips: "Be persistent, have *produced* samples on film or tape rather than scripts." Looks for "intelligence, humor, contemporary, visual and verbal skills; a fast researcher."

A/V CONCEPTS CORP., 30 Montauk Blvd., Oakdale NY 11769. (516)567-7229. Editor: Joyce W. Masterson. Produces material for el-hi students, both those on grade level and in remedial situations. 100% freelance written. Buys 25 scripts/year from unpublished/unproduced writers. Employs the media of filmstrip and personal computers. Computer—disk based—language arts, mathematics and reading. Query with resume and samples. Computer printout submissions acceptable. SASE. Reports on outline in 1 month; on final scripts in 6 weeks. Buys all rights. Catalog for SASE.
Needs: "Authors must receive a set of our specifications before submitting material. Manuscripts must be written using our lists of vocabulary words, and must meet readability formula requirements provided by us. Length of manuscript and subjects will vary according to grade level for which material is prepared. Basically, we want articles and stories that will motivate people to read. Authors must be highly creative and highly disciplined. We are interested in mature content material." Pays $100.
Software: Contact: Philip Solimene or Joyce W. Masterson. Interested in original educational computer pro-

grams for the Apple II+ 48K: language arts, math, reading.
Tips: "If possible, contact the editor or editorial department by phone and 'meet' the company through 'personal' contact."

‡BARR FILMS, 3490 E. Foothill Blvd., Pasadena CA 91107. (213)793-6153. Contact: Don Barr or Mark Chodzko. "Produces material for all age levels; grades kindergarten through college level as well as in the public library market to the same age span and adult audience. We also have interest in materials aimed at business and industry/management training programs." 20% freelance written. 100% of scripts produced are unagented submissions. Query with samples. Computer printout submissions acceptable. "We will assign projects to qualified writers. We require previous experience in film writing and want to see samples of films previously written and completed for sale in the market." Buys 2-4 scripts/year. SASE. Reports in 1 month. Catalog $1.
Needs: "We produce and distribute 16mm films in all curriculum and subject areas. We prefer a semi-dramatic form of script that entertains and provides information. Avoid excess verbiage—we produce films, not books. The length of our films is 15-24 minutes. We will also consider pure informational subjects with voice over narration. Fees are entirely negotiable. We will accept film treatments and/or completed visual and dialogue scripts. Please inquire prior to sending your materials to us."
Tips: "Meet the producer; share previous films; talk film; and be available. Your script must meet customer needs more than ever before."

BARTON FILM COMPANY, 4853 Waller St., Jacksonville FL 32205. (904)389-4541. President: Donald E. Barton. Produces material for various audiences. Works with average of 6 writers/year. Buys all rights. Computer printout submissions acceptable. Submissions returned with SASE. Reports in 1 month.
Needs: Documentary and sales-motivation material—16mm films and video tape. Query with samples. Pays $850-2,500.

BNA COMMUNICATIONS, INC., 9439 Key West Ave., Rockville MD 20850. (301)948-0540. Producer/Director: Clifton R. Witt. Produces material primarily for business, industry and government; "client-sponsored films approach specific audiences." 50% freelance written. All scripts produced are unagented submissions. Buys 7-12 scripts, works with 3-4 writers/year. Buys 1 script/year from unpublished/unproduced writer. Buys "usually all rights—but other arrangements have been made." Reports in 1 month. Free catalog.
Needs: "Presently under control." 16mm films, slides, and tapes, cassettes and videodisks. Query with samples. "Find out what we do before you query." Pays negotiable fee.
Tips: "We're looking for writers with the ability to grasp the subject and develop a relatively simple treatment, particularly if the client is not motion-savvy. Don't overload with tricks . . . unless the show is about tricks. Most good scripts have some concept of a beginning, middle and end. We are interested in good *dialogue* writers."

BOARD OF JEWISH EDUCATION OF NEW YORK, 426 W. 58th St., New York NY 10019. (212)245-8200. Director, Division of Multimedia and Materials Development: Yaakov Reshef. Produces material for Jewish schools, youth groups, temples and synagogues; for audience from kindergarten to old age. Buys 12-15 scripts/year. Submit outline/synopsis or resume. SASE. Reports in 3 months. Buys first rights or all rights.
Needs: General, educational and informational. "Generally, length is up to 20-25 minutes maximum; most material geared to 10-12 years old and up. Jewish background needed." Produces sound filmstrips, 16mm films, tapes and cassettes, and slide sets. Pays 10-15% royalty or $800 minimum/outright purchase.

BRADY COMMUNICATIONS COMPANY, INC., Routes 197 & 450, Bowie MD 20715. Publishing Director: David T. Culverwell. Produces books and computer software for professionals and paraprofessionals in allied health, nursing, emergency care and microcomputer science. Will buy rights or sign standard contracts. Free catalog. "We are always eager to develop new writers who write instructively with clarity." Query. Computer printout submissions acceptable. Produces books, manuals and computer software to accompany books.
Needs: Educational material for allied health, nursing, emergency medicine and microcomputer science. "Our company deals with instructional and informational-type projects."
Tips: "Send a resume with samples of writing ability and grasp of subject."

‡BURNS MEDIA, 5550 Main St., Amherst NY 14221. (716)632-1632. President: Jim Burns. Produces material for business, government and consumers. Buys all rights. SASE. Reports in 3 weeks.
Needs: Scripts for corporate marketing, employee relations, internal communications, and videotape productions. Produces videotapes. Query with samples. Makes outright purchase.
Tips: "Prior experience with writing scripts for productions described above is a prerequisite. We look for a command of writing in marketing/promotional language and style."

ALDEN BUTCHER PRODUCTIONS, 6331 Hollywood Blvd., Hollywood CA 90028. (213)467-6045. Personnel Manager: Cynthia Butcher. Produces material for commercial/industrial and entertainment audiences. Buys 20 scripts/year. Deals mainly with local clients. Uses *only* local writers. Buys all rights. SASE. Reports in 1 month.

Needs: "Depends upon contracts closed." Produces multimedia slide shows and some video programs. Looks for "the ability to easily communicate with an industrial client and translate that into a script that meets their communication objectives the first time." Query with samples and resume. Computer printout submissions acceptable. Pays "according to production budget on an individual basis."

Tips: "Clients are looking more and more for a production company to provide creative approaches as a part of a bidding process. Often it is important for a writer to be involved in this speculative process prior to writing the actual script. This way they can help develop the style and approach with how and what they would write in mind."

CALIFORNIA COMMUNICATIONS, 6900 Santa Monica Blvd., Los Angeles CA 90038. (213)466-8511. Editorial Director: Bill Muster. Produces material for corporations, industry and service industry. Buys 3-4 scripts/year. All scripts produced are unagented submissions. Submit resume. "No unsolicited manuscripts." SASE. Reports in 2 weeks. Buys all rights.

Needs: Produces industrial sound filmstrips, 16mm films, multimedia kits, slides, and AV multiimage shows and videotapes. "We work on assignment only." Pays in outright purchase of "approximately $100/minute minimum."

CATHEDRAL FILMS, INC., 2282 Townsgate Rd., Westlake Village CA 91359. (805)495-7418. Contact: Candace Hunt. Produces material for church and school audiences. Works with variable number of writers/year. Buys all rights and AV rights. Previously produced material OK "except from other AV media." SASE. Reports in 4 weeks on queries; 8 weeks on mss. Catalog for SAE and 54¢ postage.

Needs: Various Christian, religious, educational and/or dramatic material. All ages. Produces 16mm films, sound filmstrips and video. Submit synopsis/outline or complete script. Pays variable rates.

‡**CINE-MARK, Division of Krebs Productions, Inc.**, Suite 2026, 303 E. Ohio St., Chicago IL 60611. (312)337-3303. President: Clyde L. Krebs. Produces corporate, marketing, training, consumer material (nontheatrical) and travel promotion for agents and the general public. Buys 10-15 scripts/year. Buys all rights. Previously produced material OK. Computer printout submissions acceptable; no dot-matrix. SASE. Reports in 2 weeks. Free writer's guidelines.

Needs: 16mm films, sound filmstrips, slides, tapes and cassettes, videotape presentations. "All of our projects are specific to the sponsors' needs based upon mutual research to meet their communication objectives." Submit resume. Pays in outright purchase; varies with assignment.

CLEARVUE, INC., 5711 N. Milwaukee Ave., Chicago IL 60646. (312)775-9433. Executive Vice President: W.O. McDermed. Produces educational material for grades kindergarten-12. Buys 20-30 scripts/year. Buys all or first rights. Previously produced material OK. SASE. Reports in 2 weeks on queries; 1 month on submissions. Free catalog.

Needs: Educational material for grades kindergarten-12. Produces filmstrips (silent and sound), multimedia kits, overhead transparencies, phonograph records, study prints, tapes and cassettes. Query. Pays in outright purchase.

Tips: "Know the specific objectives of the program; have an outline of teaching experience and list of programs published." Looks for "ability to meet needs of market place."

‡**CONCEPT 80's**, 3409 West Chester Pike, Newtown Square PA 19073. (215)353-5900. Marketing Manager/Producer: Jim Higgins, Jr. Produces material for primarily corporate audiences—approximately 75% technical/industrial, 25% consumer organizations—mostly management, sales force or distributors. Buys 20-25 scripts/year. Buys all rights. No previously produced material. Computer printout submissions acceptable. SASE. Reports in several weeks. Catalog for SAE with 1 first class stamp.

Needs: Charts, silent and sound filmstrips, multimedia kits, overhead transparencies, slides, videotape presentations, multi-image. "Most projects develop, are produced and delivered within 4-6 weeks." Query with samples or submit resume. Pays in outright purchase, $200-1,000.

Tips: "Writers should have written for audiovisual or print at least 10-20 successful scripts for blue chip corporations."

CORONADO STUDIOS, #600, 3550 Biscayne Blvd., Miami FL 33137. (305)573-7250. President: Fred L. Singer. Produces material for the general public, various specialized audiences. Buys 50 commercials/year; 15 corporate films/year. "We commission custom scripts that have no value to anyone but our clients." Computer printout submissions acceptable. SASE. Reports in 2 weeks on queries; 1 month on submissions.

Needs: "We will need an indeterminate number of scripts for commercials and corporate films." Produces 16mm films, video tapes. Query with samples. Pays in outright purchase; "depends on nature of job."

‡**CORPORATE MEDIA COMMUNICATIONS INC.**, 2200 Northlake Parkway, Box 261, Tucker GA 30085. (404)491-6300. Vice President: Phil Sehenuk. Produces material for businesses. 80% freelance written. Buys 80-100 scripts/year; also uses print copy. 80 scripts produced are unagented submissions. Buys all rights. Previously produced material OK, "possibly." Computer printout submissions acceptable. SASE. Reports in 2 weeks. Free catalog.
Needs: Charts, 16mm films, silent and sound filmstrips, multimedia kits, slides, tapes and cassettes, videotape presentations, motivational material, product literature, and promotional material. "We want fresh new material with *human* orientation. We are interested in ideas for motivational show; we also make assignments." Query with samples, or submit synopsis/outline, or completed script and resume. Pays negotiable rate/project.
Tips: "Clients want choices. The options of film, video, multi-image are all becoming affordable. Communicators need to be involved in a range of media."

THE CREATIVE ESTABLISHMENT, 115 W. 31st St., New York NY 10001. (212)563-3337. Director Creative Services: Dale Wilson. Produces material for business meetings and industrial audiences. 30% freelance written. 95% of scripts produced are unagented submissions. Works with approximately 10 writers/year. Buys all rights. SASE. "We don't return unsolicited material; material is held on file." Reports "when needed. Material is always specific to project. We cannot project future needs."
Needs: 8mm and 16mm film loops, 16mm and 35mm films, sound filmstrips, slides, and multi-image and live shows. Submit synopsis/outline or completed script and resume. Computer printout submissions acceptable; no dot-matrix. Pays in outright purchase.

CREATIVE VISUALS, Division of Gamco Industries, Inc., Box 1911, Big Spring TX 79720. (915)267-6327. Vice President, Research and Development: Judith Rickey. Free catalog and author's guidelines. "Provide a list of your educational degrees and majors. Explain your teaching experience, including subjects taught, grades taught, and the number of years you have taught. Please describe any writing experience, and, if possible, include a sample of your published educational material currently on the market. We ask for this information because we have found that our best authors are usually experienced classroom teachers who are writing in their subject area. Once we have information about your background, we will ask you for the subject and titles of your proposed series." Computer printout submissions acceptable; prefers letter-quality to dot-matrix.
Software: Produces microcomputer software and sound filmstrips, cassettes and reproducible books relating to microcomputer software.
Needs: Education (grades kindergarten-12, all subjects areas). Pays royalty; usually 5 or 10% of net sales.

RAUL DA SILVA & OTHER FILMMAKERS, 137 E. 38th St, New York NY 10016. Creative Director: Raul da Silva. 10% freelance written. Produces material for business, industry, institutions, education and entertainment audiences. "We strive for excellence in both script and visual interpretation. We produce quality only, and bow to the budget-conscious clients who cannot or will not afford quality." Submit resume. "Generally work on assignment only. We have a selection of writers known to us already. Cannot handle unsolicited mail/scripts." Rights purchased vary. "If possible, we share profits with writers, particularly when resale is involved."
Needs: "We produce both types of material: on assignment from clients (one-shot communications) and proprietary AV materials which resell." Produces video, silent and sound filmstrips, 16mm and 35mm films, phonograph records, tapes and cassettes and slides. Pays 10% royalty; also pays in outright purchase of 10% of total budget. Pays in accordance with Writers Guild standards.
Tips: "We are impressed with scripts that have received recognition in writing competition. We also welcome resumes from writers who have credentials and credits with other producers. From these we will select our future writers." Looks for "knowledge of medium, structure, style, cohesiveness (mastery of continuity), clarity, obvious love for the language and intelligence."

NICHOLAS DANCY PRODUCTIONS, INC., 333 W. 39th St., New York NY 10018. (212)564-9140. President: Nicholas Dancy. Produces material for general audiences, employees, members of professional groups, members of associations and special customer groups. 90% freelance written. Buys 5-10 scripts/year; works with 5-10 writers/year. Buys all rights. Reports in 1 month. Computer printout submissions acceptable.
Needs: "We use scripts for films or videotapes from 15 minutes to 1 hour for corporate communications, sales, orientation, training, corporate image, medical and documentary." Format: 16mm films, slides and cassettes (audio tapes and videotapes). Query with resume. "No unsolicited material. Our field is too specialized." Pays in outright purchase of $800-5,000.
Tips: "Writers should have knowledge of business and industry and professions, ability to work with clients and communicators, fresh narrative style, creative use of dialogue, good skills in accomplishing research, and a professional approach to production."

ALFRED DE MARTINI EDUCATIONAL FILMS, 414 4th Ave., Haddon Heights NJ 08035. (609)547-2800. President: Alfred De Martini. Produces material for schools, colleges, universities, libraries and museums. 80% freelance written. Buys 12 scripts/year from unpublished/unproduced writers. All scripts produced are unagented submissions. "We're informal, creative, earthy, realistic, productive and perfection-oriented." Submit synopsis/outline or completed script. Computer printout submissions acceptable; prefers letter-quality to dot-matrix. SASE. Reports in 1 month. Buys all rights. Free catalog for SASE.
Needs: Subject topics include "educational material on art, travel and history from secondary to adult level." Produces silent and sound filmstrips, multimedia kits, and tapes and cassettes. Pays in outright purchase of $100-$2,500. "Fee is established in advance with writers."
Tips: Interested in "imagination, brevity, uniqueness of style and ascertaining objectives."

‡□ **DIDIK TV PRODUCTIONS**, Box 133, Rego Park NY 11374. (212)843-6839. Executive Director: Frank Didik. "All material is for either videotape productions, film productions or multimedia presentations. We produce about 25-30 TV commercials per year. The rest of the productions are industrials and training films for consumers and government." 20-25% freelance written. Most scripts produced are unagented submissions. Buys 10-15 scripts/year. Buys variable rights depending on contract. Computer printout submissions acceptable. SASE. Reporting time varies "depending on our work load." Free catalog.
Needs: 8mm film loops, 16 and 35mm films, silent and sound filmstrips, models, multimedia kits, slides, study prints, television shows/series, videotape presentations, all types of video and film. "Our main line of business is television/film production as explained above." Produces general consumer commercials for cable TV. Query with list of credits. Pay "depends on contract."

‡**DOLPHIN MULTI-MEDIA, INC.**, 1137 D San Antonio Road, Palo Alto CA 94303. (415)962-8310. President: S.C. Kondratieff. Produces material for industrial/sales/marketing/training audiences. Buys 20-50 scripts/year. Buys all rights and first rights. Previously produced material usually not applicable. Electronic submissions OK via CP/M, Eagle II or PC DOS disk; call to arrange modem. Computer printout submissions acceptable. SASE.
Needs: 16mm films, sound filmstrips, multimedia kits, overhead transparencies, slides, tapes and cassettes, videotape presentations. Currently interested in scripts for video/multi-image, high technology, also travel. Query with samples or submit completed script and resume. Pays in outright purchase, $500-5,000; depends on complexity and length.
Tips: "Most of our scripts are to specific contracts so samples of work are helpful."

THE DURASELL CORPORATION, 360 Lexington Ave., New York NY 10017. President: Albert A. Jacoby. Produces AV material for sales presentations, meetings, and training programs—primarily for consumer package goods companies. 100% freelance written. Does not buy scripts from unpublished/unproduced writers. All scripts produced are unagented submissions. Buys 30-50 scripts/year; works with 6-10 writers/year. Buys all rights. Computer printout submissions acceptable; prefers letter-quality to dot-matrix.
Needs: Video, meetings, sound filmstrips, slides and tapes. Must send letter and resume first. Pays in outright purchase. ("Freelancer sets fee.")
Tips: "Freelancers must be fast, creative, organized, enthusiastic, experienced, talented. Demonstrate heavy experience in AV sales meetings scripts and in creative multi-image sales meetings."

EDUCATIONAL INSIGHTS, 150 W. Carob St., Compton CA 90220. (213)637-2131. Director of Development: Terry Garnholz. Educational publisher. Averages 50 titles/year. Pays 5% minimum royalty; buys some mss outright. No advance. Simultaneous and photocopied submissions OK. SASE. Reports in 1 month. Free catalog.
Needs: Educational areas. Query or submit outline/synopsis and sample chapters or script.

EFC, INC., (formerly Educational Film Center), 5101 F Backlick Rd., Box 1017, Annandale VA 22003. (703)750-0560. Vice President/Script Development: Ruth Pollak. Produces dramatic and documentary material for commercial, government, broadcast, schools and communities. 80% freelance written. Buys scripts from published/produced writers only. 50% of scripts produced are unagented submissions. Works with 5-20 writers/year. Buys all rights. Computer printout submissions acceptable. SASE. Reports in 1 month.
Needs: "Strong dramatic screenplays, especially for family/children audience." Query with samples. Pays in outright purchase or by commercial arrangement.

EFFECTIVE COMMUNICATION ARTS, INC., 221 W. 57th St., New York NY 10019. (212)333-5656. Vice President: W.J. Comcowich. Produces "imaginative technical films" for physicians, nurses and medical personnel. 80% freelance written. Buys 20 scripts/year. Submit completed script and resume. Electronic submissions OK via direct modem or MCI mailbox. Computer printout submissions acceptable; prefers letter-quality to dot-matrix printouts. "Explain what the films accomplished—how they were better than the typical." Buys all rights. Reports in 1 month.

Needs: Multimedia kits, 16mm films, television shows/series, videotape presentations, interactive videodisks. Currently interested in about 15 films, videotapes for medical audiences; 6 interactive disks for medical audience, 3 interactive disks for point-of-purchase. Pays in outright purchase or negotiated rights.
Tips: "Trends in the audiovisual field that freelance writers should be aware of include interactive design."

‡**EMC CORP.**, 300 York Ave., St. Paul MN 55101. Editor: Rosemary Barry. Produces material for children and teenagers in the primary grades through high school. "We sell strictly to schools and public libraries. Because much of school buying is affected by school funding, our market changes as school funding changes." 100% freelance written by published/produced writers. All scripts produced are unagented submissions. Buys 2-3 scripts/year. Buys world rights. Catalog for 9x12 SASE. "The writer, via submitted sample, must show the capability to write appropriately for the educational market." Query with resume and one or more samples of previously published work. Computer printout submissions acceptable if upper/lower case; disk submission OK if compatible with TRS-80 III or Apple. "No unsolicited manuscripts accepted."
Needs: Career education, consumer education, special education (as related to language arts especially). "No standard requirements, due to the nature of educational materials publishing." No religious topics. Payment varies.
Software: Educational—most subject areas.

‡**MARTIN EZRA & ASSOCIATES**, 48 Garrett Rd., Upper Darby PA 19082. (215)352-9595 or 9596. Producer: Martin Ezra. Produces material for business, industry and education. Works with 4-5 writers/year. Buys all rights and first rights. SASE. Reports in 3 weeks.
Needs: Educational and informational work. Film loops, films, silent filmstrips, sound filmstrips, multimedia kits, slides, and tapes and cassettes. Query with samples or submit completed script "in writing only." Payment "varies with project."

FILMS FOR CHRIST ASSOCIATION, INC., 5310 N. Eden Rd., Elmwood IL 61529. (309)565-7722. Production Manager: Paul Taylor. Produces material for use by churches (interdenominational); schools (both secular and parochial); and missions. Most films are 20-90 minutes in length. Previously published submissions OK. Computer printout submissions acceptable; disk submissions OK if Lanier format only. Free catalog.
Needs: Produces 16mm films, sound filmstrips, slides and books. Documentaries and dramas. Particularly interested in scripts or script ideas dealing with such subjects as: Creation vs. evolution, archaeology, science and the Bible, apologetics, Christian living and evangelism. Also interested in good scripts for evangelistic children's films. Query. Prefers brief one-page synopsis. Payment negotiable.

FILMS FOR THE HUMANITIES, INC., Box 2053, Princeton NJ 08540. (609)452-1128. Vice President, Editorial: Stephen Mantell. Produces material for a junior high, high school, college, business and industry audience. Buys 50-75 scripts/year; works with 10-15 writers/year. Previously produced material OK. SASE.
Needs: Produces sound filmstrips, multimedia kits, tapes and cassettes. Submit resume and sample material; "we assign topics."
Tips: "We assign writing in line with our curriculum and editorial program needs."

FLIPTRACK LEARNING SYSTEMS, Division of Mosaic Media, Inc., Suite 200, 999 Main, Glen Ellyn IL 60137. (312)790-1117. Publisher: F. Lee McFadden. Produces training tapes for microcomputer equipment and business software. 50% freelance written. Buys 25 scripts/year; 2-3 from unpublished/unproduced writers. All scripts published are unagented submissions. Works with 10-15 writers/year. Buys all rights. Computer printout and disk submissions OK. SASE. Reports in 3 weeks. Free product literature.
Needs: Spoken voice audio cassette scripts geared to the adult or mature student in a business setting and to the first-time microcomputer user. "Programming ability may be helpful." Produces audio cassettes and reference manuals. Query with resume and samples if available. Pays negotiable royalty; buys some scripts outright.
Software: Patricia Menges, vice president for product development; CBT, geared to management training.
Tips: Looks for "ability to organize lesson content logically, develop carefully sequenced lessons and write step-by-step audio scripts in narrative form. Experience in writing training material for the adult learner is more important than a deep knowledge of the microcomputer. Business orientation is a help. We are expanding, along with the microcomputer market."

FLORIDA PRODUCTION CENTER, 150 Riverside Ave., Jacksonville FL 32202. (904)354-7000. Tampa office: 4010 N. Nebraska Ave., Tampa FL 33603. Outside Florida call (800)237-4490. Inside Florida call (813)237-1200. Vice President: Lou DiGiusto. Produces material for business, industry, government and education. Buys 24 scripts/year. Query with samples and resume. SASE. Buys all rights. Previously produced material OK.
Needs: "General script needs. Training programs and industrial motivation. Six training of 10 minutes and 10 industrial—some with image-type slant, others with informational slant." Produces 8mm film loops, silent

and sound filmstrips, 16-35mm films, multimedia kits, tapes and cassettes, slides, teaching machine programs and videotape presentations.

PAUL FRENCH & PARTNERS, INC., Rt. 5, Gabbettville Rd., LaGrange GA 30240. (404)882-5581. Contact: Wendy Schneider. 20% freelance written. Query or submit resume. Computer printout submissions acceptable; no dot-matrix. SASE. Reports in 2 weeks. Buys all rights.
Needs: Wants to see multi-screen scripts (all employee attitude related) and/or multi-screen AV sales meeting scripts or resumes. Produces silent and sound filmstrips, 16mm films, multimedia kits, phonograph records, video tapes and cassettes, and slides. Pays in outright purchase of $500-$5,000. Payment is in accordance with Writers Guild standards.

□ **FRIED PRODUCTIONS,** 768 Farmington Ave., Farmington CT 06032. (203)674-8221. President: Joel Fried. Executive Producer: Roy Shaw. Production Assistant: David Shearer. "We produce programs that are aimed at the high school/college/cable TV market." Query; "tell us what your idea is and why you can write on this particular subject." Computer printout or disk submissions OK. SASE. Buys all rights. Pays by cash and/ or royalty.
Needs: "Education is very important to us. You should be familiar with the market and what subjects are of interest to today's students. We are open to any good idea. Original script ideas for cable production also of interest." Buys 20-40 scripts/yr. Subjects include vocational education and academics, chemistry, career awareness, physics and biology, horticulture, sex education—just about any area. Produces videotapes, 6mm sound filmstrips, overhead transparencies, slides, study prints, teaching machine programs and multimedia kits. Pays by the project.
Software: "Computer software ideas are needed for the home or school market."
Tips: "Please let us hear your ideas. All queries are answered."

GESSLER PUBLISHING CO., INC., Gessler Educational Software, 900 Broadway, New York NY 10003. (212)673-3113. President: Seth C. Levin. Produces material for foreign language students—French, Spanish, German, Italian, Latin and ESL. Buys about 75 scripts/year. Buys all rights. Previously published material OK "occasionally. Do not send disk submission without documentation." SASE. Reports in 3 weeks on queries; 2 months on submissions.
Needs: "Filmstrips to create an interest in learning a foreign language and its usefulness in career objectives; also culturally insightful filmstrips on French, German, Italian and Spanish-speaking countries." Produces sound filmstrips, multimedia kits, overhead transparencies, games, realia, tapes and cassettes, computer software.
Software: Submit synopsis/outline or software with complete documentation, introduction, objectives. Pays in outright purchase and royalties.
Tips: "Be organized in your presentation; be creative but keep in mind that your audience is primarily in the junior/senior high school age bracket."

HAYES SCHOOL PUBLISHING CO., INC., 321 Pennwood Ave., Wilkinsburg PA 15221. (412)371-2373. 2nd Vice President: Clair N. Hayes III. Produces material for school teachers, principals, elementary through high school. 25% freelance written. Buys 5-10 scripts/year from unpublished/unproduced writers. All scripts produced are unagented submissions. Buys all rights. Catalog for SASE. Query. Computer printout submissions acceptable. Produces charts, workbooks, teachers' handbooks, posters, bulletin board material, computer software, and liquid duplicating books.
Needs: Educational material only. ("Particularly interested in books relating to computers.") Pays $25 minimum.
Software: Educational.

‡**ICOM INC.,** 278 N. 5th St., Columbus OH 43215. (614)224-4400. President: Phil Yoder. Produces material for corporate customers, sales people, employees. Buys 40 scripts/year. Buys all rights. Electronic submissions OK via Eagle II or 8" WordStar. Computer printout submissions acceptable; no dot-matrix except for rough drafts. SASE. Reports in 2 weeks on query; 1 month on submissions.
Needs: Multimedia kits, slides, videotape presentations, multi-image. Currently interested in hi-tech, business and sales presentations; training programs. Submit resume. Pays in outright purchase $300-2,000.

IDEAL SCHOOL SUPPLY CO., Affiliate of Westinghouse Learning Corp., 11000 S. Lavergne Ave., Oak Lawn IL 60453. (312)425-0800. Marketing Planning Analyst: Barbara Stiles. Produces material for preschool, primary and elementary students. "The majority of our product line comes from outside sources, most of them practicing classroom teachers." Occasionally these products are edited by freelance talent. Writers and editors are also used for some special development projects. Query with resume which will be filed for future reference. Free catalog.
Needs: Style, length and format vary according to grade level and subject matter of material. Produces manip-

ulatives, games, models, printed material, multimedia kits and cassette programs.
Software: Style, length and format vary according to grade level and subject matter of material.

IMAGE INNOVATIONS, INC., 14 Buttonwood Dr., Somerset NJ 08873. President: Mark A. Else. Produces material for business, education and general audiences. Query with samples. Computer printout submissions acceptable; prefers letter-quality to dot-matrix . SASE. Reports in 2 weeks. Buys all rights.
Needs: Subject topics include education, sales and public relations. Produces sound filmstrips, 16mm films, multimedia kits, ½- and ¾-inch video, and tapes and cassettes. Pays in outright purchase of $500-5,000.

IMAGE MEDIA, 3249 Hennepin Ave. S, Minneapolis MN 55408. (612)827-6500. Creative Director: A.M. Rifkin. Query with samples. SASE. Reports in 2 weeks. Rights purchased "depend on project."
Needs: Produces silent and sound filmstrips, 16mm films, tapes and cassettes, and slides. Pays in outright purchase.

IMPERIAL INTERNATIONAL LEARNING CORP., Box 548, Kankakee IL 60901. Director of Manuscript Development: Spencer Barnard. Educational AV publisher producing a variety of instructional aids for grades kindergarten through high school. 70% freelance written. Most scripts produced are unagented submissions. Draws mainly from freelance sources on an assignment basis. Seeks authors skilled in writing sound filmstrips, cassette tape and multimedia programs and microcomputer programs. "Writers should submit a query letter which includes background and professional writing experience. Indicate that you understand our particular market." Electronic submissions OK, but only programs for IBM PC or PC jr, Apple, Radio Shack, Commodore and Atari. Computer printout submissions acceptable. Reports in 6 weeks.
Needs: Sound filmstrips; slides; tapes; worksheets and teacher's manuals. Reading, math, social studies and science are main areas of concentration. Pays fee within 1 month after acceptance of ms. Contract provided.
Software: Educational programs in the areas of math, science, social studies and language arts; grades kindergarten-9. Looking for "innovative ideas to make the microcomputer challenge pupils to think; also ideas for the efficient management of instruction, testing, tracking results, etc."
Tips: "Offer concrete evidence that specific needs and requirements of the company would be met. Manuscripts need to be well researched. Stories should be intriguing with modern themes and illustrations."

‡**INDUSTRIAL MEDIA, INC.**, 6660 28th St. SE, Grand Rapids MI 49506. (616)949-7770. Contact: Jim Bartz. Produces instructional aids for vocational schools and industrial in-plant training programs. Buys all rights "usually, but other arrangements are possible." SASE.
Needs: Slide/cassette and video presentations coordinated with student workbooks and instruction guides. "We specialize in materials for training industrial equipment maintenance personnel and apprentices. Topics of particular interest to our customers include: Industrial electricity, electronics, hydraulics, mechanical maintenance, blueprint reading, welding, safety and management skills for plant supervisors. We will consider any topic with broad application in manufacturing training. We prefer to work with writers who can develop an entire, self-contained package, complete with performance objectives, script, workbooks, instruction guide and testing materials." Query.

‡**INNOVISION PRODUCTIONS**, Box 6391, Lawton OK 73506-0391. (405)357-8558. Assistant Producer: D.J. Griffin. Estab. 1983. "We aim at the 'how-to' market of hobbies and leisure time pursuits. For example, an article in an outdoor magazine brought to life on video tape for home consumers on video cassette is a good place to start. We tend to advertise in the magazine that best fits the product." Works with 3-10 writers/year. "We generate a great deal of material in house." Buys first rights. "We also retain the rights to sell to networks from the original contract." SASE. Reports in 2 weeks on queries; 2 months on submissions. Call for guidelines.
Needs: Topics include flyfishing, skiing, white water sports, backpacking, climbing, boating tips; hobbies and crafts "if they are visually exciting." Produces video cassettes for home use. Query or submit synopsis/outline and resume. "Since we look for a freestyle, it is best to use a detailed outline. The ideas are discussed with us and then the video format is decided upon. The author should also be prepared to appear on camera because it is his ideas that are being sold. Possibly, the most important thing to keep in mind is that we intend to look for the humorous and visually dramatic. We don't mean melodramatic. The idea is for the consumer to buy a tape on his favorite subject and say 'I really enjoyed that! And I learned something too!' If anything this is our main philosophy." Pays 7-12% royalty; percentage is based on retail *or* wholesale.
Tips: "We are basically looking for expertise in fields where we have none. In preparing a synopsis we need the author to mix expertise with entertainment. If the subject is active, such as kayaking, we want to make it as visually active as possible. If it's a more tedious subject, then keep it light. We need flexibility above all else. The willingness to try things. Two good programs that we tend to emulate is Bob Vila's *This Old House* on PBS and *American Sportsman* on ABC. Too many programs come off like they are absolutely planned. We want to be free-flowing and somehow enhance the consumer's dream of what this activity is all about. We need form, but a loose form. It is really important that an author be published in the last year, possibly several times. It

gives us the ability to springboard from it and gives him the ability to capitalize upon his previous success. Also, call first. We'll be glad to talk it over with authors before they prepare work."

INSIGHT! INC., 100 E. Ohio St., Chicago IL 60611. (312)467-4350. President: Neal Cochran. Produces material for all audiences, depending on type of client. 90% freelance written. Buys scripts from published/produced writers only. All scripts produced are unagented submissions. Buys over 200 scripts/year from more than 30 writers. Buys all rights. Electronic submissions OK via modem-ASCOM CP/M or 5¼" disk Apple II+ or Eagle II. Computer printout submissions acceptable. SASE.
Needs: "Depends on contract awarded to Insight! Films, videotapes, filmstrips and, most important, shows of all types." Produces 16mm films, multimedia and "book" shows. No educational materials. Concentrating entirely on film, video and shows. Query with samples. Pays in outright purchase.

INSTRUCTOR BOOKS, 1 E. 1st St., Duluth MN 55802. Editorial Director: John Bradley. "US and Canadian school supervisors, principals, and teachers purchase items in our line for instructional purposes." 35% freelance written. Buys 3 scripts/year from unpublished/unproduced writers. Most scripts produced are unagented submissions. Buys all rights. Writer should have "experience in preparing materials for elementary students, including suitable teaching guides to accompany them, and demonstrate knowledge of the appropriate subject areas, or demonstrate ability for accurate and efficient research and documentation." Query. Computer printout submissions acceptable; prefers letter-quality to dot-matrix. SASE. Free catalog.
Needs: "Elementary curriculum enrichment—all subject areas. Display material, copy and illustration should match interest and reading skills of children in grades for which material is intended. Production is limited to printed matter: posters, charts, duplicating masters, resource handbooks, teaching guides." Length: 6,000-12,000 words. "Standard contract, but fees vary considerably, depending on type of project."
Tips: "Writers who reflect current educational practices can expect to sell to us."

INTERAND CORPORATION, (formerly Instructional Dynamics Inc.), Suite 1100, 666 N. Lake Shore Dr., Chicago IL 60611. Director, Multimedia Productions: Linda Phillips. For early learning through college level. "Writer should have valid background and experience that parallels the specific assignment. Would like to have vita as first contact. We keep on file and activate as needs arise. We use outside talent to supplement our in house staff." All scripts produced are unagented submissions. SASE. Buys all rights.
Needs: Videotapes. "Requirements vary depending upon assignments from our clients. Payment depends on contractual arrangements with our client and also varies depending on medium or multimedia involved."
Tips: "We are finding that many of our clients have their own inhouse staff for scriptwriting purposes. Our business thrust is now to provide (hardware) videographic systems to the industry. On occasion we prepare sales/training tapes for our customers using a video format."

‡□ **INTERNATIONAL MEDIA SERVICES INC.**, 718 Sherman Ave., Plainfield NJ 07060. (201)756-4060. President/General Manager: Stuart Allen. Produces varied material depending on assignment or production in house; includes corporate, public relations, sales, radio/TV, CATV, teleconferencing/CCTV, etc. 60-75% freelance written. 90% of scripts produced are unagented submissions. "We normally issue assignments to writers in the freelance market who specialize in appropriate fields of interest." Buys all rights. No previously produced material. Computer printout submissions acceptable. SASE. Reporting time varies depending on job requirements and specifications.
Needs: Charts, dioramas, 8/16mm film loops, 16/35mm films, silent and sound filmstrips, kinescopes, multimedia kits, overhead transparencies, phonograph records, slides, tapes and cassettes, television shows/series, videotape presentations. "We routinely hire writers from a freelance resource file." Cable TV needs include educational and entertainment marketplaces. Query with or without samples, or submit synopsis/outline and resume. "All work must be copyrighted and be original unpublished works." Pays in accordance with Writers Guild standards, negotiated contract or flat rate.

JEAN-GUY JACQUE ET COMPAGNIE, 7026 Santa Monica Blvd., Los Angeles CA 90038. (213)462-6474. Owner: J.G. Jacque. Produces TV commercials (animation and puppet animation). Query with samples. SASE. Reports in 3 weeks. Buys all rights.
Needs: Produces 16mm and 35mm films. Pays according to Writers Guild standards.

□ **PAUL S. KARR PRODUCTIONS**, 2949 W. Indian School Rd., Box 11711, Phoenix AZ 85017. Utah Division: 1024 N. 250 E., Box 1254, Orem UT 84057. (801)225-8485/226-8209. (602)266-4198. Produces films and materials for industry, business, education, TV and cable programming. Query. "Do not submit material unless requested." Buys all rights. Works on coproduction ventures.
Needs: Produces 16mm films. Payment varies.
Tips: "One of the best ways for a writer to become a screenwriter is to create a situation with a client that requires a film. He then can assume the position of an associate producer, work with an experienced professional

producer in putting the film into being, and in that way learn about filmmaking and chalk up some meaningful credits.''

KEN-DEL PRODUCTIONS, INC., 111 Valley Rd., Wilmington DE 19804-1397. (302)655-7488. President: Ed Kennedy. Produces material for "elementary, junior high, high school and college level, as well as interested organizations and companies." Query. SASE.
Needs: "Topics of the present (technology, cities, traffic, transit, pollution, ecology, health, water, race, genetics, consumerism, fashions, communications, education, population control, waste, future sources of food, undeveloped sources of living, food, health, etc.); topics of the future; how-to series (everything for the housewife, farmer, banker or mechanic, on music, art, sports, reading, science, love, repair, sleep—on any subject); and material handling." Produces sound filmstrips; 8mm, 16mm, and 35mm films; 16mm film loops; phonograph records; prerecorded tapes and cassettes; slides and videotapes in ¾" U-matic, ½" VHS, ½" BETA cassettes.

KIMBO EDUCATIONAL-UNITED SOUND ARTS, INC., 10-16 N. 3rd Ave., Box 477, Long Branch NJ 07740. (201)229-4949. Contact: James Kimble or Amy Laufer. Produces materials for the educational market (early childhood, special education, music, physical education, dance, and preschool children 6 months and up). Buys approximately 12-15 scripts/year; works with approximately 12-15 writers/year. Buys all rights or first rights. Previously produced material OK "in some instances." SASE. Reports in 1 month. Free catalog.
Needs: "For the next two years we will be concentrating on general early chilhood-movement-oriented products, new albums in the fitness field and more. Each will be an album/cassette with accompanying teacher's manual and, if warranted, manipulatives." Phonograph records and cassettes; "all with accompanying manual or teaching guides." Query with samples and synopsis/outline or completed script. Pays 5-7% royalty on lowest wholesale selling price, and in outright purchase. Both negotiable.
Tips: "We look for creativity first. Having material that is educationally sound is also important. Being organized is certainly helpful. Fitness is growing rapidly in popularity and will always be a necessary thing. Children will always need to be taught the basic fine and gross motor skills. Capturing interest while reaching these goals is the key."

KOCH/MARSCHALL PRODUCTIONS, INC., 1718 N. Mohawk St., Chicago IL 60614. (312)664-6482. President: Phillip Koch. Produces material for teenage, health education and general audiences. 20% freelance written. Buys 3 scripts/year; 1-2 from unpublished/unproduced writers; 1-2 scripts produced are unagented submissions. Works with 5 writers/year. Buys all rights. Previously published material OK. Computer printout submissions acceptable. SASE. Reports in 6 weeks.
Needs: "We are looking for original, feature-length film scripts for both comedy and drama." Produces 16mm films. Query. Pays in accordance with Writers Guild standards.
Tips: "Submit only your very best work sample. We have a greater respect for an original idea than a commercial one. But a writer must also recognize the commercial aspect of his work." Looks for "originality, attention to craft and technique, good working attitude."

BRIEN LEE & COMPANY, 2025 N. Summit Ave., Milwaukee WI 53202. (414)277-7600. Also 33 W. 54th St., New York NY 10019. (212)307-7810. President/Creative Director: Brien Lee. Produces custom audiovisual material for business; industry; arts/non-profit; advertising and public relations agencies; business associations; special entertainment oriented projects. Buys average 5 scripts/year. Submit an example of your scripting ability as well as a resume. Computer printout submissions acceptable; disk OK if compatible. SASE. Reports in 1 month, sometimes leading to an interview and an assignment. Buys all rights.
Needs: "People who understand what 'AV' is all about . . . words, pictures, sound. Motivational, informational, clear-cut, straightforward . . . writing that is literate, but never so good it could stand on its own without the pictures or sound. Usually writing for one narrator, plus additional voices and/or characters. No hype." Produces filmstrips, multi-image presentations, and mixed media presentations, slide-sound programs.
Recent Production: AT&T International video disks.

WILLIAM V. LEVINE ASSOCIATES, INC., 31 E. 28th St., New York NY 10016. (212)683-7177. President: William V. Levine. Presentations for business and industry. 20% freelance written. Buys 4 scripts/year from unpublished/unproduced writers. Firm emphasizes "creativity and understanding of the client's goals and objectives." Will interview writers after submission of resume and/or sample AV scripts. Specifically seeks writers with offbeat or humorous flair. Buys 1-2 scripts/month. Previously published material OK. Query with resume. "We prefer New York City-area based writers only." SASE. Buys all rights.
Needs: Business-related scripts *on assignment* for specific clients for use at sales meetings or for desk-top presentations. Also uses theme-setting and inspirational scripts with inherent messages of business interest. Produces charts, sound and silent filmstrips, 16mm films, multimedia kits, tapes and cassettes, slide sets and live industrial shows. Pays $500-2,500.

J.B. LIPPINCOTT CO., Audiovisual Media Department, East Washington Sq., Philadelphia PA 19105. (215)238-4200. Contact: H.M. Eisler. Produces materials for nursing students and medical students. Buys 15-25 scripts/year. Works with approximately 25 writers/year. Disk submissions OK if compatible with TRS 80, IBM PC and Apple II. Buys all rights. SASE. Reports in 2 weeks on queries; 4 weeks on submissions. Free catalog.
Needs: "High-level instruction in medical/surgical topics for pre-service and in-service professional education." 16mm films, sound filmstrips, slides (rarely) and video materials. Query. Negotiates pay.

‡□ **LITTLE SISTER PICTURES INC.**, 1958 Glencoe Way, Hollywood CA 90068. (213)850-0473. Vice President Production: Rupert Macnee. Produces material for business and industry, home video, educational, training and instructional audience. Works with 5 writers/year. Buys all rights. Computer printout submissions acceptable. SASE. Reports in 1 month on queries; 2 months on submissions.
Needs: Videotape presentations. "We are looking for ideas to develop for the home video market, typically one hour programs that can be produced for about $60,000. We are currently developing a comedy program for cable. Also interested in variety and music programming." Query. Pays in accordance with Writers Guild standards.
Tips: "Writers should be aware of the move towards home video, the one-on-one feel that brings modular approach to information, interactive programming."

MARSHFILM ENTERPRISES, INC., Box 8082, Shawnee Mission KS 66208. (816)523-1059. President: Joan K. Marsh. Produces material for elementary and junior/senior high school students. 100% freelance written. Buys 8-16 scripts/year from unpublished/unproduced writers. All scripts produced are unagented submissions. Buys all rights. Computer printout submissions acceptable; no dot-matrix.
Needs: 50 frame; 15 minutes/script. Sound filmstrips. Query "only." Pays in outright purchase of $250-500/script.
Software: Filmstrip scripts.

ED MARZOLA & ASSOCIATES, 11846 Ventura Blvd., Studio City CA 91604. Vice President: William Case. Produces material for worldwide broadcast. Query with samples or submit resume. SASE. Reports in 2 weeks.
Needs: "We now produce television programs and feature-length films for theatrical release." Produces 35mm films and videotaped presentations. "We negotiate each case individually." Pays according to Writers Guild standards.

MAXFILMS, INC. 2525 Hyperion Ave., Los Angeles CA 90027. (213)662-3285. President: Kel Christiansen. Vice President: Sid Glenar. Produces educational material for audiences "from high-school to college graduate level in our educational film division, to all business and technical people in our industrial division. We also produce made-for-television movies and documentaries, and quality scripts and ideas in these areas are actively sought. The amount of material we use varies greatly from year to year, but on the average, perhaps 5-10 educational/industrial scripts are bought each year, with an additional 15-20 story ideas and scripts for TV movies or documentaries." Query or submit outline/synopsis, "a statement about the audience for which it is intended and the present extent of its development." SASE. Reports in 3 weeks. Rights purchased vary.
Needs: "The primary criterion for educational material is that the subject matter have entertainment as well as educational value. This does not preclude straight educational-informational scripts, but they must be entertainingly presented. Scripts or concepts for television movies must have appeal for an adult audience and have a story concept that is either unique or of current social interest. If the same concept has appeal for children as well, so much the better." Produces 16mm and 35mm films. Payment varies according to rights purchased.
Tips: "We are willing to work with new writers who show promise. About one-half of the story concepts and scripts we buy are from new writers."

‡**MEDIA FORUM INTERNATIONAL**, Box 8, Fleetwood, Mt. Vernon NY 10552. (914)667-6575. Managing Director: D.K. Bognar. Produces material for internationally active business community; international academic programs. "Our material is assigned (mostly foreign language work and translations). We usually assign translators in one or more of 16 languages used in our firm." Buys variable rights.
Needs: 16 and 35mm films, slides, videotape presentations, publications; multilingual typesetting; translations in 16 languages. Query. Pays translators by page for literary work; by word for technical work. Pay varies depending on material.
Tips: "Practice is the master." Knowledge of language is essential.

‡**MEDIA LEARNING SYSTEMS, INC.**, 1532 Rose Villa St., Pasadena CA 91106. (213)449-0006. President: Jim Griffith. Produces "custom" material for corporate, industrial, educational, product promotional audience. Buys 12 scripts/year. Buys all rights. No previously produced material. Computer printout submissions acceptable. SASE. Reports in 1 month. "Writers may contact us via the phone."

Needs: "Interactive learning is our specialty." Charts, film loops, 16mm films, sound filmstrips, 35mm slides, tapes and cassettes; teaching machine programs; television shows/series (video); videotape presentations; interactive video disks. "We develop generic programs for the educational field in general and are seeking concepts and programs for generic educational video disk production." Submit resume and technical and dramatic samples. Pay is negotiable, depends on the nature of project.

Tips: "Writers who wish to write for interactive video technology must be aware of the techniques of instructional design and technical capabilities of the new interactive media, including video disk and video tape systems."

MOTIVATION MEDIA, INC., 1245 Milwaukee Ave., Glenview IL 60025. (312)297-4740. Executive Producer: Frank Stedronsky. Produces customized material for salespeople, customers, corporate/industrial employees and distributors. 50% freelance written. Buys 100 scripts/year from unpublished/unproduced writers. All scripts produced are unagented submissions. Query with samples. SASE. Reports in 1 month. Buys all rights.

Needs: Material for all audiovisual media—particularly marketing-oriented (sales training, sales promotional, sales motivational) material. Produces sound filmstrips, 16mm films, multimedia sales meeting programs, videotapes and cassettes and slide sets. Pays $150-5,000.

Software: AV oriented.

MRC FILMS, Div. McLaughlin Research Corp., 71 W. 23rd St., New York NY 10010. (212)989-1754. Executive Producer: Larry Mollot. "Audience varies with subject matter, which is wide and diverse." 50% freelance written. Buys 20% of scripts from unpublished/unproduced writers. All scripts produced are unagented submissions. Writer "should have an ability to visualize concepts and to express ideas clearly in words. Experience in film or video scriptwriting is desirable. Write us, giving some idea of background. Submit samples of writing. We are looking for new talent. No unsolicited material accepted. Work upon assignment only." Query. SASE.

Needs: "Industrial, documentary, educational and television films. Also, public relations, teaching and motivational filmstrips. Some subjects are highly technical in the fields of aerospace and electronics. Others are on personal relationships, selling techniques, ecology, etc. A writer with an imaginative visual sense is important." Produces 16mm films, silent and sound filmstrips, video programs, and tapes and cassettes. "Fee depends on nature and length of job. Typical fees: $600-1,200 for script for 10-minute film; $1,200-2,000 for script for 20-minute film; $1,500-3,000 for script for 30-minute film. For narration writing only, the range is $300-600 for a 10-minute film; $500-900 for a 20-minute film; $600-1,200 for a 30-minute film. For scriptwriting services by the day, fee is $80-150 per day. All fees may be higher on specific projects with higher budgets."

MULTI-MEDIA PRODUCTIONS, INC., Box 5097, Stanford CA 94305. Program Manager: Mark Vining. Produces interactive instructional material for secondary (grades 9-12) schools. 99% freelance written. Buys 30-35 scripts/year; 10-15 from unpublished/unproduced writers. All scripts produced are unagented submissions. Query with samples, if available. Computer printout submissions acceptable; prefers letter quality to dot-matrix. No disk submissions. Reports in 6 weeks. Buys all rights. Free catalog.

Needs: "Sound filmstrip or video material suitable for general high school social studies curricula: history, biography, sociology, psychology, student health, anthropology, archeology and economics. Style should be straightforward, lively, objective and interactive." Approximate specifications (filmstrip): 50 frames, 10-15 minutes/program part; 1- or 2-part programs. Writer supplies script, slides for filmstrip, and teacher's manual (as per our format). Pays royalties quarterly, based on 15% of return on each program sold. "Programs with a central academic theme sell best. Program subjects should be adaptable to videotape format and to student-interactive instructional methods."

Recent Production: *Anorexia Nervosa* (sound filmstrip).

Tips: "To a certain extent, sound filmstrip topics for schools are now becoming available on videotape. There is a need for creatively produced computer software programming that gives the student user more than just rote memorizable material."

‡MULTIVISION INTERNATIONAL INC., 340 W. Huron, Chicago IL 60610. (312)337-2010. Creative Director: Michael Knab. "Most of our work is motivational/corporate image/employee communications." Buys about 50 scripts/year. Buys variable rights. Electronic disk submissions via Exxon System OK. Computer printout submissions acceptable; no dot-matrix. SASE. Reports in 2 weeks.

Needs: 16 and 35mm films, models, multimedia kits, slides, tapes and cassettes, videotape presentations, all print. Query with samples or submit synopsis/outline. Pays in royalty or outright purchase.

Tips: "We look for quality writing and imagination."

BURT MUNK & COMPANY, 666 Dundee Rd., Northbrook IL 60062. (312)564-0855. President: Burton M. Munk. Produces material for industrial, sales training, product information, and education (schools). 100%

freelance written. Works with approximately 10 writers/year. "We deal directly with writers but do not receive submissions of scripts." Buys all rights. Does not return material "all our work is 'made to order' for specific client needs—we are a custom house."
Needs: Sound filmstrips, slides, tapes and cassettes, 16mm films, videotapes. "We will contact individual writers who seem suitable for our projects." Makes outright purchase.
Software: Open for ideas.

OCEAN REALM TELEVISION, 2333 Brickell Ave., Miami FL 33129. (305)285-0252. President: Richard H. Stewart. Produces ocean-related material for broad and narrow-cast audience. Works with 8 writers/year. Buys all rights and first rights. Previously produced material OK. SASE. Reports in 1 month.
Needs: Tapes and cassettes. Query with samples.

ORIGIN, INC., 4466 Laclede, St. Louis MO 63108. (314)533-0010. President: Carla Lane. Creative Director: George V. Johnson. Produces material for corporate training, sales POP, conventions, magazine videoformat, personnel, financial, paperwork, procedures and communications testing. 10% freelance written. Buys minimal number of scripts from unpublished/unproduced writers. All scripts produced are unagented submissions. Rights purchased by assignment. SASE. Reports in 2 weeks.
Needs: "All material is produced according to client needs." Charts, films, silent and sound filmstrips, slides, tapes and cassettes, teaching machine programs, video and videodisk, and stage. Query or query with samples and resume. Pays by contract.
Tips: Looks for writers with "imagination, creativity and logical progression of thought. Have the ability to understand complicated business functions in minimum time."

OUR SUNDAY VISITOR, INC., Religious Education Dept., 200 Noll Plaza, Huntington IN 46750. (219)356-8400. Contact: Director of Religious Education. Produces material for students (kindergarten through 12th grade), adult religious education groups and teacher trainees. "We are very concerned that the materials we produce meet the needs of today's church." Query. SASE. Free catalog.
Needs: "Proposals for projects should be no more than 2 pages in length, in outline form. Programs should display up-to-date audiovisual techniques and cohesiveness. Broadly speaking, material should deal with religious education, including liturgy and daily Christian living, as well as structured catechesis. It must not conflict with sound Catholic doctrine, and should reflect modern trends in education." Produces educational books, charts, sound filmstrips and multimedia kits. "Work-for-hire and royalty arrangements possible."
Tips: "We're interested in two types of background: audiovisual and religious education. Very few people have both, and cannot be expected to perform equally well in each area. We want the best in either field."

‡**PEAK PRODUCTIONS**, Box 329, Winter Park CO 80482. (303)726-5881. President: Jim Anderson. Produces all kinds of audiovisual material. Buys all rights, first rights or variable rights. SASE. Reports in 1 month.
Needs: Tapes and cassette, television shows/series, videotape presentations. Currently interested in the following: education (12-18 minutes); news (all lengths); sports (all lengths); and promotional material. Query with samples. Pays variable rate.

‡**PHOTO COMMUNICATION SERVICES, INC.**, 6410 Knapp NE, Ada MI 49301. (616)676-1499. President: Michael Jackson. Produces commercial, industrial, sales, training, etc. material. 95% freelance written. Buys 75% of scripts from unpublished/unproduced writers. 95% of scripts produced are unagented submissions. Buys all rights and first rights. Electronic submissions OK via IBM PC format, Zenith 96 TPI format (disks); 300 or 1200 Baud Modem, or on the Source, I.D. # BBH782. Computer printout submissions acceptable. SASE. Reports in 1 month on queries; 2 weeks on scripts. Catalog for SAE; writer's guidelines for SAE.
Needs: Multimedia kits, slides, tapes and cassettes, video presentations. Primarily interested in 35mm multimedia, 1-24 projectors. Query with samples or submit completed script and resume. Pays in outright purchase or by agreement.
Tips: "There is a trend toward smaller multi-image shows."

PHOTOCOM PRODUCTIONS, Box 3135, Pismo Beach CA 93449. President: Steven C. LaMarine. Produces material for schools, junior high to university level. Query with outline/synopsis. 25% freelance written. Buys about 10 scripts/year from unpublished/unproduced writers. All scripts produced are unagented submissions. "Most writing is done inhouse or by local talent where interaction with our staff and subject matter experts is easier. However, we are willing to consider projects from any good writer." Computer printout submissions acceptable. SASE. Reports in 3 weeks. Buys filmstrip rights. Free guidelines.
Needs: "We're most interested in how-to's in vocational areas that can be used in high school shop classes or adult education classes. Material that we've been buying is 60-70 frames long and the narration runs about 8-9 minutes." Produces sound filmstrips, multimedia kits and slide sets. Pays 10-15% royalty or $200 minimum/script.

Software: Tutorials, learning games and simulations that appeal to vocational teachers. "We added educational computer software nearly two years ago and are anxious to build this line. Any programs to be considered must be accompanied by documentation and be 'user friendly': TRS 80, Apple, IBM."
Tips: "Many AV producers are taking on computer software as a logical extension of their services. This is a hot area, but with so many programs becoming available, schools are more discriminating than ever about what they buy."

‡□ **PHOTOGRAPHIC ILLUSTRATED COMPANY**, 2220 W. Magnolia Blvd., Burbank CA 91505. (818)849-7345. Executive Producer: John Denlinger. Produces material for corporate and public audience. Buys 10 scripts/year. Buys all rights. No previously produced material. Electronic submissions OK via IBM Displaywriter; computer printout submissions acceptable. SASE. Reports "as requested." Catalog for SAE.
Needs: Charts, films, silent and sound filmstrips, multimedia kits, overhead transparencies, slides, tapes and cassettes, videotape presentations, multimedia. Specific cable TV needs include projects under development. Query. Pays in outright purchase.

PHOTOSCOPE, INC., Graphic Media, Inc., 12th Floor, 12 W. 27th St., Fl. 12, New York NY 10001. (212)696-0880. General Manager: Geoffrey Carter. Vice President: Carswell Berlin. Produces material for a corporate audience. 100% freelance written. Buys 10 scripts/year from published/produced writers only. 100% of scripts produced are unagented submissions. Buys all rights. Computer printout submissions acceptable; no dot-matrix. SASE.
Needs: Produces slides and multi-image and offers computer graphic slides. Looks for "imagination, coherency, clarity." Query with samples. Buys scripts outright for negotiable rate.

PREMIER FILM & RECORDING CORP., 3033 Locust, St. Louis MO 63103. (314)531-3555. Secretary/Treasurer: Grace Dalzell. Produces material for the corporate community, religious organizations, political arms, and hospital and educational groups. Buys 50-100 scripts/year. Buys all rights; "very occasionally the writer retains rights." Previously produced material OK; "depends upon original purposes and markets." SASE. Reports "within a month or as soon as possible."
Needs: "Our work is all custom-produced with the needs being known only as required." 35mm film loops, super 8mm and 35mm films, silent and sound filmstrips, multimedia kits, overhead transparencies, phonograph records, slides, tapes and cassettes, and "LaBelle Filmstrips (a specialty)." Submit complete script and resume. Pays in accordance with Writers Guild standards or by outright purchase of $100 to "any appropriate sum."
Tips: "Always place *occupational pursuit*, name, address and phone number in upper right hand corner of resume without fail. We're looking for writers with creativity, good background and a presentable image."

PRENTICE-HALL MEDIA, INC., 150 White Plains Rd., Tarrytown NY 10591. (914)631-8300. Managing Editor: Sandra Carr Grant. Produces material for secondary, postsecondary vocational and science students. Buys 50 scripts/year. Buys all rights. Previously produced material OK. SASE. Reports in 1 month. Catalog for SAE.
Needs: "We will be looking for audiovisual treatments for high technology training." Sound filmstrips. Query with samples or submit synopsis/outline. Pays by outright purchase of $350 minimum.
Tips: "We look for clarity of language, ability to write 'visual' scripts and facility with technical subject matter."

‡□ **PRIMALUX VIDEO**, 30 W. 26th St., New York NY 10010. (212)206-1402. Director: M. Clarke. Produces industrial and training material; promotional pieces. Buys 10 scripts/year; works with 2 writers/year. Buys all rights. No previously produced material. Computer printout submissions acceptable.
Needs: Television show/series, videotape presentations. Query with samples. Pays royalty or in outright purchase.

‡**PULLIN PRODUCTIONS LTD.**, Suite 102, 617 11th Ave. SW, Calgary, Alberta T2R 0E1 Canada. (403)234-7885. Contact: Creative Director. Produces material for industrial clients. Buys average of 20 scripts/year. Buys all rights. Reports in 1 month.
Needs: "Scripts for multi-image programs on an individual basis." 16mm films and slides. Query with samples. Pays in outright purchase or determines pay by "individual negotiation."

RHYTHMS PRODUCTIONS, Whitney Bldg., Box 34485, Los Angeles CA 90034. President: R.S. White. "Our audience is generally educational, with current projects in elementary early childhood." Text 100% freelance written. All scripts produced are unagented submissions. Query. "We need to know a writer's background and credits and to see samples of his work." SASE.
Needs: Teacher resource books; phonograph records. "Content is basic to the resource books; educational

background is a necessity. For our phonograph records, we accept only fully produced tapes of a professional quality. If tapes are sent, include return postage."

SANDY CORP., 1500 W. Big Beaver Rd., Troy MI 48084. (313)649-0800. Manager of Human Resources: David Southworth. Produces material for sales and technical/automotive audiences. Works with 50 freelance writers. Buys all rights. SASE. Reports in 1 month on queries.
Needs: Articles up to 500 words on how Chevrolet or GMC truck dealers are doing an outstanding job of selling cars and trucks, servicing cars and trucks, participating in community activities, recognizing employee achievement—can use b&w glossies of story events. Produces various publications (samples on request). Submit outline/synopsis. Makes outright purchase of $100 minimum.
Tips: "Submit only if you have good relationship with local Chevrolet or GMC truck dealership and can write copy/take pictures reflecting a professional knowledge of the business."

‡**SCIENCE RESEARCH ASSOCIATES**, 155 N. Wacker, Chicago IL 60606. (312)984-7000. Script Coordinators: Matthew Kline and Walter Teague. Buys 30-40 scripts/year; works with 10-15 writers/year. Buys all rights. No previously produced material. Electronic submissions OK. Computer printout submissions acceptable; no dot-matrix. SASE. Reports in 2 weeks. Free writer's guidelines.
Needs: Videotape presentations. Currently interested in "more data processing training videotapes on IBM software products. Tapes will be 7-15 minutes and will have 50%-100% animation." Submit treatment and 3 drafts of script/storyboards. Set fee to be determined prior to agreement.

‡**SEVEN OAKS PRODUCTIONS**, 9145 Sligo Creek Pkwy., Silver Spring MD 20901. (301)587-0030. Production Manager: M. Marlow. 80% freelance written. Produces material for students, civic and professional groups, and PTA chapters. Buys 10-20 scripts from 10 writers/year. 65% of scripts are unagented submissions. Query with samples, submit outline/synopsis or submit completed script. Computer printout submissions acceptable; prefers letter-quality to dot-matrix. SASE. Reports in 2 months. Buys all rights or first rights, but rights purchased are negotiable.
Needs: Educational, medical, safety and general entertainment material. "We look for clarity in style, imagination with the ability to get information across and accomplish objectives, the ability to meet deadlines and to dig if necessary to get sufficient information to make the script better than another on the same subject. Writers should know the film format." Produces 16mm films, video disk computer active programs, multimedia kits, phonograph records, tapes and cassettes, and slide sets. Payment negotiable according to project.

‡□ **SINGER COMMUNICATIONS, INC.**, 3164 Tyler Ave., Anaheim CA 92801. (714)527-5650. Acting President: Natalie Carlton. 50% freelance written. Produces material for foreign organizations; electronic publishing (USA and foreign countries). Buys 500 scripts/year; 150 scripts/year from previously unpublished/unproduced writers. Works with 200 writers/year; represents publishing companies. Buys syndication or book rights. Previously produced material OK. Computer printout submissions acceptable. SASE. Reports in 2 weeks on queries; 3 weeks on submissions. Catalog for 9x11 SAE and $1 postage; writer's guidelines for 9x11 SAE and $1 postage.
Needs: 16mm films, overhead transparencies, slides, tapes and cassettes, television shows/series, videotape presentations, educational films for foreign TV. Currently interested in audiovisual material "of worldwide interest only for overseas TV and electronic publishing." Syndicates freelance material for the cable TV market. 98% of scripts produced are unagented submissions. Query with samples or submit synopsis/outline. Pays negotiable rate.
Tips: "Keep international market in mind."

PHOEBE T. SNOW PRODUCTIONS, INC., 240 Madison Ave., New York NY 10016. (212)679-8756. Creative Director: Deborah R. Herr. Produces material for corporate uses, sales force, inhouse training, etc. 90% freelance written. Buys 20-40 scripts/year from published/produced writers only. All scripts produced are unagented submissions. Buys all rights. Computer printout submissions acceptable; prefers letter-quality to dot-matrix . SASE. Reports in 2 weeks on queries; 1 month on mss.
Needs: 16mm films, sound filmstrips and slides. Query with samples and resume. Pays in outright purchase.
Tips: "Have some understanding of AV for corporations. This is not the educational field. We're looking for creative writers who work with speed and can take direction. Be aware of short deadlines and some low budgets."

SPENCER PRODUCTIONS, INC., 234 5th Ave., New York NY 10001. (212)697-5895. General Manager: Bruce Spencer. Produces material for high school students, college students and adults. Occasionally uses freelance writers with considerable talent. Query. SASE.
Needs: 16mm films, prerecorded tapes and cassettes. Satirical material only. Pay is negotiable.
Tips: "For a further insight into our philosophy, read *Don't Ged Mad . . . Get Even*, by our executive producer, Alan Abel."

‡**SPINDLER PRODUCTIONS**, 1501 Broadway, New York NY 10036. (212)730-1255. Creative Directors: Todd Ryan and V. Spindler. Produces material for corporate level to upper end of consumer audience. Buys 50-100 scripts/year; works with 4-10 writers/year. Buys all rights. No previously produced material. Electronic submissions OK via TRS 80, 300 Baud, 1 stopbit, 8 bit, no parity; computer printout submissions acceptable. SASE. Reports in 2 weeks. Catalog for 9x12 SAE.
Needs: Charts, film loops, 16 and 35mm films, multimedia kits, overhead transparencies, slides, tapes and cassettes, teaching machine programs, videotape presentations, AV presentations. Query with sample scripts "preferably of used/published material" or submit outline/synopsis or completed script and resume. Pays in outright purchase.

SPOTLIGHT PRESENTS, INC., 373 Park Ave. S., New York NY 10016. (212)725-5151. Producer/President: Carmine Santandrea. Produces material for corporate employees, trade association members and the general public. Query with samples and resume. SASE. Reports in 3 weeks. Buys all rights. Free catalog for SASE.
Needs: "We specialize in multi-image productions (3-30 projectors), 5-15 minutes in length. Subject topics: business, corporate image, new product introductions and general. Frequently need proposals written." Produces sound filmstrips, 16mm and 35mm films, multimedia kits, overhead transparencies, slides and video. "Freelancers supply approximately 20 scripts/year and approximately 60 proposals/year." Pays in outright purchase of $50-$125/running minute.
Tips: "Submit samples indicative of range of writing experience, e.g., proposals, multimedia and film." Writers should show "reliability, thoroughness, creativity and responsiveness to suggestions."

‡**SPOTTSWOOD STUDIOS**, 2524 Old Shell Rd., Box 7061, Mobile AL 36607. (205)478-9387. Co-owner: M.W. Spottswood. "We normally work for sponsors (not always) who seek public attention." Buys 1-2 scripts/yr. Query with resume and samples. Computer printout submissions acceptable. SASE. Reports in 2 weeks. Buys all rights.
Needs: Business, religious and general. Produces 16mm films and 8mm loops, sound filmstrips, videotape and slide sets. Pays in outright purchase price.

E.J. STEWART, INC., 525 Mildred Ave., Primos PA 19018. (215)626-6500. "Our firm is a television production house providing programming for the broadcast, industrial, educational and medical fields. Government work is also handled." Buys 50 scripts/year. Buys all rights. Computer printout submissions acceptable. SASE. Reports "when needed."
Needs: "We produce programming for our clients' specific needs. We do not know in advance what our needs will be other than general scripts for commercials and programs depending upon requests that we receive from clients." Videotapes. Submit resume only. Pays in negotiable outright purchase.

TALCO PRODUCTIONS, 279 E. 44th St., New York NY 10017. (212)697-4015. President: Alan Lawrence. Produces for TV, also videotape and films for schools, foundations, industrial organizations and associations. 20-40% freelance written. Buys scripts from published/produced writers only. All scripts produced are unagented submissions. Buys all rights. "We maintain a file of writers and call on those with experience in the general category. We do not accept unsolicited mss. We prefer to receive a writer's resume listing credits. If his background merits, we will be in touch when a project seems right." Produces sound filmstrips, films, videotapes, phonograph records, tapes and cassettes, and slide sets.
Needs: General (client-oriented productions to meet specific needs); education (peripheral market); business (public relations, documentaries, industrial); foreign language (we sometimes dub client's shows for a specific non-English speaking market). Payment runs $500 and up; usually Writers Guild minimums apply.
Tips: "We think that the Cable TV market will develop in new ways. We're watching it and indeed, working in it."

ROGER TILTON FILMS, INC., 315 6th Ave., San Diego CA 92101. (619)233-6513. Production Manager: Robert T. Hitchcox. Audience "varies with client." Submit resume. SASE. "We do not accept unrequested scripts. We will request samples if a writer is being considered." Computer printout submissions acceptable; prefers letter-quality to dot-matrix. Reports in 2 weeks. Buys all rights.
Needs: "Scripts are all on contract basis with specific details supplied by us or our clients. Subjects run full spectrum of topics and audiences." Produces sound filmstrips, 16mm, 35mm and 65mm films and video cassettes. Pays in outright purchase; "depends on project, quoted in advance."
Tips: Writers must demonstrate "ability to work within the constraints of the client."

‡**TRANSTAR PRODUCTIONS, INC.**, Suite 170, 750 W. Hampden, Englewood CO 80110. (303)761-0595. Producer/Director: Doug Hanes. Produces primarily industrial material. Buys 5-6 scripts/year. Buys all rights. No previously produced material. Computer printout submissions acceptable. SASE. Reporting time varies. Free catalog.

Needs: 8 and 16mm film loops, 16mm films, sound filmstrips, slides, tapes and cassettes, videotape presentations. Submit resume. Pays negotiable rate.

TROLL ASSOCIATES, 320 Rt. 17, Mahwah NJ 07430. (201)529-4000. Contact: M. Schecter. Produces material for elementary and high school students. Buys approximately 200 scripts/year. Query or submit outline/synopsis. SASE. Reports in 3 weeks. Buys all rights. Free catalog.
Needs: Produces silent and sound filmstrips, multimedia kits, tapes and cassettes, and books. Pays royalty or by outright purchase.

TUTOR/TAPE, 107 France St., Toms River NJ 08753. President: Richard R. Gallagher. Produces and publishes cassettes, filmstrips, software and visual aids including slides and transparencies for the college market. 50% freelance written. Half of scripts produced are unagented submissions. Buys average 5 scripts/year. "We are the largest publisher of pre-recorded educational cassettes for the college market. We are capable of handling everything from writer to recording to packaging to marketing in a totally vertically integrated production-marketing publishing organization." Send brief synopsis or short outline stating credentials, education or experience. Computer printout submissions acceptable. SASE. Reports in 1 week.
Needs: 10- to 25-page scripts for 15- to 30-minute educational messages on college topics, including business, management, marketing, personnel, advertising, accounting, economics and other related material. We also seek remedial and study skills material useful to college students and suitable for audio presentation. Pays 15% royalty or in outright purchase.
Software: College subjects.
Tips: "Writers should submit material relevant to students in college who need assistance in passing difficult courses, or interesting material which supplements college textbooks and enhances class work."

UNIVERSITY OF WISCONSIN STOUT TELEPRODUCTION CENTER, 800 S. Broadway, Menomonie WI 54751. (715)232-2622. Director of Instructional Television: David Conyer. Produces instructional TV programs for primary, secondary, post secondary and specialized audiences. 10% freelance written. Buys scripts from published/produced writers only. All scripts produced are unagented submissions. "We produce ITV programs for national, regional and state distribution to classrooms around the US and Canada." Query with resume and samples of TV scripts. Computer printout submissions acceptable; prefers letter-quality to dot-matrix. SASE. Buys all rights.
Needs: "Our clients fund programs in a 'series' format which tend to be 8-12 programs each." Produces only with one-inch broadcast quality. "I need materials from writers who have experience in writing instructional TV. I have an immediate need for writers with elementary teaching experience who can write a primary level reading series. Only the 'pros' need apply. We also have a need for writers in Wisconsin and Minnesota whom we can call on to write one or multi-program/series in instructional television."
Recent Production: *Let Me See* (5-time national award-winning first grade science series)
Tips: "Freelance writers should be aware of the hardware advances in broadcast and nonbroadcast. There are new avenues for writers to pursue in adult learning, computer assisted programming and interactive programming."

VIDEOCOM, INC., 502 Sprague St., Dedham MA 02026. (617)329-4080. President: Clifford Jones. Executive Producer: Karen Clair. Produces materials for broadcast, industrial and educational audiences. Buys 25 scripts/year. Query with samples. Buys all rights.
Needs: "Scripts and copy for broadcast and industrial clients ranging from commercials to marketing and training programs and printed materials. We look for originality in the ability to understand problems and in the design of a solution." Produces videotape (all formats), films, slide presentations and printed materials. Pays by outright purchase.

VISUAL EDUCATION CORP., Box 2321, Princeton NJ 08540. Vice President: William J. West. Produces material for colleges, elementary and high schools. 80% freelance written. Query with resume, samples and range of fees. Submissions will not be returned; "we like to keep a file of freelancers on whom we can call." Computer printout submissions acceptable; prefers letter-quality to dot-matrix. Reports in 1 month. Buys all rights.
Needs: Editorial developers of college and high school textbooks. Need editors and writers with the ability to write clearly to the grade level. Produces textbooks, sound filmstrips, films, teacher's guides and student activity material, multimedia kits. Pays variable fee based on the length of chapters assigned.

VISUAL HORIZONS, 180 Metro Park, Rochester NY 14623. (716)424-5300. President: Stanley Feingold. Produces material for general audiences. Buys 50 programs/year. Query with samples. SASE. Reports in 5 months. Free catalog.
Needs: Business, medical and general subjects. Produces silent and sound filmstrips, multimedia kits, slide sets and videotapes. Payment negotiable.

VOCATIONAL EDUCATION PRODUCTIONS, California Polytechnic State University, San Luis Obispo CA 93407. Contact: Rick Smith. "We specialize in agricultural media." 80% freelance written. Buys 10-20 scripts/year from unpublished/unproduced writers. All scripts produced are unagented submissions. Query. Electronic submissions OK on Apple II disk. Computer printout submissions acceptable. SASE.

Needs: Produces sound filmstrips, multimedia kits, tapes and cassettes, and 35mm slide sets. "We usually furnish script development pages for the typing of final drafts, just to make it easier to work with the script. Our productions deal almost exclusively with agricultural subjects. Since we sell around the world, we cannot focus on a limited regional topic. Total length of our filmstrips is about 10 minutes or 50-70 frames. Avoid talking down to the viewer. Technical accuracy is an absolute must." Pays $300/script for a series of 3-6; $400-600 for a single script.

Recent Production: *The Beef Management Practices Series.*

Software: Agriculture related.

Tips: "Video is the coming thing in AV formats."

‡**WREN ASSOCIATES, INC.**, 208 Bunn Dr., Princeton NJ 08540. Copy Department Head: Mr. Udi Shorr. Produces material for employees and sales people, and various sales and corporate presentations for Fortune 500 corporate clients. 20% freelance written. Buys 30-40 scripts/year from published/produced writers only. All scripts produced are unagented submissions. Buys all rights. No previously published material. Electronic submissions OK over Compuserve network, on IBM/Compaq, MS word, and Radio Shack TRS 80 II diskette. Computer printout submissions acceptable. SASE. Reports in 3 weeks. Catalog for #10 SAE and 1 first class stamp.

Needs: Produces 8mm film loops, 16mm films, sound filmstrips, multimedia kits, slides (multiprojector shows); tapes and cassettes, television shows/series (corporate networks); videotape presentations; and interactive video on a project-by-project basis for clients. "We need freelance writers who can assimilate technical or business-oriented subject matter (e.g., telecommunications services, automotive). They must be able to present this material in a clear, entertaining presentation that *sells* the product." Query with samples. Pays $400-7,000/job.

Tips: "Freelance writers should be aware of interactive video disk, tape trend. It's the coming wave in training and P.O.P. sales."

‡**ZM SQUARED**, Box C-30, Cinnaminson NJ 08077. (609)786-0612. Contact: Pete Zakroff. "We produce AVs for a wide range of clients including education, business, industry and labor organizations." Buys 10 scripts/year; works with 4-5 writers/year. Buys all rights. No previously published material. Electronic submissions OK via Apple system. Computer printout submissions acceptable. SASE. Reports in 2 weeks on queries; 1 month on submissions. Free catalog.

Needs: Silent filmstrips, kinescopes, multimedia kits, overhead transparencies, slides, tapes and cassettes, videotape presentations. Query with or without samples. Pays 3-10% royalty or by outright purchase $150-750.

Playwriting

"This season needs a play with teeth," wrote Walter Kerr, reporting on last year's theatre season in *The New York Times*. But producers would probably agree with the statement *any* season. No matter how many plays *with teeth* are on Broadway, they'll want more of them there. That's the constant challenge of a theatrical career.

Today's playwrights have more outlets than ever for their work. Community theatres, regional ones, and university theatre departments show that audiences aren't ready to trade stages for movie screens. But few seasons at local or regional theatres can rely on classics like *A Streetcar Named Desire*. Audiences want to see new works on stage. New York producers now review regional productions, looking for that special play to bring to the Big Apple.

Playhouse managers continue to stress involvement with theatre if you plan to write for theatre. Attend plays at the house you're interested in; watch audience reaction to characters and themes. Know the theatre's stage and casting limitations. Inquire about internships at the theatre. Enter playwriting competitions. Participate in workshops to get professional criticism.

Some universities offer playwright-in-residence grants. Investigate the options in your area and be willing to travel if necessary. As a beginning playwright *you* must find stages and actors to present your work.

While Shakespeare may not have written plays with production costs in mind, today's playwright must. The play that demands expensive sets and "a cast of thousands" is less likely to land on stage. High production costs are bringing back the concept of the one-person play. Stage props are simpler (though expressive). In the case of one touring company, the director wants productions that can be transported in a station wagon.

Regardless of the stage perimeters, new plays must offer fresh, unclichéd looks at life. "Playwrights are writing pieces that are too bizarre, just trying to come up with something new and imaginative," says one playwright coordinator. "Many times they are trying to make statements that no one cares about, and we've found that many times we don't care about the characters being written about."

Dramatic yet believable characters can make an audience care. In fact, some producers are more interested in characterization than in involved, contrived plots, observes one play publisher.

Another play publisher sees the "empowerment of young people" as a trend for playwrights to watch. Audiences want "recognition of young people's vast intelligence." Theatregoers also want accurate information about mankind, the world, and the universe, he says.

Playwrights must test the *worlds* they write about by staging readings. Whether in classrooms or living rooms, readings enable playwrights to *hear* their words. Beautiful lines on paper may sound unrealistic when an actor says them, point out playwrights.

Organizations like New Dramatists (424 W. 44th St., New York City 10036) sponsor readings and encourage new playwriting talent. "We offer script-in-hand readings of our members' plays, panel discussions, writer studios, free theatre tickets, a national script distribution service and exchanges with theatres," says Richard L. LeComte, assistant to the director of Script Development and Marketing.

Showcase theatres are also invaluable to playwrights. AMAS Repertory Theatre, Inc. (1 E. 104th St., New York City 10029), for example, is a professional off-off-Broadway showcase theatre that produces three original musicals each season. *Bubbling Brown Sugar* and others have gone on to commercial productions. The group also presents two children's theatre productions and one summer tour.

Experience and exposure to sophisticated theatre audiences pay off for the playwright, even when little or no pay is promised.

"The big question with so many places isn't money," says one playwright. "What it boils down to is what kinds of rights are they going to want to retain to your work. That's the thing the playwright has to be very, very careful about."

The closest thing to a playwright's Bible is the *Dramatists Sourcebook* (Theatre Communications Group, 355 Lexington Ave., New York City 10017). It lists theatres that consider unsolicited playscripts, festivals and contests, conferences and workshops, and playwriting opportunities in film, radio and video. A useful directory is the *Theatre Directory* (Theatre Communications Group) listing nearly 200 professional nonprofit theatres. The Alliance of Resident Theatres—New York (formerly the Off Off Broadway Alliance) will provide general information to playwrights and consultations only for members. The alliance (Room 315, 325 Spring St., New York City 10013) also has information on its 85 member theatres.

The somewhat large number of production outlets shouldn't fool you into thinking you've chosen an easy career. Many producers might read your play before you get a "yes" letter; you may never get a "yes."

For an aspiring playwright with a few rejection slips, it's easy to forget why you're writing. If that happens, go to the theatre; *feel* the strong, emotional teeth of the play on stage. Then use your own story line to go for your audience's hearts.

ACADEMY THEATRE, 1137 Peachtree St. NE, Atlanta GA 30309. (404)873-2518. Artistic Director: Frank Wittow. Produces 10 plays/year. 20% freelance written. 5% of scripts produced are unagented. Plays performed in Academy Theatre—415 seats thrust stage, and in Academy Lab Theatre, 100 seats, flexible stage. Professional productions tour the Southeast for elementary, high school, college and community audiences. Works with 2-5 unpublished/unproduced writers annually. Submit complete ms. "We accept unsolicited, year-round submissions." Computer printout submissions acceptable. Reports in 4 months. Buys negotiable rights. Pays negotiable royalty. SASE.

Needs: "Full length plays, one acts, children's plays, adaptations, translations, original plays of contemporary significance, plays that go beyond the conventions of naturalism; Transformational plays: actors playing multiple roles. Prefer small cast; unit set. Follow standard playwright submission guidelines and standard preparation of script." No sitcom love affairs, triangles; plays with very large casts. Special programs: "Academy Playwrights Lab is an ongoing program of workshop productions of previously unproduced full length and one act plays by Southeastern playwrights. Deadline is open. The Atlanta New Play Project is sponsored each June by the Academy and other local theatres. The project includes staged readings, workshops, full productions as plays in progress with a forum for discussion of new works. Southeastern playwrights are specifically desired for this project."

Tips: "Writers should be aware of the obvious trends in funding for the arts; and therefore, submit scripts which might be within reason for production. Few region theatres around the country are in a position to produce large cast, multi-set, multi-media extravaganzas; and what's more *our* theatre audiences don't expect or want that from live theatre productions."

ALASKA REPERTORY THEATRE, Suite 201, 705 W. 6th Ave., Anchorage AK 99501. (907)276-2327. Artistic Director: Robert J. Farley. Produces 4-5 plays/year. Professional plays performed for Alaskan audiences. Submit complete ms. Reports in 5 months. Pays 3% + royalty "depending on work." SASE.
Needs: Produces all types of plays.

‡**AMAS REPERTORY THEATRE, INC.**, 1 E. 104th St., New York NY 10029. (212)369-8000/8001. Artistic Director: Rosetta LeNoire. Produces 6 plays/year. 80% freelance written. 90% of scripts produced are unagented submissions. "AMAS is a professional, off-off-Broadway showcase theatre. We produce three showcase productions of original musicals each season; these are presented for a sophisticated New York theatre audience. A number have gone on to commercial productions, the best known of which is *Bubbling Brown Sugar*. We also present two children's theatre productions and one summer tour." Works with 1-2 unpublished/unproduced writers annually. Query with synopsis or submit complete script with cassette tape of score or of partial score. Computer printout submissions acceptable; prefers letter-quality to dot-matrix. Reports in 2 months. "Be prepared to wait at least one year or more between acceptance and production. Our standard contract calls for a small percentage of gross and royalties to AMAS, should the work be commercially produced within a specified period."
Needs: *Musicals only*; in addition, all works will be performed by multi-racial casts. Musical biographies are especially welcome. Cast size should be under 15 if possible, including doubling. Because of the physical space, set requirements should be relatively simple."
Tips: "AMAS is dedicated to bringing all people—regardless of race, creed, color or religion—together through the creative arts. In writing for AMAS, an author should keep this overall goal in mind."

‡**AMERICAN CONSERVATORY THEATRE**, Plays-in-Progress Division, 450 Geary, San Francisco CA 94102. (415)771-3880. General Director: William Ball. Director, Plays-in-Progress Division: Janice Hutchins. Produces 9 plays on main stage (Geary Theatre, 1,450 seats) for 18,000 subscribers to repertory season; 3-5 new plays (Playroom Theatre, 50 seats) for 800 subscribers to experimental program. Query with synopsis; submit complete script, submit through agent. "We judge the quality of the play as a whole (theme, characterization, structure, etc.) and for that reason prefer that a playwright send the play itself instead of a synopsis. We accept scripts September through May." Reports in 3 months. "If the script is chosen for production in the experimental, Plays-in-Progress program, the playwright grants A.C.T. an option to enter into a Standard Dramatist Guild Production contract. Option must be exercised within 60 days after final performance at A.T.C." Pays $750 license fee for no less than 7 and no more than 14 separate performances. Offers Playwright-in-Residence Program to playwrights selected for Plays-in-Progress covering duration of rehearsals and performances (about 5 weeks.).
Needs: American realism, comedy/drama/adaptations, farce, satire, abstract. Full length and one acts, but no musicals or children's plays. "As the size of the Experimental Theatre is small, our production elements minimal, we usually produce plays with small casts and production values. We are receptive to many different forms and structures of the drama. If the manuscript exceeds our producing capabilities in the New Plays Division, and we admire the writing, we attempt to schedule a staged reading as an alternative to production."

AMERICAN THEATRE ARTS, Dept. W, 6240 Hollywood Blvd., Hollywood CA 90028. (213)466-2462. Submit to Literary Manager: Pamela Bohnert. Artistic Director: Don Eitner. Produces 7 plays/year. 15-25%

freelance written. Plays performed in 2 Equity Waiver theatres (55 and 70 seats) for the general public. Works with 1-2 unpublished/unproduced writers annually. Submit complete ms. "Submit script-sized SASE for return of manuscript. Submit copies only—not original manuscripts. Submit bound copies, not loose pages secured only with paper clips or rubber bands." Reports in 4 months. "If show goes on to full Equity production, percentage arrangement is worked out with author." Pays $100 minimum royalty. SASE.
Needs: No restrictions as to genres, topics or styles.

ARENA STAGE, 6th and Maine Ave. SW, Washington DC 20024. Works with 1-2 unpublished/unproduced writers annually in Play Development project. Wants original plays, solicited or submitted through agents. Otherwise, writers may submit a letter of inquiry with a synopsis of the play. "Plays with relevance to the human situation—which cover a multitude of dramatic approaches—are welcome here." Produces 8 works a year; 15% musicals, 85% non-musicals. 25% are originals. Pays 5% of gross. Query. Computer printout submissions acceptable, "as long as they are easily readable"; no dot-matrix. Reports in 4 months. SASE.

‡**THE ARKANSAS ARTS CENTER CHILDREN'S THEATRE**, Box 2137, McArthur Park, Little Rock AR 72203. (501)372-4000. Artistic Director: Bradley Anderson. Produces 5 mainstage plays, 4 tours/year. Mainstage season plays performed at The Arkansas Arts Center for Little Rock and surrounding area; tour season by professional actors throughout Arkansas and surrounding states. Mainstage productions perform to family audiences in public performances; weekday performances for local schools of grades 3 through senior high school. Tour audiences generally the same. Submit complete script. Computer printout submissions acceptable. Reports in several weeks. Buys negotiable rights. Pays $250-1,000 or negotiable commission. SASE.
Needs: Original adaptations of classic and contemporary works. Also original scripts. "This theatre is defined as a children's theatre; this can inspire certain assumptions about the nature of the work. We would be pleased if submissions did not presume to condescend to a particular audience. We are not interested in 'cute' scripts. Submissions should simply strive to be good theatre literature. No cardboard and paste plays of the kind currently in abundance for children."
Recent Title: *The Thirteen Clocks* (Thurber).
Tips: "We would welcome scripts open to imaginative production and interpretation. Also, scripts which are mindful that this children's theatre casts adults as adults and children as children. Scripts which are not afraid of contemporary issues are welcome."

ART CRAFT PLAY CO., Box 1058, Cedar Rapids IA 52406. (319)364-6311. Averages 5-10 plays/year for junior and senior high school. 100% freelance written. 99% of scripts produced are unagented submissions. Query or send complete ms. Buys amateur rights. Pays $100-1,000.

‡**ARTREACH TOURING THEATRE**, 3936 Millsbrae Ave., Cincinnati OH 45209. (513)351-9973. Director: Kathryn Schultz Miller. Produces 4 plays/year to be performed in area schools and community organizations. "We are a professional company. Our audience is primarily young people in schools and their families." Submit complete ms. Reports in 6 weeks. Buys exclusive right to produce for 9 months. Pays $4/show (approximately 150 performances). SASE.
Needs: Plays for children and adolescents. Serious, intelligent plays about contemporary life or history/legend. "Limited sets and props. Can use scripts with only 2 men and 2 women; 45 minutes long. Should be appropriate for touring." No cliched approaches, camp or musicals.
Tips: "We look for opportunities to create innovative stage effects using few props, and we like scripts with good acting opportunities."

ARTS CLUB THEATRE, 1585 Johnston St., Vancouver, British Columbia, Canada V6H 3R9. (604)687-5315. Artistic Director: Bill Millerd. Produces 14 plays/year. 100% of new material is freelance written. 25% of scripts produced are unagented submissions. Plays performed in 3 theaters seating 500, 200 and 225 respectively, for a diverse adult audience. Stock professional company operating year-round. Tours British Columbia and occasionally goes on national tours. Works with 1 unproduced/unpublished writer annually. Submit complete ms. Computer printout submissions acceptable; prefers letter-quality to dot-matrix. Reports in 2 months. "If interested, we ask for first production plus future rights." Pays 8% royalty, or commission: from $1,000-5,000. SASE or SAE and IRCs.
Needs: Full-length plays for adult audiences. Comedies and plays about concerns of the region. Well-made plays as opposed to experimental; realistic over fantasy. "We are interested in plays that are well-suited to our 200 seat intimate space. Such plays usually are one-set, and have limited number of characters (not more than 8) and have a strong story line."
Recent Production: *Talking Dirty*, by Sherman Snukal ("a sexual satire which takes a close look at the contemporary lifestyles of hip, young sophisticates who inhabit the trendy neighborhoods of Canadian cities").
Tips: "As a theatre that operates in Canada, we are of course more interested in Canadian works. But we are definitely interested in good plays no matter where they are written. We are *not* a theatre that only does Canadi-

an work. We are also very interested in original revue material (both musical and non-musical) to suit our new 225-seat Arts Club Revue Theatre.''

‡**ASOLO STATE THEATRE**, Postal Drawer E, Sarasota FL 33578. (813)355-7115. Artistic Director: John Ulmer. Produces 7 plays/year. 75% freelance written. About 50% of scripts produced are unagented submissions. A LORT theatre with an intimate performing space. "We play to rather traditional middle class audiences." Works with 5-10 unproduced/unpublished writers annually. Submit complete script. Computer printout submissions acceptable; prefers letter-quality to dot-matrix. Reports in 2 months. Buys negotiable rights. Pays negotiable rate. SASE.
Needs: Play must be *full length*. "We do not restrict ourselves to any particular genre or style—generally we do a good mix of classical and modern works."
Tips: "We have no special approach—we just want well written plays with clear, dramatic throughlines."

‡**AT THE FOOT OF THE MOUNTAIN THEATER**, 2000 S. 5th St., Minneapolis MN 55454. (612)375-9487. Managing Director: Phyllis Jane Rose. Produces 2-3 plays/year. 20% freelance written "with anticipated increase." All scripts produced are unagented submissions. "Plays will be performed in our 'black box' theatre by a professional acting company. Plays submitted to our *Broadcloth Series* (a sampler of new scripts by women writers) will be given staged readings by our professional ensemble." Works with 4-6 unpublished/unproduced writers annually. Submit complete script. Computer printout submissions acceptable; no dot-matrix. Reports in 6 months. Pays $10-30/performance. Submissions returned with SASE.
Needs: All genres. "We are mainly interested in plays by and about women and prefer to produce plays with predominantly female casts. Plays with a feminist approach to the world; plays which work at creating new forms." No sexist or racist plays.
Tips: Send inquiries to Judith Katz, literary manager. "Trends in the American stage include feminism; use of imagery; departure from realism."

‡**AVILA COLLEGE PERFORMING ARTS DEPT.**, 11901 Wornall Rd., Kansas City MO 64145. (816)942-8400. Artistic Director: W.J. Louis, PhD. Produces 6 plays/year. 10% freelance written. 33% of scripts produced are unagented submissions. Performs collegiate amateur productions (4 main stage, 2 studio productions) for Kansas City audiences. Query with synopsis. Computer printout submissions acceptable; prefers letter-quality to dot-matrix. Reports in 3 months. Buys rights arranged with author. Pays rate arranged with author. SASE.
Needs: All genres with wholesome ideas and language—musicals, dramas. Length 1-2 hours. Small casts (2-5 characters), women casts; few props, simple staging. No lewd and crude language and scenes.
Tips: Example of play just done: *Towards The Morning*, by John Fenn. Story: "Mentally confused bag lady and 17-year-old egocentric boy discover they need each other; she regains mental stability; he grows up a bit and becomes more responsible. Trends in the American stage freelance writers should be aware of include (1) point-of-view one step beyond theatre of the absurd—theatre that makes light of self-pity; and (2) need for witty, energetic social satire done without smut in the style of *Kid Purple*, by Don Wollner, The 1984 national competition winner of the Unicorn Theatre, Kansas City, MO."

‡**RAN AVNI/JEWISH REPERTORY THEATRE**, 344 E. 14th St., New York NY 10003. (212)674-7200. Artistic Director: Ran Avni. "We are an Equity non-profit theatre, Mini-contract." Produces 5 plays/year. Query with synopsis. Reports in 1 month. Pays $25-50/performance. SASE.
Needs: "Plays in English that relate to the Jewish experience."

BAKER'S PLAY PUBLISHING CO., 100 Chauncy St., Boston MA 02111. Editor: John B. Welch. Plays performed by amateur groups, high schools, children's theater, churches and community theater groups. "We are the largest publisher of chancel drama in the world." Works with 2-3 unpublished/unproduced writers annually. Submit complete script. Computer printout submissions acceptable. Publishes 18-25 straight plays; all originals. 80% freelance written. 90% of scripts produced are unagented submissions. Pay varies; outright purchase price to split in production fees. SASE. Reports in 2-3 months.
Needs: "One-acts (specifically for competition use). Quality children's theater scripts. Chancel drama for easy staging—voice plays ideal. Long plays only if they have a marketable theme. Include as much stage direction in the script as possible." Emphasis on large female cast desired. No operettas for elementary school production.
Recent Title: *Love is Murder*, by Tim Kelly.

‡**MARY BALDWIN COLLEGE THEATRE**, Mary Baldwin College, Staunton VA 24401. (703)886-6277. Artistic Director: Dr. Virginia R. Francisco. Produces 5 plays/year. 10% freelance written. An undergraduate women's college theatre with an audience of students, faculty, staff and local community (adult, conservative). Query with synopsis or submit complete script. Computer printout submissions acceptable. Reports in 3 months. Buys performance rights only. Pays $10-50/performance. SASE.

Needs: Full-length and short comedies, tragedies, musical plays, particularly for young women actresses, dealing with women's issues both contemporary and historical. Experimental/studio theatre not suitable for heavy sets. Cast should emphasize women. No heavy sex; minimal explicit language.

‡**BEAR REPUBLIC THEATER**, Box 1137, Santa Cruz CA 95061. (408)425-1725. Artistic Director: Michael Griggs. 15% freelance written. 1-2 of scripts produced are unagented submissions. Produces 7 plays/year. Year-round, semi-professional productions. Four plays performed in the 81-seat Art Center Theater; 3 each summer at the 178-seat Barn Theater. "We also do new script readings and a late-night workshop program. They are intended for a general audience with a progressive slant. We are considered a socially-conscious, alternative theatre." Works with 1-2 unpublished/unproduced writers annually. Query with synopsis. Computer printout submissions acceptable; prefers letter-quality to dot-matrix. Reports in 2 months. Buys first production rights, first refusal rights on touring or regional professional productions, income participation and credits in future professional productions. Pays $15-50/performance. SASE.
Needs: "We are interested in full-length plays, one-acts, translations, adaptations and children's plays; serious plays and comedies dealing with social issues. We want plays suitable for touring to elementary schools, Spanish-English bilingual plays and Latin-American plays. Budget limitations make small-cast, simple-set shows easier, but we have no preset limitations."

‡**BERKSHIRE THEATRE FESTIVAL, INC.**, E. Main St., Stockbridge MA 01262. Artistic Director: Josephine R. Abady. 25% freelance written. Submit complete ms. Reports in 4-6 months. Produces 10-14 plays a year (5 are mainstage and 5-9 are second spaces). Submissions by agents only.

‡**BROADWAY PLAY PUBLISHING, INC.**, 249 W. 29th St., New York NY 10001. (212)563-3820. Estab. 1982. Publishes 15-20 plays/year. 10% of scripts published are unagented submissions. Works with 5 unpublished/unproduced writers annually. Query with synopsis. Computer printout submissions acceptable. Reports on submitted mss in 3 months. Buys stock, amateur, acting edition publishing rights. Pays 10% on book royalty; 90% stock; 80% amateur. SASE.
Needs: New contemporary American plays—use of language. No autobiography, domestic realism, adaptations or translations. Musicals must be accompanied by cassette. No single one-acts.
Tips: "Trends in the American stage freelance writers should be aware of include death of domestic autobiography."

JAN BRUNGARD, Box 1452, Haines City FL 33844. (813)422-4042. Artistic Director: N.R. March. Produces 3 plays/year. "We have a 500-seat auditorium for our community theater. We play to a large segment of retired people who are primarily from the Midwest and eastern seaboard." Query with synopsis or submit complete ms. Computer printout submissions acceptable. Reports in 3 weeks. Pays $25-50/performance. SASE.
Needs: Comedies and dramas; 3 acts only. "We want plays that deal with the interaction of the older generation and the younger one, or simply with the problems the younger generation has in dealing with life. We are particularly looking for a 'love in the mobile home park' play—one that might deal with a widow and widower and the problems inherent with that type of romance." Prefers one set or simple unit sets. "Not too heavy on the men; no costume or period plays. No political or religious plays. No obscenity beyond a possible 'hell or damn.' Innuendos are fine. No overt sex. Difficult to cast blacks, but we would welcome a play that shows them in roles other than domestics."
Tips: "We have decided to produce 1-2 plays by new writers in a season. A play where old age is presented with humor and dignity, as well as a few tears thrown in would be a sure winner. Frantic comedies are also well accepted (boy meets and loses girl through mix-ups, etc.). Our audience wants a happy ending. If the play has a message, it must be one with hope, not futility. Strong characters with well-defined personality traits (whiner, yeller, nervous, etc.) are popular with both our actors and the audience."

GERT BUNCHEZ AND ASSOCIATES, INC., 7730 Carondelet, St. Louis MO 63105. President: Gert Bunchez. "We feel that the time is propitious for the return of stories to radio. It is our feeling that it is not necessary to 'bring back' old programs and that there certainly should be contemporary talent to write mystery, detective, suspense, children's stories, soap operas, etc. We syndicate radio properties to advertisers and stations. Requirements are plays with sustaining lead characters, 5 minutes to 30 minutes in length, suitable for radio reproduction. Disclaimer letter must accompany scripts." SASE.

CASA MANANA MUSICALS, INC., 3101 W. Lancaster, Box 9054, Fort Worth TX 76107. (817)332-9319. Producer/General Manager: Bud Franks. Produces 12 plays/year. "All performances are staged at Casa Manana Theatre and are community funded." Query. Computer printout submissions acceptable. No disk submissions. Reports in 2 months. Produces summer musicals (uses Equity people only), Theatre for Youth and new plays. Theater-in-the-round or proscenium.
Needs: Scripts of all kinds.

THE WORLD'S LEADING MAGAZINE FOR WRITERS

Would you like to:

- get up-to-the-minute reports on where to sell what you write?

- receive the advice of editors and professional writers about what to write and how to write it to increase your chances for getting published?

- read interviews with leading authors that reveal their secrets of success?

- hear what experts have to say about writing and selling fiction, non-fiction, and poetry?

- get a special introductory price for all this?

(See other side for details.)

Close-up

Stephen Metcalfe
Playwright

When Stephen Metcalfe delivered lines on paper, he got a curtain *call* that actors couldn't get—Manhattan Theatre Club asked to produce his play, *Vikings*. It shifted his dreams from acting to writing.

Metcalfe now writes plays and screenplays full time. He also observes his plays in rehearsal at theatres across the country. "You learn so much from the rehearsal process," he says.

Before *Loves and Hours*'s premiere last spring, he finetuned the play during rehearsals—to clarify the small but important points. "Sometimes some moments (or beats, to use a director's term) are better than others and so what you want to do is be as precise and understandable with each individual beat, especially the important moments in the play," says the 1984 recipient of a National Endowment for the Arts grant in playwriting. "That's where the reworking comes in." He'd heard that Arthur Miller reworked small details of *Death of a Salesman* for its 1984 Broadway run.

Metcalfe strives to define characters very quickly in his scripts. "With the playwrights that I like, you have a sense of a character within the first three times they open their mouths."

Dialogue is more than lines recited to an audience. "You are creating action on a stage with dialogue. Very often actors and directors will ignore any stage directions you give them, so really what you have to move them around the stage is dialogue."

Reading a play aloud helps the playwright write good dialogue, suggests Metcalfe. "Words that can read beautifully do not sound real when they come out of an actor's mouth."

Melodrama will also make a play unrealistic. "There is a fine line between heightened realism and outright melodrama. You want to take it to a kind of an edge." Beyond that edge "it becomes unreal," he says.

"It's easy to start a play; it's hard to finish it," says the author of *Half a Lifetime*, *Strange Snow*, and *White Linen*. "The more I work at it, the less satisfied I am with my own work; that's a good thing."

He wants each play to be an *event* for audiences. "What makes a play so very exciting is the sense of event about it," he believes. "The plays that mean something are plays where what happens to the characters is going to affect them in a way that nothing will ever be the same again afterward."

Metcalfe stresses that playwrights must work to get their *events* on a stage. "The very first plays I did were in New York where I and directors and actors I knew literally found spaces and put on our own work."

Playwrights should showcase their work regardless of low or no pay. "An audience is definitely a part of putting the play together," says Metcalfe. "They become the final piece in the puzzle."

And so he watches his audiences, listens for their reactions, and tries to bring this awareness to each script. "A funny thing about the theatre is that if everything works, then everyone gets the credit," he says. "But very often if nothing works, the playwright gets all the blame."

CASSETTE BOOK COMPANY, Box 7111, Pasadena CA 91109. (213)799-4139. Produces material for all ages. 10% freelance written. All scripts produced are agented submissions. Buys 12-20 mss/year. Buys all rights. Previously produced submissions OK. Computer printout submissions acceptable. Works with 6-10 unpublished/unproduced writers annually. SASE. Reports in 1 month on queries; 2 months on mss. Free catalog. Writer's guidelines available for SASE.
Needs: "The only mss we buy are romance stories." Query. Pays royalty or in outright purchase.

‡**CATALYST THEATRE**, 10645 63rd Ave., Edmonton, Alberta T6H 1P7 Canada. (403)434-1007. Artistic Director: Jan Selman. Produces 4 adult, 3 school, 8 special interest audience plays/year. 40% freelance written. 1 of scripts produced is unagented submission. Plays performed for general Edmonton adult public (some tour Alberta); Alberta schools and conferences, workshops, group homes, worksite, etc. Works with 4 unpublished/unproduced writers annually. Query with synopsis. Computer printout submissions acceptable; no dot-matrix. Reports in 2 months. Pays 8-10% royalty or $20-40/performance (schools). SASE.
Needs: Special issues. "We're interested in theatre which is a catalyst for discussions—i.e., we do not wish to 'solve' with theatre but we do wish to challenge." General public: full-length; special audience: 30-60 minutes; school: 30-90 minutes. "Some productions tour. We prefer less rather than more." One set or open staging. No extremely complex (technical) plays, essay drama, prescriptive approaches, fluff.
Recent Production: *It's About Time* (participational for prisoners).

THE CHANGING SCENE THEATER, 1527½ Champa St., Denver CO 80202. Director: Alfred Brooks. Year-round productions in theatre space. Cast may be made up of both professional and amateur actors. For public audience; age varies, but mostly youthful and interested in taking a chance on new and/or experimental works. No limit to subject matter or story themes. Emphasis is on the innovative. "Also, we require that the playwright be present for at least one performance of his work, if not for the entire rehearsal period. We have a small stage area, but are able to convert to round, semi-round or environmental. Prefer to do plays with limited sets and props." 1-act, 2-act and 3-act. Produces 8-10 nonmusicals a year; all are originals. 90% freelance written. 65% of scripts produced are unagented submissions. "We do not pay royalties or sign contracts with playwrights. We function on a performance share basis of payment. Our theater seats 76; the first 50 seats go to the theater, the balance is divided among the participants in the production. The performance share process is based on the entire production run and not determined by individual performances. We do not copyright our plays." Works with 3-4 unpublished/unproduced writers annually. Send complete script. SASE. Reporting time varies; usually several months.
Recent Title: *False Colors*, by Eugene Drabent.
Tips: "We are experimental: open to young artists who want to test their talents and open to experienced artists who want to test new ideas/explore new techniques. Dare to write 'strange and wonderful' well-thought-out scripts. We want upbeat ones. Consider that we have a small performance area when submitting."

CHELSEA THEATER CENTER, Third Floor, 407 W. 43rd St., New York NY 10036. Artistic Director: Robert Kalfin. General Manager: Steve Gilger. 50% freelance written. Looking for full-length plays "that stretch the bounds of the theatre in form and content. No limitation as to size of cast or physical production." Works with 1-3 unpublished/unproduced writers annually. Pays for a 6-month renewable option for an off-Broadway production. Works 12 months in advance. No unsolicited mss. Essential to submit advance synopsis. Computer printout submissions acceptable if "readable." SASE.
Recent Production: *Shades of Brown*, by Michael Picardie (man's psycholgical struggle of the aparthied).

CHILDREN'S RADIO THEATRE, #302, 1609 Connecticut Ave. NW, Washington DC 20009. (202)234-4136. Artistic Director: Joan Bellsey. Produces 10 plays/year. 50% freelance written. "Children's Radio Theatre produces plays to be broadcast on radio nationwide. The plays are intended for a family listening audience."
Needs: "We like to receive a sample script and specific treatments." Reports in 3 months. "Each project is negotiated separately. We produce half-hour radio plays covering a wide range of topics including fairy tales, folk tales, musicals, adaptations, pop, original and commissioned plays. We are interested in material targeted for children 5-12. There are character limitations in radio plays—no more then 5 major characters. Works with 2-3 unpublished/unproduced writers annually. Contact Children's Radio Theatre before sending *any* material."

‡**CIRCLE IN THE SQUARE THEATRE**, 1633 Broadway, New York NY 10019. (212)581-3270. Artistic Director: Theodore Mann. Literary Advisor: Robert Pesola. Produces 3 plays/year. Theatre for subscription audience and New York theatre-going public. Query with 1-page synopsis only. Reports in 3 months. Pays royalty. SASE.
Tips: "We produce full-length new plays and musicals."

CIRCLE REPERTORY CO., 161 Avenue of the Americas, New York NY 10013. (212)691-3210. Associate Artistic Director: Rod Marriott. Associate Literary Manager: Ari Roth. Produces 5 Mainstage Plays. 5 Projects in Progress/year. No longer accepts unsolicited mss.

CIRCUIT PLAYHOUSE/PLAYHOUSE ON THE SQUARE, 2121 Madison Ave., Memphis TN 38104. (901)725-0776. Artistic Director: Jackie Nichols. Produces 2 plays/year. Professional plays performed for the Memphis/Mid-South area. Member of the Theatre Communications Group. A play contest is held each fall. Submit complete ms. Reports in 3 months. Buys "percentage of royalty rights for 2 years." Pays $500-1,000 in outright purchase.
Needs: All types; limited to single or unit sets. Cast of 20 or fewer.
Tips: "Each play is read by three readers through the extended length of time a script is kept. Preference is given to scripts for the southeastern region of the US."

‡I.E. CLARK, INC., Saint John's Rd., Box 246, Schulenburg TX 78956. (409)743-3232. Publishes 15 plays/year for educational theatre, children's theatre, religious theatre, regional professional theatre, amateur community theatre. 20% freelance written. Two-thirds of scripts produced are unagented submissions. Works with 3-5 unpublished/unproduced writers annually. Submit complete script. Computer printout submissions acceptable. Reports in 6 months. Buys all available rights; "we serve as an agency as well as a publisher." Pays book and performance royalty, "the amount and percentages dependent upon type and marketability of play." SASE.
Needs: "We are interested in plays of all types—short or long. We seldom publish musicals. We prefer that a play has been produced (directed by someone other than the author); photos and reviews of the production are helpful. No limitations in cast, props, staging, etc.; however, the simpler the staging, the larger the market. We insist on literary quality. We like plays that give new interpretations and understanding of human nature. Correct spelling, punctuation and grammar (befitting the characters, of course) impress our readers."
Tips: "Don't be afraid to experiment; we like new ideas, new ways of doing things. Theatre is a fine art, and art must be creative. However, the play must be stageable; that's why we seldom publish a play that has not been successfuly performed."

THE CLEVELAND PLAY HOUSE, Box 1989, Cleveland OH 44106. (216)795-7010. Literary Assistant: Arthur Knight. Plays performed in professional LORT theatre for the general public. "Ours is a long-standing resident company performing in 3 theatres presenting an eclectic season of commercial plays, musicals, and contemporary and traditional classics with occasional American and world premieres." Works with 2-3 unpublished/unproduced writers annually. Submit letter of inquiry and synopsis. Computer printout submissions acceptable; prefers letter-quality to dot-matrix. Produces 8 musicals (12%) and nonmusicals (88%) a year; 25% are originals. 25% freelance written. Very few scripts produced are unagented submissions. Buys stock rights and sometimes first class options. Payment varies. SASE. Reports in 6 months.
Needs: "No restrictions. Vulgarity and gratuitous fads are not held in much esteem. Cast size should be small to moderate. Plays intended for arena stages are not appropriate. Musicals should be geared for actors, not singers. One act plays are rarely performed. Plays of an extremely experimental nature are almost never selected." No first drafts; works-in-progress; unfinished manuscripts.

‡COACH HOUSE PRESS, INC., #718, 53 W. Jackson Blvd., Chicago IL 60604. (312)922-8993. President: David Jewell. 100% freelance written. All scripts produced are unagented submissions. Publishes trade paperback originals. Averages 3-5 plays/year. Works with 3-5 unpublished writers annually. Pays 5-15% royalty on book receipts; 50% on performance royalty. Simultaneous and photocopied submissions OK. Computer printout submissions acceptable; prefers letter-quality to dot-matrix. SASE. Reports in 2 weeks on queries; 2 months on mss.
Needs: Drama. Plays for children's theatre and older adult theatre. Books on theatre. Publishes for theatre producers and recreation specialists.
Recent Title: *Acting Up!*, by Telander, Quinlan and Verson.

THE CRICKET THEATRE, 528 Hennepin Ave., Minneapolis MN 55403. (612)333-5241. Associate Artistic Director: Sean Michael Dowse. Audiences consist of adults and students. Works with 2-4 unpublished/unproduced writers annually. Submit complete ms. Computer printout submissions acceptable; no dot-matrix. "Must include SASE." Reports in 6 months minimum. Buys production rights for selected dates. Produces 6 plays, main stage; 5-7 plays, Works-in-Progress; musicals (14%) and nonmusicals (86%) a year; 40% are originals. 10-20% freelance written. Produces primarily plays by living American playwrights. Only full-length plays will be considered for production.
Needs: "There are no content or form restrictions for scripts of the main season. For Works-in-Progress, any kind of a script is welcomed provided there is a spark of a good play in it. Works-in-Progress presentations are readings, staged readings and stage 2 productions. The focus is on the text and not the fully staged, polished performance as with the main season. All Works-in-Progress playwrights are brought to Minneapolis to join in

the play's rehearsal and revision process. Works-in-Progress cannot use plays currently under option or that have had full professional productions. Such plays will be considered only for the main season." No children's plays or large Broadway-type musicals. Cast limit: 9.

Tips: "Trends in the American stage freelance writers should be aware of include the drift from naturalism; the tendency not to give unsolicited manuscripts much attention; the passing of programs to develop new playwrights; the tendency to search for the next hit; and the boredom of two-character plays."

‡**DELAWARE THEATRE COMPANY**, 303 French St., Wilmington DE 19801. (302)658-6448. Artistic Director: Cleveland Morris. Produces 5 plays/year. "Plays are performed as part of a five-play subscription season in a 180-seat auditorium. Professional actors, directors and designers are engaged. The season is intended for a general audience." Query with synopsis. Reports in 6 months. Buys variable rights. Pays 5% (variable) royalty. SASE.

Needs: "We present comedies, dramas, tragedies and musicals. All works must be full-length and fit in with a season composed of standards and classics. All works have a strong literary element. Plays with a flair for language and a strong involvement with the interests of classical humanism are of greatest interest. Single-set, small-cast works are likeliest for consideration."

DENVER CENTER THEATRE COMPANY, 1050 13th St., Denver CO 80204. (303)893-4200. Artistic Director: Donovan Marley. Produces 12 plays/year. Professional regional repertory plays (LORT-B) performed in the only major regional theatre in the Rocky Mountain West. Also, professional tours possible, both regionally and nationally. Submit complete ms. Reports in 2 months. Buys negotiable rights. Pays negotiable royalty. SASE.

Needs: "One act and full length comedies, dramas, musicals and adaptations. The Denver Center Theatre Company is especially eager to see plays of regional interest."

‡**DODD, MEAD & CO.**, 79 Madison Ave., New York NY 10016. Senior Editor: Allen T. Klots. "We're only interested in playwrights after professional production, who promise to contribute to the literature of the theatre." Royalty negotiated. Buys book rights only. Reports in about 4 weeks. SASE.

‡**DORSET THEATRE FESTIVAL**, Box 519, Dorset VT 05251. (802)867-2223. Artistic Director: Jill Charles. Produces 6 plays/year. A professional (equity) theatre, season June-Sept. or Oct. Audience is sophisticated, largely tourists and second-home owners from metropolitan New York and Boston areas. Query with synopsis; submit through agent. Computer printout submissions acceptable; prefers letter-quality to dot-matrix. Reports in 2 months. Buys negotiable rights. Pays negotiable rate; minimum $250 for 11 performers. SASE.

Needs: Full length plays (2 acts); any genre, but should have broad audience appeal; generally realistic, but *not* "kitchen dramas." Will consider musicals; must have accompanying cassette. Cast less than 10; single or unit (flexible) settings preferred. "We lean toward *positive* plays, whether comedy or drama. No family melodrama.

Tips: "Best time to submit plays is from September to January. (Plays received after March 1 may not be read until fall).

THE DRAMATIC PUBLISHING CO., 4150 N. Milwaukee Ave., Chicago IL 60641. (312)545-2062. Publishes about 40 new shows a year. 60% freelance written. 40% of scripts published are unagented submissions. "Current growth market is in plays and small cast musicals for stock and community theatre." Also has a large market for plays and musicals for children and for amateur theatre (i.e., junior highs, high schools, colleges, churches and other theatre groups). Works with 4-8 unpublished/unproduced writers annually. Submissions must be clearly typed or computer printed and at least 30 minutes playing time. Reports in 3 months. Buys stock and amateur theatrical rights as well as rights for cable TV. Pays by usual royalty contract or by occasional outright purchase.

Tips: "Avoid stereotype roles and situations. Submit cassette tapes with musicals whenever possible. Always include SASE if script is to be returned. There is an apparent swing away from sensational situations toward a more carefully developed interrelationship between characters. There is also a length change—one intermission (if any) in a show running up to two hours."

EAST WEST PLAYERS, 4424 Santa Monica Blvd., Los Angeles CA 90029. (213)660-0366. Artistic Director: Mako. 90% freelance written. Produces 5-6 plays/year. Professional plays performed in an Equity waiver house for all audiences. Works with 2-3 unpublished/unproduced writers annually. Query with synopsis or submit complete ms. Reports in 3 weeks on query and synopsis; 2 months on mss. "High majority" of scripts produced are unagented submissions. Buys standard Dramatist's Guild contract rights. Pays $200 in outright purchase or 2-6% of house receipts (ticket prices vary). SASE.

Needs: "We prefer plays dealing with Asian-American themes. The majority of the important roles should be playable by Asian-American actors; our acting company is 98 percent Asian." No fluff, TV sitcom-type material.

Tips: "East West Players was founded by a group of Asian-American actors weary of playing stereotypes in theatre and film. Submitting writers should bear this in mind and refrain from wallowing in 'exoticism.' There appears to be a minor burgeoning of interest in Asian American writers and themes—witness David Henry Hwang's success on the East Coast, the continuing success and influence of East West Players on the West Coast and establishment theatres developing Asian American material (e.g., The Mark Taper Forum in Los Angeles working on a stage adaptation of Maxine Hong Kingston's works), etc."

ELDRIDGE PUBLISHING CO., Drawer 216, Franklin OH 45005. (513)746-6531. Editor/General Manager: Kay Myerly. Plays performed in high schools and churches; some professional—but most are amateur productions. Publishes plays for all age groups. Publishes 15-20 plays/year; (2%) musicals; 100% originals. 100% freelance written. All scripts produced are unagented submissions. Works with 10-12 unpublished/unproduced writers annually. Send synopsis or complete script. Computer printout submissions acceptable; prefers letter-quality to dot-matrix. Buys all rights "unless the author wishes to retain some rights." Pays $100-125 for 1-act plays; $350 for 3-acts. Also royalty contracts for topnotch plays. SASE. Reports in 60 days.

Needs: "We are looking for good straight comedies which will appeal to high school and junior-high age groups. We do not publish anything which can be suggestive. Most of our plays are published with a hanging indentation—2 ems. All stage, scenery and costume plots must be included." No run-of-the-mill plots. Length: 1-acts from 25-30 minutes; 2-acts of around 2 hours; and skits of 10-15 minutes.

Recent Title: *Dickerson for Senate*, by Ev Miller (comedy-drama).

THE EMPTY SPACE, 919 E. Pike, Seattle WA 98122. (206)325-4379. Artistic Director: M. Burke Walker. Produces 6 plays/year. Professional plays for subscriber base and single ticket Seattle audience. Query with synopsis before sending script. Computer printout submissions OK. Reports in 3 months. LOA Theater. SASE.

Needs: "Other things besides linear, narrative realism; but we are interested in that as well; no restriction on subject matter. Generally we opt for broader, more farcical comedies and harder-edged, uncompromising dramas. We like to go places we've never been before. Theatre is in the process of moving to larger space. Call for any details; mail will be forwarded from old address." No commercial musicals.

ENCORE THEATRE, c/o D.B. Clarke Theatre, 1455 de Maisonneuve Ave. W, Montreal, Quebec H3G 1M8 Canada. (514)737-1738. Artistic Director: Jack Roberts. Produces 6-8 plays/year. 1-2 scripts produced are unagented submissions. Plays performed on proscenium arch stage in a theatre of 380-400 seats. Audience is subscription based. Associated closely with students of Theatre Arts Department of Concordia University. Works with 0-1 unpublished/unproduced writer annually. Submit complete ms. Computer printout submissions acceptable; no dot-matrix. Reports in 6 months. Buys performance rights in the municipality of Montreal for a minimum of 18 months. Pays 7-10% royalty. Fully professional (CAEA) company.

Needs: Full length plays of all genres. No restrictions as to style or topic. No plays requiring more than 10 actors.

Tips: "In the Canadian Theatre, we are increasing in need of scripts that are attractive to a broad range of audience members. Subject matter should pertain to a Canadian based theme or one that can be international."

ETOBICOKE CHILDREN'S THEATRE, Box 243, Etobicoke, Ontario M9C 1Z1 Canada. (416)626-1963. Artistic Director: Mary E. Miller. Produces 5 plays/year. 50% freelance written. Produces 1 unagented submission each year. Plays are produced professionally with nonunion performers for children, families and seniors. Performed on tour to schools, libraries, senior citizen's homes, community centers, etc. Works with 1 unpublished/unproduced writer annually. Query with synopsis or submit complete ms. Computer printout submissions acceptable; prefers letter-quality to dot-matrix. Reports in 2 months. Rights revert to author. Pays $10-20 for 30-80 performances. SASE.

Needs: "For children—must be entertaining plot plus underlying social or moral values. Any 'lessons' must be learned through what happens, rather than by what is said. For seniors—must be highly entertaining; variety format is good." Length: 45-50 minutes. Cast limited to 3-5 performers. "Plays must require no definite set. Props and costumes must fit into the back of a station wagon."

Tips: "Trends in Canadian stage and screen that freelance writers should be aware of include 'Money is tight'—material must sell—and that a cast of two or three is about all that is being produced by children's touring companies."

‡**FOLGER THEATRE**, 201 E. Capitol St. SE, Washington DC 20003. (202)547-3230. Artistic Producer: John Neville-Andrews. Produces 5 plays/year. A Lort D regional theatre for general audience, classically oriented. Query with synopsis; submit through agent. Reports in 3 months. Buys negotiable rights. Pays negotiable rate. SASE.

Needs: Classics and new adaptations of classics only.

‡**GEORGETOWN PRODUCTIONS**, 7 Park Ave., New York NY 10016. Producers: Gerald Van De Vorst and David Singer. Produces 1-2 plays/year for a general audience. Works with 1-2 unpublished/unproduced writers annually. Submit complete ms only. Computer printout submissions acceptable; prefers letter-quality to dot-matrix. Standard Dramatists Guild contract. SASE.
Needs: Prefers plays with small casts and not demanding more than one set. Interested in new unconventional scripts dealing with contemporary issues, comedies, mysteries, musicals or dramas. No first-drafts; outlines; 1-act plays.
Tips: "Freelance writers should be aware of trend toward tryouts in regional theatres."

‡**GEVA THEATRE**, 168 Clinton Ave., Rochester NY 14604. (716)232-1366. Literary Director: Ann Patrice Carrigan. Produces 6 plays/year. Query with synopsis. Reports in 4 months. Buys theatre options for 1st- and 2nd-class productions; percentage of author royalties 5 to 10 years from closing product at GeVa Theatre. Pays 5% royalty. SASE.
Needs: "Plays done here run 2-2½ hours. We do one classical piece of world literature, one American classic, three relatively current plays that have made an impact in resident professional theatres across the country and one new work. Those works are normally comedies and dramas in a realistic/impressionist style." Limited to cast of 6 actors, 1-3 set changes. "The priority at GeVa is for scripts that touch people's heads and emotions through vital characterization and a significant storyline. We look for scripts that challenge through entertaining audiences. We are interested in scripts that would stretch the company artistically and the audience imaginatively. We would not be interested in a play whose theme, characterization and structure are not of a piece."
Tips: "Many scripts that come in are scripts for television. The writing is bald and the structure is episodic, and there is the definite logic and texture of a TV movie. Writers have to make TV writing work in terms of theatre. Often, they do not."

‡**HEUER PUBLISHING CO.**, 233 Dows Bldg., Box 248, Cedar Rapids IA 52406. Publishes 3-5 plays/year. 100% freelance written. 99% of scripts produced are unagented submissions. Amateur productions for schools and church groups. Audience consists of junior and senior high school students and some intermediate groups. Need 1- and 3-act plays. Prefers comedy, farce, mystery and mystery/comedy. Uses 1-act plays suitable for contest work (strong drama). "We suggest potential authors write for our brochure on types of plays." No sex, controversial subjects or family scenes. Prefers 1 simple setting and noncostume plays. Current need is for plays with a large number of characters (16-20). One-act plays should be 30-35 minutes long; 3-act, 90-105 minutes. Most mss purchased outright, with price depending on quality. Minimum of $500 usually. Copyrighted, however, contract stipulates amateur rights only, so author retains professional rights to TV, radio, etc. Query with synopsis only. Computer printout submissions acceptable; prefers letter-quality to dot-matrix. SASE. Reports in 6 weeks.
Recent Title: *Pick A Boy—Any Boy*, by Frank Priore (plot line along humorous witchcraft).

‡**HONOLULU THEATRE FOR YOUTH**, Box 3257, Honolulu HI 96801. (808)521-3487. Artistic Director: John Kauffman. Produces 6 plays/year. 50% freelance written. All scripts produced are unagented submissions. Plays are professional productions in Hawaii, primarily for youth audiences (youth aged 2 to 20). Works with 2 unpublished/unproduced writers annually. Query with synopsis. Computer printout submissions acceptable; prefers letter-quality to dot-matrix. Reports in 3 months. Buys negotiable rights. Pays $1,000-2,500. SASE.
Needs: Contemporary subjects of concern/interest to young people; adaptations of literary classics; fantasy including space, fairy tales, myth and legend. "HTY wants well-written plays, 60-90 minutes in length, that have something worthwhile to say and that will stretch the talents of professional adult actors." Cast not exceeding 8; *no* technical extravaganzas; *no* full-orchestra musicals; simple sets; props, costumes can be elaborate. No plays to be enacted by children or camp versions of popular fairytales.
Tips: "Young people are intelligent and perceptive, if anything more so than lots of adults, and if they are to become fans and eventual supporters of good theatre, they must see good theatre while they are young."

WILLIAM E. HUNT, 801 West End Ave., New York NY 10025. Interested in reading scripts for stock production, off-Broadway and even Broadway production. "Small cast, youth-oriented, meaningful, technically adventuresome; serious, funny, far-out. Must be about people first, ideas second. No political or social tracts." No one-act, antiblack, antisemitic or antigay plays. "I do not want 1920, 1930 or 1940 plays disguised as modern by 'modern' language. I do not want plays with 24 characters, plays with 150 costumes, plays about symbols instead of people. I do not want plays which are really movie or TV scripts." Pays royalties on production. Off-Broadway, 5%; on Broadway, 5%, 7½% and 10%, based on gross. No royalty paid if play is selected for a showcase production. Reports in "a few weeks." Must have SASE or script will not be returned.
Recent Production: *Miss Stanwyck Is Still in Hiding*, by Larry Puchall and Reigh Hagen.

‡**ILLUSION THEATER**, Suite 205, 528 Hennepin Ave., Minneapolis MN 55403. (612)339-4945. Artistic Director: Michael Robins. Produces 3-9 plays/year. "We are a professional acting company performing usual-

ly in a studio space seating approximately 90 people. Occasionally productions are moved to larger theatre spaces, and also tour to colleges and high schools. Audience is generally between ages 18-40." Query with synopsis or submit complete ms. Reports in 3 months. "Work we do with playwrights is collaborative. Agreements pertaining to rights are made on an individual basis depending on the project." Pays fee plus royalty. SASE.

Needs: "Our plays range from adaptations of works of literature (*Spring Awakening*, *Orlando*) to plays created around the history of the acting company's grandparents (*Becoming Memories*) to plays dealing with social issues. The resident company is 6 actors although the theatre does hire additional artists when needed." Playwrights should send general business letter introducing themselves and their work and include resume if possible.

Tips: "The theatre is not interested in children's plays, religious plays, or plays suitable for the commercial dinner theatre type audiences. Also not interested in plays that are sexist or abusive towards a specific group of people. Our theatre most frequently works with playwrights to collaborate on plays. While the theatre is interested in reading manuscripts to get a sense of the playwright's writing ability and style, the theatre rarely commissions works already complete."

‡**THE INDEPENDENT EYE**, 208 E. King St., Lancaster PA 17602. (717)393-9088. Artistic Director: Conrad Bishop. Produces 4 plays/year (plus revivals in tour). 75% freelance written. A few scripts produced are unagented submissions. Professional non-Equity theatre performances for general audience interested in progressive contemporary work; on tour for wide range of arts series, colleges, social agencies, etc. Works with 0-2 unpublished/unproduced writers annually. Query with synopsis. Computer printout submissions acceptable; prefers letter-quality to dot-matrix. Reports in 2 months. Buys rights for production for current season only. No claim on subsidiary rights. Pays 5% gross royalty or $20-35/performance. "We have small seating capacity so flat payment usually." SASE.

Needs: "Work that's very personal and strongly felt; work that aims for strong response, comic or otherwise; work—of many styles—whose style is very organically related to content. We ask what story it's telling, whether it's worth telling and why it's told this way." Small cast; no plays with realistic box sets. "No commercial comedies. No work narrowly focused on parent/child conflict (that's about 75% of our submissions). No work by someone who's unwilling to consider suggestions for rewrites."

‡**INDIANA REPERTORY THEATRE**, 140 W. Washington, Indianapolis IN 46204. (317)635-5277. Artistic Director: Tom Haas. Produces 10 full-length, 9 90-minute Cabarets/year. Plays are professional productions, Lort B and C contracts, in 3 theatres. Mainstage seats 600, Upperstage seats 250, Cabaret seats 150. Subscription audience composed of cross section of Indianapolis community. Query with synopsis. Reports in 3 months. Retains right for first- or second-class production with 60 days after production closes; retains percent on subsequent productions elsewhere. Pays 5% royalty; $500-1,000 nonrefundable advance over royalties. SASE.

Needs: "On our Mainstage we produce exclusively classics, with a heavy emphasis on American work, adaptations of classic work or new translations of classic work; also produce one musical yearly (often new musical). Upperstage produces new work of a smaller scale. Cabaret produces exclusively small cast (5 or less) satirical musicals. Prefer under 10 casts, staging which can be adapted—that is, not rigidly realistic; prefer one set or unit set which can be adapted. We tend to be attracted to plays that display an acute interest in using language vigorously, that exhibit an awareness of political thinking without being imitative of political situations. We are interested in epic proportion and in plays that speak very directly to concerns of 1980s. No TV scripts, movie scripts or things that rely on dated techniques like flashbacks; plays which depend on excessive profanity or explicit sexual behavior; one acts."

INVISIBLE THEATRE, 1400 N. 1st Ave., Tucson AZ 85719. (602)882-9721. Artistic Director: Susan Claassen. Produces 5-7 plays/year. 1% freelance written. Semiprofessional regional theatre for liberal, college-educated audiences. Plays performed in 70-100 seat nonequity theatre with small production budget. Query with synopsis. Computer printout submissions acceptable; no dot-matrix. Reports in 6 months. Buys non-professional rights. Pays 10% of royalty.

Needs: "Two act plays, generally contemporary, some historical, comedies, drama, small musicals, wide range of topics. Limited to plays with small casts of 10 or less, strong female roles, simple sets, minimal props." No large musicals, complex set designs, casts larger than 15.

Tips: "Trends in the American stage freelance writers should be aware of include substantial roles for women, especially over 35."

‡**LAMB'S PLAYERS THEATRE**, 500 Plaza Blvd., Box 26, National City CA 92050. (619)474-3385. Artistic Director: Robert Smyth. Produces 8 plays/year. 40% freelance written. 3 of 7 scripts produced are unagented submissions. A semi-professional resident company with a year-round production schedule. Audience is varied; high percentage of family and church interest. Works with 2-3 unpublished/unproduced writers annually. Submit complete script. Computer printout submissions acceptable. Reports in 2 months. Buys first pro-

duction rights, touring option. Pays $250-1,000. SASE.

Needs: "We produce all genres, both one-act and full-length. While not necessarily interested in 'religious' plays, our productions often come from a Christian world-view. With new material, we are primarily interested in work that presents a broad based Christian world-view." Prefers smaller cast (2-10); adaptable staging (arena stage). "We are not interested in material that is 'preachy', or material that's intention is to shock or titilate with sex, violence or language."

Tips: "Trends freelance writers should be aware of include productions which offer hope without being cliche or sentimental; productions needing small cast and imaginative yet inexpensive sets; an interest in presentational style pieces—acknowledgment and/or interaction with the audience."

‡**LILLENAS PUBLISHING CO.**, Box 527, Kansas City MO 64141. (816)931-1900. Editor, Lillenas Drama Resources: Paul Miller. Publishes 4 collections composed of 25 short plays/year (total). 95% freelance written. All scripts published are unagented submissions. "Because we are a religious music and play publisher, most of our works will be performed by churches and church-related schools." Submit query and synopsis or complete ms. "Both are acceptable when the writer is aware of our market." Computer printout submissions acceptable; prefers letter-quality to dot-matrix. Works with 25 unpublished/unproduced writers annually. Reports in 2 months. "On short plays that become a part of a collection (Christmas, Easter, Mother's Day, etc.) we obtain first rights; on full length plays (or serious one-act plays and sketches) we negotiate with the author. Generally, the work is copyrighted in the author's name." Pays 10% royalty on full length plays and collections by one author, no advance; or pays in outright purchase from $5/double-spaced, typed ms page. SASE.

Needs: *Full length plays*: "This is a new venture; we are looking for biblical and contemporary themes. Prefer characterization and thought over settings and large casts." *Short plays and skits*: Primarily seasonal. Children and teen actors (some adults OK). "We are interested in chancel drama, reader's theatre, and choral speaking pieces, as well as traditional staged scripts." Stylistic concerns: Thorough knowledge of proper script format; complete listing of cast, props; set requirements; approximate timing. Likes to have a summary paragraph for the reader. Taboos—"good guys" drinking and smoking; put-down of church." No short plays and skits dealing with "the real meaning of Christmas;" a secular approach to Easter and Christmas (Santa Claus, Easter Bunny), fantasy; religious themes that "drip with sentimentality and the miraculous;" plots that depend upon the coincidental and plots that have too many subthemes. "We want one strong idea."

Tips: "We are distributed in 10,000 Christian bookstores in North America and other areas of the English-speaking world. We also deal with musicals that have religious themes (again, both biblical and contemporary)."

‡**LOS ANGELES THEATRE CENTER**, Contact: Los Angeles Actor's Theatre, 1089 N. Oxford Ave., Los Angeles CA 90029 through January 1985. New name and address begins February: 514 S. Spring St., Los Angeles CA 90013. (213)464-5603. Artistic Director: Bill Bushnell. Produces 20-30 plays/year. 90% freelance written. 50% of scripts produced are unagented submissions. A professional theatre for a general metropolitan audience. Works with 1 or 2 unproduced writers annually. Query with synopsis plus first 5-10 pages of script. *No unsolicited ms.* Send script inquiries to Adam Leipzig, dramaturge/associate director. Reports in 4-6 months. Buys 1st production rights, options to extend and move, subsidiaries. Pays 4-5% royalty. SASE essential.

Needs: Plays with social or political awareness preferred. 10 actors maximum. No "TV scripts or movies pretending to be theatre."

LUNCHBOX THEATRE, Box 9027, Bow Valley Sq. II, Calgary, Alberta T2P 2W4 Canada. (403)265-4292. Artistic Director: Bartley Bard. Produces 8 plays/year. 12.5% freelance written. Varying number of scripts produced are unagented submissions. Professional company performs at lunchtime for downtown workers, shoppers, school groups—everyone. Submit complete ms. Reports in 2 months. Pays $25 and up/performance. Returns scripts once or twice a year. "In the meantime, we mail out letters."

Needs: One-acts only. "Must be 40-50 minutes in length. Emphasis on fast-paced comedies. Small cast plays given more consideration. Generally, *one* set. No 'dead baby' plays, plays containing overt physical violence, 'prairie dramas' or 'kitchen sink dramas'."

MAGIC THEATRE, INC., Bldg. D, Fort Mason, San Francisco CA 94123. (415)441-8001. General Director: John Lion. Administrative Director: Marcia O'Dea. Dramaturge: Martin Esslin. "Oldest experimental theater in California." For public audience, generally college-educated. General cross-section of the area with an interest in alternative theater. Plays produced in the off Broadway manner. Cast is part Equity, part non-Equity. Produces 8 plays/year. 50% of scripts produced are unagented submissions. Works with 4-6 unpublished/unproduced writers annually. Submit complete ms. SASE.

Needs: "The playwright should have an approach to his writing with a specific intellectual concept in mind or specific theme of social relevance. We don't want to see scripts that would be television or 'B' movies-oriented. 1- or 2-act plays considered. We pay $500 against 5% of gross."

Recent Productions: *Fool for Love*, by Sam Shepard.

‡**MANHATTAN PUNCH LINE**, 3rd Floor, 410 W. 42nd St., New York NY 10036. (212)239-0827. Artistic Director: Steve Kaplan. Produces 6 plays/year. Professional off-off Broadway theatre company. Submit complete ms. Reports in 2 months. Buys rights for Broadway and off-Broadway productions, and a share of future subsidiary rights. Pays $325-500. SASE.
Needs: "Manhattan Punch Line is devoted to producing comedies of all types. We are a developmental theatre interested in producing serious plays with a comedic point of view. No comedies aimed at a dinner-theatre audience or TV sit-coms."
Tips: "Don't worry about being funny, just try to be honest. The most important and successful playwrights (Durang, Wasserstein, Innaurato) are all writing comedies."

MANHATTAN THEATRE CLUB, 321 E. 73 St., New York NY 10021. Literary Manager: Jonathan Alper. A three-theatre performing arts complex classified as Off-Broadway, using professional actors. "We present a wide range of new work, from this country and abroad, to a subscription audience. We want plays about contemporary problems and people. Comedies are welcome. No verse plays or historical dramas or large musicals. Very heavy set shows or multiple detailed sets are out. We prefer shows with casts not more than 15. No skits, but any other length is fine." Payment is negotiable. Query with synopsis. Computer printout submissions acceptable; no dot-matrix. SASE. Reports in 6 months. Produces 10 plays/year. All freelance written. A few of scripts produced are unagented submissions.
Recent Production: *Other Places*, by Harold Pinter.

TOM MARKUS, Artistic Director, Virginia Museum Theatre, Boulevard and Grove Ave., Richmond VA 23221. For public, well-educated, conservative, adventurous audiences. Professional resident theater. Standard format of presentation. Light comedies, musicals and dramas with small casts. 2-act and 3-act plays considered. No 1-acts. Payment is negotiable. For a premiere, theater requires share in future income. Produces one new script/year. Send complete script. Reports in 3-5 months. SASE.

MIDWEST PLAY LAB PROGRAM, (formerly Midwest Playwrights' Program), 2301 Franklin Ave., Minneapolis MN 55406. (612)332-7481. Artistic Director: Carolyn Bye. "Midwest Play Lab is a 2-week developmental workshop for new plays. The program is held in Minneapolis-St. Paul and is open by script competition to playwrights who live/work in the 13 midwestern states. It is an extensive two-week workshop focusing on the development of a script and the playwright. The plays are given staged readings at the site of the workshop and an additional reading (some staged, some informal) at a prestigious regional theatre." Submit complete ms—work in progress. Announcements of playwrights in 5 months. Pays a small stipend; room and board; partial travel. SASE.
Needs: "We are interested in playwrights with talent, ambitions for a professional career in theatre and scripts which could benefit from an intensive developmental process involving professional dramaturges, directors and actors. A playwright needs to be affiliated with the Midwest (must be documented if they no longer reside in the Midwest); MPL accepts scripts after first of each year. Full lengths and one acts. No produced materials—"a script which has gone through a similar process which would make our work redundant (O'Neill Conference scripts, for instance)."

BRUCE E. MILLAN/DETROIT REPERTORY THEATRE, 13103 Woodrow Wilson, Detroit MI 48238. (313)868-1347. Artistic Director: Bruce E. Millan. Produces 4-5 plays/year. 50% freelance written. 50% of scripts produced are unagented submissions. Plays performed professionally. "Our audience is mixed: 60% black, 40% white; mostly middle class professionals with college backgrounds." Works with 0-1 unpublished/unproduced writers annually. Submit complete ms. Computer printout submissions acceptable. Reports in 6 months. Pays for production plus $15-25/performance. SASE.
Needs: "We interracially cast without bloodline or sex distinctions when and where possible." No one-acts or musicals. Special consideration to Michigan playwrights.

DICK MUELLER/THE FIREHOUSE THEATRE, 514 S. 11th St., Omaha NB 68102. (402)346-6009. Artistic Director: Dick Mueller. Produces 7 plays/year.
Needs: "We produce at the Firehouse Dinner Theatre in Omaha. Our interest in new scripts is the hope of finding material that can be proven here at our theatre and then go on from here to find its audience." Submit complete ms. Reporting times vary; depends on work load. Buys negotiable rights. Pays $100/week or negotiable rates. SASE.
Tips: "We are a small theatre, certainly size and cost is a consideration. Quality is also a consideration. We can't use heavy drama in this theatre. We might, however, consider a production if it were a good script and use another theatre."

NASHVILLE ACADEMY THEATRE, 724 2nd Ave. S., Nashville TN 37210. (615)254-9103. Artistic Director: Dr. Guy Keeton. Produces both amateur and professional productions in a studio situation and in a 696-seat theater. Age groups performed for are: kindergarten through 4th grade, 5th grade through 8th, and 9th grade to adult. "We are considered a family theatre. Although we select plays for different age groups, we feel that any age should enjoy any play we do on some level. In the past we have produced murder mysteries, Shakespeare, plays of the supernatural, fairy tales, *The Mikado* dance-drama, musical comedy, serious drama, chamber theatre, contemporary children's drama—almost anything you can think of." Reports in 2 months. Produces 4 musicals (15%) and nonmusicals (85%) a year; 15% are originals. 15% freelance written. 25% of scripts produced are unagented submissions. Buys exclusive performance rights for middle Tennessee, one year prior to and during their production. Pays $10-35/performance. Works with 1 unpublished/unproduced writer annually. SASE.

Needs: "We prefer a variety of styles and genres. Length is usually limited to one hour. We are interested in quality new scripts of the old fairy tales for our younger audiences. There is no limit on topics. Interested in musicals also." Wants a richness of language and mood in their productions. No intermissions. Fluid and fast moving. Must have at least some literary merit. No or little obscenity. Cast size: 5-10 players. No limits in staging.

‡**NATIONAL ARTS CENTRE-ENGLISH THEATRE CO.**, Box 1534, Station B, Ottawa, Ontario K1P 5W1 Canada. (613)996-5051. Theatre Producer: Andis Celms. Produces and/or presents 12 plays/year. 0-5% freelance written. All scripts produced are agented submissions. Professional productions performed in the theatre and studio of the National Arts Centre (also, workshop productions in a new theatre space). Audience ranges from young/middle-aged professionals (especially civil servants) to students. Works with 1-2 unpublished/unproduced writers annually.

Tips: "The general public prefers to see a presentation which has a beginning, a middle and an end."

THE NEW AMERICAN THEATER, 118 S. Main St., Rockford IL 61101. (815)963-9454. Producing Director: J.R. Sullivan. Produces 6 mainstage plays in ten-month season. "The New American Theater is a professional resident theater company performing on a thrust stage with a 270-seat house. It is located in a predominantly middle class midwestern town with significant minority populations." Submit complete ms March through June with replies in 6 months. Buys negotiable rights. Pays royalty based on number of performances. SASE. No limitations, prefer serious themes, contemporary pieces. Open to format, etc. No opera.

Recent Title: *Amadeus, Have You Anything to Declare?*

Tips: "We look for 'well-made' plays exploring past and present American and international social themes. We produce at least one premiere each season."

‡**NEW PLAYS INCORPORATED**, Box 273, Rowayton CT 06853. (203)866-4520. Artistic Director: Patricia Whitton. Publishes average 4 plays/year. Publishes plays for producers of plays for young audiences and teachers in college courses on child drama. Query with synopsis. Reports in 2 months. Agent for amateur and semi-professional productions, exclusive agency for script sales. Pays 50% royalty on productions; 10% on script sales. SASE.

Needs: Plays for young audiences with something innovative in form and content. Length: usually 45-90 minutes. "Should be suitable for performance by adults for young audiences." No skits, assembly programs, improvisations or unproduced manuscripts.

Tips: Free catalog available on request.

THE NEW PLAYWRIGHTS' THEATRE OF WASHINGTON, 1742 Church St. NW, Washington DC 20036. (202)232-4527. Artistic Director: Harry M. Bagdasian. Literary Manager: Ms. Lloyd Rose. Produces 5 musicals (20%) and straight plays (80%) and 20 readings/year. 100% freelance written. 15% of scripts produced are unagented submissions. "Plays are produced in professional productions in the 125-seat New Playwrights' Theatre in the Dupont Circle area of the city for a subscription audience as well as large single-ticket buying followers. Works with varying number of writers annually; mostly unpublished (approximately 30%), 65% unproduced. Prefers query with synopsis or submit complete ms, "typed to form, suitably bound." All musicals must be accompanied by cassette tape recording of songs in proper order. Reports in 2 weeks on synopsis; 6-8 months on scripts. "Rights purchased and financial arrangements are individually negotiated." SASE, acknowledgement postcard. No rights requested on readings; buys 7% of playwright's future royalties for 7 years, and first production credit requested for plays or musicals offered as full productions. Pays 6% royalty against a $300/week minimum.

Needs: "All styles, traditional to experimental, straight plays to musicals and music-dramas, revues and cabaret shows, and full-lengths only. No verse plays, children's plays, puppet plays or film scripts. Cast: maximum of 12. Staging: performance space adaptable.

Tips: "We prefer a strong plot line, be the play realistic, expressionistic or non-realistic, with a positive outlook on life. We prefer not to receive, but will accept plays of the 'theatre of the infirm.' Would like to find some good, new, funny plays; nothing too far out, surrealistic or avant garde. We will absolutely not accept adaptations or plays written by other than American citizens."

‡**NEWBERRY COLLEGE THEATRE**, Dept. of Theatre, Newberry SC 29108. (803)276-5010. Artistic Director: Kenn Robbins. Produces 6 plays/year. Performs plays in Chapel Theatre (175 seats) and Rast Memorial Lab Theatre (flexible seating) for Newberry students and community. Submit complete script (bound only). Reports in 6 weeks. Buys production rights only. Pay 50/25 royalty. SASE.
Needs: "Plays that are suitable for college student performance inside a liberal arts context; we are supported by the Lutheran Church. We are particularly interested in student written plays that qualify for ACTF playwriting awards; also will consider second and third productions. The piece need not be a world premiere." No gratuitous sex or profanity. "Do not care to see plays with propaganda as main motive."

NORTHLIGHT REPERTORY THEATRE, 2300 Green Bay Rd., Evanston IL 60201. (312)869-7732. Artistic Director: Michael Maggio. "We are a LORT theatre with a subscription audience using professional artistic personnel. Our season runs from September through June. We are committed to producing new plays, translations and adaptations from other literary forms." Audience is college age and over, broad range of socio-economic backgrounds. Works with approximately 5 unpublished/unproduced writers annually via studio readings/staged readings. Query with synopsis. Computer printout submissions acceptable; prefers letter-quality to dot-matrix printouts. Reports in 3 months. Produces 5 mainstage a year; 35-50% are originals. 35% freelance written. Rights purchased vary. SASE.
Needs: "New plays and small production music theatre. Plays may vary in genre and topic. Full-length and prefer a cast size of 10 or less without doubling. Though accessibility is an issue, we rate substance as a higher concern for our audience. We have a 298-seat house with a small, extended apron proscenium stage allowing for some use of multiple sets but only the suggestion of levels, e.g. a second story home, etc. Our budget and other resources restrict very elaborate staging but we are fortunate to have talented and creative designers. Solely commercial work or dinner theatre material is not appropriate for our audiences. We emphasize work which speaks to the human condition and is often contemporary."
Recent Title: *What I Did Last Summer*, by A.R. Gurney, Jr.

ODYSSEY THEATRE ENSEMBLE, 12111 Ohio Ave., Los Angeles CA 90025. (213)826-1626. Artistic Director: Ron Sossi. Produces 12 plays/year. Plays performed in a 3-theatre facility. "All three theatres are Equity waiver; Odyssey 1 and 2 each have 99 seats, while Odyssey 3 has 72-90 seats. We have a subscription audience of 1,800 who subscribe to a six-play season, and are offered a discount on our remaining non-subscription plays. Remaining seats are sold to the general public." Query with synopsis. Reports in 8 months. Buys negotiable rights. Pays 5-7% royalty or $25-35/performance. SASE. "We will *not* return scripts without SASE."
Needs: Full-length plays only with "either an innovative form or extremely provocative subject matter. We desire more theatrical pieces that explore possibilities of the live theatre experience."

OLD GLOBE THEATRE, Box 2171, San Diego CA 92112. (619)231-1941. Artistic Director: Jack O'Brien. Produces 12 plays/year. "We are a LORT B professional house. Our plays are produced for a single ticket and subscription audience of 250,000, a large cross section of southern California, including visitors from the LA area." Submit complete ms through agent only. Reports in 2 months. Buys negotiable rights. Pays 6-10% royalty. SASE.
Needs: "We are looking for contemporary, realistic, theatrical dramas and comedies and request that all submissions be full-length plays at this time." Prefers smaller cast and single sets, and "to have the playwright submit the play he has written rather than to enforce any limitations. No musicals or large cast historical dramas."
Tips: "Get back to theatricality. I am tired of reading screenplays."

OLD LOG THEATER, Box 250, Excelsior MN 55331. Producer: Don Stolz. Produces 2-act and 3-act plays for "a professional cast. Public audiences, usually adult. Interested in contemporary comedies. No more than 2 sets. Cast not too large." Produces about 14 plays/year. Payment by Dramatists Guild agreement. Send complete script. SASE.

ONE ACT THEATRE COMPANY, 430 Mason St., San Francisco CA 94102. (415)421-6162. Artistic Director: Ric Prindle. Produces 30 plays/year. Professional productions performed for a subscription and community audience—35-50 age group, especially. Reports in 6 weeks. Buys negotiable rights. Pays negotiable rate. SASE.
Needs: "One-act plays only: 60 minutes maximum. Comedy and drama, wide stylistic range. We will consider plays with provocative themes."
Tips: "Don't overwrite. Make sure there is conflict and resolution. Make your characters believable. Create a plot, a genuine problem."

O'NEILL THEATER CENTER'S NATIONAL PLAYWRIGHTS CONFERENCE, Suite 901, 234 W. 44th St., New York NY 10036. (212)382-2790. Artistic Director: Lloyd Richards. Develops staged readings

of 12 stage plays, 4 teleplays/year for a general audience. "We accept unsolicited mss with no prejudice toward either represented or unrepresented writers. Our theatre is located in Waterford, Connecticut and we operate under an Equity LORT(C) Contract. We have 3 theaters: Barn-250 seats, Amphitheatre-300 seats, Instant Theater-150." Submit complete ms. Computer printout submissions acceptable. Decision by late April. "We have an option on the script from time of acceptance until one month *after* the four-week summer conference is completed. After that, all rights revert back to the author." Pays $200 stipend plus room, board and transportation. SASE. "Interested writers should send us a self-addressed-stamped envelope and request our updated guidelines. We accept script submissions from September 15-December 1st of each year. Conference takes place during four weeks in July and August each summer."
Needs: "We do staged readings of new American plays. We use modular sets for all plays, minimal lighting, minimal props and no costumes. We do script-in-hand readings with professional actors and directors."

‡**OPERA VARIETY THEATER**, 3944 Balboa St., San Francisco CA 94121. (415)566-8805. Director: Violette M. Dale. 100% freelance written. All scripts produced are unagented submissions. Plays to be performed by professional and amateur casts for a public audience; all ages, generally families; upper educational level. Works with 1-3 unpublished/unproduced writers annually. Submit complete script. Produces 2-3 musicals (50% or more) and nonmusicals (1-2) a year; all are originals. "Everyone (cast, author, technical people, publicity, etc.) receives percentage of box office." SASE. Reports in 6 months.
Needs: "Prefer musicals (but must have musically challenging, singable, tuneful material; arranged, ready to cast). Plays or music on most any theme that conservative audiences would enjoy. Must have substantial, believable plot and good characterizations. Must be simple to produce; fairly small cast, easy setting, etc. (small backstage area limits cast, props, staging, etc.). Emphasis is on entertainment rather than social reform." Length: 1, 2 or 3 acts. "No vulgarity in language or action; no wordy preaching."
Recent Production: *The Making of Perpeople*, by Hulsebus (comedy on creation story).

‡**ORACLE PRESS, LTD.**, 5323 Heatherstone Dr., Baton Rouge LA 70820. (504)766-5577. Artistic Director: CJ Stevens. Publishes 10-15 plays/year. 90% freelance written. 90% of scripts produced are unagented submissions. Plays performed by college, high school and other amateur groups. Works with 20-30 unpublished/unproduced writers annually. Query with synopsis. Computer printout submissions acceptable; no dot-matrix. Reports in 6 weeks. Copyright in name of playwright; performance rights referred to playwright. Pays 10% royalty. SASE.
Needs: "Production must be playable *on stage*. Will not publish gratuitous filth or obscenity."
Tips: "The trend which we find deplorable is that of writing everything for Broadway; hence, small casts, limited sets. College and high school groups frequently desire just the opposite."

JOSEPH PAPP PRODUCER, New York Shakespeare Festival, 425 Lafayette St., New York NY 10003. (212)598-7100. Literary Manager, Play Department: William Hart. Interested in full-length plays and musical works. No restrictions as to style, historical period, traditional or experimental forms, etc. New works produced on 5 stages at the Public Theater. Produces about 20 plays/year; 90% are originals. Unsolicited material accepted *only* if recommended by legitimate source in theater, music or other professionally related fields. Standard option and production agreements. Reports in 6 weeks. SASE.

PEOPLE'S LIGHT & THEATRE COMPANY, 39 Conestoga Rd., Malvern PA 19355. (215)647-1900. Producing Director: Danny S. Fruchter. Produces 6 full-length, 10-12 one-act plays/year. Approximately 20% of scripts produced are unagented submissions. "LOA Actors' Equity plays are produced in Malvern 30 miles outside Philadelphia in 350-seat main stage and 80-seat second stage. Our audience is mainly suburban, some from Philadelphia. We do a 6-show subscription season which includes a New Play Festival each summer." Works with 2-4 unpublished/unproduced writers annually. Query with synopsis and cast list. Computer printout submissions acceptable; prefers letter-quality to dot-matrix. SASE is a must. Reports in 10 months. Buys "rights to production in our theatre, sometimes for local touring." Pays 2-5% royalty.
Needs: "We will produce anything that interests us." Prefers single set, maximum cast of 12 (for full length), fewer for one act. No musicals, mysteries, domestic comedies.
Tips: "Freelance writers should be aware of trend away from naturalistic family drama and smaller cast size."

‡**PERFORMANCE COMMUNITY/NEW TUNERS**, 1225 W. Belmont Ave., Chicago IL 60657. 312)929-7367. Artistic Director: Byron Schaffer, Jr. Produces 3-4 new musicals/year. 80% freelance written. "Nearly all" scripts produced are unagented submissions. Plays performed in a small off-Loop theater seating 148 for a general theatre audience, urban/suburban mix. Submit complete ms and cassette tape of the score, if available. Reports in 6 months. Buys exclusive right of production within 80 mile radius. "Submit first, we'll negotiate later." Pays 5-10% of gross. "Authors are given a stipend to cover a residency of at least two weeks." Computer printout submissions acceptable; prefers letter-quality to dot-matrix. SASE.
Needs: "We're interested in traditional forms of musical theatre as well as more innovative styles. We have less interest in operetta and operatic works, but we'd look at anything. At this time, we have no interest in nonmusi-

cal plays unless to consider them for possible adaptation—please send query letter first. Our production capabilities are limited by the lack of space, but we're very creative and authors should submit anyway. The smaller the cast, the better. We are especially interested in scripts using a younger (35 and under) ensemble of actors. We mostly look for authors who are interested in developing their script through workshops, rehearsals and production. No interest in children's theatre. No casts over 15. No one-man shows, please."

PERFORMANCE PUBLISHING CO., 978 N. McLean Blvd., Elgin IL 60120. Editor: Virginia Butler. "We publish one-, two- and three-act plays and musicals suitable for stock, community, college, high school and children's theater. We're looking for comedies, mysteries, dramas, farces, etc. with modern dialogue and theme. Plays for and about high school students are usually the most remunerative and we publish 50% high school, 15% children's theater and 35% for the balance of the market. The new writer is advised to obtain experience by limiting himself to one-acts until he has been published. We offer a standard royalty contract for amateur, stock and community theatre licensing rights." Publishes 40 plays/year; (15%) musicals and (85%) straight plays. 75% freelance written. 80% of scripts published are unagented submissions. Works with 12-15 unpublished/unproduced writers annually. Authors should retain a copy of any script mailed. Computer printout submissions acceptable. Include SASE. Reports in 3 months.
Needs: "Budgets are limited and production costs are escalating. Sets should be kept simple but innovative."
Recent Title: *Sister, Sister*, by Karen Tate (family drama).
Tips: "There is more emphasis on character delineation, more realistic situations, less structure and a free and imaginative approach to staging and costuming. There is a trend toward more conservative thinking, just beginning to exert as influence on producers. The writer will be verbally walking a tightrope."

PIONEER DRAMA SERVICE, 2171 S. Colorado Blvd., Box 22555, Denver CO 80222. (303)759-4297. Publisher: Shubert Fendrich. Plays are performed by high school, junior high and adult groups, colleges and recreation programs for audiences of all ages. "We are one of the largest full-service play publishers in the country in that we handle straight plays, musicals, children's theater and melodrama." Publishes 15 plays/year; (40%) musicals and (60%) straight plays. 20% freelance written. 100% of scripts published are unagented submissions. Submit synopsis or complete script. Computer printout submissions acceptable; prefers letter-quality to dot-matrix. Buys all rights. Pays "usually 10% royalty on copy sales; 50% of production royalty and 50% of subsidiary rights with some limitations on first-time writers." SASE. Reports in 30-60 days.
Needs: "We are looking for adaptations of great works in the public domain or plays on subjects of current interest. We use the standard 1-act and 3-act format, 2-act musicals, melodrama in all lengths and plays for children's theater (plays to be done by adult actors for children)." Length: 1-acts of 30-45 minutes; 2-act musicals and 3-act comedies from 90 minutes to 2 hours; and children's theater of 1 hour. No "heavily domestic comedy or drama, simplistic children's plays, shows with multiple sets or that hang heavily on special effects, plays with a primarily male cast, highly experimental works, or plays which lean strongly on profanity or sexual overtones."
Recent Title: *Tumbleweeds* (musical based on the Tom Ryan comic strip), by Tim Kelly, Arne Christiansen and Ole Kittleson.
Tips: "We believe writers should obtain the amateur rights to prominent properties—books, TV shows, comic strips, etc., adapt and present the material by a local group and then market the show. It is becoming more and more difficult to 'create' a market for material which lacks familiarity."

PLAYERS PRESS, INC., Box 1132, Studio City CA 91604. Senior Editor: Robert W. Gordon. "We deal in all areas and handle works for film, television as well as theater. But all works must be in stage play format for publication." 80% freelance written. Works with 1-10 unpublished/unproduced writers annually. Submit complete ms. "Must have SASE or play will not be returned, and two #10 SASE for update and correspondence. All submissions must have been produced and should include a flyer and/or program with dates of performance." Reports in 3 months. Buys negotiable rights. "We prefer all area rights." Pays variable royalty "according to area; approximately 10-75% of gross receipts." Also pays in outright purchase of $100-25,000 or $5-5,000/performance.
Needs: "We prefer comedies, musicals and children's theatre, but are open to all genres. We will rework the ms after acceptance. We are interested in the quality, not the format."
Recent Titles: *A Matter of Degree*, by Anson Campbell; and *The Berringsford Experiment*, by Marvin R. Wilson, Jr.

PLAYS, The Drama Magazine for Young People, 8 Arlington St., Boston MA 02116. Editor: Sylvia K. Burack. Publishes approximately 80 1-act plays each season to be performed by junior and senior high, middle grades, lower grades. Can use comedies, farces, melodramas, skits, mysteries and dramas, plays for holidays and other special occasions, such as Book Week; adaptations of classic stories and fables; historical plays; plays about other lands; puppet plays; folk and fairy tales; creative dramatics; and plays for conservation, ecology or human rights programs. Mss should follow the general style of *Plays*. Stage directions should not be typed in capital letters or underlined. No incorrect grammar or dialect. Characters with physical defects or speech impediments should not be included. Desired lengths for mss are: Junior and Senior high—20 double spaced ms pages (25 to 30 minutes playing time). Middle Grades—12 to 15 pages (25 to 20 minutes playing time). Lower Grades—6 to 10 pages (8 to 15 minutes playing time). Pays "good rates on acceptance." Reports in 2-3 weeks. SASE. Sample copy $3; manuscript specification sheet sent on request.

PLAYWRIGHTS' PLATFORM, INC., 43 Charles St., Boston MA 02114. (617)720-3770. Artistic Director: David Moore, Jr. Develops and presents 30 plays/season. "Selected scripts are developed through cold, rehearsed and staged reading, as well as no-frills productions. All activities professional. Audiences general and professional." Indicate with synopsis if Massachusetts or New England writer; submit complete ms if Massachusetts writer. Reports in 5 months. Program credit given only (in case of eventual fall production or publication). Playwright honoraria *average* $20 for script program.
Needs: Seeking new voices, unusual visions. Readings and workshops employ minimal props, costumes, lights, sets.
Tips: "Playwrights of real promise afforded access to first-class directors and actors with considerable dramaturgical support available. Theatrical characters and events are *not* ultimately 'real', but rather of extraordinary human circumstance and values."

RAFT THEATRE, 432 W. 42nd St., New York NY 10036. (212)947-8389. Artistic Director: Martin Zurla. Produces 5 plays/year. Plays performed are professional: showcase (AEA), with mini-contract, Off-Broadway; intended for general audiences. Submit complete ms. Computer printout submissions OK. Reports in 2 months. Pays on year option and royalty (on individual basis).
Needs: "We have *no* restrictions on content, theme, style or length. Prefer scripts that have six or *fewer* characters and limited set and scene changes (due to performing space); and scripts that are typed in professional playscript format (theme, structure, format, etc.)."
Tips: "We are looking for writers tht respect their craft and present their work in like manner. We prefer works that set their own trends and not those that follow other trends. We normally look for scripts that deal with human issues and cover a wide scope and audience, and not the so-called commercial property."

READ MAGAZINE, 245 Long Hill Rd., Middletown CT 06457. (203)347-7251. Editor: Edwin A. Hoey. 10% freelance written. For junior high school students. Biweekly magazine; 32 pages. Circ. 500,000. Rights purchased vary with author and material. May buy second serial (reprint) rights or all rights. Byline given. Buys 10 mss/year. Pays on publication. Free sample copy and writer's guidelines for SASE. Will consider photocopied submissions. No simultaneous submissions. Reports in 6 weeks. Submit complete ms. SASE.
Drama and Fiction: First emphasis is on plays; second on fiction with suspense, adventure or teenage identification themes. "No preachy material. Plays should have 12 to 15 parts and not require complicated stage directions, for they'll be used mainly for reading aloud in class. Remember that we try to be educational as well as entertaining." No kid detective stories or plays. No obscenity. Pays $50 minimum.

‡ROUND HOUSE THEATRE, 12210 Bushey Dr., Silver Spring MD 20902. (301)468-4172. Artistic Director: Jeffrey B. Davis. Acting Arts Coordinator: Linda Yost. Produces 6 mainstage plays at the Round House Theatre, a non-Equity professional theatre company (considered a Stock house by NY); also tours. Equity performers used thru Guest Artist contract thru U/RTA in New York. "Our subscriber base age range is 35-60 but becoming younger as the years pass." Submit complete script with SAS postcard for acknowledgment and SASE for script return. Reports in 12 months. Buys "exclusive production rights in Washington metropolitan area if the decision is made to produce the play." Pay varies depending on individual contract.
Needs: "We produce a wide variety of productions. We take risks. If the play is *extremely well written* and able to be produced in our theatre space, then we will consider it. We do not have fly space; cast limit is 18; single unit set is best."

‡ST. BART'S PLAYHOUSE, 109 E. 50th St., New York NY 10022. (212)751-1616. Artistic Director: Tom Briggs. "Will accept synopsis only of inherently American musicals from which artistic director will solicit scripts, if interested. Do not call."

SEATTLE REPERTORY THEATRE, Seattle Center, 155 Mercer St., Seattle WA 98109. (206)447-2210. "The Seattle Repertory Theatre is currently looking for new, unproduced plays for its main stage and for its New Plays in Process Project. Playwrights should not send script but should submit professional resume, plot synopsis and 15 pages of dialogue from the front of the play to Alison Harris, Literary Manager."

SOHO REPERTORY THEATRE, 19 Mercer St., New York NY 10013. (212)925-2588. Co-Artistic Directors: Jerry Engelbach and Marlene Swartz. Produces 4-10 full productions and 8-10 staged readings/year. 15% freelance written. All of scripts produced are unagented submissions. Plays performed off-off-Broadway. "The audience is well-educated, mature and composed of regular theatregoers. Our playwrights have usually been produced, and some published, previously." Query with synopsis. "We prefer that queries/synopses be submitted by a director interested in staging the play, but will accept author queries, too." Computer printout submissions acceptable; no dot-matrix. Reports in 6 weeks. Rights for full-length plays: percentage of author's royalties on future earnings, credit in published script and on future programs; for staged readings: none. Pays up to $200 for limited run performance rights. Pays $500 for future right to option. SASE.

Needs: "Unusual plays not likely to be seen elsewhere; including rarely produced classics; revivals of superior modern works; new plays that utilize contemporary theatre techniques; and musicals and mixed media pieces that are noncommercial. Writers should keep in mind that our stage is a thrust, not a proscenium." Desires "full-length works that are physical, three-dimensional and that use heightened language, are witty and sophisticated, and that demonstrate a high quality of dramatic craft. No sitcoms, featherweight pieces for featherbrained audiences, drawing room plays, pedantic political pieces, works that do not require the audience to think, or pieces more suited to television or the printed page than to the live stage."

Tips: "Most of the plays submitted to us are too conventional. Look us up in the Theatre Communications Group's *Theatre Profiles* to see what kind of work we have done, and use the most unusual productions as a guideline. The most interesting contemporary theater pieces are stylistically eclectic and very active. Dialogue is terse and direct. Sets are rarely realistic. The audience's imagination is constantly challenged, and they leave the theater feeling that they've had a physical, as well as intellectual/aesthetic, experience. Such works are rare, which is why we reject a thousand scripts for each one we produce."

SOUTHEASTERN ACADEMY OF THEATRE AND MUSIC INC., DBA ACADEMY THEATRE, 1137 Peachtree St. NE, Atlanta GA 30309. (404)873-2518. Artistic Director: Frank Wittow. Produces 10-16 plays/year. Plays performed on a professional mainstage for the Academy's Theatre for Youth and Children's Theatre, and for the Academy's School of Performing Arts lab theatre. Query with synopsis or agented submissions. Reports in 6 months. Buys "usually sole and exclusive right to produce play within a 100-mile radius of the metro Atlanta area for up to 3 years." Pays 5% royalty or $5-100/performance. SASE.

Needs: "Full-length, small cast shows which provide interesting challenges for actors. Plays which deal with new approaches to naturalism, transformational plays. One-acts considered for lab theatre (minimal royalty)." Cast: 12 maximum. Minimal or simple sets. "Deal with basic, honest emotions. Delve into social issues in a subtle manner. Provide thought-provoking material which deals with the human condition and allows for greater self-awareness." No frivolous, light comedies.

Tips: "The Academy Theatre is devoted to exploring human behavior, through physical and emotional involvement, for the purpose of greater self-awareness, for the purpose of making people more social, more able to live with each other."

STAGE ONE: The Louisville Children's Theatre, 721 W. Main St., Louisville KY 40202. (502)589-5946. Producing Director: Moses Goldberg. Produces 6-7 plays/year. 20% freelance written. 15-20% of scripts produced are unagented submissions (excluding work of Playwright-in-Residence). Plays performed by an Equity company for young audiences aged 4-18; usually does different plays for different age groups within that range. Submit complete ms. Computer printout submission acceptable. Reports in 4 months. Pays negotiable royalty or $25-50/performance. SASE.

Needs: "Good plays for young audiences of all types: adventure, fantasy, realism, serious problem plays about growing up or family entertainment." Cast: ideally, 10 or less. "Honest, visual potentiality, worthwhile story and characters are necessary. An awareness of children and their schooling is a plus." No "campy material or anything condescending to children. No musicals unless they are fairly limited in orchestration."

STAGE WEST EDMONTON, 16615 109th Ave., Edmonton, Alberta T5P 4K8 Canada. (403)484-0841. Director of Production: William Fisher. Produces 6 plays/year. Plays performed in dinner theatre. Submit complete ms. Reports in 2 months. Pays 6% royalty. SASE or SAE and IRCs.

Needs: Comedies, musical comedies, mystery-thrillers. Cast: 9 maximum. Stage lights: 52. About 100 minutes playing time: preferably 3 acts. "No commentary or political plays, unless in a humorous vein."

CHARLES STILWILL, Managing Director, Community Playhouse, Box 433, Waterloo IA 50704. (319)235-0367. Plays performed by Waterloo Community Playhouse with a volunteer cast. "We are one of few community theaters with a commitment to new scripts. We do at least one and have done as many as four a year. We are the largest community theater per capita in the country. We have 5,000 season members." Average attendance at main stage shows is 5,600; at studio shows 2,240. "We try to fit the play to the theater. We do a wide variety of plays. Looking for good plays with more roles for women than men. Our public isn't going to accept nudity, too much sex, too much strong language. We don't have enough black actors to do all-black shows. We have done plays with as few as 2 characters, and as many as 61." Produces 15 plays (7 adult, 8 children's); 1-3 musicals and 7-12 nonmusicals a year; 1-4 originals. 17% freelance written. Most of scripts produced are unagented submissions. "On the main stage we usually pay between $300 and $500. In our studio we usually pay between $50 and $300. We also produce children's theater. We are looking for good adaptations of name children's shows and very good shows that don't necessarily have a name. We produce children's theater with both adult and child actors. We also do a small (2-6 actors) cast show that tour the elementry schools in the spring. This does not have to be a name, but it can only be about 45 minutes long." Works with 1-4 unpublished/unproduced writers annually. Send synopsis or complete script. Computer printout submissions acceptable. SASE. "Reports negatively within 10 months, but acceptance takes longer because we try to fit a wanted script into the balanced season."

Recent Title: The US premiere of *Think Again*, by Patricia Joudry (satire on modern medical practice).

‡**THE STRAND STREET THEATRE**, 2317 Mechanic St., Galveston TX 77550. (409)763-2032. Producing Director: Robert Tolaro. Produces 7 plays/year. 15% freelance written. 1 of scripts produced is unagented submission. Professional non-Equity performances for a local audience as well as tourists. New playreading series once a month. Works with 12 unpublished/unproduced writers annually. Submit complete script. Reports in 1 month. Buys negotiable rights. SASE.
Needs: Full-length plays, small cast, unit set. "Our stage is very small—no multilevel sets will work. Think conservative—absurd is fine." No highly offensive language or action.

‡**THEATRE RAPPORT**, 8128 Gould Ave., Hollywood CA 90046. (213)462-9656. Artistic Director: Crane Jackson. Equity company. Produces contemporary (no costume) full-length plays only (no one-act plays) using one set. Produces gutsy, relevant plays on highly artistic level and true subjects. No unjustified homosexuality, nudity or profanity; realistic acceptable—also hard-hitting biography. For a sophisticated, educated, nonfad, conservative (although venturesome) audience looking for something new and different. Not avantgarde, but a strong point of view is an asset. Approach must be unique. All plays must be West Coast premieres. Pays 20% of gross. Send complete script with past reviews, if available (good or bad). Response if interested. All mss read, but *none are returned*. Produces 6 plays a year. "Preference is given to previously produced shows."
Recent Production: *Arbuckle's Rape*, by Lewis Phillips.

‡**THEATRE THREE**, 2800 Routh, Dallas TX 75201. (214)651-7225. Artistic Director: Norma Young. Produces 11-12 plays/year. 8% freelance written. 3 of scripts produced are unagented submissions. Plays in an arena house to a general audience using professional actors. Works with approximately 2 unpublished/unproduced writers annually. Submit complete script. Computer printout submissions acceptable. Replies in several months. Buys performance/staged reading rights for productions at Theatre Three only. Pays 6% royalty or honorarium for readings. SASE.
Needs: Full-length plays. "We produce a wide range of genre including musicals. Our house is inappropriate for spectacle-type shows. Multiset and large cast shows can be cost prohibitive."

VANCOUVER EAST CULTURAL CENTRE, 1895 Venables St., Vancouver, British Columbia V5L 2H6 Canada. (604)254-9578. Contact: Artistic Director. Presents 3-8 plays/year. Professional plays performed for all audiences. "We have produced in Vancouver, Toronto, New York, London, Los Angeles and many points in between." Submit complete ms or good ideas. Computer printout submissions acceptable. Reports in 2 months. Buys production rights only and option for further productions. Pays 6-9% royalty. SASE or SAE and IRCs.
Needs: "New, innovative, populist entertainment with content of relevant social issues." Small stage. "Three hundred seats means financial restraint."

‡**VIRGINIA STAGE COMPANY**, 108-14 E. Tazewell St., Norfolk VA 23510. (804)627-6988. Artistic Director: Charles Towers. Produces 8 plays/year. 20% freelance written. 10% of scripts produced are unagented submissions. A professional regional theatre serving the one million people of the Norfolk area. Plays are performed in LORT B proscenium mainstage or LORT D flexible second stage. Works with 2 unpublished/unproduced writers annually. Query with synopsis; "sample scene or dialogue may be included." Computer printout submissions acceptable; no dot-matrix. Reports in 2 months. Buys negotiable rights. Pays negotiable rate. SASE.
Needs: "Primarily full-length dramas and comedies which address contemporary issues within a study of broader themes and theatricality. A small cast and limited staging is preferable but not necessary. Material must be inherently theatrical in use of language, staging or character. We do not want to see material which offers simplistic solutions to complex concerns, is more easily suited for television or film or whose scope is *limited to* specific contemporary topical issues."

‡**WEST COAST PLAYS**, Box 7206, Berkeley CA 94707. (415)841-3096. Editor: Robert Hurwitt. Publishes 14 plays/year (2 volumes, 7 plays each). 100% freelance written. 1/2-3/4 of scripts published are unagented submissions. Plays are for general audience, professional use (through theaters), and academic use (some volumes get used as texts). No unproduced writers. "Half to three-fourths of the writers we publish each year (up to 14) may be previously unpublished." Submit complete script. Computer printout submissions acceptable. Reports in 6 months. Buys one-time publication rights with right to reprint the anthology as a whole but not the individual play. Pays royalty: .7% of list price on first 2,000 copies sold; 1.4% after that. Advance on royalties from

$50 for a one-act to $100 for a full-length play. SASE.

Needs: All types: one-acts, full-length plays; children's plays, experimental, epic or realistic; musical, comedy, drama; third world, women's, gay, straight. "We try to cover the spectrum of what is most exciting in new plays from the Western US. We *only* publish plays that have had their first US production in the western United States, roughly anywhere from Denver to the coast." No scripts that have not yet had a full-scale production.

‡**WOOLLY MAMMOTH THEATRE COMPANY**, 1317 G St. NW, Washington DC 20005. (202)393-3939. Artistic Director: Howard Shalwitz. Produces 5-6 plays/year. Produces professional productions for the general public in Washington, DC. Query with synopsis. Reports in 2 weeks on synopsis; 6 weeks on scripts. Buys first and second class production rights. Pays 5% royalty. SASE.

Needs: "We look for plays that depart from the traditional categories in some way. Apart from an innovative approach, there is no formula. One-acts are rarely used." Cast limit of 12; no unusually expensive gimmicks.

‡**WORKSHOP WEST PLAYWRIGHTS' THEATRE**, 9510-105th Ave., Edmonton, Alberta T5H 0J8 Canada. (403)429-4251. Artistic Director: Gerry Potter. Produces 5 plays/year. 50% freelance written. 20% of scripts produced are unagented submissions. Professional productions performed in 200-300 seat houses for middle-of-the-road urban audiences, many from university. Works with 1 or 2 unpublished/unproduced writers annually. Submit complete ms. Computer printout submissions acceptable. Reports in 2 months. Buys various rights "though we try for Canadian rights for 1 year." Pays 8-11% royalty vs. guarantee. SASE.

Needs: Emphasis on Canadian plays. "Various genres, though we avoid commercial comedy, musicals and absurdist work. Interested in innovative works, historical subjects, (especially Canadian or Western Canadian). Normally full-length." Cast: 7 maximum. "Socially-aware drama and modern poetic drama." No Broadway musicals.

Tips: Freelance writers should be aware of "renewed emphasis on story and character, but away from naturalism."

Screenwriting

If you only *dream* of walking up to the Academy Awards podium to receive an Oscar, you'll never write the "great American film." The tuxedoed and gowned recipients look so glamorous, but for every jewel and cummerbund there are thousands of lonely, uncertain hours that those recipients spent at the typewriter, on the set, and maybe in the cutting room. Don't just envy them; they work 14-hour days sometimes. Learn to do the same—and to produce scripts that people and producers will respond to. "People want to laugh, and they want to cry, and they do respond openly and honestly when writers write from the heart," says one producer. "*Silkwood* is a good example; so is *Terms of Endearment*, since it is a 'people story' that never resorts to gratuitous violence."

The most memorable screenplays start with a good idea, one free from stereotypes and clichés. "More and more stories are being produced about social themes and significant issues of the day," say producers. "Some of these stories have a timeless quality to them and a universal theme which can touch audiences all over the world."

Unlike playwriting and educational/industrial scriptwriting, there aren't many accessible local TV and film markets. For writers without a Los Angeles connection, breaking in may be as difficult as a pro winning an Oscar.

Fortunately, the growth of the cable TV market has opened additional opportunities for scriptwriters. Some cable services originate local programming; in fact, cable TV contracts with some communities require that there be local programming access to cable subscribers. Learning what opportunities are available in your own community is the first step.

The concept of cable is that viewers should be able to watch what they want to watch when they want to watch it. This is reflected in the specialty networks in the market—business, health, religion, entertainment, and other special interests. The ability of viewers and the cable industry itself to accommodate and sustain the volume of material will determine how many networks will survive.

It is unclear, yet, just how big the cable market will be for freelance scriptwriters.

It may be that much already-produced material will be used. Keep in touch with industry trends in the business pages of *The New York Times* and the weekly arts tabloid, *Variety*.

Production companies interested in receiving scripts for cable TV are identified with a box (□) to the left of the listing. Sometimes these local independent producers feed a particular cable network by doing scripts for which the network itself has neither facility nor equipment. Many of these markets are interested in how-to and educational programming.

The largest number of independent producers per square mile is located in Los Angeles. If you have some other writing credits, you might want to approach them. It's a good idea to register your script with the Writers Guild of America (8955 Beverly Blvd., Los Angeles 90048, or 555 W. 57th St., New York City 10019) prior to submitting it. Often ideas, rather than entire scripts, are sold to networks or producers—so don't be surprised if *your* dialogue doesn't make it to the screen.

Some producers seek only scripts submitted through agents. (See the Authors' Agents section for more information.)

Format for the screenplay calls for a typed, single-spaced (triple-spaced between the dialogue of different characters) manuscript. Set margins at 15 and 75 (pica)—18 and 90 (elite) and allow 125-150 pages for a two-hour feature film (90 pages for 90 minutes).

If you can handle characterization, dialogue, plot construction, conflict, and resolution—and continue to work on these skills—you won't have time to dream of awards. And that's usually when an award-winning work will emerge.

‡ARKOFF INTERNATIONAL PICTURES, 9200 Sunset Blvd., P.H. 3, Los Angeles CA 90069. (213)278-7600. Director of Production: Rhonda Bloom. 2% freelance written. 100% of scripts produced are agented submissions. "We do not look at unsolicited manuscripts. We work through agents and attorneys only."

‡THE CHAMBA ORGANIZATION, 230 W. 105th St., #2-A, New York NY 10025. President: St. Clair Bourne. Produces material for "the activist-oriented audience; the general audience (PG), and in the educational film market we aim at high school and adult audiences, especially the so-called 'minority' audiences. Assignments are given solely based upon our reaction to submitted material. The material is the credential." 100% freelance written. 10% of scripts produced are unagented submissions. Buys 2-4 scripts/year. Works with 3 unpublished/unproduced writers annually. Query with a brief description of plot, thumbnail descriptions of principal characters and any unusual elements. Computer printout submissions acceptable. SASE.
Needs: "I concentrate primarily on feature film projects and unique feature-length documentary film projects. We prefer submission of film treatments first. Then, if the idea interests us, we negotiate the writing of the script." Payment negotiable according to Writers Guild standards.
Recent Production: *On the Boulevard* (fiction).
Tips: Trends in the American stage and screen include "a critical examination of traditional American values."

□ CHRISTIAN BROADCASTING NETWORK, Virginia Beach VA 23463. (804)424-7777. Director of Program Development: David Freyss. Produces material for a general mass audience as well as Christian audiences. Second largest cable network in the nation. Producer of *Another Life* and *700 Club*. 20% freelance written. 60% of scripts produced are unagented submissions. "We are planning over 12 different programs: some one-shot, some series, women's programs, dramas based on Bible characters and holiday shows. Mostly staff-written but will consider freelance treatments." Buys negotiable rights. Works with 5 unpublished/unproduced writers annually. Previously produced material OK. Computer printout submissions acceptable; prefers letter-quality to dot-matrix. Send to Tom Rogeberg, Director of Operations, CBN Cable Network. SASE. Reports in 2 weeks.
Needs: Secular and Christian. Dramatic, service, educational, children's, feature films, informational shows, film adaptations of books. Query and request release form to submit an idea or script. Buys some ideas outright; flat fee for treatment, outline or script.
Tips: "We're looking for writers with strong television/film background who have screenwriting experience. A basic belief in the *Bible* is necessary."

□ Open box preceding a listing indicates a cable TV market.

CINE/DESIGN FILMS, INC., 255 Washington St., Denver CO 80203. (303)777-4222. Producer/Director: Jon Husband. Produces educational material for general, sales training and theatrical audiences. 75% freelance written. 90% of scripts produced are unagented submissions. Buys 8-10 scripts/year. Phone query OK: "original solid ideas are encouraged." Computer printout submissions acceptable. Rights purchased vary.
Needs: "Motion picture outlines in the theatrical, documentary, sales or educational areas. We are seeking theatrical scripts in the low-budget area that are possible to produce for under $1,000,000. We seek flexibility and personalities who can work well with our clients." Produces 16mm and 35mm films. Pays $100-200/screen minute on 16mm productions. Theatrical scripts negotiable.
Tips: "Understand the marketing needs of film production today."

CINETUDES, 295 W. 4th St., New York NY 10014. (212)966-4600. President: Christine Jurzykowski. Produces material for TV. Works with 20 writers/year. Query with samples or submit resume. SASE. Reports in 2 weeks. Buys all rights.
Needs: Feature length screenplays (theatrical/TV); theatrical shorts; children's programming. "We look for the willingness to listen and past experience in visual writing." Produces 16mm and 35mm films and videotape. Pays by outright purchase or pays daily rates.

‡□ **ROBERT COOPER PRODUCTIONS INC.**, 78 Scollard St., Toronto, Ontario M5R 1G2 Canada. (416)926-1841. Executive Assistant: Marlee Novak. Produces material for theatrical, pay television, syndicated TV, etc. audience. Buys 3-5 scripts/year. Buys all rights. No previously produced material. No electronic or dot-matrix submissions. SASE. Reports in 2 months.
Needs: 35mm films. Submit complete script and resume. Pays in royalty or outright purchase.

DILLY INTERNATIONAL PRODUCTIONS, 1055 St. Paul Pl., Cincinnati OH 45202. (513)281-5900. Contact: Millard Segal. Produces material for a general TV audience. Buys all rights. Reports "immediately or takes option."
Needs: Magazine-format shows—visually interesting. "You must know the structure of TV scripting. Take college courses to learn before submitting." Submit treatment. Pays negotiable royalty; buys some scripts outright for a negotiable rate; "guaranteed deal for a series."
Tips: "There is not much money in writing for cable TV now, but in a couple of years there will be."

‡**DSM PRODUCERS**, Suite 1204, 161 W. 54th St., New York NY 10019. (212)245-0006. Produces material for consumer, trade and executive audiences. Works with 7-12 writers/year. Previously produced material OK. SASE. Reports in 1 month.
Needs: Phonograph records, tapes and cassettes. Currently interested in commercial material for all segments of the music industry i.e., record acts; commercials/film/radio-TV/industrial/trade. Submit cassette/video or completed script and resume. Pays in royalty or in accordance with Writers Guild standards.

□ **ETERNAL WORD TELEVISION NETWORK**, 5817 Old Leeds Rd., Birmingham AL 35210. (205)956-9537. Director of Programming: Dick Stephen. Produces material with a Catholic focus on everyday living. "Spiritual growth network which airs 2 hours Catholic and 2 hours family entertainment nightly. This network does not solicit funds on the air. Support comes from donations. Founded by Mother Angelica who has an active book ministry." Computer printout submissions acceptable; no dot-matrix. SASE. Reports in 4 months.
Needs: "We would like to see scripts in all forms and formats: drama, talk shows, panel discussions and original ideas." Half-hour programs or specials for cable television with uplifting, inspirational themes. Submit synopsis/outline of script. "May hold the script for up to 1 year."
Tips: "We want scripts that promote strong social values, or with religious themes."

□ **FILMCREATIONS, INC.**, 6627 Kentucky Dr., West Jordan UT 84084. (801)969-5798. Producer/Director: Robert N. Hatch. Produces material for feature release, TV—commercial, cable and public and educational. 50% freelance written. About half of scripts produced are unagented submissions. Works with 1-4 writers/year; 1-2 unpublished/unproduced writers. Submit synopsis/outline or complete script. Computer printout submissions acceptable; prefers letter-quality to dot-matrix. SASE. Reports in 3 months. Buys all or first rights.
Needs: "Material should be suitable for television special or pilot programming, or suitable for public television or educational film release. Drama is preferable." Buys scripts outright for $500-50,000. "All material is purchased on a submission basis."
Tips: "Submit stories, outlines or screenplays that explore the human condition and deal with meaningful life-changing events occurring in characters with whom a broad range of today's people can closely relate. The treatment or script should probe the human psyche and provide heretofore unexplored revelations concerning human motivations, behaviors and relationships. The ideas should be multi-dimensional and have repercussions of deep relevance to modern humankind. Such material should involve true-to-life action, characters and dialogue, and should develop strong lines of conflict pointing to a final crisis and climax fraught with emotion, insight and meaning."

GOLDSHOLL ASSOCIATES, 420 Frontage Rd., Northfield IL 60093. (312)446-8300. President: M. Goldsholl. Query. Buys all rights.
Needs: Scripts for industrial PR films. Also interested in original screenplays and short stories to be made into screenplays. "Describe your material before sending it. Do not send 'fantasy' scripts!" Produces sound filmstrips, 16mm and 35mm films, multimedia kits, tapes and cassettes, and 35mm slide sets. Pays 5-10% of budget.
Tips: "Write your ideas clearly. Know the visual world."

LIROL TV PRODUCTIONS, 6335 Homewood Ave., Los Angeles CA 90028. (213)467-8111. Contact: Sandra Murray. Computer printout submissions acceptable. 25% freelance written. Writers worked with "varies from year to year"; published/produced writers only. Buys all rights.
Needs: Nonfiction material, TV syndication, presentations for industrial clients and commercials. Submit synopsis/outline. Pays in accordance with Writers Guild standards.

‡□ **THE LITTLE RED FILMHOUSE**, Box 691083, Los Angeles CA 90069. (213)855-0241. Producer: Larry Klingman. Produces material for kindergarten through adult audience. 60% freelance written. 80% of scripts produced are unagented submissions. Buys 3 scripts/year. Buys all rights and makes work-for-hire assignments. "We purchase specific rights if we are adapting published work." Works with 2-3 unpublished/unproduced writers annually. No previously produced material. Computer printout submissions acceptable. SASE. Reports in 2 weeks on queries; 1 month on submissions. Free catalog.
Needs: Motion pictures, television shows/series. Produces fiction aimed at the following groups: 7-10-year-olds, 11-14-year-olds, young adults. "We are looking for good stories, humor and cross-cultural materials with the potential for serializing." Same requirements for cable TV. Query with brief (1-2 paragraphs) outline. Pay varies with the project.
Tips: "Spend more time with the end users to get a feel for the materials they are demanding. Become market driven! Please don't tell us what the market *should* want, give us what the market *is demanding*."

‡□ **LEE MAGID PRODUCTIONS**, Box 532, Malibu CA 90265. (213)858-7282. President: Lee Magid. Produces material for all markets, teenage-adult; commercial—even musicals. 50% freelance written. 80% of scripts produced are unagented submissions. Buys 20 scripts/year; works with 10 writers/year. Works with "many" unpublished/unproduced writers. Buys all rights. Previously produced material OK. Electronic submissions acceptable via VHS video or cassette/audio; requires hard copy also. SASE. Reports in 6 weeks.
Needs: Films, sound filmstrips, phonograph records, television shows/series, videotape presentations. Currently interested in film material, either for video (TV) or theatrical. "We deal with cable networks, producers, live-stage productions, etc. Market is still questionable as to monies to be paid." Submit synopsis/outline and resume. Pays in royalty, in outright purchase, in accordance with Writers Guild standards, or depending on author."
Tips: "We like comedy, real-life drama that all can relate to."

‡**MARGIE-LEE ENTERPRISES**, 56 W. 56th St., New York NY 10019. President: Lee Levinson. 25% freelance written. Two scripts produced annually are unagented submissions. Produces material for network television and motion picture audiences. Buys 6 scripts/year. Buys TV and motion picture rights. Works with 6 unpublished/unproduced writers annually. No computer printouts or disk submissions. SASE. Reports in 2 weeks on queries; 4 weeks on submissions.
Needs: Screenplays, treatments, outlines. Query first with samples, or submit synopsis/outline or completed script. "All synopses, outlines, treatments and scripts must be copyrighted or registered with Writers Guild of America. No material will be returned without SASE." Pays in accordance with Writers Guild standards. "All submissions must include a signed release. Will not accept certified or registered mail. No phone calls or deliveries."
Recent Production: *The Legend of Walks Far Woman* (winner of the Western Heritage Award).
Tips: "More and more stories are being produced about social themes and significant issues of the day. Some of these stories have a timeless quality to them and a universal theme which can reach out and touch audiences all over the world. People want to laugh, and they want to cry, and they do respond openly and honestly when writers write from the heart. We look for positive, upbeat, reaffirming themes about the human condition. No horror stories or violent stories."

‡□ **MEDIACOM DEVELOPMENT CORP.**, 4545-5N Industrial St., Simi Valley CA 93063. (213)552-9988 or (805)583-3108. Director/Program Development: Felix Girard. 80% freelance written. Buys 10-20 scripts annually from unpublished/unproduced writers. 50% of scripts produced are unagented submissions. Query with samples. Send queries to Box 1926, Simi Valley CA 93062. Computer printout submissions acceptable. SASE. Reports in 1 month. Buys all rights or first rights.
Needs: Produces charts; sound filmstrips; 16mm films; multimedia kits; overhead transparencies; tapes and cassettes; slides and videotape with programmed instructional print materials, broadcast and cable TV pro-

grams. Publishes software ("programmed instruction training courses"). Negotiates payment depending on project.
Tips: "Send short samples of work. Especially interested in flexibility to meet clients' demands, creativity in treatment of precise subject matter. We are looking for good, fresh projects (both special and series) for cable and pay TV markets. A trend in the audiovisual field that freelance writers should be aware of is the move toward more interactive video disk/computer CRT delivery of training materials for corporate markets."

METROMEDIA PRODUCERS CORP., 5746 Sunset Blvd., Hollywood CA 90028. (213)462-7111. Story Editor: Michael Brown. "We use a lot of material. All material must be represented by a literary agent or an established production company." Buys negotiable rights; "depends on the project." Previously produced material OK, "as we are also a distributing company." Reporting time "depends on volume. If it's something we really like, we may call the writer the day material is received."
Needs: Wide variety. TV. Query with samples and resume, or submit synopsis/outline or completed script. Pays in accordance with Writers Guild standards.
Recent Production: *Little Gloria, Happy At Last* (NBC mini-series).

□ **NICKELODEON, Warner Amex Satellite Entertainment**, 1133 Avenue of the Americas, New York NY 10036. (212)944-4250. Manager of Program Services and Commercial Clearance: Ann Sweeney. Produces material for age-specific audience aged 2 to 15. Now in 18 million homes. Buys negotiable rights. SASE. Reports in 1 month.
Needs: "Full channel children's programming for cable TV. Value filled, non-violent material desired." Submit resume and programming ideas (2-3 page explanations). Pays variable rate.

□ **PACE FILMS, INC.**, 411 E. 53rd Ave., New York NY 10022. (212)755-5486. President: R. Vanderbes. Produces material for a general theatrical audience. Buys all rights. Previously produced material OK. SASE. Reports in 2 month.
Needs: Theatrical motion pictures. Produces 35mm films, cable tapes and cassettes. Query with samples; submit synopsis/outline or completed script. Pays in accordance with Writers Guild standards.

PAULIST PRODUCTIONS, Box 1057, Pacific Palisades CA 90272. (213)454-0688. Contact: Story Department. "*Insight* is geared toward older teens and adults of all faiths. Our 'Capital Cities Family Specials' are geared towards senior high school students." Buys 15-20 ½-hour scripts/year. SASE. Reports in 1 month. Catalog for 10x14 SAE and 88¢ postage.
Needs: 16mm films and television shows. Submit completed script through agent only. "We are not interested in unsolicited manuscripts. *Insight* scripts are donated. Our teenage specials allow for small stipend to writer."
Tips: "Watch *Insight* and our 'Capital Cities Family Specials' enough so that you have a strong sense of the sort of material we are interested in producing." Looks for "wit, originality of theme and approach, an unsentimental, yet strong and hopefully positive manner of approaching subject matter. Intelligent, literate, un-cliche-ridden writing."

□ **RESTON REPERTORY TELEVISION THEATRE**, Box 2400, Reston VA 22090. (703)437-0764. Executive Producer: Sharon Cohen. Produces material for a cable audience. Buys 2-3 scripts/year. "We negotiate with playwright on the basis of a percentage of resulting sales; no outright purchase or rights." SASE. Reports in 3 weeks on queries; 4 months on submissions.
Needs: "Original scripts—no adaptations. Casts should be kept small and playing time may be 30 minutes to 2 hours. All scripts considered within the limits of good taste." Produces ¾" tapes and cassettes. Submit complete script. Pay "negotiable with playwright."
Tips: "We are especially looking for writers who understand how to use the medium of television to its best advantage."

BOB THOMAS PRODUCTIONS, INC., Box 1787, Wayne NJ 07470. (201)696-7500. New York Office: 60 E. 42nd St., New York NY 10165. (212)221-3602. President: Robert G. Thomas.
Needs: Scripts for "made-for-TV" films and *only* through registered agents.

□ **UNITED JEWISH APPEAL/FEDERATION OF JEWISH PHILANTHROPIES**, 130 E. 59th St., New York NY 10022. (212)980-1000. Public Relations: Art Portnow. Produces material for people interested in Jewish topics and a Jewish audience. 30% freelance written. All scripts produced are unagented submissions. Buys 4 TV ideas and 2-3 scripts/year. Buys negotiable rights. Previously produced material OK. Computer printout and disk submissions acceptable; prefers letter-quality to dot-matrix printouts. Reports in 1 month.
Needs: Audiovisual materials for group showing, scripts for commercial and cable TV and radio programs. "Writer must be well-versed in Judaic tradition and customs." Produces slides/sound shows, video, radio, films. Query with sample or resume and sample of script from a completed program. Does not return samples. Buys scripts outright for $100-500; "varies with length and requirement of the script."

Tips: "Unique ideas are welcome here. New angles on holidays are always of interest. Additional per diem freelance writing assignments for news release work and the like is also available."

UNITED PRODUCTIONS LIMITED, Box 5756, Sherman Oaks CA 91413-5756. Contact: Patrick Roberts. Buys "several" scripts/year.
Needs: Produces 35mm films and TV. 75% freelance written. 75% of scripts produced are unagented submissions. Not interested in plays, period pieces, musicals. "Interested in mostly location shootings. Keep budget in mind!" Works with 15-20 unpublished/unproduced writers annually. Submit synopsis or complete script. Computer printout submissions acceptable; no dot-matrix. "No certified or registered mail will be accepted." Pays negotiable royalty.
Tips: "My advice to novice scriptwriters is to concentrate on content. Don't worry about camera angles, scene numbers, etc. The director will take care of that. Just give me a good story and a strong believable character—one that the reader will immediately 'care' for."

WORLD WIDE PICTURES, 2520 W. Olive, Burbank CA 91505. (213)843-1300. Executive Producer: Bill Brown. Produces material for a Christian audience. Produces 2-3 documentaries/year and 1 feature film every other year. Buys first rights. SASE. Reports in 1 month.
Needs: Religious material, church history, Biblical subjects, prophecy, evangelistic topics, Christian living material. Produces documentaries for TV, feature films for theater and church. Submit treatment. Pays in negotiable outright purchase.
Tips: Worldwide Pictures is a branch of the Billy Graham Evangelistic Association. Stories must be consistent with Dr. Graham's theology. "We do not usually select material sent on submission but assign projects to freelance writers."

Gag Writing

What do you get when you cross a store manager (who writes gags in his free time) with a cartoonist? Cartoons, you say?

The first question may be time-worn, but collaboration between cartoonists and gag writers and between comedians and gag writers happens often. For most of them, it means working weekends and evenings; few make a living in the *gag* field.

Gag writers have told us how much they rely on *Writer's Market* to help them find gag markets. That's why this year we conducted a national search for cartoonists, comedians, and syndicates which buy freelance gags. Our work led to first-time listings for comedian Joan Rivers and well-known cartoonists Dave Gerard, Randy "Harris" Jay Glasbergen, Rex May, and others. (Please note, however, since this section did not run in *Writer's Market* last year, in a sense *all* the gag writing listings are new and we have not marked any with a ‡ symbol.)

Cartoonists and comedians may appear easy-going, but don't think you can peddle your second-rate gags to them. Most buyers are very selective, and many will hold gags up to a year, until they find the perfect market for them.

The first step in writing gags is to decide what audience and medium you're aiming for. Comedians, for example, need one-liners (that they can enhance with the *right* facial expressions and tone of voice).

Cartoonists need visual gags; they can't use gags suited for night-club monologues. "I prefer understated or exaggerated gags where the gag itself is not funny unless and until the reader sees the picture—a marriage of words and drawing—that appeals to a broad audience," says one cartoonist.

To write gags for a cartoonist, you need not be an artist. A submission does not need an elaborate drawing or a paragraph explaining the gag *if* that gag is truly funny, points out one cartoonist. Cartoonists like to illustrate a *funny* gagline without seeing someone else's drawing of it. In fact, a gag on a 3x5 card that says, "Man says to woman: . . . (the gag)," is sufficient.

Captions—if used—should be simple and fairly universal. You can get more mileage out of a gag by initially directing it toward a specific audience (a farm journal, for example) and altering it somewhat for a more general market, such as a family magazine.

Be brief—and amusing. Go for the big laugh—and not one that has been done so many times it belongs in the early talkies.

Next time you're browsing the library or bookstore, look for cartoonists' work in books and magazines. Get a feel for their styles. Consult their requirements in *WM* and write accordingly.

Submit gags on 3x5 cards or slips, one per card. Include an identification number on the upper left-hand corner, and type your name and address on the back of the card. You must also include a self-addressed, stamped envelope any time you send material to a cartoonist. Submitting 10-20 gags at one time is standard.

Good gags will prompt people to laugh at—and learn about—themselves and everyday life. Insulting people's religions and nationalities doesn't work, says one gag writer. Instead, most cartoonists and comedians want timely gags focusing on audiences' newest crazes.

"You change with the times. . .beatniks gave way to hippies, hippies gave way to punkers; life goes on," says one cartoonist. "Cartoons must mirror the times."

And, points out another gag buyer, ". . . they must deal with those things that remain constant—taxes, courts, family, schools, church."

As for money matters, gag writers are paid after the cartoonist receives a check from the publication. Magazines may pay anywhere from $10 to about $300 per cartoon. The writer usually earns 25% commission on the selling price; 50% if the cartoonist submits a rough sketch and sells only the writer's idea, not the finished cartoon, to a publisher.

One-liners for comedians may merit $10. A few entertainers have reputations for paying more; some pay less.

To expand the number of markets you sell to, consider other outlets. Magazines buy short humor, anecdotes and jokes. Greeting card publishers need humorous verses. Syndicates will review cartoons with gags. And don't overlook local outlets. The hometown newspaper may want to editorialize on recent city council actions with a short, to-the-point caption and drawing. Local stand-up comedians may need rousing one-liners.

Writing and marketing gags is serious work. In fact, writers should ask themselves, "Do I think writing humor is easier or less important than other types of writing?" suggests one humor magazine editor.

If the answer is "yes," then you shouldn't write for that editor—or any cartoonist or comedian.

PAUL M. ARCHETKO, Box 90631, Rochester NY 14609. (716)467-1046. Began selling cartoons in 1980. Holds 100 gags/year. Sells to men's publications. Recently sold material to *Hustler*, *Swank*, *Harvey*, *Easyrider*, *Geneses*, *Velvet* and *High Society*. Works with 4-6 writers annually. Submit gags on 3x5 slips. Reports in 1 week. Sells cartoons for $75-150. Pays 25% commission. SASE.
Needs: "I deal only in men, girlie magazines and am only interested in this type of gag. Off-the-wall, unusual, short captions do the best; no caption, highly visual do better. Will look at hardcore sex, biker, fetish material etc. Anti-religious gags do nothing for me; no market for generals etc. Anything from mild to rough sex or related is fine. Color application is important; I do quite a bit of it."
Tips: "The shorter the gag the better; get to the point. Drop the 'stage setting' and leave it to the cartoonist. Gags must be funny, highly visual, and unusual or unique in that I wouldn't have thought of it myself. Include 'rejection slip' with gags."

EDGAR ARGO, 6504 Langdale Rd., Baltimore MD 21237. Holds 500 gags/year. Sells to a wide range of magazines, newspapers, etc. "Creatively I'm very liberal—I will consider *anything* if there is a market for it." Recently sold to *Penthouse*, *Omni*, *Swank*, *Stag*, *Easyriders*, etc. "I've just begun to concentrate on generals and trades." Submit gags on 3x5 cards. Rough sketch with caption preferred. (Stick figures OK). No limit on number of gags submitted. "Average I receive is 10-20." Reports in 1 week. Pays 25% commission or standard rate at the time. SASE.
Needs: "I work very fast and in a variety of styles. I will illustrate any gag that I think is *funny* and *salable*. There are *no* restrictions. No tired old cliches, no puns. I am in the process of developing 2 comic strips. I will consider any new ideas for humorous strips. I will provide talented writers with information on the strips once contact is made—if I like their work."
Tips: "Typing is not necessary, but the gags must be legible. I won't struggle to read them. I want economy of words. I prefer gags with rough sketches. (This saves the writer a lot of words.) Must have SASE."

EDOUARD BLAIS, 2704 Parkview Blvd., Minneapolis MN 55422. (612)588-5249. Began selling cartoons in 1981. Holds 250 gags/year. Sells to mens, sports, fitness, health, education, family, outdoor, camping and fishing publications. Recently sold material to *Running and Fitness*, *Gallery*, *Harvey*, *Iron Horse*, and *Easyriders*. Submit gags on 3x5 slips; 10-12 in one batch. Reports in 1 week. Sells cartoons for $10-75. Pays 25% commission. SASE.
Needs: Erotic, sports, health, fitness, education, family, outdoor, camping, and fishing gags, etc. No "science or computer gags or 'in' type humor such as *New Yorker* uses." Looks for sight gags—no captions or minimum amount of words.
Tips: "Gag writers should be aware of what's going on in all phases of society, the style of language being used, and new development (like fast food, microwave, G-spot, etc.). I am relatively new to cartooning (and will complete my second year this March) my 'sell' ratio isn't that good, but I am making progress. Therefore, I feel I cannot offer a writer too much of a guarantee that I will be able to sell his ideas."

DAN BORDERS, 191 Alton Rd., Galloway OH 43119. (614)878-3528. Began selling cartoons in 1982. Holds 35 gags/year. Sells to computer magazines of all kinds, trade journals, many general interest and electronic gags. Recently sold material to *Computer World*, *Info World*, *Dr. Dobb's Journal*, *Radio-Electronics* and *Reader's Digest*. Works with 5 writers annually. Buys 50% of the gags received from freelance writers. Submit gags on 3x5 cards or slips. Submit 15 gags in one batch. Reports in 2 weeks. Sells cartoons for $10-35. Pays 25% commission. SASE.
Needs: Electronics and computer gags, and environment, family and angel gags. No "girlie gags." Looks for humorists with dry humor.

Tips: "Many computer magazines are buying computer cartoons. Also electronic 'toons' are selling well. I am always ready to see good, well-thought-out ideas."

HARVEY BOSCH, 7925 Densmore N., Seattle WA 98103. (206)525-6438. Holds 200-300 gags/year. Works with 25-50 gagwriters/year. Sells to general, male, family and women's magazines. Has sold to *National Enquirer*, *Saturday Evening Post*, *Rotarian*, King Features, *New Woman*, *Forum* and *American Legion*. Submit on 3x5 slips, 20-40 gags in one batch. Reports in 2 days. Pays 25% commission. SASE.
Needs: Mostly male gags. General, family and women's gags also. "I will look at anything."
Recent Cartoon: Emergency ward nurse to patient: "It may be a few minutes . . . would you like to wait in the bar?" (Rex Stein, gagwriter).
Tips: "It is important to keep the description short. Many gagwriters turn the description into a short story. By the time the cartoonist gets done reading it and the other hundred or so he receives a day he has no time for cartooning."

BILL BOYNANSKY, Apt. 13/20, Ansonia Hotel, 2109 Broadway, New York NY 10023. (212)870-5238, "Please phone after 2 pm." Works with 35-60 gagwriters/year. Holds over 1,000 gags/year; sells between 800-900 cartoons/year. Submit 15-20 gags at one time. Reports in 3 days to 2 months. Pays "25% for regular, 35% for captionless; all others—regular payment." SASE.
Needs: General, male, female, sexy, girlie, family, children's, adventure and medical. "No overdone girlie gags, overdone family gags, TV, parking the car, woman nagging husband, etc. Prefer to see captionless gag ideas on all subject matters, but no beginners; only those who know their business. I prefer to deal with cartoonists by letter or phone because it saves me time."
Recent Cartoon: Scene: Man (in great anger) breaking up a TV set with a baseball bat: "I'm sick of this damn violence—on T.V.!!!"

ASHLEIGH BRILLIANT, 117 W. Valerio St., Santa Barbara CA 93101. Sold about 315 cartoons last year. Sells regularly to Tribune Media Services Inc. Reports in 2 weeks. Pays $20.
Needs: "My work is so different from that of any other cartoonist that it must be carefully studied before any gags are submitted. Any interested writer not completely familiar with my work should first send $1 for my catalog of 1,000 copyrighted examples. Otherwise, their time and mine will be wasted."
Recent Cartoon: "I have seen the future: Go back!"

LEONARD BRUCE, AKA "LEO", 22A Brianfield Cove, Jackson TN 38305. (901)668-1205. Holds 20 gags/month. Sells to newspapers, charity publications, space publications, science fiction and science fiction movie magazines, comic book publications and animal care publications. Recently sold material to *Starlog*, *Comics Collector*, *Space Age Times*, *Kind Magazine*, *World Wildlife Newsletter* and *Shelter Sense Magazine*. Submit gags on 3x5 cards. Submit 12 gags in one batch. Reports in 2 weeks. Pays 10% commission. SASE.
Needs: Looking for gags on science fiction movie themes, comic book hero themes, themes on space travel, UFOs, life on other planets, "aliens" trying to cope with our world. Also a Berry's World theme; one guy in crazy situations. No political, foreign affairs or white collar themes. Will consider gags for cartoon strips: Leotoons (science fiction "alien" themes); Fred (space exploration themes); and It's a Mad World (crazy situations in our insane world). Looks for offbeat gags, "taking normal situations and turning them into 'sight gags' or word gags. As an example: Berry's World or Herman gag themes."
Tips: "Gagwriters should be aware that gags *have* to be very funny or the whole cartoon doesn't work or sell. The gag is the main reason a cartoon sells nowadays."

FORD BUTTON, 3398 Chili Ave., Rochester NY 14624. (716)889-3045. Holds 75-100 gags/year. Sells to general interest, education and fraternal publications, newspapers and book publishers. Recently sold material to *Good Housekeeping*, *National Enquirer*, *School Board News*, *Saturday Review* and *Phi Delta Kappan*. Submit gags on 3x5 cards or 3x5 slips. Submit 12-15 gags in one batch. Reports in 1 week. Pays 30% commission; 50% on reprints. SASE.
Needs: "I am constantly looking for fresh and funny situations about home, kids and family. I also am in need of gags slanted toward education. Overworked situations here are the report card and 'old fashioned' school teacher. I look for inside stuff—administration jargon, curriculum development spoof, sacred cows in decision making and school board problems with budget and discipline. No pornography. I am not a girlie cartoonist. Most of my work is slanted toward everyday situations that aren't cliche-ridden—kangaroo pouch mother, marriage counselor and psychiatrist, desert island, cannibal pot, water cooler, sugar daddy, and 'we can't go on meeting like this' get quick rejection. I like Herman situations. If at all possible I like action in the picture. I want something I can draw about. Illustrated jokes have their place, but the gag line must be hilarious."
Tips: "All I ask is correct punctuation and a complete sentence. There must be a complete thought. Writers should be aware of a trend in gagwriting toward positive thinking! Let's get some joy back into humor! Let's laugh and like it. Heavy gruesome humor is tiresome."

W.J. CHAMBERS, Apt. 1, 416 W. Division, Villa Park IL 60181. Holds 400 gags/year. Sells to farm and general interest magazines. Works with 5 writers annually. Buys 50% of the gags received from freelance writers. Submit gags on 3x5 cards or slips, 12 in one batch. Reports in 1 week. Sells cartoons for $10-50. Pays 25% commission. SASE.
Needs: Farm and general.

THOMAS W. DAVIE, 28815 4th Place S, Redondo WA 98054. Buys 100 gags/year. Works with 15-20 gagwriters/year. Has sold to *Medical Economics*, *Sports Afield*, King Features, *Chevron USA*, *Rotarian*, *Saturday Evening Post*, *Ladies' Home Journal*, *Playgirl* and *Boys' Life*. Gags should be typed on 3x5 slips. Prefers batches of 5-25. Pays 25% commission. Reports in 1 month. SASE. No IRC.
Needs: General gags, medicals, mild girlies, sports (hunting and fishing), business and travel gags. No pornography.
Recent Cartoon: Scene: old man with long beard on desert island shakes hands with seaplane pilot. Caption: "I never would have guessed I'd be rescued by you guys! Which one are you . . . Orville or Wilbur?" (Steven Sauter, gagwriter).
Tips: "I'm often overstocked—please don't flood me with gags."

ED DAVIS, 69 Wind Whisper Court, The Woodlands TX 77380. (713)363-9264. Holds 30 gags/year. Sells to men's, women's, management and general publications. Recently sold material to *Easy Rider*, *Hustler*, *National Enquirer*, *Graphic Arts Monthly* and *Printer's News*. Submit gags by any method. Submit reasonable number of gags; no limit. Reports in 5 days. Pays 25% commission; "will work out better terms for writers in sync with my humor." SASE.
Needs: "Prefers any gag to deal with American themes. I sell more erotic material than anything. Also need management/business, printing/graphic arts, cowboy/western, sports, animals, working women (cosmopolitan) and general material. I have markets for any *good* material."
Tips: Looks for "professionalism in material submitted for consideration."

LEE DeGROOT, Box 115, Ambler PA 19002. Pays 25% on sales.
Needs: Interested in receiving studio greeting card ideas. "I draw up each idea in color before submitting to greeting card publishers, therefore, giving the editors a chance to visualize the idea as it would appear when printed . . . and thus increasing enormously the chances of selling the idea." Please enclose SASE.

MIGUEL "MIKE" ESPARZA, 17157 E. Milan Circle, Aurora CO 80013. (303)693-9296. Holds 200 gags/year. Works with 20 gagwriters/year. Has sold to both men's and women's publications, general interest magazines and some trade journals. Buys 4% of the gags received from freelance writers. Submit on 3x5 cards, 12 or more gags in one batch. Sells cartoons for $15-70. Reports in 2 weeks. Pays 25% commission. SASE.
Needs: "Material for markets such as *Wall Street Journal*. Also gags for *National Enquirer*." Holds gags for family, girlie and general magazines. Willing to consider any material in good taste.
Tips: "I prefer visual gags that are easily understood. Gaglines without visual support are not held."

FEATURE ASSOCIATES, Apt. 16, 520 Canal St., San Rafael CA 94901. (415)459-6190. "We usually put a gag or writer together with an illustrator or cartoonist for team cartooning and team work. Though we've less need for what we call library material than ever before, we continue to encourage submissions for syndication (distribution) on a panel and package basis. In this way we are secondary market. Most recent sales are to *Fresno Bee*; other material and periodicals include business magazines and regional magazines, certain city magazines, and many special markets including, of course, newspapers." Submit gags on 3x5 cards. "We like to get a letter or a postcard to see how the artist works." Send gags with art only, "unless you seek an artist. In the event they are gags alone, we are an unlikely market." Reports in 6 months or sooner. Pays 50% commission. "Usually we don't guarantee a return; send nothing that must be returned."
Needs: "We have not recently received material that requires a gag writer, nor gags. We have received some illustrated material that might require a short synopsis of a humorous nature. These are usually the kind of thing like story line art without the words."
Tips: "These days, as most days, we're concerned with who owns the copyright and if by origination the gag does work. Funny stuff is what we like."

JO-ANN FEISTNER, 1502 E. Cheery Lynn, Phoenix AZ 85014. (602)274-1743. Began selling cartoons in 1972. Holds 75 gags/year. Sells to women's publications and general interest magazines. Recently sold material to local publications. Works with 6 writers annually. Buys 10% of the gags received from freelance writers. Submit gags on 3x5 cards or slips. Submit 12-24 gags in one batch. Reports in 7-10 days. Sells cartoons for $20-200. Pays 25% commission. SASE.
Needs: General gags suitable for family magazines.

DAVE GERARD, Box 692, Crawfordsville IN 47933. (317)362-3373. Holds 200 gags/year. Does Citizen Smith (daily syndicated newspaper panel—Register and Tribune Syndicate, Inc.) and 30-40 freelance cartoons per month for magazines and periodicals. Recently sold material to *National Enquirer*, *Friends*, *D.A.C. News*, *Golf Digest*, *Wall Street Journal*, *Good Life*, *Medical Economics*, and King Features' Laff-A-Day. Works with 8-10 writers annually. Submit gags on 3x5 cards; 10 in one batch. Reports in 2 weeks. Sells cartoons for $50-300. Pays 25% commission; $7.50 flat rate for Citizen Smith gags. SASE.
Needs: General interest and sports, business, family and upbeat gags on pertinent and timely topics, like taxes, inflation, computers, etc. No "prisoners hanging on wall, kings and queens, talking animals, or put-down humor. I will be frank if material is not what I like. No erotic material." Citizen Smith proof sheet available upon request if feature is unfamiliar.
Tips: "I like good sight gag material and short captions; also no-captions gags. Writers should be aware that subject matter changes along with the lifestyles of Americans, which, of course, change yearly. Gagwriting is stuck, in many cases, on old material."

RANDY JAY GLASBERGEN/a.k.a. "Harris" for The Better Half, Box 687, Earlville NY 13332. Began selling cartoons in 1972. Has sold more than 6,000 cartoons. Holds variable number of gags. Sells to popular magazines worldwide (25 countries), women's magazines, men's magazines, family, general interest, children's. Cartoons appear in 200 daily and Sunday newspapers. Also sells material for greeting cards, books and other special projects. Recently sold material to *New Woman*, *The Wall Street Journal*, Hallmark Cards, *National Enquirer*, *Saturday Evening Post*, *Woman's World*, *Penthouse*, *Playgirl* and *Good Housekeeping*. Submit gags on 3x5 cards or slips. (They must be typed or printed clearly.) Submit 10-20 gags in one batch. Reports in 2 days. Sells cartoons for $15-300. Pays 25% commission. "I occasionally pay $10 for gags used in *The Better Half* which I write and draw under the pseudonym "Harris." I write 11 gags per week for the panel which appears in about 200 papers daily and Sunday. SASE.
Needs: Anything suitable for active cartoon-buying publication. "I sell to them all (except small trade journals). Clever family, kid, animal, erotic, off-beat, sophisticated, silly—I consider them all. I would like to see more gags suitable for publications like *New Woman*, one of my very best markets, but with a difficult slant."
Tips: "Don't type up the first thing that pops into your head and then call yourself a gagwriter. The gag your friends laugh at will probably bomb with a cartoonist. This is a highly competitive business—cartoonists are fussy and editors are even fussier. Be original and unique. No matter what slant you're writing, always try to comment on human behavior. People like to read about people. I'm more apt to take commentary than 'pie in the face' humor. I'm also looking for people who can write greeting cards."

CHARLES HENDRICK JR., Old Fort Ave., Kennebunkport ME 04046. (207)967-4412. Buys several gags/year; sold 50-60 cartoons last year. Works with 5-6 gagwriters/year. Sells to newspapers, magazines and local markets. Submit 8 gags at a time. Sells cartoons for $25-400. Pays 50% net of commission or negotiates commission. Reports in 10-30 days. SASE.
Needs: General family, trade (hotel, motel, general, travel, vacationers). Safe travel ideas—any vehicle. Gags must be clean; no lewd sex. Mild sex OK.
Recent Cartoon: Laughing Eskimo ladies sitting inside refrigerator. Frantic salesman says "but ladies, that is *not* a mobile home!"

WAYNE HOGAN, P.O. Box 842, Cookeville TN 38503. Began selling cartoons in 1982. Holds 200 gags/year. Sells to general interest magazines, trade/professional journals and newspapers. Recently sold material to *Lone Star* (magazine), *Herald-Citizen* (newspaper), *Quarterly Journal of Ideology*, and *Journal of Irreproducible Results*. Submit gags on sheets of white typing paper; 10-15 in one batch. Reports in 2 weeks. Pays 25% of each paid use of cartooned gag. SASE.
Needs: General gags, social science-related gags, academic-related gags, and "mostly any sort of understated humor relating to mundane affairs of life." No "gallows/black" humor or erotica.
Recent Cartoon: Patty Lou, a single-panel cartoon strip "for which I'll consider gags depicting the female character associated with everyday, mundane activities/events/phenomena."
Tips: "I look for conceptually clever and to-the-point gags."

ELLSWORTH E. JACKSON, 19304 Revere, Detroit MI 48234. (313)893-0820. Began selling cartoons in 1981. Holds 50-100 gags/year. Sells to general interest magazines, trade journals, hard-core girlie magazines, and "where ever I can make a sale." Recently sold material to *Cartoon Carnival*, *Personnel Journal*, *Referee*, *Eros*, *Harvey*, *Soft Key*, *Physician and Patient*, *Easyrider* and *Baltimore Bulletin*. Works with 10-12 writers annually. Submit gags on 3x5 cards or slips; 10-15 in one batch. Reports in 2 days. Sells cartoons for $15-50. Pays 25% commission. SASE.
Needs: "I'm open from religious gags to hard-core girlies. My best success is with personnel-related gags,

computers, sport officiating (show sports officials in *positive* light), singles living, hard-core girlies and medical gags. No farm gags and no excremental stuff for the girlie magazines. No *offensive* gags on being black or Catholic."

Tips: "I look for succinct captions; no cartoonist likes typing or writing long captions. I especially like good captionless gags (who doesn't?). Writers should get a working knowledge of computers and/or preventive medicine and try to work a computer theme or medicine theme into anything from religion to hard-core girlies. I am eager to correspond with other black gag writers and/or cartoonists. If I reject you three times in a row without a hold, we're probably wasting each other's time."

FRED ("FREJAC") JACKSON III, 70 Illinois, Pontiac MI 48053. Holds 150 gags/year. Sells to girlie magazines, computer magazines, general interest magazines, religious publications, business publications, women's publications, children's magazines, farm magazines. Has sold to *Ahoy, Woman's World, Radio-Electronics, Computerworld, Wallace's Farmer, Creative Computing*, and others. Works with 100 writers annually. Buys 20% of the gags received from freelance writers. Submit gags on 3x5 slips. Reports in 1 month. Sells cartoons for $10-100. Pays 25-35% commission; 35% for captionless and major market sales. SASE. "I hold unsold gags indefinitely until sold."

Needs: Girlie (both X-rated and softcore), computer, office, general, business, humor through youth, animals, family, farm, video game, captionless, cable and pay TV, liberated woman, the sciences, electronics gags. "No old, tired gags, please. I've seen them all before."

Tips: "I need a constant supply of computer, girlie, and humor through family gags. I look for gags that are very visual, clever sight gags. I like offbeat, off-the-wall humor—wild and wacky stuff. Go crazy. The wilder, the better. I like the use of fantasy elements in standard situations."

JOHN E. KARP, 3305 S. 61st Court, Cicero IL 60650. (312)652-9787. Holds 50 gags/year. Sells to model railroad magazines, business and office magazines, some general interest magazines such as Charlton Publications, fillers for publication, *Model Railroader, Instant Printer*. Works with 3 writers annually. Submit on 3x5 cards or slips. Submit 20 gags/batch. Reports in 1 week. Sells cartoons for $10-35. Pays 30% commission. SASE.

Needs: Model railroad, office and business, instant printing. "I have more erotic gags than I can sell. Also, I am doing mostly model railroad cartoons."

REAMER KELLER, 4500 S. Ocean Blvd., Palm Beach FL 33480. (305)582-2436.
Needs: Prefers general and visual gags. Pays $25.

MILO KINN, 1413 SW Cambridge St., Seattle WA 98106. Holds approximately 200 gags/year; sells 100-200 cartoons/year. Has sold to *Medical Economics, Computerworld, Infoworld, Review of the News, Charlton* and many farm publications and trade journals, etc. Works with 8-10 writers annually. Buys 25% of the gags received from freelance writers. Sells cartoons for $15-100 "and up on occasion." Pays 25% commission. SASE.

Needs: Medical, computer, dental, farm, male slant, girlie, woman, captionless, adventure and family gags. Sells girlie, farm, medical, office and general cartoons.

Tips: "The cartoon should be a funny picture or situation—not just 2 people talking. The gag should be a single caption-(not 'he' or 'she')—not just a joke, but a 'comic picture'! Try to slant to certain fields but must also fit 'general' category (not too technical) so they can go to more markets."

FRANK LENGEL, Box 890, Leesville SC 29070. (803)532-3259. Holds 100 gags/year. Sells to trade journals, general interest and men's magazines. Recent sales to *Saturday Evening Post, Accent on Living, Managing, National Enquirer, Hustler* and *Good Housekeeping*. Works with 3-4 writers annually "but will work with more." Buys 5% of the gags received from freelance writers. Submit on 3x5 slips in batches of 15-20. But "also would look at a gag submitted on a brown paper bag if it's a gem!" Reports in 1 week. Pays 33⅓% commission "upon receipt of my check from the publication." SASE. Submit seasonal material 4-6 months in advance.

Needs: General interest, family, business, handicapped people, religious. "I will look at almost anything if it is fresh and funny." Rarely considers word-play or multi-panel cartoons.

Tips: "My subject matter needs have remained relatively constant in the sense that I like family, religion, etc., material. Of a secondary nature, I have noticed a slight increase in sales in subjects dealing with the family in hi-tech (computers), gardening and home repair. The gagwriter mirrors society in a creative way. As society changes, gags change; however, they must deal with those things that remain constant, i.e., taxes, courts, family, schools, church, etc. I prefer understated or exaggerated gags where the gag itself is not funny unless and until the reader sees the picture—a marriage of words and drawing—that appeals to a broad audience."

LO LINKERT, 1333 Vivian Pl., Port Coquitlam, British Columbia V3C 2T9 Canada. Has sold to most major markets. Works with 20-25 gagwriters/year. Prefers batches of 10-15 gags. Returns rejected material in 1 week. Enclose SAE and 35¢ US postage. Sells cartoons for $50-600. Pays 25% commission.
Needs: Clean, general, topical, medical, family, office, outdoors gags; captionless, pro woman sophisticated ideas. "Make sure your stuff is funny. No spreads." Wants "action gags—not two people saying something funny. No puns, dirty sex, drugs, drunks, racial or handicapped."

LOS ANGELES TIMES SYNDICATE, 218 S. Spring St., Los Angeles CA 90012. (800)528-4637. "We don't hold gags; we contract with cartoonists to produce cartoons, and unless they're unacceptable to newspapers, we use all of them." Sells to newspapers (comics and editorial pages) and newspaper Sunday magazines. Recently sold to major newspapers. Submit photocopies of 24 daily strips and 4 Sundays. Reports in 3 months. SASE.
Needs: "We are looking for comic strips, panels and political cartoons. We especially need strips that are funny, well-drawn, and have interesting characters whom readers will love. Also, the work should be original (no ripoffs of strips or panels already in existence). We need cartoonists who can meet regular and frequent deadlines and are very prolific (a strip cartoonist will produce 52 Sunday strips and well over 300 daily strips per year). On strips and panels, since we sell to newspapers read by entire families, be careful with sex, booze gags, graphic or grotesque violence and so on. Politics is OK if you don't get strident or overdo it. (One gag making fun of Ronald Reagan every month is fine, but five a week gets monotonous.) On political cartoons, the market is very competitive; you must have your own voice, gag sense, drawing style, etc., or you could be lost in ghe crowd." Looks for "freshness, economy and lovable characters. Anything that's been overdone will not sell well. Strips are printed 6⁷/₁₆x2", panels 3¹/₈x4", political cartoons only slightly larger. Anything with too many words or details will have a hard time being reproduced."
Tips: "Too many writers are too eager to please, so their work becomes bland, over-affable, soft and dull. They copy what seems to sell. Remember, there was not much like Garfield on the market before that strip started; the same is true of Doonesbury, Peanuts, or many other top strips. Although it's bad to be so wild that the strip is incomprehensible or offensive, being boring is much, much worse. We're very open to hearing from cartoonists. Our phone number is toll free. To speak to the comics editor, call between 8 a.m. and 6 p.m. Pacific time and ask for David Seidman (pronounced Seedman), extension 5198. Also, we only match writers with artists or vice versa; usually we like cartoonists to be able to give us a nearly finished product."

ART McCOURT, Box 210346, Dallas TX 75211. (214)339-6865. Began selling cartoons in 1950. Sells 700 cartoons/year to general/family, medical, farm and male magazines. Recently sold material to *Ford Times*, *Furrow*, *Agway Coop*, *Medical Management*, McNaught Syndicate, *National Enquirer*, *American Legion* and King Features. Works with 12 writers annually. Buys 25% of the gags received from freelance writers. Submit 15-20 gags at one time on 3x5 cards or slips. Reports in 2 days. Sells cartoons for $15-340. Pays 25% commission. SASE.
Needs: Family/general, medical (no gripes about doctors' bills), male and farm gags. "Something unique and up-to-date." No "crowds, ghouls, TV, mothers-in-law, talking animals or desert islands."
Recent Cartoon: Female stork nagging her husband who has put human baby in the nest: "How many times I gotta tell ya not to bring your work home with you?"
Tips: "I look for original, crisp wordage and fresh approach with minimal descriptions. Don't just send a punchline that has no background. Read the newspapers; be topical. Writers shouldn't be impatient; gags can make the rounds for several years."

JOE McKEEVER, Box 829, Columbus MS 39701. Began selling cartoons in 1971. Holds 100 gags/year. Sells to religion pages of newspapers and religious newspapers and magazines. Recently sold material to *Leadership*, *Pulpit Helps*, Copley News Service and many denominational publications. Submit gags on 8½x11 pieces of paper; 3-4 in one batch. Reports in 1 week. Makes outright purchase of $10. SASE.
Needs: Humorous religious situations involving pastors, people in the pews and committee members or anything that comments on our culture—television watching, marital relations, etc. "Don't get too involved in gags, the simpler the better."
Recent Cartoon: "Pews" (syndicated religious cartoon panel sold by Copley News Service).
Tips: "I look for humor that fits all people of various religious denominations, that offends no one and that may have a moral to it."

ROBERT MAKINSON, GPO Box 3341, Brooklyn NY 11202. (212)855-5057. Began buying gags in 1979; bought 150 least year. "I publish *Latest Jokes* and *Jokes by Contributors*. Jokes are used by comedians, disc jockeys and public speakers." Submit gags on 3x5 slips in batches of 10-20. Reports in 2 weeks. Makes outright purchase of $1/joke. "SASE should always be included."
Needs: "We want jokes that relate to current trends but which do *not* mention the names of current famous personalities. I'll look at anything. Keep practicing and submitting."

Tips: "There's a trend toward bad taste in humor. A writer can go along with the trend, or he can try to swing back toward more healthy humor."

MASTERS AGENCY, Box 427, Capitola CA 95010. (408)688-8396. Director: George Crenshaw. Buys 200+ gags/year. Sells to magazines, newsletters, trade journals, house organs and newspapers worldwide. Submit sketched or finished roughs only. Submit 12-24 gags in one batch. "Don't overwhelm us." Reports in 1 week. Pays $10-15. SASE.
Needs: Banking, hospital, Christmas/holidays, industrial safety, automation/computers, farm and factory gags. " 'Oldies' are OK with us if they're funny, but nothing prior to 1960, as humor then is now obsolete. We will also pay $25-30 for *finished roughs*. Especially interested in material of this type."
Tips: "We hope we can use finished roughs as is, but if quality is under-par and we have to re-draw, then rate is minimum of $10-15. We will also purchase already published clips on above outlined topics or *any* other topics, paying $10-15 each on fast acceptance."

ENRIQUE BRAXTON MAY, 511 Washington St., Westfield NJ 07090. (201)232-4473. Submit gags on 3x5 slips. Reports in several months. Pays 25% commission.
Needs: "As a starting cartoonist I'm interested in all sorts of gags, including soccer gags and sports gags for children. Also, I'm interested in ideas for short films and possibly children's stories for creating book/film ideas."
Tips: "I like visual gags that move. I am producing my own short animated films and would like to develop a children's book/film/song package to publish overseas."

REX F. MAY (BALOO), Box 2239, West Lafayette IN 47906. (812)533-1786. Began selling cartoons in 1975. Holds 500 gags/year. Sells to general interest and some girlie magazines. Recently sold material to *Good Housekeeping*, *National Enquirer*, *Hustler*, *Cavalier*, *Woman's World*, *Wall Street Journal*, King Features, *Medical Economics*, *Saturday Evening Post*, *Easyriders*, *Datamation*, *Leadership*, *New Woman*, *Changing Times* and *Christian Science Monitor*. Submit gags on 3x5 slips; no more than 100 in a batch. Reports in 2 weeks. Pays 25% commission. SASE.
Needs: "I don't need many gags. A top gagwriter myself, I write 15,000 gags a year for many top cartoonists. I still use gags by others if they fit my style. You probably should look my style over before you submit. I don't do much background or use many props. It's a very simple style. What I want is general-to-wierd material. I sell weird non-girlie stuff to the girlie magazines, so don't send standard girlies. Simplicity and shortness of caption are the way to go.
Tips: "Writers should be mindful of a tendency to overdescribe. ('A woman sitting in an easy chair to husband sitting in another chair reading a newspaper with a surprised expression on his face' can be condensed to 'woman to husband.') Avoid doing material that has already been done; the only way to do this is to destroy any material that you even *suspect* has been done before. You can't get rich writing gags, but it can be a fun, profitable hobby. It takes me about three years currently, to try a cartoon from the top to the bottom markets, so be patient."

RAY MORIN, 140 Hamilton Ave., Meriden CT 06450. (203)237-4500. Holds 5+ gags/year; sells 90+ cartoons/year. Has sold to *Boys' Life*, *Wall Street Journal*, *National Enquirer*, *Saturday Evening Post*, McNaught Syndicate and King Features. Works with 1-2 writers annually. Buys 3% of the gags received from freelance writers. Submit 7-10 gags at one time. SASE. Sells cartoons for $25-300. Pays 25% commission. Holds gags "indefinitely," trying to redraw the cartoon from a different angle.
Needs: General, family, children's, medical and business. "I do 95% of my own gags, but am willing to look."
Recent Cartoon: Man and wife emerging from movie theater. Wife says: "Remember how shocked we were when Clark Gable told Vivien Leigh, 'Frankly Scarlett, I don't give a damn'?"

GEORGE HOEY MORRIS, 1234 Shawnee, Houston TX 77034. (713)944-9217. Began selling cartoons in 1982. Holds 300 gags/year. Sells to newspapers and fantasy and space magazines. Recently sold material to *Times Picayune Newspaper*, *The Atlanta Journal*, and *Rocky Mountain News*. Submit "unlimited" number of gags in "any manner." Reports in 1 week. Makes outright purchase of $10 minimum. SASE.
Needs: "General gags which may be transformed into comic-strip drawings. All gags are acceptable, but the space-age theme is preferred. I can especially use jokes which pertain to outer space, other planets or 'spacey' themes." Will consider submissions for the cartoon strip, *Space Case*. "I can use computer jokes since one of my characters is a computer."

DAVID MURRIETA, 9302 W. Adams, Tolleson AZ 85353. (602)936-5439. Began selling cartoons in 1982. Sells material on general interest, adult humor, Hispanic situations, teenage situations. Recently sold material to *Arizona Republic*, *Cartoon Showcase* and *Westsider Newspaper*. Submit gags on 3x5 slips; 10-20 in one batch. Reports in 1 week. Pays 25% commission. SASE.
Needs: Gags for general magazine, newspapers, trade journals and ethnic magazines. Any jokes, gags and

subjects are acceptable. Looks for "very humorous, easy-to-understand gags."
Tips: "Writers should be mindful of computers, lowriders, modern versus old-time traditions and teenagers."

RICHARD ORLIN, #10-G, 550 Olinville Ave., Bronx NY 10467. (212)882-6177. Began selling cartoons 1978. Holds 1,500 gags/year. Sells to trade journals, family and general magazines. Recently sold material to *Good Housekeeping*, *Better Homes & Gardens*, *National Enquirer* and *Datamation*. Submit gags on 3x5 slips, 20 or less to a batch. Works with 6 writers annually. Buys 10% of the gags received from freelance writers. "Most of the gags I receive are illustrated jokes. Anybody can do that. I look for a fresh approach to an established cliche." Reports in 2 days. Sells cartoons for $50-300. Pays 25% commission. SASE.
Needs: "I'm looking for captionless, sophisticated, fresh humor that, with the right treatment, can sell to the major markets. Also likes twisted cliches. Stay away from the illustrated joke. I'm particularly interested in captionless gags based on a cliché taken to extremes."
Tips: "I think most gag writers are still doing the 1950's *Saturday Evening Post* style of 'Big Foot' gags. A cartoonist has to change with the times and not be afraid to break new trails."

IRV PHILLIPS, 2807 E. Sylvia St., Phoenix AZ 85032. Recently sold material to *Saturday Evening Post*, *New Yorker*, *National Enquirer*, *Modern Maturity*, King Features and McNaught Syndicate. Submit 10-20 gags in one batch. Reports in several weeks or months, depending on circumstances. Pays minimum 25% commission on book material; makes outright purchase on syndication material.
Needs: General and pantomine gags. No pornography. Looks for funny, offbeat, *visual* gags; short, with new twists. Also interested in book material possibilities.
Tips: "All material for me personally send to above address. Anyone wishing to collaborate with beginning cartoonists can send material to Irv Phillips, Art Department, Maricopa Technical Community College, 108 N. 40th St., Phoenix AZ 85034."

THOMAS PRISK, Star Rt., Box 52, Michigamme MI 49861. Holds 300 "and up" gags/year. Sells mostly to general interest magazines. "But I also sell cartoons to trade journals (mostly doctor, computer-oriented cartoons)." Sells to *The Bulletin of The Atomic Scientists*, Charlton Publications, *Medical Economics*, *Creative Computing*, etc. Holds with the *Saturday Evening Post*, *National Enquirer*, *Good Housekeeping*, etc. Worked with more than 130 writers last year. Submit gags on 3x5 slips, 10 or more to a batch. Reports in 1 week. Sells cartoons for $7.50-250. Pays 25% commission. SASE. "Foreign writers, please use only American postage; I don't have the time or patience for the postal coupons."
Needs: "Off-the-wall, offbeat general humor, captionless and with short captions. Would like to see doctor and computer gags. Will look at mild sex (*No* hardcore). Would also like religious gags." No anti-religious, hardcore porno or gags containing racial prejudice.
Tips: "I look for well-written gags that are short and to the point. I like a nice fresh approach to old themes. Please be sure name and address are stamped on each gag slip, *SASE must be included in batch*. Include blank slip for comments. Unless gags are legibly handwritten, they should be typed out. Writers shouldn't be too impatient with long holds; gags will circulate until sold or until I lose interest in the gag's possibility of being sold. I seem to be selling more to the girlie markets over the past year, so through 1985 I will probably concentrate more on this area. Material I receive from writers should be in this vein. The gags I hold are slanted to my style and market needs. Rejected gags are not necessarily considered unsalable."

ART REYNOLDS, Box 226, Vader WA 98593. (206)295-3736. Began selling cartoons in 1977. Holds 50 gags/year. Sells to general interest magazines and trade magazines, particularly on the logging industry at present. Recently sold material to Creative Communications Publishers, *The Northern Logger & Timber Processor*, *Timber/West Magazine*, *Loggers World Magazine* and *Christian Logger Magazine*. Submit gags on 3x5 cards; 10-15 in one batch. Reports in 1 week. Pays 25% commission. SASE.
Needs: General and family gags that appeal to *Saturday Evening Post*, *Saturday Review*, *Good Housekeeping* and *Better Homes & Gardens*. Also gags with outdoor emphasis. Presently needing gags pertaining to the logging industry. No overworked themes or sex and girlie-girlie gags. "Inquire with SASE. I'll furnish sample and information on cartoon strips and panels I'm working on. I look for fresh, short and snappy, and funny gags."
Tips: "Seek or inquire about information from cartoonist. It pays to know."

JOAN RIVERS, Box 49774, Los Angeles CA 90035. Write first for a release form. Submit gags on 8½x11 paper, typed in duplicate with name and address on each page. "Must have a release form with each submission." Reports in 2 months. Pays $10/one liner. SASE.
Needs: "Always looking for *new* topics—not usual themes. Anything and everything. No "Liz Taylor, fat, Bo Derek, dumb or age" gags.
Tips: "Submit good *one-liners*. If it is long, a story, a monologue, a riddle, question and answer, it won't work."

TER SCOTT, Box 305, Lake Nebagamon WI 54849. (715)374-2525. Began selling cartoons in 1979. Holds 100-300 gags/year. Sells to trade journals, newspapers and advertisers. Recently sold material to *Multi-Level Marketing News*, *Salesman's Opportunity*, and *Michigan Health Director*. Submit gags on 3x5 slips; 10-25 in one batch. Reports in 2 weeks. Pays 25% commission plus occasional bonuses. SASE.
Needs: "I will look at anything but hardcore, girlies and racial prejudice and prefer general, religious, farm, sales and trade journal material. I provide a list of markets and currently submit cartoons to my regular gagwriters as these accounts become stocked or change often. I always need topical and seasonal material for Classified Comics newspaper strip and ideas for all occcasion cards directed to business and sales people: sales promotion, announcements, collections, thank you and birthday cards."
Tips: "Gagwriters should try to visualize their idea in cartoon form to know if it's feasible. Then toss the caption around a while for best wording. Be aware that I may reword and/or rework a gag to better fit the cartoon on occasion but gagwriter will still receive full commission. Send printed or typed material with return address stamped on each submission. I'm also available to work with writers who need a cartoonist for their specific needs such as cartoon markets they've pioneered, ads and story books."

JOSEPH SERRANO, Box 725, Capitola CA 95010. Has sold to most major and middle markets. Pays 25% commission. SASE.
Needs: General and topical material.

GODDARD SHERMAN, 1214 McRee Dr., Valdosta GA 31602. Holds 200 gags/year. Sells to general, medical and youth publications. Recently sold material to *National Enquirer*, *Saturday Evening Post*, *Boys' Life*, *Medical Economics*, *Modern Maturity* and *Woman's World*. Submit gags on 3x5 slips; 15-20 gags in one batch. Reports in 1 week. Pays 33⅓% commission. SASE.
Needs: Prefers captionless gags, or very short captions; funny action in picture. No overly technical settings, e.g., "inside machine shops or steel mills. I have no familiarity with them so I cannot draw them accurately." Gags should be in good taste.
Tips: "I reject many good gags because they are *too* current. For example, I received several plays on the TV commercial 'Where's the Beef?' but magazines work 6 months ahead—by that time the gag is passe."

JOHN W. SIDE, 335 Wells St., Darlington WI 53530. Interested in "small-town, local happening gags with a general slant." Pays 25% commission. Sample cartoon $1. Returns rejected material "immediately." SASE.

JEFF SINCLAIR, c/o Kartoonings Creative Studio, 7811-126 A St., Surrey, British Columbia V3W 7M2 Canada. (604)581-1239. Sells to newspapers, magazines, greeting card companies, T-shirt companies, advertisers. Submit on 3X5 cards or slips; "submit greeting card and T-shirt ideas with small sketch letting me know what the writer is thinking—stick men OK!" Submit 10-20 gags/batch. Reports in 1 week. Pays 30% commission; $50 for card ideas; $25 for T-shirt ideas. SASE.
Needs: General, medical, topical, family, outdoors, sports, hunting, fishing, sexy (not erotic), *National Lampoon* humor, men, women, children's, adventure, business, travel, dental, farm, teenager, hospital, TV, offbeat, whimsy. "No racial, dumb or worn-out themes. For more youth-oriented publications (e.g., *National Lampoon*). Be zany and weird, smutty! Be creative but not totally sick. No heavy drug-related themes. Always willing to collaborate with writers on good new features for syndication; also, anyone with a new unique slant on children's writing, cartoon books, humorous poetry. I will read and critique any and all material coming through my mailbox. Will hold unsold gags indefinitely. Will return gags on request. SASE.

SINGER COMMUNICATIONS, INC., 3164 Tyler Ave., Anaheim CA 92801. (714)527-5650. "Our firm represents over 80 cartoonists. We do not buy gags but many of our participating artists do. We add about 500 cartoons each year." Cartoons sold to all types of publications throughout the world. Recently sold material to *Business Today*, *She Magazines* and *Signature*. Submit very good copies; no originals.

STEWART SLOCOM, (signs work Stewart), 18 Garretson Road, White Plains NY 10604. (914)948-6682. Holds 25-30 gags/year. Sells to general interest, women's and sports publications. Recently sold material to *Good Housekeeping*, *Ladies Home Journal*, *National Enquirer*, *Cosmopolitan*, *Golf Journal*, *Tennis*, Kings Features and McNaught Syndicate. Submit gags on 3x5 slips; 10-15 in one batch. Reports in 2 days. Pays 25% commission. SASE.
Needs: General, family, women-in-business, computer and sports gags.
Tips: "I look for *originality* (even on overworked themes) and for the prospect of a funny picture. Writers should be mindful of computers, women's lib (business, home, sports, etc.) and older persons in gagwriting."

The double dagger (‡) before a listing indicates that the listing is new in this edition. New markets are often the most receptive to freelance contributions.

Close-up

George Hartman
Editor
Cartoon World

The gag writer *to be funny* can't rely on someone else's artwork. As *Cartoon World* editor George Hartman has learned, "A good gag will sell a poor drawing, but a poor gag won't sell a good drawing."

Readers want surprises, something more than ordinary, a reversal. "Gag writers should study what a funny idea is," says Hartman, who has sold an estimated 10,000 cartoons to trade journals and farm publications. Read Mark Twain; analyze gags in today's magazines.

Publishing the monthly newsletter *Cartoon World* "without a miss" for more than 40 years, Hartman helps gag writers, cartoonists and mankind. "If you can make people get a healthy laugh, you're actually helping mankind, right?" he says.

Hartman's gift to gag writers and cartoonists has been the markets he lists in *CW*. "If I can't bring new markets and new ideas to make money at cartooning, I've failed." He does "extensive pioneering" (as he calls it) to find new markets. The drawback to Hartman's asking editors if they'll consider cartoons, though, has been the "tremendous" postage bill.

"The most rewarding part of *CW* is the fact that I've actually helped people get started at cartooning or given them advice which led to a full-time job," says Hartman, who began studying cartooning at age 12. "Many former subscribers are now comic-strip artists."

Few people, though, earn a full-time living from gag writing or cartooning, points out Hartman. It takes hard work, patience and postage.

One cartoonist, for example, sold a cartoon for $50 after getting 25 rejection slips on the cartoon.

Gag writers' most common mistake is sending *general* cartoon gags to cartoonists and magazines, he says. There are an estimated 15,000 trade journals, each with a different slant. Hartman extracts these slants by thumbing page by page through a magazine. He writes down every subject covered in articles and ads and then develops ideas from these gag "kernels."

When looking for a cartoonist to "draw" your gags, ask him what kind of cartoons he draws best, suggests Hartman. Work with cartoonists whose drawings will complement your gags and vice versa.

Gag writers with a reliable cartoonist can approach editors with a typer (a term Hartman coined 25 years ago). The writer sends a typed idea—a typer—to an editor with a sample of the artist's work and a self-addressed, stamped envelope. In the center of the 3x5 card, type the situation to be illustrated, with the caption at the bottom of the card and the writer's name and address in the upper left-hand corner or on the back. If the editor says "yes " to the typer, the artist will then draw the cartoon. The gag writer and cartoonist split the check.

Gag writers and cartoonists must work hard—"this is a competitive field"—but must also enjoy the work. Laugh often and don't quit. Like Hartman, always look for people who will *buy* your humor. "I'm too stubborn to quit. Many months I made nil on *CW* but kept on anyway. No secret at all. Just do it . . . the secret is never to say, 'die'."

SUZANNE STEINIGER, 9373 Whitcomb, Detroit MI 48228. (313)838-5204. Holds 100+ gags/year. Sells to farm magazines, sex-type periodicals, women's and general interest magazines and Charlton Publications. Submit gags on 3x5 cards or 3x5 slips. Submit 30 or more gags in one batch. Reports in 1 week. Pays 25% commission. SASE.

Needs: "For the present I would like to see gags *National Lampoon* style. I guess you could say general interest, but I'm looking for crazy *new* ideas. I like to see everything except detailed scenes. Writers should simplify their words and scenes. I am working on a cartoon strip. I will not say what the strip is about for fear of someone accidentally getting the same idea. I am looking for a patient writer, someone I can discuss my idea with and someone to *help*. I do like gags that are funny and less detailed. For example, a writer should say 'man to woman in restaurant' instead of 'man in crowded restaurant, waiter looking surprised to the woman next to him.' There should be less confusion. I like quick and simple gags the best."

Tips: "Today the gags are funnier visually. The scene should have fewer props. Fewer props made the great comics such as the Marx Brothers very funny and popular, not to mention Peanuts. There should be fewer details and more concentration on the joke, the entire *gag*. I like writer's who do a good job of writing and leave the drawing to us (cartoonists)."

JOHN STINGER, Box 189, Stewartsville NJ 08886. Interested in general business gags. Would like to see more captionless sight gags. Currently doing a syndicated panel on business. Has sold to major markets. "Index cards are fine, but please keep short." Pays 25% commission; "more to top writers." Bought about 25 gags last year. Can hold unsold gags for as long as a year. SASE.

FRANK TABOR, 2817 NE 292nd Ave., Camas WA 98607. (206)834-3355. Began selling cartoons in 1947. Holds 200 gags/year. Sells to trade journals. Recently sold material to *Medical Economics, American Medical News, American Machinist, Basic Computing, Infoworld, Chesapeake Bay, Tooling & Production and True Detective*. Submit gags on 3x5 slips; 10 in one batch. Reports in 2 days. Pays 25% commission. SASE.

Needs: Computers, police, detective, fishing, salesman, medical (must be funny for the doctor—no gags on big doctor bills), industrial (slanted to the industry executive) and flower shop gags. "Cartoon spreads are wide open." No gags on subjects not listed above. "I look for situations in which the cartoon carries the punch; I don't care for the one-liner or illustrated joke. I need trade gags by writers who know or who will study the trade they're writing about."

Tips: "Not enough writers are trying to write for the trades. They're too easily won over by the big rates at the major markets. I have lots of trades paying $35 to $225, and they're begging for cartoons."

ISSAM TEWFIK, #701, 2400 Carling Ave., Ottawa, Ontario K2B 7H2 Canada. (613)828-5239. Holds 300 gags/year. Sells to general interest magazines, trade journals, men's and women's publications and newspapers. Recently sold material to *Hospital Supervisor Bulletin* and *Accent on Living*. Submit gags on 3x5 slips. Submit 10 or more gags in one batch. Reports in 1 week. Pays 25% commission. SASE.

Needs: General, family, erotic, sports, law, military, insurance, medical, computers, children, detective, cars, old age, management, outdoor, money, trucking, etc. Prefers gags that are slanted towards a specific subject and a magazine. Research the magazine and slant towards its requirments. "I will consider eagerly a well conceived strip or panel with well-defined characters and theme (e.g., family, animal, professional, children and single people)."

Tips: "Identify a need either in a specific magazine or a syndicate and let us work together to produce something marketable. Slanting to the different publications is the key to success."

BOB THAVES, Box 67, Manhattan Beach CA 90266. Pays 25% commission. Returns rejected material in 1-2 weeks. May hold unsold gags indefinitely. SASE.

Needs: Gags "dealing with anything except raw sex. Also buy gags for syndicated (daily and Sunday) panel, *Frank & Ernest*. I prefer offbeat gags for that, although almost any general gag will do."

MARVIN TOWNSEND, 631 W. 88th St., Kansas City MO 64114. Holds 25-30 gags/year; sells 300 cartoons/year. Sells to trade and business publications and church and school magazines. Works with 15-20 writers annually. Buys 3-4% of the gags received from freelance writers. Prefers batches of not over 20 gags. Sells cartoons for $20-80. Pays 25% commission. SASE.

Needs: Interested in gags with a trade journal or business slant. Such as office executives, professional engineers, plant managers, supervisors, foremen, safety engineers, etc. "Religious and children gags also welcome. Captioned or captionless. *No general gags wanted*. Don't waste postage sending general gags or worn-out material."

Tips: "Cute or mildly funny ideas don't sell. They must have a real punch or unusual twist to them. I discourage contributions from gag men not capable of creating the particular slant I need."

JOSEPH F. WHITAKER, 2522 Percy Ave., Orlando FL 32818. (305)298-8311. Began selling cartoons in 1960. Holds 100 gags/year. Sells all types of gags. Recently sold material to *Star, National Enquirer, National*

Catholic News, McNaught Syndicate and women's magazines. Submit gags on 3x5 slips; 10-15 in one batch. Reports in 4 days. Pays 25% commission. SASE.
Needs: All types of gags.
Tips: "I look for captionless gags."

ART WINBURG, 21 McKinley Ave., Jamestown NY 14701. Has sold to *National Star*, *American Medical News*, *VFW Magazine*, *Physician's Management*, *American Legion*, *Modern Medicine*, *New Woman*, *Medical Month*, and *Highlights for Children*. Sells cartoons for $15-225. Pays 25% commission. Returns rejected material "usually within a week, sometimes same day received." Will return unsold gags "on request. Always a possibility of eventually selling a cartoon." SASE.
Needs: All types of gags; general, family, trade and professional journals, adventure, sports, medical and children's magazines. Gagwriter should "use variety, be original, and avoid old cliches." Would prefer not to see gags about "smoke signals, flying carpets, moon men, harems or cannibals with some person in cooking pot."
Tips: "Most gag writers don't know how to slant. They should see and study what the magazines use. Most gags submitted to me are dull, pointless, some not even a gag."

MARTIN YOUNG, Box 7415, Orlando FL 32854. (305)423-3409. Holds 250-300 gags/year. Sells to men's and women's publications, general interest magazines, trade journals and newspapers. Recently sold material to M.A.D.D. (Mothers Against Drunk Drivers), *Saturday Evening Post*, *Charisma*, *Hi-Res/Computer* and *Orlando Sentinel*. Submit gags on 3x5 cards. Submit 15-20 gags in one batch. Reports in 3 days. Pays 25% of cartoon sale. SASE.
Needs: Computer (home/office); religious (no anti-religious); *Saturday Evening Post* type; hospital/doctor/nurse; family humor; humor though youth; school/teachers/kids; and off-the-wall general gags. No political or sex gags, no overworked gags or cliches. "I currently have a cartoon strip called Fish Tales. It deals with some well established characters that live in the ocean. Please write for further details."
Tips: "I very much like *strong, very funny*, straight-to-the-point gags. I have been getting too many weak, overworked themes. Try to be original. Gagwriters should keep up with the times. Their gags will reflect how current they are on what's happening in the world around them."

Greeting Card Publishers

Today's textured reproductions of lace replace yesterday's antique lace cards, but the messages inside haven't changed. Greeting card writers are writing about the same subjects: love, friendship, sympathy, birthdays and anniversaries. Yet there's no reason to not search for new ways to express these timeless sentiments.

In browsing through card shops, you'll find that writers are also coming up with new subjects: "Congratulations, you've got your driver's license" and "Keep up the good work on your diet."

For the aspiring verse writer, researching the greeting card market is fun and essential. Study the card racks. Observe what cards people are buying. Read card verses and observe how the verses complement the artwork.

When you visit a card shop, discuss with store managers what kinds of cards sell best. Ask them if there is any type of card that companies don't print that customers ask for, and why. Contact greeting card companies for their guidelines or current needs lists. Read *A Guide to Greeting Card Writing*, edited by Larry Sandman (Writer's Digest Books).

To submit conventional greeting card material, type or neatly print your verses on either 4x6 or 3x5 slips of paper or file cards. For humorous or studio card ideas, either fold sheets of paper into card dummies about the size and shape of an actual card, or use file cards. For ideas that use attachments, try to get the actual attachment and put it on your dummy; if you can't, suggest the attachment. For mechanical card ideas, you must make a workable mechanical dummy. Most companies will pay more for attachment and mechanical card ideas.

Neatly print or type your idea on the dummy as it would appear on the finished card. Type your name and address on the back of each dummy or card, along with an identification number (which helps you and the editor in keeping records). Always maintain records of where and when ideas were submitted; use a file card for each idea.

Submit 5-15 ideas at a time (this constitutes a "batch"). Quality, not quantity, should be your guideline. Keep the file cards for each batch together until rejected ideas are returned. You may want to code each submission so you can identify how many you have sent and where.

Listings below cover publishers' requirements for verse, gags, and other product ideas. Artwork requirements are also covered when a company is interested in a complete package of art and idea.

AMBERLEY GREETING CARD CO., Box 36159, Cincinnati OH 45236. Editor: Ned Stern. 95% freelance written. Submit ideas in batches of 5-20 on regular 3x5 cards. No conventional cards. Bought 200 freelance ideas/samples last year. Buys all rights. SASE. Reports in 3-4 weeks. Free market list revised about every 6 months (include SASE with request).
Humorous, Studio and Promotions: Buys all kinds of studio and humorous everyday cards. "Birthday studio is still the best selling caption. We never get enough. We look for belly laugh humor. All types of risque are accepted. No ideas with attachments. We prefer short and snappy ideas. The shorter gags seem to sell best. No seasonal cards. Buys 200 items/year. Studio and humorous cards sell best. Pays $40."

ARTFORMS CARD CORPORATION, 725 County Line Rd., Dearfield IL 60015. (312)272-9844. Editor: Ms. Bluma K. Marder. Buys "about 60-70 messages"/year. Submit ideas in batches of 10. Submit seasonal/holiday material 6 months in advance. SASE. Reports in 3 weeks. Buys common law and statutory copyright rights. Market list available for legal size SASE.
Needs: Conventional; humorous; informal; inspirational; sensitivity; studio; messages for Jewish Greeting Cards such as Bar/Bat Mitzvah, Jewish New Year and Chanukah; Wedding, Sympathy, Anniversary, Get Well and Birthday. No insults or risque greetings. Length: 2 lines minimum, 4 lines maximum. Pays $15-25/card idea.
Other Product Lines: Gift wrap for Chanukah and year 'round use.

Recent Verse: "Praying that you/And the ones you hold dear/Will all be inscribed/For a Happy New Year."
Tips: "Do research on Judaism so greeting is not questionable to a religious market; also, if Biblical quotes are used, make sure references are correct. We look for simple messages that pertain directly to subject matter. Humorous cards are selling well."

CAROLYN BEAN PUBLISHING, LTD., 120 2nd St., San Francisco CA 94105. (415)957-9574. Chief Executive Officer: Lawrence Barnett. 90% freelance written. Bought 400 freelance ideas/samples last year. Buys exclusive card rights; negotiates others. Pays on acceptance or publication. Submit seasonal/holiday material 18 months in advance. SASE. Reports in 6 weeks. Free writer's guidelines.
Needs: Conventional holiday and occasions; humorous; informal; studio; general, occasion-oriented messages. Looks for sophisticated, witty and/or sensitive material. No "Hallmark-type, hearts and flowers" messages or heavy Christian messages. Occasion-oriented cards sell best. Pays $15-30. "These terms are negotiable."
Tips: "The greeting card market has become more traditional in the last year."

BLUE MOUNTAIN ARTS, INC., Dept. WM, Box 1007, Boulder CO 80306. Contact: Editorial Staff. Buys 50-75 items/year. SASE. Reports in 3-5 months. Buys all rights. Pays on publication.
Needs: Inspirational (without being religious); and sensitivity ("primarily need sensitive and sensible writings about love, friendships, families, philosophies, etc.—written with originality and universal appeal"). Pays $150.
Other Product Lines: Calendars, gift books and greeting books. Payment varies.
Tips: "Get a feel for the Blue Mountain Arts line prior to submitting material. Our needs differ from other card publishers; we do not use rhymed verse, preferring instead a more honest person-to-person style. We use unrhymed, sensitive poetry and prose on the deep significance and meaning of life and relationships. A very limited amount of freelance material is selected each year, either for publication on a notecard or in a gift anthology, and the selection prospects are highly competitive. But new material is always welcome and each manuscript is given serious consideration."

‡BO-TREE PRODUCTIONS/CARD DIVISION, Suite E, 1137 San Antonio Rd., Palo Alto CA 94303. (415)967-1817. Editor: John C.W. Carroll. Estab. 1983. "We expect to publish 300 new images/year, of which many will be freelance." Submit seasonal/holiday material 1 year in advance. SASE. Reports in 6 weeks. Buys card rights. Pays on acceptance. Free writer's guidelines; annual market list.
Needs: Conventional, humorous, informal and invitations. Pays $20-50 or maybe royalty; "depends on nature of submission and amount of writer's involvement."
Tips: "We look for simplicity, sincerity, appropriateness."

BRILLIANT ENTERPRISES, 117 W. Valerio St., Santa Barbara CA 93101. Contact: Editorial Dept. Buys all rights. Submit words and art in black on $5\frac{1}{2}$x$3\frac{1}{2}$ horizontal, thin white paper in batches of no more than 15. Reports "usually in 2 weeks." SASE. Catalog and sample set for $1.
Needs: Postcards. Messages should be "of a highly original nature, emphasizing subtlety, simplicity, insight, wit, profundity, beauty and felicity of expression. Accompanying art should be in the nature of oblique commentary or decoration rather than direct illustration. Messages should be of universal appeal, capable of being appreciated by all types of people and of being easily translated into other languages. Since our line of cards is highly unconventional, it is essential that freelancers study it before submitting." No "topical references, subjects limited to American culture or puns." Limit of 17 words/card. Pays $40 for "complete ready-to-print word and picture design."
Recent Verse: "Maybe I'm lucky to be going so slowly,/Because I may be going in the wrong direction."
Tips: For further tips, study Ashleigh Brilliant's book: *I May Not Be Totally Perfect, But Parts of Me Are Excellent*.

‡COMEDY FARM GREETING CARDS, c/o ComCo Inc., Box 5159, Springfield IL 62705. Editor: Keith Colter. Estab. 1983. SASE. Reports in 1 week. Rights purchased negotiable. Pays on publication or negotiates. Sampler available on request.
Needs: Humorous, studio and comedy-oriented. Pays flat fee or royalty to be negotiated.
Other Product Lines: Postcards. "Will look at book ideas."
Tips: "Make it funny."

CONTENOVA, 1239 Adanac St., Vancouver, British Columbia V6A 2C8 Canada. (604)253-4444. Editor: Ethel Bluett. 100% freelance written. Bought 60 freelance ideas/samples last year. Submit ideas on 3x5 cards or small mock-ups in batches of 10. Reports in 3-6 weeks. Buys world rights. Pays on acceptance. Current needs list for SAE and IRC. Do *not* send US postage stamps.
Needs: Humorous, studio, both risque and nonrisque. "The shorter, the better." Birthday, belated birthday, get well, anniversary, thank you, congratulations, miss you, new job, etc. Seasonal ideas needed for Christmas

by March; Valentine's Day (September). Risque cards and birthday cards sell best. Pays $50.
Tips: "In Canada, the increased postal rates have affected Christmas card sales. We need to refine the Christmas card line—it's now more competitive."

‡**CURRENT, INC.**, Box 2559, Colorado Springs CO 80901. (303)594-4100. Editor: Nancy McConnell. Buys 2 or 3 children's book manuscripts/year. "We do *not* purchase greeting card sentiments as all our needs are met in-house." Submit seasonal/holiday material 18 months in advance. SASE. Reports in 3 weeks. Buys all rights. Pays on acceptance. Writer's guidelines for business-size SAE and 1 first class stamp. Pays approximately $300 for 1,500-word ms. "We do not pay royalties."
Tips: "Read our direct mail catalog."

DRAWING BOARD GREETING CARDS, INC., 8200 Carpenter Fwy., Dallas TX 75247. (214)637-0390. Editorial Director: Jimmie Fitzgerald. Submit ideas on 3x5 cards, typed, with name and address on each card. SASE. Reports in 2 weeks. Pays on acceptance.
Needs: Conventional, humorous, informal, inspirational, everyday, seasonal and studio cards. No 'blue' or sex humor. Pays $30-80.
Other Product Lines: Calendars. Pays $200-600.

D. FORER & CO., INC., 105 E. 73rd St., New York NY 10021. (212)879-6600. Editor: Barbara Schaffer. SASE. Reports in 2 weeks. Not copyrighted. Pays on acceptance. One-time market list for SAE and 1 first class stamp..
Needs: Humorous, studio. Pays $20.

FRAN MAR GREETING CARDS, LTD., Box 1057, Mt. Vernon NY 10550. (914)664-5060. President: Stan Cohen. Buys 100-300 items/year. Submit ideas in small batches (no more than 15 in a batch) on 3x5 sheets or cards. SASE. "Copy will not be returned without SASE enclosed with submissions." Reports in 1-2 weeks. Buys all rights. Pays on the 15th of the month following acceptance. Market list for SASE.
Needs: Invitations (all categories), thank you notes (all categories), humorous pads and stationery.
Other Product Lines: Stationery, novelty card concepts, captions, and novelty pad captions. Pays $25/card idea.
Recent Verses: Pad concept: (pad all green except for 2 eyes at the bottom). Caption: "This is not a pad, somebody squashed my froggie." Invitation: "A surprise party/Come help us surprise the pants off—."
Tips: Send "short copy—with a punch. Pads should be functional and/or funny."

‡**THE GRAPHIC ARTISAN, LTD.**, 40 Robert Pitt Dr., Monsey NY 10952. (914)352-3113. Editor: Peter A. Aron. Annual amount of freelance purchases $1,000-5,000. Submit seasonal/holiday material 6-9 months in advance. SASE. Reports in 1 month. Buys all rights (one-time payment). Pays on acceptance.
Needs: Announcements, conventional, humorous, informal, juvenile and studio. Pays $10-25/card idea. Also reviews bumper stickers, calendars, gift books, greeting books, plaques and postcards. "Payment would vary with the complexity and completeness of the individual item."
Tips: "Material must be tasteful. Note that this does *not* mean noncontroversial, nonsexy, or anything like that—must not be libelous or disgusting for the sake of shock. It's a tough world out there—but originality and first rate work still make it."

‡**THE GREAT AUSTRALIAN CARD CO.**, 46 Clayton Rd., Clayton North, Victoria 3168 Australia. (03)543-2022. Editor: Graeme Venn. Freelance material purchases total $250,000-500,000/year. Submit seasonal/holiday material 12-16 months in advance. SAE, IRCs. Reports in 2 months. Buys Australia and New Zealand rights. Pays on acceptance. Free writer's guidelines; market list regularly revised.
Needs: Announcements, conventional, humorous, informal, inspirational, invitations, juvenile, sensitivity, soft line and studio. "In all cases simplicity, witty or sophisticated theme catering for an up-market image. No localized American or specific American occasion." Pays $50-150 or 5-6% royalty; "may be mixture of both, design/card and royalty."
Other Product Lines: Calendars, promotions (pays $50-250), gift books, greeting books (pays $50-500); plaques, posters, stationery packs and gift wrap (pays $50-150).
Tips: "Cater for international taste—avoid local idioms, etc."

HALLMARK CARDS, INC., Humor Department, #303, Box 580, Kansas City MO 64141. Contact: Humor Editor. 30% freelance written. Submit ideas either on card mock-ups or 3x5 cards; 10-20/batch. SASE. Reports in 2-3 weeks. Buys all rights. Pays on acceptance. Market list for SASE.
Needs: Studio cards. Pays $136.50 maximum. "Avoid heavily masculine humor as our buyers are mostly female."
Recent Verse: "You're at that perfect age!/Somewhere between 'I Can't Wait a Minute!'/ and 'Wait a Minute, I Can't!'/Happy Birthday!"

Tips: "Don't send nonhumorous material. The funnier the better: material with a good me-to-you message sells best for us."

LEANIN' TREE PUBLISHING CO., Box 9500, Boulder CO 80301. (303)530-1442. Contact: Editor. Submit verses (not more than 15) on 3x5 cards. SASE. Reports in 3 months. May hold good verses indefinitely. Pays $35 on publication; $10 for reuse. Market list and verse writer guidelines for SASE.
Needs: Birthday, friendship, get well, anniversary, thank you, sympathy, wedding, romantic love, Christmas, Valentines, Easter, Mother's Day, Father's Day and all-occasion Christian.
Tips: "We publish western, Christian and contemporary friendship (not studio) cards. Humor preferred in western card line. Please do not send art suggestions. Become familiar with our card lines before submitting."

MAINE LINE CO., Box 418, Rockport ME 04856. (207)236-8536. Vice President: P. Ardman. 100% freelance written. Buys 300 card designs (copy and artwork)/year. Submit seasonal/holiday material 1 year in advance. SASE. Reports in 1 month. Buys negotiable but primarily greeting card rights. Pays ½ on acceptance and ½ on publication. Current market list for 9x12 SAE and 60¢ postage.
Needs: Humorous, informal, inspirational (not religious, but spiritual and motivational OK), sensitivity, Christmas, Valentines and Mother's Day. Pays $10-50 or 2.5-5% royalty. "Our fees/advances/royalties are individually negotiated. Basically, flat fee paid for executing our idea; advance/royalty for freelancer's concept/ execution. Humor cards with appeal to women or with slightly suggestive copy and attractive, creative visuals sell best."
Tips: "We most often do a series, so submitting a concept and some examples is better than random lines. Cards do not need rhyming verses, but *sendable* funny or thought-provoking words, with universal appeal. The newer and more original the better—nothing you've seen before. We are looking for unusual, highly imaginative writers, especially humor writers who can provide witty copy for contemporary women 25-40 years old. There's more demand on occasion cards, clever original copy, woman-to-woman friendship cards and contemporary women's issue cards. Also, there's more demand for freelance copy from people who have an interesting perspective on modern life that can be expressed in a unique way and understood by many people." Send SASE for guidelines.

OATMEAL STUDIOS, Box 138, Rochester VT 05767. (802)767-3325. Editor: Helene Lehrer. 90% freelance written. Buys 150-250 greeting card lines/year. Bought 200 freelance ideas/samples last year. Submit material for birthday, friendship, anniversary, get well, etc. Also Christmas, Chanukah, Mother's Day, Father's Day, Easter, Valentine's Day, etc. Pays $25-50. SASE. Reports in 3 weeks. Pays on acceptance. Current market list for SAE and 40¢ postage.
Needs: Humorous material (clever and *very* funny) year-round. "Humorous tongue-in-cheek-type humor, conversational in tone and format, sells best for us."
Tips: "We are looking for writers to send us copy that will be funny enough to knock us off our feet, something with some zing to it. The greeting card market has become more competitive with a greater need for creative and original ideas. It creates a greater challenge while opening up more doors for the freelance writer to sell his or her work."

PORTAL PUBLICATIONS, LTD., 21 Tamal Vista Blvd., Corte Madera CA 94925. (415)924-5652. Editor: Nancy Dunwell. 100% freelance written. Buys 150 greeting card lines/year. SASE. Reports in 8 weeks. Pays $50/sentiment. Free guidelines.
Needs: Light humor and conversational, prose and verse sentiments. Young adult sending situations. Everyday and seasonal ideas. General birthday and friendship cards sell best. Submit one idea/3x5 card with name and address.
Tips: "Our greeting card products are developed to meet the needs of the young professional woman. This is an expanding market segment. Conversational prose and soft humor are the major types of sentiments we use."

‡POST-OP-PRODUCTIONS INC., Box 2178, Reston VA 22090. Editor: Phillip Corrigan. Estab. 1982. Submit seasonal/holiday material 9 months in advance. SASE. Reports in 2 weeks. Buys product rights. Pays on acceptance. Free writer's guidelines; one-time market list.
Needs: Humorous "different, unusual." Pays $25-75 or 2.5% royalty.
Other Product Lines: Postcards, posters. Payment varies, $25-75 or 2.5-5% royalty.

REED STARLINE CARD CO., 3331 Sunset Blvd., Los Angeles CA 90026. (213)663-3161. Submit seasonal/holiday material 1 year in advance. SASE. Reports in 2 weeks. Pays on acceptance. Free market list.
Needs: Announcements, humorous, informal, invitations and studio. No verse or jingles-type material. Pays $40/card idea.
Tips: "Study the current trends on card racks to determine the type of card that is selling."

‡**ROCKSHOTS, INC.**, 51 W. 21st St., New York NY 10010. (212)741-3663. Editor: Tolin Greene. "We buy 75 greeting card verse (or gag) lines annually." Submit seasonal/holiday material 1 year in advance. SASE. Reports in 1 month. Buys use for greeting cards. Pays on acceptance. Writer's guidelines for SAE and 1 first class stamp; market list regularly revised.

Needs: Humorous ("should be off-the-wall, as outrageous as possible, preferably for sophisticated buyer"); informal, invitations (funny, off-beat); soft line; combination of sexy and humorous come-on type greeting ("sentimental is not our style"); and insult cards ("looking for cute insults"). No sentimental or conventional material. "Card gag can adopt a sentimental style, then take an ironic twist and end on an off-beat note." Pays $75-150; 5% royalty offered when a series of cards is done.

Other Product Lines: Posters. Pays $100-250. Also note pads, decorative matches, wrapping paper.

Tips: "Think of a concept that would normally be too outrageous to use, give it a cute and clever wording to make it drop-dead funny and you will have commercialized a non-commercial message. It's always good to mix sex and humor. Our emphasis is definitely on the erotic. Hard-core eroticism is difficult for the general public to handle on greeting cards. The trend is toward 'light' sexy humor, even cute sexy humor. 'Cute' has always sold cards, and it's a good word to think of even with the most sophisticated, crazy ideas. Remember that your gag line will probably be illustrated by a cartoonist, illustrator or photographer. So try to think visually. If no visual is needed, the gag line *can* stand alone, but we generally prefer some visual representation."

VAGABOND CREATIONS, INC., 2560 Lance Dr., Dayton OH 45409. Editor: George F. Stanley Jr. Buys all rights. Submit seasonal material any time; "we try to plan a great deal in advance." Submit on 3x5 cards. "We don't want artwork—only ideas." Reports in same week usually. May hold ideas 3 or 4 days. SASE for return of submissions.

Needs: Christmas, Valentine's, graduation, everyday, Mother's Day and Father's Day verse. "The current style of the new 'Sophisticates' greeting card line is graphics only on the front with a short tie-in punch line on the inside of the card. General rather than specific subject matter." Buys 50 items/year. Pays $10 "for beginners; up to $15 for regular contributors."

Other Product Lines: Interested in receiving copy for mottos, humorous buttons and postcards. "On buttons we like double-entendre expressions—preferably short. We don't want the protest button or a specific person named. We pay $10 for each button idea." Mottos should be written in the first-person about situations at the job, about the job, confusion, modest bragging, drinking habits, etc. Pays $10 for mottos.

Tips: "Our audience includes college students and their contemporaries . . . and young moderns. Writers can tailor their efforts by checking racks in college bookstores and discussing what college students are requesting with card buyers in these stores."

‡**WARNER PRESS, INC.**, 1200 E. 5th St., Box 2499, Anderson IN 46018. (317)644-7721. Editor: Jane L. Hammond. Annual amount of freelance purchases $2,000-3,000. Submit seasonal/holiday material 9-12 months in advance. Reports in 6 weeks. Usually buys full rights. Pays on acceptance or sometimes on publication. Free writer's guidelines. Market list revised regularly.

Needs: Announcements; conventional ("majority of what we purchase is conservative"); inspirational (looking for 6-8 line inspirational poems); juvenile; sensitivity (with a religious touch); and soft line (thought-provoking and inspirational). No off-color humor. Pays $1-$1.50/line for most verses; longer poems $25-30/poem. Also reviews other products. Pays $10-15 for plaques; $2-4 for postcards; and $3-10 for posters.

Tips: "Send verses on 3x5 cards; avoid the use of 'we' or 'us' when possible; remember religious basis for Warner Press though individual verses do not need to be extremely religious. Writers should be aware of trend towards reflective thoughts and free verse though strict poetry is still in demand in some markets."

Syndicates

When readers await a newspaper column each day—and discuss that day's column at home and at work—that columnist has the ability syndicates want.

What syndicates aren't looking for is a writer who writes only about what *he* is interested in. "Half the people in America would like to be paid to go to the movies or to do celebrity interviews, read books and travel . . . but that sort of thing is very easily done," says one syndicate editor.

Syndicates use this "glamorous" type of material, but if they already have a respected columnist writing movie reviews, your query offering to write reviews probably won't bring a "yes." Send editors *fresh*, well-researched reader-geared material that will outshine the unsolicited material in every editor's daily mail.

Syndicates and news services sell material to newspapers, trade journals and company publications. They handle humor articles, commentary, advice columns, travel, personal finance, health, and other special interest material. Names like Russell Baker, Sydney Harris and Erma Bombeck immediately come to mind.

There is generally not much room for syndicating fiction and poetry. And for beginning writers there is probably not much room in the top-notch syndicates. (Of course, there are exceptions. A woman named Jory Graham—who had some previous experience in newspaper work—approached the managing editor of the *Chicago Daily News*, later to be the *Chicago Sun-Times*, about writing a column that spoke to cancer patients. She wanted to write for and about people, like herself, living with the disease. The weekly column was syndicated in 25 newspapers around the country until Graham died in May, 1983.)

The best way to gain the attention of a syndicate is by writing for your local newspaper. Write about what you know, what you are, or what you do well—always with the reader in mind. Even a column written gratis may get you the clips you need to gain a syndicate's interest. If you are not working at a newspaper, at least read the syndicated columns in as many newspapers as you can. Notice length, style and audience slant.

Syndicated material is generally short (500-1,000 words/column), objective, and carefully documented. Since syndicates sell primarily to newspapers, "terse" newspaper style is appropriate, even for features. Remember that smaller syndicates and news services often handle specialized material (health, religion, career, business) for a well-targeted audience.

Some syndicates market one-shot (as opposed to continuous columns) articles; others handle article series. News services often concentrate on syndicated news and information to industry or trade publications.

Syndicates sell your copy (columns, features, puzzles, news, etc.) for a commission. The writer receives from 40% to 60% of the gross proceeds, though some syndicates pay the writer a salary and others buy material outright. The syndicate's percentage covers costs of promotion, mailing, staff, etc. Writers of top syndicated columns can earn more than $50,000 a year, though most syndicated writers can't expect to see anything near that figure.

Consult the following listings for the topic and form of submissions preferred by syndicates. Listings also cover the syndicate's outlets. Most, as mentioned above, sell to newspapers, but many also sell to magazines, and to radio stations that use syndicated material as "brights"—that is, lively, interesting facts and anecdotes. For more information about the titles of columns and features handled by particular syndicates, consult the *Editor and Publisher Syndicate Directory* (11 W. 19th St., New York City 10011). For a list of newspapers published in the U.S. and Canada, see *Ayer Directory of Publications* in your library.

Most syndicate editors prefer that you query them with about six sample columns or features. Enclose a self-addressed, stamped envelope with all queries and submissions.

For some already syndicated columnists, computer technology can change the way they submit material. ". . . All our writers and editors will eventually be connected to us by computer," points out one syndicate editor.

Some writers self-syndicate their material, earning 100% of the income, but also bearing the expense of soliciting clients, reproducing and mailing the features, billing, etc.

ADVENTURE FEATURE SYNDICATE, Suite 400, 329 Harvey Dr., Glendale CA 91206. (213)247-1721. Editor: Orpha Harryman Barry. Syndicates to newspapers. SASE. Reports in 1 month. Buys all rights. **Needs:** Action adventure, romance, mystery and science fiction. Pays 50% commission. Currently syndicates *Strange Encounters*, by Barry and Hull (mystery).

AMPERSAND COMMUNICATIONS, 1507 Madrid St., Coral Gables FL 33134. (305)445-9236. Editor: George Leposky. Marketing Director: Rosalie Leposky. "We are a small, exclusive organization. Our emphasis is on building a personal relationship with and aiding the professional development of each of our authors. We began by marketing our own travel articles. Now we're expanding to other subject areas, and accepting work from other writers." Syndicates to average of 50-60 newspaper travel sections and magazines (to a lesser extent). Electronic submissions OK "if compatible with our system; contact us for details"; requires hard copy also. Computer printout submissions acceptable. SASE. Reports in 3 months, "sometimes longer if we're swamped with manuscripts." Acquires all rights; will consider reprint rights on occasion, usually when first rights in author's hometown newspaper don't preclude marketing elsewhere. Send original ms with submission and publication history.
Needs: Magazine features, newspaper features: "Travel, science and health, and cooking with 'natural' foods are fields in which we're working now and would welcome submissions from authors." Length: travel, 800-1,200 words; science and health, 800-1,500 words; cooking, 800-1,200 words. "One-shot destination articles on travel—typically about places off the beaten track, or popular locations described in some unusual way. Example: How to see Disney World with young children. We concentrate on Florida, so writers approaching us with other material will have better luck. We market travel primarily—but not exclusively—to newspaper travel sections. Travel should be upbeat and positive but not puffy—tempered with caveats and criticism where appropriate." Submit complete ms with photos. SASE required for return. Science and health: "We market features to consumer magazines, newspapers and newspaper Sunday magazines. What sells in this field is the ability to translate jargon into English and explain intricate concepts and procedures meaningfully to a lay audience." Submit complete ms with photos and SASE. Cooking: "We're interested in marketing authoritative, well-written material on 'natural' foods to a non-health-food audience. If recipes aren't original, cite source and demonstrate that reprint rights have been obtained." Submit complete ms with SASE. Pays 50% of net after production, average $12-175. No additional payment for photos accompanying ms. Currently syndicates one-shot travel features to newspaper travel sections; developing a natural food column for syndication to newspaper food sections. Send SASE for contributors' guide and photo guide.

AUTHENTICATED NEWS INTERNATIONAL, ANI, 29 Katonah Ave., Katonah NY 10536. (914)232-7726. Editor: Sidney Polinsky. Syndication and Features Editor: Helga Brink. Supplies book review material to national magazines, newspapers, and house organs in the United States and important countries abroad. Buys exclusive and non-exclusive rights. Previously published submissions OK "at times." Reports in 3 months. SASE.
Nonfiction and Photos: Can use photo material in the following areas: hard news, photo features, ecology and the environment, science, medical, industry, education, human interest, the arts, city planning, and pertinent photo material from abroad. 750 words maximum. Prefers 8x10 b&w glossy prints, color transparencies (4x5 or 2¼x2¼, 35mm color). Where necessary, model releases required. Pays 50% royalty.

AUTO NEWS SYNDICATE, Box 835, Flagler Beach FL 32036. (904)439-2747. Editor: Don O'Reilly. Unsolicited material is acknowledged or returned within a few days, "but we cannot be responsible for loss." SASE. "We are not often in the market for freelance offerings."
Nonfiction and Photos: Syndicated articles, photos on automotive subjects and motor sports. Newspaper columns ("Dateline Detroit" and "Inside Auto Racing"). Magazine articles. Radio broadcasts ("Motorcade USA"). 50% commission. "Payment is made between acceptance and publication." No flat fees.

BUDDY BASCH FEATURE SYNDICATE, 771 West End Ave., New York NY 10025. Publisher: Buddy Basch. Buys all rights. Will consider photocopied submissions, but not of anything previously printed. Query or submit complete ms. Computer printout submissions acceptable; no dot-matrix. Reports in 1 week to 10 days. Must enclose SASE for answer or return of material.
Nonfiction, Humor, Photos, and Fillers: News items, nonfiction, humor, photos, fillers, puzzles, and col-

umns and features on travel and entertainment. "Material is mostly staff written at present. Query."
Tips: "Come up with something really unique. Most writers have the same old hackneyed ideas (*they* think are original) which no one can use. Just because someone in the family or a friend said, 'What a great idea,' doesn't make it so."

CALLIE-PEARL INTERNATIONAL SYNDICATE FEATURES, Box 56, Sunderland MA 01375. Editor: Wilesse Comissiong. 90% freelance written. "We review each submitted sample carefully, and answer each query. Our writers are regarded respectfully and personally since their success is our success. As a young syndicate we are open and receptive to new ideas and concepts. Our organization syndicates to newspapers, radio (some magazines, but primarily newspapers and radio). In order to mobilize our writers' work our syndicate is not bound to only syndicated material, and will use submitted material in brochures, newsletters and paperback type publications—the how-to and self-improvement variety. All of our writers have been seasoned professionals; however, we encourage new writers." Computer printout submissions acceptable. Reports within one month. For writer's guidelines or queries include SASE. Currently syndicates 33 features. Payment is individually considered, based on circulation. Contracts generally are 70/30%.
Tips: "We buy innovative, untried features older syndicates cautiously avoid. We publish a syndicate marketing newsletter to apprise writers of marketing techniques and tips. For a sample copy send SASE."

CITY NEWS SERVICE, Box 86, Willow Springs MO 65793. (417)469-2423. Editor: Richard Weatherington. 90% freelance written. Buys 100+ features/year; 25+ column/department items/year; 75+ fillers/year. Works with 50 previously unpublished writers annually. "We syndicate stories slanted toward small business in all trades." Computer printout submissions acceptable. SASE. Reports in 1 week on queries; 4 months on mss. Buys syndication rights. Writer's guidelines for SAE and 1 first class stamp.
Needs: New product, technical, business articles (1,500-3,000 words). No opinion or first-person narratives. "Will review any column which relates to small business (1,000-1,500 words)." Also uses fillers: Short Business Tips and Inside Techniques (100-250 words). Especially interested in business, finance, law, computer, security and management material. Query or submit complete ms. Send sample of 3 columns. Pays 50-75% commission on articles and columns; 50% on fillers.
Tips: Subjects should be well researched and specific. "We tailor each story to fit the market we service. We are not a mass syndicate. We are more like a custom editorial service and use the freelance material as a base for tailoring. If the writer knows the subject, we will take care of the tailoring for the specific market."

CITY NEWS SYNDICATE, 149 Ravenwood, Dickson TN 37055. (615)446-0257. Editor: Larry Irons. Estab. 1983. Buys approximately 1,200 submissions/year. "It is still growing, we need more. We syndicate to newspapers; however we have submitted to various magazines. It really depends on the article, length, nature and topic." SASE. Reports in 2 months. Buys first North American serial rights and second serial (reprint) rights. Free writer's guidelines.
Needs: Fillers, magazine columns, magazine features, newspaper columns, newspaper features and news items. "We market feature stories throughout the US so submissions must have a universal human interest appeal." Buys single features and article series. Travel, women's issues, fashions, sports, newsbreaks, etc. All must have universal appeal. Submit complete ms. Pays 50% for newspapers; 90% on magazine articles; normally 95% on sales under $50. No additional payment for photos. Currently syndicates *Bookcase*, by Aaron Caplan (book reviews).
Tips: "Be honest, write as if you were talking on the phone to a friend. The reader should walk away with something—an understanding of how to cope with a problem, laughter or happiness; or should learn something new. If and when we receive a letter seeking freelance material from any of our accounts, we get in touch with a writer we feel could fill that need. We also do a large number of newsletters for various associations. Often there is no byline in these for the writer, but the pay is usually good."

COLLEGE PRESS SERVICE, 2629 18th St., Denver CO 80211. (303)458-7216. Editor: Bill Sonn. 25% freelance written. "We work with about 10-15 previously published freelancers a year." Sells to average 500 outlets. Initial written query is imperative. Computer printout submissions acceptable; prefers letter-quality to dot-matrix. SASE. Reports in 2-4 weeks. Material is not copyrighted.
Needs: Magazine and newspaper features; news items. "All our material is somehow related to colleges, students, higher education, faculty members, research, etc. We use only reportage, no opinion or commentary pieces." Pays 5¢/word.

CONTINUUM BROADCASTING NETWORK/GENERATION NEWS, INC., Suite 46, 345 W. 85th St., New York NY 10024. (212)580-9525. Executive Editor: Donald J. Fass. Broadcast Producer: (Ms.) Sandy Benjamin. Broadcast Feature Producer: Deanna Baron. 60% freelance written. Buys 300 features/interviews/year. Works with 20-30 previously unpublished writers annually. Syndicates to newspapers and radio. SASE. Reports in 3 weeks. Buys all rights. Writer's guidelines for business-size SAE and 40¢ postage.
Needs: Newspaper columns (all kinds of weekly regular features for newspapers); radio broadcast material

(90-second and 2½-minute regular daily radio features: lifestyle, comedy, music and interview—scripts as well as taped features); 30-minute and 60-minute specials. One-shot features for radio only-for 30- and 60-minute specials; scripts and completed productions. Query with clips of published work and summary only on articles. Demo tape and/or full script for broadcast; not necessary to query on tapes, but return postage must be provided. Pays 25-50% commission or $25-175, depending on length. Offers no additional payment for photos accompanying ms. Currently syndicates *Getting It Together* (weekly youth-oriented music and lifestyle column; *American Weekend* (radio feature magazine program); *Keeping Fit* (daily series); *Taking Off* (daily travel series); *The Eighties* (daily radio lifestyle features) and *On Bleecker Street* (weekly program on the sixties—interview and music show hosted by Don Fass and Deanna Baron).

Tips: "Chances are very good to excellent, particularly in radio syndication. For both newspaper and radio, it must be a unique or very contemporary concept that can be sustained indefinitely. It is helpful to have a backlog of material and good subject knowledge, combined with good research skills."

CROWN SYNDICATE, INC., Box 99126, Seattle WA 98199. President: L.M. Boyd. Buys countless trivia items and cartoon and panel gag lines. Syndicates to newspapers, radio. SASE. Reports in 1 month. Buys first North American serial rights. Free writer's guidelines.

Needs: Filler material used weekly, items for trivia column, gaglines for specialty comic strip (format guidelines sent on request). Pays $1-5/item, depending on how it's used, i.e., trivia or filler service or comic strip. Offers no additional payment for photos accompanying ms. Currently syndicates puzzle panels and comic strips, by Crown contributors (daily strip).

CURIOUS FACTS FEATURES, 6B Ridge Ct., Lebanon OH 45036. (513)932-1820. Editor: Donald Whitacre. 43% freelance written. Buys 175 articles, features and fillers/year. Works with 65% previously unpublished writers annually. Syndicates to 55 newspapers; columns that contain oddities of all kinds, especially oddities about laws. Computer printout submissions OK; "typewritten," better. SASE. Reports in 6 weeks. Buys all rights. Writer's guidelines for 4½x9½ SAE and 2 first class stamps.

Needs: Fillers (maximum 50 words; oddities of all types); and newspaper features (maximum 400 words; strange laws of the world; strange animals of the world). "We are always interested in 'Strange Anomalies of Medicine'—Questions and Answers dealing with Oddities in the World. We purchase all kinds of oddities (no copyrighted material)." Pays 50% commission. Submit 4 columns (complete ms).

Photos: No additional payment for photos accepted with ms. Currently syndicates *Curious Facts . . . ,* by Donald Whitacre (oddities of all kinds).

Tips: "We use true oddities, which can be cut if they are too long." Average length: 30-300 words.

EDITORIAL CONSULTANT SERVICE, Box 524, West Hempstead NY 11552. Editorial Director: Arthur A. Ingoglia. 15% freelance written. "We work with 75 writers in the US and Canada," previously published writers only. Adds about 3 new columnists/year. Syndicates material to an average of 60 newspapers, magazines, automotive trade and consumer publications, and radio stations with circulation of 50,000-575,000. Query. Computer printout submissions acceptable; no dot-matrix. SASE. Reports in 2-3 weeks. Buys all rights. Writer's guidelines for SASE.

Needs: Magazine and newspaper columns and features; news items; and radio broadcast material. Prefers carefully documented material with automotive slant. Also considers automotive trade features. Will consider article series. No horoscope, child care, lovelorn or pet care. Author's percentage varies; usually averages 50%. Additional payment for 8x10 b&w and color photos accepted with ms. Submit 2-3 columns. Currently syndicates *Let's Talk About Your Car*, by R. Hite.

FACING SOUTH, Box 531, Durham NC 27702. (919)688-8167. Editor: Joycelyn Moody. 75% freelance written. Buys 52 columns/year for syndication to 50-60 newspapers; "stories with a clear, lively human interest angle, but which don't condescend to the reader by attempts to be 'cute.' " Works with about 10 previously unpublished writers annually. Query or submit complete ms. Computer printout submissions acceptable—"as long as they are double-spaced and clearly legible"; prefers letter-quality to dot-matrix. SASE. Reports in 5 weeks. Buys all rights.

Needs: "700-750-word columns focusing on a Southern individual, allowing that person to tell a story. We need portraits of activists, innovators, and artists; also of ordinary Southerners creatively involved in their communities. Each week a different writer does a column, although we will use more than one column by the same writer—just spread them over several months." No Horatio Alger themes, Southern stereotypes, or "sentimental glorifications of Southern life 'the way it used to be'; or slick tributes to the wonders of Sun Belt prosperity. Writers should avoid these simplistic extremes." Pays $50 for each column published. "Writers must send for our guidelines before attempting a column." Submit 1-3 columns. No payment for photos; "we just need some kind of a snapshot that our artist can use to do an illustration."

Tips: "We seek diverse subjects and writers; strong emphasis on details."

FICTION NETWORK, Box 5651, San Francisco CA 94101. (415)552-3223. Editor: Jay Schaefer. 100% freelance written. Syndicates to newspapers and regional magazines. Buys 150 features/year. Works with 25 previously unpublished writers annually. Computer printout submissions acceptable; prefers letter-quality to dot-matrix. SASE. Reports in 2 months. Buys first North American serial and second serial (reprint) rights. Sample catalog of syndicated stories $4; free writer's guidelines.
Needs: All types of fiction under 2,500 words. "We specialize in quality literature." Submit complete ms. "Send one manuscript at a time; do not send second until you receive a response to the first." Pays 50% commission. Currently syndicates short fiction only; authors include Alice Adams, Ann Beattie, Max Apple, Andre Dubus, Lewis Burke Frumkes, Joyce Carol Oates, and others.
Tips: "We seek and encourage previously unpublished authors."

FIRST DRAFT, Box 191107, Dallas TX 75219. (214)358-2271. Editor: Sheri Rosen. 75% freelance written. Buys 60 articles/year. Syndicates to corporate and organizational employee publications. Electronic submissions OK—ASCII compatible or MCI Mail. Computer printout submissions acceptable. SASE. Reports in 6 weeks. Buys all rights. Writer's guidelines for business-size SAE and 1 first class stamp.
Nonfiction: News items of 500 words (the effect of what's happening in the world on working people and businesses). May be universal or limited by industry. Buys one-shot features. Query with published clips or submit complete ms. Pays flat rate of $100 on acceptance.
Tips: "Most freelancers we use are business writers or former company publication editors."

GENERAL NEWS SYNDICATE, 147 W. 42nd St., New York NY 10036. (212)221-0043. 20% freelance written. Works with 12 writers/year; average of 3 previously unpublished writers annually. Syndicates to an average of 12 newspaper and radio outlets averaging 20 million circulation; buys theatre and show business people columns (mostly New York theatre pieces). Computer printout submissions acceptable; no dot-matrix. SASE. Reports in 3 weeks. Buys one-time rights. Submit 1 column.

HARRIS & ASSOCIATES PUBLISHING DIVISION, 247 S. 800 East, Logan UT 84321. (801)753-3587. President: Dick Harris. Rights purchased vary with author and material. Buys first rights. Does not purchase many mss per year since material must be in special style. Pays on acceptance. Not necessary to query. Send sample or representative material. Reports in less than 30 days. SASE.
Nonfiction, Photos, and Humor: Material on driver safety and accident prevention. Humor for modern women (not women's lib); humor for sports page. "We like to look at anything in our special interest areas. Golf and tennis are our specialties. We'll also look at cartoons in these areas. Will buy or contract for syndication. Everything must be short, terse, with humorous approach." Action, unposed, 8x10 b&w photos are purchased without features or on assignment. Captions are required. Pays 10¢ minimum per word and $15 minimum per photo.
Tips: "Submit *good* photos or art with text."

HERITAGE FEATURES SYNDICATE, 214 Massachusetts Ave. NE, Washington DC 20002. (202)543-0440. Managing Editor: Andy Seamans. 2% freelance written. Buys 3 columns/year. Syndicates to over 100 newspapers with circulations ranging from 2,000-630,000. Works with previously published writers. SASE. Reports in 3 weeks. Buys first North American serial rights. Computer printout submissions acceptable.
Needs: Newspaper columns (practically all material is done on assignment). One-shot features. "We purchase 750-800 word columns on political, economic and related subjects." Query. Pays $50 minimum. Currently syndicates *The Economy in Mind*, by Warren Brookes (economics); *A Minority View*, by Walter E. Williams (social issues); and *Main Street U.S.A.*, by William Murchison (general); *Man and His Universe*, by Milt Copulos (energy, environmental and scientific); *From Abroad*, by Anthony Lejeune (foreign affairs); *Of Consuming Interest*, by editors of Consumers' Research; and *Washington Window*, by M. Stanton Evans.
Tips: "Freelance writers can best break in to the syndicate market by being published in a local newspaper, being a working journalist, and gaining some degree of public notice in another media, such as authoring a book."

HISPANIC LINK NEWS SERVICE, 1420 N St. NW, Washington DC 20005. (202)234-0280. Editor/Publisher: Charles A. Ericksen. 80% freelance written. Buys 156 columns and features/year. Works with 50 writers/year; 5 previously unpublished writers. Syndicates to average of 193 newspapers and magazines with circulations ranging from 5,000 to 300,000. Computer printout submissions acceptable; prefers letter-quality to dot-matrix. SASE. Reports in 2 weeks. Buys second serial (reprint) or negotiable rights. Free writer's guidelines.
Needs: Magazine columns, magazine features, newspaper columns, newspaper features. One-shot features and article series. "We prefer 650-700 word op/ed or features, geared to a general national audience, but focus on issue or subject of particular interest to Hispanic Americans. Some longer pieces accepted occasionally." Query or submit complete ms. Pays $10-150. Currently syndicates *Hispanic Link*, by various authors (opinion and/or feature columns).
Tips: "Provide insights on Hispanic experience geared to a general audience. Eighty-five to ninety percent of

the columns we accept are authored by Hispanics; the Link presents Hispanic viewpoints, and showcases Hispanic writing talent to its 193 subscribing newspapers and magazines. Copy should be submitted in English. We syndicate in English and Spanish.''

HOLLYWOOD INSIDE SYNDICATE, Box 49957, Los Angeles CA 90049. Editor: John Austin. 40% freelance written. Purchases mss for syndication to newspapers in San Francisco, Philadelphia, Detroit, Montreal, London, and Sydney, etc. Works with 1-2 previously unpublished writers annually. Query or submit complete ms. Previously published submissions OK, if published in the US and Canada only. Computer printout submissions acceptable; prefers letter-quality to dot-matrix. SASE. Reports in 4-6 weeks. Buys first rights or second serial (reprint) rights.
Needs: News items (column items concerning entertainment—motion picture—personalities and jet setters for syndicated column; 750-800 words). Also considers series of 1,500-word articles; "suggest descriptive query first." Pay negotiable. Pays on acceptance "but this is also negotiable because of delays in world market acceptance and payment."
Tips: "Study the entertainment pages of Sunday (and daily) newspapers to see the type of specialized material we deal in. Perhaps we are different from other syndicates, but we deal with celebrities and particularly not 'I' journalism such as when 'I spoke to Cloris Leachman.' Many freelancers submit material from the 'dinner theatre' and summer stock circuit of 'gossip type' items from what they have observed about the 'stars' or featured players in these productions—how they act off stage, who they romance, etc. We use this material."

INDEPENDENT NEWS ALLIANCE, 200 Park Ave., New York NY 10166. (212)557-2333. Executive Editor: Sidney Goldberg. 25% freelance written. Supplies material to leading US and Canadian newspapers, also to South America, Europe, Asia and Africa. Works with 30 previously unpublished writers annually. Rights purchased vary with author and material. May buy all rights, first rights, or second serial (reprint) rights. Pays "on distribution to clients." Previously published submissions OK "on occasion." Query or submit complete ms. Computer printout submissions acceptable; prefers letter-quality to dot-matrix. Reports in 2 weeks. SASE.
Nonfiction and Photos: In the market for background, investigative, interpretive and news features. Lifestyle, trends, the arts, national issues that affect individuals and neighborhoods. The news element must be strong and purchases are generally made only from experienced, working journalists and authors. Wants timely news features of national interest that do not duplicate other coverage but add to it, interpret it, etc. Wants first-class nonfiction suitable for feature development. The story must be aimed at newspapers, must be self-explanatory, factual and well condensed. It must add measurably to the public's information or understanding of the subject, or be genuinely entertaining. Broad general interest is the key to success here. Length: 500 to 1,500 words, on occasion longer. Rarely buys columns. Looking for good 1-shots and good series of 2 to 7 articles. Where opinions are given, the author should advise, for publication, his qualifications to comment on specialized subjects. The news must be exclusive to be considered at all. Rate varies depending on interest and news value. Pays $75-300. Buys 8x10 glossy photos when needed to illustrate story; pays $25-50.
Tips: "Be space conscious—newspapers want a quick lead, fast follow-up. No leisurely developed stories. Write tight, clean copy. The target should be page one or the lead feature page of the paper—not 'any old' story."

INTERCONTINENTAL MEDIA SERVICES, LTD., Box 75127, Washington DC 20013. (202)638-5595. Editor: Dr. Edward von Rothkirch. Buys 500 features, 1,200 syndicated columns/year. Syndicates primarily to newspapers, some magazines. "In addition we syndicate 6 radio programs and are now going into 3-6 TV vignettes." SASE. Reports in 1 month. Buys all rights when available. Writer's guidelines for SAE and 1 first class stamp.
Needs: Newspaper columns (travel, collectibles, medical—500 to 700 words); newspaper features (travel, unusual subjects—1,500 words); news items (political backgrounders on foreign countries and personalities); radio broadcast material (travel, book reviews, science—length 2-3 minutes). One-shot (sometimes) and article series. "We will consider 400-1,500 words on foreign politics or personalities, travel to out of the way or unusual places, collectibles of all kinds, science or medical subjects." Submit complete ms. Pays 50% of net; $50-500 (special) flat rate. Pays $25-100 for photos. Currently syndicates *Magic Carpet*, by Edward R'Church (travel).
Tips: "If the material is well prepared, the approach is new or different, and there is a substantial segment of potential readers that have an interest in the subject, there is a good chance for syndication. The writer should indicate what the market potential is for the material."

INTERNATIONAL ECO FEATURES SYNDICATE, Box 69193, W. Hollywood, Los Angeles CA 90069. Editor: Janet Bridgers. 90% freelance written. Syndicates to newspapers. Works with approximately 3 previously unpublished writers annually. SASE. Reports in 2 months. Buys first worldwide serial rights. Writer's guidelines for business size SASE with 20¢ postage.
Needs: Newspaper columns specializing in environment, ecology and animal rights. Op-ed articles, 800-1,200 words; features, 1,500-2,000 words with photos. Query with clips of published work. Pays 50% com-

mission. "We will ask a higher price from newspapers when photos are accepted with manuscripts."
Tips: "We specialize in material about ecology, the environment and animal rights. We are not interested in material that is not about these subjects. We are *particularly* interested in op-eds on regional environmental issues."

INTERNATIONAL MEDICAL TRIBUNE SYNDICATE, Suite 700, 600 New Hampshire Ave. NW, Washington DC 20037. (202)338-8866. Editor: Keith Haglund. 75% freelance written. Buys about 100 articles/year. Works with a few previously unpublished writers annually. Syndicates to small- and medium-sized newspapers, daily and weekly; magazines; computer news service; specialty publications in the health field. Computer printout submissions acceptable. SASE. Reports in 3 weeks. Buys all rights.
Needs: Fillers (250-400 words on medical or health developments); newspaper features (1,000-1,500 words; relatively complete treatment of an area of medicine or health); news items (straight news story filed within 1 week of event covered, etc., average 500 words). One-shot features on any topic in medicine and health; 1,000 to 1,500 words. Query with clips of published work or submit complete ms. "Call with idea." Pays 15¢/word for straight news; 20¢/word for features. Offers kill fee if assigned story. Offers no additional payment for photos accompanying ms.
Tips: "Our syndicate is an excellent opportunity for freelancers, but clear, concise and LIVELY writing is a must. Strongly suggest query first, by mail or phone."

INTERPRESS OF LONDON AND NEW YORK, 400 Madison Ave., New York NY 10017. (212)832-2839. Editor: Jeffrey Blyth. 50% freelance written. Works with 2-3 previously unpublished writers annually. Buys British and European rights mostly, but can handle world rights. Will consider photocopied submissions. Previously published submissions OK "for overseas." Query or submit complete ms. Pays on publication, or agreement of sale. Reports immediately or as soon as practicable. SASE.
Nonfiction and Photos: "Unusual stories and photos for British and European press. Picture stories, for example, on such 'Americana' as a five-year-old evangelist; the 800-pound 'con-man'; the nude-male calendar; tallest girl in the world; interviews with pop celebrities such as Yoko Ono, Michael Jackson, Tom Sellick, Cher, Priscilla Presley, Cheryl Tiegs, Liza Minelli; cult subjects such as voodoo, college fads, anything amusing or offbeat. Extracts from books such as Earl Wilson's *Show Business Laid Bare*, inside-Hollywood type series ('Secrets of the Stuntmen,' 'My Life with Racquel Welch'). Real life adventure dramas ('Three Months in an Open Boat,' 'The Air Crash Cannibals of the Andes'). No length limits—short or long, but not too long. Payment varies; depending on whether material is original, or world rights. Pay top rates, up to several thousand dollars, for exclusive material. Photos purchased with or without features. Captions required. Standard size prints. Pay $50 to $100, but no limit on exclusive material."
Tips: "Be alert to the unusual story in your area—the sort that interests the American tabloids (and also the European press)."

KING FEATURES SYNDICATE, INC., 235 E. 45th St., New York NY 10017. (212)682-5600. Editor: James D. Head. 10% freelance written. Syndicates material to newspapers; "today it is the consumer-oriented column—anything about ways to save money, ways to find and hold jobs." Works with 10-15 previously unpublished writers annually. Submit "brief cover letter with samples of feature proposals." Previously published submissions OK. Computer printout submissions acceptable. SASE. Reports in 2-3 weeks. Buys all rights.
Needs: Newspaper features and columns. Will consider article series. No travel; wine or general humor columns; restaurant, theatre or movie reviews; or fad-oriented subjects. Pays "revenue commission percentage" or flat fee. Special single article opportunity is *Sunday Woman* a weekly supplement distributed nationally. Buys one-time rights to articles on beauty, health, grooming, fashion, coping, money management for women, career guidance etc. Query with SASE to Merry Clark, senior editor.
Tips: "Be brief, thoughtful and offer some evidence that the feature proposal is viable. Read newspapers—lots of them in big and small markets—to find out what already is out there. Don't try to buck established columns which newspapers would be reluctant to replace with new and untried material."

KNOWLEDGE NEWS & FEATURES SYNDICATE (K.N.F.), Box 100, Kenilworth IL 60043. (312)256-0059. Executive Editor: Dr. Whitt N. Schultz. Rights purchased vary with author and material. Will consider photocopied submissions. Previously published submissions OK. Computer printout submissions acceptable; prefers letter-quality to dot-matrix.
Business Features, Photos and Nonfiction: News items; humor; fillers; business, knowledge and education articles; "success stories." Syndicates how-to columns (e.g., *How to Develop Your Personal Potential*). Payment negotiable. Submit 6 columns. Currently syndicates *How to Improve Your Career*, by Whitt N. Schultz. Photos purchased with features and also on assignment. Captions required. Buys 8x10 glossy photos. Payment negotiable.
Fillers: Short humorous articles. "We like definitions, epigrams, puns, etc." Also short business articles. Pays negotiable fee.

Tips: "Clear, crisp, concise, cogent writing—easy to read—Open—Spotlight success, inspiration; positive news features. Material should be typed and submitted on standard size paper. Please leave 3 spaces between each item. Unused material will be returned to the writer within a few days *only* if SASE is enclosed. We do *not* send rejection slips. Please do *not* send us any material that has been sent to other publications. If SASE is not enclosed, all material will be destroyed after being considered except for items purchased. When phoning, please call person-to-person. If editor is not available, leave call-back number with long distance operator."

MIDCONTINENT FEATURES SYNDICATE, INC., Box 1662, Pittsburgh PA 15230. Editor-in-Chief: John D. Paulus. 15% freelance written. Buys 30-40 features/year. Syndicates to 550 daily newspapers in the 50,000-and-down circulation (home town America). Works with 10-20 previously unpublished writers annually. Computer printout submissions acceptable; prefers letter-quality to dot-matrix. SASE. Reports in 1 month. Buys all rights.
Needs: Newspaper columns, newspaper features. Submit complete ms. Pays 50% net after syndication expenses. Offers no additional payment for photos accompanying ms. Currently syndicates *Staying Healthy*, by Clarke Hankey, MD (medical/health column); *Everybody's Business*, by John Douglas Paulus (economics); and *Read'n & Writin*, by Mildred H. Paulus (book review column), and features in travel, religion, retirement, food, home, decoration, science, etc.
Tips: Writing bought by this syndicate "must cater to 'hometown' America."

NATIONAL NEWS BUREAU, 2019 Chancellor St., Philadelphia PA 19103. (215)569-0700. Editor: Harry Jay Katz. "We work with more than 200 writers and buy over 1,000 stories/year." Syndicates to more than 1,000 publications. SASE. Reports in 2 weeks. Buys all rights. Writer's guidelines for 9x12 SAE and 54¢ postage.
Needs: Newspaper features; "we do many reviews and celebrity interviews. Only original, assigned material." One-shot features and article series; film reviews, etc. Query with clips. Pays $5-200 flat rate. Offers $5-200 additional payment for photos accompanying ms. Currently syndicates *En Route*, by Andy Edelman (travel).

NEW YORK TIMES SYNDICATION SALES CORP., 200 Park Ave., New York NY 10166. (212)972-1070. Vice President/Editorial Director: Paula Reichler. 50% freelance written. Syndicates approximately "three books per month plus numerous one-shot articles." Also included in foreign newspapers and magazines. Prefers world rights but often buys North American second serial rights; for books, "first, second or both" rights. Computer printout submissions acceptable; no dot-matrix.
Needs: Wants magazine and newspaper features; magazine and newspaper columns; and book series. Recently syndicated Richard Nixon's *Real Peace*. "On syndicated articles, payment to author is 50% of net sales. We only consider articles that have been previously published. Send tearsheets of articles published. Photos are welcome with books and articles."

NEWS AMERICA SYNDICATE, (formerly Field Newspaper Syndicate), 1703 Kaiser Ave., Irvine CA 92714. President/Chief Executive Officer: Steven Jehorek. Syndicates material to newspapers. Submit "examples of work with explanatory letter to Submissions Department." SASE. Reports in 1-2 months. Rights purchased vary. Free writer's guidelines.
Needs: Newspaper columns (should be 500-800 words in length and should appeal to a wide audience. Subject matter should not be too specialized because syndicates sell columns to newspapers all over the US and Canada). Submit minimum 10 columns. Currently syndicates *Ann Landers*, by Ann Landers.

NEWS FLASH INTERNATIONAL, INC., 2262 Centre Ave., Bellmore NY 11710. (516)679-9888. Editor: Jackson B. Pokress. 10% freelance written. Supplies material to Observer newspapers and overseas publications. Works with 6 previously unpublished writers annually. "Contact editor prior to submission to allow for space if article is newsworthy." Photocopied submissions OK. Computer printout submissions acceptable; no dot-matrix. Pays on publication. SASE.
Nonfiction: "We have been supplying a 'ready-for-camera' sports page (tabloid size) complete with column and current sports photos on a weekly basis to many newspapers on Long Island as well as pictures and written material to publications in England and Canada. Payment for assignments is based on the article. It may vary. Payments vary from $20 for a feature of 800 words. Our sports stories feature in-depth reporting as well as book reviews on this subject. We are always in the market for good photos, sharp and clear, action photos of boxing, wrestling, football, baseball and hockey. We cover all major league ball parks during the baseball and football seasons. We are accredited to the Mets, Yanks, Jets and Giants. During the winter we cover basketball and hockey and all sports events at the Nassau Coliseum."
Photos: Purchased on assignment; captions required. Uses "good quality 8x10 b&w glossy prints; good choice of angles and lenses." Pays $7.50 minimum for b&w photos.
Tips: "Submit articles, which are fresh in their approach, on a regular basis with good quality b&w glossy pho-

Close-up

Leighton McLaughlin, Editor
News America Syndicate

Leighton McLaughlin supervises a coast-to-coast newsroom. It's the kind (without walls) that thousands of writers want to work for. "But before lunch every day, we have more submissions than we're going to syndicate in a year," says the News America editor.

Still, he looks for the six to eight *new* people each year whose work will go nationwide through syndication.

A brief, bright, thought-provoking and modern writing style will get McLaughlin's attention. "This person has to be very good at what he does; his timing has to be such that somebody needs what he does at the time that he presents it," says the newspaperman of 27 years, who joined the syndicate five years ago. "Gimmicks don't work. It needs to be a difference of substance or difference in subject matter.

"Some of the material we get here is empty. Rather than doing the hard legwork to have something to say in a column, writers want to make it up, write off the top of their heads," he says. "They want to take one fact and build a column around it rather than finding out all the ramifications."

And too many writers try to imitate News America columnists Erma Bombeck and Ann Landers, he points out. "We're not going to imitate a successful feature and compete for its space and with ourselves."

To merit syndication, aspiring columnists must woo more than a local readership. In fact, the columnist has to please three audiences in sequence: News America, newspaper editors, and readers. "We have to be successful with newspaper editors before we have a chance at being successful with the general public," he says.

Once newspaper editors buy a syndicated column, their readers must like it. "Newspapers will carry their own people for lots of reasons that they would not carry an outside columnist."

That's one problem that syndicated columnists face—they must be commercially successful. "If a column is not making money for a syndicate, the syndicate knows it every month on its statement," says McLaughlin. "As columns start costing us money, we no longer carry them." Fifty percent or less of syndicated material stays in syndication, he estimates.

News America Syndicate (formerly the Field Newspaper Syndicate) syndicates 90 columns, features and comic strips. The firm also acquires one-time features for syndication.

McLaughlin hasn't seen any changes that might affect writers since the syndicate's change of ownership last year. He is still editing (though lightly) the work of about 30 columnists. He'll contact them to clarify information, though the syndicate retains the right to edit all columns.

"Our philosophy here is the less editing, the better," he says. "Good writers have a personal style; we don't want to mess with their style."

As for meeting deadlines, syndicated columnists have habits as varied as the subjects of their columns—some work months in advance; others submit their work at the last minute. "It's just like a newsroom, only our reporters, if you will, are scattered all over the country," says McLaughlin.

tos if possible; include samples of work. Articles should have a hard-hitting approach and plenty of quotes and short terse sentences."

NEWSLINK AFRICA, Suite 411, London International Press Centre, 76, Shoe Lane-Fleet St., London EC4 England. Tel. (01)353-0186. Telex: 23862 (Attn: Newsafrica). Managing Editor: Shamlal Puri. 60% freelance written. Buys about 300 features/year (200 written inhouse). "We work with very few previously unpublished writers annually, but we like to encourage writers (whether published or unpublished) to provide copy on African affairs. So, if they are unpublished on Africa (but have written generally), we are prepared to give them a break provided they have the potential." Computer printout submissions acceptable; prefers letter-quality to dot-matrix. Syndicates to magazines, newspapers, radio, reference libraries. SASE. Reports in 3 months. Buys all rights.
Needs: Fiction, fillers, magazine columns, magazine features, newspaper columns, newspaper features, radio broadcast material. "We concentrate on African affairs or how world events affect Africa, and are (reportedly) the only syndicate dealing in African affairs exclusively in Britain, Europe and Canada. We look at events in Africa as Africans would do. We do not like 'injecting' Western influence or values into our output. Our agency is run by Africans whose sole motive is dissemination of news and information. We are not backed by any multi-national or political party. We'd prefer specialists in African affairs. We try to avoid academic writing style—simplicity is the main prerequisite." One-shot features and article series (about 1,000-2,000 words). "Topics should include Africa (economics, commerce, politics, social scene or any topic having a bearing on Africa)." Query with clips of published work or submit complete ms. "Material accepted on speculation also. Enclose IRC/check for return postage. Work accepted purely on merit. Our payments start from 5-200 pounds sterling for 1,000 words." Currently syndicates *African Culture* Series, by T. Ankrah.
Photos: "We prefer negatives to make more prints. Send negative with each print."
Tips: Encourages objectivity, sticking to details and simple language. "You must know your subject well. In our field, we prefer specialists in African affairs."

NEWSPAPER ENTERPRISE ASSOCIATION, INC., 200 Park Ave., New York NY 10166. (212)557-5870. Editorial Director: David Hendin. Executive Editor: Sidney Goldberg. Managing Editor: Diana Drake. "We provide a comprehensive package of features to mostly small- and medium-size newspapers." Computer printout submissions acceptable. SASE. Reports in 6 weeks. Buys all rights.
Needs: "Any column we purchase must fill a need in our feature lineup and must have appeal for a wide variety of people in all parts of the country. We are most interested in lively writing. We are also interested in features that are not merely copies of other features already on the market. And the writer must know his or her subject. Any writer who has a feature which meets all of those requirements should simply send a few copies of the feature to us, along with his or her plans for the column and some background material on the writer." Current columnists include Bob Walters, Bob Wagman, Julian Bond, Dr. Karen Blaker, Dr. Lawrence Lamb, Tom Tiede, Murray Olderman, Dick Kleiner, Rusty Brown and William Rusher. Current comics include *Alley Oop*, *Born Loser*, *Frank & Ernest*, *Levy's Law*, *Eek & Meek*, *Kit 'n' Carlyle*, *Bugs Bunny*, *Berry's World*, *Our Boarding House* and *The Great John L*.
Tips: "We get enormous numbers of proposals for first person columns—slice of life material with lots of anecdotes. While many of these columns are big successes in local newspapers, it's been our experience that they are extremely difficult to sell nationally. Most papers seem to prefer to buy this sort of column from a talented local writer."

NORTHWEST EDITORIALS, 2464 33rd Ave. W., Box 181, Seattle WA 98199. (206)282-4777. Editor: Patrick Johnston. Estab. 1983. Buys 200-250 articles/year. "We distribute unpublished and previously published material to publications, the media and to syndicates in foreign countries"; magazines 90%, other 10%. SASE. Reports in 2 months. "We do not need North American rights, but all other rights must be intact."
Needs: "We are especially looking for celebrity pieces with photos. These must be of good character—sensationalism must be done with integrity and with tongue-in-cheek. *No* muckraking. Also, general interest/human nature features; family life; American adventure and travel; sports and athletes; trends; fads; and topical pieces." Length: 500-3,000 words. One-shot and article series. "These particular items will be considered from queries, from previously published material, and from assignments." Query with or without published clips; "unsolicited manuscripts will not be accepted or returned." Pays 50% commission, salary up to $1,200-1,500 depending on material. Usually pays additional rate for color transparencies and 8x10 b&w prints. Payment varies with country, type of photo. Must be of high quality. "We do not syndicate features at this time."
Tips: "Writer's chances are excellent for the foreign market. Submit query (detailed)."

NUMISMATIC INFORMATION SERVICE, Rossway Rd., Rt. 4, Box 237A, Pleasant Valley NY 12569. Editor: Barbara White. Buys 5 features/year. Query. Computer printout submissions acceptable. SASE. Reports in 1-2 weeks. Buys all rights.
Needs: Newspaper columns (anything related to numismatics and philately, particularly the technical aspects of the avocations); news items (relative to the world of coin and stamp collecting); and fillers (on individual

coins or stamps, or the various aspects of the hobbies). No fiction or get rich schemes. Pays $5/500 word article; 50¢ additional payment for b&w photos accepted with ms.

OCEANIC PRESS SERVICE, Box 6538, Buena Park CA 90622-6538. (714)527-5650. Editor: John Taylor. 90% freelance written. Buys from 12-15 writers annually, "using their published work" for use in some 300 magazines, newspapers or books with a circulation range of 1-15 million. Works with 10 previously unpublished writers annually. Buys timely topics with universal appeal. Averages 9 new writers/year. Query with clips of published work. Computer printout submissions acceptable; no dot-matrix. SASE. Reports in 3 weeks. Buys all rights, or second serial (reprint) rights. Writer's guidelines $1.

Needs: "We like authors and cartoonists but, for our mutual benefit, they must fit into our editorial policies. The following list will give an idea of the kind of materials we want: interviews or profiles (world figures only); recipes, with color transparencies or b&w pictures; home building and home decoration features with photos; hairstyle features with photos; interviews with movie and TV stars with photos; current books to be sold for translation to foreign markets: mysteries, biographies, how to do, self improvement, westerns, science fiction, romance, psychological, and gothic novels; features on family relations, modern women, heroism, and ecology; features on water sports, with color transparencies; and newspaper columns with illustrations. We are always happy to obtain reprint rights, especially book excerpts or serializations. Payment is outright or on a 50/50 basis; range is $25-3,000. We take care of foreign language translations. Submit a varied sampling of columns, tearsheets preferred."

PHOTO ASSOCIATES NEWS SERVICE, INC., Box 306, Station A, Flushing NY 11358. (212)961-0909. Editor-in-Charge: Rick Moran. "We work with 25 writers, doing 350 stories/year." Syndicates to domestic and international magazines and newspapers. SASE. Reports in 1 week. Buys variable rights "depending on material submitted." Free writer's guidelines.

Needs: Rita C. Allen, features and general interest material. Maurice Kessler, entertainment and paparazzo. Rick Moran, public safety issues. Magazine features, newspaper columns, newspaper features and news items. "Photo Associates is looking for stand alone features on a wide variety of topics. We have some very good contacts in Asia and South and Central America who are looking for all kinds of material. They want regular syndicated columns on education, health, science, entertainment, etc. They also want bright travel pieces and features on virtually any topic you can imagine. We also have many domestic clients, including several in the public safety area. Writers specializing in public safety issues (police, fire, ambulance, paramedics) are also needed. One area that is in big need all the time is celebrity material, interviews, etc. Our clients simply can't get enough. We are always looking for new ideas, something fresh that is not already in wide distribution over the wires. The sheer weight of the material sent overseas by us each week is overwhelming, yet our clients are always looking for more when it comes to the movies, theatre, music and entertainment, so we are always looking for a fresh look from a new name." Buys single features and article series. Query with published clips. "A good photocopy is OK, if you do not have published work, but want to show us something, we are always willing to take a look, but obviously, we are looking for writers with the staying power for the long haul. We will handle one time sales, but prefer opening up a long term relationship with the writer." Pays 65% commission, reporting monthly. Pays extra for photos with mss. Currently syndicates *Police Story*, edited by Rick Moran (public safety).

Tips: "We are very interested in meeting new talent. We prefer writers who can also provide us with illustrative photos, but do not rule out anyone with a talent for writing."

THE REGISTER AND TRIBUNE SYNDICATE, INC., 715 Locust St., Des Moines IA 50304. (515)284-8244. President: Dennis R. Allen. Submission Editor: Thomas E. Norquist. 25% freelance written. Buys material for syndication in 1,700 daily newspapers, television, product licensing outlets. Works with many previously unpublished writers depending on subject matter. Submit complete ms. Submission not returned without SASE. Photocopied submissions required. Computer printout submissions acceptable "if legible and easy to read"; no dot-matrix. Reports in 6 weeks. Buys all rights.

Needs: News items (nonfiction); and photos (purchased with written material); items reflecting topical trends and needs with ability for sustaining on-going column. Buys article series "from 500-700 words/column on current topics. Most submissions require at least 6-weeks worth of column copy or artwork in near finish form. Don't send original work." Pays in royalties or commissions. Pays on publication.

Tips: Especially interested in self-help topic matter. "Study articles and series currently appearing in newspapers; follow successful format and topic matter for self-help."

RELIGIOUS NEWS SERVICE, 104 W. 56th St., New York NY 10019. Editor and Director: Gerald Renner. 50% freelance written. Supplies material to "secular press, religious press of all denominations, radio and TV stations." Previously published submissions OK. "Confer first on electronic submissions. We prefer electronic transmission only from those with whom we have a working relationship." Computer printout submissions acceptable. SASE for return of submissions.

Nonfiction and Photos: "Good news stories on important newsworthy developments. Religious news. No devotional, inspirational, advocacy or first person accounts; news stories only." Will buy single features "if they have news pegs. Most of our article series are produced by our own staff." Length: 200-1,000 words. Pays 3¢ a word and up. Photos purchased with and without features and on assignment; captions required. Uses b&w glossy prints, preferably 8x10. Pays $25 minimum.

SINGER COMMUNICATIONS, INC., 3164 Tyler Ave., Anaheim, CA 92801. (714)527-5650. Editor: Jane Sherrod Singer. 50% freelance written. Buys 500 features, 300 books/year. Works with 5 previously unpublished writers annually. Syndicates to magazines, newspapers, radio, TV, book publishers and businesses. Computer printout submissions acceptable; prefers letter-quality to dot-matrix. SASE. Reports in 1 month. Buys all rights, first North American serial, second serial (reprint), and world rights. Writer's guidelines $1.
Needs: Fiction (with universal appeal, contemporary romance, westerns); fillers (gags and jokes); magazine columns; magazine features; newspaper columns (with universal appeal); newspaper features (worldwide interest, no political); radio and TV broadcast material; merchandising and marketing items for manufacturing. One-shot features and article series. "We will consider any feature with a worldwide interest that has a timeless quality. We service the entire free world and therefore stay away from features and columns if they are geared only for US consumption." Query with published clips. "We prefer published work for foreign reprint." Pays 50% commission, or flat rate or minimum guarantee depending on material; books negotiable. Pays additional rate for color transparencies or b&w line drawings. Currently syndicates *Solve A Crime*, by B. Gordon (crime column) and 100 other columns.
Tips: "Find a niche in a specialized field which is not over-run; interview important people."

SYNDICATED WRITERS GROUP, Box 23, Boyertown PA 19512. (215)367-9496. Editor: Daniel Grotta. Estab. 1983. "We will work with a maximum of 24 contract writers in each subject category." Syndicates to newspapers and magazines. Electronic submissions OK via modem or Model I, III in TRS80 single density, or 5" or 8" CP/M IBM-formatted, Kaypro, Osborne, TRS80 Model II, or Xerox format. Computer printout submissions acceptable. Reports in 1 month. Maintains exclusive rights for the length of the contract. Free writer's guidelines.
Needs: Magazine columns, magazine features, newspaper columns, newspaper features. "SWG is presently expanding into all 'soft' editorial areas." One-shot and article series. Will consider "special, unique articles not available elsewhere, or by exceptional, well-known or prominent writers not wishing longer term commitments." Query only; include resume, letter and specific proposal. Pays 50% commission; 80% when SWG acts as agent for specific assignment. Pays additional rate for photos sold with ms. Currently syndicates *The Endless Winter*, by Ted Heck (ski column).
Tips: SWG is an electronic editorial syndicate, and all our writers and editors will eventually be connected to us by computer. We work *only* with writers under direct contract to us. However, we will consider freelance writers as potential contract writers as vacancies open. Develop a column format with at least 13 (weekly) or 6 (monthly) samples, plus an accurate description of the column, and a biography/resume. Have something very unusual or brilliant to say, with style and consistency. Be expert in your chosen field."

TEENAGE CORNER, INC., 70-540 Gardenia Ct., Rancho Mirage CA 92270. President: David J. Lavin. Buys 122 items/year for use in newspapers. Submit complete ms. Reports in 1 week. Material is not copyrighted.
Needs: 500-word newspaper features. Pays $25.

TRIBUNE COMPANY SYNDICATE, 220 E. 42nd St., New York NY 10017. Editor: Michael Argirion. Supplies material to Sunday supplements and newspapers in North America and abroad. Buys worldwide rights, where possible; must have North American rights to be interested. Submit at least 6 samples of any submission for continuing feature. SASE for return of submissions.
Columns, Puzzles: No fiction. Material must be extremely well-written and must not be a copy of something now being marketed to newspapers. Length varies, though columns should generally be 500 words or less. Pays variable rate, depending on market; usually 50-50 split of net after production on contractual material. Submit cover letter and 3 columns.

UNITED FEATURE SYNDICATE, 200 Park Ave., New York NY 10166. Editorial Director: David Hendin. Executive Editor: Sidney Goldberg. Managing Editor: D.L. Drake. Supplies features to 1,700 US newspapers, plus Canadian and other international papers. Works with published writers. Query with 4-6 samples and SASE. Computer printout submissions acceptable. Reports in 6 weeks.
Columns, Comic Strips and Puzzles: Current columnists include Jack Anderson, Judith Martin, Donald Lambro, Ben Wattenberg, Martin Sloane, Barbara Gibbons. Comic strips include *Peanuts*, *Nancy*, *Garfield*, *Drabble*, *Marmaduke*, *Tarzan*, and *Ben Swift*. Standard syndication contracts are offered for columns and comic strips.
Tips: "We buy the kind of writing similar to major syndicates—varied material, well-known writers. The best

way to break in to the syndicate market is for freelancers to latch on with a major newspaper and to develop a rabid following. Also, cultivate new areas and try to anticipate trends."

UNITED PRESS INTERNATIONAL (UPI), 1400 Eye St., Washington DC 20005. Editor-in-Chief: Max McCrohon. Seldom, if ever, accepts material from other than UPI staff.

UNIVERSAL PRESS SYNDICATE, 4400 Johnson Dr., Fairway KS 66205. Buys syndication rights. Reports normally in 1 month. Returned postage required.
Nonfiction: Looking for features—columns for daily and weekly newspapers. "Any material suitable for syndication in daily newspapers." Currently handling James J. Kilpatrick and others. Payment varies according to contract.

WORLD-WIDE NEWS BUREAU, 309 Varick St., Jersey City NJ 07302. Editor: Arejas Vitkauskas. "Our multiple writeups (separate, and in our weekly columns) start in greater New York publications, then go simultaneously all over the US and all over the world where English is printed. News from authors, literary agents or publishers on books planned, ready or published. Anything from poetry and children's books to space technology textbooks. We cover over eighty different trade fields." No book mss.

Services & Opportunities

Authors' Agents

You're thinking about hiring an agent but are afraid: Will he improve your writing career or become another business expense? *That* we can't tell you, because it depends on what you write and the agent you hire.

What we do know is that the role of the agent is expanding. As technology shrinks the distance between continents, authors pursue opportunities overseas. "There is an increasing international market," points out one agent, "which only an experienced agent is able to penetrate."

Agents assume several roles in the publishing world. "Increasingly, agents serve as a screening process for editors and publishers in terms of new writers," says another agent, "and agents further serve as the source for creating and developing book ideas with their established authors."

Ideally, an agent should be your trusted business (and creative) partner. "As editors and publishers keep shifting from one house to another, the one constant in a writer's life without question has become his or her agent," says an agent, who represents more than 50 clients.

Beginning writers shouldn't rush to agents' offices thinking an agent will make them better writers. On the other hand, if you have sold a reasonable number of articles, stories, or book manuscripts on your own, you may want to consider the services of an agent. He will handle the marketing of your work so you have more time to write.

An agent is a literary broker, a middleman, who gets your manuscript to the right editor at the right time. He makes the sale and negotiates the best possible deal for you. If you live in the Midwest, for example, and are interested in contacting publishers in New York, you may do well to have an agent. He is often close to the action in the publishing world. Because of his experience in teaching, writing or editing, he knows the ins and outs of the industry. He relies on contacts within the industry to know what a publishing house wants before it makes its announcements public. Some writers consider the services of an agent invaluable.

But an agent is not for everyone. Many writers prefer to do their own marketing. They look for publishers; hire attorneys for advice and contract review; and keep the 10-15% agent commission on domestic sales for themselves.

Other writers cannot find an agent to handle their work. Few agents will handle anything shorter than a book-length manuscript. Others deal only with scriptwriters who have previous credits. Many are looking for published writers or take on new clients only through referrals from other writers/editors.

Getting an Agent

If you are hunting for an agent, the search won't be easy. But if you have good ideas (preferably book-length ones), and if you are persistent, the search can be successful. The most direct approach is to contact an agent by mail with a brief query letter (not to exceed two single-spaced typewritten pages) in which you describe your work, yourself, and your publishing history. For a nonfiction book, add an outline; for fiction, a few sample chapters (up to 50 typed, double-spaced pages) will tell an agent whether the book is no or go. Generally, treatments or even concepts are preferred for television or films. Your letter should be personalized—not a photocopied form letter with the agent's name typed in, and *always include SASE* with enough postage for a reply plus return of materials. If you don't hear from an agent within six weeks, send a polite note asking if the material has been received—and include a photocopy of your original query plus materials and another SASE. If you hear nothing within four months, send a note withdrawing the material—and immediately contact another agent using the same method.

Agents and the Market Today

Literary agencies generally come in three sizes: small (handling up to 60 clients), medium (up to 100), and large (over 100). An agent should not be measured by the number of clients, or even the number of sales made in a given time period, but rather by the number of deals and dollars that he makes for his clients. Agents work for *additional* sales of your manuscripts. No good agent will be satisfied selling your novel to a hardcover publisher, for instance; he'll invest some time in selling it to a paperback house, to a movie producer, to a newspaper syndicate for serialization, to a book club, to a foreign publisher. To do this, the agent exercises energy, ideas, connections, and business experience the writer probably doesn't have.

Most agents do not handle magazine articles, poetry or essays. There is not enough revenue generated from such sales to make them worth an agent's time. Most writers develop their own rapport with the people who edit such publications and sell to them directly. Later, when a writer is doing books, his agent may handle such small sales—as a professional courtesy, not an income maker. Autobiography is almost impossible to sell today, unless you are well known in some area of endeavor. Thin books (manuscripts of less than 200-250 pages) do not sell easily either; most agents refuse to handle them because publishers are not likely to be interested. If you are writing genre fiction—such as mysteries, science fiction or romances—you may have to get a couple of book sales behind you before an agent will handle your work. Most publishers who do genre fiction are generally receptive to hearing from authors directly anyway.

Some agents specialize. The most recent specialists are those agencies representing writers of computer software. Some agencies have broadened their clientele by taking on writers of computer-related books. Other agent specialties are indicated in the listings that follow. Most of the agents in this section are members of the Independent Literary Agents Association (55 5th Ave., 15th Floor, New York City 10003), or the Society of Authors' Representatives (Box 650, Old Chelsea Station, New York City NY 10113).

Fee-Charging Agents

Agents shouldn't sell unsalable work; teach a beginner how to write salable copy; act as editor of the writer's work; solve the author's personal problems or lend money; be available outside of office hours except by appointment; or perform the functions of press agent, social secretary or travel agent. In other words, having an agent is *not* the final solution to your writing problems. An agent can aid and simplify your career, but ultimately your career is in your hands.

Some agents do charge fees. Claiming that reading new material consumes time that might otherwise be spent selling books, they have to charge the fee or stop reading unsolicited material, they say. An estimated 70 percent of agents refuse to read unsolicited manuscripts; 78 percent of those agents willing to read manuscripts by as-yet-unpublished authors charge the writer in some way, according to Author Aid Associates. "About 39 percent of all agents charge fees for some of their services in addition to the traditional commission, which is edging up toward 15 percent (and in a few cases runs as high as 25 percent)," says Arthur Orrmont, Author Aid editorial director. "Of the agents who charge no fees in addition to their commission, 97 percent provide no special services such as manuscript critiques or editorial assistance to their clients."

Here are some questions to ask about reading fees:

Is it a one-time fee, or will you have to pay again on subsequent submissions?

Will you have to pay the fee again when resubmitting a revised manuscript?

Will the fee be refunded if the agent decides to represent you?

Will the agent waive the fee if you have already had work published, or if you have particular expertise in the area you are writing about?

What do you get for the fee? Just a reading, or some criticism and analysis?

Agents may offer suggestions on how a book might be rewritten to be made salable, but under no circumstances do legitimate agents charge a fee for editing your manuscript. *Editing should be done by editors—after the book is sold.*

Remember, though, that there are agents who don't charge a reading fee, and you should try to work with those agents first. Consult the *Literary Agents of North America: 1984-85 Marketplace* (for price information, write Author Aid/Research Associates International, 340 E. 52nd St., New York City 10022) for a list/index of more than 670 currently active agents (including those who do and do not charge and *sometimes* charge for their services) in the U.S. and Canada.

The Pseudo-Agent

Do not confuse true literary agents with other individuals or "agencies" that advertise as "consultants" offering manuscript criticism or "literary services" for a fee that may cover a critique, an edit, or a rewrite of your manuscript. In order to offer some "protection" to our readers, *none of the agents listed here charge reading fees, to the best of our knowledge.* In addition, *Writer's Market* does *not* include any agent who charges postage, criticism, editing, marketing, or *any other fees.* Ask anyone who claims to be an "agent," or who uses agent-like phrasing ("We like your manuscript and we think it is marketable—of course, some revisions will be necessary to make it professionally acceptable," etc.) when discussing a fee of any sort, to give you a list of *recent* book sales. If an agent has not sold three books to established publishing houses in the previous year, he is probably out of the publishing market mainstream. Make sure you can afford such literary services. Fees may range from several hundred to several *thousand* dollars—and there is no guarantee that the arrangement will result in a sale to recoup your investment. Such firms and individuals may make their profits from reading and criticism and editing fees—not from sales to publishers.

Contract Considerations

Be careful, too, in signing any contract with an agent. Many legitimate agents conduct business with a handshake, believing that a contract will neither solidify a good relationship nor help a bad one. They want to be free to drop (or add) clients as relationships develop. Other agents—and many pseudo-agents—require a contract that should be studied carefully with an attorney before signing. Know what rights the agent is handling for your material, and check that no charges are made for services that you do not fully understand and agree to. Some agencies charge for criticism or impose a "marketing fee" for office overhead, etc. If you pay such a fee, you are entitled to see any correspondence that such a marketing endeavor would produce.

Legitimate agents will discuss marketing problems a manuscript might be having. If you have any doubts about where (or whether) your manuscript is being marketed, ask to see the mail between your agent and the publishers he claims to be showing your work to. If you have paid a marketing fee, it is illegal for the agent to withhold a prepaid service longer than three months—unless the customer is allowed to cancel the order and get a refund. An agent who breaks this law can be sued by the writer.

The best way to avoid such complications—legal or otherwise—is by selecting your agent carefully.

DOMINICK ABEL LITERARY AGENCY, INC., 498 West End Ave., New York NY 10024. (212)877-0710. Obtains new clients through recommendations and solicitation. Will not read unsolicited mss; will read unsolicited queries and outlines. SASE. Member ILAA. Agent receives 10% commission on US sales; 20% on foreign.
Will Handle: Book-length adult fiction and nonfiction.

EDWARD J. ACTON, INC., 928 Broadway, New York NY 10010. (212)675-5400. Contact: Inge Hanson. Member ILAA. Obtains new clients through referral, generally by editors and other writers. Represents 100 clients. Will read—at no charge—unsolicited queries and outlines. SASE. Agent receives 15% commission on domestic and dramatic sales; 19% on foreign sales.
Will Handle: Nonfiction books and novels.

ADAMS, RAY & ROSENBERG, Penthouse 25, 9200 Sunset Blvd., Los Angeles CA 90069. Obtains new clients through recommendation only. 5% of clients are new/unpublished writers. Will not read unsolicited mss. Reports in 2 weeks on queries; 1 month on submissions. Agent receives 10% commission.
Will Handle: Novels (motion picture, publication and TV rights), motion pictures, stage plays (film rights), and TV scripts. Percentage of mss handled: 3% nonfiction; 9% fiction; 3% stage plays; 85% screenplays.

DOROTHY ALBERT, 162 W. 54th St., New York NY 10019. Obtains new clients through recommendations of editors, educational establishments,,contacts in the film industry, and inquiries. Writers should send letter of introduction, description of material, and list of previous submissions, if any. Will not read unsolicited mss; will read unsolicited queries and outlines. SASE a must! Agent receives 10% on domestic sales; 15% on Canadian; 20% on foreign. No reading fee.
Will Handle: Novels, motion pictures (completed, no treatments), stage plays (musicals), and TV scripts. No poetry, short stories, textbooks, articles, documentaries, or scripts for established episode shows. "We are interested in novels which are well-plotted suspense, quality drama, adult fiction and human relations. The writer should have some foreknowledge of structure and endurance, whether it be motion pictures, television, or books."

MAXWELL ALEY ASSOCIATES, 145 E. 35th St., New York NY 10016. (212)679-5377. Contact: Ruth Aley. Represents 37 clients. Prefers to work with previously published authors; 10% of clients are new/unpublished writers. Query with a brief biographical background sketch first. Do not send complete ms. Computer printout submissions acceptable; no dot-matrix. SASE (include return postage if sending outlines). Reports in 1 month on queries, or sooner if negative. Member ILAA. Does not charge fee "unless special circumstances warrant." Agent receives 15% commission on domestic sales; 20% on foreign.
Will Handle: Only exceptional fiction, but preferably nonfiction books, if useful.

ALLEN & YANOW LITERARY AGENCY, Box 5158, Santa Cruz CA 95063. (408)427-1293. President: Mort Yanow. Vice President: David Allen. Will read mss, queries, outlines. Computer printout submissions acceptable. SASE. Reports in 2 weeks. Agent receives 10% commission on domestic and dramatic sales; 20% on foreign sales.
Will Handle: Films, nonfiction books, novels (no genre). Percentage of mss handled: 60% nonfiction; 35% fiction; 5% screenplays.

JAMES ALLEN, Literary Agent, (in association with Virginia Kidd Literary Agents), 538 E. Harford St., Milford PA 18337. (717)296-7266. Obtains new clients "preferably by reference from someone already on my list or from an established professional in the field." Represents 32 clients. "Writer must have minimum

$3,000 earnings from writing in the previous year; a sale in the area they bring to me is a help, i.e., a mystery writer bringing a mystery novel stands a better chance of being taken on than, say, an anthropologist with publishing credits in his field who brings me a first mystery novel." Will read queries and outlines. Will not read unsolicited mss. SASE. Agent receives 10% commission on domestic sales; 20% on dramatic and foreign sales.

Will Handle: Magazine fiction, nonfiction books and novels. "If the work from a prospective client is a 'near miss' I tell him/her why, in varying degrees of detail; likewise for authors on my list. I do not, per se, have a critiquing service."

Tips: "Get at least a couple of sales, even of shorter-length material, before seeking representation. For me at least, proper manuscript preparation and careful proofreading before I see material is very important. Manuscripts riddled with errors give a bad impression."

MARCIA AMSTERDAM AGENCY, 41 W. 82nd St., New York NY 10024. (212)873-4945. Contact: Marcia Amsterdam. Obtains new clients through client or editor referrals. Will read queries, partials and outlines. Computer printout submissions acceptable; no dot-matrix. SASE. Agent receives 10% on domestic sales; 15% on British; 20% on foreign.

Will Handle: Novels, nonfiction books, teleplays, screenplays. Percentages of mss handled: approximately 5% nonfiction; 80% fiction; 2% screenplays; 3% juvenile. "This varies, of course."

THE ARTISTS AGENCY, 10000 Santa Monica Blvd., Los Angeles CA 90067. (213)277-7779. Obtains new clients through referrals. Will not read unsolicited mss. Agent receives 10% commission on sales.

Will Handle: Films, novels, stage plays and TV scripts.

THE BALKIN AGENCY, 850 W. 176th St., New York NY 10033. President: Richard Balkin. Obtains new clients through recommendations, over-the-transom inquiries, and solicitation. Currently represents 45 clients. 10% of clients are new/unpublished writers. Will not read unsolicited mss; will read unsolicited queries, or outlines and 2 sample chapters. Computer printout submissions acceptable; prefers letter-quality to dot-matrix. Reports in 2 weeks on queries; 3 weeks on submissions. SASE. Member ILAA and Authors Guild. Interested in new/beginning writers. Agent receives 10% commission on domestic sales, 20% on UK, 25% on foreign.

Will Handle: Magazine articles (only as a service to clients who primarily write books), nonfiction books, textbooks (college only), and professional books (on occasion). Specializes in adult nonfiction. Percentage of mss handled: 100% nonfiction.

Tips: "Query with: A) Description; B) What is unique about the work; C) How it differs from competing or overlapping titles; D) Audiences/Market; and E) Size, amount of art work, if any; and completion date."

LOIS BERMAN, The Little Theatre Building, 240 W. 44th St., New York NY 10036. Obtains new clients by referral. Currently represents 25-30 clients. Member SAR. Agent receives 10% commission.

Will Handle: Dramatic writing for theatre and film only. No novels or other narrative work.

BLOOM, LEVY, SHORR & ASSOCIATES, 800 S. Robertson Blvd., Los Angeles CA 90235. (213)659-6160. Obtains new clients only by referral from clients, directors, producers, and studio executives. 50% of clients are new/unpublished writers. SASE. Reports in 1 month. Agent receives 10% commission.

Will Handle: "We will read only completed motion picture screenplays. This may include screenplays for feature films as well as movies made for television. We will not read outlines, treatments, or scripts for episodic or situation comedy television." Percentage of mss handled: 5% fiction; 95% screenplays.

GEORGES BORCHARDT, INC., 136 E. 57th St., New York NY 10022. (212)753-5785. Obtains new clients "mainly through authors already represented by us who refer others." Potential clients "must be highly recommended by someone we know." Reads unsolicited queries from well-established writers. 1% of clients are new/unpublished writers. Reports immediately on queries; 3 weeks on submissions. Interested in new/beginning writers "but we only consider their work if they have been recommended." Currently represents 200 clients. Member SAR. Agent receives 10% commission.

Will Handle: Magazine articles and fiction, novels, and nonfiction books. Specializes in "possibly the kinds of books that might or should win major awards." Percentage of mss handled: 60% nonfiction; 38% fiction; 1% poetry; 1% juvenile.

Tips: "Get your manuscript in the best possible shape and enlist the help of an established author of your acquaintance."

BRANDT & BRANDT LITERARY AGENTS, INC., 1501 Broadway, New York NY 10036. (212)840-5760. Represents approximately 150 clients. Query. Computer printout submissions acceptable; prefers letter-

quality to dot-matrix. SASE. Member SAR. Agent receives 10% commission on domestic rights; 15% on British rights; and 20% on other foreign rights.
Will Handle: Novels and nonfiction books.

BRISK, RUBIN, STEINBERG LITERARY AGENCY, 838 Michigan, Evanston IL 60202. (312)864-7222. Operating Partner: Michael Steinberg. Obtains new clients through referrals. Represents 20 clients. 60% of clients are new/unpublished writers. Clients must show evidence of "good, lucid writing and some indication that they have studied the market they are trying to sell to." Will read queries and outlines. Prefers outline and consecutive sample chapters. Reports in 2 weeks on queries; 6 weeks on submissions. Computer printout submissions acceptable; prefers letter-quality to dot-matrix. SASE (mandatory). Does not charge fee, "though this may soon change." Agent receives 15% commission on domestic and dramatic sales, 15-20% on foreign sales.
Will Handle: Nonfiction books (quality writing, demonstrating expertise in area, or imaginative non-books); novels (creative, commercial writing; mainstream, science fiction welcome; some experimental; few romances, gothics, creepy weepies); and textbooks (subjects not out of date each year, preferably landmark text). Percentage of mss handled: 40% nonfiction; 60% fiction.
Tips: "Query first. Be sure to include return postage. Don't oversell in your cover letter; the work speaks for itself. When sending a sample, always include consecutive portions and outline. Mention previous publishing history, and do not be afraid to answer 'none.' "

BROOKE DUNN OLIVER, Suite 202, 9165 Sunset Blvd., Los Angeles CA 90069. (213)859-1405. Contact: James Brooke. Obtains clients through recommendations. Currently represents 10 clients—25% stage play mss; 75% screenplays. Member Writers Guild. Agent receives 10% commission on domestic sales.
Will Handle: Screenplays; TV scripts (movies; no episodic material); stage plays.

CURTIS BROWN, LTD., 575 Madison Ave., New York NY 10022. (212)755-4200. President: Perry H. Knowlton. Curtis Brown Associates, Ltd: James Oliver Brown, President. Books: Peter L. Ginsberg, Emilie Jacobson, Perry H. Knowlton, Marilyn Marlow, Clyde Taylor, Maureen Walters. Film and TV rights: Timothy Knowlton. Query by letter only. Computer printout submissions acceptable; prefers letter-quality to dot-matrix. Unsolicited manuscripts will be returned unread. Member SAR. Agent receives 10% commission on domestic rights; 20% on foreign rights; 10% on film rights (film commission sometimes varies in particular circumstances).
Will Handle: Novels and nonfiction books.

PEMA BROWNE LTD., 185 E. 85th St., New York NY 10028. (212)369-1925. Contact: Pema Browne, Perry J. Browne. Obtains new clients through editors' and authors' referrals and directory listings. Represents 20 clients. 20% of clients are new/unpublished writers. Will read queries or outlines. Computer printout submissions acceptable; prefers letter-quality to dot-matrix. Reports in 1 week on queries; 2-3 weeks on mss. "Author must send SASE for reply." Agent receives 15% commission on domestic and dramatic sales, 20% on foreign sales. No unsolicited mss.
Will Handle: Films (treatments only); nonfiction books (how-to, illustrated: general subjects); novels (category, not "middle books"); stage plays (treatments only); syndicated material (columns, comic strips); and TV scripts (treatments only). No poetry. Percentage of mss handled: 50% nonfiction; 50% fiction.
Tips: "Seek the services of a consulting editor before sending manuscript. Obvious pitfalls are thereby avoided, as well as expense of mailing, etc."

SHIRLEY BURKE AGENCY, 370 E. 76th St., B-704, New York NY 10021. (212)861-2309. Obtains new clients through recommendations. Preferably potential clients must have published at least one book. 5% of clients are new/unpublished writers. Will not read or return unsolicited mss (do not send without approval or SASE); will read unsolicited queries. SASE. Reports within 10 days on queries. Agent receives 10% commission.
Will Handle: Magazine fiction, novels, and nonfiction books.

JANE BUTLER, ART AND LITERARY AGENT, Associate: Virginia Kidd Agents. 538 E. Harford St., Box 278, Milford PA 18337. (717)296-6205 or 296-7266. Contact: Jane Butler, independent associate. Estab. 1980. Obtains new clients through referral and queries. Represents 25 clients. "Last year our clients earned an average of from $5,000 to $10,000." A writer must have previous sales of $2,000. Will read—at no charge—unsolicited queries and sample chapters with SASE. Send tearsheets for art. Author should enclose SASE for return of submission. Agent receives 10% commission on domestic sales; 15% commission on dramatic sales; 20% commission on foreign sales; 20% commission on art; 30% commission on art (foreign).
Will Handle: Science fiction, fantasy, horror genre titles. Also genre—cover art; interior illustration.

RUTH CANTOR, LITERARY AGENT, 156 5th Ave., New York NY 10010. Literary Agent: Ruth Cantor. Foreign Rights: Nurnberg. Movies and Television: Al Jackinson. Obtains new clients through recommendations by writers, publishers, editors, and teachers. Potential client "must be of proven competence as a writer. This means either some publishing record or a recommendation from someone likely to be a competent critic of his work—a teacher of writing, another writer, etc." Will not read unsolicited mss; will read unsolicited queries and outlines. SASE. "Send a letter giving publishing history and writing experience, plus concise outline of proposed project or of ms you want to send. Do not phone." Agent receives 10% commission on domestic sales; 20% on foreign.
Will Handle: Novels, nonfiction books and children's books. Currently handles 20% nonfiction; 80% fiction.

MARIA CARVAINIS AGENCY INC., 235 West End Ave., New York NY 10023. (212)580-1559. President: Maria Carvainis. Member-at-large The Authors Guild, Inc., Signatory to Writers Guild of America, East, and member of Romance Writers of America. Obtains new clients "through recommendations of current authors, editors, and letters of query." 25% of clients are new/unpublished writers. Represents over 60 clients. "I look for the strengths of the projects I read for representation and then consider how extensive the market is for these fiction or nonfiction projects. Will read queries. Computer printout submissions acceptable; no dotmatrix. Reports in 1 month on queries; 2 months on submissions. SASE. No unsolicited manuscripts. Agent receives 15% commission on domestic sales, 10% on dramatic sales (for WGA writers), 20% on foreign sales.
Will Handle: All kinds of fiction from serious to commercial (specializing in contemporary women's fiction and historicals and young adult fiction); nonfiction books (serious to commerical projects); movie and television scripts and treatments (preferably but not exclusively the writer should have some credits); and poetry (writer must have some published poems). Will also handle magazine articles and fiction for book authors represented. Percentage of mss handled: 40% nonfiction; 40% fiction; 9% screenplays; 1% poetry; 10% juvenile.
Tips: "There are many good agents in the field and it is important once an author has confidence in the agent's abilities to carefully assess whether he/she feels comfortable working with that agent in a creative writing and business relationship."

HY COHEN LITERARY AGENCY, LTD., 111 W. 57th St., New York NY 10019. (212)757-5237. President: Hy Cohen. Currently represents 25-30 clients. 50% of clients are new/unpublished writers. Obtains new clients through recommendations. Will read unsolicited mss, queries and outlines. Mail mss to 66 Brookfield Rd., Upper Montclair NJ 07043. SASE. Reports almost immediately on queries; 1 month on mss. Interested in new/beginning writers. Agent receives 10% commission.
Will Handle: Magazine articles and fiction, novels, and nonfiction books. Percentage of mss handled: 30% nonfiction; 70% fiction.

JULIA COOPERSMITH LITERARY AGENCY, 312 E. 23rd St., New York NY 10010. (212)505-5784. Contact: Julia Coopersmith. Obtains new clients through referral. Represents 40 clients. Query first. SASE. Agent receives 12% commission on domestic sales; 20% on foreign sales.
Will Handle: Nonfiction books and novels.

JOAN DAVES, 59 E. 54th St., New York NY 10022. Contact: Joan Daves. Obtains new clients through recommendation by clients and editors. Represents 80 + clients. Will read—at no charge—queries and outlines; will not read unsolicited mss. SASE. Agent receives 10% commission on domestic and dramatic sales; 20% on stock, amateur and foreign sales.
Will Handle: Nonfiction books and novels.

ANITA DIAMANT: THE WRITERS WORKSHOP, INC., 310 Madison Ave., New York NY 10017. (212)687-1122. President: Anita Diamant. Obtains new clients through recommendations by publishers or other clients. Potential clients must have made some professional sales. Will not read unsolicited mss; will read unsolicited queries. Computer printout submissions acceptable; prefers letter-quality to dot-matrix. SASE. Reports in 2 weeks on queries; 1 month on submissions. Member SAR and Writers Guild. Interested in new/beginning writers. Agent receives 15% commission to first 10,000; 10% thereafter.
Will Handle: Adult fiction, novels, nonfiction books, motion pictures, and TV scripts. Percentage of mss handled: 40% nonfiction; 60% fiction; "Screenplays handled by our Hollywood representatives."

EDUCATIONAL DESIGN SERVICES INC., Box 253, Wantagh NY 11793. (516)221-0995, (212)359-7714. President: Bertram L. Linder. Obtains new clients through inquiries, referrals and selective advertising. Represents 28 clients. Will read—at no charge—unsolicited mss, queries and outlines if accompanied by

SASE. Agent receives 15% commission on domestic sales; 20% on foreign sales.
Will Handle: Textbooks—kindergarten-college, educational materials only.

ANN ELMO AGENCY, INC., 60 E. 42nd St., New York NY 10165. (212)661-2880. Obtains new clients through writers' queries. Sales average about a book a month. Will read queries and outlines at no charge. SASE. Member SAR. Agent receives 10% commission for domestic sales and 20% for foreign sales.
Will Handle: Magazine articles (only strong ideas); magazine fiction (very few short stories); novels, nonfiction books; stage plays; and occasional TV scripts.

KAREN EMDEN, Literary Agent, (associated with Virginia Kidd Literary Agents), Box 278, Milford PA 18337. (717)296-6205, 296-7266. Estab. 1983. Member SFWA. Obtains new clients by referral, occasionally from unsolicited sendings. Represents 15 clients. "Writer must have at least $3,000 writing income, half in fiction, in past year; must have at least one major work ready for submission; market own nonfiction articles; have preferred referral from recognized professional in field." Will read queries. Will not read unsolicited mss. SASE. Agent receives 10% on domestic sales; 15% on dramatic sales; and 20% on foreign sales.
Will Handle: Magazine fiction (no gratuitous sex or violence); nonfiction books (of wide general interest, no specialty fields); novels (virtually any type provided they are written well. "I prefer speculative fiction."); poetry (collections of previously placed work only, from regular clients). No reading fee at this time. Provides one-time critique of fiction, short stories and novels. No fee at this time.
Tips: "Submit material which you feel is ready for submission, use a standard format, wide margins, clean cover sheet, headings, no typos or grammar errors, and accompany partials with *short* synopsis."

JOHN FARQUHARSON LTD., #1914, 250 W. 57th St., New York NY 10107. (212)245-1993. Contact: Deborah Schneider. Member of SAR and ILAA. Will read—at no charge—queries. No unsolicited manuscripts. SASE. Agent receives 10% commission on domestic and dramatic sales; 20% on foreign sales.

THE FOLEY AGENCY, 34 E. 38th St., New York NY 10016. (212)686-6930. Contact: Joan and Joe Foley. Obtains clients through recommendation "and our interest." Currently represents 30 clients. Maximum of 2% of clients are new/unpublished writers. "Query first with *all* details and a self-addressed stamped envelope (no reply without the latter). We handle only books." Will read queries; will not read unsolicited mss. SASE. Reports in 1 month. Agent receives 10% commission on domestic, dramatic, and foreign sales (plus sub-agent 10%). Charges messenger fees and expenses "in connection with sales."
Will Handle: Nonfiction books and novels. Percentage of mss handled: 75% nonfiction; 25% fiction.

THE FROMMER PRICE LITERARY AGENCY INC., 185 E. 85th St., New York NY 10028. (212)289-0589. Contact: Diana Price. Obtains new clients "mainly by referral." Represents 60 clients. 10% of clients are new/unpublished writers. "Previously published writers preferred, but will consider any queries." Will read queries and outlines. Reports immediately on queries; 1 month on submissions. SASE. Agent receives 15% commission on domestic and dramatic sales, 20% on foreign sales.
Will Handle: Nonfiction books and novels (adult only). Percentage of mss handled: 75% nonfiction, 25% fiction.
Tips: "The most important criterion is trust."

HERB GALEWITZ, AGENT, 299 Madison Ave., New York NY 10017. (212)490-0785. Contact: Herb Galewitz. Obtains some new clients through referrals. Represents 4 clients. Query with outline and first few chapters "at least and return postage." Agent receives 10% commission on domestic sales; 20% on foreign sales.
Will Handle: Nonfiction books and novels.

JAY GARON-BROOKE ASSOCIATES, INC., 415 Central Park West, New York NY 10025. (212)866-3654. President: Jay Garon-Brooke. Obtains new clients through referrals. A small percentage of clients are new/unpublished writers. Will not read unsolicited mss. "New authors must query by mail, providing their backgrounds and outlines of their projects."
Will Handle: General fiction and nonfiction suitable for hardcover or paperback publication, as well as paperback mass-market category fiction; theatrical and television film scripts, and computer books.

GOODMAN ASSOCIATES LITERARY AND SOFTWARE AGENTS, 500 West End Ave., New York NY 10024. (212)873-4806. Contact: Arnold P. Goodman, Elise Simon Goodman. "Small, personal agency. One partner is a lawyer. No unsolicited mss. Query letter should contain brief bio of author and enough about project to interest us." Computer printout submissions acceptable; prefers letter-quality to dot-matrix. Reports in 1 week on queries; 1 month on submissions. SASE. Member, Governing Board of ILAA. Interested in and supportive of new writers. Currently represents 50 clients. 10% of clients are new/unpublished writers. Percentage of mss handled: 65% nonfiction; 35% fiction.

Will Handle: Adult book-length fiction and nonfiction, computer books and software. No textbooks, juveniles, science fiction, plays, screenplays.

KEITH GORMEZANO, #7WMLA, 2921 E. Madison St., Seattle WA 98112-4237. (206)322-1431. Estab. 1983. Obtains new clients by word of mouth, advertising, direct mail. Represents 5 clients. Will read queries "provided business-size SASE is enclosed." Will read submissions at no charge, but may charge criticism fee. Will not read unsolicited mss. SASE. Agent receives 8-11% commission on domestic sales; 12-14% on dramatic sales; and 17-19% on foreign sales.
Will Handle: Films; magazine articles; magazine fiction; nonfiction books (mass market); novels (historical, erotic); poetry; radio scripts (1940s style); stage plays (contemporary); syndicated material (humor, political, ethnic); textbooks (college); and TV scripts (comedies).
Tips: "Don't send a form letter, send resume; it makes you seem more personable."

SANFORD J. GREENBURGER ASSOCIATES, 55 5th Ave., New York NY 10003. (212)206-5600. Agents: Heide Lange, Peter L. Skolnik, Lucy Stille. Member ILAA. Obtains new clients mostly through referrals from authors and editors. Represents 300 clients of which about 150 are actively writing. Will read—at no charge—queries and outlines. SASE. Agent receives 15% commission on domestic and dramatic sales; 19% on foreign sales (10% to sub-agent in foreign territory).
Will Handle: Nonfiction books and novels.
Tips: "Send a query letter first. Try to work out with an agent—ahead of time—what an agent can or can't do for you in order to establish realistic expectations. Compatibility is helpful."

REECE HALSEY AGENCY, 8733 Sunset Blvd., Los Angeles CA 90069. (213)652-2409. Contact: Dorris Halsey. Obtains clients through direct referral from existing clients. Will read—at no charge—queries only. "Do not send any material until it is requested." SASE. Agent receives 10% commission on domestic sales.
Will Handle: TV scripts (movies of the week; no episodic series).

HEACOCK LITERARY AGENCY, INC., Suite 14, 1523 6th St., Santa Monica CA 90401. (213)451-8523, 393-6227. Authors' Representatives: James or Rosalie Heacock. Obtains new clients through "referrals from publishers, recommendations of our authors, referrals from book publicists and editors, listings in *Writer's Market* and *Literary Market Place*, and from public speaking as times permits. (Also from ILAA membership list.) Represents 65 clients. 20% (nonfiction only) of clients are new/unpublished writers. Member ILAA. "The majority of our clients have been previously published, but we will also read queries from authors who have a strong background in writing and a sense of craft and originality. Unpublished novelists should not query unless their book is finished; partials cannot be considered until you have a publishing track record. A good query letter tells us much about a person's ability to express thoughts. Treat your query with as much care as your manuscript; include brief biographical data and tell us why you wrote the book and why it's important to you." Will read—at no charge—queries, outlines, first 20-30 pages of manuscript. Computer printout submissions acceptable; no dot-matrix. SASE. Reports in 1 month on queries; 6 weeks on nonfiction mss, 2 months on fiction mss "depending on work load." Agent receives 10% commission on domestic sales, 20% on foreign sales, and 15% on first-time novelists..
Will Handle: Nonfiction books "of all sorts; we especially like new idea books and new ways to solve old problems, significant books likely to endure"; novels "either literary or well-crafted novels of mass market appeal, romances and big mainstream novels"; textbooks "*only if they have the potential to reach into the general trade market*"; and screenplays. Percentage of mss handled: 85% nonfiction; 10% fiction; 5% screenplays.
Tips: "Revise and polish your manuscript until it shines like a bright jewel before you even consider seeking an agent. The old adage 'Writing is rewriting' is appropriate here. When you're convinced that your book is the best of which you're capable, query with SASE." Free agency brochure for SASE.

HEINLE & HEINLE ENTERPRISES, 29 Lexington Rd., Concord MA 01742. (617)369-4858. Managing Director: Charles A.S. Heinle. President: Beverly D. Heinle. Client contact: Beverly D. Heinle. Obtains new clients through word-of-mouth, *Writer's Market*, *Literary Market Place*, and recommendations by clients. Currently represents 40 clients. Majority of clients are new/unpublished writers. Will not read unsolicited mss; will read unsolicited queries, outlines, and full-length proposals. Reports in 2 weeks on queries. No multiple submissions. All submissions and letters must be originals, not photocopies, and must offer an exclusive right to consider the proposal for at least 30 to 60 days. Computer printout submissions acceptable; prefers letter-quality to dot-matrix. SASE. Percentage of mss handled: 90% nonfiction; 10% fiction. "We are particularly interested in writers who take a professional interest in their work." Agent receives 10% commission on regular book placements, although on some special placements, the commission will be 15-20%.
Will Handle: Nonfiction of all kinds, text materials at college and adult levels, children's and young adult fiction, and novels of a serious nature. "We will read nonfiction and YA from an unpublished author, but we will not read adult fiction by an unpublished writer unless the request is accompanied by a recommendation from someone in the writing or publishing business. We do not handle poetry, short stories, or magazine articles. We

do not supply criticism or undertake rewrite assignments. We are most interested in materials with a New England theme or slant; past, present, or future; but, of course, good writing is the main consideration. We handle textbooks in the foreign-language area also."

Tips: "Write a query letter describing the project and including an outline or synopsis. Indicate orientation as a writer, and pertinent background information. Supply sample material only when requested."

HINTZ LITERARY AGENCY, (Associated with Larry Sternig Literary Agency and Ray Peekner Literary Agency), 2879 N. Grant Blvd., Milwaukee WI 53210. Obtains new clients through queries and referrals from clients and editors. Currently represents 25 clients. 15% of clients are new/unpublished writers. Will not read unsolicited mss; queries only. Computer printout submissions acceptable; prefers letter-quality to dot-matrix. SASE. Reports in 1-3 weeks on queries; 1 month on mss. Agent receives 10% commission.
Will Handle: Trade fiction and nonfiction; juvenile. Percentage of mss handled: 20% nonfiction; 60% fiction; 20% juvenile.
Tips: "Writers should put all their enthusiasm into a query or synopsis and should always include an author's sheet on themselves." Prefers concise, informal queries and no statements like, "This will make both of us a lot of money."

MICHAEL IMISON PLAYWRIGHTS LTD., (a subsidiary of Dr. Jan Van Loewen Ltd.), Suite 10G, 150 W. 47th St., New York NY 10036. (212)921-2128. Contact: Michael Imison. Member of SAR. Obtains new clients mostly by personal recommendation. Represents 80 clients. "Before sending scripts writers should submit brief letter about themselves and their material." SASE. Agent receives 10% commission on dramatic sales; 12.5% on foreign sales.
Will Handle: Stage plays, "preferably plays with an international appeal but plays for local US markets also of interest. We do not handle novels or work other than drama."

J. DE S. ASSOCIATES, Shagbark Rd., Wilson Pt., South Norwalk CT 06854. (203)838-7571. President: Jacques de Spoelberch. Obtains new clients through other clients, publishers' recommendations and directory listings. Represents 60 clients. Less than 10% of clients are new/unpublished writers. Will read mss, queries and outlines. SASE. Agent receives 15% commission.
Will Handle: Nonfiction books and novels.

JET LITERARY ASSOCIATES, INC., 124 E. 84th St., New York NY 10028. (212)879-2578. President: Jim Trupin. Obtains new clients through referrals. Represents 70 clients. "Writer must have a book publishing credit." Will read queries. SASE. Will not read unsolicited mss. Agent receives 15% commission on domestic sales, 20% on dramatic sales, 25% on foreign sales.
Will Handle: Nonfiction books and novels.

VIRGINIA KIDD, Literary Agent, 538 E. Harford St., Milford PA 18337. (717)296-6205; 296-7266. "Obtains new clients by referrals, mostly." Represents 30 active clients; 30 mostly inactive. "I prefer that the writer should have earned at least $3,000 through his/her writing during the previous year, and/or have published at least one book, and/or at the very least come to me recommended by someone whose opinion I highly value. (I probably won't accept, but will recommend to my associates.)" Query. SASE. Will read unsolicited mss. Agent receives 10% commission on domestic sales; 15% on dramatic sales; and 20% on foreign sales.
Will Handle: Magazine articles, magazine fiction, nonfiction books and novels ("I specialize in science fiction, but I am not limited to any one field.") "I work through a Hollywood agent for dramatic rights in the literary properties I sell. I do not send out any submissions without having read it first and I may critique a given work for a client—never for a nonclient."
Tips: "Don't phone; inquire with SASE, listing your achievements and citing your earnings; do not send a sample unless encouraged to do so. If you are a new unpublished writer, go it alone for a while until you can demonstrate that you are of interest."

DANIEL P. KING, LITERARY AGENT, 5125 N. Cumberland Blvd., Whitefish Bay WI 53217. (414)964-2903. Contact: Daniel P. King. Member Crime Writers' Association (England). Obtains clients by referral from current clients; members of writers' clubs. Currently represents 70 clients. 10% of clients are new/unpublished writers. "We will read all query letters and outlines and if we are interested, we will represent without previous credits. We have a good overseas market for previously published material." Will not read unsolicited mss. Computer printout submissions acceptable. Reports in 1 week on queries; 2 months on submissions. SASE. Agent receives 10% commission on domestic sales; 10% on dramatic sales; 20% on foreign sales.
Will Handle: "While we handle all material, we are especially interested in crime and mystery fiction and nonfiction: book-length or short story/article length." Magazine articles (true crime); magazine fiction (mystery, spy, sci-fi); nonfiction books (crime); novels (mystery, spy, sci-fi, mainstream). Percentage of mss handled: 20% nonfiction; 80% fiction.

Tips: "We like to see a concise query letter—no more than a page typed in a professional and coherent manner."

HARVEY KLINGER, INC., 301 W. 53rd St., New York NY 10019. (212)581-7068. President: Harvey Klinger. Obtains clients through referrals from existing clients and from editors. Currently represents over 50 clients. 10% of clients are new/unpublished writers. "Must have completed or have close to completion a full length novel, screenplay, or nonfiction work." Will read queries and outlines. Computer printout submissions acceptable; no dot-matrix. SASE. Reports in 2 weeks on queries; 6 weeks on submissions. Agent receives 15% commission on domestic and dramatic sales; 25% on foreign sales.
Will Handle: Films (completed screenplay or film treatment); nonfiction books (query first, with complete description of the book); novels (query first; may include brief synopsis); TV scripts (completed script or treatment). Percentage of mss handled: 60% nonfiction; 40% fiction.

MICHAEL LARSEN/ELIZABETH POMADA LITERARY AGENTS, 1029 Jones St., San Francisco CA 94109. (415)673-0939. Contact: Elizabeth Pomada, fiction; Michael Larsen, nonfiction. Member ILAA. Obtains clients through recommendations from other clients, publishers and writers, listings in LMP, yellow pages, ILAA list, etc. Currently represents over 120 clients. 50% of clients are new/unpublished writers. Will read—at no charge—queries. Reports in 1 month. Computer printout submissions acceptable; no dot-matrix on mss; prefers letter-quality on queries. SASE. Agent receives 15% commission on domestic sales; 10% on dramatic sales; 20% on foreign sales.
Will Handle: Nonfiction books ("proposals—a page, a chapter in outline, and as many sample chapters as possible by authors with published articles are acceptable"); and novels ("send query and first 30 pages *only*, with SASE). Percentage of mss handled: 75% nonfiction; 25% fiction.
Tips: "Writers have to do their homework better—they have to be more aware of the market and more educated about the publishing process. Send SASE for our brochure."

THE STERLING LORD AGENCY, INC., 660 Madison Ave., New York NY 10021. (212)751-2533. Vice President: Patricia Berens. Member SAR. Obtains new clients through "recommendation of clients, editors, word of mouth." Will read queries and outlines. Reports immediately on queries. SASE. Agent receives 10% commission on domestic sales, 20% on British, dramatic, and other foreign sales.
Will Handle: Nonfiction books and novels.

MARGARET MCBRIDE LITERARY AGENCY, Box 8730, La Jolla CA 92038. (619)459-0559. Associate: Winifred Golden. Member ILAA. Obtains clients "usually by recommendation of other clients." Currently represents 25 clients. "Should have been previously published or have professional or educational credentials." Will read queries; will not read unsolicited mss. Computer printout submissions acceptable; no dot-matrix. SASE. Agent receives 15% commission on domestic sales; 10% on dramatic sales; 20% on foreign sales.
Will Handle: Films, nonfiction books, novels.

HAROLD MATSON CO., INC., 276 5th Ave., New York NY 10001. (212)679-4490. Query. No unsolicited mss. SASE. Member SAR. Agent receives 10% commission.
Will Handle: Novels and nonfiction books.

GEORGE MICHAUD AGENCY, Suite 1, 4950 Densmore, Encino CA 91436. (213)981-6680. Literary Agent: Arthur Dreifuss. Obtains clients through Writers Guild publication. "Will consider new writers." Will read—at no charge—queries; "will respond with instructions and requirements." SASE. Reports in 6 weeks on queries; 3-6 months on submissions. Interested in new/beginning writers. Agent receives 10% commission on domestic sales.
Will Handle: TV and movie screenplays, treatments and original stories. Percentage of mss handled: 1% stage plays; 99% screenplays.

HENRY MORRISON, INC., 58 W. 10th St., New York NY 10011. (212)260-7600. President: Henry Morrison. Obtains clients by recommendations from editors, direct approach, from other writers, etc. Currently represents 51 clients. Will read queries. SASE. Agent receives 15% commission on domestic and dramatic sales; 20% on foreign sales.
Will Handle: Films, nonfiction books, novels.
Tips: "Many of our present writers were unpublished when they came to us."

MARVIN MOSS INC., 9200 Sunset Blvd., Los Angeles CA 90069. President: Marvin Moss. Licensed Writers Guild of America. Obtains new clients through referrals usually. Represents 20 clients. Will read—at no charge—unsolicited mss and outlines. "No materials or query letters accepted without a signed release form." Agent receives 10% commission on domestic and dramatic sales; 20% on foreign sales.
Will Handle: Films, nonfiction books and novels.

MULTIMEDIA PRODUCT DEVELOPMENT, INC., 410 S. Michigan Ave., Room 828, Chicago IL 60605. (312)922-3063. President: Jane Jordan Browne. Obtains new clients through recommendations and word-of-mouth. Currently represents 95 clients. 5% of clients are new/unpublished writers. "Multimedia handles only works of professional writers who make their living as authors. The rare exceptions are celebrity autobiographies and the 'new idea' nonfiction book." Will read unsolicited queries and outlines. Computer printout submissions acceptable; prefers letter-quality to dot-matrix. SASE. Reports in 2 weeks on queries; 1 months on submissions. Agent receives 10% commission on domestic sales; 15% on domestic sales for first-book authors; 20% on foreign.
Will Handle: Novels, nonfiction books, screenplays, juvenile. No poetry, plays, articles or short stories. Percentage of mss handled: 65% nonfiction; 25% fiction; 5% screenplays; 5% juvenile.

JEAN V. NAGGAR LITERARY AGENCY, 336 E. 73rd St., New York NY 10021. (212)794-1082. Contact: Jean Naggar. Obtains new clients through recommendations. Query with outline and brief biographical sketch. Computer printout submissions acceptable; no dot-matrix. SASE. Reports in 2 days on queries; as soon as possible on submissions—"sometimes a long wait." Member ILAA. "I am taking on *very few* new writers at this time. Only the best!" Agent receives 15% commission on domestic sales; and 20% on foreign sales.
Will Handle: Novels and nonfiction books. Percentage of mss handled: approximately 30% nonfiction; 70% fiction. Specializes in a "broad range of fiction, from literary to historical to science fiction, etc. with many in between. Some prior writing credits are a help." Sales include *The Clan of the Cave Bear* and *The Valley of Horses*, Books I & II in "Earth's Children," by Jean M. Auel (Crown).

NEW WAVE, Authors' Representatives, 2544 N. Monticello Ave., Chicago IL 60647. (312)276-5685. Client contact: Gene Lovitz. Represents over 50 authors. "Interested in promising new writers and ideas providing the text is on par with *The Manual of Style*. Queries, outlines, sample chapters and/or completed manuscripts welcomed *only* if sent with SASE (otherwise they will not be returned)." No fee. Agent receives 10% commission on domestic sales; 20% on foreign.
Will Handle: Adult trade novels, adult nonfiction and experimental. No magazine articles, poetry, juveniles, TV or film scripts.
Tips: "If you use ellipses improperly, tossing them about like golf balls, do not send."

MARY NOVIK, LITERARY AGENT, 5519 Deerhorn Lane, North Vancouver, British Columbia V7R 4S8 Canada. (604)987-4982. 50% of clients are new/unpublished writers. Agent receives 10% commission on North American sales; 20% on foreign sales.
Will Handle: "The agency will read *romance novels* only. No reading fees are charged. Interested writers should submit the first three chapters (or 50 pages) with synopsis of rest. Computer printout submissions acceptable; prefers letter-quality to dot-matrix. Enclose SASE (check or International Reply Coupons since US stamps cannot be used from Canada). Keep in mind that Canadian postage is considerably higher than American. Reports in 1 month on queries; 6 weeks on submissions. Writers are advised to study the market carefully before submitting to make sure that their novels keep pace with current trends."

FIFI OSCARD ASSOCIATES, INC., 19 W. 44th St., New York NY 10036. (212)764-1100. Contact: Literary Department. Obtains clients through recommendations. Prefers to work with authors who have previously published articles or books. Will read—at no charge—synopses. Computer printout submissions acceptable; prefers letter-quality to dot-matrix. SASE. Reports in 2 weeks. Member SAR and Writers Guild. Agent receives 10% commission on domestic sales.
Will Handle: Material in all areas.

O'TOOLE AGENCY, 5 South Winds, St. Peters MO 63376. (314)278-4144. Literary Agent: Rosie O'Toole. 90% of clients are new/unpublished writers. Will read queries, book mss if accompanied with outline or synopsis, and screenplays if accompanied with outline and synopsis. SASE. Reports in 2 weeks. Agent receives 10% commission on both domestic and dramatic sales.
Will Handle: Screenplays and books (nonfiction, fiction, juvenile). Percentage of mss handled: 10% nonfiction; 70% fiction; 10% screenplays; 10% juvenile.

RAY PEEKNER LITERARY AGENCY, 3210 S. 7th St., Milwaukee WI 53215. Contact: Ray Puechner. Associated with Larry Sternig Literary Agency, Hintz Literary Agency, Bill Kruger Agency, Lee Allan Agency (films). Obtains new clients through referrals from clients and editors. Currently represents 60 clients. 2% of clients are new/unpublished writers. Will not read unsolicited mss. No multiple queries. Computer printout submissions acceptable; no dot-matrix. Reports in 2 weeks on queries; 1 month on submissions. Member MWA, WWA, RWA, SCBW and SFWA. Interested in new/beginning writers "if recommended by an editor, or well-established writer." Agent receives 10% commission.
Will Handle: Booklengths only, fiction and nonfiction, adult and young adult. Percentage of mss handled: 20% nonfiction; 40% fiction; 40% juvenile.

RODNEY PELTER, 129 E. 61st St., New York NY 10021. (212)838-3432. Contact: Rodney Pelter. Obtains new clients through referrals from people in publishing (editors, publishers, etc.) plus referrals from writers, etc. Represents 15-20 clients; "most have work in progress." Query first. SASE. Agent receives 10-15% commission on domestic sales (graduated scale, depending on size of advance); 10-20% on dramatic sales (depending on size of option or sale); and 20% on foreign sales.
Will Handle: Nonfiction books and novels.
Tips: "Write an intelligent query letter (with SASE). Give casual background summary; details of experience in writing or lack of it; and include first 25 pages or first chapter of manuscript to be submitted."

MARIE RODELL-FRANCES COLLIN LITERARY AGENCY, 110 W. 40th St., New York NY 10018. (212)840-8664. Contact: Frances Collin. Query. Computer printout submissions acceptable; prefers letter-quality to dot-matrix. Reports in 1-2 days on queries; 1 month on submissions. SASE. Member SAR. Agent receives 15% commission for domestic sales; and 25% for foreign. Currently represents 75 clients. 3-5% of clients are new/unpublished writers.
Will Handle: Trade novels and trade nonfiction books. Percentage of mss handled: 55% nonfiction; 40% fiction; 5% juvenile.

ROSENSTONE/WENDER, 3 E. 48th St., New York NY 10017. (212)832-8330. (201)568-8739. Contact: Felicity Rubinstein, Leah Schmidt, Virginia Read. Member of Society of Authors' Representatives. Obtains new clients through client inquiries. Will read unsolicited queries, outlines. Reports in 1-8 weeks. Agent receives 10% commission on domestic and dramatic sales; 20% on foreign sales.
Will Handle: Films, magazine articles, magazine fiction, nonfiction books, novels, stage plays and TV scripts.

MARY JANE ROSS AGENCY, 85 Sunset Lane, Tenafly NJ 07670. (201)568-8739. Contact: Mary Jane Ross. Obtains new clients usually by recommendation. Represents authors and also numerous small publishers on subsidiary rights. Will read queries at no charge "but must enclose SASE." Agent receives 15% commission on domestic and dramatic sales; 25% on foreign sales.
Will Handle: Nonfiction books and novels. No juvenile.
Tips: "Send query letter first with SASE. Manuscript must be legible, double spaced, but do not send the original; stamps for returning must be enclosed. Writer must be patient while decision is made. I require exclusivity."

ELEANOR MERRYMAN ROSZEL, 1710 Bolton St., Baltimore MD 21217. (301)669-8326. Literary Agent: Eleanor M. Roszel. Obtains clients through publisher referrals, client referrals, and some by word-of-mouth. 1% of clients are new/unpublished writers. "I am interested in any writing credits if they exist." Will read queries; "prefer NOT to have mss sent to me prior to a query with SASE." Computer printout submissions acceptable; prefers letter-quality to dot-matrix. Reports in 2 weeks on queries; 3 weeks on submissions. Agent receives 10% commission on domestic sales; 20% on foreign sales.
Will Handle: Fiction and nonfiction books, adult and juvenile ("query letter with table of contents and introduction, for starters"). Percentage of mss handled: 50% nonfiction; 50% fiction—3% juvenile.

JANE ROTROSEN, 226 E. 32nd St., New York NY 10016. (212)889-7133. 4 agents. Represents 100 clients. "We're looking for people who can make a career of writing. While we are always interested in new/unpublished writers, we do not formalize arrangements with an agency agreement until we have effected an acceptable contract on the writer's behalf." Query. Reports in 2 weeks on unsolicited queries; 6 weeks on submissions. SASE. Member ILAA.
Will Handle: Novels and nonfiction books. Percentage of mss handled: 30% nonfiction; 70% fiction.

GLORIA SAFIER, 667 Madison Ave., New York NY 10021. (212)838-4868. Contact: Gloria Safier. Represents 45 clients. 20% of clients are new/unpublished writers. Query. Reports in 1 week on queries. SASE. Member SAR. Agent receives 15% commission.
Will Handle: Trade novels and nonfiction, films and plays. Percentage of mss handled: 10% nonfiction mss; 60% fiction; 25% stage plays; 5% screenplays.
Tips: "Write a good letter, one that describes the book you want the agent to read (never write a letter that says just, 'I've written a book, would you like to read it?'—this sort of letter is useless) and reveals something about your background."

ARTHUR SCHWARTZ LITERARY AGENT, 435 Riverside Dr., New York NY 10025. (212)864-3182. Obtains new clients through "letter inquiries from professional writers." Must be established writer. Will read unsolicited queries. Computer printout submissions acceptable; prefers letter-quality to dot-matrix. SASE. Member ILAA. Agent receives 12½% commission.
Will Handle: "We seek any commercially-oriented fiction and nonfiction for books, especially adult-oriented

romantic fiction, family sagas, women's historical romantic fiction and commercial nonfiction. We do not handle plays, poetry, articles for magazines, romance novels or screenplays, but do place motion picture/film rights from book. A letter of inquiry should be made first to our agency. We accept only manuscripts sent by first class mail (please do not register, certify, or insure; you must retain the original ms for your file); and enclose a manuscript size SASE. Our agency specializes in representing well-known professionals and professors who write solidly-grounded but popularly-oriented nonfiction. Particularly interested in sociology, psychology, medicine, business and science.''

JAMES SELIGMANN AGENCY, Suite 1101, 175 5th Ave., New York NY 10010. Contact: James F. Seligmann. Obtains new clients through recommendation, personal contact, or solicitation. Will not read unsolicited mss; will read unsolicited queries and outlines. Computer printout submissions acceptable; prefers letter-quality to dot-matrix. SASE. Member SAR. Agent receives 15% commission.
Will Handle: Novels and nonfiction books. "Please, no poetry, drama or film or TV scripts, science fiction, mysteries, suspense novels, or books for children under 12.''

BOBBE SIEGEL, RIGHTS REPRESENTATIVE, 41 W. 83rd St., New York NY 10024. (212)877-4985. Contact: Bobbe Siegel. Obtains clients by referral, usually by editors or writers. Currently represents 50 clients. 40% of clients are new/unpublished writers. Will read manuscripts, queries, outlines, proposals. "Send query letter first.'' SASE. Reports in 2 weeks on queries; 2 months on submissions. Agent receives 15% commission on domestic sales; 10% on dramatic sales; 20% on foreign sales (10% of which is for foreign agent).
Will Handle: Nonfiction books, novels. Percentage of mss handled: 55% nonfiction; 45% fiction.
Tips: "Freelance writers will have a tougher time without an agent. They will have to do more research to establish which houses will view their material without an agent.''

SOFTWARE AGENCY, 928 Broadway, New York NY 10010. (212)675-5400. Principal: Edward J. Acton. Estab. 1983. Obtains new clients by referral. Currently represents 35 clients. 10% of clients are new/unpublished writers. Will read ms, queries, outlines. Computer printout submissions acceptable; prefers letter-quality to dot-matrix. SASE. Reports in 1 week on queries; varying time on submissions. Agent receives 15% commission.
Will Handle: Computer books, software programs only.

RENEE SPODHEIM, 698 West End Ave., New York NY 10025. (212)222-4083. Contact: Renee Spodheim. Obtains new clients through referrals. Represents several American clients, many foreign, especially French. Will read—at no charge—queries and outlines (about 50 pages). Agent receives 15% on domestic sales; 20% on dramatic and foreign sales.
Will Handle: Nonfiction books and novels.

GLORIA STERN LITERARY AGENCY, 1230 Park Ave., New York NY 10028. (212)289-7698. Contact: Gloria Stern. Represents 34 clients. 40% of clients are new/unpublished writers. "For fiction, only serious fiction, authors who have been published in magazines or have had a book published; for nonfiction, the author must have particular expertise in the field he plans to write about.'' Query. No unsolicited mss. Computer printout submissions acceptable; no dot-matrix. SASE. Reports in 3 days on queries; 3 weeks on submissions. Member ILAA. Interested in new/beginning writers, but "only fiction writers who have been published in quality literary or commercial magazines. Nonfiction needs some established expertise in subject.'' Agent receives 10-15% commissions.
Will Handle: Novels, trade nonfiction books. No self-publications. "Prefers serious literary fiction.'' Percentage of mss handled: 85% nonfiction; 15% fiction.

LARRY STERNIG LITERARY AGENCY, 742 Robertson St., Milwaukee WI 53213. (414)771-7677. "I am unable to take on new clients.'' Currently represents 40 clients—20% nonfiction mss; 80% fiction mss. Will not read unsolicited mss. Agent receives 10% commission.
Handles: Magazine articles and fiction, novels and nonfiction books.

GUNTHER STUHLMANN, AUTHOR'S REPRESENTATIVE, Box 276, Becket MA 01223. Contact: Ms. Barbara Ward. Obtains new clients through "personal recommendation from clients, publishers, editors.'' Will not read unsolicited mss. SASE for queries and outlines. Reports in 1 week on queries; 3 weeks on submissions. Agent receives 10% commission on domestic and Canadian sales; 15% on British and 20% overseas.
Will Handle: Novels, nonfiction books, motion picture, TV and serial rights based on established properties only. "We do not handle individual original plays, TV scripts or film scripts. We handle such rights only on the basis of established properties, i.e., as subsidiary rights to books we handle.''

ALFONSO TAFOYA, #212, 655 6th Ave., New York NY 10010. (212)929-1090. Director: Alfonso Tafoya. Obtains new clients through referrals. Represents 30 clients. Writers should have some prior publishing. Will read queries at no charge. Agent receives 10% commission on domestic sales; 20% on dramatic and foreign sales.

Will Handle: Films (treatments); magazine articles; magazine fiction; nonfiction books (query); novels (query); syndicated material (must have major experience); and TV scripts (treatments). Author must have "track record" in these areas.

Tips: "Have *one* very good, very polished, completed project. Be patient."

TEAL & WATT LITERARY AGENCY, 2036 Vista del Rosa, Fullerton CA 92631. (714)738-8333. Partners: Patricia Teal and Sandra Watt. Member ILAA. Obtains new clients through *Writer's Market, Literary Market Place* and referrals. Currently represents 60 clients. 50% of clients are new/unpublished writers. Will read—at no charge—unsolicited queries consisting of outlines and sample chapters. Does not charge fee unless special circumstances warrant. Will not read unsolicited mss. Computer printout submissions acceptable; no dot-matrix. SASE. Reports in 2 weeks on queries; 6 weeks on submissions. Agent receives 15% commission on domestic sales, 15% on dramatic sales, and 20% on foreign rights.

Will Handle: Full-length adult fiction and nonfiction. Percentage of mss handled: 40% nonfiction; 60% fiction. Specializes in romance literature. No short stories, articles, poetry, scripts or syndicated material.

SUSAN P. URSTADT INC., 125 E. 84th St., New York NY 10028. (212)744-6605. President: Susan Urstadt. Member ILAA. Obtains new clients "usually through reference." Represents 15-20 clients. 5% of clients are new/unpublished writers. Will read queries and outlines. Computer printout submissions acceptable; prefers letter-quality to dot-matrix. SASE. Reports in 2 weeks on queries; 6 weeks on submissions. Agent receives 10% commission on domestic sales, 15% on dramatic sales, 20% on foreign sales.

Will Handle: Nonfiction books and quality fiction (not science fiction, romance or horror); also illustrated books (art, antiques and horses). Percentage of mss handled: 40% nonfiction; 40% fiction; 20% juvenile.

JOHN A. WARE LITERARY AGENCY, 392 Central Park W., New York NY 10025. (212)866-4733. Contact: John Ware. Obtains new clients through referrals, speaking engagements, inquiries. Represents approximately 50 clients. 50% of clients are new/unpublished writers. Will read mss (strongly prefer query first), queries and outlines. Reports in 1 week on queries; 3 weeks on mss. SASE. Agent receives 10% commission on domestic and dramatic sales, 20% on foreign sales.

Will Handle: Nonfiction books and novels. Percentage of mss handled: 75% nonfiction; 25% fiction.

WRITERS AND ARTISTS AGENCY, 162 W. 56th St., New York NY 10019. (212)246-9029. West Coast office: 11726 San Vicente Blvd., Brentwood CA 90049. Contact: Jonathan Sand, Carol Reich (NY); David Hoberman, Dan Ostroff (LA). Obtains clients through reading (solicited only) manuscripts and attending plays. Currently represents 80 clients. Will read 2-page synopsis and resume. Will not read unsolicited mss. Agent receives 10% commission on domestic, dramatic and foreign sales.

Will Handle: Plays, films, nonfiction books, novels and TV scripts (NY office). TV scripts and screenplays (LA office).

WRITERS HOUSE INC., 21 W. 26th St., New York NY 10010. Contact: Linda Robbins. Member ILAA. Obtains new clients "mostly by referrals and recommendations." Represents 240 clients. 10% of clients are new/unpublished writers. Will read queries, outlines and sample chapters. Computer printout submissions acceptable; prefers letter-quality to dot-matrix. Reports in 2 weeks on queries; 6 weeks on submissions. SASE. Agent receives 10% commission on domestic sales, 15% on dramatic sales, 20% on foreign sales.

Will Handle: Novels, nonfiction, juvenile. "Prefer seeing a detailed synopsis and a sample chapter or two." Percentage of mss handled: 40% nonfiction; 30% fiction; 30% juvenile.

WRITERS' PRODUCTIONS, Box 5152, Westport CT 06881. Contact: David L. Meth. New clients obtained through "word of mouth and professional listings. No phone calls, please." 50% of clients are new/unpublished writers. Limited client list. Will read mss (sample of 25-50 pages only); queries and outlines. Computer printout submissions acceptable; no dot-matrix. SASE. Reports in 1 week on queries; 1 month on submissions. Agent receives 10% commission on domestic and dramatic sales, 10-20% on foreign sales (depending on foreign agent's fee).

Will Handle: Nonfiction books (intriguing, sensitive subjects, nothing technical); novels (sensitive, provocative fiction of the highest quality). Percentage of mss handled: 5% nonfiction; 95% fiction.

Tips: "We are looking for writers who deal with their subjects sensitively and compassionately, and whose characters will live beyond the time the book is put down. Always send the *best* work possible as an example of your talent and skill."

GEORGE ZIEGLER AGENCY, 160 E. 97th St., New York NY 10029. (212)348-3637. Proprietor: George Ziegler. Obtains new clients through referrals and submissions. Represents 24 clients. 50% of clients are new/unpublished writers. "Writers should send query first, with brief synopsis/description of book." SASE. Reports in 1 week on queries; 6 weeks on submissions. Agent receives 15% commission on domestic and dramatic sales, 20% on foreign sales (if subagent used).

Will Handle: Nonfiction books (for general trade only); novels (non-genre, no romances); stage plays (full-evening-length, contemporary or historical, *realistic*).

Tips: "It's at least twice as hard as it was 7 or 8 years ago to get a publisher to take the leap for a talented unknown unless the book is potential top of the list. It's even hard for the writer who has one book under his/her belt if the book didn't get favorable critical attention."

Contests and Awards

Writers *compete* whenever they submit material for publication. But with most contests, awards and fellowships, writers have the benefit of written rules.

Contests enable writers to compete with one another on similar terms. Some competitions focus on a form (like poetry, perhaps) or a subject (like science). In other awards, the theme or approach doesn't matter; the object for judges is to find *the best*—the best article, play, or first-time novel.

Contests offer writers a variety of benefits. Aside from the monetary rewards from many writing prizes, there is satisfaction and the incentive to excel further. There is exposure and recognition. Distinction in a playwriting contest may lead to staged readings of a script; a winner of an American Book Award may see increased sales of his novel.

Most of the contests listed here are annual competitions. *No contest that charges the writer an entry or reading fee has been included.* Contests for both published and unpublished work are listed.

Some competitions do not accept entries or nominations directly from writers; we've included them for their national or literary importance. If you want your work to be considered for one of these competitions, tell your publisher/editor about the contest and your interest in it.

We've listed contests by name, address, contact person and type of competition. If a contest sounds interesting to you, send a self-addressed, stamped envelope to the contest contact person (if listed) for contest information and rules. In fact, don't enter any contest without seeking this information; some contests have very detailed instructions and requirements.

Two guides that offer additional information about writing contests are *How to Enter and Win Fiction Writing Contests* and *How to Enter and Win Nonfiction and Journalism Contests*, both by Alan Gadney (They are available from Facts on File, 460 Park Ave. S., New York City 10016 for a fee).

This year's *Writer's Market* includes a sampling of opportunities for writers interested in pursuing fellowships and grants for their writing projects. Fellowships may include stipends, writing residencies and/or cash awards to be used for professional advancement. Requirements and eligibilities are unique to each program. Funds for writers to practice their craft *are* available; the key is knowing where to look. Become familiar with these two resources available in most large public libraries: *Annual Register of Grant Support* (Marquis Professional Publications, Marquis Who's Who, Inc., 200 E. Ohio St., Chicago IL 60611) and *Foundation Grants to Individuals* (Foundation Center, 79 5th Ave., New York City 10003). The former is a guide to grant and fellowship support programs in government, public and private foundations, companies, professional associations, and special interest groups. A detailed subject index will lead you to writing-related programs. The Foundation Center directory lists approximately 1,000 foundations and application procedures for grants offered to individuals. Included are scholarships, fellowships, residencies, grants to needy writers, and a bibliography of other funding information.

If you don't win the first contests or fellowships you apply for, don't get discouraged. Some entries can be so close in merit that judges must reread each one numerous times. (We experienced this at *Writer's Market* in selecting the ten essays for this edition. The eleventh or twelfth best essays, say, merited publication too, but all competitions must draw a line somewhere.) In all contests, judges weigh what is said in an entry (content) *and* how it is said (form). Analyze the content and form of your writing *before* judges do.

A.I.P.—U.S. STEEL FOUNDATION SCIENCE WRITING AWARD, Public Information Division, American Institute of Physics, 335 E. 45th St., New York NY 10017. Physics and astronomy.

AAAS SOCIO-PSYCHOLOGICAL PRIZE, American Association for the Advancement of Science, 1776 Massachusetts Ave. NW, Washington DC 20036. (202)467-4470. Assistant to the Executive Officer: C. Borras. Psychology/social sciences/sociology.

AAAS-WESTINGHOUSE SCIENCE JOURNALISM AWARDS, American Association for the Advancement of Science, 1515 Massachusetts Ave. NW, Washington DC 20005. (202)467-4483. Administrator: Grayce A. Finger. Science, technology and engineering (newspaper, magazine, radio and TV).

ACTF STUDENT PLAYWRITING AWARDS, Producing Director, American College Theatre Festival, John F. Kennedy Center for the Performing Arts, Washington DC 20566. (202)254-3437. Student-written play.

HERBERT BAXTER ADAMS PRIZE, Committee Chairman, American Historical Association, 400 A St. SE, Washington DC 20003. European history (first book).

AID TO INDIVIDUAL ARTISTS FELLOWSHIP, Ohio Arts Council, 727 E. Main St., Columbus OH 43205. (614)466-2613. Contact: Susan Dickson or Lance Kinz. Nonfiction, fiction, criticism, poetry and plays. (Ohio resident, nonstudent).

ALBERTA NEW NOVELIST COMPETITION, Alberta Culture, Film and Literary Arts, 12th Fl., CN Tower, Edmonton, Alberta T5J 0K5 Canada. (403)427-2554. Award Director: John Patrick Gillese. Unpublished first novel (Alberta resident).

ALBERTA NON-FICTION AWARD, Alberta Culture, Film and Literary Arts, 12 Fl., CN Tower, Edmonton, Alberta T5J 0K5 Canada. (403)427-2554. Award Director: John Patrick Gillese. Nonfiction by Alberta author.

ALBERTA REGIONAL HISTORY AWARD, Alberta Culture, Film and Literary Arts, 12 Fl., CN Tower, Edmonton, Alberta T5J 0K5 Canada. (403)427-2554. Award Director: John Patrick Gillese. History and heritage.

THE NELSON ALGREN AWARD, *Chicago* Magazine, 3 Illinois Center, 303 E. Wacker Dr., Chicago IL 60601. (312)565-5000. Award Director: Christine Newman. Unpublished short story.

AMERICAN OSTEOPATHIC ASSOCIATION JOURNALISM AWARDS, 212 E. Ohio St., Chicago IL 60611. (312)280-5800. Director, Communications: Al Boeck. Medical journalism (print and broadcast).

AMERICAN RADIO THEATRE ANNUAL RADIO SCRIPT WRITERS COMPETITION, The American Radio Theatre, Suite 104, 1616 West Victory Blvd., Glendale CA 91201. (213)246-6584. Contest Director: Ed Thomas. Radio scripts (unpublished author).

AMERICAN-SCANDINAVIAN FOUNDATION/TRANSLATION PRIZE, American-Scandinavian Foundation, 127 E. 73rd St., New York NY 10021. (212)879-9779. Contact: Publishing Division. Contemporary Scandinavian fiction and poetry translations.

AMERICAN SPEECH-LANGUAGE-HEARING ASSOCIATION (ASHA), NATIONAL MEDIA AWARD, 10801 Rockville Pike, Rockville MD 20852. (301)897-5700. Speech-language pathology and audiology (radio, TV, newspaper, magazine).

ANNUAL INTERNATIONAL NARRATIVE CONTEST, Poets and Patrons, Inc., 13942 Keeler Ave., Crestwood IL 60445. Chairman: Mary Mathison. Narrative poetry.

ANNUAL INTERNATIONAL POETRY CONTEST, Poet's Study Club of Terre Haute, Indiana, 826 S. Center, Terre Haute IN 47807. (812)234-0819. President: Esther Alman. Serious poetry, light verse, and traditional haiku.

THE ANNUAL NATIONAL BIBLE WEEK EDITORIAL CONTEST, The Laymen's National Bible Committee Inc., Suite 512, 815 2nd Ave., New York NY 10017. (212)687-0555. Contact: Executive Director. Unpublished editorial (journalism students only).

ANNUAL W/P POETRY CONTEST, WP, Box 119, Ft. Campbell KY 42223. (615)645-1916. Contest/Award Director: Richard L. Evans. Estab. 1983. Poetry or nature.

RUBY LLOYD APSEY PLAYWRITING AWARD, University of Alabama, Department of Theater and Dance, University Station, Birmingham AL 35294. (205)934-3236. Contest Director: Dr. Rick L. Plummer. Unpublished plays by New American playwrights.

ASSOCIATION FOR EDUCATION IN JOURNALISM AWARD, Magazine Division, Southern Connecticut State University, 501 Crescent St., New Haven CT 06515. Professor of Journalism: Ms. Robin Glassman. Unpublished nonfiction magazine article. Students only.

THE AUTHOR OF THE YEAR AWARD, American Society of Journalists and Authors, 1501 Broadway, New York NY 10036. (212)997-0947. Executive Director: Mary Sutherland. Nonfiction book or body of work.

THE AXIOS AWARD, Axios Newsletter, Inc., 800 S. Euclid Ave., Fullerton CA 92632. (714)526-2131. Contest/Award Director: Daniel John Gorham. Orthodox Catholic religion in America (secular magazine article).

THE ALTHEA BANTREE MYSTERY CONTEST, Winston-Derek Publishers, Box 90883, Nashville TN 37209. (615)329-1319; 356-7384. Contest/Award Director: James W. Peebles, publisher. Unpublished mystery book.

GEORGE LOUIS BEER PRIZE, Committee Chairman, American Historical Association, 400 A St. SE, Washington DC 20003. European international history (scholarly work).

ALBERT J. BEVERIDGE AWARD, Committee Chairman, American Historical Association, 400 A St. SE, Washington DC 20003. American history of US, Canada and Latin America (book).

BITTERROOT MAGAZINE POETRY CONTEST, Write: Menke Katz, Editor-in-Chief, *Bitterroot*, Spring Glen NY 12483. Poetry.

BLACK WARRIOR REVIEW LITERARY AWARDS, *Black Warrior Review*, Box 2936, University AL 35486. (205)348-4518. Contact: Editor. Unpublished poetry and fiction.

BOLLINGEN PRIZE IN POETRY OF THE YALE UNIVERSITY LIBRARY, Yale University Library, New Haven CT 06520. (203)436-0236. Secretary, Yale Administrative Committee: David E. Schoonover. American poetry (book).

BOSTON GLOBE-HORN BOOK AWARDS, Stephanie Loer, Children's Book Editor, *The Boston Globe*, Boston MA 02107. Poetry, nonfiction and illustrated book.

BOWLING WRITING COMPETITION, American Bowling Congress, Public Relations, 5301 S. 76th St., Greendale WI 53129. Feature, editorial, local association, and news.

BROADCAST PRECEPTOR AWARDS, Broadcast Industry Conference, San Francisco State University, 1600 Holloway Ave., San Francisco CA 94132. (415)469-2184, 469-1148. Contact persons: Janet Lee Miller, Donald E. Gibson. Broadcast industry (book); academic, production and performance (tape).

BULTMAN AWARD, Chairman, Department of Drama, Loyola University, New Orleans LA 70118. Unpublished and professionally unproduced plays under 1 hour written by college students.

CANADIAN BOOKSELLERS ASSOCIATION AUTHOR OF THE YEAR AWARD, 49 Laing St., Toronto, Ontario M4L 2N4 Canada. Contact: Board of Directors of the Association. Book by Canadian author.

RUSSELL L. CECIL ARTHRITIS WRITING AWARDS, Arthritis Foundation, 1314 Spring St. NW, Atlanta GA 30309. (404)872-7100. Contact: Public Relations Department. Medical (news stories, articles, and radio/TV scripts).

CHAMPION MEDIA AWARDS FOR ECONOMIC UNDERSTANDING, Administered by The Amos Tuck School of Business Administration, Dartmouth College, Hanover NH 03755. (603)643-5596. Contest/Award Director: Ms. Jan Brigham Bent. Business and economics (newspapers, magazines, syndicates, wire services, TV and radio).

CHILDREN'S SCIENCE BOOK AWARDS, New York Academy of Sciences, 2 E. 63rd St., New York NY 10021. (212)838-0230. Public Relations Director: Ann E. Collins. General or trade science books for children under 10 years.

COLLEGIATE POETRY CONTEST, *The Lyric,* 307 Dunton Dr. SW, Blacksburg VA 24060. Editor: Leslie Mellichamp. Unpublished poems (32 lines or less) by fulltime undergraduates in 4-year US or Canadian colleges.

THE BERNARD F. CONNERS PRIZE FOR POETRY, Poetry Editor, Editorial Office, *The Paris Review*, 541 E. 72nd St., New York NY 10021. Unpublished poetry over 300 lines.

ALBERT B. COREY PRIZE IN CANADIAN-AMERICAN RELATIONS, Office of the Executive Director, American Historical Association, 400 A St. SE, Washington DC 20003. History, Canadian-US relations or history of both countries (book).

HAROLD C. CRAIN AWARD IN PLAYWRITING, Department of Theatre Arts, San Jose State University, San Jose CA 95192. (408)277-2763. Contest Coordinator: Dr. Howard Burman. Full-length plays.

CUMMINGS-TAYLOR PLAYWRITING AWARD, Sierra Repertory Theatre, Box 3030, Sonora CA 95370. (209)532-3120. Producing Director: Dennis C. Jones. Full-length plays.

THE DISCOVERY/NATION 1985, The Poetry Center of the 92nd Street YM-YWHA, 1395 Lexington Ave., New York NY 10128. (212)427-6000, ext. 176. Poetry (unpublished in book form).

JOHN H. DUNNING PRIZE IN AMERICAN HISTORY, Committee Chairman, American Historical Association, 400 A St. SE, Washington DC 20003. US history monograph.

EDUCATOR'S AWARD, Executive Secretary, Delta Kappa Gamma Society International, Box 1589, Austin TX 78767. Education, teaching (book by woman or 2 women from country in which Society is established).

JOHN K. FAIRBANK PRIZE IN EAST ASIAN HISTORY, Committee Chairman, American Historical Association, 400 A St. SE, Washington DC 20003. Book on East Asian history.

THE FORUM AWARD, Atomic Industrial Forum, 7101 Wisconsin Ave., Washington DC 20814. Contest Coordinator: Suzann Powers. Nuclear energy (print and electronic media).

GLCA NEW WRITERS AWARDS IN POETRY AND FICTION, Great Lakes Colleges Association, Wabash College, Crawfordsville IN 47933. (317)362-1400, ext. 232. Director: Donald Baker. Poetry or fiction (first book; novel or volume of short fiction).

GREAT AMERICAN PLAY CONTEST, Actors Theatre of Louisville, 316 W. Main St., Louisville KY 40202. (502)584-1265. Literary Manager: Julie Beckett Crutcher. Unproduced, workshopped or university-produced plays. (US citizens only).

GUIDEPOSTS MAGAZINE YOUTH WRITING CONTEST, Guideposts Associates, Inc., 747 3rd Ave., New York NY 10017. Senior Editor: James McDermott. Memorable true experience. Unpublished first person story by high school juniors, seniors or students in equivalent grades overseas.

CLARENCE H. HARING PRIZE, Committee Chairman, American Historical Association, 400 A St. SE, Washington DC 20003. Book on Latin American history by Latin American author.

NATE HASELTINE MEMORIAL FELLOWSHIPS IN SCIENCE WRITING, Council for the Advancement of Science Writing, Inc., 618 North Elmwood, Oak Park IL 60302. Executive Director: William J. Cromie. Science journalism.

ERNEST HEMINGWAY FOUNDATION AWARD, P.E.N. American Center, 47 5th Ave., New York NY 10003. First-published novel or short story collection by American author.

SIDNEY HILLMAN PRIZE AWARD, Sidney Hillman Foundation, Inc., 15 Union Square, New York NY 10003. (212)242-0700, ext. 235. Social/economic themes related to ideals of Sidney Hillman (daily or periodical journalism, nonfiction, radio and TV).

HOUGHTON MIFFLIN LITERARY FELLOWSHIP, Houghton Mifflin Co., 2 Park St., Boston MA 02108. Literary projects (fiction or nonfiction finished ms or work in progress).

HOW-TO-DO-IT CONTEST, The Krantz Company Publishers, 2210 N. Burling, Chicago IL 60614. (312)472-4900. Publisher: Les Krantz. Reference book material (original question-and-answer combinations, or questions only and answers only).

INTERNATIONAL FILM LITERATURE AWARDS, International Film Literature Society, #27, 8695 Via Mallorca, La Jolla CA 92037. Narrative, criticism and technical.

INTERNATIONAL IMITATION HEMINGWAY COMPETITION, Harry's Bar & American Grill, 2020 Avenue of the Stars, Los Angeles CA 90067. (213)277-2333. Contest/Award Director: Mark S. Grody, Grody/Tellem Communications, Inc., Suite 200, 9100 S. Sepulveda Blvd., Los Angeles CA 90045. (213)417-3038. Unpublished one-page parody of Hemingway.

INTERNATIONAL SHAKESPEAREAN SONNET CONTEST, c/o Nolan Boiler Co., 8531 S. Vincennes, Chicago IL 60620. Contest Chairman: Anne Nolan. Unpublished sonnet by nonmembers of Poets Club of Chicago.

IOWA SCHOOL OF LETTERS AWARD FOR SHORT FICTION, Iowa School of Letters, University of Iowa, Iowa City IA 52242. (319)353-3181. Award Director: John Leggett. Short story unpublished as a book.

JOSEPH HENRY JACKSON/JAMES D. PHELAN LITERARY AWARD, 8th Floor, 500 Washington St., San Francisco CA 94111. (415)392-0600. Assistant Coordinator: Susan Kelly. Jackson: unpublished, partly completed book-length fiction, nonfiction, short story or poetry by author with 3-year consecutive residency in N. California or Nevada; Phelan: unpublished, incomplete work of fiction, nonfiction, short story, poetry or drama by California-born author. Age 20-35.

JACKSONVILLE UNIVERSITY PLAYWRITING CONTEST, Davis Sikes, Director, College of Fine Arts, Jacksonville University, Jacksonville FL 32211. (904)744-3950. Unproduced one-act and full-length plays.

ANSON JONES AWARD, c/o Texas Medical Association, 1801 N. Lamar Blvd., Austin TX 78701. (512)477-6704. Health (newspaper, magazine, radio and TV).

THE JANET HEIDINGER KAFKA PRIZE, English Department/Writers Workshop, 315 Frederick Douglass Bldg., University of Rochester, Rochester NY 14627. (716)275-2340. Chairman: Prof. Rowland L. Collins. Administrative Secretary: Anne M. Ludlow. Book length prose fiction (novel, short story or experimental writing) by US woman citizen.

THE AGA KHAN PRIZE FOR FICTION, Editorial Office, *The Paris Review*, 541 E. 72nd St., New York NY 10021. Unpublished short story.

MARC A. KLEIN PLAYWRITING AWARD, Department of Theatre, Case Western Reserve University, 2070 Adelbert Rd., Cleveland OH 44106. (216)368-2858. Unpublished, nonprofessionally produced full length plays, evening of related short plays, or full length musical by students in American college or university.

LAMONT POETRY SELECTION, Academy of American Poets, 177 E. 87th St., New York NY 10128. (212)427-5665. Contest/Award Director: Nancy Schoenberger. Second book of poems. (American citizens.)

HAROLD MORTON LANDON TRANSLATION AWARD, The Academy of American Poets, 177 E. 87th St., New York NY 10128. Poetry translation into English (book-length poem, collection, or verse drama translated into verse).

STEPHEN LEACOCK AWARD FOR HUMOUR, The Stephen Leacock Associates, Box 854, Orillia, Ontario L3V 6K8 Canada. (705)325-6546. Chairman of Award Committee: Mrs. Jean Bradley Dickson. Humorous works by Canadian authors.

NORMAN LEAR AWARD FOR ACHIEVEMENT IN COMEDY PLAYWRITING, Producing Director, American College Theatre Festival, John F. Kennedy Center for the Performing Arts, Washington DC 20566. (202)254-3437. Plays produced by participating ACTF college or university.

JERRY LEWIS/MDA WRITING AWARDS, Craig H. Wood, Director, Department of Public Health Education, Muscular Dystrophy Association, 810 7th Ave., New York NY 10019. Works contributing to public understanding of muscular dystrophy and related neuromuscular diseases (all media).

HOWARD R. MARRARO PRIZE IN ITALIAN HISTORY, Office of the Executive Director, American Historical Association, 400 A St. SE, Washington DC 20003. Work on epoch of Italian history, Italian cultural history or Italian-American relations.

MASSACHUSETTS ARTISTS FELLOWSHIP, The Artists Foundation, Inc., 110 Broad St., Boston MA 02110. (617)482-8100. Funded by the Massachusetts Council on the Arts and Humanities. Director: Lucine A. Folgueras. Poetry, fiction and playwriting. (Massachusetts residents.)

MELCHER BOOK AWARD, Unitarian Universalist Association, 25 Beacon St., Boston MA 02108. Staff Liaison: Dr. David B. Parke. Religious liberalism (book).

MENCKEN AWARDS, Free Press Association, Box 1743, Apple Valley CA 92307. (415)834-6880. Contest/Award Director: Jeff Riggenbach. Defense of human rights and individual liberties (news story or investigative report, feature story, essay or review, editorial or op ed column, editorial cartoon; and book).

KENNETH W. MILDENBERGER MEDAL, Office of Research Programs, 62 5th Ave., New York NY 10011. Teaching foreign language and literatures (book or article).

JAMES MOONEY AWARD, The University of Tennessee Press/The Southern Anthropological Society, Department of Anthropology, University of North Carolina, Greensboro NC 27412. Contact: Harriet J. Kupferer. Unpublished book-lengh ms describing and interpreting New World people or culture—prehistoric, historic or contemporary.

FRANK LUTHER MOTT-KAPPA TAU ALPHA RESEARCH AWARD IN JOURNALISM, 107 Sondra Ave., Columbia MO 65202. (314)443-3521. Chief, Central Office: William H. Taft. Research in journalism (book).

MS PUBLIC EDUCATION AWARDS CONTEST, National Multiple Sclerosis Society, 205 E. 42nd St., New York NY 10017. Contact: Public Relations Director. Reporting on facts and consequences of multiple sclerosis (newspaper, magazine, radio or TV).

MYSTERY NEWS SHORT STORY CONTEST, *Mystery News*, Box 2637, Rohnert Park CA 94928. (707)584-4843. Contest Director: Patricia Shnell. Estab. 1984. Unpublished mystery, suspense or crime story.

NATIONAL HISTORICAL SOCIETY BOOK PRIZE IN AMERICAN HISTORY, 2245 Kohn Rd., Harrisburg PA 17105. American history (first published book).

NATIONAL JEWISH BOOK AWARD—CHILDREN'S LITERATURE, Jewish Book Council, 15 E. 26th St., New York NY 10010. Children's book on Jewish theme.

NATIONAL JEWISH BOOK AWARD—FICTION, WILLIAM AND JANICE EPSTEIN AWARD, 15 E. 26th St., New York NY 10010. Jewish fiction (novel or short story collection).

NATIONAL JEWISH BOOK AWARD—HOLOCAUST, 15 E. 26th St., New York NY 10010. Nonfiction book on some aspect of Nazi holocaust period.

NATIONAL JEWISH BOOK AWARD—JEWISH THOUGHT, FRANK & ETHEL S. COHEN AWARD, 15 E. 26th St., New York NY 10010. Book dealing with some aspect of Jewish thought, past or present.

NATIONAL ONE ACT PLAYWRITING CONTEST, Dubuque Fine Arts Society, 422 Loras Blvd., Dubuque IA 52001. Dubuque Fine Arts Players: Contest Director. Unpublished plays (new and innovative drama).

NATIONAL PLAY AWARD, Box 71011, Los Angeles CA 90071. (213)629-3762. Program Manager: Emily Schiller. Unpublished, nonprofessionally produced plays.

NATIONAL PLAYWRIGHT COMPETITION, Unicorn Theatre, 3514 Jefferson, Kansas City MO 64111. (816)531-7529. Unpublished, unproduced plays. (US residents only.)

NATIONAL SOCIETY OF PROFESSIONAL ENGINEERS JOURNALISM AWARDS, 2029 K St. NW, Washington DC 20006. (202)463-2354. PR Director: Leslie Collins. Engineering and technology in contemporary life (articles in general interest magazines and newspapers).

ALLAN NEVINS PRIZE, Professor Kenneth T. Jackson, Secretary-Treasurer, Society of American Historians, 610 Fayerweather Hall, Columbia University, New York NY 10027. American history (doctoral dissertation on arts, literature, science and American biographies).

NEW WRITERS AWARDS, Great Lakes Colleges Association, c/o English Department, Wabash College, Crawfordsville IN 47933. (317)362-1400, ext. 232. Director: Donald W. Baker. Poetry or fiction (first book).

NEW YORK STATE HISTORICAL ASSOCIATION MANUSCRIPT AWARD, Box 800, Cooperstown NY 13326. (607)547-2508. Director of Publications: Dr. Wendell Tripp. Unpublished book-length monograph on New York state history.

NEWCOMEN AWARDS IN BUSINESS HISTORY, c/o *Business History Review*, Harvard University, Gallatin D-126, Soldiers Field, Boston MA 02163. (617)495-6154. Editor: Richard S. Tedlow. Business history article.

NMMA DIRECTORS AWARD, National Marine Manufacturers Association, 353 Lexington Ave., New York NY 10016. (212)684-6622. Boating and allied water sports.

NORTH AMERICAN ESSAY CONTEST FOR YOUNG MEN AND WOMEN OF GOODWILL, *The Humanist Magazine*, 7 Harwood Dr., Box 146, Amherst NY 14226. (716)839-5080. Contest/Award Director: Lloyd Morain. Unpublished essay by writers age 29 or younger.

NORTHWEST PLAYWRIGHTS CONFERENCE, Empty Space, 95 S. Jackson St., Seattle WA 98104. Unpublished plays by residents of Washington, Oregon, Idaho, Montana and Wyoming.

OGLEBAY INSTITUTE, TOWNGATE THEATRE PLAYWRITING CONTEST, Oglebay Park, Wheeling WV 26003. (304)242-4200. Contest Director: Jennifer Coffield. Unpublished, nonprofessionally produced full length plays.

OPEN CIRCLE THEATRE PLAYWRIGHTS AWARD, Goucher College, Towson MD 21204. Director: Barry Knower. Unpublished, unproduced plays. (50% of major roles must be for women.)

THE C.F. ORVIS WRITING CONTEST, The Orvis Company, Inc., Manchester VT 05254. (802)362-3622. Contest/Award Director: Tom Rosenbauer. Outdoor writing about upland bird hunting and fly fishing (magazine and newspaper).

OSCARS IN AGRICULTURE, DeKalb AgResearch, Inc., Sycamore Rd., DeKalb IL 60115. (815)758-3461. Director of Corporate Public Relations: Ron Scherer. Agricultural news reporting (newspaper, magazine, TV and radio).

FRANCIS PARKMAN PRIZE, Professor Kenneth T. Jackson, Secretary, Society of American Historians, 610 Fayerweather Hall, Columbia University, New York NY 10027. Colonial or national US history (book).

PEN/FAULKNER AWARD FOR FICTION, PEN American Center and PEN/South, c/o Folger Shakespeare Library, 201 E. Capitol St. SE, Washington DC 20003. (202)544-7077. Contact: Katharine Zadravee. Fiction by American author.

PEN TRANSLATION PRIZE, PEN American Center, 47 5th Ave., New York NY 10003. Contact: Chairman, Translation Committee. Book-length translation into English. (No technical, scientific or reference.)

THE MAXWELL PERKINS PRIZE, Charles Scribner's Sons, 597 5th Ave., New York NY 10017. (212)486-2706. Contest/Award Director: Charles Scribner Jr. Unpublished non-genre fiction (first novel).

PLAYWRITING FOR CHILDREN AWARD, Community Children's Theatre, 8021 E. 129th Terrace, Grandview MO 64030. (816)761-5775. Unpublished plays for grades 1-6.

EDGAR ALLAN POE AWARDS, Mystery Writers of America, Inc., 150 5th Ave., New York NY 10011. Mystery novel published in America, first mystery novel by American author, fact crime book, juvenile mystery, paperback mystery, mystery short story, mystery motion picture, and TV mystery.

PULITZER PRIZES, Secretary, The Pulitzer Prize Board, 702 Journalism, Columbia University, New York NY 10027. Awards for journalism, letters, drama and music in US newspapers, and in literature, drama and music by Americans.

ERNIE PYLE MEMORIAL AWARD, Scripps-Howard Foundation, 1100 Central Trust Tower, Cincinnati OH 45202. Newspaper writing exemplifying work of Ernie Pyle.

THE RAINBOW COMPANY CHILDREN'S THEATRE NATIONAL PLAYWRITING CONTEST, 821 Las Vegas Blvd. N, Las Vegas NV 89101. (702)386-6553. Artistic Coordinator: Brian Strom. Unproduced plays for young people.

REAL ESTATE JOURNALISM ACHIEVEMENT COMPETITION, National Association of Realtors, 777 14th St. NW, Washington DC 20005. Contact: Lou Dombrowski or Dr. Paul Snider, Bradley University, Peoria IL 61625. Real estate reporting, writing and broadcasting.

RECREATION VEHICLE INDUSTRY ASSOCIATION DISTINGUISHED ACHIEVEMENT IN RV JOURNALISM AWARD, Recreation Vehicle Industry Assn., 14650 Lee Rd., Chantilly VA 22021. (703)968-7722. National Director of Public Relations: Gary M. LaBella. RV industry.

REGINA MEDAL, Catholic Library Association, 461 W. Lancaster Ave., Haverford PA 19041. Literature for children.

RHODORA PRIZE FOR WOMEN'S LITERATURE, Rhodora Books, Box 10197, Stanford CA 94305. Director: Marilyn Yalom. Unpublished women's literature (novel, stories, essays, memoirs, etc.).

FOREST A. ROBERTS PLAYWRITING AWARD, In cooperation with Shiras Institute, Forest A. Roberts Theatre, Northern Michigan University, Marquette MI 49855. (906)227-2553. Award Director: Dr. James A. Panowski. Unpublished, unproduced plays.

ST. LAWRENCE AWARD FOR FICTION, Joe David Bellamy, Department of English, St. Lawrence University, Canton NY 13617. First collection of short fiction.

ROBERT LIVINGSTON SCHUYLER PRIZE, Committee Chairman, American Historical Association, 400 A St. SE, Washington DC 20003. Modern British, British Imperial, and British commonwealth history by American citizen.

SCIENCE IN SOCIETY JOURNALISM AWARDS, Administrative Secretary, National Association of Science Writers, Box 294, Greenlawn NY 11740. Physical and life sciences investigative and interpretive reporting (newspapers, magazines, and TV-radio)

SCIENCE-WRITING AWARD IN PHYSICS AND ASTRONOMY, Director, Public Information Division, American Institute of Physics, 335 E. 45th St., New York NY 10017. Physics and astronomy work. (Physicists, astronomers or members of AIP and affiliated societies only.)

THE SCRIBNER CRIME NOVEL AWARD, Charles Scribner's Sons, 597 Fifth Ave., New York NY 10017. (212)486-2706. Contest/Award Director: Charles Scribner Jr. Estab. 1981. Unpublished first crime novel.

SERGEL DRAMA PRIZE, The Charles H. Sergel Drama Prize, The Court Theatre, 5706 S. University Ave., Chicago IL 60637. Plays.

MINA P. SHAUGHNESSY MEDAL, Office of Research Programs, 62 5th Ave., New York NY 10011. Research in teaching of English language and literature (book or article).

SINCLAIR PRIZE FOR FICTION, Sinclair Research Ltd., 50 Staniford St., Boston MA 02130. (617)742-4826. Contact: Public Relations Manager. Unpublished novels.

BRYANT SPANN MEMORIAL PRIZE, Eugene V. Debs Foundation, c/o History Dept., Indiana State University, Terre Haute IN 47809. Corresponding Secretary: Donald Jennermann. Social criticism in the tradition of Eugene V. Debs.

STANLEY DRAMA AWARD, Wagner College, Staten Island NY 10301. (212)390-3256. Award Director: J.J. Boies. Unpublished and nonprofessionally produced plays by American playwrights.

JESSE STUART CONTEST, Seven, 3630 N. W. 22, Oklahoma City OK 73107. Unpublished poems in the Jesse Stuart tradition.

THE TEN BEST "CENSORED" STORIES OF 1984, Project Censored—Sonoma State University, Rohnert Park CA 94928. (707)664-2149. Contest/Award Director: Carl Jensen, PhD. Current stories of national social significance that have been overlooked or under-reported by the news media.

TOURNAMENT GAMING WRITING AWARDS, International Gaming Promotions, Inc., #107, 20201 Sherman Way, Canoga Park CA 91306. (800)GAMES 84, (213)998-2121. Vice President: John Romera. Tournament gaming (consumer magazine article).

HARRY S. TRUMAN BOOK PRIZE, (formerly David D. Lloyd Prize), Harry S. Truman Library Institute (Independence MO), Chairman of the Committee, Professor Thomas C. Blaisdell Jr., Department of Political Science, 210 Barrows Hall, University of California, Berkeley CA 94720. Presidency of Harry S. Truman.

UFO RESEARCH AWARD, (formerly Alvin H. Lawson UFO Research Award), Fund for UFO Research, Box 277, Mt. Rainier MD 20712. (301)779-8683. Contact: Executive Committee, Fund for UFO Research. UFO phenomenon research or writing.

UNIVERSITY OF MISSOURI BUSINESS JOURNALISM AWARDS, University of Missouri, School of Journalism, 100 Neff Hall, Columbia MO 65211. (314)882-7862. Director: James K. Gentry. Business and economics (newspaper and magazine).

EDWARD LEWIS WALLANT BOOK AWARD, Mrs. Irving Waltman, 3 Brighton Rd., West Hartford CT 06117. Fiction with significance for the American Jew (novel or short stories).

PAT WEAVER/MDA BROADCAST JOURNALISM AWARDS, Department of Public Health Education, Muscular Dystrophy Association, 810 7th Ave., New York NY 10019. Director: Craig H. Wood. TV and radio programming on muscular dystrophy and related neuromuscular disorders.

WESTERN WRITERS OF AMERICA SPUR AWARDS, Jean Mead, 2231 Fairview Ave., Casper WY 82609. Western novel, historical novel, nonfiction, juvenile (fiction or nonfiction), short subject (fiction or nonfiction), TV script, movie script, and cover art.

WICHITA STATE UNIVERSITY PLAYWRITING CONTEST, Wichita State University Theatre, WSU, Box 31, Wichita KS 67208. (316)689-3185. Contest/Award Director: Bela Kiralyfalvi. Unpublished, unproduced one-act and full-length plays. (Graduate and undergraduate US college students.)

BELL I. WILEY PRIZE, National Historical Society, 2245 Kohn Rd., Box 8200, Harrisburg PA 17105. (717)657-9555, ext. 2801. Civil War and Reconstruction nonfiction (book).

WISCONSIN ARTS BOARD FELLOWSHIP PROGRAM, 123 W. Washington Ave., Madison WI 53702. (608)266-0190. Director of Grants Programs: Mary Berryman Agard. Awards for artistic works and activities for professional advancement. (Wisconsin writers.)

WORLD HUNGER MEDIA AWARDS, World Hunger Year/Kenny & Marianne Rogers, 350 Broadway, New York NY 10013. (212)226-2714. Director: Bill Ayres. Critical issues of world hunger (newspaper, periodical, film, TV, radio, photojournalism, book and cartoon, plus special achievement).

CAPTAIN DONALD T. WRIGHT AWARD, Southern Illinois University, Edwardsville IL 62026. Contact: John A. Regnell. Maritime transportation (newspaper and magazine, book, photos and photo essays, tapes, videotapes and films).

WRITER'S DIGEST CREATIVE WRITING COMPETITION, *Writer's Digest*, 9933 Alliance Rd., Cincinnati OH 45242. Unpublished article, short story, script and poetry.

WRITERS GUILD OF AMERICA WEST AWARDS, Allen Rivkin, Public Relations, Writers Guild of America West, 8955 Beverly Blvd., Los Angeles CA 90048. Scripts (screen, TV and radio). Members only.

Appendix

The Business of Freelancing

Every profession has rules. They may not be written rules, but every pro in the field knows them. The writing business is no different. Send a manuscript on yellow paper, and editors know you've been writing more for yourself than for readers. Whether you write books, gags, or short fiction, many of the same rules apply, like enclosing a self-addressed, stamped envelope with all submissions. This appendix includes these general rules of the writing trade. They are guidelines that publishing professionals follow—tips and treatments that editors expect you to know. Learn these rules first (they won't hinder your creativity), then call on editors (in writing, of course).

Manuscript Mechanics

Most writers dream of bylines in major magazines, but those who publish in them set aside those dreams long enough to write. When you trade dreams for words on pages, you must know what format to put your words into. Without manuscript mechanics, the most gifted work might get tossed aside by an editor who refuses to read hand-writing. A manuscript typed in brown ink or with coffee-stained pages is no way to show your creativity.

Following these basic rules will help you to submit your manuscript in its best form to an editor.

Type of Paper. The paper you use must measure 8½x11 inches. That's a standard size and editors are adamant—they don't want offbeat colors and sizes.

There's a wide range of white, 8½x11 papers. The cheaper ones are wood content. They will suffice, but they are not recommended. Your best bet is a good 25 percent cotton fiber content paper. It has quality feel, smoothness, shows type neatly, and holds up under erasing. Editors almost unanimously discourage the use of erasable bond for manuscripts, as it tends to smear when handled. Don't use less than a 16-pound bond paper, and 20-pound is preferred.

File Copies. Always make a carbon or photocopy of your manuscript before you send the manuscript off to a publisher. You might want to make several photocopies while the original manuscript is fresh and crisp looking—as insurance against losing a submission in the mails, and as a means of circulating the same manuscript to other editors for reprint sales after the original has been accepted for publication. (Inform editors that the manuscript offered for reprint should *not* be used before it has first appeared in the original publication buying it, of course.) Some writers keep their original manuscript as a file copy, and submit a good-quality photocopy of the manuscript to an editor, with a personal note explaining that it is *not* a simultaneous or multiple submission. (The quality of photocopies varies from ones with gray streaks to those that look like the original manuscript. Visit print shops in your area until you find one with a copier that makes *perfect* copies.) Some writers tell the editor that he may toss the photocopied manuscript if it is of no interest to him, and reply with a self-addressed postcard (also enclosed). This costs a writer some photocopy expense, but saves on the postage bill—and may speed the manuscript review process in some editorial offices.

Type Characters. Another firm rule for manuscripts is to always type double space, using either elite or pica type. The slightly larger pica type is easier to read and many editors prefer it, but they don't object to elite. They *do* dislike (and often will refuse) hard-to-read or unusual typewritten characters, such as script, italics, Old English, all capitals, or unusual letter styles.

Page Format. Do not use a cover sheet; nor should you use a binder—unless you are submitting a play or television or movie script. Instead, in the upper left corner of page one list your name, address and phone number on four single-spaced lines. In the upper right corner, on three single-spaced lines, indicate the approximate word count for the manuscript, the rights you are offering for sale, and your copyright notice (© 1985 Chris Jones). It is *not* necessary to indicate that this is page one. Its format is self-evident.

Now, flip the lever to double-space and center the title in capital letters halfway down the page. To center, set the tabulator to stop in the exact left-right center of the page. Count the letters in the title (including spaces and punctuation) and backspace half that number. Centered one double-space under that, type "by" and centered one double-space under that, your name or pseudonym.

Now, after the title and byline block, drop down three double-spaces, paragraph indent and start your story.

Margins should be about 1¼ inches on all sides of each full page of typewritten manuscript. Paragraph indentation is five or six letter spaces, consistently.

On every page after the first, type your last name, a dash, and the page number in the upper left corner (page two, for example, would be: Jones—2). Then drop down two double-spaces and begin copy. If you are using a pseudonym, type your real name, followed by your pen name in parentheses, then a dash and the page number in the upper left corner of every page after page one. (page two, for example, would be: Jones (Smith)—2)

Carry on just as you have on the other pages after page one. After your last word and period on this page, however, skip three double-spaces and then center the words "The End" or, more commonly, the old telegrapher's symbol—30—meaning the same thing.

If you are submitting novel chapters, leave one third of the first page of each chapter blank before typing the title. Subsequent pages should include in the upper left margin the author's last name, a shortened form of the book's title, and a chapter number. Use arabic numerals for chapter titles.

How to Estimate Wordage. To estimate wordage, count the exact number of words on the first three pages of your manuscript (in manuscripts up to 25 pages), divide the total by 3 and multiply the result by the number of pages. Carry the total to the nearest 100 words. For example, if you have a 12-page manuscript with totals of 303, 316 and 289 words on the first three pages, divide your total of 908 by 3 to get 302. Now multiply 302 x 12 pages and you get 3,624. Your approximate wordage, therefore, will be 3,600 words. On manuscripts over 25 pages, count five pages instead of three, then follow the same process, dividing by 5 instead of 3.

Special Points to Remember. Always use a good dark black (*not* colored) typewriter ribbon and clean your keys frequently. If the enclosures in the letters a, b, d, e, g, etc. get inked-in, your keys need cleaning. Keep your manuscript neat *always*. Occasional retyping over erasures is acceptable, but strikeovers are bad and give a manuscript a sloppy, careless appearance. Large white-out splotches (to hide typos) make your work look amateurish. Sloppy typing is viewed by many editors as a hint

Jones--2

Title of Manuscript (optional)

    Begin the second page, and all following pages, in this manner--
with a page-number line (as above) that includes your name, in case
loose manuscript pages get shuffled by mistake. You may include the
title of your manuscript or a shortened version of the title to identify
the Jones manuscript this page 2 belongs to.

Chris Jones
1234 My Street
Anytown, U.S.A.
Tel. 123/456-7890

About 3,000 words
First Serial Rights
©1985 Chris Jones

YOUR STORY OR ARTICLE TITLE HERE

by
Chris Jones

    The manuscript begins here—about halfway down the first page.
It should be cleanly typed, double spaced, using either elite or
pica type. Use one side of the paper only, and leave a margin of
about 1-1/4 inches on all four sides.

NEATNESS COUNTS. Here are sample pages of a manuscript ready for
submission to an editor. If the author uses a pseudonym, it should be
placed on the title page only in the byline position; the author's real name
must always appear in the top left corner of the title page—for manuscript
mailing and payment purposes. On subsequent pages, list the real name,
then the pen name in parentheses, followed by a dash and the page number.

of sloppy work habits—and the likelihood of careless research and writing. Strive for a clean, professional-looking manuscript that reflects pride in your work.

Computer-related Submissions. Because of the increased efficiency they afford the writing, revising and editing process, computers (word processors) are a tool of the writing trade. Hard-copy computer printouts and disk submissions are the result of the computer revolution's impact on writers.

Most editors are receptive to computer printout submissions if the type is letter-quality (as opposed to dot-matrix); double-spaced with wide margins; and generally easy to read. Fewer editors at this point are ready to accept disk submissions because some computer systems are not compatible with others. Manuscripts submitted in disk form will likely become more popular with writers and editors as the interfacing of equipment becomes more sophisticated. Those editors who welcome disk submissions often request that a hard copy of the manuscript accompany the disk and that the writer make prior arrangements before submitting a disk.

Many listings in this edition of *Writer's Market* include information about computer-related submissions. If no information is given, it usually means the editor will not accept computer-related submissions. Check with an editor before sending a computer printout or disk submission.

Mailing Your Manuscript. Except when working on assignment from a magazine, or when under contract to do a book for a publisher, always enclose a self-addressed return envelope and the correct amount of postage with your manuscript. Manuscript pages should be held together with a paper clip only—never stapled together. When submitting poetry, the poems should be typed single space (double space between stanzas), one poem per page. Long poems requiring more than a page should be on sheets paper-clipped together.

Most editors won't object if manuscripts under six pages are folded in thirds and letter-mailed. However, there is a marked *preference* for flat mailing (in large envelopes) of manuscripts of six or more pages. You will need two 9x12 gummed or clasped mailing envelopes: one for the return of the manuscript and any accompanying material, and another to send out the manuscript, photos and return envelope. It is acceptable to fold the 9x12 return envelope in half to fit inside the outer envelope. To prevent accidental loss of stamps, affix—don't paperclip—them to the return envelope.

Mark your envelope, as desired with FIRST CLASS MAIL, or SPECIAL FOURTH CLASS RATE: MANUSCRIPT. First Class mail costs more but ensures better handling and faster delivery. Special Fourth Class mail is handled the same as Parcel Post, so wrap it well. Also, the Special Fourth Class Rate only applies in the U.S., and to manuscripts that weigh one pound or more (otherwise, there is no price break).

For lighter weight manuscripts, First Class mail is recommended because of the better speed and handling. First Class mail is handled the same as Air Mail and is forwarded or returned automatically; however, Special Fourth Class Rate mail is not. To make sure you get your submission back if undeliverable, print "Return Postage Guaranteed" under your return address.

For foreign publications and publishers, including the expanding Canadian markets, always enclose an International Reply Coupon (IRC), determined by the weight of the manuscript at the post office.

Insurance is available, but payable only on typing fees or the tangible value of what is in the package, i.e., writing paper, so your best insurance is to keep a copy of what you send.

Cover Letters. At the Special Fourth Class rate, you may enclose a personal letter with your manuscript, but you must also add enough First Class postage to cover the letter and mark FIRST CLASS LETTER ENCLOSED on the outside.

In most cases, a brief cover letter is helpful in personalizing the submission. Nothing you say will make the editor decide in your favor (the manuscript must stand by itself in that regard), so don't use the letter to make a sales pitch. Tell an editor (concisely) something about yourself, your publishing history, or any particular qualifications you have for writing the enclosed manuscript. If you are doing an ex-

Postage by the Page

By Carolyn Hardesty

To assist you in using the right amount of postage for your manuscript's journey to and from an editorial office, consult the rates listed below. This chart is designed to tell you the correct amount of postage for manuscripts up to 70 pages. The weight of paper used to determine these figures was 20 pound, a paper with a respectable heft for impressing editors plus enough strength to tolerate repeated paper clip snaps if the piece is sent to several publications.

The chart shows current first-class mailing costs plus the increased rates *if* a three-cent proposal is enacted. (At press time, the post office couldn't say whether there would be a 1985 increase.) The second and third columns give number of pages plus mailing envelope and SASE, and number of pages plus SASE (for return trips).

On the odd chance you mail very short manuscripts in large envelopes or perhaps submit a few large photos, you will be assessed an additional seven cents* under the regulations for odd-sized mail (large envelope, two ounces or less).

Beyond the first 20¢ ounce, the increments are by 17¢ leaps. The exception is the fee for oversized envelopes; if this applies to you, add that denomination to your cache.

FIRST-CLASS POSTAGE RATES

ounces	9x12 envelope, 9x12 SASE number of pages	9x12 SASE (for return trips) number of pages	first-class postage	Proposed first-class postage*
2	1 to 4	3 to 8	$ .37	$ .40
3	5 to 10	9 to 12	.54	.57
4	11 to 16	13 to 19	.71	.74
5	17 to 21	20 to 25	.88	.91
6	22 to 27	26 to 30	1.05	1.08
7	28 to 32	31 to 35	1.22	1.25
8	33 to 38	36 to 41	1.39	1.42
9	39 to 44	42 to 46	1.56	1.59
10	45 to 49	47 to 52	1.73	1.74
11	50 to 55	53 to 57	1.90	1.93
12	56 to 61	58 to 63	2.07	2.10

For short manuscripts or long queries, use a business-size envelope and up to five pages with a 20¢ stamp. If you are including a business-size SASE, four pages is the limit.

● First class packages weighing more than 12 ounces are charged according to geographical zones. This is true also for all weights of fourth class (or book rate) mail.

● Four captionless 5x7 photographs or two 8x10 photographs will increase the weight of your package by one ounce.

● Insurance (to recover typing fees) is 45¢ for a $20 liability, 85¢ for up to $50, and $1.25 for coverage to $100.*

● Certified mail costs 75¢.*

● International Reply Coupons (IRCs) for Canadian and overseas submissions are generally available only at larger post offices. See glossary.

*These costs may be higher depending upon the proposed 1985 first-class mail increase.

Carolyn Hardesty *is a freelance writer whose tendency to "overstamp" led her to develop the time- and money-saving "Postage by the Page."*

posé on, say, nursing home irregularities—it would be useful to point out that you have worked as a volunteer in nursing homes for six years. If you have queried the editor on the article earlier, he probably already has the background information—so the note should be a brief reminder: "Here is the piece on nursing homes we discussed earlier. I look forward to hearing from you at your earliest convenience."

If the manuscript is a photocopy, indicate whether it is a simultaneous submission. An editor is likely to assume it is, unless you tell him otherwise—and many are offended by writers using this marketing tactic (though when agents use it, that seems to be OK).

When submitting a manuscript to a newspaper—even the Sunday magazine section—include a cover note inquiring about the paper's rates for freelance submissions. Newspaper editors are deluged regularly by PR offices and "free" writers who submit material for ego and publicity purposes. Make sure your submission is not part of that crowd, or you may find it in print without an acknowledgment—much less a check.

Query Letters. If you have an article idea that seems "right" for a particular publication, you should contact the editor with a query. A query letter is a powerful tool. It can open doors or deny entry to the published land. Though no query alone will sell a manuscript, a bad one may squelch your chances of even a cursory look from an editor. A good query letter can be your right of passage.

Granted, the specifics of a query depend on your manuscript content, the audience you hope to reach, and the particular slant you are taking. But some general guidelines may help you structure your book or article proposal in a way that reflects your professionalism.

● A query letter should inform and excite an editor—not only about an article/book idea, but about the prospect of your writing the manuscript.

● The lead paragraph may either succinctly capsule the idea, your slant and intent; or show the editor the topic and your style with a representative sample. (The latter type of lead paragraph would be double-spaced; with the rest of the query single-spaced.)

● Subsequent paragraphs should provide examples, names of people you intend to interview, and facts and anecdotes that support the writing of the manuscript. All of this should verify your ability/qualifications to do it.

● The closing paragraph might include a direct request to do the article/book; it may specify the date the manuscript can be completed and possibly suggest a proposed length.

In general, query letters are single-spaced; and whenever possible, they should be limited to one typed page. They should be addressed to the current editor by name and be accompanied by SASE. Published writing samples and a list of credits may also be attached if appropriate. Accuracy in spelling, grammar and writing mechanics is essential.

See the sample query letter that resulted in a story sold to *Woman's Day*.

Submitting Photos by Mail. When submitting black and white prints with your manuscript, send 8x10 glossies unless the editor indicates otherwise. Stamp or print your name, address and phone number on the back of each print or contact sheet. Don't use a heavy felt tip pen because the ink will seep through the print.

Buy some sturdy 9x12 envelopes. Your photo dealer should have standard print mailers in stock; some may be pre-stamped with "Photos—Do Not Bend" and contain two cardboard inserts. You can also pick up corrugated cardboard inserts from your local grocery store. Place your print(s) between two cardboard inserts, wrap two rubber bands around the bundle, and enclose it with your manuscript in the envelope.

When sending many prints (say, 25-50 for a photo book), mail them in a sturdy cardboard box; 8x10 print paper boxes are perfect. Add enough cardboard inserts to fill the carton after the prints and manuscript are in place, and cover the box with wrapping paper. Send rare or extremely valuable photos only when an editor specifically requests them; then send them in a fiberboard mailing case with canvas straps,

Query Letter Sample

Jane Chesnutt
Health and Medical Editor
Woman's Day
1515 Broadway
New York, New York 10036

Dear Ms. Chesnutt:

A young mother wheeling her baby in the sunshine looks perfectly ordinary; so does a teenager shooting baskets in his high school gym. The fact that there's nothing unusual in either one's appearance is a miracle, for they both have scoliosis, a lateral curvature of the spine. Without recently developed surgical techniques to correct this disorder, neither the baby nor the baskets would have been possible. Pregnancy-related back strain would have crippled this mother, and the teen would have spent his high school years encased in a body cast.

Scoliosis affects 10 percent of all school age children; of those affected 85 percent are girls. Cases can range from mild to severe, and many scoliosis victims share a common destiny. If the curvature is left untreated, deformity and disability occur. The disorder often creates psychological problems as well as physical ones, including feelings of isolation and rejection. However, debility can be prevented by early treatment.

An article about scoliosis makes good sense for two reasons. First, the topic insures audience interest, since many readers of Woman's Day have children who are approaching the vulnerable years for this disorder. Second, scoliosis is newsworthy because several exciting, new treatments are supplanting older, incapacitating therapies.

The article would include a description of the early signs of scoliosis, instructions to parents about screening their children for symptoms, a summary of standard treatments and the latest information about medical advances against scoliosis, such as electrical stimulation, an improved version of the Harrington rod and electro spinal instrumentation. Several case histories, including those of the young mother and the teenager mentioned above, would add interest. The teenager's situation is especially remarkable, as he plays sports in school during the day and plugs himself into a small transmitter at night for treatment of his curvature with internal electric stimulation.

Among the physicians I expect to interview are: Dr. Martin Gruber, who recently performed the first experimental electrical implant surgery for scoliosis on Long Island; Dr. Morley Herbert, a Canadian research scientist who invented the surgical implant technique, and Dr. Walter Bobechko, a surgeon who has performed over 200 operations for scoliosis using the improved Harrington rod.

I hope you'll agree that this topic will make an informative, interesting article. I'm looking forward to hearing from you about it.

Sincerely,

Adrienne

Adrienne Popper

Ms. Popper's actual letter, of course, carried her address and the date. The query letter is used with her permission.

available at most photo stores. Tell the editor to return the photos in the same case or return the empty case itself if the photos are kept.

For color transparencies, 35mm is the universally accepted size. Few buyers will look at color prints. (Check each market listing individually for exact preferences from editors). To mail transparencies, use slotted acetate sheets, which hold twenty slides and offer protection from scratches, moisture, dirt and dust—available in standard sizes from most photo supply houses. Do not use glass mounts. Put your name, address, and phone number on each transparency. Mail the transparencies just as you would prints, using corrugated cardboard. If a number of sheets is being sent, use a cardboard box. Because transparencies are irreplaceable (unless you have internegatives or duplicates made), insure the package.

One additional note about photo submissions. When you mail photos or transparencies to an editor, you are giving him permission to use any or all of the visuals according to the conditions and payment rates he has included in his *Writer's Market* listing. If he says, "We would like to consider these indefinitely," he may use them at any time—unless you respond in writing, voicing an objection or asking for their return.

Photo Captions. Prints and transparencies should always be captioned when submitted for consideration with a manuscript. For prints, type the caption on a sheet of paper and tape it to the bottom of the back of the print. The caption should fold over the front of the photo so that the buyer can fold it back for easy reading. Masking tape allows the editor to easily remove the copy for typesetting.

You can also type the captions on a separate sheet of paper, and assign each an index number corresponding with its photos. A third method, but not generally preferred, is to tape the caption to the back of the print.

Captions for transparencies 2¼x2¼ or larger can be typed on thin strips of paper and inserted in the acetate sleeve protecting the transparency. For 35mm transparencies, type the captions on a separate sheet and assign corresponding numbers.

Enclosing return postage with photos sent through the mail is more than a professional courtesy; it also helps assure that you'll get the photos back. Most writer/photographers enclose a self-addressed stamped envelope (SASE—same size as the envelope used for the submission) with their material. Never drop loose stamps into the original envelope, nor fasten them to one of the prints with a staple or paper clip. You can, however, enclose a small coin envelope (available at hobby stores) with return postage in it rather than attaching stamps to the return envelope.

Once your photos are properly packaged, speed and safe handling in the mail will be your main concerns. Most writers prefer First Class mail because it ensures both speed and safety of prints, but a cheaper rate can be allowed for the return of the material. A cover letter and manuscript can be mailed with any package sent first class. More information is available from the Postal Service.

Mailing Book Manuscripts. Do not bind your book manuscript pages in any way. They should be mailed loose in a box (a ream-size stationery box is perfect) without binding. To ensure a safe return, enclose a self-addressed label and suitable postage in stamps clipped to the label. If your manuscript is returned, it will either come back in your original box, or—increasingly likely today—in an insulated bag-like mailer, with your label and postage used thereon. Many publishing houses open the box a manuscript is mailed in, and toss the box (if it has not already been damaged in the mails, or in the opening); they then read and circulate the manuscript as necessary for editorial consideration, and finally route it through the mail room back to you with a letter or rejection slip. This kind of handling makes it likely that a freshly typed manuscript will be in rough shape after one or two submissions. So it is wise to have several photocopies made of a book-length manuscript while it is still fresh—and to circulate those to publishers, rather than risk an expensive retyping job in the midst of your marketing effort. As mentioned above, indicate in a cover note that the submission is not a multiple submission if such is the case.

Book manuscripts can be mailed Fourth Class Manuscript Rate, but that can be slow and have an additional mauling effect on the package in the mails. When doing so, if you include a letter, state this on the outer wrapping and add appropriate postage to your manuscript postal rate. Most writers use First Class, secure in the feeling that their manuscript is in an editorial office within a few days. Some send book manuscripts using the United Parcel Service, which can be less expensive than First Class mail when you drop the package off at UPS yourself. The drawback here is that UPS cannot legally carry First Class mail, so you will have to send your cover letter a few days before giving UPS the manuscript, and both will arrive at about the same time. Check with UPS in your area to see if it has benefits for you. The cost depends on the weight of your manuscript and the delivery distance.

The tips and recommendations made here are based upon what editors prefer. Give editors what they prefer and you won't be beginning with a strike or two against you before the manuscript is read.

The Waiting Game. The writer who sends off a story, article or book manuscript to an editor should turn immediately to other ideas and try to forget about the submission. Unless you are on assignment, or under contract to do a book—in which case, a phone call to your editor saying the manuscript is in the mail is quite appropriate—it's best to use your time productively on other writing projects. But one day you realize it's been too long. According to the *Writer's Market* listing, your editor responds to submissions in a maximum of four weeks—and it's been six already, and you haven't heard a word. Will inquiring about it jeopardize a possible sale? Are they really considering it, or has the editor had an accident and your manuscript is at the bottom of a huge stack of unread mail?

If you have had no report from a publisher by the maximum reporting time given in a *WM* listing, allow six weeks' grace period and then write a brief letter to the editor asking if your manuscript (give the title, a brief description, and the date you mailed it) has in fact reached his office. If so, is it still under consideration? Your concern at this point is the mails: Is the manuscript safely delivered? Don't act impatiently with an editor—who may be swamped, or short-staffed, or about to give your manuscript a second reading. The wrong word or attitude from you at this point could be hazardous to your manuscript's health. Be polite, be professional. Enclose another SASE to expedite a reply. This is usually enough to stir a decision if matters are lagging in an editorial office, even during rush season (which is year-round).

If you still hear nothing from a publisher one month after your follow-up, send the editor a short note asking if he received your previous follow-up, and include a photocopy of that second letter. If, after another month, you are still without word, send a polite letter saying that you are withdrawing the manuscript from consideration (include the title, date of submission, and dates of follow-up correspondence), and ask that the manuscript be returned immediately in the SASE your original correspondence included.

Rejection Slips. It is possible you will get a quick response from an editor in the form of a rejection. Rejection slips or letters should not be taken as a *personal* rejection. Direct your energy toward writing manuscripts, not writing attacking letters.

Whether disappointment comes from delayed editorial responses or rejection—never write in anger. Be cool, professional, and set about the business of finding another publisher for your work. The advantage of having a clean photocopy of the manuscript in your files at this point cannot be overstated. Move on to another publisher with it, using a personal cover letter and the same methods outlined above. In the meantime, continue working on other writing projects.

The Business of Writing

Writing is an occupation with many hidden costs. In addition to the time a writer spends at a typewriter actually *writing*, many hours and miles are logged doing research, soliciting materials, conducting interviews, communicating with editors, and rounding out the corners of a manuscript. While readers, and to some extent editors, are oblivious to these background tasks, the Internal Revenue Service need not be. Such costs can become deductible writing expenses at income tax time.

For the Records. Though the deadline for filing your tax return is April 15, you should maintain careful records all year. To arrive at verifiable figures, you will need two things: *records and receipts.* For tax purposes, good records are not only helpful; they are *required* by law. Receipts are the foundation that careful recordkeeping is built upon.

At tax time each year, a freelance writer normally reports his business activities on tax Schedule C ("Profit or Loss From Business or Profession"); the resulting figure for income is entered on Form 1040. In addition, if your writing or editing work nets you $400 or more in earnings, you must file a Schedule SE and pay self-employment tax, which makes you eligible for Social Security benefits. Furthermore, if you think your taxes from freelancing will be $100 or more, you are required to pay your taxes in quarterly installments. To do this, you file a declaration of estimated tax using Form 1040-ES ("Declaration Voucher") and use the envelopes the IRS provides to mail in your estimated taxes every three months.

It's not as complicated as it may sound, but one thing is certain: to document all these tax liabilities at the end of the year, you must have accurate records.

Tax laws don't require any particular type of records, as long as they are permanent, accurate and complete, and they clearly establish income, deductions, credits, etc. It's remarkably easy to overlook deductible expenses unless you record them at the time they are paid and keep receipts for them. Since some assets are subject to depreciation (typewriter, desk, files, tape recorder, camera equipment, etc.), you also need records of the purchase prices you used to determine depreciation allowances.

Finally, you need good records in case the IRS audits you and asks you to explain items reported on your return. Memos, scribbled notes, or sketchy records that merely approximate income, deductions, or other pertinent items affecting your taxes are simply *not* adequate. You must have a record supported by sales slips, invoices, receipts, bank deposit slips, canceled checks, and other documents.

Records for Credit Purposes. You and the IRS are not the only ones interested in the well-being of your business. Banks, credit organizations, suppliers of materials, and others often require information on the condition of your finances when you apply for credit—if, for example, you want to buy a house.

In fact, freelance writers, in the eyes of many lending institutions, might as well be totally unemployed. Some writers have taken on full-time jobs just to qualify for financing for a home, even when the "steady" job might produce less income than freelancing.

A Simple Bookkeeping System. There are almost as many ways of keeping records as there are recordkeepers to keep them. For a freelance writer, normally a simple type of "single-entry" bookkeeping that requires only one account book to record the flow of income and expense is completely adequate. At the heart of this single-entry system is the journal. It is an accounting book, available at any stationery store (the *Writer's Digest Diary* can be used, too), in which all the everyday transactions of your freelance business are recorded. Each transaction is set forth clearly, including the date, a description of the transaction, and the amount entered in the proper column—either "income" or "expense."

Income entries will include funds you receive, either by cash or check. Expense entries might include payments you make for writing supplies, photocopying, postage, repairs, dues paid to writers' organizations, travel expenses, books and magazine subscriptions, photo developing and printing, etc.—whatever you have to spend as a business expense.

The Receipt File. For each income entry you make, keep a copy of a receipt, an invoice, or other record to substantiate that entry. For each expense entry, keep a canceled check, a receipt, or other document. By keeping your record complete with some type of document to support *every* entry, your record is foolproof.

A partitioned, envelope-type folder works well for keeping receipts in order. If a receipt does not clearly indicate which entry it refers to, make a note on it and date it before filing it. That way, you can locate it quickly.

Business Banking. To record your income as accurately as possible, it is best to deposit all the money you receive in a separate bank account. This will give you deposit slips to verify the entries in your journal. Furthermore, you should make all payments by check, if possible, so that your business expenses will be well documented. If you have to pay cash, keep receipts on file.

Any record must be retained as long as it may be material to the administration of any law. Statutes of limitations for various legal purposes vary from state to state, but if you keep your records on file for seven to ten years, you will seldom run into difficulty. Records supporting items on a tax return should be kept for at least three years, although keeping them indefinitely is a good idea.

What's Deductible. Among your deductible expenses, don't overlook the following writing-related costs:

• **All writing supplies**, including paper, carbons, pens, ribbons, envelopes, copying costs, postage, photo developing and printing costs, and recording tapes.

• **Repairs and maintenance of writing equipment**, including typewriter, word processor, tape recorder and camera.

• **Courses and conferences attended to enhance you as a professional writer.** It's important to realize, though, that you can't deduct courses you take to *become* a writer. The IRS rule is that courses must be "refresher" or professionally improving in nature to count. Besides deducting the costs of these, also deduct mileage (at 20.5¢ a mile)—or actual car expenses, whichever is greater—cost of tickets for public transportation; cost of hotel/motel rooms; and costs of meals.

• **Courses taken as research on subjects you are writing about.** To establish that a course is for research, it would help if you had documentation from the potential publisher of your writings—such as a favorable response to a query. Even if the magazine should not publish what you write, the response will show the research was done in good faith.

• **Writing books, magazines and other references.**

• **Dues paid for membership in writers' organizations.**

• **Home office expenses.** In the past, writers using a portion of their home dining room or living room have been allowed to deduct a percentage of home costs as "office" expenses. This is no longer allowed. To take a home office deduction today, you must have a portion of your dwelling set aside *solely for writing on a regular basis.* The same rule applies to a separate structure on your property. For example, you may not use a portion of your garage for writing and a portion for parking your car. If your car goes in, your home office expense is out.

If you rent a five-room apartment for $300 a month and use one room exclusively for writing, you are entitled to deduct one-fifth of the rent which comes to $60 a month, or $720 a year. Add to this one-fifth of your heating bill and one-fifth of your electric bill and watch the deductions mount up. Keep a list, too, of long-distance phone bills arising from your writing.

If you own your home and use one room for writing, you can deduct the allocated expenses of operating that room. Among these allowable expenses are interest on mortgage, real estate taxes, repairs or additions to the home, cost of utilities, home insurance premiums, and depreciation on the room.

If you own a seven-room house with one room used for writing, one-seventh of the total cost of the house can be depreciated, as well as one-seventh of the above mentioned expenses.

There is a limit to home office expenses. You may not exceed in deductible expenses the amount of your gross income. If you made $1,000 last year, you can't deduct any more than that in home office expenses—no matter how much they came to. Just $1,000 in this case.

• **Mileage.** Take 20.5¢ a mile for the first 15,000 miles you travel on writing-related missions and 11¢ a mile for miles traveled over 15,000. Or you may take the actual cost of operating your car—gas, oil, tires, maintenance and depreciation. (See be-

Date	Description	Expense		Income	
JAN. 4	Regional Supply – 1 ream of paper	5	80		
5	Photocopying – _Analog_ story		95		
5	Postage – story sent to Analog	1	15		
8	_Economic Bulletin_ – for March article & photos			450	00
10	Billy's Bookstore – 1985 Writer's Market	19	95		
14	Reed Real Estate – for editing 4th-quarter newsletter			225	00
15	Renewal of _WD_ subscription	17	00		
18	Billy's – 20 manila envelopes	1	80		
21	Mountain Press – for editing _Survival Handbook_.			575	00
21	Aardvark & Son – for developing photos for _Am. Horse J._ article	9	55		
25	Regional Supply – Typewriter ribbons	15	20		
28	Fee for Western Writer's Conf.	24	50		
30	_American Horse Journal_ – for February article			325	00
	JAN. TOTALS	96	50	1,575	00

A typical single-entry page in a bookkeeping journal that records a freelance writer's income and expense transactions.

low for figuring depreciation.) If you use your car 100 percent for writing; the total cost of operating it is deductible. Compare mileage deduction to cost deduction, and use the one that gives you the bigger break.

What May Be Depreciated. You can count depreciation of your typewriter, desk, chair, lamps, tape recorder, files, camera equipment, photocopier, word processor, or anything else related to your writing which costs a considerable amount of money and which has a useful life of more than one year.

You have a couple of ways to recover these capital expenses. For most property placed into service after 1980, costs can be recovered in a relatively short period of time using the Accelerated Cost Recovery System (ACRS). Under this system, eligible capital expenses can be recovered by applying pre-determined percentages over a 3-, 5-, or 10-year period, depending on the category into which your property falls. Most of a writer's tangible property would likely be considered 3- or 5-year property. The accelerated cost recovery of 3-year property is 25% of its original cost in the first year; 38% in the second year; 37% in the third year. For 5-year recovery property, deductions are 15% the first year; 22% the second year; and 21% for each of the last 3 years.

An additional deduction called an investment tax credit (ITC) has been subject to considerable change in the last few years. Consult your tax adviser for information that is up-to-date and pertinent to your situation.

The IRS gives you yet another option for recovering your capital expenses. For tax years beginning after 1981, you may deduct up to $5,000 of normally depreciable property in the year you buy the typewriter, word processor or whatever. However, if you elect to take this deduction, you forfeit the investment tax credit.

There are other options, requirements and regulations that can affect the figuring of your taxes. It's wise to consult with a tax professional who is aware of the current percentages and category definitions involved in figuring your taxes. It will be important to calculate your tax both ways—using the $5,000 deduction and the ACRS/tax investment credit combination—in deciding which method best fits your situation.

Self-Employment Earnings. If after deductions you earn $400 or more, you are required to pay a Social Security tax of 14.0% of the first $37,800 of your earnings. And you must fill out and submit a Schedule SE (for "self-employment"). A credit is allowed against self-employment taxes equal to 2.7% for 1984, 2.3% for 1985, and 2% for 1986 through 1989 of the self-employment income of the individual for the tax year.

Finally, save your rejection slips. Though they may be unpleasant reminders, keep them in a folder. Look at them as professional communiques from publishers, not personal rejection letters. If you are subjected to a tax audit, these letters will help establish you as a working writer.

Rights and the Writer

Selling Rights to Your Writing. The Copyright Law which went into effect January 1978 said writers were only selling one-time rights to their work unless they agreed otherwise in writing with a publisher. In some cases, however, a writer may have little say in the rights sold to an editor. The beginning writer, in fact, can jeopardize a sale by arguing with an editor who is likely to have other writers on call who are eager to please. As long as there are more writers than there are markets, this situation will remain the same.

As a writer acquires skill, reliability, and professionalism on the job, however, that writer becomes more valued to editors—and rights become a more important consideration. Though a beginning writer will accept modest payment just to get in print, an experienced writer soon learns that he cannot afford to give away good writing just to see a byline. At this point a writer must become concerned with selling reprints of articles already sold to one market, or using sold articles as chapters in a book on the same topic, or seeking markets for the same material overseas, offering work to TV or the movies. Such dramatic rights can be meaningful for both fiction and nonfiction writers. James Michener's bestselling *Space* was bought by CBS for a ten-hour mini-series. The movie *Doctor Detroit* is based on a story that appeared in *Esquire* magazine.

What Editors Want. You should strive to keep as many rights to your work as you can from the outset, because before you can resell any piece of writing you must own the rights to negotiate. If you have sold "all rights" to an article, for instance, it can be reprinted *without* your permission, and without additional payment to you. What an editor buys, therefore, will determine whether you can resell your own work. Here is a list of the rights most editors and publishers seek.

● **First Serial Rights.** The word serial does not mean publication in installments, but refers to the fact that libraries call periodicals "serials" because they are published in serial or continuing fashion. *First serial rights* means the writer offers the newspaper or magazine (both of which are periodicals) the right to publish the article, story or poem the first time in the periodical. All other rights to the material belong to the writer. Variations on this right are, for example, First North American

Serial rights. Some magazines use this purchasing technique to obtain the right to publish first in both America and Canada since many American magazines are circulated in Canada. If an editor had purchased only First U.S. Serial Rights, a Canadian magazine could come out with prior or simultaneous publication of the same material. When material is excerpted from a book which is to be published and it appears in a magazine or newspaper prior to book publication, this is also called First Serial Rights.

• **One-Time Rights.** This differs from First Serial Rights in that the buyer has no guarantee he will be the first to publish the work. One-time rights most often applies to photos, but occasionally writing, too.

• **Second Serial (Reprint) Rights.** This gives a newspaper or magazine the opportunity to print an article, poem or story after it has already appeared in another newspaper or magazine. The term is also used to refer to the sale of part of a book to a newspaper or magazine after a book has been published, whether or not there has been any first serial publication (income derived from second serial rights to book material is often shared 50/50 by author and book publisher).

• **All Rights.** Some magazines, either because of the top prices they pay for material, or the fact that they have book publishing interests or foreign magazine connections, buy All Rights. A writer who sells an article, story or poem to a magazine under these terms forfeits the right to use his material in its present form elsewhere himself. If he signs a "work-for-hire" agreement, he signs away all rights and the copyright to the company making the assignment. If the writer thinks he may want to use his material later (perhaps in book form), he must avoid submitting to these types of markets, or refuse payment and withdraw his material if he discovers it later. Ask the editor whether he is willing to buy only first rights instead of all rights before you agree to an assignment or a sale. Some editors will reassign rights to a writer after a given period—say, one year. It's worth an inquiry in writing.

• **Simultaneous Rights.** This term covers articles and stories which are sold to publications (primarily religious magazines) which do not have overlapping circulations. A Baptist publication, for example, might be willing to buy Simultaneous Rights to a Christmas story which they like very much, even though they know a Presbyterian magazine may be publishing the same story in one of its Christmas issues. Publications which will buy simultaneous rights indicate this fact in their listings in *Writer's Market*. Always advise an editor when the material you are sending is a simultaneous submission.

• **Foreign Serial Rights.** Can you resell a story you have had published in America to a foreign magazine? If you sold only First U.S. Serial Rights to the American magazine, yes, you are free to market your story abroad. Of course, you must contact a foreign magazine that buys material which has previously appeared in an American periodical.

• **Syndication Rights.** This is a division of serial rights. For example, a book publisher may sell the rights to a newspaper syndicate to print a book in twelve installments in, say, each of twenty United States newspapers. If they did this prior to book publication it would be syndicating First Serial Rights to the book. If they did this after book publication, they would be syndicating Second Serial Rights to the book. In either case, the syndicate would be taking a commission on the sales it made to newspapers, so the remaining percentage would be split between author and publisher.

• **Dramatic, Television and Motion Picture Rights.** This means the writer is selling his material for use on the stage, in television, or in the movies. Often a one-year "option" to buy such rights is offered (generally for 10% of the total price); the interested party then tries to sell the idea to other people—actors, directors, studios or television networks, etc.—who become part of the project, which then becomes a script. Some properties are optioned over and over again, but fail to become dramatic productions. In such cases, the writer can sell his rights again and again—as long as there is interest in the material. Though dramatic, TV and motion picture rights are more important to the fiction writer than to the nonfiction writer, producers today are increasingly interested in "real-life" material; many biographies and articles are being dramatized. For example, motion picture rights to Nicholas Gage's book, *Eleni* (an account of his mother's life and torture by Communists in a post-World War II Greek village), were bought for $850,000.

Communicate and Clarify. Before submitting material to a market, check its listing in this book to see what rights are purchased. Most editors will discuss rights they wish to purchase before an exchange of money occurs. Some buyers are adamant about what rights they will accept; others will negotiate. In any case, the rights purchased should be stated specifically *in writing* sometime during the course of the sale, usually in a letter or memo of agreement. If no rights are transferred in writing, and the material is sold for use in a collective work (that is, a work that derives material from a number of contributors), you are authorizing unlimited use of the piece in that work or updates of the work or later collective works in the same series. Thus, you can't collect reprint fees if the rights weren't spelled out in advance, in writing.

Give as much attention to the rights you haven't sold as you do the rights you have sold. Be aware of the rights you retain, with an eye for additional sales.

Whatever rights you sell or don't sell, make sure all parties involved in any sale understand the terms of the sale. Clarify what is being sold *before* any actual sale, and do it in writing. Communication, coupled with these guidelines and some common sense, will preclude misunderstandings with editors over rights.

Keep in mind, too, that if there is a change in editors from the edition of *Writer's Market* you're using, the rights bought may also change.

Copyrighting Your Writing. The copyright law, effective since January 1, 1978, protects your writing, unequivocally recognizes the creator of the work as its owner, and grants the creator all the rights, benefits and *privileges* that ownership entails.

In other words, the moment you finish a piece of writing—whether it be a short story, article, novel, poem or even paragraph—the law recognizes that only you can decide how it is to be used.

This law gives writers power in dealing with editors and publishers, but they should understand how to use that power. They should also understand that certain circumstances can complicate and confuse the concept of ownership. Writers must be wary of these circumstances or risk losing ownership of their work.

Here are answers to commonly asked questions about copyright law:

● **To what rights am I entitled under copyright law?** The law gives you, as creator of your work, the right to print, reprint and copy the work; to sell or distribute copies of the work; to prepare "derivative works"—dramatizations, translations, musical arrangement, novelizations, etc.; to record the work; and to perform or display literary, dramatic or musical works publicly. These rights give you control over how your work is used, and assure you (in theory) that you receive payment for any use of your work.

If, however, you create the work as a "work-for-hire," you *do not* own any of these rights. The person or company that commissioned the work-for-hire owns the copyright. The work-for-hire agreement will be discussed in more detail later.

● **When does copyright law take effect, and how long does it last?** A piece of writing is copyrighted the moment it is put to paper. Protection lasts for the life of the author plus 50 years, thus allowing your heirs to benefit from your work. For material written by two or more people, protection lasts for the life of the last survivor plus 50 years. The life-plus-50 provision applies if the work was created or registered with the Copyright Office after Jan. 1, 1978, when the updated copyright law took effect. The old law protected works for a 28-year term, and gave the copyright owner the option to renew the copyright for an additional 28 years at the end of that term. Works copyrighted under the old law that are in their second 28-year term automatically receive an additional 19 years of protection (for a total of 75 years). Works in their first term also receive the 19-year extension but must still be renewed when the first term ends.

If you create a work anonymously or pseudonymously, protection lasts for 100 years after the work's creation, or 75 years after its publication, whichever is shorter. The life-plus-50 coverage takes effect, however, if you reveal your identity to the Copyright Office any time before the original term of protection runs out.

Works created on a for-hire basis are also protected for 100 years after the work's creation or 75 years after its publication, whichever is shorter.

● **Must I register my work with the Copyright Office to receive protection?** No. Your work is copyrighted whether or not you register it, although registration offers certain advantages. For example, you must register the work before you can bring an infringement suit to court. You can register the work *after* an infringement has taken place, and *then* take the suit to court, but registering after the fact removes certain rights from you. You can sue for actual damages (the income or other benefits lost as a result of the infringement), but you can't sue for statutory damages and you can't recover attorney's fees unless the work has been registered with the Copyright Office *before* the infringement took place. Registering before the infringement also allows you to make a stronger case when bringing the infringement to court.

If you suspect that someone might infringe on your work, register it. If you doubt that an infringement is likely (and infringements are relatively rare), you might save yourself the time and money involved in registering the material.

● **I have an article that I want to protect fully. How do I register it?** Request the proper form from the Copyright Office. Send the completed form, a $10 registration fee, and one copy (if the work is unpublished; two if it's published) of the work to the Register of Copyrights, Library of Congress, Washington, D.C. 20559. You needn't register each work individually. A group of articles can be registered simultaneously (for a single $10 fee) if they meet these requirements: They must be assembled in orderly form (simply placing them in a notebook binder is sufficient); they must bear a single title ("Works by Chris Jones," for example); they must represent the work of one person (or one set of collaborators); and they must be the subject of a single claim to copyright. No limit is placed on the number of works that can be copyrighted in a group.

● **If my writing is published in a "collective work"—such as a magazine—does the publication handle registration of the work?** Only if the publication owns the piece of writing. Although the copyright notice carried by the magazine covers its contents, you must register any writing to which *you* own the rights if you want the additional protection registration provides.

Collective works are publications with a variety of contributors. Magazines, newspapers, encyclopedias, anthologies, etc., are considered collective works. If you sell something to a collective work, state specifically—*in writing*—what rights you're selling. If you don't, you are automatically selling the nonexclusive right to use the writing in the collective work and in any succeeding issues or revisions of it. For example, a magazine that buys your article without specifying in writing the rights purchased can reuse the article in that magazine—but in no other, not even in another magazine put out by the same publisher—without repaying you. The same is true for other collective works, so always detail *in writing* what rights you are selling before actually making the sale.

When contributing to a collective work, ask that your copyright notice be placed on or near your published manuscript (if you still own the manuscript's rights). Prominent display of your copyright notice on published work has two advantages: It signals to readers and potential reusers of the piece that it belongs to you, and not to the collective work in which it appears; and it allows you to register all published works bearing such notice with the Copyright Office as a group for a single $10 fee. A published work *not* bearing notice indicating you as copyright owner can't be included in a group registration.

Display of copyright notice is especially important when contributing to an uncopyrighted publication—that is, a publication that doesn't display a copyright symbol and doesn't register with the Copyright Office. You risk losing copyright protection on material that appears in an uncopyrighted publication. Also, you have no legal recourse against a person who infringes on something that is published without appropriate copyright notice. That person has been misled by the absence of the copyright notice and can't be held liable for his infringement. Copyright protection remains in force on material published in an uncopyrighted publication without benefit of copyright notice if the notice was left off only a few copies, if you asked (in writing) that the notice be included and the publisher didn't comply, or if you register the work and make a reasonable attempt to place the notice on any copies that haven't been distributed after the omission was discovered.

Official notice of copyright consists of the symbol ©, the word "Copyright," or the abbreviation "Copr."; the name of the copyright owner or owners; and the year date of first publication (for example, "©1985 by Chris Jones").

● **Under what circumstances should I place my copyright notice on unpublished works that haven't been registered?** Place official copyright notice on the first page of *any* manuscript, a procedure intended not to stop a buyer from stealing your material (editorial piracy is very rare, actually), but to demonstrate to the editor that you understand your rights under copyright law, that you own that particular manuscript, and that you want to retain your ownership after the manuscript is published. Seeing this notice, an editor might be less apt to try to buy all rights from you. Remember, you want to retain your rights to any writing.

● **How do I transfer copyright?** A transfer of copyright, like the sale of any property, is simply an exchange of the property for payment. The law stipulates, however, that the transfer of any exclusive rights (and the copyright is the most exclusive of exclusive rights) must be made in writing to be valid. Various types of exclusive rights exist, as outlined above. Usually it is best not to sell your copyright. If you do, you lose control over use of the manuscript, and forfeit future income from its use.

● **What is a "work-for-hire agreement"?** This is a work that another party commissions you to do. Two types of for-hire works exist: Work done as a regular employee of a company, and commissioned work that is specifically called a "work-for-hire" in writing at the time of assignment. The phrase "work-for-hire" or something close must be used in the written agreement, though you should watch for similar phrasings. The work-for-hire provision was included in the new copyright law so that no writer could unwittingly sign away his copyright. The phrase "work-for-hire" is a bright red flag warning the writer that the agreement he is about to enter into will result in loss of rights to any material created under the agreement.

Some editors offer work-for-hire agreements when making assignments, and expect writers to sign them routinely. By signing them, you forfeit the potential for additional income from a manuscript through reprint sales, or sale of other rights. Be careful, therefore, in signing away your rights in a "work-for-hire" agreement. Many articles written as works-for-hire or to which all rights have been sold are never resold, but if you retain the copyright, you might try to resell the article—something you wouldn't be motivated to do if you forfeited your rights to the piece.

● **Can I get my rights back if I sell all rights to a manuscript, or if I sell the copyright itself?** Yes. You or certain heirs can terminate the transfer of rights 40 years after creation or 35 years after publication of a work by serving written notice to the person to whom you transferred rights within specified time limits. Consult the Copyright Office for the procedural details. This may seem like a long time to wait, but remember that some manuscripts remain popular (and earn royalties and other fees) for much longer than 35 years.

● **Must all transfers be in writing?** Only work-for-hire agreements and transfers of exclusive rights *must* be in writing. However, getting any agreement in writing before the sale is wise. Beware of other statements about what rights the buyer purchases that may appear on checks, writer's guidelines or magazine mastheads. If the publisher makes such a statement elsewhere, you might insert a phrase like "No statement pertaining to purchase of rights other than the one detailed in this letter—including masthead statements or writer's guidelines—applies to this agreement" into the letter that outlines your rights agreement. Some publishers put their terms in writing on the back of a check that, when endorsed by the writer, becomes in their view a "contract." If the terms on the back of the check do not agree with the rights you are selling, then change the endorsement to match the rights you have sold before signing the check for deposit. Contact the editor to discuss this difference in rights.

● **Are ideas and titles copyrightable?** No. Nor can information be copyrighted. Only the actual expression of ideas or information can be copyrighted. You can't copyright the idea to do a solar energy story, and you can't copyright information about building solar energy converters. But you can copyright the article that results from that idea and that information.

● **Where can I get more information about copyright law?** Write the Copyright Office (Library of Congress, Washington, D.C. 20559) for a free Copyright Information Kit. Call (not collect) the Copyright Public Information Office at (202)287-8700 weekdays between 8:30 a.m. and 5 p.m. if you need forms for registration of a claim to copyright. The Copyright Office will answer specific questions but won't provide legal advice. For more information about copyright and other laws, consult *Law and the Writer*, edited by Kirk Polking and Leonard S. Meranus (Writer's Digest Books).

How Much Should I Charge?

The editors of magazines in this directory spell out very clearly what their rates are for manuscripts, so the writer doesn't have much to say about setting his own price. But what do you do when you are asked to handle a writing or editing assignment for a local company or a regional organization? Or, if you have decided to aggressively pursue some writing jobs in your community on a part-time or seasonal basis, how do you know what your time is worth? What follows is a checklist of writing jobs you might want to consider in your own corner of the world—and rates that have been reported to us by freelancers doing similar duties in various parts of the United States. Prices quoted here are by no means fixed; the rates in your own marketplace may be higher or lower, depending on demand and other local variables. Therefore, consider the rates quoted here as guidelines, not fixed fees.

How do you find out what the local going rate is? If possible, contact writers or friends in a related business or agency that employs freelancers to find out what has been paid for certain kinds of jobs in the past. Or try to get the prospective client to quote his budget for a specific project before you name your price.

When setting your own fees, keep two factors in mind: (1)how much you think the client is willing or able to pay for the job; and (2)how much you want to earn for your time. For example, if something you write helps a businessman get a $50,000 order or a school board to get a $100,000 grant, that may influence your fees. How much you want to earn for your time should take into consideration not only an hourly rate for the time you actually spend writing, but also the time involved in meeting with the client, doing research, and, where necessary, handling details with a printer or producer. One way to figure your hourly rate is to determine what an annual salary might be for a staff person to do the same job you are bidding on, and figure an hourly wage on that. If, for example, you think the buyer would have to pay a staff person $20,000 a year, divide that by 2,000 (approximately 40 hours per week for 50 weeks) and you will arrive at $10 an hour. Then add another 20% to cover the amount of fringe benefits that an employer normally pays in Social Security, unemployment insurance, paid vacations, hospitalization, retirement funds, etc. Then add on another dollars-per-hour figure to cover your actual overhead expense for office space, equipment, supplies; plus time spent on professional meetings, readings, and making unsuccessful proposals. (Add up one year's expense and divide by the number of hours per year you work on freelancing. In the beginning you may have to adjust this to avoid pricing yourself out of the market.)

Regardless of the method by which you arrive at your fee for the job, be sure to get a letter of agreement signed by both parties covering the work to be done and the fee to be paid.

You will, of course, from time to time handle certain jobs at less than desirable rates because they are for a social cause you believe in, or because the job offers you additional experience or exposure to some profitable client for the future. Some clients pay hourly rates, others pay flat fees for the job; both kinds of rates are listed when the data were available so you have as many pricing options as possible. More details on many of the freelance jobs listed below are contained in *Jobs for Writers*, edited by Kirk Polking (Writer's Digest Books)—which tells how to get writing jobs, how to handle them most effectively, and how to get a fair price for your work.

Advertising copywriting: Advertising agencies and the advertising departments of large companies need part-time help in rush seasons. Newspapers, radio and TV stations also need copywriters for their smaller business customers who do not have an agency. Depending on the client and the job, the following rates could apply: $10-$45 per hour, $100 per day, $200 and up per week, $100-$500 as a monthly retainer.

Annual reports: A brief report with some economic information and an explanation of figures, $20-$35 per hour; a report that must meet Securities and Exchange Commission (SEC) standards and reports that use legal language could bill at $40-$50 per hour. Some writers who provide copywriting and editing services charge flat fees ranging from $1,500-$10,000.

Anthology editing: 3%-15% of royalties.

Article manuscript critique: 3,000 words, $30.

Arts reviewing: for weekly newspapers, $15-25; for dailies, $45 and up; for Sunday supplements, $100-$400; regional arts events summaries for national trade magazines $35-$100.

Associations: miscellaneous writing projects, small associations, $5-$15 per hour; larger groups, up to $60 per hour; or a flat fee per project, such as $250-$500 for 10-12 page magazine articles, or $500-$1,500 for a 10-page booklet.

Audio cassette scripts: $150 for 20 minutes, assuming written from existing client materials, no additional research or meetings; otherwise $75-$100 per minute, $750 minimum.

Audiovisuals: $300 per day plus travel and expenses for consulting, research, producing, directing, soundtrack oversight, etc. Audiovisual writing: $150 per scripted minute. Includes rough draft, editing conference with client, and final shooting script. See also filmstrip script; slide film script; and video script.

Book, as-told-to (ghostwriting): author gets full advance and 50% of author's royalties; subject gets 50%. Hourly rate for subjects who are self-publishing ($8-$30 per hour).

Book, ghostwritten, without as-told-to credit: For clients who are either self-publishing or have no royalty publisher lined up, $5,000 to $30,000 with one-fourth down payment, one-fourth when book half finished, one-fourth at three quarters mark and last fourth of payment when manuscript completed; or chapter by chapter.

Book content editing: $10-$25 per hour and up; $600-$3,000 per manuscript, based on size and complexity of the project.

Book copyediting: $7.50-$9 per hour and up; occasionally $1 per page.

Book indexing: $8-$15 per hour; $1.50 per printed book page; or flat fee.

Book jacket blurb writing: $60-$75 for selling front cover copy plus inside and back cover copy summarizing content and tone of the book.

Book manuscript criticism: $125 for outline and first 20,000 words.

Book manuscript reading, nonspecialized subjects: $20-$50 for a half page summary and recommendation. *Specialized subject:* $100-$350 and up, depending on complexity of project.

Book proofreading: $6-$9 per hour and up; sometimes 40-50¢ per page.

Book proposal consultation: $25-$35 per hour.

Book query critique: $50 for letter to publisher and outline.

Book research: $5-$20 per hour and up, depending on complexity.

Book reviews: byline and the book only, on small papers; to $25-$125 on larger publications.

Book rewriting: $12-$30 per hour; sometimes $5 per page. Some writers have combination ghostwriting and rewriting short-term jobs for which the pay could be $350 per day and up.

Business booklets, announcement folders: writing and editing, $25-$1,000 depending on size, research, etc. Average 8½x11" brochure, $150-$250.

Business facilities brochure: 12-16 pages, $1,000-$4,000.

Business letters: such as those designed to be used as form letters to improve customer relations, $20 per hour for small businesses; $200-$500 per form letter for corporations.

Business meeting guide and brochure: 4 pages, $150; 8-12 pages, $300.

Business writing: On the local or national level, this may be advertising copy, collateral materials, speechwriting, films, public relations or other jobs—see individual entries on these subjects for details. General business writing rates could range from $20-$50 per hour; $100-$200 per day, plus expenses.

Catalogs for business: $60-$75 per printed page; more if many tables or charts must be reworked for readability and consistency.

Collateral materials for business: see business booklets, catalogs, etc.

Comedy writing for night club entertainers: *Gags only,*$2-$10 each. *Routines:* $100-$500 per minute. Some new comics may try to get a five-minute routine for $150; others will pay $1,500 for a five-minute bit from a top writer.

Commercial reports for businesses, insurance companies, credit agencies: $6-$10 per page; $5-$20 per report on short reports.

Company newsletters and inhouse publications: writing and editing 2-4 pages, $200-$500; 12-32 pages, $1,000-$2,000.

Church history: $200-$1,000 for writing 15 to 50 pages.

Consultation on communications: $250 per day plus expenses for nonprofit, social service and religious organizations.

Consultation to business: on writing, PR, $25-$50 per hour.

Consumer complaint letters: $25 each.

Contest judging: short manuscripts, $5 per entry; with one-page critique, $10-$25.

Corporate history: up to 5,000 words, $1,000-$3,000.

Corporate profile: up to 3,000 words, $1,250-$2,500.

Dance criticism: $25-$400 per article (see also Arts reviewing.)

Direct-mail catalog copy: $10-$50 per page for 3-20 blocks of copy per page of a 24-48 page catalog.

Direct-mail packages: copywriting direct mail letter, response card, etc., $300-$3,000 depending on writer's skill, reputation.

Direct response card on a product: $250.

Editing: see book editing, company newsletters, magazines, etc.

Educational consulting and educational grant and proposal writing: $250-$750 per day and sometimes up to 5-10% of the total grant funds depending on whether writing only is involved or also research and design of the project itself.

Encyclopedia articles: entries in some reference books, such as biographical encyclopedias, 500-2,000 words and pay ranges from $60-$80 per 1,000 words. Specialists' fees vary.

English teachers—lay reading for: $4-$6 per hour.

Family histories: See histories, family.

Filmstrip script: $75-$100 per minute, $750 minimum.

Financial presentation for a corporation: 20-30 minutes, $1,500-$4,500.

Flyers for tourist attractions, small museums, art shows: $25 and up for writing a brief bio, history, etc.

Fund-raising campaign brochure: at least $2,000 for 20 hours' research and 30 hours to write, get it approved, lay out and produce with printer.

Gags: see comedy writing.

Genealogical research: $5-$25 per hour.

Ghostwriting: $15-$40 per hour; $5-$10 per page, $200 per day plus expenses. Ghostwritten trade journal article under someone else's byline, $250-$400. Ghostwritten books: see book, as-told-to (ghostwriting and book, ghostwritten, without as-told-to credit).

Ghostwriting a corporate book: 6 months' work, $13,000-$25,000.

Ghostwriting speeches: see speeches.

Government public information officer: part-time, with local governments, $10-$15 per hour; or a retainer for so many hours per period.

Histories, family: fees depend on whether the writer need only edit already prepared notes or do extensive research and writing; and the length of the work, $500-$5,000.

House organ editing: see company newsletters and inhouse publications.

Industrial product film: $1,000 for 10-minute script.

Industrial promotions: $15-$40 per hour. See also business writing.

Job application letters: $10-$25.

Lectures to local librarians or teachers: $50-$100.

Lectures to school classes: $25-$50.

Lectures at national conventions by well-known authors: $300-$1,000 and up, plus expenses; less for panel discussions.

Magazine, city, calendar of events column: $150.

Magazine column: 200 words, $25. Larger circulation publications pay more.

Magazine editing: religious publications, $200-$500 per month.

Magazine stringing: 20¢-$1 per word based on circulation. Daily rate: $200 plus expenses; weekly rate: $750 plus expenses. Also $7.50-$35 per hour plus expenses.

Manuscript consultation on book proposals: $25-$35 per hour.

Manuscript criticism: $20 per 16-line poem; $30 per article or short story of up to 3,000 words; book outlines and sample chapters of up to 20,000 words, $125.

Manuscript typing: 65¢-$1.25 per page with one copy.

Market research survey reports: $10 per report; $15-$30 per hour; writing results of studies or reports, $500-$1,200 per day.

Medical editing: $15-$25 per hour.

Medical proofreading: $10-$12 per hour.

Medical writing: $15 per hour.

New product release: $300-$500 plus expenses.

Newsletters: see company newsletters and retail business newsletters.

Newspaper column, local: 80¢ per column inch to $5 for a weekly; $7.50 for dallies of 4,000-6,000 circulation; $10-$12.50 for 7,000-10,000 dailies; $15-$20 for 11,000-25,000 dailies; and $25 and up for larger dailies.

Newspaper reviews of art, music, drama: see arts reviewing.

Newspaper stringing: 50¢-$2.50 per column inch up to $4-$5 per column inch for some national publications. Also publications like *National Enquirer* pay lead fees up to $250 for tips on page one story ideas.

Newspaper ads for small business: $25 for a small, one-column ad, or $10 per hour and up.

Novel synopsis for film producer: $150 for 5-10 pages typed single-spaced.

Obituary copy: where local newspapers permit lengthier than normal notices paid for by the funeral home (and charged to the family), $15. Writers are engaged by funeral homes.

Opinion research interviewing: $4-$5.50 per hour or $15-$25 per completed interview.

Permission fees to publishers to reprint article or story: $10-$100.

Photo brochures: $700-$15,000 flat fee for photos and writing.

Poetry criticism: $20 per 16-line poem.

Political writing: see public relations and speechwriting.

Press background on a company: $500-$1,200 for 4-8 pages.

Press release: 1-3 pages, $50-$200.

Printers' camera-ready typewritten copy: negotiated with individual printers, but see also manuscript typing services.

Product literature: per page, $100-$150.

Programmed instruction consultant fees: $300-$700 per day; $50 per hour.

Programmed instruction materials for business: $50 per hour for inhouse writing and editing; $500-$700 a day plus expenses for outside research and writing. *Alternate method:* $2,000-$5,000 per hour of programmed training provided, depending on technicality of subject.

Public relations for business: $200-$400 per day plus expenses.

Public relations for conventions: $500-$1,500 flat fee.

Public relations for libraries: small libraries, $5-$10 per hour; larger cities, $35 an hour and up.

Public relations for nonprofit or proprietary organizations: small towns, $100-$500 monthly retainers.

Public relations for politicians: small town, state campaigns, $10-$30 per hour; incumbents, congressional, gubernatorial, and other national campaigns, $25-$75 per hour.

Public relations for schools: $10 per hour and up in small districts; larger districts have full-time staff personnel.

Radio advertising copy: small towns, up to $5 per spot; $20-$40 per hour; $100-$250 per week for a four- to six-hour day; larger cities, $250-$400 per week.

Radio continuity writing: $5 per page to $150 per week, part-time.

Radio documentaries: $200 for 60 minutes, local station.

Radio editorials: $10-$30 for 90-second to two-minute spots.

Radio interviews: for National Public Radio, up to 3 minutes, $25; 3-10 minutes, $40-$75; 10-60 minutes, $125 to negotiable fees. Small radio stations would pay approximately 50% of the NPR rate; large stations, double the NPR rate.

Readings by poets, fiction writers: $25-$300 depending on the author.

Record album cover copy: $100-$250 flat fee.

Recruiting brochure: 8-12 pages, $500-$1,500.

Research for writers or book publishers: $10-$30 an hour and up. Some quote a flat fee of $300-$500 for a complete and complicated job.

Restaurant guide features: short article on restaurant, owner, special attractions, $15; interior, exterior photos, $15.

Résumé writing: $45-$100 per résumé.

Retail business newsletters for customers: $175-$300 for writing four-page publications. Some writers work with a local printer and handle production details as well, billing the client for the total package. Some writers also do their own photography.

Sales brochure: 12-16 pages, $750-$3,000.

Sales letter for business or industry: $150-$500 for one or two pages.

Script synopsis for agent or film producer: $75 for 2-3 typed pages, single-spaced.

Scripts for nontheatrical films for education, business, industry: prices vary among producers, clients, and sponsors and there is no standardization of rates in the field. Fees include $75-$120 per minute for one reel (10 minutes) and corresponding increases with each successive reel; approximately 10% of the production cost of films that cost the producer more than $1,500 per release minute.

Services brochure: 12-18 pages, $1,250-$2,000.

Shopping mall promotion: $500 monthly retainer up to 15% of promotion budget for the mall.

Short story manuscript critique: 3,000 words, $30.

Slide film script: $75-$100 per minute, $750 minimum.

Slide presentation: including visual formats plus audio, $1,000-$1,500 for 10-15 minutes.

Slide/single image photos: $75 flat fee.

Slide/tape script: $75-$100 per minute, $750 minimum.
Software manual writing: $15-$50 per hour for research and writing.
Special news article: for a business's submission to trade publication, $250-$400 for 1,000 words.
Special occasion booklet: Family keepsake of a wedding, anniversary, Bar Mitzvah, etc., $115 and up.
Speech for owners of a small business: $100 for six minutes.
Speech for owners of larger businesses: $500-$1,500 for 10-15 minutes.
Speech for local political candidate: $150-$250 for 15 minutes.
Speech for statewide candidate: $500-$800.
Speech for national candidate: $1,000 and up.
Syndicated newspaper column, self-promoted: $2-$8 each for weeklies; $5-$25 per week for dailies, based on circulation.
Teaching adult education course: $10-$60 per class hour.
Teaching adult seminar: $350 plus mileage and per diem for a 6- or 7-hour day; plus 40% of the tuition fee beyond the sponsor's breakeven point.
Teaching college course or seminar: $15-$70 per class hour.
Teaching creative writing in school: $15-$60 per hour of instruction, or $1,200 for a 10-session class of 25 students; less in recessionary times.
Teaching journalism in high school: proportionate to salary scale for full-time teacher in the same school district.
Teaching home-bound students: $5 per hour.
Technical typing: $1-$4 per double-spaced page.
Technical writing: $15-$50 per hour.
Trade journal ad copywriting: $250-$500.
Trade journal article: for business client, $500-$1,500.
Translation, commercial: a final draft in one of the common European languages, 2½-4½¢ per English word.
Translation for government agencies: $20-$60 per 1,000 foreign words into English.
Translation, literary: $40-$60 per thousand English words.
Translation through translation agencies: less 33⅓% for agency commission.
TV documentary: 30-minute five-six page proposal outline, $250 and up; 15-17 page treatment, $1,000 and up; less in smaller cities.
TV editorials: $35 and up for 1-minute, 45 seconds (250-300 words).
TV instruction taping: $150 per 30-minute tape; $25 residual each time tape is sold.
TV news film still photo: $3-$6 flat fee.
TV news story: $16-$25 flat fee.
TV filmed news and features: from $10-$20 per clip for 30-second spot; $15-$25 for 60-second clip; more for special events.
TV, national and local public stations: $35-$100 per minute down to a flat fee of $100-$500 for a 30- to 60-minute script.
TV scripts: 60 minutes, prime time, Writers Guild rates effective 7/1/84-2/28/85: $9,420; 30 minutes, $6,983.
Video script: $75-$100 per minute, $750 minimum.
Writer-in-schools: Arts council program, $130 per day; $475 per week. Personal charges vary from $25 per day to $100 per hour depending on school's ability to pay.
Writer's workshop: lecturing and seminar conducting, $100 per hour to $400 per day plus expenses; local classes, $50 per student for 10 sessions.

Glossary

All Rights. See "Rights and the Writer" in the appendix.

Assignment. Editor asks a writer to do a specific article for which he usually names a price for the completed manuscript.

B&W. Abbreviation for black & white photograph.

Beat. A specific subject area regularly covered by a reporter, such as the police department or education or the environment. It can also mean a scoop on some news item.

Bimonthly. Every two months. See also *semimonthly*.

Bionote. A sentence or brief paragraph about the writer at the bottom of the first or last page on which an article or short story appears in a publication. A bionote may also appear on a contributors' page where the editor discusses the writers contributing to that particular edition.

Biweekly. Every two weeks.

Blue-penciling. Editing a manuscript.

Book packager. Draws all the elements of a book together, from the initial concept to writing and marketing strategies, then sells the book package to a book publisher and/or movie producer.

Caption. Originally a title or headline over a picture but now a description of the subject matter of a photograph, including names of people where appropriate. Also called cutline.

Chapbook. A small booklet, usually paperback, of poetry, ballads or tales.

Clean copy. Free of errors, cross-outs, wrinkles, smudges.

Clippings. News items of possible interest to trade magazine editors.

Column Inch. All the type contained in one inch of a typeset column.

Compatible. The condition which allows one type of computer/word processor to share information or communicate with another type of machine.

Concept. A statement that summarizes a screenplay or teleplay—before the outline or treatment is written.

Contributor's copies. Copies of the issues of a magazine sent to an author in which his/her work appears.

Co-publishing. An arrangement (usually contractual) in which author and publisher share publication costs and profits.

Copyediting. Editing the manuscript for grammar, punctuation and printing style as opposed to subject content.

Copyright. A means to protect an author's work. See "Rights and the Writer."

Correspondent. Writer away from the home office of a newspaper or magazine who regularly provides it with copy.

Cutline. See *caption*.

Disk. A round, flat magnetic plate on which computer data may be stored.

Dot-matrix. Printed type where individual characters are composed of a matrix or pattern of tiny dots.

El-hi. Elementary to high school.

Epigram. A short, witty, sometimes paradoxical saying.

Erotica. Usually fiction that is sexually-oriented; although it could be art on the same theme.

Fair use. A provision of the copyright law that says short passages from copyrighted material may be used without infringing on the owner's rights.

Feature. An article giving the reader background information on the news. Also used by magazines to indicate a lead article or distinctive department.

Filler. A short item used by an editor to "fill" out a newspaper column or a page in a magazine. It could be a timeless news item, a joke, an anecdote, some light verse or short humor, a puzzle, etc.

First North American serial rights. See "Rights and the Writer."

Formula story. Familiar theme treated in a predictable plot structure—such as boy meets girl, boy loses girl, boy gets girl.

Gagline. The caption for a cartoon, or the cover teaser line and the punchline on the inside of a studio greeting card.

Ghostwriter. A writer who puts into literary form, an article, speech, story or book based on another person's ideas or knowledge.

Glossy. A black and white photograph with a shiny surface as opposed to one with a non-shiny matte finish.

Gothic novel. One in which the central character is usually a beautiful young girl, the setting is an old mansion or castle; there is a handsome hero and a real menace, either natural or supernatural.

Hard copy. The printed copy (usually on paper) of a computer's output.

Hardware. All the mechanically-integrated components of a computer that are not software. Circuit boards, transistors, and the machines that are the actual computer are the hardware.

Honorarium. A token payment. It may be a very small amount of money, or simply a byline and copies of the publication in which your material appears.

Illustrations. May be photographs, old engravings, artwork. Usually paid for separately from the manuscript. See also *package sale.*

Interactive fiction. Works of fiction in book or computer software format in which the reader determines the path that the story will take. The reader chooses from several alternatives at the end of a "chapter," and this determines the structure of the story. Interactive fiction features multiple plots and endings.

International Reply Coupon (IRC). Can be purchased at larger post offices for 65 cents each. Must be enclosed in mailings to Canadian and overseas publishers to ensure return reply.

Invasion of privacy. Cause for suits against some writers who have written about persons (even though truthfully) without their consent.

Kill fee. A portion of the agreed-on price for a complete article that was assigned but which was subsequently cancelled.

Libel. A false accusation; or any published statement or presentation that tends to expose another to public contempt, ridicule, etc. Defenses are truth; fair comment on the matter of public interest; and privileged communication—such as a report of legal proceedings or a client's communication to his lawyer.

Little magazine. Publications of limited circulation, usually on literary or political subject matter.

Machine language. Symbols that can be used directly by a computer.

Microcomputer. A small computer system capable of performing various specific tasks with data it receives. Personal computers are microcomputers.

Model release. A paper signed by the subject of a photograph (or his guardian, if a juvenile) giving the photographer permission to use the photograph, editorially or for advertising purposes or for some specific purpose as stated.

Ms. Abbreviation for manuscript.

Mss. Abbreviation for more than one manuscript.

Multiple submissions. Some editors of nonoverlapping circulation magazines, such as religious publications, are willing to look at manuscripts which have also been submitted to other editors at the same time. See individual listings. No multiple submissions should be made to larger markets paying good prices for original material, unless it is a query on a highly topical article requiring an immediate response and that fact is so stated in your letter.

Novelette. A short novel, or a long short story; 7,000 to 15,000 words approximately.

One-time rights. See "Rights and the Writer."

Outline. Of a book is usually a summary of its contents in five to fifteen double-spaced pages; often in the form of chapter headings with a descriptive sentence or two under each one to show the scope of the book. Of a screenplay or teleplay is a scene-by-scene narrative description of the story (10-15 pages for a ½-hour teleplay; 15-25 pages for a 1-hour teleplay; 25-40 pages for a 90-minute teleplay; 40-60 pages for a 2-hour feature film or teleplay).

Over-the-transom. Refers to unsolicited material submitted to a book publisher, magazine editor, etc., by a freelance writer. These submissions are said to come in "over-the-transom."

Package sale. The editor wants to buy manuscript and photos as a "package" and pay for them in one check.

Page rate. Some magazines pay for material at a fixed rate per published page, rather than so much per word.

Payment on acceptance. The editor sends you a check for your article, story or poem as soon as he reads it and decides to publish it.

Payment on publication. The editor decides to buy your material but doesn't send you a check until he publishes it.

Pen name. The use of a name other than your legal name on articles, stories, or books where you wish to remain anonymous. Simply notify your post office and bank that you are using the name so that you'll receive mail and/or checks in that name.

Photo feature. A feature in which the emphasis is on the photographs rather than any accompanying written material.

Photocopied submissions. Submitting *photocopies* of an original manuscript; are acceptable to some editors instead of the author's sending his original manuscript. See also *multiple submissions.*

Plagiarism. Passing off as one's own the expression of ideas and words of another writer.

Postal Money Order. Available at all post offices. Useful for writers who send longer manuscripts to publishers outside the United States since they are more economical than International Reply Coupons (IRCs). Money orders up to $25 may be purchased for 75 cents.

Program. A series of instructions written in symbols and codes that a computer "reads" to perform a specific task.

Public domain. Material which was either never copyrighted or whose copyright term has run out.

Publication not copyrighted. Publication of an author's work in such a publication places it in the public domain, and it cannot subsequently be copyrighted. See "Rights and the Writer."

Query. A letter to an editor aimed to get his interest in an article you want to write.

Reporting times. The number of days, weeks, etc., it takes an editor to report back to the author on his query or manuscript.

Reprint rights. See "Rights and the Writer."

Round-up article. Comments from, or interviews with, a number of celebrities or experts on a single theme.

Royalties, standard hardcover book. 10% of the retail price on the first 5,000 copies sold; 12½% on the next 5,000 and 15% thereafter.

Royalties, standard mass paperback book. 4 to 8% of the retail price on the first 150,000 copies sold.

Royalties, trade paperback book. No less than 6% of list price on first 20,000 copies; 7½% thereafter.

SAE. Self-addressed envelope.

SASE. Self-addressed, stamped envelope.

Screenplay. Script for a film intended to be shown in theatres.

Second serial rights. See "Rights and the Writer."

Semimonthly. Twice a month.

Semiweekly. Twice a week.

Serial. Published periodically, such as a newspaper or magazine.

Sidebar. A feature presented as a companion to a straight news report (or main magazine article) giving sidelights on human-interest aspects, (or) sometimes elucidating just one aspect of the story.

Simultaneous submissions. Submissions of the same article, story or poem to several publications at the same time.

Slant. The approach of a story or article so as to appeal to the readers of a specific magazine. Does, for example, this magazine always like stories with an upbeat ending? Or does that one like articles aimed only at the blue-collar worker?

Slides. Usually called transparencies by editors looking for color photographs.

Slush pile. A collective term for the stack of unsolicited, or misdirected manuscripts received by an editor or book publisher.

Software. Programs and related documentation for use with a particular computer system.

Speculation. The editor agrees to look at the author's manuscript with no assurance that it will be bought.

Stringer. A writer who submits material to a magazine or newspaper from a specific geographical location.

Style. The way in which something is written—for example, short, punchy sentences of flowing, narrative description, or heavy use of quotes of dialogue.

Subsidiary rights. All those rights, other than book publishing rights included in a book contract—such as paperback, book club, movie rights, etc.

Subsidy publisher. A book publisher who charges the author for the cost to typeset and print his book, the jacket, etc., as opposed to a royalty publisher which pays the author.

Syndication rights. A book publisher may sell the rights to a newspaper syndicate to print a book in installments in one or more newspapers.

Synopsis. Of a book is a summary of its contents. Of a screenplay or teleplay is a summary of the story. See *Outline.*

Tabloids. Newspaper format publication on about half the size of the regular newspaper page, such as *National Enquirer.*

Tagline. A tagline has two definitions in the writing world: a caption for a photo or an editorial comment appended to a filler in a magazine such as those used in *The New Yorker.*

Tearsheet. Page from a magazine or newspaper containing your printed story, article, poem or ad.

Teleplay. A dramatic story written to be performed on television.

Transparencies. Positive color slides; not color prints.

Treatment. Synopsis of a proposed television or film script (40-60 pages for a 2-hour feature film or teleplay). More detailed than an outline.

Uncopyrighted publication. Publication of an author's work in such a publication potentially puts it in the public domain.

Unsolicited manuscript. A story, article, poem or book that an editor did not specifically ask to see.

User friendly. Easy to handle and use. Refers to computer hardware designed with the user in mind.

Vanity publisher. See *subsidy publisher.*

Word processor. A computer that produces typewritten copy via automated typing, text-editing, and storage and transmission capabilities.

Index

F

N

O

U

X-Y-Z

Other Books of Interest

General Writing Books
Beginning Writer's Answer Book, edited by Polking and Bloss $14.95
Getting the Words Right: How to Revise, Edit and Rewrite, by Theodore A. Rees Cheney $13.95
How to Become a Bestselling Author, by Stan Corwin $14.95
How to Get Started in Writing, by Peggy Teeters $10.95
If I Can Write, You Can Write, by Charlie Shedd $12.95
International Writers' & Artists' Yearbook, (paper) $11.95
Knowing Where to Look: The Ultimate Guide to Research, by Lois Horowitz $16.95
Make Every Word Count, by Gary Provost (paper) $7.95
Teach Yourself to Write, by Evelyn A. Stenbock $12.95
Treasury of Tips for Writers, edited by Marvin Weisbord (paper) $6.95
Writer's Encyclopedia, edited by Kirk Polking $19.95
Writer's Market, edited by Paula Deimling $19.95
Writer's Resource Guide, edited by Bernadine Clark $16.95
Writing for the Joy of It, by Leonard Knott $11.95
Writing From the Inside Out, by Charlotte Edwards (paper) $9.95

Magazine/News Writing
Complete Guide to Marketing Magazine Articles, by Duane Newcomb $9.95
Complete Guide to Writing Nonfiction, by the American Society of Journalists & Authors, edited by Glen Evans $24.95
Craft of Interviewing, by John Brady $9.95
Magazine Writing: The Inside Angle, by Art Spikol $12.95
Magazine Writing Today, by Jerome E. Kelley $10.95
Newsthinking: The Secret of Great Newswriting, by Bob Baker $11.95
1001 Article Ideas, by Frank A. Dickson $10.95
Stalking the Feature Story, by William Ruehlmann $9.95
Write On Target, by Connie Emerson $12.95
Writing and Selling Non-Fiction, by Hayes B. Jacobs $12.95

Fiction Writing
Fiction Is Folks: How to Create Unforgettable Characters, by Robert Newton Peck $11.95
Fiction Writer's Help Book, by Maxine Rock $12.95
Fiction Writer's Market, edited by Jean Fredette $17.95
Handbook of Short Story Writing, by Dickson and Smythe (paper) $6.95
How to Write Best-Selling Fiction, by Dean R. Koontz $13.95
How to Write Short Stories that Sell, by Louise Boggess (paper) $7.95
One Way to Write Your Novel, by Dick Perry (paper) $6.95
Secrets of Successful Fiction, by Robert Newton Peck $8.95
Storycrafting, by Paul Darcy Boles $14.95
Writing Romance Fiction—For Love And Money, by Helene Schellenberg Barnhart $14.95
Writing the Novel: From Plot to Print, by Lawrence Block $10.95

Special Interest Writing Books
The Children's Picture Book: How to Write It, How to Sell It, by Ellen E. M. Roberts $17.95
Complete Book of Scriptwriting, by J. Michael Straczynski $14.95
Complete Guide to Writing Software User Manuals, by Brad McGehee (paper) $14.95
Confession Writer's Handbook, by Florence K. Palmer. Revised by Marguerite McClain $9.95
The Craft of Lyric Writing, by Sheila Davis $16.95
Guide to Greeting Card Writing, edited by Larry Sandman (paper) $7.95
How to Make Money Writing . . . Fillers, by Connie Emerson $12.95
How to Write a Cookbook and Get It Published, by Sara Pitzer $15.95
How to Write a Play, by Raymond Hull $13.95
How to Write and Sell Your Personal Experiences, by Lois Duncan $10.95
How to Write and Sell (Your Sense of) Humor, by Gene Perret $12.95
How to Write "How-To" Books and Articles, by Raymond Hull (paper) $8.95

How to Write the Story of Your Life, by Frank P. Thomas $12.95
Mystery Writer's Handbook, edited by Lawrence Treat (paper) $8.95
On Being a Poet, by Judson Jerome $14.95
Poet and the Poem, revised edition by Judson Jerome $13.95
Poet's Handbook, by Judson Jerome $11.95
Programmer's Market, edited by Brad McGehee (paper) $16.95
Sell Copy, by Webster Kuswa $11.95
Successful Outdoor Writing, by Jack Samson $11.95
Travel Writer's Handbook, by Louise Zobel (paper) $8.95
TV Scriptwriter's Handbook, by Alfred Brenner $12.95
Writing and Selling Science Fiction, by Science Fiction Writers of America (paper) $7.95
Writing for Children & Teenagers, by Lee Wyndham. Revised by Arnold Madison $11.95
Writing for Regional Publications, by Brian Vachon $11.95
Writing for the Soaps, by Jean Rouverol $14.95
Writing to Inspire, by Gentz, Roddy, et al $14.95

The Writing Business

Complete Handbook for Freelance Writers, by Kay Cassill $14.95
Freelance Jobs for Writers, edited by Kirk Polking (paper) $7.95
How to Be a Successful Housewife/Writer, by Elaine Fantle Shimberg $10.95
How You Can Make $20,000 a Year Writing, by Nancy Hanson (paper) $6.95
Profitable Part-time/Full-time Freelancing, by Clair Rees $10.95
The Writer's Survival Guide: How to Cope with Rejection, Success and 99 Other Hang-Ups of the Writing Life, by Jean and Veryl Rosenbaum $12.95

To order directly from the publisher, include $1.50 postage and handling for 1 book and 50¢ for each additional book. Allow 30 days for delivery.

Writer's Digest Books, Department B
9933 Alliance Road, Cincinnati OH 45242
Prices subject to change without notice.

Notes

Notes

Notes